The Wise Garden Encyclopedia

The Wise Garden Encyclopedia

A Complete, Practical, and Convenient Guide to Every Detail of Gardening Written for All U.S. Climates, Soils, Seasons, and Methods

Edited by E. L. D. Seymour, B.S.A.

Grosset & Dunlap

A NATIONAL GENERAL COMPANY

New York 1970

FRONTISPIECE: Begonias. These delicate blossoms are a summer garden favorite. They are as easy to grow as they are beautiful.

DISTRIBUTED BY

Grosset & Dunlap, Inc., New York, N.Y.

Printed in the United States of America

1972 PRINTING

FOREWORD

THE GARDEN ENCYCLOPEDIA has been prepared with the aim of presenting in simple, practical, interesting and helpful form the information that will enable any person with a garden to get the most out of it.

The returns—or should we call them rewards?—that one gets from a garden are of various kinds. There are the material products—flowers, vegetables, fruits—to be enjoyed through the several senses, or shared with others and thereby doubly enjoyed. There is the physical benefit and enjoyable recreation to be gained from garden work. There is the pride of ownership of something fine and beautiful, and the inspiration of working hand in hand with Nature in creating it. Perhaps there is the thrill of an award or other recognition for something unusually good; always there is the well-merited satisfaction of accomplishing something that benefits the community—of taking a step, however small, toward that noble goal, a more beautiful America.

But these rewards are not to be had for the wishing. The smallest garden no less than the most elaborate estate represents the result of the combination of four basic elements. They may be called (1) the *materials* of gardening; (2) the *means* to gardening; (3) the *methods* of gardening, and (4) the *background* of gardening. Those elements—and the all-important and all-essential human factor—have been kept in mind throughout the preparation of this book. One way to tell what THE GARDEN ENCYCLOPEDIA is and how the reader can use and enjoy and benefit by it, is to discuss those four elements in relation to its contents.

Materials. These are, first, the plants that make gardens and, second, the soil in which they grow. In the plant articles the objective has been to describe or picture the subject (whether a single plant or a group such as botanists call a *genus*), then to give simple cultural directions and finally to list and describe briefly the more important or promising kinds available for garden use.

In nearly every instance, a plant (or a genus) is listed twice—once under its correct botanical name, and again under its common name. Sometimes these are the same, as Chrysanthemum or Zinnia; but sometimes a plant has a botanical name and also two or even more common names, under each of which it appears. The main discussion of a plant may occur under either botanical or common name, whichever is the more familiar. This is usually the latter, as Apple, Oak, Peony; but it may be the scientific name, as Delphinium, Petunia, Salvia. In either case, the other name appears as a cross reference—which may often supply the information immediately desired, leaving the other, longer article to be read when more facts are needed or there is more leisure.

Study the style in which the plant names are printed. A complete botanical name always appears in italics, as *Rosa rugosa;* but the name of a genus alone (as Rosa) does not. Except when emphasized, as in a definition, a common name is not capitalized; but both capitals and hyphens when used in a name have significance. For example, Regal Lily and English Holly are so printed because they belong to the true Lily and Holly genera respectively; but Trout-lily and Mountain-holly are hyphenated because they are not members of those genera. Similarly Horse-chestnut is so written because the tree is not a true Chestnut and because the name is easily said as one word. In these respects, and in the simplification of botanical names by dropping the last of two final i's and by keeping the first letter of all specific names small, THE GARDEN ENCYCLOPEDIA has followed the style of "Standardized Plant Names" in an endeavor to make the problem of correct plant naming easier for the average gardener. Unless otherwise noted "Hortus" has been followed as the authority for plant identity.

Garden soils are, of course, a subject in themselves. Their treatment here seeks to make their use and (where necessary) their improvement as simple and as much a part of the ordinary garden routine as possible.

Means to gardening. These are the implements, accessories and aids with which gardens are made and cared for and plants are grown. They include tools, fertilizers, spray materials, hotbeds—in fact, all objects that are neither plants nor part of the soil. The articles dealing with them should be read in connection with the cultural notes on the various plants and with the articles of the third group, namely—

Methods. These include all such details as *design* or *planning, construction* or *planting* and *maintenance* or *culture.* Here, too, different related articles should be read so as to get a complete understanding of any one subject. Seeking information on pruning a rosebush, for example, the reader should consult not only directions under ROSE, but also the separate articles on PRUNING, SHEARS, SHRUBS, etc. This is especially true in the case of plant enemies and their control, the notes under each plant or genus being supplemented in many instances by more detailed accounts of the more serious diseases or pests and directions for the use of sprays or dusts. All this material has been prepared by Dr. Cynthia Westcott so as to present in one volume what must usually be sought in several. Naturally one need not fear to find in one garden or on a particular plant or crop all the enemies that might attack it; but with knowledge of what may happen and what to do in that emergency, the gardener is forewarned and forearmed to a degree that can prevent much unnecessary loss and disappointment.

Background. This refers to the relation of individual plants and gardens to others, and to various outside factors. It includes elementary basic facts about the science of botany, which underlies all plant growing; it touches on theory and principle, and also the agencies and institutions from or through which the gardener can obtain information and assistance. It seeks to give to the manual work in the garden a larger outlook, a broader horizon, such as a general college education gives to an otherwise limited commercial or industrial life.

But, after all, gardens themselves furnish a background for life, a rich and inspiring one; a common background for all who are interested in growing things. With this in mind, THE GARDEN ENCYCLOPEDIA applies (with such minor modifications as may be required on account of· climate and environment) to all parts of the United States. However, because of local differences in soil, rainfall, temperature, etc., and also because commercial plantsmen are constantly producing new and improved plants, this book does not, except in a few cases, attempt to recommend varieties, types or strains. That is the function of the catalogs issued seasonally by seedsmen and nurserymen; rich in suggestions and possibilities, they should be consulted in connection with the fundamental facts and directions provided by THE GARDEN ENCYCLOPEDIA.

In presenting a book of nearly a million words that treats several thousand items and covers the multiple phases of such a complex subject as gardening, it is impossible to express fully and in detail the thanks due all who have helped make it possible. All that can be done is to name below those whose part in building THE GARDEN ENCYCLOPEDIA is most gratefully acknowledged, and to record special appreciative indebtedness to Miss Carol H. Woodward for her untiring, invaluable editorial assistance both in perfecting the preliminary layout of the book and in carrying it to completion.

Editorial Aides: Margaret McKenny; W. L. Parker; Daniel T. Walden.

Contributors: Dorothea J. Blom; Clement G. Bowers; Sarah V. Coombs; John S. Doig; H. E. Downer; Arthur G. Eldredge; Gerald English; Richard Ferris; Grace H. Gaines; Elizabeth Gibbons; Walter J. Guille; Elisabeth S. Harrold; Ethel Bailey Higgins; Maurice G. Kains; Mary D. Lamson; Margaret McKenny; Nellie D. Merrell; Richard T. Muller; Guy G. Nearing; Maynard A. Nichols; Ida M. Pattison; I. George Quint; Robert Snedigar; the late G. A. Stevens; Grace Tabor; F. E. Taylor; Ernest K. Thomas; Daniel T. Walden; Cynthia Westcott; Walter B. Wilder.

Artists: Laurence Blair; Alma W. Froderstrom; Dorothy Handsaker; Robert Rotter; Meta P. Shirrefs; Margaret Sorensen.

THE PUBLISHERS

KEY TO THE SYMBOLS FOR PRONUNCIATION

The purpose of this key is to indicate the pronunciation of botanical names accurately without requiring the learning of hundreds of special symbols. This is a book for gardeners, not elocutionists, hence the symbols are limited to those listed below. Only the major accent is indicated; it is felt that *Acalypha* is represented satisfactorily by (ak-ah-ly'-fah) and that the use of double and single accents to indicate major and secondary stress would lead to confusion.

"Rules" for making the botanical names self-pronouncing are not supplied. In those books which undertake to supply them the rules are so affected by exception, qualification, etc., that they are of little use.

a	*a* in c*a*tch	m	*m* in sa*m*ple
ah	*a* in b*a*rge, when accented. When unstressed *a* as in *a*nemone or zinni*a*	n	*n* in sa*n*d
		ng	*ng* in si*ng*er or fi*ng*er
au	*au* in s*au*cer	o	*o* in h*o*t
ay	*a* in br*a*ve	oh	*o* in cl*o*ver
b	*b* in *b*ig	oi	*oi* in s*oi*l
		oo	*oo* in bl*oo*m
c	not used alone	ou	*ou* in s*ou*th
ch	*ch* in whi*ch*	p	*p* in o*p*en
d	*d* in par*d*on	q	not used
e	*e* in p*e*n		
ee	*e* in c*e*dar	r	*r* in pu*r*e
eu	*u* in p*u*pil	s	*s* in pur*s*e
f	*f* in o*f*ten	sh	*sh* in cu*sh*ion
g	*g* in *g*o (see also *n* for combination)	t	*t* in gar*t*er
		th	*th* in pa*th* or ra*th*er
h	*h* in be*h*ave (see also *a, c, o, s, t,* for combinations with *h*)	u	*u* in b*u*t (see *a, e,* and *o* for combinations with *u*)
i	*i* in d*i*m (see also *o* for combination)	v	*v* in se*v*en
		w	*w* in s*w*im
j	*g* in ra*g*e or *j* in e*j*ect	x	not used
k	*c* in a*c*orn or *k* in li*k*e	y	*y* in t*y*pe or *y*ank
l	*l* in pa*l*e	z	*z* in da*z*e

LIST OF HALFTONE ILLUSTRATIONS

LIST OF HALFTONE ILLUSTRATIONS

LIST OF HALFTONE ILLUSTRATIONS

LIST OF HALFTONE ILLUSTRATIONS

___

Acknowledgment for the use of photographs is hereby made to: The General
Electric Company (Plate 15); Lord and Burnham Company (Plate 25); Nellie
D. Merrell (lower illustration, Plate 23); Richard Averill Smith (Plate 28);
and the New York Botanical Garden, Walter Beebe Wilder and the A. T. De La
Mare Company for the remainder of the plates.

LIST OF COLOR ILLUSTRATIONS

LIST OF COLOR ILLUSTRATIONS

The Wise
Garden
Encyclopedia

A

AARONS BEARD. Common name for several garden plants, including one of the St. Johnsworts (*Hypericum calycinum*) because of its numerous stamens; the Strawberry-geranium (*Saxifraga sarmentosa*) perhaps because of its trailing branches of small white flowers; and the Kenilworth Ivy (*Cymbalaria muralis*) because of its many thread-like runners. The Aaronsbeard Cactus is *Opuntia leucotricha*.

ABELE (a-beel′ *or* ay′-bel). A name for the white poplar (*Populus alba*), a large tree with coarsely-lobed, triangular leaves, hardy even along the N. Atlantic coast. Its var. *nivea*, with leaves white and cottony beneath, is sometimes, but wrongly, called "silver-maple." See POPLAR.

ABELIA (a-beel′-i-ah). A genus of several small shrubs, natives of Asia and Mexico, and with one or two exceptions not hardy N. They thrive best in a sunny, sheltered location. A well-drained sandy loam, into which plenty of leafmold or peat has been worked, encourages growth. Flowers are rather small, tubular or bell-shaped, abundantly produced in summer on young growth, and vary in color from white to pink or rose.

Cuttings taken in late summer root readily under glass. Young plants wintered in a cool greenhouse and planted out in spring grow and flower well that year.

SPECIES

A. engleriana, from China, hardy in Mass., grows from 3 to 6 ft. and bears rosy-pink flowers in early summer.

grandiflora. To 6 ft. A semi-evergreen hybrid, the leaves taking on a lovely bronze tone in fall. Flowers, pink and white, from June to November. Wood injured by severe cold.

floribunda. A handsome evergreen from Mexico. Not hardy N. of Washington, D. C., but sometimes grown in a cool greenhouse. Flowers larger than most, nodding, purple-rose, blooming in June and July.

ABIES (ay′-bi-eez). Botanical name of the genus Fir (which see), large evergreen conifers of the Pine Family, some species native to U. S. and a number valuable as ornamentals, especially when young.

ABOBRA (a-boh′-brah). A tropical, tuberous-rooted, flowering vine, suitable for greenhouse culture. See CRANBERRY-GOURD.

ABRONIA (ah-broh′-ni-ah). Sand-verbena. Low or trailing native herbs with fragrant white, pink, or yellow flowers. Grown as annuals and good for open, sunny places in light soil, or for vases, rockwork, and baskets. Sow seed, after peeling off the husk, outdoors after danger of frost; or in pots or frames in early fall for planting out the next spring. In mild climates plants will survive the winter or may self-sow. *A. umbellata*, 9 in. tall, with pink flowers, is the best known species; *A. latifolia*, prostrate, has yellow flowers, and *A. mellifera* is a stouter, white-flowered Pacific Coast form. Blossoming all summer, the plants are pleasingly fragrant in the evening.

ABRUS (ay′-brus). Tropical creeping or climbing woody herbs grown in the S. for screens and sometimes in greenhouses for ornamental effect and the interesting, bead-like seeds, which, however, are poisonous. Raise from seed (preferably soaked before sowing), or from cuttings rooted under glass. *A. precatorius*, to 10 ft. but usually trailing, has white to rose flowers and scarlet, black-spotted seeds. These are used in making Buddhist rosaries, hence the plant's common name, Rosary-pea. It is also called Crabs-eye vine, and, sometimes, Weather-plant because it droops or "goes to sleep" during storms.

ABSINTH (ab′-sinth) or ABSINTHE. The shrubby, aromatic, herb *Artemisia absinthium* (which see) ; or, more correctly, a strong alcoholic, highly-intoxicating green liquor made from it.

ABUTILON (ah-beu′-ti-lon). A genus of tropical or semi-tropical plants, shrubby, or less often herbaceous, known as Flower-

---

Opposite. Cottage tulips are among the last tulips to bloom in the spring, and are distinguished by their graceful flowers, frequently with reflexed, pointed petals.

ing-maple. Many species produce numerous, long-lasting beautiful blossoms—red, yellow, white or striped. Some species are erect, tree-like and handsome. Others resemble miniature maple trees in form and leaf, which explains the popular name. These are grown as house plants, being treated like geraniums or fuchsias; that is, placed outdoors in the summer and brought indoors when the weather becomes cold. The long-stalked, vine-like leaves are usually edged or mottled with white. The pendent flowers, 1 to 3 in. long, vary in color from red to yellow and white, with many intermediate hues and tints.

ABUTILON BLOSSOM
The profusion of handsome flowers, produced nearly all year around, makes the abutilon a favorite shrub for indoor bloom.

Valuable plants for the greenhouse, window box or conservatory, they are equally suited for use in hanging baskets, vases or the summer bedding garden. Indoors they require a temperature of 60 to 70 deg. F., full exposure to light and frequent watering. They are easily grown from seed, and if started outdoors as annuals may be lifted, cut back and potted in the fall. So treated they will bear flowers during the winter, growing to a height of 3 to 4 ft. and making charming ornaments for the living room. They may also be propagated from green-wood cuttings taken in autumn. From these new plants other cuttings may be taken and rooted any time during the winter. Thus one plant will produce a large supply for planting outdoors the following summer. Young plants are likely to become spindling unless the tip shoots are pinched back frequently to induce formation of side branches.

ENEMIES. A virus disease called "infectious chlorosis" causes a variegation or mosaic of the foliage, but since the variegated forms are considered desirable from an ornamental standpoint the disease is intentionally fostered and transmitted by budding or grafting chlorotic stock on normal green plants. One type of chlorosis may be transmitted by seeds. Leaves showing irregular brown spots (caused by the fungus) should be removed and destroyed; so should entire plants if they show signs of Fusarium wilt or Corticium stem rot (which see). For infestations of tortoise scale, mealy bugs and white fly, spray with a strong nicotine-soap or pyrethrum-soap solution as recommended under Greenhouse Pests. Fumigation also will clear up scale, white fly and young (not adult) mealy bugs.

PRINCIPAL SPECIES

A. hybridum. Leaves slightly 3-lobed or unlobed and spotted; flowers of various colors. Actually a group of developed types to which most garden forms belong.

indicum. A shrubby perennial growing to 5 ft.; leaves entire or toothed, 4 in. across; flowers yellow, 1 in.

insigne. Leaves 4 in. long, wavy-toothed, not lobed; flowers white or rose with dark veins, 2½ in.

megapotamicum. Of drooping form with 3-in. unlobed leaves often arrow-shaped; flowers 2 in. with yellow petals and red calyx; stamens exserted as in fuchsias.

mollissimum. Grows to 10 ft.; leaves ovate, pubescent; 6 in. long, flowers yellow, ½ in.

pictum. Three-lobed, toothed, leaves green or variegated; flowers orange or yellow with crimson veins, 1¼ in.

pleniflorum. Resembles *pictum* except that leaves are green and flowers double.

theophrasti. An annual herb to 5 ft.; leaves pubescent, nearly entire or toothed, to 1 ft. across; flowers yellow, ¾ in.

vitifolium. Leaves 3 to 7 lobed, to 5 in. across, the underside woolly; flowers light blue, 3½ in.

ACACIA (ah-kay'-shah). Trees and shrubs distributed over the warmer parts of the world, belonging to the Pea Family, about 500 species having been described. It is a variable group and serves many purposes, both useful and ornamental. Certain kinds provide forage, fibres, gums, medicine, tannin and valuable wood, some of which is scented. In tropical America there is a group known as Bull-horn Acacias, remarkable for their large inflated spines which are inhabited by fighting ants.

From a horticultural view-point the most important species are those from Australia, where the "Wattle-blossom" is held in high regard. A few kinds are grown in greenhouses, and a number have taken kindly to outdoor cultivation in the warmer parts of the United States, particularly in Calif. Some kinds will stand a few degrees of frost.

Acacias are fast growing and certain kinds make good shade trees for immediate effect; but they are not long-lived. The great variation noted in leaf form is of interest not alone to botanists. The normal leaf is bipinnate and gives a light feathery appearance, but in many cases the leaves have been reduced to flattened stems (known as *phyllodes*) which function as leaves. In a few species the leaves have been further reduced to spines.

Most kinds are very floriferous, with flowers in shades of yellow or rarely white. The flowers are very tiny but numerous, packed closely together to form fluffy balls or short round spikes.

CULTURAL NOTES. Propagation is by seeds and cuttings. For pot culture young plants from cuttings are freer-flowering than seedlings. Cuttings of half-ripened wood taken with a heel are the best. Use a mixture of peat and sand and keep in a close, shaded place in a cool temperature until rooted.

Seeds germinate readily if sown as soon as ripe. If kept the seed coats get very hard and germination is likely to be irregular and poor. Soaking dry seeds until soft in hot water is a help.

When grown under glass, Acacias must be kept cool and will not stand forcing. They flower in March and April and are not difficult to manage. If planted in a border they must have good drainage. The plants need plenty of water, but the soil should never became waterlogged. A sandy loam with some leafmold suits them well; it should be well firmed. Those which make long shoots are well-adapted to clothe pillars and rafters, while those of more bushy habits make neat pot plants. Cutting back should be done right after

flowering; this is also the time for any repotting or soil renovation. When the weather is settled it is well to plunge them outside for the summer.

Rust occurs on *A. farnesiana* in the S. W. The Calif. and Fla. red scales common on citrus trees may also infest Acacia; control them by spraying with oil emulsions. See SCALE INSECTS.

PRINCIPAL SPECIES

A. armata (Kangaroo-thorn). A large spreading shrub when it has room to fully develop, but it can be grown as a good, compact pot plant. It has dark-green half-

ABUTILON OR FLOWERING-MAPLE
Many hybrid forms with colored veining, bearing pink, yellow or white flowers, are available for indoor bloom in a large sunny window.

rounded phyllodes and globular flower heads.

baileyana. A shrub or small tree with attractive feathery gray foliage and a shower of golden flower-heads.

calamifolia (Broom Wattle). A tall shrub or small tree with slender upright branches and narrow phyllodes. One of the most decorative species.

cultriformis. A tall shrub with bluish knife-shaped phyllodes and crowded heads of flowers in a terminal raceme.

decurrens (Green Wattle). A handsome tree with feathery foliage and racemes of fluffy flower-heads. Var. *dealbata* (Silver Wattle) is a beautiful tree with silvery feathery leaves and soft yellow flowerheads. Sprays (mostly from California) are sold by florists as "Mimosa."

drummondi. A handsome species with feathery leaves and drooping spikes of pale lemon flowers. One of the best for pot culture.

farnesiana. A thorny shrub growing in Texas. Its fragrant flowers are used in perfumery.

longifolia (Sydney Golden Wattle). A handsome shrub or small tree with long phyllodes and a long season of bloom with flowers in long loose spikes.

melanoxylon (Blackwood). A street tree in California, with wide phyllodes.

pravissima (Screw-pod Acacia). A small tree with long drooping branches terminating in finger-like divisions; seed pods are twisted.

pubescens (Hairy Wattle). A graceful plant with feathery leaves and fluffy heads. One of the most decorative.

podalyriaefolia. Attractive with gray branches overlaid with soft white downy hairs and phyllodes silvery. Fluffy yellow flowers freely borne in clusters.

riceana. A tall shrub with slender drooping branches giving a weeping willow effect. It has narrow phyllodes, and flowers in loose spikes.

tenuifolia. An everblooming shrub of low-branching habit with fragrant flowers. One of the easiest to grow from seed.

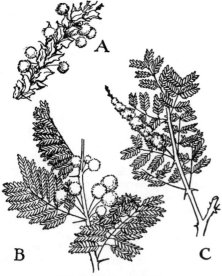

SPRAYS OF ACACIA
A. Acacia armata, showing the presence of phyllodes instead of true leaves. **B.** Acacia decurrens, in florist shops ordinarily called "Mimosa." **C.** Acacia senegal, a tropical African tree for greenhouse use.

verticillata (Star-leaved Acacia). A spreading, prickly shrub of graceful habit with flowers in spikes.

False-, Black- or Yellow-acacia is Robinia pseudoacacia, and Rose-acacia is R. hispida. See ROBINIA.

ACAENA (a-see'-nah). An attractive group of more or less trailing perennial plants of the Rose Family, used in mild climates in the rock garden or as a ground-cover over bulbs. They are occasionally grown in the N. if winter protection can be given. They are used principally on account of their attractive divided leaves and bristly fruits, for the flowers are quite inconspicuous. Easily propagated by seeds, division or cuttings.

A. argentea from Chile has a creeping stem and silvery leaflets. *A. microphylla* (New-Zealand Bur) has stems that hug the ground and rounded heads of flowers with purplish-red spines. There are species native in Calif.

ACALYPHA (ak-ah-ly'-fah). A genus of tropical- and temperate-zone, rather weedy, herbs or shrubs of the Spurge Family. Of the many species a few are grown as greenhouse or conservatory plants in the N. and as bedding plants or hedges in the S. From these many varieties and forms have been developed that are valued for their ornamental foliage, or for the showy bracts which surround the clusters of inconspicuous flowers.

For bedding purposes, plants from 4 in. pots should be set out at the end of May. They are easily propagated by cuttings either taken from outdoor plants in the fall, from such plants taken indoors and cut back, or, in summer, from plants kept over a second year indoors. The latter method which provides well-ripened wood, is preferred. In the greenhouse the plants should be guarded against red spider, mealy bug and scale. Control Cercospora leaf spot and Rhizoctonia stem rot by sanitary measures, such as removing spotted leaves and destroying wilted plants.

A. wilkesiana (Copper-leaf) is a shrub to 15 ft. with bronzy-green leaves, often variegated or margined with red, purple or copper. There are numerous varieties with variegated foliage.

hispida (Chenille-plant or Red-hot-cattail) is a shrub of about the same size with flowers red or purple in drooping spikes 1½ ft. long. Var. *alba* has cream-white flowers.

godseffiana, bushy and dense, has green leaves with white margin; they are sometimes cut or ragged in appearance.

ACANTHOLIMON (ak-an-thol'-i-mon). A genus of hardy, evergreen European and Asiatic perennials of the Plumbago Family, known as Prickly-thrift They are similar to the ordinary thrift (see STATICE) except that the leaves are much stiffer and sharp-pointed. The flowers are rose or white in tightly compressed heads or clusters. Excellent for the sunny rock garden, plants may be propagated by cuttings or layering.

A. venustum grows 8 in. high and the prickly leaves have a marked bloom. The flowers are rose or purple in racemes. It blooms from July to September when flowers are needed in the rock garden.

ACANTHOPANAX (ak-an-thop'-an-ax). Deciduous shrubs and trees from Asia, with ornamental foliage and prickly stems. The most striking in appearance is *A. ricinifolium,* a tall tree with large and handsome dark-green leaves, resembling those of the castor-bean. Flat clusters of white flowers are borne in summer, followed by small black fruits. *A. sieboldianum* (also known as *A. pentaphyllum* and *Aralia pentaphylla*) is a bushy shrub with slender, arching branches. It thrives in shady places and is sometimes used as a hedge plant. During May and June terminal leaves are frequently injured by the sucking of the four-lined plant bug (which see); they can be protected by using rotenone dusts.

ACANTHORHIZA (ah-kan-thoh-ry'-zah). A genus of fan-leaved palms native to Mexico and S. America and commonly known as Rootspine Palms. The fan-shaped leaves, cut into many segments, are bluish-green above and pale beneath, and the slender trunk is covered, especially toward the base, with a network of aerial roots which have hardened into dark-brown spines. The species most widely known, *A. mocinni,* a tree growing 30 ft. in its native habitat, has white or pink flowers, followed by clusters of small white fruits. It is frequently grown outdoors in S. Fla., and, as it will endure several degrees of frost, it could be used in the garden still farther N. It thrives in rich humus soil in a partially shaded spot. In the N. it is grown in the cool greenhouse or as a potted plant in the window. In either case shade it from direct sunlight,

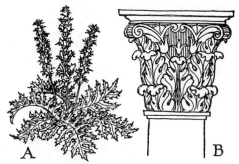

ACANTHUS IN NATURE AND IN ART
"Bears Breech" is the name that we give today to the Acanthus (A), whose decorative leaves provided the pattern for the capitals of the Corinthian columns (B).

water well, but never so much that water stands about the roots, and shift only when absolutely necessary. Repotting should be done only when the roots are active in spring or summer.

ACANTHUS (ah-kan'-thus). Bears breech. Perennial herbs or thistle-like small shrubs of the Old World about 3 ft. tall, with leaves from 12 to 24 in. long and 6 to 12 in. wide, and whitish, rose, or lilac flowers borne on spikes 18 in. long. They are semi-hardy, do best in rich, well-drained soil and full sunlight, and are especially useful for background plantings. Although semi-hardy, they need heavy winter protection in the N. Seed may be sown in late April; plants will flower in August. Propagation by division of the roots may be done in spring or early autumn. The more useful species are:

A. mollis. To 2 ft. tall, the spineless leaves 2 ft. long. Flowers rose, lilac or whitish. A pretty plant but somewhat tender. Var. *latifolius* is hardier, has even larger leaves, grows to 3 ft. and is much better for U.S. gardens.

montanus. Spiny leaves 1 ft. long. Rose-tinted flowers are borne on terminal spikes about 10 in. long.

spinosus. Flowers purplish, on dense spikes. The lobed leaves of this S. European species were the inspiration for important forms in early art, including the Greek Corinthian column.

ACAULESCENT. A term sometimes used to describe plants, flowers, etc., that are stemless or that have very short, not evident, stems. Compare CAULESCENT.

ACCENT PLANTS. Individuals planted singly or in small groups for emphasis in the garden picture. Usually kinds having marked characteristics of form or color are chosen, though any plant may become an accent when in strong contrast with its surroundings. Great discretion is needed to introduce an accent at the proper place and not to overdo the idea.

ACCENT PLANTS SERVE VARIOUS PURPOSES

Even in this little border planting, the light clump of alyssum marks a corner, the dark hollyhock spires against the house prevent monotony, and the tall red-cedar (or it might be a Lombardy poplar) rises at the far end to keep our eyes and attention from wandering.

Among trees the spire forms such as the Lombardy poplar, red-cedar, arborvitae, Lawson cypress, Italian cypress, upright Japanese yew, and, to a slightly less degree, the ginkgo, are notable for use as accents. Yet an accent is not necessarily the exclamation point which these forms contribute to the landscape, although it is true that similar forms among flowers furnish effective emphasis. Hollyhocks, foxgloves, delphiniums, yuccas, lupines, false dragonhead, red-hot poker and Kansas gayfeather are examples. But among the flowers useful for accent, color is as important as form; therefore it is not possible to limit the desirable kinds to any one shape, size, foliage type, or form of inflorescence.

An accent is needed in garden composition (a) to introduce life where the effect may otherwise be monotonous; (b) to em-phasize a change in the character of the planting, or in the grade or ground levels; (c) to draw attention to desirable vistas or other features; and (d) occasionally to neutralize the bad effect which some element which cannot be eliminated would otherwise produce.

ACER (ay'-ser). Important genus of hardy native and foreign trees valuable in woodlots as a source of timber and sugar and many species grown and planted for ornament and shade in grounds, parks and roadsides. See MAPLE.

A C E R A N T H U S (ay-ser-an'-thus). Hardy herbaceous perennials for semi-shady locations. See MAPLEWORT.

ACHENE (ay-keen'). A small, dry, hard, one-seeded fruit with no fissure or "valve" along which it opens. An example is the tiny seed of a strawberry, many of which are imbedded in the fleshy edible part that is actually the swollen receptacle of the flower.

ACHILLEA (ak-i-lee'-ah). Hardy herbaceous composite perennials known as Milfoil or Yarrow. They are easily recognizable by their bitterish, aromatic odor and taste, and their leaves and flowers have been used for centuries (and still are used in Europe) in medicines.

Easily grown in any good garden soil in a sunny location, the plants bear, from June to August or later, clusters of small white and yellow flowers excellent for cutting. If seeds are planted indoors in March or early April in leafmold, sand and garden soil well mixed and finely sifted, and set outdoors early in May, the plants will probably flower the first season. Seed may also be started outdoors in May and the plants set in their permanent places in September or October to blossom next year. They grow to a height of from 18 in. to 3 ft. and should be set about 1 ft. apart. They may also be propagated by root division. A handful of bonemeal around every plant in May will promote growth. Control rust and powdery mildew with sulphur dust. Plants showing the presence of Corticium stem rot (which see) should be destroyed.

A. ptarmica (Sneezewort) has white flowers and includes a popular, much grown double-flowered var., the Pearl, which makes plants 2 ft. high.

ageratum (Sweet Yarrow) bears yellow, pleasantly scented blossoms on more compact plants.

millefolium (Common Yarrow) has finely cut foliage and yellow flowers. Its var. *roseum* bears dense heads of rosy-pink flowers from July until late fall.

tomentosa, with woolly foliage, grows 10 in. to 12 in. and bears yellow flowers in July.

ACHIMENES (ah-kim'-e-neez). A genus of tropical American plants of the Gesneria Family grown in greenhouses for their showy flowers and occasionally planted out in the garden in the summer. They have thick tuberous roots and gloxinia-like flowers in red, white and violet. Propagated by division, or by cuttings.

A. longiflora (Trumpet Achimenes) has attractive, long-tubed violet flowers, each one growing from the axil of a leaf.

swainsoni is a horticultural (developed) form with pale-lavender spotted flowers.

ACHLYS (ak'-lis) *triphylla.* A Pacific Coast herb sometimes planted in rock gardens, etc. See DEERFOOT.

ACHRAS (ak'-ras) *zapota.* A large evergreen tree of tropical America where it is grown in frost-free regions for its edible fruit. Its common names are Marmalade-plum and Sapote, which see. Do not confuse it with another tree so closely related that it was formerly called by botanists *Achras sapota,* but which is now *Sapota achras,* the Sapodilla, which see.

ACIDANTHERA (as-id-an'thee-rah). A genus of tender summer-blooming herbaceous plants of the Iris Family native to tropical and S. Africa. One species, *A. bicolor,* is sometimes grown in gardens, being handled like the gladiolus or, where the season is too short for that, grown in pots or tubs outdoors over summer and brought indoors to bloom. The cream-colored long-tubed flowers with dark centers up to 2 in. across droop on short slender stalks from a 12 to 18 in. stem.

Propagation is by seeds or the numerous cormels that form about the gladiolus-like corm, which should be dried off promptly after the flowers have faded, whether grown indoors or in pots, as it is likely to rot if stored away moist.

ACID PHOSPHATE. A term sometimes used, but less than formerly, for the chief source of phosphoric acid in commercial fertilizers. Now called superphosphate (which see), it is made by treating phosphate rock with sulphuric; however, it does not cause soil acidity as the term might suggest.

ACID SOIL (and ACID-SOIL PLANTS). In addition to exhibiting differences in texture (or physical condition) and in fertility, soils may be either acid, neutral or alkaline. The degree of acidity or alkalinity has an important bearing on the health of many plants.

Acids and alkalis are opposite and if mixed together tend to neutralize each other, so that a combination may be neither acid nor alkaline, but neutral. A well-known acid (acetic) is that which gives sourness to vinegar; lime in its various forms is a familiar, mild alkali; caustic soda is a more powerful sort. Compounds containing both lime and the acetic acid of vinegar occur in soils, but acid soils contain more of carbonic, humic, tannic and other acids, many of which are complex and not yet well understood.

Where underlying rocks are quartz, granite, gneiss, mica schist, sandstone, shale or slate, the soil above or derived from them is usually acid, though sometimes shales and sandstones are neutral or moderately alkaline instead. The soil above limestone, marble or serpentine, on the contrary, is nearly always alkaline. Where drinking-water from shallow wells is "hard" expect the soil nearby to be alkaline. If this "hard" water is used in sprinkling, it may injure acid-soil plants.

The soil condition may be roughly guessed at from the kind of plants which grow naturally upon it; where acid-soil plants predominate, look for acid soil, while alkaline plants indicate soil-alkalinity. It is often said that where you find sheep-sorrel the soil is acid, but this weed is not a reliable indicator. Swamps are usually acid unless surrounded by limestone land. Poor sandy soils are often acid, also peat or muck soils.

To decide definitely whether a soil is acid, neutral, or alkaline, samples may be tested by the old litmus method, slips of red or blue litmus paper (obtainable at drug stores) being inserted in a slit made in a cupful of moistened soil. If the blue paper turns red, the soil is acid; if the red paper turns blue, the soil is alkaline; while if either paper turns purple it indicates a neutral condition. Much more satisfactory are compact testing sets sold at seed stores, which by means of a color chart, show the degree of acidity.

WHAT pH MEANS. Soil acidity is measured by what scientists call its *hydrogen ion concentration* and designated for convenience as pH. The scale reads from 1 to 14; 7 is neutral, and readings above that point show alkalinity, below it, acidity. Tests even more accurate than those of the testing sets may be had by sending soil samples to the State experiment station or agricultural college.

To make an alkaline or neutral soil acid, or to increase acidity in one already on the acid side, chemicals may be added, commonly aluminum sulphate, sulphur, or tannic acid. Aluminum sulphate should be used cautiously, not more than 5 lbs. per 100 sq. ft. at one application, spread evenly and watered in. Sulphur, also dangerous in excess, should be scattered at the rate of not more than 3 lbs. per 100 sq. ft. Tannic acid may be used rather liberally—1 part to 50 of water.

For ordinary gardening it is better and perfectly safe to use such acid materials as the following spaded into the soil and also as a mulch: Peat (peat moss), oak or pine leafmold, well-rotted hardwood sawdust, or pomace (dried pulp from cider mills), all applied as necessary.

It is not known for certain whether the demand of acid-soil plants is for acidity or for other soil conditions which go with acidity; until this important question has been decided, natural acid materials such as those just specified should be supplied to their soil rather than chemical acids. The type of soil desired by such plants is loose, light, moist and largely organic, and rich in thoroughly decayed leaves, wood and other vegetable substances. The acid-forming materials should be dug into the soil in quantities depending on its original nature; poor ground where the topsoil has been removed requires at least an equal bulk of peat or leafmold to give it a proper consistency or friability, while a rich, light topsoil needs only enough added to create distinct acidity. One part each of peat, leafmold and sand mixed make an excellent soil for acid-soil plants in pots or as a bed.

When making an acid-soil bed on strongly alkaline soil (that testing pH 8 or more), the peat and other materials should not be dug in or placed in a hole, but incorporated in a raised bed on top of the natural soil; more acid material should frequently be added as a mulch to maintain the acidity. Unless the bed is kept raised, the natural "sweetness" of the surrounding soil will encroach upon it. If the local water is alkaline, such beds should be sprinkled only with collected rain water, which is always acid.

ACID-SOIL PLANTS

Lists of plants requiring acid soil have been published from time to time, but are often contradictory. Most plants grow equally well in neutral, mildly alkaline, or mildly acid soils, varying from 6 to 8 pH readings, or even 5 to 9. With these we are not now concerned. Real acid-soil plants prefer a soil that tests not over 6.5, and thrive best at a pH of 4 to 6. Acidity below pH4 is too extreme even for most acid-soil plants.

Plants which seem to need a decidedly acid soil include:

Andromeda	Lupine
Azalea	Lily
Baptisia	Magnolia
Bayberry	Marigold
Blackberry	Mountain-laurel
Blueberry	New-Jersey-tea
Butterfly-weed	Oak
Cardinal-flower	Orchid
Chrysanthemum	Pieris
Cranberry	Pine
Dutchmans Breeches	Platycodon
Fir	Radish
Flax	Raspberry
Galax	Rhododendron
Ground-pine	Sourwood
Heath	Sweet-fern
Heather	Sweet Pepperbush
Hemlock Spruce	Spicebush
Hickory	Spruce
Huckleberry	Swamp Ferns
Lady-slipper	Trailing Arbutus
Leather-leaf	Wintergreen
Ledum	Yew
Leucothoë	

Most extreme in their demand for acid soil, and most frequently injured by alkalinity, are plants of the Heath Family, especially Rhododendrons. Injury often follows their use as foundation-planting material. House builders are likely to throw at the base of the wall and cover with earth pieces of lime, concrete, mortar, stucco and plaster, all of which are poisonous to acid-soil plants. Even evergreens of the Pine Family, most of which prefer mildly acid soil, are often harmed and even killed by such alkaline materials. Consequently, before planting any acid-soil plant near the foundation, dig out all filled earth and either reject it or screen it to remove the débris. If the wall is concrete, stucco, brick, or stone with mortared joints, the drip from it will cause the soil close by to become gradually alkaline. To prevent this, keep the planting well forward from the wall, use peat or leafmold frequently, and water often; or strew aluminum-sulphate close to the wall.

Signs of alkaline poisoning in acid-soil plants are: drooping, yellowing and falling of leaves; lack of root development; poor health not otherwise explainable. If emergency measures are called for, water with a solution of 1 part commercial tannic acid to 50 parts water. Also never use lime, bonemeal or chemical fertilizers on acid-soil plants, except fertilizers known to contribute to acidity, as sulphate of potash, ferrous-sulphate or superphosphate. Even these should be used with caution.

See also ALKALINE SOIL; NEUTRAL SOIL.

ACONITE (ak'-oh-nyt). Genus Aconitum. Herbaceous perennials of the Buttercup Family that derive their common name, Monkshood, from the characteristic hooded or helmet-shaped sepals of the large showy flowers, usually blue. Roots (and sometimes flowers) contain violent poisons and therefore should not be placed in the mouth; nor should plants be grown near the vegetable garden. The best-known (and most poisonous) species is the European *A. napellus,* which yields the drug aconite. (See illustration, Plate 39.)

Seed (which germinates slowly) may be sown outdoors in rich soil and partial shade in May or June or it may be started indoors in March or April, though the plants do better if not moved. When well up they should be thinned to stand 18 in. apart. Bought plants should go into the garden in May or September and if transplanting is done it should be done in September or October, enriching the soil with bonemeal.

Flowers, blue or white, borne in July, August and September of the second year on plants that attain heights of 3 to 6 ft., are excellent for cutting. The plants do best under trees or in other semi-shaded locations, though they sometimes do well in rear borders, forming bushy clumps. Feed with bonemeal dug carefully in around the plants once every six weeks as well as when setting out. Tall, slender varieties of the Fischeri group require staking.

ENEMIES. Sudden wilting of plants may be due to crown rot (which see) or to the Verticillium wilt (recognized by brown or black streaks seen in the tissues when a stem is cut slantwise). In either case remove diseased plants with the soil around their roots and burn them. Then drench the area from which they were taken with a 1-1000 solution of corrosive sublimate. Dust with sulphur to control powdery mildew beginning when the disease first appears. A drying of the lower leaves seen in many plants is apparently a physiological symptom due to hot dry summers and too-exposed locations. The cyclamen mite blackens and distorts the buds. See also Enemies under DELPHINIUM.

Propagation is by seeds, as noted, or by divisions of the thickened, tuberous roots. Among the more important species are:

A. anthora (*A. pyrenaicum*) (Pyrenees Monkshood). It has pale yellow flowers, with rounded helmets produced into short beaks. Var. *aureum* has deeper yellow flowers.

fischeri. To 6 ft.; flowers blue or white, with helmets as wide as they are long produced into spur-like visors. This group is extremely variable and includes many named garden sorts.

napellus. To 4 ft.; blue flowers with wide helmets and beak-like visors. Var. *album* has white flowers and var. *bicolor* blue and white blossoms.

uncinatum. To 5 ft.; native from Pa. to Wis. and La. Partially climbing; flowers blue with decurved beaks.

The plant called Winter-aconite is really Eranthis, which see.

ACORUS (ak'-oh-rus). The name of a few, hardy, swamp-loving herbs of the Arum Family. They have slender, grassy leaves and inconspicuous, greenish flowers on a thick spike (*spadix*) partly surrounded by a bract (*spathe*). They are often planted in the bog garden and are increased by division. *A. calamus,* the Sweet Flag, grows as high as 6 ft. with attractive, long, narrow foliage and a spadix 4 in. long. The roots are dug by country people and boiled in syrup to make a spicy candy.

A. gramineus and its var. *variegatus* are much smaller plants and are often used in hanging baskets, in the rock garden, and for cutting. They are sometimes grown as house plants.

ACROCLINIUM (ak-roh-klin'-i-um). The seedsmen's name for an annual plant bearing white to deep-rose flowers of the "everlasting" type, now called by botanists Helipterum, which see.

ACROCOMIA (a-kroh-koh'-mi-ah). A genus of the palm trees of tropical America, characterized by handsome crowns of feathery leaves, and tall, sometimes swollen trunks often covered with sharp-pointed spines. Some of the species are grown in Calif. and Fla. *A. aculeata* (Grugru or Groo-groo Palm), a W. Indian species often sold in this country as *A. sclerocarpa,* grows to 40 ft. and has leaves to 10 or more ft. long with 2 to 3 ft. leaflets, dark green above, and whitish beneath. The nuts hang in long clusters and yield an oil used for making toilet soap.

A. mexicana (Coyol Palm) has a brown, woolly trunk, covered with long prickles, and at the summit a regally handsome, symmetrical crown of foliage. It is frequently grown in Calif., but is tender and should not be exposed to frost or cold winds.

A. totai, from S. America, has a trunk to 30 ft., at first covered with sharp spines, but later, because of the dropping of the leaf-stalks, almost smooth. It is surmounted by a decorative crown of bluish-green leaves. Widely grown in Fla., this species is hardy as far N. as Jacksonville. Plant in a protected position and, to produce fine specimens quickly, feed frequently, always giving a mulch of well-rotted manure during the rainy season.

See also PALM.

ACROSTICHUM (a-kros'-ti-kum). A genus of ferns (which see), chiefly tropical and including many diverse forms, all having the fruit dots spread over the entire under surface of the upper part of the fertile fronds, occasionally on the upper surface as well. All require much moisture at the roots, fibrous compost, and greenhouse conditions. Principal species are:

A. aureum. Erect, bright green, 4 to 6 ft., fronds once-pinnate, the pinnae stalked. Suitable for warm temperatures.

canaliculatum. A climbing form, the rhizomes with spiny scales and the 3 to 4 ft. fronds glossy, dark, 3-pinnate. Excellent for clothing the stump of a dead tree-fern or any foundation of bark.

crinitum (Elephants Ear Fern). A handsome form with broad, entire, leathery, dull-green blades, 1 to 2 ft. long, covered with black hairs. Needs careful watering to prevent leaf-spotting, hence a small pot is desirable.

nicotianae folium. One of the easiest to grow, it has glossy 2 to 5 ft. fronds, once-pinnate and with a long terminal segment, growing from a woody rhizome.

peltatum. A dwarf form for warm conditions. The leathery sterile fronds 3 to 6 ins. tall are compoundly forked, and the fertile fronds contracted into broad disks 1 in. in diameter. Very decorative and of easy culture.

scandens. A graceful, drooping form, with 2 to 3½ ft. fronds, once-pinnate, the pinnae waved and sometimes eared.

ACTAEA (ak-tee'-ah). A few species of herbaceous perennials of the Buttercup Family commonly called Baneberry, Cohosh or Actea. The small white flowers borne in showy terminal clusters in spring develop into bright-colored or white berries in summer and fall. Growing to a height of 2 ft. the plants are admirably adapted to rockeries, wild gardens or borders; they are vigorous growers in shady locations. Seed may be sown in late fall or spring. Propagation generally is by root division in spring. The popular species for gardens are: *alba* (White Baneberry) with white berries; *rubra,* with red berries; and *spicata* (Herb Christopher), with flowers white or bluish and berries of purplish-black.

ACTINIDIA (ak-ti-nid'-i-ah). Deciduous climbing shrubs of twining habit and vigorous growth. Several of the species thrive in northern gardens. They grow well in good garden soil and are equally at home in sun or partial shade. Well adapted to clothe arbors and pergolas, to be trained on a wall, or to trail up a tree. Propagation is by seeds, cuttings and layers.

PRINCIPAL SPECIES

A. arguta grows to more than 50 ft. Attractive large green leaves and small clusters of whitish flowers. Bears edible fruit resembling a gooseberry, but not all plants fruit as some have flowers of one sex only.

chinensis. The most handsome, but not reliably hardy in the North. Red hairs clothe the branches when young, and it bears the largest flowers and fruit.

kolomikta, to 18 ft., is the shortest grower. The male plant is handsome with pink and white variegated leaves.

polygama (Silver-vine). As it attracts cats, this species may need protection from

Upper left: The early spring flowering shadbush (Amelanchier canadensis). Upper right: The ever-useful rose-of-sharon or shrub-althea (Hibiscus syriacus). Insert: the lily-of-the-valley-like flowers of one of the andromedas (Zenobia pulverulenta). Bottom: The splendor of a spreading shrubby azalea.

their attentions. Young leaves of male plant are silvery.

ACUMINATE. A term applied to leaves that taper to a long, slender tip; often called *attenuate.* The leaf of *Celtis occidentalis,* the hackberry, is described as *long-acuminate.*

ACUTE. Sharp; said of a leaf (as of the chestnut) that ends decisively in a point, the apex forming an angle of less than 90 deg. Compare ACUMINATE.

ADAM - AND - EVE. One common name for *Aplectrum hyemale,* a small, terrestrial orchid bearing dull-yellowish flowers in a raceme in May or June.

ADAMS NEEDLE. Common name for *Yucca filamentosa,* with its needle-pointed leaves from the edges of which hang curly thread-like fibres. See YUCCA.

ADDERS TONGUE. An early spring bulbous plant of the Lily Family, also known as dog-tooth violet. See ERYTHRO-NIUM.

ADDERS TONGUE FAMILY. Common name of the *Ophioglossaceae,* a family of ferns sometimes planted as curiosities.

ADDERS TONGUE FERN. Common name for *Ophioglossum,* a genus of ferns native throughout most of U. S. and a possible, though somewhat difficult, subject for garden or terrarium. From a brief fleshy rootstock arises an erect, entire, ovate-or-kidney-shaped sterile blade, and a taller fertile blade altered into a naked stipe terminating in a narrow cylindrical fruiting spike formed of two rows of naked spore clusters. The common species, *O. vulgatum,* 2 to 12 ins. high, with a sterile blade attached halfway on the fruiting stalk, grows in moist pastures and meadows, rarely on dry slopes, and because of its size is difficult to locate; not recommended except for experienced fern growers. Needs damp, heavy soil and half-shade, preferably with low-growing wild flowers. *O. vulgatum minus,* a smaller, N. E. variety, does better in sandy soil.

ADELIA (a-dee'-li-ah). Former name of a genus of deciduous and evergreen ornamental shrubs or trees belonging to the Olive Family, now called Forestiera, which see.

ADENANDRA (a-den-an'-drah). Small, tender, evergreen shrubs belonging to the Rue Family, natives of the Cape of Good Hope region of S. Africa. Of the 20 or more species known, some are found in large greenhouse collections. *A. fragrans* (Breath of Heaven) is grown in Calif.; and the species *A. amoena* (with flowers white above, red below), *coriacea* (pink), and *umbellata* (pink, fringed) are occasionally found in botanical gardens where they are wintered under glass and grown outdoors in summer. Propagation is by cuttings of half-ripened wood, rooted in a fibrous loam.

ADENANTHERA (a-den-an-thee'-rah). A genus of evergreen tropical trees of the Pea Family commonly known as Bead-trees. They have compound leaves and slender clusters of white or yellow flowers followed by narrow pods of brightly colored seeds. *A. pavonina* (Red Sandalwood Tree or Peacock Flower-Fence) grows to a large size in the tropics. It is frequently grown in the open in the far S. and sometimes in greenhouses in the N. principally because of the interesting bright-red lens-shaped seeds borne in the 7 in. pods. They are sometimes called "Circassian seeds" and used for beads in necklaces.

ADENOCALYMMA (a-den-oh-kal'-i-mah). S. American, mostly Brazilian, shrubby climbers related to the Bignonia with more than 50 species. The orange or yellow flowers are large and trumpet-shaped, with five lobes; they are followed by long, woody seedpods. In temperate climates plants are grown in moist greenhouses and propagated by cuttings rooted in a mixture of sand and peat in a frame.

ADENOCARPUS (a-den-oh-kahr'-pus). Small deciduous or evergreen shrubs of the Pea Family, from warm temperate countries. They are sometimes grown in a cool greenhouse; outdoors only where frosts are not severe.

Their habit of growth is somewhat spreading. They require a light well-drained soil and a sunny location. The yellow pea-like flowers are borne in terminal racemes, followed by glandular pods

A. decorticans is perhaps the best-known species. It is not unlike the Gorse (see ULEX) but is spineless.

ADENOPHORA (ad-e-nof'-oh-rah). A genus of perennial herbs of the Campanulaceae or Bellflower Family. Called Ladybells and very similar to the Campanulas, they are but little known in U. S. gardens. The flowers are bell-shaped, blue, nodding, in erect panicles, or in racemes. They are propagated by cuttings or seeds as they resent disturbance of their roots when well established. *A. lilifolia* grows 3 ft. high. The flowers are pale blue, 1¼ in. long, fragrant and borne freely in late summer.

ADENOSTOMA (a-den-os'-toh-mah). Evergreen shrubs of Calif., belonging to the Rose Family, but of heath-like appearance. Only two species are described. Both have white flowers in terminal racemes, and make a handsome appearance when in bloom.

A. fasciculatum, the hardiest, is said to withstand several degrees of frost. *A. sparsifolium,* found in Lower Calif., sometimes grows into a small tree.

ADIANTUM (a-di-an'-tum). Maidenhair. A genus of ferns (which see) of widespread distribution, including some hardy species of temperate zones, and even more tender species from the tropics, especially the W. Indies. Distinguished by their wedge-shaped, stalked pinnules which bear the fruit dots under brief reflexed marginal segments. The root stems creep just below the surface; the fronds are usually forked, and the stipes and main branches shiny brown-black or purplish, and wiry.

The clean-cut delicacy and distinctive form of the Maidenhair has long made it one of the most popular plants in cultivation, both the native forms of American woods, and the tender species, with their horticultural varieties, which are among the staples of the florist both for pot culture and for use with cut flowers. Some of these have streaked and variously colored fronds, others often produce crested forms.

Hardy sorts respond readily to careful cultivation; they grow in moist woods, prefer limestone, and require half-shade, good drainage and a little fibre. Avoid acid conditions, such as soil under oaks and conifers. Do not water directly on the fronds. Protect with leaf cover in winter. Dust with hellebore if attacked by slugs or canker worms.

Greenhouse specimens require leafmold, dislike peat moss, and are vitally dependent upon a careful and regular watering, rest in summer, and a warm, moist atmosphere.

Species

A. aethiopicum. From S. California with 1 to 1½ ft. fronds, 3 to 4 pinnate.

capillus-veneris (Southern Maidenhair; Venus-Hair Fern). Widely distributed throughout the world, this species includes numerous varieties. A luxuriant and familiar fern in the far S., it clothes the old gate of St. Augustine, Fla., and lines the moat of Fort Marion and is common N. to Va. Fronds 1 to 2 ft. long simply-pinnate above, with pinnules smooth and incised, rise from running rhizomes that firmly attach themselves to any material at hand. It is more of a rock plant than the N. species, and is usually pendent on dripping shaded cliffs; hence fine for shaded damp places in S. rockeries, especially walls. Protect in winter except in Far S. Greenhouse varieties will grow much larger but small specimens are good for terraria, needing warm, moist air, shade and a temperature of 50 to 60 deg. Var. *daphnites* has erect 8 to 12 in. fronds, dull green, the terminal pinnules larger, crisped and waved. Var. *imbricatum,* a dwarf, barren form good for terraria.

caudatum. Pendent fronds to 1½ ft. long, are tip-rooting, once pinnate, not forking, gray-green. Var. *edgeworthi* is smooth, bright green, ideal for baskets.

concinnum. With twice-pinnate fronds (except at tapering tip) it is highly decorative.

cuneatum (Delta Maidenhair). Exotic from Brazil, this is an old favorite, a standard for the greenhouse, and the best tender sort for dwellings. Fronds are 1 to 2 ft., 3 to 4 pinnate. There are many varieties as: *gracillimum,* with minute leaflets; *grandiceps,* tasseled; *lawsonianum,* with scattered, narrow pinnules.

diaphanum. Erect, 6 to 10 in., delicate textured, branched at base of blade. Ex-

AN ADIANTUM FERN FOR INDOORS
This tender form of Maidenhair (A. cuneatum) makes a pretty pot plant and the cut fronds are decorative.

A HARDY NATIVE ADIANTUM
The American Maidenhair (A. pedatum) is a fine
subject for a shady spot in the wild garden.

cellent for edging greenhouse benches or
beds.

farleyense. From Barbados and perhaps
the handsomest of all. Has broad, massive, drooping, 2 to 3 ft. fronds, 4-pinnate;
likes abundant light; pinnules are pink-margined when young.

formosum. Erect, branching, 1½ to 3
ft., 4-pinnate, with pinnules oblique. Of
easy cultivation under glass; reproduces
freely.

jordani (California Maidenhair). Native in S. W. States, like *A. capillus-veneris* and requires same care.

pedatum (Northern Maidenhair). Sometimes called "American Maidenhair" to
distinguish it from the European species,
which corresponds to our S. Maidenhair.
Native and hardy throughout U. S. except
in far S. and in prairies; rarer in far W.
Fronds 1 to 2 ft., branching at summit of
stipe, recurved branches bearing several
slender pinnae on upper side; pinnules cleft
on outer margin.

tenerum (N. American Brittle Fern).
Fronds 3 to 4 ft., 3 to 4 pinnate, brilliant
green; pinnules black-stalked. Native in
deep South, excellent for greenhouse.

tinctum. A dwarf from Peru, 6 to 9
in. with narrow, 2-pinnate fronds rosy red
when young.

venustum. Dwarf, hardier than the last;
one of the best for terraria.

ADLUMIA (ad-leum′-i-ah). A hardy
biennial vine, native in E. N. America. *A.
fungosa* (formerly known as *A. cirrhosa*)
is known as Allegheny Vine, which see.

ADNATE. A term applied to unlike
structures closely united to form what appears to be a single part or organ; the

ovary of the apple flower is said to be
adnate to the calyx-tube within which it
is buried.

ADOBE (ah-doh′-bay) **LILY.** Common name for *Fritillaria pluriflora,* a pinkish-purple-flowered bulbous plant of the
Lily Family, native to California.

ADOBE SOIL. A type of soil found in
the arid regions of Texas, Mexico and
Central America. It is of a clayey nature
and its origin has been largely due to wind
action. Both the physical and the chemical properties of adobe combine to give it,
in general, a high agricultural value if
rightly handled and supplied with sufficient
moisture. Because it can be "puddled" and
baked hard, it is also used to make a type
of brick from which small buildings are
made. See also SOIL.

ADONIS (ah-doh′-nis). Pheasants-eye. Annual and perennial herbs from
temperate Europe and Asia, named after
the youthful hunter of mythology beloved
by Aphrodite. Both kinds prefer light,
sandy soil.

The annual type is hardy and grows
well under trees or in other shaded locations. The foliage is dark green and finely
cut, and the terminal flowers, solitary crimson or scarlet with a dark-colored base,
appear in May or June. Plants grow about
1 ft. tall and are good for border use.
Seeds may be sown outdoors in late April,
or started indoors or in frames a month
earlier.

The perennial Adonis is also desirable as
a border plant, growing a foot tall and
producing large yellow flowers in May or
June. It may be grown from seed sown
in spring or fall; or the roots may be
divided in spring.

Of the half-dozen or more species, the
more popular are:

A. aestivalis (Summer Adonis). Annual.
Bears scarlet flowers from June to August.

autumnalis (Autumn or Flos Adonis).
Annual. Small crimson flowers with dark
centers from May through July.

vernalis (Spring Adonis). Perennial.
Delicate foliage and yellow flowers in May
or June.

ADVENTITIOUS. A term applied to
a plant part or organ that appears otherwise than in its regular position, such as
a bud arising from a root, a leaf or the
trunk of a tree. Less commonly it means
a foreign plant that has been introduced
but has not become naturalized.

AECHMEA (ek-mee'-ah). Highly ornamental South American herbaceous epiphytes (air plants) belonging to the Pineapple Family (Bromeliaceae). About 60 species are known, of which perhaps 10 are occasionally found in greenhouse collections. They are grown like Bromelias (which see) in a soil rich in sphagnum moss and old roots of ferns, or other similar fibrous material. They require abundant water in the summer—their growing season. The flowers are produced in the spring, at which time the tops of the plants should not be wet.

AEGOPODIUM (ee-goh-poh'-di-um). Fast-growing weedy, perennial herbs of the Parsley Family, natives of Eurasia. They have creeping rootstocks, much-divided leaves and very small white or yellow flowers clustered in umbels. Weedy in growth, they are easily increased by division of the roots. *A. podagraria* (Goutweed or Bishops-weed) has white flowers and grows 14 in. high. Its var. *variegatum* has leaves margined with white and makes mats of attractive foliage. It will grow in shady places by buildings or in soil too poor for other plants. It is often found naturalized in eastern U. S.

AEONIUM (ee-oh'-ni-um). A genus of shrubby, succulent, flowering plants with woody stems, belonging to the Houseleek Family (Crassulaceae) and natives of Morocco, Madeira and the Canary Islands. Of the 10 or more species recognized, some are grown in the open in S. Calif. In colder regions they make interesting greenhouse subjects with flowers mostly yellow but sometimes orange, pink, or red. They should receive the same treatment as Sempervivum, which see.

AERATION. The healthy growth of plants is dependent to a considerable degree on the aeration or air-content and circulation of air in the soil. While soil may appear solid and compact, actually, unless it is waterlogged, there is air in the myriads of tiny spaces between the soil particles. This air is one of the sources of the oxygen that plants must have. Also, by supporting certain kinds of bacteria, it facilitates the formation of nitrates and thereby renders the other fertilizing constituents of the soil more easily soluble.

To insure good aeration there must be proper drainage, so that excess water can pass through freely and allow fresh air to enter. Cultivation and the maintenance of a loose, friable condition also helps.

In general, a light sandy soil is likely to be better aerated than a heavy, stiff clay soil. See also SOIL.

AERIDES (ee'-ri-deez). A beautiful genus of tropical evergreen epiphytal orchids, much admired for their beautifully arranged, curving, leathery leaves, and the long graceful spikes of sweetly scented, soft-colored flowers. They closely resemble those of another genus (Gastrochilus or Saccolabium) but are distinct in the form of the flower. This has a long stem to the column to which the base of the "lip" is fixed, so as to form a spur underneath, at the back. The numerous species and varieties are natives to India, Eastern Asia, Malay Archipelago and Japan. *A. odoratum* is one of the best free flowering sorts. See also ORCHID.

AESCULUS (es'-keu-lus). The Horsechestnut or Buckeye. Deciduous trees or large shrubs ornamental in leaf; conspicuous panicles of flowers, and large spiny fruit burs. Of fairly rapid growth; most of the 20-odd species are hardy. See HORSECHESTNUT.

AETHIONEMA (ee-thi-o-nee'-mah). A genus of dwarf, sometimes woody, herbs, of the Mustard Family. Commonly known as Stone-cress, they include annual, biennial and perennial species. They are closely related to the perennial candytuft and have similar little 4-petaled flowers usually in charming shades of pink, lilac or purple, occasionally white, and very seldom yellow. Less well known than the candytufts, they are really superior to them for cut flowers, lasting much longer in water. They have small, narrow leaves, often with a bloom, and as they are natives of hot dry countries, they enjoy a sandy, gritty soil in a sunny position in the rock garden, in a dry wall facing south, or along the edge of the border. The perennials are increased by cuttings and division in the summer and by seeds in the spring. The annuals and biennials are increased by seed. Old· plants are hard to transplant, but if given good drainage will grow bravely for many years.

All the following useful species are perennial:

A. armenum is excellent to place in rock crevices. It grows but 3 or 4 in. high and has blue-gray foliage and veined pink flowers in rounded heads.

grandiflorum (Persian Stone-cress). Grows 1 ft. high and has 1 ft. long slender branches that lie among the rocks. The handsome rose-colored flowers grow in racemes at the ends of the branches. It is one of the best species for both the rock garden and dry wall with a south exposure.

coridifolium (Lebanon Stone-cress). Has smaller, less showy, rosy-lilac flowers in shorter racemes. An excellent plant for edging the border.

pulchellum is very much like the preceding, but more branching and trailing in habit. The heads of pale-pink flowers appear early in the summer.

AFRICAN CHERRY-ORANGE. The genus Citropsis, Tropical African small, thorny trees belonging to the Rue Family (Rutaceae). They bear cherry-like clusters of small fruits of attractive odor and flavor, and may be grown as ornamental plants. However, their chief interest and possibilities are as stocks upon which some citrus fruits have been successfully budded. On the other hand, buds of the cherry-orange thrive on stocks of species of the genus Citrus, which see.

AFRICAN CORN FLAG. Common name for *Antholyza aethiopica,* a member of the Iris Family with red or yellow flowers in summer.

AFRICAN DAISY. Common name applied to two annuals of the Composite Family. One, with white and violet flowers, is *Arctotis stoechadifolia* (or *grandis*) from S. Africa; the other, with yellow flowers, is *Lonas inodora* from the Mediterranean region. The name is sometimes (though incorrectly) given to other S. African composites, particularly *Gerbera jamesoni* (Transvaal Daisy), the genus Dimorphotheca (Cape-marigold), and *Felicia amelloides* (Blue Daisy).

AFRICAN GOLDEN DAISY. Common name for some species of Dimorphotheca, a genus of S. African annual and perennial herbs, also known as Cape-marigold, which see.

AFRICAN-HOLLY. Common name in S. Calif. for *Solanum giganteum,* a prickly-leaved shrub growing to 25 ft.

AFRICAN LILY or LILY-OF-THE-NILE. Common names for *Agapanthus africanus,* a semi-hardy African herbaceous subject which forms rhizomes with thick fleshy roots. Growing to 3 ft., it is a popular plant for house decoration and cool

conservatories, grown in large pots or tubs; and for outdoors in warm sections. The large umbels of funnel-shaped bright-blue flowers appear above strap-shaped leaves. There are varieties with dark-blue, and also white, flowers and with striped foliage. Easily propagated by division of roots, plants can be allowed to bloom for several years without shifting if fed with liquid manure.

AFRICAN MARIGOLD. A common name for *Tagetes erecta,* a tall, sturdy type of Marigold, which see. The name reflects the former belief that the plant is native to Africa instead of Mexico, the true habitat of the genus.

AFRICAN VALERIAN (*Fedia cornucopiae*). An annual herbaceous plant native to the Mediterranean basin. Related to the common Corn-salad (Fetticus) of the kitchen garden, it, also, is sometimes eaten as a salad. Or it may be grown as an ornamental plant (as it is in European gardens) for its fine, though small, red flowers and shining foliage. See CORN-SALAD.

AFRICAN- or USAMBARA-VIOLET. Common names for *Saintpaulia ionantha,* a tropical African perennial with deep violet flowers suitable for greenhouse or window-box culture.

AGASTACHE (a-gas'-ta-kee). A group of tall, perennial North American herbs with the 4-sided stems and opposite leaves characteristic of the Mint Family. They are weedy plants of little beauty or interest, the flowers being small, yellowish, blue or purplish in spikes. Too coarse for the border, plants are occasionally used in the wild garden.

A. nepetoides, found from Que. to Ga. and Ark., grows 5 ft. high, and the wands or spikes of tiny greenish-yellow flowers are sometimes 1½ ft. long.

AGAVE (ah-gah'-ve). A genus containing many species of handsome plants with long, stiff evergreen leaves forming clumps or rosettes from which rise the tall, bare flower stems. They belong to the Amaryllis Family and are natives of warm arid and semi-arid regions of America. They are of great economic importance, rope being manufactured from the fibre, and food, beverages, soap and other products from the pulp. Some bloom annually, but most of them at much longer intervals and some species die after flowering. In the S. some kinds are planted as lawn specimens or about the foundations of houses, but only the species *A. americana* is common as a house or porch plant in the N. Agaves are variously propagated—by seed, from the bulbels formed in the flower clusters, from suckers, or by underground stems. The soil should be a mixture of sand and loam and thoroughly drained.

If anthracnose spots occur on the leaves, these should be removed and burned.

A. americana, called Century-plant, in the erroneous belief that it blooms only when 100 years old, has leaves sometimes 6 ft. long and a flower stalk up to 40 ft. high. As a matter of fact, it does not bloom until after it is 10 or more years old; it then dies, but new plants develop irom suckers at the base. The flowers, about 2½ in. across, are greenish and borne on many horizontal branches at the top of the stalk. (See illustration, Plate 50.) This species is often used as a potted specimen in the N., especially the var. *marginata* which has white-margined leaves.

Other interesting and economically interesting species are: *A. atrovirens,* or Pulque Agave, from which an alcoholic Mexican drink is made; *A. fourcroydes,* or Henequen, source of a Yucatan fibre; and, especially, *A. sisolana* or Sisal-hemp, whose habitat is unknown but which is extensively cultivated for its fibre largely used in rope making. Smaller species may be used in rock or desert gardens.

AGAVE CACTUS (*Leuchtenbergia principis*). A true Cactus, but showing features of the Agaves. Bearing striking, yellow flowers, it is a greenhouse plant requiring the same treatment as the Echinocactus, which see. It is propagated by offsets which should be well dried at the base, and potted in soil of broken brick and peaty loam; or seeds which must be sown as soon as ripe in shallow pans over heat.

AGERATUM (a-jer-ay'-tum). Flossflower. An attractive herbaceous annual grown from seed and also easily propagated by stem cuttings. One of the most popular summer-flowering plants grown from seed, it is covered with blossoms from early summer until frost and is excellent for borders, edgings or pots. The taller varieties are good for cutting, though most species, ranging from 3 in. to 10 in. tall, have stems too short for that purpose. Most varieties bear blue flowers, but white and pink are produced by some. The individual flowers, small in size and ball-shaped, last for a long time after being cut. While most of the common annuals are too spreading to permit them to be used in a small rockery, the dwarf forms of this Mexican plant are ideally adapted for such use and will give a quick effect at trifling cost. It is of the Composite Family.

For early flowering, seed should be started indoors in March or April and plants set out 9 to 12 in. apart in May. Seed may be sown outdoors in May, but the plants will not flower until August or later. The popularity of Ageratum is due not only to the profusion with which it bears flowers but also to the fact that rain does not fade or otherwise spoil the blossoms. After their season of bloom has ended, take up the smallest plants, cut them back severely and pot them up for the winter, placing them in the smallest pots available and setting these in a shady spot in the garden. The plants will take hold quickly and then may be brought indoors, where they will flower until the weather becomes dull.

In the greenhouse or home Ageratum is often infested with white fly, mealy bugs and red spider. Spray frequently with clear water or, if the pests become serious, use control measures given under GREENHOUSE PESTS. Pale-green caterpillars called leaf-tyers may attack plants both under glass and outdoors. Dusting with a mixture of arsenate of lead (1 part) and fine sulphur (4 parts) will kill the caterpillars and also prevent rust. Plants affected by Corticium stem rot (which see) should be removed and burned.

A. conyzoides, 1½ to 2 ft., bears blue or white flowers in heads ¼ in. across all summer long.

houstonianum (or *mexicanum*) has flowers mainly blue and larger than those of the preceding species. The dwarf var. *nanum* is especially adapted to rockeries.

The so-called Hardy- or Perennial-Ageratum is really Eupatorium, which see.

AGLAONEMA (ag-lah-oh-nee'-mah). An evergreen shrub of China and the East Indies with attractive sometimes variegated foliage. Small branches or rooted cuttings kept in water or wet soil make decorative house plants. See CHINESE EVERGREEN.

AGRICULTURAL LIME. A general term sometimes applied to standard hydrated or slaked lime (which see), but more often to a low grade commercial product of variable composition resulting from the grinding of unburned cores of lime kilns, mixed with more or less air- or water-slaked lime, etc. It may carry from 40 to 70% of calcium oxide, and its action may be slow or rapid depending upon the relative amounts of raw ground limestone and slaked lime it contains. When it can be obtained at a low price and applied rather heavily well in advance of a crop, it should prove a satisfactory and economical soil sweetener.

AGRICULTURE, DEPARTMENT OF. The large important administrative branch of the Federal Government called the U. S. Department of Agriculture touches the interests of the home gardener and renders valuable service in many ways that are not generally appreciated even if realized. Established in a small way in 1862, it has grown steadily in size, scope, activities and effect upon everyday garden operations. The information and help it offers is available to every citizen and those who fail to make the most of it have only themselves to blame.

The Department's work is of three main types—administrative or regulatory, investigational, and informational. It is carried on, under the direction of the Secretary of Agriculture (a cabinet officer) and various assistants, directors, legal officers, etc., by a number of subdivisions called in different cases Bureaus, Services or Administrations. Those that directly serve gardeners are the Bureaus of Chemistry and Soils, of Entomology and Plant Quarantine, of Home Economics, and of Plant Industry; the Forest Service, the Weather Bureau, and the Offices of the Directors of Extension Work and Information.

Less direct, but highly important, service to gardeners, as citizens, is rendered by such agencies as the Bureaus of Public Roads, Agricultural Engineering and Agricultural Economics, the Food and Drug, and Agricultural Adjustment Administrations, etc.

The work of the Bureaus ranges from purely scientific research, survey and analysis, to thoroughly practical application of the facts learned as to soils and their handling, plants and their cultivation, insects and diseases and their control, forest conservation and utilization, road building and maintenance, weather forecasting, and so on. Application and enforcement of plant quarantines, both foreign and domestic, with its inspections, permits and other regulatory requirements, is part of the work of the Bureau of Entomology and Plant Quarantine and, while there is considerable controversy regarding the need for and merits of certain orders or their administration, the protection afforded plantsmen against enemies is of unquestionable value.

The dissemination of the vast amount of information obtained by the Department is effected in many ways—through free publications and others for which nominal charge is made; through press releases; through regular weather and market reports; through motion pictures and radio broadcasts, and, by means of a close tie-up with State and local activities, through the Office of Experiment Stations and an army of county agents and other workers.

Gardeners should get to know the Department—through personal visits and contacts when possible, and through correspondence; they should apply to those Bureaus dealing with the matters that underlie their problems; they should frequently secure from the Office of Information current lists of free publications and from the Superintendent of Documents, Government Printing Office, Washington, D. C., price lists of bulletins, circulars, etc., for which a charge is made.

STATE DEPARTMENTS. Modeled somewhat after, and conducted more or less like, the Federal Department, are those of the several States. Located at the State capitols they restrict their activities in some cases to regulatory work leaving research and education to the State Experiment Stations and Agricultural Colleges. But most of them issue helpful publications and are usually prompt in rendering any help they can. They, too, are operated for the benefit and in the interests of citizens whose privilege and opportunity it is to make use of them.

AGRIMONY (ag'-ri-moh-ni). The common name for Agrimonia, a genus of European herbs of the Rose Family. The small flowers, in a loose cluster, with their 5 petals look like tiny single yellow roses. They are not showy flowers, but plants are occasionally grown in the herb garden because of their aromatic, astringent leaves used in making a tonic tea. They are easily increased by root division. *A. eupatoria* grows 2 to 3 ft. high in small clumps.

As the yellow petals fall the calyx forms a little green bur armed with hooked bristles.

AGROSTEMMA (ag-roh-stem'-ah). A small Old-World genus of herbs, one species (*A. githago*), a weedy but showy plant, being common in fields as Corn Cockle (which see), and sometimes grown in gardens.

AGROSTIS (ah-gros'-tis). A group of tufted annual and perennial grasses, widely distributed throughout the world. They include important lawn grasses, some ornamental garden subjects and also hay and pasture grasses. See BENT GRASS; LAWN; ORNAMENTAL GRASSES.

AILANTHUS (ay-lan'-thus). A genus of Asiatic trees, one of which (*A. altissima*), called Tree of Heaven, is widely planted and especially useful for city yards. It grows rapidly and may attain 60 ft.; is hardy, deciduous and of tropical appearance. The pinnate compound leaves (resembling those of Sumac) have an unpleasant odor when crushed but are little troubled by insects or disease and highly resistant to smoke and dust. The staminate flowers have a strong odor, offensive to some, so it is best to plant the female tree which bears large panicles of persistent red fruit. A high hedge may be made quickly by setting trees close together and topping them at the desired height each spring. Easily grown from seed, the Ailanthus frequently self-seeds so freely as to become a nuisance. It may also be propagated from root cuttings.

Although considered particularly healthy because of its ability to withstand city smoke and insect attacks, the Ailanthus is sometimes killed by Verticillium wilt (which see). Nectria canker and a Cercospora leaf spot may also occur.

AIR-LAYERING. A method of propagating certain woody plants by causing the formation of roots at some point along a tall erect stem which is then severed just below them so as to produce two shorter, stockier plants. Also called "pot-layering," it is a common and simple treatment for a rubber-plant (which see) that has become "leggy." The stem is notched or cut about a quarter through and a splinter of wood or small pebble is placed in the cut to keep it open. Then one of three things can be done: (1) A large handful of sphagnum moss placed about the stem at this point and bound in place with cord or raffia; (2) a 3- or 4-in. flowerpot split in half vertically, placed about the stem, filled with sphagnum, peat moss or light absorbent soil, and bound in place; or (3) a special layering-pot made with the slit in one side slid on to the stem and similarly filled and tied. With the material kept moist, roots will soon develop; when they are abundant, filling the sphagnum ball (or pot), the entire upper

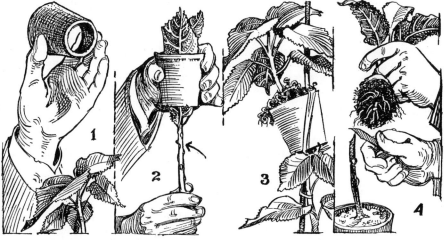

FOUR STEPS IN AIR-LAYERING A PLANT

1, Knock most of the bottom out of a 2½ or 3 in. pot. 2, Fold up the leaves of the tall "leggy" plant after notching the stem (see arrow) where roots are desired. 3, Place pot at that point. fill it with sphagnum or peat moss and tie it in place—a stake will help support it. 4. When roots fill the pot break and remove it, cut the new plant from the old stem and pot it up.

portion is cut away and treated as a new plant to replace the old one, unless the lower portion bears enough leaves and is sufficiently attractive also to be grown on. See also LAYERS AND LAYERING; PROPAGATION.

AIR PLANTS, or in scientific language *epiphytes* (of which the term is a direct translation or derivation), are specialized plants which fasten themselves upon the trunk or branches of another plant, usually a tree, drawing some of their subsistence from the air and, occasionally, rain. Some of them put out air-roots or scale-like organs to absorb air and moisture and various kinds are frequently grown as curiosities in the greenhouse. They are not parasites or saprophytes, which also attach themselves to other plants (live ones in the former case and dead ones in the latter) and live upon their sap and tissues respectively. In other words, air plants use other plants merely as supports whereby to reach a situation which assures sufficient air and light.

The epiphytes include representatives of the ferns, mosses, lichens, bromeliads and orchids, all of which see.

AIR - POTATO. Common name for *Dioscorea bulbifera,* a climbing plant of Asia and the Philippines, related to the sweet-potato (which see) and which develops tubers in the axils of its leaves. See DIOSCOREA.

AIZOACEAE (ay-y-zoh-ay'-see-ee). Botanical name of the Carpetweed Family, a group of low, usually fleshy, herbs and sub-shrubs widely distributed but principally in warm regions where they inhabit deserts and seashores. The family is of garden interest principally on account of a few useful plants, among them Tetragonia (New-Zealand spinach), a hot-weather pot-herb, and Mesembryanthemum, the best-known genus, prized for its fine flowers which open only in the sunshine. (*M. crystallinum* is the common ice-plant.) Aridaria, Conophytum, Dorotheanthus, and Oscularia, formerly classed under Mesembryanthemum, are other cultivated genera.

AJUGA (a-jeu'-gah). A group of annual and perennial herbs, used in rock gardens. See BUGLE.

AKEBIA (ah-kee'-bi-ah). Hardy deciduous or semi-evergreen twining shrubs from China and Japan. Their habit of growth is light and graceful and extends to about 12 ft. They appear to advantage on arbors and pergolas and are useful for clothing stumps, or sprawling over rocks. They will grow in any fairly good soil, and produce their dark-colored flowers in early spring. Male and female flowers are separate in the same cluster, the latter being larger, darker in color and opening first. The grayish-purple, sausage-shaped fruits are attractive but seldom seen. Apparently hand-pollination of the flowers is necessary to produce them. Sweet and pulpy, they are eaten in Japan; and the pliable stems are much used in wicker-work.

The best known species is *A. quinata,* with five-foliate leaves and chocolate-purple fragrant flowers. *A. trifoliata* (better known as *A. lobata*) has three leaflets and smaller flowers.

ALBIZZIA (al-biz'-i-ah). Small deciduous trees or shrubs, belonging to the Pea Family, closely allied to the Acacias. Being natives of tropical and subtropical regions, they can be grown outdoors only in the warmer parts of the U. S. One or two species are sometimes grown in greenhouses. They have graceful feathery foliage and clusters of tassel-like flowers, followed by strap-shaped dry pods. They are easily raised from seed under glass.

The three principal species are:

A. julibrissin (Silk-tree). Handsome tree, 30 to 40 ft., grown as far north as Washington, and some hardier forms to Boston. The flowers are pale pink. Var. *rosea,* with brighter-pink flowers, is dwarfer and hardier than the type.

lebbek is called Woman's-tongue-tree because of the rattling seed-pods. A common tree in the tropics, growing to 50 ft. with greenish-yellow flowers and pods a foot long.

lophantha, called Plumed-acacia, is naturalized in S. California and often seen in greenhouses. It has yellow flowers in short spikes.

ALBUCA (al-beu'kah). Greenhouse bulbs of the Lily Family, natives of the Cape of Good Hope region and allied to Ornithogallum, which see. About 20 species are known, and many hybrids have been produced. Blooming in the late spring or early summer, with large white or yellow flowers, they are grown in a compost of loam, peat and sand. The bulbs should be set deep in the pots and these kept in the dark until growth begins. Propagation is also by seeds or offsets taken in the spring.

ALCHEMILLA (al-ke-mil′-ah). A genus of herbs belonging to the Rose Family and commonly known as Ladys Mantle, which see.

ALDER. Common name for the genus Alnus. A member of the Birch Family, it includes some 20 species and numerous varieties of hardy, deciduous trees and tall shrubs. Associated with cool, temperate climates, they grow mostly in cool, moist or even wet soils. They are all decorative plants with attractive stems, foliage and flowers. The staminate catkins blossom very early in the spring; the pistillate catkins are woody, resembling small pine cones. In using alders we may take a lesson from nature in grouping plants suited to the same conditions. Intermingled with huckleberry, Cornus and sweet pepperbush, the Speckled Alder (*A. incana*) lines pond margins and makes colorful copses in grass-grown wet meadows. Its dense root system retains the banks of swift streams and makes it a friend and ally in landscaping such places. Where logs are needed to build walks or retaining edges in wet soil, alder may be used as it will not decay easily when continually wet.

Two species, *A. incana* and *A. maritima*, will grow in wet soil; both are bushy and may attain 25 ft. Others, which grow best in moist soil, are the native Green Alder (*A. crispa*), a shrub to 10 ft.; *cordata*, a round-headed tree to 50 ft. not hardy North; *rugosa*, the Smooth Alder, a hardy tree to 25 ft.; *vulgaris*, the Black Alder, an attractive tree to 70 ft., with many varieties showing interesting leaf forms, and *japonica*, a pyramidal form to 80 ft. conceded to be the most beautiful of all. In groups along the garden boundaries alders combine well with related trees such as birches, hornbeams and hazelnuts.

Propagation is by seeds gathered in the fall, kept dry and sowed in moist shady soil in the spring. The shrubby species grow from hard-wood cuttings and suckers, while the rarer varieties are grafted on potted seedlings indoors.

ENEMIES. Alders growing wild are generally infested with insects but grown as ornamentals they are rarely seriously injured. A lace bug may discolor the foliage and mites may cause galls on the leaves. Spraying with lead arsenate will keep the dark-blue flea-beetles from skeletonizing the leaves. Contact insecticides will kill the alder-blight aphids which form woolly masses on the stems. A leaf rust occurs in the West and a powdery mildew of the female catkins in the East. Deformed catkins are also sometimes caused by hypertrophying fungus; while these may not endanger the life of the plant, they should be removed, if only for esthetic purposes. Several other fungi cause leaf spots but do no great damage. The same blackrot that causes a canker of apple sometimes affects alder. See Enemies under APPLE.

ALETRIS (al′-ee-tris). A genus of herbs of the Lily Family, found from Me. to Ark. Small white or yellow flowers are borne on erect stems above clumps of grass-like foliage. Good for naturalistic plantings in moist, sunny locations. One of the plants called Star-grass, which see.

ALEXANDRIAN-LAUREL. Common name for *Danaë racemosa*, a hardy evergreen Asiatic shrub of the Lily Family, bearing red berries and sometimes planted for its ornamental effect. See DANAË.

ALFALFA or LUCERNE (*Medicago sativa*). A long-lived, perennial, leguminous forage plant with deeply penetrating roots. A native of the Old World, it is extensively grown for hay and pasture and sometimes as a cover crop on farms throughout the U. S. but especially in irrigated regions. It grows from 1 to 4 ft. high, bearing small divided leaves, small, purplish, clover-like flowers, and spiral pods. See also MEDICAGO.

ALFILARIA (al-fil-ah-ree′-ah). Redstem Filaree. A low-growing annual herb of S. Europe grown for forage and range pasture in the S. W. States. A species of Heronsbill or Erodium, which see.

ALGAE. Simple aquatic plants including the seaweeds and pondscums. They and the fungi make up the Thallophyta, or first great group of plants.

ALICES FERN. A local name for *Lygodium palmatum*, or the Climbing Fern.

ALISMA (ah-liz′-mah). A genus comprising two species of hardy aquatic perennial herbs of the Water-Plantain Family. Varying but slightly, both are used for planting along stream or pond margins or in bogs because of their decorative foliage and attractive bloom. The flowers are small, usually white although sometimes tinged with rose. The large, heart-shaped leaves, either floating or rising well above the water on long stalks, are effective. Propagated by root division or from seed.

ALKALINE SOIL (and Alkaline-soil Plants). Alkaline soil, the opposite of acid soil (which see) is usually found in limestone country and is associated with "hard" water. Extreme alkalinity, as found in the western "bad lands," is injurious to most plants. It follows lack of enough rain to wash away the alkali salts, and long-continued irrigation with hard water which, evaporating, leaves a constantly increasing accumulation of the salts. To discover whether a soil is alkaline or acid, tests should be made as described under acid soil; readings higher than pH 7 (there explained) show alkalinity. But a slight tendency in this direction is no disadvantage in gardening except where certain acid-loving plants are to be grown. In fact, it has long been customary to add lime to cultivated soils. See soil.

Much of such benefit comes from changes in soil texture and the release of mineral foods; but there is also an increase in pH reading, as the acid soil is made neutral or alkaline. Old, exhausted soil is usually acid (sour), and here lime is particularly valuable to increase fertility. Sometimes a soil is acid because it is not well drained, in which case ditching or underdraining will help neutralize the acidity. When peat, tree-leaves, leafmold, or other acid materials are used in growing alkaline-soil plants, lime, limestone or bonemeal should be added immediately in quantity sufficient to counteract the acidity.

Alkaline-soil Plants

Moderately alkaline soil favors the growth and productiveness of many garden plants; others prefer acidity or are apparently indifferent. The use of lime creates or increases alkalinity; but it must be renewed, as rains wash it away, allowing a naturally acid soil again to become acid. Clovers and other members of the Pea Family usually require an alkaline soil to aid the nitrogen-collecting bacteria in their roots. These and other alkaline-soil plants may become stunted, sickly and yellow or reddish in acid soil. They include:

Alyssum	Celery	Parsnip
Asparagus	Cucumber	Pea
Bean	Geum	Phlox
Beet	Iris	Rhubarb
Cabbage	Lettuce	Salsify
Carnation	Mignonette	Squash
Canteloupe	Nasturtium	Sweet Pea
Cauliflower	Onion	

ALKANET (al'-kah-net) or Alkanna. Name of a red dye made from the root of species of Anchusa and therefore applied also to the plant. Formerly a name for Puccoon (*Lithospermum canescens*), the roots of which were similarly used by the Indians. See anchusa.

ALKEKENGI (al-kee-ken'-ji). One of the common names for *Physalis alkekengi,* also called Strawberry-tomato, and Chinese Lantern Plant.

ALLAMANDA (al-ah-man'-dah). Shrubs or climbers from Brazil, grown in greenhouses in the N. and planted out by walls and fences in the far S. They belong to the Milkweed Family and have large yellow or showy purplish flowers followed (when grown outdoors) by large prickly fruits. Propagated by cuttings of new or old wood, the plants should be generously fed during the growing season (from late winter to autumn). They should then be kept nearly dry until February or March, cut back, watered, started into growth and repotted before the new shoots have made much headway.

A. cathartica (Common Allamanda) has golden-yellow flowers 3 in. across; in several varieties the flowers show various markings in their throats.

neriifolia (Oleander Allamanda) is lower growing, to 3 ft. and semi-erect.

ALL-AMERICA SELECTIONS. The name given to a plan, sponsored first by the Southern Seedsmen's Association in 1932 and, since 1933, by the American Seed Trade Association, for the registration, testing, scoring, and promotion through publicity, of new flower and vegetable varieties commonly grown from seed. It is governed by a Council (whose members also serve as judges) under a Constitution and By-laws which give the object as: "to encourage the development and distribution of new and better flowers and vegetables." The Council endeavors to obtain from all parts of the world seed of new, worthy varieties the season before their expected introduction. Samples of the seeds submitted are sent to 12 trial grounds in different parts of the U. S. to be planted under number, grown in open-field competition, judged, and scored. On the basis of the ratings given, the varieties are awarded gold medals, awards of merit, special mentions, or other recognition which is then featured in news stories released by the Council and in the advertising

of the introducers and distributors of the
seed. The Council also recommends a
minimum price at which seed of All-America
varieties should be sold during their
first season of general introduction.

In 1939, the idea was expanded to include
garden roses and an organization of
commercial rose plant growers was formed
to sponsor and conduct similar registration,
trial, scoring and recognition, except that,
for roses, the procedure covers two years.
W. Ray Hastings, Box 675, Harrisburg,
Pa., is chairman of both All-America organizations.

ALLEGHENY-SPURGE. A popular
name for *Pachysandra · procumbens,* a
perennial herb used as a ground cover in
shaded places.

ALLEGHENY VINE (*Adlumia fungosa*).
Known also as Climbing Fumitory
and Mountain Fringe. An attractive biennial
vine related to the Bleeding Heart. Of
frail and delicate appearance it clambers to
a height of 15 ft. It is tolerant of shade
and prefers a moist soil with protection
from wind. With delicately cut leaves and
a profusion of pale-pink flowers it makes a
charming picture, especially when draping
an old bush with its light festoons. Propagation
is by seeds, often self-sown.

ALLIGATOR-PEAR. A c o m m o n
(fruit-stand) name for the oily edible fruit
of *Persea americana,* the Avocado (which
see), and also sometimes applied to the tree
itself.

ALLIUM (al'-i-um). A genus of strong-smelling
bulbous herbs of the Lily Family
(including onions, leeks, chives, and their
relatives). Some 300 species are known in
north temperate regions, and about 70 of
these are cultivated, all in the open ground,
mostly as vegetables, but a few as ornamentals.
A few species of Asian origin are
treated as greenhouse plants. The hardy
varieties have flat or tubular leaves with
tapering tips and flowers at the end of
erect bare stems in spherical clusters or
slender spikes—the colors ranging from
white to yellow, and through pinks to
purple. Alliums require a rich, loamy soil.
They can be grown from seeds, offsets, or
small, aerial bulblets in the flower heads.
(See illustration, Plate 6.)

ALLOPLECTUS (al'-oh-plek-tus).
Tropical evergreen shrubby plants belonging
to the Gesneria Family. They do well
in the warm greenhouse under the same
cultural treatment as Gesnera, which see.

THE FLOWERING ALMOND
A shrub in full bloom in early spring, and a
branch of double flowers.

The leaves are opposite, one in each pair
being smaller than the other. The tubular
flowers are mostly red and yellow.

ALLSPICE. Common name for *Pimenta
officinalis,* an evergreen tree of tropical
America, and also its dried, unripe,
berry-like fruits used for flavoring. See
PIMENTA. Carolina-allspice is the common
name for *Calycanthus floridus,* a sweet-scented
shrub. See CALYCANTHUS.

ALLUVIAL. Water-formed. A term
applied to deposits of soil formed by the
action of water, whether in valleys and
river beds or on the site of ancient lakes.
Depending on the method of formation
they may be of loam, clay, gravel, etc.,
washed down from the higher grounds or
accumulated as sediment in still waters.
See also SOIL.

ALMOND. The name of two groups of
plants of the genus Prunus, one of value in
gardens, the other primarily an orchard or
commercial subject.

The garden or ornamental sorts are
small to medium-size shrubs that cover
themselves in early spring with pink or
white, single or double flowers about the
size of pompon or "button" chrysanthemums.
The commoner species are *P.
glandulosa* and *P. triloba; P. japonica* and
P. nana (the true dwarf almond) are not
often seen. Hardy as far north as Massachusetts,
the first-named thrives in any
well-drained soil but does best in sandy
loam. Grown on its own roots (that is,
not grafted), it becomes bushy and, even
under neglect, blooms profusely. If grafted
(usually on plum stock) two things must
be watched: shoots from the plum root,
which must be promptly removed; and
attacks by peach borers (which see).

These, entering the tree at or just below the ground, can soon weaken and may kill it. Grafted plants should therefore be carefully examined for signs of borer infestation before planting; if free, the point of graft union should be planted at least 6 in. deep to encourage the development of many stems from dormant buds of the almond. "Worming" of grafted plants (that is the killing of any borers that may enter later, by thrusting a pointed, flexible wire into their burrows) should thereafter be done annually in late fall. See PEACH.

The other almond species is *P.* (formerly *Amygdalus*) *communis,* a small, peach-like tree which produces the familiar thin-shelled nuts. These are really the pits of the small, peach-like but thin-fleshed, inedible fruits. Grown commercially in California, it is frequently planted elsewhere for its abundant, large pink flowers. Double varieties are even more popular, but are sterile. (See illustration, Plate 41.)

The Indian- or Tropical-almond is a plant of a different family, *Terminalia catappa* (which see).

ALNUS (al'-nus). Generic name of an important member of the Birch Family. See ALDER.

ALOCASIA (al-oh-kay'-zhi-ah). Tropical herbs of S. Asia and the East Indies. Belonging to the Arum Family, they are allied to Colocasia and to Caladium, both of which are sometimes called Elephants Ear. They are grown under glass for their ornamental foliage—the large, hanging green leaves being veined, spotted, and marbled with striking colorings and sometimes showing a metallic gloss. About 40 species are known, and, with the hybrids which have been developed, a collection of 100 or more kinds is possible. The species fall into two divisions, one evergreen, and the other herbaceous; the latter has a resting period each year, during which it sheds its leaves. They require a night temperature of not less than 60 deg. When active growth begins in March, abundant water should be given, and the temperature control set at 70 deg. (night) and 85 deg. (day).

The soil for the evergreen kinds is made up of two parts of fibrous peat and sphagnum moss and one part of chunks of fibrous loam with small broken charcoal intermixed. The herbaceous kinds require two parts of a good, fibrous loam with one part of old, well-rotted cow manure. Perfect

drainage is required, and on the surface of the pots holding the evergreen sorts sphagnum moss should be packed up conically around the stem. Propagation is by suckers or cuttings of the roots, planted in pots which are plunged in sand, with bottom heat. Seeds of new hybrids are sown in a bed kept at 75 deg.

ALOE (al'-oh). A genus of perennial succulent herbs, native to the Cape of Good Hope and belonging to the Lily Family. They should not be confused with the Agaves of America which they somewhat resemble. Their leaves are fleshy, stiff, and spiny along the edges, often large, and crowded together into a rude but picturesque rosette, making them attractive ornamental plants. The flowers, produced in irregular showy spikes, sometimes extending 20 ft. above the ground, are mostly of reddish shades, a few being yellow, orange, or whitish green. Upwards of 150 species and hybrids are recognized, many of which appear in large collections, but only a few are in common decorative or garden use.

The plants are grown in pots, in a sandy loam soil with a little peat and old manure added and some small chunks of old limemortar. As this is filled in about the roots, bits of broken bricks are added, the coarser pieces being placed at the bottom. The soil must be compactly rammed snugly about the roots. Unless active growth is evident, very little water is given and plants should remain in the same pots and soil for several years. Propagation is by suckers, cuttings or sprouts at the base of leaves, or seeds.

Water-aloe is a name sometimes given to *Stratiotes aloides,* the Water Soldier, which see.

ALONSOA (al-on-soh'-ah). A genus of herbs and small shrubs of the Figwort Family (Scrophulariaceae). Native to tropical America, they are grown in the garden as annuals and also indoors. Known as MASK-FLOWER, which see.

ALOYSIA (al-oh-i'-si-ah) *citriodora.* Former botanical name for Lemon-verbena, which is now included in the genus Lippia, which see.

ALPINE-AZALEA (ah-zay'-le-ah). A procumbent, evergreen, shrubby mountain plant with glossy foliage. See LOISELEURIA.

ALPINE PLANTS. In American gardening this means not strictly plants native to the Alps, but rather those kinds which grow naturally on the rocky slopes above the mountain meadows at timber-line or higher. Here the growing season is very short (100 to 120 days) and the winters are long and cold with a profuse fall of snow which affords ample winter protection. During the short summer the plants are exposed to brilliant sunlight, but the nights are cold, and the roots are kept constantly supplied with ice-cold water from the melting snows above. They are generally of miniature growth and often shrubby; many are perennial, though there are a few attractive annuals. They often make brilliant displays of color, as one species sometimes covers a wide area of ground, blooming profusely through the short season.

From among the alpines come our choicest rock-garden subjects, although the true alpine garden is only a special form of rock garden, perhaps forming a part of a rock garden and differing from the rest because it is usually provided with a system of underground irrigation.

The alpine garden, if not a part of the rock garden, should have a northern exposure and be built of rocks placed in as natural a manner as possible, preferably resembling the prevailing rocky formation of the neighborhood. Paths made of flat rock should lead from point to point so that all parts may be easily reached. The large boulders should be covered at least two-thirds with the soil and smaller ones placed among them to provide pockets to hold the alpine treasures.

The soil in different sections of the area may vary to suit acid- or alkaline-loving plants, but a good general mixture consists of the following: Mix ⅓ peat moss, ⅓ leaf-mold, ⅓ ordinary garden loam, then count this as ⅓ of the final mixture, the remaining ⅔ consisting of chip rock and sand. Combine thoroughly and place this soil 18 in. deep over the whole alpine garden, ramming it well into the pockets between the rocks. The peat moss should be well soaked before being incorporated in the mixture. The rock chips should be of granite in the portion devoted to acid-loving plants and of limestone where the lime-lovers are to grow. Correct soil and suitable moisture can make many plants feel at home in spite of a lack of real alpine altitude.

All ordinary alpines will grow in a garden of this type, but for the rarer sorts, more difficult to handle, that come from very high altitudes and need not only a constant supply of water, but also a cool soil, a moraine or scree garden must be constructed. This may have beneath the top-soil a system of perforated water-pipes which can be turned on or off at intervals or it can be made without an underground supply of water and watered from the top with a watering-can.

The moraine is usually made on a slight slope. The ground is excavated to the depth of 2 to 2½ ft. and the bottom covered with coarse rubble-stone in order to pro-

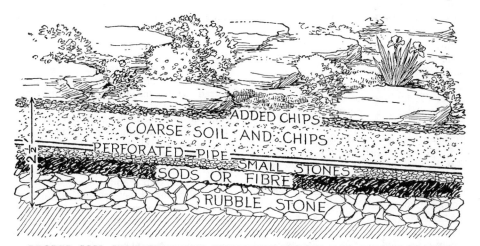

PROPER SOIL STRUCTURE AND WATERING SYSTEM FOR ALPINE PLANTS
A perforated pipe, a foot beneath the surface, will provide moisture when needed, while rubble stone at the bottom will drain off excess water. A layr of sods, then one of small stones, covered with coarse soil and chips, with a layer of stone chips over the top, will more or less duplicate alpine conditions.

vide adequate drainage. On this stone place sods or cocoanut fiber, then a layer of small stones, not over 2 in. in diameter. The remaining space is then filled with the soil mixture above described, with an additional sprinkling of rock chips. The monotony of the surface may be broken by irregular boulders placed here and there; these prevent the soil from slipping and provide shelter for many tiny plants. Here rare alpines which have sulked or died in the ordinary alpine garden will thrive, bloom, and increase rapidly.

It is almost impossible to have a garden of this type on the Atlantic seaboard, in the southern states, or in coastal California, but where the altitude is high or the growing season short, an alpine collection is a source of great pleasure and interest.

See also MORAINE GARDEN.

A few choice alpines are listed below:
Aethionema schistosum
Androsace primuloides, sarmentosa and maxima
Campanula waldsteiniana
Dianthus neglectus
Edraianthus dalmatica
Eritrichium nanum
Gentiana verna, septemfida, farreri, sino-ornata
Iris gracilipes
Lewisia howelli and tweedyi
Phyteuma comosum, hemisphaericum
Saxifraga apiculata, godseffiana and haagi
Silene acaulis
Soldanella alpina

ALPINIA (al-pin'-i-ah). A genus of Asiatic leafy perennial herbs of the Ginger Family, grown for their showy flowers borne in racemes and also for their handsome foliage. They are subjects for outdoors in the tropics and subtropics and, farther N., for greenhouses where they require moist air, a temperature of 60 deg., a rich soil, and abundant water. They are propagated by division in the spring.

A. speciosa (Shell-flower) grows 10 to 12 ft. high. The leaves are long and veined and the flowers are white, tinged purple with a lip crinkled and variegated red and brown. Grows well in southern Calif.

ALSIKE (al'-sik) or ALSIKE CLOVER. Common name for *Trifolium hybridum,* which originated in the Alsike parish of Sweden. A tall, slender-stemmed, perennial clover with white blossons. Valuable on cool, moist lands and excellent for hay,

pasture and, if sown thickly, as a cover crop, which see.

See also TRIFOLIUM.

ALSINE (al-sy'-nee). Former name (still occasionally used) for annual and perennial species of the Pink Family (Caryophyllaceae) which botanists now place in two other genera, viz., Arenaria and Stellaria, which see.

ALSOPHILA (al-sof'-i-lah). A genus of tree ferns, often elaborately pinnate, chiefly from the tropics and suitable only for greenhouse culture.

ALSTROEMERIA (al-stre-mee'-ri-ah). A genus of S. American greenhouse plants of the Amaryllis Family that grow from tuberous roots which are treated like bulbs. They require deep planting in a deep rich soil. They are sometimes planted outdoors in a moist, fairly sunny spot, but the tender ones must be brought to a fairly warm storehouse when cool weather comes. Whether grown in pots or in the soil, the tuberous roots need dividing once a year. Plants raised from fresh seed sown in August or later in pots in a good rich soil will bloom the next summer in the garden. *A. aurantiaca* (see below) requires a slightly heavier soil than the others.

The flowers, from 1 to 2 in. long and usually some shade of red, purple or yellow heavily spotted with other colors, occur in clusters.

Alstroemerias are sometimes called Herb-lilies.

A. pulchella, with dark red flowers tipped with green and spotted with purple, has long been known as a garden plant. *A. chilensis,* the rose-red Chilean-lily, *A. aurantiaca* with yellow flowers, *A. haemantha,* copper-colored, its var. *rosea,* rose or pink, and *A. pelegrina,* lilac-colored, spotted with dark purple, have all been grown successfully outdoors without special winter protection, in the vicinity of Boston. *A. pelegrina,* var. *alba,* is recommended for greenhouse use.

ALTERNANTHERA (al-ter-nan-thee'-rah). A genus of tender shrubs or herbs of the Amaranth Family some of which, much used for carpet-bedding, are placed by botanists in two other genera (Achyranthes and Telanthera), though still called Alternantheras by gardeners. The flowers are minute, the plants being grown for their variously colored leaves, and kept dwarf and compact by shearing. They grow best where they have full sun, and are easily propagated by division (the preferable method) or by cuttings made in the garden in August and kept over winter in the greenhouse or hotbed. Cuttings may be subject to damping off (which see).

A. amoena, a very dwarf plant from Brazil, includes garden forms as *rosea* and *amabilis.* It has leaves with conspicuous green veins, variously marbled with red and orange.

bettzickiana has narrow leaves, variegated with creamy yellow and red. Most of the forms seen in gardens are included under its varieties *aurea, magnifica, spathulata,* etc.

versicolor (Copper Alternanthera) has roundish leaves of copper or blood-red.

besteri var. *mosaica* is a light-yellow marbled with crimson.

ALTERNARIA (al-ter-nay'-ri-ah) **BLIGHT.** A disease caused by various species of the fungus genus Alternaria. On potatoes and tomatoes it is called early blight and appears as brown spots on the leaves; on some other vegetables and fruits it produces a soft rot. It also causes leaf spotting of many ornamentals, especially carnation, violet and zinnia. The spots are usually light-colored, often with concentric rings or circles. The dark centers are due to the growth of the brown fungus mycelium and spores. Control by cleaning up all old plant débris· and spraying affected plants with bordeaux mixture.

ALTERNATE. An arrangement of leaves placed singly at different heights along the axis. *Leaves opposite* refers to two leaves arising from two sides of the same node or stem joint; more than two leaves arranged at the same point are said to be *whorled.*

ALTHAEA (al-thee'-ah). A genus of annual, biennial or perennial herbs, found in temperate regions, belonging to the Mallow Family. They are of easy cultivation, and often grown in flower gardens. Do not confuse with Shrub-althea which is a hardy, summer-flowering shrub, *Hibiscus syriacus,* also called Rose-of-Sharon, illustrated on Plate 1.

A. ficifolia (Antwerp Hollyhock) is biennial, growing to 6 ft., with leaves deeply 7-lobed, and spikes of large showy lemon-yellow or orange flowers.

officinalis (Marsh Mallow) is a perennial, growing to 4 ft., with leaves entire or 3-lobed, and blush or rose flowers an inch across, clustered in the leaf-axils. A Euro-

pean species, this has become naturalized in moist places in the E. part of the country. But this is not the same as *Hibiscus moscheutos,* a native herbaceous species of Rose Mallow also sometimes called Marsh Mallow. Common in marshes along the Atlantic Coast, it bears typical mallow flowers but of great size—up to 6 in. or more across—at the top of the tall stiff stems.

rosea is the Hollyhock (which see), a Chinese biennial or semi-perennial, occurring in many forms and colors in cultivation. An annual strain has recently been introduced.

ALTHEA (al-thee'-ah) **SHRUB-** (*Hibiscus syriacus*). Well-known hardy summer-flowering shrub, the Rose-of-Sharon. (See illustration, Plate 1.) See HIBISCUS.

ALUMINUM SULPHATE. A chemical used to acidify a neutral or alkaline soil in order to make it suitable for acid-loving plants such as rhododendrons, azaleas and other members of the Heath Family. It should be applied at the rate of "up to a pound" to the square yard on loams of ordinary fertility and thoroughly mixed with the soil which should then be watered well. So used, it also causes hydrangea plants to produce blue flowers instead of pink ones.

It may also be used to overcome excessive alkalinity or "hardness" of water which sometimes is injurious to plants.

ALUM-ROOT. Common name for *Heuchera americana,* a widely distributed woodland plant of the Saxifrage Family. False-alum-root is *Tellima grandiflora.*

ALYSSUM (ah-lis'-um). Madwort. Annual and perennial herbs of the Crucifer Family, easily grown from seed in any good garden soil and especially suited to rockeries and edges in open sunny situations. The foliage tends to be grayish and the flowers are white or yellow.

The popular Sweet Alyssum is botanically *Lobularia maritima,* a perennial; but it is generally referred to as Alyssum and grown as an annual. The plants grow only 4 to 10 in. tall. As seed does not always germinate well in the open ground, it is sometimes best started indoors and the plants set out about the middle of April. It flowers freely from early spring until late summer; is of uniform height and habit and is sweet-scented. It can be grown by the beginner with assurance of success, being equally at home in beds, pots or boxes. Some varieties, especially the double white, can be propagated only by cuttings. These may be taken any time during the summer and will root easily in a cold-frame or even in the open border in a somewhat shaded location.

Perennial Alyssum, besides being valuable in the rockery and for edging, is excellent for window boxes, baskets and vases and for lines in carpet beds. It blooms very early, when other flowers are scarce. About 10 in. in height, it grows readily from seed and may also be propagated by cuttings or layering. Seed may be sown out of doors after danger from frost is over, in beds of finely pulverized soil, covering to a depth four times their size with light soil. Thin out the seedlings as it becomes necessary and transplant to permanent positions as soon as they are large enough, so they can become thoroughly established before winter. Seed may also be sown in early fall, the plants being wintered in a coldframe and transplanted outdoors in spring.

Both types of alyssum may be lifted, potted, and taken indoors in the fall; cut them back to induce new growth and winter bloom.

ENEMIES. A fungus on Sweet Alyssum that causes a water-soaked and scalded appearance and rots the leaves, can be checked by spraying 2 or 3 times with bordeaux mixture. The little black flea beetle that infests young cabbages and turnips bothers this plant, but may be controlled by dusting with fine ashes mixed with tobacco dust. Alyssum, like other crucifers, is subject to club-root (which see).

The best-known species in the present genus Alyssum are:

A. saxatile. The spring-flowering perennial known as Golden Tuft, Gold Dust, Basket of Gold, or Rock Madwort. One of the most popular early rock-garden subjects, about 1 ft. tall; flowers bright yellow, abundant; foliage grayish, persistent.

argenteum (Yellow Tuft). Grows to 15 in. and flowers later than *A. saxatile* but is used in same manner.

spinosum. Low, branching, spiny plant with white or pinkish flowers.

AMARANTH. Common name for the genus Amaranthus, which includes some coarse annual warm-climate herbs grown in the garden for their colorful foliage and, in the case of some species, for the showy, tassel-like heads made up of a great many red or brownish-red flowers which, individually, are tiny and unimportant. The genus also includes some bad weeds, such as pigweed and tumble-weed, which fact may be one reason why the ornamental kinds are not more popular. The poorer the soil the more brilliant the foliage of the amaranthus; if the soil is very fertile the gardener is likely to be disappointed. The plants grow readily from seed and prefer a sunny spot in the garden. They may be started in the open in May and June but as they require considerable space should be thinned or transplanted to stand at least 18 in. to 2 ft. apart.

Of the 50 or more species two are well known and satisfactory for garden use. *A. caudatus* (Love-Lies-Bleeding or Tassel-flower) reaches heights of from 3 to 6 ft., growing coarsely and branching freely. Its odd crimson flower-spikes have a texture like that of chenille, and may be either long and drooping or thick and short.

A. tricolor (Josephs Coat) is erect, growing from 1 to 4 ft. with gay leaves 2 to 4 in. wide, of green, yellow and scarlet sometimes blotched or splashed, which give it its popular name. A dwarf variety (*nanus*) called Fire Amaranth because of its brilliant coloring, the leaves being carmine with spots of yellow, red and dark green, is especially good for potting. The var. *angustior* (or *salicifolius*) is called Fountain-plant on account of the drooping habit of its leaves, which are orange and bronze. It grows to 3 ft. Oriflamme, another new variety, is featured by its pyramidal growth to 5 ft. It has large leaves of a glossy maroon and the central and side branches are topped with bright-scarlet leaves.

A. hybridus is a common weed, but its var. *hypochondriacus,* called Princes Feather, is more graceful and has much-branched showy panicles.

The so-called Globe-amaranth belongs to the Amaranth Family but a different genus. It is grown mainly for its "everlasting" qualities. See GOMPHRENA and EVERLASTINGS.

In the S. Amaranthus may be a host of the red- and black-spotted Harlequin bugs which are pests of cabbage and other crucifers (which see). The roots are sometimes attacked by the carrot beetle but there is no satisfactory control measure. Stem rots caused by fungi are best controlled by sanitary measures. See CORTICIUM and SCLEROTINIA.

AMARANTHACEAE (am-ah-ran-thay'-see-ee). The Amaranth Family. An extensive family of weed-like herbs, resembling those of the Goosefoot Family (Chenopodiaceae), mostly native to warm regions. The flowers are small, petal-less, usually green or white of a somewhat shriveled texture, and usually in terminal spikes or heads, made showy by the chaffy bracts or scales. While many members of the family are weeds, others are popular flower-garden subjects, and a few pot-herbs. All are easily grown, either from seeds or cuttings, in an open, sunny position. Among the principal cultivated genera are Amaranthus, Celosia (Cockscomb), Iresine, Gomphrena and Nototrichum.

AMARCRINUM (am-ahr-kry'-num). A group or genus of hybrids produced by crossing plants of the genera Amaryllis and Crinum. One species, *A. howardi,* has soft-pink, fragrant flowers in large clusters on a 4 ft. stalk. Suitable for pot culture.

AMARYLLIDACEAE (am-ah-ril-i-day'-see-ee). The Amaryllis Family. A large group of widely distributed perennial herbs growing from bulbs, rhizomes or fibrous roots, and differing from the Lily Family by having the ovary below the floral parts (*inferior*) rather than above them (*superior*). This family is associated with warm, dry climates, some of its members often bearing leaves only during the rainy season. Here belongs the agave, an important source of fibre, and some of the most attractive and useful of garden and greenhouse genera, such as Amaryllis, Amarcrinum, Clivia, Cooperia, Curculigo, Eucharis, Furcraea, Galanthus, Haemanthus, Hippeastrum, Hymenocallis, Hypoxis, Manfreda, Narcissus, Nerine, Pancratium and Polianthes.

AMARYLLIS (am-ah-ril'-is). A genus of S. African bulbous plants which bear several large lily-like pink, white, rose-red or purple flowers on a single, solid stem in mudsummer. The only true species is *A. belladonna,* the Belladonna-lily, which grows well and blooms freely outdoors in Calif. In the E. it seems to defy every attempt to establish it outdoors. For indoor flowering it requires a soil of fibrous loam, leafmold and sand, with liquid manure during the blooming season.

Many closely related subjects are also commonly known as Amaryllis, especially

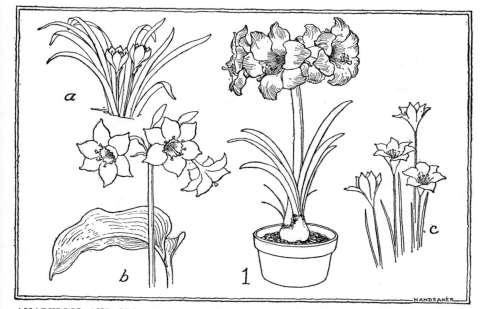

AMARYLLIS AND ITS RELATIVES GIVE BRIGHT-COLORED BLOOM IN SUMMER
Best known in the Amaryllis Family is the red and white Hippeastrum, commonly known as Amaryllis (1). The yellow-flowered Sternbergia (a) is hardy. The Amazon-lily (b) with fragrant white flowers is for southern gardens. Zephyr-lilies (c) are fairly hardy small plants with dainty pink, red or yellow flowers.

certain species and many hybrids of the genus Hippeastrum.

AMARYLLIS HYBRIDS (Hippeastrum). Bulbs of these hybrids are now being commercially produced in enormous quantities in our S. states. For outdoor planting in those localities, and for greenhouse and home flowering in the North, there is nothing among the bulbous plants that is as readily handled or that produces more effectively showy flowers. The blossoms range in color from pure white through various shades of pink to deepest red. In the South the foliage, except when cut down by frost, is evergreen.

The bulbs must be lifted and stored in dry sand over winter. When new bulbs are received they should be potted at once, and maintained in an even temperature of about 65 deg. F. The flowers often appear before the foliage. After blooming, the potted plant may be plunged outdoors when the weather becomes warm. Taken in again in the fall, it will be ready to flower again in the early spring.

Because propagation by natural division of the bulbs is very slow, the common method of increase is by seed which produces flowering size bulbs in from 2 to 4 years. Artificial increase of the bulbs is practiced to a limited extent but requires special knowledge and equipment.

The foregoing cultural directions also apply to the different species, the more important of which are the following:

Amaryllis equestre (*Hippeastrum puniceum*). A beautiful soft-pink variety that grows abundantly in Fla. and other S. States and adapts itself well to home and greenhouse conditions in the N.

formosissima. Called by botanists *Sprekelia formosissima* and commonly known as Jacobean-lily, this is a native of Mexico. It forms black-skinned bulbs and bears bright-crimson flowers above strap-shaped foliage.

halli. This is called by botanists *Lycoris squamigera,* which see.

johnsoni (Hippeastrum). Has large red flowers with white veins.

DISEASES. The leaf scorch common on Narcissus also occurs on Amaryllis, the fungus apparently overwintering on the bulbs, which should be treated with a disinfectant. Bulbs showing the black resting bodies (sclerotia) of the botrytis fungus should be discarded.

See BULBS; DISINFECTION.

AMARYLLIS SOCIETY, AMERICAN. This society was organized in 1933 to devote itself to the advancement of amaryllis culture in all its branches and to the holding of exhibitions of amaryllis, both national and regional. The membership includes horticulturists, amateurs and professional growers.

The Society publishes a yearbook, free to paid-up members, which is devoted to amaryllis culture in its various phases, reports of exhibitions and regional activities, standardization of color descriptions, and other information of interest and educational value to amaryllis growers and lovers.

The annual dues are $2. The secretary is Wyndham Hayward, Winter Park, Fla.

AMATEUR. In gardening, as in other fields, this term refers to activities carried on, not for material profit or monetary reward, but for the personal satisfaction derived—in other words, "for the love of it" (which is an apt phrase since the word is derived directly from the Latin *amo,* meaning "to love"). Thus, in a flower show, garden competition or any other horticultural event in which prizes are offered, it is customary to designate classes for *amateur* exhibitors, meaning those who have never sold their garden products or received remuneration for their efforts as gardeners or show judges or for any other services directly related to plant growing or exhibition. Some organizations make a further distinction, grading amateurs according to the number of plants (as dahlias) that they grow. Also the schedules of some events require that an amateur shall not previously have won an award in certain advanced classes; this, however, is ordinarily considered the measure of a "novice" rather than an amateur.

As distinguished from the amateur gardener, there are: first, the professional or private gardener, who receives pay for his work, but who does not market the products he grows; and second, the commercial grower, who grows plants for sale whether as florist, seedsman, or nurseryman. He may specialize on a single kind of flower, on a general line of greenhouse or outdoor stock, on vegetables, perennials or fruits or in any other horticultural line; but in any case it is a business venture, involving perhaps the issuing of a catalog or price list, but in any case the exchange of plant merchandise for money.

It is—or should be—clear, therefore, that the term is by no means one of reproach, depreciation or criticism. On the contrary, amateur gardeners, individually and collectively, may be regarded as the real backbone of the fine art of gardening, and take pride in their status. Not only do they compose a vast army of enthusiasts whose efforts are making their homes and communities—and consequently the whole country—better and more beautiful to live in; but also, through their constant desire for new and better plant materials, they provide a powerful stimulus for commercial plantsmen, assisted by professional plant hunters, scientific plant breeders and others, to discover, create, reproduce, make available, and disseminate new, exotic, and improved kinds of plants and flowers with which to brighten human life and its environment.

AMAZON-LILY. Common name for *Eucharis grandiflora,* a bulbous plant of the Amaryllis Family. Native to Colombia, it is grown in hothouses in temperate zones.

AMBERBOA (am-bur-boh'-ah). Rather weedy annual plants of the Composite Family with jaggedly cut or divided leaves and purple, blue, or pink flowers in heads. They resemble Bachelors Buttons and are occasionally grown in the flower garden. Their culture is simple; the seed should be sown where the plants are to flower. *A. muricata* is the most attractive species, growing 2 ft. high and having narrow leaves and heads of pink or purple flowers. It is native to Spain and Morocco.

AMELANCHIER (am-e-lan'-ki-er). (See illustration, Plate 1.) Shadbush. Shadblow. Service - berry. June - berry. Hardy deciduous shrubs or small trees of the Rose Family. About 25 species, most of them native in N. America. Their racemes of white flowers freely produced in early spring, rank them amongst the most conspicuous of woody plants at that season. The flowers open in advance of, or with the unfolding of, the leaves. In most species the young leaves attract attention by reason of a covering of soft woolly white hairs. In the fall the tinted foliage adds to the display of that season. Some (noted in the list below by F after the name) are grown for their edible fruits, which are purple-black juicy berries. These are usually the stoloniferous kinds, which soon make a large patch.

Amelanchiers are not especially particular as to soil, but have a liking for lime-stone. Some prefer a moister place than others, but in general the group is very tolerant.

Propagation is by seeds, layers, and, in some obvious cases, by suckers.

ENEMIES. Yellow spots on shadbush leaves indicate infection by one of the Juniper rusts (*Gymnosporangium* sp.). If it is present in abundance and if the two kinds of plants are growing close together, the best procedure is to remove all the plants of the least valuable kind. Pruning out excessive, bushy twig growths (known as "witches' brooms") will control the fungus causing them. Blighted twigs (see FIRE BLIGHT) should also be removed. Clearing away fallen leaves and fruits will tend to prevent fruit and twig blight. (See also BROWN ROT of stone fruits.) Insect mines, frequently seen in the leaves, do not seriously affect the tree.

PRINCIPAL SPECIES

A. stolonifera. F. A twiggy shrub of eastern N. America, spreading by suckers to form a thicket about 4 ft. high.

humilis. F. Very similar to the preceding. Grows well in dry soil and ripens its fruit a little later.

sanguinea. F. Found across the northern part of the country. A slender shrub, 6 to 8 ft., also doing well in dry soil. One of the best for fruit.

florida. Native of the Northwest. It makes a clump of upright stems to 8 ft. or more. Rich-yellow foliage in the fall.

bartramiana. A good bushy shrub from 2 to 8 ft., found naturally in boggy places from Labrador south. Very free-flowering.

alnifolia. F. A shrub or slender tree to 25 ft. Widespread in the region of Lake Superior. Has the largest fruit of any kind, up to ¾ in. across. Long an important food tree for the Indians of that region.

oblongifolia. F. The largest of the shrubby species, common in eastern N. America. Conspicuous in spring with its flowers and whitish leaves, in June with its abundant fruit, and in fall with its richly tinted leaves.

canadensis (formerly *A. botryapium*). A bushy tree 30 ft. or more, widespread in the eastern U. S., and the earliest species to bloom. Both sides of the young leaves are covered with short, dense, woolly hairs, giving the tree a very silvery appearance for a short time.

laevis. F. One of the most graceful and attractive of N. American small trees. Especially beautiful in spring with its nodding racemes of white flowers among the bronze-tinted young leaves, which are a distinguishing feature.

grandiflora. A natural hybrid between the two preceding species. A small tree with the largest flowers of any American shadbush. It grows wild near Rochester, N. Y. A form (var. *rubescens*) has rose-tinted flowers.

ovalis (*A. rotundifolia. A. vulgaris*) (European shadbush). Usually a shrub, but occasionally a tree to 25 ft. Has the largest flowers of any species. The young leaves have such a coat of woolly hairs that the plant appears to be mantled in white. From this it is, in Europe, called Snowy-mespilus.

asiatica (Oriental Shadbush). A small tree of slender graceful habit to 30 ft. or more. Native of Japan and Korea. The fruits do not ripen until fall, and sometimes hang on during most of the winter.

AMENDMENT, SOIL. This is any material added to a soil to act as an indirect fertilizer, influencing plant growth favorably through its effect on the soil texture or quality rather than by actually adding plant food, as would a fertilizer. It might also be called a soil conditioner.

Beneficial effects of so-called soil amendments are: The conversion of unavailable into available plant food; the improvement of the physical condition of the soil; the neutralizing of a too acid condition in the soil; the making of neutral or alkaline soils more acid and thus more favorable for certain plants such as the rhododendron and blueberry.

Lime in various forms, muck, peat moss, salt, sulphate of iron, soot, coal ashes and aluminum-sulphate are all soil amendments. See also SOIL.

AMENT. The botanical name for a catkin (which see), the blossom of certain kinds of trees.

AMERICAN BEAUTY. A variety of hybrid perpetual (H.P.) rose bearing large, fragrant, light crimson-carmine flowers. It is the "state flower" of the District of Columbia. Originated in France in 1875 as Mme. Ferdinand Jamin, it was introduced into the U. S. in 1886 and renamed American Beauty. For years it was the most glamorous, most favored and most expensive commercial cut-flower rose, but it is now almost obsolete being grown in only a few greenhouses.

AMERICAN COWSLIP. A small perennial of the Primula Family, widely distributed throughout N. America. See DODECATHEON.

AMERICAN HORTICULTURAL SOCIETY. This society was organized in 1922 through the merging of two previous groups, in the interests of American horticulture. Membership is largely amateur although many leading commercial and professional horticulturists belong and contribute to its scholarly and finely illustrated quarterly publication, *The National Horticultural Magazine*. The reprinting and distribution of articles, bulletins and leaflets are other of the Society's services. Its meetings, flower shows and other activities are held mainly in Washington.

The annual dues are $3 and sustaining, life and patron memberships are available. The secretary is Mr. C. C. Thomas, 821 Washington Loan & Trust Bldg., Washington, D. C.

AMERICAN IPECAC. Common name for *Gillenia stipulata,* an erect, hardy perennial herb that grows abundantly in the S. States.

AMERICAN PARSLEY FERN (*Cryptogramma acrostichoides*). A small rock fern of the N. States, with narrow pod-like segments on the fertile fronds. Difficult of cultivation.

AMIANTHIUM (am-i-an'-thi-um). A perennial, bulbous herb of the Lily Family. See FLY-POISON.

AMMOBIUM (a-moh'-bi-um). Annual Australian herbs grown as everlastings. The name, a combination of Latin words meaning sand and life, indicates that the plant prefers a definitely sandy soil. Easy to grow, it bears a profusion of small white flowers with yellow centers, which brighten the garden. Plants are 18 in. tall and seed may be sown either in the spring, or in the fall for next season's bloom. Flowers remain white if cut before they have reached full bloom and hung in a shady, airy place to dry; later they become yellowish. *A. alatum,* the Winged Everlasting, derives its name from the peculiar winged formation of the branches. It grows to a height of 3 ft. and its flower-heads are almost 2 in. across. See also EVERLASTING.

AMMONIUM SULPHATE. A chemical, obtained as a by-product in the manufacture of coke and illuminating gas, used both as a fertilizer (which see) and to control weeds in lawns. Containing about 20 per cent of nitrogen in comparatively available form, it is, as a plant food, classed among the quick-acting, nitrogenous materials such as nitrate of soda. Its continued use tends to make the soil acid, which renders it very satisfactory for ericaceous plants (rhododendrons, etc)., for bent grasses and for other subjects that prefer an acid condition.

For the control of weeds it is scattered over the turf at the rate of 6 lbs. to 1000 sq. ft. of area in the early spring or late fall. Let it remain for a day, then water it in thoroughly. Unless the tendency to acidity above referred to is counteracted by the use of some form of lime, this use of ammonium-sulphate will be detrimental to a lawn made largely of blue grass, whereas it will encourage a bent grass turf.

AMMOPHILA (a-mof'-i-lah). A genus of tall, perennial grasses with long, creeping, rootstocks useful in gardens near the water. *A. arenaria* is common along the N. Atlantic coast and shores of the Great Lakes. See BEACH-GRASS.

AMOLE (ah-moh'lay). A common name for *Chlorogalum pomeridianum*, also known as Soap-plant (which see). A tall, branching plant growing from a very large bulb, the juice of which is used in Mexico for soap-making.

AMOMUM (a-moh'-mum) *cardamon.* A perennial E. Indian herb of the Ginger Family grown for its attractive foliage in warm regions, and occasionally N. in indoor collections. It yields medicinal products, the seeds especially being sometimes substituted for those of *Elettaria cardamomum,* the true Cardamon, which see.

AMORPHA (ah-mor'-fah). False-indigo. Deciduous shrubs of N. America, members of the Pea Family, not reliably hardy north of Mass. They prefer a sunny location and can stand a dry soil better than many shrubs. They are summer-blooming, with small dark-blue or purple flowers in dense terminal spikes. Old plants get straggly, but can be renewed with good growth by hard pruning in spring. The foliage is fine and fern-like, turning yellow in the fall. The two best known species are *A. canescens,* 2 to 3 ft. (Lead-plant), and *A. fruticosa,* 6 to 18 ft. (Bastard-indigo).

AMORPHOPHALLUS (ah-mor-foh-fal'-us). Large, tropical, Asiatic herbaceous plants of the Arum Family, having immense, bulb-like, tuberous roots. The very large, funnel-shaped flowers (resembling huge Callas in shape) are thrust up from the bulb on a long, naked stem in advance of the three-parted leaves which may be 3 ft. or more across. The flower is of a chocolate, or reddish-maroon, and in some species emits a nauseous odor. In temperate regions, these plants are grown in tubs, as greenhouse curiosities, and sometimes transplanted to the open in summer and allowed to dry off under the greenhouse bench in the fall. The soil required is a mixture of light, sandy loam, leafmold and rotted manure. Propagation is by the small tubers that offset from the parent root. These should be placed in pots just large enough to hold them, and shifted as they grow. The common name is Krubi. The plant called Devils Tongue (*Hydrosome rivieri*) was formerly listed as Amorphophallus.

AMPELOPSIS (am-pe-lop'-sis). Tendril-climbing deciduous shrubs, native in N. America and Asia, belonging to the Grape Family. About 20 species are known, not all of them hardy North. Not particular as to soil and situation, they are useful in gardens to cover walls, arbors or trelliswork, and to ramble over rocks. Propagated by seeds, cuttings and layers.

PRINCIPAL SPECIES

A. humulifolia. Very like the true Vitis (which see), with handsome leaves of firm texture, whitish beneath. Fruit is small, pale yellow or pale blue. *A. micans* is very similar, but with dark blue fruit. Both native to China.

A. brevipedunculata (formerly known as *A. heterophylla* var. *amurensis*) is one of the best of the Asiatic species. A strong grower, well adapted to clothe low walls and sprawl in rocky places, it is beautiful in fall with its berries varying in color from pale lilac through copper green to turquoise blue. Var. *elegans* (or *A. heterophylla tricolor*) makes a lovely porch vine, being a smaller and slower grower. The young leaves show white, green and pink variegation.

A. cordata. A high climber, native to Ill. and Ohio, has roundish leaves sometimes slightly 3-lobed. Fruit is blue or greenish blue.

A. delavayana. A vigorous climber from China with 3-lobed leaves and young growth covered with reddish hairs. Fruit dark blue or blue-black.

A. arborea (Pepper-vine). Native of the S. States, not quite hardy N. Of slender, graceful habit, with finely cut leaves. Fruit dark purple.

A. aconitifolia. A slender grower with dissected leaves. Fruit first bluish, then yellow or orange. China.

A. japonica. Somewhat tender, with a tuberous root. Handsome with lustrous, finely cut leaves. Fruit small, blue.

A number of species formerly included in this genus are now referred to Parthenocissus (which see). The chief distinction seems to be that in the latter the tendrils have adhesive tips, while those in Ampelopsis do not.

ENEMIES. A fungous leaf spot may prove serious in wet seasons. If it is unchecked the leaves become very unsightly. The brown spot, sometimes angular, is dotted with the black pin-point fruiting bodies of the fungus. Where the vines are attached to walls, effective protective measures are difficult, but spraying several times with bordeaux mixture, beginning early in the season, will help. Wherever possible remove and burn infected leaves. The same control measures may be used to prevent the shot-hole effect caused by two other leaf-spotting fungi. Hand picking is the best control for caterpillars banded in black, white and orange that feed on the foliage and sometimes strip the vines. If leaf-hoppers are numerous, spray with nicotine-soap solution. If grape flea-beetles and rose chafers attack Ampelopsis, use control measures recommended under GRAPE. Use a dormant oil-spray to get rid of the cottony maple scale.

AMPHICARPA (am-fi-kahr′-pah). A genus of perennial vines of the Pea Family (Leguminosae) known as Hog-peanut. Natives of E. N. America and India, they have little horticultural interest. The flowers, white or purple, are of two sorts —the upper ones showy, the lower ones without petals but followed by rather conspicuous pods. *A. monoica* has rose-colored blossoms and can be used to trail over a bulb bed in a shady spot.

AMSONIA (am-soh′-ni-ah). Perennial herbs of the Milkweed Family, growing 1 to 3 ft. high, and having peculiar tough bark and quite narrow leaves. The panicles of inconspicuous blue or bluish flowers are followed by rather attractive milkweed-like

pods. Occasionally they are planted in the border or amongst shrubbery, for some of them hold their leaves well into the fall. They will grow in ordinary garden soil and are increased by division, cuttings in summer, or by seed.

A. tabernaemontana grows 2 to 3 ft. high and has soft-blue flowers, hairy outside, in dense clusters, from May to July. It is found in low ground, N. J. to Fla. and Tex.

AMYGDALUS (ah-mig′-dah-lus). The former botanic name of the Almond, which is now listed as *Prunus communis,* one of the species of stone fruits. See ALMOND and PRUNUS.

ANACARDIACEAE (an-a-kahr-di-ay′-see-ee). Botanical name of the Cashew Family, a group of trees or woody shrubs found mostly in the tropics, with acrid, resinous or caustic juice. Some kinds are grown for their plum- or cherry-like fruit which encloses a nut; others for ornament or tanning or medicinal products. The principal genera are *Rhus* (sumac, poison ivy and the lacquer-tree), *Pistacia, Anacardium, Schinus,* and *Spondias.*

ANACHARIS (an-ak′-ah-ris). A generic name sometimes applied to the Waterweed or Ditchmoss, *Elodea canadensis.*

ANAGALLIS (an-ah-gal′-is). Pimpernel. A genus of low-growing annual, biennial or perennial herbs of the Primrose Family. They have delightful little star-like flowers of red, blue, or white which grow out of the axils of the leaves on hair-like stems. They are free-flowering plants, some species most attractive in the rock garden. They require the simplest culture, for the annuals may be sown where the flowers are to grow and the perennial kinds are easily increased by root division and cuttings. They thrive in a loose, warm soil.

A. arvensis. Called the Poor Mans Weatherglass because the flowers close at the approach of bad weather, has trailing stems and scarlet or white flowers ¼ in. across. An annual native to Eurasia, it has run wild in N. America. Var. *caerulea* has blue flowers.

linifolia. Perennial or biennial. Has a woody stem which sometimes grows 1½ ft. high, and blue flowers, reddish beneath.

ANANAS (ah-nay′-nas) *sativus.* A stiff perennial herbaceous plant, native to tropical America; the Pineapple, which see. For culture, see BROMELIA, to which it is related.

ANAPHALIS (ah-naf'-al-is) *margarit-acea.* A hardy herbaceous woolly-foliaged perennial of the Composite Family commonly called Pearl, or Pearly Everlasting, because of the prominent whitish bracts in the small flower heads; being persistent, they make the plant valuable for dried bouquets. For such use, the flower stalk is cut just before the flowers mature. Plants attain a height of 3 ft. and with their leafy stems and woolly appearance are good subjects for hardy borders and rock gardens.

ANCHISTEA (an-kis'-tee-ah). A genus of ferns, represented by only one species suitable for gardens, namely, the Virginia Chain Fern, usually placed in the genus Woodwardia, which see.

ANCHOR-PLANT. Common name for *Colletia cruciata,* a stiff, spiny shrub of S. America, sometimes cultivated as a curiosity.

ANCHUSA (an-keu'-sah). From a Greek word meaning "paint for the skin," the Ancients having made a kind of rouge from the root of the plant. Also known as Alkanet, Bugloss, and Summer-forget-me-not. Hardy, easy to grow perennial and biennial herbaceous plants, excellent for the summer border in a sunny location. They make good sized clumps of rather coarse, usually hairy foliage, from which rise 1½ ft. to 5 ft. leafy stalks bearing, from mid-July to September or later, loose masses of small flowers usually blue and often in intense, striking shades. Anchusa does well even in ordinary soil, but given plenty of well-rotted manure it proves a heavy feeder and responds vigorously. It is grown from seed sown in spring (in hotbed or frame) or in early summer (outside). The biennial kinds are usually treated as annuals and may be sown where they are to bloom and the plants later thinned to 1 ft. apart. Otherwise, transplant them early in fall or spring, handling carefully so as not to break the tap-root and setting 12 to 18 in. apart. (Some species self-sow freely in mild locations.) After flowering, cut off the flower stems and give a little fertilizer or liquid manure to stimulate a second blossoming until frost. Then cut back again. In severe locations, after the ground freezes, mulch with straw or leaves—but lightly to avoid rotting the crown.

A member of the Borage Family (Boraginaceae), Anchusa is related to forget-me-not, heliotrope, mertensia, pulmonaria and other useful garden plants.

A. capensis (Cape-forget-me-not). Biennial. 1½ ft.; offered by seedsmen as an annual; blue flowers, red-edged with white throats.

italica. Perennial. 5½ ft. blue; the varieties Dropmore (deep blue) and Opal (lighter) are especially popular.

myosotidiflora. Perennial. 1½ ft., good for rock gardens; small flowers in summer resemble forget-me-nots. (Botanists now call it *Brunnera macrophylla.*)

barrelieri. Perennial. 2 ft. blue flowers with white and yellow centers, in spring.

officinalis. Perennial or biennial. 2 ft. bright blue or purple flowers, summer and autumn.

ANDROMEDA (an-drom'-e-dah). Common name for a group of attractive shrubs of several genera in the Heath Family. (See illustration, Plate 1.)

Also the botanical name for 2 dwarf hardy evergreen shrubs of the same group, commonly called Bog-rosemary. They grow naturally in peaty bogs of the temperate and colder regions of the northern hemisphere. In habit rather thin, they are interesting when clumped in front of evergreens or azaleas. They need a moist peaty soil in a partly shaded position, as they will not stand becoming dry at the roots.

A. polifolia, 1 to 2 ft., is found in Europe, Asia and N. America. It has small narrow leaves, glaucous beneath. The pinkish urn-shaped flowers are in clusters at the end of the branches. *A. glaucophylla,* native only in N. America, is very similar, but the leaves are white beneath.

Other species formerly in this genus are now included under Cassiope, Chamaedaphne, Leucothoë, Pieris and Zenobia. Among them is Japanese Andromeda (*Pieris japonica*).

Armillaria root rot (which see) has been found killing Andromeda in New Jersey and red leaf spot of Blueberry (which see) distorts its foliage.

ANDROSACE (an-dros'-ah-see). A genus of true alpine, annual or perennial plants of the Primrose Family, known as Rock-jasmines. They grow naturally in the rocky stretches above timber-line, and many of them require special treatment in the alpine or rock garden. Their leaves, which are often very woolly, are usually tufted or in rosettes. The small flowers—

pink, red, or lavender—are usually borne in rather flattened rounded clusters. They are grown from seeds, division or cuttings, and require a dry, gritty soil and good drainage, though they must never suffer from drought.

PERENNIAL SPECIES

A. carnea. Forms close-set groups of rosettes in which the leaves are narrow, smooth and bright green. The rose-pink flowers with a yellow throat, 3 to 7 in number, grow in a loose umbel on a stalk 3 in. high. Should be given exceedingly good drainage.

chamaejasme. The hairy leaves grow in rather large rosettes. The flowers are ½ in. across and grow 1 to 5 in. high in umbels. Provide a light loam sprinkled with rock chips in full sunlight.

lanuginosa. Has narrow foliage covered with silvery, woolly hairs. It is a trailer and the flowers are in dense umbels on stems 2 in. high. Should be grown in a sandy soil in a sunny, sheltered position.

sarmentosa. Has woolly leaves clustered at the base and increases by rooting stems which end in new rosettes. The many rose-pink flowers appear on stems sometimes 5 in. high. Easily grown in gritty soil.

sempervivoides. Forms fleshy dark green leaves in rosettes. The flowers are rose-color, ¼ in. across, in umbels on stems 4 in. high. Grown in gritty soil, it may be readily increased by pegging down the runners.

ANNUAL SPECIES

lactiflora. Sometimes 1 ft. high, it has smooth, narrow leaves in rosettes. The flowers are large, ½ in. across, pure white, in dense clusters. Easily grown in any sunny spot in the rock garden. It frequently self-sows.

ANDROSTEPHIUM (an-droh-stee'-fi-um). A genus of bulbous plants, closely related to the brodiaeas, and belonging to the Lily Family. They are sometimes known as Babys Breath, though this name is more commonly given to Gypsophila. They have small flowers in partly flattened heads and very narrow leaves at the base of the stem. Natives of southwest and central U. S. they should be planted in light, sandy soil and given a sunny position in the wild garden. They are increased by division of the bulb or by seed.

A. caeruleum grows 8 in. high and has lilac or violet flowers 1 in. long.

ANEMIA (ah-nee'-mi-ah). A genus of comparatively dwarf, slow growing, tropical ferns, of the "flowering" type, with spore clusters borne in a separate panicle. Difficult to grow and for the greenhouse only. Do not wet the fronds. *A. phillitidis,* the hardiest, attains 2½ ft.

ANEMONE (ah-nem'-oh-ne). Wind flower. A large genus of perennial herbs with cup-shaped white, purple, or red flowers, different species being suitable for the border, the wild garden, or the rock garden. The most popular types are the autumn-flowering, fibrous-rooted Japanese Anemone, and the spring-flowering, tuberous-rooted Poppy Anemone; the best rock-garden sorts are among the less known kinds.

JAPANESE ANEMONE
A favorite autumn-flowering plant.

The Japanese Anemone (*A. japonica*) and its attractive varieties with pink and white flowers, are most decorative subjects, beautiful in the border and when naturalized, the graceful flowers on slender stems rising above sturdy clumps of good-sized leaves. They should be planted in moist soil, rich in humus (including well-rotted manure) in a rather shaded portion of the border or beneath a vine-covered pergola. Never allow the plants to dry out in summer; frequent watering and a mulch of decayed leaves will materially increase the beauty of the flowers. The clumps with their fibrous roots may be increased by division in spring, although plants resent disturbance.

The Poppy-flowered Anemones, such as *A. coronaria, A. hortensis* and *A. fulgens,* are very beautiful, with both single and double flowers shaped like large buttercups, and of many colors. But they are more difficult to grow, except in equable climates, as they succumb to the heat of summer as well as to severe cold. In the E. they are occasionally planted outdoors: either in the open, in a shady, sheltered spot and covered over winter with a thick but loose layer of leaves, held in place with evergreen boughs; or in a coldframe. Set the tubers in leafmold and sand, and in the spring sift rich soil around those growing in the coldframe, giving them frequent ventilation and removing the frames after the danger from frost is over. At the same time remove the leaves from those growing in the open. Poppy Anemones may be increased by division of the tubers or from seed.

ENEMIES. A smut sometimes causes abnormally large and deformed flowers of *A. nemorosa;* and diseased plants should be destroyed. In California *A. coronaria* is severely attacked by a rust which causes the leaves to become abnormally thickened, puffy and rigid, and to die prematurely. This rust passes another stage on stone fruits (as almond, apricot, cherry, peach, etc.). To control it, promptly remove infected plants and avoid growing alternate hosts in the same locality. Blister beetles which may harm *A. japonica* are difficult to control, but spraying with lead arsenate checks them somewhat. See BLISTER BEETLE for other measures.

AUTUMN-FLOWERING SPECIES

A. japonica (Japanese Anemone), to 3 ft., has flowers white, or tinged with rose, or purplish, to 3 in. across, blooming from Sept. to heavy frost. Among the numerous varieties are: *alba,* pure white; *rosea superba,* rose, and *rubra,* waxy red. Other horticultural forms found in catalogs include: Queen Charlotte, semi-double, white; Alice, rose-pink, lilac center; September Charm, silvery pink. The plant listed as *A. hupehensis,* with pink or mauve flowers shaded lavender-rose on the reverse, is now considered a dwarf, early flowering form of this species.

SPRING-FLOWERING SPECIES

A. coronaria (Poppy-flowered or Poppy Anemone), to 1½ ft., is one of the tuberous-rooted type; it has finely cut leaves and bears solitary flowers to 2½ in. across, in white and brilliant shades and combinations of purple, red, and blue. St. Brigid is a strain much used, most frequently for forcing by florists, and also for outdoor culture in the S. and W.

hortensis (Broad-leaved Garden Anemone), to 10 in., differs from *A. coronaria* in having broad, irregularly cut leaves and slightly smaller flowers in shades of red, rose-purple or white. It also is used for forcing and many garden forms have been evolved.

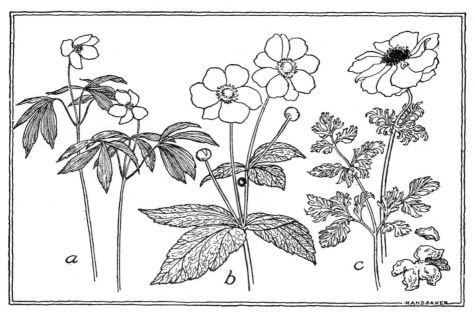

ANEMONES FOR ALL SEASONS IN THE GARDEN
The windflower (a) is a delicate accompaniment of spring; the tall Japanese anemone (b) blossoms in the fall; and the St. Brigid anemone (c) brightens the border in June with its broad flowers of red, blue and white. Two of the latter's curious corms are shown beside the stem.

fulgens (Flame or Scarlet Anemone), to 1 ft., is also frequently forced. The flowers, to 2 in. across, are vivid scarlet with numerous black stamens.

ROCK-GARDEN SPECIES

A. pulsatilla (Pasque Flower of Europe), to 1 ft., has hairy foliage and blue, or purplish, bell-shaped flowers. Appropriate for the rock garden in dry, rocky soil. (See illustration, Plate 44.)

patens var. *nuttalliana* (American Pasque Flower), 4 to 9 in., with silky, hairy foliage and bluish-purple, erect flowers, followed by plumed seeds. It should be placed in a low spot in the rock garden in full sun.

nemorosa (European Wood Anemone), to 8 in., with delicate airy white flowers 1 in. across, is best used in the rock garden or in a shady part of the border. Var. *robinsoniana* has larger flowers, occasionally blue; var. *alba*, with white flowers, has a semi-double horticultural form which is very beautiful.

quinquefolia (American Wood Anemone), of E. U. S., is much like the preceding and, like it, is often called Windflower.

vernalis, to 6 in., with flowers white, should also be grown in the rock garden.

ANEMONOPSIS (a-nem-oh-nop'-sis) *macrophylla*. A beautiful perennial herb of the Buttercup Family from Japan. It closely resembles the Japanese anemone in manner of growth, but is smaller in every part, having finely cut leaves and drooping flowers of a pale-purple color about 1½ in. across. It thrives best in rich soil in a shady position and is increased by root division, or from seed. If fresh seed is sown in the fall or early spring, flowers may be seen the following summer. Has flowers borne in loose racemes; the petals do not spread but form a half-closed bud-like cone within the sepals.

ANGELICA (an-jel'-i-kah). A genus of herbs of the Parsley Family, resembling the common cow-parsnip or poison hemlock, a species of Delphinium, which see. Several of them are natives of N. A. and other temperate parts of the world. They have large, much-divided leaves and large umbels (flattened rounded clusters) of white or greenish flowers on tall stout stalks. They are easily propagated by seed or division, and are sometimes planted in the border where height is needed, or along roadsides for the bold, striking, almost tropical effect of their profuse foliage. The name was given them because they were once supposed to have angelic healing properties.

A. curtisi grows from 2 to 5 ft. high from Pa. to N. C., with finely cut, ample foliage. The flowers are white and in umbels 6 in. across.

archangelica, a stout herb to 6 ft., grows in low ground and makes a striking picture by the side of a stream.

rosaefolia has scrambling stems 5 ft. long and the umbels or flower heads are 3 in. across.

ANGELICA-TREE. One name for Aralia spinosa. The Chinese Angelica-tree is *A. chinensis;* the Japanese Angelica-tree is *A. elata.* See ARALIA.

ANGELS EYES. One of the common names for *Veronica chamaedrys,* the blue germander speedwell of Europe, naturalized in North America. See VERONICA.

ANGELS TRUMPET. Common name for *Datura arborea,* a small tree bearing long, pendent, solitary, white flowers of musk-like odor.

ANGIOPTERIS (an-ji-op'-ter-is). A genus of greenhouse ferns of large size and robust habit. The best species, *A. evecta,* attaining a length of 16 ft., is a standard greenhouse plant, and gives a very tropical effect to the large conservatory. Provide fibrous loam, peat moss, coarse sand, and plenty of water, as this fern grows naturally in swamps.

ANGRAECUM (an-gree'-kum). A genus of tropical epiphytal orchids peculiar in construction and make-up, but beautiful and always attractive. They have a strong robust habit of growth, for which they are greatly admired, even when not in flower. The strong leathery leaves are arranged in two-ranked (*distichous*) form along the stem and the flowers are borne on long stalks out from the axils of the leaves. The flowers, mostly waxy white in all the species, have a long spur; this gives one species its name—*sesquipedale,* meaning "a foot and a half." They are widely scattered, but the majority are native to S. Africa, Madagascar, etc. *A. eburneum* is a very fine type, producing long upright racemes of beautiful white flowers which are very fragrant.

See also ORCHID.

ANGULOA (an-geu-loh'-ah). These are very handsome terrestrial orchid plants of temperate regions, with large pseudo-bulbs and broad leaves about 12 in. long. The flower spikes are about the same height as the foliage, which comes from the base of the bulb just as they begin to grow. The beautiful solitary flowers appearing in May and June have thick, fleshy sepals arching inward so as to give the blossoms a globular appearance which, although not graceful, have a solid, massive beauty. The flower somewhat resembles a bull's head, and for that reason, in its native home in the Andes of Colombia, S. A., it is called "El Torita." The principal species, *A. clowesi,* has yellow flowers; *A. ruckeri* is somewhat smaller and the flowers are olive-green. For culture, see ORCHID.

ANIMALS IN THE GARDEN. In any such discussion many angles and arguments for and against a particular species necessarily present themselves. The relationship of the animal in question to other living creatures in the garden and to the plant material comes first to mind. Fortunately facts and statistics from scientific works can settle very nicely all such questions and definitely indicate who should be allowed to stay in the garden and who should be snubbed and discouraged.

The question of economic value has great weight, of course, but it must be balanced against another more important though capricious factor, namely: How much, and in what way, does the animal's presence add to or detract from the garden's attractiveness and its owner's pleasure?

Unfortunately, some of the most worthy garden residents from the economic point of view are the ones most likely to upset the gardener's nerves and destroy his peace of mind. In such cases, it might pay him to try to overcome his prejudice and cultivate the acquaintance of a useful helper. At other times, a creature of attractive appearance and manner will prove somewhat of a rascal and the gardener will have to decide whether the pleasure of his company is sufficient recompense for the damage he does.

SQUIRRELS AND CHIPMUNKS are a case in point. Attractive and certainly amusing, they add a flashing bit of color and life to any garden; their noise is not unpleasant and most species tame readily. Their foraging for seeds, nuts, acorns, berries, insects, etc., can usually be overlooked as they are not particularly destructive to

plant material. The fact that one of their weaknesses as to food is a liking for the eggs and fledglings of insect-destroying birds is the thing most likely to make them unwelcome.

The red squirrel, commonly called the chickaree, is probably the worst offender in this respect. The most widespread of all the tree squirrels, its varieties are found in wooded areas from coast to coast. Its size and rusty-red coloring, its scolding and its curiosity readily distinguish it from its larger and more wary cousins, the fox and gray squirrels. In some of the E. States, the last named is more numerous. He is larger, with long, flat, bushy tail, common in the parks of most large E. cities. Being of a slightly less nervous temperament than the chickaree, it is more easily tamed; it is also reputed to be less destructive to bird life.

The chipmunks, found in some form throughout most of the U. S., are bright, alert, and active, and, being easy to tame, are easily observed and studied. They make interesting pets. The chipmunk's food is largely vegetable, principally seeds, berries, nuts, grain, etc., with the addition of insects, young mice, etc., and probably small bird eggs.

THE MOLE is a less spectacular garden resident and one rather unjustly blamed for damage he doesn't do. His presence is usually known only by the raised ridges of turf or earth pushed up from beneath as he burrows. These are unsightly in the midst of an otherwise well-kept lawn and are often disastrous beneath a recently planted row of lima beans, etc., provoking the gardener to great efforts to combat an evil more fancied than real. It is true that the grass roots die out above the burrows (because the moisture supply is interfered with) causing yellow streaks to appear, but it is a mistake to take it for granted that the mole is feeding on the roots. He takes nothing in the way of plant food and his activities are entirely concerned with the hunt for worms, insects and even mice which *are* destructive to plant roots and bulbs as well as tree trunks. He is a powerful destroyer of beetle larvae and in his favor also is the fact that he is not an enemy of the birds, the toads and other natural insect pest controls. See MOLES for control measures.

GOPHERS. Another group of burrowing animals, the pocket gophers, have almost nation-wide distribution. They, in contrast to the mole, live strictly on vegetable material and are destructive to a wide range of plant life. Their burrows are deeper and the only surface indication of their presence is the scattered mounds of pushed-up earth where they enter and leave. Roots, bulbs and tubers, including potatoes and other garden vegetables, suffer from their depredations. In addition, surface vegetation, such as grains and the bark of trees (especially apple, pear, almond, fig, etc.), is the victim of their voracity. Irrigated regions have still another grievance since the gophers' burrows in ditch banks may cause washouts, floods and water-scarcity representing thousands of dollars loss to a community. In these irrigated districts public feeling has swung from fear and hatred of snakes to an appreciation of them, and they are now protected because of the warfare they wage against these most destructive rodents.

RABBITS. Another eater of green vegetation who may possibly visit or take up residence in the garden is the cottontail rabbit, of which varieties are found throughout the U. S. Here is another case of the gardener's choice: Is the company of this timid and beautiful little creature worth his board in bark, grass, foliage and vegetables? He has nothing in his favor except attractive appearance and engaging manner unless it is the fact that he is nobody's enemy. He is not an insect eater, nor does he prey on foes of insect pests.

BATS. It is not uncommon to see at dusk, flying about the garden pool or at the edge of the marsh, one of man's small unappreciated friends—a bat. The bat is not a bird but a highly specialized, warm-blooded mammal whose front legs and feet have been modified into the wings with which it flits and darts about in its nightly insect hunt.

Bats are not attractive, it is true, but they are harmless and need cause no alarm even when they enter the house. Here they are apt to be disconcerting with their dizzy swooping and erratic flight which, however, is partly due to fright. Usually if the lights are turned out for a moment the creature will zip out the door or window by which it entered. Let the thought that the bat's nightly hunting saves the itch of many a mosquito bite mitigate any unpleasant feeling the animal's proximity may give.

SKUNKS. Almost every garden is visited now and then by a skunk. Fortunately he is not at all likely to take up permanent residence there and his visits are usually nocturnal. The efficiency of his unique means of defense is reflected in the skunk's slow, deliberate movements and his calmness in situations which, to a less well protected animal, would be terrible emergencies. Confident of his ability to control and dominate almost any situation which may arise, he behaves accordingly. Hence, it is inadvisable to try to hurry his departure from your grounds should you encounter him. He won't tarry long after having been disturbed in his search for mice and other small game, but he will not be hurried. He will depart only with dignity or else ——! So remember that skunks are helpful to the gardener in that they assist in the elimination of the several types of mice which are so often a nuisance.

MICE. Of the many species found in the U. S. only two are of real economic importance in crop destruction. The meadow mouse, which makes well-defined runways through the grass, lives in large colonies which sometimes attain nuisance proportions. Although small, this mouse, when present in great numbers, may do severe damage not only to grass, hay and other surface vegetation but to the bark of trees, flowering shrubs, etc. Unfortunately, its pernicious activity around the roots of trees and shrubs is carried on ordinarily beneath the surface of either snow or earth and the damage has usually gone too far to be remedied before it is discovered. Tubers and bulbs are also damaged, though this work is often blamed on the mole. Valuable trees, especially newly planted fruit trees may be protected by wrappings or guards of wire, wood veneer, etc., but natural agents that hold the meadow mouse in check are hawks, owls, snakes, skunks and, near ponds, the bullfrog. See also MICE.

TOADS, FROGS AND LIZARDS. That familiar and friendly dweller in garden and field, the toad, although still regarded by the uninformed with suspicion, has been proved to be a most valuable gardener's helper. Indeed, in the garden, its place as a beneficial animal cannot be overemphasized. A large series of examinations of stomach contents of toads has revealed that they devour nightly an astonishing variety and quantity of material. Upwards of 3,000 insects or their larvae may be destroyed by a single toad in a summer month and in this insect harvest ants, ground beetles, click beetles, weevils, sowbugs and cutworms are prominent.

The many species of tree toads and tree frogs are also powerful enemies of insect pests and definitely an asset in the garden. Their place is, of course, at the edge of the water garden, in the pool or in the bog garden. There, besides their usefulness, their amusing behavior and bright colorings make them an attractive decorative feature.

In the S. and W. States lizards of several species sometimes frequent gardens in search of food. As this is composed of insects and insect larvae, their presence should be welcomed. They are all absolutely harmless and the gardener should try, for his garden's sake, not to give in to the prevailing prejudice against them, however unattractive they may be.

SNAKES. It is this prevailing prejudice against reptiles that makes the consideration of snakes in gardens particularly difficult. Among the many species found in the U. S. only four are poisonous. The others are harmless and many of them are powerful aids in the control of insect and animal pests.

Of the four that are not wanted around, the rattlesnake is easily recognized by its characteristic warning sound. In color it varies according to region but generally is yellowish or brown with cross bands and markings of darker brown or black. The sides are lighter in color and the body darkens toward the tail. The head is of the so-called "diamond" shape common to many species of poisonous snake.

The copperhead, dangerous because of its habit of striking without warning and often apparently without due provocation, is found from the N. E. part of the U. S. to Wis. and southward, usually in rather damp places. It sometimes strays into gardens, yards or even into outbuildings. Of a distinct reddish coloring, it has hazel-brown saddle markings and copper-yellow shading along the sides and head. Many examinations of stomach contents have shown it to be extremely useful in the destruction of insect and animal pests but its careless use of a dangerous weapon necessarily calls for its elimination from any haunt of man.

The other two poisonous N. American snakes occur only in the far S. and are not likely to get in the gardener's way. The water moccasin or cottonmouth, related to the rattler and the copperhead, doesn't often stray from the deep swamps. The tiny coral snake might possibly be encountered by a Florida gardener, but its bright colors and the warnings of the local wiseacres should make its recognition easy.

BENEFICIAL SNAKES. The harmless garter snake, found throughout the U. S. in various forms, is the one most commonly found in gardens. It is entirely harmless, although when cornered it manages to put up a good fight. However, it is scarcely able to break the skin with a bite and it is only necessary to treat such a wound as an ordinary scratch. Its food is composed largely of insects and small animals such as mice, frogs, toads, etc.

The two snakes whose presence causes the least consternation and which are often cherished as pets by country children, are the green snake and the grass snake. Both are strictly insect and insect-larvae eaters and are harmless to man or animal. Unfortunately, they are the prey of many of the smaller carnivorous animals and of flesh eating birds.

Probably the most maligned of all the snakes beneficial to the gardener and farmer is the milk snake. Despite the old superstition that it hangs about barns and houses in order to steal the milk from the family cow, it has no interest in milk whatever. Its prey is the rats, mice, gophers, etc., infesting the buildings and vicinity. Although its reddish coloring and black markings frequently lead this snake into being mistaken for a copperhead, the milk snake really belongs to the same family as the king snake, a redoubtable killer of rattlers and copperheads; in all probability, it also accounts for more than a few dead young rattlers on its own score.

Among the other snakes found in close proximity to man and his activities, the black snake, the pilot black, the hog-nosed snake, the pine snake and the corn snake all have good points and bad, depending entirely on the point of view. One, with no redeeming feature whatever, is the common water snake. In any of its many widely distributed varieties it is not poisonous, but can give a vicious bite—and does so on the slightest provocation. Squat and ugly in appearance it preys almost entirely on the life of ponds and streams. Frogs and the young of any water-fowl are common victims.

With snakes as with other animals the gardener must make a choice. If his dislike of them is so intense as to make them objectionable, he owes it to his own pleasure and that of his guests to rid his premises of them. However, before doing this and depriving himself and his plants of the material help of some species in pest control, the development of a little familiarity might breed—not contempt, but tolerance and perhaps even respect and liking. A little study of Ditmars' "Reptile Book," in which many of the N. American species are pictured and described, might help.

ANISE (an'-is). Common name for *Pimpinella anisum,* a herb of the Parsley Family, the leaves and seeds of which are used in cookery for flavoring, and in medicine. It is an annual plant to 2 ft. with small white or yellow clustered flowers, easily grown from seed in the herb garden. Seed should be planted in April in rows in mellow soil where the plants are to stand.

Anise is sometimes incorrectly applied to Foeniculum or Fennel (which see). Staror Chinese-anise is *Illicium verum.*

ANNONA (a-noh'-nah). A group of S. American, mostly tropical small trees and woody shrubs, grown in warm sections for their edible fruits. A few of the 50 or more species are grown in S. Calif. and Fla. where they require a light, well-drained soil. The most popular of these is *A. cherimoya,* the Cherimoya, which see. Others are *A. glabra,* the Pond-apple, grown mainly as a stock for grafting; *A. muricata,* the Soursop; *A. squamosa,* the Sweetsop or Sugar-apple, and *A. reticulata,* the Custard-apple or Bullocks Heart.

ANNUALS. Plants which grow from seed, attain their growth, flower and produce seed in one year (or less), then die, having completed their life-cycle. Annual is derived from the Latin word meaning a year, and is, of course, used as an adjective as well as a noun. Many annuals are apparently perennial, seeming to live on from year to year; in reality they self-sow (that is, scatter seed which lives over winter and gives rise to new plants) and thus perpetuate themselves. In gardening many plants of the biennial or perennial classes, but which bloom the first year from seed, are considered and used as annuals; directions for their culture, which is similar to that given the true annuals, are included in this article.

Annuals come to us from almost all parts of the world, and like all cosmopolitans are most adaptable. Properly chosen, they can provide bloom and fragrance in the garden from early spring to late fall. As they come in many forms, heights and colors, they lend themselves to many uses, and a very brilliant effect can be secured from a few packets of seeds. Some are excellent in beds or borders, either massed by themselves, in varied combinations, as fillers among perennials or to follow springblooming bulbs. Others are attractive vines; many are suitable for screens for window boxes and hanging baskets, and still others can be used for edging and for prolonging bloom in the rock garden after the normal season of many of the best rock-garden subjects. They are invaluable as cut flowers, and some can be used in winter bouquets.

BASIC PRINCIPLES. Two things must be remembered in growing annuals. The first is the necessity of obtaining the best seed from a well-known, established firm, if possible. These seedsmen have a pride in the purity of the strains they offer, and the gardener can more safely count on the right color and the desired quality in plants which grow from their carefully grown and selected seeds. The second thing to remember is that if you wish to prolong the blooming period of an annual the flowers must be picked before they fade (or immediately thereafter) in order that no seed may form. A true annual has a slight root system, as it stores no food for future seasons and it lives to bloom quickly, set seed, and finish its existence; therefore constant picking conserves its energy and stimulates it to use this energy in producing new blossoms as fast as the old ones are removed.

Annuals may be divided into three classes: (1) *Hardy,* which can withstand a light spring frost, and can therefore be started from seed sown in the open as soon as the soil can be worked; (2) *half-hardy,* which require a long season to attain maturity, and therefore must be given an early start under glass; and (3) *tender,* which require a still earlier start in the greenhouse, or hotbed, or indoors and which cannot be transplanted to the open until the ground is warm and all danger of frost is over.

HARDY ANNUALS. The seed of hardy annuals sown in the open should be planted in well-prepared loamy soil into which well-rotted manure has been dug the fall before. The surface soil should be so light and fine that the tender seedlings may penetrate it easily. If the soil is stiff, or heavy, an admixture of sand or any sort of humus will help lighten the texture. No commercial fertilizer should be used in this seed-bed, however, excepting perhaps bonemeal.

Annuals of which seed may thus be sown outdoors in early spring include:

African Daisy (Arctotis and Dimorphotheca), Alyssum, *Anchusa capensis,* Babys

in flats in the greenhouse or hotbed. If a few plants only are desired, use the pots. First scrub them clean, then place a piece of broken crock or a pebble over the hole in the bottom and fill to within 4 in. of the top of the pot with coarse soil. The next 2 in. should be finely sifted soil composed of equal parts garden loam, humus, and sand. Plant the seeds in this mixture, scattering them thinly over the surface if very fine and planting larger seeds in a spiral row in order to have room for weeding. Very fine seeds should be pressed into the soil and not covered; larger ones should be covered according to their size—about as deep as their diameter is a com-

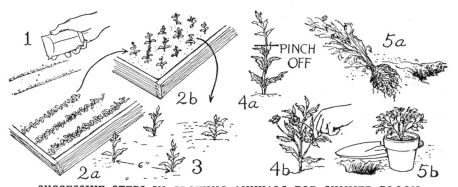

SUCCESSIVE STEPS IN GROWING ANNUALS FOR SUMMER BLOOM
(1) Sowing seeds from a packet into shallow drills in a seed box or flat. (2a) The seedlings are first "pricked out" and set an inch apart in another flat or hotbed, shown at 2b. Thence, when hardened off, they are transplanted to the garden after danger of frost is past (3). To prevent lanky growth pinch off the top (4a) to make the plant branch. To keep the plants blooming remove faded flowers promptly (4b). In the fall pull up and destroy all plants that have lived their lives (5a); but small stocky ones from late-sown seed that have not flowered can be cut back, potted, and brought indoors for winter bloom (5b).

Breath, Bartonia, Bachelors Button, Cacalia, Calendula, California Poppy, Calliopsis, Candytuft, Celosia, Chinese Delphinium, Clarkia, Cosmos, Dianthus, Euphorbia, Evening-primrose, Evening Stock, Gaillardia, Gilia, Globe-amaranth, Godetia, Kochia, Larkspur, Leptosyne, Lupine, Mallow, Marigold, Nigella, Pansy, Petunia, Phlox, Poppy (Opium and Shirley), Portulaca, Prickly Poppy, Scabiosa, Sunflower, Sweet Pea, Verbena, Viscaria and Zinnia.

Some of the above annuals resent transplanting and should, if possible, be planted in the spot where they are to grow. Among them are: California Poppy, Lupine, Mallow, Mignonette, Poppy and Sweet Pea.

HALF-HARDY ANNUALS. These can be started in pots or boxes of well-pulverized soil in a sunny window in the house, or

mon rule. Water, if necessary, with a fine spray. A piece of glass may now be placed over the top of the pot, which should be shaded with newspaper until germination takes place, then the paper and glass should be removed and the pot brought into full sunlight.

If a greater quantity of plants is desired use boxes or flats about 4 in. deep, making sure there is adequate drainage. Partly fill the boxes with coarse soil, finishing as in the pots, with an inch of the soil mixture given above. Sow the seeds in rows 1 in. apart. Very fine seeds may be covered with burlap, which is watered often enough to stay moist and left in place until germination takes place.

Some of the annuals, and plants treated as annuals, which profit by an early start are: Aster, Browallia, Butterfly-flower,

Chinese Delphinium (*D. grandiflorum*), Flax, Floss-flower, Hop, Immortelle, Lobelia, Ornamental Tobacco, Painted Tongue, Pansy, Petunia, Phlox, Sage, Snapdragon, Swan River Daisy, Sweet Sultan, Torenia, Verbena and Wallflower.

TENDER ANNUALS. These should be started in the same way as the half-hardy sorts, but earlier—in February in the greenhouse, or in March in the hotbed. Among those requiring this early start are: Annual Poinsettia, Balsam, Balsam-apple, Browallia, Butterfly-flower, Canary bird-vine, Castor-bean, Chrysanthemum (annual), Cup-and-saucer-vine, Dwarf Morning-glory, Floss-flower, Gourd, Hyacinth-bean, Lace-flower, Mignonette, Monkey-flower, Nasturtium, Rainbow-corn, Scarlet Sage, Scarlet Runner bean, Sensitive-plant, Spider-flower, Stock, Swan River Everlasting, Toad-flax, Torenia and Verbena.

In starting all seeds in flats it is necessary to place the ones which germinate rapidly in one flat and those slow to appear in another, in order that they may receive the same sort of care.

Seedlings started indoors benefit and are made more stocky by being shifted at least once before being set outdoors. As soon as several true leaves have appeared the seedlings should be "pricked off" into small individual pots or into another box or flat. An old kitchen fork is an excellent tool to use in this work, or a small garden label with the end notched. These transplanted seedlings form a better root system and grow compact and sturdy instead of tall and spindly as they would if left in a crowded row. By the middle or end of May these plants, which should have been gradually hardened off by increasing ventilation and exposure to the outdoor temperature, should be ready to set in the open. They should then be watered, and also the spot where they are to be planted, several hours before they are moved. Separate the little plants carefully and set them far enough apart in the ground to allow them to develop without crowding.

Some of the hardy annuals may be started in the fall; so handled they will flower much earlier than those grown from spring-sown seed. Among them are: Alyssum, Bachelors Button, California Poppy, Candytuft, Cosmos, Gaillardia, Godetia, Larkspur, Nigella, Petunia, Poppy, Portulaca, Snapdragon, and Sweet Pea. Ordinarily they can be sown slightly deeper than in spring planting. The idea is not to get them above ground in the fall, but to get the seed in place and ready to grow with the first favorable weather of spring, even before the soil could normally be worked. For this reason some protection applied after the soil freezes, so as to prevent excessively deep freezing, is a good idea. Fall-planted sweet peas are usually sown at the bottom of a trench 4 to 6 in. deep which is filled about one-third full of soil and the rest with litter or manure until spring, when it is removed and the soil gradually cultivated in to fill the trench as the plants grow.

ANNUALS FOR COLOR. Annuals run the gamut of the spectrum, in both brilliant and pastel shades, from darkest purple to white. While individual taste naturally will dictate the arrangement of flowers with regard to color combinations, attention should also be paid to harmony. Beautiful effects are obtained by massing of colors. The following combinations have been tested and found to produce excellent results:

maroon and white: Scabiosa and Nicotiana; Black Prince Snapdragon and Sweet Alyssum.

blue and yellow: Calliopsis and Centaurea; dwarf Zinnias and Larkspur.

pink and yellow: Snapdragon and Marigold; Verbena and Calendula; *Phlox drummondi* and Snapdragon; Scabiosa and Marigold.

pink and blue: Phlox drummondi as edging for Larkspur; pink and blue Larkspur; Dianthus and Ageratum.

orange and red: Calliopsis and Nasturtium; Marigold and Salvia; Zinnia and Marigold; Gaillardia and Marigold.

These combinations are suggested for the gardener who is beginning. The experienced grower will learn from experience which colors are harmonious, as well as the annuals which are best suited to his special purposes.

Before deciding on plants for specific uses, however, the gardener should be certain that he has a liberal quantity of the most *practical* annuals. That question has been discussed for many years, almost always with different, though interesting answers. The most *practical* plant, of course, is the one that provides the most bloom over the longest period with least effort. For display alone the petunia seems to carry the greatest favor. It gives greater bloom over a longer period than any other annual, with the least amount of attention and is of great value for flower arrangements. For beauty of display, for cutting and for a long flowering season the zinnia is a general favorite. Close behind are marigolds, which are limited in color to varying shades of yellow, orange and brownish reds, and poppies, which, however, have a short season. For cutting alone, asters are very highly regarded, but they do not flower until late summer.

All these annuals, however, should be in every garden, for they come in a wide range of form, color and height, the zinnia being produced from the tiny buttons of the lilliput type to the mammoth forms that rival dahlias. Marigolds range from the tiny flowers that spangle the fern-like foliage of the dwarf *Tagetes signata* var. *pumila* to the huge globes of the African type. Others that are special favorites in American gardens are larkspur, scabiosa, salpiglossis, ageratum, and lobelia.

Once having grown these annuals, the gardener should specialize in one or two particular plants, growing the improved varieties which are listed from year to year. Some of these should be grown in the general garden, while others should have a place in the special garden for cutting.

Annuals for Cutting

One may have a cutting garden where annuals are grown in rows like vegetables, and spaced and cultivated in the same manner. In a garden of this type they will develop to perfection and one may pick without thought of marring the effect of the garden picture in order to have an abundance of blossoms for the house and for gifts. The desirability of asters and zinnias as cut flowers has been mentioned. Other annuals which make excellent cut flowers include the following: African Daisy, Annual Carnation, Babys Breath, Bachelors Button, Chrysanthemum (annual), Cosmos, Everlastings, Godetia, Grasses, Larkspur, Love-in-a-mist, Lupine, Marigold, Mignonette, Mourning Bride, Nasturtium, Painted Tongue, Pansy, Petunia, Phlox, Pinks, Poppy, Stocks, Sweet Pea, Sweet Sultan, Verbena.

Annuals for Shade

Many gardens do not have sun all day, and it is often necessary to select annuals that will grow well in shade. While most of them must have some sun and hardly any will thrive in dense shade, there are a number that do well in locations which get only a little sun. Among them are: Aster, Centaurea, Forget-me-not, Godetia, Monkey-flower, Nemophila, Pansy, Schizanthus, Snapdragon, Sweet Alyssum, and Torenia.

For Rock Gardens

While the rock garden is a permanent planting and the backbone of its planting scheme should consist of carefully selected perennials, there are a number of annuals which will lend it color, especially at those times when the perennials are not in bloom. In choosing annuals for the rock garden it is necessary to consider their growing habits. While most of them are a bit too spreading to be ideal, there are many that can be extremely useful, providing quick effect for small cost. A few annuals which give bloom in the rock garden without dominating it are: Baby Blue-eyes, Babys Breath (*Gypsophila muralis*), Meadow Foam, Musk, Pimpernel (*Anagallis arvensis,* var. *phoenicea*), Stonecrop (*Sedum caeruleum*), and Violet-cress or Diamondflower.

Climbing Annuals

Annual vines are ideal as a cover for fences or unsightly objects, or to form a screen for privacy. They grow quickly and provide beauty while performing these utilitarian purposes. Annuals are especially suitable for such purposes in the case of persons who rent and do not own their property. They are also useful while evergreen and hardy vines are becoming established.

One of the most beautiful is the Moonflower vine, whose fragrance resembles that of the magnolia. Its white blossoms, from 5 to 6 in. across, are in bloom from late afternoon to early morning and make good cut flowers in the evening. With its clusters of purple and white flowers resembling hyacinths, the Hyacinth-bean vine is a favorite, as is the Canary Creeper, also useful for cutting, with its canary-colored flowers resembling tiny birds in flight. One of the fastest growing climbers is the Cup-and-saucer vine whose purple and white blossoms, resembling Canterbury Bells, are borne profusely. Nor can one ignore the old-fashioned Morning-glory, which is too well known to require description. Other climbers include Balloon-vine, Balsam-apple or Balsam-pear, Cardinal Climber, Cypress-vine, Gourds, Nasturtiums, Scarlet Runner, Sweet Pea, and Wild-cucumber.

Hanging baskets and window boxes are often a feature of the home, either indoors or on the porch. Annuals which may be used in these baskets and boxes include: Clock-vine, Kenilworth Ivy and Maurandia for the basket and, for window boxes, Alyssum, Browallia, Dusty Miller, Dwarf Zinnias, Floss-flower, Lobelia, Madagascar Periwinkle, Marigolds (French and Mexican), Nasturtium (Tom Thumb), Nemesia, Pansy, Petunia, Phlox, Portulaca, Verbena, Wishbone-flower.

Vacation Garden

Many people, feeling that they will leave their winter home before annuals can flower and too late to start a garden at their summer location, deprive themselves unnecessarily of the joy of flowers. The ease with which annuals can be grown makes it a simple matter to have a garden while on vacation. The air at high altitudes is usually cool and that near the water ordinarily moist and a large number of annuals grow better under such conditions than where it is hot or dry. Quick-growing hardy types should be chosen, including Alyssum, Bachelors Button, Calendula, Candytuft, Cosmos, Larkspur, Marigold (French, African and Mexican), Mignonette, Mourning Bride and Nasturtium.

Annuals for Edging

The appearance of the herbaceous border may often be improved by the planting of a few annuals in the foreground; or a bed of geraniums or other plants may have its beauty enhanced by an edging of low growing annuals. Perhaps attractive low plants may be wanted for lining a garden path. Such situations offer some of the best uses for annuals. There is perhaps no more satisfactory edging plant than alyssum, covered from spring to frost with a sheet of bloom. White varieties are best, though some of the lilacs and pinks are often grown to advantage. Among the whites Little Dorrit, Benthami and Little Gem are unsurpassed for edging. Other annuals suitable for such purposes include Anagallis, Pimpernel, Brachycome or the

Swan River Daisy, Lobelia, Dwarf Nasturtium, Nemesia, Nemophila, and Pansy.

A garden designed especially for twilight and evening enjoyment can be made doubly attractive by the use of annuals notable for their fragrance, for the perfume is always more intense as the dew begins to fall. Some fragrant annuals are: Alyssum, Candytuft, Dianthus, Evening Stock, Mignonette, Petunia, Snapdragon, Stock, Sweet Pea, Tobacco (Nicotiana), Verbena, Wallflower. See also EVENING GARDEN; FRAGRANT GARDEN.

Annuals for Children's Gardens

To attract and hold the interest of children, plants should be brilliant and attractive, quick growing and of easy culture, yielding prompt and generous returns for the care they receive. Annuals are especially suited for such use, and in addition they are obtainable in inexpensive packets of seed, or as low-priced seedling plants. They thrive and bloom quickly even when planted in ordinary soil, from seed sown either shallow or deep, require no staking, and suffer less than other plants from improper watering or from prolonged drought. Examples of such annuals are: Aster, Calendula, Calliopsis, Cornflower, Gaillardia, Petunia, Marigold, Nasturtium, Portulaca and Zinnia.

For Dry Soil

For gardeners who are at a loss as to what to grow in dry soil the following annuals are recommended: African Daisy (*Arctotis*), Browallia, California Poppies, Calliopsis, Candytuft, Cosmos, Cynoglossum, Amabile, Gaillardia, Mexican Zinnia, Nigella, Prickly Poppy, Red Flax.

For Damp Soil

Where opposite soil conditions prevail, and it is difficult to get the earth dry, the following annuals will thrive: Myosotis or Forget-me-not, Pansy, Phlox, Sanvitalia, and Schizanthus.

In the Bulb Bed

When the spring-flowering bulbous plants fade it is necessary to fill the space with something that will grow quickly and not leave the bulb bed barren. It is not necessary to buy plants, for annuals, sown before the bulbs bloom, will be ready when they decline. Any annuals that can be started outdoors may be used for this purpose, and some of them may even be sown the preceding fall. In tulip beds a fine sowing of Shirley poppies is especially good. The seed will germinate either in the fall or early in the spring and the plants will grow quickly enough to hide the tulip leaves as they turn brown. Plant larkspur only among the early tulips, for their thick growth crowds the late types before their bloom is past.

Annual Everlastings

There are a large number of annuals that may be grown not only for their color in the summer but also to be preserved for winter bouquets. These are known as Strawflowers or Everlastings (which see).

Annual Grasses

There are many annual grasses of considerable beauty, valuable for mixing with fresh flowers and equally suited for drying for winter use with everlasting flowers. Though they do not retain their color when dried, they are easily dyed, taking dye much more satisfactorily than many of the everlasting blossoms. There is one exception, *Briza Maxima,* which must be treated to remove its glossy surface before it will take dye. All dried grasses are useful even without coloring. Any of them may be preserved if cut at the proper time, the requirement being to gather them just before the flowers open. Then tie the grasses in small bunches and hang them in the shade where there is good ventilation. When thoroughly dry pack the bunches away, not in a dusty place. Cutting the grasses at various stages of growth will provide variety. In transplanting seedlings to the open ground, space them about 8 in. apart. This seems a great distance but the plants grow rapidly and if placed closer together they will be crowded when they develop. Among the best of the annual grasses are:

Agrostis nebulosa (Cloud Grass). Fine, light and graceful, the panicles, resembling mist-like veils, add airiness to bouquets.

Briza minor (Little Quaking Grass) to 1½ ft. has pale green nodding spikelets in panicles to 5 in. long.

Briza maxima (Quaking Grass), to 2 ft., has bronzy spikelets in panicles to 3 in. It is one of the most decorative species.

Coix lachryma-jobi (Jobs Tears), to 4 ft., with peculiar, large, hard, shiny seeds which are used for beads.

Pennisetum ruppeli (Fountain Grass) to 4 ft., with rose, copper, or purple spikes to 1 ft. long, is excellent for massing.

See also EDGING PLANTS; CUT FLOWERS; EVERLASTINGS; BIENNIALS; PERENNIALS.

ANTELOPE-BRUSH. Common name for *Purshia* (or *Kunzia*) *tridentata,* a hardy, scraggy, evergreen shrub native in the Rocky Mountain region of Oregon and California; sometimes transplanted to gardens. See PURSHIA.

ANTENNARIA (an-te-nay'-ri-ah), Perennial herbs of the Composite Family commonly known as Everlastings or Pussy-Toes. The white-woolly leaves are clustered at the base of the stem and the flowers are in heads. Antennarias are common field plants, only occasionally offered by dealers for planting in the wild or rock garden; sometimes they are grown for dried winter bouquets. They will grow in poor soil and are easily propagated by seed or division.

A. plantaginifolia (Ladies-tobacco) makes broad patches in old fields and pastures, with woolly leaves and small flowers appearing in early spring. It provides attractive foliage for a dry stone wall or rock garden.

rosea grows to 1½ ft., spreading by means of underground stems. The foliage is distinctly white-woolly and the bracts of the flowerheads are rose-colored. Found in W. America.

ANTHEMIS (an'-the-mis). Perennial herbs of the Composite or Daisy Family with scented and finely cut foliage and solitary flowers with yellow disks. The two most-grown species are known as Golden Marguerite and Chamomile. The bushy plants 2 to 3 ft. tall, thriving in any soil and requiring full sun, grow compactly and are covered with white or rich yellow flowers good for cutting. Seed should be sown out of doors late in April or early in May, but it can be started earlier indoors. When transplanting to their places in the garden, thin plants to stand at least 9 in. apart. They flower profusely from June to September or even until frost. Mature plants may be increased by division of the roots.

Species commonly cultivated include:

A. cinerea. Spreading to 1 ft., grayish woolly foliage. Large heads with white ray flowers longer than the disk diameter.

montana. To 10 in., with silky foliage and white ray flowers.

nobilis (Chamomile). To 1 ft. White

ray flowers but those of var. *grandiflora* are larger and sometimes yellow, while var. *flore-pleno* has double flowers. The flower buds of this species are the source of the chamomile used in medicine.

tinctoria (Golden Marguerite). To 3 ft. with golden yellow ray flowers 2 in. across.

kelwayi. May be a separate species or a form of *A. tinctoria* with more finely cut foliage and flowers of a deeper yellow.

ANTHER. A two-celled sac borne on the thread-like stalk of a stamen located just within the floral envelope. At maturity each cell splits to release pollen grains containing the male or germ elements of the plant.

See FLOWER.

ANTHERICUM (an-ther'-i-kum). A genus of tuberous-rooted herbs of the Lily Family with racemes of small white lily-like flowers and long narrow grassy leaves; sometimes known as St. Brunos Lily or St. Bernards Lily. In mild climates Anthericums may be grown in the open and in the N. they will live through the winter in the border if given protection. They also make decorative subjects for the cool greenhouse and for use in lawn vases in the summer. Of easy culture, they should be grown in rich fibrous loam. When in bloom they require a plentiful supply of water. They are easily increased by cuttings of the stolons or by division. *A. liliago* (St. Bernards Lily) to 3 ft. with clustered flowers 1 in. across, is the plant more frequently grown, but *A. bicheti* from Africa, with variegated leaves, is occasionally seen.

ANTHOLYZA (an-thoh-ly'-zah). A S. African genus of leafy-stemmed herbs of the Iris Family; plants growing from corms, flowering in summer and resembling gladiolus. They have narrow leaves and red or yellow flowers on spikes to 4 ft. tall. The corms are planted out in the spring and taken up in the fall; or for early bloom they can be started under glass and set out about June 1. The best known species is *A. aethiopica* to 4 ft. with leaves to 1½ in. wide and reddish-yellow curved flowers to 2½ in. long. *A. cunonia* and *A. caffra,* growing only about 1 ft. tall, have brilliant red flowers. There are numerous hybrids.

ANTHRACNOSE (an-thrak'-nohs). A term originally used in France to designate the slightly raised, scab-like leaf spot of grapes, caused by the "birds-eye" fungus. Later it was applied in America to the sunken black spots on bean pods. At present the word anthracnose usually means a certain fungous disease, in which circular leaf spots with a gray or white center and a reddish border are typical, especially on rose and grape. On beans the black pod spots are more prominent than the angular leaf lesions. Anthracnose diseases of shade trees are widespread. Sycamore and oak are particularly subject to them, but the same type of disease occurs on maple, horsechestnut and linden. Large areas on the leaves appear brown and scorched and there may follow defoliation, twig and limb blights and, sometimes, the death of the tree. In general, anthracnose diseases are treated by spraying with copper fungicides such as bordeaux mixture. See also the various host plants for detailed symptoms and control measures.

ANTHURIUM (an-theu'-ri-um). A genus of tropical plants of the Arum Family, grown for their ornamental, usually heart- or arrow-shaped leaves, and gayly colored spreading spathe or flower bracts from which protrudes a slender spike of contrasting color, usually yellow. They are greenhouse plants requiring a high temperature and can be grown from seed, suckers, or root-cuttings. The best soil is a rough, fibrous loam. Though not common garden or house plants the cut flowers and foliage are popular material for modernistic table and mantel arrangements.

A. andraeanum has leaves 1 ft. long and 6 in. wide; the spathe, spreading 6 in., varies from orange-red to rose and white.

scherzereanum has narrow leaves to 8 in. long and a spathe 3 in. long, from red to rose and white in color.

magnificum. The leaves to 1½ ft. long, are olive-green with white veins. The recurved spathe 8 in. long, is green or reddish.

ANTIGONON (an-tig'-oh-non). A tendril-climber belonging to the Buckwheat Family. Grown in the North as a greenhouse vine, it is a popular, hardy climber in the South, where it has a long season of bloom. It will grow more than 30 ft. in good soil, but if over-fed it makes a rank growth.

In the greenhouse it needs plenty of light and not too much root run. It blooms in the summer, and needs plenty of water when growth is active, supplemented with liquid manure if in a tub or pot. It makes a large tuberous r o-o t, a n d m u s t be kept dry during the resting period in winter.

The chief species is *A. leptopus,* called Mountain-rose and Coral-vine. T h e handsome rose-pink flowers are borne in racemes. V a r. *albus* has white flowers.

ANTIRRHINUM, OR SNAPDRAGON, RUST Causes faint spots on upper leaf surfaces and more pronounced ones on under leaf surfaces and stems.

ANTIRRHI- N U M (an-ti-ry'-num). A genus of the Figwort Family, comprising a number of species of erect, trailing or half-shrubby plants, usually treated as annuals if grown in garden or greenhouse.

A. majus, known as Snapdragon (which see), is the most important species. This is a perennial to 3 ft. with white to purplish red flowers to 1½ in. long. Many beautiful intermediate shades have been developed by hybridists and are grouped according to height, as Dwarf or Tom Thumb, 6 to 9 in.; Intermediate or Half-dwarf 15 to 18 in.; and Tall, 2 to 3 ft.

Other species of interest are: *A. coulterianum* (Chaparral S.) to 3 ft. from Calif., having small flowers varying from white to purplish; and *A. orontium,* a Eurasian species, occasionally found as an escape in N. America.

ANTS. These familiar garden inhabitants vary in size, color and to some extent habits, but all kinds have a well-developed social organization with a queen and workers. The majority of the larvae hatched from the eggs are sterile workers but a certain percentage are winged males and females. After mating the male dies while the female flies to a suitable site, tears off her wings, makes a small nest and lays eggs. The whitish maggot-like grubs (young larvae) are cared for by the females until they are full-grown workers, when they in turn care for the queen and her young.

ANTS AS PESTS. Ants do not feed on plants but become garden pests because of the unsightly hills or nests they form in lawns and especially because of their habit of fostering aphids. The ants often seen swarming over the succulent tips of plants are there to obtain the aphid excreta called honeydew. The relation between ants and the corn- and strawberry-root aphids benefits both. In the autumn ants carry the aphid eggs underground and nurse them over the winter; in the spring they carry them to some succulent weed host where the young can obtain nourishment. Later they carry the adult aphids around and "pasture" them on corn roots. The aphids have become so dependent on ants for transportation that they have practically lost the means of locomotion.

CONTROL. If the ant nest can be located fumigation is probably the best method of control. Make holes 8 to 10 in. apart with a sharp stick deep enough to reach the center of the nest (3 to 6 in.) and place about an ounce of carbon-bisulphide in each hole; then cover with earth and spread burlap over the area. When the colonies cannot be located, or if there are many small nests, it is better to use a poison syrup bait slow enough in its action to allow the worker ants to carry it back to the queen and her young. A syrup frequently recommended is made by boiling together for 30 minutes:

Granulated sugar	1¼ lbs.
Water	1¼ pints
Tartaric acid (crystalized)	1 gram
Benzoate of soda	1 gram

Then dissolve ⅛ oz. of sodium-arsenite in hot water, stir well and, when cool, add to first solution. Finally add ⅔ lb. strained honey and mix well. The chemicals may be purchased from the druggist, who should weigh them out.

The syrup may be put on bits of sponge and left out in perforated tin boxes, which will keep it away from birds and animals. Various proprietary compounds in paste, jelly and "trap" forms, containing thallium-sulphate are effective and save labor.

So-called "white ants" are really Termites, which see.

APETALOUS. Without petals; when a flower is lacking one set of floral leaves, it is customary to regard the missing set as the corolla even though the remaining set may be petal-like. See FLOWER.

A P H E L A N D R A (af-ee-lan'-drah). Evergreen shrubs of tropical America. A few species grown in choice collections of warm greenhouse plants. They are prized for their handsome leaves which, in some kinds, are variegated. All have showy terminal flower spikes, in shades of orange or scarlet, often supplemented by large colored bracts more lasting than the flowers. The usual flowering time is fall and winter. Old plants may be cut back when rested and grown on again, or young plants may be grown annually from cuttings.

APHIDS. A world-wide group of insects popularly called plant lice, attacking nearly every garden and greenhouse crop. Small, soft bodied, they are usually green but may be brown, yellow, pink or black. They feed by thrusting a sharp-nosed stylet from their beaks into the plant cells and sucking out the sap. The plant's resulting loss in vitality is shown by discolored areas on the foliage, curling of leaves and blighting of buds and fruits. Even more disastrous is the propensity of the aphid to transmit plant diseases such as fire blight and mosaic.

LIFE-HISTORY. Aphids winter as fertilized eggs on stems and in bud crevices of some perennial plant.

ANT NURSE CARRYING AN APHID

By harboring aphids from which they secure a secretion called honeydew, ants are partly responsible for the spread of the pests.

In spring wingless young (called nymphs) hatch out and quickly grow to full size becoming so-called "stem mothers," which produce living female young without a mating or an exposed egg stage. At the end of a week or so these young in turn reproduce in the same manner so that great colonies are quickly formed. Some of the females (called spring migrants) develop wings and fly to a different type of plant known as the summer host. More generations are produced until finally, at the approach of cold weather, an entire winged group is born, containing males as well as females. These last females fly back to the same type of perennial plant from which their ancestors came and there produce wingless nymphs, which mate with the winged males of the preceding generation. After mating the females lay from one to four eggs and die.

HONEYDEW. Aphids excrete a sticky substance called honeydew which furnishes nutriment for the sooty mold fungus (so prominent on tulip trees and some others) and for ants. The latter keep aphids (as men keep cows for their milk) and may pasture them out on corn and strawberry roots. See ANTS.

All shade trees, shrubs, ornamental plants and vegetables suffer to some extent from aphids. In greenhouses the females continue to produce generations without mating. Spruce galls, cockscomb gall of elm, and phylloxera of grapes are caused by aphids. Purplish-red aphids, covered with a white felty mass, curl and deform apple and elm leaves in early spring. Black snowball and cherry aphids cause the same type of injury. Green aphids suck the juice from succulent rose shoots.

CONTROL. Aphids are controlled by using contact insecticides (which see). For the spruce gall aphid and the bark aphid which cause cottony flecks on pine trunks, use a dormant oil spray containing nicotine-sulphate and apply just before new growth starts in the spring. To control rosy and woolly apple aphids, spray just when the tips of the buds show green. For ordinary garden crops spray with nicotine-sulphate and soap whenever the young first appear. Nicotine dust may be more desirable for low growing crops. Pyrethrum, derris or rotenone compounds may also be used (see special crops for detailed instructions). Natural predatory enemies (such as ant-lions and lady-bird beetles) and parasitic wasps help to reduce the aphid population.

APICRA (ah-py'-krah). A name of Greek derivation, meaning not bitter, given to a genus of small succulent plants of the Lily Family, native to the Cape of Good Hope, probably to distinguish them from the aloes, which they resemble. They are grown indoors in cactus or succulent collections and may be used in rockeries in the summer. Grown in pots in a soil of peat and sandy loam, plants do well in the same soil and pot for years. Propagation is by suckers, by cuttings of the young growths, or by seeds if they can be had.

APHIDS A COMMON GARDEN PEST

Left, aphids on a rose stem; right, a small section enlarged.

APIUM (ay'-pi-um). A genus of annual or biennial herbs of the Parsley Family (Umbelliferae), native in the Mediterranean region of Europe. One species (*A. graveolens*) includes two familiar vegetables: celery, which is the var. *dulce;* and celeriac, which is the var. *rapaceum.* See CELERY and CELERIAC.

APOCYNACEAE (ah-pos-i-nay'-see-ee). Botanical name of the Dogbane Family, a group of herbs, shrubs or trees of wide range but most abundant in the tropics, grown for ornament and, in a few cases, for their edible fruit and drug products. The juice of some species is an acrid, poisonous secretion. The principal cultivated genera are *Apocynum,* the common Dogbane; *Vinca* (Periwinkle), *Oleander, Nerium* and *Tabernaemontana.*

APOCYNUM (ah-pos'-i-num). A genus of perennial herbs commonly known as Dogbane (which see), because the milky juice of the stem is supposed to be poisonous to dogs. *A. cannabinum* is also called Indian-hemp or Hemp Dogbane.

APONOGETON (ah-poh-noh-jee'-ton). Perennial Asiatic aquatic plants forming the only genus of the Aponogeton Family. They are grown in indoor pools, in aquaria and also outdoors in the summer in the N. Propagated by seed, division or offsets, the plants should be grown in pots 18 to 24 in. deep in water. To favor seed production, hand pollinate the flowers and keep them out of the water.

A. distachyus (Cape Pond-weed or Water-hawthorn) has flowers with prominent white bracts and a delicious hawthorn-like fragrance. Even in the N. it may be grown in a protected pool without lifting and keeping indoors over winter.

fenestralis (Lace- or Lattice-leaf), the most popular species, has broad, elliptic, lacy leaves that float just under the water and show only a network of veins. It should be grown in a tub in a warm (65 to 70 deg.) greenhouse or in a heated aquarium.

See also AQUARIUM.

APOROCACTUS (a-poh-roh-kak'-tus) *flagelliformis.* This species of cactus, nowhere known in its wild state, is supposed to have been introduced into cultivation from South America about 1690. It is often seen in Mexico growing in a cow's horn hung at the side of the house and called "flor de querno." In European countries it has long been popular, and is some-times to be seen completely curtaining a window with its pendent stems, upon which are borne its rose-colored blossoms. From the shape of its stem it is often called the "rat-tail cactus." It grows best when grafted upon some larger stem like that of *Nyctocereus serpentinus,* cut sufficiently high to allow for its drooping growth.

See also CACTUS.

APOTHECIUM (ap-oh-thee'-si-um). A cup-shaped, open, fungus fruiting body lined with sacs (*asci*) containing the sexual spores.

See FUNGI; compare PERITHECIUM.

APPLE. This is the most important temperate-climate fruit, measured by the extent of its culture, the number of uses to which it is adapted and the length of the season covered by its varieties, ripening successionally, and without the aid of commercial cold storage. The tree (botanically *Pyrus malus* or, according to some, *Malus sylvestris*) is presumably a native of Europe and adjacent Asia whence also come the true crabs (*P. baccata*) with which it has probably been hybridized to produce some of the larger crab apple varieties. The apple blossom is the state flower of Ark. and of Mich.

VARIETIES

One variety of apple, the Paradise, of bush-like form and stature, is used as a dwarfing stock on which to graft choice dessert varieties so that the trees will be adaptable in size to garden rather than orchard planting. For the standard or naturally growing apple tree often exceeding 50 ft. in height and spread unless controlled, is not a subject for small properties. Moreover, unless grafted to several varieties, a standard tree would produce too much fruit for the average family at one time and none the rest of the season. A full-grown apple tree may produce 50 bushels in a single season.

Of all fruits the apple has developed the largest number of varieties, American lists totaling more than 3,000 and European countless others, with new ones being introduced annually. Of the domestic kinds scarcely more than two score are commercially prominent. For home gardens, however, where high eating quality rather than heavy bearing or mere appearance and shipping quality of the fruit is the important factor, several hundred others are well worth consideration. For here none but the choicest dessert varieties should have a place; garden space is too valuable to devote to culinary staples and these may be bought in unlimited supply in the markets and stores. Dessert kinds never reach the market in condition comparable with that of home-grown fruit. They are gathered before they have developed the fragrance and flavor which characterize full ripeness and which are easily attained in the home garden.

To help the novice choose desirable dessert varieties a suggestive list is given. As probably less than half of these are listed by most nurseries (even though all are familiar, time-tried sorts), the gardener will have to secure scions and graft his own trees. (See GRAFTING.) Doubtless the best sources of scions or of information as to where they can be obtained are the State Experiment Stations and the U. S. Department of Agriculture. Here are recommended home varieties:

Benoni, Blenheim, Chenango, Cox Orange, Early Joe, Early Strawberry, Esopus, Fall Pippin, Fameuse, Gravenstein, Grimes Golden, Hawley, Hubbardston, Jonathan, Louise, MacIntosh, Mother, Newtown, Northern Spy, Peck, Pomme Gris, Porter, Primate, Red Canada, Red June, Ribston, Roxbury, Saint Lawrence, Shiawassee, Smokehouse, Stayman, Sutton, Swaar, Swazie, Sweet Bough, Wagener, Wealthy, Williams, Winesap.

In choosing other varieties from nursery catalogs (as he may prefer or have to do), the novice may well be guided by the following considerations: Avoid all varieties described as "commercial" or "culinary" unless they are also rated as of dessert quality. Avoid culinary winter kinds because these may always be had in the stores. Choose varieties that, ripening successionally, will cover the season between midsummer and the following spring; and, if garden space permits, include among them one tree each (not more) of summer and early autumn culinary kinds which are seldom obtainable in choice condition in stores. So far as possible choose varieties that begin to bear while young, avoiding those that require many years to reach bearing age.

For the home garden dwarf apple trees are ideal. First, because no one tree is likely to ripen more fruit than can be used during its season; second, because an "orchard" of 16 to 25 trees may be grown in the space that would be required by one standard apple tree; third, because the succession of varieties may cover the entire season; and, fourth, because dwarf apples properly managed normally begin to bear the second or third year after planting, whereas very few standards start sooner than the fifth year and some not before the tenth.

In all the States and most of the Canadian Provinces apples of some kinds can be grown; however, varieties suited to the S. require too long a season to ripen in the N. and are likely to be injured if not killed by N. winters. On the other hand, N. varieties tend to ripen earlier the farther they are taken southward. To illustrate, the Northern Spy which ripens late and keeps well as a winter apple in N. New York, matures so much earlier in the lower Hudson Valley that it can rarely be kept in home storage after Christmas; and in Delaware it is a fall variety.

CULTURE

Though some varieties of applies grow best and yield the best quality fruit only when grown on a certain kind of soil (and are therefore planted commercially on such soils), practically all kinds will do fairly well on any type of soil the average home garden may have. However, best results are secured on a deep, fairly rich, well-drained soil. If choice is possible, a clayey loam, rich in humus and underlaid with gravel or shale, is excellent; but many orchards do fully as well on light, sandy soils.

So far as the small home planting is concerned, it makes little difference what method of propagation—budding or grafting—the nursery used, so long as the trees are delivered in good condition with well-ripened wood. However, for cold climates, the grafting of hardy varieties on small pieces of seedling apple root (called "nurse stocks") has the advantage of encouraging the hardy scions to form roots above the graft union; thus they become "own rooted" and, therefore, hardier than if all the roots of the tree were on the stock, probably of unknown hardiness.

Though many commercial apple growers plant trees two years old from the bud or graft, many object to them because they have usually been allowed (or even encouraged) to form branches in undesirable positions and must therefore be cut back severely in order to develop new ones. In many cases this means that all the branches with their vigorous buds must be destroyed and the inferior latent buds of the previous year forced to grow; all too often these produce mis-shaped trees! No such objection can be made against one-year trees because they are usually unbranched "whips" and are under the planter's control as to where the branches shall be allowed to form right from the first. Moreover, yearling trees usually cost less both to buy and to transport; they must be thrifty to be salable at that age; they transplant more successfully and they usually grow more promptly and vigorously.

Today, as a result of carefully planned experiments, the approved method of developing sturdy trees is to start with *freshly dug* unbranched whips, *plump to the very tip bud, which must be intact.* Then, after planting, choose groups of three buds, the first at the height where the lowest main branch is wanted, the others at 12 in. intervals up to the tip well distributed around the stem, not all on one side. All other buds are destroyed by cutting them across with a sharp knife. The selected buds are allowed to develop branches during the first season but all except the desired ones are pruned off the following spring; the ones chosen and left are those that point in different directions.

During the second year buds on the frame (sometimes erroneously called "scaffold") branches and on the yearling growth of the leader or main trunk are chosen in the same way as during the first year. Thus the tree is made architecturally or structurally strong, well balanced and symmetrical. When the desired height of trunk has been reached the leader or tip bud is destroyed to stop increase of height.

When trees are started and trained as thus described, the suppression of undesired branches obviates their later removal after they have taken a certain amount of strength and sustenance. This prevents the possibility of throwing the tree out of balance and thus favors the early development of the fruit-bearing habit. In spite of such training, however, some branches may develop where not wanted—where they would interfere with others; or they may become diseased beyond aid. In such cases the sooner they are removed the better. See PRUNING.

Always it is advisable for the home gardener to buy his apple trees in the autumn and have them delivered as soon as they have dropped their leaves *naturally.* This "naturally" is important. It means that the tree has ripened its tissues in preparation for winter. No impatience to have his order delivered should tempt a tree buyer to have the leaves stripped or cut off, because the trees would probably suffer from, if not succumb to, excessive loss of water through the little leaf wounds.

The most important advantages of autumn buying are:

1. The buyer is far more likely to get the varieties he desires than in the spring because nurseries propagate so few trees of the non-commercial kinds that they are soon sold out.

2. To fill autumn orders the trees are usually chosen individually from the nursery row and dug by hand instead of being dug by machine and snatched from a pile during the rush of the spring shipping season.

3. Being freshly dug they arrive in better condition than do those stored over winter in even the best-managed nursery storage house, and are likely to make a better start than stored trees and to maintain this advantage all season.

4. In localities where the winters are not severe they may be planted upon arrival and thus start to form roots long before spring planting time; and where the winters are severe the trees may be stored by heeling-in (as described below) and planted in earliest spring, often before a winter- or spring-placed order could be delivered.

Heeling-in for winter storage is best done in well-drained, bare ground by digging a trench running east and west with its north side vertical and its south a long slope. The trees are laid singly but close together with their roots against the vertical side and their trunks on the slope. Earth is then shoveled in to cover completely the roots, trunks and lower parts of the branches (if any). All litter is removed to prevent mice from forming nests near-by. As further protection 12-in. boards may be set on edge to form a tight pen around the trees and thus shut mice out. Dormant nursery stock will pass the winter in perfect condition heeled-in and be better to plant in spring than stock stored in nursery storage houses.

Temporary heeling-in—for a few weeks —need not be so thorough; it is enough to cover only the roots and the lower parts of the trunks.

In order to avoid the common mistake of tree crowding it is important to know how

When one-year trees are planted they need no pruning of the tops and rarely any of the roots—only the removal of any broken or mangled tips. Two-year and older trees must have any injured roots shortened to sound wood and the tops re-

A NEGLECTED APPLE TREE BEFORE AND AFTER PRUNING
The strongest boughs are kept, but weak and interfering branches are removed in order to stimulate fruit production. Very severe pruning is best spread over 2 or even 3 years.

widely each variety of tree will spread *when mature.* Varieties differ in this respect; for instance, the erect growing Wagener will spread about 35 ft., whereas the sprawling Rhode Island Greening often exceeds 50 ft. Trees should always be planted as far apart as they are likely to spread. While they are young the spaces between them may be utilized for other plantings—preferably annual vegetables or strawberries. Bush fruits are good for from 5 to 10 years; but as the tree branches extend, the areas so planted must be reduced annually until, in 10 or 15 years, the trees themselves will occupy all the space.

Often small-growing, short-lived trees such as peach, nectarine and sour cherry are planted as "fillers" between the slower-growing kinds to utilize the space while the large trees are developing. These fillers must be ruthlessly destroyed without delay as soon as they begin to crowd the large ones or they will do more or less damage.

Dwarf apples properly managed may be kept 15 ft. or even as little as 10 ft. tall, but if neglected as to pruning, they may strike root above the graft and grow as large as standards. The principal attention required is to cut all roots that start to form *above* the graft union. This is best done late each spring by hoeing away the earth from the base of the trunk and cutting the roots close thereto.

duced sufficiently to balance the unavoidable loss of roots suffered in digging.

Though commercial orchards are generally cultivated from spring to midsummer and then planted to a cover-crop (which see), they are also successfully managed under a "sod mulch." This means that grass, clover or alfalfa is grown between the trees and cut two or three times a year while green and either allowed to decay where it falls or raked beneath the trees and left there. In the home garden also, either of those methods may be followed; or the trees may stand in a closely mowed lawn, preferably with a foot-wide circle of bare earth around the base of each trunk to discourage the attacks of the flat-headed apple-tree borer.

If a cover-crop is grown it should be fertilized so as to increase the amount of humus it will provide and, indirectly, the amount of plant food in the soil. In the other event, the trees must be liberally fed with manure or other nitrogenous fertilizers. A mature apple tree should receive 6 to 10 lbs. of nitrate of soda or sulphate of amommnia annually; young ones proportionately less—a five-year tree, 1 to 2 lbs.; a ten-year tree, 3 or 4 lbs. Such concentrated fertilizers must be distributed not close to the trunks, but in a ring or belt perhaps a yard wide beneath the outer ends of the branches where the feeding roots are located.

As apple trees approach bearing age they develop short, stubby twigs with rounded "cluster" buds at their tips. These "fruit spurs," as they are called, must not be broken or cut off because they may bear fruit for ten or more years. Each rounded bud may contain few to many flowers surrounded by leaves. Usually only one or two fruits develop from each flower cluster, the others being crowded off while small during early summer. When this "June drop" occurs the novice may fear that he will have no fruit left. Usually even then there are too many specimens for all to develop perfectly. Therefore to get the choicest fruit thinning is adopted. This consists in removing all defective, wormy and undersized fruits and reducing the clusters to one apple to a spur.

The benefits of thinning are: that the size and quality of the remaining fruits is enhanced without appreciably reducing the quantity matured; that the vigor of the tree is maintained because fewer fruits (and especially seeds) are developed; that it distributes the load and thus prevents breakage of branches; that it reduces damage by insects and diseases because the defective specimens can be gathered and burned before the pests mature in and emerge from them; that when the practice is started and maintained with young trees it tends to establish regular, annual, instead of biennial, bearing, thus providing a supply of fruit each year instead of "a feast or a famine."

Most summer and early autumn varieties ripen during several weeks, so may be picked and used as they mature. Under home conditions this early fruit can rarely be kept longer than a week or two without serious deterioration. Late autumn and winter varieties may be gathered as soon as the seeds in sample specimens have turned brown and while the fruit is still firm. Care must be exercised to prevent bruising by rough handling because though apples are apparently hard, such bruises turn brown and injure the appearance of the fruit if they do not actually lessen its keeping quality. As soon as gathered the fruit should be placed out of the sun and, as soon as possible, removed to a cold cellar. Apples keep best at 33 or 34 deg. F. See STORING CROPS.

Apple trees are sometimes planted as ornamentals for their bloom and, less often, for their highly colored fruits. Favored positions are in borders where their fallen fruit will not be objectionable. When specimen trees are to be placed on lawns or near the house they should be of late fall or winter varieties because there will be relatively fewer specimens dropped during the time when the lawn must be mowed or otherwise used. Summer and early fall varieties are highly objectionable in such places for this reason. Most of the flowering crab apples belong in the late class.

ENEMIES AND THEIR CONTROL

DISEASES. Of the diseases that affect apple trees, scab is the most important, economically speaking; it may cause losses up to 50 per cent of the crop in some States. Early, uncontrolled infection on the fruit stems may almost entirely prevent the setting of fruit; later infection by the scab fungus affects chiefly fruit and leaves, and severe leaf infection seriously weakens a tree and results in reducing successive year's crops.

APPLE SCAB
Careful spraying will prevent spots like these on apples.

On the leaves scab shows first as dull, smoky areas, later becoming olive-colored and velvety as masses of dark-colored spores develop. Typical fruit-scab spots are olive-black surrounded by papery broken skin. As the fruit grows the center of the spot cracks disclosing brown corky tissue. The fruit may also be stunted.

The fungus overwinters in old leaves on the ground; in the spring spores are carried by air currents to newly opened leaves. To prevent this infection trees should be kept protected with a fungicide during the six to eight weeks' period when these spores are maturing. Later (secondary) infection is by summer spores developed on leaves or young fruit. Control of apple scab requires correct timing of sprays in relation to the growth of the trees. Get advice from county agents or State Experiment Stations to supplement the general spray schedule given below.

Fire blight (caused by *Bacillus amylovorous*), which attacks apples, pears, quinces and many ornamental trees and shrubs, comes next in importance. Blossoms, leaves and twigs may appear to have been burned by fire, and cankers may be formed on larger limbs and trunks. The disease organism is spread by splashing rain and insects, especially bees. Although spraying during the open blossom period is usually avoided because it tends to interfere with fruit setting, a 1-3-50 bordeaux mixture (which see), applied when 50 per cent of the blossoms are open, has been found to check fire blight considerably without seriously affecting the fruit set. Blighted twigs and limbs should be removed but with sanitary precautions as directed under FIRE BLIGHT.

The three apple rust diseases are caused by fungi which live part of their lives on red cedar and the remainder largely on apple, hawthorn and quince. Rust spots on fruit are orange with small fungus cups. The most effective control is the eradication of red cedar for at least a half mile around apple orchards. Spraying trees with lime-sulphur or with a wettable sulphur (which see) when the petals fall seems to help reduce fruit infection. See JUNIPER.

Black rot causes the so-called New-York apple-tree canker on the limbs, a blossom-end rot on the fruit and a "frog-eye" leaf spot. The fungus enters through wounds so all injured or dead branches should be removed and the wounds carefully painted and the spray schedule given below followed.

Bitter rot of apple causes brown rotted spots filled with pink spore masses on the fruit and cankers on the limbs. Remove the cankers and paint the wounds and follow the spray schedule.

Blotch causes cankers on twigs, small light brown spots on the leaves and dark blotches on the fruit, but it is not important in properly sprayed orchards.

INSECT PESTS. Many of the sucking insects, including San José, oyster-shell and scurfy scales (see SCALE INSECTS) and the common apple aphids, are controlled by a delayed dormant spray as described below. The principal aphids are the rosy apple aphid which has a pinkish coating and causes clusters of puckered "aphis-apples"; the woolly apple aphid which migrates from elm to apple and forms a bluish white cottony growth around scars and wounds often causing galls; and the green apple aphid which causes the familiar curling of the leaves and tender shoots.

The European red mite is responsible for rusty brown foliage in midsummer and may call for a summer application of lime-sulphur. See MITES.

Where apple trees are desired for shade or ornamental effect, so that the loss of a single tree is a tragedy, it is particularly important to examine them frequently for borers. The flat-headed apple-tree borer which works in the sapwood of unthrifty trees—oak, apple, maple and many other kinds—is distributed throughout the U. S. The larvae construct broad feeding tunnels under the bark until late summer when they bore into the sapwood and form pupal cells in which they pass the winter; the adults appear from May to July as dark copper-colored beetles about $\frac{1}{2}$ in. long. The appearance of sawdust in or below holes in the bark indicates the presence of the borer which may be killed by running a wire into the burrow or by injecting carbon-bisulphide or nicotine paste. Since borers do not work in healthy sapwood, the best control is prevention, that is, the promotion of vigor in your trees by feeding, watering, and pruning them. A lead-arsenate lime-sulphur wash may also be applied to the trunk.

The round-headed borer which makes nearly round holes in the main trunk, sometimes seriously injuring young trees, is the larva of a long-horned gray, white-striped beetle about an inch long. The shot-hole borer makes many small holes and burrows (filled with fine sawdust) up to 4 in. long; the adult, a small black beetle, is called the fruit-tree bark beetle. Control by stimulating the tree with a heavy spring application of nitrogenous fertilizer. See also BARK BEETLES; BORERS.

Chewing insects may attack twigs, leaves, or fruit. Weevils or snout beetles cut off small branches, buds and newly set fruit. Leaves may be skeletonized by the spring or fall canker worm, or the apple-leaf skeletonizer which also webs two or three leaves together. Pistol and cigar case-bearers feed on the leaves and young buds; the budworm webs over the buds and the eastern tent caterpillar, if neglected, forms large webs and defoliates the tree in spring as does the fall webworm in late summer. (For control measures see BUDWORM; CASE-BEARER; TENT CATERPILLAR.) Other insects eating leaves are the tussock, brown tail, and gypsy moths while the Japanese beetle attacks both leaves and fruit.

Among the insects injurious to fruit the codling moth (which see) is undoubtedly the best known. This pinkish brown-headed worm burrows to the core leaving brown castings protruding from the holes. The plum curculio (see CURCULIO) injures early set apples with its crescent-shaped punctures; such fruit usually falls. The apple curculio causes knotty apples, as does the red bug (which see). The yellowish-white apple maggot or railroad worm makes slender brown twisting mines through the fruit, especially of early sweet apples. The adult is a 2-winged fly, somewhat smaller than a house fly, with conspicuous dark bands across the wings.

PROTECTION PROGRAM. The production of sound healthy apples calls for a complicated spray schedule which is financially profitable only to the commercial grower. It pays him to continue spraying throughout the season, but the returns will not compensate the small gardener for the cost of such elaborate efforts. And in addition to the cost, there is the question of spray residues which make it necessary for the commercial orchardist to install equipment with which to wash the fruit before selling it.

In small home orchards or fruit gardens 4 or 5 sprays properly timed will insure healthy trees and the production of fruit in fair condition. The following general schedule should be modified to conform to local conditions in accordance with advice that can be secured from the various State Experiment Stations; see accompanying illustration:

1. *Delayed dormant spray.* May start when the fruit buds become silvery and must end before the leaves show ¼ in. To control scales, European red mite, aphis and scab. For 10 gals. spray use 1 gal. concentrated lime-sulphur and 5 tablespoons nicotine-sulphate. Or use a lubricating-oil emulsion following manufacturer's directions.

2. *Pink bud spray.* When the fruit buds show color. To control curculio, scab and chewing insects such as tent caterpillars and canker worms. Lime-sulphur 1 qt., powdered lead arsenate, 1⅓ cups.

3. *Petal-fall or calyx spray.* Immediately after petals fall and *before* calyx closes. For codling moth, curculio, scab. Lime-sulphur 1½ pts. and lead arsenate 1⅓

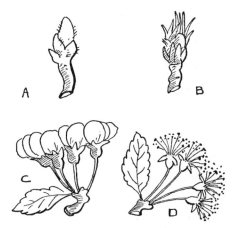

APPLE BUDS SHOWING STAGES FOR SPRING SPRAYING
A, beginning, and, B, end of "delayed dormant" period. C, pink bud stage. D, petal-fall or calyx stage. See directions under Apple enemies.

cups. Or use dry lime-sulphur mixture as recommended locally.

4. *Ten days after petals fall.* Same as 3.

5. *Three or four weeks after petals fall.* Same as 3.

Where it is necessary to call in professional tree experts to do the spraying and desirable to reduce the number of sprays to the minimum to cut the expense, the most important sprays to have applied are 1 and 3, the delayed dormant and the calyx. The former is necessary for the general health of the tree and the latter is the most important spray for codling moth; without it the apples are almost sure to be wormy.

See also CRAB; PYRUS.

Wood-apple (which see) is *Feronia limonia.*

APPLE-OF-PERU. Common name for *Nicandra physalodes,* a spreading annual herb with blue flowers, native to Peru. Occasionally grown under glass in the N., it was formerly popular in S. gardens from which it escaped and has become a weed.

APRICOT. A tree (*prunus armeniaca*) grown for its fruit—one of the stone fruits—which resembles a small, yellow, sweetish peach and which is used for dessert, drying, canning and preserves. Though the so-called Russian varieties of this species are hardier than the commercial sorts developed from it, they bear smaller, less desirable fruit. The Japanese apricot (*P. mume*), also hardy, is more often planted for ornament than for its fruit.

Though apricots are grown commercially on the Pacific Coast and in parts of the Rocky Mountain region, they are less popular than they deserve to be in home gardens elsewhere in America. This is partly because the flowers open so early that spring frosts often destroy them, and partly because the fruit that reaches the eastern markets from the West is gathered while so immature that when eaten it gives a poor impression and does not inspire people to plant apricots even where they could be grown. By planting the trees where their buds may be retarded—that is, on a northern slope or the north or west side of a building or shaded by tall trees to the eastward, a crop can sometimes be obtained where otherwise it would be impossible.

The choicer varieties are distinct acquisitions to home gardens, first, because of their beautiful, early, pink blossoms; second, because of their attractive form and foliage; and third, because their fruit, in successively ripening varieties, links the season of late strawberries with that of early peaches.

Apricot varieties are budded or grafted on either seedling apricot, peach, or plum stocks. The first two are to be preferred for planting on light soils; plum stocks will do better on heavy soils. However, it is better to use whichever kind is available, regardless of soil type, than to forego the planting of a few trees for the home fruit garden.

One-year trees are better for planting than older ones because they may be trained as desired. Each should be allowed a spread of 25 ft. during the first five years, clean cultivation until midsummer and cover-cropping after that, at least as far as the branches spread, is highly desirable. This tends to develop deep rooting and helps the trees withstand dry weather. After the fifth year heavy mulching is satisfactory and saves labor. Should growth not be as good as desired manure (about a bushel to the square yard) may be applied in spring; if this is not obtainable at reasonable cost, a general fertilizer may be applied at the rate of 5 lbs. per tree.

Training young trees consists in developing three to five well-spaced frame limbs and removing branches that crowd more desirable ones. See PRUNING; TRAINING OF PLANTS.

ENEMIES. In general apricots are attacked by the same enemies as plums, but the green rot is especially characteristic of this host although also found on almonds, lemons and figs. Partial or complete blighting of the young fruit while still enclosed in the calyx sometimes results in entire crop losses in California, and in the bad years spraying does not control. In other years the disease presents no problem. Plum curculio and San José scale are often destructive. For further discussion of the enemies of stone fruits see PRUNES.

AQUARIUM. Whether the prime interest of the gardener who is also an aquarium enthusiast is the keeping and breeding of fish or the culture of aquatic plants, he must reconcile himself to the paradox that if he wants fish he must raise

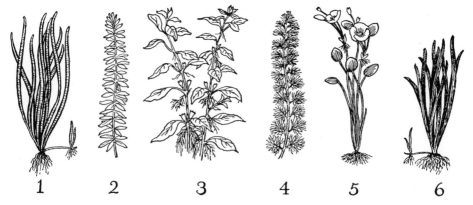

POPULAR AQUATIC PLANTS FOR THE HOME AQUARIUM
(1) Vallisneria or eel-grass; (2) Elodea (waterweed), sometimes sold as Anacharis; (3) Ludwigia, also known as Isnardia; (4) Cabomba, a feathery-leaved relative of the water-lily; (5) the water-poppy whose yellow flowers open above the surface; (6) the under-water form of one of the arrow-heads.

plants, and its complement, that if he wants plants, he must keep fish.

In simple terms, the principle underlying this interdependence of plant and animal life boils down to the fact that, in the small aquarium especially, fish and plants have something to give each other and that the exchange is vital to the health of both. The gills of fish extract oxygen from the water much as our lungs take oxygen from the air; like us, fish breathe out carbon dioxide. In a limited space, carbon dioxide saturates the water and, if there is no purifying agent, the fish die of suffocation. With plants, the reverse is true: They absorb and use the carbon dioxide and give off oxygen.

A "balanced" aquarium is, therefore, one in which plant and animal material are so adjusted that no outside agent (jet of air or running water) is needed to keep it healthy for both.

Aquatic plants (which see) vary considerably in the amount of oxygen they liberate. Certain of them, particularly rich in output, have been labelled "oxygenators" and are used either alone or in combination with others, less efficient but decorative, to keep the "balance." Any fish dealer can supply one or more of the staple oxygenating plants, namely, Vallisneria (Tape- or Eel-grass); Sagittaria (Arrow-heads); Elodea; Myriophyllum and Cabomba.

USEFUL OXYGENATING PLANTS. Vallisneria and Sagittaria, both powerful oxygenators and beautiful in foliage and bloom, may be used in the tank alone or as a background planting for smaller and more unusual plants, especially if these be of uncertain oxygenating power. Both should be rooted in the sand of the tank bottom or grown in tiny buried pots.

Elodea, Cabomba and Myriophyllum, all well-known as oxygenating plants, can be grown successfully either floating free or rooted. They are particularly good as a "cover planting" to keep the tank healthy and rich in green while rarer and more interesting plants are being grown. Cabomba, with tiny leaflets branching from a heavy stem, is attractive in appearance but has an unfortunate tendency to break up and discolor unless conditions are exactly right for its growth. However, it is cheap, almost always in the market and may easily be replaced as it decays. Elodea is a quick grower and a good oxygenator and will probably be of greater satisfaction for general use. Myriophyllums are the most feathery of the aquatics and, since two varieties are common—a red and a green —they offer an opportunity for color arrangement.

Fish fanciers ordinarily confine their planting to a selection of the foregoing standbys, but the aquarist interested in plant culture has many unusual and beautiful plants at his disposal. The rarer Cryptocoryne is a good oxygenator with broad leaves and the ability to grow beautifully in less light than most of the aquatics require.

In addition to the submerged plants, a well-planted aquarium needs its assortment of floating plants. These may range in size from the tiny duckweeds and Salvinia to such flowering plants as the floating-hearts (Nymphoides) and, if the tank is large enough, perhaps even waterlilies.

AQUATIC PLANTS. The term "aquatic" applies not only to those plants which live entirely submerged beneath the water, but also to those which, like the waterlilies, root in the bottom, but project stems, leaves and bloom up to float on, or stand above, the surface. It also includes those plants which can adapt themselves to either a terrestrial or an aquatic life.

The true aquatics (those which grow entirely submerged) are for the most part plants of simple structure whose greatest use is in oxygenating (keeping supplied with oxygen from the air) tanks or pools in which fish are kept without artificial aeration. (See AQUARIUM; also FISH.) However, these water plants are almost without exception extremely decorative when seen through the sides of a glass tank which harbors also a few colorful fish, and thus may well be a charming and satisfying solace for the winter-frustrated gardener.

Outside, in the natural pond, water course or artificial pool, the greenery of these submerged plants helps to create a setting for the bloom of surface plants and effectually to camouflage or hide the unsightly boxes or other containers in which the larger waterlilies, etc., are usually planted.

For this outdoor use, many of the plants discussed under Aquarium are suitable. Elodea, Cabomba, Myriophyllum, Vallisneria and Hornwort (all of which see) are good oxygenators of easy cultivation. Indeed, they are more likely to need restraint than encouragement.

Other submerged plants are of less interest and value to the gardener than to the aquarist within whose field they properly come. The gardener, being concerned with a decorative effect, naturally turns his attention to the great body of floating aquatics. These range from the tiny, bright green leaves of the duckweed to the gigantic leaves (up to 7 ft. in diameter)

VICTORIA REGIA, A MIGHTY AQUATIC
The leaves of this tropical water-lily are large and heavy enough to support a child.

and enormous white blooms of the royal *Victoria regia*. There are appropriate water plants for any area, situation or temperature from a tub on a city roof to a wilderness lake.

Obviously, these factors of situation, temperature range and size determine the selection of proper material. Wild ponds in regions of hard winters are hardly suitable homes for the sweet-scented exotic lilies but quite right for the hardy yellow lotus, the spatterdock or cow-lily, the lavender-flowered pickerel-weed and other natives. Among them and in such a setting, the exotics would be inappropriate, hard to care for and very likely would not succeed.

See POND; see also the illustration on Plate 2 for some of the standard aquatic plants described below.

WATERLILIES AND LOTUS

In the sheltered garden pool, formal or informal, the tender tropical lilies show to best advantage. Necessarily, in a pool in which waterlilies (Nympheas) and lotus (Nelumbiums) are used, they are the feature and other material is selected to supplement them. The surrounding shrubbery and trees, the border planting and the other water material must all be considered, not solely for its own sake. but for what it

contributes to the setting and well-being of the lilies. Cold northeast winds in the spring just after the lilies have been set in the pool may seriously check their growth and bloom. If the pool is not naturally sheltered, a windbreak planting of evergreens, or, if space permits, of large deciduous trees such as oaks, lindens, poplars, etc., is desirable. This may be supplemented and graded down to the pool by a marginal planting of laurel, rhododendrons, etc. The southern exposures should be clear and unshaded to allow the maximum of sun to reach the pool; hence large marginal planting should be confined to the north and northeast and, if cold winds may be expected from that direction, the northwest.

Even if the situation of the pond, by reason of latitude or exposure, is unsuited to the tender tropicals, there is a wide variation in the form and color of the hardy Nympheas. The large white pond-lily of the eastern states (*Nymphaea odorata*) is most desirable. From its hybrids and the hybrids of the Mexican, European and Chinese species a selection of hardy varieties can be made that will equal in beauty of leaf and bloom a similar selection of tropicals.

The water gardener usually finds it advisable to plant his pool with both hardy and tropical lilies. A wider range of color (there are no hardy blue lilies and no tropical yellows) and variation in height of bloom above the water is thus obtained.

To grow waterlilies and lotus and their appropriate companions, good rich soil in abundance is imperative. If the soil is not sufficiently rich, the plants will produce but small flowers and their foliage, instead of making rich patterns against the water, will be spare, sick looking, yellow and blotchy.

In large ponds it is sometimes necessary to plant directly in the pond bottom but, if possible, this should be avoided. It is much easier to properly enrich the soil in a box or tub than that of a whole pond bottom. Too, the unrestricted roots of certain species of lilies spread so as to crowd out and stunt less robust, but perhaps more desirable, varieties. So for all except a few of the larger aquatics, container planting in rich soil is best. In boxes, tubs or pots, lilies and other aquatics may be rearranged, moved to other pools without check, or brought indoors to the greenhouse pool in the fall, whereas, growing free, these shifts are not easily possible. See NYMPHAEA; also NELUMBIUM.

PLANTS FOR SHALLOW WATERS

Aquatics other than lilies and lotus suitable for tub or pool comprise two general groups: those forming masses of foliage and bloom above the water surface and those floating upon it. From the first group come the plants for marginal and island planting. From the second, those for breaking the surface of the water into attractive arrangements of leaf and bloom.

The marginal aquatics are, as one might expect, shallow-water plants and are best handled in pots submerged a couple of inches. Many of them, besides being useful outdoors, are excellent house plants; the plants need only to be removed from the pool (in the pots), repotted if necessary, and taken indoors in the fall. There, with their pots set in a tray or in saucers kept filled with water, such plants as the umbrella-palm (*Cyperus alternifolius*), pickerel-weed (*Pontederia cordata*), water-canna (*Thalia dealbata*), primrose-willow (*Jussiaea longifolia*) and others make up a most attractive indoor garden. Good soil, a sunny, warm window and plenty of water are, of course, essential.

Among the most graceful of the high growing shallow-water plants are the umbrella-palm (above mentioned) and its cousin the papyrus (*Cyperus papyrus*). The latter with its mass of tall stems, each topped with a star of grass-like leaves, makes as much as 15 ft. of growth in a summer and is particularly suited for a place at one end of the large pool.

Another tall grassy plant for the water's edge or island planting is wild-rice (*Zizania aquatica*). It grows as much as 10 ft. during the summer; seeds itself, and, besides having ornamental value, its grain attracts the birds, water-fowl particularly. A native American plant, it is especially suited to the wild pond.

The cat-tails (*Typha latifolia*) and (*T. angustifolia*), are both native swamp plants of particular value for planting in the shallows at the edge of pool or water-course. Their narrow, dark green leaves and familiar cylindrical soft, brown seed-heads form a pleasant contrast to the broad, drooping leaves and gay blue-violet spikes of the pickerel-weed and the distinctive leaves of the arrow-heads (Sagittaria) with their white bloom. The latter as generally used vary in size from a few inches high to one species (*S. montevidensis*), the giant arrow-head, which grows as high as 6 ft.

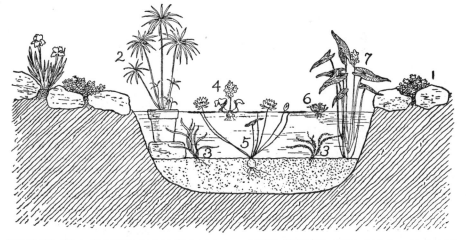

SECTION OF A SIMPLE GARDEN POOL SHOWING USEFUL AQUATIC PLANTS AND WHERE THEY SHOULD BE PLACED

At the pool's edge (1) suitable rock-garden plants are appropriate, especially those liking constant moisture about their roots. The umbrella-plant (2) is best kept in a pot with its rim at the water level. Certain aerating (oxygenating) plants (3), such as eel-grass and hornwort, help to keep the water clear. The water-hyacinth (4) floats at the surface by means of inflated leaf bases. Water-lilies (5) root in the bottom of the pool, and develop their leaves and flowers just at or above the surface. Water-lettuce (6) is a free-floater which requires some shade. Arrowheads (7) take root in the bottom and open both leaves and flowers well above the surface.

Any list of shallow-water plants would hardly be complete without a mention of the water-loving iris. Both the yellow flag (*Iris pseudacorus*) and the blue flag (*I. versicolor*) planted in a few inches of water make fine heavy clumps of sword-like leaves and flower profusely.

The sweet flag (*Acorus calamus*) of the Arum Family has lance-shaped, erect leaves several feet high; it takes its common name

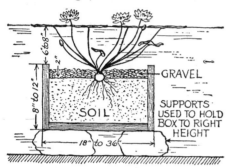

A GOOD WAY TO PLANT A WATER-LILY
If planted in a box supported at the proper height, it is happiest. The soil does not dirty the pool, and the whole box can be removed indoors over winter.

from the aromatic root-stock. Its smaller variety, *variegatus,* with yellow-striped leaves, is more common in cultivation.

Another member of the Arum Family good for planting in the shallows and with particularly handsome foliage is the water- or arrow-arum (*Peltandra virginica*). Its leaves are large, arrow-shaped, dark green and held well above the water on long stems. Similar in use and value are the water-plantains, species of Alisma.

The several species of Colocasia, known as Japanese-taro and elephants ear, have become popular for their rich foliage, not only for shallow-water planting, but also as house plants. Their large leaves give to a pool a definitely tropical air, as does *Thalia dealbata,* sometimes called the water-canna, with its long stems and large leaves.

Among the shallow-water plants remarkable not only for beauty of foliage but for their bloom as well, are the marsh-marigold (*Caltha palustris*) with its bright yellow flowers and luxuriant green leaves; the primrose water-willow (*Jussiaea longifolia*), whose tall stems bear charming yellow flowers in the axils of the reddish, willow-like leaves; the hardy golden club (*Orontium aquaticum*) with its spike of golden

flowerets and handsome leaves; the flowering-rush (*Butomus unbellatus*) with clusters of rose flowers held high above the clumps of three-cornered leaves, and the lizard tail (*Saururus cernuus*) with heart-shaped leaves and curved, lizard-tail spikes of tiny, fragrant white flowers.

The several floating hearts (Nymphoides) are splendid for planting not only in the shallows but in water up to a couple of feet deep. Their profusion of bloom and foliage makes them particularly good in the small tub garden. Under favorable conditions, they are more likely to need restraint than encouragement.

Another small, attractively flowered plant suitable for the shallow water of the pool, for the tub garden or, in winter, the sunny aquarium, is the water-poppy (*Hydrocleis nymphoides* or *Limnocharis humboldti*). Growing quickly, it rewards the gardener with a summer-long profusion of poppy-like yellow bloom, held well above the masses of floating green foliage. *Limnocharis flava* (or *emarginata*), one of its relatives, has small very light yellow flowers set among the masses of heart-shaped leaves which rise from 1 to 2 ft. above the surface. It, likewise, is excellent for the pool.

PLANTS FOR DEEPER WATERS

The deeper waters may receive as their portion, not only the lotus and the water-lilies, but a sizable group of charming floating plants. (See illustrations, Plate 23.)

The lotus, in any of its several species, presents large and beautiful blossoms that tower above masses of enormous blue-green leaves. They are at their best if planted by themselves in a pool where the long roots may run at will. However, if this is not practical, they are quite successful planted in large containers and submerged in the deeper waters of the pond. They are also good subjects for the tub garden; one tuber may be planted in a tub or half barrel filled to within 5 or 6 in. of the top with rich soil and then filled with water. With the exception of the yellow American lotus (*Nelumbium luteum*) the forms of lotus range from pure white through many of rose shades.

The American lotus and the cowlily (also called Spatterdock) with its yellow, cup-shaped flowers and 12 in. heart-shaped leaves, are both hardy and especially suited to planting directly in the bottom of the wild type of pond, which see.

Plate 2.   AQUATICS MERIT ATTENTION

Upper left: The fast-growing water-hyacinth (Eichornia crassipes).   Upper right: The brilliant blue pickerel-weed (Pontederia cordata) growing with the lavender water-hyacinth.   Center: Well-spaced planting of waterlilies.   Lower left: The happy, yellow blooms of water-poppy (Hydrocleys nymphoides).   Lower right: The spiritual beauty of a single waterlily.

The fragrant waterlilies (Nymphaea) are roughly divided into two groups: the tender ones (tropical and sub-tropical in origin) and the hardy ones. The latter may be planted directly in the bottom of large, natural ponds if the more desirable container-planting is out of the question; unless actually frozen, plants will survive over the winter. The tropical kinds are usually grown from seed each year and set out in the pool as soon as the weather permits.

The hardy lilies present a wide variety of shapes, colors and sizes of bloom, and it is among them that the best yellows are found. In some the flowers float on the water surface; other kinds raise the blossoms slightly above the water. The tropicals are the more spectacular in size of bloom and leaf, and their flowers are displayed on fine, erect stems well above the water. They offer fine blue shades not to be found in the hardy sorts and also the fragrant exotic charm of the night-blooming varieties.

See NYMPHAEA, also illustration, Plate 2.

The water-hawthorn or cape pondweed (*Aponogeton distachyus*), with its hawthorn-like scent, is a fine aquatic for the deeper waters. The blunt lance-shaped leaves, 3 to 6 in. long, float beside twin spikes of fragrant white flowers lifted slightly above the surface. Although tender in the N., the cape pondweed is easily naturalized in S. waters.

The most common and showy of the large floating plants is the water-hyacinth (*Eichhornia crassipes*). Naturalized in Fla., it has spread so rapidly there as to be a serious and expensive obstruction to navigation in certain waters. It is much used both in outdoor pools and in aquaria. It blooms more profusely in waters shallow enough to permit the mass of hanging roots to make fast than in places where it floats free. The plant and its spike of yellow-blotched blue flowers are kept afloat by curious bladder-like inflations of the leaf stems.

Another floating plant useful either indoors or out is the water fern (*Ceratopteris thalictroides*). In warm water and bright sun, it quickly builds up a large mass of lettuce-green foliage, tiny new plants rapidly developing along the margins of the older leaves.

The floating shell-flower or water-lettuce (*Pistia stratiotes*) likes a shady place in which to display its rosette of elegantly fluted gray-green leaves. Its cluster of hanging roots makes a splendid nursery for very young fish.

Of the small floating plants useful either in the pool or the aquarium, *Azolla caroliniana* is one of the most curious and interesting. A small moss-like plant, it divides and propagates rapidly. Since in bright sun it takes on a reddish tinge, it can be used as an indicator to show whether or not the tank or pool is getting enough direct light.

Its larger relative (Salvinia) quickly forms large patterns of soft, velvety green on the surface of warm, sunny waters, while the duckweed (*Lemna minor*), a little smaller than Salvinia, shows as confetti-like spots of bright green floating about.

See also AQUARIUM; BOG GARDEN; GARDEN POOL; POND; WATER GARDEN.

AQUIFOLIACEAE (ak-wi-foh-li-ay'-see-ee). Botanical name of the Holly Family, a group of generally distributed trees and shrubs often preferring moist woodlands. The two principal genera, Ilex (Holly) and Nemopanthus (Mountain Holly), are widely used in horticulture as ornamental shrubs because of their glossy, handsome foliage and small, bright, berry-like fruits. Useful for wood and wood-products, some species of Ilex are also sources of beverages. "Appalachian tea" is derived from the Dahoon Holly (*I. cassine*), and the well-known yerba de maté from *I. paraguariensis*.

AQUILEGIA (ak-wi-lee'-ji-ah). Columbine. (See illustration, Plate 8.) This is one of the most valuable of hardy perennials for its exquisite, durable, lobed foliage which often turns to rich colors in autumn, and its spurred, gracefully hung blossoms produced in early summer. In many sections of the U. S. it is incorrectly known as Honeysuckle.

The sepals as well as the petals are colored, and each of the latter has a downward extension which forms a hollow spur.

There are few spots in the garden to which some form of Aquilegia is not appropriate—the perennial border, the cutting garden, the wild garden, and the rockery.

Seed sown in spring or early summer will give plants which can be set into their permanent quarters in September. The following spring they will bloom abundantly, growing generally from 1 to 3 ft. high. The seed may be slow to germinate, but it

is reliable, pro-
vided the soil is
kept fairly moist
and shaded.

Young plants,
too, s h o u l d be
shaded, and when
they are trans-
planted (prefer-
ably to rich humus
to w h i c h bone-
meal or well-de-
cayed manure has
been added) they
should be given
only partial sun and protection from wind.

**A LEAF OF AQUI-
LEGIA (COLUMBINE)**
Showing the serpentine tun-
nels eaten by a leaf miner.

Most Aquilegias (especially the garden
hybrids) may also be propagated from root-
divisions. Made in the autumn, these will
produce well-established plants ready for
flowering in the spring. To keep one's
supply intact, it is well to raise several
new plants each season, as hybrid Aquilegias are often short-lived.

ENEMIES. When borers (salmon-brown
caterpillars of a moth) are found in the
crowns, pull up and destroy infested plants
and burn in fall all waste grass, weeds and
other débris on which the eggs of this pest
spend the winter.

A leaf miner often eats tunnels in the
leaves, making winding white markings.
Pick and burn such leaves and, if the infestation is heavy, spray several times at
3- or 4-day intervals with a contact insecticide such as a solution of 40% nicotine-
sulphate.

Plant tops may be killed by either crown
rot or stem rot (both of which see); remove and destroy infected clumps. Powdery mildew on the foliage may be controlled by dusting with fine sulphur.

SPECIES. Native American species with
their numerous varieties are most used in
this country, though some of the European
and Asiatic species are also available—
and desirable.

AMERICAN SPECIES

A. canadensis. The dainty scarlet and
yellow Columbine of middle W. and E. U.
S.; smaller but more brilliant in color than
the long-spurred hybrids. Especially attractive on a semi-shaded hillside, it self-
sows readily, and blooms from May to
July.

caerulea (Colorado Columbine). Generally taller than *A. canadensis,* bearing

large showy blue flowers from April to
July. Hybrids in white or in combinations,
sometimes with pink or yellow, are available. This is the Colorado state flower.

chrysantha (Golden Columbine). Tall,
branched plant bearing yellow flowers with
long spurs, a Rocky Mountain native,
blooming from May to Aug. Its var.
jaeschkani is smaller and has red spurs.

formosa (Sitka Columbine). A N. W.
species (Calif. to Alaska), whose red and
yellow, short-spurred flowers appear from
May to Aug.

skinneri (Mexican Columbine). Growing in warm countries to 3 ft., this S.
mountain species opens its pale-red and
greenish-yellow flowers from July until
Sept.

FOREIGN SPECIES

A. glandulosa. Native to Siberia, this is
sometimes a difficult subject to keep, but
worth an effort, because of its bluish foliage and blue flowers tipped with white.
It prefers a deep, sandy soil.

alpina. An excellent rock-garden plant
from central Europe, low-growing with
large deep blue flowers in midsummer.

vulgaris. The common Columbine of
Europe; blue flowers with short, knobbed,
incurved spurs appearing in midsummer.

sibirica (Siberian Columbine). Large
lilac-blue flowers; in var. *spectabilis* the
petals tipped with yellow.

In addition to these well-known species,
all of which have undoubtedly contributed
to the garden hybrids, several new species
which give promise for the alpine garden
have lately been introduced. Among these
are *buergeriana,* a Japanese plant 1 ft. high
with large purple and yellow flowers; *discolor,* a blue and white alpine flower from
Spain; *leptoceras,* a small Siberian species
with flowers of greenish-yellow and violet;
and *jonesi,* a minute mountain Aquilegia,
blue-flowered, native N. from Wyo.

ARABIAN-GENTIAN. A catalog name
for species of Exacum (which see), especially *E. affine,* a biennial with lilac flowers, native to an island in the Arabian Sea.

ARABIS (ar'-ah-bis). Rock-cress. A
genus of annuals, biennials and perennials
of the Mustard Family including delightful,
low-growing border and rock-garden plants
of easy culture. Reaching heights of from
6 to 12 in., they bear a profusion of white,
pink, or purple flowers in April, May and

into early summer. They prefer a sunny location but will get along in partial shade. Given a light, sandy soil enriched with bone-meal worked in around each plant when it is set out, these charming plants produce an abundance of blossoms and attractive mats of foliage later in the season after the blossoms.

Seed may be sown out of doors in late April or early May; it should be covered to a depth twice its diameter. Mixing a little sand with the seeds will facilitate even sowing. Bought plants should be set out in September, at which time plants grown from seed should be shifted to their permanent locations to flower the second season. They should stand 6 in. apart. Propagation is by division of roots soon after flowering; lift the plant and separate the mass of roots by pulling it apart gently and using no knife unless necessary. Cuttings may be made of green growth, as with Chrysanthemums, which see. Spraying with bordeaux mixture every 10 days from April to September will keep plants healthy. After flowering cut established plants back, and when the ground freezes cover them with two or three inches of leaves.

There are 100 or more species, a few native to America. The following perennials are the most useful for gardens:

A. albida (Wall Rock-cress), to 1 ft.; with whitish woolly foliage and white flowers, sometimes double, in early spring.

alpina (Mountain Rock-cress), white flowers and silvery-gray foliage; blooms for 6 to 8 weeks; 6 in. tall, more slender than preceding.

hirsuta, to 10 in.; tufted at base; hairy foliage; flowers white or rose; biennial.

ARALIA (ah-ray'-li-ah). Ornamental herbs, shrubs or small trees, most of them hardy North. In some the stems are spiny; and they send up suckers for a considerable distance around the parent plant. They thrive in any good soil, and the larger species give a very imposing effect when grouped on the lawn or used as accent plants in the shrub border. The doubly pinnate leaves may exceed 3 ft. in length and 2 ft. in width. This fine foliage, together with the large clusters of small creamy-white flowers at the end of the summer, creates a marked subtropical effect. The fruit is a soft, black, juicy berry.

Propagation is by seeds, root-cuttings and suckers.

PRINCIPAL SPECIES

A. chinensis (Chinese Angelica-tree). A large shrub to 20 ft. or more, with spiny stems. Leaves 2 to 4 ft., usually without prickles. Flower panicle nearly 2 ft. long in Aug. and Sept.

elata (Japanese Angelica-tree). A large shrub, or tree to 50 ft., with usually spiny stems. Leaflets are somewhat smaller than in the preceding species. Flower clusters are as large and come about the same time.

spinosa (Angelica-tree; Hercules Club; Devils Walking-stick). Native of Southeastern U. S. Tree to 40 ft., with very spiny stems and upper leaf surface. Leaves somewhat smaller but flower clusters larger than in the above species; opening in Aug. Suckers very freely and may become troublesome in consequence.

cordata (Udo). A perennial herb from Japan, growing 4 to 8 ft. The young blanched shoots in spring are edible.

racemosa (Spikenard). A perennial native herb, growing 3 to 6 ft. The rootstock is used in medicine.

hispida (Bristly Sarsaparilla). A native herb or sub-shrub, 1 to 3 ft., with bark of medicinal value.

Several shrubby tender plants known as Aralias and grown in greenhouses for their ornamental foliage are now placed in other genera—Panax, Polyscias, and Dizygotheca.

ARALIACEAE (ah-ray-li-ay'-see-ee). Botanical name of the Aralia or Ginseng Family, a group of widely distributed, mostly woody herbs, shrubs and trees, including a number of good garden subjects of ornamental foliage; some species yield medicinal products. Flowers, whitish or greenish, small and regular, are borne in close heads as in the Parsley Family (Umbelliferae), which this family resembles. The foliage of many species is aromatic. The variable Aralia (including the Devils Walking-stick and the Wild Sarsaparillas) is one well-known genus, and others are Panax (the source of ginseng root), Hedera (English Ivy), Acanthopanax and Dizygotheca.

ARAUCARIA (ar-au-kay'-ri-ah). Evergreen trees of the Pine Family, natives of the South Temperate zone, much planted as ornamental specimens in the S. and in Calif. and deservedly popular in juvenile form as house plants. For the latter purpose they are usually bought in pots from florists, but they can be propagated by cuttings, from seed or by stem-rooting in a cool greenhouse. They will not endure crowding or exposure to burning sunlight.

ENEMIES. Whitish, dusty-appearing mealy bugs (*Pseudococcus citri*) suck the sap from the axils of leaves and branches, often causing considerable injury. Spray with an oil emulsion or pyrethrum-soap. See GREENHOUSE PESTS.

SPECIES

A. excelsa (Norfolk-Island-pine), which in its native habitat grows to a height of 200 ft., is one of the most widely grown species for house plants and especially for Christmas decorations. Though stiff and rather formal, it is graceful with its branches in distinct whorls and its bright green needles. It is easily raised from seed, but as the seedlings do not make graceful plants (the spaces between the tiers of branches usually being too great) cuttings are made from the "leader" growth of young plants. These cuttings root easily, have a compact form and remain small plants for many years. Var. *albo-spica,* a most attractive variation, is known as the Silver-star Araucaria.

auracana (Monkey Puzzle) is a stiff, ungainly tree with heavy, brittle branches and sharp-pointed, overlapping leathery needles which are supposed to make it a puzzle for even a monkey to climb. The hardiest of the species, it is grown in the open in the south of England and Ireland and also in W. U. S. Native in Chile. It is often listed as *A. imbricata.*

cunninghami (Hoop-pine) is a less symmetrical tree than the Norfolk-Island-pine. In its native Australia it reaches 200 ft. and has spiny, needle-like leaves.

ARBOR. Primarily, today, a shelter from the sun composed of vines trained over a framework or so interwoven that they support themselves. The primitive form of arbor consists of the trunks of trees grown in regular ranks and a convenient distance apart, with the tops cut off at the desired height where stubs of the branches are left. Over these grapevines are trained and woven into a green canopy from which the clusters of fruit depend. In Eastern Mediterranean countries olive trees and grapes are planted in this manner, which is occasionally seen in this country where Mediterranean peoples have established their homes. But here generally an open, light structure is built to provide support for the vines used.

Since "arbor" is from the Latin word for "tree" and thus relates intimately to the natural shelter idea, it is evident that whatever structure is built it should be inconspicuous and shadowy in character rather than striking or flamboyant. Its primary purpose is to support vines and thus provide a cool retreat. This should be its suggestion and its invitation through simplicity of form and design and also color. Indeed, it can be said that the ideal arbor is so secondary to the vines which clothe it that its structural existence is hardly considered. In this it contrasts with the Summer House or Pavilion, designed to adorn the garden and also provide shelter from storm. The arbor shelters as a tree does, and no more.

In a garden lacking trees an arbor will provide shade within a single season and at the same time furnish opportunity to grow decorative climbing plants not otherwise possible; or to cultivate grapes if these are preferred. (See illustrations, Plate 24.)

See also GARDEN SHELTERS; OUTDOOR LIVING-ROOM; PERGOLA; PLEACH; RUSTIC WORK; SUMMER HOUSE; TRELLIS.

ARBORETUM. A collection of growing trees and other woody plants used for scientific and educational purposes. An arboretum may be started on a natural wooded site, the existing trees and shrubs being preserved and added to, or it may be an entirely new planting; in either case it is gradually supplemented, not only by other trees of the immediate region or country, but also by those from all over the world that are hardy in and adapted to that particular environment.

To be of maximum value to the public an arboretum should be arranged by families and, as far as possible, in generic groups, with the hybrids of the first group near their parent species, then hybrids between the first and second groups adjacent to their parents, and so on. Such an arrangement gives the student a clearer picture of the plant relationships, and more information about the plants' habits, and enables him to make better comparisons.

Due consideration should be given also to the ecology of the planting, that is, the different associations of trees, shrubs and herbs as they grow naturally in relation to the features of the environment, as soil, altitude, topography, etc. This, of course, can be observed more easily, in the part given over to the native, rather than the exotic species. The latter are to be studied principally for their adaptability in adjusting themselves to new conditions.

The arboretum in reality is an outdoor laboratory where the plants may be observed growing under varying but entirely natural conditions. Here may be studied the growth of trees suitable for ornamental purposes or for timber, some planted in the open to show how they spread and the shapes they take, others close to one another, to show the resulting self-trimming, or mutual protection against severe cold or wind. The behavior of native plants moved from the wild can be noted, and new species of ornamental shrubs planted in several situations may be studied so as to learn their value in the garden; for an exotic may thrive on a dry rocky hillside and yet perish in the mellow soil of a border.

An arboretum may be an outdoor museum only, or there may be maintained in connection with it buildings with offices for the director and his assistants, a library, a herbarium or collection of dried specimens, a laboratory for research work, and collections of drawings, paintings, photographs and other material. Besides the director and the men employed in the physical upkeep of the planting, there may be a force of research workers engaged in classifying specimens. There may also be field-workers or collectors, who are sent to various parts of the world to bring back additional plants. (See EXPLORATION FOR PLANTS.) Bulletins are often issued and books sometimes published dealing with new horticultural discoveries of importance based on the arboretum's work.

But, besides utilizing these considerable aids to plant knowledge, gardeners should make more personal use of arboreta by visiting them frequently, through all the seasons; by becoming familiar with the plant materials—old and new, domestic and exotic—in their various phases; by coming to regard arboreta not as cold, scientific institutions, but as splendid, living adjuncts of their own garden properties and, like them, rich in practical information, enjoyment and inspiration.

Probably the first arboretum was made early in the middle of the 16th century in France, at Touvoye; no trace of it remains. In England, in the Royal Horticultural Society Gardens at Kew, is found perhaps the finest collection of trees and shrubs of the temperate zone. In the U. S. the first arboretum (though probably not dignified by that title) was started near Philadelphia in 1728 by John Bartram. Some of the original trees are still living and the site of "Bartram's Garden" is now a park maintained by the city of Philadelphia. The extensive plantings of some of the old-time nurseries, especially those of Prince and Parsons on Long Island, N. Y., and of Ellwanger and Barry in Rochester, N. Y., rendered service as arboreta in disseminating knowledge of new species of trees to the public.

The Arnold Arboretum, at Jamaica Plain, Mass., started in 1872 and developed under the directorship of the late Charles Sprague Sargent, now occupies 220 acres of meadows and wooded land and is world famous both for the beauty of the site and its treatment, and the extent of the collection. It is also noteworthy for the many plants brought from the Far East by the late E. H. ("Chinese") Wilson, intrepid plant explorer.

Another important collection of woody material is in Highland Park, Rochester, N. Y., and the Morton Arboretum at Lisle, Ill., contains numerous interesting trees and shrubs. Other arboreta are maintained in connection with the various botanic gardens or separately. One of the most recent and most ambitious involves the development along arboretum lines of several thousand acres including part of the campus of Cornell University at Ithaca, N. Y., and extensive adjacent land owned by it. There is also under way a National Arboretum, for which land has been purchased along the Anacostia River near Washington, D. C., where it is planned to create a vast collection of plants that will be given added value by its proximity to the immense facilities of the U. S. Department of Agriculture.

See also list under BOTANIC GARDEN.

ARBORICULTURE. This is the culture of trees in all its aspects including propagation, planting, pruning, repair, protection from weather and from insects, etc. To be successful it requires a study of soil conditions such as acidity, alkalinity, drainage, fertility and physical texture, as well as climate, exposure, topography, etc. It involves the selection of the most desirable trees for a given location and knowledge of how to maintain them, and it leads to the extension of all these divisions into the horticultural field, both esthetically, as in garden making, and commercially, as in the production of fruits or the multiplication of plants in nurseries for landscape-gardening purposes. Associated terms are *Silviculture,* which pertains to the processes by which a forest may be efficiently operated and developed as regards lumber production; *Dendrology,* which is the science or study of trees; *Taxonomy,* which is the science of classifying woody plants.

ARBORIST. Literally, this means one who "does something" to trees, that is, one who practices arboriculture. However, of

more tender plants. When so used in an exposed location they are aided by a few wind-loving Austrian pines planted to break the wind for them. They are also most excellent hedge material, requiring little clipping because of slow growth and compactness. There are dwarf forms particularly desirable for borders, providing a substitute for Box in colder latitudes.

In foundation plantings it is a common error to plant closely for immediate effect and fail to separate the plants every two or three years. Another failure is to arrange the tall-growing varieties and the dwarfs in correct relation to the house. The result is

ARBORVITAE CAN BE USEFUL AND EFFECTIVE IN VARIOUS FORMS
1. As a hedge.   2. A sheared, pyramidal specimen for lawn or background.   3. Even old, neglected trees have a quaint homely character.

late it has come rather to mean a professional, trained tree expert who specializes in diagnosing sick trees, developing means of saving them, and doing all kinds of protective work such as spraying, bracing, cavity filling, etc. as well as the general care of healthy trees. Leaders in this field have organized the National Arborist Association to raise its standards, protect its interests, and gain increased public appreciation of the services it can render.

ARBORVITAE (ahr-bor-vy'-tee). Common name for the genus Thuja, a group of hardy evergreen trees of compact pyramidal or columnar form. They grow best in cool locations, either in wet soil, sandy loam or sand with water near the surface, but suffer from both heat and cold in dry situations. The foliage is dense, scale-like, waxy to the touch and fragrant. The lower branches are retained even in severe exposures but growth is more luxuriant in sheltered positions. (See illustration, Plate 15.)

Garden plans have found extensive use for arborvitaes as screens and shelters for

unsightliness and overcrowding which often is difficult or impossible to remedy.

Propagation is by seeds, cuttings and grafting. The smaller sizes are readily transplanted because of a fibrous root system. In dry locations plants sometimes become infested with red spider during warm weather. These can be destroyed by spraying with a strong stream of cold water followed by a suitable miscible oil.

ENEMIES. The American Arborvitae of the Eastern States has no serious diseases, the brown leaves so often seen being due to winter drying and sun scorch. Black leaf spot is very destructive to the Giant Arborvitae of the West. To control, spray young trees with bordeaux mixture in late spring and summer. A white or brown condition of the tips may be due to the leaf miner (*Argyresthia thuiella*). Insects winter in the mines and emerge in late spring to deposit eggs on the leaves which the young larvae enter in early summer. Spraying at this time with nicotine and soap may help. The bag-worm (which see)

TRAILING ARBUTUS OR MAYFLOWER
The sort of vigorous plant that grows in suitably acid soil.

often causes extensive defoliation. Red spider (which see) causes a mottled brown or gray discoloration of the leaves. See also diseases and their control under EVER-GREENS.

SPECIES

The American Arborvitae (*T. occidentalis*) often grows to 60 ft., retaining its dense pyramidal form. It thrives in all the Northern States and in higher cooler ridges south to N. Carolina. There are many desirable varieties such as *robusta* with even denser foliage; *riversi*, pyramidal with yellow-green foliage; *rosenthali*, a columnar form with dark green foliage; *vervaeneana*, pyramidal with more slender twigs, leaves somewhat yellow; *douglasi pyramidalis*, of particularly slow growth, forming a narrow dense pyramid; *globosa* var. Tom Thumb, a very dwarfed, globular form carrying both adult and juvenile foliage simultaneously and useful in rock gardens or borders.

The Oriental Arborvitae (*T. orientalis*) is an attractive tree much used because of its dense, vertically arranged foliage, distinct from previously mentioned forms. It is hardy, ranging about the same as *T. occidentalis*. Var. *elegantissima* makes a compact pyramid with bright-yellow foliage in spring, later becoming more green; var. *conspicua* is a golden yellow shaded green, having a compact columnar form.

From Alaska along the Pacific Coast and to Montana we get the Giant Arborvitae (*T. plicata*), hardy over the same range as the Oriental. In the wild it grows to 180 ft. but as cultivated it is smaller.

It would be suitable to use in garden compositions with smaller species.

False or Hiba-arborvitae is *Thujopsis dolobrata*, which see.

ARBUTUS (ahr'-beu-tus). Evergreen trees and shrubs of the Heath Family that, in the North, can be grown only under glass. Attractive outdoors in warm-temperate regions, with red-barked branches and dark-green foliage.

The best known is *A. unedo*, the Strawberry-tree, a native of Ireland and southern Europe, with several attractive varieties. The drooping clusters of white or pinkish flowers appear in the fall, along with the ripe strawberry-like berries from flowers of the previous year. These are edible but lack flavor. *A. menziesi*, a native of California, is the largest of the family, growing to 100 ft. A destructive leaf-spot (which see) disease may cause defoliation in the Pacific N. W.

ARBUTUS, TRAILING, also called Mayflower, is *Epigaea repens*, a trailing evergreen belonging to the Heath Family. One of the choicest wild flowers of the E. United States, it is the state flower of Mass. It is not a common plant in cultivation in spite of the many attempts to establish it in gardens. It requires an acid, peaty soil in a shady place, and seems to like association with Hemlock. As plants from the wild seldom get established, it is best in every way to get nursery-grown plants. Prepare a good station in a moist place and work in plenty of peat moss and sharp sand.

Propagation may be achieved by divisions and layers, but the best plants are obtained from seed. This should be sown as soon as ripe, using a mixture of peat moss and sand in a well-drained flat. Cover with a shaded pane of glass and look for the seedlings in about 4 weeks. When large enough to handle, put them singly into small pots, plunge these in moss and keep cool and shaded at all times. When this method is followed they usually begin to flower in their third year.

ARCHONTOPHOENIX (ahr-kon-toh-fe'-niks). Called the Majestic Phoenix or King Palm, this is the most elegant of the Feather Palms, having stout ringed stems and feathered leaves drooping from the smooth green sheaths. The flowers, usually white, are succeeded by small red fruits. Natives of the Far East, the palms of this genus are grown outdoors in subtropical regions. In the N. they need a temperate greenhouse and a rich fibrous soil. They are grown from seed which must have heat and moisture.

Among the best known species *A. cunninghamiana* (Picabeen-pine), with lilac flowers, is usually called *Seaforthia elegans* by florists who grow or handle it. *A. alexandrae,* the tallest type, growing to 80 ft., has white or creamy flowers.

ARCTIC DAISY. Common name for *Chrysanthemum arcticum,* a low-growing perennial species found in the Arctic, with white or lilac flowers resembling asters.

ARCTOSTAPHYLOS (ark-toh-staf'-i-los). Evergreen shrubs or small trees of the Heath Family, mostly natives of California. The best known is *A. uva-ursi,* the Bearberry, a prostrate species with rooting branches, widely spread throughout the northern hemisphere. Being a trailing evergreen only a few inches in height, it is a valuable ground-cover plant for northern gardens where suitable soil conditions can be provided. The soil can be quite gritty, provided plenty of leafmold or peat is worked in. Like other members of the family it objects to lime.

The bright-green leaves are small and leathery, taking on a bronzy tone in fall. The small flowers, white to rose, open in spring and are followed by mealy red berries, said to be enjoyed by bears. Cuttings of mature growth root readily under glass in late summer in a mixture of sand and peat. It is best to establish them in pots previous to planting outside.

A. manzanita, the native Manzanita of California, is a large and crooked-branched shrub of distinct appearance, with drooping panicles of white and rose flowers.

ARCTOTIS (ahrk-toh'-tis). Attractive daisy-like, half-hardy annuals from S. Africa especially valuable as a source of cut flowers, whose use is limited to the daytime because they close at night. The somewhat white-woolly plants bearing solitary flowers ranging from white through orange to brown and purple, grow from 6 in. to 3 ft. high, and can be planted in any part of the garden. They grow luxuriously in any good garden soil and a sunny position and are easy to start from seed either indoors or outdoors. Seeds germinate quickly, the plants grow rapidly and flowers are borne all summer and fall. When cut, they last from a week to 10 days. An interesting feature of this plant is

that undeveloped buds brought indoors and placed in water in a sunny window will open.

The best known species is the African Daisy (*A. grandis* or *stoechadifolia*), a bushy plant 2 to 2½ ft. tall, with 4 in. toothed leaves. The ray flowers are white on the upper surface and lilac-blue beneath and the center or disk is steel blue, giving rise to another common name, Blue-eyed African Daisy. The flowers, sometimes 3 in. across, are borne on strong stalks well above the leaves. Other species are *A. breviscapa,* dwarf, with 6 in. leaves and 2 in. flowers with orange rays and dark centers, and *A. gumbletoni,* to 1 ft. with very short stems, leaves 1 ft. long and 3 in. flowers, deep orange-red with brown basal markings.

ARCTOUS (ahrk'-toh-us). A low-growing deciduous shrub known as Black Bearberry and a member of the Heath Family. One species (*A. alpinus*), native of the N. regions of Europe, Asia, and N. America, is seldom cultivated but useful as a ground-cover plant for a cool shady place in the rock garden. The bright-green leaves turn red in autumn. The small white flowers, tinged pink, are sparsely borne in terminal clusters, and followed by black fruits. Propagated by seeds and cuttings.

ARDISIA (ahr-diz'-i-ah). An extensive genus of ornamental evergreen trees and shrubs of subtropical and tropical regions. Only one species usually grown in U. S. This is *A. crispa* (better known as *A. crenulata* or *crenata*), one of the best red-berried greenhouse plants for Christmas decorations. The berries are very durable, sometimes hanging on until the next crop is ripe.

After about three years the plant becomes "leggy," but when this happens, the tops may be girdled and bound with moss which is kept damp. In a warm house they soon root and may be cut off and potted; they should be kept in a close atmosphere until the roots are active. The old plant may then be cut back low so it will form a new head, first allowing it to get dry to prevent bleeding. Young shoots can be rooted as cuttings. The old plant can be shaken free of old soil, repotted and grown on to a good specimen. Equal parts loam and peat, with some sharp sand, suits them well. At the final potting some old crumbly manure may be added to advantage.

Seeds germinate in a few weeks; the seedlings need to be grown in a warm house to make much progress the first year.

Ardisia is subject to attacks of the common large brown scale insect. See GREENHOUSE PESTS.

ARECA (ar'-e-kah). A genus of graceful, slender-stemmed feather-palms from the Malayan peninsula, now much at home in S. Fla. Outdoors the smooth ringed trunks to 100 ft. are topped by a feathery cluster of leaves to 6 or 8 ft. long; the flowers are white and heavily fragrant, and the fruit is orange-colored. In the N. Arecas are grown under glass as pot plants and decorative material, in a rich fibrous soil. These palms have several commercial uses. The seeds contain a dye, the fibrous spathes and fruit-husks are used in packing, and the species *A. catechu* or *cathecu* (Betel Palm) produces the betel-nut commonly chewed by the natives of the Far East.

AREGELIA (a-ree-jee'-li-ah). A genus of tropical epiphytes or air-plants (which see) belonging to the Bromeliads (the Pineapple Family) and native to Guiana and Brazil. The leaves, toothed along their edges, form a rosette, and the flowers (white, blue or violet) are densely grouped within the innermost leaves. Greenhouse subjects in the N., the plants are commonly grown in pots filled with fibrous material, and freely supplied with water in summer. A night temperature of 50 to 75 deg. is required in winter. They bloom in March.

ARENARIA (ar-e-nay'-ri-ah). Sandworts, a genus of the Pink Family, so named because they prefer a sandy soil. They constitute a large group of low-growing herbs, annuals and perennials, native around the world except in the tropics, and including many true alpines found only at high altitudes. Upwards of 120 species have been recognized, but comparatively few, chiefly perennial sorts, are grown in gardens. Their habit of growth in dense mats, picturesque tufts, or graceful trailing creepers, has commended their use in carpet bedding and in rock gardens. Most of the perennial sorts bear small white flowers, but red and purple flowers may be had if truly alpine conditions can be provided. They are quite indifferent as to soil, so long as it is light and sandy and free from standing water. Propagation is by division, or by seeds; in the case of rare forms, cuttings are rooted in sand, under glass.

ARETHUSA (ar-ee-theu'-sah). A lovely wild hardy terrestrial orchid, which grows in the boglands of New England from bulbous roots which give the name of the one species *A. bulbosa*. The flowers, generally borne singly on stems 6 to 10 in. long, are rose-purple in color. The flowers are very noticeable because of their distinct shape and the fact that the lip has a bearded appearance. The beautiful Arethusa may be found in cranberry bogs beside bushes of Labrador-tea and rose pogonia. For culture, see ORCHID.

ARGEMONE (ahr-je-moh'-nee). Prickly Poppy. A free-flowering hardy annual of the Poppy Family (Papaveraceae), with large flowers resembling white, yellow or purplish poppies, and slender prickles on the leaves which resemble those of the thistle. The generic name comes from the Greek word for a disease of the eye that the plant was supposed to heal.

Plants grow from 2 to 4 ft. tall and if set 10 in. apart in rows make a good low screen or hedge, especially attractive when topped by their beautiful flowers. Thriving in any soil and a sunny exposure, they are grown from seed that should be sown where the plants are to grow, as they resent transplanting. They blossom all summer.

Some of the best species are:

A. alba. 3 ft. Foliage pale or covered with whitish "bloom." Flowers white.

grandiflora. 3 ft. Leaves white-veined. White flowers, 2 in. across, the sepals with stout, long tips.

mexicana. 3 ft. Leaves white-veined. Flowers 2 in. across, yellow or orange.

platyceras. (Crested Prickly Poppy.) The most commonly cultivated species. 4 ft. Flowers white or sometimes purple. Var. *hispida,* known as the Hedgehog Poppy, is densely bristled besides having yellow prickles. Var. *rosea* has brownish-purple flowers.

ARGYREIA (ahr-ji-ree'-ah). Tropical shrubby twining plants of the Convolvulus (Morning-glory) Family, with silvery leaves, hence known as Silverweed. In cultivation, they are mostly grown in greenhouses as robust and extensive climbers, needing plenty of room in which to grow before producing their colorful flowers. They need a light rich soil-mixture, and are propagated by cuttings.

A. cuneata does not exceed 5 ft. and is very free flowering. *A. speciosa,* with long woolly leaves, and *A. splendens,* with somewhat smaller but more silvery and silky leaves, are two of the showiest of the stronger-growing kinds.

ARISAEMA (ar-i-see'-mah). A genus of tuberous-rooted perennial herbs of worldwide distribution, belonging to the Arum group, the most familiar example being the common Jack-in-the-pulpit (*A. triphyllum*). About 60 species are known, some of which are successfully transplanted to gardens if a moist, shaded place can be given them. Some varieties are grown in pots, in a soil-mixture of loam and peat. Propagation is by division of the tubers, and by seeds. See also JACK-IN-THE-PULPIT.

ARISTOLOCHIA (ar-is-toh-loh'-ki-ah). Birthwort. A genus of nearly 200 species of evergreen and deciduous shrubs, widely distributed throughout the temperate and warmer parts of the earth. Most are climbers of twining habit, usually grown in greenhouses. They do best when planted out in rich soil, although some are grown successfully in pots, when well fed. The flowers are remarkable for their extraordinary formation and peculiar coloring. In some species they are very large with a long tail-like appendage, and most kinds have an offensive odor. Propagation is by seeds and cuttings.

PRINCIPAL SPECIES

A. durior (better known as *A. sipho*) is the Dutchmans Pipe. A hardy native vine, tolerant of shade and dry soil and with large leaves, it is one of the best for screening. The small flowers lack the pronounced unpleasant family odor ; their form gives the species its common name.

elegans (Calico-flower) is a well-known greenhouse climber, hardy south of Washington, D. C. The flowers are freely produced, about 3 in. across, purple-brown with white markings and no bad odor.

goldieana. A herbaceous species, with a fleshy rootstock that should be kept dry in winter. Its flowers, greenish-yellow with chocolate markings, are sometimes 1 ft. across and 2 ft. long.

grandiflora is called Pelican-flower, the flower bud resembling the body and neck of a large bird at rest. The expanded flower is several inches across, heavily blotched and veined with purple on a white ground, and terminates in a slender tail. The var. *sturtevanti* has flowers over a foot across, splashed with velvety crimson and with a tail 3 ft. or more in length.

ARISTOTELIA (ar-is-toh-tee'-li-ah). Evergreen trees and shrubs, native in the southern hemisphere and grown in S. California. The foliage is handsome, but the flowers are small and not showy, with male

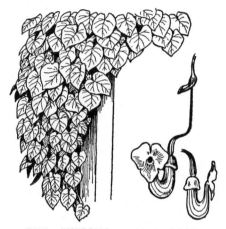

THE CURIOUS ARISTOLOCHIA
The Dutchmans Pipe Vine makes a quick-growing screen for porches.

and female often separate. The principal species is *A. racemosa,* the New-Zealand Wineberry, which makes a small tree with thin glossy leaves and dark-purple berries the size of a pea.

A. macqui is a large shrub, native of Chili, but able to stand a few degrees of frost. It has purple-black berries and there is a golden variegated variety.

The genus is named in honor of Aristotle, the Greek philosopher.

ARMED. Provided with spines, thorns, prickles, bristles or any other kind of sharp defense.

ARMERIA (ahr-mee'-ri-ah). Former name for part of the genus Statice (which see), comprising dwarf perennials with evergreen leaves in rosettes and numerous flower-heads on wiry stems from spring to autumn. They are called Sea-pinks and Thrift.

ARMILLARIA (ahr-mi-lay'-ri-ah) **ROOT ROT.** Also called Mushroom or Shoe-string Root Rot. A root and trunk decay of conifers, broad-leaved forest trees fruit trees and shrubs caused by the mush-room *Armillaria mellea,* often called the Shoe-string fungus or Honey agaric. The symptoms are decline in vigor and tardy growth, followed by rotting of the bark and finally death of the tree. The fungus is seen as a white mycelium between bark and cambium; also as black shoe-string strands (rhizomorphs) growing out from the trunk and roots and through the soil; and finally as honey-colored mushrooms growing in clusters around the trunk of the tree. The latter do not usually appear un-til the tree is almost or quite dead, which may be three or four years after the first signs of decline.

To prevent this rot, avoid planting trees in recently cleared lands. Instead, grow farm crops for a season or two first. Keep-ing trees in a vigorous condition by proper feeding and watering will render them less liable to attack by the fungus, which is a very weak parasite. Treat a diseased tree by digging the soil away from the crown, cutting affected bark back to healthy tis-sue, and painting the wounds with a disin-fectant. Keep the rhizomorphs from grow-ing through the soil to other trees by dig-ging a trench one foot wide and two feet deep around the affected tree.

ARMY WORM. *Cirphis unipuncta.* Striped caterpillars up to two inches long which move in ranks like armies from one field to another are called army worms. In certain seasons entire crops of corn, tim-othy, millet, blue grass and small grains may be devastated, when the hungry worms move from grain fields to attack orna-mental plants. Wintering as partly grown larvae the caterpillars begin to feed early in the spring, then pupate just below the surface of the soil and emerge in two weeks as pale-brown or grayish moths with a wing-spread of 1½ in. There are two to three generations a year but the first brood of caterpillars, hatching from the greenish-white eggs laid on grasses, does the most damage. This is usually during June in the middle W. and July in the E. Army worms are similar to cutworms (both be-longing to the family Noctuidae) but they are more apt to feed in the daytime and are more conspicuously striped. Control by broadcasting poison bran bait or by making a narrow band of the bait around the plots to be protected. See CUT-WORMS.

The FALL ARMY WORM is a similar in-sect of a different genus (*Laphygma frugi-perda*). In the N. there is usually but one generation a year, but there may be five or six in the S. Except in cold wet springs parasitic enemies keep this pest down to moderate numbers. It attacks nearly all field and vegetable crops but prefers grasses and is often called the grass-worm.

ARNEBIA (ahr-nee′-bi-ah). Easily cul-tivated border or rock-garden plants of the Borage Family, thriving in ordinary garden soil and a sunny location. From 1 to 2 ft. tall, and equally wide, they bear all summer long a profusion of beautiful yellow flowers which undergo a character-istic change in color. On opening, the blossoms are primrose-yellow with black or purple spots. After the second day the black spots in the annual species (*A. cor-nuta*) known as Arabian-primrose, become maroon and then disappear, leaving clear yellow blooms. The purple spots of *A. echioides,* the perennial species, known as Prophet-flower, fade away entirely, leaving the blossoms yellow. Plants are propa-gated by seeds, divisions or cuttings.

ARNICA. A genus of perennial herbs of the Composite Family having clustered basal leaves and bright-yellow flowers on long stalks. Only a few species are grown in the border or rock garden, though some of those native to the W. States are effec-tive when colonized in the wild garden. Arnicas grow readily in any good garden soil and spread so rapidly that they are most frequently propagated by division rather than by seeds. *A. montana* (Moun-tain-tobacco, Mountain Snuff) is an Old-World plant to 2 ft. tall, the source of the medicinal tincture of arnica; it has large heads of yellow ray and disk flowers, 3 to 4 in a cluster, and is attractive in an open sunny border. *A. alpina,* to 15 in. with soft-hairy foliage and heads of yellow flowers to 2 in. across, is excellent in the sunny rock garden.

AROID (ar′-oid). Any plant of the Araceae, or Arum Family, such as the Calla, Jack-in-the-pulpit, Tail-flower, and similar plants, characterized by having extremely small, simple unisexual flowers crowded around a column, called a *spadix,* which is surrounded by a broad, petal- or leaf-like, often colored organ called a *spathe.*

ARONIA (a-roh′-ni-ah). Hardy native deciduous shrubs, belonging to the Rose Family. Valuable in the shrub border for all round effect. See CHOKEBERRY.

ARRANGEMENT, FLOWER. The art of utilizing flowers and foliage for (a) the decoration of one's environment, (b) personal adornment, or (c) the expression of tribute, friendship, etc., is not exactly a phase of gardening, but is intimately related to it and makes possible its increased enjoyment. See FLOWER ARRANGEMENT and Plate 12.

ARROW ARUM (ay'-rum). Common name for *Peltandra virginica,* a perennial herb of the Arum Family, found in bogs from Me. to Fla. and westward to Mo. It has glossy, dark-green leaves shaped like an arrow-head on long leaf-stalks, and bears white flowers, and is sometimes grown in gardens, as an ornamental plant. Propagation is by division of the tuberous root, and by seeds.

ARROW-HEAD. Common name for the genus Sagittaria of the Water-plantain Family, comprising perennial aquatic herbs with white buttercup-like flowers and, generally, arrow-shaped leaves. They are most attractive planted on the edge of a pond, and some of the species are excellent in aquaria. They are propagated by division, by seeds, and by tubers.

S. sagittifolia, the Old-World Arrow-head, grows as high as 4 ft. The white flowers are spotted with purple and the underground tubers are eaten in E. Asia.

engelmanniana is excellent for naturalizing in colonies in shallow water, the arrow-shaped leaves and clustered white flowers creating a most pleasing effect.

montevidensis, the Giant Arrow-head, is often grown in aquaria and lily ponds. It has large, white flowers and sometimes reaches a height of 6 ft. It is tender N., but has become naturalized S. in the U. S., both east and west.

ARROW-ROOT. Common name for *Maranta arundinacea,* a tropical American herb with starchy roots which yield the arrow-root and tapioca of commerce. Growing to 6 ft. and with leaves 1 ft. long and 4 in. wide, it bears white flowers but is grown only for its edible product. An acre of arrow-root will commonly yield about 14,000 lbs. of rootstocks, from which about 2,100 lbs. of the dry starches will be obtained. See MARANTA.

ARROW-WOOD. Common name for *Viburnum dentatum,* a small tree to 15 ft., with circular, toothed leaves, and white flowers in late spring, followed by black berry-like fruits. See VIBURNUM.

ARSENATE OF LEAD. A stomach poison used to protect plants against chewing insects. See ARSENICAL POISONS.

ARSENICAL POISONS. Some form of arsenic is most commonly used as a stomach poison against chewing insects, white arsenic (arsenious oxid) being the basis of manufacture of arsenical sprays.

ARSENATE OF LEAD, the best known and most widely used stomach poison, comes in two forms, basic and acid. The former is less apt to burn tender foliage but stays in suspension poorly and kills insects more slowly. Most commercial preparations are the acid form, usually sold as a powder, sometimes as a paste. For general spraying use the powder at the rate of 3 lbs. to 100 gallons of water; or, in small quantities, one heaping tablespoon to one gallon of water. (Certain plants, such as stone fruits, require modifications of this.) If the paste form is available, use twice the amount recommended.

Lead arsenate may safely be combined with nicotine, oil emulsions, bordeaux mixture and lime-sulphur. It should *not* be used with sodium or potassium sulphide nor with soaps. It may be used as a dust by combining the powder (one part) with five or six parts of hydrated lime or sulphur that serves as a carrier.

ARSENATE OF LIME (calcium arsenate) is frequently used in dust form. Though cheaper than lead arsenate, it is not stable and should be used only when fresh. It is likely to burn tender foliage and should not be used on stone fruits. It is of especial value in cotton boll weevil control, being dusted over the fields from airplanes. As a spray for vegetables it is used in the proportion of 3 lbs. calcium arsenate, 3 lbs. hydrated lime, and 100 gallons of water. As a dust for cucumber beetles 1 lb. is mixed with 15 lbs. of gypsum.

PARIS GREEN (aceto-arsenite of copper) was the first arsenical spray to come into general use, but it has since been largely superseded by lead arsenate. It may safely be used with bordeaux mixture but never with sulphur or soaps. Now it is chiefly used in poison baits, as is white arsenic.

Arsenate of soda is used in poison baits and arsenite of soda as a weed killer. (See WEEDS.) Arsenite of zinc, sometimes used as a spray for potatoes, has a tendency to burn foliage.

MAGNESIUM ARSENATE is safer than lead arsenate on tender bean foliage and is extensively used in the control of the Mexican bean beetle. As a dust 1 lb. is used to 5 lbs. of hydrated lime; as a spray 3 lbs. plus 2 lbs. of calcium caseinate and 100 gallons of water.

London Purple is a calcium-arsenic compound formerly recommended. It burns foliage easily and is now little used.

CAUTION. All arsenical sprays leave a poisonous residue on leaves and fruits. The gardener must, therefore, discontinue their use some weeks before fruits or vegetables are mature. Fruit grown commercially goes through a special washing process, usually with diluted hydrochloric acid, before its sale on the market is permitted. Take care in using arsenicals not to leave the poisons around where children or pets can get them; and do not use mixing vessels for other purposes without thorough washing.

ARTABOTRYS (ahr-ta-bo'-tris). Tail-grape. Tropical evergreen climbers sometimes grown in warm greenhouses for their fragrant flowers. The common name refers to the way in which the fruit is supported by the curious hooked tendril. The principal species, *A. odoratissimus,* has greenish-yellow flowers with thick petals, and is extremely fragrant. In Java the leaves are considered to be a preventative of cholera. *A. suaveolens,* the Buffalo-thorn, is grown in the tropics to form barriers against cattle. It has small yellow, and also very fragrant, flowers.

ARTEMISIA (ahr-tee-miz'-i-ah). Wormwood. A genus of hardy aromatic usually perennial herbs or small shrubs of the Composite Family whose small white or yellow heads are composed entirely of disk (tubular) flowers. Grown chiefly for their aromatic and medicinal qualities, the plants are also garden subjects, being ornamental in the rear of the border and good for cutting. They thrive in any average soil and the species vary widely in shape and size, ranging from 6 in. to 12 ft. high. They bloom from August through September. The foliage of many species is so densely hairy as to appear white. Propagation is generally by division, sometimes by seed. The 50 or more species include the native sagebrushes of the W. one of which, *A. tridentata,* is the state flower of Nev. The following species are among the most satisfactory for U. S. gardens:

A. albula (Silver King). One of the showiest of the Wormwoods, native to S.W. U. S. but hardy N. and growing 3 ft. or more tall. The leaves, white and finely hairy and less dissected than in other species, are often used in winter as well as in fresh bouquets. It requires considerable moisture.

lactiflora (White Mugwort). Tall, with deeply-toothed, smooth-green foliage. The masses of white flower-heads, appearing in September, are fragrant.

vulgaris (Mugwort). A tall plant, with the stems often purple and fragrant divided leaves green above, white beneath. Flower-heads yellow, in spikes.

abrotanum (Southernwood, Old Man). Shrubby green plant, with leaves divided into thread-like segments.

stelleriana (Beach Wormwood, Old Woman, Dusty Miller). Native to N. temperate coastal regions, this is especially suitable to seaside rock gardens. The foliage is densely woolly.

frigida (Mountain Fringe, Fringed Wormwood). Decorative in borders, 15 in. tall, with delicate, velvety leaves.

sacrorum (Russian Wormwood). Leaves whitish. Its tall, drought-resistant var. *viride* (Summer-fir), with finely cut, dark-green leaves, is used in borders and as lawn specimens.

gnaphalodes. Tall, silvery-white; excellent in borders.

pontica (Roman Wormwood). Leaves finely cut, whitish below. Though it seldom flowers, it is effective as foliage in a rock garden.

pedemontana, a silvery-leaved plant, is similarly used.

absinthium (Absinth, which see). Shrubby plant with silky-white segmented leaves. One of the sources of absinthe.

dracunculus (Tarragon). The long, narrow, smooth, green leaves are used as seasoning.

ARTHROPODIUM (ahr-throh-poh'-di-um). A genus of tufted perennials of the Lily Family closely related to Anthericum. They have white or purple flowers in clusters and grass-like leaves. Grown in greenhouses in the N. and in the open in the S., they are easily propagated by stolons, divisions or seeds. The two best-known species are *A. candidum,* growing 14 in. high with pure-white flowers in graceful clusters; and *A. cirrhatum,* which is taller and has larger flowers in 1 ft. panicles.

ARTICHOKE. Name given to plants (and their edible products) of three genera.

—Cynara, Helianthus and Stachys. The first two, of importance as garden crops, are discussed separately following this article. The Chinese or Japanese Artichoke (*Stachys sieboldi*) also called Chorogi, Knot-root and Crosnes du Japan, is an erect, hairy, herbaceous perennial to 1½ ft. that has been grown in this country for its edible, slender, knotty, white tubers, but it has no special value.

GLOBE, FRENCH, or BUR ARTICHOKE is a thistle-like perennial (*Cynara scolymus*) grown for its edible flower-bud scales and "bottoms" and young suckers which when blanched are eaten like asparagus. Though not hardy in the N., it has been wintered safely in Mass. by placing peck-size peach baskets over the crowns to prevent smothering and covering these with deep mulch.

When seed is sown indoors in early spring, seedlings, pricked into small pots, hardened off and later planted outdoors, often produce heads by fall. Outdoor-grown seedlings rarely bear until the following summer. Set plants 3 × 3, or 2 × 4 ft. in rich soil and give clean cultivation. Gather flower-heads before they bloom and cut back the stalks that bore them to the ground to conserve the plants' strength and encourage sucker production. As plants rarely continue productive more than two or three years, and as seedlings vary greatly, suckers of the best ones should be used each spring to start new plantings. The most popular varieties are Large Green Globe and Large Green Paris.

JERUSALEM ARTICHOKE. An American perennial sunflower (*Helianthus tuberosus*) growing to 6 ft. with coarse, hairy foliage surmounted by bright-yellow flowers 2 to 3 in. across but grown more as a vegetable than for ornament. Its potato-like tubers, when escalloped or steamed and served with a cream or a hollandaise sauce, compare with cauliflower in delicate but distinct flavor. When cooked it differs from potato and sweet potato in never being mealy. It also makes a delicious pickle.

As it often becomes a pestiferous weed it should always be planted where it can do no harm—as in a corner, or around the compost heap. Here it will bloom profusely in late summer and produce tubers abundantly without jeopardizing the garden. It produces no seeds. When the tops die cut them down and use them (with dead leaves and other garden refuse) to cover the patch and prevent deep freezing of the ground

so tubers may be dug as needed all winter. This is better than digging and storing a supply in the fall because the tubers shrivel in storage. One planting will last indefinitely without care, though feeding will improve the size and yield of tubers. Enough tubers are always left in the ground when digging to stock the bed for another year.

ARTILLERY-PLANT. Common name for *Pilea microphylla*, a low-growing herb of tropical America, grown as a pot-plant or along the edge of benches in greenhouses and as a border plant in the S. So called because the staminate flowers "shoot out" their pollen when dry.

ARTOCARPUS (ahr-toh-kahr'-pus). A genus of tropical trees of the Mulberry Family, now widely distributed throughout the torrid zone, where the species *A. communis* (Breadfruit) is grown for its prickly edible oval fruit to 8 in. through. Specimens are rarely seen in botanical gardens or in S. U.S. as curiosities. In the usually cultivated form, the fruits are fleshy and seedless but one seed-bearing form is

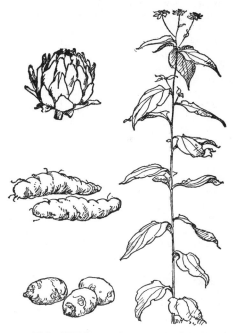

ALL THESE ARE ARTICHOKES
French or Globe Artichoke; fleshy green bracts Upper left, the edible young flower-head of this surround the bud of a huge thistle-like flower. Center left is the edible tuber of the little grown Chinese Artichoke (Stachys sieboldi). Lower left, delicately flavored tubers of the Jerusalem Artichoke, a kind of small-flowered sunflower, of which a stem is shown at the right.

called breadnut, although this name is also given to a related plant, *Brosimum alicastrum*. The large seeds of both are eaten roasted or boiled. Propagation of the breadfruit type is by suckers and root cuttings and of the breadnut type, by its seeds.

Another Malayan species (*A. integra*) of less importance is called Jakfruit or Jackfruit.

ARUM (ay'-rum). A genus of tuberous herbs from Europe and Asia from which the large family of Aroids takes its name (Araceae). The plants resemble and are often spoken of as Callas (which are, however, Zantedeschia), and are sometimes called Wild-ginger because of the acrid-tasting roots, in some species poisonous. They have large leaves and variously colored spathes, as the bracts surrounding a flower-spike are called. Some species are tender and should be grown in the greenhouse, the tubers being planted deep in rich soil so that roots may form near the top, and the plants being shaded from intense sun and watered freely. The outdoor species should also have rich soil and shaded position and a leaf mulch in the fall is very beneficial. They are propagated by offsets of the tubers or by seeds.

A. italicum has a yellowish or white spadix, sometimes green or purplish. Though hardy it is often grown in pots.

maculatum is the Lords-and-Ladies or Cuckoo-pint, often mentioned in English poetry. It grows to 1 ft. high with both leaves and spathe 10 in. long, the latter green, spotted and margined with purple. It is hardy.

palaestinum, known as Black Calla, or Solomons-lily, has a greenish spathe, black-purple within. It is grown in pots as an oddity.

Arrow-arum (which see) is *Peltandra virginica;* Ivy-arum (which see) is *Scindapsus;* Twist-arum (which see) is *Helicodiceros muscivorus;* and Water-arum is a name for *Calla palustris.*

ARUNCUS (ah-run'-kus). A genus of hardy, herbaceous plants of the Rose Family, with dense spikes of small white flowers; commonly called Goats Beard, which see.

ARUNDINARIA (ah-run-di-nay'-ri-ah). One of the most important of several genera of tall-growing, woody members of the Grass Family, to all of which is given the common name Bamboo, which see. Arundinarias are tree-like with smooth,

round, jointed stems, and often form great forests in the tropics from sea level to 15,000 ft. Some of the smaller, hardier species used in the garden are the following: *A. nitida* to 20 ft. with graceful arching purple canes and leaves 3 in. long, deep green above with a bloom beneath. One of the hardiest of the bamboos, it thrives in an alkaline soil, near water and in partial shade. *A. fastuosa,* another hardy and very vigorous species, growing to 40 ft. with canes marked purplish brown and leaves lustrous green above with a bloom beneath. *A. macrosperma* (Southern Cane), a native swamp form, forming immense "canebrakes" in the S. States. *A. tecta,* somewhat similar but smaller, is considerably hardier, growing as far N. as Md. and Ind.

ARUNDO (ah-run'-doh) *donax.* Commonly known as the Giant Reed, this is, with the exception of the Bamboos, the tallest of the ornamental perennial grasses. It is useful for bold effects in warm climates, sometimes reaching a height of 20 ft. The stem is woody, the leaves broad, and the plum-like panicles of flowers often 2 ft. long. See GIANT REED; also ORNAMENTAL GRASSES.

ASARUM (as'-ah-rum). A genus of native, perennial herbs, the common "wild ginger" of moist woodlands, sometimes transplanted to gardens. See GINGER.

ASCLEPIADACEAE (as-klee-pee-a-day'-see-ee). Botanical name of the Milkweed Family, a group of widely distributed plants characterized by an abundant milky juice; the production of pollen grains in waxy masses; and a fruit which is a pod opening when ripe along one side to discharge flat, light seeds tufted with long silky down. Generally herbs or shrubs, they vary widely, some genera being vines, like Hoya; or leafless and fleshy, as Stapelia. Many have medicinal properties and some are grown for ornament, as Asclepias, Stephanotis, Vincetoxicum.

ASCLEPIAS (as-klee'-pi-as). A genus of perennial plants with milky juice commonly known as Milkweed or Silkweed. Many of them have gay flowers and attractive seed-pods and are easily cultivated in the border and wild garden. They are propagated by division or seeds.

A. tuberosa, the Butterfly-weed, sometimes called Pleurisy-root, is a rough-hairy plant growing 3 ft. high with brilliant orange flowers in umbels (flattened clusters). Frequently found in dry places in E. U.S. it is most effective when planted in masses in the border or wild garden, but also excellent as a cut flower. Var. *sulfurea* has primose-yellow flowers.

incarnata, the common Swamp Milkweed, grows to 4 ft. and has rose-purple flowers; occasionally a white form, var. *alba,* is seen.

syriaca is the species seen by the roadside in E. N. America, growing to 5 ft. with green or purplish flowers and interesting seed-pods which release masses of light, flat seeds with long, delicate silky tassels.

curassavica (Blood-flower) is a tropical species which may be grown in the greenhouse in the N. and easily naturalized in the wild flower garden in the S. It has brilliant flowers of orange and reddish-purple.

ASCOCHYTA (as-koh-ky'-tah) **BLIGHT.** Various species of the imperfect fungus Ascochyta cause such diseases as a leaf spot and stem rot of clematis, a ray blight of chrysanthemum flowers and a wilt of cucurbits. This blight is serious on peas, where it causes a leaf spot, a stem and root rot and a pod spot somewhat similar to anthracnose of beans. Species of this fungus also cause diseases of alfalfa and other legumes, aster, columbine, cyclamen, hollyhock, horse-radish, okra, rhubarb, strawberry, sweet pea, tomato and walnut. See CHRYSANTHEMUM, CLEMATIS and PEA for special control measures.

ASCUS (as'-kus). In the group of fungi called Ascomycetes, a sac containing the sexual spores, usually eight. See FUNGUS.

ASCYRUM (a-sy'-rum). Low-growing (to 2½ ft.), evergreen shrubs, fairly hardy in the N. if protected and useful in the S. in landscape gardening. The species *A. hypericoides* is called St. Andrews Cross, which see.

ASEXUAL REPRODUCTION. The propagation of plants by vegetative means, not by seed; that is, by such processes as grafting, cutting, budding, layering and division, which involve the use of an actual piece of the growing tissue of the plant increased. Plants so produced are "true to type" that is, to those so increased, whereas reproduction by seed may give rise to progeny quite different from its parents. See PROPAGATION.

ASH. Common name for the genus Fraxinus, a group of hardy, deciduous trees

of moderately rapid growth. There are three native species of importance, namely, the White, Black, and Blue Ashes. The White Ash (*F. americana*), grows in average soils to over 100 ft. having usually a long oval shape, which makes it desirable for lawns because grass will grow well beneath. Its pinnate foliage is dense and generally free from insects. Autumn turns the leaves to brilliant yellows and shades of violet.

ENEMIES. Although rust, leaf spots and cankers may occur, the white heartwood decay is the only disease especially destructive; it is chiefly found west of the Mississippi. Control by keeping the trees fed and in a vigorous condition. Several insects find the ash a favorite host, especially the oyster-shell scale (see SCALE INSECTS) and the carpenter worm. Dress trunk wounds caused by this and other borers carefully; also seal carbon bisulphide (which see) into the large holes. The mite which causes the flower galls of white ash should be controlled with a dormant spray of miscible oil.

The Black Ash (*F. nigra*) is naturally a swamp tree but will grow in average soils if grafted on White Ash roots. It is a broad-headed tree much planted for shade; its characteristics are open branching with few twigs; flowers appear before leaves.

The Blue Ash (*F. quadrangulata*) is a large tree found chiefly in the Miss. Valley on limestone soils. It is adapted to the northern prairies with their trying conditions, where it will provide good garden shelter from the wind. From Europe comes *F. excelsior,* a large tree to 140 ft. preferring a moist limestone soil; it and its several varieties are much used for landscape gardening, particularly the weeping types. The Flowering Ash (*F. ornus*), which also comes from Europe, has fragrant blossoms, averages 25 ft., is round in form and well-suited to garden uses.

All of the Ashes are propagated easily from seed. They belong to the Oleaceae or Olive Family, other members of which are Lilac, Fringe-tree and Privet.

Wafer-ash is *Ptelea trifoliata;* Prickly-ash is *Zanthoxylum americanum;* Mountain-ash is Sorbus.

ASHES. Wood ashes, if not leached, contain all the mineral elements that were in the wood in the form of oxides or carbonates. Potassium carbonate and calcium carbonate or calcium oxide are present in comparatively large quantities giving the ashes a strongly alkaline reaction and the power to neutralize acid soils. However, the value of wood ashes as a plant food depends more on the potassium they contain than on the lime content.

At one time wood ashes were the chief source of potassium and much used in farming and horticulture. At present, the supply is small and they are not an important fertilizer though valuable for use in gardens where they can be obtained cheaply— or better from the home fireplaces. Good quality unleached wood ashes contain 5 to 7% potash and 1.5 to 2% phosphoric acid; leached ashes contain about 1% potash and 1 to 1.5% phosphoric acid; and both have 25 to 30% calcium compounds. Hardwood ashes contain more potassium than those from softwood lumber. Either kind loses much of its value if exposed to the weather so that the soluble chemicals are leached out.

Wood ashes should be applied to a soil some time in advance of planting and should not be mixed with manure or other nitrogenous material except in the soil. In view of their low plant-food value they can be used in any quantity without danger. An average application would be 5 to 10 lbs. per 100 sq. ft. scattered on the freshly dug surface and raked in. Wood ashes should not be used on lawns (which see) or around any acid-loving plants (which see).

Coal ashes may be useful to mix with a heavy clay soil to improve its texture. From the fertilizer standpoint the amount of potassium or phosphorus they contain is insignificant. Screened coal ashes are used on greenhouse benches under potted plants to assure good drainage. Or they can be placed at the bottom of borders or beds to protect roses or other plants against "wet feet" in heavy or poorly drained soil.

ASIATIC BEETLES. Three beetles of Japanese origin occur in the Eastern States. One is the Japanese beetle (which see); a second (*Anomala orientalis*) is the Asiatic beetle; and the third (*Aserica castanea*) is known as the Asiatic garden beetle.

The Asiatic beetle is particularly injurious to lawns. The adult beetles (about ⅜ in. in length, varying greatly in color and markings) emerge in late June and July and soon lay their eggs about 6 in. deep in the soil. In three or four weeks the recently hatched grubs ascend and begin to feed on grass roots near the surface;

ASIATIC GARDEN BEETLES
Dark tan in color, they are called "Aserica castanea" by scientists, and an increasingly troublesome lawn pest by gardeners.

in late fall they descend a foot into the soil to hibernate. They again ascend to the surface in April, feed until early in June and then pupate at a 6 in. depth. Thus there is only one generation a year. Protect lawns by broadcasting lead arsenate at the rate of 3 lbs. to each 100 sq. ft. of surface. See LAWN.

The Asiatic garden beetle (which has been accurately described as an "animated coffee-bean") may also feed on grass but is particularly injurious to garden crops such as aster, bean, chrysanthemum and dahlia, often feeding at night when also it may be seen in great numbers around street lights. The dull, cinnamon-brown beetles, about the size of the Japanese beetles, can be found in the daytime only by digging into the soil around plants. Control by spraying plants with lead arsenate when the beetles are numerous. If this will seriously deface especially beautiful plants by staining, treat the soil with lead arsenate as recommended above.

ASIMINA (ah-sim'-i-nah). Deciduous or evergreen shrubs or small trees, native of N. America. Only one species, *A. triloba,* the Pawpaw of N. America, is hardy North. This is a small deciduous tree to about 30 ft., with large drooping leaves and curious purple flowers of disagreeable odor, opening before the leaves. The fruit is 3 to 5 in. long and almost black when ripe, with a highly aromatic flavor. The plant thrives best in rich moist soil, suckering freely, but it is not easy to transplant. It is propagated by seeds, best sown in the fall; also by layers and root-cuttings. Compare PAWPAW.

ASPARAGUS. A genus of about 150 species of Old-World perennial herbs, shrubs and vines of which several are cultivated as ornamentals and one as a vegetable (see below).

The "smilax" of florists (*Asparagus asparagoides*) has been extensively grown in greenhouses as a "green" but is now supplied mainly by outdoor plantings in Florida. Several varieties of asparagus-fern (*A. plumosus*), a twining vine, are cultivated commercially under glass for their cut sprays and "strings" of lacy foliage which long continues attractive. This is a favorite florists' green for use with cut flowers and in table decorations.

Asparagus plumosus in the S. may be seriously troubled by a blight which causes the smaller branches to dry and to be shed prematurely. Control by spraying frequently with a 1-1-50 bordeaux mixture.

Sprengers asparagus (*A. sprengeri*), the most satisfactory species for house culture, is easily grown from seed sown during February. At living-room temperatures the seed usually takes about a month to sprout. When the seedlings are 2 or 3 in. high prick them into moderately fertile potting soil in small flower pots. Shift to larger pots when the roots form mats around the soil ball. Established plants bear open racemes of small, pinkish, fragrant flowers in May or June and coral-red berries about Christmas time.

GARDEN ASPARAGUS. Most extensively grown of all is *A. officinalis.* This choicest of spring vegetables should be grown in every home garden as better quality can be produced there than can usually be bought. Once established it requires less cultural attention than any other vegetable and, well fed and properly attended to, it is a lifetime investment, annually producing successive crops of stalks for six to ten weeks.

The annual stems or "spears" of this perennial plant develop from subterranean "crowns," from which thick, fleshy roots spread in all directions. Because of this horizontal root-development the old-fashioned method of burying a 12 or 18 in. layer of manure 3 or 4 ft. deep in the asparagus bed is a waste of energy and plant food.

Field-culture methods (rarely feasible in home gardens) consist of plowing under a heavy dressing of manure, setting the plants 4 ft. asunder in rows 6 ft. apart and thereafter cultivating with horse or tractor. In home gardens the best plan is to plant in a single row along the border of the area and not closer than 4 ft. from other permanent plants such as rhubarb, artichoke and currant, and still farther away from grapevines and trees. The space between need not be idle; seed of short-season vegetables —radish, lettuce, spinach, etc.—may be broadcast, or onion sets planted, in early spring on the freshly prepared bed and the plants, after the necessary thinning, harvested before the asparagus needs the area.

PLANTING. A trench is dug about 15 in. deep in fall or spring and well-rotted manure is tramped down to make a layer 3 or 4 in. deep, then covered with 4 to 6 in. of rich garden loam or compost. On this the plants are placed 18 to 24 in. apart, with their roots spread widely and their crowns (the buds) pointing upward. They are then covered with only 1 or 2 in. of soil packed carefully but firmly around them. They will thus be about 6 in. below the ground level but with only a thin layer of earth over them. In fall planting the trench is then filled with leaves or litter to be removed in spring.

As the growing season advances the soil in the trench must be slightly stirred with a narrow hoe or other implement about twice a week. This kills weeds and works down a little earth from the sides each time, gradually increasing the covering over the roots and assuring better plant-development than if the trench is completely filled at planting time. By the close of the season the trench will have been filled and the plants well established.

In many cases "beds" are preferred to rows. Preparation of the soil is the same, except that all the earth is removed to the full width (5 ft.) and depth (15 in.) of the bed. The manure is spread and tramped down over the whole area, then covered with rich soil. One row of plants is placed down the center and one on each side 18 in. from it and 12 in. from the edge. As in a garden row set the plants closer together (18 to 24 in.) than in field planting, then compensate for this by intensive culture and lavish feeding. Though many beds are set with plants less than a foot apart, larger, finer quality spears are produced if the distance is 18 to 24 in.

In a heavy clay loam soil, especially if not naturally well drained, it is advisable to dig the trenches deeper than 15 in. Place the good topsoil in a pile by itself and replace part of the poorer subsoil with drainage material such as gravel, stones or cinders. Then fill in with manure and rich compost to the planting level and later use the topsoil originally removed in gradually leveling off as already outlined. If an outlet can be had, a line of tile may be placed below the trench. See DRAINAGE.

BUYING PLANTS. Beginners often make the mistake of buying two-year-old and older plants. Although these almost always cost more than yearlings of the same variety, they never give as satisfactory results because they have lost proportionately more roots and consequently take one or two years longer to produce usable stems. When buying yearling plants, do not only select the highest grade stock, but also get 25 to 50 per cent more plants than are actually needed and discard the poorest when planting to assure a uniform stand in the bed. The discarded plants may be planted in some odd corner, where usable shoots may appear a year or two later than those in the bed.

CUTTING AND AFTER-CARE. Avoid cutting spears sooner than the third spring after planting; otherwise the plants will suffer and will not yield so well in after years. Do not cut too liberally the first crop-year; three cuttings is enough. Cutting too late in any season reduces the yield of sprouts in the season following; it should stop as soon as early peas in local gardens are ready for the table, so as to give the plants time to store up food for the next year's crop.

Careless cutting often injures or destroys sprouts still undeveloped below the surface. The right way is to push the knife vertically down beside the sprout and, at the desired depth, give it a slight twist so the point will cut only the desired spear. Or, better still, snap off the sprouts by bending them across the finger with the thumb. This prevents injuring other sprouts and secures only the tender, edible parts of the stalks.

Blanching to make the shoots white, by mounding the soil up around them as they grow, was formerly a common practice, especially with asparagus for canning. Modern preference is for natural green shoots produced by level cultivation.

FEEDING. At the close of each season the tops should be cut close to the ground as soon as they have turned yellow or the berries become red. Avoid breaking off and scattering the berries, for any seeds that grow would become "weeds.". Then spread on the bed a heavy dressing of fresh manure, if available, to serve as a mulch and to enrich the soil. Too much can hardly be used because asparagus is a gross feeder and responds with more and better spears. In the spring remove the coarse, strawy part of the cover and fork the fine material into the upper 2 or 3 in. of soil. If fresh manure is not available in the fall, any coarse litter can be used as a mulch

and well-decayed manure spread and forked in when spring opens. Poultry, pigeon, and pulverized animal manures may be liberally used in spring or early summer.

Chemical fertilizers may be used as follows: Nitrate of soda (not later than July) one pound to 200 sq. ft.; superphosphate and potash (either muriate or sulphate) one pound of each to 100 sq. ft. In addition to the fertilizers the plants may be given annual top-dressings of compost or other humus. Salt was formerly recommended as a dressing because the crops from farm home beds where the brine from pickled meat was emptied in spring were found to be superior to those from other beds. The salt was undeservedly given the credit due the saltpeter (niter) in the brine. As good asparagus may be grown without salt as with it.

The varieties now most popular are the rust-resistant Washington strains—Mary, Martha, and Pedigreed—developed by the U. S. Department of Agriculture. Plants may be purchased from specialist asparagus plant growers and leading seedsmen. Growing asparagus from seed in the home garden is not advisable. It demands patience and skill because (1) the seed is slow to germinate and the seedlings are hard to see when they appear; (2) weeding is tedious; (3) it takes the seedlings an entire season to develop to transplanting size, and (4) the number of plants needed for the home garden is in most cases too small to warrant the bother entailed.

ENEMIES. Rust (*Puccinia asparagi*), formerly a serious enemy, has been rendered far less prevalent by the development of resistant varieties of the Washington type. It may be recognized by

ASPARAGUS BEETLES
Adults of two common types are shown and between them a section of asparagus stalk with an adult and a grub (larva) at work, and two clumps of the tiny cylindrical eggs.

dusty reddish pustules of summer spores and black pustules of winter spores. If susceptible varieties are grown, dust with fine sulphur three weeks after the last cutting and again a month later. Cut and burn all tops in the fall.

Fusarium wilt and stem rot seems to be increasing. If beds are badly diseased start healthy stock in a different location. Destroy all wilted plants, including roots, as soon as noticed.

Two species of beetles feed on asparagus tops. The common asparagus beetle is blue-black with three white spots and an orange margin on each wing. The adult hibernates under rubbish, emerges in spring, feeds on tender shoots and lays eggs. These hatch into gray, black legged grubs which attack the leaves and stalks. There are from two to five generations. The 12-spotted asparagus beetle is reddish-brown or orange with 6 black spots on each wing cover. The adults may eat the shoots but the larvae feed on the berries of the fruiting plants. There are two generations a year.

To fight both kinds, protect new beds by spraying or dusting with arsenate of lead. Cut older crops clean every few days to remove the eggs before they hatch. Destroy all volunteer plants except a few left as traps and kept sprayed or dusted. After the cutting season spray or dust two or three times with lead or calcium arsenate. Poultry allowed the run of the asparagus patch will keep beetles under control, but in this case do not spray with poisons.

ASPARAGUS-BEAN. One of the common names for *Vigna* (formerly *Dolichos*) *sesquipedalis,* a leguminous herb related to the cowpea. It is grown in warm places as a pole bean though oftener as a curiosity, under the name of Yard-long bean, its pods being 1 to 3 ft. long.

ASPARAGUS-FERN. A common but erroneous name for the foliage of Asparagus (chiefly *A. plumosus,* a tender species) because its minutely divided leaves suggest fern fronds.

ASPEN. One common name for the genus Populus, also called Cottonwood and Poplar, but generally applied to the smaller growing species and particularly to those having flat leaf-stems which cause the leaves to shake and flutter with the slightest breeze. They are hardy and widely distributed through the temperate zone. *P. grandidentata* (Large-toothed Aspen) of the Atlantic Coast, and *P. tremuloides* (Quaking Aspen) of N. America generally are the native species. *P. tremula,* the European Aspen (but found also in Asia and N. Africa), has three varieties including one, *pendula,* with drooping branches. *P. sieboldi* is the Japanese Aspen.

See POPLAR.

ASPERULA (as-per'-eu-lah). Woodruff. A genus of small herbs of the Madder Family with leaves in whorls and small lily-shaped flowers of white, blue or pink. They are used in the rock garden or for carpeting shady places, thrive in moist soil, and are of the easiest culture, being propagated by seeds or division of the plants.

A. odorata (Sweet Woodruff), a perennial growing 8 in. high, has fragrant white flowers and sweet-scented foliage. It makes an excellent ground-cover for bulb beds. It is used to crown the Queen of the May in Denmark and to flavor wine in Germany. *A. orientalis,* an annual, grows to 1 ft. and has sprays of dainty blue flowers, and is the best species for the open border. *A. suberosa,* a tiny plant growing only 2 in. high, is suitable for the rock garden. The leaves are grayish with soft-hairs and the flower rose.

ASPHODEL (as'-foh-del). An ancient name that rather confusingly applies to plants of two genera—Asphodeline and Asphodelus. All are, however, members of the Lily Family—hardy herbs with fleshy roots, narrow leaves and lily-like flowers.

The asphodels are easily grown, preferably in a rich sandy loam, and propagated by seed or division of roots. *Asphodeline lutea,* also called Kings Spear, grows 2 to 4 ft. high and has leafy flower-stems and fragrant, yellow flowers in racemes 6 to 18 in. long. It thrives in a partially shaded border. *A. balansae* grows 2 ft. high and has small white flowers.

Asphodelus differs from *Asphodeline* only in having leafless flower-stems, the foliage being clustered at the base. The culture is similar. *A. ramosus* grows to 5 ft. with sword-shaped leaves and flowers in branching clusters.

ASPIDISTRA (as-pi-dis'-trah). Thick-rooted perennial herbs of the Lily Family, valuable and much used as foliage plants in homes and for window and porch boxes. They have stiff, glossy, evergreen leaves and will withstand much heat and dust, poor soil and dim light. The flowers are dark colored; and, borne close to the ground where they are hidden by the foliage, they are not effective and are usually not noticed. Aspidistras are propagated by dividing the roots in early spring.

A. elatior is the species commonly grown by florists. The leaves last well when cut and therefore are sometimes used as foliage in arrangements with cut Amaryllis blossoms. In Fla. they are extensively grown commercially in unheated plant-sheds, but they will thrive luxuriantly there on banks of streams or ditches. Var. *variegata,* with leaves striped green and white, is occasionally seen, but the variegation rapidly disappears if the plant is given rich soil. The species is sometimes listed as *A. lurida.*

ASPIDIUM (as-pid'-i-um). A large genus of ferns, which are now included by most botanists in the genus Dryopteris.

ASPLENIUM (as-plee'-ni-um). A genus of ferns, mostly lime-loving, distributed well over the world and represented in America by several species known popularly as Spleenworts. They are characterized by their tufted growth, wiry, usually black or polished brown stipes, and rather large and sparse linear or crescent-shaped fruit-dots. Both botanical and common names refer to alleged "anti-splenetic" curative properties.

Among our most charming and distinctive rock plants, one or more species are found in nearly all mountainous parts of the country. Dealers in rock plants can supply the more common species. When transplanting from the wild, chip away surrounding rock to avoid breaking the deep roots. They require well-drained rock soil, not too rich, with ⅕ lime added, and they do best in pockets between stones. Careful drainage is essential. Do not remove old fronds, and protect with leaves in the fall.

Greenhouse species require shade, perfect drainage and a soil of fibrous loam, peat, and sand in equal proportions.

For Silvery Spleenwort and Narrow-leaved Spleenwort see ATHYRIUM.

HARDY SPECIES

A. bradleyi (Bradleys Spleenwort). Has 2 to 8 in. oblong-spear-shaped fronds with blackish stipes and green rachis, once pinnate, the pinnae all of equal size, with a few toothed lobes and very short stalks. Found on rocks from N. Y. to Ala. and W. to Mo., it is the only native species not requiring a lime soil.

montanum (Mountain Spleenwort). Broadly spear-shaped. Fronds, 3 to 5 in. long, once pinnate, but with the lowest pinnae deeply cut into toothed lobes; the stipes brown at base; the rachis flattened and green. A difficult fern to grow, it should have half crushed-stone and half sand.

parvulum (Little Spleenwort). Closely resembles the Ebony Spleenwort (below) but fronds are not over 4 in. tall, more coarse and rigid; more common in the S.

pinnatifidum. Lance-shaped fronds, 2 to 9 in. long, pinnate below only, tapering above with roundish lobes, the apex sometimes taking root, as in the Walking Fern. Stipes brownish, rachis green. A very rare fern, found on cliffs. Not recommended for gardens.

platyneuron (Ebony Spleenwort). Erect, narrow fronds, 8 to 20 in. tall, the fertile conspicuously taller, with polished blackish-purple stipes and rachis; once pinnate, the oblong pinnae not stalked, and with a little ear at the base on one or both sides; the sterile fronds evergreen. Occasional forms have deeply serrated or plumed pinnae. Found often on banks beside wood-roads, it likes the proximity of stones but does not demand the exclusively rock surroundings of other species.

ruta-muraria (Wall-rue). A delicate tufted species, 2 to 4 in. high, with linear forking fronds, native in N. States on ledges.

trichomanes (Maidenhair Spleenwort). Fronds 3 to 8 in. long, in dense tufts; pinnae like those of *A. viride,* but stiff, leathery and darker green; the delicate stipe and rachis wiry and shining purple-brown. One of the best for garden culture and good in terraria. Do not crowd.

viride (Green Spleenwort). Small linear, pale-green and softly herbaceous fronds, 2 to 5 in., with green stipe and rachis, and roundish-oval, short-stalked pinnae. A gem, found only in far N. States, at high altitudes, but excellent in a cool greenhouse. Requires plenty of air and a bricky, sandy soil.

TENDER SPECIES

A. attenuatum. Dwarf, rigid, pinnate only at base.

avis-nidus (Birds-nest Fern). The most reliable for house culture. Produces broad, entire, 1 to 3 ft. fronds symmetrically from a single crown in open vase-shape. Requires little soil but much peat or sphagnum, taking its nourishment from surface rootlets.

belangeri. Plumed, 2-pinnate, 1½ ft., green stipes.

bulbiferum. Spear-shaped, 1 to 2 ft. fronds, rooting at the tip. Grow in peat and sand only.

caudatum. Fronds 1½ to 2 ft., suddenly narrowed at apex and terminating in a tail-like extension.

goeringianum. Superb in color, with a grayish band in center of each frond, reddish stipe and rachis. This rare species can also be grown outdoors in the climate of New York.

hemionitis. Fronds 6 to 10 in., broadly triangular and deeply lobed.

incisum. The best for baskets, 2 to 3 ft. fronds.

rutaefolium. Leathery 4 to 6 in. fronds, with much-divided blades.

ASTER. This name, meaning star, refers to two distinct genera of plants, both of which are, however, members of the Composite or Daisy Family. First, it is the botanic or generic name of the true, hardy asters, also called Starworts or Michaelmas Daisies and many of which are native to the temperate zone of the U. S. Secondly, it is the popular name of the tender, so-called China Asters, natives of China and Japan, which have been developed until they now provide us with some of our finest and most popular garden annuals. The botanical name of the China Aster is *Callistephus chinensis;* its culture, enemies, types, etc., are treated in the latter part of this article.

HARDY ASTERS

Hardy asters are usually characterized by leafy stems, and opposite, often spear-shaped leaves, ranging from 1 in. to 3 or 4 in. in length. The small flowers are daisy-like with yellow or orange centers and fine, often thickly growing petals. The stems are frequently much branched near the top, producing large clusters of flowers which individually range from less than 1 in. to 2 in. across. The colors range from deep purple through lavender, blue, pink and rose to white. Most varieties bloom in the late summer and fall when many other plants have finished blooming. For this reason and because of their variation in height (from 6 in. to 6 ft.), which makes them adaptable to so many purposes, they are rightly considered plants of outstanding value.

These asters have been developed and used far more extensively abroad than in

FLOWERS OF ASTERS IN WILD AND CULTIVATED FORMS
The native New England Aster (1) is known as Michaelmas Daisy in its many cultivated forms. China Asters (Callistephus) (2) have been developed into a number of types, three of which are: the rounded Invincible (A), the loose Comet or Crego (B), and the semi-double star or Sunshine (C).

America, in spite of the fact that some of the principal parents used in creating the modern forms are natives of the U. S. However, many gardens in this country have under cultivation wild species. These are principally *A. novae-angliae* (the New-England aster) and *A. novi-belgi* (the New-York aster). Both of these are attractive in their wild state and improve considerably when planted in a good soil and given food and attention. Both are also parents of many fine varieties. With the numerous superior varieties now on the market and being developed, it is to be hoped that American gardens will benefit by their increasing use.

CULTURAL DIRECTIONS. Most of the asters under cultivation like full sun. Many of them enjoy a moist situation (although they do not like to have their roots stand in water), but they will usually accept the average garden condition with an open exposure. A good average garden soil is more satisfactory than one which has been made very rich by much fertilization.

Asters are happily used for several purposes. In the flower border, the taller varieties may be usel as background flowers, with smaller ones in front of them, arranged according to their respective heights. As the taller varieties naturalize well, they may be satisfactorily used along the edge of fields, to divide the mown lawn from the uncultivated areas. They are also delightfully effective as well as happy at the edge of a natural pond, bog, or brook, as long as their roots are above the water line.

The dwarf sorts make ideal rock-garden subjects, some blooming in the fall when there is a scarcity of flowering plants in this type of garden, and others flowering in early summer.

Wherever planted, the effect of asters is charming rather than striking; they blend with the landscape, yet are very much in evidence. When planted in the border the taller varieties will often need staking because the heavily branched spikes have a tendency to weight themselves down.

Asters are easily raised from seed, almost invariably blooming the next year after a spring sowing. In the case of *A. novae-angliae,* var. *roseus,* even fall-sown seeds will give flowering plants the following year although the plants in bloom may be only 18 in. high in contrast with the 5 ft. height attained by older plants of the same variety. However, in this case the seedlings bloom later than the older plants, extending the fall season of bloom. Named varieties cannot be depended upon to come true from seed, so they must be procured as plants. Because of their late-flowering habit, these plants should be set out in spring.

Mature specimens should be spaced at least 2 ft. apart, except in the case of the dwarf and alpine sorts which need be only 8 in. apart. Most hardy asters thrive best when they are divided each year, in spring, and in this way the supply can be increased rapidly. Also, they can be increased by cuttings made later in the spring when the growth has reached a height of about 3 in. These cuttings should be placed in damp sand in a coldframe which is kept closed to maintain a humid condition. They will root readily and a large per cent will bloom in the fall of the same year. However, division is the more common and simpler method.

The hardy asters are comparatively insect and disease free. Occasional attacks of rust and mildew can be controlled with fine sulphur dust. Michaelmas Daisies may suffer from a wilt disease which first mottles the leaves, then causes the lower ones to turn bright yellow and later die. Destroy diseased plants, use healthy suckers for propagation; avoid excessive watering.

In general these plants can be considered among the most desirable perennials from the point of view of simplicity of culture as well as from an esthetic point of view.

HARDY ASTER SPECIES AND VARIETIES

A. alpinus (Mountain Daisy). Suitable as rock-garden subject and edging plant; violet-blue flowers, one blossom to a stem, in early summer, 6 to 10 in. tall. Var. *albus* has white flowers.

amellus (Italian Starwort). A semi-dwarf species, 2 ft. tall, large purple flowers in late summer. Var. King George has violet-blue flowers in early fall.

cordifolius (Blue Wood Aster). To 5 ft. Pale lavender flowers on graceful sprays in October.

ericoides (North-American or Heath Aster). To 3 ft. Flowers white or pinkish in the fall.

novae-angliae (New - England Aster). Much grown in the U. S. To 5 ft. Deep purple flowers in the late summer. Var. *roseus* has rose flowers. Other vars. are:

Barrs Pink, 4½ ft., rose-pink flowers in September; *Mrs. F. W. Raynor,* 5 ft., reddish-rose flowers in September and October; *Mrs. S. T. Wright,* 3 ft., rose-mauve flowers in the fall; *Roycroft Pink,* 4 ft., bright-pink flowers in the fall.

novi-belgi (New-York Aster). Also popular in this country. To 3 ft. with bright blue-violet flowers in the fall. Some vars. are: *Anita Ballard,* 4½ ft., cornflower-blue flowers in early fall; *Beauty of Colwell,* 4 ft., soft-lavender flowers in early fall; *Blue Gem,* 4 ft., rich blue in late fall; *Climax,* 5 ft., clear blue flowers on long sprays in late fall; *Glory of Colwell,* 4½ ft., pale silver-mauve flowers in late fall; *King of the Belgians,* 5½ ft., lavender-blue flowers in the fall; *Nancy Bullard,* 3½ ft., pink flowers in late fall. *Peggy Ballard,* 3½ ft., rosy-mauve flowers in late fall; *St. Egwin,* 3 ft., rosy-pink flowers in summer.

subcaeruleus. Large, pale-blue, solitary flowers in midsummer, on branchless stems 2 ft. tall; the plants form thick mats.

tataricus. A very late blooming species from Siberia; violet flowers, 6 ft. high.

yunnanensis. To 15 in.; soft-blue flowers in late spring.

mauve cushion. A horticultural variety which makes large cushion-like plants; valuable as a fall-flowering plant in the rock garden; to 9 in.; flowers of soft mauve.

The China Aster

In the late nineteenth century, the blossom of the *Callistephus chinensis* was a simple, single, little yellow-centered lavender flower. Today, with its varied double and greatly enlarged forms, it is a lush and frequently spectacular annual. The plants grow from 1 to 2½ ft. tall and are much branched. The flowers average 2½ or 3 in. across and often are so heavy that their weight is all the wiry stems can hold. They come in all shades of lavender, purple, rose, pink, crimson, and white. The foliage, plentiful near the base of the plant, is scanty or absent along the flower stems.

CULTURAL DIRECTIONS. Best results are attained with China Asters when they are grown in a little shade, although they often prosper in full sun. A moderately rich soil to which wood ashes have been added in early spring or at least two weeks before planting is most satisfactory. In the absence of wood ashes, well-rotted manure or a manure substitute can be used to advantage, but either of these is best applied in the fall previous to planting. A "light snow" of lime sprinkled on the soil surface a few weeks before planting is beneficial, as the China Asters like a sweet (alkaline) soil.

China Asters are relatively easy to grow in a soil comparatively insect and disease free. In fact, their chief drawback is their susceptibility to insects and diseases. However, healthy plants given a good start usually escape trouble and seed growers and breeders are making valuable progress in developing increasingly resistant forms or strains.

The most important point in growing China Asters is to see that, once started from seed, they do not suffer from any check or set-back until they have reached maturity. Set-backs usually occur as a result of overwatering, or overcrowding of seedlings, and from drought.

Seeds may be started indoors in a flat in early spring or out of doors in the open after danger of heavy frosts has passed. In flats they will want a soil mixture of one-third garden soil, one-third sand, and one-third humus or leafmold. It is a wise precaution to free this soil of possible insect and disease organisms by disinfecting it. (See STERILIZATION; SOIL.) The seeds germinate quickly and the seedlings should be transplanted at least once to stimulate growth. After they have been planted in their permanent position it is important to cultivate and water them regularly. In cultivating remember that the fine roots are shallow and must not be disturbed or broken; this makes *shallow* cultivation near the plants essential. Plants should be set to stand 1 ft. apart when mature.

Whether the first crop of seeds is started early indoors or later outdoors, succession sowings should be made every 2 weeks for a period of at least 6 weeks in order to have a long season of bloom. The individual plant is short lived. Early and late varieties are available on the markets and by using both the season can be lengthened to some degree.

There are several features which make the modern China Aster one of the most desirable of annual cut-flower subjects. These are their long stems, their excellent lasting quality, and the fact that they are not easily damaged. However, if leaves are allowed to stand in water for some time they decay and emit a foul odor; they should be removed from all parts of the stems which will stand under the water.

ASTER ENEMIES

INSECT PESTS. The most serious of the insects which attack the China Aster is the tarnished plant bug, a flying creature about ¼ in. long, difficult to control, and most likely to be present in long dry spells. The insects puncture new growths just below the flower buds, which droop or become deformed. Spraying or dusting with a tobacco preparation is the most effective treatment but the destruction of weeds in which the insects can live and breed is a good preventive measure. These bugs do not seem to do their work in the shade.

The large black or gray aster beetles (or blister beetles), which eat both foliage and flowers, will drop off a plant when disturbed. Holding a can of kerosene or kerosene and water under a plant as you tap the plant with a stick will destroy many. Both blister beetles and grasshoppers can also be killed on foliage with a spray of arsenate of lead, and on the flowers with nicotine sulphate or a pyrethrum-soap solution. Root lice (aphids) occasionally attract weak plants, sap their strength and stunt them. Tobacco dust worked into the soil, or nicotine-sulphate solution poured in a depression around the crown is helpful. It is advisable not to plant China Asters in the same place the year following a bad infestation with this pest.

DISEASES. A virus disease, called *yellows*, is responsible for severe aster losses. The dwarfed plants turn yellow and if the flower-heads open at all they are malformed and greenish. The virus overwinters in various weed hosts and is carried back to new aster plants in the spring by leafhoppers that attack them. Fall destruction of weed hosts plus spraying or dusting to destroy the insect carrier gives some control; use a contact insecticide to kill the hopper or bordeaux mixture to repel it. However, the greatest protection is obtained by growing asters under tents made of cheesecloth runing 22 threads to the inch. Besides keeping off the insects and preventing inoculation with the disease, this protects the plants from hot sun, hail, wind, etc., and results in the production of finer flowers.

Stem rot, also called Wilt, caused by a fungus (*Fusarium conglutinans*) that lives in the soil, is a serious disease among the China Asters. The fungus attacks the roots first, then advances up the stem, which becomes black at the soil surface just as the buds form. The leaves wilt and subsequently the whole plant wilts and dies, though sometimes only one of the branches becomes infected. Soil sterilization, and seed disinfection (which see) with a 1 per cent solution of formaldehyde, are useful preventives. But the best plan is to secure and grow only wilt-resistant aster varieties of which seed is now obtainable on the market.

Orange-colored patches on the under sides of leaves are caused by rust fungi. See DISEASES, PLANT; FUNGOUS DISEASES.

While modern China Asters have all been developed from the one species, *Callistephus chinensis,* the nomenclature, as far as types and varieties go, is rather confused. However, the following notes will help the gardener in selecting from the many kinds offered in the seed catalogs.

In this discussion varieties over 2 ft. are considered "tall," and those under 2 ft., "dwarf." Each of the types or varieties has its own list of segregated colors; many have more than a half-dozen different shades and tones.

The *Branching* type offers a compact pyramidal plant with many lateral branches; unless otherwise specified, it is late blooming. The flowers are loose and full. There are "non-lateral strains" which have no side buds. The *Giant Branching* type has exceedingly long stems. Both it and the type previously mentioned are extremely vigorous and easy to grow. Blooms cut just before they are mature will last almost two weeks, if the water is changed daily and if the lower leaves are not allowed to foul it.

The *Comet* type may be either early or late, tall or dwarf. The flowers are large and the petals fine and slightly curled, giving a feathery appearance. The *Crego* is usually considered an improved Comet, or in cases where the term "giant" is used, a branching Comet. *Giants of California* or *California Giant Asters* (an improved form of Crego), are exceedingly tall, with perhaps the largest flowers obtainable in the aster clan, and with long stems excellent for cutting. They bloom in mid-season. Although "earliest blooming" claims are made for other varieties, *Queen of the Market* is usually figured to open the China

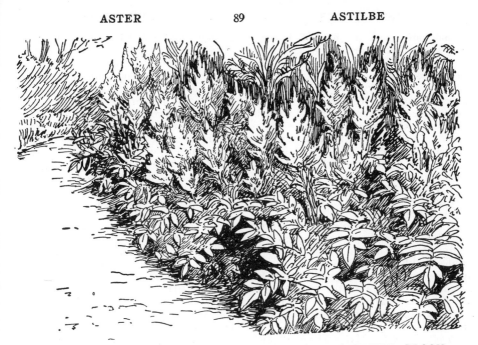

ASTILBE PROVIDES A HANDSOME BORDER FOR MIDSUMMER BLOOM
An excellent shrubby plant with filmy flowers of white or pink, Astilbe (by florists called **Spirea**) may be used in the garden as well as in the house.

Aster season. It is a dwarf and loosely branched kind, with neat, compact and full flowers. The *King* aster is the modern form of the *Victoria* or *needle* type. The flowers are fairly flat and neatly formed and the petals are semi-quill-like, opening in a spiral swing. This fairly dwarf aster has a tendency to be upright and unbranched except when otherwise noted.

The *Mammoth Peony-flowered* is the modern improvement of the *Truffaut* or peony-flowered aster of yesterday. The flowers are globular, like a florist's chrysanthemum, exceptionally large and borne on long stems; the plants themselves are extremely tall and late. *The American Beauty* aster has flowers of much the same appearance as the peony-flowered. However, it blooms earlier, is much branched and, although one of the taller varieties, is not so tall as the Mammoth Peony-flowered.

The *Sunshine* aster in its improved form (*Giant California Sunshine*) has very large flowers, with a center of quills which radiate outward over a single row of ray petals of a contrasting shade.

Although the single asters of today are large and fine and come in many colors, they do not enjoy the popularity of the above described various double forms. They are usually medium height and bloom in mid-season, and are to be recommended.

ASTILBE (a-stil'-be). Strong herbaceous perennials of the Saxifrage Family, growing from 1 to 6 ft., bearing feathery trusses of tiny whitish, pink or red flowers and with pleasing finely cut foliage. At one time a favorite garden and house ornament, especially popular at Easter, the astilbe was then for many years neglected; now it is coming into its own again. Easy to grow, in either a sunny or a partly shady location, it does best in rich soil if supplied with great quantities of water. It may be grown in the open border or forced in the greenhouse, when it requires from 10 weeks to 4 months to come into flower. Its propagation may be either by seeds or by division.

A. japonica, probably the most common species, is often called Spirea, to which it is somewhat related, though Spirea belongs to the Rose Family. After it has flowered in the house, a plant should be set out in the perennial border, where it will adapt itself and blossom year after year.

In growing astilbes for forcing, the gardener should plant the roots in 7 in. pots in the fall, and plunge the pots into the ground until about the first of January. They should then be brought indoors, given plenty of light and, preferably, a temperature between 50 and 60 deg. F. Constant moisture is necessary, and the pots should be kept in saucers filled with water. Grown indoors, the flowers are larger and purer in color than when grown outdoors. Plants should be washed at least once a month to control red spider.

There are a dozen or more species and many variable forms and hybrids grown by florists and frequently offered by them as Spireas. In addition to *A. japonica,* good garden species are:

A. arendsi. Really a group of hybrids with flowers from purplish to almost white.

astilboides. To 3 ft. Foliage sharp-toothed and hairy. Flowers white, crowded in dense spikes. From Japan.

biternata. Native to the mountains of the S. Atlantic States. To 6 ft. Leaves 2 ft. across. Numerous yellowish-white flowers.

davidi. To 6 ft. Hairy foliage; flowers rose-pink with dark-blue anthers. This and the next two from China.

grandis. 6 ft. Somewhat hairy. Flowers creamy-white.

rivularis. 5 ft. Spreads by means of creeping rhizomes. Flowers yellowish-white.

rosea. Hybrid of *A. japonica* which it resembles but with pinkish flowers. Includes several named varieties as Peach Blossom (light pink) and Queen Alexandra (deeper pink).

simplicifolia. To 1 ft. With star-like white flowers. This and the next are Japanese species.

thunbergi. 2 ft. With toothed and hairy foliage and white flowers which often become pink.

ASTRAGALUS (as-trag'-ah-lus). A group of herbs of the Pea Family with deeply cut leaves and purple, white or yellow flowers in spikes or racemes. They are commonly known as Milk Vetches and only a few species have beauty enough to be grown in the border or rock garden. They thrive in light, sandy soil and are propagated by seeds or by division in the spring. *A. mollissimus* is sometimes called Loco-weed, but the western prairie plant of that name which poisons cattle and horses belongs to Oxytropis, a related genus.

ASTRANTIA (as-tran'-shi-ah). A genus of perennial Eurasian herbs of the Parsley Family with deeply-lobed or cut leaves and flowers in flattened clusters. Commonly called Masterworts. One species, *A. major,* growing 1 to 3 ft. high with pink, rose, or white flowers, is occasionally planted in borders, but more frequently by the side of moist, shady woodland walks. The botanical name is from *astra,* a star, in reference to the star-like umbels or flower-heads. Propagated by seeds or division.

ATAMASCO-LILY (a-tah-mos'-koh). Common name for *Zephyranthes atamasco,* a bulbous herb of the Amaryllis Family, found from Pa. southward. It has grassy leaves to 1 ft. and funnel-shaped flowers to 3 in., white, purple-tinged, in spring.

ATHANASIA (a-thah-nay'-zhi-ah). Former botanical name for a yellow-flowered annual, one of the plants called African Daisy but now known as *Lonas inodora.*

ATHYRIUM (ah-thir'-i-um). A genus of large ferns represented by three species native to the N. and E. States, distinguished by their small crescent-shaped fruit dots borne profusely on the segments of the pinnae.

SPECIES

A. acrostichoides (Silvery Spleenwort). 2 to 3 ft. tall, once pinnate, the pinnae cut nearly to the mid-rib; the fruit-dots, white during the summer, give the fronds a silvery color when the wind bends them over. Of easy culture in rich, moist woods soil.

angustifolium (Narrow-leaved Spleenwort). A rather rare wood fern, with fronds 2 to 3 ft. long, once pinnate, the sterile fronds taller and with much narrower pinnae. Desirable for the garden as the only native once-pinnate hardy tall species. Give rich, deep soil and protect in winter. Fronds are especially subject to frost and storm damage.

cyclosorum. A tall and handsome form of moist, cool canyons in the far W., resembling *A. angustum* and needing the same culture.

asplenoides (Lowland Lady Fern). 1 to 3 ft. tall, 2-pinnate, the pinnules often prominently toothed. This and the next are among the most common, varied and satisfactory of native ferns. They are not fastidious but prefer a rich woods soil and half-shade. They will bear watching because they are rank growers; and they tend to look rusty after midsummer. This and the following species together are called by some botanists *A. filix-femina.*

angustum (Upland Lady Fern). Much like the foregoing but found usually farther N. and having reddish stipes.

ATRAGENE (a-traj'-ee-nee). A former generic name (still found in some catalogs) now referred to Clematis. It applied chiefly to *C. alpina* and *C. verticillaris.*

ATRIPLEX (at'-ri-pleks). A group of scaly herbs or shrubs of the Goosefoot Family, going in some sections by the common name of Salt-bush, as they are usually found growing in salty situations. Of the many species the great majority are weeds, though a few are valued as forage in arid regions, a very few are grown as ornamentals and one, *A. hortensis,* a native of Asia, is cultivated as a green, like spinach, under the name Orach (which see). *A. breweri* is sometimes grown as a hedge plant in Southern California, and *A. lentiformis* goes by the name Quail-bush.

AUBRIETIA (au-bree'-shi-ah). Originally spelled Aubrieta. Known as False- or Purple Rock-cress, this low-growing perennial of the Mustard Family (Cruciferae), is an excellent spreading plant for the border, bed or rock garden, doing well in semi-shade. Growing to a maximum height of only 12 in., the attractive silvery-green foliage covers spaces between rocks and along borders. In spring and early summer the flowers, when grown in masses, form a blanket of rosy-purple, blue or lilac. They look especially well combined with arabis or alyssum. Plants are grown from seed sown the previous season; or they may be propagated by layering the trailing shoots, or by division of the mats or clumps. The various improved forms grown in gardens are varieties or strains of one species, with lilac flowers (*A. deltoidea*). Some of the more popular are: *bougainvillei,* dark blue; *graeca,* light blue, 6 in.; *leichtlini,* bright reddish crimson, 8 in.

AUCUBA (au'-keu-bah). A name latinized from the Japanese Aokiba. Evergreen shrubs tolerant of shade, with large and ornamental leaves, able to withstand a smoky atmosphere. Not reliably hardy N. of Washington, D. C. Often grown in pots or tubs in the N. for porch or terrace decoration during the summer. Can be wintered safely in a cool place if kept on the dry side. Male and female flowers are borne on separate plants. To insure a display of the attractive scarlet berries the female flowers must be fertilized with pollen from the male plants. If kept dry, pollen retains its power for several weeks. The principal species is *A. japonica,* of which there are many handsome varieties; the best known (*variegata*) is called Gold-dust-tree. Aucuba belongs to the Dogwood Family.

AUDIBERTIA (oh-di-ber'-shi-ah). A genus of plants, sometimes shrubby, of the Mint Family, closely related to Salvia. The leaves are often white-woolly, or wrinkled and sage-like; the flowers are crimson, purple, or white. Occasionally they are grown in the border, but their chief use is as bee-plants. They require the usual culture for perennials, which see.

A. stachyoides (Black Sage) makes a stiff, shrubby growth up to 3 ft. and the flowers are white or lilac. An important bee-plant in Calif.

grandiflora (Crimson or Bee Sage) has dense clusters of brilliant-crimson flowers.

polystachya (White Sage) grows up to 10 ft. and has white-woolly leaves and white flowers. It is known as "greasewood" in W. America.

nivea (Purple Sage) has white-woolly leaves and purple flowers.

AURICULA (au-rik'-eu-lah). Common name for *Primula auricula,* a hardy primrose of the European Alps but in the U. S. grown more as a pot plant than in the rock garden where it suffers from the summer heat. See PRIMROSE.

AUSTRALIAN BLUEBELL-CREEPER. Common name for *Sollya heterophylla,* an evergreen climbing shrub, useful as a fence or bank cover in the South.

AUSTRALIAN BRUSH - CHERRY. Common name for a small tropical tree, *Eugenia paniculata* var. *australis* (formerly *E. myrtifolia*). See EUGENIA.

AUSTRALIAN PEA-VINE. Common name for *Dolichos lignosus,* an evergreen perennial leguminous climber, with white or purplish flowers.

AUTUMN CROCUS. A common name for Colchicum (which see), which bears large white to purple flowers directly from the corm in the autumn, after the leaves have died. Do not confuse with the autumn-flowering species of the true crocus. (See illustration, Plate 45.)

AUTUMN EFFECTS IN THE GARDEN. This may refer to those effects which autumn produces; or to effects which the gardener plans for the autumn season. Each meaning is important and must be considered.

NATURAL EFFECTS. Of the effects which autumn produces on all vegetation it is hardly necessary to say that the garden may be greatly enriched by tree, shrub and flower arrangements designed to take advantage of the changing color due to the seasonal ripening and gradual cessation of growth. In selecting material for such a composition it is necessary to know the color which each individual will contribute, and also to know the sequence in which one will follow another in the color procession; precisely as one must know the colors of each kind of flower in a mixed border and when each will bloom.

EVERGREENS. It is well to bear in mind that in natural landscapes the color pageant of autumn is greatly enhanced when the deep accents of evergreens appear occasionally. These bring a sustained quality into the changing effects, and by this contrast rest the eyes, and through the eyes the consciousness, which otherwise becomes exhausted with the struggle to take in and assimilate. There should always be enough evergreen material mingled in such a planting to give accent, relieve monotony, and give depth to the composition. But its proportion to other growth must be considered from the picture aspect, not from the number of plants used nor the plan of the ground. Depending on the size of the garden one evergreen shrub, one small evergreen tree, or one forest conifer well placed in relation to the rest of the plantation may bring into the picture a one-tenth portion of green; yet it may not represent one-twentieth of all the things planted. It is the green mass or bulk viewed in elevation that counts, not the specimen as a unit. In general one-tenth evergreen, to nine-tenths deciduous, color foliage is ample and in a small garden even this may be reduced, since spaces and distances are reduced and color masses are not likely to be overwhelming.

PLANNED EFFECTS. Coming to those effects which are planned for the autumn season, it is naturally the chief purpose to carry bloom to the latest date possible. This places dependence largely upon plants which blossom late in the season. Though comparatively few in number, they make up for this in abundance of bloom and in brilliance of color; it is easily possible to devote an entire garden to them if desired, without sacrificing its general excellence and beauty. There are also many spring-blooming shrubs which belong in an autumn-effect composition because of the ornamental fruits they bear at the end of the season. So it is hardly possible to limit effect to autumn only.

In addition to these ornamental berry-bearing shrubs and small trees, the apple, pear and quince are desirable in an autumn-effect garden; because fruits of one kind or another are essentially the expression of autumn. In relation to Michaelmas daisies, hardy chrysanthemums, monkshood, heleniums, torch-lily, fragrant artemisias, steeple bellflower, turtle-head, bugbane, tufted pansies and the persistent blossoming of hybrid tea roses (which continues until winter blasts the buds), a laden apple tree is not merely beautiful; it is distinguished.

Note that in all the flowers mentioned the colors of autumn predominate. This suggests following the lead of Nature even in the planned autumn effects. As we observe how the yellows, reds, purple-reds, scarlets and bronzes (running into browns) which clothe the earth at this season are persistently carried into autumn's flowers, it is hard not to believe that these colors have a special value at this season, even as do the distinctive spring colors at the beginning of the growing season.

See also BERRY-BEARING PLANTS; COLOR IN THE GARDEN; LANDSCAPING; NATURALIZING; PLANTS FOR SPECIAL PURPOSES; TREES IN THE GARDEN.

AUTUMN WORK IN THE GARDEN

The conscientious gardener places as much emphasis on fall gardening tasks as on those of the spring season. Indeed, many of the most essential operations of all must be—or should be—taken care of in the fall. In spite of which, spring always catches many gardeners unprepared, and many important things have to be neglected or overlooked in consequence. Much of *next* year's garden success depends upon the careful preparations made *this* fall; so now is a good time to go over your garden thoroughly, analyzing any mistakes of the past season and making plans to prevent their repetition.

Autumn work may be divided into two classes: (1) The completion of the summer's activities, including harvesting, storing, clearing up, putting away tools for the winter, etc. (2) Preparations for another spring, as planting bulbs, transplanting evergreens, trees, shrubs, and vines and so on. Perennials should be divided and reset so they can become established before cold weather. Flower and shrubbery beds and borders are to be mulched (after the ground freezes) and tender shrubs, roses, and broad-leaved evergreens must be protected against cold, drying winter winds, as well as the destructive effects of alternate freezing and thawing. The preparation of soil for new lawns and garden features such as beds for lilies or roses, etc., is best done in the fall.

GARDEN AND GROUNDS. As the ornamental aspects of a garden are, perhaps, most common and closest to the hearts of home owners, they will be mentioned first, to be followed by brief discussion of "chores" in the vegetable and fruit gardens.

Mulch rhododendrons, azaleas, mountain-laurel and other shrubs of the Heath Family with a heavy covering of oak leaves. As this decays it helps maintain the acid condition needed by this class of plants, besides providing winter protection and a cooling ground-cover in summer. Place a wind-break in front of the rhododendrons if necessary, using cut boughs of conifers, burlap screens or reed mats. Similarly protect tender evergreens, especially those in exposed locations. Cover bulb beds with a mulch—preferably of coarse manure or salt hay—as soon as the ground is frozen.

Any herbaceous plants that are prone to die off during the winter should be lifted and placed in a coldframe.

Take up waterlilies; move them to a frame or cool greenhouse and dry them off slowly so they will ripen gradually. Cut dahlia plants to within a few inches of the ground after a blackening frost and dig the roots carefully within a week or ten days. Lift corms of gladiolus, tuberose, and cannas, and store in a cool cellar.

The winter sun is apt to injure boxwoods, so give them a light protection of burlap or evergreen boughs arranged over a frame so it and the winter snows will not break down the bushes. Canterbury bells, fox gloves, delphiniums and Oriental poppies need only a light covering, but cover chrysanthemums with coarse manure. Hardy roses appreciate a heavy manure-covering and litter on top of that, mainly to check evaporation. The more tender bush roses should be mounded up with soil to half the height of the branches, while tender climbers and standards should be buried. To do this, rake away the soil at one side near the stem, then bend the plant gently

down in that direction and cover it with earth, manure, and, last of all, litter.

But *don't start mulching too early.* A little freezing is less harmful than keeping the plants soft and tender or stimulating them to start new growth at this late date.

Pull out all dead annuals and burn them to kill the eggs of insects and the spores of disease. The ashes can be added to the compost heap along with all succulent garden rubbish that is reasonably certain to be free from pests, such as lawn clippings.

If barnyard manure is to be used in the garden next season it is well to secure it now and compost it by piling it in alternate layers with leaves, sods, and other humus forming material. An occasional sprinkling of lime will help break down such a mixture, while the addition of some acid phosphate now and then will increase its plant-food value. A compost heap is invaluable to a garden and should receive additions of suitable material at any and all seasons.

Cut away dead wood from shrubs and trees before the leaves fall, when it can be more easily distinguished. Cut the suckers from about the shrubs and make hardwood cuttings. Prune the roots of trees that you intend to move during winter or next spring by digging a trench around them and filling it up again.

Spray for scale, using lime-sulphur, after trees and shrubs become dormant. Search boxwoods for signs of leafminer or red spider; if infestation is found, spray or dust with sulphur; all pines can well be treated the same way.

Drain all pools and bird baths, for if heavy ice forms in them the concrete or stone may be cracked. Wooden covers over the empty basin or pool are a wise protection.

Build rock gardens so the soil will have a chance to settle before spring planting time. Label all bulbs and roots as they are dug up for winter storage; also mark places where bulbs and perennials are being planted so that they will not be disturbed during early spring activities.

Move all garden furniture into a dry sheltered place for the winter. Examine it for any necessary repairs and make any that are called for. A coat of paint now is good insurance. Gather up all stakes and poles and put them away where they will be handy when needed again. Look over all seeds gathered from the garden and see that they are free from visible pests or diseases; then put them in tight tin boxes correctly labeled to be kept in a dry place until spring.

Repair old coldframes or build new ones. They will be needed to shelter some half-hardy subjects over winter, for the storage of hardy bulbs wanted for winter forcing and to receive seedlings started next spring indoors. An early fall sowing of spinach often gives a crop before severe winter weather; but if it doesn't it will be ready for use much earlier in spring than if planted then. Cabbage, lettuce, and cauliflower are other vegetables that can be sown in coldframes to be protected and grown on for spring use. Pansies and various perennials can be carried along in the same way.

Fill boxes with leafmold, good garden soil, and sand and store them so the material will be unfrozen and ready for use next spring when planting seeds in flats and boxes.

While nitrogenous fertilizers should not be applied to the soil in fall, as much of the plant food will be lost by leaching over winter, phosphorus and potash are not so lost, but become available slowly so that it is often wise to apply them in the fall.

There is no better time for preparing the soil than in the fall. Spade up every bit of unused ground in the garden and leave it open. By spring the frost action will have mellowed it and killed many insects and their eggs. If a soil needs humus, sow any vacant spaces to a cover-crop (which see). Overhaul and clean up the perennial beds. Fork in manure around chrysanthemums. Clear out the old hotbeds, adding the spent manure for the new flower beds. But do not allow manure to touch the roots of peonies or bearded irises, planted now or at any other time. Prepare rose beds and, if possible, plant roses of greater profusion of bloom next summer.

Now is an excellent time to make or repair lawns. Don't mow too late or too close, but on the other hand, don't leave a long, unkempt, unsightly crop of grass. Top-dress the lawn with compost, humus or thoroughly rotted, screened manure. The former practice of applying a heavy mulch of coarse manure is no longer recommended. Reseed bare or patchy-looking places, if there is time for the seed to germinate, fitting and feeding the soil first. Clip or trim any formal hedges that need it before freezing weather.

Evergreens can be transplanted now. Dig them with good balls of earth, keep them watered well and shielded from sun and wind, and mulch carefully after they are in place.

Transplant ferns and wild flowers.

Plant all kinds of hardy, Dutch or spring-flowering bulbs as hyacinths, jonquils, lilies-of-the-valley, tulips, crocus, snowdrops, grape-hyacinths, etc. Madonna lilies and other hardy kinds and also bleeding heart should be in the ground well in advance of frost so as to get established. The other bulbs can be planted until hard freezing prevents, even until Christmas.

Some kinds of annuals (which see) can be sown now for spring blooming; cover them lightly with screened, rotted manure. Plant sweet peas late in a deep trench; if they sprout, keep covering them with soil as they grow until the ground freezes. In planting bulbs where field mice are troublesome it may be necessary to surround the beds with "fences" of $\frac{1}{2}$ in. wire-netting sunk 6 or 8 in. in the ground but extending only a little above the surface or the mulch on it.

Freesias, narcissi, amaryllis, hyacinths and tulips desired for indoor blooming should be potted and the pots buried in a frame or other cool place from which they can be removed to the house in midwinter. Repot house plants in good rich soil and compost and move them to a protected place for a day or two before bringing them inside, so as gradually to accustom them to house conditions. Pot up a few plants of parsley to be grown in a sunny kitchen window.

Fruits and Vegetables. Taking up now the autumn work in vegetable and fruit gardens, the following tasks should be kept in mind:

Do not let pears ripen on the trees, but pick them while still firm. Pick apples as they ripen but before frost strikes them. Dig carrots and beets and store them in a moist cellar at just above freezing temperature. Salsify and parsnips can be left in the ground and dug as wanted. Pull onions, clean them, spread out thinly for a day or two, then store in a dry cool place, not the root cellar. Blanch endive by tying the leaves together on top. Dig potatoes as soon as the tops have died, especially if the season is a wet one. If cabbage heads begin to crack, bend them so as to break the roots on one side.

Just before a frost pull up tomato vines and hang upside down in shed or garage where many of the immature fruits will ripen. Parsley, sage, thyme, sweet marjoram, and other herbs should be cut and hung up to dry. Mature cabbage should be pulled and stored in the root cellar or in a pit with a dry sandy bottom; here they are placed with the roots up and covered with hay. Brussels sprouts and kale can be left in the ground and harvested as needed. Spinach can be taken up, roots and all, and put in a pit or box of sand. Put pumpkins and squash in a cool dry place.

The root cellar should be below the frost line or insulated against freezing temperatures, have a dry floor and be divided into bins 3 or 4 ft. square. It should be provided with a ventilation system that will prevent excessive moisture and insure circulation of air.

After the first real cold spell take up the celery. A good way to store it is to clean out a hotbed and put one foot of sand in the bottom; then cut off about 6 in. of the celery leaves, and place the bunches upright on the sand and close together. There should be several inches of air between the tops of the celery and the glass sash, which should be covered with wooden shutters. Large wooden boxes with sand on the bottom placed in the root cellar can be used instead of a hotbed.

Divide and replant rhubarb roots. Cover the asparagus beds with manure after a heavy frost, to be dug in next spring.

After currant and gooseberry bushes have lost their leaves they can be taken up, divided and replanted in good loose soil. Fork up the raspberry and blackberry beds, and cut out all wood that bore the past summer except in the case of everbearing kinds. Pull up the new sprout growth, leaving only 4 or 5 canes to a plant. If more plants are wanted, those pulled out can be used.

Buy apple, pear and quince trees and set them out at once; plums, cherries and peaches are better planted in spring. Any time after the leaves fall, fruit trees can be pruned to better shape. Pinch or prune off the runners from strawberries planted in August so as to throw the energy into a single crown for next season's fruiting. Mulch strawberries after the ground freezes, being careful that no manure comes in contact with the crowns of the plant;

rye straw or salt hay is often preferable. Raspberries, blackberries, gooseberries, and currants should all be thoroughly mulched as they are not deep rooting and are apt to be injured otherwise.

Finally, assuming that you have finished all the fall work that can be done, be sure to gather up all tools and put them safely away for the winter. But first they must be cleaned; rust, if present, removed with kerosene, all working parts oiled, and metal parts, such as blades and ferrules of hoes, etc., smeared with heavy oil or grease. It helps prolong the life of tools if the handles are kept painted. Don't forget to clean (and perhaps paint) the wheelbarrow, plant boxes, ladders and other wooden articles. Wash clay pots and sterilize them in hot water if you have had trouble with any sort of infection in the plants grown in them.

See also BULBS; MULCH; PROTECTION; SPRAYING, DORMANT; STORING OF CROPS; WINTER WORK IN THE GARDEN.

AUXIN (ox'-in). A chemical manufactured in the growing tips of plants. As the substance travels down through the plant it stimulates the growth of the cambium or living tissue just under the bark, causing the stem to become larger and thicker. Eventually it reaches the root where it stimulates the formation of new roots by increasing the rate of cell development.

In their search for natural plant hormones, or auxins, scientists have isolated three substances, namely, auxin a, auxin b, and hetero-auxin. Auxin a was first isolated from urine in 1933 and auxin b was found in corn germ oil in 1934. These are closely allied chemical compounds, very unstable, and found in minute amounts of one or two parts in 100,000,000 parts of plant tissue. A third substance, subsequently found in both plant and animal tissue and found to have growth-promoting properties, was named hetero-auxin and later identified as beta-indoleacetic acid.

See CHEMICALS IN GARDENING and ROOT-FORMING SUBSTANCES.

AVAILABILITY. A plant food is said to be available when it is in such form that plants can promptly take it up and make use of it when it is added to the soil or other medium in which they are growing. A soil may contain great quantities of plant foods chemically speaking, but they may be in such forms or combinations with other materials as to be useless to a crop.

Examples of plant foods immediately or readily available are: nitrate nitrogen, as found in nitrate of soda; the phosphorus and calcium in acid calcium phosphate, and the potassium in potassium chloride (muriate of potash), potassium sulphate or potassium carbonate. All these compounds are soluble in water and thus quickly become part of the soil solution which is the source of a plant's sustenance.

Plant foods not immediately available are the organic nitrogenous fertilizers such as dried blood, fish scrap, cottonseed meal, etc., which are insoluble in water. Under the action of certain bacteria their nitrogen is changed into the available nitrate form. Under usual conditions, the nitrogen in such substances, when applied to soils in spring, becomes completely available in time to be used that season. Thus, for practical garden purposes, much of the nitrogen in such fertilizers is available. Fresh stable manure contains no immediately available plant food, but, as it ferments and decays, the bacteria gradually bring about the change just described.

Strictly speaking, a fertile soil is one which contains abundant plant food in available form. Obviously, proper cultural practices that favor the growth of the nitrifying micro-organisms are essential to the maintenance of such a condition, as is the constant addition of plant food in various forms to make up for that which is removed by the growing plants.

See also FERTILIZERS; SOILS.

AVALANCHE-LILY. Common name for *Erythronium montanum,* a species of Adders Tongue or Dogtooth violet, a white-flowered bulbous plant of the Lily Family, native to Ore. and Wash.

AVENS (av'-enz). Former name, still in occasional use, for the genus Geum, which see.

AVIGNON-BERRY (ah-vee'-ni-on). Common name for one species of Buckthorn (*Rhamnus infectoria*). See RHAMNUS.

AVOCADO (a-vo-kah'-doh). A much branched, evergreen tree (*Persea americana*) of tropical and subtropical America which in nature often exceeds 50 ft. but in cultivation is kept below 30 ft. As it is tender its range is confined to frostless areas. In S. Fla. and Calif. it has become commercially important for its fruits which are called alligator-pears. They differ as to size and colorings, but are in general large, thick skinned, green or olive-colored

AN AVOCADO AS A HOUSE PLANT
Buy an "alligator pear," enjoy it in a salad and save the seed. Stick three toothpicks into the broad end to support it in a tumbler, keep the water level just touching the base and when top and roots have developed, pot up the plant.

and globular, oblong or pear-shaped. The one big seed (the size of a plum) is imbedded in yellow, buttery flesh which is eaten as a salad.

As garden subjects the trees deserve to be planted for both fruit and ornament wherever they can be grown. They are best dug in spring while small, with good balls of earth; banked with shavings in lath-houses; and syringed daily for two or three weeks before planting. Each tree should be allowed at least 30 ft. in which to spread. Well-drained fertile soil suits them best. They should begin to bear in three or four years. They grow easily and fast and make interesting and useful additions to the home grounds where the fruit becomes everyday fare.

None but named varieties (budded on seedling stock) should be planted. These constitute three groups: Guatemalan, which ripen from early winter to spring; Mexican, from late spring to early autumn; and West Indian, late summer to early winter. The first may be grown halfway up the Florida peninsula; the second, only near the tip; and the third, within the range of the sweet orange.

An interesting house plant can be grown by thrusting three toothpicks radially into the broad base of an avocado seed so it can be supported above a tumbler or wide-mouthed jar kept full of water, so that the bottom of the seed just touches the surface. Within a few weeks the seed will sprout, first thrusting a long white root into the water and then a stem, bearing handsome glossy leaves, straight upward. It can be grown thus for some months; then by gradually adding soil to the water the plant can be transferred from a water to a soil medium and then carefully potted. If protected from frost it can be grown to a good-sized plant or shrub, which can be plunged, pot and all, in the garden over summer and brought back indoors in the fall.

AWN. A bristle-like appendage, especially one of those at the tip of the bracts or "glumes" of grasses, which collectively make up the "beard" of barley, certain kinds of wheat, etc.

AXIL. The angle formed by a branch, leaf- or flower-stalk with the stem or another branch.

AXIS. The main line of development of a plant, as the principal root and its continuation, the stem; or the line of support of an organ or group of organs, such as stem, branch or shoot. Also the main or base lines upon which a garden design or other landscape plan is built up. See GARDEN DESIGN.

AZALEA (ah-zay'-le-ah). A kind of Rhododendron. While some of the forms are evergreen, the common hardy sorts drop their leaves in the fall or are merely semi-evergreen. Greenhouse races exist. (See illustration, Plate 1.)

Azaleas are among the most beautiful flowering shrubs in existence. In size they range from dwarf plants 1 ft. high to tall bushes of 20 ft. Most forms produce flowers abundantly in spring or early summer; their colors range through the pink, red and purple shades to white, yellow, orange and scarlet, with all intermediate hues. Many are delightfully fragrant. When not in bloom their foliage is good and in winter, when the leaves are gone, the branching habit of most species is very interesting and useful in the landscape. The low-growing kinds are useful as small shrubs or as 2 ft. ground-cover material.

Azaleas require an acid soil, prepared as described for rhododendrons, which see. Directions as to site and culture are also similar, although the hardy, deciduous American azaleas will withstand considerably more wind and sunshine than the evergreen rhododendrons. For abundant blooming, azaleas should have a little more light than the "true" rhododendrons, but all do well in conditions of semi-shade. An oak-leaf mulch is decidedly beneficial to all and is very important for Ghent azaleas or for any that are grown in full sunlight. Much alleged "tenderness" of azaleas is due to dryness in summer rather than winter

cold, and the mulch or irrigation maintains the needed uniformity of soil moisture.

Enemies that attack both azaleas and rhododendrons are discussed under the latter heading. A few warrant special mention here.

Leaf scorch (caused by a fungus) is a generally destructive azalea-disease of both outdoor and greenhouse plants. Small indefinite yellow or red areas are followed by browning of larger areas and defoliation. As the fungus overwinters in the fallen leaves, clean up all plant débris; and spray plants with copper ammonium silicate.

A flower-spot disease of cultivated azaleas has, since 1931, spread throughout the S. states from N. C. to Texas. Small pale spots on the petals enlarge to blotches and the corolla collapses, though it may remain clinging to the twig. Hard black sclerotia overwintering in diseased petals in the soil produce, in the spring, fruiting bodies which discharge spores that cause initial infection of healthy plants. Secondary infection comes from spores spread by wind, rain, insects, especially bees. The fungus is carried on blooming plants or in soil moved with dormant plants. Control with copper sprays or dusts applied at three-day intervals from first coloring of buds to full opening of flowers. Destroy infected flowers and replace surface soil around sick plants with fresh earth or a thick leaf mulch.

A fungus bud and twig blight threatens cultivated and wild azaleas, especially in Mass. Prune out promptly diseased portions and dust with copper-lime dust or spray with bordeaux mixture 5-5-50. Destroy leaves swollen into galls by another fungus. Control the mildew often prevalent in late summer by dusting with sulphur.

The azalea lacebug resembles and acts like the lacebug that attacks the rhododendron, which see. Around New York City there are three broods from June into September, each requiring a well-timed contact spray. In the S. spray with a white oil emulsion (3 tbls. oil, 2 tbls. powdered derris and 1 tsp. nicotine sulphate per gal. of water) right after blooming, again late in May, and late in September. The same spray controls mealybugs, mites, peony scale and thrips.

GARDEN EFFECTS. The Azalea Garden at Magnolia, S. C., is famous for its huge Indian azaleas set in a grove of live oaks.

While identical conditions cannot be reproduced in the North, gorgeous effects may be obtained by the use of hardy azaleas in a woodland setting. Several hardy sorts grow to 12 or 15 ft. and are very colorful, while there are many more which will exceed 6 ft. and a number of smaller ones. If dark-colored forms cannot be obtained, a few of the richly colored hardy "true" rhododendrons may be included in the collection. Any partly shaded area or corner of the home grounds, especially if hedged or encircled by tallish plantings of shrubs or trees, or a partly cleared patch of woods, makes a fine spot for an azalea garden which is easy to maintain when established. Azaleas may also be used in the shrubbery border and for many other purposes. By the use of early and late blooming sorts flowers may be secured successively from April first until August at New York City. The possibilities of azalea gardens for the North are not yet fully realized. Time, of course, is needed to develop big plants.

HARDY SPECIES. In New England and the region described as (AA) for hardiness in the article on rhododendrons, the following species of azaleas are recommended: *R. calendula-ceum* (orange, yellow or scarlet), *R. arbores-cens* (white), *R. roseum* (rose), *R. vaseyi* (pink), *R. kaempferi* (cerise or salmon-rose), *R. japonicum* (orange, apricot or yellow), *R. viscosum* (late white), *R. atlanticum* (dwarf white), *R. poukhanense* (low lilac), *R. schlippen-bachi* (blush), *R. mucronulatum* (magenta-rose), *R. canadense* (light lilac) and the hardiest of the Ghent and Mollis hybrids (from deep red to white and yellow).

To this list may be added several more when New York City or its equivalent, the (A) region, is considered: *R. mu-cronatum* (white) and its pink, spotted or lilac varieties, *R. pentaphyllum* (bright rose), *R. obtusum,* vars. *hinodegiri* and *amoenum* (crimson), *R. poukhanense* var. *Yodagawa, R. pulchrum* var. *Maxwelli, R. indicum* vars. J. T. Lovett and *Balsaminae-florum* (deep rose) as well as the Malvatica hybrids and forms of *R. mucronatum* known as Indicum-Roseum or Magnificum hybrids. Several in this list are commonly advertised as "hardy" but are not reliably hardy in New England or equivalent climates. This should be borne in mind and only the (AA) sorts purchased for regions which are truly cold.

LESS HARDY KINDS. For Philadelphia and southward, as well as warm gardens elsewhere, the Kurume azaleas may be added to the list. There is a possibility that a few of these may be developed into sorts hardy at New York, but they are tender now unless protected in winter. In the Lower S. many varieties of the hybrid Indian Azaleas, with forms *R. pulchrum,*

ATTRACTIVE AZALEA PLANTS CALL FOR SKILLFUL HANDLING
1, A rooted cutting left alone might make a growth like this in a season. But instead it is pinched back (or perhaps grafted) to give a stocky plant (2) shown in a 2½ in. pot. Such a plant, fed, watered, repeatedly pinched back and repotted as necessary, becomes a plant like that in (3) and finally a fine flower-loaded specimen like the Kurume hybrid shown in (4).

R. *mucronatum, R. simsi* and *R. indicum* are used. Old forms of these grow at Magnolia, and similar varieties have been planted elsewhere in S. C., Ga., Ala. and Fla. For this same region, several native species, tender in the N., are useful. These include *R. prunifolium, R. speciosum, R. canescens,|R. austrinum* and *R. serrulatum*.

AZALEAS FOR FORCING. The so-called Indian Azaleas, which are mostly hybrids of *R. simsi* (not *R. indicum*) have long been used as florists' pot plants for winter forcing. There are two general kinds, early and late blooming. The early sorts may be forced for Christmas or midwinter, while the late ones are mainly for Easter and early spring. These azaleas are all named clonal varieties (see CLON)· propagated by grafting upon seedling stock or stock from vigorous cuttings. They are propagated mainly by specialists, so the methods will not be described here.

In forcing, the plants are left out in coldframes or put into a very cold greenhouse (40 deg. F.) until December or January, when they are taken into a 60 deg. house and kept at this temperature until they bloom. Of course, the time of commencing as well as the temperature is varied somewhat to fit the desired time for bloom. Azaleas, however, are cool-house plants and should not be forced at high temperatures. The varieties of early blooming Indian Azaleas include: Mme. Petrick, Pres. Oswald de Kerchove, Simon Mardner and Vervaeneana. The later varieties include Blushing Bride, Empress of India, Jean Haerens, Mme. Van der Cruysen and Professor Wolters.

KURUMES. Kurume Azaleas are a race developed in Kurume, Japan, from forms of *R. obtusum*. They are dwarf, twiggy and compact, blooming when small, forcing well and easy to propagate from cuttings in sand and peat. They are used for forcing as pot plants, or grown outdoors in the S. Popular florists' varieties are: Bridesmaid, Cherry-blossom, Christmas Cheer, Coral Bells, Hinodigiri, Salmon Beauty and Snow. They are forced much like the Indian Azaleas.

The Sander Hybrids are intermediate between Indian and Kurume azaleas, but with gorgeous rich colors. Some of the best for forcing are, perhaps, Ruby, Uncas, Black Hawk and Hexe.

Among the hardy hybrid azaleas the Ghent Azaleas are pre-eminent. They were developed from *R. calendulaceum, R. nudiflorum, R. arborescens* and other American species crossed with *R. luteum*. Some of them may be tender, but many of them are entirely hardy. The secret of growing them is to keep them adequately supplied with water in dry summer weather. Pallas, Daviesii and Coccinea Speciosa are varieties which will withstand 20 deg. below zero. Others recommended for the N. are Dulcinee, Unique, Bijou de Gendbrugge and Raphael de Smet, Mercene, Narcissiflora and Rosette have double flowers. Another race with larger flowers is known as Mollis Hybrids. Most of the hardy forms have much "blood" of *R. japonicum* in them; and seedling forms of *R. japonicum* are frequently as good as the hybrids. Miss Louisa Hunnewell, Anthony Koster, Hugo Koster and Brilliant are all good, mostly yellow or orange in color.

Azaleas now constitute a "Series" within the genus Rhododendron. While there is a great difference between the American forms of Azalea and Rhododendron, there are all sorts of intermediate grades between them in other parts of the world, so that no line of separation can be drawn which will put them into separate genera. Accordingly all are regarded as Rhododendrons. Azaleas are subdivided into Subseries under the names of the following species, which act as centers for their respective groups: Canadense, Luteum, Nipponicum, Obtusum, Schlippenbachi and Tashiroi. All native American azaleas, except *R. canadense* and *R. vaseyi*, are members of the Luteum Subseries.

Descriptive notes on the various species are given under the title RHODODENDRON.

Alpine-azalea is a hardy, ericaceous, low-growing shrub. See LOISELEURIA.

AZALEA AND CAMELLIA SOCIETY OF AMERICA. This body was organized in 1932 to create a greater interest in these plants (particularly in the Camellia), and to attempt to straighten out and standardize the names of many varieties, about which there is great confusion. The membership is mainly amateur. Through its encouragement camellia shows have been held in a number of cities and towns throughout the S. and in California.

The Society's Annual supplies news of the organization as well as material on the cultivation of azaleas and camellias and descriptive listings of species and varieties of both subjects.

The annual dues are $1. The secretary is Mr. H. T. Conner, Box 478, Macon, Ga.

AZALEAMUM. Name given by some plant dealers to their strain of the compact, hardy, early flowering garden chrysanthemum Amelia, even better known as Pink Cushion 'Mum, because the low-growing, densely flowered plants form mounds of color suggestive of the old-fashioned azalea.

AZARA (ah-zah'-rah). Evergreen shrubs native of Chile. Can be grown outdoors only in warm-temperate regions. They are handsome shrubs of elegant habit, with small but fragrant flowers without petals. *A. microphylla,* the best known, is prized for its orange-colored berries as well as its graceful habit. It is hardy as far north as Washington, D. C., and is occasionally found in greenhouse collections in northern gardens. *A. gillesi,* with more conspicuous flowers, and holly-like leaves, is considered the showiest member of the genus. Propagation is by seeds or cuttings of mature wood.

AZOLLA (ah-zol'-ah). A small group of moss-like floating aquatics with divided, leaf-like stems and tiny greenish or reddish leaves. The plants multiply rapidly by self-division, and, if not disturbed, will completely cover the water surface where they appear. *A. caroliniana,* found floating on still water from Fla., Canada to Mexico, has been used in Panama to prevent the breeding of mosquitoes; it is sometimes grown on the surface of aquaria and conservatory tanks or pools.

B

BABIANA (bab-i-ay'-nah). Baboon-root. The botanical name comes from a Dutch word for baboons, which eat the bulbs. A genus of low-growing S. African plants of the Iris Family with sword-shaped, hairy leaves and a loose spike-like cluster of showy red or purplish flowers in early spring. Grown from seeds or, more often, corms, they succeed in very sandy soil. Being tender they are grown in the North only indoors or in protected cold-frames; plant 3 to 5 corms in 4 in. pot. In the South plants can remain outdoors untouched, but are better replanted every other year. The varieties obtainable (usually in mixtures) are probably all of the species *B. stricta*, 1 ft. or less high, with red or purple to bluish and yellow flowers.

BABIES SLIPPERS. One name for *Lotus corniculatus* (Birdsfoot Trefoil), a low, hardy, yellow-flowered plant good for dry banks and rock work. See LOTUS.

BABOON-ROOT. Common name for Babiana (which see) applied to both the plant and its corm.

BABY BLUE-EYES. Common name for *Nemophila insignis*, a pretty, low-growing, spreading annual with bell-shaped blue flowers. See NEMOPHILA.

BABYS BREATH. A name sometimes applied to Muscari (Grape-hyacinth) because of its fragrance, but commonly given to *Gypsophila paniculata*, the popular, easily grown perennial having clouds of fine white flowers; attractive in borders and for bouquets with other flowers. (See GYPSOPHILA.) Do not confuse with False-babys breath, which is *Galium aristatum*.

BABYS TEARS. A common name for *Helxine soleirdi*. See CREEPING-NETTLE.

BACCHARIS (bak'-ah-ris). Ornamental shrubby plants of the Composite Family attaining heights of 5 to 12 ft. A few species are native to the U. S. but more than 200 are native to S. America. Most of the garden forms mentioned below are easily grown in almost any well-drained soil in a sunny position and will do well even on dry, rocky slopes and in seashore plantings. Others are marsh plants. All have small white or yellowish flower heads borne in panicles or corymbs in late summer. Thereafter the glistening white bristles (pappus) of the fruits make an attractive, showy effect. Propagated by seeds and cuttings under glass.

B. halimifolia, the Groundsel-bush, a deciduous form growing to 12 ft. and found in marshes and along the coast, New England to Texas, is the hardiest, best known and most used; very attractive when in fruit.

pilularis, 5 ft., is a handsome evergreen found on dry hills, Calif. and Ore. Not entirely hardy.

angustifolia (8 ft.), *douglasi* (5 ft.), and *glomeruliflora* (10 ft.) are lowland or marsh forms.

BACHELORS BUTTONS. One of several common names for *Centaurea cyanus* (Cornflower). Also sometimes applied to *Gomphrena globosa* (Globe-amaranth) and to the double form of Buttercup (*Ranunculus acris*). See CENTAUREA and GOMPHRENA.

BACKGROUND PLANTING. This term seems to explain itself, but actually it refers to a variety of materials and involves several important principles. In a garden bed or border the background may be simply the larger, taller annuals or perennials used. Or it may be a permanent arrangement of shrubs, or a hedge, or a wall. The hedge may be informal or it may be symmetrically sheared to provide a setting for a statue, pool, garden seat or other feature. In a larger way, a tree, a group of trees, or even a piece of woodland may be needed to supply an adequate background for a building, a specimen plant, an entire lawn, or a broad vista.

The background planting, whether natural or planned, should combine and harmonize with and balance the other elements of the garden picture—not only in type of material, but also as to size, form, etc. For a small, intimate arrangement the plants should be selected that will not grow out of proportion or unduly crowd or starve out those in front of them. For large effects they should be so chosen and arranged as to maintain the desired results with a minimum of care and protection against insect and disease enemies. In short, although a successful background planting is itself inconspicuous, it plays an exceedingly important part and can do a great deal toward making or marring the ultimate effect of a garden layout.

See also BEDDING; BORDER; GARDEN DESIGN; GARDEN WALLS; LANDSCAPING.

BACTERIA. Microscopic, single-celled organisms placed by botanists at the bottom of the plant kingdom in the lowest class of the first division (Thallophyta) which includes also the fungi, slime-molds, seaweeds, etc. They are of many kinds, occur in many forms (round, rod-shaped, spiral, etc.), and are normally present almost everywhere. Though far too small to be seen with the naked eye, they make their presence known and felt in various ways.

As the cause of diseases in humans, animals and plants, bacteria are popularly called "microbes" and "germs" and rightly regarded as dangerous. But there are also many forms that are vitally useful in their relation to soil fertility and plant growth, and therefore to gardening. Some of them break down complex substances in the soil and in fertilizers and help convert them into simpler forms that the plant roots can take up as food. Others have the unique power of taking free nitrogen from the air and "fixing" it so that plants can use it, as in the nodules found on the roots of legumes (which see). Still others are essential agents of fermentation, as in vinegar and wine making.

It is one of the gardener's tasks and opportunities to try to increase and make use of the helpful bacteria and to control or eliminate the harmful ones. This calls for a knowledge of the conditions that favor bacterial growth and activity—that is, moisture, the correct temperature-range, and, in most cases, the presence of air; also knowledge of how to create and maintain such conditions—or correct them, as circumstances may require. It may mean (1) the sterilization or disinfection of seeds, soil or plants; (2) the development of more resistant plant varieties; or (3) the inoculation of soils or seeds with beneficial bacteria in the form of commercial preparations called "cultures" so as to bring about or hasten the desired growth stimulus or other effect.

See also DISEASES, PLANT; DISINFECTION; IMMUNE; INOCULATION; PLANT FOODS; RESISTANCE; SOIL; STERILIZATION.

BACTERIAL DISEASES. Many serious plant diseases are caused by bacteria. While the symptoms may be similar to those of fungous diseases, the latters' characteristic signs, such as fruiting bodies and spores, are absent. The following kinds of symptoms are typical of those shown by bacterial diseases. (See DISEASES for definition of these symptoms):

Blights, such as fire blight of apples and ornamentals, bean blight, bacterial blight of lilacs; *rots,* such as soft rot of iris, black rot of crucifers; *wilts,* as cucumber wilt; *leaf spots,* as black spot of delphinium; *overgrowths,* such as gladiolus scab, crown gall.

Bacteria that cause plant disease may be spread by the carelessness of the gardener, especially during wet weather; by wind-splashed rain; and by insects, sometimes within them as in the case of cucumber wilt, and sometimes on the outside of their body as the iris borer spreads bacterial soft rot. Fortunately bacteria that cause plant disease are not of the group that forms resistant resting bodies called "spores," so the spread of bacterial diseases through the air is not as common as that of fungous diseases, whose spores may be carried long distances by wind and air currents.

As these diseases in plants are difficult, if not impossible, to cure, precautions should be taken to avoid them, by preventing infection and by developing immunity or increased resistance to the organisms in improved varieties of plants.

See references under BACTERIA.

BAERIA (bee'-ri-ah.) Commonly known as Goldfields. Small annual plants of Calif. belonging to the Composite Family, about 1 ft. high and bearing many-flowered heads of small, yellow, daisy-like flowers in late spring and summer. Grown from seed sown in spring as edging plants or "everlastings" for cutting, they are treated like any annuals. Of the 20 or more species only three appear to be cultivated: *B. aristata,* with heads ½ in. across on 10 in. stems; *B. chrysostoma,* with heads up to 1 in. and stems 12 in. long; and *B. macrantha,* sometimes growing 12 in. tall.

BAGWORM. The larva of a moth that spends much of its life inside its "house" or bag 2 in. long. As a worm, it is a destructive shade-tree and shrub pest in the

BAGWORM ON A TWIG

Pick off these small pouches, made of silk and bits of leaves and twigs, and destroy them, preferably by burning.

E. and S. E. States, with special fondness for arborvitae, red cedar, willow and maple. It lives in, and carries around as it feeds, a spindle-shaped bag made of bits of leaves and twigs and lined with silk. When the worm is full grown it attaches its house to a twig and pupates inside. In three weeks the males emerge and mate (inside their bags) with the females, which do not emerge until egg laying is completed. Control consists of hand picking and burning the conspicuous bags and spraying infested plants with arsenate of lead during the feeding period of the larvae.

BAHIA (ba-hee'ah). A dozen species of perennial herbs or shrubby plants of the Composite Family native to S. America and Calif. They have gray, woolly, much-divided leaves and yellow flowers. Though little known in gardens they can be grown without difficulty in the open sunny border in a light well-drained soil in mild regions. Increase by seed or division of old plants in early spring. *B. lanata* of Calif. is the most common form.

BAKED-APPLE-BERRY. One of the common names for *Rubus chamaemorus,* also known as Cloudberry; used in rock-gardens. See RUBUS.

BAKING. A clay or silt soil is said to be baked when it becomes thoroughly dried out, as during a period of drought or under a strong sun. Under such conditions (especially if "puddled" before-hand by being worked while wet) it becomes as hard as raw bricks, and often as it shrinks deep cracks develop through which evaporation of water from below is hastened. Only a generous amount of humus, well worked in over an extended period, can bring such a soil back into friable condition.

Baking by electricity (or in the case of small quantities of soil, in the oven) is a method often used for the sterilization of soil previous to seed sowing or planting. This destroys weed seeds and disease-causing organisms such as bacteria and fungous spores, but it has the disadvantage of also destroying certain beneficial soil organisms as well. To effectively sterilize a soil it should be heated to a temperature of from 180 to 200 deg. F. for one to two hours. See also DISINFECTION.

BALD or DECIDUOUS CYPRESS. Common names for *Taxodium distichum,* a member of the Pine Family, but which, though it resembles an evergreen, sheds its leaves in the fall. See TAXODIUM.

BALL. The rounded mass of roots of a plant, shrub or tree removed from a pot or tub or dug from a bed or nursery row, together with the soil enclosed by or adhering to it. Successful transplanting is promoted by keeping this ball intact so that the fine feeding-roots will be injured as little as possible and subjected to a minimum of light and drying wind. To this end com-

YEW TREE BALLED AND BURLAPPED
Firmly wrapped and strongly tied, with a good ball of earth around the roots, a plant will travel safely. The burlap needs only to be loosened when the tree is set in the ground

mercial plantsmen and nurserymen wrap the balls of plants (if small) in heavy tough paper or (if more than a few inches in diameter) in squares of coarse burlap which is gathered tightly together and fastened with cord, wire, or nails.

Shrubs and trees so prepared for delivery to a customer or to his home, or for shipment, are said to be "balled and burlapped" and in many catalogs are designated by the term "B & B." A plant with its mass of roots so protected is much better fitted to go right on growing than is a specimen dug from the wild, inevitably with considerable injury to its root system.

When planted, balled and burlapped plants can be placed in the prepared hole (see PLANTING) with the burlap intact; the wrapping can then be undone and all the loose part cut away or merely folded back, if the ball is very heavy, as it will in time decay so the roots can spread.

To form a good root ball a soil should be somewhat heavy; a loose sandy soil will fall from the roots unless firmly wrapped. However, a soil too "sticky," because of excess clay and insufficient humus, is likely to pack and bake into a hard mass when balled and burlapped.

The Horticultural Standards (which see) adopted by the American Association of Nurserymen set the following minimum depths for balls of different sizes as necessary to insure lifting enough of the feeding root system to enable the plant to recover from the shock of transplanting: Diameter of ball 20 in. or less—depth must be 75 per cent of it; diameter 20 to 30 in.—depth $66\frac{2}{3}$ per cent; diameter 31 to 48 in.—depth 60 per cent.

To estimate the weight of such a ball of average soil, the following formula can be used: Square the diameter; multiply by the depth (both in inches); subtract one-third; multiply the remainder by .075 and the result will be the weight of the ball in pounds. For example, taking a ball 12 in. across and 12 in. deep,

```
12 x 12 x 12 = 1728
1728 x ⅓ = 576
1728 − 576 = 1152 cu. in.
1152 x .075 = 86.4 lbs.,
the weight of the ball.
```

BALL FERN. Common name for the genus Davallia, which see.

BALLOON-FLOWER (*Platycodon grandiflorum*). A useful hardy herbaceous perennial so named on account of the shape of its buds, which resemble little balloons. The flowers, borne at the end of slender, leafy stems, are bell-shaped or star-shaped, large and rich blue in the species and white in the var. *album*. The plants, growing from 1 to 2 ft. tall, are especially adapted for use in rockeries or garden borders. There are also dwarf forms and some with semi-double flowers. Many gardeners consider this the most beautiful hardy plant in cultivation. It thrives best in deep, well-drained, sandy loam soil and is easily grown from seed sown in early spring or propagated by division at that time.

BALLOON-VINE. Common name for *Cardiospermum halicacabum,* an attractive vine of tropical America but frequently grown in gardens as an annual climber on account of its interesting inflated fruits. See CARDIOSPERMUM.

BALM, LEMON BALM. Common names for *Melissa officinalis,* an aromatic, sweet herb of the Mint Family grown in the herb garden for seasoning, and also used in liqueurs and for medicine. It grows to 2 ft. tall and has small 2-lipped flowers in late summer, and leaves of a decided lemon odor and flavor. Of Old-World origin it is widely naturalized in America. Var. *variegata* has variegated leaves and is sometimes used in the border. It is easily increased by division or by seeds sown in the hotbed or coldframe.

Bee Balm is *Monarda didyma.* Canary Balm is *Cedronella triphylla.* Horse-balm is *Collinsonia canadensis.* Molucca Balm is *Molucella laevis.*

BALM OF GILEAD. Common name sometimes given to *Populus balsamifera,* the Balsam Poplar, but correctly applied to *P. candicans,* a strong-growing but not long-lived species of poplar with large dark-green leaves downy beneath, and large sticky aromatic buds in spring. See POPLAR.

BALSAM-APPLE. Common name for *Momordica balsamina,* an annual herbaceous climber, bearing egg-shaped, orange-colored fruits following white or yellow flowers. Sometimes incorrectly applied to Echinocystis, the Wild-cucumber.

BALSAM, GARDEN. Common name for *Impatiens balsamina,* an annual, ornamental herb native to the tropics and subtropics. Requiring a fertile but light, sandy soil, it grows to $2\frac{1}{2}$ ft. and, combined with Alyssum or Verbena, is best used as a border subject. Its double blossoms, from white to red, purple or yellow, are borne close to the stems and overtopped by leafy shoots. It is ornamental and an old flower-garden favorite. As it is decidedly tender it should be started in the garden from seed after all danger of frost is over. For best development the plants should be spaced about 2 ft. apart and the stout central stem should be kept clear of side branches so that it will produce a profusion of flowers in midsummer. Grown alone, Balsam is suitable for low hedges because of its upright habit. It is a fast grower and will respond to extra attention such as addition of fertilizer to the soil, the best enrichment being liquid manure. Full exposure to the sun and an adequate supply of water are also essential to best results. Many gardeners have produced shorter plants with flowers more double than normal by transplanting two or three times during the summer. When grown in the greenhouse balsams can be increased by cuttings.

See also IMPATIENS.

BALSAMORRHIZA (bahl-sam-oh-ryz'-ah). A genus of American plants called Balsam-roots because of their large, resinous tubers which exude a thick, pitchy juice when broken and which were formerly used by the Indians for food. They belong to the Composite Family and have sunflower-like blossoms. *B. hookeri* has long, deeply cut white-woolly leaves and yellow flowers 4 to 12 in. high. It grows on the prairies of W. U. S. and is useful to plant in dry situations in the wild garden.

BALSAM-PEAR. Common name for *Momordica charantia,* an annual herbaceous climber, bearing oblong, orange-yellow fruits.

BAMBOO. Common name for several genera making up a tribe (Bambusae) of the Grass Family. They comprise giant ornamental grasses, sometimes woody and tree-like. The most important genera, from the American gardener's point of view, are Arundinaria, Bambusa, Dendrocalamus, Phyllostachys and Sasa. Chusquea is a subtropical American genus of shrubby or vine-like forms. These are distinguished from one another by botanical rather than horticultural characters or uses. In general, plants of the genus Arundinaria have cylindrical stems; those of Bambusa have stems growing in a zigzag manner; those of the Dendrocalamus are exceptionally large; Phyllostachys contains plants with canes flattened on one side; and Sasa includes dwarf (or at least not tall) shrubs, with cylindrical stems similar to those of Arundinaria. (See illustration, Plate 37.)

Bamboos are of great importance in the tropics (especially in Asia) where they are used for many purposes as food products, building materials, etc. Some species lend grace and beauty to gardens in mild climates and a few are hardy as far N. as Philadelphia. In the S. and in the Pacific States they are much planted, their delicate stems and graceful, feathery foliage adding much to the garden picture, especially when grown against a background composed of evergreens.

Bamboos thrive in partial shade and need a rich deep loam and an abundance of moisture, preferably a supply of pure underground water; some species grow in marshes. It takes at least three years to establish a good-sized clump, and until the plants are growing strongly and have sent their roots into the earth firmly, they are greatly benefited by a constantly renewed mulch of well-rotted manure. They also need protection from harsh cold winter winds, except the few species that will stand close to zero weather.

The larger sorts in time form excellent shelter belts, while some of the smaller, slower-growing kinds make beautiful specimens in conservatories; or they may be used outdoors as potted plants in tubs and wintered on the sun porch or cool greenhouse. It is difficult to secure seed as the plants are unreliable and uneven seed-bearers, therefore stock should be increased by dividing the clumps before the year's growth starts, potting up the small pieces and placing them in the greenhouse to form roots. They may be propagated also by layering young shoots. Spring is the best time for planting out, pruning, and propagating by layering or division. In pruning off old canes, take care not to leave stubs

A DWARF HARDY BAMBOO
While some bamboos grow to tree size in the tropics, a few small ones may be used for their foliage effect in northern borders.

that will decay and threaten the life of the plant.

BAMBOO FERN (*Gymnogramma japonica*). A robust and ornamental fern for the cool greenhouse or conservatory with dark, once-pinnate fronds of stiff erect habit. Use half peat and half loam, and give plenty of water.

BAMBUSA (bam-beu'-sah). Woody grasses mostly of tropical and subtropical regions, numbering more than 200 species, one of the several genera known as Bamboo. Their stems are straight, tall, resilient

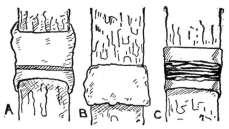

TWO WAYS OF BANDING TREES
A strip of cotton batting or burlap tied in place (A), then folded down (at B) for catching insects. (C) Tar-paper smeared with tanglefoot as a trap for crawling pests.

and of great strength. They grow rapidly making very dense thickets, the different species thriving in all kinds of soils from wet to dry, and in localities from sea level to mountain slopes.

Among the important species are: *B. arundinacea,* a tree-like form with yellow culm (or "trunk"), dying after flowering; *B. vulgaris* (Feathery Bamboo), with yellow-striped culm and smooth broad leaves; and *B. nana,* 10 ft. or less high, the leaves normally bluish but also appearing with yellow, rose and silvery markings. Many new varieties suitable for the S. States and Calif. have been introduced in recent years by the Department of Agriculture. See also BAMBOO.

BANANA. A large, perennial, tropical herb (see MUSA) whose stem and leaf sheaths become tree-like with a crown of long, broad leaves. From this crown hang the fruits, in a bunch made of successive ranks or "hands," the whole cluster often weighing more than 50 pounds. After bearing, the stem and leaves weaken or die; however, a sucker develops from the base and in its turn bears and ripens fruit about a year later. In commercial plantations each plant may thus produce fruit for four or more years.

As edible bananas produce no seed, suckers are used for propagation. Plants of the Chinese or Dwarf Banana (*M. cavendishi*) are set 10 ft. apart; those of standard varieties 15 to 20 ft. The plants thrive best in deep, rich, well-drained soils sheltered from hot sun and strong winds which break the leaves.

Dwarf Bananas are somewhat grown in the Gulf States, also in S. California, but the fruit and even the stems are sometimes destroyed by frost. However, unless the underground parts are frozen, new shoots usually develop.

The Abyssinian Banana (*M. ensete*), which bears inedible fruit but is one of the most ornamental species, is often grown from seed which, being very hard, should have holes filed in them or be soaked for 48 hours in warm water before being planted in a propagating bench with bottom heat. The young plants should be potted up in good soil and kept at a night temperature of 65 deg. F. While small they may be used outdoors during the frost-free months for tropical effects; but in time they become too large to move in and out conveniently for any but the largest conservatories.

BANANA FAMILY. Common name of the Musaceae, a family of stout tropical herbs, including *Musa paradisiaca* var. *sapientum,* the source of the popular fruit.

BANANA-SHRUB. Common name for *Michelia fuscata,* on account of the banana-like fragrance of the flowers.

BANDING, TREE. Used to trap and destroy insects which infest trees by crawling up the trunk. Bands are of no value against flying insects and, as they may, if neglected, harbor certain pests, they should not be used indiscriminately. The simplest band, for catching caterpillars and wingless moths, is made by tying a strip of burlap or cotton batting, 6 to 8 in. wide, tightly around the trunk; place the string about the center and fold the upper half down to form a flange. Wire screening, cut to fit the tree at the top but allowed to flare at the bottom, is good. Bands of tar building-paper painted with sticky material made for the purpose may be tied around the tree over a layer of cotton which will fill in the bark crevices, but sticky material applied directly to the tree may be injurious. A new and promising material called Balsam Wool combines a tough, brown bark-like outer layer over a soft, fibrous base and should prove excellent for banding trees where appearance is important. Such a paper band applied in early spring is effective against the spring canker worm, and in the fall against the fall type; it is also useful in fighting severe codling-moth infestations. All bands should be examined frequently and the trapped insects removed and destroyed to keep later arrivals from ascending over the bridge formed by the accumulated earlier victims.

BANEBERRY. A common name for Actaea (which see) a native genus of useful herbaceous perennials also known as Cohosh.

BANKSIA (bank′-si-ah). A genus of Australian shrubs belonging to the Protea Family, named in honor of Sir Joseph Banks, one of the most distinguished patrons of natural history. A few species have been cultivated but seldom outside of botanic gardens. The plants are noted chiefly for their handsome foliage, which is mostly long and narrow, dark green above and silvery white or brownish beneath. But they are not easy to propagate and grow.

BANKSIA ROSE. A climbing evergreen Chinese rose species (*Rosa banksiae*), tender but much grown in Calif. and other warm sections for its attractive foliage and small white or yellowish blossoms. See ROSE.

BANYAN (ban′-yan). A species of fig (*Ficus benghalensis*) growing in the tropics, noted for the great age and size which trees attain. Roots which descend from the branches develop into supplementary trunks and extend the tree until it covers a large area, giving it a striking characteristic form. See FICUS.

BAPTISIA (bap-tiz′-i-ah). Sturdy, perennial leguminous herbs called False- or Wild-indigo. Natives of the U. S. and growing wild from Penn. to Texas, they often reach a height of 6 ft. With deep-green cut foliage and indigo-blue, white, or yellow flowers resembling lupines in form and produced in long terminal racemes, these plants are imposing members of the border or wild garden. The flowers are good for cutting and the period of bloom is from late spring to midsummer. The blossoms are followed by short, plump pods that become black. Easily grown from seed in any good garden soil, but preferring partial shade, plants should be started in the open ground.

B. australis, the tallest species, bears profuse blooms and has leaves 2½ in. long.

bracteata. To 2 ft.; leaves 4 in. long; flowers cream-colored in May and June.

leucantha. To 4 ft.; leaves 2 in. long; white flowers in June-July.

leucophaea. To 2½ ft.; leaves 4 in. long; white or cream flowers in May-June.

perfoliata. To 3 ft.; leaves 2 in. long; yellow flowers in May-June.

tinctoria. To 4 ft.; leaves only 1 in. long; flowers bright yellow in June-July.

BARBADOS - CHERRY (bahr-bay′-dohz). Common name for *Malpighia glabra,* a small tree of tropical America producing edible fruits.

BARBADOS - GOOSEBERRY. Common name for *Pereskia aculeata,* a tropical American shrubby or vine-like cactus sometimes called Lemon-vine.

BARBADOS-LILY. Common name for *Hippeastrum puniceum* (formerly *H. equestre*) a member of the Amaryllis Family native in Mexico, Brazil and Chile.

BARBADOS PRIDE, or BARBADOS FLOWER-FENCE. Common names for *Poinciana pulcherrima,* a prickly shrub of the tropics with shining leaves and striking orange flowers.

BARBAREA (bahr-ba′-ree-ah). A genus of European biennial and perennial herbs of the Mustard Family commonly known as Winter- or Upland-cress. A few of the species are grown for ornament in the border, others are somewhat grown as pot-herbs or salads, and still others are roadside weeds. The cultivated species are easily grown in any rich garden soil and increased by seed. *B. rupicola* grows to 1 ft., forming mats or sods covered with rather large yellow flowers. *B. vulgaris,* the Common Winter-cress, to 2 ft., the species most commonly cultivated for salad, has escaped and become a troublesome field and roadside weed in America. Its var. *variegata* with leaves variegated with yellow is often grown in the border for its foliage. See also CRESS.

BARBE DE CAPUCIN (bahrb d′ kapeu-san′). Common name for *Cichorium intybus,* or Chicory (which see), adapted from the name of the French salad made from the blanched leaves of the plant.

BARBERRY. Common name for the genus Berberis. Evergreen or deciduous spiny shrubs with yellow inner bark and wood. About 175 species, mostly in Asia and S. America, but a few in N. America,

Europe and N. Africa. They are among the most useful and ornamental shrubs, with a good habit of growth. The flowers are not large, but numerous enough in many cases to be attractive in spring or early summer. Some of the deciduous kinds rank among the best berried shrubs, and the leaves of several are brilliantly colored before falling. The evergreen species are not entirely hardy North, although a few manage to survive the severe winters in more or less satisfactory condition if given a sheltered position.

Barberries are of easy cultivation and adapted to various soils and situations. Propagation is by seeds, cuttings, suckers, and layers. Grafting may be resorted to with rare kinds, but keep a watchful eye on sucker growth. The raising of barberries from seed has interesting possibilities. Some beautiful forms have originated in this way and been given distinctive names; they can be reproduced true only by vegetative means.

ENEMIES. Some relation has long been suspected between the common barberry and the black stem rust of wheat. Barberry eradication legislation was passed in France in 1660 and in Connecticut, Rhode Island and Massachusetts in the middle of the eighteenth century, but it was not until 1865 that it was definitely proved that the rust on barberry and on wheat were stages in the life cycle of the one fungus. Destruction of the common barberry in important wheat sections remains the chief means of control of the rust; its effectiveness is seen in the reduction of losses from 57 million bushels in 1916 to about nine million in 1930.

As Japanese Barberry (*B. thunbergi*) is *not* attacked by rust it may safely be used for ornamental plantings. It is subject to a Verticillium wilt and a bacterial leaf spot. Destroy wilted plants and diseased leaves.

PRINCIPAL SPECIES

Evergreen, mostly from China, and all with purple or blue-black berries:

B. buxifolia. A Chilean species of upright habit, to 10 ft. Flowers solitary or in twos. Var. *nana* is a useful dwarf and compact form. Var. *pygmaea* is a low tufted form with unarmed branches. Amongst the hardiest.

darwinii. Another Chilean species, one of the most beautiful. Can withstand only a few degrees of frost. Has lustrous dark-green leaves and clusters of golden flowers.

gagnepaini. A bushy grower to 6 ft. with yellowish stems armed with slender spines, and narrow spiny leaves with rolled edges. Barely hardy North.

julianae. A tall erect-grower with light colored branches and spines. The dark-green spiny leaves are up to 3 in. long. One of the hardiest.

sargentiana. A spreading bush to 6 ft. with branches reddish when young. One of the hardiest.

stenophylla. A garden hybrid between *B. darwinii* and *B. empetrifolia*. A grace-

VARIATION IN THE JAPANESE BARBERRY
Right, the ordinary Berberis thunbergi in its spreading, irregular form. Left, a recently developed, strongly erect variety especially good for hedges.

ful shrub with slender arching branches but not reliably hardy.

triacanthophora. A very graceful species with slender spreading branches and narrow, bright-green leaves, whitish beneath.

verruculosa. Of low dense habit with glossy green leaves, whitish beneath. In fall they assume a lovely bronzy tone. The golden flowers are solitary or in twos.

Deciduous species, from W. China unless otherwise noted:

B. *aggregata.* Of dense bushy habit, 5 to 6 ft. Flowers open late, in close panicles toward the end of the branches. Fruit coral-red. Var. *pratti* is more profuse in flowers and fruit.

amurensis. A tall upright grower from Japan and Korea, with flowers in drooping racemes to 4 in. long and bright-red berries. Var. *japonica* (B. *regeliana*) has larger leaves, shorter racemes and orange-red fruit.

aristata. From the Himalayas but hardy. Reputed the strongest grower, to 12 ft. or more. Has arching branches and red to purplish fruits.

canadensis (Allegheny Barberry). A native species of slender, upright growth. Often confused with B. *vulgaris,* but dwarfer. Leaves turn scarlet in fall, and the scarlet berries persist a long time.

diaphana. A low, rounded dense bush. The leaves are very late in starting and turn crimson in fall.

dictyophylla. Of graceful habit and outstanding with its young shoots and undersides of leaves covered with a white bloom. The leaves assume a lovely old-rose tint in fall.

koreana. A Korean species of vigorous upright growth, with large leaves, brilliantly fall-colored. The clusters of bright-red berries persist long.

polyantha. A large rounded shrub, with yellow flower panicles to 6 in. long, and grape-like clusters of salmon-red berries. Not reliably hardy North.

sieboldi. A rather dwarf and slow-growing Japanese species. The young leaves are purplish, turning wine-red in the fall. The red berries retain their color and form until spring.

thunbergi (Japanese Barberry). A popular hedge plant and useful in general planting. Leaves open early in spring and color brilliantly in fall. The red berries hang until spring. Var. *atropurpurea,* with lus-

trous bronzy-red leaves, is one of the best shrubs with colored foliage. Var. *minor* (Box Barberry) of low, dense form makes a useful edging plant. Var. *erecta* is a recent introduction that gives promise of being much better for hedges than the type.

vernae. A shrub of spreading habit with slender branches, and dense racemes of small flowers, followed by small round red berries.

vulgaris (Common Barberry). A European species that is naturalized in America. One of the most ornamental, with drooping clusters of coral-red berries, but its cultivation in wheat-growing regions is prohibited by Federal quarantine regulations because it is a host to wheat rust. Var. *atropurpurea* is one of the best purple-leaved shrubs.

wilsonae. A half-evergreen of low bushy habit with clusters of salmon-red berries. Well suited for the rock garden but not always hardy North.

mentoriensis is a new hybrid, the product of crossing B. *julianae* and B. *thunbergi.* It is said to be evergreen and very hardy.

Holly-leaved Barberry is *Mahonia aquifolium.* See MAHONIA.

BARBERRY FAMILY. Common name of the Berberidaceae (which see), a family of mostly spiny, hardy herbs and shrubs much used for ornamental hedges.

BARBERRY-FIG. Common name for *Opuntia vulgaris,* one of the cacti of the hardy "prickly-pear" group.

BARBERTON DAISY. A common name for *Gerbera jamesoni,* also known as Transvaal Daisy, an African daisylike plant grown (principally under glass) for its flowers in many pastel colors. See GERBERA. (See also illustration, Plate 19.)

BARIUM FLUOSILICATE. A chemical compound in powder form used chiefly as a dust against the Mexican bean beetle. In using mix 1 lb. with 5 lb. hydrated lime. See also FLUORINE COMPOUNDS.

BARK BEETLES. A number of species of small black or brown beetles attack the bark of trees unthrifty because of lack of moisture, insufficient food, disease and other causes. They feed in the cambium making many fine burrows in various interesting and significant designs that eventually cut off the sap flow and kill the tree. The females lay eggs along the sides of burrows in the inner bark through which the grubs tunnel for 2 to 3 in. When full grown they change to beetles, emerge through small holes which they cut in the bark and fly to other trees.

The peach-tree bark beetle attacks nearly all the stone fruit. The hickory bark beetle causes serious damage (see HICKORY). The smaller European elm bark beetle is particularly important because it carries the fungus that causes the Dutch elm disease (which see). Bark beetles attacking conifers carry blue-staining fungi.

Control is limited to keeping trees in a vigorous growing condition and pruning out each winter or early spring all dead, dying or injured wood.

BARK BOUND. An uncommon condition caused when the wood of a tree expands faster than the bark, causing the latter to split. An artificial slit may be made part way the length of the trunk, to allow the bark to expand and the inner bark to grow over the wound. This should be painted with melted grafting wax or other wound dressing.

BARLERIA (bahr-lee'-ri-ah). A large genus of tropical herbs or shrubs, belonging to the Acanthus Family. A few have been grown in warm greenhouse collections for their ornamental flowers, and may be grown outdoors in warm climates. They do well in pots filled with equal parts loam and peat, with some old manure added. Old plants may be cut back after flowering and grown on again. Cuttings rooted in spring make neat flowering plants in 5- or 6-in. pots early the following year. The principal species are *B. flava,* with yellow flowers; *B. cristata,* with dense spikes of purplish-blue, and *B. gibsoni,* pale purple.

BARREN- or FALSE-STRAW-BERRY. Common name for *Waldsteinia fragarioides,* a species of creeping, strawberry-like plants of the Rose Family found in woods from N. B. to Ga. and Minn. The flowers, in sprays, are yellow but there is no edible fruit. They are attractive little trailers for the rock garden, or for rocky ledges, banks or dry walls, forming a leafy mat. To increase the plants, divide the roots in March and plant out in the permanent position in full sunlight.

BARRIER. In addition to natural barriers such as streams, lakes, mountains, etc., which retard the spread of plant enemies, man-made barriers are sometimes useful. For example, a deep-plowed furrow around a field will maroon army worms, and a log dragged back and forth in it will destroy millions. Chinch bugs will not pass over an inch-wide line of crude creosote spread on the earth. Similarly soil containing 2 to 4 per cent sulphur, crude carbolic acid, or waste motor oil, rows of sorghum or open trenches may prevent spread of the cotton root rot fungus. A combined natural and man-made barrier zone along the eastern border of New York State has for some years successfully prevented the spread of the gypsy moth (which see) westward out of New England.

BARTONIA (bahr-toh'-ni-ah) *aurea.* Former name, still used in catalogs, for a popular annual now correctly called *Mentzelia lindleyi.*

BASAL ROT. A serious fungous disease of the narcissus, crocus, hyacinth and freesia (especially the first named), which rots the basal plate and sometimes the whole bulb, dwarfs the growth of the plant and cripples the flower, if any. For control measures see Bulb Enemies under BULB.

BASIC SLAG. (Also known as Thomas phosphate powder, basic-iron slag, and phosphate slag.) A by-product obtained in the manufacture of steel from pig-iron containing about 16 to 20 per cent of phosphoric acid as well as compounds containing calcium, magnesium, iron, manganese and silicon. Used as a fertilizer, basic slag has given good results on acid soils, especially those of swampy and wet nature. Because it contains from 40 to 50 per cent calcium and magnesium compounds (largely in the form of oxides), it has the same effect as an equal amount of quicklime in neutralizing soil acidity or in making a neutral soil alkaline or in affecting the physical condition of a soil.

See also FERTILIZER.

BASIL (baz'-il). The common name for *Ocimum basilicum,* a popular sweet herb of the Mint Family esteemed for flavoring and formerly used for medicinal purposes. An annual of the tropics, it is tender and should not be attempted outdoors until the weather is warm. It grows easily from seed which may be sown in the garden or started indoors. Plants should be transplanted or thinned to stand 6 to 10 in. apart; they prefer a quick light soil in a warm location. The small flowers are white or purple, but the plant is grown for its sometimes purple-tinged leaves, which are cut during the growing season and dried in bundles. If the soil is rich, a plant cut back will develop successive crops of foliage until fall. At that time roots of strong plants can be lifted and potted up to supply a winter crop.

See HERBS; OCIMUM.

BASKET-FLOWER. Common name for *Centaurea americana* (see illustration, Plate 9); also for *Hymenocallis calathina,* a species of Spider-lily, which see.

BASKET GRASS. The common name for *Oplismenus compositus,* a member of the true Grass Family (Gramineae). Most of the perennial and annual species of this tropical and subtropical genus are of little interest horticulturally, but this one is used as an ornamental edging in the greenhouse or in hanging baskets, and is easily increased by seed or division. Its trailing stems are sometimes 3 ft. long. Var. *vittatus* has leaves striped pink and white.

BASKET-OF-GOLD. Common name for *Alyssum saxatile,* the yellow, perennial species of this favorite, low-growing border plant. See ALYSSUM.

BASKET-PLANTS. Plants especially grown (or suitable) for use in hanging baskets. They may range from ornamental, more or less upright foliage or flowering subjects, to slender trailing or drooping plants especially valuable for planting the edges of such containers. For treatment and suggestive lists, see HANGING BASKETS.

BASSWOOD. A common name for the genus Tilia, consisting of many uncommonly handsome trees of the N. Temperate zone, known also as Linden (which see); in England referred to as Lime-tree. Also the common name of the family Tiliaceae (which see) to which this genus belongs.

BAUHINIA (bau-hin'-i-ah). Mountain-ebony. Tropical trees, shrubs or vines, belonging to the Pea Family. Rarely seen in warm greenhouses; grown outdoors in the warmer parts of the country where they make a good showing with their colorful racemes of white, purple, or yellow flowers. The two most common and hardiest species are *B. purpurea* and *B. variegata,* natives of India but able to withstand a few degrees of frost. *B. purpurea* is a small, quick-growing tree, bearing an abundance of large purplish flowers over a long season. *B. variegata* is similar in habit but with varied colored flowers in rose, red, and yellow. In India the bark is used in tanning and dyeing, and the leaves and flower buds as a vegetable.

BAYBERRY. Common name for *Myrica caroliniensis,* a handsome native shrub with dark-green leaves which emit a resinous fragrance when crushed, and clusters of gray berries whose waxy covering is used in New England in making fragrant candles.

BAY-TREE, SWEET BAY. Common names for the genus Laurus (Laurel), evergreen shrubs or trees with long, oval, glossy green leaves. The name Sweetbay is also given to *Magnolia glauca,* a shrubby tree native from Mass. to Fla. and Texas. See LAURUS; MAGNOLIA.

BEACH-ASTER. One of the common names for *Erigeron glaucus,* a perennial species of Fleabane, also known as Seaside Daisy. Native along the Pacific Coast. See ERIGERON.

BEACH GRASS. Common name for Ammophila, a genus of tall perennial grasses valuable for sand-binding. They have been extensively used for that purpose in Europe, on Cape Cod, in Mass. and in Golden Gate Park, Calif. Either start seed in flats of mixed sand and leafmold and set out the small plants directly in the sand, or sow seed where the grass is to grow. In both cases throw evergreen boughs or straw over the area planted in order to hold the sand in place and provide a little protecting shade. When the seedlings have taken hold, remove the protection and reinforce them with plantings of low-growing grasses.

A. arenaria (Marram Grass, Sea Sand-reed, or Psamma) grows to 3 ft. and has panicled flowers to 1 ft., and very long, hard, branching rootstocks that make it an excellent sand-binder. *A. breviligulata* (American Beach Grass) grows abundantly and to nearly 2 ft. on the shores of the Atlantic and also near the Great Lakes. It is another fine sand-binder.

BEACH-HEATHER. Common name for a small group of heath-like shrubs, growing near the seacoast of eastern N. America. See HUDSONIA.

BEACH PLUM. The common name for *Prunus maritima,* a native shrub useful for seaside plantings. The dark-purple fruit is very ornamental, and makes an excellent preserve.

BEAD FERN. A name for various species of Gleichenia, tropical ferns of branching habit, suitable only for greenhouse conditions where space and good ventilation are assured.

BEAD-PLANT. Common name for *Nertera depressa,* a slender creeping perennial, native of the S. hemisphere but sometimes grown in greenhouses in the N., where it merits attention as a window plant. In regions where the climate is not severe, it makes a good ground-cover plant for shady places, showing to advantage in the rock garden. It requires a sandy soil with leafmold. The flowers are inconspicuous, but the orange-colored berries make it a handsome little plant when in fruit. Propagated by seeds or division.

BEAD-TREE. Common name for two genera—Adenanthera and Melia (which see), the former grown under glass (or outdoors in the S.) for its ornamental seeds, the latter a shade tree in warm sections.

BEAM-TREE. A name applied to the Mountain-ash (which see), especially the species *Sorbus aria,* also known as White Beam-tree.

BEAN. The name of many herbs of the Legume or Pea Family and their edible pods and seeds, but also loosely applied to the pods or seeds of various trees and shrubs (as tamarind-coffee). In America, when used without qualification the term refers to horticultural varieties of *Phaseolus vulgaris.*

KIDNEY OR COMMON BEANS

To this most important species belong all the common garden, snap, string, and stringless beans whose immature pods are boiled and served as a vegetable and whose dried seeds (in the case of the field bean, of which the smallest are called navy, Boston pea, and California tree beans) are also baked. The fully-formed but unripe seeds of the larger seeded varieties are often "shelled," and cooked like garden peas. To this same group belong the French haricots, the Spanish frijoles and the English kidney beans, so called because of their shape. In America the term "kidney bean" is limited to those varieties whose large, purplish-brown seeds are used ripe, like navy beans.

As these names suggest, the species has been greatly modified by man, so much, in fact, that its original wild form is not known, though it is believed to be native to the American tropics. The plants range in habit of growth from low and bushy forms to tall and climbing "pole" beans, with many gradations between. They also vary in foliage and seed characters, the latter especially as to size, color and markings—large and small, mottled, "eyed," and self colors in white, black, brown, red and yellow. About 200 "types" have been distinguished and at least 500 varieties introduced. See PHASEOLUS.

Beans of this group are popularly classified as "field" and "garden" varieties. Each of these classes is subdivided into "bush," and "pole" or "climbing." The kidney varieties include also "green" and "butter" (or "wax") podded sorts. Of all these the bush varieties are the most important.

Other terms are used to distinguish special uses. "Snap" or "string" is applied to those varieties whose freshly gathered, immature pods, while thick and meaty, will break cleanly across when bent without leaving a "string" along the back. "Shell" applies to those large-seeded varieties whose immature, but fully-formed, seeds are removed from the pods to be cooked like green peas. Beans allowed to mature fully are called "dry." There are also the double terms, "green shell" and "dry shell," which are often used in descriptive literature, as seed catalogs. Many varieties, particularly of the white-seeded kinds of garden beans are highly valued in all three stages—snap, shell and dry. Limas (discussed below) are never used as snap beans because they are more highly valued for their shelled seeds and because the pods, when large enough to be worth gathering, are too fibrous and tough.

In common with other legumes, beans are able to obtain much of their nitrogen from the air. For this reason they do not deplete the soil but leave it in better condition for a succeeding crop than do non-leguminous crops. Hence they are rated as soil-improving, not soil-impoverishing, crops. When only the pods and their contents are gathered young, they consist mainly of water and cell-tissue, and the harvest takes only trifling amounts of the mineral plant-food elements from the soil—especially if the vines are plowed under. However, gathering the beans while immature stimulates the plants of many kinds to continue producing pods over a much longer season than if the first-formed pods are allowed to mature.

LIMA OR SUGAR BEANS. Ranking second in America is the lima or sugar bean (*P. lunatus* var. *macrocarpus*), of which there are both climbing and dwarf forms whose seeds are white, either small or large, flat or plump. The tall, climbing "pole" limas are slow growing and the beans ripen late; hence they are often killed by early fall frosts before their pods mature. The earlier dwarf varieties are therefore more reliable.

The lima bean is thus an improved variety of the sieva or civet bean (*P. lunatus*), whose slender, bushy or low-climbing plants bear smaller pods containing two or three small beans which when ripe are either white, brown or mottled. These varieties, popular in warm countries, mature even earlier than the dwarf limas and much earlier than the pole varieties.

Garden Bean Growing

The two classes of garden beans cannot stand frost, but their varieties display wide differences in ability to resist cold and heat. In cold, wet soil the seed of many sorts is almost sure to decay; that of others will germinate and grow. Also low temperatures over several days, even though well above freezing, will chill and stunt the plants of some varieties more than of others. The flowers of many kinds are often blasted by hot, dry weather, particularly in arid southwestern sections.

Excessive moisture in soil or air, and poor air circulation (particularly where the soil is rich), tend to cause lush growth and to favor diseases of foliage and pods. Hence the importance of selecting varieties and strains reputed to be resistant to these drawbacks, and of testing various kinds and strains so as to determine which are most satisfactory for any particular locality or expected set of conditions. For the same reasons it is rarely advisable to sow beans before the weather becomes settled and the ground warm in spring; this means not more than a week earlier than the usual local date for the latest spring frost. (See illustration, Plate 54.)

Soils. When a choice of soil is possible, select strong loams, especially those underlaid by limestone; second best are sandy or gravelly loams. Where no choice is possible, the garden soil, no matter what its character, can usually be improved sufficiently to meet the plants' needs. The soil *must* be well drained, fairly well supplied with humus and moderately rich. If too rich in nitrogenous plant food the plants are likely to make excessive leaf and stem development and produce few or no beans. So far as possible rotate beans with other garden vegetables so as to help maintain soil fertility.

See ROTATION OF CROPS.

VARIATION IN FORM OF BEAN PLANT AND PRODUCT

Pole and bush beans (left) are both valuable home-garden types. These close-ups show (above) limas and ordinary string or wax beans; (below) a pod of the historic Broad bean (Vicia faba), and (right) the curious and accurately named Yard-long-bean (Vigna sesquipedalis).

MANURES AND FERTILIZERS. Though beans gather much of their nitrogen from the air, they are benefited, particularly from the time buds form, by a top-dressing of nitrate of soda (1 or 2 oz. to 25 ft. of row). Apply this to bush varieties after the plants are growing well and give pole varieties, especially limas, two or three such dressings at intervals of three or four weeks. Beans need potash and phosphorus more than nitrogen, so these elements should be supplied in preparing the soil. Use 1 to 2 lbs. each of muriate of potash and superphosphate per 200 sq. ft. of ground.

Where well-decayed stable or cow manure is available it may be plowed or dug in at the rate of a ton (or two-horse load) to 2,000 sq. ft. Fresh manure is best applied and turned under late the previous autumn. Pulverized sheep manure (1 lb. to 10 sq. ft.) is best used as a top dressing after the ground has been dug; or it may be applied beside the plants. Use proprietary (mixed) fertilizers carefully and never more than the manufacturer's directions advise.

Bush-bean plants vary considerably in size so the plant and row spacing should vary in proportion. In drills the seeds should be sown at least 2 in. apart, and preferably 4 or 6 in.; hills should be not less than 8 in. apart and each should support only two or three plants. The hill method facilitates hand hoeing and is believed to produce larger and finer beans than can be grown in drills, which however, for hoe and wheelhoe culture may be as close as 15 in. for the smaller-growing varieties and 18 in. for the large kinds. For horse or garden tractor-tillage 30 in. is about the minimum.

The depth to plant seed varies with the season and the character of the soil. Plant deeper in light loams, shallower in heavy ones. In general, early in the season, while the soil is moist, 2 in. or less is desirable; later, in dry soil, plant deeper and firm the soil by tramping directly on the rows and afterward raking the surface loosely to prevent evaporation.

In home gardening beans are often soaked in water over night before sowing to "give them a start." As they often swell to twice their dry size, provide plenty of water. Before planting, pour off any excess water and air-dry the beans for an hour or so to facilitate handling. As much as a week may be gained by doing this, but if cold, wet weather occurs soon after sowing, the seed is almost sure to decay. Therefore do not try it until the weather has settled and the soil dried out somewhat.

Many varieties of bush beans mature as snap beans in six to eight weeks, so successional sowings may well be made at two-week intervals until only enough time is left between the sowing date and the probable first local frost for the pods to reach edible size. Soaking the seed and thoroughly firming the soil when planting will hasten this last crop. In the North the seasons are too short for successful successional sowings of dwarf limas; one main sowing should be made as early as it can safely be done.

CULTIVATION. Soils containing considerable clay tend to form crusts after hard rains; bean seedlings find it difficult to break through such a crust, so it is important (especially with limas and other large-seeded varieties) to loosen the soil carefully above the seeds as soon as it is no longer sticky but before it bakes and becomes hard. After the plants are up use the weeder along the rows, preferably in midafternoon when the plants are more limber and less likely to be broken than when full of water in the morning or late in the day.

Cultivation should be continuous, thorough and clean, so as to destroy weeds and maintain a loose, open surface, thus conserving soil moisture. It must not be deep because beans are shallow-rooting plants. The "scuffle hoe" (or "sweep") and the "three gang cultivator" attachments of the wheelhoe are best for this as they may be set to straddle the rows and work close to the plants without injuring them. For the last cultivation use the "shovel" or hilling attachment to ridge up the soil and help support the plants. (See illustration under HOE.)

Never cultivate, weed-pick or do any other work—or even walk—among the bean rows or hills while the plants are wet with dew or rain, because the spores of bean canker or anthracnose are thus spread from plant (or soil surface) to plant. (See ENEMIES, below). Attacking the green parts of the plants, this disease renders them unsightly and sometimes unfit for food.

HARVESTING. Gather snap beans while the seeds within are too small to give the pods an uneven outline; pick all of edible size so as to encourage continued pod production. For shell beans, leave the pods on the plants until the seeds are full size but not hard. If dry beans are wanted, leave the plants until they have dropped their leaves. Then pull them by hand or cut with a bean harvesting machine and lay them in shallow piles or windrows to cure for a few days before placing them under cover. Should rain occur during this time, spread the piles out or turn them over each day for several days thereafter so they will dry out evenly. (See illustration under HARVESTING.)

GROWING POLE BEANS. Climbing beans, especially pole limas, require rich, warm soil and ample space. If they are to be grown on upright poles, the latter should be 8 or 9 ft. long, stout and rough barked to aid the vines in clinging. Set them at least 4 ft. apart as the centers of hills and drive them fully 15 in. or more into the ground. Light bamboo poles thrust slantingly in the ground beside four adjacent hills and lashed together at the top will form a wigwam of vines much less likely to be blown over than single poles.

Temporary trellises may be made of woven wire fencing or by stretching stout cords, zigzag, between two strands of No. 10 wire fastened to firmly set posts 15 to 20 ft. apart. Let the lower wire be about 6 in. above the ground and the upper one 5 or 6 ft. All stakes, poles and trellises should be placed before the seeds are sown or immediately afterward to avoid injuring the plants. Sow four or five seeds to each hill; or in rows, let the plants stand a foot apart. Sowing limas and other broad and large beans with the "eye" down, especially in heavy soil, is generally recommended, but it is not essential. Thousands of acres of broad-seeded beans are planted by machines annually without any attention to this point. Cultivation is the same as for bush varieties.

ENEMIES. Unless precautions are taken, these may destroy a large part of a crop. The chief symptoms of anthracnose (a fungous disease) are black, oval, sunken cankers (which may ooze salmon-colored spots in the center) on pods, stems and cotyledons. Leaf symptoms are black marks on the veins. Control by selecting seed from healthy pods, by using seed of resistant types or seed from Calif. where the disease does not exist. *Avoid working*

BADLY DISEASED

The bean-pod (a) is afflicted with anthracnose; (b) with bacterial blight.

in the bean rows during wet weather since this spreads the spores from one plant to another.

Bacterial blight produces large brown blotches on the leaves, which may drop off, stem-girdling so that the whole plant may topple over, and indefinite reddish-edged spots on the pods. Kidney beans are especially susceptible. Since the bacteria may enter the seed without infecting the pod, selection of clean pods does not insure healthy seed. The safest plan is, therefore, to use disease-free seed grown in Idaho and Calif.

Mosaic is caused by a virus that lives in the seed and is carried from diseased to healthy plants by sucking insects. The variety Robust Pea is fairly resistant. A dry root rot (*Fusarium sp.*) results in stunting, wilting and yellowing of plants. Proper disposal of infected bean refuse and a long (six-year) rotation are control measures.

Anthracnose is often referred to as rust but true rust is recognized by brown or black pustules on the leaves. Some varieties are resistant.

In rainy seasons the seed-corn maggot may destroy germinating seeds. To check it plant shallow and avoid using barnyard manure. The bean weevil is a serious garden pest in the S. and often infests stored beans anywhere. Destroy it by fumigating in the fall with carbon bisulphide (1 oz. per bushel of beans) in a tight container for 36 hours. Fumigated beans do not germinate well and should not be used for seed.

In cold, moist weather lima beans are particularly subject to downy mildew, which covers the pods with white downy patches and distorts young shoots. Long rotation, use of healthy seed and destruction of diseased vines in autumn are control measures.

INSECTS. The Mexican bean beetle (*Epilachna corrupta*) is exceedingly destructive. The adults (tan with eight black spots on each wing cover) hibernate in plant rubbish and appear about with the first bean leaves. After eating for a week or two they lay yellow eggs in clusters on the undersides of the leaves. Repulsive yellow larvae covered with spines hatch in 6 to 14 days, and eat all of the leaves but the veins and upper epidermis. After three to five weeks they pupate, the beetles emerging about a week later. There are two or more generations. Stomach poisons will control both larvae and beetles. Since lead arsenate injures tender bean foliage, magnesium arsenate may be used as a spray (1 lb. to 50 gal. water), or as a dust (1 lb. to 4 lbs. hydrated lime). Calcium arsenate (1 lb. to 7 lbs. lime), is also used as a dust, as is barium fluosilicate (1 lb. to 5 lbs. lime). On string beans use a pyrethrum or derris preparation, not a poison, after the pods form.

MINOR BEAN SPECIES

Among the many less important plants known as beans, grown for food or ornament, are the following:

The Scarlet Runner Bean (*Phaseolus multiflora*), a tall-climbing twiner, like its white-flowered variety, the Dutch Caseknife Bean, has a tuberous root in the tropics where it is a perennial. In cool climates it is treated as an annual and often grown as an ornamental for its long, naked racemes of large, brilliant-red flowers. The 3 to 6 in. pods contain three or four large seeds which, if shelled and cooked while "green," are delicious; if allowed to approach ripeness, they are more or less unattractive because of their color—brown, red and black.

The Tepary Bean (*P. acutifolius*) has long been cultivated in the arid Southwest where it is native and highly prized as a vegetable. The plant is an erect grower on poor soils but rather spreading on better ones. It bears short pods with two to seven white, yellow, brown self-colored or dotted seeds, about the size of navy beans.

The Hyacinth-bean (*Dolichos lablab*) is grown in its native tropics for its edible pods and seeds. In temperate climates it is popular as an ornamental because of its rapid growth (often 20 ft. in a season), its abundant, large leaves and its purple or white flowers.

The tropical Chickasaw-lima or Jack-bean (*Canavalia ensiformis*) is often grown in the Southern States for its immature pods which are used as snap beans. The plant is bushy, the flowers purple, the pods often more than a foot long, and the white seeds are attached about at right angles to the pods.

The Soy- or Soja-bean (*Glycine max*), a native of Japan and China, is a bushy annual, 2 to 6 ft. high, with clusters of small, white flowers in the leaf axils and little, pendent pods which contain small yellow, brown, green or black seeds. In the Orient the ripe seeds are largely used for oil making and as human food, not, however, as a vegetable, but in fermented form, mainly as a sauce or as a protein substitute for meat. In America (except for soy sauce in Chinese menus) these uses are almost unknown, but the plant is an important animal forage and a soil improver, being grown as a green manure and as a cover-crop. See SOY-BEAN.

The Velvet-bean (*Stizolobium* species, especially *deeringianum*) is an Old-World tropical plant grown somewhat in the Southern States for ornament but more for cattle forage. It is a rank-growing vine often 60 to 100 ft. long, with ample foliage, clusters of large purple flowers and small pods containing only two or three, nearly globular seeds. It is rarely grown in northern gardens and then only for ornament or curiosity.

A BAD BEAN PEST

The Mexican bean beetle, of which eggs, larvae and adults and their work, are shown here, soon destroys plants unless vigorously fought.

The Asparagus- or Yard-long bean (*Vigna sesquipedalis*), though grown somewhat as a curiosity, is too unproductive to become popular. Its close relative the cow-pea (*V. sinensis*) is often called "bean" and is widely used as forage, fodder, and green manure crops.

The Broad Bean (*Vicia faba*), the "bean of history," variously known as field, tick, Windsor, English dwarf and horse bean, is a native of Southwestern Asia and Northern Africa where it has been cultivated from prehistoric times and whence it has spread throughout the world to be grown in cool climates and seasons for forage and human food. The plant differs from the other beans here discussed in being hardy. It is stiffly erect, has thick, very leafy, angular stems, 2 to 4 ft. high, with clusters of dull-white flowers, each with a blue-black spot on the "wing," large thick pods from 2 or 3 to 16 or more inches long, and flat angular seeds larger than limas and six to eight weeks earlier in maturing. Though extensively grown in the E. hemisphere, the Broad Bean is little planted in the U. S., mainly because it fails when treated like other beans. Unless planted in earliest spring, it usually succumbs to aphis, blister beetles or hot weather and sets no pods. It succeeds, however, in the Canadian Maritime Provinces, British Columbia and the States of Washington and Oregon. Also in parts of California it is grown as a winter vegetable.

BEARBERRY. The common name for *Arctostaphylos uva-ursi*, also called Red Bearberry. Black-bearberry is *Arctous alpinus*.

BEARDTONGUE. Common name for the large American genus Pentstemon (which see) of the Figwort Family. It comprises upwards of 70 species of herbaceous perennials or shrubs, the cultivated varieties being mostly hybrids of the hardier sorts.

BEAR-GRASS. A name sometimes given to Turkey-beard (which see), a plant of the Lily Family, *Xerophyllum tenax*.

BEARS-BREECH. Common name for the genus Acanthus, perennial herbs or small shrubs that bear long, erect, showy spikes of flowers, white to rose and purple.

BEARS-FOOT FERN. Common name for *Davallia tyermanni*, a greenhouse fern.

BEARS-PAW FERN. Common name for *Polypodium meyenianum*, an interesting hothouse fern for culture in large baskets, in peaty soil. The upper part of its frond, fertile and contracted, suggests an open claw.

BEARS-TAIL, CRETAN. Common name for *Celsia arcturus*, an ornamental herb from Asia Minor, bearing yellow and purple flowers in long racemes.

BEAUFORTIA (boh-for'-shi-ah). Australian shrubs belonging to the Myrtle Family. One species, *B. purpurea*, sometimes grown as a cool greenhouse plant, or outdoors in a favorable climate, is a small shrub with wand-like branches and narrow rigid leaves. The small reddish flowers, with conspicuous purple stamens, are borne in dense heads in spring. It requires a mixture of loam and peat, with sand, and is propagated by cuttings of maturing shoots.

BEAUMONTIA (boh-mon'-shi-ah). Vigorous woody vines of the tropics. One species, *B. grandiflora* (Heralds Trumpet) is sometimes grown in warm greenhouses or outdoors in the S. Under glass it is not happy when confined in a pot, doing better when planted out in a solid bed or border of good soil and trained to the roof. It has large oval leaves, and large white, fragrant trumpet-shaped flowers, borne in terminal clusters in spring. The wood needs to be well ripened to induce flowering; afterwards a hard pruning should be given to produce laterals for the next season's bloom. Propagated by cuttings.

BEAUTY-BERRY. Common name for the genus Callicarpa, a decorative group of fairly hardy shrubs and trees of the Verbena Family.

BEAUTY-BUSH. (*Kolkwitzia amabilis*). A hardy, deciduous, upright shrub of twiggy habit from China, belonging to the Honeysuckle Family. A very desirable subject growing 5 to 8 ft., it has a particularly graceful habit with good foliage value throughout the season. Both the young leaves and branches are hairy when young. It does not flower until really well established, but then becomes one of the freest and loveliest of flowering shrubs in May and June. The bell-shaped flowers are soft pink with a yellow throat and distinction is added by the white bristly hairs with which flower stalks and sepals are clothed. Propagation is by cuttings of growing wood in late summer. The plant flowers best in poor soil in an exposed situation.

BEAVER-TREE. A common name for *Magnolia glauca,* also known as Sweet-bay, a shrubby tree, evergreen in the S., bearing fragrant white flowers. See MAGNOLIA.

BEDDING and BEDDING PLANTS. Bedding in garden language is a term used to denote the massing of plants for showy flower or foliage effects. It is not of such importance in the garden picture of the present time as it has been in years gone by. The style does not fit in so well with the prevailing informal plantings and, while very showy, it is the most expensive form of outdooi floral decoration. Many of the plants best suited to bedding are tender and their period of effectiveness comparatively short. However, there are certain formal areas in parks, and in connection with certain types of architecture, where it is very fitting, and, if well carried out, worthy of commendation. There are four main divisions—spring bedding, summer bedding, subtropical bedding, and carpet bedding. (See illustrations, Plate 20.)

A SPRINGTIME BED OF TULIPS
Arabis has been used here to cover the bare
ground between them.

Spring Bedding. This style gives showy floral effects early in the season, and features such hardy bulbs in variety as crocus, hyacinth, narcissus, and tulips of both the early and late-flowering groups. Other plants used in connection with these are aubrietia, alyssum, arabis, bellis, myosotis, primulas of the polyanthus type, and pansies. One simple but effective combination is to carpet a bed of yellow tulips with forget-me-notes. As soon as the display is over these spring plants are usually removed and replaced with others which have been brought along under glass for summer display. Where bulbs alone are used they may be planted over with annuals, either transplanted or sown in place.

Summer Bedding. Plants for summer display are set out as soon as danger from frost is past. This group comprises tender perennials propagated from cuttings, and perennials or annuals raised from seed sown early in the year indoors or in hotbeds. Among the tender perennials that give a good floral display and that are usually grown from cuttings are the so-called geraniums (actually pelargoniums) in variety, heliotrope, lantana, cuphea, and fuchsia, the last named for shady places.

Plants raised from seed include such kinds as ageratum (in both compact and spreading forms), varieties of *Begonia semperflorens,* California poppy (Eschscholzia), dahlias of the Coltness and other dwarf strains, annual gaillardias, lobularia (better known as sweet alyssum), Japanese pinks, Drummond phlox, bedding petunias, sanvitalia, varieties of *Tagetes erecta* and *T. patula,* torenia, garden verbenas and *Verbena venosa,* which is sometimes hardy but succeeds best if handled as an annual.

For foliage effects named varieties of coleus grown from cuttings are colorful in sunny situations. Good gray-leaved plants, popularly known as Dusty Millers, are *Centaurea cineraria,* and *C. gymnocarpa;* and another gray-leaved plant is *Senecio leucostachys,* all usually raised from seed sown early in the year. Forms of *Chrysanthemum parthenium* (commonly called Golden Feather or Feverfew) are attractive with their golden leaves, often finely cut.

Subtropical Bedding. This term is applied to the arrangement of tropical plants in beds or groups outdoors for the summer months. Bold and luxuriant effects may be obtained for a short season, and for best results sheltered positions should be selected. Certain more or less permanent occupants of the conservatory or greenhouse may be given a turn outdoors for the summer, such as tree ferns, palms, crotons, dracaenas, abutilons, acalyphas, cycads, and pittosporum. These are best plunged in the garden without being removed from their pots or tubs; thus they are easily returned under glass on the approach of cold weather. Certain kinds are easily and quickly grown from seed. Amongst these are amaranthus, *Albizzia lophantha, Eucalyptus globulus, Grevillea robusta,* melianthus, *Nicotiana sylvestris,* ricinus, and various species of solanum, such as *S. marginatum, S. aculeatissimum, S. sisymbrifolium,* and *S. warscewiczi.* Cannas fit in very well with this group, giving strong flower and foliage effects. Good grasses are the various forms of pennisetum and miscanthus.

Carpet Bedding. This style has almost disappeared from the home garden as far as the elaborate, geometrical layout of beds and intricate design of the plant arrangements, featuring coats-of-arms and similar picture work are concerned. Examples are still to be seen in parks and other public places, especially as welcoming tributes to

Plate 3.   BEDS AND BORDERS

Top: A formal treatment of beds suited to a garden near a dignified house.   Lower left: The charmingly planned casualness of a mixed perennial border on the edge of a winding walk.   Lower right: A border with an excellent background, well-placed groups and a pleasingly varied edging.

organization conventions or other large gatherings. While a most expensive and unnatural style, it calls for a high degree of technical skill in design, selection of plant material and continuous attention in the form of pinching to keep the pattern well defined. The color effects in this style of planting are obtained from foliage rather than from flowers. Alternanthera, coleus, iresine, santolina, and dwarf forms of feverfew are good examples. *Antennaria dioica* and *Herniaria glabra* are useful edgers, as are also such succulents as *Sedum acre, S. lydium, S. hispanicum, Aptenia cordifolia variegata, Senecio succulentus* and various echeverias and sempervivums.

An outstanding example of carpet bedding is the floral clock in the public gardens in Edinburgh, Scotland.

THE CARE OF BEDS

SOIL PREPARATION. To obtain the best results from bedding plants one must give the preparation of the soil adequate attention. The effort expended in deep cultivation will be well repaid, as it is the best insurance against drought. This means providing good friable soil to a depth of at least 12 to 18 in., and for most plants it should be well enriched with real old manure or leafmold. Succulents, and such flowering plants as geraniums and nasturtiums, do best in a rather lean (sandy) mixture.

Good drainage is essential, and if the subsoil is heavy and retentive it can be greatly improved by digging in some sand, gravel, or coal ashes. If on the other hand it is of a leachy character, a 6 in. layer of old sod or half-rotted leaves buried about 18 in. deep will offset this poor condition. Beds that are vacant over winter will be improved by double digging (which see) in the fall; at this time manure should be worked in and the surface left rough until planting time. The action of frost renders it more friable.

PLANTING. Perhaps the first planting will be done in early spring, using such things as pansies, daisies and forget-me-nots that have been wintered in frames. Later on these would be replaced by more tender plants for summer display that have been brought along under glass and held until danger from frost is safely past. It is well that all such plants be somewhat "hardened off" before planting by giving them increasing ventilation. If cloudy or showery weather threatens about planting time, try to make the most of such favorable conditions for moving the plants.

As a rule it is helpful to first lay out the plants in position, then make any necessary rearrangements, and finally begin to plant, working from the center of the area to the edges. In most cases the planting shows to best advantage when the center of the bed is somewhat raised. After planting, unless rain falls promptly, give a good soaking to

FORMAL BEDDING ARRANGEMENT FOR FLOWER AND FOLIAGE EFFECT
Large-leaved cannas and elephants ears in the center are surrounded by lower-growing annuals and the whole is enclosed in a sheared temporary hedge of summer-cypress (Kochia) with low clumps of alyssum between each two plants.

nicely settle things in place. As to future waterings there can be no set rule except that in general it is well to defer applying water as long as possible—that is, until the plants definitely need it, and then to soak the soil well when it is undertaken.

AFTER-CARE. Tidiness means a good deal in the success of a bedding scheme. Keep the soil lightly cultivated as long as it can be done without danger of injuring the plants; and pick off the withered leaves and flowers as they appear. In some cases some pinching back of wayward shoots may be necessary from time to time, especially if the design is formal; but this is less needed if the right kinds of plants are chosen and if they are good, uniform stock. Neatly kept edges add much to an attractive appearance.

On the approach of frost, cuttings of tender perennials in the beds may be taken as a source of future stock; or some old plants may be lifted and potted up to provide cuttings at a later date. When the summer flower display is finally over, the beds should be well dug, and either planted to hardy bulbs for spring effects, or left in a rough state as already mentioned until planting time the following season.

BEDSTRAW. Common name for the genus Galium, small herbs with filmy white flowers, occasionally grown in rock gardens; the cut flowers are used in bouquets.

BEE BALM. A common name for *Monarda didyma,* also known as Oswego-tea and Fragrant Balm, a perennial plant bearing terminal clusters of scarlet flowers with reddish bracts. See MONARDA.

BEECH. The genus Fagus, a group of hardy deciduous trees belonging to the same family as the Oaks and Chestnuts. The name is said to be derived from a Saxon word meaning book, as records were written on the bark and on tablets made of its wood. There are several species, all natives of the north temperate zones of America, Europe and Asia, but only two, with their numerous varieties, are much grown in gardens.

All are round-headed, spreading trees growing to 80 ft. or more, with light-colored, smooth bark. It is customarily stated that they are partial to limestone soil but fine specimens and large stands are found on acid soils, preferring rather dry hillsides. Hard-wooded and long-lived, the trees are particularly free from dead branches, insect pests and fungi. They

are among the most decorative of garden subjects in form, color, cleanliness and grace. The species are much alike but the varieties include forms with brilliantly colored and finely cut leaves, weeping or pendulous branches and other interesting characters. Spring fills them with heads of staminate flowers which are followed by three-cornered burry nuts containing edible kernels.

The beech thrives best where the soil is protected by a mulch of its own leaves. It is propagated by seeds stratified over winter and sown in spring. Seedlings should be frequently transplanted to prevent the development of long tap-roots, since the trees suffer if these are injured.

A serious bark disease, associated with the presence of the beech scale, prevalent in Canada, has spread through Maine. Use a dormant application of an oil spray to check the scale and also to control the woolly aphis which covers the under surface of leaves of the European beech with disfiguring white masses. Nicotine-sulphate can also be used when the young leaves first appear.

A mottle-leaf or scorch disease, resulting in premature leaf fall, is prevalent on American beech, but the exact cause is not yet known.

PRINCIPAL SPECIES

F. grandifolia (American Beech) grows to 75 ft., has a clean gray trunk and limbs. It is strikingly beautiful, particularly in winter but makes an effective background for early-flowering shrubs and perennial borders.

sylvatica (European Beech) has darker bark and smaller, darker green, shining leaves that turn reddish brown in fall and remain on the tree most of the winter. It is less sensitive to unfavorable conditions and there are numerous varieties of great merit. These include *atropunicea,* the Purple Beech, whose leaves become very dark purple; and of this there is a variety that comes out delicate copper color, while still another has light purple foliage turning to green. Var. *pendula* forms a large, broad pyramid with weeping branches that make a dense growth right to the ground. A cut-leaved form (var. *laciniata*) has drooping branches and forms a broadly columnar tree of marked grace and beauty. All upright forms may be clipped, forming excellent hedges.

BLUE-BEECH is a Hornbeam (which see), *Carpinus caroliniana.*

BEECH FAMILY. Common name of the Fagaceae, which see.

BEECH FERN. Common name for N. American species of the genus Phegopteris, which see. They are small deciduous ferns, useful for underplanting in woods soil, well drained.

BEES. The lifework of bees is the storing up of honey which they collect, as nectar, from blossoms. Visiting flower after flower they are constantly brushing against, first, the stamens (or male organs) of one blossom and then the pistil (or female organ) of another. From the former they pick up on their body or legs a sprinkling of pollen which they later carry to and deposit upon the stigma (sticky tip) of the second flower's pistil. This brings about the pollination or fertilization of the second flower and results in the development of seed or fruit.

Owing to the numbers and ceaseless activity of bees—both wild and "domesticated"—the service they unintentionally render becomes a most important factor in the production of good crops in orcharding, gardening and the growing of certain vegetables, notably tomatoes, cucumbers and melons—especially in greenhouses, where wind (the other important natural pollinating agent) cannot act. Because most wild bees are of what is called the "solitary" type, living alone or in small groups, the "social" bees, of which the honey bee is the most important, play by far the larger part in the work described.

BEES AS GARDEN HELPERS. Although many gardeners and orchardists do not appreciate the debt they owe to bees, others do, and are capitalizing it. To insure the maximum fertilization of their crops, they maintain colonies of honey bees in their orchards, gardens or greenhouses. In the latter case this practice has largely done away with the former hand-pollinating of tomatoes—a slow, tedious procedure now restricted to special hybridizing activities.

A second benefit derived from bees is, of course, the surplus honey which, even from a single hive, will, in the course of a year, represent a welcome, wholesome addition to the family diet. Finally, a small apiary (as a collection of beehives is called) can be a source of much pleasure and interest to anyone to whom natural history appeals; it supplies a picturesque feature in the garden or landscape; and it calls for but little work, and that of a pleasant and not arduous nature. A modest start in beekeeping can be made at nominal cost—say, $25—for a colony or "nucleus" of bees (including the essential queen or "mother of the hive"); a modern sectional hive with brood frames (in which the bees raise their young) and "supers" (in which the surplus honey is stored); a second, reserve hive; and a few necessary accessories. From such a start, with a little study and average success, it should not be difficult to build up as extensive an enterprise as may be desired with the knowledge that, meanwhile, the garden and orchard are being greatly assisted. Anyone planning to go into beekeeping will find detailed instructions in bulletins obtainable from the U. S. Department of Agriculture and the Agricultural Experiment Stations in a number of States.

BEES NOT HARMFUL. Bees are sometimes thought of by the uninformed as harmful to plants and gardens. As a matter of fact, their good qualities more than make up for any occasional shortcomings. Growers of greenhouse cut flowers may complain that bees invade their structures and, by pollinating their crops, cause them to mature more quickly, thereby lessening their keeping qualities and market value. This effect, should it threaten to become serious, can always be prevented by screening the greenhouse ventilators.

Fruit growers occasionally claim to have seen bees biting or stinging fruits and sucking the juices—but the probable facts in all such cases are that the bees observed were merely sucking up juice as it oozed through breaks in the skin of the fruit already made by bird, wasp or, possibly, a blow.

One kind of solitary bee (the leaf-cutter bee) cuts small pieces out of the leaves of roses and other shrubs with which to line its tunnels, but this damage is rarely serious. As to any fears on the part of garden visitors that the presence of bees necessarily means stings, it can safely be said that a colony (or several colonies) of bees in an out-of-the-way corner of the garden, correctly handled and not molested, is very unlikely indeed to be responsible for any promiscuous stinging. Anyone who has ever watched an expert beekeeper work, unprotected, among his hives is likely to agree with the assertion that the modern, improved races of bees are just about as domesticated and deserving of a place in the garden as poultry or birds. And always, it must be remembered, they are more than "paying their way" in useful service.

See also FERTILIZATION OF FLOWERS; INSECTS.

BEE-SAGE. Common name for *Audibertia polystachya* (formerly *Salvia apiana*), a shrubby herb of Calif., with white flowers, also known as White-sage and sometimes called Grease-wood. See AUDIBERTIA.

BEET. The name of about 15 Old World species of mostly biennial herbs of the genus Beta (which see). One (*B. vulgaris*) is of economic importance as the progenitor of the common garden beet, sugar and foliage beets, Swiss chard and mangel-wurzel (see also CHARD and MANGEL), which have been cultivated for centuries.

Garden beet varieties are of two classes —long- and turnip-rooted. The former require five or more months to mature; with the "half-long" sorts they are famous for their fine flavor. The latter, developed mainly within the past 50 years, and reaching edible size in three or four months, include some varieties that compare favorably. But since turnip-rooted sorts, if spring sown, are likely to become tasteless and woody by fall, it is best to make succession sowings every fortnight or so; or at least a second, midsummer, sowing to provide a late fall and winter crop.

Beets are semi-hardy and seed may be sown as early in spring as the ground can be worked; also the roots may be left in the ground until heavy frosts threaten. They should then be pulled, the tops cut (leaving an inch of stem), and the beets stored in pits or a cellar like potatoes. See STORAGE OF CROPS.

SOIL AND PREPARATION. Though beets do best in deep, light, sandy loams, they will yield satisfactorily in any well-drained, properly managed garden. In soils underlain by hardpan or rock, grow only turnip-rooted varieties, for in shallow soil the longer roots are likely to be deformed, rough and of poor quality.

Soil preparation is the same as for other vegetables except that lime should not be added; it tends to cause the "scab" disease. Unrotted stable manure is undesirable as it tends to develop excessive tops at the expense of the roots; if well decayed, it is excellent. As a manure substitute, cover-crops or green manures and commercial fertilizers may be used. One pound of high grade, complete fertilizer to 50 sq. ft. of surface is a good dressing, either plowed or dug under or raked into the seed-bed. Three weeks after sowing seed a top-dressing of 1 lb. of nitrate of soda to 400 sq. ft. may be made, and a month later a second such application.

SEED SOWING AND FUTURE CARE. Strictly speaking, beet "seed" is dried, shriveled fruits in which as many as eight seeds may be embedded. This explains the importance of thin sowing; also why seedlings appear in clusters even after thin sowing.

In home gardens seed is usually sown where the plants are to remain. However, if hotbed or coldframe is availabe, crops may be started four or six weeks before the season opens and the seedlings transplanted outdoors when the first sowing is made there. Or an even earlier crop may be grown to maturity in a hotbed or frame, if space can be spared. In transplanting beets the taproots should be extended straight down in the holes, not doubled up.

Sowing should not be deeper than 1 in. while the soil is moist in early spring; in fact the seed need only be firmed into the ground and lightly covered. In midsummer, the drier soil should be freshly turned and raked; the seed may then be covered 2 in. deep and the rows should be tramped firm and loose soil lightly raked over them to serve as a mulch and insure a good stand of plants.

The distance between rows will depend upon the tillage methods and tools. In large scale operations horse- or tractor-cultivation may require 24 to 30 in. spacing. In the small garden 15 to 18 in., or even less, gives room for wheelhoe or hand implements.

Thin when the plants are about 4 in. high. Those removed may be transplanted, or cooked like "greens." The distance left between plants varies with the variety; small-topped, globular sorts may stand as close as 3 in., while large, flat-rooted kinds need at least 5 in.

Among the many varieties offered these have long been popular: Bassano, Crimson Globe, Edmands Blood Turnip, Crosbys Egyptian, Early Eclipse, Lentz, Bastians Half-long and Long Dark Blood.

ENEMIES. A leaf spot is common but not serious. Destroying diseased leaves will usually be enough control. Potato scab also occurs on beets (see POTATO). To prevent fungous diseases of seedlings dust seed with mercury or copper compounds (see SEED DISINFECTION). Curly-top, a virus disease of sugar beets causing great damage in the semi-arid western regions, is spread by means of a leafhopper. It causes dwarfed plants, curled leaves and irregularly swollen veins. No certain control is known but early planting helps.

BEETLES. The popular name for members of the order Coleoptra—the largest of all the insect groups. (Two out of every 5 insects discovered and named are beetles.) They usually have hardened outer skins or shells. The front pair of wings is veinless and thickened, forming two convex shields (called *elytra*) which, when the insect is at rest, meet in a straight line down the back, covering the folded, membranous, veined, hind wings, with which the creature flies. In flight, the elytra stand out stiffly sidewise like the wings of a monoplane. The mouth parts are of the typical chewing type (see INSECTS), except in one group, the snout beetles, in which they are greatly reduced in size and placed at the end of a slender trunk-like snout.

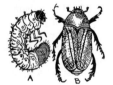

Beetles, in growing, go through a "complete metamorphosis" (see INSECTS). The larvae are worm-like grubs, usually with six true legs (like the adult), though the snout beetle maggot is legless. The head of the grub is always distinct from the body and is usually dark in color. The pupa or resting stage is a brown shiny oval object with a slight but peculiar squirming or wiggling ability. These pupae are not enclosed in dense silky cocoons like those of most butterflies and moths, but may be found unprotected in the soil or in burrows in infested trees or plants.

JUNE BEETLE
(A) The destructive white grub. (B) Its harmless but annoying adult, also called June-bug.

Since both larvae and adults have chewing mouth-parts, beetles are commonly injurious in both stages, but in a few cases one stage is injurious while the other is beneficial. Adult blister beetles, for instance, feed on foliage and flowers but the grubs are helpful because they eat the grasshopper eggs in the soil. Lady beetles and ground beetles (which see) are highly beneficial since, both are larvae and as adults, they devour other insects that are injurious to the garden.

Since beetles are chewing insects the general recommendation for control is the use of a stomach poison, such as arsenate of lead, calcium, or magnesium. There are, however, many cases when this rule should not be followed. Foliage can usually be protected with lead arsenate, but spraying flowers with this material is often undesirable or inadvisable. Hence flower-loving beetles, such as the Japanese beetle, the blister beetle and the rose chafer, are best destroyed by hand picking, or by knocking them off into a pail of water with a layer of kerosene on top.

Grubs of the Japanese and Asiatic beetles, as well as white-grubs (which see), can be poisoned by applying lead arsenate to the soil or killed by injecting carbon bisulphide into it (see INSECTS: CONTROL). The elm leaf beetle is readily kept from defoliating trees by spraying them with a stomach poison, but beans in the vegetable garden cannot be protected from the Mexican bean beetle in this way except while the plants are small because of the danger of arsenical residue on the beans. In this case contact insecticides are resorted to for the later sprayings.

Small active beetles such as flea beetles are often warded off by a repellent such as bordeaux mixture or may be sprayed with a contact insecticide. Bark beetles or borers can be destroyed only by mechanical means or by fumigation.

See INSECTS; also ASIATIC, BARK, BLISTER, CLICK, FLEA, GROUND, LADY AND SNOUT BEETLES; CURCULIO; WEEVILS; WIREWORMS.

BEGGARWEED. Common name for *Desmodium purpureum,* a plant of the Pea Family, a native of the West Indies, with blue or purple flowers, followed by twisted pods which adhere like burs. It is grown as a cover crop in S. U.S., reaching a height of 8 ft. Once seeded it will reseed itself year after year.

BEGONIA (be-goh'-ni-ah). A large and varied group of succulent herbs or partly shrubby plants, widely distributed in warm regions of the earth. A great many species have been introduced into cultivation, and countless hybrids and forms have been developed in gardens. Some are grown for their handsome foliage, and many others for their showy flowers, either for summer bedding outdoors or for summer or winter flowering under glass. Many are fine plants for the window garden.

They are divided roughly into three main sections—fibrous-rooted, rhizomatous, and tuberous-rooted, but due to intermingling the lines are not clearly defined in all cases. Male and female flowers are borne separately in the same cluster. They mostly dislike full exposure to sun or very dry conditions, and thrive best in a mixture of fibrous loam, with leafmold, some old cow manure and sand added.

ENEMIES. The leaf nematode disease is a serious problem on the semi-tuberous type of begonia. The feeding of the eelworms results in small brown spots on the under sides of the leaves followed by dying of foliage and stunting of plants which may mean the destruction of the entire stock of greenhouse. To prevent this, take cuttings only from healthy stock; discard infested soil; place pots so that leaves of neighboring plants do not touch; isolate infected plants; remove and burn infected leaves; and, most important of all, *do not wet the foliage when watering.* Plants may be treated with hot water at 117 deg. F. for 3 minutes.

To avoid bacterial leaf spot and resultant defoliation, Botrytis blight, and Pythium stem rot, keep plants well spaced and the humidity not too high. To prevent nematode root knot use soil free from infestation or sterilize it. See NEMATODE; SOIL; STERILIZATION. To control aphids, white flies and mealybugs, spray with nicotine-sulphate and soap or pick off the last named with a cotton swab dipped in alcohol.

Begonias are propagated by seed, which is extremely small and should not be covered with compost; also by stem and leaf cuttings, and by division of the rhizomes and tubers.

PRINCIPAL SPECIES

Fibrous-rooted and of more or less shrubby habit:

B. coccinea has tall smooth stems, oblique angular leaves with red margins, and drooping clusters of coral-red flowers.

dichroa is of pendulous habit with large green leaves and brick-red flowers. A good basket plant.

fuchsioides has tall slender stems, small leaves tinged red when young, and drooping scarlet fuchsia-like flowers.

foliosa is a small grower with slender stems, small glossy green drooping leaves, and small whitish flowers tinged pink. A good basket plant.

haageana is a tall handsome red-hairy species, with large hanging clusters of rose-pink flowers.

maculata has woody branching stems, with wavy green leaves blotched silvery-white, and drooping clusters of pink flowers.

corallina (considered to be a form of the last mentioned) grows to 10 ft. or so, with glossy green leaves and clusters of coral-red flowers. It is one of the best to train against a pillar or over rafters.

metallica is atttractive with green leaves shaded a dark metallic color and clusters of blush flowers.

nitida has woody stems with large shining green leaves and pale-pink flowers.

polyantha is an erect free-branching grower with green stems red at the nodes, rich-green leaves and a profusion of pink flowers in winter.

phyllomaniaca is a curious species with thick fleshy hairy stems and large fringed leaves bearing buds which produce young plants. It bears a profusion of small pink flowers.

sanguinea is smooth and shining, with thick green leaves, red beneath, and small white flowers.

semperflorens is a dwarf compact grower almost everblooming. It is a popular summer bedding plant and also for winter-flowering under glass, occurring in many named forms.

venosa is an interesting upright species with thick fleshy leaves covered with silvery-gray scales, and which can be distinguished by very large veined stipules or basal appendages.

Fibrous-rooted hybrids, more or less shrubby:

B. argenteo-guttata has leaves of shining green thickly spotted white, and blush-pink flowers.

carminata is a fine erect plant with light-green deeply toothed leaves and massive clusters of carmine-pink flowers.

digswelliana has large green leaves tinged red, and pendulous rosy-scarlet flowers.

ingrami has small green leaves, tinted red in the sun, and large rose-colored flowers on horizontal side branches.

lucerna is of strong shrubby habit, with leaves heavily spotted white and large showy bright-pink flowers.

margaritae is a vigorous grower with hairy purple stems, green and purplish leaves, red beneath, and pale-pink flowers.

manicata has thick fleshy shining green leaves with stems covered with scale-like hairs, and loose panicles of small pink flowers. Var. *aureo-maculata* is a form with leaves blotched yellowish-white, while *crispa* has leaves with heavily crinkled margins.

rex is a dwarf species with large wavy leaves of metallic green with purple mar-

BEGONIA FLOWERS HAVE BEEN DEVELOPED INTO MANY FORMS
At the left is a typical branch of one of the Christmas-flowering begonias; at the right, various
doubled and fringed flowers found in hybrids, many of which are easily raised in the house.

Mme. de Lesseps is a strong upright grower with large, lobed leaves and clusters of large white flowers.

President Carnot is one of the showiest and best. It is a strong shrubby grower with large leaves and large clusters of brilliant rosy-carmine flowers.

Rhizomatous Section:

B. feasti has thick roundish leaves, red beneath, with hairy margin and bright-pink flowers on long stems.

glaucophylla has somewhat pendulous stems, with glaucous wavy-margined leaves and red flowers. A good basket plant.

heracleifolia has large bronzy-green palmate leaves and rose-colored flowers on long hairy stems.

gin and silvery zone above, and red beneath. It is the chief parent of the many named forms of the beautiful colored-leaved Rex begonias. While often grown in pots these forms do much better when planted out in a greenhouse, where they show to advantage in rockwork with ferns or planted under the staging.

ricinfolia is a vigorous grower with large, lobed bronzy-green leaves and small rose-pink flowers on long stems.

scandens has glossy green leaves and small white flowers in round clusters. It is an excellent basket, window box, and climbing plant.

verschaffeltiana has large, green, ovate, lobed leaves, and large clusters of rose flowers.

Tuberous or semi-tuberous and bulbous section:

B. *tuberhybrida* is a class name for the showy and beautiful summer-flowering tuberous begonias in both single and double vars. These have been developed from the following species native in the Andes of Peru: B. *cinnabarina,* B. *clarkei,* B. *boliviensis,* B. *davisi,* B. *roseflora,* B. *pearcei,* and B. *veitchi,* which are interesting and beautiful in themselves, but seldom seen outside botanic gardens. Tuberous begonias may be raised from seed, a good strain giving fine form and color variation. The tubers will be good for several years. Started early in spring they make good plants for summer flowering under glass or for bedding out in moist and partly shaded places.

evansiana is not showy but is unusual in being able to stand some frost. It has lobed leaves, red beneath, and flesh-colored flowers. It is propagated by bulblets from the leaf-axils.

gracilis, also increased by leaf bulblets, has erect succulent stems, lobed heart-shaped leaves, and pink flowers in summer.

dregei grows to 3 ft., has small thin leaves and a profusion of small white flowers.

weltoniensis is a Dregei hybrid with pink flowers; an old-time favorite in window gardens.

froebeli has green heart-shaped leaves with fleshy purple hairs and large scarlet flowers in loose drooping clusters.

socotrana is a bulbous species about 1 ft. high, with large dark-green round leaves and large rose-pink flowers in winter. After flowering, a cluster of bulbs is formed at the base of the stems from which new plants are started. Crossed with other species and varieties it has produced some remarkable hybrids. The fine winter-flowering var. Gloire de Lorraine, good in pots or baskets, and producing a wealth of bright-pink flowers, was the result of a cross with B. *dregei.* Glory of Cincinnati, a larger form, is a well-known Christmas plant. B. *socotrana* crossed with B. *subpeltata* gave the magnificent Gloire de Sceaux, a half-shrubby grower to 8 ft., with large dark metallic-green leaves, red beneath, and rose-pink flowers. Crossed with large-flowering tuberous varieties, B. *socotrana* produced that fine

race known as Winter-Flowering Begonias. These are stout erect plants of compact growth, with handsome dark-green foliage and colorful flowers in single, semi-double and double forms. It is an interesting fact that the named varieties Ensign, Winter Perfection, Ideala, and Success were derived from a single seed-pod. Plants of this group, although they make tubers, are best propagated annually by leaf-cuttings.

BELAMCANDA (bel-am-kan'-dah) *chinensis.* A hardy Chinese plant of the Iris Family, grown in old gardens and naturalized in the U. S., and known as Blackberry-lily, which see.

BELLADONNA (bel-ah-don'-ah). Common name for *Atropa belladonna,* also known as Deadly Nightshade, a European perennial herb which is not a garden subject but important as the source of atropine. All parts of the plants are poisonous, and the leaves and roots are used in medicine. Growing 3 ft. tall, it is a coarse plant producing dull-purplish flowers 1 in. long, either solitary or paired, and nodding in habit. The fruits are nearly globular, shiny, brownish-black berries. The name Belladonna is often mistakenly applied to the Garland Larkspur (*Delphinium cheilanthum*).

BELLADONNA-LILY. Common name for *Amaryllis belladonna,* a bulbous herb that bears large, fragrant flowers, from white through rosy-red to purple, in summer.

BELLFLOWER. Common name for the genus Campanula (which see), a group of excellent plants for garden display and of easy culture. It is generally applied to the perennial species as differentiated from the biennial Canterbury Bells.

Chilean-bellflower is *Lapageria rosea.* Giant-bellflower is *Ostrowskia magnifica.* Gland-bellflower is a catalog name for the genus Adenophora, also known as Ladybell.

BELLFLOWER FAMILY. Common name of the Campanulaceae (which see), a family including many attractive and important ornamental herbs.

BELL-GLASS. A glass vessel more or less bell-shaped usually with a handle at the top, used in the propagation shed for covering seeds, grafts, cuttings, etc., that need a close, moist atmosphere, and in the garden to cover seedlings to protect them from frost and hasten growth. See also CLOCHE ; FORCERS, PLANT.

BELLIS (bel′-is). Herbaceous annuals or perennials of the Composite Family, growing in tufts or with branching stems. The solitary daisy-like heads have yellow disks and white, pink, or red rays. Though only one species (*B. perennis*) is correctly named English Daisy, this term has become associated with all the species, many catalogs listing them as such.

THE SHRIMP PLANT
Beloperone guttata deserves wider use as a sun-room subject.

They need a fertile, moist soil and plenty of sun, but are easily grown from seed sown in the fall; wintered over in a cold-frame, they flower early the next season. However, they will bloom the first season if seed is sown very early in the spring. The blossoming period is from May to August. Because of their dwarf nature—they are only 6 to 8 in. tall—they are best used for edgings, low beds and colonizing in lawns, though they also are satisfactory for borders and potting. Special varieties are best propagated by division in cool weather as they do not always come true from seed. (See illustration, Plate 44.)

Of the two leading species, *B. perennis* produces heads 2 in. across in spring and early summer, in red, rose and white. Var. *ranunculiflora* is double. *B. rotundifolia* has longer-stalked, coarsely-toothed leaves and heads somewhat smaller than in *B. perennis* and usually white. A var., *caerulescens*, bears flowers with blue rays.

BELLIUM (be′-li-um). A genus of small European daisy-like plants of the Composite Family suitable for planting in the rock garden or between stones in a paving-stone walk. They have small heads of yellow disk flowers, surrounded by white rays, tinged purple or blue on the back. They grow well in a mixture of sandy loam and leafmold and are propagated by division or from seed. *B. minutum* grows to the height of 3 in. and has heads ½ in. across. The rays are tinged with blue on the reverse. The tiny daisies are in bloom from May to September.

BELL-VINE, PURPLE. Common name for *Rhodochiton volubile*, a free-flowering, graceful vine of Mexico with purplish-red flowers.

BELLWORT. Common name for the genus Uvularia, a group of herbs of the Lily Family with drooping yellow, bell-shaped flowers; also sometimes used in catalogs for Codonopsis, a genus of herbs of the Campanulaceae or Bellflower Family.

BELOPERONE (be-loh-pe′-roh-nee) *guttata*. This native of the American Tropics is less frequently cultivated than its interesting form deserves, though it is sometimes seen in the open ground in the S. States or as a house plant in other sections. Related to the Acanthus, though much more slender, the tubular 2-lipped flowers in long curving spikes are made showy by brick-red overlapping bracts which give the plant its common name, Shrimp-plant. Growing 18 in. tall the plant requires a rich, well-drained soil and delights in full sunshine and considerable warmth. It is propagated by cuttings or by seed, although it is difficult to raise from seed.

BELVEDERE. A common name for *Kochia scoparia*, also called Summer-cypress, an annual that forms symmetrical, bush-like plants and whose light-green foliage turns purple-red in autumn.

BELVEDERE. A permanent garden shelter of distinct architectural design, roofed over but open at the sides and placed on an eminence so as to command a broad extensive view. See GARDEN SHELTERS.

BENINCASA (ben-in-kay′-sah) *hispida*. An annual pumpkin-like vine belonging to the Cucumber Family. Called by various names such as Wax, or White Gourd of India, Chinese-watermelon, Preserving-melon, etc., it is much grown in China and India for the large (up to 16 in.), hairy, white-fleshed, oblong fruit, which is used in the making of preserves and sweet pickles and sometimes eaten raw. It succeeds under the same treatment as muskmelon.

BENJAMIN-BUSH. One of the common names for the native Spicebush, *Benzoin aestivale*.

BENT GRASS. Common name for Agrostis, a large genus of mostly low-growing and spreading sorts including some valuable, high-class lawn grasses as well as the important pasture grass, Redtop. The species are annual or perennial, have somewhat rough, flat or slightly rolled leaves and bear loose panicles of small reddish flowers. While some of the forms are grown from seed, those used for fine lawns and putting greens are of the creeping type and are increasingly being grown from stolons, which are simply the chopped-up running stems. A good bent grass turf is a joy to the eye as well as to walk on, but it calls for very well prepared soil and also for constant, intelligent attention. Bent grasses will do well, in sun or partial shade, but are not in any sense shady-spot sorts. The soil should be well supplied with thoroughly rotted manure and receive a good application of a balanced complete fertilizer before planting time. In sowing use about 1 lb. of seed per 250 sq. ft.; if stolons are used fit the soil and broadcast them at the rate of 25 sq. ft. of stolons per 200 sq. ft. of area. They must then be covered lightly with soil, rotted and watered.

Bent grass seed is part imported, especially from Germany, and part domestic, being produced mainly in the Pacific N.W. and in Rhode Island. The production of stolons is purely a domestic activity, and several improved strains have been developed, including the Metropolitan and the Washington. Botanically, the principal bent grass species are the following:

A. palustris (Redtop), a European grass now naturalized in N. America and considerably used in pasture and somewhat in lawn-seed mixtures.

capillaris (Rhode-Island Bent), similar to redtop, but smaller and with redder panicles. It is a good lawn grass, particularly in more acid soils than blue grass will stand. Sulphate of ammonia at the rate of 5 lbs. per 1000 sq. ft., applied before the seed is sown, is a helpful stimulant.

maritima (Creeping Bent) is the type to which the best of the fine-lawn bent grasses

belong. It is smaller and more stoloniferous in habit than redtop. Both it and Rhode-Island bent withstand close cutting well.

nebulosa (Cloud Grass), a dwarf annual species with panicles 6 in. long, composed of many fine branches, and *A. retrofracta*, a taller annual, to 2 ft., with leaves 8 in. long, and 1-ft. panicles with hair-like branches are good ornamental subjects. *A. hiemalis* (Hair or Silk Grass) is a perennial ornamental to 2 ft., with short, narrow, basal leaves and delicate purplish panicles up to 1 ft. long.

See also LAWN and ORNAMENTAL GRASSES.

BENZOIN (ben'-zoin). Deciduous or evergreen aromatic shrubs or trees, native in Asia and N. America, belonging to the Laurel Family. Only one or two of the nearly 60 known species are hardy in cold regions. *B. aestivale* (Spicebush, Benjamin-Bush, Fever-bush, Wild Allspice) is a hardy, deciduous shrub to 15 ft., growing in moist places from New England S. Flowers are minus petals but numerous enough to be conspicuous in spring before the leaves. The plant is attractive again in fall with its clear yellow leaves and scarlet fruits. *B. grandifolium* is a large evergreen shrub or tree from China, not hardy N. Has large lustrous leaves and black fruit. *B. obtusifolium* is a tall and spreading shrub with handsome lobed leaves, native of Japan and Korea and hardy in Mass. in sheltered places.

BERBERIDACEAE (bur-ber-i-day'-see-ee). Botanical name of the Barberry Family, a group of herbs or shrubs, many of them ornamental, native to the N. hemisphere. Their spiny stems, black, red·or yellow berries and attractive small leaves, often held late into the winter, make them widely popular for hedges. The majority are deciduous and hardy; the evergreen kinds are not hardy. One genus, Berberis, includes species that are host-plants for the fungus causing wheat rust; the elimination of these species is an important step in its control. Principal genera are Berberis, Mahonia, Nandina, Epimedium, Podophyllum.

BERBERIDOPIS (bur-ber-i-dop'-sis). Coral-plant. An ornamental evergreen shrub from Chili with climbing habit. A good plant for the cool greenhouse and for outdoor planting in warm-temperate regions. Only one species is known, B.

corallina. It has glossy prickly leaves, and bears racemes of drooping coral-red flowers. Propagation is by cuttings of growing shoots or by layers.

BERBERIS (bur-ber'-is). A genus of about 175 species of evergreen and deciduous spiny shrubs. Valued in gardens for their good habit, handsome foliage and attractive fruit. See BARBERRY.

BERCHEMIA (bur-kee'-mi-ah). Deciduous twining shrubs of the Buckthorn Family. They are of slender habit with graceful foliage, suitable for trellis-work in a sunny place, but not reliably hardy North. The flowers—greenish-white in terminal panicles—appear rather insignificant, but the berries are attractive. *B. racemosa,* a native of Japan, is the hardiest and runs up to about 15 ft. The berries change from green to red to black. *B. scandens* (Supple Jack), a native of the S. States, has bluish-black fruit.

BERGAMOT (bur'-gah-mot). Common name for *Citrus bergamia,* grown in Europe for its perfume-yielding oil, and in the U. S. as a curiosity. Wild-bergamot is another common name for Horse-mint (*Monarda fistulosa*).

BERGAMOT MINT. Common name for *Mentha citrata,* a European perennial herb naturalized in N. America. The odor of its foliage resembles that of bergamot. See MENTHA and MINT.

BERGENIA (ber-jee'-ni-ah). A genus of hardy perennial herbs closely related and quite similar to the Saxifrages, but with much larger leaves. They rapidly increase, when planted in the border, into large clumps or colonies. The large flowers are pink or white, and come quite early in the spring. The leaves are almost evergreen and make good points of accent when planted at corners. They will grow well in ordinary garden soil and are increased by seed or division.

Most species have large, fleshy, shining, almost evergreen leaves, and clear rose flowers on stems 1 ft. or more tall, often partly hidden by the lush foliage. Natives of Asia, they are often listed as Saxifraga or Megasea.

BERGEROCACTUS (bur'-jur-oh-kaktus). A genus of cacti represented by a single species, *B. emoryi.* Found in small groups, near the coast and border of San Diego County, Calif., and extending into Lower California, it is usually of low growth but sometimes forms thickets up to 8 ft. high. Its light bright-green color is modified by the completely enveloping yellow spines. The blossoms appear along the side of the stem, greenish yellow in color. The dry fruit, resembling a chestnut bur, is persistent, so that buds, blossoms and fruit are found together. Easily cultivated, but not particularly desirable in the garden unless as part of a large collection. See also CACTUS.

BERMUDA GRASS. The common name for *Cynodon dactylon,* a creeping perennial grass that grows from seed but spreads by means of runners or stolons. The narrow leaves, to 2 in. long, are rough on top. Bermuda Grass might be called the "Kentucky blue grass of the S.," for it is one of the most important pasture and lawn grasses for that region.

Preferring a fertile, rather heavy soil that is not too wet, but able to grow on light sand and to stand a more alkaline condition than most crops, it thrives throughout the hot weather but cannot survive hard freezing. Lawns can be started from stolon cuttings (as is done with bent grass, which see), but seeding is preferable, using 25 to 30 lbs. per acre, or 4 lbs. or more per 1000 sq. ft. The soil should be thoroughly warm and well prepared, and the seed, after being broadcast, should be covered very lightly.

Established from Va. southward and westward to Ariz. and Calif., Bermuda grass is widely used for athletic fields and golf courses as well as lawns, but owing to its persistent character in frost-free sections it sometimes becomes a bad weed in cultivated fields; however, it can be killed by shading or crowding out by other crops.

See also LAWN.

BERMUDA LILY. A name given to *Lilium harrisi,* a strain of *L. longiflorum,* var. *eximium.* The bulbs are grown in Bermuda, and forced in U. S. greenhouses. See LILY.

BERRY. A term commonly and loosely applied to a number of different kinds of small, pulpy, often compound fruits. Examples are: strawberry—which is a swollen "receptacle" on the outside of which the partly exposed seeds (achenes) are embedded; blackberry—a union of many small fruits or "drupelets"; mulberry—resembling the blackberry but actually composed of flesh-covered achenes; checkerberry (or wintergreen)—a swollen calyx

Plate 4.   BERRIES—BETTER THAN YOU BUY

Top: The high-bush blueberry, a native shrub with delicious fruit, that should be grown in more gardens. Left: Red raspberries—a wealth of fragrant lusciousness. Center right: Vine-ripened strawberries develop maximum flavor. Lower left: Strawberries ripen earlier in a coldframe. Lower right: Blackberries of melting richness.

containing seeds; coffee—a one- to three-seeded, cherry-like fruit or drupe; and cereal grains, such as rice, wheat, etc.

Botanically, the term is limited to fruits with thin skin, fleshy throughout, developed from one pistil and containing one or more seeds, but no "stone." By such definition, currant, grape, blueberry, tomato—and even banana (!) are true berries. See FRUIT.

BERRY-BEARING PLANTS. In garden making this term is used to designate in particular those ornamentals which produce their seed within brightly colored seed vessels and are therefore in many cases decorative throughout the winter; that is, it does not apply to the edible bush fruits of the garden although they, too, are "berry bearing." The garden use of berry-bearing shrubs and small trees has grown with the developing appreciation of their value in winter landscapes and also with the increasing interest in bird life and its conservation until it is now usual for nursery catalogs to list the type and color of berry yielded by each as well as the period of bloom. Not all produce showy flowers, but most of them are sufficiently attractive to warrant their generous use in shrubbery plantings for their bloom as well as for their colorful berries; and they are a necessity in plantings for autumn effects.

According to whether the berries are especially favored by birds for food or are merely decorative, these plants fall into two groups. It is an advantage to the garden effect that the berries of some are almost never eaten by birds; these retain their decorative quality all winter. But because of the importance of bird-life conservation to gardeners as well as to farmers, it is short-sighted to use only those which the birds do not like. A few may go into prominent places where all-winter color is greatly desired, but in backgrounds and thickets those which provide well for birds are more desirable.

Most notable of these are the dogwood or cornel group, the flowering dogwood being the finest native berry-bearing tree. Native hawthorns, viburnums, chokeberries, June-berries or shadbush, buckthorn and bayberry all include varieties that will provide growth from low up to 20 ft. in height. All wild or species roses have bright fruits, many large and brilliant in color. And all barberries are richly bespangled with their vivid berries.

See also EVERGREEN GARDEN; HEDGE; LANDSCAPING: NATURALIZING; PLANTS FOR SPECIAL PURPOSES; ROADSIDE PLANTING; WILD GARDEN; BIRDS IN THE GARDEN.

BERRY (or **BULBLET**) **BLADDER FERN.** Common names for *Cystopteris bulbifera,* a hardy garden species of fern.

BERTOLONIA (ber-toh-loh'-ni-ah). Dwarf herbs of S. America, sometimes grown in the warm greenhouse for their beautifully marked leaves, young plants being more colorful than old ones. To be seen at their best they require dense shade and a close moist atmosphere; often the only way to provide the proper conditions is to place them under a bell-glass. They thrive in a soil of equal parts peat, leafmold, and sand. Propagation is by cuttings. *B. maculata* and *B. marmorata* are the principal species, and several hybrids with even more handsome leaves than these have been raised in Europe.

BESCHORNERIA (be-shohr-nee'-ri-ah). A genus of succulent desert plants of the Amaryllis Family, native to Mexico and related to and resembling the agave. The rough-edged leaves are covered with a whitish bloom, and rise from a tuberous rootstock forming a striking rosette. Reddish-green flowers are borne on erect stems to 6 ft. or so tall. The several species, which are rather confused, succeed well in S. Calif. and other warm, dry sections, where they bloom every year. In colder regions, treated as greenhouse plants, they flower only at long intervals. They call for the same treatment as agaves, but will stand a soil made richer with humus and bonemeal.

BESSERA (bes'-er-ah) *elegans.* A name under which the native bulbous plant *Milla biflora* (which see) is often grown and sold. The common name is Mexican Star.

BETA (bee'-tah). Beet. A genus of Old-World herbs, mostly annual and biennial, as grown for their edible roots or foliage. The most important species (*B. vulgaris*), naturally a perennial, has four main botanical varieties: *crassa* (Beet-root), grown for its thick roots used as a vegetable or, commercially, as a source of sugar; *cruenta* (Victoria or Foliage Beets), small-rooted plants with large, brilliantly colored foliage; *cicla* (Swiss chard), small-rooted plants whose large thick-stemmed leaves are used as "greens"; and *macrorhiza* (Mangel-wurzel), enormous-rooted plants grown for cattle feeding.

BETHLEHEM-SAGE. Common name for *Pulmonaria saccharata,* a species of Lungwort. Growing to 1½ ft., it has white spotted leaves and flowers described as whitish- or reddish-violet.

BETONY (bet'-oh-ni). One common name for species of Stachys (which see), a genus of colorful herbs of the Mint Family; and especially for *S. officinalis.* Wood-betony is another name for the Lousewort (*Pedicularis canadensis*), a group of herbs of the Figwort Family. See PEDICULARIS.

BETULA (bet'-eu-lah). A group of hardy, but mostly short-lived, deciduous trees of distinct decorative value. Many have conspicuous bark and characteristic catkins. See BIRCH.

BETULACEAE (bet-eu-lay'-see-ee). Botanical name of the Birch Family, a group of hardy trees native to the cooler portions of the N. Temperate zone and prominent as producers of timber, some edible fruits and medicinal oils and, in many cases, as ornamental forms. One or two species of the genus Betula (Birch) are planted extensively as ornamentals; Carpinus is the ornamental Hornbeam, a small tree with smooth, fluted bark; Ostrya is the Hop-hornbeam or Ironwood; Corylus (Hazlenut) includes. both ornamental shrubs and nut producers.

BICHLORIDE OF MERCURY. A virulent poison used as a garden disinfectant for seeds, tools, etc., in gardening; also called corrosive sublimate (which see). See also MERCURY COMPOUNDS.

BIDENS (by'-denz). Plants of this genus of the Composite Family, variously called Bur-marigold, Stick-tights and Tickseed, are closely related to Cosmos, and resemble it in having divided leaves and clustered heads with yellow or white ray flowers. As they are of weedy growth, they are seldom used in the flower garden. In the wild they grow principally in moist places throughout N. America, springing up readily from seed. *B. ferulaefolia* (Fern-leaved Bidens) is an annual of Mexico, with branching, divided leaves and bright-yellow flowers less than 1 in. across.

BIENNIAL. A plant which, started from seed, requires two seasons to come to maturity. The first year it makes top growth, and usually, a fleshy root. The second year it produces flowers and seed, living on the food stored up in the root and then dying. Some biennials will bloom the first year if sown early enough indoors or in a hotbed. Some perennials are so short-lived that they virtually become biennial when cultivated. Examples of typical biennials are Canterbury bells, foxglove, pansy, hollyhock, parsnip and cabbage. In sections where winter-killing or rotting of the crowns is not feared, biennials may be grown in the open garden from seed to maturity, seed being sown in June or July and seedlings transplanted later to permanent locations. As cold weather arrives a loose mulch of leaves or straw should be given, though where the winter rosette of leaves is formed these must be protected from the matting of the mulch, by placing twigs or berry baskets under it. Where mulching is impracticable, plants can be wintered in a coldframe. Biennials as a class require no different culture from that given other plants; they can be treated as annuals if desired and started early.

Compare ANNUAL and PERENNIAL.

BIGNONIA (big-noh'-ni-ah). A genus formerly comprising several species, but now reduced to only one, *B. capreolata* (Cross-vine or Trumpet-flower), an evergreen climber growing to 50 ft. or more. It is found from Va. south and west, but will grow considerably further north as a trailing plant. The rather stiff leaves end in a branched tendril, which clings by means of small disks. In flower it is a very showy vine with large clusters of yellowish-red tubular blossoms in early summer. It is a very good wall plant, and as a robust trailer would show to advantage among boulders, in a well-drained position.

As a trained plant on a wall it should be pruned hard after flowering; later some of the weakest shoots should be thinned out. It is propagated by cuttings of half-ripened wood, and by layering.

Two plants well known in cultivation as Bignonias are the Cats-claw (*Doxantha unguis-cati,* formerly *Bignonia tweediana*) and *Pyrostegia ignea,* formerly *B. venusta.* These are vigorous vines with showy flowers, but they can be grown in the N. only under glass.

BIGNONIACEAE (big-noh-ni-ay'-see-ee). Botanical name of the Bignonia or Trumpet-creeper Family, a large group of trees, shrubs and woody vines, characterized in most cases by the beauty and profusion of the large, showy, often trumpet-shaped flowers. Preferring a moist, rich soil, members of the family are found chiefly in the tropics, but a few genera extend into temperate climates. Bignonia and Tecoma are evergreen vines extensively used as ornamentals, most species of Bignonia being hot-house climbers. Other cultivated genera are Catalpa, Doxantha, Pyrostegia, Pandorea, Eccremocarpus, Incarvillea, Crescentia (Calabashtree), Campsis and the handsome-foliaged Spathodea and Jacaranda.

BIG TREE. The name commonly given to *Sequoia gigantea,* a giant W. Coast member of the Pine Family. Can be grown, if protected, to 30 ft. or more in Central States and possibly lower N. Y. See SEQUOIA.

BILBERRY. Common name for species of Vaccinium, Bog Bilberry being applied to *V. uliginosum,* and Dwarf Bilberry to *V. caespitosum.*

BILLARDIERA (bi-lahr-di-ee'-rah). Apple-berry. Evergreen climbing shrubs with twining stems, native of Australia. Ornamental plants for greenhouse culture, and can be grown outside in warm climates. The fruit is a fleshy, blue edible berry. Propagated by seeds and cuttings.

B. scandens bears flowers cream to purple, sometimes two together; *B. longiflora* bears flowers solitary, greenish-yellow changing to purple; *B. cymosa* bears violet-blue flowers in clusters.

BILLBERGIA (bil-bur'-ji-ah). A genus of herbaceous epiphytes (air-plants) of tropical America, belonging to the Pineapple Family. Several species are grown in warm greenhouses, and also make good house plants. They thrive in a mixture of fern-fibre and sphagnum moss with broken charcoal, and require an abundance of water during the summer. They have long stiff leaves, usually spiny, in basal rosettes, and showy flowers mostly with colorful bracts. Propagated by suckers.

PRINCIPAL SPECIES

B. liboniana has spiny green leaves and upright spikes of red and blue flowers, without showy bracts.

moreli has green leaves, with few spiny teeth, and drooping spikes of red and blue flowers with long red bracts.

nutans has narrow long-pointed leaves and a loose drooping cluster of nodding green and blue flowers with red bracts.

pyramidalis has finely-toothed leaves to 3 ft. long, and a mealy erect flower-cluster

composed of red violet-tipped flowers with red bracts.

sanderiana has leathery leaves 1 ft. long, and nodding racemes of green blue-tipped flowers and rose bracts.

speciosa has strap-shaped green leaves, striped on the back, 2 ft. long, with large and loose drooping clusters of pale-green blue-tipped flowers and rosy bracts.

zebrina has leaves to 3 ft. long, spotted and banded with gray-white, and greenish-yellow flowers with salmon-pink bracts.

BILLBUGS. Black or clay-colored beetles with long slender snouts, injurious to corn, chiefly in the S. The larvae are dirty white grubs with brown heads. Corn billbugs eat holes across the leaves, causing the stalks to become distorted and dwarfed. They can be controlled by crop rotation. Grass and rush billbugs, common through grassy and lowland areas, feed on corn planted there. Where they are bad do not plant corn on newly plowed sod land.

BINDING PLANTS. A varied group of plants which, by reason of their underground running stems, or above-ground creeping and often rooting stems, are valuable in binding loose shifting sands and light soils subject to erosion.

In Europe and along sections of our own coasts, Beach-grass (Ammophila) has done wonders in holding shifting sands in place. Creeping Willow (*Salix repens*) is equally effective under the same conditions. The White Willow (*S. alba*) has been used to advantage in checking sliding banks along streams, and may be established by sticking large pieces of stem into the banks to take root.

In dry, sandy regions Gray Birch and Pitch Pine are good. Black Locust is one of the most effective plants to use in almost any kind of soil subject to erosion. For dry banks, Rose-acacia and other shrubby plants of the Pea Family, are both effective and decorative; and almost any shrub of spreading habit may be used where the soil is not too dry. Vines such as Kudzu, Japanese Honeysuckle, Bittersweet, and Virginia Creeper are first rate to cover large slopes. In sandy areas bearberry and heather are useful and attractive. Many other binding plants are available.

BINDWEED. Common name for the genus Convolvulus, which includes some troublesome weeds, as well as a few species resembling Morning-glories that are sometimes planted in gardens, hanging baskets, etc. These should be watched and kept from spreading too much.

BIO-DYNAMIC GARDENING AND FARMING. A name given to a system of soil and plant management originated in Europe by Dr. Rudolf Steiner and being taught and advocated by Dr. Ehrenfried Pfeiffer, of Switzerland, and disciples of the system in various parts of the world. In the U. S. considerable work has been done by, and information can be obtained from, Mr. Frederick Heckel, Threefold Farm, Spring Valley, N. Y.

The system is built around the concept that any farm or garden is a biological, organic unit in which all elements involved in its operation—as cropping, tillage, manuring, protection against pests and diseases, management of livestock, etc.—are interrelated and interdependent, rather than a series of unconnected processes. It is the contention of advocates of bio-dynamic methods that when a garden or farm is operated on that basis, "it will be seen that that which is biologically correct, is also economically the most profitable." Also that only through a thoroughly "natural" type of husbandry such as this can lands now fertile and productive be maintained in that condition and lands that have been brought to an infertile state through misuse and mismanagement, be restored to a productive condition.

Bio-dynamic agriculture does not introduce any methods new or contrary to principles long accepted as advisable; but it does carry certain practices much farther, and, at the same time, it places no dependence upon the use of inorganic chemicals, either as fertilizers or spray materials. Its most fundamental consideration is the maintenance of the productive life and "health" of the soil through the constant addition of humus. And to the bio-dynamic gardener humus means a very carefully and systematicaly prepared product. While he emphasizes the great importance and value of manures as a source of humus, he insists that they shall be applied to the land only when thoroughly "ripened" by means of careful composting. Hence the compost heap, with its proper construction and handling (including its treatment with certain organic preparations or "leavens" designed to hasten its ripening) and its correct use in relation to the crops that make up a desirable rotation, becomes perhaps the most vital single factor in the bio-dynamic garden or farm.

Another carefully considered factor is crop rotation; still another is the influence different plants have on one another when grown in close proximity. Thus kohlrabi is said to be harmful to tomatoes grown close by; radishes are benefited by a companion crop of chervil, or of lettuce; leeks and celery, carrots and peas, cucumbers and corn, onions and beets are other mutually beneficial combinations. And this type of farming goes farther, directing the way in which crops shall be fed to cattle and other animals so that they, too, shall share the benefits of a "natural" progression from the soil and back to it again.

The logical approach of bio-dynamic arguments is suggested by the following "four chief causes for trouble in an orchard" as noted in a textbook on the subject: "(1) Too strong fertilizing, especially if this has been done with fresh, raw manure; (2) too thick a stand of tree, which permits too little light and too little movement of air; (3) the wrong tree stock for the tree in question; (4) the use of a variety of fruit tree on a soil and in a climate to which it is not suited." Certainly there is nothing there to antagonize any good fruit grower as measured by commonly accepted standards. However, as the proponents of this type of farming point out, "the farmer who wants to convert his farm in accordance with the new bio-dynamic points of view has first to work on himself, to learn to think along different lines." And the same thing would apply to the gardener who wants to see what this theory might do for him. Actually, given willingness to proceed slowly and gradually, the steps in a bio-dynamic program do not sound difficult when summed up as follows:

First, gather together and carefully nurture all organic fertilizer material at hand, to insure the production of humus in the soil. Next, establish and practice a correct, soil-conserving crop rotation. Third, work to improve any livestock kept, since these are the source of future "raw material" and their fitness carries on through the manure they produce. Finally, develop or reshape if necessary the whole biological unity of the garden (or farm) through the harmonious practice of the foregoing steps. In short, make of the gardening operations a big, unified, policy of soil conservation.

BIOLOGICAL CONTROL. The forces of nature, left to themselves, tend to balance each other. If injurious insects increase abnormally in a region over a period of years, certain natural forces, such as climatic conditions, parasitic and predacious insects, birds, and fungous diseases, ultimately get to work and reduce the population to normal or subnormal numbers for a time. The ten-year cycle of tent-caterpillar infestation in the N.E. is a familiar example of such alternating gradual increase and sudden reduction. When man employs or fosters natural agencies in his warfare against insects and diseases, he is said to be practicing the "biological method of control." The use of certain fungi to fight citrus whitefly, of the lady-beetle against cottony cushion scale on citrus plants, of the so-called "milky disease" of Japanese beetle larvae in the control of that pest, and of the ground beetle against the gypsy moth are a few successful examples of this type of control. See also INSECTS, BENEFICIAL.

BIOTA (by'-oh-tah). Former name for *Thuja orientalis,* a species of Arborvitae (which see), still used in nursery catalogs. The so-called Biotas are less hardy than the American Arborvitae (*T. occidentalis*) but include a number of popular varieties showing a wide diversity of form and foliage color.

BIRCH. Common name for the genus Betula, of about 28 species of hardy deciduous trees generally of tall and narrow form. The ten native species and their horticultural varieties are all effectively used in the garden plan. Their delicate flexible branches and conspicuous bark, ranging from white through shades of orange to black, give them an individual and distinctive charm in the dormant season.

As a background they combine well with flowers of the woodland type and particularly with a naturalistic rockery. All young birches have dark-colored bark; the characteristic colors do not mature until the trees are several years old.

In landscape planting it is always appropriate to place them near water. There can hardly be a more charming picture than the reflection of a birch with its autumn gold. Nature often crowds them so closely along both sides of a woodland road that their white boles have the effect of a colonnade and in autumn it becomes a bower of golden light. The suggestions found in the natural landscape may be effectively applied in the home grounds by using birches—singly or in groups—to mark entrances or curves in a drive where they are especially helpful at night. Planted against an evergreen background they create a stimulating picture at any season.

Most of the birches thrive in moist sandy loam with sandy or rocky subsoil, some others in dry locations. All bear catkins and soft cones and are propagated by seed sown or stratified in sandy soil; also by layers or greenwood cuttings under glass and by grafting or budding. The genus supplies the name for the Birch Family (*Betulaceae*), to which belong also the Hazelnut, Alder and Hornbeam.

ENEMIES. Several leaf diseases are common but not serious; wood-decays attack old trees; European canker (caused by a fungus) produces a large open canker with concentric rings of dead callus. It is serious only in weak, unthrifty trees, so feed them properly and dress any wounds. Presence of the bronze birch borer is indicated by dying tops and tortuous galleries formed underneath the bark. Dead or dying trees or parts of trees should be cut and burned in early spring before the beetles emerge. Later spraying with lead arsenate may help. The recently-introduced European birch sawfly or leaf miner has spread rapidly and may defoliate many kinds of birches. Since the larval and egg stages occur within the leaves, control is difficult. Spray choice specimen trees with nicotine-sulphate 1-800, without soap, weekly during

WEEPING BIRCH
One of the many and varied forms of birch, useful as a specimen tree.

the first and second generations. (In the E. this means from the middle of May to about the first of July.) About every 11 years in the N. States the birch leaf skeletonizer defoliates many trees. Spray with lead arsenate about the middle of August.

PRINCIPAL SPECIES

B. papyrifera (Canoe or Paper Birch) grows to large size, has chalky white bark and thick, dark-green leaves, and is probably the most showy; var. *occidentalis* has orange or brown bark.

pendula (European White Birch) grows to 60 ft. with drooping branches and a white bark that peels easily. There is a var. *fastigiata* of narrow columnar form and another, *gracilis*, with finely dissected leaves.

nigra (Red or River Birch) is a moisture-loving species with a glowing, ragged, orange bark. It likes the rocky places beside streams and in youth is usually a dense growth of small branches.

lenta (Sweet or Cherry Birch) grows with a clean smooth dark bark like that of the garden cherry. It is often wide branching with a high head, giving shade but admitting sun and air below.

lutea (Yellow Birch), which often attains large size in the wild, has a very attractive frayed bark, silvery without but in orange shades where it peels.

maximowicziana may attain great size. It has unusually large leaves (to 6 in.), a smooth orange bark and reddish-brown twigs. Its cones are about 3 in. long. Because of its rapid growth and hardiness it is a valuable lawn tree.

From the Artic region comes the exceedingly hardy species *nana*, a little birch that lies flat against the soil and is useful in cool rockeries because of the slowness of its growth.

BIRCH FAMILY. Common name of the Betulaceae (which see), a family of cold-climate trees composed of the Ironwoods (Ostrya), Birches (Betula), Hazelnuts (Corylus), and Hornbeams (Carpinus).

BIRD-FLOWER. Name sometimes given to *Heterotoma lobelioides,* a Mexican perennial with flowers of yellow and orange.

BIRD - OF - PARADISE FLOWER. Common name for *Strelitzia reginae,* a perennial herb of S. Africa whose highly colored, oddly shaped flowers resemble a bird

JAPANESE BIRCH
White bark and slender branches characterize this tree, which is beautiful at all seasons.

taking flight. Often featured in florists' windows and at flower shows, but not much grown outside of Calif.

BIRDS-EYES. Common name for *Gilia tricolor,* annual Calif. herbs bearing flowers of lilac, yellow and purple. The name is also given to *Veronica chamaedrys,* the Germander Speedwell.

BIRDSFOOT TREFOIL. A common name for *Lotus corniculatus,* a perennial leguminous plant of Europe and Asia, sometimes grown for forage.

BIRDSFOOT VIOLET. Common name for *Viola pedata,* a native species with fragrant flowers with dark upper and pale lower petals, found from Mass. and Minn. to Fla. See VIOLET.

BIRDS IN THE GARDEN. The lure of growing things—especially in gardens—is largely esthetic. The esthetic value of birds—with their sprightly actions, their vigorous, usually pleasing songs and their dashing colors—cannot fail to attract attention and add to the pleasure of a garden. Birds add charm and character to even the smallest plot, their subtle instincts often astounding the intelligence of observers. They also interest by posing, preening, courting, mating, and nesting within the garden.

But efforts should be made to attract and protect these feathered creatures for economic reasons as well as for their charm and beauty. No one is in a better position than the gardener to appreciate the vast contribution birds make to our economic life. Insects form a large part of avian sustenance and birds are most numerous and active just at those times when harmful insects are at their height. They search every plant, tree and shrub meticulously and materially check the rising tide of harmful insect life. Birds also consume large quantities of weed seeds at a time when fall winds threaten to broadcast them over the land. Furthermore small rodents troublesome in the garden form a large part of the diet of birds of prey. For all these reasons the service of birds in the interest of mankind and their appeal to his affections must be acknowledged by the gardener.

Protecting the Birds

Before birds are encouraged to enter the garden they must be assured all possible protection. They are exceedingly wary and individual specimens that are molested quickly communicate their caution to an entire flock. Months may pass before birds of some species will trespass where one of their number has been killed or injured.

The most effectual type of protection is a fence around the entire garden. It will serve a double purpose if it is set upon a 4 in. curb of concrete extending at least 6 in. into the ground. Where this is not practical, heavy gauge, heavily galvanized wire may extend into the ground. With four rows of barbed wire attached to supports projecting outward horizontally or diagonally from the top of the posts, such a fence will exclude both digging and climbing animals. If it is impossible to provide a fence, tree guards should be placed around all trees and nest-box posts. These guards made of sheet metal should extend 8 in. or more from the tree in an inverted cone shape and be placed about 6 ft. above the ground.

Cats, boys with sling-shots and guns, red squirrels, and snakes are the most troublesome enemies of birds in the garden. Birds of prey are active chiefly in rural sections. The abundance and voracious habits of some small birds frequently present serious local problems; the English sparrow and European starling are common offenders.

Estimates place the number of birds killed annually by each house cat at 50;

the toll taken by half-wild cats doubtless is many times as heavy. Cats should never be allowed to run at large in gardens. Those that cannot be confined may wear a small bell attached to the collar to warn birds of their approach.

The persecution of birds by boys may be overcome by education. Once boys learn the value of birds and come to know their interesting habits, they will love live birds rather than dead ones.

English sparrows (which as an "introduced" foreign species have become a nuisance) can be eradicated or driven away by breaking up their nests before they are completed, setting baited wire traps, or scattering poison grain. Unpoisoned grain should be scattered in the same place for several days until the sparrows are attracted to it before setting the poison grain. There is then less chance of poisoning other birds. Clean up carefully any remaining poison so other birds cannot get it after the sparrows are disposed of. This entire process should be detailed to responsible hands and children should have no part in it.

The European starling is generally regarded with suspicion but the harm it does by molesting other birds is negligible compared with the good it does in destroying insects. Its tendencies for harm result chiefly from its flocking habit where it preys upon small fruits. It also usurps nesting sites of many native song-birds. Providing nesting boxes (for other birds) with entrances not larger than 1½ in. in diameter will prevent starlings from entering. They are easily frightened and a clap of the hands or the discharge of a gun is usually sufficient to teach them to shun the garden. There are local areas at present where they are detrimental to horticulture but steps to eradicate them are not recommended except when they become bold. Leaflet No. 61 entitled "English Sparrow Control" published by the U. S. Biological Survey, Washington, D. C., contains detailed information for exterminating undesirable birds.

The extensive use of poisonous insecticides is also taking its toll of our birds. Many dead ones are found in rainy weather after spraying programs have been conducted over wide areas. No statistics are available regarding the number of fatalities but the evidence is enough to entitle the subject to consideration. The use of the various effective non-poisonous insecticides now available is therefore recommended wherever practical. Nicotine in solutions used for spraying plants is not fatal to birds.

ATTRACTING BIRDS TO THE GARDEN

Once birds are given protection from their enemies they are as quick to rely upon the friendship of man as they were to elude him before. Thus the bird population can be increased from year to year where the environment is congenial. Any doubt that individual birds return to the same locality from year to year may be dismissed. Investigations by the Biological Survey show that many birds return three and four years to the same stations while some return six or even eight years. Water and food are the most potent attractions and bird life is always abundant where these factors are assured.

Water for drinking may be supplied in shallow pans deepening gradually toward the center, but cement or clay is better material for the bird-bath as metal presents too smooth a surface for secure footing. The bath should be placed in the open away from shrubs or trees that might harbor enemies. Elevated positions are to be preferred, but the bath may be placed on the ground if in the open. The nesting population of the garden especially will increase where a constant supply of water is assured.

The birds' food supply in the garden may be classed as (a) artificial and (b) natural. The simplest types of artificial food accepted by all birds are bread crumbs and small grains. Others include suet, meat scraps, coconut meat, nut meats (especially peanuts), cereals, peppers and a large variety of vegetable seeds. Many and various devices are on the market for offering these foods to the birds. A food-shelf either attached at a window-sill or supported on a short pole is practical, though at times wind and rain will sweep food from the shelf. A roof of some sort to make a kind of "feeding house" will protect the food as well as provide shelter for the birds. Another type is set upon a pivot and equipped with a vane so that it is turned by the wind, the opening thus being kept on the leeward side. A very simple feeder can be easily made from a coconut by boring a 1½ in. hole at one end. Leave the meat in the shell and scatter seeds inside,

fasten a wire around it, and support it from the limb of a tree.

Artificial foods are taken readily in winter when other types of food are scarce, but summer feeding presents other problems. Wild small fruits and weed seeds form a large part of the birds' diet whenever they are available. But gardens and vacant lots in urban localities are often so thoroughly cultivated or cleared of wild growth that these natural sources of supply are entirely eliminated. Birds especially enjoy uncultivated headlands along fences and property lines. Hedgerows of wild fruits and flowering shrubs will furnish food as well as nesting sites. Providing food for seed-eating birds presents some difficulty; they feed upon weeds which, obviously, are not cultivated. However there are a number of annuals which will prove attractive to this group if they can be sown in out-of-the-way corners and allowed to go to seed. These are zinnia, bee balm (Monarda), sunflower, centaureas, millet, asters, poppies, portulaca, myosotis, and amaranthus. Other annuals adapted to local conditions may be added to this list by observing birds as they feed upon the plants. Cedars, pines, ashes, alders, larches and birches are the trees most attractive to the seed-eating birds.

Catering to the needs and desires of fruit-eating birds is most important in gardens where fruit trees and small fruits are cultivated and must be protected. The raids of birds in gardens that have only one or two fruit trees are far more disastrous than those in orchards. The orchard provides many trees and generally the stealing is scattered over the whole area, whereas in the garden, one tree is usually stripped when the fruit is half ripe.

The following fruit trees and shrubs (listed in the order of their value) will furnish food for the birds and help to protect cultivated trees: Mulberry, bayberry, blackberry, honeysuckle (*Lonicera tatarica* and others), wild grape, blueberry, sumac, dogwood, blackhaw (*Viburnum*), elder, dwarf apples, hawthorn, sassafras, holly, mountain-ash, and spicebush. The widely planted Japanese barberry (*Berberis thunbergi*) frequently advocated by nurserymen as providing bird food is actually of little value for this purpose. Wild cherries are excellent bird food, but in many sections the trees are unpopular as hosts for tent caterpillars. In selecting varieties to protect cultivated fruits, try to use the wild forms of the same kinds that are cultivated and choose those that ripen *earlier* than the cultivated crops if possible. Additional information on feeding birds may be obtained from Farmers Bulletins 621 and 1644 issued by the U. S. Department of Agriculture.

NESTING AND NEST BOXES

Birds arrive from the South in large flocks in the spring. The males of many species come several days in advance of the females and promptly begin to look about for nesting sites and mates. As they find mates they abandon the flock and find a territory of one half acre or more to which they lay claim. They are at this time more evenly distributed over the land and many birds will fight to drive others of the same species from the land that they have laid claim to. This "claim" will be their nesting site, and if a garden offers the proper protection, water, and food it will probably have several bird tenants.

It is during the nesting season that the greatest mortality occurs. Therefore the utmost precaution for the birds' protection should be exercised at this time. The growing nestlings consume enormous quantities of insects which are generally gathered from a comparatively small area around the nest. Hence the garden with several nests will reap the greatest benefits.

Birds that prefer holes in trees for nesting can be induced to accept nesting boxes. Bluebirds, house wrens, swallows, woodpeckers, and chickadees are some of the common birds that nest in bird houses. The boxes, which should be about 6 by 6 by 8 in. with a round hole 1½ in. in diameter for the entrance, may be placed in trees or on poles at least 6 ft. in height. Houses for purple martins may contain many compartments. They are placed in the open on poles 10 or 12 ft. in height. Boxes for other birds should have but one compartment.

Many types of bird houses are offered for sale or may be made at home without difficulty. The roof should pitch sharply, the eaves should extend well beyond the box, and the entrance should be placed well up under the eaves.

Several species will nest about buildings, among them phoebes, chimney swifts, robins, barn swallows, and owls. Owls usually select cavities in trees but no specific method can be given to induce owls to nest about the garden. However, they prefer to nest and live close to the habitations of man. They are especially valuable in the garden, as moles, field mice and other small rodents form the greater part of their diet.

Cedars and other coniferous trees are preferred by tree-nesting birds which always select a dense growth in which to hide their nests. Closely planted trees and shrubs will not fail to attract them.

Ground-nesting birds like grassy fields and unless the garden is a large one it is not likely to offer sites favorable to this class. Song sparrows will accept conditions offered in the garden more readily than other ground-nesting birds. As many as three families of song sparrows are often found in a garden where grass and low shrubs are allowed to grow wild along the borders.

SPECIES OF BIRDS COMMON IN GARDENS

The early settlers in America are largely responsible for naming many of our native birds and the names they gave, while often misleading, have become as firmly fixed as the common name of many garden flowers. Thus the robin is not really a robin but rather a true thrush. There are 75 families containing more than 800 species of birds found in the United States. Seven families are classed as shore birds; 5 as game birds; 5 as birds of prey; and 36 as land birds.

The land birds are of the greatest importance to the garden; from 60 to 75 different species may be identified in the average garden throughout the four seasons of a year.

The cuckoos are evenly distributed over their geographical range. They usually keep out of sight but their strange though well-known notes always betray (even though they do not reveal) their presence. They are highly beneficial, feeding largely on caterpillars of the hairy type. The stomach of one cuckoo examined contained 250 tent caterpillars and that of another 217 fall webworms.

The woodpecker family includes 25 species found in the U. S. They wage their warfare chiefly against woodboring larvae and devour many insect eggs deposited under the bark of trees. Some woodpeckers (notably the flickers) consume large quantities of ants. One flicker is known to have taken 5,000 ants at a single meal!

The goatsucker family (Caprimulgidae) —so called because of an old but mistaken notion that its members sucked the milk of goats—includes a diverse group as far as appearance is concerned. Night hawks, whippoorwills, poorwills, swifts and humming birds belong to this group. All are insect eaters, taking large numbers on the wing, and one characteristic of the larger birds of the family group is their night-flying habit. The humming birds gather minute insects from the corolla of flowers. Contrary to the usual supposition, it is more often insects that they subsist on rather than the nectar of flowers.

Flycatchers are the hawks of the insect world. They perch on limbs where there is little foliage, constantly watching for their prey. After capturing insects on the wing, they return, as a rule, to the same perch, this being a characteristic habit of the members of this family. The common birds included in the group are the crested flycatcher, kingbird, phoebe, and wood pewee. On an average, 95 per cent of the food of these birds consists of insects.

There are six members of the crow or raven family (Corvidae) in this country. They are all severely criticized and for the most part the criticism is justified. However, as far as gardens are concerned, the good they do will balance the evil. Crows and ravens mainly restrict their depredations to farms and rural sections. Blue jays are more frequent visitors to the garden but do little damage unless present in considerable numbers.

Blackbirds, like starlings, gather in large flocks but fortunately these are formed only in the fall and winter when there is little in the garden for them to damage. Small groups of ten or more may descend upon fruit trees, and measures should be taken to prevent such raids where they become troublesome. The meadow lark, bobolink, cowbird, and orioles are related species. Their habits are beneficial excepting the cowbird's bad trait of laying its eggs in the nests of smaller birds, leaving to them the responsibility of raising its young. Where identification is certain the cowbird's egg may be removed from the nest.

The native sparrows (which do *not* include the English sparrow) form the largest and most interesting group of birds as well as the most beneficial to the garden. When the migrant sparrows have departed in the fall, others take their places so that some sparrows are present throughout the year. A few species are permanent residents in most localities. The song sparrow

LET THE BIRDS FIND A PROTECTED RETREAT IN YOUR GARDEN
A well-placed bird-bath, a bird house in a tree, and a metal guard around the trunk to keep cats from climbing up, will make a bird sanctuary out of the home grounds.

Name, Marks, Size	Haunts and Habits	Nesting Sites
Downy woodpecker Black and white; smaller than robin.	Trunks and large limbs of trees in orchards and open woods. Frequents gardens in winter. Tame.	Holes in trees, orchards or open woods.
Flicker Yellow-lined wings, white rump; larger than robin.	Roadside trees, woods, gardens in summer.	Cavity in tree any distance from ground.
Phoebe Dull olive above, whitish below; sparrow size.	Flirts tail nervously. Friendly, found a b o u t buildings o r bridges.	Barns, bridges and porch rafters.
Wood pewee Olive gray; sparrow size.	Open woods. Perches on dead limbs and sings for long periods.	Open woods and orchards.
Blue jay Blue and white; larger than robin.	Open woods, gardens. Very active. Occasionally robs birds nests. Will feed from window shelf in winter.	Pines, cedars and shrubs 4 to 8 ft. above ground. Roadsides, gardens and open woods.
Starling Greenish-black, spotted yellowish; robin size.	Flocks about building and roosting places. Voracious. Sometimes drives away native songbirds.	Holes in trees or buildings.
Junco Slate-gray, white outer wing-feathers; sparrow size.	Common about feeding stations and door yards in winter. Gentle.	On the ground near stones or in a clump of weeds or under a small bush.
Song sparrow Brown and white stripes, spot on center of breast.	Found in bushes, vines or hedges about houses.	On the ground or in low bushes.
Chewink Black and white and red; between robin and sparrow.	Pastures and open woodlands. Ground birds, usually found scratching in bushes.	On the ground; rarely in low bushes.
Purple martin Purple-black; sparrow size.	About cities and towns. Usually on the wing.	Prefer dwellings especially built for them with many rooms.
Barn swallow Black above, reddish-brown below; sparrow size.	Skim over meadows, fields and lakes. Perch about door yards near old buildings.	Beams and rafters of old buildings and open sheds and bridges.

the American Ornithologists' Union)

Type of Nest	Eggs	Food	Economic Status
Holes in trees. Eggs laid upon bare wood.	White, 4 to 6.	Insects, grubs and larvae present under bark of trees.	Useful as destroyer of harmful insects found in decaying wood.
Sparsely lined with chips of wood.	White, 5 to 10.	Insects, larvae, grubs, ants.	Useful as destroyer of harmful insects.
Grass and hair, lined with mud, covered with lichens.	White with brown spots.	Insects caught on the wing.	Useful as destroyer of harmful insects.
Grass lined with moss, covered with lichens.	White with ring of light-brown markings.	Insects.	Useful as destroyer of harmful insects.
Twigs, sticks with a few bits of paper or leaves.	Greenish blue speckled with brown.	Nut meats, beetles, grain.	Doubtful.
Grass with feathers, paper, roots and miscellaneous material untidily arranged at bottom of hole in tree.	4 to 6 pale blue, unspotted.	Large variety of insects, beetles, fruit.	Highly valued as destroyer of harmful beetles and insects.
Grass lined with fine grass; bowl-shaped.	3 or 4 white speckled with brown.	Weed seeds, crumbs and insects.	Destroys weed seeds and insects.
Grass lined with fine grass; bowl-shaped.	4 or 5 bluish white spotted with brown.	Small seeds and insects.	Useful as destroyer of harmful insects.
Bark, grass and leaves.	White with reddish brown spots.	Seeds, wild fruits and insects.	Useful as destroyer of harmful insects.
Straw, paper, rags, etc. Nest in colonies usually in multiple-room bird-houses.	White.	Insects.	Useful as destroyer of harmful insects.
Mud lined with feathers into bowl-shaped nest.	5 to 7 white, spotted with brown.	Insects.	Useful as destroyer of harmful insects.

Name, Marks, Size	Haunts and Habits	Nesting Sites
Red-eyed vireo Greenish olive, white-eyebrow stripe; sparrow size.	Near homes and gardens. Frequent outer branches of tall trees.	Fork of limb 20 to 30 ft. above ground near tips of branches, usually Norway maple.
Baltimore oriole Golden-orange and black; between robin and sparrow.	Intimately associated with mankind. Always about tree tops near houses.	Near the end of branches of tall trees close to houses.
Gold finch Yellow with black cap and wings; canary size.	Sociable, breeding in communities and flocking in gardens in fall and winter.	Forks of bushes, willows or alders preferably near water.
English sparrow Olive-brown, black bib on male.	About door yards and city streets. Noisy and dirty; often fighting and driving away native song-birds.	Buildings, trees and nestboxes. Cavities in trees.
Tree sparrow Red-brown cap, white wing bars, one spot on breast.	Frequent fields and gardens where weeds are standing above the snow.	On ground or in low bushes.
Chipping sparrow Red-cap, unspotted breast; smaller than English sparrow.	Orchards, yards and fields. Active, found on the ground or in tree tops.	Bushes, trees and vines near dwellings.
Black and white warbler Black and white stripes; canary size.	Gardens, woodlands. Creeps over trunk and larger limbs of trees in search of insects. Unsuspicious.	On ground near tree-trunk stump or rock.
Yellow warbler Yellow, streaked reddish-brown on breast; canary size.	Woodland, park, orchard and gardens. Found in leafy parts of trees.	Forks of small limbs, at low elevations in gardens or orchards near ponds or rivers.
Myrtle warbler Slaty-blue, spotted yellow on rump and wings; canary size.	Active, darting from limbs to catch insects in air. Found everywhere during migration.	Low evergreen trees placed a few feet from ground.
Northern yellow throat	Common in swamps, shrubbery along roadsides and gardens. Inquisitive and without fear.	Clumps of weeds on the ground or 6 in. above the ground.

Type of Nest	Eggs	Food	Economic Status
Bowl-shaped basket woven around fork of limb. Bark, paper and fibres, grass-lined.	3 to 5 white, with black specks on large end.	Insects.	Useful as destroyer of harmful insects.
Deep basket hanging 8 or 10 inches below the branch swinging with the wind.	5 or 6 white scrawled with blackish brown.	Insects, seeds and fruits.	Useful as destroyer of harmful insects.
Plant fibres, grasses and thistledown, neatly constructed.	4 or 5 pale blue.	Seeds, especially sunflower seeds.	Useful as destroyer of harmful insects **and** weed seeds.
Loosely constructed of grass, straw and rubbish. Usually unsightly.	5 to 7 white, with black markings.	Large variety of small grain seeds, insects, fruit and buds of trees.	Doubtful.
Fine grasses.	Greenish blue.	Seeds of weeds and insects.	Useful as destroyer of weed seeds and insects.
Grass and root fibres lined with horse hair.	Greenish blue with cinnamon markings.	Insects and small seeds.	Controls multiplication of weeds and insects.
Grass, strips of bark.	4 or 5 white, scrawls of brown around large end.	Insects and larvae.	Useful as destroyer of harmful insects.
Solid structure closely woven of plant fibres; bowl-shaped.	4 or 5 grayish white or pale green, sprinkled with spots of brown wreathed at large end.	Insects.	Useful as destroyer of harmful insects.
Loose and bulky, of dead twigs lined with fine roots, hair and feathers.	3 to 5 dull white, creamy, spotted with brown.	Insects.	Useful as destroyer of harmful insects.
Neatly woven of grape-vine bark and grasses.	4 or 5 white with brown specks.	Insects.	Useful as destroyer of harmful insects.

Name, Marks, Size	Haunts and Habits	Nesting Sites
Mocking bird Slate-gray; about robin size.	Gardens, pastures and open woods. Friendly to man.	Dense thickets or hedges. Sometimes in open places in the garden.
Catbird Gray, black cap, brownish under tail; smaller than robin.	Gardens, swamps and pastures. Perch for an hour or more singing.	Hedges or thickets, gardens, roadsides and open woods.
Brown thrasher Red-brown, striped back; larger than robin.	Scrub fields, farms, open woods and gardens.	Hedges, thickets, low trees or thorn bushes.
House wren Ashy brown above, whitish below; canary size.	Gardens and open woods. Friendly, bold, prefer to associate with man.	Bird-boxes, holes in trees and crevices.
Black-capped chickadee Gray, black m a r k e d, whitish below, smaller than sparrow.	Gardens, open woods, roadsides. Friendly.	Cavities in trees and crevices usually near ground.
Robin Grayish-brown a b o v e, reddish below.	Gardens, farms and parks. Well known. Usually on lawns or singing from trees.	Crotch of trees near houses; 6 to 25 ft. above ground.
Bluebird Blue above, red below; between robin and sparrow.	Farms and orchards. Friendly; less frequent about houses and gardens.	Cavities in trees; bird-boxes.

and its subspecies are the most widely distributed, with the junco, tree sparrow, and chipping sparrow following closely in numbers. All are essentially seed eaters, consuming quantities of weed seeds. In summer they vary their diet with insects such as grasshoppers, wasps, aphids, etc., so that they may well be considered beneficial to man.

In general they are easily distinguished from their unwelcome immigrant cousins by their quieter, less quarrelsome demeanor. The cheerful, companionable conversation of a group of them is as delightful as the noisy bickering of English sparrows is irritating.

The tanagers and swallows are of great value as insect eaters. The latter especially wage an unceasing aerial warfare, coursing over land and water in gathering many plant pests.

The vireos and warblers are other large

families nearly as widely distributed as the sparrows. They are absent in winter from the northern part of their range and their presence in large numbers during the other three seasons is often unsuspected due to their small size, their habit of keeping among the small twigs and foliage of the tree tops, and their inconspicuous vocal efforts. Insects that commonly attack foliage, such as plant lice, scale insects and caterpillars, are devoured by them in numbers almost beyond conception. The chickadees, titmice and kinglets confine their work more to the bark of trees, gathering insects and their eggs from cavities and crevices. This group, including the creepers and nuthatches, is more friendly and better known than that of the warblers although in most sections the latter outnumber them.

Wrens, thrashers, mocking birds, and catbirds are fruit eaters, but the good they

Type of Nest	Eggs	Food	Economic Status
Twigs and roots lined with black rootlets.	4 or 5 bluish green with blotches of reddish brown.	Beetles, insects and fruit.	Useful as destroyer of harmful insects.
Twigs and rootlets.	4 or 5 greenish blue.	Fruit, beetles and insects.	Useful as destroyer of harmful insects.
Twigs, rootlets and grasses.	4 or 5 bluish white with fine dots.	Beetles, grubs and insects.	Useful as destroyer of harmful insects.
Grass or weeds loosely laid in box or crevice.	4 to 6 white, fine dots of brown.	Insects.	Useful as destroyer of harmful insects.
Sparsely lined.	4 white, speckled with brown.	Insects.	Useful as destroyer of harmful insects.
Grass and coarse fibres lined and cemented together with mud.	4 or 5 bluish green.	Insects, grubs, worms and fruit.	Useful as destroyer of harmful insects.
Lined with grass.	4 or 5 pale blue.	Insects and grubs.	Useful as destroyer of harmful insects.

do compensates for all the fruit they take. They are delightful vocalists and are often encouraged to stay about homes solely on account of their songs.

The thrush family includes the best-known birds, robins and bluebirds being the most friendly and familiar species about our homes. The wood thrush, hermit thrush, and veery are also woodland birds.

While the robins are numerous in the southern part of their range, they have for the most part a wider esthetic appeal than any other of the land birds. There are birds with more brilliant plumage, of greater economic value, with more striking songs and more interesting habits, but there are none whose bearing is more distinguished and whose songs are more emotional or make a stronger appeal to the higher aspirations of mankind than the birds of the thrush family.

Some Native Shrubs Attractive to Birds
NATIVE KINDS

Red Chokeberry (*Aronia arbutifolia*) and Black Chokeberry (*A. melanocarpa*). Aronias hold their fruit well into the winter and 13 kinds of birds are known to eat it, including the most desirable meadowlark and brown thrasher.

Shadbush (*Amelanchier canadensis*). Bears little reddish fruits highly enjoyed by 40 kinds of birds including the flicker, oriole, cedar waxwing, hermit thrush, veery, and robin.

Spicebush (*Benzoin aestivale*). The berries are eaten by 17 kinds of birds, the most desirable being the kingbird, red-eyed vireo, catbird and veery.

False-bittersweet (*Celastrus scandens*).

Dogwood (*Cornus*). 86 kinds of birds are known to eat the fruit of various species of dogwood, especially Flowering

Dogwood (*C. florida*) with red fruits, Alternate-leaved Dogwood (*C. alternifolia*) berries blue with red stems, Silky Dogwood (*C. amomum*) fruit pale blue, Panicled Dogwood (*C. paniculata*) fruit white with red stems, Red Osier (*C. stolonifera*) berries dull white.

Inkberry (*Ilex glabra*) and Winterberry (*I. verticillata*). 48 kinds of birds are known to eat the berries of these and other hollies.

Bayberry (*Myrica caroliniensis*). Of the 75 kinds of birds that eat the berries the most desirable are bobwhite, myrtle warbler, phoebe, chickadee, chewink, tree swallow, downy woodpecker and flicker. American Mountain-ash (*Sorbus americana*). 14 kinds of birds, among them the cedar waxwing, evening grosbeak and pine grosbeak eat the fruit of this small tree.

Black Elderberry (*Sambucus canadensis*). The berries are eaten by 106 kinds of birds.

Viburnum. At least 28 kinds of birds eat the fruits of the Black haw (*V. prunifolium*). Other species valued for their berries include: Dockmackie (*V. acerifolium*) with dark-violet blue berries; Hobble-bush (*V. alnifolium*) coral-red berries; Witherod (*V. cassinoides*) berries yellowish and pink when young, turning blue-black with a bloom; Arrow-wood (*V. dentatatum*) berries deep blue-black; (*V. lentago*) berries cadet-blue with a bloom; American Highbush-cranberry (*V. opulus america*) berries scarlet-red.

BIRDS-NEST FERN. Common name for *Asplenium nidus-avis,* an excellent house fern, having broad, entire bright-green fronds with dark midribs, growing in a crown. It likes peat and a little lime.

BIRD-TOBACCO-TREE. Common name for *Nicotiana glauca,* a S. American, quick-growing, treelike species of tobacco which has become naturalized in Texas and the S. Calif. foothills and is sometimes used as an ornamental for quick, if short-lived, effects.

BIRTHROOT. One name for Trillium (which see), known also as Wake-robin, a genus of perennial woodland herbs, sometimes transplanted to the wild garden.

BIRTHWORT. A common name for Aristolochia (which see), in reference to supposed medicinal virtues.

BISHOPS CAP. Common name for the genus Mitella, a group of small native woodland herbs occasionally transplanted to the wild garden.

BISHOPS-WEED. A common name for *Aegopodium podagraria,* also called Gout-weed, a coarse herb of Europe naturalized in N. America. Sometimes used as an edging in shady situations.

BITING INSECTS. Those with biting or chewing mouth parts which gnaw or devour plant parts are usually controlled with a stomach poison. See INSECTS; INSECTICIDE.

BITTER CRESS. Common name for the genus Cardamine (which see), whose chief cultivated species (*C. pratensis*) blooms in the spring with pinkish flowers; good for rock gardens or moist borders. In Europe its leaves are used for salad.

BITTERNUT. Common name for *Carya cordiformis,* a species of Hickory (which see), bearing a small nut, nearly round, and of very bitter taste.

BITTER-ROOT. Common name for *Lewisia rediviva,* a deciduous member of the Portulaca Family. Native from British Columbia southward, it is a good rock-garden subject if given a sunny position

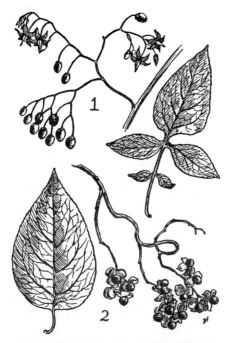

TWO VINES CALLED BITTERSWEET
1. Flowering and fruiting spray and leaf of the attractive but poisonous weed, Solanum dulcamara. 2. The native Celastrus scandens, with red fruits enclosed in three-lobed orange husks, a vigorous vine useful for home planting.

and a deep, loose soil, moisture retaining but gritty. The State flower of Montana.

BITTERSWEET. A name given to two unrelated shrubby climbers or twining shrubs. One, a member of the nightshade group, is *Solanum dulcamara.* The other, highly prized for its colored fruits, is *Celastrus scandens* or Waxwork, which should properly be called False-bittersweet. See CELASTRUS and SOLANUM.

BIXA (bik′-sah) *orellana.* A tree of tropical America commonly called Annatto, grown in S. Fla. and elsewhere for the orange-hued dye of that name obtained from the pulp surrounding the seeds in its small fruits; it is used to color butter and cheeses, and, to some extent, silks. Sometimes grown from cuttings of flowering branches as greenhouse plants. Outdoor trees are usually grown from the seeds.

BLACK-ALDER. A common name for *Ilex verticillata,* a hardy deciduous shrub whose persistent, attractive red berries give it also the name of Winterberry. These are much used in winter bouquets or to brighten up evergreen wreaths.

BLACKBERRY. Various tall, upright to trailing perennials with thorny biennial stems. All are "Brambles," that is, members of the genus Rubus and therefore closely related to the Raspberries. The Dewberry (which see) is sometimes called "trailing blackberry." With two notable exceptions (the Oregon Evergreen and the Himalaya, recently imported from Europe), blackberry varieties grown in America have been developed, since about 1850, from native species, of which there are several score. (See illustration, Plate 40.)

CULTURAL DIRECTIONS. Blackberries thrive in well-drained, preferably clay-loam, soils liberally supplied with humus and moisture. They are propagated by suckers and root cuttings. Plants are set in early spring 3 ft. asunder in rows 8 ft. apart. Clean cultivation until midsummer, when a cover-crop (which see) is sown, is the common practice, but in home gardens deep mulching with cut weeds, lawn clippings and any other vegetable debris available is preferable.

When the young shoots reach 30 to 36 in. in length the tips should be pinched off to develop low branches and make the stems so stiff that they will need no supports. The following spring the branches may be shortened to 18 in. or less while the plants are dormant and again after the blossom

buds have formed. However, cutting back too severely while dormant, may destroy so many blossom buds as to seriously reduce the yield of fruit. After they have fruited, the old stems should be cut out as already noted. They will die during the winter anyway, so their prompt removal and burning helps to clean up the patch, admits more air and light into the bushes and controls plant diseases and insects.

ENEMIES. The underside of the leaves is often covered with a bright-orange rust. This fungus is perennial in the underground parts of the plants so the only remedy is to pull up and burn diseased specimens. Crown gall is also common (see RUBUS) and rose scale may be present (see SCALE). Remove and burn canes infested with cane- and root-borers at the annual pruning. Spray with nicotine-sulphate and soap for leaf miners.

PROBLEMS OF BLACKBERRIES

As a home-garden fruit the blackberry deserves high standing because so grown the berries can be had in the perfection of full ripeness—which they do not have when bought because berries for market must be picked while still hard, rather acid and lacking the delicious flavor that characterizes the best varieties when fully ripe. At this stage they drop into the hand at a slight touch.

On the other hand, blackberries offer three disadvantages—as the plants are ordinarily treated. (1) The stems are often winter-killed, sometimes to the ground, so that no fruit forms the following summer. (2) Unless properly managed the plants are likely to spread in all directions by means of suckers and form impenetrable thickets. (3) The plants languish and the fruit shrivels in hot, dry seasons (and in the arid Southwest), though this tendency may be partially overcome by mulching and by irrigation.

Winter-killing may be partially, if not wholly, prevented by growing only varieties known to be generally hardy in the region, by cutting out all old canes and puny young shoots immediately after the fruiting season so as to direct the plant food and water they would consume into the sturdy canes chosen to bear fruit the following season, and by ripening the wood of these canes.

This ripening of the canes is dependent upon the amount of water and the quantity and character of plant food in the soil from

TWO BLACK-EYED SUSANS
Below, the common field flower, Rudbeckia. Above, the silky yellow and brown flower of a choice greenhouse vine, Thunbergia.

midsummer to early fall. When water is ample during this period the plants develop strongly. When, however, it is insufficient then, but is abundant later in the autumn, the plants are likely to make additional growth which, failing to ripen, is killed by the winter. Also when nitrogenous plant food is too abundant from early fall onward, the canes continue to grow too late to become mature before winter with the same result. It is, therefore, important to avoid supplying strongly nitrogenous fertilizers after May, but to be liberal with potash and phosphatic plant food from late summer into fall, because these tend to ripen the canes and to make them hardy.

The problem of suckers springing up between the rows and in other places where they are not wanted can be largely solved by correct cultural practices. First, to get rid of such suckers *pull them up* while less than a foot high; *do not cut them off* with hoe, scythe, etc., as new ones soon sprout from their cut stumps. Second, to prevent excessive suckering, avoid cutting or in-

juring the plant roots in the space between the rows. That means do not cultivate too deeply. As a matter of fact, a deep mulch left from year to year is even better than clean cultivation, as it not only lessens the chance of suckers but also maintains the cool moist soil-conditions that blackberries prefer.

See also RUBUS.

BLACKBERRY-LILY. Common name for *Belamcanda chinensis,* a favorite flower in old gardens that has become naturalized in some parts of N. America. Belonging to the Iris Family, it has iris-like leaves, orange flowers, red-spotted, and ornamental black fruit resembling a large-seeded blackberry. A strong-growing perennial, it delights in a rich sandy soil in an open border in full sunlight and is easily propagated by division or seeds. It is often sold under the name Pardanthus and is sometimes referred to as Leopard-lily.

BLACK COHOSH (koh'-hosh) or BLACK SNAKEROOT. Common names for *Cimicifuga racemosa,* a tall perennial herb useful for background planting.

BLACK-EYED SUSAN. Common name for *Rudbeckia hirta* (sometimes called Yellow Daisy), a native rough, hairy biennial bearing heads of deep yellow rayflowers around a purple-brown center; it is the State flower of Maryland. The name is also given to the Clock-vine, *Thunbergia alata.* See RUDBECKIA; THUNBERGIA.

BLACKHAW. Common name for *Viburnum prunifolium,* a large shrub ranging from Conn. to Fla. and Tex. The species *V. rufidulum,* known as Southern Blackhaw, is found from Virginia southward. See VIBURNUM.

BLACK HELLEBORE (hel'-ee-bor). Common name for *Helleborus niger,* also known as Christmas-rose (which see), a plant of the Buttercup Family, blooming in late winter or early spring.

BLACK-LILY. Common name for *Fritillaria biflora,* with flowers of a deep chocolate tint; also applied to *F. camschatcensis,* of a dark maroon shade. Both species flower in early spring.

BLACK SPOT OF ROSE. A fungus disease causing black spots on the leaves followed by yellowing and defoliation. Probably the most widely distributed and generally destructive rose disease. See ROSE, ENEMIES.

BLACKTHORN. Common name for *Prunus spinosa,* also called Sloe; an ornamental, thorny shrub of the Old World, often with purple leaves and sometimes with double flowers which are white, appearing before the leaves. The smooth fruit, about ½ in. in diameter, is blue or black.

BLADDER FERN. Common name for the genus Cystopteris, which see. Two native species do well in proper garden soil.

BLADDER-NUT. Common name for the genus Staphylea, a group of mostly hardy ornamental shrubs bearing panicles of white flowers in early summer, followed by inflated fruits.

BLADDER-POD. Common name for the genus Vesicaria, embracing annual and perennial herbs native to Central Europe and the Mediterranean shores. Of the 20 known species, nearly all of which bear yellow flowers, *V. utriculata* is the one usually grown, because of its inflated seedpods. Although a perennial, it is grown outdoors in America as an annual, blooming in May or June. It is not particular as to soil. The perennial sorts are propagated by division; the annuals, by seeds.

BLADDER-SENNA. Common name for the genus Colutea, ornamental hardy shrubs with pea-like flowers.

BLADDERWORT. Common name for aquatic or terrestrial herbs of the genus Utricularia. Few are of interest horticulturally, except to the collector, but the native species are occasionally collected and used in aquaria. The flowers are not showy but have floating bladder-like leaves equipped with valve-like openings which trap small aquatic creatures when searching for food. The tropical species are terrestrial or epiphytic with beautiful orchid-like flowers; they are frequently grown in greenhouses under the same conditions as orchids.

U. vulgaris is a hardy Old-World aquatic plant with floating leaves provided with many bladders. The flowers are yellow on stalks 6 to 8 in. high. Var. *americana* is the form found in this country. *U. longifolia* is a tropical species having beautiful violet and orange flowers 2 in. across. It should be grown in the greenhouse in baskets containing a compost of sphagnum moss and sand.

BLADE-APPLE. A common name for *Pereskia aculeata,* a vine-like, leafy cactus with yellow, pink or white flowers.

BLANCH. Blanch is the process of whitening the shoots, leaves or stems of plants or of preventing their becoming green by excluding light. Its main objectives are: to modify the appearance, tenderness, pungency, acidity, bitterness or other characteristics, improve quality and thus enhance their palatability.

The desired results are attained by such methods as boarding up or earthing up (which see) such plants as celery, leek, cardoon, and Florence fennel; by breaking or tying the leaves of cauliflower and romaine lettuce over the newly forming heads; by covering endive plants with flower pots a week or two before they are needed during summer and fall; by covering sea-kale and rhubarb clumps with barrels, boxes, tile or large flower-pots in early spring (the rhubarb does not exactly whiten but becomes paler and tenderer); and by forcing chicory roots in a dark cellar to produce *barbe de capucin* (or, if they are buried in manure or other soft material to produce witloof or "French endive"). See CHICORY; WITLOOF.

The principal precaution to observe in blanching is to see that free moisture is not enclosed in the blanched parts, where it may cause decay and spoilage.

BLANDFORDIA (bland-for'-di-ah). A genus of fibrous-rooted herbs of the Lily Family from Australia. The large leaves are borne mostly at the base of the 2 to 3 ft. stems, which bear the large showy flowers, usually orange-red and yellow-tipped, in drooping terminal spikes. Small bright fruits succeed the bloom. A plant for the greenhouse or for mild climates, it is difficult to grow. Air and moisture are essential but drafts are fatal, and plants must be carefully shaded during the growing season. Soil should be chiefly peat with a little loam and charcoal. Plants should be potted in early spring after flowering and left undisturbed for two years. *B. flammea,* var. *princeps,* is one of the best forms.

BLANKET-FLOWER. Common name sometimes used for the genus Gaillardia, more particularly the perennial species *G. aristata* and the annual *G. pulchella,* both popular garden flowers.

BLAST (BLASTING). Term often applied to the blighting or sudden death of young buds, flower-clusters (inflorescences), or fruits. It may be a symptom or result of disease, or may be caused by some external influence, as weather, excess or insufficient moisture, etc.

In another sense, blasting (by means of explosives) is sometimes employed as a preparatory step in garden making or tree planting. One objective might be the breaking up of a layer of so-called "hard pan" between the top-soil and a desirably porous subsoil. The shattering of the impervious formation opens up channels for drainage and aeration without disturbing the general land surface. The same method may be used in place of a subsoil plow, to loosen a deep hard subsoil. In either case small charges (half a stick or less of 20% dynamite) are placed 2 to 3 ft. deep and 10 to 15 ft. apart.

Sometimes where rock formations come near the surface it is necessary to blast holes for special trees, or a trench for hedge plants; explosives are also useful in breaking up large stumps or boulders and making them easier to remove preparatory to constructing a garden in cut-over timber land or other uncultivated areas. Such operations are more in the nature of engineering than of gardening and should either be entrusted to specialists or attempted only after securing detailed instructions from firms making explosives or from State Agricultural Experiment Stations.

BLAZING STAR. Common name for the genus Mentzelia, especially *M. laevicaulis*, a W. biennial herb with large white flowers. The name is also applied to other genera, namely Liatris (Gayfeather or Button-snakeroot), Kniphofia (Torch-lily) and Chamaelirium (Fairy-wand), all of which see.

BLECHNUM (blek'-num). A genus of ferns comprising several species suitable only for greenhouse culture; among them are tree ferns and some dwarf ferns of possible value in the terrarium.

B. lanceolatum. Evergreen, entire, 4 to 6 in. fronds of leathery texture, from a creeping rhizome; blades are bright green; fruit-dots form a continuous band of dark brown along the mid-rib.

longifolium. 9 to 12 in., once-pinnate fronds; fruit-dots as in preceding species.

occidentale. Fronds 9 to 15 in., once pinnate, the pinnae entire; scaly stipes. The easiest to grow, unusually free from insect pests.

spicant. Now referred to the genus Lomaria, which see.

BLEEDING. The exudation of sap from any wound, especially one made in pruning. Contrary to popular belief it is not harmful, because whatever moisture is thus visibly lost is only part of what would normally have been distributed to the removed branches and in due course given off through their leaves. Hence no treatment such as the formerly recommended searing with a hot iron need be given to stop or check it. When cavities develop in trunks of trees and are "treated" by amateurs or incompetent workers, a "slime flux" condition and decay may follow imperfect work. Such cases should be treated by a competent tree expert.

BLEEDING HEART. Common name for *Dicentra spectabilis,* a well-known and popular hardy perennial, often grown in old gardens, with rosy-red flowers of peculiar form that suggest the name. There is also a white variety. (See illustration, Plate 39.)

BLESSED THISTLE. Common name for *Cnicus benedictus,* and for *Silybum marianum,* which is also called Holy Thistle, St. Marys Thistle or Milk Thistle. See CNICUS and SILYBUM.

BLETILLA (blee'-til-ah). A genus of terrestrial and epiphytical orchids, some of which are hardy as far north as New York, though not recommended for general planting outdoors except in favored locations. They grow well in the cool greenhouse, and are useful because of their highly colored flowers. *B. striata* or *hyacinthina* is one of the hardiest species. Set the bulbs in pots just beneath the surface of the soil; place the plants outdoors after flowering, plunging the pots in ashes and leaving the foliage exposed to the sun. Move them back indoors before cold weather sets in. The name was formerly Bletia. See also ORCHID.

BLIGHT. A term commonly used to describe the browning of foliage, blossoms or shoots suddenly killed by pathogenic (disease-causing) organisms. The word usually indicates death of plant tissues over an extended area rather than a local lesion. such as a leaf spot or canker, and is applied to various types of diseases, such as fire blight of pears and apples, chestnut blight, and botrytis blight, etc. See DISEASES, PLANT.

BLISTER BEETLES. Black, gray or striped beetles, common garden pests about ¾ in. long, which feed voraciously on a number of garden and field plants. They are especial pests of asters and Japanese anemones. Their blood contains an oil (cantharidin) with caustic or blistering properties which become apparent if a beetle is crushed on the skin. In the last century blisters prepared from the insects were used as external local irritants, especially in veterinary practice. At present the oil has a certain limited use in internal treatment. Blister beetles in the flowers are difficult to control. If they are numerous knock them off into a pail of kerosene. Dusting with sodium fluosilicate or spraying with lead arsenate will protect foliage.

BLISTER BEETLE Shake this black pest of asters into a pan of kerosene.

BLISTER-CRESS. Common name for the genus Erysimum, a group of herbs with yellow, blue or lilac flowers closely related to the wallflowers.

BLISTER MITE. A small insect that causes black, blister-like galls on pear leaves and yellow blisters on apple leaves. See MITES; PEAR.

BLOOD, DRIED. This fairly quick-acting organic or nitrogenous animal fertilizer is prepared by evaporating, drying and grinding blood and non-fatty refuse at slaughter houses. Varying in color from red to black, it also contains a varying but generally large amount of nitrogen, ranging from 13 to 15%. The red product is of better quality than the black, which is often mixed with more or less hair, dirt and other useless or undesirable material and of which the nitrogen content is rarely above 12%. Dried blood is usually applied to the soil as a constituent of a prepared, complete fertilizer mixture. But as a nitrogenous "tonic" it can be worked into the soil at the rate of 3 to 5 lbs. per 100 sq. ft. 3 or 4 times during the growing season. It can also be mixed with potting soil at the rate of a 6 in.-potful to each bushel of soil.

See also FERTILIZER.

BLOOD-FLOWER. Common name for *Asclepias curassavica,* one of the Milkweeds, with purple and orange flowers.

BLOOD-LEAF. Common name for the genus Iresine, climbing or erect herbs or shrubby plants, native to tropical or semitropical regions, and belonging to the Amaranth Family. They have inconspicuous flowers but are grown as bedding and house plants because of their ornamental foliage; they were much used in the days when carpet-bedding (see BEDDING) was popular. They are grown in much the same way as coleus and are propagated by cuttings. *I. lindeni* has narrow, sharp-pointed red leaves; *I. herbsti,* to 6 ft., has notched leaves, purplish-red or green veined with yellow; its var. *aureo-reticulata* has greenish-red leaves veined with yellow.

BLOOD-LILY. Common name for Haemanthus, a genus of showy S. African, bulbous plants of the Amaryllis Family, grown indoors in the N. for spring and summer bloom. The flowers, in dense ball-like clusters, are usually blood red, and often precede the broad, luxuriant leaves. There are a number of species and various named forms. One of the most beautiful is *H. katharinae* with large, apple-green leaves to 14 in. long and 6 in. broad, and brilliant-red flowers in round clusters sometimes 9 in. across.

Pot the bulbs in the fall in equal parts peat and loam, made friable with sand, covering the lower half of the bulb only. Water frequently and syringe the foliage daily until the blooms begin to fade. Then gradually dry off the plants, leaving the bulbs undisturbed in the pots, and store until the following autumn. They are increased by offsets.

BLOODROOT. The common name for *Sanguinaria canadensis,* a North American plant of the Poppy Family. Its red juice was formerly used by the Indians in decorating themselves for war. It grows in rich, moist woodlands in eastern and central N. America and is easily transplanted to the wild garden where it may be propagated by seed or division. It has attractive white flowers in April and May on stems 8 in. high; large, lobed leaves; and a prominent rootstock.

BLOODTWIG DOGWOOD. Common name for *Cornus sanguinea.* See DOGWOOD.

BLOOM. This term has several meanings in gardening, namely: (1) the blossom of a seed-bearing plant, generally used collectively, as "spring bloom"; (2) the flowering period, as "an orchard in bloom"; (3) the grayish or "dusty" surface-coating of various fruits (such as plum) and leaves (such as cabbage).

BLOOMERIA (bloo-mee'-ri-ah). A genus of S. California herbs of the Lily Family. *B. aurea,* the species usually

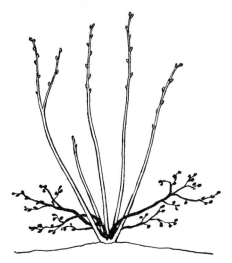

BLUEBERRY PRUNING—I

At the end of the first year in the garden, cut out the low bushy side-growth (shown in black), leaving erect stems to form the plant.

grown, with orange-yellow, striped-flowers in clusters, is generally called Golden-stars.

BLOOMING SALLY. A common name for *Epilobium angustifolium,* a species of Willow-herb (which see), also known as Fireweed; a tall-growing perennial bearing long spikes of purple flowers in July. See EPILOBIUM.

BLOTCH. A symptom of disease in plants consisting of a dark lesion or wound area usually with an irregular margin; it appears on fruit and sometimes on leaves. The disease called apple blotch takes its name from this symptom. See also APPLE.

BLOTTER GARDENING. A variation or extension of an old method of testing viability of seeds (see Seed Testing, under SEEDS, AND SEEDING) wherein a dilute nutrient solution is used to secure a somewhat extended growth of seedlings, preparatory to planting them in a permanent culture. See also CHEMICAL GARDENING.

BLUE AMARYLLIS. Common name for *Griffinia hyacinthina,* a summer-flowering bulb from S. America with broad-bladed leaves and large, lily-like flowers shading from white to lilac or rose. The difficulty of cultivation and the high cost of sizable bulbs keep these beautiful plants from being more generally used. They should be grown under glass until warm weather in spring and brought in again for winter storage before the first fall frost.

BLUEBEARD. The genus Caryopteris. Showy shrubs, valuable for their colorful lavender or white flowers late in the season. The tops are usually killed back during northern winters, but young shoots that spring up from below as the weather becomes warm flower the same season These shrubs require a well-drained light soil in a sunny position, and show to advantage in the flower garden. The leaves are aromatic and of an attractive grayish tone. The dense-flowered clusters appear in September, a season when any new flower in the garden is most welcome.

C. incana, formerly known as *C. mastacanthus,* and often called "blue-spirea," is the best known. The flowers are lavender blue. Var. *candida* is white, and a pink form has recently been offered. *C. mongolica* has bright-blue flowers, not as freely produced, but larger. *C. tangutica* has flowers of violet-blue.

BLUEBELL. Common name applied to several plants, principally species of Campanula and especially *C. rotundifolia.* California-bluebell is *Phacelia whitlavia.* English-bluebell is *Scilla nonscripta* and

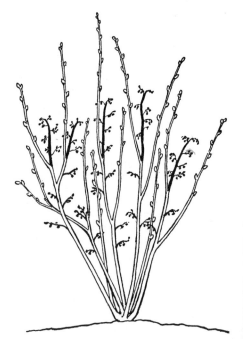

BLUEBERRY PRUNING—II

For the best crop of fruit, the shorter branches (in black) should be pruned off to give the strong young side-shoots a chance.

Spanish-bluebell, *Scilla hispanica.* Virginia-bluebell is *Mertensia virginica.*

BLUEBERRY. A name given to various American species of Vaccinium (which see) especially the Highbush Blueberry (*V. corymbosum*). This, during the present century, has produced several varieties of great prolificacy and varied season with fruit of high quality and great size. These have been mainly the result of work by Dr. F. V. Coville, botanist of the U. S. Department of Agriculture, and Miss Elizabeth C. White of New Jersey. The former proved that the blueberry requires an acid soil in which to grow and developed methods of propagation; the latter applied the facts he discovered, found and propagated native bushes of outstanding merit and did much to popularize and distribute them.

Blueberries fail in alkaline and neutral soils, such as those of ordinary vegetable gardens. The ideal medium for them is a mixture of peat and sand, well drained and aerated but with an ample supply of water a foot or more below the surface during the growing season. However in limestone regions and areas of alkaline and neutral soils, plants may be grown in pockets filled with a peat and sand mixture or one of 4 parts rotted oak leaves to 1 part sand. (See ACID SOIL.) No manure or alkaline fertilizers must be used—only those that give an acid reaction. See FERTILIZER.

Though improved sorts can be propagated by budding, this work is difficult if not impossible under ordinary garden conditions. Also it is hard to successfully transplant plants from the wild. Therefore plants of named varieties should be bought from reliable sources, set 8 ft. apart and given clean cultivation. Mulching with oak leaves, peat moss or sawdust will help keep the soil of the desired texture and acidity. The plants should begin to bear during the third year and by the fifth be in full bearing. (See illustration, Plate 4; also under BUD.)

Though the terms blueberry and huckleberry are frequently confused and used interchangeably, they actually refer to entirely different and easily distinguished plants as explained under HUCKLEBERRY.

The "rose bloom" disease of cultivated blueberries reddens, curls and distorts the leaves. Two rusts, one of which causes a witches' broom effect, also attack the blueberry. Cut out infected parts. Breeding

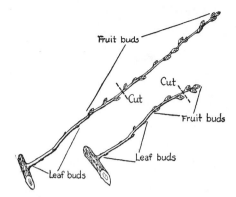

TO PRODUCE BETTER BLUEBERRIES
The fruit buds should be in proportion to the leaf buds on a branch. Hence varieties making long shoots should be pruned more severely than those making short ones, as indicated at the points marked "cut."

of resistant varieties offers a possible control of mildew.

Of the many blueberry insects, the fruit-fly maggot, akin to the apple maggot, is a serious pest of commercial crops. In Me., where the berries are canned and spray residue can be washed off, the bushes are dusted with calcium arsenate twice in July. In N. J., where the fruit is marketed fresh, airplane dusting with nonpoisonous derris has been successful. Lead arsenate applied early in the season will control flea beetles and other chewing insects, and the custom of burning over the fields helps control spittle bugs and thrips. Poison baits are best for the various species of cutworms.

BLUE-BLOSSOM. Common name for *Ceanothus thyrsiflorus,* a small Pacific Coast evergreen tree with shiny foliage, bearing flowers blue, or sometimes white.

BLUEBONNET. A common name for *Lupinus subcarnosus,* an annual native to, and the state flower of, Texas.

BLUEBOTTLE. A common name for that old garden favorite, *Centaurea cyanus* or Bachelors Button. See CENTAUREA.

BLUE COHOSH (koh'-hosh). Common name for *Caulophyllum thalictroides,* a native plant of the Barberry Family, of great beauty in the wild garden. The plants grow 3 ft. tall, and the small, yellowish-white flowers are followed, after the foliage dies in September, by brilliant blue fruits. The plants are easily moved into the garden from the wild, and can be increased from seed or by division. They prefer partially shaded rich wood soil.

BLUECURLS. Common name of *Trichostema lanatum,* a shrubby perennial of the Mint Family, suitable for the wild garden, or as a background plant for the rock garden. The plant reaches the height of 4 ft. and has narrow leaves, downy beneath, and attractive blue flowers ½ in. long, covered with blue or purple wool. In its native Calif., it is known as Ramero.

BLUE DAISY. Common name for species of Felicia, tender African subshrub, also called Blue Marguerite. It bears solitary heads with yellow disk- and sky-blue ray-flowers. See FELICIA.

BLUE DAWN-FLOWER. Common name for *Ipomoea leari,* one of the Morning-glories; its very large blue flowers gradually turn to pink.

BLUE-DICKS. Common name for *Brodiaea capitata,* an herb of the Lily Family, hardy along the Pacific Coast and in the S. Growing to 2 ft., it bears clusters of blue flowers.

BLUE-EYED-GRASS. Common name for herbs of the genus Sisyrinchium of the Iris Family; they are small perennial plants with fibrous roots, grass-like foliage, and small blue or yellow flowers. Growing wild in rich meadows or swamps, they make most attractive colonies in an open, rather moist spot in the wild garden. They are easily transplanted from the wild, and are increased by seed or division. *S. angustifolium* grows to 2 ft. and has deep violet-blue flowers. *S. californicum,* to 1 ft., has bright-yellow flowers. *S. graminoides,* to 1½ ft., has pale-green leaves and blue flowers ¾ in. across; it is occasionally cataloged as *S. graminea.*

BLUE-EYED MARY. Common name for *Collinsia verna,* a native, hardy herbaceous annual found from N. Y. to Wis. and Ky., with blue and purplish flowers.

BLUE FAIRY-OF-THE-VELDT. Common name for *Heliophila,* a genus of small blue-flowered annuals from S. Africa.

BLUE GRASS, KENTUCKY BLUE GRASS. Common names for *Poa pratensis,* also called June Grass, the standard lawn grass in temperate regions. Though native to Europe and Asia, it has become naturalized in N. America and has become a valuable feature of the rich meadows and pastures of some sections of the country, especially the State whose name it bears.

It is a hardy tufted perennial which, uncut, may grow to 3 ft. in favorable locations, with leaves ½ in. wide and 6 in.

long. The inflorescence or seed-head is a panicle to 8 in. long.

Blue Grass does best in a slightly sweet (alkaline) soil in a moist, moderately cool climate, forming a thick, even turf which is self-perpetuating under favorable conditions. Irrigation may be required in hot, dry summers. It does not do well where continued use of ammonium fertilizers tend to create an acid soil condition.

Blue Grass lawns or pastures are grown from seed, sown alone or mixed with redtop and white clover. The seed is light, weighing only from 14 and 21 lbs. to the bushel. It is sown at the rate of 2½ to 3½ bu. per acre or 4 lbs. or more per 1000 sq. ft. In mixtures, 2 to 5 parts are used to 1 of redtop; the clover may be included or sown separately at the rate of 1 or 2 qts. to the acre.

For soil preparation, sowing, care, etc., see LAWN.

Canada Blue Grass (which see) is a related species, *Poa compressa.*

BLUE GUM. Common name for *Eucalyptus globulus,* the most common species of Gum-tree in U. S. A rapid grower in dry locations. Juvenile forms are used for gray-foliage effect in N. greenhouses. Var. *compacta* is dwarf, round-headed and densely branched. See EUCALYPTUS.

BLUE LACE-FLOWER (formerly *Didiscus* but now *Trachymene caerulea*). A handsome Australian annual herbaceous plant at one time a garden favorite, then for several years neglected and forgotten, then taken up again and offered as a novelty and at present popular once more. The dainty plant, growing 2½ ft. tall, blossoms from July to November. Its flat or rounded clusters of clear-blue flowers with slender tubes suggest miniature lace parasols, or delicately formed and colored heads of the familiar wild carrot or "queens lace handkerchief." (This resemblance is explained by the fact that both plants belong to the Carrot Family.) The blossoms make graceful cut flowers, and are extensively grown by florists to supply city trade.

However, the plant is also a good garden subject of easy culture although it is best placed in a moist and cool (though not shady) location. Seed should be sown outdoors where the plants are to stand as soon as danger of frost has passed; later they should be thinned so as to have a foot of room. As seed germination is slow it is sometimes advisable to start plants indoors in pots so they can be set outdoors with the least possible disturbance of the roots. For winter flowering in the greenhouse or conservatory, plants may be grown from seed in the bench; or carefully potted up from the garden before frost occurs.

BLUE-LOTUS-OF-EGYPT. Common name for *Nymphaea caerulea*, not a species of Lotus but a tender waterlily with light blue, white-centered morning-blooming flowers. Compare LOTUS.

BLUE OXALIS (ok'-sa-lis). Common name for *Parochetus communis*, also called Shamrock-pea (which see), a trailing plant of the tropics with shamrock-like leaves and rich blue flowers.

BLUE PALM, MEXICAN BLUE PALM. Common names for *Erythea armata*, a sturdy palm of Mexico and Lower Calif., the trunk of which is covered with a thick ruffle of old leaves.

BLUE-PALMETTO. One name for *Rhapidophyllum hystrix*, also known as Needle Palm (which see), a native dwarf palm of the coastal region from S. C. to Miss.

BLUE-SPIREA (spy-ree'-ah). A name sometimes applied to *Caryopteris incana*, more commonly known as Bluebeard (which see), a handsome, semi-hardy shrub bearing lavender-blue flowers profusely in autumn.

BLUESTAIN. Several species of fungi (usually following attacks of bark beetles) stain the wood of living trees or fresh lumber in yards a gray or blue color. Pines are especially subject to it. See BARK BEETLES.

BLUESTONE. A common name for copper sulphate (which see) or blue vitriol, an important fungicide, especially as used with lime in making bordeaux mixture, which see.

BLUETS. Common name for *Houstonia caerulea*, a blue, spring-blooming, perennial herb of S. U.S. forming low, rounded tufts, and useful in the rock garden. Mountain-bluet is *Centaurea montana*.

BLUE-WEED. Common name for *Echium vulgare*, also known as Vipersbugloss, a native of Europe and Asia, but widely naturalized in the U. S. See ECHIUM.

BOCCONIA (bok-oh'-ni-ah). A genus of trees, shrubs or perennial herbs of the Poppy Family which because of their stately appearance are especially desirable for background planting. Catalogs gener-

ally regard Bocconia as one with the genus Macleaya, and most gardeners regard the two as the same. In general characteristics they are almost identical, except that Bocconia has a yellowish juice. The one species, *frutescens*, which is occasionally planted in the S., is a shrub or tree reaching a height of 25 ft. and bearing leaves up to 16 in. long and small petalless flowers in terminal, branching panicles. Other listed species—*cordata* (Plume-poppy, which see), *japonica* and *microcarpa*—are all considered botanically as species of Macleaya, which see.

BOEHMERIA (bu-mee'-ri-ah). Herbs, shrubs or trees, mostly found in warm countries, belonging to the Nettle Family, but without stinging hairs. The most important species is *B. nivea*, the source of the valuable fibre known as ramie. It is a perennial with a woody base, making long annual shoots 6 ft. or more. It is extensively cultivated in the Southern United States. *B. argentea* is a small Mexican tree, with large silvery leaves to 1 ft. long.

BOGBEAN, BUCKBEAN. Common names of the herb *Menyanthes trifoliata* of the Gentian Family, a native of cool bogs of the northern hemisphere, and excellent for planting in the bog garden. The starry white flowers, with a beard on each petal, are most pleasing, and the glossy trifoliate leaves make a good ground-cover. It can be moved from the wild, and is easily increased by division or seed.

BOG GARDEN. This means just what the name implies—the usually low, and always wet, ground where plants that need such conditions are cultivated. There have been artificially contrived bog gardens, but it is not satisfactory, from either the artistic or the practical standpoint, to violate the natural conditions as much as the artificial creation of such a feature requires. On the other hand, land naturally boggy is such a difficult problem for the gardener that to make a virtue of necessity and develop it as the site for the delightful and rare (to the garden at least) moisture-loving plants which will not grow elsewhere is the rational thing.

SITE AND CONSTRUCTION. For success in such a special undertaking it is important to have a genuine bog- or swamp-condition, or a little brook which may be slightly dammed and induced to saturate an area outside its natural banks. Merely low-lying land where water settles at rainy seasons only to disappear altogether as the summer advances will not suffice. Hence it is desirable that there shall be a spring or springs to maintain the constant supply. Lacking these natural conditions it is not advisable to attempt this really exacting feature. Given them, however, it is sometimes well to excavate enough at the lowest portion of the land to provide moderate drainage for the entire space. Of course such excavation, filling with water, will form a naturalistic little pool which then will become a feature of the composition. Since it is necessary to walk intimately among the plants in order to enjoy them as well as to tend them on occasion, pathways are important. In such conditions stepping stones justify themselves as nowhere else, because they provide the dry and firm footing which no other kind of path can give. They should be evenly and securely set with their surfaces 2 in. above the earth—more, if the water sometimes rises above its normal level. The local conditions must govern this, of course.

PLANT MATERIALS. Trees especially adapted to sodden earth conditions are sour gum, black willow, swamp white oak, willow oak, hornbeam, black ash, bald cypress, white and red birch, larch and black spruce. Shrubs that thrive in such places are alder, spicebush, button-bush, sweet pepperbush, clammy azalea, elder, steeple-bush and arrow-wood. These shrubs and trees are not only able to do well in unusually wet soil but they bring the associated idea of natural bogs and swales into the composition. Therefore they may be said to belong in such a garden or in the approach to such a garden, even though they also grow well under less saturated ground conditions. Naturally they will be used as boundary planting rather than within the bog garden itself where the smaller things will be used.

Bog plants themselves require special study—as does all unusual and out-of-the-ordinary vegetation. Of them all perhaps the marsh-marigold and the pitcher-plant are most generally known. The cardinal-flower would certainly come next and, though lacking conspicuous blossoms, the native sweet flag. Others include the two native irises (known as the slender and the large blue flag), ironweed, possibly bladderwort, perhaps rose mallow (if not too far north), and countless other quaint and interesting lesser plants.

See also GARDEN DESIGN; WATER GARDEN; WILD GARDEN.

BOIS D'ARC (bwah dahrk). French name (meaning "bow-wood") for *Maclura pomifera,* the Osage-orange (which see), given by early American settlers, because Indians made their bows from it.

BOISDUVALIA (bwah-deu-vay′-li-ah). Annual herbs or subshrubs, native to the W. Coast region, belonging to the Evening Primrose Family. One species, *B. densiflora,* may be grown in sunny places in the flower border. It is an annual, growing to 5 ft. high, with narrow hairy leaves, and small light purple flowers in leafy clusters.

BOLANDRA (boh-lan′-drah). A genus of the Saxifrage Family embracing two species native to Washington and Oregon. They are small delicate herbs grown chiefly in wild gardens and moist rockeries. The leaves are lobed and picturesquely slashed, and the flowers are deep purple.

BOLTONIA. A genus of tall perennial herbs of the Composite Family easily grown in the border or in groups in the wild garden, and known as False-chamomile. *B. asteroides,* of the E. States, growing to 8 ft., has small heads of aster-like flowers with white, purple, or lavender ray-flowers. *B. latisquama,* of the S. W., has larger blue-violet ray-flowers.

B O M A R E A (boh-may′-ree-ah). S. American twining plants, sometimes grown in the cool greenhouse, or outdoors in warm climates, where they prefer partial shade. They make good pot plants with liberal feeding, but do best under glass when planted in a bench or bed. Fibrous loam, leafmold and sand, with some old manure added, make a suitable compost. They need plenty of water when growing. Propagated by seeds or rooted divisions of the underground stems.

Of the principal species, *B. carderi* has large pendulous clusters of bell-shaped flowers, rose colored, with dark-purple spots; *B. edulis* has tubers said to be edible, and bears short clusters of rose flowers, tipped green; *B. oligantha* has few-flowered clusters of dull red and yellow blossoms, spotted brown; while *B. multiflora* bears dense clusters of reddish flowers also with brown spots; *B. vitellina* is one of the showiest, with large drooping clusters of orange-yellow flowers.

BONAVIST (boh-nah-vist). A common name for *Dolichos lablab* commonly called Hyacinth-bean (which see), an ornamental climbing perennial, generally grown as an annual.

BONEMEAL. This rather slow-acting organic fertilizer (which see) is valuable principally for the phosphorus it contains and which may range from 23 to 25%. But it also contains from 1 to 3% nitrogen in readily available form. Depending on the fineness to which it is ground, bonemeal requires from 1 to 3 years or even more for its plant-food elements to become available. While not, therefore, a source of a quick supply of phosphorus, it is a useful and popular fertilizer for garden use.

It is generally applied at the rate of about 10 lbs. per 100 sq. ft. and is especially satisfactory for roses and other plants that prefer a neutral or slightly alkaline soil. It is absolutely safe and causes no burning such as may result from the heavy use of more rapidly available plant foods. It is a somewhat more expensive form of phosphorus than acid phosphate (superphosphate) which is the most common phosphatic ingredient of mixed fertilizers, but is a good material to keep on hand and use in the potting-soil mixture, in preparing garden soil, and in top-dressing perennials and other established plants.

See also FERTILIZER; PHOSPHORUS.

BONESET. Common name for *Eupatorium perfoliatum,* a shrubby herb of waste lands, with flowers of dull white or bluish-purple.

BOOTTS SHIELD FERN. Common name for *Dryopteris bootti,* a hardy garden species of fern.

BORAGE (bur'-ahj). Hairy Mediterranean herbs, one of which, a low-growing perennial, *Borago laxiflora,* with blue flowers is recommended and offered for rock gardens. Another, *B. officinalis,* is a rank-growing annual 2 to 3 ft. high whose young leaves, in Germany, are used for "greens." In the U. S. it is sometimes planted as a honey plant and rarely for its ornamental loose racemes of blue flowers.

BORAGINACEAE (boh-raj-i-nay'-see-ee). The Borage Family, a widely distributed group of plants grown in some cases as pot-herbs, in others for their ornamental foliage and sometimes for their bright, usually small flowers. Mostly bristly herbs, a few are woody; the herbaceous kinds bear the numerous small flowers on one side of a shortened shoot resembling a spike, which, at first rolled up, straightens as the flowers develop.

Among the genera of ornamental value are: Echium, Heliotropum, Borago, Onosmodium, Myosotis (Forget-me-not), Mertensia (Virginia-bluebells).

BORDEAUX (bor-doh') **MIXTURE.** One of the oldest and most widely used fungicides, whose efficacy was discovered by accident. The vineyardists near Bordeaux, France, sprayed their vines with a bluish mixture of lime and copper sulphate to simulate a poison and thus prevent theft of the grapes. In 1882 a scientist (Millardet) reported that the mixture also protected the plants from downy mildew. Bordeaux mixture was introduced into the United States in 1885.

The present-day standard formula for general use is 4-4-50, meaning 4 lbs. copper sulphate (bluestone or blue vitriol), 4 lbs. hydrated lime and 50 gals. water. The mixture is made by thoroughly dissolving the copper sulphate in several gallons of water in an earthernware or wooden container, mixing the lime with a like quantity of water in another vessel, then pouring the two into the spray tank or other receptacle in which is enough water to make up the full 50 gals., stirring constantly meanwhile. Properly prepared, the mixture is of a light blue color; it should be used within a few hours of mixing and be constantly agitated.

On certain crops the standard-strength mixture may cause burning of the foliage or russeting of fruits, which may be mistaken for pest or disease injury. See SPRAY INJURY. Danger of such burning may be lessened by increasing the amount of lime so as to prevent the possibility of there being any free copper in the mixture, and by increasing the amount of water. Thus a 4-6-50 formula is quite popular. To make a small quantity of this strength, dissolve 2 oz. of the copper sulphate in 1 gal. of water (in earthenware, glass or wood); mix 3 oz. of lime in 1 gal. of water in a second vessel; pour the two together, stirring well, and spray. Or stock solutions of 1 lb. of copper sulphate per gallon of water, and 1 lb. of lime per gallon of water, can be made up and kept in separate tight containers (preferably glass). When 1 gal. of a 4-6-50 mixture is wanted, pour ½ pint of the copper sulphate stock solution and ¾ pint of the lime solution into 6½ pints of water in a third container, stir and spray. To make a "weak bordeaux mixture" as recommended for certain blights, reduce the amounts of the two materials one-half.

Prepared bordeaux mixture, in either dry or paste form, which needs only the addition of water according to directions on the package, is obtainable at garden supply stores and is convenient and economical in caring for the small garden.

BORDEAUX PAINT. Used for painting wounds caused in pruning and by the removal of diseased limbs or malformations of various kinds, this consists of dry bordeaux mixture (powder) moistened with linseed oil until a paste of the proper consistency results.

BORDER. (See illustrations, Plates 3 and 31.) In gardening, borders are special plantings located: primarily, on the margins of open areas; secondarily, beside drives and walks; and, thirdly, around buildings, though these last are usually termed "foundation" or "base" plantings. In marginal cases borders form the "frame" in which the garden "picture" is set. Here they are of artistic value in proportion to their mass, background and perspective effects rather than because of individual specimens, which may, however, appear as accents and points of special interest. Beside drives (and still more beside walks) they are used more to display individual and grouped specimens than for framework and background effects. Around buildings their chief purpose is to break up and soften hard, straight lines and abrupt angles as at wall corners and between walls and the ground level.

Borders have two outstanding advantages over flower beds: First, they avoid any spotty, uneasy cramping and polka-dot effects; second, they afford far greater opportunities for the expression of personal taste, variety and enlarging experience with plants and plant arrangements, since flower beds are frequently limited to a few subjects which have short seasons of beauty and long periods of ugliness when not in flower. Of course, if a border is made exclusively of the same kinds of plants as are ordinarily used in flower beds, it may be just as unsightly when not in bloom. But plant materials offer such wide choice that such cases need not occur.

One border may be composed of evergreens, coniferous, broad leaved, flowering, or a mixture of all three; another may be of deciduous shrubs; a third, of hardy perennials; a fourth, of native wild plants; a

fifth, of annuals and bedding plants. But such "defined" borders are usually less effective—and some of them much more insistent upon cultural attention—than combined ones. And innumerable pleasing combinations may be made with plants belonging to the distinctive groups mentioned. Moreover, changes may be made occasionally, or even annually, among the minor subjects, so that though the background remains more or less constant, the border as a whole will present new effects each year. Thus the well-planned, well cared for mixed border offers the greatest opportunities for the expression of personal taste, experiment and experience.

ANNUAL AND BULB BORDERS. If a border is to consist exclusively of annuals the ground may be prepared in spring if the soil is light; if it is heavy, late autumn fitting is preferable. In the latter case leave the ground rough so the winter weather will break up and "mellow" the clods. If the border is to contain hardy, large-flowering bulbs such as tulip, hyacinth and crown imperial followed by annuals or bedding plants, the soil should be prepared in autumn prior to bulb-planting time. The bulbs may either be left in the ground from year to year or dug after their tops have died down, dried, cleaned, stored and replanted the following autumn. Though such borders are attractive while in bloom they are less continuously interesting and involve more work each year than do borders of perennials or shrubs.

PERENNIAL AND SHRUB BORDERS. As perennial and shrubbery borders are permanent investments, they deserve thorough preparation. This means deep digging and preferably trenching (which see) for deep rooting, long lasting subjects such as peony and gas-plant. Also it means thoroughly mixing abundant humus (compost, leaf-mold, commercial humus or peat moss) with the soil when forking it over. Should the soil be heavy these materials (and also sifted coal ashes) will help lighten and loosen it. So will late fall digging, leaving the clods over winter and, in spring, scattering lime or wood ashes on the surface (about a pound to 10 sq. ft.) before-raking. Should the soil be wet it must be drained; should it be naturally dry some kind of irrigation should be provided. Humus will also give "body" to a loose sandy soil and increase its ability to retain moisture.

DESIGN AND CARE. In laying out a border it is important to locate the largest-growing subjects, especially the shrubs, first. They should go mostly in the background and always far enough apart to permit development to full size without crowding. Next, the plants that attain only medium size and those that grow rapidly should be similarly placed with respect to the large ones and to each other. In this way all the permanent plants are properly placed, regardless of how sparsely populated the border may appear at first. For while the permanent plants are developing to normal stature and spread, any blank or bare spaces between them may be filled with annuals, bedding stock and bulbous plants, such as lilies, of which there are many, both tall and dwarf growing, to choose among.

During the growing season keep borders neat and clean by staking tall plants, destroying weeds, removing dead flower stems, feeding when necessary, stirring exposed soil areas to keep them loose and friable and soaking the soil well whenever it becomes too dry. Just before winter but only *after* the ground freezes, apply a deep mulch, preferably of strawy stable manure, leafmold or both, if available at reasonable cost, or otherwise of leaves, straw, compost or any loose material. In spring the coarse material, together with all tops or other vegetable debris not previously removed should be raked off and added to the compost pile and the fine stuff (or an application of pulverized manure and ground bone) worked into the soil by shallow forking. The only time a spade should be used in a border is when changes are to be made and plants removed, replaced or reset.

Winter mulches that mat down, become sodden and freeze solid should be avoided, especially where herbaceous perennials with leafy crowns are used. Evergreen branches and other loose materials are good; and a deep covering of loose snow is an unexcelled natural blanket.

See also ANNUALS; BEDDING AND BEDDING PLANTS; HERBACEOUS BORDER; BULBS; PERENNIALS; SHRUBS.

BORECOLE (bohr'-kohl). A European name for the loose-leafed, green or purple "peasant's cabbage" (*boor's cole*) grown in America as Kale (which see).

BORERS. Insects which bore or tunnel through the trunk or branches of trees or stalks of herbaceous plants. The adult stage in some cases is a beetle (order Coleoptera); in others, it is a moth (order Lepidoptera).

Flat-headed tree borers make shallow mines in the bark and sapwood of the trunks and larger branches of shade and fruit trees, generally on the south and southwest sides. The grayish white grubs have a pronounced flattened enlargement of the body just back of the head. The adults are flattened beetles with a metallic luster. In this group are the flat-headed apple tree borer and the bronze birch borer. See under APPLE and BIRCH.

Long-horned or round-headed borers may extend the mines into the solid wood. Their grubs are not flattened and the beetles are more or less cylindrical and often beautifully colored. The group includes poplar, locust, elm and apple borers. Linden, maple, oak, hickory and willow are also subject o attack.

The presence of a borer is generally indicated by a pile of sadwust outside of the hole on the rough bark or perhaps on the ground below. Probing with a flexible wire will sometimes kill the borers within.

THE STALK BORER
Destroy him inside of dahlia and other stems by slitting them—and him—with a sharp knife.

With a machine-oil can carbon bisulphide may be injected into the opening, which should be closed with a wad of clay or putty; or a proprietary nicotine paste may be used without closing the aperture. If fumigation does not succeed, borer-infested stems of dogwood, lilac, rhododendron and other shrubs should be cut out and burned.

To prevent borer attack, newly transplanted trees should have their trunks wrapped with burlap or paper to be left on for two years. Double craft crepe paper, with a layer of asphaltum between made in strips for this purpose, wound spirally downward from the lowest branches to the ground and tied with twine spiralled in the opposite direction, gives good protection. Or sheets of ordinary heavy wrapping paper can be used, tied around every foot or so. Wax emulsion sprays used to prevent drying out of plants, offer some slight resistance to borers. A repellent soap wash recently recommended consists of 10 lbs. C.P.O. soap, 4 lbs. Bentonite, and 2 lbs. napthalene flakes mixed with water to a thin paste to be applied every 2 or 3 weeks during June and July. Paradichlorobenzene, much used against the peach-tree borer, is being replaced by ethylene dichloride emulsion. See under PEACH.

Since borer attack is correlated with lack of tree vigor due to drought or malnutrition, proper feeding and watering are excellent preventive measures. The Iris borer should be cut out as soon as the plants have finished flowering (see IRIS). The various stalk borers may be kept under control by pulling up annuals and cutting off above-ground parts of perennials in late fall and burning all this debris and all weeds.

BORER CONTROL
Protect newly set shade trees with a well-tied spiral wrapping of kraft-paper.

BORONIA (boh-roh'-ni-ah). A genus of dwarf Australian shrubs of elegant habit belonging to the Rue Family. In cultivation they are usually grown as pot plants under cool greenhouse conditions. They have small fine leaves, and are valued most for the delightful fragrance of their small flowers, which are mostly of red or purple tones. Propagation is by seeds or cuttings, and they bloom freely when young.

After flowering they should be cut back to encourage a good, bushy growth. They can be plunged outdoors for the summer, but it should be kept in mind that they will not stand drought. At the same time, good drainage is necessary in the pots as they object just as much to being waterlogged.

Principal Species

B. heterophylla. The best from a decorative viewpoint. It has pinkish drooping flowers that stay partly closed.

elatior. Flowers (not opening wide) are rosy red or purple in dense clusters along the ends of the branches.

megastigma. Flowers (more open, and noted as the most fragrant) are purplish maroon on the outside and yellow on the inside.

alata. Bears terminal clusters of wide open fragrant pink flowers.

pulchella. One of the prettiest species with a profusion of rose-pink flowers in spring.

BOSTON FERN (*Nephrolepis exaltata* var. *bostoniensis*). One of the best-known and most satisfactory ferns for indoor cultivation, obtainable in numerous varieties, and able to withstand neglect as no other fern will. The original plant appeared in a Boston (Mass.) greenhouse as a sport of the common *N. exaltata* of the W. Indies and S. Fla. Although it originated only about 30 years ago, it is estimated that over a million plants are now sold annually in the E. States alone. It seldom produces spores but multiplies from running stolons. Subsequently other varieties developed, some of them 4- and 5-pinnate, others dwarf, plumed, waved, forked, etc., but none of these have the great stamina of the simple-leaved varieties. The true Boston fern has fronds 2 ft. or more long and 3 to 6 in. broad, the pinnae slightly toothed and sharp pointed, and the upper side of each eared. The stipes are scaly, from a compact crown.

For best results provide a light, porous soil, a north exposure (as for all ferns) and plenty of water at the roots. Repot regularly each spring, and rest in shade through the summer.

Varieties

Some popular varieties are: Mill's Boston Fern, compact, low growing, once pinnate; Verona Fern, with variable, 3-pinnate, fronds, 1 ft. tall, and one of the hardiest; var. *piersoni*, deeply cut, 2-pinnate; var. *craigi*, 5-pinnate, very feathery; and var. *whitmani*, 3-pinnate.

BOSTON IVY. A common name for *Parthenocissus tricuspidata*, sometimes called Japanese Ivy. See IVY.

BOTANIC GARDEN. A botanic garden is an institution in or by which are maintained collections of living plants, and usually a collection of dried specimens of plants known as a herbarium; also a library, greenhouses, museums, and laboratories for research work in botanical science and the application of horticultural skill.

These gardens, supported by public or private funds, are generally open to the public and are by most people regarded and enjoyed as parks where beautiful trees, shrubs, flowering plants and lawns may be enjoyed, and where special types of gardens may be seen, such as rose gardens, perennial or annual gardens, rock, water, wild-flower and herb gardens. Students and other advanced horticulturists of course make greater use of their scientific facilities.

The education of the public in the knowledge and appreciation of the plant world and in the encouragement of practical gardening is now regarded as just as important a function of a botanic garden as the advancement of botanical science. The greatest institutions of this kind which have contributed most to botanical science and which have been consistently supported are those which have always recognized this two-fold opportunity.

Botanic gardens are training schools for advanced students in botany, horticulture and forestry but many also offer elementary courses in these and related subjects and conduct series of popular lectures for the benefit of the general public, including school children. Scientific literature and popular bulletins, too, are issued regularly by many botanic gardens to their members, who pay various annual dues for different privileges. Some of them are also obtainable free or for a nominal sum by the public.

The most important botanic gardens in the United States are the New York Botanical Garden, the Brooklyn (N. Y.) Botanic Garden and the Missouri Botanic Garden in St. Louis. There are many others (as listed below) of varying degrees of size, completeness, scope and scientific rank. Wherever they are, and in whatever stage of development, they merit the support of the gardening public, both moral and, if possible, financial. Besides contributing to the advance of botanical science, they give full return for such support in the form of direct and indirect help to even small garden owners who will take the time and trouble to visit and use them.

There are many more botanic gardens in Europe than in the United States. One of the oldest, and according to many scientists the greatest in the world, is the Royal Botanic Gardens at Kew, London, Eng. From as early as 1772, Kew-trained men have been sent on plant-exploration trips to many parts of the world in search of plants that would be of interest to agriculture, horticulture and botanical science. And other graduates of these gardens are found in important horticultural positions and as superintendents and gardeners of the finest estates in many parts of this country as well as abroad.

Considering the growth of botanical gardens and arboretums as a national movement, an important step was taken in September, 1940, in the organization, at Cleveland, O., of the American Association of Botanical Garden and Arboretum Executives designed to promote the interchange of information and materials between such institutions and the correlation of their efforts and investigations. The secretary of the new group is Mr. G. E. Godshalk, Morton Arboretum, Lisle, Ill.

The following list of the botanic gardens in the U. S. and Canada, which includes also establishments more correctly called Arboreta (see ARBORETUM), is given so that garden lovers located near them can become acquainted and then familiar with them and the service they can render toward more serious and more enjoyable gardening. A few public parks are also included where these contain exceptionally interesting or valuable collections of trees, shrubs, and other plant materials.

(P—*Indicates private gardens or collections;* Pro —*Indicates proposed;* U—*Indicates new, under construction.*)

UNITED STATES

Alabama—
  Birmingham: Arboretum (U).
Arizona—
  Phoenix: Botanical Garden in Papago Park (Pro).
  Superior: Boyce Thompson Southwest Arboretum.
  Tucson: Carnegie Institution Desert Botanical Laboratory; Univ. of Ariz.
Arkansas—
  Fayetteville: State Agricultural Experiment Station, Univ. of Ark.
California—
  Anaheim: Rancho Santa Ana Botanic Garden (P).
  Berkeley: Univ. of Calif. Botanical Garden.
  Carmel: Carnegie Institution Acclimatization Garden; Point Lobos Reserve.
  Chico: U. S. Dept. of Agriculture Plant Introduction Station.
  Hueneme: Botanic Garden (P).
  Lompoc: Purisima Mission.
  Los Angeles: California Botanic Garden; H. W. O'Melveny Estate (P).; Univ. of Calif.
  Mandeville Canyon: Aboretum.

Palo Alto: Leland Stanford Univ., Pacific Botanical Garden.
Placerville: Institute of Forest Genetics.
Riverside: Albert White Park.
San Diego: Balboa Park; Mission Cliff Gardens.
San Francisco: Golden Gate Park.
San Marino: Huntington Botanical Gardens.
Santa Barbara: Blaksley Botanic Garden; Montarioso Botanic Garden; Carnegie Institution of Washington, Mission Canyon.
Santa Maria: Succulent Garden, Santa Maria Inn; Botanical Collection, Legion Memorial Building.
Sierra Madre: Los Angeles County Arboretum.
West Los Angeles: A Stephen Vavra Garden (P).

Colorado—
Colorado Springs: The Myron Stratton Home.
Manitou: Carnegie Institute of Washington.

Connecticut—
Fairfield: Pinetum of George P. Brett (P).
Greenwich: Montgomery Pinetum (P).
Hartford: Elizabeth Park; Batterson Park Arboretum; Estate of Charles F. T. Seaverns (P).
New Haven: Marsh Botanic Garden at Yale Univ.; Osborn Botanical Laboratory Garden.
New London: Arboretum at Connecticut College.

District of Columbia—
Washington: National Arboretum; Rock Creek Park Arboretum; U. S. Botanic Garden; Washington Cathedral Gardens.

Florida—
Coconut Grove: Botanical Garden; U. S. D. A. Experiment Station; Brett Palm Collection (P); Coconut Grove Palmetum (P); Fairchild Tropical Garden.
Coral Gables: Matheson Hammock County Park.
Gainesville: State Agricultural Experiment Stations.
Jacksonville: Oriental Gardens (P).
Lake Wales: The Mountain Lake Sanctuary and Singing Tower.
Miami: Everglades National Park Project.
Sebring: Florida Botanical Garden and Arboretum.
Vero Beach: McKee Jungle Gardens.
Winter Park: Meade Botanical Garden (U).

Georgia—
Athens: The University of Georgia.
Atlanta: Botanic Garden (Pro).
Savannah: Wormsloe Gardens (P).
Wormsloe: Wormsloe Gardens (P).

Idaho—
Moscow: Univ. of Idaho Experiment Station; School of Forestry University of Idaho.

Illinois—
Bloomington: Arboretum on the grounds of the Bloomington and Normal Sanitary District.
Chicago: Marquette Park; Park System Greenhouses; Garfield Park Conservatory.
Joliet: Park System, including Pilcher Arboretum.
Lisle: Morton Arboretum.
Lombard: Lombard Park District (Lilac Collection).
Urbana: Univ. of Illinois Arboretum (Pro).

Indiana—
Huntington: Botanic Garden and Arboretum of Huntington College.
Indianapolis: Riverside Park; Botanical Garden in Halliday Park; Botanical Garden of Butler University.
Michigan City: International Friendship Gardens (P).
Muncie: Botanical Garden at Ball State Teachers College.
Porter County: Dunes State Park.

Iowa—
Ames: Iowa State College Botanic Garden.
Grinnell: Grinnell College Botanic Garden.

McGregor: Iowa Memorial Arboretum Association Arboretum; State Park System—38 or more.

Kansas—
Belle Plaine: Bartlett Arboretum (P).
Lawrence: University of Kansas Botanical Garden.
Topeka: Indian Hill Arboretum, North Topeka (P).

Kentucky—
Lexington: Translyvania Univ. Botanic Garden; Univ. of Kentucky Experimental Station; Kentucky Botanic Garden at Univ. of Kentucky.
Louisville: Bernheim Arboretum (Pro).

Louisiana—
Avery Island: Jungle Gardens (P).
New Orleans: Subtropical Arboretum of New Orleans.

Maine—
Thomaston: The Knox Academy of Arts and Sciences.
Warren (Thomastown): Knox Academy Arboretum.

Maryland—
Baltimore: Johns Hopkins University, Botanical Department and Botanical Garden.
Bell Station: U. S. D. A. Experiment Station.
College Park: Univ. of Maryland Experiment Station; Univ. of Maryland Arboretum and Botanical Garden.

Massachusetts—
Boston: Park System; Boston Park Department.
Cambridge: Botanic Garden and Museum, Harvard Univ.; Farlow Reference Library and Herbarium; Gray Herbarium of Harvard Univ.
Groton: Lowthorpe School of Landscape Architecture.
Jamaica Plain: Arnold Arboretum.
Lexington: The Lexington Botanic Gardens, Inc.
Northampton: Smith College Arboretum; Smith College Botanical Garden.
Petersham: Harvard Forest.
South Hadley: Mt. Holyoke College; Dwight Botanical Garden and Talcott Arboretum.
Springfield: Riverside Park.
Topsfield: Proctor Arboretum (P).
Wellesley: Alexandria Botanic Garden and Hunnewell Arboretum at Wellesley College (P).

Michigan—
Ann Arbor: Univ. of Michigan, Nichols Arboretum and Botanic Garden.
Augusta: W. K. Kellogg Bird Sanctuary and Arboretum (Pro).
Battle Creek: Park Department, Leila Arboretum.
Charlevoix: Hemingway Evergreen Aboretum (Pro) (P).
Detroit: Palmer Park Arboretum.
East Lansing: Mich. Agricultural College, Beal Arboretum; Beal Botanical Garden.
Hillsdale: Slayton Arboretum and Botanical Garden.
Presque Isle: Peninsula State Park.

Minnesota—
Lake City: Lake City Arboretum; Underwood Arboretum and State Game Refuge.
Minneapolis: Park System; Univ. of Minnesota; Wild Botanic Garden; The Eloise Butler Wild Garden at Glenwood Park; Rose Garden at Lyndale Park; Univ. of Minnesota Greenhouse Gardens.
Northfield: Carleton College Arboretum.

Missouri—
Florida: Mark Twain Memorial Park.
St. Louis: Missouri (Shaw's) Botanical Gardens.

Nebraska—
Nebraska City: Arbor Lodge State Park.

New Jersey—
Gladstone: Willowwood Farm Arboretum (P).

BROOKLYN BOTANIC GARDEN
CO-OPERATION WITH OTHER INSTITUTIONS

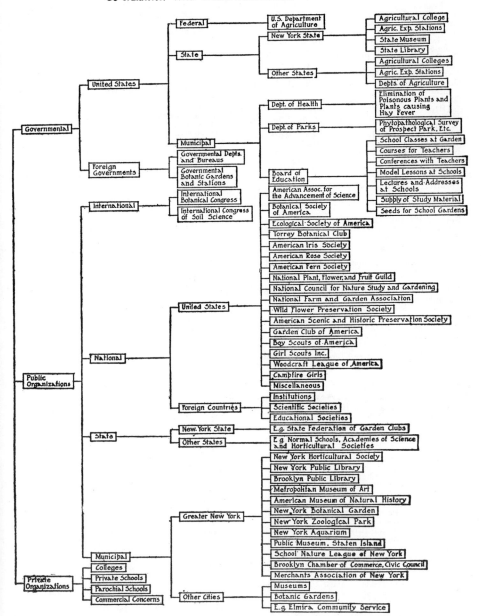

HOW A BOTANIC GARDEN CO-OPERATES WITH OTHER INSTITUTIONS FOR THE
BENEFIT OF THE PUBLIC
(Courtesy of the Brooklyn Botanic Garden)

New Brunswick: State Agricultural Experiment Station.
Washington Crossing: Washington Crossing State Park.

New York—
Albany: Park System.
Beacon: Craig House.
Brooklyn: Brooklyn Botanic Garden.
Brookville: T. A. Havemeyer Arboretum (P).
Buffalo: South Park Conservatory.
Castile: Letchworth State Park.
Farmingdale: State Institute of Agriculture.
Fishkill Landing: Wodenethe (Sargent Estate).
Geneva: New York State Agricultural Experiment Station.
Glen Clove: Dosoris Arboretum (Dana Estate) (P).
Irvington: Hamilton Arboretum of Columbia Univ.
Ithaca: Cornell Univ. Campus and Arboretum.
Locust Valley: Hodenpyle Estate (P).
New York: Bronx Park; Central Park; Inwood Park; New York Botanical Garden.
Oakdale: W. B. Cutting Arboretum (P).
Palisades: Interstate Park.
Portageville: Letchworth Park Arboretum.
Poughkeepsie: Vassar College Gardens.
Rochester: Highland Park, Durand-Eastman Park, etc.
Roslyn: Pinetum Claytonense (P).
Sterlington: Skylands Nursery (Lewis Estate) (P).
Syracuse: State College of Forestry; Pinetum in Thornton Park.
Yonkers: Boyce Thompson Institute for Plant Research.

North Carolina—
Chapel Hill: Univ. of N. C. Coker Arboretum; Southeastern Aboretum.
Mars Hill: Mars Hill College Arboretum.

North Dakota—
Fargo: State Agricultural Experiment Station.
Rolla: International Peace Garden.

Ohio—
Cincinnati: Mt. Airy Forest Arboretum; Spring Grove Cemetery; The Stanley M. Rowe Arboretum.
Cleveland: Fine Arts Garden; Holden Arboretum (Kirtland Hills).
Columbus: Botanic Garden of Ohio State Univ.
Kent: John Davey Memorial Arboretum.
Newark: Dawes' Arboretum.
Northfield: Rocky Run Arboretum (P).
Oberlin: Oberlin College Hall Arboretum.
Wooster: State Agricultural Experiment Station.
Yellow Springs: Arboretum, Bryan Park; Antioch College.
Youngstown: Mill Creek Park.
Zoar: Zoar Gardens.

Oregon—
Corvallis: State Agricultural College Forestry Arboretum; Percy Arboretum at Oregon State College, School of Forestry.
Portland: Portland Civic Arboretum; Hoyt Park Arboretum.

Pennsylvania—
Bethlehem: Lehigh Univ. Arboretum.
Bryn Mawr: Bryn Mawr College Botanic Garden.
Chestnut Hill: Boxley Arboretum; Compton Arboretum; Morris Arboretum (P).
Elizabethtown: Masonic Homes.
George School: George School.
Harrisburg: Breeze Hill (J. H. McFarland) (P).
Haverford: Haverford College.
Kennett Square: Longwood (P).
Lima: Painter Estate Arboretum.
Marshalltown: Humphrey Marshall Arboretum.
Merion: Barnes Foundation Arboretum.
Mont Alto: Mont Alto State Forest Arboretum.
Narberth: Narberth Park; Narbrook Park Improvement Association.

Philadelphia: Aldie Arboretum (P); Bartram's Garden; Awbury Park (Germantown); Cheltenham; Curtis Arboretum; Fairmount Park (Germantown); Univ. of Penn. Botanic Garden; Woodland's Cemetery; Hemlock Arboretum (P); Morris Arboretum, Univ. of Pennsylvania.
Pittsburgh: North Park Arboretum (Pro); Schenley Park; Phipps Conservatory.
Radnor: John Evans Arboretum (Smith Estate) (P).
State College: Arboretum (Pro).
Swarthmore: Swarthmore College Arboretum.
West Chester: Josiah Hoopes Pinetum.
Westtown: Westtown Friends School Arboretum.

Rhode Island—
East Greenwich: Goddard Park.
Potowomut: Goddard Park.
Providence: Roger Williams Park.

South Carolina—
Augusta: Goshen Plantation (P).
Charleston: Cypress Gardens; Magnolia Gardens (P); Middletown Place Gardens (P).
Columbia: Univ. of South Carolina Arboretum.
Oakley: Cypress Gardens (P).

South Dakota—
Brookings: State Agricultural Experiment Station.

Tennessee—
Knoxville: A. F. Sandford Arboretum (P).
Madison: Madison College Arboretum.
Memphis: Park System.
Sewanee: Univ. of the South.

Texas—
Austin: University of Texas Botanical Garden.
Beaumont: Texas State Univ. Botanic Garden; Botanic Garden in Tyrrell Park (Pro).
College Station: Helge-Ness Arboretum of Agricultural Experiment Station.
Fort Davis: County Court House Arboretum.
Fort Worth: Nature Trails, Fort Worth Botanic Garden.
Houston: Herman Park Botanical Garden; Botanic Garden in Memorial Park (Pro).
Longview: Roger Lacey Gardens.
Marble Falls: Sanctuary for Native Wild Flowers.

Utah—
Logan: Smith Arboretum (P).

Virginia—
Blacksburg: Virginia Polytechnic Institute.
Boyce: Blandy Experimental Farm, Univ. of Virginia.
Mount Vernon: Mount Vernon.
Richmond: Maymount Park (Dooley Estate).

Washington—
Carson: Wind River Arboretum (Pacific Northwest Forest Experiment Station).
Seattle: Univ. of Washington Arboretum.

West Virginia—
Wheeling: Oglebay Farm Arboretum (P).

Wisconsin—
Lake Geneva: Wynchwood.
Madison: Wisconsin Pharmaceutical Garden; Univ. of Wisconsin Arboretum.
Milwaukee: County Arboretum at Whitnall Park.

Canada—
Hamilton: Royal Botanic Garden.
Montreal: The Botanical Garden.
Morden, Manitoba: Dominion Experimental Station.
Ottawa: Dominion Arboretum and Botanic Gardens.
Vancouver, B. C.: Botanical Gardens at Univ. of B. C.

Hawaiian Islands—
Honolulu: Pan-Pacific Union Research Institute.

West Indies—
Cuba: Atkins Institution of the Arnold Arboretum.

Some of the other important botanic gardens outside the United States are located in Dublin, Ireland; Edinburgh, Scotland; Cambridge, England; Paris, France; Berlin, Germany; Tokyo, Japan; Genoa, Italy; Copenhagen, Denmark; Athens, Greece; Ghent, Belgium; Vienna, Austria; and Groningen, Holland.

BOTANY. Botany is the science which teaches us about the vegetable kingdom in all its various forms, from the lowest kinds of plant life (which are so small they cannot be seen without the aid of a microscope) to the highest forms of flowering and seed-bearing plants such as we use for the beautification of our gardens.

The science is divided into various parts and a study of at least some of these—such as that which teaches us how plants live, is of great interest to gardeners. In fact, gardening itself may be considered as a practical application of botanical science.

Scientists have divided the study of botany into parts, each having to do with some particular phase of plant life as follows:

PLANT MORPHOLOGY. The study of the various forms and structures of plants, and their comparison, covering all phases of plant life from the lowest to the highest. This is usually divided again into *Anatomy,* or the study of the larger structures of the parts; *Histology,* or the study of the more minute tissues; *Embryology,* or the study of the embryo or rudimentary plant as formed in a seed; *Morphogenesis,* or the beginning of forms and their development or evolution; and *Cytology,* the study of the cells of plants, their division and development.

PLANT PHYSIOLOGY. The study of the vital actions or functions of all parts of a plant, and the plant as a whole.

GENETICS. The study of inheritance or genealogy in plants.

PLANT ECOLOGY. The study of plant life in relation to its environment, and the effect of environment in modifying or changing the appearance of plants.

SYSTEMATIC BOTANY or TAXONOMY. The classification of plants, noting similarities and differences, which results in grouping them according to the resemblances and relations one to another. This is the study in connection with which plants are given their botanical names and arranged in groups and sub-groups such as *Rosa setigera,* the Prairie Rose, which belongs to the genus Rosa and, with other genera, to the Rosaeae or Rose Family.

The English or common name (Prairie Rose) is not official but the result of custom and it may be more or less local; yet it may also be more familiar to many than the correct scientific name. There may be a dozen or more common names given to the same plant, and this leads to confusion unless the scientific name is used to identify it in each case. It is therefore highly desirable that gardeners should learn the correct botanical names of plants and be able to use them, as well as common names.

PLANT GEOGRAPHY. This teaches us about the distribution of plants in space or over the earth's surface.

PALEOBOTANY. The study of the distribution of plants in time. Sometimes called "fossil botany" meaning the study of plants or their remains in the geological rock strata of the earth's crust.

MYCOLOGY. The study of Fungi (which see) such as mushrooms and the organisms that cause rusts and mildews.

ECONOMIC BOTANY. The study of the products of plants that are of use to man, such as food, fibres, lumber, medicine, etc.

Agriculture and its divisions that relate to plants, including gardening, horticulture, floriculture, pomology and forestry, may be regarded as applied botanical science.

See also FLOWER; PLANT; PLANT NAMES AND CLASSIFICATION.

BOTRYCHIUM (boh-trik'-i-um). A genus of fern allies, closely related to the Adders Tongue. The name (from the Greek *botrys,* a bunch of grapes) refers to the appearance of the fruiting spike. They have fleshy erect fronds from a brief rootstock, the fertile and sterile parts united below; the fertile segment bearing a panicle of naked globular spore clusters; and the leafy sterile part being thrice divided. Several species are native to open woods and pastures in this country, so in growing them simulate their habitat, giving well-drained but moist soil in semi-shade.

SPECIES

B. lunulatum (Moonwort). A diminutive species, 3 to 10 in. high, the sterile segment oblong with 3 to 8 pairs of moon-shaped or fan-shaped divisions, the fertile fronds taller and 2- to 3-pinnate. A charming and curious little fern, confined to the N. States, growing sometimes in dry pastures, but seldom thriving in gardens.

obliquum (Grape Fern). 2 to 12 in. tall, the leafy segment triangular, three

branched, spreading horizontally, bronzed
in the fall; the lower branches once pinnate, the upper 2-pinnate or nearly so.
There are many variations, some with 2 to
3 fruiting clusters and a form (var. *dissectum*) with finely cut pinnules, known as
the Cut-leaved Grape Fern.

virgianum (Rattlesnake Fern). 1 to 2 ft.
fronds, forking well above the ground, the
sterile part leafy, triangular, 3-branched
and 2-pinnate, the pinnules deeply cut and
toothed. The fertile spike, which withers
after maturity in late June, is narrowly
branched and close set, perhaps suggesting
a rattler's tail and giving the plant its common name. This species is supposed to
frequent the neighborhood of certain valuable herbs and for that reason in some
places is called "Indicator Fern."

BOTRYTIS (bo'-tri-tis). A minute
fungus responsible for many destructive
blights. The genus Botrytis is one of the
"imperfect fun-
gi" (see FUN-
GUS) but many
of its species are
part stages in
the life-history
of other fungi.
The characteris-
tic brownish-
gray mold of
Botrytis blights
is produced by
spores borne in
clusters on little
stalks all over
the infected sur-
faces. (The
name comes
from the Greek
botrys and
means a grape-
like cluster.) A
black resting
body (*sclero-
tium*) is also typical of this genus; it is
the form in which the fungus lives over
the winter on infected plant parts or
débris in the soil. Certain Botrytis species, such as those which blight peony, lily,
and tulip (which see) can attack only their
respective host-plant types, but *Botrytis
cinerea* attacks many, causing gray-mold
rot of geranium, primrose and other greenhouse plants, blossom blights of such garden flowers as rose, zinnia and marigold,
a rot of lettuce and storage rots of fruits.

BOTRYTIS

The gray mold spreads over
peony stems and leaves and
blasts the buds. The hairy
objects are spore-bearing
bodies.

SURE SIGNS OF DISEASE

Botrytis blight attacks young peony shoots, first
wilting them and turning them black. If not
controlled, it later causes bud blast.

In general, to control Botrytis troubles
burn all diseased plant parts; remove from
the beds all old plant débris in autumn;
spray young shoots with weak bordeaux
mixture in early spring. Avoid wetting
leaves in watering greenhouse plants. For
special treatments see under the different
plants affected.

BOTTLE-BRUSH. Common name
given to two Australian genera of shrubs
and trees, both members of the Myrtle
Family and both having dense cylindrical
flower spikes responsible for the title.
These are Callistemon and Melaleuca, both
of which see.

BOTTLE-BRUSH GRASS. Common
name for *Hystrix patula,* a tall, perennial,
ornamental grass, grown to some extent for
use in bouquets.

BOTTLE GENTIAN. A common name
for *Gentiana andrewsi,* also known as the
Closed Gentian, as its purplish-blue flowers
borne in terminal clusters are nearly or
quite closed.

BOTTLE-TREE. Common name for
Brachychiton, a genus of Australian trees
grown for ornament in the warmer sections
of the U. S. The name refers to the
peculiarly swollen trunk of some species.

BOTTOM HEAT. The warmth artificially applied beneath seeds, cuttings or
plants to hasten germination or rooting and
favor growth as distinguished from the heat
of the sun or the air. It may be provided
by fermenting material (as manure in a
hotbed); warm flues (in sweet-potato plant

production) ; hot water or steam pipes or radiators (as in dwellings or propagating benches) ; or by electricity carried by wires, plates or grids below the soil surface. The expression "degrees of bottom heat" means the increase in temperature over that of the adjacent air. Generally, however, the heat applied to or needed in the soil or bed is specified, as 60 deg., 70 deg., etc.

BOUGAINVILLEA (boo-gin-vil'-ee-ah). Also spelled Buginvillaea. Strong-growing shrubs from S. America. In the North grown as greenhouse climbers or in standard or bush form in pots. In Fla. and Cal. among the most showy plants with which to clothe porches and pergolas, or drape tree trunks. The flowers are small and inconspicuous; it is the surrounding large bracts which make the gaudy display. Easy to grow, they are lovers of sunshine. In the tropics Bougainvilleas may be seen planted as hedges and subjected to hard trimming.

Propagation is by cuttings of young shoots or half-ripened wood. Young plants for flowering in pots may be planted outside for the summer, then lifted and potted in the fall. For early blooming keep them in pots, but plunged outside during the summer. They can be kept in a dormant state for some time by withholding water.

PRINCIPAL SPECIES

B. glabra. A free-flowering shrub with magenta colored bracts that is trained as a vine or kept dwarf in pots. Var. *sanderiana* is even more floriferous and will bloom in small pots. Var. *cypheri* is larger with bright rose bracts. Var. *variegata* is a neat plant with creamy-white foliage.

spectabilis is a stronger grower, reaching to a great height in the tropics by means of its stout, hooked spines. It has large deep rose colored bracts, in large panicles. Var. Crimson Lake has large crimson bracts. Var. *lateritia* has even showier bracts of a brick-red color.

BOULDER FERN. Common name for *Dennstedtia punctilobula,* a very graceful, light-colored fern native to many parts of the U. S., in woods and pastures, often clustering about boulders. Fronds are 1 to 3 ft. tall, 2-pinnate, the pinnules lobed and bearing the minutely cup-shaped indusia at the base of each lobe; the rootstock creeping extensively. Excellent for naturalizing in fields and open woods (as it prefers

some sunlight), or under large shrubs; but too rampant for planting with other ferns or herbaceous plants. The fronds emit a pleasant odor when crushed, hence another name, "Hay-scented Fern."

BOUNCING BET. A common name for *Saponaria officinalis,* an Asiatic herbaceous perennial species of Soapwort, widely naturalized in N. America. It has pinkish flowers in crowded terminal clusters from May to September.

BOUQUET. An arrangement of cut plant materials considered as a unity exclusive of any container or support. It may consist of cut flowers—with or without foliage—of branches of shrubs bearing cones, berries or fruit, or of stems of grasses or everlastings, combined in various ways. The arrangement may be formal or informal but it should always have due regard for the underlying principles of design, rhythm, balance, and unity of composition as well as color harmony.

Bouquets may be carried or worn on the person, or arranged in appropriate receptacles, as vases, bowls, baskets, etc. Those to be carried may range from the stiff mid-Victorian or Colonial type, with close-set rows of solid, double buds, surrounded with smaller, lighter ones such as violets or forget-me-nots, and finished with a ruff of paper or real lace, to the typical bride's shower-bouquet of lilies-of-the-valley or orchids, or the casual appearing but carefully selected and arranged sheaf of blossoms and foliage to be carried, presented or worn as a corsage decoration. For suggestions as to the arrangement of bouquets in appropriate receptacles, see FLOWER ARRANGEMENT.

BOURBON ROSE. Common name of a group of old-fashioned garden sorts represented by a few named varieties, some of the bedding, and others of the climbing, type. The species *R. borboniana* to which the name particularly applies is a hybrid of *R. chinensis* (the China Rose) and *R. gallica* (the French Rose) and it in turn has been much crossed with other species to produce hybrids from which the Remontant or hybrid perpetual sorts have been developed. Bourbon Roses are generally fairly continuous bloomers but some have only a single short flowering period. The hybrids are hardier than the species itself. See ROSE.

BOUSSINGAULTIA (boo-sin-gaul'-ti-ah). Tropical American perennial vines.

of which one species, *B. basselloides,* is frequently grown as a porch vine in the North as Mignonette- or Madeira-vine (which see).

BOUVARDIA (boo-vahr'-di-ah). Small shrubs, mostly native to Mexico and Cent. America, belonging to the Madder Family. They are not grown as much to-day as they formerly were, but are still interesting shrubby plants for winter flowering in the greenhouse. Florists grow them for the rather waxy white flowers with four stout petals. Some bear yellow or red flowers. Those in cultivation are mostly sports or hybrids.

Bouvardias thrive in a mixture of fibrous loam, leafmold and sand. After they have flowered keep them cooler and dryer for a few weeks, then cut back and start into new growth in heat and moisture. The shoots should be pinched from time to time to induce a good habit and free flowering. During the growing period they need plenty of water; it is helpful to occasionally color the water with liquid manure. Plants can be flowered in pots or in the bench. Old plants can be set outdoors for the summer; if carefully handled and potted in the fall, kept in a close temperature and shaded for a few days, such specimens will produce a good supply of flowers for cutting. Propagation is effected by young stem cuttings taken with a heel; also by cutting up pieces of the thickest roots into 2 in. lengths.

B. humboldti is perhaps the most handsome species. It differs from most in having opposite glossy green leaves, and in flowering before winter. It has white fragrant flowers borne in a large terminal cluster. *B. triphylla,* with leaves in 3's, was the earliest to be introduced, late in the 18th century. It has scarlet flowers and has played an important part in the production of the improved forms now grown.

BOWER-PLANT. Common name for *Pandorea jasminoides,* an evergreen climbing shrub of Australia, with pink-throated white flowers.

BOWMANS-ROOT. Common name for *Gillenia trifoliata,* also known as Indian Physic, an erect, branching herb of E. N. America, with loose clusters of white or pinkish flowers, easily grown in rock or wild gardens.

BOWSTRING-HEMP. The common name for the genus Sansevieria, to which belong the sturdy, stiff-leaved, popular house plants popularly known as "snakeplants." It is not related to the true hemp, but belongs to the Lily Family.

BOX. About 30 species of evergreen shrubs or small trees found in N. Africa, Cent. America, and different parts of Europe and Asia comprise the genus Buxus of the Box Family (Buxaceae) named after it. They have small, leathery leaves and inconspicuous flowers. The hard and closegrained wood is prized in engraving and the finer wood work.

Box (or Boxwood) grows in any well drained soil, and seems to prefer partial shade. In the North, winter protection from sun and wind is usually necessary, and even then injury is likely to show after a severe winter. It is slow growing, but valued in gardens for its many uses. In one very dwarf form it has been grown for centuries to edge walks and flower beds. In another form it grows into billowy mounds, well suited to be used in association with the noblest architecture. It is also amenable to hard trimming and can be cut into various shapes and figures if desired. See TOPIARY WORK.

Only one or two species are generally cultivated, but of these there are numerous varieities. Propagation is by cuttings of mature shoots in early fall. Box edging may be increased or renovated by division in spring.

ENEMIES. Boxwood canker (caused by Nectria, a fungus, is becoming increasingly prevalent and serious in the eastern states. In early summer infected twigs show feeble growth and pale-green foliage; later twigs and branches show a conspicuous die-back, the leaves fading and withering. Sometimes a branch suddenly turns straw colored. On the undersides of leaves and on twigs and trunks appear salmon-pink pustules containing thousands of spores which may be washed or carried by air currents to other branches or plants. Infection may also be carried by the gardener working among the plants. Plants weakened by starvation and severe cold weather are especially susceptible; but, contrariwise, much loss attributed to winter injury is primarily due to Nectria canker.

The fruiting bodies of another fungus appear as conspicuous black dots on the under-surfaces of straw-colored leaves but this is not serious.

Gray mottling of the leaves is likely to be due to spider mites (see Mites). The

BOX   171   **BOX-THORN**

boxwood psylla, a small greenish sucking insect which causes the tips of the leaves to curl, may be controlled with a nicotine spray. The leaf miner or midge which is the worst pest of box is a tiny orange fly which lays eggs in punctures in the lower leaf-surface. The small maggots, which cause oval, blister-like areas, winter in the leaves, and the young flies emerge in late May or early June. A special spray program is needed to protect the plants during the three weeks the flies are active. Spray thoroughly, *especially the lower surfaces and interior of the bushes* with a mixture of 1 gallon spray-molasses, 4 or 5 gallons water and 6 to 8 teaspoonsful of nicotine-sulphate. Apply as the first flies are emerging and keep the plants covered by spraying again after each rain.

A PROTECTIVE PROGRAM. A general program for the control of boxwood enemies starts in spring with prunning out dead branches and, with a whisk broom, brushing out dead leaves fallen into the crotches. In competent hands a dormant application of an oil spray may be made to control scale, but it is safer to use nicotine-sulphate later as a summer spray. If canker is present spray several times during the season with lime-sulphur (1-50) or 1½-1½-50 copper ammonium silicate (see COPPER COMPOUNDS). Lime-sulphur also controls mites, but if an oil spray was used in winter, wait a month before applying any form of sulphur. In pruning out infected wood always disinfect the pruning knife between cuts to prevent spreading infection. This is so important that such work is ordinarily better left to plant experts; if the life of valuable old plants is at stake, the expense involved is fully justified.

PRINCIPAL SPECIES

B. sempervirens (Common Box). A shrub or small tree to 25 ft., found in S. Europe, N. Africa, and W. Asia. Long in cultivation. There are several forms, variable in size, color and shape of the leaves. Var. *arborescens* is the typical large form. Var. *rotundifolia* makes a rounded bush, has broadly oval leaves, and is hardier than most. Var. *handsworthi*, an upright bushy form with very dark green leaves, is considered the best for a hedge. Var. *myrtifolia* is a dwarf form with narrow leaves. The larger leaves of var. *bullata* give a puckered appearance. Var. *angustifolia* has leaves long and narrow. Var. *suffruticosa*

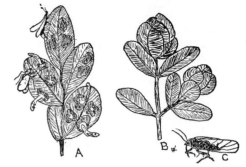

TWO INSECT PESTS OF BOX
(A) The leaf miner, showing the injured leaves, pupa cases, and the adult flies. (B) The cupped terminal leaves of box caused by the psylla shown at (C).

is the Edging Box, a real old-time garden plant, seen in southern colonial gardens. Vars. *argenteo-variegata*, with leaves edged white, and *aureo-variegata* with yellow variegated leaves are sometimes grown, but do not color well in the shade.

microphylla. This is a compact shrub from Japan. It grows to 3 ft. but is often prostrate. Var. *japonica* grows to 6 ft. and is distinct, with spreading branches and light-green foliage. Var. *koreana* is a small shrub to 2 ft. This species and its two varieties are the hardiest of the boxes.

balearica, a tender species from Spain, grows up to 30 ft. and has leaves up to 2 in. long, which is large for the family.

Brisbane-box is *Tristania conferta;* Victorian-box is *Pittosporum undulatum.*

BOXBERRY. A name sometimes applied to *Gaultheria procumbens,* better known as Checkerberry, Wintergreen or Teaberry; a creeping evergreen plant with small nodding flowers and scarlet fruit.

BOX-ELDER. Common name for *Acer negundo,* a degenerate species of maple, possessing none of the virtues of its relatives except that it propagates easily from seed and grows rapidly under unfavorable circumstances. It is therefore used for windbreaks in the prairie region, but leaves drop early after attaining a sickly yellow color and trunk decay follows rapidly after injuries. See also MAPLE.

BOX-THORN. Common name for the genus Lycium, also known as Matrimonyvine, a group of ornamental shrubs with long flowering branches, some climbing, others requiring support.

BOYKINIA (boi-kin'-i-ah). A genus of perennial herbs of the Saxifrage Family sometimes known as Therofon. Natives of the mountains of N. America, they are used principally in the rock and wild garden and are propagated from seed or by division of the creeping rootstocks. The small, white or greenish flowers grow in panicles or cymes. *B. rotundifolia* growing to 2 ft., has white flowers in clusters; *B. tellimoides,* to 3 ft., has greenish flowers.

BRACHYCHITON (bra-ki-ky'-ton.) A group of trees native to Australia, grown for ornamental effects in California and the S. In some species the trunks are swollen at the ground level. Others, constricted both at the ground and near their tops, are swollen between, whence the common name, Bottle-tree. They have large, heavily-lobed leaves, some with showy flowers of red or scarlet. They succeed well in the soil of the high pine-lands of Florida. Propagation is by seeds, or cuttings of the ripe wood.

BRACHYCOME (brak-i-koh'-me). Herbaceous annuals and perennials of the Composite Family with generally branching stems and solitary or loosely-clustered heads of daisy-like flowers. *B. iberidifolia* is the Swan River Daisy, which see.

BRACHYSEMA (brak-i-see'-mah). A genus of tender evergreen, semi-climbing shrubs having red, sweet-pea-like flowers and, generally, silvery-hairy leaves. Attractive in flower and foliage, the plants are grown outdoors in Calif. and used as pillar-climbers in greenhouses in the N. *B. acuminatum* and *B. lanceolatum* are the species most frequently grown.

BRACKEN. Common name for the fern genus Pteridium which is closely allied to the Brakes (Pteris). It is often used especially for *P. latiusculum,* the commonest species, which has coarsely triangular fronds, 1 to 3½ ft., three-branched, on erect stipes; the branches 2-pinnate, the lower pinnae nearly 3-pinnate, and the fruit dots borne in a continuous line under the reflexed margins of the entire frond, which renders the fertile fronds narrower in appearance. The bracken is one of the commonest ferns of N. America, occurring in thickets, open woods and pastures (sometimes covering acres of dry soil), and flourishing abundantly in waste lands. It is not generally desirable in gardens, being much too vigorous a weed and turning brown late in summer. But for covering difficult dry land or forming a dense background in large rockeries it is unsurpassed.

The very similar W. species, *P. aquilinum,* is also common in Europe, and its variety *pseudo-caudatum,* with forked pinnules, is more common in the S.

BRACKET FUNGI. These are shelf-like fruiting bodies of certain kinds of mushrooms (fungi) growing from the trunks of trees. They may be soft, fleshy and sometimes edible but they are commonly hard and woody. They are always an indication of diseased heartwood. See FUNGUS; DISEASES, PLANT.

BRACT. A small modified leaf, with or without a stem; particularly one of the smaller scale-like leaves in a flower cluster. A bract's usual function is to protect the delicate tissue of the bud, over which the bracts overlap, the so-called "chaff" of wheat is an illustration. Some bracts are large and showy resembling petals, as in the poinsettia and water-arum.

BRAKE. A term loosely used for any coarse fern but rightly the common name for the genus Pteris comprising mostly tropical ferns, some of which are grown in fern dishes for table decoration. It is sometimes used as a synonym for Bracken, a widely distributed hardy coarse fern (*Pteridium aquilinum*), formerly classed as a Pteris. See BRACKEN and PTERIS.

BRAMBLE. A common name for the genus Rubus (which see) which includes Raspberries, Dewberries, Blackberries, Loganberries and other small fruits. Thus it applies both to plants bearing thorns (with which the name is generally associated) and to certain species or forms that are relatively or entirely thornless.

BRAN MASH, POISON. This is used as a bait to destroy cut-worms, army-worms, grasshoppers and other chewing pests that attack young crops in the garden. To make it mix 4 oz. white arsenic or Paris Green with 5 lbs. dry bran. When these are thoroughly mixed, grind two lemons or oranges and stir them into 2 qts. water sweetened with about 1 pint cheap molasses. Then wet the bran mixture with the water, stirring well, until it is of a crumbly—*not pasty*—consistency. More water can be used if necessary. Place a tablespoonful of the mash beside each large plant in the early evening, or scatter it along a row or among small plants. In the morning gather up or cultivate under any that remains, so chickens or birds cannot get it. When more is needed, mix a fresh batch.

BRASENIA (bra-see'-ni-ah) *schreberi.* An aquatic herb growing often in deep water, native in N. America and elsewhere. Comomnly known as Water Shield, which see.

BRASSAVOLA (brah-sav'-oh-lah). A genus of orchids native to Brazil, the West Indies, Venezuela and a few species to Mexico. They are not often met with in orchid collections except those of very large amateur establishments, and then only a few of the showiest varieties. They require very tropical conditions, as will be readily understood considering their native habitat. The flowers are greenish white in color, and very fragrant and the foliage is rush-like in appearance. *B. acaulis* flowers in September and remains in bloom for a long time. For culture, see ORCHID.

BRASSIA (bra'-si-ah). This orchid genus is often called the Spider Orchid, the flower having long narrow sepals and petals, greenish-yellow in color with brown spots. It is not generally considered a valuable orchid, yet it is attractive and easy to grow. Several species are grown, *B. caudata,* native to the West Indies, and *B. guttata,* native to Guatemala, being two of the most popular. For culture, see ORCHID.

BRASSICA (bras'-i-kah). A genus of about 50 annual and biennial herbs and an important branch of the Crucifer Family, the Mustards. Mostly they are natives of the Old World but many are naturalized elsewhere as bad weeds. Others are among the most important food plants of cool climates and seasons.

The roots of the annual species are fibrous, spreading and shallow; those of the biennials, deep penetrating and thickened; the foliage is mostly coarse or fleshy; the yellow flowers are borne usually in erect racemes. All parts of the plants have a characteristic, pungent flavor. The seeds of several species, especially *B. nigra* and *B. alba,* produce commercial mustard and the oil of mustard.

Under cultivation various species tend to thicken diverse parts. *B. rapa,* the common Turnip and *B. napobrassica,* the Swedish Turnip or Rutabaga, form bulb-like roots; *B. pekinensis* (Pe-Tsai or Chinese Cabbage), forms a loose, cylindrical head like Cos lettuce; *B. juncea* (Chinese Mustard), has large tufts of leaves used as greens; the closely related *B. chinensis* (Pak-choi), has cabbage-like leaves and swollen, tuberous roots; *B. caulorapa* (Kohlrabi), has swollen, globular stems.

B. oleracea, however, has the widest series of variations in the following varieties: *acephala* (Kale or Borecole), has loose, large, spreading leaves; *botrytis* includes Cauliflower, which forms a thickened, white, solid head of its flower-clusters, and Broccoli, which produces several smaller, looser heads, either white or green; *capitata* (Cabbage), forms dense, firm heads of the leaves; and in *gemmifera* (Brussels Sprouts) the axillary buds develop into little heads.

BRAZILIAN PEPPER-TREE. Common name for *Schinus terebinthifolius,*

THE BRASSICA GROUP PROVIDES MANY VALUABLE VEGETABLES
Here are shown, from left to right, heads of the closely related cabbage, kale, broccoli, cauliflower, brussels sprouts and collards; also, in the foreground, kohlrabi and turnips.

also known as Christmas-berry-tree, a sub-tropical tree reaching 20 ft. in height, and bearing drooping clusters of small bright-red fruits that last well and make attractive indoor decorative material.

BREADFRUIT. Common name for both the tropical tree, *Artocarpus communis,* and its large seedless pulpy fruit or thickened stalk on which its cluster of flowers is produced; this after cooking is eaten by the native Malayans. The tree is cultivated only in moist sections of the tropics, and, as a curiosity in large green-house collections. A form of this species bears seeded fruits which are called bread-nuts.

BREAK. Term applied to the starting of a new shoot with the appearance of buds or leaves; or of a new growth after a stem has been "pinched" or "stopped," or the normal growth has been otherwise interfered with.

BREAKING (OF TULIPS). Segregation of the color pigment into irregular stripes or flecks. Variegated tulips, thought by early growers to be special types or species, were encouraged and favored, but the condition is now known to be caused by a virus disease, or mosaic, transmitted by aphids. Apparently two distinct viruses may cause breaking: one results in loss of flower color, yellow-striped or mottled leaves, general stunting and loss of vigor; the other causes darker streaks of color and seems not to have appreciable effect on the general health of the plant. Control by prompt removal of diseased plants and use contact insecticides against aphids. See MOSAIC; VIRUS DISEASES.

BREATH-OF-HEAVEN. Common name for *Adenandra* (or *Diosma*) *fragrans,* a small, tender, summer-blooming shrub of the Rue Family, native of S. Africa, sometimes seen in California. It is also applied to other species of Diosma.

BREEDING, PLANT. See PLANT BREEDING.

BREVOORTIA (bree-voor'-ti-ah). Floral-firecracker. A distinctive genus of the lily family native to California and consisting of a single species, *B. ida-maia,* which because of its close relationship to the brodiaeas is sometimes listed as *Brodiaea coccinea.* The slender stems rise to 3 ft. from the narrow, grass-like basal leaves and terminate in a pendulous cluster of crimson-red, tubular flowers tipped with green. Grown from small corms the plants

are half-hardy and do well in the border, requiring partial shade and a deep loose soil thoroughly drained, with some leaf-mold.

BRICKELLIA (bri-kel'-i-ah). Herbs or shrubs of high altitudes in N. America, belonging to the Daisy Family. *B. grandiflora* (Tassel-flower), which appears to be the only one in cultivation, is a perennial, growing to 3 ft., and suitable for a moist shady border. It bears drooping heads of yellowish-white flowers in large panicles. Propagated by cuttings, under close conditions.

BRIDAL WREATH. Common name for *Spiraea prunifolia;* also incorrectly applied to *Francoa ramosa.* Korean Bridal Wreath is *Spiraea trichocarpa.*

BRIER or **BRIAR.** A term commonly applied to prickly bushes, especially brambles, as in the Blackberry Family. The name Greenbrier is applied to the genus Smilax, the following native species being designated as particular kinds: *S. rotundifolia* (Horse-brier); *S. Bona-nox* (Saw-brier); *S. glauca* (Cat-brier); *S. laurifolia* (False China-brier).

In Europe certain kinds of wild roses are known as Briers: Wild Brier (*Rosa canina*); Sweet-brier (*R. rubiginosa*); Austrian Brier (*R. foetida*). French-brier is a trade name for the root of a European species of heath (*Erica arborea*) used in making pipes; but in U. S. brier-root may refer to that of mountain-laurel (*Kalmia latifolia*) or to species of Smilax.

BRIER GRAPE. Common name for *Vitis davidi,* on account of its prickly stems,

BRIER ROSE. A name given to different kinds of shrub roses, principally two species and their descendants. The Sweet-brier or Eglantine is *Rosa rubiginosa,* a European form growing 8 ft. tall with pink flowers 2 in. across. It has become naturalized in U. S. and is common in fields and hedgerows. It has given rise to a number of delightful named hybrids. The Austrian Briers have developed from the very old, hardy, Asiatic *Rosa foetida,* which attains 10 ft. and is characterized by gloriously yellow flowers 3 in. across but of unpleasant odor.

The name Brier-rose is also applied to a species of bramble, *Rubus coronarius.* See ROSE; RUBUS.

BRISBANE-BOX. Common name for *Tristania conferta,* an Australian flowering tree of the Myrtle Family. Attaining 150

ft. in its native habitat, it is sometimes planted in other warm climates.

BRITTLE FERN (*Cystopteris fragilis*). A finely divided fern, 6 to 18 in. tall, native to wet rocky slopes and wooded cliffs in the E. States and excellent for shaded, moist places in the rockery. It likes leaf-mold and a little lime, and produces a second crop of fronds late in the summer.

BRIZA (bry'-zah). A genus of Old-World and S. American grasses some of which are grown as ornamentals under the name Quaking Grass, which see.

BROAD BEAN. An Old-World vegetable and forage plant (*Vicia faba*) also called Windsor or Horse Bean. See BEAN and VICIA.

BROADCAST. To scatter seed by hand or machine instead of sowing in rows or "drills." In gardening it is most practiced in lawn making, in sowing cover-crops and in starting very small seeds in flats for later pricking out, which see. Outdoors the seed is generally scratched, raked, brushed or rolled into the freshly loosened soil surface; in flats, loose soil is sifted lightly over the seed, or the latter may be merely pressed into the surface with a board or wooden block. See DRILL.

BROCCOLI (brok'-oh-li). Formerly this name referred to a race of very late or long-season Cauliflower (which see) which, in mild climates, is left in the ground over winter to mature its heads in spring. It is now more commonly applied to a closely related plant long popular as a vegetable in Europe, but now gaining in popularity in U. S. although as yet grown less in gardens than as a commercial vegetable crop. This is the Italian, Sprouting, or Asparagus Broccoli, or Calabrese (*Brassica oleracea* var. *italica* or *asparagoides*) which produces, not a thick, solid, white head like cauliflower, but a number of smaller, looser, green heads. These develop first on the thickened main stem and later on the side branches. They, with the smaller surrounding leaves, are boiled and served as "greens" with a cream or hollandaise sauce. Broccoli is grown like cabbage, which see. Sow seed in late winter, under glass, or outdoors from the time the soil can be worked until July. In the garden space the plants about 2 ft. apart and keep the ground cultivated. Light frosts improve rather than injure the heads, so harvesting may be continued well into the winter.

The diseases and pests of cabbage and cauliflower (which see) are often found on broccoli. Ring spot, a leaf disease, occurs in the West. See also enemies under CRUCIFER.

Another plant of the cabbage group (*Brassica oleracea* var. *septiceps*) is sometimes wrongly called Broccoli or Italian kale. Actually it is an edible-leaved turnip, which see.

BRODIAEA (broh-di-ee'-ah). Known by a wide variety of common names, these cormous herbs of the Lily Family, native to the W. Coast, are hardy there and in the S. They can also, with careful culture, be used in rock gardens in other regions. Delicate of flower, they are excellent for naturalizing. Growing from 6 in. to 3 ft. tall, they thrive in any soil that is not too moist or heavy. They dislike rich manure or other organic fertilizer, but given a good deal of sunshine they will produce loose umbels of pretty funnel-like flowers in spring and summer. The few grass-like leaves grow at or near base of plant.

Brodiaeas are also grown occasionally in pots indoors. Propagation is by seeds, though seedling plants take several years to flower; or by offsets when these are produced.

Among the most popular species are:

B. capitata (Blue-dicks). Also known as *Milla* or *Dichelostemma capitata*. Growing to 2 ft. and bearing blue flowers ¾ in. long in head-like umbels, these are excellent border plants.

coronaria. To 1½ ft. tall, the violet-purple flowers nearly 2 in. long.

crocea. A dwarfer species, to 1 ft. with bright yellow flowers ¾ in. long.

hendersoni. Large yellow flowers on plants 9 in. tall, a purple band in the center.

ixioides (Pretty Face) also known as *Calliprora ixioides*. To 1½ ft., the salmon-yellow flowers ¾ in. long, veined with dark purple.

lactea (Wild-hyacinth). Sometimes classified as *Hesperoscordum hyacinthinum*. To 1½ ft., with white or lilac flowers ½ in. long.

laxa (Triplet-lily, Grass-nut or Ithuriels Spear). Known also as *Triteleia laxa*, this sturdy plant 1 to 2 ft. tall bears variable purple or white flowers nearly 2 in. long.

uniflora (Spring Star-flower). Also classed in the genera Milla, Triteleia and Leucocoryne. Growing to 8 in. and distinguished by an onion-like odor, it is fairly hardy, and grown also as a pot-plant. The solitary white flowers 1 in. long are tinged with blue. Two popular colored varieties are: *caerulea* and *violacea. volubilis* (Snake-lily). Grows upright to 3 ft., or twining to 8 ft., with pink flowers ¾ in. long.

BROME GRASS. Popular name for the genus Bromus, a group of annual and perennial grasses with flat leaves and nodding spikes of bloom, natives of the north temperate zone of Europe, and naturalized in America. While most of them are of a weedy character, some have a special value as forage grasses on dry soils of the Middle W. and S. *Bromus inermis,* known as Awnless or Hungarian Brome Grass, is useful for its ability to hold earth banks in shape. There are several ornamental species valuable in the border: *B. brizaeformis,* or Quake Grass, forms effective clumps with long spikes of nodding bloom which, dried, are also useful in winter bouquets; *B. madritensis* has a feathery bloom of much beauty, and *B. macrostachys,* though less striking than the others finds a place both in the garden and in dry bouquets.

BROMELIA (broh-mee'-li-ah). A genus of tropical American perennial herbs with long stiff leaves with spines along the margins set in an imposing basal rosette from which rises the 4 ft. flower-stem crowned with flat heads of bloom. They succeed outdoors in subtropical climates but are greenhouse plants in the N. They require a well broken-up loam enriched with about a quarter decayed manure. Water should be given sparingly in winter. They are propagated by suckers. Of the two dozen species *B. pinguin,* the Pinguin or Wild-pine of Jamaica, is the showiest. Its 6 ft. leaves with hooked prickles turn from bright green to pink and red with age and its red flowers are followed by an edible, plum-like fruit.

BROMELIACEAE (broh-mee-li-ay'-see-ee). Botanical name of the Bromelia or Pineapple Family, a group of herbs or subshrubs of the American tropics with persistent, stiff, channeled leaves in rosettes, crowded into a basal sheath. The bright flowers, provided with large, often colored and showy bracts, are borne in dense heads or spikes. Many Bromeliads (as the members of the family are called), grow on other plants, but some, like the Pineapple

(Ananas) are terrestrial. They show great diversity, including such different forms as the Pineapple, Spanish-moss (Tillandsia), and Water-hyacinth (Eichhornea). In greenhouses some are grown in pots and baskets making showy and effective subjects. Genera grown for ornament and not already mentioned include Vriesia, Aechmea, Billbergia, Nidularium, Cryptanthus.

BRONZE-LEAF. Common name for *Rodgersia podophylla,* a hardy, perennial herb of S. America, with 5-lobed foliage which turns to a metallic bronze in summer.

BROOM. A common name for two genera of woody plants, Cytisus and Genista. Spanish- or Weavers-broom is *Spartium junceum.* Butchers-broom is *Ruscus aculeatus.*

BROOM-CROWBERRY (*Corema conradi*). A small evergreen heath-like shrub, found from Newfoundland to N. J. in rocky and sandy places. It is rarely cultivated, but might be of value as a ground-cover in poor soil. It is of upright twiggy habit, to 2 ft. high. Male and female flowers are borne on separate plants, only the former, with long purple stamens, being at all conspicuous. Propagated by cutting of almost mature wood, under glass.

BROUSSONETIA (broo-soh-nee'-shi-ah). Paper Mulberry. Deciduous trees or shrubs belonging to the Mulberry Family, native in E. Asia where the bark is used in paper making. The best known is *B. papyrifera,* which grows into a broad rounded tree to 50 ft., with smooth gray bark and large oval leaves, usually lobed. It is hardy from N. Y. south, and has been used to some extent as a street tree. In some sections it has become naturalized. Var. *laciniata* is conspicuous because of its finely dissected leaves.

BROWALLIA (broh-wal'-i-ah). Annual free-flowering bedding plants of the Nightshade Family (*Solanaceae*) 1 to 1½ ft. tall, used with best results in the blue section of the garden, where the winged flowers, of an intense blue color covering the plant, provide beauty throughout the summer and fall. Native to tropical America, this plant is easily cultivated in any good garden soil, needing practically no care so long as it has a sunny spot and the plants are at least 6 in. apart. Lifted in the fall, potted, cut back and brought indoors, Browallia will bloom during the winter.

The species *B. americana* is the usually cultivated garden plant; it has white and dwarf varieties. *B. speciosa,* with its larger flowers and often reaching a height of 4 to 5 ft., can be used in hanging baskets and vases.

BROWN CANKER. A very serious disease of rose canes. See under ROSE.

BROWN PATCH. A disease of grasses caused by a common soil fungus (*Rhizoctonia solani*). Definite, rather circular spots, bordered by a dark green ring, appear suddenly in the lawn during warm humid weather. They may vary from an inch or so to several feet in diameter. Small brown patch (caused by another species of the same fungus) is characterized by light brown patches never more than 2 in. across. For further notes and control methods, see LAWN.

BROWN ROT. A fungus disease of stone fruits—peaches, cherries, plums, prunes, nectarines and apricots—and, to a slight extent, pome fruits. Symptoms appearing at different times in the season are blossom blight, twig blight, fruit rot and canker.

The fungus (*Sclerotinia cinera*) winters in the cankers and in the hard, wrinkled fallen fruits called "mummies." When the flower buds begin to show color, small mushroom-like cups (*apothecia*) grow out from the mummies. In moist weather millions of spores are literally shot from these cups and carried by air currents to the blossoms, which turn brown and wither. The disease then progresses down the twigs and eventually to the trunk, forming a canker there. Gummy substances on the twigs, cankers and (sometimes) fruits are also evidence of brown rot. Gray spore tufts (masses of summer spores or *conidia*) which appear on the blighted blossoms and on mummies that cling to the trees over winter, are sources of infection of the young fruit, which, soon covered with its own crop of spores, continues to spread infection throughout the season.

Sanitary measures are the best means of control. Knock clinging mummies from the trees, then plow under or rake up and burn them and all fallen mummies and plant debris. Consult your county farm bureau agent or state experiment station about a spraying or dusting program for your locality. The first spray is generally applied when the blossoms are at the pink stage, the second when the petals are falling, the third two or three weeks later, and the fourth three or four weeks before the fruit ripens. Dry mixed lime-sulphur is replacing the older self-boiled lime-sulphur spray. Sulphur (which see) dust may also be used.

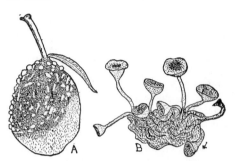

A SERIOUS PLUM DISEASE

Brown rot spoils the fruit, covers it with gray masses of fungus (A), and finally turns the plum into a mummy (B) from which rise mushroom-like spore-bearing organs (apothecia).

BROWN TAIL MOTH. An important pest of deciduous shade and fruit trees in New England and south-eastern Canada. Also a nuisance because of the painful irritation and rash caused by a poison in the hairs of both caterpillars and moths. The insect (*Nygmia phaeorrhoea*) hibernates as a colony of tiny caterpillars in small web-like nests on the outer twigs of trees. In spring they begin to feed on young leaves, returning to the nest at night until full grown (1½ in. long), when they are dark brown with a broken white stripe on each side of the body and bright red tubercles on the 11th and 12th segments. The moths (after three weeks of pupation) have white wings and a brown abdomen with a tuft of chestnut colored hairs at the tip; this gives the insect its name. They fly in large swarms at night. The eggs, laid in small masses covered with hairs from the female, hatch in late summer and the young feed on branch tips before spinning their winter webs.

Control by pruning off and burning the nests during winter and by spraying in early spring to destroy the caterpillars while small. Use 4 to 5 lbs. lead arsenate to 100 gallons of water. With the spread of certain diseases that attack it, the brown tail moth is becoming less important.

BROWNING. A condition often seen on evergreens, especially arborvitae, in which the foliage becomes rusty and brownish. It varies in extent and degree from place to place, season to season and year to year, and may indicate natural or abnormal conditions. In early fall it commonly accompanies the natural shedding or pruning of the older foliage (3- and 4-year-old needles) comparable to what occurs in deciduous trees. A browning in very early spring may be caused by transpiration of moisture by the foliage faster than the roots can take it up from frozen soil. Shading from direct sunlight and protection against prevailing winds at this season to check excessive drying may be warranted in the case of valuable specimens. Summer browning is usually caused by insects, especially spruce mite (controlled by dusting with sulphur), scale, and root and gall aphids; by unfavorable planting sites, hot, dry weather, or failure of newly transplanted trees to become established.

BRUNELLA (broo-nel′-ah). A sometimes-used spelling of Prunella (which see), a genus of hardy, low, weedy perennials suitable for borders.

BRUNFELSIA (brun-fel′-zi-ah). A genus of showy, winter-blooming shrubs and sub-shrubs of Tropical America, members of the Nightshade Family (Solanaceae). Grown in the open in the subtropics, they need a temperate greenhouse (50 deg. at night) in the N. The large funnel-shaped flowers, usually fragrant, grow singly or in loose terminal clusters. Brunfelsias need a rich loose compost and plenty of food while growing; they bloom better when pot-bound than when newly started. Propagate from cuttings of ripened wood in spring or autumn.

Typical species are B. americana (Lady-of-the-night), to 8 ft., with solitary flowers white fading to yellow, fragrant at night.

calycina and several varieties have flowers of rich purple and violet to lavender-blue with a white eye.

undulata, to 15 ft. Strong-growing evergreen, flowers creamy-white with wavy margins. Magnificent species.

BRUNNERA (broo-nee′-rah). The genus to which, according to present botannical classifications, the plant generally called Anchusa myosotidiflora belongs. See ANCHUSA.

BRUNSDONNA (bruns-don′-ah). A synthetic name for hybrids produced by crossing Amaryllis belladonna and Brunsvigia josephinae; those in which the

amaryllis has been used as the seed-bearing parent are usually considered superior.

BRUNSVIGIA (bruns-vi-ji-ah). A genus of tender, S. African bulbs from which grow strap- or tongue-shaped leaves and orange-red flowers in umbels or flattened clusters. They are occasionally grown in the greenhouse. Pot the bulbs in rich, sandy soil, water frequently and give plenty of sunlight and heat. Rest the bulbs after flowering and increase by offsets. B. josephinae, with umbels of 20 to 50 red flowers, and B. gigantea, having fewer, paler blossoms, are the species most commonly grown. For cultural details see the related genus, AMARYLLIS.

BRUSSELS SPROUTS. One of the seven distinct vegetables (the others being broccoli, cabbage, cauliflower, collards, kale and kohlrabi) developed from the original wild cabbage (Brassica oleracea). It is the variety gemmifera and is distinguished, as the plants mature, by the "sprouts," which are small, compact, more or less globular heads (really swollen buds) borne along the elongated, erect stem in the axils of the leaves. Its seeds and young plants cannot be told from those of the other vegetables mentioned. The plant is entirely hardy. For culture, see CABBAGE.

Sprout formation starts near the ground and progresses steadily up the stem. As the buds approach edible size (1 to 2 in.) the lower leaves should be removed from the plant to make harvesting easier. More leaves—and sprouts—develop above as the stalk grows until finally there remains a tall, lanky stem with a tuft of leaves at the top just above the remaining sprouts. Sprouts may be gathered from late September until well into winter. Or plants can be dug with some soil before the ground freezes and transplanted to a cool, moist cellar or deep coldframe. Here, if the soil is kept damp, many sprouts too small to use at transplanting time will develop to edible size, extending the crop season.

The varieties offered by seedsmen differ mainly in the height to which they grow and the spacing of sprouts on the stalk.

The diseases and insect pests of brussels sprouts are those of cabbage and other crucifers, which see.

BRYONIA (bry-oh′-ni-ah). A genus of Old-World perennial vines of the Gourd Family, only occasionally grown in this country in collections under the common name Bryony. They have large, fleshy roots, sometimes used for medicines; large, rough 5-lobed leaves, pale beneath; and greenish-white flowers in long-stemmed clusters. They grow rapidly in warm, light soil and soon make a thick screen over fences or walls. *B. dioica* grows to 10 or 12 ft. and has greenish flowers, followed by a smooth red berry 1½ in. in diameter. It is a common plant along English highways.

Bryonopsis laciniosa is an annual vine sometimes grown in the greenhouse and occasionally (incorrectly) listed as *Bryonia laciniosa.* Black-bryony of Great Britain is *Tamus communis.*

BRYOPHYLLUM (bry-oh-fi'-lum). A small genus of fleshy perennials of the Figwort Family native to the tropics of the Old World and closely related to the Stone crops, Hens-and-chickens, etc. The nodding, clustered flowers are like tiny lanterns, paper-thin in texture and of a pale-green color shaded with red or purple. The fleshy leaves are scalloped or notched along the edges and a detached leaf laid on damp sand—or even pinned on the wall—will soon begin to develop a little new plant in each of the scallops. As soon as they are large enough to handle they may be separated from the parent leaf and potted. This odd character is responsible for the generic name, which is from Greek words meaning "sprouting leaf." Bryophyllums grow rampantly outdoors the year around in warm regions but in the N. must be housed for the winter. They like a rich, well-drained soil and will thrive in shade or sun given sufficient heat and moisture. They can be propagated by stem-cuttings, seeds or divisions, as well as by the leaves but the latter method described above is the simplest.

B. pinnatus (Life-plant, Air-plant, Floppers and, sometimes, Lantern-plant). The common type, to 6 in., with purplish or reddish flowers to 3 in. long.

crenatum to 3 ft., with smaller flowers, pink and red.

BUCKBEAN. Another name for *Menyanthes trifoliata,* also called Bogbean, which see.

BUCKBERRY. Common name for *Gaylussacia ursina,* a species of Huckleberry native to the Carolinas.

BUCKEYE. While this name can refer to the whole Horsechestnut genus (Aesculus), it is applied mostly to the southern species (*A. arguta* and *A. discolor*) and

the native Ohio member (*A. glabra*). All have large, showy clusters of flowers in various combinations of white, yellow, green, pink, scarlet or red. They vary from shrubs to trees of majestic proportions (100 ft.). See HORSECHESTNUT.

The Texas-, Mexican- or Spanish-Buckeye is an entirely different, unrelated plant (*Ungnadia speciosa*) belonging to the Soapberry Family. A shrub or small tree (to 30 ft.) native from Texas to Mexico, with glossy leaves and rose-colored flowers, it is occasionally planted in the far South.

BUCKLER FERN. Another name for the Shield Fern, now placed in the genus Dryopteris, which see.

BUCKTHORN. Common name for Rhamnus, a genus of shrubs or small trees. False-buckthorn is Bumelia. Sea-buckthorn is *Hippophaë rhamnoides.*

The Buckthorn Family, named after this genus, is Rhamnaceae.

BUCKWHEAT. A quick growing annual herb (*Fagopyrum esculentum*), grown as a farm crop for its seed which is ground into a dark colored flour famous for making pancakes. It is also an important bee plant, though buckwheat honey is sometimes considered dark and rather strong-flavored.

Because it is not particular as to soil, buckwheat is popular as a "first crop" on newly cleared land and in improving poor soil. So used (and also in orchards and gardens) it is grown as a green manure or cover-crop (see both titles) to be dug or plowed under while still green and succulent.

It is usually sown about midsummer either broadcast at the rate of 4 pecks per acre, or scattered among growing annual crops at the rate of 1 oz. to about 50 sq. ft. The first frost will kill the plants but the stems will catch and hold fallen leaves (which when the land is dug or plowed in spring will also increase the humus content of the soil), as well as the winter's snow, which as it melts will add to the soil's supply of moisture.

Buckwheat straw (from mature plants grown for the seed) provides probably the best fall mulch for strawberry plants, because the stems become brittle over winter and break up readily when raked between the rows. Buckwheat hulls are also excellent mulch material for all kinds of perennial plants in both vegetable and

BUDS ARE OF TWO TYPES
1. A blueberry twig in spring with two flower buds at the tip and two leaf buds just below.
2. The same branch in July, bearing the fruit which has followed the flowers.

flower gardens, especially around roses. They are light, clean, and convenient to use; do not mat down and freeze, or blow away; prevent evaporation and conserve moisture, and can be dug in to the soil to decay and increase the humus supply.

Wild-buckwheat is Erigeron; Russian-buckwheat is Polygonum.

BUCKWHEAT FAMILY. Common name of the Polygonaceae, which includes plants cultivated for edible fruits and many ornamental subjects.

BUCKWHEAT-TREE. Common name for *Cliftonia monophylla,* a small evergreen tree or shrub which grows wild in swamps from Ga. to La. but is hardy to Philadelphia. The white or pinkish, delicately fragrant flowers are borne in racemes in early spring. Sometimes transplanted to gardens, it would be a desirable plant for more general cultivation. Preferring moist sandy and peaty soil, it can be raised from seed and possibly by cuttings of partly ripened wood.

BUD. An incipient shoot together with the rudimentary leaves (or leaf-parts in the form of scales) that invest and protect it. All growth of stems, foliage branches and flower-bearing shoots occurs from buds.

At the end of a season's growth the stem has formed at its tip a leaf-bearing shoot which, the following season, will continue the lengthwise growing of the stem; this is the *terminal bud.* But whereas it has one terminal bud, each stem has numerous *axillary buds* which, formed in the upper angle between each leaf and the stem, may develop leaf shoots and flower shoots. Accompanying an axillary bud may be one or more *accessory buds,* as in the red maple.

A bud is composed of embryonic leaves grouped about the growing point. Over winter this whole tiny shoot is covered by scale-like leaves of the past season's growth which persist until the following season. The most conspicuous and highly specialized buds of temperate-climate shrubs and trees are the so-called "resting buds" which are remarkably well adapted to resisting unfavorable weather conditions. Many times they are covered with resinous secretions, hairy growths, waxy layers, etc., which protect them from unfavorable growing conditions, prevent their drying out, and guard them against premature development. It is these buds which, by refusing to grow until a certain period of cold weather has elapsed, make it difficult to force some kinds of plants or their branches into flower indoors in the winter; however treatments are being discovered which overcome this natural tendency to seasonal dormancy.

See also DORMANT; REST-PERIOD; FLOWER; PLANT.

BUDDING. A special form of grafting (which see) in which only a single bud of a desired variety with little or no wood is inserted in the stock. It is preferred to grafting for many species of plants, gives less satisfactory results with others, and works about equally well with still others. There is no general rule by which decision can be made. See PROPAGATION.

Though perhaps a dozen methods of budding are used in special cases, the one by which millions of plants are annually propagated is "shield budding," so called because the scion bud is an elongated oval.

Budding is usually done outdoors from midsummer until early autumn, while the bark of the plants to be "worked" will readily separate when gently pried from the young wood beneath. These "stocks" should be ½ in. or more in diameter and, to facilitate the work, be stripped of their lower leaves for about 6 in. As near the ground as possible, and where the bark is smooth, a vertical cut about 2 in. long is made with a budding knife and at its upper end a horizontal cross cut. The two cuts forming a T, must not be deeper than the bark or the wood may be wounded. The two upper corners of bark are then gently pried up just enough to permit insertion of the bud.

"Bud sticks" (as the young twigs of the current season's growth are called) are cut from the variety it is desired to propagate and the leaves are cut off so that only about ½ in. of the stems are left. To prevent shriveling they are wrapped in wet burlap or stood in water.

To cut a bud, start the knife about ¾ in. below it, pass it upward through the bark and beneath the bud and bring it out about ¼ in. above, producing a shield-shaped sliver of bark and wood with a bud near its center. This, held by the stump of its leaf-stem, is pushed down—bud pointing upward—beneath the raised bark of the T-cut. Its under side thus presses against the *cambium* or layer of growing wood of the stock. The operation is completed by wrapping raffia, adhesive grafting-tape or a rubber strip around the stock to hold the bud in place but not so as to cover it.

If raffia (or any other tier that will not stretch as the stem grows) is used, it must later be cut through on the side opposite the inserted bud; an elastic tier will "give" and need not be cut. Buds that have "taken" or united with the stock will remain plump and later begin to grow; if the operation fails the bud dies. In such a case the stock may be rebudded.

When, the spring after the budding is done, the stocks begin to leaf out, they must be cut to 4 to 6 in. above the bud. In cold climates this will still be dormant, but it will start to grow soon after the stock is cut back. Within three weeks the stubs should be cut off about ½ in. above the new shoot which, during the season may grow from 2 to 6 ft. depending on the kind of plant, the growing conditions, etc. All other sprouts that appear along the stock must be rubbed off while small and soft so all the plant food will go into the bud shoot. At the end of that season or during the following spring the young budded plants may be transplanted.

BUDDLEIA (bud'-lee-ah). Butterfly-bush. (See illustration, Plate 39.) Deciduous or half-evergreen shrubs or trees belonging to the Logania Family. The 70 or so species are found in tropical and temperate regions of America, Asia and S. Africa. Only a few species are cultivated, and with one or two exceptions they are not hardy North. Fast, rather coarse growers, with usually quadrangular stems. Buddleias delight in rich, well-drained soil in a sunny position. The individual flowers

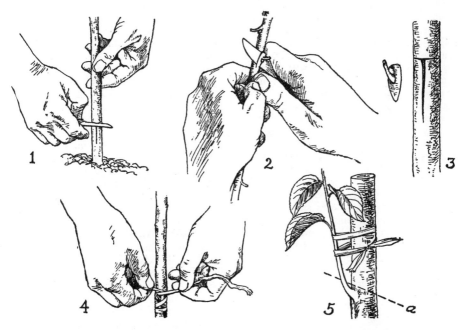

STEPS IN PROPAGATING A WOODY PLANT BY BUDDING
1. Making a T-shaped slit in the bark of the stock. 2. Cutting a bud from the plant to be propagated. 3. The bud ready to be inserted under the loosened bark. 4. Tying the bud in place with raffia. 5. After the bud has "taken", and begins to grow, support the young shoot by tying it to the stock which, the next year, is cut off (a).

are small, but produced in great profusion, mostly in long dense racemes. Shades of lilac and purple predominate, but some have white and yellow flowers. Nearly all have a prominent orange eye and are sweetly fragrant. Butterflies attracted to the plant in gardens add to its interest. Propagation is easily effected by cuttings taken in early fall and wintered over in a cool house.

PRINCIPAL SPECIES

B. alternifolia. A good-looking Chinese shrub to 12 ft., with wide-spreading arching branches. It is the hardiest species as well as the only one with alternate leaves. The long arching shoots of the previous year are studded with compact clusters of lavender-purple flowers in early summer. Shoots of the current season may flower later in the summer.

Davidi (V. variabilis) (Summer-lilac). A native of China, it is one of the best known but is not absolutely hardy North. Given a protection of litter the rootstock will survive most winters and send up vigorous shoots that flower in late summer. It is best to defer cutting them down until Spring. The lilac-colored flowers are produced in terminal tail-like spikes a foot or more long. Var. *magnifica* gives larger spikes and deeper colored flowers with crinkled and slightly reflexed petals. Var. *superba* is very similar but with straight petals and even larger spikes. Var. *veitchiana* is the earliest to bloom, and has arching clusters of bright-mauve flowers. Var. *wilsoni* is the latest, and produces flowers of rosy lilac in loose drooping spikes 2 ft. or more long. Var. Ile de France, the dwarfest of the group, has shorter spikes of reddish-violet flowers all summer.

asiatica, a tender species from India, makes a good winter-flowering shrub for the cool greenhouse. Bears slender spikes of sweetly scented white flowers. Spring rooted cuttings may be grown along in pots, or the young plants can be set out in the open ground and lifted before frost.

officinalis. A tender Chinese species, bearing short clusters of very fragrant lilac flowers.

farquhari. A hybrid between the two preceding species. Very like *asiatica* in habit and treatment but has pale-pink flowers.

colvilei. A large tender shrub or small tree to 30 ft. native in the Himalayas. Said to be the most handsome of all, with dense spikes of purple or crimson flowers with a white eye.

globosa (Orange Ball). A handsome half-evergreen shrub from Chili; able to withstand a few degrees of frost. Very striking in bloom with the long-stalked, round heads of orange-yellow flowers.

BUD MOTH. A pest of fruit and ornamental plants from Nova Scotia to Mass. and westward to Wash. Half-inch long, cinnamon brown caterpillars attack expanding buds of apple, pear, quince, plum, peach, cherry, wild plum and hawthorn, and tie the leaves together with silk; they also eat shallow cavities in the young fruits. The adult moth is dark ash gray, with a broad cream-white band. Control by spraying with lead arsenate added to the pink and calyx sprays as discussed under APPLE.

BUD-WORMS. Caterpillars that bore in buds. The greenish tobacco bud-worm chews holes in the leaf buds causing misshapen leaves. Arsenate of lead (1 part in 75 parts of cornmeal) may be sprinkled directly on the buds. The spruce bud-worm, a dark brown caterpillar covered with yellow warts, causes affected trees to appear as if scorched by fire. See under SPRUCE. The apple bud-worm usually goes under the name of bud-moth, which see, and the corn ear-worm (see under CORN) is sometimes called false-bud-worm.

BUFFALO-BERRY. Common name for *Shepherdia argentea*, a very hardy, small, thorny tree of N. America with leaves silvery on both sides, grown as a hedge plant in the N.W. and sometimes for its fruits which can be made into jelly.

BUGBANE. Common name for the genus Cimicifuga, tall-growing temperate region perennials of the Crowfoot Family. Preferring a partially shaded spot and rich soil, they bear long spikes of white flowers in late summer.

BUGLE, BUGLE-WEED. Common name for Ajuga, a genus of herbaceous plants of the Mint Family especially suitable for growing in the rock garden though often used in the border; the name is also sometimes applied to species of Lycopus, or Water-horehound.

Growing from 6 to 14 in. tall, Ajugas bloom early, generally in May and June, and occasionally again in the fall, bearing blue, purple, rose or white flowers in dense whorls in terminal spikes. Of simple cultivation and thriving in any ordinary garden soil, they will do well in shade or sun. Propagated by seeds and division.

Among the perennial species in general cultivation are:

A. genevensis (Geneva Bugle), a tall species often used as a ground cover for shady places, the flowers blue; and *A. reptans* (Carpet Bugle), the stems to 12 in. long though somewhat prostrate, the flowers white, blue or purplish. Varieties include: *atropurpurea,* blue flowers and bronze leaves; *multicolor,* foliage red, brown and yellow; *rubra,* dark purple; and *variegata,* leaves splotched and bordered with cream.

ENEMIES. *A. reptans* is particularly subject to the fungus disease known as crown rot. In humid weather the white mycelial growth quickly creeps over the crowns of the plants often destroying large areas in a few days. Remove diseased plants and sterilize soil as recommended under CROWN ROT.

A. metallica var. *crispa* is a dwarf horticultural form with metallic-blue flowers.

BUGLE-LILY. Name given by some horticulturists to the genus Watsonia, a S. African member of the Iris Family.

BUGLOSS (beu'-glos). A common name for Anchusa, a genus of hairy herbs grown for their bright blue (or occasionally white) flowers.

Vipers-bugloss is Echium.

BUGS. Although the layman is accustomed to call all insects "bugs," the only true bugs, as the entomologists knows them, are those insects that belong to the order Hemiptera (meaning "half-winged"). Most of them have scent glands which give them a distinct and often offensive odor. They are sucking insects with a gradual metamorphosis (see INSECTS). The front pair of wings is thickened and quite stiff for the basal half, the rest being thinner and usually membranous; this distinctive structure is responsible for the family name. The various species attack a wide variety of plants; some of them belong to the following families: The stink bugs (Pentatomidae), leaf bugs (Miriade), lace bugs (Tingididae), chinch bugs (Lygaeidae), squash bugs (Coreidae). See also TARNISHED PLANT BUG; HARLEQUIN BUG and RED BUG.

BULBIL, BULBLET. A small bulblike bud, produced generally in the axil of a leaf (as in the tiger lily) or in place of the flower (as in the multiplier onion), and capable, when planted, of developing into a new plant.

BULBINELLA (bul-bi-nel'-ah). Perennial herbs of the Lily Family, natives of S. Africa and New Zealand. They have fleshy tuberous roots, grass-like leaves and bright yellow or white flowers in dense clusters at the top of bare stalks. They should be planted in spring in a warm sheltered place in the border or at the corner of the rock garden where a note of height is needed. They are increased by division in the spring. *B. hookeri,* to 3 ft., has bright yellow flowers in 10 in. racemes. *B. latifolia* is white-flowered and grows but 1 ft. high.

BULBOCODIUM (bul-boh-koh'-di-um) *vernum.* A small bulbous plant resembling a crocus, blooming very early in the spring in advance of the leaves. The rosy-purple, funnel-form flowers appear above ground as early as the snowdrops. Plant the bulbs early in the fall, about 4 in. below the surface in good, well-drained soil in a sheltered spot in the rock garden and mulch lightly with decayed leaves.

BULBS. A bulb is an encased leaf bud, or flower bud, or sometimes a combination of the two, surrounded by fleshy layers or scales fastened upon a fibrous base from which the roots are produced. The onion is a typical example of a true bulb. Some bulbs, such as the Hyacinth or Tulip, have the thickened fleshy layers wrapped all around them, while others, such as the Lily, have overlapping scales.

A great many other floral subjects, because of their resemblance, are commonly known as bulbs but their true classifications are as follows:

CORMS. A corm, of which the Gladiolus and Crocus are typical, is a solid object, usually quite hard, instead of being formed of layers or scales like a true bulb. The method of growth is also entirely different. A true bulb may live indefinitely as a single unit or may increase by splitting itself up, but a mature corm actually withers and dies after a year of growth, being replaced by a new corm or corms that form usually on top of the old one but sometimes beneath or alongside it.

TUBERS. These are shortened, congested or swollen parts usually (though not always) produced underground. They may be modified stems, in which case they bear leaf buds or "eyes" in regular arrangement over their surface (the Irish Potato is an example) ; or they may be swollen roots without eyes, as in the Dahlia and Sweet-potato, which sprout from buds on the stem end or "neck" of the tuber. The function of these fleshy tubers is to serve as reservoirs of plant food upon which the new shoots can subsist until their new rooting system is able to provide it by absorption through the root hairs.

RHIZOMES. A rhizome or rootstock is a thick fleshy root that usually grows horizontally and often quite near the surface of the soil. The German Iris is a typical example.

A definite advantage of planting true bulbs for flower production is the fact that their flower buds, in well-matured, full-sized specimens, are actually encased within the bulb at the time of planting and surrounded with stored-up food material. That is why some kinds need little else than water to flower them perfectly. Hyacinths, Narcissus, and Amaryllis can be flowered in water alone, and the Autumn Crocus (Colchicum) will sometimes bloom if the temperature is favorable without even soil or water. The bud within a dormant bulb was created while the foliage was maturing the season before. It is therefore important to remember that, in all true bulbs, next year's flowers are being produced while this year's foliage is maturing. Therefore just as much care should be given to bulbs *after* they flower as before.

This condition does not prevail with corms, tubers or rhizomes, which have what can be called a progressive flower embryo. The treatment these subjects receive during their early growth determines to a great extent that same season's flowering results.

CLASSES OF BULBS. Seasonally, this whole group of bulbs and related subjects is usually divided into two main groups— the first being generally termed "fall bulbs" which means those that are dormant and should be planted in the late summer and fall; and the second being called "spring bulbs," meaning those that are dormant over the winter and must be planted in the early spring. Fall bulbs include such well-known items as Tulip, Narcissus, etc., while the spring group includes Gladiolus, Dahlia, and the like.

There is another important division of this whole group into "hardy" and "tender" sorts. When a bulb—like any other plant —is spoken of as being hardy, it means that it will survive the usual winter weather experienced in our temperate zone; tender subjects will not do this and therefore must not be allowed to freeze—either in the ground or out of it. Included in the so-called fall bulb class are many that are hardy and thus capable of remaining in the open ground during the winter, among them the whole group of Dutch bulbs (which see). On the other hand, very few of the spring bulbs are hardy, which means that most of their group must come out of the ground in fall and be placed in frost-free storage during the winter.

PLANTING AND GROWING FALL BULBS

September and October are the best months for planting. While the period can be extended into November or early December if the ground is still open, early planting is best as it provides sufficient time for rooting before the soil gets too cold. Spade the location thoroughly and if the soil is impoverished work in liberal applications of bonemeal or well-rotted manure.

Bulbs should be spaced in accordance with the floral effect that is desired. Generally speaking, a good plan to follow is to allow twice the diameter of a bulb between every two and to plant so that the top of the bulb is about 3 in. below the ground when covered, in the case of most of the larger bulbs, and 1½ to 2 in. below for smaller kinds, as Crocus, Galanthus, etc. Lily bulbs should go considerably deeper, as noted in the article on Lily. Since no bulb can flourish if crowded by other plants, it is important to select a location that provides ample light and space.

In the N. States a winter covering is essential if the bulbs are to do their best and for this purpose light strawy manure, hay or leaves can be employed. It should be removed as the bulbs start peeping through in the spring and after danger of heavy frost is past. This covering is not intended to prevent frost from reaching the bulbs or even going below them, but it does prevent the alternate freezing and thawing which heaves the ground and injures many plants.

As the bulbs develop top growth in the spring, the soil should be continually loosened on the surface but not deep enough to damage the roots. This treatment should

Plate 5.   THREE DIFFERENT EFFECTS WITH BULBS

Top: A border of Narcissus and early Tulips. Inset: Tulips with an edging of Hyacinths.
Bottom: A naturalized planting of Narcissus.

be continued through the whole period of their growth and stopped only after all the foliage has completely died down. Remember that after the flower is spent, the bulb is making its flower bud for the next season, so it is important that the foliage be encouraged to stay green as long as possible. With bulbous subjects that make separate flower-stems and leaves, such as Narcissi, the picking of the flowers has only a slight effect on the building up of a flower bud for the next season. But with bulbs that bear flowers and leaves on the same stem, such as Tulips, any cutting of of the flower that removes part of the foliage is detrimental to the next season's flower in proportion to the percentage of foliage removed. Whatever the type, the flowers, as they wither, should be cut off near the top of the stem; this prevents the flower from going to seed, which draws heavily upon the stored-up vitality of the bulb.

After the foliage has completely matured—usually during July—the bulb is dormant. If the planting is a recent one and the bulbs have not become crowded by increasing, they may remain in the same spot for years. But when they have increased considerably (which will be shown by much additional foliage and fewer flowers), they should be taken up, separated by pulling apart those that hang loose and then either immediately replanted (which is best) or stored over the summer months, then replanted in the early fall, as indicated above. A change of location when replanting is always beneficial.

TO GET GOOD BLOOMS FROM BULBS
Sometimes a hyacinth flowers poorly just above ground (A). To prevent this, place a cone of paper (open at the top) over the bulb for a fortnight (B). This "draws" the bud up and gives a bloom as shown at (C).

PLANTING AND GROWING SPRING BULBS

It has been pointed out that a great many subjects commonly known as "spring bulbs" are not true bulbs at all but either corms, tubers, or rhizomes. Since these do not have their flower buds encased within them, but depend for their bud development to a great extent upon the treatment they receive after planting, it is apparent that considerable care and attention must be given their culture if the best flowering results are to be obtained. Select a spot that is fully exposed to the sun for at least three-quarters of the day, well away from tree or other roots that continually rob the soil of its moisture and vitality. Spade the location thoroughly and deeply and as before directed mix in well liberal applications of bonemeal or well-rotted manure. No simple rule for spacing can be given as this will depend upon the size of the growing plant. Gladioli can be planted 6 in. apart, while Dahlias should have at least 3 ft. between them.

Practically all these subjects can be planted as soon as the soil is warm in the spring and from then on the soil must be kept thoroughly loosened at the surface; this provides a mulch which prevents the evaporation of moisture. Never disturb the soil deep enough to destroy any roots. Continue this treatment throughout the summer, and provide water whenever necessary. Applications of liquid manure aid greatly in producing extra fine blossoms. Successive plantings can be made during the early summer of such subjects as Gladiolus; they will provide a continuity of blooms over a much longer period than if all the bulbs are planted at the same time.

Some of the species will start to die off in the early fall, while others will remain in full growth until cut down by frost. In any case the bulbs should be lifted immediately and the top growth cut off with a sharp knife or shears. Then store the bulbs in a frost-free location for the winter. A hot dry cellar is not a desirable storage place and if it is the only location available, the bulbs should be wrapped in several thicknesses of old newspaper to prevent evaporation of moisture. An ideal location is a part of the cellar partitioned off from any heating apparatus or pipes where a constant temperature of about 45 deg. can be maintained with sufficient moisture in the atmosphere to preserve the roots in a plump condition the whole winter through.

Growing Bulbs in the Home or Conservatory

For indoor (home) culture, true bulbs are the easiest to flower successfully, because, as previously explained, they contain their flower buds within them. However, the light and atmospheric conditions that prevail in the modern home tend to greatly limit the subjects that can be readily flowered there. A very dry atmosphere is a handicap to most plants and fatal to many. It can be overcome to some extent by placing water in suitable receptacles in out-of-the-way places, as behind radiators. As it evaporates it creates much better conditions for plant life. A uniform temperature is also very desirable. Rooms that are maintained at the usual 70 deg. temperature in the daytime and allowed to fall much lower at night are not conducive to best results. Freedom from drafts is also important. To summarize, the ideal room for indoor flower gardening is one that is light and airy, free from gas fumes, where a uniform temperature of about 65 deg. is maintained and where sufficient moisture is being freed at all times to create a moist atmosphere, and where some sunlight penetrates. The following is a list of the more popular bulbous subjects that can be readily flowered in the home:

NARCISSUS. The Polyanthus, or many-flowered, varieties of the species *N. tazetta* include (1) the pure white Paper-white Grandiflora, (2) the dark yellow Soleil d'Or, and (3) the two-toned yellow var. *orientalis,* commonly known as Chinese Sacred-lily or Joss-flower. The culture of all three kinds is simple. The dormant bulbs are available from August to January and may be planted at any time during that period. The earlier plantings will take several months to flower, while those made in December or January take only two or three weeks. This is because the flower bud progresses as the season advances. Water (and the right temperature) is all that is necessary to flower them perfectly, so any other material used in the container simply serves as a root anchorage to prevent the plants from toppling over after they have attained some height.

The usual method of planting is to place a thin layer of gravel, stones, sand, peat moss or similar material in the bottom of a bowl, then arrange the bulbs in an upright position in the manner desired, then fill in the spaces around the bulbs with the same material, allowing the tops (or so-called "noses") of the bulbs to protrude. Water is then added, after which the bulbs will start to grow immediately. Small pieces of charcoal placed in the bowl will prevent the water from souring but this condition can also be corrected by changing the water (which should be at room temperature) every few days.

Placing the bowl containing the planted bulbs in a dark place while the bulbs make their first root growth is sometimes recommended, but it is not desirable as it tends to create abnormally tall foliage and flower stems. So simply place the bowl in a light, sunny window, and, except for the addition or change of water as mentioned above, no other attention is needed.

AMARYLLIS are among the showiest and easiest of bulbous flowers to successfully grow in the home. For cultural instructions see AMARYLLIS.

FALL-FLOWERING CROCUS. Both this type of true Crocus and Colchicum (which see) are desirable house subjects. The bulbs are dormant for only a short time in late summer and will produce flowers even without being planted. But the results are much better if the bulbs are properly planted in shallow bowls and barely covered with peat moss which should be lightly soaked. Add additional water as evaporation occurs. Because they have no foliage the beauty of the flowers and the general effect will be much enhanced if a little lawn-grass seed is planted in the bowls with them and at the same time.

ZEPHYRANTHES (Rain-lily or Fairy-lily). All the Zephyranthes (which are related to the Amaryllis) are good house subjects and can be treated the same as Crocus.

HYACINTHS. The French White Roman Hyacinths adapt themselves well to house culture. The bulbs should be planted in early fall in well-dampened peat moss, then stored away in a dark closet. Water should be added as it evaporates. In early December they can be brought out to a light sunny window where they will flower about Christmas time. Dutch hyacinths, while often recommended for growing in water in such receptacles as hyacinth glasses or milk bottles, are really quite difficult to handle in this manner. If the bulbs are not planted until late November or early December, the chances of success are much improved. In any event, after planting, they should be placed in a cool dark closet and allowed to remain there until considerable root growth develops and the foliage and bud has attained a height of 1 or 2 in. The containers can then be removed to a light, sunny window in a warmer room.

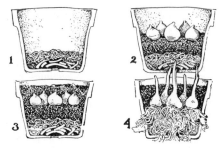

FOUR STAGES IN POTTING BULBS
1. Broken crocks, then dried leaves or moss in the bottom of the pot. 2. A layer of earth with the bulbs set at the proper height. 3. More earth to cover the tips of the bulbs. 4. The bulbs well rooted and beginning to sprout, ready to be brought into the warmth and light.

LILY-OF-THE-VALLEY, while grown from a "crown" or "pip," not a bulb, is easily flowered in the home and may well be mentioned here. The pips are held in a frozen condition in cold storage by importers and bulb dealers from one season to the next and are therefore available for forcing every day in the year. Their culture is most simple. The fibrous roots are usually too long for use in the popular shallow bowls but may be partially trimmed off to fit into such receptacles without suffering any damage. A bowl 6 in. in diameter can well accommodate 10 or 12 pips which are placed in an upright position with their shoots extending above the top of the bowl. Pack sphagnum moss, sand or peat moss firmly around the roots. Fill with lukewarm water and the pips will start to grow immediately; they will flower within three or four weeks in the usual room temperature.

With some preliminary outdoor handling the list of bulbs that can be flowered in the home may be greatly enlarged. In view of the fact that any true bulb, *if well rooted,* can be brought into a heated room and flowered, a preliminary outdoor planting and storage followed by subsequent removal into warmer quarters, duplicates what greenhouse growers call "forcing"—

which merely means the flowering of any plant before its normal period.

Practically the whole list of Dutch bulbs (which see) and, in fact, nearly all true bulbs can be handled in this manner.

The cultural details are as follows: In early fall plant the bulbs in the desired receptacle. An ordinary clay flower pot with a drainage hole is best but even fancy bowls without drainage can also be employed. (For commercial crops of forced cut flowers plain wooden boxes or "flats" are commonly used.) When clay pots are used, water well, then plunge or bury the whole pot outdoors from 1 to 2 ft. deep and cover it with ashes, soil, leaves or straw. The latter is best as it can be more readily removed. A deep, unused coldframe is a good place for this "conditioning process." Leave the pots and bulbs undisturbed until February or early March when the bulbs will have put out a good root system which is the secret of this whole operation. They are then ready for removal to a warmer temperature indoors.

When fancy bowls without drainage are used, the bulbs should be planted in dampened peat moss and the pots either plunged outdoors (which is best) or kept in a cool, dark place such as a root or fruit cellar. As before, when the bulbs are thoroughly rooted, they are transferred to the warmer location. The indoor temperature should at first be between 45 and 50 deg.; it can be stepped up after the foliage and buds develop.

This method of indoor winter gardening is much employed in Europe, where it provides flower lovers with a succession of blooming plants during the late winter and early spring months.

All the foregoing is intended only for those who have the average home conditions or equipment. Where conservatories or light, sunny porches are available, the list of bulbous plants that can be successfully flowered is very much greater. Such subjects as Callas, Freesias, Orinthogalums, etc., can then be employed.

BULB PROPAGATION

Nearly all the plants referred to in this article increase naturally, the extent depending upon the locality and the conditions under which they are grown. The more care and attention they are given the greater will be the increase, the larger the size and higher the quality of the bulbs.

Plate 6.   THERE IS AMAZING VARIETY IN BULBS

Upper left: Narcissus (Bicolor Trumpet). Lower left: Tiger Lily (Lilium tigrinum). Upper right: Hyacinths (Giant Pink Italian). Center right: Darwin Tulips. Lower right: Allium (The Garden Onion).

In addition, most of these subjects produce seed. While patience is needed to grow many of them from seed in that it takes years to produce a flowering-size bulb, it is an interesting work and often results in producing a hybrid variety of considerable beauty and value. The small bulbs that are produced from seed can be handled in the same way as the parent stocks. See PROPAGATION.

BULB ENEMIES

Bulbs are subject to a number of diseases and to attack by several serious insect pests, all of which make rigid care necessary.

VIRUS AND BACTERIAL DISEASES. Most bulbous plants have some form of virus disease (which see). *Mosaic* produces mottling of the foliage, poor flowers and stunted plants and is often called the gray disease. *Breaking* (which see) refers to a change from a solid color to a streaking or splashing of the flowers; it is responsible for the variegated tulips that were formerly thought to be distinct varieties or types. A third kind of virus disease is typified by the "yellow-flat" disease of lily (which see). *Roguing,* which means a periodical inspection of plantings and the removal and destruction of every diseased individual, is the only control method available against such diseases.

Hyacinth yellows, a bacterial disease, is confined to that genus (see HYACINTH), but bacterial soft rot is found in many types of bulbs, particularly Callas, which see.

FUNGOUS DISEASES. Fungi of the Botrytis group cause a blight, or "fire disease" of lily, tulip, hyacinth, crocus and narcissus. The most typical sign of the disease is the fuzzy grayish mold produced on leaves and flowers, but small black resting bodies (*sclerotia*) may be found on the bulb scales and on plant debris in the soil. Sanitary measures (removing all blossoms as soon as they fade and cutting off the leaves at the surface of the ground as soon as they ripen) are the best means of control. Spraying with a weak bordeaux mixture several times in the spring, starting when the young shoots first appear is beneficial. See BOTRYTIS.

A basal bulb rot causes serious losses among narcissus, crocus, hyacinth and freesia bulbs. The fungus rots the basal plate (or the entire bulb), dwarfing the plant and causing crippled flowers. Discard badly diseased bulbs and soak the rest in a 1 to 1000 solution of corrosive sublimate for 1 hour, or in 0.25% liquid Semesan for 6 hours. Where basal rot threatens, the hot water used to treat narcissus, iris, etc., for the control of nematodes and bulb flies, as directed below, should contain a fungicide such as 1 oz. Semesan to 4 gals. water or 1 oz. corrosive sublimate to 8 gals. water.

BULB FLIES. The greater narcissus fly (*Merodon equestris*) attacks narcissus, hyacinth, amaryllis, galtonia and other bulbous plants over most of the United States. The adult is a shiny, yellow and black, hairy fly, resembling a small bumble bee. It lays eggs in the base of the leaves or in the neck of the bulb which, usually, is penetrated by a single whitish or yellowish maggot. As the latter grows, perhaps to ¾ in. in length, it may consume most of the bulb, which becomes soft and shows brown scars on the outer scales. Examine bulbs that are either bought or dug up in the garden, and destroy any showing distinct evidence of fly infestation.

To sterilize the remainder, place them in a loosely woven bag, wood or wire rack or other open container, and suspend in a tank of water kept at a constant temperature of 110 deg. F.—for 2½ hours. (More time will be necessary with very large bulbs.) If any bulbs then develop poorly or fail completely in the spring, dig and destroy them immediately.

The lesser narcissus fly (*Eumeris strigatus*) causes somewhat similar injury and the control measures are the same. The adult is a blackish-green small fly; the maggots, grayish or yellowish-gray with wrinkled bodies, can sometimes be found in narcissus, hyacinth, amaryllis, onion, shallot or iris bulbs.

MITES. The bulb mite attacks practically all types of bulbs, but is a special pest of narissus, tulip, hyacinth, crocus, lily, amaryllis, orchids and dahlias. It is very minute, whitish, eight-legged and usually visible only with the aid of a hand lens. The female lays from 50 to 100 eggs on the surface of a bulb; they hatch in 4 to 7 days, and the young mites burrow into the bulb, growing rapidly as they feed on scales or root tissue. Preferring healthy bulbs, they migrate through the soil from decaying to sound ones. Infested bulbs stored under favorable conditions for the mites deteriorate rapidly. Control by burning all soft and rotted bulbs. Others may be immersed in a 1-400 solution of nicotine sulphate; or in a 2% solution of formaldehyde which is held at 122 deg. F. for 10 minutes. Or they may be treated with hot water at 110 deg. F. for 2½ hours, as directed above, under Bulb Flies. These methods are safe for dormant bulbs but will kill young roots.

EEL-WORM OR NEMATODE. The bulb or stem nematode (*Anguillulina dipsaci,* formerly *Tylenchus dipsaci*) is a microscopic round "eel-worm" that burrows through the cells and eventually destroys the bulb, which usually shows concentric brown rings when it is cut across. Use the hot water treatment above described, being careful to maintain the exact temperature and plant treated bulbs in fresh or sterilized soil. See NEMATODE.

BULL-BAY. Common name applied to *Magnolia grandiflora,* and to *Persea borbonia.* See both those genera.

BULRUSH. Common name for herbs of the genus *Scirpus* of the Sedge Family. Having grass-like leaves and bearing flowers in spikelets. Some of the species are grown in the bog garden or in ponds in shallow water, and one in the greenhouse. They are increased by division, by seeds or by suckers. *S. cernuus,* to 1 ft., with many drooping stems and solitary spikelets, is grown in the greenhouse in damp pots and is prized because of its graceful drooping habit of growth. *S. lacustris* grows to 9 ft. and is apparently leafless, making a mass of spikes terminating in dense head-like clusters. *S. tabernaemontani* grows to 2 ft. and the spikelets are in flat-topped clusters; its var. *zebrinus* has white-banded stems. *S. holoschoenus* is stiff and rushlike with a few narrow leaves and spikelets in dense heads. *S. acutis* reaches to 9 ft. and has spikelets either in clusters or solitary. *S. atrovirens* has leafy stems to 4 ft. and spikelets in heads.

BUNCHBERRY. A common name for *Cornus canadensis,* the Canadian, or Dwarf Dogwood, a woody plant but a few inches tall, bearing dense heads of pale flowers followed by small red berries. See DOGWOOD.

BUNCH-FLOWER. Common name for *Melanthium virginicum,* a perennial herb of the Lily Family. Colonies of it are often used in the wild or bog garden, as it is easily increased from seed or by division

BUNCHBERRY, A MINIATURE SHRUB
This low dogwood (Cornus canadensis) has, first, white flowers and later a tight cluster of red berries in the center of the leaf rosette. A tiny treasure for the wild garden.

of the large, stout rootstocks. It has a cluster of narrow leaves at the base and outstanding greenish or white flowers in panicles on a stalk 5 ft. high.

BUNYA-BUNYA (bun'-i-ah). Common name for *Araucaria bidwilli,* a thick-leaved evergreen tree of the Pine Family, from Australia.

BUPHTHALMUM (beuf-thal'-mum). A genus of showy composite plants from Europe and W. Asia, growing from 2 to 4 ft. high, with large, rather coarse leaves and large yellow flowers. The name, from the Greek, means Ox-eye, which is the common name for the group. Of easy culture, requiring only a dry sunny position and well-drained soil, the plants are useful for bold mass effects towards the back of the perennial border. They may be increased by division in spring or by spring-sown seed, which frequently blossoms the first year.

B. speciosum, to 4 ft., blooming in June, is probably the best species. *B. speciosissimum,* to 5 ft., flowers in July or later. *B. salicifolium,* to only 2 ft., is a root-runner and spreads rapidly.

BUPLEURUM (beu-ploor'-um). A genus of Old-World perennials and subshrubs of the Parsley Family (Umbelliferae), commonly known as Thoroughwax. They have coarse leaves and heads of yellow flowers on long stems, and their weedy habits make them suitable for planting only on dry sterile soil in waste corners. They may be planted in autumn or spring.

B. fruticosum, to 6 ft., is a more or less evergreen aromatic shrub, valuable for its hardiness in seashore gardens; the flower clusters are to 4 in. across.

BUR. A common name for any fruit (botanically speaking) that has a rough or prickly exterior, whatever part of the flower it may be developed from. Examples are Burdock, Bur-marigold, Cocklebur, and Chestnut. The word is also applied to weeds or other plants that produce such fruits.

BUR- or **STAR-CUCUMBER** (*Sicyos angulatus*). An annual climbing plant, native of N. America, belonging to the Cucumber Family. It is a fast grower, to 20 ft. or more, and is useful for screening purposes. It has sharply angled or lobed leaves, small whitish flowers, and short spiny fruits.

BURDOCK. Common name for the genus Arctium, comprising coarse, strong-smelling biennials or possibly perennials of the Composite Family. They have large leaves and small, purplish flowers followed by bur-like heads, armed with hooked bristles which aid in spreading them. Old-World plants, they are now widely distributed and some species are much despised weeds, especially *A. minus,* the Common Burdock, which is widely naturalized in this country. *A. lappa,* the Great Burdock, to 8 ft., with large, heart-shaped leaves, white-wolly beneath, is less common in the U. S. but in Japan it is cultivated for the large, edible root called "gobo." See also WEEDS.

BURGUNDY MIXTURE. A copper spray which leaves no stain and can be used as a substitute for bordeaux mixture on small fruits and other plants which do not burn easily. Use 1 lb. copper sulphate, 1½ lbs. sodium carbonate (sal soda) to 50 gals. of water. Proceed as in making bordeaux mixture (which see). This spray cannot safely be combined with lead arsenate but may be used with calcium arsenate.

BUR-MARIGOLD. One of the common names for the genus Bidens, also known as Tickseed and Stick-tights. Weedy relatives of Cosmos, the plants bear yellow ray-flowers, and seeds which hook on to passing objects.

BURNET (bur'-net). Common name for plants of the genus Sanguisorba of the Rose Family—hardy perennial herbs with, usually, white, greenish, purple or crimson flowers in heads or spikes, sometimes reaching the height of 6 ft. Most of the species are grown as ornamental plants in the border; one (*S. minor*) for its leaves, which are used as a flavoring. They are increased from seeds and by division. *S. officinalis* grows to 5 ft. and has dark purple flowers in short spikes. An Old-World plant, it has often escaped in America. Closely related to Poterium, which see.

BURNING. A term for several types of plant injury. Literally, fermenting fresh manure in soil or hotbed may generate enough heat to injure nearby tender feeding roots. Concentrated commercial fertilizers (plant foods) may cause the "burning" of seeds, roots or bulbs with which they come in contact. Being soluble they are quickly taken up by the soil moisture which may thus become a more concentrated solution than is the cell sap in adjacent root hairs and other plant tissues. If this happens, the thinner sap is drawn by the physical process osmosis (which see) out of the plant cells into the soil solution. This abnormal action kills cells subjected to it and if enough are destroyed, the plant will be injured or even killed. To prevent this trouble, do not apply commercial fertilizer where it can touch plant parts; spread it evenly and cultivate it at once into the soil; and water well immediately to dilute the enriched soil solution to keep it in proper relation to the cell sap.

Injury resembling, if not actual, burning may be done to plant foliage and stems (including tree trunks) by insects, diseases, drying winds, brilliant winter or spring sunlight, and, paradoxically, by intense cold; also by certain spray mixtures wrongly prepared or applied at the wrong time, that is, under unfavorable temperature and moisture conditions.

BURNING-BUSH. A common name for *Euonymus atropurpureus;* also one of the names for Dictamnus, both of which see.

BURSTWORT. Common name for Herniaria (Herniary), a genus of low growing, greenish-flowered herbs of the Pink Family.

BUSH-CLOVER. Common name for the leguminous genus Lespedeza; some species are forage crops and a few hardy ones are grown as ornamentals.

BUSH-HONEYSUCKLE. Common name for Diervilla, an American genus of low, spreading shrubs closely related to Weigela. Forming a mat of underground stems, they are useful in holding banks in shape.

BUSH-POPPY (*Dendromecon rigida*). Known also as Tree-poppy. This is a Californian shrub of stiff habit, evergreen or nearly so, growing to 10 ft. high. It is not hardy in severe climates, but can stand some frost if given protection, such as is afforded by a wall. It has narrow, leathery, glaucous leaves with prominent veins, and the golden-yellow flowers are very like single poppies. Propagated by seeds, which are very slow to germinate.

BUTTERCUP FAMILY. Another name for *Ruscus aculeatus,* also known as Box-holly. A small-leaved European shrub of the Lily Family, whose cut sprays are dyed and used by florists for decorative work.

Climbing-butchers-broom is *Semele androgyna.*

BUTOMUS (beu'-toh-mus) *umbellatus.* An erect aquatic herb of Europe and Asia, with 3 ft. leaves. Hardy and easily grown in ponds as Flowering-rush, which see.

BUTTER-AND-EGGS. A common name for *Linaria vulgaris,* also known as Toadflax, a hardy field and roadside plant with flowers of orange and yellow.

BUTTER-BUR. Common name for the genus Petasites, hardy large-leaved, early-blooming plants adapted for rough, difficult locations.

BUTTERCUP. Common name for the genus Ranunculus (also called Crowfoot), familiar as a flower of fields and meadows and including a score or more of improved horticultural subjects.

BUTTERCUP FAMILY. Another name for the Crowfoot Family, which includes many favorite garden subjects. See RANUNCULACEAE.

BUTTERFLIES. These attractive, graceful insects, often brilliantly colored, are the adult form of various caterpillars. Thus (and in other respects) they resemble moths, which also belong to the Order Lepidoptera. But they differ from moths in flying only by day, in having more slender bodies, and clubbed or hooked (never feathery) antennae, and in folding their broad wings together vertically when at rest instead of horizontally. Butterflies are themselves harmless, and even as the parents of potentially destructive caterpillars only one is responsible for serious damage to crops. This is the Cabbage-butterfly, introduced from Europe in 1868, and now wide-spread over the country. It lays its eggs in young plants of various members of the Cabbage Family and the larvae feed on the heads as they form, being protected by the outer leaves. Pyrethrum-soap spray or hellebore dust helps to keep them down.

BUTTERFLY-BUSH. A common name for the genus Buddleia.

BUTTERFLY-FLOWER. Common name for Schizanthus, a S. American genus of graceful, free-flowering annuals and biennials of the Nightshade Family, which have given rise to many showy hybrids. The name is also applied to *Bauhinia monandra,* the Jerusalem-date, a leguminous tree of N. Africa.

BUTTERFLY-LILY. A common name for Hedychium, also called Ginger-lily, a tropical genus of perennial herbs of the Ginger Family, with showy, fragrant flowers. Grown as a greenhouse plant except in frostless regions.

BUTTERFLY ORCHID. Common name for *Oncidium papilio,* a Venezuelan species having a single leaf and bearing 2½ in. solitary yellow and brown flowers on 3 ft. stalks throughout the year.

BUTTERFLY-PEA. Common name for Clitoria, a genus of perennial herbs and small shrubs of the tropics (and one species in S. Atlantic States), sometimes grown in the South, but more often in N. greenhouses as an ornamental. Also applied to Centrosema or Conchita, another tropical legume of which some species are grown as cover crops.

BUTTERFLY-TULIP. Common name for *Calochortus vestus* and *C. venustus,* both white-flowering species of the Mariposa-lily or Globe-tulip, a member of the Lily Family.

See CALOCHORTUS.

BUTTERFLY-WEED. Common name for *Asclepias tuberosa,* a handsome, summer-blooming herb of the fields, from Me. to Fla. and Ariz., belonging to the Milkweed Family. Its brilliant orange flowers attract butterflies. It has been called America's finest wild flower.

BUTTERNUT. A large, deciduous tree of the Walnut genus (*Juglans cinerea*) and its nuts, which have always been esteemed. They are customarily pickled while young and green. The hard wood is used for furniture and interior trim. The sap, bark, and all green parts of the tree have the characteristic staining properties of the tribe, the juice quickly oxidizing to a dark brown color on exposure to the air. See WALNUT.

BUTTERWORT. Common name given to the plants of the genus Pinguicula, members of the Bladderwort Family. They are small, stemless herbs with flat leaves covered with a sticky substance to which insects adhere. The pretty little solitary flowers are variously colored, yellow, purple or white. They can be grown only on rocks in the bog garden, or in a moist part of the rock garden. They are increased by seed or offsets. *P. vulgaris* growing to 6 in. and with violet or purple flowers ½ in. long; *P. lutea,* to 1 ft., with flowers golden-yellow, 1½ in. long and broad; and *P. grandiflora,* to 8 in., with wavy-lobed violet flowers, are the principal species.

BUTTON-BUSH. Common name for Cephalanthus, a genus of five or six species of shrubs found in Asia, Africa and N. America, belonging to the Madder Family. The one found in this country is widespread in swampy places. This is *C. occidentalis,* a deciduous shrub to 12 ft. or more, and apparently the only one in cultivation. While found naturally in swampy places, and therefore well suited for wet places in gardens, it will grow in any good garden soil. It has good glossy foliage. The small tubular white flowers are densely packed in long-stalked globular heads, and open after midsummer.

BUTTON-SNAKEROOT. A common name for Liatris, a genus of hardy N.

American Composite herbs with attractive rosy-purple or white flowers in late summer. Known also as Gayfeather and Blazing Star, they are sometimes transplanted to the wild garden. The name is also used for *Eryngium aquaticum,* a perennial herb of E. U.S. belonging to the Parsley Family.

BUTTONWOOD or **BUTTONBALL.** The common name of a native species (*occidentalis*) of Platanus, spectacular when dormant with its white upper branches shading to green and brown toward the base. The brittle bark peels off each year as it is not able to expand with the growth of the trunk. In the wild it is found in the wet rich soil of valleys, river floodplains and lake shores. But it endures city conditions well and has been extensively planted with fine effect on streets and avenues and in parks as well as about home grounds. It stands pruning well and the tops are sometimes sheared to fit into formal landscape treatment of small areas.

See also PLANE.

BUXACEAE. The Box Family, comprising some half dozen genera of trees, shrubs or herbs that retain their foliage from year to year. Boxwood and Pachysandra are its best known representatives.

BUXUS (buk'-sus). A genus of slow-growing ornamental evergreen shrubs and small trees. See BOX.

C

CABBAGE. A biennial herb (*Brassica oleracea,* var. *capitata*) whose thick, rounded, strongly veined leaves are compressed itno a huge bud or compact "head" on a short, stout stalk. Its numerous horticultural varieties include early and late sorts; smooth or crinkly and green or purple ("red") leaves; and oblong, conical, globular or flattened heads. Chinese or celery cabbage (which see) is a different species (*B. pekinensis*).

REQUIREMENTS AND VARIATIONS. To grow best, cabbage requires full exposure to the sun and a soil abundantly supplied with plant food and moisture. The soil may be of any type—sandy, clayey, even mucky or gravelly—but can hardly be made too rich with stable manures and leguminous green manures. Without ample soil moisture the plants suffer and make few, poor or no heads; but in poorly drained soil they also fail. Hence the importance of good drainage (which see).

Cabbage varieties display perhaps wider variation than those of any other vegetable, and not only in the ways already mentioned. Early sorts (mostly of high quality) may form their small heads in less than 100 days from seed-sowing and require only a square foot each in which to develop; late ones need twice as long and three times as much space. The former do best if planted in early spring, as they prefer cool, moist conditions; mid-season varieties should be started equally early to give them a good start before hot weather which they stand better than do the early kinds; late sorts are usually started in May or June and harvested in October or November. They are less susceptible to heat than the earlier kinds and make their heads during the cool fall weather.

For the home garden early and mid-season kinds are better than the late ones, because they require less space and because late cabbage is a staple market vegetable. If any late variety is desired in the home garden, first choice should be one of the Savoy sorts, all of which are of the highest quality and seldom seen in the markets.

GARDEN CULTURE. For the earliest crop sow seed under glass in seed pans or flats. When the seedlings have developed their second pair of true leaves, prick them off about 2 in. apart into other flats. The soil should be friable but not rich so that strong roots rather than large tops will develop. Keep where the night temperature is below 60 deg.—even down to 50—and give abundant air. When the plants are well established place the flats in a coldframe and gradually harden the plants in readiness

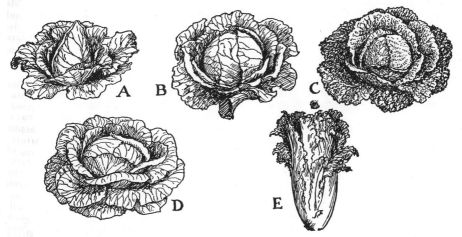

CABBAGE VARIETIES HAVE BEEN ON RECORD FOR NEARLY 2,000 YEARS
Among several hundred types known to growers today are the following: (A) Conical or Wakefield; (B) Round; (C) Savoy, with crinkled leaves and often superior flavor; and (D) Dutch or flat-headed. These are all forms of Brassica oleracea. The Chinese or celery cabbage (E) made recently popular in America, is of a different species.

for transplanting them out of doors. Vigorous, stocky subjects more easily transplant and grow rapidly when properly handled. It is well to wrap a 2 in. wide strip of paper around each stem at ground level or use the flat disks of tar paper to outwit cut-worms, which see.

CABBAGE WORM AND BUTTERFLY
Only careful spraying or dusting will keep the voracious green larvae of the white cabbage butterfly in check.

Distances between plants will vary with the variety, the soil and the method of cultivation. Set early kinds 12 in. or even less asunder in rows 18 in. apart for wheelhoe or hoe culture; leave 30 in. between rows if horse or garden tractor is used. Cultivate twice a week until there is danger of injuring the plants with the tools.

For the late crop sow seed about June 1st in rows a foot or less apart in outdoor beds. Dig the soil freshly and rake it finely; it should be only moderately fertile. If the seed is sown thinly the plants, without thinning, will grow sturdy and stocky enough for direct transplanting to the garden within a month after sowing the seed.

HARVESTING. It is usually advised to pull the plants up by the roots when wanted. However, if cut so as to leave a few inches of stalk, several small, loose heads may form along the stem for later gathering. The outer leaves and stems of large heads should be fed to live stock or poultry or chopped up and buried in the compost pile so as to destroy insect pests which are very likely to be present in the leaf axils. Cut early cabbage only as needed as it does not keep well after cutting; to prevent excessive growth and splitting, bend or twist

the stems of the largest heads so as to break or loosen some of the feeding roots. Harvest late cabbage as late as possible before freezing. Trim off the outer leaves and store for winter use. See STORING OF CROPS.

ENEMIES. The diseases and insect pests of cabbage are treated under CRUCIFERS.

CABBAGE PALMETTO. One common name for *Sabal palmetto,* a species of fan palm found from N. C. to Fla. and better known as Palmetto, which see.

CABBAGE ROSE. The common name for *Rosa centifolia,* an old-time species from the Caucasus. A popular garden aristocrat since late in the sixteenth century, it is still valued for the delicious fragrance and clear pink color of its individual, nodding flowers. These are very double and globular, opening from blunt buds. The bush, of rather spreading form, may grow as high as 5 or 6 ft. One of its varieties is *muscosa,* called the Moss Rose because of the roughened, mossy quality of its calyx and flower stem.

CABOMBA (kah-bom'-bah). A small genus of aquatic plants popularly called Fanwort and Water Shield, native to the W. hemisphere and belonging to the Waterlily Family. The floating leaves are rounded and entire but those below the surface are finely cut. *C. caroliniana,* the species chiefly grown, is found in ponds and slow streams from Ill. southward and can easily be established in garden pools. It can also be used in aquaria but, unless it can root in soil, it lasts only a few weeks. Propagation is by cuttings, division and seeds.

CACALIA (kah-kay'-li-ah). Former generic name (still found in some catalogs) for *Emelia sagittata,* the Tasselflower or Floras Paintbrush. See EMILIA.

CACAO (kah-kay'-oh). Common name in the tropics for the Cocoa- or Chocolate-tree (*Theobroma cacao*). A native of Central and S. America, it is extensively cultivated for its seed, the source of cocoa and chocolate. A wide branched evergreen to 25 ft. it bears seed-pods to 1 ft. long and 4 in. thick with a hard leathery shell, containing up to 40 "beans," some an inch wide. These are prepared for manufacture by washing and fermentation. Propagated generally from seeds, trees when 1 to 2 ft. high, are planted 10 to 15 ft. apart; they bear in about 4 years.

CACTUS. (See illustrations, Plate 7.) The Cactus Family (Cactaceae) stands apart, with little to connect it with other families of plants.

It is dicotyledonous (that is, its seeds have 2 seed-leaves), perennial, and enjoys the distinction of being succulent in all its members. (Succulent in this connection means capable of storing within itself sufficient moisture to enable it to withstand drought or arid conditions. In cacti this stored moisture is mucilaginous, which tends to retard evaporation.)

Plants vary in shape from huge columnar branched or unbranched forms, to slender vines; from tree-like growths to the small, flat, rounded forms of the Mammillaria (which see). Leaves, except in rare cases which will be noted, are conspicuous by their absence. When present, they are small and inconspicuous and soon fall. The roots also vary greatly; in most cases they are fibrous, but some are tuberous, some are aerial, and sometimes there is a tap-root.

The blossoms are usually large and showy, with many petals and numerous stamens. The petals and sepals often intergrade and are usually referred to as inner and outer perianth segments, the perianth being the floral envelope which includes both corolla and calyx. The fruits are berries with no paritions between the seed. In many cases they are edible.

The cacti have one distinguishing mark, found in no other plants, in the form of specialized organs whence spring branches, flowers, spines, glochids (barbed hairs) and, when present, leaves. These centers of growth are called *areoles*. Their position and number are determining factors in differentiating species, as are also the number, form and position of the spines. See illustration, page 203.

Cacti (with a single doubtful exception, a species of Rhipsalis) are native to the W. hemisphere. In N. America their habitat extends into Canada, to Nova Scotia and British Columbia, and throughout the U. S., especially the Southwest. (Mexico is undoubtedly entitled to be called "Cactus Land," leading all other localities in the number and variety of kinds found there.) There are also distributed over many parts of S. America, whence come some of our most interesting species.

KINDS OF CACTI

Originally only a few species were known; these were then grouped under a single genus, Cactus. As our knowledge of these plants has grown and new species have been discovered, there have come to be recognized some 1500 species and subdivisions, and changes in nomenclature have been many. As, to American readers, the "Manual of Cacti" by Britton and Rose is the standard authority, and that most generally accepted, its names and classifications will be followed in this article and other articles discussing cactus genera throughout this book.

The three tribes which form the first great subdivisions are:

(1) PERESKIAE. In this true leaves are persistent and there is more or less resemblance to other plants; hence by the uninitiated they are often referred to other families. They will be briefly considered under the heading Pereskia.

(2) OPUNTIAE. This includes the genus Nopalea, the Prickly-pear, and the Cholla,

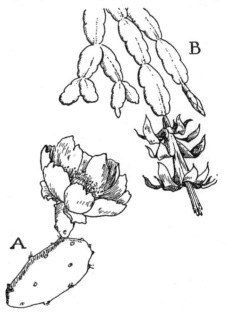

B

A

VARIATION IN CACTUS FLOWERS
A. The large cup-shaped blossom typical of Prickly-pear and some other species. B. The drooping, "hose-in-hose" bloom of the popular Christmas or Crab Cactus.

familiar to many. These will be briefly considered under the heading Nopalea and at greater length under Opuntia.

(3) CEREI. This is a very large and diverse section, divided into 8 subtribes and including the huge columnar giants, the

slender climbing plants (some of which are known as "the night-blooming cereus and frequently cultivated as house plants), the Echinocereus types, delightful with their interesting spines and their lovely, colorful flowers, the Ferocacti, including some of the most interesting specimens in the list of those we wish in our homes, the Coryphanthenae, including the largest single group—the Neomammillarias, which lend themselves delightfully to use in even the smallest of dish gardens, the Epiphyllums, those wondrously beautiful things that are claiming the attention of professional and amateur alike, and the unique and curious Rhipsalis.

Among these numerous representatives of the Cactus Family, there are many that are but little known, many others that are difficult or impossbile to obtain, and still others whose cultivation would be impossible and interest in which is necessarily confined to the botanist. Therefore, in considering cultural possibilities, the field is much narrowed, and in this discussion attention will be confined to those which hold interest for cultural purposes, either in the garden or in the home. Yet even this list will be found to be surprisingly large and varied, with specimens to meet every need, large or small, and almost any cultural condition.

The choice of what to grow will, of course, depend upon climatic conditions and the space to be devoted to the cactus garden (or to house culture).

Cacti in the Garden

In considering the culture of cacti, we find that the plants naturally fall into two classes: (1) those which have their origin in the arid desert, and (2) those that are native to the tropics and find their habitat in the jungle, perhaps climbing over the trunk of a dead tree, and blooming along with an orchid for company. This latter class, whose members are semi-epiphytic in their habits, include some of those longest known in cultivation, and dearest to plant lovers; some of those we dub "night-blooming cereus," epiphyllums, etc., all lath-house or greenhouse subjects. Manifestly, different cultural conditions and methods are required than are called for by our ordinary garden subjects.

All cacti, however, are succulent; built to store up any moisture obtainable, and to take it up sometimes too greedily. So

the one essential factor in the culture of all cacti is absolutely good drainage. Under no circumstances will they tolerate a soggy soil; a choice plant may be ruined in a single day by water standing at its roots.

In planning a cactus garden, a gentle slope is absolutely ideal. The ground must be dug up and a substratum of stones, broken brick or similar substance placed. It should be filled in with gravel and topped with a good sandy loam. Whether fertilizer should be used is a moot question. Some workers answer absolutely and emphatically "no"; while others go contrary to this advice and use a richer soil with such success that their experience goes to prove the lack of wisdom in absolute prohibition, at any rate. There is a commercial plant food now on the market which seems to be very successful, the difference in the growth of plants with and without it being very noticeable. Most desert cacti like an alkaline soil and it is good practice to use slaked lime in small amount, mixing it well into the soil.

Climatic conditions vary so greatly over this broad country, that it is hard to make any rule that is applicable to them all. In the more northern and colder states, few cacti are hardy in the ground, but even up into Canada come Opuntias are found; so that a nucleus of native growth may be had. *O. opuntia* (*O. compressa*), for instance, is found along the sandy Atlantic Coast. Of somewhat straggly growth, it has a beautiful rose-like flower, of a clear yellow.

With this as a starting point, the more hardy varieties may be potted and sunk into the ground—but here double care must be taken with drainage, first, in the pot and also in the bed into which it is sunk. In the colder season, of course, these potted plants must be removed and taken indoors or otherwise protected.

In the warmer climates the hardier specimens may be planted in the garden and allowed to remain there. Under such conditions a wider choice of plants may be indulged in; not only may larger growing species be included but also larger specimens may be used than when they are grown in pots which must be removed from the ground.

In planning such a garden, as when using other plants, it is well to study the future stature of the specimens used, so that one which grows or spreads rapidly will not crowd out its slower growing neighbor. Thus is harmony and balance preserved. In this connection, however, remember that some of the smaller ones like partial shade, so try and give them this help by planting them where it will be provided by their larger neighbors.

A cactus garden is often so planned as to include other succulent plants requiring similar treatment. In this case it is advantageous to have some low-growing plant, succulent in character, as a ground cover.

The rock garden is a subject in whose name many crimes are committed. Too often a few boulders or cobblestones are strewn about, some cacti planted hit-or-miss, and the result is dubbed a rock garden! Rocks are *not* necessary to a cactus garden (except as a substratum for drainage), but if used, they should be carefully selected and placed as though they had been "growing" in their places these many years. Only exceptional rock gardens are artistic, especially those in which cacti are used.

CARE: WATERING. The care of the cactus garden after planting is simple. Weeds should be kept out, of course. The important question is watering—when to do it, how often, and how much?

Do not water cacti from above, especially those showing a depressed crown where the water might stand; even standing drops of water can cause burning, the injury later leading to rot.

Do not overwater. The amount required varies with climatic conditions—a drier atmosphere meaning a larger amount of water. It also varies with the closeness of the planting. Some workers prefer to give a light watering about once every two weeks; others advocate a thorough watering once a month or six weeks. A good rule is: moist but not wet. These directions apply to the blooming and growing season. After that is over, little water should be given.

Of all things to be guarded against, rot easily takes first place. A touch will sometimes disclose that a cactus is completely rotted inside; in that case, nothing can save it. This is due to insufficient drainage or gross overwatering. On the other hand, a cactus in which rot has barely started, as the result of an abrasion, may be saved if the trouble is not too far ad-

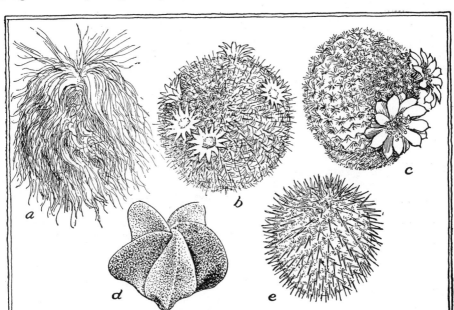

SOME OF MANY REMARKABLE FORMS FOUND AMONG THE CACTI
And almost equaled by their names! Here are shown: a, the Old Man Cactus (Cephalacereus senilis) with long silky hairs; b, Neomammilaria longicoma; c, Rebutia minuscula; d, Astrophytum myriostigma; and e, Neomammilaria parkinsoni.

vanced. Cut away all infected tissue; or, if the injury is at the base, cut back to healthy tissue, leave to callus a few days and treat as a cutting (see below).

INSECT PESTS. Some insect pests must be guarded against. Cacti are susceptible to scale, mealy bug, aphis, and (in the case of the Opuntias) the cochineal insect.

First-aid against scale may be had in an alcohol spray. Soapy water (particularly if whale-oil soap is used) is usually effective; it may be applied with a brush or, if necessary, as a spray. Use an oil-emulsion spray as a last resort, but only then, as it often spoils the appearance of the plants.

Mealy bugs or aphids are sometimes found on the roots of cactus plants. If an unthrifty appearance of the plant warrants suspicion of this possibility, investigate; if the insects are found, wash them off thoroughly with a brush, and treat, for mealy bug, with a reliable oil emulsion, and, for aphis, with nicotine-sulphate solution.

The presence of ants about the plants is often a sign or warning of the presence of scale or aphis. It is well to keep some kind of ant poison about the plants at all times.

CACTI FOR THE GARDEN. The choice of cactus plants for garden culture will of necessity vary with such considerations as amount of space to be used, climatic conditions, etc. However, some that may be used can be suggested, and a consultation of catalogs will permit additions to the list.

For the summer garden where plants must be grown in pots and protected in winter, there might be used some of the smaller growing Opuntias, Neomammillarias, Echinocacti and Echinocerei such as:

O. erinacea, whose white spines give it the name of "grizzly bear cactus."

O. pottsi, a small-growing plant with pink, rose-like flowers.

O. microdasys, with its golden glochids.

O. subulata, with its persistent awl-like leaves.

O. santa-rita, with colored pads.

O. leptocaulis, with persistent colored fruits.

Pediocactus simpsoni (Plains Cactus).

Neomammillaria applanata, like a little Christmas wreath.

Ferocactus uncinatus, with colored spines and chocolate flowers.

Echinocactus johnsoni, with large yellow flowers having maroon center.

Lophophora williamsi (Dumpling Cactus).

Ariocarpus fissuratus (Living Rock).

Echinocereus rigidissimus (Rainbow Cactus).

E. reichenbachi (Merry Widow).

E. fendleri, with large violet-purple blossoms.

In the more permanent garden, where pots need not be used and plantings can be made directly in the ground, we may add such plants as:

Opuntia monacantha, a S. American species of rapid growth, and free blooming.

O. basilaris, a mound of beauty when blooming.

Lophocereus schotti, with its curious gray spines.

Trichocereus spachianus, with its crown of white flowers.

Echinocereus engelmanni, with rose-purple blossoms.

E. straminius, with straw-colored spines and yellow flowers.

And, as a crowning glory, *Echinocactus grusoni,* forming a perfect ball of gold.

CACTI IN THE HOME

To by far the greater number of us, a garden is that which is seen only in our dreams; but the cactus fan need spend no time in regrets, for to him may be given the opportunity to really possess beauty rivaling that of his seemingly more fortunate garden-minded friend.

Even with a single plant—were he so limited—he may have a thing of unrivaled beauty. This would be in the way of one potted plant—which is an ideal way in which to begin a cactus collection. In this way the habit of the subject may be studied, and the knowledge thus gained and applied through more intelligent care will prevent the loss of choice specimens later on.

The initial choice will probably govern the future character of the collection. Such a beginning may be with a Heliocereus or an Epiphyllum, whose wonderful floral beauty may make you the envy of some orchid-conscious friend, for it can prove a rival indeed. It may be a Christmas Cactus which will provide unique holiday-season beauty, and later will lead to experimentation in that fascinating subject of grafting. Or it may be that object of beauty already mentioned — *Echinocactus*

Plate 7.   CACTI ARE FULL OF CHARACTER

Top: Exquisite, satiny blossoms contrast curiously with these squat, spiny plants.   Bottom: A garden of cacti and succulents demonstrates interesting possibilities of these desert plant types.

grusoni, a ball of gold, truly a delight to the eye.

Whatever the choice, one plant possessed will surely mean desire for others. And a group of cactus plants, potted and arranged on shelving, will occupy little space but give enough variety to provide unflagging interest.

If there should not be space available for such shelving, an inside window garden may be constructed, using iron brackets and plate glass for shelves. This may well provide for a most interesting grouping, with, perhaps, a drooping Aporocactus at one corner and the center space filled with low-growing specimens. An outside window garden, if feasible, will allow of the inclusion of specimens of greater height, thus rendering possible a more effective arrangement. A miniature glass-house, placed upon a table, affords opportunity for the display of smaller specimens. See page 204.

Plants suitable for such culture include such subjects as the smaller growing Opuntias, Echinocerei, Echinopses, Neomammillarias and Coryphanthas, which have been mentioned under garden culture. Some other plants ideal for such use but that have not already been suggested are:

Neomammillaria hahniana, covered with white hair; it multiplies rapidly and may be propagated by separation.

N. elegans, and *N. parkinsoni,* a beautiful plant.

Astrophytum myriostigma (Bishops Cap).

A. asterias, sometimes likened to a sea-urchin.

Dolichothele longimamma, with large clear yellow blossoms; this is unique in that it can be propagated by rooting a single tubercle.

Coryphantha aggregata.

C. macromeris, with a pink blossom as large as the plant itself.

Mamillopsis senilis.

CARE OF POTTED CACTI. In the culture of potted plants the same care as to drainage must be exercised as outdoors. Fill the pot ¼ to ⅓ full of broken pot, stone or other material (it is well to include pieces of charcoal), fill in with gravel and upon this substratum place the soil prepared according to the needs of the subject to be planted.

In the case of desert cacti, little or no fertilizer should be added, but a little slaked lime (about a spoonful to a medium-sized pot) will help the soil, which should be a good sandy loam. With Epiphyllums and cacti of similar habit, after the substratum of drainage insurance is provided, use rather a rich loam containing peat moss.

Watering a cactus in a pot is rather different from the practice in garden planting since the roots are confined to a small space rather than permitted to reach out for moisture. Generally speaking, to treat them much as other plants is sound practice. Watch at all times to detect any sign of overwatering, and err on the side of too little rather than too much. In this connection cacti will bear neglect to a surprising degree. They require more water during the blooming and growing periods than at other times; it is well to give them a decided rest after this time has passed.

THE CACTUS DISH GARDEN. If space or inclination will not permit of so ambitious a project as is implied in any of the foregoing suggestions, there still remains the dish garden. Some of these arrangements are charming, and in a room or apartment prove an ideal solution of the problem of what will provide the most interest and require the least time for care and attention.

In the interest of the beautiful plant which you are to grow, let the container be a double dish such as are now obtainable, or one that in some other way provides for the all-important drainage. Otherwise the specimen is doomed to death. That essential point settled, one can go on with enthusiasm.

Special attention should be given to the selection of plants, for as they are limited in the matter of variety, choice specimens must be chosen to compensate by giving all possible beauty.

The dish may be tiny, accommodating only one or two small subjects, or up to a foot or more in diameter, thus offering a possibility of interesting variety.

As to arrangement, it might be suggested that at one side there be placed a specimen of comparatively greater height, smaller ones being used at the other side and in the foreground. To give the required height, there might be selected a specimen of the Old-man Cactus, or one or more joints of one of the more decorative Opuntias (*O. microdasys* is a favorite for this purpose, or that rare and interesting one, *O. vestita* may be used).

For a tiny dish there might be suggested *Neomammillaria elongata* for height and in the foreground some of the tiny ones such as *Escobaria sneedi,* growing in clusters; possibly the smallest we have.

Neomammillaria denudata.

N. lasiacantha.

N. plumosa, a little ball of soft feathers.

Chamaecereus silvestri, called the Peanut Cactus, from the size and shape of its joints.

Epithelantha micromeris (Button Cactus), with tiny scarlet fruits like little jewels.

In making up a dish garden it is usually the practice to include some other succulent plants; for a ground cover between the plants some low-growing sedum, or something similar, can be used.

Propagating Cacti

It is inevitable that, once interest in these plants is aroused, the question of propagation should arise. Most of those subjects suited to house or small garden culture can be propagated from cuttings, or from offshoots which are treated as cuttings. The handling of cuttings is very simple and with the observance of a few simple precautions, success is assured.

Cuttings. It is usually best to leave the cuttings exposed to the air for a few days to callus, before planting them. They may be rooted in boxes prepared for this purpose and later transplanted to the pots in which they will be left. In the former case, prepare first by attending to the detail of drainage, as is necessary in any cultivation of cacti. Then fill the box with sand and powdered charcoal; dampen it slightly; insert the cuttings, and water sparingly or not at all until roots begin to form. In case of a tall cutting or a top-heavy one, put a support deeply into the soil and tie the cutting (that extends only a little way into the soil) to it.

If it is preferred to root a cutting in the pot in which the plant will remain, prepare the pot as for a growing plant, make a little pocket and fill this with prepared sand and charcoal, and place the cutting therein.

Cacti from Seed. The raising of cacti from seed by professional growers has come to be necessary; indeed, it is the only way in which rare kinds may be propagated. Government regulations as to the importation of plants are very stringent; only for propagation purposes and under rigid inspection and supervision, may they be had.

Even with our native plants, restrictions are being more tightly drawn. Interstate quarantine is one factor which prevents their former easy transportation. The spoilation of our desert flora by wholesale and ruthless collection has aroused local action in the interests of conservation, with

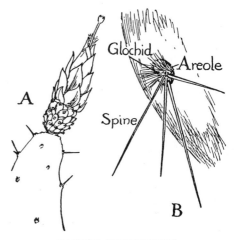

CACTUS CURIOSITIES
A. The details of the flower of Nopalea. B. Only cacti have areoles, which are specialized organs from which arise short fine bristles (glochids) and long sharp spines.

more and more rigid enforcement of state laws to that end. Seeds, on the other hand, are available to all growers from practically everywhere. And with greater familiarity with cactus seedlings has come the impulse to try raising them oneself. Hence the propagation of cacti from seed has come to be considered one of the most interesting details of their culture.

A seed bed may be a small box with holes in the bottom, a flower pot, a fern dish, or a regulation seed flat. As in all cactus operations, provide perfect drainage. Fill with a light mixture of sand, loam and peat; wet thoroughly and let stand over night; plant seed; cover by dusting lightly with a little fine gravel; place a glass over the seed bed, elevating it slightly as seed begins to sprout. Never allow the soil to dry out; but, while keeping it moist, do *not* keep it wet.

Cactus seed, for the most part, germinates quickly. The great danger is in "damping off," or the sudden killing of young seedlings by a rapid spreading fungus. If there is any indication of this, use some disinfectant sold for the purpose.

When rare seeds are being sown, it is a good plan to place them individually in small pots and sink these in the propagating sand or peat.

The greatest requisite in raising cactus seedlings is patience, for though, as noted, most seed germinates quickly, many species are of very slow growth.

GRAFTING THE CACTUS. In the culture of the cactus, the desirability or even the necessity of grafting, will early present itself. The object may be to increase rapidity of growth, to induce a form of growth which will better display the plant, the preservation of a delicate and rare specimen which may be suffering from rot, or some other important reason. Still another object in grafting (which will only be mentioned since it is not likely to appeal to the normal mind) is the creation of fantastic growth.

Whatever the purpose, the method is simple. Implements needed are a sharp knife and a few cactus spines of the long slender type which provide the best possible means of fastening the scions in place; *do not use metal pins.* Requisites to success are absolute cleanliness; clean, sharp cuts; immediate contact of cut surfaces. Also cactus grafting should be done in the growing season.

The cuts may either form flat surfaces, as might be used in grafting a small globose specimen to a columnar stock of similar diameter, in order to raise it above

CACTI PUT TO USE
They are especially satisfactory for small homes, growing very slowly and withstanding well the hot dry air of apartments and flats.

the danger point for rot; or the scion may be cut in wedge shape and inserted into a notch of similar size cut in the stock.

Grafting stock is somewhat varied, depending upon the scion to be used, the result to be obtained, the method used and other details. In common use are Opuntia, Acanthocereus, *Nyctocereus serpentinus, Selenicereus macdonoldiae,* Pereskia, and others. It should be a well-rooted cutting of appropriate size, and should be dry when the graft is made.

Plan the operation so that there will be no delay in bringing the cut surfaces in contact; fasten the stock and scion in place, and union will soon take place.

As examples of the desirable results possible, an Aporocactus ("Rat-tail") may be grafted upon a columnar stock of suitable height so that a drooping effect may be had; or upon a quick-growing stock so that its influence will cause more rapid growth. Similarly, joints of Christmas Cactus (Zygocactus) may be grafted to form a pyramid, or at intervals along a climbing stem, or an erect stem, of Pereskia, etc. Epiphyllums especially are often grafted upon a quick-growing stock to stimulate and quicken growth.

HINTS TO CACTUS BUYERS

In purchasing stock, there is possible choice between collected specimens and those which have been propagated from seed. Under the first heading come native plants only, imported specimens not being available except for propagation or scientific purposes.

If purchased from a responsible and reputable dealer, collected plants may safely be chosen; such dealers usually have their stock regularly inspected so that diseased plants are not maintained or sold.

A CASE FOR THE CARE OF CACTI
Thus are these semi-tropical succulents protected from drafts and assured a favorable atmosphere. Fresh air is admitted by partially lifting the lid.

If any plants are received showing broken or injured roots, trim these off and plant with a view to developing new roots. Do not plant injured specimens and run the risk of rot appearing at the root. If a bruise appears on the body of a plant, treat it with powdered charcoal and watch carefully to guard against that same foe—rot.

Large shipments of desert plants are sometimes thrown on the market at low and tempting prices. Beware how such bargains(?) are purchased. Not only are the specimens offered usually unattractive, mutilated and worthless, but they may carry disease that will spread to and ruin other really valuable plants.

Seedlings are now generally considered more worth-while subjects. The plants are more shapely and more perfect, and do not carry the possibility of disease or of loss from rot following mutilation. And, as has been said, production from seed is the only way in which the rarer species can be obtained.

(For descriptive and cultural information about different kinds of cacti, see articles under the various generic names referred to above.)

CACTUS AND SUCCULENT SO-CIETY OF AMERICA. This body was organized in 1929 with a membership including both amateurs and professionals, in all parts of the world. It publishes a monthly magazine, the *Cactus and Succulent Journal,* a subscription to which is included with membership. It has also been reissuing in installments "The Cactaceae," the outstanding authoritative work on cactus, by N. L. Britton and J. N. Rose, long out of print. Back issues, bound, can be bought by new members who wish to have this monograph complete as published. The annual dues are $3. The secretary is Mr. Boyd L. Sloan, Pasadena, Calif.

CAESALPINIA (sez-al-pin'-i-ah). A genus of tropical evergreen trees and shrubs of the Pea Family. A few species are climbers and some are armed with prickles. They bear loose clusters of showy yellow, orange and red flowers, followed by conspicuous, usually flattened, seed pods. They are grown as ornamentals in frostless regions or occasionally in greenhouses elsewhere. They require a rich, sandy soil and are propagated by seeds which are best soaked before planting. Pot up as soon as seedlings can be handled.

CAJANUS (kah-jay'-nus). Pigeon-pea or Cajan. A tropical shrub of the Pea Family. One species (*C. cajan,* formerly *C. indicus*) is widely cultivated in tropical countries for its nutritious seeds, good for man and beast. It grows to 10 ft. in height and its stems, leaves, and seed pods are covered with soft, velvety hairs. The purple-spotted yellow flowers are produced over a long season. It is often grown from seeds as an annual.

CAJUPUT - TREE (ka-jeu'-put). A common name for *Melaleuca leucadendra,* an Australian tree not uncommon in Calif., conspicuous because the bark shreds in strips. Also called the Punk-tree.

CALABASH-GOURD (kal'-ah-bash). Common name for the hard-shelled fruits of *Lagenaria leucantha,* an Old-World tropical vine of the Cucumber Family. Of easy culture, the plant is widely grown for its fruits which, occurring in various shapes, are used for different purposes as dippers, bowls, etc.

CALABASH-TREE. Common name for *Crescentia cujete,* a tropical American tree of the Bignonia Family. Attaining 40 ft. with broad head and spreading branches, it is grown for the smooth, globular fruits, which may measure 1 ft. or more across, and the hard woody shells which are made into water vessels, "calabash pipes" and other objects. The shell may be made to assume various forms by constricting with bandages while growing.

CALACINUM (kal-ah-sin'-um). Wireplants. Twining prostrate or climbing woody plants native to the S. Temperate zone, belonging to the Buckwheat Family. They have wiry stems, alternate leaves and small unisexual flowers in short clusters followed by berry-like fruits. Sometimes seen in greenhouses, they are also sometimes grown in hanging baskets and outdoors in warm climates. Propagated by cuttings. The principal species of the genus (which was formerly called *Muehlenbeckia*) are:

C. complexum (Wire-vine, Maidenhair-vine, Mattress-vine). A thickly interlaced twining plant from New Zealand, best grown in hanging-baskets under glass. A popular plant in California, where it has proved drought resistant, and is used to cover embankments and as a high climber. The greenish-white flowers are inconspicuous, but the female flowers develop into fleshy white cups holding the seed.

axillare is a prostrate twining plant or sprawling bush that makes a low, matted clump.

CALADIUM (kah-lay'-di-um). A genus of striking, large-leaved herbs of the Arum Family, native to tropical America, and grown for their ornamental veined and

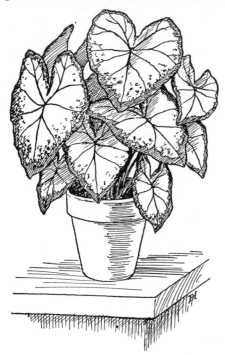

FOR DECORATIVE FOLIAGE

Fancy-leaved Caladiums, in red, white and green together, make attractive pot-plants for house or conservatory.

marbled foliage as bedding plants, or more commonly in the greenhouse and conservatory. The principal species is *C. bicolor,* from which have been developed many varieties and hybrids with brilliantly colored and variously marked leaves.

For outdoor planting the dormant tubers should be set out about 2 in. deep as soon as danger from frost is over, in a semi-shaded position. Plants started in the greenhouse as directed below, and gradually hardened off may be used instead of the tubers, setting them 12 to 24 in. apart. Cultivate and water frequently.

Indoors caladiums can be started from seed but they are usually grown from bulbs planted one to a 3- or 4-in. pot in a mixture of 1 part light sandy soil and 4 parts humus. This should be kept moist and

the temperature should not go below 70 deg., while it can go as high as 100 deg. without injury. When 3 or 4 leaves have developed, repot; then continue to shift as necessary, making the soil a little heavier each time by adding more loam and feeding with liquid manure every 2 or 3 weeks. Whether indoors or out, caladiums need plenty of food, plenty of moisture in the loose, friable soil and, preferably, a humid atmosphere.

A plant known as Elephants Ear and formerly included with the Caladiums as *C. esculentum,* is really a species of Colocasia, which see.

CALAMINT (kal'-ah-mint). Common name for *Satureja calamintha,* a perennial aromatic species of Savory, which see.

CALAMONDIN (kal-ah-mon'-din). A small, tropical and subtropical, evergreen tree (*Citrus mitis*) noted for its relative hardiness, ornamental form and foliage, and its small, juicy, acid fruits of which the skin is orange-red and the flesh deep orange, which are used for making ades and preserves. It may be grown where the kumquat and the Satsuma orange thrive. See CITRUS.

CALANDRINIA (kal-an-drin'-i-ah). A genus of low-growing, spreading, fleshy herbs of the Portulaca Family, native from British Columbia to S. America. They are occasionally grown as annuals in rock gardens, or as edging plants in borders, where they require a sunny location. The flowers, which are of short duration, range from orange-yellow and coppery-rose to brick-red, or from crimson-magenta to light purple. Propagation is by cuttings or seeds.

CALANTHE (kah-lan'-thee). A genus of tropical, mostly terrestrial orchids, which have become very poplar during the past decade. Once their cultural requirements are understood, they are easy to grow, and their beautiful long racemes of white, rose, or pink flowers well repay the grower for any special care that he gives them. *C. domini* was the first hybrid raised in England by the late Mr. Dominy, of the famous Veitch Nursery. Another fine old hybrid is *C. veitchi. C. vestita,* a species of rare beauty, is native to India. For culture, see ORCHID.

CALATHEA (kal-ah-thee'-ah). A genus of perennial plants of the Maranta Family having attractively colored foliage and flowers in cones among the leaves. They are tropical plants and should be grown in a close, moist greenhouse with a night temperature not lower than 65 deg. F. The soil should be a mixture of loam, leaf mold and sand, and the plants should be shaded from hot sun. In mild climates Calathea may be grown outdoors with winter protection. Propagate by division of crowns, by cuttings in spring, or by tubers. There are numerous species with leaves colored green, red, brown, yellow or white. *C. zebrina*, the Zebra-plant, from Brazil, has velvety green leaves marked above with crosswise bands of pale yellowish-green and olive-green, and purplish beneath.

CALCEOLARIA (kal-se-oh-lay-ri-ah). A genus of chiefly greenhouse-flowering plants of the Figwort Family, bearing large numbers of mostly red and yellow spotted flowers, each with a large inflated pouch like a slipper-toe or purse.

Natives chiefly of S. America, they have been so extensively hybridized that few original species are seen in cultivation. In England, the small shrubby types with mostly yellow or white unspotted flowers are frequently used as edging plants, and these should be equally suitable on the W. Coast of N. America. Otherwise, Calceolarias are distinctly florists' plants, their exacting demands, especially when young, keeping them confined to commercial greenhouses or those on large estates.

They require a low temperature (not over 60 deg.) and a N. exposure for the germination of seeds. March to July is the best time for sowing, and the recommended soil mixture is ⅖ sand, ⅖ loose peat and ⅕ charcoal, all sifted. After the small seeds are pressed into the surface, they should be covered with fine sphagnum and the seed-pan should be moistened by setting it in a tub of water. The seedlings need fresh air constantly, but will not stand sun until autumn, when they demand an abundance of it. As the plants grow, dried cow manure and loam should be added to the mixture, until at the final shift they are potted in ⅕ manure, ⅖ sand and peat with a little charcoal, and ⅖ fibrous loam. When about to flower, they relish a dose of liquid cow manure twice a week.

When cuttings are used for propagation, they are rooted in sand in the early fall and thereafter treated the same as the seedlings.

Green-fly, as professional gardeners often call aphis, is the most persistent enemy of calceolaria; they favor fumigating with nicotine preparations and placing tobacco stems around the pots. If white fly attacks the plants, careful fumigation (which see) with hydrocyanic gas is the only effective measure.

Gray mold (Botrytis blight) of leaves and flowers is kept down by removing infected parts and keeping foliage dry. Stem rot is reduced by clean culture, making sure that the hard black sclerotia (resting bodies) do not fall from infected stems to the moist soil or cinders in the benches and there produce fruiting bodies and start general infection.

CALCIUM. This is one of the dozen or so chemical elements essential to the

MANY FINE FORMS ARE BEING BRED AMONG CALCEOLARIAS
For example, the two plants shown here at left and right were crossed, and produced the splendid hybrid shown in the center.

growth and health of plants. In its pure state—as a light, silvery white, soft metal—it is rarely seen outside laboratories and it never occurs in that form in nature. It is, however, present in many other forms in most soils except those that are definitely sour; and in some mineral formations, such as limestone. In fact, calcium is best known in one form or another of lime (which see), which may be the simple oxide (CaO), which we call quicklime, or hydrated or slaked lime (Ca(OH)$_2$), or the carbonate (CaCO$_3$) which is raw limestone.

While the exact way in which calcium serves the plant is not fully understood, it is accepted that the element is an essential plant food. However, as there is usually plenty of it in most soils in forms that plants can use, it is rarely if ever necessary to apply lime to the soil as a fertilizer.

Its great usefulness is as a soil amendment (which see), or conditioner or modifier, and it is in that capacity that calcium is added to soils as ground limestone, or hydrated or agricultural lime; or, sometimes, in the form of ground shells, marl, bonemeal, etc.

See also LIME.

CALCIUM ARSENATE. A white substance, called also arsenate of lime, similar to lead arsenate, used especially to control the cotton-boll weevil and some vegetable insects. It is cheaper than lead arsenate but more apt to burn foliage. *It must not be used on stone fruits.* For a spray use 1 lb. calcium arsenate, and 1 lb. hydrated lime in 33 gals. water. As a dust (especially for cucumber beetles), mix 1 lb. calcium arsenate with 15 lbs. gypsum. See also ARSENICAL POISONS.

CALCIUM CASEINATE. A finely ground mixture obtainable under various trade names, containing about 20% casein and 80% hydrated lime, used in combination with various spray materials, at the rate of 1 oz. to 12 gals. as a spreader (which see), to get a more even distribution of the spray material, and as a sticker, to make it more adhesive.

CALCIUM CHLORIDE. A commercial chemical product, white, light, flaky or granular, and strongly hygroscopic, that is, with the ability to absorb and dissolve itself in, moisture from its surroundings. For this reason it is sprinkled on dirt surfaces, such as walks, drives, tennis courts, etc. to prevent dust, which it does by absorbing moisture from the atmosphere and transferring it to the surface layer of the gravel, soil, sand, etc. As it kills plant life it is also sometimes used in such places as a weed killer; but for large scale weed control it is less used than some other preparations. See POISON IVY; WEEDS. Indoors, calcium chloride is used to dry the air of damp basements, storage rooms, etc., to hasten the setting of concrete, to prevent the freezing of water in fire pails, for refrigeration, and for other purposes. The home owner can also use it to remove ice on steps, porches, brick and cement walks, etc. It can be bought at hardware stores, from dealers in builders' supplies and similar sources.

CALCIUM CYANIDE. A source of the deadly poisonous hydrocyanic acid gas used in fumigation, superseding liquid hydrocyanic acid and sodium and potassium cyanide because of its gerater safety and ease of use. Offered in commercial forms as cyanogas and calcyanide. Used in greenhouse and soil fumigation, in citrus scale control and to some extent in dusting horticultural crops. See CYANIDE COMPOUNDS; FUMIGATION.

CALCIUM SULPHATE. Commonly known as gypsum or land plaster, this is a powder used as a filler in making dust mixtures of calcium arsenate, and also with calomel. It is sometimes recommended for treatment of iris rot, the rhizomes being rolled in it before being replanted.

CALENDULA (kah-len'-deu-lah). This genus of the Daisy Family includes several species of herbaceous annuals and perennials, but to gardeners the name means the old favorite, *C. officinale,* called by Shakespeare "Marygold," and now known as Pot-marigold. This is one of the easiest of annuals to grow. Although of tropical origin and therefore happy in the heat, it will flourish almost anywhere and bloom satisfactorily even in cool areas. In the S. it blooms practically throughout the year; in the N. from May to frost. Its yellow or orange heads of ray and disk flowers in both single and double varieties are borne on plants 1 to 2 ft. high. It does well under any average soil conditions and in either full sun or semi-shade. The flowers close at night.

Valuable for cutting, the calendula may also be used for pot culture, the smaller plants being cut back in fall and potted up; they will bear flowers indoors for several weeks. Easily started from seed sown in the spring indoors or outdoors, the plants should be thinned to about 9 in. A second sowing in June will be of advantage to the gardener who wants garden color when many other plants have faded.

Under crowded conditions in greenhouse beds plants may be affected near the ground with a soft stem rot. Stripping the lower leaves helps to control the trouble, which soil sterilization (which see) will prevent. Mosaic (which see) and yellows (see under ASTER) may also occur. Aphids, especially troublesome in the garden, are controlled with any contact insecticide applied regularly.

A recent novelty in calendulas is the chrysanthemum-flowered or shaggy type, which in 1934 and 1935 received high rating in the All-America seed trials. Quite different from the earlier forms, it has long, deeply fringed petals overlapping one another in irregular manner. A two-tone effect is produced by the shading of the petals from deep orange to pale orange in the center. It is catalogued as *C. officinalis* var. *chrysantha*.

The name Calendula comes from the Latin *calendae*, meaning the first day of the month, for it was formerly supposed that some species bloomed every month of the year. In our forefather's time, the Potmarigold, was highly regarded not only for its medicinal qualities, but also as a flavoring for soups and stews.

Other species of calendula are: *C. eriocarpa*, branching with yellow heads 1 in. across; *C. stellata*, 1 ft. with rough foliage and yellow heads 1 in. across; *C. suffruticosa*, 1 ft., woody at base, with woolly, toothed leaves and profuse, bright yellow heads 1 to 2 in. across; *C. maderensis*, 2 ft. with rough leaves and yellow flowers; this last is a perennial.

CALICO-BUSH. A common name for *Kalmia latifolia*, or Mountain-laurel, the attractive evergreen of wooded uplands in E. U.S. The name was given in the early days because of the fancied resemblance of the odd pink and white flowers in both color and pattern to the then new calicos.

CALICO-FLOWER. Common name for *Aristolochia elegans*, a slender tropical vine with large purplish-brown flowers.

CALIFORNIA-BLUEBELL. Common name for *Phacelia whitlavia*, an annual herb with blue flowers.

CALIFORNIA CHAIN FERN. Common name for *Woodwardia radicans*, a very tall, hardy fern of the Far West, with arching fronds. Best grown in fibrous peaty soil.

CALIFORNIA-FUCHSIA (feu'-shiah). Common name for *Zauschneria californica*, a perennial, usually trailing herb with scarlet, fuchsia-like flowers.

CALIFORNIA-GERANIUM. A common name for *Senecio petasitis*, a lusty perennial with heads of yellow flowers.

CALIFORNIA-LAUREL. Common name for *Umbrellularia californica*, a tall evergreen tree of the Laurel Family, native in Calif. It sometimes attains a height of 90 ft., and is a very handsome subject, with a dense head of lustrous foliage. The leaves are rather narrow, to 5 in. long, and highly aromatic. The yellowish-green flowers are followed by pear-shaped yellowish or purple fruit.

CALIFORNIA-NUTMEG. Common name for *Torreya californica*, a species of N. American evergreen related to the Yew.

CALIFORNIA PEPPER-TREE. Common name for *Schinus molle*, a subtropical tree extensively planted in Calif. Ornamental but subject to black scale. See PEPPER-TREE.

CALIFORNIA-PHLOX. Trade name for one species of Linanthus (which see) sometimes classified as *Gilia densiflora*.

CALIFORNIA PITCHER-PLANT. Common name for *Darlingtonia californica*, so-called because of the form of the leaves which, erect and hollow, hold moisture in which insects trapped by the plant are drowned and gradually dissolved so they can be digested.

See also INSECTIVOROUS PLANTS.

CALIFORNIA POPPY. Popular name for *Eschscholtzia californica*, a hardy golden-flowered annual of the Poppy Family. It grows wild in Calif., where it is the State flower, and is popular the country over as an attractive garden plant. See ESCHSCHOLTZIA.

CALIFORNIA-ROSE. Common name for *Convolvulus japonicus*, a species of bindweed; it is a perennial vine with bright pink flowers.

CALIMERIS (kal-i-mer'-is). A genus of about ten hardy perennial Asiatic herbs, resembling the N. American perennial asters, but of lower growth, and blooming somewhat earlier. They are useful for massing or grouped in front of taller growths in the border. The species usually found in cultivation is the Siberian *C. incisa,* with large ray flowers of purple or white, having yellow centers. Cultivation is the same as for native asters, and propagation is by seeds or division of the clumps.

CALLA. A name applied to plants of several genera of the Arum Family, especially the native water-loving herb, *Calla palustris* and species of the genus Zantedeschia, which are S. African tuberous-rooted plants cultivated in the garden and greenhouse and often called Calla-lily.

Calla palustris (Water arum or Wild Calla) to 12 in., grows in cold bogs in the N. temperate regions. It has a white spathe, or flower-like bract, greenish outside, surrounding a yellow spadix or flower spike, which later bears a dense cluster of bright red berries. It is frequently transferred from the wild to the margin of the bog garden.

Zantedeschia aethiopica (the Calla of florists) is a sturdy bulbous plant growing to 2½ ft. It also has large smooth, arrow-shaped leaves and a creamy-white flaring spathe with a pointed tip, surrounding a yellow spadix. There are a number of horticultural forms, such as vars. *minor* and *devoniensis,* both smaller than the type. The calla is much grown in greenhouses

CALLAS OF TWO KINDS
The upper flower is the familiar tropical white Calla (Zantedeschia); the lower one is the Wild Calla or Water-arum (Calla palustris).

as a pot plant and for cut flowers, as a perennial outdoors in mild climates, and in the N. for summer bloom in the garden, the tubers being wintered indoors. In the latter case, plant the tubers after danger of frost is over in moist ground near a pool. The plants will bloom profusely during the summer, and the tubers should be lifted before cold weather in the fall. After being rested for a month or two, they can be potted in soil made rich with well-rotted manure, placed in a fairly sunny spot in the cool greenhouse, watered daily and given an occasional watering of weak liquid manure. With this treatment they will later bloom in late winter or early spring even in a shaded spot. Plants received as gifts in winter can likewise be rested after blooming, then planted in the garden to flower in early fall.

Z. elliottiana (Golden Calla) with a rich glowing-yellow spathe and large, somewhat oval leaves, mottled or spotted with white, requires a leaner soil mixture and rather more heat than the foregoing. Pot the tubers at the end of October for March and April bloom, or in spring for winter flowers, and keep them dark and slightly dry until the roots begin to form. When they have outgrown their pots, shift them into the next size, using a fibrous soil with plenty of leafmold and no manure, and grow in a moderately warm temperature, feeding with liquid manure from the time the flower stalks appear. After the flowering season is finished, ripen off the tubers in the pots by gradually withholding water, then store in a dark, cool place.

ENEMIES. A fungus is responsible for stunting and dry rot of calla roots, accompanied by yellowed foliage and reduction in bloom. A bacterial soft rot causes rotting of plants at the surface of the soil, blighting of leaves and a slimy decay of the corm. Discard badly diseased corms and cut out diseased areas in others. To control both dry and soft rots soak corms in formalin (1 part of commercial formaldehyde to 50 parts water) for one hour, or in 1 to 1000 solution of corrosive sublimate for two hours. If aphids are troublesome on calla leaves spray with nicotine-soap solution.

Black-calla is *Arum palaestinum;* Red-calla is a name sometimes given to varieties of *Sauromatum guttatum.*

CALLA-BEGONIA. Common name for a red-flowered variety of the familiar, herbaceous, fibrous-rooted semperflorens, or everblooming, begonia (which see), in which the mature leaves are white-veined, while the center cluster of young leaves is pure white and shaped like a calla. Although a handsome subject for winter blooming, it is rarely seen in commercial greenhouses anywhere or in house plant collections except in kitchens of farm homes in New England and upper N. Y., where it thrives in the warm, moist air, especially if kept in a north window. It needs water sparingly on the roots and not at all on the leaves; a good plant is to set the pot in peat moss in a larger container and apply water only to the moss.

CALLICARPA (kal-i-kahr'-pa). Beauty-berry. Deciduous or evergreen shrubs or trees found in tropical and subtropical regions of Asia, Australia, N. and Central America; members of the Vervain Family. The flowers are small, borne in short clusters in summer and the plants are grown chiefly for their bright lilac or violet colored berry-like fruits, very conspicuous in late autumn. Only a few of the species are at all hardy North, and in severe winters these are generally killed back close to the ground. However, in such cases, new, vigorous shoots start from below the following spring and usually flower and fruit the same season. They like rich soil in a sheltered place and are tolerant of shade. Propagated by cuttings of growing and mature wood, layers and seed.

Principal Species

C. americana (French-mulberry) is found from Va. south, growing to 6 ft. It has bluish flowers and in fruit is one of the showiest; the fruit is violet in the species and white in var. *alba*. Not hardy North.

dichotoma. A Japanese species formerly known as *C. purpurea.* It grows to 4 ft. and has pink flowers and lilac-white fruit borne in clusters in the leaf axils. It is one of the hardiest.

japonica. A shrub to 5 ft. with pale-pink flowers and violet fruit, is fairly hardy.

giraldiana. A Chinese species to 10 ft. has pink flowers and violet fruit. Hardy N.

CALLIOPSIS (kal-i-op'-sis). Another name for the genus Coreopsis (which see) but commonly used for the annual species, especially *C. tinctoria.* They are hardy, easily cultivated, and bright, cheerful garden subjects.

CALLIRHOE (kal-ir'-oh-ee). Popularly known as Poppy-mallow, this is a genus of nine species of N. American annual and perennial herbs. They have picturesque lobed foliage and showy flowers of pink, red or reddish-purple which bloom through most of the summer. They thrive in poor soil, and their deeply penetrating, often tuberous, roots make them suitable for dry situations. Trailing perennial forms are useful in the rock garden. Propagation is usually by seeds, but the perennial sorts may also be increased by cuttings and divisions.

CALLISTEMON (kal-i-stee'-mon). Bottle-brush. Shrubs or small trees of Australia, belonging to the Myrtle Family. They have been much planted in California, and are sometimes grown under glass. They have narrow leathery leaves and remarkable showy cylindrical spikes of red or yellow flowers, mostly composed of stamens; these and the general shape of the spike combine to suggest the popular name "Bottle-brush." They grow well in any good soil and are propagated by seeds or cuttings of ripened wood. To secure seed for spring sowing gather the fruits in summer and keep in boxes or wrapped in paper until they open.

C. speciosus grows to 40 ft. and is the showiest species. The dense spikes bristle with bright red filaments tipped with yellow anthers. *C. salignus* also grows to 40 ft. and bears loose spikes of yellow or pink. *C. brachyandrus* is a slender shrub with stiff needle-like gray leaves, and spikes of dark red filaments bearing golden anthers.

CALLISTEPHUS (ka-lis'-te-fus) *chinensis.* The botanical name for the erect, branching Asiatic plant of the Composite Family from which have been developed the many improved forms of the popular garden annual known as China Aster. See under ASTER.

CALLITRIS (kah-ly'-tris). A genus of several tender evergreen trees of the Pine Family and known as Cypress-pines. Natives of Australia, some of the species are grown in Calif. and Fla. for ornament or timber.

CALLUNA (kah-leu'-nah). The genus that comprises the true (hardy) Heathers. The heaths or florists' heathers belong to the genus Erica. See HEATH ; HEATHER.

CALLUS (kal'-us). A growth, sometimes more or less protuberant, of hard or tough protective tissue developed over or about a wounded surface, such as that formed over the end of a cutting and from which roots develop, or over a smooth wound caused by pruning. See PROPAGATION; PRUNING.

CALOCEPHALUS (kal-oh-see'-fal-us). A genus of tender annual Australian herbs or small shrubs with white, woolly foliage and terminal clusters of white tubular flowers. One species (*C. browni*) is somewhat grown in Calif. in carpet bedding (which see), or as an edging plant. It is propagated by cuttings.

CALOCHORTUS (kal-oh-kohr'-tus). A genus of W. American plants of the Lily Family growing from corms and bearing bell-shaped, lilac, white, or yellow flowers. Known as Mariposa-, Butterfly-, Globe-, and Star-tulips, Mariposa- and Sego-lilies, and Fairy Lantern, the numerous species are of great beauty, showing many exquisite tints and markings, and varying greatly in flower form. See illustration below.

The plants are hardy in the N. E. States but must be protected against alternate freezing and thawing in winter. They need an open sunny position in a light soil, made so, if necessary, with sand or sifted coal ashes. If not planted in the rock garden in a spot where good drainage is

assured, it is wise to raise the level of the bed where they are to be grown a few inches above the surrounding surface. Plant in the fall just before freezing weather or just after the first light freeze so as to prevent an autumn growth of foliage which would be killed during the winter. After they have flowered in the spring, the corms should be dug and stored in a dry place until the following autumn as is often done with tulip bulbs. Calochortuses may be grown in pots, the same care being given as to soil and drainage, but they do not force readily.

PRINCIPAL SPECIES

These are divided into 3 sections. The first comprises the Globe-tulips, which have a single grassy leaf from the base, and rounded, nodding flowers on a graceful leafy stem. The most beautiful and interesting are *C. albus* (Fairy Lantern) to 2 ft. with hanging satiny white blossoms, fringed with hairs, one of the most charming of the species; *C. amabilis* (Golden Globe-tulip) to 1½ ft. with golden yellow flowers and a stout 2-branched stem; and *C. amoenus* (Purple Globe-tulip) to 1½ ft. with purplish-rose flowers which, unlike those of the other two, open as they mature.

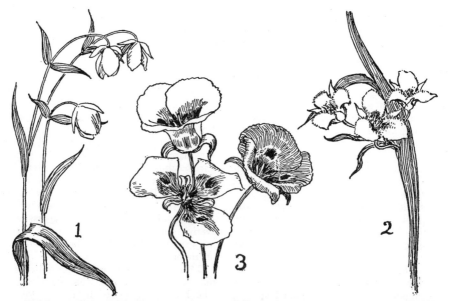

CALOCHORTUS PRESENTS MANY INTERESTING FORMS FOR THE GARDEN
(1) Typical of the group known as Globe-tulips is C. albus. (2) The Star-tulips, often with curiously hairy petals, are characterized by C. maweanus. (3) Types of the Mariposa- or Butterfly-tulip include C. vesta (above) and C. venustus variety El Dorado.

The second section is made up of the Star-tulips, which are similar to the Globe-tulips, but smaller and more slender. Among them are: *C. monophyllus* (Yellow Star-tulip) to 10 in. with dainty, bright yellow cups, often marked with brown or black at the base, opening wide when in full bloom; *C. uniflorus* (often listed as *C. lilacinus*) to 10 in. with handsome fragrant lilac flowers also opening wide; and *C. maweanus* and its var. *major,* with white flowers fringed with decilate lavender hairs. Still others provide variations from purple to rose.

The third section includes the many species of true Mariposa-, Meadow-, or Butterfly-tulips, all lovely in coloring and growth. Those named below have been successfully grown in E. gardens; other species are hardy but require special care to protect them from too much moisture. *C. venustus* var. *citrinus* to 10 in. is a hardy plant with yellow flowers with a dark eye; the var. listed as *oculatus* has white or cream blossoms to 4 in., tinted with purple and rich dark markings at the base of each petal. *C. nitidus* to 1½ ft. has wide-flaring lavender or purple flowers, marked with a deep lilac eye. *C. clavatus* to 3 ft. has large golden-yellow flowers and stout stem. *C. eurycarpus* to 1½ ft. is a hardy species having an umbel of white, lavender-tinged flowers, marked dark bluish-purple. *C. nuttalli*, the Sego-lily, with white flowers lined and spotted in the center with purple, is the State flower of Utah.

CALOMEL (kal'-oh-mel). Common name for the chemical compound, mercurous chloride, which is used particularly in the treatment of lawns to cure the fungous disease, brown patch. It may be used alone or in combination with mercuric chloride. See LAWN. It is also used mixed with gypsum (4 oz. calomel to 6 lbs. gypsum) as a dust to be applied on the soil around cabbage plants to prevent injury by the cabbage root maggot.

CALONYCTION (kal-oh-nik'-ti-on). Tropical American vines of the Bindweed Family formerly placed with the morning-glories in the genus Ipomoea. Their large trumpet-shaped white flowers with a broad flat rim give them the common name Moon-flower, which see.

CALOPHACA (kal-oh-fay'-kah). Deciduous shrubs found from S. Russia to E. India, belonging to the Pea Family. *C. wolgarica*, the best known, is a small shrub

of spreading habit, requiring a well-drained soil in a sunny place, and well placed on a sandy slope. It has grayish-green compound foliage and racemes of bright yellow flowers in summer. It is propagated by seeds, and is sometimes grafted high on Laburnum to form a graceful small tree.

CALOPOGON (kal-oh-poh'-gon). A genus of hardy terrestrial orchids formerly

A FRAGRANT SHRUB
Carolina-allspice (Calycanthus floridus) has flowers that are brown and inconspicuous but of deliciously sweet odor.

known by the name Limodorum, which comes from Greek words meaning "a gift from the meadows." They are found in the sphagnum swamps of New England. The most remarkable thing about these hardy orchids is that the flowers open up one at a time on a stalk; as soon as one fades another opens, thus prolonging the flowering period. *C. pulchellus* (still sometimes listed as *Limodorum tuberosum*) is the Grass-pink Orchid, growing to 14 in., with violet-rose flowers, and used in bog and rock gardens. For culture, see ORCHID.

CALTHA (kal'-thah). Small, perennial, succulent herbs chiefly natives of N. America, members of the Crowfoot Family. They are at their best in marsh land near running water, but may be grown successfully in moist spots in the border. They are especially useful in plantings near water gardens, where they bloom abundantly in the spring, and usually again in the fall. The flowers are without petals, but their yellow, white, or pink sepals are brilliantly showy and, because of their lasting quality, make good cut flowers. *C. palustris* is the familiar Marsh-marigold, found in wet ground from the Carolinas to Canada and westward and sometimes called cowslip. A double-flowered variety is especially attractive for planting at the edge of a pond. Propagation is by division of the roots in autumn, or by seeds freshly gathered.

CALYCANTHUS (kal-i-kan'-thus). Sweet- or Sweet-scented-shrub. Ornamental deciduous shrubs of N. America, favored for their aromatic fragrance. They grow as well in shade as in open situations, and prefer a rather rich soil that does not get too dry. Propagated by seeds, layers and division. The principal species are:

C. floridus (Carolina Allspice). A shrub to 6 ft. or more, of rather open habit. The best-known and hardiest species, it is beloved for its dark reddish-brown, spicily fragrant flowers.

fertilis. Of more bushy habit than the previous one, with leaves to 6 in. long, glaucous beneath, it bears chocolate-purple flowers a little later. But it is not quite as hardy.

occidentalis (California Allspice). The tallest grower with leaves to 8 in. long. The flowers are light brown and continue to late summer. Not hardy North.

CALYPSO (ka-lip'-soh). A genus of hardy terrestrial orchids native to the northern New England States. They have small bulbous roots and, growing in boglands, are sometimes planted in places with similar moist conditions. The flowers, purple, yellow, and white, are borne singly on stems 3 in. to 6 in. long. There is but one species, *C. bulbosa.* For culture, see ORCHID.

CALYX (kay'-liks). The outer set of small leaf-like parts which, with the corolla, comprises the *perianth* or floral envelope of a flower. The individual leaves, called *sepals,* usually green, are sometimes fused to form a tube but more often are distinct. In some flowers, like the lily, the sepals may be petal-like and the calyx and corolla similar in appearance. See FLOWER.

CAMASSIA (kah-mas'-i-ah). (Sometimes spelled Quamassia.) A genus of N. American bulbous plants of the Lily Family, having blue or white flowers in graceful racemes and narrow grass-like foliage. They are perfectly hardy and should be planted in groups of 9 or more, 3 or 4 in. apart in the border, or the smaller species in the rock garden. The bulbs were formerly valued by the Indians for food. The plants can also be increased by seed. *C. quamash,* the common Camass, grows 2 to 3 ft. with flowers varying from white to deep blue. *C. leichtlini* is a stouter plant with more regular flowers, white to purple. *C. esculenta,* growing from 12 to 18 in.

and bearing light-blue flowers, is the form most suitable for the rock garden.

CAMBIUM (kam'-bi-um). The layer of living tissue just below the bark, whose growth results in the increase in thickness of stems and perennial roots. In woody stems its annual alternating growth and resting periods lead to the formation of the familiar annual rings seen in the cross section of a tree trunk.

CAMELLIA (kah-mel'-i-ah). Evergreen trees and shrubs, native of Asia, belonging to the Tea Family. They have long been prized for their handsome glossy-green leaves and showy single, semi-double and double flowers of white and shades of pink or red. In sheltered places they can stand some frost, but where winters are severe they need the protection of a greenhouse for a good part of the year. Attractive small specimens can be grown in large pots or tubs; they also do well planted out in a bed in the cool conservatory.

CULTURAL NOTES

POT CULTURE. Under these conditions they are not difficult to grow and flower, providing strict attention is paid to certain cultural details, especially watering. Bud dropping sometimes causes a considerable loss of flowers, and perhaps the chief reason for this is dryness at the roots, particularly after the buds have set. In pots or tubs the soil and roots are very likely to become compacted into a hard ball which gets dry in the center. When this occurs the container should be completely immersed in water for a few hours so that the soil will be well soaked throughout.

While the plants need to be maintained in a moist state at the roots, perfect drainage is essential, as a sodden soil will also cause trouble. Equal parts of turfy loam and peat, with a liberal dash of sharp sand, make a good potting mixture. Camellias do not require frequent repotting and should never be over-potted. When repotting is called for, the best time to do it (or to renovate the soil) is immediately after flowering. This is also the time to thin out any overcrowded shoots and shorten back any straggly growth. The plants object to being forced into bloom, but can stand heat and moisture after the flowers have passed and new growth is being made. When this is complete, harden them off by degrees. Those in pots or tubs will appreciate being outdoors for the summer in a partly shaded place. With a collection it is possible to have flowers over a period of several months from October on.

OUTDOOR CULTURE. Camellias do well outdoors in the S., and grow in quite poor soil providing it is of a somewhat acid character. But they are very slow growers unless well cultivated and fed. A mulch of leafmold or real old cow manure helps to maintain cool and moist conditions at the roots, besides providing some food. A little commercial fertilizer now and then, with thorough waterings in a dry time, will also aid materially in promoting vigorous and healthy growth. The flowering season in the S. is from October until hot weather comes, and the flowers are more satisfactory if the plants are in a somewhat shaded and moist place.

Propagation is by seeds (which are slow to germinate), cuttings, layers, and, in the case of choice varieties, by grafting.

Leaf spots may follow frost injury and wounds may serve as starting points for cankers. Treat all large wounds with a mercury disinfectant and paint with a wound dressing. A flower blight occurs in Calif. The only remedy is sanitation, consisting of the removal of all fallen blossoms for several consecutive seasons. In the S. spraying early in April and late in September with a white-oil emulsion (3 tbsp. oil to 1 gal. water) controls various scales and also mites.

PRINCIPAL SPECIES

C. japonica (Common Camellia) grows to 40 ft. under very favorable conditions. It has given rise to a great many forms of single, semi-double and double named varieties, in white, pink, red and variegated colors.

sasanqua is a shrubby species of a rather loose habit of growth, with single white, or sometimes pink, flowers. This also runs into several forms with semi-double and double flowers.

reticulata makes a large shrub or small tree, and is distinguished from the others by dull green instead of glossy leaves. It has very large semi-double rose-colored flowers to 7 in. across. They bear more resemblance to a semi-double peony than to the stiff and formal flowers of the japonica type.

CAMELLIA SOCIETY. The full name of this organization is the Azalea and Camellia Society of America, which see.

CAMOMILE (kam'-oh-myl). One form of spelling Chamomile—which is Anthemis nobilis and also a name given to species of Matricaria.

See ANTHEMIS and MATRICARIA.

CAMPANULA (kam-pan'-eu-lah). (See illustration, Plate 8.) A genus of biennial and perennial herbs, and a few annuals, commonly known as Bellflower, Harebell or Bluebell. The attractive bell- or wheel-shaped flowers are white, blue, purple or yellow in color, and show lovely shades of deep rose and pink in the biennial types. With their great variations of size, Campanulas form most desirable groups of garden flowers, and are deservedly popular. The tall perennials, such as the Chimney, and Peach-leaved Bellflowers and C. lactiflora, with its milky-white or pale-blue flowers, are excellent for the background of the border; the profusely blooming Canterbury Bells show most interesting variation; the Cup-and-Saucer Bellflowers with their showy flowers in midsummer are most desirable in masses; while the low-growing perennials, including the Carpathian Harebell, and the Scotch Bluebell, are among the most charming plants for the rock garden.

The perennials and biennials are started from seed sown in the open in summer or under glass in early spring; the perennials are also increased by division. The annuals start readily from spring-sown seed, sown either under glass or where they are to grow. Where the winters are severe, the biennial Canterbury Bells should be mulched with leaves.

A rust has one stage of its life cycle on pine needles and the other on Campanula leaves, so cut and destroy all tops of the latter in the autumn. To control slugs, which are fond of the young plants, sprinkle air-slaked lime around, or spray plants with lead arsenate.

PRINCIPAL SPECIES

C. medium (Canterbury Bells). Biennial bushy plants to 4 ft., loaded with large bell-shaped flowers, white, blue, lavender or pink in color. Var. calycanthema (Cup-and-Saucer Bellflower) has the calyx colored and flattened below the flower. If started very early Canterbury Bells will bloom the first summer, but they produce much more profuse and handsome flowers the second year from summer-sown seed.

persicifolia (Peach-leaved Bellflower) is the most beautiful of the perennial sorts, bearing in June or July a profusion of delicate blue blossoms on 3 ft. branching plants. They should be separated and reset in early fall or spring in order to keep them growing vigorously.

carpatica (Carpathian Harebell) is a low-growing perennial with broad tufts of heart-shaped leaves and charming, widely bell-shaped blue flowers, blooming all summer on the edge of the border and in the rock garden. Var. *alba, coelestina* and *turbinata* are desirable variations.

pyramidalis (Chimney Bellflower), to 4 ft. or more, of spire-like growth, has small saucer-shaped pale-blue flowers. Most effective in the border, it is still lovelier grown as a potted plant for the sun-porch, where the flowers, not being pollenized by insects, remain unfaded for days.

roundifolia (Bluebell or Harebell, the "Bluebells of Scotland"). Perenniel 1½ ft. Slender, wiry stems bear clear blue, dainty bells in long, loose clusters, reaching their greatest beauty in June, but often blooming sparingly throughout the summer. An interesting variety is var. *soldanellaeflora,* which has partly double flowers, slit into shreds.

Among the few annual Campanulas, blossoming in six months from seed, is *C. macrostyla* with blue-purple flowers on 2 ft. branching plants. Named varieties are Angelus Bell, deep rose, and Liberty Bell, violet-blue.

Species especially adapted for the rock garden include: *C. portenschlagiana,* with blue-purple flowers, delighting in stony soil in a half-shady spot in the rock garden, where it forms attractive clumps of very dwarf foliage; *C. garganica,* with wheel-shaped dainty flowers, thriving in a rock crevice in full sun; *C. pusilla,* which is very dwarf and covered with exquisite milky-white bells, growing profusely in gritty soil; *C. abietina,* very low-growing with flat blue flowers on delicate stems.

Other interesting species include *C. isophylla* var. *alba,* a tender perennial with starry white flowers, exceedingly effective when used in window or porch boxes with a northern exposure.

CAMPANULACEAE (kam-pan-eu-lay'-see-ee). Botanical name of the Bellflower Family, so-called from the shape of the blossoms, whence comes the term *campanulate.* Cultivated species are erect, frequently with a milky juice; the characteristic showy flowers are usually blue but sometimes white or pink. The family includes herbs, shrubs or rarely trees, widely distributed in both temperate and tropical regions, many of them fine ornamentals, such as Phyteuma, Wahlenbergia, Campanula, Adenophora, Symphyandra, Specularia, Platycodon.

CAMPERNELLE (kam'-per-nel). Common name for forms of *Narcissus odorus,* one of the jonquil types of the genus. See NARCISSUS and JONQUIL.

CAMPHOR-TREE. Common name for *Cinnamomum camphora,* formerly the chief source of camphor. See CINNAMOMUM.

CAMPION (kam'-pi-un). A common name applied to the genus Silene (Catchfly) and also to several species of Lychnis, European herbs which have escaped in the U. S. Both belong to the Pink Family.

CAMPSIDIUM (kamp-si'-di-um). An evergreen climbing shrub, related to the Bignonia, sometimes grown in the S. and propagated by greenwood cuttings rooted under glass. It has orange flowers about 1½ in. long followed by narrow pods or capsules to 4 in. long.

CAMPSIS (kamp'-sis). Vigorous woody plants, bushy shrubs or climbers, belonging to the Bignonia Family. The several species included were formerly placed in the genera Bignonia and Tecoma. See TRUMPET-CREEPER.

CAMPTOSORUS (kamp-toh-soh'-rus). A genus of ferns, including one American species (the Walking Fern of the E. woods), which root at the tips of the small fronds. Of use in the rock garden in shade and rich soil.

CANADA BLUE GRASS. Common name for *Poa compressa,* a close relative of Kentucky Blue Grass, than which it is coarser textured. However it it more adaptable to varying soil and climatic conditions and, though not so highly thought of, is much used in lawn-seed mixtures. It also is a perennial, to 2 ft. tall, with creeping rootstocks of a bluish-green tinge; the leaves are 4 in. long, and the flower panicles 3 in. in length.

See also BLUE GRASS ; LAWN.

CANAIGRE (ka-nay'-ger). Common name for a Dock (*Rumex hymenosepalus*) found in S.W. U. S. Tannin is obtained from the roots.

Upper left: Graceful and lovely in its fall bloom is the Japanese Anemone. Upper right: The airy grace of the columbine adds a peculiar charm to the border. Bottom: Canterbury bells (Campanula media) and the foxglove spires mingle in this planting.

CANARY-BALM. Common name for *Cedronella canariensis*, a fragrant shrubby herb of the Mint Family, native to the Canary Islands. It has been referred to as *C. triphylla* and also placed in another genus as *Dracocephalum canariense*. The flowers, white or lilac, are borne in loose terminal spikes. The plant is not quite hardy, but may be grown in the border in the S. States. In the N. it is occasionally grown in the greenhouse. Propagation is by cuttings.

CANARY-BIRD FLOWER. Common name for *Tropaeolum peregrinum*, a popular quick-growing annual climber. Belonging to the garden Nasturtium genus, this vine bears curiously-cut yellow flowers with curved green spurs, the entire blossoms vaguely resembling canary birds in flight. Native to Peru and Ecuador, this plant has been adapted to American gardens and will grow in almost any soil. It is ideal for covering trellises, often reaching a height of 15 ft.

CANARY-GRASS. Common name for *Phalaris canariensis*, a European annual naturalized in N. America, whose glossy yellow seeds are fed to cage birds.

CANDLENUT, or **CANDLEBERRY-TREE.** Common name for *Aleurites moluccana*, an Asiatic tree sometimes planted in the far S. Its seeds yield a valuable oil.

CANDLE-PLANT. Common name for *Senecio articulatus*, a S. African composite plant whose white flower-heads are composed solely of disk-flowers.

CANDLE-TREE. Common name for a tropical, spiny small tree (*Parmentiera cereifera*) of the Bignonia Family, occasionally planted for ornament in S. Fla. The flowers are white and the hanging, yellowish, cylindrical fruits, sometimes 4 ft. long, resemble huge candles.

CANDLEWOOD. A common name for the small genus Fouquieria, spiny shrubs or small trees (to 20 ft.) found in Mexican deserts and S.E. U. S. Commonly planted as a hedge in Mexico they form a barrier that man or beast cannot pass. In the dry season their leaves fall and the slender, erect stems appear like dead sticks. But in the rainy season they flame with brilliant flowers borne in slender panicles or racemes to 10 in. long. The chief species is *F. splendens* called also Ocotillo, Coachwhip, Vine-cactus, and Jacobs-staff. Its stem is furrowed and the scarlet flowers are about 1 in. long.

CANDYTUFT. (See illustration, Plate 40.) The common name for Iberis, a genus of half-hardy annuals and evergreen perennials of the Mustard Family (Cruciferae). The botanical name is derived from Iberia, as Spain, its native home, was formerly called. Originally white, it has lent itself well to hybridization and now comes in many pastel tints. Used in the rock garden or as an edging plant, the annual varieties (some of which are fragrant) will bloom throughout the season if not allowed to seed, though successive sowings are advised for best results. The perennial variety blooms only in the spring. Both types are low-growing, thrive in any ordinary garden soil, and require little special care.

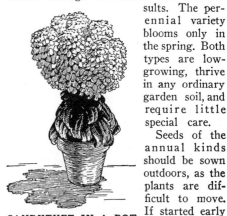

CANDYTUFT IN A POT
Though usually seen in the garden, a variety like Little Prince is also interesting grown indoors.

Seeds of the annual kinds should be sown outdoors, as the plants are difficult to move. If started early in the spring, plants will bloom within two months, as germination and growth are rapid. Keep the soil loose around the plants and to produce large flowers thin out the buds.

The perennial candytuft is a low-growing, compact plant somewhat woody at the base, with white flowers that become lilac with age. Seeds may be sown in the fall for next season's early bloom or propagation may be accomplished by dividing the roots. There are about 20 species of candytuft, the following being the most satisfactory in the U. S.:

I. affinis. Closely branching annual, to 16 in. Flowers white with lilac tinge, often slightly fragrant.

amara (Rocket Candytuft). Smaller, slightly hairy annual. Flowers large, white, fragrant.

corifolia. Evergreen perennial with white flowers in close clusters.

gibraltarica (Gibraltar Candytuft). Evergreen perennial with light-purple or lilac flowers in flat clusters.

sempervirens (Edging Candytuft). Evergreen, with white flowers in raceme-like heads.

umbellata (Globe Candytuft). Annual, to 16 in., branching freely. This is the common garden annual, numerous named varieties having flowers of pink, violet, purple, red or carmine.

CANE. In horticulture this may refer to (1) a slender jointed, woody, hollow or pithy, more or less flexible plant stem, as of bamboo or rattan; (2) the leafless yearling stems of grape and bramble fruits from which "bearing-" or "fruiting-wood" is chosen; (3) bamboo rods used for staking which see.

CANE-REED or **SOUTHERN CANE.** Common name for *Arundinaria macrosperma*, a tall grass native to wet ground from Va. to the Gulf States. Compare BAMBOO.

CANESCENT (kah-nes'-ent). Covered with a gray or whitish hoar formed by a coating of fine hairs, as on twigs and leaves.

CANISTRUM (kah-nis'-trum). A genus of tropical herbs of Brazil, some of which are occasionally grown in the greenhouse. Members of the Bromelia Family, some are air-plants; others root in the ground. The plant forms a rosette of long, pointed leaves having little spines along the edges; from the center of the rosette rise stems bearing flowers which are generally green, but which may be yellow, blue or white in different species. They are usually grown in wire baskets of sphagnum moss, or in pots with fibrous loam. Propagation is by suckers, or sprouts which appear following a blooming period.

CANKER. Strictly speaking this is a localized lesion or wound area resulting in the destruction of tissue, with the final production of an open wound, generally on woody tissues. Loosely the term has been used to cover many types of lesions on woody or semi-woody parts of plants. Certain diseases are frequently named after this symptom, as chestnut canker, brown canker of rose, etc.

CANKER WORMS. Several kinds of smooth, rather small caterpillars commonly known as measuring worms due to their habit of arching up the middle of their body when crawling. They feed on the foliage of apple, elm, maple and many other fruit and shade trees, appearing early in the spring and causing greatest damage

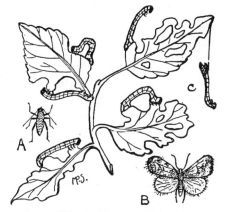

THE CANKER WORM
A. Wingless female, often seen on tree trunks in late fall. B. Winged male, also harmless. C. Canker worm grubs, a kind of "measuring worm" may defoliate shade trees in spring.

about the time the trees obtain full foliage, often skeletonizing the leaves. When a caterpillar is disturbed it drops from the leaf or twig and hangs suspended by a silken thread.

There are two common canker worms, the so-called spring canker worm (*Paleacrita vernata*) and the fall canker worm (*Alosphila pometaria*). Both kinds are green or brown, sometimes slightly striped, and about an inch long when full grown. The adults are moths.

The spring canker worm passes the winter as a pupa, 1 to 4 in. deep in the soil about the base of trees. The wingless females crawl up the trees in early spring to lay clusters of yellowish-green oval eggs, which hatch about the time the buds break. The moths of the fall canker worm emerge from the soil in the autumn and lay their eggs which do not hatch until the following spring.

Since the females are wingless they can be prevented from ascending trees and laying eggs by keeping sticky bands around the trunks from September until April. See BANDING. Such bands, however, afford no protection against young caterpillars carried by the wind or dropping from other trees, and rarely reduce infestation more than 10 per cent. It is far better to rely on a thorough spraying with lead arsenate when the trees first come into leaf.

CANNA (ka'-nah). A genus of tropical summer-flowering plants of the Banana Family, growing from thick, fleshy tuber-like roots. They are valued for both their large tropical-appearing foliage and their brilliantly colored blossoms. In the hands of modern hybridists flowers have been developed in tones ranging from ivory and yellow through rose and salmon to crimson and scarlet. The foliage is either green or bronze. In the tropics and subtropics where they grow wild, they range from 2½ to 10 ft. in height. In the N. where they are tender and handled as annuals, they rarely exceed 5 or 6 ft. Few of the true species are grown in gardens, the cultivated sorts being mainly hybrids and strains. Because of the hard bullet-like seeds produced, any of these kinds are often called "Indian Shot," though correctly this name applies only to *C. indica*. A wild species (*C. flaccida*) with small yellow flowers native to S. C. and Fla. is one of the principal parents of the modern kinds, but these have become so enlarged and glorified in the hands of hybridizers that there is no longer much resemblance.

Cannas show to best advantage when massed plantings are made in formal beds; thus their use is to a great extent confined to parks and larger gardens. However their bold colorful foliage provides good background material in formal effects. The roots should be planted as soon as the soil is warm in the early summer. Select an exposed spot and space them 18 in. apart.

TALL CANNAS FOR A BORDER
Always good foliage plants where bold massing is desired, the modern canna is also showy in flower.

As they require an abundance of plant food, the soil must be well and deeply prepared and generously enriched. After growth gets under way, they also require considerable water. In the fall when the foliage starts to wither or is cut down by frost, the roots should be lifted and stored away from frost in a root cellar.

Propagation is easily done by division of the roots, as these grow rapidly. Plants may also be grown from seed, which should be soaked in warm water, or notched with a file, to hasten germination. Started in February or March in flats or pots (which are kept on a radiator or warm greenhouse bench), seeds may give blooming plants the first year. They may not, of course, be the same as their parents, but interesting new kinds may result.

ENEMIES. Infection with a bacterial bud rot disease starts while the leaves are still rolled in the bud. When they unfold they are either covered with minute white spots or partially or wholly blackened. The flowers may be ruined and the whole stalk killed. To avoid this trouble select root stalks from healthy plants. Sterilize dormant corms by soaking for two hours in a 1 to 1000 solution of corrosive sublimate. In greenhouses keep young growth dry and the humidity of the air low; out-of-doors set only disease-free plants and space them far apart. Be careful not to overwater.

Japanese beetles (which see) may feed on the blossoms.

The garden sorts are sometimes grouped under the species name *C. generalis,* which naturally shows great variation. *C. edulis* of the W. Indies and S. America produces edible tubers called in those parts "Tous-les-mois." *C. flaccida* of S.E. U. S. grows to 5 ft. and *C. indica,* the other kind found wild in U. S. attains 4 ft. and has brilliant red flowers. *C. orchiodes,* the Orchid-flowered Canna from Australia, has large (6 in.) flowers that open wide with reflexed petals after the first day of blooming.

CANNABIS (kan'-ah-bis). A genus of annual Asiatic herbs cultivated for centuries and in all parts of the world for their fibre, hemp. In the Far East they are also cultivated as a source of the narcotic drug, hashish; and in this country small patches are sometimes grown, surreptitiously and illegally, for the same purpose, under the name "mariahuana" or "mariahuana-weed." The single species (*C.*

sativa) has numerous forms that have been given different names. Some of these are occasionally grown in gardens as ornamental screen or background plants. Requiring no special care or soil conditions, beyond a good supply of humus and moisture, they are raised from seed sown in spring outdoors or, earlier, in flats. The most common type, known as *C. gigantea,* may attain 10 ft. or more.

CANOE BIRCH, PAPER BIRCH. Common names for *Betula papyrifera,* a tree growing to 100 ft. in light and rocky soils of N. N. America. Its bark is chalky white and its foliage larger and of better quality than in most native species. It shines in bold groups on hillsides and graces the banks of streams. Many people cannot resist the temptation to peel its beautiful bark and usually peel it so deep that later a black band develops, spoiling the tree's appearance and leaving a record that says, "A destroyer has passed this way, indifferent to the preservation of Nature's beauty." See BETULA.

CANTALOUPE. Strictly, the pale green or yellow fruit of the hard-rinded, ribbed or warty type of musk melon (*Cucumis melo*); derived from Cantalupo, Italy, where it was first grown in Europe. In America, popularly, any kind of Muskmelon. See CUCUMIS; MELON.

CANTERBURY BELLS. Common name for *Campanula medium* and its horticultural forms. They are imposing, profusely blooming biennial plants, having large, pendent, white, blue or pink bells and long, wavy leaves. They prefer a medium rich soil and will thrive in semishade, blooming in June and July. See CAMPANULA. (See illustration, Plate 8.)

CANTUA (kan'-teu-ah). Erect evergreen shrubs from S. America, belonging to the Phlox Family. Although usually grown as greenhouse plants, they will thrive outside where but little frost is experienced. The principal species (*C. buxifolia*) is a handsome shrub to 10 ft. The branch tips and young leaves are downy and the showy red drooping flowers are borne in a short terminal leafy cluster. Propagated by cuttings under close, humid conditions.

CANYON or MATILIJA (mah-til'-ee-hah) **POPPY.** The common name for *Romneya coulteri,* a showy plant of the Poppy Family, native of California. It grows to a height of 8 ft. with many branches, and has large, white flowers with thick, crinkled petals, 6 in. across. The foliage is attractive, the leaves being much cut and having a slight bloom. Difficult to raise in the E. States, it should be given a warm, sheltered position in light, rich soil and full sun. It may be increased by root-cuttings or by seed, but the seedlings take several · years to attain blooming size. Plants should be cut back to the ground before being translpanted, but even then failure is likely to result when they are moved.

CAPE BULBS. A popular name for various bulb-like and bulbous plants from the Cape of Good Hope region in S. Africa, such as Amaryllis, Tritonia, Ixia, Watsonia, Lachenalia, etc. They are being increasingly grown in the U. S. as more is learned about their cultural needs and also about their characteristic beauty, both as plants and as sources of cut flowers.

See also SOUTH AFRICAN PLANTS.

CAPE-COWSLIP. Common name for Lachenalia, a genus of small bulbous herbs of the Lily Family from the Cape of Good Hope, with broad basal leaves and 9 in. spikes of red, yellow or white bell-shaped blossoms, either erect, or cylindrical and drooping. They are easily flowered in a cool greenhouse in winter and will give six weeks of bloom. Many are suited to the window-garden or hanging-basket. Plant in August, ½ in. deep, using 6 bulbs to a 6 in. pot, in a rich loam soil with leafmold, peat and sand, adding 1 part of bonemeal to 50 of soil. Store in a well-protected coldframe until late November, when pots may be brought inside. Water weekly with liquid manure when growth starts. After bloom is over and the leaves and stems wither, water must be gradually withheld. When thoroughly dry, the bulbs should be stored in their pots until the following August. The bulblets should then be removed and placed in separate pots. Ripened seed germinates readily, blooming the first season.

L. tricolor, with yellow, red-tipped flowers, is the best-known species. It has varieties with interesting color variations.

CAPE-FORGET-ME-NOT. A common or catalog name for *Anchusa capensis.*

CAPE-FUCHSIA (feu'-shi-ah). Common name for the genus Phygelius, a group of small S. African shrubs of the Figwort Family and therefore related to penstemon. Once widely cultivated but now seldom

seen, they are hardy as far N. as Philadelphia but need greenhouse protection in
more severe climates. They require a loose
rich soil and are propagated by seeds or
by cuttings of ripened wood in autumn. Of
the two species, *P. capensis* is the more
familiar. It grows to 3 ft. with long narrow leaves and purple-scarlet blooms in
drooping panicles to 1½ ft.

CAPE-GOOSEBERRY. Common name
for *Physalis peruviana,* a form of Husk-
tomato with edible yellow berries. The
Dwarf Cape-gooseberry or Strawberry-
tomato, is the closely similar *P. pruinosa.*

CAPE-HONEYSUCKLE (*Tecomaria
capensis*). A half-climbing evergreen shrub
of S. Africa, belonging to the Bignonia
Family. It is a good porch or trellis plant
for the warmer parts of the country. It
has handsome pinnate leaves and clusters of
showy orange-red flowers, produced almost
continuously. Spring pruning insures a
good growth of flowering wood. Propagation is by seeds and cuttings.

CAPE IVY. Common name for *Senecio
macroglossus,* a climbing perennial herb
with yellow flowers.

CAPE-JASMINE. Common name for
Gardenia jasminoides, an evergreen shrub
with large waxy-white fragrant flowers.

CAPE-MARIGOLD. Common name
for Dimorphotheca, also called African
Daisy. South Africa contributed this
choice and colorful group of flowers to our
gardens. They are herbaceous or sub-
shrubby annuals and perennials bearing
solitary terminal heads of ray and disk
flowers in orange, yellow, purple, blue or
white and ideally suited to low beds or
borders or the rock garden as a source of
color late in the season. Growing from 1
to 2 ft. tall in warm sunny locations, they
do best when given a long season, flowering from early summer until frost. The
plants, spreading in habit, are covered with
an abundance of large daisy-like blossoms
which generally expand in the sunlight but
close toward evening.

In Calif. and other mild States they are
splendid winter plants if seed is sown in
late fall, but in the rest of the U. S. seed
is generally sown indoors in early spring
or outdoors in April or May. The perennial species are propagated by cuttings.

The more important species include:

D. annua, a rough, hairy annual plant,
the rays being white or yellowish above
and purplish on the under side. Var.

ligulosa is double, with white rays which
are yellow or violet on the under surface.
Var. *ringens* has a deep-blue ring around
the center.

aurantiaca, a perennial, often shrubby,
which blossoms the first season. Rays
orange-yellow. There are many hybrids in
white, sulphur-yellow, golden-yellow, salmon, rose, apricot and ecru.

ecklonis, a perennial, to 2 ft. Upper side
of rays white, under side steely lavender;
the disk is dark and ringed with blue.

calendulacea, a hairy annual with orange-
yellow flowers.

cuneata, a small, branching, sticky shrub
with yellow flowers.

CAPE-PONDWEED. Common name
for *Aponogeton distachyus,* a plant with
long floating leaves grown in aquaria.

CAPE-PRIMROSE. Common name for
Streptocarpus, a genus of choice herbaceous
plants from S. Africa and Madagascar,
akin to Gloxinia and Saintpaulia and
usually stemless, with showy blue or purple
blooms and broad basal leaves, and capsular seed-pods (the name of the genus coming from Greek words meaning "twisted
fruit"). Cape-primroses are easy to grow,
thriving in a cool greenhouse if given a
rich loose soil with sand. Seed sown in
February or thereabouts should produce
blooming plants by the following winter,
which should be discarded after flowering.
Plants may also be increased by leaf-cuttings and division.

S. dunni has single leaves to 3 ft. long,
and flowers rose or reddish on 1 ft. stems.
S. rexi bears several leaves to 8 in. long;
the flowers are mauve on 1 ft. stems. *S.
kewensis,* a hybrid between the foregoing
species, has leaves 2 to 3 ft. and numerous
mauve-purple flowers with striped throats
on 1 ft. stems. *S. wendlandi,* like *S. dunni,*
produces a single leaf to 2 ft. long, and
violet-blue flowers on stems to 2½ ft. high.
This last species is the most striking of
this handsome family.

CAPER-BUSH (*capparis spinosa*). A
spiny shrub of straggling habit about 3 ft.
high, found in the Mediterranean region,
valued chiefly for its flower buds, which
are pickled and sold as capers. It may be
grown as a greenhouse plant North, and
outdoors in the warmer parts of the United
States. It is deciduous with roundish
leaves. The most conspicuous feature of
the fleeting white flowers is the mass of
purple-tipped stamens.

CAPITATE (kap'-i-tayt). Arranged in a very dense head, like that of the teasel.

CAPRIFOLIACEAE (kap-ri-foh-li-ay'-see-ee). Botanical name of the Honeysuckle Family, a group of widely distributed, largely woody shrubs, many of which are cultivated in N. America for their showy and fragrant flowers, and for medicinal purposes. Among the cultivated genera are Sambucus (Elder), Viburnum, Leycesteria, Linnaea, Symphoricarpos (Snowberry and Coral-berry), Lonicera (Honeysuckle), Abelia, Diervilla.

CAPSICUM (kap'-si-kum). Red-pepper. A genus of plants of the Nightshade Family, mostly grown as annuals, although in their native warm countries they are actually shrubs. They bear small white or slightly tinted flowers and attractive fruit in the form of edible, many-seeded berries varying in color, size, form and flavor from very hot to mild or sweetly pungent.

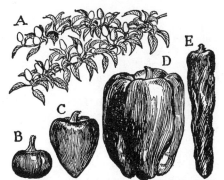

PEPPERS—SWEET, HOT, ORNAMENTAL

Most varieties of Capsicum frutescens are garden vegetables, but a few make handsome house plants (A). Their fruits range from small to large, round to slender, cream color to deep red, mild-flavored (C and D) to intolerably hot (B and E).

There is only one important species, the Bird-pepper (*C. frutescens* formerly *C. annuum*), but it has numerous varieties, some grown as vegetables or condiments (see PEPPER), some as ornamental pot plants, and some for both purposes. The type or species has erect, oblong, usually red fruit to ¾ in. long. In var. *cerasiforme* (Cherry-pepper) the fruits are erect or bending, rounded to 1 in. across, yellow or purple, very pungent; in var. *conoides* (Cone-pepper) they are erect and conical to 2 in. long; in var. *fasciculatum* (Red Cluster-pepper) they are erect, slender, to 3 in. long, red and very hot; in var. *grossum* (the Bell- or Sweet-pepper of seed catalogs), the bush is stout and the fruit large, soft, irregularly compressed, red or yellow, and mild; in var. *longum* (Long-pepper) which includes the Chili and Cayenne sorts, the fruit is pendent, slender, tapering to 1 ft. long, and very hot.

The plants are tender and must be started under glass. For edible peppers, plants are set out when the weather is warm; for pot plants they are grown and repotted as necessary to fruit in 5 in. pots with rich soil and adequate drainage.

Pimento, from the Spanish word for pepper (*pimiento*) is sometimes applied to the genus or to certain cultivated varieties; but it is also a common name for *Pimento officinalis* or Allspice, a tropical American aromatic tree.

CAPSULE (kap'-seul). A dry, pod-like fruit developed from a compound pistil and usually opening when mature. The pod or "fruit" of the poppy and of the day-lily are examples.

CARAGANA (kar-ah-gay'-nah). A genus of hardy deciduous shrubs or small trees mostly from Cent. Asia, belonging to the Pea Family. See PEA-TREE.

CARAUNDA (kah-raun'-dah) or **KARANDA.** Common name for *Carissa carandas,* an evergreen shrub or small tree of the East Indies, cultivated for its acid fruit.

CARAWAY (kar'-ah-way). A biennial or annual umbelliferous herb (*Carum carvi*) whose seeds are used to flavor bread, cakes, confections and cheese. Easily grown in any garden soil. Sow seed in early spring where the plants are to remain for two seasons, adding a few radish seeds to mark the rows. The young shoots and tender leaves may be used to flavor salads. The seeds are produced the second summer.

CARBOLIC ACID EMULSION. A preparation occasionally recommended as a foliage spray for aphids, soft scales and similar insects; also as a soil treatment for the cabbage maggot. To make the foliage spray, dissolve 4 lbs. fish-oil soap in 4 gals. boiling water, add ½ gal. crude carbolic acid and boil 20 minutes; for use, dilute this stock solution with 20 parts of water. For soil treatment, dissolve 1 lb. hard soap in 1 gal. hot water, add 1 pint carbolic acid and churn until an emulsion is formed; for use, dilute with 30 parts of water.

CARBON. This is one of the most important of all the chemical elements. It makes up about one-half of the dry matter in plants, which obtain it partly from the soil but chiefly from the carbon-dioxide of the air. Also combined with other elements it forms the various carbonates and other compounds of importance in plant growth and soil handling.

CARBON BISULPHIDE (also spelled *di*sulphide). A heavy, colorless, vile-smelling liquid which changes to a gas on exposure to air and which is used to destroy insects when the temperature is that at which they are active. It is especially important as a fumigant for use against insects in soil or in bins of seed or grain, and against borers (as well as rodents and other animals) in their burrows. *The gas is highly inflammable and explosive and deadly to human beings if inhaled in large quantities. Hence it should be used with great care and never in the presence of fire.*

For ants in lawns a teaspoonful of the liquid may be squirted into nest openings from an oil can. If a mound has been made, make holes into the center of the nest with a slender stick and pour about a tablespoonful down each hole; then plug the holes with a bit of sod. For moles inject a teaspoonful every five feet into the runways, closing the openings with dirt as before mentioned. Injecting the liquid into borer holes in trees kills grubs within 6 to 10 in. of the opening.

Carbon bisulphide emulsion may be purchased, or made by churning together 1 gal. rosin fish-oil soap and 3 gals. water; than add 10 gals. carbon bisulphide, churning until a creamy emulsion is formed. For use dilute 1 part with 200 parts of water and apply at the rate of 1 qt. per square foot of soil area. This treatment gives good control of the root knot nematode in greenhouses, while flooding soil with the emulsion kills wireworms and Japanese beetle grubs. See FUMIGATION; GREENHOUSE PESTS; JAPANESE BEETLE.

CARDAMINE (kahr-dam'-i-nee). A genus of annual, biennial and perennial herbs called collectively Bitter-cress. Members of the Mustard Family, there are many species, some of them rather showy, but only one, *C. pratensis,* known as Ladys Smock or Cuckoo-flower, is often cultivated. It is a perennial with white or rose-colored flowers on stems 1 to 1½ ft. high, blooming very early in the spring. It should be grown in moist places in the border or rock garden. or on the edge of the bog garden, and is easily increased by division.

CARDAMON (kahr'-dah-mun). Common name for *Elettaria cardamomum,* a species of perennial herb native in India and belonging to the Ginger Family. The plants, which are not hardy N., should be grown in moist shady places. They are propagated by root division and by seeds. They attain 10 ft. with large leaves, hairy beneath, and white flowers with a lip striped yellow and blue. The aromatic seeds, which are used as a spice and in medicine, are contained in a capsule ¾ in. long. The seeds of a related plant, *Amomum cardamon,* having similar properties, are sometimes offered and used as cardamon seeds in place of the real article.

CARDINAL-CLIMBER. Common name for *Quamoclit sloteri,* a hybrid annual vine of the Morning-glory Family with white-throated crimson flowers.

CARDINAL-FLOWER. Common name for *Lobelia cardinalis,* a N. American wet-ground perennial with spikes of brilliant red flowers.

CARDIOSPERMUM (kahr-di-oh-spur'-mum). A genus of hardy annual or perennial ornamental vines known as Heart-seed or Balloon-vine. They are excellent for covering wire fences or trellises and with support will grow to a height of 10 ft. The seed-pods are inflated like balloons, and each black seed is marked with a white, heart-shaped spot. The quick-growing vines are graceful with their deeply cut leaves, and small white 4-petaled flowers.

Seed should be sown where the plants are to grow, or it may be started indoors in the spring, the plants later put outdoors, preferably in a light soil, and in a sheltered spot. Plants may self-sow in mild regions. *C. halicacabum* (true Balloon-vine), also called Love-in-a-Puff, is the most commonly grown. Other species include *C. grandiflorum,* with larger white flowers and pods to 2 in. long; and *C. hirsutum,* with densely hairy stems.

CARDOON (kahr-doon'). A sturdy, thistle-like composite plant (*Cynara cardunculus*) closely related to the globe artichoke (*C. scolymus*) but grown for its blanched stalks and thick main roots. Sow seed in early spring where plants are to stand, either in hills 18 to 24 in. asunder or in rows 3 to 4 ft. apart. In either case, thin the plants so they stand only one at a place. Water in dry spells, as lack of moisture makes the stalks pithy or hollow. In autumn tie the mature leaves together, wrap them in blanching paper or straw and bank them with earth. About a month later the stalks are ready to cut and use like celery or endive.

CARDUUS (kahr'-deu-us). A genus of vigorous herbs of S.E. Asia popularly known as Plumeless Thistle because the flowers forming the composite head are without the hairy plume of the true thistles. They are robust, spiny-leaved, annual and perennial plants with purple tubular flowers. Striking in both flower and foliage, some species are distinctly ornamental. They grow well in ordinary garden soils and are propagated by seeds or division. They have escaped from gardens and become naturalized in parts of N. America.

CARE OF THE GARDEN. Routine work necessary for the proper growth of plants is discussed under GARDEN MAINTENANCE. See also SPRING, SUMMER, AUTUMN and WINTER WORK IN THE GARDEN.

CAREX (kay'reks). A large genus (some 900 species) of grass-like perennials found in marshy places and known as Sedge (which see). Some are planted by ponds, in rock gardens and bog gardens or used for naturalizing.

CARICA (kar'-i-kah). A genus of tropical tree-like herbs of which *C. papaya* is grown for its fruit, the Pawpaw.

CARICATURE - PLANT. Popular name for *Graptophyllum pictum,* a shrub of New Guinea, with large green or purplish leaves marked with yellow blotches which often suggest the profile of a human face. It has large wide-open flowers of purple or crimson, and is sparingly cultivated as a greenhouse curiosity. Propagation is by cuttings.

CARISSA (kah-ris'-ah). Evergreen shrubs from S. Africa, Asia, and Australia, much branched and spiny. Grown as hedge plants, and for the edible fruits in regions where only light frosts occur. The principal species are:

C. grandiflora (Natal-plum). A large S. African shrub with glossy leathery leaves, fragrant white star-shaped flowers, and scarlet plum-like fruit. A good hedge plant, tolerant of hard shearing.

carandas (Karanda). A native of India, growing to 20 ft. in the warmer parts of the United States. It has white or pink fragrant flowers, and cherry-like fruits used in jelly-making or pickled when green.

CARLINA (kahr-ly'-nah). A genus of European and Asiatic hardy herbs of the Daisy Family. They have deeply cut thistle-like foliage and large stemless white, yellow, or purple flower heads closely set in the center of the flat rosette of foliage. Sometimes grown in the rock garden, they do well in ordinary soil but need a warm sunny exposure. Seeds may be sown in late summer or the perennials may be increased by division.

CARLUDOVICA (kahr-leu-doh-vy'-kah). A genus of stemless, shrubby or herbaceous plants with palm-like leaves, native to tropical America. Some have climbing stems which send out air-roots that attach themselves to other plants; these, and others, can be grown as greenhouse plants in winter and set in the open ground in summer. They require an abundance of water but good drainage. Panama hats are made of fiber from the leaves of *C. palmata.* Propagation is by division, or by thoroughly washed seeds sown on crumbled sphagnum moss.

CARMICHAELIA (kahr-my-kah-ee'-li-ah). Tender deciduous shrubs, native of New Zealand, belonging to the Pea Family. May be grown outdoors in California. Remarkable for their mostly leafless appearance. The leaves fall off quite young, their function thereafter being performed by the flattened or cylindrical green branches. The principal species are:

C. flagelliformis, a much-branched spreading shrub to 8 ft. with tiny pinkish pea-shaped flowers smothering the branches; *C. ensyi,* which makes a dense mat only a few inches in height, and has reddish flowers; *C. grandiflora,* which grows to 6 ft. and has purple and violet flowers; *C. odorata,* which grows to 18 ft. with drooping branches and many-flowered racemes of white or lilac flowers.

CARNATION. Common name for *Dianthus caryophyllus,* also known, because of its fragrance, as the Clove Pink. While general usage associates the name with the greenhouse (florists') carnation it properly belongs to all forms of the species, some of which are grown outdoors.

Native to the S. part of Europe and in cultivation for more than 20 centuries, the carnation has become generally known in N. America as a plant 2 to 3½ ft. tall, with a brittle, slightly branching stem, narrow opposite leaves, and large terminal double flowers, usually ruffled or toothed, in which red, white, and pink predominate, with occasionally yellow or purple. Variegations occur but usually on body colors of yellow or white. "Selfs" are the flowers of one solid color; the flowers are known as *flakes* when striped with one color, *bizarres* if striped with two or three, and *picotees* if the petals are merely edged or bordered with another color. The Grenadins include strongly perfumed flowers of one color; the Flamands, large flowers, always double, and higher in the center.

There are two main groups among the highly developed large-flowered forms, the outdoor or border carnations, including the "marguerite" type, which are delightful though seldom grown in the U. S. as they require cooler summers than we can offer; and the florists' or greenhouse carnations, among which the perpetual-flowering type is known as the American carnation. The red form of this type is the State flower of Ohio.

As a greenhouse crop carnations are grown from cuttings about 3 in. long taken from the base or stems of stock plants in late fall and early winter. Inserted in sand kept moist and over mild bottom heat, they are sufficiently rooted for potting up in a month and are shifted to larger pots from time to time as necessary. About April they are hardened off so they can be set out in the field in May. After a summer outdoors, they are benched in July or early August so as to come into bloom as the weather gets cold. Some growers get excellent results by growing their plants under glass the year 'round, thus avoiding the planting out in spring and the moving indoors in fall.

ENEMIES. The stem rots or wilt diseases are probably the most serious carnation troubles. Brown lesions appear on the stem at the surface of the soil, followed by wilting and yellowing of leaves. Remove diseased plants or parts as soon as noticed and use only healthy plants for propagation. Soil sterilization with a formaldehyde drench is of some help. Care should be taken to prevent wounding plants by rough handling or too close cultivation.

Blight or leaf spot, also known as branch rot, shows as ashy-white, circular spots on the leaves, the centers of the spots being covered with dark fungous growth. It may cause girdling and death of the branches. Spray plants with bordeaux mixture containing a good spreader before they are placed in the benches and every two or three weeks thereafter.

Yellowish or reddish brown pustules on the backs of leaves and on stems are symptoms of rust. Hand-pick infected leaves before the pustules break. Spray regularly with bordeaux mixture or lime-sulphur, or dust with sulphur. These measures will also prevent other minor leaf spots. In greenhouses try to keep proper humidity and dry foliage.

Red spider (which see) may be kept down by dusting with sulphur or spraying with a weak solution of lime-sulphur. Recent commercial control methods for this mite include the use of a selenium spray,

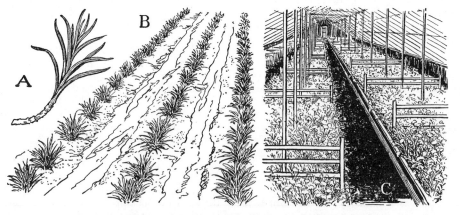

THREE STAGES IN THE GROWING OF CARNATIONS
Which are primarily a commercial, florists cut flower crop. A, typical cutting as taken from the side shoot of an old plant ready to be rooted in sand. B, young plants from rooted cuttings growing in the field until early or mid-summer. C, plants from the field benched in the greenhouse coming into bloom in winter.

and of a dinitro-ortho-cyclo-hexylphenol dust, and napthalene fumigation, the latter safe only in houses where carnations are the sole crop.

CARNATION SOCIETY, AMERICAN. An organization of commercial growers and carnation enthusiasts formed about 1892 to promote the welfare and improvement of the flower as a greenhouse crop. It gives its attention to problems of nomenclature, types and standards of culture and exhibition, the control of pests and diseases, the production of improved sorts, and the development of public interest in what its admirers call "the Divine Flower." The Society holds an annual convention and show and issues an annual report for its members. The secretary is Francis A. Baur, Indianapolis, Ind.

CARNEGEIA (kar-nay-gee′-ah) *giganteus*. A large columnar cactus of the S.W. desert country called Suwarro and Desert Cactus, whose 4 in. white blossom is the State flower of Arizona. Its erect stem, often 2 ft. through and attaining 60 ft. is heavily ribbed and covered with stout spines, and sometimes has a few branches jutting outward and upward. Occasionally transplanted to gardens or show collections, but not easy to cultivate. Formerly placed in the genus Cereus as *C. giganteus*.

CAROB (kar′-ob). Common name for *Ceratonia siliqua*, also called St. Johns Bread. A handsome evergreen tree, reaching a height of 50 ft. and native to the E. Mediterranean country, it is now widely cultivated in warm regions; it withstands a few degrees of frost and succeeds in Fla. and Calif. As an orchard crop, grown for its large protein-rich pods, the trees are set 40 ft. apart. The pods, besides being eaten greedily by all kinds of live stock, are an acceptable human food, and are also used to make a nourishing, fermented drink. On arid soils the carob yields a much larger quantity of food than any other crop. Propagation is from seeds started under glass, and, in the case of preferred varieties, by budding.

CAROLINA ALLSPICE. Common name for *Calycanthus floridus*, a hardy shrub of N. America, bearing large, deep maroon or reddish-brown flowers of spicy fragrance.

CAROLINA MOONSEED. Common name for *Cocculus carolinus*, a species of Snailseed (which see). It is a twining plant bearing bright red berries found along streams from Va. to Fla. and Tex., and hardy farther N.

CAROLINA-VANILLA. Common name for *Trilisa odoratissima*, a shrub of the Composite Family, growing to 3 ft. high with foliage vanilla-scented when bruised. Though hardy as far N. as New York, it is not often planted in gardens. The flowers, in purplish heads without rays, appear in the fall. It grows best in a light soil and is propagated by seed sown in the autumn, or by division.

CAROLINA YELLOW JESSAMINE (*Gelsemium sempervirens*). An evergreen twining shrubby plant found from Va. to Central America; the State flower of S. Carolina. It bears a wealth of yellow, very fragrant flowers, and is useful for draping porches or covering banks. It is propagated from cuttings.

CAROSELLA (ka-roh-sel′-ah). Common name for *Foeniculum vulgare piperitum*, a variety of Fennel (which see), grown for the young stems which are eaten.

CARPEL (kahr′-pel). The ovule-bearing unit of a flower, comprising ovary, style, and stigma. A *simple pistil* consists of one carpel; a *compound pistil* is composed of several carpels, the ovaries of which are fused, whereas the styles and stigmas may be either fused or independent. See PISTIL.

CARPENTERIA (kahr-pen-tee′-ri-ah). Californian Mock-orange. An evergreen shrub native in California, belonging to the Saxifrage Family. The one species (*C. californica*) is a most attractive shrub, growing to 10 ft. and requiring a well-drained soil in a sunny sheltered location. It has long narrow leaves, whitish beneath. The pure-white fragrant flowers with golden anthers resemble a single rose. They are 2 to 3 in. across and are borne in clusters at the ends of the shoots.

CARPENTER WORM. The larva of a moth which is common on many shade trees, especially oak, chestnut, maple, locust and cottonwood. Trees are rarely killed but the wide burrows (sometimes an inch or more in diameter), generally in the trunk of the tree and often at the lower end, produce serious deformities. Signs of infestation are wilting of the twigs, accumulations of sawdust and a discharge of dark-colored sap from the openings on the trunk. The full grown worm is a large (3 in.) reddish-white caterpillar, greenish underneath, with a shining black head. The life cycle covers three years, the large moths mottled gray tinged with yellow, being about most of the summer. They lay eggs in crevices in the bark, preferably in old wounds, and the young borers work into the wood immediately on hatching. Here they live, grow and finally pupate.

Control is difficult. Since the moths prefer roughened places for egg-laying, smoothing off such areas and treating them with grafting wax or a wound dressing may help. Trunk wounds should be treated promptly (see TREE SURGERY). Carbon bisulphide (which see) can be injected into the borer openings, which are then plugged with putty.

CARPET-GRASS. Common name for *Axonopus compressus,* a perennial herb of the Grass Family. Formerly regarded as only a pasture grass in the S., it is being increasingly used for lawns there as it retains its color well in cool weather. It spreads by stolons, cuttings of which are used for planting. See also GRASSES; LAWN.

CARPETWEED FAMILY. Common name of Aizoaceae (which see), a family

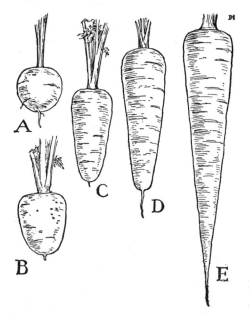

GOOD CARROTS OF MANY FORMS
(A) French forcing type, also good for an early outdoor crop; (B) Oxheart, another type early to mature; (C) Chantenay; (D) half-long Danvers, one of the most popular in market-gardening; and (E) long Danvers, a standard main crop sort.

characterized in general by the grotesque forms it gives to desert vegetation. Tetragonia and Mesembryanthemum are the genera most widely cultivated.

CARPINUS (kahr-py'-nus). Generic name of the Hornbeams, hardy, deciduous trees of the northern hemisphere, members of the Birch Family. Mostly small or medium sized, of ornamental value. See HORNBEAM.

CARPOBROTUS (kahr-poh-broh'-tus). A genus of plants of the Carpetweed Family having fleshy leaves, showy, yellow to reddish and purple flowers, and edible fruit. They are used in mild climates as a ground-cover, but are not hardy N. If grown in pots they should have a light soil, full sunlight and ample drainage. *C. edulis,* the Hottentot-fig, has yellow flowers varying to rose-purple, opening to 3 in. wide. It is frequently raised under glass and much planted in California where it has become naturalized in many places.

CARRION-FLOWER. Common name for *Smilax herbacea,* a native black-fruited form of Greenbrier; also applied to the genus Stapelia, whose flowers have an offensive odor.

CARROT. A biennial herb (*Daucus carota* var., *sativa*) whose cultivated forms are supposed to have been developed from the wild carrot, a bad weed in improperly managed land. Large-rooted, late kinds are used for stock feeding; small ones as a vegetable and for flavoring soups, stews and salads.

Carrots do best in deep, light, rich soils. As the seedlings are hardy, sow seed thinly as soon as the soil can be worked. Make the rows 12 to 15 in. apart for hand tillage and 30 in. for power implements.

Because carrot seed sprouts slowly, sow some lettuce or forcing radish seed with it; these plants, appearing quickly, mark the carrot rows and permit early cultivation so as to forestall weeds. The radishes or lettuce can be used within a month or removed when the carrots are thinned to stand not less than an inch apart. Thin a second time a month later, leaving the plants 3 or 4 in. apart. Roots of the early or forcing varieties pulled at the second thinning should be large enough to cook.

For autumn and winter use, a more tender- better-quality crop can be secured by sowing a forcing variety during August in freshly dug soil, tramping the seed firmly on the rows, then raking the surface ½ in.

loose so as to promote germination and growth despite summer heat. Dig the winter crop before cold weather sets in, cut the tops half an inch from the root-crown and store in a root cellar or a pit. See STORING OF CROPS.

ENEMIES. Bacterial soft rot is of importance both in the field and in storage. It occurs on many other vegetables and on some ornamentals, iris particularly, and causes a soft slimy disintegration of the tissues accompanied by a very disagreeable odor. Generally the outer skin is left intact. To prevent, practice long crop rotations and in storing dry the roots in the sun and save only perfectly healthy roots.

Two leaf blights turn leaves and petioles first yellow and then brown and one may kill the whole plant. The disease is worse in damp localities near large bodies of water. If necessary spray with 4-4-50 bordeaux mixture or dust with 20-80 copper-lime dust. Destruction of diseased carrot refuse and planting on high, well-drained ground are aids.

The carrot rust fly, a small, shining, dark green fly with yellow head and red eyes, may be serious on carrots, celery and parsnips. Its ¼ in. long, slender, dark brown larvae feed on the roots, and the injured plants show a rusty appearance. In the vicinity of New York State planting the main crop after June 1st eliminates danger of infestation by the first brood, and harvesting early in September prevents destruction by the second. In the home garden where this pest is bad carrots may be grown under a cheesecloth screen; or the growing plants may be treated with calomel, used at the rate of 3 or 4 oz. to ten gallons of water; or crude naphthalene may be broadcasted between the rows.

Proper rotation of crops will prevent injury by the larvae of the dark brown carrot weevil and destruction of weeds and decaying vegetation will keep down the reddish-brown carrot beetle.

CARROT FAMILY. A common name for the Umbelliferae or Parsnip Family, a group of hollow-stemmed herbs including important vegetable root-crops, such as carrot and parsnips, herbs, as caraway and coriander, and several ornamentals.

CARROT FERN. A name for *Onychium japonicum,* a fern for the cool greenhouse and living room; also known as Japanese Claw Fern, which see.

CARTHAMUS (kahr'-tha-mus). Popularly known as Safflower, this group of 20 species of spiny-leaved annuals of the Composite Family is native to the region extending from the Canaries to Central

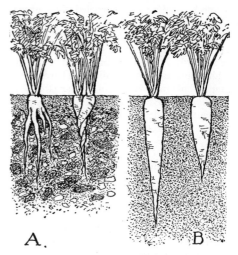

GOOD CARROTS NEED CARE
A. Stones, clods and lumps of manure cause poor, forked roots, and failure to thin young plants leads to twisted, inferior ones. B. Deeply prepared, uniform, friable soil produces clean, well-developed roots like this.

Asia. The flower-heads are purplish or yellow and the plants form ornamental clumps in the garden. *C. tinctorius,* known commonly as False-saffron, yields two dyes from its florets: one, a tint of orange, soluble in water, is used for coloring soups and pickles; the other, a resinous red, affords shades of pink to cherry-red which are used in dyeing silks and, when mixed with talc, for making rouge. Seeds are sown in April where the plants are to bloom.

CARYA (kay'-ri-ah). A genus of native hardwood, deciduous trees including the Hickory and Pecan (both of which see), belonging to the Walnut Family. They have pinnate (deeply divided) leaves with 3 to 17 leaflets, and bear nuts which in some species are sweet and edible, in others exceedingly bitter; the nuts range from very hard and rough-shelled, to smooth and thin-shelled. Their golden autumn foliage and rugged form makes them desirable for ornamental purposes, while improved named varieties (especially of pecan) bearing edible nuts of high quality are planted in orchards.

PRINCIPAL SPECIES

C. pecan (Pecan). Grows to 150 ft. in nature but not when grown as an orchard crop. A most valuable nut tree; but it is only half hardy. It is extensively planted in the S. for its sweet-kerneled, light-brown to reddish nut.

ovata (Shagbark Hickory) to 120 ft.; an ornamental tree with a broad open head. It is hardy N. and is much planted for its white nuts of good quality. There are a number of improved named varieties.

laciniosa (Big Shellbark Hickory) to 120 ft.; a handsome tree with a yellowish-white, sweet-kerneled nut, pointed at both ends.

cordiformis (Bitternut) to 90 ft., one of the fastest growing species under cultivation; excellent for park planting.

alba (Mockernut) to 90 ft., with leaves white-downy beneath and a nut with a small sweet kernel.

glabra (Pignut), small tree to 40 ft., bearing a ridged nut with a bitter. kernel.

aquatica (Bitter Pecan) to 90 ft., with shreddy light-brown bark and an angled, ridged nut with a very bitter kernel.

cathayensis (Chinese Hickory) to 60 ft., with leaves yellowish beneath and the nut somewhat oval.

See also HICKORY; PECAN; SHAGBARK.

CARYOPHYLLACEAE (kar-i-oh-fi-lay'-see-ee). Botanical name of the Pink Family, a group of widely distributed herbs and sometimes sub-shrubs most abundant in temperate and cold regions. The stems are characteristically swollen at the joints and the flowers bright-colored and mostly regular. The family contributes many fine annuals and perennials to the garden as well as the greenhouse, the perennials being extensively used in borders. Among the cultivated genera are Tunica, Dianthus (Carnation), Gypsophila, Saponaria, Silene, Lychnis, Cerastium, Stellaria, Spergula.

CARYOPTERIS (kar - i - op' - ter - is). Bluebeard. Small deciduous shrubs or herbs from Asia, belonging to the Vervain Family. See BLUEBEARD.

CARYOTA (kar-i-oh'-tah). A genus of trees popularly known as Fish-tail Palms because of the graceful, wide-spreading tips of the leaves. They have ringed, brown trunks, smooth after the leaf-sheaths have fallen, and unarmed (free from spines). They bear flowers in the axils of the leaves, in very large clusters or flowing plumes, suggesting horses' tails, 12 ft. long. The trees do not bloom until maturity and die after fruiting. Although natives of Asia and Australia, they are easily grown in S. Fla., if given sufficient water and food, thriving in sun or shade; potted specimens are most attractive in the patio. Because of their large size, they are more appropriate for conservatories than for the house when grown in the N.

The most widely known species is *C. urens* (Wine Palm), reaching 60 ft. with dark green leaves to 20 ft. long and 10 to 15 ft. broad, the leaflets stiff and prominently toothed. A graceful, decorative tree, it is frequently planted outdoors on the W. Coast of Fla., where it grows to perfection. From this tree in India is obtained toddy or palm wine (some trees yielding 100 pts. in 24 hours), and many other commercial products, such as sago, fibre, etc. Other species less well known are *C. rumphiana* and *C. mitis,* the latter sometimes grown outdoors in Fla.

See also PALM.

CASE-BEARERS. Small, mottled gray moths whose larvae construct cigar- or pistol-shaped cases from the woolly hairs of leaves. Apples particularly, but also quinces, plums and cherries, are attacked, the larvae feeding on as much of the leaf or fruit as they can reach by leaning out of the case. Rarely abundant enough to cause serious damage, these insects are controlled by the regular fruit tree spray program outlined under APPLE.

CASEIN (kay'-seen). A substance obtained from milk and added to certain spray materials and dusts to increase their spreading and sticking qualities. See SPREADERS and STICKERS.

CASHEW (kah-shoo'). Common name for *Anacardium occidentale,* the most prominent of eight species of tropical trees, grown in the U. S. only in S. Florida. The tree is a spreading evergreen to 40 ft. with a milky juice which yields a gum used in making a varnish that protects woodwork and books against insects. It is propagated by seeds, shield-budding or mature wood cuttings under glass. The nut, about the size of a kidney bean, is borne on the end of a red or yellow, fleshy edible cashew "apple." The nut yields an oil and also is edible when roasted.

CASHEW FAMILY. Common name of *Anacardiaceae* (which see), a mostly tropical family of trees and shrubs, familiar members of which are poison ivy and sumac; others less known yield pistachio and cashew nuts, and the mango.

CASSABANANA (kas-a-ba-nah'-nah). A common name for *Sicana odorifera*, which is also called Curuba. This is a fast growing and lengthy vine from S. America, belonging to the Cucumber Family. It can be grown in this country as an annual and is of interest chiefly for its decorative fruits. These are smooth, slender and nearly cylindrical, up to 2 ft. long; orange-crimson in color, edible, and with a strong aromatic fragrance.

CASSAVA (ka-sah'-vah). Common name for *Manihot esculenta*, a tropical shrub important as a source of tapioca and cassava. Other species are of tree form. See MANIHOT.

CASSENA (ka-see'nah). A common name for an evergreen holly (*Ilex vomitoria*) of the S., also called Yaupon. See HOLLY.

CASSIA (kash'-ah). A genus (of about 400 species) of herbs, shrubs and trees native in tropical and temperate regions, belonging to the Pea Family. See SENNA.

CASSIA - BARK - TREE or CASSIA-FLOWER-TREE. These are common names for two tropical trees of the genus Cinnamomum: *C. cassia* and *C. loureiri* respectively.

CASSINIA (kah-sin'-i-ah). Evergreen shrubs from New Zealand and Australia, belonging to the Daisy Family. A few species are grown outdoors in California. They range from 3 to 6 ft. high, are very much branched, and flower in late summer. The principal species is *C. fulvida*, with yellow stems and small green leaves yellowish beneath. The small, white, daisy-like flowers are borne in clusters at the ends of the shoots. *C. leptophylla* is distinguished from *C. fulvida* by the grayish-white tone of the leaves.

CASTANEA (kas-tay'-ne-ah). Generic name for the Chestnut, an important group of hardy, deciduous trees and shrubs in the Beech Family. Valued for ornament and its edible nuts. The name is sometimes applied to the Brazil- or Para-nut, produced by a tropical tree (*Bertholletia excelsa*). See CHESTNUT.

CASTANOPSIS (kas - tah - nop' - sis). Evergreen trees and shrubs belonging to the Beech Family. Several species are found in Asia and one (*C. chrysophylla*)

in W. N. America. This, called Giant Chinquapin and Golden-chestnut, is variable in size and habit, sometimes a large shrub, and again a tree of 100 ft. or more. It has showy lustrous green leaves, golden beneath. The male and female flowers are mostly borne on separate catkins, and the fruits, which resemble small sweet chestnuts, ripen in the second year.

CASTILLEJA (kas-til-ee'-yah). A genus of herbs of the Figwort Family variously known as Painted Cup or Indian Paintbrush. The brilliant, orange, red or rose bracts surrounding the small flowers are striking and would seem to offer excellent color effect possibilities in gardens; but the plants are not seen in cultivation because it is exceedingly difficult to transplant them from the wild or to grow them from seed, as they are either parasitic on the roots of other plants or depend for their food on the presence of the roots of certain fungi in close contact with their own—a condition called mycorrhizal association (which see). *C. coccinea* (Scarlet Paint-brush), native to damp meadows, is the State flower of Wyoming; and *C. californica* is the gaudy red Indian Paint-brush of the W. coast.

CASTOR-BEAN, CASTOR-OIL PLANT, PALMA CHRISTI. Various common names for *Ricinus communis*, a plant of the Spurge Family naturalized in the tropics and other warm regions and used for both ornamental and medicinal purposes there and in the N. where it is treated as an annual and planted as a foliage specimen or a screen. In such locations it rarely reaches a height of more than 12 ft. but in the tropics it becomes a tree to 40 ft.

For garden plants seeds may be started under glass and transplanted in May to the place where they are to stand. The soil may be a clay or sandy loam but should have good drainage. In the typical Castor-bean (*R. communis*) the leaves are large, sometimes 3 ft. across, and divided into from 5 to 11 lobes. The flowers, without petals, are borne in panicles covered with dark brown spines; the fruit is a capsule containing three large seeds which yield the castor oil of commerce and which are recommended for ridding gardens of moles (which see). There are numerous forms differing greatly in appearance. Var. *africanus* has very large green leaves; *macrocarpus* has purple-red foliage; *cambodgensis* has blackish-purple stems and leaves; *sanguinea* is red-leaved; *gibsoni* is dwarf and has dark red foliage with a metallic lustre; and *borboniensis arboreus,* one of the largest types, has red stems and red leaves with a bloom.

CATALPA (kah-tal′-pah). Common and generic name for deciduous, hardy, native and Asiatic trees, ornamental because of their large, long-stalked leaves, showy terminal clusters of white or pinkish flowers in late spring, and long, slender pods. The six species found in the north temperate zone are rapid growers and thrive in any good soil. Catalpas are popular for lawn and avenue plantings, especially where a formal or exotic effect is desired. Propagated from seed sown in spring with a little bottom heat; also from cuttings of ripe or green wood or roots.

C. speciosa (Western Catalpa) is the most commonly planted in the North. A very rapid grower in favorable locations, it has leaves to 1 ft. across, fuzzy beneath and bears many panicles of brown-spotted white flowers 2 in. across.

bignonioides (Common Catalpa or Indian-bean), a native of the South, bears large panicles of striped and spotted flowers and is ornamental on lawns or in a garden background. Var. *nana,* a dwarf form, develops a dense round head and is often grafted on 6 ft. straight stems for use along paths, at doorways, etc. So used it is often wrongly called *Catalpa bungei* after another Chinese species.

fargesi and *ovata* are other Chinese species, and *C. hybrida* (the product of crossing *bignonioides* and *ovata*) is a popular form, with leaves purplish when young.

ENEMIES. Two leaf-spot fungi form circular brown spots on the leaves and larger dead areas and defoliation may follow. The primary cause of such spots may be the catalpa midge which may also cause distorted seed pods and excessive branching. The minute, delicate, yellow midges deposit great quantities of eggs on the buds and young leaves in late spring; the white to orange maggots are ⅛ in. long. Spray for them with a nicotine-molasses solution as recommended for the boxwood leaf miner. See under BOX.

The catalpa sphinx, a 3-in. long, green-marked caterpillar with a horn at its rear end, may defoliate trees in the Middle West. Spray with lead arsenate. In large areas airplane dusting has given good results. Control the mealy bug which infests

catalpa from New York City southward by using a dormant spray of oil or lime-sulphur, after clearing away the litter at the base of the branches with a wire brush. A forcible spray of water will wash off many insects of the later broods, particularly the third brood in August.

CATANANCHE (kat - ah - nan′ - kee) *caerulea.* A hardy perennial from S. Europe growing to 2 ft., bearing blue daisy-like heads from June to August and grown as a garden subject and for its "everlasting" cut flowers known as Cupids Dart, which see.

CATASETUM (kat-a-see′-tum). A fine genus of very beautiful, tropical, terrestrial orchids with yellow, greenish, brown and reddish colored flowers, but rarely seen in amateur collections. There are about 40 known species, natives of Tropical America and Mexico. A remarkable thing about these orchids is that the male and female flowers, produced on different plants, are so different that they have been mistaken as belonging to distinct genera. The plants need little water when growing, and only enough to keep the bulbs from shriveling when resting. The stamen-bearing column is so constructed that when its sensitive elongations or appendages are touched, the pollen masses fly out or are forcibly ejected. For culture, see ORCHID.

CAT-BRIER. Common name for *Smilax glauca,* a trailing plant of the Lily Family, with oval leaves, sometimes covered with a bloom, and black berries. It grows in thickets of eastern N. America, spreads rapidly by underground runners and may cause great annoyance in shrubbery plantings in dry ground or around the edge of a garden because of its strong, smooth, almost wiry, stems armed with needle-sharp spines. It is a hard pest to eradicate; determined grubbing out of the roots is probably the best method of extermination.

CATCH-CROP. A farming term applied to any crop used to occupy ground between the harvesting of one more important crop and the planting of another, as for instance, between the harvesting of early potatoes and the sowing of winter rye. Its purpose is to make maximum use of the land and if it cannot be grown long enough to yield a useful product itself—whether vegetable, seed, foliage or flower—it can at any rate be plowed or dug under to improve the soil, when it is called a cover-crop or a green manure (see both titles). Sometimes catch-crop is used as a synonym for companion-crop, which see.

In vegetable gardening such quick-maturing crops as radishes, onion sets and spinach are often used as catch-crops in spring or autumn. An effective way to use catch-crops in the home garden is to sow the short-season crops and others mentioned between the asparagus rows in early spring. They do not interfere with the harvesting of the asparagus shoots and by the time the asparagus tops begin to shade the ground, they will have been harvested.

CATCHFLY. Common name for the genus Silene (which see) of the Carnation Family. It comprises many species of annual or perennial herbs with red or white flowers. German-catchfly is *Lychnis viscaria.*

CATERPILLAR. Popular term for a young insect (larva) of the order Lepidoptera (see INSECTS), the adult form of which is a moth or a butterfly. It has a soft, cylindrical body composed of 13 segments besides the head. The first three of these segments have one pair of jointed appendages (legs) each, which sets all caterpillars apart from the true worms which they somewhat resemble. The abdominal segments usually bear soft fleshy projections called *prolegs*—usually five pair. Although larvae of several insect orders may have prolegs, only in caterpillars are they armed with fine hooks called *crochets.* Caterpillars also are characterized by the presence, near the jaws, of *spinnerets* from which issues the excretion that hardens to form silk of which the creature spins its cocoon. The larvae of beetles (Order Coleoptera) are called grubs; they may resemble caterpillars, but they never have more than one pair of prolegs, which lack crochets.

CATESBAEA (kayts'-bee-ah). A spiny shrub (*C. spinosa*) from the West Indies. See LILY-THORN.

CATHEDRAL BELLS. Catalog name for *Cobaea scandens,* a tropical vine with large bell-shaped flowers, useful as a garden annual and probably better known as Cup-and-saucer-vine.

CATKIN. One of the blossoms or flowering parts of certain kinds of trees, notably willow, poplar and birch. It consists of a number of small flowers closely clustered on a drooping, tassel-like spike. But only the reproductive parts of these flowers, that is, the stamens and pistils are present; they are protected, not by petals and sepals, but by scaly bracts. Catkins are either staminate (male) or pistillate (female), the two types being sometimes borne on separate trees, and sometimes on different parts of the same tree. In botanical language a catkin is an *ament.*

Plants bearing catkins usually bloom very early and are largely dependent on wind pollination for fertilization and seed production. The male catkins fall after the pollen has been scattered and the female catkins develop the seeds.

CATMINT, CATNIP, CATNEP. Common names for *Nepeta cataria,* a hardy perennial herb of the Mint Family, with pungent fragrance which is highly attractive and exciting to cats.

CATS-CLAW. Common name for an evergreen vine (*Doxantha unguis-cati*) so-called because of the claw-like tendrils with which it clings. This plant is better known in gardens by its former botanical name, *Bignonia tweediana.* It is usually grown in the greenhouse, but can stand a few degrees of frost outside. It is too robust a grower for pot culture, but the roots need to be somewhat restricted, either in a long box or narrow border, in order to induce free flowering. The bright yellow, trumpet-shaped flowers are up to 4 in. across.

CATS-EAR. Common name for species of two genera—Antennaria and Hypochoeris—of the Composite Family, both characterized by woolly leaves; also applied to *Calochortus caeruleus,* whose blue flowers have hairy petals.

CAT-TAIL. Common name for tall, perennial, swamp herbs of the genus Typha. They have creeping rootstocks, narrow, flat leaves and odd brown flowers in dense, blunt spikes on unbranched stems up to 10 ft. tall. They are often planted in the bog garden, or in colonies along streams or ponds for their stately and decorative effect. The leaves are used for chair seats or in basketry. The plants grow readily and increase naturally, but they may be propagated more rapidly by division or by seeds planted in pots kept in water. *T. angustifolia,* to 10 ft., has spikes light brown in color and leaves not over ½ in. wide. *T. latifolia,* not quite so tall, has dark brown spikes and broader leaves, to 1 in.

CATTLEYA (kat'-lee-ah). A genus of tropical American, epiphytic orchids with

BLANCHING CAULIFLOWER

To develop a tender, white head, just as the flower-cluster begins to show, gather the leaves up around it—when it and they are dry—and tie them with raffia.

exceedingly showy purple, lavender, rosy-violet, yellowish-brown or greenish blossoms. The flowers, borne singly or in clusters, above 1 to 3 leathery leaves, have beautifully waved petals, large 3-lobed lips, the margins often crisped, and throats often spotted or streaked with other colors. These orchids, grown extensively in the greenhouses of the N., are the most popular type for personal adornment.

Many species and hybrids are grown, the hybrids being frequently richer in color and more floriferous than the parents. *C. warscewiczi* var. *gigas* (formerly *C. gigas*) a widely grown species, has rosy-lavender petals and sepals and a deep-purple wavy lip with 2 yellow spots at the throat. There is a very beautiful pure white form, the rarest of the Cattleyas. The flowers of *C. trianaei,* also exceedingly popular, are pale-rose to white, 6 in. across, with crisped petals, a rather narrow lip, the middle lobe purple and the throat streaked with yellow. Hybrids developed from *C. trianaei* show endless variation in the delicate colors of the parent.

CAULESCENT. Having an obvious stem; a term used in describing plants or flowers. Compare ACAULESCENT.

CAULIFLOWER. A biennial herb (*Brassica oleracea,* var. *botrytis*) developed from the wild cabbage but distinguished from cultivated cabbage by its swollen flower-stems which form white heads and suggest its name "stem-flower."

Of all the members of the cabbage group cauliflower is the most finical. When conditions are right, even the novice may succeed with it; otherwise, even the skilled grower may fail. The plant resents heat and dryness and cannot be grown as a summer crop; a voracious but "choosy" feeder, it must have a deep, rich, loamy soil abundantly supplied with quickly available plant food. Well-decayed horse manure is its best fertilizer though green manures make fair substitutes.

After the ground is plowed or dug, but before planting, apply 1 lb. to 100 sq. ft. of a quickly available chemical fertilizer mixture analyzing 4% nitrogen, 8% phosphorus and 10% potash, and preferably consisting of nitrate of soda, superphosphate and sulphate of potash. Give a second application beside the plants when the heads begin to form.

For an early crop start the plants under glass a week later than early cabbage, prick them into flats when the second true leaf forms, keep them growing steadily and set them out a week or ten days later than cabbage. For a late crop sow the seed thinly in partial shade about June 1st, in moderately rich, friable, moist soil. Manage like late cabbage, setting the plants in the open in early July, 24 in. asunder for hand tillage but leaving 36 in. between rows for horse or garden tractor.

Cultivate at least weekly till the leaves shade the ground and in dry weather soak the soil weekly either by irrigation (which see) or by filling bowl-like hollows of hoed-up loose earth around the plants. When the "buttons" or young flower-heads are egg-size, fold (or tie with raffia) some of the leaves up over them to keep them white. See BRASSICA and CABBAGE.

ENEMIES. The black leaf-spot of cabbage causes brown spots on cauliflower heads, and a ring spot disease is sometimes destructive in the West. Circular and irregular spots occur on the leaves causing them to die prematurely. Use seed from healthy plants or treat it with hot water as directed under CRUCIFER.

CAULOPHYLLUM (kau-loh-fil'-um). A genus of small-flowered perennial herbs, commonly called Blue Cohosh, which see.

CAVITY TREATMENT. Cavities in tree trunks and limbs are caused by gradual decay of the wood under the action of fungi which gain entrance through some type of wound, such as a broken branch stub, bark split or torn during ice, wind or hail storms, frost cracks, abrasions made by wires and moving objects and holes made by boring insects. To prevent them try to avoid wounding trees, and protect all wounds that are made (as in pruning) with disinfectants. There are two main ways to treat cavities: They may be left open, after the diseased wood has been removed and the surface treated with a wound dressing; or they may be filled and sealed in such a way that the original form is restored and callus (new bark) formation over the area is encouraged. Proper cavity work requires the services of an expert tree surgeon. See TREE SURGERY; WOUNDS.

CEANOTHUS (see - ah - noh' - thus). Nearly 50 species of ornamental deciduous or evergreen shrubs of N. America, native chiefly in the Pacific Coast area. Belonging to the Buckthorn Family, they are handsome, free-flowering shrubs, with dense panicles of small blue, white or pink flowers. Only one or two can be grown outdoors in the North. The evergreen species flower in spring, and in favored climates make bushes up to 20 ft. The deciduous kinds flower late in the season, and so should be pruned fairly hard in spring to encourage good flowering shoots. They do best in a sunny sheltered position and well-drained light soil.

The principal evergreen species are:

C. thyrsiflorus, the hardiest of the tall evergreen sorts, a handsome free-flowering shrub with pale-blue flowers.

rigidus, a much-branched shrub of stiff habit, bearing long spikes of purple-blue flowers.

veitchianus, a hybrid of the above two with dense clusters of deep blue flowers.

Deciduous species of importance are:

C. americanus (New-Jersey-tea). This is a low shrub of slender upright growth, bearing clusters of white flowers in summer. Several hybrids have been raised, but they are only half-hardy North. However, it is possible to carry them over by digging them in the fall and wintering them in a frost-proof place.

fendleri, a native species of sprawling habit, useful for planting on dry sandy banks. It has white flowers, and is hardy.

ovatus, found from New England to Texas. It is an upright shrub to 3 ft. with flowers similar to those of *C. americanus,* but smaller.

caeruleus, a tender Mexican species with deep blue flowers. It is the parent of several beautiful and hardier forms.

delilianus, a hybrid between *C. americanus* and *C. caeruleus.* There are various named forms, one of the most notable being the bright blue, late flowering "Gloire de Versailles."

pallidus, a hybrid of *C. delilianus* and *C. ovatus.* Here again there are named forms, one of the best being "Marie Simon," with flesh-colored flowers.

CEDAR. Properly used, this is the common name for the coniferous genus Cedrus. But it is often applied (usually with some descriptive adjective) to trees or plants of other genera (see below) as follows: Canoe-cedar (*Thuja plicata*); Cigar-box-cedar (*Cedrela odorata,* also called Spanish- or West-Indian-cedar); Ground-cedar (*Lycopodium complanatum*); Incense-cedar (*Libocedrus*); Red-cedar (*Juniperus lucayana, J. scopulorum,* and *J. virginiana*); Stinking-cedar (*Torreya taxifolia*); White-cedar (*Chamaecyparis thyoides, Tabebuia pallida* and *Thuja occidentalis*).

Several species of the true Cedar, and the many varietal forms of the Red- and White-cedars, are most valuable from the horticultural standpoint, providing much of the ornamental evergreen material used in gardens, park and cemetery plantings.

The four species of Cedrus, of Asiatic and N. African origin, provide large widespreading evergreen trees with stiff "needles" in clusters and small erect cones. Though not really hardy, all but one will, if protected, stand normal winters up to S. New England. These are *C. atlantica,* the Atlas Cedar, with feathery bluish-green leaves less than 1 in. long, cones to 3 in. and several varieties showing differences in form and coloring; *C. deodara* (see illustration, Plate 17), the Deodar Cedar from the Himalayas, with graceful drooping branches, leaves to 2 in. long, 5 in. cones, and several varieties; and *C. libanotica,* the famous and beautiful Cedar of Lebanon in which the dark green leaves are 1 in. and the cones 4 in. long. In recent years a mountain type of the last mentioned species has proved hardy in the Arnold Arboretum, giving promise of a useful addition with wider range to this valuable and beautiful group.

The common Red-cedar (*Juniperus virginiana*) is a native tree (Me. to Fla.)

widely used in the garden and in landscape work. It is quite variable, grading in size from the type which grows to 100 ft. with wide-spread or upright branches, to very dwarf columnar forms. It is frequently used for bordering *allées,* for framing vistas, or as a background planting for garden features, such as fountains, benches or statuary at the end of an axis. It should not be planted near trees or shrubs of the Apple Family as it is a host for one stage of the apple rust (which see). *J. scopulorum* (Colorado or Rocky-mountain Red-cedar) to 30 ft. or over is very similar to *J. virginiana,* and is used horticulturally in the same way in the W. States. *J. lucayana* (Southern Red-cedar) native from Ga. to Tex., attains 50 ft., is of drooping form, has light green foliage, and is suitable only for use in the extreme S.

Chamaecyparis thyoides (White-cedar, sometimes called Swamp White-cedar) is a handsome tree to 80 ft., thriving in moist soil and able to grow in very swampy land. It is often planted to screen off unsightly marshes.

Tabebuia pallida (White-cedar) is not an evergreen but a member of the Bignonia Family, growing to 50 ft. with large white, pink or rose flowers, nearly 3 in. long. It is somewhat planted in S. Fla.

Thuja occidentalis (White-cedar or, correctly, Arbor-vitae) may grow to 60 ft. and, with its many varieties, provides much valuable evergreen material for the landscape architect with an infinite variety in shape, color or foliage and size, suitable for backgrounds, hedges and accents. The dwarf forms are admirable material for carrying out designs or for foundation planting.

Thuja plicata (Canoe- or Red-cedar), to 200 ft., is a West Coast tree, not hardy N. It has great drooping fern-like branches and will not endure close shearing as will the E. form.

Cedrela odorata (Cigar-, Spanish- or West-Indian-cedar), to 100 ft., is a tropical tree not of the Pine but of the Mahogany Family, bearing yellowish flowers in loose clusters. Grown in the W. Indies and S. America, it provides the fragrant wood extensively used for making cigar-boxes.

Libocedrus decurrens (Incense-cedar, sometimes called Western-cedar), to 200 ft., forms a somewhat narrow graceful head and has light yellowish-green foliage.

Although a native of the W. Coast, it has proved hardy in the E. States in sheltered positions. Its dwarf and variegated forms are very useful in horticultural work.

Lycopodium complanatum (Ground-cedar) is not a tree at all, but a species of club-moss (which see), the common name being suggested by its upright, sometimes fan-shaped, scale-covered branches.

Torreya taxifolia (Stinking-cedar), to 40 ft., is a somewhat spreading tree of Fla., a member of the Yew Family and with yew-like foliage which when bruised emits a fetid odor. It bears dark purple drupe-like-fruits. It is a handsome evergreen in its region but is not hardy N.

See also CONIFER and the various genera referred to above.

CEDAR-APPLE. A gall, formed from an overgrown, distorted cedar leaf and caused by the apple-rust fungus. Cedar galls are brown, more or less globose and ¼ to 1 in. in diameter. During wet weather in the spring they put forth numerous orange-colored gelatinous horns in which the spores of the fungus are borne. See JUNIPER; RUSTS.

CEDAR OF LEBANON (leb'-ah-nun). Common name for *Cedrus libanotica,* a highly ornamental evergreen conifer from Asia Minor. See CEDAR.

CEDRELA (se-dree'-lah). Several species of mostly subtropical or tropical deciduous or evergreen trees of the Bead-tree Family, with colored, fragrant wood of commercial value. The foliage resembles that of Ailanthus, and some of the species are grown for ornament in warm places. *C. odorata* of W. Indies and S. America is commonly called West-Indian-cedar, Spanish-cedar and Cigar-box-cedar, the latter name indicating its most extensive use. *C. sinensis* from China grows to 50 ft., has long panicles of white flowers and is hardy in S. New York State and S. N. England. *C. toona* from the Himalayas often attains 70 ft. and has white fragrant flowers. It has been planted in S. Fla.

Cedrelas are propagated by seeds, cuttings of mature wood and root cuttings over heat.

CEDRONELLA (see-droh-nel'-ah) *canariensis.* A perennial shrubby herb of the Canary Islands, with loose sprays of white or lilac flowers; called popularly Canary-balm, which see.

CEDRUS (see'-druss). Four species of Asiatic and N. African trees of the Pine

Family (Pinaceae). They are ornamental but not entirely hardy. See CEDAR.

CEIBA (say-ee'-bah) *pentandra.* A very large (to 120 ft.) tropical tree with wide-spreading branches and thin buttresses or surface roots that may extend 30 ft. Its seed fibres produce the kapok used in cushions. See SILK-COTTON-TREE.

CELANDINE (sel'-an-dyn). Common name for *Chelidonium majus,* a weedy biennial or perennial herb of the Poppy Family, occasionally grown in the wild garden. It grows to 4 ft. and has deeply divided leaves, yellow flowers, sometimes double, in small umbels, and slender fruits to 2 in. long. Of Old-World origin, it is widely naturalized in eastern U. S. The juice of the plant is orange colored. Var. *laciniatum* has finely cut leaves. Lesser-celandine is *Ranunculus ficaria.* Tree-celandine is *Macleaya cordata.*

CELANDINE-POPPY. Common name for *Stylophorum diphyllum,* a perennial herb of the Poppy Family growing 1 to 1½ ft. and having deep yellow flowers 2 in. across, in clusters. It blooms in early spring and is quite charming in the wild garden. It is easily transplanted and grows readily in rich soil where there is partial shade. The European *Chelidonium majus* or true Celandine is also sometimes called by this name.

CELASTRACEAE (sel-as-tray'-see-ee). Botanical name of the Staff-tree Family, a widely distributed group of trees and shrubs, often climbing. The name, signifying evergreen, refers to the bright fruits which persist through the winter; they are really pods, splitting at the summit to reveal red seeds. The genus Pachistema is sometimes cultivated, principally in borders; species of Celastrus, Maytenus and Euonymus are grown chiefly as ornamental wall shrubs and trellis covers.

CELASTRUS (se-las'-trus). Staff-tree. Mostly deciduous shrubs of usually twining habit, found in Asia, N. America and Australia. Some are very hardy and ornamental, being most effective late in the season, when their leaves turn yellow and the yellow fruits open up to reveal the crimson-coated seeds. They are useful to cover walls and trellis work, and especially attractive when allowed to clamber up through an old tree, or to ramble at will in rocky places or over rough banks.

They are not particular as to soil or situation, and grow as well in sun or shade.

Male and female flowers are borne separately, mostly on the same plant but sometimes on separate plants. This accounts for the non-fruiting of certain plants. Propagated by seeds sown in fall, by root cuttings, and stem cuttings of soft or mature wood.

Bittersweet is frequently infested with the euonymus scale. Control with a dormant application of an oil spray in early spring. See SCALE.

PRINCIPAL SPECIES

C. scandens (Wax-work or False-bittersweet). A native shrub, climbing to 20 ft. or more. The fruiting branches make attractive and lasting decorative material for the home; on this account the plant is rapidly disappearing from the countryside.

articulatus. This Japanese species (often listed as *C. orbiculatus*) is a vigorous climber or rambler to 40 ft. It is distinguished from the native species by more roundish leaves and shorter fruit clusters.

angulatus is a Chinese climber to 20 ft., with angular branches and large handsome leaves. It is not quite hardy North.

hypoleucus, also from China and not quite hardy, grows to 15 ft. and is distinguished by large leaves bluish-white beneath.

flagellaris is a hardy Korean vine to 25 ft. It has short hooked spines, small fruits, and orange-red seeds.

CELERIAC (se-ler'-i-ak). A variety of celery (which see) grown for its thickened, turnip-like roots. Seed is sown in spring and the crop grown during summer like celery, but it requires much less work because it needs no hilling up or blanching and its roots are much easier to store safely. They may be sliced and eaten raw with salt, used for flavoring soups and stews, boiled like turnips and served with a cream or a hollandaise sauce, or served as a salad with French or mayonnaise dressing.

CELERY. A biennial herb (*Apium graveolens*) of the Parsley Family, whose crisp, blanched leaf stalks are a table delicacy plain and in salads and also as flavoring in soups and stews.

Commercially the crop is grown mainly on reclaimed muck lands with special equipment, but better quality celery may be produced by home gardeners who will give it the necessary attention and whose soil is rich and well supplied with moisture.

EARLY CELERY. For this crop use a self-blanching variety. Starting in February or early March, fill a seed pan with well-firmed, finely sifted soil. Scatter the seed thinly on the surface; barely cover with sifted soil; press firmly; sprinkle and then keep covered with newspaper and a

BLANCHING CELERY

An easy method is to set planks on edge close to, and on either side of, the row and hold them in place with soil at the bottom, cleats across them, or strong supporting stakes driven into the ground outside them.

pane of glass until sprouting starts (in about a month). Then remove the paper but retain the glass for a week or two. If moisture condenses on it, raise one side lightly for ventilation but not enough to dry the soil. When the seedlings are an inch tall prick them out 2 x 2 in. apart in flats of similar soil; place the flats in a coldframe or hotbed until weather and soil conditions permit setting them outdoors. At each transplanting pinch off the outside leaves.

From then on the so-called "new celery culture" (which demands less work than the old style) is as follows: Having, in early spring, enriched the soil of a 4 ft. wide bed—preferably with well-rotted stable or poultry manure—by forking it in 10 or 12 in. deep, rake the surface 6 in. very fine. Set the plants from the hotbed 6 in. asunder in rows 10 in. apart and shade with screens of plaster laths an inch apart placed on stakes 18 to 24 in. above. Plants so treated will blanch themselves, but if desired they may be set farther apart and blanched individually with tiles or paper celery-blanching tubes obtainable in seed stores.

LATE CELERY. For an autumn crop sow seed thinly and shallow in April or early May outdoors in finely prepared, moderately fertile soil. Make the drills 8 or 10 in. apart. After sowing, firm the soil with the back of the rake and spread burlap

snugly over it to check evaporation; water only when the burlap begins to get dry. When the seed starts to sprout remove the burlap but provide partial shade for a week or two. When the seedlings are 2 in. high thin them, setting out the thinned ones so that all the plants stand 1 to 2 in. apart in a similar seed bed.

About mid-July prepare a space in the garden where a well-fertilized early crop of some sort has been grown and harvested. Before digging, manure it heavily and apply wood ashes (1 lb. to 10 sq. ft.) if available. If manure is scarce or costly, dig a trench 8 or 10 in. deep, place the manure in the bottom and cover with rich soil until nearly level full, mixing the ashes with the soil, though not directly on the manure. The bed is then ready for the young plants; however, several hours before transplanting soak the soil in the seed bed so the plants will be full of water when moved. Trim them as they are lifted and set them 6 in. apart in rows 10 to 18 in. asunder depending upon the blanching method used. Firm the soil well around them. Keep cultivated until the cool fall days when blanching time arrives.

BLANCHING LATE CELERY. This may be done with tiles or blanching tubes (as for the early crop) but boards or earth are more often used. Lay 12 in. boards flat on the ground on each side of a row, raise them on their edges, work them into the soil a little and hold them a few inches apart with wire hooks laid across or wooden strips nailed across their upper edges. This method is not safe with early celery because the plants might decay. It is less work than earthing up, which, however, produces the finest quality celery and is done as follows:

First, run the wheelhoe with cultivator teeth attached down each side of the row and close to it. Gather the stalks of celery in one hand and pack enough earth around their bases to hold them erect. Then with hand hoe or wheelhoe (with plow attachment) throw more earth against the plants. Repeat this "handling" process two or three times, raising the soil higher each time. Dig the crop before cold weather sets in. Never allow it to freeze.

STORAGE. Here are two ways to store celery for winter: 1. In late fall as you dig the plants, transplant them closely together in deep boxes of soil in a cool, moist, frost-proof cellar. Here they will continue to grow and to blanch. 2. Dig and replant them closely in a trench a foot deep or deeper, and at the approach of cold weather cover with an A-shaped board roof with closed ends. Before hard winter sets in, cover this roof with 6 or 8 in. of manure or other litter. By making the roof in sections a part of the trench may be emptied at a time without risk of freezing the rest of the crop.

ENEMIES. Three separate blights (all of which can be controlled in the same way) attack celery. (1) Early blight (caused by *Cercospora apii*) produces dead or ashen gray velvety areas; (2) late blight (due to *Septoria apii*) causes brown spots containing tiny black fruiting bodies on leaves and stem; (3) bacterial blight (caused by *Bacterium apii*) produces reddish-brown spots with a yellow halo but without the black fruiting bodies. These symptoms may appear on leaf blade, petiole or stalk at any stage of the plant's growth. To prevent infection select for the seed bed soil which has not grown celery for at least three years and is free from celery refuse. Spray seedlings weekly with a 5-5-50 bordeaux mixture or dust with 20-80 copper-lime dust.

Punctures made by the tarnished plant bug (which see) may cause serious damage. Dust plants with sulphur or spray (so as to hit the bugs) with a strong pyrethrum spray. Hand-picking is the only control measure necessary in the case of the celery worm (*Papilio polyxenes*), which is a smooth caterpillar about 2 in. long, green with cross bands of black. The adult is the common black swallow-tail butterfly and there are two broods a year.

CELERY CABBAGE. A name for the species of Brassica commonly called Chinese Cabbage, but properly Mustards, and particularly the kind listed in catalogs as Chi-hi-li. See BRASSICA; CHINESE CABBAGE; MUSTARD.

CELLAR GARDENING. At the end of the outdoor gardening season, a number of products for kitchen use besides mushrooms (which see) can be raised in a cellar which is always cool but never freezing. French endive, blanched asparagus and turnip greens may be grown, as well as blanched rhubarb and such garnishing greens as parsley and chives.

The latter are merely dug as clumps from the garden with plenty of soil about their roots and set in boxes in the basement window. To have French endive for salads all winter long, bring in the witloof chicory roots, with the tops cut 1 in. above the crown, trim the roots down to less than 1 ft., and pack horizontally in layers in apple boxes laid on their sides. When filled, set the boxes upright, so that the roots are vertical like stalks of asparagus in a bunch, and cover 6 to 8 in. deep above the crowns. Kept moist, these roots will give several cuttings of endive during the winter.

Roots of asparagus 4 or more years old brought inside and covered with 1 ft. of rich soil and manure, equal parts, will give good blanched asparagus if watered fre-

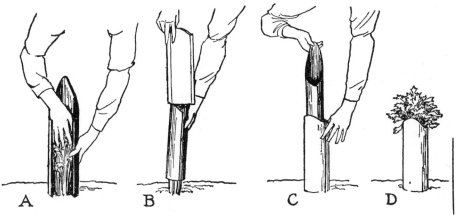

ANOTHER HANDY WAY TO BLANCH CELERY
Using aids to be had at seed or garden supply stores, it involves (A) placing a springy metal guard around a plant; (B) slipping a tough paper cylinder around the firmly held stalks; (C) sliding the metal holder from within the paper bleacher, which keeps light from all but the uppermost foliage.

quently. Good sound turnips need only to be set in soil, crowns up, and covered with 5 in. of soil to provide tender blanched buds to be cooked and used in salads. Rhubarb roots 4 years old or more with the soil around them should be allowed to freeze outdoors either before or after they are lifted. Then, planted in deep boxes in the cellar with plenty of rich soil below them and over their crowns, they will produce an abundance of stalks, slender and pale in color but of excellent quality.

CELOSIA (se-loh'-shi-ah). Popular herbaceous annuals of the tropics belonging to the Amaranth Family and the best known forms being commonly known as Cockscomb or Chinese Wool-flower. Easily grown from seed, they do best in a fertile soil supplied with plenty of moisture. There are two forms, both producing large ornamental heads and both good for either pot culture or garden beds. The cockscomb varieties (belonging to the species *C. argentea*) terminate in dense, plush-like spikes sometimes in pyramid shape and sometimes grotesquely flattened like the comb of a rooster, or ruffled. There are also feathery or plumed varieties with large globular heads like balls of wool-chenille. The former are usually red or golden, the latter bright red. Plants of the cockscomb type grow from 12 to 18 in. tall and those of the plumed type from 2 to 3 ft. Individually the flowers are small and not showy, but the crests, besides being colorful and interesting outdoors, can be dried for winter bouquets. Seed should be started indoors in March to provide plants to set in the garden in May.

The forms offered under such names as *cristata, childsi, plumosa,* etc., all belong in the species *argentea*.

C. floribunda is a much branched shrub to 12 ft., with numerous flowers in tight panicles sometimes grown in S. Calif.

CELSIA (sel'-si-ah). A genus of biennial or perennial herbs from Asia and the Mediterranean region with yellow flowers in tall upright spikes. They resemble the mulleins, to which they are closely related and cross with them to make interesting hybrids. Not quite hardy, they are started under glass and planted in the open in early summer. They can also be propagated by cuttings.

CELTIS (sel'-tis). A genus of mostly hardy, usually deciduous trees of the Elm Family, including several species of large trees valuable for shade and ornament. See HACKBERRY.

CENTAUREA (sen-tau-ree'-ah). (See illustration, Plate 9.) A genus of composite herbaceous annuals and perennials with purple, blue, yellow, rose or white flowers, both single and double and sometimes plume- or pompon-like. Known by many common names, the different species are used for many garden purposes, especially in borders, mass plantings or carpet bedding. All are hardy and will thrive under ordinary conditions in any good garden soil if given a sunny location. Flowering from July to frost, they produce a profusion of blossoms excellent for cutting and are remarkably resistant to disease. In some species the gray or whitish leaves provide pleasing contrast with other plants.

The annuals are grown from seed started indoors in early spring or in the open ground about mid-April. The foliage types are increased from cuttings taken in September and carried over the winter indoors; or from seed sown in August. Perennial sorts may be started from seed in early spring or by root division in April or May. The annuals especially often self-seed.

Centaurea is subject to rust, as shown by reddish pustules on both surfaces of leaves and on stems. Control by dusting with sulphur. Pull up and burn plants affected with root rot and disinfect the soil with 1-1000 corrosive sublimate (see MERCURY COMPOUNDS). Yellowed, sickly plants may have "yellows." See under ASTER.

Of the nearly 50 varieties the most populare are the following:

ANNUALS

C. americana (Basket-flower). To 6 ft., bearing solitary, thistle-like flowers generally of rose or flesh color often 5 in. across. Var. *alba,* called Star-thistle, bears white, fluffy double flowers.

cyanus (Bachelors Button, Bluebottle or Cornflower). To 2 ft. Hardy. Often reseeds itself. Single and double varieties with 1½ in. flowers in blue, white, rose, purple and mauve shades. The plants are woolly white only when young. There are dwarf varieties 10 in. high.

moschata (Sweet Sultan). 2 ft. The fragrant, white, yellow or purple solitary flowers are 2 in. across; often beautifully soft and fluffy.

imperialis (Giant Sweet Sultan). Hybrid between *C. moschata* and its var. *alba.* To

Plate 9.   AN INTERESTING QUINTET OF CENTAUREAS

Upper left: The yellow-flowered Centaurea macrocephala from Armenia. Upper right: The Sweet
Sultan (C. moschata), one of the loveliest and most fragrant of the group. Center left: The Mountain-
bluet (C. montana), a graceful type with silvery foliage. Lower left: A double form of the well
known Bachelors Buttons. Lower right: Flowers of the American Basket-flower (C. americana),
last long when cut.

4 ft., with fragrant flowers, white, rose, lilac and blue.

PERENNIALS

C. cineraria (Dusty Miller). To 1 ft. with woolly white foliage and large yellow or purple flowers.

gymnocarpa (also called Dusty Miller). To 2 ft. Densely woolly foliage; flowers in panicles, rose or purple, but mostly hidden by leaves.

macrocephala. To 3 ft. Yellow flowers 4 in. across in July and August.

montana (Mountain Bluet or Perennial Cornflower). To 1 ft. Leaves silvery-white when young. Flowers violet-blue, purple, rose, and white in the several var.

nigra (Knapweed, Hardheads). To 2 ft. Coarsely woolly; solitary flowers rose-purple, about 1 in.

CENTAURIUM (sen-tau'-ri-um). Century. Small annual or perennial herbs of the Gentian Family, growing from 4 to 8 in. tall, thriving in light sandy soil and requiring protection from full sun and cold weather. Bright red or rose flowers resembling pinks are produced in midsummer in broad flat clusters. The plants are especially suitable for rock gardens or borders. The annuals are propagated by seed sown indoors or outdoors, the perennials by seeds, division or cuttings. There are only a few perennial species and it is best to treat most of the species as annuals or biennials. *C. conferta* is a fleshy-leaved species, native in England or S. W. Europe. The species best known in the U. S. is *C. venustum,* 8 in. tall, bearing rose flowers with white throats spotted red.

CENTIPEDE (from two Latin words for "hundred" and "feet"). Hard-shelled brown, yellow or orange, swift-moving, wormlike insects of the Order Myriopoda. Most of the segments forming the body carry two pairs of legs, longer than the body width. The bite of some of the larger forms is painful and may be poisonous.

The true centipede, which has 15 to 24 segments, preys on the smaller garden type, which has only 12 pairs of legs and which attacks greenhouse, and occasionally truck, crops in the E. and middle W. and is a major pest of vegetables in Calif. especially asparagus. Plants are stunted and often killed by it. Greenhouse control is by means of steam sterilization or soil fumigants such as paradichlorobenzene or carbon bisulphide. Outdoors, in Calif., flood-ing the fields for several weeks is the most practical measure. Do not confuse Centipede with Millepede (which see)—a related but smaller insect with many more body segments and much shorter legs, which moves more slowly and is a real pest, feeding upon plant roots, bulbs, etc.

CENTIPEDE GRASS (*Eremochloa ophiuroides*). A grass introduced from Asia and recommended for lawns and pastures in the South, where it has been tested by the Florida Experiment Station. It spreads by means of runners; is able to withstand drought, and is propagated by cuttings (called stolons) which are planted in spring and summer in well-prepared soil. See also LAWN.

CENTIPEDE-PLANT. One of the common names for Homalocladium (Ribbon-bush), a curious and interesting plant with flattened, jointed stems. It is grown in the far S. and sometimes as a pot plant.

CENTRADENIA (sen-trah-dee'-ni-ah). Small evergreen shrubby plants from Central America. Very ornamental for warm greenhouse culture, with colorful leaves, small pink or white flowers and capsular fruits. They grow best with plenty of leafmold and sand in the soil, and appreciate liquid manure when established. Propagated by cuttings. The principal species are:

C. floribunda, with slightly angled reddish stems, leaves red beneath, and clusters of pink flowers.

grandifolia, with 4-winged stems, larger leaves bright red beneath, and showy clusters of light rose flowers. Cut sprays are very decorative and last well.

CENTRANTHUS (sen-tran'-thus) or KENTRANTHUS. A genus of annual and perennial plants of the Valerian Family, long popular for use in the garden. The small flowers are white or red and borne in dense terminal clusters. The plants grow well in the open border and are easily increased by seed or division. *C. ruber* (Jupiters Beard or Red Valerian) was a very common feature in old gardens. It is a handsome perennial growing to 3 ft. and blooming all summer. There is a white-flowered form, var. *albus. C. angustifolius,* also perennial, to 2 ft., has clear rose flowers that are very fragrant. *C. macrosiphon* is an annual growing to 2 ft. and bearing very pretty rose flowers.

CENTROPOGON (sen-trop'-oh-gon). Tropical American shrubby plants of somewhat scandent (climbing) habit, belonging to the Lobelia Family. In cultivation they are usually grown in a warm greenhouse, showing to good advantage in hanging-baskets. Propagated by cuttings, they thrive best in a sandy fibrous loam. The best known is *C. lucyanus,* said to be a hybrid. It has shiny green, fine-toothed leaves, and long tubular rosy-carmine flowers at the ends of the shoots.

CENTROSEMA (sen-troh-see'-mah). Butterfly-pea. Twining plants of the Pea Family, chiefly grown as cover-crops in the tropics. One species, *C. virginianum,* found from New Jersey S., is a perennial vine with white to purplish flowers, blooming the first year from seed.

CENTURY-PLANT. (See illustration, Plate 51.) Common name for *Agave americana,* a plant of the Amaryllis Family, which was formerly thought to have to attain the age of 100 years before blooming. The name is loosely applied to other plants of similar appearance. See AGAVE.

CEPHALANTHUS (sef-ah-lan'-thus). A small genus of hardy trees and shrubs, popularly known as Button-bush, which see.

CEPHALARIA (se-fah-lay'-ri-ah). A genus of Old-World annual and perennial coarse herbs bearing, from June to August, flowers much like those of scabiosa and both effective in the open garden and lasting well when cut. The colors range from creamy-white through various tints of yellow. Ordinary garden soil is satisfactory, and propagation is by seeds or cuttings.

CEPHALOCEREUS (sef-ah-loh-see'-re-us). Members of this genus of the Cactus Family are mostly columnar in habit. Sometimes there is developed a mass of wool at or near the top, or long wool or hair may grow from the areoles. *C. senilis* is well known as the "old man cactus." The long white hair that covers the young plants is parted at the top. Considered a great curiosity it commands a ready sale, though is usually quite high in price. It grows wild in great abundance in the State of Hidalgo, Mexico, and, though it grows to great size, it can be easily cut, as it contains very little woody fibre. It is usually seen as a small specimen, but the Huntington Botanical Gardens near Pasadena, Calif., have large specimens which have flowered.

See also CACTUS.

CEPHALOTAXUS (sef-ah-loh-tak'-sus). Plum-yew. A few species of ever-green trees and shrubs from Asia, hardy into N. Y. and New England. Desirable ornamental material, coarser than the Yew (Taxus) but more graceful and bearing reddish-brown, plum-like fruits 1 in. long. Cultural methods are those of conifers.

C. drupacea is a tree to 30 ft., with several varieties. Hardy in sheltered positions but slow-growing.

C. fortuni has slender branches and is the most graceful; in nature a tree, under cultivation it usually remains shrubby. *C. oliveri* is still smaller with small, closely set, spine-pointed leaves.

CEPHALOTUS (sef-ah-loh'-tus). A genus of interesting, insectivorous plants related to the Saxifrage Family. The one cultivated species (*C. follicularis*) is not a garden subject but can be raised under a bell-jar in a cool greenhouse. The potted plants should be set in saucers of water and the soil should be covered with peat moss to prevent its dying out. Plants produce a few true leaves, then a set of richly-colored little pitcher-shaped leaves ½ to 1½ in. long. They are covered with glands which serve to attract insects, which are caught, and digested in the fluid secreted in the pitchers. The plants are increased by separating pieces of the rhizome or by seed.

See also INSECTIVOROUS PLANTS.

CERASTIUM (se-ras'-ti-um). Hardy herbaceous annuals and perennials, valuable for their spreading, mat-forming habit, and attractive silvery-white foliage and showy white, star-shaped flowers in May and June. When plants, which are only 3 to 6 in. high, are in full bloom, their creeping stems covering the ground, the effect is that of a snowdrift, which accounts for the name Snow-in-Summer, given to *C. tomentosum,* the most popular and widely grown species. Because of the nature of its growth, this plant is especially fitted for a place in the rock garden; and because of its preference for a sunny location and a dry soil it is valuable as a ground cover. It also does well in the border or in beds as an edging plant. Propagation is by seeds, division or cuttings taken aften flowering. The genus as a whole is called Mouse-ear Chickweed. In addition to *C. tomentosum,* some useful perennial species are:

C. alpinum. Native to Arctic N. America and Europe; 6 in.; with silky hair.

arvense (Starry Grasswort). 10 in.; densely tufted, with erect or rising stems;

flowers white, numerous and very early (April and May).

grandiflorum. 8 in.; creeping; grayish leaves; flowers transparent white.

lerchenfeldianum. 8 in.; erect.

CERASUS (ser'-ah-sus). Formerly the name of a genus in which were grouped several species now included under Prunus, it is still so used in some nursery catalogs in connection with certain forms of ornamental "flowering cherries." However, it is now the accepted specific name for the sour cherry, *Prunus cerasus.*

CERATONIA (ser-ah-toh'-ni-ah). Siliqua. An evergreen tree native to the Mediterranean region, cultivated in S. Calif. and Fla. for its edible flattened pods called St. Johns Bread. The plant is also known as Carob, which see.

CERATOPHYLLUM (ser-ah-toh-fil'-um) *demersum.* Known by several common names, the most used being Hornwort (which see), this aquatic is found growing in ponds of all regions of the U. S. Its principal use is the unheated aquarium.

CERATOPTERIS (ser-ah-top'-ter-is). A genus of small, mostly tropical ferns suitable only for specialized greenhouse conditions. See FLOATING FERN.

CERATOSTIGMA (ser-ah-toh-stig'-mah). A small group of hardy perennial herbs of the Leadwort Family (Plumbaginaceae), with shining leaves, natives of the Orient. They are of dwarf habit—from 6 to 12 in.—and are especially desirable in the rock garden, where they continue in bloom late into the fall. The saucer-shaped flowers are blue. One species, *C. willmottianum,* is a shrub attaining 5 ft. and producing bright blue flowers from July to November. They require good drainage. Propagation is by division, or by cuttings rooted under glass during July and August.

CERATOZAMIA (ser-ah-toh-zay'-mi-ah). A group of handsome Mexican plants with stiff, palm-like leaves in a whorl at the top of a short trunk. The young leaves are a rich bronzy, chocolate tint, which later changes to olive green. Six species are recognized, but only two or three are grown. A peaty soil with some sand is best. Propagation is by suckers, or from the rarely formed seeds.

CERCIDIPHYLLUM (ser-sid-i-fil'-um) *japonicum.* A bushy, deciduous tree from Japan, hardy in New England and preferring rich, moist soil. Ornamental and desirable for street and garden planting. See KATSURA-TREE.

CERCOCARPUS (ser-koh-kahr'-pus). A genus of small trees, often evergreen, of the N. W. succeeding in dry sunny places and sometimes used as shrubs. See MOUNTAIN-MAHOGANY.

CERCIS (sur'-sis). A genus of trees and shrubs of the Legume Family native in N. America, S. Europe and Asia, bearing pink or red flowers before the leaves. Common names are Judas-tree and Redbud, which see.

CERCOSPORA (sur-kos'-poh-rah) **LEAFSPOT** (also called cercospora blight). A plant disease caused by various species of the imperfect fungus, cercospora. The spots on leaves are generally reddish-brown, of irregular shape, often with a purplish margin. As they grow older they become ashen gray at the center because of the presence of spores. This fungus causes many common leaf spots on trees and shrubs, vegetables and ornamentals; that on beets and the early blight of celery are among those economically important. Zinnia leaf spot is very disfiguring. For control measures see under FUNGUS and the various plants especially affected.

CEREUS (see'-re-us). A genus of cacti; but many of the plants formerly listed under this heading are now called by other names, as for example: Aporocactus, Heliocereus (Sun-cereus), Selenicereus (Moon-cereus), Hylocereus, *Carnegeia gigantea,* the Arizona state flower, which used to be *Cereus giganteus,* etc. It is true that those accustomed to the old names still retain them, calling them all "cereus."

One species that still rightfully retains its name is a common plant in cactus gardens old and new, *Cereus peruvianus.*

See also CACTUS; CARNEGEIA.

CERIMAN (ser'-i-man). Common name for a tropical, woody climber with large leaves irregularly cut and perforated; grown in greenhouses as a curiosity. See MONSTERA.

CERINTHE (se-rin'-thee). A genus of Old-World herbs with yellow flowers easily grown from seed. See HONEYWORT.

CEROPEGIA (see-roh-pee'-ji-ah). A group of about 100 species of herbs or sub-shrubs belonging to the Milkweed Family, native to tropical Asia, Africa and the Malay Peninsula. In temperate regions they are greenhouse plants, in most cases twining, but some species are erect. Their flowers, more curious than beautiful, are often swollen at the base. They require a peaty loam with some sand and fragments of charcoal, and are propagated by cuttings of small sideshoots in the spring, rooted in sand over bottom heat.

CESPITOSE (ses'-pi-tohs). Growing in tufts or dense bunches; or thereby forming mats or turf, like the Maiden Pinks (*Dianthus deltoides*), or *Phlox subulata*.

CESTRUM (ses'-trum). Shrubs or small trees of the Nightshade Family, natives of tropical America. A few species are grown in greenhouses and outside in the warmer parts of the United States. As pillar or wall plants under glass they are attractive in winter with their bright flowers. Propagation is by cuttings. Principal species (the first two of which were formerly put in the genus Habrothamnus) are:

C. elegans. A tall and slender halfclimber, with loose clusters of red-purple flowers produced over a long season. Var. *smithi* has flowers of pale rose.

fasciculatum has larger flowers in more compact and leafy clusters. Var. *newelli* has larger and more brilliant flowers.

diurnum (Day-jessamine). A tall evergreen shrub with thick glossy leaves and white flowers, fragrant in the day.

nocturnum (Night-jessamine). A bushy shrub with slender branches and creamywhite flowers, fragrant at night.

CEYLON-CREEPER. A common name for the genus Scindapsus, better known as IVY-ARUM, which see.

CEYLON-GOOSEBERRY. Common name for *Dovyalis hebecarpa*, a small tree of Ceylon and India that bears an edible fruit resembling a ripe gooseberry.

CHAENOMELES (ke-nom'-el-eez). Flowering-quince. Formerly, and still sometimes, classified as Cydonia, this is a genus of hardy deciduous or half-evergreen shrubs of the Rose Family. Highly ornamental with their glossy leaves, showy flowers in early spring, and hard green fruits that resemble quinces and give use to the common name, Flowering-quince, they are useful in shrub borders, for a hedge, or trained against a wall. They thrive in any good soil, doing best in a sunny place; and are propagated by seed, root-cuttings, and grafting. The fruits are not edible raw but are occasionally used in preserving.

C. lagenaria (Japanese-quince), is often listed as *C. japonica*. It is a vigorous spiny shrub to 6 ft. or more, with lustrous leaves held late, and large scarlet-red flowers in the type species. There are many named varieties with flowers of varying shades, from pure white to deep scarlet, and some with semi-double flowers.

japonica (formerly *C. maulei*) is a low, spreading grower, with spiny branches and bright orange-scarlet flowers. Var. *alpina* is a dwarf form with prostrate branches, very free in fruiting.

sinensis (Chinese-quince) grows to 20 ft. and is spineless. It has light pink flowers and leaves which turn scarlet in late fall. It is not hardy N. See also QUINCE.

CHAENOSTOMA (ke-nos'-toh-mah). A genus of African herbs or shrubby plants of the Figwort Family grown in the greenhouse in the N. and occasionally planted out in mild climates. The flowers are showy, white, yellow or reddish, somewhat starry in shape, and grow in racemes. The plants are propagated by seeds or cuttings. *C. hispidum* grows 2 ft. high and is a perennial, sometimes assuming shrubby growth. The flowers are pinkish or white, profusely produced. It is frequently planted in California.

CHAFER, ROSE. This insect, known also as the Rose Beetle and, in some localities, as the Hessian Bug, is a troublesome garden enemy, though not as serious as it used to be before improved cultural methods and the use of modern spray materials became so general in average garden practice. The long-legged, lanky, awkward beetles, $\frac{1}{3}$ to $\frac{1}{2}$ in. long and of a light molasses-yellow color, attack buds and open flowers, eating right into the heart and resisting all but the most persistent attempts to fight them with poison sprays. They also attack grapes (both foliage and the young fruit), apple trees, peonies and other garden plants.

When not too numerous they can be kept down by hand-picking into a vessel of kerosene. As they are clumsy and slow to fly, many can be jarred onto sheets of papers spread under bushes or vines. As the grubs or larvae spend the winter in the ground (they closely resemble the common white grubs, which see) many can be destroyed by digging the soil late in the fall and exposing the grubs to freezing weather (They are especially numerous in sandy soils.) Also, if hens or ducks can be

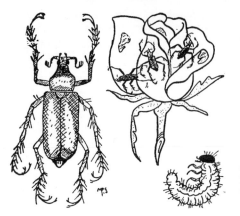

ONE OF THE ROSE'S WORST PESTS

The rose chafer. Left, the beetle enlarged. Right, its larva. Above, how it attacks and ruins roses.

allowed to run among the plants in early June when the young beetles are emerging, they will devour large numbers.

While it is impossible to recommend any one spray material as positively, invariably, and entirely effective against this pest, various practical gardeners frequently report gratifying success with different kinds of poisonous sprays and dusts and also some of the newer non-poisonous or contact sprays. So if one kind does not seem to give control, try others. In any case spraying (or dusting) must be done frequently and thoroughly from the time the first beetles appear until they vanish early in July after laying eggs. Soil poisoning, as recommended in the control of Japanese beetles (which see), should also prove helpful by destroying the grubs.

There is a related but somewhat smaller and broader beetle of another species known as the European Rose Chafer which, though less common in this country, is also a pest. The same measures should be used against it.

CHAIN FERN. A common name for the genus Woodwardia, which includes three American species found in acid soil.

CHALICE VINE (*Solandra*). Stout climbing shrubs belonging to the Nightshade Family. Sometimes grown in warm greenhouses, and outside in the warmer parts of the United States, they like plenty of sunlight at all times and a soil not too rich, as rank growth produces few flowers. The growing and flowering season under glass is from fall to spring.

While the plants are resting in summer keep them on the dry side. They object to much root disturbance, but top-dressings of new soil will suffice for two years or more. Propagated by cuttings of half-ripened shoots taken with a heel.

S. grandiflorum, from the W. Indies, is the tallest grower, reaching 30 ft. or more. It has thick leathery leaves and fragrant white or yellowish flowers, nearly a foot long.

guttatum, from Mexico, growing to 12 ft. or more, has leaves to 6 in. long, and yellow fragrant flowers spotted purple, about 9 in. long.

CHAMAECYPARIS (kam-ee-sip'-ah-ris). A genus of evergreen plants of the Pine Family, commonly called False cypress. Young plants, like those of the genus Thuja, differ in appearance from the older plants and for that reason certain species were formerly placed in a separate genus called Retinispora. Though still so used in catalogs, that name really means juvenile forms of the two genera.

All five species of Chamaecyparis grow naturally to great size—100 ft. or more, but for garden use the shrubby, compact forms are more useful and better known, being especially desirable for hedges or foundation plantings. Partly shaded and sheltered locations and plenty of room between plants give the best results. Plants are not hard to move if dug with a large ball of earth properly wrapped in burlap, and if the roots are kept from drying or exposure to the sun. The foliage may burn in winter in exposed places or if the soil gets too dry. Choice specimens should therefore be protected by screens or tents of burlap and the soil should be well supplied with water in late fall to prevent such injury. Light shearing in alternate years improves the form and texture.

ENEMIES. Two Gymnosporangium rust diseases may cause deformation or death of white-cedar. One, causing witches' brooms, must be fought by removing the alternate hosts nearby, namely bayberry, sweet-fern and wax-myrtle. The other rust, causing swelling of the branches, has for its alternate host the shadbush (Amelanchier). Juniper blight (see JUNIPER) may cause serious damage following winter injury.

The bag-worm is sometimes found on this host but on the whole Chamaecyparis is exempt from insect attack.

For cultivation see EVERGREENS.

PRINCIPAL SPECIES

Of the half-dozen species, *C. thyoides* (White-cedar) is valuable for planting in wet ground. It grows naturally in the North in swamps, often making dense, almost impenetrable, stands. The light, elastic and durable wood is particularly suited for making trellises and arbors; even untreated it will endure for many years without decaying.

C. lawsoniana is a beautiful tree with horizontal, spreading, usually drooping branches, frond-like foliage and bright red catkins. There are more than 60 cultivated varieties with variously colored or marked foliage and differing habits. *C. obtusa* (Hinoki-cypress) is much used in the varietal forms which accentuate the fan-shaped structure of the sprays. *C. pisifera* (Sawara-cypress) has several slow-growing varieties with varying types of foliage.

CHAMAEDAPHNE (kam-ee-daf'-nee). A hardy native evergreen shrub whose one species (*C. calyculata*) is called Leatherleaf, which see.

CHAMAEDOREA (kam-ee-doh'-ree-ah). A genus of slender, shade-loving palms, found from Mexico S. The stems are mostly ringed or jointed like reeds, and some species take on a climbing habit. A few species are sometimes grown under glass, thriving best under warm, moist, shady conditions. *C. desmoncoides* has leaves to 3 ft. long, with narrow drooping leaflets, and stems which eventually climb. *C. elegans* is a graceful grower to 8 ft., sometimes with clustered stems. *C. glaucifolia* grows to 20 ft. and is one of the most decorative, with long glaucous leaves divided into 70 to 80 leaflets. *C. graminifolia* is considered the most graceful, having leaves composed of many grass-like leaflets, which give it a very plumy appearance.

CHAMAELIRIUM (kam-ee-li'-ri-um) *luteum.* Popularly known as Blazing Star, or Devils Bit, this is a tuberous-rooted perennial belonging to the Lily Family, found from W. N. Y. to Ill. and from Mass. southward to Fla. and Ark. It grows to a height of 4 ft., and bears bright, yellowish-white flowers in spike-like sprays from May to July. It needs a moist, peaty soil and a shady location. Propagation is by offsets which are taken at the close of the blooming season.

CHAMAEPERICLYMENUM (kam-ee-per-i-kly'-men-um). Alternative name for *Cornus canadensis,* the Bunchberry. See CORNUS.

CHAMAERANTHEMUM (kam-ee-ran'-the-mum). A group of 6 dwarf evergreen herbs with handsome foliage, natives of Brazil. They are essentially greenhouse plants, and are rarely found in cultivation. Their flowers are small, the plants' attraction lying in the ornamental markings of the large leaves—with veinings, stripings, marblings and edgings of white, silvery gray, orange or red. The species most often seen is *C. igneum,* with dark green leaves margined with bands of orange or yellow. They require a fibrous, loamy soil with some sand. Propagation is by cuttings rooted in sand over bottom heat.

CHAMAEROPS (kah-mee'-rops). The European Fan Palm is a small member of that group, usually growing in clumps, but sometimes rising with a single trunk to a height of 20 ft. *C. humilis,* a single species with many varieties is the only palm native to Europe. It has large, round leaves, cut to the center and is widely grown in the garden and under glass. It is the hardiest palm, a specimen having lived outdoors as far N. as Edinburgh, Scotland. It is easily grown in Fla. and Calif. and is most effective when grouped as a foreground planting. Mulching with well-rotted manure during the rainy season, and occasional applications of commercial fertilizers, are beneficial practices.

CHAMISO (chah-mee'-soh). Common name for the genus Adenostoma, a group of heath-like S. Calif. shrubs grown in sunny positions for their white flowers.

CHAMOMILE (kam'-oh-myl) or CAMOMILE. Common name often applied to the two genera Anthemis and Matricaria, both of which have scented foliage and the typical daisy-like flowers of the Composite Family. Sweet Camomile and Scentless Camomile are species of Boltonia and Matricaria.

CHARCOAL. This material is of value in plant growing as a soil amendment (which see). That is, it does not contribute any of the essential plant-food elements, but tends to have a beneficial effect on the general chemical condition of a soil. Made up mostly of carbon, it may contain very small quantities of phosphoric acid (.16%) and potash (.4%), but its usefulness lies in its ability to absorb impurities from the soil solution.

It is therefore often mixed with the soil in which plants are to be grown in pots, especially orchids, ferns and bulbs. Or in somewhat coarser form it may be mixed with the drainage material in the bottom of the pots. A bit of charcoal placed in the water in a vase will also serve to keep conditions sweet, thereby preventing mold and the unpleasant effects of decay.

CHARD, SWISS. This plant, often called Leaf Beet, or Sea-kale Beet, is a variety of the common beet (*Beta vulgaris,* var. *cicla*), grown for its large leaves and broad, thick, pale or white leaf stalks. The former are used as greens, the latter like asparagus. In a newly introduced strain, the stalks and larger leaf veins are dark, rich ruby red, resembling those of rhubarb and suggesting the variety's trade name, Rhubarb Chard. While equally as good for eating as the type, it is also a brilliantly ornamental plant while growing and will probably prove popular for use in "flower" arrangements. Culture is the same as for beets except that the plants should be at least 12 in. asunder in rows at least 18 in. apart. As the outer leaves attain usable size they may be cut or broken off close to the crown. Others will develop from the center so one planting will yield from midsummer until frost. Both leaves and stems are keenly relished by chickens. See BETA (VULGARIS) and BEET.

CHARIEIS (kay-ry-ee'-is). A S. African genus of the Composite Family containing one species, *C. heterophylla.* The plants grow 6 to 12 in. high and bear daisy-like flowers with blue or yellow rays and yellow disks. It is a pretty little annual of the easiest culture, for the seeds may be sown where the plants are to grow, or started early in the spring in a hotbed and transplanted to the open. It is excellent as an annual filler in the dry rock wall. It is sometimes listed in catalogs as *Kaulfussia amelloides.*

CHARITY. A common name for *Polemonium caeruleum,* also known as Jacobs Ladder and Greek Valerian, a perennial herb with blue, lilac, and white flowers, easily grown in good soil.

CHARLOCK. One of the common names for *Brassica arvensis,* an annual weed of the Mustard Family, which spreads rapidly through fields and waste places and along roadsides. It has small, yellow flowers and its seeds are sometimes used as a substitute for table mustard.

CHASTE-TREE. One of several common names for *Vitex agnus-castus,* a rather tender shrub or small tree with leaves dark green above and grayish-woolly beneath. The lavender or white flowers are borne in spikes to 7 in. long.

CHAYOTE (chah-yoh'-tay). One of the names given to *Sechium edule,* a vine of the Gourd Family (Cucurbitaceae), much planted in Tropical America for its edible tubers and fruit, which is also known as Christophine or Chuchu, and in other places as Vegetable-pear. It is perennial in warm climates and suitable for growing in both Fla. and Calif., and, if treated as annual, even farther N. if the growing season is rather long. The fruit is pear-shaped, green or white, 3 to 4 in. long and contains one large seed. The tubers are harvested after two years' growth, the leaves supply forage, the young parts are used as greens, or pot herbs, and the fruit is much esteemed boiled and prepared in various ways. Start plants where they are to stand, 8 to 12 ft. apart, planting the whole fruit.

CHECKERBERRY. A common name for *Gaultheria procumbens,* a creeping, evergreen shrub of E. U. S. It is also called Teaberry, but more generally Wintergreen.

CHECKERBLOOM. Common name for *Sidalcea malvaeflora,* a Calif. perennial with rosy-purple flowers resembling those of the mallow.

CHECKERED-LILY. Common name for *Fritillaria meleagris* (also called Snakes-head), hardy bulbous herb whose flowers are checkered with maroon.

CHEDDAR (ched'-ahr) **PINK.** Common name for *Dianthus caesius,* a European hardy species forming compact mats of foliage and bearing fragrant, rose-colored flowers on 3 to 12 in. stems.

CHEESES. The common name, especially among children, for the round, flattened green seed-pods of *Malva rotundifolia,* a spreading weedy plant of the Mallow Family. See MALVA; also WEEDS.

CHEILANTHES (ky-lan'-theez). Lip Fern. A genus of ferns, several of which are common in various parts of the United States. They are chiefly small, britle plants, bearing their fruit dots toward the margin of the pinnae so that when ripe they are party covered by their rolled back edges. The indusia form little pouches, suggesting the name Lip Fern. The American species grow on trap rock, and are hairy or woolly, with much-divided leaves. They require some sunlight, as their hairiness retards evaporation. Excellent for rockeries, walls, and places too dry for other ferns. Do not wet the fronds, use porous soil, and add a little charcoal from time to time. Several exotic species are available for greenhouse cultivation, their undersides having a golden or silvery farina much resembling those of the genus Gymnogramme.

SPECIES

C. alabamensis. A S. type, 2 to 10 in., 2-pinnate, with shiny black petioles and black stipes, woolly below. The only one with smooth fronds.

lanosa or *vestita* (Hairy Lip Fern). A New England species, 7 to 15 in. tall, with rough, brownish stipes, and 2-pinnate blades.

tomentosa (Woolly Lip Fern). 8 to 18 ins., the terminal pinnules longer than the others, and all thickly covered with whitish wool. From Ky. through Tex. to Ariz.

feei (Slender Lip Fern). 3 to 8 ins. long; fronds 2 to 3 pinnate, forming tangled mats on dry cliffs in the Middle W. and S. W.

californica or *gracillima* (California Lace Fern). Densely tufted, glossy, 5 in. fronds, deeply cut, and produced from deep roots.

CHEIRANTHUS (ky-ran'-thus). A genus of garden perennials of the Crucifer Family, several species of which rank among the showiest members of the group. The Wallflower which accompanies the daffodils in every English garden is *Cheiranthus cheiri,* occurring in tones from bright yellow through rich maroon to brown and occasionally purple, and growing from ½ to 2 ft. high. *C. allioni,* properly *Erysimum asperum,* is the brilliant orange Siberian Wallflower. *C. kewensis* is a hybrid of bushy character with brownish flowers, used for indoor bloom. There are other species, some of which are confused with Mathiola (which see) also Erysimum, with which Cheiranthus hybridizes. See WALLFLOWER.

CHELIDONIUM (kel-i-doh'-ni-um) *majus.* A biennial or perennial herb sometimes grown from seed in wild gardens for its yellow flowers and commonly called Celandine, which see.

CHELONE (ke-loh'-nee). A group of N. American hardy, herbaceous perennials closely resembling Penstemon, belonging to the Figwort Family and known as Turtlehead from the shape of the flowers. They are, appropriately, grown in the wild garden in a damp situation in partial shade and are propagated by seed or division.

C. glabra (White Turtle-head or Snakehead) grows to 3 ft., the flowers being white or pinkish.

lyoni, which also grows to 3 ft., has rosepurple flowers. Though found wild in the mountains of N. C., S. C. and Tenn., it is perfectly hardy in the N. and makes an interesting variation planted with the white-flowered species.

CHEMICAL GARDENING. All gardening is fundamentally chemical gardening. The plant absorbs through the roots certain inorganic chemical substances that are essential for growth and production. This is true whether the plant is growing in a soil as such, in water, or in sand, gravel or cinders. Specifically however, the term has come to be applied to a method of growing plants in nutrient solutions in some inert material such as those just mentioned.

The study of the growth of plants has always interested farmers and scientists and certain facts about the fertilization of plants have been known for ages. But it was not until comparatively recent times (late in the 18th century, in fact) that scientific reasoning came into the picture. About the middle of the nineteenth century, as knowledge of chemistry and botany advanced, plants were grown in solutions whose chemical relationships were carefully worked out, and through the work of those early investigators, many facts pertaining to plant growth became known. There are certain chemical elements that are necessary in relatively large amounts. Certain other elements, just as necessary but only in very minute amounts are called, therefore, trace elements, which see. About 1914, more intensive researches into the nutrient requirements of plants were begun and finally, several investigators in their publications suggested, as a result of their work, that there were possible practical applications of the laboratory method of growing plants in nutrient solutions.

This suggestion, given wide publicity, captured the popular imagination and led both to another new industry—the compounding and sale of chemicals for growing plants—and to the writing of many books upon the subject for amateurs and commercial plant growers.

It should be understood at the beginning that chemical gardening is not a panacea

READY TO PLANT

Sown on a blotter, seeds will sprout and seedlings will grow if supplied with nutrient solution. The method is not practical for growing plants to maturity. After the seedlings are a few inches tall, it is easier to care for them in sand or soil, and they can then be transplanted.

for all plant growing ills. Unless all the environmental factors, such as light, temperature, etc., are satisfactory, plants will grow no better in chemical gardening than in soil gardening. Furthermore, the nutrient solutions used are generally satisfactory only in sand, gravel, cinders or water culture. For gardening in soil, the general run of familiar commercial fertilizers will yield more satisfactory results. The nutrient solutions of chemical gardening may be used in the soil only after considerable knowledge of plant growth has been obtained and only with experience.

Chemical gardening should be attempted usually only under controlled conditions, that is, in the house where the plants can be observed frequently and certain environmental factors can be kept under control. If plant growing is practiced out of doors in summer, it should be done, not in the open ground, but in containers in a situation where air currents and the moisture condition of the root medium can be controlled.

ADVANTAGES. Chemical gardening as applied to growing plants in a house—whether dwelling or greenhouse—has certain advantages over soil culture. Sand, cinders, or water are more readily obtained, especially by amateur or home gardeners, than is good soil. Such a medium does not have to be changed as frequently as does soil. Diseases and insect pests, frequently encountered in soil, are not (or are very rarely) present in sand, cinders, or gravel. In soil, the organic material (humus) needed to maintain its physical condition must be renewed and the soil itself changed frequently. In chemical gardening, the supply of mineral elements may readily be adjusted to the condition of growth of the plant and the amount of sunlight. If the supply of nutrients is too great, they can be flushed out; if more or less of any particular elements is needed, this modification can easily be made. In sand and cinder cultures moisture relationships and the aeration of the root medium are better than in soil. In extensive operations the cost of chemicals and their application is lower than in the case of soil. Plants in chemical culture make a more uniformly developed and sometimes larger and more compact root system, but will nevertheless grow in a smaller root area because of the efficiency and ready availability of the nutrient supply. The plants, however, require just as much space in one method as in the other.

DISADVANTAGES. Chemical gardening has certain disadvantages, too. The cost of plant growing containers or vessels may be higher, as they must be waterproof; however, plants can be grown in the regulation type flower-pot. Provision, either temporary or permanent as a part of the plant growing structure, must be made for the drainage of excess solution. The plants in sand or cinders may require more frequent attention than those grown in soil, in order to keep the root medium moist; however, in large scale operations this can often be handled mechanically. More attention must be given to the pH reaction (alkalinity or acidity) of the medium, than is usually the case with soil.

REQUIREMENTS FOR THE GROWTH OF PLANTS

Growing plants is an art, the art of adjusting the supply of plant food materials and the environment to secure a balance that will result in good plants. Knowledge enabling one to do this can be obtained only in part by reading; much of it must come from experience, the observation of the subject and its environment, and then correct interpretation of cause and effect.

There are certain fundamental facts that every plant grower should appreciate. First of all, the growing plant is a wonderful, complex organism. The great bulk of it is water, and of the solid substance, by far the greatest part is made up of carbonaceous materials, which are manufactured as simple sugars in the leaves, by the process of photosynthesis, which see. This implies, then, that a very small proportion of the dry matter consists of the mineral elements taken in through the roots.

The simple sugars are soluble and move about through the plant. Part are transformed into more complex sugars and starches, some of which are stored for future use (as in the sugar beet and sugar cane). Part of the sugars are transformed into fats and oils, and into starches. Other parts may be changed into cellulose of various types that make up the "skeleton" or stiff framework of the plant, and which furnish the vegetable fibers used in commerce, as hemp, flax, sisal, cotton.

A portion of the sugars is transported to the roots, and combined with nitrogen, which is taken into the plant as ammonia or as nitrate, to form amino acids or proteins. Some of the proteins are stored at once for future use (as in seeds, such as beans and peas) while others are used to make up the protoplasm or living stuff that fills the plant cells. A portion of the amino acids is transported to the leaves to maintain the green coloring matter (chlorophyll). If anything should happen to the roots so that nitrogen is not absorbed, the leaves of the plant will become yellow. One factor that contributes to this condition is lack of aeration in the root medium. Most plants require air about the roots, from which they absorb oxygen; sufficient air cannot enter soil that is very fine and dense, or too wet, and as a result the leaves of plants growing in such soil turn yellow.

Besides the proper amount of nutrients, an adequate water supply, and the air supply about the roots, there are other environmental factors that have a bearing upon the growth of plants. First, and perhaps most important, is an adequate amount of *direct sunlight*. Sunlight is vital in providing the energy source for photosynthesis. One reason why plants do not flower well in the house is lack of sunlight. Even when placed near a window in a dwelling, flowering plants cannot receive all the sunlight they need for growth and reproduction. How much less they receive when drapes or curtains are interposed is evidenced in the poor growth they make.

Some of the foliage plants, on the other hand, such as ferns, do well with a minimum amount of sunlight, and will often thrive where the only light received is reflected from the sky, as in a north window.

Next in order of importance, perhaps, is *temperature*. During the day time, plants manufacture and elaborate foods and to do this, the proper room temperature is necessary. If it is too low, nitrogen cannot be utilized. For most plants which we may reasonably expect to grow in the house, a room temperature of 70 deg. F. is adequate, provided sunlight and atmospheric humidity are also right. It is the night temperature, perhaps, that has the greatest bearing upon the health of plants, for it is

CHEMICAL GARDENING IN THE HOME
A simple set-up in which the nutrient solution in inverted globe is fed by a wick to the plant and then drains into the jar below.

during the night that plants make most of their growth. If the temperature is too high, so much growth is made that the plant will be succulent or soft, and this will mean the utilization of the reserves of stored food. The plant is not able to manufacture sufficient food during the day time, and the result will be a leggy specimen. Night temperatures should be between 45 and 55 deg. F. during the season of the year when the sunlight is of low intensity.

Another important matter is *humidity*. The air contains at all times varying amounts of water. The relation between the temperature of the air and the amount of moisture held in the air is called relative humidity. It and the moisture requirement of plants are closely related and strongly influence the type of growth made as well as upon the composition of the plant tissue. When the moisture content of the air is high, the amount of water transpired by the leaves will be relatively low. Ferns require a relatively high humidity, about 45 per cent. During the summer they may grow well, but when brought indoors in the autumn, after the fires are started, they will practically stop growing, because the relative humidity will be only around 20 to 25 per cent. Plants grown in a high humidity are soft, succulent, and contain a comparatively high percentage of water. If grown in relatively low humidity, the leaves are smaller, the growth is harder, and the leaves do not wilt so readily, because they have little water to lose and give it up slowly. A florist, growing crops to sell, keeps his plants in a high humidity because, through his ability to control other factors of the environment, he gets faster growth. When such plants are transferred to the ordinary household, quick wilting follows, because the humidity is too low. When plants are grown in groups close together, there is less danger of wilting, because of the amount of water vapor transpired by them. A plant by itself is apt to wilt more quickly. Frequent syringing with a fine spray will also help to maintain humidity. Also when a plant that has been grown in a relatively high humidity is subjected to a draft or current of air, it will wilt quickly, because the moving air dries out that around the plant. Plants can adapt themselves to changes, sometimes by actually changing the structure or reducing the size of new leaves. But this can only come about gradually, by what is known as a hardening-off process in which temperature and humidity are gradually decreased until the plant loses its extreme succulence.

All the factors mentioned are interdependent. The plant must have an adequate supply of mineral nutrients in proper balance in an adequate supply of water, in air of the proper temperature and humidity, in the presence of an adequate amount of direct sunlight and with the leaves clean so that the carbon dioxide of the air may enter. If any one of these factors is out of adjustment, the plant does not grow well.

Science gives us these organized facts. He who would grow plants must take them and fit them to his circumstances. The art of growing plants is derived from the adjustment of conditions so as to secure optimum results.

HANDLING PLANTS IN CHEMICAL GARDENING

When first attempting to grow plants by this method, it is suggested that the simplest and easiest way be tried first.

The first step is to provide the proper sort of receptacle and to decide what technique is to be followed. For the beginner, a flower pot, either a rough, unglazed, clay florist's pot, or an ornamental glazed pot would probably be the best container to start with. For an individual plant a 6, 8 or 10 in. pot is recommended, the size referring to the *inside* diameter of the top. It should be provided with a drainage hole, so that excess solution may drain away. If it has a tight bottom, salts will accumulate, causing injury to the roots and hence to the whole plant. Under the receptacle should be placed some vessel to receive the drainage. A simple way would be to use a pan large enough to contain all the solution that will run through and place the plant container in it but upon pieces of brick so that its bottom will be above the level of the liquid at all times, permitting free drainage.

Next is the selection of the root medium. Again, for the beginner, it is suggested that sand of a coarse concrete grade or fine cinders be used. With either of these materials, fairly rapid drainage with good aeration follows the application of the solution; yet both of them hold sufficient water to maintain turgidity in the plant. For specific directions for preparing the sand and cinders, see SAND CULTURE and CINDER CULTURE.

CONSTANT-DRIP METHOD. As to the manner of supplying the nutrients, the constant-drip method is recommended until the operator becomes familiar with the growth and appearance of the plants under his care, when some other can be followed. The object of the constant drip method is to apply to the material in which the plant is growing, drop by drop, about a quart of nutrient solution a day. As it drains through the root medium, the solution draws fresh air after it, thus providing good aeration. Some sort of reservoir should be elevated just above the edge of the vessel used for growing; it can be set upon a stand, or a bracket can be attached to the edge of the culture vessel. A good type of reservoir is made by inverting a quart fruit jar filled with the nutrient solution in a finger bowl. Agate pans or pottery bowls may be used, but it is advisable to cover them to keep dust out. From the reservoir the solution is siphoned over onto the material in the culture vessel and the siphon may be constructed in several ways. The one used in technical work is made of 2-millimeter-bore glass tubing with an inch or so of 0.6-millimeter capillary tubing attached at the end by means of a piece of rubber tubing. By lengthening or shortening this tube, the flow of the solution may be adjusted; the longer it is, the faster the flow. Another and very efficient form of siphon easy to construct is made of bandage gauze, rolled. The number of thicknesses and the tightness of the roll needed will be governed by the coarseness of the weave. One end of this wick is placed in the solution in the reservoir and the other end upon the root medium.

The next step is the preparation of the plants. Seedlings can be started to give a basis for the work. They enable the operator to follow the cycle of plant growth from beginning to end and can be grown by the blotter method or by the sand culture method, both of which see. They may even be raised in soil according to common practice. Another, quicker way to secure results is to buy plants already partly grown.

If the seedlings are started in soil, or if plants grown in soil are purchased, the first step is to wash all soil from the roots. This can be done with least damage to the root system by immersing the root-ball in a pail of water, and, after the soil has become saturated, swishing the plant around until all adhering particles of soil and other materials have been removed. Then rinse in clear water and the plant is ready to set in place. First flush the medium with nutrient solution until it is saturated. Then open up a hole large enough to receive the root system, insert it, and flush

HOW SOILLESS GARDENING WORKS
Here the wire tray filled with excelsior which supports the plants has been raised above the tank to show how the feeding roots extend through the wire into the nutrient solution. This is one way to give them necessary occasional aeration.

again so that the particles are washed in closely around the roots. It may be necessary to stake large plants for a few days until the roots become established, but the support can soon be removed.

Now all that is necessary is to provide the proper light conditions, temperature, fresh air and atmospheric humidity, and make sure that the plant roots secure the nutrient solution. This, as it filters through the gravel or sand, can be saved and used repeatedly for 3 or 4 weeks. But after the plant has been growing about two weeks, it is wise to give the medium a flushing with several quarts of clear water to wash out any possible accumulations of undesirable salts. After flushing with water, it is advisable to flush with a quart of nutrient solution, which, as it comes through, should be discarded, as it is diluted. Then the siphon may be started in operation again. This cleansing flushing should be repeated every two or three weeks.

"SLOP" METHOD OF FEEDING. After the operator has mastered the growing of plants through the constant-drip method, some other technique may be tried. The simplest is the "slop" method. The culture is set up as suggested, with a container to catch the drainage. Then, as often as the plant seems to need it, a pint, quart or even more (depending upon the size of the container and the season of the year as governing the growth of the plants) is slopped or poured over the medium. No harm will come to the plant if some of the solution gets on the leaves, as it is very dilute. The frequency of application will depend upon the amount of sunlight, the temperature, the relative humidity of the air—as governing growth—and the porosity of the medium. If the medium is very coarse, as cinders or fine gravel, two or three applications may be needed daily. In sand, there may be seasons of the year when one application will be all that will be needed for two or three days. Here is one place where the judgment of the operator is of more weight than any printed directions. The solution may be used repeatedly for sometimes 5 or 6 weeks, depending upon the activity of the plants. Periodical flushing should be practiced as suggested above.

All this time the grower is learning about the behavior of plants. His adventure has intrigued him and he is ready for wider experience. Now he is ready to exercise his own ingenuity in the devising of soilless window boxes (which see) and will perhaps try subirrigation, which see. At any rate, his close contact with growing plants will bring to him an appreciation of the marvels of nature, to a better comprehension of the Supreme Mind that planned it all. It will be a hobby, and a worth while hobby for any person. In a hobby, one puts away the cares of the world and thereby secures a better balance to his personality.

See also CINDER CULTURE; NUTRIENT SOLUTION.

CHEMICALS IN GARDENING.

Chemicals in some form or other influence and control the growth of all plants (see CHEMICAL GARDENING; PLANT FOOD, etc.). But many discoveries have been made during recent years regarding the application of different chemicals to promote or alter plant development. Although practical application is being made of some of these materials, others are still of only theoretical or unknown value. For the most part, the place of practically all of them is in the laboratory, the experimental garden, or the gardens of advanced amateurs who want to do their own experimenting.

Vitamin B_1, Vitamin B_2 (Riboflavin), Vitamin B_6, Nicotinic Acid, and Vitamin C have all proved to be essential plant growth needs. Some plants require but one of the vitamins for healthy growth; others seem to need a combination of two or more to get the same result. Most plants, growing normally, make all they need in their own leaves and roots, but sometimes sick plants or plants grown under unfavorable conditions are benefited by the addition of more vitamin material when water is applied.

HORMONES. Another group of chemicals of economic importance are the so-called plant hormones (which see) or growth substances. The first pure chemical used to stimulate root growth was carbon monoxide gas. The natural course of investigation led to the finding of other chemicals which are more easily applied and have greater potency and a wider range of effectiveness. Indolebutyric Acid (which see) is one of the most valuable of these root growth stimulating chemicals in general use and is readily applied to cuttings, either in solution or in powder form. Indoleacetic Acid (which see) has been considered the natural hormone, but it has not yet been isolated from, or identified in, green plant tissue though found in both animal and fungi plant tissue. It is not as effective or as valuable a root-inducing substance as indolebutyric acid. Alphanaphthaleneacetic Acid is considered one of the most potent of the root-inducing substances, but its use has been limited, in some cases, by a narrow range of effectiveness.

Uses other than to facilitate the rooting of cuttings have recently been found for some of the more active of these hormone-like materials. Naphthaleneacetic acid, at the rate of 1 part to 100,000 parts of water, has shown promise when sprayed on fruit trees to prevent the early drop of apples and peaches. It has also been applied to retard fruit-bud development until the dangers of late spring frosts have passed. Injuries to trees are healed rapidly by covering the wound with a lanum paste containing 1 per cent of the acid. It is said that the shattering of Christmas wreaths of holly, etc., can be checked by treating them with the material.

Two other chemicals of this group which may also have similar uses are phenylacetic acid and indolepropionic acid. It is thought that the former may be used to break the dormancy of tubers, bulbs, and corms so that they will start readily earlier in the season.

colchicine (which see) is an important chemical because of its apparent ability to affect the plant chromosomes and thereby bring about hereditary changes and create new varieties. It can be applied either by treating seeds with a solution, or by applying it directly to the growing plant tips in a lanum paste or water solution. Care should be exercised in handling colchicine because of its poisonous nature.

apiol, obtained from the seeds of parsley, is used for the same purpose as is colchicine. It is relatively nonpoisonous, but not very effective.

allantoin apparently has some action on the flowering process in plant life. Injection of this chemical in solution into the bulbs and branches of flowers has caused earlier and larger flowers.

thiourea has been used experimentally, in combination with certain of the growth substances discussed above, as a cutting and seed treatment. It also prevents cut fruit from discoloring.

humic acid is a product of rotting and decaying vegetation, especially grass. It helps break down the resultant material into plant food and is supposed to be able to impart a fine green color to growing plants.

traumatic acid is a plant wound hormone. When a plant is cut or bruised this substance collects at the point of injury and helps heal the wound.

biotin is one of the active substances in liquid manure. Also it is said to be stored in various seeds as an essential agent for stimulating the growth of the seedling after germination.

adenine is a leaf growth substance. Produced in considerable quantity within a well-fed plant, it in turn, makes large healthy leaves.

NUTRITIONAL MINERAL DEFICIENCIES

The Everglades in Florida were very unproductive when first reclaimed. The usual fertilizer applications failed to make their soil productive for many crops. It was found, for instance, that potatoes could be grown successfully only if sprayed with bordeaux mixture. Subsequently, it was found that some of the soils became highly productive when treated with copper sulphate (contained in bordeaux) and other minerals. From 30 to 100 lbs. of copper sulphate are required to bring an acre of deficient soil of this type into productive condition.

Where organic or mineral soils are not sufficiently acid to dissolve manganese compounds, growing crops are apt to be affected with chlorosis, giving the leaf a mottled yellow-green appearance. A fertilizer supplying 50 to 100 lbs. of manganese sulphate to the acre is sufficient to correct this condition in most soils. Sulphur is sometimes added in somewhat similar amounts to increase the soil acidity and aid in the solubility of the manganese compounds.

Some response to the addition of zinc has been noted where copper and manganese do not completely correct unproductivity. From 10 to 20 lbs. of zinc sulphate should be applied per acre. Response is also obtained by spraying affected plants with a solution containing 2 lbs. of zinc sulphate in 50 gals. of water at the rate of 50 gals. per acre.

Raspberry, pear, and peach chlorosis can be controlled from year to year by applying a solution of iron sulphate (1 lb. to 2 gals. water) to the soil in the early spring; for individual trees, 5 to 10 lbs. can be used for the same purpose. Foliage can be sprayed to correct chlorosis with a solution of 1 oz. to 7 gals. of water.

SEED TREATMENTS. Various chemicals are used to prevent the "damping off" of seedlings and others to rid the soil or seed of other pests or diseases, and to kill weeds. Treating soil or seed before planting can well be considered "seed insurance."

See DISINFECTION; WEEDS; and various materials therein referred to.

CHEMI-CULTURE. One of several terms applied to the growing of plants in sand, gravel, or other inert material, through the use of nutrient solutions made up of chemicals. See CHEMICAL GARDENING.

CHEMOTHERAPY. The treatment of internal disease by chemicals. With the introduction of many new chemicals research into the possibility of curing various tree wilts by chemical injections is being pursued with increased emphasis. Although a failure against chestnut blight, the method is now successfully used in treating chlorosis and other physiological diseases. There seems reason to hope that methods eventually may be perfected that will defeat the now incurable diseases caused by fungi, bacteria and other organisms.

CHENILLE-PLANT (she-neel'). A common name for *Acalypha hispida,* a shrub for S. gardens or N. conservatories and also known as Red-hot-cat tail. It is interesting chiefly for its long red spikes that resemble those of amaranthus.

CHENOPOD (kee'-noh-pod). Common name for any member of the Goosefoot Family, Chenopodiaceae, which see.

CHENOPODIACEAE (kee-no-poh-diay'-see-ee). The botanical name of the Goosefoot Family, so called because of the shape of the leaves of some species. It is a widespread group of about 75 genera of weedy herbs and shrubs, often succulent, a few of which are grown for food or ornament. A few have medicinal properties. The flowers, which have no petals, are very inconspicuous; plants are sometimes found in salty locations. Principal horticultural genera are Atriplex (Saltbush), Beta (Beet), Spinacia (Spinach), and Kochia (Burning-bush). Many others include pestiferous weeds of world-wide importance, such as Winged Pigweed, Mexican-tea and Russian-thistle.

CHENOPODIUM (kee-no-poh'-dium). A genus of plants commonly known as Goosefoot or Pigweed, and giving its name to the Goosefoot Family (Chenopodiaceae). A few are grown for ornament in the garden and for pot herbs and others are used in medicine or for greens, or as salad; but they are mainly weeds with mealy foliage, often found in the vegetable garden.

C. bonus-henricus (Good King Henry, occasionally called Mercury). A perennial to 2½ ft. with arrow-shaped leaves, sometimes cultivated as a pot herb.

botrys (Feather-geranium or Jerusalemoak). An annual with pretty, feathery spikes to 2 ft. tall used for cut flowers, and oval or oblong leaves.

album (Lambs-quarters or Pigweed). A common annual weed from 1 to 10 ft. in rich soils, which when gathered young makes excellent greens.

purpurascens. An annual formerly much grown in old gardens for its foliage, which is covered with a crystal-like, violet-purple substance.

ambrosioides (American Wormseed or Mexican-tea). A strong-smelling herb used for medicinal purposes.

CHERIMOYA (cher-i-moi'-ah). A S. American tropical tree (*Annona cherimola*) grown in warm countries, including the Florida Keys and S. Calif., for its heart-shaped, fragrant acidulous, white-fleshed fruits. These range from the size of an orange to 16 lbs. weight or more and are considered almost as delicious as the mangosteen (which see). The tree, which often reaches 30 ft., has drooping branches and oblong leaves. Its flowers, when abundant, are almost overpowering in their delightful fragrance.

CHEROKEE ROSE. Common name for *Rosa laevigata,* a Chinese climbing evergreen species with glossy leaflets and solitary fragrant white flowers to 3 in. or more across. Too tender for garden use N., it is an attractive and popular climber in the S. where it attains 15 ft. or more and has become naturalized. It is the State flower of Ga. See also ROSE.

CHERRY. The name of various Old and New World trees of the genus Prunus (which see). Two of the Old-World species have been cultivated for their fruit for centuries, and a few of the New-World kinds have been grown to a limited extent within recent years. Several others (see below) are cultivated for the ornamental effect of their early spring blossoms.

KINDS OF SWEET CHERRIES. The sweet or dessert cherry (*Prunus avium*) is a native of S. Europe and Asia Minor. Its tall, pyramidal trees sometimes attain heights of 100 ft., spreads of 75 ft. or more, and ages of a century or more. The following four classes of varieties have originated from it directly or (in the case of one group) by hybridization with the sour cherry.

1. *Mazzards,* whose young seedlings are used as stock for propagation of named varieties of both sweet and sour kinds and whose mature trees are common in fence rows and other uncultivated areas.

2. *Hearts* or *Geans,* which bear soft-fleshed, juicy fruits.

3. *Bigarreaus,* whose fruits are firm-fleshed and less juicy.

4. *Dukes* (the name being derived from that of the variety May Duke which is a corruption of Médoc where the variety originated); their sub-acid fruit, intermediate tree size, and other characteristics

indicate these varieties to be hybrids between the sweet- and sour-fruited species. Both the hearts and the bigarreaus are subdivided into varieties with light-colored and dark-colored juice.

SOUR CHERRY TYPES. The sour or pie cherry (*P. cerasus*), called "probably the most widely distributed of all tree fruits," is a native of S. W. Asia and adjacent Europe. Its several hundred varieties are divided into two groups which differ most conspicuously in their fruit characters. One is the *Amarelles,* with pale red fruits, colorless juice, moderate acidity and whitish flesh; the other is the *Morellos,* with dark-colored fruits, red juice and often keen acidity. Though the fruit of neither can be ranked as of dessert quality, that of the former is sometimes moderately pleasing eaten out of hand when fully ripe.

Amarelle trees sometimes exceed 30 ft. in height, 20 ft. or more in spread and are more erect and larger growing than the morellos, which are often not taller than long-established common lilac bushes.

Of all culinary fruits deserving a place in the home garden the sour cherry should rank first because its ripe fruit can rarely be obtained from stores and markets in good condition unless produced locally and marketed carefully and quickly. Most of such fruit is picked before it has reached full size or developed the characteristic rich flavor of full ripeness. Moreover, unless used within a day of being gathered it loses flavor and before long begins to decay. In the home garden it may be gathered when ripe as wanted and used at once.

Because the sweet cherry tree attains great size it is not suited to small properties, unless budded on a dwarfing stock. Even then it is less satisfactory than the dwarf pear or even the dwarf apple because it may die or become own-rooted, and then, in time, grow to standard size. The sour cherries, especially the morellos, being much smaller than the sweet kinds, are suited to small grounds, both as sources of fruit and as ornamental material; for they are beautiful in flower and in fruit.

SOME NATIVE SPECIES. In addition to the above mentioned two Old-World species

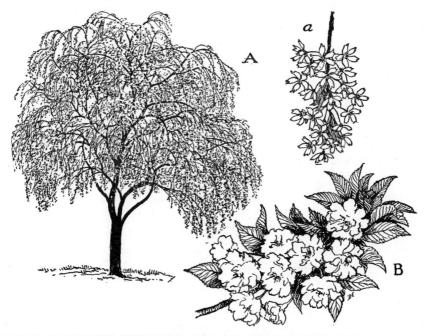

JAPANESE FLOWERING CHERRIES—ONE OF THE ORIENT'S LOVELIEST GIFTS TO WESTERN GARDENS

A, the Rosebud Cherry (Prunus subhirtella), a graceful small tree, weeping in some forms, with delicate single blossoms (a); and P. serrulata with white and pink, often double flowers (B) are only two of a host of charming varieties.

and their countless varieties, two American species are somewhat grown for their fruit. The Bessey cherry (*P. besseyi*) is the parent of the dwarf Rocky Mountain cherry and of its hybrids (with apricots, plums, peaches and other cherries) originated by Prof. N. E. Hansen of S. Dak. These are valuable acquisitions in the Prairie States where the sour cherry is not fully reliable and the sweet cherry fails.

The Choke cherry (*P. virginiana*) is somewhat cultivated in Quebec, N. Ontario and other cold parts of the continent for making jellies, jams, sauces and liqueurs; its improved varieties are grown to some extent for eating raw.

When these native species are included, it is correct to say that cherries can be grown in every State and adjacent Canadian Provinces. However, as the sweet cherry is almost as tender, both in wood and in flower bud, as the peach, it fails where the winters are very cold and the air is dry as in the Prairie States. It is also susceptible to heat and does not thrive in the S. or the arid S. W. Its most successful areas are the Hudson Valley, the Great Lakes section and the Pacific Coast States, especially Calif. and Ore.

How to Grow Cherries

Sour cherries are much more adaptable and have a wider range—from New England southward along the coast to Del. and in the mountains to the Carolinas; from the Great Lakes down the Mississippi Valley, and especially in N. Y., O., Ind., Mich. and Pa.

The sweet cherry is "finicky" as to soil. As it resents excess moisture the soil must be well drained; nothing suits it better than deep, gravelly or shaly loams from which surplus water quickly disappears while the moisture supply from below is continuous but not excessive. The sour cherry is far more cosmopolitan and, though it prefers the types of soil just mentioned, will make the best of whatever ground it is placed in, producing good crops even in rather dry and cold regions, provided the supply of soil moisture is adequate. Moreover, it is not attacked by San José scale and is less subject to other pests that attack the sweet cherry.

WHAT AND HOW TO PLANT. Sweet and sour cherry trees are both budded on two kinds of stock—mazzard and mahaleb. Though trees budded on the former may cost somewhat more, they should always be given the preference. With nurserymen, mazzard stock is somewhat unpopular because budding it is more difficult than working the mahaleb; also because the resulting young trees are less satisfactory as to appearance in the nursery rows. But commercial cherry growers prefer mazzard stock because the trees develop better than do those on mahaleb stock and are more productive and longer lived; furthermore, the mahaleb, being a dwarfing stock, tends to reduce the size of trees budded upon it, whether sour or sweet varieties. If it is not possible to purchase trees on mazzard stocks, the next best thing is to plant the mahaleb budded trees deeply enough so they will develop roots above the point of union and thus become "own-rooted." The point of union can easily be recognized; it shows as a slight crook in the stem 6 or 8 in. above the roots.

As in the case of the apple (which see) it is important to plant one-year sweet cherry trees rather than older, larger specimens because the branches can then be developed where they are wanted. But as one-year sour cherry trees are generally much smaller, it is advisable to plant them about 4 ft. apart in a row and give them clean cultivation for one year before transplanting them to their permanent positions. This reduces the danger of possible damage to such small trees if set out the regulation distance apart; it also facilitates training them to good form as already described.

Sour cherry trees are able to set fruit even when standing alone; but many varieties of sweet cherries fail to bear, not only as isolated trees but also when other varieties growing near-by cannot provide the necessary cross pollination. Three varieties incapable of pollinating themselves or each other are Lambert, Bing and Napoleon. When planting either one of them it is necessary to have good pollinizers, such as Black Republican, Windsor or Black Tartarian growing near-by. Experiments in Ore. have shown that especially good pollinizers for Lambert and Napoleon are Coe and Norma; for Bing, Elton is good; Black Republican has given fair results with Napoleon and Lambert, but poor ones with Bing.

When grown in gardens, morello cherry trees should be given 20 ft. of space; amarelles, 24 ft., dukes, 30 ft. and sweet cherries 35 to 40 ft. In commercial plantings the distances are usually much less because the trees are kept severely pruned.

Though the best cherry-orchard management involves clean cultivation and cover-cropping, sweet cherries will do fairly well planted in a lawn. The sour cherry, being less deep rooting, is less successful in sod but will produce moderately well if bearing trees are fed 2 to 3 lbs. of nitrate of soda in early spring as recommended under Apple. Such feeding is necessary for the development of the terminal growths.

PRUNING. When two-year cherry trees are planted the number of branches should immediately be reduced to the 3, 4, or 5 best-placed ones, but these should not be cut back because the terminal buds are the most important ones in young trees. Little or no pruning (except the removal of interfering branches) is needed until after the trees begin to bear; some of the interior, heavily shaded branches may then be removed to let light and air into the center of the trees.

When short fruit spurs crowd in sour cherry trees, they may be thinned; also when the terminal growths become long, wiry and naked, they may be cut back to their bases or even farther—into larger branches if these are also rather bare. Both these practices tend to stimulate the development of new shoots; but do not shorten the terminal growths until the trees begin to spread widely, and then prune them only enough to keep the trees shapely and within bounds.

The cultivated sweet cherries are distinctly dessert fruits, to be eaten out of hand or stoned and sugared for the table. Stewing and ordinary canning dissipates their delicate flavor and makes them "flat." Their flavor is less impaired when they are made into cobblers and deep-dish pies than by any other mode of cooking.

Most sour cherries are too tart to eat raw until "dead ripe" when also they are in best condition for canning and for pies; but even when not fully mature they are excellent for stewing and for pies. For wine-making the riper they are the better both for flavor and color.

HARVESTING. When cherries are to be used within a few hours it is advisable to pick them without stems because this lessens the chances of breaking the fruit spurs upon which the crop of the following season depends. In picking cherries for sale, the stems (or part of them) must be left attached to the fruit to prevent "bleeding" and to avoid leaving wounds through which decay fungi might enter. Some commercial growers use shears to cut the stems close to the fruit which is allowed to fall on sheets stretched beneath the trees. Sour cherries may sometimes be allowed to hang on the trees for two to four weeks after they are fully ripe; but this calls for special spraying or dusting with non-poisonous materials in order to prevent damage by insects and by brown rot, which is worst during wet or muggy weather.

The fact that a well-grown, intelligently cared for mature sweet cherry tree will yield from 1 to 3 bushels of fruit in favorable seasons suggests that one tree each of an early, a midseason and a late variety will produce enough fruit for the ordinary sized family. Dukes, being large trees, bear nearly as well. Amarelles are much smaller, so rarely yield 3 bushels, and morellos smaller still, seldom exceed 2 bushels. However, since the sour cherries may be used for making jam, wine and preserves as well as for canning, two trees each of early, mid-season, and late varieties will probably produce enough for all average families.

CHERRIES FOR THE HOME GARDEN. High-quality cherry varieties suited to home use (in addition to those already mentioned) include: *Sweet varieties*—Windsor, Governor Wood, Ida, Yellow Spanish, Schmidt, Lyons. *Dukes*—May Duke, Late Duke, Reine Hortense, Abbesse d'Oignies. *Amarelles*—Early Richmond, Montmorency, Late Montmorency, Carnation. *Morellos*—Ostheim, Olivet, Vladimir, English Morello, Riga. As few nurserymen carry all these varieties the reader should adopt the method of obtaining them as outlined under Apple.

Cherry species of less horticultural importance include the American natives, Bessey cherry (*P. besseyi*), the Pin cherry (*P. pennsylvanica*), and the Sand cherry (*P. pumila*) which are planted mainly for ornament, though they are also used to some extent for stocks.

FLOWERING CHERRIES

Within recent years varieties developed by the Chinese and the Japanese from the

Oriental cherry (*P. serrulata*—often improperly listed as *P. pseudocerasus*) and from the Nanking cherry (*P. tomentosa*) have attracted wide attention in the U. S. because of the trees presented by the Japanese Government to this country and planted near the Lincoln Memorial in Washington, D. C. Though other trees of these types have existed much longer in this country, interest in them has greatly increased their popularity. They are of two general forms: erect but more or less spreading, and weeping; both among the most beautiful of all flowering trees.

As many of them are grafted or budded, care must be exercised to prevent the stock from developing undesirable shoots, especially when weeping forms are united with erect stems. Should any shoot or stem develop below the point of union (it is usually erect) it must be immediately removed, for if allowed to develop it will perhaps replace and destroy the valuable part of the tree. Every spring after growth has well started the trees should be carefully examined and all sprouts from the stock rubbed off before they become woody—while they are soft.

ENEMIES. The commonest disease of cherry is brown rot, causing blossom and twig blight and particularly rotting of the fruit. The fruit turns brown and soft and is often covered with a grayish mold. For control see BROWN ROT.

A leaf-spotting fungus may cause almost complete defoliation of trees in years favorable to it. Small purplish or reddish spots appear on the leaves in early spring and later may fall out causing a "shot-hole" effect. Leaves turn yellow and fall about the time the fruit ripens and this early defoliation weakens the trees and makes them liable to winter-killing. The fungus overwinters on fallen leaves and the fruiting bodies mature during the tree's blossoming period, shooting out spores during rainy periods. These are carried up to the tree by air currents; and from spots formed on the under surfaces of the leaves spores are carried by wind and rain to healthy leaves. The disease occurs on both sweet and sour cherries but is worse on the latter.

A yellow-leaf of cherry, resembling leaf spot in some respects, is due to an injured or inefficient root system. Winter-injury, wet feet, drought, or unfavorable soil conditions may cause defoliation.

Black knot (see PLUM) is frequently found on sour cherry. Abnormal branching, known as witches' brooms, is caused by one of the leaf-curl fungi. Cut off affected branches several inches below the brooms.

Powdery mildew, which often covers leaves on tips of the branches with a white coating, is controlled by the regular spray schedule for cherries given below.

Under insect enemies, the black cherry aphis may cause serious injury to sweet cherries but is seldom serious on sour. Shining black eggs that winter on smaller branches near buds hatch as the buds are opening, and the aphids reproduce rapidly (see APHIS). Their presence and feeding cause the leaves of the terminal shoots to curl; and the fruit clusters are covered with insects which secrete a honeydew in which grows a sooty mold fungus.

Wormy cherries are due either to the plum curculio (which see) or to fruit flies, of which there are two species: one with an entirely black abdomen, and one marked by a series of white crossbands. Both kinds attack cherry, pear and plum in the northern U. S. and Canada. Ten months are passed in the soil in a brown pupa case, the flies emerging in early summer and laying eggs in the fruit. The eggs hatch into very small whitish, legless maggots which burrow through the flesh. The surface of the fruit appears normal until the maggots are nearly grown, when sunken spots appear. When full-grown the maggot eats its way out, falls to the ground and enters the resting stage.

SPRAY PROGRAM. The following is a general spray schedule for the control of the common cherry diseases and pests. Modifications for local conditions may be obtained from the state experiment stations or county agents.

1. When the bud scales separate and show green.—1 part lime-sulphur to 40 parts of water. For sweet cherries add 1 teaspoon nocotine-sulphate per gallon.

2. Just as the hucks split from the fruit: lime-sulphur 1 to 40 with 1 tablespoon lead arsenate per gallon.

3. Ten days later—same spray as 2.

4. After harvest (necessary only in years when leaf spot is bad)—1-40 lime-sulphur.

A sulphur (90 parts)-lead arsenate (10 parts) dust may be substituted as a spray for spray 2 and an 80 to 10 dust for spray

3. In home orchards where the fruit may not be thoroughly washed, poison sprays that may be used for the fruit fly leave an unsafe residue on the fruit and therefore have not been included in the above schedule.

Wild cherries are favorite hosts for the eastern tent caterpillar (which see). Unless carefully watched and used as lures on which the moths will lay eggs which will be destroyed over winter, such trees should be destroyed.

Plants of other genera to which the name cherry is applied include: Bardados-cherry, which is *Malpighia glabra;* Cornelian-cherry, *Cornus mas;* Ground-cherry, species of Physalis; Indian-cherry, *Rhamnus caroliniana;* Jerusalem-cherry, *Solanum pseudo-capsicum;* Madden-cherry, *Maddenia hypoleuca;* Spanish-cherry, *Mimusops elengi;* Surinam-cherry, *Eugenia uniflora;* Winter-cherry, *Physalis alkekengi.*

CHERRY-LAUREL. Common name for ornamental species of Prunus, particularly *P. laurocerasus,* a native of E. Europe and the Orient grown in the S. and Calif.

CHERRY PIE. An old-time name for the popular old-fashioned Heliotrope—suggested, perhaps, by the resemblance of its flowers to marbled violet tints produced when cream is poured upon black-cherry pie.

CHERVIL (chur'-vil). A name for two vegetables, both members of the Parsley Family (Umbelliferæ), but neither much grown in U. S. Salad chervil (*Anthriscus cerefolium*) is an annual herb 18 to 24 in. high, whose parsley-like leaves are used for flavoring salads. Seed sown in early spring or in early autumn in any good garden soil, preferably in partial shade, will yield leaves ready for gathering in six to ten weeks.

Turnip-rooted or tuberous chervil (*Chærophyllum tuberosum*) is a biennial whose roots resemble parsnip but are grayish, smaller (4 to 5 in.) and with yellowish and more floury flesh. They are used for flavoring soups and stews, and served like carrots. If seed is allowed to become dry it germinates poorly or not at all. Therefore it is best sown in the fall, preferably where the plants are to mature. The seedlings will not appear until spring when they should be thinned like carrots. Seed may be kept moist over winter by stratification (which see), but must not be allowed to freeze and thaw alternately. Four or five months after the seedlings appear roots may be dug as needed. Like parsnips they may be left in the ground over winter but a spring crop must be used soon or it will go to seed.

Sweet Cicely, a form of Myrrh (which see), is sometimes called Sweet-scented Chervil.

CHESTNUT. Common name for the genus Castanea, comprising a number of handsome, hardy, deciduous trees of the N. hemisphere, valuable for their decorative effect in the home grounds and, both there and in the wild, for the edible nuts borne in prickly burs. Members of the Beech Family, they have long, rather slender, toothed leaves and attractive blossoms in the form of catkins. They grow readily in any strong well-drained soil and even in drier, rocky situations. Propagated easily from seed, they can also be budded or grafted, though not always successfully. When a tree is cut down, numerous shoots usually develop, often making an ornamental clump.

While the native species (the first of those noted below) is one of the best of all, it has been almost exterminated throughout its E. range by the deadly and as yet uncontrollable chestnut blight. However some of the foreign species found to be more or less immune to the disease, are gradually being introduced both as garden subjects and as material for breeding work with the production of resistant hybrids in view.

PRINCIPAL SPECIES

C. dentata (American Chestnut) is a vigorous, moderately rapid growing tree, attaining 100 ft., perfectly hardy but extending as far S. as Ala. and Miss. The flowers are delightfully fragrant, and the nuts, though smaller than those of European or Japanese species, are of much better flavor. This is the valuable species that has been almost wiped out in the N. E. by the blight. See CHESTNUT BLIGHT.

sativa (Spanish Chestnut). Growing to 80 or 100 ft., this is somewhat more tender than *C. dentata.* The nut is large, over 1 in. in diameter. There are a number of garden forms, var. *asplenifolia* having lobed leaves.

mollissima (Chinese Chestnut). Attaining 60 ft. and bearing large nuts, this has proved perfectly hardy in the Arnold Arboretum in Mass.

pumila (Chinquapin or Chinkapin). Another native species found from Pa. to Texas, this makes a shrub or small tree to 30 ft. and is useful for planting on dry banks, or in rocky, open woods. The abundant light green burs are very attractive in autumn.

crenata (Japanese Chestnut). A small tree to 30 ft., it sometimes retains a shrubby form. Bearing nuts when only a few years old, it is especially valuable for the home grounds.

Horsechestnut (which see) is Aesculus; Water-chestnut (which see) is Trapa.

CHESTNUT BLIGHT. A fatal disease attacking all native American chestnut species and responsible for the practical extermination of Sweet Chestnut and Chinkapin trees throughout most of the E. States. The cause is a parasitic fungus (*Endothia parasitica*) which gains entrance through wounds or insect-injuries in the bark, and girdles the stems and trunks of trees of all ages, killing them in a few years. The sticky spores of the fungus are spread by the wind, rain, insects, birds, small animals and by the transportation of diseased plants, timber or cordwood from which the bark is not removed.

Believed to have been brought from Japan, the disease was first observed in New York City in 1904 although it was probably established by that time in the surrounding countryside. Spreading rapidly, it killed trees over a steadily increasing territory in spite of investigations begun a few years later by Pennsylvania and then by the U. S. Department of Agriculture and other States, and their vigorous efforts to control it. No cure has yet been found and owing to the many distributing agencies it is practically impossible to keep the trouble within any limited area.

The measures employed by the various departments in fighting it have therefore consisted of cutting down diseased trees and burning the bark before using the timber; and of investigating the possibility of developing resistant or immune forms of improved chestnut. Japanese species appear to be highly, if not completely, resistant, and work is continuing with the objective of developing by hybridization new forms that will combine the high nut quality of the American, with the resistance of the Japanese species. Considerable progress has been made experimentally, but it is not yet possible anywhere in eastern United States to secure and plant chestnut trees with any real assurance of escaping this disease.

See also DISEASES; CHESTNUT.

CHESTNUT OAK. A true Oak (*Quercus montana*) of E. U. S., so-called because its leaves closely resemble those of the chestnut. Growing to 100 ft. it is, like most of its relatives, an ornamental tree. See OAK.

CHEWING INSECTS. Those with biting mouth-parts and which actually devour leaves and other plant parts. Such pests are killed and kept under control by spraying the plants they feed on with so-called stomach poisons. See INSECTS; INSECTICIDES.

CHICK-PEA. Popular name for *Cicer arietinum,* also known as Garbanzo; a bushy, hairy, annual herb of the Pea Family. It is native to S. Europe and India, where it is extensively grown as a garden vegetable, the seeds being eaten boiled like peas or roasted like peanuts; more thoroughly roasted, they make an acceptable substitute for coffee. As a field crop they are grown as a food for horses. Cultivation is the same as for bush beans.

CHICKWEED. Common name for *Stellaria media,* a member of the Carnation Family, but a bad weed growing to 2 ft. high with opposite leaves and small white flowers. It is very troublesome in the rich soil of the border or vegetable garden and in frames, spreading fastest during the cool months of the growing season. Sometimes it is allowed to form a cover-crop in orchards or vineyards, but it is never deliberately planted. It is an Old-World plant, but has become naturalized over much of America.

Mouse-ear Chickweed is the common name for the genus Cerastium, which see. See also WEEDS.

CHICORY or SUCCORY. A perennial European herb (*Cichorium intybus*) common as a weed in temperate climates, but whose thick, cultivated roots are roasted and used as a coffee substitute. The leaves of seedlings are used as greens; sometimes those of older plant are blanched like celery, either in autumn or early spring. During fall and winter the roots are forced by one method to produce loose, white or pink leaves called "barbe de capucin," and by another to yield witloof or so-called French endive; both are used as salads. In America chicory is most used as witloof.

CULTURE. For these winter salads sow seed thinly in well prepared, rich, deep soil in earliest spring, making the rows 15 or 18 in. apart. Thin when the seedlings are 4 in. high, using the thinnings as greens and leaving plants 6 in. asunder in the rows. Keep cleanly cultivated till the leaves meet between the rows. In late autumn dig the roots and, after cutting the tops an inch above the root crown, bury them in a pit or in moist sand or earth in a coldframe or root cellar.

WITLOOF. To produce witloof heads, shorten the parsnip-like roots from below to 8 or 9 in. long; bury them upright in damp sand or soil and cover the tops with as much more. Keep the temperature at about 60 degrees. In two or three weeks blanched heads 5 or 6 in. long may be cut for use. The roots are of no further use.

BARBE DE CAPUCIN. To produce this, place the trimmed roots *horizontally* on a bed of moist soil in a dark celler, their stem ends pointing outward. Cover with 3 in. of soil then place a second layer of roots 3 or 4 in. back from the first. Add alternate layers of roots and soil until a pyramidal or conical pile is formed 2 or 3 ft. high. Keep the soil moist and the temperature about 60 deg. F. In two or three weeks cut the loose leaves that appear on the outside of the pile. If the roots are not disturbed several cuttings may be made. See ENDIVE.

CHILDREN'S GARDENS. Every child should have a garden. Preparing the soil, sowing the seed, and caring for the growing plant make up an experience which leads to a realization of oneness with Nature more than any other activity of childhood. Through this work the child can be led to understand that, without gardens, man would be still living in a cave, precariously gathering chance fruits, nuts and grains; that through agriculture and horticulture, where man works in cooperation with Nature, he has become the civilized being he is today.

A child's garden is a laboratory where may be studied not only the phenomena of plant life, but also the interdependence of plant and animal life. After seeing the development of the seed into the plant, he watches the flowers unfold, and learns that the bright petals attract certain insects which carry the pollen which insures fertile seed, the promise of future harvests. He becomes aware of the ravages of harmful insects, which, in their struggle for existence, work havoc among planted crops and call for various defensive, protective or curative measures; and he learns to cherish his friends the toads and harmless snakes, and the multitude of birds, which so materially aid in keeping the balance of nature.

The child's first garden should be a small plot which he feels is his very own; a piece of fertile, easily-worked soil, not shaded by trees, where plants given ordinary care will grow and flourish, not languish and die, as often happens when a piece of poor ground "not needed for anything else" is turned over to the child for his first attempts.

Every child should come to this first garden bright with interest. If he is not fortunate enough to have grown up in an atmosphere of gardening, his interest should be aroused while he is very young— even before the plot of ground is given him—by letting him grow easily-handled bulbs, like the paper-white narcissus, in fibre or water indoors. Their fragrant blooms are so certain to appear that this first adventure will be attended by success; and this is important psychologically, for children are always discouraged if their first attempts do not produce results. The ability to look ahead and wait patiently are not attributes of childhood, but they are qualities which the love of gardening will develop.

Contrary to the usual practice, the first garden need not necessarily be grown from seed. A few easily grown perennials, even a small shrub (old enough to bloom the next spring) or a few bulbs, will lead toward the desire to plant and care for a garden of annuals or vegetables.

Suppose that, in the early fall, a plot of ground 8 by 10 or 12 ft. is selected. It should be thoroughly dug over and some well-rotted manure should be spaded into it by an adult, the reason for the steps being explained. The child should then be shown how to rake it free of all lumps to a smooth, fine surface. If the child is old enough, he should draw a little plan, then be shown how to plant a few perennials for a border. White rock-cress, set at intervals, with plants of forget-me-nots, or

FORETHOUGHT
Carefully weeded and watered, plants will in
due course yield an abundant harvest.

the old-fashioned viola, known to generations of children as "Johnny-jump-up," are
excellent selections, with perhaps, a little
bush of double-flowering-almond at the
back. Among the border plants let him
tuck yellow and purple crocus and snowdrops, with a group of five daffodils at
each corner. Here is a charming combination which will be sure to blossom in
the spring and make the advance to seed-
planting operations a matter of intense interest.

In the early spring the unplanted part
of the plot should be marked off according to the previous design, or divided into
rows, and the seeds of annuals sown.
Choose those most likely to succeed and
give a wealth of bloom, such as alyssum,
bachelors buttons, calendulas, California
poppies, cosmos, dwarf nasturtiums, larkspurs, love-in-a-mist, marigolds, petunias,
phlox, poppies, portulaca, and zinnias (especially the dwarf Mexican type). Many
combinations can be worked out, as a center of calendulas, surrounded by California
poppies and these edged with alyssum; or
blue larkspurs, surrounded by mixed phlox;
or poppies, interplanted with a few gladioli, and edged with petunias. Or—which
is simpler and better for younger children
—the seeds may be planted in rows and the
flowers used principally for cutting.

For some children the vegetable garden
will make the strongest appeal. Leaf lettuce, radishes, carrots, onion sets, beets and
Swiss chard are easily grown and will give
a sure reward for the work expended. To
these, if the plot is large enough, may be
added bush and pole beans, tomatoes, cucumbers and bush summer squash, the
whole edged with parsley, alternated with
clumps of chives, to give something of
decorative interest. Tomato plants are best
purchased unless some are being grown for
the main garden. The cucumbers should
be planted at the back of the bed where
they will not overrun it, and they can be
trained on a little trellis of intertwined
brush.

Show the child how to plant each kind
of seed, explaining that the fine seed should
be sifted on the surface and pressed gently
into the soft soil, while the larger seeds
are lightly covered and firmed into the
ground. Too deep planting has caused
many a disappointment. After the seedlings appear, explain the necessity of thinning and cultivating and demonstrate
watering methods. As the plants develop
call the child's attention to the changes as
buds, flowers, and fruits form and mature.

Let the child truly own his garden and
do all the work possible in it, but do not
hesitate to give, surreptitiously, any assistance that will contribute to its success.
A sense of joyful achievement the first

REALIZATION
Gathering the fruits of the well-tended garden.
Care is needed here, too.

year will almost invariably lead to permanent future interest in gardening.

This article deals with the individual garden for a single child, but splendid work is being done throughout the country by schools, botanic gardens, garden clubs, women's clubs, publications and other agencies in connection with large neighborhood or community gardens for the instruction and interest of classes, groups or clubs of boys and girls. This is a field in itself of vast and useful possibilities.

CHILEAN-JASMINE (*Mandevilla suaveolens*). A woody vine from S. America, belonging to the Dogbane Family. It is sometimes grown in the greenhouse and outdoors in warm regions. It does not take kindly to pot culture. The large fragrant white funnel-shaped flowers are borne in racemes.

CHILE-BELLS. Common name for *Lapageria rosea*, which is also called Chilean-bellflower. A tall, twining, half-hardy, summer-blooming plant, the leaves and tendrils indicating its relation to the smilax, and its large showy lily-like flowers drooping in rosy, spotted bells, suggesting its membership in the Lily Family. However, there is no bulb, the flowers ripening into fleshy, beaked fruits, and propagation being by seed, cuttings or by layering shoots in sandy peat. The shoots, sometimes 20 ft. long, climb on walls or trellises. This is a choice subject for cool greenhouses, or gardens in mild climates, but its culture is exacting. Sharply-drained soil is essential, with shade and careful watering. The single species, which has a number of lovely varieties, was named in honor of Napoleon's wife, Josephine de la Pagerie.

CHILE-HAZEL, CHILEAN-NUT. Common names for *Gevuina avellana,* an evergreen tree of Chile, sparingly grown in S. Calif., and hardy throughout the South. It reaches a height of 40 ft. and, following the white flowers in axillary spikes, bears coral-red fruits enclosing a seed whose edible kernel tastes like a hazel-nut. The tree is sometimes grown as a greenhouse ornament. The soil preferred is a fibrous loam with some fresh humus added. Propagation is by seeds, or by cuttings of green wood, rooted under glass.

CHILE-NETTLE. A common name applied to species of Loasa, herbs or small shrubs of Mexico and S. America, which have stinging hairs.

CHILICOTHE (chi-li-koth'ee). Common name for *Echinocystis macrocarpa,* a hardy perennial climber with large lobed leaves and white flowers.

CHILOPSIS (ky-lop'-sis). Desert- or Flowering-willow. One species (*C. linearis*) found from Texas to Calif. and in Mexico, and a member of the Bignonia Family, is a deciduous shrub or tree to 20 ft., bearing narrow leaves to 1 ft. long, and handsome crimped, trumpet-shaped flowers. These are lilac-colored with two yellow stripes inside, and are borne in short terminal racemes.

CHIMAPHILA (ky-maf'-i-lah). A genus of evergreen N. American herbs or small shrubs popularly known as Pipsissewa (which see). Found in the woods from Me. to Ala., it is a favorite plant for half shady spots in wild gardens.

CHIMNEY BELLFLOWER. Common name for *Campanula pyramidalis,* a perennial bearing pale blue or white bells.

CHINA ASTER. The annual, garden or so-called cultivated aster which, botanically, is *Callistephus chinensis.* See ASTER.

CHINA-BERRY. A common name for *Melia azedarach,* also called China-tree, Pride of India, Umbrella-tree, and Indian-lilac. The genus Melia (which see) is called Bead-tree.

CHINCH BUG. This small bug is notorious in the S., where it attacks St. Augustine-grass, in the Middle W., where it ravages corn and small grains, and during recent years it has become a troublesome pest on lawns in the E., especially in New England and on Long Island, where it causes ugly brown patches. It becomes abundant with a succession of hot dry summers, and both young and adult bugs puncture grass stems and suck the juices. The leaves become red-stained and in severe infestations large areas of turf may turn brown. The adult bug is ⅕ in. or less long, but has a conspicuous black body with white wings; the young are reddish. If its presence is suspected, flood a piece of lawn and watch for the bugs to climb the grass stems.

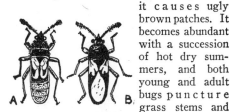

CHINCH BUGS
A, short-winged and B, long-winged forms. Both injure farm crops and, in the East, lawns.

As the adults winter over in waste grass and rubbish, this should be cleaned up and destroyed in the fall. A nicotine-sulphate spray, or a tobacco dust, can be used on lawns, but a special derris dust, analyzing 1 per cent rotenone, is considered most effective if applied at the rate of 25 lbs. per 1000 sq. ft. (if put on by hand) or 8 to 10 lbs. if a dusting machine (which can be rented from an insecticide company) is used. Apply first in June as soon as chinch bug activity is noted and again in late summer if necessary for the second brood.

CHINCHERICHEE (ching-ker-i-chee') or CHINKERICHEE. This is the common name for *Ornithogalum thyrsoides* var. *aureum,* a S. African bulbous herb bearing many brilliant yellow long-lasting flowers; related to Star-of-Bethlehem, it is a greenhouse subject in the U. S.

CHINESE-ANISE, STAR-ANISE. Common names for *Illicium verum,* a species of aromatic evergreen trees and shrubs from China, often planted as an ornamental in warm regions.

CHINESE BRAKE. Common name for *Pteris serrulata,* an excellent and easily grown house fern, with much branched slender divisions and papery texture. Needs subdued light and some sand.

CHINESE CABBAGE, CELERY CABBAGE. These are popular names for oriental species of the genus Brassica which are really mustards rather than cabbages. In America the best known are Pe-tsai (*B. pekinensis*), Pak-choi (*B. chinensis*), Wong-bok, and Chi-hi-li. Unlike true cabbages, these species quickly run to seed in warm weather without making much leafage (for which they are valued). For early use, sow outdoors in earliest spring; for a fall crop, sow after midsummer. In either case make the rows 18 to 24 in. apart and thin the plants when to 4 to 6 in. high; use the thinnings for greens or salad and leave the permanent plants 8 to 12 in. apart in the row. In 60 to 70 days the heads will be ready for use, either raw for salad or slaw, or boiled. Late maturing heads stored in moist, cool (but frostproof) quarters, will keep about two months. See CABBAGE; MUSTARD.

CHINESE EVERGREEN. (*Aglaonema modestum*). A desirable and popular house plant of African origin valued for its large glossy dark green leaves, two, three, or occasionally more of which grow on the top of a talk, with, rarely, a side shoot. The stalk is thick and solid; height on an average, 15 inches. A bloom like a small green calla appears rarely, seemingly stimulated by an over-crowded root system which has been in the same pot a number of years.

This plant is often grown in water only; sometimes in potted soil or peat moss. It thrives best in a vase of soil mixture (⅓ sand, ⅓ garden soil, ⅓ compost) kept flooded by water. Charcoal may be added to keep the soil mixture sweet. This plant has no use for the direct rays of the sun and prospers in hallways or room corners where many other house plants would fail. Stalks may be encouraged to grow in interesting and grotesque curves by placing them sideways in a bowl.

CHINESE LANTERN PLANT. One common name for a hardy perennial species of Physalis (*P. alkekengi*), known also as Winter-cherry, grown for its balloon-like husks which turn to orange-red flaming lanterns when ripe. Ranged along stiff stems, they are effective for indoor winter decoration. Plants grow 18 in. to 2 ft. tall, developing pods the second year on dense bushes. Propagation from seed is easy, and the plants often self-sow. The rhizomes may be divided or cuttings taken as additional means of propagation.

Several species of tortoise beetles (such as those which feed on sweet potato) may

THE CHINESE EVERGREEN
This shade-loving aroid is a splendid foliage plant for the house, thriving in water or planted in peat moss kept wet.

severely infest the plants. Potato beetles (which see) may also be troublesome. For both, spray with lead arsenate. To prevent a Verticillum wilt, first reported in 1938, from causing severe losses, remove and destroy infected plants and surrounding soil.

CHINESE MUSTARD. A name loosely applied to various Asiatic species of Brassica, the plants somewhat resembling celery cabbage, but forming loose open heads. The leaves are used as potherbs. *B. juncea,* or leaf mustard, is more commonly grown in U. S. for this purpose than are the strictly Chinese forms, *B. chinensis, B. pekinensis,* etc.

CHINESE PARASOL-TREE. Common name for *Firmiana simplex,* a deciduous tree, to 50 ft. with leaves 1 ft. across, resembling those of the sycamore. In a variety (*variegata*), these are marked with white. Native to China and Japan, it is grown in the South as a shade tree for street or lawn. Propagated by seeds. It is also called the Phoenix-tree.

CHINESE SACRED-LILY. Common name for *Narcissus tazetta orientalis,* one of the tender, polyanthus (many-flowered) forms of which the familiar Paper-white is another. It has large bulbs, rather broad flat leaves and 3 or 4 creamy white and yellow flowers clustered at the end of slender 12 in. stalks. They are popular throughout the Orient, and as a garden subject on the Pacific Coast; and widely grown indoors in bowls of water in which the bulbs are supported by pebbles, the bowls being placed in a cool dark closet for about two weeks, or until the roots have started. If the bulbs are large and very firm, the outer segments may be carefully slit with a penknife to hasten the growth, care being taken not to injure the flowering stalks within. They may also be grown in earth like other narcissi, requiring little heat to force them into bloom. Bulbs are grown on a large scale in Fla. See also NARCISSUS.

CHINESE SCHOLAR-TREE. Common name for *Sophora japonica,* an ornamental leguminous tree from China and Korea, also called Japanese Pagoda-tree.

CHINESE SILK-PLANT. Common name for *Boehmeria nivea;* a tall-growing herb of S. Asia, from the stem of which is obtained the fibre, ramie.

CHINESE TALLOW-TREE. Common name for *Sapium sebiferum,* also known as Vegetable Tallow, a tree of the Spurge Family growing to 40 ft. with a milky poisonous juice, sharp-pointed leaves turning a bright crimson in age, and flowers in spikes. These are followed by fruits containing seeds covered with wax which is used in China for making candles, as a dressing for cloth and for soap. Somewhat resembling a poplar, it is now grown in many tropical countries. In the S. States, where it is planted as a shade and ornamental subject, it has become widely naturalized. It is propagated by seed or cuttings.

CHINESE-WATERMELON. A common name for *Benincasa hispida,* also called Tunka and Wax Gourd; a running annual vine bearing large gourd-like fruits.

CHINESE WOOLFLOWER. A common and catalog name for one type of *selosia argentea* var. *cristata.*

CHINQUAPIN (ching'-kah-pin) or CHINKAPIN. Common names for *Castanea pumila,* a S. species of Chestnut. Giant-chinquapin is *Castanopsis chrysophylla,* a near relative. Water-chinkapin is *Nelumbium luteum,* the American Lotus. See CHESTNUT; CASTANOPSIS; NELUMBIUM.

CHIOGENES (ky-oj'-e-neez). A genus of tiny, creeping evergreen plants of the Heath Family, growing in cool, acid soil and meriting more frequent use as a ground-cover in peaty soil in a moist part of the rock garden. *C. hispidula* (Creeping Snowberry) has small bell-shaped flowers in May and June, followed by dainty white berries clustered among the glossy leaves. It can be propagated by seeds, divisions or cuttings.

CHIONANTHUS (ky-oh-nan'-thus). Two species of hardy deciduous trees or large shrubs with showy panicles of white flowers in early summer. See FRINGE-TREE.

CHIONODOXA (ky-on-oh-dok'-sah). Glory-of-the-snow. A genus of small bulbous plants of the Lily Family from the mountains of Asia Minor. They are among the most beautiful of our very early spring-flowering bulbous subjects, their brilliant blues, sometimes varied with white, brightening the garden when few other subjects are seen. Perfectly hardy, they can be planted in any well-drained fertile spot and need no protection. The bulbs should be planted in the early fall 2 or 3 in. deep and 1 or 2 in. apart; natural increase will provide plenty of offsets or new stock can be grown from seed. Massed plantings around shrubbery or evergreens, and naturalized groups in meadows or on grassy slope, create a fine effect. The trap-shaped leaves appear at the same time as the flowers. Replanting every third year is advisable though not always essential. To keep the plants strong and vigorous, the foliage must be left to ripen.

Chionodoxa is subject to Botrytis blight and may be attacked by a smut. Control by sanitary methods.

C. luciliae, of which there are many horticultural varieties, some introducing tones of red, is the most widely grown species. Among its hybrids is *C. grandiflora,* the largest flowered of all. *C. tmolusi* blooms later than the others.

CHIVES (chyvz). (Sometimes spelled CIVES.) A perennial, hardy species of onion (*Allium schœnoprasum*), whose small, slender, hollow leaves, chopped fine, are used for flavoring salads, stews and soups. Handled like onions (which see), the small oval bulbs multiply rapidly, form clumps, develop abundant foliage 6 to 8 in. high and small round heads of tiny lavender flowers. As both foliage and flowers are attractive in appearance (though onion-scented), the plants are often used for edging flower beds; but unless the flower-heads are cut and the seed is gathered promptly, self-sown seedlings may prove troublesome weeds. For best results the clumps should be divided every second or third year.

CHLORIS (kloh'-ris). A genus of annual and perennial grasses of warm regions and known as Finger Grass. It includes species grown for forage and in the garden for ornament and as everlastings for winter bouquets. The spikelets are borne in two compact rows along one side of each flowering stem.

C. gayana is Rhodes Grass, a perennial forage crop, to 4 ft. with leaves 1 ft. long and ½ in. wide, and 4-in. spikes. *C. polydactyla,* a perennial to 3 ft., has 2-ft. leaves and 6-in. spikes; *C. truncata,* a dwarf perennial to 1 ft., has short leaves and 6-in. whorled spikes; *C. paraguayensis,* an annual to 2 ft., has 4-in. flat or folded leaves and 2-in. purplish spikes in umbels; and *C. virgata,* a tropical plant, either annual or perennial, grows to 3 ft., with 4-in. leaves and 2½ in. white or purplish spikes. See also ORNAMENTAL GRASSES.

CHLOROCODON (kloh-roh'-coh-don) *whitei.* A vine of tropical Africa belonging to the Milkweed Family, grown in the S. or under glass, and known as Mundiroot, which see.

CHLOROGALUM (kloh-roh-gal'-um) *Pomeridianum.* Popularly known as the Soap Plant (which see), or Amole. This is a bulbous herb of Calif. belonging to the Lily Family.

CHLOROPHYTUM (kloh-roh-fy'-tum). A group of 60 tropical herbs of the Lily Family, closely resembling Anthericum (which see); natives of the warm sections of Asia, Africa, and America. In cooler sections they are grown as greenhouse plants. The flowers are borne in graceful sprays of white, green, or cream, and the foliage of some species is strikingly banded with yellow. Occasionally grown as border plants, they are more commonly used as pot plants or in vases. They are readily multiplied by seeds, suckers, or offsets from the lower stem, and by division in the spring.

CHLOROPICRIN. A heavy, colorless, pungent liquid, the active ingredient in tear gas, now used in soil sterilization. See DISINFECTION.

CHLOROSIS (kloh-roh'-sis). A reduction in the amount of chlorophyll or green coloring matter in a plant, resulting in the paling of its normal green color to yellow, or even white. The foliage may be uniformly yellow or variegated. In food plants any type of chlorosis is considered detrimental because lack of chlorophyll means reduced photosynthesis which is essential to normal plant life and development. But certain ornamentals with variegated (chlorotic) foliage are purposely propagated. Infectious chlorosis, transmitted by budding or grafting or occasionally by seed, is usually due to a virus. See VIRUS DISEASES.

Environmental conditions that cause chlorosis include lack of essential elements, such as nitrogen, magnesium, or iron in the soil; excessive soil alkalinity which renders the iron present unavailable to the plant; and excess water. Too alkaline a soil can be acidified by means of sulphur or aluminum sulphate; see ACID SOIL. Chlorotic trees sprayed with iron in the form of ferrous sulphate or injected with ferric phosphate frequently resume their normal green color. See CHEMOTHERAPY; PHYSIOLOGICAL DISEASES.

CHOCOLATE-LILY. A common name for *Fritillaria biflora,* a small bulbous plant of the Lily Family. See FRITILLARIA.

CHOCOLATE-TREE. Common name for *Theobroma cacao*, a tropical tree from which chocolate is obtained. See CACAO.

CHOISYA (choi'-zi-ah). An evergreen shrub, native of Mexico, belonging to the Rue Family. See MEXICAN-ORANGE.

CHOKEBERRY. Common name for the genus Aronia with its three species of native deciduous shrubs, useful in the shrub border and for grouping in the wild garden. They are not specially particular as to soil and situation, but thrive best in rich soil, on the moist side. The white flowers are attractive in spring, and the leaves are colorful in autumn. Propagated by seeds, cuttings, suckers and layers.

A. arbutifolia (Red Chokeberry) grows to 10 ft. and bears a profusion of red berries which remain colorful most of the winter.

atropurpurea (Purple Chokeberry) grows to 12 ft. and has dark purple fruits which ripen in Sept. but soon shrivel.

Melanocarpa (Black Chokeberry) grows to about 4 ft., with shining black fruits ripe in Aug. but dropping early. Var. *grandifolia* is much more vigorous and outstanding with lustrous leaves.

CHOKE CHERRY. Common name in E. U. S. for the wild *Prunus virginiana*, and in the W. for *P. demissa.*

CHOLLA (chohl'-i-ah). Common name for *Opuntia fulgida*, one of the tree cacti of the Arizona plains. See CACTUS; OPUNTIA.

CHORIZEMA (koh-ri-zee'-mah). Small evergreen shrubs with prickly leaves, native of Australia and belonging to the Pea Family. They rank with the most attractive hardwood plants for spring flowering in the cool greenhouse, and can be grown outdoors in the far South. Under glass they are sometimes trained to wire forms, though generally allowed to grow in a natural loose manner. Neat little plants in 5 in. pots can be grown from cuttings in a year. They do best at first in a mixture of peat and sand; then later in fibrous loam and peat with a little sand. Potting must be firmly done at all times. Established plants do best plunged outdoors for the summer. Propagated by seeds, and cuttings in spring.

There has been much confusion in the naming of species and forms. The one commonly grown as *C. ilicifolium* (but now referred to by botanists as *C. cordatum*) is a medium shrub with weak slender branches, very showy in bloom with its profusion of orange and red-purple flowers. Var. *splendens* has larger and showier flowers.

There are several forms of *C. varium*, the one known as *chandleri* being one of the showiest, with numerous flowers of red and yellow.

CHRISTMAS-BERRY. Common name for *Heteromeles arbutifolia*, also called Toyon (which see), a berry-bearing evergreen of S. Calif.

CHRISTMAS-BERRY-TREE. Common name for *Schinus terebinthifolius*, the Brazilian Pepper-tree, which is attaining increasing popularity in Calif. See PEPPER-TREE.

CHRISTMAS CACTUS. Common name for *Zygocactus truncatus*, referring to the approximate time of its blooming. Also known as the Crab Cactus. See CACTUS; ZYGOCACTUS.

CHRISTMAS-CHERRY. One common name for *Solanum pseudocapsicum*, also known as Jerusalem-cherry, which see.

CHRISTMAS CACTUS
An excellent winter-flowering plant. This one is grafted and trained to standard or tree form.

CHRISTMAS FERN. Common name for *Polystichum acrostichoides*, a familiar native fern suggesting the Boston fern, but hardy and evergreen in the N. States.

CHRISTMAS - FLOWER. Common name in Mexico for *Euphorbia pulcherrima*, the Poinsettia. See EUPHORBIA; POINSETTIA.

CHRISTMAS GREENS. At least part of the festivity of the Christmas season is due to Christmas decorations, which are usually in evidence whether or not there is a Christmas tree. The abundance, beauty and variety of such decorations can often be enhanced by a judicious use of material obtained from the garden.

The collecting of material on the home place may also serve a second purpose, namely, in the pruning of the shrubs and trees which supply it. In pruning to secure Christmas greens (as well as at other times) the natural growth tendency of each kind of plant must be appreciated and respected. (See PRUNING.) Thus the home decorator need not stick to the time-honored supplies, such as laurel and holly. If there is a plentiful supply of these, he will want to make use of them; but he should use his ingenuity in making use of other available material. Almost any of the evergreens—balsam, fir, white pine, pitch pine, red-cedar, common juniper, white and red spruce, Canada, Western or Japanese yew, and evergreen honeysuckle—make good material. With them may be used the red tips of sweet brier, sumac, barberry, bittersweet, shrub roses or any of the red-berried hollies. Or, if there are no colorful berries in the garden, various kinds can be purchased to supplement the evergreen foliage —leafless sprays of *Ilex verticillata,* drooping clusters of the California pepper-tree, etc. Pine cones, grotesque twigs, and various seed-pods painted with or dipped in different colors, silver and gold, add variety and character.

Christmas wreaths are not hard to make on wire hoops from 10 to 14 in. in diameter. These should be padded or "mossed" as the florists say, with sphagnum moss, held by string wound around in spiral fashion; the evergreen sprays, twigs, etc., are then thrust into this base and held with strong thread or fine wire. Ropes of green for the mantel, staircase, balustrade or passageway can be made on a piece of clothesline, one long piece of string being wrapped spirally (and knotted when necessary) to bind the greens.

Two or three handsome decorative pieces are always more effective than many unrelated bits scattered about the house. And wreaths and roping tend to be more beautiful and dignified if made of a few kinds of material rather than a promiscuous variety. Arrangements of evergreen materials in bowls are always in order and, of course, there are the appropriate Christmas-season flowering pot plants.

CHRISTMAS-ROSE. Common name for *Helleborus niger,* a perennial herb of the Buttercup Family. It has excellent bright colored, divided foliage and large attractive white, greenish or slightly purplish flowers resembling wild roses or anemones, with prominent yellowish stamens.

They appear in late winter (thus explaining its name) or very early spring. It should be planted in partial shade in rich, moist soil and should not be disturbed when once established; a fern bed gives excellent protection both winter and summer. It is also an excellent plant in a shrubbery border, or for the rock garden. If the flowers are wanted primarily for cutting, plants should be grown in beds in a soil of good garden loam mixed with sand, and top-dressed with well-rotted manure. If it is desired to force plants under glass, strong specimens should be selected, potted up in late summer or fall and gradually brought into a warmer temperature. The flowers, which may thus be secured at any period of the winter, last well when cut. Propagation is by division of the root or seed, the seedling bearing flowers the third year.

There are a number of interesting varieties. Var. *maximus,* a horticultural form, has flowers 3 to 5 in. across, with, sometimes, several on the same stem. Var. *praecox* is especially early, blooming from Sept. to Feb. See also HELLEBORE.

CHRISTMAS TREES. In different parts of the country, different kinds of evergreen trees are used for Christmas celebration, but almost without exception they are of the coniferous type. In the S. and Central States the red-cedar is most often used, or sometimes the scrub pine. In the W. the Douglas fir is considered the ideal tree, but the N. E. markets are usually supplied with balsam fir and spruce, both the red and the Norway species, from N. New England, Canada and N. N. Y. As sold, the trees vary from 3 to 35 ft. or more in height. More than 8 million trees are used every year.

The question is often raised whether the practice of cutting so many trees every year is not wasteful and destructive, but foresters contend that, rightly done, it is a phase of good forest management. Therefore, whether Christmas trees are cut and sold in the course of thinning and improving a forest, or grown especially for the holiday trade as a commercial project, in either case their sale may be regarded as legitimate. The growing of Christmas trees in pastures that are going back to forest or on other nonagricultural or marginal land, has become a real business. Seedling trees may be obtained at cost from the Conservation Departments of several States or in larger sizes from commercial nurseries, and information as to the planting and care may be obtained from the State Foresters and State Colleges of Agriculture.

There has developed during recent years a decided sentiment in favor of the use of living Christmas Trees. It has spread throughout the country and led many nurserymen to grow stock especially for this purpose, to be sold in pots, tubs and containers.

Potted trees of various sizes may now be obtained, decorated and enjoyed over the Christmas holidays and later planted out in the ground in a place previously mulched to prevent its freezing. Or the gardener may set aside an area in which spruce or fir trees can be grown, then potted in late fall in preparation for the holiday season.

CHRISTOPHINE (kris'-toh-feen). A common name for *Sechium edule*, a tall, climbing cucurbitous vine of tropical America, also known as Chayote, which see.

CHRISTS-THORN. A common name for *Paliurus spina-christi*, a spiny tree of S. Europe and the Orient. It is also applied to *Carissa carandas*, a spiny, fragrant-flowered shrub of India. See PALIURUS; CARISSA.

CHRYSALIDOCARPUS (kri-sal-i-doh-kahr'-pus) *lutescens*. One of the Feather Palms, this species, commonly known as Yellow-bamboo or Areca Palm, has many stems growing in clumps, sometimes 25 ft. high and with a spread of 15 ft. The plants are covered nearly to the ground with unarmed (spineless) graceful, erect leaves with yellow leaf-sheaths. The Areca Palm is grown extensively in S. Fla., thriving best in the shade and in a rich, mucky soil. It is extensively grown by florists as a decorative plant, being started easily from seed. But though frequently sold as a house plant, it does not long endure the hot, dry atmosphere of the average living-room.

Larger species, *C. lucubensis* and *C. madagascariensis* are also grown in southern Florida.

CHRYSALIS (kris'-al-is) (plural, *chrysalids*). The pupa or transformation stage of a butterfly or moth into which the full-grown caterpillar turns. It is oval or cigar-shaped with a horny covering of hardened glue-like substance exuded from the skin of the larva. The pupae

of butterflies are naked chrysalids; those of many moths are enclosed in a soft but tough silken cocoon.

CHRYSANTHEMUM (kris-an'-the-mum). A large genus of annual and perennial herbs, some of them slightly woody or shrubby at the base, members of the Composite Family. Certain of its more valued species, especially the pyrethrum and shasta daisy, bear ornamental flowers during the summer. The most famous member, the garden chrysanthemum, is undoubtedly the showiest of all autumn blossoms. Its plants are mostly musk-scented and somewhat coarse of growth, with blooms of amazing diversity in sizes and forms. Its colors vary from white to pale, delicate pastels, tawny bronzes, yellow-purplish, and red. No blue or true purple ever appears, but blends are numerous, and floral production is liberal.

In view of the great popularity of the garden chrysanthemum (colloquially termed "mum") a discussion of its history is important. The plant has a long romantic history of Asiatic origin. *C. indicum*, a tiny yellow daisy, was known to Confucius in China after 550 B.C., and seeds from Korea were dispatched to Japan in 386 A.D. In all those countries many new types were developed, and the chrysanthemum became Japan's national flower. *C. morifolium*, in its double form, first appeared in Japan, and became the parent of all future double varieties. The Japanese are still very active in breeding, but their exotically-shaped, often mammoth flowers bloom too late for most of the United States.

In 1764 the chrysanthemum reached England and later France, but its late flowering reduced it to a greenhouse flower. A French baker is credited with developing the first seeds leading to earlier varieties, as his plants, next to a warm oven, escaped frost injury. Other French breeders continued, and the pompon, or small, rounded type of blossom, also was brought from China. After 1847 some American gardens had chrysanthemums, chiefly very late pompons called "Artemisias".

Because of late blossoms, invariably nipped by hard frosts, and mediocre growth habits, the chrysanthemum held only moderate popularity until 1933. In that year a Connecticut nurseryman introduced his first creation of the set called Korean Hybrids. He had bred the wild but vigorous *C. sibiricum* (then known as *C. coreanum*) with existing garden varieties to achieve earlier, much hardier, more floriferous kinds of exquisite shadings. The chrysanthemum quickly came into prominence. While the original Korean Hybrids were of single or daisy flowers, they were intensely bred further into doubles as well. Nearly all recent varieties have lineage going back to the Korean Hybrids. *C. articum, C. rubellum,* and *C. nipponicum* have also been utilized by hybridizers, but with less spectacular results.

Shortly after the Korean Hybrid's debut a chance seedling appeared in a Texas nursery; it was low and broad, but covered with hundreds of double pink flowers. Because it resembled a florist's azalea in habit and prolific bloom, it was called "Azaleamum". This led to the very widely-grown class known as cushions (azaleamum is a trademarked name) and still more fame for the chrysanthemum. Very early to flower, the cushions were also easily grown and well suited for small spaces, including foundation plantings. Many varieties will bloom by late July after their first year.

USES. Especially in September and October the garden needs chrysanthemums. In sunny, well-drained borders individual specimens or groups, set at two-foot intervals, become masses of bloom when little else remains, for they withstand light frosts. Since heights usually vary from one to three and a half feet, judicious selection of varieties enhances the whole width of the border. Low growers, as the cushions, are fine as edgings, in urns and tubs, in rock gardens or foundation plantings next to evergreens. Chrysanthemums may also be moved while in full bloom if care is taken. If dug up with a ball of soil around them, they can be planted wherever desired. So they may be grown all summer in a reserve area, like a vegetable garden, and then moved in the fall.

Most chrysanthemums of taller stature are superb for cutting, and the flowers will last two or three weeks in water but leaves should be removed from the submerged portions of the stem. They are also good when arranged with fall foliage or berried branches. Countless late-blooming varieties are used by commercial greenhouses for bouquets and potted plants. And some compact outdoor types with good color are often lifted with a ball of soil, placed in large pots, and brought indoors for added weeks of bloom.

Most late outdoor varieties can be grown in the South and Far West due to milder climate. In the North varieties not flowering by October 15 are likely to become frozen unless protected on cold nights. Repeated temperatures below 27° F. badly damage most varieties.

CLASSIFICATION BY BLOOM TYPES. Following are the general classifications for the amateur; the connoisseur further subdivides some classes into groups by floral sizes and petal characteristics.

1. *Single.* Daisies, like the original Korean Hybrids, with not more than five rows of straplike florets surrounded by a central disk. They are airy and fine in bouquets, but are no longer in great demand.

2. *Semidouble* or *Duplex.* More than five rows of florets and prominent disk.

3. *Anemone.* No more than five rows of ray florets, but also with disk florets as a pad or cushion in the center of each flower. Today's earlier varieties have vastly increased garden usage.

4. *Pompon.* Neatly rounded flowers, usually 1½ to 2½ in. in size, trim looking and excellent to cut. "Buttons" are smaller, like 1 in. globes.

5. *Commercial.* The "football mum," 4 to 8 in. across, fully double. The large perfect blossoms are usually achieved by disbudding in greenhouses. However, some are found in gardens in New York and to the South. This class requires special attention in growing, as explained further along in this article under the heading Disbudding. If petals curve inward, the flower is "incurved;" if they curve outward, it is "reflexed."

6. *Decorative.* The most popular garden type, with fully double blooms of long, strap-like petals, generally 2 to 4 in. long.

7. *Spoon.* Florets open at the ends to form tips like a spoon or a chemist's spatula. This unique formation is greatly favored for flower arrangements.

8. *Spider.* Very exotic, with long, curved, twisted, tubular florets tending to

Plate 10. THE CHRYSANTHEMUM TAKES MANY FORMS

Upper left: A single pink variety typical of the newer garden sorts. Upper right: The Cascade form adapts chrysanthemums to the rock garden. Center left: Mammoth blooms as grown under glass with special care. Center right: The simple grace of an outdoor pompon variety. Bottom: Hardy chrysanthemums bring glory to the late autumn border.

droop. While they grow very large if disbudded, the flowers bloom too late for northern autumns unless protected.

The garden chrysanthemum is becoming extremely popular and important. Hundreds of fine varieties are being produced commercially. Further breeding among the various classes is under way, and in time some of the allied species may prove successful in crosses.

Greatly improved techniques of shading and heating now allow "Year Round" production of bloom. Potted plants or cut flowers are available at Florists all year. Rooted cuttings for such propagation are also constantly in supply. Thus, the renewed availability has catapulted the plant to top status in popularity.

In gardens, increased use of the low, colorful cushions is evident. Also more plants are sold each fall in full display, for instant garden results.

Chrysanthemum Culture

Garden chrysanthemums prefer predominantly sunny exposures and a well-drained soil of moderate humus content. Ground capable of sustaining good vegetables is suitable. Each plant requires about a tablespoonful of a complete fertilizer when set out, but this should not actually touch the roots. If growth is poor in August, a feeding with modern, quickly available, soluble fertilizer is most helpful.

Planting time is in the spring, after danger of night frosts has ended; in the North May 15 to July 1 is the favored period. New plants may be placed in small pots, as rooted cuttings without soil or as divisions of older plants. They should be placed 18-24 in. from neighboring material and watered heavily. Wilting plants should be covered with baskets or other protection for a few days, but remove the cover at sundown. As soon as the roots take hold, cover is unnecessary.

When growth reaches four to six inches, the tips of each shoot are pinched off; this encourages a bushy development and avoids the need for staking. Also many more stems of flowers will appear. The pinching is repeated after each additional four to six inches of growth until mid-July. From then on blossom buds start forming. While chrysanthemums are relatively tolerant toward drought, some heavy waterings in dry periods are prudent, especially as the mass of bloom opens.

Plants with larger flowers can be damaged by frosts when fully open, particularly after softening warm spells. Frosts as low as 27° may only brown the petals, while new buds continue unfolding. Temperatures around 22° may freeze buds. If frost is predicted for any given night, shelters of plastic, burlap, heavy cloth, thick paper, etc., often save the plants. Such shelters should be erected on sticks or poles, as canopies or tents, a few inches above the flowers. If these shelters actually touch the blooms, they act as frost conductors rather than insulators. The covers should drape all the way to the ground. Remove them the next morning.

DISBUDDING. To achieve especially large, perfect flowers, like those grown commercially in greenhouses, quantity must be sacrificed for quality. This is easily done outdoors. The plant is trimmed to one to four stems in August, and is staked as the stems elongate. When buds form, all are removed except the top or crown buds on each stem. That bud gradually swells to abnormal size, as all the strength goes into it. Frequent attention is required to remove all new side buds and other strength-taking growths from leaf axils. When bloom is full such fine blossoms deserve protection from frosts and also from heavy rains.

SHADING. This practice is largely for the commercial grower, who seeks to force plants into earlier bloom. Amateur gardeners may also do this on a smaller scale. Since the chrysanthemum normally blossoms in the fall when the days are shorter, the light period largely governs the time of flowering. So by covering the plants with dark shade cloth or plastic from about 7 P.M. to 7 A.M. each day, the daily light period is considerably shortened. Structures of lath or poles can be erected around large plantings; smaller box-like frames will do for single clumps. Cloth is draped completely over and around the group or plant to be forced. When buds are nearly ready to show color, shading is halted.

About sixty days of such shading is required to bring a plant into bloom a month ahead of the usual time. Thus if a variety normally flowering October 20 was desired to bloom September 15, shading should be commenced July 15.

POT PLANT GROWING. Some gardeners enjoy later flowering chrysanthemums in pots for indoor display; commercial growers raise large quantities of them under careful repotting schedules. There is a simple procedure for the average amateur. Plants may be set out, pinched, and grown just as for the garden. When cold weather approaches, these plants are carefully dug up with a ball of soil and placed in eight to nine inch pots. After a thorough watering they may be brought inside into a fairly sunny, reasonably cool room. Further watering will be necessary about every third day.

ENEMIES. Aphis, red, green, or black, and red spider, both sucking insects, sometimes appear in hot weather. Many insecticides can control them. Various chewing insects, such as beetles, chafers, and tarnished plant bugs, occasionally injure buds and early flowers. Midge is troublesome on rare occasions; small lumps or swellings on leaves signify their presence as eggs are laid inside. If allowed to go unchecked, the whole plant can be disfigured and crippled. An insecticide called Malathion works well against all these pests.

Leaf nematodes can be very serious, but happily are not too common. Tiny, invisible insects inside the leaves can suck these leaves dry and brown from ground up. In wet weather, the nematodes actually swim up the stem. Without good foliage, flowers are largely ruined.

Symptoms are basically brown areas between leaf veins, which gradually spread and increase. Best cures comes from systemic poisons, such as P-40, a powdered form of sodium selenate. These are applied to the ground, as recommended, and absorbed by plant, which is then nematode-resistant. Very poisonous, these compounds are to be kept from pets and human mouths. Leafy vegetables are best not grown in the same area for several years.

DISEASES. Leaf spot is the most common, especially on crowded or starved plants. A fungicidal spray or dust prevents spread of the brown blotches, and diseased leaves should be removed. Mildew, a white coating, sometimes appears after cold wet nights and can be eradicated by sulfur or specific anti-mildew sprays.

There are also several other diseases less common to the amateur's garden than to more extensive commercial plantings. Among these is Stunt, a virus, which threatened to become serious a few years ago but is now under control, due to sanitation and to careful roguing of diseased propagating stock. Stunt, like aster yel-

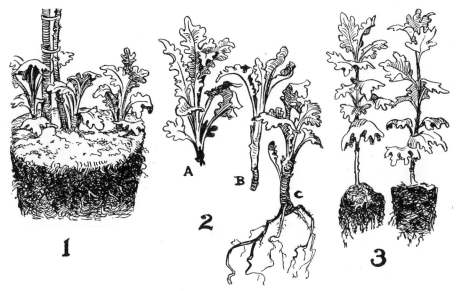

RAISING NEW CHRYSANTHEMUMS FROM CUTTINGS

1. An old plant showing the new root shoots or suckers which are cut off to make cuttings. 2. A cutting (A) freshly taken, (B) trimmed for insertion in moist sand, and (C) when roots have developed and new growth has started. 3. Vigorous young plants from cuttings ready to be trained to single stems for exhibition blooms, or pinched back if bushy plants are wanted.

lows, is evidenced in the garden by runted plants only a few inches tall, small yellow foliage, and premature, undersized, off-color blossoms. Since it is probably passed on by aster leaf-hoppers and by contact with other plants, such sick specimens should be dug up and burned. The disease appears most serious in gardens near weedy fields or roadsides; aster leaf-hoppers evidently bring the virus from diseased weeds. Hence clean cultivation is helpful. Commercial growers, however, are reducing the risk of purchasing diseased stock by careful choice of propagating stock.

WINTER PROTECTION. Most garden chrysanthemums are inherently hardy against cold, but like other shallow-rooted plants they can heave out of the ground if not protected against thaws. Also they do not like constant wetness. Therefore steady winter drainage is the keynote to wintering success. In late fall cut the stems down to about 4 in. When the ground is frozen hard, a mulch of 3 to 4 in. of hay may be loosely applied. Clumps can be stored in coldframes if desired. Or clumps can be dug up in late fall with a ball of soil and left to freeze atop the ground. When frozen hard, a light cover of hay will keep the plants dry and firm until spring.

When spring arrives, the covering is loosened and gradually removed. All chrysanthemums, except cushions whose summer bloom comes only on older plants, should be properly divided each spring. When shoots are one to two inches high, the clumps are lifted and strongly-rooted outer stems are torn or cut off. The young divisions are replanted, and the old clump's center is discarded; healthier, less woody plants result if this is done. Undivided plants become lanky, straggly, and may blossom poorly.

Cuttings may also be made, of two to three inch soft tips in spring. These root readily in sand, peat, perlite or a blend thereof.

PROPAGATION. If seed is sown by early May, the resulting plants should bloom that autumn, but the extremely hybrid nature of the modern variety means wide variations. Stem cuttings are easily rooted in sand during late spring and may then be planted directly into the border, but must be carefully watered. Division, described above under Winter Protection, is not only desirable but also affords speedy increase. Cuttings are increasingly employed, as tissues are soft and eager to grow.

PRINCIPAL ANNUAL SPECIES

C. carinatum (Tricolor Chrysanthemum). 2 to 3 ft. heads 2 to 2½ in. across have white, red, yellow, or purple rays with a colored ring around the purple disk. An excellent garden subject.

coronarium (Garland Chrysanthemum or Crown Daisy). Stout and branching to 3 or 4 ft. Leaves deeply and compoundly cut. Many yellow or whitish heads 1 to 1½ in. across. Ideal for the garden. Var. *spatiosum*, 2 ft., and heavy-leaved, has light yellow flowers.

segetum (Corn Marigold). 1 to 2 ft., with small yellow to white heads terminating many branches. Includes several named varieties.

PRINCIPAL PERENNIAL SPECIES

C. articum (Arctic Chrysanthemum). 12 to 15 in. Thick leathery leaves. Very hardy. White to lilac daisies 2 in. across blossom in profusion in October. Used by breeders as parent of Northland Daisies.

cinerariaefolium (Dalmatian Chrysanthemum). 1 to 2 ft. Many stems. Silvery, slashed leaves, and 1 in. white flower heads, often dried and ground to make Persian insect powder. Blooms early summer.

coccineum (Pyrethrum, Painted Daisy). 2 to 3 ft. An excellent perennial. Blooms profusely in June-July, often later, with flowers in various shades of pink, red, and white. It may be single, semi-double or double. An ideal cutflower, excellent in borders, especially in groups of 3 to 6, in good sunlight and average soil. Fern-like foliage, hardy. Clumps should be divided and reset every three or four years, best in midsummer. Seeds germinate easily, but may not give flowers for several years. Many named varieties available.

frutescens (Marguerite, Paris Daisy). To 3 ft. Not hardy. Many white, pale yellow or pink daisies on branchy plant, woody at base. Familiar as florist's pot plant and cutflower.

maximum (Shasta Daisy). 2 to 3 ft. Very popular garden plant but often short-lived. Blooms exclusively white, 2 to 4 in. across, in single, semi-double, frilled, lacinated, or double forms. Blooms much of the summer. Long, glossy leaves and heavy clumps. Superb cutflowers, excellent in borders. Needs protection from dampness in winter. Many named varieties in great demand. Division every second year is essential to prevent its dying out. Seed is easily raised in the spring.

morifolium (Commercial or Florist's Chrysanthemum). 2 to 4 ft. An original species. 2 in. daisies in several colors. Interesting as parent of garden chrysanthemums. Most fine greenhouse varieties, for cutting or pot plant use, are derived from the double form, which has been vastly improved.

nipponicum (Nippon Daisy). 1½ to 2 ft. White heads 1½ to 3½ in. across, from late summer on. Thick, spatulate leaves and woody stems. Fine Japanese plant, especially near U.S. seacoasts. Used somewhat in hybridizing, to no apparent avail.

parthenium (Feverfew). 1 to 3 ft. Bushy, with abundant, ferny, often yellowish foliage. Clusters of small heads, single or double, white or yellow, excellent for summer cutting. Dwarf varieties good in border but short-lived unless divided annually. Also grown from seed.

rubellum (*C. erubescens*). 2 to 3 ft. Very hardy, quite branching. Floriferous clump blooming in early autumn. Long pinnate foliage. 2 to 3 in. daisies, pink or rose-red. Often an important parent in hybridizing and has led to Rubellum Hybrids, mostly rather coarse singles.

sibiricum (*C. coreanum*) (Korean Daisy). 2 to 3 ft. Very hardy and floriferous. 2 to 2½ in. heads white or rose tinted. Best known as parent of Korean Hybrids. Useful for a wild garden.

uliginosum (Giant Daisy, Hungarian Daisy). 4 to 7 ft. Tall, late-blooming European species often incorrectly listed as *Pyrethrum uliginosum*. Good background plant, 1 to 3 in. heads of white, slender cut foliage. Its tolerance for wet soils interests hybridizers.

CHRYSANTHEMUM SOCIETY, NATIONAL. Organized in October, 1944, the purpose of the Society is the promotion of all activities relating to the Chrysanthemum. The Society publishes a quarterly bulletin and a handbook. Secretary: Mrs. George S. Briggs, 8504 La Verne Drive, Adelphi, Maryland 20783.

CHRYSOBALANUS (kris-oh-bal'-ahnus). Shrubs or small trees of the Rosaceae, or Rose Family, native in the American and African tropics. The chief species

is *C. icaco* (Coco-Plum), sometimes an evergreen tree to 30 ft., but only a bush in its northern range, which is Florida, where it grows on the coast and along streams. It has thick leathery leaves and small white flowers. The rather dry and insipid plum-shaped fruits are sometimes used for preserves.

CHRYSOGONUM (kris-og'-oh-num) *virginianum*. A perennial herb found wild from Penn. to Fla. and sometimes transplanted to gardens. Its yellow composite heads fit its popular name, Golden Star, which see.

CHRYSOPHYLLUM (kris-oh-fil'-um) *cainito*. A tropical American evergreen tree sometimes grown in S. Fla. for ornament and its edible fruit. It is commonly called Star-apple, which see.

CHRYSOPSIS (kris-op'-sis). Golden aster. A group of daisy-like plants of the Composite Family, with yellow flowers on stems 1 to 3 ft. high. They are occasionally grown in the border, though more at home in the dry, sunny part of the wild garden. They are easily increased by seed or division. *C. graminifolia* has silvery hairy foliage and bright yellow flowers ½ in. across.

CHRYSOSPLENIUM (kris-oh-splee'-ni-um). A genus of little creeping herbs of the Saxifrage Family, called Golden-saxifrage. Their only value horticulturally is in the bog garden where they can be planted as a ground cover. *C. americanum*, with small roundish leaves, and inconspicuous flowers, grows best in damp soil in partial shade.

CHUFA (choo'-fa). Common name for *Cyperus esculentus*, a moisture-loving, reed-like herb sometimes called Earth-almond. The many roots are hard, little tubers, often spoken of as nuts, and may be eaten roasted or cooked. Chufas are grown in the southern states chiefly as food for poultry and pigs.

CHURCH GARDENS. An interesting suggestion, reflecting the increasing thought being given to the larger possibilities of gardening, has recently been offered through different channels in N.J., to the effect that the grounds of many churches might well be improved and put to increased use, both esthetic and practical. It is pointed out that, although the former use of these choice community locations as burying grounds has been almost entirely given up, they have been almost as completely left out of America's outdoor life and garden picture. The idea contemplates both the development of small church yards as quiet, secluded garden spots for rest, relaxation, and communion with nature, and the beautification of larger areas with a view to their frequent use for church socials, bazaars, festivals, etc. and even weddings and other happy social functions in which the church plays a major part. There is also the further possibility that in favorable locations, a small part of a church yard could be planted and maintained as a source of flowers for use on the altar, later, perhaps, to be sent to the ill and the old of the parish. The discussion of the plan aroused considerable favorable response and evidence that it was already being successfully carried out in some places. Those interested in securing further information can probably obtain it from the editor of *The Shade Tree,* published by the N. J. Federation of Shade Tree Commissions at Kearny, N. J.

CIBOTIUM (si-boh'-shi-um). A genus of tropical ferns, named from the Greek word for "casket," referring to the indusia. Closely related to Dicksonia, it is composed largely of tree ferns requiring excellent warm-greenhouse care.

CICADA (si-kay'-dah). The correct name of a genus of large, wide-headed, membranous-winged insects well known for their loud, insistent, buzzing noise in midsummer, and yet usually called by either of two names to which they are not entitled, namely, "harvest fly" and "locust." They are not flies at all but members of another insect order (Homoptera); and Locust (which see) is the correct name of what are popularly called grasshoppers. The cicadas are not usually serious pests, although when present in large numbers the adult females in laying their eggs may injure young fruit trees, while the grubs sometimes do damage by gnawing plant roots. They are familiarly regarded as signs of hot weather, which they are to the extent that they appear and begin to "sing" only when summer is well advanced and heat can logically be expected.

There are several kinds of cicadas, distinguished chiefly by the length of time (ranging up to 17 years) that elapses between broods. The periodical cicada (*Magicicada septendecim*) or "17-year locust" has a dark colored body about 1¼ in. long, two pair of transparent wings,

reddish legs and sucking mouth parts (see INSECTS). Injury to trees, especially young fruit trees, is caused by the egg-laying female splintering the wood of the smaller branches with her tough horny ovipositor (egg-laying apparatus). The male's peculiar "song," of great volume and intensity, is produced by a complicated system of vibrating body membranes.

This species has the longest developing period of any known insect. The eggs, laid (400 to 600 by each female) from late May to early July, hatch in six or seven weeks. The young (nymphs) drop to the ground, enter the soil and there feed on roots of plants for 17 years before working their way to the surface again. Because they grow so slowly they do not cause much injury. At the end of the period they emerge in large numbers—as many as 20,000 to 40,000 from under a single tree—crawl up on tree trunks or weed stems, gradually work out of their old skins over night and, by the next day, are ready for flight as mature cicadas.

There are several broods maturing in different years in different sections. Their habits have been carefully studied and the years and dates when the insects may be expected to appear can be obtained in advance from the State experiment stations. Since they never fail to appear on schedule, young orchards should not be set out the year a large brood is due to emerge. However, young trees can be protected by covering them with cheese-cloth while the adult cicadas are on the wing; after they have disappeared prune off and burn any damaged weakened limbs.

A similar cicada, but with a 13-year cycle, is common throughout the South. The short-cycle, "dog-day cicada" appearing every year over a large area, is larger than the periodical, but does very little damage.

CICER (sy'-ser) *arietinum.* An annual legume, grown in the Old World as a food crop and popularly known as Garbanzo or Chick-pea (which see).

CICHORIUM (si-koh'-ri-um). A genus of Old-World herbs of the Composite Family. Both of the two principal species are grown in the vegetable garden. *C. endivia* (Endive) is an annual or biennial with much curled and cut leaves which are blanched and used as a substitute for lettuce in hot weather when ordinary lettuce fails to head. *C. intybus* is Chicory or

Succory, the large roots of which are used, ground, as an adulterant of coffee, and also lifted and forced to produce hard tight heads of white leaves which are called Barbe de Capucin or Witloof Chicory and used for salad. The flowers of both species are a beautiful shade of blue and the plants are sometimes used in the border. Succory is widely naturalized in eastern N. A. See CHICORY; ENDIVE.

CICUTA (si-keu'-tah). A genus of moisture-loving native perennial herbs, with small white strongly scented flowers in flat clusters. The roots are poisonous, but it is sometimes transplanted to bog-gardens or moist spots in the wild garden. See WATER-HEMLOCK.

CIGAR-FLOWER. Common name for *Cuphea platycentra,* a tender Mexican herb easily grown as an annual in greenhouses. The flowers have no petals but a slender bright red calyx tipped with white and gray suggesting the popular name.

CILIATE. Fringed with small hairs.

C I M I C I F U G A (sim-i-sif'-eu-gah). (Bugbane). A genus of plants of the But-tercup Family. They are woodland, tall-growing, herbaceous perennials with long wands of very small white flowers. Use-ful in the back of a hardy border or in semi-shade locations in the wild garden, they are easily increased by seed or di-vision. *C. racemosa* (Black Cohosh or Black Snakeroot), grows to a height of 8 ft. in rich, moist woodland soil. The odor of its flowers is not pleasant. *C. sim-plex* is of lower growth, not exceeding 3 ft. and is the most effective for planting in the shady border, blooming in autumn.

CINDER-CULTURE. The use of cin-ders as a root medium for growing plants with nutrient solutions has given rise to this term. Cinders, readily available, are a good material to use. Those from bitu-minous coal are considered somewhat su-perior to those from anthracite, but require thorough leaching before using. This type of material is suitable for use in the larger home gardening containers, such as window boxes and large pots. Nutrients may be applied by subirrigation or by the flush method. See CHEMICAL GARDENING; NUTRI-ENT SOLUTION; WINDOW BOX.

CINDERS. Coarse cinders are excel-lent drainage material for the bottom of walks and drives, or even in the bottom of beds, borders, trenches, or rose gardens in heavy, stiff soil. Fine, sifted cinders can

be worked into a clay soil to improve (lighten and loosen) its texture. While cinders do not furnish plant food, save pos-sibly a small amount of sulphur, they have some garden value because of their effect on the physical conditions surrounding the plants.

CINERARIA (sin-e-ray'-ri-ah). This is the former name, still used by florists for *Senecio cruentus,* a short-stemmed woolly perennial which they grow as a winter-flowering pot plant in a cool part of the greenhouse. In warm regions it can be and is grown successfully outdoors. The large velvety leaves, generally toothed, are often completely obscured by the daisy-like flowers in shades and combinations of purple, red, blue, pink, and white. Native to the Canary Islands, the species is the parent of many hybrids that grace green-houses and homes with even larger and more brilliant blossoms.

While Cinerarias can be carried over, fresh stock is usually grown every year from seed sown in April, May or June, depending on the season in which flowers are wanted. The soil should be a fine sandy loam containing about one-third leaf-mold. When seedlings are large enough to handle they should be potted up and kept moist and cool. Liquid manure is bene-ficial *after* the buds appear. Double-flow-ered varieties are also propagated by cut-tings of strong shoots that arise after the flowering tops are removed.

The Star Cineraria (known to growers as *C. stellata*), of more open habit to 2 ft. tall, has single, smaller flowers. All cinerarias are subject to attack by green aphids which are most often seen on tender shoots and the under leaf surfaces. The greenhouse leaf tyer and white fly may also be injurious. For control measures see GREENHOUSE PESTS.

Two other species of Senecio: *S. cin-eraria* and *S. leucostachys,* often called Dusty Millers because of their whitish woolly foliage, are sometimes spoken of as cinerarias.

CINNAMOMUM (sin-ah-moh'-mum). Evergreen trees and shrubs of Asia and Australia, with aromatic leaves and wood. They are mostly of economic rather than horticultural value, although one or two species are grown in Fla. and Calif. for ornamental and shade purposes. The prin-cipal species are *C. camphora* (Camphor-tree). A tree to 40 ft. with glossy green leaves which turn yellow to crimson before dropping off. This happens just as the unfolding young leaves are a soft rose-pink shade, quite outclassing in beauty the small yellow flowers. Commercial camphor is extracted from the wood.

C. zeylanicum (Cinnamon-tree). Small tree with long stiff leaves; the bark yields the cinnamon of commerce.

C. cassia (Cassia-bark-tree). Handsome tree to 40 ft., whose bark is used as a substitute for cinnamon.

CINNAMON FERN (*Osmunda cinnamomea*). A common and handsome fern of the E. States, doing excellently in ordinary garden soil. It has broad 3 to 4 ft. fronds. The fertile ones, appearing after the sterile ones and altered into flowerlike sprays of spores, soon wither. It prefers a peaty soil, much water, and good drainage.

CINNAMON-TREE. Common name for *Cinnamomum zeylanicum,* an evergreen E. Indian tree of the Laurel Family, the bark of which supplies commercial cinnamon.

CINNAMON-VINE (*Dioscorea batatas*). A tall climbing plant from China with slender twining stems, useful as a porch vine where a heavy screen is not desired. It is tuberous-rooted and fairly hardy North, where it is herbaceous. It has attractive shining leaves, conspicuously ribbed and veined, and bears small clusters of cinnamon-scented white flowers in the axils. Little tubercles are formed in the axils of the leaves and from these new plants can be started.

See also DIOSCOREA.

CINQUEFOIL (sink'-foil). Common name for Potentilla, a large genus of herbs and shrubby plants of the Rose Family, with yellow, red, or white flowers. Mostly they are hardy N. and effective in beds, borders or rock gardens.

CION (sy'-on) or SCION. In grafting, the shoot or bud of a plant that it is desired to propagate. It is inserted in stem or branch of another growing plant, called the *stock.* Thus a rare or improved, but weak-growing, variety can be established on the roots of a strong-growing but less desirable kind.

See GRAFTING.

CIPURA (sy-peu'-rah). A small group of tropical American herbs belonging to the Iris Family and closely related to Marica (which see). They bear clusters

of white or blue 6-petaled flowers which quickly wither. In the S. they are grown in the open; in the North, under glass. They require a sandy fibrous loam, and may be propagated by seeds or by offsets from the corm.

CIRCAEA (sur-see'-ah) *lutetiana.* A weedy herb of the Evening-primrose Family with very small white flowers. It is known as Enchanters Nightshade, which see.

CIRSIUM (sur'-si-um). Plumed Thistle. A genus of rank-growing, prickly plants of the Composite Family with spiny leaves and purple, yellow and white flowers in heads. A few species are grown for their bold ornamental effect in the wild garden and are easily increased from seed. *C. occidentale* is a striking form growing 3 ft. high and having silvery white foliage topped with large rose or purple heads. *C. lanceolatum,* the common pasture or bull thistle, grows to 5 ft. high and has purple heads of fragrant flowers.

The true or Scotch thistle is *Onopordum acanthium,* which see.

CISSUS (sis'-us). Tendril-climbing shrubs from tropical regions, belonging to the Grape Family. A few are grown in greenhouses for their decorative foliage or interesting habit, and outdoors in the warmest parts of the country. Most of them have been known and described as Vitis (which see). Propagated by cuttings. Principal species are as follows:

C. discolor. A popular warm house foliage plant from Java. The oblong leaves of velvety green are mottled with white and pink on the upper surface, and reddish-purple beneath.

incisa (Marine Ivy). A tall climber of the Southern States, with fleshy leaves which are divided.

antarctica (Kangaroo-vine). A shrubby climber from Australia with thick glossy leaves. Cannot stand frost.

capensis. A strong growing evergreen S. African vine, much planted in S. Calif. The fruit is used in jelly making and the tuberous roots are said to make good cattle fodder.

quadrangularis. A curious succulent climber with 4-angled and winged stems.

CISTUS (sis'-tus). Low upright shrubs, evergreen or partially so, native of the Mediterranean region, belonging to the Rock-rose Family. See ROCK-ROSE.

CITRANGE (sit′-ranj). A "made name" for hybrids (produced by Walter T. Swingle of the U. S. Department of Agriculture) between the common orange and the hardy but inedible trifoliate orange (*Poncirus,* formerly *Citrus, trifoliata*). While dormant the trees are hardier than oranges, often surviving temperatures lower than 15° F. For home gardens in climates similar to that of the Cotton Belt they are ornamental in flower and fruit; the latter, though not large or generally marketable, makes good beverages and marmalade. There are several varieties all of which are worked on trifoliate stock.

Citrangequats are the yellow or orange fruits 1½ to 2 in. in diameter borne by even hardier hybrids of the citrange and the kumquat (which see). Also used in beverages and for cooking.

CITRANGEDIN (sit-ran′-jee-din). A hybrid citrus fruit whose parents are the calamondin and the citrange (both of which see). The tree is relatively hardy, having successfully withstood temperatures of 12 deg. F., so may be grown in gardens as far N. as the kumquat (which see) or even farther. The fruit makes an excellent drink which suggests limeade. See also CITRUS FRUITS.

CITRON (sit′-ron). Generally refers to a large, lemon-like citrus fruit whose thick peel is candied for use in cakes and confectionery. Also the shrub or small tree (*Citrus medica*) that bears it, which is so tender that its cultivation is limited to southern Florida and southern California. In the latter state a few citron orchards are managed like those of lemons. The name "citron," is also applied to the preserving melon (*Citrullus vulgaris* var. *citroides*) a variety of watermelon. See also CITRUS FRUITS.

CITRONELLA (sit-run-el′-ah). The common name for *Collinsonia canadensis,* a coarse plant of the Mint Family, growing 5 ft. high in rich woods. It has small yellow flowers and large lemon-scented leaves, but is of little interest horticulturally.

CITRULLUS (si-trul′-us) *vulgaris.* The botanical name of the Watermelon. Its var. *citroides,* the Citron or Preserving Melon has a small fruit with firm white flesh which is used only candied or preserved.

CITRUS FRUITS. These form the most important group of tropical and sub-tropical fruit trees of the world. In the U. S. some of them may be grown as garden subjects in warm and favored areas from Fla. to Calif. and occasionally as ornamental greenhouse or house plants in the N. Commercially their culture is restricted to S. Fla., the Mississippi Delta, the lower Rio Grande Valley and S. Calif.

In varying degree frost injures all the citrus species. The lime (which see) is the tenderest, being killed by even slight freezing temperatures; the kumquat (which see) is one of the hardiest, withstanding temperatures of 15 or even 12 deg. F. Hardiness of tender sorts can be measurably increased by budding or grafting on seedling stocks of the trifoliate orange, a species hardy even as far north as Washington, D. C. Hybrids of this with the sweet orange are hardy in the warmer parts of the cotton belt (see CITRANGE) where the fruits are used for making ades and preserves.

Citrus fruits will grow in any well-drained garden soil from sandy to clayey, though these extremes are less desirable than a medium loam. In the former it is difficult to maintain the necessary humus and plant food, and the latter are harder to work, besides being more difficult to drain.

Propagation is usually by shield budding on two-year or three-year-old seedlings of various stocks, mostly sour orange for good land, rough lemon for sandy soils, and trifoliate orange for heavy ones.

Planting is generally done in winter, the larger species (grapefruit and orange) requiring 25 to 30 ft. each way, medium species (tangerines and lemons) 20 to 25 ft. and small ones (kumquat) 15 ft. To maintain the necessary humus in the soil cover-crops and green manures are necessary. From Fla. to Tex. velvet beans, cowpeas and beggarweed are used as summer crops to absorb rainfall; in the arid but irrigated sections, Canada field peas, bur clover and vetch are grown. In the S. E. though the trees are sometimes grown in sod, clean cultivation is usually practiced from early spring until the beginning of the rainy season; in the S. W. it is carried on until fall when a cover-crop is sown.

In the E. complete fertilizers are generally applied three times—February, June and September or October. A popular formula for young trees is 4 to 5 lbs. of a mixture containing 6 per cent phosphoric acid, 5 per cent potash, and 4 per cent ammonia; one for bearing trees is 8 per cent phosphoric acid, 10 per cent potash and 3 per cent ammonia in amounts up to 50 lbs. or even more to individual old trees. Calif. soils are thought to contain enough phosphoric acid and potash, so only nitrogenous fertilizers are generally used there.

When the trees are planted they are generally cut back to 18 or 24 in. to assure low branching. Should sprouts develop from below the bud union they should be rubbed off while succulent because the wounds will heal more quickly than if they have become woody. After the trees are well established, the branches should be thinned so as to leave only 4 or 5 for framework limbs. After this they normally form shapely heads with little or no pruning except the removal of dead branches and of excessive shoots, preferably while succulent. Should frost kill parts of the trees, pruning should be delayed until new shoots appear when the dead parts should be cut out. Heading back will often reclaim and rejuvenate neglected trees.

See also CITRANGEDIN; GRAPEFRUIT; KUMQUAT; LEMON; LIME; LIMEQUAT; MANDARIN; ORANGE; POMELO; PUMMELO; SHADDOCK; TANGELO; TANGERINE.

ENEMIES. Citrus canker, a bacterial disease, resembles chestnut blight as chiefly of historical importance; but in its case the fight was won, not lost. Brought, apparently, from the Orient to Texas about 1910, it four years later was raging through the Gulf States and threatening the entire citrus industry of Fla. However, heroic efforts by the growers, aided later by large sums appropriated by . the Government, finally stamped it out and at the same time proved the value of strict sanitary measures in dealing with infectious plant diseases. Inspectors wore white suits dipped in bichloride of mercury, and had their faces, hands, shoes and leggings disinfected as well. When an infected tree was found it was not touched but immediately destroyed by being sprayed with a flaming mixture of kerosene and crude oil. Other diseases of citrus plants—scab, melanose, brown rot and *mal di gomma*— are chiefly of importance to commercial growers who should get detailed advice from their experiment stations.

The most destructive citrus insects are the armoured purple, and California red, scales, the unarmoured black scale and mealy bugs; but red spiders, thrips and white flies may at times become serious. In Calif. fumigation under tents has been the chief method of control for some 40 years. But resistant strains of scale insects have gradually been built up so that oil sprays are now preferred, both there and in Fla. An agricultural inspector in each district sees that spraying or fumigation is properly done and that growers do not let orchards become so infested that they are a menace to the community. The Mediterranean fruit fly (which see) was found in Fla. in 1929 but prompt steps were taken to destroy all probably infested material and to prohibit the transportation of dangerous material.

CITY GARDEN. In the less densely populated cities gardens do not differ essentially from gardens in towns and villages. Hence the reference here is to the type of garden which has been developed in consequence of congested conditions. Such gardens have necessarily very limited area and are usually surrounded by high walls or high buildings, which also limit both daylight and direct sunlight. They are rarely open to the street but lie back of the dwelling in practically every case. This arrangement leads to a reversal of the typical American city house plan which placed the kitchen at the rear, substituting the plan of Old-World cities which places the kitchen and service elements on the street and puts living rooms in the quieter seclusion of the rear overlooking the garden.

Perhaps no one knows just where and when the first city garden was made in this country. In New York City private individuals began here and there to do a little with their individual . back yards; others living around one city block combined all of these into a community garden; still others, realizing the advantages of flat, open spaces on their roofs took up residence there and thus the penthouse, with accompanying roof garden, became a feature of city living. As landscape architects were called upon the possibilities were more and more realized. And under professional demand, real study of the plant material adapted to the atmosphere and soil conditions of cities was undertaken and the plant possibilities were definitely worked out. In this study the gradually increasing city garden clubs naturally took a leading part, developing also interest and belief in the city garden idea until this became general. Thus the city garden has come to be something as definite as any other distinct type.

The chief problem in the city garden now is likely to be entirely outside the garden maker's control—especially the individual garden maker. This is less the case in community or neighborhood enterprise because the initial step of taking down barriers and uniting several plots into a common holding eliminates much of the ugliness in any such area. But towering buildings, presenting unattractive surfaces or forms, may still intrude; so it is always true that in developing the garden design any such intruding elements must be kept in mind continually, in order to design them out of the composition so far as possible. If they cannot be successfully eliminated by screen planting, arbor or trellis, the next best thing usually is to make a virtue of necessity and incorporate them into the picture—force them to become an asset by framing them into it in such a way that even the ugliness which they seemed to represent takes on character and interest. Surprising though it be, this can be done oftener than is suspected.

In spite of the strict limitations of land area and surrounding walls, there are opportunities for original ideas in city garden design; indeed, innumerable such gardens of great distinction and charm exist. Wall surfaces, for example, are opportunities which the city garden enjoys oftener than that in the country. And though generally the treatment must be architectural (because a garden in a city is a unit in one great architectural whole), this does not by any means deny it trees and shrubs and flowers. It merely implies and demands that, even without them, it shall be interesting and pleasing and a fitting extension out of doors of the dwelling.

Restraint is necessary in selecting plant material. Usually the best effects are the result of using very few kinds; which means, of course, that a great many plants of the kinds chosen are possible. This, in turn, emphasizes them, and in this emphasis lies the important rhythm which is as necessary to a garden as to any other art form. Reliance should be placed mainly on those things which have been tried and

proven. At the same time independent try-outs are not undesirable; they may well yield further material for any particular garden. Just keep the trial plantings on a small scale and inconspicuously placed in any given season.

See also GARDEN DESIGN, SHELTERS, WALLS; OUTDOOR LIVING-ROOM; PATIO GARDEN; PLANTS FOR SPECIAL PURPOSES; SCULPTURE; TERRACE GARDEN; WATER IN THE GARDEN.

CITY GARDEN CLUBS. The first organization to be formed in the United States by garden enthusiasts in a large city for the discussion and study of garden problems peculiar to such an environment, appears to have been the Society of Little Gardens, started in Philadelphia in 1914. Some of the groups formed subsequently on similar lines are the City Gardens Club of New York (1918), the San Francisco Garden Club (1926), the Beacon Hill Garden Club of Boston, Mass. (1928), and the Down-Town Garden Club of Cleveland, O. (1933).

While at first the "city gardening" to which these clubs gave attention was inter-

A CITY GARDEN
It is not the amount of space, but rather the way it is used and cared for, that counts in planting in a crowded area.

preted as merely the beautification of individual front or back yards, the growing of plants in pots or window boxes at the members' homes, and the like, it has gradually taken on a broader, more civic, or community-minded meaning. Thus while the individual's interests and problems are still fully considered, projects for the greater use and enjoyment of trees and plants throughout the city itself have been carried out; street tree, and neighborhood window box planting campaigns have been promoted, garden centers established and maintained, public lectures, demonstrations, and exhibitions have been sponsored, aid to school nature study work given, and an active part taken in conservation movements and endeavors to create wider public appreciation of plants in public places—with a corresponding reduction of ignorant or wilful destruction of such plants. The scope of these activities is well expressed in the Constitution of the New York City club which states that its object is: "to make New York a more livable place by encouraging and assisting the members of the Club and other persons to transform backyards into gardens; to improve public spaces and vacant lots; to develop roof gardens and, in general, to arouse interest in planting and caring for trees, plants, and grass in New York City; and to do such other work as may be convenient or necessary in carrying out such objects."

CLADANTHUS (klah-dan'-thus). An annual herb with strongly odorous foliage, native of S. Spain and Morocco, sometimes grown in the border. The species usually cultivated (*C. arabicus*) has finely-cut, smooth, waxy leaves, and bears its yellow ray-flowers at the tips of the branches. Seeds are sown in April, in ordinary soil.

CLADRASTIS (klah-dras'-tis). Generic name for a native hardy, decorative tree with fragrant flowers, called Yellowwood (which see). It is a member of the Pea or Legume Family.

CLAMMY AZALEA (ah-zay'-le-ah). One of the common names for *Rhododendron viscosum*, a species usually found in swampy places, with pink or white, fragrant, sticky blossoms in midsummer.

CLAMMY LOCUST. Common name for *Robinia viscosa*, a small tree of the Pea Family, whose young growth and pods are covered with sticky hairs.

CLARKIA (klahr'-ki-ah). A hardy annual herb of the Pacific Coast popularly known as Rocky Mountain Garland because in form and color it resembles a garland of almond blossoms. Easily cultivated in sunny locations in any light garden soil, it produces graceful, showy blossoms delicately rose or purple. Excellent for mass planting, it grows 2 ft. tall (or man-high in a greenhouse), with flowers borne along slender upright branches. The long, graceful buds that resemble those of the fuchsia, open in July and August. The flowers are valuable for cutting as they will last a long time if gathered while in bud. This makes clarkia an important greenhouse crop as well as a popular garden subject. Plants seem to thrive better if seed is sown late in April or early in May where plant is to grow, though seed may be sown in the greenhouse in January and the seedlings transplanted in May to stand 9 in. apart, for late spring bloom.

The commonly grown species is *C. elegans,* which has smooth reddish stems and attains a height of 3 ft. under favorable garden conditions and more when grown under glass. Recently there have been developed several double varieties in salmon, crimson, purple, scarlet and white. *C. pulchella* is a lower-growing species with more slender leaves and flowers ranging from lilac to white.

CLARY (kla'-ri). Comomn name for *Salvia sclarea,* a hardy, biennial, scented-leaved plant, with bluish flowers.

CLASPING. Said of a stalkless leaf which wholly or partly surrounds the twig, as in the Toad-lily or the New-England Aster.

CLASSIFICATION. The orderly and systematic arrangement of plants, without which their proper identification and intelligent use is impossible, is based upon their relationship as determined by similarities in structure in relation to their evolution or descent from common ancestors.

The plant kingdom is divided by scientists into four great groups, in which there is a progressive tendency toward increasing complexity and differentiation. Each group is further divided and sub-divided as may be illustrated by Group IV, comprising plants with stems, leaves and roots, and that bear seeds, as follows:

The initial division is into two sub-groups, one of which, called the *Gymnosperms,* contain plants (such as the conifers) that bear their seeds in an exposed situation; examples are the naked seeds lying on the segments of a pine cone. Plants of the other group—the *Angiosperms*—bear their seeds enclosed in an ovary. This sub-group is divided into two classes, differentiated by basic structural differences and called *Monocotyledons* and *Dicotyledons* (both of which see). Each of these classes is made up of *orders,* which are composed of related groups called *families.* Each family generally embraces two or more closely related *genera.* The Genus Rosa, the Genus Prunus, the Genus Crataegus, all belong to the Rose Family, called Rosaceae. And each genus is composed of a number of (rarely one) *species,* which represent the practical unit of plant classification. For a more extended discussion see PLANT NAMES AND CLASSIFICATION.

CLAUSENA (klau-see'-nah) *punctata.* A small Chinese, fruit-bearing tree of the Rue Family, commonly known as Wampi and sometimes grown in the S. as an ornamental plant.

CLAW FERN (*Onychium japonicum*). A good cool-greenhouse fern, with 1 ft. feathery fronds, the tips of whose fertile pinnules somewhat suggest a claw. Pot loosely in fibrous soil, with coarse sand. It is imperative to keep the fronds dry, watering only on the surface of the soil.

CLAY. In the gradation of soil types on a basis of texture, clay is at the extreme of fineness. Even though a garden soil rarely contains any pure clay—which is Kaolinite or the material from which fine pottery is made—a clay type soil will show the characteristic clay qualities in greater or less degree. These are: a smooth greasiness to the touch, especially when moist; a tendency to become more compact when wet—that is to "puddle"; a tendency to then dry into a hard, solid consistency like unbaked brick, and in so doing to shrink so that broad, deep cracks form in the surface. Through these cracks more moisture from below is lost, depriving the plants growing in the soil (if any) and rendering the soil even less fit for cultivation. The result of digging or plowing a clay soil when wet is even more disastrous as it produces large clods or lumps which dry into almost unbreakable solidity. A soil in this condition is almost useless and can be gotten back in shape only after much hard work and long delay.

What is generally called a clay soil, will contain about 30% real clay. It will hold moisture tenaciously, taking a long time to dry out, often because of poor drainage below. Where a clay "hardpan" underlies a loam or sandy soil, this same condition of poor drainage is almost sure to exist.

While some plants will do fairly well in a clay soil, provided the latter is correctly handled, the aim should be to make such a soil more friable, more easily handled and "warmer." This can be done by gradually incorporating sand, sifted coal ashes, or quantities of humus—either manure, compost, peat moss or whatever is available. In doing this take care to work the soil only when it is fairly dry. Also frequently vary the depth to which it is plowed or dug so that a smooth, impervious surface will not be created just below the improved, arable layer.

To break up a stiff clay subsoil, the use of a deep, subsoil plow, trenching (which see), or blasting (see BLAST) can be resorted to.

See also CULTIVATION; SOIL.

CLAYTONIA (klay-toh-ni-ah). Spring Beauty. Spring-flowering native perennials that delight in damp, rich soil and partial shade and are especially adapted to rock gardens. Plants are dwarf, rarely attaining a height of more than a foot; they bear white or rose-colored flowers. They grow from deep-seated hard corms or tubers but are related to the Portulaca of gardens. The most frequently cultivated species are: *C. caroliniana,* to 1 ft. in height with 1-2 in. broad leaves, and pink flowers; and *C. virginica,* not over 8 in. with narrower, longer leaves and white flowers tinged with pink.

CLEAR-WING. Name given to a kind of moth with transparent wings; it is the adult stage of certain borers.

CLEMATIS (klem'-ah-tis). (See illustrations, Plate 11.) A genus of herbaceous perennials or woody climbing plants of the Buttercup Family, widely distributed in temperate regions. They thrive in a well dug and enriched light loamy soil, to which lime should be added if lacking, and appreciate an annual dressing of rotted manure.

There are many species of varying habit and widely differing flower forms, and in addition many beautiful hybrids. The bushy kinds are well placed in the flower-border. The woody small-flowered kinds are adapted for use on fences, arbors or porches, or to ramble in rocky places. The large-flowered hybrids show to advantage on trellises or posts, while some of the less vigorous kinds are well suited for pot culture under glass.

For those which flower off the old wood, pruning consists in removing weak, straggly and superfluous shoots when dormant.

CLEMATIS IN TWO FORMS

Left, blossoms of a large-flowered sort, such as C. jackmani; center, spray of the small-flowered Virgins Bower (C. paniculata) and, right, as the latter covers a trellis with a filmy white mantle.

Those which flower from young basal shoots should have all the growth cut back in spring.

ENEMIES. Leaf spot and stem rot appear differently on different hybrids. In the garden the stem near the soil line is usually the only part affected. In greenhouses water-soaked spots, later becoming tan-colored with red margins, occur on the leaves while the girdling lesions at the base of the stem cause the death of the shoots. Supporting the vines and spacing them far enough apart to prevent them matting together will often keep the disease from becoming serious. Remove diseased leaves and infected stubs; take cuttings from disease-free plants; grow young stock in clean beds; spray lightly with a good sulphur fungicide (see SULPHUR) or with bordeaux mixture.

The clematis borer is a white, brown-headed grub about ⅔ in. long that infests roots and crowns and sometimes hollows out bases of stems, especially in C. virginiana and C. jackmani. The adult is a clear-winged moth, the fore wings blackish or violet, the hind wings transparent with dark margins. Moths emerge from June to August and lay eggs, the resulting lar-

vae wintering in the roots. Cut out the borers and destroy badly infested plants.

For red spider syringe plants with a forceful stream of water, spray with a summer oil or dust with sulphur, taking care to coat the undersides of leaves.

Dusting with sulphur will also tend to prevent the ravages of the tarnished plant bug, which see.

Propagation is by seed, layers, division, cuttings under glass, and grafting.

HERBACEOUS NON-CLIMBING SPECIES

C. heraclaefolia is of stout erect habit with a woody base, large leaves of 3 leaflets, and clusters of lilac flowers in late summer. Var. *davidiana* is of more slender habit with fragrant flowers of deep blue.

recta grows to about 4 ft. and produces many-flowered panicles of white fragrant flowers in early summer.

CLIMBERS

C. montana is a vigorous grower, bearing fragrant white anemone-like flowers in May and June. In var. *rubens* the young growth is reddish and the flowers rose or pink.

flammula is a slender grower to 15 ft., with a wealth of small white fragrant flowers in late summer.

paniculata, a vigorous grower, and one of the hardiest and easiest to grow, is conspicuous in late summer wtih many-flowered panicles of white fragrant flowers.

virginiana (Virgins Bower) is a native vine, very attractive in the hedgerows in midsummer with its long festoons of white flowers in leafy panicles. Good to ramble over slopes and rocky places.

vitalba (Travelers Joy) is a vigorous grower to 30 ft., with dull-white fragrant flowers in summer, and later feathery seed heads, called "old man's beard."

texensis is of moderate growth, with handsome solitary nodding urn-shaped flowers in summer.

tangutica is a very handsome species growing to 10 ft., with golden flowers in June and again in fall, when the feathery fruits are also attractive.

lanuginosa grows to 6 ft., bearing in early summer flat lavender or white flowers to 6 in. across.

viticella grows to 12 ft., with blue, purple or rosy-purple flowers in summer, to 2 in. across. From these two species have been derived the beautiful Jackmani type

Plate 11.   CLEMATIS FORMS AND ENGLISH IVY

Upper left: The starry blooms of Blue Gem, a large-flowered variety of Clematis.   Upper right: The friendly, feathery Clematis paniculata envelopes its support in a mist of bloom.   Lower left: English ivy will cover a house or—(Lower right) trained on chains close to the ground it will neatly outline a path.

of hybrids. The popular and widely grown *C. jackmani* was one of the first of these, and is still one of the best in its color— rich violet-purple. Of the numerous forms, the following are well tried and reliable: Mme. Andre, deep rich crimson; Mme. Baron Veillard, rosy-lilac; Henryi, white; Ramona, with sky-blue flowers to 10 in. across; Duchess of Edinburgh, double white; and Star of India, purple barred with red. There are many others which deserve to be better known.

CLEOME (klee-oh'-me). Herbs or small shrubs of the tropics with white, green, yellow or purple flowers, whose feathery petals and long stamens give them the appearance of orchids. They are members of the Caper Family. Seed sown outdoors in May will germinate quickly. When seedlings are 3 or 4 in. high thin them out to 2 ft. apart. The one annual species grown in northern gardens is *C. spinosa,* known as Spider-flower and often listed in catalogs as *C. gigantea* or *C. pungens,* because of its odor, which is strong but not unpleasant. The plant grows 4 ft. tall, has rose-purple or white flowers and is best used in the border in sandy soil. It is a terrific spreader, self-sowing unless care is taken to remove the seed pods before they ripen.

CLERODENDRON (klee-roh-den'-dron). Glorybower. Deciduous or evergreen trees or shrubs with white, violet or red flowers, found mainly in the tropics and belonging to the Vervain Family. Most of these can be grown only in the greenhouse or outdoors in warm regions. One or two grow and flower fairly well North if given a sheltered position and well-drained soil. Propagated by seeds and cuttings. The principal species are as follows:

C. trichotomum. A Japanese tall shrub or small tree with large soft leaves. It is conspicuous in late summer with loose clusters of fragrant white flowers set off by red calyxes. The latter persist and make a pleasing contrast with the bright blue fruits. Var. *fargesi* from China is somewhat similar but has smaller leaves. Also the calyx, green when the flowers open, later turns reddish-purple to set off the turquoise-blue berries. Both these forms are hardy North, although the tops may be killed back in severe winters.

foetidum is a Chinese shrub of medium height, not quite hardy. It has rosy-red

flowers and the leaves give off an unpleasant odor when bruised.

fragrans is a useful small shrub for the cool greenhouse; it has fragrant white flowers.

speciosissimum, a shrub from Java with scarlet flowers, is often grown in warm greenhouses; it is better known as *C. fallax.*

thomsonae is a popular evergreen twiner for the warm greenhouse. The crimson flowers are set off by white calyxes which persist for a long time, eventually turning purple.

CLETHRA (klee'-thrah). White-alder. Deciduous or evergreen shrubs or small trees found in E. N. America, Asia and Madeira. They are closely allied to the Heath Family, and grow best in a rather moist and lime-free soil with peat or leafmold. Only a few species are hardy North, but these are favored for their spikes of white fragrant flowers in summer. They are propagated by seeds, cuttings of young shoots, layers and division. The principal species are as follows:

C. alnifolia (Sweet Pepper-bush). Found in moist places from Me. to Fla., this is an upright grower to 10 ft., producing erect racemes of white fragrant flowers in July and Aug. It is subject to red spider if grown in dry places.

tomentosa is very similar, but flowers later, and the leaves are white beneath. It is found from N. C. to Fla.

acuminata grows to 15 ft. or more and has nodding racemes. It is found in the mountains from Va. to Ga.

barbinervis, a large shrub or small tree from Japan, is the earliest to bloom.

arborea (Lily-of-the-valley-tree) is a handsome small evergreen tree of Madeira, not hardy North.

CLIANTHUS (kly-an'-thus). Gloryvine. Tender half-trailing shrubs of Australia and New Zealand, belonging to the Pea Family. They are usually grown in the greenhouse, trained to trellis-work or light stakes, but can be grown outdoors in a warm climate.

C. dampieri (Glory-pea) has large showy flowers of remarkable appearance. They are bright red with a velvety dark purple blotch in the centre, borne 5-6 in a drooping raceme. This plant is difficult to grow on its own roots. The usual and most satisfactory method is to graft it on a plant of a different genus, *Colutea ar-*

borescens. This is done by wedge-grafting a tiny seedling on to a seedling Colutea cut off near the soil. See GRAFTING.

C. puniceus (Parrots-bill) is a shrubby branched plant to 6 ft. with 8 or more crimson flowers in a raceme. It is easily propagated from cuttings and is a good outdoor shrub in California.

CLICK BEETLE. A hard-shelled, slender, brownish, gray or black beetle, about ½ in. long. It is the adult of the wireworm (which see), and gets its name from the fact that when it falls or is placed on its back it will throw itself several inches into the air causing a sharp "click" in doing so. If it comes down right side up it hurries away; if not it tries again and again, as it cannot roll over.

CLIFF BRAKE. Common name for Pellaea, a genus of small, rock-loving ferns, including several native to the U. S., but difficult of cultivation.

CLIMATE. This is the general average of weather in a given locality. Climates commonly considered are tropical, temperate and arctic, progressing from hot at the equator to cold at the poles. But temperature is much influenced by other factors. The higher the elevation above sea level, the colder the climate, so that even at the equator, mountains 3 or 4 miles high are capped with perpetual snow. Thus a mountain (alpine) climate brings within 6 miles going upward, changes that correspond roughly to those met in going 6,000 miles northward. In other words a mile of altitude nearly equals 1,000 miles latitude in lowering temperature.

There are also wet and dry climates, with rainfall varying from several hundred inches a year at some points in the tropics to practically none in certain deserts. Nearness to the ocean or to large lakes causes not only increase in moisture supply, but also moderation in temperature—making it less cold in winter, and less hot in summer. Climate on or along an ocean (or other large body of water) shows least change in temperature; a continental climate far from the ocean exhibits the greatest extremes of both heat and cold, especially in deserts, for vegetation, too, moderates climate to some extent.

Island climates are like that of the ocean, as are climates along the coast of a continent where the winds blow prevailingly from the water. Such climates are further affected by currents of warm water flowing away from tropical seas, the Gulf Stream in the Atlantic (which warms the British and Norwegian coasts), and in the Pacific the Japan current which helps to give temperate climates in the N.W., even up to Alaska. How much of the result is due to warm currents, and how much to prevailing W. winds is not known. But the S.W. coast of England, where ice seldom forms, has about the same latitude as Labrador and Winnipeg, while there are open seaports in Norway farther N. than Hudson Bay and the Yukon.

CLIMATE AND PLANTS. Since garden plants come from different parts of the earth, their cultivation will be simplified by knowledge of the native climates. Plants from the Pacific Coast usually prove tender at corresponding latitudes in the E., unable to endure the extreme cold and heat of a continental climate to which they were not subjected in their W. ocean climate blown to them out of the Pacific.

Plants from S. Europe, S. Japan, E. China, Australia, New Zealand and S. Africa can often be grown in the S. Atlantic, Gulf and Pacific States, but rarely in Central or E. sections. From Central Europe, N. Japan, Korea and N. China come plants hardy on the Atlantic coast, in the Ohio valley and in the Great Lakes region; while in the N. plains, only plants from Siberia or N. Europe can be expected to survive.

Tropical plants are given conditions in the greenhouse which create as far as possible a replica of tropical climate. These necessarily fall short in the matter of sunlight which at 50 deg. N. in December is but a small fraction of that under the equator.

Plants grown from seeds collected in foreign countries often require more care than those of the same species which have become acclimated by growing for one or more generations in the new locality. Those from island climates like England and Japan should be sheltered from cold winds, given as much moisture as possible, and shaded from the summer sun. Alpines need excessive moisture in the soil during the growing season, but little protection from wind and sun. Species from the far N. must have ample moisture and also shade, as they suffer most from heat. Some arctic plants winterkill in temperate climates, because accustomed to a deep protective blanket of snow, hence unable to endure snowless cold. On the other hand cacti and other desert plants (succulents) can often bear extreme cold, but may rot from continued dampness.

See also PROTECTION; SHADE; WEATHER.

CLIMBERS. In the popular sense, climbers are any plants used to cover walls, arbors or trellises, regardless of whether they provide their own means of attachment, or have to be fastened to their supports. A more limited definition restricts the term to those plants which attach themselves by means of tendrils, stems or aerial roots, and excludes those which raise themselves above the ground by twisting their stems about a support, being therefore known as "twiners."

The climbers form a useful group of plants that do not always receive all the care they deserve or need to do their best, either in the matter of soil preparation, or growth regulation and help. When planting a climber close to a wall or old tree-trunk, it pays to prepare a place much larger than just big enough to hold the roots. Break up the soil at least 2 ft. deep and enrich with old manure or leafmold. This helps to provide moisture (or at least prevent excessive dryness) just at the time when growth is most active. In pruning or thinning climbers the main point is to consider the flowering habit, that is, whether the flowers are produced on old or young wood.

See also VINES; PRUNING; TRAINING.

CLIMBING - BUTCHERS - BROOM (*Semele androgyna*). A tender shrubby vine, which in a warm climate may attain a height of 50 ft. or more. What appear to be leaves are really leaf-like branches known as *cladodes*. The leaves are represented by minute scales, from the axils of which arise the cladodes which are 3 to 4 in. long, and carry the small yellow flowers along their margins. The general effect is like that of a giant smilax.

CLIMBING-DAHLIA (*Hidalgoa wercklei*). Tender herbaceous vine from Central America, belonging to the Daisy Family. It has compound leaves and climbs by means of the coiled leaf-stalks. The showy flowers of orange-scarlet, over 2 in. across, resemble single dahlias. The plant is hardy only in the warmest parts of the country.

CLIMBING FERN. Common name for the fern genus Lygodium, comprising

mostly tropical species, but one hardy in New England and southward.

CLIMBING FUMITORY (feu'-mi-toh-ri). One common name for *Adlumia fungosa,* which is also called Mountain Fringe and Allegheny-vine, which see.

CLIMBING HEMPWEED (*Mikania scandens*). A native twining plant belonging to the Daisy Family. It is closely allied to eupatorium, and has very small flowers, white or pinkish, borne in dense clusters. It is useful for colonizing in moist places that are not cultivated or disturbed.

CLIMBING HYDRANGEA (hy-dran'-je-ah). A common name for two closely related plants which are often confused. These are *Hydrangea petiolaris* and *Schizophragma hydrangeoides.* They are described under their generic names.

CLIMBING-LILY. Common name for *Gloriosa superba,* a climbing greenhouse or warm region plant belonging to the Lily Family; a species of Glory-lily, which see.

CLINTONIA (klin-toh'-ni-ah). A group of hardy herbs of the Lily Family, spreading by long rhizomes or underground stems, with broad leaves, and most appropriate for colonizing in the wild or rock garden. The berries, which follow the small white or yellow flowers, are most attractive. Clintonias should be grown in rich, moist wood soil in shady spots; they are increased by seed or division of roots. The genus was named for Governor Clinton, one of the early governors of the State of New York, in recognition of his interest in gardening and botany.

C. andrewsiana, to 1½ ft., has rose-purple flowers; *C. borealis,* common in northeastern woods, and the best for naturalizing, has brilliant blue berries; *C. uniflora,* a western plant with large, starry white flowers, should be grown in peaty soil.

CLINTONS SHIELD FERN. A large variety of the Crested Fern. See DRYOPTERIS.

CLITORIA (kly-toh'-ri-ah). Butterfly-Pea. Perennial herbs or shrubby climbers, mostly of the tropics, belonging to the Pea Family. One or two are grown under glass, and outdoors in the warmest parts of the country. Propagated by seeds and cuttings.

C. ternatea is the best for garden use in the far S., where it is hardy. It makes an attractive twiner for the greenhouse, with showy blue flowers.

CLOTH SHADE PROTECTS PLANTS AND IMPROVES THEM
When grown under a light cloth structure like this, asters, for instance, are kept free from insect injury, from the yellows disease, and from damage by wind, rain and hail; also their flowers are larger and finer.

arborescens is also a good shrubby twiner for the greenhouse, bearing showy pinkish flowers.

mariana is a low twining perennial with light blue flowers in summer, found from N. J. south.

C L I V I A (kly'-vi-ah). Kafir-lily. A genus of fleshy-rooted evergreen African plants of the Amaryllis Family, extensively grown in the N. as house plants and greenhouse subjects and in the S. in shady places outdoors. They are exceedingly decorative, with large reddish orange or scarlet, lily-like flowers borne in umbels, at right angles to the rather stiff stalks that rise above the strap-shaped, drooping leaves. They are easily raised from seed and many interesting hybrids have been developed in this way. They may also be increased by division in the spring, although plants do best if not disturbed for several years. The potting soil should be of rich loam and sand with charcoal added to prevent it from becoming acid. During the growing period water freely and feed with liquid manure. During the resting season keep the plants in a cool greenhouse and give little if any water. The usual species in cultivation is *C. miniata,* the flowers of which are scarlet, yellow inside; they are followed by bright red berries.

The most troublesome pest in winter is the mealy bug (which see). Remove these small, fleshy, sucking insects which are enveloped in a mealy white, spongy, wax-like substance, with a forceful stream of water, or with a soft toothbrush and soap suds; or spray with a contact insecticide.

CLOAK FERN. Common name for the fern genus Notholaena, several species of which, native to the S. W. States, can be grown in gardens there. Others are greenhouse subjects.

CLOCHE (klosh). A French name for a more or less bell-shaped glass contrivance made to be placed over a plant or hill of plants in the garden to protect it from frost in early spring and thereafter to hasten its growth. Though popular in Europe, cloches are not often seen in the U. S., though the same results are obtained by means of different kinds of plant forcers. See FORCERS.

CLOCK-VINE. Common name for the genus Thunbergia, which see.

CLON (klohn) or CLONE. A clone or clonal variety is a named variety of plant, the members of which have all originated from the multiplication of a single plant by vegetative (asexual) means, such as grafting, budding, cutting or division, rather than from seed. In reality, therefore, they all comprise separate pieces of one original individual.

A *clon* implies an individual. A *race* or *strain,* or a variety reproduced from seed, on the other hand, implies a population or group of individuals. Plants whose distinguishing characters fail to come true from seed or which are incapable of producing seedlings, are generally propagated as clons.

CLOSED GENTIAN (jen'-shan). Common name for *Gentiana andrewsi,* a perennial native to E. N. America having dark-blue partially or entirely closed flowers. See GENTIAN..

CLOTH SHADE. The practice of shading tobacco crops with white cloth is a well-established means of improving the quality of the leaf as well as protecting it against rain, hail, etc. Cloth of any sort is often draped over a border of late Chrysanthemums to ward off early frost and permit the plants to continue in bloom. In recent years the protection of asters with cloth has won favor since it excludes the small leaf hopper that carries the aster yellows disease and also helps to produce finer blooms. Shading plants (chiefly in greenhouses) with opaque black cloth so as to change their periods of light and dark has recently been found an effective way to both advance and retard flowering dates. See also LIGHT; SHADE. (See illustration, page 291.)

CLOUDBERRY. A common name for *Rubus chamaemorus,* a hardy herbaceous species of bramble with white flowers and orange-red fruit; a good rock-garden plant.

CLOVE. One of the segments or bulblets of a garlic or similar bulb. For clove, the spice of commerce, see EUGENIA.

CLOVE PINK. One common name for *Dianthus caryophyllus,* the true Carnation. See CARNATION; DIANTHUS.

CLOVER. A common name for the genus Trifolium, but loosely applied to many other legumes (members of the Pea Family) and some plants that are not of that group but that resemble the true clovers, either in having rounded 3-lobed foliage, or in other respects. Clovers are annual, biennial and perennial herbs, some low-growing and trailing, some to 3 ft. tall. The leaves are normally 3-parted, and the small flowers—white, pink, or red— are borne in dense, soft, rounded or elongated heads; the small seed-pods are often enclosed in the dried calyx.

The most important clovers are forage and pasture crops such as Red Clover (*Trifolium pratense*), which is the State flower of Vt.; Crimson Clover (*T. incarnatum*), and Alsike Clover (*T. hybridum*); but White Clover (*T. repens*), a low, creeping perennial with small round white heads, is much used in lawn seed mixtures to give a quick effect for the first few years and help shelter the slower growing grasses while they are getting established. The usual allowance is 5 per cent of the total amount of seed sown, or about ¼ lb. per 1000 sq. ft. If sown alone, as is sometimes done, twice as much must be used. A distinct type of *T. repens* called Kentish wild white, produced on old pastures in Kent, Eng. is recom-

mended (when available) as superior to the usual form because it lasts longer and, in lawns, blossoms much more sparsely, and later.

Any of the kinds named, and some other less common species, such as *T. rubens,* can also be used in the flower garden, either in borders or in the rock garden, depending on their size and habits. Like all the legumes, clovers are nitrogen fixers and soil improvers and are therefore advantageous to grow, whatever the primary purpose of the crop.

Clovers are commonly grown from seed sown early in the spring, although White Clover can also be propagated from its runners. They are not particular as to soil so long as it is not sour or wet. Gardeners can achieve pleasing results by planting clumps of Red Clover in the border, masses of Crimson Clover in the wild garden and bits of the smaller sorts among their rocks plants.

ENEMIES. Diseases of clover and alfalfa are not usually important in the garden, but the characteristics of the more common of them are worth noting.

Leaf spot shows as small, brownish-purple spots each with a central disk-like fruiting pustule on the upper surface. The leaves turn yellow and often drop off. Early cutting is recommended. The leaves of red clover are frequently whitened by powdery mildew and may serve to infect cowpeas, larkspur, lima and string beans, lupines, peas, and turnip.

Several species of rust cause pustules on the leaves but they are not dangerous.

Early mowing provides the most satisfactory control of most insect pests of clover, such as the greenish white clover-head caterpillar, which feeds in the flower heads of red clover; the clover leaf hopper, which sucks the sap from the leaves causing white spots; the clover leaf weevil, a brown beetle with dark brown stripes which eats notches in the leaves; the pea aphid (see APHIS) and the clover mite (see MITES). The greenish clover bud weevil which cuts slits in the stem just above the lateral buds is the most destructive pest of clover in the Middle West and there is no satisfactory control.

Other plants called Clover are: Sweetclover (Melilotus), Owls-clover (Orthocarpus), Prairie-clover (Orthocarpus or Petalostemum), Bur-, Bokhara-, and Hubam-clover (Melilotus), Bush- and Japan-

clover (Lespedeza), Tick-clover (Desmodium), Holy-clover (Onobrychis) and Mexican-clover (*Richardia scabra*).
See also LAWN; TRIFOLIUM.

CLOVE-TREE. Common name for *Eugenia aromatica,* a tropical tree to 30 ft. whose dried flower buds are the spice of commerce called cloves.

CLUB GOURD. One common name for *Trichosanthes anguina,* also called Serpent Gourd, which see.

CLUB-MOSS. Common name for the genus Lycopodium (which see), comprising a number of interesting evergreen herbs sometimes grown as cover-plants and some collected from the wild for use as Christmas greens.

CLUB ROOT. Also called finger-and-toe disease and by numerous other descriptive names. A swelling or distortion of the roots of cabbage and other members of the Mustard Family caused by a slime mold and resulting frequently in a decline in vigor and often in the death of affected plants. Practically all the cultivated species of crucifers are subject to it, including pepper-grass and alyssum.

CLUBS. See GARDEN CLUBS AND OTHER ORGANIZATIONS.

CLYTOSTOMA (kly-tos'-toh-mah). Evergreen climbing shrubs from S. America, belonging to the Bignonia Family. Closely related to plants of the Bignonia genus, they have been grown and described as such. Under tropical or subtropical conditions which are necessary for their growth, they are vigorous growers, climbing by leaf-tendrils, and bearing handsome funnel-shaped flowers.

Two species are known: *C. callistegioides,* with wavy leaves and pale purple streaked flowers; and *C. purpureum,* with leaves sometimes toothed and flowers mauve colored with a white throat.

CNICUS (ny'-kus) *benedictus.* Popularly known as Blessed Thistle, this is a hardy branching, thistle-like, composite annual, native to the Mediterranean region and the Caucasus. It reaches a height of 2 ft., bears large heads of yellow flowers, and is utilized to good effect in the rock garden or in the wild garden. The seeds are sown in the open ground in April, where the plants are to bloom.

COACH-WHIP. One of the common names for *Fouquieria splendens,* a striking desert plant best known as Ocotillo. It is a species of Candlewood, which see.

COAL ASHES. These have long been known as valuable for lightening heavy, stiff soils, making them more friable and improving the drainage conditions. For use in the garden they should be from a good grade of hard coal, preferably with a low sulphur content, and should be sifted free from dust and clinkers, unless from the smallest sizes of coal. A screen of ¼ to ⅜ in. openings is suitable. As a result of studies carried on at Mellon Institute under an industrial fellowship, advantages of using hard coal ashes on either heavy or very light garden soils are given as: Improved texture and workability; better moisture absorption; reduction of erosion; improved drainage and aeration; and increased resistance to drought conditions. Ashes can also be used in soilless gardening (see CINDER CULTURE); as mulching material; for underdrainage; in greenhouse benches to support pots and flats; and for forcing rhubarb clumps indoors. See ASHES.

COAT-FLOWER or TUNIC-FLOWER. Common names for *Tunica saxifraga,* a purplish flower used as edging or in the rock garden.

COBAEA (koh-bee'-ah). Climbing plants of tropical America, belonging to the Phlox Family of which they are the only climbers. While perennial under tropical conditions, they are usually grown as annuals. They grow readily from seeds, best results being obtained by setting the large flat seeds on edge. In the North they should be started under glass so as to have well-established plants in pots ready to set out when all danger of frost has passed.

CLUB ROOT OF CABBAGE
A microscopic organism causes large root swellings that prevent normal life functions. Heavy liming of the soil helps to prevent the trouble.

The principal species is *C. scandens,* often listed as Cathedral Bells or Cup-and-saucer-vine, a rapid and graceful grower to 25 ft. or more, climbing by leaf-tendrils. The large violet-colored bell-shaped flowers are set off by a large leafy calyx, the structure suggesting the second common name above-mentioned. There is a white flowered form (*C. alba*) also one with variegated leaves, which must be propagated by cuttings. If planted in a sheltered corner the flowers continue for some time after the early frosts.

COBNUT. Common name for a variety of the European Hazelnut (*Corylus avellana,* var. *grandis*). See HAZELNUT.

COBWEB HOUSELEEK. The common name for *Sempervivum arachnoideum,* a plant of the Orpine Family characterized by the silky, web-like strands enveloping the small rosettes of succulent leaves.

COCA (kok'-kah) COCAINE-PLANT. Common names for *Erythroxylon coca,* a shrub reaching 12 ft., native of W. S. America and the W. Indies. It is cultivated in S. America for the narcotic drug, cocaine, which is secured from the leaves. The leaves dried and mixed with a little lime, have long been chewed by Peruvian natives to prevent hunger while on journeys. The plant is sometimes grown as a greenhouse plant in the North. Propagation is by cuttings rooted over bottom heat.

COCCINIA (kok-sin'-i-ah) *cordifolia.* A tropical vine from Asia. See IVY GOURD.

COCCOCYPSELUM (kok-oh-sip'-see-lum). A small genus of soft-wooded, trailing plants belonging to the Blackberry Family, natives of Central America and the W. Indies. They bear funnel-shaped flowers of white or purple, followed by hollow, berry-shaped fruits which, in some species, are of a decorative blue color. They are useful as ground covers or as drooping plants in baskets.

COCCOLOBA (ko-kol'-oh-bah) or COCCOLOBIS. A large genus of tropical and sub-tropical woody plants, some native along the Fla. coast and a few grown outdoors in frostless regions, or under glass in the north as ornamentals. The best known is *C. uvifera,* the Sea- or Shore-grape, which has large, handsome, glossy leaves veined with red, and grape-like clusters of edible fruit. The slightly larger pear-shaped fruits of the Pigeon-cherry (*C. floridana*) are also edible. Both species

do best in rich, sandy soil and are propagated easily from seed and also by cuttings of ripe wood or by layering.

COCCULUS (kok'-eu-lus). A genus of native and Asiatic shrubs, one of which is the Carolina Moonseed. See SNAILSEED.

COCHLEARIA (kok-lee-ay'-ri-ah). A small biennial or perennial herb sometimes grown for salad and commonly called Scurvy-grass, which see.

COCHLIOSTEMA (kok-li-oh-stee'-mah). A group of curious and handsome greenhouse herbs, native to Brazil and Ecuador, with very short stems and foliage forming a rosette. Two species are in cultivation, one with leaves which are deep red on the underside. The flowers of both are violet-blue, and borne freely in branched clusters. The soil, which should be a fibrous loam with peat added, must never be permitted to dry out. The plants also need a humid atmosphere. Propagation is by seeds, which should be sown as soon as ripe. Hand-fertilization is necessary.

COCHLOSPERMUM (kok-loh-spur'-mum). Tropical evergreen trees or shrubs, little known in cultivation. One species (*C. vitifolium*) has been introduced into S. Calif. This is a tree to 40 ft. with large 5-lobed leaves and bright yellow flowers 4 in. or more across, borne in terminal clusters.

COCKSCOMB. Common name of the most commonly grown of the Celosias, *C. argentea,* var. *cristata.* See CELOSIA.

COCKS-EGGS. Common name for *Salpichroa rhomboidea,* a perennial vine of the Nightshade Family, native to Chile. It is planted extensively in the tropics for fence and wall coverings as it makes a dense screen of leaves in a short time. Growing from a heavy, woody root with a strong odor, it bears small white flowers, followed by yellowish or whitish berries which are sold in Paraguay as "cocks-eggs." Plants are increased by seed or by cuttings of half-ripened wood. It is sometimes listed in catalogs as *Withania origanifolia.*

COCKSFOOT. Another name for Orchard Grass (which see), which is botanically known as *Dactylis glomerata.*

COCOA-TREE, or CHOCOLATE-TREE. Common names for the tropical tree, *Theobroma cacao.* See CACAO.

COCONUT. The fruit of a tropical palm (*Cocos nucifera*) which grows both along coast lines and inland; and the name applied to the tree itself. Important as a source of four commercial products (the sap, used as a beverage; the husk fibre, called coir, used in making cord, brushes, etc.; the mature fresh edible nut, and the dried nut meat, called copra), the tree is ornamental in its youth, providing an effective screen for windy locations, and in old age its tall stems are picturesque accents in any tropical garden plan. Although it grows by the seashore, its roots require fresh water supplied by seepage from higher levels. An annual rainfall of 40 in. or more is necessary for continuous thrifty growth. Propagation is only from seed (the nut) which takes several months to germinate. Protected by its hard shell and thick husk, a nut can float in the ocean for hundreds of miles and yet give rise to a tree when finally cast ashore.

The genus Cocos, which now is considered to have only the one species already mentioned, formerly included numerous palms grown in northern greenhouses as house plants and for decorative purposes. They may be placed out of doors (preferably in pots or tubs) over summer, or may be grown as garden, park or avenue subjects in warm sections. One of the most important of these is *Syagrus weddelliana* (formerly called *Cocos weddelliana* and still so listed by florists) which is much used in its younger stages.

See PALM; SYAGRUS.

COCONUT FIBRE. Where obtainable, this by-product is a cheap and useful material in which to plunge young stock in pots in propagating houses and frames. It is also good as a rooting medium for cuttings of many soft-wooded plants. The fresher it is, the better for these purposes. It also makes an excellent mulch and a good material to work into stiff soils to make them more friable.

COCOON. The soft but tough case woven about itself by a full grown caterpillar before transforming into a pupa. It is made of silk, which is hardened saliva secreted by larva, but may be strengthened by bits of leaf, twig, sand or other material. The pupa of a butterfly is usually a naked, hard-shelled chrysalis (which see), not a cocoon.

COCOZELLE (koh-koh-zel). Popular name for a bush vegetable marrow or summer squash (*Cucurbita pepo* var. *melopepo*) whose elongated, green, striped fruits, picked while the rind can be easily indented with the finger nail, are sliced and fried like egg-plant. Common in foreign section city markets, but well worth growing. See SQUASH.

CODIAEUM (koh-di-ee'-um). A genus of shrubby plants of the Spurge Family, much grown in gardens in the S. and under glass in the N. for their brightly colored foliage but generally referred to as Crotons, which see.

CODLING or CODLIN **MOTH.** The most important insect pest of the apple in America, and the most common cause of the familiar "wormy" fruit. It also attacks pear, quince, English walnut, crabapple and wild haws. The larva is a pinkish-white caterpillar with a brown head, about ¾ in. long, which bores into the core of an apple, eating out an irregular cavity and filling it with a dark brown mass of excrement or "frass." Later it leaves through the blossom end of the fruit, a large hole filled with brown particles marking its exit. Young larvae often disfigure fruit by eating shallow or deep tunnels in its sides.

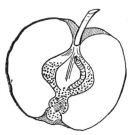

ORCHARD MEN'S ENEMY
The familiar worm in the apple is the larva of the codling moth.

The moth is dark gray with wavy lines giving a "watered silk" appearance on the fore wings each of which at the tip bears a large brown spot or "ocellus." Moths appear as the apple blossoms open and are at their height about one week after the petals fall, laying small white flattened eggs on the leaves. The larvae hatch in about a week and enter the young apples (usually) by the blossom end. Emerging after 25 to 30 days, and falling or crawling to the ground, they spin cocoons beneath flakes of bark or sticks. Sometimes there is a second generation, the moths emerging from cocoons in midsummer and the larvae entering the well-advanced apples through the sides.

The standard control measure is spraying with lead arsenate, 1½ lbs. of powder or 3 lbs. of paste to 50 gals. of water. The most important application is the "calyx spray," made when three fourths of the petals have fallen. Poison must not be used when trees are in full bloom because of the danger of poisoning bees which aid in pollinating and setting fruit. For the number and times of later sprayings it is well to consult the nearest experiment station or county agent; another spraying 3 to 4 weeks after the first is always in order.

Other measures in codling moth control consist of: Removing all dead branches and stubs from trees; cleaning up and burning all brush, decaying wood and weeds; scraping loose bark from trunk and larger limbs; and banding mature trees with chemically treated paper bands during the summer months. (As such bands may injure young, smooth barked trees, these should be banded with untreated corrugated paper. These bands should be examined every ten days and the worms beneath them killed.) See APPLE; INSECTICIDE; SPRAYING.

CODONOPSIS (koh-doh-nop'-sis). A group of plants of the Bellflower Family, some of them vines, others upright in habit. They can be grown in the border but require winter protection in the N. They are increased by seed or cuttings. *C. clematidea*, to 3 ft., has charming white, bell-shaped flowers. *C. ovata*, to 1 ft., is best suited to the rock garden, where it should be planted at the higher levels in order to show the full beauty of the flowers, steel-blue, spotted yellow and white inside. *C. silvestris* is a climber; its foliage has a bloom and the solitary flowers are pale yellowish-purple.

COELOGYNE (see-loj'-i-nee). A genus of tropical epiphytic orchids with long racemes of white or greenish-yellow flowers, the petals and sepals being alike and the keeled lip sometimes fringed or spotted. Native to the tropics of the E. hemisphere, they are grown under glass in the N., in a moderately warm atmosphere, often suspended in baskets, or in pots or pans, in a mixture of osmundine and sphagnum moss, which should always be well aerated. As Coelogynes are evergreen orchids, they should never be allowed to dry out entirely, and should be well watered when coming into bloom; they benefit greatly from applications of weak manure water. They are increased by division immediately after flowering, or by removing and potting the back bulbs.

Of the numerous species grown, *C. cristata*, with its lovely clusters of pure white flowers with orange keels, is one of the most charming and most easily handled. *C. dayana* is another good one, especially for growing in baskets hung from the rafters of a warm greenhouse.

See also ORCHIDS.

COFFEE. The common name of the genus Coffea, a group of evergreen shrubs and trees belonging to the Madder Family, native to the tropics of Asia and Africa. More than 25 species have been recognized, some of which are found in greenhouse collections and outdoors in warm climates. Coffee is grown as a shrub for its handsome, shining leaves, fragrant white flowers, and attractive red berries. The species grown commercially is *C. arabica*, the "beans" being the seeds formed within a pulpy fruit; the several distinct varieties have their own peculiar flavors. Soil for these plants should be half peat and half loam. Propagation of the ornamental species is by cuttings of ripe wood rooted under glass in moist heat.

COFFEE-BERRY. Common name for *Rhamnus californica*, a tender, evergreen, berry-bearing shrub, cultivated in Calif.

COFFEE FERN. Common name for *Pellaea andromaedifolia*, a small W. fern of the Cliff-brake group, with dark stems and deep rounded lobes. Prefers light rocky soil, well drained.

COFFEE-TREE, KENTUCKY. Common name for *Gymnocladus dioica*, a large sturdy tree of the Pea Family, growing to 100 ft. and native to the E. and Central States. It is much used for its bold decorative effect in large plantings. It has coarse twigs and few branchlets and large compound leaves. The greenish-white flowers in large clusters borne at the ends of the branches are followed by thick curved pods containing dark seeds 1 in. broad, the pods remaining on the tree all winter. Growing luxuriantly in rich soil, it is propagated by seed or cuttings.

COHOSH (koh'-hosh). A common name for Actaea, a genus of native herbaceous plants having feathery white flowers and ornamental red or white berries; good for shady spots in the garden. Other common names are Actea and Baneberry.

Black-cohosh is *Cimicifuga racemosa* and Blue-cohosh is *Caulophyllum thalictroides*.

COIX (koh'-iks). The name Jobs-tears is given to one species (*C. lacryma-jobi*) of this genus of tall, broad-leaved grasses. It is a popular ornamental garden subject. Although a perennial, it will not stand N. winters, so is generally grown as an annual. Seeds should be planted in the open ground in the not-too-early spring. Plants grow about 4 ft. high with leaves 2 ft. long and 1½ in. wide. The peculiar large, grayish, round seeds hang in clusters from the sheaths, and it is these seeds, which can be used as beads, that make the grass attractive and give it its common name. The sprays of seeds, but before they shatter, and dried, are good ornamental material combined with Everlastings. See also ORNAMENTAL GRASSES.

COLCHICINE (kol'-ki-seen). A fine, yellow, very bitter and very poisonous powder obtained from corms of the autumn-crocus (*Colchicum autumnale*). It is a powerful drug and, in minute doses, has been used as a remedy for gout for many years. Quite recently it has come into the horticultural limelight on account of its newly discovered power to modify the development of plants to which it is applied.

Plants are made up of cells or box-like structures of minute size which, multiplying naturally by self-division, cause the plants to grow larger. Each cell contains a nucleus which has within it microscopic bodies called *chromosomes* which are responsible for the plant's inherited characteristics and also for the passing on of these characters to succeeding generations. As growth takes place, each cell, and each chromosome in it, splits into two and thus, by a complicated process involving the rearrangement of the multiplied bodies, new complete cells are formed. This division, called *mitosis,* is the stabilizing process insuring the perpetuation of the structure and habits of the parent plants.

When colchicine is applied to a plant part it sometimes so interferes with this normal process as to cause the formation of new cells which may have twice, or some other multiple, of the original number of chromosomes, a condition called *polyploidy,* which see. This leads to marked changes in the structure, size, appearance, etc. of the plant and, in some cases, even in its reproduction powers, so that a formerly infertile hybrid may become fertile. Increased flower size has been one of the results thus far.

COLCHICUMS IN AUTUMN
The big silky cups cover the ground in the fall, but no leaves appear until spring.

Thus new varieties or strains of plants bearing blossoms of near giant size have been produced by treating the seed or sections of a plant itself with a solution or a lanum paste containing specified amounts of colchicine. Some plants after treatment grow with increased vigor even though multiplication of the chromosome count has not been achieved. It is predicted that colchicine may cause radical changes in plant types and lead to the development of vegetables and flowers having new tastes, odors, or size. But, because the whole field is new, unexplored, and experimental, and because of the highly, dangerously poisonous nature of colchicine, its use in trying to create unusual plants is definitely not for the amateur or home gardener.

COLCHICUM (kol'-ki-kum). Autumn-crocus or Meadow-saffron. A genus of cormous plants of the Lily Family. Not related to the true crocus, though the flowers of the two plants look alike. The species most frequently cultivated (*C. autumnale*) bears clusters of large, pale-lavender blossoms in the fall. The coarse grassy foliage appears the following spring, dying down before midsummer. (See illustration, Plate 45; also under CROCUS.)

The corms are hardy enough to winter over with little or no protection in the temperate zone and, left undisturbed, they will flower freely for years. Some can be dug during the dormant season (June and July) and kept for indoor blooming as they are effective and exceedingly easy to handle. Planted in peat moss in shallow bowls they will blossom with moderate heat and moisture. Indeed, so strongly inclined to flower are they that they are sometimes advertised as "bulbs that will flower without soil or water." Of course, while this may happen, the results are inferior.

There are many varieties, including double forms in purple and white. Other autumn-flowering species include *C. parkinsoni* and *C. bivonae,* both with checkered markings on the purple petals; *C. sibthorpi,* with large cup-shaped flowers; *C. speciosum,* with large violet or pink flowers in clusters; *C. decaisnei,* very late-blooming, with flesh-colored flowers; and *C. alpinum,* bearing small lilac flowers, often in pairs.

Of the less common spring-blooming species, the more important are *C. montanum,* which also blooms again in the fall; and *C. luteum,* the only yellow-flowered member of the genus.

Do not confuse Colchicums with the autumn-flowering forms of the true Crocus, which see.

COLDFRAME. A bottomless box placed on the soil or over a pit, and in which plants may be started, grown, or stored. It may be covered with a more or less transparent top to develop and maintain warmth within it; with some solid protective cover to keep out cold and withstand snow, or with a slat or other type of screen to give shade. (See illustration, Plate 4.)

Standard dimensions are 6 by 12 ft.; such a frame can be covered with a regulation sash, either glazed or made with one of the several glass substitutes available, which are lighter and not breakable but less transparent. The length of a coldframe is set by the number of plants it is to hold and the space available. While the coldframe protects plants and promotes their growth, the only heat it receives or supplies to them is that of the sun. In this respect only do coldframes differ from hotbeds, which are heated from below.

Coldframes may be used: (1) To start seedlings in advance of the outdoor season, though not so early as in hotbeds. (2) To receive seedlings or other small plants shifted from hotbeds or greenhouses to flats or flower pots, before they can be set in the open ground; that is, to "harden them off." (3) To shelter seedlings of hardy plants over winter until they can be planted outdoors in spring. (4) To store hardy and semi-hardy plants during the winter months. (5) To store hardy bulbs planted in flower pots or flats during their root-forming periods. (6) To propagate plants from cuttings, especially during summer.

To be successful, a coldframe must be placed on a well-drained site. This should

A CONVENIENT METHOD OF VENTILATING COLDFRAME OR HOTBED
By means of a cord and pulley arrangement one sash or more can be raised and lowered with ease and need not be removed. At the left is a slat frame for shading.

be fully open to the sun for forcing purposes and preferably in partial shade if protection during summer is wanted. However, as noted, shade may be provided by screens of various kinds. It is important that protection from cold winds be supplied, either natural (as by woods or a hill) or artificial (as by a hedge, a high, tight board fence or a building). Nearness to the residence, greenhouse or potting shed and to a supply of water is also important so the plants can be cared for without trouble. While coldframes are often permanent features of commercial establishments, they can be temporary, movable aids at home. See also HOTBED.

COLD STORAGE. A general term for methods of storing indoors perishable products, such as fruits, flowers and vegetables, at temperatures that retard the maturing processes and thus extend their period of usefulness. The keeping of potatoes, cabbage, root crops, etc., in an outdoor pit serves this same purpose as well as that of preventing injury by freezing. But cold storage is generally associated with the idea of keeping a room or compartment at a uniform, fairly low temperature by some more or less artificial or mechanical means.

Small scale cold storage may be provided by insulating a' room (preferably in the basement of an unheated building or the north side of the house cellar), and providing an in-take cold-air flue which discharges at the floor and an outlet at the ceiling, each provided with a damper to control the flow of air.

The floor should be of earth or porous brick laid in sand to maintain the desired degree of humidity. If possible, it should have no obstructions to interfere with handling the stored product and with cleaning and disinfecting the surroundings. Portable floor racks, crates and boxes are better than bins. Fumigation or spraying with a fungicide at both the beginning and the close of the storage period are highly important as a means of destroying plant disease organisms and preventing rot, etc.

COLEUS (koh'-lee-us). Tender annual or perennial herbs of the Mint Family, with brilliantly variegated foliage, which surpasses that of other garden plants for color. Indispensable for grouping on lawns or for ribboning, excellently adapted to window-box culture and suitable for potting and bedding, they grow luxuriant foliage, of maroon, green, crimson, yellow and combinations of these colors. Their blue or lilac spiked flowers are unimportant.

Natives of Africa and the East Indies, they are cultivated with ease in American gardens, and may be propagated by cuttings rooted in sand at any time. Growing Coleus from seed, however, is fascinating, as the seedlings vary greatly in foliage design. Long branches should be pinched back to shape the plants gracefully.

Mealy bugs, recognized by their soft, white, waxy covering, frequently infest the foliage and should be controlled as soon as they appear. Wilt or black-leg caused by a fungus may blacken the tissues of single stalks or rot the entire plant. See under GERANIUM.

Greenhouse orthezia and whitefly are common on plants under glass. See GREENHOUSE PESTS; SCALE INSECTS.

COLLARDS. A tall-growing form of kale (2 to 4 ft. high) whose coarse leaves, borne in tufts, are eaten like greens. Georgia collards, the standard variety, are grown mostly in the South, where seedlings are started like cabbage in February or March for spring use. In the North, for a fall crop, sow in midsummer. The plants are later set 3 x 4 ft. apart and cultivated like cabbage. The name collards is also loosely applied to cabbage seedlings grown without transplanting, harvested before heads form, and used as greens. Where heading cabbage is successful, true collards are not popular. See BRASSICA; CABBAGE.

COLLETIA (ko-lee'-shi-ah). Curious, almost leafless shrubs from S. America, belonging to the Buckthorn Family. They are remarkable for their odd appearance and stiff spiny habit. They can be grown outdoors where frost is light. Propagated by cuttings of side-shoots taken with a "heel."

C. armata has strong straight spines and urn-shaped waxy-white flowers late in the season.

cruciata (Anchor-Plant) has flattened branches with broad spines and small creamy-white flowers in fall.

infausta has stiff green branches armed with round spines, and bears greenish-white flowers in spring.

ephreda is a small stiff spiny shrub with flattened branches, with white flowers in spring.

COLLINSIA (ko-lin'-si-ah). Hardy, herbaceous, attractive, free-blooming annuals of the Figwort Family, used in rock gardens and edgings. Named for Zachary Collins, an American naturalist, they are pretty, low-growing plants with many colored, two-lipped flowers in whorls of five or six blossoms, and three or more whorls on every flower stem. Colors include rose, white, lilac, violet, and blue. Seeds may be sown outdoors in the fall if the young plants can be well protected, but spring sowing as usually done with annuals is the general practice. The plants prefer a dry location.

PRINCIPAL SPECIES

C. bartsiaefolia (Seaside Collinsia). 1 ft. tall; sticky stems; flowers whitish with lilac or purple markings and short upper lip.

bicolor. 2 ft.; sticky; lower lip of flower violet or rose-purple, upper lip white. Var. *candidissima* has all white, and var. *multicolor,* variegated flowers.

grandiflora (Blue-lips). 15 in.; lower lip of flowers blue or violet; upper lip white or purple.

tinctoria. 2 ft.; sticky; flowers pale purple or nearly white and streaked. Upper lip very short.

verna (Blue-eyed Mary). 2 ft.; lower flower-lip bright blue, upper lip white or purplish.

COLLINSONIA (ko-lin-soh'-ni-ah). A genus of weedy, aromatic, perennial plants of the Mint Family often called Horse-balm, Horse-weed, Stone-foot, and, in the case of *C. canadensis,* Citronella. They are not subjects for the border, but can be grown in the background of the wild garden where bold foliage is desired. They are most easily cultivated, growing rankly in rich, woodland soil.

COLLOIDS. Gelatinous substances of the type of albumin, gelatine, or starch, but with characteristic qualities that make them distinct. The protoplasm of a plant is of a colloid nature and therefore cannot diffuse through the cell walls. In the soil, colloids surround the soil particles and absorb the nutrient materials, placing them closer and more accessible to the feeding roots of the plants. For spraying, colloidal forms of certain materials, such as sulphur (which see) and possibly certain arsenates, offer special advantages because of their exceedingly fine structure which enables them to remain in suspension in a liquid longer than can coarser materials.

COLLOMIA (ko-loh'-mi-ah). A genus of pleasing, easily grown annuals of the Phlox Family, with yellow, red, or white flowers. They are easily grown from seed which should be started in the border or wild garden where the plants are to stand. *C. biflora,* the showiest of the species, has scarlet flowers and grows 2 ft. high. *C. grandiflora,* with salmon-colored flowers, is suitable for the wild garden.

COLOCASIA (kol-oh-kay'-shi-ah). A genus of large-leaved tropical herbs of the Arum Family, some being grown in warm climates for their edible, starchy tubers and others as garden subjects for their ornamental foliage. These are known as Elephants Ears, which see.

COLORADO POTATO BEETLE. The common yellow and black striped beetle, chiefly a pest of potato, but also found on other plants of the same family, such as egg-plant, tomato, tobacco and some weeds. For control, see under POTATO.

COLOR IN THE GARDEN. One thing which should be the foundation of all efforts towards a standard of excellence in handling color in the garden seems to have been generally overlooked. This is the simple fact that in Nature, where every possible color as well as all the tints and shades of colors, exist, *there is no such thing as antagonistic color.* All colors are in harmony and are to be seen with all other colors, on occasion (although not always), without unpleasant results. However extraordinary this seems, in view of much popular prejudice and some facts relating to color when pigments are its medium of expression, it is undeniably true.

Its realization brings the further realization that existing taboos against particular colors and color combinations have been established arbitrarily—presumably by those whose personal taste they have affronted. Nothing more. For this reason it is important to forget, if possible, the inhibitions which such teachings have sought or tended to establish, and to advance as a pioneer. For in this realm each may pioneer according to individual fancy in the certainty of doing no real harm, and in the hope of greatly enriching—the garden? Possibly. But himself beyond doubt. One may give free rein to imagination within the broad limits of just one generalization about color, and still be assured of producing excellent color compositions.

THE SPECTRUM. The spectrum "scale" or sequence reveals violet, indigo, blue, green, yellow, orange, red. Setting down these color names equal distances apart around the circumference of a circle, gives, of course, no end or beginning in the sequence. And thus we have a generalization in two parts, namely: (a) each color has greater affinity with the colors on either side of it than with any of the others; (b) but there is growing affinity between it and all others as these others are attenuated, thinned out, or (as the formula would be if pigments were involved) made into *tints* by the admixture of white.

Thus there appears to be a kind of natural rule or guiding principle, something like this: To accompany a dominant color, seek the most agreeable color within the group of either of its neighbors; and use any or all other colors in tints only. (A "tint" always means a color made *lighter;* a "shade" always means one made *darker*.)

Is there verification of this broad natural rule? Let us examine the painter's palette. Here three colors stand out because from them all others may be composed. These three *primary colors* are red, blue and yellow. If these are set like wedges in a circle, with equal open spaces between them, and these open spaces are then filled with the color produced by mixing the two primary colors on either side, the same sequence will occur as that revealed by the spectrum; namely, red, orange, yellow, green, blue, purple (indigo *and* violet in the spectrum) to red again, the primary and secondary alternating just as they do in the spectrum. So here again is the same guiding principle, but carried a little further. For now it appears that each color leads to the next inevitably through the color made up of the two united—a perfectly natural progression. And the original rule is supplemented by proof that, in the garden, one strong color may be led into another equally strong color by planting between them flowers showing the color of the two intermingled.

This last needs emphasis with special reference to a theory popularized by some,

that white flowers may serve as transition between two strong colors. There could not be a greater fallacy. Because white flowers are themselves the strongest color of all, if we use "color" in its fullest sense, which evaluates it as Light. Consequently, white flowers divide, never reconcile. Where contrast between two colors in the garden is so strong that reconciliation is felt necessary, it can be accomplished by the natural progression just explained and *in no other way.*

Red flowers are carried to blue or "reconciled" with them in a sequence that begins at red-purple, goes on through pure purple to violet, thence to violet-blue and at last reaches pure blue. Yellows are carried to reds through orange; and blues are carried to yellows through the leafage itself—in other words, through green, that interesting color which comes midway of the spectrum.

THE IMPORTANCE OF COLOR. This brings into consideration another phase of the subject. The most obvious and notable thing that the eye observes, look where it will, is color. Long before the form of an object is noted or recognized, its color has registered in the consciousness; and the last lingering mental vision of it is normally in color rather than form. This seems to be a pretty definite indication of the importance of color apart from its esthetic values. That it has greater importance to the human organism than accustomed association realizes or even suspects, also seems probable; this inference being drawn from consideration of color in its aspect as Light.

Science has as yet unearthed only a few of the things which there is reason to believe lie in the realm of this phenomenon. Two or three decades back it was discovered that sick people exposed to certain colors (usually in the form of light) were affected definitely by them—favorably by some, unfavorably by others. Then workers on plates for use in color photography were found to be very much affected, both mentally and physically, by the color of the light under which they had to carry on certain technical processes in the preparation of the plates. Animals and insects, too, react unmistakably to colors. Butterflies show preference for mauves and lavenders; bees show great fondness for blue and make savage onslaughts against anyone rash enough to wear a red garment around the hives. Tests with containers made by one of the great English jam and marmalade manufacturers has developed that, "everything else being equal, the house fly prefers white light to colored light, and red and yellow are the best deterrents. Blue and green are not nearly so effective. The loss in illumination with red glass being too great for general use, it appears that yellow is the best.

This is all suggestive, but the inferences that follow are just as applicable in the garden as in the laboratory. The significant thing seems to be that there are elements in color which involve other nerve reactions than the familiar one of vision; and that these reactions may be favorable or unfavorable according to the color stimulus. It is amusing and perhaps a little startling to discover that they are in accord with the emotional associations that tradition has always assigned to colors. Evidently the human race learned some things without waiting for the revelations of science.

RED FLOWERS AND THEIR PLACE. When the spectrum came along it revealed that the color red (which had always stood for physical strength, especially as it asserts itself when activated by the baser motives) was *lowest* in the scale of colors. But had men not always known this? A common phrase is that men "see red" when infuriated; and the sight of red infuriates not only the most savage of animals as well as the bee and the wasp, but sometimes human beings—especially the mentally unstable ones and the primitive.

There are not many red flowers. Nature seems restrained in the use of this color as if it were, indeed, a little dangerous. Touches of it appear in the first vegetation to pierce the earth in early spring—red life itself, that will not be denied. But these change rapidly to the soberer green. Ripening fruits show it again, richly and more permanently; from which it would appear that at the proper time and seasons, and in moderate amount, it is desirable.

That is undoubtedly true of red in the garden. Red flowers are favorable for the weak and ailing to sit among, for rapid growing children below the physical norm to play in the midst of, for the aged and feeble to dwell with. We gather that it is an unfavorable color for general use, how-

ever, because the tendency (previously mentioned) of workers under red light was to irritability and quarrelsomeness; not until they were removed from it or allowed to spend part of their time in the "blue" room did they become normal.

THE PART BLUE FLOWERS PLAY. There is an old-wives' tradition that blue flowers will allay fevers and cool the blood. Certainly all are familiar with the expression "blue with the cold." (And note that it was to the blue light that those workmen were transferred when the effects of the red stimulation became intolerable.) Those facts suggest a "blue garden" for the nervous and highly-strung, for the tired business man, for the child given to violent outbursts. Being the antithesis of red, blue is not a stimulating color and should be kept out of a garden if sluggish temperaments are in need of stirring and awakening. But it may prove of great help to the student or any desirous of contemplative retreat.

YELLOWS. Rarest and most elusive of all colors in the flower world is yellow— the pure yellow uncorrupted by red and so made orange. Though it may definitely appear in the bud, it is, oftener than not, altogether gone in the flower; as witness the yellow roses. A truly yellow rose is most coveted, yet least often produced by the men whose lives are spent in rose breeding. Painters have ever used yellow to delineate the halo shining from the head of saint and martyr; hence it is associated with spiritual qualities, purity and shining legions. In the garden, too, it may yield unusual and ethereal beauty if well handled. But it is almost necessary to intensify it through the liberal use with it of white—a fact which might seem odd unless, as before, we think of the color white as, and compare it with, Light. Think of the characteristics of each and see how they correspond: White is dazzling, sharp, and draws the eye from all else, even the most vivid color; and its presence, like that of light, intensifies the quality of other colors everywhere— among flowers in the garden as well as elsewhere.

WHITE—A POWERFUL ELEMENT. That is why white is such an effective aid and accompaniment to yellow, the delicate and evanescent color. It intensifies it, not merely through contrast, but by "lighting it up," as it were. White affords desir-

PLATE 1.   **AZALEAS OF DIFFERENT TYPES**

At the upper left and lower right are examples of the hardy Ghent hybrids. At the upper right is the Kurume Azalea "Snow," and in the lower left is one of the Sander hybrids.

T. H. Everett

PLATE 2.   AZALEA MOLLIS

A race of Azaleas with larger flowers than the Ghent hybrids is the Mollis hybrids. Many hardy varieties have been developed and can be used with striking effect, as in this planting.

Wayside Gardens Company

PLATE 3. TUBEROUS BEGONIAS

Among the showiest of flowers are the Tuberous Begonias which may be grown from seed or tubers, and which do well under glass or bedded out in the summer time.

W. Atlee Burpee Co.

PLATE 4.   SETTING OUT THE BORDER

In transplanting seedlings into the border, it is helpful to indicate the area to
be covered by the adult plants by furrows, as has been done here. In this way
straight lines and formal effects are avoided.

T. H. Everett

PLATE 5.   **CANDYTUFT**

A striking member of this well loved flower for the rock garden or low border is
the Hyacinth-Flowered Candytuft.

W. Atlee Burpee Co.

PLATE 6.   **TWO FINE VEGETABLES**

Above, is a fine head of cauliflower, not the easiest of vegetables to grow, but fine when conditions are right. Below, a fine plant of Rhubarb Chard, a variety of Swiss Chard which is ornamental as well as delicious as a vegetable.

W. Atlee Burpee Co.

PLATE 7.   GARDEN CHRYSANTHEMUMS

A representative collection of early flowering varieties which make a fine showing
in the autumn garden.

Wayside Gardens Company

PLATE 8.   AN AUTUMN DISPLAY
A border of Chrysanthemums, in some of the newest and best of the garden
varieties, provides the last mass color effect in the garden year.
T. H. Everett

PLATE 9.   CLEMATIS LAWSONIANA
One of the older of the large-flowered species, the color of this Clematis is surpassed by some of the newer hybrids.

Bobbink and Atkins

PLATE 10.   YELLOW COSMOS

This new development of an old fashioned garden friend is an unusual change
from the familiar white and rosy colors.

W. Atlee Burpee Co.

PLATE 11.   PINK TRUMPET DAFFODILS

Among the newest additions are the Pink Trumpet Daffodils. Reading down the
left side are Pink Select, Cannes, Siam and Mentone. In the same order on the
right are Champagne, Pink Favorite, Pink Fancy, and Pink Glory.

Wayside Gardens Company

PLATE 12. DWARF PINK

This member of the large Dianthus family is especially suited to the rock garden, where its mass of bright blossoms makes a pleasing spot of color.

T. H. Everett

RED SPIDER DAMAGE
While not ordinarily a serious pest except on house plants, the red spider can cause serious damage to evergreens, as illustrated here.

T. H. Everett

PLATE 13.   WINTER BURN ON IVY

Winter injury can be a matter of many effects short of actually killing the plant. Here only certain parts of the ivy plant have been damaged, while the plant generally remains in good shape.

T. H. Everett

PLATE 14.   EVERGREENS FOR EDGINGS

Four unusual evergreens which may be used for low hedges and borders. From the top down are Taxus Canadensis Stricta, Pachistima Canbyi, Teucrium Chamaedrys, and Salix Purpurea Nana, the Dwarf Blue-leaf Arctic Willow.

Wayside Gardens Company

PLATE 15.   SPRING-FLOWERING FORSYTHIA

One of the earliest of the showy spring shrubs, Forsythia does well in many
situations and under most conditions.

T. H. Everett

PLATE 16.   RICHLY COLORED GLOXINIAS

Ordinarily grown in the greenhouse, Gloxinias can be grown in the garden in warm climates or used as potted plants in northern gardens.

W. Atlee Burpee Co.

able qualities for use with high or pale tints of all colors, to be sure; but its association with yellow brings superlative effects.

As a matter of fact, a flower of pure white probably does not exist—never did and never will. Even though the petals of what are called white flowers may not be pencilled or powdered with faint colors wholly unsuspected unless searched out, there are the golden stamens and a warmth in the depth or heart of the flower structure which seems like a stain that they have left there. So there is inevitably departure, even if slight, from flawless white. Yet notwithstanding this, the dazzling quality remains and white flowers are a class apart from all others. Presumably this is the reason why only those high and attenuated tints which are in accord with its fluorescence and that consequently do not offer violent contrast with it, give the most satisfactory and lovely effects in combination with it.

An undertone of purple and a measure of violet are desirable accompaniment to all colors, because these are shadow tones and so provide the accent which every planting needs. Whatever the dominant garden color may be, they bring depth and atmosphere into the composition. Use them freely.

Reference to color in the garden is not complete without mention of the two general classifications to which all flowers are assigned according to their color. These divisions were made by the Swiss botanist, de Candolle, and are based on the presence in certain flowers of a trace of blue—giving the "cyanic group"—or in others a trace of yellow—resulting in the "xanthic group."

It is a peculiarity of the flowers in each group that, while they may pass into red or white they cannot pass over into the other group. That is, a xanthic cannot become cyanic, nor a cyanic develop a variety of xanthic coloring; but white flowers or red flowers may appear in both divisions. There are many large families of flowers which show every imaginable tint and shade in one or the other of these divisions. Asters belong in the cyanic group, chrysanthemums in the xanthic group—and so on endlessly. The whole matter is of deep significance to the plant breeder. To the gardener it is interesting but has little practical application.

The Color Garden may properly find place in this discussion, since it offers suggestion regarding use of color in a special manner. As the name implies, it means a garden or distinct garden unit wholly planted with flowers of a chosen color or with colors which blend into a common tone. It is not as often seen here as in England, where it frequently is an element

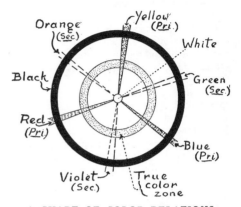

A CHART OF COLOR RELATIONS

Red, blue and yellow are the primary colors, and orange, green and violet, midway between, are the secondaries. In any color, as the amount of white decreases and that of black increases, the shade becomes darker until it merges into black, the "true color" being approximately midway.

or unit in a large garden wherein diverse concepts are expressed, each perhaps cunningly secreted from the rest and furnishing a lively series of surprise compositions.

Often very subtle color schemes are chosen, the whole idea being to introduce a precious quality into the garden aspect. Lavenders and mauves, and gray and misty tints, and foliage designed to produce a wraith-like, shimmering, ghostly beauty haunt the memory; white and creamy-white and pale yellow flowers are eloquent of moonlight and bewitch the senses when seen under moonlight; a famous color garden all in blues, from the softest, fleecy cloudy tints to the deeps of the sea and the sky, was taken bodily from Sandringham Palace gardens and given to a musician friend by the late Queen Alexandra who had created it.

One really notable example in this country is doubly a color garden. For on the hot and sunny side of the Italian dwelling are only the hot, vibrant salmon pinks which burnished copper holds—flowers of this color surrounding a large round pool with a broad, shallow copper tazza (a saucer-like receptacle set on a pedestal) at the center, over whose rim the water spills continually like a veil. On the cool and shadowy side of the house, facing the blue sea and tumbling white surf, plantings of blue flowers and white ones echo the natural features. A great artist, famous as a colorist, made this garden for his own home. It proves once and for all that the method chosen by inspired genius is to work *with* the natural light and conditions, intensifying every element until it is dramatized and brought to a climax. Then how Nature aids, as if she rejoiced at being thus understood!

It is not necessary, however, to possess exceptional gifts in order to study and analyze conditions and color combinations in Nature, and to try to create garden effects that are similarly pleasing. In fact, the study of Nature is the best schooling possible for adventures with color in the garden. Mistakes do not occur; discords are not found. Nevertheless, remarkable combinations appear. Note all of these and seek to discover why they are invariably effective.

Note especially proportions. They will be found to have great significance when colors commonly regarded as hostile are found in combination. There are no hostile colors—this bears repeating every little while. But there are sometimes combinations or couplings which distress the eye when they are not handled with understanding. Complete understanding that prevents such results is the result of closely observing how Nature proportions one of these colors to the other, when they appear together. The gardener who endeavors to be as adroit in this as Nature is, no matter how "radical" his or her garden arrangements and activities may appear at first glance, will acquire a sound and highly flexible criterion for the use of color.

COLQUHOUNIA (kohl-koo'-ni-ah). One or two species of evergreen shrubs from Asia, belonging to the Mint Family. They are rarely grown in greenhouses or outdoors in warm regions. *C. vestita,* the best known, is an upright shrub of medium height with white woolly growth and orange-scarlet flowers borne in dense whorls. *C. coccinea* is a twining climber with scarlet flowers in whorls approximating a spike. Apparently it is seldom seen in cultivation.

COLTSFOOT. The common name for *Tussilago farfara,* a plant of the Composite Family, often planted as a groundcover or to hold sandy banks. The yellow flowers, which are like small dandelions, appear very early in the spring before the leaves, opening on stalks 1½ ft. high. The leaves, which appear later, are very large, to 7 in. across. Propagation is by seed and root-cuttings.

Sweet-coltsfoot is *Petasites fragrans.*

COLUMBINE (kol'-um-byn). Common name for the popular, hardy, spring-flowering perennial, Aquilegia (which see). One of the native, W. species is the State flower of Colo. Feathered-columbine is *Thalictrum aquilegifolium,* one of the Meadow-rues.

COLUMN. A body formed by the union of the pistil with fertile or sterile stamens and a characteristic of the orchid flower; also the body formed by stamens alone, as the tube formed by a union of stamens in the mallows.

COLUMNEA (koh-lum'-nee-ah). Tropical American vine-like plants belonging to the Gesnera Family. In cultivation they are usually grown in a warm greenhouse, either drooping in hanging-baskets or upright, being attached to a branch covered with fibrous peat.

C. aurantiaca has showy flowers of rich orange color. *C. gloriosa* has leaves covered with purple hairs, which make a rich setting for the scarlet and yellow flowers.

COLUTEA (koh-leu'-te-ah). (Bladdersenna.) Deciduous shrubs belonging to the Pea Family, found from S. Europe to the Himalayas. They are fast growers where winters are not too severe, and thrive in almost any soil in a sunny position. The yellow, red or brownish flowers, borne throughout the summer, are followed by inflated pods even more decorative than the flowers. Propagated by seeds or cuttings of half-ripened shoots. Principal species are:

C. arborescens, a tall shrub to 15 ft. with dull green leaves and yellow flowers.

orientalis, which grows to 6 ft. with grayish-white foliage and flowers of red and yellow.

media, a hybrid from the above two species, which grows to 10 ft. and has grayish-green foliage and reddish-brown flowers.

COMFREY (kum'-fri). The common name of a group of Old-World perennial herbs forming the genus Symphytum of the Borage Family, some of which were once thought to be of medicinal value. A few are now used in the border for the sake of their large, hairy foliage, which is much more beautiful than the small, blue, purplish or yellow flowers. They are easily grown in any good garden soil and are tolerant of shade. Remove the flower stalks of those grown for their foliage and propagate by division, root-cuttings or by seed. The principal species are S. asperum, the Prickly Comfrey, which grows to 5 ft. and is sometimes used as a forage plant; and S. officinale, the Common Comfrey, growing to 3 ft., which has escaped from cultivation in parts of America. The var. variegatum has very ornamental leaves variegated with white.

COMMELINA (kom-e-ly'-nah). A genus of perennial herbs of the Spiderwort Family with jointed stems, grass-like leaves, and short-lived flowers which are generally blue. Called Day-flowers, some are weedy, but others can be used as ground-covers in the greenhouse or outdoors. Propagation is by seeds, sown in spring or fall, also by cuttings rooted over heat. Two Mexican species, C. coelestis and C. tuberosa, both suitable for the greenhouse, develop tubers which may be divided.

C. angustifolia is a plant of S. U. S. with blue flowers in purple sheaths. C. nudiflora, a creeping perennial with small blue flowers, can be grown outdoors as far N. as N. J. In Fla. it is the most important weed host for celery mosaic disease, hence all mottled or otherwise infected plants should be destroyed.

COMMELINACEAE (kom-e-lin-ay'-see-ee). Botanical name of the Spiderwort Family, so-called from the spiderlike appearance of the hairy flower stalks inclosed at the base by flat sheathing leaves, as in Tradescantia. The family, which is herbaceous and widely dispersed but principally in the tropics, yields a number of ornamental subjects, chiefly grown under glass in the N. The genus Tradescantia (Spiderwort) includes common greenhouse basket plants and hardy border subjects; Commelina (Day-flower) is grown as a ground cover; other cultivated genera are Dichorisandra, Rhoeo and Zebrina (Wandering Jew).

COMMERCIAL FERTILIZER. A fertilizer (which see) is any material applied to the soil to increase its supply of the chemical elements needed by growing plants. Commercial fertilizer is a term used for inorganic, mineral, chemical or otherwise manufactured plant-food substances as distinguished from organic or "natural" plant foods, such as all kinds of manures, leafmold, and decomposed vegetable and animal substances.

A commercial fertilizer may be a single substance, such as nitrate of soda or muriate of potash, or it may be a combination of such materials so chosen and proportioned that the mixture contains a definite ratio of the three main plant-food elements, namely, nitrogen, phosphorus and potassium. Such a mixture is said to be "complete." And if the proportions of the three elements are such as to meet the full needs of a certain plant or crop under normal conditions, that fertilizer is said to be "balanced" as well as complete.

A gardener who knows the various individual commercial-fertilizer materials, how to mix them, and how much of them to use to get certain results, can buy them separately and prepare his own plant food. But the task is not an easy or pleasant one and it needs expert knowledge; so it is far easier and usually more economical to buy a commercial fertilizer ready mixed, of a reliable brand and a definitely stated, guaranteed analysis. This will be given in various forms according to the legal labeling requirements of different states, but the vital facts to look for are the percentages of nitrogen (N), phosphoric acid (P_2O_5—the fertilizer form of phosphorus), and potash (K_2O—the fertilizer form of potassium). While special crops and soils may call for special analyses, one that carries a total of 20 or more "units" or percents of those three materials in approximately these proportions: 4—12—4, or 5—10—5, will be of real help if added to a soil in good physical condition.

As the plant food compounds in commercial (manufactured) fertilizers are generally in highly available (soluble) form, these materials should not be applied too heavily or allowed to come in contact with plant parts. Small, frequent applications are safest and least wasteful as they give less chance for the soluble salts to be dissolved and leached out of the soil before the plant roots can get them. It is usually advisable to water the soil after adding commercial fertilizer, both to put the latter in solution so the plants can take it up, and to prevent its absorbing the moisture in the soil and, perhaps, thereby depriving the plants.

COMMUNITY GARDENS. In the main the reference is to such garden enterprises as developed largely during the first World War. It early became evident that gardening was an activity in which, under some circumstances, group effort afforded advantages over individual or solitary effort. Emergency food conditions made it important for communities to avail themselves of these advantages, and the community gardens were a natural result.

Thus there came about organization, through which permission to use undeveloped and waste lands owned by township, village or city (and also vacant land privately owned) was obtained, usually free of charge. School authorities cooperated enthusiastically with teachers of gardening and definite garden work for student gardeners; this led often to family interest and desire to join the effort. Industrial firms gave employees the use of idle land within their domain, often contributing its preparation on a large scale for the later seeding, planting and cultivation by individuals of their respective plots. Everywhere Farm Bureaus and County Agents and other extension workers were active, often in response to calls for help.

AFTER THE WAR. As emergency measures the majority of these projects lasted only "for the duration" of the emergency. But their values were too apparent to many who had taken part in the work as leaders or gardeners for the idea to be altogether given up. Hence there gradually developed from the wartime projects more or less permanent community gardens here and there, especially where daylight saving time has persisted. Originally advocated largely because of the added daylight hours it gave office and factory workers for activities in their wartime food gardens, this forward shift of the clock's hour hand at the beginning of the growing season is ardently approved and urged wherever the value of the garden is appreciated as it is by community gardeners.

While it has been upon the economic aspect of community gardens that most emphasis has fallen, social advantages of major importance have too often accrued to be disregarded, even in a cursory examination of the subject. The most outstanding of these during the wartime garden activities was the fraternizing, in the gardens and in regard to garden work, between families of foreign-born at that time racially antagonistic by reason of the war. Many of the major industries employing thousands of workers, where these racial antipathies smouldered and constantly

COMPANION CROPPING IN A BACKYARD GARDEN
Making the most of his space, the gardener is growing here, from left to right, rows of corn, gladiolus (where early peas had been), carrots, lettuce, a second sowing of lettuce, and another (later) planting of gladiolus.

threatened to break into disastrous action, found the reconciling effect of community garden endeavor so impressive that gardening found thereafter a permanent place in their social-service programs.

Similarly in the school gardens it was discovered that a real sense of citizenship and responsibility for, and to, the neighbor, was a result of garden ownership and responsibility. And in at least one community enterprise—the Rockefeller's Children's Gardens in the congested east side of New York City—the records show a steady movement of a percentage of the families whose children have had gardens there, to homes of their own in the country. Thus the community garden proves its influence in the decentralization problem.

ORGANIZATION SYSTEMS. Two systems of community garden organization are possible. Each has advantages and either may be preferable for a given community according to its character, preferences and working conditions. In one the members are allotted individual gardens based on a fixed unit per person to be provided for; here they plant and tend according to their own taste and choice, under broad community regulations. In the other, broadscale work is done on crops grown in large blocks or field rows, as in a commercial truck garden; time records are kept of each worker's hours in the garden, and each receives in the form of the garden produce he or she prefers, the value of the time put in. Occasionally the two systems are combined so that field crops are grown in an area cultivated by all alike on the time basis, while separate plots for the culture of the smaller or more personally favored vegetables are individually allotted.

In a secondary sense the term Community Garden is described under CITY GARDEN, which see.

COMPANION CROPPING. The practice of growing on a given area alternate plants or rows of two or more crops that require different lengths of time to mature. By the time the short season plants are ready to harvest, the longer season ones are ready to use the increased space so provided. Each crop is cultivated normally and harvested in its turn as the remaining plants need more room.

COMPASS-PLANT. Common name given to *Silphium laciniatum,* a Rosinweed, because the leaves point N. and S.

COMPATIBILITY. In spraying to control plant enemies certain insecticides and fungicides are often combined to save labor. Some combinations are safe, others are not, for they may cause severe injury by burning the foliage. The combinations used in proprietary compounds are usually carefully worked out for safety, but in making combinations at home in following one kind of spray with another certain precautions should be observed. The main "don'ts" are (1) that lime-sulphur should *never be mixed with soaps or oils,* and (2) that *arsenicals and soaps should never be combined,* as this produces injurious free arsenic. The following summarizes some of the possible and some of the injurious combinations:

Copper sprays are compatible with arsenates, nicotine-sulphate, flour and caseinate spreaders. Soaps and oils should *not* be used with bordeaux mixture, but a copper-silicate spray has been developed which may be combined with an oil emulsion.

Sulphur sprays (and dusts) *but not lime-sulphur* are compatible with arsenates and nicotine-sulphate; and with flour, caseinate and soaps as spreaders and stickers.

Lime-sulphur is compatible with lead and calcium arsenates, nicotine-sulphate and flour or caseinate spreaders but *not* with Paris Green, and *never* with soaps or oils.

Nicotine-sulphur is apparently compatible with any fungicide or insecticide or soap.

Lead and calcium arsenate may be combined with sulphur sprays and dusts, bordeaux mixture and nicotine-sulphate, but *not* with soaps and oil sprays.

Soaps are compatible with certain sulphur sprays, nicotine-sulphate and basic lead arsenate, but *not* with acid lead arsenate or other arsenicals, or with lime-sulphur or bordeaux mixture.

Oil sprays are *not ordinarily compatible* with sulphur, lime-sulphur, bordeaux mixture or arsenicals.

If trees have been given a dormant oil spray, sulphur sprays or dusts should not be used until from 2 to 4 weeks have elapsed. If roses are dusted with sulphur-lead-arsenate dust, any spray containing soap (as for aphids) should not be used until several days have elapsed.

See also DUSTING; SPRAYING; SPRAY INJURY.

COMPETITIONS, YARD AND GARDEN.

A yard and garden competition in any community is a desirable civic activity which may be organized by the chamber of commerce, one of the service clubs, such as the Lions, Rotary, Kiwanis, Town Criers, or the horticultural society, garden club, newspaper or magazine.

Any community in which a well organized garden competition is conducted, will be benefitted in many ways, for when interest is aroused in the improvement of the home surroundings, it leads to a desire on the part of the people to make the whole community more beautiful.

When the grounds of a home property are made attractive by the planting of trees, shrubs, flowers and lawns, the real estate value of the property is increased. A small bungalow which won a prize in a garden contest was sold for $1,000 more than the property could have brought before the improvements were made. Another home on which only $26 was expended for garden improvements was valued at $500 more after they were made. But in addition to such material benefits, there is a satisfaction and pride that comes from making and keeping the home grounds attractive that cannot be measured in dollars and cents. More than that, the attractive, well-kept home with a beautiful garden setting is a powerful example and stimulus for the entire neighborhood, especially if it enjoys the distinction of having won a prize in competition. Thus it is not only the awards but also the prestige and respect that they bring that makes participation in a yard and garden competition worth while—not to mention the pleasure of having done a good job.

In organizing a competition and in judging the results, it is important that expert advice be secured. For judge, a man of long experience and excellent professional training in horticulture and landscape work is necessary, and he should be given full authority to make decisions.

The Yard and Garden Contest Association of Davenport, Iowa, conducts a nationwide contest in the improvement of home grounds. More than 700 organizations conducted such contests under the auspices of this association last year. This is a non-profit organization and, for a nominal sum of $5, window cards, publicity, lantern slides, rules, judging book, entry blanks, awards of merit, prizes and suggestions for organizing a garden contest are furnished. The plan provides for those who have small home grounds and who do all of the work themselves, as well as for large properties where expert gardeners may be employed.

The New York Herald Tribune conducted for some years a yard and garden competition within an area of fifty miles from New York City. This plan provided for classes based on the size of the home grounds beginning with 6,000 square feet or less, up to 40,000 square feet or more. There was also a class for roof gardens. Community grand prizes were awarded.

The Better Homes and Garden Magazine of Des Moines, Iowa, conducts a nationwide "More Beautiful America" contest. This is designed for communities as a whole rather than individual home garden contests. A small park or recreation center, highway beautification, improvement of school grounds, railroad stations, municipal gardens, forests and woodland trails, and civic improvements of all kinds are the types of projects that may be entered for the prizes offered.

The contest is divided into classes based on the population of the communities taking part.

This same magazine conducts a contest in which boys and girls participate. Details of these contests, with rules and suggestions for organizing them, may be secured by writing to the magazine.

The Extension Service of the Colorado Agricultural College at Fort Collins, Colorado, assists local groups in that state to conduct garden contests.

The state colleges and universities in every state, through the extension departments, will be able to give valuable assistance in yard and garden contests to civic clubs or local organizations desiring to organize such an activity. (See Government Agencies for the address of each state institution.)

COMPOST.

A term applied to a rich, loose, friable soil-preparation resulting from the making of a "compost heap" of alternate layers of fresh manure and any suitable absorbent material. Added to the soil it supplies both humus and plant food elements in safe, convenient form. The exact materials used, the thickness of the layers and details of handling vary with local circumstances, but in general the procedure is as follows:

The basic layer 4 to 6 in. deep is of inverted sods, chopped cornstalks or other coarse material. The pile is usually oblong, not over 6 ft. wide, as long as desired and conveniently high—rarely over 5 ft. On this first layer is spread a 3 or 4 in. layer of manure, preferably cow manure, but pig, sheep, horse or poultry manure will do; the latter two kinds heat rapidly so should not be deeper than 3 in. Continue the alternating layers, using in the soil layer lawn cuttings, leaves or any sort of vegetable refuse that is not infected with plant diseases. To accelerate the

ing a variety of materials and mixing them.

As the pile is built, the top should be kept flat or slightly concave so as to collect rather than shed rain. If the weather is dry, the pile should be wet down with a hose or several pails of water once a week. If such a pile can be built all at one time, it should be spaded over and repiled in the same shape after about 2 months. This will hasten uniform decomposition and after being turned once again 4 to 6 weeks later, the compost should be ready for use. If, however, the heap is built gradually as the

HOW AND HOW NOT TO MAKE A COMPOST PILE

Indiscriminate accumulation of garden waste (left) is unsightly, makes poor compost and often carries over insects and diseases from one season to another. A good compost pile (right) is built carefully of alternating layers of vegetable refuse (B), and manure (C) with an occasional sprinkling of lime or superphosphate. The top (A) is kept concave to catch and hold rain or water applied with the hose.

break-down of the pile and also to reinforce and increase its plant-food value, sprinkle each such layer with agricultural lime, bonemeal, superphosphate, or, better still, one of the following: (1) a complete, balanced commercial fertilizer; (2) this mixture of chemicals—sulphate of ammonia 60 lbs., ground limestone 50 lbs., superphosphate 30 lbs. and muriate of potash 25 lbs., the above amount being sufficient for one ton of dry straw or other vegetable matter. The foregoing formula is that of the N. Y. State Agricultural Experiment Station. There is also on the market a special trade-marked preparation invented and made for the purpose that, at slightly greater cost, will save the gardener all the trouble of secur-

materials accumulate, it may take 6 months to a year for it to become big enough and sufficiently decayed for use. Even a pile of fallen leaves, lawn clippings, pea vines, etc., if sprinkled occasionally with lime or fertilizer, kept moist and forked over now and then, will give a valuable supply of compost in a year or two.

If a concrete or other pit is available for making the compost much valuable liquid plant food that would otherwise leach away can be saved. In such a case, the mixture can be made even richer by adding all liquid manure from horse or cow stalls. On a much smaller scale, a supply of compost can be built up in a back yard, by using a partly buried box or even an old barrel.

For garden use compost can be applied just as it is dug from the well-rotted heap. In making potting soil or filling greenhouse benches or coldframes, it is best to screen the compost through ½ in. mesh wire to remove any stones, sticks or coarse rubbish. The latter can sometimes be utilized for mulching or as the bottom layer of a new compost heap. As compost cannot burn or otherwise injure plants, it is one of the best forms in which to supply plant food, especially to small or delicate plants which might be harmed by manure.

COMPOSITE. A composite flower is a compound flower or, more accurately, a head or compact assembly of many small flowers, surmounting or surrounded by leafy bracts forming the *involucre*. The small flowers may be all of one kind, or of different kinds as in the daisy, which is a typical composite flower. Here the central part is of tiny tubular disk flowers, while the rim is of ray flowers whose one petal is greatly enlarged and strap-shaped.

This type of flower gives its name to the Composite Family (Compositae), which comprises many genera all having their flowers in heads as above described. This family is supposed by some botanists to be best suited to surviving in the temperate zones, because of the clustered growth of the flowers and the abundant production of seeds, which are often crowned with scales, barbs or hairs which assist in their wide distribution. It includes some of our most popular garden plants such as the dahlia, chrysanthemum, aster, gaillardia, sunflower, etc., many common vegetables, as lettuce, salsify and chicory, and a number of widespread troublesome weeds, such as thistle, burdock, hawk-weed and field daisy.

COMPTONIA (komp-toh'-ni-ah) *asplenifolia.* ·A fragrant, deciduous, hardy native shrub. See SWEET-FERN.

CONANDRON (koh-nan'-drun) *ramondioides.* A dwarf, tuberous-rooted herb, native to the mountains of Japan, but in this country not hardy above N. C. It bears a profusion of white or pink flowers with purple eye and yellow throat, in loose, drooping terminal clusters rising about 1 ft. in height. The plant is suitable for partially shaded locations in rockeries.

THE CHARACTERISTIC COMPOSITE FLOWER IN SEVERAL FORMS
Left, the head of a sunflower, composed of both ray- and disk-flowers; a tiny disk-flower from the center enlarged below. The ray-flowers of this plant do not bear seeds. Center, the head of a dandelion, composed entirely of ray-flowers, one of which is enlarged below. Right, part of a cluster of flower-heads from Eupatorium; below, a single head greatly enlarged, consisting only of disk-flowers; above, a single disk-flower enlarged.

CONCRETE. Artificial stone composed of Portland cement, sand and gravel (or broken stone, or cinders), mixed in various proportions (depending upon the purpose sought) with water, and allowed to "set" after being poured or placed in some wooden or metal form. It has many uses in and around the garden, as for making hotbed frames, walks, fence posts, retaining walls, summer-house floors, pools, stepping stones, vegetable pits and the like. It can also be used for making urns, pedestals and other ornamental articles though its use for making statuary should be undertaken, if at all, with care and artistic restraint. With proper machine forms it can be made into building blocks, and flower pots.

Concrete can be made at any time except during freezing weather. It is essential to have clean sand and gravel (if they are not clean they must be washed). They and the cement must be correctly measured and proportioned. A convenient method is to use a bottomless box of known capacity (say 2 cu. ft.) which can be filled 3 times with gravel, twice with sand and once with cement for a 3-2-1 mixture, and so on. The materials must be thoroughly mixed dry; then the mixing must be continued (shoveling over is the best way) as water is added gradually—enough to make a perfect mix, but not enough to give a sloppy consistency.

Complete and very helpful directions for all kinds of concrete work, of which generous use should be made, can be obtained from cement manufacturers (or the service bureaus of their associations), often with blue prints and specifications.

CONE. A compact arrangement of stiff, somewhat leaf-like scales beneath which the reproductive bodies are borne. Cones thus form the reproductive processes (or "flowers" of the plants called Gymnosperms. They are of two kinds, *pistillate* (or female) cones bearing naked ovules and *staminate* (or male) cones bearing sacs containing pollen. The staminate cones are shed after pollination takes place, while the larger pistillate cones become hard and woody and remain on the tree for some time.

CONEFLOWER. Common name given to three different genera of composites. See ECHINACEA, LEPACHYS and RUDBECKIA.

CONE-HEAD. Common name for the genus Strobilanthes (which see); this name comes from Greek words meaning "cone" and "flower."

CONE-PLANT. A name given to the genus Conophytum of the Carpet-weed Family (Aizoaceae), formerly considered a branch of the Fig-marigold group or Mesembryanthemums. The plants are not of horticultural interest except to the collector; they are merely small, fleshy bodies which produce stemless flowers, rosy, magenta, yellow, red, or white. (See illustrations under SUCCULENTS.)

CONFEDERATE-JASMINE or JESSAMINE. One of the common names for *Trachelospermum jasminoides,* an evergreen vine of the Dogbane Family, with fragrant white flowers, widely grown through the S.

CONIFER. This is a tree that bears woody cones containing naked seeds. Pines, hemlocks, firs, larches, etc., are familiar examples. Popularly the term is used and supposed to refer to any kind of narrow-leaved evergreen, but actually some genera of conifers are deciduous, as, for example, the larch (Larix) and the bald-cypress (Taxodium).

Conifers make up the most valuable softwood forests of the world, and also they include some of the most valuable plants used in landscape work, in the shrubbery border and in the rock garden. The pines, hemlocks, spruces, firs, junipers and cedars are used as windbreaks, in groves, as boundary outlines, for backgrounds, as specimens, and hedges, and in many other situations. They furnish a quiet note of green that frames or sets off the garden design, acting as an excellent foil for the contrasting texture of deciduous trees and shrubs and the brilliant bloom of smaller growing perennials, annuals, etc.

The coniferous genera most commonly used in gardening are, in the N.E. States, Abies, Chamaecyparis, Juniperus, Larix, Picea, Pinus, Pseudotsuga, Taxodium, Taxus, Thuja and Tsuga (all of which see) ; and, in the S. and W., various species of the above not hardy N. and such other genera as Araucaria, Cedrus, Cryptomeria, Cunninghamia, Sequoia. There are many species and numerous varietal and horticultural forms that furnish a multiplicity of material from which the landscape architect and home gardener may choose.

Conifers require little pruning. All that is necessary is to nip out the central bud of lower branches in order to encourage a bushy growth. Many take kindly to severe, repeated shearing and therefore make excellent formal hedges or special garden features.

If the soil is well supplied with humus and the trees are consistently mulched, conifers require little fertilizer, beside an occasional application of well-rotted manure or bonemeal. Often it is better not to encourage too rapid growth, as conifers that grow too rapidly are inclined to be spindly. Also certain kinds, especially among the pines, are adapted to and do well in sandy or otherwise rather poor soils.

Conifers should be moved in early spring before the new growth starts, or in late summer or early fall after the season's growth has ripened. In transplanting, never allow the roots to dry out, and avoid injuring them as this reduces the food and moisture-obtaining mechanism. For this reason balled and burlapped specimens from the nursery are more likely to grow than specimens dug up in the field or wood lot where the roots are less compact and much more likely to be injured. Plant firmly, loosening but not removing the burlap if needed to hold the soil around the

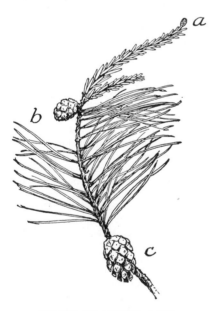

CONES OF THREE AGES

A terminal spray of a 2-needled pine showing (a) a young seed-bearing cone at the tip of the scale-covered shoot. (b) a one-year-old cone; and (c) a two-year-old cone partly open to facilitate distribution of the seeds.

roots. Fill the hole with good top-soil and water well when planting. Thereafter water frequently until the plant is well established, and mulch with rotted leaves or peat moss for the first year or two.

Propagation (which see) is by seeds, cuttings, or grafting.

See also EVERGREENS and the various genera mentioned.

CONIUM (koh′-ni-um) *maculatum.* A coarse, biennial herb of the Parsley Family, sometimes called Winter-fern, but more often Poison-hemlock, which see. In England hemlock means this plant, not the evergreen that we know by that name and that Europeans call spruce or, sometimes, hemlock spruce.

CONSERVATION OF NATIVE PLANTS. Within recent years there has been an awakening of public opinion as to the immediate necessity of preserving, not only our forests and other natural resources, but also many of our beautiful native plants, now on the verge of extinction. The Government has led the way in the National Parks by forbidding the picking of wild flowers, thus preserving for everyone's enjoyment acres of loveliness. In the E. States plants that have suffered particularly at the hands of ruthless pickers are the mayflower (*Epigaea repens*), dogwood (*Cornus florida*), mountain-laurel (*Kalmia latifolia*), holly (*Ilex opaca*), and ground-pine (*Lycopodium obscurum*), the latter three being used extensively for Christmas greens and the others largely for decorative effects at weddings, banquets, etc. Through the efforts of garden clubs, wild flower preservation societies, women's clubs and kindred organizations, a campaign of conservation education has been launched, and now in many States laws have been passed for the protection of these and other native plants which always have been or are rapidly becoming rare.

Past generations have been most wasteful of our national heritage of this natural beauty, but with the present generation aroused to the need of preserving what remains, thinking people all over the country are realizing that this can best be done through the schools. Nature camps have been established in various sections where teachers are taught how to inspire in their classes the intelligent love for Nature which is the true foundation of conservation. At the same time commercial nurserymen and florists are being urged to grow and distribute the plant materials formerly obtainable only from the wild, thus making it possible for people to enjoy them without defacing the countrysides.

Other movements backed by various organizations are the issuing of wild flower charts, the exhibition of nature work done by school children, the making of surveys of natural resources, the building of nature trails, and wild flower and bird sanctuaries, the promotion of campaigns for proper use of Christmas greens and for the use of living Christmas trees, and promotion of legislation for the preservation of roadside beauty.

CONSERVATORY. A small greenhouse (or glasshouse) attached to or part of a house for the special purpose of raising or showing decorative plants is generally termed a conservatory. Likewise, a section of a large greenhouse devoted to the display of foliage and flowering plants when they are at their prime may also be so called. In order to keep plants in good condition for the longest possible time, a conservatory must be kept cooler than a greenhouse. But the ventilation must be indirect and carefully arranged so that no drafts will strike the plants. The subjects displayed must be watered regularly according to their individual needs. If the conservatory is used solely for display, sun is not as essential as where the plants are growing, but it should not be excluded entirely. An adjustable slat shade outside is more desirable than whitewash on the glass.

Artistry in the arrangement of plants on display is an important factor in the enjoyment of the conservatory. Plenty of foliage plants should be used, but not too many with variegated leaves. Inharmonious reds should be kept apart, though they may often be gradually blended into one another by the use of intermediate tones combined with white and set apart, if necessary, with foliage plants. Some variation in height is desirable in a display of plants of the same type. If they have all grown the same size, some of them may be set on inverted flower-pots or wire stands. Tender vines, such as Clerodendron, will give a good showing of flowers in the conservatory for a large part of the year besides their foliage effect; but vines should not be used to the extent that they shade the lower specimens, espe-

cially the flowering plants. (See illustration, Plate 25.)

CONTACT POISON. An insecticide (which see) used against insects (and other creatures such as mites) that have sucking mouth parts and, therefore, cannot be controlled with a poison applied to the

A TINY CONSERVATORY
This glazed and ventilated metal frame can be bolted to a house around an existing window to provide a handy compact "window greenhouse."

surface of the plant, but must have it come in direct contact with their bodies. Nicotine, pyrethrum, rotenone, sulphur and some oils are used as contact insecticides, in either dust or liquid form. See IN-SECTICIDE.

CONVALLARIA (kon-va-lay'-ri-ah) *majalis.* The small, hardy, graceful, white-flowered herb of the Lily Family widely grown and loved as Lily-of-the-valley, which see.

CONVOLVULACEAE (kon-vol-veu-lay'-see-ee). The Morning-glory Family, a widely distributed group best known horticulturally as twining herbs, but including some erect herbs, shrubs and rarely trees. The juice is characteristically milky; the flowers are often large and bright-colored, the petals united into a funnel-form corolla with a flaring limb. The sweet-potato (*Ipomoea batatas*) belongs to this family; some forms are of medicinal value, and others are grown for ornament. Among the cultivated genera are Convolvulus, Calonyction, Quamoclit, Ipomoea, Porana. Some species are obnoxious weeds, particularly the parasitic dodders (Cuscuta) and many species of Convolvulus such as the field bindweed.

CONVOLVULUS (kon-vol'-veu-lus). Bindweed. Annual or perennial herbs, mostly trailing or twining and named from the word convulvo, meaning to entwine. The plants bear funnel-shaped flowers resembling those of the true morning-glory (Ipomoea) to which they are closely related, differing partly in that their flowers remain open all day. In catalogs they are often referred to as morning-glories. Dwarf species may be used for bedding, for which they are excellent because of their season of bloom which continues all summer. The tall sorts are good for covering fences or walls and the tender kinds are grown in the greenhouse. The blue tones are the most satisfactory shade.

Full sunshine and not too much water are their sole requirements. Propagation is by seeds, division, and cuttings of the young wood. Their planting and spreading should be watched with care as they sometimes develop into annoying weeds.

Species giving best results include: *C. tricolor* (Dwarf Morning-glory), an annual, 6 to 12 in. tall, often branching, covered with brown hairs, the blue flowers with a yellow and white throat; *C. sepium* (Rutland Beauty), a trailing perennial, to 10 ft., flowers white, or pink striped with white; *C. japonicus* (California Rose), a twining perennial, to 20 ft., with bright pink flowers.

COOLHOUSE. Name given to a greenhouse or section of one kept especially for growing plants that thrive best in temperatures ranging from 35 to 40 deg. at night to not over 60 deg. during the day. Most enclosed porches or small lean-to conservatories answer to this description. Flowers thriving best under the temperature conditions mentioned include sweet peas, mignonette, violets and hardy annuals or perennials grown from seeds. Pot-plants doing well under similar conditions include old favorites like geraniums, fuchsias, etc., as well as various members of the Azalea group.

Some coolhouses are used entirely for carrying plants through their dormant seasons. Agaves, bay-trees, cacti of certain kinds and other pot-plants that cannot survive freezing temperatures outdoors find congenial winter quarters in a coolhouse.

Where it affords bench space, it may even be used for starting extra-early hardy vegetables, such as lettuce, cabbage, endive, parsley, etc.

Coolhouses are maintained at very small expense and require very little attention. They prove valuable for carrying over quantities of semi-hardy pot-plants which ordinarily are plunged outdoors during late spring, summer and early fall.

See also CONSERVATORY; GREENHOUSE; HOTHOUSE.

COON-TAIL. One of the common names of *Ceratophyllum demersum,* an indoor aquarium plant, known also as Hornwort, which see.

COONTIE. Common name applied to species of Zamia, especially *Z. floridana* and *Z. integrifolia,* fern- or palm-like plants of the Cycad Family, with underground, tuber-like trunks and handsome, dark green, feather-shaped leaves forming tufts about 2 ft. high. They are grown out of doors in the S. where they are especially useful in low plantings, and under glass in the N. where they should be planted in peat, sand and loam and given much moisture and shade. They are propagated by suckers, seed, or by starting them from pieces sliced from the trunk. The leaves are largely used by florists as the background of decorations and funeral pieces, as they are long lasting and do not wither.

COOPERIA (koo-pee'-ri-ah). A genus of bulbous-rooted, night-blooming herbs of the Amaryllis Family. Popularly known as Prairie-lily or Rain-lily, which see.

COPPER BEECH. A beautiful variety (*cuprea*) of the European Beech (*Fagus sylvatica*), in which the new leaves are brilliantly copper-colored. Mentioned in English books, it is apparently not grown commercially in U. S. The Purple Beech (*Fagus sylvatica* var. *atropunicea,* formerly var. *atropurpurea*) is sometimes known as the Copper Beech in the E. States.

COPPER COMPOUNDS. The most familiar form of these materials, used chiefly as fungicides, is *bordeaux mixture,* which has been a standard since 1882 when its fungicidal value was discovered by accident in the vineyards of France. When solutions of copper sulphate and hydrated lime are mixed fine membranes are formed, which cover and protect the foliage. They are practically insoluble in water but, in the presence of a germinating fungus spore or bacterial thallus, they release enough toxic material to kill the disease organism. Bordeaux mixture may be purchased in either paste or powder form, to be diluted according to the manufacturer's directions; or it may be prepared at home from previously prepared copper sulphate and lime (called "instant bordeaux"); or it may be made of copper sulphate crystals (bluestone) and slaked lime. (For directions see BORDEAUX MIXTURE.) The solution must be applied immediately and kept agitated while in the sprayer. One of the best general fungicides, it is used generally at a 4-4-50 dilution (4 lbs. copper sulphate, 4 lbs. lime, 50 gals. water) for the control of many leaf spot diseases and blights; and also in weak concentrations ($1\frac{1}{2}$-$1\frac{1}{2}$-50) as a spray for various Botrytis blights and for fire-blight of apple. (See APPLE). Powdered bordeaux mixture mixed with linseed oil is a valuable wound dressing.

There is some danger of injuring tender foliage with bordeaux mixture; since apple and other fruit leaves are often russetted by it, sulphur sprays are usually substituted. Continued use of bordeaux causes the leaves of certain rose varieties to turn yellow and fall. Bordeaux mixture may be combined with insecticides such as lead or calcium arsenate and nicotine-sulphate. It acts as a repellent to drive away certain insects—leaf hoppers in particular. For plants with waxy leaves some type of spreader (which see) should be added.

Burgundy mixture (which see), a combination of copper sulphate with sodium carbonate, is used as a substitute for bordeaux mixture on small fruits (when ripening) and some other plants. It leaves no stain or residue.

A proprietary compound of copper silicate has been used successfully as a spray for apples in certain parts of the country and may sometimes replace bordeaux for use on ornamentals. The great advantage is that it does not discolor the foliage to any extent and may be combined with an oil emulsion.

Ammoniacal copper carbonate (made by dissolving 1 level teaspoon of copper carbonate in 2 tablespoons of ammonia and adding 1 gallon of water) should be used immediately. It is used on ornamentals because it does not stain, but it does not adhere as well, and is not as efficient, as bordeaux mixture. A proprietary compound of copper and ammonia used in combination with lead arsenate and a contact insecticide appears highly efficient in preventing rose diseases, with no resulting injury or unsightliness.

A copper-lime dust, applied when the plants are wet with dew, forms a protective bordeaux membrane on the plant. The usual formula is 20 parts copper sulphate to 80 parts hydrated lime. Or 10 parts lead arsenate may be substituted for an equal amount of lime. See also DUSTING.

Copper sulphate, besides being used to make copper sprays, was formerly used for treating seed before planting, but at the present time copper carbonate dust is more generally used. *Red copper oxide* (cuprous oxide) is a new disinfectant of much promise for treating seeds of various vegetables and ornamentals. See DISINFECTION.

COPPER-LEAF. Common name for *Acalypha wilkesiana,* a shrub of the Spurge Family, grown in the greenhouse N. and much planted in the S. States and Calif. for hedge and lawn plants.

COPPER OXIDE (CUPROUS OXIDE). A chemical used in a stable red-powder form as a seed disinfectant. See DISINFECTION.

Its use as a spray (1 oz. in 3 gals. water, or 1 lb. in 50 gals.) is being recommended to prevent damping-off, stem canker, and leaf diseases of seedlings grown in greenhouses and tomato plants raised in flats for setting outdoors. Unlike bordeaux mixture, it never stunts the plants. A proprietary grade is now obtainable that mixes with water and stays in suspension better than the pure chemical.

COPPERTIP. A name given to *Crocosmia aurea,* a showy African plant of the Iris Family, closely resembling the gladiolus, but of branching habit and with few leaves. It blooms in the fall, the bright orange-yellow flowers being borne on stalks 4 ft. high. In the N. it is not hardy and the corms should be planted in a warm spot after danger of frost is over, lifted in the fall and stored over winter in sphagnum moss to prevent their drying out.

COPROSMA (kop-ros'-mah). Tender shrubs or small trees from New Zealand. The male and female flowers, borne on separate plants, have no decorative value; this is found, however, in the foliage and colored berries. The plant can be grown outdoors only in warm regions. The principal species are:

C. baueri, an evergreen growing to 25 ft., with glossy leaves and orange-yellow berries. It is a useful hedge plant in California.

acerosa, a low spreading shrub about 6 in. high with attractive light blue berries.

lucida, which grows to 15 ft., with shining leathery leaves to 5 in. long. The berries are orange-red.

COPTIS (kop'-tis). A genus of small, hardy perennial herbs of the Buttercup Family, popularly known as Goldthread

CORAL-GEM. Common name for *Lotus bertholeti,* a shrub of the Pea Family having scarlet flowers and silvery foliage. See LOTUS.

CORALLITA (koh-ra-ly'-tah). Another name for *Antigonon leptopus,* the Coral-vine. Do not confuse with White Corallita, which is *Porana paniculata.* See ANTIGONON.

CORAL-PLANT. Common name for *Jatropha multifida* of the Spurge Family, a shrub or tree with scarlet flowers; also

THE CORDON IS A SIMPLE STYLE OF TRAINED FRUIT TREE
(A) The simplest of all—a single stem trained horizontally. (B) A 2-armed horizontal cordon. (C) A modification of (B) creates a lattice effect against a wall.

(which see). The slender rootstocks yield a rich yellow dye.

CORAL-BEAN. A name sometimes applied to Erythrina, the Coral-tree, which see.

CORAL-BELLS. Another common name for Alum-foot, which is the genus Heuchera (which see); and especially for *H. sanguinea.*

CORAL-BERRY or INDIAN CURRANT. These are common names for *Symphoricarpos orbiculatus,* a hardy native shrub of the Honeysuckle Family, with white flowers and purplish-red berries.

CORAL-BLOW or CORAL-PLANT. Common names for *Russelia equisetiformis,* a rush-like shrub of the Figwort Family.

CORAL-BUSH (*Templetonia retusa*). An Australian shrub belonging to the Pea Family. It is a tall grower with leathery leaves and red flowers. In S. Calif. it succeeds in fairly light soil and blooms in winter.

CORAL-DROPS. A common name for Mexican Star (which see), classified by some authorities as *Bessera elegans,* but more recently as *Milla biflora.*

for *Russelia equisetiformis,* a rush-like shrub of the Figwort Family.

CORAL-TREE. Common name for thorny trees of the genus Erythrina. Members of the Pea Family, they are grown in the open in the S. and in Calif. In the tropics some species are used for shade trees in coffee and cacao plantations and are known as "immortelles." Coral-trees are easily propagated from seed or by cuttings of growing wood.

E. crista-galli (Common or Cock-spur Coral-tree) is a small bushy tree with brilliant scarlet, sweet-pea-like flowers. Native to Brazil it requires a hot summer in order to develop bloom in full beauty.

poeppigiana, a prickly tree to 60 ft., used as a "nurse tree" in the coffee plantings in the W. Indies and often grown for ornament in S. Fla.

CORAL-VINE. A common name for *Antigonon leptopus,* which is also called Pink-vine, Corallita, Confederate-vine, and Rosa de Montana.

CORCHORUS (kaur'-koh-rus). Tropical herbs of commercial but no horticultural value. *C. capsularis* is the principal source of jute fibre and its young shoots are eaten as pot-herbs. Corchorus is also a former generic name, still used in some trade lists, for Kerria (which see), an ornamental, hardy, deciduous shrub.

CORDATE. Heart-shaped; particularly a leaf more or less egg-shaped in general outline, but notched at the base, like that of the four o'clock. Compare OVATE.

CORDIA (kaur'-di-ah). A large genus of tropical trees and shrubs, some vine-like, belonging to the Borage Family. A few may be found in greenhouse collections, or growing outdoors in the warmest parts of the country. They thrive in any light rich soil, and are propagated by seeds and cuttings.

C. sebestena (Geiger-tree) is a large evergreen shrub or small tree of the Florida Keys. It has bell-shaped orange-scarlet flowers in large terminal clusters. C. greggi var. palmeri is a Mexican shrub, with white fragrant flowers in loose clusters.

CORDON. (See illustration, Plate 52.) A fruit tree (usually dwarf) trained to 1, 2 or more straight, unbranching stems which are supported upright, horizontally or obliquely on a trellis or against a wall in more or less geometrical regularity of design. The cordon is sometimes considered a simple form of espalier (which see). Its advantages are the saving of space and the production of superior fruit which, borne close to the stems just where wanted, is given maximum room and sunlight to develop to perfection. While all of the stone fruits can be so trained, the fruits most commonly handled in this way are the apple and pear, especially the latter. See also TRAINING OF PLANTS.

CORDULA (kaur'-deu-lah). A large genus of Old-World, tropical, terrestrial and epipyhtic orchids called Venus and Lady-slipper (which see) from the characteristic form of the showy greenish, yellowish, or white flowers with their large inflated, sac-like lips. Numerous species and many named hybrids are grown in the greenhouse, and are among the easiest of orchids to handle. Consequently they are frequently seen in exhibitions and in the florists' windows. C. insignis and its var. sanderae are very easily grown either in the greenhouse or as house plants. For culture see ORCHIDS.

CORDYLINE (kaur-di-ly'-nee). Ornamental trees or shrubs belonging to the Lily Family and closely related to Dra-

caena. As a matter of fact Cordylines are better known in cultivation and in the florist trade as Dracaenas, the differences being only slight botanical details of flower and fruit. They grow stiffly erect, becoming branched in age. The long drooping leathery leaves are crowded at the top of the stem, giving a palm-like effect. Small plants, especially the richly variegated forms of C. terminalis, make very ornamental subjects for the warm greenhouse. For cultural details and descriptions see DRACAENA.

COREMA (koh-ree'-mah) conradi. An evergreen, heathlike small shrub useful as a ground cover. See BROOM-CROWBERRY.

COREOPSIS (koh-ree-op'-sis). Tickseed. Annual and perennial herbs of the Daisy Family (Compositae), grown as much for cutting as for their long season of garden decoration. Both kinds succeed in any good soil, ranging in height from 1½ to 4 ft., and bearing flowers, yellow, orange, red or brownish-purple, from June to frost. They need a sunny location.

The annual species, known as Calliopsis, provide some of the gayest, hardiest and most easily grown of garden materials. Their yellow, maroon and crimson flowers on wiry stems make excellent bouquet material. Grown from seed sown outdoors in late April (because of difficulty of transplanting), plants should be thinned to stand 10 in. apart. The perennial forms may be started from seed, from cuttings of growing wood taken in summer, or by divisions of the roots made in April or May. In the border they make a brilliant showing, the toothed petals forming a ring around a darker colored disk. Tall varieties are effective grouped with dwarf compact types as edgings.

COREOPSIS IMPROVEMENT
Typical single flowers at right and, at left, those of one of the new improved double forms.

A dark, bronze-green leaf beetle with two cream colored stripes, that sometimes attacks Córeopsis, should be controlled with lead arsenate.

Of the 30 or more species the following are the most popular:

C. drummondi (Goldenwave Calliopsis). To 12 ft.; golden yellow; especially good for cutting, border or bedding.

tinctoria, elegans or *marmorata* (Calliopsis). Rays yellow, crimson-brown at base, disk brownish-purple. Taller than *C. drummondi.* Does best in sunny borders.

lanceolata. Perennial, with large orange-yellow heads 2 in. across, on long, graceful stems. Var. *flore-pleno* has double flowers.

CORIANDER (koh-ri-an'-dur). An annual or biennial herb (*Coriandrum sativum*) of the Parsley Family (Umbelliferae), grown for its aromatic seeds which are used for flavoring liquors and confections. The plants, which grow about 2 ft. high, are cultivated in rows about 18 in. apart from seed sown in early spring. The seed heads which ripen about midsummer are gathered and dried on sheets, then beaten with light rods or flails to separate the seeds. See HERBS.

CORIARIA (koh-ri-ay'-ri-ah). A small genus of herbs or shrubs, grown chiefly for their ornamental berries. They grow well in good garden soil in a sunny place, but are not hardy where frosts are severe.

C. japonica, the best known, is a shrub of medium height, with pale-green, frond-like stems and leaves. The bright red berries in summer later turn black.

terminalis is usually herbaceous and has black fruit. Var. *xanthocarpa* has translucent yellow berries that remain decorative for a long time.

myrtifolia (Myrtle-leaved-sumach or Tanners-tree) is a good-sized shrub bearing poisonous black berries.

CORKSCREW-FLOWER. A common name for *Phaseolus caracalla,* also known as Snail-flower, a climbing vine with flowers in which the keel or lower petal is curiously twisted after the manner of a snail shell.

CORK-TREE. Common name for the genus Phellodendron, a member of the Rue Family (Rutaceae), native to eastern Asia. Ornamental trees with particularly attractive aromatic foliage, they bear abundant black fruit which remains for a long time after the leaves have fallen. They are hardy and adapted to a wide variety of soils, growing vigorously when young. The species commonly listed are all desirable for landscape planting, varying from 30 to 50 ft. in height, with broad, round heads. These are *P. amurense, P. chinense, P. japonicum* and *P. sachalinense,* the latter being the most planted. They are propagated from seed, by hardwood cuttings over heat, and by root cuttings.

CORM. A shortened, fleshy, erect underground stem with inconspicuous scale-like leaves. It closely resembles, and is often mistakenly called, a bulb (as the "bulbs" of Gladiolus and Crocus), but actually it is distinguished by being more definitely a modified stem. The stem character of bulbs is obscured by their very fleshy leaves. From the prominent terminal bud and smaller ones in the axils of its scale-like leaves, corms develop new plants, and often small, subsidiary corms known as *cormels.* Gladiolus, Colchicum and Caladium all grow from corms.

CORN or MAIZE. An annual American cereal grass (*Zea mays*). Its "field varieties" are grown for fodder and grain; its "sweet" kinds for their "ears" of immature seeds; certain "popping" sorts for making "pop-corn," and a few kinds as ornamentals on account of their attractive foliage.

Sweet corn (*Z. mays,* var. *rugosa*) is horticulturally the most important, being grown in every State, in Mexico and in bordering Canadian provinces, and having many varieties with differing characteristics—size of plant, color, size and arrangement of seeds, etc.

CULTURAL REQUIREMENTS. Sweet corn thrives best in warm, well-drained soils, especially those enriched by plowing under heavy clover sod or lavish dressings of manure. The soil can hardly be too rich and the crop will not thrive on poor, thin soils without liberal feeding. In such places a generous dressing of complete, quickly available commercial fertilizer composed of nitrate of soda, muriate of potash and superphosphate may make possible fairly successful results.

Soil preparation is the same as for early spring garden crops, but should be done immediately before seeding if possible. As all varieties are tender, it is risky to have seedlings appear before the last spring frost; but in the home garden the satisfaction of occasionally pulling an extra early crop through, is well worth the small cost of seed and labor. Similarly, it is worth risking the loss of a late crop by sowing even after midsummer, provided an early maturing variety is chosen that will perhaps reach an edible stage before the first frost. Sometimes a crop may be saved from an early fall frost by cutting and standing the stalks in shocks; many of the ears will continue to ripen to edible condition.

In the case of small plots, time can be gained by soaking the seed overnight, by sprouting it for a week before sowing, or by starting plants indoors or in hotbeds in dirt bands or paper or clay pots and transplanting to the garden after the weather has become settled.

Planting in hills for cultivation in both directions with horse or tractor is admissible on large areas of rough, stony or gravelly land, but in small plots and well tilled soils sowing in drills and leaving the plants of dwarf varieties 6 or 8 in. apart in the rows and of tall ones 8 to 12 in., will yield the most and best corn with the least work, especially if the wheelhoe is used at weekly or ten-day intervals. The distance between rows will depend upon the size of the varieties and the tools used —from 18 to 24 in. for dwarf sorts to 30 to 36 in. for all kinds.

HARVESTING. Corn is ready for the table when shortly past the "milk stage," which can easily be recognized after a little practise. The silks should be dry and black and the husk leaves will have a characteristic appearance of maturity. In general if the ear feels plump and firm when grasped it is ready. For home use it is better to harvest too young than too old.

In gathering grasp the stem just below the ear with one hand and the ear butt with the other and twist in opposite directions. The ear will then break off at a joint just below it. The shorter the time between gathering and serving the better, because the sugars in the kernels rapidly change to other, less flavorful compounds. After gathering the last ear on a stalk bend the latter down and break or cut it off close to the ground. Left standing it would use water and plant food to no purpose; cut while still green it can be fed to animals or used as the basis of a compost heap.

POP-CORN (*Z. mays,* var. *everta*) is sown at the same time as the first sweet corn, and given the same cultivation. It is allowed to mature fully, then cut and shocked like field corn so as to dry out thoroughly. The ears are then removed, shucked and stored in dry quarters such as a warm attic.

"RAINBOW" OR ORNAMENTAL CORN is a variously variegated plant about 5 ft. high. It is often grown to divide the vegetable garden from the ornamental grounds.

ENEMIES. The many diseases and insect pests of corn are usually controlled on commercial crops by cultural methods, crop rotation, and the destruction of all refuse or waste materials which might harbor pests. In the home garden special efforts may be possible and well worth while.

Bacterial wilt known as "Stewart's disease" attacks all varieties of sweet corn but is most destructive on the early yellow types. Favored by high temperatures it results in plants that are dwarfed, wilted and dried up, looking as though they had been frosted. Small drops of yellow slime may ooze from the cut ends of stalks. The causal bacterium is carried in the seed and

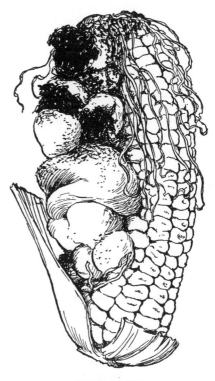

CORN SMUT

This common disease spoils the whole ear, swelling the kernels and filling them with the black dust-like spores of the fungus.

in old plant refuse and may be transmitted by the 12-spotted cucumber beetle (see below) and by flea beetles. To avoid the disease use seed from healthy plants; where it is severe, plant late varieties. Seed of fairly resistant strains developed by crossing may be purchased.

Corn smut caused by a fungus is usually seen wherever corn is grown as black swellings on ear and tassel. The first symptom is a pale, shining, swollen area; the white covering membrane becomes darker and finally bursts, releasing a powdery mass of black spores. Gather and burn smutted ears and stalks before this happens.

The corn ear worm begins to injure plants when the ears are in silk, continuing active until harvest time. Its presence is evidenced outside by moist castings on the silk; inside the husk the grains may be eaten down to the cob. And molds may follow the feeding of the larvae. The worm, which is 2 in. long when full grown, light green to brown with alternating light and dark lengthwise stripes, may attack other plants such as tomato, tobacco and cotton. Dust the corn silks while green with a mixture of 2 parts arsenate of lead to 1 part hydrated lime or flour. Spade the land deeply in autumn.

Bent or broken tassels indicate the presence of the well-known European corn borer, a flesh-colored worm with fine black dots, about 1 in. long when full grown. It attacks many herbaceous plants, especially corn, sorghum, smartweed, pigweed and dahlias. It has spread rapidly S.W. from the New England States and the Great Lakes corn areas in spite of a Federal plant quarantine that for several years regulated the movement of host plants. Full grown larvae hibernate in the stems of weeds and corn stalks, pupating in late spring. The moths, yellowish-brown with irregular, wavy, darker bands, emerge from June to August and lay eggs on the undersides of the leaves. When the eggs hatch (in a week or less) the larvae soon bore into leaves, leaf stems, stalks and corn ears. In most of the infested area there is but one generation; in New England there are two.

The most effective control measure is to destroy all corn stalks and weeds in the fall, cutting the corn as close to the ground as possible and in any case not more than 2 in. above it.

The southern corn root worm is the larve of the 12-spotted cucumber beetle already mentioned, which injures corn and other food plants, such as peanuts, beans and cucurbits, in the S. The grubs feed on the roots and buds, boring through the crown at the base of the plant. Insecticides are futile against this rootworm stage but may be used to destroy the beetles as they feed on above-ground portions of the plants. Crop rotation helps to control the pest.

For other corn insect pests see ARMYWORM; BILLBUG; CHINCH BUG; CUTWORM; GRASSHOPPER; JAPANESE BEETLE; WIREWORM; WHITE GRUB.

CORNCOCKLE. Common name for *Agrostemma githago,* a common weed found in abundance in grain fields. When its seeds become mixed with the grain they render the flour or meal unwholesome. The plants are tall, erect, branching, grayish, and silky. They are sometimes cultivated in the garden for their flat-topped purplish-red flowers, 1 in. across.

CORNEL (kaur′-nel). Another name for *Cornus mas,* the Cornelian-cherry. Dwarf Cornel is *Cornus canadensis.*

CORNELIAN-CHERRY. The common name for *Cornus mas,* a tall shrub or small tree of Europe and Asia, the first of the Dogwoods to come into flower, and one of the earliest of spring-flowering shrubs. Its small but very numerous yellow flowers appear before the leaves. They are followed by large edible berries that ripen in late summer. It is valuable to plant in shady places and can stand dry soil better than most Dogwoods.

See also DOGWOOD.

CORN-FLAG. Common name for *Gladiolus segetum,* a purple-flowered species sometimes grown in gardens in the S.

CORNFLOWER. One common name for *Centaurea cyanus,* also called Bachelors Button, Ragged Sailor, etc. See CENTAUREA. (See also illustration, Plate 9.)

CORN-MARIGOLD. Common name for *Chrysanthemum segetum,* an annual growing from 1 to 2 ft. tall, greatly branching in habit. Flower heads, yellow to whitish, are as much as 2½ in. across. There are many varieties of this species in common cultivation, known by a large number of names, such as White Glory, Morning Star, Evening Star, Gold Star and Northern Star. Cultivation is the same as for annual species of Chrysanthemum, which see.

CORN POPPY. Common name for *Papaver rhoeas,* the red field poppy of Europe and Asia.

CORN SALAD. Also called Fetticus, Vetticost, and Lambs-lettuce. This is an annual (*Valerianella locusta,* var. *oiltoria*) grown in late fall and early spring as a pot-herb or salad. Seed sown broadcast in early fall in rich soil should produce some plants large enough to use before winter. With light mulching the smaller ones may be easily wintered for earliest spring use.

In early spring seed may be sown thickly in drills 12 to 15 in. apart. Given clean cultivation, this crop should be ready for use within two months. Sown late it is rarely satisfactory since the plants cannot stand hot weather. As the leaves are almost tasteless they are usually mixed with more piquant plants—mustard, peppergrass or watercress—to enhance their flavor. Italian Corn-salad is *V. eriocarpa.*

See GREENS; VALERIANELLA.

CORNUS (kaur'-nus). Dogwood, Cornel. A genus of ornamental shrubs or small trees, found in temperate regions of the northern hemisphere. They are mostly deciduous and serve many useful purposes in garden and landscape plantings. The foliage is handsome, in some cases variegated, and in others very colorful in fall. Some kinds are noted for the bright effects of their colored stems in winter, and all have attractive flowers and fruits. They thrive in almost any soil, and seem to be as happy in shade as in the open. Propagation is by seeds, best sown in fall, by cuttings of mature wood, and by layers.

See DOGWOOD; BUNCHBERRY; CORNELIAN-CHERRY.

COROKIA (koh-roh'-ki-ah). Evergreen shrubs of New Zealand, belonging to the Dogwood Family. They are of easy culture in good garden soil, but only hardy where frosts are light. The small yellow fragrant flowers opening in spring are followed by orange or red berries. *C. cotoneaster* is the most attractive species. It has wiry branches much interlaced, small leaves whitish beneath, and bright yellow star-shaped flowers.

COROLLA (koh-rol'-ah). The inner set of floral leaves or *petals,* which are of delicate texture, usually brightly colored and often scented. See FLOWER.

CORONA (koh-roh'-nah). In a flower an outgrowth of the receptacle forming a

crown around the stamens, on or just inside the corolla, as the conspicuous cup of the daffodil or the fringed crown of the passion flower; or an outgrowth of stamens united to form a tube, as the hood crowning the stamen tube of the milkweeds.

CORONILLA (kor-oh-nil'-ah). Shrubs and herbs from the Mediterranean region and W. Asia, belonging to the Pea Family. The shrubby species, deciduous or evergreen, are very attractive in form, with

NATIVE DOGWOOD FOR THE GARDEN
Several species of Cornus are suitable for transplanting. The dense whitish flower-cluster (left) is followed by a bunch of berries (right).

pinnate leaves and tufts of yellow flowers. They grow well in sandy loam in a warm sunny place, but are not entirely hardy where frosts are severe. Principal species are:

C. emerus (Scorpion-sema). This medium sized shrub is deciduous or evergreen, according to climate. It is in flower most of the summer.

glauca is an attractive evergreen of medium height, with glaucous leaves and fragrant clear yellow flowers, produced over a long season.

varia (Crown-vetch). A straggly European herb, naturalized in some parts of this country, and effective when planted on banks. The pinkish-white flowers are borne in dense heads all summer.

CORREA (kor'-ee-ah). Tender Australian shrubs belonging to the Rue Family. They are good decorative plants for the greenhouse, making shapely free-flowering specimens. They grow best in a mixture of fibrous peat and sharp sand, and the shoots need pinching to induce a good bushy growth. They are propagated by cuttings, or by grafting the choicer kinds on seedlings of the species *C. alba.*

C. speciosa is the best known. It is a slender grower and a profuse bloomer, with nodding tubular flowers of scarlet, tipped yellowish-green. There are several good forms. *C. alba* grows more compactly with smaller white flowers. It is a good stock on which to graft the showier kinds.

CORROSIVE SUBLIMATE. One name for a chemical compound, also known as mercuric chloride and bichloride of mercury, that has many uses as a disinfectant. It is available at drug stores in convenient tablet form, one tablet to a pint of water making a 1 to 1,000 dilution. This strength is used to disinfect soil from which diseased plants have been removed, and to disinfect plant parts such as iris rhizomes, pruning and budding tools or anything that might carry infection. A dilution of 1 to 2,000 (half a tablet to a pint of water) is often poured around the base of living plants for the control of such stem and root rots as crown rot, sclerotinia rot and rhizoctonia rot. *Corrosive sublimate is a virulent poison and care should be taken to wash the hands after handling the tablets.* In making solutions, always use an agate or glass container since the solution corrodes metals.

See also DISINFECTION.

CORTADERIA (kor-ta-dee'-ri-ah). A genus of large perennial grasses called Pampas Grass (which see), frequently grown for ornament.

CORTICIUM (kohr-tis'-ee-um). A minute, partially saprophytic fungus, the cause of the Rhizoctonia disease of potatoes, and one of the fungi causing damping off in seedlings, and also stem and root rot. Plants in the garden most likely to be attacked belong to the Pink, Mustard, Pea, Nightshade and Composite Families.

To discourage attacks of this fungus in seed-beds avoid a high temperature, water from below, give excellent ventilation without drafts, and spread a thin layer of dry sand over the surface of the soil between the seedlings.

See RHIZOCTONIA; DISEASES, PLANT.

CORTUSA (kor-teu'-sah). A small genus of dwarf, perennial, hairy herbs belonging to the Primrose Family, natives of Europe and N. Asia. *C. matthioli,* occasionally seen in cultivation, is used in shady spots in the rock garden. Its small, rosy-purple nodding flowers appear early in the spring. Culture is the same as for primroses, but Cortusa must have winter protection in the N. Propagation is by division of the roots.

CORYDALIS (koh-rid'-al-is). A group of herbs of the Fumitory Family (Fumariaceae) with interesting, irregular yellow, blue, purple or rose flowers resembling those of the bleeding heart. They are easily cultivated in any ordinary garden soil, being increased by seed or division, and some species by tubers. *C. thalictrifolia* is a perennial growing 1 ft. with yellow flowers in spreading racemes and delicately-cut foliage like that of meadowrue. *C. sempervirens* is an annual occasionally growing 2 ft. high with brilliant pink and yellow flowers.

CORYLOPSIS (koh-ri-lop'-sis). Winter-hazel. Ornamental deciduous shrubs of Asia, belonging to the Witch-hazel Family. They thrive in a light rich soil, and, where winters are severe, prefer a protected position. The delicately scented flowers are borne in nodding clusters, and open in advance of the leaves. Propagated by seeds or layers. The principal species are:

C. pauciflora, of a spreading habit to 6 ft. tall. It has pale yellow flowers, larger than the other kinds.

spicata, with heart-shaped leaves about 4 in. long, and bright yellow flowers.

gotoana, is the largest grower and the hardiest of the group. It has flowers of pale yellow.

CORYLUS (kor'-i-lus). A genus of shrubs or small trees native to the N. Temperate zone and belonging to the Birch Family. They bear edible nuts and are popularly known as Filbert or Hazelnut, which see.

CORYMB (kor'-imb). A broad, more or less flat, cluster of short-stalked flowers the outer ones blooming first. The blossoming progresses toward the center of the cluster. Contrast CYME.

CORYPHA (kor'-i-fah). One of the Fan Palms, a tree to 80 ft., popularly known as Talipot Palm, native of Ceylon and the Malabar Coast. It has a stout, ringed trunk, and leaves, from 12 to 16 ft. across, unarmed, (spineless) except on the stalks, very light in weight and easily folded up like a fan. (The number of these gigantic leaves carried before a person in Ceylon is indicative of his social status and is settled by law.) After reaching maturity, at from 20 to 80 years, the tree produces a large cluster of creamy blossoms, dying after the seeds ripen. Talipot Palms are occasionally planted in S. Fla., where they require a fertile, moist soil to which ground limestone has been added. They are seldom grown for greenhouse plants.

CORYTHOLOMA (koh-ri-thoh-loh'-mah). A large genus of tuberous-rooted herbs of tropical S. America, having leafy stems and hairy leaves, and bearing tubular 2-lipped flowers in terminal clusters or sprays. Related to gloxinias. *C. macropodium* has red flowers spotted with purple. They require a light, rich soil in a warm location, with plenty of water (which when applied should not be allowed to touch the foliage). After blooming, the plants should be dried off in their pots for the winter. Propagation is preferably by cuttings of young shoots, but may also be from seeds sown in March under glass.

COS or ROMAINE **LETTUCE.** A group of lettuces of a single variety (*Lactuca sativa* var. *longifolia*) which grow 12 to 24 in. high and form cylindrical or conical heads which tend to blanch at the center. They are more valued in England than in America, and few of them are grown here because our hot summers do not favor them. These few, however, are gaining in popularity as both greenhouse and outdoor crops. Seed may be sown outdoors at any time from early spring until late summer and well-formed heads gathered in ten weeks or less. See LETTUCE.

COSMIDIUM (koz-mi'-di-um). Former name, still used in many catalogs, for a species of a coreopsis-like annual, Thelesperma, which see.

COSMOS (koz'-mos). Tall annual herbs of the Composite Family, native in Mexico and Central America, with feathery foliage and light, airy blossoms with broad silky rays usually white to rosy-lilac. Reaching a height of from 3 to 10 ft., they are grown for late summer bloom in the tall border, where the late-flowering species withstand first frosts.

Thriving in average soil, but preferring a light, rather poor texture, and flourishing in either sun or partial shade, Cosmos should be started from seed outdoors late in April or early in May and covered to a depth of ¼ in. When the plants are 3 in. tall, thin out to not less than 2 ft.

apart. As they reach a height of 2 ft. pinch the tops so that they will branch out. Frequent cultivation around the base of plants is of benefit so long as it is not deep enough to injure the roots. Double varieties, in which the yellow disk-flowers have been displaced by florets the color of the rays, have been recently introduced. An excellent new single variety called Orange Flare grows 4 to 6 ft. tall with large, brilliant, orange flowers.

Stem blight attacks mature plants (both indoors and out) but not young ones. Infection appears first as small brown spots, which gradually enlarge until the stem is girdled, after which the parts above suddenly wilt and die. Remove diseased branches as they appear and pull up and burn all plants and plant parts in the fall. Wilting of plants may also follow injury caused by the stalk borer discussed under DAHLIA.

C. bipinnatus is the principal species grown. It is extremely tall, sometimes 10 ft., with white, pink, lilac or crimson heads 3 in. across with yellow disks. There are early and late varieties in double as well as single forms. *C. diversifolius* is a low tuberous-rooted perennial grown as an annual, reaching 16 in. The velvety-red rays, with red disks, are sometimes tinged dark purple; *C. sulphureus*, to 6 ft., has heads 3 in. across, the rays pale yellow and disk of darker yellow.

COSTMARY. Common name for the plant *Chrysanthemum balsamita*, formerly placed in the genus Tanacetum.

COTINUS (koh-ty'-nus). The genus in which the Smoke-tree, formerly *Rhus cotinus*, is now placed. See SMOKE-TREE.

COTONEASTER (koh-toh-ne-as'-ter). Deciduous or evergreen shrubs, found in the temperate regions of Europe, N. Africa, and Asia (mostly in China), belonging to the Rose Family. Most of them are hardy N., and rank amongst the most useful of shrubs for ornamental planting. They are outstanding for their attractive habit of growth and colorful fruits. A few, white-flowered species are conspicuous in bloom, and in some the foliage takes on brilliant coloring in fall. All kinds thrive in an open sunny position and well-drained soil. In general plants from pots are the most easily established.

The sudden death and blackening of shoots from the tips may be due to the bacterial disease, fire blight, which see.

Remove carefully all infected branches, cutting with pruning shears *that have been dipped in a disinfectant* several inches below the visibly affected portion. San José scale (which see), a small, circular, dark gray scale, is frequently present. Spray with lime-sulphur (1 to 7) or a miscible oil before growth starts. See also SCALE INSECTS; SPRAYING.

Propagation is effected by seeds, cuttings and layers. There are many species, of which the more important for garden use can be grouped in four classes according to their size, habits and other characteristics.

GROUP 1. *Dwarf or prostrate growers of spreading habit, with small dark green leaves, sometimes evergreen, and red fruits. They are well suited for planting on slopes and in rock gardens.*

C. adpressa hugs the ground, the stems often rooting. It has pink flowers and the leaves turn dark red in the fall.

horizontalis has a distinct two-ranked habit of branching. It makes a good wall plant and is effective when sprawling over a boulder in the rock garden. It has pinkish flowers. Var. *perpusilla* is a dwarfer form.

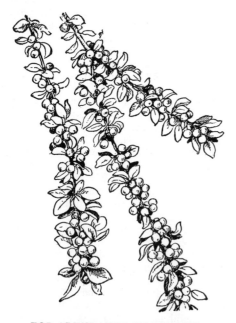

FOR ABUNDANCE OF BERRIES
Among the Cotoneasters, C. racemiflora var. songarica is rated as one of the finest for northern gardens, both when in bloom and in fruit. It is a large, fine-leaved shrub with arching whip-like branches.

dammeri (also known as *C. humifusa*) is a low evergreen with long trailing branches that root as they go, and white flowers.

microphylla is a dwarf evergreen of dense spreading habit, also with white flowers. Var. *glacialis* (also known as *C. congesta*) is a dwarfer and more compact form. Var. *thymifolia* is another dwarf form with very narrow leaves.

GROUP 2. *Large shrubs with white flowers and red fruits.*

C. hupehensis is a medium-sized shrub of graceful habit, with conspicuous clusters of flowers in spring and large bright red berries which drop in Sept. The leaves remain green late and finally turn yellow.

multiflora is similar in appearance but not very free fruiting; in this respect var. *calocarpa* is better than the type.

racemiflora is a good-looking shrub of spreading habit to 8 ft. Var. *songarica* is one of the showiest of all when in fruit.

frigida grows to 20 ft. and is one of the most beautiful in flower and fruit; but it is not hardy N.

pannosa is another outstanding species, not hardy N. It grows to 6 ft. with graceful arching branches and leaves white beneath.

salicifolia var. *floccosa* is regarded as the best of the tall evergreen species to grow as far north as Mass. It has dark green leathery wrinkled leaves, and flower clusters about 2 in. across.

simonsi is a handsome semi-evergreen upright grower.

GROUP 3. *Species with reddish flowers and fruits.*

C. divaricata makes a dense wide-spreading bush to 6 ft. with shining dark green leaves.

dielsiana is very similar, but of a looser habit, with arching branches to 10 ft.

francheti is a densely branched upright evergreen of graceful habit, not quite hardy N.

integerrima is of bushy rounded form to 6 ft., with short stiff branches.

bullata is also a broad round-topped bush, the tallest of the red-fruited kinds. Var. *floribunda* has arching branches and deeply wrinkled leaves.

zabeli is a medium-sized shrub with slender arching branches and dull green leaves which turn yellow in the fall. Var. *miniata* has orange-red fruits and is one of the outstanding berried shrubs.

rosea is of graceful habit, growing to 8 ft., very striking in fruit.

GROUP 4. *Species with reddish flowers and black fruits. These are the least showy in fruit, but some are desirable for their good vigorous habit, and often brilliant leaf coloring in the fall.*

C. acutifolia var. *villosula* is a handsome upright grower to 12 ft.

foveolata is another vigorous grower, outstanding in the fall when its leaves turn orange and scarlet.

nitens is a handsome grower with slender arching branches and lustrous leaves of dark green.

lucida is a strong upright grower, holding its lustrous green leaves till late in the season.

COTTON. Shrubs or woody herbs of the genus Gossypium of the Mallow Family and their product which is one of the world's most important crops. The plants have lobed leaves and large, white, yellow or purplish flowers, succeeded by "bolls" or seed capsules; the seeds are attached to a fibrous fleece for which several species are grown commercially. Though seldom used as ornamentals, cotton plants are attractive with their large mallow-like flowers. Two species are occasionally grown in mild climates for their decorative effect: *G. davidsoni,* which has yellow flowers, purple at the base, and *G. sturti* with large purple flowers with dark center, a native of Australia. Sometimes plants of the commercial types are grown as pot plants to be exhibited at flower shows, etc.

Lavender-cotton is *Santolina chamaecyparissus.*

COTTON FERN. Common name for *Notholaena newberryi,* a S. Calif. fern that thrives in half shade.

COTTON-GRASS. Common name for the genus Eriophorum. Not true grasses but members of the Sedge Family (Cyperaceae). They are natives of bogs of the N. Temperate and Arctic zones. They are sometimes planted along the edge of ponds or in the bog garden for their ornamental cottony seed-heads. See ERIOPHORUM.

COTTON ROOT ROT. A fungous disease attacking not only cotton but some 1700 other plants in arid parts of the S.W. See PHYMATOTRICHUM ROOT ROT.

COTTON-ROSE. Common name for *Hibiscus mutabilis,* a shrub or small tree of the Mallow Family having large pink or white flowers, grown in the S.

COTTONSEED-MEAL. This organic fertilizer is the ground residue of cottonseed, after the oil has been extracted. When of good quality, it contains 6.5 to 7% nitrogen, about 3% phosphoric acid and 2% potash which while not immediately available as in commercial fertilizers is more so than in manure. Cottonseed-meal is a valuable fertilizer for acid-loving plants, as it tends to keep the soil acid, in addition to supplying food. It can also be broadcast on lawns in the spring before a rain, at the rate of 3 to 5 lbs. per 100 sq. ft. It is a popular constituent of high-class complete plant-food mixtures.

See also FERTILIZER.

COTTON-WEED. Common name for *Diotis candidissima,* a dwarf perennial of the European coast, belonging to the Daisy Family. It has somewhat woody stems and small leaves of a white cottony appearance and is used for edgings and in rock gardens. Propagated by seed and cuttings.

COTTONWOOD. One common name for the genus Populus, and especially for *P. balsamifera* and related native species. It relates to the abundant cottony or silky hairs that clothe the seeds and that sometimes litter up the lawn unpleasantly around pistillate trees. The white wood is coarse and of poor quality, but the trees are rapid growers in almost any soil and are widely used for windbreaks where better subjects will not thrive, and to some extent for ornament. Cottonwoods are easily propagated by hardwood cuttings or from seed.

See POPLAR.

COTULA (kot'-eu-lah). A genus of annual or perennial herbs, native in the S. hemisphere and belonging to the Daisy Family. One or two species are sometimes grown in rock gardens for their low mats of interesting foliage. They need a light sandy soil and are propagated by seed and division. *C. dioica* makes stems about 1 ft. long, with small dark green, somewhat divided leaves, and small heads of pale yellow flowers. It was formerly much used in carpet-bedding. *C. squalida* has soft hairy stems and much divided, fern-like leaves.

COTYLEDON (kot-i-lee'-dun). The first leaf of a germinating plant commonly called seed leaf because it exists in embryo form in the seed, as the two halves of a bean or pea. Cotyledons contain stored food and nourish the young seedling until it has developed true leaves.

COTYLEDON. A genus of succulent herbs, native mostly to S. Africa and the Mediterranean region and belonging to the Orpine Family. Many species formerly listed here are now referred to other genera. They thrive under the same treatment as crassula and similar succulents.

C. cooperi is a small plant with a short stem and 5 to 6 rounded spotted leaves near the base. It bears 6 to 10 red and greenish tubular flowers.

orbiculata grows to 4 ft., with flat glaucous red-margined mealy leaves, and panicles of red drooping flowers.

semenovi grows to 18 in. with narrow sharp-pointed leaves and with flowers which turn reddish.

umbilicus (Navelwort, Pennywort, Penny Pies) grows to 12 in., with fleshy shield-shaped leaves and drooping yellowish-green flowers.

COUCH GRASS. Common name for some species of grasses of the genus Agropyron; a number are valuable forage crops, though considered weeds in the garden. See WEEDS.

COVER-CROP. Any crop sown toward the close of the growing season, either where a temporary crop has been harvested or between permanent plants, to cover the ground until early spring. It benefits the garden in one or more of several ways: it may (1) prevent the loss of surface soil and plant food, especially on slopes, from soil washing; (2) prevent the loss by leaching of soluble plant food which it takes up and later adds again to the soil; (3) check the growth of and tend to ripen woody plants by using up some of the available plant food from midsummer on; (4) add humus to the soil as it decays after being turned under; (5) increase the supply of available nitrogen in the soil—this especially when a legume (see INOCULATION) or nitrogen-producer is grown; (6) reduce the supply of available nitrogen and check woody growth—when a nitrogen-consuming (non-leguminous) crop is grown; (7) hold leaves over fall and winter and thereby provide more humus when they are all turned over; (8) prevent or reduce the effects of alternate freezing and thawing during winter and the possible resulting damage to crop roots.

In vegetable gardens a cover crop may be sown broadcast among the rows or growing crops any time after midsummer. Though much of it may be destroyed in harvesting the late crops, what survives will be worth more than its cost. A cover-crop should always be turned under in spring while still green and succulent; otherwise the work is harder to do and the crop breaks down and decays slowly.

Good nitrogen-consumer (non-leguminous) crops are buckwheat, turnips, rape, barley and rye; nitrogen-gathering (leguminous) crops are crimson clover, winter vetch, Canada field peas, beggarweed. See also GREEN MANURE.

COWANIA (kou-ay′-ni-ah). Evergreen shrubs of the S. W. States and Mexico, belonging to the Rose Family. *C. stansburiana,* the best known kind, is a very ornamental aromatic shrub, requiring a sunny position and well-drained soil. The fragrant white or pale yellow flowers are borne singly, and followed by feathery fruits.

COWBERRY. Common name for *Vaccinium vitis-idaea,* a trailing evergreen shrub of the Heath Family having dark red, acid berries. See VACCINIUM.

COW-HERB or COW SOAPWORT. Common names for *Saponaria vaccaria,* an annual herb of the Pink Family having deep pink flowers in clusters, widely naturalized in N. America.

COW-LILY. The common name for *Nymphozanthus advena* (sometimes listed as *Nuphar advena* or *Nymphaea advena*), the yellow pondlily; or, as it is also called, the Spatterdock. This N. American waterlily is found in stagnant waters and still pools in which mud bottoms offer its heavy creeping rootstocks foothold and supply nourishment. Flat, green, heart-shaped leaves float or stand slightly above the water to frame the groupings of cup-shaped yellow "lilies." In northern regions, the pure yellow species is replaced by a variety tinged with purplish tones.

In cultivation, the yellow pondlily responds to the same methods and treatment used for other hardy waterlilies and lotus. See NYMPHAEA; also NELUMBIUM.

COW MANURE. Because, when fresh, this type of organic fertilizer contains a large amount of moisture, its average plant food analysis is rather low—about .4 per cent nitrogen, .2 per cent phosphoric acid and .1 per cent potash. However, it is of what is called a "cold" character, that is, it does not tend to ferment and create heat as does horse manure, so it can be used with greater safety on many crops. It is especially good for heavy feeding plants such as roses, asparagus, cabbage, etc., but for best results it should be mixed with plenty of bedding or litter, such as straw, peat moss, or shredded cornstalks (*not* sawdust or wood shavings) that will absorb the valuable liquid portions before they are lost. Mixing cow and horse manure, equal parts, is good practice as the former checks the rapid fermentation of the latter while at the same time its own decomposition is hastened. If applied alone it gives up its plant food to the soil slowly, hence it should be applied as far as possible in advance of the planting of a crop. If it can be spread in the fall and turned under either then or in early spring, so much the better. It can be applied in the form of a 4 in. deep layer, or at the rate of 5 lbs. or more per sq. ft. of soil surface. Or it can be made a large part of a compost heap to good advantage.

See also MANURE.

COW-PARSNIP. Common name for Heracleum, a genus of perennial or biennial herbs, native in the N. hemisphere and belonging to the Parsley Family. They are coarse growers with large lobed or compound leaves and large flattened clusters of white or purplish flowers, well suited for bold effects in the wild garden or along the water-side. Propagated by seed and division.

H. lanatum is a native species growing to 8 ft., with large leaves white beneath, and umbels of white flowers 1 ft. across. *H. mantegazzianum,* a Caucasian species, grows to 9 ft. or more, with deeply cut leaves 3 ft. long, and large white flowers in umbels 4 ft. across.

COWPEA. A tender annual legume (*Vigna sinensis*) from Asia, with several varieties ranging from bush-like to trailing, not climbing, vines. As a farm crop it is grown chiefly in the S. for forage and green manuring. But in the N. it is often grown in the summer for green manure (which see), being sown in spring after danger of frost has passed, and plowed or dug under when the ground is needed, but in any case before pods form. As it grows rapidly it can thus be used to follow crops of early maturing vegetables, as radishes, spinach or lettuce, as a soil-improving measure. Sow 1 oz. to 25 or 30 sq. ft. broadcast on small areas, or drill in at the rate of about 5 pecks per acre on larger spaces.

COW-POISON or POISON LARKSPUR. Common names for *Delphinium trolliifolium,* a weak-stemmed herb with blue and white flowers, occasionally planted, but usually found in the wild along the W. Coast, where it causes great trouble among herds of horses and cattle.

COWSLIP. This name, of ancient Anglo-Saxon origin, has become associated with several plants of four different families. The commonest and most accepted use is for *Primula veris* (also called *P. officinalis*), the low-growing, yellow-flowered hardy primrose of Europe. The American Cowslip is Dodecatheon, a genus of N. American perennials sometimes cultivated in wild gardens under the even more popular name of Shooting-star. These two genera belong to the Primrose Family. The name also refers to the native Marsh-marigold (*Caltha palustris*) of the Buttercup Family, especially when the tender young leaves are used for culinary purposes. The Cape-cowslip is Lachenalia, a bulbous plant of the Lily Family native to S. Africa and grown in this country as a greenhouse plant. The name is also applied to Virginia Bluebells (*Mertensia virginica*), herbaceous perennial of the Borage Family found from N. Y. to Tenn., and a popular subject for shady parts of the garden.

See DODECATHEON; LACHENALIA; MERTENSIA; PRIMROSE.

CRAB or CRAB APPLE. Popular name for any small-fruited variety of apple used for jelly making; among nurserymen, various species of shrubs and trees of the genus Pyrus (which see), planted for their showy flowers, or fruits, or both; among botanists, the Siberian Crab (*P. baccata*) and its small-fruited varieties or hybrids. All do well in the N. States and adjacent Canada, but not in the South, except in the mountains. They constitute one of the most useful spring-flowering groups of ornamentals. Their culture, training and pruning are the same as those of the apple, which see.

Both wild and cultivated varieties (and especially Transcendent) are susceptible to fire blight, which see. The Wild Crab (*Pyrus coronaria*) was probably the first host of the apple and cedar rust (see under JUNIPER), but Bechtels Crab is always severely rusted when grown in close proximity to red-cedar. Since crab apples are subject to most of the insect pests attacking apple (which see), wild crabs near an apple orchard should be cut down to remove sources of infestation.

The fruit of any of the species that bear (some kinds have sterile flowers) may be used for jelly making, each species having a more or less distinctive flavor; some sorts are so small, however, as hardly to be worth using. For ornamental plantings, practically any crab is attractive, but the following brief notes on species offered by American nurseries may be a helpful guide to size of plant and color of flowers.

SPECIES

Southern crab (*P. angustifolia*) semi-evergreen, 25 ft., large, pink or rose flowers; Carmine crab (*P. atrosanguinea*) 15 ft., deep, unfading rose; Siberian crab (*P. baccata*), 40 ft., small, white flowers; Garland or sweet crab (*P. coronaria*), 30 ft., large, rose flowers changing to white; Japanese flowering crab (*P. floribunda*), 25 ft., profuse, large red flowers, paling to almost white; Hall crab (*P. halliana*), 18 ft., large, deep rose; Parkman crab, a double-flowered variety (*parkmani*) of *P. halliana;* Prairie crab (*P. ioensis*), 30 ft., white or bluish flowers—the latest to bloom; Chinese apple or Ringo crab (*P. prunifolia* var. *rinki*), 15 ft., white; Sargent crab (*P. sargenti*), 6 ft., large white flowers; Siebold or Toringo crab (*P. sieboldi*), 15 ft., blush-pink flowers; Showy crab (*P. spectabilis*), 25 ft., extra large, pink or rose flowers; Rivers crab (a variety of *P. spectabilis*) with double pink flowers.

See also PYRUS.

CRAB CACTUS. A name often applied to the Christmas Cactus, *Zygocactus truncatus* (which see), on account of the fancied resemblance in shape or color of its irregular pink to red flowers. Also called the Lobster Cactus. See also CACTUS.

CRAB GRASS. Common name for *Eleusine indica* and *Panicum sanguinale,* both members of the Grass Family and natives of the Old World but also extensively naturalized in the U. S. Here, while occasionally used for ornament and in pastures, they are in general obnoxious weeds, especially in lawns.

The leaves and flower-bearing stems bend before the lawn mower, making it very difficult to cut off the seed-bearing tops. Moreover, pieces of crab grass scattered by the mower are likely to take root where they fall. However, the pest can be controlled by raking the sod vigorously with a steel rake so as to loosen the plants and make them stand upright, when they can more easily be mown, or, better, cut by hand. Areas so treated should be re-seeded with good grass seed in the fall as this as well as other weeds can be crowded and kept out by a dense vigorous sod. If raking and mowing is not effective, the grass should be cut out with a hoe or pulled up by hand before the plants go to seed. Still another method is to squirt a few drops of carbolic acid into the heart of each tuft. If seeding is prevented, any of the above methods should clean a lawn of the weed in 2 or 3 seasons.

See also WEEDS.

CRABS-EYE-VINE. A common name for *Abrus precatorius,* also called Rosary-pea, a vine of the Pea Family having white, red or purple flowers, followed by pods filled with brilliant red seeds, sometimes used as beads.

CRADLE ORCHID. Common name for the genus Anguloa of the Orchid Family, terrestrial plants from S. America, grown N. in a cool greenhouse.

CRAMBE (kram'-bee). A genus of cruciferous herbs grown sometimes for ornament. One species, *C. maritima* commonly called Sea-kale (which see), is raised for its young shoots which are blanched and used like asparagus.

CRANBERRY. Several trailing, evergreen species of Vaccinium, which see. The Mountain Cranberry, Cowberry or Foxberry (*V. vitis-idaea*) is a low-growing creeper often used as a ground cover among shrubbery, attractive in its little, shiny leaves and small dark red berries which often persist until spring. The "small" or European Cranberry (*V. oxycoccus*) forms plants with small leaves, dark green above and powdery-white below, and bears little red berries. The "large," American or Trailing Swamp Cranberry (*V. macrocarpon*) with longer stems (often 4 ft.), larger leaves and much larger fruits, is the species cultivated commercially for its berries used in making jelly or sauce inseparably associated with turkey. It is grown in specially constructed, sand-covered "bogs," provided with ditches and dams to permit flooding or draining as needed. Cape Cod in Mass. and parts of N. J. and Mich. are the leading cranberry-producing regions. This plant is not grown in gardens for its fruit and rarely, if ever, as an ornamental. But with the discovery that the tops of the plants cut off in the fall make an excellent mulch for perennial beds and borders, the cranberry has attained new importance in the eyes of gardeners, and a new business—the gathering, baling, and selling of this mulching material—has developed. Cranberries, like other plants of the Heath Family, require acid conditions for growth.

The name is believed to be a corruption of "crane berry" in allusion to the curved neck-like form of the flower-bud stem.

False blossom, a virus disease causing malformation of the flower, stunting of the plant and a "witches' broom" effect is transmitted by the blunt-nosed leaf hopper, a small, active insect. Control the latter (and thereby prevent the spread of the disease) by spraying with pyrethrum compounds or by flooding the bog with water. Flooding until late May also helps control the black and yellow-headed cranberry worm and the cranberry fruit worm.

CRANBERRY-BUSH or TREE. Common name for *Viburnum trilobum,* sometimes listed as *V. americanum,* a shrub of the Honeysuckle Family having clusters of white flowers, the outer rows sterile, followed by brilliant red cranberry-like fruit. It is also known as High-bush-cranberry. The European Cranberry-bush is *Viburnum opulus.*

CRANBERRY-GOURD. Common name for *Abobra tenuifolia,* a S. American tuberous-rooted vine, belonging to the Cucumber Family. Sometimes grown under glass, it may also be grown outdoors in summer and the roots dug and stored like dahlias. The stem grows to 20 ft. bearing leaves 5-lobed or much divided, small greenish fragrant flowers, and small scarlet ovoid fruits. Easily grown from seed.

CRANESBILL. Common name for the genus Geranium, which comprises a number of species of annual or perennial herbs with pink or purple flowers.

CRAPE-JASMINE (*Ervatamia coronaria*). A shrub 6 to 8 ft. high, sometimes grown as a pot plant in greenhouses, and a good outdoor shrub in the warmest parts of the country. It has glossy green leaves and waxy white flowers about 2 in. across, clustered in the forks of the branches.

The double-flowered (var. *florepleno*) is the form mostly grown. It is easily propagated from cuttings.

CRAPE-MYRTLE. Common name for the deciduous shrub, *Lagerstroemia indica,* a member of the Loosestrife Family. Growing to 20 ft., it has attractive flowers with fringed petals in panicles; there are numerous varieties as: var. *alba* with white flowers; *purpurea,* purple; *rosea,* pink; and *rubra,* reddish-purple. It is a Chinese plant but is grown widely throughout the S. States, where it blooms profusely for several months, as specimen shrubs, as hedges and for background planting; in many places it has become naturalized. In the N. it may be grown in a pot or tub in a cool greenhouse, and if cut back severely will bloom several times through the year. As far N. as Mass. it is root hardy, if given winter protection. Though it dies to the ground, it will send out a vigorous growth in the spring and bloom profusely. It is easily raised from seed, the young plants blooming the first summer; also from cuttings of ripe wood.

Powdery mildew is common on this plant in the Gulf States. Minute, deformed shoots, covered with a white coating appearing in early spring, are followed by circular white patches on the young leaves; the white coating then spreads over all of the shoots. In midsummer the disease is not conspicuous but it reappears in the fall. A single application of commercial lime-sulphur, diluted 1 to 80, made as soon as the buds burst in the spring will control it.

Aphids, if abundant, may cause defoliation; also the honeydew that they secrete supports the sooty-mold fungus which gives the leaves a black, smutty appearance. Spray with nicotine sulphate or other contact insecticide to control both troubles.

CRASSULA (kras'-eu-lah). (See illustration, Plate 51.) A genus of succulent herbs and shrubs, mostly from S. Africa, belonging to the Orpine Family. They have opposite fleshy leaves, and clusters of small white, rose or yellow flowers. They are sun-lovers, and thrive best in sandy loam with a small proportion of leafmold. During the growing season they may be watered as freely as ordinary plants, but in the resting period they should be kept on the dry side. Propagated by cuttings of stems and leaves.

PRINCIPAL SPECIES

C. arborescens is a sturdy shrub to 10 ft., with thick stems and roundish glossy leaves, because of which it is sometimes called "wax-plant" though this name belongs rightly to *Hoya carnosa*. In flower, covered with clusters of small rose-colored blossoms, a plant is very attractive; but as a house subject it does not often bloom being of value mainly as a foliage plant.

FOR SPRINGTIME BLOOM
Hawthorn (Crataegus) includes some of the handsomest trees and shrubs. In May the young leaves are often entirely hidden by the flowers.

cordata makes a slender shrub to 3 ft., with heart-shaped dotted leaves and white to pink flowers.

portulacea is shrubby to 10 ft., with thick shining leaves and rosy-red flowers.

falcata grows to 10 ft., has thick gray sickle-shaped leaves, united at the base, and bright flowers, crimson, rarely white.

lactea is shrubby to 2 ft., with rather narrow leaves grown together at the base, and spotted along the margins; it bears white flowers in winter.

multicava has oval, spotted leaves and white flowers, freely produced in spring.

lycopodioides has slender prostrate stems, with overlapping scale-like leaves in 4 ranks.

CRASSULACEAE (kras-eu-lay'-see-ee). Botanical name of the Orpine Family, a group of characteristically fleshy plants included by gardeners among the "succulents." Herbs and shrubs of wide distribution (but chiefly in dry places), they yield medicinal products and a good many horticultural subjects. Their flowers are notably symmetrical, for the most part in shades of yellow and red combined with green, and arranged in flat heads or, rarely, solitary. Many are grown under glass as pot plants; the hardy ones as borders or in rock gardens. Important cultivated genera are Crassula, Rochea, Sedum (Stonecrop), Sempervivum (Houseleek), Cotyledon, Echeveria, Bryophyllum.

CRATAEGUS (krah-tee'-gus). Generic name of the Hawthorn or Thornapple, derived appropriately from the Greek word meaning "strength." For the trunks frequently have a muscular appearance, the wood is hard and the branches are exceedingly tough. A member of the Rose Family, this extensive group includes many native species valuable for ornamental planting, nearly all hardy and all attractive in habit of growth, in blossom and in fruit, long lived and slow growing. The efficient thorns make the plants useful as boundary barriers. See HAWTHORN.

CRAZY PAVING. Pavement of irregularly shaped flagstones fitted to each other in laying just as they come, without dressing or breaking them. Distinguished from "random paving," in which dressed and squared flagstones of different sizes are laid with all joints lined up parallel or at true right angles, crazy paving shows joints running in all directions in conformity with the angles of the stones used. See GARDEN PATHS AND DRIVES.

CREAM-CUPS. Common name for *Platystemon californicus,* a low annual herb, native in Calif., and belonging to the Poppy Family. It has narrow or oblong entire leaves, and white to pale yellow flowers 1 in. across, borne singly on long stems. It is sometimes grown in flower gardens.

CREEPERS. As generally regarded creepers are not especially different from climbers and vines. To some any plant that is or can be used to cover a wall is a creeper. A closer definition limits the term to those plants of trailing habit which root along the stem. These range from little plants which creep along the ground, such as *Veronica filiformis,* up to a plant like the English Ivy (*Hedera helix*) which is both a good ground cover and a high climbing vine.

Plants to which the term creeper has become firmly attached are *Parthenocissus quinquefolia* (Virginia Creeper), *Tropaeolum peregrinum* (Canary Creeper), *Lysimachia nummularia* (Creeping Charlie or Creeping Jenny), and *Chiogenes hispidula* (Creeping Snowberry).

CREEPING CHARLIE or CREEPING JENNY. Common names for *Lysimachia nummularia,* a creeping herb of the Primrose Family, carpeting damp ground with its round shiny leaves and yellow flowers. *Pilea nummulariaefolia* of the Nettle Family, a tender perennial with creeping stems, is also known as Creeping Charlie.

CREEPING FORGET-ME-NOT. Common name for the Navelwort, *Omphalodes verna,* which bears blue forget-me-not-like flowers in early spring.

CREEPING-NETTLE. Common name for *Helxine soleiroli,* a small creeping herb with rooting stems, from Corsica and Sardinia, belonging to the Nettle Family. It is also called Paddy's-wig or Irishman's-wig. Useful as a ground cover in greenhouses and window gardens, it also makes a dense mat of bright green in the rock garden in mild regions. Easily propagated from pieces of stem.

CREEPING-SNOWBERRY. Common name for *Chiogenes hispida,* an evergreen creeping plant of the Heath Family having white fruits.

CRENATE (kree'-nayt). Term given to the toothed margin of a leaf when the teeth are rounded and point toward the apex of the leaf; sometimes it is used to include all leaf margins with rounded teeth, in which case it may be combined with another term to complete the description. Thus the leaf of black cottonwood is finely crenate-serrate, that is, with small round teeth pointing toward the tip. See LEAF.

CREOSOTE AND RELATED COMPOUNDS. These are bituminous substances used as disinfectants and insect repellents. Crude tar, obtained from the distillation of bituminous coal, petroleum, and wood is named coal-tar, oil, oil-tar or wood-tar according to its source. In the further distillation of crude tars, oils of different weights, and pitch are obtained. The oils lighter than water are known as *creosotes.* Carbolineum is a trade name for a coal-tar creosote. Crude coal-tar is frequently used for wound dressings. Creosote is used in trenches as a barrier around a field against chinch bugs, for killing egg masses of the tussock and gypsy moths, for impregnating wood against termites, and in combination with coal-tar in painting wounds. Asphaltum is a pitch-like compound used in many tree paints. See WOUNDS; TREE SURGERY.

CREPIS (kre'-pis). A genus of the Composite Family including herbs with red or yellow flowers commonly known as Hawksbeard, which see.

CRESCENTIA (kre-sen'-ti-ah). Botanical name for a tropical American tree of the Bignonia Family commonly known as Calabash-tree, which see.

CRESS. Various annual and perennial herbs of the mustard family used as salads and garnishes and characterized by their piquant flavors.

In America the best known is Watercress (*Nasturtium officinale*), a low, trailing European perennial naturalized in springs and wet ground in temperate climates. Though easily grown from seed it is usually propagated by bits of stem which readily take root in wet soil and need no further attention. Its season is from mid-autumn until spring. After its flower buds appear the leaves become too rank in flavor to be edible.

Garden Cress or Pepper-grass (*Lepidium sativum*) an Asiatic annual widely popular in Europe, deserves to be better known in America. No vegetable grows more quickly or easily, or is more attractive as a garnish or a salad. The richer the soil the better. Sow seed thickly in narrow drills 10 or 12 in. apart in earliest spring and at weekly intervals until mid-May. If sown later than this the plants become strong flavored and quickly run to seed. Seedlings appear in three or four days, grow rapidly and may be cut with shears in three or four weeks. If the cutting is not too close two or three more may be made. In common with other crucifers, cress may show prominent white blisters on the leaves—the so-called white rust (*Albugo candida*). To prevent it destroy infected refuse; keep down cruciferous weeds; practice crop rotation.

Upland or Winter cress (*Barbarea vernapraecox*) is a hardy European biennial naturalized in many parts of America. If sown in earliest spring in rich ground the leaves may be used shortly after midsummer. As the plants are hardy they need no winter protection. In spring, use them before their flower stems develop.

Bitter-cress is a small, spring-blooming perennial (*Cardamine pratensis*) sometimes grown in rock gardens. Blister-cress is a name for some popular garden flowers, species of Erysimum, including relatives of the wallflower, stock, etc.

Indian-cress is another name for "nasturtium" (*Tropaeolum majus*) the popular annual. Though mainly grown for its flowers, the leaves and blossoms can be eaten as salad and the immature ridged seeds pickled like capers. Penny-cress is a name for several annual and perennial species of Thlaspi grown in rock gardens or for "winter bouquets." Rock-cress is a term applied to many species of Arabis grown for their flowers. Stone-cress refers to numerous dwarf flowering herbs and sub-shrubs of the genus Aethionema, and the name Wart-cress is given to several small annual and biennial species of Coronopus used as ground covers.

See separate articles on the different kinds of Cress that are merely mentioned here.

CRESTED DOGS-TAIL. A perennial Old-World species of grass (*Cynosurus cristatus*) often used in lawn and pasture mixtures and naturalized in parts of E. N. America. It starts early in spring, low-growing and tough and a turf stands hard wear. It is particularly useful for mixing with Kentucky blue grass (especially for shady places), because its color is the same and its habit of growth similar. *C. elegans,* a related annual species, is sometimes grown for its loose panicles which are often used for "dry bouquets."

CRESTED FERN (*Dryopteris cristata*). A native fern of the E. States, distinguished by its nearly horizontal pinnae. Excellent in the garden in woods soil.

CRETAN BEARS-TAIL. Common name for *Celsia arcturus,* a tall herb of the Figwort Family having clear yellow flowers in long racemes. Cretan Mullein is *Celsia cretica.*

CRETAN BRAKE. Common name for *Pteris cretica,* a good indoor and greenhouse fern, with long toothed segments on straw-colored stipes. Likes a little lime.

CRIMSON CLOVER. An erect annual legume (*Trifolium incarnatum*), growing 24 to 36 in. high and bearing handsome, elongated dark red flower-heads. It is much used in orchards and gardens as well as in farm rotations as a cover-crop (which see), being sown in midsummer so it can become well established before cold weather. It is ideal for sowing among garden vegetables that will be gathered during autumn, scattering 1 oz. of seed to 150 or 200 sq. ft. Enough plants should survive even the digging of such crops as potatoes and parsnips to make a worthwhile stand. Again, even though the winter may kill it, the vegetable matter it provides is a valuable source of humus (which see), while its ability (as a legume) to gather nitrogen from the air makes it still more useful in increasing the soil fertility. If the cover crop survives the winter it must be dug or plowed under while only a foot or so high before the stems become woody.

Crimson clover is sometimes grown in wild gardens or as background material for the ornamental effect of its crimson blossom heads. See also CLOVER.

CRIMSON FLAG. Common name for *Schizostylis coccinea,* also known as Kafir-lily, a tender plant of the Iris Family having narrow leaves and showy crimson flowers. It is planted out in late spring and if placed in rich soil will bloom profusely in the summer. If taken up and potted in September it will bloom again during the winter in the greenhouse.

CRIMSON-GLORY-VINE. A name sometimes given to a Japanese species of grape (*Vitis kaempferi*), the leaves of which turn brilliant red in the fall. Do not confuse with the tender, leguminous glory-vine, Clianthus, which see.

CRINKLE-BUSH. Name given to dyed sprays of an Australian shrub (*Lomatia silaifolia*) which are used by florists and decorators.

CRINKLEROOT. Another name for the Pepper-root or Toothwort, *Dentaria diphylla,* a native plant having small white or lilac flowers and tuberous white roots. Useful for colonizing in the wild garden.

CRINODONNA (kry-noh-don'-ah). A "made name" for hybrids produced in Europe by crossing Amaryllis (especially *A. belladonna*) and Crinum. The name, though sometimes seen, has been superseded by Amarcrinum (which see) given to hybrids of similar ancestry produced in Calif.

CRINUM (kry'-num). A genus of bulbous plants, usually evergreen and fragrant, one of which is native to our S. States. The leaves are thick and strap-shaped. All through the extreme S., Crinums are seen flourishing in a great many gardens. They seem to withstand neglect and severe treatment and still bloom and propagate profusely. They are tender subjects which will not winter over in our

N. States unless special preparation for winter protection is made, and for this reason, together with the fact that they resent disturbance and re-establish themselves slowly when started from dry bulbs, their use in our N. gardens is very limited. As a greenhouse item they occupy more space than their value warrants.

There are many species and varieties ranging from trumpet- to star-shaped flowers but always characterized by a very long flower-tube. The colors range from pale pink to wine red and white.

Because of the many hybrids, Crinums are difficult to name. *C. americanum* is the native Florida Swamp-lily. The white *C. asiaticum* var. *sinicum* (sometimes called *C. pedunculatum* Hort.), one of the most important in the American trade, is known as St.-Johns-lily. The true species *C. pedunculatum* has greenish-tinged white flowers with bright-red anthers.

CRITHMUM (krith'-mum) *maritimum.* A perennial herb called Samphire (which see), occasionally grown as a salad.

CROCK. As a noun, this refers to a bit of broken flower pot or other pottery placed over the hole in the bottom of a flower pot or other plant receptacle to prevent the soil from washing through without interfering with drainage. As a verb, it is the process of providing drainage by the use of one or more crocks in plant containers. Often a little sphagnum moss, excelsior, partially rotted leaves, or other vegetable material is placed over the crocks to prevent a fine soil from being washed down among them and defeating their purpose. The crock (or the first one if several are used in a large pot) should be placed with the piece *concave* side upward over the drainage hole; other pieces are then similarly placed on and around it.

CROCUS. (See illustration, Plate 45.) A genus of hardy cormous or bulbous herbs of the Iris Family, comprising many species from which the modern varieties have been developed. Seasonally, crocuses are divided into two main groups—those that bloom in the fall, and the much more important and better known spring-flowering crocuses. The former type must not be confused with the Colchicum (which see), a member of the Lily Family but called Autumn-crocus because of the similar appearance of the flowers.

FALL CROCUSES. Corms of the autumn-flowering crocus are obtainable in July and

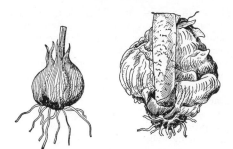

TWO AUTUMN CROCUSES
At the left is the corm of the Saffron Crocus; at the right, the corm of the crocus-like Colchicum, also a fall-blooming plant.

August and should be planted during those months or their flower buds may start to develop and spoil while the bulbs are out of the ground. They flower in advance of the foliage and, being mostly of the rosy lavender shades, make bright spots of color in the early fall garden. The slender leaves appear in spring and if allowed to develop and die down naturally, store up food for a crop of flowers for the ensuing fall. If uncrowded the bulbs can remain undisturbed for years, but when they become too thick they should be taken up and respaced.

SPRING CROCUSES. Because of their brilliant coloring in the very early spring before most other flowers appear, the spring crocuses are deservedly extremely popular. The best effects are obtained when they are massed, but informal plantings of individual colors may also be made in front of shrubbery or evergreens, on the edge of perennial borders, or scattered through grass that can be left unmowed for several weeks. If the foliage is left uncut to die down naturally, the corms will increase from year to year and continue to bloom profusely until they become crowded, when, as suggested above, they should be dug up and replanted while dormant in midsummer. Since the corms are inexpensive, some gardeners plant them directly in the lawn, mow them down along with the grass after the flowers fade, and plant a new crop of bulbs year after year.

Corms of spring-flowering crocuses should be planted not later than November, spaced about 3 in. apart and set about 3 in. deep. Where the winters are severe, some protection is advisable until the plants are well established.

Crocus colorings range from pure yellow through the various lavender and blue shades to pure white. There is a constant improvement in varieties, so current bulb catalogs should be consumed in order to locate the finest kinds.

Of the 40 or more species, the best known for spring flowering are the yellow *C. susianus* (Cloth-of-gold Crocus), the lilac or white *C. imperati;* the lilac or white, often purple-striped, *C. vernus;* and the yellow Dutch Crocus, *C. moesiacus.* A great many hybrids of these and others are on the market. The best autumn-flowering species are *C. sativus,* the Saffron Crocus, usually bright lilac in color, whose stigmas furnish the medicine, dye, and seasoning known as Saffron; and *C. speciosus,* with feather-veined, lilac flowers.

While crocuses grown as undisturbed perennials in lawns, borders and gardens do not usually call for insect or disease control measures, darker flecks on the flowers indicate the presence of a virus disease resembling the "breaking" of tulips, which see. A decay of the bulbs is caused by a Fusarium fungus, and a storage rot by Botrytis. (See BULB ENEMIES.) The fungus causing dry rot of gladiolus corms also affects crocus.

CROPPING SYSTEMS. A term applied to planting schemes or arrangements by which advantages are gained in the way of soil improvement or the maintenance of fertility, pest control, economical and intensive use of land, etc. They fall into two general classes, one involving the sequence of crops and the other their interrelations, as follows:

1. CROP ROTATION. This consists mainly of growing successionally, either during one season or over a series of years, crops that make different demands upon the soil. Plants differ widely in their food requirements, leaf crops (such as cabbage) needing relatively large quantities of nitrogen, root crops (as beets) requiring abundant potash, and seed or fruit crops (as tomatoes, beans, etc.) demanding ample supplies of phosphorus. Crops of the same type planted consecutively on the same area deplete it unevenly and cannot, themselves, make the most and best growth. A good rotation would be (a) early cabbage, (b) tomatoes and (c) a mixture of rye and winter (hairy) vetch broadcast in early fall among the tomatoes to serve as a winter cover-crop. See COVER-CROP.

Trouble with certain weeds, insects and plant diseases may also be largely or wholly prevented by rational crop rotation, though this aspect is of more importance to growers of large areas of vegetables (truck farmers) than to home gardeners. However, by varying the crops in a rotation various insects, weeds and plant diseases that especially attack specific crop types can be "starved out." A good illustration is found in "club root" discussed under enemies of Crucifer, which see.

2. INTENSIVE CROPPING means making the greatest possible use of limited soil areas. It includes the following plans:

A. *Marker cropping,* or the sparse sowing of some quick-germinating seeds at the same time and in the same row with those of a slow germinating crop (such as parsnip), or one whose young seedlings are hard to see (as onion.) Forcing-varieties of radish are best for this purpose because their seed leaves are conspicuous and appear within four days of sowing. The main object of marker cropping is to promptly indicate the planted row so that cultivation may begin within a week of sowing, before weeds can get a start. The radishes may be removed and used within a month at the time when the permanent crop is first thinned.

B. *Inter-cropping,* or the growing of two or more crops on a specific area during one season. It is of three types:

a. *Partnership cropping* is the growing simultaneously of two crops of about the same rate and season of growth, but of different habits and requirements. Popular examples are winter squash or pole beans with tall growing corn.

b. *Companion cropping* is the sowing or planting together (as alternate plants or rows) of two or more crops that require different lengths of time to mature. For instance, rows of transplanted cabbage might alternate with rows of lettuce plants. These rows in turn might also alternate with some other quick maturing crop, as spinach or radish.

c. *Succession cropping* is the replacement of an early maturing crop by one planted or sown after the first is removed. For instance, a crop of early lettuce might be followed by tomatoes; then spinach could be broadcast among the tomato plants in late summer, to provide a late fall crop. Or pea vines, from which a crop has been harvested, may be dug under, thereby improving the soil in preparation for the planting of celery or other late crop.

CROP ROTATION. The practice of alternating different crops on a given area so as to avoid the sometimes injurious effects of continuously growing plants with similar food requirements, insect or disease susceptibilities, etc. on the same land. See ROTATION OF CROPS; also CROPPING SYSTEMS.

CROSS. Another name for a hybrid, which see. "To cross" is to hybridize. See also PLANT BREEDING.

CROSS-VINE. A common name for a native S. vine also known as Trumpet-flower. See BIGNONIA.

CROSSWORT. Common name for Crucianella, a genus of annual or perennial herbs, belonging to the Madder Family. *C. stylosa* is sometimes grown in the rock garden, where it thrives in light soil and partial shade. Although a perennial, it is usually grown as an annual. Of prostrate habit and light growth, it bears round heads of small deep-pink flowers. Propagated by seed and division.

CROTALARIA (kroh-tah-lay'-ri-ah). A genus of the Pea Family comprising a large number of species of shrubs and herbs, some of them grown for ornament and others for forage crops, popularly known as Rattlebox, which see.

CROTON (kroh'-tun). Common name for Codiaeum, a genus of tropical shrubs belonging to the Spurge Family which are extensively grown in warm regions and under glass for their highly colored ornamental foliage, which is extremely variable in form and color. Massed in a sunny place outdoors during summer they give a rich tropical effect, and are also useful for vases and window boxes. Young plants are preferable under glass, although with feeding they may be kept healthy in fairly small pots for some time. A mixture of fibrous loam with leafmold and sand suits them well. In the early stages of growth they need very warm and moist conditions. While good light is needed to induce bright coloring, some shade may be necessary under clear glass during the brightest weather to prevent leaf-burning.

Crotons are subject to leaf spots and rust which, however, are not often serious. Remove badly spotted leaves and dust rusted plants with sulphur.

Propagation is by cuttings of half-ripened shoots under warm and close conditions. Substantial young plants may be secured from old specimens by air-layering (which see) well-colored tops.

Most of the many, many named varieties in cultivation are considered to have originated as seedling forms or sports of *Codiaeum variegatum* var. *pictum*. They vary greatly in foliage, the leaves ranging from large entire or deeply-lobed to long, narrow and often twisted. The color combinations are often very striking, involving shades of green, yellow, orange, pink, red and crimson.

Many "best twelves" could be selected, and the following are mentioned as some good examples: *Broad-leaved kinds, not lobed: andreanum,* yellow with red veinings; B. Compte, yellow with red blotches; Mrs. Iceton, dark red with rose mottlings; *reidi,* yellow and red with rosy tints. With large lobed leaves: *evansianum,* yellow, veined and mottled red; Lord Derby, yellow with bright red suffusion.

With long and more or less narrow leaves: chelsoni, with drooping and often twisted leaves of yellow, tinted bright orange, and shaded crimson; *insigne,* narrow deep green with red margin, and yellow midrib and veins; *interruptum,* twisted yellow leaves with red markings, and an extended midrib; *hanburyanum,* olive-green with yellow markings and rosy blotches; Lady Zetland, yellow with red margin and veins; Queen Victoria, with leaves about 12 in. long and 2 in. wide, yellow mottled green, with margins banded carmine, and veins magenta to crimson.

Croton is also the botanical name of a large genus mostly of trees and shrubs belonging to the same family but of no particular garden value. *C. tiglium* is a small tropical tree which yields the powerful purgative croton oil. *C. eleuteria* is the source of cascarilla bark, also used in medicine.

CROWBERRY (*Empetrum nigrum*). This is a hardy evergreen much-branched prostrate heath-like shrub, widely distributed in the northern hemisphere, and found all across the northern part of this country. It has inconspicuous flowers, the male and female forms being borne on separate plants, and the pistillate (female) flowers being followed by black berries. It is a good plant for the rock garden, and thrives in a lime-free soil of sandy loam with plenty of peat or leafmold. It is propagated by cuttings.

CROWFOOT. A common name for many buttercups, herbs of the genus Ranunculus, which see. Also one common name for the Buttercup Family (Ranunculaceae, which see), of which Ranunculus is an important genus.

CROWN. This term has three different meanings in connection with plants. (1) The part of a plant, particularly a tree, above the first branching of the stem; hence its foliage- and flower-bearing region. In this sense, in a bulb, corm or tuber, or budded rhizome, it is the summit from which the green leaves or the main stem arises.

(2) An organ or group of organs formed in a circle, like the cup of a daffodil or the whorl of leaves above the flowers of crown imperial.

(3) In any herbaceous perennial, as delphinium, the portion of the plant at, or just below, the surface of the ground, where the stem emerges from the root.

CROWN DAISY. Common name for *Chrysanthemum coronarium,* a shrubby annual chrysanthemum for outdoor use, with yellowish or white daisy-like flowers and deeply cut leaves. The tender young shoots are frequently eaten in the Orient.

CROWN GALL. A bacterial disease manifested on various woody or herbaceous plants in the form of tumor-like enlargements at the crown or on aerial portions, or else by an excessive production of roots and shoots. Other names for the gall formations are crown knot, root knot and

CROWN GALL ON RASPBERRY
Note the large, hard, black swelling at the crown or base of the stem and the younger, lighter-colored ones at points along the roots.

cane galls; excessive root development usually goes under the name of hairy root. The latter is common on fruit trees, especially apple, but the galls are found on many ornamental plants—roses, blackberries, raspberries, grapes and daisies being particularly susceptible. They are irregularly globular, with a more or less convoluted surface, and may vary in size up to 6 to 10 times the diameter of the stem from which they originate.

To control crown gall clean nursery stock must always be planted. Diseased and healthy stock should never be mixed, nor should plants be heeled in soil which may have produced plants with crown gall, since the bacteria live in the soil. If there is any doubt as to the health of the stock purchased for the garden, place it in a copper sulphate solution (1 oz. to 4 gal. of water) for one hour before planting it. Prevent wounding plants when cultivating them. Galls on aerial portions may be removed, but disinfect the pruning knife used with corrosive sublimate (which see) and paint the pruning wound with bordeaux paint, which see.

CROWN IMPERIAL. Common name for *Fritillaria imperialis,* a showy bulbous plant with a terminal cluster of nodding bell-shaped flowers, usually orange and red.

CROWN-OF-THORNS. A common name for *Euphorbia splendens* given because of the plant's curving stems 3-4 ft. long, which are thickly covered with stout spines an inch or so in length. See EUPHORBIA.

CROWN ROT. This disease also called root rot or sclerotium rot, is very prevalent on ornamentals in the N. E. States and occurs to some extent also in the Middle West. It has been reported on Aconite, Ajuga, Aquilegia, Campanula, Cosmos, Delphinium, Dianthus, Dracocephalum, Erigeron, Eupatorium, Hosta, Iris, Pentstemon, Phlox, Physostegia, Trillium, Valeriana and Viola, and nearly a hundred other plants are known to be susceptible. The name of the fungus that causes it (*Sclerotium delphinii*) is indicative of the heavy losses in delphinium beds. Another species (*rolfsii*) is responsible for a similar disease of many S. plants.

The first symptoms, usually appearing with the beginning of warm, humid weather at the end of June or early in July, are a sudden yellowing of the shoots followed by rapid wilting and drying. Sometimes the rapid decay of the crown causes the plants to topple over without preliminary wilting. When plants are crowded or cover the ground closely (as does *Ajuga reptans*) large plantings seem literally to disappear in the course of two or three days, only a few black, dried strands being left where there was luxuriant green growth a few days before. As the plants wilt, the crowns and surrounding soil are overrun with white fungus threads (*mycelium*) in which the resting bodies (*sclerotia*) are formed. The latter are about the size and shape of mustard seed, are first white, then reddish brown. They may be so numerous as to make the ground look red.

The sclerotia are able to remain alive in the soil for months or even years. So if there has been continued trouble from crown rot, the best control is to destroy all of the plants and either replace the soil or disinfect it with a formaldehyde drench (see DISINFECTION). Since this is not often feasible in a perennial border, the next best method is to remove and burn the diseased plants and drench the soil and crowns of neighboring plants with corrosive sublimate at a 1 to 1,000 dilution (1 tablet to 1 pint of water). Naphthalene crystals (ordinary moth flakes procurable at drug or department stores) applied at the rate of 8 oz. per square yard and lightly worked into the soil will prevent the spread of the disease in many cases.

Constant vigilance is necessary during the humid summer months to make sure that this dread disease does not ravage the entire perennial border. The corrosive sublimate and naphthalene treatments will stop the spread of disease during a single season, especially if repeated once or twice, but they are no guarantee against a recurrence another year.

CROWN-VETCH. Common name for *Coronilla varia,* a sprawling herb with pinkish-white, pea-like flowers, now widely naturalized through N. America.

CRUCIANELLA (kroo-shan-el'-ah). A genus of the Madder Family commonly known as Crosswort (which see), comprising small herbs often grown in the shady rock garden.

CRUCIFER (kroo'-si-fur). Any plant belonging to the large and important Mustard Family, which includes among its 1800 or more species many valuable vegetables, a number of useful garden flowers, and also some troublesome weeds. A few

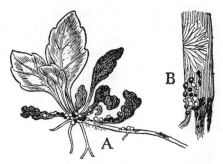

CROWN ROT, BANE OF PERENNIALS
(A) An Ajuga with several leaves killed and blackened, or dying, and the fungus spore bodies (sclerotia) on the crown and along the runner. (B) Base of a diseased iris leaf showing the fan-shaped mycelium of the fungus; and below, where the tissue is rotting, light- and dark-colored sclerotia.

of these are Alyssum, Arabis (rock-cress), Iberis (candy-tuft), Cheiranthus (wallflower), Mathiola (stock), and Brassica, (including mustard, turnip, and the rest of the cabbage tribe). The term, and the botanical family name (Cruciferae) from which it comes, are derived from Latin words meaning cross-bearing, and refer to the fact that the flowers of all members of the family (which may be white, yellow, orange, rose or purple) are composed of four petals arranged in the form of a cross. These are followed by characteristic, usually slender, pointed seed pods. A sharp, peppery flavor or fragrance is also characteristic of many plants in this useful and widely distributed group.

ENEMIES. In general the diseases and pests of one crucifer are found on many other plants of the family. Black-leg is widely distributed and attacks all varieties of cabbage as well as many other Brassicas, sometimes causing a 50 to 90 per cent loss in commercial cabbage and cauliflower crops. The plants may be infected in the seed bed or later, the first symptoms being oval, depressed, light brown cankers near the base of the stem. As these enlarge, the stem is girdled and the dead tissue turns black, giving the disease its name. Small black dots (the fungus fruiting bodies), in the lesions on leaves and stems also identify the disease. The fungus lives over on the seed and in cabbage refuse. To avoid the trouble use healthy seed, such as is produced in the Puget Sound region where the disease does not normally occur; and practice a 4 yr. crop rotation. Treat seed that may be diseased by tying it in cheesecloth bags and suspending these for half an hour in a solution made of 1 corrosive-sublimate tablet to each pint of water. After immersion rinse the seed thoroughly in clear water and spread out to dry. A surer method of killing the fungus (but one that causes some loss in germination) is as follows: Place the bags of seed in water held constantly at 122 deg. F. for 30 minutes, keeping the water stirred. Then dip in cold water and spread the seed out to dry. In some States the experiment stations give this hot-water-treatment for growers.

Black rot, a bacterial disease, causes dwarfing and rotting of plants, spotting or blighting of leaves and sometimes death. Practically all crucifers are affected, cauliflower being particularly susceptible. The disease may affect seedlings or appear after the plants are set out into the field; the first symptom is a yellowing of the leaves accompanied by the blackening of veins, which begins at the leaf margin or around an insect injury. Disinfect seed by either treatment recommended above for blackleg; use clean or disinfected soil in the seed bed; practise a 4- or 5-year crop rotation; control insect pests, and promptly remove and burn diseased plants.

Club root (called finger-and-toe disease in England and cabbage hernia in some other countries) may occur wherever cabbage is grown. Nearly all kinds of crucifers may be affected, but while some varieties of turnips and radishes are very susceptible others are practically immune. Above the ground the main symptom is a wilting of the tops on hot days followed by partial recovery at night; leaves may appear yellowish and sickly; young plants may die outright and older ones may fail to produce marketable heads. The roots of diseased plants will be found much enlarged and malformed, the enlargements varying from small swellings to huge clubbed masses, often ten times normal size, cracked and furrowed on the surface; later they decay, giving off bad odors.

This is one of the few diseases of economic plants caused by a slime-mold whose spores are liberated in vast numbers into the soil when the diseased roots decay. These spores can live in the soil for at least 7 years and attack susceptible plants at any time during that period. To avoid the disease start the seed in soil in which cabbage has never been grown and set the plants in soil that has been heavily limed 3 to 6 months before planting. Apply corrosive sublimate (1 tablet to a pint of water, or 1 oz. to 10 to 12 gallons of water) to the plants in the seed bed and, later, to those in the field once a week for several weeks; use 1 gal. of the solution for 20 to 40 ft. of row. Cultivate the crop thoroughly, destroying all cruciferous weeds.

Cabbage yellows (caused by the fungus Fusarium) which also affects cauliflower and kale, is of particular importance in the S. Central States, since the fungus, which lives in the soil, develops best at temperatures of 80 to 90 deg. F. Diseased plants are sickly, yellow and dwarfed with pinkish spore masses on the stems. Resistant strains of cabbage are being developed by selection and seed of such kinds adapted for a grower's locality can often be obtained from state experiment stations.

Several important insect pests occur on cabbage and related vegetables. The imported cabbage worm is common throughout the U. S. and most of Canada. The velvety green worms with a slender orange stripe down the middle of the back, which grow up to 1¼ in. long, riddle the first formed leaves of cabbage and cauliflower and destroy so much leaf tissue that the heads are stunted or do not form at all. The adult is the familiar white cabbage butterfly, which emerges in spring and lays several hundred eggs on the underside of leaves. The young green caterpillars hatch in about a week and there are from 3 to 6 generations in a summer. To fight this pest, spray or dust the plants with lead- or calcium-arsenate. Dust sticks to the leaves better, and a good mixture is 1 part calcium arsenate and 3 parts hydrated lime. While such arsenicals can be safely used on cabbage (since the outer poisoned leaves are discarded), those who prefer to can use one of the new dusts with a pyrethrum or rotenone base. In the case of collards, kale, mustard or cauliflower discontinue any spraying or dusting treatment four weeks before the crop is gathered. In some sections natural enemies of the cabbage worm keep the pest from becoming serious.

The cabbage looper which attacks cabbage in the same manner as the cabbage worm, is a light green caterpillar with four thin lengthwise white lines, that moves by humping or looping up the middle of the body like other "inch worms" (which see).

It winters in a white cocoon attached to a leaf and the adults are night-flying inconspicuous grayish-brown moths. There are three or more generations a year. The same control measures are used as for the cabbage worm but the spraying or dusting must be thoroughly done since the worms are very active.

Two species of aphis—the dusty gray cabbage aphis and the green turnip aphis —attack cabbage, cauliflower and related crops feeding on the underside of the leaves, which crinkle and curl, forming cups completely lined with aphids. The plants are dwarfed and form light heads. Heavy dusting with nicotine will kill both pests.

The cabbage maggot infests the stems of early set cabbage and cauliflower plants as well as early turnips and late radish crops. The worms work in the stems just below the soil surfce, causing the plants to wilt and die without forming heads. They hatch from eggs laid on the soil by slender gray flies which emerge in late spring, the winter being passed in the pupal stage in the soil. There are three broods each year. Control by placing a tarred paper disk around the stem of each plant when setting it out; or by applying half a cupful of calomel solution (1 oz. to 10 gals. of water). Corrosive sublimate at the same dilution may be used but 2 or 3 applications may be necesasry. Where only a few plants are grown they may be screened with cheesecloth to keep the flies from laying eggs near them.

Larvae of the striped cabbage flea beetle, which is very small and black with wavy yellow stripes, feed on the roots of cabbage, radish and wild mustard. Cheesecloth screens afford protection as does a heavy application of fine tobacco dust when the plants first appear.

The gaudy, red and black spotted Harlequin bug (which see) is an injurious pest of crucifers in the S. Newly set plants or seedlings grown in the garden can be protected against cutworms (which see) by means of paper collars or poison bran mash, which see.

CRYOLITE. A chemical compound combining fluorine (which see) and silica, used as a stomach poison for insect pests. It may be procured in natural or synthetic form.

C R Y O P H Y T U M (kry-oh-fy'-tum) (formerly Mesembryanthemum). A genus of the Carpetweed Family comprising a number of species of biennial or annual herbs, often low-growing, with solitary red, yellow or white flowers with numerous petals, and leaves usually covered with crystalline drops, giving them a glistening icy appearance. The species best known is *C. crystallinum* (Ice-plant, which see) an annual, easily grown from seed and used for a ground-cover in mild climates or in porch and window-boxes in the N.

CRYPTANTHUS (krip'-tan-thus). A genus of small tropical foliage plants, belonging to the Pineapple Family. Air plants in their native habitat, they are often grown in warm greenhouses being effective in pans, and thriving in a mixture of fern-fibre and sphagnum moss with broken brick and charcoal. Plenty of water is needed in the growing season, but very little in winter. The stiff and spreading leaves, with spiny edges, are in the form of a rosette, in which the small white flowers in dense heads are almost hidden. Propagated by division.

C. acaulis has wavy recurved dark green leaves, white and scurfy beneath.

C. bivittatus has leaves brown beneath, dull green above and marked with two buff or reddish longitudinal bands. *C. zonatus* has crinkly leaves marked with transverse bands of white, green or brown.

CRYPTOCORYNE (krip-toh-ko-ry'-nee). A submerged aquatic plant of the Arum Family which is taking a first rank among choice aquarium plants. Two types, one with broad, somewhat heart-shaped leaves and one with straplike leaves, are now in fairly common use. It is of especial value in the indoor aquarium which receives too little light to produce the best growth of the more common aerating plants. Its reddish flower resembles a small calla.

CRYPTOGRAMMA (krip-toh-gram'-ah). Rock-brake. A genus of small ferns growing on limestone, and closely related to the Pellaeae or Cliff-brakes. The fertile blades are somewhat contracted by the revolute edges which cover the fruit dots. Lovely, gem-like ferns, but difficult to establish in gardens. Try a mixture of loam, peat, and chips of stone or brick, but be careful of lime as it is apt to burn the very fibrous rootlets.

SPECIES

C. acrostichoides (American Parsley Fern, or Little Fern). 6 to 8 in., with very dissimilar fertile and sterile fronds, the former having linear pod-like segments, the latter obtuse toothed lobes. Confined to N. regions, as Canada, Lake Superior, Colo., and N. Calif.

densa (Dense Cliff Brake). 3 to 9 in. tall; 3-pinnate below; stipes wiry, light brown. For N. States only.

stelleri (Slender Cliff Brake). 3 to 6 in. tall, thin and narrow with round-lobed pinnae. Native New England to Pa. and N. W.

CRYPTOMERIA (krip-toh-mee'-ri-ah). A Japanese member of the Pine Family having no common name, and only one species, with numerous varieties. It attains a height of 125 ft. in its native land. In the U. S. it grows as far N. as Mass. in sheltered locations near the coast, but suffers in severe winters, the foliage being occasionally killed in irregular patches. From Philadelphia S. it develops into a beautiful tree.

The angular, pointed foliage is arranged spirally around the stem; growing in tufted masses, it creates a distinctive and attractive effect. As cold weather approaches it takes on a purple hue like that of the native junipers. This tree, suitably located, adds interest and beauty to any garden. Both its color and the modeling of the foliage masses are immediately noticeable and set it off from other evergreens. It is propagated by seeds or cuttings from green wood.

CRYPTOSTEGIA (krip-toh-stee'-ji-ah). Tropical climbers of the Milkweed Family, grown for ornamental or economic purposes. See RUBBER-VINE.

CRYSTAL-TEA. Common name for *Ledum palustre,* shrub of the Heath Family, having small white flowers and narrow, evergreen leaves, covered with rusty down beneath.

CUBAN-LILY. Inappropriate but frequently used name for *Scilla peruviana,* a bulbous plant of the Lily Family, bearing a heavy spike of reddish, white or purple flowers; native of the Mediterranean region.

CUBÉ (koo'-bay). A tropical leguminous plant which, pounded up and thrown into streams by savages of countries where it grows, kills or paralyzes fish so they can be easily caught. Though harmless to man, the poisonous principle in the plant (known as *rotenone*) is an effective insecticide. Extracted from the cubé roots, it is used in the making of contact,

and to some extent stomach, poisons for plant protection. See DERRIS; INSECTICIDE.

CUCKOO-FLOWER. A common name for *Cardamine pratensis,* a perennial Bitter-cress, with white or rose flowers, sometimes grown in the rock garden. It is also called Ladys Smock.

CUCKOO-PINT. A common name for *Arum maculatum* (sometimes called Lords-and-ladies), a moisture loving plant of the Mediterranean region with 10-in. leaves and a flower bract (spathe) resembling that of the calla but edged with green and sometimes purple-spotted.

CUCUMBER. An Asiatic trailing or tendril-climbing annual herb (*Cucumis sativus*) grown for its immature, green fruits which are used as pickles, in salads and, sometimes, cooked. Cultivated varieties are of two general classes: (1) English forcing—long, slender (often more than 3 ft.), few seeded and nearly spineless; (2) common or garden cucumbers of several types and many sizes. The former are grown only under artificial conditions, that is, in greenhouses; the latter in hotbeds, coldframes, outdoor home gardens and largely on market gardens and truck farms.

PLANT REQUIREMENTS. Cucumbers being tender can be grown outdoors only in frostless weather. As they transplant with difficulty they are generally grown from seed sown where the plants are to remain. Plants can, however, be started under glass in flower pots (clay or paper) or berry boxes or in the soil of inverted sods. They require warm soil—preferably a sandy loam—full sun, abundant, quickly available plant food and protection from insects and diseases, especially cucumber beetles, which, besides feeding on them, spread the destructive wilt disease.

CULTURE. Enrich the ground and prepare it for seeding after the weather has settled. Make hills 4 by 4 ft. apart for early, small kinds, and 4 by 6 ft. for large, late ones. If the soil is naturally poor or lacking in humus work a forkful of well-decayed manure into each hill. Scatter a dozen seeds in a 1 ft. circle in each hill, and bury them ½ in. deep. It is advisable to cover each hill with a melon plant protector until after the vines begin to "run" to keep out cucumber beetles. When the plants are nicely under way, thin out the inferior ones, leaving not more than five to the hill. Keep the soil cultivated as long as it can be done without injuring the spreading vines, and spray as described below.

HARVESTING. For small pickles (gherkins), gather the cucumbers when only 2 or 3 in. long—about six weeks from sowing; for "dill" size pickles, harvest when 4 to 6 in. long; for slicing, when they are plump and cylindrical but before they bulge in the middle or show a yellowish tinge at the blossom ends. Daily picking during hot weather will prolong the fruiting season. (See illustration, Plate 55.)

To force garden cucumbers under glass, start the plants in flower pots of good soil two weeks before their spaces in the greenhouse will be ready. Transplant into beds of rich soil, 18 to 24 in. asunder in rows 30 to 36 in. apart. Train the vines on rough cords suspended from the roof or a framework. With proper care good plants should begin to bear in 6 or 8 weeks and yield perhaps 100 fruits each.

English frame cucumber plants for winted cropping are started in the fall 80 to 100 days before the fruits are wanted. If grown for spring and early summer, sow seed in February or March. When bees are not available in the house, the pistillate flowers must be hand pollinated.

Cucumbers are subject to bacterial wilt, mosaic, anthracnose, and angular leaf spot. The most troublesome pests are pickle worm, squash bug, cucumber beetles and aphids. For control measures see Enemies, under CUCURBITA.

Mock- or Wild-cucumber, an American annual climber, is often planted to cover arbors because of its profuse, small flowers and large foliage. See ECHINOCYSTIS.

Bur- or Star-cucumber is an annual vine (*Sicyos angulatus*) which makes a good, temporary screen but is prone to become a weed.

Squirting-cucumber is a herbaceous perennial trailer (*Ecballium elaterium*). It is grown for its odd, yellow fruits which when ripe "squirt" out their seeds.

CUCUMBER-ROOT. Common name for *Medeola virginiana,* a native perennial herb with an edible tuberous root, belonging to the Lily Family. It is found in moist soils, and has slender stems to 3 ft. with leaves borne in 2 whorls, the lower with 5 to 9 leaves to 5 in. long, the upper one with 3 to 5 smaller leaves. The small greenish-yellow flowers appear in the upper leaf-whorl in early summer, and are followed by dark purple berries.

CUCUMBER-TREE. Common name for *Magnolia acuminata,* a hardy pyramidal tree to 100 ft. bearing large green flowers and conspicuous seeds. *M. macrophylla,* called Large-leaved Cucumber-tree, is smaller (50 ft.), with larger leaves and white flowers. See MAGNOLIA.

CUCUMIS (keu'-keu-mis). A genus of tender, mostly Asiatic and African, vine-like herbs. Four of them are grown in America for their variously formed succulent fruits which are edible, interesting, or both. The most important species are *C. sativus,* the cucumber (which see), and *C. melo,* the melon (which see), also called muskmelon.

C. sativus includes the various garden kinds of cucumber, while its var. *anglicus* is the strong-growing English forcing type with long, almost spineless, fruits.

C. melo is widely cultivated in many forms which are popularly and indiscriminately classed as "cantaloupes," although that name correctly applies only to the little grown var. *cantaloupensis* with hardy, scaly or warty rind. Other varieties are: *chito,* the mango- or orange-melon or lemon-cucumber, whose small, firm fruits are used as pickles or preserves; *conomon,* the oriental pickling melon similarly used, but little grown in this country; *dudaim,* the dudaim melon, sometimes grown for its marbled, highly fragrant fruits; *flexuosus,* the snake or serpent melon which produces curious long, coiled or twisted fruits; and *inodorus,* the winter or cassaba melon, a strong-growing kind whose large, mildly scented fruits keep well into winter.

C. anguria (West-India or Bur Gherkin), grows wild in Fla. and Tex.; its odd small prickly fruits are sometimes used as pickles. *C. dipsaceus* (Hedgehog or Teasel Gourd), from Arabia, has a hard bristly bur on account of which it is grown as curiosity or ornament.

CUCURBITA (keu-kur'-bi-tah). A genus of the Gourd Family (Cucurbitaceae). They are tendril-bearing, annual or perennial, vine-like herbs, which, except in cultivated bush varieties, root at the joints. A member of the genus is called a *cucurbit.*

C. pepo includes common summer and autumn pumpkins, vegetable marrows, bush pumpkins, pattypan, scallop (or simlin), and summer crookneck squashes; also yellow-flowered gourds. *C. moschata* embraces the winter crookneck, Canada or cushaw pumpkins and the so-called sweet-potato, Quaker, or Japanese squashes (or pumpkins). *C. maxima* is the parent species of Mammoth Chile, Hubbard, Boston Marrow and the curious turban (or "squash-within-a-squash") types. *C. fici-folia* or Malabar gourd, a native of Eastern Asia, is grown for ornament. *C. foetidis-sima* (or *C. perennis*), the Mexican cala-bazilla which grows wild as far N. as Ne-braska, bears inedible fruits. See also GOURD; PUMPKIN; SQUASH.

ENEMIES. Bacterial wilt is one of the most serious troubles of cucumber, squash, muskmelon and pumpkin E. of Kan. and N. of Tenn. The bacteria clog and destroy the sap tubes of stem and leaf, frequently causing a crop loss of 20 per cent. Start-ing with a single leaf, the wilting gradually spreads through the entire plant. The bacillus that causes it can overwinter only in the digestive tract of the 12-spotted cu-cumber beetle hence control of the disease is directed largely at control of the beetle (see below). Pull up and burn diseased plants and, to protect healthy ones, follow spray schedule below.

Anthracnose is usually more severe on watermelons than on other cucurbits but sometimes occurs in epidemic form on cu-cumbers and muskmelons. All parts of the plant above ground may be affected show-ing (1) yellow and water-soaked spots on the leaves, later enlarging and turning brown; (2) a blackened or scorched con-dition of the vines; (3) on fruits, water-soaked sunken spots covered with masses of buff-colored spores. Control by crop rotation, seed treatment (5 minutes in a 1 to 1000 corrosive sublimate solution), and spray with bordeaux mixture (see be-low).

Downy mildew produces irregular yellow spots on leaves which later curl and die. Spray with bordeaux mixture every week or ten days.

Mosaic, a virus disease also known as "white pickle" is, next to bacterial wilt, the most important cucurbit disease. The leaves are dwarfed and distorted, the plants stunted, and the fruit blotched with yel-low and green and knotted. Cucumbers and squash are seriously affected, and muskmelon vines are stunted, but water-melon is only slightly susceptible. There are several weed hosts—milkweed, poke-berry, ground cherry and wild-cucumber—from which the disease is carried by in-sects, particularly the melon aphis (see be-low). Such hosts should be destroyed in and around the garden.

Of many insects that attack cucurbits, the most serious is probably the striped cu-cumber beetle. Overwintering yellow, black-striped adults devour leaves and stems of tender young plants and may in-fect them with cucumber wilt. To prevent this plants may be covered with cheese-cloth on frames, or dusted frequently on warm days with a 3 to 4% nicotine lime dust. Burn all old vines and trash at the end of each season.

The following schedule is useful against the beetles, wilt and other diseases:

1. During first week after plants come up—Dust with 1 part calcium arsenate to 15 parts gypsum, or dust with a 3 to 4% nicotine dust.

SQUASHES AND PUMPKINS ARE FAMILIAR MEMBERS OF THE CUCURBIT FAMILY
This group of plants includes such useful vegetables as (from left to right) the smooth Hubbard squash; two summer squashes, the scallop or patty-pan above and the yellow crookneck below; the pumpkin; the warted Hubbard squash; and the vegetable marrow. Gourds (which see) are another group of Cucurbits.

2. When plants are a week old—Spray with bordeaux mixture (4—4—50 for cucumbers, 3—6—50 for muskmelons) plus 2 lbs. calcium arsenate; or dust with copper sulphate 25 parts, calcium arsenate 20 parts, hydrated lime dust 55 parts.

3. Repeat above spray or dust every four to eight days.

The 12-spotted cucumber beetle, which feeds on a large number of food plants, is more serious in the S. Control measures are as for the striped beetle.

The pickle worm, another S. pest, is a slender green worm with a row of black spots. To control it, plant early and destroy waste materials and old vines by burning.

The squash vine borer (*Melittia satyriniformis*), a white grublike caterpillar with a dark head, prefers squash and pumpkin but may attack all cucurbits. It tunnels in the main stem near the ground and may be killed by slitting the stem with a knife. Spraying plants with nicotine-sulphate will kill most of the eggs and reduce infestation.

The melon aphis or louse, which attacks a large number of plants but is most troublesome on cucumber and melon, feeds on the under side of leaves, causing them to curl. Spray or dust thoroughly with nicotine compounds.

The squash bug, also called stink bug because of its offensive odor, lives over the winter in trash and attacks plants as soon as they are up by puncturing the leaf tissues and petioles. Although a sucking insect the rusty brown adult is resistant to contact sprays. Control by hand picking adults and by spraying as for aphis to kill the young nymphs.

CUCURBITACEAE (keu-kur-bi-tay'-see-ee). The botanical name of the Gourd Family, to which the Cucurbits and many other useful plants belong. Besides the genus Cucurbita, it includes many genera grown for edible fruits and ornamental vines, among them Luffa, Benincasa, Citrullus (watermelon), Cucumis (melon and cucumber), Lagenaria, Sechium; chiefly ornamental are Sicana, Bryonia, Coccinea, Ecballium, Cyclanthera, Echinocystis, Melothria, Abobra, Monordica, Trichosanthes. Mostly tropical herbs and erect shrubs, the horticultural kinds are all herbaceous, tendril-climbing vines (except Ecballium), and are mostly tender and rapid growing. The gourd or characteristic fruit of the family, from which it derives its common name, is botanically a *pepo*.

CULINARY HERBS. Plants whose seeds, leaves, bulbs or roots are used for flavoring cooked viands and salads; also applied (though incorrectly) to various garnishes and pot-herbs. In European cookery many are highly prized for their ability to add zest and flavor and make "made-over dishes taste like new." In America they deserve—and are slowly gaining—similar recognition and importance.

The Mint Family (Labiatae) includes the largest number of species whose leaves are the parts used—e.g., balm, basil, chervil, clary, hyssop, marjoram, lavender, parsley, pennyroyal, rosemary, sage, savory, spearmint and thyme. Next in number are members of the Parsley Family (Umbelliferae) whose seeds are used, as angelica, anise, caraway, coriander, cumin, and dill. The Lily Family (Lilaceae) contributes chives (whose leaves are used) and shallots and garlic (grown for the bulbs). The Sunflower Family (Compositae) is represented by tarragon (leaves) and marigold (flower-heads). The Mustard Family (Cruciferae) provides the roots of horse-radish. The Crowfoot Family (Ranunculaceae) has the fennel-flower of which the seed and the whole plant are used; the Borage Family (Boraginaceae) supplies borage leaves; and the Rue Family (Rutaceae) yields rue leaves.

Some of these (and several others), though somewhat used in cookery, are more often employed in confectionery and cake baking, as angelica (the stems), anise, caraway, coriander, horehound (or hoarhound), peppermint, lovage, southern-wood.

PLANT REQUIREMENTS. All culinary herbs thrive best and develop the finest flavor when grown in moderately fertile, fibrous garden loam fully exposed to the sun. If shaded or grown in too rich soil, the leafage may be great but the flavor is likely to be weak. Except for spearmint and peppermint (which prefer actual dampness) the soil should be only moderately moist.

CULTIVATION. As the seed of most species is small and slow to germinate, sow it in seed pans or flats before the season opens and keep these in a hotbed or a coldframe. Prick the seedlings into flats while small, grow them on for two or more weeks, and harden them well before transplanting outdoors in finely prepared soil soon after spring opens. Keep the soil well cultivated.

Sage (Holt's Mammoth, the best variety) and tarragon produce no seed so must be bought as plants or propagated from layers or cuttings—as may also other perennial herbs.

HARVESTING. Gather leaf herbs before the first blossoms begin to open, and *in the early morning*—as soon as the dew is off. They then contain the largest percentage of flavoring oils. Spread them thinly on sheets or trays in shady, airy, warm places to dry. When the leafy parts become crisp, rub them to powder and store this (discarding the stems) in sealed jars to prevent loss of flavor. Keep in the dark to preserve the color.

As soon as the heads of seed herbs ripen, gather them after the dew is off and spread them loosely on strong sheets or on sailcloth placed where a constant current of warm, *not hot,* dry air will pass over them. Never pack them down as heating may result, causing loss of flavor, if not actual decay. When the smaller stems are brittle, dry, rub with the hands or thresh with light rods, a small quantity at a time. After threshing, spread very thinly for further drying and turn over daily for at least a week. Hang in cotton sacks (like sugar or salt bags) in a warm, dry attic or loft for a month, then store in sealed jars.

See also HERBS; HERB GARDEN; KITCHEN GARDEN; BORAGE; CARAWAY; CHEVIL; CHIVES; DILL; FENNEL; GARLIC; HORSERADISH; MARJORAM; MINT; PARSLEY; SAGE; SAVORY, SUMMER, and SHALLOT.

CULTIGEN. A plant or group of plants that exists, so far as known, only in cultivation; as opposed to *indigen,* one that is indigenous, which means native, or a part of the wild flora. Highly improved varieties or strains, as in pansies, potatoes, peaches, etc., are cultigens, whereas their original, ancestral species are indigens of the region in which they were first found growing.

CULTIVAR. A term, proposed in 1923 by Dr. L. H. Bailey, to be used to designate "a botanical variety or race subordinate to a species that has originated and persisted under cultivation," but that is not necessarily referable to any recognized botanical species. Thus it practically corresponds to the term "variety" except that

the origin of the plant to which it is applied is not known. It has been proposed that such cultivars be designated, not by botanical names, but by popular names, such as Petunia Rosy Morn.

CULTIVATION. In its broadest sense, this term covers all tillage operations from the preparing of the land by digging or plowing through the various stirrings of the surface soil up to the time a crop is "laid by" prior to harvesting. More specifically, it means merely the manipulation of the surface soil after crops have been sown or planted in order to kill weeds, break the crust that forms where wet soil dries, aerate the ground, and establish and maintain a dust mulch to conserve moisture in the ground.

When the area involved is extensive enough to permit the use of horse- or tractor-drawn implements, the customary order of procedure in preparing the land for planting on sod land in heavy soil is as follows: 1, Plowing; 2, drag harrowing in the direction of the furrows; 3, disk or cutaway harrowing also in the direction of the furrows; 4, disking at right angles to the furrows; 5, dragging across the disk marks; 6, if necessary, disking a second time at right angles to the first; 7, using a smoothing harrow back and forth until the surface 2 or 3 in. of soil are finely pulverized.

When the area is too small to warrant or permit the use of power implements it must be dug by hand, preferably with the spading fork. This is better than a spade (except in loose, sandy soil), first because it is lighter to use, and second because with it a better job can be done; a glancing blow struck with the tines slices the clods into fragments with less effort than is required to smash them. The steel garden rake is next used to fine the surface 2 or 3 in. deep and to smooth the surface for sowing or planting.

If newly prepared ground must remain idle for several days before sowing or planting is done, its surface should be stirred with weeder attachment on the wheelhoe or with the steel garden rake often enough to prevent the formation of a crust but, more important, to destroy weed seedlings as they start to grow. It is much better, however, to dig and prepare only so much ground as can be planted the same day while the seed-bed is loose and moist.

Cultivation proper should start immediately after the seed has been sown or the plants transplanted to the garden; the purpose here, too, is to keep the soil from crusting and to destroy weeds while they are small. From that time forward this soil stirring should be repeated as soon after every rain as the ground becomes dry enough so that it does not "puddle" (which see) when worked. If no rain occurs and the ground cannot be watered artificially, it is advisable to cultivate once every week or ten days until the plants are large enough to shade the ground and prevent weed growth, or until the roots are likely to be injured by the operation.

Except under special conditions and for particular purposes, level cultivation is unquestionably better than hilling or ridging. Exceptional conditions under which the latter practices are advisable are: Wet land, when hilling and ridging will aid in drying out the surface soil; in wet seasons, for the same reason; in order to eradicate (by burying them) weeds that have gotten too much of a start, due to wet weather or neglect; and in order to "hill" such crops as potatoes and celery, in the first case to avoid sun-burning of the tubers; in the second to blanch the crop.

The early cultivations between rows of plants may be as much as 2½ in. deep, but they should gradually become shallower as the season advances so as to avoid, as much as possible, injury to the crop roots. The width of the strip cultivated between the rows should also decrease as the plants grow and shade the ground.

Cultivation of large areas is generally done by power implements (see CULTIVATOR); small scale work is often done with the wheelhoe (which see), especially where the rows are long. In the average small home garden, or where a wheelhoe is not available, the usual tools for cultivating are some form of hand hoe, the steel rake, and the hand weeder. The hoe and the weeder are of course also used for killing large isolated weeds and for thinning out excess plants in rows grown from seed. This and all other hand work is done most effectively and with least expenditure of effort while the plants and the weeds are very small—preferably before the latter have become visible on the surface. At that stage the steel garden rake is even better than the ordinary hoe; however, several types of scuffle hoe which do not have to be lifted from the ground and which leave a smooth mulch are available.

Cultivation should never be done while the soil is wet. Occasionally this rule may be almost disregarded when the soil is very sandy and well drained, but it must be rigidly enforced in connection with all heavy clays, or otherwise fine-textured. For all soils containing large proportions of clay are not only heavy and sticky to

CONTRASTING METHODS IN CULTIVATION
The old-fashioned hand hoe (left) is still a supremely effective tool for certain tasks, but the wheelhoe (right) takes much of yesterday's drudgery out of vegetable gardening.

handle when wet, but, what is still more important, tend to puddle, bake and form hard, brick-like clods if manipulated while so moist that a fresh cut surface glistens. Such a soil should never be stirred or if possible walked on until after this glary sheen has disappeared.

Also, cultivation should not be done when the plants in the rows are wet with rain or dew; as the implement or its operator brushes against them, fungous disease spores are likely to be scattered or picked up from diseased plants and carried to healthy ones, where the moist foliage provides the best possible conditions for storing new infections.

See DIGGING; MULCH; TOOLS.

CULTIVATOR. Any implement used to loosen the soil and destroy weeds around crops grown either in drills or in hills. Formerly known as "horse-hoe," it consists of various types of replaceable, adjustable "teeth" attached to a frame, which can be manipulated to fit the width to be covered and the depth the teeth are to penetrate. In large-scale operation it is drawn by horses or a tractor, and may work two or more rows simultaneously. The operator may walk or ride. In small gardens the cultivator is replaced by the wheelhoe, which see.

The work done varies according to the styles of teeth used. Some have only one type of teeth, usually spikes or shovels; others have several interchangeable teeth, including rakes, spikes, shovels, disks and cutaways (disks with deep notches cut in their margins). Each type has its special advantages.

Rakes and spikes do the best work on light soils in which they scratch the surface and destroy weeds; rakes kill weeds while sprouting, spikes kill them when larger. Disks, usually set at a slight angle to the direction of pull, slice the surface and throw the soil either toward or away from the rows of plants. They are useful also (especially when weighted) for cutting and mixing sod with surface soil. Shovels, according to their "set," are useful in the same way, either hilling the plants or raising the soil between the rows. Cutaway teeth break down clods of heavy soil and reduce the surface to an even level and texture.

The rototiller, a comparatively new implement introduced from Europe, is becoming increasingly popular in America. It consists essentially of a gasoline motor and various types of narrow teeth which, rotating at high speed, break up and stir the soil, incorporating manure, etc., without the preliminary operation of plowing. Also the "push" of the revolving teeth imparts a forward motion and lightens the load on the propelling motor.

See also TOOLS.

CULVERS-ROOT, CULVERS PHYSIC. Names for *Veronicastrum virginicum* (formerly listed as *Veronica virginica*), a herbaceous perennial, native from New England S. It is a robust plant of stiff habit to 7 ft., and thrives best in rich soil and an open situation. The leaves are in whorls, and in late summer it is conspicuous with dense spikes of small white or pale-blue flowers. Good in the wild garden.

CUMIN (kum'-in). The common name for *Cuminum cyminum*, a small annual herb of the Old World belonging to the Parsley Family, with finely cut leaves and clusters of small white or rose flowers; also the name for its seeds, which are used as an ingredient in curry powder, and for flavoring pickles and soups. Plants are easily raised from seed.

CUNILA (keu-ny'-lah) *origanoides*. A perennial herb of the Mint Family having small purplish-pink flowers; popularly known as Maryland Dittany or Stone-mint, which see.

CUP-AND-SAUCER BELLFLOWER. Common name for *Campanula medium* var. *calycanthemum*, a biennial form of bellflower in which there is a flaring, colored calyx below the bell-shaped corolla. See CAMPANULA.

CUP-AND-SAUCER VINE. A common name for the attractive, useful, annual vine, *Cobaea scandens*. See COBAEA.

CUP FERN. A common name for *Dennstedtia punctilobula*, more commonly known as the Boulder Fern. One of the most robust and rampant native American plants. The finely divided fronds, light green in color, form dense tangles. It is one of the best for naturalizing in open, half-shaded places.

CUP-FLOWER (*Nierembergia*). Low-growing, tender, S. American perennials, generally treated as annuals in the U. S. They will flower the first season from seed sown indoors early. The plants require a warm, protected situation, especially during the early stages of their development.

Excellent in the rock garden because of their dwarf stature—seldom more than 6 in. —they are also used in the open border and, because of their numerous pale-violet or white flowers of slightly irregular cup-shape and sometimes with purple centres, they occasionally are grown as pot plants. Few plants are better for baskets and vases.

If grown indoors or in warm regions as perennials they may be propagated by cuttings, though *N. rivularis* (White-cup) may be increased by division of the creeping stems where they have rooted. There is one tall species, *N. frutescens,* that reaches 3 ft. and is shrubby and branching. Its flowers are white with lilac or blue tints and yellow throats. *N. gracilis,* like *N. rivularis,* is a creeping type.

CUPHEA (keu'-fe-ah). A large genus of tropical and subtropical American herbs, belonging to the Loosestrife Family. Only a few kinds have been generally grown and these mostly in greenhouses or outdoors in warm regions. The herbaceous sorts are easy to raise from seed as tender annuals, and the shrubby kinds from cuttings. The principal species are the following:

C. ignea (Cigar-flower). This, the best known and most attractive, is sometimes known as *C. platycentra.* It is a free flowering little shrubby plant, useful for greenhouse decoration, and it can be used outside as a tender bedding plant. The flower is without petals, the color being furnished by the calyx tube, which is bright scarlet, tipped with black and white.

hyssopifolia is a narrow leaved little shrub, bearing 6-petaled flowers of pale pink with a green calyx.

miniata (also known as *C. llavea*) has distinctive flowers, with a green and purple calyx and two large scarlet petals.

hookeriana has flowers with a red calyx and 2 large and 4 small deep purple petals.

CUPIDS-DART or BLUE CUPIDONE (*Catananche caerulea*). A herbaceous perennial distinguished by narrow leaves borne near the base of the stems and by long-stalked blue, chaff-like heads of ray and disk flowers. Growing 2 ft. tall and blossoming from June to August the first year from seed, the plants are excellent in beds and borders and are good for cutting. The flowers may be dried for winter-use as everlastings (which see). Well-drained soil and sun are required. Propagation is by seed or by division, though the best method is to treat them as biennials, sowing seed outdoors for the following season's bloom. Var. *alba* has white flowers, and var. *bicolor* has blue rays edged with white.

CUP-PLANT or INDIAN CUP. Common name for *Silphium perfoliatum,* a tall stout perennial herb of the Composite Family, sometimes used in the wild garden. It is a species of Rosin-weed, which see.

CUPRESSUS (keu-pres'-us). Generic name for the large group of trees known as Cypress, belonging to the Pine Family, but adapted only to mild and warm regions. See CYPRESS.

CURCULIGO (kur-keu'-li-goh). A genus of tropical plants belonging to the Amaryllis Family. They are dwarfs of palm-like appearance, with arching corrugated leaves. Useful ornamental subjects for the warm greenhouse, they can stand heavy shade. They thrive in a mixture of fibrous loam, old cow manure and sand. Propagated by division.

C. capitulata (formerly *C. recurvata*), the principal species, has dark green leaves to 3 ft. long, and a dense spike of yellow flowers, recurving and usually just above the ground. Its var. *striata* has a central band of white down the leaves, and var. *variegata* has pure white stripes.

CURCULIO (kur-keu'-li-oh). A name for various kinds of snout beetles or weevils, some of which are troublesome fruit pests. The plum curculio, a native species, attacks plum, peach, apple, pear, and other stone and pome fruits and is generally distributed east of the Rocky Mountains from Canada S. The adult, about ¼ in. long, is brown, mottled with gray, and has four humps on its back. It feeds on the blossoms to some extent but the chief injury is the shallow feeding cavities and crescent-shaped scars on the fruit caused when the female lays an egg in a cavity and then, just in front, makes a crescent-shaped slit which leaves the egg in a kind of pocket. The young larvae, grayish-white with a small brown head, eat into the flesh of the fruit, causing it nearly always to fall to the ground before they have completed their growth. After two to four weeks the larvae leave the fruit, burrow into the soil and pupate in earthen cells, the adult beetles emerging in about a month.

Besides being, probably, the chief cause of wormy cherries when grown in small orchards or in cities, the plum curculio is harmful in that it spreads spores of the brown rot fungus. See BROWN ROT.

Because of a peculiar habit of feigning death when disturbed by drawing their legs and snout close to the body and falling to the ground, curculios can be controlled by what is known as the "jarring method." A sheet is placed under the tree whose trunk is hit with a wooden or cloth-covered mallet; the insects fall onto the sheet and can be destroyed. Jarring trees each morning for six weeks after blossoming has been recommended. Lead arsenate as spray or dust is effective but must be used with hydrated lime to prevent burning tender fruits. Consult local experiment stations or county agents for detailed advice. Generally, the first spray should be applied just as the husks split from the young fruits, and the second two weeks later. Badly infested trees need further applications. Clean cultivation around the trees is an important measure and all early "drops" of peaches, plums or apples should be raked up and destroyed.

The apple curculio, a less important pest, resembling the plum curculio, makes a large number of skin punctures close together and causes apples to become misshaped and knotty. General orchard sanitation methods should be practiced and wild hawthorns and crabs (which are the curculios' native food plants) should be cut down over half a mile area around an orchard.

See also SNOUT BEETLES.

CURCUMA (kur-keu'-mah). A genus of vigorous tropical herbaceous plants, belonging to the Ginger Family. They may be grown outdoors in warm regions, but they thrive in rich soil in a warm greenhouse. They have a thick tuberous rootstock, and stems which grow to 10 ft., with large leaves which dry off soon after flowering. The flowers are borne in showy spikes, each flower surrounded by a leafy

PLUM CURCULIO

An adult of this weevil-like pest, and two of the crescent-shaped wounds it makes in fruit.

bract, and the whole spike crowned with a colored tuft. During the plant's resting stage the soil should not be kept bone dry or the tubers will shrivel. Propagated by division or tubers in spring.

C. petiolata (Queen-lily) has dense spikes of pale yellow flowers and rosy-purple bracts. *C. longa* has long-stalked leaves and spikes of yellow flowers with green and pink bracts. The dried rhizomes yield the turmeric of India, used as a condiment and dye. *C. zedoaria* has leaves silky beneath and yellow flowers, the lower bracts being green and the upper ones white tinged with carmine.

CURLY-GRASS (*Schizaea pusilla*). A minute and thread-like fern found only in the N. J. pine barrens and in Nova Scotia. The sterile fronds are grasslike, 1 to 2 in. tall; the fertile ones are 3 to 4 in., bearing about 5 pairs of tiny contracted fruiting pinnae. A possible subject for the bog garden, in sandy peat, but requiring very special conditions.

CURLY TOP. Name of a virus disease of the beet, which see.

CURRANT. This is the name of two popular, unrelated fruits and the plant that produces one of them. The first is the dried fruit of small grapes (a variety of *Vitis vinifera*) exported from the Mediterranean region of Europe; the name is a corruption of Corinth whence the product was originally shipped. The second kind of currant is the small, red, white or black, globular berry borne in clusters by various species of Ribes (which see). The former are rarely grown in America; the latter are found in both home and commercial plantings throughout the N. two-thirds of the U. S. The red and white varieties, both developed from the European species *R. sativum,* are the most important in home gardening and the reds as a market fruit. The black currant (*R. nigrum*) is only occasionally seen in American gardens though it is fairly common in Canadian home grounds, especially those owned by Scotch, English and Irish people, who enjoy the peculiar flavor of its jam and jelly. As one of the chief alternate hosts of the destructive white pine blister rust disease, it is being exterminated by government agencies and outlawed by nurserymen in many States.

Currant bushes are of outstanding hardiness; even the blossoms which appear in early spring being able to withstand frosts that destroy the flowers of other fruits. They are grown successfully almost to the Arctic Circle, but are at their best where the soil is moist and the air cool and humid, as along the sea and the Great Lakes shores. They cannot, however, stand either heat or dryness, so except in the mountains, or under shade and irrigation, they fail in the hotter, drier parts of the country.

The soils best suited to currants are moist but well-drained silt and clay loams, especially those well supplied with humus. On lighter (sandy) soils they are usually less successful. All too often they are neglected in home gardens, the bushes being choked with worthless stems, grown up with sod and weeds and the prey of currant worms, which strip off the foliage, plant lice which suck the juices of the leaves, and borers which destroy the older stems. This is the reason for the frequent small yields of inferior fruit. Yet no bush fruit is easier to keep free of such enemies and to maintain in high productivity of choice fruit.

The most effective management allows only the best two of each year's usually numerous young shoots to remain; the inferior ones are cut out right to the base shortly after midsummer so as to concentrate all the plant food in the selected stems which thus become sturdy and highly productive. These stems begin to bear the second season, increase their yield the third and reach their maximum the fourth; thereafter the quantity, size, and quality of the berries rapidly declines. Hence the importance of cutting out the oldest stems after they have borne their third crop—that is at the end of their fourth summer. All cut stems should be burned at once to destroy any borers that may be present in them. This method restricts the number of stems left after the summer pruning to a maximum of 8.

Currant varieties differ widely in their habit of growth, some being erect, others sprawling, and it is important to know what type you are planting before deciding upon the distance to allow between bushes. Unless this is watched out for, difficulties will arise later in connection with the cultivating and especially the gathering of the fruit. Erect varieties may be planted 6 ft. apart; sprawling ones should be not less than 8 ft. Whenever possible the bushes should be planted in checks so they may be cultivated in two directions. A path border along one or both sides is also good, provided the bushes are planted at least 4 ft. from the edge of the turf or walk. The worst position for currants is beside a fence or other property boundary because there cultivation is most likely to be neglected and harvesting most difficult.

When allowed to develop naturally, currant bushes extend their roots too close to the soil surface for best results; therefore during the first two years the tillage between the plants should be deep (6 or 8 in.) so as to encourage deep-rooting. Beginning the third season this deep digging or cultivation should be restricted to a narrow central strip between the rows and the plants, the balance being cultivated only 2 to 4 in. deep. Thus supplemental root development in the tilled area is encouraged after the third year and the productive power of the plants is augmented.

When stable manure or other mulching material is available, it may well be applied to help keep the soil moist and cool; preferably this should be postponed until early summer to give opportunity for as much deep rooting as possible. The mulch may be dug or plowed under in early autumn and a cover-crop (which see) sown between the plants and rows if the soil is in need of humus. The cover-crop should be one that will be killed by the winter cold; this will avoid the necessity of digging it under early in the spring before it grows up and threatens to smother the plants.

ENEMIES

DISEASES. Cane blight or wilt (caused by a fungus) may be very destructive. The canes die suddenly while loaded with fruit and leaves and fruiting bodies of the fungus show as small black cushions on the canes. No protective measures have been worked out so plants should be examined three or four times during the summer and all canes showing signs of disease cut out immediately.

Leaf spot or anthracnose spots occur and may cause extensive defoliation. Control by spraying 3 to 5 times during the season with 5—5—50 bordeaux mixture (which see) or with lime-sulphur (which see) 1 to 50.

Currants are particularly important as alternate hosts of the white pine blister rust. (See PINE; also RUSTS.) The black currant is most susceptible and in some states its cultivation is prohibited by law, while many nurserymen no longer grow or offer it.

INSECT PESTS. Small green, black-spotted larvae of the currant worm whose adult is a sawfly (which see), feed on the foliage. To control the first brood spray the bushes with lead arsenate (1 oz. to 2½ gals. of water) as soon as the foliage is well developed. If a second brood appears after the fruit is formed spray with fresh hellebore (4 oz. to 2 gals. of water or use is as a dust, mixing 1 lb. with 5 lbs. of flour or lime) ; or spray with rotenone.

The currant borer causes the same symptons as wilt. Cut off and burn sickly appearing canes. This is also a control measure against the currant stem girdler, another sawfly which lays an egg in a new shoot and then cuts it off above the egg thus destroying sometimes all the young growth.

The currant aphid which causes curling and blistering of tender terminal leaves, has several generations. Spray thoroughly, with nicotine soap solution, beginning when the new leaves first appear.

The four-lined plant bug (which see) attacks many plants, but has been consid-

TO KEEP CUT FLOWERS FRESH
Half-an-inch or so should be cut each day from stems of roses and other flowers. A dull knife is bad; scissors are worse as they crush the tissues. The device shown cuts diagonally with a guillotine-like action of a razor-thin blade.

ered a special pest of currants. Affected leaves are covered with depressed circular areas and are deformed. Spray with nicotine or pyrethrum soap solution or kerosene emulsion, or dust with rotenone.

Besides the species already mentioned the following American species are grown, mainly for ornament: Swamp Red Currant (*R. triste*), with purple flowers and red fruits; American Black Currant (*R. americanum* or *R. floridum*), with creamy flowers and black fruit; Golden Currant (*R. aureum*), with yellow flowers and purplish fruit; and Buffalo Currant (*R. odoratum*), with fragrant yellow flowers and black fruit. None of these has been much improved by man as far as the edibility or yield or its fruit is concerned.

The Indian-currant is *Symphoricarpos orbiculatus,* a species of Snowberry. See SYMPHORICARPOS.

CURRANT TOMATO. The common name for *Lycopersicon pimpinellifolium,* a spreading, rather weak-growing species of tomato native to Peru and producing clusters of from 10 to 25 fruits, only slightly larger than currants and used mainly for *hors d' oeuvres* and garnishing. The plants are sometimes grown as curiosities or ornamentals. They also make an excellent summer cover for unsightly piles of brush.

CURUBA (koo-roo'-bah). One of the common names for *Sicana odorifera,* the Cassabanana, which see.

CUSHAW (ku-shau'). A common name for *Cucurbita moschata,* a species of Squash of variable form but mostly oblong with a large smooth crookneck. It is used in fall and winter hence another common name is Winter Crookneck Pumpkin. See SQUASH and PUMPKIN.

CUSH-CUSH. Common name for *Dioscorea trifida,* a yam cultivated in the S. for the small edible tubers; also known as Yampee.

See DIOSCOREA.

CUSHION FERN. *Dicksonia culcita.* A large, cool-greenhouse fern from the Azores, taking its name from the dense woolly substance which abundantly covers the crowns and bases of the fronds. Should have chiefly peat moss, and a rather small pot so that the soil about the roots is constantly moist.

CUSHION PINK. Common name for *Silene acaulis,* a species of Catchfly or Campion, having reddish-purple, short-stemmed flowers. See SILENE.

Upper left: The dainty, fragrant blooms of sweet peas, ideal for cutting. Upper right: Shirley poppies, exquisite in their color tones and shades. Lower left: Star dahlia lends itself to unusual flower arrangements. Lower right: The gladiolus—often lovelier cut than in the garden.

CUSTARD-APPLE. One of the common names for *Annona reticulata,* also called Bullocks Heart, a tropical, half-evergreen tree, bearing an edible fruit.

CUT FLOWERS. (See illustrations, Plates 12, 28 and 61.) If people could be made to realize that flowers are living, breathing things thriving under proper care and fading and dying with neglect, the problem of how to keep flowers fresh for a reasonably long period would be solved. Like human beings, they respond to attention, and through the observance of some simple fundamental rules paralleling those of human health, they can be made to live longer than if permitted to shift for themselves like neglected children.

GATHERING. Before bringing them into the house, however, thought should be given to the method of cutting them from the plants in the garden. Different kinds of flowers have their own requirements and should be cut at the proper stage of their development; gladiolus when the first bud opens, peonies as the outer petals unfold, roses when the buds are fairly soft, poppies the night before they open, asters when about half open, and most other flowers just before reaching full bloom. Cut the stems with a *sharp knife,* not with dull scissors; many blossoms do not last well if broken from the plants. Flowers which are susceptible to wilting should be cut in the morning or evening, when the tissues are filled with sap.

Having cut a flower and thereby wounded the stem, treat the wound as you would that of a human—but with a difference. When you cut your hand, nature begins to heal the wound or bruise, by sealing it against possible infection from the air. A cut flower, permitted to have its stem exposed to the air even for only a few minutes, might almost as well never be placed in water, for the healing or sealing action of nature begins to work at once. Therefore, plunge the stems into water almost to the base of the blossoms immediately after they are cut. Do not attempt to arrange flowers for at least two hours. Certain flowers "bleed," among them the dahlia, oriental poppy, euphorbia and poinsettia. In their case it is well to sear the ends by passing them through a flame or dipping them in boiling water for a moment before putting them in water.

In placing flowers in a container be sure it is spacious enough to permit circulation of air and proper absorption of water. Jamming them into a narrow vase "chokes" the flowers and shortens their life.

CARE. Flowers should not be kept in the draught of an open window or door, or an electric fan. Nor should they be exposed to bright sunlight. In winter do not keep them close to a hot radiator, and, if possible, keep the air in the room humid. Illuminating gas or fumes from a furnace, range or oil burner quickly cause flowers to wilt or "go to sleep" and most pot plants to droop and shed their leaves. The cooler the room in summer, the longer flowers will live.

Water in vases or other containers should be changed daily to prevent accumulation of bacteria making the water foul. It can be kept pure by adding a bit of charcoal or three drops of formalin to a quart of water. The addition of salt, aspirin and other chemicals is sometimes recommended but as yet there is no scientific proof of their practical use, although one experiment station has reported favorable results from the addition of "2 eyedroppers of sulphurous acid per pint of water" in which cut flowers are kept. When changing the water, cut half an inch or so from the ends of the stems with a clean, *slanting* cut. This reopens the water absorbing vessels and enables the flowers to take in a new supply. Stems cut squarely are likely to rest flat on the bottom of the container and defeat this objective.

Leaves which would be submerged should be removed from stems, especially in the case of asters, calendulas, chrysanthemums and dahlias, which become foul quickly.

If low, broad vases or containers are used, fresh water should be added frequently to make up for the increased evaporation.

If it is possible to place the vase in a refrigerator over night, do so, for the low temperature will keep the flowers from opening too quickly and thereby prolong their life. But this does not mean the excessive dry cold of an electric refrigerator; a cool, moist cellar is much safer and more satisfactory.

Many times flowers which have been kept out of water longer than usual and which, as a result, show signs of wilting, can be revived by a simple method. Place the stems in water in a broad receptacle such as a pail or the sink, and cut the stems an inch or so back *under water* and with a sharp knife; then do not remove them from the water until they have revived. Another method is to plunge the stems into very hot water and then into cold water. A third procedure is to plunge the stems into deep, cold water, almost up to the blossoms but not so as to wet the flowers. Then place the container in a cool, dark, draughtless room for several hours. It is reported that tulip stems will stiffen and strengthen if immersed in a solution of calcium nitrate, 2 oz. in 5 gals. of water.

Corsages, bouquets and other made up flower arrangements to be worn or carried should be left in the florists' box as received until time to use them. The box should be kept in a cool place or, if necessary, the ice box (so long as it is not open). If there is likely to be a delay of a day or more, it may be well to open the box, sprinkle the paper lightly without disturbing the flowers, then close and replace it in a cool place.

ARRANGEMENT. In arranging cut flowers for home decoration two cardinal principles should be followed depending upon the effect desired. If the chief wish is to obtain the most artistic effect without special regard to length of time the flowers last, the total height of the container and flowers should be 2½ times the height of the container alone. If the container is 12 in. high, the tops of the flowers should be about 30 in. above its base. If, however, the desire is to keep flowers alive as long as possible, irrespective of the artistic effect, there should be as much of the stem under water as there is above it.

If there are too many flowers on hand for one vase, use two, or even three. *Do not crowd the flowers.*

See FLOWER ARRANGEMENT.

The so-called flower calendar, of use in arranging birthday dinners, has attracted considerable attention. Here are the birth month flowers according to this system: January, carnation; February, primrose; March, violet; April, daisy or lily; May, hawthorn or lily-of-the-valley; June, rose; July, waterlily; August, poppy; September, dahlia; October, begonia; November, chrisanthemum; and December, poinsettia.

CUTTING GARDEN. A section of the garden, preferably in a secluded but sunny spot, devoted to flowers to be used for cutting. Thus the main border need not be denuded when flowers are desired in the house. For names of plants suitable for the cutting garden see lists under ANNUALS, PERENNIALS, and PLANTS FOR SPECIAL PURPOSES.

NEW PLANTS FROM LEAVES
From the notches around the edge of a leaf of Bryophyllum, many vigorous plantlets arise. Some begonias are increased in the same way.

CUTTINGS. Parts of plants cut (or sometimes broken) from a parent plant and inserted in water, sand, soil, peat moss, or some other medium where they form roots and become new plants are known as cuttings. By this method of propagation (which see) as well as by division, layering or budding (all of which see), plants which are identical with the parent are reproduced. In this way new forms, which have been created by hybridization or discovered as variations or "sports" (which see) from the normal type, are increased and a stock of plants built up. Seeds from such new forms, if produced (sometimes such plants are sterile), are apt to revert to a previous type, but cuttings will reproduce in kind the plant from which they were severed. And they provide a simple, convenient and inexpensive method for increasing one's stock of a particular plant. Most plants are easily multiplied by this method; some are increased more favorably by division, layering, or grafting or budding; and though herbaceous plants are commonly propagated by seed, many may also be grown from cuttings or layers when desired.

Cuttings may be classified either according to the plant parts used—as roots, tubers, rhizomes, stems or leaves—or according to the stage of development of the parts—as dormant, ripe or hardwood cuttings or active, that is, green, immature or softwood cuttings.

HARDWOOD CUTTINGS. Hardwood cuttings are generally used in propagating grapes, such soft-wooded trees as willows and poplars, and bushes such as gooseberries and currants. In late autumn after the leaves have fallen the stems are cut to the desired length (generally 6 to 10 in.), tied in bundles and buried, butt-ends upward, below the frost line in the soil. Or, they may be taken in winter and buried in sand, peat moss or sphagnum moss and kept moist and cool in a cellar. These fall- and winter-made cuttings form good calluses (protective coverings of new cells on the cut surfaces), and therefore root more freely than cuttings made in spring.

When spring comes, the calloused hardwood cuttings are unearthed and planted, usually 4 to 8 in. apart, erect or slanting, preferably in light, well-drained soil with adequate moisture provided for the butt. Both root and stem development will be facilitated if the lower buds on the cuttings, especially on short-jointed stock, are removed. Plants grown outdoors from such ripe or hardwood cuttings may be transplanted to nursery rows or (in the case of grapes, especially) to permanent quarters after the first season.

SOFTWOOD CUTTINGS. Green or softwood cuttings are generally rooted in greenhouses or coldframes or, on a small scale, in boxes or pots in a warm room in the dwelling. The "wood" should be taken from vigorous plants at a stage when it breaks with a snap when bent. If it merely crushes between the fingers, it is too young

to use; if it bends without breaking, it it too old and tough. After a little practice, the favorable stage can be recognized without difficulty.

Convenient lengths for greenwood cuttings are 2 to 4 in. The base should be cut straight across just below a node, or joint. The top should be cut slanting with a bud (or a node from which a bud will sprout) just below the tip. There should be two or three nodes on each cutting. Lower leaves are usually cut off, both to facilitate handling and to reduce transpiration. If the remaining leaves are large, as on a begonia, from a third to a half of each is cut away to prevent too much water from being evaporated from their surface. But some leaf surface should be left to carry on the life processes while the cutting is forming roots.

Because it provides perfect drainage, sand or fine gravel which is quite free from clay or decaying organic matter, is a favorite medium in which to root softwood cuttings. Sterilization (which see) by baking, boiling water, steam, chemicals, or electricity reduces the possibility of damping-off (which see)—the decay of seedlings and cuttings by various fungi at the ground surface. Much experimenting is being done and mixtures of peat moss and sand and even peat moss alone are being found highly satisfactory for certain kinds of plants.

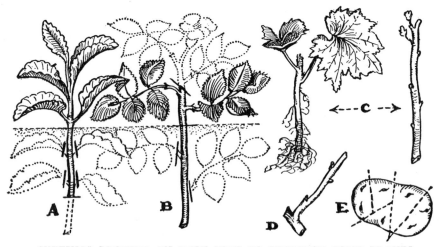

CUTTINGS PROVIDE AN EASY WAY TO INCREASE SOME PLANTS
(A) A greenwood Coleus cutting inserted in sand to root. (B) A hardwood rose cutting similarly handled. In each case, first trim off parts shown by dotted lines. (C) Two grape cuttings after 6 weeks in sand; the one without any leaves failed to make roots. (D) A "mallet" cutting taken with a bit of the parent stem is sometimes used. (E) Pieces of "seed" potato are also cuttings.

To prepare a propagating bed for rooting cuttings, level the sand perfectly, water it, and pack it firmly by pressing it with a level board. Then take a straight-edged board and at regular intervals with a blunt-tipped dibber make holes for the insertion of the cuttings. Press each cutting gently but firmly against the flat bottom of the hole, and bring the loose sand around it so that it can stand alone. The sand in the whole bed must always be kept level. Except for the cuttings of certain plants, such as cacti, which need to be calloused before they are started in sand, softwood cuttings should be transferred as rapidly as possible from parent plant to and into the propagating bed. They should be kept cool and shaded while the work is being done, but should not be placed in water with the idea of keeping them fresh.

When they are all in place in the bed of sand, drench them with water from a fine rose sprinkler and cover them lightly with newspapers to give shade and reduce transpiration until the roots begin to form. When the root system develops, they can take in from the soil all the water they need, and can then be given more sunshine to aid their growth. But during the first two weeks they need protection from strong light, as well as good ventilation and constant moisture. If given moderate bottom heat (which see) roots will form more quickly.

When roots are ¼ to ½ in. long, the cuttings may be transferred to 2-in. flower-pots, one to a pot, and again given plenty of water to encourage their growth. When the roots fill these pots, the young plants should be shifted to the next size larger, and so on until they reach the largest size pot required or until they are set outdoors. See POTTING; POT PLANTS.

On a small scale, greenwood cuttings may be started in soup-plates or saucers ⅔ full of sand and kept brimming with water. Shading is not so essential with these.

LEAF CUTTINGS. Cuttings may often be made from leaves of certain plants that are succulent or fleshy. A mature leaf of the Rex begonia can be cut from a plant, slashed at each point where two large veins unite, placed flat on wet sand and weighted down with pebbles. If handled from this stage like a softwood cutting, such a leaf will develop tiny new plants at many if not all of the points where cuts were made.

Some leaves, when treated thus, should be pulled from the parent plant with a bit of the main stem adhering to the base. This stump should be buried, and the leaf itself held flat on the sand by the pebbles or with little pegs. Gloxinia leaves, when

THE UBIQUITOUS CUTWORM
One of the commonest and most exasperating enemies of young plants. If disturbed when at work it curls up and "plays possum"—which is a good time to dispose of it.

inserted in sand, form tubers at the base of the stem. When dried and rested for a while, they can be planted like ordinary tubers. Hyacinth leaves placed in wet sand often develop bulblets at their base.

ROOT CUTTINGS. Root cuttings may be used to propagate plants which naturally produce suckers from their roots—such as red raspberries and blackberries. In a sense, these are simply small divisions (which see). Bits of a root the size of a lead-pencil 2 to 4 in. long are stored over winter to form calluses, then planted in spring in a horizontal position, about 2 in. deep, preferably in sandy soil.

Rhizomes, which are underground stems, are treated similarly. The potato (which see) is the best example of cuttings made from a tuber.

See also PROPAGATION; DIVISION.

CUTWORM. A name given to the larvae or caterpillars of many species of moths, which cause various types of injury on many kinds of plants except those with woody stems. Crops seriously affected (especially in young stages) are beans, cabbage, corn, cotton, tomatoes, tobacco and clover, but newly set out ornamental seedlings are also often attacked.

The worms usually winter as small larvae in the soil under plant débris. In the spring the smooth, dull gray, green or brown, ravenously hungry caterpillars clean up tender young plants as they are set out. Generally they cut them off at or near the surface of the ground, but some species of cutworms climb up and eat the leaves. If disturbed, they curl up and "play dead" until unobserved, then swiftly burrow out of sight. In early summer the worms pupate, the somber colored moths emerging shortly afterward. Usually there is but one generation a year.

When numerous, cutworms can be most effectively fought by scattering a poison bran mash (see BRAN MASH) among newly set plants in the early evening, since the worms are night feeders. Any bait left in the morning should be gathered up or cultivated under before chickens are allowed near. Individual plants, like cabbage, tomatoes, etc., can be protected by wrapping the stems in 6-in. long strips of paper a couple of inches wide so that half will be below and half above ground level; small tar-paper disks, which can be homemade or bought at seed stores, can also be slipped about the stems. Spraying larger plants with a poison such as arsenate of lead will control the climbing species that feed on leaves and flowers.

CYANIDE COMPOUNDS. Hydrocyanic acid gas, a deadly posion for all forms of life, used chiefly for fumigation, may be liberated from sodium, potassium, or calcium cyanide or from liquid hydrocyanic acid. Calcium cyanide (available in proprietary form), in addition to its use as a fumigant, is sometimes used as an insecticidal dust against chinch bugs, pear psylla and aphids on some horticultural crops. See FUMIGATION.

CYANOTIS (sy-ah-noh'-tis). Perennial herbs with weak or creeping stems, native in warm countries, belonging to the Spiderwort Family. They resemble tradescantia (which see) and are grown under similar conditions in the greenhouse.

C. barbata has long branching stems, narrow leaves and blue flowers. *C. kewensis* is prostrate, with reddish-hairy stems and rosy-purple flowers. *C. somaliensis* has narrow-triangular leaves, and dense heads of blue flowers.

CYATHEA (sy-ath'-e-ah). A genus of ferns, with cup-like indusia. Generally tree ferns. They are suitable for the warm greenhouse only.

CYCAD (sy'-kad); **CYCADACEAE** (syk-a-day'-see-ee). Common and family names for an ancient and primitive group of plants, interesting and decorative, of slow growth, and often grown in greenhouses in pots or tubs, or planted out in conservatory beds. In warm regions they make good specimen plants outdoors, and in the N. they are effective plunged outside for the summer in subtropical arrangements.

In pots or tubs they thrive in good fibrous loam with sand; while good drainage is essential, they need abundant moisture in the growing season. The long pinnately-divided stiff evergreen leaves are arranged in rosette form at the top of a short stout trunk; in some species they are cut and used for decorative purposes. Propagation is by seeds and also by suckers, which are best taken from dormant plants and from which the old leaves are removed.

The following genera (which see) are well known in cultivation—Ceratozamia, Cycas, Encephalartos and Zamia, the last one known popularly as coontie.

CYCLAMEN (sik'-lah-men). A genus of European and Asiatic plants with attractive flowers whose petals are sharply reflexed (as in the shooting-star) and whose heart-shaped leaves are mottled with white along the veins. They grow from corm-like tubers.

The large-flowered cyclamens of the florists, which come in all shades of red as well as white, are hybrids developed from *Cyclamen persicum* (formerly *C. indicum*) by constant breeding and selection. Started from seed, which comes true to color, cyclamens take from 15 to 18 months to reach maturity. The tubers which they produce do not make as free-flowering plants as the specimens raised from seed, hence tubers are seldom used in growing the commercial florist's varieties.

In Europe, however, the tubers of the small, rose-purple flowered *C. europaeum* are gathered from the wild and planted in gardens. When obtainable in America, this species blooms in Aug. in rock gardens in the N. States and Canada. *C. neapolitanum*, with pink and white flowers, blooms still later.

Great care must be exercised in the raising of cyclamens in the greenhouse, as they have numerous enemies (see below). Seed sown in early winter will germinate after the tuber has formed below ground, in about 2 months. When 2 leaves appear, set several plants in a 4- or 5-in. pot. A fresh, fibrous, well-drained loam containing one-fifth well-rotted horse manure is best for their potting mixture. Move each plant to a 3-in. pot when root growth

A PERFECT CYCLAMEN
High class seed and intensively careful culture are needed for such results.

demands the space. The plants may be set outdoors in the summer and shifted again while there. They require abundant light but some shading on hot summer days.

DISEASES. A soft, slimy, bacterial rot that affects the crowns of cyclamens results in stunting, wilting and loss of leaves. Destroy infected plants. See that healthy ones are not too wet and that there is proper ventilation. Various fungi, including gray mold or botrytis blight, may also appear on the leaves of plants kept too wet. Destroy infected parts, clean up rubbish around the pots, ventilate to keep surface of plants free from moisture and use care in watering. Young plants may be sprayed with bordeaux mixture.

Another fungus causes conspicuous stunting and reddish-brown diseased areas in the corms, but rarely kills plants. The only control measure yet discovered is to plant seeds from healthy plants in new or sterilized soil.

INSECT PESTS. Knotty growths or galls on the roots may be due to nematodes (which see).

The cyclamen mite is serious on both greenhouse and out-door plants. This minute animal feeds in the crevices of the tips of plants or buds, resulting in stunted and distorted plant growth. Severely infested plants do not flower. The broad mite, a related species, often causes a downward puckering of the leaves, and a silvery, blistered appearance on the under side. Dusting frequently with fine sulphur is somewhat effective. Potted plants

may also be immersed for 15 minutes in water at 111 deg. F. Balls of paradichlorobenzene, about ¾ in. in diameter, may be placed in the pots every two weeks. Strict greenhouse sanitation is important and fumigation may be practiced if necessary. See GREENHOUSE PESTS.

To control the black vine weevil which, common on Yew (which see), may chew cyclamen roots, work lead arsenate into the soil.

CYCLANTHERA (sy-klan-thee'-rah). Annual or perennial vines, native mostly in tropical America, belonging to the Cucumber Family. One or two species are grown as ornamental vines for screening purposes, being treated as tender annuals. They climb by tendrils.

C. explodens, growing to 10 ft., with 3-angled or lobed leaves, bears short spiny, usually curved fruits, which burst open when ripe. *C. pedata,* growing to 10 ft. or more, has leaves of 5 to 7 narrow leaflets, and oblong fruit about 2 in. long, often with soft prickles.

CYCLOPHORUS (sy-kloh-foh'-rus). A small genus of ferns, suitable for the greenhouse. The fronds are variously shaped according to the species, but all are simple and long and tapering at each end, from ½ to 3 ft. long. The best known species is *C. lingua,* the Felt Fern or Tongue Fern. The compost should be mostly peat, with some sand.

CYCLAMEN FLOWERS
From the original simple flower (a), plantsmen have developed numerous bizarre effects, as in in the Rococo type (b).

CYDONIA (sy-doh'-ni-ah). A shrub or small tree (*C. oblonga*) from Persia and Turkestan, belonging to the Rose Family. It has long been cultivated for its fruit, which is used in the making of choice preserves.

See QUINCE.

The so-called Japanese- or Flowering-Quince, often listed as Cydonia, is now placed in the genus Chaenomeles; in this book it is, however, also treated under QUINCE.

CYMBALARIA (sim-bah-lay'-riah). A group of creeping herbaceous perennials of the Figwort Family, formerly classed as Linaria. The plants are tender in cold climates, but seed themselves and thrive in moist and partly shaded positions. Some are grown as ground covers in the open or in the greenhouse, or in vases or hanging baskets or on walls. Propagation is by seeds or by division of the long stems. The best known is Kenilworth Ivy, *C. muralis*, a shade-loving plant, bearing lilac-blue flowers with yellow throats. There are several varieties: *alba* has white flowers, *maxima* is a larger form, and *rosea* bears pink blossoms.

CYMBIDIUM (sin-bi'-di-um). A genus of decorative epiphytic orchids having long arching or erect spikes of white, dull-purple or greenish-yellow blossoms. Some of the species are native of the high mountains of Asia and therefore succeed best in an intermediate temperature. While growing, water the roots plentifully, but after growth is completed decrease the supply of moisture, allowing them to rest during the months of Sept. and Oct. After the period of rest they will bloom, the charming flowers lasting in perfection for a number of weeks.

One of the loveliest species is *C. eburneum* with ivory-white flowers, occasionally tinged with pink, about 3 in. across, appearing in Apr. and May. There are also many remarkably fine hybrid forms with delicate, soft colorings, among them *C. alexanderi*, a cross between *C. veitchi* and *C. insigne*.

CYMBOPOGON (sim-boh-poh'-gon). A genus of tall, mostly perennial, grasses, natives of the tropics, and useful for border planting. They grow to a height of 6 ft., and have fragrant leaves to 3 ft. long and ¾ in. wide, covered with a whitish bloom. The flower clusters may be 2½ ft. long. *C. nardus* (Citronella Grass) has tapering, lance-like spikelets, while those of *C. citra-*

tus (Lemon Grass) are linear and not tapering. *C. choenanthus* (Camel-hay) is a dwarf species, to 2 ft., with the joints of its flower clusters covered with hair. Citronella oil, used as a deterrent against mosquitoes, is derived from *C. nardus* and other species.

See ORNAMENTAL GRASSES.

CYME (sym). A more or less flat-topped, often branched cluster of flowers in which those in the center bloom first. The blossoming moves outward toward the perimeter of the cluster. Contrast CORYMB.

CYNANCHUM (sy-nan'-chum) *acuminatifolium*. A hardy Japanese herb of the Milkweed Family bearing white flowers in summer; the Mosquito-trap, which see.

CYNARA (sin'-ah-rah). A genus of about a dozen Old World thistle-like perennial herbs with large purple, blue, or white flowers. Two species frequently grown in gardens as vegetables are *C. scolymus*, the French or Globe artichoke, and *C. cardunculus*, which is cardoon. See ARTICHOKE; CARDOON.

CYNOGLOSSUM (sin-oh-glos'-um). A genus of stiffly-hairy herbs of the Borage Family, popularly known as Hounds Tongue, which see.

CYPELLA (sy-pel'-ah). Bulbous plants of S. America, belonging to the Iris Family. They may be grown outdoors in the summer and lifted and stored over winter. Propagated by offsets and seeds. *C. herberti* has narrow plaited leaves about 1 ft. long, and a flower-stem to 3 ft., with several rather fleeting yellow flowers about 3 in. across. *C. peruviana* is smaller, with yellow brown-spotted flowers.

CYPERACEAE (sy-pur-ay'-see-ee). The Sedge Family, a group of perennial grass-like herbs but distinguished from the grasses by their solid three-angled stems, the leaves borne in closed sheaths and the very different flowers borne on spikes. Distributed around the world, the sedges are commonly found in low marshy places, whence their principal use as ornamentals in the water garden. Species of only a few genera are cultivated, principally Cyperus, Carex, Scirpus and Eriophorum.

CYPERUS (sy-pee'-rus). Two species of this genus of moisture-loving sedges are probably the most commonly encountered cultivated members of the Sedge Family. Both are perennials.

C. alternifolius is a splendid plant for the shallow water at the edge of the pond, or for the large aquarium. It requires a rich soil and, as long as its roots are wet, thrives equally well indoors or outside. Indeed, it survives as a house plant under conditions other plants find impossible. Growing to 3 or 4 ft. high, in appearance it resembles a miniature clump of palm trees and well deserves its popular name of Umbrella-palm. The leaf crown will produce new plants if cut off and pressed flat into damp sand or moss. The var. *gracilis* is smaller and perhaps more suited to the aquarium.

C. *papyrus* (formerly *Papyrus antiquorum*), the plant from which the ancient Egyptians made paper, grows from 10 to 15 ft. tall in a summer and displays at the top of each giant stem a mop-like crown of fine, grassy leaves. It should be planted in a box of rich soil and submerged in shallow water. As it is tender, this will facilitate its removal indoors at the approach of frost. Propagation is by division of the root clump in the spring or early summer while the plant is in a vigorous growing condition, or from seed.

See also AQUATIC PLANTS.

CYPRESS. Common name for genus Cupressus, about 12 species and many varieties of evergreen tree, members of the Pine Family, native in N. America, Europe and Asia. Some have very dark foliage and are very distinctive in form, attaining 80 ft. Most of them are hardy only in the Gulf States and in Calif. They thrive in deep sandy loam soil, are ornamental in youth and picturesque in maturity, living to a great age. Some are dense and bushy; some flat topped with horizontal branching, while others are sharply pyramidal and compact. Age gives to them all a singular beauty that lends itself to a garden of simple design. Like other long-lived trees, the Cypress should be given more consideration in garden design, for it helps place the gardener in his true position as a creator of enduring pictures. It is propagated from seed.

DISEASES. Pecky heartwood decay is the only important fungous disease attacking the common bald cyprus (Taxodium). It causes a worm-eaten appearance familiar to all who handle cypress timber. But, strangely enough, the presence of the fungus brings about a sort of preservative action that enables the rest of the wood to resist ordinary rots. For this reason the so-called "pecky cypress" lumber is exceptionally durable and especially favored for building greenhouse benches, hotbed frames and other structures where strength and appearance are secondary factors.

The canker disease of Monterey cypress (*C. macrocarpa*) in some sections of the W. coast kills the top branches and patches

AN AGED CYPRESS, DWARFED
The Japanese are masters of the art of growing a tree for scores or even hundreds of years in a flower pot. Their products make interesting subjects for indoor decoration.

of bark; trees may be killed or so deformed as to lose their ornamental value. Remove all affected branches promptly.

PESTS. Cypress is comparatively free from insect pests but the larvae of a small moth may brown the foliage of bald cypress by feeding on it. Control by spraying early in the season with lead arsenate. The cypress bark-scale turns the limbs of Monterey cypress yellow, then red or brown, and may seriously damage thickly planted hedge rows. It may also attack the Arizona and Guadaloupe cypress and Incense-cedar. Spray in August and again the latter part of September with a miscible oil emulsion.

PRINCIPAL SPECIES

The Macnab Cypress (*C. macnabiana*) grows to 20 ft. and has fragrant foliage. It is the hardiest species for, although native to southern Oregon and Calif., it is hardy from Mass. to Mo. and southward. Bushy and of slow growth, it is especially valuable in garden design. The Monterey Cypress (*C. macrocarpa*) is found only along the coast of S. Calif., but will grow throughout the Southern States as far north as Va. Attaining a height of 75 ft., it is pyramidal in youth, becoming flat topped in old age with ascending branches and a bare high trunk. It would fit in well with dwarfer evergreens of similar character, and lends itself to dry rock gardens near the sea.

The Arizona Cypress (*C. arizonica*), being native to the S. half of Arizona, is particularly adapted to dry soils and drought conditions; it is hardy from Va. to Ark. and southward. Narrowly pyramidal to a height of 40 ft., it can be effectively used to frame entrances and doorways and to terminate axes. *C. sargenti,* with about the same range, is another fragrant-leaved species growing only to 16 ft.; also useful as a foil and hedge.

The Italian Cypress (*C. sempervirens*) to 80 ft. is hardy from N. C. to Ark. and southward. In its native S. Europe and W. Asia, it is famous as a garden subject, having been used for centuries. Its foliage is dark green and its form like that of the Lombardy Poplar; the narrow columnar variety, *stricta,* has been extensively used in Calif. gardens.

The Pond, Ball, and Montezuma Cypresses are species of Taxodium; False-cypress is Chamaecyparis; Standing-cypress is *Gilia rubra,* and Summer-cypress is *Kochia scorparia.*

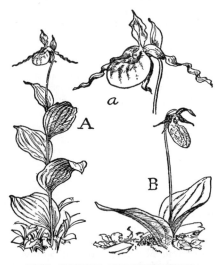

TWO NATIVE CYPRIPEDIUMS
The large yellow Lady-slipper (A) with its interesting flower (a) is charming when carefully brought from the woods into the wild garden. The pink Stemless Lady-slipper (B), however, should not be uprooted, as it will not stand transplanting. Because of their rarity, neither should be picked.

CYPRESS SPURGE. Common name for *Euphorbia, cyparissias,* a small fine-leaved perennial useful as a ground cover.

CYPRESS-VINE. An annual tropical, quick-growing member of the Morning-glory Family, known also as Star-glory, formerly listed as *Ipomoea quamoclit,* but now as *Quamoclit pennata.*

CYPRIPEDIUM (sip-ri-pee'-di-um). A genus of hardy orchids, commonly known as Lady-slippers, having white, yellow, pink or rose-purple flowers with large sac-like lips. They may be naturalized in the wild or bog garden, the different species often having quite different cultural and soil requirements. They are best increased by division as it is exceedingly difficult to grow them from seed.

C. acaule (Stemless Lady-slipper; Pink Moccasin-flower) to 12 in., has two deeply ridged, oval leaves, flat on the ground, and a single rose-pink or purple blossom, with a very large pouch netted with purple veins. Occasionally a pure white form is found. Usually growing in shady woods in very acid soil, this stately flower is difficult to transplant, and should not be carelessly uprooted, but left to multiply in its native habitat. See WILD GARDEN.

parviflorum (Yellow Lady-slipper) has 1 to 2 flowers on a leafy stalk, sometimes 2 ft. high. The flowers are yellow and the golden lip is smooth and egg-shaped. Taking kindly to cultivation and growing well in ordinary garden soil, this graceful, bright-colored flower may be easily naturalized in a sheltered spot in the wild garden, the clumps increasing constantly in size and beauty of flower.

reginae (Showy or Queen Lady-slipper) has a handsome leafy stalk to 3 ft. surmounted by 1 or 2, occasionally 3 or 4, white-petaled flowers, having large, almost round lips, flushed or veined with pink. Native of bogs and moist woodland, this strikingly beautiful orchid may be easily naturalized on hummocks in lightly shaded spots in the bog garden, where it gets constant moisture and perfect drainage. It grows luxuriantly in limestone regions, but also thrives in neutral soil. This species, formerly known as *C. spectabile,* is the State flower of Minn.

CYRILLA (si-ril'-ah). A deciduous or semi-evergreen shrub or tree commonly known as Leatherwood, which see.

CYRTOMIUM (sir-toh'-mi-um). A genus of ferns with rounded indusia. The best species is *C. falcatum,* the Tender Holly Fern, an excellent house plant with glossy distinct pinnae and chaffy stipes. Give leafmold and sand and rest it occasionally. (See illustration, Plate 18.)

CYSTOPTERIS (sis-top'-ter-is). Bladder Ferns. A genus of ferns whose scientific and common names both refer to the swollen indusium. The two species native and hardy in this country do well in the garden, in proper soil. The first of these is *C. fragilis* (Fragile Bladder Fern). With oblong spear-shaped fronds, 5 to 15 in. tall, 2-pinnate, the cutting varying greatly; the stipes long, brittle and often dark brown; the fruit-dots dark, small and inconspicuous. Common in rocky woods, especially near waterfalls. Needs dampness and shade, prefers limestone. The second is *C. bulbifera* (Berry Bladder Fern). Tapering, 1 to 3 ft. fronds, clear light green and rippled, often reclining; 2-pinnate, pinnae rather distant and toothed; fruit dots as in *C. fragilis.* Rachis and pinnae often bear green bulblets beneath, which drop and give birth to new plants. One of the most graceful of our native ferns, splendid for clothing slopes in shade, it spreads rapidly. It prefers woods soil near rock, preferably limestone.

CYTISUS (sit'-i-sus). Broom. Attractive shrubs, native in Europe, Asia and Africa, belonging to the Pea Family. The species are deciduous or evergreen, and in some cases almost leafless. One or two are popular greenhouse plants, and several can be grown outdoors in the North if given suitable conditions. They require full exposure to sun and wind and perfect drainage at the roots, and prefer poor soil to rich. The taller kinds are likely to become straggly unless pruned back after flowering. Small plants are easier to establish than large ones. Propagated by seeds, cuttings, layers and grafting. Following are the principal species:

C. scoparius (Scotch Broom; sometimes locally called Shower o' Gold), is a European shrub to 10 ft. that has become naturalized in some parts of N. America. It is of value for planting on dry gravelly banks, and makes a good showing with its bright green stems and yellow flowers. Var. *andreanus* has very striking flowers of yellow and crimson, but is more tender.

C. supinus (better known as *C. capitatus*) is a hardy low shrub of dense habit, with terminal heads of yellow flowers in summer. *C. nigricans* is a slender grower to 4 ft. with spikes of clear yellow flowers in midsummer, and *C. multiflorus* (White Spanish Broom) is a slender grower to 3 ft. bearing a profusion of white flowers. One of the showiest is *C. praecox,* a vigorous growing hybrid to 10 ft. with a mass of sulphur-yellow flowers.

C. albus (creamy-white), *C. ardoini* (deep yellow), *C. beani* (golden yellow), *C. kewensis* (creamy-white), and *C. purpureus* (purple) are all of somewhat prostrate habit, and suitable for planting in rock gardens or on slopes where hardy.

C. canariensis is the well-known Genista (which see) of the florist. *C. racemosus* is very similar. Both are popular evergreen shrubs for winter and spring flowering under glass. They grow well in a sandy loam. After plants have flowered, trim them back to compact shape and plunge outdoors during the summer.

DABOËCIA (da-boh-ee'-si-ah) *cantabrica*. A low evergreen shrub, native in Ireland and S. W. Europe and belonging to the Heath Family, hence commonly called Irish or St. Dabeocs Heath. It is suitable for planting in the rock garden, thriving in peaty soil; but it requires winter protection N. It grows a foot or more high, with small shining green leaves, whitish beneath, and nodding purple flowers. Var. *alba* is a white-flowered form, and var. *bicolor* has flowers striped white and purple. It is propagated by cuttings of half-ripened shoots under glass. The plant was formerly listed as *Daboëcia* (or *Menziesia*) *polifolia*.

DACRYDIUM (da-krid'-i-um). Evergreen trees of New Zealand and Tasmania, with scale-like leaves, belonging to the Yew Family. In their native climate they grow to 100 ft. high, but they are hardy only in the warmest parts of this country. *D. cupressinum*, the Red-pine or "Rimu" of New Zealand, has long graceful pendulous branches when young. *D. franklini*, the Huon-pine of Tasmania, is conspicuous because of its slender thread-like drooping branchlets.

DACTYLIS (dak'-ti-lis). A genus of tall perennial grasses of which the most important is *D. glomerata*, a pasture and forage plant known as Orchard Grass, which see.

DADDY-LONG-LEGS. A common or child's name for insects belonging to the spider group and also called harvestmen. They resemble round-bodied, very long-legged spiders, the legs being carried with the "knees" high. It is not known whether this creature feeds on injurious insects enough to be called beneficial, but it does not bite, sting or injure plants so it is certainly not harmful or objectionable.

DAFFODIL. (See illustrations, Plates 5, 6 and 50.) Common name often applied indiscriminately to any kind of Narcissus (which see), but which correctly refers to several of the hardy types, especially the larger, single flowered trumpet sorts. It is not the same as Jonquil, which see.

Peruvian-daffodil is *Hymenocallis* (formerly *Ismene*) *callathina*, a species of the S. American bulbous plant spider-lily, which see.

DAFFODIL POISONING. An irritation of the skin of hands and arms caused by the juice from daffodil leaves and flowers, occasionally troublesome to those who pick or handle them in quantity. Like the effects of other poisonous plants (which see), it is not fully understood and, although various treatments have been recommended, there does not seem to be any known sure cure. One florist has suggested: (1) Scrub hands with soap and water as hot as can be borne as soon as possible after handling daffodils (or Primula obconica). (2) Rub hands if infected with 3 per cent carbolated vaseline to stop itching and check the poisoning. (3) Wash affected parts in a solution of 1 to 2 teaspoonfuls of permanganate of potash in 1 gallon of water. It is reported that there are immunizing drugs that can be taken internally to prevent such poisoning, but any such precautions should be taken only under a doctor's direction.

DAGGER FERN (*Polystichum munitum*). A tall fern of the Far West, with simple pointed pinnae of coarse texture, good for the garden in woods soil and shade. The name is used also for other species of Polystichum, which see.

DAHLIA (dal'-yah). (See illustrations, Plates 12 and 13.) A genus of tender herbaceous perennial plants growing from tuberous roots, not hardy in the colder climates of the U. S., where they are treated more as annuals, the tubers being stored over winter and planted after danger of frost has passed. The color range of the dahlia blossom is wide, embodying practically all colors and combinations of colors except blues.

Discovered in the mountains of Mexico in the 16th century by a Spanish physician sent by King Philip II to study the natural history of that country, it was first described under the native name of Acoctii. Some two centuries later—about 1789—plants and seeds were first sent to various parts of Europe, some of them going to Andreas Dahl, a Swedish botanist and student of the great Linnaeus. He became so interested in the plant and so identified with its culture and development, that later, in his honor, the name Dahlia was given to the genus. He is also sometimes, though erroneously, given credit for its discovery. The original species was at that time named *D. variabilis* and aptly, since today thousands of its named hybrids exist as the result of its variability. The name has since been changed to *D. pinnata*. The parent of the cactus form (*D. juarezi*) likewise originated in Mexico but at a much later date—1879.

CULTURAL DIRECTIONS

SOIL AND SITE. There is a common, but erroneous, impression that the plant is not particular about soil or location. Since it is native to a hot, high, dry climate, a dahlia, however variable, needs a soil that is well drained. In wet, heavy, poorly drained soils where water settles, plants cannot thrive and will almost surely die. But under favorable conditions, a single tuber, planted at the beginning of the growing season, will show an increase of from 5 to 15 tubers (depending upon the variety planted), forming a clump by the end of the growing season. This shows the gross feeding capacity of the plant, whose rootlets shoot out from the tubers in all directions. Briefly, well-drained, loamy soils in which quantities of humus or well decayed leafmold have been well mixed is the soil best suited to dahlias.

PLANTING. Planting time is mid-spring after all danger of frost has passed, the exact dates depending, of course, on the locality and season. Being of tropical or subtropical origin a dahlia plant can be easily and sometimes seriously checked and stunted if hit by a late freeze or a spell of cold, wet weather in early spring. Sufficient space should be allowed in planting. 36 in. between plants in the row and at least the same distance between the rows are minimum dimensions for the taller growing decoratives, etc. For the miniatures, this space may be less; but for best results dahlias, no matter what the type, should never be crowded.

After the soil has been prepared and stout stakes driven at the correct distances *before planting* (so that the roots will not be injured), the soil should be drawn away from a stake, and a tuber laid flat on the soil with the new growth or sprout end nearest the stake. The depression must be deep enough so that when the soil is all replaced (this is done gradually as growth proceeds) at least 6 in. of soil will cover the tuber. As the

plants grow, the stems should be securely (but not tightly) fastened to the stakes, preferably with some wide material; strips of strong cloth about 1 in. wide will prevent the destruction of many of the hollow, pithy stalks during storms or high winds. Cord is not suitable since it will often cut through the hollow stalk. See TYING.

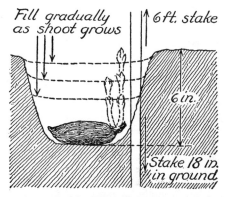

HOW TO PLANT A DAHLIA TUBER
Put the stake in place beside the 6 in. hole. Then lay the tuber horizontally with stem and near stake and gradually fill the depression with soil as the young shoots grow.

DISBUDDING. When plants reach a height of 1 ft.—about July first—the tips, if desired, may be pinched out, leaving two sets of two leaves each remaining upon the plant. At the junction of each of these four remaining leaves with the main stem, a new flowering branch will take the place of the single main stem whose tip was removed. This will retard the flowering season from 10 days to 2 weeks, which is desirable, since the finest flowers are always produced upon the younger, more tender growth. All flower buds should be removed until August first, after which time they may be allowed to mature.

As growth proceeds, at the end of each flowering stalk, flower buds will appear, a center bud and two side buds, and at the junction of each leaf and stalk below the tip, three more buds will appear, the leaves being upon opposite sides of the stalk and the flowering buds always appearing in threes. For large exhibition flowers, allow the tip or center bud to remain, pinching out the two side buds. The two series of buds next below the terminal or tip bud should then be removed taking care that the leaves are not injured, since foliage counts for points as well as flowers in the exhibitions. This disbudding should give the terminal bud a stem 18 to 24 in. long. It may be further lengthened by removing the third series of buds.

Disbudding, as described, relates only to the decorative forms (both formal and informal), to straight and incurved cactus forms and to the peony-flowered types. It should not be practiced with the collarettes, miniatures, etc., where a wealth of bloom is desired rather than size of bloom.

FEEDING AND CULTIVATING. As to food —assuming the soil contains plenty of humus-making material and is well drained —the plants will require regular applications of a complete fertilizer at intervals of about one month, beginning when the plants are 1 ft. high. Such a fertilizer should be high in its phosphoric acid and potash content, and relatively low in nitrogen, since the dahlia plant is naturally leafy. Under no circumstance should ordinary horse manure alone be used, as it would produce a rank growth of foliage and but insignificant flowers, if any.

Cultivation must follow every application of fertilizer and every rain so that a dust mulch (not over an inch or two deep) is maintained at all times. This makes

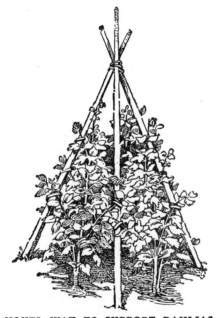

NOVEL WAY TO SUPPORT DAHLIAS
One grower sets tall stakes in a triable, ties them together at top, and plants three tubers at the base of the pyramid, and ties side branches to the stakes. But don't let the foliage get so dense that pests and diseases are encouraged under the "tent."

the plant food available for the roots and keeps weeds in check. Green cover-crops (which see) of rye, vetch, etc., grown over the winter and turned under in the early spring to decay will keep dahlia soil in ideal condition.

Where it is desired to hasten growth for backward plants or to meet exhibition dates, this result may be brought about by the use of liquid manures. Sulphate of ammonia, nitrate of soda, or urea may be used at the rate of not more than 1 teaspoonful to a gallon of water and applied at intervals of two or three weeks. These are not complete foods, however, and will not take the place of the complete formulas; they supply nitrogen only and are used solely for forcing purposes.

FALL CARE. After plants have been cut down by a killing frost, remove the tops leaving stubs 6 in. tall. Allow the clumps to remain in the soil for 10 days or 2 weeks to thoroughly ripen, after which time they may be removed. But use great care so that the narrow neck which connects the tuber and the clump is not injured or the tender skin of the neck broken, otherwise a blind tuber results. When the clumps have dried out so the soil shakes freely from them, they may be stored for the winter in quarters where they will neither freeze nor dry out as a result of exposure to the air. A cellar that will keep potatoes in good condition will answer the purpose. The clumps may be packed in boxes or barrels, either covered with any light, perfectly dry material such as bran or sawdust, or wrapped well in dry newspapers, and then stored where they cannot absorb dampness. Cold rooms partitioned off in the cellar where the temperature may be kept in the forties prove ideal locations.

ENEMIES

INSECT PESTS. Dahlias are sometimes attacked by common stalk or stem borers— grayish-brown, white-striped larvae which cause wilting and sometimes the death of plants. Their presence can often be detected by finding a small hole and exudations of sawdust near the base of the stem. If discovered in time they can be killed and the plant saved, by carefully slitting the stem lengthwise with a sharp knife, by probing with a flexible wire, or by injecting carbon bisulphide or nicotine-sulphate paste. As the insects attack many weeds and the inconspicuous adult moths

Plate 13.   DAHLIAS—A DELIGHT IN THE FALL GARDEN

Upper left: An unusual form of white dahlia. Upper right: Informal decorative. Center left: Pompon dahlias are of compact growth, long lasting in the garden and when cut. Center right: The oddly quilled Cactus type. Bottom: Dahlias in the border provide a wealth of glowing color.

lay their eggs on them in the fall, keeping all weeds cut down in and around the garden will largely control this pest.

Over much of the N. Atlantic region, and especially in the New England States, the European corn borer is becoming an increasingly serious dahlia pest. Its control is difficult because it attacks so many hosts, including both useful plants and weeds. Suggestions are given under CORN, but wherever the insect is prevalent the state agricultural experiment station or county agent should be applied to for the latest information and advice. It is reported that rotenone sprays will kill young borers before they enter the stalks.

Chewing insects, such as the grasshopper, will attack at times but may be held under control or prevented by spraying with a stomach poison. See INSECTICIDE.

Plants which are stunted by the feeding activities of other insects (leaf hoppers, thrips, or plant bugs) will recover if these are destroyed with pyrethrum or other suitable sprays. The active tarnished plant bug (which see) causes blackening or unequal development of the flower buds; cleaning up garden rubbish where the insect may winter is one control method.

DISEASES. Dahlia stunt—which makes the plants short and bushy with an excessive number of side branches—may be caused by the feeding of insects or by mosaic disease. The latter is characterized by yellowish or pale green bands along the leaf veins or by general mottling, roughening, curling or crinkling of the leaves. Affected plants do not recover so should be destroyed. The disease is carried in cuttings and root divisions and by aphids, but not in seed; and it does not persist in the soil. Varieties known to be relatively resistant should be grown.

Three wilt diseases may affect dahlias. One is a soft, wet bacterial soft rot, showing a yellow ooze when the stem is cut; the other two are fungous diseases which cause browning of the stem tissues and a decay of stored tubers. Remove wilted plants and the soil immediately surrounding them immediately on discovery and select healthy plants for propagation. To prevent the rotting of the tubers in storage the clumps may be dusted with sulphur.

Mildew, a white coating over the leaves, may appear late in the season, but it is not particularly serious and is readily controlled by dusting with sulphur.

PROPAGATION METHODS

Dahlias may be propagated by division of the clumps, by cuttings taken from growing plants, and by seed. The dahlia does not grow from an eye like the potato; growth starts only at the junction of the narrow neck of the tuber and the tough wood of the old stem or stalk. In dividing a clump, therefore, each individual tuber must be cut in such a manner that some portion of the old stalk is attached to the neck of the tuber and with the skin about the neck unbroken, otherwise no growth will result. Growth of the sprouts in early spring is a guide to the division of the clumps which is the method usually followed by the amateur.

The commercial grower subjects the clumps to heat, light and moisture during February or early March, when growth quickly starts. When a new sprout has formed at least 2 sets of leaves, it may be cut off cleanly with a sharp knife or razor blade; cut close up to but just below the first set of leaves nearest the tuber. With the sharp blade remove, without tearing, the first or lower set of leaves and insert the resulting cutting up to the second set of leaves in sand in a hot bed or propagating box. The cuttings root readily in moist sand and will soon need to be transplanted into light soil and kept shaded for a few days to prevent wilting; it is well to spray them with a gentle spray two or three times a day until they are well started. Thereafter gradual exposure to sun and air will soon harden them off ready for their permanent bed.

Cuttings may also be taken from green, growing plants during August or early September. Taken from non-flower-bearing branches, they should be treated as above described, started in the smallest sized pots, shifted when necessary into the next larger size and encouraged to grow until the tops are cut down by frost. The tubers remain in the pot and are thus stored for the winter. Taken out at planting time, although they may have taken on curiously twisted shapes from having grown in a pot, they may be treated like any other tuber. Tubers from divisions of the clumps or developed from cuttings, either spring or fall, will all reproduce true.

Dahlias may also be propagated from seed sown in early spring under glass and planted out at the usual time. They will

THE MODERN DAHLIA OFFERS A VARIETY OF FLOWER FORMS

Here are shown the following types: (I) Cactus, (II) Single, (III) Pompon, (IV) Formal
Decorative, (V) Informal Decorative, (VI) Collarette, (VII) Anemone-flowered, and (VIII)
Peony-flowered.

bear flowers and from tubers during the same growing season but they will not reproduce true to the parent. Unless systematically handcrossed by experienced breeders, seedling plants rarely have exceptional value; if not superior (or at least equal) to existing varieties, such plants should be destroyed. Experienced growers, knowing that a change of soil, different climatic conditions and excessive food are all important factors in producing variability of this remarkable plant, use such knowledge in the further production of new and interesting varieties.

Blooms for Exhibition

Exhibition blooms to be in best form should be cut in the early morning or late evening, never during the heat of the day. Garden shears, if keen and sharp, should be used, and the cut made on a long angle so water may be freely taken up through the cells of the stem. If the stem is cut squarely across or torn or pinched together by a dull knife, water cannot be absorbed freely. As soon as cut the bloom should be deeply immersed in plain cold water and placed in a cool, dark, shaded position for 6 hours. In this time it will have absorbed all the water needed and be ready for showing or decorative use. If the stem is shortened daily by about one inch, if the cut is always made on a long angle and if fresh water is supplied, flowers should stay in perfect condition five days.

Classification of Dahlias

For exhibition purposes the American Dahlia Society has recently reclassified dahlias and its classification is now in general use, as follows:

Class 1, Incurved Cactus. Fully double flower with the margins of the majority of the floral rays revolute (rolled or quilled) for one-half or more of their length; the floral rays tending to curve toward the center of the flower.

Class 2, Recurved and Straight Cactus. Fully double flowers with the margins of the majority of the floral rays revolute for one-half of their length or more; the floral rays being recurved or straight.

Class 3, Peony. Open centered flowers with not more than three rows of ray florets regardless of form or number of florets, with the addition of smaller curled or twisted floral rays around the disk.

Class 4, Semi-cactus. Fully double flowers with the margins of the majority of the floral rays revolute for less than one-half their length.

Class 5, Formal Decorative. Fully double flowers, rays generally broad, either pointed or rounded at tips, with outer floral rays tending to recurve and central floral rays tending to be cupped, all floral rays in somewhat regular arrangement.

Class 6, Informal Decorative. Fully double flower, floral rays generally long, twisted or pointed and usually irregular in arrangement.

Class 7, Ball. Fully double flowers, ball shaped or slightly flattened, floral rays in spiral arrangement, blunt or rounded at tips and quilled or with markedly involute margins; 2 in. or more in diameter.

Class 8, Anemone. Open centered flowers with only one row of ray florets regardless of form or number of florets, with the tubular disk florets elongated, forming a pin cushion effect.

Class 9, Single. Open centered flowers, with only one row of ray flowers regardless of form or number of florets.

Class. 10, Duplex. Open centered flowers, with only two rows of ray florets regardless of form or number of florets.

Class 11, Pompon. Fully double flowers, ball-shaped or slightly flattened, floral rays in spiral arrangement, blunt or rounded and quilled or with markedly involute margins; less than 2 in. in diameter.

Class 12, Collarette. Open centered flower with only one row of ray florets, with the addition of one or more rows of petaloids, usually of a different color, forming a collar around the disc.

Class 13, Miniature Decorative. All dahlias which normally produce flowers that do not exceed 3 in. in diameter, pompons excluded, to be classified according to the foregoing definition.

Species

As already noted, the parent species of the familiar garden dahlias is *D. pinnata* (or *variabilis*), and that of the cactus dahlia, *D. juarezi*. Several other species are recognized and occasionally grown by specialists or in botanical collections. Though not really garden subjects, they merit mention, the principle ones being:

D. coccinea. Slender, to 4 ft.; single, typically 8-petaled flowers, scarlet above, lighter below.

excelsa (Flat Tree Dahlia), *imperialis* (Bell, Tree, or Candelabra Dahlia), and *maxoni*—all three tall, more or less woody forms to 20 ft. with single, usually 8-petaled flowers in pinks, reds and lavenders. Sometimes grown in S. Calif.

mercki (Bedding Dahlia), slender to 3 ft. with finely cut foliage and erect, single, lilac flowers.

popenovi. Bushy, to 4 ft. with scarlet single flowers with 8-quilled petals. It is thought to be an even older form than *D. juarezi* and is possibly the ultimate ancestor of the cactus dahlia.

DAHLIA SOCIETY, AMERICAN. Organized in 1915, this society has a nationwide membership of which about two-thirds are amateur growers. (There is also a separate smaller organization of commercial growers only.) Dedicated to the production of finer flowers, the standardization of types, the testing and appraising of new varieties, the dissemination of dahlia information and the stimulation of interest in and appreciation of dahlias, the Society publishes a quarterly bulletin, conducts one or more trial grounds, and holds one or more exhibitions annually, offering medals, cups and other trophies in many classes. Its membership includes active, life and honorary membership and the headquarters and secretary's office are at 251 Court St., New Haven, Conn.

DAHOON (dah-hoon'). Common name for *Ilex cassine,* an evergreen holly, native from Va. southward. See HOLLY.

DAISY. Now a common name for many Composite flowers, this originally meant the low, cheerful *Bellis perennis,* the "daisy" of poetry and literature but in America known as "English Daisy." In this country "Daisy" alone more often refers to *Chrysanthemum leucanthemum,* a European perennial that is now one of our most widespread pestiferous weeds on waste or mismanaged land; this same plant is also called Ox-eye Daisy and Whiteweed, though the former term more correctly belongs to *Rudbeckia hirta,* also known as Yellow Daisy and sometimes as Black-eyed-Susan.

"Daisy Family" is a term sometimes popularly used instead of the botanical term "Composite Family."

The name Daisy qualified by various words is applied to plants that belong to different genera and species mostly of the Composite Family as follows:

Paris Daisy or Marguerite (*Chrysanthemum frutescens*), a favorite pot plant much grown by florists.

African Daisy (*Arctotis staechadifolia* and also *Lonas inodora,* called by florists *Athanasia annua*); the Dimorphotheca of the garden is also often called African Daisy, but more properly Cape-marigold.

Blue Daisy (*Felicia amelloides*).

Barberton, or Transvaal Daisy (*Gerbera jamesoni*).

Michaelmas Daisy (*Aster tradescanti*).

Orange Daisy (*Erigeron aurantiacus*).

Seaside or Double Orange Daisy (*E. glaucus*).

Globe-Daisy (*Globularia trichosantha*).

Swan River Daisy (*Brachycome iberidifolia*).

Turfing Daisy (*Matricaria tchihatchewi*).

White Daisy (*Layia glandulosa*).

Crown or Garland Daisy (*Chrysanthemum coronarium*).

High or Giant Daisy (*C. uliginosum*).

Nippon Daisy (*C. nipponicum*).

Painted Daisy or Pyrethrum (*C. coccineum*).

Native Daisy of New Zealand (*Lagenophosa forsteri*).

Easter Daisy (*Townsendia exscapa*).

DAISY-TREE. A common name for a genus of evergreen shrubs and trees of the Composite Family, also called Tree-aster. See OLEARIA.

DALEA (day'-lee-ah). A genus of leguminous herbs or shrubs of N. and S. America, found in dry or even desert locations and bearing pea-like flowers of purple, white, or yellow. Sometimes used in gardens where conditions resemble their native habitat, but not important horticulturally. The species *D. spinosa,* an ashy gray, large, gaunt shrub of Colo. called Smoke-tree should not be confused with *Cotinus coggygria,* the Old-World deciduous shrub frequently seen in N. and E. gardens and called by the same common name because of its fluffy "smoky" appearance following its blossoming.

DALECHAMPIA (day-le-cham'-pi-ah). Mostly climbing shrubs of the tropics, belonging to the Euphorbia Family. Only one species appears to be in cultivation. This is *D. roezliana,* a small upright shrub, grown in warm greenhouses for its large and attractive rosy-pink bracts. Inside the two large outer bracts are smaller ones, placed among the small male and female flowers, which are of curious shape and yellowish in color. It requires perfect drainage, and a mixture of sandy loam, peat and leafmold. Propagation is by cuttings.

DALIBARDA (dal-i-bahr'-dah) *repens.* A N. American low-growing hardy herbaceous perennial, belonging to the Rose Family. It is of tufted creeping habit, with heart-shaped leaves and white strawberry-like flowers in summer. It is sometimes grown in the rock garden or border, thriving best in a rich woodsy soil.

DAMASK ROSE. Common name for *Rosa damascena,* a supposedly Asiatic bush species with flattish clusters of fragrant, pale pink or red, double flowers used for making attar of roses.

DAMES ROCKET or DAMES- or DAMASK-VIOLET. A coarse, branching perennial with fragrant, purple to white, single and double flowers. See HESPERIS.

DAMMAR- (dam'-ahr) **PINE.** Common name for the genus Agathis, comprising tall evergreen trees of the Pine Family native to the S. Hemisphere. They have broad leathery leaves, bear round or oval cones to 4 in. long, and yield a pitchy sap from which is obtained dammar resin. They are not hardy N., but are occasionally cultivated in the conservatory and grown outdoors in Calif. *A. australis* (Kauri-pine) growing to 150 ft. is a native forest tree of New Zealand; leaves on young trees are sometimes 4 in. long, while those on older trees are less than half as long. *A. robusta,* to 130 ft., is an Australian species with rather wide-spreading, horizontal branches, frequently seen in Calif.

DAMPING-OFF. A name given by gardeners to the wilting and death of seedlings just before or just after they emerge from the soil. When, instead of the uniform well-filled rows of seedlings one expects in a flat or seed bed, one finds rows thin and broken by many bare spots; or when many of a good stand of seedlings suddenly collapse or fall over on the ground and die it is usually the disease called damping-off that is responsible.

The cause is not one specific organism, as with most plant diseases, but may be any one of several fungi which live in the soil near the surface and, under favorable conditions, enter the plants just as they come out of the ground. The slender, tender stems shrivel up and the plants topple over. Too thick planting and high humidity are factors favoring the development of these fungi which may cause losses up to even 90 or 100 per cent of an entire planting.

There is no way to cure or save a seedling affected by damping-off. But if the disease appears in the corner of a hotbed, it can sometimes be prevented from spreading by prompt action to correct the conditions that favor it. Ventilate and dry off the bed; remove the dead plants with some of the soil if they are restricted to a limited area. A practice among commercial growers is to heat some fine sand in the oven and sprinkle it lightly on the soil among the uninfected seedlings with a view to killing or preventing the spread of the fungus.

Damping-off may be largely prevented by treating—before sowing—either the soil or the seed with heat or with chemicals. In greenhouses where steam is available, it is the best means for soil sterilization. Recently electrical equipment giving at least partial sterilization or pasteurization of soil has been perfected. Such sterilizers may be purchased or directions for making them at home can be obtained from state experiment stations.

For treating small lots of soil at home

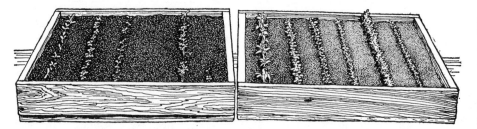

DAMPING-OFF CAN BE PREVENTED BY SOIL DISINFECTION
Equal quantities of the same kinds of seed were sown in these two flats, which were handled alike except that the soil in the right-hand one was treated with formaldehyde dust. Note the fine stand of seedlings there, as compared with the loss caused by the damping-off fungus in the untreated soil.

the simplest method is probably baking in an oven. The time required is that needed to bake a potato in the center of the flat or pan of soil.

Formaldehyde is the chemical most often employed for damping off. Mix 2½ tablespoons of the commercial or 40 per cent liquid formaldehyde with 5 or 6 times the amount of water, sprinkle over a bushel of soil and mix well. Formaldehyde dust may be used at the rate of 8 oz. of 6 per cent dust to a bushel of soil. Seeds may be sown 12 to 24 hours after the flats have been treated and thoroughly watered.

For treating seed various proprietary organic mercury compounds are on the market. Red copper oxide (purchased as cuprous oxide or under various trade names) markedly improves the stand of many vegetable and flower seedlings. Use at the rate of only a small pinch of the material to an ordinary packet of seeds, shaking the seeds and dust together in a bottle. Red copper oxide as a spray (4 tsp. to 3 gals. water) is also useful in preventing damping off of young seedlings. Spray surface of soil immediately after first watering, and the plants as they appear above ground. See also DISINFECTION.

DANAË (dan'-ay-ee). Alexandrian-laurel. A small S. European evergreen shrub belonging to the Lily Family. *D. racemosa,* with glossy green spiny leaves on long arching stems, seems to be the only species cultivated. It is a good shrub as far as withstanding the shade and drip of trees is concerned, but it is not hardy where frosts are severe. The flowers are inconspicuous, but are followed by bright red berries.

DANDELION. Common name for *Taraxacum officinale,* a stemless herb of the Composite Family, with leaves in deeply cut spear-shaped rosettes, and flat solitary bright yellow heads of exclusively disk flowers on naked hollow stems. It is a plant of Old-World origin, but now naturalized in almost every temperate climate and often an annoying weed especially in lawns. It is collected from the wild for "greens" and sometimes cultivated for that purpose, many European growers having developed special strains, some with very large and very curly leaves. Dandelion roots and leaves are also used for medicinal purposes.

When grown as a salad or pot herb crop, dandelions should be planted 1 ft. apart each way in light fertile loam. A light crop of leaves may be gathered the first fall after seeding, but plants are usually allowed to stand until the following spring when the leaves are harvested like spinach; or they may first be blanched by gathering and tying the leaves together, placing pots over the plants, or covering them with sand. The blanching process gives them a less bitter flavor. Dandelions may also be handled like chicory, *i.e.,* the roots dug in the fall and forced in a cellar or hothouse to produce blanched heads resembling *barbe de capucin,* which see.

As a weed, the dandelion has spread over vast areas by means of its small plumed seeds that are carried by the lightest breeze. When once established, plants are hard to dislodge because of their long fleshy tap-root which, when just the tops are cut, promptly send out new leaves and flowers, the latter if cut in full bloom will sometimes mature seeds while lying on the ground.

The only practical way to eradicate dandelions from a lawn is to pull out each plant, root and all, by hand if the grass is very young and the turf tender, or, in firmer sod, with two spades or a weeding spud. This should be done before the plants have bloomed. The roots should be promptly burned or otherwise effectively disposed of. Another method is to put a skewer dipped in carbolic acid into the heart of each plant or to use one of the implements like a sharp pointed hollow cane that inserts acid or other weed killer into the plant. Afterwards go over the lawn, remove the dead weeds and fill the holes they leave with a bit of soil and a pinch of grass seed.

Dwarf-dandelion and Mountain-dandelion are common names for the genus Krigia, also of the Composite Family, comprising annual and perennial yellow-flowered herbs, resembling Taraxacum, though some species have leafy stems. They have bright flower heads about 1 in. across and, as they do not become weedy as does the ordinary dandelion, some of the species make excellent rock-garden subjects. They grow readily in any pocket of light sandy loam and are increased by seed. *K. virginica,* an annual to 1 ft., has oval, cut leaves to 8 in. and reddish-orange or orange flowers. *K. montana,* a perennial to 1 ft., has very narrow leaves, sometimes cut, and bright golden flowers.

See also WEEDS; CULINARY HERBS.

DAPHNE, A HIGHLY PRIZED SHRUB
At the left, one of the fragrant lilac flower-clusters enlarged; right, a plant suitably placed in a rock garden.

DANGLEBERRY. Colloquial name for *Gaylussacia frondosa*, a deciduous shrub with bell-shaped purplish flowers and blue fruit.

DAPHNE (daf'-nee). Small deciduous or evergreen shrubs, native in Europe, N. Africa and Asia. They are chiefly valued for their fragrant flowers (sometimes resembling those of candytuft) and thrive best in well-drained sandy loam well supplied with leafmold. Not all are hardy North, and *D. odora* and its varieties are sometimes grown as winter-flowering plants in a cool greenhouse. Propagation is by seeds, cuttings, layers, and sometimes by root-grafting on *D. mezereum.*

Dieback of *D. cneorum* is now believed due not to a disease-causing organism but to lack of calcium in the soil. If the soil tests acid apply lime. *D. mezereum,* exceedingly subject to scale, should be sprayed with a miscible oil or lime-sulphur in early spring. Crown rot, which ,see, has been reported on *D. odora* on the W. Coast.

Principal Species

D. mezereum is a neat little European deciduous shrub that has become naturalized in some parts of the N. States. Its fragrant lilac-purple flowers appear early, before the leaves, and in the summer it is attractive with scarlet fruit. Var. *alba* has white flowers and yellow fruit.

genkwa is a slender deciduous shrub from China, with pale lilac flowers before the leaves, not entirely hardy N.

alpina is a rare little deciduous shrub for the rock garden, bearing clusters of fragrant white flowers in May. It has a downy covering on the lower surface of the leaves.

cneorum (Garland-flower) is a choice low evergreen with dense clusters of fragrant pink flowers in spring, and often a second crop in the fall. Light soil or peat moss spread over the base of a plant induces stem rooting and the development of a larger clump.

blagayana is a hardy dwarf evergreen with clusters of creamy-white fragrant flowers.

laureola (Spurge-laurel) is an evergreen shrub to 4 ft. with large shining green leaves and yellowish-green flowers in early spring. It grows best in partial shade and moist soil, and is not entirely hardy North.

odora is an evergreen to 4 ft. with dense heads of very fragrant white or purplish flowers. Not hardy N., but a good plant for the cool greenhouse.

DAPHNIPHYLLUM (daf-ni-fil'-um). Handsome small evergreen trees or shrubs, natives of China and Japan, belonging to the Euphorbia Family. They are of slow growth and can be cultivated only where frosts are light. A partly protected place in rich moist soil in which lime is present suits them best. *D. macropodum,* to 30 ft., is the best-known species. Its twigs are red when young, and the large handsome leaves, glaucous beneath, somewhat resemble those of a Rhododendron. The flowers are not conspicuous, but the fruits are bloomy black. *D. humile* is dwarf, with oval leaves and dark-blue fruit.

DARLINGTONIA (dahr-ling-toh'-ni-ah). A genus of insectivorous plants of the Sarracenia Family, occurring only in the mountain swamps of Calif. and S. Ore., but of late offered by florists as house plants throughout the country. Their leaves, from 3 to 30 in. long, grow from a rootstock in an annual rosette, and are modified into a pitcher-shape, the fused half of the leaves forming a lid decorated with an attractive crimson and green tongue-like appendage. The leaves are hollow and fascinatingly colored and covered with honey-glands so that insects are lured within them and drowned in the liquid secreted at the hollow base.

Darlingtonias are not considered hardy N., but in several instances have wintered over. They are generally grown in greenhouses under the sáme conditions as Sarracenia and other allied species, in a soil composed of fern fibre, silver sand and chopped sphagnum. A constantly moist atmosphere must be maintained and the plants shaded. A glass case, well-ventilated is desirable. They must never be allowed to dry out, and to prevent this the pot they are in should be placed in a larger pot or deep saucer and the space between be filled with sphagnum moss which will retain moisture. They may be increased by division or by seed.

D. *californica* has tubular leaves with an arched hood marked with translucent areas which admit light into the interior. The yellowish to brownish-red flowers on a stem 2 ft. long are 1¼ in. across and bloom from May to July. See also INSECTIVOROUS PLANTS.

DASHEEN (da-sheen'). Natural or forced sprouts of *Colocasia esculenta*, a tropical herb introduced in the S. by the Dept. of Agriculture and commonly called Taro, which see.

DASYLIRION (das-i-li'-ri-on). Sotol. Desert plants of N. America and Mexico, belonging to the Lily Family. They are short trunked plants of stiff habit, with many long and narrow leaves crowded near the top to form a more or less dome-shaped head. Very striking in bloom, with dense panicled racemes of small whitish flowers towering high above the crown of leaves. Sometimes grown in pots or tubs for formal decoration. Propagated by seed.

D. *glaucophyllum* has glaucous leaves to 4 ft. long, the margins armed with small teeth. The flower stem grows 12 to 18 ft. high. D. *longissimum* has dull green leaves to 6 ft. long, and a flower stem sometimes as high as 20 ft. D. *wheeleri* has leaves to 3 ft. long, armed with brown-tipped teeth, and with long usually drooping racemes on stems 9 to 15 ft.. The leaves of this species have become popular for use in flower arrangements; they are collected and sold in large numbers, with their broad, cup-shaped, ivory bases highly polished, as "spoon-flowers," which see.

DATE. A species of palm tree (*Phoenix dactylifera*) cultivated in arid regions since prehistoric times for its fruit, to which the term is also applied. Though dates have been grown in Florida, California and some other parts of the U. S. for more than a century, the trees yield poorly because the temperatures are not continuously high enough to ripen the fruit.

Commercial date growing in America, which started about 1890 in Arizona, was stimulated by importations of superior varieties by Walter T. Swingle of the U. S. Department of Agriculture. Today it is well established and increasing in importance in irrigated sections of the hot and arid Southwestern States. As the male and female flowers are borne on different trees, and as only inferior, seedless dates develop from unpollinated flowers, natural fertilization is supplemented by the grower, who ties branches of male flower clusters among the female flower clusters at the proper times.

Propagation of choice varieties is by suckers which develop at the base of and as much as 10 ft. up the trunk. When three to six years old these are moved in spring to favored locations in warm soil and their tops reduced. Such trees should bear at 5 or 6 years old and when 10 or 15 be producing 100 to 200 pounds of fruit a year. The fruit clusters are generally cut before they are fully ripe and matured somewhat like bananas in a warm room. See PHOENIX.

A TRAP FOR INSECTS
Darlingtonia, the California Pitcher-plant, attracts, then catches and "digests" insects inside its hollow leaves.

DATE-PLUM. Common name for *Diospyros lotus,* a small deciduous Asiatic tree, a species of Persimmon, which see.

DATE-YUCCA. Common name for the genus Samuela, of yucca-like trees. See YUCCA.

DATISCA (dah-tis'-kah). Generic name for two species of herbs, one of which, the Asiatic *D. cannabina,* of hemp-like habit, is sometimes grown for ornament.

DATURA (dah-teu'-rah). A genus of annual or perrennial herbs, shrubs or trees, found in the warmer parts of the earth, belonging to the Nightshade Family. They are mostly coarse, strong-smelling plants, but a few are grown for the sake of their large trumpet-shaped flowers. They are of easy cultivation, some being treated as tender annuals. The woody species are propagated by cuttings.

PRINCIPAL SPECIES

D. arborea (Angels Trumpet) is tree-like to 15 ft., with soft-hairy leaves to 8 in. long, and white green-veined flowers to 9 in. long.

cornigera grows to 4 ft., and is almost entirely covered with soft down. The leaves are chiefly at the ends of the branches, and the white or creamy flowers are very fragrant at night. The floral lobes are terminated by a long spreading or recurved point.

metel (known to many gardeners as *D. cornucopia*) is an annual to 5 ft., with large often double flowers, whitish inside and violet outside, with a purple calyx.

stramonium (Thorn-apple, Jimson-weed) is a tropical annual to 5 ft., naturalized in parts of this country. It has erect white or violet flowers and a very prickly fruit.

suaveolens, tree-like to 15 ft., is often grown in tubs under glass, and frequently confused with *D. arborea.* However, it has larger and smoother leaves and distinguishing sweet-scented flowers to a foot long, with an inflated calyx.

DAUCUS (dau'-kus) *carota* var. *sativa.* Botanical name of the common carrot, which see.

DAVALLIA (dah-val'-i-ah). A genus of excellent greenhouse and indoor ferns, chiefly evergreen, and especially good for baskets. Broadly triangular fronds rise from a thickened, hairy, creeping surface rhizome, that suggests the common name, Hares Foot Fern. The fruit-dots are close

to margin, with indusia round or kidney-shaped and generally united. Pot carefully so as not to bury the rhizomes, in a soil of 3 parts fibrous peat, 1 part leaf mold, and 1 part sand. Water from below, but sparingly in rest periods. Give plenty of N. light.

SPECIES

D. bullata (Squirrels Foot Fern). Fronds 8 to 12 in. long, 4-pinnate, dark, shining green, delicately curled; rhizomes covered with red-brown scales. The formerly popular "fern ball" is made from this species, by bending rhizomes when wet over a wire frame filled with moss; these the roots penetrate while the fronds are born abundantly over the whole surface. Dip the ball in water for a few minutes daily throughout growing season, less often later.

canariensis (Hares Foot Fern). Fronds 1 to 1½ ft. long, from rhizomes covered with pale brown scales, which creep down and overhang the pot. The best species for living rooms.

divaricata. A large species, for greenhouse only; 2 to 3 ft. fronds, 3-pinnate and deep red when young, from woody, twisted rhizomes with rusty scales. Very shallow rooting.

fijiensis. Very feathery, with fronds gracefully drooping and growing freely. For warm greenhouse only but splendid for exhibition.

pallida. For the warm greenhouse. Fronds 2 to 3 ft. long, 3- to 4-pinnate, on thick rhizomes with dark brown scales. A rapid grower.

solida (Glossy Davallia). Fronds 1 to 1½ ft. long, glossy, bronzy green, broad and 3-pinnate, from supple rust-colored rhizomes.

tyermanni (Bears Foot Fern). A dwarf form, with broad, bright green, 4-pinnate fronds, and rhizomes covered with silvery scales.

DAVIDIA (dah-vid'-i-ah) *involucrata.* A Chinese pyramidal tree, bearing dense heads of cream-colored flowers. It is hardy in S. New England. See DOVE-TREE.

DAWN-FLOWER. A common name for *Ipomœa leari,* a tropical American twining perennial vine with blue flowers becoming pink. See IPOMŒA, also MORNING-GLORY.

DAY-FLOWER. Common name for the genus Commelina, mostly blue-flowered herbs of the S. Temperate zone, grown in greenhouses and outdoors.

DAYLILY. (See illustration, Plate 28.) Common name for Hemerocallis, an important genus of showy perennial herbs of the Lily Family. They bear large yellow, orange, or, in the newest hybrids, red flowers, chiefly in June and July.

The name Daylily is also sometimes applied to the Plantain-lily (which see) of the genus Hosta which is characterized by broad plantain-like leaves, fibrous roots, flat winged seeds, and flowers of white, blue or lavender in simple unbranched racemes. The flowers of Hemerocallis occur on either branched or unbranched stalks; the black seeds are either round or angled, never winged; and the roots are often tuberous.

Extremely hardy and free from the many diseases which attack most true lilies, Hemerocallis is a favorite with gardeners who find the former difficult to raise. These daylilies are effective in borders, as specimen plants and for naturalizing. Beyond a well-drained soil, they demand little attention, thriving almost anywhere, sending up a satisfactory clump of sword-shaped leaves and a leafless stalk of large lily-like flowers.

While each flower of the daylily stays open only for one day, there is always abundant bloom on the plant throughout the flowering season.

Daylilies which produce seeds (which not all of them do) may be easily increased by sowing these in the open ground in May or June. Two or three years are generally required to produce flowering plants, and then, because most of the garden forms are hybrids, they are not likely to resemble the immediate parent. The common practice, therefore, is to increase a stock by division of the roots or rhizomes, setting them out in August or September for the following summer's bloom.

Daylilies are known that range in height from 7 in. to 7 ft. The small ones, however, are not yet in extensive cultivation, but may prove useful parents for new rock-garden subjects. While most varieties are at the height of their bloom in early summer, some fall-flowering varieties are being gradually introduced. Rose-pink, crimson and mahogany are some of the tones of red featured in recent Hemerocallis hybrids.

Principal Species

A. flava (Lemon- or Custard-lily or Tall Yellow Daylily). Early-flowering, robust plant with fragrant, uniform yellow flowers showing above the mass of foliage, the scape being about 3 ft. tall.

fulva (Tawny or Fulvous Daylily). Tall vigorous flower-scapes ascending far above the lax spears of foliage, the soft orange-colored flowers (July) having a fulvous

A NEW HYBRID DAYLILY
Mikado. with flowers 5 in. across, has a blotch of mahogany-red at the base of each petal. The plant's habit of growth is shown at the right.

cast. Propagated entirely by division of the fast-growing rhizome.

aurantiaca (Orange-fulvous or Golden Summer Daylily). Resembles the Fulvous Daylily, blooming at the same time, but paler in color, not quite so tall, the petals narrower, and the foliage darker and, in the S., evergreen.

thunbergi (Thunbergs or Late Yellow Daylily). Flowers clear lemon-yellow, green-tinged on the outside, July, on scapes 3 ft. tall; intolerant of heat.

middendorfi (Broad Dwarf, Middendorfs or Amur Daylily). Orange flowers 3 in. across clustered at the top of an unbranched scape 3 ft. high and overtopping the leaves. Buds and seed-capsules are prominently ridged and the roots are slenderly cylindrical, not fleshy.

dumortieri (Narrow Dwarf or Dumortiers Daylily). Clear orange flowers, 2 to 4 clustered compactly, opening from brownish-red-tinged buds in May. The coarse leaves and flowers both stand about 2 ft. high. Hybrids derived from this species are more vigorous.

citrina (Long Yellow or Citron Daylily). A tall night-blooming species, with many fragrant pale yellow flowers, the outer segments of which are tinged with green and tipped with purplish.

Hybrids

The hybrids of Hemerocallis offer most interesting subjects for garden use, though some of the new reds are not yet on the market. Varieties now available and to be recommended include:

Anna Betscher, large empire-yellow flower, late July and early August; Apricot, early-flowering and semi-dwarf; Aureole, with abundant large flowers of rich cadmium-yellow, July; Bijou, a new race with an abundance of small flowers in orange and fulvous-red on 2-ft. scapes, mid-July; Cinnabar, cadmium-yellow overlaid with a unique dark red; Dawn, large bell-shaped flowers combining sulphur, crimson, and rose-buff; Estmere, graceful, semi-dwarf plants with medium flowers of orange-yellow; Florham, large flowers 6 in. across in yellow and orange; Gay Day, tall plant with yellow flowers, August and later; Gold Dust, compact plant, semi-dwarf, the yellow flowers long-blooming; Lemona, large plant, night-blooming, with yellow flowers; Mikado, large flowers of rich orange with mahogany-red blotch, vigorous, July; Ophir, tall, showy, clear orange-yellow, July; Queen of May, tallest of May-flowering varieties, with yellowish-orange flowers; Soudan, gold-glistening yellow, blooming later than the Lemon Daylily; Sunkist, large rose-bronze flowers, August; Tangerine, semi-dwarf plant, dark orange flowers, red buds, opening early; Wau-Bun (Winnebago name for early morn), light cadmium-yellow veiled with fulvous-red, large flowers with petals folded back and twisted.

DEAD-NETTLE. Common name for the genus Lamium, a member of the Mint Family, comprising annual and perennial herbs of the Old World, a few of which are grown as hardy plants in the border and rock garden. The forms cultivated in this country, of which *L. maculatum* with white-striped leaves is the most common, though not the most striking in appearance, grow 1 ft. or more tall. The

opposite, toothed leaves, though resembling those of nettle, are not prickly to the touch. The whorled flowers, usually purple-red or white, are hooded.

Dead-nettles are of easy culture and are increased by division and seeds. Some varieties have naturalized themselves in this country and become weeds.

DEBREGEASIA (dee-bree-je-ay'-si-ah). Trees and shrubs of Asia and Africa, belonging to the Nettle Family. One species, *D. longifolia,* is sometimes grown as an ornamental. It is a large deciduous shrub or small tree, easy to grow, but not hardy where frosts are severe. It is conspicuous on account of its foliage, the large handsome leaves being dark lustrous green above and white beneath. The flowers are tiny and inconspicuous, but the orange-red mulberry-like fruits are decorative.

DECAISNEA (de-kays'-nee-ah). A genus of Asiatic shrubs, the species *D. fargesi* being the best known in cultivation. This is a tall upright deciduous shrub, native to China. It likes a rather light soil with plenty of leafmold, and though hardy needs a sheltered position in the North. It is of outstanding appearance, with large drooping pinnate leaves 2 ft. or more in length. The nodding greenish-yellow flowers are borne in long racemes, followed by curious deep blue fruits about 4 in. long. These are edible but insipid.

DECIDUOUS (dee-sid'-eu-us). This describes trees, shrubs or vines that shed their leaves in winter, as opposed to EVERGREENS (which see), which hold their leaves throughout the year. The word is also used by botanists to describe any portion of a plant which falls off in natural course, as flower parts, bud-scales, fruits, etc. Shedding the leaves lessens the breaking and uprooting force of the wind, and saves trees much effort repairing leaf-damage due to wind and frost. It also saves trouble for the gardener, who can transplant most deciduous trees easily while dormant, without the necessity of keeping the roots moist with a ball of earth.

DECIDUOUS CYPRESS. Common name for *Taxodium distichum,* a deciduous tree growing as far north as N. Y. City and Central Ill. Also called Bald Cypress. See TAXODIUM.

DECODON (dek'-o-don) *verticillatus* This perennial herb of the Loosestrife Family is called Swamp Loosestrife, and also commonly Water-willow. It sometimes grows quite tall and its showy clusters of magenta flowers are a common sight along marshy pond edges and in swamps of E. U. S. during the summer months. It is a desirable plant for colonizing about ponds and in very wet places.

DECUMARIA (dek-eu-may'-ri-ah). Climbing shrubs, one species native in N. America and one in China, belonging to the Saxifrage Family. The native kind, *D. barbara,* grows well in a rich moist soil and partial shade. It is a handsome shrub to 30 ft., climbing by aerial rootlets, and clinging firmly to walls and tree-trunks. It has glossy leaves and produces a mass of small fragrant white flowers in early summer. *D. sinensis,* from China, is very similar, but much smaller and less hardy.

DEERBERRY. The common name for *Vaccinium stamineum* (which see) ; in England applied to Partridge-berry (*Mitchella repens*).

DEERBRUSH. Common name for *Ceanothus integerrimus,* a Calif. shrub with mases of fine white, blue or pink flowers.

DEER FERN (*Lomaria spicant*). An erect rigid comb-like fern, not native to this country, but excellent for the cool greenhouse or for the garden in mild moist sections, where it needs shaly or gravelly soil.

DEERFOOT. Common name for *Achlys triphylla,* a low perennial herb, native in W. N. America, belonging to the Barberry Family. It is found in shady woods, and is sometimes planted in rock gardens. The leaves are divided into 3 fan-shaped leaflets, and it has a short spike of small flowers minus petals.

DEER-GRASS. A common name for Rhexia, a group of native perennial herbs better known as Meadow Beauty, which see.

DEHISCENCE. The method or process by which (1) a seed pod or (2) the anther of a flower opens to discharge its contents, which are seeds in the first case and pollen grains in the second.

DEHORN. An animal-industry term applied to the severe cutting back of tree branches (especially of peach), to mere stubs to force the development of shoots from which to select such as will make a new well-formed top.

DELONIX (de-loh'-niks). A genus of small tropical trees, belonging to the Pea Family, formerly included in the genus Poinciana. *D. regia* (Royal Poinciana, Peacock-flower, Flamboyant) is one of the most brilliant of tropical flowering trees, commonly planted in warm countries. It is a widespreading tree to 40 ft., with leaves 2 ft. long, comprising 10 to 20 leaflets, and bright scarlet flowers 3 to 4 in. across in clusters, followed by flat woody pods to 2 ft. long.

DELPHINIUM (del-fin'-i-um). (See illustration, Plate 14.) This important genus includes both annual and perennial herbs commonly known as Larkspur. Although the most widely known form is the popular garden delphinium with dense or branched spires of most attractive blossoms in shades of blue, or, in the hybrids, lavender, purple or rosy-mauve, rising from 3 to 8 ft. high, there are smaller, more delicate, less important species having yellow, white or red blossoms. The flowers of all species are somewhat irregular, the sepals forming the spur and petal-like outer parts, while the small petals, clustered around the stamens, form the "bee," so prominent in some forms. The leaves, usually much cut, are clustered at the base or are on the flowering stalks.

In this article only the highly developed perennial garden hybrids are being treated. For other species of delphinium and their culture see LARKSPUR.

Even casually grown, delphiniums are extremely hardy and make satisfactory garden plants, but if given a little special consideration, they reward the grower many times over. Fine plants depend upon sun, circulation of air, and a rich, light, alkaline soil. To insure air circulation, mature plants should stand at least 2 ft. apart. To maintain a highly alkaline soil condition it is advisable to sprinkle a "light snow" of agricultural lime over the soil once or twice during the growing season. A well balanced commercial fertilizer (containing about 5% nitrogen, 10% phosphates, and 5% potash, should be given the plants in the early spring, following the directions supplied by the manufacturer.

The popular garden varieties, if cut to the ground after blooming, will often produce a second set of blossoms later in the summer. A second feeding should be given after a ten-day rest period following the cutting down. It is almost a necessity to stake the taller varieties early in the season to prevent damage by high winds and storms. Although certain diseases (see below) are almost always associated with delphiniums, if the plants have all the sun, air and lime they need and are well watered during prolonged dry spells— that is, if they are kept strong and vigorous—infection is rare. Except in the most extreme climates winter protection is not needed.

Although nothing can take the place of delphiniums in the herbaceous border, they are usually at their best when grown in rows by themselves. In either case, madonna lilies, canterbury bells, daylilies, or some other plant which enjoys or tolerates the same conditions, may be planted in front of them for decorative effect, allowing the 2 ft. clearance for circulation of air.

By sowing seeds in an outdoor frame, sheltered from the sun, in midsummer when the first crop of seed has ripened, one may have, the following year, small plants which will blossom in between the first and second flowering of the older stock.

A coldframe, or wooden flat with the bottom knocked out and set into the soil, is ideal for summer-sown seed, as it simplifies the matter of giving protection against storms or intense heat with stretched burlap. After the seed is sown the bed should not be allowed to dry out. The plants will be large enough to move by early fall, but still should be given the protection of a coldframe or mulch of leaves. Transplanting should be done at least a month before frost to give the seedlings time to establish themselves. As few delphiniums can be depended upon to come true from seed, all the young plants should be taken care of to permit a selection of the best colors and types later on. By late spring set in their permanent places in the garden.

Seeds may be sown in frames in the early fall when rains and the lack of intense summer heat make an ideal condition for their growth. In spring the young plants may be set in rows in the propagating bed or in the vegetable garden until of sufficient size to place in the border.

Old established plants in the garden will begin to bloom in June, and will often bloom again in September. For July and

HYBRID DELPHINIUMS ARE AMONG THE MOST MAJESTIC OF GARDEN FLOWERS
Under favorable conditions, they will often grow well over 6 ft. tall. In the center is a branching spike of a single-flowered type, showing the characteristic "bee" in the center of each blossom. At the right is a heavy spike of double flowers, the "bee" no longer visible.

August flowers, seeds may be sown in the greenhouse or hotbed in February, the seedlings pricked out into pots, and the young plants set out in the garden in May in a bed made rich with rotted cow-manure. When an old clump of delphinium becomes so thick that air cannot circulate through the stalks, it should be lifted and divided into three clumps of approximately the same size. See DIVISION.

ENEMIES

Black-spot, a bacterial disease that causes irregular black spots on the upper leaf surfaces and sometimes on the stems, is unsightly but not often serious. The similarity between its name and the term "blacks" used to describe mite injury (see below) has confused many lecturers and writers, so that the wrong remedy is often recommended for mites. To control the bacterial black spot, remove all old plant parts in autumn and drench the crowns in early spring with a 1 to 2,000 solution of corrosive sublimate. Remove infected leaves as soon as noticed. If much injury has been noted in previous years spray two or three times during the spring with bordeaux mixture.

A most serious fungous disease of delphiniums is crown rot (which see). Plants suddenly wilt or topple over, and at the crown may usually be seen the small red resting bodies and the white mycelium of threadlike vegetative part of the fungus. Carefully remove each diseased plant with surrounding soil and drench the vacant space and adjacent plants with 1 to 1,000 corrosive sublimate solution. It is important to take care of infected plants immediately since the fungus is able to infect a great many other perennials.

Other root rots are due to various bacteria, fungi, or other organisms and cultural defects such as too high soil temperature, insufficient moisture, too compact a soil, and the use of manure too close to plant crowns. Rots following cutting back of flower stalks may be somewhat prevented by disinfecting tools between cuts.

Mildew, prevalent on the W. Coast and, late in the season, in Eastern gardens, is controlled with either sulphur or copper fungicides.

Stunt, or chlorosis, a virus disease, causes dwarfing of the plant and flower heads and mottling of the foliage. Remove and destroy diseased plants.

DEFORMED DELPHINIUM LEAVES
The delphinium mite, which can be controlled with a nicotine spray, has caused this unsightly distortion.

The cyclamen mite causes very severe injury, curling and distorting the leaves, blackening the flower buds and generally stunting the plant, which is said to have "the blacks." The mites are too small to be seen with the naked eye and since the general appearance is that of a disease rather than insect injury the wrong control measures are frequently applied. Remove infested parts and spray frequently, both early and late in the season, with rotenone. Dusting with sulphur between sprays may also help.

Leaves which are cupped downward probably have aphids clustering underneath. Spray the under surfaces promptly with a contact insecticide.

Slugs may be at least partly controlled by sprinkling lime or spreading sifted coal ashes around the plants.

From the species *D. elatum,* commonly called Bee or Candle Larkspur or Delphinium, an erect perennial with spire-like clusters of rather small flowers, many of the tall garden varieties have been derived. *D. cheilanthum,* called Garland Larkspur or Delphinium, a tall branched sort, originally from Siberia, is supposed to be the parent of *belladonna,* a low-growing plant with light blue blossoms, of *bellamosum,* with deep blue blossoms, and also of the varieties *coelestinum* and *formosum.* As these two groups are so confused by long cultivation and interbreeding they are often listed under the head of *D. cultorum.*

Among the best known hybrid strains are the Wrexham Hybrids, called Hollyhock-flowered, and those sent out by Blackmore and Langdon. These two strains were developed in England; other interesting hybrids have been produced by both French and American growers.

DELPHINIUM SOCIETY, AMERICAN. This society was organized in 1926 to promote the hybridizing of domestic and foreign delphiniums and their related species, to hold shows, award medals and certificates of merit, provide for proper classification and nomenclature and disseminate information on the culture of the flower. By far the greater proportion of members is amateur.

Members are entitled to exhibit in, and to attend, its shows. They also receive its illustrated bulletin which is published three times a year. The annual dues are $2 and the secretary is Fred C. Schnelz, Royal Oak, Mich.

DENDROBIUM (den-droh'-bi-um). A genus of epiphytic orchids from the tropics of the E. hemisphere usually having long drooping racemes of showy blossoms. The flowers, in shades of rosy-purple and mauve, white or pale green, have a sac or spur, and a lip, entire or 3-lobed, the lobes sometimes hairy or fringed. A large number of species and varieties are included in this genus, some of them exceedingly popular for greenhouse decoration. For the grower's convenience they may be divided into two sections, the evergreen and the deciduous.

The evergreen types, *D. thyrsiflorum, D. densiflorum* and *D. fimbriatum* require a moist warm temperature. The deciduous species, of which *D. nobile* is an example, require a high moist temperature during the growing season, but a cooler and drier treatment during the late fall, winter and early spring months. *D. nobile* is easily grown by the amateur.

For further details of culture see ORCHIDS.

DENDROCALAMUS (den-droh-kal'-ah-mus). A genus of tree-like bamboos. *D. membranaceus,* with bright green mature culm (or "trunk"), will grow up to 70 ft. in protected spots in Calif.; *D. strictus* (Male Bamboo) is 20 to 50 ft. high when mature. See BAMBOO.

DENDROMECON (den-droh-mee'-kon) *rigida.* Bush-poppy (which see) or Tree-poppy. A leathery-leaved shrub with yellow flowers, native to Calif.

DENNSTEDTIA (den-stet'-i-ah). A genus of ferns, including the common Boulder Fern of the E. States, excellent for naturalizing in open places, but too rampant for the garden.

DENTARIA (den-tay'-ri-ah). A genus of small white or purple-flowered woodland herbs of the Mustard Family commonly known as Toothwort, which see.

DENTATE. Toothed; particularly a sharply toothed leaf with teeth somewhat large and at right angles to the blade.

DEODAR (dee-oh'-dahr). (See illustration, Plate 17.) Common name for *Cedrus deodara,* a handsome, graceful evergreen tree hardy only in the S. States and S. Calif. See CEDAR.

DERRIS (der'-is). A genus of tropical leguminous plants formerly known as Deguelia, one or two species of which contain a resinous substance which is used by natives of the tropics to temporarily poison streams and simplify the catching of fish which are paralyzed by it. In recent years the roots of *Derris elliptica* have been made into powders or extracts and offered under various proprietary names as contact insecticides. The active principle (rotenone) though not poisonous to humans and domestic animals, seems to have some possibilities as a stomach poison as well as a contact insecticide. The proprietary compounds on the market sometimes contain rotenone in combination with other insecticides, and sometimes with a fungicide. See also CUBE; INSECTICIDE.

The purple-flowered species of Derris sometimes grown in warm climates is *D. scandens* or Malay Jewel-vine, which see.

DESERT-CANDLE. Common name for Eremurus, a genus of Asiatic, semi-hardy perennials with basal rosettes of leaves and tall stalks clothed with usually white, pink, or yellow flowers. (See illustration, Plate 19.)

DESERT GARDEN. This may be a reproduction of desert landscape; or it may be a garden wherein plants native to the desert are collected and grown. The first would of course imply the second, whereas the second does not of necessity imply the first. There is a third reference sometimes to miniature indoor gardens which cleverly portray desert scenes, using the diminutive forms of desert growth; this type of gardening probably approaches more nearly than any practice anywhere else in the world to the dwarf trees and dwarf tree landscapes of the Japanese garden artists.

Some are unwilling to admit that a desert garden has beauty. Judged by ordi-

Upper left: Varied forms and colors in one of the new English hybrids.   Center left: Compact, many-flowered spires of delphinium.   Upper right: The tall spires of delphinium give dignity to the garden. Lower left: Sweet William (Dianthus barbatus) with its many brilliant shades adds a note of cheer. Lower right: The massed blues of delphinium create an outstanding effect.

nary standards of garden excellence it has not, of course. But the desert garden is so entirely different from any other type that it cannot be classed with others in respect to its qualities or its excellence. This means, naturally, that it cannot compete with other forms, and therefore must never be associated with them in the garden composition or, one might add, in garden or flower show competition. Even more than the rock garden, the desert garden requires to be set apart—even secreted—so that comparison is avoided; so that its own grim and sometimes terrible beauty dominates completely. None can deny that it is a fascinating and wonder-inducing place when it is thus rightly handled and placed, just as no one will deny the superlative beauty of many desert plants' blossoms. (See illustrations, Plate 7.)

It is not for the sake of the bloom however that enthusiasts develop desert gardens. Rather it is the strangeness of the plant forms and the mystery of how and why they have become what they are, that intrigue the imagination; also the tremendous contrast to the usual and normal things, common everywhere, which they and their desert environment provide. To spend an hour in a well planned, well executed desert garden is as refreshing as a cruise to foreign lands—even as to emerge from such a garden and the scene it presents, and again experience the refreshment and sense of reassurance which accustomed things bring, is like a long anticipated home coming.

THE DESERT GARDEN'S PLACE. This is a highly specialized form of gardening, making its appeal usually and especially to tnose of scientific tastes or interest—not scientists, but gardeners who have a scientific curiosity. The plants employed provide material for endless research; for fascinating experiments in plant breeding; for limitless study and speculative thought as regards adaptation of form and color, and the influences of environment.

Where there is a real enthusiasm for the idea, combined with a real taste for plant study and plant collecting, the desert garden may prove the one best thing to do with a dry, arid, sun-baked area such as gardens in warm regions often possess. But without this taste (which alone will prompt the effort to study the plants to their minutest detail and spare no pains to discover personally their requirements) it is the last thing in the world to undertake. For it is never enough to take another's word—except in the most general way—about the strange plant individualists that grow in such a garden. Different situations may alter the conditions completely, hence each particular desert garden must be worked out individually.

If, in making such a garden, it is intended to duplicate a desert landscape, only a limited number of kinds of plants may be introduced; for these limitations are strictly the rule of desert survival. So it is necessary to recognize at the beginning that true desert landscape will not permit indulging the collecting instinct which may be the gardener's motive. But it is possible to modify the realism of the composition enough to admit the many things which a collector is bound to acquire, without wholly destroying the desert suggestion, if a plant that prevails in the actual desert is used freely and so allowed to dominate the planting. The variety existing in the balance of the plant material will not then be as noticeable.

See also CACTUS; GARDENING IN DIFFERENT SECTIONS.

DESERT- or **FLOWERING-WILLOW.** Common names for one species of Chilopsis, which see, a deciduous shrub found from Calif. to Texas and in Mexico.

DESFONTAINEA (des-fon-tay'-nee-ah). An interesting evergreen shrub from S. America. *D. spinosa,* apparently the only species in cultivation, is not hardy where frosts are severe. In favored places it grows to 6 ft. or more, thriving in a somewhat porous soil with plenty of humus. It has leathery, holly-like leaves and very showy tubular flowers of scarlet and yellow, produced over a long season.

DESIGN OF GARDENS. See GARDEN DESIGN.

DESMODIUM (des-moh'-di-um). A genus of herbs and shrubs of the Pea Family known as Tick-trefoil or Tick-clover; one species is called Beggarweed because of the twisted pods which cling like burs and may be carried long distances by animals or people. The species nearly all grow in dry woods and fields, and are sometimes used in the border or wild garden, though their chief use is as forage plants. They are easily grown from seed.

D. gyrans (Telegraph-plant) is a tender Asiatic species with purple flowers sometimes grown as an oddity in the greenhouse because of the leaflets which have the power of moving in several directions. Though a perennial it is treated as an annual and grown from seed.

rigidum, a native N. American species, grows 3 ft. high. It is a stiff plant with small purple flowers.

purpureum (Beggarweed, which see) is a forage plant grown on moist land in the S. U. S.

DEUTZIA (deut'-si-ah). A genus of deciduous shrubs, native in Asia and belonging to the Saxifrage Family. They are attractive in early summer with their wealth of flowers, mostly white but some tinged pinkish. They do best in well-drained soil with plenty of humus. In the N. some need a protected position, and even then are not entirely hardy in severe winters. Numerous hybrids and varieties have been developed.

Two fungous leaf spots may attack deutzias. Protect them by spraying with bordeaux mixture. Root knot may be caused by nematodes, which see. The sudden death of branches in midsummer may be due to injury suffered the previous winter. See WINTER INJURY.

Propagated by seed, cuttings of green and hard wood, and layers.

PRINCIPAL SPECIES

D. gracilis is one of the best dwarf shrubs, of graceful habit and bearing large clusters of pure white flowers.

parviflora is of vigorous upright habit with dense flower-clusters, and one of the hardiest.

lemoinei, a hybrid between the two species named above, makes a broad rounded bush with large clusters of white flowers, and is also very hardy. It has several good forms, of which Boule de Neige is outstanding.

scabra is a tall shrub with reddish branches, rough leaves and erect clusters of white flowers often tinged pink. The form known as Pride of Rochester has large double white flowers tinged rose.

longifolia is a tall handsome shrub with large lance-shaped leaves and clusters of large flowers tinted light purple. Not entirely hardy.

vilmorinae is somewhat hardier and is likewise a tall graceful grower, with loose clusters of white flowers.

purpurascens is a rather tender species of spreading habit, with slender branches and large open flowers tinged purple outside. It has been used for hybridizing with good results. Crossed with *D. gracilis* it gave several good white- and pink-flowered forms.

kalmiaeflora is considered the best of the *D. purpurascens* hybrids, obtained by crossing with *D. parviflora.* It is of graceful habit, with cup-shaped flowers colored carmine on the outside.

DEVIL-IN-A-BUSH. A common name for *Nigella damascena,* also called Love-in-a-mist, an annual with white or blue flowers inclosed in a lacy network of finely divided bracts.

DEVILS-BIT. A common name for *Chamaelirium luteum,* a native herb of the Lily Family called also Blazing Star. Also a common name for *Hieracium aurantiacum,* a species of Hawkweed (which see).

DEVILS PAINTBRUSH. Another common name for *Hieracium aurantiacum,* just referred to and which is a serious pest in meadows and hayfields in some sections.

DEVILS TONGUE. Common name for *Hydrosme rivieri,* a large, tropical herb of the Arum Family with leaves to 4 ft. long cut into segments. The large calla-like flowers are 1 ft long, green spotted with purple; they appear before the leaves and have an offensive odor. The plant is sometimes grown as an oddity in the greenhouse, where it requires a soil rich in humus and a high temperature.

DEVILS WALKING-STICK. A common name given to *Aralia spinosa,* a gaunt but interesting shrub on account of the spines on the slender, woody stems.

DEVIL-WOOD. A common name for *Osmanthus americanus,* an evergreen tree of the Olive Family found from Va. to Miss. It has leaves to 7 in. long and fragrant greenish flowers.

DEWBERRY. A popular name for forms of trailing blackberries (mostly *Rubus flagellaris*) and their fruit. Plants root at joints and tips and are propagated by the latter instead of by suckers as in blackberries. Also they bear earlier by a week or two than the upright, non-trailing forms. Cultivated like blackberries, dewberries require support for their long slender stems.

They deserve a place in home gardens because the fruit may be allowed to ripen fully, thus excelling that bought. Plants should be set 5 to 7 ft. apart during early spring, in light, well-drained loam, and the young shoots tied to poles the first year. The second spring these stems should be shortened to 4 or 5 ft.; in summer new shoots should be pinched to 5 ft. and only four to six allowed to grow. The best known varieties are Lucretia, Austin, Primo and Bartel. To assure pollination and resulting good yields several varieties should be planted in proximity.

DIAMOND-FLOWER. Common name for *Ionopsidium acaule,* a small annual of the Mustard Family, which produces tiny violet or white flowers in profusion. It requires moist soil, partial shade and protection from drying winds. Seed may be sown in early spring for summer blossoming and in midsummer for the fall. Plants started in the fall may be kept over winter in pots for spring use.

DIANELLA (dy-ah-nel'-ah). A genus of fibrous-rooted perennials of the Lily Family, with grass-like leaves and whitish or blue flowers in loose clusters followed by blue fruits. In mild climates the plants may be grown outdoors but elsewhere a greenhouse or other frostproof location is necessary.

DIANTHUS (dy-an'-thus). (See illustration, Plate 14.) In this genus are grouped a large number of mostly hardy perennial and annual herbs, known by many common names. Whether it be Carnation (which see), Picotee, Sweet William or Pink—virtually every species of Dianthus is a fragrant, beautifully flowered plant.

With the exception of a few alpine species, which thrive best in the N., Dianthus may be raised almost anywhere with confidence. Enjoying sunshine and delighting in a moist soil of ordinary garden composition, the plants bloom generally in the spring in rose, pink, red and white combinations with occasional yellow.

The old-fashioned Grass Pinks, universally cultivated in borders, are mostly *D. plumarius,* distinguished by a clove-like fragrance. The familiar Sweet William, almost equally popular, is *D. barbatus.* Annual pinks are *D. chinensis,* really short-lived perennials, blooming the first season from seed. *D. caryophyllus,* known as Carnation (which see), including the Picotee and other types, is treated separately as it requires special cultivation.

The Grass Pinks have been hybridized into a wide range of large-flowering varieties with colors running from white to rich crimson, with beautiful zonings or stripes. Combining this group with the Carnation has resulted in a hardy strain called Allwoods (*D. allwoodi*), after the original hybridizers, the Allwood Brothers of England.

It is best to increase the perennial kinds by layering or by cuttings (taken with a heel), though seed can be used; planted in spring or summer, it gives flowers the second season. Cuttings will sometimes root better if taken from the new growth of plants grown in pots. The annuals are propagated by seed sown in spring.

Anthracnose causes death of the branches of hardy pinks, the leaves first turning yellow and then brown. Spray wtih bordeaux mixture. Sudden wilting or rotting at the base of the plants may be due to root or crown rot, which see. See also CARNATION for notes on other diseases and insect pests.

Though there are more than 120 species of Dianthus, those listed below are of the greatest importance to the average gardener.

PRINCIPAL SPECIES

D. allwoodi. This hardy hybrid race of *D. plumarius* crossed with *D. caryophyllus* comes in a wide range of colors with petals entire or variously fringed. The tufted foliage generally is firm and broad and somewhat glaucous. These pinks have the free-blooming habit and clove-scent of *plumarius* with the heavy texture of carnations. There are many named varieties, but mixed seed produces fine quality flowers on plants that can be propagated from cuttings. The period of bloom is from June to late July. Var. *alpinus* has shiny leaves, large rose and pink flowers in July and August, and is an excellent rock-garden plant. It prefers soil containing lime.

barbatus (Sweet William). This faintly scented species grows about 2 ft. tall, has smooth, broad, green, flat foliage and bears flowers of purple, red, rose or white in large bracted heads. Some forms are double. There are many excellent named varieties, which bloom in spring and early summer. Though perennial, the plants are best treated as biennials. There is also an annual group about 15 in. tall, which blooms in late summer and early fall the first year from seed.

plumarius (Grass Pink). Mat-forming plants with smooth whitish foliage, growing to 18 in. high, with simple or branched stems and 2 or 3 highly fragrant flowers with fringed petals, rose, purple, white or particolored, blooming from early June to midsummer. There are many named varieties, one of the most popular being *semperflorens*. Some are double. The Grass Pinks may be grown very easily from seed which germinates in less than a week. They prefer a rich, well-drained soil containing lime, though they will thrive almost anywhere in a sunny location. Frequent cutting as soon as flowers begin to fade will prolong the period of bloom. An excellent garden practice is to edge paths with these pinks.

Among other desirable rock-garden pinks are *D. caesius* (Cheddar Pink) with fragrant rose-colored flowers, the petals toothed; *D. arenarius,* with fragrant white flowers, the petals deeply cut; *D. deltoides* (Maiden Pink), with small deep red, crimson-eyed flowers on numerous branchlets, fragrant; *D. alpinus,* with odorless, dark-colored, crimson spotted flowers and shining green foliage; *D. glacialis* var. *neglectus* (Glacier Pink) with small, odorless red-purple flowers, the toothed petals tawny beneath.

chinensis (Annual Pinks). Though called annual because they will flower from seed the first season, they are really short-lived perennials. The foliage is glabrous, green

and tufted; the plants are from 12 to 18 in. tall, and the stems are somewhat branching. The flowers are solitary or loosely assembled, only slightly fragrant if at all, and 1 in. across in tones of red, lilac or white. There are many fine hybrids, of which var. *heddewigi,* with rich velvety flowers, is one of the best.

DIAPENSIA (dy-ah-pen'-si-ah). Small tufted evergreen plants found in N. America, N. Europe and Asia. *D. lapponica,* found on mountain tops of New York and New England, is sometimes grown in rock gardens. It requires a cool situation, in a gritty soil with peat or leafmold and under favorable conditions forms a low dense tuft, usually only an inch or two high, with white bell-shaped flowers.

DIAPENSIACEAE (dy-ah-pen-si-ay'-see-ee). The Diapensia Family, so named by Linnaeus because the parts of the flower are in fives. The members of the family are low growing, perennial and evergreen, woody shrubs or herbs restricted to the N. temperate zone. Diapensia, Pyxidanthera, Galax and Shortia are genera some-

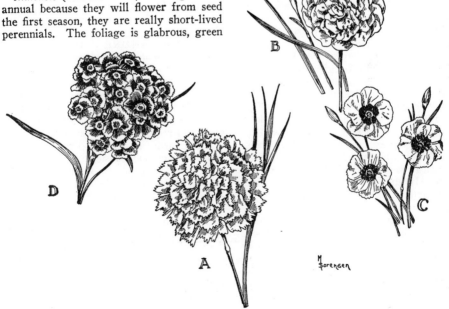

DIANTHUS PRESENTS FORMS FOR BORDER, ROCK GARDEN AND GREENHOUSE
(A) The carnation, raised in commercial greenhouses for cut-flower use. (B) One of the border carnations with rounded petals, especially suitable for growth far north. (C) One of the small alpine Dianthus species, much used in rock gardens. (D) Sweet William, long a favorite in gardens.

times cultivated as ground covers and in rockeries.

DIASCIA (dy-ash'-i-ah) *barberae*. A small half-hardy S. African annual of the Figwort Family. From the round teeth or spurs on the lower petals of the rosy pink flowers with a yellow spot in the throat, it gets the common name of Twinspur, which see.

DIBBER, DIBBLE. A pointed tool, often merely a short, stout stick, but often with a bent handle or grip and a metal-shod point, used to make holes in soft ground for planting bulbs or setting small plants. The term is also used as a verb, meaning the practice of using the tool. To do this correctly, thrust the dibber into the soil, remove it, lower the plant roots into the hole, then press the earth firmly against them all the way to the bottom. Unless this is done carefully an air pocket may be left below the surface in which the roots will hang and dry, injuring and possibly killing the plant.

DICENTRA (dy-sen'-trah). A genus of charming hardy, long-lived, perennial herbs commonly known as Bleeding Heart. They have attractive fern-like foliage, and their dainty heart-shaped blossoms with spurred petals are usually rose or white but in some species yellow or straw-colored. Dicentra was formerly known as Dielytra and plants are still frequently listed in catalogs under that name.

The old-time garden favorite is *D. spectabilis*, which forms a leafy clump to 2 ft. tall that in May is covered with drooping clusters of bright-pink drooping blossoms held gracefully above the finely cut foliage. It grows best in deep, mellow soil, in a sunny sheltered spot in the border and increases in beauty year after year if undisturbed but well cared for. It is easily increased by division of the crown or the roots. If the roots are cut into 3 in. pieces and set in rich loam, new plants will soon start.

Another interesting species for the border native to Calif. and recently introduced as a garden subject is *D. chrysantha* (Golden Eardrops). It has numerous golden erect flowers in panicles and pale bluish-green cut leaves. Other species suitable for the wild garden and rock garden are:

D. cucullaria (Dutchmans Breeches) with small white yellow-tipped flowers having widely spreading spurs. Growing 10 in.

high, it is a native species easily naturalized in rich soil in open rocky woods.

canadensis (Squirrel-corn) has greenish-white flowers nodding in loose sprays. The root consists of many small tubers, which give rise to the common name.

eximia is the native wild Bleeding Heart with nodding dull rose-pink blossoms with rounded spurs. It grows readily in cool, moist soil in the wild garden or a sheltered corner of the rock garden, and if watered will bloom all summer.

formosa (Western Bleeding Heart) is very similar to *D. eximia,* but varies in color from white to deep rose.

oregana (sometimes listed as *D. glauca*) is another W. Coast plant with cream and rose flowers in nodding clusters.

ochroleuca has yellow or cream-colored blossoms.

uniflora is a tiny plant for the rock garden. Its white or pink flowers rising singly 3 in. above the ferny leaves have recurved petals and rounded, sack-like spurs.

DICHLORETHYL ETHER. A heavy colorless or yellow-green liquid with a strong ether odor. In emulsified form it can safely be used as a soil disinfectant around growing plants. It has been successful against garden centipedes and sod webworms. See DISINFECTION; FUMIGATION.

DICHORISANDRA (dy-koh-ri-san'-drah). A genus of herbaceous perennial herbs from tropical America, belonging to the Spiderwort Family. One or two are sometimes grown in the warm greenhouse, and outdoors in warm regions. They thrive in a mixture of loam and leafmold with sand, and require a liberal supply of water when growth is active. Propagated by seed, cuttings and division.

D. mosaica grows to 18 in. high, with spotted stems and large oval dark green leaves marked with numerous short transverse white lines, the under side being deep reddish purple. It has bright blue and white flowers in a short spike. *D. thyrsi-flora* grows to 4 ft., with large glossy green leaves and rich dark blue flowers with yellow stamens in a dense compound inflorescence.

DICKSONIA (dik-soh'-ni-ah). A genus of ferns closely related to Cibotium and including many tree ferns. For cool greenhouse or hothouse only. See CUSHION FERN; TREE FERN; VEGETABLE LAMB.

DICOTYLEDON (dy'-kot-i-lee'-dun). A member of one of the two great classes of Angiosperms, or flowering plants, the other being the Monocotyledons. Dicotyledons are distinguished by (1) two plump wing-like embryo- or seed-leaves (cotyledons); (2) leaf-veins forming an open network and ending freely at the leaf-margin; (3) flowers typically (though not necessarily) with parts grouped in series of four or five; (4) the food or water vessels in the stem arranged concentrically, forming the "rings" of woody stems. See also MONOCOTYLEDON.

DICTAMNUS (dik-tam'-nus) *albus*. A bushy hardy perennial with numerous common names including Burning-bush, Fraxinella, Dittany and Gas-plant. It is notably long-lived but resents transplanting after it is once established; growing in a sunny position, a plant has been known to outlive three generations of one family. The rather strong-smelling plants, which are about 3 ft. high and as broad, make a fine display all summer and are especially striking when the loose spires of white flowers surmount the foliage. On sultry summer evenings the volatile oil emitted as a vapor by the flowers will flash when touched off with a lighted match; this unique property gives rise to two of the popular names—Burning-bush and Gas-plant.

Seed sown an inch deep in the open ground as soon as ripe in autumn will sprout well the following spring. Seedlings should be transplanted to stand 4 to 6 in. apart when a few inches tall and again spaced 12 in. apart the following spring. Give clean cultivation both years and set the plants in their permanent positions (preferably in a sunny spot) the third spring. From that time forward they should bloom every year.

DICTYOSPERMA (dik-ti-oh-spur'-mah). A genus of feather-leaved tropical trees, known as Linoma Palms, and sometimes erroneously, as Arecas. They have trunks to 40 or 50 ft., crowned with long drooping unarmed (spineless) leaves with red or yellow nerves and stems. *D. album* found in the Mascarene Islands of the Indian Ocean, is a stately tree with graceful feathered leaves, glossy above, the stems covered with white down. It is extensively planted in S. Fla. where it is sometimes called White Areca Palm, and grows well in sun or shade. Young plants of its var. *rubrum* have beautiful red veined and mar-

gined glossy, deep-green leaves. It thrives in sandy soil or in limestone foundations and needs shade when the plants are young. In the N., Linoma Palms are grown in a warm greenhouse, with a day temperature of not less than 75 deg. and never less than 60 deg. at night. They should be planted in peat and loam, or loam and sand

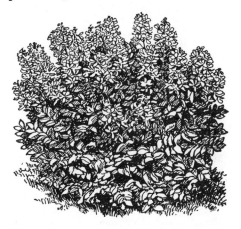

THE GAS-PLANT
Both flowers and lemon-scented foliage of this interesting old-fashioned perennial, Dictamnus, are decorative features in the border.

mixed with well-rotted cow manure and receive frequent waterings. The plants are most attractive when young used as table decorations.

DIDISCUS (di-dis'-kus). Former name of the genus now called Trachymene; one species (*T. caerulea*) is the popular Blue Lace-flower, which see.

DIEBACK. A symptom of plant disease consisting of the progressive death of a terminal shoot from the tip backwards. This may be caused by an organism, insufficient moisture, or severe temperatures. Many plants of indeterminate annual growth normally die back to some extent over the winter, but an abnormal amount of dying back in roses or other woody shrubs may be due to insufficient maturing of tender growth before cold weather starts. Feeding of such plants too late in the season (especially with nitrogenous substances) may cause this. See DISEASES, PLANT.

DIEFFENBACHIA (deef-en-bak'-i-ah). Tropical American upright shrubby evergreen plants with fleshy stems, belonging to the Arum Family. They are usually grown in warm greenhouses for their large soft handsome leaves, that are variously spotted and feathered with white, cream, or yellow markings. They thrive in a mixture of fibrous loam and peat with sand, and are appreciative of a little real old manure. A bacterial, leaf disease produces reddish spots with yellow margins, often followed by wilting. Don't crowd plants and avoid overhead watering. Propagation is by cuttings of the leafy top or by cutting up the old stems into short pieces. Be cautious in handling the plant as the juice is very acrid and poisonous. Principal species are the following:

D. bausei is a showy hybrid, with broad yellowish-green leaves, blotched dark green and spotted white, on white stems. *D. picta* is very showy, with shiny green leaves blotched white and yellow. It runs into several handsome forms with varying leaf markings. *D. seguine* has dark green leaves spotted with transparent white blotches. It is known as Dumb-cane, because the acrid juice causes temporary loss of speech if applied to the mouth. *D. imperialis* has handsome shining green leaves, marked yellow and white, up to 2 ft. long and a foot wide.

DIELYTRA (dy-el'-i-trah). Former name (still used in some catalogs) for the genus Dicentra, commonly called Bleeding Heart.

DIERAMA (dy-e-ray'-mah). A genus of bulbous plants of S. Africa, belonging to the Iris Family. They can be grown outdoors in mild climates, and are sometimes grown in cool greenhouses. They thrive under the same treatment as Ixia, which see.

D. pendula has narrow leaves and lilac flowers on stems to 4 ft., drooping at the ends. *D. pulcherrima* has narrow sword-shaped leaves drawn to a slender point, and reddish-purple drooping flowers borne on spikes to 6 ft. long.

DIERVILLA (dy-er-vil'-ah). A genus of deciduous shrubs of N. America, belonging to the Honeysuckle Family and commonly called Bush-honeysuckle. The more showy plants now classed as Weigela (which see) were formerly included in this genus. Diervillas are useful little shrubs for massing, or to edge the front of shrubberies. They are not particular as to soil, do well in partial shade and are propagated by suckers. There are three species.

D. lonicera, native from Newfoundland to N. C. and often listed as *D. trifida,*

grows to 3 ft., with oval long-pointed leaves to 4 in. long, and small yellow flowers, usually in 3's in early summer. *D. sessilifolia* is native from N. C. southward but is fairly hardy N. It grows to 5 ft., has 4-angled stems, leaves to 6 in. long, and pale yellow flowers in 3- to 7-flowered clusters in early summer. *D. rivularis* has the same range in habitat and hardiness. It grows to 6 ft., has smaller leaves, and few-to-many-flowered clusters of yellow flowers in late summer.

DIFFUSE. A widely or loosely spreading habit; a term applied to plants or parts of extensive open growths.

DIGGING. The preliminary step in preparing a limited area of soil for planting, by means of the spade or the spading fork. See SPADES AND SPADING; TRENCHING.

DIGITALIS (dij-i-tay'-lis). A genus of bienniel and perennial herbs with tall heads of handsome flowers; commonly called Foxglove (which see), they are popular herbaceous border subjects.

DIGITATE. In the shape of a hand; particularly applied to a leaf like that of the Buckeye, in which all 5 leaflets arise from the same point at the apex of the stalk, the general appearance being hand-like or, as it is termed, *palmately compound.* See PALMATE.

DILL. An Old-World annual or biennial herb (*Anethum graveolens*) of the Parsley Family, grown for its bitter seeds which are used for flavoring the popular dill (cucumber) pickles. Sow in drills 15 to 18 in. apart in early spring in warm soil and a sunny place. Thin the seedlings while small to stand 8 or 10 in. asunder. Cultivate frequently. In midsummer cut the ripening heads and spread thinly on sheets. When dry, thresh with light rods. Clean and store the seed in cotton sacks in dry quarters. See HERBS; CULINARY HERBS; HERB GARDEN.

DILLENIA (di-lee'-ni-ah). A genus of Australasian trees, one of which, *D. indica* (or *D. speciosa*), is grown in the warmest parts of the U. S., for its large, showy white or yellow flowers, often exceeding 6 in. in diameter and its tart fleshy fruits. While normally evergreen it is likely to drop its leaves in dry seasons.

DILLWYNIA (dil-wy'-ni-ah). Small heath-like shrubs of Australia, belonging to the Pea Family. They may be grown as pot plants in the cool greenhouse, or outdoors in warm regions. They thrive under the same conditions as Chorizema, which see. The pea-like flowers of yellow or orange-red are very showy. The principal species are:

D. ericifolia, with yellow flowers in short clusters; *D. floribunda,* with yellow flowers in pairs; *D. hispida,* which bears red and purple flowers in terminal heads, and *D. juniperiana,* with orange and red flowers, also in terminal heads.

DIMORPHOTHECA (dy-mor-fo-thee′-kah). A genus of S. African annuals and perennials commonly known as Cape-marigold, which see.

DINGLEBERRY. Colloquial name for *Vaccinium erythrocarpum,* a deciduous shrub, native from Va. to Ga., with pink flowers and red to purplish fruits.

DIOECIOUS (dy-ee′-shus). A term applied to plants in which the two kinds of sex organs are borne on different individuals. The flowers bearing only the male reproductive elements are called *staminate* flowers; those bearing the female egg-cells are *pistillate* flowers. In contrast, *monoecious* plants are those which bear both kinds of flowers in the same individual. These terms apply only to plants in which the stamens and pistils occur in separate (*unisexual*) flowers. In so-called "perfect" (*bisexual*) flowers, the male and female organs are found together in a single blossom.

See also FLOWER.

DIONAEA (dy-oh-nee′-ah) *muscipula.* An insect-eating plant native to the Carolinas. See VENUS FLY-TRAP; INSECTIVOROUS PLANTS.

DIOSCOREA (dy-os-koh′-ree-ah). Yam. Herbaceous twining vines from warm regions, closely related to the Lily Family. Several species are cultivated in the tropics for their large edible tubers, which are handled and used like potatoes. A few are grown in greenhouses for their handsome foliage. Easy to grow, they are propagated by seeds, tubers and cuttings. The principal species are as follows:

D. alata is distinguished by 4-winged or angled stems. It bears tubers up to 8 ft. long and weighing up to 100 lbs.

batatas (Cinnamon-vine or Chinese Yam). A hardy, useful vine of light growth. The edible tubers grow up to 3 ft. long, deep in the ground.

bulbifera (Air-potato). A tall slender climber, remarkable for its large angular stem tubers which may become a foot long

and several pounds in weight. The root-tubers, when produced at all, are small.

discolor. A decorative greenhouse species with leaves mottled in several shades of green, white along the mid-rib and rich purple beneath.

multicolor. Another ornamental-leaved, tender species with several forms, showing variegations in silvery white, yellow, red, green and pink.

See CINNAMON-VINE; SWEET POTATO; YAM.

DIOSMA (dy-oz′-mah). A heath-like shrub of S. Africa, belonging to the Rue Family. The one species (*D. ericoides*), known as Buchu, is sometimes grown under glass, also outdoors in the warmest parts of the country. When grown in a pot it requires a mixture of fibrous loam, with peat or leafmold and plenty of sharp sand. Plants should be cut back hard after flowering to induce a good bushy habit. The foliage is pleasantly aromatic, and the small white flowers, freely produced, are useful as fillers in table decorations. Propagation is by cuttings of young wood.

Because a related plant, *Adenandra fragrans,* was formerly known as Diosma fragrans, its common name, Breath-of-Heaven, is frequently applied to this plant, too.

DIOSPYROS (dy-os′-pi-ros). A genus of widely scattered trees and shrubs mostly ornamental and interesting but some grown for their fruits. See PERSIMMON.

DIPELTA (dy-pel′-tah). Deciduous shrubs of China belonging to the Honeysuckle Family. They are fairly hardy North, and grow well in any good soil in a position that does not get too hot and dry. Propagated by cuttings of half-ripened and mature wood.

D. floribunda is the hardiest, and makes a large handsome shrub to 15 ft. In early summer it produces a profusion of clusters of fragrant funnel-shaped pale rose flowers with orange markings. Large conspicuous and persistent bracts are borne at the base of the clusters.

ventricosa grows to more than 15 ft., but is not quite as hardy. It has darker colored flowers.

DIPLADENIA (dip-lah-dee′-ni-ah). Twining evergreen shrubs from S. America, belonging to the Dogbane Family. They are handsome and showy flowering plants for the intermediate greenhouse, where they may be grown either in a border and trained to the roof, or in pots trained on stakes or a wire form. They thrive in a mixture of fibrous peat and loam, with coarse sand and broken charcoal added. Keep them moderately warm and dry during the resting stage in winter. In early spring when new growth shows signs of starting, prune back the side branches and repot, or renovate the soil. Give a little extra heat until growth is well under way. Root cuttings with bottom heat.

D. boliviensis and *D. splendens* are the species usually grown. There are also numerous named forms of garden origin, with clusters of large showy funnel-shaped flowers in white and shades of pink, with yellow markings.

DIPSACEAE (dip-say'-see-ee). The Teasel Family, a group of herbs bearing dense heads or spikes of small flowers subtended by stiff hooked bracts. The common name is derived from the use of the dry, ripe spikes of species of Dipsacus (the "teasels" of commerce) for fulling or "teasing" the nap of cloth. A few other genera are ornamental subjects, such as Scabiosa, Cephalaria and Morina.

DIPSACUS (dip'-sah-kus). A genus of tall hairy or prickly, thistle-like herbs whose dry bristly flower-heads are used in the textile industry for raising a nap on fabrics. See TEASEL.

DIPTERONIA (dip-tur-oh'-ni-ah). Small deciduous trees from China, belonging to the Maple Family. *D. sinensis,* apparently the only species in cultivation, is an ornamental tree, not particular as to soil, but not hardy North. It has long attractive leaves, composed of 9 to 15 leaflets. The small and inconspicuous flowers are followed by clusters of peculiar winged seeds.

DIRCA (dur'-kah). Two species of N. American shrubs of interesting habit and valued for the early flowers. See LEATHER-WOOD.

DIRT BANDS. Small bottomless and topless, generally square, paper pots or boxes, each to be filled with soil and used in starting individual seeds or growing on seedling plants. Usually they are fitted closely together in flats which are kept in greenhouses, hotbeds or coldframes until time to set the plants in the open. Then the little pots may either be removed and used over again or set in the ground along with the plants they contain so as to avoid disturbing the roots. In moist soil they will break down and permit the roots to spread naturally. See FLOWER POTS, PAPER.

DISBUDDING. The practice of destroying buds or young shoots for some desired end, usually the enhancement of the quality and size of flowers. For instance, bush roses normally develop several flower buds on each stem. If all are allowed to bloom the flowers will be small and imperfect; but if all except the terminal bud are destroyed as soon as they can be reached with the finger-nail, the single flower remaining will be larger and more perfect in form, and will have a longer stem. Early disbudding also tends to foster quick new growth lower down on the plant and helps maintain a succession of bloom the whole season through. Chrysanthemums, dahlias and various other plants produce "specimen" and "exhibition" blooms when their flower and branch buds are so treated.

Newly planted grape-vines are often allowed to develop a shoot from each of two or three buds, only to have all but one cut off the following spring. It is better practice to "disbud" all but the strongest of such shoots, leaving only one leaf on each, as soon as the base of the selected shoot has become partially woody. It thus gets most of the available plant food and usually becomes strong enough to bear fruit the next season—a year earlier than under usual practice. For the same reason during the second and third years shoots that start at a point lower than is desirable for arms, and those between the upper and lower arms, are destroyed when an inch or less in length. The sooner they are removed the better.

Recent experiments have proved that fruit trees may be made much stronger structurally if disbudded instead of being permitted to branch at will. The practice starts with the unbranched one-year tree—the "whip"—with its terminal bud intact and *plump.* Groups of three buds located at the heights desired and a foot or more apart are chosen for development and all others except the terminal or topmost one are destroyed. These selected buds may all be expected to develop branches. In the spring of the second year the most favorably placed and best developed branch in each group is chosen to form a part of the permanent framework of the tree, the others being cut back close to the trunk. The same practice when repeated on the main branches tends to make a symmetrical, well balanced, structurally strong tree. See also PINCHING.

DISEASES, PLANT. Disease in plants is most simply defined as "any deviation from a normal condition." Generally this means an injurious condition or process caused by the continued irritation of some chief factor which may be either an environmental condition or a living organism. Diseases due to environmental conditions such as drought, excessive moisture, lack of proper nutrients or overfeeding, improper soil acidity, too low or too high temperatures, gas or electrical injury or injury resulting from industrial processes, are called *Physiological Diseases.* A group of diseases difficult to classify and known as *Virus Diseases* (which see), are due to some transmittable infectious principle the true nature of which is as yet unknown, perhaps because it is too small to be seen even with an ultra-microscope or is unrecognizable. Comparable virus diseases of man include sleeping sickness and infantile paralysis, and those of animals, rabies. In plants virus diseases are recognized chiefly by a "mosaic" or mottled effect on the foliage or by a yellowing and stunting of the plant.

Plant injury caused by the chewing and sucking of insects and other animals is not considered true plant disease; but the disturbance caused by nematodes (eel-worms) resulting in typical symptoms such as browning of the tissues and gall formation, *is* generally so considered. Plant parasites that cause disease in the generally accepted sense are bacteria, slime molds, fungi and a few higher plants such as dodder and mistletoe, which see.

Symptoms are evidences of plant disease produced in or by the plant itself; *signs* are evidences of the *pathogene,* or disease-producing organism, such as fruiting bodies or mycelium (see fungi). It is necessary for the gardener to recognize a plant disease or the group to which it belongs, if he is to select and apply proper control measures. An understanding of a few of the fundamental symptoms and signs will help in consulting the literature concerning specific diseases and in asking for special help. In writing to experiment stations and other sources of information about garden troubles send a typical specimen of the affected plant whenever possible. In any case send a complete, careful description of the symptoms and signs noted. Too often such a query takes the form: "My elm is sick; what shall I do about it?"

COMMON SYMPTOMS OF PLANT DISEASE

Symptoms may be either *local,* such as a spot or canker; or *general,* as in the case of wilt or damping-off. They are classed as *necrotic,* which means resulting in death of the tissues involved; *hypoplastic,* resulting in underdevelopment; or *hyperplastic,* resulting in overdevelopment of tissues or functions. (Become familiar with those terms.)

Some common *necrotic symptoms* are:

Scorch—sudden death and browning of large areas of leaves or fruits—due to drought, heat or spray injury.

Blight—sudden killing of shoots, foliage or blossoms by a pathogenic organism.

Spot—a more or less circular, dead area developed in leaves or fruit; usually brown in the center but often surrounded by reddish or yellow zones.

Die-back—the dying backward from the tip of twigs and branches of trees and shrubs. May be a symptom of winter injury, of fungus attacks, or of wet soil.

Shot-hole—a spotting of leaves followed by dropping out of diseased areas; certain kinds of leaves, such as cherry, have a special tendency in this direction. May be due to fungi or to spray injury.

Canker — sunken lesions in stems, branches, trunks or roots of trees or shrubs.

Rot—dead tissue in a more or less advanced stage of decomposition. Rots may be soft, hard, dry or wet, and caused by either bacteria (e.g., soft rot of iris) or by fungi (e.g., crown rot of ornamentals).

Mummification—wrinkling and drying of fruits into a hard mass called a "mummy," consisting of an intermingling of host plant and fungus tissue. See BROWN ROT.

Damping-off—the rapid rotting at the base, or wilting, of seedlings. They may be damped-off in such a young stage that they do not even emerge from the soil.

Wilt—the clogging or poisoning of the vascular (circulatory) system of a plant, resulting in drooping or die-back and usually the death of the entire plant.

Among the common *hypoplastic symptoms* (those showing underdevelopment in size or differentiation of organs) are some particularly characteristic of virus diseases, as:

Chlorosis—subnormal development of the green color in a plant.

Mosaic—a mottling or incomplete chlorosis.

Yellows—a general chlorotic condition.

Stunting—a reduction in size.

Rosetting—the crowding of the foliage into a rosette due to the shortening of the internodes of the stems.

Examples of *hyperplastic symptoms* (those showing overdevelopment in size or differentiation of organs) are:

Tumefaction—tumor-like swellings or galls produced on woody portions of plants due to the action of bacteria or fungi.

Curl—abnormal bending, curling, or crinkling of leaves due to overdevelopment of one side.

Scab—definite, usually circular, somewhat raised lesions on fruits, tubers, stems and leaves.

Callus—tissue overgrowth in response to wounding.

Fasciculation or witches' brooms—clustering of organs due to adventitious development of shoots.

SIGNS OF DISEASE-CAUSING AGENTS

There are various signs of disease producing organisms, such as

Mycelium—a white weft at the base of the plant (as in Sclerotinia rot) or dark radiating strands in a leaf spot disease such as black spot or rose. The mycelium is the growing part of a fungus.

Sclerotia—hard, more or less spherical, resting bodies of a fungus, black in the case of botrytis blight of peonies, reddish brown in crown rot.

Fruiting bodies (see FUNGI)—These may be soft brown cups arising from mummies on the ground (see BROWN ROT); small black dots in the center of stem or leaf lesions; or large *sporophores* coming out of tree trunks (see BRACKET FUNGI).

Spores—These may appear as grayish mold on buds (as in botrytis blight), gray pustules on fruit (in brown rot), reddish pustules on stems and leaves (in rusts), or black sooty masses (in smuts).

Exudation—A mixture of plant sap and the disease-causing organism, as illustrated by the bacterial ooze seen on fire-blight cankers and the gummy substance formed in brown rot.

Odors—These are characteristic of certain diseases, especially the soft rot of iris.

Despite popular belief to the contrary, the prevalence of plant disease is nothing new; some of the present day troubles go back to the earliest records of man. But the spread of plant disease has kept pace with the advance in methods of transportation and the severity of its attacks with the more intensive culture of special crops. Disease-producing organisms are transported in or on seed, tubers, nursery stock, and soil and plant débris by boat, train, automobile and airplane as well as by the older natural forces of air and water currents, birds, and insects.

Local dissemination of plant disease is accomplished by wind and wind-splashed rain, by insects—the honey bee is responsible for spreading fire-blight organism and aphids and leaf hoppers carry the virus of certain mosaics—and by animals, dogs, cats, field mice and, especially, man. Gardeners themselves (through their hands, clothing and tools) are often unwittingly responsible for spreading disease around their own and their neighbors' gardens. Hence, always take sanitary precautions when working with diseased plants. If you cut off a blighted peony bud covered with spores, do not carry it openly around the garden on the way to the trash pile; put it in a paper bag immediately. If you pull up a slimy diseased iris plant do not touch a healthy one until you have washed your hands thoroughly with soap and water or dipped them in a disinfectant. Above all do not divide your iris and give to your neighbors without disinfecting the rhizomes and fans (see IRIS). Likewise disinfect pruning tools after cutting off a diseased plant part before touching them to a healthy subject. See DISINFECTION; SANITATION.

The control of plant disease is accomplished by four principle methods: (1) exclusion, (2) eradication, (3) protection and (4) immunization. *Exclusion* means keeping the pathogene out of a disease-free area as by quarantine regulations or by disinfecting seeds or plant parts before planting. *Eradication* depends on removal and destruction of infected plants or plant parts, or the application of a fungicide strong enough to kill the pathogene in its position on the host plant. Generally this means applying a dormant spray, such as 1 to 7 lime-sulphur for peach leaf curl, though sometimes fungi (especially mildews) may be killed by applying summer strength fungicides during the growing season. Sometimes an important factor in an eradication campaign is the control of insects that help spread it.

Protection is the most usual method of control in gardens. Plants are dusted or sprayed with a protective material designed to *prevent* the growth of the pathogene and its entrance into the plant. For this reason protective measures must always be started *early in the season,* before the pathogene is disseminated. See SPRAYING; DUSTING; FUNGICIDE.

Immunization as a means of control consists chiefly in the breeding, multiplication and distribution of immune varieties. This is a relatively new means of fighting plant disease among ornamentals, but recent developments in the production of wilt-resistant asters and rust-proof snapdragons show that progress is being made.

DISHCLOTH-GOURD. Common name for Luffa (which see), a genus of tropical vines of the Cucumber Family, some of which bear large hard shelled fruits, the fibrous absorbent interior of which is used as a wash rag.

DISINFECTION. This means the direct destruction of a disease-producing organism while in any way associated with the host plant or present in its immediate environment. The term includes (1) disinfection of the plant in a dormant condition (as in spraying for peach leaf curl) or in an active condition (as when dusted with sulphur to control powdery mildews); (2) disinfection of plant parts such as seeds, bulbs and tubers, and (3) soil disinfection.

SOIL DISINFECTION may be accomplished by heat or with electricity or chemicals. Partial sterilization by heat may be accomplished by baking the soil in an oven, by heating it with electricity, or by treating it with hot water or steam. It is not desirable to completely sterilize soil, since that means killing *all* living organisms, those that cause disease and those that are harmless or even beneficial. The destructive organisms should be destroyed, but if all organic life ceases the soil is rendered infertile.

Baking is a simple method of treating a few flats of soil for the home gardener. The soil (in a metal container) should be left in the oven until a medium sized potato placed in the center of the pot or pan is baked. The same effect can be obtained in seed beds out-of-doors by covering the loosened soil with straw or brush and keeping up a hot fire for an hour or so. Burning over stubble and plant débris in the fall so as to destroy various disease-causing organisms is also helpful. Recently electric cookers have been de-

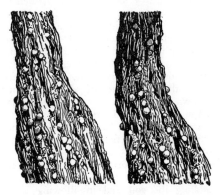

CROWN ROT ON IRIS
This shows the base of two leaves badly rotted by this serious fungus. The small light and dark-colored spots are the sclerotia (resting bodies) of the fungus.

vised and put on the market for partially sterilizing small quantities of soil. In some places, electrically treated soil can be purchased for use in flats or seed beds.

Steam is probably the most satisfactory means of heat sterilization, although it is usually applicable only to large greenhouses unless a portable boiler is available for treating outdoor seed beds. Steam may be applied either through loose tile or perforated pipe buried in the soil or by means of a large inverted pan. Limited amounts of soil can be sterilized in a large pressure cooker as used for canning operations.

Hot water at boiling temperature can be used for soil disinfection where only a small area is to be treated, but has the disadvantage of puddling the soil. Enough must be applied to thoroughly saturate the soil—about 7 gals. per cu. ft. This method controls nematodes and soil fungi near the soil surface, but is not very successful for deep sterilization. Small (4-in.) flower pots full of soil can be sterilized by a 5-minute immersion in boiling water and trays from one to two inches deep by a slightly longer period of treating.

Of the chemicals used for soil disinfection, formaldehyde is the commonest. It can be applied to soil outdoors where steam is not generally available, but must be used only when all living plants have been removed. Dilute one part of commercial formalin (40% formaldehyde) with 50 parts of water and apply ½ to 1 gal. to each square foot of soil after loosening it up. Cover the ground immediately with canvas or heavy paper for a day, then remove the covering, and wait for about 2 weeks before planting—until all odor has evaporated. Formaldehyde dust, purchased ready for use, is convenient for preventing damping-off and killing other soil organisms; thoroughly mix 8 oz. of 6 per cent dust with each bushel of soil. Seed may be sown in such soil at once and the flats thoroughly watered afterwards; *but if rooted plants are to be planted,* the formaldehyde odor must first be allowed to disappear.

A new liquid formaldehyde method has the same advantages as the dust in not puddling the soil and in allowing immediate seeding, but is cheaper and seems more effective. With a soil mixture of equal parts sand and top soil, 2½ tablespoons of formaldehyde are used for each bushel of soil; these are diluted with 5 or 6 times as much water, sprinkled over the soil and mixed in. The dosage for the average flat is 1 level tablespoonful. Seeds may be sown in soil so treated in 12 to 24 hours, after which the flats should be watered thoroughly. It is essential that the soil be in proper condition for seed sowing—as regards both moisture content and friability—before it is treated.

A new combination formaldehyde-and-steam method of sterilizing soil in greenhouses to control wilt and club root was, in 1940, reported by commercial Ohio growers as "unusually effective" and causing considerable saving in time and coal consumed. By means of a simple apparatus, the chemical is fed into the steam as it is carried to the pipes that distribute it through the soil in the beds.

Acetic acid is sometimes used for disinfecting soil in which no plants are growing. A commercial grade containing 56 per cent acid is diluted at the rate of 1 part to 50 parts of water and applied at the rate of ½ gal. per square foot. Wait two weeks before planting in the soil.

Various chemicals have been used to prevent damping off of coniferous seedlings. Sulphuric acid diluted at the rate of 1 pint to 2 to 4 gals. of water can be applied over 8 to 10 sq. ft. of area right after the seed is sown. Aluminum sulphate—1 lb. to 30 sq. ft.—can be used as a dust or sprinkled on; also diluted acetic acid—1 qt. of a ½ per cent solution per square foot.

Sulphur may occasionally be used as a soil fungicide, especially for the suppression of common scab of potatoes. Apply 1 lb. to 100 sq. ft. and thoroughly cultivate it in advance of planting. The amount of sulphur may have to be varied somewhat to correspond with the initial acidity of the soil.

Zinc oxide (obtainable cheaply at paint stores as "zinc white") may be applied to soil as a supplementary treatment to control above-ground damping off; enough of the chemical (½ to 1 oz. per square foot) is applied to the soil surface thickly enough to make a smooth white layer over the ground. For best results seed should not be sown deeper than ¼ in. If used around transplanted plants apply only on cool, cloudy days or in late afternoon.

Mercuric chloride (better known as corrosive sublimate, which see) is mostly used as a disinfectant for plant parts but can be used in borders to control various crown and root rots. When a diseased plant is removed, the soil in and around the resulting hole should be drenched with a 1 to 1000 solution of the chemical. Mild infections may sometimes be overcome by applying one of the proprietary organic mercury compounds to the soil, but these are usually used for treating seed (see below).

Napthalene flakes worked into the soil around plants will frequently prevent the spread of crown rot. Other soil fumigants, used in most cases for the control of nematodes and insects, are carbon bisulphide, chloropicrin, methyl bromide, ethylene dichloride and dichlorethylether. See those subjects and FUMIGATION.

TREATING PLANT PARTS. Disinfection of seeds and other plant parts is accomplished with hot water or various chemicals. Hot water seed treatment is practiced mainly by farmers in protecting grains against loose smut. Cabbage seed is sometimes treated for black rot by being soaked for 30 minutes in water held at 122 deg. F. Hot water is also used to destroy nematodes, flies and mites in bulbs, especially narcissus and other flowering sorts. The usual procedure is 3 hours at 110 deg. F. See ENEMIES under BULBS.

Sodium chloride was first found to be a seed disinfectant when a cargo of wheat, lost off the coast of England in the seventeenth century, was later salvaged in good condition—freed from the smut fungus by the immersion in salt water. Copper sulphate, next developed as a cereal seed disinfectant, has since been largely replaced by copper carbonate dust, used at the rate of 2 to 3 oz. per bushel of seed.

Formaldehyde is also used to treat seed (which is soaked for 10 minutes in a solution of 1 pint to 40 gals. water), but it is apt to cause injury unless the seed is washed with water afterwards. Formaldehyde is also often used on potato tubers affected with scab and rhizoctonia. They are soaked in a cold solution of 1 pint formalin in 30 gals. water for $2\frac{1}{2}$ hours; or in a solution of 2 pints formalin in 30 gals. for $2\frac{1}{2}$ minutes, water at 122 deg. F. The seed is then covered with canvas or burlap for 1 hour. *Formaldehyde should not be used for treating flower seed.*

Corrosive sublimate (above refererd to) also can be used for soaking potato tubers for $1\frac{1}{2}$ hours in a cold 1 to 1000 solution (1 oz. to 7 gals. water). Cabbage and cauliflower seed are treated for 15 to 20 minutes with the same solution, which may also be used to free seeds of such organisms as cause bacterial spot of tomato, tobacco wild-fire, and celery blight. Iris rhizomes may be washed in the solution for 20 to 30 minutes to free them of soft rot bacteria.

Various organic mercury compounds under proprietary names such as uspulun and semesan have been successfully used to control damping-off of vegetable and flower seedlings. In using such materials, follow the manufacturer's directions exactly.

Red copper oxide (cuprous oxide) is now being successfully used in treating seeds to prevent damping-off. It must be purchased in a stable red form and no more should be used than necessary. On a commercial scale, 1 level teaspoonful of the dust is added to 1 lb. of small seed or 5 lbs. of large seed, and the seed and dust shaken together in a bottle. For a packet of seed, a small pinch is sufficient. This same material is being recommended for use as a spray (supplementing seed treatment) to prevent stem-cankers and leaf diseases as well as damping-off in seedlings

in greenhouses. Weekly applications of 1 oz. red copper oxide to 3 gals. water (1 lb. to 50 gals.), or $1\frac{1}{2}$ oz. of a newly perfected proprietary form of the chemical, are suggested by the N. Y. Experiment Station.

Disinfectants such as corrosive sublimate, mercuric cyanide, bordeaux paint and creosote compounds, are also used in the treatment of wounds and cleaned out cavity surfaces. See TREE SURGERY.

Wherever there is a possibility of infection being carried by pruning knives and other garden tools, they should be treated. Corrosive sublimate is generally effective for steel instruments.

DISK-FLOWER. One of the individual florets which make up the center of the flower-head of such composite plants as the daisy. They are so small and so compactly arranged that the whole head, whether or not it has a border of strap-shaped, petal-like ray-flowers (which see), has the appearance of, and is often mistaken for, a single flower.

Disk-flowers are tubular in shape; usually yellow, brown or purple, rather than colorful; and contain both male and female elements, that is stamens and pistils. When associated with ray-flowers, as in the daisy head, sometimes they alone are fertilized and develop seed, the ray flowers in such a case being imperfect.

DISPORUM (dy-spoh'-rum). A genus of liliaceous perennial herbs with drooping white or yellowish flowers found in woods and sometimes grown in wild gardens as Fairy Bells, which see.

DISSEMINATION. In gardening this means the distribution of plants or seeds to the public. The word originally meant broadcast sowing, but is now used figuratively. Dissemination is accomplished by the nursery, seed, and florist trades, which are organized into propagators, growers, wholesalers and retailers who use salesmen, catalogs, and advertising to reach one another and the public. New plants introduced by large growers are usually sold to local retailers before they reach the ultimate buyer.

See also INTRODUCTION, ORIGINATION.

DITCH-MOSS. Common name for *Elodea canadensis,* an aquatic perennial with whitish flowers that float on the surface.

DITTANY (dit'-ah-ni). A common name for *Dictamnus albus,* a shrubby per-

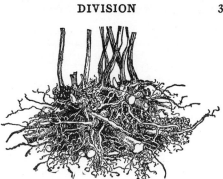

DIVIDING A PEONY CLUMP—I
Soil has been washed from the mass of roots,
which are to be cut into sections, each of which
will produce a new plant.

ennial with white, rosy or purplish flowers,
also called Gas-plant, Burning-bush, etc.,
because of the inflammable vapor given off
by its flowers.

Maryland-dittany (which see) is *Cunila
origanoides,* a low-growing herb of the
Mint Family.

DIVISION. A form of plant propagation in which new plants are not grown
from seeds or bulbs but separated from
the parents; also any such part or new
plant is called a "division." There are
several types. Parts already naturally
rooted (as strawberry runners, blackberry
suckers) may be severed from the original specimen and transplanted. Or there
may be simple separation of parts not
already rooted (as tulip bulblets and hen-
and-chicken offsets) but which take root
readily after being removed from the parent, especially at the close of the growing season. Similarly certain types of cut-
tage as in handling cannas, rhubarb and
various herbaceous perennials in which
parts are simply cut or torn from the main
clump of roots and crown, are kinds of
division.

Methods of division vary widely. Rough
division consists in using a sharp spade
to cut across large clumps of such plants
as phlox and rhubarb or an axe for shrubs
such as Diervilla and Philadelphus. The
pieces are then dug and replanted. Finer
practices include digging and breaking the
clumps apart with the hand or the fingers
or cutting them apart with a sharp knife.
Suckers which develop from plants such as
red raspberry and snowberry are dug individually. Stolons (slender branches)
which naturally take root (as in red osier
dogwood) are similarly cut apart. Crowns

or rooted buds which form (usually at
the tips of rhizomes) toward the close of
the growing season and push forward in
the soil, are often severed and planted;
the best example of this type is lily-of-
the-valley, millions of whose "pips" are
forced annually by florists. Tubers (short,
thickened parts of subterranean branches
such as dahlia or Jerusalem artichoke)
are broken apart from the main stems and
clumps and then planted separately. Still
more specialized instances of division or
separation are the bulblets formed in the
leaf axils of Tiger Lilies and other kinds,
the plantlets formed in the margins of bryophyllum leaves, and the fronds of various
ferns.

Taken as a whole, division and separation are two of the easiest methods of
propagation which amateur gardeners can
utilize in increasing plants suited to these
types of multiplication. See LAYERING;
PROPAGATION.

DOCK. One common name for species
of the genus Rumex, often used to include
those called Sorrel (which see), a large
group of biennial and perennial herbs, with
stout taproots, large, smooth leaves, usually
with wavy margins, placed alternately on
tall stems, and greenish flowers without
petals arranged in whorled clusters and
followed by fruits of leathery red or brown.
Most of them are troublesome weeds, common in pastures and along roadsides, but
the Great Water Dock of Europe (*R. hy-
drolapathum*) growing 4 to 6 ft. high, is
sometimes used with good effect in land-

DIVIDING A PEONY CLUMP—II
Eight new plants can be grown from these divisions made from the single peony plant shown in
the preceding illustration.

scaping along water courses. Some of the dock roots yield a dye, and astringent medicines are made from others. Roots of Canaigre (*R. hymenosepalus*) contain tannin used in preparing leather.

DOCKMACKIE (dok'-mak-i). A common name for *Viburnum acerifolium,* a white-flowered shrub with maple-like leaves and purplish black fruits.

DODDER. One of the very few higher plants that are true pathogenes, that is, cause disease. Species of the genus Cuscuta, the Dodders or Love-vines (also called Strangle-weed, Gold Thread, Devils Hair, and Hell-bind) are closely related to the morning-glory; but they are leafless, twining, parasitic seed plants without chlorophyll, which attach their yellow, orange or pink thread-like stems to various cultivated and wild plants, taking their food from these hosts by means of sucking organs (*haustoria*).

Especially menacing to clovers, alfalfa, and flax, dodders are sometimes found on ornamentals, having been seen strangling chrysanthemum, dahlia, helenium, petunia, Virginia-creeper, trumpet-vine, English ivy, and other vines. The dodder flowers, small, white, pink or yellowish, appear in clusters from early June to the end of the growing season. The seeds, ripening from July until frost, are produced in great abundance and only clover or alfalfa seed free from dodder seed should be purchased. Seed firms use special apparatus to remove it, but if there is doubt as to the purity of seed intended for planting, send it to your state seed laboratory for testing. Portions of ornamentals attacked by dodder should be freed of it or removed before it sets seed.

DODECATHEON (doh-de-kath'-e-on). Shooting Star, American Cowslip. A genus of small American perennial herbs of the Primrose Family with basal leaves and nodding cyclamen-like flowers in rounded clusters. The flowers are white, rose or purple with reflexed petals, the joined stamens making a beak-like projection which gives the plant its common name of Shooting Star.

Dodecatheons grow naturally in half-shady woodland or rather damp mountain meadows, hence should be planted in moist soil, rich in humus, in the rock or wild garden in partial shade, taking care that there is good drainage. They are propagated by division or by seed.

PRINCIPAL SPECIES

D. meadie, to 2 ft., is one of the largest, with rose-colored flowers, white at the base, and leaves up to 6 in. long. It runs into many forms, among which are vars. *alba* and *superba.*

jeffreyi, also tall, has erect leaves to 1 ft. and a many-flowered umbel of deep rose-red flowers with a purple beak.

clevelandi, to 1½ ft., has rather small leaves and purple flowers with a yellow base and beak, the color occasionally varying to white.

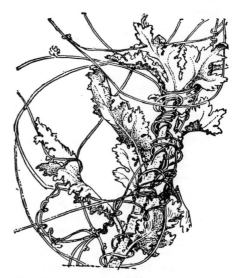

THE WELL NAMED STRANGLE-WEED
Dodder enveloping a chrysanthemum shoot. Unless removed it will both choke the host and rob it of sap.

hendersoni is similar, except that the beak is deep purple.

latilobum, to 1 ft. or more, has leaves to 10 in. and yellowish-white flowers, 2 to 4 in a cluster, with very short beaks.

poeticum, with leaves to 4½ in., has prettily colored flowers, rose-pink with concentric circles of yellow and crimson.

radicatum is a plant with smooth light-green leaves and rose-red flowers on a stout stem, particularly suited to the rock garden.

DODGES HYBRID FERN. A wood fern native to the N. E. States and excellent for garden use. It is a cross between *Dryopteris marginalis* and *D. cristata.* The upper part is like the former parent, 2-pinnate and leathery, the lower part like

D. cristata, with horizontal, broader and distant pinnae. Its culture is the same as for all Dryopteris.

DOGBANE. Common name for the genus Apocynum, represented especially by the native perennial Spreading Dogbane (*A. androsaemifolium*), a shrub-like herb with milky juice and small pink bell-shaped flowers in loose flat clusters. Although attractive in the border where it will stand drought and poor soil, it must be watched because it increases rapidly and may prove a nuisance, crowding out more desirable plants.

DOGBANE FAMILY. Common name of Apocynaceae (which see), a widely distributed family of herbs, shrubs and trees, grown mostly for ornament, but in some cases for their fruit.

DOG ROSE. Common name for *Rosa canina,* an Old-World shrub or bush species with mostly single, pink or white flowers. A good, hardy sort, it has run wild to some extent but is not much grown in gardens. It had been used extensively in Europe as a stock for grafting, and some growers in parts of this country like it for certain varieties of roses for outdoor growing.

DOGS, PROTECTING PLANTS FROM. Injury caused by dogs running through gardens and flower beds, or by burying (and later digging up) bones in the soft, tilled ground can, of course, be prevented only by fencing the planted areas or by restraining the animals or training them to know their place in the garden.

The more common and more serious killing or disfiguring of the lower branches of valued evergreens by dogs wetting on them can be prevented in several ways. Commercial (40%) nicotine-sulphate sprayed on the plants at the rate of 1½ teaspoonful to a gallon of water, is claimed to have quite a lasting effect in repelling both dogs and cats—besides its value as a contact insecticide. There are also several preparations obtainable in collapsible tubes or other containers which, hung among the branches with the stoppers removed, slowly evaporate and act in the same way. There are also on the market inconspicuous, slender, spreading wire devices which, thrust into the soil at the base of plants, serve to mechanically repel animals that get close to them. Supplementing any of the foregoing methods, steps, porches, and other parts of the dwelling, or garden furniture, can similarly be protected by spraying with gasoline in which is dissolved as much napthalene or paradichrolobenzene (which see) as it will take up. But this, though an effective repellent, will injure plants and should not be applied to them.

DOGSTOOTH-VIOLET. A common but misleading name for *Erythronium denscanis* (also called Adders Tongue), a hardy perennial herb with yellow flowers. It is a member of the Lily Family and not related to the violets.

DOGWOOD. Cornus. The Dogwoods are among the most useful of hardy ornamental woody plants. One or two are herbs (see *C. canadensis* below), and some grow to be fair sized trees, but most of them are free growing shrubs. The native Flowering Dogwood (*C. florida* in the list of species below) is one of the most beautiful features of the early spring landscape in the Atlantic Coast States and a favorite for garden planting wherever it will grow.

Dogwoods are adapted for many garden purposes, and grow well in ordinary soil. For shady places few shrubs are better, but the variegated leaved forms are brighter in the open. The forms with colored stems are very effective in winter, and grow and show to good advantage when grouped near water, especially if a good portion of old wood is cut out every year.

Fresh seeds sown in the fall in a coldframe, usually germinate the following spring. *Cornus alba* and other kinds with rather soft wood can be easily propagated from cuttings of mature shoots, or by layering.

DISEASES AND PESTS

A crown canker has been killing trees on Long Island and is reported in Mass. Symptoms include dieback of the crown with defoliation. Leaves are small, chlorotic, and sparse, but fruit is abnormally abundant; slime flux sets in where bark is ruptured. As yet, no control is known. A twig blight may be checked by pruning out infected twigs and feeding trees to increase vigor. Check leaf spots by spraying in spring with bordeaux mixture and, in fall, collecting and burning fallen leaves.

Twigs attacked by borers may be cut and burned; bark borers are controlled by removing dead outer bark containing larvae in the spring just after the leaves appear. The cottony maple scale on flowering dogwood and scurfy scale on some of the shrub forms are controlled with a miscible oil spray in early spring. See also SCALE INSECTS.

PRINCIPAL SPECIES

C. alba (Tatarian Dogwood) is an upright shrub from W. Asia, growing to 10 ft. and conspicuous with its blood-red branches. Its flat heads of creamy-white flowers are followed by clusters of white or bluish tinted fruits. Var. *sibirica* is a less vigorous grower with coral-red branches. Good variegated leaved forms are *argenteo-marginata,* with leaves edged white; *gouchalti,* leaves variegated yellowish and pink; *spaethi,* leaves broadly edged yellow.

amomum (Silky Dogwood), a vigorous shrub with purple branches, found from Mass. to Tenn. It has yellowish flowers and blue or partly white fruits and its leaves are hairy or silky beneath.

baileyi, found from Ont. to Pa., has reddish branches which take on vivid coloring in winter. The leaves are white beneath and brilliantly colored in fall. The fruit is white.

stolonifera (Red-osier Dogwood), found from Nfd. to Va., spreads by underground stems. It has dark red branches and white or bluish fruits. Var. *flaviramea* is outstanding in winter with its yellow branches.

racemosa, found from Me. to Ga., is a gray-branched, good looking shrub of dense habit, with attractive white flowers in early summer. It is of striking appearance in the fall with its white fruits on red stems, which are colorful long after the fruits have gone.

rugosa, growing from N. S. to Va., is big and vigorous, fine to plant for a compact mass effect. The branches, green with purple blotches when young, become entirely purple with age. It has compact clusters of creamy-white flowers followed by bright blue or whitish fruits.

sanguinea (Blood-Twig Dogwood) is a European species with dark red branches and leaves deep red in fall. It has greenish white flowers and black fruits. Var. *viridissima* has green branches instead of red and also green fruits.

alternifolia (Pagoda Dogwood), found from N. B. to Ga., is a handsome large shrub or small tree, whose whorled branches in horizontal tiers give it a distinctive appearance. It has dark blue fruits.

controversa is the Asiatic form of the preceding species; it grows much larger and flowers several days earlier.

mas (Cornelian-cherry) is a large European shrub, conspicuous in early spring

FLOWERING DOGWOOD
One of America's finest native trees, beautiful with its mantle of flowers in the spring and its sprays of red leaves and berries in autumn.

with small clusters of yellow flowers opening and fading before the lustrous leaves, which remain green until late in the fall. It bears large red edible fruits in late summer. Var. *aureo-elegantissima* has leaves variegated creamy-white and pink.

officinalis, the Asiatic form of the Cornelian-cherry, is hardy in New England. It differs most noticeably in the bark which in *C. mas* is of close texture and dark colored and remains on several years; the bark of *C. officinalis* is reddish and peels into papery shreds about the second year.

florida (Flowering Dogwood) found from Mass. to Fla. is one of the most beautiful of small trees. It is handsome in early spring with its four white, blunt ended bracts surrounding the dense heads of small greenish flowers, and again in fall with scarlet fruits and gorgeous leaf coloring. The flower buds are conspicuous all winter. Var. *rubra* has showy pink bracts; var. *pendula* is a curious weeping form; var. *plena* has double white flowers, and var. *xanthocarpa* has yellow fruits.

kousa, a large shrub or small tree from Asia, is conspicuous in June with showy white bracts that are pointed and not rounded as in the Flowering Dogwood. The fruits are crowded together to form a round scarlet head. (See illustration, Plate 49.)

nuttalli, native of W. N. Amer. is the giant of the Dogwoods, growing to 75 ft.

or more, and considered the most beautiful of the genus. But it is not hardy North. It bears four to six bracts, white or pinkish, about 6 in. across, and bright red or orange fruit.

paucinervis is a handsome medium sized shrub from China, not quite hardy North. It flowers late in the summer and has black fruits.

capitata, a tender species from the Himalayas, is a partly evergreen large shrub or small tree with pale-yellow bracts and red strawberry-like fruits.

canadensis (Bunch-berry) is a native herb growing only a few inches high. It requires a cool rich soil in a partly shaded place and is often slow in getting established in gardens. It has a whorl of about six leaves, from the center of which come the tiny greenish flowers surrounded by four to six white bracts. Later it bears round scarlet berries in tight clusters.

DOLICHOS (dol'-i-kos). Tropical twining plants, belonging to the Pea Family. In the tropics several species are grown for food, and as forage and cover crops; in the U. S. one or two are grown in gardens for ornamental purposes. They are rapid growers, to 10 ft. or so, with wistaria-like flowers of red or white followed by attractive seed pods. They do best if planted where they are to stand.

D. lablab (Hyacinth-bean, Bonavist or Lablab), though a perennial, is grown as an annual. It is not particular as to soil, and can be sown outdoors when the weather becomes warm or started in pots under glass. It has large three-part leaves and stiff spikes of reddish-purple flowers. Var. *giganteus* is of larger growth with white flowers. *D. lignosus* (Australian Pea), another perennial, evergreen in warm regions, has much smaller leaves than the preceding species and rosy-purple or white flowers. It is a useful trellis vine.

DOMBEYA (dom'-bi-ah). Shrubs or small trees of Africa, sometimes grown in greenhouses, and one or two outdoors in the warmest parts of the country. They are rapid growers, with mostly large heart-shaped or palmate leaves and umbels of showy flowers. Propagation is effected by seeds or cuttings.

Of the principal species, *D. natalensis* is large shrub or small tree with poplar-like leaves and fragrant white flowers. A good winter-flowering subject in S. Calif. (*D. punctata*) grows to 10 ft. or more, with angled leaves white beneath, and pink flowers. *D. mastersi* is a small shrub with velvety leaves and fragrant white flowers. *D. wallichi* is the largest and showiest. It grows to 30 ft., with large velvety leaves and drooping red or pink flowers.

DOODIA (doo'-di-ah). A genus of small ferns from Australia, useful in the cool greenhouse for edging and underplanting, as they will tolerate overhead watering and prefer shade. There are a half-dozen species available from the trade, all rather similar, forming compact bushy plants from 8 to 24 ins. tall, with once pinnate fronds, colored red, violet or bronze when young, and often in fancy crested, plumed and pendulous forms. Must have perfect drainage. The most reliable species (*D. lunulata*) known as the Hacksaw Fern, has spear-shaped fronds, 1 to 2 ft. long, once pinnate, of a soft red when young. The stipes are suffused with pink.

DORMANT. A living plant or seed capable of active vegetative growth, but in an inactive state, due to the effect of unfavorable environmental conditions. Although a plant's rest-period (which see) may be completed, it may still remain dormant if the weather is hostile to growth. Dormancy, therefore, is controlled by external factors, such as temperature and moisture, whereas the rest period is controlled by internal factors. A plant will remain dormant because of the weather, but during its rest period it will not grow anyway, regardless of the weather.

DORONICUM (doh-ron'-i-kum). A genus of perennial daisy-like yellow-flowered herbs of the Composite Family, natives of Europe and temperate Asia. Commonly known as Leopards-bane, they are among the earliest of the family to bloom in gardens in the spring. The leaves are oval or slightly heart-shaped, numerous and with petioles at the base, thinning out and often stemless along the flower stalks. Doronicums thrive under average conditions but prefer a rich loam and full sun. Stock can be increased readily by yearly divisions, after the plants are through flowering, or grown from seed.

D. plantagineum, the best known and most grown species, grows 5 ft. high and bears large solitary flowers 2 to 4 in. across; the roots are tuberous.

caucasicum grows 2 ft. high with flowers one to a stem; the leaves are coarsely toothed.

clusi to 2 ft. also has solitary flowers but the basal leaves are not heart shaped as in the preceding species.

cordifolium is an alpine species growing only 5 in. high.

pardalianches to 4 ft. has hairy stems bearing up to 5 flower heads.

DORYANTHES (doh-ri-an'-theez). A genus, commonly called Spear-lily, of large succulent plants of the Amaryllis Family, native in dry regions of Australia, and sometimes seen in greenhouse collections. They usually attain a good size before flowering, and when fully grown may have as many as 100 leaves 6 ft. long. Propagation is by suckers.

D. excelsa has sword-shaped leaves to 4 ft. long, and a flower stem to 18 ft. bearing scarlet flowers 4 in. across in a round head. *D. palmeri* has arching leaves to 6 ft. long, and a many-flowered panicle of funnel-shaped red flowers, whitish on the inside, on a tall stem.

DORYCNIUM (doh-rik'-ni-um). Herbs or small shrubs from southern Europe, belonging to the Pea Family. *D. suffruticosum,* the best known, is a hardy, much branched deciduous shrub growing about 2 ft. high, and requiring a sunny position in rather light soil. It has attractive silvery clover-like leaves, and flower heads of pinkish-white flowers produced all summer. It is easily grown from seed.

DOUBLE COCONUT. Common name for *Lodoicea maldivica,* a species of Fan Palm, remarkable for bearing the largest known seeds. These are massive 2-lobed fruits, 12 by 18 in. in size; sometimes called *Coco de Mer* or "fruit of the sea," because, falling from trees into the ocean, they may float for miles and germinate when finally washed ashore.

DOUBLE DIGGING. A seldom used term that means digging two spade depths deep. See TRENCHING.

DOUBLE FLOWER. A flower in which the petals are multiplied beyond the usual number found in the species. Doubling is usually an inherent character, that is, not susceptible to modification by culture or environment. The extra petals often appear to replace stamens or pistils which have become suppressed or transformed into the petal-like shape or condition.

DOUBLE ORANGE-DAISY. A name for *Erigeron aurantiacus,* a Turkestan species of Fleabane attaining 10 ft. in height

and used as tall background material in perennial borders.

DOUGLAS-FIR. Common name for *Pseudotsuga douglasi,* also called Red-fir, a tree of the Pine Family reaching, in its natural habitat (the Rocky Mountain region), a height of over 200 ft. It has beautiful bluish-green needles on pendent branchlets, and bears drooping brown cones. In age it sometimes has a trunk 12 ft. in diameter with 2 ft. thick cinnamon-brown bark and no branches up to 100 ft. from the ground, but as a young tree it makes a regular pyramidal growth with branches that sweep the ground. It is a valuable timber tree in W. America, and from the horticultural standpoint one of the most useful and beautiful evergreens for landscape work, on account of both its form and its fine-textured dense foliage. It grows best in a light, rather acid, sandy loam, and groups do better than single specimens, because of the mutual protection afforded against high winds. It is propagated from seed, which should be secured from the E. limit of its range in Montana; otherwise the seedlings are not hardy. Trees transplant easily and grow rapidly. There are a number of varietal forms which are grafted on seedling stock of the species.

A fungous disease in Conn. causes yellowish color and heavy defoliation; another, prevalent in the N. W., turns the needles reddish-brown. Dislodge and destroy affected needles.

DOUGLASIA (dug-las'-i-ah). A genus of small alpine herbs of the Primrose Family, differing from Primula and Androsace mainly in having a branching growth. They bear yellow or rose flowers, solitary or in somewhat rounded flat clusters, and are suitable for the rock garden. They should be planted in pockets of well-drained soil which should never be allowed to dry out, entirely; they are increased by division and cuttings, as well as by seeds. In *D. vitaliana* the stems lie on the ground and are tipped with small rosettes of leaves and nearly stemless, yellow, long-tubed flowers.

DOVE-TREE. Common name for *Davidia involucrata,* a deciduous Chinese tree, exceedingly beautiful when in bloom, the dense heads of small, inconspicuous flowers being surrounded by very large, creamy-white, drooping bracts, converging in such a way as to resemble a white dove, and giving rise to its popular name. The tree, hardy as far N. as Mass., grows to a height of 50 or 60 ft. and has graceful, oval leaves, 6 in. long, silky beneath, and green, plum-like fruit, 1½ in. long. It is propagated by seed, layering, and cuttings of half-ripened wood.

This interesting tree, so spectacular in bloom, was discovered in China in 1869 by the Abbé David, for whom it was named. In 1901, the late E. H. Wilson, plant explorer, on an expedition sent out by a large English nursery firm, rediscovered it and introduced it into cultivation in England in 1902, and into the U. S. via the Arnold Arboretum, two years later.

DOWNINGIA (dou'-ning-i-ah). A genus of small annual herbs of the Lobelia Family with blue, white or yellow 2-lipped flowers. They are attractive little plants seldom seen in cultivation, but suitable for the edge of the border as they never grow over 10 in. high. They are propagated by seed.

D. pulchella has small simple leaves and deep blue flowers marked with yellow, white and purple. Grown as a pot plant or in a hanging basket, its rather straggling growth is not objectionable. *D. elegans* is a delightful little plant with sky-blue flowers with white throats, easily grown in a moist sunny spot in the wild or rock garden.

THE NEVER-FAILING DRACAENA
It will thrive even in sunless rooms, and is brave in the face of neglect.

DOWNY MILDEW. The common name of fungi which produce loose white tufts or downy masses on the surface of the host. Control as directed under MIL-DEW. See also FUNGI.

DOWNY MYRTLE (*Rhodomyrtus tomentosa*) is also called Hill-gooseberry. It is an Asiatic shrub of some economic value, and has been introduced into Fla. and Calif. It is ornamental in bloom, with rose-pink flowers resembling small single roses; is not very particular as to soil, and can stand some frost. The dull purple fruits, about the size of gooseberries, are used for pies and preserves.

DRABA (dray'-bah). A large group of small tufted hardy annual or perennial herbs, belonging to the Mustard Family. They are useful in the rock garden, having a neat habit, flowering early and thriving in porous soil and a sunny position. They are propagated by seed and division.

D. aizoon grows about 4 in. high, with narrow rigid hairy leaves and pale yellow flowers. *D. azoides* makes a low tuft, with narrow acute leaves and yellow flowers. *D. olympica* makes a dense little cushion-like tuft, and has orange-yellow flowers; it grows well in pieces of tufa. *D. fladnizensis* sends up greenish-white flowers from a cushion-like tuft. *D. sibirica* has creeping stems to 12 in. long, making a soft green mat studded with bright yellow flowers. *D. verna* (Whitlow-grass) is a low annual with small white flowers in early spring.

DRACAENA (drah-see'-nah). Dracena. Ornamental plants with brilliant, often variegated foliage belonging to the Lily Family; widely distributed in the tropics. Many properly belong to the closely related genus, Cordyline, but are sold and grown as Dracenas. One or two may be grown outdoors in the warmest parts of the country, but they are mostly popular as ornamental greenhouse foliage plants.

These are easily grown but need a light rich soil and, to promote a quick growth, plenty of heat and moisture. They do not need large pots, but to maintain the bright leaf colors of the variegated forms good light is needed in winter. When established, they can stand ordinary greenhouse conditions, and some of them (notably *D. fragrans* and *D. godseffiana*) tolerate living-room conditions fairly well. They are subject to red spider, scale and mealy bugs. For control and preventive measures, see under HOUSE PLANTS.

Dracaenas are easily propagated. The leafy tops of "leggy" plants can be taken as cuttings or made into new specimens by "air-layering" (which see). Young plants are obtained by cutting up the old stems into pieces an inch or so long, but better ones in shorter time come from the underground "toes" or fleshy extensions of the stem.

PRINCIPAL SPECIES

D. draco (Dragon-Tree). A long-lived tree to 30 ft. or more with sword-shaped leaves of bluish-green. It can be grown outdoors in Calif. A famous specimen at Teneriffe (Canary Is.) 70 ft. high, with a trunk diameter of 15 ft., was one of the oldest trees ever known.

fragrans is a popular decorative plant with handsome shining green recurved leaves. Var. *lindeni* has marginal bands of creamy-white or yellow. Var. *massangeana* has a broad yellow stripe down the center.

godseffiana, one of the best house plants, is a slender bushy plant with leaves freely spotted white.

goldieana is a magnificent foliage plant. The handsome leaves are marked with alternate cross bars of dark green and silvery gray.

sanderiana, a slender grower, has leaves marked with broad white margins. It soon becomes "leggy" and should be frequently propagated.

terminalis, properly a Cordyline, runs to many handsome variegated forms, which are the popular Dracenas of cultivation.

indivisa (properly *Cordyline indivisa*) is the hardiest of the group. In one or more of its forms it is a familiar plant in subtropical bedding arrangements. It is also used to plant vases and window-boxes in the North.

DRACOCEPHALUM (dray-koh-sef'-ah-lum). A genus of hardy annual and perennial herbs with blue, purple, or white flowers, popularly called Dragonhead, which see.

DRACUNCULUS (dra-kun'-keu-lus). A genus of tuberous herbs of the Arum Family, native in the Mediterranean region. *D. vulgaris,* which is sometimes grown as a curiosity in greenhouses, or outdoors in a mild climate, has interesting leaves divided into 10 or more segments from a bow-shaped base, and a large purple spathe of vile odor.

DRAFTS. Plants are as sensitive as human beings to drafts if not more so. In both greenhouse and dwelling they must be fully protected from direct currents of cold air. The retarding of growth and subsequent stunting, or the sudden dropping of leaves on apparently healthy, otherwise well-kept plants may be caused by nothing more than a chilling breeze from an open window. For this reason, plants should never be placed in winter where the air from an outside door can strike them; the hall is therefore a place for only the toughest kinds. In the modern greenhouse, the ventilation is so regulated that direct air currents do not reach the plants; yet it provides for the admission of enough fresh air to keep the plants healthy. Ventilation should be given if possible when the outdoor temperature has warmed up, and never during storms or high winds.

The advent of many diseases in greenhouses—mildew infection particularly—is ascribed to drafts since sudden currents of air may carry fungus spores either from plant to plant inside the house or from some diseased weed-plant growing outside.

DRAGONHEAD. Common name for Dracocephalum, a genus of hardy annual or perennial herbs of the Mint Family with blue, purple and sometimes white, 2-lipped flowers borne in whorls in the axils of the leaves or in spikes. These plants are not of great horticultural value, but sometimes make pretty groups in a rather moist shady part of the border. They are easily raised from seed or cuttings but their flowers are very fleeting, not lasting at all in hot exposed situations.

D. moldavica, the only annual listed here, is a charming species with blue or white flowers in long leafy racemes. *D. ruyschiana,* has bluish flowers in spikes; *D. speciosum,* has round wrinkled leaves and hairy purple blossoms; *D. grandiflorum,* 1 ft. tall, has hairy blue flowers in spikes 3 in. long; *bullatum,* with almost round hairy leaves and bright blue flowers, is an excellent subject for a shady corner of the rock garden; *forresti,* a trifle larger, has much-cut leaves, white-hairy beneath, and whorled, blue-purple flowers; *nutans,* 1 ft. tall has rather large bright blue flowers in drooping spikes nearly 6 in. long.

False-dragonhead is Physostegia.

DRAGON-ROOT. Common name for *Arisaema dracontium,* a tall tuberous herb with greenish flower-like bracts within which are produced orange-red berries. It is related to Jack-in-the-Pulpit.

DRAGONS BRIDGES. Another name for the Sensitive Fern, which see.

DRAGON-TREE. Common name applied to Daemonorops, a genus of climbing palms; and also to *Dracaena draco,* a large-leaved tree of the Canary Islands which can be grown in Calif.

DRAINAGE. The removal of excess water. Most plants and trees—except aquatics (which see)—will die if water stands on the roots for any length of time. Their root development is also hampered by too much moisture in the subsoil even where the surface conditions are satisfactory. To remove excess water, gardeners use various forms of drainage, the simplest of which is to plant on sloping ground. Swamps or flat ground in danger of flooding may be ditched, the ditches leading to an outlet; or if no outlet is available, a large "dry" well is dug through the subsoil and hardpan to some more porous layer beneath. This is usually filled with stones, topped with cinders or gravel.

LAWNS AND GARDENS. For lawns and gardens where ditches are objectionable underdrainage is used. Narrow ditches are partly filled with stone, cinders or coarse gravel and a layer of straw or other material to prevent the replaced topsoil from washing down into the drainage and clogging it. Or porous drain tiles are laid end to end in the ditch with joints uncemented but covered with enough cinders or gravel (or strips of building paper) to prevent the soil washing in and "silting" them up. The ditch is then filled with soil. Where there is any considerable flow of water, as under land that has springs and wet spots, or in soils so heavy that they become strongly acid and do not warm up in the early season, tile drains are better than stone, and should be spaced only a few feet apart and placed deep enough so as not to be disturbed in cultivating the soil. But in regions where plenty of flat stone is available, skilful men can build good permanent drains to carry any flow of water by laying two rows of stones in the bottom of the ditch and capping these with larger flat stones, preferably two or three layers.

In hard soils a measure of temporary underdrainage can be secured with dynamite. (See BLASTING.) Holes are made with a crowbar, and charges of half a stick or less exploded at a depth of several feet. The concussion opens channels through the subsoil by which soil water may drain away for a time. This is one way to break up a hardpan which may prevent what would overwise be adequate drainage.

For rock gardens and alpine gardens, drainage material is often laid under the entire area, sometimes in conjunction with an underground irrigation system. Sloping ground may be dug out to a depth of 2 ft. or more and the excavation half filled with cinders and stone chips. Perforated water pipes are then laid so that a continual flow of water seeping out of the small holes will drain away rapidly, thus simulating the water from melting snow which trickles through the ground all summer on high mountains. Pipes and drainage are covered with alpine soil. See ALPINE PLANTS.

Beds and borders can be drained by merely raising them 3 or 4 in. above the lawn, so that an inch or two of flood water from a sudden rain cannot cover them. This is particulary important on level grounds in winter. When there is frost in the ground, water cannot soak away, but accumulates on the frozen surface, and unless surface drainage has been arranged, it may form an ice-cap ruinous to perennials, and, if long continued, even to hardy evergreens and lawns.

PATHS AND DRIVES. Driveways and paths should be so laid out that the surface water will drain away, either by rounding up the center (crowning) or by making gutters at the side. Where there is likelihood of water accumulating during a heavy rain, a drain of vitreous tile with closed bell joints should be installed with gratings at suitable intervals. In the N. underdrainage is necessary to prevent frost damage. A bed of stone and cinders 1 ft. deep is usually enough under plants, but driveways should have double that depth if they are to last. Whether the surface is cement, brick, asphalt, crushed stone, gravel or sod, underdrainage should be provided.

Drainage for potted plants is taken care of by the hole in the bottom of the pot; a piece of broken pot (potsherd) is laid over it concave side down to prevent the soil slipping out. For alpine plants several potsherds are thrown in, sometimes enough to half fill the pot. This is called "drainage," but its purpose is as much to furnish a reservoir of moisture as to drain, for the fragments of pot soak up quantities of water and remain damp a long time, affording good root-hold for alpines. The same practise is followed in seed-pans and flats, especially for alpines and plants of the Heath Family. Cinders and stones are often used in the drainage instead of potsherds, but best of all, because of the large amount of water absorbed, is broken soft brick.

See also IMPROVEMENT OF SOIL.

DRAWN. A term applied to seedlings or plants which have become thin and spindly through overcrowding, lack of sufficient air and light, or other unfavorable conditions.

DRESSING. A general term for an application of any such material as manure, compost, fertilizer, lime, gypsum, etc., spread over land to increase its crop-producing power; sometimes substituted for manure by those who dislike to use that good old garden word. See TOP-DRESSING. Also applied to materials used in treating wounds or cavities in trees to stimulate healing and prevent infection by disease organisms.

DRILL. This may refer to (a) any kind of machine for sowing seed in rows; (b) a row thus sown; or (c) the act or method of sowing seed in rows, either by hand or by machine. It has distinct advantages over broadcasting (either by hand or machine) in that when it is carefully done the seedlings will be more evenly spaced and concentrated in narrower areas, where they can be weeded, thinned, fed, and watered with less labor and have a better chance to grow well. See BROAD-CAST; SEEDS AND SEED SOWING.

DRIVES, CONSTRUCTION OF. See under GARDEN PATHS AND DRIVES.

DROPWORT. Common name for *Filipendula hexapetala,* a species of Meadow sweet. It is a tall perennial herb of Europe and Asia with fern-like leaves and white flowers. See FILIPENDULA.

DROSERA (dros'-er-ah). A genus of native, swamp-loving, mostly perennial herbs with basal leaves covered with sticky hairs which catch insects, and small white, red, or pink flowers. They are known as Sundews (which see). See also INSECTIV-OROUS PLANTS.

DRUPE. The term for a fruit developed from one carpel or ovary cell in which the outer part is soft and fleshy and the inner part is a single hard seed or "stone," the shell enclosing a "kernel." Typical drupes are cherry. almond, and peach.

Various drupe-like fruits—coconut, walnut—are intermediate between nuts and drupes; others (the fruits of hawthorn) though resembling drupes are pomes. Blackberries and raspberries are composed of many small drupes or "druplets" joined together.

See FRUIT.

DRYAS (dry'-as). Mountain Avens. Dwarf evergreen prostrate plants with a somewhat shrubby base, belonging to the Rose Family. They are far northern or mountain plants of N. America, Europe and Asia, well suited for the rock garden, forming a low ground cover and white or yellowish solitary flowers. They require a well-drained porous soil, in a position not too hot and dry. It is well to shade them from winter sun to preserve the leaves from scorching. Propagated by division, cuttings or seed.

D. octopetala, the best known, has dark green wrinkled leaves, whitish beneath, and white strawberry-like flowers that stand erect.

drummondi has yellow nodding flowers, often not opening well.

suendermanni, a hybrid of the above two, has nodding flowers, yellow in the bud, but white when open.

DRYING-OFF. The practice of reducing the moisture in pots or other plant containers in order to ripen bulbs or give plants a "rest" between periods of forcing. It is usually done gradually; often the containers are laid on their sides or tilted under greenhouse benches or in the shade outdoors.

DRYOPTERIS (dry-op'-ter-is). A large genus of ferns, distributed in nearly all wooded parts of the world, including many species of temperate regions, of robust habit and excellent for garden culture. The sterile fronds of most species are evergreen and from 1 to 4 ft. tall, with running underground stems, and terminal crowns; the indusia are disposed variously, but all are shield- or kidney-shaped. Plants prefer well-drained fibrous woods soil with some sand, in rather dense shade, and much water during growing season. See FERN.

SPECIES

D. bootti (Boott's Shield Fern). Fronds 1 to 3 ft., 2-pinnate below with cut pinnules; sori small, each side of mid-vein and often scattered on lowest pinnules; very closely resembles *D. spinulosa* but is narrower, and grows in more moist localities.

cristata (Crested Fern). Fronds 1 to 2½ ft., the fertile taller, once pinnate with rounded lobes and acute tips and the pinnae turned horizontally like slats of a shutter.

erythrosora (Japanese Shield Fern). A foreign species but hardy as far N. as N. Y., and a distinct addition to the fern garden because of its color. This is bright claret when young, mottled violet and bronze as the ferns grow, and clear glossy green when mature. The fruit-dots are whitish with orange centers, turning to rich cocoa-violet as they ripen in early July. Fronds are 2 to 2½ ft., on smooth blackish stipes with a few hairs.

fragrans (Fragrant Fern). A rare dwarf variety, found on cliffs and often in bright sun. Confined to N. States and difficult to establish. The fronds emit a strong violet or primrose scent.

goldiana (Goldies Shield Fern). The largest and handsomest of our native species, 2 to 4 ft. long, 1 ft. broad, once pinnate, with large indusia close to the mid vein. Grows from Canada to Ky. in deep moist woods.

marginalis (Marginal Shield Fern, Evergreen Wood Fern). The best of the shield ferns for general use; broad, 1 to 3 ft. fronds, rather leathery, of a rich bluegreen, paler below, with large fruit-dots in dense rows on the edge of each pinnule.

sieboldi (Siebolds Shield Fern). An odd, triangular-leaved species, with a few large and broad pinnae, contracted on the fertile fronds, 1 ft. tall, not native to this country but a good house plant if allowed to rest in summer.

spinulosa var. *intermedia* (Toothed Wood Fern). One of the commonest; the so-called "fancy fern" of the florist, 1 to 2 ft. fronds, with finely cut and toothed pinnae. Of easy culture, responding to a rich, fibrous wood soil.

spinulosa var. *americana* (Mountain Shield Fern). A similar variety, found in the N. States and in upland rocky woods. The broader and larger fronds have wider basal pinnae, and on these the second pair of inferior pinnules are conspicuously elongated. One of the best for gardens N. of Washington, D. C.

viridescens (Glossy Shield Fern). A species from China; 1 to 2 ft., pale green at first, 3-pinnate and toothed. For cool greenhouse or home use if given a prolonged rest in summer.

DRY-SIDE. To "keep on the dryside" is a gardener's term for keeping a plant (or a greenhouse) slightly drier than is ordinarily required to promote good growth. This means the maintenance of a relatively small amount of water in the soil in which plants are growing. It is accomplished either by reducing the amounts of water applied or watering at longer intervals than usual.

DUCKWEED. Common name for Lemna, a genus of tiny, floating aquatic plants, one of which, *L. minor,* is in common use in the indoor aquarium and the outdoor pool. Individual plants of the Duckweed are most insignificant, very small and simple in structure; but, under favorable conditions with plenty of light and warmth, a colony of them soon forms attractive floating patterns of rich green on the surface of the water. It is necessary, in the aquarium especially, to thin its masses periodically lest fish and submerged plant material suffer from the lack of light and the reduction of oxygenating surface. Some species of fish use the duckweed as an occasional article of diet.

DUDLEYA (dud'-li-ah). A genus of succulent perennials, native in the W. coast region of N. America and belonging to the Orpine Family. Most of the species were formerly listed in two other genera, Cotyledon and Echeveria. The plants have flat, narrow to oval leaves in basal clumps or rosettes.

D. farinosa has white-mealy, tongue-shaped leaves, and yellow flowers on stems a foot or more high.

lanceolata has narrow leaves to 6 in. long, and reddish-yellow flowers on stems to 2 ft.

lurida has narrow green leaves which turn bronze, and reddish flowers on stems to 20 in.

pulverulenta has rounded mealy leaves, and red flowers on stems 2 ft. long.

septentrionalis produces a compact rosette of white-powdered, oval leaves, and bears yellowish-green flowers on a short stem.

DUMB CANE. A common name in tropical America for *Dieffenbachia seguine,* an ornamental shrub grown in greenhouses in the N.

DUNE GRASS. A common name for *Elymus arenarius,* a perennial grass of the temperate zone grown as a soil binder especially on sandy shores and also as a background in borders. See ELYMUS.

DURANTA (deu-ran'-tah). Tropical American woody shrubs or small trees belonging to the Verbena Family. One or two species are grown in the warmest parts of the country and occasionally in greenhouses. They are propagated by seed or cuttings.

D. repens (Golden Dewdrop, Pigeonberry, or Sky-flower) was formerly known as *D. plumieri*. Branches are sometimes spiny, flowers lilac-colored borne in loose panicled racemes. Fruit yellow.

D. stenostachya has spineless branches, flowers lilac-colored in slender racemes with yellow fruit.

DUSTING AND DUSTERS. Dusting is the application of pesticides in dry form with a stream of air as the propellent, as opposed to spraying (which see), to plants to prevent or control harmful organisms. The ancients scattered lime and other materials on plants to protect them against disease, and the use of dry sulphur in the control of powdery mildew on grapes was common in this country as early as 1848.

Most of the pesticides alone and in combination commonly recommended for gardeners can be bought in either spray or dust form. This leaves the gardener the choice of fighting plant pests either by spraying or dusting or both. The advantages and disadvantages of each method may help in making a choice:

ADVANTAGES OF SPRAYING

1. Garden supply stores generally stock a greater variety of spray materials than dusts.
2. Sprays leave a less conspicuous residue on the foliage.
3. Plant diseases are more easily controlled by spraying because sprays adhere longer and therefore less frequent applications are needed.
4. Weather conditions do not limit spraying as much as dusting which is less effective in windy weather or on dry foliage.
5. Sprays can be directed higher and more accurately and do not drift as much as dusts, hence they can be used on trees more effectively.
6. Dust clouds tend to drift and settle in places other than those to which they

are being applied, so that there is a greater possibility of irritation and harm to people, animals, or plants from poisonous dusts than from poisonous sprays. Because of this, weed killers should not be applied as dusts or fine mists and respirators should be worn with all dangerous materials.
7. For effective coverage of a given area spraying is more economical than dusting.

DUSTING SHOULD COVER THE LEAVES
Both surfaces should be reached. Use a duster that will send a cloud of the fungicide or insecticide upwards as well as downwards.

ADVANTAGES OF DUSTING

1. Dusts are much lighter than sprays (one pound of dust equals about 5 gals. of spray in coverage). This makes them, and the dusters, much easier to handle.
2. With dusts there is no messy measuring or mixing. You simply put them in the duster and proceed.
3. Dusts may be left in the duster ready to use again with little likelihood of damage to the duster whereas sprays, being corrosive, must be carefully cleaned out of the equipment after each use.
4. Dusting equipment is usually simpler and easier to operate.
5. One can do a thorough job of dusting much more quickly than spraying.
6. Dusts penetrate dense foliage and reach the undersides of foliage more readily than sprays.
7. Dusts are less likely to injure foliage than sprays.
8. There is less danger of poisonous residues remaining on fruit or vegetables from dusts because dust washes off more readily.
9. Though dusts cost more, there is a saving of time and labor in application.

Wet dusts or spray-dust applications that combine many of the advantages of both spraying and dusting are possible with certain types of equipment available. The application process involves driving a stream of dust at high velocity past a liquid spray nozzle near the outlet of a tube so that the liquid becomes finely atomized and coats or blends with the dust. Better coverage and carrying distance may be obtained by placing the above spray-dust nozzle in the large outlet of a low velocity, high volume blower. A highly refined emulsifiable spray oil in water (1 quart of spray oil in 1 gal. of water) is generally used for coating the dust.

Dusts for horticultural use are made to contain active pesticides such as methoxychlor, lindane or rotenone for insects or copper, sulphur, captan, or maneb for diseases. The pesticides are mixed with or impregnated in suitable carriers or diluents namely walnut shell flour, talc, pyrophyllite or clay to make even-flowing dusts of the right air buoyancy to produce maximum coverage.

Many general-purpose dust mixtures that will control most foliage chewing and sucking pests as well as diseases are available as labor savers for use on ornamentals, vegetable-rose dusts, fruit-tree dusts, vegetable garden dusts, floral dusts, tomato dusts, and general garden dusts.

Typically they contain such combinations as methoxychlor, rotenone and captan; captan or ferbam and sulphur; methoxychlor, malathion and captan; and methoxychlor, rotenone, ferbam and sulphur. Many combinations are available for home garden use in refillable container-dusters of the squeeze or hand pump type.

Plants are best dusted when they are damp or wet and the weather is calm. That usually means waiting until evening or early morning for best results. Always dust lightly but thoroughly coating the entire plant (and especially the undersides of leaves) with a thin layer of dust. Repeat weekly or as often as necessary to keep the growth covered. A heavy application of dust is not only unsightly but may also be injurious.

APPLICATION EQUIPMENT. Equipment for applying dusts ranges from the primitive and wasteful can with small holes punched in the cover through hand and power dusters to airplane and helicopter devices for dusting forests and large acreages of crops. Small plastic bottle squeeze-dusters are the most simple and easy devices to use when only a few plants are concerned. They tend to pour when held pointing downward and should not be held in that position.

For larger areas a number of various types of small hand dusters of the plunger dustgun or bellows type are available. The best types have easier action than others, produce a better and more uniform dust cloud, do not pour dust when held downwards, and are equipped with an extension tube with a fish tail dust nozzle for directing dust to the lower parts of plants and the undersides of low-growing leaves.

One of the best of the small hand dusters is of the rotary fan type. These are light-

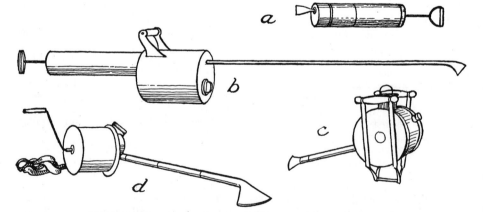

FOUR KINDS OF HAND-OPERATED GARDEN DUSTERS
The simple plunger type suitable for small gardens is shown in two sizes at (a) and (b). The bellows type is at (c) and the fan or rotary type at (d), the latter giving a continuous dust discharge. Note the extensionpipe and the broad nozzle on (d).

weight and easily held in one hand while turning a crank with the other. The air blast produces a continuous even dust cloud that will reach plants up to 10 feet tall with a minimum of effort. A considerable amount of plants and shrubbery may be dusted in a short time with this type of duster. A flashlight battery driven one is also on the market.

The larger knapsack dusters suitable for gardens up to several acres are of two types, the rotary-fan type operated by a crank and the bellows type operated by a lever. They are supported by shoulder straps and fit quite comfortably at first but operation for any extended length of time is quite wearing on the operator. The rotary-fan type is most suitable for row crops, while the bellows type is best suited for individual plants, small trees and shrubs. Also available are motorized knapsack dusters in which the fan is driven by a lightweight engine. They are both easy and convenient to use in gardens where expensive motorized dusters drawn by tractors are impractical.

A number of types of engine-driven power dusters are made for large truck farms and orchards. Airplane or helicopter dusting has been used successfully for a number of years in inaccessible forested areas and on large fields of crops. Such pests as the gypsy moth, the spruce bud worm, the cotton boll weevil, the insects and diseases of forage and orchard crops and many others have been successfully controlled by dusting from the air. It should be done with care when treated plants may poison bugs, birds and animals.

DUSTY MILLER. A common name given to various plants with white woolly foliage, but most frequently to *Senecio cineraria* and its variety (*candidissima*) which has very white foliage. These are tender herbaceous perennials of the Composite Family. The foliage is finely cut and the small yellow or cream-colored flowers are borne in small compact cymes. It is used as a bedding foliage plant in annual borders and thrives best in full sun. Increase by cuttings or seed.

Also known as Dusty Miller are *Artemisia stelleriana*; *Centaurea cineraria*, *C. gymnocarpa*; and *Lychnis coronaria*.

DUTCH BULBS. The popular, hardy bulbs that are planted in the fall for spring bloom have become known as Dutch Bulbs. This is not because these flowers had their origin in Holland, but for the reason that Holland adopted them, and has grown them for centuries to a greater extent than any other country, and to a greater degree of perfection.

Principally the group includes tulips, hardy narcissi, hyacinth, crocuses and, to a lesser extent, the bulbous irises, scillas, chinodoxas, eranthis, muscari and galanthus.

The bulb fields of Holland comprise an area approximately fifty miles long, and two miles wide, along the North Sea coast. Situated mainly below sea-level, and protected by man-made dikes, they are crisscrossed with canals which provide a constant source of moisture (water table) at a controlled depth. These conditions permit what is probably one of the finest examples and highest types of mass horticultural development in the world. Holland's annual crop of some three billion bulbs is sold the world over. The Netherlands' government insists on maintaining rigid inspection in the fields, and at all distribution points, and strictly enforces standards of size and quality which bulbs must meet to qualify for export.

American gardeners now take more than 500 million bulbs from Holland each year, of which about one-third are tulips. Most of these bulbs are planted in gardens to bloom for a period extending from a few seasons to many years, depending on the particular type of bulb, and the care with which it is tended.

Dutch bulbs are among the easiest flowers to grow and demand little in preparation or special materials. While soil preparation and enrichment are always of value in cultivating any plant life, they are, strictly speaking, not necessary in the case of bulbs. All the latter require is average soil, and simple cultivation methods.

Bulbs have been constructed by nature so that they carry their own food for the period of germination and preliminary growth. Actually they are whole but dormant plants—roots, stems, leaves and blossom—telescoped into a bud-like structure. The bulb itself consists mostly of plant food. Depending on the particular flower, bulbs are planted from three to six inches deep and about five to six inches apart, for normal growth.

In addition to outdoor planting, a large number of each year's crop of bulbs is sold to commercial growers to be forced into flower in greenhouses, and are then made available to the public through the florist trade.

DUTCH ELM DISEASE. This very serious disease of elms was first observed in 1919 in Holland, whence its name; but its original home is not known. Four infected trees were found in Ohio in 1930, the number later increasing to eleven. It is now believed that the fungus (*Graphium ulmi* and in the perfect stage *Ceratostomella ulmi*) entered this country in elm logs imported from Europe for making furniture veneer (now excluded by a Federal quarantine) and shipped to factories in a number of eastern and central cities.

The fungus is known to be parasitic only on the elm and the related zelkova. The disease may occur in either acute or chronic form. In the former, wilting begins in the younger leaves and advances rapidly down the branches; an entire tree may be near death in as short a period as four weeks. In the chronic form wilting occurs in one or several branches of the tree following conspicuous yellowing of the foliage. This yellow "flag" is one of the chief symptoms looked for in scouting for infected trees. Such a tree may live for three or more years before its inevitable death.

If twigs from a diseased tree are cut across, a brown discoloration is seen in the sapwood. The same discoloration may be present in the case of Verticillium wilt (which see) or Dephalosporium dieback.

Several elm insects are probably carriers of the fungus. The most important in America is a small bark beetle, *Scolytus multistriatus*. Adult beetles emerging from diseased wood during the summer months feed in the crotches of young twigs or in leaf axils, chewing through the bark to the cambium, wounding the tree and inoculating it with the disease fungus. Later they go again to dead or dying parts of weak trees and lay their eggs in vertical galleries; the larvae eat their way sideways from the main gallery and pupate, and later the beetles chew their way out, leaving exit holes.

Dutch elm disease has been held at reasonable levels in communities with a program combining sanitation, spraying and chemotherapy. In sanitation, pruning and removal of all unhealthy wood or trees is attempted and the bark on the removed material rendered innocuous by burning or spraying with a strong fungicide. In spraying, trees are protected against the elm bark beetle by dormant applications of fungicides so formulated to be effective in this particular use. In chemotherapy eightquinolinol benzoate or other chemotherapeutant is forced around the root system in aqueous solution. The latter measure is costly and is usually reserved for particularly valued trees.

DUTCHMANS BREECHES. Common name for *Dicentra cucullaria,* a dwarf hardy perennial, with finely-cut graceful foliage. The racemes of yellow-tipped, white flowers, shaped somewhat like those of the related Bleeding Heart, appear in early spring. It is found growing in semi-shady woodlands of eastern North America. Plant in groups among rocks in a wild garden. It is easily propagated from seed.

DUTCHMANS PIPE, PIPE-VINE. Common names for *Aristolochia durior,* a hardy woody climber with large rounded leaves that make it an excellent screen plant for arbors and fences. The pipe-shape flowers are greenish-yellow in color. Plant in well-drained garden soil. Under ideal conditions it will grow to 30 ft. Propagate by seed. It is very hardy and free of insects and diseases.

DWARF-ALDER. A name sometimes given to the genus Fothergilla, but an unfortunate one as these plants do not even belong to the same family as the Alder (Alnus). See FOTHERGILLA.

DWARF CORNEL. A common name for *Cornus canadensis,* better known as Bunchberry. See DOGWOOD.

DWARF DANDELION. Name sometimes given to a small, annual herb, *Krigia virginica,* native from Ontario to Texas and occasionally grown for its bright orange flower heads. Except that both are members of the Composite Family, it is not related to the true dandelion.

DWARF PLANTS AND DWARFING. Dwarf plants are of interest and value for garden planting, especially in restricted areas. Dwarf forms of species may occur naturally, or be developed by man through plant breeding. Certain plants are also dwarfed by mechanical manipulation, such as grafting on stocks of a dwarfing nature, by stem and root pruning, or by otherwise interfering with the normal process of growth.

In the case of annuals, or plants grown as such (whether flowers or vegetables), it is a real triumph for the plant breeder to get a dwarf strain that will reproduce true from seed. In recent years our gardens have been greatly enriched as the result of much painstaking work along these lines.

In the case of dwarf forms of perennials, either herbaceous or woody, that may not reproduce true from seed (or in some cases not set seed at all), propagation may be effected by cuttings or by some other vegetative method. Dwarfing by manipulation has been carried to the greatest perfection by Chinese and Japanese gardeners, in their handling of Chamaecyparis, junipers, pines, and other evergreen and deciduous shrubs and trees. By a carefully studied system of pruning and training, watering and feeding, they have been able to keep specimens of these naturally large-growing plants dwarfed and in small containers to a ripe old age.

Hedges are good examples of plants dwarfed by pruning. For example, a hemlock hedge may be only 4 ft. high at 30 yrs. old, while a few feet away there may be an isolated specimen of the same age, left over or set out by itself when the hedge was planted, that stands more than 30 ft. high.

The dwarfing of fruit trees has long been a subject of interest in gardens. The old system was to practice severe repressive pruning on the top growth, and to restrict the root run, even to the extent of root pruning. Much of this is no longer necessary on account of a better knowledge of stocks. Apples are dwarfed by being budded on stocks or the Paradise or Doucin apple varieties, which are geographical forms of the apple with a shallow fibrous root system, minus the deep anchor roots of the ordinary apple seedling. These dwarf stocks are themselves variable and are classified into types used for carrying different varieties according to their strength of growth and the purpose of the grower. In recent years, investigation has revealed the superiority of a group of root stocks of English origin which are identified by the name Malling, with different numerals added to indicate the several types.

Quince is a dwarfing stock for pear, but certain varieties of pears do not unite readily with quince. In such cases the grower first buds a pear that will readily unite with quince, then the next year the difficult variety is budded to the other pear. This process is known as "double working."

The Mahaleb Cherry as a stock has a dwarfing influence on other cherry varieties. The Sand Cherries (*Prunus pumila* and *P. besseyi*) have been used as stocks for plums, to develop both hardiness and dwarfing. The St. Julien Damson also has a dwarfing effect on plums. The Myrobalan Plum (*Prunus cerasifera*), has a dwarfing influence on peach, apricot, and nectarine.

DYCKIA (dike'-i-ah). A genus of tropical S. American perennial herbs belonging to the Bromeliaceae or Pineapple Family. Dyckias have stiff rather succulent leaves, edged with sharp spines. Native principally to Brazil, but also found in other southern S. American countries, it lives in open semidry areas mostly in rocky territory. Flowers, generally yellow or orange, are borne on tall spikes produced from a compact rosette. Excellent subjects for tropical rock gardens or as house plants with treatment similar to cacti and other succulents, except that Dyckias prefer a more acid soil than do cacti. Propagated by offshoots or seeds.

D. brevifolia, long known as *D. sulphurea*. Is excellent for succulent collections. Forms a compact rosette that divides and subdivides, and, eventually, becomes large masses; leaves green, heavily spined. Flowers yellow on tall spikes.

fosteriana. A compact, ball-rosette of many silvery, deeply serrated leaves, 3 to 5 in. long. Flowers orange on a 12-inch spike. Striking and showy, excellent as house plant or in tropical rock garden.

DYERS GREENWEED. Common name for *Genista tinctoria*, a shrub with yellow pea-like flowers.

DYERS WOAD. Common name for *Isatis tinctoria*, a biennial herb with yellow mustard-like flowers. Its leaves supplied the blue dye, called woad, used by the ancient Britons to stain their bodies.

EARDROPS. A name sometimes applied to Fuchsia because of the pendent, jewel-like blossoms. Golden Eardrops is *Dicentra chrysantha,* a tall graceful perennial of Calif., related to Bleeding Heart.

EARTHING-UP. Hilling or heaping soil around the roots of plants. The purpose may be to increase root-hold, as with corn; to cover the tubers of potatoes to prevent sun scorch and to give drainage between the rows in heavy soil; to bleach the stalks of celery, or to protect half-hardy plants in winter. Fig trees and European varieties of grape grown in the N. are sometimes laid flat and completely covered with a mound of soil in autumn. Some vigorous but tender shrubs and perennials also winter more safely when earthed-up, but this must be done with caution in poorly drained, heavy soils.

An all too common garden practice is to hill or earth-up the soil around specimen shrubs and, especially, along hedges, the theory being that it "looks well." Actually this is definitely harmful, as the mound or ridge of soil in time becomes full of fine

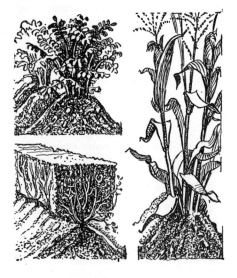

EARTHING-UP
A desirable practice in growing corn (right) to prevent its being blown over, and with potatoes (upper left) to protect the tubers from sunburn, earthing-up should **NOT** be done with hedges (lower left) as it exposes the roots to injury by drying.

feeding roots which are necessarily close to the surface. When droughts occur, these roots cannot get moisture and if the sun is strong they may be actually "cooked," seriously injuring the plant.

EARTHWORMS. These familiar denizens of the garden, known also as land worms or "fishing worms," belong to a group of low animal life called Annelida. They are segmented worms that live in moist soil containing decaying organic matter, crawling out at night to feed or when the burrows are filled with water as during heavy rains. The worm eats the soil through which it burrows and its digestive juices break down and dissolve bacteria, leafmold and other organic matter in the soil. The indigestible remainder is discharged in the form of "castings" which may be abundant on the surface of the soil. It has been estimated that earthworms in an acre of land thus bring more than 35,000 lbs. of soil to the surface in a year. This type of soil working and conditioning is of great value in the garden and earthworms should be left alone wherever possible. However, too many present in lawns, golf greens, etc., mar the beauty of the turf and sometimes call for control or extermination.

To accomplish this mix 1 lb. lead arsenate with a peck of soil or compost and apply so that 5 lbs. of the poison is distributed evenly over each 1000 sq. ft. of lawn. Then water well. On a heavy soil a second application may be necessary. A second remedy is corrosive sublimate (which see). Dissolve 3 oz. in 50 gals. of water for each 1000 sq. ft. of surface. After applying wash it into the soil with at least twice the quantity of water. Or this poison may be applied dry by mixing 3 oz. with 2 cu. ft. of sand, to be scattered over 1000 sq. ft. and followed by very liberal watering. The worms, which soon start coming to the surface, should be swept up and destroyed lest birds eat them and die from the poison in their bodies. A commercial vegetable preparation called mowrah meal (which see) is also recommended for worm control.

See also LAWN.

EARWIGS. Chewing insects of the order Dermaptera, meaning skin wing, re-

sembling beetles in their hard wing covers but distinguished from them by pincer-like appendages at the tail end. The hind wings are folded both length-
w i s e   a n d   crosswise.
E a r w i g s are troublesome plant pests in the
S. and on the Pacific
Coast, feeding on the
petals of flowers and on
fruits and vegetables.
They may be controlled
by means of poison baits
such as are provided for
cut-worms, which see.
The name refers to the
belief that these insects
creep into the ears of
sleeping persons.

EARWIG
Troublesome in N.W. gardens, but not harmful to humans.

EASTER BELLS. Common name for *Stellaria holostea*, a root-creeping perennial of the Pink Family (Caryophyllaceae), with erect downy stems to 2 ft. tall, bearing in May and June numerous small white flowers in terminal clusters. A native of the Old World, it has escaped from gardens in the U. S. It is allied to cerastium and arenaria but tends to spread too freely for general garden use. It should be reserved for planting on arid banks where grass will not grow.

EASTER CACTUS. Common name for *Schlumbergera gaertneri*, referring to its time of blooming. It resembles the Christmas Cactus (which see), but has regular flowers.

EASTER DAISY. Local name (in Colo.) for the native Townsendia, a perennial herb with pink or purple flower-heads.

EASTER LILY. A name originally applied to *Lilium longiflorum*, a tender, white-flowered Asiatic species and especially to the variety developed and grown commercially in Bermuda. Today it is applied to any of the many forms of tender white-flowered lilies forced for Easter bloom. See LILY.

EAST INDIAN FLAX. A common name for *Reinwardtia indica*, better known as Yellow Flax, which see.

EBONY. A name applied to the wood of a number of trees and hence to the trees themselves, especially Asiatic species of Diospyros. Green-ebony is *Jacaranda acutifolia*, native of S. America and sometimes grown in N. greenhouses. Mountain-ebony is *Bauhinia variegata*, native of India and China, and now widely planted

in Fla. Natal Ebony is *Maba natalensis*, an evergreen shrub, planted for ornament in the S. See the genera above mentioned.

ECBALLIUM (ek-bal'i-um) *elaterium*. A perennial trailing vine of the Gourd Family, native to the moist forests of the middle and E. Mediterranean region and popularly known as the Squirting Cucumber because, when the fruit is ripe, the seeds are violently squirted out of the pod, along with the semi-liquid jelly surrounding them. It is commonly grown as an annual, in S. gardens, for its curious seed-throwing propensity. A powerful cathartic known as elaterium is made from the fruit juice. Propagation is by seeds.

ECCREMOCARPUS (e-krem-oh-kahr'-pus). A climbing vine of Chile, with tubular orange flowers; popularly known as Glory-flower, which see.

ECHEVERIA (ek-e-vee'-ri-ah). (See illustration, Plate 51, also page 414.) A genus of succulents of the Orpine Family, having leaves in rosettes and small flowers usually in spikes. They closely resemble the houseleeks and cotyledons, and like them are grown indoors in pots and dish arrangements and sometimes bedded out in summer. Echeverias require a light sandy or gritty soil and excellent drainage; they are easily increased by seed or offsets. For cultural notes see SUCCULENTS.

E. gibbiflora, to 2 ft., has leaves to 7 in. long, often rose-tinted, and red flowers. Var. *metallica* has foliage with a purplish metallic lustre.

secunda, with broadly oval, sharp-pointed, grayish blue leaves, bears reddish flowers on stems to 15 in.

glauca has nearly round leaves, pale green with a bloom, and bears yellow and pink flowers on reddish branches.

ECHINACEA (ek-i-nay'-she-ah). A genus of native perennials of the Composite Family, closely related to Rudbeckia, of bushy growth with showy, daisy-like flower-heads ofter 6 in. across, with raised bronzy centers. A fine source of cut flowers and for bold landscape effects, giving two months or more of bloom. They like rich, sandy loam and thrive in dry or exposed spots. Spring-sown seed will give bloom the following year; clumps may be divided but this should not be done too often. One of three genera called Cone-flower (which see) this one gets its botanical name from a Greek word for hedgehog, suggested by its bristly seed heads.

E. angustifolia, to 2 ft., has leaves lance-shaped and heads light purple with dark disk flowers often 1 in. high. *E. pallida,* to 3 ft., has rose-purple or white flowers with long, drooping rays. *E. purpurea* (Purple Coneflower), to 5 ft., has broad, oval leaves, and purplish-rose to white flowers also with drooping rays.

ECHINOCACTANAE (ee-ky-noh-kak'-tan-ee). A division (sub-tribe) of the Cereeae, a group of cacti. It includes not only the Echinocactus, sometimes known as the hedgehog cactus, but many others of considerable interest. Some of these genera and representative species are: Ariocarpus —*A. fissuratus* (Living Rock); Lophophora—*L. williamsi,* the famous and much discussed Peyote or Mescal Button, an Aztec narcotic; Astrophytum, including the much prized "Bishops Cap"; Epithelantha (Button Cactus); Homalocephala (Devils

ECHEVERIA, EVER ORNAMENTAL
This small succulent plant has leaves of various shapes, colors and texture, generally smooth but sometimes hairy as shown here in E. setosa. It bears a tall curving spray of red and yellow flowers.

Pincushion); Ferocactus, to which belongs the Barrel Cactus.

See also CACTUS.

ECHINOCEREUS (ee-ky-noh-see'-ree-us). Confined to W. U. S. and Mexico, this genus of cacti contains some of the most desirable forms for cultivation. They are fairly hardy, desert species which need little care and reward the grower with most beautiful flowers. The blossoms are for the most part large and brilliant—rose, magenta, carmine, red-violet, a few yellow and, in two cases, smaller and green. One of the distinguishing characters of the genus is the feathery green stigma lobes, which set off the coloring and add just the finishing touch to what already approaches perfection. Many of the species are small enough to be effectively used as dish plants; other larger ones make excellent pot plants. Most species of this genus bear edible fruits which earn for them the name of Strawberry Cactus.

ECHINOCYSTIS (ee-ky-noh-sis'-tis). Wild-cucumber, Wild Balsam-apple. Annual and perennial vines, native to both N. and S. America. *E. lobata,* a fast-growing annual species, is widely distributed in eastern N. America and is useful as a temporary screen for unsightly objects, or to drape fences and arbors. It has deeply lobed leaves, clusters of small white or greenish flowers, and egg-shaped prickly fruit. Plants are easily grown from seed.

ECHINOPS (e-ky'-nops). A genus of thistle-like perennial and biennial plants of the Composite Family with flowers in round heads; the scales surrounding the flowers are often metallic-blue in color. They are commonly known as Globe Thistles and because of their bold prickly white-woolly foliage, as well as their flowers, are most decorative as background plants in the border or when planted among shrubbery. They are easily grown from seed or increased by division and root cuttings.

E. sphaerocephalus (Great Globe Thistle), to 8 ft., has white or bluish heads to 2 in. and somewhat cobwebby stems and rough-hairy leaves. *E. ritro* (Small Globe Thistle), to 2 ft., with finely-cut, white downy leaves and steel-blue flowers, blossoms all summer. *E. humilis,* to 4 ft., with silvery, cobwebby foliage and large blue heads of flowers, is a native of Siberia.

ECHINOPSIS (ee-ky-nop'-sis). This cactus genus is the S. American version of the N. American Echinocereus. It is very desirable in cultivation and well suited for use in dish gardens. *E. multiplex* is the species most often seen. Its blossom is a beautiful pink; as it rises from the little round cushion on its long, slender tube, it seems nothing short of a miracle. The plant multiplies rapidly and can be propagated by separation. *E. eyriesi* is another very desirable species having white flowers with a delicate fragrance. For cultural directions see CACTUS.

ECHINOSTACHYS (ee-ky-noh-stay'-kis). A small group (5 or 6 species) of handsome herbaceous perennials belonging to the Bromelia Family and allied to Aechmea (which see), with which they are sometimes classified. They are spiny-leaved plants native to S. America. The flowers are brilliant in color, and the leaves darken in tint after flowering. The plants require hothouse conditions and a fibrous loam with fresh humus added.

ECHITES (ee-ky'-teez). Twining shrubs of tropical America, belonging to the Dogbane Family. They succeed under the same treatment as Dipladenia, which see. *E. tomentosa* (Savannah-flower) is a very hairy plant with yellow and red flowers. *E. nutans* has beautiful leaves of pale green with transparent red veins and bears panicles of yellow nodding flowers. *E. umbellata* has white or pale yellow flowers in umbels.

ECHIUM (ek'-i-um). A genus of rough-hairy or bristly, annual, perennial and biennial herbs belonging to the Borage Family and known as Vipers Bugloss. They have purple, rose or white flowers in coiled racemes or showy spikes. Some of the species from the Canary Isles are much planted in California. All thrive and flower well in poor soil in open, sunny situations; they produce only a profusion of leaves if planted in too rich ground. The annual and biennial species are increased by seed, and the perennial sorts by seed, layering, or cuttings.

E. vulgaris (Blueweed), a biennial to 2½ ft., is an Old-World plant with panicles of blue flowers following rose-pink buds. In the eastern U. S. it has escaped and become a troublesome weed in open fields.

candicans, a shrub to 6 ft., has white-hairy foliage and white or blue and white flowers in profuse spikes.

bourgaeanum, a shrub to 11 ft., has very narrow leaves and rose-colored flowers.

fastuosum, a shrub to 6 ft., has purple or dark blue flowers in dense spikes.

wildpreti, a biennial to 3 ft., has white-hairy foliage and rose-colored flowers in large flat-topped clusters.

giganteum, a shrub to 10 ft., has white-hairy leaves and white flowers.

plantagineum has been extensively hybridized, with larger red as well as blue and purple flowers developed.

EDELWEISS (ay'-del-vys). Common name for *Leontopodium alpinum,* a perennial, tufted herb of the Composite Family, with white-woolly foliage and inconspicuous flowers in heads surrounded by floral leaves in star-like clusters resembling "pearly everlastings." Native to high mountains of Central Asia and Europe and especially associated with the Swiss Alps, it is a favorite truly alpine subject for rock gardens though sometimes grown in pots. It requires a rough, sandy loam, plenty of room in the rock pockets for its wide-spreading roots, and full sunlight. It will also grow in the border. Division of the roots is not often successful, so it is better to grow the plants from seed.

EDGEWORTHIA (ej-wur'-thi-ah). Asiatic shrubs, closely allied to Daphne, but not hardy N. See PAPER-BUSH.

EDGING. The act or practice of attractively and appropriately defining the edge of a flower bed or border, or of a lawn, path, driveway or other specific area of a garden or home property; also, the material used for that purpose (see EDGING PLANTS). In a well-kept garden, such a boundary or division line between lawn and path, lawn and border, path and border, etc., is neat and definite without being stiff, harsh or obtrusive in the garden picture.

It may be marked (1) by the simple margin of the turf itself, either cut to a vertical edge with a sod cutter (see over) or kept sheared to a soft rounded slope; (2) by a strip of grass between bed and path; (3) by a hedge of low-growing, closely clipped evergreens or a row of other dwarf plants; (4) by a narrow strip of wood; (5) by bricks or concrete blocks; (6) by a concrete curb; (7) by a strip of steel or other patented device; or (8) by an informal line of irregularly shaped, unpainted stones among which small rock plants can be grown. Shells, painted or white-washed stones, and other fancy materials are occasionally used, but they are likely to detract from the dignity of a garden.

To maintain the symmetry and neatness of the grass edge, various tools have been designed, among them a very narrow lawn-mower and a device with a revolving very sharp-edged disk; but the ordinary half-moon-shaped edging iron or sod cutter, sharpened on the rounded edge, best used with a tightly stretched guide line, is one of the best. In maintaining a low-growing evergreen hedge, such as box or yew, close shearing is necessary to keep it in close, symmetrical shape.

For a permanent straight wooden edging, 2 x 4's can be used, set almost flush with the grass or path, and held in place by being nailed to flat pegs driven at regular intervals. For a curving line 4 in. stock not over 1 in. thick must be used. This is an inexpensive edging and quite lasting if made of a long-lived wood like cypress.

The brick edge is more conspicuous and formal, but appropriate when it is in harmony with the architecture of the house, and supplements a path, terrace or wall made of this material. The bricks are sometimes set at an angle giving a sort of saw-tooth effect, but the preferable method is to place them end to end on edge. Bricks are durable, dignified and desirable.

If the paths are of concrete, a raised edge of the same material makes a simple, lasting division for either formal or informal borders. This concrete edge is also excellent for bordering driveways. The patented steel edging is easily set, durable and inconspicuous, but more expensive than the other types mentioned.

An edge of irregular rounded stones is excellent for a herbaceous border or informal path in the small place as it gives an opportunity to grow rock-garden plants when there is no space for a regular rock garden. The stones should be well sunk in the soil, the edging effect being secured by the dwarf plants.

EDGING PLANTS. Plants used along the margins of beds or borders or otherwise to outline definite areas should be of small, compact growth. If annuals, they should have a long season of bloom and be easily kept within bounds; if perennials or of shrubby form, they should be sufficiently dwarf, and tolerant of clipping or pruning if necessary. Edging plants are used in both formal and informal plantings. For the formal bed a grass strip or a close-clipped hedge of a low-growing evergreen, such as box or dwarf barberry, are appropriate. For the shrubbery border, Japanese-spurge, Japanese yew, or myrtle (Vinca) are often used. The more infor-

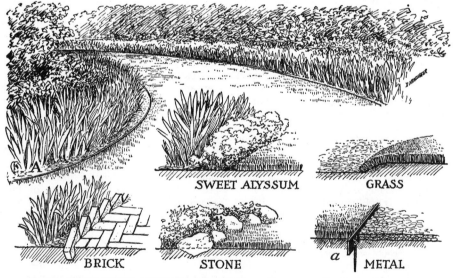

NEAT, WELL-KEPT EDGINGS ENHANCE THE GARDEN'S APPEARANCE AND SIMPLIFY ITS CARE

Here are a number of suitable types, such as close-trimmed grass, dwarf flowering plants, bricks on edge or diagonally laid like dominoes, irregular stones interplanted with a ground cover, and a metal strip such as is shown above (A) and in detail below (a).

mal herbaceous border is often edged with a combination of low-growing perennials such as perennial candytuft, rock-cress, dwarf phlox, pinks or violas, while for the annual border sweet alyssum, lobelia, ageratum, candytuft, torenia and many other low-growing annuals make a charming transition from the higher-growing flowers to the path. (See illustration, Plate 8.)

See also PLANTS FOR SPECIAL PURPOSES.

EDRAIANTHUS (ed-ray-an'-thus). A small group of low-growing perennial herbs belonging to the Bellflower Family, native to the Mediterranean region. They are very like and sometimes classified with Wahlenbergia (which see). They bear nodding bell-shaped flowers of blue, violet, or purple, and are useful in the rock-garden, where they should be given a light soil rich in new humus, and watered freely. Propagation is by division, or by seeds.

EDUCATION IN GARDENING. Considerable skill in gardening can be developed through actual experience alone (especially if under the guidance of an expert), but a real knowledge of both theory and practice can best be obtained through some of the numerous agencies interested in helping the general public to an understanding of the subject. In the primary schools, garden education has experienced a remarkable development within the last 30 years. In New York City alone the School Garden Association has a membership of over 10,000 and under the supervision of nature-study teachers, school children in the most crowded parts of the city raise gardens on plots of ground which would otherwise lie idle, often as unsightly waste space. This Association, with plans to extend its work over the country, has been endorsed by and named state directors in, Ala., Calif., Fla., Ind., Ga., O., Ore., N. Y., Ia., La., Md., Mich., Mont., Pa., R. I., Texas, Ky., Mass., and Wis.

In many cities newspapers are working in connection with the School Garden Associations, encouraging the formation of local junior garden clubs and giving regular space to their activities.

The Junior Garden Clubs of America, a movement sponsored by the *Better Homes and Gardens* magazine, with a view to presenting gardening to children more as an alluring adventure than as a task, has spread all over the U. S., its activities having been made part of the school curriculum in many places. Adult garden clubs, 4-H Clubs, Campfire Girls, Boy Scouts, Girl Scouts, children in orphans' homes and crippled children's hospitals have joined in the work which now has a membership of over 20,000.

Many museums, botanical gardens, and city parks have organized children's gardens in connection with their regular curricula. The Brooklyn (N. Y.) Botanic Garden outlines their objective as follows: "to increase the child's knowledge in the subject of gardening, to open his eyes to the outdoor world, prepare him for the study of botany in high school, and through the work develop certain character traits."

The 4-H Clubs, which are a part of the Extension Service of State Agricultural Colleges and Farm Bureau activities, have organized plans for teaching gardening to children of high school age. See GOVERNMENT AGENCIES; EXTENSION COURSES.

Much serious work in gardening in its practical horticultural sense, and also in its higher meaning as it relates to civic and highway beautification and conservation, is being done through the senior garden club organizations. The development of these clubs has done much to spread the desire for knowledge of gardening throughout the country. See GARDEN CLUBS AND OTHER ORGANIZATIONS.

Horticultural societies extend many opportunities to the student of gardening through their excellent libraries, series of lectures and demonstration courses and the like. Some of them employ garden consultants to answer questions and help garden owners solve their problems. Special exhibitions at frequent intervals and sometimes annual flower shows sponsored by some of these organizations are truly educational as well as beautiful.

Garden centers in many communities help the amateur gardener to a knowledge of facts, local conditions and possibilities. Radio programs on garden subjects, sponsored by garden clubs, agricultural colleges, museums, botanical gardens and even some commercial firms, feature garden authorities, and greatly enlarge their fields of service. Garden articles in general magazines and whole magazines devoted to garden matters provide much interesting and helpful material, especially about new and promising plants.

Botanic gardens and arboreta (both of which see) give courses in nature study (especially plant identification) and even in practical horticulture, some planned for the aspiring amateur, others for more or less trained professional gardeners. Also they issue bulletins, books and pamphlets either free or for a reasonable sum, and the libraries and herbaria are always accessible as are members of the staff who can answer garden questions.

Special courses in gardening and landscape architecture are given by State colleges of agriculture and universities whose extension services carry the information

EEL-WORMS. Popular name for nematodes (which see), microscopic eel-like organisms which normally infest soils, plant and animal tissues, etc. While many kinds are apparently harmless, some are destructive plant pests—true plant parasites, causing diseases of various kinds, such as root knots, leaf galls, bulb injury, etc., in many ornamental and economic plants.

EGG-FRUIT. One of the common names for *Lucuma nervosa*, another being Canistel. This is a small tree to 25 ft.

CHILDREN'S GARDENS ARE GOOD FOR THEM AND FOR THE COMMUNITY
In every section where they have been established, a vital interest has been manifested by the small gardeners, proving the success of the project.

right into the homes both by visiting agents and through bulletins.

The U. S. Department of Agriculture at Washington, D. C., is a mine of information for gardeners, its publications, motion picture films, radio talks and other services covering all phases of horticulture.

Every year flower shows are staged by institutions, or associations of gardeners, florists, and nurserymen, usually working in cooperation. Here the public may see new and rare species of plants, examples of garden planning and demonstrations of improved methods which include civic beautification and roadside conservation as well as the development of the individual home garden.

EEL-GRASS. Common name for either of the two species of Vallisneria (which see), an aquatic plant much in favor among aquarium keepers.

native in S. America, but naturalized in southern Florida. It will grow in rather poor soil, has long leathery leaves, and is esteemed for its edible fruit, which is orange-yellow, about 3 in. long, with a dry or mealy orange sweet flesh.

EGG-PLANT. Also called Guinea-squash. An Old-World, tropical perennial or sub-shrub (*Solanum melongena*, var. *esculentum*) grown in vegetable gardens as an annual for its large pear-shaped purple (or white) fruits which are used as a vegetable.

The plants are tender, slow-growing and easily checked and stunted by temperatures below 50 degrees F. In the N., therefore, they must be started under glass 4 to 6 weeks before they can safely be planted outdoors. To lessen the shock of transplanting, when the seedlings have developed their third true leaves shift to 2½ or 3 in. flower pots, either paper or clay. Shift again to a larger size when necessary and set in the garden 2 to 3 ft. apart after the weather has become warm. The soil should be warm, well drained and light, but rich. Thereafter they need clean cultivation, watering in very dry weather and protection against potato beetles. In the South, seed may be sown in an outdoor seed-bed and the seedlings, when 6 in. high, moved directly to the garden.

Well-grown plants in good soil will produce two to five large fruits, so the number needed may thus be calculated. Fruits may be used when sufficiently large, and richly colored in the case of the purple kinds, and as long as the seeds are soft. When fall frost threatens cut them with several inches of stem, place in ventilated baskets and store in a cool, moist cellar where they should keep until Christmas.

Egg-plant may be subject to the same bacterial wilt as that which affects tomato (which see). For a fungus that causes a fruit rot, leaf spot and stem blight soak seed before planting in a 1 to 1000 corrosive-sublimate solution for 5 minutes, then wash in water. Spray plants with bordeaux mixture weekly for five weeks after setting them out.

The egg-plant flea beetle punctures the leaves and stunts plants in the seed-bed. Spray with bordeaux mixture to which calcium arsenate has been added at the rate of 1 part to 25 parts of spray. Or dust with copper-lime-calcium-arsenate dust. Spray with nicotine-sulphate to keep down the egg-plant lace bug. The Colorado potato beetle is frequently injurious and should be fought with arsenates (see POTATO), and tortoise beetles (which see) may be destructive in the S.

OTHER TYPES. The Serpent Egg-plant has fruits a foot long and an inch thick with curved tips. The Scarlet or Tomato Egg-plant (*S. integrifolium*) is a spiny ornamental annual to 3 ft., with clusters of white flowers and scarlet or yellow fruits to 2 in. across. See SOLANUM.

EGLANTINE (eg′-lan-tyn). Another popular name for Sweetbrier, which is the rose species *Rosa eglanteria,* formerly called *R. rubiginosa.* The term Eglantine, from a French word meaning prickly, dates back to the 16th century, when the English monarchs were crowned with Sweetbrier. The plant is a dense shrub with hooked prickles, the leaves dark green above and

pale beneath. Its flowers, borne in groups of 1 to 3, are bright pink and occasionally double. They are followed by fruits (hips) of orange-red or scarlet. The foliage exhales a dainty aromatic odor. A number of interesting hybrids have been obtained. See aso ROSE.

The term Eglantine has also been applied to a species of blackberry and, rarely, to a species of Honeysuckle (*Lonicera periclymenum*), also called Woodbine.

EGYPTIAN-LOTUS, or WHITE-LOTUS OF EGYPT. Popular names for *Nymphæa lotus,* a waterlily of Egypt, with large floating leaves and white flowers. The true Lotus is Nelumbium.

EHRETIA (e-ree′-ti-ah). Deciduous and evergreen trees and shrubs of tropical and subtropical regions, belonging to the Borage Family. They are not particular as to soil, but with one or two exceptions can be grown only in the warmer parts of the country.

E. thyrsiflora, hardy to Mass., is a small tree with large oblong saw-edged leaves, and big panicles of small white scented flowers in summer.

EGG-PLANT IN THE GARDEN
Left, a young pot-grown plant of the right size to set outdoors. Right, a mature fruit at the end of the summer.

dicksoni, smaller and more tender, has large roundish hairy leaves and clusters of white fragrant flowers.

microphylla (Philippine-tea) is a large tender shrub with smaller leaves in clusters, and flowers singly or 2 to 4 together.

EICHHORNEA (yk-haur′-ni-ah) *crassipes.* The beautiful floating Water-hyacinth (which see), which grows luxuriantly in Fla. freshwaters and is cultivated in N. ponds and aquaria.

ELAEAGNACEAE (el-ee-ag-nay'-see-ee). Botanical name of the Oleaster Family, a group of trees and shrubs mostly distributed in the tropics of the N. hemisphere, usually covered with silvery or yellow-brown scales. The flowers are without petals and the fruit is a berry-like structure imbedded in the fleshy calyx. The three genera—Elaeagnus (Oleaster), Hippophaë (Sea-buckthorn) and Shepherdia (Buffalo-berry)—are grown for ornament and somewhat for their fruit.

ELAEAGNUS (el-ee-ag'-nus). A genus of ornamental N. American, European and Asiatic small trees and shrubs of the Oleaster Family, generally slow growing, some with spiny branches. They are easy to grow and bear fragrant, inconspicuous flowers followed by fruits of various colors, sometimes edible. Some species are hardy N., and deciduous; others are southern evergreens. A sunny position in well-drained soil is most favorable. Propagated by seed, cuttings of mature or half-ripened wood and by grafting.

E. angustifolia (Oleaster or Russian-olive) is hardy, deciduous, to 20 ft. with small, gray-green leaves, silvery beneath, forming rather dense masses. It is a pleasant tree for the garden border, changing from silver to green in gentle breezes. In early summer the tubular flowers, silver without and yellow within, emit a delicious, spicy fragrance of great carrying power. If pruned severely it will make a dense plant suitable for screens and windbreaks.

argentea (Silver-berry) attains 12 ft. and is found from E. Canada to Utah. Its axillary, fragrant flowers are followed by short-stemmed silvery fruit.

glabra, growing to 20 ft. and somewhat climbing in habit, is a desirable evergreen for S. gardens.

latifolia, a warm-climate form from India, that may be either erect or climbing, bears red fruit to 1½ in. long.

macrophylla, another S. evergreen to 12 ft., is a highly ornamental with large, broad shining leaves, silvery beneath. These, combined with the red fruit that follow the autumn flowers, make a brilliant picture.

multiflora (Gumi) is a useful N. shrub to 6 ft. with fragrant flowers but most conspicuous for its long stemmed, spotted scarlet edible fruit.

pungens is a tall evergreen shrub for the S., with fragrant flowers in autumn followed by red fruit having silvery and brown scales. There are several varieties with leaves margined yellow, white, etc., that are often raised under glass in the North.

ELAEOCARPUS (el-ee-oh-kahr'-pus). A genus of Old-World tropical trees and shrubs, grown extensively in the S. states and in California, and occasionally under glass in the N. They have showy flowers in racemes and are propagated by cuttings or by seed. *E. cyaneus,* treated as a shrub in the greenhouse, has cream-white flowers and blue fruit; *E. dentatus,* a tree to 60 ft., has leathery leaves, white flowers in drooping racemes, and purplish-gray fruits; *E. hookerianus,* a tree to 40 ft., has greenish-white drooping flowers.

ELDER. Common name for Sambucus, a widely distributed genus of mostly large and rather coarse deciduous shrubs, with compound leaves, showy clusters of white flowers, and attractive red or black berries. They are very effective when planted in groups, and while not particular as to soil and location, do especially well in partial shade and rich moist soil. Most species are hardy N. The berries of *S. nigra* and *S. canadensis* are prized in some localities for the making of elderberry wine and for combining with applies in pies. Propagated by seeds, cuttings, and some kinds of suckers.

A dark blue beetle, orange yellow at the base of the wing covers, may be seen on flowers and foliage, but the grubs work in the stems. Cut out and burn infested wood. The currant borer may also attack elder. For control see CURRANT.

PRINCIPAL SPECIES

S. nigra (European Elder) grows to 30 ft., and bears yellowish-white flowers in clusters to 8 in. across, followed by shining black berries. Vars. *albo-variegata* and *aureo-variegata,* are sometimes grown for the sake of their white and yellow variegated leaves. The color is more intense when they are planted in a sunny position. Var. *laciniata* is an attractive form with leaves regularly and finely dissected.

canadensis (American or Sweet Elder) grows to 12 ft., and suckers freely. It is the most handsome in bloom, with flower clusters to 10 in. across; later it hangs heavy with purplish-black berries. Var. *aurea* has leaves of golden yellow and red berries.

pubens (American Red Elder). To 15 ft., bears rather loose pyramidal, not very showy, flower clusters to 4 in. across. But when the scarlet berries ripen in early summer it is one of the outstanding shrubs of the countryside. Var. *chlorocarpa* is a form with white berries.

AN ORNAMENTAL SHRUB
The native elderberry makes a handsome shrub with broad white flower-clusters and luscious shining blackish fruits.

racemosa (European Red Elder). Grows to 12 ft., with dense oval flower clusters about 3 in. long and showy scarlet berries in June and July. Var. *plumosa* is a cut-leaved form with the leaflets divided to about the middle.

caerulea (Blue Elder). From the W. part of the country, sometimes grows to 50 ft. The branches are bloomy when young and the blue-black berries are covered with a heavy bloom. Hardy as far N. as Mass. Adams Elderberry is an improved variety with larger berries and extra large fruit clusters. Plants grow 5 to 6 ft. tall.

ELECAMPANE (el-e-kam-payn'). Common name for *Inula helenium*, a hardy, herbaceous perennial of the Com-posite Family, bearing large clusters of yellow flowers.

ELECTRICAL INJURY. When tree branches come in contact with service wires carrying electric current the plant tissues are actually killed by the heat produced when the current encounters the high resistance of the tissues.

The same thing happens when a tree is struck by lightning. Alternating current of low voltage carried in insulated wires does little damage except where the insulation is rubbed away by contact with the tree; then the rough open wounds on the branches provide entrance for wood-decaying fungi. High voltage, uninsulated wires carrying direct current, will cause local burning but not necessarily kill a tree.

Lightning injury is usually a groove plowed down the trunk through the bark and wood, but it may mean the stripping of all bark from the tree, or the shattering of the top or base of the tree. Rare or exceptionally valuable ornamental trees should be equipped with lightning rods.

ELECTRICITY IN THE GARDEN. Electricity has become an almost indispensable tool for every home gardener. It is not only used as a source of power for many work-saving tools and appliances; it also operates many types of automatic controls; supplies a source of heat for hot-beds and greenhouses; and, by lighting the garden at night, helps extend the number of hours available for enjoying its beauty.

This type of garden lighting, once limited to expensive professional installations on large formal estates, can now be put in around any home at modest cost. Specially designed weatherproof fixtures are widely available everywhere. They can be spiked into the ground where needed, or can be attached to trees, fences or other outdoor structures. Groups of them can be used to light up anything from a small flower bed to an entire yard. Many are designed for use on terraces and patios—in line with the modern trend toward outdoor living.

To provide for maximum convenience, a number of weatherproof outlets should be installed around the outside walls of the house and in various locations throughout the garden. These outlets will not only provide a source of current for outdoor lighting, they will also permit the home-owner to make use of electric trimmers, mowers, sprayers and power saws.

The simplest and least expensive type of outdoor outlet that can be installed is one which is cut into an exterior wall of the house itself—preferably opposite an existing indoor junction box from which the cables can be drawn. Special plug-in receptacles are used which have rubber-lined cover plates and screw-type caps over the outlets to protect them against the weather when they are not in use.

For bringing current to an outlet in a remote part of the garden away from the house itself, special plastic covered electrical cables are available which are approved for direct burial underground in most communities. Known as Type UF, this neoprene-jacketed wire is available as either two-conductor or three-conductor cable, and is much less expensive to install than lead cable or metal conduit. It should be buried in a trench at least 12 inches deep and should be covered with a protective board before the earth is replaced. Wherever it comes up out of the ground it must be enclosed with rigid metal conduit to protect it. For installations requiring more than just one or two of these outlets the safest and most advisable procedure is to have a professional electrician run direct wires from the main fuse box so that all outdoor outlets are on their own, separately fused circuit.

For lighting up the garden at night there are a great many different types of fixtures available. The most versatile are the small floodlights and spotlights. These are usually housed in bullet-shaped shields which extend several inches in front of the bulb so that there is no glare unless the unit is viewed head-on. They are available with different kinds of mountings or base plates. Some have spikes which permit pushing them into the ground wherever needed. Others can be clamped to any upright pole or screwed to the side of large trees or buildings. All can be tilted and swiveled so that the light may be aimed in any direction. Though most use standard 150 watt reflector spot or floodlamps, mercury vapor bulbs are also available for an unusually striking effect on dark green foliage.

Other fixtures in popular use are the low, mushroom lamps or path lights which vary from two to four feet in height and can be spiked into the ground at any convenient location. They throw most of their light downward, away from the eyes, and use standard indoor bulbs up to 100 watts in size. Most come equipped with long weatherproof cords which can be laid over the top of the ground so that the lamps can be moved about as requirements vary.

There are also tall, pole-type work lights which can be spiked into the ground wherever needed to provide a brilliant overhead light for working in the garden during the cool evening hours. And, to lend an unusually festive touch to the home grounds there are decoratively shaped hanging lights of various kinds which can be suspended from the branches of a tree or from an overhanging roof.

Garden lighting should be planned to provide for an interesting interplay between light and shadow. No attempt should be made to floodlight the entire area. Illuminate only the most attractive portions, and direct the lights in such a manner as to avoid glare in the eyes of the observer. Where possible, camouflage the source of light by hiding the fixtures behind trees or convenient clumps of shrubbery. Avoid too much front lighting —side lighting and back lighting create a much more interesting effect. Use a few lights shining upward from the ground to create unusual highlights and to outline the branches of tall trees. Generally speaking, stay away from colored lighting effects. Nature's colors look their best under plain white light.

Since night-flying insects will inevitably be attracted to the bright lights, place them as far from the terrace or patio as possible. Where practical, light up these outdoor living areas by means of high, overhead lights which are off to one side so that the insects will be attracted away from the immediate vicinity where guests may be sitting. As additional protection, use yellow or amber colored bulbs in all patio lamps, and in back or side door lights. Insects are practically blind to this color and can scarcely see these bulbs.

Special electrically-powered, insect-killing lanterns are also available. They look like a decorative hanging light—but are surrounded by wire grills which are electrically charged. The current is small enough to be harmless to humans, yet powerful enough to kill instantly all insects on contact. A tray at the bottom catches the dead insects as they fall for disposal purposes.

Plate 15.   ELECTRICITY—A MODERN GARDEN GENIE

The allure of moonlight nights is always possible in the flood-lit garden. Here, electricity transforms the informal garden into fairyland.

Electric lights can also be used in greenhouses or propagating rooms to help stimulate early plant growth and to help force plants into blooming at special seasons. Fluorescent lights are most popular for this. They are usually hung approximately three to four feet above the plants. When there are a great many such artificially lighted plant boxes to be handled at one time, stack them on shelves one above the other. Fasten 40 watt fluorescent strip lights to the bottom side of each shelf directly above the plants.

Lights are usually turned on just before sunset each day. They may be turned off after several hours by a manual switch or by electric time clocks. The circuit should be wired so that a single master switch can turn all lights on or off at one time. In addition, each light should also have its own individual switch so that the amount of exposure given some plants can be varied when necessary.

Artificial lighting can also be used to make certain types of plants bloom later than usual. Many late blooming plants (such as carnations) do not flower until the daylight hours are shorter by a specific amount than the hours of darkness. To fool these into blooming later than usual, additional light can be added for a few hours every day after the sun has set. Not until the hours of light are reduced to match those of a normal autumn day will flowers be produced.

Electricity also provides an extremely convenient source of heat for hotbeds or for greenhouse propagating boxes. Banks of incandescent lights can be used in some cases to provide overall heating. However, electric heating cable provides the most reliable and easily controlled source of bottom heat—the type which is ideal for propagating tender young plants.

The heating cable is sold in complete kits of various size. They contain the flexible lead-covered heating wires, a thermostat, and all necessary instructions for wiring and installation.

Commercial and scientific use of electricity in relation to plants include the killing of insect pests by electric current; also the increasing of the rate of growth and the development of new forms of plants by exposing them to X-ray currents. This last work is still exclusively in the hands of scientists, but the results of the present-day experiments will no doubt eventually be seen and used by every-day gardeners.

ELEPHANTS EAR. Common name for tropical herbs of the genus Colocasia, a member of the Arum Family; and also for a tropical American tree, *Enterlobium cyclocarpum;* it grows to 50 ft., bears bent or coiled pods that are fed to cattle, and belongs to the Pea Family. Colocasias are grown in N. and S. gardens for their ornamental foliage, the large heart- or shield-shaped leaves being sometimes 3 ft. long. *C. esculenta* (Taro, Eddo or Dasheen) is widely grown on the Islands of the

ELEPHANTS EARS GROW LARGE AND FAST
The stout bulbs of Colocasia develop enormous leaves in a few weeks when planted out in summer.

Pacific for its large edible tubers. *C. antiquorum* is an ornamental species with very large leaves; in its varieties these show margins and veinings of purple. This is probably the elephants ear formerly known and sometimes still listed as *Caladium esculentum.*

ELEPHANTS EAR FERN (*Acrostichum crinitum*). A greenhouse fern with broad entire fronds, 1 to 2 ft. long; requires fibrous soil and constant care.

ELETTARIA (el-e-tay'-ri-ah). A small group of perennial aromatic herbs of the Ginger Family, native to the E. Indies,

including the species which produces the Cardamon "seeds" of the drug trade (actually, the dried seed capsules). The plants are occasionally found in greenhouse collections, as they bear vari-colored flowers in great profusion. See also CARDAMON.

ELK (or STAGS) HORN FERN. Common name for the large-leaved, deeply forked ferns of the genus Platycerium, excellent for greenhouse and house culture.

ELM. Common name for Ulmus, a genus of hardy, ornamental deciduous trees native of the N. Temperate Zone and extensively planted as lawn and street trees. While the destruction of vast numbers of elms in Europe by the Dutch elm disease (which see) and the appearance of that trouble in E. U. S. has tended temporarily to check their popularity, it is to be hoped that the success of efforts to exterminate or control the disease will make possible and desirable the continuance of this, one of the most beautiful of trees.

In the main, elms are tall and of outstanding dignity, but the different species have their own distinctive characters and types of beauty. The vase-shaped American Elm (*U. americana*), also called the White, or Water Elm, with its straight gradually branching trunk and broad, gently rounded head, is the characteristic New England tree, though found throughout the E. part of the country, and both home properties and community parks and greens are made lovely by its presence. It is well worth the attention required to fight the rather numerous enemies noted below. The other species mentioned hereunder are perhaps less striking but nevertheless desirable.

Elms are propagated by seeds sown as soon as ripe; also by layering and by green-wood cuttings. Varieties are grafted on seedling stock, usually of *U. americana, U. campestris* or *U. glabra.*

DISEASES. One of the most serious diseases affecting the elm is the so-called Dutch elm disease, which see. Although no means of control is known, and although it has resulted in the loss of a great many fine trees in several European countries, the prompt and vigorous measures that have been employed toward its eradication in N. E. U. S. since its discovery in 1930 and their success, give reason to hope that it may be stamped out before this country suffers serious loss of one of its most beautiful shade trees. Incidentally, the campaign against it stresses the care and protection of healthy elms (and indirectly other trees), which should also have a valuable effect. In particular, a leaf spot trouble, characterized by hard black spots, can be controlled by destroying all fallen infected leaves.

Two other elm wilts are difficult to distinguish from the Dutch elm disease without laboratory culture and study of the fungi (Verticillium and Cephalosporium) that cause them. Trees affected by them may die or may recover naturally. A new virus disease, called phloem necrosis, that is moving along the Ohio River into W. Va., Ind., Ill., and Ky., had, by 1941, killed two-thirds of the elms along the streets of Chillicothe, O. No control is known except the removal of diseased trees.

INSECT PESTS. These are many, and since any agent weakening the tree predisposes it to the Dutch elm disease, it is particularly important to protect the trees against insect attack. Canker worms, destructive early in the season, should be controlled by spraying with arsenate of lead just after the leaves open. This spray (or possibly a second one) will also check the elm leaf beetle, which is especially destructive in dry seasons. The beetles winter as adults, eat holes in young foliage in early spring and lay rows of tiny pear-shaped, orange eggs on the underside of the leaves in June. The spring grubs feed there, skeletonizing the leaves, then transform to yellow pupae in bark crevices at the base of the tree to produce the yellow or green black-striped ¼ in. long beetles. A midsummer spray of lead arsenate may be needed to prevent the ravages of the Japanese beetle in its area. Larvae of the white-marked tussock moth, the gypsy moth, the spiny elm caterpillar (which develops into the mourning cloak butterfly), the fall webworm and the bagworm all feed on elm foliage. The leopard moth tunnels in small twigs and larger branches, but the elm borer, a small gray, red-marked, black-spotted beetle, is restricted to diseased or dying areas of bark.

Dormant spraying with a miscible oil will control the elm scurfy scale, and the chocolate brown European elm scale and possibly the woolly apple and elm aphid which curls and deforms the leaves in early spring. The latter are difficult to fight, but a nicotine spray *before* the leaves

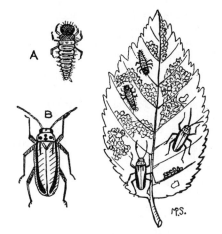

THE ELM LEAF BEETLE
In early spring the adult (B) chews the leaves; later, until July, grubs (A) which hatch from eggs laid on the leaf also attack and skeletonize the foliage.

curl is helpful. The cockscomb elm-leaf gall, which causes red-tipped elevations between the leaf veins, can also be controlled with a dormant spray.

PRINCIPAL SPECIES

U. americana (American Elm) to 120 ft., with light gray, fissured bark and upward sweeping branches with long pendent branchlets forming the typical "vase" form. Var. *aurea* with yellow leaves and var. *pendula*, of distinctly drooping habits, are nursery forms.

campestris (English Elm) to 130 ft., has a straight trunk with erect branches forming an oval head, less graceful than the American tree. Among the varietal forms are *argenteo-variegata* with leaves variegated with white; *purpurascens,* with small purple leaves; *purpurea* with purple leaves of average size, 2 to 4 in. long; *vanhouttei* with yellowish foliage.

fulva (Slippery Elm) to 70 ft., is a wide-branching, flat-topped tree, occasionally used for street planting.

glabra (Wych Elm, Scotch Elm) to 120 ft., forms a rather oblong-shaped head with spreading branches. As it does not sucker, it is a valuable tree for lawn planting, especially popular in some of its varietal forms, such as: *atropurpurea* with purple leaves; *camperdowni* (Camperdown Elm) with a globose head of pendulous branches; *crispa* (Fernleaf Elm), slow-growing, with drooping branches and leaves much cut on the margins; *fastigiata* (Exeter Elm) of erect habit; *lutescens* with yellow foliage); *nana* (Bush Elm), a very dwarf form; *pendula* (Tabletop Elm), a dwarf with horizontal branches, stiffly pendent; and *variegata* with leaves mottled white and green.

hollandica (Holland or Dutch Elm), a hybrid species to 100 ft., is a vigorous tree with short trunk and broad head with smooth glossy foliage. Among its varieties valuable for street planting are *klemmeri,* with narrow pyramidal habit of branching, and *belgica,* with a tall trunk and wide-spread branches.

foliacea (Smoothleaf Elm) is a tall broad-topped tree, often with corky branches, frequently suckering. Varieties most suitable for avenue planting are: *dampieri,* which is slender and erect; *stricta* (Cornish Elm), erect and narrow-topped, and *wheatleyi* (Guernsey or Jersey Elm), with ascending pyramidal branches. For outlining the path in a formal garden, var. *umbraculifera* (Globe Elm) of dwarf dense growth may be used.

parvifolia (Chinese Elm) is a small, half evergreen tree useful in mild climates.

pumila, the Dwarf or Siberian Elm (sometimes mistakenly called Chinese Elm), is an erect tree introduced in recent years and favored for planting in dry, wind-swept regions.

racemosa (Rock Elm, Cork Elm), to 100 ft., a large, round-topped tree with very corky branches, excellent for street planting.

crassifolia (Cedar Elm), to 80 ft., with broad top and drooping corky branches, is frequently planted S., but tender N.

serotina (September Elm), of medium height, with short drooping branches, although native in the S. States, has proved hardy in Mass.

alata (Wahoo Elm), to 80 ft., has a round or open head and branchlets furnished with two wide corky wings. A good avenue tree for the S., but not hardy N.

ELM FAMILY. Common name of the *Ulmaceae,* which includes besides the familiar elm, a few other shade and ornamental subjects.

ELODEA (el-oh-dee'-ah). Taking its name from a Greek word meaning marshy, and known commonly as Waterweed, Ditchmoss or Water-thyme, this genus includes some of the most useful aquatics

for use in the aquarium (which see), especially where the health and well-being of fish is important. The tender, perennial, branching stems, from 3 in. to 4 ft. long, depending on the depth of water, with their small whorled or opposite leaves, form an attractive green lacework through the water. The flowers are inconspicuous. Elodea propagates freely from cuttings and may be used as either a rooted or a floating plant. For the aquarium, cultivated stock is preferable to that collected in the field.

E. canadensis (sometimes listed as *Anacharis canadensis*) is commonly found in slow moving streams and ponds throughout the summer.

ELSHOLTZIA (el-sholt'-zi-ah). Several species of herbs or sub-shrubs, belonging to the Mint Family. The most valuable for gardens is *E. stauntoni,* a Chinese hardy deciduous semi-woody shrub 4 to 5 ft. high. It grows best in a sunny position and fairly rich soil. The dense one-sided spikes of purplish-pink flowers open in Sept. and Oct. The shoots should be shortened back about half their length in spring. The name is likely to be confused with Eschscholzia, the California Poppy, unless carefully noted.

ELYMUS (el'-i-mus). A genus of tall-growing perennial grasses native to temperate regions of both hemispheres and commonly known as Wild-rye or Lyme Grass. Some of the species are planted on banks or at the back of borders in the garden. One, much planted to hold sandy soils, is *E. arenarius;* known as Sea Lyme Grass or Dune Grass, it grows to 8 ft., with leaves 1 ft. long, and beardless spikes 10 in. long. Several other species range from 3 to 10 ft. tall and bear spikes from a few to 15 in. long.

See SOIL-BINDING PLANT.

EMBRYO. A plant (or animal) in the earliest and most rudimentary stage of its development; in the flowering or seed-bearing plants it is the plantlet as contained in the seed.

EMILIA (e-mil'-i-ah). Commonly known as Tassel-flower or Floras Paintbrush, this is a genus of annual and perennial plants of low neat habit, members of the Composite Family and natives of the Old-World tropics. The slender stems are tipped by small, rayless, many-colored flower-heads surrounded by soft white bristles (pappi); they resemble tiny paintbrushes. They will grow in any sunny corner and self-sow, blooming from July to frost.

E. *sagittata*, the common garden species, is an annual to 1½ ft., with scarlet flowers in loose clusters. Var. *lutea* has yellow flowers.

E. *sonchifolia*, another annual of about the same height, has flowers rose or purple, rarely white.

EMMENANTHE (em-en-an'-thee). A genus of annual herbs of the Water-leaf Family, native to W. N. America and bearing long-lasting yellow bell-shaped flowers in drooping racemes. If started outdoors they should be given a warm sunny location and a light sandy soil. If early bloom is desired, they should be started indoors and set out after danger of frost is over. E. *penduliflora*, called Yellow-bells, Golden-bells and sometimes Whispering Bells, grows from a few inches to 1½ ft. in height and forms bushy, branching plants covered with creamy-yellow persistent flowers.

EMPRESS-TREE. Common name for *Paulownia tomentosa*, a sturdy tree with large violet flower clusters and catalpa-like leaves, excellent for seashore planting. Both generic and common names were given in honor of Anna Paulowna, princess of the Netherlands.

EMULSION. A mixture in which fatty or resinous substances are suspended in a liquid in the form of minute globules. Properly made emulsions have a milky appearance. Oil emulsions are extensively used as dormant sprays, and kerosene and carbon-bisulphide emulsions are used to some extent in the control of plant pests, all of them as contact Insecticides, which see. See also OIL SPRAYS; KEROSENE; CARBON BISULPHIDE.

ENCEPHALARTOS (en-sef-ah-lahr'-tos). Beautiful palm-like plants (Cycads) from S. Africa, with stout, usually branchless trunks and stiff, glossy, fern-like spiny-tipped foliage. Aside from their ornamental value, they are interesting botanically, being ancient forms and occupying an intermediate place between flowering and spore-bearing plants. They are grown only under glass in the N., but are successfully used out-of-doors in S. Florida. Of slow growth, they need heat, moisture, partial shade, and a rich, sandy soil containing fibre. Propagation is by suckers which sprout around the base. Of the 20 or

more species, some with trunks entirely underground and others rising to 30 ft., but few are in cultivation. E. *villosus* has an orange-yellow fruit considerably larger than a pineapple.

ENCHANTERS-NIGHTSHADE. A common name for *Circaea lutetiana*, a soft, woolly herbaceous perennial of the Evening-primrose Family, native to Europe, but naturalized in parts of N. America, mostly in moist woodlands. It is sometimes used in shady bog plantings and in moist spots in rock gardens. It may be multiplied by division or by rooting offsets in the shade.

ENDEMIC. A term applied to plants native or indigenous to a certain region as opposed to the term exotic, which signifies plants not native to a given section.

BOTH ARE ENDIVE

And both are forms of Cichorium. (A) C. endivia, often called escarole, is like a ragged, curly head of lettuce blanched in the center. (B) C. intybus is the smooth, white, forced shoot of the plant called chicory.

ENDIVE (en'-div). A hardy biennial or annual herb (*Cichorium endivia*) grown for use as salad or as a pot herb and often called escarole in markets and kitchens. For summer use sow the seed thinly in early spring in a hotbed, a coldframe, or, as soon as the garden can be dug, in a seed bed for later transplanting, or even direct in the garden rows. Make the latter 18 to 24 in. apart, and thin or set the plants 12 to 15 in. asunder. Keep cleanly cultivated.

For autumn and winter make successional sowings three weeks apart from June until August, in the North, and 4 to 6 weeks longer in the South. Though the plant is hardy, the leaves may be injured by severe frost, so protect them on cold nights. Transplanting to a coldframe as fall approaches is a favorite method.

Endive may be subject to downy-mildew and gray mold rot (see LETTUCE), and the seedlings and roots may have Rhizoctonia rot, which see. Bean, pea and lettuce aphids all feed on endive. To control them, spray with nicotine-sulphate and soap.

To blanch the inner leaves for salad, tie the outer ones together above the crowns, or cover individual plants with drain tiles or "blanching tubes." Be sure the plants are dry when this is done, or the centers may rot. Should rain occur while the blanching is going on (it requires 2 to 4 weeks), uncover the heads, let them dry, and re-cover them. Blanching is not required where the crops are grown for greens.

The long blanched heads of the Witloof chicory, *C. intybus,* are also known in many places as Endive. (See illustration, Plate 56.) See also CICHORIUM.

ENGLISH DAISY. Common name for *Bellis perennis,* a dwarf hardy perennial with rounded double flower-heads of white and pink. It is the "daisy" of literature.

ENGLISH IVY. (See illustration, Plate 11.) Common name for *Hedera helix,* generally considered a vine, but actually high-climbing evergreen shrub, clinging by aerial rootlets; it is a member of the Aralia Family. It is hardy in sheltered places as far N. as Mass., and comes through the winter in better condition in shady places.

It has many uses, from covering walls, rocks, tree trunks and trellises, to carpeting bare spots in shady places and edging beds and borders. Under glass it is useful for clothing space under benches, for growing as trained specimens, and for planting in hanging baskets. It makes a good house plant, especially to train around a window. Pieces of stem placed in water root readily and continue decorative for some time if it is not desired to plant them.

Old plants of the type produce flowering shoots of different appearance from the normal creeping or climbing growth, the familiar 3- to 5-lobed leaves being replaced by usually rounded entire leaves. The flowers are small and greenish, borne in a cluster and followed by black berries. English Ivy runs into many forms, of which the following varieties are the most outstanding: *hibernica,* native in Ireland, with larger leaves of thinner texture; *arborescens,* a shrubby non-climbing form, obtained by propagating from flowering branches; *baltica,* a small leaved and very hardy form; *conglomerata,* a very slow growing plant with small wavy leaves

crowded on the stem; *gracilis,* with slender small leaves, turning bronzy in fall; *minima,* dwarf with close-set leaves; *pedata,* with 5-lobed leaves, with the middle lobe long and narrow, and *tortuosa,* with leaves almost entire, more or less curled and twisted.

There are also variegated leaved forms, which are rather more tender. Var. *argenteo-variegata* has leaves marked white; *aureo-variegata* marked yellow; *maculata* is a form of *hibernica* spotted and striped yellowish-white; *marmorata* has leaves blotched yellow and white; and *marginata* has cream-edged leaves.

English Ivy is easily propagated by cuttings and layers, and slow-growing choice varieties sometimes by grafting. Seeds, which should be sown when ripe, are usually slow to germinate.

ENEMIES. A bacterial disease may cause spots on leaves and cankers on stems. It occurs on ivy grown outdoors in the S. and on greenhouse stock in N. Y. and N. J. Control by hand-picking infected leaves and discarding plants showing stem lesions. Greenhouse benches should be disinfected before fresh cuttings are placed where infected plants have stood. Winter injury to this plant may be severe.

The bean aphid out-of-doors and mealy bugs, soft brown scale and oleander scale indoors may infest English Ivy. Spray with nicotine-sulphate and soap. See also MEALY BUG; SCALE INSECTS.

ENGLISH WALNUT. Common name for *Juglans regia,* a handsome, semi-hardy tree planted for its decorative value as well as for its nuts; because it originated in Persia, it would be more correctly called the Persian Walnut. See WALNUT.

ENKIANTHUS (en-ki-an'-thus). Hardy deciduous Asiatic shrubs, belonging to the Heath Family. They thrive in a rather moist sandy loam supplied with peat or leafmold. In habit they are stiffly upright with whorled branches, and are distinctive in appearance the year round. The long slender clusters of nodding flowers which open in spring, while not large and showy, are most attractive and have suggested as a common name "Necklace-bush." In the fall the leaves assume gorgeous shades of yellow, red and orange. Propagation is by seeds, cuttings or layers.

Principal species are: *E. campanulatus,* a tall shrub with pendulous bell-shaped flowers, yellowish veined with red, of unusual appearance. It is one of the most brilliantly colored shrubs in the fall. *E. perulatus,* which grows to 6 ft., and has urn-shaped white flowers which open in advance of the leaves. The latter are mostly yellow in the fall. *E. subsessilis,* a larger grower with smaller white flowers. It is the least attractive in bloom, but one of the most colorful in fall, when the leaves turn brilliant red. *E. cernuus,* which grows to 15 ft. and also has white flowers. Var. *rubens,* with red flowers, is more handsome.

ENTELEA (en-te-lee'-ah). One species (*E. arborescens*) of shrub or small tree from New Zealand, belonging to the Linden Family. It has been planted in S. Calif. and is ornamental with large heart-shaped leaves, toothed and sometimes slightly 3-lobed. The white flowers are an inch across and borne in flat clusters.

ENTEROLOBIUM (en-ter-oh-loh'-bi-um). A genus of tropical trees with feather-form leaves and large pods, eaten by cattle. It is one of several plants known as Elephants Ear, which see.

ENTIRE. A term referring to any leaf or leaf-like part whose margin is continuous and not to any extent toothed or indented. While it usually means that a leaf is unlobed, it is sometimes applied for a lobed leaf to indicate that margins of the lobes are not toothed.

EOMECON (ee-oh-me'-kon) *chionantha.* A half hardy, early-blooming herbaceous perennial from China, with white, poppy-like flowers, commonly known as Snow Poppy, which see.

EPACRIS (ep'-a-kris). Heath-like evergreen shrubs of New Zealand and Australia, sometimes grown as pot plants in a cool greenhouse. They thrive under the same treatment as Ericas (which see), but are easier to propagate and grow from cuttings. *E. impressa,* the best known species in gardens, makes a very decorative winter-flowering plant. It is an erect loosely branched shrub to 3 ft., with small tubular drooping flowers of red and white. There are several good garden forms that are superior to the type species.

EPAULET-TREE. Common name for the genus Pterostyrax, comprising two hardy Asiatic species, both deciduous. *P. hispida* is a tree to 45 ft. with broad head and slender branches. The oblong leaves to 7 in. long resemble those of the Elm. And the abundant, creamy white pendulous

panicles of fragrant flowers make it decidedly desirable. The other species, *P. cormybosa,* is more shrubby with both leaves and flower clusters smaller. The two species prefer a moist sandy loam and are propagated by seeds, layers and cuttings of young wood under glass.

EPHEDRA (ef-ee'-drah). Mexican-tea, Joint-fir. Small bushy shrubs found in dry places in various parts of the world. They are of peculiar appearance, with jointed and apparently leafless green stems, somewhat resembling the Horse-tails (which see). Most kinds are tender, but a few are half-hardy. Their chief value in cultivation seems to be for planting on dry sandy banks. The flowers are inconspicuous, but some species have decorative scarlet berry-like fruits. *E. distachya, E. trifurca, E. foliata,* and *E. nebrodensis* are the hardiest and best-known species.

EPIDENDRUM (ep-i-den'-drum). A genus of epiphytic tropical orchids, mainly from Central America, having rather small yellow, white, rose, or greenish blossoms, usually in terminal racemes. The flowers have similar petals and sepals and a wide-spreading, 3-lobed lip. They are of limited importance horticulturally, their main interest lying in the rapid growth of the hybrid forms produced by crossing the different species, or by crossing Epidendrums with the better known genera, Cattleya and Laelia. For culture see ORCHIDS.

EPIGAEA (ep-i-jee'-ah) *repens.* The attractive, spring-blooming, native, creeping evergreen called Mayflower or Trailing Arbutus. See ARBUTUS, TRAILING.

EPIGYNOUS (ee-pi'-ji-nus). Term applied to a flower in which petals, sepals and stamens are inserted *above* the ovary and attached to it. In such a case (as illustrated by the iris or apple), the ovary does not appear within the flower but below it, and it is said to be *inferior.* See OVARY.

EPILOBIUM (ep-i-loh'-bi-um). A large genus of herbs or subshrubs, native in temperate regions of the world, belonging to the Evening Primrose Family. See WILLOW-HERB.

EPIMEDIUM (ep-i-mee'-di-um). A genus of hardy perennial herbs of the Barberry Family, commonly known as Barrenworts. They have small leaves, bronzy when young and almost evergreen in sheltered spots, and bear delicate, airy racemes of small, waxen, red, pink, yellow or white flowers. Because of their attractive foliage, Barrenworts are eminently suited to the rock garden, but may also be planted in a shady portion of the border or along a woodland path. They are easily increased by division of the roots.

The species most commonly grown are: *E. macranthum* (Long-spur Epimedium), to 9 in., a native of Japan, with red and violet white-spurred flowers in early summer; var. *niveum* is white, var. *roseum,* rose-red, and var. *violaceum* has purple spurs. *E. alpinum,* to 1 ft., a European species seen in gardens mainly in its var. *rubrum,* which has red-edged leaves and red flowers. *E. pinnatum* (Persian Epimedium), which has yellow, red-spurred flowers with different shades and sizes represented in several good varieties.

EPIPACTIS (ep-i-pak′-tis). A genus of small, hardy, terrestrial orchids, commonly known as Rattlesnake-plantain because of the beautifully veined and variegated leaves. Resembling in pattern the markings on a rattlesnake, they were for that reason at one time considered an antidote for the bite. The small white flowers, united above into a helmet over the unfringed lip, grow in spikes, sometimes nearly a foot high. Found generally in open woods in acid soil, Rattlesnake-plantains may be transferred to the wild garden if a plentiful supply of leafmold is taken with them and if they are placed in conditions similar to those in which they originally grew. *E. pubescens,* with leaves to 2 in. veined with white, is the commonest species in the woods of the E. States.

EPIPHYLLUM (ep-i-fil′-um). The cacti of this genus (also called Phyllocactus) occupy a place almost by themselves when it comes to their culture.

Both names (Epiphyllum meaning upon a leaf, and Phyllocactus meaning leaf cactus) are rather misnomers, for in neither case are leaves present; the leaf-like stem, upon which the flowers are borne, is responsible for the names.

These cacti are of tropical origin and proper subjects for greenhouse or lathhouse culture. The flowers of the species are large and very beautiful, and as they have been in cultivation for many years, there are many very fine hybrids. All are easily cultivated and can be propagated from cuttings. They are often the subjects of grafting operations; since they themselves are fairly rapid growers, the de-

velopment may become phenomenal when they are grafted upon a vigorous stock.

See also CACTUS.

EPIPHYTE (ep′-i-fyt). An "air plant," or organism that scarcely roots but grows upon other plants, particularly trees, without being parasitic upon them, in order to be in a better position to secure light. Air plants are variously modified to cling, to obtain and store water and to catch drifting humus, since they usually have no contact with actual soil, but only with humus which clusters about their base.

EPISCIA (e-pish′-i-ah). A genus of choice trailing greenhouse plants from Tropical America, of the Gesneria Family. The small, often hairy leaves are showy, and the white, red or purple flowers small but numerous and succeeded by leathery fruits. They are favorite subjects for hanging-baskets and for training on small wire trellises. A rich, fibrous loam, mixed with peat, leafmold and sand, and a partially shady location, give best results. Propagation is by division and cuttings.

E. chontalensis has both stems and leaves reddish purple and flowers pale-lilac or white. *E. cupreata* has a drooping habit, downy leaves with copper luster, and scarlet flowers, its var. *viridiflora* has larger flowers and green leaves. *E. fulgida* is a creeper with dark green leaves and red flowers.

EQUISETUM (ek-wi-see′-tum). A genus of flowerless plants called Scouring-rushes or Horsetails (which see), useful for holding banks and covering waste land.

ERADICATION. Meaning literally "a rooting out," this term refers to the destruction or removal of a plant enemy within an area, as opposed to *exclusion,* which refers to the prevention of its entry into the area. See DISEASES, PLANT.

ERAGROSTIS (er-ah-gros′-tis). A genus of medium-sized grasses, some annuals, some perennials, valued for their delicate ornamental sprays, which consist of small spikelets carried in open panicles. There is considerable confusion between the individual species, which grow between 1½ to 3 ft. tall, with leaves 4 to 12 in. long, and panicles 4 to 15 in. long. *E. abyssinica,* an annual to 3 ft., is known as Teff. *E. elegans, interrupta* and *japonica,* all known as Love Grass, are annuals to 3 ft., useful for bouquets.

ERANTHEMUM (ee-ran′-thee-mum). A genus of tropical herbs and shrubs, belonging to the Acanthus Family. Its botanical status and relations have been much confused and several plants long known and grown as Eranthemums, are now referred to other genera. At present the one species recognized by botanists as belonging here is *E. nervosum,* which has been known as *E. pulchellum* and also as *Daedalacanthus nervosus.* This is a good blue-flowering plant to be grown for winter bloom in the warm greenhouse, and also a popular shrub for outdoor planting in the far S. It is easy to grow from cuttings but needs good soil and plenty of water.

ERANTHIS (e-ran'-this). Commonly known as Winter-aconite, this is a genus of small, tuberous-rooted hardy perennials of the Buttercup Family. Its bright buttercup-like blooms and whorl of shiny leaves appear in earliest spring with the snowdrops. It thrives in half-shade and leafy soil and is especially happy in the rock garden. Tubers are usually planted in autumn; to avoid disturbing them, their location should be marked before the foliage dies down after flowering.

E. hyemalis, to 8 in., has long stemmed finely-cut foliage and flowers to 1½ in. across. *E. sibirica,* only about half as high, has somewhat smaller flowers with fewer petals.

ERCILLA (er-sil'-ah) *spicata.* A climbing evergreen shrub native to Chile. It can stand a few degrees of frost, is not particular as to soil, and is best planted against a wall or fence. It has dense spikes of small purple flowers and dark purple berries. Prune plants after they have flowered to keep the growth within bounds.

EREMURUS (er-e-meu'-rus). (See illustration, Plate 19.) Called by such descriptive names as Desert Candle, Foxtail-lily, and Giant-asphodel, this genus includes the hardiest of the tall desert members of the Lily Family and some of the most spectacular. Long, slender leaves spring from the fleshy rope-like roots in dense basal rosettes; above them rises the stout, sometimes to 8 ft. flower stalk, clothed for half its length with close-set starry blooms which last for several weeks. The Eremurus is steadily gaining popularity both as a stately border-subject and as a florist's flower. As seedlings develop slowly, the purchase of sizable plants is advisable. A rich, fibrous, well-drained soil containing sharp sand, and a sunny location are essen-

tial. The plant dies away after flowering but foliage growth reappears in early spring and must be protected against late frosts. A mound of wood ashes drawn over the crown or a water-tight box filled with dry leaves will give winter protection. Established plants should never be disturbed, as the roots are very brittle.

There are about 20 species all from W. and Central Asia, and many hybrids. *E. bungei* has orange-yellow flowers, *E. elwesii* has peach-pink flowers and *E. himalaicus,* the most commonly grown species, has white flowers.

ERGOT. A disease of rye and other cereals and some wild grasses, which attacks the inflorescence, replacing certain kernels with hard black or dark purple structures called ergots, which are the resting bodies (*sclerotia*) of the fungus. It is important because of the medicinal qualities of extracts of ergots and because of epidemics known as ergotism that were common among people and animals in the Middle Ages but that are rare today although the feeding or ergotized grain affects cows, horses, chickens and other domestic animals. Ergot-free seed should be used for planting and susceptible grasses in the vicinity of cereal fields should be mowed before they blossom.

ERIANTHUS (er-i-an'-thus). A genus of tall-growing plants of the Grass Family, collectively known as the Plume Grasses, and making good subjects for the border or the background of lawns from N. Y. southward. They are perennials, but are mostly grown as annuals, attaining a height of 10 to 12 ft. in a season, with long flat leaves. *E. ravennae* (Ravenna Grass), the tallest, has leaves 3 ft. long and about ½ in. wide; the plume-like panicles may be as much as 3 ft. long. *E. divaricatus* and *saccharoides,* usually not more than 10 ft. tall, have panicles about 1 ft. in length. See ORNAMENTAL GRASSES.

ERICA (er'-i-cah). A large genus of evergreen shrubs of the Heath Family, native in Europe and S. Africa. In mild regions they are attractive for outdoor grouping, and they were formerly very popular as pot plants. Only a few are fairly hardy N. See HEATH. HEATHER.

ERICACEAE (e-ri-kay'-see-ee). Botanical name of the Heath Family, an important group of shrubs and small trees widely distributed but strongly preferring regions with acid-soil conditions. A large, much varied family, some species, as the blueberry, are grown for food and many others as highly ornamental subjects grown for foliage and showy flowers; some members furnish the finest broad-leaved evergreens.

ERICACEOUS PLANTS. These are members of the *Ericaceae* or Heath Family. All are woody plants, mostly shrubs or low ground-cover materials, but sometimes small trees. Some of them are broad-leaved evergreens while others are deciduous. They include some of our finest flowering shrubs. There are about 70 genera and nearly 2,000 species in this family, more than 800 belonging to the genus Rhododendron. Other common representatives are Mountain-laurel (Kalmia), Blueberry and Cranberry (Vaccinium), Huckleberry (Gaylussacia), Trailing Arbutus, Scotch Heather, Bearberry, Wintergreen, Heath (Erica), Ledum, Andromeda, Pieris, Leucothoë, Enkianthus and the Azaleas. They come from all parts of the world, many being mountain plants.

Ericaceous plants almost invariably prefer acid soils and most of them will tolerate nothing else. Although some prefer open situations, nearly all will do well in semi-shade and many, particularly the evergreen sorts, need protection from sweeping winds. As a general rule, the cultural directions given for Rhododendron (which see) apply to the other ericaceous plants, all of which prefer peaty soils.

ERICAMERIA (er-i-kah-mee'-ri-ah) *ericoides.* A tender evergreen shrub of Calif., belonging to the Daisy Family and formerly known as *Alopappus ericoides.* It is commonly called Mock-heather.

ERIGENIA (er-i-jee-ny'-ah). A low-growing, tuberous native herb bearing white flowers in small clusters early in the season and popularly called Harbinger-of-Spring, which see.

ERIGERON (e-rij'-er-on). (See illustration, Plate 45.) A genus of aster-like annual and perennial plants of the Composite Family, commonly known as Fleabane. They have flowers in heads with white, rose or violet ray-flowers and yellow disk-flowers. Some of the species are cultivated in the border, others are naturalized in the wild garden, and a few are grown in the rock garden. They should be planted in warm sandy soil in full sun. Fleabanes are easily increased from seed or division.

Aster yellows (see under ASTER), a virus disease, causes yellowing and stunting; control it by removing and burning infected plants.

PRINCIPAL SPECIES

E. speciosus, perennial to 2 ft., violet-rayed flowers to 1½ in. across in flat-topped clusters, blooms over a long period.

karvinskianus, perennial to 18 in., a trailing alpine with white or pink daisy-like flowers all summer and autumn. It blooms the first year from seed and should have winter protection in the N.

aurantiacus (Double Orange Daisy) to 9 in., with brilliant orange blossoms, blooms throughout the summer and is a very showy plant in the rock garden at a time when bloom is needed.

alpinus, to 3 in., has delicate pink daisy-like flowers.

compositus, to 2 in., has feathery gray foliage and pale lavender flowers.

caucasicus, to 10 in., has rosy lavender flowers blooming in profusion all summer.

ERINUS (e-ry'-nus) *alpinus.* A hardy European mountain perennial of the Figwort Family, that forms low dense tufts and is commonly grown in the dry rock wall or in crevices in the rock garden. It bears early in April small rosy-purple flowers rising 3 to 4 in. above the matted foliage. It is easily grown from seed and self-sows readily. Color forms are: var. *alba* with white flowers and var. *carmineus* with deep rose flowers.

ERIOBOTRYA (er-i-oh-bot'-ri-ah) *japonica.* A white-flowered evergreen Asian shrub sometimes called Japan-plum but popularly known as Loquat, which see.

ERIOCEPHALUS (er-i-oh-sef'-ah-lus). Shrubby evergreen S. African plants belonging to the Daisy Family. *E. africanus,* the best known, may be grown in the greenhouse, or outdoors in California. It is a much branched shrub with pleasantly scented, silvery leaves, and heads of white and purple flowers. It is propagated by cuttings, and grows best in a mixture of sandy loam and peat.

ERIOGONUM (er-i-o-goh'-num). Herbs or subshrubs belonging to the Buckwheat Family and native in the western part of the country. One or two species, sometimes offered by dealers in native plants and rarely grown in rock gardens, require a well-drained peaty soil in a sunny position. *E. compositum* is a little tufted

Plate 16.   EXHIBITING—AN AIM OF MANY GARDENERS

Top: The peony lends itself admirably to exhibition purposes. Insert: There are always rose classes for all sorts of gardeners. Bottom: The chrysanthemum exhibition provides a glorious finale for the outdoor garden season.

woolly-leaved plant, with heads of small dull-white or pinkish flowers. *E. umbellatum* has leaves white beneath, and umbels of deep yellow flowers. The larger (to 3 ft.) *E. fasciculatum* of Calif. and Nev. with white flowers is called Wild Buckwheat.

ERIOPHORUM (er-i-o-foh'-rum). A genus of N. hemisphere perennial sedges found in marshy places and attractive in bog gardens and around ponds because of their cottony flower heads. See COTTON-GRASS.

ERIOPHYLLUM (er-i-oh-fil'-um). Annual or perennial herbs or subshrubs, native in W. N. America, belonging to the Daisy Family. They are not widely cultivated, but are useful for planting in dry regions where hardy.

E. caespitosum is a low tufted herbaceous perennial, with leaves deeply lobed, woolly beneath, and yellow flowers. *E. confertiflorum* (Golden-yarrow), is a somewhat larger growing perennial with finely cut leaves, woolly on both sides.

ERIOPSIS (er-ri-op'-sis). A small genus of epiphytic orchids from S. America bearing racemes of small but attractive brownish or yellowish-green flowers with 3-lobed lips. They should be grown in a cool greenhouse, given full exposure to the sun, and frequently watered. *E. rutidobulbon* has brownish-yellow flowers 1½ in. across, with a white lip spotted purple. *E. biloba* is another good sort. For further details of culture see ORCHIDS.

ERIOSTEMON (er-i-oh-stee'-mon). Small evergreen shrubs of Australia, belonging to the Rue Family. Some are listed for garden use in Calif., but they are usually grown as cool greenhouse plants for winter flowering. They do best in a mixture of fibrous peat and loam, with sharp sand. Trim back to shape after flowering, and when growth is well advanced it is well to place them outdoors for the summer to insure better flowering wood. Propagated by cuttings taken in spring.

E. buxifolius has small box-like leaves and pale pink flowers. *E. salicifolius* has willow-like leaves and pink flowers. *E. myoporoides* has slender leaves, tapering each way from the middle, and white or pink flowers.

ERITRICHIUM (er-i-trik'-i-um). A small genus of handsome low-growing annual and perennial herbs, natives of mountainous regions of Europe and members of the Borage Family. Some of them are covered with woolly hairs, giving them a whitish appearance. The blue flowers are small, but often of brilliant shades; one species has a yellow eye. They are useful in the rock garden. Propagation is by division, or by seeds.

ERLANGEA (er-lan-jee'-ah). Herbaceous or shrubby plants from Tropical Africa, belonging to the Daisy Family (Compositae). The shrubby species (*E. tomentosa*) is a good winter flowering plant for the cool greenhouse. Excellent plants can be grown from spring-rooted cuttings to flower within the year. Year-old plants cut back and planted outdoors for the summer make good specimens by early fall when they should be lifted, moved back into the greenhouse and grown on as a source of cut flowers. This species has gray scented leaves and clusters of mauve or lilac flowers in small heads. *E. cordifolia*, an erect, hairy herb with purple to lavender flower-heads, is said to have been grown in Calif.

ERODIUM (e-roh'-di-um). A genus of the Geranium Family comprising a number of annual and perennial species, commonly known as Heronsbill, a few of them used in the garden, but the greater number planted as forage crops. Those species cultivated on the edge of the border or in the rock garden, should be planted in gritty loam to which a little lime has been added, and given a sunny position. Valuable because of their long blooming period, they are increased by seed or division. The following list includes those, mainly perennial, of horticultural interest:

E. manescavi, the tallest, reaching 1 ft. or more, a European species with magenta flowers to 1½ in. across, a vigorous plant rather difficult to combine with others because of the strong color of the blossoms.

cheilanthifolium, to 4 in., with silvery fern-like leaves and white flowers veined with rose to ¾ in. across, a charming alpine species from Spain and Morocco, perfectly hardy N.

trichomanefolium, to 5 in., another good rock-garden subject, the violet flowers veined with pink.

corsicum, to 6 in., forming rosettes of downy foliage covered with pink, rose-veined flowers all summer.

macradenum, to 1 ft., has pale lavender blossoms, the two upper petals marked with large purple spots.

cnamaedryoides, to 3 in., with white flowers veined with rose, in bloom nearly all the year, is a dainty alpine, suitable for a shady corner in the rock garden.

EROSION. This refers to two distinct actions, one constructive and a phase of soil formation, the other destructive, contributing to the injury of soil.

Weathering, disintegration and washing or blowing away of rocks and soil represents the first type. Rocks are split and chipped by frost and by plant roots, dissolved by chemical action of rainwater and soil seepage, worn away by stream action or by sand blown in the wind. The resulting finely powdered rock, mixed with humus or decayed vegetable and animal matter, is soil.

Soil erosion, meaning the washing or blowing away of the topsoil (and sometimes even the subsoil) is a great destructive force, requiring the expenditure of large sums of public money in agricultural areas. It is most rapid on cultivated, sloping land, where heavy rains wash out channels and carry off many tons per acre of the best topsoil; also in drought times the wind whirls such soil away as dust.

Preventive measures include the planting of hills, slopes and banks with trees, shrubs, forage crops, permanent groundcover or strong grass; the clothing of less steep inclines with permanent sod; and the plowing of sloping land only when in good condition and when it is to be quickly replanted. Erosion channels while still small should be blocked with stones, brush, anchored straw and fast-growing trees; otherwise they deepen to torrent beds. Where possible, hillsides that must be cultivated should be terraced to break the flow of water; or level trenches may be plowed or strips of sod left at right angles to the slope. The best control for wind erosion is permanent planting of any vegetation with strong roots.

While the suggestions given are commonly used on large areas, the same principles of checking the surface movement of water, of keeping the soil more porous by supplying plenty of humus, and of keeping loose soils planted to a thickly fibrous-rooted crop as much as possible, can all be applied to even the most restricted garden area where erosion may threaten.

The widespread occurrence of erosion, its importance as a threat to the nation's soil, crop, and food resources, and the proven value of conservation methods led to the establishment of the Soil Conservation Service as a division of the U. S. Department of Agriculture. This agency, in cooperation with the States, the C.C.C., etc., is carrying on a many sided constructive program which includes investigation of causes and cures, study and testing of erosion-preventing crops and their production when necessary, demonstration of erosion-control methods of farming, and assistance of farmers and communities in putting them into practice, both on individual properties and throughout extensive areas. For information on all such matters, apply to the Soil Conservation Service in Washington, D. C. or your local or State coordinator.

ERUCA (ee-roo'-kah). A genus of the Crucifer or Cabbage Family. The species *E. sativa* is grown (as *Rocket-salad* or *Roquette*) for use as greens. See ROCKET-SALAD.

ERVATAMIA (er-vah-tay'-mi-ah). A tropical shrub belonging to the Dogbane Family, formerly known as *Tabernaemontana coronaria.* See CRAPE-JASMINE.

ERYNGIUM (e-rin'-ji-um). A genus of mostly perennial plants of the Parsley Family with spiny leaves and flowers in dense heads or spikes, generally known as Eryngo or Sea-holly. The steel-blue or gray foliage of the larger species is most attractive in the border, while the smaller kinds are well suited to the rock garden. The taller types provide excellent cut flowers that can be dried for winter bouquets. Eryngos should be planted in light rich soil in an open sunny position; they are easily increased by seed sown as soon as ripe, and by division.

E. maritimum (Sea-holly) to 1 ft., with broad spiny grayish-blue leaves, bears pale blue heads of flowers surrounded by spiny bracts.

amethystinum, to 1½ ft., has small blue flowers surrounded by narrow bracts.

oliverianum, to 3 ft., has broad cut leaves and blue flowers 1½ in. long, surrounded by very narrow stiff bracts.

ERYSIMUM (e-ris'-i-mum). A genus of hardy annual, biennial or perennial herbs of the Mustard Family, closely resembling wallflowers, and commonly known as Blister-cress. They have white, yellow or lilac flowers, and some of the smaller species are excellent subjects for the rock garden or the edge of the sunny border. They are easily cultivated, the seeds of the annuals being planted where the plants are to stand, and the perennials being increased from seed and from root division in the spring.

Among the species used in the rock garden are: *E. pulchellum* (P.) to 1 ft. or more, which has mustard-yellow flowers and blooms profusely in early spring; *E. pumilum,* perennial, having clear yellow flowers in broad clusters, and *E. purpureum,* a low-growing Asiatic species with purple flowers, also perennial.

ERYTHEA (er-i-thee′-ah). A group of Mexican fan-palms, often planted outdoors in the warmest parts of this country, and sometimes seen as small specimens under glass.

E. armata (Blue Palm) is a robust grower to 40 ft., the trunk being covered with fibrous material and carrying a heavy crown of bluish-green leaves. The leaf-stems are armed with stout hooked spines.

brandegeei grows to 125 ft., with a slender trunk and dark-green leaves pale beneath. The stems are edged with recurved spines.

edulis (Guadalupe Palm) has a stout trunk to 30 ft. or more, and a crown of much-divided leaves with few prickles on the stems. Clusters of the shining black fruits with a sweet pulp, are said to grow up to 50 lbs. weight.

elegans is dwarfer and of slow growth, with glaucous leaves and spiny stems.

ERYTHRINA (er-i-thry′-nah). A leguminous genus comprising trees, shrubs and sometimes herbs, with showy flowers and pods. The tree species are known as Coral-tree, which see.

ERYTHRONIUM (er-i-throh′-ni-um). A genus of bulbous early spring-blooming herbs of the Lily Family, with graceful nodding flowers, and often richly mottled leaves. Common names are Dogs-tooth-violet, Fawn- or Trout-lily and Adderstongue, and others are applied, locally. The plants are particularly attractive in the rock garden or naturalized in masses in the wild garden, and should be planted in light soil full of humus in partially shaded places. Unless they are given a natural woodland condition, a winter mulch of decayed leaves and coal ashes is beneficial.

Erythroniums are increased by seed and some species spread naturally by means of underground rootstocks. The best time for obtaining new stock or for replanting is when the leaves die away after flowering. The bulbs should be planted not less than 3 in. deep and finer effects are obtained by massing or planting them in groups rather than as individual plants.

ENEMIES. Speckling of leaves, followed by shriveling and falling over on the soil, is caused by a fungus that develops resting bodies (sclerotia), which produce spores in the spring. Remove and destroy infected plants, taking the adjacent soil with them. Then drench the spot with corrosive sublimate, which see.

PRINCIPAL SPECIES

E. americanum (Trout-lily) to 12 in. is the species commonly known in the E. The leaves are richly mottled and the yellow flowers have recurved petals. It often grows in great colonies on the edge of the woodland, and increases rapidly by offsets.

californicum (Fawn-lily), to 1 ft. with cream-colored flowers and richly marked leaves, is a W. species which may naturalize very easily. Var. *bicolor* (white or yellow) is very fragrant.

giganteum, to 1½ ft. with beautifully mottled brown and green leaves and large creamy flowers touched with maroon at the base, is one of the most beautiful of the species. It is also listed as *E. watsoni.*

grandiflorum (Glacier-lily), to 2 ft. has green leaves and bright buttercup-yellow flowers. Var. *robustum* is a large form.

citrinum, to 8 in. has white flowers marked at the base with deep citron yellow.

hendersoni, to 1 ft. with mottled leaves, has strongly recurved purple flowers.

multiscapoideum, to 6 in., a dainty species, with creamy-white flowers with yellow centers is generally sold as *E. hartwegi.*

revolutum, to 1 ft. has white flowers tinted lavender or purple. Var. *johnsoni* has dark rose flowers.

montanum (Avalanche-lily), to 1½ ft. with slightly recurved white flowers, grows in profusion on the high slopes of far W. mountains, but because it starts so late it is difficult to cultivate in the E.

dens-canis (Dogs-tooth-violet), to 6 in. with mottled leaves and rose or purple flowers, is the Eurasian form commonly grown abroad.

ESCALLONIA (es-kah-loh′-ni-ah). Handsome shrubs of S. America, mostly evergreen, belonging to the Saxifrage Family. They can stand some frost, but are not hardy where winters are severe. When well suited as to climate, and in a rather light and well-drained soil, they make dense, mound-like bushes from 6 to 15 ft. or more in height. They thrive near the seaside. Some species have been successfully used as hedges, and also trained as vines. In most cases the young growth glistens with resinous glands. The flowers, usually tubular in shape, are borne in clusters of white, pink, or red. Most of the species are summer bloomers, but one or two flower in autumn. They are easily propagated by cuttings.

PRINCIPAL SPECIES

E. floribunda grows to a large bush with very sticky branchlets. The long and narrow glossy green leaves are finely toothed, and the flowers are white.

montevidensis is very similar but not sticky. Its leaves, slightly notched at the tip, are distinctive, and it has larger flowers.

virgata is a much branched deciduous species with white flowers in leafy racemes, and the hardiest of the group.

macrantha is of dense spreading habit, with thick oval shining leaves and clusters of rosy-crimson flowers. A good hedge plant where hardy.

langleyensis is one of the best of the hybrid forms. It has graceful arching branches, small leaves, and short racemes of rosy-carmine flowers.

ESCAROLE. A name used (mainly by greengrocers and cooks) for the salad or pot herb *Cichorium endivia,* more commonly known as endive (which see).

ESCHSCHOLZIA (esh-sholt′-zi-ah). Sometimes spelled ESCHSCHOLTZIA. A genus of annual or perennial herbs of the Poppy Family, commonly grown as annuals, the most widely known and popular species being the California Poppy (*E. californica*). The plants sometimes grow to 2 ft., but are usually lower and spreading, with bluish-green, finely-cut foliage, and attractive satiny-petaled flowers to 2 in. across, varying from pale cream to deep orange. The flowers, which are slender rather than cup-shaped as in other poppies, vary considerably in form as well as color, double forms occasionally occurring.

California poppies are attractive border or edging plants, blooming profusely all summer and even after the first frosts. They thrive in ordinary good garden soil and are easy to grow. Seed can be sown

very early in spring (or later if desired), where the plants are to stand. They should be thinned out later, since they will not stand transplanting. If well protected with a light loose covering of leaves, plants will often winter over and bloom extra early the following spring; plants also may develop from self-sown seed.

Other species sometimes seen in gardens are: *E. tenuifolia* to 1 ft. with small light yellow flowers, and *E. caespitosa* to 9 in. with golden yellow blooms to 2 in. across.

ESPALIER (es-pal′-yer). This term is used both for a trellis or lattice on which a fruit tree is trained and for a tree so handled. The practice, which is much commoner abroad than in America where the long, hot growing season is not so well adapted to keeping the plants under strict control, has the advantages of saving space, of giving the trees maximum care and, when necessary, shelter, and of helping produce high quality fruit. It is therefore sometimes followed in small gardens or in sections of large estates that are in charge of expert gardeners skilled in the art.

In employing the espalier system dwarf trees (mainly pear or apple, but any of the stone fruits if desired) are used, and the branches, restricted to a definite, symmetrical number, are trained, in a single plane parallel to the support, either horizontally, vertically or in diagonal directions. The branching is started low and by constant heading back, pinching of unwanted shoots and tying of the stems to the trellis, the desired form and design of branches is developed, the fruits being allowed to form on selected spurs at uniform intervals.

This training and spacing results in giving all the fruit maximum light and air; trees on espalier trellises are therefore less likely to suffer from abrupt temperature changes than those grown close against walls. (See illustrations, Plate 52; also page 438.) See also TRAINING OF PLANTS.

ETHYLENE DICHLORIDE. A colorless liquid with an odor like chloroform, used by commercial growers (1) with rotenone in a spray recommended for mites and thrips, or (2) emulsified with soap to control the peach tree borer.

ETIOLATED. Blanched or whitened from lack of sunlight. The term is generally applied to plants that have been grown in darkness and in whose tissues the green color bodies (*choroplasts*) have been changed to white *leucoplasts.*

EUCALYPTUS (eu-kah-lip'-tus). A genus of rapidly growing broad-leaved evergreen trees of subtropical and warm-temperate climates, many of them commonly known as Gum Trees. Members of the Myrtle Family, they grow to great size and are of ornamental value for street and lawn, having attractive gray-green or bluish, lance-shaped or ovate leaves on pendulous twigs. Some are profuse bloomers, bearing umbels of white or pink flowers which are a valuable source of honey. There are dwarf types of some species, while of others juvenile forms are grown as greenhouse foliage plants. Some kinds endure extremes of heat, as well as cold, and the whole group is notably free from insects because of the strong aromatic oil in the wood. Propagated by seed sown under screens.

Among the many species in use are:

E. globulus (Blue Gum), the species most planted in Calif., is particularly suited to dry soil and makes a fine windbreak. A majestic tree, it grows to 300 ft. and bears flowers 1½ in. across. Var. *compacta* is well suited to garden use, being dwarf with a round compact form.

rostrata (Red Gum), growing to 200 ft., is also resistant to drought and withstands great heat, yet endures some frost. It will thrive in an alkaline soil and stand flooding for a prolonged period.

sideroxylon (Red Ironbark), a tall tree with dark, persistent bark, has a var. *rosea* with rose-colored flowers and another var. *pallens* with red blossoms, both profuse bloomers and of desirable form for W. grounds.

EUCHARIDIUM (eu-ka-ri'-di-um). Attractive, low-growing California annuals of simple culture, with leafy stems and showy flowers succeeded by small bright fruits. They are of the same Evening-primrose Family as Clarkia and have the same requirements, namely partial shade and a rich, well-drained soil. Seed should be sown in early spring and the plants undisturbed.

E. breweri (formerly called Clarkia), or Fairy Fans, grows to 9 in.; its flowers are

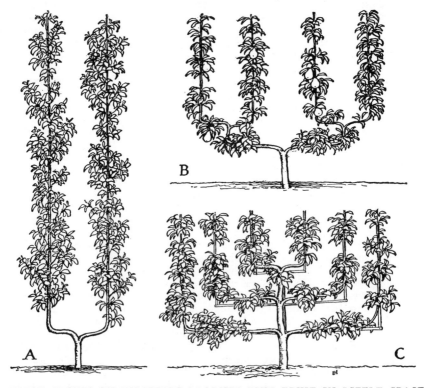

TREES GROWN ON ESPALIERS PRODUCE FINE FRUIT IN LITTLE SPACE
(A) A simple U-form espalier useful for apple trees in narrow spaces, as between windows. (B) A pear tree trained to a double U-form espalier. (C) A 6-armed espalier adaptable to a broad, low wall.

deep pink with a honeysuckle fragrance. *E. concinnum* (Red Ribbons) to 2 ft., has rose-purple flowers, the petals bearing tiny claws.

EUCHARIS (eu'-kah-ris). A genus of bulbous herbs of the Amaryllis Family from the Colombian Andes, with broad, long-stemmed basal leaves and clusters of fragrant, dazzling white flowers. A greenhouse subject except in subtropical climates, it is unrivaled for its beauty and freedom of bloom. The bulb should be planted in coarse fibrous soil with charcoal and sand. Flowering is stimulated by free watering and full sunshine. After a shaded resting period, during which water must be withheld, it may flower again. Syringe frequently for red spider. *E. amazonica* (Amazon-lily) has leaves 1 ft. long with stems of equal length. The flowers are up to 3 in. across and borne on stalks 2 ft. high.

EUCOMIS (eu'-koh-mis) *punctata.* A S. African herb of the Lily Family with greenish flowers in a spike topped with a cluster of leaf-like bracts. Commonly known as Pineapple-flower, which see.

EUGENIA (eu-jee'-ni-ah). Evergreen trees and shrubs of the tropics, belonging to the Myrtle Family. Many species are grown in the tropics for the edible fruits, much used for jellies and confections. Some have been introduced into the warmest parts of this country, chiefly for ornamental purposes. They are of easy culture, and propagated by seeds and cuttings. The principal species include the following:

E. jambos (Rose-apple) is an ornamental tree to 30 ft. much planted in California, as far north as San Francisco. It has long narrow leaves, rose-tinted when young, conspicuous greenish-white flowers, and creamy-white fragrant fruits. *E. uniflora* (Surinam-cherry) is a large shrub or tree to 25 ft. that bears fragrant white flowers and edible red berries with a spicy flavor. It makes a very attractive pot plant. *E. myrtifolia* (Australian Brush-Cherry), a tall tree in Australia, is much used in California as a hedge plant and for topiary pieces. The red-tinted young growth gives a lovely effect, and later the leaves are glossy green. *E. aromatica* produces the "cloves" of commerce, these being the dried flower buds,

EULALIA (eu-lay'-li-ah). Common name for *Miscanthus sinensis*, one of the best ornamental grasses (which see) for N. regions. It makes attractive clumps for the border or around the lawn and, once established, will remain for years. Any good soil is suitable. It grows from 4 to 10 ft., with leaves to 3 ft. long and 1 in. wide having a striking whitish midrib. The silky, plume-like panicles grow to 2 ft. long. The leaves of var. *gracillimus* are narrow, and channeled; those of var. *variegatus* have white or yellow stripes, and those of var. *zebrinus* (Zebra Grass) yellowish bands. Eulalia sometimes grows wild as an escape from gardens. (See illustration, Plate 37.)

EUONYMUS (eu-on'-i-mus). Spindletree. Deciduous or evergreen shrubs or small trees, widely distributed in temperate and warmer regions, belonging to the Staff-tree Family. They are mostly of upright habit, a few prostrate species do well in sun or partial shade, and are not particular as to soil. The flowers are inconspicuous, but most kinds have colorful fruits. Most of the deciduous kinds and a few of the evergreen are hardy N. The latter make good hedges, and thrive under city and seaside conditions. Propagated by seeds, layers and cuttings.

Euonymus stems are often afflicted with aerial crown gall tumors (see CROWN GALL); the only remedy is the cutting out of infected portions. Various leaf spots of minor importance may disfigure foliage. Mildew, prevalent in the S. and W. can be controlled with sulphur fungicides, or sometimes merely by a stream of water directed against the shrub under high pressure.

The chief pest is the euonymus scale, which is common on most species and also on bittersweet. The female resembles the oyster-shell scale (which see); the male is white and slender; the young appear in early spring, and successive generations feed on both wood and foliage until late fall. Spray thoroughly in early spring with a miscible oil, and, in the summer as the young scales hatch, with a white-oil emulsion plus nicotine sulphate. Do not use an oil spray if the temperature is nearing 90 deg. F. and follow manufacturers' directions carefully.

PRINCIPAL SPECIES

E. americanus (Strawberry-bush) is a native deciduous shrub to 8 ft. Not of very distinguished habit, but showy in fall with pink warty fruits and scarlet covered seeds.

obovatus (Running Strawberry-bush) is a native creeping species with rooting stems about 1 ft. high. Useful as a ground cover in shady places.

atropurpureus (Wahoo or Burning-bush) is a large native deciduous shrub or tree to 25 ft. The leaves turn yellow in fall, and the fruit is scarlet.

SPRAYS OF EUONYMUS
Left, E. alatus, with curiously winged stems and purplish fruit. Right, E. radicans, a small, useful, evergreen climber.

europaeus is a European deciduous shrub or tree to 25 ft. It is very showy in the fall with smooth pinkish-red fruits. There are forms with fruit of varying color, from white to crimson.

The following are all native in Asia:

E. alatus is a wide-spreading deciduous shrub to 8 ft. or more, distinguished by its winged branches. The leaves turn old rose to crimson in the fall, and when these have fallen the small but numerous brightly colored fruits are conspicuous. Var. *compactus* is a dense rounded form, suitable for a hedge.

latifolius is a vigorous deciduous shrub or tree with large leaves, and large pendulous pink fruits with winged lobes.

bungeanus, with its slender branches, has a rather loose and graceful appearance. It produces an abundance of yellowish fruits which remain on the branches long after the leaves have fallen. Var. *semipersistens* holds its leaves longer.

patens is a handsome, nearly evergreen species, with fairly conspicuous clusters of greenish-white flowers after midsummer, and showy pinkish fruits with orange covered seeds late in the fall. It is hardy to Mass. in sheltered places.

japonicus is a tender evergreen (not hardy N. of Philadelphia), growing to 15 ft., with dark green glossy leaves. It is a good screen or hedge plant for seaside gardens. There are numerous forms with white and yellow variegated leaves.

radicans is a trailing evergreen that can climb to 20 ft. or more on a rough surface by means of stem rootlets. It is very variable and useful in all its forms. Var. *vegetus* has larger leaves of dull green, makes a good low-spreading bush, tight hedge, or high climber on a wall, and is very hardy and handsome in fruit. Var. *carrierei* is somewhat similar but with lustrous leaves and not such a good climber. Var. *acutus* is a glossy pointed-leaved form, useful as a ground cover or to clothe a low wall. Var. *coloratus* is similar but the leaves turn reddish-purple in fall. Var. *minimus* (sometimes called *E. kewensis*) has tiny dark green leaves, marked white along the veins. It is well placed in the rock garden.

EUPATORIUM (eu-pah-toh'-ri-um). A large genus of the Composite Family comprising a number of plants which are ornamental in the border or wild garden and a few in the greenhouse.

The hardy sorts are of very easy culture, thriving in ordinary good light garden soil, and while they may be grown from seed, they are usually increased from root division in spring.

Two root and crown diseases, crown rot and Rhizoctonia rot (both of which see), may be responsible for the sudden wiping out of stands of this plant. At the first indication of wilting remove all diseased plants and drench the areas where they grow and surrounding plants with 1 to 1000 corrosive sublimate solution.

A Botrytis (which see) blight may kill tops back to a lesion a few inches from the ground but prompt removal of infected portions often allows side shoots that grow from below the lesion to continue blooming.

Principal Species

E. coelestinum (Mist-flower) to 3 ft., a native plant having azure blue to violet flowers in delicate fluffy heads, growing in sun or shade, and making a pleasing color combination when planted in a sunny border with bright-hued Mexican zinnias. Closely resembling ageratum, although taller, it blooms from the end of August until late in the fall.

purpureum (Joe-Pye-weed), a tall rank-growing species with old rose or rose-purple flowers in large open clusters, useful for naturalizing in the wild garden in low marshy ground. The common name was given because it was believed that the plant was used medicinally in early days in Mass. by an Indian doctor called Joe Pye. Other similar species known as Joe-Pye-weed are the smaller *E. maculatum* to 6 ft. and *E. verticillatum* to 8 ft. with purple flowers in rounded clusters.

urticaefolium (White Snakeroot), to 4 ft. with massed heads of white flowers. It was formerly used medicinally, and is an attractive plant in the wild garden.

perfoliatum (Boneset or Thoroughwort) 2 to 3 ft., has grayish-white flowers in flat-topped clusters. It was formerly used medicinally and is often seen in old gardens.

ianthinum, with violet clustered flowers, is a tender Mexican species easily grown in the greenhouse N. It is readily propagated from cuttings.

EUPHORBIA (eu-faur'-bi-ah). Spurge. A very large and diverse genus, widely distributed in tropical and temperate regions. Some are desert plants and assume a cactus-like form; some are leafy tropical shrubs; and others are hardy herbaceous perennials and annuals. They have abundant milky juice, which in many species has poisonous properties. The fleshy kinds are grown under conditions similar to those required by cacti, and add interest to a collection of succulents. They thrive in a porous and not very rich soil. Propagated by cuttings, which are best allowed to dry somewhat before being placed in a mixture of sand and charcoal.

E. pulcherrima, the Poinsettia (which see) is the best known of the shrubby kinds, principally as a greenhouse pot plant for the Christmas holiday season. Old plants may be cut back after a rest period and grown on again, but usually young plants are grown annually from cuttings. These are rooted at intervals from April on, to secure different sized plants. They may be grown outdoors during summer in the N. (in Fla. they are hardy), but require uniform conditions of warmth and moisture after being transferred to the greenhouse.

The herbaceous perennials are propagated by seed or division. There are one or two annual kinds easily grown from seed and useful for the flower garden.

Principal Fleshy Species

E. lactea is a fast grower of candelabrum form, with 3- to 4-angled branches marked with a white band down the middle. It is much used for hedges in warm regions.

grandicornis is one of the most striking in appearance, with broadly winged angled stems and large spines.

canariensis grows to 20 ft. and has thick 4- to 6-angled stems and black spines.

triangularis is a tree-like species with 6-angled stems which later become rounded.

tirucalli (Milk-bush) grows to a small tree with a dense head of slender round branches, whose sap is poisonous.

splendens (Crown-of-Thorns) has flexible stems to 4 ft. long, well armed with stout spines. It may be trained to a form and is attractive with its bright red bracts produced most of the year.

FOUR WIDELY VARIED TYPES IN THE CURIOUS GENUS EUPHORBIA
From left to right (1) the middle-western native with white-edged leaves called Snow-on-the-Mountain, frequently cultivated in gardens; (2) a cactus-like Euphorbia from the East Indies; (3) the florists' Poinsettia, the "flower" of which consists of showy red bracts; (4) the Crown-of-thorns, a spiny red-flowered vine from Madagascar, often used as a house-plant and mistakenly called a cactus.

meloformis (Melon Spurge) is a curious deeply angled melon-shaped plant, often with small offsets attached.

SHRUBBY SPECIES

E. pulcherrima (Poinsettia) is a shrub to 10 ft. or more outdoors in warm regions. It is grown in quantity under glass for its large rich red bracts at Christmas time. In var. *plenissima* some of the flowers have been transformed into red bracts, giving the appearance of doubling. Var. *alba* and *rosea* are forms with white and pink bracts respectively.

fulgens (Scarlet Plume) is a small shrub with slender drooping branches bedecked with small orange-scarlet bracts, very decorative and lasting as cut sprays. It is best grown from cuttings annually and kept along under warm conditions.

HERBACEOUS SPECIES

E. myrsinites is a fleshy prostrate grower with gray-green leaves and attractive yellow flowering heads in early spring. It shows to good advantage in stony places.

epithymoides forms a rounded clump a foot or more high. It is very attractive in the spring flower garden with its yellow floral leaves.

corollata (Flowering Spurge), a native to 3 ft., makes an attractive showing in the flower border with its white bracts, and is useful for cutting.

cyparissias has long been cultivated and is now naturalized in E. U. S. It is a good ground cover on dry banks, its narrow dark green leaves giving it a moss-like appearance.

marginata (Snow-on-the-Mountain) is an old annual flower-garden favorite, with white bracts and the upper leaves margined white.

heterophylla (Mexican Fire-plant) is a bushy annual growing to 3 ft. with leaves of varying shapes, the upper marked red.

EUPHORBIACEAE (eu-faur-bi-ay'-see-ee). Botanical name of the Spurge Family, an important group of herbs, shrubs and trees of varied habit, including many ornamental forms and many plants of economic importance, that yield edible nuts and fruits, rubber and valuable medicinal products. Some are cactus-like, and most are characterized by a milky, acrid juice. The flowers vary widely in form: in Poinsettia the showy parts are actually colored bracts. Among the cultivated genera are Euphorbia, Pedilanthus, Phyllanthus, Breynia, Sapium, Aleurites, Codiaeum, Ricinus, Manihot, Acalypha, Hevea.

EUPHORBIA SOCIETY, THE INTERNATIONAL. This society was organized in 1934 by a small group in California for the purpose of directing the study and collection of these plants, and to act as a medium of contact between growers in various countries. It publishes an illustrated quarterly magazine. The membership includes both amateurs and professionals. The dues are $2 in the U. S. or $2.25 elsewhere. The Secretary is Mrs. J. M. Warner, 3744 Seneca Ave., Los Angeles, Calif.

EUPTELEA (eup-tee'-lee-ah). Deciduous shrubs or small trees of Asia, hardy in favored spots as far north as Boston. They thrive in a loamy soil that does not get too dry. The flowers, which appear before the leaves, are without sepals and petals, but are conspicuous because of their bright red anthers. *E. polyandra* is a small bushy tree; its young growth is reddish in spring and in fall the bright green leaves of summer turn red and yellow. *E. francheti* is quite similar, but a larger grower.

EURYA (eu-ry'-ah). A Japanese evergreen shrub, allied to the Camellia and thriving under similar conditions. *E. japonica,* the one usually grown, is a tall shrub or small tree. The handsome glossy leaves are either roundish or long, with toothed edges. The var. *variegata* is a handsome decorative plant for the cool greenhouse, thriving in sandy loam, with peat or leafmold. The flowers are small and inconspicuous.

EURYALE (eu-ry'-ah-lee). A genus of waterlily represented in cultivation by the single species, *E. ferox,* which is somewhat like *Victoria regia* in type of leaf and manner of growth, but with much smaller flowers. Its leaves are from 1 to 4 ft. across, round, deep green above, spiny and rich purple beneath (like those of Victoria). The flowers are small (about 2 in. across), deep purple in color. In India, its home, the plant is cultivated for the edible seeds. A self-sowing annual, it is hardy even N. of Washington, D. C.

See also AQUATIC PLANTS.

EUSTOMA (eu'-stom-ah) *russellianum.* A showy wild herb of S. W. U. S. with pale purple flowers, sometimes grown in gardens and commonly called Prairie-Gentian, which see.

EUSTREPHUS (eu'-stree-fus). Australian twining plants belonging to the Lily Family. They are easy to grow in pots or a greenhouse border, or outdoors in a warm climate. The light blue flowers are clustered in the axils of the leaves, and are followed by orange-colored berries. This plant provides good material for decorative work.

EUTERPE (eu-tur'-pee). A genus of slender Feather Palms, popularly known as Assai Palms, having erect trunks, often in clumps, and showing the ringed scars of fallen leaves. The leaves themselves are spineless and feathery. Natives of warm parts of S. America and the West Indies, these palms are not reliably hardy even in Fla., but they are much grown in conservatories, where they require moist air and a rich soil, supplemented with overhead sprinkling. *E. oleracea* is the wild Cabbage Palm of which the terminal shoot or bud is cut out and eaten; this causes the death of the plant. *E. edulis,* grown occasionally in Fla., has clumps of slender trunks to 60 ft., wide-spreading leaves and large clusters of purple-black fruit.

EVENING GARDEN. This designates a garden planned and planted with a view to emphasizing those aspects which do not depend entirely upon vision for their appeal to our appreciation. It may be as large or as small as circumstances dictate; and evening effects may of course occur in the midst of any general composition if there is no room or desire for a separate feature devoted to them.

There are two ways of creating an evening garden. The older, natural way relies wholly upon plant material and the manner of handling it in the design. The other resorts to special and spectacular effects through artificial lighting, and gives less attention to the plant material—although this should be selected with care to complement the light. Each type is good when well done. But the introduction of light may so easily be all wrong, and consequently very bad instead of even tolerably good, that its successful application demands extremely careful study and a high degree of artistry.

THE NATURAL UNLIT GARDEN. Where reliance is wholly upon the plant material and the design or general scheme of the garden with reference to its free enjoyment in twilight or darkness, the gardener must keep three things in mind. (1) Everywhere there must be safe and agreeable footing so that walking about in darkness shall offer no difficulties; this means level, smooth pathways of material that will remain dry under heavy dew. (2) Overhead must be open sky in order to give free view of the stars and moon when she sails above, as well as to admit all of the light diffused from even the night sky. (3) Flowers must be distinguished for their fragrance more than for any other attribute, and preferably be of a pale color, or white, in order to be perceptible.

In the details of composition, special consideration of the skyline—the silhouette or profile of the trees and shrubs surrounding the Evening Garden, as they rise against the sky—is important. Irregularity is here preferable to an even height; if it is possible, an opening so placed as to catch the first glimpse of the rising moon between masses of dense growth will provide a charming feature. Seats under a shelter opposite this vista and a little outside the open area are a requisite, since it is not always agreeable to linger in the open even on warm nights, owing to dampness.

THE ILLUMINATED GARDEN. The evening garden that is planned for artificial lighting does not need to be fully open to the sky; nor are perfectly smooth pavements so important, since there will be no necessity to walk about in darkness. Scented flowers are equally desirable, however, there being an especial quality in fragrance at night which gives character to the entire concept.

As to the lighting itself, two things are definitely to be avoided. One is the use of ordinary flood lighting, the other is lighting with colored lamps or screens. Flood lighting not only gives the effect of an arena or other public space, but it is bleak in quality and subtracts all nuances of shade and shadow from the scene, reducing it to a hard, flattened, one-dimensional prospect. Colored lights blur and deaden all flower colors—even white—as well as the greens which are so essential as a support for the flowers; hence they result in effects as distressing to the eye as they are contrary to every principle of color composition. Modern lighting engineering is capable of introducing marvellous night effects into the garden, but these are always based on recognition of this fact: that daylight cannot be artificially created out of doors under the darkened dome of the night sky; hence daylight effects are not possible and should not be attempted by means of electricity.

The artist takes advantage of this and turns what appears to be the liability of darkness into the asset of wholly new and strangely beautiful scenes which emphasize the night, and the reversed conditions which absence of light overhead involves. Thus the Evening Garden becomes totally different from the daytime picture, even when it is in the identical spot and when the same flowers are blooming in it.

See also ELECTRICITY IN THE GARDEN; FRAGRANT GARDEN.

EVENING-PRIMROSE. Common name for the genus Oenothera (which see) comprising a number of showy plants used in the border and rock garden. The plant most commonly known as Evening-primrose is *O. biennis* with yellow flowers, often found as an escape in the U. S.

The Evening-primrose Family is Onagraceae, which see.

EVENING-STAR. Common name for *Cooperia drummondi,* a night-blooming bulbous plant with grass-like foliage and large flowers—a species of Rain- or Prairie-lily, which see.

EVERGREEN GARDEN. Depending upon latitude, this reference varies. In the north it implies a garden devoted to those hardiest species, mostly arboreal or tree-like, which have needle or scale-like leaves, and bear cones. In southern regions where there are many types of trees, shrubs and climbing plants which do not shed their leaves and remain dormant during a part of the year, the term embraces widely different species and varieties. These two groups are distinguished as "conifers" and "broad-leaved evergreens," which is not as exact as a botanist would wish but serves the layman for all practical purposes.

Old time gardeners realized the opportunities which the use of evergreens alone afforded, and some of the finest early work in this country was executed exclusively in such material—patterned no doubt on the Old-World gardens wherein boxwood and yew often furnished all the planting. Even in the restricted and severely cold sections where only a few kinds are to be relied upon to endure the winter rigors, the richness which these bring into the composition, merely through repetition, is unique. And for the very busy gardener the serene and quiet beauty of an evergreen garden is the ultimate triumph.

See also EVERGREENS; PINETUM.

EVERGREEN-GRAPE. Common name for *Cissus discolor,* an old-fashioned greenhouse vine from Java with handsome foliage.

EVERGREENS. A term applied to plants which hold their foliage from season to season, often for a long period of time, some pines retaining their needles for 15 years. Eventually the leaves are shed and replaced by new ones, but so gradually that the loss is not noticed. Climatic conditions have a great deal to do with whether a plant is evergreen or not; it may retain its foliage in a mild climate, but shed its leaves in winter when planted in the N. even though it is perfectly hardy. Common privet (*Ligustrum vulgare*) is entirely evergreen in the S. but only partially so N. of Philadelphia.

For horticultural purposes evergreens may be conveniently divided into two classes; the conifers, or narrow-leaved evergreens, plants with needle-like, scale-like or flat leaves; and the broad-leaved evergreens. The word conifer (which see) means strictly trees bearing woody cones containing naked seeds; it is often considered synonymous with evergreen, but botanically it includes a few trees, such as the larches, which are distinctly deciduous.

From the horticultural standpoint, that is, for garden use, the coniferous and other narrow-leaved evergreens are outstandingly valuable. They vary in type from the dwarf trailing juniper used for ground-cover or in the rock garden, to the towering pines, firs, spruces and hemlocks planted as windbreaks, groves, and backgrounds. They also constitute some of our most valuable forest trees. Their flowers are inconspicuous, but their fruits whether cones or small berry-like drupes are most attractive and interesting. Think, for instance, of the erect, often blue or purple cones of the firs, the tiny, multitudinous cones of the hemlock, the graceful drooping tassels of the white pine, the brilliant blue berries of the juniper, and the showy red drupes of the yews.

Broad-leaved evergreens also vary greatly in size and form from the pink-flowered trailing arbutus (*Epigaea repens*) and the glossy running myrtle (*Vinca minor*) used for ground covers, to the tree-like forms of *Ilex opaca* (American Holly)

Plate 17.   THE VARIED CHARM OF EVERGREENS

Upper left: The symmetrical, pyramidal form of evergreens makes an admirable foil for deciduous trees and flowering shrubs.   Upper right: The feathery-foliaged deodar (Cedrus deodara) is delightfully decorative where it can be grown.   'Center right: The Colorado blue spruce, interesting and useful as an accent.   Bottom: This cascade of living green is one plant of the dwarf form of the hemlock (Tsuga canadensis).

and the majestic *Quercus virginiana* (Evergreen Oak) and *Magnolia grandiflora* (Bull Bay) of the S. which attain to a height of nearly 100 ft. Among them are found some of our showiest flowering shrubs and trees, the rhododendrons and kalmias in the N. and, in the S., the camellias and many genera that bear brilliant fruit which adds to the garden value and beauty in the winter; holly, mahonia and euonymus are three popular kinds. A few evergreen vines are also included, as English ivy (*Hedera helix*) and *Euonymus radicans.*

Conifers (which see) have innumerable uses in landscape work and in the garden, especially the slow-growing kinds that are also long-lived, giving stability to the landscape design or garden picture. There is great variation in their color, from the sombre green of some of the spruces to the frosty silver of many of the firs and the bronze and purple hues of the junipers, while horticultural varieties provide "gold" and white effects, especially valuable as accent points and for contrast. The larger species are best used for windbreaks, for outlining an estate, or for specimens in large lawns or other expanses where they increase in stateliness and beauty through the years and form an appropriate background for the more fleeting flowers and the brightly colored autumn foliage of deciduous trees and shrubs; or for the contrasting texture and lavish bloom of the broad-leaved evergreens.

SOME CONIFEROUS EVERGREENS. The coniferous trees used in the N. E. States belong mainly to the genera listed below (for details see each genus), many species of each now being available for horticultural work. (See illustration, Plate 21.)

Abies (Fir) used for shelter belts and specimens and preferably planted in soil rich in humus and without too much clay. Chamaecyparis (False-cypress or White-cedar) of which some species are especially adapted for growing in low damp situations. Juniperus (Red-cedar) particularly *J. virginiana,* for dry hillsides, backgrounds, allees and accents. Picea (Spruce) for windbreaks, specimens and hedges, thriving in cool, sandy loam. Pseudotsuga (Douglas-fir) for specimens and park planting, demanding a sheltered position and moist cool soil, rich in humus. Thuja (Arbor-vitae) for windbreaks, backgrounds, hedges and accents, tolerant of clipping and growing well in rich, loamy soil, or in damp situations. Tsuga (Hemlock) for backgrounds, groves, hedges and lawn specimens, delighting in humus and tolerant of northern exposures and shade conditions.

All the above have numerous species and varieties which supply an infinite variety of choice for shrubbery borders or foundation plantings. Many of the varieties are procumbent, drooping or very dwarf, especially in the younger stages. Thuja and Chamaecyparis show in the seedling stage numerous interesting variations, so widely differing from mature specimens that for a long time they were thought to belong to a distinct genus and were given the name Retinispora (which see).

Farther S. and in the Western States a number of other conifers and additional species of those already named not hardy in the N.E. States can be grown. But as coniferous evergreens grow most abundantly in the temperate regions, the gardens of the far S. and the tropics exhibit a preponderance of broad-leaved evergreens.

SOME BROAD-LEAVED EVERGREENS. The only broad-leaved evergreens that reach tree-like dimensions in the N.E. States are *Ilex opaca* (American Holly) which in its southern range reaches a height of 50 ft., and *Rhododendron maximum,* attaining 35 ft. But there are many evergreen shrubs, most of them having flowers or fruit as well as foliage of great beauty. The following are reliably hardy under conditions such as are found in the N.E. States: Glossy Abelia (*A. grandiflora*), to 6 ft., a graceful shrub for the border; Barberry (species of Berberis); Common Box (*Buxus sempervirens*) for hedges and borders, accent plants and specimens; species of Cotoneaster (which see), for the shrubbery border and foundation planting; *Daphne cneorum,* growing to 1 ft., for the rock garden; *Euonymus radicans* var. *vegetus* and var. *carrieri* for underplanting in shady spots or on the N. side of buildings; American Holly (*Ilex opaca*), for hedges, specimens and the shrubbery border; Japanese Holly (*I. crenata* var. *microphylla*), for backgrounds, specimens and foundation planting; Inkberry (*I. glabra*), for the wild garden and N. shaded exposures; Mountain-laurel (*Kalmia latifolia*); for planting in masses in combination with rhododendrons or alone; Labrador-tea

(*Ledum groenlandicum*), for the edge of the bog garden in acid peaty soil; Sand-myrtle (*Leiophyllum buxifolium*), in the rock garden or border in acid, sandy soil; Drooping Leucothöe (*L. catesbaei*), in peaty soil in a protected situation in background of rock garden; species of Privet (Ligustrum), only semi-evergreen but useful for hedges and windbreaks; Holly Mahonia (*Mahonia aquifolium*), for mass planting in situations protected from burning sun and wind, and most satisfactory where there is a heavy snowfall; *Pieris floribunda,* growing to 6 ft., requiring part shade and acid soil; *P. japonica,* to 10 ft.; many species of Rhododendron, for mass planting under shade of conifers, or at the N. of buildings, and requiring acid soil rich in humus; *Yucca filamentosa* and *Y. glauca* for accents and bold massing.

The following can be used for ground covers: Bearberry (*Arctostaphylos uva-ursi*), in acid, sandy soil, in the open or under trees; Pipsissewa (*Chimaphila maculata*), in the wild garden under conifers; Creeping Snowberry (*Chiogenes hispidula*), for the wild garden in acid soil; Trailing Arbutus (*Epigaea repens*), in acid soil in the shade; Wintergreen (*Gaultheria procumbens*), in acid soil under trees or in the open; Evergreen Candy-tuft (*Iberis sempervirens*), in the open; Partridge-berry (*Mitchella repens*), in the shade or in partially exposed portion of rock garden; Japanese-spurge (*Pachysandra terminalis*), under trees; *Pachistima*

canbyi, for rock or wild gardens in ordinary soil; Myrtle (*Vinca minor*), under trees.

Evergreen or semi-evergreen vines include: Five-leaf Akebia (*A. quinata*) and Three-leaf Akebia (*A. trifoliata*); Climbing Euonymus (*E. radicans*); English Ivy (*Hedera helix*); species of Honeysuckle (Lonicera), which are semi-evergreen; and Japanese Memorial Rose (*Rosa wichuriana*), for banks in the open.

PLANTING AND CARING FOR CONIFERS

The best time to transplant conifers is the spring when buds are swelling, or in August and September after the new growth has ripened. Late fall planting is often disastrous, as the plants have not time to become established before freezing weather sets in.

Nursery-grown specimens are much more easily transplanted than those collected from the wild, for in the nursery the root system has been kept compact and bushy by repeated transplantings. Also the plants are delivered with a ball of earth wrapped in burlap which prevents the roots from drying out. Dig a hole considerably larger than the burlapped ball and, without removing the covering, set the plant in the hole at just about its previous level. Then unfasten, open out and, if desired, cut away the burlap, although it will rot in time anyway. Some of the encasing earth can be removed with a fork or weeding tool (especially if the exterior has been plastered with clay). If this soil seems poorer than that available for filling the hole, remove more of it, straighten out the roots without exposing them to the sun, then quickly fill the hole with good top-soil, watering at the same time so as to settle the soil in and around the fibrous roots. Be sure the earth is well settled, so as to leave no air pockets. Then spread an inch or so of loose, dry earth or a mulch of peat moss on the surface to prevent evaporation of moisture from the roots. If the weather

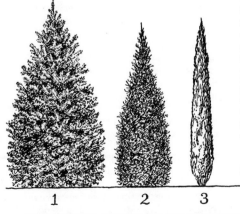

| 1 | 2 | 3 | 4 | 5 | 6 |

THE VARIED FORMS OF EVERGREENS MAKE THEM WIDELY ADAPTABLE

For backgrounds and specimens, the tall-growing (1) and the medium-sized pyramidal forms (2) are admirable, while the narrow-pyramidal or columnar form (3) is essentially an accent in the landscape. For rock gardens or for border plantings, or among a group of other shrubbery specimens, the globular form (4) is desirable. The half-erect type (5) fits well into foundation planting, while creeping varieties (6) make interesting evergreen ground covers.

is warm, dry or windy, spray the foliage and trunk thoroughly and frequently to aid in the conservation of moisture. See that there is a slight depression rather than a mound about the plant; this will hold the water instead of shedding it. Water daily if necessary until the plant is well established. The drying out of newly planted evergreens is a common cause of loss, for they have a small root system compared with their large leaf area which is constantly transpiring moisture—often more rapidly than it can be absorbed by the roots in their new location. If conifers are deeply mulched the ground will not freeze so far down and the plants will be able to secure moisture from the soil even in winter, which, since they have no true dormant season, is most helpful. An extra heavy mulch should be partially removed in early spring so that the surface soil will thaw more quickly and be in shape to absorb the early spring rains. It should be stirred and loosened before a new mulch is applied.

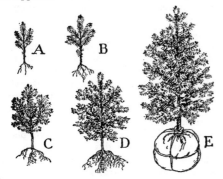

STAGES OF GROWTH IN A CONIFER
(A) 1-year old seedling. (B) 2 years' growth.
(C) 4 or 5 years old and once transplanted.
(D) 5 to 7 years and again transplanted to induce a compact, fibrous root system. (E) 7 to 10 years, with a good "ball" for planting, and properly "balled and burlapped" for delivery to the gardener.

Well-rotted manure is probably the best fertilizer for evergreens. Sometimes a balanced plant food or one rich in nitrogen is given to stimulate growth. This should be dug into the soil, and the area well watered; or it may be applied in solution; or it may be applied in crow-bar holes driven at 2 ft. intervals down to the feeding roots.

Broad-leaved evergreens are handled essentially in the manner described but tender species can be dug and heeled in over

winter where they will not be injured by hard freezing and set out again in the open in the spring. Specimens planted in spring or early fall are the most likely to make rapid growth; as with conifers, properly balled nursery-grown plants are more successfully moved than collected stock from fields and woods.

Many of the broad-leaved evergreens belong to the Heath Family, the rhododendrons and kalmias being outstanding examples. These plants thrive best in an acid soil and for the most part require partial shade. Therefore the ground should be prepared with great care and a suitable situation selected. They should be planted in soil free from lime, rich in humus, and provided with good drainage; if possible, a position under the light shade of high conifers should be given. After planting, water them thoroughly and spray the foliage, and mulch heavily with leaves, preferably oak leaves because they last longer and contribute more to the acid condition. An occasional top-dressing of well-rotted manure can be given, but if the soil is well supplied with humus and if a plentiful leaf mulch is maintained, any special feeding is best done with fertilizers of an acid-forming nature. After the plants have become established the soil surrounding the plants should be disturbed as little as possible, for the roots are very near the surface and it has recently become known that there is a definite mycorrhizal association (which see) between the feeding roots of ericaceous plants and certain fungi.

Among the hollies the American species (*Ilex opaca*) is especially difficult to move. Early fall is the most propitious time to transplant it and even then great care should be taken in preparing the roots and moving them to prevent their exposure to wind or sun. Many growers advise stripping off a considerable portion of the leaves to lessen the transpiration area, but if the plants are cut back rather severely, and the foliage frequently sprayed with water for several weeks after planting, this stripping is not usually necessary.

As noted, most shrubs and small groundcovers of the Heath Family require an acid soil, but the cotoneasters, euonymus, the privets, *Pachysandra terminalis* and *Vinca minor* grow readily in any good garden soil.

Evergreens are grown from seed, cuttings and layers; also they are frequently grafted, especially the improved varieties of various coniferous sorts. While propagation of a number of kinds is not especially difficult and decidedly interesting, the different genera and species require definite and particular methods, and special facilities such as propagation boxes and bottom heat are often necessary. The work is therefore not an ordinary gardening activity although full of possibilities and rewards for those who can and care to give it study and attention.

ENEMIES

PHYSIOLOGICAL TROUBLES. Some of the most conspicuous diseases of conifers are due not to fungi, bacteria or other living organisms, but to physiological conditions.

Trees which retain their foliage throughout the year need a constant supply of moisture. Winter drying, resulting in a reddening or browning of the needles, is caused by the rapid loss of water from the leaves when the water in the soil is frozen and can not be taken up by the roots. Root freezing or other injury has the same result and strong winds or intense sunlight may increase evaporation to such an extent that parts of the plant wilt and die. When limbs or trunk previously shaded are suddenly exposed to full sunlight, there may be actual scorching of the bark due to rapid drying out of the tissues. Needles when sun-scorched turn a bright wine red.

Mulching to prevent root freezing and excessive evaporation of water from the

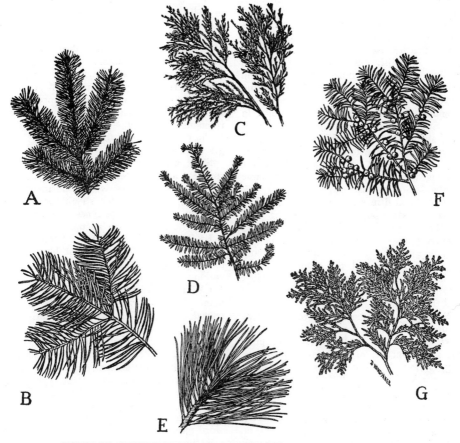

FOLIAGE DIFFERENCES IN SEVEN FAMILIAR EVERGREENS

A. The spruce has bristly needles all around the twig. B. In fir, they are longer, softer and not so dense. C. Juniper has tiny, wiry, sharp-pointed needles. D. Hemlock is characterized by flattened rows of short, thin leaves. E. Pine always bears its long slender needles in bundles, the number differing with the species. F. In the Yew the leaves are broad, glossy and usually give an effect of flatness. G. Arborvitae bears its minute, scale-like leaves compacted in graceful, fan-like sprays.

soil; watering evergreens generously late in the fall; and, sometimes, shading by means of a wind-break, bamboo mats, cut evergreen boughs, etc., against early spring sun and wind, will all aid in protecting valuable evergreens from such troubles.

FUNGOUS DISEASES. Needle cast (as defoliation of conifers is called) is caused by several fungi. The needles show yellowish or brown bands and later turn entirely yellow or brown and drop off; sometimes they exhibit the round or oblong black fruiting bodies of the fungus. Young trees (which are more subject to these diseases than old ones) should be sprayed with bordeaux mixture before rainy periods when the spores are most likely to be spread and so start new infections.

Heartwood and root decay, though most serious in forests, may damage specimen trees. The most destructive of the heartwood type is the pecky wood decay which gives the heartwood around the decayed area a purplish tinge, fills the affected reddish wood with holes or pockets and produces a triangular shelf-like fruiting body (see Bracket Fungi) at old branch wounds. Another wood decay common in W. States appears as large, rusty-brown, hoof-shaped fruiting bodies emerging from branch stubs. The interior of this body is a bright rusty red and Indians used it for making warpaint, hence the popular name "Indian-paint fungus."

Heartwood diseases may be prevented to a great extent by careful pruning and proper care of all wounds, especially broken branch stubs. (See TREE SURGERY.) All broken limbs should be sawed off evenly against the tree and the wound, if over 2 in. across, covered with a dressing. Cavities should be properly cleaned out and treated.

Basal decay is usually more important among ornamental conifers than are the wood rots. One kind occurring in pine, fir, larch, spruce, hemlock and arborvitae may spread from the roots upward into the trunk for several feet. The usual result is the uprooting of the tree in a heavy wind. The soft, red-brown, umbrella-shaped fruiting bodies grow from exposed or lightly buried roots. The mushroom root-rot is common on many kinds of coniferous trees. See ARMILLARIA. The control of root diseases is somewhat difficult. Remove diseased parts of roots and the fungus fruiting bodies; dig an "isolation ditch" around diseased trees to prevent the spread of infection.

Various blister rust fungi occur on needles and bark of conifers but they usually require some deciduous plant (alternate host) on which to complete their development. Control consists in eradication of the alternate host. See RUSTS; also directions under PINE; SPRUCE; FIR; LARCH; HEMLOCK.

INSECT PESTS. All types of evergreens are subject to attacks by spider mites (see MITES; RED SPIDER) which give the plants a brownish or grayish pale appearance. Examined closely, the needles are seen to be mottled brown or gray and covered with fine webs. Small reddish eggs and the tiny mites may be seen with a reading glass. Occurring abundantly with the approach of warm weather, mites may cause serious injury. Spray early in the season, before new growth starts, with a miscible oil or an oil emulsion diluted according to manufacturer's directions for evergreens (see SPRAYING, DORMANT). After growth starts, syringe forcibly with the hose, dust with sulphur on warm days, or spray with lime-sulphur (summer strength) or with a rotenone compound. Spraying with glue (1 lb. powdered glue to 10 gal. water) has given good results.

Scale insects (which see) attack pines, spruces and junipers especially. Spray before growth starts with a dormant oil. Lime-sulphur (1 to 9) should be substituted in spraying those types of Juniper in which the leaves form a cup.

EVERGREEN SHIELD FERN (*Dryopteris marginalis*). A beautiful, blue-green, native American wood fern, of easy cultivation; discussed under DRYOPTERIS.

EVERLASTING-PEA. One common name for *Lathyrus latifolius,* the broadleaved, tall growing perennial relative of the familiar sweet pea. Sometimes applied to other species of Lathyrus.

EVERLASTINGS. Flowers of papery quality which are extensively used for permanent winter bouquets because when they are dried they retain their form and color. Many of them also are attractive subjects for garden or greenhouse. The French word *immortelles,* which is used for one or sometimes all of them, corresponds to our word "everlastings."

Most everlastings of the hardy garden belong to the Composite Family. What appear to be the ray florets of the flower-heads are actually greatly enlarged papery bracts in delicate colors, the true florets being hidden at their base. These everlastings include *Catananche caerulea* (Cupids Dart); *Ammobium alatum* (Winged Everlasting); *Helichrysum bracteatum* (the Strawflower, in many varieties, which is the most frequently grown everlasting in America); *Xeranthemum annuum* (Immortelle) with its varieties in lilac and purple and rose; species of Podolepis (Australian annuals with pink, yellow, purple or lavender flower-heads), and of Helipterum (all small plants, one of them, called the Swan River Everlasting, formerly known as Rhodanthe, and another as Acroclinium). All are easily grown in a sunny spot in ordinary soil and, whether annual or perennial, they all give bloom the first year from seed sown in spring outdoors or earlier indoors.

Statice or Sea-lavender (species of Limonium, especially *L. latifolium, L. sinuatum,* and *L. suworowi*); Globe-amaranth (*Gomphrena globosa*) and Babys Breath (*Gypsophila paniculata*) comprise the other everlastings most frequently grown in American gardens. These, with their variously arranged clusters of flowers, enhance the form of the dried bouquet. They also are of fairly easy culture, either outdoors or in. Some of the sea-lavenders, besides making attractive groups in the rock garden, are admirable greenhouse subjects. *L. suworowi* retains its close parallel spikes of lavender blossoms indoors over many months. The short blue spikes of *L. sinuatum* make it a good edging plant, treated as an annual. Babys Breath is well known for its use in the border, rock garden and greenhouse, its small white flowers on stiff, slender, almost leafless branches, giving a misty effect in garden or bouquet. A thoroughly hardy perennial, it likes a dry, rather limy soil. The Globe Amaranth, with its papery clover-like heads of lilac, rose, orange, yellow or white, gives a long season of bloom in the annual border from seeds sown indoors and transplanted outside when warm weather is established.

DRYING AND USING. While the Composite everlasting should be picked when the flowers first open from the bud, to prevent their spreading wide and appearing brown, Gomphrena should be picked only when the flowers are well matured. Babys Breath and the Sea-lavenders may be picked whenever the flowers are of suitable form, and may be used at once in dry bouquets.

To prepare other everlastings, strip off their leaves and hang them upside down in small bunches held together with elastic bands. Do not attempt to arrange them in vases until the artificial indoor heat has drawn the last vestige of moisture from their stems. In order to vary for variety in the form of curving sprays, a few fresh stems can be hung singly over a rounded surface, such as may be made by tacking heavy paper to the edge of a shelf, rounding it out well and tacking the lower edge to the under side of the shelf. In arranging dried flowers in bouquets, a bunch of dried sphagnum moss or shredded paper, or a few inches of clean dry sand will help keep them in place.

Many grasses and seed-pods are also used in everlasting bouquets. For treatment of these, see ORNAMENTAL GRASSES.

EVODIA (ee-voh'-di-ah). Numerous deciduous and evergreen trees and shrubs, native of Asia and Australia, belonging to the Rue Family. Three or four species from China are the hardiest; but they are not extensively planted as yet. They are small trees distinguished by their handsome compound and aromatic leaves. The small whitish flowers are borne in panicles in summer and followed by showy black seeds. They grow well in ordinary garden soil, and the seeds germinate readily.

E. glauca has leaves of 7 to 15 leaflets, whitish beneath. *E. hupehensis* has smooth leaves of 5 to 9 leaflets. *E. velutina* has soft hairy leaves of 7 to 11 leaflets.

EVONYMUS (ee-von'-i-mus). One form of spelling Euonymus (which see) used in 1753 by Linnaeus who later wrote it Euonymus, which is the generally accepted name at the present time.

EXACUM (eks'-a-kum). Summer-blooming Old-World annual, biennial or perennial herbs of the Gentian Family, with white, lilac or purplish-blue, flat-petalled flowers in branching clusters at the top of leafy stems. They are usually grown from seed as pot-plants, though hardy in warm climates. Seed may be sown in light well-drained soil in March or for larger specimens the previous August. Shade from hot sunlight.

E. affine, with bluish flowers, and *E. macrantha,* whose purplish-blue flowers are ringed with yellow in the throat, are both biennials about 2 ft. high. *E. zeylanicum* is an annual with smaller, blue flowers with blunter petals.

EXHIBITING. (see illustrations, Plates 16 and 56.) Sooner or later the plant grower faces the question of exhibiting garden products. To one unfamiliar with the subject, the whole idea may seem difficult or complicated. But it is really not difficult at all, for as any structure must be built on a foundation, so exhibiting comes back to its separate exhibitors, who are the garden owners, the ones who grew the plant material.

WHY EXHIBIT? It is perfectly natural, if one has grown a beautiful rose or dahlia, a fine egg-plant or a good bunch of grapes, to enjoy showing it in competition with similar products grown by others. It is like a game of skill and has all the amusement and interest that comes from pitting oneself against others on more or less equal terms. There is a great thrill in taking a prize in a flower show or at a county fair and the blue, red, and yellow ribbons, for first, second, and third prize respectively, which are often the only awards at amateur shows, are as highly regarded by many exhibitors as more valuable prizes. The contest has all the joy of pure sport.

As interest in growing flowers, fruits and vegetables of many kinds has spread, the opportunities for exhibiting offered to the amateur have increased greatly. Garden clubs are scattered from one end of the country to the other, many of them grouped in State Federations; and all, practically, hold flower shows. States and counties have annual fairs; horticultural societies and special flower organizations hold exhibitions, and there are other displays of many kinds. An enterprising store will often stage some sort of contest, and large banks, insurance companies and business institutions of many kinds encourage their employees to stage flower shows. The opportunities are indeed many, and no one should be afraid to try his or her luck, for the rules are simple and the reward in pleasure or profit is great.

There are still other results. A garden-lover meets many people who have the same interests and benefits from the friendliness and exchange of ideas. One always learns something at an exhibition and each new contact helps to raise one's standard a little higher. Thus, in the end, the whole country will be more beautiful and interesting because many thousands of garden-minded people are growing their plants a little better each year and striving to improve their communities in many ways. There is an appeal to patriotism in

A SIMPLE, EFFECTIVE WAY TO EXHIBIT FLOWERS

An inexpensive, temporary background for single variety or color classes is made by inserting ¾ in. dowels, in pairs (held together with caps), in holes bored in the table. A lengthwise slot sawed in each dowel receives the edge of a sheet of heavy poster board of any desired color. The resulting concave display space depends on the distance between the dowels.

it—the wish to make America truly "the beautiful."

THE SEASONS' SHOWS. To come down to the practical side of exhibiting, shows are held most commonly in spring and autumn, some in summer, a few in winter. In each community, the times are chosen when there is the greatest chance for a large number of exhibits. The spring and early summer shows are almost entirely flower shows. Late summer and autumn shows will also have many classes for fruits and vegetables. Winter shows will consist largely of flower arrangements; these will be scheduled as, for example, "Arrangement for a Christmas Dinner Table"; or "Conservation Christmas Wreaths," in which only the greens permitted by the conservation associations are utilized; or "Winter Bouquets" made of such materials as bayberries, pods of honesty (Lunaria), dried grasses and the many wild seeds and berries to be found growing in fields and by the roadsides. Some people may have forced bulbs in shape for a winter show, at first Roman hyacinths, or Paper-white or Soleil d'Or narcissus, and later such things as Dutch hyacinths, tulips, freesias and daffodils. Rare plants or well-grown house-plants can be used. Anything that makes our homes more attractive in winter is to be desired. Groups in even the smallest places could have exhibitions planned by themselves which would encourage the growing of better plants.

In the spring or autumn shows are many classes. One who has never exhibited is sometimes timid, but he should remember that each exhibitor was in his class once. Most shows now include a few classes for novices, so that the beginner is pitted only against others as new to the work as he. When he sees how simple it is, he will not be afraid later to try his luck in the other classes. Why should he be afraid? His gladiolus or larkspurs or pumpkins or pears are probably as good as his neighbors'.

At first an exhibitor will probably take to a show the material he ordinarily grows. This may be above the average; or it may be just the commoner varieties or sorts grown without extra care. At the show, in a class for daffodils, perhaps, someone takes the prize who has some of the newer varieties. They were probably no harder to grow but were of more beautiful shapes

and colors. If, in an autumn show, there was a class for vegetables where points were given for arrangement, someone may have taken the prize who showed an artistic display of well-grown and well-scrubbed roots, tiny tomatoes in bunches like grapes, egg-plants and purple and green cabbage and beets and turnips and beans and corn, arranged to make a handsome color group. That sort of thing is contagious. Next year the prize-winner is likely to have some new competitors. Seed and bulb catalogs are available to all and anyone willing to dig and fertilize and cultivate and spray will have a chance at the prizes. Judges like to reward quality.

SELECTING EXHIBITION MATERIAL. If an exhibitor wishes big flowers of dahlias and chrysanthemums and asters and others of that type, he should, early in the season, cut off close to the stem all buds but the one terminal (end) one. The plant will send all its vigor into that one flower. If he wants his cosmos and hardy chrysanthemums and French marigolds to bear masses of flowers, pinching back the shoots early in their growth will make the plants spread and have many branches.

He need never be afraid that the ground will be too rich. Only the exceptional gardener need fear that. If the added plant food is only soap-suds from the kitchen sink, plants will use it; and they are grateful for bonemeal, wood ashes and, in fact, any bit of fertilizer they can get. And they will reward the owner with exhibition blooms if they are well fed.

With plenty of food, they will often withstand attacks of pests and disease successfully, but spraying will often prevent trouble and will keep the foliage in good condition, an important point with judges. A contact spray, such as the nicotine preparations for sucking insects, a poison, such as arsenate of lead for the chewing kinds, and bordeaux mixture for rust and other fungus diseases will work wonders. There are many good spray materials and any seedsman will give directions for their use. There is no magic spell in the production of good flowers. Like children, if they have comfortable homes, good food, loving care and protection against disease, they will flourish and repay you a thousand times.

GATHERING AND PREPARING EXHIBITS. So much for growing the plants. The next step is the gathering of the material so that the exhibitor will have it in its very best condition when judged. The judge must give his decision on the exhibit as it is' at the moment he judges it; not as it may have been in the early morning or as it may be in an hour or two. So it is important that the tulips should not lay their heads on the ground, that the dahlias should not wilt, that the gladiolus should make a good showing as to the number of flowers open, and that even the poppies should be induced to hold up their heads.

Flower stems should be cut on a slant with a sharp knife. The slanting cut keeps the stems from resting flat on the bottom of the container, which may prevent water from entering. If the weather is very hot and the flowers have drooped or threatened to open too soon, shading the plants lightly for a day or two before the show will often save them. It may also protect them from damage by storms. If frost is predicted, a light cloth thrown over the plants at night (or over a frame built around them) will probably protect them.

Some flowers should have their stems cut again *under water* as otherwise air enters the stems and prevents free passage of water through them. This is particularly the trouble with more or less woody stems, such as those of chrysanthemums, peonies or hollyhocks.

The flowers should be gathered the day before the show, preferably in the late afternoon. They should be set in water up to their necks and put in a cool, semi-dark place, away from drafts. Gathering even a day earlier is advisable for tulips. This gives them time to decide what they are going to do with their stems; some, which insist on assuming artistic but not horticultural curves, may be successfully used in arrangement classes, where their curves will be attractive. Sometimes the stems are tied together or they may be laid flat, side by side, and the flowers sprinkled, but in that case you cannot always be sure of their last minute "flop."

Peonies may also be gathered 48 hours before the show and wrapped lightly in soft paper. With gladiolus, too, the open flowers may be wrapped; this may prevent their fading before the later ones open. Peonies which bloom too early are sometimes cut and sent to a cold storage establishment. They should be gathered just when the color shows at the tip.

A red- or orange-cupped narcissus should be cut just before it opens, as the sun fades the color. A white one should be cut when it is fully open and after the sun has bleached out the yellow tones.

If the weather is hot, roses should be brought to the show in bud.

Dahlias should be cut after sunset, when in full bloom. Their stems should be burned (see below) and they should be set in cool water up to their necks, away from drafts, which wilt them badly.

Iris should be cut in bud but not too tight a bud or it will not open. Poppies should be cut in bud and the stems dipped in boiling water or burned.

To burn flower stems, wrap stems and blossoms in a cloth or paper, leaving 2 in. exposed. Hold the ends horizontally over a hot flame until they are red hot, then set them in deep water for an hour before using. This burning makes carbon of the stem end and this, being porous, admits the water. The stem-ends may also be held in boiling water for a moment or two, protecting the flowers from the heat during the treatment.

Some plants have a milky juice which hardens over the cut end of the stem so water cannot enter. An alkali such as salt or ashes may be used to melt this sap.

Leaves should be wet directly by holding the stems upside down and pouring water over the foliage. When in place, spraying with a very fine spray will help to keep them in good condition.

Experiments appear to have proved that chemicals such as aspirin do not prolong the life of flowers to any extent.

Be sure the flowers are clean. Rub dirt off with your fingers or with a fine water-color brush dipped in water. Stains made by bordeaux mixture may be removed with a weak solution of vinegar.

Fruits and vegetables should be cut or dug with great care. Any that bruise easily must be laid separately on trays or wrapped in paper. Green leafy ones like spinach or parsley should be set in water or washed. Carrots, turnips, etc., should be well-scrubbed. Onions should have the soiled outer skin removed. Perishable fruits like grapes and raspberries should be protected from shaking, which would dislodge or crush the fruit.

Transport your entries, especially flowers, very carefully. If going by auto to a show, you can stand them in a pail of wet sand with a wire mesh stretched over the top.

To carry dahlias, pad a long box well with paper and lay the flowers so that they will not bruise each other; then tie the stems in the center of the box so they will not shift.

Perishable fruits should be transported with great care, peaches, plums, apples, etc., being wrapped in paper to avoid bruising.

FLOWER SHOW CLASSES. Flower shows have two divisions, cultural and artistic. Such classes as those for gardens come under both heads, being planned for artistic beauty as well as for horticultural perfection. They are generally classed as "cultural exhibits."

Cultural classes, or straight classes as they are called, are judged for the excellence (or lack of it) in the growth. A gladiolus, for instance, would be judged for the size of the flowers according to its variety, the number open at once, the arrangement of the flowers, the general appearance, the leaves, stem and condition. Each kind of flower would be judged according to its quality as a specimen and as a type. Groups would be judged in the same manner, with points given also for special excellence in variety, rarity, etc.

In the artistic-arrangement classes the perfection of the flowers is not as impor-tant as in the straight classes, though still considered. The emphasis is on the artistic beauty of the whole. There must be a good and attractive combination of color in flowers and container and a proper relation of the parts to one another; that is, the flowers must not be too large for the container nor must they look lost in it. They should not look so tall as to be top-heavy nor so short as to look insignificant; they should never be so badly balanced as to look as if they were falling over.

Flowers of coarse texture like zinnias look well in peasant pottery. Fine-textured flowers like roses look well in fine Venetian glass. Flowers must be fresh and in good condition when shown.

If the arrangement is for a special purpose, as "for a luncheon table," the imaginary people sitting at the table should be able to see each other through or above it. An arrangement to be set on a mantel would be seen from an entirely different point from one set on a low table, and should be planned according to the place where it would be used.

ARRANGEMENT HINTS. There are some generally accepted rules, but they are not hard and fast ones and may be broken for good reason. A good arrangement is about one and one half times the height of the vase or other container; that is, if the container is 1 ft. high, the whole arrange-

EXHIBITING OFFERS OPPORTUNITIES TO ALL
The successful entry—whether of flowers (left) or fruit (right), whether large or small, simple or complex, in novice class or for the sweepstakes trophy—is a real achievement and a step toward more and better gardens.

ment would be 2½ ft. from the base to the top of the flowers. If the container is a low broad one, the height should be about one and a half times its diameter.

Do not overcrowd a container. Most arrangements have too many flowers. You should be able to see the beauty of the flowers, stems and leaves, which may be lost in a crowded arrangement. In what are known as "period arrangements," such as Victorian, French or Flemish, which often imitate old paintings, crowding is allowed, since it was the style of the time.

Flower stems should not be all the same length so that the top makes a flat line. They should not be placed one above another like steps. The stems should not be exactly parallel. It makes an awkward-looking arrangement. Stems should not cross.

Cut the stems to different lengths and arrange the flowers loosely. After a little practice, studying the effect produced, you will see the beauty of the flowers. If you study the line effects in arrangements made by the Japanese, it will teach you many points. They show vitality, simplicity and beauty of line.

The background should be considered when you arrange flower exhibits in the home. In certain cases (in flower shows) it must be considered also, and there are sometimes extra articles included. A class might be for "An arrangement showing flowers in tones of red and orange, against a background. Shown in a shadow-box, with accessories." A shadow-box is usually about 15 by 18 by 12 in. or larger; sometimes it is equipped with artificial lights. The background may be of any material (unless specified) as silk, satin, brocade, wall-paper, etc. The accessories are small appropriate objects—a small book, a box, a string of beads, a small image. The whole arrangement is supposed to make a picture so all objects should be good in color and in relationship to the size of the space and to each other.

A favorite class is one for "miniature arrangements" in which flowers and container are both very small. One should try to have a true relationship in size between flowers and container and not overcrowd.

There are many interesting arrangement classes such as: flowers in glass or metal containers; flowers in shades of one or different colors; seasonable flowers, alone

or in combination; arrangements for formal and for informal meals, indoors and outdoors; arrangements for a hall-table or a bedside- or a porch-table; flowers in front of a mirror; breakfast and tea trays; bridge-luncheon tables; wall-vases and tall ones to stand on the floor; small bouquets, terrariums, aquariums and bird-feeding stations—the great variety possible makes flower shows continually interesting.

FLOWER SHOW JUDGING. In flower shows, classes are judged by scales of points. Certain qualities are valued, the entry is penalized for shortcomings and the net result gives the final score.

A good general score-card for cut flowers follows:

Cultural perfection	80
divided as follows:	
Distinction of species or variety .. 20	
Size according to species or variety 20	
Form, color, substance and abundance of bloom 20	
Foliage and stem 20	
Condition	20
	100

For arrangement classes, a good general score-card is:

Color combination	25
Relation to container	10
Proportion and balance	25
Distinction and originality	20
Suitability of combination of material ..	10
Condition	10
	100

These show perfect scores. The judge (or judges) takes off points where the exhibit falls below perfection.

HOW TO STAGE A SHOW. It is perfectly possible for a garden group to plan a flower show. Those who were the pioneers had no rules to guide them. Now that shows are held in so many parts of the country, much information may be had. Garden clubs and horticultural societies and agricultural experiment stations or colleges are anxious to help. A list of classes is called a "Schedule" and should be planned to bring out as many exhibitors as possible. Start with a short list for the first show. Have a well-lighted room and do not crowd the exhibits. Have committees to do the work which is divided up as follows:

Flower Show Chairman—in charge of show.
Schedule Committee—to decide on the classes (suggestions are asked for from all the chairmen)
Entry Committee—takes the entries as they come in, in a book. Each exhibitor is given a card with name, class and number in class, which is placed with his exhibit.

Classification Committee—places exhibits on the day of the show and decides doubtful cases. This work needs the best horticulturist of the group.

Staging Committee—chooses the place, prepares for the show, providing everything necessary, such as tables, containers for the flowers in the cultural classes (milk and cream bottles are often used), etc.

Judging Committee—will find the judges and arrange to meet them at bus, train or boat, if they are not coming by auto.

Hospitality Committee—may be combined with judging committee. Judges of amateur shows are not paid but they are generally entertained at luncheon.

There should be clerks (one or two) to accompany each group of judges, to answer questions, to list the prize-winners and put stickers or ribbons on the entry cards which are then taken out of their envelopes so the contestant's name can be seen. There are usually two sets of judges, three judges for the cultural classes and three for the artistic or arrangement classes.

Groups soon learn to have good flower shows. There are many helps available for garden-lovers but experience is a good teacher. Try to interest the children in showing. Call their section "classes for Juniors" (*not* "Classes for Children"). Do not have them exhibit wild flowers; instead teach them not to destroy native plant treasures. With a little encouragement they will enjoy making arrangements, and setting a doll's table with a little bouquet, or a small tea-tray. Older children will also enjoy making posters for the show, which also can be judged for ribbons or prizes.

Try to get the men interested. They are grand workers when they get started and they like flowers, fruits and vegetables as well as the women do even if they do not say so or realize it. You will find great satisfaction in flower show work, and after a few years you will find that your whole community is better for what you have done.

Flower-loving groups branch out in a few years and try to improve their communities. Avenues of trees are planted; village or town or city parks and squares are improved; garden centers are established where new gardeners may obtain practical information on all garden subjects; conservation groups watch the street and park trees for signs of disease or pests and set the authorities at work to protect them or interest themselves in laws to be passed to protect the wild flowers and birds. Garden-lovers, in short, are always

ready and eager to make their home communities more beautiful places to live in, and exhibiting at shows is an important part of this movement. For the flower show is generally the starting point from which gardeners branch out to encourage other forms of civic beauty.

EXOCHORDA (ek - soh - kaur' - dah). Pearl-bush. Hardy deciduous shrubs of Asia, belonging to the Rose Family and resembling some of the spireas. They grow best in a rather light rich soil in a sunny place, and are among the most attractive of spring-flowering shrubs. Their white flowers in terminal racemes are followed by capsular fruits with winged seeds. Straggly shoots should be cut back and some old wood removed after flowering to keep them in good shape. Propagated by seeds, cuttings of soft wood under glass, and layering. Among the principal species are the following:

E. racemosus, of rather slender spreading habit to 10 ft., bears racemes of pearly buds and pure white flowers. *E. giraldi* is very similar but a more vigorous grower; its var. *wilsoni* is stronger still and more floriferous—the best of the group. *E. korolkowi,* one of the earliest shrubs to leaf out in spring, has darker and denser foliage than the others but is not so floriferous. *E. macrantha,* a hybrid between *racemosa* and *korolkowi,* resembles the first named parent, but is more upright and vigorous.

EXOTIC. Not native; a term (used both as a noun and as an adjective) applied to a plant introduced from a foreign country. *Mesembryanthemum pomeridianum* is *native* to S. Africa, but *exotic* elsewhere; goldenrod is *native* to the U. S., but an *exotic* garden plant in Europe. In contrast with exotic as a noun we have *indigen* (which see), of which the corresponding adjective form is *indigenous.*

EXPERIMENT STATIONS. There is at least one agricultural experiment station located in each of the United States, supported by federal and state funds. The activities of these stations (which, in most cases, are connected with the State Agricultural Colleges) are supervised by the Office of Experiment Stations of the U. S. Department of Agriculture, Washington, D. C. In Canada, there are five similar institutions with headquarters at the Central Experiment Farm, Ottawa.

Research work in all phases of agricultural science is carried on continuously by these stations. While not a great deal of their work has concerned gardeners or ornamental horticulture in the past, several stations are now carrying on research work that is of great value and interest to home gardeners as well as farmers—whom the stations were established to serve.

The study of insect pests and plant diseases and their control is an example of such work; so are the extensive soil and fertilizer (plant food) investigations. Plant breeding studies have resulted in the development of new and improved varieties which can be grown by amateur gardeners as well as commercial growers. New fruits, such as the Latham and Chief raspberries developed by the Minnesota Station, the Oriole and Golden Jubilee peaches of the New Jersey Station, and new grapes and strawberries of the New York Station, new sweet corn produced at the Connecticut Station, improved types of vegetables originated by the Iowa, Louisiana and Wisconsin Stations, and hardy roses by the South Dakota Station, are examples of the practical results of this kind of work.

The California Station is doing considerable research with flowers. Its plant breeding work has resulted in developing strains of snapdragon which are resistant to the rust disease. The wilt of asters, the rust of hollyhocks, and mildew on delphiniums are being investigated with much promise of the development of strains that will be immune to these diseases. The gladiolus thrips, the inheritance of doubleness in nasturtiums, double flowering in stocks, and the development of strains of verbena with better colors are subjects of other investigations now being carried on and of much interest to all.

The New Jersey Station maintains large plantings of ornamental plants and was the first to employ a research specialist on diseases of ornamentals on a full time basis. The Massachusetts Station maintains a collection of hardy flowers, and publishes information on their care. The New York Station has published many monographs on such flowers as iris, peony and gladiolus. It has developed the "Massey Dust" largely used to control black spot of roses. Studies on the fertilization of shade trees, methods

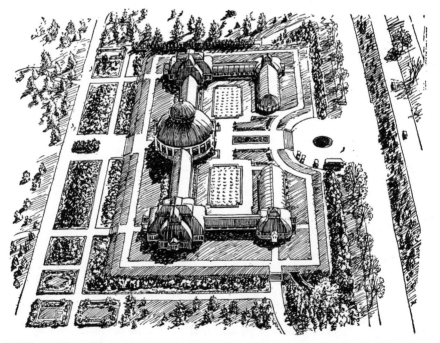

A TRUE CENTER OF GARDEN INFORMATION AND HORTICULTURAL KNOWLEDGE
Drawn from an airplane photograph of a small part of the New York Botanical Garden, this shows the main conservatory range, surrounded by plant collections. pools, and demonstration plantings from which extend the deciduous and evergreen tree collections—all planned and developed to help people know and appreciate plants.

of propagating nursery stock, and electrical hotbed heating are also carried on there, as well as investigations on annuals and perennials, including bulbs.

The Ohio Station has made many studies of ornamental plants, including the effect on growth and flowering of increasing or decreasing the amount of light, the adaptability of new species and varieties, the effects of shading, etc. The Michigan and Wisconsin Stations have encouraged gardening by the publication of bulletins on the improvement of home grounds and the former has developed a method for the rapid propagation of dahlias.

The Iowa Station is studying the best methods of propagating ornamental plants while the Indiana Station has done work in breeding disease-resistant asters and antirrhinums. The Rhode Island Station has made studies of lawn grasses, ornamental shrubs, and other matters of interest to the amateur gardener. The Florida, Tennessee and Virginia Stations are studying ornamental plants, and testing new species and varieties. A number of stations have under way studies of soil acidity and alkalinity in relation to plant growth, including that of annuals and perennials.

The foregoing are only a few of the many research projects of value to the amateur gardener carried on by these institutions. The rapidly growing interest in gardening all over the country will undoubtedly result in many more being undertaken from time to time.

Publications—some of a scientific nature, but in many instances popular bulletins—giving the results of their work, are issued by the stations regularly. The Office of Experiment Stations in Washington, D. C., issues mimeographed lists of all such bulletins published by the stations and copies may be secured by writing to that Office. The bulletins desired may then be secured by writing to the stations publishing them; they cannot be obtained from the office in Washington.

Amateur gardeners should write to the experiment station in their own state, and ask to be placed on its mailing list to receive any publications as issued on subjects in which they are interested. They should also inquire as to special services rendered to citizens of the state, such as the free testing of soil or seeds, the analysis of fertilizers, spray materials, etc., consultation and advice about plant, crop or garden

problems, the supplying of new plant varieties for trial, and the like. Tax-payers are entitled to whatever aid of this sort the station can give; it may enable them to gain much more success and satisfaction from their gardening efforts.

Following are the names and addresses of all experiment stations in the United States. Address communications in each case to the Director, and give the name of the town or post office address.

STATE EXPERIMENT STATIONS

Alabama—Auburn
Alaska—College
Arizona—Tucson
Arkansas—Fayetteville
California—Berkeley
Colorado—Fort Collins
Connecticut—State Station, New Haven; Storrs Station, Storrs
Delaware—Newark
Florida—Gainesville
Georgia—State Station, Experiment; Coastal Plain Station, Tifton
Hawaii—Honolulu
Idaho—Moscow
Illinois—Urbana
Indiana—Lafayette
Iowa—Ames
Kansas—Manhattan
Kentucky—Lexington
Louisiana—Baton Rouge
Maine—Orono
Maryland—College Park
Massachusetts—Amherst
Michigan—East Lansing
Minnesota—University Farm
Mississippi—State College
Missouri—College Station, Columbia; Fruit Station and Poultry Station, Mountain Grove
Montana—Bozeman
Nebraska—Lincoln
Nevada—Reno
New Hampshire—Durham
New Jersey—New Brunswick
New Mexico—State College
New York—State Station, Geneva; Cornell Station, Ithaca
North Carolina—State College Station, Raleigh
North Dakota—State College Station, Fargo
Ohio—Wooster
Oklahoma—Stillwater
Oregon—Corvallis
Pennsylvania—State College
Puerto Rico—Federal Station, Mayaguez; Insular Station, Rio Piedras
Rhode Island—Kingston
South Carolina—Clemson College
South Dakota—Brookings
Tennessee—Knoxville
Texas—College Station
Utah—Logan
Vermont—Burlington
Virginia—College Station, Blacksburg; Truck Station, Norfolk
Washington—College Station, Pullman; Western Washington Station, Puyallup
West Virginia—Morgantown
Wisconsin—Madison
Wyoming—Laramie

See also EDUCATION IN GARDENING; GOVERNMENT AGENCIES; RESEARCH IN GARDENING.

EXPLORATION FOR PLANTS. The seeking of new plants of potential value as garden subjects or for other purposes, in all parts of the world, has long been carried on by intrepid botanists and plantsmen both as a hobby and as a scientific, professional, or commercial venture. Sometimes these "plant hunters" operate on their own initiative; in other cases they are sent out by leading seed or nursery firms, by government agencies, or by institutions of research, teaching, etc., which test, propagate and disseminate worthy discoveries or use them in plant breeding work. They have rendered and are rendering a great service to horticulture and the story of their work and achievements is a bright page in the annals of plants and their use. See PLANT EXPLORATION.

EXTENSION COURSES. Instruction in various phases of gardening and horticulture is included in many extension courses offered by high schools, colleges and universities, as a supplement to their resident courses, and also by some state departments of education and public institutions. Some extension courses may be taken by mail; others by attendance at special classes (often evening classes for the benefit of those who work by day), and others (known also as "short courses") by a few days or weeks of concentrated study in connection with lectures and demonstrations in a given subject. Summer extension courses are also given and in some cases members of the staff of the institution travel over large areas visiting the homes of the students, or they may be located at outlying points, as in the county farm bureau headquarters. Such workers are called extension specialists.

As noted, extension courses are not a part of the regular curriculum of an educational institution; they are given rather for those people who have not the scholastic requirements, the desire, or the time or money to enroll in a full course; they usually emphasize the practical side of the subjects treated. Among the horticultural subjects included in extension courses are general gardening practices; soil diagnosis, testing and preparation; prevention and cure of pests and diseases of plants; raising and marketing of flower, fruit, and vegetable crops; greenhouse practices; raising exhibition flowers and vegetables; principles of landscape gardening; care of house plants; pruning, training, grafting, fertilizing; protecting plants over winter; principles of rock gardening; identification of garden flowers, weeds, shrubs and trees; the sciences underlying the practice of gardening, and many others. A postcard directed to the nearest educational institution —government agency, local school, state agricultural college or university, etc.—will bring information about extension courses that are within reach of practically every gardener and that can greatly aid gardeners in achieving success in their hobby or profession.

See also GOVERNMENT AGENCIES; EXPERIMENT STATIONS; EDUCATION IN GARDENING.

EYE. A term variously applied in horticulture as (1) to the dark center of such flowers as Black-eyed Susan (Thunbergia); (2) to the sunken buds on certain tubers, as the "Irish" potato; (3) to the branch buds on stems of shrubs, trees and woody vines and the shoots of herbs asexually propagated. In cases (2) and (3) the term is most frequently used in connection with propagation, as single-eye or two-eye cuttings, etc.

EYEBRIGHT. Common name for the genus Euphrasia, a large group of low-growing annual herbs of the Figwort Family, more or less parasitic on the roots of other plants. It is derived from their former reputed ability to cure blindness. They are found widely distributed throughout the temperate and colder sections of the globe but are of little horticultural value except that the white, yellow, and purple flowers of a few species might be useful in an alpine garden.

F

FABIANA (fa-bi-ay'-nah). A genus of small heath-like shrubs of the Nightshade Family, and native to S. America. *F. imbricata,* the best-known species, is sometimes grown in a cool greenhouse, and also outdoors in mild climates. It is a much-branched shrub to 8 ft., with small overlapping scale-like leaves, and small white flowers freely produced. Propagation is by cuttings.

FAGACEAE (fa-gay'-see-ee). Botanical name of the Beech Family, which includes Fagus (beech), Quercus (oak), and Castanea (chestnut), all woody trees or shrubs distributed for the most part in the temperate and subtropical regions of the northern hemisphere. Male flowers are borne in catkins; female flowers are clustered or solitary; the fruit is a nut enclosed in a cub or bur. The family furnishes many desirable species for ornament and shade; some yield valuable timber, edible nuts, and medicinal and dye products.

FAGUS (fay'-gus). A genus of hardy deciduous trees of the N. temperate zone; hard wooded, long lived and beautiful in their light gray bark and various forms. See BEECH.

FAIRY BELLS. Common name for plants of the genus Disporum, members of the Lily Family. They are perennial herbs with slender rootstocks, leafy stems and drooping flowers solitary or borne in clusters and followed by attractive red or yellow berries. They are very lovely in the wild garden, especially when in fruit, and similar to Solomons Seal in growth, but usually grow in drier situations. They can be increased by seed or division.

D. oreganum, to 2 ft., has creamy-white flowers. *D. smithi,* to 3 ft., has whitish flowers to 1 in. and bright yellow berries. *D. hookeri,* to 2 ft., has green flowers and scarlet berries. *D. maculatum,* to 2 ft., has yellowish flowers dotted with black. *D. lanuginosum* has greenish flowers and red fruit.

FAIRY FANS. Common name for *Eucharidium breweri,* a Calif. herb with showy deep pink flowers in clusters.

FAIRY-LILY. A common name for Zephyranthes, a genus of small Amaryllis-like bulbous herbs with variously colored funnel-shaped flowers. See ZEPHYRANTHES.

FAIRY-WAND. A common name for *Chamaelirium luteum,* a native perennial herb good for shady places.

FALL. One of the three outer segments of an iris flower, each of which is hanging or reflexed. Compare STANDARD; see IRIS.

FALLOW. Originally, this term meant fields plowed up after harvest and left unplanted; popularly, it is applied to any plowed land so left for several to many weeks. In a still more restricted sense, it is land allowed to lie uncultivated (or with only enough surface tillage to kill weeds) during one or more seasons in order to build up its productive capacity or starve out some particular pest, disease or weed. Though an important farming practice, fallowing is of limited application in home gardening, where it is much more desirable to keep idle ground under a cover-crop.

FALLUGIA (fal-oo'-ji-ah). A genus of one species (*F. paradoxa*) native in the W. part of the country, and a member of the Rose Family. It is a low spreading deciduous shrub, bearing white flowers, and later attractive heads of feathery-tailed fruits. Hardy as far N. as Mass., it requires a well-drained limestone soil in a warm sunny position. Propagated by seeds.

FALSE-ACACIA. A common name for *Robinia pseudoacacia,* a species of Locust, which see. Also known as Black-acacia and Yellow Locust, it is a tree of E. and Central U. S. to 80 ft. with spiny branches, fragrant white flowers, and reddish-brown, flattened pods that hang on over winter.

FALSE-ALUM-ROOT. Common name for *Tellima grandiflora,* a small perennial plant of N. W. America, belonging to the Saxifrage Family and having almost round, toothed leaves. Its greenish flowers, becoming red, have fringed petals and are borne in racemes resembling graceful sprays of green lily-of-the-valley. The W. representative of the bishops-cap (Mitella) of the E., it is charming naturalized in the wild garden, where it should be given a partially shaded situation and a moist soil rich in humus. It is increased by seed or division.

FALSE BABYS BREATH. A common name for *Galium mullugo,* a white-flowered perennial often mistaken for *Gypsophila paniculata.*

FALSE - CHAMOMILE. A common name sometimes applied to the genus Boltonia, but more often to *Matricaria chamomilla* and *M. inodora,* the former being the "sweet" the latter the "scentless" False-chamomile.

FALSE-CYPRESS. Common name for trees of the genus Chamaecyparis (which see), a member of the Pine Family.

FALSE-DRAGONHEAD. C o m m o n name for Physostegia, a genus of attractive tall hardy perennials with loose spires of pink, white or purple flowers borne in late summer.

FALSE-HEATH. A common name for the genus Fabiana, small greenhouse shrubs with little white flowers.

FALSE-HELLEBORE (hel'-ee-bor). Common name for the genus Veratrum, a group of stout herbaceous perennials with greenish or purplish flowers and poisonous roots.

FALSE - INDIGO. Common name for two leguminous genera, Amorpha and Baptisia, both of which see. The former comprises shrubs with small flowers in dense terminal spikes; the latter, herbs with flowers in loose clusters.

FALSE - MALLOW. Common name for the genus Malvastrum, a member of the Mallow Family including herbs and shrubby plants with purple, red or yellow mallow-like blossoms. Many of the species are excellent plants for the border, but in the N. others must be grown in the greenhouse. They are readily propagated by seed or from cuttings under glass. *M. coccineum* (Prairie-mallow), 6 to 10 in. tall, is a native plant with brick-red flowers almost 1 in. across; *M. capense,* to 4 ft., is a shrubby S. African plant with purple flowers; *M. fasiculatum* is a tree-like species with hairy leaves and clusters of rose-purple flowers; native in S. W. U. S.; *M. hypomadarum,* to 10 ft., from S. Africa, has attractive white flowers with a rose-purple center.

FALSE - MITREWORT. C o m m o n name for Tiarella (which see), a genus of perennial herbs with brilliant fall colors, especially suited to shady places in the wild garden.

FALSE-OLIVE. Common name for *Elaeodendron orientale,* a semi-tropical plant with small leathery leaves, remarkable for the way they change from a narrow slender form with a red midrib in the juvenile stage to the broad blunt leaves of the mature plant. It has small yellowish-green flowers followed by fruit the size and shape of an olive. Grown as a pot plant under glass in the N., it is propagated by single-eye cuttings.

FALSE-SOLOMONS-SEAL, or **FALSE-SPIKENARD.** Common name for the genus Smilacina of the Lily Family, comprising a number of perennial herbs with creeping rootstocks, leafy stems, small white or greenish flowers in terminal clusters, followed by conspicuous red or greenish berries. They are easily colonized in the wild garden and are increased by division or seed. *S. racemosa,* to 3 ft., found all over N. America, has a plume-like cluster of creamy-white flowers and red berries; *S. amplexicaulis,* to 3 ft., a W. species, has large panicles of white flowers followed by red berries spotted with purple; *S. stellata,* to 20 in., which has a few-flowered cluster of starry blossoms, will grow in the shade of evergreens.

FALSE-SPIREA (spy-ree'-ah). This name is given to several Asiatic shrubby plants, belonging to the Rose Family, formerly classed with the true spireas but now put in the genus Sorbaria. They are not particular as to soil and can stand some shade, but thrive and show to best advantage near water. They have handsome pinnate leaves, and large plumes of creamy or white flowers in summer. Propagated by suckers and root and stem cuttings.

Of the principal species, *S. sorbifolia* grows to about 6 ft. and spreads freely by suckers. It is one of the earliest shrubs to unfold its leaves in spring, and has plumes of creamy-white flowers in June. *S. arborea* is the tallest and most handsome, growing to 15 ft. or more. It has large drooping panicles of pure white flowers in July and August. *S. aitchisoni* grows to 10 ft. and is conspicuous with bright red young stems and very handsome foliage. It flowers from July to September. *S. lindleyana* is a large handsome grower with big panicles of flowers, but it is too tender to grow in the N.

FALSE-TAMARISK (*Myricaria germanica*). This deciduous shrub, a native of Europe and Asia and allied to the Tamarisk, thrives in sandy soil, and is a good seaside plant. The wand-like branches are furnished with small grayish leaves, and bear dense racemes of small pinkish flowers. Old gaunt specimens can be renovated by hard pruning in spring. It is propagated by cuttings.

FAME-FLOWER. Common name for the genus Talinum of the Purslane Family, comprising a number of small fleshy perennial herbs with erect clusters of pink, red, or yellow flowers that last but a short time. Some of the species are hardy and grown in the rock garden or the border; others are grown in pots or tubs as house plants. They are increased by seed or division. *T. paniculatum,* to 2 ft., with red to yellowish flowers in clusters to 10 in. long, has a form with white-edged leaves that is often grown indoors. *T. triangulare,* to 1½ or 2 ft., with flowers red or yellowish in long racemes, a native of tropical America, is an excellent border-plant and also used as a pot-herb.

FAMILY. A group of plants comprising few or many genera, the members of which are sufficiently alike in general characteristics to show somewhat close relationship and to justify their being classed together. In some families (known as *natural families*), such as the grasses, the composites and the crucifers, the similarities and relationship are obvious. In other families such evidences are obscure even to botanists and the affinities so doubtful that the grouping of the genera is more or less tentative.

Generally, the characteristics identifying a family are indicated in one prominent genus which gives the family its name. Thus Rosaceae is the Rose Family. Names of plant families can easily be recognized because they all end in *-ae* as in Rosaceae, Labiatae, Rubiaceae, etc.

See also CLASSIFICATION; GENUS; SPECIES; VARIETY.

FAN-PALMS. Common name given to a number of palms having broad, fan-shaped leaves, sometimes cut all the way to the center into many segments. Well known examples are the Palmetto, the European Fan-Palm, the Washingtonia, and the Talipot, which latter produce the largest fans known.

FANWORT. Common name for *Cabomba caroliniana,* an aquatic with finely divided submerged leaves, decorative in indoor aquaria. Also called Water Shield, Fish-grass, and Washington-plant.

FAREWELL-TO-SPRING. Common name for *Godetia amoena,* a slender Pacific Coast annual with large crimson, white, or pink single and double flowers.

FARFUGIUM (far-feu'-ji-um). Former name (still found in catalogs) for the Leopard-plant, a Japanese herbaceous perennial, now placed in the genus Ligularia, which see.

FARKLEBERRY. A common name for *Vaccinium arboreum,* a large white-flowered, black-berried shrub, evergreen in the S.; also called Sparkleberry.

FASCIATION (fash-i-ay'-shun). A botanical term for a common malformation in plant stems resulting in an enlargement and flattening as if several stems were fused together.

FASTIGIATE (fas-tij'-i-ayt). Erect, narrowing toward the top. A term applied to trees of slender or pyramidal form in which the branches spring from a single trunk, gradually lengthening from top to bottom, as contrasted with the vase-form of the American elm.

FATSIA (fat'-si-ah) *japonica.* An evergreen shrub or small tree belonging to the Aralia Family. It has large glossy, deeply lobed leaves, and long panicles of white flowers. Sometimes grown under glass in the N., it makes a stately plant of subtropical appearance outdoors in mild climates. Propagated by seed and cuttings.

FAWN-LILY. Common name for *Erythronium californicum,* a creamy-flowered, bulbous, spring-flowering perennial herb of the Lily Family, native to Calif.

FEATHERED-COLUMBINE. Common name for *Thalictrum aquilegifolium,* an Old-World species of Meadow-rue. See THALICTRUM.

FEATHERFLEECE. Common name for *Stenanthium robustum,* a tall liliaceous herb with white or greenish flowers in clusters; sometimes planted in wild gardens or borders.

FEATHERFOIL. A common name for Hottonia (which see), a genus of water plants of the Primrose Family, sometimes used in aquaria for their attractive bloom.

FEATHER-GERANIUM. A common name for *Chenopodium botrys,* a strong-smelling Old-World annual sometimes listed in catalogs as *Ambrosia mexicana.*

FEATHER GRASS. A common name for stipa (also called Spear Grass), a genus of tall grasses grown mainly for ornament; one species, *S. tenacissima,* called Esparto Grass, is grown for its fibre.

FEDERATED GARDEN CLUBS. After the formation in 1913 of the Garden Club of America (which see), garden clubs

DON'T STRANGLE YOUR TREE
Any wire tightly wrapped around the trunk will, in time, cut through the growing bark, always defacing and usually killing the tree.

sprang up rapidly in the various States. As the number of clubs included in the Garden Club of America was strictly limited, the other widely distributed groups, feeling the need of concerted action, organized themselves into State Federations. Virginia was the leader in this move, its Garden Club Federation being organized in 1920. New York and New Jersey soon followed suit and now more than 30 States have federated their clubs. Today many other organizations, such as horticultural societies, belong to these Federations; in addition, at least half of the member clubs of the Garden Club of America belong to them and work actively with them, thus making possible concerted action on a very large scale when needed to support or oppose legislation or to assist in the work connected with flower shows. In order to obtain still greater solidarity, these State Federations in many cases have joined the National Council of State Garden Club Federations. At present those so affiliated are the Federations of Alabama, Arkansas, California, Colorado, Connecticut, Florida, Georgia, Illinois, Indiana, Iowa, Kansas, Kentucky, Maine, Maryland, Massachusetts, Michigan, Mississippi, New Hampshire, New Jersey, New York, North Carolina, Ohio, Oregon, Pennsylvania,

Rhode Island, South Carolina, Tennessee, Texas, Virginia, Washington, West Virginia, Wisconsin and Wyoming.

FEIJOA (fay-shoh'-ah). This S. American genus, sometimes called Pine-apple-guava, is represented in this country by *F. sellowiana*, a beautiful evergreen shrub from Brazil, belonging to the Myrtle Family. It was introduced into California chiefly for its aromatic and edible fruits, but apart from this it is a worth-while ornamental. Growing to about 15 ft., it can stand a few degrees of frost, and thrives best in a loamy soil with plenty of humus. The oval glossy green leaves are silvery beneath, and it has cup-shaped flowers of white and crimson, with a conspicuous cluster of dark red stamens. The egg-shaped fruit is green with a red flush. Propagated by seeds, cuttings and layers.

FELICIA (fe-lish'-i-ah). A genus of herbs or subshrubs of the Daisy Family, natives of Africa. The shrubby species, which can be propagated by cuttings, are sometimes grown under glass for winter bloom, and outdoors in warm regions. The annuals, easily grown from seed, are useful fillers in the rock garden.

F. amelloides (Blue Marguerite), a low shrubby plant, is an old-time greenhouse favorite valued for its sky-blue flowers on long wiry stems. *F. petiolata* is also shrubby but with prostrate branches useful for hanging baskets. *F. tenella* is an annual with weak spreading stems and pale blue flowers. *F. bergeriana* (Kingfisher Daisy) is a low spreading annual with bright blue flowers of a rather unusual shade.

FELT FERN (*Cyclophorus lingua*). One of a genus of ferns suitable for greenhouse cultivation, having simple, oblong, or linear fronds, 6 to 10 ins. tall, rarely lobed, and rather fleshy and hairy. The rooting stems require shallow pots, as they creep on the surface. Provide peaty soil with some coarse sand.

FENCES, GARDEN. As distinguished from large-scale fencing around estates or farms and meadows, the reference may be regarded as limited. Yet it includes every sort of protective barrier which may be set along the boundaries of home grounds, as well as the lesser or secondary barriers, dividing, within its boundaries, one part of a place from another. Railings of all types, solidly boarded walls, low lattice or trellis, wire fencing and palings or "picket" fences, are all included, since any of these may be used in or around a garden.

Little by little the desire for protection around the home grounds is beginning to reassert itself, after several decades of inertia. At the beginning of the fairly long interval all the fences in the land were laid low—literally swept off the landscape in response to a craze for wide open spaces without obstructions which had seized the country.

This craze had its inception in the mistaken idea that to remove the visible sign of separation between neighboring lands, as well as between private land and the highway, would make each man's property appear larger than its actual size. Far from this being the case, the contrary is true. Well defined boundary treatment around a garden that is well designed actually tends to make the area seem more spacious than it really is.

The realization of this as well as the desire for privacy and seclusion throughout all of one's domain is responsible for today's restoration of the garden fence or other permanent boundary feature. As with all structural elements in the garden, the house must govern choice in every respect. This means, not that fence must match house in any particular, but that it must bear out the house character. Furthermore, it must do this in such a way that it will always remain secondary to all parts of the garden picture. The garden fence which draws attention to itself in any way is a virulent example of bad design. See GARDEN WALLS.

FENDLERA (fend-lee′-rah). A medium-sized graceful shrub from the S. W. part of the country, belonging to the Saxifrage Family. Of the two species, *F. rupicola* is the better known, but it is not entirely hardy N. It needs a light rich loam with plenty of humus, and a sunny place. Its slender branches bear small grayish leaves and white or rose-tinted cross-shaped flowers in June. Propagated by seeds or cuttings.

FENNEL. A hardy, perennial European herb (*Foeniculum vulgare*) grown as an annual for its aromatic seeds and fragrant young leaves, both of which are used for flavoring. As the seed is slow to

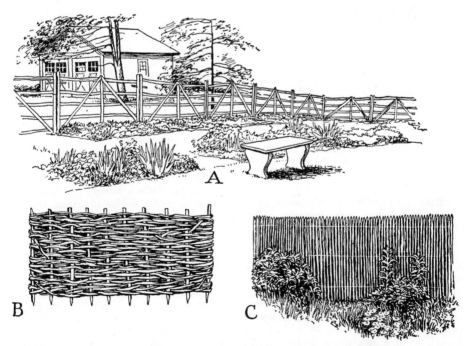

A FENCE CAN BE MADE AN EFFECTIVE GARDEN FEATURE
Portable types are often especially useful. Chestnut hurdles (A) give an open, rural effect but do not afford the protection or privacy of the woven wattle type (B) or the close wire-woven chestnut Sapling fence (C) obtainable in various heights.

sprout, sow it in early spring. The plants require full sunlight but only the simplest culture in any good garden soil. In places it has become a pestiferous weed, giving an unpleasant flavor to the milk and butter of cows that eat it, as do garlic and wild onion.

In Florence or Sweet Fennel (var. *dulce*) the greatly enlarged leaf bases form a bulb-like structure 3 to 4 in. in diameter and called the "apple." When blanched by earthing up it is cooked as a vegetable, but the stalks, resembling anise-flavored celery, can also be eaten raw. As the plants grow rapidly, make successional sowings two weeks apart.

Giant-fennel (*Ferula communis*), a thick rooted Asiatic perennial, often 10 ft. high, is grown for its ornamental foliage and umbels of yellow flowers.

FINOCCHIO, OR FLORENCE FENNEL
The enlarged anise-flavored basal portions of the stalks of Foeniculum vulgare var. dulce are eaten like celery.

FENNEL-FLOWER. Common name for Nigella (which see), a genus of attractive annuals with white, blue or yellow flowers.

FERNS. (See illustration, Plate 18.) Among non-flowering plants, the ferns and their relatives represent the highest development. Instead of growing from seeds, as do flowering plants, ferns come from simple spores, which are borne in spore-cases on the under side of a leaf (or *frond*) or in a specialized portion of the frond, or on a separate stalk which develops brown spore-cases instead of a green leaf.

A distinguishing character of ferns is the fact that the leaf or frond is rolled up in the bud with the tip at the very center; this is true of the leaves of no other plants. Another characteristic is the usually 2-forked veining.

The bare stalk of the frond is called the *stipe;* where it continues through the center of the leaf it is called the *rachis.* Each major lobe or division of a fern frond is a *pinna,* and each secondary division a *pinnule.*

It is the shape and position of the spore-cases (or *sporangia*) on the backs of the pinnae or on separate structures that largely determine the classification of ferns. All gardeners interested in raising ferns, either outdoors or in the house, will profit by knowledge of not only their natural surroundings and hence their requirements, but also their names and botanical relationships. Accordingly, at the end of this article, descriptions are given by which one can distinguish the hardy ferns of N. America. Descriptions of greenhouse subjects will be found in articles under the name of each.

The reproduction of ferns by spores differs from that of flowering plants by seeds in that it interposes a half step between each two generations. The single spore, a very minute body, germinates in dampness and shade, producing a little flat leaf-like body called the *prothallium.* On the underside of this the sex organs develop, and fertilization occurs at this stage. Then, after a long period, varying usually from 2 to 6 months, the first young fronds of the true fern appear.

FERN USES. Thoreau said: "Nature made ferns for pure leaves." And it is primarily for the great beauty of their leaves, the endless variety of forms, the range of subtle shades of green, that we treasure these plants. A well-grown specimen is always pleasing, not depending upon any special season for its chief appeal, as flowering plants do. Ferns are comparatively easy to grow; they give us perfect foliage in a brief time. In the city and suburban garden they bring in a suggestion of the woods; in rockeries they are invaluable for softening the junctures of stone and soil and providing a foil for other plants. A collection of various kinds in a separate fern bed has constant interest.

Moreover, many excellent sorts are ours for the trouble of transplanting them. They are long-lived and remarkably free from pests. Some ferns are practically evergreen the year round, and some are valuable for attracting birds because of the woolly substance which clothes the uncoiling fronds and is much prized as nesting material. Above all, ferns prefer a diffused light, and some will endure dense shade, thus serving us in places that no other plants will tolerate.

In general, we may expect success with two types: the species strictly native to our own region or to a similar climate and soil, and those coming from somewhat more southerly latitudes, such as the Boston fern and the Cretan brake, which will not endure freezing but can be wintered indoors. To expect the same ferns to do service both indoors in winter and out of doors in summer is unreasonable. Many house ferns will send up a fresh and vigorous growth when planted in the garden, but they will die down in the fall when you want them for the living-room. The best plan is to re-pot house ferns in May or June, put them in the shade, and give them a summer's rest, meanwhile turning your attention to hardy ferns in the garden.

Hardy Ferns for the Garden

Moisture and protection from the direct rays of the sun are the two prime requisites of fern culture. This does not mean that we can expect ferns to survive in soggy soil or almost total darkness. Whether in pots or in the open ground, indoors or out, they must have drainage to carry away excess water from their roots, and must have diffused light, at least during the warm season. The first requirement can be satisfied by a proper soil texture. With qualifications for certain kinds, the general rule is a mixture of equal parts of leafmold, garden loam, coarse sand, and peat moss. If you haven't the moss, use 2 parts of well-rotted leafmold. The watering pot or hose must be liberally used, even in periods of rest, but never to the point where standing water may turn the soil sour. A slightly sloping site is excellent. Surface cultivation is not desirable because many ferns have fine roots close to the top-soil, but a thin covering of sand or a leaf mulch will maintain moisture under ground. A northern exposure is much the best, an eastern one next best, and a southern one to be

absolutely avoided. If the only space available faces south and you must have ferns, construct a lath-house or trellis and interpose the shade of some luxuriant vines.

TRANSPLANTING. Transplanting native ferns is best accomplished in early spring, as the "crosiers" (young fronds) unroll. The ground is then cold and wet and there is less danger of the roots drying out. However, ferns will stand removal at any time until midsummer, and the period from mid-May to mid-June, when a good growth has been made, has the advantage of enabling you to estimate the mature height and size of the plant. Proper spacing is important, both to set off the plant to advantage and to prevent the unhealthy, over-damp condition which may result from crowding. When transplanting a large specimen, it is well to observe and mark its approximate orientation (the way it sets with relation to compass directions) and re-set it facing the same way. Three ft. apart is not too much for large osmundas and 2 ft. for the shield ferns. Smaller kinds may be spaced proportionately closer, and may be so arranged that by midsummer the overarching fronds of the larger types will partially shade the smaller.

CINNAMON FERN
A rank-growing native, easily transplanted to a shady garden.

FUTURE CARE. Dig your bed to 12 in., cover the bottom with coarse gravel and broken pots, add a layer of well-decayed leafmold and refill with the prepared soil as specified above. The texture should not be too fine; a fistful should break apart readily but not run off when the hand in unclenched. Note the natural depth of the fern before lifting and re-set it in the same fashion. *Do not bury the crowns.* Cover running underground rhizomes to a depth of an inch or two and peg down any surface runners until they have taken hold. The more woods soil you can introduce the better; if possible add to it from year to year.

When the planting is completed, wet thoroughly with a fine spray and cover the surface with an inch of coarse sand. Do not remove fronds for bouquets too often, and in the late summer and fall allow all dead fronds, as well as the stubby bases of severed fronds, to remain until spring, because these act as natural insulation for the crowns through the cold months. Throughout the summer keep the bed mulched, and water it well into November. After a hard frost, cover lightly with leaves or evergreen boughs and do not remove this protection until all risk of recurring cold is past, as the new growth of many of our hardiest ferns is very susceptible to spring freezes.

When planting ferns in the rock garden have the pockets of earth deep enough— at least 12 in.—to accommodate the far-reaching roots and keep them cool. See that the natural drainage runs towards the roots. Rock ferns require a less rich soil than border ferns. Use very little peat moss and mix in a fifth part of lime or finely crushed old mortar.

HARDY BORDER FERNS. Adders tongue, beech fern, bladder fern, Bootts wood fern, boulder fern, brittle fern, chain fern, Clintons wood fern, California chain fern, Christmas fern, cinnamon fern, cloak fern, crested fern, dagger fern, deer fern, Goldies wood fern, grape fern, harts tongue, holly fern, interrupted fern, lady fern, lip fern, maidenhair, male fern, marginal shield fern, marsh fern, mountain holly fern, mountain wood fern, New York fern, oak fern, ostrich fern, polypody, rattlesnake fern, royal fern, sensitive fern, shield fern, silvery spleenwort, walking fern, woodsia.

HARDY ROCK-GARDEN FERNS. Beech fern, bladder fern, boulder fern, brittle fern, Christmas fern, cliff-brake, cloak fern, harts tongue, holly fern, lip fern, maidenhair, oak fern, polypody, rattlesnake fern, resurrection fern, rock-brake, rock spleenwort, walking fern, woodsia. *For the far West add:* Birds foot fern, coffee fern, cotton fern, golden-backed fern, lace fern, limestone polypody.

CHOOSING GARDEN FERNS. Not all native ferns lend themselves to cultivation. The climbing fern, the adders tongue, and the grape ferns are usually difficult to establish. The harts tongue and several of the rock spleenworts are best left alone,

at least until one has successfully grappled with other sorts. On the other hand, the New York fern, the bulblet bladder fern, the boulder, marsh, and sensitive ferns, are apt to become a nuisance and over-run the whole garden. The lady fern, too, is a rank grower. The New York fern and the bulblet bladder fern make excellent ground covers in a large foundation planting or border of shrubs. The lady fern and the ostrich fern have an unfortunate habit of getting rather brown and ragged toward the end of summer, for which reason do not give them too conspicuous positions. Wild asters, snake-root, or such garden plants as *Lilium henryi* may be planted among them and will tend to veil their unsightliness after mid-August.

As a rule, however, both for esthetic and horticultural reasons, it is better to keep flowers and ferns apart. They are two distinct types of beauty. Some charming effects can be made by planting such wild flowers as Jack-in-the-pulpit, Solomons seal, snakeroot, columbine, and wild orchids among ferns; but garden flowers seldom look well.

SOIL PREFERENCES. A more important reason than appearance is the fact that ferns demand a soil and situation undesirable for many garden plants. The chemical composition of soil is a big factor in success with ferns. Many sorts will grow well in ordinary soil, but for excellent results, favor them with their own individual preferences. The rock spleenworts must have some lime, although the ebony spleenwort will tolerate a neutral condition. The wood ferns and osmundas like a rather neutral or slightly acid soil, supplied by leaf humus and peat. Goldies fern and the woodwardias like one definitely acid. Woodsias and lip ferns usually grow on shale and traprock, but will endure the conditions suitable for wood ferns, especially if broken stone and more sunlight are afforded them; and they will also stand the lime soil required by spleenworts. Charcoal pleases them, as it does also the purple cliff-brake. Christmas and holly ferns will adapt themselves to either condition, though they prefer limestone.

PROPAGATION. Under cultivation, ferns generally prove to be less fertile, but they will increase by root division, and some kinds can be artificially propagated. Those which form a compact crown can be divided and cut apart with a sharp spade;

Plate 18.   FERNS FOR GARDEN AND HOME

Upper left: The stately fronds of ostrich fern unfurl near the margin of a lake or stream.   Upper
right: Softening the rocky boulder in the wild garden, grows the erect leathery polypody.   Center
left: The marginal shield fern enjoys a roothold in an obscure rock crevice.   Center right: The filmy
lace-like fronds of the tender maidenhair.   Lower left: The delicate, yellow-green lady-fern outlined
        against a rocky hillside.   Lower right: The odd, pointed leaves of the tender holly fern.

those with creeping rhizomes can simply be cut, and the severed section with its young fronds and roots held down until firmly rooted. The osmundas form large

FRUIT DOTS ON A FERN
Arranged on the back of each fertile pinna of a fern like Dryopteris are small fruit-dots containing the reproductive spores.

and definite crowns; some of the wood ferns can be divided. The rock spleenworts, woodsias, and lip ferns form densely matted tufts of wiry rootlets which can be occasionally pulled apart, if overgrown. All the other common sorts possess definitely creeping roots or surface stems. The polypody grows in such tangled mats over large areas that sections of it can be cut and rolled up like sods. The bulblet bladder fern is unique in bearing green "berries" on the under-side of the frond, which increase the species in all directions.

Indoor or House Ferns

The modern steam-heated home is too dry and too warm for the successful culture of native ferns. Besides, most of these are deciduous and normally dormant through the winter. The most reliable house ferns are therefore those more tender varieties from southern latitudes, many of which will thrive if the atmosphere is kept moist and the temperature above 50 and under 80 deg. F.

Potting Ferns Cleanliness of soil, pots, and leaves is imperative. Thoroughly wash the pots with soap and hot water, and have them quite dry before filling. Set a concave piece of broken pot over the drainage hole and fill with an inch or so of potsherds and gravel. Over this place a layer of moss, and then a soil composed of leafmold, good garden earth (the blacker the better), and coarse sand, in equal parts, adding lime for the rock ferns. Sterilization, by baking the soil in an oven for an hour, will destroy any soil pests present.

Have the earth neither too dry nor too wet when put in the pot; if too wet it will tend to cake. Loosen the old soil around the roots of the plant and spread out exposed roots. Select a pot just large enough to accommodate the plant with an inch of soil all around, and no larger. Gauge the depth by the rooting habit; most ferns do not need deep pots. Ferns like Davallias and Gleichenias, with surface rhizomes, naturally will require wider pots and less depth. Allow an inch of space for watering between the top of the rim and the soil level, and be sure the crown of the plant is not buried. Cover the surface with sand or moss and water well.

Do not wet the leaves often: this tends to turn them yellow. Rather water on the soil surface or by standing the pot in a bowl of water until saturated. It is dangerous to leave standing water in the saucer or to keep the soil too soaking wet. Water thoroughly every few days, then not again until the soil apparently needs it, meanwhile keeping the surface from drying out by a light surface stirring or a mulch of moss.

Through the winter see that the outer surface of the pot is kept clean of scum, and wash the leaves once a month, *never letting them dry in hot sun.* Always use water at room temperature. Keep the plants out of drafts; if in a conservatory or special room, give them fresh air by indirect ventilation now and then. Do not rotate the pot. Do not give them strong fertilizers. A weak sodium-nitrate solution is beneficial, and a teaspoonful of lime occasionally for the lime-loving kinds. Few ferns will require repotting more than once a year; and you can do this for all of them regularly before placing them (in their pots) outdoors to rest over summer.

House ferns should never be placed in direct sunlight. A north window is always best; an eastern one good. If your room has only southern windows let them stand well at the eastern side, where only the late afternoon rays will strike them.

Best Ferns for Indoors. Birds nest fern, Boston fern and its varieties, Cretan brake, hares foot fern, maidenhair, stags horn fern, tender holly fern. *More difficult subjects are:* Asplenium, Davallia, Dryopteris, Lomaria, Lygodium, Pityrogramma, Polystichum; for their culture, see under those titles.

With constant care it is possible to grow a few of our hardy ferns in the living-room. The best for this purpose are: ebony spleenwort, maidenhair spleenwort, northern maidenhair, Christmas fern, and purple cliff-brake. But you will need to let them rest in summer, watch them constantly, and provide plenty of moisture in the atmosphere.

Of late years the Wardian case or its offspring, the terrarium, has had a great vogue. Many choice little ferns may be grown in these containers or miniature greenhouses. The best of them are the following: beech ferns, cliff-brake, Cretan brake, ebony spleenwort, filmy ferns (difficult), fragile fern, grape fern, green spleenwort, hares foot fern, Japanese claw fern, maidenhair, maidenhair spleenwort, oak fern, polypody, rattlesnake fern, Scotts spleenwort, tender holly fern, Venus-hair fern, walking fern wall-rue.

FERN BALLS AND BASKETS. There are many fascinating methods of aerial fern culture for proper conditions indoors. Hanging baskets of wire or wood lined with moss; suspended coconut shells, and cork or bark wall-pockets are especially good for ferns with creeping roots, like maidenhair, as these will push through crevices and develop new fronds on all sides. The fern-ball, formerly much more popular than now, is made of the hares foot fern, whose freely branching thick and hairy rhizomes, pliable when wet, are bound over variously shaped wire frames filled with sphagnum moss. The roots penetrate the moist moss and delicately curled fronds develop over the whole surface. The moss acts as a sponge and will hold water for a long time. These "balls" are sometimes made in varied, humorous, and even grotesque forms, such as boats, animals, etc.

ENEMIES OF FERNS

Ferns, both outdoors and in, are comparatively free from troubles, but there are some diseases and pests that should be watched for and fought whenever discovered so they will not become bad enough to necessitate destruction of the victims. In general, ferns in the greenhouse or dwelling need about the same care and protective measures as other plants grown there, but special problems may require special treatment.

Brownish or ashy spots on fronds may be caused by an Alternaria fungus, but by ventilating well and refraining from syringing for a time one can often stave

off an attack. Yellow areas on Christmas fern leaflets are likely to be caused by the Taphrina leaf-spot that occurs in gardens along the N. Atlantic Coast. Spraying with bordeaux mixture will control it along with tip blight and some other fungous troubles. Scale insect infestations (see below) may bring black molds which live on the honeydew exuded by the scales and, if abundant, tend to "suffocate" as well as disfigure the ferns. Anthracnose affects Boston ferns, causing frond tips to turn brown and shrivel. Remove diseased fronds, give the plants plenty of space and keep their tops dry until the trouble is checked.

Several blister-rust fungi of fir (which see) have different ferns as their alternate hosts; that is, spores from fir trees infect and cause small reddish or yellowish spots on the fronds in midsummer, overwinter there, and in spring produce other spores that reinfect fir trees. Spraying with bordeaux mixture should help here. See RUST FUNGI.

Of the insects, one of the most noticeable outdoors is the yellow, hairy "woolly

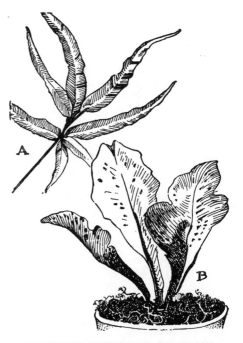

EELWORM SYMPTOMS ON FERNS
Note blackened leaf bases and spots on bird's-nest fern (left), and brown bands on frond of the Cretan brake (right).

bear" caterpillar that feeds on ferns and verbena. Hand pick, or spray with lead arsenate. In greenhouses at least two kinds of thrips may attack ferns. Prompt, thorough, repeated spraying with any good contact insecticide may clean up a light infestation, but a plant overridden with thrips is best discarded and burned.

Several kinds of scale are bad fern pests. The fern scale, common on the underside of Boston fern fronds, is small and pure white in the case of the males and about $\frac{1}{12}$ in. long, pear-shaped and light brown in the case of the females. The hemispherical scale, much larger, convex, and brown, appears on both fronds and stems of various ferns. The soft or terrapin scale, oval, flat and semi-transparent, infests rubber plants, ivy and other house plants as well as ferns. And related mealy bugs may cause trouble. Sometimes scales are carried by ants, so if the latter are numerous, poisoning them with one of the preparations made for the purpose may help to keep the ferns cleaner. An old but still approved scale control is spraying with lemon-oil in warm water, then washing it off after 3 or 4 hours. Some of the improved white oils can be used, except on susceptible ferns such as the maidenhair. In greenhouses, fumigation (which see) may be the most effective and convenient measure.

A disease caused by nematodes or minute eelworms (which see) can be recognized as brownish or blackish bands extending between the side veins of the fronds, or in some cases by irregular discoloration which may spread over an entire leaf, killing it. There is no cure, so infected leaves, or even plants, should be promptly removed and burned. Attacks on the bird's nest fern can sometimes be cured by putting the whole top of the plant in hot water (110 deg. F.) for not more than 15 minutes. Of course, only nematode-free plants should be used in propagating.

Growers of ferns from spores may be bothered by various fungi that attack the prothallium or first stage. As some

FERN SCALE
Do not confuse the grayish-brown hemispherical scale-insects common on house ferns with the fruit-dots which some species bear.

of these are borne by soil or the water in it, fern spores should be sown only in sterilized soil. Another fungus appears to be transmitted on old frond fragments, so it is well to sift spores free of all such material before sowing them.

CLASSIFICATION OF FERNS

Though the study of the classification of ferns may be looked upon as a matter for the scientist, it is not essentially difficult, and will add interest to the growing of these decorative leafy plants.

As already stated, the minute spores, which correspond in a way to the seeds of flowering plants, are borne in spore-cases (*sporangia*) which in turn are clustered into plainly visible fruit-dots, called *sori* (one alone is called a *sorus*). These are the brown dots found on the backs of the leaves of such ferns as the holly fern and lady fern; halfway up the frond in what look like brown crumpled leaves in the interrupted fern, and on a separate stalk in the grape fern and others. Each sorus is usually covered by a lid called an *indusium,* which splits or falls off when the spores are ripe.

While the veining and cellular structure of the fronds and the habits of root and stem growth also affect the determination of genera and species of ferns, for the practical gardener's purposes, the fruit-dots and indusia alone serve as a reliable index to the classification of the hardy native ferns he is apt to grow in his garden.

Among the more common ferns, the polypodies, the beech ferns, and the cloak ferns plainly exhibit their yellowish or brownish spore-clusters on the underside of the fronds, without protecting indusia.

The bracken and its related greenhouse species, also the various hardy and hothouse maidenhairs, the cliff-brakes, and the lip ferns have their naked spore-clusters disposed under the backward-curling edge of the pinnae.

The wood ferns or shield ferns, of which the "fancy fern" of the florist is typical, have very distinctly marked indusia, either kidney-shaped or nearly round with a depression on one side. The common wood fern, the mountain wood fern, the male fern, the marginal shield fern, Goldies fern, the fragrant fern, the crested fern, the New York fern, and the marsh fern are of this type, the last two having much smaller fruit dots than the others.

By their circular indusia, attached at the centers, the popular Christmas fern of our E. woods, its Canadian cousins, the holly ferns, and the various dagger ferns of Florida and the West Coast are recognized. From one of this genus the usually sterile Boston fern of greenhouse origin was derived. Smaller indusia, that appear to the eye as mere dots, mark the delicately-cut bladder ferns.

Circular indusia fastened all round their edge and splitting at the top when ripe into irregular lobes that fold back and suggest a crude star pattern, distinguish the rock-loving woodsias.

The large group of spleenworts possess rather large and prominent, separate and sparsely scattered, indusia, usually linear and sometimes slightly curved. The harts tongue fern (rare in this country) resembles the spleenworts in fructification, but is a larger and entire-leaved species.

The "flowering ferns" are so called because of their habit of producing fertile fronds so contracted and altered in appearance, at least in the fruiting part, as to lose all suggestion of a leaf and rather to resemble a flowerlike spray or cluster of seeds. The royal fern, the cinnamon fern, and the interrupted fern are the only N. American species of this genus, but they are among our most valuable garden ferns.

Rattlesnake ferns, grape ferns, and adders tongues form another related group: low-growing types with naked spore clusters held erect in little spikes or panicles and with almost always a single frond forking into fertile and sterile segments.

FERN SOCIETY, AMERICAN. This group was organized in 1893 with nine members as the Linnaean Fern Chapter of the Agassiz Association, and became the American Fern Society in 1905, when its membership was about 150. Its purpose is to extend to its members both technical and · popular information about ferns and related plants.

The Society maintains an herbarium of 5,000 sheets and a lending library. Members exchange specimens and make field trips together. The Society publishes the *American Fern Journal*, an illustrated quarterly.

Annual dues are $1.50. The secretary is Mrs. Elsie G. Whitney, New York State Museum, Albany, N. Y.

FEROCACTUS (fer-oh-kak'-tus). A cactus genus of very spiny, often large forms including the so-called Barrel Cacti which in most cases are so large that they are suitable only for very extensive and complete collections. Other of the smaller growing species may well, however, be included in any collection, where they will prove very desirable plants, either for pot or garden culture.

F. johnsoni has beautiful large yellow flowers.

F. uncinatus wrighti is one of the smaller sorts; its beautiful spines make it most interesting, even without considering its unusual flowers which are of a peculiar reddish chocolate marked with white lines. *F. grusoni,* one of the most beautiful, is completely covered with yellow spines that make it a veritable ball of gold. Although it attains large size a small specimen forms a most attractive plant.

All these are of the desert type and fairly hardy. For cultural directions see CACTUS.

FERRARIA (fe-ray'-ri-ah). A genus of small bulbous plants from S. Africa, belonging to the Iris Family. If planted 6 in. deep in a warm sunny border, they will survive winters if not very severe. In cold regions they may be lifted and stored like gladiolus. The flowers last but a few hours, but open in succession.

F. undulata has wavy leaves about 1 ft. long, and greenish-brown flowers 2 in. across. *F. atrata* has ribbed leaves and dark reddish-purple flowers. *F. uncinata* has narrow leaves, hooked at the top, and flowers of greenish-brown.

FERTILITY. In gardening this may refer either to the ability of a plant to bear good crops or flowers, seeds, or fruits, or to the state of the soil as regards its plant-food content and a physical condition that makes this food available to plants. In general a soil is fertile when (a) it is well supplied with plant food, part of which is in available form; (b) it is well supplied with humus (which see); (c) it is well drained but at the same time assured of a sufficient supply of moisture for the needs of the plants; (d) it is well aerated; (e) it contains the microscopic organisms (bacteria, etc.) necessary to vigorous, healthy plant growth; and (f) it is free from substances that interfere with plant growth, such as toxins, alkali, excessive acidity, or harmful bacteria, fungi or insects.

One of the principal tasks of the gardener is to endeavor to get his soil into that condition and then maintain it so.

FERTILIZATION (of flowers). The union of male reproductive body (pollen) with female reproductive body (eggs) to produce offspring (seeds). Do not confuse with pollination (which see) or with fertilizing in the sense of improving soil by increasing its fertility or supply of available plant food.

FERTILIZER. Any material which supplies nutrients to growing plants is a fertilizer. Strictly speaking, the term includes farm manure which must first be decomposed before the nutrients become available to the plant. Most gardeners, however, make a distinction between manures and fertilizers. In classifying fertilizers, such terms as artificial, natural, mineral, chemical, prepared, and manufactured, all have their limitations, and even the terms organic and inorganic must be qualified. Commercial fertilizer is generally thought of as manufactured or processed material sold in bags (or bulk loads), as contrasted to fresh or rotted unprocessed manure sold in bulk. Manure which is dried, shredded and bagged is a commercial fertilizer.

ORGANIC AND INORGANIC

Organic fertilizers are substances produced by animals or derived from plants and include animal excrement, carcasses, blood, bone, and other packing house by-products, refuse from fisheries and fish oil factories, and oil meals left after extraction of vegetable oils (e.g. castor pomace, cottonseed meal), and brewery and tobacco wastes. Among the sewage sludges, activated sludge is a fertilizer, but digested sludge is not, as it is used primarily to improve the physical condition of the soil. Materials such as straw, leaves, garden refuse and garbage, when composted, are known as artificial manures.

Inorganic fertilizers include products derived from natural mineral deposits (e.g. Chilean nitrate of soda), manufactured or synthetic products (e.g. Arcadian nitrate of soda), and by-products of steel mills and factories.

Materials used primarily to improve the soil's physical condition, or to change its reaction, are considered soil amendments, but to the extent that they supply a needed nutrient they are also fertilizers. Most fertilizers furnish one or more of the three elements most commonly deficient in soils; namely, nitrogen (denoted by the chemical symbol N), phosphorus (P), and potassium (K). These are not present in elemental form, of course, but are chemically combined with oxygen and/or other elements, both in the fertilizer bag and in the soil. It is the custom in the U.S. to give the analysis of fertilizers in terms of nitrogen (N), phosphoric acid (P_2O_5), and potash (K_2O), and these major nutrients are always listed in that order. Thus the figures 5-10-5 mean: 5 per cent nitrogen, 10 per cent phosphoric acid, and 5 per cent potash. A fertilizer analysis shown as 0-15-30 means no nitrogen, 15 per cent phosphoric acid, and 30 per cent potash. Fertilizers which contain all three nutrients are known as complete fertilizers. Those with only one or two nutrients are called incomplete or special fertilizers.

No fertilizer nutrients come in pure form. They all contain other substances some of which may play only a minor role in plant nutrition, have no value, or may be harmful in certain situations. For example, muriate of potash is an excellent source of potassium, but the chloride it contains is injurious to certain crops.

MAJOR NUTRIENTS

Nitrogen. Generally speaking, nitrogen is considered to be the most important of the three major plant nutrients for these reasons: (1) The quantities ordinarily procurable by plants from natural sources for immediate use are limited; (2) the nitrogen demands of plants are often in excess of the supply in the soil; (3) it has always been the most expensive of all plant foods to purchase; (4) at the same time it is the only plant-food element that can be procured and whose supply can be maintained in the soil by cultural practices.

Nitrogen Fertilizers. Listed in the approximate order of interest to home gardeners, they are:

Nitrate of soda (16 per cent N, all water-soluble). This is a popular, quick-acting nitrogenous fertilizer. As it is fully soluble it can be leached out readily by rains or heavy irrigation. It is best applied as a side dressing (on the surface along the side of the row) during the growing season. Apply small doses at 2 to

4-week intervals. This fertilizer leaves a basic residue, hence tends to make the soil more alkaline. It also has a tendency to destroy the granular structure of the soil, and result ultimately in a puddled condition. Used in moderation, however, the effect is slight and can be ignored. Formerly, all nitrate of soda came from natural deposits of crude nitrate in Chile; but now much of the commercial supply is synthetic, being produced by fixation of nitrogen obtained from the atmosphere.

Ammonium nitrate (33½ per cent N, fully water-soluble). One-half of the nitrogen is in the form of ammonia which becomes partially fixed (chemically combined) in the soil and does not readily leach out. For most crops the ammonia must be oxidized to the nitrate form by soil bacteria before it is taken up by the plant roots. Thus it is slower acting than nitrate of soda. Ammonium nitrate increases soil acidity, requiring about 36 pounds of limestone for each 100 pounds of fertilizer to counteract the acid residue.

Ammonium sulfate (20-21 per cent N, fully water-soluble). As all of it becomes partially fixed in the soil it is slower acting than ammonium nitrate. Ammonium sulfate leaves a strong acid residue in the soil, 100 pounds of the fertilizer requiring about 106 pounds of limestone to counteract this acidity. Where an increase in acidity is desired, ammonium sulfate is an excellent material to use, providing the presence of the additional nitrogen is not objectionable.

Urea (40-46 per cent N, is a water-soluble, organic form of nitrogen). Like ammonium sulfate it is partially fixed in the soil. Because its nitrogen has to be converted first to ammonia, and then to nitrates, urea is more slowly available than is ammonium sulfate. Under favorable conditions of temperature and moisture, however, the process is fairly rapid. Urea is acid-forming to about the same degree as ammonium nitrate.

Cyanamid (21 per cent N, it contains calcium cyanamide and hydrated lime). Cyanamid is a synthetic product having a non-protein form of nitrogen which, when added to the soil, is not readily leached by rain until it is converted into available form (nitrates), a process that takes place slowly. Cynamid has a neu-

tralizing effect on the soil, 100 pounds being equal to about 62 pounds of calcium limestone. Cynamid is toxic to plants for a short period after application, and can be used to kill weeds. It will kill desirable vegetation if used carelessly and at sufficiently high rates. To obtain maximum benefits and avoid injury to plants, follow the directions.

Urea-formaldehyde compounds (38 per cent N, only slightly water-soluble). These materials are designed to release their nitrogen slowly, one application supposedly being sufficient for the entire growing season. In this respect, the product compares favorably with such organic nitrogen fertilizers as cottonseed meal, castor pomace and activated sludge. As urea-formaldehyde compounds are comparatively new, there is more to be learned of their performance.

Calcium nitrate (nitrate of lime), 15 per cent N; and Ammonium nitrate and lime, 20.5 per cent N (sold as ANL), are synthetic products containing lime. The nitrogen is quickly available and the fertilizer does not change the acidity of the soil.

Organic nitrogen fertilizers include the following products which vary in nitrogen content from about 5 to 10 per cent: castor pomace, cottonseed meal, linseed oil meal, tankage, fish meal and activated sludge. Blood meal, and hoof and horn meal usually contain about 13 per cent nitrogen. All of these materials tend to release their nitrogen rather slowly, and they all contain 1 to 2 per cent phosphoric acid. All but activated sludge contain about 1 per cent potash.

Phosphorus. Phosphorus promotes root development in young seedlings and the production of fruit and seed in older plants. It is usually present in the soil in inadequate quantities, hence must be included in most fertilizer programs. Phosphorus compounds are fixed (i.e., chemically combined in the soil) thus do not leach out readily. For this reason they may be applied at any season except when the ground is frozen.

Phosphorus fertilizers are listed as follows for home gardeners:

Superphosphate, 16-20 per cent available phosphoric acid is made by treating raw rock phosphate with sulfuric acid to make the phosphorus more available.

Superphosphate consists of mono-calcium phosphate and gypsum. Although strong acid is used in its manufacture, the end products are natural salts; and for this reason superphosphate has relatively little effect on soil acidity.

Raw bone meal, contains 3-4 per cent nitrogen, and 20-25 per cent phosphoric acid. *Steamed bone meal,* contains 1.5-2.5 per cent nitrogen and about 20-25 per cent phosphoric acid. The latter is more quickly available than the raw product.

Rock phosphate, 25-40 per cent total phosphoric acid. This is the basic material in the manufacture of superphosphate, and is sometimes applied in finely ground form directly to the soil. Because of its low rate of availability, rock phosphate seldom supplies enough phosphorus to meet the needs of a rapidly growing crop.

Basic slag, 14-16 per cent available phosphoric acid, is not usually obtainable for home garden use.

Precipitated bone phosphate, 30-42 per cent available phosphoric acid, is more likely to be used by farmers than by the home gardeners.

Potassium. Potassium is less likely to be deficient in the average soil than is nitrogen or phosphorus, especially in regions of low rainfall. However, in humid climates, and especially where root crops and legumes are grown, potassium is very much needed, particularly on sandy and peaty soils. Potassium performs vital functions in plants, especially in the formation and movement of carbohydrates.

Potassium fertilizers are listed as follows for home gardeners:

Muriate of potash or potassium chloride, 50-60 per cent potash, is the most common potash fertilizer, and is suitable for virtually all crops. In those situations where chlorine is objectionable, such as tobacco culture, growers use *sulfate of potash,* 48-50 per cent potash. Either form is suitable though for the average home gardener.

Sulfate of potash-magnesia and *potash manure salts* are additional sources of potassium, but are not generally available to the home gardener.

Potassium glass or frit, 35 per cent potash is a newly developed, slowly available potassium fertilizer. It offers much promise for use in greenhouses, on house

plants, and in small gardens, but it is not likely to become popular for farm use because of its high cost.

Granitestone meal has been found in some instances to be a satisfactory source of potassium provided it has a potash content of at least 7 or 8 per cent. Because of its slower availability rate, it is necessary to use rather high applications —around 100 pounds per 1,000 square feet.

Woodashes, when protected from leaching by rain, contain 4 to 7 per cent potash, and 1 or 2 per cent phosphoric acid, and are a good source of potassium. They also contain lime which is equivalent to about 60 pounds of limestone per 100 pounds of dry ashes; but when lime is not wanted it is advisable to use woodashes sparingly, if at all.

Leached woodashes may contain only 1 per cent potash and 30 per cent limestone equivalent, hence are of less value as a source of potassium. Leached woodashes are about half as effective as unleached ashes for supplying lime.

SECONDARY AND TRACE ELEMENTS

Calcium, magnesium and *sulfur* are called secondary nutrients (elements) because they are usually less likely to be deficient in the soil. They are just as essential to plant growth, however, as are the major nutrients. A deficiency of one or more of the secondary elements may limit plant growth even though the major nutrients are abundantly present.

Trace elements are nutrients required in extremely small quantities, although they are as essential to plant growth as the major and secondary nutrients. In some cases as little as a pound or two to the acre spells the difference between crop success or failure. Manufactured mineral fertilizers are apt to be lower in trace element content than those fertilizers derived from either natural mineral ores or organic materials. The trace elements that are essentials to plants are: boron, cobalt, copper, iron, manganese, molybdenum, and zinc.

FACTORY-MIXED FERTILIZERS

Factory-mixed fertilizers are indispensable to modern agriculture and very useful to the home gardener as well. Home mixing is possible, and in some instances may result in a cost saving, but the labor involved seldom justifies the practice. Factory-mixed fertilizers usually contain a number of products so selected as to provide the various nutrients in the proportions required for any particular analysis. Choice of ingredients is governed in part by their blending properties and, of course, cost is an important factor. Frequently the same nutrients is a single mix come from several different materials. For example, nitrogen may be supplied by nitrogen solution alone (concentrated form of soluble nitrogent), or it may come from urea and sulphate of ammonia, or from urea, ammonia nitrate and castor pomace.

Fillers are usually included in mixed fertilizers, not as adulterants, but as conditioners and dilutants—substances which are quite essential to the mixing of commercial fertilizer. The fillers in present-day fertilizer mixes usually contain lime and organic material such as dried, digested sludge, rather than sand, as was formerly the case.

Labels. The purchase of fertilizers should be governed by the chemical analysis of the product as shown on the label rather than by brand name. State laws require the registration of fertilizers, and a package label giving the guaranteed analysis, i.e., the percentage of nitrogen, available phosphoric acid, and water-soluble potash present. In the case of organic materials, the label must state the total, rather than available, phosphoric acid content.

Brand Differences. Differences between fertilizer brands having the same analysis lie chiefly in the choice of ingredients used rather than in overall quality. These differences have little significance for ordinary use, and a 5-10-10 of one brand is likely to be as good as the same analysis of any other brand. However, in the more specialized fields, differences in fertilizer ingredients need to be taken into account. For example, the grower who wants a fertilizer containing slowly acting organic nitrogen needs to know whether the nitrogen comes from urea or a more slowly available material such as castor pomace or blood meal. Unfortunately this information is not usually provided. Claims of trace elements in fertilizer may be discounted.

Fertilizer Use

Slowly available organic nitrogen is recommended for lawns, or slow-growing ornamental shrubs and trees. The alternative is to apply a mineral fertilizer in smaller repeat doses. This will supply the needs of the plant during the growing season without having too high a concentration when the plants are small.

Soil tests and the crop grown should be the basis for determining the fertilizer analysis required. However, in the small garden, a general purpose mix such as 5-10-5, 5-10-10, or 5-8-7 will usually be satisfactory. The large garden or lawn may have need for more than one grade of fertilizer. Because soils, crop requirements, climate and weather differ widely, it is impossible to give specific directions on fertilizer usage, and unwise to generalize. However, a rough guide is as follows:

Annual flower and vegetable crops—30 to 50 pounds of 5-10-10 fertilizer per 1,000 square feet, worked into the soil before seeding or planting. If farm manure is used, cut the fertilizer treatment in half.

Biennial and perennial plants—20 to 30 pounds of 5-10-10 per 1,000 square feet broadcast on the surface between plants in the early spring and worked in well with a hoe.

Lawns—10 pounds of 10-10-10 or 10-5-5 per 1,000 square feet in early spring, followed by 2 or 3 applications of about 8 pounds each, using same material. If a highly organic material is used, one 20- to 25-pound application may be sufficient for the season.

Flower pots—½ to 1 tablespoon of 5-10-10 for 5 and 6 inch pots, or use soluble fertilizers. The latter are fertilizer materials which come in either dry powders which can be dissolved completely in water, or as concentrated liquids which must be diluted with water. While both are expensive, the quantity required per application is relatively low.

FERULA (fer'-oo-lah). A genus of perennial herbs of the Parsley Family most of which are valuable only as sources of gums or medicinal products. One species (*F. communis*) known as Common Giant-fennel, is sometimes planted for ornament. It has finely cut leaves, bears flattish clusters of yellow or greenish flowers, and makes a striking background in the wild garden. It is easily started from seed sown in rather moist ground. Near a pond or streamside the foliage produces a charming effect.

FESCUE (fes'-keu). Common name for Festuca, a genus of temperate-zone perennial grasses some of which have become naturalized in N. America. They will grow in sandy soil and moderate shade and for this reason some of them are frequently used in lawn seed mixtures for these special conditions. With one exception, however, the fescues, though low growing and durable, tend to form tufts or bunches unless sown very thickly or with other quicker-growing kinds.

The exception is Chewings Fescue, a creeping New Zealand variety (*fallox*) of the Red Fescue (*F. rubra*). It forms a low dense mat-like turf of fine, bristly leaves brownish green in color and long wearing even under hard usage. It is therefore popular for lawns, putting greens and golf course fairways. There is another creeping type of Red Fescue, but being less dwarf and coarser than Chewings it is less desirable, even though a brighter green.

The other species most often used are: Sheeps Fescue (*F. ovina*), Hard Fescue (*F. duriuscula*), and Tall or Meadow Fescue (*F. elatior*). All these tend to form a bunchy turf and are therefore unsuited for lawns though sometimes used in grass mixtures for shady places and for meadows and pastures.

FETTER-BUSH. Common name for *Lyonia lucida,* an evergreen shrub of the Heath Family with white or pink flowers; found from Va. to La.

FETTICUS (fet'-i-kus). Another popular name for Corn-salad (which see), a pot herb or salad plant, botanically a variety of *Valerianella locusta.*

FEVER-BUSH. A common name for *Benzoin aestivale* also called Spicebush, a native yellow-flowered, red-berried shrub found from Me. to Tex.

FEVERFEW. Common name for *Chrysanthemum parthenium,* a hardy perennial of shrubby, leafy habit, strong-smelling but an old-time garden favorite. There are several varieties showing variation in height (1 to 3 ft.), color of foliage, and the form of the white flowers from single to double. Readily grown from seed.

FEVERWORT. A common name for Triosteum, a genus of weedy perennials with inconspicuous yellowish or purplish flowers, commonly called Horse-gentian.

FICUS (fy'-kus). The Fig. Trees, shrubs, and woody vines, widely distributed in tropical and warm-temperate regions, belonging to the Mulberry Family. Some are grown as ornamental plants under glass and outdoors in the warmest parts of the country where *F. carica* is grown for its sweet edible fruits. Propagated by cuttings and layers.

PRINCIPAL SPECIES

F. benghalensis (Banyan) is a large tree of India, growing to 100 ft. high, and with a huge spread when its aerial roots take hold in the soil to form secondary trunks. It is one of the wonders of the plant world.

benjamina (Benjamin-tree) makes a small neat tree for the greenhouse, with slender drooping branches and thin shining leaves.

carica is the common Fig (which see), often grown in pots or borders under glass, and outdoors in mild climates for its edible fruit.

elastica grows to 100 ft. high in the tropics but is largely grown under glass as a decorative pot plant familiar to all as the Rubber-plant, which see.

pumila (Creeping Fig) is a prostrate or climbing shrub with close-clinging stems and small leaves. Good on greenhouse walls and useful in hanging-baskets. The fruiting branches have much larger leaves and stand erect.

quercifolia is a more or less prostrate grower with oak-like leaves.

lyrata is a vigorous attractive house plant with large fiddle-shaped leaves, often called by its former name, *F. pandurata.*

religiosa (Peepul-tree) is the Sacred Tree of India, growing to 100 ft. high.

rubiginosa is a large Australian tree which extends its top by aerial roots like the banyan. It has leathery leaves, covered with a rusty down beneath, and makes a good pot plant when small.

parcelli is a bushy plant with thin light green leaves, marbled with creamy-white; the best of the variegated-leaved species.

sycamorus (Pharaohs Fig) is the sycamore of the ancients. It is a large round-headed tree native in Egypt and Syria, and will grow outdoors in Fla.

FIELD-BALM. A common name for *Nepeta hederacea,* also known as Ground-ivy, a hardy, useful ground cover.

FIELD MOUSE. A common enemy in orchards and less so in gardens, injuring trees and smaller woody plants by gnawing the bark at or near the ground surface in winter. For control see MICE.

FIESTA-FLOWER. Common name for *Nemophila aurita,* a purple or blue flowered annual which blooms from spring to fall.

FIG. A small tree or large spreading bush (*Ficus carica*) of warm-temperate climates grown for its pear-shaped, so-called "fruit." This is actually a swollen, hollow receptacle with a small opening in the end opposite the stem, completely lined with tiny flowers which develop into the true fruits—the "seeds" of the fig.

Though under favorable conditions the plant will stand temperatures of 20 or even 15 degrees F., and though it has been wintered successfully as far north as Conn. and S. Mich. when protected by being laid down and covered with earth, it cannot be counted a good risk north of Washington, D. C. From the Chesapeake peninsula S. along the Coastal Plain, in the Gulf States and on the Pacific coast it is a favorite garden and local market subject and from the warmer parts of these regions the fresh fruit is to some extent shipped to N. markets. In California the Smyrna fig is grown commercially for drying. (See below.)

North of Washington, D. C., plants are sometimes grown outdoors during summer and dug in late fall with large balls of earth which are kept moist in a cool cellar until spring; the plants are set outdoors again when the weather becomes settled. They may also be grown in tubs moved in and out as the weather demands, and they are often grown in greenhouses, being treated like hothouse grapes with their branches trained horizontally to save space and in-crease the yield. So handled, a plant may be expected to ripen two or even three crops in a year.

Though figs may be grown from "seeds" taken from fresh "fruits" the product of the resulting plants is so variable that desir-able varieties are propagated mainly from dormant wood cuttings taken from mature trees in winter or early spring. For best results these should be 4 or 5 in. long, cut through their nodes and set with their tips even with the soil surface. In good soil

they will be ready to transplant to the nursery row (and set 2 ft. apart) the fol-lowing spring; the next year they can be planted in their permanent positions 18 to 25 ft. apart.

Though the fig does best in heavy soils well supplied with moisture, especially in

THE LUSCIOUS FIG
Ornamental and useful in mild sections. Left, fruiting branch with its characteristic leaves; right, an ancient tree, still bearing.

the Gulf States, it may be grown success-fully in a sandy soil if firmly packed, as in door-yards, and kept moist by occasional watering. Under these conditions eel-worms (see NEMATODES) give less trouble than in light, loose, dry soils. Shading the soil, mulching deeply, and irrigating during dry spells also promote growth and fruit production.

Ordinary figs produce fruit anywhere in the regions mentioned, but the high quality Smyrna fig fails except where a small wasp (see below) is present in numbers. It enters the immature figs, pollinates the flowers and causes the development of the fleshy fruit to edible size. Since the dis-covery of the part this insect plays in fig production and the development of methods of raising it and establishing it in orchards, the growing of Smyrna figs for drying has become a large, successful commercial activity in S. Calif.

FIG-MARIGOLD. Common name for the large and variable genus of mostly S. African, drought- and heat-resistant plants called Mesembryanthemum, which see.

FIG WASP. The palatability of the Smyrna fig depends on the pollination of the flowers (which line the *inside* wall of the so-called fruit) by a small wasp (*Blas-tophaga psenes*) imported from Asia Minor for this purpose. If the flowers are *not* fertilized seeds do not form and the characteristic flavor is lacking. The female fig wasp comes from the male tree (called the caprifig) covered with pollen, to lay her eggs in the fleshy receptacles borne by the female trees, where the pollen is dropped or rubbed off against the flowers. The male wasps are wingless and never leave the tree in which they develop from larvae in small galls. The females gnaw their way out of their galls, and become covered with pollen as they emerge and seek the small opening at the end of a fig. Formerly figs containing mature wasps were strung among the branches of the Smyrna fig trees, but because this spread brown rot, a fungous disease, the wasps have of late years been reared in sterile incubators, taken to fig orchards and there released.

FIGWORT. Common name for Scrophularia, a genus of strong-smelling herbs or subshrubs, widely distributed in the N. hemisphere, and so named because of their supposed medicinal value in cases of scrofula. They are scarcely showy enough for the flower garden, but are suitable for the wild garden.

S. lanceolata is a native species growing to 8 ft., with rather narrow leaves and clusters of small green and purple flowers. *S. marilandica,* also a native, grows to 10 ft., with grooved stems, large dark green leaves, and dull purple or greenish flowers.

FIGWORT FAMILY. Common name of the Scrophulariaceae (which see), a family of temperate zone herbs furnishing many subjects of horticultural importance. Flowers are characterized by having the 5 petals fused into 2 lips of unlike form.

FILAMENT. A thread-like body; particularly the anther-bearing stalk of a stamen. See FLOWER.

FILAREE (fil-ah-ree'). Common name for *Erodium cicutarium* (called Red-stem Filaree or Alfilaria) and *E. moschatum* (called White-stem Filaree). Both are European herbs, closely related to the Heronsbills. See ERODIUM.

FILBERT. A common name for the genus Corylus, also called Hazelnut, which see.

FILIPENDULA (fil-i-pen'-deu-lah). A genus of hardy perennial herbs of the Rose Family resembling certain spireas, having very finely cut leaves and small white, pink or purple flowers borne in clusters. They are showy, easily grown plants for the

border, and some species are of such robust growth that they may be naturalized by the borders of streams or ponds. One species, *F. purpurea,* should be given winter protection in the N. It is often forced in pots. All are easily increased by seed or by division.

F. hexapetala (Dropwort), 2 or 3 ft. tall, has a tuberous rootstock, beautiful fern-like foliage, and sprays of delicate white flowers in June and July; *F. rubra* (Queen-of-the-Prairie), growing man-high, a native from Pa. to Ky., has large clusters of small flowers of an exquisite peach-blossom pink; *F. camtschatica,* still taller, has lobed leaves and white flowers; *F. ulmaria* (Queen-of-the-Meadow), an escape in the E. States, has cut leaves, white-woolly beneath, and white flowers in dense clusters; *F. purpurea,* to 4 ft., one of the handsomest of the species, has pink or purple flowers, while var. *alba* has white blossoms, and var. *elegans* white flowers with prominent red stamens.

FILMY FERNS. A family of delicate, usually diminutive, plants having a single layer of cell tissue, which produces a transparent texture through which the veining and bristle-like receptacles for the fruit dots can be seen. They include only two genera, Hymenophyllum and Trichomanes, distinguishable only by very minor characteristics. Dripping cliffs and dank ravines are their habitat, and a moisture-laden atmosphere is quite essential for their growth. Hence the few temperate-zone species are far more abundant in S. England and Ireland than in America.

Plants of both genera require the same treatment: shallow soil, sand-stone chips, and fine peat; and species of Trichomanes need a sandstone rock on which to take foothold. The difficulty is to keep the soil from going sour under the necessarily copious sprinklings and syringings; the chief safeguard against this is a very fine light soil. The terrarium is the obvious and most suitable place for growing these plants. Specialists can supply several species, but all are much alike. Of those listed below the first is the most difficult to grow, but too famous to be omitted from a collection.

Hymenophyllum tunbridgensis (T u n - bridge Fern). One of the smallest, native in England and the Azores and the W. Indies. Oblong pointed fronds, 1 to 3 in. long, with compound forking pinnae and very delicate threadlike stipes.

demissum. A gem from the S. Seas, having 6 to 12 in. fronds, narrowly triangular and fruiting copiously.

Trichomanes radicans (Irish Fern, Killarney Fern). A native of S. U.S., having 4 to 10 in. fronds, deeply cut, from threadlike creeping stems.

The large New Zealand Filmy Fern belongs to the genus Todaea (which see). It takes its common name from its transparent texture.

FINGER-AND-TOE DISEASE. A common name given to club root of cabbage and other crucifers. See CLUB-ROOT; CRUCIFER.

FINGER GRASS. Common name for Chloris (which see) a genus of ornamental and forage grasses. See also ORNAMENTAL GRASSES.

FINOCCHIO (fi-noh'-ki-oh). Native (Italian) and popular name for Sweet or Florence Fennel (*Foeniculum vulgare,* var. *dulce*), grown for its edible thickened leaf stalks. See FENNEL.

FIR. Common name for the genus Abies, hardy evergreen trees of the Pine Family and mostly of cool latitudes. They are generally conical and of particular beauty in youth. Their upright cones and flat leaves distinguish them from the Spruces, which have pendant cones and angular leaves. New cones are showy, varying with different species through bright shades of purple, violet, blue, red-brown and green. Their branches are stiff and the foliage is bristly to the touch.

Firs are attractive in the garden while young, but they should be carefully placed if you do not intend to move them later. In the lawn they are more suitable for grouping in the background than for use as specimens in open area. If happily situated as to soil and exposure, some species maintain their fine appearance into maturity while others become thin and unsightly. Their fibrous root system permits transplanting them even in large sizes. Most firs prefer moist soil which is kept cool by shading from the sun. Like most other evergreens they are not often pruned but may be made denser by removing the terminal buds of the branches, which causes the laterals to develop side branches of their own. Species are propagated from seed and the varieties by grafting.

ENEMIES.—Firs are subject to all the common wood and root diseases of conifers (see EVERGREENS) but though important in

forests and wood lots, they are rarely serious in ornamental plantings.

Eight species of blister rust fungus occurring on needles of fir require certain ferns (Aspidium, Polypodium, Onoclea, Phegopteris, Asplenium and Osmunda) as alternate hosts. Another rust fungus of fir causes a witches' broom disease of species of Vaccinium. In the West still another rust fungus completes its life cycle on poplar.

The most important of the rust diseases is a witches' broom which dwarfs young twigs and causes upright laterals to develop into a broom-like growth. Species of Stellaria and Cerastium (chickweed) are alternate hosts so should be destroyed. Prune off all infested fir branches.

A needle-cast disease of Douglas fir causes yellow tips on the older needles during the winter and brown mottling in the spring. Remove and destroy infected needles and spray with bordeaux mixture in the spring.

Of the few insects that attack ornamental firs, the spruce budworm may injure balsam fir and the spruce mite attack various kinds. See EVERGREEN; MITES; SPRUCE.

PRINCIPAL SPECIES

A. alba (Silver Fir), whose lustrous green needles are whitish beneath, becomes a large tree but is not good in the E. States, usually losing its lower branches and becoming thin at the top.

balsamea (Balsam Fir) is a very hardy species, common in wet soils northward. Attractive in youth it loses its lower branches, particularly in warmer regions and drier soils. Its dwarf var. *hudsonia* is even better for home grounds.

cephalonica (Greek Fir) does best from N. Y. southward but is susceptible to sunburn in winter, so prefers a sheltered location on a wooded north slope.

concolor (White Fir) is one of the most desirable species, holding its dense lower branches to maturity in a rich well mulched soil and enduring heat and dry weather in a good moist location. Its needles are bluish and the new growth is light colored, giving it a more cheerful appearance than that of most evergreens. This is enhanced by the smooth and light gray trunk and branches. There are varieties with golden-yellow needles when young (*aurea*), with pale yellow needles (*wattezi*), with shorter thicker needles than the type (*brevifolia*) and of globular form especially suitable for the garden (*globosa*).

homolepis (Nikko Fir) from Japan is hardy and much planted. Symmetrical and attractive while young, it becomes more open and develops a rounded head with maturity.

TWO ORNAMENTAL FIRS
Above, a branch of the Balsam Fir, with violet-purple cones; below, one of the White Fir, whose numerous varieties have needles in silvery, yellow, and bluish tones. At the right, a fir in its typical mature form.

lasiocarpa, an alpine fir, thriving in the N. W. and Canada, is a good tree for large groups. var. *compacta* is dwarf, compact and of slow growth, suiting it to limited garden areas.

nordmanniana (Nordmanns Fir), a hardy decorative tree from the Caucasus, is rather slow growing and needs protection from strong winter sun; it may lose some foliage in New England in severe winters.

pinsapo (Spanish Fir), not entirely hardy but suitable where there is some shelter.

spectabilis (Himalayan Fir), ornamental with its large, violet-purple cones and good for the central S. States.

veitchi, a hardy species from Japan, particularly ornamental in its youth especially if made denser by trimming. The unusually long needles are crowded together giving it an appearance of great density. The large purple cones are borne on quite young trees. Var. *olivacea* has green cones and is particularly attractive because of its rich olive color.

China-fir is Cunninghamia; Douglas- or Red-fir is Pseudotsuga; Joint-fir is Ephedra; Summer-fir is *Artemisia sacrorum* var. *viride*.

See also ABIES; PSEUDOTSUGA.

FIRE or FIRE DISEASE. A name given to the botrytis blight of tulip, which see.

FIRE BLIGHT. A serious bacterial disease affecting apples, pears, quinces and many ornamental shrubs, among them shadbush, Japanese quince, cotoneaster, hawthorn, evergreen California holly, species of prunus, firethorn, rose and spirea. Affected portions are black or brown with the appearance of having been scorched. In spring the blossoms may be blighted and the twigs die back rapidly, with dark, drooping leaves. During the summer infection may spread to the larger limbs and main trunk where "hold over" cankers may form in which the bacteria may survive the winter. The disease is spread chiefly by insects, especially bees, and by wind-blown rain.

The blossom blight phase may be controlled by spraying with a weak bordeaux mixture (1-3-50) just when the blossoms are entering the full bloom stage. Otherwise eradication is the chief means of control. To effect it break off or prune out blighted blossom clusters and remove all diseased limbs and twigs, cutting *several inches* below the visibly blighted part. After each cut disinfect the pruning tool. Corrosive sublimate alone (1 to 1000 dilution) may be used, but the following formula is better for the tools; corrosive sublimate 1 oz.; mercuric cyanide 1 oz.; add this to 4 gals. of a mixture of 3 parts glycerine and 1 part water.

Large cankers may be treated with zinc-chloride during the dormant season as fol-

FIRE BLIGHT ON APPLE TWIG
This serious disease strikes first at the ends of twigs and shoots whence it spreads to the larger branches unless wilted parts are promptly pruned off with sterilized tools.

lows without resorting to surgery: to 1 qt. hot water (*in an enameled container*) add 3 oz. concentrated hydrochloric acid and stir thoroughly; in this dissolve 9 lbs. dry zinc chloride powder; when cool mix with 7 pints denatured alcohol. Store this mixture in tightly stoppered glass containers and apply with a paint-brush to the cankered area and to apparently healthy tissues for 6 to 10 in. beyond the margin of any canker.

FIREBUSH. Another common name for the genus Pyracantha better known as Firethorn, which see.

FIRE-PINK. Common name for *Silene virginica,* a native perennial species of Catchfly or Campion, with sticky-hairy foliage and scarlet or crimson flowers all summer.

FIREPLACES, GARDEN. These bring to gardens the same vital element which the indoor fireplace brings to a room. Besides being a never failing source of interest and pleasure as a center around which to congregate (especially at night), an outdoor fire is a genuine convenience when entertaining. Such fireplaces may be of simplest construction, of any suitable material available, though rough stones merit first choice. These are best laid dry; cement blocks or bricks will require laying with mortar.

As always, the draft is important, since a fire burns no better outdoors than in, if it is faulty. Face the open side—which must be open from the ground up—towards the prevailing summer wind (normally this blows from the south and southwest), and place an iron grill or grate from an old stove at the height it is desired to have the fire itself. The grate is held in position by the next course (or courses) of stone, which must extend at least 10 in. higher. Upon these, across the top, broilers are laid for cooking.

FIRETHORN. Common name for Pyracantha, a genus of shrubs, mostly thorny, native in S. Europe and Asia, belonging to the Rose Family, and sometimes known as Firebush. Where hardy they are beautiful shrubs for various purposes—as climbers against a wall, for forming a hedge, or as dense bushes in the shrub border. They show to particularly good advantage on a slope. A sunny position in well-drained soil suits them best. Sudden browning or blackening and die-back of twigs is due to fire blight (which see), a bacterial disease

common on apple and several ornamental shrubs. Prune out diseased shoots well below the infected area with pruning shears dipped in a disinfectant, such as a mercuric bichloride solution, between each two cuts. Lacebugs, especially prevalent in the Midsouth, are controlled with contact insecticides.

Only *P. coccinea* and its varieties can stand much frost, these being fairly hardy

SCARLET BERRIES ALL WINTER
Mantled with white bloom in early summer, the firethorn in fall becomes studded with orange-red fruits that stay for months.

as far N. as Mass. Propagated by seed, cuttings, layers and grafting.

PRINCIPAL SPECIES

P. coccinea grows to 6 ft. as a bush, or to 20 ft. against a wall. It has oval leaves an inch or more long, and is of striking appearance in fruit, with berries of bright red. Var. *lalandi* is hardier, more vigorous, and has showy orange-red fruit.

angustifolia has long slender, often prostrate branches, narrow leaves gray beneath, and bright orange or brick-red berries.

gibbsi grows to 10 ft. or more, with shining leaves and large red berries in abundance. Var. *yunnanensis* has smaller red berries which ripen later and remain until spring.

crenulata grows to 20 ft., with lustrous bright green leaves and orange-red berries. Var. *flava* is a form with yellow fruit.

FIREWEED. Common name for *Epilobium angustifolium,* a species of Willowherb, which see.

FIRMIANA (fur-mi-ay'-nah). A genus of Asiatic trees of the Sterculia Family, resembling plane trees and grown as lawn specimens in the S. Known also as Phoenix-tree or Chinese Parasol-tree, which see.

FISH. In any decorative body of water —artificial pool, natural pond, tank or water course—it is essential to establish and maintain a colony of fish to check the breeding of pest insects, mosquitos particularly. The mosquito must have water in which to breed; the rafts of its tiny eggs hatch in 15 days and the wriggling larvae, unless eaten by fish or other aquatic creatures or killed by oil on the water surface (a measure certainly not to be considered in the lily pond), soon change into the vicious (and sometimes disease-bearing) winged state.

The usefulness of fish in eliminating this insect hazard has been officially recognized by many really garden-minded communities whose ordinances require any builder of a garden pool or other water feature to stock it with an adequate number of fish.

The choice of fish is wide but, naturally, species should be selected that will not injure the roots of delicate plant material. The goldfish is by virtue of its hardiness, cheapness and varied beauty of color and form, the most practical. In a pond of any size, with half-way decent protection from enemies, goldfish breed prolifically and are able to subsist entirely on the natural food —mostly insect larvae—of the pond.

The many interesting and pretty species of tropical fish now available and the popularity of the indoor aquarium has led to the widespread practice of using tropicals in the outdoor pool during the summer for mosquito control and keeping them in the indoor tank during the winter months for their decorative qualities. Large fish breeding establishments now sell unnamed tropicals under the term "mosquito fish."

FISHBONE THISTLE. Common name for *Cirsium diacantha*, one of the Plumed Thistles; a coarse prickly biennial herb of Asia with purplish heads.

FISH-GRASS. A common name for *Cabomba caroliniana*, an aquarium plant also known as Fanwort, which see.

FISH-HOOK CACTUS. Common name for species of Ferocactus, because of their hooked or barbed spines.

FISH-OIL SOAP. Made by combining fish-oil with water and caustic potash, and often called "whale-oil soap," this material was formerly used as a contact spray; it is now used chiefly as a spreader for nicotine sprays and as a flux for oil sprays. See INSECTICIDES; SOAPS.

FISH SCRAP (dried ground fish, acidulated fish, fish guano). This fertilizer consists of by-products from fish-oil works, fish-canning factories and fish-salting plants, dried, ground or otherwise treated. It varies considerably in composition, containing 8 to 9.5% nitrogen and 5 to 9% phosphoric acid, but gives quick results and is a useful form of organic fertilizer where its characteristic odor does not render it unsuitable for garden use. See FERTILIZER.

FISHTAIL PALM. Common name for decorative trees with leaves spreading at the tips like fishes' tails, belonging to the genus Caryota (which see). Natives of Asia and Australia, some species are planted outdoors in Fla.

FITTONIA (fi-toh'-ni-ah). A genus of tropical perennial herbs of the Acanthus Family grown for their hairy beautifully veined foliage. The small 2-lipped flowers are quite inconspicuous being borne in slender spikes beneath bracts. Fittonias are useful low or creeping foliage plants, often grown beneath the benches in the greenhouse or in shaded parts where few other plants thrive. They should be potted in a soil of equal parts loam, leafmold and sand, kept shaded and grown in a temperature never lower than 55 deg.

F. verschaffelti has dark green leaves beautifully veined with red; its var. *argyroneura* has white-veined leaves, and in var. *pearcei* the leaves are hairless beneath and with carmine veins. *F. gigantea*, to 1½ ft., has short-pointed leaves veined with rosy red.

FIVE-FINGER. Common name for Potentilla (which see), a genus of N. temperate herbs and shrubs of the Rose family, grown in gardens as Cinquefoil.

FIVE-SPOT. Common name for *Nemophila maculata*, a delicate Calif. annual with white flowers bearing a purple spot on each of the 5 lobes.

FLACOURTIA (flah-koor'-ti-ah). A genus of tropical shrubs and trees, sometimes spiny, of no particular ornamental value. One shrubby species has been introduced into California for its edible fruit. This is *F. indica*, to which is given the common names of Ramontchi, Governorsplum, and Batoko-plum. It is not particular as to soil, but cannot stand frost. The small yellowish flowers are followed by cherry-like dark pulpy fruits, used far jams and preserves.

FLAG. A name given to various plants, most commonly to *Acorus calamus*, the Sweet Flag, which see.

The Yellow Flag (*Iris pseudacorus*), not native but naturalized in the N. E. States, grows from 2-3 ft., bearing branched clusters of bright yellow flowers in May and June. It forms large clumps, excellent for margins of water. Varieties are available in the trade.

The Corn Flag is a local name for Gladiolus, which see.

Cat-tail Flag (*Typha latifolia*), more often called simply Cat-tail, is a common luxuriant swamp herb, with long rush-like leaves, a few stem leaves, and the flowers minute, densely clustered in brown cylindrical spikes. It is useful in water gardens and for dried bouquets.

FLAG-OF-SPAIN. A common name for *Quamoclit lobata,* a tropical climbing vine of the Morning-glory Family with crimson flowers turning pale yellow, thus representing the Spanish national colors.

FLAGSTONE PLANTING. This refers to the use of certain special kinds of plants which may be set in the earth in the joints or cracks between flagstones laid, without cement, as pavement. The conditions demand a growth of very low creeping habit and one which is dense and strong in character; for the plants must not be an annoyance underfoot nor be injured by being trodden upon. (See illustrations, Plates 21 and 59.)

Providing it is not overdone, the effect of such planting is very delightful. By limiting the plant surface (after the plants have matured) to one-tenth of the total pavement space there is assurance against overcrowding. Set plants in the middle of the wider joints exactly as if in a border, after lifting the stones on either side; then replace these and tamp them gently down to settle them.

See also PLANTS FOR SPECIAL PLACES.

FLAMBOYANT. A common name for *Delonix regia,* the Royal Poinciana of Fla.

FLAME POPPY. Common name for *Meconopsis heterophylla,* also called Wind Poppy. An annual with purple-centered red flowers.

FLAME-TREE. Common name for *Brachychiton acerifolium,* a genus of Australian trees of the Sterculia Family.

FLAMINGO-FLOWER. Common name for *Anthurium andraeanum,* a tropical American perennial herb, popular for greenhouse culture, bearing large heart-shaped leaves and a brilliant orange-red to white calla-like bract surrounding the flower.

FLANNEL-BUSH (*Fremontia californica*). A handsome evergreen shrub or small tree of California. Though not hardy N., it can stand a few degrees of frost, but in such regions it should be given a sunny position against a wall. A rather dry soil suits it well. It has small lobed leaves resembling those of a palm and produces a mass of large cup-shaped yellow flowers in early summer. Propagated by seeds and cuttings.

FLAT. A shallow box (a) in which seed is sown (usually indoors), (b) to which seedlings are transferred (pricked-out) as soon as they are large enough to handle, and (c) from which such seedlings are transplanted to a hot bed, frame or outdoors when of suitable size. Flats are especially handy for the small gardener as they make possible more and better work in a given time than any other means of handling seedlings. Back-breaking labor over a frame is eliminated, for they may be brought indoors where sowing and transplanting can be done on tables or benches of convenient height, regardless of the weather. Moisture control is easier than in outdoor beds, with a resulting bonus in better plants. If evenly spaced, the number of plants in flats of uniform size may be estimated at a glance. When it comes time to transplant, each plant may be lifted from the flat with ample soil around its roots.

Flats made from cigar boxes, soap boxes and other miscellaneous containers may be

CONSTRUCTION OF A FLAT

Note space between, or holes bored in, bottom boards to provide drainage. A layer of sphagnum moss prevents loss of soil layer which is two layers—coarse below, fine on top. Leave space between top of soil and edge of flat and use glass cover to promote early growth.

satisfactory in themselves, but they are objectionable because the irregular sizes tend to waste space and because being made of light, cheap lumber, they are not durable. "Standard" flats bought "knocked down" at reasonable prices are much better because they are made of strong wood (cypress or redwood) and cut to fit regulation hotbeds, coldframes and greenhouse benches. Three flats of the usual 16 by 22½ in. size will fit a standard (6 ft. wide) frame with but little waste space. In depth, flats vary from 2 to 4 in., the most useful for vegetable and flower seedlings being 2 or 2½ in. inside measurement. As the seedlings are removed while small, no greater depth of soil is necessary; and any more simply means more weight to carry about.

The bottom boards should be separated by ¼ in. cracks to provide drainage; otherwise several ½ in. well-spaced holes should be bored in the bottom. In preparing a flat for planting, these holes are covered with bits of broken flower pots, just like the hole in a flower pot. A layer of sphagnum moss is then spread over the bottom to prevent the soil washing through. On this, loose friable soil (⅓ loam, ⅓ leafmold or other humus, and ⅓ sharp sand well mixed and sifted) is spread to within ½ in. of the top. After this has been firmed with a brick or block of wood (especially in the corners), a thin (⅛ in.) layer of even finer soil, resifted, is spread loosely on the surface in which the seed is sown. Prior to sowing, however, the soil should be well moistened either with a fine spray or by placing the flat half its depth in water until the soil is saturated; then let it dry until in good shape for sowing.

As the seedlings do not remain long in the flat, the soil mixture needs little or no fertilizer added to it; it is simply a medium for seed germination and as such needs only to maintain the required moisture and temperature conditions.

FLAX. Common name for the genus Linum, from one species of which (*L. usitatissimum*) both linen and linseed oil are derived. Several others are favorite flower-garden subjects, bearing numerous delicate 5-petaled flowers in blue, yellow, white, or red on extremely slender stems.

Placed in full sun in the garden, the plants will bloom abundantly, but will not stand frost. Seeds of the annual species may be sown where the plants are to stand, or they may be sown indoors with the perennials and set in the garden later. Some perennials will bloom the first year from seeds.

L. grandiflorum, with its varieties, is most often seen. This and the blue-flowered flax of commerce are the only well-known annual species. *L. flavum,* with bright yellow flowers, is an excellent half-hardy border perennial. *L. virginianum,* more hardy, but with smaller yellow flowers, is also recommended. *L. monogynum* from New Zealand, with large white flowers, and *L. salsoloides* from the Alps, with white flowers with a purple eye, are showy species although seldom grown. *L. perenne* with blue flowers, sometimes white, is the most reliable hardy perennial of the group. *L. narbonnense* is considered the best of several rock-garden types. The large sky-blue flowers are white in the center and have white stamens.

East-Indian-flax (also known as Yellow-flax, which see) is *Reinwardtia indica.* New-Zealand-flax is *Phormium tenax.* Toad-flax is *Linaria vulgaris.*

FLAX-LILY. A common name for the genus Phormium and sometimes applied to Dianella.

FLEABANE. Common name for Erigeron, a genus of easily grown aster-like annuals and perennials of the Daisy Family.

FLEA BEETLES. A name applied to small beetles which have the hind legs enlarged and can jump vigorously when disturbed. They injure plants by eating very small holes through and into the leaf so that it looks as if peppered with fine shot. The foliage of many garden plants may be so badly eaten that the plants die. Some flea beetles spread diseases by picking up the organisms causing them when feeding on an affected plant and carrying them to healthy plants. Thus the potato flea beetle is known to spread early potato blight. In most cases different kinds of flea beetles attack only closely related plants, but some are general feeders. The adults are small (1/16 to ⅕ in. long), oval in shape and yellowish brown or black in color. The larvae are delicate, whitish, slender, cylindrical worms not over ⅓ in. long, with brownish heads and small legs.

Flea beetles are difficult to control since they do not readily eat foliage sprayed with arsenicals. However, they dislike leaf surfaces covered with any foreign substance, so repellents applied before they do much injury are usually effective. Bordeaux mixture plus arsenate of lead or calcium arsenate applied at ten-day intervals is recommended; or, for dusting, tobacco dust with lime, or a calcium arsenate and monohydrated copper sulphate dust with lime, is suggested by the N. Y. Agricultural Experiment Station.

FLEA BEETLE WORK
The active black beetles, pin-head size, eat many tiny holes in the foliage. Poison sprays kill them, bordeaux mixture repels them.

Seedbeds can be protected with screens of gauze or thin cheese-cloth. Keeping down weeds on which the flea-beetles live in and around the garden is one of the best ways to keep them in check.

FLEECE-FLOWER or FLEECE-VINE. Common names for *Polygonum auberti* and *P. baldschuanicum,* attractive, rapid-growing hardy vines with large clusters of small flowers white and pinkish respectively.

FLEUR-DE-LIS. This, the royal emblem of France, is the conventionalized flower of the so-called German variety of Iris (*I. germanica* var. *florentina*). Loosely the name has come to be used for other Iris species.

FLIES. These are insects of the Order Diptera (meaning two-winged) which includes also the mosquitoes, gnats and midges. This is the most dangerous insect order as far as the carrying of human and animal diseases is concerned, but it numbers comparatively few crop pests. Among those injurious to plants are certain gall flies like the Hessian fly, many fruit flies, various bulb flies, the cabbage, apple, and onion maggots, some root maggots, and a few leaf miners and borers in the stems of plants. Certain flies are beneficial, the so-called syrphid flies being predaceous and the tachinids being parasitic on certain injurious insects. See also INSECTS, BENEFICIAL.

The adult fly is distinguished from other insects chiefly by the single pair of wings; its three body regions are very distinct, and the mouth parts are of the piercing-sucking type. The larvae are legless maggots with chewing mouth-parts, which seldom feed externally on plants, usually living buried in decaying vegetable matter or inside the plants. In certain families the skin of the last larval stage is retained about the pupa as a cocoon; it is called a puparium.

FLOATING FERN. Common name for Ceratopteris, a genus of small ferns chiefly of the tropics, having inflated stipes with large air cells and succulent fronds. Found in ditches and swamps, and suitable only for specialized greenhouse conditions.

FLOATING HEART. Common name for Nymphoides (which see), a genus of aquatic plants of the Gentian Family, much like the large waterlilies in habit of growth, but with small leaves and flowers.

FLOPPERS. A common name used in Bermuda for *Bryophyllum pinnatum,* a fleshly tropical perennial so called from the "dancing in the breeze" of the inflated greenish or yellowish flowers.

FLORAL FIRECRACKER. Common name for *Brevoortit ida-maia,* a Calif. herb of the Lily Family with tubular green-tipped scarlet flowers in nodding clusters.

FLORAS PAINTBRUSH. Common name for *Brevoortia ida-maia,* a Calif. Old-World annual of the Daisy Family, with small red flowers in loose clusters. Also called Tassel-flower.

FLORET. One of the individual usually small flowers that make up a dense flower cluster; in particular one of those comprising the head of a Composite or the spike of a grass. See FLOWER.

FLORIBUNDA. Name given to a type of garden rose by the late J. H. Nicolas, its developer. The combination of especially hardy Hybrid Tea varieties with varieties rich in polyantha or Rambler blood, and careful selection, gave rise to this useful form in which large, brilliantly colored flowers ranging from single to many petalled are borne in clusters over a long season on sturdy, bushy, low-growing plants with handsome foliage. The inappropriateness of the name "Baby Rambler," which some applied to the early developments in this direction, led to Dr. Nicolas' search for a better name for what he considered was a really new and improved race of garden roses, and which is now pretty generally accepted as such.

FLORICULTURE, COMMERCIAL. The growing of flowers for sale, including both cut flowers, potted plants for ornament, and various kinds of decorative material. Flowers are grown either outdoors or under glass, but in many cases greenhouse flowers have largely replaced those grown in the open, because they are available at all seasons, more perfect, and freer from injury by wind and insects. Enclosures of cheesecloth or cotton netting are sometimes used for summer flowers, especially asters; besides protecting from the elements and improving quality, they exclude insect pests that may do actual damage or carry serious diseases.

The bulk of the perhaps 100 million dollars invested in floriculture is devoted to forcing plants for winter trade, the peak demand coming at Easter, with secondary peaks at Christmas and other holidays. There is much variety in the flowers used, with fashions changing from year to year, but with the rose, carnation, lily-of-the-valley, violet, snapdragon, sweet pea, azalea, orchid, narcissus, geranium, tulip, fern and others permanent favorites. Some flowers have special seasons due either to the nature of the plant or to public preference, as the poinsettia for Christmas, the lily for Easter, and established national customs. Growers have learned to hasten or hold back flowering with accuracy for the seasonal trade. They usually locate near large cities and ship to city wholesalers, who distribute to the florist shops. The most important special uses for cut flowers are for funerals, weddings and social events, but the public is gradually, if slowly, coming to the realization that if flowers are an appropriate means of expressing congratulations, condolences and other sentiments, they are also logical and desirable subjects with which to brighten and cheer the home surroundings at all times. And the florist industry's objective is to provide the wherewithal to make this possible.

FLORIDA OLEA. A common name for *Osmanthus americanus,* or Devil-wood, an evergreen tree, native from N. C. to Tex., with fragrant greenish flowers.

FLORIDA SWAMP-LILY. Common name for *Crinum americanum,* an amaryllis-like bulbous herb of the Gulf States with showy white flowers in winter and spring.

FLORIPONDIO (floh-ri-pon'-di-oh). Common name for *Datura sanguinea,* a Peruvian shrub with shining leaves and drooping yellow-nerved, bright orange scentless flowers followed by narcotic seeds.

FLOSS-FLOWER. A seed catalog name for Ageratum, a genus of attractive annuals with fluffy heads of blue or white flowers.

FLOSS-SILK-TREE. Common name for *Chorisia speciosa,* a member of the Bombax Family having narrow toothed leaves, and conspicuous yellow flowers 3 in. across striped with brown at the base; they are followed by pear-shaped capsules filled with seeds covered with cottony or silky floss which is used to stuff pillows. A medium-sized tree from S. America, this plant is frequently cultivated in warm climates, including S. Calif., and sometimes grown under glass in the N. It is propagated by seed or cuttings.

FLOWER. From the gardener's standpoint, the flower is one of the most important features of plant material because of its esthetic qualities—color, texture, fragrance, form, etc. But to the plant it has a different and even greater significance, for it constitutes the reproductive apparatus by means of which the higher plants propagate themselves through fertilization—that is, the union of reproductive bodies—and the production of seed containing new plants in embryo.

The typical flower consists of distinct parts called *calyx, corolla, stamens,* and *pistil,* all borne on the swollen tip (called the *receptacle*) of the stalk. To find these parts look, for example, at one of the phloxes in the garden. Pick off a single flower and examine it carefully. At its base, surmounting the very short stalk (called a *pedicel*), is a green cup which expands and splits into 5 segments. Each of these segments is a *sepal;* the whole structure is the *calyx.*

Just above, or within, the calyx is the colored portion of the flower, the *corolla,* which expands at the top into 5 lobes, each representing a *petal.*

Pull the flower gently apart, and within the corolla, you will find 5 slender stalks, each with a heavy head covered with masses of powder, usually yellow. These are the *stamens.* Their slender stalks are called the *filaments,* because they are usually threadlike, while the powdery mass exuding from the swollen heads (or *anthers*) is the *pollen*. Each grain of pollen is a so-called male reproductive cell, capable, under the right conditions, of fertilizing a female cell and thus creating a seed which gives rise to a new plant.

But how does it do this?

In the center of this little phlox flower you will find a flask-shaped structure, with a bulbous base, a long stalk, and an expanded tip. This is the *pistil*, or female reproductive organ. The bulbous base is the *ovary*, containing the ovules, which after fertilization become the *seeds*. The stalk is called the *style* (the name comes from a Greek word meaning "pillar"), and the expanded tip, the *stigma*.

When the flower is at the right stage for fertilization, the stigma is covered with a sticky substance that holds any pollen-grain that comes in touch with it. Such a grain from a nearby phlox flower is brought there, perhaps, by an insect. Once in place on the sticky stigma, it commences its true life function. It begins to develop a tube-like projection, which pushes itself through the surface of the stigma, extends in length, pushing ever downward, growing through the entire length of the style, until it reaches the ovary at the base. There it seems to seek out an ovule, touches it, and, through a microscopic change in the cells of both the ovule and the tube at the point of contact, fertilizes the ovule, which then develops into a seed.

Many such pollen-grains may light on the stigma of a single flower, send their elongating tubes into the ovary, and thus bring about the development of perhaps a whole capsule-full of seeds. Every plump pea in a pod has been fertilized in this manner; the small flat ones are the ovules which no pollen-tube has reached. Every ripe kernel of corn has been touched by a pollen-tube which has grown all the way down the "silk"—each strand of which is the style of a flower of corn.

Every mature seed gathered from the garden in the fall has become a seed, capable of developing into a new plant, because it has been fertilized by this process just described.

FLOWER TYPES

Not every flower, of course, has its parts arranged like the phlox. Examine a blue-

bell (Campanula), and you will find the ovary as a swollen portion of the receptacle just below the calyx instead of inside the corolla. An ovary so placed is called *inferior*; if it lies within the flower as in the phlox, it is said to be *superior*. In the evening-primrose, the ovary is still farther down, for the calyx forms a long tube with, at the top, 4 green sepals, and, at

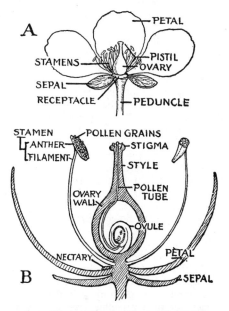

THE STRUCTURE OF A FLOWER
(A) A longitudinal section of a typical flower, showing the sepals, petals, stamens and pistil (the swollen lower part of which is called the ovary), and the receptacle on which the structure rests. The "stem" of the flower is called a peduncle. (B) Detailed structure reveals the nectar frequently found at the base of a petal, the stamen composed of a filament (or "stem") and an anther which bears the pollen grains; the pistil composed primarily of stigma, style and ovary, but showing also the pollen tube which has extended down the style to fertilize the ovule within the ovary.

the base, the 4-celled ovary. All parts of the evening-primrose are in multiples of 4: there are 4 separate petals in the corolla; 8 (2 times 4) stamens are attached to them at the base, and the stigma expanding in the very center is divided into 4 sections.

Flowers of the buttercup have a less definite number of parts. While the sepals are usually 5, the number of petals in different species ranges from 5 to 20; the stamens are numerous and of indefinite number, and the ovary is split into many single-celled units called *carpels,* which arise in a thimble-like mass from the receptacle.

In the Lily Family, the flower-parts run characteristically in 3's. Think of the Easter lily which adorns the table in spring. Or look closely at one of the scillas when it comes up in the garden in spring; or, in midsummer, one of the tiger lilies in the border. In either of these you will find no definite calyx, but only a spreading, funnel-shaped corolla with 6 pointed lobes. Botanists call 3 of these lobes the calyx and the other 3 the corolla, but the word *perianth* (which in any flower refers to the calyx and corolla, or "floral envelope," together) is a more convenient term.

In flowers outside the Lily tribe, if either the calyx or corolla is apparently lacking, scientists always assume that it is the corolla that is missing, and call the existing part of the perianth, even though it be colored, the calyx. Such is the case in many members of the Crowfoot Family —anemones, marsh marigolds, and most species of clematis. The showy colored portions of these flowers are therefore not petals, but sepals.

In some cases, the showy parts of the flower are neither petals nor sepals, but still different structures known as *bracts,* which stand between the true leaves of the plant and the perianth of the flower. Sometimes they resemble leaves, as in the leafy branch half-way up the stem of an anemone. Sometimes they resemble sepals, lying close beneath the flower, as in hepaticas. In other cases they resemble petals, as in dogwood and poinsettia.

A large aggregation of bracts, such as that which upholds the flower-head of a chrysanthemum or thistle, is called an *involucre.*

The Composite "Flower"

In the Composite, or Daisy Family, to which asters, chrysanthemums, thistles and many other familiar plants belong, each "flower" is really a *head* consisting of innumerable flowers, or *florets,* as can be seen in the common field daisy. Each tiny part in the golden center of the head is a complete and perfect flower, called a *disk-flower,* with a calyx consisting of a narrow crown; a tubular corolla with 5 teeth to indicate the petals; usually 5 stamens, and a pistil containing a single ovule, with a style cleft into 2 arms.

Also, every white strap-shaped "petal" bordering the daisy is a separate flower, sometimes simpler in structure than those in the center, but a flower nevertheless and known as a *ray-flower.* The dandelion head consists of ray-flowers exclusively; so do those of most "double" chrysanthemums and dahlias. The ageratum head, on the other hand, consists only of disk-flowers, and thistles, ironwood, and gayfeather are also in this class. In the cornflower (Centaurea), the marginal flowers take on the aspect of rays, but retain the tubular character of the disk-flowers. The head is one of several ways in which flowers may be arranged. For others see INFLORESCENCE.

"Regular" and "Irregular"

A glance at the flower of an apple tree, a petunia, or tulip, reveals each part duplicated around the circle. That is, all the petals are alike in form, and other parts correspond to them. This symmetry gives them the name of *regular* flowers. In an *irregular* flower there is variation in the shape. An orchid, for instance, has one petal often developed into a lip, as in the cattleyas, or into a pouch, as in the lady-slippers.

The snapdragon and lobelia are other types of irregular flowers; in them, 2 petals are united into an upper lip and 3 petals into a lower lip of distinctive form. In the sweet pea (in virtually all members of the Pea Family, in fact), while the sepals are fairly regular, 2 of the petals are united to form an upright "keel" which encloses the stamens and pistil; 2 more form "wings," one at either side of the keel, and a fifth is broadened out to form the "standard" or "banner," which stands at a right-angle to the keel. Flowers of the garden nasturtium are made irregular chiefly by the spur, which is an elongated nectar sac developed from one of the sepals.

Inducements for Pollination

If one considers the plant's supreme need to propagate itself, one can find a reason for every type of flower, for with few exceptions each modification is adapted to suit and promote the method of pollination or mode of seed-distribution upon which that flower largely depends.

It is presumed that the showy portions of the flower are designed to attract insects needed to carry pollen on their rough bodies from the anthers of one flower to

Plate 19.   A FOURSOME OF FAIR FLOWERS

Upper left: Glamour, as well as dignity, is added by the foxglove's wands.   Upper right: In spring
the stately Eremurus towers high above other bulbous plants.   Lower left: The clear blue of the
forget-me-not is charming both in the garden and in the house.   Lower right: The long-stemmed
gerbera is rich in mellow shades of orange and apricot.

the stigma of another. The glands of fragrant nectar found in some flowers doubtless serve the same purpose. A moth or a bee or a humming-bird comes to sip the nectar, catches the loose grains of pollen on his body, flies to another flower for another delicious drink, and unwittingly leaves the pollen on the sticky stigma there.

Some flowers have neither petals nor sepals, but seem to rely for attractiveness on a large sail-like organ called a *spathe*. This is the "flower" of the calla, the jack-in-the-pulpit, the scarlet anthurium of florists, and other aroids. In these plants, the actual flowers are minute structures of the simplest sort—a cluster of stamens comprises a male flower, a single-celled ovule, a female flower, and many of these are crowded on the columnar *spadix,* which the spathe more or less completely surrounds.

Some flowers are so particular as to the type of insect performing the pollination that they are especially constructed to respond only to certain ones. The snapdragon, for instance, has a mouth which can be opened only by a bee; a crawling ant can not gain entrance there. Some tropical plants have a throat so long that only a certain moth with a long proboscis can reach the pollen. In the iris, the stigma has been developed into 3 widely separated parts, resembling 3 extra petals, and bearing the sticky surface for receiving pollen more or less underneath a protective shelf. The adaptations of the orchid to pollination by special insects have been the subject of volumes of scientific writing.

The majority of flowers produce more vigorous seed when they have been *cross-pollinated*—that is, received pollen from another plant of the same kind; or at least *close-pollinated* by another flower from the same plant. Yet some are so formed that only the pollen from their own stamens can reach their pistils. Such flowers are said to be *self-pollinated*.

Each kind of flower has its own peculiarities in this respect, and many are the devices employed to fulfill these requirements. In certain flowers, to induce cross-pollination, the stigma does not become sticky until after the pollen is shed; while in others, the stigma may ripen first, receive pollen from outside sources, then, its function completed, dry up at the time the stamens within the same flower begin to shake out their pollen.

When time comes for seed dispersal, some plants provide their seeds with feathery wings (as the dandelion and milkweed), while others, especially such trees as maple, ailanthus, and elm, send their seeds abroad with an airplane style of wing. Other plants arrange to have their seeds carried by means of burs. Seeds of aquatic plants usually have special apparatus for floating, while seeds of some plants (garden-balsam and witch-hazel, for example) are shot out with such force when their capsule bursts that they fall clear of the parent plant where they can start into growth under favorable circumstances or perhaps be carried elsewhere.

Seldom-seen Flowers

One must not think of flowers as confined to those charming blossoms one sees in the garden, fields and woods. All weeds have flowers; all grasses bear flowers, otherwise we could have no grain, for grains (including rice and corn) are the seeds of various grass plants.

All trees have flowers, too; even the pines and spruces, junipers and yews, their flowers developing into cones or "berries" which bear the seeds. All nuts are preceded by flowers which often bloomed unnoticed on the trees.

The flowers of weeds are apt to be inconspicuous and ugly—as in ragweed, pigweed, and plantain; but they are all highly specialized for prolific reproduction—which is what makes these very plants pernicious weeds. In eradicating weeds, especially annuals that reproduce only by seeds, it is therefore necessary to destroy the weeds before the flowers and seeds can form.

The tassels which hang from the oak trees and maples in early spring are the flowers of these trees—one flower being provided with pistils and another with stamens, but no petals being present. Their pollen is always carried by the wind; therefore their fertilization is facilitated by their blooming before the leaves open.

The pussy willows of late winter days are the flowers of willow trees. Each furry "pussy" consists of anywhere from 50 to several hundred flowers. But in this case one tree will bear *only* pistillate flowers, while another will bear only staminate ones. Thus, to have seeds produced there must be a staminate and a pistillate tree near enough for the wind to carry the pollen from one to the other.

FLOWER CLASSIFICATION

The form of the flower is the basis of classification. By this method, orders, families, genera, species, and varieties of plants are identified and named. (See the article PLANT NAMES AND CLASSIFICATION). But is is chiefly the genera and species which are of concern to the gardener, though the identification of certain varieties means recognition of often superior plants for garden use, while a knowledge of the main families of flowering plants is helpful in recognizing and choosing new garden subjects and estimating what may be expected of them.

house, in attempting to develop new forms by the simplest plant-breeding methods.

See also BUD; FRUIT; INFLORESCENCE; LEAF; PLANT; PLANT BREEDING; SEEDS AND SEEDING.

FLOWER ARRANGEMENT. (See illustration, Plate 12.) The varied material for making artistic arrangements of flowers may come from the flower beds of the garden or from the florist shop, from branches of shrubbery or trees, from special types of foliage and berries, and from wayside gleanings. But even if one possessed a wealth of such material, beautiful and artistic arrangements would not be possible unless there were suitable containers in

GOOD FLOWER ARRANGEMENT DEMANDS SKILL—BUT ACCESSORIES HELP
Left, an all too common effect—flat, crowded, ugly. Right, a graceful grouping of the same material. Center, one ingenious type of support that makes artistic effects possible.

Flower characters are fairly constant; yet it is the chance of change that spurs professional horticulturists—and sometimes amateur gardeners—to the eternal effort to produce superior new forms.

Sometimes these appear spontaneously as "sports" or "mutations." Again they may—and often do—result from hybridizing; that is, breeding together different species and varieties (see HYBRIDIZATION). And it is even possible to stimulate changes by subjecting plants to X-rays, radium waves, or other such forces. This last is, however, a new and but little understood field for scientific work and there is plenty of opportunity for the interested amateur, right in his own garden or green-

which to place it, a variety of blocks or holders to support it, and a very sharp knife (that is better than scissors) to clip stems to desired lengths.

CONTAINERS—Pewter vases, tankards, and dishes make charming receptacles for many flowers (notably petunias) white flowers combined with gray foliage and flowers in rich warm shades of red. Copper and brass harmonize well with zinnias in shades of orange—brown and yellow; they are also specially suited to wild asters, autumn leaves, the wayside flowers of summer and early fall and the branches of flowering shrubs and trees.

The stems of flowers may be beautiful seen through water and a clear glass vase,

ROSES FROM THE GARDEN
In a glass bowl, the stems of flowers (with leaves removed) are often an attractive part of the picture.

but if they have a tendency to grow slimy, or the water to become putrid, it is better to place them in a vase where the stems cannot be seen. Mignonette, asters and chrysanthemums are among the worst offenders in this class. Pottery and delicate china are prime favorites and artistic effects can be produced by using dishes that were designed for other purposes, as for example an old china sugarbowl, an opaque green glass salt cellar of chalice shape, old fashioned bottles, jugs, and compotes. Even chargers of pewter or glass may serve as beautiful frames for flowers.

It is necessary to have vases of all sizes, for the quantity of available material as well as its stature varies with the season. There must be plenty of little containers for the first delicate flowers of spring and the last gleanings from the fall garden. Also large dishes for the days when the spring-flowering shrubs come, many and varied vases for the outburst of June and always something slender for the occasional flower that is rare.

As to arrangement itself, everyone experienced in this art knows that it is easier to get a good result with garden flowers than with those bought from the florist. That is in part due to the fact that the seller of flowers tends to discard flowers with curving irregular stems, preferring neat bunches of a dozen blooms with stems of equal length. A dozen "perfect flowers" (from the commercial standpoint)

may bring flowers into the room, but the result is seldom artistic; it is more of a grower's exhibit than a work of art. As a rule, several kinds of flowers combined produce a more interesting result than when all the flowers in a vase are alike.

It is often said that the total height of the flowers above the vase should be one and a half times the height of the vase itself, but that cannot be considered a hard and fast rule. Great latitude must be allowed owing to the variable character of the material. Whenever possible cut the flowers with long stems; they can always be shortened if necessary. Start with the strongest flowers with the greatest height and gradually build up around them, being careful to maintain a center of interest. Add the flowers one at a time, putting each where it is needed and serves a purpose, clipping the stem to the right length. See that there is greater weight below the center of the composition to give stability; slender delicate flowers help to make an interesting silhouette. Do not allow the stems to crosscut, that is, intercept one another; or, if they must, conceal the fact with a spray of leaves or flowers. Take care that the heavier flowers do not make a silhouette that appears to be a series of steps. The block or holder must not be seen unless it is in itself beautiful and actually contributes to the beauty of the arrangement. This it may do in a study where line is emphasized more than form and color, as it is in some Japanese arrangement.

Treat the vase and the flowers as one. This may be done by allowing some of the leaves or the flowers to hang over the edge of the container. A good effect may be achieved by using a leaf or a vine spray of totally different character from the flowers themselves. The leaf of a hosta, a spray of vitis or clematis, or even the coarse leaf of the thistle, the soft gray foliage of the mullein or even the red-green leaf of the garden beet can add a note of real distinction to a vase of flowers that without it looked quite meaningless. Flowers taken at different stages of their development, as buds partly open, flowers in full bloom, and seed-pods likewise add to the interest of the composition.

Choose flowers that will harmonize with the color scheme of the room and the decorations where they are to be placed. If several arrangements are to go into one room see that they are placed where they do not clash. Large and daring combinations can be used on terraces or verandas and baskets of wire or reed grass are good for these; sometimes such receptacles can be made to hold all the flowers that "had to be picked," whereas a daintier container indoors will need much more restraint and selection if it is not to appear overcrowded. Judges' arangement-classes at flower shows have decreed that babys breath (Gypsophila) obscures the main design and produces a saccharine result. However, if not bound by such formal considerations one can create real beauty with a vase of gypsophila framing Shirley poppies in a variety of colors or delicate and fragrant sweet peas.

Endless combinations can be made with grasses, weeds, and seed-pods; lasting longer than most cut flowers, these subjects are especially good for winter effects. Smartweed, tansy and marsh grasses are beautiful together. Whereas a favorite combination of early spring flowers is pansies, in shades of blue and purple, with forget-me-nots for delicacy and wallflowers to lend a dash of color. Pink tulips with white narcissus and bleeding hearts placed in a white alabaster vase or bowl make an equisite effect.

When the irises come, place them in heavy pottery dishes, tall and with not too large an opening. Combine them with other flowers on the large side such as delphiniums or foxgloves, with a few peonies to "hold them down." Geraniums are generally regarded as purely garden decoration subjects, but if a dozen plants are planted in the picking garden where they can be cut from at will, beautiful arrangements can be made with the sprays. This illustrates how a single variety of flower can be placed so as to achieve a beautiful result, due to the interesting line of its branches.

A nicotiana, inclined to look aggrieved a good part of the day in the garden, remains beautiful all day in the house and its graceful branching leaves are most lovely in a green wall-pocket of pottery. Huge gladiolus and dahlias are better as garden decorations than when brought into the house, but primulinus varieties of the former may lend a style to an arrangement as well as a lovely bit of color. Single small dahlias also have unlimited possibilities; their foliage is interesting, the buds add a charm, and their great variety

of color and the grace of the individual flower combine to make them general favorites for interior decoration. Single red dahlias and white eupatorium in a black bowl make an interesting, if simple, combination.

Clusters of bright berries invariably add to the beauty of an arrangement of fall flowers, and a wooden bowl is a good receptacle for a collection of berries of different sizes and colors such as those of bittersweet, euonymous, snowberry, yew, *Ilex verticillata*, and bayberry. Barberries with their bright leaves and berries combine well with the dark wine color of the sumach, the brown balls of the button-bush and a few sprays of corydalis leaves to give delicacy. The whole group would look well rising from a low cluster of gray mullein leaves.

These are but a few of the countless combinations that may be made. A little ingenuity and some experience will enable one to make beautiful pictures of flowers and leaves, that add an air of distinction to the rooms in which they are placed.

HINTS ON FLOWER CARE.—Cut flowers and branches (except those of the so-called everlastings, dried grasses, etc.) will keep fresh and attractive only so long as they are able to take up water from the container in which they are arranged. This they do only through the cut ends of the stems; leaves and small stems immersed in the water do not help, but, on the contrary, tend to decay and produce an ugly appearance and unpleasant odor. They should therefore be removed when the arrangement is made up. If more support is needed than can be given by a basal flower holder, dry stems, twigs or even crumpled paper (if kept out of sight) can be thrust into the container between and around the stems.

The absorption of water by the stems may be interfered with by (1) the normal closing up (callusing) of the ends of the vessels, (2) the growth of a film of bacteria over the cut ends, or (3) the entry of a bubble of air. Cutting off half an inch of each stem every day or two if possible with a very sharp knife blade (scissors tend to crush and close the tubes) removes the sealed up end and any accumulation of bacteria, and gives the flowers a fresh chance to take up water. If this cutting is done *under* water, air is prevented from entering and the beneficial effect is increased. Stem ends should always be cut slanting; this exposes a larger absorbing surface and also makes it impossible for a stem to rest flat on the bottom of a container, thus practically sealing up the tubes.

Some flowers (for example, dahlias, poppies, poinsettias and heliotrope) wilt quickly unless the ends of their stems are seared in a flame or dipped for a few moments in boiling water. In doing this, do not let the heat affect the blossoms. Flowers with woody stems, such as chrysanthemums, benefit from having the end of the stem slit upward for half an inch or so. Some authorities advocate the use of small amounts of different substances such as salt, aspirin, Epsom salts, sugar, etc., dissolved in the water to prolong the life of cut flowers, but others deny that there is any experimental evidence of their beneficial action. Probably the best policy is to employ any such method that you find effective. Certainly, however, a bit of charcoal or other harmless preservative will help to keep the water sweet. In any case, even if the water in a vase is not replaced and the stems cut every day, it is advisable to make the rounds of all the containers in the house each morning with a pitcher of fresh cool water and see that each receptacle is filled to the brim. See also CUT FLOWERS.

FLOWER-FENCE. One of the common names for *Poinciana pulcherrimia;* also, as Peacock Flower-fence, for *Adenanthera pavonina.* See those genera.

FLOWER GUILD. See NATIONAL PLANT, FLOWER AND FRUIT GUILD.

FLOWERING DOGWOOD. Common name for *Cornus florida,* one of the handsomest of native trees, bearing white-, pink-, or red-bracted flowers in spring and red berry-like fruits in the fall.

FLOWERING-MAPLE. Common name (suggested by the leaf form) for Abutilon, a genus of herbs and small shrubs grown, usually as annuals, in greenhouse or garden.

FLOWERING RASPBERRY. A common name given to *Rubus odoratus,* an erect, thornless bramble of the E. half of the U. S. with red, dry, unpalatable berries, but sometimes grown for ornament; also sometimes to *R. deliciosus,* a hardy, also thornless, Colo. species grown for its roselike blossoms.

FLOWERING-RUSH. Popular name for *Butomus umbellatus,* an erect, hardy, perennial aquatic of the Old World but escaped from cultivation in New England. It has leaves 2 to 3 ft. long, resembling those of the iris and rose-colored flowers 1 in. across borne in clusters at the top of a 4 ft. stem. It is readily grown in ponds, or in a moist rich loamy soil. Propagation is by division.

FLOWERING SPURGE. Common name for *Euphorbia corollata,* a white-flowered perennial native from Ont. to the Gulf States.

FLOWER-OF-AN-HOUR. Common name for *Hibiscus trionum,* an annual species of Rose-mallow, growing to 2 ft. and bearing yellow or white, dark-centered flowers.

FLOWER-OF-JOVE. Common name for *Lychnis flos-jovis,* a woolly perennial herb with small pink flowers.

FLOWER POT. Flower pots are containers in which plants are grown, either temporarily or permanently. They are generally made of clay, but for various special purposes may also be made of concrete, peat moss, paper, glazed crockery, glass or wood. Large wooden pots, sometimes square and also called tubs, are used for large foliage plants such as palms, particularly in hotel lobbies and large reception rooms.

Porous clay pots are the standard plant containers the world over. They come in many sizes, from 1 in. in diameter up to 1 ft. or more, and in slightly different shapes adapted to the root systems of various plants. All have a drainage hole in the bottom. The standard and commonest shape is about twice as wide at the top as at the base and as deep as the top is wide.

Seed "pans," bulb "pans" and azalea "pans" are actually shallow clay pots varying from 2 to 6 in. deep and from 6 to 8 in. across. They are used for starting small seeds, rooting cuttings, forcing bulbs and growing shallow-rooted plants.

USING CLAY POTS. Before using new clay pots soak them in water for at least half a day to fill the pores; otherwise they will draw water from the soil and rob the plants. Never pot a plant in an old pot covered with dirt or green growths, either material is unsightly, and interferes with plant growth and may contain disease organisms. Therefore clean used pots thoroughly by scrubbing with a stiff brush (wire if necessary) and hot water. Or the following easier method can be used:

Fill a large crock with as many pots (nested if possible) as it will hold and cover them with water. Add slowly ⅒ as much commercial sulphuric acid as there is water. Let the pots soak for a day or longer, then remove, rinse, scrub with a stiff brush and water, and soak again in clean water to remove all traces of acid. The acid solution may be used for several lots of pots before it loses its strength.

TEMPORARY POTS. Pots made of compressed peat moss are sometimes used for starting plants that do not like to have their root system disturbed when transplanted. They retain moisture and the roots easily

increasing use, especially for house plants. Extensive experiments have revealed interesting facts about the distribution of roots in the soil in porous and non-porous containers, the different rates of evaporation from them, and other factors affecting plant growth. It seems clearly proved that, whereas in greenhouses where the air is moist and conditions are kept uniform, the old style clay pot is entirely satisfactory; for dwellings, hotels and offices, etc., where the air is almost always dry and the temperature liable to fluctuate, the non-porous type requires less attention and less frequent watering, and insures better results

MODERN TYPE FLOWER POTS FOR HOUSE PLANTS
In the dry air of homes, the cement pot (center) and glazed non-porous containers in many attractive styles (right) are found to give better results than the standard porous clay pot (left). The geraniums shown are of the same age and were handled alike in the three pots.

penetrate their walls, which become soft and disintegrate into the soil when they are set out in the ground.

PAPER POTS, made of thin but strong waterproof flexible cardboard or roofing paper, also are used for growing (and especially for shipping) young plants, such as vegetables and annual and perennial ornamentals. Made with interlocking but easily opened bottoms, they too can be left on the plants when they are set out so as to keep the root ball intact. The rim, if allowed to stand slightly above the soil level, helps ward off cut-worms. Some kinds of paper pots will in time break down and let the roots spread into the soil.

NON-POROUS POTS. Non-porous pots of glazed crockery or glass are a rather recent development but they are coming into

and stronger, more vigorous plants. The glazed pots are also more durable and, being available in an almost limitless range of colors and designs, they can be fitted into home decoration schemes and obviate the need for jardinieres or fancy pot covers.

FLOWER SOCIETIES. Growers and lovers of many kinds of flowers have organized to promote the welfare of their favorite subjects. This they do in various ways: By holding exhibitions at which representative specimens of standard and new varieties are shown at their best, singly or in arrangements for the public to see; by offering prizes for the best entries in various classes; by stimulating the production of new, improved sorts; by seeking to standardize types, names and other factors; by conducting trial grounds; by holding conventions designed to bring together those interested; by publishing bulletins or other periodicals and otherwise carrying on educational publicity for the flower involved.

Some of these organizations are composed exclusively of commercial growers; others are mainly of amateur gardeners; still others (probably the majority) have members in both fields. The greater number of these groups are national, but there are some of local scope. Varying greatly in membership, age, scope and influence, activity and other respects, these flower societies as a whole are doing splendid work for horticulture, for gardening and

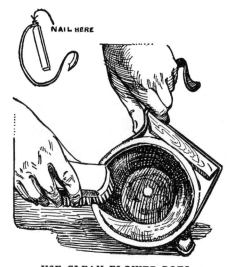

NAIL HERE

USE CLEAN FLOWER POTS
A handy holder for a pot while being scrubbed is a short piece of wood beveled at one end where a 2 ft. length of strap is nailed. Place it around the pot and grasp the free end as shown.

for individual gardeners, who will find themselves well repaid for taking up membership and taking the active part in the societies' work that such membership implies.

The following organizations are briefly discussed in this book under their respective names as given:

Amaryllis Society, American.
Azalea and Camellia Society of America.
Cactus and Succulent Society of America.
Carnation Society, American.
Chrysanthemum Society of America.
Dahlia Society, American.
Delphinium Society, American.
Euphorbia Society, International.
Fern Society, American.

Fuchsia Society, American.
Gladiolus Society, American.
Gourd Society, New England.
Iris Society, American.
Orchid Society, American.
Peony Society, American.
Rock Garden Society, American.
Rose Society, American.
Sweet Pea Society, American.
Watsonia Society of America.
Zinnia Society, National.

FLUORINE COMPOUNDS. Sodium fluoride is used to control household insects, but cannot be used as a spray on plants because of the danger of burning.

Recently, various fluosilicates (compounds of fluorine and silica) have appeared promising as stomach poisons. Barium fluosilicate (1 lb. to 5 lbs. of lime) is used successfully as a dust against the Mexican bean beetle.

Cryolite (sodium fluo-aluminate) is being tried, especially in the West, as a substitute for lead arsenate in the control of codling moth on fruit trees. It has also given excellent results when used for the Mexican bean beetle. Both natural and synthetic cryolite are on the market.

FLY-POISON. Common name for *Amianthium muscaetoxicum,* a member of the Lily Family, with grass-like leaves 2 ft. long and small white flowers in clusters to 4 ft. high. Grown in the wild garden, it should be given a light sandy soil and an open sunny position. It is increased by seeds or division. Both foliage and bulb are poisonous and in the S. a fly-poison is made from the bulb.

The name Fly-poison-plant is given to *Nicandra physalodes,* also called Apple-of-Peru, a coarse, weedy, S. American herb of the Nightshade Family. Formerly grown in S. gardens from which it seems to have escaped in parts of the S. E., it is credited with strong fly-killing powers. Leaves and shoots are pounded up, mixed with milk in a shallow dish, and placed by a door or wherever flies are numerous. The insects are said to consume the bait greedily and shortly to succumb to its effect.

FLY-TRAP, VENUS. Comomn name for *Dionaea muscipula,* an insect-eating perennial found only in the Carolinas. See VENUS FLY-TRAP; INSECTIVOROUS PLANTS.

FOAMFLOWER. Common name for *Tiarella cordifolia,* a species of falsemiterwort, a hardy herbaceous perennial of E. U.S., good for shady places in the rock or wild garden.

FOENICULUM (fee-nik'-eu-lum). A genus of Old-World herbs, of which the species *F. vulgare,* or Fennel (which see), is grown as an annual for its aromatic seeds which are used as a flavoring. Its var. *dulce* known as Florence Fennel or Finochio, is grown for the swollen leaf bases which are cooked like kohlrabi. The young stems of another variety (*piper-itum*), called Carosella, are eaten like celery.

FOLIAGE PLANTS. Under this heading is included a wide range of plants which are grown for the decorative value of their leaves rather than for their flowers. In some cases the foliage is highly and variously colored, as in the genus Codiaeum, the various forms of which are best known in gardens as Crotons. With many others, while the foliage may be green, their general habit of growth, as well as the pleasing character of the individual leaves, renders them of outstanding decorative value.

Foliage plants associate well with flowering plants, and serve to show off their floral beauty to better advantage. In general, they are of a much more permanent character than flowering plants, and on the whole require less cultural skill to secure effective results.

A great many are available for the adornment of greenhouses and conservatories, ranging all the way from such large and permanent occupants as palms, down to the lowly but colorful forms of Rex begonias and the deciduous caladiums. While some of the woody foliage plants require good light conditions to develop their best color, a great many will thrive under shadier conditions than is suitable for most flowering plants. An annual repotting is usually sufficient to keep them in good condition, supplemented by feeding when growth is most active. A sharp lookout should be kept at all times for such insect pests as scale, red spider, mealy bug, and thrips, and appropriate means of control should be adopted as soon as their presence is detected.

PALMS (which see). In general, palms are of easy culture, obtainable in various forms, and most useful and lasting in decorative groups or as single specimens. In large glass structures they may be planted out in beds, but most kinds can be maintained in good condition for some time in comparatively small pots or tubs. They appreciate feeding and should never be allowed to get really dry. The following are good examples, and details concerning them will be found under the respective genera:

Archontophoenix cunninghamiana, Caryota urens, Chamaedorea glaucifolia, Chrysalidocarpus lutescens, Cocos plumosa, Howea belmoreana, Geonoma riedeliana, Licuala grandis, Livistona chinensis, Phoenix roebeleni, Rhapis flabelliformis, and *Thrimax radiata.*

FERNS (which see). This great group of flowerless plants contains a great many notable for their grace of habit and beauty of leaf form. Ferns are highly valued to combine with both flowering plants and cut flowers. In view of their diversity of form and varied shades of color, a greenhouse devoted entirely to ferns can be a place of the utmost attractiveness the year round. The following are mentioned as good examples in their respective groups:

Alsophila australis, Cibotium schiedei, Cyathea dealbata, Dicksonia antarctica, and *Blechnum gibbum.* All these develop trunks of varying length in maturity, and are known as Tree Ferns. Large and well grown specimens are very imposing, and keep in better condition if the trunks are kept moist.

One of the most remarkable of the entire fern family is the Staghorn Fern (*Platycerium bifurcatum*). With its large shield-like sterile fronds and antler-like fertile fronds it makes a noble-looking specimen. The Gold and Silver Ferns (*Pityrogramma calemolanus* and var. *aureo-flava*) are interesting and beautiful, with the white or yellow mealy powder covering their fronds. They keep their color better when not subjected to spraying or drip.

Asplenium bulbiferum has an additional feature of interest in the young plantlets which are formed on the arching fronds; and *Woodwardia orientalis* is another very decorative fern, which produces numerous buds on the upper surface of the fronds from which young plants may be obtained.

Polypodium aureum and the wavy-leaved var. *mandaianum* are vigorous and attractive with their large glaucous leaves: and *P. subauriculatum* makes a very handsome specimen with its long fronds. Very graceful are the various Maidenhairs. *Adiantum cuneatum* and its varieties, *A.*

formosum, A. tenerum var. *farleyense,* and *A. trapeziforme* are of outstanding merit.

Davallia dissecta, D. fijiensis, and *Microlepia platyphylla* are interesting and attractive with their creeping rhizomes and finely divided fronds. There are enough forms of the Sword Fern (*Nephrolepis exaltata*) to make a good collection, and several of the species of Pteris are commonly grown to furnish fern-dishes and are best known in the small state. Forms of *P. cretica, P. serrulata,* and *P. tremula* are well worth growing on to larger sizes.

Selaginella is a genus of fern-like plants, and at least two species are well worth including in any list of foliage plants. *S. emmeliana* makes a compact feathery plant of light green, and *S. wildenovi* can be grown to form a bronzy-blue screen to 20 ft. or more.

HERBS WITH SHOWY LEAVES. Most of those mentioned below grow best under warm greenhouse conditions, where plenty of atmospheric moisture abounds and the light is somewhat subdued. Some are useful grown as ground covers for edging beds or walks, as they are cultivated on benches in pots or pans. Among these are *Fittonia verschaffelti,* with leaves veined deep red, and its var. *argyroneura,* veined white. Colorful forms of Wandering Jew (*Tradescantia fluminensis* and *Zebrina pendula*) grow well beneath benches as well as in more favored places. The striped-leaved forms of *Chlorophytum elatum* are equally good in this respect. Rex begonias in variety and *Peperomia sandersi* show to good advantage planted out in rockwork as well as on the plant tables in pots.

Alocasias make very handsome pot plants. *A. cuprea, A. lowi, A. sanderiana,* and various hybrids are distinguished for the size, shape, and beautiful markings of their leaves. *Anthurium crystallinum, A. magnificum, A. veitchi* and *A. warocqueanum* are magnificent foliage plants when well grown. Fancy-leaved caladiums, forms of *Caladium bicolor* and *C. picturatum,* are showy for conservatory decoration, and may also be used outdoors in subtropical bedding. Calatheas (most of which were formerly called Marantas) can stand a lot of shade and occur in good variety; *C. ornata, C. roseo-picta, C. veitchiana* and *C. zebrina* are among the best.

Cissus discolor shows its highly colored leaves to advantage either trained on a form or grown as a vine. The many colorful forms of *Coleus blumei* may be quickly grown into large handsome specimens for conservatory decoration; they are also grown in large quantity for summer bedding. The Velvet-plant (*Gynura aurantiaca*) produces leaves of good color when grown in a light position in the greenhouse. *Monstera deliciosa, Philodendron andreanum, P. verrucosum,* and *Xanthosoma lindeni* are interesting and attractive members of the Arum Family, well worth a place in choice collections.

SHRUBBY FOLIAGE PLANTS. Some of these are hard-wooded, and while they may be kept in fairly good condition for some years, it is a good plan to keep young plants coming along from cuttings.

Abutilon savitzi is a rather dwarf member of the group, but attractive with silvery-edged leaves, and useful as a summer bedding plant as well as for greenhouse adornment. *A. striatum* var. *thompsoni* is a strong grower with large lobed leaves blotched creamy-white and yellow. The variegated form of *A. magapotamicum* is very useful and attractive for furnishing baskets and vases. *Acalypha wilkesiana* and its varieties make good bushy plants with handsome bronzy-green leaves, blotched or mottled with coppery, orange, red, and crimson shades. *Begonia argenteo-guttata, B. metallica,* and *B. sanguinea* are shrubby species well worth growing for their foliage alone.

The garden crotons (forms of *Codiaeum variegatum*) offer wide variety in leaf-form and coloring. Good companions for them are the highly colored forms of *Cordyline terminalis,* often known as dracenas. Of the true drace-genus, *D. fragrans, D. godseffiana, D. goldieana,* and *D. sanderiana* are outstanding. *Dizygotheca elegantissima, D. veitchi* and *Polyscias guilfoylei* (formerly listed in the genus Aralia) have long been popular for their graceful foliage and in a small state are much used in table decorations. The same is true of the Silk-oak (*Grevillea robusta*) young plants of which are easily raised from seed. The common Rubber-plant (*Ficus elastica*) and its variegated form have long been known for their ability to stand tough treatment; and the same is true of *F. lyrata.* The showiest of the family is *F. parcelli,* but it is not of such robust growth, and its thin leaves, blotched with creamy-white, are rather tender. *Hibiscus rosa-sinensis* var. *cooperi* has leaves marked with crimson and white variegations that are especially showy in young plants. The Screw-pines—species of Pandanus—are very useful decorative plants in the juvenile state, and make imposing specimens when planted out with plenty of room to develop. *P. baptisti* is the easiest to handle, having no prickles; but *P. veitchi* and *P. sanderi* are very popular in spite of their spiny character. *Paullinia thalictrifolia* has delicate fern-like foliage that shows to best advantage when the stems are trained to a trellis. *Sanchezia nobilis* var. *glaucophylla* and *Strobilanthes dyerianus* make handsome plants, with the best leaf-coloring found in young specimens.

ANNUALS (or plants that may be grown as such). A number of good foliage plants, of particular value in summer bedding arrangements, may be raised annually from seed sown under glass early in the year. Gray-leaved plants are always most effective, and prominent among them are the so-called Dusty Millers, including *Senecio cineraria* and its varieties, *S. leucostachys, Centaurea cineraria* and *C. gymnocarpa*. Feverfew or Golden Feather (*Chrysanthemum parthenium*) occurs in various forms of neat compact plants with yellow foliage. For dark crimson foliage effects the highly developed, colored-leaf forms of the garden beet (*Beta vulgaris*) are most effective. *Amaranthus tricolor* var. *splendens* is a striking and colorful plant with leaves of rich red marked with yellow and bronzy-green. Summer-fir (*Artemisia sacrorum* var. *viride*) and Summer-cypress (*Kochia scoparia*) make very neat compact specimens with feathery foliage.

Albizzia lophantha, with straight stem and finely cut leaves, gives a very graceful effect, and young plants of the Blue Gum (*Eucalyptus globulus*) are very striking. *Melianthus major* is attractive with light green leaves of good size cut into 9 to 11 leaflets, while the various forms of the Castor-bean (*Ricinus communis*) are outstanding for bold and stately effects.

HARDY FOLIAGE PLANTS. A number of herbaceous perennials and sub-shrubs with good foliage value could be selected for use in flower gardens and shrub borders. A few examples are cited as suggestions: Old Man (*Artemisia abrotanum*), Old Woman (*A. stelleriana*), and *A. albula,* known as Silver King, give bushy gray and silvery effects. Lavender (*Lavandula*

spica) and Lavender-cotton (*Santolina chamaecyparissus*) are also effective silvery sub-shrubs, good in connection with rock-work. *Cerastium tomentosum* and *Stachys lanata*—the latter better when the flower stems are cut off early—are good for low silvery mats and patches. The old-fashioned Pink (*Dianthus plumarius*) would be well worth growing for its glaucous foliage, even if it never flowered. In some places the blue-green of Rue (*Ruta graveolens*) can be used to produce an unusual effect. The Plume-poppy (*Macleaya cordata*) is too big and spreading for the average flower border, but a clump in a corner, or with shrubs, may be one of the most effective things in the garden, both when in bloom and at other times.

FOLLICLE. A type of simple seed-pod opening to emit its seeds along only one suture. It may occur alone, as in the milkweed, or as one section of a compound ovary, as in delphinium or peony.

FONTANESIA (fon-tan-ee'-zi-ah). A genus of deciduous shrubs of W. Asia, resembling privet in their leaves and clusters of small white flowers. (Both plants belong to the Olive Family.) These shrubs are easily grown in ordinary garden soil, and are readily increased by seed or cuttings. There are only two species, *F. phillyreoides* to 10 ft., only half-hardy N., with small grayish-green leaves; and *F. fortunei,* a taller shrub with glossy leaves held until late in the fall, hardy as far N. as Mass.

FORAGE PLANTS. These are plants grown as feed for cattle whether consumed green or cured as hay. Hence, they concern the farmer rather than the gardener. The principal forage plants belong to the grasses, cereals and herbaceous legumes, especially alfalfa, various clovers, peas, vetches, and peanuts. Some forage crops are also grown as green manures and cover-crops (which see), especially those of the legume group, as they help build up soil by taking nitrogen from the air. See LEGUME.

FORCERS, PLANT. These are appliances by which plants are started, developed, or matured under unnaturally stimulating or favorable conditions; in particular, this means protection from cold and the providing of extra heat, either natural (that of the sun), or artificial (caused by fermentation, fire or electricty). Though this broad definition includes coldframes, hotbeds, and greenhouses, the term is generally restricted to smaller appliances, of which there is a wide variety.

The most familiar style is a small square wooden frame (about 15 by 15 in.), with a tilted, removable glass top, to be placed over cucumber or melon hills in early spring. By its use plants may be started two to four weeks earlier than would be safe or even possible in the open. Besides protecting the plants against frost, it keeps out injurious insects, especially if, as the weather warms up, the glass cover is replaced by wire netting. Such forcers should be opened slightly to provide ventilation on sunny and warm days, otherwise sufficient heat may be developed within them to "cook" the plants. With equal care they must be closed on cold nights.

COLLAPSIBLE PLANT FORCER

The legs of the wire frame are thrust in the soil. The waterproof paper sides and back and the adjustable glass front concentrate heat around the plant.

Other plant forcers include bell glasses or cloches (which see) and numerous patented appliances, some made of cloth, others ("hotkaps") of waxed paper, some of waterproofed cardboard and glass (as illustrated above), etc.

FORCING. Strictly speaking, this means the growing of plants during other than their natural seasons. By extension, it may mean making them grow, bloom, or ripen fruit earlier than they normally would outdoors in the locality. To accomplish these ends the plants may be either merely protected from the rigors of the weather as in coldframes and greenhouses warmed solely by the heat of the sun; or they may be stimulated by increased warmth obtained from artificial sources—fermenting materials (as in manure-heated hotbeds), fires (as in flue, hot water and steam-heated greenhouses), or electricity applied by means of incandescent light bulbs, or specially designed heating cables, plates or other elements.

Imitation of natural growth conditions is not necessarily forcing; it may constitute only the maintenance of favorable conditions during seasons when the plants would normally be active in their native environment—as, for instance, when growing tropical plants in greenhouses during northern winters. On the other hand, the growing of summer-blooming temperate-climate plants during winter is true forcing because it is making them grow during what is for them an unnatural season.

A special application of the term forcing refers to the development of flowers in much shorter time than they would normally require. Subjects so treated are mostly bulbs, corms, tubers and rhizomes which contain stored-up food on which they live while developing the blooms that are often already present in embryo form (see BULB). To force these, about all that is needed is moisture and extra heat, which in many cases develop the flowers before much of a root system has formed. Chief among these plants are lily-of-the-valley, the so-called "Dutch" bulbs (which see) and some tender species of narcissus.

Commercial forcing of flowers and vegetables involves the investment of many millions of dollars. The principal forced plants are roses, carnations, violets, lily-of-the-valley, hardy bulbs, lettuce, tomatoes, cucumbers and radishes. In home greenhouses, forcing pits, hotbeds and coldframes many other flowers and vegetables may be grown. Some of the fruits may also be ripened out of season or earlier than normal — especially strawberries, grapes, loquats, dwarf pears, peaches, nectarines and plums.

Greenhouses devoted to promoting plant development are often called "forcing houses" simply because they are so used. Though commercial vegetable forcing is

HOW PLANT FORCERS HELP

These two cucumber plants are the same age but that at (2) was started early under an individual glass shelter while that at (1) was planted when the weather was warm and grown unprotected.

done in specially adapted houses, amateurs can get good results in any type of greenhouse available and in any climate; other conditions being equal, production will be easier and less costly where the forcing seasons are mild and sunny rather than excessively cold, cloudy or dark because of very short days.

The basic soil mixture for all forced crops should be light, well drained and easily worked; it should contain ample humus to hold moisture and, when possible, be sterilized to rid it of plant disease germs, insects and other enemies (see DISINFECTION). Its plant food content must vary to meet the needs of individual crops, but in general be balanced to promote normal growth. It should be relatively high in nitrogen for "leaf" crops such as lettuce, spinach and cauliflower; stronger in phosphorus and potash for tomatoes, and so on. In addition to meeting these basic requirements, however, the operator must understand the requirements of the plants he wants to grow; for attention to details is far more necessary than when the same plants are being grown outdoors.

The vegetables best suited to home forcing are those classed as "cool plants" because outdoors they can withstand temperatures down to freezing, or even a little lower, without damage if in unheated greenhouses, pits and coldframes. They thrive best under night temperatures of 40 to 55 deg., and the day temperature on sunny days when there is ample ventilation should not exceed 10 to 15 deg. higher than that.

Though all "cool" vegetables may be so grown, the home gardener will naturally limit his choice to those kinds that mature quickly and to varieties whose quality is higher than that available in the market during their forcing season. The vegetables most easily grown include globe beets, forcing carrots, cauliflower, peppergrass, mustard, corn-salad, lettuce, onion sets, parsley, radish, spinach, watercress, sage and chives.

To supply the ordinary sized family one or two rows of seed in a flat will provide enough seedlings of most kinds. These should be pricked out and reset about 2 in. apart in other flats as soon as they have formed their second pair of leaves; about a month later they are again transplanted either into small flower pots or direct into the benches or beds.

Where a night temperature of 55 to 70 deg. can be maintained, "warm plants" may be grown successfully. These include stringless green and wax beans (not limas because they require too long a season), cucumbers, muskmellons, tomatoes, eggplants, peppers, New Zealand spinach, summer squash and vegetable marrow. Two or three plants each of these last two should produce enough for a family.

The beans are sown direct in the benches; all the others are started individually—in small flower pots, paper pots or old berry boxes—and transplanted to the beds when they have developed good balls of roots. They must at no time be checked by a draft or suddenly lowered temperature or they may "sulk" and recover slowly.

Besides these vegetables which are grown from seed to maturity under forcing conditions, there are several others which must be started and grown in the open ground for from one to several years before they are forced. The more important of these are chicory, asparagus, rhubarb and seakale. The first is grown as an annual, seed being sown outdoors in early spring and the roots being dug in late autumn for forcing to produce either *barbe de capucin* or witloof (see CHICORY).

The other three are perennials which must be grown on for at least two years in rich soil and with good care. In late autumn after the tops have died down plants are dug with large clumps of earth, which are allowed to freeze solid (preferably in a coldframe so as to be within convenient reach). Here they remain until 4 to 8 weeks before their shoots are wanted. Then they are brought into warm quarters and planted in soil, peat moss, sand or sifted coal ashes and kept moist. Stalks will develop more or less rapidly according to the degree of heat and moisture supplied. In general, but especially in the case of rhubarb, the forced stems will be found of higher quality and greater tenderness than those developed outdoors.

As the four vegetables last mentioned can be forced without the aid of light they may be handled beneath greenhouse benches or in cellars where the temperature conditions are suitable. The products of such forcing are paler in color as well as more delicate in flavor than those grown outdoors. After being forced, clumps and roots are worthless, so must be thrown away, new ones being dug another year.

FORESTIERA (foh - res - ti - ee' - rah). Trees and shrubs, sometimes evergreen, but not particularly ornamental, belonging to the Olive Family. Those usually grown are deciduous shrubs native from Ill. south. They have inconspicuous yellowish flowers before the leaves, and later dark-purple berry-like fruits. Thriving best in moist locations, they are propagated by seeds and layers. *F. acuminata*, a large native shrub, is hardy in sheltered positions as far north as Mass. *F. ligustrina* is smaller and more tender.

FORESTRY. This embraces the study and practical management of forests, which are plantations of trees grown for timber. It includes not only consideration of kinds of trees in relation to localities, soils, etc., but also details of planting, feeding and protecting from insects and diseases (which activities comprise *silviculture*). It differs from *arboriculture* in that the latter deals with trees in general, or as individuals, not especially in forests.

Forestry has three important divisions: (1) the preservation of standing forests— in small areas or woodlots by systematic thinning and feeding, and in large areas, principally by protection from fire; (2) forestation, or the planting of new forests, not only as sources of timber but also as shelter-belts to check winds and prevent soil drying and blowing, or to help prevent soil erosion and floods; (3) reforestation, the restoring of lands not needed or suited for other crops to woodland conditions. The subject merits mention even in a garden book because of the tremendous value of forests as a natural resource. Forestry is an important department of government activity in relation to the management of private woodlots, to the development of great sections of forest land set aside as public property, and to vast water supply and power site projects, etc., which are directly influenced by forest conditions.

FORGET-ME-NOT. (See illustration, Plate 19.) Common name for Myosotis (which see), a genus of hardy annual, biennial and perennial low herbs, desiring moist soil and partial shade. It is the state flower of Alaska. Cape- or Summer-forget-me-not is *Anchusa capensis;* Creeping-forget-me-not is *Omphalodes verna,* or Navelwort, which see.

FORMALDEHYDE. Also called formalin. A chemical compound valued as a disinfectant and fumigant; first used for seed disinfection purposes in 1895. Today it is used extensively in the treatment of seed potatoes for scab and rhizoctonia, for treatment of grains, and as a soil disinfectant. Commercial strength liquid formaldehyde contains 37 per cent of the chemical. For drenching the soil it is usually used in solution at the rate of 1 part to 50 parts of water. Formaldehyde may also be purchased in dust form under various proprietary names. See DISINFECTION.

FORMAL GARDEN. (See illustration, Plate 20). This designates a garden of geometrical and balanced design, in which plant material chosen for its adaptability to the design's demands, rather than for its own qualities, is used. It is true that between every house and its garden (if the latter is well designed) there exists a space partaking of the character of each, which may properly become a formal garden if desired; for close intimacy with the house is the inception of formal design, of whatever extent. But in the strict sense the term applies to more elaborate treatments than such space is usually accorded, and the broad parterres of palatial grounds are usually the standard by which all formal gardens are judged or considered.

Yet a formal garden is especially adapted to the strict limitation of small dooryard gardens in cities and suburbs, the entire area then becoming an out-of-doors, ground-level extension of the house. The surroundings also make formal design the truly appropriate design here; for this type especially expresses that decorum which is demanded by slight acquaintance as distinguished from the freedom from restraint which prevails between intimates.

Formal garden design must always proceed from the dwelling, taking its rise from the garden front of the house—either by means of a center axis projected from the doorway, the steps or whatever feature gives access to the garden; by a pair of such lines leading from a pair of steps or doorways, if these exist; or perhaps by the extension of wall lines, either in the form of growing hedges, or in the wall material itself. Symmetry and perfect balance are both required in the basic terms; but the pattern may vary in the detail figures or elements—the beds where flowers are planted, or where ornaments of one kind or another find their setting.

It is in the formal garden only that flower beds of definite form, usually numerous

Plate 20.   THE FORMAL GARDEN FOR SMALL SPACES

Top: The close-clipped hedge and the geometric shapes of the flower beds complement the architectural features of the house. Bottom: Colorful and as harmoniously designed as a Persian carpet.

and composing an interrelated and organized pattern when taken together, are truly appropriate. The simplest example possible is furnished by the square or rectangle divided by a cross of walks which may or may not support a central feature where they cross; this walk division produces in turn four lesser squares or rectangles in each corner of the larger or total area. Elaboration of such a balanced and symmetrical basic design would break up these four corner beds or spaces into smaller beds or parts shaped to fit into one another in outline and separated in their turn by walk spaces narrower than the main walks.

This division and multiplication of plots could go on indefinitely if a start were made with a large enough space, and in vast formal gardens it actually is carried to extremes, until the mosaic effect created often suggests a splendid rug or tapestry. Such gardens have indeed been designed deliberately to produce such an effect. But the truly formal garden also finds expression in the much simpler plan of a rectangle or square of greensward filling the central space, with a walk passing around this and borders of flowers on the outer side of the walk. Or a similar effect may be obtained with a circle or ellipse of turf likewise encircled by a flower-bordered walk.

Forms as simple as these are not generally associated in the popular mind with formal gardens, it is true. But *it is never the elaborateness of the design* which determines the type of a garden, whether it is formal or not. It is its character, its true balance and symmetry, the exactness of form in its entirety and in the component parts and details. The importance of form is, of course, paramount in all "form-al" things. And in the formal garden success requires that everything about it be laid out carefully and exactly in the beginning; and that it be thereafter maintained with scrupulous care so that the lines and forms are never impaired.

Ornaments and sculpture, benches, dials, fountains, pools, rills led in definite architectural channels or canals, casinos and every kind of garden shelter may find a place in a formal garden, depending, of course, upon the garden's size and elegance. The smallest city garden may center a pool and a bench and be delightful; while the broad areas of an estate may afford space for all the features named above without crowding or the deplorable effect of clutter. In this regard it is the same with formal gardens as with informal and every other kind: good taste always imposes restraint —restraint in design lest it become over-elaborate and ostentatious; restraint in the introduction of ornament lest a museum collection result; restraint in the choice and use of plant material lest this suffocate the whole, including itself.

Three sets of plants are needed in formal garden making; spring bulbs, early bedding annuals, and late ones, so as to insure all-summer perfection. The flower spaces are therefore completely worked over and newly enriched at least twice during the summer season. This makes unnecessary the continual weeding and cultivating required by the perennial border; and this saving in labor compensates for the extra work of replanting.

See also PLANTS FOR SPECIAL PURPOSES; FOUNTAIN; GARDEN POOL; PARTERRE; TERRACE GARDEN. Compare INFORMAL GARDEN; WILD GARDEN.

FORSYTHIA (for-sy'-thi-ah). Golden Bell. Hardy deciduous shrubs of Asia, belonging to the Olive Family. With their wealth of brilliant yellow flowers appearing before the leaves, they are among the showiest of spring-flowering shrubs. They are not particular as to soil, and do well in partial shade as well as in the open. They have very good foliage value, the slender, clean-looking leaves being carried late into the fall and sometimes becoming handsomely olive or purplish in color. They are propagated by cutting of green or mature wood, and by layers.

Nodular outgrowths, or galls, $\frac{1}{4}$ to 1 in. in diameter caused by a fungus may occur along forsythia stems which should then be removed and burnt.

PRINCIPAL SPECIES

F. suspensa grows to 8 ft. or more, with slender branches often bending to the ground and rooting at the tips. In bloom it forms a golden yellow mound. Var. *sieboldi* has more slender branches, and can be used effectively to clothe a wall or arbor. It is also very effective when trailing over a rock or wall. Var. *fortunei* is a vigorous upright grower, with finely arching branches.

intermedia, a hybrid of *F. suspensa* and *F. viridissima*, includes several useful forms. Among them var. *spectabilis* is a strong grower with the largest and showiest flowers of the group. Var. *primulina* has flowers of a pleasing pale yellow color.

viridissima is conspicuous with its bright green stems and because its leaves turn dark purple in the fall. It is of rather stiff habit, more tender than most, and later to bloom.

ovata is a Korean species, the hardiest and also the earliest to bloom. It has amber-yellow flowers borne singly.

FORTUNELLA. A genus of small tropical evergreen trees related to citrus. See KUMQUAT.

FOTHERGILLA (foth-er-gil'-ah). Deciduous shrubs of N. America, belonging to the Witch-hazel Family. They are well branched, of medium height, and thrive best in moist sandy loam with plenty of peat or leafmold. The flowers, though without petals, present very conspicuous clusters of long white stamens, tipped with yellow anthers. In the fall the leaves assume very colorful tones. Propagated by seeds, cuttings of ripened wood, and also by layers which are slow to root.

F. major, the best known, is a compact roundish shrub to 10 ft. or more. The leaves turn orange yellow in fall. *F. monticola* is of a looser and more spreading habit, with somewhat larger flower clusters. Its leaves turn scarlet and yellow. *F. gardeni* is of dwarf slender habit, with smaller flower clusters, opening before the leaves, which turn crimson in fall.

FOUNDATION PLANTING. (See illustration, Plate 21.) This means the treatment along the foundations of buildings where it is necessary or desirable to hide unsightly cellar walls and that barren stretch along the foot of the wall where it is seldom possible to induce grass or other ground cover to grow. The need for covering or masking walls is growing less as architects and home builders tend to lower house foundations until the first floor of the dwelling is virtually on the ground level. But even so, the judicious arrangement of well-chosen plant material is often highly desirable (if not demanded) to frame the building, tie it to the site, and make it appear an intrinsic part of its environment.

There has been an unfortunate and rather general feeling that foundations are, in themselves, eyesores and ought to be completely hidden from view all the year around. This is the belief that brought about the use of masses of evergreens along buildings of various kinds everywhere. Whether it is a sound theory and whether it is reasonable to use evergreen material in such close relationship to buildings are questions that need earnest study and frank answers.

Of course, there are foundation walls that are ugly and that seriously detract from the appearance of the building they support. But to hide completely an element that is as vital to the permanence and soundness of a structure as the base on which it stands is illogical. There must appear openly, at certain points anyway, enough of the base to reassure the eye.

Granting, then, the necessity for covering as much as may reasonably be hidden, the question remains: How is this to be done? What shall decide *where* the foundation shall remain visible and where it shall be covered? What proportions shall there be of the two areas?

Here the ground plan, or form, of the building comes into the picture. For it is the outside corners of this plan that furnish the starting points from which planting shall advance along each of the walls. But it is not enough merely to set a row of plants from each corner each way along each wall. *Never plant in straight rows anywhere along a foundation.*

Instead, start at the corner with a group of plants pointing like an arrow from the corner outward. The distance along each wall to which these plant groups should extend may be determined by the general lines of the building as viewed from a little distance, the door and window openings and other details being also taken into consideration. On a long stretch, it is well to leave an opening and then plant a lesser group for a distance of perhaps not quite twice the opening's length. The grade may influence these; likewise such a break as the wing of a building which will form an inner corner or, more properly, a bay.

This brings up a second important consideration, namely: *Inside angles or bays should invariably be kept free of planting altogether.* The only possible exception is an ivy or other wall-climbing plant, set far enough from the corner itself to insure this being always free, clear and clean-cut straight to the ground.

The second question stated early in this article referred specifically to evergreens.

but it is really concerned with the type of plant material most suitable for use in foundation planting. It may be said promptly and emphatically that deciduous shrubs provide the ideal material, and that *nothing else will ever fit the situation as well* as selections from this great group. The available variations in size and in form; the individuality which is interesting yet not aggressive; the diversified texture of foliage and leaf color in summer and equally diversified and often brilliant coloring of the bare branches throughout the winter; the delight of spring and summer bloom, and the added beauty of many extremely decorative fruits or berries which remain throughout the winter—all these things combine to insure true picture composition.

For example, in planting from an outer corner each way along two walls, as well as directly outward from the corner itself (as explained above), the taller shrubs would first be used at the corner itself. Lower ones would take their places against these and still lower kinds against these here and there to bring the mass down to the ground as it comes outward from the building. This is the guiding principle in such a planting; yet it does not imply a regular descent. Fortunately, the inherent irregularity in the shrubs and the tendency of certain species to grow into different shapes as they mature help overcome such a tendency. In brief, a foundation planting suggestive of a natural thicket growth disciplined to a moderate degree furnishes more perfect reconciliation of house to ground than any other treatment. It serves to hide foundations (where this is desired) as effectively as the once popular evergreen mixtures.

In such a mass planting shrubs of the largest size (at maturity) which will occupy rear positions, may stand 3½ to 4 ft. apart. Others will need to be placed not more than 3 ft. apart on the average. Remember that none are planted to develop as fine specimens; each is secondary in importance to the thicket or mass effect. When that reaches maturity it should present uninterrupted continuity.

It is occasionally not amiss to introduce an evergreen a little apart from such a group but in relation to it though not directly against the foundation wall. When placed near buildings these subjects are likely to outgrow their positions in a very little while; then they have to be taken out or cut back, which mars the composition irreparably. Also it should be remembered that the needle-leaved evergreens are always a sharp accent, in their form as well as in their color, wherever they appear. And while there are appropriate places in the garden for accents, as well as for accent groups, a series of accents is not desirable anywhere, and is never the proper treatment for a foundation or other wall.

See also SHRUBS; PLANTS FOR SPECIAL PURPOSES.

FOUNTAIN. In its broad sense this means, rightly, a *source* of water; common usage applies it more especially to flowing water itself as it issues in a jet or bubbles from an aperture. At one time popular in the jet form as a feature set in the midst of a lawn without regard to any further garden elements or design, fountains were rather speedily abandoned in America, partly because of their extravagant demands for water, and also because of difficulties caused by severe winter weather. In the modest garden, largely because of the first of the two reasons given, they have been too ambitious an undertaking for many to attempt.

However, it takes very little water to maintain a dripping overflow from the basin of a wall fountain into a lower spill-basin or small pool, once these have been filled. Or to permit the spilling over of a broad, low bowl set on a pedestal in the midst of a pool of slightly greater circumference into which its contents fall. This is called a *tazza,* and owing to its still serenity as well as the fascinating sense of abundance which its ever brimming lip inspires, it is perhaps the best form of fountain to be chosen for a garden of limited area and intimate surroundings.

FOUNTAIN GRASS. Common name for *Pennisetum ruppeli,* a perennial grass related to millet but grown for ornament.

FOUNTAIN-PLANT. A common name for *Russelia equisetiformis;* also called Coral-plant or Coral-blow; a tropical American shrub with clustered, tubular red flowers, popular in S. gardens and also grown in N. greenhouses.

FOUQUIERIA (foo-ki-ee′-ri-ah). A genus of somewhat cactus-like plants of the semi-tropical, desert Southwest. See CANDLEWOOD.

FOUR-LEAF WATER-CLOVER. A common name for a species of Pepperwort

Plate 21. FOUNDATION PLANTING HELPS A HOUSE

Top: Harsh corners are softened and too great height brought down by the aid of carefully chosen plant material. Bottom: Smoothly shorn shrubs accent the doorway's welcome, while well-placed plants give unity to the picture of house and grounds.

(which see). It is a small aquatic plant with four clover-like floating leaves.

FOUR-LINED PLANT BUG. This sucking insect, one of the true bugs (which see) is generally considered an enemy of currants but it also attacks many weeds, ornamentals, garden vegetables and even fruit trees E. of the Rocky Mountains. The young nymphs are bright red and the adults greenish yellow with four distinct black stripes down

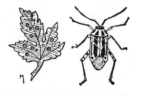

4-LINED PLANT BUG
The injury it causes on a chrysanthemum leaf (reduced) and the pest itself (twice natural size).

the wing covers. The eggs winter over in slits in the canes of currants and other plants and hatch in late spring. The feeding of the young bugs causes small whitish dots on the upper surfaces of the leaves, which may turn brown and drop off while new growth may wilt. Kerosene emulsion, nicotine and pyrethrum sprays may be used to kill the nymphs, but frequent and thorough sprayings will be necessary. Nicotine dust may prove effective.

FOUR-O'CLOCK. A common name for *Mirabilis jalapa,* a tender tuberous-rooted perennial usually grown as an annual. The name refers to the fact that its variously colored flowers open in late afternoon. It is also called Marvel-of-Peru. See MIRABILIS.

In some places the same name is given to spiderwort (*Tradescantia virginiana*).

FOUR-O'CLOCK FAMILY. Common name of Nyctaginaceae, represented in gardens by *Mirabilis jalapa,* the Marvel-of-Peru.

FOXBERRY. A common name for *Vaccinium vitis-idaea,* a hardy mat-forming shrub with white or pink flowers and red berries of cranberry flavor.

FOXGLOVE. (See illustration, Plates 8, 19, 29.) Common name for Digitalis, erect biennial or perennial herbs whose stately spires have been favorites in gardens for many generations. Natives of Europe and W. Asia, they have been widely and successfully grown in N. America, and have occasionally become naturalized. Their long spikes on stems 3 or more ft. high are crowded with large thimble-like flowers all drooping toward

one side and beautifully spotted on outer or inner surface. Foxgloves are useful for naturalizing among shrubs or placing in the background of a hardy border. *D. purpurea* has important medicinal use as a heart stimulant.

Easy to grow in the garden, so long as they have some shade, foxgloves will thrive in any ordinary soil. They are generally propagated by seeds or by division following the cultural rules for perennials. Seed for biennial species may be sown in the spring or summer, producing flowering plants the second season.

Leaf spot may be prevented by spraying with bordeaux mixture. Remove and destroy plants affected with Rhizoctonia stem rot, which see.

PRINCIPAL SPECIES

D. purpurea, the old-fashioned foxglove, may be found growing wild along shaded country roads in England. Four feet tall, this species has flowers 3 in. long, purplish in color and somewhat spotted. Var. *alba* is white, and an improved variety, known as *gloxinaeflora,* has wide-mouthed flowers and longer spikes than others of the species.

ambigua (Yellow Foxglove). A perennial or biennial, growing to 3 ft., with hairy foliage. The flowers are 2 in. long, yellowish marked with brown.

ferruginea (Rusty Foxglove). A perennial or biennial to 6 ft. The flowers are rusty-red, downy outside and the lower lip bearded.

laevigata. A perennial, to 3 ft. with yellow flowers, spotted purple.

lanata (Grecian Foxglove). A perennial or biennial, to 3 ft. with flowers 1 in. long, nearly white with fine veins.

lutea (Straw Foxglove). A perennial, to 2 ft., whose flowers are yellow to white, ¾ in. long.

nervosa. Perennial, with small, yellowish flowers in long dense racemes.

sibirica. A hairy perennial with yellowish flowers.

Mexican-foxglove is *Allophyton mexicanum,* a greenhouse subject. False- or Wild-foxglove is Aureolaria, a tall, yellow-flowered native, partially parasitic, and not yet "domesticated." All, including Digitalis, belong to the Figwort Family.

FOXTAIL-LILY. A common name for Eremurus (which see), a genus of tall desert plants of the Lily Family, effective in perennial borders.

FRAGARIA (fra-gay'-ri-ah). The botanical name for the Strawberry.

FRAGILE BLADDER FERN or BRITTLE BLADDER FERN. Common name for *Cystopteris fragilis,* one of two American species that do well in good garden soil.

FRAGRANT FERN (*Dryopteris fragrans*). A sweet-scented and rare fern of rocky ledges in the N. States, difficult to grow.

FRAGRANT GARDEN. It would seem impossible to have a garden without fragrance; yet this pleasing feature may be lacking to a surprising degree, if not definitely included in the planning. The many flowers offered each year with descriptive superlatives referring to their size, color, display and responsiveness to culture, tend to focus interest on these qualities and away from the thing that is, after all, the soul and essence of a flower. If they are used at the expense of others the garden suffers. It is easier to overcome or prevent this if the desire for fragrant flowers is cultivated actively, and if the possibilities of a fragrant garden are studied.

There are certain flowers and groups of flowers that have always been famous for their sweet odors. In planning a fragrant garden a selection will naturally be made from among these first; it will, perhaps, include all that are adapted to the garden's place and circumstance. Two groups make up the list, according to the character of fragrance. One—by far the larger—may be designated the harmonious group, made up of flowers whose fragrance blends. The other is the contrasting group—flowers whose fragrance remains distinct and claims recognition no matter how many other odors are perceived at the same time. This is rather a fine point, but it merits attention and sometimes governs selection, or, more particularly, grouping.

As a rule it is better to allow each strongly fragrant kind its undisputed sway without interference from any other, than to attempt combinations. Yet the hovering sweetness of lavender or eglantine (sweetbrier) is never out of place, partly because it seems to float over and around other scents, and partly because its own character is so distinct without being strident. It is individual, it neither mixes nor overpowers; it drifts and accompanies, forming an obligato so to speak.

The pleasure to be gained from fragrance is a most personal thing, so each gardener must select his or her flowers and develop a fragrant garden according to individual taste and preference. The generally acclaimed and prized fragrant things will, of course, provide the beginning, but the planting should be "individualized" by further and special attention. Any and all scents of personal association ought to be included.

One feature that should not be overlooked is the pathway set with sweet herbs that merely creep on the surface of the ground. Few things are more delightful than thyme when it is trodden upon; or one of the mints overrunning its bed so that it is brushed against in passing. And such inconspicuous but stimulating things as lemon verbena, placed where a leaf may be pinched or plucked in passing, are a delightful touch never forgotten by visitors nor by the garden's owner. The fragrant garden gives opportunity for the play of many delicate little fancies.

Finally, in selecting plant material for fragrance in the garden it must always be remembered that certain notably fragrant flowers, which yield definite fragrance when cut and brought indoors or when held to the nostril, do not diffuse this sweetness sufficiently to make their contribution outdoors in the garden at all impressive. It is not enough that a flower shall itself be deliciously scented; its scent must be freely diffused out of doors and linger in the air.

FRAGRANT-OLIVE. Common name for *Osmanthus fragrans,* an Asiatic tree of the Olive Family with small fragrant creamy flowers; popular as a greenhouse plant.

FRAME. An abbreviated name for a coldframe (which see), a topless, bottomless box used to grow plants. The standard single size is 6 to 12 ft. Compare HOTBED; PROPAGATING BENCH.

FRANCOA (fran-koh'-ah). A genus of perennial herbs with mostly basal leaves, native in Chile and belonging to the Saxifrage Family. They are useful border plants in mild regions, and are sometimes grown in a cool greenhouse. Propagated by seed and division.

F. conchifolia has leaves with rounded lobes and leaf-stalks strongly winged at the base. It bears a long-stemmed raceme of pink flowers. *F. ramosa* is taller, with a more woody base and arching spikes of white flowers on a branching stem.

FRANGIPANI (fran-ji-pan'-i). Common name for the genus Plumiera, and for the perfume derived from some of its species. They are tropical American shrubs and trees with milky juice and large, fragrant, funnel-formed flowers.

FRANKINCENSE FERN. Common name for *Mohria thurifraga,* a graceful basket fern for the greenhouse, from Madagascar. The only species in the genus, it has fronds 1 to 2 ft. long, 3-pinnate, and emitting a spicy fragrance when crushed. Grown in peat, fibrous loam and a little sand. Do not water overhead. See also FERN.

FRANKLINIA (frank-lin'-i-ah). The original name of a shrub now placed in the genus *Gordonia* (*G. alatamaha*). Native, but very rare, in Ga., it is a splendid garden plant, half-hardy to Mass. Growing from 6 to 20 ft. tall, with smooth, shiny, bright green leaves, the shrub bears large waxy-white flowers in the fall. Plant in November or April in moist peaty soil in a protected place. All garden plants of this species are thought to have come from the original tree in John Bartram's 18th-centurn garden near Philadelphia.

FRAXINELLA (frak-si-nel'-ah). A common name (and formerly the specific name) for the Gas-plant, *Dictamnus albus,* a long-lived, lemon-scented perennial herb, also called Burning-bush because it gives off a volatile oil or vapor which, on hot nights, will flare up when ignited with a match.

FRAXINUS (frak'-si-nus). A genus of large deciduous trees of the Olive Family. Mostly hardy, they are important landscape subjects and are also sources of timber. See ASH.

FREESIA (free'-zih-ah). A genus of S. African bulbous plants which, while important as commercial florists' cut flowers, are of limited interest value to the home gardener on account of the special conditions and handling needed to flower them.

The bulbs are produced commercially in S. Calif., where also freesias are a popular and beautiful garden flower, being planted outdoors in early fall and blooming profusely in midwinter. As a conservatory or home greenhouse subject the bulbs can be planted in pots, boxes, or benches in the early fall to flower in about 3 months. Their success is largely governed by correct regulation of the temperature, which should be maintained at about 50 deg. F.

Also plenty of ventilation should be given and a well-drained soil. After they flower and the foliage becomes yellow, the corms are dug, dried out and kept for replanting the next fall. Handled in this manner they can be grown year after year with no deterioration.

The fusarium corm disease or rot (see ENEMIES under BULBS), to which the variety Purity is especially susceptible, has been so destructive in certain greenhouses that freesia growing has been practically given up there. The dry rot fungus of gladiolus also attacks freesia, and breaking, a virus disease, shows in freesias as a concentration of color in certain areas on the blossoms. See BREAKING OF TULIPS.

The many kinds of Freesia available, ranging from pure white through yellow, orange, opal, lavender and pink, with some interesting combinations, are either forms or hybrids of two principal species. These are *F. armstrongi* (with flowers white, shaded with orange and purple) and *F. refracta,* the latter with vars. *alba* and *xanthospila* (both white), *lechtlini* (pale yellow) and *odorata* (bright yellow). The hybrids are constantly showing improvement in form and habit and interesting variations in color, doubleness and fragrance.

FREMONTIA (fre-mon'-ti-ah). A genus of S. Calif. shrubs with showy yellow flowers. See FLANNEL-BUSH.

FRENCH-HONEYSUCKLE. Common name for *Hedysarum coronarium,* a perennial herb with fragrant red pea-like flowers.

FRENCH MARIGOLD. Common name for *Tagetes patula,* popular garden annual used for borders and cutting, growing 1½ ft. tall and greatly branching in habit. Solitary heads, to 1½ in. across, have many rays, yellow, marked red. For cultural directions, see MARIGOLD.

FRENCH-SPINACH. Another name for *Atriplex hortensis,* an edible herb commonly known as Orach, which see.

FRIENDSHIP GARDEN. A living plant is a definite and peculiar link to all the associations and legends clustered around it; it is forever particularly eloquent of them. So all gardeners rightly prize—and have always prized—plants from special places or people. Long ago, indeed, all gardens were largely planted with flowers, and shrubs, and even trees, obtained through friends, as witness the contributions of Lafayette to General

Washington's garden at Mount Vernon. Nothing seen there is so intimate a revelation of the two men and their friendship; nothing else brings them as close to human fellowship with men of today.

This is the significance of the friendship garden. It extends the souvenir idea into the best possible form for infinite development. All is grist that comes to its mill —seeds in a letter from the other side of the earth; a rose from the originator, perhaps; a choice bulb dug by its owner during a stroll through the garden; potted lilies of Easter greeting or a shrub or fern or evergreen sent to recall a happy trip or adventure. Even cut flowers will sometimes strike root, if the stems are plunged into sand kept evenly moist and warm, and thereby perpetuate what might have been merely an ephemeral memento. Keep a garden journal detailing the story of each thing, even though your memory is good. It makes excellent reading.

FRINGEBELL or FRINGED-GALAX (gay'-laks). Common name for small perennial herbs of the genus Schizocodon. They have fringed, nodding, bell-shaped flowers, 4 to 6 in a cluster, on a stem only a few in. high, surrounded by leathery, evergreen, long-stemmed leaves. They are increased by division and should be given an acid soil full of humus in a sheltered spot in the rock garden. *S. soldanelloides* has deep rose flowers 1 in. across, whitish at the finely-fringed edges, like the soldanellas of the Alps. The evergreen leaves become more or less bronzy in autumn like those of galax, to which the plant is related.

FRINGED MILKWORT or FRINGED POLYGALA (poh-lig'-ah-lah). Common names for *Polygala paucifolia,* also called Flowering-wintergreen and Gaywings. It is a low perennial with rosy-purple flowers, abundant in moist woods in N. and E. U. S.

FRINGED ORCHIS (aur'-kis). Common name for the genus Habenaria, terrestrial orchids, mostly native to N. America, grown in moist and boggy ground for their variously colored flowers.

FRINGE-TREE. Common name for the genus Chionanthus, a member of the Olive Family, comprising two species of trees or large shrubs with deciduous leaves, and fluffy clusters of very small white flowers, followed by a dark-blue olive-like fruit. The Fringe-trees are hardy N. if

FRINGE-TREE IN FLOWER AND FRUIT
This fine hardy native bears a shower of white blossoms in late spring and in late summer a mass of purplish-blue fruits. A single flower half natural size is shown at the right.

given sheltered positions and winter protection, and should be planted in a warm sandy loam in an open sunny position and never allowed to suffer for lack of water. They are propagated by seeds sown in the fall or stratified; also by layers and cuttings, and occasionally they are grafted on the ash, which belongs to the same family. *C. virginica,* a shrub or tree to 30 ft. having panicles to 8 in. long of fine white flowers, is the American species and makes a fine lawn or shrub border specimen. *C. retusa* grows to 20 ft. with shorter panicles of flowers; it is a Chinese species, but has proved hardy in Mass.

FRITILLARIA (frit-i-lay'-ri-ah). Fritillary. A large genus of bulbous plants of the Lily Family with drooping bell-shaped flowers, in many cases checkered in greenish, brown or purple.

The showiest species, *F. imperialis,* commonly known as Crown Imperial, makes a large cluster of yellow, orange or crimson bell-shaped flowers tightly grouped around the top of a stem 3 or 4 ft. high. It requires wide spacing and deep planting in exceedingly rich soil.

The other fritillaries, of which *F. melea-gris* (Snakes-head, Checker-lily or Guinea-hen-flower), with its many varieties, is the most commonly grown, have fewer, more scattered flowers and the plants are much smaller. They are generally hardy. Bulbs should be planted in early fall for flowering the next spring. Numerous native western species of attractive coloring—such as *recurva*, orange and scarlet; *lanceolata*, green and purple or brown; *parviflora*, purplish; and *pudica*, golden yellow—are offered in the trade.

The gray bulb rot of tulips (which see) may attack Fritillaria, as may the lily mosaic disease. Plants that are stunted with mottled flowers should be discarded.

FROG SPITTLE. A white frothy mass often found in summer on stems of grass and other low growing plants popularly believed to have been left by a frog, but in reality foamy secretion produced by small sucking insects. See SPITTLE BUG.

THE CROWN IMPERIAL
A stately flower of spring is the towering Fritillaria imperialis, with its crest of flame-colored bloom.

FROND. The entire leafy portion of any fern, including (1) the apparent stem, (2) the mid-rib, or extension of the apparent stem, and (3) the green blade. The true stems of the ferns are either below or on the surface, sometimes abbreviated into a mere surface base for the fronds. A frond differs from a leaf in that it may bear reproductive cells on its surface, and develops from a coil. See also FERNS.

FROST. A freezing condition. Frost in the ground is the part frozen solid, usually at the surface. In British writings the phrase "degrees of frost" means degrees below the freezing point. Thus 12 degrees of frost means, not 12 above zero, but 12 below 32, or 20 deg. Fahrenheit. Hoar frost or white frost is a fuzz of small ice crystals formed on the ground, on plants or other objects in certain weather. A black frost is one in which plants freeze without the appearance of hoar frost.

WHAT FROST DOES. Frost in the ground causes heaving (which see), crumbles unplanted banks, and cracks and eventually destroys foundations of buildings, walls, roads and rock-work. Damage may be put off hundreds of years by starting stone construction below the average frost line, and by good drainage. Posts may be lifted and thrown out by the action of frost in a few seasons unless set deep. Young plants or those with weak roots are often pushed completely out of the ground by alternating frosts and thaws of winter and early spring. Most subject to this injury are primrose, columbine, campanula, and any small seedlings transplanted in fall into damp, heavy soil.

Strawberry plants if small may also be uprooted; if large, their root systems may be torn apart. Use of loose, sandy soil will lessen heaving as will the use of a mulch, not by protecting the soil against cold, but by keeping the cold in, once it has frozen, and thus preventing alternate freezing and thawing. In the rock garden, a close mulch of rather large stones should keep down most plants. But in soils which heave badly, fall planting should be avoided.

At times, early fall frost occurring just after good growing weather will split the bark or wood of shrubs and trees, causing serious injury, especially to evergreens. For this reason, woody plants should never be fertilized later than early summer with growth-forcing chemicals such as nitrate of soda; or with fresh manure, the strength of which will last until fall. Nor should any fertilizer or manure mulch be applied between midsummer and Thanksgiving. Cultivation of the soil also should be discontinued during this period, watering restricted after September, and the soaking in preparation for winter delayed until all likelihood of stimulating growth has passed. Warm spells in winter, by bringing up the sap in such trees as maples, and followed by intense cold, cause frost-cracks to open in the trunks, through which much sap is afterward lost. As a treatment or partial remedy for frost-cracks in any bark or wood, filling with tallow and wrapping has been recommended. Better is prevention, by placing species likely to make fall growth or early sap flow where they will not feel the warmth of the sun, and where the ground will remain frozen late, as on a north slope or at the north side of a building or woodland. This is a common method of preventing the killing of peach buds in early spring. A heavy mulch also helps delay spring growth, but should not be placed till early winter.

The steady frosts of midwinter do less damage than late spring and early fall frosts, which find plants unprepared. Injury in autumn however is expected, and seldom causes much concern. Late apples are sometimes frozen on the tree, chrysanthemums often cut down while in flower, and the vegetable garden yields little after killing frost. But some flowers as chrysanthemum, pansy, violet, and varieties of phlox, pink, candytuft, etc., may continue to open after frost, while the Christmas-rose and some witch-hazels flower in spite of heavy freezing. Parsnips and salsify roots are benefited by frost.

Most hardy plants prepare for the cold season; perennials by withdrawing their sap into the roots, woody plants in several ways. The new growth is hardened and drained of excess sap so that freezing will not burst the cells; winter buds are formed with scales and often dense coverings of protective wool or gum; deciduous trees drop all their leaves, and evergreens the older ones. If heavy or killing frosts come before these preparations are finished, injury results.

But the chief damage occurs in spring, when sap is flowing, buds are bursting their covers, and flowers are opening. Fruit crops may be completely destroyed by killing frost after the flowers have opened; this damage runs into millions of dollars a year, and is the reason for the United States Weather Bureau's program of issuing systematic frost warnings.

WHY FROST OCCURS. In order to foresee and combat frost, its nature must be understood. A storm is normally followed by clear weather and (in the N. hemisphere) northerly winds—masses of cooler air moving in with the higher air-pressure. The sky clears. Toward evening the wind drops to a dead calm, and, if the temperature at sunset is 40 deg. or lower, frost may be expected. The clearer the sky, the greater is the probability of frost; it increases with high barometer and absence of wind. Under these conditions heat is lost rapidly from the surface of the ground, from plants and other objects, by radiation. Plants are still further cooled by evaporation of their moisture, and the drier the air, the faster the evaporation and consequent cooling will take place. Frost is likely to occur at any time during the night and may last all night. Although high ground is normally colder than low, low ground feels the frost first, because with no wind blowing, air cooled by contact with the chilled ground flows down the slopes, displacing the warm air in valleys and lowlands and making the lowest spot the coldest. Since warm air always tends to rise above cold, the currents of warmer air rising along the slopes prevent frost there. Where a valley narrows abruptly or is crossed by a belt of woodland, or where valleys come together, floods of cold air dam up as water would do, and in such spots, known as "frost holes" or "frost pockets," frosts occur more often than anywhere else in the neighborhood. Small frost pockets appear on relatively flat ground where no such explanation will show these pockets to be points where currents of down-flowing air meet or accumulate.

If there is a lake or wide stream in the valley, it lies naturally at the lowest point, to which the chilled air flows. But the water in late spring has a higher temperature than this air, and quickly warms it, lessening the frost probability. Also some mist usually rises from the water, spreading over the valley and checking both radiation and evaporation, the two forces which create the frost condition. Clouds in the sky also stop radiation at the earth's surface, and anything between the ground and sky, even the bare branches and twigs of a tree, serve the same purpose. When wind is blowing, it prevents separation of the air into warm and cold layers, and makes frost unlikely. In or near a city two circumstances prevent frost: the warmth of heated buildings takes the chill from the air around them, and the smoke from chimneys hangs overhead to give the same protection as a cloud. Any wind tends to disperse the heated air and the smoke, but itself prevents frost. On farms even the character of the soil, particularly where exposed in a plowed field, influences frost;

occur only in winter and are rare, but their very rarity results in extensive damage, lemon, grapefruit and orange groves suffering severely. The fruits themselves are sometimes frozen and lost; the trees, which are evergreen, may be partly or wholly killed. Farther N. the greatest damage is done later to the flowers of apple, peach and related fruits, resulting in loss of a season's crop, but seldom injuring the trees if varieties have been well chosen. These trees blooming during the season of probable frost are so constantly in danger that the owners, aided by government forecasts,

FROST RECORDS TELL GARDENERS WHEN TO SET OUT TENDER PLANTS
Based on many years' data, this map shows the areas where severe late spring frosts do not, as a rule, occur after March, April, May or June. respectively, when tender plants can usually be set out. Of course, exceptions occur and must be watched for.

heavy, wet soil chills the air more because of greater evaporation, while light, sandy soil remains warmer.

FROST PRECAUTIONS. Tables and charts giving the normal expected dates for the first frosts in fall and the last in spring, have been published by the Weather Bureau and other agencies, but as frost occasionally comes weeks beyond these dates, their value is only approximate. However, they indicate, for instance, the earliest advisable planting time for lima beans, corn, squash, cantaloupe, tomato, etc. In the extreme S. of Fla., Tex. and Calif., frosts

are on the alert all through the spring months. Small fruits, especially cranberries which are grown in low bogs, may also be injured, as may young or newly set out vegetable or ornamental plants. Magnolia flowers in the N. are cut by frost more often than not and blossoms of the flowering dogwood are occasionally nipped.

Frost injury may be lessened by choice of site for garden or orchard. Fruit trees or other vulnerable plants should be placed on rising ground rather than at the bottom of a valley. A hilltop or N. slope will also protect by holding back the bursting of buds in spring until there is less likelihood of cold. In planting in natural frost pockets, frost-resistant varieties should be used. Or the atmospheric condition can be changed by building an artificial lake (which must be at the low spot).

WARDING FROST OFF. Frost can be fought with fire and smudges, an ancient and world-wide practice lately improved and made both easy and inexpensive. Commercial orchards use it on a large scale, and by it a gardener can often save sensitive flowers and vegetables. Wood fires last so short a time that it would be necessary to stay up all night tending them, which few small-scale gardeners are in a position to do. Instead, fuel oil, obtainable wherever oil-burning furnaces are used, is now burned in cheap metal containers holding a gallon or more each, enough to last the night. Gallon buckets are usually placed 25 or 30 ft. apart, and burn from the surface, which is lighted with a torch. As frosts often recur the second and even the third night, a supply of oil for three or four nights is kept on hand.

Other means of fighting frost are recommended. Sprinkling with water may prove effective with light frosts if continued all night. Since any covering above the ground will check radiation, small plants may be protected to a certain extent by inverted flower pots, tents of paper, boxes, or any like device. Straw scattered to a depth of several inches is often effective. For taller plants burlap shades may be arranged. Choice small flowers or even whole rows of flowers or vegetables may be shielded by panes of glass mounted on wire frames, as has been done in England.

It should be remembered that stopping radiation from the root of a plant does not prevent air cooled by radiation a few inches away from flowing in around the plant and freezing it. Flower pots, boxes, and straw are therefore more effective than covers open at the sides. But even slight protection may be enough to maintain a non-freezing temperature in the warmer season. Potted plants may be brought under shelter at any threat of frost, and when danger is evident, it may even pay to take up newly transplanted ornamentals of a tender nature, carry them under shelter till the cold wave has passed, then set them in the open again.

CARE OF FROSTED PLANTS. Potted and movable plants that have been frozen should be taken immediately, *before the sun strikes them and they have a chance to thaw,* to a shaded coldframe or lighted cellar, where the air, though above freezing, is cold; there they may be allowed to thaw as slowly as possible. Annuals once badly frozen can seldom be brought back to health, and should be thrown away. House plants frozen by heater failure or other accident should be removed immediately to a cool cellar and there allowed to thaw slowly. If the freezing has not been severe, they may be returned to their places next day with little injury, but usually should be allowed two or three days in cool and rather dark conditions. Then, if they are badly disfigured, cut them back.

Plants of doubtful hardiness that have passed a severe winter in the open and been injured, may not entirely recover their vigor during the following season of growth, and will almost certainly die the next winter if unprotected after their "frost injury." Where possible these should be wintered in a greenhouse or coldframe to regain strength before again facing the full severity of the climate.

Plants frozen in shipment should be left packed and kept in a cool place to thaw gradually, then unpacked and well watered. If they have a ball of earth, thawing will take longer, perhaps as much as two or three days. If planting must then be done in the open and there is frost in the ground, great care must be taken to tamp and pack the soil so that no air pockets remain among the lumps. Repeated heavy waterings and a thick mulch of straw or leaves will be needed. Where possible it is better to delay planting until the ground has thawed.

Frost warnings are printed in newspapers with the weather forecast and, in farm sections, released by radio. Local information about probable dates of frost may be secured from the U. S. Weather Bureau at Washington or any of its branches, or from agricultural colleges and experiment stations.

See also WINTER PROTECTION.

FROST INJURY. Injury resulting from low temperatures after plants have started growing in the spring or before they have matured in the fall, as distinguished from that occurring during the dormant period and termed winter injury (which see). Frost injury involves frost-sensitive annuals or foliage, blossoms and young fruit of perennial plants. Leaves may be yellowed, crinkled or curled and the buds and blossoms may be blighted with resulting failure to set fruit. Even mild frost injury may permanently dwarf and cripple sensitive annuals.

Although it is beyond the gardener's power to control the temperature outdoors, he can take steps to protect some plants against changes, within certain limits. He can place temporary tents of newspaper, etc., or protectors (which see) of more permanent nature over individual plants; or he can erect cloth tents or some sheds over whole beds, borders or large areas. Also, since the occurrence of frost depends on humidity as well as temperature, he can raise the frost point by increasing the moisture content of the air, as by spraying from hose on evenings when a mild frost is probable. Any circulation of air tends to prevent frost as does the presence of vapor or smoke as from a bonfire or so-called smudge pots.

See also PROTECTION OF PLANTS.

FRUIT. In the widest, most general sense, any plant product of use or benefit to man—as "the kindly fruits of the earth." Less broadly it may be applied to the ripe or ripening reproductive part of any plant together with the part containing it—as wheat, barley, almond, blueberry, peach. Popularly the term is applied to any sort of fleshy or succulent tree-, bush-, or vine-product usually eaten raw or as a dessert and thus distinguished from "vegetable."

Botanically and strictly, fruit is the ripened ovary of a flower (which see), including its contents and any closely adhering parts. Examples are cucumber, pepper, tomato, apple, plum, raspberry. Or it may refer to a specialized reproductive body of any kind (as the spore of a fungus) including any modified plant part in which it is developed. Or even, by extension of this thought, it may refer to various consolidated forms of inflorescence, the cone of a pine being an example.

See DRUPE; POME; VEGETABLE.

FRUITING BODY. A structure in which spores of a fungus (which see) are borne. A mushroom is an example of the larger, more complex types.

FRUIT IN THE GARDEN. (See illustration, Plate 22.) Why are so many garden owners afraid to plant fruit-bearing nursery stock? Why do they so often limit their plantings to ornamental subjects? Probably the main reasons are a number of deep-seated but largely unwarranted beliefs such as the following: that years must elapse before fruit can be gathered from home plantings; that fruit trees, bushes and vines will occupy too much space and use up too much plant food; that other plants near them will be overshadowed by their branches or robbed of plant food by their hungry roots; that pruning is a mysterious process which only the chosen few can understand; and, finally, that noxious insects are so numerous and plant diseases so virulent that there is little or no hope of making the fruit plants grow, much less bear fruit.

WHY FRUITS BELONG IN GARDENS. Of course, saying that such fears are unfounded does not imply that fruits should be grown exclusively, or at the expense of ornamental plants. But when the plants selected will *also* bear fruit—and better quality fruit than can usually be bought in the stores and markets—why not choose more of them to grace the garden picture and augment its delight? An apple or a sweet cherry tree properly placed will in time provide just as good shade as a maple or a basswood; blackberry and raspberry bushes in full blossom are as beautiful as *Spiraea vanhoutei* or many another white-flowered shrub; grape-vines trained on verandas, pergolas and summer-houses are as attractive and ornamental as Dutchmans pipe or akebia whose flowers are inconspicuous; and blueberry bushes compare favorably in their brilliant autumn color with the winged euonymus (*E. alatus*) or other shrubs planted especially for autumn effects. And, in addition, the fruit-bearing plants *bear luscious fruit* which the merely ornamental plants do not!

Moreover, when varieties of high quality are grown, the home gardener can provide his table (and please his friends) with better fruit than can ordinarily be purchased. For in general the kinds grown commercially are "good lookers" and good shippers even if inferior in flavor; and harvested for marketing they are all too often picked before the highest degree of palatability has been attained. Moreover, where sufficient space is available and storage facilities are adequate, and where the gardener selects varieties that ripen successively, the supply of home-grown fresh fruit may start with the earliest straw-berries and continue without a break throughout the year until the earliest strawberries are again ripe in the follow-ing year, not to mention the additional pleasure of canned and preserved delicacies at any time.

Fruit-bearing trees, shrubs and vines may be placed in almost all the positions in which non-fruiting specimens may be artis-tically or appropriately placed. For obvious reasons the one place where a shade tree is preferable to—or shall we say safer than

—a fruit tree is beside a public sidewalk! Similarly, a fruit tree should not be placed where its fallen fruit will be unsightly or otherwise objectionable on a lawn path, or similar service or ornamental area.

This latter caution applies with special force to the mulberry tree, which drops its rather messy fruit for several weeks. The best place for it is, therefore, in the poultry yard (if there is one) or in the shrubbery border. In the former position the fowls will eat the otherwise wasted fruits and benefit thereby; in the latter the fallen

A HOME GARDEN PLANTING PLAN THAT INSURES FRUIT IN VARIETY AND ABUNDANCE

On a lot 48 ft. square, apples, cherries, peaches, plums, and small fruits can be raised successfully if the arrangement is properly spaced. Here apple trees (A) are placed at the four corners and a sweet cherry (SwCh) is placed in the center. Four peaches (PE) and four plums (PL) and twelve dwarf trees (D) are also indicated. Between the trees on the left are gooseberries (g) and between those on the right and down the center, black raspberries (br). A row each of red (rr) and purple raspberries (pr), dewberries (d) and blackberries (b) is marked by a dotted line, on either side of which stands a temporary row (t) either of vegetables or regular strawberries, except for the left-hand row, which contains ever-bearing strawberries (e).

berries will not be seen. Plum, cherry and other stone-fruit trees are also well placed in the poultry yard, both because the fowls will catch and eat many curculios whose larvae are responsible for "wormy" fruits —and because the poultry manure will enrich the soil and help feed the trees.

As nearly all fruit trees are beautiful when in blossom, they should be placed in conspicuous positions so they may be enjoyed either from the house or from other points of vantage on the grounds. (Though some varieties of peaches have small, poorly colored, insignificant flowers, others have large, brilliantly colored ones; therefore, before placing any peach tree with the idea of its proving ornamental, find out which group it belongs to; then locate it accordingly.) Raspberry, dewberry and blackberry bushes may be grouped around the borders of the property just as "flowering shrubs" are grouped in borders; grapevines, though aided if supported on trellises where they may be pruned and managed with ease, can be trained against house walls, and along the sides and eaves of verandas, porches, and summer-houses and thus provide shade as well as fruit.

It is advantageous to place fruit trees adjacent to the borders of the property; first, because such locations permit the maximum utilization of one's own available ground and secondly, because the roots may gather plant food from the soil beyond the property boundaries.

Currant and gooseberry bushes are the only temperate-climate fruit plants that have neither attractive flowers nor ornamental foliage. Moreover they drop their leaves rather early in the autumn without having developed any brilliant colors. Therefore, they should not be placed in conspicuous positions. The blueberry, on the contrary, though it develops inconspicuous flowers, is attractive when loaded with fruit and still more so in autumn when its foliage turns brilliant purple or deep red; and also during winter when its young branches stand out in their redness against the snow. It therefore deserves a prominent place within sight of the house windows.

A Practical Home Fruit Garden

When a separate clear area 48 by 48 ft. in extent can be devoted to a fruit garden, space may be economized by the plan described hereunder and pictured on page 519,

without jeopardizing the success of any of the plants during their normally productive lives:

Place four standard apple trees, one at each corner of the square. Each tree should be of a different variety; or, better still, should be grafted to two, three or four varieties preferably kinds that ripen over a long season. This grafting (which see) should be done after the trees are well established, using carefully selected scions. In this way successional yields of 4 to 16 varieties of applies may be secured from the four trees.

In the center of the square place a sweet cherry tree. This will thus be approximately 36 ft. distant from each of the apple trees—a liberal distance, even without training and pruning, until all five trees have attained full development, at say 20 to 30 years of age. Systematic training and pruning, however, will prevent their crowding even at their maturity and if properly managed they should each bear fruit for 50 or more years. If desired, standard pear trees may be planted instead of the apple and sweet cherry trees, or some of them, but, even when full grown, they will not fill the space so completely. Midway between each two apple trees on the sides of the area and between the apples and the sweet cherry on the diagonals, 4 peach and 4 plum trees can be located. And in the spaces between them, dwarf fruit trees of any desired kind can be set. If preferred, the spaces devoted to plums and peaches may be filled with sour cherries or dwarf fruit trees. The dwarf trees shown at D in the plan are too close to the other trees to allow of satisfactory substitution of other fruit trees, though berry plants might take their place.

While these larger, permanent trees are developing, the spaces between them need not be idle but may be devoted to shorter-lived tree and bush fruits with strawberries and annual vegetables between the rows for the first two or three years, as indicated on the chart.

The continuous rows of brambles (berries) may start with 16 red raspberry plants set 3 ft. apart or 24 at 2 ft. The spaces between these plants can be filled with sucker plants produced by the original setting. Likewise 8, 12, or 16 blackberry plants may be planted 6, 4 or 3 ft. apart and their suckers allowed to fill the row. Purple raspberries (preferably Columbian,

Plate 22.

THE HOME FRUIT GARDEN

Top: The apple's crimson globes add color and satisfaction to the autumn border.   Lower left: The snowy wreaths on ancient pears enframe the garden path.   Center right: The profuse bloom of the symmetrically trimmed young pear tree foretells abundant fruit.   Lower right: A marvel of fragrance and beauty, this apple tree speaks eloquently of the fall harvest.

because it is the most prolific and largest-fruited variety) should be 6 ft. apart because of the exceptional size they attain. Eight dewberry plants should be trained to stakes the same distance apart since, if allowed to sprawl upon the ground, they will interfere with cultivation. Black raspberries need the same spacing but need not be trained to stakes because by training (see under RASPBERRY) they can be made tree-like in form.

In addition to economizing space through such an arrangement of a plantation, one gains much in economy of effort needed to cultivate the area. When vegetables and strawberries are grown between the bush, berry, and tree rows, cultivation may be done in one direction with a wheel-hoe, thus reducing the amount of hoeing and weeding that must be done by hand. If neither vegetables nor strawberries are grown in these interspaces, the cultivation can be done in two directions with wheel-hoe, horse-drawn or power-driven tools, thus cutting down the amount of hand work still further. In each case it is evident that the total amount of cultivation will be less than where no concentration of planting is practiced.

GETTING MAXIMUM RESULTS

As to the time one must wait for fruit, much depends not only upon the species but also upon the varieties chosen. Everbearing strawberries planted in spring and properly managed (see STRAWBERRY) will begin to bear shortly after midsummer of the same season and continue until cold weather.

Raspberries, blackberries, dewberries, currants, gooseberries and blueberries generally begin to yield the summer after being spring-planted, and should be in full bearing the succeeding summer. Grapevines often start to bear the year after the vines have been planted. Though peach and nectarine trees sometimes produce a few fruits the second summer, they generally do not bear until the third summer. Plums, apricots and sour cherries sometimes start to bear during the third summer; usually not before the fourth. Sweet cherries and pears may begin during the fourth year but usually the fifth.

The apple shows the widest range of all; some precocious varieties begin during the third, or even the second year after planting; others require ten years or even

longer. The late bearers may well be the first varieties to omit from a list of fruits to be grown for home use, though careful training rather than vigorous pruning will shorten the time one has to wait.

Selection of varieties is certainly the most important problem in attaining success in home fruit growing. They should be chosen so as to give the longest possible succession. Few people realize that by proper selection (and proper storage after the harvest period ends) it is possible to have strawberies from June until November; raspberries from July to October; cherries, apricots, gooseberries, currants and blueberries from late June until mid-August; mulberries from June to September; plums, peaches and nectarines from late July until October, and in some cases even until Christmas; pears from late July or early August to March; grapes from

Fruits and Their Bearing Habits.

Kind of Fruit	Starts to Bear in — Years		Bears for — Years	
Apple	3	to 10	50	to 100
Apricot	3	" 4	10	" 25
Blackberry	2	" 3	5	" 10
Cherry, sour	3	" 4	15	" 25
Cherry, sweet	4	" 5	25	" 75
Currant	2	" 3	5	" 10
Dwarf fruit trees	See note below			
Gooseberry	2	to 3	5	to 10
Grape	1	" 3	10	" 50
Peach and Nectarine ..	2	" 3	5	" 15
Pear	3	" 5	25	" 75
Plum	3	" 4	10	" 20
Quince	3	" 4	10	" 20
Raspberry	1	" 2	5	" 10
Strawberry (potted plants fall-planted) ..	⅔	" ¾	1	" 2
Strawberry (runner plants spring-planted)	1½		1	" 2
Strawberry (Everbearing)	⅓		1	" 2

NOTE: Dwarf fruit trees usually start to bear one to three years sooner than standards of the same variety, but are not usually as long lived.

late August until February, March or even April; apples from late July to late May or early June.

When selecting varieties to meet such specifications the gardener will do well to give preference to the highest quality and the softest textured kinds because these are the ones rarely obtainable in the markets and stores or from local growers all of whom are interested in commercial, staple kinds. Except where ample space is available purely culinary varieties should be ruled out of the home planting, because needed supplies of such can be bought in unlimited quantity.

Another point to keep in mind where space is at a premium is the selection of fruit varieties that ripen when the stores and market supplies of those kinds are short; as for instance, summer apples and pears and late varieties of peaches and plums. In these ways the home table can not only have abundance of choicer fruit than the commercial sources can supply, but also be well provided for when the market is bare of such fruits. For instance, there are usually abundant Bartlett pears available, either from Calif. or from local sources, for 6 weeks or two months; later in the autumn pears are scarce. Yet there is a score of varieties far superior to the Bartlett that ripen during autumn and early winter. Similarly the market is flooded with grapes in September and early October, but practically bare after the Concord season has ended; yet there are at least two dozen varieties superior as dessert fruit to the Concord—varieties that will continue the grape season until late winter or even permit a supply of stored fruit until early spring. Somewhat similar statements might be made concerning other fruits.

See HARVESTING GARDEN CROPS; STORING OF CROPS; DISEASES; PESTS; PRUNING; PROPAGATION; SPRAYING; MAINTENANCE OF THE GARDEN.

FUCHSIA (feu'-shi-ah). Natives of Mexico, S. America and New Zealand, Fuchsias (sometimes called Ladys Eardrops because of the form of the flowers) long have been favorites both in the garden and indoors. They are shrubs or trees in their countries of origin, but in the U. S. they generally are cultivated in the house (or in the cool greenhouse) as pot plants. However, they often are bedded out over summer in N. gardens, while in milder climates they are cultivated outdoors the year round.

The species differ widely in their appearance and habit of growth, some being only 18 in. tall and others reaching 20 ft. or more. In the commonly cultivated species, the maximum height is about 12 ft. All species are shrubby, grow rapidly, are generally of erect form and produce long branches, from the extremities of which droop the beautiful, pendulous flowers in great profusion.

Fuchsias are often trained and pruned to form standards, or large pyramids with one central stem. In developing the latter

shape, all shoots except the leader must be pinched in, carefully and systematically. So rapid is the growth of the fuchsia that where it can be treated as an outdoor plant it can be used to cover walls and fences.

FUCHSIA, A FAVORITE
The gracefully drooping flowers of crimson and violet are shown in the center. The plant is grown in both bushy form (left) and standard or "tree" form (right).

Medium-rich garden soil, containing some leafmold, is best; the plants also like a rather humid atmosphere and partial shade. The foliage is simple, generally small, and the flowers, produced outdoors in July and August and indoors nearly the entire winter, range through rose, red and purple to white. The calyx, consisting of four parts, generally is reflexed and so colored as to contrast beautifully with the corolla, also of four parts.

Plants grown from seed should be started in the greenhouse in January or February; and the plants can then be set out in May. Propagation, however, is most often done by cuttings of soft greenwood handled as follows:

After the plants have finished blossoming indoors they should be "rested" by putting them in a cool, dry place and withholding water, except for the small amount needed to keep the wood from drying. Start watering and feeding them again in December, and by February there will have developed enough new shoots for cutting. Do not use hard-wood. Take cuttings with two joints and root them in the propagating bed. As soon as they are rooted, they should be potted in 2 in. pots of rich soil composed of loam and leafmold with a slight quantity of sand. Shift to larger pots as growth makes it necessary and in repotting cut back the branches slightly. Pinch off the ends of the new growth frequently to produce stocky plants. Cuttings so handled should make good plants in 6 in. pots the following fall. Full exposure to the light, a moist atmosphere and water as needed are essential, especially when the plants are young. Cuttings of outdoor-grown plants may be taken in the fall.

Control red spider by syringing the plants occasionally with water. For measures to use against greenhouse whitefly and the mealy bug see GREENHOUSE PESTS.

PRINCIPAL SPECIES

Florists today grow few of the natural species, most of their attention being centered on the hybrids, the number of which is increasing. Most catalogs list only hybrid varieties. One of the best is *F. hybrida,* probably derived from *F. magellanica* and *F. fulgens.* Its leaves are 4 in. long and the flowers have crimson calyx and purple petals (sometimes rose or white). The flowers, often 3 in. long, are sometimes double. This is the common conservatory and window fuchsia. Other important species are:

F. magellanica. Usually a low shrub but growing to 20 ft. when trained on walls. Leaves 2 in. long; flowers ½ in., with red calyx and blue petals. This species, which has numerous varieties, is commonly grown outdoors in California.

arborescens. Another tall species, reaching 18 ft., with leaves 8 in. long but flowers only ½ in., pink or purplish.

fulgens. To 4 ft.; leaves 7 in.; flowers 3 in., red.

splendens. Flowers scarlet with small, greenish petals and long, protruding stamens.

triphylla. To 1½ ft.; leaves small; flowers 1½ in., cinnabar red.

The name California-fuchsia is sometimes applied to *Zauschneria californica.* Capefuchsia (which see) is *Phygelius capensis.*

FUCHSIA SOCIETY, THE AMERICAN. Organized in 1930 in the interest of Fuchsias in America, this society is made up of both amateur and professional members.

In 1934 it issued and distributed to its members a reprint of an illustrated article on fuchsias from *The National Horticultural Magazine.* While available, copies are given to new members as they join.

The annual dues are $1. The secretary is Miss Alice Eastwood, Academy of Sciences, Golden Gate Park, San Francisco, Calif.

FUMARIACEAE (feu-may-ri-ay'-see-ee). The Fumitory Family, the name, which means smoky, being perhaps derived from the odor of some species of Fumaria. The members are delicate herbs native to the N. temperate zone and closely related to those of the Poppy Family but differing in having a watery instead of a milky juice. Leaves are deeply cleft and the flowers are very irregular. Adlumia and Dicentra (which includes Dutchmans breeches and the popular bleeding heart) are the chief cultivated genera; and Fumaria was once considered of medicinal value.

FUMIGATION. The control of undesirable plant infesting (or other) undesirable organisms by toxic fumes given off by substances called fumigants. Fumigation is particularly valuable in greenhouses and other enclosed spaces, but has some use out-of-doors in treating trees under tents and for destroying insects or other animals in burrows in wood and in the soil.

GREENHOUSE FUMIGATION. The first step is the careful calculation of the space to be treated. For even-span houses multiply the length by the width to get the area and this by the average height to get the contents in cubic feet. To get the average height measure at highest and lowest points, add together and divide by two. In odd-span houses the area of the end (or cross-section) must be calculated by dividing it into two units by a vertical line from the highest point, finding the area of each unit by multiplying its width by its average height, and adding the two areas together; then multiply this area by the length of the house. The dosage of the chemical to be used is determined partly by the kinds of plants and insects to be treated and partly by the tightness of the house.

The deadly fumes of hydrocyanic acid gas and of nicotine are most commonly used; those of naphthalene sometimes. Sodium, potassium, or calcium cyanide give off the first mentioned gas. The first two, which must be used in combination with

sulphuric acid, have been largely superseded by the more easily and more safely
used calcium cyanide, but the method is
given here for reference: Use 3-gal. or
4-gal. earthenware crocks. Put the proper
amount of water (according to the capacity of the house and the formula given
below) in each, pour in the sulphuric acid
slowly and carefully, then, beginning at
the far end, quickly drop in the right
amount of sodium cyanide wrapped in tissue paper. Work rapidly toward the door
and leave the house *immediately* the cyanide is added to the crocks. Lock the
door for the fumigation period, and do
not re-enter until the house has been well
aired.

The generally safe dosage for greenhouses containing growing plants is water
½ fluid oz.; commercial sulphuric acid ¼
fluid oz., and sodium cyanide ⅛ oz., for
each 1000 cu. ft. of space. The cyanide
may be purchased in a one ounce compressed form known as a "cyanegg."

Calcium cyanide, though also poisonous,
is much easier to use and safer for the
operator as it acts more slowly. It is
applied merely by sprinkling it over the
walks, where, taking up moisture from the
air, it releases the gas. It is obtainable
in three forms: a dust, fine granules, and
flakes. The granular G grade powder
(containing 40 to 50 per cent calcium
cyanide) is preferable for greenhouse fumigation, the standard dosage being ¼ oz.
per 1000 cu. ft. of space. If there is much
leakage more will be necessary, but the
grower should start with the normal dosage and increase gradually in successive
treatments until a dosage is found which
will kill the insects and not injure the
plants. In a house of tender plants, such
as sweet peas, asparagus fern and snapdragon, start with a ⅛ oz. dosage. Hardy
plants like gardenia, cyclamen and begonia
will stand a ½ oz. rate. The frequency
of treatment depends on the insects to be
controlled, but in general fumigation every
ten days or two weeks will keep a house
free of insect pests.

After ascertaining the number of ounces
required for one treatment, place this
amount of calcium cyanide in a container,
such as a screw cap fruit jar, with holes

FUMIGATION, AN EFFECTIVE WAY TO FIGHT GREENHOUSE PESTS
A modern method employs a nicotine preparation sold in cans from which, when punctured, issue
clouds of an insect-destroying vapor that penetrates all parts of the greenhouse structure.

punched through the cap from the inside out. (By marking the jar and keeping it for the same house, subsequent weighings will be unnecessary.) Begin at the end farthest from the door and scatter the material even over the center walk; or if the house is large, let two operators work simultaneously down two walks. As before, leave immediately, lock the house and do not enter until it has been aired. If it is desired to fumigate an empty greenhouse to clean up a severe insect infestation, use 1 to 2 lbs. of calcium cyanide for each 1000 cu. ft. and expose for at least 24 hours. Air out well before replanting.

CAUTION. In fumigating with cyanide compounds, take these precautions:

Use great care in handling the poison. Do not breathe fumes or dust. Wash hands thoroughly after handling.

Remove all goldfish, birds or other pets before starting fumigation. Do not fumigate greenhouses or conservatories attached to dwellings that will be occupied during the fumigation.

Make sure that everyone except the operator is out of the house before starting to fumigate. Close and lock the doors immediately and post a danger sign.

Fumigate only at night, starting about one hour after sundown, and select a night free from wind, rain or other abnormal weather conditions. Close all transoms and other openings to prevent rapid loss of gas. If possible, arrange so that the ventilators can be opened *from the outside* after the treatment and before the house is entered. However with the dosages of calcium cyanide safe for plants, this is not absolutely necessary *if the house is not opened until next morning.*

The plants in the house must be dry since moisture on them absorbs the gas and may cause burning. Do not water for 24 hours before fumigation and do not fumigate with calcium cyanide while there is any copper dust or spray from a previous treatment on the plants, since a chemical reaction will occur which is injurious to the plants.

The temperature during the fumigation should not be lower than 60 deg. F. and preferably not below 70 deg.

NICOTINE FUMIGATION. This is more expensive than using cyanide but is safer in the case of tender plants and in houses where the required dry conditions cannot be obtained. It may spot sweet pea and

cyclamen blossoms, which should therefore be cut just before the fumigation. Violets and maidenhair ferns should *not* be fumigated with nicotine.

Nicotine is effective against aphids and thrips but does not control white fly and scale as well as cyanide. It may be used in liquid, powder or paper form. The liquid, containing 40 to 50 per cent nicotine, and used at the rate of 1 oz. to 4000 cu. ft., is painted on the steam pipes or heated in shallow pans. Commercially prepared nicotine papers (which should be purchased as needed and used fresh) may be suspended from wire plant stakes hung over the sides of the benches; light the lower edge, then blow the flame out so that the paper smoulders. Nicotine powders consist of ground tobacco with extra nicotine added. The amount needed depends on the brand used and tightness of the house. Of brands containing 12 per cent nicotine, use about 4 oz. for each 5000 cu. ft. or, approximately, a 2½ in. flower pot heaping full. Pour the powder on a small wire screen bent down at one end to keep it off the ground and provide draft, and light it. Nicotine fumigation is most effective on still damp nights.

NAPHTHALENE FUMIGATION. This is effective against red spider and thrips. Use 1½ to 2 oz. per 1000 cu. ft. and evaporate slowly over an electric hot-plate. Begin not later than 5.30 p. m. and start ventilating the house by 7 a. m. next morning. A temperature above 70 deg. F. and a dry atmosphere are necessary.

SULPHUR is sometimes used as a fumigant for mildew (which see). Make into a paste form with water and paint it on the steam pipes while the heat is on. Sulphur at high concentrations may also be used as a powerful disinfectant for *empty* houses. Burn ⅓ lb. for each 1000 cu. ft. in wide, deep, metal pans distributed evenly through the house. Keep the house closed tightly for 12 hours, then open and air.

FUMIGATION OF TREES. In California scale insects on citrus trees are largely controlled by fumigation. Heavy canvas tents are placed over the trees and charges of hydrocyanic acid gas or calcium cyanide dust released within these shelters. Commercial fumigating companies or coöperative societies bring the equipment and do the work.

SOIL FUMIGATION. The three materials usually applied to the soil to rid it of insects and rodents are carbon bisulphide, calcium cyanide and paradichlorobenzene (see each material). Carbon bisulphide is of value in treating small lots of soil but is too expensive to use on a large scale. For potting soils distribute a pound for each cubic yard, keeping it at a temperature above 50 deg. F. for 48 hours. Lawns and golf greens may be treated with carbon-bisulphide emulsion (which see) to control beetle grubs. Mix 1 qt. of emulsion with 50 gals. water and apply at rate of 3 pints to each square foot to grass which has been kept moist for several days previous. Carbon bisulphide may be injected from an oil can into ant hills and mole runs. (See ANTS; MOLES; LAWN.)

Calcium-cyanide dust is used to destroy wireworms, chinch bugs, ants. For wireworms a trap crop is planted which will collect the worms about the roots, then apply the cyanide at the rate of 200 lbs. per acre. Give this treatment in the spring in advance of the planting of the main crop. To control chinch bugs on lawns, dust the cyanide on at the rate of 50 to 75 lbs. per acre, making three or four applications at intervals of two or three days. Control rodents and ants by blowing or pouring a small amount of the dust into the burrows or nests.

Paradichlorobenzene (popularly called PD benzene) is used chiefly to kill the larvae of the peach tree borer. Scrape away the soil for an inch or so, then apply the heavy white crystals in a ring encircling the trunk between 1 and 3 in. from it. Use ½ oz. for each tree under 3 years old; ¾ oz. for each tree 3 to 6 years old, and 1 to 1½ oz. for each older tree. Fall is the best time to give this treatment. Apply to the nearest State Experiment Station as to the proper dates.

Being somewhat safer and effective over a greater temperature range, ethylene dichloride emulsion has, of late, been replacing paradichlorobenzene in peach-borer control. It must be used in accurate dosages that have been worked out for trees of every age and size. It can be bought as a commercial preparation with complete directions for use. See PEACH.

Chloropicrin, or tear gas, is now probably the best complete soil fumigant known. Properly applied it will kill all soil insects and many nematodes, weed seeds, fungi, and soil bacteria. Being poisonous to plants, it cannot be used around growing crops nor in a closed greenhouse containing plants. And treated soil cannot be planted until all fumes have disappeared—usually two or three weeks later. Before using tear gas cultivate the soil until it is friable, and firm it; then inject the chloropicrin at the rate of 2 to 4 cc. per sq. ft. The material is sold under a trade name together with a special injector, and detailed directions.

Methyl bromide (which see) can be used on soil in which plants are growing. It is now the chief fumigant for treating stock to be shipped out of the Japanese beetle area. Applied as an emulsion around plants, it gives a fair control of various soil insects.

Dichlorethyl ether (which see) although not especially good for fumigating fallow soil, is useful, in emulsion, to apply around living plants. It shows real promise in the control of the sod webworm and garden centipede.

Naphthalene flakes worked into the soil have a limited use in the control of the fungous disease, crown rot, which see. Ground tobacco stems similarly used are of some value in controlling root aphids.

FUMIGATION OF BURROWS. Some borers in tree trunks may be controlled by injecting carbon bisulphide into the holes with a machine-oil can and plugging up the opening with wet putty. This will kill borers within a few inches of the opening. A nicotine paste may also be injected into the burrows.

FUMITORY (feu'-mi-toh-ri). Common name for the genus Fumaria, a member of the Fumitory Family, and especially applied to *F. officinalis,* a plant 2 or 3 ft. tall, with finely cut leaves and racemes of small flesh-colored or purplish flowers tipped with crimson. Fumitory was once considered of medicinal value, and is sometimes found as an escape, but it has little horticultural value. Climbing-fumitory is *Adlumia fungosa.*

FUNGICIDE. A material used to protect plants against, or to inactivate or kill fungi, primarily those that cause plant diseases. Fungicides are of two kinds: *eradicants,* materials used to kill or inactivate the fungi or bacteria existing in the soil, on seed, on the plant, or in the

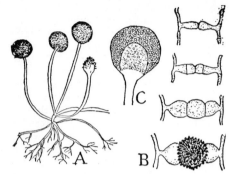

KINDS OF FUNGI—I

The bread-mold fungus represents the Zygomycetes of the Phycomycete Class. A, a group of spore-bearing bodies (sporangia). C, one sporangium enlarged to show mass of spores. B, steps in development of a sexual spore (zygospore). (This and the five subsequent fungus diagrams show microscopic subjects greatly magnified. **See text for definition of terms).**

plant (chemotherapy); and *protectants,* materials used to protect susceptible plant parts externally or internally in advance of the invasion of fungi or bacteria.

Eradicants used in treating soil and seed are formaldehyde, steam, hot water, and various fumigants. Generally the treatments must not be made on soil with growing plants.

A dormant application of lime-sulfur is an eradicant for the peach leaf curl fungus that clings to the buds. Sulfur dusts or sprays kill out powdery mildews on the rose, phlox, sweet william and many other plants. Certain organic mercury compounds and dichlone are useful as eradicants on the apple scab fungus.

Chemotherapy is a relatively new approach to plant disease control through internal chemical cure. The chemicals that have curative value may also have immunization effects depending upon how long they remain in active form within the plant. Most success has been attained in the control of such nutrient deficiencies as iron, zinc, copper, and boron through root feedings, foliage sprays, or trunk injections.

Most fungicides used on plants are *protectants,* and the spray or dust must be on the plant before the disease-producing organism arrives in order to halt its progress. The protective fungicides may be divided into three groups: the copper compounds, the sulfur compounds, and the newer organic com-

pounds. The copper compounds are divided into the old *Bordeaux* mixture (copper sulfate and hydrated lime), and the fixed or low soluble coppers such as tri-basic copper sulfate, copper oxychloride, and yellow copper oxide. The sulfurs consist of liquid lime-sulfur, dry lime-sulfur, sulfur pastes, powders and dusts.

Among the newer organic fungicides are the dormant dinitro compounds under trade names; the dithiocarbamic acid derivatives; the phenyl mercury compounds under trade names, and others.

See also SPRAYING AND SPRAYERS.

FUNGOUS DISEASES. Maladies caused by various kinds of fungus, which see. The majority of plant diseases come in this category. They may be recognized by their symptoms, such as leaf spot, wilt, rot or blight (some of which may resemble symptoms of bacterial diseases); and especially by their signs, which include the fungus fruiting bodies or spores. For positive identification it is often necessary to examine these spores under the microscope or to grow the fungus from material taken from the diseased plant, in the laboratory, on artificial culture media. See also DISEASES.

FUNGUS (plural *fungi*). A member of a low order of plants, more complicated in structure and therefore higher up the scale than bacteria and slime molds, but lower than mosses, ferns, and flowering

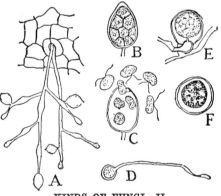

KINDS OF FUNGI—II

The potato-blight fungus represents the Oomycete division of the Phycomycetes. A, sporangia at the end of sporangiophores emerging from a leaf. B and C, a sporangium germinating by swarm spores. D, spore germinating by a germ tube. E, contents of oogonium and antheridium uniting to form mature oospore (F).

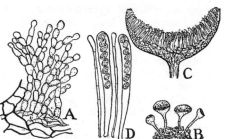

KINDS OF FUNGI—III
The brown rot fungus represents the Discomycete division of the Ascomycete Class. A, asexual spores—conidia formed in chains. B, apothecia. C, section through a single apothecium showing fruiting layer of asci. D, two asci, each with eight ascospores.

plants. Fungi vary widely in size, form and appearance, but all are characterized by lack of chlorophyll, the green substance that gives the higher plants their characteristic color. Because chlorophyll is essential to the manufacture of food in the leaf (see *photosynthesis*), fungi cannot make their own food but must obtain it from other plants (or animals), which are called *hosts*. Fungi which live on dead tissues, whether animal or vegetable, are called *saprophytes;* those that derive their food, ready prepared, from living organisms are called *parasites* (which term is also applied to animals that do the same thing). Many are both parasitic and saprophytic at different stages in their life cycle. And a few—such as the rusts, smuts and mildews—are known as *obligate parasites* because direct contact with living tissue is necessary if they are to make any growth.

One group of fungi—the mushrooms—includes valuable edible, or interesting ornamental forms; others are familiar to most of us as the molds and mildews that appear on spoiled foodstuffs or in damp places. But in horticulture, fungi are of greatest significance as the cause of the majority of plant diseases.

CHARACTERISTICS OF FUNGI

Fungi are characterized by the presence of (1) a *mycelium,* or growing, vegetative part, made up of fungus threads (*hyphae*), and (2) spores, which are reproductive bodies corresponding to the seeds of higher plants and of importance because their characters are factors in the classification of fungi. These spores vary greatly in function and in the manner in which they

are borne. In general, there are two types, (1) *sexual spores* (also called mature or winter spores), which result from a union of two kinds of cells (considered male and female); and (2) *asexual* ("without sex") *spores* (called summer spores), which are formed directly from the mycelium without a fertilization process.

A fungus has two or more distinct stages in its life history: one is the *perfect* stage, during which the sexual spores are produced; and the other is the *imperfect* stage, during which asexual spores are produced. These two stages may follow each other on a host so that the connection between them is easily seen, or they may appear as two separate fungi whose respective parts in the life-cycle of a single fungus must be demonstrated by experiment. When the perfect or sexual stage is known, the correct scientific name of the fungus is the name first given that stage. The fact that the imperfect stage of certain fungi causing the plant diseases may have been known and described before the complete life-history of the organism was understood accounts for the different names found in different accounts of some fungi. For example, the fungus causing black-spot of rose was first named *Actinomena rosae,* but when the winter, or perfect, spores were finally seen the name was changed to *Diplocarpon rosae,* since, as noted, the classification of fungi depends on the spore characters of the sexual stage.

Fungi are classified under three main groups: the *Phycomycetes* or mold fungi; the *Ascomycetes* or sac fungi; and the *Basidiomycetes,* or mushroom group. A

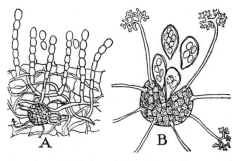

KINDS OF FUNGI—IV
Powdery mildew of lilac is a Pyrenomycete, also of the Ascomycete Class. C, a magnified weft of the fungus on leaf surface showing the mycelium bearing chains of conidia and one round perithecium. B, the perithecium enlarged showing the appendages that help to anchor it and the emerging asci containing spores.

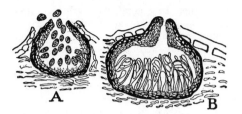

KINDS OF FUNGI—V

The fungus causing black rot of apples is another Pyrenomycete. A, pycnidium and spores issuing from it. B, perithecium with asci containing spores.

fourth group (the *Fungi imperfecti*) consists of those forms in which the perfect stage is wanting—either it is as yet undiscovered or it has been lost in the course of their evolution.

CLASSES OF FUNGI

PHYCOMYCETES. These are the lowest forms of true fungi. Growing best under moist conditions, they differ from the higher fungi in that the mycelial threads lack cross walls (*cepta*). The asexual spores are born singly or in groups known as *sporangia*. The sexual spores may be *zygospores* (produced by the union of two fertilizing hyphae of equal size), or *oospores,* formed by the union of two cells of unequal size, which we call male and female. Spores germinate by putting forth a tube, called a *germ tube,* just as a seed sends forth a sprout; but in the Phycomycetes many spores break up into swimming animal-like bodies called *zoospores.* The classical example of the Zygomycete group is the common black mold which grows on bread. The Oomycetes, or oospore-producing types, include several fungi capable of causing plant disease, especially the damping-off (Pythium) and stem-rotting (Phytopthora) fungi and the downy mildews, including the potato blight fungus (see POTATO) and that causing grape mildew (see GRAPE). A few members of this group that are parasitic on insects may be regarded as beneficial from that standpoint. (See illustrations I and II.)

ASCOMYCETES. The sac fungi are so called because their sexual spores are borne in sacs called *asci.* These may be produced in an open layer as in the leaf curl fungus (see PEACH); in an open cup called an *apothecium* (fungi of this sort form a subdivision called Discomycetes); or in a closed receptacle called a *perithecium* (this

group being named Pyrenomycetes). The cups arising from fruit mummied by the brown rot fungus (see BROWN ROT) are apothecia; they may be ¼ to ½ in. and plenty large enough to be seen with the naked eye, but a microscope is needed to see the asci and spores. Perithecia are smaller and are usually seen as black dots nestling in a white weft of mildew mycelium or in the center of leaf or stem lesions. The asexual spores (*conidia*) may be borne in chains on the surface of plants or in enclosed receptacles similar to perithecia and called *pycnidia.* Probably the majority of plant diseases are caused by Ascomycetes, the group including every type of disease—leaf spots, cankers, blights,

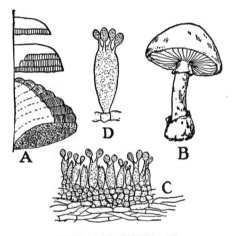

KINDS OF FUNGI—VI

Mushrooms, shelf fungi and other large types are members of the Basidiomycete group. A, diagrams of shelf- or bracket-fungi showing the pores. These, like the gills of the various mushrooms (B), are lined with basidia as shown at (C). D, a single basidium enlarged showing spores at its apex. (See text for definition of the various terms.)

rots, wilts and so on. (See illustrations III, IV and V.)

BASIDIOMYCETES are characterized by having their sexual organs borne on club-like cells called *basidia.* Here belong the primitive forms such as the rusts and smuts (which see) and the true basidiomycetes which are composed chiefly of the bracket of shelf fungi and the mushrooms. In this latter group it is the fruiting body and not the fungus itself or the disease it causes which is large and conspicuous. These fruiting bodies, called *sporophores,* bear their spores on a fruiting layer (*hy-*

menium), which may be a flat surface or may take the form of teeth or pores, as in the bracket fungi, or gills as in the mushrooms. In either case, there are always openings so arranged that the spores can drop out easily. Poisonous forms of the gill fungi are called "toadstools" by the layman, but all are mushrooms to the scientist. One important root rot (see ARMILLARIA ROOT ROT) is caused by a mushroom, but many of the disease-producing Basidiomycetes belong to the "bracket fungi" group which cause heartwood and sapwood rot of trees. Other disease-producing Basidiomycetes have less conspicuous fruiting bodies, forming merely a fruiting layer over the diseased portion of host plants. Species responsible for some types of damping-off and stem rots and for brown patch of grass, are found here; also the fungus causing crown rot (which see), although its life-history is not completely known.

FUNGI IMPERFECTI. In this group are many of the fungi that cause leaf spots and stem lesions, but that need some investigator to work out their life history. When this has been done they will be given the genus name of the sexual stage and be removed from this group to one of the other three.

FUNKIA (fung'-ki-ah). Former name (still found in catalogs) of the genus Hosta, the Plantain-lily, which see.

FURCRAEA (fur-kree'-ah). A genus of succulent desert plants from tropical America, belonging to the Amaryllis Family. They resemble agaves, and are grown under similar conditions. Their flowering size and age is very uncertain, and once they send up their tall stems bearing many greenish-white flowers in loose panicles they usually die. Numerous bulblets are borne in the flower clusters, by which they are easily propagated. For cultural directions, see AGAVE.

F. bedinghausi has a trunk to 3 ft., with leaves 33 ft. long, 30 to 50 in a rosette, and a flower stem 12 to 15 ft. high.

F. cubensis has a rosette of 25 to 30 bright green leaves, with edges armed with brown hooked prickles. The flower stem grows to 15 ft.

F. gigantea has a short trunk, a rosette of 40 to 50 leaves to 8 ft. long, and a wide-spreading flower panicle on stems to 30 ft. high.

FURNITURE FOR THE GARDEN. See GARDEN FURNITURE.

FURZE. A common name for Ulex (which see), a genus of spiny shrubs with yellow pea-like flowers.

FUSARIUM (feu-say'-ri-um). A soil fungus, with various species which are widespread and which cause wilts in a great variety of plants. The symptoms are root or stem rots. The white vegetative portion (*mycelium*) and the spore masses usually have a pink or purple cast. Some of the serious fusarium diseases are aster wilt, cabbage yellows, and wilts of flax, potato, tomato and cotton. Control lies in soil disinfection and in the planting of improved, resistant varieties.

G

GAGEA (gay'-jee-ah). A genus of small bulbous plants, native in Europe, Asia, and N. Africa, belonging to the Lily Family. Formerly included under the genus Ornithogalum, they require the same treatment as plants of that group. The flowers are mostly yellow and open in spring.

G. lutea (Yellow Star-of-Bethlehem) has 3 to 4 flowers in a flat cluster, yellow with a green back, and opening only in the forenoon. *G. bracteolaris* has umbels of pale yellow flowers; the stem leaves are fringed with long hairs.

GAILLARDIA (gay-lahr'-di-ah). Blanket-flower. A genus of American herbaceous annuals, biennials and perennials of the Composite Family. Much grown cut flower favorites, they do best in full sunlight in a light, open, well-drained soil. The hardy annual kinds, reaching a height of 2 ft., bear large, showy, solitary heads with yellow or reddish rays and purple disks from June to frost. All types produce their flowers on long stems, which makes them ideal for indoor decorative purposes. The annuals are more beautiful than the other types, and the double varieties are considered handsomer than the singles. Grown alone, in the border or in beds, the flowers with their contrasting colors make an effective display.

The annuals and biennials are grown from seed sown indoors or in the open garden; the perennials can be propagated by seeds, division of the roots, cuttings taken in August or September, or root cuttings taken in early spring. Plants occasionally self-seed.

Of the annual species *G. pulchella* is the most popular; its heads are 2 in. across and the ray flowers yellow shaded with rose-purple at the base. The var. *picta* produces even larger heads in varied shades; while var. *lorenziana* shows enlarged and tubular rays.

In the perennial group *G. aristata* (to 3 ft.) is one of the last plants in the garden to die. Its flower heads are often 4 in. across; the ray flowers are yellow. The best red or brownish-red species is *G. amblyodon*, an annual, rather hairy.

GALACTITES (ga-lak'-ti-teez). A genus of annual or biennial thistle-like herbs from the Mediterranean region, be-longing to the Daisy Family. *G. tomentosa,* the best known, has spiny-pointed lobed or divided leaves, spotted white above, covered with cottony-down beneath, and heads of purple flowers. It is sometimes grown for ornament.

GALANTHUS (gah-lan'-thus). A genus of small hardy bulbous plants of the Amaryllis Family that bear drooping bell-shaped white flowers on stalks 1 ft., more or less, tall, above a few basal leaves. Their chief value is their extreme earliness, for they bloom before any other bulbous subject, often before the snow disappears. This and the little blossoms both suggest the common name, Snowdrop.

The bulbs should be planted 3 or 4 in. deep in early fall in their permanent location, for they much resent disturbance. They naturalize readily in semi-shaded locations, in meadows or on grassy slopes

GAILLARDIAS DO DOUBLE DUTY
Both annual and perennial forms bloom brightly in the summer garden, even in the face of poor soil and extreme heat, and are excellent for cutting.

and, left alone, will bloom profusely from year to year without further attention. The common snowdrop is *G. nivalis,* but *G. elwesi* is much larger, and there is also a double form. All three have white flowers with greenish stripes on the petals. They are perfectly hardy and can be planted outdoors without protection.

Snowdrops are susceptible to gray mold (Botrytis blight), so don't plant any bulbs harboring the minute, hard, black resting bodies (sclerotia). But if these are solely on the outer scales, the latter can be removed and the naked bulb saved for planting.

GALAX (gay'-laks) *aphylla.* A stemless perennial herb, with stiff shining heart-shaped or rounded leaves up to 5 in. across, and small white flowers in a spike from 9 to 15 in. high. Native from Va. to Ga. and belonging to the Diapensia Family, it is fairly hardy N., thriving in sandy loam with peat or leafmold and suitable for a ground cover in a partly shaded place. Propagated by division.

Galax leaves gathered in large quantities from wild plants in the mountains of Va. and N. C., are much used by florists for wreath making and other decorative work. They keep well in cool storage and take on a bronzy tint in fall that makes them additionally attractive.

GALEGA (gah-lee'-gah). A small genus of bushy perennial herbs with white, purple or blue pea-like flowers in thick clusters which are good for cutting. Two species are grown in America. *G. orientalis,* from the Caucasus, and *G. officinalis* (Goatsrue), from Europe and Asia, with its four botanical varieties, *alba,* white; *compacta; hartlandi,* lilac; and *carnea,* rose.

GALIUM (gay'-li-um). A genus of slender temperate-climate herbs, some with square stems, all with stalkless leaves in whorls, and abundant clusters of very small white or yellow flowers. They are grown mainly in rock gardens for the light airy effect similar to that of babys breath. The species best known in America are *G. mollugo* (known as Wild Madder, Great or White Bedstraw, or False-babys-breath), a 3 ft. perennial weed introduced from Europe to E. U. S.; *G. boreale* (Northern Bedstraw), native over much of N. America and popular for use in rockeries; and *G. verum* (Yellow Bedstraw), a good rock and bank plant, but sometimes becoming a weed in E. U.S.

GALLS. Deformations or overgrowths of plant tissues caused by the irritation produced by bacteria, fungi or insects. Bacteria cause the tumors on the stems and crowns of such plants as blackberries and roses (see CROWN GALL). The cedarapple (see JUNIPER) is a single cedar leaf deformed by a rust fungus. Such galls as the cockscomb gall of elm and the hard spruce gall are due to aphids. A group of plant lice called Phylloxera cause the leaf galls abundant on some trees and -on grapes. A large group of insects called gall wasps cause various types of deformations, particularly on oaks, among them the familiar oak-apple.

The life history of some of these gall makers has what is known as alternation of generations, the second generation producing a gall very different from the first, but the third resembling the grandparents. The gall midges (Itonidae) most frequently attack herbaceous plants such as chrysanthemum; to prevent these conical leaf galls, the grower must watch for and destroy the mature insects when they emerge, which is always between midnight and 4 a. m.

GALTONIA (gaul-toh'-ni-ah). Giant Summer-hyacinth. A small genus of S. African bulbs of the Lily Family which produce, in midsummer, tall spikes bearing fragrant, white or greenish drooping bell-shaped flowers. The basal leaves are stout and strap-shaped. The bulbs are tender in the temperate zone and must either be heavily mulched (after being planted in a protected location) or dug up in early fall, stored in a frost-free place over winter and planted out when the soil warms in the spring. They increase naturally by offsets, but can also be raised freely from seed. The principal species is *G. candicans* (formerly *Hyacinthus candicans*), whose white flowers are borne on stems 3 ft. high.

GALVEZIA (gal-vee'-zi-ah). An evergreen shrub belonging to the Figwort Family, native on the islands off California. *G. speciosa,* the one mostly grown, was formerly known as *Antirrhinum speciosum.* It grows up to 7 ft. tall, has leaves in 3's, and scarlet flowers about an inch long in a terminal inflorescence.

GAMBOGE-TREE (gam-bohj'). Common name for *Garcinia morella,* a broad-leaved, slow growing tree from Asia grown in West Indies and sometimes in S. Fla., bearing fruit the size of cherries. Its juice yields the coloring matter (gamboge) of commerce.

GAMOPETALOUS. Term applied to a flower with petals wholly or partly fused to form a more or less tubular organ, as in the morning-glory or salvia. Gamopetalous corollas are differentiated into two regions, the tube and the more or less flaring portions, called the limb, which see.

GARBANZO (gahr-bahn'-so). A common name for *Cicer arietinum* or Chickpea, which see.

GARBERIA (gahr-bee'-ri-ah). A branching shrub of medium height, native of Florida, belonging to the Daisy Family. The one species (*G. fruticosa*) is rarely used in ornamental plantings. It does best in a dry sunny place and has pale leathery leaves and dense heads of pinkish flowers.

GARDEN-BALSAM. The accepted common name for *Impatiens balsamina,* a popular colorful annual, but sometimes given to a species of tropical water-willows (which see), *Dianthera pectoralis.*

GARDEN CLUB OF AMERICA, THE. This organization was formed in 1913 by a group of women inspired by Mrs. John Willis Martin of Philadelphia. Its purpose and the objective which the many member clubs strive to attain is "to stimulate the knowledge and love of gardening among amateurs, to share the advantage of association through conference and correspondence in this country and abroad, to aid in the protection of native plants and birds, and to encourage civic planting."

The main office of the Garden Club of America is in New York City at 598 Madison Avenue, but through its various committees the Club wields a nationwide influence in the esthetics of gardening. Through its Conservation and Roadside Committee it aids materially in protecting birds and wild life, in conserving native plants, in spreading knowledge of the proper use of Christmas green so as to avoid exterminating the wild materials, in preserving the beauty of our waysides, and, through education, in inspiring a true appreciation of plant life and beauty among children in schools.

Through its Horticultural Committee it seeks to advance the knowledge of plants and planting through study and through encouraging a closer contact with horticultural societies and botanic gardens. Through its National Parks Committee it watches legislation which deals with the control of the areas of the public domain in which are preserved the country's heritage of wild life, both plant and animal.

Through other powerful Committees and numerous other activities—especially the highly educational exhibitions it stages in the large flower shows held in various cities—it has awakened the public to the wide scope of the true art of gardening.

GARDEN CLUBS AND OTHER ORGANIZATIONS. The garden club movement represents a definite step upward in the development of this country; it is evidence of a decided gain in appreciation of the esthetic rather than of the strictly utilitarian. Agricultural and horticultural societies marked earlier stages of this progress. The former were naturally interested primarily in farming; the latter in the growing of fine vegetables, fruits and, to a less extent, flowers considered as specimens.

Garden clubs are interested in gardening in the highest and broadest sense: as a means to the esthetic development of the members, as a community asset, and as a concerted movement for the preservation and development of the natural beauty of the country as a whole. These clubs were started by women, and for a number of years the movement was purely feminine, but of late years more and more men have become active members; in some localities, men's garden clubs (which see) have been organized and are functioning enthusiastically and successfully.

The movement, moreover, is typically American. In no other country is there anything comparable to it. In every portion of the U. S. the garden club is now an integral part of the community life. And though the individual clubs vary in size from a village or neighborhood group to the large coordinated federations of clubs with national membership, all have a share in the general upbuilding of civic and national beauty. Indeed, so valuable is this movement considered by leading thinkers that garden clubs have been and are being sponsored by newspapers, garden magazines, and even by commercial and industrial organizations, such as big railroad and life insurance companies.

The first step was taken in 1860 when the Horticultural Garden Club was organized at Sandy Springs, Md. This was followed in 1892 by the organization of the Ladies' Garden Club of Athens, Ga. The first garden club to have a constitution, by-laws and officers, this body is still in active existence.

In 1893, the National Plant, Flower and Fruit Guild (which see) was organized by Mrs. John Wood Stewart as a purely philanthropic organization, its object being to see that the poor of city tenement districts, and the inmates of hospitals and insane asylums might share in the bounty of the more fortunate through the distribution of contributed plants, flowers and fruit.

In 1913 the Garden Club of America (which see) was organized by a group of women inspired by Mrs. John Willis Martin of Philadelphia. At the first meeting held May 1, 1913, 12 clubs were represented. Today the Garden Club of America has 105 member clubs and more than 7000 individual members, and is national in its membership and international in its influence on horticulture and gardening.

Thereafter garden clubs were gradually organized in all parts of the country and in 1920 a number of groups in Virginia, seeing the need of concerted action when civic, state or national legislation was required, formed themselves into the first Garden Club Federation. In 1924 the clubs of the State of New York followed suit, and since then 30 or more Federations have been formed in the various states. See FEDERATED GARDEN CLUBS.

The National Council of State Garden Club Federations was next formed on May 1, 1929, with 13 states represented. Its by-laws state that it was organized "to bring into relations of mutual helpfulness the State Federations of Garden Clubs, and to make combined action possible when deemed expedient."

In the meantime, in 1914, another important organization was formed—the Women's Farm and Garden Association. Its stated objects were: "To stimulate an interest in and love for country life; to cooperate with Federal and State agencies for the improvement of rural conditions, to assist the woman on the farm and the woman in the city to a realization of their interdependence, and to a better understanding of their mutual and individual problems; to help women through scholarships and expert advice to the best training in agriculture, horticulture and the related professions, and to develop oppor-

tunities for women so trained; to furnish to its members all possible opportunities for the marketing of farm and garden products, including some types of handiwork, and to set forces in motion which will bring producer and consumer together; to offer opportunities for the exchange of members' ideas by means of correspondence, by arranging meetings and by forming branches in various parts of the country." The membership now numbers about 5000 and the headquarters are at Dearborn, Mich.

In 1924, the General Federation of Women's Clubs recognized the significance of the general garden interest and added a garden department to their study groups. It also instituted National Garden Week.

On March 15, 1928, the first Men's Garden Club was organized in Chicago, carrying out an idea conceived by Mr. Leo W. Nack of that city. Four years later, the Chicago club and three others launched the Men's Garden Clubs of America, which grew so rapidly that at its eighth annual convention in 1940 the roll call included 29 groups in 15 States. The secretary at that time was G. B. Dobbin, 212 W. Jackson Ave., Jackson, Mich.

Other interesting related activities include City Garden Clubs (which see) made up, as the name indicates, of urban dwellers, and Junior Garden Clubs, now being established and fostered by many of the Federated Garden Clubs, by schools and departments of education, sometimes through playground and recreation centers, and in some cases by magazines and newspapers that give more or less attention to garden matters.

GARDEN CRESS. An annual herb (*Lepidium sativum*), a species of peppergrass. Easily grown during cool weather for its peppery flavor as a salad. Sometimes called Upland Cress, which name is better applied to Barbarea. See CRESS.

GARDEN DESIGN. This embraces, first, the elements which go to make up the "plan" or form on the ground of a garden and their details; and, also, the resulting forms in elevation (that is, actual pictures) when the ground plan is carried out. To develop a plot of ground, large or small, for any purpose whatsoever, requires planning it out to suit this purpose. When such a plan is put down on paper, it becomes definitely a design. Whether it is geometrical and formal, or casual and wholly informal has nothing to do with the case. Wherefore it is at once evident that garden design does not mean stilted effects when the work is carried out; hence it is nothing to fight shy of or fear.

Rather it is an imperative necessity if a garden is to be successful. For without it endless mistakes are inevitable, and these will mean hurried replanting and changing about later on when they are recognized; that is hard on plants, expensive, and never wholly satisfactory. While it is true that the importance of a plan or a garden design is recognized by many people, it is also true that the most serious fault in American gardens generally and throughout the country, is lack of just such a plan or design. In the mistaken belief that a design will hamper freedom and lead to formalities he wishes to avoid, the novice plunges into gardening with ostentatious defiance of the idea. The truth of the matter is that the "naturalistic beauty" for which certain gardens are notable is the result of planning or designing of the very highest order. Anyone with knowledge of how to handle a T-square and a triangle may take these implements and lay out straight-line-and-angle plans. But to develop scenes of picturesque and natural beauty and charm such as Nature offers when at her very best and richest, and to relate these so closely with a dwelling that each seems an integral part of the other, requires vision, imagination, the soul of artist and poet, too, and infinite patience and capacity for taking pains—in other words, for genius. Planning of this kind is what every garden demands and can receive—can express if given it; the art which conceals art. Nothing is more artful in the world, nothing demands such study and care—such careful designing.

FIRST THINGS. Coming from the general to the particular, what is the first essential in garden design? It is precisely the same as in the design of a building. The first essential is always *advance knowledge* of the things to be provided for—the needs and desires of the home of which the garden is to be a part. Just as the architect, in making a design for a house, must know in advance how many rooms to provide and what these rooms are to be, in order to meet the needs and desires of the family, so the person who is to make a garden design must have advance knowledge of the house it is to com-

plement. He must know about its rooms, for they look out upon the outdoors; and about the people who will live there and use the garden and *how* they will use it—whether there will be children needing play spaces, or young people wanting a place for games, or elderly people desiring only lovely retreats and beautiful pictures to contemplate; or, perhaps, all of these.

THE MAP. Garden design itself starts with a map of the ground, drawn to scale and showing in their exact positions all existing features that are to be permanent. This, of course, includes the buildings if these are already present. If no buildings exist the first need of all is the careful study of the area as it lays spread out in its entirety in map form, so as to discover and determine the best place for the dwelling and its appurtenances. This study should be made with particular regard to two basic and important considerations: the *orientation* and the *approach*.

ORIENTATION. This deals with the position of a building with reference to the points of the compass, more particularly the east, but this of course implies the others also. Because this affects the winter and summer exposure of every room—exposure to the sun, to prevailing summer breezes, to the bitter storms of winter—it determines for all time the aspect of every room, of every door and window opening. Indeed, it is the most influential factor in the success of every room and, therefore, in the success of the entire house.

Consequently, when garden design can start at the beginning—that is, with land not yet built on—it concerns itself first of all with this placing of the dwelling in relation to the factors of climate, weather, storm and sunshine. Such a program provides ideal conditions for the production of a perfect composition—a house and a garden in right relation, fully complementing one another and, together, forming an idyllic home.

APPROACH. This deals with the relation of the dwelling (and of the entire place) to the highway; also with the means of passing to and fro between house and highway—in short, with driveways and walks. Do not regard these as undesirable necessities any more than as features to be especially stressed and (mistakenly) treated as decorative elements. Think of them for what they are—reasonable utilities which may easily make or mar the entire enterprise according to whether or not they are hospitable, spacious, and easily negotiated. This viewpoint is a real help in planning them along the best possible lines.

Both walks and driveways should follow the line of least resistance between the points which they connect; *or they should be made to seem to do this.* It is important to recognize the psychology underlying movement between two points and to cater to the ever dominant instinct to "take a short cut." This need not result in actual short cuts, although these utility features should be as direct as possible, should never intrude upon the garden pictures, and should never *unnecessarily* use up ground space.

Curves are not in themselves preferable to straight lines, nor vice versa. The general conditions determine preference for one or the other in any particular place; and by general conditions we understand the general lay of the ground and the character of the property—that is, whether it is level and a plot of geometric form making up, with similar plots, a community or neighborhood, or instead, an irregular piece of land situated in the midst of naturalistic surroundings with perhaps irregularities of levels or contours. There is nothing more foolish than an entrance walk curving needlessly to the front door on the average suburban place. All the conditions demand straightforward entry and this means a walk rationally located to provide the most direct way from sidewalk to the door, no matter from which direction along the street the visitor may approach.

This requirement is as true of a driveway as it is of a walk; but because driveway traffic makes demands which foot traffic does not, it is nearly always necessary to consider a change in direction in planning a driveway. It is *not* desirable to drive up straight to a door and stop there—unless it is the door of the garage. On small areas the latter arrangement is often the logical (and therefore the *right*) thing to do. In this connection it may not be amiss to note how much ground can often be saved for other and better purposes than driveway, if the garage or automobile room is made a part of the house, instead of being detached and placed toward the rear of the plot. In more and more plans for modern and model houses, this is being done; and not only as a ground economy measure, but for the convenience of

being under cover when going to and from the car. Sometimes nothing can equal the advantage of driving literally, "into the house."

Where there is an appreciable amount of ground so that a choice between several routes for the driveway is possible, choose the most direct. Then remember that changes in direction should always be made easily and on wide curves. Parking space, if provided, is best when it is merely a widened portion of the driveway requiring no turning around or backing up to depart from it; the ideal turn-around space admits of driving around rather than stopping, backing and working painfully out of a pocket. A radius of not less than 30 ft. is required in which to make an easy turn and the entire space within this circle should be clear. If a central grass plot or specimen tree is desired, the circle should spring from a radius 15 to 20 ft. greater.

We have dealt at some length with driveways and walks because these affect all other elements in the design of a garden. Carelessly and improperly placed they make it impossible to proceed with a design, since they interfere with distribution and arrangement of other spaces and with the entire composition to such a degree that no continuity is possible. And, lacking continuity, a garden lacks that flowing and gracious quality which should always distinguish gardens, great and small.

GROUND PLAN. With the dwelling properly oriented and the entrances determined, the design itself is reached. Primarily, as noted at the outset, garden design is ground plan—the layout on the ground of the desired elements or features. From such plan rises the effect in elevation—the various garden pictures—that become the secondary part of the design. This does not mean that they are less important than the plan, but only that they are consequent upon the development of it, and dependent upon the materials with which it is carried out.

FEATURES. Ground plan begins with consideration of the features which it is desired to include in the garden. For the average home a complete and suitable layout will include (1) a terrace or level outdoor transition space uniting house and garden; (2) a lawn space of modest size, with trees and shrubbery (or other enclosing and screening boundary treatment); (3) space for a herbaceous border (perennial flowers); (4) space for cutting flowers, which may be annual or perennial or both; (5) a service area (which, like a driveway, is utilitarian but essential); (6) adequate space for growing, at least, the choicer vegetables or those most favored by the household, some tree and bush fruits and grapes; and (7) as many sheltered retreats as it is possible to provide without cluttering up the whole layout or destroying the desired wide, open-space effects.

Incidental to the essential garden elements just listed are such things as rock gardens, rose gardens, lily pools and all the special features which go to enhance and distinguish the individual place. To many home owners these represent their chief delight, whereas to many others they would be an undesirable burden. They are, therefore, the things to be individually decided upon and planned *after* the fundamentals are arranged.

BEGIN AT THE HOUSE. However large or small a garden may be, it should invariably have its definite beginning at the house. Hence that is where garden design begins. Failure to recognize this fact is the most frequent cause of failure in design generally. For no matter how well proportioned and well planted, in and by itself, a garden may be, it falls short of the standard of excellence by which all gardens must be judged if it lacks one-ness with the dwelling which is, after all, the reason for its existence.

THE AXIS. Because great and famous gardens—classic examples—have been designed with careful regard to axial lines, projected (which in non-technical language means carried on or extended) from a source which is some feature of the dwelling; and because it is true that an axis on which the house and at least the beginning of the garden are united, is an admitted necessity, for these reasons the axis has come to be a veritable obsession in many places and with many designers. This is a pity, for slavish adherence to axial lines inhibits the play of fancy, and imagination ceases to function. Because imagination is the heart and flame of garden design just as of everything else in the world, the loss in such case is too great.

Yet the fault is not in the axis nor what it stands for, but in failure to correctly estimate its function and appreciate the

GARDEN DESIGN AIMS TO FIT THE GARDEN TO THE SITE AND TO THE NEEDS AND DESIRES OF THOSE WHO USE IT

In this instance formal treatment involving different levels is appropriate and effective; elsewhere something entirely different would be necessary. The wide range of possible results is one of the alluring features of designing garden pictures.

rigidity which it will impose upon design if it is not restrained. So let us not devaluate the garden axis, but estimate it truly. It is admittedly the essential link between two forms—in this instance, between house and garden. Now, because the function of any link—as in a chain—is simply to reach between the two things which it unites, there is no reason for projecting an axis to extreme limits in order to have it create the desired unity between house and garden.

Let us, therefore, set it down as a definite rule of good design that while there is required a close relationship on a common axis between house and garden *where they meet,* such axis need continue only far enough to establish this relationship. It then should (or may) disappear as far as any definite influence on the further design is concerned. Sometimes it may well be picked up again at a distance by placing some garden feature on it—a statue, sun dial, birdbath, or what you will—but over the intervening space no suggestion of it whatsoever should be allowed.

Very often it is desirable to lead out from the house with just a simple lawn space, rectangular in form or perhaps oval or circular. In these circumstances it may appear at first glance that there is no axis uniting the indoors with outdoors. But if the lawn space is itself recognized as the garden feature that may share a common axis with the house, and in consequence is balanced on the axis of whatever architectural feature gives access to it—a simple door perhaps, or a French window that extends to the ground or possibly a porch or loggia—then the sought-for unity is perfectly accomplished. Beyond this lawn feature the garden may go its various ways, disregarding further axial considerations altogether; or, if not wholly disregarding them, proceeding from one to another of its divisions by means of successive, lightly emphasized, but never elongated axial links that serve merely to hold the design together. No hard formality will result when design is developed in this way, for there is so little of geometrical line actually shown that geometrical forms cannot occur, nor even a suggestion of them.

BOUNDARIES. Until the limits of a garden whether large or small are defined and made evident, there can really be no garden in the true sense. For the very word garden means a place apart, protected and enclosed. And that is what every garden should be in order to be inviting and to provide the delightful recreational opportunities which are one of the reasons for having a garden. Compare a garden which affords its owner the keen pleasures of day-by-day use and intimate enjoyment, with even the finest sweep of lawn open to the surroundings and merely enveloping the dwelling, and it at once becomes clear why people tend to keep within the seclusion of the porches in the latter type of place. Seclusion, privacy and a resulting intimate home-sense are the very essence of a true garden. The place which stimulates such feelings is irresistible; everyone's instinct is to go out and spend every possible moment in the fascinating surroundings it provides. Whereas instinct is equally opposed to the public parade which even the crossing of an unprotected dooryard lawn suggests.

Objections to walls, fences or dense plantings designed to shut off the garden from the outside world are, in some places, based on the mistaken idea that it is not in keeping with the American principles of living to retain a landscaped area around one's home and not share its beauty with all who pass along street or highway. If this were a valid objection to privacy in the garden it would apply equally to drawing the curtains before the windows of the house and thus shutting the public out from the interior and from sharing the beauties of the furnishings and the home life within. This also is contrary to democratic ideals—*if* garden privacy is.

There are, of course, appropriate treatments of highways designed to make them attractive and enjoyable for those who use them; but this is a problem wholly apart from the gardens which are, first of all, parts of the homes that they belong to and only secondarily a part of the public arteries of travel and convenience. It is an unbalanced misconception to claim for the public generally a right to intrude within the very heart and inner sanctuary of anybody's home—even though it is an intrusion limited to vision alone.

A second objection to enclosing garden walls or planting sometimes raised is that a desirable air of spaciousness is preserved by the elimination of boundary lines between properties; by the continuous sweep of a cleared lawn space throughout a community, so that everyone's land runs undefined into the neighboring plots and up to the common sidewalk line. Possibly this objection is based upon the idea that all boundary barriers between properties must appear simply as divisions—bare fences that merely set each plot apart from its neighbors. As a matter of fact, that is exactly how the undeveloped or unlandscaped fence *does* appear; and where nothing better has ever been seen or imagined the objection is understandable even though we may not sympathize with it. In such instances it is not the fault of the boundary itself, but rather that of the way of handling it.

It may be considered an aphorism of garden design that every element or feature must be reconciled with the earth and with its surroundings so completely that it will form a distinct and valuable contribution to the landscape picture as well as serve its useful purpose (if it has one). In other words, it must be an esthetic asset, as well as a practical utility. Thus the garden boundary must be a decorative background for all the garden features within it, as well as a barrier affording protection to the entire garden and the home. Under this concept and the treatment required to bear it out, every boundary in such a community as was just referred to will appear not so much as a separation between one area and the next as a union between the home, the earth and the sky—carrying the vision skyward by means of its lifting growth against which the garden's loveliest treasures will be displayed.

Such a background is quite as important as the foreground in every garden view or picture—even more important, perhaps, because background provides its own individual features in addition to a setting that enhances the display of other things. It is therefore capable of being, in itself and without the aid of foreground elements, an important decorative adjunct. The subjects in the foreground, on the other hand, are dependent upon support from behind to bring them into true focus and set their value adequately in the composition.

Boundary treatment may be of several kinds, depending upon individual circumstances. Walls of masonry lead everything else as far as permanence, picture effect and general desirability are concerned. Excellent effects are possible with wood; some of the modern synthetic building materials offer new ideas and ways of carrying them out; and the simple wire fence, masked with a trimmed hedge or with flowing lines of shrubbery, is inexpensive and easily erected. Whether wall or fence is chosen, its color is easily the paramount consideration when the garden effect is being calculated. The glare of white or light colors—except such light, earthy shades as stones sometimes introduce—is never good because it is conspicuous and too sharply limiting. Depth of shadow and inconspicuous blending with shadow constitute the boundary ideal, and anything that runs contrary to this should be avoided.

INNER DIVISIONS. Within the garden's boundaries divisions may and usually do occur, requiring expression in one way or another. These are similar to the division into rooms of the floor space within the house; and just as a few, finely proportioned rooms in a given number of square feet, are preferable to many smaller, petty ones, so the garden divisions should avoid pettiness and the sense of clutter which comes of overdoing even a very good thing.

Here is the place for a finely discriminating sense of scale or proportion to assert itself. The eager desire of most garden enthusiasts to include within their own domain as many beautiful features and as many varieties of plant material as can be crowded into it, needs to be sternly kept in check. The possibilities of the garden's area should be studied with nothing between the designer and his design but the cool, pure light of restrained reasoning and a consequent exercise of reasonable restraint.

GARDEN DETAILS. While it is not possible to lay down definite laws or rules to govern such highly individual matters as the details of any particular garden, it is perhaps safe to say that all but the very smallest imaginable garden area may have two distinct divisions; and should have at least two. Above this, the number will depend upon both the size of the place, its character and those of its surroundings and of the dwelling in its midst. Consideration of a basic two will here make it possible to arrive at the underlying principles which apply to any number of parts that may be desired, or possible.

Contrast is an important quality or characteristic in garden design when it is not overdone and when it is achieved without forced effect. These are nice qualifications

Plate 23.   PLEASURES OF A GARDEN POOL

Top: Circular form follows circular form, ranging symmetrically around the central jewel, the formal pool. Bottom: Dark water and cool green foliage so well placed that all thought of design is lost in the satisfying whole, are shown in the informal pool at Cronamere, Greens Farms, Conn.

and mean that garden contrasts must be well studied, carefully weighed and adroitly introduced so that they seem inevitable as well as desirable and delightful. Taking up the minimum two divisions which it is suggested that every garden shall have, it is desirable that they shall show contrast —first in size; not greatly, perhaps, but definitely, so that the more important expresses greater importance, even as the more important rooms of a house unmistakably express their functions and status. Contrast in treatment is next in importance; contrast in mood is a rare and subtle distinction.

Under the first—size—come such matters as the plant material. Perhaps there will be brilliant flowers in one, no flowering material at all in the other; perhaps evergreens, shrubs, special kinds of flowers, as roses or rock plants, or other favorites assembled for comparative observation and to enrich each other by the emphasis which such assemblage lays on particular beauties and qualites.

Under the heading of contrast of mood in garden detail, come such matters as color and direct full light, shade, shadow, and half-light—with these can be calculated the natural and unconscious reaction which normal human beings will feel to these various gradations. It is of special interest and significance that whatever harmonizes with a given mood in the garden will actually call up that mood in the normal person who comes within the influence of the garden. Gaiety, pensive quiet, still expectancy, solemn and philosophic meditation—sadness, if you will—all are within the range of the garden's special expression. Every emotion, indeed, which the human heart is capable of entertaining may find expression there, to make in turn its appeal emotionally.

Recognition of this and the consequent study of the possibilities latent in garden design as a form of creative expression, unfold to the designer endless resources as well as give assurance of effects in his finished work of marked individuality and significance. Yet it is an aspect of garden design which cannot be more than suggested, since each design itself offers a new problem, and demands a new approach and a new solution in order to weave into the concept such an inspiring thought-pattern.

As a final word, it is to be remembered that such mood stimulation is inevitable whether it is calculated by the designer or not. But if it is *not* so calculated and carefully planned out, it is as likely to be an undesired mood (and an undesirable one) as it is to be the contrary. Hence it is essential to the ultimate success of a garden that we concede these mood potentialities; that we study the meaning and the effect of every detail proposed; and that we adopt and make use of those which seem to promise the desired result. As with every sort of garden activity, it is sometimes only by the trial and error method that results can be arrived at; but the important thing is to know that such results *are possible,* for this will induce persistent effort until they are achieved.

CONTOURS AND GRADES. While a certain amount of smoothing down and ironing out of the wrinkles of the earth where it meets the house may be needed on land that is violently irregular, much more so-called "grading" is done on the general run of places of this type than need be. Adaptation of garden design (and house design, also, of course) to land irregularities is a rare privilege and opportunity to the really creative designer; every effort should always be made to preserve the marked individuality which is inherent in such sites. The purpose of true grading is not to level to a commonplace and insignificant standard of similarity, but to adjust house and garden and all appurtenances to the land; to insure convenient approach, entrance and exit; and to preserve intact everything else that is unique and individual in the land formation.

SUMMARY. In garden design *Proportion, Mass* and *Perspective* are responsible for the results, precisely as in painting on a canvas. The garden design must set forth in its plan for the ground, such an assemblage of garden elements as will furnish *mass* (of dark, light, and high-light as provided by complete shade, shadows and open spaces) correctly *proportioned* to each other and to the whole, when viewed in elevation—or *perspective.* Thus created, these perspectives, elevation views or pictures will inevitably be harmonious and beautiful.

See also ACCENT PLANTS; CITY GARDEN; FORMAL GARDEN; GARDEN PATHS AND DRIVES; GARDEN WALLS; INFORMAL GARDEN; LANDSCAPING, etc.

GARDENERS GARTERS. Another name for the Ribbon Grass (*Phalaris arun-*

dinacea var. *picta*) an ornamental grass whose long narrow leaves are striped white and green; an old time garden favorite. See PHALARIS.

GARDENERS, NATIONAL ASSOCIATION OF. Organized in 1910, this body seeks to develop and maintain higher standards for professional gardeners, to assist student gardeners in securing the necessary theoretical and practical training, and to promote the mutual interests of gardeners and their employers. The membership is composed of active members, who are private or professional gardeners; associate members, who are men and women engaged in pursuits pertaining to gardening; and sustaining members including estate owners and others interested in gardening.

The official organ of the society is the monthly magazine, *The Gardeners' Chronicle of America.* The Society sponsored and was instrumental in establishing the International Peace Garden, on the boundary between North Dakota and Manitoba, the development and maintenance costs of which are supplied by an endowment fund made up of voluntary contributions. It also maintains a service bureau through which qualified superintendents and gardeners are supplied to employers.

The annual dues for active and associate membership are $5, and for sustaining members $10. The secretary is Mrs. Dorothy E. Hansell, 1270 Sixth Ave., New York City.

GARDEN FIXTURES. All permanent construction in the garden, as distinguished from plant or horticultural elements, is covered by this term. Summer houses, arbors, pergolas, walls, gazebos, fountains come within it; likewise sculpture, benches, and other ornaments when these are permanently fixed in place. By extension, removable or portable objects are generally included although they are not garden fixtures in the strict sense of the words.

In either case they are mostly useful things which are capable of becoming ornamental when artistically developed and treated. It can never be too strongly emphasized that in developing or selecting any of them, the simplest designs and generally subdued and inconspicuous coloring should prevail. The object is always to fit them into the garden picture as a whole; never to allow them to dominate it. For this reason it is seldom that arbors or summer houses can be painted white or any light color with good effect unless they are to be masked with vegetation, and in that case any essential spraying of the foliage is likely to stain light colored paint. The soft shades of blue-green which vanish in the shadows of vegetation, or colors like the brown of old wood or the gray of tree bark are much to be preferred and are appropriate always and anywhere, even with old-fashioned white houses.

GARDEN FURNITURE. This term is loosely applied to anything structural in the garden, but properly it includes only such things as seats, benches, tables, sun-umbrellas, swings and articles of similar purpose—those things which are for personal use as distinguished from things introduced wholly or mainly for decorative purposes, as sculpture, sundials, fountains, etc.

It goes without saying that garden furniture should be as comfortable to use as furniture in the house; no design is good which does not provide for this. It should further be impervious to the elements, as to both material and construction. This means that it must be so shaped and put together that it will shed water instantly and completely after a drenching. Particular pains must be taken to eliminate even very insignificant corners and pockets from which water cannot freely drain away.

Light weight is an important factor in the case of articles that are to be moved about; and the importance of forms free from projections both at the ground level or higher up, cannot be too strongly emphasized. Projections, however decorative they may seem to be, become dangerous traps if at or near the ground where they can be stumbled over, or if they are at a higher level where they may catch and tear garments.

These considerations demand the simplest designs, smooth surfaces everywhere and careful finishing. While freakish forms are undesirable, this does not mean that novelties may not sometimes be excellent, *if* they are structurally sound.

The development of light, strong, weather-resistant metals has provided material for garden furniture which meets every requirement—esthetic and practical. The simple, clean-cut lines of modern designs executed in such metals probably account in large measure for the better designs now available in wooden furniture.

These newer forms have rightly super-seded the cumbersome and decidedly un-comfortable pieces of so-called rustic con-struction, which were supposed to be especially appropriate to garden use. Actually they never were, for rusticity and the degree of cultivation represented by even a naturalistic, informal garden are incompatible.

The best placing of furniture in the garden will suggest itself as the design of a garden progresses, or as the contours of the land are studied and desirable loitering spots are revealed. Naturally a terrace, that links house with garden, demands tables and seats and full provision for as constant use as an indoor living room. Here, if there is lack of shade, umbrellas are especially appropriate. Once this area is passed, it is better not to introduce anything more until a place sufficiently remote from the house to make a resting spot desirable is reached. Too many places are so "adorned" with garden furniture as to defeat a main purpose of the plan, which is to provide a definite and separate outdoor living room. In a large garden there may be several such places, but they should be completely isolated and not visible one from another. In small gardens it is not desirable to develop more than one such general gathering center, though in all gardens the need to provide a resting spot wherever an attractive scene or vista may be enjoyed, is sufficient reason for placing an unobtrusive bench or settee wherever desired.

Dark colors are usually preferable to light ones or white for painted furniture, and even for trellises, arbors, etc. For these things are all incidental to the garden, not important features of it, and light colors emphasize them unduly and draw attention away from the garden scenes, compositions, and plant materials. Of colors to choose, the best three are deep bottle green, weathered gray, and the shadowy soft blue that is a little deeper than the horizon color on a summer day. For painting (or repainting) garden furniture only the best quality outside-paint should be used; when several coats are applied, each must be allowed to dry thoroughly before putting on the next. This insures a hard, durable surface which will not become sticky in damp weather.

GARDEN FURNITURE MAY SUIT ONE'S WHIM OR THE LOCATION OR BOTH
I. The rustic chair—if comfortable—belongs in a simple, old-fashioned garden. II. For a garden nook or "outdoor living room" the white-painted wooden bench is highly appropriate. III. Metal furniture is durable, inconspicuous, and more comfortable than might be expected. IV. For luncheon, tea or bridge on the patio or lawn, modernistic metal chairs and a shaded table are hospitable and add a note of interest.

THE GARDEN GATE SHOULD HARMONIZE WITH THE BARRIER OF WHICH IT IS A PART

When a close-clipped hedge surrounds the property, a wooden gate with hand-wrought hinges (a) is appropriate. For the rough stone wall, a simple barred wooden gate (b) is suitable. Ironwork (c) fits in with the severity of the plain brick wall. A suburban garden or entire property is often enclosed in a light but durable fence and gate (d) of heavy wire.

GARDEN FURNITURE MATERIALS

WOOD. Adaptable to every place and condition, according to. design, which near dwellings or garden structures will preferably be restrained though it may well be thoroughly modern. Farther away the design may become more tricky and fanciful if desired. Advantages of wood are low cost, fairly light weight and, for the home-craftsman, ease of construction. A disadvantage is the necessity for frequent repainting if exposed to the weather.

METAL. Expressing artful simplicity, modern metal furniture is appropriate to terraces, perfect lawns under the shade of trees or lawn shelters, and all architectural sites. It is *not* in harmony with remoter parts of the garden since inherent in its form and material is a sophistication and degree of elegance which implies restraint as opposed to the casual abandon of purely natural surroundings. Its advantages are permanence, ease of handling and freedom from maintenance demands. Its disadvantages are negligible, cost being the chief difficulty; but this is largely nullified by its lasting qualities.

STONE. A material "of the ages," this implies grave and classical environment when in definite forms. Yet rude stones may be set up to form seats and tables in the midst of wholly wild and naturalistic surroundings with better effect than any other material. Sculptured stone furniture demands splendid settings rarely possible except in large and splendid gardens. Its advantages of permanence and fixed position are obvious. Its disadvantages consist mainly in its dwarfing effect on everything around, which makes insignificant all that is not scaled to its own dignity and splendor. It is a material wholly out of key with small-scale things and does not suit the average modest garden.

FABRIC. Informality, freedom from restraint and general abandon to the moment are associated with this type. For carrying about as fancy dictates, chairs, settees, etc., of canvas slung on frames are ideal. But they are hardly furniture in the strict sense and it is impossible to assign them any particular place. However, every garden might well keep a supply in reserve in a convenient and sheltered place, whence one piece or several may be picked up and taken anywhere on occasion. In small gardens they are indispensable. Their advantages lie in their flexibility of use; their disadvantages in the necessity of keeping them under cover during bad weather.

Satisfactory garden furniture in various styles and materials and at a wide range of prices is now so generally obtainable that it rarely pays to make it at home—unless as a hobby. In such case the work should be carefully and strongly done; nails (or preferably screws) that will not rust and cause stains should be used, or, better still, pins, wedges, dowels, tenons, and other wooden fastenings, so as to eliminate all metal parts.

GARDEN GATES. Entrance gates from the highway should be substantial and designed to express something of the importance associated with portals to a special domain. Gates within that lead from one division to another should similarly express, in their proportions, in the material of which they are made, and in the degree to which they attract attention, the relatively less important purposes which they serve. They should be "in scale."

However unimportant it may be relatively, a garden gate must never stand alone. It exists to provide a way through a barrier of some kind—hedge, wall, shrubbery thicket, hedgerow, or fence. Without such a positive barrier it is an absurd affectation. But when correctly placed and built it may provide greater interest and charm than any other equally simple garden detail; for it both forbids and invites, thus appealing to any imagination.

In a barrier of natural vegetation, simple, sturdy, inconspicuous gates of wood are most suitable. For clipped hedges or fences, a design which is restrained and conventional is best, while a gate through a thicket may indulge in fantasy without becoming unpleasant. Special devices, or the owner's monogram or initials, cut with a jigsaw and mounted within the frame are interesting and sometimes amusing. The construction must be in keeping with the protective character of the gate.

Wooden gates, when heavily constructed, are good in stone and brick walls, although wrought iron is more often seen. Annual painting of both kinds is highly desirable and gate posts should be examined and trued up each spring in cold regions.

GARDEN-HELIOTROPE. A common name for the *Valeriana officinalis*, a popular tall hardy perennial with clusters of numerous small white, pink or lavender highly fragrant flowers.

GARDENIA (gahr-dee'-ni-ah). A genus of shrubs or small trees, native in subtropical regions of the E. hemisphere and belonging to the Madder Family. They will grow outdoors in the warm parts of this country, but are also extensively grown under glass for their cut flowers, popular as corsage material, mostly produced in winter.

Under glass they need warm moist conditions during their growing season and young plants (preferably not over 2 years old) give best results, although it is possible to keep old plants going. They are grown in pots or benches, and thrive best in good fibrous loam, with one-third old cow manure and a little sand. Propagation is by cuttings rooted under close conditions in winter. But with these great care should be taken not to infect them with Phomopsis canker which appears as brown, dead areas containing black fungus fruiting bodies on stem and branches. Use a very sharp knife and dip the cuttings in a fungicidal dust or, preferably, plant them in a sterilized rooting medium.

Owing to the fact that gardenias seem fussy and sometimes refuse to do well even for expert greenhouse growers, professional gardeners are loath to recommend them for house culture because of the dry heat and varying conditions found in most dwellings. Yet many home owners manage to keep plants in good condition for years and to get successive crops of the popular, sweet-smelling flowers. The secret is largely one of keeping the atmosphere sufficiently moist; giving the plant enough, but not too much, water in the soil and spraying it often; protecting it from drafts and temperature changes of any kind, and giving it a bright, sunny location during the winter and one with slight shade part of the time in summer, but not out in the garden where winds can buffet it.

Leaf spots are checked by sanitary measures such as removal of spotted leaves. Use of sterilized soil prevents root knot (see NEMATODES). Bud drop, a non-parasitic disease, is induced by too high temperature and humidity, and sometimes by overfeeding. Too alkaline a soil may produce chlorotic leaves.

The gardenia grows best in a definitely acid soil, one with a pH of 5.0 to 5.5. White flies, mealy bugs, and soft scale may be controlled with a special greenhouse white-oil spray.

PRINCIPAL SPECIES

G. jasminoides (formerly known as *G. florida*). This is the Cape-jasmine which makes a bushy shrub to 6 ft., with thick glossy evergreen leaves and waxy-white, heavily scented flowers with 9 petals. The double-flowered varieties are the most popular, and some growers have developed specially selected forms with larger flowers. It is also extensively grown in greenhouses for cut flowers sold by florists, and as a pot plant.

thunbergiana has long leaves and large 8-parted white fragrant flowers, long-tubed and with a spathe-like calyx.

rothmannia has distinctive leaves with hairy glands along the midrib, and 5-parted short-tubed flowers of pale yellow with purple markings.

GARDENING IN DIFFERENT SECTIONS. Dividing the country roughly into sections that seem to have certain distinguishing characteristics that influence garden types and methods, this article deals briefly with the following: California—Florida—the Mississippi Valley—the Mountain States Region—New England—the Northern Region—the Pacific Northwest—the Southeastern Section—the Southwestern Section, in that order.

CALIFORNIA

Two seasons instead of four are a distinguishing climatic feature that directly influences gardening in this State. The rainy season extends from October to May; the dry one covers the balance of the year. This makes autumn comparable to spring elsewhere as regards favorable planting and sowing conditions, and the Calif. spring a poor time, especially for planting. Extremes of heat and cold which the length of the State (nearly 800 miles from N. to S.) would seem to imply, are surprisingly equalized by moist winds from the Pacific; also by the mountain ranges, which constitute roughly half the area. Thus the average temperature variation between N. and S. in the coastal regions is only about 12 deg. F. The interior of the State is much warmer than the coast, as the mountains cut off the ocean winds, yet the temperature is similarly equalized so that here, too, N. and S. have about the same amount of heat. In other words, throughout the State it is not latitude that counts so much as distance from the ocean.

These conditions, plus low humidity during the heat of summer, make plant material of widely different kinds useful in places not far apart. Hence probably a greater variety of plants can be grown in Calif. than in any equal area elsewhere in the world. This seeming advantage horticulturally has led to an extravagant use of exotics from every warm region of the world, to the consequent neglect of fine native material. As most of these exotics require copious watering during the long dry season, it is impossible to combine them with the drought-resisting native plants, which, therefore are simply left out of many gardens. However, a strong corrective influence is beginning to assert itself through the splendid Blakesley Botanic Garden at Santa Barbara, where only native material, handled to show what its possibilities are in the garden as well as in the landscape, is grown. As a result more new gardens, like the best of the older ones, show a combination of native plants with exotics from regions of similar climatic conditions.

As the garden has no season of real rest, gardeners have no season of idleness. They must have plant material in shape to produce bloom throughout the year. This demands careful planning and vigorous execution of plans. The best authorities advise disregarding such distinctions as "annual" and "perennial" among flowers and using both according to their bloom only, accompanying them with early- and summer-flowering bulbs.

Mr. Sidney Mitchell has pointed out ("Gardening in California") that in northern Calif. (and northward to Vancouver Is.) the climate resembles that of S. England and Ireland; while from the central part southward it repeats conditions of the Riviera, Italy, N. Africa and Madeira. The vegetation that characterizes those regions does extremely well in the corresponding regions of Calif. and the similarity of climate to that of S. Africa and parts of Australia explains the success of the Cape bulbs (which see) and of many Australian shrubs and vines and trees. Of the latter, the eucalyptus is now so abundant as to seem native.

FLORIDA

Variability of climate and of rainfall (which, however, is generally heavy), characterizes this peninsula thrust between the Atlantic Ocean and the Gulf of Mexico. Rain is unevenly distributed also throughout the season, and occasionally over periods of several years. Normally it is dry, or comparatively dry, through the autumn and winter, and especially dry in spring and sometimes well into June; from then on to October come heavy rains, summer being definitely a rainy season.

Plant material from dry climates cannot be expected to succeed under these circumstances and is rarely used except in isolated places where the adverse conditions are modified by purely local influences. In many places it is almost a necessity to provide drainage in the garden in order to succeed with even the appropriate garden plants. Either open ditches or deep ditches filled to within 20 in. of the surface with loose stones covered with straw over which the earth is leveled, are considered better than tile drains. The depth of ditch is determined by the level at which it is desired to maintain the water table; this is usually from 36 to 40 in. below the surface.

Variations of temperature are often extreme; as wide a range as 60 deg. is sometimes recorded within a 10 day period in spring. This may be fatal to that class of plants which respond quickly to spring warmth; beginning to grow prematurely, they are often caught by subsequent cold spells. Hence only plant material that remains dormant until the weather has "settled," can be relied on.

Fla. soils are mainly neutral or acid rather than alkaline. But fortunately the chief ornamental plants useful here are acid-loving, notably much of the material from China and Japan, as well as many ornamentals available only as greenhouse material in the N. The addition of lime to the soil is a relatively unknown practice and Mr. H. H. Hume ("Gardening in the Lower South") warns that it may do more harm than good to practically the entire range of plants in which Fla. gardeners are interested.

Planting of most things is best done in late autumn and winter, or at the season of most complete dormancy in the plant in question. For those that shed their leaves (deciduous kinds), December and January are usually the best season; in the case of broad-leaved evergreens, the work may be done either then or as the rainy season comes on, whichever is most convenient. When moved without balls of earth, broad-leaved evergreens are generally stripped of their leaves. Careful gardeners bind a 1 in. layer of sphagnum moss to the trunks and branches of all transplanted trees and keep it moistened and in place until new growth starts.

MISSISSIPPI VALLEY

Throughout this section the early traditions of a landed aristocracy have left a very definite mark. Dwellers in the country, the rich slave-owning planters who built splendid mansions, also made some of the finest gardens the country has had, and the gardens found there today reveal the same appreciation of stately effect and haughty dignity that distinguished the gardens of long ago.

The short springtime of the upper portion, with correspondingly long hot summer during which rainfall is sometimes very meager, has led to the practice of summer mulching-over the roots of many plants, to protect them from both sun and wind. Farther southward, vegetation grows more luxuriant as the soil grows heavier and more acid, until, approaching the Gulf, subtropical conditions are reached, where, in La. the influence of the early French settlements is seen in both garden design and the use of plant material.

The native material of the entire section is especially rich and useful for ornamental planting, from the varied plants (both woody and herbaceous) of Ky. to the splendid material of the southern portion. Here roses bloom throughout the year; camellias, magnolias, pomegranates, oranges and other citrus fruits are cultivated; and gardens in general are distinguished by that careless opulence expressive of southern climes and subtropical places.

MOUNTAIN STATES SECTION

As is to be expected, all this region is distinguished by that wide divergence in temperatures, rainfall and other climatic conditions that accompany alternating high and low altitudes. The natural conditions are such that land is largely devoted to stock raising, and practically all that is not used for this purpose is agriculturally worked for the commercial growing of grains, fruits and vegetables. Thus there is no reason for the growth of large towns and cities; and where these do not exist, with their accompanying desire for luxurious living, gardening naturally does not develop to any extent. Except in Colo., therefore, it is hardly to be expected that this section shall have developed a distinguishing type of garden activity.

Nevertheless, much of the fine ornamental tree and shrub material in cultivation comes from that State. And the flora of the entire region is finding its way into cultivation, as the knowledge of plants and their needs grows and the interest in rock gardens and alpines increases and is shared by gardeners throughout the country. So it may be in gardens in other sections that the plant material of this intensely interesting but difficult portion of the United States will be best known. Gardening may never be highly developed here, however keen the interest and enthusiasm of individuals. For notwithstanding the work of these people, it requires more than an occasional fine garden to establish in any given section a truly representative standard.

New England

In this region gardening enjoys great advantages even though it must contend with some difficulties. The latter are principally concerned with the hardiness of garden material under the somewhat unstable conditions of the New England winter, which goes to extremes but seldom stays there as long as one could wish. Even the hardiest plants cannot endure fickleness of weather beyond a certain point.

It is a particularly happy circumstance for New England gardeners that the Arnold Arboretum at Jamaica Plain, just outside of Boston, has for many years been collecting and testing out the finest exotic material that the world affords. Trees and shrubs that pass this test and go abroad or into gardens as "hardy at the Arboretum" may be used by gardeners throughout New England—save in the most northerly parts —in full reliability regardless of the land of their nativity.

As might be expected, tradition and the example of old gardens exert a strong influence on modern gardening as regards both design and plant materials. Restoration of historic dwellings is now usually accompanied by restoration of their gardens where there are any remaining traces to build on; and the interest which this enterprise always arouses in a community stimulates garden thinking and doing and directs these in the main along the original lines. Thus the flavor of early New England prevails so that most of its gardens express something of the earlier life and its customs.

A further advantage to this close-knit region is the fact that the first great landscape architect of this country, Frederick Law Olmsted, did his greatest work from here, and established the sound principles of the then new art which he represented. In such examples of his genius as the Arnold Arboretum, the parks of Cambridge and Boston, and countless private estates, superlative excellence prevails; and through day-by-day, habitual contact its merits were early recognized. So while it is true that his influence extended across the Continent and to centers of garden interest north and south along the way, it was unquestionably in New England that it first made itself felt in the environment of small and average homes. His declaration, made in reference to his plans for his own first garden, that "the lawn is to be the grand feature of my gardening," may be taken as a summary of what he taught the average home owner and home gardener—namely, the importance of the open-lawn-boundary-frame principle. And this principle is universally applicable.

Gardening in New England today may be said to have been wisely approached and to be wisely carried out, because it is grounded in sound underlying principles absorbed quietly but surely over a period of half a century. The Olmsted influence, supplemented by the work of Prof. Charles Sprague Sargent, first director of the Arnold Arboretum, has developed a rich horticultural consciousness in the region and a profound appreciation of native plants and their possibilities in the garden. Hence there is extensive use of plant material suited to the extremes of the climate rather than reliance upon elaborate winter protection. And native trees and shrubs are extremely popular with gardeners however they may also prize such exotics as are suitable.

Northern Region

This refers to the Great Lakes territory (except that part adjacent to Lake Erie) and the region in general above 43 deg. of latitude. It includes an isolated bit— the northern plateau—of north-eastern N.Y., practically all of Mich., all of Wis., a strip of Ia., all of Minn. and so westward, until gardening gives way to agriculture and the great plains dominate and in fact are the landscape. Variations in temperature are great and summers are, for the most part, short, although in the immediate region of any large body of water, the rigors of climate are greatly tempered.

Rainfall, upon which the garden development of any region must depend, however important irrigation may be, is notably irregular in N. Y., whereas in Minn. it is not only adequate but evenly distributed throughout the season. Next as an influence upon garden development comes such growth of industrial cities as has occurred during later years in the lower portion of Mich.; for such business growth invariably brings a corresponding growth in fine residence and estate development. It is not surprising, therefore, to find in this region gardens famous everywhere, not only for their extent and fine design but for the variety and excellence of the plant material used. The availability of this wealth of material is partly due to the natural advantages of climate and the great variety of soils; its artistic use and wide appreciation is in part due to the influence upon landscape design emanating from the State University at Ann Arbor where an excellent course in landscape architecture carries on the best traditions of the art.

In general, as in all sections where winters are long and severe and the growing season is correspondingly shortened, the attention of flower lovers and gardeners is concentrated on doing superlatively those things that it is possible to carry through with success; they will tend to disregard the plants which cannot, in the nature of things, yield satisfactory returns. Also as the fruit grown in severe climate is usually finer flavored, of higher quality and more vividly colored, so are the flowers which succeed in these northern regions of exceptional character. Hence gardening has as great rewards for its enthusiastic disciples here as in any other portion of the country. As fruits themselves are important products of the region, the ornamental development of many of this type of plant has been carried to a high degree. The flowering season of such things as hawthorns (Crataegus), crabapples, and related subjects is one of rare and distinguished display, peculiar to gardening throughout this austere and occasionally inhospitable region.

PACIFIC NORTHWEST

This entire section is virtually divided into two parts by the Cascade Range of mountains. It may, in consequence, be said to enjoy what amounts to two climates. The great gardening development has occurred on the western side of this range, toward the coast. Here the growing season is characterized by a low rainfall and warm temperature, while winter brings excessive rain, generally cloudy conditions but never extreme cold and rarely wind. Changes in temperature are gradual instead of sudden.

These conditions are most favorable to gardening, especially the cultivation of special things. The roses, both of municipal plantings and of individual gardens throughout the Pacific Northwest, are proverbial for both quantity and quality; with regard to requirements of this flower, the conditions are strikingly similar to those in England where tradition has always placed it first.

Passing across the Strait to Vancouver Island and the city of Victoria, this likeness in climate becomes still more marked. The island conditions in themselves insure the same tempering of extremes, while the proximity of the Japan Current acts precisely here as the Gulf Stream acts on the British Isles. As a consequence, throughout the upper portion of the Northwest, gardening has much in common with that in England. The general effect and the broad impression it gives are reminiscent, even though they are never imitative. This is especially true of the fine rock gardens, built on absolutely natural formations, characteristic of the region, and where nothing but a rock garden would be appropriate— or, in some cases, possible.

On both the mainland and Vancouver Island bulb growing is rapidly becoming an industry of great importance and plant material in general is of exceptionally fine quality regardless of species or variety. In addition to the exotic things which thrive here there is native material of great value capable of development (if not already sufficiently perfected) and desirable in garden planting. One of the most delightful of American flowers is the erythronium of this section, which grows in abundance over wide areas.

SOUTHEAST SECTION

From the earliest days of the colonies established here by the British, gardens have flourished and gardening has been an art worthy of attention. Every great plantation developed gardens to accompany the mansion-house as a matter of course; and proprietors were proud to entertain visitors from the motherland across the sea with the same elegant pageant of fine lawns, splendid trees, rare and "outlandish" plants (as they called the more unusual exotics), and elaborately designed parterres as they were accustomed to at home. The plantation home was the rule and cities did not exist throughout this section unil the Spanish influence that came northward from Florida established itself. It is still discernible in such gardens as Charleston and Savannah are noted for.

This overlapping of Mediterranean feeling upon the thought and customs of a wholly different race (which also occurs in the Mississippi Valley) has resulted in what might be called a garden model of great charm. The seclusion which the British required because of their normally exclusive attitude, was required for the actual protection it afforded in the Latin countries. The walls of the Charleston gardens were designed as much to repel invading parties as to afford privacy and elegant seclusion to the household.

It is such things that establish a tradition which inevitably prevails. Here gardens that are hidden away and unsuspected are the consequence of an instinct which derives from this early need for real protection; and gardening is thus a very real and precious home accomplishment, even as music or painting or fine needle-work. It is instinctive in people of this region to know cultivated plants and how to plant and tend them. And from this it is natural for them to enter actively upon organized work designed to promote further the cause of horticulture and gardening and the general beauty of the land. Thus the entire section is energized by a gardening consciousness and enthusiasm that is rooted deep in yesterday though it is a growth of today. The excellent things of gardening then are combined with the excellencies of now with admirable results.

SOUTHWEST SECTION

Differing from all the rest of the country more than any other section, this portion affords unparalleled extremes of arid desert and well-watered mountain lands within short range of each other. New Mexico is considered to be at the very heart of the arid section, yet its climate is rather more temperate than otherwise, owing to the generally high altitude. Temperate region plants do better than those from farther south, while such things as palms are too tender to endure the winter temperature though they grow well during summer.

It is in general the soil that here offers to the gardener the most acute problem. Every possible kind exists, but it is the adobe type which is especially difficult. Gardening must therefore be worked out according to the immediate local conditions in any case. This tends to develop initiative and a high degree of individuality in gardeners, who must devise their own ways for overcoming their own special difficulties.

Perhaps nowhere in the country has the rapid advance of the garden club idea been of greater value than throughout this section. For it brings together, for the benefit of all, the gardeners of each separate and different part; and there is being worked out, through the comparing of results and exchange of experiences, a set of methods which will apply generally wherever the same conditions occur.

GARDEN PATHS AND DRIVES.

While these are as utilitarian in character as similar features elsewhere, they should adorn as well as serve—provide a beauty of their own. Yet in good garden design a path is never introduced merely for effect —it must be essential to the comfortable, pleasant and convenient enjoyment of the garden and the surrounding grounds.

DESIGN OF PATHS

Next in importance to the need for a path is its *directness*. It must never follow a line less direct than circumstances force it to follow. Its purpose is to connect two points (sometimes more than two) and afford passage between them. Let it do this without evasive uncertainty.

Observation of any casual trail across a meadow will reveal that such natural footways depart from a perfectly straight line only when irregularities in the ground, accumulations of water or other obstacles (such as a tree, a clump of bushes or a boulder) interrupt. Note that where these occur the path swings off while still some distance away and forms what landscape architects call an "eye-sweet" line or curve —a streamline—sweeping back to its straight course in similar manner.

From this it is evident that curves and straight lines are equally naturalistic; that there is no greater artistry inherent in the one than in the other. It is wholly a matter of the conditions generally, which in any given place, must determine what shall be used. On level ground a straight course will be better than a winding one; on irregular ground where one must go around obstacles, a curved or even a winding course will be appropriate.

INTENTIONAL OBSTACLES. Sometimes there may be important reasons for making a path curve even on flat ground where no natural obstacles exist. In that case obstacles must be provided. Put trees or shrubs or both along the line of direct progress between the two points to be connected, and make the path go around them.

But when doing this, study the whole situation carefully in order to introduce planting that will seem natural and always to have been there. An arrangement of a single tree backed or accompanied by 4 or 5 shrubs, planted directly in the straight course with one or two more trees farther on and a group of shrubs opposite to prevent the path from going too far along the new direction once the obstacle is cleared, will do the work naturally and simply. (See illustration, page 553.)

UNWARRANTED INTERRUPTION. Free and uninterrupted progress between the points which a straight path connects is, however, essential. To put sundials, bird-baths, fountains, pieces of sculpture or clumps of plant material in the middle of a straight path anywhere along its length is poor design and therefore wrong. Such features belong only at its termination or, if midway, at one side where, though they may invite a pause, they do not suggest an interruption.

PROPORTIONS. The width of a garden path must be sufficient for free use, and may be as much more, within reason, as space allows. Straight paths appear narrower than they are because of perspective. A minimum width of 4 ft. is therefore usual except for slight footpaths such as sometimes connect two entrances of a house. Between a double border of flowers greater width is desirable, the maximum depending largely upon the path's length. A good rule is to start at 4 ft. wide for a 50 ft. length and increase the width by 6 in. for every 50 ft. in length. (That is, of course, the length of the entire path.)

Curving paths do not need to be made wider the longer they are, since only a short distance is ever seen from any one point. However, 4 ft. remains the minimum, this being requisite for two persons to walk abreast.

PATH CONSTRUCTION AND MAINTENANCE

MATERIALS. Near the dwelling it is appropriate to use brick, flagstones or cobblestones—the latter bedded in cement. As the distance from the house (and the freer spirit of the garden) increases, less architectural or artificial paths are preferable. Properly laid, cinders make an excellent path; if edged with brick or stone they become sufficiently conventional for use even around the dwelling. Well-kept gravel is always appropriate and stepping stones are good anywhere.

CONSTRUCTION. Excavate not less than 4 in. for the simple cinder path, up to 12 in. or a calculated requirement for brick, flagstones, etc. To make a cinder path put down a 2 in. (when well tamped) base layer of coarse cinders. Over this spread evenly a layer of fine cinders or cinders and coal ash mixed; wet this by spraying (to prevent washing) and tamp down to 2 in. thick. This alone makes an excellent path but it will be more permanent (especially on a slope) if, after it has dried for several days, a surface binder such as parkways are dressed with, is applied. Follow the directions accompanying such material and take special pains to apply it well out to the edges of the paths.

For a path of cobblestones or pebbles bedded in cement the excavation needs to be at least 5 in. deep. Start with the 2 in. base layer of coarse cinders, well tamped; over it spread an inch of ash and cinder mixture, wet down and tamped; cover this with 2 in. of a dry mixture of sand, 2 parts, and cement, 1 part. On this place the cobblestones by hand, pushing them down into it and setting them as close together as possible; or, if pebbles are used spread them lightly over it, after washing off any soil and letting them dry, and roll or tamp them into it. With the top material in place, spray the whole gently and long enough so that the water penetrates the dry cement and wets it thoroughly. It cannot be made too wet. Then cover the path with burlap or light litter and keep this moist by spraying twice daily (or oftener depending on the weather) for ten days, by which time the cement will have "cured."

Brick and flagstones give best effects when laid dry, which means without cement. A cinder or ash foundation layer at least 3 in. deep after tamping is required. On this spread a 1 in. even layer of fine screened sand to receive the bricks or stones,. when these are placed sift more sand over the surface and brush it into the joints until they are filled. For flagstone paths excavate the thickness of the stones plus 4 in. Bricks are 4 in. deep when laid on edge, and 2 in. when laid on the side or broad surface.

Stepping stones may be let into the earth of a lawn without any foundation. Arrange them in place, a standard pace apart on centers, and carefully cut through the sod around their edges. Then lift them out of the way, and take up the sod with enough earth so that the surface of each stone will be even with the ground around. If the soil is very stony or gravelly, it may be advisable to take out more and provide a smooth 1 in. bed of sand. Then lay the stones in place and firm them down well so they do not tilt when trod on.

MAINTENANCE. Brick and stone paths afford lodgement in their crevices for weed and grass seeds, so they, like gravel paths, will need regular spraying with one of the weed killers obtainable at seed and garden supply stores (see WEEDS).. Or spaces between flags may be made wider and planted with low growing subjects especially suited to give this pleasing effect which is especially fitting in rock gardens. Paths treated with a binder and the cobblestone or pebble path will not permit growth of any kind in their midst. Unsurfaced cinder paths are not usually very troublesome, but may need treatment with weed killer two or three times during the growing season. Hollow places that develop in cinder paths should be filled annually and the general surface kept level and smooth to prevent water seeping into the interior and undermining the foundation.

GARDEN DRIVES

All that has been said about garden paths applies equally to drives. Here especially the surface finish must express or harmonize with garden feeling rather than suggest public domain. Bluestone and gravel are so formal as to usually be out of order except immediately around the dwelling. Cinders or red ash held firmly by a binder are neat and yet not artificial

or stilted. Tanbark, if available, is extremely good.

The roadbed excavation must go down from 12 to 20 in. to insure a permanently sound, well drained and even result. Or foundation and surface together must be this deep if laid on top of the ground, as they may be if the general level is being built up. The latter method is advisable where the drainage problem is difficult, as it insures a well-drained drive *if this is properly crowned.*

A very old method of road building remains the easiest, simplest and best for private grounds of modest proportions. First the earth of the roadbed or foundation is drawn up from the sides to form a ridge down the middle—the basis of the crown. A layer of rye straw, from 4 to 8 in.. deep depending upon the character of the dirt itself as well as upon the general drainage conditions, is then laid crossways of the roadway, the butt ends meeting and overlapping a little at the middle. This must be done evenly and carefully so that there are no bunches or tangled masses and the surface is level. On top of the straw

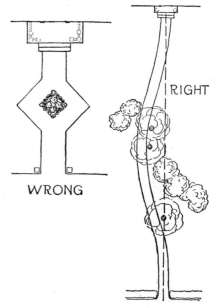

GOOD TASTE IN GARDEN PATHS
A path is for a purpose—to get from one point to another. It should be direct, but pleasingly so. An aimless interruption of its course, especially if short, is wrong, as shown at the left. A longer path can be gracefully curved—but the curve should be justified by shrubs and trees placed naturally, as at the right.

go coarse cinders which are rolled down firmly to a 2 in. depth, and on these goes the surface material whatever it may be—preferably fine cinders or red ash. Finally this in turn is rolled and if possible treated with a binder as suggested for cinder paths.

Rye straw so used is practically indestructible and laid across a crowned road-bed it carries water quickly to the outer edges where it can flow away. Consequently even a dirt surfaced road built in this way will quickly dry out after rain; and mud holes in it are impossible. For the moderate traffic within the garden or private grounds, this type of road is as permanent as it is pleasing to look at or drive over.

GARDEN POOL. (See illustration, Plate 23.) Water in some form is craved wherever outdoor pictures are being made and wherever it is proposed to gather for social enjoyment. Rarely, however, are the advantages of a natural body of water available in the average garden; hence the garden pool, which satisfies this craving in any kind of garden—the very small and modest one as well as the one that is large and stately.

One's choice of the type of pool depends on the type of the particular garden as well as upon the position of the pool in it. It might be expected that a naturalistic garden would require a pool naturalistic in form, but this is true only when the pool is remote from the dwelling or from a garden structure. For even in a generally naturalistic setting a pool must be of exact form if it is situated near the house and in close relationship with it. (A possible exception might occur in rough and unimproved terrain such as a summer home or camp sometimes occupies—but this location is likely not to include a real garden at all, and so does not come within the scope of this article.)

It is important to note that while a naturalistic, irregular form is appropriate only in surroundings that are, or seem to be, in a natural state, the circular form is suitable in *any* surroundings. How and why is this so? Because the circle is a nature form and as appropriate to naturalistic surroundings as to the most formal environment. Hence to make a pool exactly circular is no violation of Nature's laws. Whereas to lay out on level ground, which in itself furnishes no reason for irregularity, a pool that is irregular in form or outline, *is* a violation of natural law. In nature it is the contours of the land that produce irregularly shaped bodies of water—whether puddles, pools or lakes; if such contours are lacking, irregularity disappears.

CONSTRUCTION. In building a pool of whatever form perhaps the most important single thing is to make its inner sides slope *outward* from bottom to top. This is sound construction as regards strength and resistance to pressure; it also prevents damage by expansion due to freezing if the water is left in the pool, as is usually most convenient. Outward slanting walls offer no resistance to the outward thrust of ice as it expands since the mass will ride or slide up the slope.

Pools may be most simply constructed by excavating the desired space 3 to 5 in. deeper and wider in all directions than the finished work is to measure inside; then lining the space with chicken wire, old metal lath or other reinforcement, laid carefully against the earth and fitted by clipping wherever necessary; and covering this with two coats of cement. For the first or under coat, mix equal parts clean gravel and sand, then mix 3 parts of that (dry) with 1 part portland cement. When the latter is evenly distributed through, add water slowly (continuing the mixing), until the mass is evenly wet enough to spread and trowel to a smooth surface without being sloppy; this layer should be from 3 to 4 in. thick depending on the size of the pool. The second layer, of 2 parts sand to 1 part cement, should be applied when the other is wet, to a depth of about an inch. When it is firm (but not dry) it is well to apply a final thin coat of plain cement and water, using a large brush rather than a trowel.

Do the entire job of each layer without interruption, working from the center of the pool outward and up to its margin. Allow the first layer to season for three days, wetting it down morning, noon and night to prevent cracking, before applying the second coat, and let the latter harden for a day or so before giving the final coat. The thickness of the finished walls and over the bottom should be about 5 in. diminishing to 3 in. at the edge.

Do not put fish into a new pool as soon as it is hard and dry. It should be thoroughly soaked to free it of lime before either plants or fish are introduced. Special containers for dirt are usually convenient in small pools and where plants that have to be removed indoors over winter are to be used. The earth in these boxes can be covered with sand and gravel to keep it from escaping and muddying the water. In simple reflecting pools it is better to omit plants altogether; or to use only the smaller floating aquatics (which see) and these in small quantity. Around the margin any low creeping mint or other small plant is attractive; or simply the turf of the lawn growing right to the water's edge, which produces a delightful effect of brimming coolness.

A definite coping or edging of brick or concrete is undesirable except around formal and somewhat elaborate pools, for it implies a considerable elaboration in all the surroundings. Unless a pool is large and intended for swimming rather than for garden ornamentation, the close relationship between natural growth and the water which the absence of a coping allows is most attractive.

Leaves and litter in the water are unavoidable and not unhygienic, but they can be scooped out with a net whenever it seems desirable and added to the compost heap. The green or brown algae or "scum" that appears in many pools is also harmless, but if sufficiently abundant to make the water cloudy and unsightly, steps can be taken. Since the cause of the algae is too much sunlight, enough plants should be grown in the pool so that 60 to 75 per cent of the surface will be covered. To destroy and clear out the algae, the pool may be treated with potassium permanganate at the rate of about 4 parts per million; the crystals are dissolved in hot water and enough of the solution poured into the pool and stirred around to color the water a light pink. Or copper sulphate (blue vitriol) can be used at the rate of 2 lbs. per million gals. of water, the simplest way being to put the crystals in a cheesecloth bag and pull it around the pool with a stick or fishing pole. But this chemical can not safely be used if there are fish in the pool, and it may even injure lilies growing there.

GARDEN SHELTERS. In its broadest sense this includes every kind of retreat in the garden which is protected overhead. But as it is generally understood to imply shelter from storm as well as from the sun, it is applied particularly to roofed structures. These are given different names by landscape architects and garden designers to denote differences in type and character, such as casino, belvedere, gazebo, loggia and bower.

The first and last of these—*casino* and *bower*—are applied to just a simple summer pleasure house; such a structure as any garden may have. A *belvedere* is an open structure standing on an eminence

THE FORMAL GARDEN POOL
Two papyrus plants flank arrowhead and water-hyacinth in the background, while waterlilies adorn the surface with their leaves and flowers.

from which it may command a fine wide-spreading view, the name also implies definite architectural treatment and the use of permanent materials, such as brick or stone. A *gazebo* is also elevated, but not necessarily to command a view. It is a development from the watch tower on a mediaeval wall and consequently today is part of a garden wall over which it enables a watcher to look out. Examples are seen along the brick walls of the gardens at Mount Vernon.

The *loggia* is more pretentious and majestic, virtually an outdoor sitting room, usually enclosed on one side and having a row of columns on the other to support the roof. Architecturally it is presumed to conform to the house, of which it may be a part; or it may be built any distance away from it. Sometimes it furnishes a portion of garden boundary. It is a monumental concept and requires a generous amount of land on all sides to furnish an appropriate setting. Hence it is suitable only for large estates and gardens of ambitious proportion, design and execution.

Because a garden shelter is designed to be an outdoor sitting room secluded and as far apart from the dwelling as possible (in order to afford complete change of environment), it is the circumstances of each particular given garden that must determine whether it is a reasonable project there. In most gardens spots can be found that fit the requirements, or that may be made to fit them; but in some gardens, small ones especially, this may not be true. If a garden shelter looks, or is, crowded into the composition, it may be set down as a failure. There must be open space enough to avoid any appearance of crowding; also it must be sufficiently separated and secluded by well-executed and abundant planting as to produce an effect of pleasant surprise.

The best spot for a garden shelter can be determined only by a study of the ground itself while a tentative ground plan is being worked out. Regardless of its character and whether it is elaborate or primitive, it should stand where all the circumstances of the garden require it to be in order that it shall fulfill its purpose. This means that it must occupy that spot which most persuasively invites one to loiter—a spot easily discovered usually by the simple expedient of wandering around in the garden and deciding where it would be most agreeable to rest on a hot day. This will mean a breezy spot as well as one away from the workaday things; yet one not so remote that when weariness overtakes the gardener he must go too far in order to rest there.

The simplest form and materials are most desirable for the average garden shelter. The aim is a finished structure which sinks into the garden picture rather than stands out of or against it. Details of height and pitch of roof repay careful study as these are dominant when the whole is viewed from a distance.

GARDENS, TYPES OF. Although it may not be spontaneously realized, it should be apparent that there may be many types of gardens, even as there are many types of dwellings. Enthusiasm for a particular aspect of nature may lead to its adoption as a garden theme. Or limitations of soil, site and climate may compel choice of a type of garden suited to such limitations. Special types of architecture demand special garden treatment, just as personal preference for wilderness or for directly contrasting sophistication seeks expression in natural surroundings in the one case, or in a formal design executed in trained plant material, in the other. Again, the uses to which a garden is put and the way and amount in which it is enjoyed are powerful determining factors.

A generally familiar example of a definite type of garden is the Rock Garden,

SOLVING THE PROBLEM OF AN INVOLUNTARY GARDEN WALL

A garden wall you build yourself is one thing. But when a neighbor's garage (or your own) forms one of your garden boundaries, it may present difficulties. Here is such a problem delightfully solved by means of built-in beds, a vine-covered fountain feature (not necessarily attached to the building) and a couple of accent trees at the ends. Could one ask a more pleasing terminus for a small formal arrangement?

(which see). But there are many others, not as well known as their merits and possibilities would seem to warrant. Each requires special study as to the design which will best express the theme or type, and usually as to the plant material used, although this does not always have to differ from that used in gardens generally. Sometimes, as in a Desert, Bog, or Evergreen garden, the available plant material may in itself provide the reason for the kind of garden. In care and management also special type gardens present particular problems and definite requirements which should be taken into consideration before they are undertaken.

As an illustration, an Alpine Garden is a garden devoted to the culture of mountain plants, "alpines" being plants native to the mountain ranges of the world at large. Many of these grow in crevices and crannies in the rocks high up on the steep faces of mountains. Others are native to high plateaus or broad, meadow-like areas which occur at lower, but still mountainous, levels. Thus some are true rock plants while others have no direct or intimate association with rocks. Rocks are not therefore necessarily a part of the Alpine Garden, although they may be. Perhaps more essential is a correct soil type, a system for insuring sufficient moisture below, rather than above the surface, and a reasonable duplication of climatic conditions and exposure as found at high altitudes.

For further discussion of types of gardens, see articles under these headings: BOG; CHILDREN'S; CITY; COLOR (COLOR IN GARDEN); COMMUNITY; DESERT; EVENING; EVERGREEN; FORMAL; FRAGRANT; FRIENDSHIP; HERB; INFORMAL; JAPANESE; KITCHEN; MORAINE; PATIO; ROCK; ROOF; SEASIDE; SUBSISTENCE; SUNKEN; TERRACE; VEGETABLE; WALL; AND WATER.

GARDEN WALLS. This means true walls of stone, brick or other similar material (as distinguished from fences) built around a garden or an estate or a portion of either, for the purpose of protecting the cultivated plants grown within. In the old days such protection was needed from poachers or from small animals, such as rabbits, as well as from the larger deer and domesticated animals allowed to stray. Hence the garden wall was originally a practical necessity, and has come to be regarded as a luxury only now.

A different but very real advantage of this sort of substantial protection is becoming apparent as the pressure of city population impinges upon the countryside and trespassers upon private grounds grow bolder and more ruthless. However, the extremely high cost of building masonry walls works against their restoration to the important place which they once held,

PRACTICAL AND PICTURESQUE
The garden wall is, primarily, a boundary and a protection. But it can also be pleasing to the eye, whether rough and informal, as shown here, or more severely simple as when made of brick, cement blocks or cut and fitted stone.

and it is probable that other protective barriers will come into use as need for protection or desire for it grows.

The enclosing or protective type of garden wall has been omitted from gardens in America almost universally, and to come upon a real "wall garden" is now fairly unusual, outside of some really large estate. Perhaps it was the abundance of wood and the ease of preparing it for use which was responsible for railings and fences taking the place here of walls such as those common in England.

Apart from the need for protection, there are two occasions when a wall demands consideration as a feature in or adjacent to, the garden. The most common of these results from the proximity of buildings on adjoining property. Walls of garages (especially) often abut on the garden of the small home and force themselves into the garden plan. Other walls are required by changing levels, when it becomes necessary to hold back the earth on higher portions from lower areas. Such retaining walls are essential in irregular, hilly surroundings; and they have become a popular garden feature wherever grading can bring about even a slight change in ground levels, because they afford opportunity for the culture of unusual plants in their crannies.

Because stone is a natural material and takes its place easily and naturally in garden surroundings, it is always acceptable for walls, whatever the material of the dwelling and other buildings. Brick is similar in this respect though it carries a suggestion of formality which stone—especially rough stone—does not. This makes brick especially appropriate to use in walls near to or leading from the house—walls in the intimate portions of the garden—and also for small areas, where it carries the appropriate scale.

Walls of stone may be laid either dry or with cement; brick walls of course require mortar. Dry walls afford great opportunity for the culture of those special plants which delight to grow in crannies between stones. Such plants should be placed as the wall is being laid. Or seed may be sown in the crannies by mixing it into a ball of moistened earth or mud and thrusting this mud-ball back in the cranny, into the earth behind the stones. See WALL GARDEN.

There is no better way to unite a house with its garden and reconcile it with its site and surroundings, than to build a wall of the same material as a continuation of the house wall. Brick, stone, stucco concrete or wood—each is capable of excellent effect. Especially good are the cinder-concrete blocks in random shapes and sizes which are so generally employed in fine building. Some of the recently evolved fabricated materials give promise of excellent effects also.

The best solution of the vexing problem presented by a neighboring garage abutting on the garden will be found in accepting its wall as the beginning of an extended structure of similar material along at least that side of the garden. Such a wall space broken by a niche holding a small image or a wall fountain, is a charming asset anywhere. And to take advantage of threatened liabilities of this kind which are forced upon the garden, and turn them into assets, is the very essence of good garden design in limited surroundings. By observing the principles of proportion (which means both relative size of garden space and relative character of material

for construction) and by giving thought to the surface texture or finish and to the color of the wall, and by such planting as shall enhance the value of these things without obscuring the structure, it is possible to immeasurably increase the beauty of a garden by putting a wall around it.

See also FENCES; HEDGE; WALL GARDEN.

GARLAND-FLOWER. Common name for *Hedychium coronarium*, a tropical Asiatic perennial, a species of Ginger-lily; also often applied to *Daphne cneorum*, an attractive, low-growing evergreen shrub bearing fragrant pink flowers in spring. See DAPHNE; HEDYCHIUM.

GARLIC. A hardy perennial bulb (*Allium sativum*), native to the Mediterranean region of Africa and Europe. The bulb, unlike that of its close relative, the onion (which see), separates beneath a papery, superficial skin, into divisions or so-called "cloves" which are used mainly for flavoring meats, dressings and sauces; and also for planting. This is done in spring in rows of 18 to 24 in. apart with the cloves 6 in. asunder. The plant, which rarely produces seed, is of easiest culture and does best in only moderately fertile soil. In rich soil the tops become overdeveloped. In autumn when the leaves have died the plants are dug, braided by their tops and hung in an airy place to dry.

False-garlic, a rarely grown liliaceous herb with yellow flowers, is Nothoscordum, which see.

GARRYA (gar'-i-ah). Silk Tassel-bush. Ornamental evergreen shrubs of W. N. America, not hardy North. They are distinctive because of the long drooping catkins of greenish-white flowers borne on shoots of the previous year, the male and female forms on separate plants. The male catkins are larger and of more striking appearance. Plants are propagated by cuttings or layers; they are not easy to transplant except from pots.

G. elliptica, the best-known species, grows to over 10 ft. in favorable localities, and is good looking with dark green oval leaves, gray on the under side.

GAS INJURY. Leakage of illuminating gas from mains into the soil injures herbaceous and woody plants growing in streets, gardens and greenhouses. Probably the most damage done is to shade trees. A slight leakage results in a cumulative asphyxiating and poisoning effect on

A HANDSOME GREENHOUSE PLANT
Clerodendron thomsonae is a handsome plant which is ordinarily grown in a warm greenhouse, but with care and appropriate conditions it may be grown as a house plant.

T. H. Everett

PLATE 17.   PINEAPPLE-FLOWER
This attractive, half-hardy bulb, may be grown out of doors in the South, but in the North is usually found as a greenhouse or house plant.

T. H. Everett

PLATE 18.   TWO TYPES OF IRIS

At the top are two fine specimens of the Bearded Iris, at the left, Prairie Sunset,
and at the right, Sable. Below is a group of Iris Kaempferi, the Japanese Iris.
Wayside Gardens Company

PLATE 19.   REWARDS OF THE VEGETABLE GARDEN
Above, one of the fine varieties of leafing lettuce which may be grown in the
home garden. Below, a fine plant of Zucchini, one of the summer Squashes,
sometimes called Italian Squash.

W. Atlee Burpee Co.

PLATE 20.   THE REGAL LILY

One of the handsomest and yet easily handled lilies for the garden, the Regal Lily
is well worth attention.

Wayside Gardens Company

PLATE 21.   CRIMSON KING

Something new in hardy shade trees is a maroon leaved Norway Maple which is
a recent importation to this country. It is as satisfactory as the ordinary green-
leaved Norway Maple, and retains its color throughout the summer.

Wayside Gardens Company

PLATE 22.   MARIGOLDS IN VARIETY

One of the earliest grown of garden annuals, Marigolds are available in a number
of forms developed from the original African and French types. Above, is a dish
of "Flare." Lower left, "Buff Beauty," and lower right, "Naughty Marietta."

W. Atlee Burpee Co.

PLATE 23.   HEAVENLY BLUE
One of the most striking of the Morning Glories, this variety is an excellent one
to form a handsome screen.

W. Atlee Burpee Co.

PLATE 24.   SECRETS OF SUCCESSFUL GARDENING

Above, a well handled mulch around young plants to protect their growth. Below,
a fine compost heap will repay the gardener's efforts by enriching the soil in the
best possible way.

T. H. Everett

PLATE 25.   A SPRING PICTURE

Narcissi and Daffodils, naturalized or massed in the border, are a rewarding
sight in the spring.

Associated Bulb Growers of Holland

PLATE 26.   NARCISSI AND DAFFODILS

At the top are five sweer-scented Poetaz Narcissi. From left to right, top row, are
Glorious, Orange Prince and Helios. In the second row, Early Perfection and
Innocence. At the bottom are two Trumpet Daffodils, Statendam and Mt. Hood.
Wayside Gardens Company

PLATE 27.   **A FINE CLIMBING NASTURTIUM**

The climbing nasturtiums make an attractive covering for a trellis or fence, and
provide cut flowers as well.

W. Atlee Brupee Co.

PLATE 28.   STAKING PEAS

Twiggy branches or saplings make the best brush for peas, and should be placed before the peas have reached any height.

T. H. Everett

PLATE 29.   INTERESTING HOUSE PLANTS

These exotic Pelargoniums, close relatives of the Common Geranium, are natives of South Africa, and like their relative, easy to grow as house plants.

T. H. Everett

PLATE 30.   **PETUNIAS FOR BEDDING DISPLAYS**

Here are three of this favorite summer flower in both single and double varieties.
At the top is a group of Pink Sensation. At the lower left is Rose Marie, and at
the right Silver Medal.

W. Atlee Burpee Co.

PLATE 31.   PHLOX FOR THE BORDER

Among the showiest of plants for the border is the Hardy Phlox, which comes in a multitude of colors and color effects. Here is a representative group of the best modern varieties.

Wayside Gardens Company

PLATE 32.   PLANTING SEEDS

Proper preparation of the ground is essential if the seeds are to germinate properly.
After the deep spading and enriching which is required, the surface of the ground
should be raked to a finely-pulverized state. Then the drills are made, using a
sharp tool or the handle of a hoe or rake. If the ground is dry and rain is not
expected, it is a good plan to water the drills before placing the seed. And last of
all, the seed is scattered as evenly as possible in the drill. After this, the soil is
raked over the seeds and the area watered well if no shower is expected.

T. H. Everett

the roots, the tree not showing it until some time has elapsed. Then the foliage turns yellow and trunk and root tissues die and turn brown. Conifers are fairly resistant and may recover even after such symptoms are pronounced, but deciduous trees are less likely to. With pronounced leakage, injury may develop very rapidly. The only remedy for gas injury is to stop the leak, aerate the soil with compressed air until all the gas has been forced out, and then water the area heavily.

Effects of gas injury other than those on shade trees are prevention of germination of seeds, abnormal curvatures and swelling of young rootlets, production of excess root tissue, retarded growth, wilting and falling of foliage, undeveloped and distorted flowers and often death of herbaceous plants. A characteristic response of leaf stems called *epinasty* causes them to be turned *downwards* and helps growers to recognize the trouble. When tomato plants are used as "gas detectors" in greenhouses it is this downward bending of branches of otherwise vigorous plants that gives the first but a positive indication of gas leakage. Tomatoes are so sensitive that they respond to as little as 1 part of illuminating gas in 100,000 parts of air. (The familiar orange fruited house plant, Jerusalem-cherry, a relative of the tomato, is also highly susceptible to gas fumes and a disappointing shedding of the leaves is often caused by a leak in a gas range or other fixture even when the odor is not noticeable.)

Injury from gases contained in smoke is described under smoke injury, which see.

GAS LIME. This by-product of the manufacture of illuminating gas results when quicklime (which see) is used to remove impurities from the gas. When it is exposed to the air these impurities gradually change into harmless calcium sulphate or gypsum (which see) rendering the material a low-grade form of slaked lime mixed with land-plaster. Although seldom obtainable in the U. S., it is excellent, when applied fresh, for killing slugs, insects and plant diseases in the soil. Planting must not be done for 6 weeks.

GAS-PLANT. A popular name given to *Dictamnus albus,* a hardy attractive perennial, because on hot evenings the lemon-flavored volatile oil given off by the fragrant flowers will flash into flame when a lighted match is thrust against the stem.

GASTERIA (gas-tee'-ri-ah). A genus of small succulent plants of the Lily Family, native in S. Africa. A few species are grown in succulent collections under glass, and also make good window plants. Their leaves are thick and fleshy, more or less tongue-shaped and rough, and either 2-ranked or in rosettes. The flowers are red or pinkish, somewhat inflated and borne in loose clusters on arching stems. They need good drainage and do well in pans, in a mixture of sandy loam with broken brick and a little leafmold.

G. maculata has leaves of shining green to 6 in. long, in a rather twisted arrangement and with large white spots. *G. pulchra* has glossy dark green leaves to 1 ft. long in spiral ranks, with white spots. *G. sulcata* has short dull green strap-shaped leaves with greenish dots. *G. verrucosa* has dull gray leaves to 6 in. long, rough with many small white warts.

GATES. See GARDEN GATES.

GAULTHERIA (gaul-thee'-ri-ah). Evergreen shrubs, erect or prostrate, widely distributed in N. and S. America, Asia and Australasia, belonging to the Heath Family. They are well adapted for rock garden and evergreen shrub border planting, growing best in sandy peaty soil and a rather moist and partly shaded situation. Propagated by seeds, cuttings, layers and division.

PRINCIPAL SPECIES

G. procumbens (Wintergreen, Checkerberry) is a low plant with creeping stems, native from Canada to Ga. It has oval leathery leaves, nodding white flowers borne singly, and edible, scarlet berry-like fruits.

shallon (Salal) native in the western part of the country, grows to 2 ft. or more, and makes a good under shrub. It has rather large heart-shaped leaves, panicles of pinkish-white flowers, and dark purple fruits.

miqueliana is a Japanese species growing about 1 ft. high, with racemes of white flowers and white fruits.

veitchiana, native in China, is a neat shrub to 3 ft., with lustrous dark green wrinkled leaves, short dense racemes of white flowers, and indigo-blue fruits.

GAURA (gau'-rah). A small genus of perennial N. American herbs with spikes or clusters of rose or white flowers, occasionally planted in wild gardens or hardy borders. *G. coccinea,* a midwestern plant, grows to 2 ft. and has white, pink, or scarlet flowers; *G. lindheimeri,* native from La. to Tex., grows 4 ft. tall and has loose clusters of white flowers.

GAYFEATHER. A common name for Liatris (also called Blazing Star), a genus of tall showy tuberous-rooted hardy perennials wtih slender purple or white flower spikes in late summer which have the unusual habit of opening at the top first, the bloom progressing downward.

GAYLUSSACIA (gay-lu-say'-shi-ah). A genus of N. American berry-bearing shrubs valuable for both foliage effect and fruit and commonly called Huckleberry, which see. *G. frondosa* is the Dangleberry, and *G. ursina,* the Buckberry.

GAYWINGS. A common name for *Polygala paucifolia,* a trailing perennial of N. U. S. sometimes planted along the edge of woodlands. A species of milkwort, it is also called Flowering-wintergreen or Fringed Polygala. See POLYGALA.

GAZANIA (gah-zay'-ni-ah). A genus of low herbs, annual or perennial, of S. Africa and belonging to the Daisy Family. Old-time favorites for flowering in the cool greenhouse and for summer bedding outdoors, they have rather narrow leaves of varying form, mostly covered beneath with dense white woolly hairs. The flowers range from white through orange and yellow to scarlet and are beautifully spotted at the base of the petals. Like many S. African flowers they close at night. Sandy loam with humus, and a sunny place, suit them well. Propagation is by seed, division and cuttings.

PRINCIPAL SPECIES

G. longiscapa is an annual, with orange-colored flowers and dark spots.

rigens has a short branching stem, and showy flowers of orange with basal markings of brown, black and white.

uniflora has a woody base and yellow flowers free of markings. Good hybrid strains with brilliant flowers have originated by crossing with *G. rigens.*

splendens, reputed to be of hybrid origin, is of trailing habit, and has showy orange flowers with black and white basal markings.

GAZEBO (gah-zee'-boh). A type of garden shelter forming part of a garden wall or terrace out over which the occupant can look. It is a development of the watch tower in a medieval palace wall or battlement. See GARDEN SHELTERS.

GELSEMIUM (jel-see'-mi-um) *sempervirens.* A twining evergreen shrub of S.E. U. S. grown in mild places as a cover plant and sometimes in greenhouses. Its fragrant funnel-shaped yellow flowers are followed by beaked seed capsules. See CAROLINA YELLOW JESSAMINE, which is the S. Carolina State flower.

GENIP, GENIPAP (jen'-ip, jen'-i-pap). Common names for *Genipa americana,* a tropical American tree with large yellowish or white flowers and large (3 in.) brown berries that may be eaten fresh, preserved or used in beverages. The name Genip is also applied to *Melicocca bijuga,* another—but unrelated—American tree grown in warm countries for its smaller fruit.

GENISTA (je-nis'-tah). Broom. A genus of deciduous or half-evergreen shrubs of the Pea Family found in Europe, Asia and Africa. They are closely allied to Cytisus, several species having been referred to that genus; the common Genista grown by florists especially for Easter is *Cytisus canariensis* or *C. racemosus.*

Genistas are ornamental shrubs with showy yellow or white flowers, well suited for dry sandy soil in mild climates, and appearing to good advantage on sunny banks. They are not quite hardy N., but one or two species may survive in favored positions with winter protection. Propagated by seeds, cuttings and layers.

PRINCIPAL SPECIES

G. hispanica (Spanish Broom) is a densely branched prickly shrub to 3 ft., with clusters of golden-yellow flowers in May and June.

tinctoria (Dyers-greenweed) is an upright slender grower to 3 ft., with striped branches and many-flowered terminal clusters. Var. *plena* is a form with double flowers.

germanica is an upright spiny little shrub with rather small flowers, but one of the hardiest.

pilosa is a small prostrate grower with rooting branches and short clusters of yellow flowers in May and June.

sagittalis is another dwarf species, featured by 2-winged branches.

silvestris, var. *pungens,* formerly *G. dalmatica,* is a spiny little shrub usually only a few inches high.

The last three mentioned are among the hardiest, and well suited for sunny positions in the rock garden.

GENTIAN (jen'-shan). Common name for herbs, mostly perennial, of the genus Gentiana, which gives its name to the Gentian Family. They have purple or yellow flowers and opposite leaves and are grown principally in the rock or alpine

THE GOLDEN GENISTA

An especially popular subject for the Easter season, this compact, shapely little plant, botanically known as Cytisus, is smothered in long-lasting, yellow, pea-shaped flowers.

garden, and a few in the border or wild garden. All require good drainage, nearly all resent extremely hot weather, and a few can be grown only with special treatment. The best method of propagation is by seeds, which should be as fresh as possible. These seeds are extremely small, and usually slow to germinate, and seedlings will not bloom until the third year. Among the gentians we find some of the finest blues of nature, and the plants are so beautiful and interesting that they repay the trouble taken to grow them.

Taller Growing Species

Among the higher growing and more easily raised species are the following, all perennial:

G. lutea. To 6 ft., with yellow flowers in which the calyx resembles the spathe of a jack-in-the-pulpit. The root is sometimes used for medicinal purposes.

andrewsi (Closed Gentian). To 2 ft., with purple-blue flowers, almost or entirely closed. It is especially good in colonies in the wild garden. Var. *alba* is the white form.

macrophylla. To 1 ft., with pale blue flowers in clusters.

septemfida. To 1½ ft., with clustered flowers of clear soft blue 2 in. long. It should be grown in peaty soil and protected from extreme sunlight.

sceptrum. To 4 ft., with dark blue flowers, sometimes spotted greenish.

saponaria. A native species to 2½ ft., with blue flowers 2 in. long. It grows well planted in rich humus near water and may be increased by both seed and division.

asclepiadea. To 1½ ft., with dark blue flowers 1½ in. long growing from the axils of the leaves. It requires a deep, rich, moist soil.

porphyrio. To 1½ ft., with beautiful clear light-blue flowers 2 in. long produced in autumn. A native of the pine barrens, it requires a light, acid, sandy soil.

bigelovi. To 1 ft., with a many-flowered spike of purple blossoms. An interesting Colorado form which makes attractive clumps in the wild garden.

Rock Garden Species

Gentians of lower growth and best suited for the rock or alpine garden include the following, all perennial except the Fringed Gentian:

G. acaulis. To 4 in., the blue gentian of the Alps. When properly grown, it forms sheets of dark blue flowers, and is one of the finest rock-garden species. It needs ample drainage and a mulch of *well-rotted* manure, both spring and fall. A white form (var. *alba*) is now listed.

oregana. To 2 ft., with light blue flowers 1½ in. long, is rather hard to grow in the E. States.

GENTIANS ARE GARDEN GEMS

And, even if difficult to succeed with, are worth the effort. At left is the Closed, or Bottle Gentian with deep blue, non-opening flowers. At right, the lovely shy Fringed Gentian of lighter, brighter blue. Don't try to transplant it from the wild; get plants from a specialist and take pains to give them the conditions they need.

calycosa. To 1 ft., with dark blue flowers, sometimes spotted with green, is another western plant that should be grown in cool, acid, boggy soil and shaded from afternoon sun.

sino-ornata. To 7 in., has flowers of yellowish-white blotched with purple and increases by stolons. It must be grown in peat moss and leafmold.

farreri bearing lovely blue flowers with a white throat is one of the lime-loving plants.

lagodechiana low-growing with large pale blue flowers is easily handled in the rock garden.

phlogifolia to 10 in. has clear blue flowers in flat-topped clusters.

altaica to 4 in. is of dense tufted growth with trumpet-shaped flowers violet-blue.

rochelli to 2 or 3 in. has clustered evergreen leaves and trumpet-shaped blue flowers.

crinita (Fringed Gentian). To 3 ft. with large clear blue flowers 2 in. long with beautifully fringed lobes. Difficult to transplant because of the long slender roots, it may be increased by scattering seed near the parent plant as soon as they are ripe and moving the seedlings in clumps as soon as they appear to be thinned later. Plants may also be started in pots as follows: Mix equal parts of pure sand and soil from beneath blooming plants (thus securing the fungus associated with the gentian's root system). Put 1 in. of broken crocks in a 12 in. pot, cover with 1 in. of fine gravel, then fill with the above soil mixture. Gather seed as soon as ripe (in September) and sow on the surface of the soil, firming lightly. Water daily by setting the pot in a deep basin of water. Germination soon occurs, and as soon as the second leaves have formed, but before the long tap-root has started, prick out the tiny plants into individual paper pots which should be placed in a cold frame or in flats with moistened sphagnum between them. Before freezing weather, set the plants (in the pots) where they are to bloom, preferably in conditions like those of a damp meadow, and cover with light straw and leaves. The plants should winter well, grow vigorously in the spring, and in September send up blossoming stalks, thus, though they are really biennials, giving blossoms the first year.

Arabian-gentian is the catalog name for *Exacum affinis,* and Horse-gentian is *Triosteum.* See these genera.

GENTIANACEAE (jen-shi-ah-nay'-see-ee). The Gentian Family, an almost wholly herbaceous group principally native to temperate climates. The flowers are regular and bisexual with fused petals; they exhibit some of the best blues known to horticulture. Otherwise the family is of minor importance, only a few genera being in cultivation, principally Exacum and Nymphoides; many species of Gentiana are valued but difficult to grow.

GENTIANELLA (jen-shan-el'-ah). A common name for *Gentiana acaulis,* which means "stemless gentian" (another common name). It is a low alpine form of this popular perennial with large, single dark-blue flowers.

GENUS (plural *genera*). A group of plants constituting a subdivision of a family, and containing groups of species more or less closely related and having certain obvious structural characteristics in common. Like a species, a genus is a somewhat arbitrary concept designed to simplify identification and indicate relationship; hence its definition is subject to differences of opinion. Members of a genus resemble each other more than they do members of other genera; all oaks, for example, are more alike than they are like any of the willows.

The first part of a plant's botanical or "scientific" name is that of the genus to which it belongs; the second part, a qualifying adjective indicating *what kind,* is the species name. Thus *Betula* is the name of the genus to which all birches belong, and *Betula lutea* indicates the Yellow Birch, a particular kind. See CLASSIFICATION; FAMILY; SPECIES; VARIETY.

GEONOMA (jee-on'-oh-mah). A genus of small shade-loving palms from S. America. A few are grown under glass, being most attractive in a young state. They need an abundance of water.

G. elegans grows to 6 ft., with a slender reed-like stem and leaves 1 ft. long, usually divided into 5 to 7 segments, or rarely 3. *G. gracilis* is very graceful, with dark green arching leaves of many narrow leaflets. *G. schottiana* grows to 15 ft., with leaves to 3 ft. long, divided into many narrow leaflets tapering to a tail-like point.

GERANIACEAE (jee-ray-ni-ay'-see-ee). The Geranium Family, so called from the Greek word for crane, suggested by the beaked capsular fruit. Widely distributed herbs, a few are woody. Most of the cultivated kinds are grown solely for ornament but some species of Pelargonium

STARTING A POT PLANT ANEW
A. Old, leggy geranium showing where stems should be cut—each just above a bud; b, plant as cut back; c, same plant after new growth has developed.

furnish the perfumery oil called rose geranium. The nearly regular flowers have 5 petals, 5 sepals, a lobed ovary and stamens 1, 2 or 3 times the number of petals. The house and bedding plants commonly known as geraniums are species of Pelargonium; the genus Geranium and another, Erodium, are hardy plants of simple culture.

GERANIUM (jee-ray'-ni-um). A large genus of herbs, widely distributed in temperate regions of the earth and commonly called Cranesbill. (Both names refer to the long beak-like projection on the seed.) They have mostly lobed or divided leaves and showy flowers of various colors, sometimes to 1½ in. across, but mostly under ½ in. They are useful plants for the rock garden and flower border, growing well in any good soil, and some are well adapted for naturalizing. Propagation is by seeds and division.

The so-called geraniums of the florist, including the familiar house and bedding sorts, belong to the genus Pelargonium, which see.

For enemies also see PELARGONIUM.

PRINCIPAL SPECIES

(Perennial unless otherwise specified)

G. grandiflorum grows 1 ft. or more high, with deeply 5-lobed leaves and pale-lilac flowers.

ibericum grows to 18 in., with leaves deeply 7-lobed and showy panicles of violet-purple flowers in midsummer. Var. *album* is a good white form.

pratense grows to 3 ft., with 7-lobed leaves and large bluish-purple flowers.

maculatum is the common American species, thriving in moist places showy in summer with pale rosy-purple flowers.

sanguineum makes a rounded plant about 18 in. high, with leaves 5 to 7 lobed and large reddish-purple flowers. Var. *prostratum* (often grown as *G. lancastriense*) is a small compact form with rosy-pink flowers.

psilostemon is a vigorous and free-flowering species from Armenia, with dark red flowers spotted black.

argenteum is perennial or biennial, growing only a few inches high, with divided silvery leaves and large pink flowers.

robertianum (Herb Robert) is a little native annual or biennial species with small bright crimson flowers. It colonizes readily from seed.

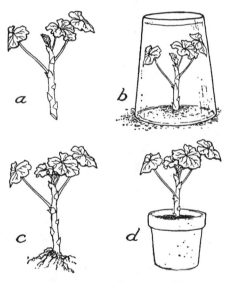

PROPAGATION BY CUTTINGS
A, Geranium "slip" trimmed of superfluous leaves; b, slip inserted in soil and covered with tumbler or jelly glass to keep air moist and conserve heat; c, cutting after formation of roots, and d, "potted up" as a new plant.

The name Geranium is also applied to several unrelated plants (treated under the generic names given) as follows: Beefsteak-geranium, *Begonia rex-cultorum;* California-geranium, *Senecio petasites;* Feather-geranium, *Chenopodium botrys;* Mint-geranium, *Chrysanthemum balsamita;* Strawberry-geranium, *Saxifraga sarmentosa.*

GERBERA (ger'-be-ra) *jamesoni.* (Sometimes spelled *Gerberia.*) (See illustration, Plate 19.) Transvaal or Barberton Daisy. A tender S. African perennial which has attained tremendous popularity as a florists' cut-flower, following the introduction of an improved, large-flowered scarlet type and the development of variously colored hybrids. Usually grown as greenhouse or window plants, where they flower over a long winter season, they produce long-petaled daisy-like flowers 2 to 4 in. across on exceedingly long stems. The flowers are excellent for cutting and stand well above a rosette of gray-green leaves and are solid colored in many pastel shades, from pale amber through salmon and rose to rich ruby red.

Raising plants from seed is not difficult, except that germination is uncertain and careful handling is required. For this reason propagation is generally by cuttings of side shoots. In sowing seed, start them in slight heat, such as a sunny window, hotbed or greenhouse, in well-drained sandy peat soil. The fuzzy, pointed end of the seed should come just above the soil surface. About two weeks after they germinate the seedlings should be put into pots and repotted occasionally as the plants develop. A temperature of about 70 deg. is best. Flowers appear in six to nine months after sowing, and plants will continue to bear for years if given winter protection in the garden or wintered over in the coldframe.

GERMANDER (jer-man'-der). Common name for the genus Teucrium, a group of showy-flowered mint-like plants, some grown in gardens and others in greenhouses.

GERMAN IRIS. A name formerly applied to the tall bearded group of Irises and the species *I. germanica,* one of those from which the group developed. While still used occasionally, it has no geographical or other basis and is rapidly being discarded.

GERMAN IVY. Common name for *Senecio mikanioides* (often incorrectly

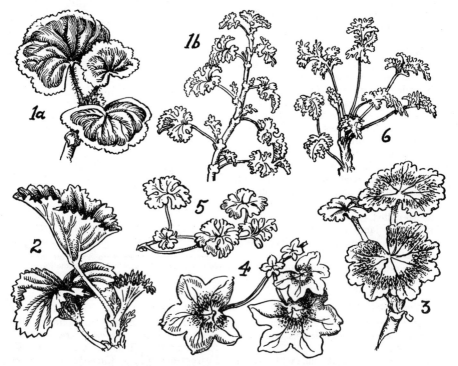

LEAF FORM VARIATIONS IN THE GERANIUM FAMILY

1, 2, 3, and 4 are Pelargoniums: 1a, the rose- or scent-leaved P. Mrs. Wm. Langeith and 1b, P. "crispum" of the same group; 2, P. Lady Washington; 3. the Zonale or Bedding P. Poitevive; 4, the Ivy-leaved P. Alliance. 5. is "Geranium farreri," and 6 is a heronsbill, "Erodium chellanthefolium."

called *S. scandens*); a popular tall-climbing window-garden and conservatory plant, with small heads of yellow flowers.

GERMINATION. Popularly speaking, the beginning of plant growth from a seed. Botanists give it more specific meanings: (1) the resumption of growth by the dormant embryo in a seed under the favorable combined influence of moisture, heat and oxygen-laden air; (2) the start of growth from a seed or a spore; (3) by extension, though less correctly, the resumption of activity by a dormant or latent bud. See SEEDS AND SEED SOWING; SEED TESTING.

GESNERIA (jes-nee'-ri-ah). Former name for certain tropical American tuberous-rooted herbs with red, two-lipped tubular flowers. They are now placed in the genera Naegelia and Corytholoma, which see.

GESNERIACEAE (jes-ner-i-ay'-see-ee). The Gesneria Family, a group of mostly herbaceous plants, widely distributed in the tropics. The stems are commonly fleshy and prostrate, but in the woody kinds are erect and climbing. A number are frequently cultivated for their very large, showy tubular flowers, mostly under glass. Among these are Corytholoma, Isoloma, Episcia, Sinningia, Achimenes, Naegelia, Alloplectus, Trichosporum; Streptocarpus, Saintpaulia.

GESNOUINIA (jes-noo-i'-ni-ah). Shrubs or trees of the Canary Isles, belonging to the Nettle Family. One species (*G. arborea,* formerly *Parietaria arborea*) has been planted in S. Calif. for ornamental purposes. It is a large shrub or small tree, with attractive long lanceolate leaves that are white beneath.

GEUM. (jee'-um). Avens. Easy-to-grow perennial of the Rose Family, erect and generally dwarf, excellent for cutting and adapted to the rock garden, borders or beds. Bearing yellow, red or white flowers freely from May to October, the plants thrive best in light, rich, well-drained soil in open, sunny situations. Propagation is by seeds sown in the open ground in the spring or by division of the roots in the fall. There are a score or more species and about 25 varieties are cultivated in the U. S. The following species are the most satisfactory:

G. chiloense. A hairy plant 1 to 2 ft. high. The leaves have a large terminal leaflet and many smaller lateral leaflets.

GERBERAS FOR THE GARDEN
Called Transvaal, or Barberton, Daisies, these long-stemmed, slender-petaled flowers in pastel shades are being increasingly grown in florists' greenhouses, but they seem to be hardy, with winter protection, as far North as New York City.

The dazzling scarlet flowers, at their best in June and July, are 1½ in. across. Var. *plenum* is double. Probably the most popular catalog variety is Mrs. Bradshaw, which blooms all summer, bearing fully double, brilliant orange-scarlet flowers. Lady Stratheden is a double yellow, and Orange Queen a double orange-scarlet.

bulgaricum. To 2 ft. The large terminal leaflets are heart-shaped. Flowers bright yellow or orange.

coccineum. With similar foliage. Flowers bright red, 1 in. across. The double var. (*flore pleno*) is best used in the border.

montanum. To 1 ft., has golden-yellow flowers 1½ in. across; a form with orange-red flowers is sometimes listed as a species, *G. heldreichi.*

pecki. To 2 ft., has few, if any, lateral leaflets. Yellow flowers are 1 in. across.

reptans. The 6-in. plants develop long runners and have 1½ in. yellow flowers.

strictum. To 5 ft., with yellow flowers, is good at the back of borders.

GHERKIN (gur'-kin). A small-fruited variety of cucumber, or the small, immature fruit of an ordinary variety harvested early for pickling. See CUCUMBER.

GHOSTWEED. A common name for *Euphorbia marginata,* popular garden annual, better known as Snow-on-the-mountain.

GIANT-BELLFLOWER. C o m m o n name for *Ostrowskya magnifica,* a stately herbaceous perennial of the Campanula Family, native in Asia. It is hardy N. with protection, but likely to be short-lived. A sunny slope of light sandy soil, with humus added, is about the best position. It has a thick fleshy root-stock, from which young growth starts so early in spring that it may need protection from late frost. It grows to 5 ft. or more, with whorled leaves and pale lilac flowers about 4 in. across. Propagation is by root or top cuttings. Seeds are slow to germinate and seedlings slow to grow.

GIANT DAISY. A common name for *Chrysanthemum uliginosum,* a 6 ft. European perennial, much branched, bearing large white flowers.

GIANT-FENNEL. Common name for *Ferula communis,* a 12 ft. tall, thick-rooted perennial with finely divided foliage and large yellow-flowered umbels.

GIANT FERN-PALM. A common but misleading name for Macrozamia, a genus of plants which are neither palms nor ferns, but huge members of the group called Cycads, which see.

GIANT GROUNDSEL. Common name for *Ligularia wilsoniana,* a 5 ft. perennial herb with yellow flowers in heads.

GIANT REED. Common name for *Arundo donax,* which, with the exception of the Bamboos and Uva Grass (which see), is the tallest of the perennial grasses. Coming from the warmer regions of the Old World, it grows from 8 to 20 ft. in height according to location and soil, and bears loose, feathery flower spikes 1 to 3 ft. long. It is from the stems of this plant that the reeds of musical instruments are made.

Several varieties are available: *A. donax* var. *versicolor* will grow to 12 ft. with white-streaked leaves, is less hardy than the parent species, although both should be protected in the N. States during the winter months. Var. *macrophylla* has

wide, glossy, green leaves and conspicuously close-jointed stems.

GIANT SUMMER-HYACINTH. Common name for *Galtonia* (formerly *Hyacinthus) candicans,* a tall bulbous, summer-blooming herb with a stout spike of bell-like white flowers.

GILIA (jil'-i-ah). A genus of annual, biennial or perennial herbs, mostly of W. N. America, belonging to the Polemonium Family. They are of easy culture in the flower garden, and seeds may be sown where the plants are to bloom.

PRINCIPAL SPECIES

G. capitata, an annual to 2 ft. or so, has dense roundish heads of light blue flowers.

laciniata is a dwarf annual with finely-divided leaves and few-flowered clusters of rose, blue, or lilac flowers.

achilleaefolia is a bushy annual to 2 ft. or more, with finely-divided leaves and dense clusters of blue or purple flowers.

tricolor (Birds-eyes) is an annual to 3 ft., with loose clusters of lilac or violet flowers marked yellow, very freely produced.

aggregata is a biennial to 2 ft., with showy flowers of scarlet ranging to white.

rubra (Standing-cypress) is biennial or perennial, growing to 6 ft., with finely-dissected leaves, and a narrow panicle of scarlet flowers with orange or yellow markings.

GILLENIA (ji-lee'-ni-ah). A genus of rosaceous herbs with pinkish or white flowers. Two American species, *G. stipulata* (American Ipecac) and *G. trifoliata* (Indian Physic), are attractive hardy border and rockery plants.

GILLIFLOWER (ji'-li-flou-er). A corruption from the French Giroflée, sometimes spelled Gillyflower and Gilloflower. The name is said to have been first given in Italy to plants of the Pink Family (Caryophyllaceae), especially the carnation. The Gilliflower of Chaucer and Shakespeare also was the carnation (*Dianthus caryophyllus*). Today the name is applied chiefly to stock (*Mathiola incana*) and sometimes to wallflower (*Cheiranthus cheiri*). In England in the 17th century the name Queens-gilliflower was applied to *Hesperis matronalis.*

GILL-OVER-THE-GROUND. A common name for *Nepeta hederacea,* a creeping, mat-forming, blue-flowered perennial grown as a ground cover in shady places.

GINGER. The ginger of the market consists of the dried rhizomes of a tropical plant, *Zingiber officinale,* which is grown commercially in the E. and W. Indies, Africa, and China, the Jamaica ginger being regarded as the best.

Wild-ginger is the common name for the genus Asarum, of which *A. canadense* is common in woods of the E. States. A low herb with kidney-shaped leaves, and chocolate-colored flowers borne close to the ground, it is a good ground-cover plant for moist shady places.

GINGER FAMILY. Common name of the *Zingiberaceae,* a tropical family of rhizomatous herbs, providing commercial ginger and several ornamental greenhouse plants.

GINGER-LILY. A common name for the genus Hedychium, tropical herbs with stout root stocks, leafy stems, and showy fragrant flowers.

GINKGO (gink'-goh). An Asiatic genus of hardy deciduous trees represented by one species, *G. biloba,* often called Maidenhair-tree because its attractive foliage resembles in form that of the popular Maidenhair fern (Adiantum). It grows to 120 ft. with characteristic diagonally upright form and flowers in loose catkins, followed (in the case of pistillate trees) by yellowish, foul-smelling fruit. It is native to northern China and Japan and is the sole survivor of a family widespread in early geologic times.

The Ginkgo is much used as a street or park tree, or for planting as a specimen where a picturesque effect is desired. It is hardy N. and because of the rather leathery texture of the leaves practically free from insect pests and disease. It is easily propagated from seeds (which should be stratified in the fall), by layers and cuttings, and, in the case of varieties, by budding or grafting. Because of the ill-smelling fruit of the pistillate tree, the last two methods are more generally employed. Of the different forms available, var. *aurea* has yellow leaves; *fastigiata* is especially upright in growth; *laciniata* has cut leaves; *macrophylla* has larger leaves than the type; *pendula* has drooping branches, and *variegata* has yellow and green leaves.

GINSENG (jin'-seng). The common name of a genus (Panax) of Asiatic and N. American perennial herbs valued by the Chinese as medicine. The only species of interest are the Asiatic (*P. schinseng*), the Dwarf or Groundnut Ginseng (*P. trifolium*), and the American (*P. quinquefolium*). The last mentioned is gathered wild (and also occasionally grown) for export. At one time exploited, it has today little status as a garden crop.

The plants require cool, moist, deep, well-drained soil and shade supplied either by tall forest trees or slat sheds. Seed sown as soon as gathered may germinate the following spring; if allowed to dry it requires a year longer. Seedlings may be sold or transplanted in fall or spring when one or two years old. Roots four or five years old may be dug for export.

GINSENG or ARALIA FAMILY. Common name of Araliaceae (which see), a family of herbs, shrubs and trees whose small, regular flowers are borne in close heads, and which often have aromatic foliage.

THE MAIDENHAIR-TREE

Ginkgo biloba is so called because the leaves are shaped like those of the maidenhair fern. It makes a handsome lawn specimen, but the fruits are ill-smelling; therefore, plant staminate trees.

GIRASOLE (jir'-ah-sohl). A tall growing perennial sunflower (*Helianthus tuberosus*) whose potato-like tubers are a delicious fall, winter and early spring vegetable, escalloped or steamed and served with a cream or a hollandaise sauce. It is more familiar to many (and usually listed in catalogs) as Jerusalem Artichoke —which is a misnomer because it is neither an artichoke nor does it hail from Palestine but is a native of North America! See under ARTICHOKE.

GLABROUS. A term meaning "not hairy," as illustrated by the stem of the bush poppy or the leaves of the orpine (*Crassula portulacea*). It is often incorrectly used to mean *smooth,* which properly refers to plant parts which are not only free from hairs, but also not rough or gritty to the touch. Do not confuse with GLAUCOUS.

GLACIAL SOIL. A type of soil widely distributed over those parts of N. U. S. once covered by the prehistoric ice sheet. Resulting from the grinding, mixing and carrying action of that vast glacier as it alternately advanced and receded, the soil is a mingled, unsorted mass of fine and coarse particles including rock fragments and even large boulders. Naturally its fertility and value for plant growing varies from place to place according to its condition and its constituents. See SOIL.

GLACIER-LILY. Common name for *Erythronium grandiflorum,* a 2 ft., bulbous, spring-blooming herb with yellow lily-like flowers.

GLADIOLUS (glad-i-oh'-lus). A genus of tender cormous plants of the Iris Family. Leaves are sword-like and grow fan-shaped. Flowers are borne on tall, upright spikes having as many as 25 flowers a spike under ideal culture. Flowers open from the bottom upward, five to ten being open at one time.

Gladiolus fall into three general classifications: the tender small spring flowering ones having their origin in tropical Africa; the winter-hardy species from the Mediterranean regions of Europe; and the summer flowering ones having their origin in southeast Africa. These last are by far the most popular. The spring-flowering types have value only as greenhouse subjects and are not widely grown by amateur gardeners. The winter-hardy ones are available only as species and have not been developed or improved by hybridization. The summer flowering gladiolus, on the other hand, have been widely hybridized and greatly improved from the original species.

These modern summer flowering gladiolus may be found in hundreds of varieties and still new ones appear each year from hybridists' gardens. They cover an unusually wide range of size, color, and petal formation. In size they range from the miniatures, some of which have florets little more than an inch in diameter, to the giant size ones which may produce florets up to ten inches in diameter. Varieties may be found in almost every color and shade from pure white through the deep black reds. Many popular ones are bicolor, and some have blendings of several colors and are known as smokies. There is no

true blue-colored gladiolus, but many of the violet shades approach the blue. The gladiolus is one of the few flowers whose blossoms include the color green.

Most varieties have round, rather broad petals which may be plain, ruffled, crinkled, or needlepointed. In addition, others are laciniated, some are orchid-like, and still others doubled. Fragrance in gladiolus has been an elusive quality, but in recent years breeders have been able to produce that in a few cases.

HISTORY OF GLADIOLUS

The hybridization and improvement of the gladiolus began at least as far back as 1807 when William Herbert produced seedlings from some of the African species then being brought to England. Interest thereupon developed rapidly in both England and on the continent. The modern summer flowering gladiolus had its real beginning with the introduction of the hybrid *G. Gandavensis* which had been developed by Bedinghaus, gardener for the Duc d'Aremburg. The species *G. psittacinus,* a summer flowering species, entered into this new gladiolus and from that time on interest turned from the spring flowering types to the summer flowering ones.

In America the John Lewis Child's firm on Long Island was one of the first to popularize and improve the gladiolus. Luther Burbank included this flower among his many hybridizing projects. In 1908 Lemoine of France introduced the first of the *G. primulinus* hybrids, and these, because of the elements of grace, soft clear coloring, and ease of growth and propagation, revolutionized gladiolus breeding. When crossed with other types the Primulinus produced many new and beautiful forms. In 1932 Prof. E. F. Palmer of Canada introduced the variety *Picardy,* the first very large flowered variety to result from the crossing of the Gandavensis and Primulinus strains.

GLADIOLUS CULTURE

Few flowers are as adaptable to various climates and soil conditions as the gladiolus. Its cultural requirements are rather simple. It will grow well in almost any type of rich soil if it has the two absolutely necessary features of full sun and good drainage. It will not compete with roots from woody plants and it will not remain healthy in water-logged soil. The corm from which the gladiolus grows is tender and in most areas will not winter over in the ground, although this has been done successfully in mild climates or where winter protection has been given. The general practice, however, is to lift the corms each fall and to plant them again the next year.

The corms may be planted in the spring as soon as the soil is warm. Plantings may be continued up to within 90 days of heavy freezes.

The corms are planted in trenches about four or five inches deep, depending on size of corm, in soil that has been well worked. A slightly acid state is best. Moderate fertilization is desirable; the fertilizer should have a low nitrogen and a high phosphate content, a formula of 3-8-6 being good. The soil around the plants should be kept loose and friable at all times for best results.

Plenty of water given either naturally or by irrigation is helpful in growing top quality blooms. The feeding roots of the gladiolus grow out from the plant toward the middle of the rows. Therefor fertilizer is best fed in ribbons about 8 in. from the row, and when the plant has made fair growth cultivation should be shallow.

When gladioli are grown as cut flowers the removal of any part of the foliage (with the spike) interferes with the normal development of the new corm. If two or three of the broadest leaves at the base of the plant are allowed to remain, a fair crop can result, but maximum corm development can only come if the whole plant is left intact. After the flowers wither the spike should be removed as the development of a seed-pod draws heavily upon the whole plant structure and in time decreases the size of the new corm.

About six weeks after the blooming period is over the corms will be ready for digging. With spading fork or other convenient tool loosen the soil around the plant and lift it free. The old tops are then cut off close to the top of the new corm. These corms are set out to dry in a warm airy place, not in full sun, and permitted to dry for about three weeks. Then the old corm may be broken from the new and discarded. These new corms are then stored in suitable containers in a basement or other quarters that are fairly cool. It is important that corms be stored so that air may move around them during the storage period. This storage period is a period of rest for the corms and corms should not be planted until they have gone through this period of rest.

SMALL CORMS GIVE GOOD BLOOMS. Corms that measure 1½ in. in diameter are known in the trade as "first size" in the case of most varieties; and this size is recommended for general garden use. However, under good cultural conditions, corms of much smaller size will flower equally well, for the flower bud is a progressive one and will develop from even a small cormel when the right conditions prevail. The age of the corm, which can be determined by the size of the root plate or flattened basal area from which roots arise—the smaller the root plate the younger the bulb—is almost as important in determining the quality of the corm as is the size. For, after they attain their normal growth, gladiolus corms do not continue to improve with age but, on the contrary, become less valuable. The corm that is planted is not the one that is harvested, for the old corm withers up during the growing period, a new one forming on top of it.

THREE GLADIOLUS GENERATIONS
This popular plant renews itself annually. The corm you dig up in the fall (a) is actually a new one developed on top of the one you planted in the spring (b) now black and shriveled. At (c) are two small cormels, also the fruits of a year's growth; grown on for two seasons they become flowering-size corms—an easy way to work up a stock of a variety.

SUCCESSION OF BLOOM. Gladiolus varieties are fairly regular in the number of days they take to bloom each season. Some bloom in as short a period as 60 days; others take up to 100 days or more.

Catalogs usually indicate the number of days for each variety. Sometimes, instead of giving the approximate number of days, they will use general terms, such as *early, medium, late,* or *very late.* Early means from 60 to 75 days, medium from 75 to 85, late 85 and more, and very late as many as 120 days.

A succession of blooms may be had by planting varieties with different length blooming seasons. The same end is accomplished by planting the same variety at different times. The first planting may be made as early as the soil is dry enough in the spring, and additional plantings made at various dates up to within about 75 days of the first killing frost. The blooming season may also be lengthened by using corms of different sizes. In a given variety medium sized corms will take about ten days longer before blooming than will large ones. Small corms will take even longer and sometimes fail to bloom at all.

All the foregoing applies to the well known large type of hybrids, but there are several of the original species that are still considered valuable. The most prominent is *G. tristis* of which there are several varieties ranging from pure yellow and citron white, to one that has a yellow background with brown spots. There is also a group called *G. colvillei,* of which *tristis* is one of the parents. Because of their small wiry stems and small flowers, members of this species are quite generally called Baby Gladiolus. They seem to be semi-hardy and for best results must be planted in the fall and given some winter protection. They make no cormels like the larger hybrids, and propagation is confined to the making of two or three new corms on top of the old one.

PROPAGATION

Propagation of the gladiolus is by means of growing into corms the small hard shelled cormels that are found attached to the mother corm at digging time. Some varieties produce these cormels in greater profusion than others, and some produce cormels which will germinate much more readily than do others. In general cormels that are large and soft shelled will germinate more readily. Hard-shelled types may be encouraged to germinate by soaking them in water for several hours before planting, or by cracking the shell.

Cormels are planted in trenches about two inches deep. The soil must be packed firmly about them and kept fairly moist until germination has been induced. During the storage period these cormels should be kept in as cool temperatures as possible but above freezing. Quarters that are too warm will throw them into deep dormancy. Cormels are treated as other corms at digging time. They will reach full-size corms in about two years on the average.

Because of their interest in gladiolus and the ease with which the mechanics of hybridization are carried out, many amateur gardeners carry out their own breeding programs. Each gladiolus flower bears both the anthers or pollen bearing organ and the stigma or female part. Cross pollenization is accomplished by dusting the pollen from the anthers of the pollen parent on the stamen, the end portion of the stigma, of the seed bearing parent. Pollen must be dry to be useful. Parent selections are made according to the aims and judgment of the breeder.

After fertilization has taken place the seed will develop in the ovaries. It is permitted to ripen on the flower stem. After it is ripe it is gathered, kept over winter, and in the spring planted about ½ inch deep in a specially prepared seed bed. A majority of the seed will grow into small corms the first season. Over winter these are handled just like regular corms and are planted the next spring in the garden. Selection is made as the flowers bloom and propagation of the selected flowers is repeated by growing cormels as directed above.

Hybridization calls for good judgment in the defining of aims, in the selection of parents for the desired qualities you want to combine, and in knowing when real improvement has been achieved.

ENEMIES

The most important insect enemy of gladiolus is thrips, a small blackish insect which may be seen with the naked eye as it is about $\frac{1}{16}$ of an inch in length. It causes damage by sucking the juices from the growing plant, especially from the flower spike as it is developing, thus producing a brownish or blasted effect. Modern insecticides have made control measures comparatively easy. For the storage period a specially prepared dust can be purchased and put on the corms to kill any thrips that they may harbor. Corms are planted with the dust on them.

Gladiolus should be treated with a good

insecticide, such as 10 percent, Chlordane dust or Malathion spray, beginning after the plants have reached a height of eight to ten inches. Spray or dust at ten day intervals until bud spikes begin to appear. The life cycle of the thrips is about ten to twelve days so it is more effective to follow a short concentrated spray schedule than it is to spray sporadically throughout the season.

The diseases of gladiolus may be divided into three general classes: fungus diseases, bacterial diseases, and virus. *Fusarium yellows* is one of the most prevalent of the fungus diseases. It causes a slowing down of growth and a yellowing of the leaf between the veins. Later the yellow turns to brown as the disease spreads and eventually the plant dies.

Other fungus diseases are rots of one kind or another. The amateur gardener will have trouble distinguishing which is which, but general rules for treatment will hold for all.

Dry rot, *Sclerotinum gladioli,* causes dark corky lesions to appear on the dormant corms. The growing plant may show a rotting at the neck, where the stem joins the corm.

Hard rot, *Septoria gladioli,* produces hard lesions on the corms. Small brown spots may appear on the leaves above ground level. The best way to handle any cases where fungus trouble is suspected is to rogue (which see). Also remove some of the soil where the plant was growing. Good drainage of the soil is very important. Quick drying of the corms at digging time is another disease preventative measure. Storage should be in a location which is not overly damp. The use of a good fungicide on the corms or in the soil at planting time will also aid in preventing disease. Bortran and Morsodren are fungicides now available.

Two forms of blight caused by fungus may be encountered. These are Red Spot, *Stemphylium leaf blight,* and Botrytis, *Botrytis gladioli.* Each causes small spots of rotting on the foliage and on the flowers. These lesions in Red Spot have a tiny red center. In Botrytis the spotting is dark brown with a lighter brown center. Both Stemphylium and Botrytis have much the same effect of making the flowers useless. And both spread rapidly only under foggy or humid conditions. Neither

disease is prevalent under most conditions. At least partial control can be achieved by a spray of Dithane-78 used in a proportion of 2 lbs. to 100 gallons of water. In climates where humidity is a special problem only varieties known to resist these diseases should be planted.

There are two forms of virus which attack gladiolus. One is known as Mild Mosaic and may be identified by the white flecking on the leaves. In most cases the flower is not harmed. The other form of virus is White Break which causes a white woody breaking of the color on flowers and a narrowing and stunting of the leaves. There is no known cure for these virus diseases. Diseased plants should be rogued to prevent spread of the virus to other plants which have not yet been attacked.

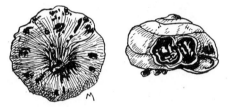

SCAB ON GLADIOLUS CORMS
If husks show infection spots (left) remove and burn them in fall. Otherwise the corm tissue may be attacked (right). Precautionary disinfection before planting is always advisable.

Fortunately most gladiolus varieties are not affected by viruses. Gardeners will have little trouble with gladiolus diseases if they begin with healthy stock, rogue any affected plants that show up, spray or dust during the growing season, and make certain that corms are planted in well drained locations.

GLADIOLUS COUNCIL, NORTH AMERICAN. The registrar of the North American Gladiolus Council is Mr. Lawrence R. Rupert, Sardinia, N. Y. 14134. The Society has an annual convention and makes awards for outstanding new varieties.

Mr. Rupert can furnish information on American and foreign suppliers and other specialized information on gladiolus.

GLADWYN (glad"n). The common name for *Iris foetidissima,* an evergreen species grown for its large attractive seedpods which contain globular scarlet seeds. The leaves emit an offensive odor when bruised.

GLAND-BELLFLOWER. A catalog name for Adenophora, a campanula-like, hardy perennial with drooping blue flowers in loose, branching spikes.

GLASS-HOUSE. A general term for any structure designed for the growing of plants, such as a greenhouse or conservatory (which are discussed under those headings).

Poppy Family, native to Europe. There are annual, biennial, and perennial species, but all are usually grown as annuals from seed in sunny locations, where their large orange, yellow or red flowers and their dissected bluish leaves adorn the garden throughout the season. Their common names are Horned Poppy and Sea Poppy.

G. corniculatum, the annual sort, grows

SOME POSSIBLE USES FOR STRUCTURAL GLASS IN THE GARDEN
Left above, corrugated, reinforced glass as a background and shelter; left below, plate glass protection against sea winds and spray.   Right, glass building block steps in a modern type garden.

GLASS IN THE GARDEN. In recent years many gardeners, especially those whose gardens are in close proximity to ocean winds or other strong breezes, have discovered the usefulness of glass for garden walls and screens. Glass, whether transparent or translucent, corrugated or flat, has the advantage of allowing light to enter the garden, while still offering maximum protection from strong winds and the sand, salt, and other undesirable elements often carried by them. Even greater sturdiness can be obtained by using wire-reinforced glass.

GLASTONBURY THORN. A British name for a variety of *Crataegus oxyacantha,* one of the Hawthorns.

GLAUCIDIUM (glau-sid′-i-um). A small genus of oriental herbs of which one, *G. palmatum,* from Japan, is sometimes grown in rock gardens for its maple-like foliage and its violet flowers.

GLAUCIUM (glau′-si-um). A genus of easily cultivated garden flowers of the

to 1½ feet and has red flowers, each petal with a black spot at the base.

flavum, biennial or perennial, is taller to 3 feet, with yellow flowers followed by long, slender seed pods.

leiocarpum, the perennial species, also has yellow flowers, but is less than 2 feet tall.

GLAUCOUS. Covered or whitened with a bloom that rubs off. A term used to describe the surface texture and appearance of leaves, stems, fruits, etc. Do not confuse with GLABROUS.

GLAUX (glauks) *maritima.* A small succulent perennial herb common to the salt marshes along the coasts of the N. hemisphere. Sometimes it is planted where the soil is fed by brackish water, for its pale, bloomy foliage and inconspicuous white or purplish flowers.

GLEDITSIA (gle-dit′-si-ah) formerly spelled Gleditschia. A genus of broad-headed, deciduous, mostly thorny trees of the pea family commonly known as Honey

Locusts and planted as shade and lawn specimens and for the decorative effect of their finely cut foliage. They have smooth bark and small greenish flowers and bear large numbers of large glossy brown ornamental pods. The strong sharp thorns are often branched. Honey Locusts are propagated by seeds which should be soaked in hot water before being sown; choice specimens can be increased by grafting on seedlings of *G. triacanthos.*

G. aquatica (Water or Swamp Locust) to 60 ft. is a low-branching tree with spiny trunk growing in swamps of the S. States. *G. triacanthos* (Honey or Sweet Locust) 70 to 140 ft. and found from Pa. to Tex., is a fine lawn or avenue tree; its var. *inermis* is quite thornless. *G. sinensis, G. delavayi* and *G. horrida* are Asiatic trees, grown in the S., but tender N.

GLEICHENIA (gly-kee'-ni-ah). Bead Fern, Umbrella Fern. A genus of ferns, suitable only for cool-greenhouse conditions. The fronds vary from 1 to 6 ft. tall in different species and differ from all other ferns in their development. Each forks and produces a bud in the fork, from which another forking frond appears. The elongated-globular, clustered fruit dots suggest beads. The rhizomes are surface-creeping and should be pegged down in wide pots. Provide rough peat, sand, and perfect drainage, as they require much water at the roots. Wet sparingly from above, and give plenty of light and air. The best species are *G. circinata,* an airy plant, with short blades and narrow pinnae on long stipes; *G. dicarpa,* with pendulous pinnae; and *G. flabellata,* two or three times forked and very large, with narrow comb-like pinnae; also the most dependable.

GLIRICIDIA (gli-ri-sid'-i-ah). Trees or shrubs of tropical America, belonging to the Pea Family. One or two species are grown outdoors in the warm regions of the country. *G. sepium,* commonly called Madre, is the best known. It is a tree growing to 30 ft., with racemes of pink or white flowers freely produced in advance of the pinnate leaves. Later it has flat pods about 5 in. long.

GLOBE-AMARANTH (am'-ah-ranth). Common name for *Gomphrena globosa,* an erect rather stiff branchy annual with variously colored flowers which when dried are used for everlasting bouquets.

GLOBE-DAISY. Common name for *Globularia trichosantha,* a dwarf perennial with small blue flowers in ½ in. rounded heads.

GLOBE-FLOWER. Common name for *Trollius europaeus;* also for a double-flowered form of *Kerria japonica.*

GLOBE-MALLOW. Common name for the genus Sphaeralcea, consisting mostly of warm-region herbs and shrubs of which half a dozen species are grown in gardens for their red or violet flowers.

GLOBE THISTLE. Common name for Echinops, a genus of tall biennial and perennial and annual herbs with large dense spherical heads of flowers.

GLOBE-TULIP. Common name for certain species of Calochortus, a W. American genus of liliaceous herbs from whose slender, graceful stems droop single, nearly globular flowers of fine white, yellow or rose color.

GLOBULARIA (glob-eu-lay'-ri-ah). Little shrubby plants found mostly in the mountains of S. Europe and Asia. They have small blue (or rarely white) flowers in rounded heads and are sometimes grown in rock gardens, where they need a well drained soil in a moist and partly shaded place. Propagated by division or seed. *G. trichosantha* (Globe-daisy) is a neat little plant a few inches high, with toothed leaves about an inch long, and small heads of pale blue fluffy flowers on leafy stems. *G. nudicaulis* is very similar but a bit larger and with naked flower stems. *G. cordifolia* is a tiny prostrate grower, with leaves notched only at the tips, and tiny heads of blue flowers on short stems.

GLORIOSA (gloh-ri-oh'-sah). A genus of tropical tuberous-rooted climbing herbs with lily-like yellow or red flowers. See GLORY-LILY.

GLORYBOWER. Common name for Clerodendron or Clerodendrum, a genus of herbs, shrubs and trees with showy red, white or violet flowers in terminal clusters; grown under glass or outdoors in the S.

GLORY-BUSH. The common name for Tibouchina, a genus of tropical American shrubs, grown under glass or outdoors in the far South. They are handsome plants for conservatory decoration, grown either in bush form, or to adorn a wall or pillar; in the first case, pinch the strong shoots now and again and train in shape. They grow easily from cuttings, and thrive in a rich loamy soil.

T. semidecandra, the principal species, grows to 10 ft. or more and has soft hairy leaves and showy violet-colored flowers up to 5 in. across. It is sometimes used in summer bedding arrangements, and as a terrace plant in pots or tubs. *T. elegans* is a much smaller plant, with stiff leaves and purple flowers an inch or so across.

GLORY - FLOWER. (*Eccremocarpus scaber*). A climbing shrub from S. America, belonging to the Bignonia Family. In the North it can be grown as an annual. It flowers well if sown early and grown in light rich soil in a warm position. It has bipinnate leaves with a branching tendril at the end by which it climbs. The orange-red flowers are about an inch long, and borne in loose racemes.

GLORY-LILY. Common name for Gloriosa, a genus of climbing herbaceous plants with tall weak stems, native in tropical Africa and Asia, belonging to the Lily Family. They grow from long tubers, and are attractive summer-flowering climbers under glass. In the S. they grow well outdoors and plants may be bedded outdoors in N. Y. for summer flowering, though the growth under such conditions is short and less floriferous. The dormant tubers are started in pots early in the year. They do best in a rather rough turfy loam with leafmold, and appreciate liberal feeding when growth is well under way. The flowers are very colorful and of curious form, with wavy reflexed segments and long spreading stamens. Propagation is by tuber division or by offsets.

G. superba (Spider-lily) has orange and red flowers with narrow crisped segments. *G. rothschildiana* has crimson flowers with oblong, strongly reflexed segments, margined yellow and broadening to a yellow base. Var. *citrina* is a form with pale yellow and reddish-purple flowers.

GLORY-OF-THE-SNOW. Common name for Chionodoxa, a genus of hardy early spring-blooming bulbs with blue or white flowers in loose open spikes.

GLORY-PEA, or GLORY-VINE. Common names for *Clianthus dampieri*, an Australian trailing shrub, grown in warm countries for its large, showy scarlet flowers in drooping clusters.

GLOXINIA (glok-sin'-i-ah). Commonly accepted name for *Sinningia speciosa*, which is usually listed as *Gloxinia speciosa*. The garden or greenhouse gloxinias are Brazilian herbs with richly colored, showy, bell-shaped flowers, violet, purple, white or reddish, often marbled or spotted with darker shades, rising to 6 in. above the large, downy, conspicuously-veined leaves.

Florists usually start gloxinias in Feb. in a warm greenhouse, planting seed in shallow flats in soil composed of equal parts of finely sifted leafmold, silver sand and peat. Later the seedlings are potted in equal parts of leafmold, loam and peat, shifting several times, shading the plants from direct sunlight and taking care not to wet the leaves when watering. The plants bloom in August and after the flowers and leaves have matured, water is withheld in order that the tubers may ripen. When mature they are stored in sand for the winter in a temperature of 45 deg. F. These tubers will start into growth the following spring. The rare varieties are grown from leaf or stem cuttings.

If gloxinias are infected with the spotted wilt virus, remove and burn diseased plants.

GLUE. A good, if somewhat messy, contact spray used to control mites on evergreens. Dissolve 1 lb. cheap powdered glue in 1 gal. boiling water and dilute to 10 gal.

GLYCERIA (gly-see'-ri-ah). A genus of rather tall coarse perennial grasses, commonly known as Manna Grass, used for landscape effects or border-planting in wet places. Their elongated flower clusters, usually purple, are borne in terminal branching racemes. *G. grandis* (Reed Meadow Grass or American Manna Grass) grows to 5 ft. with leaves 1 ft. long and ½ in. wide, rough on the top side. Its European relative, *G. aquatica,* is similar. Multiplication may be from division of clumps, offsets, or by seed.

See ORNAMENTAL GRASSES.

GLYCOSMIS (gly-kos'-mis). Evergreen shrubs or trees belonging to the Rue Family. One species, *G. pentaphylla,* from the tropics, has been introduced into cultivation in this country and may be grown under glass or outdoors in the far South. It is a bushy plant with dark green glossy leaves of 1 to 7 leaflets, and panicles of small white fragrant flowers. These are followed by pink translucent berries.

GNAPHALIUM (nah-fay'-li-um). A genus of woolly herbs, widely distributed throughout the world, belonging to the Daisy Family. They have small heads of mostly yellow flowers, resembling tiny everlastings. Only a few have been cultivated, and the best known are now referred to other genera. *Helichrysum petio-*

latum was formerly *G. lanatum; Leonto-podium alpinum* (Edelweiss) was formerly *G. leontopodium;* and *Antennaria marga-ritacea* was formerly *G. margaritacea.*

GOATSBEARD. Common name for the genus Aruncus, hardy herbaceous perennials of the Rose Family, with white flowers in clusters of spikes; also for Tragopogon, a group of biennials and perennials with large purple or yellow flowers in heads, belonging to the Composite Family and including Salsify, which see.

GOATS-RUE. Common name for *Galega officinalis,* a hardy perennial with pea-like flowers.

GODETIA (goh-dee'-shi-ah). A genus of annual herbs of the Evening-primrose Family with red, white, lilac or purple flowers in leafy clusters. Most of the species grown in the border are native to Calif. and should therefore be given a light warm soil and a sunny exposure. They come readily from seed and will often self-sow. Start seed where the plants are to grow or, for early bloom, under glass.

G. grandiflora, to 1 ft., the species most frequently cultivated, has rose-red flowers with a dark blotch at the center of each petal; it is known in several forms.

amoena (Farewell-to-Spring), a common wild flower of the Western States, grows to 3 ft. and has flowers varying from rosy-purple to white, frequently double. It is an easily grown annual, blooming freely although not showy.

GOLD AND SILVER FERNS. Names given to various tender ferns whose under surfaces are coated with white or colored powder or, in other cases, with colored hairs. See GYMNOGRAMMA; NOTHOLAENA; CHEILANTHES.

GOLD - DUST - PLANT. A common name for *Alyssum saxatile,* a spring-blooming perennial with abundant small yellow flowers.

GOLD-DUST-TREE. Common name for *Aucuba japonica* var. *variegata,* a mild climate evergreen shrub bearing bright red fruit.

GOLDEN-ASTER. Common name for the genus Chrysopsis, hardy perennial herbs with yellow flowers in heads.

GOLDEN-BACKED FERN. A common name for the Calif. Gold Fern, *Gymnogramma triangularis,* also known as *Pityrogramma triangularis.*

GOLDEN-BELLS. Common name for Forsythia, the popular early spring flowering shrub; also for *Emmenanthe penduliflora,* an annual herb sometimes called Yellow-bells.

GOLDEN-CHAIN. Common name for *Laburnum anagyroides,* a hardy deciduous tree with long pendulous racemes of yellow flowers.

GOLDEN-CLUB. Common name for *Orontium aquaticum,* a handsome native perennial of the Arum Family. Its conspicuous feature is the 2 in. long, narrow spadix, or spike-like flower part, covered with minute golden-yellow blossoms, which gives the plant its popular name. The elliptical leaves are rich, dark green and grow to a foot in length. Perfectly hardy, it is well suited to the edge of the pond or any marshy spot. See also AQUATIC PLANTS.

GOLDEN-CUP. Another name for the Tulip poppy (*Hunnemannia fumariaefolia*), a Mexican perennial, that blooms over a long season when grown as an annual in N. gardens.

GOLDEN DEWDROP. A common name for *Duranta repens,* a subtropical American shrub or small tree with lilac flowers and yellow berries; also called Sky-flower and Pigeon-berry.

GOLDEN-DROP. Common name for the genus Onosma, mostly Mediterranean herbs suitable for rock gardens and borders, with flowers hanging from a one-sided raceme.

GOLDEN EARDROPS. Common name for *Dicentra chrysantha,* a perennial herb with yellow heart-shaped flowers.

GOLDEN EGGS. Common name for *Oenothera ovata,* a stemless perennial of W. America, whose yellow flowers when in bud lie like eggs in a nest of leaves. A good rock-garden subject.

GOLDEN-FEATHER. A common name for *Chrysanthemum parthenium* var. *aureum,* the yellowish-leaved variety of Feverfew (which see). It is a bushy perennial with white flower heads.

GOLDEN GLOW. This popular, somewhat coarse, hardy perennial with its abundant golden yellow double flowers is a variety (*hortensia*) of *Rudbeckia laciniata,* a species of Coneflower, a member of the Composite Family. Growing to a height of 6 ft. or more, it is best used in the background of the perennial border. It prefers a sunny location but will thrive in any garden soil. The blossoms, up to 4 in. in diameter, provide welcome color in the garden and bright flowers for cutting from

July until October. Plants are easily grown from seed or cuttings and large clumps can—and indeed should be—divided from time to time. Otherwise they sometimes overrun a bed and encroach on other subjects.

A bothersome enemy of this plant is the red aphis, which infests the tips of growing shoots in great numbers, retarding their growth and making the flowers unpleasant to pick and use in the house. Persistent use of a nicotine or other contact spray with soap added will usually keep them under control. Dust with sulphur to control the white powdery mildew that is an almost inevitable accompaniment of humid weather in August.

See also RUDBECKIA.

GOLDEN-LARCH. Common name for *Pseudolarix amabilis,* one of the few deciduous members of the Pine Family. The feathery needle-like leaves in dense bundles are pale green in summer and turn golden-yellow in autumn. The tree is graceful with whorled branches, slender and drooping. Although a native of China it is hardy N. and quite free from insect pests and diseases. It should be planted

GOLDENROD
One of America's most noteworthy wild flowers, Goldenrod is more appreciated as a garden subject in Europe than in this country.

in moist, well-drained soil in a sheltered sunny position, and is particularly beautiful when placed in front of dark green evergreens. It is increased by seed.

GOLDEN MARGUERITE. Common name for *Anthemis tinctoria,* a perennial with yellow flowers in heads.

GOLDENPERT. A common name for *Gratiola aurea,* a low annual herb with small golden-yellow flowers, indigenous in wet grounds from Me. to Fla., useful for clothing damp banks of ditches and ponds. Also called Golden Hedge-hyssop.

GOLDEN POLYPODY. (*Polypodium aureum*). A fern for the warm greenhouse having a long terminal segment and brilliant yellow fruit dots. Needs much water and occasional weak manure.

GOLDEN-RAIN-TREE. Common name for *Koelreuteria paniculata,* a tree to 30 ft., of the Soapberry Family, bearing compound leaves and large clusters of showy yellow flowers followed by 3 parted bladdery capsules. A tree from eastern Asia, hardy N. as far as Mass. (in sheltered position), it is rather short-lived and likely to be killed back by severe cold spells. But it is a rather compact roundheaded subject, adaptable in its soil requirements and resistant to drought so it is much planted in the S. Central States. It is increased by seeds planted in autumn or stratified over winter, and by root cuttings. Catalogs occasionally list this tree under the name of Varnish-tree, which properly applies to *Rhus verniciflua.*

GOLDENROD. Common name for the genus Solidago, a member of the Composite Family consisting of many species of perennial herbs with clustered yellow, rarely white, flowers which brighten the countryside in many parts of N. America. In a popular canvass conducted by a magazine, the goldenrod was approved as the National flower of the U. S. but it has not been officially recognized as such. However, three species are official State flowers, namely *S. canadensis* for Alabama, *S. patula* for Kentucky, and *S. serotina* (the November Goldenrod) for Nebraska. The goldenrods are used extensively in combination with the fall asters or Michaelmas daisies in the border in English gardens, and the finer species should be more widely used in this country. A collection of goldenrod and asters in the wild garden is easily made, as both plants are moved very readily and increase rapidly. They become weedy in rich soil, however, and should therefore be handled with care in cultivation. They bloom the second year from spring-sown seed. Old clumps should be divided in the spring. Since golden-rod, like aster, is host for an orange rust of pine needles during part of its life, plants should be removed from the vicinity of valuable stands of pine-trees. See PINE; RUSTS.

S. altissima, which grows from 3 to 6 ft. high, is one of the handsomest species with large pyramidal panicles of small golden flowers; *S. speciosa,* also tall, has nearly smooth leaves and bright yellow flowers in a compound panicle; *S. nemoralis,* to 2 ft., has grayish soft-hairy leaves and long-lasting flowers in a one-sided panicle; *S. odora* (Sweet Goldenrod) 1½ to 4 ft. high, has anise-scented leaves and flowers in panicles lasting many weeks; *S. caesia* (Wreath Goldenrod) growing about 2 ft. tall in semi-shade, has smooth foliage, sometimes with a bloom, and flowers in the axils of the leaves or in terminal clusters; *S. canadensis,* usually 3 or 4 ft. tall, is one of the commonest species, with large pyramidal panicles of very small flowers; *S. bicolor* (Silverrod), smaller, has white flowers crowded on a slender spike.

GOLDEN - SAXIFRAGE. C o m m o n name for Chrysosplenium, a genus of semi-aquatic herbs with little greenish flowers, suitable for a ground-cover in a bog garden.

GOLDEN-SEAL. Common name for *Hydrastis canadensis,* also known as Orange-root, a member of the Buttercup Family growing nearly 1 ft. tall with a thick yellow rootstock, broad basal leaves, and inconspicuous greenish-white flowers, followed by beautiful raspberry-like fruits. When commercial plantings of Golden-seal are made for its medicinal roots, the beds are covered with laths to give the proper shade. Occasionally grown in gardens for the beauty of its leaves and fruits, it should be planted in rich moist soil in a partially shaded position and liberally mulched with humus. It is increased by division or by seed.

GOLDEN-SHOWER. A common name for the greenhouse tree, *Cassia fistula,* a species of Senna (which see), with large leaves and pale yellow pea-like flowers in loose clusters.

GOLDEN SPIDER-LILY. Common name for *Lycoris aurea,* a half-hardy oriental bulbous plant whose red or yellow flowers appear at the top of a stout scape after the leaves have disappeared.

GOLDEN-STAR. Common name for *Chrysogonum virginianum,* a low-growing, hairy perennial Composite. Native in dry soil from Pa. to the Gulf States.

GOLDEN-STARS. Common name for *Bloomeria crocea,* a half-hardy member of the Lily Family, growing 1 ft. or more tall from a fibrous corm, and bearing grass-like leaves and umbels of bright orange flowers with dark stripes. They may be grown in the open in mild climates, but in the N. should be planted early in the fall in light sandy soil in a sheltered position and heavily mulched with leaves, or, better still, grown in a coldframe. They force easily and are most successfully raised in pots in a cool greenhouse.

GOLDEN THISTLE. A common name for *Scolymus hispanicus,* also called Spanish-oyster-plant. It is a thistle-like biennial with toothed leaves and a long tap-root grown and used like the true oyster-plant or salsify (which see), but somewhat milder in flavor.

GOLDENTOP. Common name for *Lamarckia aurea,* an annual, tufted, ornamental grass, native of California. Growing to 1 ft. tall with soft glabrous leaves 6 in. long and ¼ in. wide, it bears awned spikelets, purplish or golden-yellow in color, in clusters in one-sided glossy panicles 4 in. long. See ORNAMENTAL GRASSES.

GOLDEN-TUFT. One of the common names for *Alyssum saxatile,* a bright yellow spring-flowering plant perennial much used in rock gardens.

GOLDEN-WAVE. A common name for *Coreopsis drummondi,* an annual with 2 in. heads of yellow and brown-purple flowers.

GOLDEN-YARROW. Common name for *Eriophyllum confertiflorum,* a 2 ft. perennial with yellow flowers in heads.

GOLDEN-YELLOW HAWKWEED. Catalog name for *Tolpis barbata,* a 12 in. annual with yellow flowers, occasionally grown for ornament.

GOLDFIELDS. Common name for Baeria, a genus of Calif. herbs with yellow flower-heads.

GOLD-FLOWER. Common name for *Hypericum moserianum,* an ornamental shrub to 2 ft. with loose clusters of yellow flowers.

GOLDIES FERN. Common name for *Dryopteris goldiegna,* a splendid American

GLOBE-AMARANTH

Gomphrena globosa an attractive rose-purple annual, is also useful as an everlasting.

wood fern, the tallest of all, liking moist shaded situations in rich woods soil.

GOLDILOCKS. Common name for *Linosyris vulgaris,* an Old World, 2 ft. perennial aster with small heads of yellow flowers in clusters. A good late summer flowering plant that thrives in any soil.

GOLD-MOSS. Common name for *Sedum acre,* a creeping evergreen stonecrop bearing abundant little yellow flowers. The small leaves are succulent.

GOLDTHREAD. Common name for the genus Coptis, small perennial herbs of the Crowfoot Family, with slender yellow root-fibers and white or yellow flowers on long stalks. Two species are planted somewhat in shady, damp places in peaty soil— *C. groenlandica* and *C. trifolia.*

GOMPHRENA (gom-free'-nah). A genus of herbs with white, red or violet heads which somewhat resemble those of clover, useful both for bedding and for cut flowers as well as for drying as everlastings (which see). Propagation is by seed which should be started indoors as it does

not germinate well in the open ground. Remove the cottony coating before sowing.

G. globosa (Globe amaranth), the best known species, is an annual, erect and branching, 18 in. tall. Flowers for drying should not be picked until well matured, toward the end of summer. Protect them while drying from rats which are fond of the seeds.

GOOBER. Colloquial name in the S. for Peanut, which see.

GOOD-KING-HENRY. Common name for *Chenopodium bonus-henricus;* a perennial herb also called Mercury and Markery. Its young stems are used in early spring like asparagus and later its leaves are used like spinach.

GOODYERA (good'-ye-rah). Former name of orchids now classified as in two other genera—Epipactis and Haemaria. They are dwarf terrestrial types grown with difficulty in shade and more for their variegated leaves than their flower spikes. The best known species is *Epipactis pubescens,* or Rattlesnake-plantain, native from Newfoundland to Mich. and Fla.

See also ORCHID.

GOOSEBERRY. Various species of thorny bushes closely related to the currants and generally included with them in the genus Ribes; some botanists, however, separate them into the genus Grossularia. Some of the species (namely two), have produced improved varieties whose fruit is used in America while immature for making jam, jelly and pie and in Europe when ripe as a dessert. American varieties (developed from *Ribes hirtellum*) are mostly inferior in size and quality to European kinds (developed from *R. grossularia*) some of which are almost as large as hen's eggs. In America these so-called English Gooseberries fail to produce well partly because of our hotter, drier summers and partly because of their greater susceptibility to mildew, but mainly in many cases because of neglect! Given proper care they are fairly successful.

The bushes are exceedingly hardy and can be grown in very cold climates; in warm ones they must be sheltered from the heat. Rich, heavy, but well-drained soils suit them best. They should stand 6 ft. apart to favor cross cultivation and facilitate fruit picking. Each year several to many shoots grow from the base of the bush; if allowed to remain they reduce the quantity and lower the quality of the berries; therefore, all but the two sturdiest should be removed not later than when the fruit is harvested. At this time also the stems that have borne three times should be cut out because thereafter they decline in productiveness.

For general cultural directions, see CURRANT, where also are found control measures to use against anthracnose, leaf spot and powdery mildew, and also the imported currant worm. The gooseberry fruit worm causes infected berries to color prematurely, then either dry up or decay. Such fruit should be gathered promptly and destroyed.

The term "Gooseberry" with qualifying words is applied to several plants not related to the real gooseberry as follows: Barbados-gooseberry, *Pereskia aclueata;* Cape-gooseberry, *Physalis peruviana* and *P. pruinosa;* Ceylon-gooseberry, *Davyalis hebecarpa;* Hill-gooseberry, *Rhodomyrtus tomentosa;* Otaheite-gooseberry, *Phyllanthus acidus;* Southern-gooseberry, *Vaccinium melanocarpum.*

GOOSEBERRY-TREE. A common name for *Phyllanthus acidus,* a tropical tree grown in the W. Indies for its tart fruit, used for pickles and preserves. It has been naturalized in S. Fla.

GOOSEFOOT. The name for various species of Chenopodium, a genus of glandular, shrubby herbs, with insignificant flowers but with medicinal and culinary uses.

GOOSEFOOT FAMILY. Common name of the Chenopodiaceae (which see), which includes beets, spinach, some ornamental plants for gardens and many troublesome weeds.

GOPHER. Name given to several species of small, burrowing, pouched rodents of the country W. of the Mississippi which, collectively, have been called the "western gardener's public enemy No. 1." Although, like the earthworm, this animal performs a service by stirring and mixing the soil and making it arable, it is better known and hated because of the damage it does to agricultural crops of all kinds, including grains, orchard and forest trees, vegetables, flower bulbs in gardens, etc. Also its shallow burrows and the mounds of earth surrounding the tunnel openings, injure and disfigure fields, pastures and lawns, are a danger to live stock, and sometimes weaken the banks of irrigation ditches. Gardeners therefore go to considerable trouble to keep them out of their gardens or to combat them by various means. Their presence is revealed by the loose mounds of fresh soil pushed out of their runs and no time should be lost in fighting them.

Among the methods employed are: (1) traps, usually placed at the tunnel entrances and fastened there so they will not be dragged far into the burrows; (2) gopher-guns which are set at the entrances to shoot off when sprung a blank cartridge which kills by concussion; (3) smoke bombs, to be set inside the entrances which are then plugged with soil; (4) gas led through a hose from an automobile exhaust into the burrow; (5) flooding the burrow with a garden hose and watching for the emergence of the animal which is killed with a shovel, stick or other weapon. The last mentioned method is said to be most successful if practiced early in the morning and in the evening, the hunter watching the burrow openings from ten or fifteen feet away. The gopher snake, a valuable help in controlling this pest, should not be killed or harmed but on the contrary encouraged to live in western gardens.

In the N.W. the term gopher is applied to a striped ground squirrel, and in the Gulf States to a burrowing turtle, neither of which are of particular importance to gardeners.

GORDONIA (gor-doh'-ni-ah). A genus of evergreen or deciduous trees or shrubs of the Tea Family, having glossy decorative foliage and flowers resembling camellias. They should be planted in moist acid soil and can be propagated by greenwood cuttings under glass, or by seeds or layering. The most attractive species is *G. alatamaha* (or mistakenly *altamaha*) a tree to 20 ft., but usually grown as a shrub. It was discovered in the woods of Ga. in the 18th century by John Bartram of Philadelphia, who named it *Franklinia alatamaha* in honor of his friend, Benjamin Franklin. It was again seen in the same region in 1790 by Bartram's son, William, but it has never since been seen growing wild in its natural habitat and it is known as "The lost Franklinia." All the plants now existing (and renamed Gordonia) are supposed to have been propagated from the original shrub now dead, brought back by John Bartram to his Gardens. It has bright green leaves to 6 in. long that turn red in the fall, and large cup-shaped creamy-white flowers with profuse yellow stamens borne close against the stems in the autumn. It is hardy as far N. as Mass. if given a sheltered position. *G. lasianthus* (Loblolly-bay), an evergreen tree to 60 ft. not hardy N., has glossy dark green leaves and long-stemmed white flowers 2½ in. across.

GORDONIAS SHOULD BE GROWN MORE
The shrub is hardy and handsome, but wants an acid soil. The glossy leaves turn red in fall. The abundant short-stemmed white gardenia-like flowers with yellow centers are borne all summer until frost.

GORMANIA (gor-may'-ni-ah). A genus or low perennial plants, native in W. N. America, belonging to the Orpine Family. Most botanists place them in the genus Sedum. The best known is *G. oregana*, a small creeping evergreen with fleshy shining green leaves, often tinged red, and clusters of yellow flowers. It makes a good mat in partial shade and fairly moist soil.

GORSE. A common name for Ulex (which see), a genus of spiny, semi-hardy shrubs, also called Furze and Whin.

GOSSYPIUM (go-sip'-i-um). A genus of tropical woody herbs, several species of which are grown as an annual field crop to furnish commercial Cotton (which see), and sometimes in N. greenhouses for interest or educational purposes. The purplish or yellow flowers are followed by fruits called "bolls," within which the seeds are covered with a lint.

GOURD. A name formerly applied to the plants and fruits of any species of the Gourd Family (Cucurbitaceae), including pumpkin, squash, cucumber and melon. It is now restricted (in N. America) to the ornamental, inedible-fruited species of cucurbits, of which the following are most popular: the yellow-flowered varieties of *Cucurbita pepo,* var. *ovifera;* the white-flowered ones of *Lagenaria leucantha,* to which also belong the dishcloth, maté (or utensil gourd of Paraguay), the calabash and some of the serpent or snake gourds (other varieties of serpent gourds are forms of *Trichosanthes anguina*); wax or white gourds, *Benincasa hispida;* gooseberry gourds, *Cucumis anguria;* hedgehog gourds, *C. dipsaceus;* cranberry gourds, *Abobra tenuifolia;* and ivy gourds, *Coccinia cordifolia.* The true calabash is not a gourd, but the fruit of a tropical tree (*Crescentia cujete*) of the Bignonia Family.

All these gourds are tender annuals, either trailing or climbing by means of tendrils. They thrive in the full sun, in well drained, rich soil. Usually the seed is sown where the plants are to remain, but sometimes, to save time, it is started on inverted sods or in small flower pots, the plants being set outdoors after danger of frost has passed. The plants are rapid-growing and, having good foliage, are often planted for summer screens to be trained on trellises or strings against porches facing south. Powdery mildew frequently appears as a white coating on the leaves. To control it, dust with fine sulphur. For other diseases and insect and control measures see CUCURBITA. The ripe fruits of many small varieties are of odd shapes and markings so are often used as curiosities or ornaments. A growing practice is to clean and varnish or shellac them for use in table centerpiece arrangements. Some of the larger ones are used for dippers, wren houses, wash-rags and other purposes. See CUCURBITA; LAGENARIA; SERPENT GOURD.

GOURD SOCIETY, NEW ENGLAND. The headquarters of this group of people interested in the growing and utilization of gourds, especially for ornaments and decorative purposes, is in Mass. and can be reached through the Horticultural Society of that State, at Horticultural Hall, Boston.

GOUTWEED. A common name for *Aegopodium podagraria,* a coarse herbaceous perennial with yellow flowers in umbels.

GOVERNMENT AGENCIES—HOW THEY HELP HOME GARDENERS.

FEDERAL AGENCIES. The U. S. Department of Agriculture, Washington, D. C., carries on many activities of interest to the home gardener. Much research work is done by experts in its various bureaus on soils, fertilizers, insecticides, fungicides, grasses, injurious insects, plant diseases, erosion control and soil conservation, etc. It also has charge of the recently authorized National Arboretum. See ARBORETUM.

The U. S. Forest Service, a branch of the Department of Agriculture, issues for general distribution many interesting bulletins, particularly on the care, use and protection of trees. It also has sets of lantern slides and films which are available for the use of schools, organizations, etc.

Plant-quarantine regulations designed to prevent the importation from foreign countries and the spread within this country of injurious insects and diseases, are promulgated by the Secretary of Agriculture and administered by the Bureau of Entomology and Plant Quarantine, often in cooperation with the departments of agriculture, the experiment stations or special quarantine officials of the different states. The Office of Plant Introduction of the Department sends specialists to all parts of the world in search of new plant material which may be of economic importance or ornamental value to the farms and gardens of the United States. It also conducts trials of such material in different parts of the country.

Popular bulletins on garden topics published by the Department may be secured from the Superintendent of Documents, Government Printing Office, Washington, D. C., either free or at a slight cost. A list of the available bulletins may be obtained there without charge.

Lantern slides, moving picture films, and film scripts on garden topics are also distributed by the Department through its Information Service and other agencies.

The U. S. Department of Commerce administers the Plant Patent Act which encourages and protects the originator of a new plant with a view to insuring him deserved financial return from his ingenuity and effort. See PATENT, PLANT.

The U. S. Botanic Garden in Washington, for many years administered by the Congressional Committee that has charge of the Congressional Library, contains much interesting plant material but has never been developed to function as a real botanic garden should. The question of how it can be made of more practical value is being given consideration.

The National Park Service now has charge of the parks in the District of

SOME GROTESQUE GOURDS

Besides the squashes, melons, pumpkins and other edible sorts, the Gourd Family includes a host of curious types in many sizes, shapes and colors. Grow a collection—for table decorations, dippers, washcloths, pipe bowls and other odd uses.

Columbia as well as the National Parks in various parts of the country. Interesting publications and motion pictures on the parks and the flora and fauna in them, are available for distribution.

The U. S. Department of the Interior, through its Bureau of Education, cooperates with the State Department of Education in providing vocational education work in agriculture in high schools. Gardening or horticulture is a phase of the instruction given.

STATE AGENCIES. The state departments of agriculture, located at the several state capitals, administer various regulatory and "police" measures such as state and local plant quarantines, the suppression of injurious insects and plant diseases, inspection and licensing of nurseries, analyzing of fertilizers and spray materials, licensing of arborists or tree experts, etc., all of which is of interest to gardeners. In some states, these departments also carry on educational work, including the publication of bulletins and lectures on gardening or horticultural topics.

State departments of education sometimes sponsor extension courses in gardening in connection with horticultural societies, schools and colleges. See EXTENSION COURSES.

The agricultural experiment stations of the several states conduct research work, much of which is of interest and value to gardeners and also publish bulletins on horticultural topics. See EXPERIMENT STATIONS.

The state extension service is a department of many state colleges or universities supported jointly by state and federal funds. Its purpose is to carry information on agricultural and home economics subjects to the people in their homes. This it does by means of trained agents, both men and women, who conduct demonstrations, give lectures, furnish publications, lantern slides, films, etc. Many counties throughout the United States have an organization known as a Farm Bureau which is a part of the state extension service and directs the activities of the county agents. This is perhaps the greatest system of practical public education in agriculture (including gardening) and home economics in the world. Every person engaged or interested in such matters should write to the Extension Director at his or her state college or university for full information about this service, including the address of the nearest Farm Bureau office.

Following are the addresses of the Extension Service headquarters in each state and territory:

Alabama: Alabama Polytechnic Institute, Auburn.

Arizona: University of Arizona, Tucson.

Arkansas: University of Arkansas, Fayetteville.

California: University of California, Berkeley.

Colorado: State Agricultural College, Fort Collins.

Connecticut: Connecticut State College, Storrs.

Delaware: University of Delaware, Newark.

Florida: Agricultural Experiment Station, Gainesville.

Georgia: State College of Agriculture, Athens.

Idaho: University of Idaho, Moscow.

Illinois: University of Illinois, Urbana.

Indiana: Purdue University, Lafayette.

Iowa: Iowa State College, Ames.

Kansas: State College of Agriculture, Manhattan.

Kentucky: University of Kentucky, Lexington.

Louisiana: Louisiana State University, Baton Rouge.

Maine: University of Maine, Orono.

Maryland: University of Maryland, College Park.

Massachusetts: Massachusetts State College, Amherst.

Michigan: State College of Agriculture, East Lansing.

Minnesota: University of Minnesota, St. Paul.

Mississippi: State College, State College.

Missouri: University of Missouri, Columbia.

Montana: State College of Agriculture, Bozeman.

Nebraska: University of Nebraska, Lincoln.

Nevada: University of Nevada, Reno.

New Hampshire: University of New Hampshire, Durham.

New Jersey: State College of Agriculture, New Brunswick.

New Mexico: College of Agriculture, State College.

New York: State College of Agriculture, Ithaca.

North Carolina: College Station, Raleigh.

North Dakota: State Agricultural College, Fargo.

Ohio: State University, Columbus.

Oklahoma: Agricultural and Mechanical College, Stillwater.

Oregon: State Agricultural College, Corvallis.

Pennsylvania: State College, State College.

Rhode Island: State College, Kingston.

South Carolina: Clemson Agricultural College, Clemson Station.

South Dakota: State College of Agriculture, Brookings.

Tennessee: University of Tennessee, Knoxville.

Texas: Agricultural and Mechanical College, College Station.

Utah: State Agricultural College, Logan.

Vermont: University of Vermont, Burlington.

Virginia: Virginia Polytechnic Institute, Blacksburg.

Washington: State College, Pullman.

West Virginia: West Virginia University, Morgantown.

Wisconsin: University of Wisconsin, Madison.

Wyoming: University of Wyoming, Laramie.

Alaska: Agricultural College, College.

Hawaii: University of Hawaii, Honolulu.

Puerto Rico: University of Puerto Rico, Puerto Rico.

There is, in many states, a State Park or Conservation System with headquarters at the capital whose officials are concerned with such subjects as trees, shrubs and flowers, especially the native flora. There is usually someone on the staff well versed in horticultural and gardening subjects.

County and municipal park systems are also frequently interested in gardening subjects. Collections of trees, shrubs, and flowers, rock gardens, water gardens, etc., may be found in many park systems whose superintendents are usually glad to assist home gardeners in solving their problems.

Municipal departments of education in some parts of the country are active in interesting young people in gardening through school and home garden projects as well as in class room work. See CHILDREN'S GARDENS; EDUCATION IN GARDENING.

GOVERNORS-PLUM. A common name for *Flacourtia indica,* an Asiatic tree, the pulp of whose maroon-colored fruit is made into jams. Has been introduced into Calif.

GRADES. Plants sold by catalog are graded according to size and quality, as Juniperus virginiana 2-4 ft. B & B; Spruce 4-5 ft., Specimen, 4 times transplanted; Apple 2 year, No. 1; Gladiolus No. 3, etc. These grades came into use naturally for the convenience of grower and customer; but variations in interpretations and misunderstandings resulted, especially in regard to the dimensions and quality of valuable evergreens. To clear up confusion, the Association of American Nurserymen compiled, adopted and recommended to the trade a list of standard grades that is now almost universally followed by the trade. It is now understood between what points the dimensions of a tree shall be measured, what constitutes a transplanting, how a peony root shall be divided, etc.

See also STANDARDS.

GRAFTING. Any process whereby a part (called the *scion*) taken from one plant, is made to unite with and grow upon another plant or part of a plant (called the *stock*). The scion may be a single bud (see BUDDING), a small twig bearing a few to several buds, a piece of stem (as of a

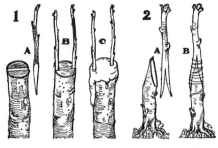

TWO SIMPLE GRAFTING METHODS
1—Cleft grafting, most popular for limbs of trees. A, stock split and scion cut wedge-shaped to fit; B, 2 scions in place; C, entire graft waxed. 2—Saddle graft, used for very small subjects. A, stock and scion prepared. B, parts fitted and tied ready for waxing.

cactus), a terminal shoot (as of an evergreen), or a fragment of root of a desirable variety. Grafting is a method of propagation (which see) in which the primary purpose is either (1) to increase the chances of the scion's making successful growth by giving it a new foundation in the form of a more vigorous root system than it had before, or (2) to change over the form, character, fruit-bearing quality, etc., of the stock plant or tree by substituting some other variety for its original top. The operation may also create a tree or plant bearing two distinct varieties of flower or fruit, or two kinds (staminate and pistillate) flowers, in which case the chances of successful pollination of the latter are increased. Grafting provides a way to work up a stock of plants that cannot successfully be increased by other asexual methods, such as division, layering, the rooting of cuttings, etc.

To be successful, grafting *must* insure and maintain intimate contact between the *cambium* tissues of scion and stock, that is the layer of growing cells that is just under the bark and outside the wood. Most grafting is done with dormant scions, which means in winter or early spring, unless the scions can be kept dormant in cold storage until the stock plants are in best condition to receive them. This is illustrated in budding, which is usually done in midsummer. Scions so kept for future use should be carefully labeled and kept moist and cool so they will neither shrivel nor start into growth.

After the scion and stock have been cut and adjusted (by any of the methods described below), they are tied in place (if necessary) after which the whole area of wounded surfaces is covered with grafting wax (which see) or wound with grafting tape to prevent the drying of the parts and to exclude moisture, and disease organisms. In recent years melted paraffin has been used in place of wax with marked success. Easy to apply, it is often spread over the entire scion as well as the graft, thereby checking evaporation of valuable moisture.

As the two parts of a graft grow together they are said to form a *union.*

Many kinds of grafting are practiced by expert plantsmen for special purposes or with specific plants, but those best suited to the average gardener's needs are *whip, cleft, side,* and *bridge grafting.*

WHIP OR TONGUE GRAFTING. In this method both scion and stock (of about the same diameter) are cut on a long slant; a slit is made in the middle of each cut surface, and the two are fitted together so that the tongue of one fits into the slot of the

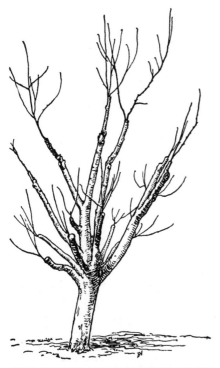

WRONG WAY TO TOP-WORK TREES
It is all right to "work over" an old tree to an improved variety, but it should be done over 3 years or more. When too many branches are treated in one year, some scions will be "drowned out," others grow rampantly, others fail to "take." Many "water sprouts" will develop and some branches or even the whole tree will die.

other. They are then bound firmly with grafting tape and, if to be exposed to the air, covered with grafting wax.

CLEFT GRAFTING. This is the simplest method, and the one generally used in working over old trees—either to make a worthless seedling or other specimen produce good fruit, or to make it possible to grow more than one variety on a tree.

Stock branches ½ in. to 2 in. in diameter are sawed squarely across with a sharp, fine-toothed saw, where the bark is smooth. These stumps are then split with a chisel and mallet to a depth of about 1½ in. and the slit is pried apart with a special grafting iron or wedge of hardwood until it will admit two scions (one at each side). These are previously cut to a slender wedge shape at the bottom; they are usually 4 to 6 in. long and bear 3 or 4 buds. Each scion is inserted in the split stock and adjusted so that its lowest bud is just above the top of the stock and on the outside. Also the scion is slanted slightly outward so that its cambium layer is certain to be in contact with that of the stock at at least one point.

Next the wedge or iron is gently withdrawn without displacing the scions. As a rule the pressure of the wood is enough to keep them in place, but the graft can be tied with cord or tape if necessary. The entire top of the stock to below the base of the split is then covered with grafting wax. If both scions grow, the weaker is cut away the next year.

The above method is the one usually used in "top-working," that is, changing over a mature tree to another, better, variety. A tree should have only 20 to 30% of its top so grafted in any one year. If more is removed in preparing the stocks, the scions will probably not "take" and the tree may die.

SIDE GRAFTING. In this method a cut is made downward into the stock just beneath the bark, and the scion (its base cut wedge-shaped) is thrust beneath the bark, tied there and waxed. The stock above the graft may or may not be cut off. This method is especially useful for developing branches at bare spaces along trunks and main limbs.

BRIDGE OR REPAIR GRAFTING. This method is used to establish new sap connections across large wounds such as those made in winter when mice gnaw the bark of trees. Water sprouts, being long and lusty, make the best scions for this work. The edges of the wound are trimmed back to healthy wood at top and bottom where slots are cut at 4 or 5 points around the trunk. The scions are cut long enough to fit in to corresponding slots above and below so as to have a slight bow outward and each scion is cut slanting at each end so that the smooth part will fit against the trunk to which it is tacked firmly. All cut and injured surfaces are then covered with grafting wax or wound with waxed cloth. Trees so treated may be saved, even though completely girdled as, in time, the scions will not only form unions at top and bottom, but will also grow together to form a new exterior trunk.

GRAFTING WAX. A more or less pliable protective material used to cover cut surfaces on woody plants, especially those made in grafting. It is usually made of resin, beeswax and beef tallow and can be bought or prepared at home. For a soft wax the amount of tallow is slightly increased; for a tough wax, which has to be warmed for use, the amount of beeswax.

All resin waxes are started by melting 3 lbs. of resin cut into small lumps over gentle heat, and adding 3 lbs. beeswax and 2 lbs. tallow. When all the ingredients are melted and stirred to a uniform consistency, the mass is poured into a container of cold water. Here it is flattened so it will cool evenly. When cool enough to handle the mass is kneaded and pulled with greased hands until like molasses taffy; it is then formed into balls or sticks for use or storage. As the task is a messy one small quantities are better bought at garden supply stores.

Grafting tape and string are made by soaking cotton strips or wicking in the wax while it is hot. In budding (which see), raffia and rubber strips are sometimes used instead of waxed tape or string. Raffia is tied firmly and usually has to be cut when the bud has "taken." The rubber strip has its ends tucked in to prevent its loosening; it is often preferred to non-elastic materials because it will "give" with the tree's growth and never "strangle" the buds.

GRANADILLA (gran-ah-dil'-ah). Common name for the edible fruit of several passion-flowers. See PASSIFLORA.

GRANITE CHIPS. Small rock fragments, usually about ½ in. on the average, are used on the surface of rock and espe-cially alpine gardens, and sometimes added to the soil mixture in such places. The object is to simulate the natural conditions under which rock and alpine plants thrive. The chips prevent the washing of the surface soil, permit surface water to quickly percolate into the soil and down to the plant roots and, where incorporated in the soil, promote good drainage. Because plants used in the kinds of gardens mentioned in general prefer acid to alkaline soil conditions, granite chips are superior to those of limestone or any type of rock that would contribute to an alkaline soil condition.

GRAPE. (See illustration, Plate 24.) A pulpy, edible berry borne in clusters on vines of the genus Vitis, which see. Its cultivated varieties belong to three important groups. The Old-World species (*V. vinifera*) with its 1,500 varieties has been cultivated in mild parts of the E. Hemisphere from prehistoric times, but in N. America it consistently failed until means were discovered (by grafting it upon American species as stocks) to prevent its destruction by the grape root louse or Phylloxera, which see. Except when grafted on such resistant stocks it still fails wherever this pest is established. It is the leading species on the Pacific Coast, especially in Calif., where 75 per cent of the nation's grape crop is produced.

NATIVE GRAPES. The most important American species, the Fox Grape (*V. labrusca*), is native from Mass. to the Allegheny Mountains and southward to Ga. Its first important variety (Catawba) was disseminated in 1823 and its second (Concord) in 1854, since when more than a thousand varieties have been introduced; yet these two are still leading commercial varieties, while the former is also a popular home garden (dessert) sort.

From the Potomac River southward the native Muscadine grape (*V. rotundifolia*) has been cultivated in gardens since colonial days. It is not grown commercially (except occasionally for a local market) because it "shatters" or drops off its clusters when ripe.

As a class grapes are ideal for the home garden. Their vines may be trained on porches, pergolas, arbors and summer-houses, where they are as attractive and useful as any other ornamental vine, not to mention their regular production of red, white, or blue fruit. By selecting varieties that ripen successively, one can make the fruiting season cover a full two months; and with simple home-storage facilities the fresh grape season may be extended to 6 months or even longer. When once planted the vines may be allowed to take care of themselves, but they will not produce as well as when trained by the easily understood and applied principles discussed be-

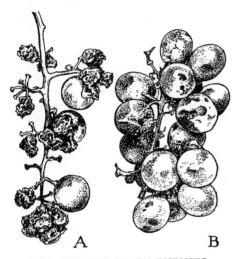

TWO SERIOUS GRAPE ENEMIES
(A) Black rot may reduce a whole bunch to a cluster of mummies. (B) Two broods of worms of the berry moth attack the young fruits and call for early spring spraying.

low. So cared for they can be kept productive 50 years or longer.

SOIL AND PLANTING. Though sandy or gravelly loams are preferred for commercial grape growing, any fairly deep, well-drained, moderately fertile soil will produce abundant crops. Soils excessively rich in nitrogenous matter are undesirable because they tend to produce a rank growth of stems and foliage, but little fruit. Distances to allow between vines (when to be trained on trellises) vary with the variety: small growing kinds (Delaware, Jessica) may stand 6 or 8 ft. apart; stronger kinds (Catawba, Concord) need 8 or 10 ft.; still stronger ones (Salem, Agawam) 10 or 12 ft., and the Muscadine varieties 12 or 15 or even 20 ft. On porches, buildings and arbors the vines may be allowed more space as they will presumably be allowed to ramble at will. Distances between rows—which rows are usuallly 8 to 10 ft. should extend N. and S.

In commercial vineyards the universal rule is to plow or disk the ground as close

as possible to the vines in early spring, practise clean cultivation until midsummer, then sow a cover-crop (which see). In home gardens where this plan is rarely feasible, the ground may be hoed or a mulch may be kept around the vines, or they may even be kept in sod, though this last is least desirable.

Fertilizers are best applied to the cover crop which is thus stimulated and, when turned under, returns the plant food to the soil to be taken up by the vines. On poor soil an application of 1 lb. nitrate of soda per vine scattered over as much ground as it is likely to cover when growth starts, will help develop shoots. An additional application of equal parts potash and superphosphate may also be given in such cases to help ripen the growth.

Commercial grape growers generally prefer for planting "first class" one-year vines because they are vigorous. Two year vines are also popular but generally cost more. It probably makes little difference which is chosen provided that the planting is done correctly and followed by good after-care. Never should vines older than two years be planted because their root systems are usually seriously reduced in digging.

BUILDING THE TRUNK. After planting, successful grape growers cut off all puny shoots and reduce the strongest one to only two or three joints, each carrying a plump bud. In vineyard practice all three buds are allowed to develop shoots, but two of these are cut off before the following spring. Then the strongest is cut back to two or three buds and the process repeated. The idea here is to get a strong trunk or main stem with which to start the third spring.

A better practice is to shorten the weaker shoots to only one joint and one leaf as soon as the lower joints of the strongest have become woody—usually after 6 or 8 weeks of growth. This concentrates the plant food in the remaining shoot, which becomes strong enough to serve as the main trunk of the vine and, the following year, perhaps to produce some fruit-bearing shoots. This method starts fruit production a year sooner than the usual vineyard treatment. The only reason for allowing the extra shoots to develop at all is to provide against loss of the main shoot by the possible accident of having it broken off.

The main shoot should be tied vertically, but loosely, to a stout bean pole or other

Upper left: The grace of the grape is as great as any flowering vine and the harvest of fruit is added bounty. Upper right: The Concord—the standby for the table or for preserving. Center: Grapes bagged to preserve them from the ravages of insects and birds. Lower left: The translucent amber globes of the hardy light red grape, Banner. Lower right: A grape arbor—a thing of beauty and an admirable support for the vine.

upright support 6 or 8 ft. long. If it grows more than 3 ft. during the first season it will be strong enough to bear some fruit the following year, but it should be cut back 30 to 50 per cent before the spring of that year opens. Vines considerably less than 30 in. long should be cut back to only three joints and made to start over again and develop stronger stems under the treatment already described.

No trellis, arbor or other permanent support need be given until the spring of the second year. Then, if the vine is in open ground, it may be merely a stout stake; or, if the plant is by a porch, veranda or arbor a heavy wire (No. 9 or 8), preferably of copper, will serve. This should be securely fastened at the ground and at the top so the main stem may go straight up and become a trunk from which the branches will be developed during the second year.

BASIC PRUNING PRINCIPLES. As in all other pruning for the production of flowers or fruit, it is essential to understand how and where the plant bears its blossoms; for upon these depend the fruit. Each year the grape-vine develops, from buds formed the previous year, long green shoots which bear leaves and tendrils. Examination of several shoots will show that a tendril occurs opposite a leaf at nearly every node (joint) and that the tendrils show many variations—including single and branched strands, some of which bear a few grapes while others have lost the tendril habit and become clusters of fruit.

All of these green parts—leaves, tendrils and clusters—are borne on shoots that start to grow in spring. Most of them develop from buds formed the previous year in the angles of the leaf stems. After the leaves fall in the autumn these buds may be easily seen at each joint on the ripe shoot (now called a "cane"), where they and the joints serve as guides at pruning time. If their number is reduced, the shoots that develop from the remainder are strengthened and made more prolific of higher quality fruit than unpruned, untrained vines can ever bear. Furthermore, the vines may be kept within desired bounds and trained in any desired direction.

Grape-vines should never be pruned during the summer; exhaustive experiments have proved this old practice to be not merely a mistake but often positively harmful to the vines. The only time when grape-vines should be pruned is during winter while they are dormant. At that time, with the above principles of growth in mind, the pruning is based on the following considerations: 1. Puny shoots bear no fruits; therefore, cut them off. 2. "Bull" canes—over-grown, burly, very long ones—also are generally sterile; therefore, cut them out at their starting points. 3. Reduce, in both number and length, those canes that are about the thickness of a lead pencil; they are the ones whose green shoots, produced the following summer, will bear fruit.

Commercial grape growers generally limit the number of canes to 2, 4 or sometimes 6, each pair trained horizontally at approximate right-angles to the main trunk, and each allowed to bear only 6 to 10 buds, depending upon the strength of the vine. They reckon upon an average of two clusters of grapes to each bud and an average of a quarter-pound to the cluster, though many clusters will weigh double that.

RECLAIMING OLD VINES. To prune a vine long neglected and that bears little or no fruit because it is choked with dead and worthless branches, proceed as follows: First cut out all dead wood and puny shoots at their starting points. Second, save the main trunk and arms but cut out all long, slender branches which have only a few young canes near and at their ends. Third, reduce the number of medium-sized canes and shorten them at least 25 per cent. The whole process consists in reëstablishing the bearing area nearer to the roots and limiting it so as to enhance both the quality and the quantity of fruit.

When such reclamation removes considerable quantities of wood the vine will probably produce many new shoots from adventitious buds (those in unexpected places). None of these are likely to bear fruit, but some of them may be saved at pruning time the following year to replace older stems that will be cut out then or later. The best positions for such shoots to appear are at and near the ground, for in such cases they may replace the old trunks. Such new canes may be treated exactly as if they were young vines. The shoots that develop on them will probably not bear any fruit because of over-stimulation by the roots; their function is to make a new top. At pruning time the following winter, the best of these can be chosen to become new arms, whose buds will produce fruit-bearing shoots. From this time forward branches on the old trunk may be reduced more or less each year and finally the old trunk itself until little or none of the old wood remains above ground.

Training (as distinguished from pruning) consists in placing the canes and shoots so as to take best advantage of sunlight and air. It allows for wide divergence of preference. However, on arbors and other high supports, the best plan is to train the main trunk direct to the top and to cut back the canes on it each year to mere "spurs" of only one to three buds —two being preferred.

KNIFFIN VS. MUNSON METHODS. The chief advantages of this method are: first, that fruit will be borne on the shoots developed from these spur buds from near the ground to the top of the vine; and, second, that the work needed for pruning, spraying and gathering the fruit will be easier and less than when the vines are allowed to clamber without restraint to the top of the arbor; moreover, this would then become unsightly, crowded with stems above, but bare below.

Trellises of 2 No. 9 hard galvanized wires strung one above the other, are most popular in commercial American vineyards. Stout posts of durable wood (locust, chestnut, cedar), 7 or 8 ft. long, are placed with their butt ends below the local frost line and no farther apart than will allow three vines to be planted and trained between them.

In what is called the 4-cane Kniffin system, the lowest wire is placed 30 in. from the ground; the upper, 60 in. The trunk is allowed to reach the upper wire and to develop *two* branches (arms), extending in opposite directions on each wire. These arms are each renewed by a one-year cane each spring, all the other growths being cut off. The selected canes are shortened to 6 to 10 buds and tied to the wires. When the buds grow the shoots are allowed to droop where they will.

In the Munson or canopy system, 3 No. 10 or 11 wires are used. The lowest is 4 or 5 ft. from the ground and on it only two yearling canes are trained. The shoots developed from their buds are allowed to pass over the other wires, which are placed 6 in. higher and attached to the ends of cross-pieces of scantling spiked to the tops of the posts to form T's. This is the preferable system for the home gar-

den because it provides for better aëration and use of sunlight, because the fruit is more easily gathered, one can easily pass from row to row beneath the trellis, and currants, gooseberries and black raspberries (*not* red raspberries, blackberries or dewberries) can be planted between each 2 grape-vines in the rows.

PROTECTING THE GRAPES
Birds often eat the seeds out of grapes, especially early white varieties. By covering the vines with mosquito netting weighted at the bottom 2 weeks before ripening time, the injury is prevented.

In vineyards the European grape-vines are cut back to from half a dozen to perhaps 2 dozen spurs at or near the head of the trunks, which in time thus become stump-like. As they are shorter-branched than American varieties they are generally grown without trellises.

HOME STORAGE. Some varieties of grapes may be stored under home conditions for several months. For one of the best methods the first requisite is that storage be attempted only with those varieties reputed to be good keepers. Thick skin does not necessarily mean long-keeping attributes, though firm-berried varieties generally keep well. The fruit should be gathered on cool, dry days or in the coolest part of the day. It must be fully ripe, sound, free from rot, mildew, and cracks or broken berries. For two or three days the clusters should lie spread out on paper-covered trays in a cool, dry, airy room until the exterior moisture has evaporated and the stems have begun to shrivel slightly. They are then placed in layers not more than 4 in. deep, on wooden trays of orange-box material with spaces between the slats for ventilation and which have previously been sprayed with a copper sulphate solution (2 oz. to 1 gal. water) and allowed to dry. This fungicide will destroy spores of mold, rot, etc.

The cellar or storage room should be well chilled before any fruit is placed in it and thereafter kept at about 38 deg. Opening the windows at night and on cold days and closing them in the day time and during warm weather, should maintain this temperature from late autumn forward. Spaces 4 to 6 in. deep should separate the trays vertically so as to permit free circulation of air.

ENEMIES

DISEASES. Black rot is the most destructive fungous disease of grapes, directly attacking and destroying the berries and spotting the leaves. The fungus lives over winters in shriveled, mummied, rotted fruit, putting out a crop of spores to infect new growth in the spring. The first control measure therefore is early spring plowing to bury the mummies. Then spray four or five times with bordeaux mixture, which see. Make the first application (a 4-6-50 mixture) when the new growth is about ½ in. long, and the remaining sprays (of 3-6-50 bordeaux) (a) when the growth is 8 to 12 in., (b) after blossom-fall, (c) ten days later, and (d) two weeks later. Applications (b) and (c) may have a heaping tablespoon of lead arsenate added for each gallon of the spray to control flea beetle, rose chafer, berry moth and root worm (see below).

Downy mildew of grapes has spread from the U. S. to Europe causing great losses. On the leaves it first shows as pale yellow spots on the upper surface accompanied by downy white tufts beneath. Later flowers and fruits are blighted and rotted. Spraying for black rot as directed will control it. Powdery mildew may occur in late summer as a fine white coating on the upper sides of the leaves but appears too late to do serious damage. Remove and burn vines affected with dead arm caused by a fungus that grows in the wood, dwarfing, yellowing and curling the leaves but not affecting the root.

PHYLLOXERA. Like downy mildew, the insect pest, phylloxera of grapes, was introduced from N. America to Europe and other parts of the world, where it is a serious menace. (In France it is known as the American blight.) The insect (*Phylloxera vitifoliae*), one of the gall aphids, causes many small galls on the foliage and more important ones on the roots that may so affect the plant's nutrition that it is stunted, rendered unproductive and often killed. In this country, especially in California, European varieties are seriously affected but the native wild grape is not much injured. If, therefore, European varieties are grafted onto American stocks the injury from the root galls is largely eliminated.

OTHER PESTS. The grape berry moth is the cause of most of the wormy grapes in this country. The grape berries are webbed together and drop from the stems when about the size of garden peas, or small holes are eaten in nearly ripened berries. The ½ in. long, greenish-gray worms with brown heads pass the winter and pupate in grayish silken cocoons, the small grayish-purple moths emerging in spring. Control by spraying with arsenate of lead (see black rot above) or, in the case of a few vines, by enclosing the bunches in bags of paper, cellophane or netting.

The adult grape rootworm, also very destructive, is a small gray-brown leaf beetle which eats chain-like holes in the leaves; the larvae devour small root fibres and the bark of larger roots. Spray foliage with lead arsenate during June and cultivate the soil to expose the pupae to its natural enemies.

The grape flea beetle, rose chafer, Japanese beetle, grape-vine beetle, sphinx caterpillar and, sometimes, the spotted grapevine beetle are pests which can generally be controlled by spraying the foliage with lead arsenate during the early part of the season. Later the foliage may be covered with lime to discourage the Japanese beetle. Even better are the derris sprays made expressly for use against this pest. They are invisible and non-poisonous but must be repeated weekly while the beetles are about. The grape leaf-hopper which sucks the sap from the leaves, causing them to turn brown, may be controlled by spraying with nicotine-sulphate and soap or other contact insecticide.

OTHER GRAPES. Evergreen-grape is *Cissus capensis;* Oregon-grape is *Mahonia nervosa;* Sea-grape is the genus Coccolobis; Tail-grape is the genus Artabotrys.

GRAPE FAMILY. Common name of the Vitaceae, a family of mostly climbing vines cultivated for their edible fruit and, in several cases, as ornamental subjects.

GRAPE FERN. Common name for Botrychium (which see), a genus of fern allies, including the Moonwort, the Rattlesnake Fern, and the Grape Fern proper (*B. obliquum*) and its varieties. The fertile and sterile parts, united at the base or mid-way, are unlike; the single barren blade is more or less 3-lobed and often again pinnate; and the fertile stem terminates in a spike or panicle of naked spores. All are low-growing, in woods or thickets or moist pastures.

GRAPEFRUIT or POMELO (pom'-e-loh). An evergreen, semi-tropical citrus fruit tree (*Citrus paradisi*), grown mainly in Fla., S. Tex. and Calif. for its large, fine-grained fruits borne in bunches which suggest huge few-berried grape clusters. The names given are often erroneously interchanged with shaddock, pummelo and pompelmous, popular names for *C. maxima* (or *C. grandis*) a related, but smaller tree scarcely known in America but readily distinguished from the grapefruit by its larger, coarse-grained fruits borne singly, not in clusters.

The grapefruit, though of increasing importance as a commercial orchard tree, is hardly a home-garden subject. For cultural notes see under CITRUS FRUITS.

GRAPE-HYACINTH. Common name for the genus Muscari, a group of important small, hardy, spring-blooming bulbs. See MUSCARI.

GRAPTOPHYLLUM (grap-toh-fil'-um) *pictum.* A tropical shrub with purple or crimson flowers known as Caricature-plant, which see.

GRASS FAMILY. Common name for the Gramineae, a large group of monocotyledonous plants, comprising more than 500 genera, a third of which grow in the U. S. Many have high agricultural value as human food plants as well as forage crops, such as wheat, corn, rice, barley, oats, rye, and other cereal grains. Others are horticulturally important as lawn grasses or as decorative subjects in the flower garden or border. Some, however, are pernicious weeds.

Grasses are characterized by their long narrow 2-ranked leaves which clasp the stem and bear a small appendage called a ligule (or sometimes a tuft of hairs) on the stem-side where the sheath flattens into the blade. The flowers, which are usually minute, are borne in spikelets, each flower consisting of 2 or more bracts. The lowest 1 or 2, always empty, are called *glumes;* the next, containing the floret, are the *lemmas,* and within is a 2-nerved bract called the *palea.* The flower has no definite perianth (calyx and corolla); the stamens are usually 3, but may be from 1 to 6. The 2 styles surmount a single 1-celled ovary containing one ovule which becomes a seed—in many cases one of the grains of commerce.

Among the ornamental grasses (which see), one group, mostly hardy annuals grown from seed, are raised for their ornamental sprays, which are used in both green and everlasting bouquets; examples are the genera Agrostis, Briza, Coix, Eragrostis, Hordeum, Lagurus, Pennisetum, and Stipa. Another group, used for outdoor ornamental effects, are mostly tall perennials, the larger varieties of which may figure in landscape design, creating a tropical effect in the garden. They like a fairly rich soil in a protected position, and are propagated by early spring division, stolons, offsets, and, in some cases, by seeds. Examples are Arrhenatherum, Arundo, Elymus, Erianthus, Miscanthus, Festuca, Gynerium, Cortaderia, Pennisetum (*P. japonicum*), Phalaris, Setaria, and Uniola, besides the bamboos.

Lawn grasses are perennials and in many cases improved or selected strains of wild species. They are chosen for their ability to make a turf of green throughout the year, and numerous mixtures are available for various locations and purposes such as in shade, for banks, seaside, southern conditions, etc. Grass-seed mixtures usually contain a quick-starting but short-lived kind to serve as a nurse crop and slower growing but more permanent kinds. Lawns are also established by planting stolons of certain kinds of grass or squares or strips of sod.

GRASSHOPPER. A name for a number of species of large, usually green or brown, winged insects which, however, are more familiar to us as remarkable jumpers, being equipped with long, powerful hind legs. The scientific name of the group is Locust, which suggests that grasshoppers may have been the destructive "locusts" of ancient times. They should not be confused with the so-called "locusts" that sing in trees in summer, which are really cicadas (which see) and considerably less harmful.

Various species of grasshoppers occur all over the world and attack a great variety of wild and cultivated crops, doing tremendous damage when in great numbers. The eggs winter over in inch-long packets an inch or so below the soil surface in uncultivated ground such as field margins, waste land, etc. The young hoppers that emerge in late May look like the adults except in size and lack of wings. They soon begin to feed and complete their growth by midsummer, but continue to feed until frost.

Control consists of fall plowing (4 in. deep) areas where eggs are laid so as to expose them to frost and to birds which eat them. In gardens, grasshoppers can be poisoned by using poison bran (see BRAN MASH). A poison bait recommended by the University of Oklahoma consists of: 10 per cent bran, 15 per cent molasses, and 20 to 25 per cent magnesium sulphate (epsom salts). Where vast swarms attack grain and grass fields, as in the West, machines or traps called hopperdozers are drawn back and forth across the fields by horses or tractors and the insects caught in them, if not killed, are then destroyed.

See also INSECTS.

GRASS-OF-PARNASSUS. Common name for Parnassia, a genus of small perennial herbs with white flowers delicately greenish-veined, often pink stamens, and a single smooth leaf on the flower-stem. Good to plant in damp spots.

GRASS PINK. Common name for *Dianthus plumarius,* a mat-forming perennial with white, rose or purple flowers.

GRASS-PINK ORCHID. An American swamp orchid, *Calopogon pulchellus,* with grass-like leaves and magenta flowers appearing in July.

GRATIOLA (gra-ty'-oh-lah) *aurea.* A low-growing, wet-ground herb called Goldenpert (which see) or Golden Hedgehyssop.

GRAVEL CULTURE. One type of what is commonly called "soilless" or chemical gardening, which see. Where subirrigation is used to apply nutrient solutions to plants growing in beds or benches, a coarser material than sand is necessary to secure rapid drainage. Fine gravel, broken rock, or cinders may be used in this method. If gravel, it should be preferably of quartz. If it contains limestone, it is

advisable, before setting plants in it, to add superphosphate and keep the medium well flushed for about two weeks; it is wise also to use a nutrient solution designed for that particular kind of medium.

GRAVELLY SOIL. Any kind of soil containing a considerable proportion of gravel or small stones or pebbles of the rounded, waterworn type. Mixed with a clay or silt loam, gravel serves to facilitate drainage and does not seriously interfere with cultivation. But present as a dominant feature, or combined with a thin, sandy soil, it is likely to cause extreme leaching and excessive drying, making difficult the growing of any but drought-resistant plants. See SOIL.

GRAY MOLD. Name sometimes given to botrytis blights because of the fluffy gray masses of spores. See BOTRYTIS; also under PEONY.

GREEK VALERIAN. Common name for *Polemonium caeruleum,* a 3 ft. perennial with drooping blue flowers in clusters. Varieties have white, and lilac, flowers and variegated leaves. Sometimes the native species, *P. reptans,* a smaller plant, is called by the same name.

GREEN-BRIER. Common name for the genus Smilax, mostly woody vines; some are grown or collected for use as decorative foliage material by florists, but others are annoying weeds.

GREEN FLY. Another name for the green plant louse or aphid, which see.

GREENHOUSE. (See illustrations, Plate 25.) A glass-roofed building used for the propagation or maintenance of plants. Though usually (and preferably) built as a separate structure with independent heating equipment, it may be combined with a garage (if small), or with the residence, especially in the form of a conservatory (which see) or sun-parlor. The use of the two latter types is largely confined to the display of plants developed elsewhere, discarded and replaced when no longer attractive. The true greenhouse has many more advantages for the amateur gardener.

During late winter and early spring it may be used to produce seedlings for later use in the outdoor garden. Ornamental plants, especially flowers, may be grown in it during the cold months. Various vegetables, such as asparagus, rhubarb, mushrooms and salad greens, and fruits such as strawberries, peaches, grapes, nec-

A SASH GREENHOUSE

Except for the ends such a house may be glazed with full or half size standard hotbed sash attached to a framework by brass screws or (preferably) bolts so it may be "knocked down" for summer storage and set up when needed.

tarines, plums and loquats may be grown in it, bringing welcome variety and luxury to the table. But the greatest pleasure a greenhouse can give the amateur gardener is in the challenge it offers to Jack Frost, and its greatest advantage is in the knowledge of plant life which it imparts to the owner and operator.

The greenhouse types of greatest interest to amateurs are the even-span and the lean-to, the former preferably extending north and south, the latter built against a wall and facing south. These basic forms are often varied to meet special needs or desires but usually the less they depart from the normal the better.

As its name implies, the even-span type is a gabled structure which, if divided lengthwise by a partition from ridge to ground would give two sections with equal areas of roof and walls. If not an isolated structure it should preferably have its north end conected with some other building. The lean-to is comparable to one of the "lengthwise halves" of an even-span house divided as just suggested. It is generally much narrower, frequently being 10 ft., or less in width.

More or less standard widths for an even-span house have been established on the basis of the experience of greenhouse operators. The "reach" of the men who work with the plants determines the most convenient width of the benches, or beds and of the space required for walks between them. Popular widths for small houses are 15, 18 and 25 ft. Other conditions being equal, the widest is the best investment. For example, a greenhouse 15

by 60 ft. or 18 by 50 ft. has an area of 900 sq. ft., whereas a 25-by-40-ft. house covers 1000 sq. ft. of ground. The latter house also has more pleasing proportions, is the most adaptable size, costs relatively less to build and is easier and more economical to operate because it encloses a greater volume of air and therefore is less susceptible to temperature changes outside which naturally affect the conditions within. Moreover, it permits taller plants.

Within reasonable limits the length of a greenhouse may consist of as many units (defined below) as are desired. Three lengths or sections are preferable for the amateur, as they permit several different temperatures suiting various classes of plants and create a form less likely to show ugly proportions in relation to adjacent structures.

The term "square feet of glass" as ordinarily used means the area of ground covered by a greenhouse, except for purposes of (1) hail insurance, and (2) working out heating requirements, when it means the total area of glass—roof, side walls and end walls.

Complete plans should be drawn before any construction gets under way. Disappointment will thus be avoided, especially if the greenhouse is to be attached to a residence. Both the design and construction and the heating of a greenhouse are technical problems for the trained greenhouse builder and engineer; neither the amateur gardener, the residence architect nor the "local builder" is competent to handle them.

A SMALL GREENHOUSE

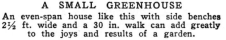

An even-span house like this with side benches 2½ ft. wide and a 30 in. walk can add greatly to the joys and results of a garden.

A convenient location (for the one who looks after it) where it will receive maximum sunlight and minimum shadow is most important. The plans should consider not only the initial house but also present and prospective grade, the shape of the area, heating arrangements, and possible enlargements.

The great demand in recent years for amateur or "home" greenhouses has stimulated leading greenhouse-construction firms to develop standard sizes and unit features which fit together somewhat like sectional bookcases. The purchaser benefits not only in reduced costs for standard sizes and equipment, but also because he can start with as few units as desired and expand as his confidence, experience and skill prompt him to.

If possible the greenhouse floor should be all on one level and several inches above the outside ground line. As a preliminary step, all surface soil should be removed from the area to be covered by the greenhouse and the space filled with several layers of wetted and tamped subsoil, gravel or sand; this prevents souring and settling, which would take place if the surface soil were left, owing to the decay of vegetable matter in it.

Foundations for walls and posts must be carefully built, for they must support the very considerable weight of the side walls and roof. They must be extended well below the local frost line, to avoid heaving, and about 2 ft. above ground level. The part below ground may be of rubble-stone or concrete but that above ground should be of brick, stone or concrete, to harmonize with other architectural features.

A combination of iron and wood is the best permanent roof construction. The iron (or steel) frame supports the weight and strain and casts the smallest amount of shadow, and the wooden sash-bars serve both as nonconductors of heat and as a setting or bed for the glass. The first cost of such construction is somewhat greater than for wood alone but is offset by lower repair costs and greater durability.

Only "double-thick" glass should be used to glaze a greenhouse roof. It weighs 24 to 26 oz. to the sq. ft. and is far more resistant to possible breakage by hail than is "single-thick" glass, which weighs about 16 oz. to the sq. ft. Variations in thickness and waves in the glass, which act as lenses, intensify the sun's rays and burn the foliage, are found in all grades and brands of glass and cannot be entirely eliminated. However, it is important to buy from a firm making a specialty of greenhouse glass. Second quality is the grade usually recommended; it is less expensive than first quality, and more desirable than lower grades.

Since rafters, sash-bars and other parts of the roof skeleton cast shadows it is highly desirable to use as large size "lights" (panes) as practicable, thus reducing the number of rafters and sash-bars. Standard widths vary from 12 to 16 in., lengths from 16 to 24 in. The most favored size is 16 x 24 in., placed the short way between sash-bars. Ribbed and rough plate glass are sometimes used in conservatories and various other greenhouses but since they require extra support because of their weight the cost of such roofs is thereby increased, usually without benefit.

A NEW TYPE OF ADAPTABLE, EASY-TO-ERECT GREENHOUSE
Glazed sections are bolted together, then put in place on a simple foundation (left), either out in the garden or attached to a garage or other building (right).

Glazing is best done by bedding the lights in first quality putty placed evenly in the rabbets of the sash-bars with not more than $\frac{1}{16}$ in. "play." The first panes are laid at the bottom. Each succeeding light is lapped $\frac{1}{8}$ to $\frac{1}{4}$ in. over the one below and held in place by zinc shoe-nails placed on each side—preferably one at the end to prevent slipping down, another near the end and a third near the middle to prevent lifting. All cracks between the sash-bars and the glass are pressed full of putty but all excess is removed so as to

factory with linseed oil and white lead and all metal parts with metallic paint. A second coat is given when the structure is up and the sash-bars are in place and a third after the glazing is completed, thin paint being used each time. If desired, some light color (but no dark) may be added. Each coat should always be thin and well brushed out; paint so applied will protect the wood and last longer than thicker mixtures or other materials and will form a better base for repainting (one coat), which should be done every second year.

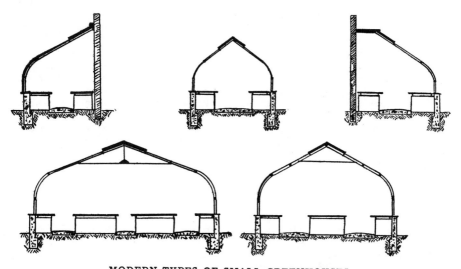

MODERN TYPES OF SMALL GREENHOUSES
All of the graceful and efficient curved-eave design, these illustrate the 2-bench lean-to style (top left and right); even-span (top center); and wider, multiple bench types (below).

leave none on the outside. As a result of the over-lapping of the panes, water condensed on the inside during cold weather can find its way out between the lights.

Various glass substitutes with and without reinforcement of fine wire netting are on the market, but glass still maintains its popularity for large and permanent greenhouses. For temporary structures such as hotbeds, coldframes, plant pits and small greenhouses whose roofs are made of hotbed sash, the substitutes are often admirable.

Because greenhouse roofs are exposed to extremes of heat, cold, wetness during winter and dryness in summer, liberal protection of the supports by painting is essential. It should start before the parts are assembled; in fact, greenhouse-construction companies prime all wooden parts in the

Ventilators, comprising about 10% of the roof area, should be placed preferably on both sides of the ridge, each side to be operated independently on the lee side of the wind so as to avoid down drafts of air during cold weather. There are several styles of regulators, made to lift several ventilators at once from a narrow crack to full capacity, thus providing for complete and immediate control of air out-go. Ventilators are often placed at the sides but such location is not as essential or as desirable as at the ridge. So much "fresh air" enters the greenhouse through cracks that no provision need be made for intakes; indeed, the latter are undesirable because of the risk of damage to the plants. The purpose of ventilation in greenhouses is to reduce the temperature of, and the water vapor in, the air.

Most commercial greenhouses are heated by steam, but small houses for amateur activities are best warmed by hot water. The open tank system is the most adaptable and so easily understood that it should have preference over other types. It requires only the most ordinary attention. At night it may be regulated to maintain a uniform temperature for 10 or more hours, thus dispensing with the services of a fireman.

One of the greatest advantages of hot water over steam is that during chilly fall and spring weather the fire may be kept very low, while still maintaining enough heat to meet cultural needs. It may even be let out and a wood fire started to take the chill off the houses. Steam systems produce no heat in the houses until the water boils and the steam begins to circulate in the heating pipes. Hot water is more costly to install and repair but the increased costs are more than offset by ease and convenience of operation, and fuel economy.

As no other one item of greenhouse construction is so important, the capacity of the heating system should always be calculated by a specialist in greenhouse heating.

The details of greenhouse management may be divided under two headings: Control of the house, and handling of the plants. The first includes:

1. Imitation of a normal day outdoors by maintaining full and continuous sunlight and providing a gradual increase in heat from early morning to early afternoon, then a gradual decrease toward evening and a minimum during the night—10° to 15° F. lower than the maximum in the shade during the day. Without such a rise and fall the plants are likely to have weak stems and produce poor flowers. It is much better to keep the temperature a little below rather than above the recommended degree, for then the plants will be sturdier and the flowers will last longer. Plants grown under too high a temperature, with too much water and too rich soil grow over-rapidly and are easily harmed, especially by cold drafts, which, in many cases, make them susceptible to mildew, green fly, and other pests. This is most likely to happen during cloudy weather.

2. Since space in the greenhouse is far more valuable than an equal area in the outdoor garden, it must be used intensively.

When a plant has passed its prime it should be replaced. Each individual plant, rather than a group or a row of plants as outdoors, demands attention. Care in this respect helps gardeners develop skill in their work outdoors, as well as in the greenhouse.

3. Because only small amounts of soil can be used in greenhouse benches and flower-pots the roots cannot forage as freely as under garden conditions. Consequently the soil must be mixed and prepared to the liking of the particular plant grown. In general, greenhouse soil must be looser and more loamy than in the garden to (1) assure good drainage; (2) retain moisture; and (3) prevent or reduce puddling (see PUDDLE). Excessive watering especially with the hose, tends to pack the soil. Hence the undesirability of excess clay and silt in the soil mixture.

Using ordinary good garden soil as a basis, "looseness" may be achieved by adding sand. The ability to retain moisture is increased by adding humus in the form of compost, leafmold, commercial humus, or peat moss, all of which also help to loosen the soil mixture. Screening to remove stones, clods and other débris and to mix the ingredients thoroughly is essential. The preliminary sifting may be through a mason's galvanized wire screen of ½-in. mesh; later sifting should be through a circular hand screen of ¼-in. mesh.

4. Watering plants during winter, especially during cloudy weather, demands the use of better judgment than any other one feature of greenhouse management. No set rules can be laid down, and allowances must be made for various circumstances. For instance, water evaporates from the top only of solid beds. In raised benches it is lost from both top and bottom, while in flower-pots, unless made of impervious materials, evaporation takes place from top, sides and bottom. The practical gardener's rule is to *water only when the plants need watering.* Do not give the plants all they can stand without being drowned! Rather keep them "on the dry side," particularly during cloudy weather and at night. On the other hand, when you water do not sprinkle; give enough to soak the soil from top to bottom, applying it to the soil, not on the plants. Then wait until the plants again show *need* of a soaking. Frequent sprinkling often does harm.

5. Because evaporation is a cooling process, do not water greenhouses, hotbeds and coldframes toward evening or when the temperature is falling. Never wet the foliage toward night. These rules are especially important for warm-house plants. For the same reasons, give water stingily or not at all during cloudy weather or when evaporation is slow.

6. Attacks by diseases and insects usually start as a result of either carelessness or error in management. Knowledge of the conditions under which such pests increase and spread, plus adherence to the above principles and precautions will reduce the danger of attack. Keep the premises clean and sweet by destroying all débris and affected plant parts. It is far easier and more important to maintain healthy conditions than to reëstablish them after infection has occurred.

Alertness in applying a remedy when an enemy is first noticed is highly desirable. Spraying (which see) with a fungicide for non-bacterial diseases, with a stomach poison for chewing insects, and with a contact spray for those that suck plant juices, is indicated in most cases, though many species of insects can be most easily and effectively controlled by fumigation (which see). Should any pest trouble get out of control, destroy all affected plants, remove all soil, give the houses drastic treatment and, if necessary, make a change from plants grown to those not affected by the pest in question.

7. As the season advances the sun is likely to burn the foliage of plants in small greenhouses as a result of waves (not bubbles) in the glass. Such injury is most severe where the rays are focused by these spots—usually fairly near them. Herein lies another advantage of the wide greenhouse, because in it the glass is farther away from the plants.

8. Shade is necessary in the spring to prevent scalded foliage due to strong sunshine following so soon after the long winter period of dull weather; the plants need an opportunity to accustom themselves to the change. Cheesecloth blinds or curtains hung parallel to the glass, either

AN IMPORTANT CORNER IN THE GREENHOUSE
The boiler on the same level as the greenhouse floor is practical with small hot water systems like the modern convenient style shown. In larger sizes and in steam-heated systems it should be several feet lower to insure correct circulation.

inside or outside the house, may be used. Usually, however, the glass is sprayed outside with whitewash, whiting, or white lead.

As most plants suffer from the excessive heat if kept in greenhouses during the summer they are usually moved out of doors. If this is not done the shade must be increased.

By autumn much of the shade material (especially if whiting or whitewash is used) will have been flaked off. The balance must be removed by scrubbing with stiff brushes.

Under the handling of plants, the following general principles are most important:

1. Practically every kind of plant grown in greenhouses has a normal period of activity and season of bloom. It is the better part of wisdom to keep conditions favorable to the plant rather than to force it to adapt itself to unnatural conditions for its growth.

2. Most plant species do not grow continuously but go through an inactive or rest period. For instance, "hardy bulbs" such as tulips rest between late spring and early autumn; cacti rest during dry seasons. Plants should be given similar rest periods when grown under the artificial conditions of greenhouse culture.

3. Each plant species must reach a definite stage of growth before it blooms. Vegetative development and reproduction rarely occur coincidentally. Woody plants such as azaleas must have "well-ripened wood" before flowers can be expected; otherwise such blooms as may develop will be inferior and short-lived. The frequency at which plants are shifted from pot to pot, particularly in the case of herbaceous plants, acts as a partial control of the time of flowering and fruit production. If kept in small pots they will blossom prematurely or die. If shifted frequently to successively larger pots, the period of vegetative growth is lengthened. Maintenance in one pot for a period of time tends to check growth and encourage flowering. Fertilizers applied during the early stages encourage vegetative growth; withheld until growth is well advanced, they induce flowering and increase the size of flowers and fruit.

4. Its natural habitat suggests the type of treatment best for each plant species. Imitation of soil, light, temperature and moisture conditions under which the plant grows naturally usually lead to success in culture. However, the fact that a plant is found naturally in a swamp, a tropical country, or on a mountain-side does not necessarily mean that it will fail under different conditions. The original habitat merely hints at the probable successful method of treatment.

5. Each plant has its own typical means of propagation, usually by seeds, but often by some asexual method such as layering, division, grafting, or cuttings (which see). The latter methods frequently produce the better plants and they are always true to variety (bud sports excepted).

GREENHOUSE PESTS. The insects and other pests that attack greenhouse plants are in many cases the same as those that attack the same or related crops in the garden, but conditions in a greenhouse are usually particularly favorable for pests whereas the ordinary control methods are difficult because of the sensitivity of many plants to sprays, used under glass. The best control is therefore prevention—which means exclusion. Houses (meaning the soil and benches as well as the rest) should be cleaned up by heat, steam or other sterilization or heavy fumigation in the intervals between crops, and all plants should be carefully inspected before they are admitted. Soil used in filling the benches should be carefully examined to see that it does not contain wireworms, white grubs, eel-worms, cut-worms and other insects. Infested soil should be sterilized by steam when possible. See DISINFECTION.

INSECTS. Among the sucking insects common in greenhouses are the scales— the small hard, brown and armored sorts and the larger soft tortoise scales common on oleander, fern, palm; soft mealy bugs that form white clusters on coleus, orchid, poinsettia, ivy and many other plants; the small dark-bodied greenhouse orthezia covered with waxy filaments; aphids of various colors which weaken the plants and distort the young growth; white flies—tiny, four-winged and snow-white, which rise up from the plants in swarms when disturbed and cover plants with a sticky material in which a sooty black fungus grows; greenhouse thrips that whiten and fleck the leaves with yellow and distort the flower buds; red spiders, tiny mites that cover the under leaf surface with fine webs and turn the upper surface yellow; and the cyclamen

Plate 25. GARDEN THE YEAR 'ROUND IN A GREENHOUSE

Upper left: The tiny lean-to greenhouse provides ample space to start seedling plants which will soon outstrip the laggard spring. Upper right: Though snow falls without, summer is trapped beneath the arching glass. Bottom: Fruit and flowers, fragrance and foliage—a greenhouse is the tropics in miniature.

mite, which blackens the buds and distorts the leaves.

Among the chewing insects troublesome under glass are the greenhouse leaf-tyer, pale-green caterpillars that enclose one or more leaves in a web; leaf rollers, which act first as miners and then as chewers; the dark-green Florida fern caterpillar; many species of cut-worms; the corn ear-worm which likes to eat chrysanthemum buds; the strawberry root worm which as a beetle feeds on rose leaves and as a grub injures the roots. The chrysanthemum midge makes cone-shaped galls on the leaves, and the rose midge distorts the flower buds. Wireworms, white grubs, sow-bugs, millepedes and the garden centipede may work in the soil feeding on the roots, while nematodes cause galls on roots or leaves, disfiguring and often killing the plants.

Many insects and related pests in greenhouses are most easily controlled by fumigation (which see). Those that work in the soil are controlled by soil sterilization with steam or chemicals (see DISINFECTION), and sometimes by the use of poison baits.

If fumigation is not possible, spraying with contact insecticides may be resorted to for the control of scales, mealy bugs and other sucking insects. A white-oil emulsion, especially prepared for greenhouse use, is most effective; but it must be diluted exactly according to manufacturer's directions, should not be used on plants in bright sunshine, and should be rinsed off with clear water after some hours.

DISEASES. The spread of plant disease is encouraged in greenhouses by the practice of overhead watering. Plants soaked with the hose, especially on cloudy days when they cannot dry off rapidly, are very apt to get botrytis blight or to become covered with mildew. Rose black spot and mildew are more prevalent in early fall before the temperature is well regulated. Painting the heating pipes with sulphur is one of the remedies for mildew. Specific control measures are given for the various diseases mentioned in the articles on the various crops, but in general removal of all diseased plant parts, spacing the plants well apart and keeping the humidity low will do much toward keeping down plant diseases under glass.

GREEN MANURE. Any crop that is grown expressly to be plowed or dug under so as to improve the soil is called a green-manure crop. The term is almost synonymous with cover-crop (which see) and the same kinds of plants are used in both rôles; however with green-manure crops any protective effect on trees or other plants among which they are grown or any soil-binding effect is secondary to four objectives: (1) to take up any available plant food and prevent its loss by leaching from uncultivated ground; (2) to add humus (vegetable matter) to the soil and improve its physical condition; (3) if a leguminous crop, to take nitrogen from the air, "fix" it in the plant roots and thus add it to the soil's supply of fertility; (4) to bring up plant food from the subsoil where it may be obtained by the deep growing roots and thus sent up to the leaves and stems to be later incorporated in the soil.

Green-manure crops are usually forage or grain crops, but there are many kinds of different degrees of value for different soils and under varying conditions. Sometimes one is wanted that will make quick, abundant growth during a short period when a piece of land is idle; again a perennial crop may be sown, to be cut as hay for a year or two, or perhaps grazed by livestock, before being turned under.

Generally speaking, legumes, such as cowpeas, sow-beans, Canada field peas, various clovers, vetches and alfalfa make the best green manures because, besides contributing their own growth, they store in their roots nitrogen taken directly from the air. Alfalfa and the perennial clovers are best for use in long rotations; cowpeas and soy-beans are good summer green manures; and winter vetch is good for fall planting.

Of the non-legumes, rye is the most used as it grows rapidly, can be sown until freezing weather occurs or very early in spring; and will do well even on light rather poor soils. Buckwheat in even more used on poor land, especially newly turned ground, but it must be sown in spring and grown in warm weather. Spurry is another forage crop that will make good growth on poor soil.

Whatever crop is sown, and at whatever season, it must be turned under while it is green and succulent if it is to promptly decay and fulfil its task as a green manure. If it makes especially heavy growth it may prove advisable to mow it before turning it under. Or, if the area is large enough, the ground can be disk-harrowed either before or just after it is plowed.

GREENS, EDIBLE. Plants whose succulent leaves and stems, steamed or boiled, are served as a vegetable. While growing, they are usually called by their popular, individual names or referred to collectively as pot-herbs. In general, as they are most in demand in early spring, the hardy annuals are often sown in the fall and wintered under mulches or in coldframes. They are also started during late winter in greenhouses, hotbeds or coldframes or sown at the earliest possible moment outdoors in spring.

As greens must be succulent and tender, the annuals must be grown rapidly in loose, very rich soil, well drained but well supplied with moisture. The perennials may be hastened by placing coldframes or plant forcers over them as soon as the ground has thawed. The latter include pokeweed, sorrel, dock, dandelion, and chicory.

Among the many weeds and wild plants used as greens are the following: Buckhorn plantain, chicory, dandelion, various cresses, dock, goosefoot (or lambs quarters), mustard, pigweed, pokeweed, purslane, sorrel and marsh-marigold.

Hardy annuals suitable for spring sowing, seed of which may be obtained at the seed stores, include: chervil, Chinese amaranth, Chinese artichoke, Chinese mustard, Chinese cabbage, corn-salad, kale, nasturtium, orach and spinach.

Species that may be sown in the fall and wintered over for spring use are spinach, dandelion, fetticus, kale and collards. For summer and autumn use the most popular are Swiss chard and New Zealand spinach. In addition, the following are often used as greens: Beet tops, turnip sprouts and thinned out seedlings of cabbage and related plants.

GREENS, ORNAMENTAL. This term applies properly to any fresh leaves or branches of plants cut for decoration. See CHRISTMAS GREENS.

GREENWEED, DYERS. Common name for *Genista tinctoria,* a yellow-flowered shrub of the Pea Family.

GREIGIA (gree'-jah). A genus of showy S. American herbs resembling the pineapple with rose-colored flowers and the foliage growing in rosettes. Sometimes included in greenhouse collections, they are grown like Bromelia, which see.

GRENADINE (gren'-ah-din). Name (from the French) for a fragrant type of Carnation, which see.

GREVILLEA (gre-vil'-e-ah). Australian trees and shrubs belonging to the Protea Family of the S. Hemisphere. One or two species are grown for ornament in this country, either under glass or outdoors in warm regions. *G. robusta* (Silk-oak) is the best known. In its native land it is a fast growing tree to 150 ft. As a greenhouse subject it is easily grown from seed, forming one of the most decorative of fern-leaved plants and doing well in 4 or 5 in. pots. In the warmer parts of the country it is used as a shade tree, and there the curiously shaped orange-yellow flowers add to the beauty of the foliage. *G. thelemanniana* is a spreading shrub to 5 ft., with finely-cut leaves and curious red flowers tipped green.

GREWIA (groo'-i-ah). Trees or shrubs found in warm regions of Asia, Africa and Australia, belonging to the Linden Family. *G. parviflora* from China and Korea, which is the hardiest, can be grown as far north as southern New England. It is a shrub up to 8 ft. with large leaves, toothed and sometimes 3-lobed, and small clusters of pale yellow flowers in summer. *G. caffra* is a S. African shrub or small tree with finely toothed leaves and purple flowers, hardy only in the warmest parts of the country.

GREYIA (gray'-i-ah). A deciduous shrub or small tree of S. Africa. *G. sutherlandi,* apparently the only species in cultivation, is sometimes grown under glass, or outdoors in the warmest parts of the country. It grows best in a light rich soil, and should be kept on the dry side when at rest. The coarsely toothed leaves are clustered at the ends of the branches, and the bright crimson flowers are borne in a long dense raceme. Propagated by seeds or cuttings of half-ripened wood.

GRINDELIA (grin-dee'-li-ah). A genus of coarse W. N. American perennial herbs, called Gum-plants. They bear large yellow, generally sticky flowers, and are sometimes planted in poor soils for ornament.

GRISELINIA (gri-sel-in'-i-ah). Evergreen trees or shrubs of New Zealand, belonging to the Dogwood Family. They can be grown outdoors only in the warmest parts of U. S. Male and female flowers are borne on separate plants; if plants of the two sexes are planted in close proximity, the female or pistillate ones bear bunches of green grape-like berries. They grow well in ordinary soil and are propagated by cuttings.

G. littoralis makes a good big shrub or small tree. It has oval pale green leathery leaves, will stand clipping, and where hardy is an excellent subject for seaside gardens. *G. lucida* is a smaller grower but with much larger leaves, up to 6 in. long.

GROMWELL. Common name for the genus Lithospermum, which includes hardy annual and perennial herbs, with heavy foliage and blue, white or yellow flowers in heavy clusters or spikes. Grown without difficulty from seeds and cuttings in any average soil, it is used in borders and rock gardens in temperate latitudes. The name False-gromwell is given to Onosmodium, a group of American plants of the same (Borage) family, sometimes transplanted to gardens but of no particular garden value.

GROSSULARIA (grohs-eu-lay′-ri-ah). Former botanical name for the Gooseberry (which see) and still used by some authors. Others now place gooseberries in the same genus (Ribes) as the currants, even though there are marked differences. The gooseberries are generally prickly and their berries occur singly or only few together, while in the currants the fruits and stems are smooth and bear their flowers and berries in loose clusters on jointed pedicels, or "stems." Under the present system the native American gooseberry, formerly *Grossularia hirtella,* is now *Ribes hirtellum* and the English gooseberry, formerly *G. reclinata,* is *R. grossularia.*

GROUND BEETLES. Fairly large beetles commonly found on the surface of the ground, lurking under stones or rubbish, or running through the grass. Most of them are shining black, but some are blue, green or brown and a few are spotted. Many species are predatory, capturing and feeding on other insects. The larvae are generally long with the body of nearly equal width throughout. They usually feed at night and are of great value in destroying certain caterpillars. Two ground beetles, the searcher and the fiery hunter, climb trees in search of their prey. The European ground beetle which feeds on the gypsy and brown-tail moths was introduced in New England to fight those pests. See INSECTS, BENEFICIAL.

GROUND-CEDAR. A common name for *Lycopodium complanatum,* a dwarf, trailing, conifer-like plant of N. woods. One of the club-mosses gathered for use as a holiday decorating material, it is sometimes called Ground-pine, which more correctly refers to *L. obscurum.*

GROUND-CHERRY. A common name for the genus Physalis, also called Husktomato, which includes the ornamental Chinese lantern-plant (which see) and several species that produce small, edible fruits enclosed in papery husks.

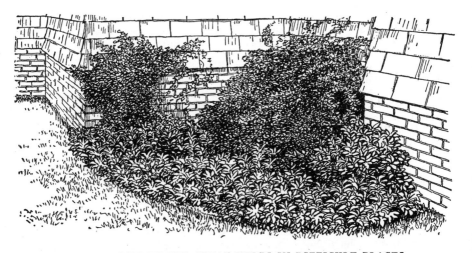

GROUND-COVERS ARE GREAT HELPS IN DIFFICULT PLACES
In shady corners, under trees and in many other situations where neither grass nor flowering plants will succeed. Pachysandra or Spurge (shown above), English Ivy, Periwinkle (Vinca) and other such low, thick-growing, evergreen subjects are invaluable—and gratifyingly easy to grow.

GROUND-COVER. A term applied to a plant or group of plants of special value for covering the ground, particularly beneath trees, or on banks where the cost of maintaining grass in good condition is excessive. This method of treatment has far greater possibilities in the way of creating pleasant little garden scenes than have yet been fully developed, but enough has been done to show its value when properly undertaken. The most common example, perhaps, is the use of Pachysandra (which see) under trees and in other shady places where it is impossible to maintain grass. *Euonymus radicans* (especially its var. *colorata*), English Ivy, and Running-myrtle, are other broad-leaved evergreens of value for use in shady and difficult situations. Trailing Junipers, Halls Honeysuckle, the Memorial Rose, and Virginia Creeper are examples of suitable plants for use on large banks. For smaller patches, several of the Sedums, Thymes, and Veronicas, as well as others, may be used to advantage.

See also PLANTS FOR SPECIAL PURPOSES.

GROUND-IVY. A common name for *Nepeta hederacea,* a hardy perennial creeper useful as ground cover because it grows rapidly and forms an attractive mat in either open or shaded locations. A member of the Mint Family, it is related to the catnip.

GROUNDNUT. A common name for various plants that bear tubers or tuber-like parts; notably *Apios tuberosa* (also called Potato-bean), *Arachis hypogaea,* the Peanut (which see), and *Panax trifolium,* a species of Ginseng, which see.

GROUND-PINE. A common name for *Lycopodium obscurum,* a club-moss distributed in cool parts of the U. S. and Asia.

GROUND-PINK. A common name for *Phlox subulata,* better known as Moss-pink, a hardy mat-forming perennial with very small leaves and abundant pink, lavender or magenta flowers.

GROUNDSEL. Common name for Senecio (which see), a large and variable genus of herbs and woody plants. Common Groundsel (*S. vulgaris*) is a bad weed in some regions. Groundsel-bush is *Baccharis halimifolia.* Giant-groundsel is *Ligularia wilsoniana.*

GROWTH-RINGS. Circular lines seen in logs of wood when trees are sawed across. They are formed at the outside of the wood of the stem or trunk, just under the bark, by the growth of the cells of the *cambium,* which is the layer of actively living, growing tissue. Thus there is one ring for each year's growth in temperate climates. Counting these rings gives the tree's age and the distance between them shows the rate of growth. These data are important to the tree planter, since each species has its own average rate, which varies with locality, soil type and condition, moisture, weather and exposure. By a study of growth-rings in similar trees, it is possible when planting a tree to predict, within limits, how large it will be at any future time.

GRUB. The larvae of an insect. Usually this term is used to specify the larval stage of a beetle, Caterpillar to specify that of a moth or butterfly, and Maggot that of a fly. See INSECTS; BEETLES; CATERPILLAR; FLIES.

GRUGRU PALM (groo'-groo). Common name for *Acrocomia aculeata,* a tree to 40 ft. with feathery foliage. It bears large clusters of small nuts which are the source of palm oil, widely used in making soap and other toilet preparations.

GUADALUPE (gwah-d'-loop'). Common name for *Erythea edulis,* a stout Palm to 30 ft. with fan-shaped leaves, which bears long clusters of sweet black fruits. Native to Lower Calif. and S., it is frequently planted in S. Calif.

GUAIACUM (gwy'-ah-kum). A genus of tropical American very hard wooded trees and shrubs called Lignum-vitae (which see). Bearing small blue or purple flowers, they are slow-growing but are sometimes seen in Calif. and Fla. gardens.

GUANO (gwah'-noh). An organic fertilizer, less used than formerly, consisting of the accumulated excrement of wild birds with some admixture of dead birds themselves, decayed feathers, fragments of fish and seaweed, etc. It is obtained from dry coastal areas (chiefly of S. America) where vast numbers of seabirds have gathered for many years. Owing to the heavy depletion of the deposits and the increasing availability of manufactured (synthetic) fertilizers it is becoming relatively unimportant.

Peruvian guano collected from a group of islands off the coast of Peru, contains about 10.5 per cent of nitrogen and 10 per cent of phosphoric acid. Guanos containing larger percentages of phosphorus come from the West Indies and from islands in various parts of the Pacific Ocean. But in general guano is considered primarily a nitrogenous fertilizer.

GUAVA (gwah'-vah). Tropical American trees (the genus Psidium) belonging to the Myrtle Family. The common guava (*Psidium guajava*) and some of its varieties, with one or two other species, are grown in the warmest parts of the U. S. for their edible fruits. They are not particular as to soil, except that it be well drained. *P. guajava* grows to 30 ft. and bears roundish yellow fruit up to 4 in. long, with white, yellow or pink aromatic flesh. The Strawberry Guava (*P. cattleianum*) is a smaller and hardier tree with purplish-red fruits; these are about half the size of the other, and their flesh is white. Propagation is by seeds or, in the case of the better varieties, by budding.

GUELDER-ROSE (gel'-der). A popular name for the common Snowball (*Viburnum opulus* var. *sterilis*), long a favorite summer-flowering shrub.

GUERNSEY-LILY. Common name for *Nerine sarniensis,* a tender bulbous plant with crimson lily-like flowers.

GUINEA-HEN-FLOWER. A common name for *Fritillaria meleagris,* better known as Checkered-lily, a bulbous herb of W. U. S. and temperate regions of Europe whose lily-like flowers are spotted and veined with purple and maroon.

GUM. A name applied, alone and in combinations, and rather loosely, to trees (and one herb) of different species, genera, and even families, which are discussed under their headings, as follows:

Gum, Cotton Gum or Tupelo Gum, is *Nyssa aquatica,* a large tree of the swamps of southern U. S.

Sour Gum, or Black Gum is the Pepperidge (*Nyssa sylvatica*), an even larger tree growing from Me. to Tex. See NYSSA.

Sweet Gum is *Liquidambar styraciflua,* a huge deciduous tree ranging from Conn. to Fla. and Mexico.

Gum-arabic-tree—a species of leguminous tree (*Acacia arabica*), grown for its sap.

Gum-plant is Grindelia, a species of western N. Amer. herbs of the Composite Family.

GUMBO. A popular name in the S. for Okra, which see.

GUMI (goo'-mi). Common name for *Elaeagnus multiflora* (sometimes given as *E. longipes*), a hardy, deciduous shrub.

GUMMOSIS (gum-oh'-sis). The formation and exudation of clear or amber-colored gums which harden into solid masses on the surface of affected parts. It is a common symptom on fruits affected with brown rot, but may also be caused by other disease-causing organisms and by nonparasitic causes such as growth in too heavy soils, winter injury or excessive pruning.

GUNNERA (gun'-er-ah). A genus of perennial herbs of the S. hemisphere, not reliably hardy N. The principal species is *G. manicata,* which has a stout creeping root-stock and huge lobed leaves to 6 ft. or more across, on prickly stems to 6 ft. high. The greenish flowers are borne in a dense tapering spike to 3 ft. long. It is a plant of majestic appearance and requires rich moist soil in a sheltered but sunny place. Propagated by seed and division.

GUZMANIA (guz-may'-ni-ah). A genus of tropical American herbs belonging to the Pineapple Family, a few of which are grown for ornament in the warm greenhouses thriving under the same treatment as billbergia. They have stiff erect leaves in basal rosettes, with the flowers usually surrounded by long showy bracts.

G. lingulata has leaves to 18 in. long, and dense drooping heads of yellow and purple flowers with red bracts. *G. tricolor* has rich green sword-shaped leaves to 18 in. long. The flower spike is longer than the leaves and is clothed with bracts of yellowish-green streaked with black, and the upper ones tinged red. The flowers are white.

GYMNOGRAMMA (jim'-noh-gram-ah). A genus of ferns, mostly from the tropics, whose fertile fronds are densely covered below with naked, brilliant yellow or orange fruit dots. Specimens with glistening whitish fruit dots are known as Silver Ferns. All the species are very ornamental and especially good in hanging baskets, where their showy undersides may be seen. They require light and a dryer atmosphere than most ferns. Use light, porous compost mostly of peat, leafmold, and coarse sand, pot loosely in small pots, and do not water from above, as this spoils the colored coating. The best known species are:

G. calomelanos with 1 to 3 ft. fronds, covered with white powder below, the stipes being polished black.

japonica (Bamboo Fern). An open once-pinnate form, requiring quantities of water.

sulphurea with 6 to 12 in. fronds, the pinnae far apart and covered with golden powder.

tartarea with 1 to 2 ft. fronds, nearly 2-pinnate, powdered snowy white below and dark dull green above.

triangularis (California Gold Fern). A small species, three branched, native to S. Calif. and of possible outdoor use there.

GYMNOSPERM (jim' - noh - spurm). This term (from Greek words meaning "naked seed") is applied to the large group of plants that produce seeds on the open surfaces of scales that go to make up a cone. The group is further distinguished from the flowering plants or *angiosperms* (which bear seeds inclosed in a case), by having evergreen, needle, scale- or fern-like leaves. The gymnosperms are a very ancient group represented today by cycads, yews, ginkgos and the conifers, like pine and spruce. See PLANT NAMES AND CLASSIFICATION.

GYMNOSPORIA (jim-noh-spoh'-ri-ah). A genus of leathery-leaved evergreen shrubs and trees of the Staff-tree Family, sometimes planted in the S. The two species most frequently seen are *G. cassinoides* from the Canary Isles, an erect shrub with small white flowers; and *G. serrata,* a spiny shrub from Abyssinia. They are propagated by seed or cuttings.

GYNURA (ji-neu'-rah) *aurantica.* A tropical member of the Composite Family, commonly known as Velvet-plant. A native of Java where it makes a branching shrubby plant to 3 ft., it is grown under glass as a pot plant for the purple velvet effect of the densely hairy foliage. The rather inconspicuous orange flower-heads consist of disk-flowers only, but the charm of the plant is in the purplish bloom on the soft green leaves. The Velvet-plant should be given rich potting soil, abundant moisture, and full sunlight to bring out the color of the foliage. It is increased by both cuttings and seed.

GYPSOPHILA (jip-sof'-i-lah). Babys Breath. Hardy annual and perennial herbs of the Pink Family, these airy plants are extremely graceful though devoid of conspicuous foliage. Bearing many tiny blossoms on delicate-appearing but sturdy, well-branched stalks, the plants when in flower produce a misty effect in the border or rock garden. They thrive in any soil

and almost any location and generally come into bloom in July, continuing through August. The plants are propagated by seeds sown in the open ground, by division and occasionally by cuttings. Gypsophila is fine for cut-flower mixtures.

G. elegans, a hardy annual growing 2 ft. tall, has been improved greatly in recent years. Paris Market is an especially good strain bearing large, single, pure white blossoms which come within 8 weeks from seed. The period of bloom is brief, so successive sowings are advised.

G. paniculata is one of the most interesting perennials, excellent as a border plant in masses, bearing white flowers on plants 3 ft. high. While the hybrids of this species are still unfixed, the plants bear a good proportion of double rose-shaped blossoms. Among the named doubles are Bristol Fairy and Ehrlei. If cut before flowers are fully open, the graceful sprays may be dried to use in winter bouquets.

G. repens is another excellent species, a perennial 6 in. tall (Creeping Gypsophila) bearing pale pink blossoms in June and July, and adapted to rock-garden use.

Other species in cultivation include:

G. acutifolia, a tall perennial, greatly branched, with larger white flowers than *G. paniculata; G. cerastioides* (Mouse-ear Gypsophila), a downy, creeping perennial to 4 in., bearing white flowers with pink veins; and *G. muralis,* an annual species to 1 ft. whose rose flowers are solitary and axillary.

GYPSUM. This material, known also as land-plaster, is chemically sulphate of lime. Containing some 23% of calcium oxide, it was formerly considered a satisfactory source of lime for soils. As a matter of fact it does serve to liberate unavailable potash, and in general improve a soil's texture or tilth. But, owing to its sulphur content, it tends to make soil acid and therefore has just the opposite effect of limestone or any of the carbonate forms of lime. Where this is not an objection it can be used, preferably in finely ground form. Gypsum forms up to 50% of most commercial acid phosphate (super-phosphate) fertilizers.

Gypsum is sometimes used as carrier for insecticide dusts. It is also mixed (as a "carrier") with calomel for use against the cabbage root maggot, and with calcium arsenate against the striped cucumber beetle. It has been recommended for dusting over iris rhizomes after soft rot and borers have been cut out.

GYPSY MOTH. Although this pest is more an enemy of forest and shade trees than of garden crops, it is worth special mention as an example of the successful prevention of long distance spread by quarantine enforcement and the maintenance of a barrier zone (which see). The

THE DANGEROUS GYPSY MOTH
A serious enemy of New England trees. Male, female and caterpillar are shown here from left to right. Destroy egg masses in winter and poison foliage in spring to control this pest.

gypsy moth was brought to Mass. in 1868 for experiments in silk worm raising and liberated by accident. By 1890 it had be come established and so destructive that the State began the work of extermination which has been in progress ever since, except for a period when, lulled by unjustified assumptions that it was beaten, the Legislature economized by failing to appropriate funds, and the pest got a fresh start.

The insect appears to be confined to New England and small areas in S. E. Canada

and N. J. Anyone finding an insect suspected of being this pest elsewhere than in those areas should immediately send it to the State entomologist.

The gypsy moth feeds on fruit and forest trees (including conifers) and attacks some garden plants and cranberries. Winter is passed in the egg stage, the oval egg masses, about 1 in. long, coated with hair and the color of chamois skin, are attached in sheltered spots to stones, buildings, stone walls, fences and tree trunks. The caterpillars hatch out about the end of April, feed voraciously and grow rapidly, being very hairy, dark colored, with blue tubercles on the front half of the body and red ones on the rear half. They form cocoons in July, from which moths begin to emerge within a month. The males are dark brown and less than an inch long; the light buff females with darker markings are heavy and able only to flutter along the ground. The spread of the insects has been largely due to the carrying of the young larvae long distances by wind currents.

Control by painting egg masses with crude creosote during winter and by banding trees in spring to prevent the caterpillars from climbing them. Examine bands daily, killing the trapped insects. Have trees sprayed with a strong mixture of arsenate of lead. Several insect parasites (see INSECTS, BENEFICIAL) are now established in the infested area and helping to keep the pest in check.

HABENARIA (ha-bee-nay'-ri-ah). A genus of hardy, native terrestrial orchids, popularly known as Fringed or Rein Orchis, having white, yellow, purple or orange blossoms with the lip of the flower often beautifully fringed and spurred. They grow on leafy stalks, the racemes or spikes of flowers sometimes reaching a height of 5 ft. The group includes some of our loveliest native orchids, nearly all of which may be easily naturalized on the edge of the bog garden in light shade, if given a strongly acid, peaty soil, kept constantly moist, but well drained.

See also ORCHID.

PRINCIPAL SPECIES

H. blephariglottis (White-fringed Orchis; Plume-of-Navarre) has feathery spires of pure white, fragrant blossoms with both petals and lip fringed. Growing in peat bogs and pine barrens, it often reaches 2 ft.

fimbriata (Large Purple-fringed Orchis) sometimes growing as high as 5 ft., has exceedingly beautiful loose racemes of lilac to white flowers, the petals toothed, and the 3-parted lip profusely fringed. An excellent species to plant on the edge of a pool or by a brook.

ciliaris (Yellow-fringed Orchis, Orange-fringe) is the only orange-colored orchid native to the N. E. States. It bears a handsome cluster of brilliant orange spurred flowers, the lip often compoundly fringed, on a leafy stalk, sometimes 30 in. tall. As it grows naturally in the open, the Orange-fringe may be naturalized in acid or sub-acid soil on the edge of a thicket in the wild garden and on hummocks in the open bog garden.

HABERLEA (ha-ber-lee'-ah). A genus of small, tufted perennial herbs with nodding blue or lilac flowers on stems 4 to 6 in. high. Natives of the Balkans, they can be grown in the rock garden with winter protection. Propagation is by seed or division. Only two species are known, *H. ferdinandi-coburgi* with dark blue irregularly-lobed flowers, and *H. rhodopensis* with pale lavender blossoms, 1 in. broad.

HABIT. In gardening, the manner of growth of a plant, whether tall, dwarf, upright, spreading, trailing, open, dense or otherwise. Also the artistic arrangement of parts, as the droop of the weeping willow, the vase-shape of the elm, the spear-head outline of a young spruce. Habit is the anatomy of plant form, a matter of utmost importance in ornamental trees, shrubs, vines and herbs, but its significance has been overshadowed by an undue emphasis on flower color. Where gardening has reached a more advanced stage, as in Japan, habit is given its rightful importance. The pattern of twig and leaf arrangement on the plant, easily seen but hard to define, is not habit but "texture," also a factor too much neglected in planning garden effects, especially of trees and shrubs.

HABITAT. The region where a plant grows naturally or is indigenous. (See INDIGEN.) The *habitat* of the persimmon is Conn. to Ia. and southward to the Gulf of Mexico; its *situation* is woods and fields. A particular spot where the persimmon is known to grow would, by botanists, be called a *station*. A plant can often be cultivated far from its habitat. Thus Oconee Bells, whose habitat is a small region in the Carolina mountains, is cultivated successfully in the N. E. States and also in Europe where it is an *exotic*.

See also ENDEMIC.

HACKBERRY. Common name for the genus Celtis, a member of the Elm Family, comprising species of trees with elm-like leaves and small cherry-like fruits. Hackberries (also called Nettle-trees) are planted as lawn or specimen subjects. Their rather wide-spreading boughs and light green foliage give them an airy, cheerful appearance, and as they are not particular as to soil they will thrive in almost any situation. They grow rapidly, especially when young; and, having a fibrous root-system, they are easily transplanted. They are propagated by seed and by layers and cuttings of ripened wood.

For the most part hackberries are free from diseases and insect pests. Of the occasional exceptions, the principal disease is a form of witches' broom (which see) with which are always associated two other organisms—a gall mite and a powdery mildew. The only control measure is to cut out the brooms and reshape the shrub. The hackberry is also a favorite host for jumping plant lice (psyllids) which cause deforming galls on foliage and twigs.

Principal species are as follows:

C. occidentalis to 120 ft. has shining green leaves, paler beneath, and orange-red to dark-purple fruit. This, the native species, is frequently planted in the E. and Middle W. States.

laevigata (Sugarberry; Mississippi Hackberry) to 120 ft. with long thin leaves and orange-red fruit becoming bluish-purple, is native in the S. and S. Central States and is occasionally planted there.

douglasi to 20 ft. is a small tree with brownish fruit, native to the W. States.

julianae to 80 ft. with yellowish green leaves, soft-hairy beneath, and brown fruit, is a Chinese tree much grown in Calif. It is not hardy N.

sinensis to 60 ft. with long, wavy-toothed leaves and orange fruit, is an Asiatic tree grown in mild climates.

australis to 80 ft. with grayish green leaves, soft-hairy beneath, and orange fruit, is suitable only for the S.

HACKMATACK. Colloquial American name for *Larix americana,* the American Larch (see LARCH). Though a member of the Pine Family and a conifer (cone-bearer) it is not an evergreen but sheds its leaves or needles in the fall.

HACKSAW FERN (Doodia lunulata). A small fern for the cool greenhouse, compact, liking shade, and excellent for edging. Fronds reddish when young.

HAEMANTHUS (hee-man'-thus). A genus of African bulbous plants of the Amaryllis Family with white or red lily-like flowers borne in compact heads on long stalks. See BLOOD-LILY; also SOUTH AFRICAN PLANTS.

HA-HA. The ejaculatory name given in England to a sunken, invisible fence or wall whose existence is unsuspected until it is reached. These structures came into use as a result of the vogue for natural effects developed early in the 19th century according to the theories of Humphrey Repton, the great landscape designer. Nothing was wanted in the landscape that might suggest man's interference; yet grazing herds had to be protected and confined. Where a deep ditch alone did not suffice, the barrier was erected in it out of sight of the dwelling or garden.

HAIRY ROOT. The excessive production of roots, especially on fruit trees, due to crown gall, which see.

HAKEA (hay'-ke-ah). Australian evergreen shrubs, belonging to the Protea Family, a few species of which are grown in Calif. for ornamental use. They are good drought resisters and can also stand a few degrees of frost. They are propagated by seeds and cuttings. The principal species are the following:

H. laurina (Sea Urchin) is a tall shrub or small tree with narrow leaves about 6 in. long, and round clusters of crimson flowers with showy yellow styles. It is the showiest of all in bloom.

elliptica is a shrub of compact habit with white flowers. The young growth opens a rich bronzy tone and is very showy.

suaveolens is a large shrub of rounded form with needle-like leaves and tiny white flowers, sweetly scented.

HALESIA (hay-lee'-zih-ah). Silverbell; Snowdrop-tree. Deciduous trees or large shrubs of N. America, valued for their handsome, drooping, bell-shaped, white flowers in early spring. They thrive in any well-drained soil, and in the N. appreciate a sheltered position. They are propagated by seed, best sown in the fall; also by layers and root-cuttings.

H. carolina is the best-known species. In a favorable climate it is a tree to 40 ft. with spreading branches, but in the N. it is usually a tall shrub. *H. monticola*

A PASTORAL EFFECT WITHOUT DANGER OF INVASION
In the days when cows and sheep were, from choice or of necessity, a part of the landscape, they were prevented from reaching the lawn by an arrangement known as a "ha-ha," the construction of which is pictured here.

grows to nearly 100 ft. in the S., and is hardy N. It has larger leaves and flowers. *H. diptera* is similar to *H. carolina,* but smaller and not so hardy.

HALF-HARDY PLANTS in a given climate are those injured by severe weather, or requiring special care part of the year. Plants which need a heated greenhouse in winter are called tender. But these terms are not used strictly, either of them being often applied to any condition short of complete hardiness. Annuals are half-hardy where they must be started indoors, not set outdoors until warm weather. Half-hardy perennials will live through some winters only to be killed by an unusually severe season. Or they may require special protection in the form of mulch, shade or wind-screen, or need to be wintered under glass in a cold frame. Such are certain Chinese primroses and encrusted saxifrages. Among woody plants and trees, those which kill to the ground but are root-hardy and spring up again, may be called half-hardy. Certain evergreens, as hollies and evergreen barberries, will shed their leaves during intense cold, but are otherwise not much injured. Judas-trees often have the ends of their branches killed. Azaleas may lose some or all of their flower buds. Heaths and other ericaceous plants sometimes have their stems split by the frost in late autumn or early winter, sub-zero temperatures occasionally reducing the wood to shreds. Any of these different types of injury may cause a plant to be described as half-hardy.

See also HARDY PLANTS.

HALIMODENDRON (hal-i-moh-den'-dron). A deciduous shrub from Central Asia, belonging to the Pea Family. See SALT-TREE.

HAMAMELIDACEAE (ham-ah-mel-i-day'-see-ee). Botanical name of the Witch-hazel Family, a group of trees and shrubs common to warm-temperate regions, and including a few ornamental genera, as Hamamelis and Corylopsis. Another, Liquidambar, is an ornamental hardwood of commercial importance. The flowers are in heads or spikes, usually with four strap-shaped petals; the fruit is a two-beaked woody capsule, borne singly or in heads, and opening at the summit to release two bony seeds

HAMAMELIS (ham-ah-mee'-lis) Witch-hazel. Hardy deciduous shrubs or small trees, native to N. America and Asia.

HALESIA, THE SILVERBELL
The pendent white flowers which cover the branches in spring make the Silverbell one of the loveliest of small hardy trees. A winged fruit is shown at the right.

They are of special interest because of their season of bloom, which is from late fall to early spring. The fragrant flowers with narrow wavy petals, are borne in clusters. Witch-hazels do well in sandy loam, and the native kinds can stand more shade and moisture than those from Asia. In habit they are vigorous and bushy, with good foliage which turns yellow and orange in the fall.

ENEMIES. Two species of plant lice that cause conspicuous galls on witch-hazel, have an alternate host, birch, on which they cause serious damage. A cone gall commonly occurs on the foliage and a spiny gall deforms the buds. There is no practical control for either.

Propagation is by seeds, which usually do not germinate until the second year, by layers, and also by grafting.

PRINCIPAL SPECIES

H. virginiana, which occurs from Canada to Fla., is a large shrub or tree to 25 ft. It is conspicuous, as the light yellow flowers appear while the leaves are falling.

vernalis, from the southern part of the country, grows to 6 ft., and opens its yellow petals from a dark red calix in winter.

japonica is a shrub or tree to 30 ft., with bright yellow petals and purplish calyx. In var. *flavo-purpurascens* the petals are reddish and rise from a deep purple calyx.

mollis, another Asiatic shrub or tree to 30 ft., is the showiest of all the witchhazels. The leaves are grayish-white beneath, and the flowers have golden yellow petals from a purplish red calyx.

HAMAMELIS, THE WITCH-HAZEL
The yellow flowers (at the right) and the hardshelled fruits (left) which shoot out their seeds like bullets from a gun, are both to be seen on the trees in autumn.

HAMELIA (hah-mee'-li-ah). Evergreen shrubs of tropical and subtropical America, belonging to the Madder Family. One or two are grown in Florida for their showy flowers and dark-colored berries. If the tops are cut down by frost, the plants sprout readily again from below. Propagation is from seed and by cuttings of halfripened wood. *H. erecta* (Scarlet-bush) is a large shrub with long leaves usually in 3s; and with branching clusters of bright orange-red flowers produced over a long season. These are followed by attractive dark berries, also very lasting. *H. sphaerocarpa* is a smaller grower with very hairy leaves and large clusters of orangeyellow flowers.

HANGING BASKETS. Hanging baskets tastefully filled with handsome thrifty foliage and flowering plants contribute to the adornment of a window or the decoration of any room.

Baskets are available in different forms and of various materials such as wire, willow or wickerwork, terra cotta and wood covered with bark, knots, etc. The wire and wicker baskets are more generally used because more easily cared for; when watering is needed, they can be plunged into the water and allowed to drain off before being put back in place. They should be lined with a thick layer of moss over which should be placed a layer of burlap or other coarse material to prevent the soil from working through. If wood, metal, or terra cotta containers are used, drainage holes must be provided. If rustic, earthenware or bark-covered baskets are obtainable containing an inner plant basin properly providing for drainage, they will be suitable.

The soil should be one-half loam, onequarter sand, and one-quarter well decayed leafmold or humus, the whole thoroughly mixed together. It should be pressed firmly around the roots so that no settling or washing out will occur.

PLANT MATERIALS. Basket effects may be made up exclusively of flowering plants, of foliage plants, or combinations of the two. In arranging the subjects in a basket, while most of the suitable plants are dwarf in growth, the center or upright plant should be the tallest, the next outer ones shorter, and the marginal ones of a trailing or drooping habit. Do not crowd the material together too closely.

For the taller growing, upright, center plants, suitable subjects of the flowering type are geranium, fuchsia, begonia, lantana and swainsona. Lower growing flowering subjects are *Primula obconica, Bellis perennis, Phlox drummondi* and dwarf alyssum. Trailing or drooping flowering plants include lobelia, *Fuchsia procumbens,* oxalis and sweet alyssum.

Desirable erect foliage plants (in addition to the smaller ferns and palms) are croton, dusty miller, coleus and *Dracaena indivisa.* For drooping foliage effects *Vinca minor,* wandering Jew, *Saxifraga sarmentosa,* English ivy, and smilax are all satisfactory. Other suitable subjects will often present themselves or a florist can be consulted, as he will usually have in stock appropriate plants for the purpose as well as ready-made arrangements.

WATERING, FEEDING, ETC. Baskets containing flowering subjects will need a sunny exposure as close to the glass as possible;

foliage-plant collections do not require or want direct sunlight. Baskets containing foliage plants exclusively may well hang at the north or shady side of the room. Watering must be attended to with care. In ordinary house temperatures (about 70 deg. in the day time and some 10 deg. less at night), baskets may be watered every second or third day if the plants are actively growing. Overwatering, so as to keep the soil in a saturated condition, is to be avoided; but, on the other hand, it should never be allowed to become bone dry. Free circulation of fresh air is as necessary as sufficient water, but this does *not* mean direct cold drafts which are distinctly harmful.

As soon as the plants in a newly arranged basket are well established and growing, the basket should be fed once each month by either dipping it in or watering it with weak liquid manure. Complete balanced fertilizers containing all the necessary plant foods can be bought in convenient form and small packages; the directions on or in the package should be closely followed.

If all faded flowers, dead leaves, etc., are kept removed and if the foliage is sprayed with clear warm water every few days, using a rubber syringe with a very fine spray, enemies—particularly red spider—should be prevented. For special control measures see under HOUSE PLANTS.

HARBINGER-OF-SPRING. Common name of *Erigenia bulbosa,* a tuberous-rooted, almost stemless, white-flowered herbaceous perennial, native in open deciduous woods from the Mississippi River eastward, blooming among the first of the spring flowers.

HARBOURIA (hahr-boo'-ri-ah). An American perennial herb of the N. Rocky Mountains, growing 1 to 2 ft. tall, with deeply cut leaves and little yellow flowers in long-stemmed clusters; it is suitable for a sunny spot in the rock garden.

HARDENBERGIA (hahr-den-bur'-ji-ah). Twining herbaceous or shrubby vines of Australia, belonging to the Pea Family. They are sometimes trained over rafters and pillars in the greenhouse; they are also grown outdoors in the warmest parts of the country. They like a peaty and well-drained soil, and under glass do better in a prepared border or solid bed than in pots. Propagation is by seeds or cuttings of young growth.

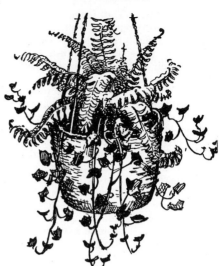

FOR A HANGING BASKET ·
Boston Ferns and English Ivy are two dependable subjects.

H. comptonia has 3 to 5 leaflets and small blue or violet flowers borne in a long raceme. *H. monophylla,* usually with but one leaflet, has rosy purple flowers.

HARDENING-OFF. The practice of "toughening" young plants started indoors or under glass, so as to accustom them to outdoor, open-air conditions, especially when these involve lower temperatures. It consists mainly of reducing the amount of water supplied and gradually increasing the ventilation until the plants (while still in hotbeds or coldframes) are open to the sky and entirely unprotected—except when the weather is unfavorable. This may be done with seedlings in flats or beds, with pot plants or with rooted cuttings, grafted plants, etc.

HARD FERN (*Lomaria spicant*). A small fern hardy in mild sections of the U. S. though not native. The bright green, rigid, comb-like fronds are fine for cutting. Prefers a gravel soil.

HARDHACK. A common name for *Spiraea tomentosa,* a low deciduous shrub of E. U. S. with rose or purple flowers in spire-like clusters.

HARDHEADS. A common name for *Centaurea nigra,* a perennial herb of Europe, naturalized in the U. S. A rather coarse relative of the familiar corn-flower, it bears reddish-purple flower-heads and is sometimes called Knapweed. See CENTAUREA.

HARDPAN. The name given to a layer of impervious soil sometimes found (and sometimes created) just below the surface or top-soil. It is usually composed largely of clay or other fine-textured soil which has become compacted or "puddled" until its particles are practically cemented together. This condition is sometimes brought about by plowing year after year to just the same depth. It may also be a result of poor drainage; or the presence of a large amount of alkali salts may be to blame. In any hardpan condition there is sure to be a lack of humus and of coarse soil particles (sand).

To remedy the condition, sub-soiling with a special plow may be enough to break up the formation. Dynamite may have to be resorted to (see BLAST). Or it may prove necessary to install tile drains or otherwise provide for the removal of the surplus water. When the hardpan has once been broken up, sand or sifted ashes can be worked into it to prevent further compacting, and as rapidly as possible generous quantities of humus should be incorporated both to improve the physical condition and to promote aeration of the soil and the other factors that constitute fertility, which see.

HARDY PLANTS are those which live and thrive in a given climate. The word hardy is most often used to mean capable of enduring cold, but as there is no word to signify ability to live through heat, wet or drought, all these conditions are sometimes included under the one word. Thus a plant hardy in Labrador, which will usually die of heat in Fla. or of drought in Ariz., may be called "not hardy" in those warmer climates.

In practice, however, writers speaking of hardy plants commonly mean those which survive the winter in the N. States and perhaps S. Canada. Plants not hardy are called half-hardy (which see) or tender. Hardy annuals are those of which seed may be sown early in the open ground, the seedlings being able to withstand spring frosts, like peas or poppies, as opposed to half-hardy and tender annuals like tomatoes or zinnias, which must be started indoors, or if outdoors, not sown till danger of frost is past. Hardy perennials such as columbine or rhubarb die to the ground in winter, but the roots remain alive to put up new growth year after year. Trees and other woody plants are hardy when the entire growth remains alive through the winter. Woody plants are so variously affected by climate that special types of hardiness are often mentioned. A plant is bud-hardy when the flower buds formed in summer or autumn to bloom the following spring pass through the winter uninjured; root-hardy when the upper part of the plant winter-kills but not the roots.

The accompanying "Hardiness Map of the U. S." is reproduced from the *Bulletin of Popular Information* of the Arnold Arboretum (Ser. 4, Vol. VIII, No. 12), having previously appeared in a book on Hedges by Donald Wyman and, in enlarged form, in the second (1940) edition of Alfred Rehder's "Manual of Cultivated Trees and Shrubs." After much study, the areas were designated on the basis of the average annual minimum temperatures as reported by the U. S. Weather Bureau. As the *Bulletin* explains, a map of such a large area cannot indicate the inevitable variations that are sure to occur within narrow territorial limitations. But the relationships of different parts of the country is brought out. The following lists of woody plants hardy in the different zones (with the exception of the Canadian Zone, No. 1) indicate in general the type of such vegetation that can be expected within the temperature ranges noted.

ZONE 2	ZONE 6
Acer negundo	Berberis buxifolia
Caragana arborescens	Bignonia capreolata
Cornus alba	Ilex crenata
Juniperus virginiana	Myrica cerifera
Prunus virginiana	Taxus baccata

ZONE 3	ZONE 7
Euonymus alata	Abelia triflora
Ligustrum amurense	Ilex cornuta
Lonicera tartarica	Prunus laurocerasus
Philadelphus coronarius	Pyracantha crenato-
Pinus strobus	serrata
	Quercus virginiana

ZONE 4	ZONE 8
Abies concolor	Euonymus japonica
Betula populifolia	Ligustrum japonicum
Juniperus chinensis	Melia azedarach
Ligustrum vulgare	Myrtus communis
Tsuga canadensis	Pittosporum tobira

ZONE 5	ZONE 9
Abelia grandiflora	Berberis darwini
Berberis tricanthophora	Cinnamomum
Ilex opaca	camphora
Pieris japonica	Cotoneaster pannosa
Taxus cuspidata	Nerium oleander
	Raphiolepis umbellata

ZONE 10

Bougainvillea spectabilis	Musa sapientum
Cocos nucifera	Roystona regia
Hibiscus rosa-sinensis	

Plate 26.

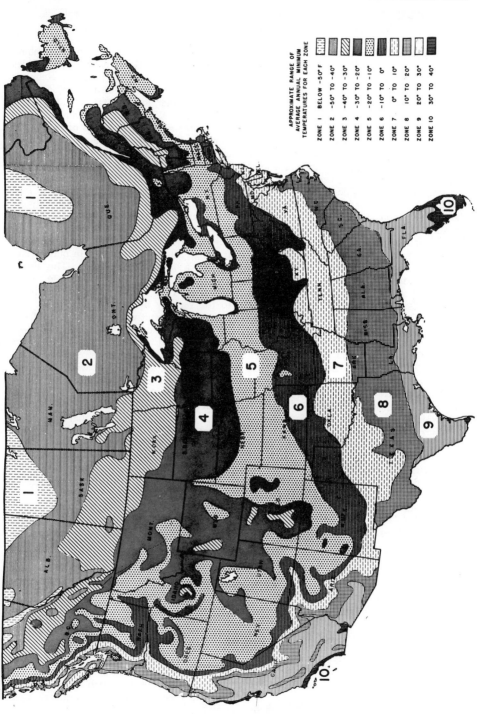

APPROXIMATE RANGE OF
AVERAGE ANNUAL MINIMUM
TEMPERATURES FOR EACH ZONE

ZONE 1   BELOW -50° F
ZONE 2   -50° TO -40°
ZONE 3   -40° TO -30°
ZONE 4   -30° TO -20°
ZONE 5   -20° TO -10°
ZONE 6   -10° TO 0°
ZONE 7   0° TO 10°
ZONE 8   10° TO 20°
ZONE 9   20° TO 30°
ZONE 10 30° TO 40°

HAREBELL (sometimes incorrectly spelled Hairbell). A common name for *Campanula rotundifolia,* also called Bluebell or Bluebell of Scotland, although one of the most cosmopolitan of all Campanulas. It is a slender perennial 1 to 2 ft. tall, with delicate blue flowers slightly drooping in loose racemes. There are varities with white and more or less double flowers.

HARES-FOOT FERN (*Davallia canariensis*). A cool greenhouse or indoor fern, having broad fronds about a foot long and furry rhizomes. Best grown in peat and sand in shallow, wide pots.

HARES-TAIL GRASS or RABBIT-TAIL GRASS. Common names for *Lagurus ovatus,* an annual grass grown for ornament in gardens and pots, but chiefly cultivated for winter bouquets. A native of the Mediterranean region and California, it prefers a warm location and well-drained soil. Reaching a height of 1 ft., it is soft and pubescent, with leaves 4 in. long and less than ½ in. wide. The spikelets have dense woolly heads, 2 in. long and rather broad. See ORNAMENTAL GRASSES; EVERLASTINGS.

HARICOT. Common name (derived from the French) for the kidney bean, *Phaseolus vulgaris.* See BEAN.

HARLEQUIN BUG. Common name for a sucking insect (*Murgantia histrionica*) which feeds on the sap of plants so that they wilt, turn brown and die. Also called fire bug or calico bug, it is especially injurious to crucifers and plants of the Nightshade Family in the S. It is gaudy, red- and black-spotted, about ⅜ in. long, flat and shield-shaped, and, on account of its unpleasant odor, included in the so-called "stink bug" group. The insects in all stages of development are found on plants by the dozen from early spring to winter. Tiny, white, black-banded eggs are laid in packets on the under side of the leaves.

There is no satisfactory spray or dust and the most effective control measures are the destruction of adults in the fall and spring by hand-picking, and the use of trap crops, such as mustard, kale, turnip or radish, which are planted early, then sprayed with kerosene and burned after the insects have congregated on them. See also CRUCIFERS.

HARLEQUIN-FLOWER. A common name for Sparaxis, a S. African genus of delicate spring-blooming herbs of the Iris Family with yellow and purple flowers. They are also called Wand-flowers.

HARTFORD FERN (*Lygodium palmatum*). The only N. American climbing fern, now rare. Bears palm-shaped blades at intervals on twining rachids. Requires rich acid soil of porous texture, and the shade of other low plants.

HARTS-THORN. A common name for *Rhamnus cathartica,* one of the Buckthorns. A widely distributed hardy deciduous shrub of the temperate zone with small greenish flowers and black fruits.

HARTS TONGUE FERN. Common name for *Phyllitis scolopendrium,* a fern found frequently in Europe but only at three known "stations" in the U. S. and in Ontario. The name comes from the unique, entire, tongue-like fronds, 1 to 2 ft. long, which vary greatly in outline and are of a glossy rich green. The linear indusia are in parallel rows oblique to the mid-rib. This fern is a distinct addition to the rockery or fern collection, but few persons have cultivated it successfully out of doors. The soil should be light—2 parts leafmold or peat, 1 part loam, 1 part sand; and the plants require a damp atmosphere and good shade, with protection in winter. A small quantity of lime and broken oyster shells have been found useful.

HARVESTING GARDEN CROPS. Strictly speaking, the term harvest means to gather ripened grain. Here it applies to gathering garden products—fruit, vegetables, flowers—primarily for immediate use, but in some cases for canning or other processing (or for storage), or for curing in preparation for later replanting.

GATHERING FRUIT. Apart from differences in varieties, one of the reasons why fruit bought in the stores and markets is disappointing is that it is picked before it has developed the essential or volatile oils upon which its characteristic flavor and pleasing texture (when ripe) depend. One of the most important reasons why every gardener should grow fruit is so he may have the choicest varieties at hand and select the individual specimens at the correct stage of their development.

This perfect stage can be recognized only after much observation and experiment for it varies more or less with every species. But the time and study required are well worth while.

In general, fruits, especially tree fruits, have a "green as grass" look until they reach the cooking stage; it then gives way to a more or less distinct color development characteristic of the variety, succeeded somewhat later in many cases by a waxy finish, polish or "bloom," that reaches a climax of beauty and then begins to wane.

One cannot be too careful when gathering apples, pears, cherries, plums and apricots. The stubby twigs or "spurs" which bear the fruit must not be broken because this would reduce the productivity of the trees; they should be removed only when they have become too numerous or too antiquated to produce good specimens. The proper way to gather apples is to give the fruit stems a twist instead of a pull. They will then separate from the spurs without breaking them. For home use and immediate consumption, plums, cherries and apricots may be gathered without stems by bending them to one side and giving them a slight pull. But if the fruit must be kept for several days or is to be sold, the stems must be left attached to the fruit and in picking bent so as to break loose from the spurs.

Pears should never be allowed to ripen on the tree because it injures their quality to do so, fruit of early varieties becoming "flat" or decaying at the core, and that of late varieties tending to become gritty as well as flavorless. The exact stage of development at which pears should be gathered is when the fruit stem and the spur will part company when the fruit is lifted upward and outward. If it is not mature enough, either its stem or the spur will break before they will separate.

To ripen pears and develop their choicest flavor store them where the atmosphere is still and the temperature uniformly mild. Examine early varieties every two or three days and remove the ripe ones for immediate consumption lest they spoil and induce spoilage of others. Late varieties must be handled as carefully as eggs, stored like apples, kept cold (just above freezing) until a week or two before needed and then brought into a living-room temperature and watched like early varieties.

Peaches for preserving whole or in halves should be gathered when their flesh will "give" somewhat when pressed with the fleshy part of the thumb while being held in the hand—*not* the tip of the thumb because that would bruise the fruit. For slicing they should be somewhat softer;

and for eating out of hand softer yet. Nectarines should be similarly treated.

For culinary purposes all tree fruits should be fully ripe but firm, and never "dead ripe" because when "mushy" they will not only break down but will have lost much of their characteristic flavor.

Grapes will not ripen when once removed from the vines so must always be allowed to become fully ripe before being gathered. It is advisable to delay picking a cluster until its slowest-ripening berries are mature. Indeed, the fruit of many varieties may be allowed to remain on the vines for a few days or even for several weeks, except when frost might injure or birds steal it, or unless the varieties are such as "shell" or "shatter," that is, drop their berries prematurely.

Currants and gooseberries, though often harvested for stewing and canning a month before they are really mature, are superior for dessert when they are "dead ripe." They make the best jelly and jam when mid-way between these two extremes. Raspberries, blackberries, loganberries and dewberries should be so ripe that they will separate from their stems with the slightest touch. If they must be "picked" they are not mature enough and have not attained the perfection of flavor characteristic of full ripeness.

Strawberries of most varieties are naturally some tint of red, the color being evenly distributed all over the fruit when

HARVESTING BEANS
To be at their best, string beans should always be gathered when young and tender. When they are picked at frequent intervals, the bearing season is prolonged.

it is ready for use. However, some varieties have light colored or even greenish tips when ripe.

To assure the finest flavor of muskmelons never wait until the fruits separate from the vines because at that stage they are usually "mushy" and "flat." Conversely, never cut them from the vines because they are not then mature enough to ripen and will not develop flavor. Always wait until cracks begin to show around the attachment of the fruit at the stem. It will then continue to develop flavor for two or three days when placed in a glass-covered cold-frame or on a sunny window-sill; but it may be stored in a cold cellar or a refrigerator for a week or longer. Since the blossom end of the fruit ripens first, it is desirable to turn the stem end toward the sun. A shingle or other small board placed under a melon will promote even ripening and tend to keep the fruit clean.

Watermelons advertise their maturity by the following signs: Disappearance of the "green as grass" look and of the whitish bloom; hardening of the rind which at maturity can be dented by the finger nail only with difficulty; blackening and drying of the tendril on the vine just opposite the fruit stem; development of a creamy color on the under side; a distinct, almost tinny "pink" when fillipped with the finger, instead of a thuddy "plunk" given out when green. To learn to recognize mature specimens while growing on the vines and to verify these color differences at a glance, "plug" a few specimens after testing and judging them by cutting out a pyramidal piece about an inch square at its base (the outside). If the flesh at the apex of the piece is whitish the fruit is not ripe and the plug should be replaced; if it is red or orange, taste it as "the proof of the pudding."

Little need be said concerning vegetables beyond that, in general, the younger the product, the more tender and delicious it is. Early root crops (carrots, radishes, beets) may be gathered as soon as they have reached edible size, while they are of much finer texture and flavor than after they have survived the high summer temperatures. Best also for canning. Late root crops can be allowed to remain in the ground until late autumn before being harvested, and some (parsnips and salsify) are improved after experiencing freezing weather. See STORING OF CROPS.

To attain their best flavor, tomatoes· should be allowed to mature on the plants; however, they may be ripened indoors if gathered any time after they have begun to turn pink. Peppers and egg-plants may be gathered and used whenever they are large enough. Pea pods should be well filled out but still bright green and crisp, but string beans are delicious in the earliest stages of development.

Sweet corn is ready when the silks have become black down to the point where they emerge from the ears. Never, if possible, should corn be gathered longer than a few minutes before it can be placed in the kettle; and the ears should be steam cooked, not "boiled" in water.

Summer squash is always best when gathered before its rind becomes hard; winter varieties to be stored are harvested after that stage has been attained.

The salad crops (lettuce, pepper-grass, endive) should always be gathered as near the time they are to be used as possible so they may be plump and crisp. Brussels sprouts and kale are not injured by freezing weather, but cabbage and cauliflower should be harvested before the ground freezes. If early cabbage is cut just below the head rather than broken or pulled up, so that several leaves are left on the stump, new, small, loose heads will form and may be cut and used as greens.

Cut flowers (which see) for gifts or use in the house should be gathered just as the buds are preparing to open and preferably in the early morning while the plants are cool and full of sap or in the cool of the evening. They should immediately be plunged deep in cold water and left in a cool place for a couple of hours before being arranged in containers. For winter bouquets, flowers should be gathered when the buds are beginning to open and hung heads downward in an airy, warm room, preferably out of strong sunlight, until dry. If too mature they will break apart and if stood to ripen "right end up" they will usually dry in crooked forms. See EVERLASTINGS.

Hardy bulbs, as tulips, if not left in the ground from year to year, should be dug when the tops die down, shaken free of soil and stored in a cool, dry, airy place. Tender sorts (gladiolus, dahlia, etc.), are dug when the tops are killed by the first frost, dried in the sun for a few hours, then stored in a frost-free place either loose in trays, or buried in peat moss, buckwheat hulls or similar material.

HARVESTMEN. Another name for the harmless long-legged insects better known as Daddy-long-legs, which see.

HASTATE. Halberd-shaped; said of a triangular leaf whose pointed basal lobes spread sideways. Compare SAGITTATE.

HAULM. Strictly speaking, straw-like stalks of grass plants such as wheat or rye; less correctly, the stalks of any sort of cultivated crops from which seeds or pods are harvested, such as peas and buckwheat. The term is often used loosely for straw and litter and may also apply to the trunks or boles of large palms.

HAUSTORIA (hau-stoh'-ri-ah). Specialized root-like sucking organs by means of which certain of the higher plant parasites, such as dodder and mistletoe and certain fungi, such as rusts and mildews, obtain their food from the tissues of the host plants on which they live.

HAW. A common name for the fruit of the Hawthorn (Crataegus). Blackhaw is a common name for *Viburnum prunifolium* and *V. rufidulum.* Possum-haw is *Ilex decidua.*

HAWKSBEARD. Common name for hardy herbs of the genus Crepis, a few species of which are sparingly grown in borders for their red, yellow or orange flower-heads. The plants thrive in light loams and should be fully exposed to the sun. Some species are widely distributed weeds.

HAWKWEED. Common name for hardy, perennial herbs of the genus Hieracium, bearing red, yellow or orange flowers in heads on slender erect stalks above flat rosettes of leaves. Some of the species have become very bad weeds in the E. States, but a few are attractive in the border. They are easily grown from seed, and increased by division of the rooting stem.

H. aurantiacum (Orange Hawkweed or Devils Paint-brush) has deep orange to flame-colored flowers. A bad weed.

venosum (Rattlesnake-weed), with bright yellow flowers, is also a troublesome weed.

villosum (Shaggy Hawkweed) to 2 ft., with golden yellow flowers and silvery white foliage, is the most desirable form for the border.

HAWORTHIA (hau-wur'-thi-ah). A genus of 60 species of S. African succulents, with thick leaves often dotted with tubercles, spotted, veined, or margined in white, red or brown; the leaves form rosettes which are sometimes rectangular instead of round. The small white or greenish lily-like flowers are borne in a loose spire on a naked stalk.

Haworthias submit to the general culture advised for succulent plants indoors, requiring a porous sandy loam with perfect drainage, ample sun, warmth and moisture during the growing period, and plenty of fresh air with freedom from draughts. They may be propagated by seeds, offsets, or cuttings.

HAWTHORN. Common name for small trees or shrubs of the Rose Family included in the genus Crataegus. They have attractive, white, pink, or ocasionally red, flowers, usually clustered, followed by small, decorative apple-like fruits; in some species these remain on the branches until midwinter, in others they are juicy enough to be made into jelly. The branches are spiny, and the deciduous foliage often turns brilliant red or orange in the fall. Of generally small size, often branching horizontally, and frequently showing symmetrical, flat-topped forms, the various hawthorns are most valuable in the shrubbery border, where their distinct planes carry up from the lower shrubs to the trees in the background. Their abundant flowers render them excellent lawn specimens, and some species make fine hedges.

Hawthorns grow readily in almost any soil, even in limey clay and thrive in open woodlands or exposed, sunny locations. If properly handled, they readily develop a fibrous root system, and when properly root-trimmed, are easily transplanted. Almost all species endure trimming, and if cut back when reset, become established quickly. In pruning, however, care should be taken to preserve the rugged character of the tree, for when leafless, the widespread, thorny branches are most picturesque in effect.

All American hawthorns come true from seed, which should be rubbed free from the pulp or separated by soaking the fruit in water until the flesh has decayed. Sow the seed in flats and keep there in a cool cellar or shade house for two years, watering them occasionally, as germination does not take place until the second spring, or sometimes the third. Transplant the seedlings within a year to encourage the formation of a fibrous root system. Rare varieties are grafted on seedling stock of the English Hawthorn, *C. oxyacantha.*

ENEMIES. The most prevalent leaf disease of hawthorn is a fungous leaf spot. The small reddish-brown spots may cover the leaves which turn yellow and drop off, sometimes until the plant is completely defoliated. Where the disease persists, the shrubs should be sprayed with bordeaux mixture several times, beginning as the young leaves form.

Several of the apple and juniper rust fungi attack this host. (See JUNIPER; also RUSTS and RUST FUNGI.) Fire blight (which see) causes twig blight and canker; prune out diseased parts.

A lace bug if abundant may turn the leaves yellow or stippled white by sucking out the plant juices. Spray thoroughly with a contact insecticide such as nicotine and soap.

Nicotine will also control the woolly apple aphid; and red spider injury may be prevented by dormant spraying with a miscible oil or controlled during the summer with a sulphur spray. Remove and burn twigs infested with the thorn limb borer.

PRINCIPAL SPECIES

C. oxyacantha, the Hawthorn or May of English literature (and the plant for which the ship Mayflower was named) grows to 15 ft., forming a bush or small tree. Its white flowers are followed by bright red fruit. Var. *pauli* has bright scarlet, double flowers and is the form most frequently seen in the U. S. It is an exceedingly showy plant and valuable for the small garden as it never becomes very large.

mollis, native to the Middle W., is a handsome species with short, stiff thorns, glossy leaves and small, scarlet, pear-shaped fruit, which, unfortunately, drop soon after ripening in August. It is the State flower of Mo.

crus-galli (Cockspur Thorn) has widespread, rigid, often drooping, branches, covered with long thorns. The showy flowers are followed by small, round, dry-fleshed, red fruits, often remaining on the tree all winter; the glossy leaves take on brilliant autumn coloration. The Cockspur thorn sometimes reaches 40 ft., but can be kept bushy by pruning, and if the plants are close-set as a hedge, the long sharp thorns produce an almost impenetrable barrier.

phaenopyrum (Washington Thorn) to 30 ft., a native of the S. States, has slender thorns and flowers in dense clusters, succeeded by lustrous, coral-like fruits which remain on the branches into midwinter. It makes an excellent hedge.

tomentosa is somewhat shrubby in growth, occasionally becoming a small tree; it bears clustered white flowers and dull yellow or orange, edible fruit.

rivularis, of the W. States, has spines 1½ in. long and red fruits that turn shiny black.

punctata (Dotted Haw), a small, wide-limbed tree to 30 ft., sometimes almost spineless; bears pear-shaped, dotted fruit.

India-hawthorn is *Raphiolepis indica,* and Yeddo-hawthorn, *R. umbellata;* Water-hawthorn is *Aponogeton distachyus.*

HAY-SCENTED FERN (*Dennstedtia punctilobula*). A graceful pale green, delicately cut American fern, common in pastures and rocky open woods; best for naturalizing because of its rampant habit. Also known as Boulder Fern, which see.

HAZEL, HAZELNUT. Common names for Corylus, a genus of hardy, deciduous shrubs or trees, native in N. America, Europe and Asia, and related to the birches. Other common names are Filbert and Cobnut. Several species are sometimes grown for their ornamental foliage, which in some kinds is colored, while in others it turns yellow or red in the fall. The golden-yellow male flowers in pendulous catkins are also attractive in early spring. Filberts have long been cultivated, especially in Europe, for their edible nuts. They thrive in any good well-drained soil and are propagated by seed, suckers, layers, budding and grafting.

ENEMIES. Two leaf spot diseases may be controlled by spraying with bordeaux mixture, first when the leaves are full grown and then two weeks later. Destroy infected leaves in the fall.

A small mite causes a bud gall and aphids may infest the leaves; a nicotine-soap-molasses solution spray will destroy the crawling mites. Nuts infested with the hazelnut weevil fall early; they should be destroyed.

PRINCIPAL SPECIES

C. colurna (Turkish Hazel) is a S. European tree sometimes growing to 80 ft., and forming a handsome pyramidal head.

chinensis (Chinese Hazel) grows to 100 ft. or more, and forms a broad oval head, with leaves 6 to 7 in. long.

maxima (Filbert) grows to 30 ft. and has many varieties grown for the large nuts. Var. *purpurea* is an ornamental form with dark purple leaves. Removing a portion of the old growth each spring induces young growth which produces larger and better colored leaves.

avellana (European Hazelnut; Cobnut) is a bushy shrub to 15 ft., occurring in many varieties and long cultivated for its nuts. Distinctive forms are *aurea*, with yellow leaves; *heterophylla*, with divided leaves; and *contorta*, with twisted and curled branches.

sieboldiana (Japanese Hazelnut) is a large bush to 15 ft., with the young leaves often marked reddish in the middle. The nuts are enclosed in a bristly constricted involucre.

cornuta (Beaked Hazelnut) is a native shrub to 10 ft., conspicuous in fruit with the bristly involucre constricted above the nut to form a long beak.

americana is the common native Hazelnut.

Other plants to which the name Hazel is applied are Chilean-hazel, *Gevuina avellana;* Winter-hazel, Corylopsis; Witch-hazel, Hamamelis; Victorian-hazel, *Pomaderris apetala.*

HEAD. A term sometimes applied to any dense flower cluster or inflorescence (which see), but generally used to refer particularly to the type found in members of the Composite Family (which see), and in clovers and a few other plants. Here many small florets without pedicels (flower stalks) are crowded together in a compact, rounded, either conical, or flattish, cluster. In the Composites a head may consist of (1) two kinds of florets—disk florets in the center with ray florets bordering them, as in most asters; the common daisy; or (2) all ray (strap-shaped) florets, as in the zinnia; or (3) all disk florets, as in Linosyris.

HEAL-ALL. Common name for *Prunella vulgaris,* commonly called Self-heal, which see. It is a low, hardy, and rather weedy herbaceous perennial with purple flowers in blunt spikes.

HEART ROT. Rot of the heartwood of a tree caused by various wood destroying fungi, mainly of the Basidiomycete or mushroom group. Their presence in apparently sound trees is frequently known by the appearance of bracket fungi which are the fruiting bodies of the fungus growing within. Infection usually takes place through wounds, such as broken branch stubs. Heart rots weaken a tree and render its timber of little value.

See also FUNGUS; TREE SURGERY.

HEARTSEASE. Old-fashioned name for *Viola tricolo* var. *hortensis,* the Pansy, which see.

TWO NATIVE HAZELNUTS
The common American hazel, Corylus americana, is at the left; the beaked hazelnut, C. cornuta, at the right.

HEART-SEED. Popular name for the genus Cardiospermum, so called from the heart-shaped white spot on each seed. Tropical herbaceous climbers, one species, *C. helicacabum,* is the popular Balloon-vine.

HEATH or HEATHER. Often used interchangeably, these names strictly refer to two distinct, but closely allied genera, namely, Erica (Heath) and Calluna (Heather). Both are members of the Heath Family (Ericaceae, which see), and are frequently confused, though they can be distinguished by flower as well as foliage characters. Heaths have needle-like or very narrow leaves, usually in whorls and spread apart; those of Heathers are shorter, overlapping and scale-like. The flower of the Heather has a colored calyx that is longer than the corolla; also at the base of the calyx are 4 small green bracts that at first glance might be mistaken for the calyx itself.

Both genera require lime-free soil and thrive where there is plenty of leafmold or peat. In general, the Heathers are the hardier, although, as noted below, several species of Erica do well N. if given a sheltered position. Several Ericas are excellent pot plants, holding their flowers well and much grown by florists for Christmas and Easter.

Heaths in pots do best when firmly potted in fibrous peat and coarse sand. To keep them shapely, trim back after flowering. The soft-wooded kinds are easier to grow than the hard-wooded ones, but any of them call for considerable attention.

Heathers should be sheared in spring to keep them compact and well furnished with flowering shoots; rabbits sometimes do all the pruning needed. Plants of both groups are propagated by cuttings of young shoots rooted under glass, and by layers.

HEATH (ERICA) SPECIES

E. carnea (Spring Heath) grows about a foot high, with leaves in 4's and reddish flowers in early spring.

vagans (Cornish Heath) grows to 1 ft. or more, with leaves in 4's or 5's and pinkish flowers in summer.

tetralix (Cross-leaved Heath) has grayish leaves in 4's and rose flowers.

cinera (Twisted Heath) is a twisted and much branched little shrub with leaves in 3's and rosy-purple flowers.

stricta (Corsican Heath) has stiff branches with leaves in 4's and is usually more upright. The flowers are rosy-purple.

The foregoing are the hardiest kinds and with the exception of *E. carnea* flower in summer. They stand fairly well N. and are well placed in sunny positions in the rock garden or on well-drained slopes. Evergreen boughs placed over them in winter will keep the foliage in good condition. The following kinds thrive only in mild regions or under cool greenhouse conditions:

E. arborea (Tree Heath) grows to 20 ft. in favored climates. It has leaves in 3's and bears an abundance of white fragrant flowers in spring. Several forms are grown.

mediterranea grows to 10 ft., has leaves in 4's or 5's and red flowers in spring. Several forms of this are grown in mild regions.

lusitanica (Spanish Heath) grows to 12 ft., with leaves from 3 to 5 in a whorl and pink flowers in early spring.

melanthera is a good species to grow in pots for winter bloom. It has leaves in 3's and bears a profusion of pinkish flowers with conspicuous black anthers.

hyemalis is a hybrid with leaves in 4's and rosy-pink flowers, tipped white. It is one of the easiest and most popular for pot culture.

cavendishiana is also a hybrid, with showy yellow flowers almost an inch long.

ventricosa has leaves in 4's and pink flowers with a swollen tube. There are several good color forms of this beautiful species.

Irish-heath is *Daboëcia cantabrica.* Spike-heath is *Bruckenthalia spiculifolia.* Prickly-heath is *Pernettya mucronata.*

HEATHER (CALLUNA) FORMS

The different forms of heather have all been derived from one species, *Calluna vulgaris.* This is native in Europe and Asia, and found in a few localities in the N. E. part of this country. Heather is hardier than any of the Heaths and well adapted to clothe dry sunny slopes. Kept sheared in spring, the plants make compact clumps, and, by planting several forms together in drifts, very pleasing foliage effects can be secured as well as flower color variations in summer. The type, *C. vulgaris,* grows to 2 ft. or more, and has rosy-pink flowers in late summer. Among the best of the numerous named forms are the following: *alba,* with white flowers; *hammondi,* one of the tallest, with bright green leaves and white flowers; *searlei,* with feathery growth and white flowers, late; *alporti,* a vigorous grower with crimson flowers; *coccinea,* a smaller form with deep

HEATHER AND HEATH
(A) A spray of the heather, Calluna vulgaris, of Scotland (and continental Europe); (B) One of the florist's Christmas-flowering heaths from South Africa, Erica melanthera.

red flowers; *carnea,* with pink flowers; *hypnoides,* with deep pink flowers; *cuprea,* outstanding with golden leaves which turn bronze in winter; *hirsuta,* forming a spreading grayish mat; and *nana,* forming low moss-like tufts of bright green.

Mock-heather is *Ericameria ericoides.*

HEATH GARDEN. A specialized type of planting consisting exclusively or mainly of members of the Heath Family (Ericaceae). These, including such popular plants as rhododendron, azalea, laurel, andromeda, leucothoë, bearberry, blueberry, trailing arbutus and their relatives, can create a garden of great beauty and distinction where soil and climatic conditions favor the different genera and species. Common to all of them is preference for an acid soil, and where this exists or can be provided, an arrangement of suitable plants (chosen also with reference to the other features of the environment) is a source of beauty and real satisfaction. In England and places of similar climate, the true heathers (Erica) are largely used. In the U. S. this genus is usually grown under glass both because it is tender in many parts of the country, and because it resents hot summer weather. However, the many other genera of the Heath Family provide abundant and varied material for the heath garden.

HEATING. As used in horticulture the term heating embraces several distinct ways of raising temperature, some of them undesirable. (1) When seed is insufficiently dry when packed it may become so hot as to start fires through spontaneous combustion. (2) When plants are improperly packed, especially when packed with bud foliage, the heat which they generate may either kill them or favor decay. (3) When seedlings are grown in temperatures too high for the species they "draw," they become spindling, weak, and unfit for planting.

Conversely, desirable heating includes the use of bell-glasses, plant forcers, and other arrangements for raising temperatures by no other agency than the sun. It also includes the use of fermenting materials such as manure in hotbeds, hot water or steam pipes connected with a furnace, and electric current passing through thermal cables and plates.

HEAT INJURY. Too high temperatures—either natural outdoors or artificial in homes or greenhouses—may result in

HOW FROST HEAVES PLANTS
When surface soil freezes (especially heavy soil) it expands and lifts, raising plants and either tearing or loosening the roots. When it thaws it settles back. Each successive freezing and thawing leaves the plants higher and more likely to die of freezing or drying.

retarded growth and failure to mature flowers and fruit; sun burn or sun scald of leaves, flowers or fruit; formation of heat cankers on stems; defoliation; premature ripening of fruits; or death of an entire plant. Tip burn of potato shows as a browning of the margins of leaves under the influence of excessive heat. Lettuce may show similar symptoms; strawberries, grapes, apples and other fruits may be scalded; and sun scald of tomatoes is common. See also DISEASES, PLANT.

HEAVENLY-BAMBOO. Nursery catalog name for *Nandina domestica,* a small Japanese evergreen shrub, popular in warm countries for its finely cut, graceful foliage, its winter coloring and its red berries, which follow loose clusters to 1 ft. long of small white flowers. It is related to the barberries, not the bamboos, and the roots are hardy as far N. as N. Y. even though the top may be killed in severe winters.

HEAVING. The lifting action exerted by a soil during the winter under the influence of alternate freezing and thawing. It is directly associated with the soil texture. A light, well-drained sandy soil or a loose, porous soil rich in humus rarely heaves; a stiff clay or silt soil, on the other hand, may heave sufficiently to lift a summer-set strawberry plant completely out of the ground, or to tear the crown of an established perennial away from its roots.

Where heaving is likely to happen, it can be largely prevented by mulching the soil after it has frozen in late fall (see MULCH). The mulch should be thick enough to "insulate" the soil against the thawing effect of mild spells. Otherwise, all beds and borders of heavy soil should be carefully examined in early spring as the frost leaves. Slightly heaved plants may be pressed back into place with hand or foot; those severely displaced are best lifted with trowel or spade and replanted.

HEBE (hee'-bee). A genus of shrubby or small tree-like plants with leathery leaves and pink, purple or white flowers borne in small clusters. Except that they are woody and usually evergreen, the plants resemble veronicas, with which they were formerly grouped. Members of the Figwort Family, they are mostly natives of New Zealand. They are valuable garden subjects for mild climates, being extensively used in Calif. and suitable for the cooler regions of the S. States. They are also sometimes grown in the greenhouse N., and are propagated by seeds and cuttings.

The best known species are *H. speciosa,* an evergreen shrub to 5 ft. with reddish purple flowers in 4 in. racemes; and *H. traversi,* a small shrub with 3 in. racemes of white flowers.

HEDERA (hed'-ur-ah) *helix.* (See illustrations, Plate 11.) The evergreen English Ivy, famous in literature as well as horticulture for its long life, its easy propagation, and its ability to cover brick and stone walls with a dense, thick mantle of glossy green. The small clusters of greenish flowers which appear in the fall are scarcely noticeable. See ENGLISH IVY; also IVY.

HEDGE. (See illustrations, Plates 27, 31, 33.) A continuous and close planting of tree, shrubs or occasionally (for temporary results) quick-, tall-growing annuals, along a boundary to protect and enclose the garden, or along a division line within the garden to set one portion apart from another. The term does not necessarily imply a rigidly pruned and restrained growth, though it is often so interpreted. But splendid walls of living green such as may be developed by proper pruning, are among the finest elements of a garden, giving dignity and repose.

The pruned and shaped hedge belongs wherever a stone or similar wall might be properly used; and it is almost as effective a protection. The unsheared casual hedge belongs to a more free-and-easy environment; also it requires more room. Yet it is not strictly "naturalistic" even though permitted to grow in a natural manner. Being composed of just one kind of plant, instead of two or more (as compose a natural thicket), it cannot give the impression of natural wild growth. So it is really sophisticated without being as dignified or refined as a clipped hedge. Bear this in mind when choosing hedge plants for any position; the untrimmed hedge may easily degenerate from a casual to an untidy and careless appearance.

PROPORTION. Along a highway a hedge can hardly be too heavy, too high or too thick and impenetrable. But one within the garden must be only heavy enough for reasonable separation of the areas which it sets apart. Otherwise it will dwarf them and create a cluttered, cramped effect.

MATERIALS. It is usually assumed that deciduous hedge plants should have small leaves, but size of leaf is not as important as certain characteristics of growth. The desired or necessary even and unbroken surface of a clipped hedge can be achieved by density of growth and by a quick even response after pruning regardless of leaf size. Slow growing materials best meet this requirement; and evergreen species better than deciduous sorts. Hence, for a clipped hedge, first choice will always be an evergreen; second will be a deciduous shrub or tree of deliberate growth. Practically all flowering shrubs are effective for untrimmed hedges.

Extensive trials of both deciduous and evergreen plants suitable for hedges were begun in Ottawa, Can., in 1889 by the late W. T. Macoun, Dominion Horticulturist, more than 100 species being planted and many being still under observation. These have yielded valuable information on which selection of material, planting methods and cultural details can well be based.

PLANTING. Hedge plants are spaced according to the type of material and the demands of the gardener. Common deciduous shrubs like privet, which grow quickly and are expected to give quick effects, are usually planted 9 in. apart. Finer deciduous material and most evergreens are better set at least 18 in. apart, while some of the larger growing evergreens will do better yet at 24 in. This insures root room for adequate feeding right from the start, and makes it unnecessary to remove alternate plants in the future as growth advances.

FORM. To insure dense growth from the ground up, deciduous plants are usually cut back to within a few inches of the ground when planted. Material especially grown for hedges in a nursery may not need such handling, but a cutting back of all over about 30 per cent of the tip growth is always needed. The properly shaped hedge is narrower at the top than at the bottom, and the top should be rounded rather than flat. The sloping sides admit abundant light to the lower branches, which is of the greatest importance in preventing them from pining away and giving the hedge that unpleasant but exceedingly common open and "leggy" look. Also a somewhat narrow and rounded top sheds snow instead of accumulating a heavy load and sometimes bending or breaking under it.

MAINTENANCE. To establish the form (described above), planting is completed by clipping along the sides of the plants but not between them. Annual clipping of deciduous hedges should be done just as the first strong growth of the season is slowing down—in May or June, depending on the locality—and again in late summer after the secondary growth is made

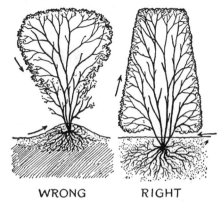

WRONG   RIGHT

HEDGE CARE

Shallow planting, moulding of the soil and failure to shear young plants often gives the sad effect shown at left. Deep planting, level cultivation, frequent trimming so the plants will be widest at the base, produce a real hedge.

if a shaggy appearance makes it desirable. Evergreens grow more slowly and usually do not need clipping until well past midsummer; and they should never be severely pruned. Simply shape them and, once they have filled out, maintain that shape.

PLANTS FOR SHEARED HEDGES

For the northern half of U. S.: Evergreen—*Chamaecyparis pisifera* var. *filifera* (Sawara-cypress), *Juniperus virginiana* (Red-cedar), *Pinus strobus* (White Pine), *P. cembra* (Swiss Stone Pine), *Tsuga canadensis* (Canada Hemlock), *Taxus cuspidata* (Japanese Yew), *Thuja occidentalis* (American Arborvitae), *T. orientalis* (Oriental Arborvitae). Deciduous—*Caragana arborescens* (Pea-tree), *Carpinus caroliniana* (Hornbeam), *Berberis thunbergi* (Japanese Barberry), *Rhamnus cathartica* (Buckthorn), *Viburnum lantana* (Wayfaringtree), *Fagus americana* (American Beech), *Quercus imbricaria* (Shingle Oak), *Larix europaea* (European Larch).

For the southern half of the U. S.: Evergreen—many of the above, also *Cupressus macrocarpa* (Monterey Cypress), *Abelia grandiflora*, *Azalea amoena*, *Euonymus japonica*, *Ilex aquifolium* (English Holly), *Osmanthus fragrans*.

For the southeastern section: *Buxus sempervirens* (True Box), *Gardenia jasminoides*, *Prunus caroliniana*. For southern coastal and Gulf regions: *Cinnamomum camphora* (Camphor-tree), *Pittosporum tobira*, *Thea sinensis* var. *bohea* (Tea), *Viburnum tinus* (Laurestinus).

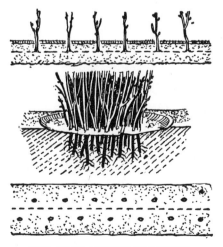

HEDGE PLANTING METHODS

Single row setting is suggested above and staggering of plants at bottom. One way to get a supply of privet for a hedge is to root cuttings in moist earth in a depressed area as shown in center.

HEDGEHOG or **TEASEL GOURD.** A common name for the curious vine, *Cucumis dipsaceus,* a relative of the cucumber and muskmelon, but grown only for ornament.

HEDGE-HYSSOP. A common name for the native genus Gratiola, of which one species, *G. aurea,* is a useful plant for wet ground. See GOLDENPERT.

HEDGE-MUSTARD. A catalog name for Erysimum, a genus of yellow and orange border plants resembling small wallflowers. Sometimes called Blister-cress.

HEDGE-THORN. Common name for *Carissa arduina,* a 10 ft. tall S. African evergreen shrub with white flowers and red fruits.

HEDRAIANTHUS (hed-ri-an'-thus), HEDRAEANTHUS. Alternative spellings for Edraianthus, which see.

HEDYCHIUM (hee-dik'-i-um). A genus of tropical herbs of the Ginger Family, mostly natives of India and popularly known as Ginger-lily, Butterfly-lily, or Garland-flower. In frostless regions they are favorites in the open garden; in colder climates they are greenhouse plants. They are robust growers, attaining 3 to 5 ft. with highly ornamental foliage similar to that of the canna, and sprays or spikes of fragrant flowers of various colors—white and cream through orange and pinks to scarlet. In the open, most of them flower in the fall; under glass, they can be coaxed to bloom almost continuously. They require a rich soil, preferably a peaty loam with a little sand and a generous proportion of well-rotted cow manure. Plenty of water must be given, with an occasional complete immersion of the pot during the growing period. An application of liquid manure should be given at intervals, and while growing the plant needs abundant light and a moist atmosphere. After blooming, the root-stocks are lifted, dried off gradually, rested in a cool place, and repotted in new soil in spring or early summer. Propagation is by division just before repotting.

HEDYSARUM (hee-dis'-ah-rum). Perennial herbs or shrubs belonging to the Pea Family and found in temperate regions of the northern hemisphere. They are good border plants, and easy to grow in light soil in a sunny place. Propagation is by seeds or division. *H. coronarium* (French-honeysuckle) is a European perennial or biennial to 4 ft., long grown in gardens. It has 3 to 7 pairs of leaflets, and bears spikes of deep red fragrant flowers in summer. *H. multijugum* is a small Asiatic shrub of rather straggly habit. It has 10 to 20 pairs of leaflets and reddish-purple spikes of flowers all summer.

HEDYSCEPE (hee-di-see'-pee) *canterburyana.* A species of feather-leaved palm, popularly known as Umbrella Palm, and frequently listed under the former generic name of Kentia. Although found wild only in Lord Howe Islands, in the S. Pacific Ocean, where its tall trunk, crowned by the broad, feathery, over-arching fronds, reaches a height of 40 ft., it has been grown successfully outdoors in S. Fla. and Calif. Thriving in rich moist loam, it should be sheltered, especially in the juvenile stage, from the direct rays of the sun. When grown under glass the Umbrella Palm requires a rather heavy potting soil, enriched with well-rotted manure, frequent watering, a night temperature never below 60 deg., and partial shading throughout the year.

HEEL. The small piece of two-year or older stem left at the base of a cutting (see CUTTINGS) taken for propagation purposes. Usually it is either the first joint of the old wood below the extension of young wood; or, when the young stem grows at an angle, it is merely a thin slice of such wood. When the cutting carries an entire short section of the older stem, it is said to be made with a mallet.

HEELING-IN. Storing dormant plants in trenches by covering them with soil until conditions are favorable for planting. It is most often practiced with dormant nursery stock received before the ground has been prepared. For winter storage dig the trenches from east to west on well drained, bare ground. Make the north side vertical; the south, a long slope. Across this slope lay a slanting row, or single layer, of plants, their roots toward the opposite (vertical) end, and only their tops extending beyond the soil level. Cover them—roots and stems, almost to the tops —with soil, sifting and packing it in around them. Lay another single row and cover it, and so on until the trench is full of overlapping, slanting alternate rows of plants and soil. The trench can be made as long as necessary by extending it at the vertical end. When heeling-in newly received small trees or shrubs, remove all packing material to prevent mice making

Upper left: The close-clipped hedge, as architectural in line as a wall, fittingly enframes the formal garden. Upper right: Severely pruned, the althea (Hibiscus syriacus) combines formality with the informality of profuse bloom. Bottom: The serried ranks of Lombardy poplars make a stately hedge and an adequate windbreak.

HEELING-IN RASPBERRY PLANTS
Plants received before the ground is ready for them are laid close together in trenches and covered with soil almost to their tops.

nests in it. Dormant, deciduous shrubs and vines so stored will pass the winter safely, but should be dug and planted in early spring before they make much growth.

HE-HUCKLEBERRY. A common name for *Lyonia ligustrina,* a tall deciduous heath-like shrub with pinkish or white flowers in clusters, found growing in moist soil from Me. to Tex., and also called Maleberry.

HELENIUM (he-lee'-ni-um). Sneezeweed. A genus of mostly perennial herbs of the Composite Family, with yellow flower-heads, borne alone or in broad flat-topped clusters. A number of the perennial species are cultivated in rich loamy soil in the border, preferably in the rear, for height and early autumn bloom. Some of the more weedy species can be massed in the wild garden. They are easily increased by seeds, division and cuttings. If attacked by white aphis on the roots, they should be lifted, the roots thoroughly washed, and the plants reset in another section of the border.

Snout beetles (which see) frequently feed on the terminal buds and leaves. They are difficult to control but spraying with lead arsenate is somewhat effective. Or the beetles may be hit with a contact insecticide.

PRINCIPAL SPECIES

H. autumnale, to 6 ft., has long, rather narrow leaves and 2-in. heads of flowers whose rays shade from lemon yellow to deep red in the varieties. Var. *grandiflorum* has larger flowers than the type; var. *nanum praecox* is dwarf and early;

var. *pumilum* only reaches 2 ft.; var. *rubrum* has red blossoms; in var. *striatum* the yellow rays are striped with red; while var. *superbum* has very large blossoms.

hoopesi, to 3 ft., has yellow flower-heads to 3 in. across, lasting well in the border and also when cut.

nudiflorum, to 3 ft., has clustered heads of flowers with brownish or purplish disks and drooping yellow, striped, or brownish-yellow rays. The var. *grandicephalum striatum* grows to 5 ft. and has heads to 2 in. across.

bigelovi, to 4 ft., is a decorative plant with richly colored flowers, the disks brownish and the rays clear yellow.

HELIAMPHORA (hee-li-am'-foh-rah). An insectivorous plant of the Sarracenia Family, native of S. America, having leaves modified to form tubular pitchers, often veined with crimson, winged down the front, hairy inside, and having a flaring mouth with a small lid. The nodding flowers are white or pale rose and grow in a cluster of 2 or 3. These rare plants which, being extremely difficult to grow, are seen only in collections, are closely related to the pitcher-plants, their name signifying "sun pitchers." They must be kept within a glass case in a greenhouse, where moist conditions may be maintained, in pots plunged in other pots filled with sphagnum and kept constantly wet with applications of warm water.

See also INSECTIVOROUS PLANTS.

HELIANTHELLA (hee-li-an-thel'-ah). A genus of W. N. American perennial herbs of the Daisy Family, with long-stemmed yellow or brownish heads of flowers from midsummer to autumn.

HELIANTHEMUM (hee-li-an'-themum). Sun-rose. There are more than 120 species in this genus of perennial herbs or low sub-shrubs, suitable for ground cover, rock gardens or border planting. Of N. American and Mediterranean origin, they thrive in a dry limestone soil and full sun, bearing yellow, rose, white or purple flowers from July to September on plants from 6 in. to 2 ft. high. The plants must be protected in winter in northern sections. Propagation is by seeds sown in spring, by greenwood cuttings, or by division of the roots.

The most common species in the North is the hardy *H. nummularium,* which is 1 ft. tall, bears yellow flowers 1 in. across. It has the numerous varieties, including:

albo-plenum, double, white; *aureum,* deep yellow; *cupreum,* copper, variegated with yellow; *macranthum,* white, with yellow blotches; *roseum,* pale rose (there is a double form); and *mutabile,* whose pale rose flowers change to lilac or nearly white.

HELIANTHUS (hee-li-an′-thus). A genus of coarse annual or perennial herbs of the Daisy Family, popularly known as Sunflowers, which see. The flower-heads, with yellow rays and yellow, purple or brown centers, range from a few inches to more than a foot in diameter. The small ones are borne in clusters, the large ones as a rule singly or at intervals along tall, stout stems. Sunflowers are easily grown from seed, but perennial kinds are also increased by division, or from offsets. They make excellent border and background material.

H. annuus, often reaching a height of 12 ft., is the common Garden Sunflower, and *H. tuberosus* is the Jerusalem Artichoke which produces edible potato-like roots. The latter has escaped from gardens in some sections and become a troublesome weed. See ARTICHOKE.

HELICHRYSUM (hel-i-kry′-sum) *bracteatum.* Strawflower. A hardy annual of the Composite Family, growing from 1 to 3 ft. tall, considered the finest of all everlastings for the home garden. These natives of Europe, called *Immortelles* by the French, are attractive in the border as well as in winter bouquets. Flowers should be cut when partially open and dried slowly in a cool place, heads downward to keep the long stems straight. The stiff overlapping scales, which form the showy part of the flower-head, come in a wide range of soft and brilliant shades. Propagation is by seed either sown outdoors or started indoors for earlier bloom; also by cuttings. A rich loamy soil is preferred.

Of the many species in the genus Helichrysum, some of them dwarf, some tender, *H. bracteatum* is the only one widely grown in America. Its stiff, shiny flowers of the Composite type up to 2½ in. across are of white, yellow, orange, red, pink or lavender. Var. *monstrosum* is large and fully double, showing no yellow disk-flowers in the center. Var. *nanum* is dwarf.

See also EVERLASTINGS.

HELICONIA (hel-i-koh′-ni-ah). A genus of tropical herbs of the Banana Family having large leaves similar to those of the banana, but bearing a capsular fruit. They are grown in the greenhouse as foliage plants, and outdoors in warm climates as specimen plants on lawns, where, if planted in rich soil and given plenty of water, they will attain great size. They are increased from seed when obtainable; otherwise by division of the roots.

H. bihai (Wild-plantain or Balisier), growing to 18 ft., has leaves up to 3 ft. long and 1 ft. wide, and red or orange flowers enclosed in scarlet or black boat-shaped sheaths. *H. illustris,* is a South-Sea plant with large pink-veined leaves.

HELIOCEREUS (hee-li-oh-see′-ree-us). Sun-cereus. For greenhouse or lath-house culture, nothing could be superior to the members of this cactus genus. Easy of culture and quick growing, their blossoms, in point of size and brilliancy, can scarcely be surpassed. One seen growing in a San Diego garden had 115 buds and blossoms at one time. The flowers, about 9 in. across, were most brilliant—crimson and violet mauve. The names of the species tell the story—*H. speciosus, H. speciosissimus, H. superbus, H. elegantissimus.* There are many hybrids, produced by cross fertilization, and especially fine buds are often grafted upon other stock. Of tropical origin, they should be treated accordingly. For cultural directions see CACTUS.

HELIOPHILA (hee-li-of′-il-ah). A genus of small S. African herbs of the Mustard Family, having racemes of blue flowers and narrow hairy leaves. They are treated as half-hardy annuals, the seed started under glass and the seedlings set out after danger of frost is over, or the seed sown in May directly where the plants are to stand. *H. pilosa,* from 6 to 24 in., has light blue flowers, varying to lilac and yellow. It may be forced in the greenhouse or used as bedding plant in the border where it will bloom in June or July.

As a greenhouse and cut-flower subject, *H. linearifolia* is desirable for its abundance of delicate sky-blue flowers, although the petals close at night.

See also SOUTH AFRICAN PLANTS.

HELIOPSIS (hee-li-op′-sis). A genus of hardy herbaceous composite perennials with yellow sunflower-like heads 2½ in. across on plants up to 5 ft. tall. Seeds sown outdoors in ordinary dry soil, even in an exposed situation, will produce flowers for cutting the second year. *H. helianthoides* and *H. scabra,* the latter with rough-hairy stems, have both given rise to a number of varieties in several tones of yellow and orange, some with double flowers.

HELIOTROPE. A half-hardy border and greenhouse plant which, because of the pleasant fragrance of its attractive clusters of small, deep violet flowers, has long been used in gardens and by florists. It is botanically the genus Heliotropium.

Somewhat woody at the base, heliotropes can be developed into standard or "tree" forms by early and continued pruning of all side branches. But they are best known as border plants, giving their fragrant bloom amid rough-veined leaves from early summer until heavy frost. Heliotropes are also used as pot-plants. They are of easy culture for any of these purposes, propagation being best accomplished from softwood cuttings placed in flats containing half leafmold and half sand. They require heavy shading for the first week, ample moisture from the very beginning, and they do best in a coolhouse. They should be potted in 10 or 12 days—or as soon as they have rooted—or they may be attacked by a destructive fungus. A light soil is best in the pots. If green fly infests them, nicotinesulphate will keep it in check.

Garden forms of the heliotrope are mostly derived from *H. peruvianum,* which is vanilla-scented, or from *H. corymbosum,* with a narcissus-like odor. The color of hybrids may vary from white to deep purple.

In the greenhouse, heliotropes may be kept in the same pots for several years; they should be given liquid manure in the growing season.

Garden-heliotrope is *Valeriana officinalis,* also known as Valerian (which see). Winter-heliotrope is a small plant of the Composite Family, *Petasites fragrans.* The Heliotrope-tree is *Ehretia thyrsiflora.*

HELIPTERUM (hee-lip'-ter-um). A genus of annuals of the Composite or Daisy Family, grown for winter bouquets as an everlasting. One of the daintiest in the annual group, it is easily cultivated. Seeds are generally sown outdoors where plants are to grow, though they may be started indoors to produce earlier flowers. Plants stand 1 to 2 ft. tall and should be placed 6 to 12 in. apart. The most popular species is *H. humboldtianum* (or *sandfordi*) which bears small flowers in clusters making balls 1½ in. across. The color is deep, rich, golden yellow, but the outer bracts have

a greenish tinge. They should be cut when the buds are opening, stripped of leaves, tied in bunches and hung in a shady place. As they dry the flowers will open. They retain their color for years. Another excellent species is *H. roseum* commonly listed in catalogs as Acroclinium. It grows 2 ft. high, with heads of rose or white flowers not clustered. *H. manglesi,* the Swan River Everlasting, which is still frequently listed by its former name, Rhodanthe, is slender, to 1½ ft. with loose heads about 1½ in. across of white to bright pink flowers. Its var. *maculata* has red spots on the white bracts.

HELLEBORE (hel'-ee-bor). Common name for Helleborus, a genus of Old-World perennial fibrous-rooted herbs of the Buttercup Family, which are perfectly hardy and bloom in earliest spring or even midwinter. One species (*H. niger*) is known as Christmas-rose, which see.

H. viridis, which, like the others, grows well in moist, rich, half-shaded spots, opens its broad, yellowish-green, buttercup-like flowers somewhat later than the Christmas-rose, yet earlier than any other spring-flowering subject in the garden. *H. orientalis,* of which there are many attractive varieties, bears purplish flowers in clusters, and also blooms early. Several species of Helleborus have become naturalized in N. America.

False-hellebore is the genus Veratrum, *V. viride* also being known as American White-hellebore and *V. album* as European White-hellebore.

The rootstocks of plants of both genera contain active poisonous properties.

HELLEBORE. An insecticide made from the roots of plants of the genus Veratrum (false-hellebore) and sold in the form of a dry powder. This is comparatively non-poisonous to man but a slow stomach poison for insects. It is an old, well-known material but expensive and not effective unless fresh. At present it is recommended only in certain cases (as in the control of the currant worm) when a dangerous poison such as lead arsenate is not advisable. It should be used as a dust or mixed with water at the rate of 1 oz. in 2 gal. See also INSECTICIDE.

HELONIAS (he-loh'-ni-as) *bullata.* A perennial bulbous herb of the Lily Family commonly known as Swamp-pink. It has thin dark-green, clustered leaves, 6 to 15 in. long and bears 30 pink or purplish flowers clustered at the summit of a stalk to 2 ft. high. Found in bogs and wet places in the E. States, it is a handsome plant for the wild garden, and very easily increased by division.

HELWINGIA (hel-win'-ji-ah). Deciduous shrubs from Asia, belonging to the Dogwood Family. The principal species is *H. japonica,* a bushy shrub to 5 ft., easy to grow and hardy as far north as Boston. It has no particular ornamental value, but is interesting because the clusters of tiny greenish-white flowers are borne *on the upper surface of the leaves.* Propagated by cuttings of side shoots.

HELXINE (helk-sy'-nee) *soleiroli.* A moss-like herb from Corsica used as ground cover in conservatories and in outdoor rockeries in frostless areas. Known as Babys Tears, Paddys or Irishmans Wig, and Creeping-nettle, which see.

HEMEROCALLIS (hem-er-oh-kal'-is). A genus of mostly tuberous-rooted perennial herbs called Daylily (which see) because their large flowers last only a day. Recent improved hybrids promise to replace the old-time favorite. (See illustrations, Plate 28.)

HEMIGRAPHIS (he-mi'-grah-fis). Asiatic herbs or shrubs belonging to the Acanthus Family. One species (*H. colorata*) is often grown in baskets or pans in warm greenhouses; in the far South it is grown outdoors as a cover plant. It is a prostrate, spreading plant with reddish-purple leaves and small heads of white flowers. Propagated by cuttings.

HEMIONITIS (hem-i-oh-ny'-tis). A genus of small ferns, one species of which (*H. palmata,* the Strawberry or Ivy-leaved Fern) is excellent for the greenhouse or terrarium, where it requires a peaty soil. The frond is composed of a 5-lobed blade and a long erect stipe.

HEMLOCK (See illustration, Plate 17). Common name for the Tsuga, a genus of coniferous evergreens with scattered horizontal branches clothed with small flat rather soft needles and bearing quantities of small cones which add to their beauty. Sometimes called Hemlock-spruce. The hemlocks are less formal in outline than the firs (Abies) and true spruces (Picea), for though their limbs spread horizontally, they branch repeatedly into many small branchlets which generally droop most gracefully. With their fine feathery foliage they are most beautiful in youth; but they

CANADA HEMLOCK
A branch of this graceful tree is shown here bearing nature cones; in the background a full grown tree suggests its typical form.

attain great dignity in age, and are among the finest evergreen trees for park or lawn planting. They will stand severe pruning, growing dense and velvety, and are therefore often used for hedges. As they have fibrous roots they can be moved easily, especially if root-pruned in preparation. They grow best in a rather acid soil well drained but with plenty of moisture.

Hemlocks are propagated by seeds or cuttings and the varieties by grafting on *T. canadensis.*

ENEMIES. In general hemlock is less attacked by fungous diseases than pine, spruce, or fir. Two species of blister rust fungi affect the leaves of Canada hemlock. (See RUSTS.) One has its alternate stage on rhododendron and vaccinium; the other completes its life-cycle on hydrangea. A third rust produces dirty white pustules on cones, twigs and needles and uses poplar as its alternate host. One rust, requiring no alternate host, may kill the needles or cause reddish, swollen pustules on them and on twigs which should be pruned off and burned.

A leaf blight occasionally defoliates hemlocks by late summer, the browned needles being covered with small black pustules. Gather and burn them in late autumn.

To control the hemlock span-worm which feeds on the new growth and sometimes completely strips trees, spray with lead arsenate.

The flat-headed spotted hemlock borer works under the bark of living, injured and dying hemlock and spruce trees. The adult beetle is bronze with three small, whitish spots on each wing cover. Cut down infested trees in late winter and burn the bark.

For control of hemlock and pine leaf scales and spruce mite, see EVERGREENS.

PRINCIPAL SPECIES

The species most grown in the E. States is the hardy *T. canadensis,* which naturally often forms groves on the N. side of ravines from Nova Scotia to Ala. Its garden forms include var. *albo-spica* with white-tipped young branchlets; *compacta,* dwarf with short branchlets and short leaves; *gracilis,* with drooping branchlets; *microphylla,* with very small needles; *nana,* a very small form suitable for the rock garden; and *pendula,* which forms a flat-topped bush with pendent branchlets. Other species are:

T. caroliniana, a smaller tree from the S., of compact growth and with dark green needles; graceful, but not always hardy. Var. *compacta* has a dense, round-topped growth.

sieboldi, from Japan, is generally shrubby as cultivated in this country.

heterophylla (Western Hemlock), to 200 ft., is a majestic tree attaining its greatest beauty and grace in the damp climate of N. W. America.

HEN-AND-CHICKENS
The house-leek, Sempervivum, is one of the plants called Hen-and-chickens, because of the way the offsets nestle close to the parent plant.

mertensiana (Mountain Hemlock), to 100 ft., has a more open pyramidal growth, bluish-green foliage, and cones to 2 in. long that are often bright violet-purple while young. This species from the Cascade Mountains is frequently grown in Europe, but is little known in the E. U. S.

Ground-hemlock is *Taxus canadensis;* Poison-hemlock is Conium; Water-hemlock is Cicuta.

HEMP. An annual herb belonging to the Mulberry Family, native to central Asia and the N. W. Himalayas, and naturalized in E. N. America. Grown commercially in Wis., Ill., and Ky., for the fibre contained in its inner bark, it is also sometimes cultivated in gardens as an ornamental. There is but one species, *Cannabis sativa,* but several variations have received specific names—as *C. gigantea,* the tall strain usually grown in gardens, reaching a height of 10 feet; and *C. indica,* which grown in torrid climates yields the narcotic drug cannabis (probably the same as the Mexican "marihuana").

Hemp requires a soil rich in humus and well supplied with moisture. The seeds are sown about 2 in. deep where the plants are to stand in April.

Other plants yielding fibre to which the name hemp has been given are: Bowstring-hemp, which is Sansevieria; Manila-hemp or Abacá, which is *Musa textilis,* a species of banana; *Sisal-hemp,* which is *Agave silalana;* and Indian-hemp, which is *Apocynum cannabinum.*

HEMP-TREE. A common name for *Vitex agnus-castus,* a S. European shrub of the Vervain Family, called also Chaste-tree and Monks Pepper-tree. See VITEX.

HEN-AND-CHICKENS. Common name for *Sempervivum tectorum* (see SEMPERVIVUM), also called Houseleek because in humid climates it often grows on roofs (the specific name is from the Latin *tectum,* meaning roof). The plant is an herbaceous evergreen perennial whose thick, succulent leaves form rosettes, from which the pink or red flowers and the more abundant "chickens" or small rosettes are produced. The latter take root and become new plants which may be separated and replanted.

This species is one of the most popular of its genus for edging beds of succulents (which see), and for planting in rockeries, carpet beds, rock walls and rock gardens. No plant is easier to grow provided the soil is not wet. It rapidly multiplies and soon forms mats of rosettes which completely cover the ground.

HENBANE. Common name for the genus Hyoscyamus, coarse, ill-smelling weedy herbs found in poor soils and waste places, occasionally grown for medicinal uses.

HENNA. Common name for *Lawsonia inermis,* a tropical shrub, widely grown for ornament in warm countries; the source of henna dye. It bears clusters of small fragrant flowers, white or rose-colored. In the W. Indies, where it has become naturalized, it is known as Mignonette-tree.

HEPATICA (he-pat'-i-kah). A genus of small herbs of the Buttercup Family, often known as Liverleaf. They have 3-lobed evergreen leaves, the new ones appearing after the flowers, and white, lavender, purple or pinkish blossoms, occasionally fragrant. Natives of open rich woodlands, they bloom in the very early spring. They may be transferred easily to the wild garden, requiring a rather neutral soil rich in humus. Propagation is by division of the roots or by seed.

Hepatica may be attacked by both rust and smut fungi. Removal of diseased leaves and dusting with sulphur will aid in their control.

H. americana has leaves with rounded lobes, while *H. acutiloba* has 3-pointed lobes, and *H. angulosa,* from Hungary, toothed lobes 3 to 5 in number, and flowers 1¼ in. across. *H. nobilis,* another Old-World plant, is similar to *americana,* but has larger flowers, often double.

HERACLEUM (her-ah-klee'-um). A genus of coarse herbaceous perennials commonly called Cow-parsnip, bearing minute white or pink-tinted flowers in enormous umbels. Some tall species are used for bold effects in wild gardens.

HERALDS TRUMPET. C o m m o n name for *Beaumontia grandiflora* (which see), a weedy greenhouse vine with showy white funnel-form flowers; grown also outdoors in warm countries.

HERBACEOUS BORDER. A border in which herbaceous plants (meaning those which die to the ground) are used rather than shrubs or evergreens. In recent years the herbaceous border has come to be a chief feature of almost every intimate garden. It may follow a path or wall, or the edge of a lawn, but it should not be placed directly in front of a newly planted shrub border, where the shrubs will quickly overhang and shade it, the roots rob it of moisture and plant food. Well-grown shrubs at a proper distance and those with restricted root systems, such as rhododendrons and azaleas, and also magnolias, hollies, etc., which root deeply, form a proper background for such a border. The neighborhood of a privet hedge, a poplar screen-planting or trees with wide-spreading, shallow root systems is least desirable, while the most satisfactory location is between a path and a wall, provided there is enough sunlight and air.

MAKING. A good depth of fertile soil should be provided, either by removing a foot or two of the natural soil and replacing with top-soil; or, if the natural soil is good, by adding and spading in leafmold, compost, rotted manure, peat, or other humus. Lime, bonemeal and complete fertilizers should not be added to the whole border if any acid-soil plants are to be used in it, but rather supplied instead to individual plants according to their needs. When finished, and after the soil has settled, the surface of the border should be 3 or 4 in. above the original soil level to assure drainage.

CARE. After planting (which is best done in spring) the border needs care in summer to keep the weeds out; the removal of dead flower-heads; the occasional division of perennials; replacing of the plants that fail; warfare against insects and plant diseases, and adequate watering during dry weather. In winter in very cold climates a mulch of loose straw or evergreen boughs may be put on *after the ground freezes,* and removed early in spring. But at best mulches are unsightly; often they become soaked and sodden and do more harm than good; and there are many hardy plants which winter more successfully unmulched. It is better to protect with small mounds of coarse litter only those perennials known to be tender. (See WINTER PROTECTION.) In the spring remove the coarse part of the mulch (if any) and fork in any fine, humus-forming residue, clean up dead stalks, and repair winter damage.

PLANTING HINTS. In the border, plants of one kind and color are usually grouped —but not too regularly—in some artistic relation to other groups, so that there is a balance of color, size and texture, giving unity to the whole. But, except that tall-growing forms must be placed at the back so the smaller ones may be seen, there are few restrictions as to the manner of planting; almost unlimited variety and the expression of individual taste is permissible. Color harmony can be planned among plants which flower at the same season, avoiding shades that clash; but colors do not conflict in the open as they do indoors, because sunlight and wind-motion affect the eye and effect a blending and softening. It is enough to remember that different shades of red seldom look well close together, and that magenta will harmonize only with white. Reds can best be separated by white or blue. Magenta is a special shade of purplish pink, and should not be confused with violet, purple, mauve, lilac and lavender, all good colors.

Bulbs, perennials and annuals may be included in the herbaceous border, and also a few woody plants if very dwarf and neat. Since bulbs begin flowering early in spring and usually die to the ground by midsummer, they are usually scattered about, rather·than massed. After them come the perennials, most of which reach a climax of bloom in May and June, with a few varieties lasting throughout the season until frost. Beginning with July, annuals give the best display, for they thrive in the heat of summer. But only a few scattered annuals should go into the mixed herbaceous border, otherwise they shade out and weaken the perennials, which are the backbone of the planting. Perennials are often said to be winter-killed when they are "summer-killed" by annuals, and merely linger on till winter in a dying condition.

A complete list .of plants for the herbaceous border would fill many pages. A few of the most commonly used are

BULBS. Crocus, hyacinth, narcissus, snowdrop, gladiolus, lily, squill, tulip.

PERENNIALS. Aster, bleeding heart, butterfly weed, campanula, candytuft, chrysanthemum, columbine, coral bells, daylily, delphinium, foxglove, gaillardia, iris, oriental poppy, peony, phlox, pink, platycodon, polyanthus, viola.

ANNUALS. Asters, calendula, coreopsis, cornflower, cosmos, marigold, pansy, petunia, poppy, portulaca, scabiosa, snapdragon, sweet alyssum, sweet-pea, zinnia. See also BORDER.

HERBALS. Books on plants written earlier than 1753, when Linnaeus founded modern scientific botany. The writers, called herbalists, discussed chiefly medicinal plants and those with curious, even imaginary forms and properties. Among the most noted herbals is that of John Gerarde, now republished in a modern edition. While the original volumes are not easy reading (many having been written in medieval Latin), and while botanically and horticulturally they are far from reliable in the light of modern knowledge, they are quaint relics of early interest in plant life and are invaluable in tracing the history of plants and of man's knowledge of them.

HERBARIUM. A collection of dried, pressed plants mounted on sheets of paper and used in the study of botany. Besides thousands of private herbaria, there are large collections in botanic gardens, natural-history museums and universities, many open to the public. Names of all plants not cross-bred nor altered from their natural state by cultivation can be found by comparing flowers, leaves, stems and seeds with herbarium specimens. Most trees, many shrubs and rock-garden plants, and all wild flowers, ferns, grasses and weeds are included in the public herbarium. Of plants altered by cultivation, all named varieties propagated by division, cuttings, layers or grafts can and should be preserved in the herbarium to avoid misnaming. Since the public herbaria seldom contain these cultivated varieties, each gardener and nurseryman should make his own. Detailed directions for pressing, mounting and labeling will be found in books on botany that can be consulted at public libraries or in the libraries of botanic gardeners or horticultural societies. It is worth-while doing the work neatly and classifying accurately. Standard sheets of mounting paper 11½ by 16⅜ in., standard labels and covers, give the herbarium value and permanence.

HERB-CHRISTOPHER. A common name for *Actaea spicata,* the Black Baneberry. Perennial herb with small white or bluish flowers and purplish-black berries.

HERB GARDEN. This is a garden (or section of a garden) devoted to the cultivation of those plants, mostly aromatic, which are used for flavoring foods, for teas or tisanes (decoctions), for medicines, for candies, and for perfume or fragrance (see HERBS).

Incidentally, the pronunciation of the word "herb" is so often a subject of controversy, that it seems desirable to note that it has long been the custom in England to sound the initial "h"; whereas in this country it has been the custom to ignore it and pronounce the word "'urb" in the ancient and original way.

DESIGN. Because of the character of most of the plant material in an herb garden, preciseness of pattern is important. Not even in the vegetable garden does each plant require such individual consideration. Vegetables may crowd each other somewhat in their rows, but herbs must never crowd, both for their success and for the best garden effect. Also, instead of the continuity of the perennial garden or other flower border, the herb garden will show great diversity and unless carefully arranged it will be just a crowded mess of ill-assorted plant material. Design and arrangement must conform to the requirements of the herbs. This means neatness and exactness, a symmetrical little plan with the plants spaced, and paired or repeated, regularly; each where it may be reached without undue effort and without interfering with the others.

To be table to step directly from the kitchen into the herb garden (or border) is an ideal arrangement, for as herbs become a regular culinary requirement (as they are sure to do, once their delights are realized) one will find that almost every meal will require a sprig of this or that, freshly plucked during the growing season. Protection from wind is desirable as well as that segregation or privacy that makes every feature of the garden doubly interesting; so a medium size hedge of any suitable plant, kept neatly clipped and in order, should enclose the area.

PLANTS AND THEIR CARE. Everyone will choose a little differently according to individual taste. But what have been called the "Great Herbs" of ancient association and acknowledged excellence may well be considered essential to every herb garden. These are basil, pot and sweet marjoram, balm, bergamot, mint, sage, hyssop, rue spike vervain, lovage (a lusty six-footer), and lavender.

Nearly all herbs may be grown from seed though some are slower to start than others. Some are not yet in the American trade but may be had from French and English seedsmen; others are offered by a few specialists in the U. S., either as seeds or as young plants or both. A well-drained soil, not too rich, is the general requirement, nearly all herbs having a tendency to overgrow and become weedy if overfed. Beyond keeping the earth free from weeds little attention is necessary.

HARVESTING. Just before the flower buds open cut off leafy branches to cure for winter use. Do this on a sunny, dry day as early in the morning as the dew is off the plants—*never while any dew remains*

on them. Take off all imperfect leaves and hang the sprays in loose bunches in the sunlight in an airy room for half an hour. Then put them out of the light to stay until completely dry. Pick the leaves from the stems which are discarded and keep the leaves of those intended for teas or decoctions as whole as possible. Rub the others as fine as desired and put away in tightly closed glass jars or canisters.

HERB MERCURY. Common name for *Mercurialis annua,* a subshrub of S. Europe belonging to the Spurge Family. Sometimes grown for medicinal purposes, which presumably explains its name, Mercury having been the god of medicine.

HERB-PARIS. Common name for *Paris quadrifolia,* a member of the Lily Family resembling Trillium but having its parts in fours instead of threes. It grows from a rhizome to a height of 6 to 12 in., the leaves being borne in a single whorl just below the yellowish-green flower, which is followed by a blue-black berry. Though of little horticultural interest, it is occasionally planted in the hardy border or wild garden. It is increased by seed or by division of the rootstock.

HERB-PATIENCE. Common name for *Rumex patientia* or Spinach-dock, a 6-ft. perennial whose young leaves are used for greens in spring.

HERB-ROBERT. A common name for *Geranium robertianum,* an attractive annual or biennial herb with deeply cut leaves and small purplish-rose flowers.

HERBS. Properly this means any plants which die to the ground, as distinguished from shrubs and trees which have woody stems living from year to year. However, the word is now infrequently used in that sense, its place taken by the more specific names of herb subdivisions—perennial, annual, biennial, bulb, etc.; it therefore usually means medicinal and pot herbs, some of which are really shrubs. An herb garden (which see) may contain: anise, balm, basil, bene, borage, caraway, catnip, chives, coriander, cumin, dill, fennel, hoarhound, lavender, mint, parsley, pennyroyal, rosemary, rue, saffron, sage savory, spearmint, sweet marjoram, tansy, tarragon, thyme, wormwood, and others.

In gardening, especially vegetable gardening, herbs are plants grown principally for flavoring food. They also include annuals, biennials, perennials as well as some subshrubs (as lavender and rosemary) whose leaves, fruits (popularly called "seeds"), or roots are so used. Often included are plants whose leaves are used for garnishing or for boiling and serving as pot-herbs. See GREENS, EDIBLE.

Without including these last, about forty species of flavoring herbs are grown in European home gardens; in America, except among residents of foreign extraction, few gardens can boast of as many as half a dozen. Yet the amateur gardener should recognize them as next to salad plants in importance, primarily because they offer a supply found in few markets with which to enhance the pleasures and economies of his table at insignificant cost.

Though often employed to flavor roast meats, they play much more important roles in improving stews, soups, stuffings, sauces, "cheap cuts" and "left-overs."

Some of the leaf herbs have such small seeds that they must be started in seed pans, the seedlings pricked into flats and, when large enough, transplanted to the garden and set about a foot apart. They need no special cultural care. All are hardy and when once established thrive with only ordinary attention. Any good garden soil suits them. When possible, however, they should be grown close to the kitchen, but where they have full sunlight for at least six hours each day.

The seed-bearing herbs (and parsley) have relatively larger seeds than most "leaf" herbs so they may be sown right in the garden in early spring. As they germinate slowly it is advisable to sow plump radish seeds of a forcing variety 3 in. apart in the same rows to mark them so that tillage may start within a week. The radishes may be used two or three weeks later and the herb plants then given their first thinning and weeding. Plants should stand from 6 to 12 in. apart. When once started, the perennial herbs may be propagated either by layers, cuttings or in some cases by division; the first method is preferred when possible because easiest, surest and least likely to injure the parent plant.

To meet the family needs for fresh leaves between seasons, plants may be transplanted from the garden in late fall to flower pots or boxes and placed in sunny windows. More often, however, the leaves or fruits are dried during summer and fall for winter use. Fully formed, dark green parsley leaves may be cut at any time after the plants have become established. The best time to gather other leaf herbs is when the flower buds are forming but before they have opened; also as soon as the dew has evaporated but before the day has become warm and begun to rob the leaves of their fragrant oil. Spread the leaves thinly on trays in a warm, airy place (*not* in an oven or a strong sunlight) and turn them daily. When dry, crumble their soft parts and remove the stems.

Cut the heads of "seeds" herbs when the change of color indicates approaching ripeness. Do this immediately after the dew has evaporated, when the fruits cling better to the stems than later in the day. Spread thinly on cloth or in sieves raised above the ground. When dry enough "thresh" by beating with light rods to separate the fruits from the husks and trash. Spread the seed very thinly and stir daily for a week or more before storing.

As paper and cardboard absorb the volatile herb flavors, never store either seed or leaf herbs in such containers but always in tight glass jars or stoppered bottles.

The seed herbs, which belong to the Parsley Family, and are discussed under their respective names, include the following: angelica, anise, caraway, chervil, coriander, cumin, dill, fennel, lovage, parsley and samphire.

Leaf herbs belonging to the Mint Family are: balm, basil, catnip, clary, hoarhound, hyssop, lavender, marjoram, pennyroyal, peppermint, rosemary, sage, spearmint, summer savory, winter savory and thyme; four belong to the Sunflower or Daisy Family—marigold, southernwood, tansy, tarragon; one is of the Rue Family—rue; one of the Borage Family—borage; and one of the Crowfoot Family—fennel-flower.

Besides these, five members of the Lily Family often used for flavoring, are sometimes classed as culinary herbs, namely chives, ciboule (Welsh onion), garlic, rocambole and shallots. All these resemble the related onion and leek but differ in character of both plant and flavor.

See also HERB GARDEN.

HERCULES CLUB. One of the common names for *Aralia spinosa,* a very spiny small tree of the Ginseng Family; also applied to *Zanthoxylum clava-herculis,* another spiny shrub or tree of the Rue Family.

HERDS GRASS. A common name (more in England than the U. S.) for *Phleum pratense* (better known here as

Timothy, which see). In Pa. it is applied to *Agrostis palustris,* generally known as Redtop (which see). The former is one of the most important hay grasses and the latter is both a pasture and lawn grass.

HERNIARY. One of the common names for Herniaria, a genus of small trailing evergreen herbs of the Pink Family, annual and perennial natives of sandy places in Europe, W. Asia, Africa and the Canary Islands. The species *H. glabra,* which forms dense mats of moss-like foliage, that turns bronzy-red in winter, is used to some extent in carpet beds and rock gardens, and in cemeteries as a cover plant for graves. The plant thrives in ordinary garden soil, and is propagated by division or by seeds.

HERONSBILL. Common name for Erodium, a genus of herbs, some perennial species of which are grown for their fine foliage and white or lavender flowers.

HERPESTIS (her-pes'-tis). A genus of low herbs, resembling the Monkey-flowers (which see), having small blue or white flowers, somewhat fleshy leaves and a creeping stem. Some of the species grow on river banks and may be readily transferred to the wild garden and planted as a ground-cover.

HESPERALOE (hes-per-al'-oh). A genus of herbs very similar to Yucca, which see. *H. parviflora,* found in Texas, has long narrow leaves to 4 ft. and nodding rose flowers. It is grown outdoors in the S. States, and under glass in the N.

HESPERANTHA (hes-per-an'-thah). A genus of small bulbous plants from Africa, having fragrant flowers, opening only in the evening, with the outer segments white, the inner, red. The culture is similar to that of Ixia, which see. The principal species are: *H. pilosa, H. falcata* and *H. graminifolia.*

HESPERIS (hes'-per-is). Rocket. Hardy biennial and perennial herbs of erect, branching habit that bear in pyramidal spikes showy white, rose, or mauve-purple flowers good for cutting, from June to August. Plants are 1 to 3 ft. tall and their effective colorful display is enhanced by the sweet fragrance of the blooms. They do best when given a sunny location in the border. Mottling of the foliage and curling of the leaves is the sign of mosaic, a virus disease. Remove and destroy infected plants. Propagation is by seed sown outdoors in April or indoors in March; the

resulting plants will flower the following season.

H. matronalis, known as Sweet Rocket or Dames-violet, is a perennial whose delightful fragrance is accentuated in the evening. Plants often self-sow but better results come from handling them as biennials, that is, sowing some seed every year for plants to blossom the next year. *H. nivalis* is also a perennial, but only about 1 ft. tall, with loose racemes of flowers so pale as to be almost white. Catalogs sometimes list this species as a white variety of *H. matronalis.*

HESPEROCALLIS (hes-per-oh-kal'-is) *undulata.* A bulbous herb of the Lily Family commonly called Desert-lily. It belongs to the Daylily group and has funnel-shaped, waxy-white, fragrant flowers, banded with green on the reverse of each petal. The blooms, in few-flowered clusters, rise 2 ft. above the long, narrow basal leaves. A native of the deserts of Calif. and Col., the plant is sometimes grown in gardens of these regions. The bulb should be set at least 6 in. deep in light dry, sandy soil.

HESPEROYUCCA (hes-per-oh-yuk'-ah). A genus of stemless plants of the Lily Family, closely resembling yucca and growing only in mild climates. *H. whipplei* from S. Calif. has creamy-white flowers on a stalk 12 ft. high and narrow rigid leaves to nearly 2 ft.

HESSIAN FLY. An inconspicuous insect seriously destructive on wheat, barley and rye. Introduced into N. America in straw bedding used by Hessian troops during the Revolutionary War, it has spread to all wheat growing areas in the world. The insect (*Phytophaga destructor*) hides behind the sheaths of lower leaves either as white or greenish maggots, or in puparia which resemble flax seeds and in which the winter is passed. Infested stems break under the weight of the heads of grain, yields often being greatly reduced. Control by (1) seeding late in the fall after the flies have emerged, laid their eggs and died; and (2) plowing under infested stubble soon after harvest.

HETERANTHERA (het-er-an'-the-rah). A genus of bog herbs with small white, blue or yellow flowers, and creeping or floating stems. There are several species; *H. reniformis* has blue flowers and *H. dubia* small yellow ones. Both grow readily in damp spots in the bog garden.

HETEROMELES (het - er - oh - mee'-leez). An evergreen shrub, formerly classed with Photinia, belonging to the Rose Family. See TOYON.

HETEROSPERMUM (het-er-oh-spur'-mum). A genus of warm-climate American composite herbs grown for their small heads of yellow flowers.

HETEROTOMA (het-er-ot'-oh-ma). A genus of annual or perennial herbs from Mexico, belonging to the Bellflower Family. One species, *H. lobelioides*, P., sometimes known as Bird-flower, has brilliant red and yellow spurred and lobed blossoms. Occasionally grown in the greenhouse for its odd-shaped flowers, it makes an interesting plant to grow in the open in summer.

HEUCHERA RAISED FRQM A CUTTING
The leaf at the lower left was stuck in sand in a coolhouse in November. By March, five new leaves had developed. The plant can soon be set in the garden for spring bloom.

HEUCHERA (heu'-ker-ah). Alumroot. Herbaceous perennials of usually dwarf, compact habit of growth, natives of W. N. America and members of the Saxifrage Family. Blooming from June to September, they are valuable for the low border or rockery. In a good loamy soil and sunny location, the plants produce mats of deep green sometimes tinged white or red, from which rise slender stalks bearing airy clusters of tiny bell-shaped flowers, which are good for cutting. Plants are propagated from seed sown in the spring, and by division in spring or fall.

H. sanguinea, commonly known as Coral Bells, is the most generally cultivated in the United States. Growing from 1 to 2 ft.

high and bearing bell-shaped flowers about ½ in. long with prominent coral-colored calyx. There are many horticultural varieties, among them *alba*, with white flowers; *hybrida*, a robust type with large flowers of various colors developed from crimson; *gracillima*, a slender form; and *maxima*, featuring dark crimson flowers.

Several horticultural forms have been given specific names, such as *H. convallaria*, whose flowers resemble lilies-of-the-valley. A number of natural species may be used in the wild garden.

HIBBERTIA (hi-bur'-ti-ah). Shrubs or sub-shrubs from Australia of which only 2 or 3 species have been grown to any extent. These are climbers or trailers to be grown in a greenhouse over most of the U. S. or outdoors in the warmest parts of the country. *H. dentata*, the best known, is a trailer or twiner, with oblong toothed leaves, and dark yellow flowers about 2 in. across, with many stamens. *H. volubilis*, a woody climber and the largest of the genus, has large yellow flowers of unpleasant odor.

HIBISCUS (hy-bis'-kus). (See illustrations, Plates 1 and 27.) Rose-mallow. A variable genus of widely distributed herbs, shrubs and small trees, of the Mallow Family. It is generally divided into 4 groups—annuals, herbaceous perennials, hardy shrubs, and tropical shrubs and trees. In recent years improved forms of the native species have been developed with large showy flowers; popularly known as Mallow Marvels and Giant-flowering Marsh-mallows, they are usually listed as *H. moscheutos* hybrids.

Several armored scale insects and the white fly attack hibiscus in the greenhouse. Fumigate with hydrocyanic acid gas or calcium cyanide.

Out-of-doors the rose of sharon (*H. syriacus*) is often seriously infested with aphids. Spray with nicotine-sulphate and soap or other contact insecticide.

The annual kinds of hibiscus are easily raised from seed; the herbaceous perennials by seed or division; the shrubby kinds by seed, cuttings, and grafting.

PRINCIPAL ANNUAL SPECIES

H. abelmoschus (Musk-mallow) grows to 6 ft. tall, with leaves variously lobed and large yellow flowers with a crimson center. Largely grown in the tropics for the musk-scented seeds.

trionum (Flower-of-an-hour) grows to 2 ft., with leaves deeply divided and sulphur-yellow flowers with dark centers. Useful in the flower border and formerly known as *H. africanus.*

manihot is a strong grower to 10 ft., with palmate leaves and yellow flowers with a dark velvety center, to 9 in. across. Perennial in the tropics, but can be grown North as an annual if seeds are sown early under glass.

esculentus (Okra; Gumbo). This is grown in the kitchen-garden for its long ribbed pods, used in cooking.

sabdariffa (Roselle) is a strong grower cultivated in warm regions for its fleshy calyces, from which sauces, jellies, and a cooling drink are made.

Herbaceous Perennial Species

This group contains some good garden forms valuable for late summer flowering. They will grow almost anywhere, but appear to best advantage in moist soil in the flower border or shrubbery.

H. coccineus is native in S. swamps, and has slender lobed leaves and large rose-red or crimson flowers. Not hardy N. but has been used as a parent in the production of garden forms.

militaris is found in wet places from Pa. south. It has halberd-shaped leaves, and large white or pink flowers with a purple eye. It has been used in hybridizing.

moscheutos (Swamp Rose-mallow) is found in swamps from Mass. to Fla. It has leaves scarcely lobed and pink flowers to 8 in. across. It has played an important part in the production of garden forms.

oculiroseus is found in coastal swamps from N. J. S. It is similar to the preceding species but has white flowers with a crimson center.

incanus also resembles *H. moscheutos,* but has smaller leaves and flowers, the latter being in pale yellow, pink or white, with a crimson eye. Found in S. swamps.

Hardy Shrub Species

H. syriacus (Rose-of-Sharon), commonly knows as Althea. A tall shrub of upright growth and rounded form, valued for its late flowering season and colorful flowers. There are numerous garden forms, the colors ranging from white to pink, red, and bluish-purple. Some have double flowers, and some variegated leaves. They thrive best in well-drained soil.

Tropical Shrub Species

H. rosa-sinensis (Chinese Hibiscus) is a shrub or tree to 30 ft. in warm countries. It is an old favorite pot plant in greenhouses, valued for its large showy flowers of various colors, some double. It is the "State" flower of Hawaii. Old plants can be cut back annually and grown on for several years. Among the numerous forms var. *cooperi* is conspicuous, with narrow leaves variegated white and small scarlet flowers.

schizopetalus is a tall shrub from tropical Africa with slender drooping branches, and curious drooping flowers of red or orange-red. The petals are recurved and deeply cut, with the stamens hanging far beyond. An interesting plant for the warm greenhouse.

HICKORY. Common name for several familiar species of hardy, deciduous trees of the genus Carya. Members of the Walnut Family, they are rather tall, somewhat slow-growing trees, much planted for their ornamental appearance and some for their edible nuts. They have large leaves and greenish flowers, followed by a large green fruit which when splitting reveals the nut. They are beautiful native American trees, and despite their slow growth, excellent for planting in parks and in the home grounds, as they have tall straight trunks and hold their foliage well above the ground.

As it is difficult to transplant them from the wild, it is better to plant seeds where the trees are to grow (if grown solely for ornament) or to buy nursery-grown stock of selected varieties or strains if nuts are the first consideration. They should be planted in rich, well-watered soil, though some of the species will grow in dry situations. The nuts form a valuable crop, and of late years many orchards have been planted.

ENEMIES. There are no serious or important diseases of hickory, but the hickory leaf aphid, the leaf stem gall and certain borers do great damage. Plant lice, causing hollow green galls on the leaf stems, may kill as much as half of the new growth. Control them with a dormant oil spray. Various twig borers and pruners can be kept in check by removing and burning infested wood. The hickory bark beetle, a close relative of the insect that spreads the Dutch elm disease (which see), is a particularly dangerous pest, its presence often not being noted until the whole top of the tree is dead. Trees found to have been entered by thousands of beetles should be cut and the bark burned before the insects can escape and attack other trees in spring. Encourage vigorous growth of the trees by plenty of food and water.

HICORIA (hi-koh'-ri-ah). Former generic name for Hickory (which see), now called Carya.

HIERACIUM (hy-er-ay'-shi-um). A genus of perennial composite herbs with red, yellow or orange flowers, often becoming a pest in fields. See HAWKWEED.

HILL-GOOSEBERRY. A common name for *Rhodomyrtus tomentosa* or Downy-myrtle, an Australasian shrub with white flowers and edible purple berries.

HILLS-OF-SNOW. Popular name for *Hydrangea arborescens* var. *grandiflora*, a profuse and early blooming white-flowered variety.

HIMALAYA-BERRY. A European, not Asiatic, species of blackberry (*Rubus procerus*), recently introduced into America for its fruit. Its long, thorny, semi-perennial canes are best grown on trellises; otherwise it is treated like the Dewberry, which see.

HIMALAYAN-HONEYSUCKLE (*Leycesteria formosa*). An attractive Himalayan deciduous shrub of medium size belonging to the Honeysuckle Family, not quite hardy North. The white flowers, tinged purple, are arranged in whorls in drooping leafy racemes. The leafy bracts are purple colored, and the flowers (which open in summer) are followed by reddish-purple berries. Plants are propagated by seeds and cuttings of green and mature wood.

HIPPEASTRUM (hip - ee - as' - trum). The genus of bulbous herbaceous plants with large lily-like flowers whose species and many hybrids are grown as house plants and summer garden subjects and commonly known as Amaryllis (which see). The strong, stout, erect stems bear several enormous flowers of white, pink, or red (or those colors combined) above a clump of broad, sword-shaped leaves. Both Hippeastrum and the true genus Amaryllis are members of the Amaryllis Family. The latter comes from S. Africa, while Hippeastrum is native only in S. America. Lycoris, a closely related genus whose flowers

are also known as Amaryllis, is native to China and Japan.

For cultural directions and description of species and hybrids of Hippeastrum, see AMARYLLIS.

HIPPOPHAE (hi-pof'-ah-ee). Sea-Buckthorn. Of these deciduous shrubs or trees with spiny branches, belonging to the Oleaster Family, *H. rhamnoides* is the one usually grown. This is a very hardy shrub or small tree of Europe and Asia. It is not particular as to soil, and often suckers freely. The narrow silvery-gray leaves make it very conspicuous. The small yellow flowers are of separate sexes produced on different plants, so it is necessary to have plants of each near-by, to insure a crop of the showy orange-colored berries. *H. salicifolia* is a tender Himalayan tree with larger leaves and pale yellow berries.

HIPPURIS (hi-peu'-ris). A genus of aquatic herbs with long tail-like stems, set with very small leaves and inconspicuous flowers. They grow in water, sometimes attaining 2 ft. in height. *H. vulgaris* is quite decorative when used in the bog garden.

HIRSUTE. Rather coarsely hairy; used particularly in reference to leaves and twigs.

HISPID. Clothed with erect, stiff hairs, as in species of Borage.

HOARHOUND or HOREHOUND. Common name for *Marrubium vulgare*, an aromatic perennial herb with woolly white foliage and whitish flowers. Its chief use is for flavoring candies and lozenges to be used for throat affections. The plant thrives in any dry soil.

HOARY. Covered with a close grayish-white down, as the fruit of the Pasque-flower or the young branches of the Silk-oak.

HOBBLEBUSH. A common name for *Viburnum alnifolium* (which see), also called American Wayfaring-tree; an attractive native shrub with white flowers in broad clusters.

HOE. A tillage tool which, in its simplest form (the draw-hoe or field-hoe) consists of a thin, flat blade set nearly at right angles to its long handle. However, there are many varied forms for special purposes. Popular styles include (1) the grub- or grubbing-hoe—a heavy, pick-axe-like tool, usually with one axe-like blade for chopping roots and the other hoe-shaped for slicing earth; (2) the Dutch, push, or scuffle hoe with a narrow blade set parallel to the ground, which is alternately pushed and pulled through the soil, as the user moves backward, and leaves the hoed surface untrodden; (3) the bayonet-hoe, whose narrow trowel-like blade is used for thinning plants in rows; and (4) the ridging hoe, a broad-bladed tool used for "earthing-up" soil around plants. Many other types are made for working specific crops.

The horse-hoe, better known in America as the cultivator (which see) and the wheelhoe (which see), have greatly reduced the need for hand hoes, but every gardener can usually find use for at least five types, namely: The flat-tined hoe resembling a digging fork with tines bent at right angles, used to level off rough newly dug or plowed ground preparatory to raking, to clear up stones and rubbish, to work between narrow rows, to dig potatoes, etc. The common hoe has a thin, sharp blade, and a solid shank (not a ferrule), and is unexcelled for general purposes. The small "onion hoe," resembles the common hoe but for lighter work. The Warren or heart-shaped hoe is used chiefly to open furrows with its "point" and to cover them with its "ears." The scuffle hoe (preferably a narrow, light one) has already been described.

Used for weeding, the common hoe should be handled as a chopping or slicing tool, not a drawing implement. Thus used it will leave a level soil surface completely loosened and with all weeds cut off and exposed to the killing rays of the sun. The various types of scuffle hoe do the same work, but are slid along just under the surface, not lifted or chopped. To do good work a hoe must be kept clean and sharp. See also CULTIVATION; TOOLS.

HOFFMANNIA (hof-man'-i-ah). Tropical American herbs or shrubs, usually grown in warm greenhouses for their colored foliage. They are easily grown from cuttings and old plants make good specimens if cut back in spring. The principal species are:

H. discolor, a dwarf hairy plant with purple stems, leaves olive-green above and rich red beneath, and small red flowers.

ghiesbreghti, which grows to 4 ft., with 4-angled stems, leaves a foot or more long, dark velvety-green above and red purple beneath, small yellow flowers, spotted red.

regalis, which has plaited leaves about 9 in. long, shining dark green above and deep red beneath.

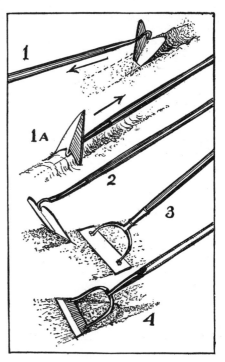

SOME HOES IN USE

From the top down, are shown: 1. Warren or heart-shaped type opening a furrow. 1A. Same type, filling furrow in which seed has been sown. 2. Common garden hoe. 3 and 4. Two types of Dutch or scuffle hoe which are pushed back and forth flat and just under the surface to destroy weeds and maintain a dust mulch.

HOG-PEANUT. A common name for *Amphicarpa monoica* (which see), a trailing perennial herb of small horticultural importance, often becoming a pestiferous weed.

HOHERIA (hoh-hee'-ri-ah). A genus of New-Zealand shrubs or small trees, white-flowered and evergreen or nearly so, belonging to the Mallow Family. They can only be grown outdoors in mild climates. *H. populnea,* the largest of the group, grows to 30 ft., has oval leaves to 5 in. long, and bears a profusion of flowers about an inch across, followed by clusters of winged seeds. *H. sexstylosa* grows to 15 ft. or more, with long narrow leaves and flowers less than an inch across. *H. angustifolia* has smaller leaves and flowers.

HOLCUS (hohl'-kus). A genus of tall, Old-World grasses with broad, coarse-textured leaves and some with large tassel-like seed-heads. There are both annual and perennial species but none are hardy. The most important of the grasses is *H. sorghum* from the stems of which sorghum syrup is pressed; it has numerous varieties, some useful forage crops, others grown for the grain or other products. These include Kafir-corn, Feterita, Durra, and Broomcorn. Other species are important S. hay or pasture grasses as Johnson, Means, or Aleppo Grass (*H. halepensis*), Sudan Grass (*H. sudanensis*) and Tunis Grass (*H. virgatus*).

OPENING A TRENCH WITH A HOE
For beans, peas, and other large seeds. Keep feet on tightly stretched line to hold it straight. Use corner of hoe.

HOLLY. Common name for the Ilex, a genus of trees or shrubs having glossy evergreen or deciduous leaves, small inconspicuous flowers, and small, usually bright red fruits. The hollies are of great ornamental value in the gardens as small specimen trees, hedges, and in the shrubbery border. As many of the species are *dioecious,* that is, have the pistillate or berry-bearing flowers on one plant and the staminate flowers on another, and as much of the charm of the plants is in the berries, care should be taken to plant (especially in the case of deciduous species) mostly pistillate specimens, with a few staminate ones to insure pollination of the others.

One of the handsomest of our native shrubs is *I. opaca* found from Mass. to Fla.

and Tex. but which has been so extensively used for Christmas greens that it has been almost exterminated in many sections; it is now protected by law in several States. Hardy as far N. as Mass. and with its spiny evergreen foliage and brilliant red berries, a well-grown specimen is most decorative in front of coniferous evergreens.

I. aquifolium (English Holly) is even more beautiful, as it bears larger, denser clusters of berries, but it is not as hardy as the native sort. An occasional specimen will survive even S. New York winters in a sheltered spot, but the species does best in the moister, more equable climate of W. Wash. and Ore.

I. glabra (Inkberry), another evergreen native species, is hardy N., and although the black fruit has not the showy effect of the red-berried species, the excellent smooth dark foliage is effective in a shady N. corner. *I. crenata* (Japanese Holly), especially the var. *microphylla,* is an exceedingly fine evergreen for general use in the garden, making a good background or formal specimen shrub.

The native deciduous species, *I. laevigata* (Smooth Winterberry) and *I. verticillata* (Black-alder or Winterberry) should be used much more extensively for the winter beauty of their clustered scarlet berries on the bare stems. The second of the two supplies berried twigs that florists use in brightening up holiday wreaths. In the wild garden they should be massed in swampy places; but they will also grow well in the border, especially *I. verticillata* if given sufficient moisture and a soil with an acid reaction.

CULTURAL NOTES

All hollies grow best in rich, rather moist soil, and, though they are slow-growing, the evergreen species make remarkably fine hedges. They should be moved in spring before growth starts or in the late summer after the season's growth has commenced to ripen. Both *I. opaca* and *I. aquifolium,* when moved in large sizes, should have most of the foliage stripped from them to check the transpiration of moisture. Or they may be moved without stripping the leaves if dug with a large ball of earth and cut back severely; when transplanted they should be sprayed daily with the hose for several weeks. Hollies are raised from seed, which should be stratified, as they do not germinate until the second year. The evergreen species are also increased by cuttings of ripened wood, placed in a coldframe and kept well moistened.

Leaf spots sometimes make holly foliage unsightly; if affected leaves are not too numerous remove and destroy them.

The chief insect pest of holly is a leaf miner which produces winding yellowish-brown mines in the green leaves. The young maggots, hatching from eggs laid on the underside of the leaves, work in the new foliage throughout the season and winter there. Therefore control by picking and burning infested leaves and spraying with a nicotine-soap solution during late spring and early summer.

Species and Varieties

In addition to the species already discussed there may be mentioned also the following forms: Horticultural varieties of *I. aquifolium,* including var. *albomarginata,* with very bright red berries and leaves with a silvery-white margin; var. *ferox* (Hedgehog Holly), whose leaves are covered with short sharp spines on the upper surface, and usually seen in a yellow leaved strain; var. *laurifolia,* having entire leaves without spines; var. *microphylla,* having very small leaves and spines; var. *princeps,* with large spiny leaves; and var. *serratifolia,* with leaves edged with small spiny teeth. All these varieties are grafted on seedlings of the species.

cornuta, to 10 ft., shrubby in growth and resembling *I. aquifolium,* but possibly more hardy in the E. States.

cassine (Dahoon) grows to 25 ft., and also in shrub form, with toothed evergreen leaves and dull red berries; extensively used in its native S. States for hedges.

vomitoria (Yaupon, Cassena), a shrub or small tree with evergreen leaves and scarlet berries, native from Va. to Fla. and Tex. A medicinal drink was formerly made from this plant by the Indians.

paraguariensis, a small evergreen tree or shrub of Brazil and southward, valued there for its leaves which are made into a stimulating beverage called Paraguay tea, or herba de maté.

Mountain-holly is Nemapanthus, another member of the Holly Family; African-holly is *Solanum giganteum;* Sea-holly is *Eryngium maritimum.*

HOLLY FAMILY. Common name of the Aquifoliaceae (which see), comprising three genera of mostly hardy, widely cultivated ornamental shrubs.

HOLLY FERN. The name given to various species of Polystichum, all glossy, prickly toothed ferns, some of them native in the N. States and good in the garden in woods soil supplied with lime. The Tender Holly Fern (which see), one of the standard house plants, belongs to another genus, Cyrtomium.

HOLLYHOCK. Common name for *Althaea rosea* and less commonly *A. ficifolia,* which differs only in having fig-like, deeply lobed leaves. Both are stately hardy biennials or semi-perennials which should be included in every garden because of their graceful, tall growth which makes them especially suitable for background borders, against walls or trellises and to screen unsightly views or fences. Attaining a height of 5 to 9 ft., they blossom from July until early September, bearing large, wide-open single or double flowers along the leafy main stem, which generally is hairy. The flowers, which may be white, red, rose, yellowish or salmon, often present beautiful delicate pastel shades. Because of their stately appearance they seem to belong especially to colonial-type houses. A tall group among shrubbery or against a clump of evergreens is most effective, and a row along a garden wall or fence with a white house as a background makes a charming picture. Many of the newer hollyhocks bear flowers the first week in July. Seed is usually sown in July in a coldframe or seed bed about ½ in. deep, and the plants set out 2 ft. apart the following spring to bloom that summer. Or they may be started in their permanent location. There is a new strain called annuals, which produces flowers the first summer if seeds are sown indoors in February.

Hollyhocks require a rich, well-drained soil, deeply dug and enriched with rotted manure. Heavy soil should be made looser by the addition of sand; very light soil should be given body by the addition of cow manure. Full sunlight and group planting are best and new plants should be grown and set out every two years, for while semi-perennial they are best treated as biennials.

A new semi-double variety (Allegheny) grows 7 ft. tall, with large flowers with fringed edges. Prince of Orange is an orange double variety, but most of the doubles are rose, maroon, pink, white, scarlet, salmon and yellow. Hollyhocks will bloom longer if dead blossoms are picked off the flower stalks, which should be cut down to the ground when all the flowers have faded, unless it is desired to save seed. As seedlings cannot be depended upon to come true to color, an unusual shade may be increased by root division in the early fall. This rather difficult operation consists of separating the auxiliary tap roots from the main tap root of an old plant.

The commonest disease of hollyhocks is rust, characterized by reddish-brown spore pustules on the under leaf surfaces. Severe infections cause yellowed foliage and very sickly looking plants. Control by careful dusting *underneath* the leaves with fine sulphur dust beginning very early in the spring and keeping the new growth protected in the fall. Cut the old flower stalks down to the ground as soon as they finish blooming and destroy the common succulent weed called "cheeses" (*Malva rotundifolia*) which is also a host for this fungus.

Several other fungi cause leaf spots, but the removal and burning of all old plant parts in the fall will keep them in check. Removal of old stalks will also keep the common stalk borer from becoming too numerous. Ten per cent lead arsenate added to the sulphur dust used against rust will largely prevent injury by slugs and other chewing insects.

HOLLY-LEAVED BARBERRY. Common name for *Mahonia aquifolium* (which see). Also called Oregon Hollygrape. An evergreen shrub with abundant yellow flowers and clusters of bloomy dark-blue berries.

HOLODISCUS (hoh-loh-dis'-kus). Ornamental shrubs belonging to the Rose Family, found in the western part of the U. S. In gardens they prefer a well-drained soil in a sunny position. They are hardy as far north as Mass. Propagated by seeds and layers. *H. discolor* (Rockspirea) is the principal species. This is a large shrub, to 9 ft., with slender arching branches, making a good subject as a single specimen on a lawn. It has rather small, somewhat lobed leaves, and is conspicuous in summer with its large drooping panicles of small creamy-white flowers. Instead of falling, these later turn an attractive tan color continuing in that condition for some time. Var. *ariaefolius* is more often cultivated, and differs from the type in having

leaves grayish-green beneath instead of white.

HOLY-GHOST-FLOWER. Common name for a S. American orchid, *Peristeria elata,* with large plaited leaves and fragrant waxy-white flowers in spikes. See ORCHIDS.

HOLY GRASS. A common name for *Hierochloë odorata* or ᵗ Vanilla Grass (which see), a fragrant perennial grass used by N. American Indians for basket and mat making.

HOLY THISTLE. A common name for *Silybum marianum* (which see), an annual or biennial thistle-like plant with rosy-purple flower-heads.

HONESTY. Common name for Lunaria (which see), especially *L. annua,* also known as Moonwort, Satin-flower, St. Peters Penny and Money-plant.

HONEY-BELL (*Mahernia verticillata*). A S. African shrub of weak straggly habit, usually grown in greenhouses as a hanging plant or trained to a form. The leaves are small and finely cut, and in spring it bears a profusion of nodding very fragrant yellow flowers. It is easily grown from cuttings. Do not confuse with Mahonia, a genus of handsome evergreen shrubs closely related to the barberries.

HONEY-BUSH. The common name for the genus Melianthus, evergreen shrubs of S. Africa, belonging to the Soapberry Family. They can be grown outdoors only in the warmest parts of the U. S. *M. major,* which grows to 10 ft. in California, has gray compound leaves a foot or more long, with a winged stem and stipules (small appendages at the base of a leaf) united at the base to form a leafy collar. The sweetly scented reddish-brown flowers are borne in racemes a foot long. *M. minor* has smaller leaves with 2 stipules *not* united, and upright racemes of dull red flowers. *M. comosus* has leaves about 6 in. long on a winged stem, 2 free stipules like the preceding species. The orange flowers, spotted red, are borne in short nodding racemes.

HONEY LOCUST. Common name for the genus Gleditsia, a member of the Pea Family, comprising species of deciduous trees, often spiny, which are used for shade trees and other ornamental purposes. It is most frequently applied to *G. triacanthos* (also called Sweet Locust), which grows to 140 ft., the trunk and branches being armed with stout, rigid, 3-forked spines,

3 to 4 in. long. The leaves are feather-form and finely-divided and the inconspicuous greenish flowers are followed by handsome flat, glossy brown or black pods. This species is much used for street and park planting, and plants when severely pruned form excellent hedges. Propagated by seeds sown in spring after being soaked in warm water.

See also GLEDITSIA.

HONEYSUCKLE. Common name for the genus Lonicera, a group of very desirable ornamental shrubs, valued for their showy, often fragrant flowers, and decorative fruits. They are mostly hardy N., of easy cultivation, not particular as to soil, and in general prefer open sunny situations, although some do well in partial shade. The bush forms are valuable for use in mixed shrub plantings or for screening purposes; some attain large size if grown as single specimens with ample room for development. The climbers are good on fences and trellises, and *L. japonica* and some others make good ground-covers though at times becoming a nuisance by spreading and choking out other plants. Honeysuckles are propagated by seed, cuttings of mature wood, and layers.

ASIATIC BUSH HONEYSUCKLES

L. fragrantissima, a stout half-evergreen shrub, to 8 ft., with handsome leathery leaves, is especially valued for its very sweet-scented creamy-white flowers in early spring and its leaves which remain green well into winter.

syringantha is of dense habit with slender, partly prostrate branches, small leaves and fragrant pale-lavender, lilac-like flowers. Var. *wolfi* is a form with narrower leaves and carmine flowers.

thibetica, to 5 ft., is of similar habit, but with lustrous dark green leaves white beneath, and pale purple flowers.

chrysantha is an upright grower, to 12 ft., with flowers yellowish-white to yellow, and bright red fruit in abundance.

gracilipes is a graceful shrub, to 6 ft., and one of the earliest to bloom. The pink to carmine flowers are mostly borne singly, and the scarlet fruit is ripe in June.

korolkowi makes a large rounded bush, to 12 ft., of distinctive appearance, with bluish-green leaves and light pink flowers.

tatarica (Tartarian Honeysuckle), one of the best known, bears a profusion of pink or white flowers, followed by dark red fruit. It is very variable, some of the best forms being var. *grandiflora,* with large white flowers; *rosea,* with flowers rosy-pink outside and paler within; *latifolia,* with larger leaves and large pink flowers; *lutea,* a form with yellow fruit.

morrowi is a widespreading shrub of distinctive habit, growing to 8 ft., with flowers white to yellow and blood-red fruit. The leaves hang on and continue green until quite late.

maacki is a stout upright grower, to 15 ft., with large dark green leaves. About the last to bloom, it is very conspicuous with large white to yellow flowers. The dark red fruit is ripe in Sept. Var. *podocarpa* is shorter and of more spreading habit, with leaves and fruit retained later.

quinquelocularis grows to 15 ft., with yellowish flowers and white translucent fruit.

nitida is an evergreen, to 6 ft., of upright habit, with small leaves, creamy-white flowers and bluish-purple fruit. It makes a good hedge in mild regions.

pileata, evergreen or partly so, of almost prostrate habit, with whitish flowers and dark purple fruit, is excellent for a shady place in the rock garden.

OTHER BUSH SPECIES

L. ledebouri is a somewhat tender Californian species, with showy orange flowers tinged scarlet, and black fruits.

alpigena is a European species growing to 8 ft., with yellowish flowers tinged red, and showy scarlet fruit in late summer.

CLIMBING SPECIES

L. japonica is evergreen or nearly so, with twining stems, to 15 ft., and fragrant white flowers tinged purple. It is a good porch vine and an excellent ground-cover, especially for steep slopes. Var. *halliana* is very similar but with flowers pure white to yellow; *aureo-reticulata* is a form with small leaves netted yellow.

henryi is a half-evergreen slender twiner with dark green leaves, yellowish to reddish-purple flowers and black berries. It makes a good ground-cover in a shady place.

sempervirens (Trumpet Honeysuckle) is a tall native climber, with dark green leaves bluish beneath, and orange-yellow to scarlet flowers.

caprifolium, a twiner, to 20 ft., with leaves bluish beneath, yellowish-white or purplish flowers, and orange-red fruit, is naturalized in parts of E. U. S.

prolifera is a native bushy twiner, to 5 ft., with glaucous leaves, pale yellow flowers with purple markings, and handsome scarlet berries.

tragophylla, a high-climbing Chinese species, with bright yellow flowers, is fairly hardy N.

heckrotti is a hybrid, supposedly between *L. americana* and *L. sempervirens*. It has purple and yellow flowers and is one of the freest flowering of the climbing kinds.

periclymenum, the Woodbine of English hedgerows, shows to best advantage when scrambling over shrubs or small trees, and is very attractive, with yellowish-white fragrant flowers.

Bush-honeysuckle is Diervilla; White Swamp-honeysuckle is *Rhododendron viscosum;* Himalaya-honeysuckle is *Leycesteria formosa;* Cape-honeysuckle is *Tecomaria capensis;* Jamaica-honeysuckle is *Passiflora laurifolia;* French-honeysuckle is *Hedysarum coronarium.*

HONEYSUCKLE FAMILY. Common name for Caprifoliaceae (which see), a family of ornamental, mostly shrubby plants.

HONEYWORT. Common name for the Old-World genus Cerinthe which means Wax-flower, given because of the old belief that bees visited the purple-tipped yellow flowers for wax. The name Honeywort is due to the abundant nectar secreted by the flowers. The plants are easily grown annuals, of which *C. retorta* is the best.

HOODIA (hoo'-di-ah). A genus of small succulent tropical herbs belonging to

the Milkwort Family. They have large showy yellow or purple flowers and cactus-like foliage. In the N. they are grown in botanical collections in the greenhouse.

HOP. The genus Humulus. Tall, vigorous vines, with rough stems and leaves. Besides being important in brewing, they are of some ornamental value. *H. lupulus,* the Common or European Hop, is an herbaceous perennial, with fast-growing twining stems, sometimes attaining 30 ft. in a season. It has become widely naturalized in N. America and is a good screen plant for the summer, interesting with its clusters of papery, pale yellow "hops," which have a distinct heavy odor. Several varieties are grown commercially in the hop-fields, being propagated by cuttings of the young shoots from the crown.

Powdery mildew may trouble hop vines but can be controlled by dusting with fine sulphur. Control the hop aphid by spraying with nicotine-sulphate and soap or by applying nicotine dust.

H. japonicus, a good and fast growing annual vine, has leaves more deeply cut than the preceding species. It will make 10 to 20 ft. of growth in a season from seed sown in May. Var. *variegatus,* with leaves streaked and blotched white, is more decorative. Seedlings of this form are likely to show considerable and interesting variations.

HOP-BUSH. Common name for *Dodonaea cuneata,* a tropical shrub, generally viscid, with small flowers and winged fruits.

HOP-HORNBEAM. Common name for *Ostrya virginiana* (also known as Ironwood), a small or medium-sized N. American tree, belonging to the Birch Family and differing but slightly from the Hornbeam (which see). It is very slow growing, but worth considering as an ornamental subject, especially for dry places. It has bright green attractive foliage, turning yellow in fall, and light green cone-like fruits consisting of nutlets enclosed in bladder-like husks. The wood is heavy and close-grained and considerably used for making tool handles and similar small objects. Propagated by seeds, best sown in fall.

HOPPERBURN. A condition caused by the feeding of leaf hoppers on potatoes; it consists of a browning of the margins of the leaves accompanied by some curling and breaking of the leaf blades. The hop-

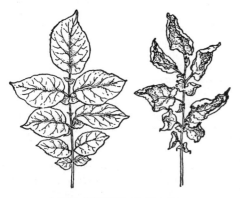

LEAF HOPPER DAMAGE
The characteristic hopperburn on potato leaves is shown at the right, in contrast to the normal, healthy leaves, left.

pers may be repelled by a bordeaux spray. See LEAF HOPPER; and under POTATO.

HOPS, SPENT. A by-product of brewing, containing small quantities of organic nitrogen. It may be used with safety in soils where acid-loving plants are to be grown and is a cheap low-grade fertilizer and source of humus in those localities where it may be readily secured from breweries.

HOP-TREE. Common name for *Ptelea trifoliata*, a N. American shrub or small tree, growing to 25 ft., and belonging to the Rue Family. It is not particular as to soil, but is partial to shade. The dark green leaves have good value in a mixed planting, and are highly aromatic. The small fragrant yellowish flowers, borne in dense clusters, are followed by interesting and decorative hop-like seeds. Propagation of the species is by seeds; of varieties, by layering or grafting. Var. *aurea*, with yellow leaves, is the best known.

HORDEUM (hor'-de-um). A genus of annual and perennial members of the Grass Family, native to temperate zones of both E. and W. hemispheres. *H. jubatum*, commonly known as Squirreltail Grass, is a biennial or perennial, to 2½ ft., grown as an ornamental. The 4-in. nodding heads have barbed beards often 3 in. long. Propagation is by seed, usually sown where the plants are to grow. Any ordinary soil is satisfactory provided there is plenty of sun. The flower spikes are gathered just after their emergence from the sheath and dried for use in winter bouquets. *H. vulgare* is the wild species from which barley, the cereal crop, has been developed. See also ORNAMENTAL GRASSES.

HOREHOUND. Another spelling for Hoarhound, which see.

HORMINUM (hor'-mi-num). A small herb of the Mint Family, sometimes used in the rock garden. The perennial *H. pyrenaicum* has bluish-purple flowers on 1 ft. stalks. It increases by seed or division.

HORMONE. A substance produced in one part of a plant that affects the function or regulates the action of another part. It is assumed by students of plant physiology that there are root-forming, flower-forming, and other process-regulating substances present in plants as hormones. Because of their characteristic actions, they are sometimes popularly referred to as "chemical messengers," and, because various chemical compounds found elsewhere than in plants or made by man have been found to have somewhat similar growth-inducing or growth-regulating effects, they, too, have been loosely called hormones. But this is inaccurate since the term strictly means only substances produced in and by plants themselves. These synthetic materials are now being used in the manufacture of proprietary liquids and powders used to stimulate or hasten growth responses, as in the treatment of cuttings to facilitate rooting; of flowers to induce the formation of fruits without pollination; of fruits to delay their fall until they are more fully ripe (and thus to partly prevent "June drop"), and so on. While much progress has been made and noteworthy results obtained in various applications of these discoveries to practical plant, flower, and fruit production, investigations are still going on and recommendations made regarding specific subjects under certain conditions should not be interpreted as applying also to other subjects and circumstances. In other words, any of the new growth substances should be used carefully and exactly in accordance with the directions supplied by the manufacturer—unless, of course, one wants to undertake experiments of his own to find out just what responses can be obtained from various plants.

Referring again to the natural or true hormones, the effect of light on the tips of growing shoots was observed many years ago. Later it was discovered that plants manufacture in their growing tips chemicals to which the name hormones was given. These hormones influence growth activity as they pass downward through the cambium tissue layer toward the root. Throughout this transport system, wherever the hormone substance is present or accumulates, there is increased cell growth. It has been found that the course downward of these substances' (and consequently their greatest effect) is mostly on the darker side of the plant away from the strongest light. The greatly increased cell growth on the dark side causes the plant to bend—or, in reality, to be actually pushed toward—the light. This is why house plants bend appreciably when grown where strong light comes from one side. This same hormone influence continues into the root system where it is essential for healthy root growth.

Since the root-forming substance is made in the growing tip and leaves of a plant

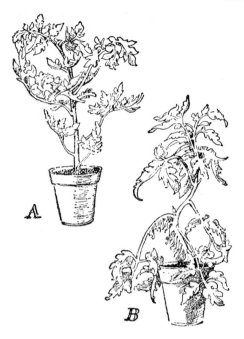

HORMONE ACTION ON PLANTS

A. A tomato plant growing normally. B. A similar plant that has had a hormone containing grease rubbed on its stem. Note the bending down of the branches (called epinasty) and the dense growth of white roots along the treated area.

and goes downward, a cut made on a twig or stem stops the downward movement, and roots tend to form just above the cut where the hormone accumulates. This is what happens when air- or pot-layering is employed in propagating a plant, such as a rubber-plant, which see.

Flower-forming hormones are also a product of the growing shoot tip. Artificially shortening the day by covering certain plants with opaque cloth during certain periods of growth induces early flowering. Lengthening the day with artificial lights causes the same kind of plants to delay their blooming period. These variations are assumed to be due to different amounts of the flowering hormone manufactured under the unnatural growing conditions created.

The most important use of hormones is as weed killers. When used in larger amounts than needed to stimulate growth, certain hormone compounds such as 2,4-D and 2,4,5-T will cause the death of certain plants to which they are applied.

COUNTER-HORMONES

The existence of counter-hormones (chemicals which temporarily hold back the action of hormones) has been shown by scientists. Counter-hormones play a role in dormancy by preventing hormones from stimulating growth. Gradually used up by exposure to cold, they then permit the plant to resume growth at the end of its dormant period.

Another interesting substance which might be considered a counter-hormone is Maleic hydrazide. This chemical checks the growth of the terminal buds of stems and of other growing parts of plants.

If Maleic hydrazide is not used in excess, the plant will gradually resume growth. Its effect is being used to hold back the growth of rough grass on roadsides, to edge lawns chemically, and to keep plants dormant in storage.

See also AUXIN; CHEMICALS IN GARDENING; ROOT-FORMING SUBSTANCES.

HORN AND HOOF MEAL. A by-product of slaughter houses made from ground up refuse that is not suitable for other purposes. If finely ground, it is a good organic fertilizer containing 10 to 15 per cent nitrogen in fairly available form and a relatively high proportion of phosphoric acid which, however, is very slowly available. The material can be used in mixing a complete fertilizer or applied alone at the rate of 3 to 5 lbs. per 100 sq. ft. It will not injure plants by burning and will tend to lighten and loosen a heavy soil. See also FERTILIZER.

HORNBEAM. Common name for the genus Carpinus, deciduous trees of the Birch Family. They are of irregular form, with delicate wiry twigs, smooth, beech-like bark, tendon-like swellings along the trunk and lower limbs, and handsome light green fruit clusters which, unlike those of the related Hop-hornbeam (which see), are not enclosed in husks or "hops." They have rounded heads of good foliage, rarely subject to insect attacks, and they assume attractive autumn tints. The withered leaves hang on the trees through the winter, providing excellent cover for birds.

The wood is exceedingly hard, justifying the name Ironwood, occasionally given; formerly used to make ox yokes, it takes on, when so used, a glossy, horn-like polish.

Some species stand severe pruning and have long been used for hedges in formal gardens. Although they grow slowly they are hardy and also of value as specimens on the lawn or for park planting, especially along brooks. They are raised from seed, which is slow to germinate; or choice individuals can be propagated by grafting on common seedings. *C. caroliniana* (American Hornbeam), a tree to 40 ft., is sometimes called Blue-beech because of its bark and bluish-green foliage; *C. betulus* (European Hornbeam), to 70 ft., the species most used for hedges, has a number of varieties, as *pendula* with drooping branches and *purpurea* with leaves purple when young. *C. japonica,* to 50 ft., is a graceful Japanese species, quite hardy in the U. S.

HORNED POPPY. One of the common names of the genus Glaucium (which see); also called Sea Poppy.

HORNED RAMPION. Common name for the genus Phyteuma, a curious member of the Bellflower Family, comprising perennial herbs with white, blue or purple flowers, ocasionally wheel-shaped, with 5 slender petals, or, more often, the petals united at the tip but so separated at the base as to form a flask-shaped flower. The inflorescence is a head, an umbel, or a usually compact spike. Phyteumas are occasionally grown in the border, but the smaller species are more suited to the rock garden, where they thrive best in fissures supplied with leafmold and sand. They are increased by seed or division.

Among the rock-garden species are: *P. charmeli,* with dark blue flower-heads; *P. scheuchzeri,* violet-blue, with exceedingly long bracts; *P. sieberi,* deep violet with fewer flowers and broader leaves; *P. hemisphaericum,* a smaller plant with blue, white or yellowish flowers, and *P. comosum,* with lilac and deep purple flowers in umbels, the styles protruding, the plant demanding a fissure in a limestone wall.

The tall-growing species, suitable for borders, include *P. canescens,* with grayish leaves and a long spike of blue flowers; *P. orbiculare,* a variable species, less tall with purple flowers; *P. scorzonerifolium,* with long spikes of bright blue flowers; and *P. limonifolium,* unique with wheel-shaped flowers in a long loose spike. Many other species are also known from mountain regions of Europe.

HOW HORNETS INJURE PLANTS
Stem of lilac with damage caused by European hornet shown at work.

HORNETS. Common name given to several species of large social wasps, especially the European hornet (*Vespa crabro*) and the bald-faced or white-faced American hornet (*Vespa maculata*). The former, which may be more than an inch long, is dark brown with bands of orange yellow. It builds nests in hollow trees and in gathering wood for their construction tears pieces of bark from the stems of lilac, boxwood, arborvitae and other trees and shrubs. The work often suggests that of a novice using a dull saw, the bark being torn away to the cambium and the stems sometimes being girdled. The hornets also appear to feed on the sap flowing from the wounds, being active in the evening until 9 o'clock or later. They can be caught in lighted traps or, if the nests can be located, the occupants can be destroyed by blowing in calcium cyanide. A derris spray, of the type recommended for Japanese beetles (which see), but used double strength, is an effective repellent.

See also WASPS.

HORNWORT. A common name for *Ceratophyllum demersum,* a most useful aquarium plant also called Mares-tail, Coon-tail and Fox-tail. Growing entirely submerged, it produces whorls of narrow, bristle-like leaves about the stem. A native

American plant, it may be found in ponds and still waters throughout the country. In use, it is best suited to the unheated aquarium and should be rooted in the sand of the aquarium bottom.

HORSE-BALM or HORSEWEED. Common name for the genus Collinsonia (which see) ; native aromatic herbaceous perennials with small yellowish flowers in clusters.

HORSE-BRIER. Common name for *Smilax rotundifolia,* a vicious climbing weed of the Lily Family, found from the Carolinas to Tex.; closely related and similar to CAT-BRIER, which see.

HORSECHESTNUT. Common name for the genus Aesculus, a group of hardy deciduous trees much planted for their shade and for their showy flowers. Native species are generally called Buckeyes especially in the Middle West, West and South. They are well worth a place in the general landscape, their pyramidal form being intensified by repetition in the large panicles of blossoms. Seen in the dusk a horsechestnut looms up in an impressive way, and the flower clusters seem to be alight. It is a desirable garden background if planted where the litter of its wiry stemmed leaves, burs and nuts is not unsightly and does not require too much work.

The large, highly varnished, sticky buds, on the terminal twigs, provide a striking winter and spring feature, as do the characteristic stout stem and branch structure, the conspicuous seasonal growth rings and leaf-scars and the sudden unfolding of the large leaves in the spring.

The most commonly planted species (*A. hippocastanum*) is too often used as a street tree, for which purpose the litter it causes makes it unsuitable. It suffers from dryness and for best results should be planted in heavy moist soil. More or less narrowly pyramidal varieties are well adapted to more confined spaces and the double flowered forms are desirable as the blossoms last longer and are not followed by burs and nuts. There are also dwarf forms suitable for general garden use.

There are numerous species native to various parts of the country, ranging in height from 7 to 90 ft., and in color of their blossoms from white through yellow, pink and greenish to shades of purple or red. Among these are the Ohio Buckeye (*A. glabra*), with yellow flowers; *octandra,* a large tree with yellow blossoms, for the south; *pavia,* a small southern tree with dark red panicles, and *wilsoni,* a large tree with white panicles a foot high.

Propagation is by seed sown in autumn or by grafting, budding, or root cuttings.

ENEMIES. Leaf scorch is a physiological disease occurring in the same trees year after year but being more pronounced in dry seasons. It is apparently due to inadequate or damaged root systems or to poor soil conditions and cannot be controlled by spraying but only by improving the soil, feeding and giving plenty of water.

Leaf blotch (caused by *Guignardia aesculi*), which is often confused with scorch, gives rise to irregular brown spots on the leaves, with small black fungus-

THE BROAD BRANCH OF A HORSECHESTNUT TREE IN FLOWER
A handsome tree in all its phases, from winter until fall, the Horsechestnut is at its best when the heavy flower spikes open in June.

fruiting bodies in the center. Defoliation follows and the overwintering spores are formed in dead leaves on the ground. Control by raking up and burning such leaves and by spraying developing foliage with bordeaux mixture. If powdery mildew appears on the leaves in late summer, bordeaux may be used.

The white-marked tussock moth (which see) thrives on horsechestnut. Collect its frothy white egg-cases over winter and spray horsechestnut foliage with lead arsenate, which will also protect against the Japanese beetle which is especially fond of this tree.

HORSE-GENTIAN. Common name for the genus Triosteum, a member of the Honeysuckle Family, comprising weedy herbs, 2 species of which are common in woods in N. America. They grow to about 4 ft. and bear inconspicuous flowers in the axils of the opposite leaves, followed by a leathery drupe. They are sometimes planted in the wild garden, but are of no special ornamental value. *T. aurantiacum* has dull-red flowers and orange-red fruit; *T. per-foliatum* has purple flowers and orange-yellow drupes.

HORSE MANURE. Once a standby in home gardening everywhere, this form of organic fertilizer is becoming scarce and hard to get except on farms. However it is valuable wherever it can be had at reasonable cost, not only as a source of heat for hotbeds where electricity is not at hand, but also as a source of plant food and humus. The average composition of horse manure is nitrogen .55%, phosphoric acid .3% and potash .4%. While fairly high in moisture, it is not as wet and heavy as cow manure (which see), and it is much quicker to ferment and break down. In doing so, it gives off much of its nitrogen in the form of ammonia compounds, as evidenced both by the odor of a fermenting heap, and by its white "fire-fanged" appearance when the fermentation has taken place under dry conditions.

To get the good from horse manure as fertilizer, therefore, it should be handled so as to prevent heating and also the leaching away of the plant food elements by the rain. One of the best ways to do this is by mixing it with cow manure, or by using it to build a compost heap which will be kept moist. Another way is to apply it to the soil while fresh *and turn it under immediately;* as some fermentation

is likely to occur even in the soil, this should not be done close to the roots of growing plants.

Well-rotted horse manure (or a mixture of horse and cow manure) can be spread on the soil to a depth of 3 to 5 in. and promptly worked in. For use in a hotbed it should, of course, be fresh and unfermented. Before putting it in the bed it should be piled, moistened, forked over and piled again until it begins to heat evenly and vigorously. It should then be thrown in the hotbed to a depth of 18 in. to 2 ft. well trodden down, and moistened again. The soil should then be spread on top and the sash put in place. When the soil temperature (which may rise to 100 deg. or more) falls to 90 deg. or below, the hotbed is ready to plant.

See also MANURE.

HORSE-MINT. Common name for the genus Monarda (which see), one species of which (*M. didyma*) is the popular, red-flowered perennial, Oswego-tea or Bee-Balm.

HORSE - RADISH. A large-leaved, hardy European perennial herb (*Armoracia rusticana*) that has become a weed in moist ground in cool parts of this country, but that is cultivated for its white-fleshed, pungent roots which when grated are used as an appetizer and condiment. It is hardly a home garden crop, for, as usually grown in gardens and allowed to remain from year to year, its roots are small, tough and fibrous in comparison with those grown commercially as an annual crop.

The plant does well in practically all deep, moist but well-drained soils of moderate fertility.

Since it produces no seed, small roots trimmed from the large ones after harvest are used to start new plantings in spring. They are cut about 6 in. long, square across the upper, and slanting on the lower end so they will be planted "right end up" in shallow furrows 30 to 36 in. apart and 10 to 15 in. asunder, with the upper ends 4 in. below the surface.

The horse-radish flea beetle feeds on this plant and water-cress. The tiny insects are black with yellowish wing covers and the larvae may burrow in the petioles killing some of the leaves. Spray foliage with lead arsenate.

HORSE-RADISH TREE (*Moringa oleifera*). A deciduous tree of the E. Indies somewhat planted in the tropics for (1) the ornamental effect of its fragrant white flowers; (2) its edible root and (3) its seeds, from which ben oil (used in the arts) is extracted.

HORSE-SUGAR. A common name for the genus Symplocus, a small group of ornamental trees and shrubs, known also as Sweetleaf, which see.

HORSETAIL. Common name for the genus Equisetum, a group of perennial rush-like herbs with creeping rootstocks, allied to the ferns and club-mosses. They have hollow jointed stems, with leaves reduced to mere scales at the joints. Spores (not seeds) are borne in conelike spikes. *E. hyemale* (Scouring-rush) is a native species, with slender evergreen stems to 4 ft. It is suitable for naturalizing.

HORTENSIS (hor-ten'-sis). Literally this means "an inhabitant of gardens." It is usually used, abbreviated to "Hort.," after certain plant names to show that while they may be in common use, they are not yet definitely established or accepted. In such cases the plant may be a product of deliberate cultivation (as *Aster alpinus* var. *superbus* Hort.) or of doubtful origin (as *Viola cornuta* var. *admirabilis* Hort.) Or our knowledge of the plant may be insufficient to classify it definitely (as *Calathea sanderiana* Hort.).

HORTICULTURAL SOCIETIES. Two distinct kinds of organization come under this head. One type consists primarily of fruit and vegetable growers, in whose interests and activities the ornamental and esthetic side of horticulture (which see) is quite subordinate to the utilitarian aspect. Such are the New Jersey and New York Horticultural Societies and those of many other important agricultural states. The other type is made up, in the main, of home owners (or, as they are called, amateur gardeners), private or professional gardeners, patrons of horticulture, and others who are most concerned with plants as ornamental materials grown to beautify home properties and for pleasure rather than for profit. The Horticultural Society of New York (not to be confused with the body named above), the Massachusetts and Pennsylvania Horticultural Societies and many, more local, groups are examples. In general they have wider fields of interest and larger membership than garden clubs, which see.

Best known in this field as far as gardening is concerned, are the state societies.

The oldest, that of Pennsylvania, was founded in 1827 when interest in gardening had not spread to the general public. The Massachusetts Horticultural Society, two years younger, has long been a leader; its publication *Horticulture* (now the organ of the New York and Pennsylvania Societies as well) is one of the few magazines in America devoted entirely to this field.

Also sometimes regarded and classed as horticultural societies are the national organizations for special plant enthusiasts, as the American Rose Society, American Rock Garden Society, and many others. Trade associations and garden clubs are considered separately.

Horticultural societies aim to promote interest in horticulture generally, or in their special fields, by holding flower, fruit and vegetable shows, issuing publications, giving lectures, and maintaining libraries. Attracting the most attention are the flower shows in large cities staged by the state societies and others, often with the coöperation of commercial interests, which hundreds of thousands of spectators pay to see, and which do more perhaps than any other institution to augment the rapidly growing enthusiasm for gardening now so evident in this country. Here both professional and amateur gardeners compete for prizes, exhibiting their skill in growing and arranging flowers and plants. Less spectacular but hardly less fruitful of results is the gathering and publishing by national societies of information on special plant groups in the form of books, periodical reports, special bulletins and other publications.

See also GARDEN CLUBS; FLOWER SOCIETIES; EDUCATION IN GARDENING.

HORTICULTURE. The cultivation of plants other than farm and forest crops. The word comes from the Latin *hortus,* meaning garden, but the term is usually taken to include ornamental and vegetable gardening, landscape planting, gruit growing and related activities both around the home and commercially as in orcharding, truck gardening, etc. There is an increasing tendency, however, to popularly restrict it to non-commercial activities.

Agriculture means farming, including the raising of animals, and forestry the raising of timber trees, but there is no sharp line between horticulture, agriculture and forestry. The manner of cultivating and the purpose for which a crop is grown, more

Plate 28.　　HEMEROCALLIS AND HOSTA ARE BOTH HARDY

Upper left: The clear lemon-yellow Taruga—a new and distinctive type of daylily or Hemerocallis. Upper right: The Soudan daylily holds its glistening golden blossoms high above arching leaves. Center: Graceful growth and a long period of bloom make the daylily valuable in the border. Lower 'eft: Bijou, another new daylily. Lower right: Hostas, admirable accent plants, grow well in the shade.

than the crop itself, decide in which division the crop belongs. Thus a 100-acre field of potatoes belongs to agriculture, and a 100-ft. row of potatoes in the vegetable garden to horticulture. White pine raised for timber comes under forestry, a specimen white pine for lawn planting, whether in the nursery or planted in the garden, under horticulture.

Horticulture, generally more intensive than agriculture, thus embraces market gardening, floriculture, nursery propagation, tree surgery, botanic gardening, plant breeding, mushroom culture, etc., and extends to the art of planning a garden, and even the arrangement of flowers in the house. As the use of the word is entirely a matter of custom, an exact definition is not needed.

HOSACKIA (hoh-sak'-i-ah). A genus of American herbs or shrubby plants of the Pea Family with butterfly-like flowers. A few species are used in the border but they have little garden value. They are increased by seed, or the woody kinds by division or cuttings. *H. gracilis*, to 1 ft., has weak stems and rose and yellow flowers.

HOSE, GARDEN. This familiar flexible tubing of rubber and fabric is one of the essential adjuncts of garden or greenhouse. Like other garden "tools" it has undergone great improvement; and like them it is all too often abused.

In the first place, good quality hose is always a good investment; cheap, flimsy hose, never. Of the two common sizes the ¾ in. is naturally heavier and bulkier than the ½ in., but except in the smallest garden it is worth the difference in cost. (Try to keep all the hose on the place of the same size; then there is no trouble with hose menders and such things not fitting.) For the small place 25 ft. lengths are satisfactory; elsewhere 50 ft. sections are plenty short enough.

To get the most use from a hose do not leave it in the sun more than necessary. Also, if it is so left on a hot summer day, see that it is left full of water. But, do not play the first water that comes out of it when next it is turned on, on valuable plants; it is often hot enough to scald them. Avoid kinks whenever possible and when they occur untwist them patiently; do not pull and jerk them as this often strains or breaks the fabric.

Before winter comes, drain each section of hose, then hang it, loosely coiled, indoors, out of the weather, but not near the furnace where the rubber will dry and crack. At all times keep the hose out of contact with any kind of oil, which rots the rubber.

HANDY HOSE HOLDER
Nozzle is held in notched block on a brick by a half inch section of old inner tube.

One of the interesting modern developments in hose is the type in which small spray nozzles are inserted every few feet. The hose thus serves as a flexible sprinkler system that can be arranged along a bed or border or across the lawn. Another is the large (4 in.) hose of porous but waterproof fabric through which the water oozes evenly so as to gradually soak the soil along its length without wasting any moisture as spray. See WATERING.

All hose as bought is equipped with standard connections for attaching it to taps, and various kinds of nozzles, sprinklers, etc. There are several handy accessory connections that greatly simplify the attachment of hose to faucet, requiring merely a contact and a single twist, or the flip of a lever. The gardener who seeks efficiency and labor-saving methods will find them worth looking into.

HOSE-IN-HOSE. A form of doubling in certain funnel-shaped or tube-shaped flowers, in which there are two single corollas, much alike, one fitted inside the other, as in the hose-in-hose polyanthus (*Primula polyantha*). More often the calyx becomes petaloid, enlarged and colored, to form the outer funnel, as in *Azalea amoena,* the crab cactus, and others. Or the stamens may grow together to make the inner funnel, as in *Datura fastuosa.* In all these cases the appearance is much the same.

HOST. An organism which harbors a parasite. Since a disease-producing organism is not always strictly parasitic (*i.e.,* obtaining its food directly from the host plant) the term *suscept* has been introduced to indicate any living organism in which disease has been introduced by another organism. However, the older word "host" is still used loosely to cover all cases of one organism victimized by another.

HOSTA (hoh'-stah). Perennial herbs with thick, durable roots, commonly known as Plantain-lily, which see. Formerly classed botanically as Funkia and sometimes popularly called Daylily, though distinct from the daylily of the genus Hemerocallis. (See illustration, Plate 28.)

HOTBED. A bottomless box with a more or less transparent, removable top used to grow plants out of local season. It differs from a coldframe (which see) chiefly in that it is artificially heated so it can be used earlier (and later) and operated during more inclement weather. When its source of artificial heat ceases or is removed, a hotbed becomes a coldframe in effect and service.

Unlike coldframes, hotbeds are always some multiple of standard glass sash, which are 6 ft. long and 3 ft. wide; and they are usually more permanent structures. Though often temporary they are generally built with a sub-frame or foundation of wood, or masonry, which extends from 12 to 24 in. below the soil surface, depending on the location and its climate. On this sub-frame rests the hotbed frame proper. Well-recognized dimensions are 18 in. high in the rear, 12 in. in front, sloping ends joining those two members, and cross-bars at 3 ft. ½ in. intervals to support the sash.

Gulf cypress is recognized as the best lumber for all wooden parts of hotbeds and coldframes, though less durable woods give satisfactory temporary results. While the frame can be built by a handy man, it is advisable to buy the ready made, cut and fitted forms as well as glazed and painted sash. The four-sash frame (6 by 12 ft.) is the favorite in home gardens,

SIMPLE HOTBED VENTILATOR
A block of 4 x 10 x 1 in. wood notched at 4 in., 6 in. and 8 in. heights will hold the sash at different positions.

especially since the introduction of electric heating, because a half or a quarter of the area may be used as a hotbed and the rest as a coldframe by placing a partition beneath one of the cross-bars extending to or into the soil.

In the past hotbeds were heated exclusively by fermenting organic materials (especially fresh horse manure), by warm air flues, hot water or steam pipes, or by warm air from a heated house basement. These sources are still used where local conditions make them economical or otherwise desirable. But in recent years electricity has proved so convenient, adaptable and satisfactory that both commercial and amateur gardeners are adopting it widely. Since improvements are constantly being made the reader is referred to bulletins and other literature issued by the Department of Agriculture, various state experiment stations, public utility corporations and the manufacturers of electrical hotbed heating equipment.

For those who can still get fresh stable manure, the method of using it may be given as follows: Pile fresh manure, preferably under cover, in heaps 4 or 5 ft. high and as long as necessary to fill the hotbed pit or sub-frame. In a few days, when it begins to steam well, fork over the pile to make a new pile in which the outside of the first is on the inside of the second. If necessary repeat this process once, twice more, until the pile is of uniform heat. Then pack it tightly in the hotbed pit, tramping it firmly along the sides and especially in the corners. The

THE PLANTAIN-LILY
Hosta, once known as Funkia, is a favorite flowering plant for shady places.

ELECTRIC HEAT FOR THE HOTBED
It is supplied by a lead-covered cable laid 6 in. below the soil surface. A thermometer and a thermostat (connected by the diagonal wire shown) automatically maintain any desired temperature.

The time to start a hotbed depends upon local conditions such as the kinds of plants wanted, the saving in time sought, the outdoor temperature to be overcome, the available heat, etc. Hardy plants can naturally be started long before tender ones, and also set out in the open ground sooner. Generally speaking hotbeds can be gotten under way 6 to 8 weeks before the soil can be dug or plowed in the garden.

Successful management of a hotbed depends mainly upon (1) providing ample space between seedling plants, (2) watering early in the day (never toward night), (3) regulation of the temperature by ventilation (except where it is electrical and thermostatically controlled) and (4) ventilating carefully, as much as is safe and increasingly as the season advances. The objects of ventilation are, first, to allow the fumes of decomposition to escape; and second, to maintain temperatures lower (rather than higher) than those recommended for each species, thereby tending to develop sturdy, stocky plants which will be nicely hardened off and able to withstand unfavorable conditions when transplanted to the open ground.

layer should be 15 to 24 in. thick, depending upon the locality—deeper in the N. When it is thoroughly and evenly packed cover it with 4 to 6 in. of finely sifted soil, put the sash on snugly and let the hotbed stand for several days—until the soil temperature falls to below 90 deg. Then it is safe to sow seed.

After sowing, water and ventilate carefully. Without enough water the young plants will be burned by the heat and the dryness; without adequate fresh air (*not* cold drafts) they will grow weak.

Ventilation is done either by raising the sash on blocks at their upper ends an inch or more, by tilting them up on the side from which the wind is not blowing, or by sliding each alternate sash a greater or

A HOTBED—AND HOW TO BUILD AND OPERATE IT
Within the frame of boards or concrete (which slopes upward toward the back) on the bottom of the 30 in. pit, is spread a 2 ft. layer of fresh horse manure (E) which is wet and trodden down to provide heat. On this goes a 4 to 6 in. layer of soil (D), the finest part on top. In this, seeds are sown or seedlings (C) are transplanted, pricked-out from flats (A) or seed pans (B) placed on the soil so as to be close to the sash when it is put on to confine and intensify the warmth.

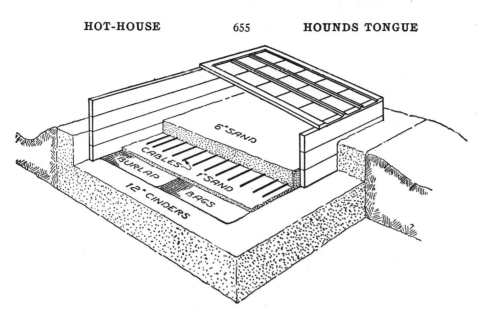

HOW TO BUILD A HOTBED FOR ELECTRIC HEATING
Cover a foot of cinders (for drainage) with 1 in. of sand spread on old burlap to prevent its sifting through. On the sand lay the electric heating cables and cover them with soil if seeds are to be sown or sand if cuttings are to be rooted. See article on Electricity in Gardening.

less distance up or down. Finally the sash can be removed altogether when weather conditions become favorable.

In severe cold weather hotbeds and coldframes may need the protection of mats held in place by wooden shutters, wires or other devices. The old-fashioned homemade straw mats have been largely replaced by manufactured kinds (quilted burlap, etc.) obtainable at garden supply stores. Hotbeds, but more often coldframes, are also sometimes covered with lath or slat lattice work frames so as to provide partial shade as the spring advances and the sun's rays become stronger.

See COLDFRAME; ELECTRICITY; VENTILATION.

HOT-HOUSE. A glass house (greenhouse) kept artificially heated for the growing of tender exotic or subtropical plants, or for the production of fruits, flowers or vegetables out of season. The temperature maintained is intermediate between that of the cool-house and that of the "stove-," orchid- or palm-house. See CONSERVATORY; COOL-HOUSE; STOVE-HOUSE and GREEN-HOUSE.

HOTTENTOT-FIG. Common name for *Carpobrotus edulis,* a perennial with fleshy leaves, large showy flowers of yellow, red or purple, and edible fruits. Grown in California; elsewhere under glass.

HOTTONIA (ho-toh'-ni-ah). A genus comprising two species of perennial water herbs of the Primrose Family sometimes used in aquaria.

The European species (*H. palustris*) is preferable to our American *H. inflata* although the latter may be gathered freely in ponds and streams of the eastern U. S. throughout the summer. The erect, submerged stems and creeping rootstocks of both these aquatics are practically leafless and of doubtful ornamental value in the tank, but the handsome spikes of pale violet flowers make up for this deficiency.

See AQUATIC PLANTS.

HOT WATER TREATMENT. A general term for different methods of disinfecting to destroy plant diseases or insect pests. They are used in the sterilization of soil, in treating seed, in treating flower bulbs for nematodes and bulb flies, and in the control of cyclamen mites. See DISINFECTION; ENEMIES under BULBS; CYCLAMEN.

HOUNDS TONGUE. Common name for the genus Cynoglossum, a member of the Borage Family, comprising a number of rather weedy plants about 2 ft. tall, with stiff-hairy leaves, the shape of which has given rise to the common name. Although of little interest in the garden, they are occasionallly grown for their blue flowers, being propagated by seeds.

C. amabile is a biennial with small blue flowers; *C. nervosum* is larger and showier; *C. wallichi,* an annual, has very small blue flowers in racemes; *C. virginianum,* a native perennial, has clusters of rather large oblong flowers ½ in. across.

HOUSELEEK. Common name for a large genus of Sempervivum, succulent evergreen herbs with leaves in rosettes.

TWO STAGES IN REPOTTING
Above: With the stem of the plant held between the first two fingers, the pot is tapped gently on the edge of the frame to make the ball of earth come out whole. Below: After proper drainage has been placed in the larger pot, the old plant is set at the proper height and fresh earth is first thrown around it, then made firm, by even pressure with the thumbs.

HOUSE PLANTS. (See illustrations, Plates 7, 15, 18.) This term refers to such plants as can be grown in the ordinary rooms of dwelling houses, rather than subjects requiring a greenhouse and expert care. They may consist of one or a few single plants, or the whole window space may be occupied. They may be hardy or tender, but they should be well adapted to withstand average house conditions—dry atmospheres, high or uneven temperatures and inadequate light. The best room for plants is the one which gets the most sunshine, and the best position is nearest the window. A saucer should be provided for each pot and small pebbles, coarse sand, or sphagnum moss in the saucer are an advantage in permitting excess water to seep

from the pot into the saucer instead of lying about the roots of the plant. As it evaporates from the saucer it helps create the moist atmosphere that most plants need.

Aside from the bulbous plants (see BULBS), there are two clases of plants to be considered, (1) those of a woody or shrubby nature which have made their growth during the summer and whose natural resting period would be during the winter; and (2) a group composed of young tender herbaceous subjects grown from cuttings made for the purpose, or recently started from seed.

The shrubby class includes most of the climbing plants as well as those of an evergreen nature, most of which do not bloom until late winter or early spring and the majority of which may be cultivated best in small pots. The aim with all such plants is to encourage summer growth in order that they be well ripened before entering their resting period. These plants require lower temperatures and much less water and light until growth starts naturally, when they should be given more heat and sunshine and water.

The young tender or soft-wood group, grown from cuttings or seed, require all possible light and heat and considerably more water at all times, since they are actively growing. Rapidly growing flowering plants especially need abundant water, heat and exposure to direct sunlight, whereas tropical plants, such as palms, ferns, dracaenas, pandanus and foliage plants generally, which normally are resting during the winter, prefer subdued light and should receive water sparingly.

Cuttings of many of the bedding plants (mostly annuals) may be started during late summer and grown on rapidly for use as house plants during the winter. Cuttings from geranium, heliotrope, begonia, fuchsia, snapdragon, etc., may be taken in August from non-flowering branches, using tips bearing two sets of leaves. Cut them just below a joint, remove the lower set of leaves, embed them in moist sand up to the second set of leaves. Kept shaded and sprayed for ten days, they should by then have formed roots, and be ready to be potted up and grown on. Seed of petunia, coleus, verbena, etc. may be sown in late summer and the seedlings grown on rapidly for the same purpose.

Soil for potted house plants should be made up generally of one half good loamy garden soil, one quarter well-rotted leaf-mold or fine humus and one quarter sand. To each wheelbarrow load of such soil should be added one 4 in. potful of a complete, high grade fertilizer, then the mass should be thoroughly mixed together and screened to get rid of stones, trash, etc.

Comparatively small pots are needed at first. Do not overpot by placing small plants in large pots; when necessary (as shown by a dense growth of roots around the "ball" next to the pot) they can be shifted into larger pots. On the other hand, do not attempt to underpot by crowding large roots into pots too small for them. In potting, do not fill a pot with soil; leave half an inch of space between soil and rim of pot for watering. But pot firmly by pressing down the soil with the thumbs as you rotate the pot until pulling a leaf from the plant will not dislodge it. Old pots should be thoroughly cleaned by scrubbing before being used, and new ones should be soaked and allowed to absorb all the water they will; but they should not be wet during the actual operation of potting. Pieces of broken pot (potsherds) must be placed over the hole in the bottom

HOUSE PLANTS THEN—
An indoor vista of a generation ago when brilliant colors and profuse forms were as popular as ruffled lace curtains.

to permit drainage while preventing the soil from escaping. In 4-in. and all larger sizes, an inch of coarse material such as broken pots, cinders, sifted ashes, etc., should be placed in the bottom to assist drainage. After being potted and given a thorough watering (until water runs through the drainage hole) the plants should be sprayed with a combined insecticide and fungicide so they will not carry any insects or plant diseases into the house and to give them a good, healthy start.

Christmas and Easter plants, poinsettia, cyclamen, primula, Jerusalem-cherry, even gardenia, and many lesser subjects all may be kept in blossom and sturdy for weeks if faded flowers, seed-pods and imperfect leaves are promptly removed and the plants are not given too sunny a position. Other plants suitable are *Asparagus sprengeri,* aspidistra, wandering Jew, *Dracaena indivisa,* sansevieria, pandanus (screw-pine), *Ficus elastica* (rubber-plant), umbrella sedge and many of the cactus and succulent groups.

If it is desired, holiday gift plants (while not really "house plants" since they come from the hot, moist atmosphere of the greenhouse to the very different conditions of the modern dwelling) may be grown on

—HOUSE PLANTS NOW
Modern taste favors simple, even severe lines, and smaller plant subjects. Glass shelves across deep window casings offer real opportunities.

for flowering another season. After flowering is over, water should be gradually withheld and the plant allowed to rest for a few weeks. They should never become bone dry at the roots, but should receive just sufficient water to keep them alive. Then, at the approach of warm weather, cut them back to a compact, symmetrical shape and plunge the pots to the rim in the garden in a semi-shaded location. As they grow, keep them pinched back to shape and in the fall, before frost, take them up and indoors. If conditions are not too difficult for them (dry air is the greatest problem), they will probably bloom again though perhaps not as early and never as satisfactorily as the first time. Consequently it is usually desirable to raise or purchase young plants for flowering in the home.

All indoor plants require additional food during their active growing and flowering seasons. At three- or four-week intervals they can receive liquid food made of a good, high-grade, commercial complete fertilizer which can be purchased in dry form to be used according to directions.

ENEMIES. Due to the dry atmospheric conditions under which most house plants are grown, the possibilities of infection by bacteria or fungi are much reduced and little attention need be paid to the control of plant diseases beyond removing and destroying an occasional infected leaf or blossom. Certain insects, on the other hand, thrive under dry house conditions, but most insects that infest such plants can be fairly easily controlled with a good contact insecticide of nicotine, pyrethrum, or derris.

ARTIFICIAL SUNLIGHT

The right size electric bulb at the right distance keeps house plants vigorous even in dim places. Combined fixtures and plant holders can now be obtained.

Plant lice (aphids) and mealy bugs (which look like small bits of cotton fluff), are best controlled on small plants by holding the hand with the stem between the second and third fingers, over the soil and dipping the whole top of the plant in a bath of the insecticide. A solution of ¼ teaspoonful nicotine-sulphate (Black Leaf-40) and ¼ oz. ivory soap in 1 qt. warm water is good for dipping. Plants which cannot be handled easily in that way can be sprayed with the same mixture. Mealy bugs are harder to control than aphids and a special white oil spray, one safe for house plants, may be needed. When the bugs are few, a soft brush dipped in soapy water can be used to dislodge them.

Scale insects on palms, ornamental citrus fruits and rubber plants can be scrubbed off the leaves or stems with a discarded toothbrush dipped in soap and water; afterward the plants should be syringed with clear water. On other plants scales should be killed while young by spraying three to five times at weekly intervals with a contact insecticide. The same treatment will control white flies which, common on greenhouse plants, sometimes infest house plants.

The mite or red spider (which see) is best controlled by increasing the humidity by setting the pots on pebbles or moss in a pan in which water is kept, by frequently syringing the foliage, or by using humidifiers in the room. If a spray proves necessary, one containing rotenone will be most effective.

Earthworms (which see) in the soil may interfere with root development of potted plants. They can be destroyed by dusting lime on the surface of the soil, by watering the plants with water containing lime, or by the careful use (starting with weak concentrations) of recommended proprietary worm eradicators.

See also GREENHOUSE PESTS.

The bulbous plants as already noted are in a class by themselves and are not included here. Generally they may be grown in sandy soils, in comparatively small pots or dishes, and allowed to make root growth in a dark cool location before being brought into the light and heat and encouraged to flower. Tulips, daffodils and hyacinths grow best in soil; paper white narcissus and the related Chinese sacred lily can be grown in bowls of water containing pebbles to support them.

See also HANGING BASKETS; POT PLANTS;
WINDOW BOXES.

HOUSTONIA (hoo-stoh'-ni-ah). A
genus of small tufted N. American herbs
of the Madder Family having pretty little
white, blue or purple flowers. Some of
the species are grown in the rock garden,
and all except *H. caerulea,* which must be
planted in the open, thrive in moist, semi-
shaded situations. They are delicate little
plants but easily transferred from the wild
and increased by division of the clumps.

H. caerulea (Bluets), a low perennial,
with solitary white, blue or violet flowers
with a yellow eye, is the common form seen
in the E. States where sometimes damp
meadows look as if powdered with a light
fall of snow because of the profusion of
blooms. *H. serpyllifolia* has larger, deep
violet-blue flowers; *H. angustifolia,* a taller
plant with white to purple flowers in flat-
topped clusters, is the species seen in the
S. States; *H. floridana* is a S. Fla. plant
with purple flowers; *H. purpurea,* from the
Central States, has purple or lilac flowers
in long clusters.

HOVEA (hoh'-vee-ah). Small ornamental shrubs of Australia, belonging to
the Pea Family. They are but rarely
cultivated and then in a cool greenhouse or,
sometimes, outdoors in warm regions. The
flowers, mostly deep blue or purple, are
small but freely produced in clusters.
When grown in pots the plants need frequent pinching when young to induce a
bushy growth. Their flowering season is
early spring, and they resent being potted
(being grown in unnecessarily large pots)
and over-watering. *H. celsi, H. longifolia,*
and *H. trisperma* are the chief species.

HOVENIA (hoh-veen'-i-ah). A deciduous tree from China, belonging to the
Buckthorn Family. *H. dulcis* (Japanese
Raisin-tree), the only species that has been
described, is a small tree to 30 ft., not
quite hardy where winters are severe. It
has toothed oval leaves over 6 in. long,
clusters of small greenish yellow flowers,
and later curious fleshy, reddish stems
partly enveloping the small berries. It is
propagated by seeds, stem and root cuttings.

HOWEA (hou'-ee-ah). A genus of
feather-leaved palms, formerly known as
Kentia, having gracefully arching, feathery,
spineless leaves over 7 ft. long (in mature
specimens) and tall trunks, ringed with
scars of fallen leaves. The two species,

A PALM FOR THE HOUSE
Howea belmoreana makes an attractive indoor
foliage plant, requiring a minimum of care.

H. belmoreana and *H. forsteriana* are
grown outdoors in frost-proof regions of
Calif., but do not grow so well in the
climate of Fla. In the juvenile state, however, they constitute two of the most popular palms for the house, standing dry conditions, dim light and even considerable
abuse remarkably well. In the greenhouse
they start readily from seed, sown in light
soil and given a bottom heat of 80 deg.
Pot the seedlings in rich soil, preferably of
rotted sod without manure, keep the air
moist, and after four months give a night
temperature of 60 deg., spraying frequently
for scale insects, the most troublesome
pests.

HOYA (hoi'-ah). Tropical evergreen,
mostly climbing, shrubs belonging to the
Milkweed Family. One or two species are
grown in greenhouses or window gardens.
They have thick fleshy leaves and umbels
of fragrant flowers of waxy texture. They
are not difficult to grow in a mixture of
fibrous loam and peat, with some charcoal.
Good drainage is important, as they will

not stand stagnating water at the roots. Keep them in the resting stage during winter but do not cut off the old flower stalks as they produce flowers for several years. Propagation is by cuttings or layers.

H. carnosa (Wax-plant) is the best known species. It is a twiner with rooting stems and grows to 8 ft. or more. The clustered flowers are whitish with a pink center. *H. bella* is a small bushy grower bearing white flowers with a crimson center. *H. imperialis* is a very tall climber, with reddish brown flowers to 3 in. across in drooping umbels.

HUCKLEBERRY. A name properly applied to species of Gaylussacia, erroneously to species of Vaccinium (especially *V. corymbosum*, the High-bush Blueberry), and in some localities interchangeably to species of both genera. The fruit of the true huckleberries is easily distinguished by the ten large, bony seeds which crack loudly between the teeth when eaten, thus suggesting another popular name "crackerberry." The seeds of blueberries (Vaccinium) are so small as to be scarcely noticeable. Also huckleberry leaves are sprinkled on the underside with resinous dots not found on blueberry-leaves. Though the huckleberry can be grown like the blueberry, its culture is not commonly attempted nor recommended. See BLUE-BERRY; GAYLUSSACIA.

Garden-huckleberry is a popular name for *Solanum nigrum;* He-huckleberry is *Lyonia ligustrina;* and reflecting the confusion above referred to, the name Hairy-huckleberry is sometimes given to *Vaccinium hirsutum* and that of Squaw-huckleberry to *V. stamineum,* correctly called Deerberry.

HUDSONIA (hud-soh'-ni-ah). A genus of hardy heath-like shrubs, comprising three species: *H. tomentosa,* growing on sandy shores and dunes near the Atlantic coast from New Brunswick southward to N. C.; *H. ericoides,* extending far to the W. in dry, sandy sections; and *H. montana,* growing in the mountains of N. C. They bear numerous bright yellow flowers, but are not often cultivated as they are short-lived. They are propagated by seeds.

HULSEA (hul'-see-ah). A genus of small sticky or woolly herbs of the Composite Family, having large yellow or purple flowers, and grown preferably as alpines. *H. nana* from Calif. has sticky and hairy finely cut foliage.

HUMBLE-PLANT. A common name for *Mimosa pudica,* a spiny perennial of interest mainly for its sensitive foliage which folds when touched. See SENSITIVE-PLANT.

HUMEA (heu'-mee-ah). Australian herbs or shrubby plants belonging to the Daisy Family. Only one species (*H. elegans*) is grown to any extent. This is treated as a biennial from seed sown in summer. Pot up the young plants and shift to larger pots as required, keeping them on the dry side in a cool house over winter. In spring shift into 8 or 10 in. pots for flowering, using rich soil and feeding well when established. The plants are of interest for summer flowering in the conservatory, or outdoors in a subtropical arrangement. The leaves are sweet scented and the flowers are borne in terminal loose branched drooping panicles, mostly brownish-red.

HUMULUS (heu'-meu-lus). Tall twining vines, native in N. America, Europe and Asia, belonging to the Mulberry Family. They are grown for ornament, and one species for its fruit, the hops used in brewing. See HOP.

HUMUS. This is the organic or non-mineral material that makes up a large part of any good, fertile, productive soil that is in good condition. It consists of the more or less decomposed remains of vegetable and animal matter—that is: plants themselves; dead animals, from microscopic organisms up to rodents, bugs or any other kind; and all kinds of manures.

Humus may accumulate in a soil naturally, as leafmold in an undisturbed forest, as dead grasses and weeds in a meadow or pasture, or as peat formed by the dying of water plants in ponds and bogs and their accumulation on the bottom. Or it may be added to and incorporated in a soil, in the form of manure, granulated peat moss, compost, green manure crops turned under to rot, or many other substances. While this variety of sources and the fact that it is constantly undergoing change makes it impossible to give any definite description of humus, its general character is that of a black or brown, loose, porous, absorbent substance such as can be scraped up from the forest floor where no fires or human interference have prevented the natural decay.

Without humus a soil would be dead and inert, like pure sand or clay, and utterly unsuited for growing plants. The services that humus renders in a soil and that make it such an essential factor are these: (1) It contains in available form several plant-food elements without which plants cannot thrive. (True, also, these are contained in the mineral part of the soil, but there they are not always available and usable.) (2) It improves the soil texture or physical condition, loosening it, admitting air and moisture and making it friable. (3) It absorbs and holds moisture, preventing the soil from drying out and, at the same time, provides a reservoir that takes up any surplus free water that might be injurious to the plants. (4) It provides congenial conditions for the growth and activity of certain bacteria and other minute organisms that prepare the plant food for crop consumption, breaking down complex insoluble chemical combinations and building up simpler, soluble ones that can be readily taken up by the plant roots as part of the soil solution. (5) It provides a medium, as well as raw material for these plant-food manufacturing operations.

How essential these functions are is being demonstrated in soils all the time and on every hand. A convincing test is to gather a handful of road dust, or beach sand or clay from a clay pit, and compare it—in appearance, in "feeling," in all respects that relate to fertility and the ability to support plant life, with a handful of soil from a well-cared-for garden, a rich perennial border, or a carefully made hotbed or greenhouse bench. The difference is obvious—and the reason is the presence of humus in the good soils. In brief, humus helps and improves thin, sandy soils by giving them more body; and improves heavy, stiff clays by loosening them and making them more open.

Consequently, one of the gardener's most important and never ending tasks is to keep his soil supplied with humus. Let him work in well-rotted manure whenever he can get it, no matter what kind. Let him carefully save every scrap of vegetable refuse—*so long as it is known not to be disease infected*—and add it to the compost heap (which see). Let him when necessary purchase supplementary supplies of humus in the form of peat moss, buckwheat hulls, etc., or promptly sow every vacant bit of garden space to some quick-growing forage crop that can later be dug or plowed under

as green manure. And let him see that his soil is sufficiently drained and correctly cultivated so that the humus in it will be able to perform its invaluable functions.

See also SOIL; PLANT FOODS; FERTILITY; GREEN MANURE; MANURE, ETC.

MEXICAN TULIP POPPY
Hunnemannia fumariaefolia, with finely cut, blue-green foliage, bears masses of cupped golden flowers from June until frost.

HUNNEMANNIA (hun-e-man'-i-ah). This Mexican perennial herb with its one species, *H. fumariaefolia,* is known also by the common names, Golden-cup, Mexican Tulip Poppy and Bush-eschscholzia since it resembles a tall, bushy California poppy. In the U. S. it is grown as an annual because plants from spring-sown seed will flower the first season, in August, continuing until cool weather. The yellow, tulip-shaped flowers 3 in. across are borne on upright plants to 2 ft. tall which need full sun but thrive in ordinary garden soil. They withstand drouth well and often will survive conditions that are fatal to many other plants. They are good for the border and for cut flowers, which if gathered before they are fully open will last more than a week indoors. Plants frequently self-seed.

HUON-PINE. Common name for *Dacrydium franklini,* a Tasmanian tree of the Yew Family.

HURDLE. A movable section of fence made of wooden rails, woven wattles or metal, originally designed to enclose a paddock, but frequently used in gardens in making permanent fences or, singly, as a gate through a thicket. See also FENCES.

HUSK-TOMATO. A common name for the genus Physalis, herbs whose two-celled berries are inclosed in a husk.

HUTCHINSIA (huch-in′-si-ah). A genus of small herbs of the Mustard Family resembling Draba (which see) and having entire or cut leaves and small white clustered flowers. *H. alpina* is a minute tufted perennial suitable for the alpine or rock garden, where its flowers appear during the spring and summer. It should be grown in a moist, semi-shaded position, and can be increased by seed or by cuttings.

HYACINTH. (See illustration, Plate 6.) The common name for a small genus of true bulbous plants (Hyacinthus) the chief of which is *H. orientalis,* a native of Asia Minor, from which most of the present-day hyacinths for outdoor and indoor use have descended. With the massive trusses of perfectly shaped flowers, in white, occasionally yellow, and many tones of red, purple and blue, hyacinths provide a distinctive type of sturdy, formal beauty in the early spring garden. As a house

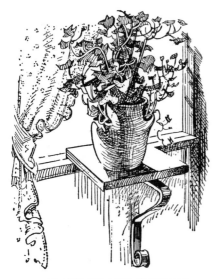

A PLANT IN THE WINDOW

Plants need light; foliage and flowers in a not too sunny window are pleasant to look at. A little bracket like this, with 2 flanges to hook over the window frame or sill and a bent metal support below, meets both requirements simply and efficiently.

plant they are easy to force in late winter and early spring, when their bright colors are truly welcome, notwithstanding the sweet, at times almost overpowering, fragrance.

DUTCH HYACINTHS IN THE GARDEN. Fresh bulbs of medium size of the so-called Dutch hyacinths, the kind universally grown in gardens, are essential for good effects. They are available from September through the fall months and should be planted as early as possible to permit root development before the ground gets cold. Prepare the soil by spading and enriching and plant the bulbs 4 in. deep and 6 in. apart for the larger sizes and correspondingly closer for the smaller ones. In the spring trusses can be picked for use as cut flowers without damage to the bulb, but the foliage must remain and be allowed to die down naturally. Nothing is to be gained by digging and replanting the bulbs unless they are being crowded out by other subjects. However, each year will likely see a diminishing of the size of the bloom; and as there is nothing that can be done to materially alter the condition, the continued production of large, full flower-trusses year after year will ordinarily require constant renewing of bulbs.

For names of the best and most popular varieties in each color, consult the current catalogs of bulb dealers who keep up with the production of new and improved kinds.

DUTCH HYACINTHS INDOORS. Hyacinth bulbs planted singly in 5 in. pots in September can be forced into bloom by Christmas time indoors. Single bulbs can also be flowered with fair satisfaction in the familiar hyacinth glasses or vases. In using pots, place broken crockery for drainage in the bottom of each pot, fill loosely with a rich mixture of leafmold, loam and sand, and press each bulb firmly into the pot until the crown is at soil level. Then bury the pots 8 or 10 in. deep in the ground or in a coldframe. In 2 months or less, when the roots are developed and a pale sprout shows well above the bulb, bring the pots indoors, but keep them in a cool, dark corner until the sprouts turn green. Thereafter good window light (but *not* extreme heat) and frequent watering will bring the flowers into bloom. Liquid manure applied from the time the buds appear will improve the flowers. If a flower shoot begins to show buds while very short, it can be drawn up to give a larger truss by placing an inverted flower pot or a cone of paper over it for a week or so.

Pots brought in from the outdoor storage at intervals will provide successive crops of flowers until spring.

ROMAN HYACINTHS. Another small class of tender hyacinths is known as the Roman, or French Roman type. Produced commercially in S. France and Italy, these bulbs are used outdoors in this country only in the extreme S. They are distinguishable from the Dutch type of N. gardens in that they produce several graceful loose-flowering spikes from one bulb instead of the usual compact single spike. The best of them, at present, are white.

For indoor growing, the bulbs can be planted from late summer through the early fall months, in bowls of peat moss and kept in a cool dark place until they are well rooted and the tops show a growth or an inch or two. Transferred then to a light window they will ordinarily bloom about Christmas time. If desired, several bulbs can be planted in a pot, the same steps being followed as recommended for Dutch hyacinths.

ENEMIES. Hyacinth yellows was one of the first diseases of plants known to be caused by bacteria. Water-soaked stripes in the foliage followed by yellowing and withering of leaves and flower stalks, and a yellow soggy rot of the bulbs are the chief symptoms. Each infected bulb, together with the surrounding soil, should be carefully removed. Another bacterial disease causes the bulbs to become a sticky white slimy mass soon after they are dug. Burn all such bulbs.

A sclerotinia rot causes yellow blotches on the leaves and small, raised, dark spore bodies (*sclerotia*) on the outer bulb-scales. Sterilize the soil to kill the sclerotia and ventilate the bulbs well during storage. For control of fusarium basal rot, see BULB ENEMIES under BULBS.

Yellowed leaves and brown rings in the bulbs may be caused by nematodes (which see) and soft bulbs may be due to mites.

HYACINTH BULB PRODUCTION. Hyacinth bulbs (except the Roman type) are produced almost exclusively in Holland, where favorable soil and climatic conditions, plus generations of experience, combine to give splendid results and a high class product. Because hyacinth bulbs do not naturally propagate fast enough for commercial growers, an artificial method of increase

involving the scooping out of the bulbs to stimulate the formation of bulblets is resorted to. This work requires expert knowledge and special treatment and is hardly an activity for the amateur.

Hyacinth bulbs are offered in catalogs in various sizes; the accepted standard for top-size bulbs is 19 centimeters in circumference, while 13 cm. is the size described as miniature. The size of a forced flower truss is almost entirely determined by the measurement of the bulb; a medium size bulb is considered best for general garden use.

The name Hyacinth is combined with other words and applied to a number of plants, including the following: Grape-hyacinth is the genus Muscari; Giant Summer- (or Summer-flowering-) hyacinth is Galtonia. Water-hyacinth is *Eichhornia crassipes*. Musk-, or Nutmeg-hyacinth is *Muscari moschatum*. Feathered-hyacinth is *M. comosum* var. *monstrosum*. Wild-hyacinth (especially in the British Isles, where it covers acres of ground in spring with blue) is *Scilla nonscripta;* Star-hyacinth is *S. amoena;* Starry-hyacinth is *S. autumnalis.*

HYACINTH-BEAN. A common name for *Dolichos lablab*, a perennial grown as an annual vine for its abundant foliage, purple flowers, and edible seeds.

HYACINTH-SHRUB. Common name for Xanthoceras sorbifolia (which see), a handsome, large, deciduous shrub whose blossoms somewhat resemble huge hyacinth flowers.

HYBRID. A variety or individual resulting from the crossing of two species; or, less strictly, the offspring of almost any two parents which differ genetically in some strongly marked characteristic. Thus a hybrid is the result of cross-fertilization; a cross. See also PLANT BREEDING.

HYBRIDIZATION. The process of bringing together parent plants of different kinds or groups for the purpose of reproducing them and creating more. See PLANT BREEDING.

HYDRANGEA (hy-dran'-je-ah). (See illustrations, Plate 48.) Deciduous shrubs, native in Asia, N. and S. America, belonging to the Saxifrage Family. They are valued for their large clusters of showy white, pink or blue flowers; very lasting, often with enlarged sterile marginal flowers, and in some cases with all flowers sterile.

They thrive best in a rich moist soil and flower freely in an open situation, but will grow under varying conditions. Rather severe pruning should be practiced and the weak growth thinned, to encourage strong shoots for good flower-heads.

Several kinds are quite hardy N., but some can stand only a few degrees of frost. In the latter group is *H. macrophylla* (better known as *H. hortensis*), a fine plant for seaside gardens in mild climates. It is sometimes preserved outdoors in colder regions by tying up the branches in late fall and banking up soil around it. It is also a good plant for forcing under glass, and is largely grown for the Easter trade. Numerous good forms have been developed.

Blue Hydrangeas are very popular and sometimes a seeming miracle takes place when plants propagated from the blue variety produce pink flowers. This is due to a change in soil acidity. *Blue flowers are produced in an acid soil.* Hence growers of pot plants often add iron filings to the soil, or water with a solution of alum at the rate of a teaspoonful to one gallon of water; or with aluminum sulphate (3 ozs. to the gal.). Outdoors a sandy soil and the addition of peat moss, leafmold or any other acid-creating material, will aid in keeping blue varieties blue.

Good plants can be grown in one year from cuttings. The young plants can be plunged outdoors in pots for the summer, or planted out in a sunny place, lifted and potted in the fall. Old plants may be cut back and planted out for another term of flowering, and either protected outside or lifted and stored in a frost-proof place.

Several leaf spots may occur on this plant but are not serious. If necessary, spray several times with bordeaux mixture. If botrytis blight causes rotting of the flowers in wet seasons, remove all infected parts.

The rose chafer (see CHAFER, ROSE) and the tarnished plant bug (which see) may also feed on hydrangea. Tip-burn may be caused by red spider which can be controlled by washing the leaves with a strong stream of water. A leaf tyer often fastens together the tip leaves of outdoor hydrangeas, but if these are promptly pulled apart and the worm is killed the bud will usually continue to develop.

Most kinds of hydrangeas are readily propagated by cuttings of half-matured shoots under glass, also by hardwood cuttings, layers, suckers, or divisions.

PRINCIPAL AMERICAN SPECIES

H. arborescens, an upright shrub to 10 ft., with rounded clusters of white flowers, only a few sterile. The var. *grandiflora* (Hills-of-Snow) is more generally planted for its large clusters of white, all sterile flowers, which turn greenish in late summer. Best results are obtained by cutting the shoots to the ground each spring.

cinerea is a spreading shrub to 6 ft., with leaves ashy gray beneath, and flat white flower clusters with only a few sterile flowers.

radiata is somewhat similar but more desirable on account of its leaves of better texture, silvery-white beneath. The flower heads have more sterile flowers.

quercifolia, a S. species but hardy to Mass., is a distinguished shrub with large-lobed leaves which turn wine-color in fall. The flowers open in early summer in long panicles, with many sterile flowers which turn purple.

PRINCIPAL ASIATIC SPECIES

H. macrophylla grows to 12 ft. in favored climates, and has broad handsome leaves, thick and shining. It occurs in forms with blue, pink, or white flowers borne in flat or rounded clusters. Many named varieties are grown, some with very large clusters of all sterile flowers of varying color shades.

bretschneideri is hardy and makes a rounded bush to 8 ft., with white flowers in slightly convex clusters.

xanthoneura is somewhat similar but with larger leaves and more vigorous growth. It has loose convex clusters of white flowers with large sterile flowers. Var. *wilsoni* is a good form with narrower and glossy leaves.

paniculata, which is one of the hardiest, may assume the size and form of a small tree. It has long panicles of white flowers with few sterile flowers and is a .. ndsome late-flowering shrub.

praecox is similar to the type but flowers in midsummer. Var. *grandiflora* has very large panicles of almost all sterile flowers. It has been planted everywhere.

davidi is a tender handsome shrub to 6 ft., with large loose clusters of bluish fertile flowers surrounded by large white sterile flowers.

sargentiana is a striking shrub with hairy stems, purplish young growth and large leaves. The large flat clusters of bluish-violet fertile flowers surrounded by sterile white flowers are very showy. Can be grown outdoors only in mild regions, and prefers partial shade.

petiolaris is a high climber, clinging firmly to walls and tree trunks by aerial rootlets. Without support it is a straggling prostrate bush. It is very slow to get established, but has good clean foliage, and is conspicuous in early summer with large white flower clusters, bearing only a few sterile flowers.

HYDRANGEA - VINE, JAPANESE. A common name for a tall-growing, climbing shrub from Japan, a member of the Saxifrage Family. See SCHIZOPHRAGMA.

HYDRASTIS (hy-dras'-tis) *canadensis.* A low herbaceous perennial with petal-less flowers, crimson berries and thick yellow rootstocks, hence the popular names Orange-root and Golden-seal, which see.

HYDRIASTELE (hy-dri-ah-stee'-lee). A genus of Feather Palms from Australia, comprising only one species, *H. wendlandiana,* formerly listed (and still sometimes referred to) as *Kentia wendlandiana.* It is frequently planted in S. Fla. where it becomes a small tree, with graceful, arching, spineless leaves and large bunches of fruit at the top of the trunk. In the greenhouse it requires an abundance of water and a temperature of about 65 deg. F. It responds well to fertilizers, especially when kept pot-bound. It makes an excellent house plant and is easily handled.

HYDROCLEIS (hy'-droh-klys) or HY-DROCLEYS. A genus of aquatic herbs with showy flowers. *H. nymphoides,* the Water-poppy (which see), is popularly grown in tubs, ponds and aquaria.

HYDROCOTYLE (hy-droh-kot'-i-lee). A genus of creeping perennials with little white flowers in small flat clusters sometimes used for carpet bedding. See MARSH PENNYWORT.

HYDROCYANIC ACID. The deadly poisonous compound that is the source of one of the most effective gases for fumigating purposes. It is produced by combining sulphuric acid and some cyanide salt such as sodium or potassium cyanide. See FUMIGATION.

HYDROPHYLLUM (hy-droh-fil'-um). A genus of half a dozen or more hardy American plants, mostly perennial, useful in the wild garden or in rich, shaded locations and commonly called Water-leaf. The perennial species are good for a planting about shrubbery where they colonize, take care of themselves and form a very attractive foliage mass. *H. canadense* is one of these. It grows to about 2½ ft. and its lobed, palm-shaped leaves are a foot across. It has clusters of small, greenish-white or violet flowers in the early summer.

HYDROPONICS. An artificial word coined specifically for the growing of plants in tanks of nutrient solution. The seeds are sown, or the young plants are set, into a layer of hardwood sawdust which rests upon a thin layer of excelsior on a tray of hardware cloth or similar material. The level of the nutrient solution is at first high enough to reach the excelsior, and the nutrient solution must be poured upon the sawdust to keep it moist; but as the roots grow down into the solution, the level is dropped an inch or two, and sometimes more, below the tray. In a tank it is possible to heat the solution by means of an electric heater such as is used for tropical fish aquaria. It may also be necessary to aerate the solution with an air pump or other device though on a small scale the necessary aeration may be accomplished by occasionally raising the tray so the roots are exposed to the air for a few moments. See also CHEMICAL GARDENING; NUTRIENT SOLUTION; SOILLESS GARDENING; SOILLESS WINDOW BOX.

HYDROSME (hy-dros'-mee). A genus or large-leaved herbs of the Arum Family, closely resembling Amorphophallus and formerly listed under that name. *H. rivieri* (Devils Tongue) has a green spathe, spotted with white and shaded with purple, and leaves to 4 ft. cut into segments.

HYLOCEREUS (hy-loh-see'-ree-us) *undatus.* This is probably the best known of that highly prized group of cultivated cacti frequently alluded to as "the night-blooming cereus." It is grown all over the world and visitors to Honolulu rhapsodize over hedges of it bearing, it is said, as many as 5,000 blossoms at a time, and scenting the air for blocks. It sends forth many aerial roots and grows readily from cuttings. In colder climates it should be treated like other species of tropical origin; and grown in a lath-house or greenhouse as conditions warrant. For soil requirements and culture see CACTUS.

HYMENOCALLIS (hy-men-oh-kal'-is). A genus of American summer-blooming bulbs with (mostly) white flowers in flattened clusters on long naked stems. Commonly called Spider-lily, which see.

HYMENOPHYLLUM (hy-men-oh-fil'-um). A genus of very small, transparently textured ferns belonging to the group called Filmy Ferns, which see.

HYOSCYAMUS (hy-oh-sy'-ah-mus). A genus of coarse herbs with funnel-formed flowers in spikes, known as HENBANE, which see.

A SHRUBBY ST. JOHNSWORT
Growing wild in the South but quite hardy North, Hypericum aureum blooms with a showy mass of yellow flowers soon after midsummer.

HYPERICUM (hy-per'-i-kum). St. Johnswort. A genus composed of a large number of perennial herbs and shrubs, some weedy, but most of them decorative, usually having bright yellow flowers with profuse stamens, and often evergreen foliage. They are grown in the rock garden and in borders and the species which sucker readily are used for ground-cover in landscape work. They grow easily in loamy or sandy soil and their blooming period is prolonged if they are given a semi-shaded position. The more tender species should be placed in the rock garden where they can have winter protection. St. Johnsworts grow readily from seed, though the creeping species are also increased by division and suckers.

PRINCIPAL SPECIES

H. kalmianum, a low hardy shrub, has narrow overgreen leaves and yellow flowers 1 in. across in flat-topped clusters.

ascyron, a perennial 2 to 6 ft. tall, has golden flowers to 2 in. across; hardy in Canada.

aureum, a deciduous shrub 3 ft. high, has bluish-green foliage and flowers nearly 2 in. across; hardy in Mass.

prolificum, a larger shrub, with smaller flowers in flat-topped clusters has narrow evergreen leaves.

lobocarpum, a hardy shrub to 6 ft. with racemes of rather small yellow flowers, should be planted in a moist spot.

calycinum (Aarons Beard or Rose-of-Sharon), a low shrub spreading by suckers, with evergreen foliage and beautiful large golden flowers, is suitable for a ground-cover and is hardy if given protection.

patulum, a shrub to 3 ft., has large solitary or clustered flowers. Var. *henryi* is a larger form needing winter protection.

moserianum (Gold-flower), a hybrid between *H. calycinum* and *H. patulum,* is an attractive shrub to 2 ft. with drooping branches and flowers to 2½ in. It is hardy only S. of N. Y., where it is most attractive massed in the border, or grown as a pot plant.

HYPOCHOERIS (hy-poh-kee'-ris). A genus of the Composite Family composed of a number of European herbs with divided foliage and single or clustered heads of yellow flowers. Known as Cats-ear, they are occasionally grown in the rock garden, being increased by division or by seeds. *H. uniflora* and *H. radicata* are perennials, the latter with white-hairy leaves; *H. glabra,* an annual, has smooth leaves and small flowers.

HYPOXIS (hy-pok'-sis). A genus of small herbs of the Amaryllis Family, native to temperate and tropical regions, and known as Star-grass, which see.

HYSSOP (his'-up). An Old-World hardy, perennial herb or sub-shrub (*Hyssopus officinalis*) grown as a culinary and medicinal herb and as an ornamental. It it readily propagated by cuttings and division, but is usually grown from seed sown in early spring, either in drills 18 in. apart and the plants thinned to 12 in., or in seed beds, the seedlings to be transplanted in early summer. Abundant light and limy soils suit it best. See HERBS.

IBERIS (y-bee'-ris). A genus of small to medium sized annual and perennial herbaceous plants of the Mustard Family, known to gardeners as Candytuft (which see). Natives of S. Europe, they are hardy and easy to grow, but the garden kinds are of two distinct types—annual and perennial.

IBOZA (y-boh'-zah). A genus of African herbs or shrubs with small flowers grown outdoors in the S. but in greenhouses elsewhere. When through blooming the plants may be cut back and treated like salvia, a closely related plant.

ICE-PLANT. Common name for *Cryophytum crystalinum,* a succulent annual formerly known (and still often listed in catalogs) as Mesembryanthemum. In S. Africa, Mediterranean regions, and S. and Lower Calif. it grows luxuriantly in barren, rocky places and dry sand, storing up moisture in its thick stems and foliage. It is therefore an ideal rock-garden plant, its prostrate growth about 6 in. high being especially adapted to dry banks and sunny spots. The foliage sparkles like ice crystals, giving rise to the common name, and as they trail over the ground the plants are decidedly ornamental. The inconspicuous flowers are pinkish white with slender petals. Easily propagated by seed, the ice-plant should be started indoors in the N., the seedlings being set out only after the weather becomes warm.

ICHNEUMON WASP (though commonly incorrectly called FLY). A parasitic insect that attacks caterpillars, though some kinds lay their eggs in the burrows of wood-boring larvae. See INSECTS, BENEFICIAL.

IDESIA (y-dee'-zi-ah) polycarpa. An Oriental deciduous spreading tree with light gray bark, grown for its attractive red-stemmed lustrous foliage and racemes of orange-red berries which are most conspicuous after the leaves fall. It is hardy in the S. and seedlings have wintered well even in Mass.

ILEX (y'-leks). A genus of evergreen and deciduous glossy leaved trees and shrubs, notable for their brilliantly colored berries and commonly called Holly (which see). They range from hardy to quite tender, but wherever they can be grown the different species are highly ornamental

for garden and lawn specimens besides having an inseparable association with the Christmas holidays.

ILLICIUM (i-lis'-i-um). Evergreen trees and shrubs, belonging to the Magnolia Family, mostly of the Orient but one or two native in S. U. S. They can be grown only in warm climates. *I. anisatum,* the principal species, is a small Japanese tree, with elliptic, aromatic leaves and yellowish-green flowers with many narrow petals. *I. floridanum,* native of Fla., is a shrub with larger leaves and many-petaled flowers of crimson-maroon. *I. verum,* the Star-anise of China, produces a star-shaped fruit cluster, used for flavoring purposes.

IMBRICARIA (im-bri-kay'-ri-ah). A former name for the genus Mimusops, a group of tropical evergreen trees somewhat planted in the S. for their thick shining foliage and sometimes edible fruit.

IMMORTELLE (i-mor-tel'). This, the French word for Everlasting, is especially applied in America to *Xeranthemum annuum,* but it is also used loosely for any of the kinds of flowers which are dried for use in winter bouquets.

IMMUNE. Exempt from disease. A plant may be *resistant* to a disease in varying degrees, but immunity implies 100 per cent resistance. See DISEASES, PLANT.

IMMUNIZATION. The art of rendering a crop immune—that is, 100 per cent resistant—to attacks by specific organisms or pests generally established in an area. Natural immunity may be developed by selection and propagation of individuals which show marked resistance, or by crossing plants that are desirable but susceptible to a given trouble with less desirable but more resistant forms. Numerous attempts at artificial inoculations have been made on plants, but so far no success has been attained.

IMPATIENS (im-pay'-shi-enz). An interesting genus of greenhouse, border, and wild-garden plants, several of which differ so in form and habit that only the spur formed by one of the three sepals and the way the ripe seed-pods quickly curl at a touch to expel the ripened seeds reveal their relationship. This latter character is responsible for the common names of the genus—Touch-me-not and Snapweed.

I. sultani (Sultan Snapweed, Sultana, or Patience) is the best-known greenhouse subject in the group. Long a favorite house plant, it is easily raised from cuttings and studded with waxy bright-rose-colored flowers nearly all year around. In summer, when a half-shaded spot can be found, it makes an excellent plant for the outdoor border, forming a good bushy growth about 15 in. high, with an abundance of bloom. Do not confuse its common name with Sweet Sultan (Centaurea).

Hybrids of *I. holsti,* with red-striped stems and flowers varying from white to scarlet, are also grown as greenhouse plants, house plants, and summer border subjects.

I. balsamina (Garden Balsam) is the species more often seen in the border, with its rose-like blooms in white, lavender, lemon-yellow, and many shades of red crowded close to the leafy spikes 12 to 18 in. tall. Lately improved new hybrids with fuller flowers of peach-blossom pink have been introduced. Though a tender subject, plants set out in June from seed sown indoors in April, will continue blooming through the autumn after most other annuals are gone. They require a rich sandy

GARDEN BALSAM
The newly improved forms of this old-fashioned border favorite bear larger, more fully double and more numerous flowers.

loam, ample moisture, some shade, and plenty of room. Several transplantings, leaving them finally 2 ft. apart, are often desirable. Pinch off the first buds, and remove sideshoots if heavy central spikes of bloom are desired.

I. roylei is a purple-flowered garden annual, grown from seed and requiring little care. Although rather coarse in habit, it serves well to fill in vacant spots in the garden in August and September.

For the wild garden, dig up in spring self-sown seedlings of the native Touch-me-not or Jewel-weed (*I. pallida* or *I. biflora*), and plant them in a wet spot on the shore of a pond or stream. During most of the summer they will bear a profusion of little golden blossoms dangling above the foliage of these bushy but watery-stemmed plants.

IMPERFECT FLOWER. One in which either stamens or pistil are lacking, in contradistinction to an hermaphrodite or perfect flower, which see. It is thus *unisexual,* as distinguished from *bisexual.* When flowers of each sex are borne separately, but on the same plant, the individual (or species, if this is a distinguishing character) is said to be *monoecious.* When the sexes are borne only upon separate plants, these plants (and the species) are *dioecious.* See FLOWER; STERILITY; SELF.

IMPROVEMENT, PLANT. There are two general ways of improving plants. The first is by providing better environmental conditions, resulting in improved growth or fruitfulness. This involves such things as nutrition, hardiness, soil chemistry, pest and disease control, propagation, and similar matters which have their theoretical basis in botanical science and their practical application in horticulture and gardening. The second means of plant improvement is by causing favorable changes in the inherent nature of the species itself. This involves the science of genetics or heredity and the practice of plant breeding. See PLANT BREEDING; STERILITY.

IMPROVEMENT, SOIL. The improvement of any soil, whether of garden or field, flower bed or farm land, may be required along either chemical or physical lines, or both. Chemically, a soil may lack one or more of the essential plant-food elements; or it may be either too acid or too alkaline for the kind of plants that are being grown in it. Physically, soil may be too wet (calling for drainage); too dry (calling for irrigation to supplement the precipitation of the region) ; too loose and sandy (so that it needs more body or water-holding capacity), or too stiff and heavy (which means that both moisture and air percolate too slowly, making it uncongenial for the growing plants). The several operations that correct these undesirable conditions are treated elsewhere under the subjects of DRAINAGE; FERTILITY; FERTILIZER; IRRIGATION; MANURE; SOIL; etc.

In addition, of course, the various operations that constitute cultivation (which see) or tillage (which see) are highly important not only for keeping a soil in good condition, but also for putting it in proper condition in the first place. How true this is is indicated by the fact that the good old garden term Manure, synonymous with something to improve the soil, comes from the same word-root as Manual, Maneuver, or any similar word referring to "work by hand."

The benefits to plant growth from commercial fertilizers, nitrate of soda, and other forcing plant foods applied to the soil last usually one season or less, and do not permanently enrich it. Hence, in conjunction with those materials soil-improvement methods should be used. These include: manuring, cover-cropping, deep plowing, and the addition of compost, humus, lime, bonemeal, and fertilizers that dissolve slowly so that their effects last more than one season.

Manure should be added every year, not so much for the ammonia, phosphoric acid and other valuable nutritive ingredients it contains, as for the supply of organic matter. The difference between topsoil and subsoil which makes the former more fertile is mainly the presence there of decayed vegetable and animal substances, and the best means of improving most soils is by increasing the amount of such decayed vegetable matter. Where the soil is not to be turned over, as on lawns, or where only the surface will be cultivated, as in the border or around specimen trees, a top-dressing of manure should be applied in winter.

As often as possible, cover or green manure crops should be grown on all or part of the vegetable garden. Sown as early as possible, among corn and similar crops—even before they have stopped yielding, these vegetable manures are plowed or dug under in spring. The best are the legumes such as crimson clover and winter or hairy vetch. Rye will produce a greater quantity of green manure, and may be sown mixed with clover or vetch.

Deep plowing further improves the soil by increasing the depth of the topsoil. Better still is subsoil spading or trenching (which see) by which the organic materials can be worked in to a depth of 2 ft. or more.

All dead leaves, stalks, grass-clippings and green garbage should be rotted down for compost (which see) rather than burned; and this compost should be added to the soil when plowing or spading or used with manure for top-dressing.

If these natural methods build up soil too slowly, humus and leaf mold may be added in any quantity desired, as they are largely organic; but if they are acid, lime must be used with them. For most garden crops, hydrated lime or ground limestone increases the effectiveness of manure and organic fertilizers. Other minerals, though ordinarily present, especially when subsoil is brought to the surface, may in time become depleted, requiring occasional additions of plant foods rich in potash, phosphorus, sulphur, etc.

When a bed or border is prepared, organic materials should be added and mixed thoroughly by deep digging especially if the bed is to be planted permanently, and for new lawns a soil as deep and rich as possible should be provided by the same means.

INARCHING or APPROACH GRAFTING. A type of plant propagation in which one plant, providing the scion, is joined to another plant, providing the stock, while each continues to grow on its own roots. When union is accomplished, the scion is severed from its original plant becoming thereafter a part of the stock plant. See GRAFTING.

INCARVILLEA (in-kahr-vil'-ee-ah). A genus of Asiatic herbs containing several showy and fairly hardy perennials that have been brought from China and established with great success in American gardens. Growing from 18 in. to 2 ft. high, the plants produce terminal clusters of red or yellow bloom above a basal group of vivid green leaves resembling those of ailanthus. The tubular flowers have a broadly expanded 5-lobed rim.

Often (incorrectly) called "hardy gloxinias," incarvilleas thrive in rich but light well-drained soil in a sunny border. Prop-

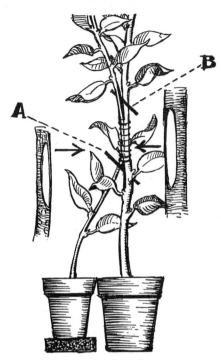

INARCHING OR GRAFTING BY APPROACH

A method used with difficult or valuable subjects because it keeps the scion on its own roots until well united with the stock. This shows the scion plant at left and, enlarged, the areas of bark cut away where the two cambium layers are to be brought in contact and firmly wrapped. When the union is complete the scion is cut from its stem at (A) and the upper part of the stock at (B) leaving the least possible stub.

agation is by seeds sown in spring and summer for bloom the following year; or by root division. Winter protection is recommended, especially in the N. The young growths forming above the rootstock in summer may be cut off and rooted as cuttings under glass.

The best-known species is *I. delavayi*, 2 ft. tall, bearing rose-purple flowers with yellow tubes. *I. grandiflora* is similar, with rose-red flowers.

INCENSE-CEDAR. Common name for the genus Libocedrus, comprising ornamental Old-World conifers with attractive foliage resembling that of arborvitae.

INCENSE-PLANT. A common name for *Humea elegans,* an Australian biennial herb growing to 6 ft. with small copper-colored flower-heads in drooping clusters.

INCH WORM or MEASURING WORM. Names for the leaf eating canker worm

(which see), referring to its method of progressing by alternately looping up and straightening out its body as though measuring off distances.

INCISED. Cut sharply and irregularly and more or less deeply, forming large jagged teeth; applied to leaves like those of red birch.

INDEHISCENT. Term applied to a fruit that does not open along an obvious suture or valve, as for instance, that of the apple or maple. Compare DEHISCENCE.

INDIAN-BEAN. Common name for *Catalpa bignonioides,* a large deciduous tree of S. E. U. S. with large, white, yellow-striped flowers in loose panicles.

INDIAN-CHERRY. Common name for *Rhamnus caroliniana,* a deciduous tree with greenish flowers and black, berry-like fruits in flattened clusters.

INDIAN-CRESS. Common name sometimes given to the flower buds and young seed pods of nasturtium (Tropaeolum) when picked and used as seasoning for salads or pickled as a substitute for capers.

INDIAN CUCUMBER-ROOT. Common name for *Medeola virginiana,* a liliaceous herb with small greenish-yellow flowers and purple berries in flat clusters. It is found in swampy land from Nova Scotia to Minn. and southward and its tuberous roots are sometimes eaten.

INDIAN CUP. Common name for *Silphium perfoliatum,* a tall, coarse, hardy perennial with large yellow flower-heads; also called Cup-plant.

INDIAN-CURRANT. A common name for *Symphoricarpos orbiculatus,* a deciduous shrub with insignificant flowers followed by attractive purplish-red fruits.

INDIAN-FIG. A common name for *Opuntia ficus-indica,* a species of hardy cactus of the prickly-pear group. It is cultivated in tropical countries for the edible fruit. See CACTUS; OPUNTIA.

INDIAN-GRASS. Common name for *Sorghastrum nutans,* a 5 ft. hardy American perennial that forms large clumps and is highly ornamental in bloom and also when the flowers turn bronzy in autumn.

INDIAN-HAWTHORN. Common name for *Raphiolepis indica,* an evergreen shrub with shining leathery foliage, pink flowers and small black fruits.

INDIAN-MULBERRY. Common name for *Morinda citrifolia,* a small tropical-region tree with white flowers which yield a red dye, and yellowish fruits.

INDIAN PAINT. A common name for *Lithospermum canescens,* a perennial hairy herb with orange-yellow flowers. A species of Gromwell, it is also called Puccoon.

INDIAN PAINT-BRUSH. Common name for members of the genus Castilleja (which see), western herbs of the Figwort Family, with brilliant orange or red flowers, especially *C. californica* and *C. coccinea,* which is the State flower of Wyoming.

INDIAN PHYSIC. Common name for *Gillenia trifoliata,* a perennial branching herb with white or pink-tinted flowers in panicles.

INDIAN-PINK. A common name for *Lobelia cardinalis,* a native perennial herb known also as Cardinal-flower; it is sometimes applied to the tropical climber *Quamoclit pinnata,* the popular Cypress-vine.

INDIAN PIPE. Common name for *Monotropa uniflora,* a leafless herb with naked stems each bearing a nodding waxy white flower. Remarkable among the higher (flowering) plants because it contains no chlorophyll or green coloring matter. Native to shady damp woods in the N. hemisphere, it is often called Ghost-plant.

INDIAN-POTATO. Early name for the giant sunflower, *Helianthus giganteus,* a N. form of which produces fleshy roots used for food by American Indians.

INDIAN-SHOT. Common name (suggested by the hard, black seeds) for *Canna indica,* a relative of the popular bedding plant; native to tropical America and naturalized in S. U. S.

INDIAN- or MOCK-STRAWBERRY. Common name for *Duchesnea indica,* an Asiatic perennial with yellow flowers and strawberry-like insipid fruit. It is useful as a hanging-basket plant and a ground-cover.

INDIAN-TOBACCO. Common name for *Lobelia inflata,* a 3 ft. hairy annual with light blue flowers, native to N. E. U. S.

INDIAN TREE-SPURGE. A common name for the poisonous African tree or shrub, *Euphorbia triucalli,* also called Milk-bush because of its milky sap. Grown outdoors in Fla. and sometimes under glass in the N.

INDIAN-TURNIP. Another common name for *Arisaema triphyllum,* the familiar, moisture-loving native herb better known as Jack-in-the-pulpit, which see.

INDIAN-WHEAT. An early name for *Fagopyrum tataricum,* sometimes called Duckwheat, a close relative of Buckwheat, which see.

INDICATOR FERN (*Botrychium virginianum*). The largest of the Grape Ferns this species is native to many parts of the U. S. and is usually known as the Rattlesnake Fern. Its frond is divided into a broad, 3-branched sterile segment, and an erect fruiting spike. Attractive under other ferns in woods soil near rock.

INDIGEN. A term applied to a plant from which originated normally in a natural habitat (to which it is said to be *indigenous*), as distinguished from a *cultigen* (which see) or plant which originated in cultivation. *Brassica oleracea* (a wild plant from which developed the cauliflower and cabbage), is indigenous to W. Europe; but cauliflower and cabbage, kohlrabi and Brussels sprouts, are cultigens derived from it.

INDIGO. Common name for Indigofera, a genus of deciduous shrubs and perennial herbs, mostly from warm regions of the world, belonging to the Pea Family. The shrubby species are attractive summer flowering shrubs of light and graceful habit. They do well in light loam and a sunny position. A few are fairly hardy N.; if killed back these usually renew themselves from the base. Propagated by seeds and cuttings.

PRINCIPAL SPECIES

I. gerardiana is a slender Himalayan shrub with leaves of 13 to 21 leaflets and long racemes of purplish-rose flowers.

amblyantha, native in China, grows to 6 ft. with 7 to 11 leaflets and slender clusters of small pink flowers.

kirilowi, from Korea, is an erect grower to 4 ft., with 7 to 11 leaflets and dense clusters of large bright rose flowers.

potanini, a Chinese species of graceful habit to 5 ft., has 9 to 11 leaflets and drooping clusters of lilac-pink flowers.

tinctoria is a small Asiatic shrub with silvery stems and reddish-yellow flowers. It was formerly the chief source of indigo and long ago was introduced into and cultivated in S. where it has since run wild.

"Indigo" is incorrectly used in the common names of several plants: Bastard-indigo is *Amorpha fruticosa;* Wild-indigo is Baptisia, and False-indigo may be either Amorpha or Baptisia.

INDOLEACETIC ACID. One of the synthetic or manufactured chemical substances which have effects on plants similar to those caused by the hormones (which see) or natural growth-regulating materials made by and within the plants themselves. Because they are not of plant origin, these substances are not true hormones although sometimes called by that name.

Indoleacetic acid has long been known to chemists but only recently, in the course of the investigations that resulted in the discovery of the auxins (which see), were its growth-promoting properties revealed. Although it has not been found, or identified, in plants, it is a natural constituent of some fungi (as yeast) and certain animal tissues. It has been and is used considerably by scientific workers, and is highly effective in producing stem curvature, as described under hormone; but it is less valuable and less used in the field of practical growth-production, such as the treatment of cuttings, etc. by amateur gardeners and commercial plant growers.

See also CHEMICALS IN HORTICULTURE.

INDOLEBUTYRIC ACID. Another of the chemical root-growth or hormone-like substances sometimes, but mistakenly, called hormones. A white or yellowish crystalline powder, soluble in alcohol but not in water, it is perhaps the most valuable of such materials as have yet been discovered. It is the active ingredient in some of the commercial preparations used to expedite the rooting of cuttings. Cell growth and the initiation of root systems are greatly speeded up by very small amounts of this material which, apparently, activates and increases the amount of natural root-forming hormones in the treated cuttings.

See also AUXIN; CHEMICALS IN HORTICULTURE; HORMONE; and INDOLEACETIC ACID, above.

INFERIOR. Beneath, below or under. An *inferior ovary* in one that appears to be beneath the flower rather than within it, because of the insertion of the calyx, corolla and stamens upon the summit of the ovary. See EPIGYNOUS.

INFLORESCENCE. Meaning, strictly, the arrangement of flowers on a plant, this term is also applied to the individual flower cluster, and, sometimes, to its manner of unfolding, or opening. The many forms of flower cluster or arrangement fall into several quite distinct groups, which provide one of the means of distinguishing flowers. The term "head" is sometimes applied to any flower cluster, but inaccurately, since a head is a special type, as noted below.

A single flower borne at the end of a stem (as in the poppy) is called "solitary." Sometimes blossoms occur in pairs, as in the twinflower (*Linnaea borealis*). Beyond this, the arrangement may take any of the typical forms briefly described below. As explained under FLOWER (which see), the stalk of a single flower or flower cluster is called a *peduncle* (except that, in bulbous plants it is usually termed a *scape*); in a cluster, the stalk of a single flower is a *pedicel*. If a cluster or a flower has neither peduncle nor pedicel, it is said to be *sessile,* meaning that it is set directly against the main stem.

Spike. This is a slender, usually erect but sometimes drooping, arrangement of flowers (either sessile or on very short stalks) along the sides of a common stem. In the spikes of timothy (herds grass) or of cat-tail, the flowers are sessile; in that of the common lavender they have short peduncles. In the spikes of the common grape-hyacinth and the hollyhock, flowers are sometimes sessile, sometimes short-stalked.

Raceme. This differs from a spike only in that the flower stalks are longer, giving a looser effect, as in the lily-of-the-valley, or fireweed.

Panicle. This is an extension of the raceme, in which the flower stalks are branched; giving a loosely pyramidal form as in oats and many other grasses, also astilbe and Hercules club (*Aralia spinosa*). When a shortening of the peduncles makes the panicle more compact, as in the lilac, the term *thyrse* is often used.

Catkin or *Ament.* This is another sort of spike, compact, sometimes short and rounded and usually supplied with a bract or scale beneath each minute flower. Birch and willow bear catkins; and the *cone* as in the pine is actually an inflorescence of this type.

Spadix. Another spike-like form. It is a fleshy column bearing densely packed sessile flowers; the whole structure usually arises from a partly enveloping sheath, called a *spathe.* Jack-in-the-pulpit and Anthurium are good examples, their large green or colored spathes being often mistaken for the corolla of a large single flower.

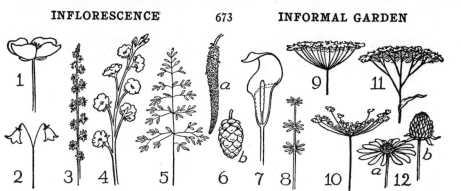

TYPES OF FLOWER ARRANGEMENT, OR INFLORESCENCE

1. The solitary flower. 2. The flowers paired. 3. A characteristic spike. 4. A raceme, a spike-like form in which each flower is on a short stem. 5. A panicle, or branched raceme. 6. Two types of cones: (a) the catkin, or ament; (b) the hard, scaly cone of an evergreen. 7. A spadix, surrounded by a leafy or petal-like spathe. 8. Diagram representing three whorls around a stem. 9. An umbel. 10. A cyme, in which the central flowers open first. 11. A corymb, in which the outer flowers open first. 12. Two types of heads: (a) of the Composite Family; (b) rounded head of certain other plants.

Departing from the spike form, there are the following familiar types of inflorescence:

Whorl. Flowers are said to occur in whorls when more than 2 surround the stem at exactly the same level.

Umbel. Here a number of flower stalks arise from a common center in such a way that the flowers are carried at about the same height, forming a flattened or slightly rounded cluster. All members of the Parsley Family (called on this account Umbelliferae), of which the wild carrot and the blue lace-flower are examples, have this sort of inflorescence. It is said to be "simple" if the peduncles are undivided, or "compound" if they are branched.

Cyme. Here again the flower stalks rise from a common point to approximately the same level, but the intermediate divisions are irregular, filling up the intervening space, as in the common elder or snowball (Viburnum). In this type the flowers at the center of the inflorescence open first.

Corymb. In this type the flower stalks, instead of arising from a common point, originate at different points along the stem; however, as the lowest are the longest, the others becoming progressively shorter, all the flowers are borne at about the same height, again forming a flattened or slightly rounded surface, as in the verbena. They differ from those of a cyme in that they open first around the margin and progressively inward. The flower cluster of the pear is an example, whereas that of the apple forms an umbel. A modification of the corymb sometimes recognized, in which

the flowers are more compactly placed, is the *fascicle,* as in sweet william.

Head. This is a dense spherical, ovoid or perhaps cylindrical flower cluster borne at the end of a stem, as in clovers, the globe-amaranth, and globe-thistle (Echinops). The name is also applied to the flower cluster of the Composite Family as illustrated by the aster or daisy, in which a compact round mass of disk-flowers (which see) may be surrounded by a fringe of flattened, strap-shaped ray-flowers (which see). Or, a composite flower-head may consist of all disk or all ray-flowers, or the two sorts may be mingled in varying proportions or modified into intermediate shapes. See COMPOSITE.

INFORMAL GARDEN. (See illustration, Plate 29.) This is an expression of garden design that is casual and not ordered in effect, yet carefully ordered in fact. Such a garden is one of the best products of that art which conceals art—the art of its design and composition veiling the art with which it is designed and executed. It is not by any means a garden which comes into existence accidentally without planning; nor is it merely a naturalistic handling of the area that surrounds and forms the setting of a dwelling (although such handling it is quite true results in informality). It may not follow naturalistic lines at all, in that it may make no effort to imitate Nature. In short, garden "informality" does not mean a lapse into jungle manners or wilderness conditions; rather it may be defined as strict discipline of these—quite as strict as the discipline of extreme formality—but strict discipline applied in such a graceful manner as to put the whole effect at ease.

FEATURES. All the things which find their places in formal gardens (which see) are equally suitable in informal gardens, the essential difference being the manner in which they are assembled. Instead of being arbitrarily related to each other according to a preconceived symmetrical plan, they are brought into mutual relationship according to the peculiarities of the situation. For every garden situation has peculiarities, even if only the result of such small things as the position of a neighboring garage or the lay of the land with reference to prevailing winds. No two gardens present even approximately the same problem. And this is fortunate, for it is this variability which makes every garden individual and delightful in its own special characters. Of course, to achieve this, the garden plan must recognize those small distinctions. And this, it may be noted in passing, no standard, stock garden plan can ever do.

ELEMENTS OF DESIGN. It is always important that the transition from the house to the garden be well marked and rightly developed. And this is especially true in the garden of informal design. Otherwise there will be a break between indoors and outdoors; a sense of separateness between the house and the garden instead of a sense of union in which they are, as they should be, two parts of a single whole.

Informality in design is not violated by this uniting link in which the formal lines of the dwelling are carried out from it by means of an arbor, terrace, hedged grass plot or wall, to where, beyond these limits, it yields to the less restricted ground forms and lines which the plan develops. Nor is it necessary to exclude from an informal design those bits of so-called formality which a rose garden, for example, represents. A rose garden need not be rectangular, to be sure; but for convenience in tending the plants and in order to save space, garden roses are usually planted in some definite order, much as vegetables are planted in orderly rows.

In the informal garden such elements are so related to the whole that they are not seen until arrived at directly; and so that their formality, such as it is, does not intrude upon the general informal effect. It is, in brief, in the manner of assembling the rose garden and the other component parts of the whole garden that the achievement of informality lies.

PLANT MATERIALS. Great freedom as regards selection of plants used is allowed in designing an informal garden. It is possible for the entire garden to be developed around a desire for certain plants or kinds of plants. Not that the entire space will be devoted solely to that one thing, but rather that all the planning will lead up to it, emphasizing its importance in the gardener's thought and sentiment.

MAINTENANCE. Permanent plantings of trees and shrubs find full expression in informal design; as such things require no special care beyond the removal of dead wood or unruly growth when it appears, one element of maintenance is reduced to a minimum. Spraying must however, be attended to regularly; weeds must be plucked; dead flower-heads must be cut and perennial borders must be gone over, lifted, thinned and replanted after the soil has been renewed or fed, at least every fourth year to keep them at their best. In other words there are definite maintenance requirements in informal as in all other kinds of gardens. But though order and discipline are just as important in the informal garden as in the most formal arrangement, the great difference and the significant thing is that one is not conscious of them.

See also PERENNIAL BORDER; SHRUBS; OUTDOOR LIVING-ROOM. Compare FORMAL GARDEN; WILD GARDEN.

INJURY. In discussing plant troubles there is sometimes confusion between injury and disease. Usually the latter is recognized as a result of some *continued* irritation by a causal factor, whereas injury is the harmful effect on a plant of some *transient* act or condition. Thus the result of the action of fungi or bacteria that infect plants is considered disease, while the biting or chewing of insects results in injury. Sudden changes in temperature and the like may result in injury, whereas a long continued irritant, such as improper soil condition, may cause a physiological disease. See BROWNING; BURNING; DISEASES, PLANT; PHYSIOLOGICAL DISEASES; ELECTRICAL INJURY; GAS INJURY; HEAT INJURY; SMOKE INJURY; SPRAY INJURY; FROST; WINTER INJURY; INSECTS.

INKBERRY. A common name for *Ilex glabra,* an evergreen, black-berried holly

Plate 29.   THE CHARM OF THE INFORMAL GARDEN

The informal garden has the lure of the unexpected.   Here, though apparently unplanned, are many satisfying combinations.   Airy, light growth is complemented by the contrast of dark green vines, and tall stalks of foxgloves make charming notes against the old stone wall.

(which see), native from Mass. to Miss. Also called Winterberry.

INOCULATION. In its relation to gardening and plant growing this term, like many others, refers sometimes to harmful and sometimes to beneficial acts and results. A simple definition is, the depositing of infectious material (called the *inoculum*) on or in an "infection court," which is any place in or on a host plant where infection can be set up; this may be a wound, a water pore, breathing pore (*stoma*), nectary, leaf surface, seed surface or root hair. An inoculum may consist of any portion of the organism causing the infection (called a *pathogene*), as spores, mycelium, bacterial thallus, insect eggs, etc.

In many—perhaps most—cases, inoculation is the first step in the development of an injurious plant disease (see DISEASES, PLANT), but there are certain infectious organisms that establish a useful or helpful relationship with the host plant that is called *symbiosis*.

In this second class are the various legume bacteria which enter the roots of leguminous plants—such as pea, bean, vetch, alfalfa, sweet clover, soy-bean, etc.—through the young root hairs and cause an irritation of the root tissues. This results in the formation of nodules or tubercles in which the bacteria find favorable conditions for rapid growth and development. Thus the plant furnishes food for the bacteria but the latter in return render an even greater service to the plant by taking nitrogen from the air and "fixing" it in available—that is, usable—form both for the infected plant and for crops which may be grown on the same land after the inoculated legume has died or been turned under.

This contribution of nitrogen-fixing bacteria is very important in keeping a soil supplied with nitrogen; and leguminous crops are frequently grown simply to be plowed under so as to increase the fertility of the soil. Since not all soils contain these useful bacteria in sufficient numbers, pure "cultures" of the organisms, grown on agar (a jelly-like substance) or on humus, are sold by seed and garden supply stores. In purchasing this material it is important to get the special strain of the organism needed; that is, a culture intended to produce nodules on sweet clover will have no effect on red clover, and the soy-bean inoculant will be useless on garden beans, etc. Also be sure the culture is fresh. (In most states the law requires that the date of preparation appear on the package.) The accompanying directions may include inoculating seed (which should be just before planting) or the soil, or both, though seed inoculation is the most common and reliable method.

Inoculated sulphur, containing sulpho-fying organisms, is sometimes applied to soil for the control of potato scab. Also bacterial cultures can be obtained that will hasten the decomposition of a compost pile or so-called synthetic manure.

INORGANIC. Not living, such as rock or sand, as contrasted with *organic,* or living matter, which comprises the plant and animal life of the world.

The mineral basis of the soil in which plants grow is inorganic; but any fertile garden soil is a mixture of such material with more or less organic constituents, such as bacteria, fungi and insects; and the decomposing remains of plants (or animals) which having once been alive are of organic origin.

Plant foods added to the soil in the form of commercial fertilizers are generally inorganic; but the same chemical elements of nutrition that they provide—such as nitrogen, phosphorus, potassium, calcium, etc.—may also be supplied to soil in the form of organic fertilizers such as manures and composts, since the plant substances composing these composts have previously obtained the chemical elements from the soil.

INSECTICIDE. An insect killer, the term usually applied to chemical compounds employed for that purpose. In the air above and around us on a summer day there are millions of insects. Most of them are harmless, a few are beneficial, particularly the bees which unwittingly and incidentally distribute pollen from flower to flower while on their food collecting rounds. But some are decidedly harmful by devouring our cultivated plants and by spreading the germs indoors. Between them, the annual loss in the U.S. runs into the millions.

Man has waged war from time immemorial on these small but inplacable enemies, and with little success until recent years. In ancient times there was little understanding of their way of life, and none of any effective insecticide.

It was only about a century ago that poisonous sprays and dusts began to be used in agriculture. Arsenic had long since been known as a potent eradicator of persons, and eventually the thought occurred that it would be worth trying on the insect plagues. Paris green and London purple are two compounds embodying it that are frequently mentioned in the older gardening books; calcium arsenate, lead arsenate, and other arsenical compounds were of great service to farmers and horticulturists, and have by no means entirely disappeared from use. An early non-arsenical, still serviceable, is Bordeaux mixture which was concocted by vineyardists of Bordeaux, France, in the late 1880's.

The once famous Persian powder, and the similar Dalmatian powder, were based on pyrethrum derived from the flowers of chrysanthemum species. Pyrethum is still a valuable insecticide, usually fortified by synergists, or activators, such as sesame oil and piperonyl butoxide, which add to its strength and prolong its effectiveness. Another plant product which is not harmful to man, but very much so to insects is rotenone, derived from the powdered roots of derris and cubé, leguminous species of the tropics, long used there to stun fish in streams.

Long ago it was obvious that insects were averse to tobacco and many a pipe was smoked against them as a fumigant or repellent; many an ounce of tobacco burned in greenhouses. What is commonly used now, in dusts and sprays, is nicotine sulphate, very effective on asphids, leafhoppers, white flies and other small pests.

In the present century, the explosive advance of technical science on all sides is seen also in the expansion of knowledge about insects and the means of controlling those that are undesirable to mankind. Their structures and habits have been intensively studied and are understood as never before. This accords with the old maxim of war that to defeat an enemy you must first know him. And in war against destructive insects, a whole new armory of weapons has been developed through the rapid and extensive advances of organic chemistry —that is, the chemistry of carbon compounds, to which we also owe plastics, fibres, explosives and a multitude of new chemicals.

None of the new insecticides made such a sensational appearance as DDT in 1944, when it was used to dust the people of Naples and elsewhere in successful efforts to restrain a threatened epidemic of typhus, one of the attendant scourges of war and spread by lice. It had been discovered years earlier in Switzerland, and in 1939 it had been tried with good results when the potato crop seemed likely to be lost to the Colorado beetle. Before long its potency against other harmful insects was demonstrated, and its value to the health and well being of mankind was recognized by the award of a Nobel Prize to Paul Muller in 1948 for its discovery and development.

ORGANIC INSECTICIDES

The new organic insecticides form two general groups of synthetic chemicals, chlorinated hydrocarbons and organic phosphates. The former are made by reacting hydrocarbon molecules, composed of carbon and hydrogen, with chlorine. The latter are obtained by combining phosphorus with certain hydrocarbon molecules. The chlorinated hydrocarbons include DDT, BHC, lindane, methoxychlor, chlordane, toxaphene, aldrin and dieldrin. Among the organic phosphates are parathion, TEPP and malathion.

DDT is a shorthand symbol for dichloro-diphenyl-trichloroethane, compounded of chlorine, benzene and alcohol, and it is now a familiar term because of its wide use, effectiveness, low cost, safety, and ease in handling. Probably 100 million pounds are used annually in the U.S. with a corresponding decrease in the use of lead arsenate which it largely replaced. Its effect on insects is to disorganize their nervous systems so that they shake, stagger and die. It may be compounded with pyrethrum, which has a faster knockdown effect but is less lethal. Some insects have developed resistance to DDT, that is, offspring of survivors. Resort must then be made to combinations, or alternative controls. Another drawback to DDT is its stability which prevents it from breaking down quickly in the soil, and an accumulation of it can have undesirable effects on some plants.

Benzene hexachloride, BHC for short, was long known in England as a chemical, but only in the 1940's were its insecticidal properties observed. It has been of great value in attacking certain insects on which DDT is not altogether successful, particularly the cotton boll worm, which can cause losses annually in the hundreds of million dollars. For use on food crops, however, it has a notable drawback in its unpleasant odor which clings to vegetables and gives them an off-flavor. This is overcome by using one of its isomers (an isomer has the same chemical structure except that the atoms are arranged differently) which has been named lindane after T. von der Linden, the German chemist who isolated it.

In 1950 a Nobel Prize was awarded to two German chemists, Otto Diels and Kurt Alder for their development of a chemical process of the type which has been used in reacting chlorine with certain compounds, thus producing another known as chlordane. It is somewhat less stable than DDT, therefore with less residual toxicity, and is largely used as a dust on lawns infested by the grubs of Japanese beetles and other pests that gnaw the grass roots.

Aldrin and dieldrin are two other hydrocarbons (named for the chemists mentioned above). Aldrin is effective against grasshoppers and certain pests of cotton, as well as a number of soil and other insects. Dieldrin is used to control chinch bugs, several fruit insects and such menaces to health as mosquitoes, chiggers, flies, ticks and fleas.

The organic phosphate compounds are generally more lethal against insects, and more dangerous to man and his animals. Parathion is fatal to a number of insects which are resistant to the hydrocarbons, either by nature, or by developed immunity, including many of the mites. In distributing parathion, protective clothing and masks are worn. One of its close relatives is TEPP (tetraethyl pyrophosphate), a more volatile compound which means that it can be used within a few days of harvesting without leaving dangerous residues. Malathion is an organic phosphate of American development, much less toxic to warm-blooded animals than the others mentioned, but highly effective against insects and mites that are not controlled by the chlorinated hydrocarbons.

Quite a different type of insecticide is known as systemic. The compounds used such as Pestox and Systox, are applied to the roots of plants so that they can be taken up in the soil solution and thus reach both chewing and sucking insects. No systemic has yet gained approval for use on food crops, but good results have been had with ornamentals and with non-food crops such as cotton.

The home gardener will seldom, if ever, use individually the compounds mentioned above, though he will frequently see their names in garden literature, and the analyses of dusts and sprays blended by manufacturers for general or special purposes. The laws are strict about labeling, thus the home gardener should follow all directions accurately.

INSECTIVOROUS PLANTS. A term applied generally to various kinds of plants which supplement the food they obtain from the soil and the air by trapping insects in their specially modified leaves, dissolving out their soluble juices by means of special secretions, and assimilating the nutrient solution so manufactured. This is especially rich in nitrogen, which these plants, growing generally in bogs and other wet places and frequently having scanty roots, are particularly in need of.

One familiar group is the Pitcher-plants of the Sarracenia Family and including the genera Sarracenia, Darlingtonia and Heliamphora (all of which see). All of these, as suggested by the common name, have leaves modified into a sort of pitcher or hooded-trumpet form, often bright colored and sometimes adorned with conspicuous appendages. The hollowed leaves may also be provided with honey glands which help to attract the insect prey. Downward-pointing hairs line the leaves and urge the trapped insects toward the accumulated liquid in the bottom of the receptacle, but prevent it from climbing up. Once "bogged" in the secretion, the victim dies, and is "digested" by the plant.

Owing to this method of feeding, Darlingtonias (California Pitcher-plants) have in recent years been put on the market in large quantities and widely advertised as "carnivorous," "meat-eating," and the like, sometimes with the unwarranted recommendation that they be fed a daily ration of raw meat.

The Sundew (Drosera) represents another type of insect-consuming plants which have small, rounded leaves covered with glistening, sticky hairs which, when an insect touches them and is caught by the sticky secretion, gradually fold over upon it until it is firmly held. The sweet secretion then changes to a sort of gastric juice which acts on the prey and prepares it for assimilation by the leaf, which later spreads out its hairs again and is ready for more "game."

Another member of the same (Sundew) family is the Venus Fly-trap (Dionaea) whose leaves are 2-lobed, covered with glandular hairs, and fringed with stiff bristles. When an insect lights on one of these leaves, the two halves come together like the jaws of a trap, the marginal bristles interlocking. The trapped insect dies, is dissolved and absorbed, after which the plant opens and "sets" its leaf trap again.

Species of all the genera mentioned can be grown in bog garden, greenhouse or even, with special care, the dwelling. Other interesting genera which also have the ability to trap and "eat" insects are Nepenthes, Urticularia and Pinguicula.

INSECT-EATING
PLANTS—I

The little Sundew attracts its prey with honey-tipped hairs, which then fold over to enclose the insect as shown by the single inset leaf.

INSECT-EATING
PLANTS—II

The Pitcher-plant induces insects to enter its tubular leaves, then drowns them in a digestive fluid secreted at the bottom.

INSECTS. More than half of the known species of animals in the world are insects. They belong in the group known as Arthropoda, meaning jointed legs. In common with spiders, mites, sow-bugs, millepedes and centipedes (which are not really insects) they have an external skeleton or hardened body wall, jointed legs

occurring always in pairs and a body made up of distinct rings or segments. True insects (class Hexapoda) are separated from the others by the definite number of legs (always six) and the presence of wings, usually two pair, in the adult form.

One group of insects (see *Hemiptera,* below) comprises what are known as the "true bugs," but the term bug is popularly applied to all kinds of insects and even to entirely different organisms such as bacteria (which see). On the other hand, the order Arthropoda, as noted above, includes some creatures that would never be mistaken for insects, such as crabs, lobsters, shrimps and other water creatures, all members of the class Crustacea, to which the sow-bugs belong.

The body of an insect is composed of three distinct regions: the head, which has one pair of compound eyes and one pair of *antennae* or feelers; the thorax, which bears the three pair of legs and, usually, two pair of wings; and an abdomen made up of segments. Insects breathe by means of *spiracles,* which are small holes or pores arranged in pairs along the sides of the abdomen and thorax. They are the openings of tubes, called *tracheae,* which carry the necessary oxygen directly to the different parts of the body. The purpose of dusting or spraying plants with certain contact insecticides is to clog up these pores and suffocate the insects.

How INSECTS GROW. All insects except those of two relatively unimportant groups go through distinct changes of form in their life cycle. This is known as *metamorphosis* and may be of two types, incomplete, or complete. In incomplete metamorphosis there are three forms: the egg, the nymph and the adult. The nymph is similar to the adult except in size and lack of wings.

As it feeds and outgrows its covering, it forms a new body wall and sheds the old one. This is called "molting." There may be several molts in the course of growth and each brings greater resemblance to the adult; the wings, which are padlike structures in young nymphs, do not expand until the last molt. Grasshoppers, aphids and leaf hoppers are examples of this type of metamorphosis.

In complete metamorphosis the egg hatches into a *larva,* or grub, which is entirely unlike the adult, often being wormlike. Larvae may be footless, may have three pairs of legs, or possess both true legs and extra clasping legs termed *prolegs.* The larvae of flies are called *maggots;* those of beetles, *grubs;* and those of butterflies and moths, *caterpillars.* A larva feeds, grows and molts much as a nymph, but it does not change its appearance or structure until it is fully grown. Then it transforms into a *pupa,* an inactive object with no resemblance to either larva or adult, within which the insect undergoes a complete transformation, emerging as an adult similar to the one which laid the egg from which it hatched. This adult may be a fly, bee, wasp, beetle, moth or butterfly. All growth takes place in the larval stage; the pupa is merely a transition stage and the adult stage is chiefly for the purpose of reproduction. The pupal stage may or may not be passed within a protective covering called a *cocoon.*

How Insects Eat. Insects may be divided into two main groups according to the nature of their mouth parts. This grouping is particularly useful to the gardener who wishes to choose the correct control method (see INSECTICIDES, CONTACT). Chewing insects obtain their food by biting

INSECT-EATING
PLANTS—III

Venus Fly-trap has hinged leaves which close together like leaves of a book, holding the insect firmly until its flesh is all digested.

off, chewing and swallowing solid particles which may be leaf, flower, fruit, stem or root tissue. In doing this they use a complicated arrangement of mouth parts made up of an upper lip (*labrum*) a lower lip (*labium*), a pair of jaws which work from side to side (*mandibles*), accessory jaws which help hold the food (*maxillae*), and two pairs of finger-like feelers. One pair (*labial palpae*) is attached to the lower lip and the other pair (*maxillary palpae*) is attached to the accessory jaws.

Sucking insects have these mouth parts so modified that they can take only liquid food. Usually the labium becomes a tube-like beak which pierces the plant tissue and through which the juices are sucked out. In butterflies and moths all the mouth parts are reduced or absent except the maxillae which are modified into a long hollow tube which, except when feeding, they keep coiled like a watch spring. As they are generally incapable of puncturing plant tissue with this organ, these insects are not injurious in the adult stage, though highly destructive in the larval or caterpillar stage. In other cases (as some beetles, which see) both stages attack plants; in still others the larvae may be comparatively harmless while the adults may be destructive pests. In no case is the pupal stage injurious; on the contrary it may have tremendous value as in the case of the silk-worm, whose cocoon (into which the larva spins itself before becoming a pupa) supplies the silk of commerce.

KINDS OF INSECTS. Insects are classified by entomologists (insect specialists) into more than 20 orders, but the forms important as plant pests fall into 7 major orders:

Orthoptera. Grasshoppers and crickets. Front wings narrow and leathery, hind wings broad and thin; typical chewing mouth parts; gradual metamorphosis.

Hemiptera. True bugs, such as squash bugs. Front wings thickened and narrowed at the base where they meet to form a triangular area, and thinner at the tips; sucking mouth parts, with beak attached to tip of head but folded back between front legs when not in use; gradual metamorphosis.

Coleoptera. Beetles (which see). Largest of the insect orders; front wings thickened and usually hardened, meeting in a straight line down the middle of the back; chewing mouth parts in both grub and beetles stages; complete metamorphosis.

Lepidoptera. Butterflies and moths. Scaly coverings on wings (often of beautiful colors) and frequently on bodies; mouth parts of adults modified to form flexible tubes coiled beneath the head, and of larvae of true chewing type; complete metamorphosis; pupae often encased in silken cocoons; many injurious species, many others which are beautiful but of no economic importance, and no beneficial forms, except the silk-worm.

Diptera. Flies. Two winged; sucking mouth parts; many of the footless larvae (maggots) live in plant tissues, but adults are rarely injurious to plants; many beneficial parasitic forms.

Hymenoptera. Bees, ants, wasps and wasp-like insects which are parasites of other insects. The narrow membranous wings are fastened together to act as a single pair; chewing mouth parts but, in the case of bees, with modifications for sucking; larvae, footless grubs, many beneficial parasitic forms and a few plant pests, besides the highly important and valuable honey bee.

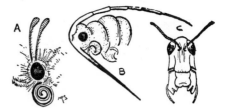

TYPICAL INSECT MOUTH-PARTS
(A) The coiled lapping apparatus of the butterfly, not injurious to plants; (B) the long piercing tube with which aphids suck up plant juices; (C) mouth-parts adapted for biting and chewing, as in the grasshopper.

Minor insect orders which include crop pests are:

Thysanoptera. Thrips (which is both singular and plural). Small slender, winged pests with rasping sucking mouth parts; one kind especially injurious to gladiolus, which see.

Isoptera. Termites or "white ants" (though not really ants at all). Yellowish white, soft bodies; biting mouth parts; gradual metamorphosis. Wood-boring and destructive to buildings.

Dermaptera. Earwigs. Similar to beetles but with pincer-like rear appendages.

Neuroptera. Aphid-lions, ant-lions. Chewing mouth parts in both larvae and adults; complete metamorphosis; being insect eaters they are chiefly beneficial.

INSECTS, BENEFICIAL. The fact that some insects are fed upon by other insects is the greatest single factor in keeping the plant-destructive kinds from over-running the world and conquering mankind by destroying his main sources of food, clothing, etc. These so-called *entomophagous* (insect-eating) insects fall into two groups: the *predators,* which catch and devour their prey (usually smaller and weaker insects), and the *parasites,* which make their homes on or in the bodies of other living organisms (called hosts), from which they get their food. Hosts are usually larger than their parasites and therefore are not necessarily killed at once; frequently they continue to live for a period, supporting themselves and the parasite until they succumb.

One of the largest and best known of the predacious insects is the preying (or praying) mantis (which see). Probably the most important of the group are the lady beetles (also called ladybirds and ladybugs), ground beetles, and the syrphid

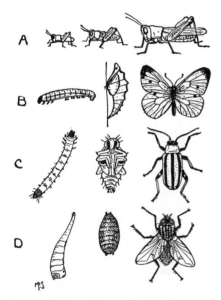

HOW INSECTS GROW
Insect development (metamorphosis) is of two types: incomplete, as illustrated by the grasshopper (A), in which the young are of the same form as the adult, increasing in size by successive moultings; and complete, as illustrated by three familiar creatures—the butterfly (B), beetle (C) and fly (D). In each, a worm-like larva, grub. or maggot (left) hatches from an egg; later becomes a pupa (center) of quite different form; and finally emerges as adult (right). The adult females lay eggs from which more larvae hatch.

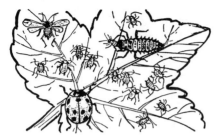

THE LADYBIRD BEETLE
The larva of this helpful insect (above at right) feeds on aphids (shown here on the leaf) and mealy bugs that infest many garden plants.

flies. Both larvae and adults of the lady beetles are active in destroying scales and aphids; they can be, and are, shipped from one place where they are easily grown to another section or country to check insect pests there. In the latter half of the nineteenth century the cottony maple scale became a most serious pest of orange groves in the U. S., threatening to wipe out the entire industry. Traced back to New Zealand and Australia this scale was found to be very destructive in the former country but causing little injury in the latter where scientists finally located a species of lady beetle as its effective natural enemy. About 500 of these beetles were shipped to California where within a year and a half their progeny had reduced the scale to negligible proportions. This same species, since shipped to many other countries, has never failed to control the cottony scale. And another species is now offered for sale and shipment to destroy woolly aphis in greenhouses.

Ground beetles (which see) are especially fond of caterpillars and have been useful in fighting the gypsy moth. In most species both larvae and adults are predacious.

Aphid lions are the larvae of lacewinged or golden flies, so called because of their delicate gauzy wings. The adults are of little or no benefit to man, but the spindle-

BENEFICIAL BEETLE
This one aids the gardener by catching and eating the destructive-canker worms.

shaped larvae grasp with their jaws and puncture the bodies of aphids or other soft-bodied insects and their eggs, then suck up the juices. Similarly in the groups known as syrphid flies, flower flies or sweat flies, only the larvae are predacious. The yellow and black, sometimes shiny, adult flies somewhat resemble house flies but with more flattened bodies; they are often seen hovering almost motionless in the air. The maggots are green, gaily colored with red, yellow or blue, pointed at the head end and broadly rounded at the rear. One larva can destroy aphids at the rate of one a minute over a considerable period. If aphid colonies are known to be infested with syrphid flies, it is a good plan to delay spraying so as not to destroy the beneficial insects.

Insects parasitic on other insects are confined chiefly to the orders Diptera and Hymenoptera. Tachinid flies are parasites of the larger caterpillars, grasshoppers and beetles. Many of the species roughly resemble bristly, grayish or brownish overgrown house flies. These adults glue their eggs to the skin of the host or lay them on foliage where the host will eat them; newly hatched larvae may also be deposited on the body of the victim or beneath its skin. The larvae feed on the muscular and fatty tissues, avoiding vital parts until the caterpillar is full grown or has pupated. But, at the end of the pupation period, it is the parasitic fly which emerges and not the host moth or butterfly which has died of the parasitism. When army worms are abundant large numbers of the syrphid flies are usually present destroying many.

INSECT DRILLING
The beneficial ichneumon fly (really a wasp) drills through tree bark to lay an egg in the body of a hidden injurious borer, which will be destroyed by the grub when it hatches.

Of the many hymenopterous parasites the most common are ichneumon, braconid and chalcid wasps and egg parasites. The latter include some of the smallest known insects; some actually live their entire life cycle *inside a single egg of another insect.* Various other species live in the eggs of moths, true bugs, grasshoppers, spiders and flies, one kind being especially useful in reducing the chinch bug population.

Many species of chalcid wasps live in the bodies or eggs of scale insects, aphids, caterpillars and flies. One species attacks the imported cabbage worm, 3,000 individuals having hatched on or within a single caterpillar. These wasps are only 1/100 to ⅜ in. in length, are usually black and with strong metallic reflections. The great majority of parasites of the smaller insects are found in this group.

Some braconid wasps cover the backs of their victims, as, for example, the tomato hornworm or catalpa sphinx, with small elongate white cocoons which look like eggs. Other species attack larvae of flies, ants, cockroaches, beetles, bees, wasps and particularly aphids. Parasitized aphids exhibit distended, shiny, grayish brown bodies, often with circular holes in their backs where the parasites have emerged.

Ichneumon wasps include both large and minute parasitic species. Often brilliantly marked, they may be recognized by their short jerky flight and constantly vibrating antennae. Most species attack caterpillars, and one, a large species, called the "longsting" because of its 3 in. long *ovipositor* or egg-laying apparatus, uses this organ to insert its eggs into the burrow of wood boring larvae.

Parasites may themselves be attacked by secondary parasites, these by tertiary and the latter even by quarternary parasites; all these three latter groups are called hyperparasites.

Insects may be of benefit to plant growers not only by destroying destructive insects but also by injuring plants which are themselves pests. Insects recently introduced into Australia give promise of exterminating the opuntia or "pricklypear" cactus which now makes thousands of square miles impenetrable. In introducing such insects to accomplish such work it is, of course, important to make sure that they will not become pests on useful plants. See also BEES.

INSERTED. Attached, as an organ to its support. The sepals, petals and stamens of Potentilla are said to be *inserted* on the receptacle *below* the ovary, making the insertion or manner of attachment what is called *hypogynous*. If they were inserted *above* the ovary, the flower would be termed *epigynous*. See also OVARY.

INSIDE-OUT-FLOWER. Common name for *Vancouveria parviflora*, a low hardy border perennial of N.W. U. S.

INTENSIVE CROPPING. Various practices designed to obtain maximum crop returns from specific areas. See CROPPING SYSTEMS.

INTERCROPPING. The practice of alternating plants or rows of different sizes or habits so as to grow two or more crops on the same area at the same time. See CROPPING SYSTEMS.

INTERRUPTED FERN (*Osmunda claytoniana*). A common large fern of wet places in the E. States. This is one of the best for ordinary garden soil. Fronds are 3 to 4 ft. high and the spores are borne on contracted pinnae half way up the fronds, hanging down like jewelry.

INTRODUCTION. As an activity, this means making a new plant available to the channels of trade, that is nurserymen, florists and seedsmen who are equipped to disseminate it to the public. Sometimes the introducer of a plant will also disseminate it. This may be a wild species never before cultivated, or a newly originated horticultural variety. The plant to be introduced (sometimes called an "introduction") is multiplied by seeds, cuttings, divisions or grafts, until there is stock enough to meet the probable public demand, then advertised for sale, exhibited at flower shows, and described in horticultural publications.

See also DISSEMINATION; ORIGINATION.

INULA (in'-eu-lah). A genus of perennial, mostly hairy, herbs of the Composite Family with usually yellow flowers in daisy-like heads. The plants are mostly hardy and thrive in average garden soil if given a sunny location. Easily grown from seed or propagated by division. Perhaps half a dozen of the 50 or more Old-World species are cultivated as showy border subjects. These include *I. ensifolia* with hairless leaves and 1½ in. heads; *I. glandulosa* (Caucasian Inula), taller growing and hairy; *I. helenium* (Elecampane) still taller, to 6 ft., with velvety leaves; *I. oculus-christi*, to 2 ft., with silky leaves.

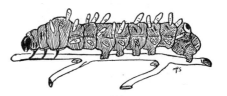

INSECT WARFARE
This injurious caterpillar is destined to be destroyed by tiny parasitic wasps whose cocoons are shown attached to its back.

I. helenium is extremely susceptible to mildew and unless protected by frequent applications of sulphur dust is likely to show a thick coating of white over the leaves by midsummer.

INVOLUCRE. A whorl or rosette of scale-like bracts around the base of a flower cluster, as in members of the Daisy and Parsley Families.

INVOLUTE. Rolled inward from each side; said of a leaf or other flat body whose margins curl inward upon the body. Compare REVOLUTE.

IOCHROMA (y-oh-kroh'-ma). A genus of sub-tropical shrubs and small trees of the Nightshade Family, somewhat grown outdoors in warm countries and in greenhouses for their showy bell-shaped or tubular flowers of purple, blue, red, yellow, or white. They can be grown from seed when it is available or propagated by cuttings in early spring. *I. coccineum,* from Central America, has woolly branches and drooping scarlet flowers 2 in. long; *I. lanceolatum,* from Ecuador, has more slender leaves and deep purple flowers 2 in. long in flat clusters; and *I. tubulosum* has smaller blue flowers in drooping clusters.

IONOPSIDIUM (y-oh-nop-sid'-i-um) *acaule.* A small Portuguese annual, grown in gardens and greenhouses for its little violet or white blossoms as Diamond-flower, which see.

IPOMOEA (y-poh-mee'-ah). A genus of mostly herbaceous plants commonly called Morning-glory, whose best known species include such important vines as the decorative Blue Dawn-flower, the useful Sweet-potato (which see), and the pernicious weed called Wild Sweet-potato-vine (see WEEDS). There is considerable confusion between this genus and Convolvulus (Bindweed), Calonyction (Moon-flower), and Quamoclit (Star-glory), and four genera being of the Morning-glory Family, and the differences being only in minor details of botanical structure. Thus species of the four groups are sometimes found under different names in different catalogs and lists.

Plants of the various species of Ipomoea are easily grown in any fairly good soil either indoors or out. The tubers of the half-hardy perennial kinds (as noted below) should be dug in fall in the N. and kept indoors away from frost over winter. When seeds are sown, germination can be hastened by filing or cutting a small notch in the horny outer coat. The perennial forms may also be increased by division, though the customary method is layering or by cuttings rooted indoors or in a hot-bed.

Many species of Ipomoea can be used to cover fences, trellises and walls or banks, and some can be grown in pots.

PRINCIPAL SPECIES

I. leari (Blue Dawn-flower). A twining perennial bearing large heart-shaped leaves and vast numbers of white-throated blue or purple flowers which turn pink with age. Good for the warm greenhouse or, in warm regions, for covering embankments.

nil (also known as *I. hederacea*). One of the most popular morning-glories in cultivation and the source of the large-flowered Japanese or Imperial forms (sometimes called *I. imperialis*), they bear flowers of blue, purple, pink or rose, and leaves varying from heart-shaped to lobed. The vines grow rapidly, often blooming in 6 weeks from seed.

purpurea (Common or Tall Morning-glory). Appearing in many color varieties, including double forms, this is the morning-glory most commonly grown. It will grow well on string or wooden trellises, wire poultry netting, old tree trunks or stone walls. Seeds may be saved from the vines for the next year's sowing.

leptophylla (Bush Morning-glory or Moonflower). Growing in exceedingly dry places, this W. native is a shrubby plant with purple-throated rose-pink flowers.

horsfalliae. One of the best of several tropical morning-glories suitable mainly for greenhouse cultivation. Flowers are pink, white or magenta.

batatas (Sweet-potato, which see). Native of tropical America, this small-flowered species is now world-wide in its cultivation and an important commercial crop.

pandurata (Wild Sweet-potato-vine, or Man-of-the-earth). A beautiful, hardy, purple-and-white-flowered vine which when cultivated frequently escapes to become one of the worst weed pests known.

IRESINE (y-re-sy'-nee). A genus of bushy or climbing herbs and small shrubs grown like coleus under glass and in summer beds for their foliage. See BLOOD-LEAF.

IRIDACEAE (y-ri-day'-see-ee). The Iris Family, a group of widely distributed, mostly low growing perennial herbs with fleshy rootstocks, corms or bulbs. The leaves are long and narrow; the flowers are subtended by bracts, with six petals and sepals inserted on the rim of the ovary; stamens are three instead of six as in the other families of the same (Lily) Order. The family yields some medicinal products, as orris root and the drug saffron, and many of the choicest ornamentals. Genera chiefly in cultivation are: Iris, Morea, Tigridia, Belamcanda, Ixia, Babiana, Freesia, Acidanthera, Sparaxis, Tritonia, Crocosmia, Crocus, Antholyza, Gladiolus, Watsonia, Lapeirousia, Marica.

IRIS. (See illustrations, Plate 30.) This is the principal genus of one of the largest and most important plant families from a garden standpoint—one to which it gives its name, Iridaceae. Another important member is the gladiolus which attained its position of permanent value in the garden before· the iris became so well diversified. Crocus, tigridia, tithonia and many other genera are included.

In ancient mythology, Iris symbolizing the rainbow, is often referred to as the "goddess of the rainbow." But she had no such important position on Olympus. She was the personal attendant and messenger of Hera, spouse of the great Zeus. Her name has been perpetuated in a great genus of plants because of their unusual color quality—a shimmering changeability under varying lights and positions, which has given us the descriptive word, "iridescent." This quality was contained in her garb, says an old author, who wrote: "Iris, of saffron wings, displaying against the sun a robe of a thousand varying colors."

The Historical Background

The iris, as we now know it and of such paramount importance in our gardens during its main season, which, over the greater part of the country comes in late May and early June, after the tulips and before the peonies and roses, is a comparatively modern type. Its development into garden material of first importance has come within about 50 years. And this development has been confined principally to one subdivision of a large number of iris types, that known as the bearded or pogon section, because there

is a strip of hairy growth—a beard—on the three divisions of the flower that usually droop or are barely horizontal and are known as the "falls."

This beard, according to botanists, is a guide or signal to insects seeking nectar. It leads them to the store hidden deep in the heart of the flower, and in going after this nectar they must come in contact with the flower's seed-producing organs. Thus they pick up and carry on their bodies some of the pollen from the stamen placed above the beard of one flower to the next flower visited, and so fertilize it. The iris is one of those flowers so constructed that they are not self-fertilizing; seed is produced only through the unintentional agency of insects (as just described) or by plant breeders who deliberately perform the same function.

These facts have resulted in the wonderful development of the modern iris, for the plant is perhaps the most easily controlled and handled for hybridizing purposes of all garden subjects. Even the most uninformed amateur (scientifically) may practice the breeding of new varieties of iris.

Along botanical lines garden irises divide themselves into two groups which are quite different as to habits and cultural requirements which are discussed farther on. These groups are (a) the bearded or pogon section just mentioned, which needs a well-drained soil and a midsummer resting period and is therefore sometimes called the "dry" type; and (b) the beardless, apogon, or "wet" section which prefers heavier soils, and moisture conditions that include actual swamps.

The iris has long been used in heraldry and for ornamental designs because of its distinct form. This consists of three upright divisions, known as the *standards;* three lower divisions known as the *falls,* and, between them, three strap-shaped divisions known as the *style branches.* It is classically represented in the *fleur-de-lis* or national symbol of the French.

IRISES OF YESTERDAY. In our ancestors' old gardens were found only a few irises. Occupying a position of rather minor importance, they were known as "flags" or flower-de-luces. There was a graywhite, the old time orris, from which was obtained the fragrant powder of orris root used in cosmetics and tooth powders. One of the oldest of common garden plants, this was known botanically as the Florentine iris (*I. florentina*).

Another was a purple iris often known as a "German iris" for no good geographical reason. This for a time gave its name to the entire section of tall bearded iris. A pale yellow was found occasionally, a yellow with brown falls and a tall handsome lavender (*I. pallida*). All these were natives of Europe.

Intercrossing them gave the start of the thousands of varieties now in commerce and cultivation. Yet the ancient varieties have taken rather a minor place in the modern iris, aside from furnishing two outstanding characteristics that make the plant of garden value—namely, hardiness and variety of coloring.

THE MODERN IRIS. The real beginning of the modern iris came with the introduction from the eastern Mediterranean countries of new species with huge flowers and tall stems, attaining heights of 4 ft. or more, a stature previously unknown in bearded irises. The first of these was *I. amas*, discovered in the province of Amasia in Asia Minor. While lacking in great height, it first brought huge flowers, and it is in the family background of many modern irises. Then came *I. trojana*, huge and tall, found near the site of ancient Troy.; *I. cypriana* from the island of Cyprus and *I. mesopotamica* and its ally, *I. ricardi*.

The finest of the modern irises contain a mixture of several of these strains.

This rather sketchy outline of the origin of the modern garden iris is given because it has a direct bearing on the garden use and value of the plant. While the oriental forms gave great height and size they also brought to the previously ironclad bearded iris an element of tenderness and some cultural difficulties which iris fanciers soon learned to know. So in obtaining irises for the garden, some knowledge of a plant's ancestry (usually available in catalogs) is essential if the gardener wishes to be assured of its successful growth.

Iris breeders, having availed themselves of the good qualities of the Asiatic forms, are now working for hardiness, vigor of growth and freedom of bloom.

THE BEARDED IRISES

The bearded iris class breaks into three rather natural divisions based on season and style of growth, both, of course, of garden importance. These are the *dwarfs*, earliest of all; the *intermediates*, a rapidly developing class; and, most important of all, the *tall* bearded class. They give a season of bloom extending from early April to mid June, one class merging into the other. The intermediates are actually results of crossing the early dwarfs and the late, tall bearded irises; they are, as the name implies, intermediate in period of bloom and in height.

THE DWARF IRISES

These furnish material for beautiful garden combinations with the daffodils and other early spring bulbs. The earliest of the type and one of the first irises grown in the gardens of the U.S., a tiny red-purple, is *I. atroviolacea*. It comes down to us from our pioneers and is delightful with yellow crocus, the forsythias and the earliest spring bulbs. Then follows a great variety of dwarfs in a fairly wide and increasing color range, all making fine material for garden pictures with the daffodils, early tulips, primroses, and other early perennials and bulbs.

The dwarfs merge into the intermediate class, which has been receiving due attention from hybridists. New and attractive varieties are intermediate both in season and in size between the dwarfs and the tall bearded class. Gardeners are using this fine type in combinations with the Darwin, Cottage and Breeder tulips to produce wonderful spring garden pictures. The intermediates have a season of about two weeks and overlap the tall bearded season by a few days, thus giving a continuous iris pageant.

SOME LATE SPRING EFFECTS

The tall bearded irises in their marvellous and gorgeous, as well as delicate and elusive, colorings, in combination with the late May and early June perennials, provide material for some of the finest garden pictures of the entire season.

Four perennials blooming at this time form the mainstay of the garden for

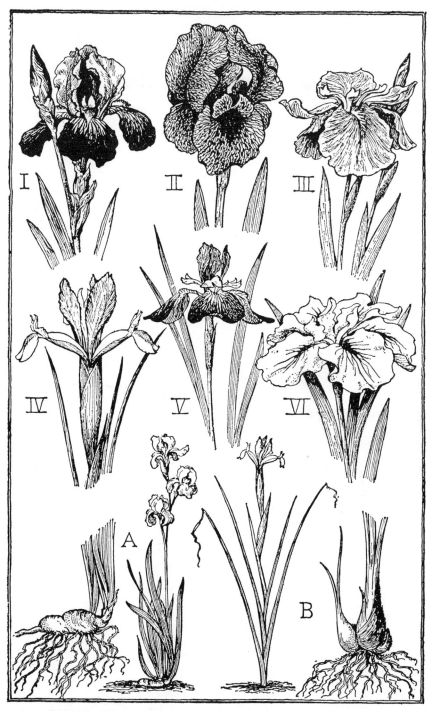

GARDEN IRISES VARY WIDELY IN PLANT AND FLOWER FORM
Those which grow from rhizomes or rootstocks (A) include: (I) slender-bearded or
Pogon; (II) broadly bearded or Onocyclus; (III) crested or Evansia; beardless
(Apogon) (V) Siberian and (VI) Japanese types. The bulbous group (B) includes
(IV) the Dutch, Spanish, and English types.

a period of about a month. These are the yellow daylilies (Hemerocallis), the painted daisies or pyrethrum, oriental poppies and columbines. The color combinations are almost unlimited. But with the tall bearded iris go also most effectively some of the smaller perennials, such as the hardy pinks, Iceland poppies, coral bells (Heuchera), and the perennial flax.

CULTURE

The culture of all classes of bearded irises is of the simplest. There are only two requirements—sun and good drainage. The plants grow well in almost any soil, but they are most satisfactory and less susceptible to disease such as root rot in soils of only moderate fertility. While they need to be fed from time to time, and while the finest quality of bloom is developed in richer soil, the soft growth that too much food produces is more susceptible to the dreaded root rot, the worst enemy the iris has to combat. A hot wet season and resulting lush growth also appear to encourage it.

The iris should not be crowded by other plants that overshadow it or mat closely about its roots and foliage. It needs air and sunshine, but half a day of full sun will suffice.

An old theory had it that bearded irises needed lime but it has been demonstrated that this is not true and that they grow well in neutral or even slightly acid soils. Only if the soil is very acid should liming be necessary. Calcium they do need but this is best applied in the form of gypsum, which see.

The bearded iris grows from a peculiar form of root known as a *rhizome,* as do many of the beardless types. This is really a fleshy underground stalk from which extend the true, stringy roots. These rhizomes branch and in time overgrow and crowd each other so that it is necessary to dig and replant the clump at certain intervals—usually from three to five years under ordinary culture. Otherwise parts of the clump become choked and cannot produce a good crop of bloom. Some growers obviate the necessity of too frequent digging and replanting and destroying the clump effect by carefully cutting out crowding rhizomes, and then working in fertilizer.

PLANTING. In planting the iris, the root should be reduced to a single section of the rhizome with a single fan of leaves. Half the length of the leaves should be cut off to balance the disturbance of the roots. The rhizome should be planted horizontally with a light covering of soil; not more than an inch and even less in light soils. An old and frequently quoted direction said: "Plant it like a duck on the water, half in and half out of the soil." But this has not worked out well, being conducive to heavy losses from heaving during the first winter after planting. If planted a little too deep, the rhizomes will work their way to the surface as the plants' needs indicate. The bearded irises should be planted after their blooming season, but the sooner thereafter the better.

SOIL AND FEEDING. Heavy clay soils must be broken up for the successful growth of the bearded iris. Washed sand and peat moss or other humic material have been found excellent for this purpose. Very light sandy soils need from time to time the addition of humus in the form of old manure, synthetic manure or peat moss; in such soils, however, the peat moss is sometimes slow to disintegrate.

As to fertilizers, bearded iris growers have learned that the earlier theories that all fertilizers are dangerous to the health of the plant are unfounded. It will not stand fresh manure except as a mulch and then only if there is no actual contact; so that any use of fresh manure on iris is inadvisable.

When an iris makes a vigorous growth and large clump but produces no bloom, the best treatment seems to be to dig, divide and replant it. If then it won't bloom, discard it.

In planting a variety of tall bearded irises pay attention to the heights of the different kinds which are usually given in catalogs. Otherwise you may find a tall variety eclipsing a lower growing beauty.

The so-called *variegata* types—those with yellow standards and darker falls—are frequently used with telling effect in modern plantings with the yellow daylilies (Hemerocallis), especially those with russet reverses. The clear yellow daylilies and medium blue toned irises are also used most effectively.

Most striking effects are attained by combining irises with the gorgeous oriental poppies in varying hues ranging from salmon and rose to orange, scarlet and crimson. In fitting the colors, avoid the association of the salmons with the lilac-pink irises. The blue tone varieties make gorgeous plantings with the orange and scarlet poppies.

Yellow irises should be used liberally, particularly with paler types. They are now obtainable in all heights and sizes of bloom where formerly we never had them much over 2 ft. The same is true of the white sorts. The development of these two classes from low-growing, small flowered forms that long resisted efforts of hybridizers to their present gigantic proportions, is an outstanding development in the tall bearded class. New varieties are being offered constantly.

An Outstanding Variety. So constantly is the standard changing in modern iris that it is hardly ever safe to specify any variety as an "all-time iris." The great iris of today is eclipsed tomorrow, and this has been going on for many years past with improvement on improvement in each year's list of new varieties.

With thousands of varieties available and scores of dealers offering good stock, selections can best be made by personal inspection and study, or from the beautifully illustrated catalogs available from growers specializing in direct mail.

The Beardless Irises

As already mentioned, the dry or bearded irises need a well-drained soil and period of rest in midsummer. The beardless, on the other hand, at all times, require moister conditions and prefer heavier soils. A few are really swamp plants and semi-aquatics, such as our wild blue flag (*I. versicolor*).

Siberian Irises. The best-known and most useful garden material in the beardless group is the large class of what is known as Siberian irises. They bloom along with the tall bearded class in white, in many tones of blue and, in the more modern varieties, there are some reddish tones. They have narrow grass-like foliage, tall slender stems and graceful blooms of medium size produced in great profusion, which make them among the

PREPARING IRIS FOR WINTER
By the end of the summer, the plants are apt to be wind-torn and choked with weeds as shown above. All grass and rubbish should be cleared from around the base in late August and the "fans" of leaves cut to about 5 in. tall, as shown below.

most ornamental of all the irises. There are many named varieties. They like a rich, heavy soil with good moisture-retaining qualities. They are very hardy and impervious to all but the most exceptional heat and drought.

Siberians should be planted in the early spring before growth gets well started, or in the early fall in time for them to become established. They like rich soil and stand some fertilizing. In masses or single clumps they are most effective, and are ideal for planting beside pools where conditions suit them excellently. They gradually form thick clumps but are best let alone as they do not require frequent division like the tall bearded types. They are as easily raised from seed as any of the common perennials.

They are among the finest of the irises for cutting purposes, being much superior for this purpose to the more fragile and rather ephemeral, tall bearded sorts. Much improvement has been made in this class, particularly in rich, dark, almost velvety types, formerly altogether lacking, also in increasing the height, which sometimes now reaches 50 in.

Species closely allied to the Siberian irises have been introduced from China, bringing new colors to this class in the way of red and yellow tones, but they have yet to show any particular garden value and ability to grow well. These include the species *I. chrysographes, I. forresti* and others.

IRIS SPURIA

As the season of the tall bearded and Siberian irises wanes there appears another highly decorative type, which produces flowers of quite distinctive and very attractive appearance, the best of all the irises for cutting. This is the *I. spuria* type. (Just why it was dubbed the "spurious" iris has never been explained.) It is represented by stately plants with fine, all-season foliage of good height; under some conditions, such as prevail in parts of California, it is so rank a grower that it is useful only in the larger gardens and estates. This is not true, however, in most portions of the country. And these irises are of the easiest culture.

The best-known and most striking of this group so far is the gold-banded iris (*I. ochroleuca*) and its variants, with huge tall-stemmed creamy blooms with a yellow patch on the falls. It is beautiful associated with delphiniums and with pink climbing roses.

Others of this group, of smaller stature but of similar grace of foliage and flower in blue and blue purple, are: Mt. Wilson, typical of the class, a pale blue frequently seen in striking combinations with umbellatum lilies; Lord Wolseley, deeper blue; and several not so well known. Finer new varieties are being added from time to time.

LOUISIANA IRIS

With the happy discovery in the Louisiana delta country and other southern sections of scores of what appear to be new beardless iris species, there was opened a prospect of an entirely new race for garden use, including hitherto unknown colors. They range from white to deep purple, with all the intermediate tones of yellows, reds and blues. In size and shape the flowers also vary, and, though native to the South, have been successfully grown all over the U.S.

The forerunners of these types, which seem to fall close to them structurally, were *I. fulva,* a coppery red native to the more southerly states but hardy in the north; *I. hexagona,* a blue-purple, and *I. foliosa,* a light blue with lush foliage and blooms hidden among the leaves.

IRIS KAEMPFERI

The foregoing types bring the unfolding pageantry of the iris to the most magnificent of them all—the Japanese type, with its ruffled blooms sometimes nearly a foot across, in all manner of blues and red-purples and white with a great variety of mottlings, speckings and stipplings as well as self colors. They require abundant moisture—indeed almost swamp conditions, during their spring growing season—and then a dryer resting season when they withstand much drought safely. But they need an acid soil in order to endure and flourish. In the average garden they will survive for two or three years, then dwindle and disappear. They are so beautiful, however, that they are well worth replacing and those whose garden conditions suit them are truly fortunate.

As they are readily grown from seed some gardeners maintain a supply by this means; but the seedlings are by no means as fine as the named varieties, carefully selected from thousands of seedlings. There is much confusion as to their names owing to carelessness of Japanese exporters who have sent the same iris under different names at different times, different irises under the same name, etc.

THE VESPER TYPE

The Japanese class carries the iris picture through July. Then, in August, comes a strange and seldom seen, slender-growing iris known as the Vesper iris. It is a 4 o'clock iris, opening late in the afternoon and the bloom lasting only one day, but there are so many of them to a stalk that the display is maintained for some time. It is excellently and effectively used with *Nicotiana affinis* (ornamental tobacco) and four-o'clocks (*Mirabilis jalapa*). It is also an excellent companion for the tall, pale yellow Hemerocallis, *H. citrina,* which also is a late afternoon bloomer. This unusual iris is easily grown from seed. As it appears short lived but is readily renewed, it seems best to treat it as a biennial. It has some variation in its lavender coloring and may yet yield a decided color range.

With the coming of the fall months, the iris procession continues with another valuable development of the hybridizers' skill—a race of autumn-blooming iris of the beardless class. It embraces dwarf, intermediate and tall sorts, all of which bloom at the same time. This class is being built up rapidly so that there are now a number of fall bloomers named and catalogued.

The fall-blooming characteristic is not fully dependable except in a few varieties. In the others it is largely a matter of cultural and seasonal conditions and latitude. In the more southerly states they are fairly dependable; in the northern tier of states they need coldframe protection in order to produce fall bloom. They also need the encouragement of preliminary growth in August to produce fall bloom while other bearded irises are resting and fairly dormant. Autumn Queen, a white intermediate and a pioneer in this class, has a record of having bloomed every month from April to December.

The Bulbous Irises

The irises so far discussed all grow from rootstocks and form what is known as the "rhizomatous group." Another important class, more of greenhouse than outdoor importance, comprises the bulbous irises. The best known and most generally known are the Spanish, Dutch and English. The Dutch type has rapidly forged to the front, being an improvement on the older Spanish which it resembles.

The Spanish and Dutch Irises

The Spanish iris was more often grown in quantity in gardens than the tall bearded up to the time of the federal quarantine that prohibited the importation of many kinds of foreign plants, and before the bearded class became popular.

It was then obtainable very cheaply and, although short lived, was easily replaced.

Now that the Dutch irises (suspected at first of being tender) have been tested by gardeners and found to be grown as easily as the Spanish, they are rapidly making their way into American gardens. Both Spanish and Dutch kinds require light well-drained soil for best growth outdoors. They also require late fall planting because of the fact they make a fall growth of foliage. The colors run white, yellow, blue and bronze.

English and Other Bulbous Sorts

The English iris (which really comes from Spain) is another handsome bulbous subject. It requires a moist, heavy soil in order to flourish. It has heavier foliage than the Spanish and in bloom is, in effect, a miniature Japanese iris. The bulbous irises referred to bloom towards the middle or end of June, just as the tall bearded are waning. But one of the earliest of spring bulbs is the netted iris

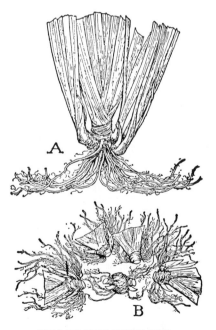

NEW PLANTS FROM OLD
Immediately after the flowering season, iris can be divided. Soil should be forcibly washed from the roots (A), and the part of the rhizome attached to each fan of leaves should be cut with a clean knife to make new divisions (B). Diseased portions must be pared off and the cut surfaces sterilized.

(*I. reticulata*). It is a little beauty in purple or blue for a sheltered corner where it will come up with the snowdrops and often bloom while the snow still lies about it.

SPECIES AND HYBRIDS

There are a number of iris species of great beauty but exceedingly difficult to grow, notably the huge, curiously marked and colored Oncocyclus irises, of which the Mourning iris (*I. susiana*) is the best known. They are subjects for the expert or for the gardener willing to give them special culture and conditions. The Regelia group also has beautiful members but is also difficult to handle. Then there are hybrids between these two difficult sections that are somewhat easier to grow. Again there are a few hybrids between the easily grown tall- and dwarf-bearded and the oncocyclus types; they exhibit great and unusual beauty and many more are likely to come into commerce, bringing new types to this remarkable race of garden plants. A good one among them is William Mohr, a hybrid between the ancient bearded iris variety, Parisiana, and the rarely beautiful species, *I. gatesi*.

The little irises dear to the heart of the rock gardener offer a field of beauty quite distinct from their more stately relatives. Our native crested iris (*I. cristata*), its fine white variety, and its smaller edition, the lake iris (*I. lacustris*) are all easily grown if given partial shade, moisture, and an occasional dressing of leafmold. The roof iris (*I. tectorum*) is another easy grower, larger in all its parts. These irises form a distinct section—the "crested" division, distinguished by the presence of a notched ridge instead of a beard.

Other little irises of the rock garden are the species *verna, gracilipes, arenaria* (now called *flavissima*); there is also a small yellow beauty, *minuta*.

The race of California native irises does not seem to thrive well in the eastern and middle states although it has been tried frequently.

Many other rare and beautiful species are in existence and are sometimes found in gardens. But they are for the collector or botanist rather than for the average garden.

IRIS ENEMIES AND THEIR CONTROL

DISEASES. Rhizome (or soft) rot, a bacterial disease (due to *Bacillus carotovorus*) common on many vegetables and some ornamental plants, causes a rotting of fleshy rhizomes and is responsible for the loss of much valuable iris. All rhizomatous kinds are susceptible. The first visible symptom is a browning and withering of the foliage tips; then follows a watersoaked appearance at the base and the collapse of leaf and shoot. A cream-colored bacterial ooze may appear on the rotting leaves and the fleshy portions of the rhizomes disintegrate into a soft, wet, slimy, yellowish, foul-smelling mass within the intact epidermis. If the rot is allowed to spread, the characteristic evil smell may make a visit to the garden anything but pleasant. Infection takes place through wounds many of which are made by the Iris borer, see below.

Combat the rot by lifting all infected plants and burning those most seriously affected. From the others cut out all soft portions, then dip in a disinfectant such as bichloride of mercury 1:1000—one tablet per pint of water. Bear in mind that this is a strong poison and must, therefore, be handled with extreme caution. If the disease has been severe, sterilize the soil with a formaldehyde drench (2 qts. per sq. ft. of a 1 to 50 solution) or with another disinfectant. Removal of the old soil and replacing it with fresh is even better when possible. Leave the treated rhizomes in the sun for a day or so and in replanting space well and be sure to leave the top of the rhizome exposed. Keep the soil light and well drained by incorporating sand or sifted coal ashes.

Leaf spot is more common and destructive to Siberian iris than is generally realized. The elliptical reddish-bordered spots with a grayish center dotted with black fruiting bodies of the fungus occur largely on the upper half of the leaf, but in severe cases all the foliage dies prematurely with consequent weakening of the rhizomes and often death of the plant in a year or two. As the fungus lives in old leaves on the ground, the most feasible means of control is the careful removal and burning of all dead and diseased leaves in the fall.

A bacterial leaf blight may be serious in midsummer in wet seasons. Sanitary measures are the chief means of control.

In crown rot (which see), which may be serious in crowded iris beds, the leaf bases and flower stalks are rotted and covered with numerous reddish brown sclerotia. Remove such leaves and stalks and drench the soil with a good disinfectant. If necessary remove and treat plants as for rhizome rot. Mosaic, a streaking of the foliage with light and dark green areas, occurs chiefly in bulbous iris.

Most iris diseases are fostered by the humidity maintained by too luxuriant foliage growth. Cutting the leaves back to 8 to 10 inch fans after flowering will aid greatly in disease control.

INSECT PESTS. The most dreaded insect pest of iris is the borer (*Macronoctua onusta*) which is not only extremely injurious itself, but which is almost inevitably followed by soft rot. Eggs laid in the fall near or on the basal leaves hatch sometime in April. The young larvae eat their way down inside the leaves increasing in size until, when they reach the rhizome, they are 1 to 1½ in. long, soft, fat, and pinkish tinge, with a brown head. They pupate in the soil near the base of the plants in August or September and the moths, violet brown with black markings, emerge in October to lay their eggs. In its early stages the borer's presence may be recognized by a wet stain along the edges of the leaves, followed by a ragged appearance. In small plantings, many of the larvae can be killed by squeezing all leaves which show the wet stain firmly between thumb and forefinger, commencing at the ground and pulling upward. Some authorities recommend covering iris beds with dry leaves in the fall and burning them over quickly to kill the eggs, but this often injures the plants. It is better to cut away the old dead leaves and thus destroy eggs which would produce borers the following season. In the spring, dust once a week with a garden dust containing DDT or the like. The best way to get rid of the borers is to dig up and examine all the plants just after flowering, cut out any borers found, then treat the rhizomes as for soft rot. If this procedure is followed every three or four years when the iris should naturally be divided, the borers should be kept fairly well under control.

Aphids when present may be controlled by spraying with pyrethrum-soap or nicotine-soap solution.

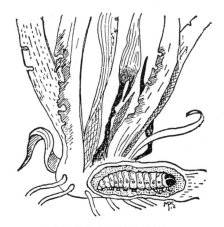

ENEMY OF THE IRIS
The iris borer first gnaws the edge of young leaves, damaging them as shown, then bores into the rhizome, not only killing many plants, but also permitting entry of destructive rots and other diseases. Careful inspection and cleanliness in the iris bed are essential.

A CHART OF THE GENUS IRIS

I. RHIZOMATOUS. Growing from rhizomes (thickened stems or rootstocks) which creep more or less horizontally below the surface of the soil or partly above it and from which the true roots descend; these rhizomes are terminated by a cluster of the leaves known as the "fan" because of their arrangement.

A. BEARDED or POGONIRIS SECTION. Each of the *falls* (or three lower divisions of the flower) bears at its base a strip of hairy growth of varying colors. Irises of this division require above all good drainage, sun, and a summer resting period.

a. *Bearded* or *Pogoniris*. Includes (1) tall bearded; (2) intermediate; (3) dwarf. They are classified as to height and blooming seasons which approximate: *tall*, late (May-early June), height, 24 to 50 in.; *intermediate*, early (to mid May), 20 to 30 in.; *dwarf*,

April, 6 to 12 in. They thrive either in alkaline, neutral or acid soils of good fertility but must not be overfed or given too strong fertilizer. Old well-made compost in the soil a few weeks before planting is excellent. Standard fertilizers are bone meal, dressings of gypsum, and balanced commercial fertilizers low in nitrogen.

b. *Oncocyclus.* Strangely marked and colored irises from western Asia having huge blooms, beards and dark signal patches about the beard. Type: *Iris susiana* (the Mourning Iris). Of difficult culture, they need special treatment such as lifting and keeping dry after their bloom and replanting in late fall and a lime soil. Season, April and May; height, 10 to 20 in.

c. *Regelia.* Closely related to the above and requiring the same conditions, but of different and distinct form and taller. Type: *Iris hoogiana.* Blooming season, April-May. Height 5 to 24 in.

Hybrids between the two above classes are known as *regeliocyclus* or *oncoregelias* and are of easier culture. Type: Hera. There are also fine hybrids between oncocyclus and pogon irises known as *oncopogons.* Type: William Mohr. They are of as easy culture as the tall bearded. Season the same. Height 12 to 30 in.

d. *Pseudoregelia.* A type related to the above, but a small class not in cultivation.

B. CRESTED or EVANSIA SECTION. The beard in this section is replaced by a toothed ridge, resembling a rooster's comb. The group includes the roof iris (*I. tectorum*), our native *I. cristata* (the Crested Iris), the lake iris (*I. lacustris*), the tender *I. watti* and others. They require moist soil, some shade and plenty of vegetable material in the soil. Season, late April and May. Height from 4 in. in lacustris to 5 to 6 ft. in watti when it grows well.

C. BEARDLESS or APOGON SECTION. The largest and most widely distributed section of the genus and, as figured by Dykes and other authorities, the oldest type of iris. The falls are smooth, that is, have no beard. In general the beardless section is the "wet class" as compared with the bearded or "dry section." Some are even aquatic. They require heavier, moister soil and a more liberal supply of moisture in order to flourish. They also thrive better with fertilizer. Some have pronounced liking for acid soil and need it. They will stand a dry spell in midsummer without damage.

a. *Sibirica.* The most widely known and grown of the beardless forms. Slender grassy foliage, wiry stems and a profusion of smaller flowers than the tall bearded. Type: Perry's Blue. The true sibiricas are blue or white; later Asiatic species bring yellow and red-purple to this section. Garden forms originate from *I. sibirica* and the closely related species, *I. orientalis,* which is taller and has red spathes. The yellow type is *I. forresti;* the red-purple type, *I. chrysographes.* Other species more or less grown are *I. bulleyana, delavayi, wilsoni, prismatica* and *clarkei,* and there are numerous hybrids among them. Season, May-June. Height, 12 to 48 in.

b. *Spuria.* Includes tall, handsome plants of increasing garden importance with decorative, all-season foliage. New forms are appearing from time to time. Types: *I. ochroleuca,* the gold-banded iris; and *I. spuria* var. Lord Wolseley. Other forms in cultivation are the species *I. aurea* and *I. monnieri* and their hybrids.

Plate 30.   SOME INTERESTING IRIS TYPES

Upper left: In the rock garden, the miniature Iris pumila is delightful in early spring.   Upper center: Iris susiana, dark and curiously veined, is only for the specialist in a mild climate.   Upper right: Gracefully carried blooms of the scented, lavender German Iris, Ballerine.   Center left: The graciously-modeled Japanese iris.   Center and center right: Two of the newly discovered Louisiana irises, I. rosiflora and I. giganticaerulea.   Bottom: Spanish iris in the border.

Season, June. Height, 2 to 4 ft. They require heavy, rich and moist soil to do their best.

c. *California types.* Fine low-growing irises that are excellent in their native section, the Pacific Coast; but they do not yield to cultivation elsewhere. Type: *I. tenax.*

d. *Longipetala.* A small division, *I. missouriensis* and *I. longipetala* being types. Both are in cultivation, resembling sibiricas in habit, season and height.

e. *Hexagona.* So named from the six-ridged seed-pods. Originally confined to three species, viz. *I. fulva, I. foliosa* and *I. hexagona,* natives of southern U.S. but hardy in the north. Many attractive native forms have been discovered in the Mississippi Delta country. *I. fulva* is a copper red—a distinctive color in the entire genus Iris. Hybrids have yielded some fine things. Type: Dorothy K. Williamson. Season, late May and June. Height, 2 to 6 ft. in their native soils. They require rich soil and abundant moisture.

f. *Japanese types.* Includes *I. kaempferi* and *I. laevigata* and the great race of Japanese garden irises, descendants of *I. kaempferi* and most magnificent of the entire genus. They require plenty of moisture throughout the period of flowering, but thereafter no more than the average border. The soil should be well provided with organic matter, and enriched with a handful of fertilizer to each clump.

g. *Miscellaneous.* A grab bag for a varied lot, a number of which are in cultivation. Most common are the *versicolors* (type: the common wild flag or swamp iris); and *I. pseudacorus,* of Europe, sometimes called the fleur-de-lis of France. The winter-blooming but tender *I. unguicularis* belongs here. Also *I. ensata. I.*

setosa, the scarlet fruited *I. foetidissima,* the handsome little *I. verna* of early spring and others of assorted heights and seasons.

D. PARDANTHOPSIS SECTION. This has only one species so far as known, the vesper iris (*I. dichotoma*) now seen occasionally, and growing easily anywhere except in light, warm soils. It opens in the late afternoon, the bloom enduring for only a day. But its numerous buds give it a long season and its lavender blue is a good garden note. It seems to be biennial or to be treated as such and is easily mantained from seed. Season, August-September. Height, 3 ft.

II. BULBOUS DIVISION. In this division the plant grows from a bulb, not a rhizome. The foliage is also distinct and different from that of the previous sections.

A. XIPHIUM SECTION. With slender, sparse and rounded foliage.

a. *Spanish iris.* A fine garden and cut flower but being supplanted by the Dutch class. Color range from yellow and white through blues and bronzes. Height 18 to 24 in. Season, June. Requires rather light, well-drained soil to be at all happy but is short lived at best. Plant bulbs about 4 in. deep and late as the plant makes fall growth which should not be too far advanced.

b. *Dutch iris.* Apparently a group of hybrids between various Spanish varieties and the much more robust and larger *I. tingitana* from Algiers. These have become staple and popular greenhouse material for cut-flower production and are making fine garden subjects now that they have been tested and found hardy. They require deeper planting (5 to 6 in.) than the Spanish, but like the same character of soil. Height, 2 to 3 ft. Season, June.

c. *English iris.* Heavier in growth than the above and requiring entirely different soil; they need a moist and heavy root medium. Resemble miniature Japanese irises in color and marking. Season, late June. Height, 10 to 14 in.

B. JUNO SECTION. Most un-iris-like of the irises, with broad, channeled foliage resembling miniature corn-stalks, the strikingly colored blooms springing from the leaf axils. The bulbs have attached to the base permanent fleshy roots which must be handled carefully as they can easily be badly damaged. There are a number of species and varieties but *I. orchioides* and *I. bucharica* are the most commonly grown, though not of general distribution. Season, May. Height, 6 to 15 in.

C. RETICULATA. The netted iris, so named because of the peculiar network pattern on the covering of the bulb. A handsome violet-flowered early spring bulb often coming while the snow is still on the ground in March. It seems to require a lime soil. There are several species and varieties but *I. reticulata* is the only one at all well known or grown in gardens. Season, March and April. Height, 2 to 4 in.

III. CORMOUS. *I. sisyrinchium* is the sole species. It grows from a solid bulb or corm and botanists are not agreed that it is a true iris. Of no garden value.

IRISH FERN (*Trichomanes radicans*). An exquisite little fern in the group called Filmy Ferns, which see.

IRISH-HEATH. Common name for *Daboëcia cantabrica,* a small half-hardy evergreen shrub of the Heath Family with loose nodding sprays of purple flowers.

IRIS SOCIETY, AMERICAN. This society was formed in 1920 for amateurs, scientific and technical workers, although its membership is now essentially amateur. Its primary purpose is to keep iris lovers here and abroad informed about what is happening in the iris world. In past years it has published an illustrated quarterly which covers selection and rating of varieties, cultural directions, historical and breeding records, garden arrangements, and many other related subjects. It is considering issuing this bulletin five times a year instead of four. There have also been occasional special publications and the Society arranges for the purchase of other iris literature published here and abroad, for members.

The Society encourages correspondence and questions in relation to iris experiences; maintains a registration file of new varieties with descriptions and ratings; and has published an "Alphabetical Check List" which includes thousands of varieties with color descriptions.

All officers and directors serve without charge. Annual membership costs $3, and a 3-year membership, $8. Sustaining, Research and Life memberships are also available. The secretary is B. Y. Morrison, 821 Washington Loan and Trust Bldg., Washington, D. C.

IRON. Besides being one of the principal commercial minerals, iron is also one of the elements essential to plant growth. However it is present in sufficient quantities in practically all soils to meet the needs of plants, so it presents no problem for the gardener in connection with the providing of plant food. In rare instances where iron deficiency is found (the Hawaiian pineapple lands are an example), small quantities of soluble iron salts can be applied. Sulphate of iron is generally used at the rate of ½ lb. to 100 sq. ft.

Iron causes some of the characteristic soil colors—red, yellow, etc.—and it is a constituent of chlorophyll, the green coloring matter of plants, without which the manufacture of food in the leaves (and, consequently, normal growth) is impossible. When for any reason plants fail to assimilate iron, their foliage becomes white, or nearly so, in mottled designs or over large areas; they are then said to be "chlorotic" or suffering from "chlorosis." Sometimes young shoots develop more rapidly than the iron salts can reach them, causing the newly formed leaves to be pale or white instead of green for a time.

Iron compounds are used in gardening to some extent as fungicides and weed killers. The most common of these is iron sulphate which is sometimes used to spray plants infected with fungi, instead of copper sulphate, though it is not as efficient.

The same material, used to kill weeds on walks and drives and in lawns, is applied as a solution of 2 lbs. iron sulphate in 1 gal. water. This will destroy chickweed, wild mustard, dandelion and similar weeds without injuring the grass, which may, however, be blackened for a time.

Iron filings, old nails, etc., having a slight acid effect on the soil, are sometimes added to it when it is desired to promote the growth of acid-loving plants (which see), or to intensify the blue color of hydrangea blossoms. However, its action is slow and somewhat uncertain so the use of aluminum sulphate or other acid-forming reagents is more effective.

IRON SULPHATE. A chemical used to destroy broad-leaved perennial weeds such as dandelion, plantain and chickweed. Obtainable at drugstores also as ferrous sulphate, copperas crystals or green vitriol. Dissolve 1½ lbs. in 2 gals. water and apply as a fine spray over 350 sq. ft. of the weed-ridden turf. If a sprinkling-can rather than a sprayer is used, reduce the strength to 1 lb. to 2 gals. water and apply to 200 sq. ft. One application in the spring before flower buds open, two more later in the spring and two in the autumn should be sufficient to keep weeds under control. The treatment may blacken the ends of the grass blades but this portion will be removed in mowing. Do not use iron sulphate during very hot dry weather and avoid getting the solution on clothing or walks as it makes a permanent yellowish-brown stain.

IRONWEED. Common name for the genus Vernonia, perennial herbs in the N. and tropical trees and shrubs in the S. Members of the Composite Family, with showy white, purple or pink flowers in heads in late summer. Some species are grown in hardy borders and wild gardens, being easily handled in a good rich soil and increased either by seed, divisions or cuttings. *V. altissima* grows from N. Y. to La. sometimes attaining 10 ft. *V. baldwini,* to 7 ft., and *V. crinita,* to 12 ft., are native from Mo. to Tex.

IRONWOOD. Common name for Ostrya (see HOP-HORNBEAM), Carpinus (see HORNBEAM), and various other trees characterized by exceptionally hard wood.

IRREGULAR. A type of flower in which not all parts are alike. Examples are those of the 2-lipped snapdragon; the highly modified orchid; the lobelia and mint with two petals distinctly unlike the other three; the nasturtium, with its long spur

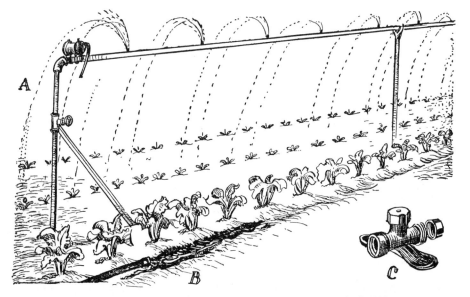

IRRIGATION THROUGH THE AIR AND ON THE GROUND
The overhead-pipe sprinkler system (A) is efficient and labor-saving, especially in vegetable gardens where water may be needed all summer. For occasional irrigation let the hose flow into a shallow furrow made alongside the crop row (B). The sprinkler head (C) is made to be inserted between short lengths of hose for use wherever needed.

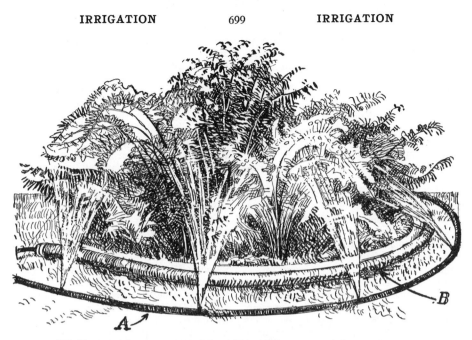

SPECIAL HOSE DEVICES FOR EFFECTIVE GARDEN IRRIGATION
A modern development of the ordinary hose (A) has sprinkler nozzles built in at regular intervals.
An even newer watering system is a large (4 in.) hose of durable, porous fabric (B), through which
water seeps slowly so as to soak the soil gently without wasting any moisture as spray. Both types
may be laid to conform to the shape of a bed or border.

formed by one sepal; the gladiolus, with
petals of different shapes, and many other
types. All these are different from any
regular flower, such as that of the apple
or potato, whose perianth is the same as
seen from every side.

IRRIGATION. A general term for the
process of watering crops by any method,
but especially that of distributing water in
quantity over land surfaces. In arid regions of W. U. S. elaborate and costly
construction and equipment including dams,
reservoirs, machinery, flumes, ditches, furrows, etc., are often employed in irrigating orchards and field crops such as sugar
beets, alfalfa and the like. In normally
humid sections where irrigation is used
more to meet drought emergencies or to
improve crop quality or hasten growth,
"overhead" or sprinkler systems are more
general, both on truck gardens and in
smaller home gardens. Here water is conducted in pipes under pressure and distributed through tiny "nozzles" to fall in
rain-like drops. Effective overhead irrigation is a valuable insurance of success in
plant growing, lawn care, etc.

Overhead irrigation presents five outstanding advantages: 1. The saving of
time in applying water. 2. Its ideal application in the form of artificial rain that does
not pack the soil or injure plants, flowers
or fruits. 3. The ability to soak the soil
in summer as soon as a crop has been
harvested and in advance of plowing or
digging for a succeeding crop, so as to
provide ideal conditions for seed germination and rapid plant growth. 4. The ability to protect tender plants such as beans
and dahlias against frost in late spring and
early autumn by creating a moist atmosphere in the evening; or to save them, if
slightly frost-bitten, by thawing them out
in the early morning before the sun strikes
them. 5. Its effect in putting applications
of plant food into solution and in washing
off any commercial fertilizer that, lodged
on the foliage, might burn it.

The horizontal pipe of a stationary overhead system is usually supported upon gas-
pipe posts with roller fittings at the top
so that the pipe can be easily rotated and
the nozzles aimed in different directions.
However, it may be concealed by being
attached along a fence, pergola, or veranda
edge, or beside a curb or walk. There are
also portable styles, usually mounted on
runners or wheels so they may be attached

to hose and easily moved from place to place. Both styles can be equipped with automatic devices (operated by the water pressure) that swing the streams back and forth over an arc of 180 degrees so as to cover a broad strip of ground on each side of the pipe. This gives uniform distribution, saves much trouble and fully justifies the small extra cost. A stationary pipe system will irrigate an area up to 30 or 50 ft. wide depending upon the water pressure and the direction and strength of the wind. In a small garden one pipe line can easily be shifted between two sets of supports (or more as may be needed) so as to cover the whole area. Connection with the main supply line (if under ground) or with the nearest faucet can be made with a length of garden hose.

HOSE IRRIGATION. A recent development in sprinkler irrigation is a hose in which nozzles are inserted at regular intervals giving, in effect, a flexible pipe system for use on the ground along curving borders. Still another novelty is a hose of large diameter (some 3 in.) made of a durable but porous material through which water seeps slowly enough so as not to wash the soil, but rapidly enough to moisten a considerable area as the water spreads sideways by capillary attraction. This can be used either on cultivated soil or on the lawn.

Another method of irrigation, especially adaptable to specimen plants, consists of sinking flower pots, tin cans with perforated bottoms, or short lengths of drain tile vertically near such plants and filling them with water as frequently as necessary. This carries the moisture down to the roots and is economical when a limited supply makes it impossible to thoroughly soak all the soil between rows or plants.

Vegetables and berry plants grown in rows can be irrigated by the western method of running water into shallow furrows beside or between the rows until the ground is soaked and then filling the furrows with loose soil to prevent the wet surface from drying hard and causing rapid evaporation.

ISATIS (y'-sah-tis). A genus of Old-World herbs of the Mustard Family commonly called Woad (which see); two species are sometimes grown as ornamentals.

ISLAY (is'-lay). A common name for *Prunus ilicifolia,* a small tree native to S.

Calif. with holly-like evergreen leaves, small white flowers and dark red, almost black, fruit.

ISMENE (is-mee'-ne). Common name for *Hymenocallis* (formerly *Ismene*) *calathina,* known as Basket-flower and Peruvian-daffodil; a species of Spider-lily (which see).

ISNARDIA (is-nahr'-di-ah). The former generic name (still found in catalogs) for *Ludwigia mulertti,* a marsh or aquatic perennial of S. America grown in aquaria and bog gardens.

ISOLOMA (y-soh-loh'-mah). A genus of tropical American herbs, several species of which and many hybrids are grown in N. greenhouses for their orange-purple or scarlet flowers.

ISOPYRUM (y-soh-py'-rum). A genus of American perennial herbs with white flowers; sometimes grown in wild gardens.

ISOTOMA (y-soh-toh'-mah). A genus of annual and perennial lobelia-like herbs with white, purple or blue flowers. *I. petraea* is sometimes erroneously listed and sold as lemon-verbena, which is really *Lippia citriodora.*

ITEA (it'-e-ah). Deciduous or evergreen shrubs, mostly from Asia, belonging to the Saxifrage Family. The one N. American species, *I. virginica* (Sweet Spire), a deciduous shrub to 8 ft., is the only one at all hardy N. The tops may die back after a severe winter, but it soon makes up from below. It is a useful summer-flowering shrub, very adaptable as to soil and situation, but best suited by moist ground. The white fragrant flowers are borne in upright racemes, and in the fall the leaves turn a brilliant red. Propagated by seed, cuttings and root divisions. *I. ilicifolia* and *I. yunnanensis* are evergreen species from China, both tender.

ITHURIELS SPEAR. Common name for *Brodiaea laxa,* a purple-flowered bulbous plant of the Lily Family, growing to 2 ft. tall in its native Calif.

IVY. When used alone, this refers to the genus Hedera, that being the ancient Latin name of Ivy; English Ivy is *Hedera helix.* (See illustration, Plate 11.) But plants with ivy-like leaves though belonging to other genera have been designated as particular kinds of Ivy. American Ivy or Five-leaved Ivy is *Parthenocissus quinquefolia,* and Boston or Japanese Ivy is *P. tricuspidata.* Cape Ivy is *Senecio macroglossus* and German Ivy is *S. mikanioides.*

Ground Ivy is *Nepeta hederacea.* Kenilworth Ivy is now *Cymbalaria muralis,* having formerly been called *Linaria cymbalaria.* Marine Ivy is *Cissus incisa;* Poison Ivy is *Rhus toxicodendron,* and the Ivy Geranium is a name given to *Pelargonium peltatum.*

IVY-ARUM. Common name for the genus Scindapsus, Malayan perennials which climb by means of stem rootlets and whose flowers are spadiceous. Two species are grown in greenhouses, *S. aureus,* with yellow blotched green leaves; and *S. pictus,* with bright green leaves spotted dark green.

IVY GOURD. Common name for *Coccinia cordifolia,* a slender tendril-climbing vine of the tropics, belonging to the Cucumber Family. It is perennial with a tuberous root, but can be grown as a tender annual, making about 10 ft., with glossy ivy-like leaves 2 in. or so across, white bell-shaped flowers in separate sexes, and smooth, short, oblong scarlet fruit.

IVY-LEAVED FERN. Another name for the Strawberry Fern, which see.

IXIA (ik'-si-ah). A genus of S. African herbs, related to the Iris. Growing from bulb-like corms, they produce slender, grass-like leaves and slender spikes of small, funnel-shaped flowers in showy colors. They are spring-flowering subjects but tender, so their use in American gardens is restricted to warm parts of the country. Like many other S. African bulbs, Ixias seem to prefer the W. Coast conditions and do splendidly there. In the E. they have proved difficult to handle.

They should be planted in late fall about 3 in. deep, with sand in the bottom of each hole. A winter covering is essential in the N. part of their range, but a coldframe can also be employed to good advantage. Spring planted corms will bloom in summer, while those planted in a cool greenhouse in early fall with provide winter flowers.

There are many horticultural forms ranging from white to pink, red, lilac and yellow. Among the species are *I. maculata,* attaining a height of 2 ft. and originally yellow flowered, but now with many hybrids in various colors; *I. columellaris,* mauve and blue; *I. speciosa,* crimson; *I. lutea,* deep yellow, and *I. viridiflora,* which has interesting flowers pale green with black throats. (See illustration.)

IXIOLIRION (ik-si-oh-li'-ri-on). A genus of Asiatic summer-blooming herbs

with bulbous rootstocks and violet or blue lily-like flowers in flattened clusters. As the species are tender the plants must be dug in the fall and the bulbs stored in frost-proof quarters until spring.

IXORA (ik-soh'-rah). Tropical evergreen shrubs, often grown in warm greenhouses and outdoors in hot climates, belonging to the Madder Family. They are among the most handsome of tropical woody plants, of good bushy habit with attractive foliage and clusters of showy flowers. They are not difficult to grow and do well in a mixture of fibrous loam and peat with sharp sand. For sizable plants use the compost in as rough a state as possible and pot firmly. Specimen plants in large pots can be kept going for several years without repotting if fed liberally with liquid manure. Give the plants a short rest after flowering and then prune to

A GREEN-FLOWERED BULB

Ixia viridiflora, with its jade-green, black-throated perianth, has no counterpart among flowers. It can be treated like gladiolus in northern gardens.

shape. Light shade is desirable during the hottest weather. Propagated by cuttings.

I. acuminata has clusters of white fragrant flowers. *I. chinensis* is a common and variable species, with flowers ranging from red and orange to almost white. *I. macrothyrsa* is one of the finest, with leaves to a foot long and immense trusses of deep red flowers. *I. fulgens* has bright clusters of handsome orange-scarlet flowers.

A number of garden forms are likely to be found in a good collection, and the following are outstanding: *I. amabilis,* with flowers of orange suffused pink; *aurantiaca,* orange-red; *chelsoni,* salmon-orange; *colei,* pure white; *splendens,* bright coppery-scarlet; *decora,* yellow splashed crimson.

J

JACARANDA (jak-ah-ran'-dah). Tropical American trees or shrubs, belonging to the Bignonia Family. One or two species are grown as street trees or lawn specimens in the warmest parts of the country. Plants are occasionally seen in the N. as small specimens in the greenhouse or used in subtropical arrangements. Propagated by seeds or cuttings of half-ripened wood.

J. acutifolia (or *mimosifolia*) has elegant finely cut fern-like leaves and loose clusters of large blue flowers. *J. cuspidifolia* has larger leaves and clusters of long-pointed violet-blue flowers.

JACK-IN-THE-PULPIT. Common name for *Arisaema triphyllum,* a member of the Arum Family, also known as Indianturnip. It is an interesting native plant ranging from 1 to 3 ft. tall, with large 3-part leaves and flowers consisting of a brown and green mottled spathe arching over a club-shaped spadix which is followed by a bunch of brilliant red berries. Jack-in-the-pulpit grows naturally in rich moist soil, but transplants easily and is tolerant of almost any average conditions. It is easily increased by seed or division.

JACOBAEA (jak-oh-bee'-ah). Former name for plants now placed in the genus Senecio, which see.

JACOBEAN-LILY or St. James Lily. Common names for *Sprekelia formosissima,* a bulbous herb of Mexico and S. America belonging to the Amaryllis Family and formerly classed as an amaryllis. Growing to about 1 ft. it bears brilliant scarlet flowers to 4 in. long. Seen in Peru by early Spanish explorers, the color reminded them of that worn by the knights of St. James, and suggested the common names. The plants are half hardy and do well in the open border in mild regions, where the bulbs should be planted in May. After they bloom in June, the bulbs are allowed to ripen until fall then lifted, dried, and stored away from frost over winter. Plants can also be grown in pots indoors, being handled like amaryllis; or, it is suggested, in glasses like hyacinths. They are easily increased by offsets.

JACOBINIA (jak-oh-bin'-i-ah). Tropical American shrubby plants, belonging to the Acanthus Family. They make attractive greenhouse plants for winter flowering in the N., and are grown outdoors in warm regions. Under glass, the best results are obtained with young plants, the young shoots of which should be pinched early to induce a bushy growth. They are not difficult to grow, and thrive in good loamy soil with extra feeding now and then. There has been much confusion regarding both the generic and specific names.

J. carnea is the best known. It will grow to 5 ft. when planted out in a conservatory bed, but good dwarf plants can be flowered in 5- or 6-in. pots. It has dense terminal heads of pale or rosy-pink flowers. *J. chrysostephana* has leaves with red markings beneath and heads of golden yellow flowers. *J. pauciflora* (long known as *Libonia floribunda*) is very free flowering with nodding tubular flowers of scarlet tipped yellow. *J. ghiesbreghtiana* makes a handsome winter-flowering plant with loose clusters of tubular scarlet flowers. *J. velutina* has soft hairy leaves and rose-colored flowers freely produced.

JACOBS LADDER. A common name for *Polemonium caeruleum,* a perennial blue-flowered herb also called Greekvalerian and Charity.

JACOBS ROD. Common name for the genus Asphodeline. See ASPHODEL.

JACOBS STAFF. A common name for *Fouquieria splendens,* a spiny, cactus-like shrub of the S. W. and Mexico, called also Ocotillo and Coach-whip. See CANDLEWOOD, which is a common name for the genus.

JACQUEMONTIA (jak-we-mon'-shi-ah). A genus of subtropical and tropical climbing plants, belonging to the Morningglory Family. They can be grown outdoors in the South. The principal species is *J. pentantha,* a twining perennial with a shrubby base, bearing loose clusters of violet-blue flowers. Propagated by seeds or cuttings.

JAK-FRUIT or JACK-FRUIT. The common name for *Artocarpus integra,* a tropical Asiatic tree related to the Breadfruit, which see.

JAMBOS (jam'-bohs) or JAMBOLAN-PLUM. Common names for *Eugenia jambos* and *E. cumini* respectively, species of tropical Asiatic trees producing edible fruits used in making preserves and confections.

JAMESIA (jaym'-si-ah). Deciduous shrubs, native in the Rocky Mt. region, belonging to the Saxifrage Family. *J. americana* is hardy N., and thrives in any well-drained garden soil in a sunny place. It grows to 4 ft. and bears short clusters of white flowers in early summer; var. *rosea* has pink flowers. Propagated by seeds or cuttings of ripened wood.

JAMESTOWN - WEED. A common name (usually shortened to Jimson-weed), for *Datura stramonium,* a coarse, strong-smelling annual with large white or violet flowers most fragrant at night. Like other daturas, it has strong narcotic qualities and is poisonous in large quantities.

JANUSIA (jan-oo'-si-ah). A genus of trailing and twining plants, one species of which, native from Tex. to New Mex. is planted in S. Calif. for ornament.

JAPANESE (CHINESE) **ARTICHOKE.** Common name for *Stachys sieboldi,* a plant of the Mint Family with an edible root once introduced into eastern U. S. but of little garden importance. See ARTICHOKE.

JAPANESE BARBERRY. Common name for *Berberis thunbergi,* a hardy deciduous species deservedly popular for hedges and especially valuable because, unlike many other barberries, it is not an alternate host for the black-stem rust of wheat. It has some interesting varieties and is the parent of several attractive hybrids. See BARBERRY; RUSTS.

JAPANESE BEETLE. This beetle (*Popillia japonica*), a native of Japan, was first found in the U. S. in 1916 around Cinnaminson, N. J. (not far from Philadelphia). It has since been distributed by automobiles, shipments of plant products, etc. over a large part of N. E. U. S. The natural spread of the beetle (by flight)

JAPANESE BEETLE Adult (left) and larva (right), both about twice actual size. The two white spots on tip of adult are important distinguishing features.

has been slow, so the zone of dense infestation has moved each year only from five to ten miles outward. The beetles, coming into hitherto uninfested areas, increase very rapidly—over a period of about three years—and then decrease again to a point where control is comparatively easy. Persons situated in regions which are now subjected to this devastating scourge may therefore confidently hope that in a year or two the wave of great abundance will have passed; and, so far as past experience shows, it will not come back.

A partial list of food plants particularly favored by the adult Japanese beetle would include: *Trees*—American elm, chestnut, European white birch, horsechestnut, linden, sassafras, willow; *fruits*—quince, apple, plum, cherry, peach, blackberry, raspberry, grape, cranberry, blueberry; *shrubs and vines*—alder, kerria, Virginia creeper, button-bush, elder; *flowers*—rose, hollyhock, canna, evening-primrose, mallow and others with striking light colored blossoms; *vegetables*—corn and soy-bean. The grubs damage lawns particularly and sometimes vegetables and low-growing fruits.

The beetle is nearly ½ in. long; bright, shining green with bronze or reddish wing covers. Along the sides of the abdomen are five white spots made of tufts of white hairs; and two distinct white spots show at the tip of the abdomen below the tips of the wing covers. The larva is a white grub resembling that of the common May beetle or June bug, but only about half as big. There is one generation a year. The beetles begin to emerge from the soil the latter part of June and may be present until the first of October, but the period of greatest density lasts only from the middle of July to early August. The eggs, laid in the soil chiefly during July and August, hatch in 12 days and the grubs soon begin to feed on grass roots near the surface. Toward winter they move downward about a foot to hibernate. In the spring they ascend, again feed on roots, and pupate for 2 weeks in late May or early June. (See illustration.)

CONTROL. Control of the beetle lies in (1) the protection of favorite food plants by sprays, (2) the use of traps, (3) handpicking and (4) the destruction of grubs. Just before the beetles are scheduled to emerge (your Agricultural Experiment Station can advise you) spray the favored food plants thoroughly with: lead arsenate (2 oz. of the powdered acid type) and 1½ oz. cheap wheat flour in 1 gal. water. Fruits, such as peaches, that would be injured by strong lead arsenate or on which the use of poison is inadvisable, may be kept coated with: hydrated lime (5 oz.)

and wheat flour (2 oz.) in 1 gal water.
Or the lime may be applied dry to form a
thick white dust over the plants (this, of
course, as a repellent and not a stomach
poison). The
coated lead-
arsenate spray,
formerly rec-
ommended, is at
present not so
popular. Derris
sprays, often
combined with
a rosin residue,
and manufac-
tured expressly
for the Japanese
beetle, are effec-
tive, non-disfig-
uring and non-
poisonous, but
the application
must be re-
peated weekly
during the bee-
tle season. An-
other repellent
spray on the
market has a
base of tetra-
methylthiuram
disulphide. Bee-
tle traps baited
with a geraniol
compound are
useful in re-
gions of heavy infestation but will attract
more beetles to the area where they are
used than would normally be present. *Do
not place traps near valuable ornamentals*
since more beetles will stop and feed on the
plants than will find their way into the
traps. Planting some crop attractive to
the beetle near the trap as a lure is a good
idea. Tests have shown yellow traps to be
far more attractive to beetles than those
painted any other color. During the period
of heaviest infestation (4 to 6 weeks) a
daily tour of the garden should be made
and as many beetles as possible knocked or
picked off into a jar of water with a layer
of kerosene on top.

Valuable sod land may be "grub-proofed"
by applying 5 to 10 lbs. powdered lead
arsenate, mixed with several times its
weight of sandy soil, evenly over each 1000
sq. ft. The best months for this are May
and September. (See LAWN.) Grubs in

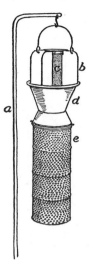

INSECT TRAP
Improved model for catching
Japanese beetles. Suspended
from 6-ft. iron stake (a), it
has 4 metal wings (b) radiating from a perforated cylinder (c) in which is a jar
of volatile liquid which attracts the insects. Hitting
the wings, they fall through
the metal funnel (d) into the
container (e) which is perforated so rain water can
drain off.

garden or potting soil may be killed by
injecting 1 lb. of carbon bisulphide per
cu. yard. (*This liquid is highly inflammable,* poisonous to animals and injurious to
plants; *use it with care.*) The soil may
also be flooded with carbon bisulphide
emulsion. See CARBON BISULPHIDE; DISIN-
FECTION.

Japanese beetle larvae are preyed upon
by several natural enemies, including parasitic wasps (which are being colonized in
beetle regions), nematodes, and bacteria.
The latter, which causes a milky disease
of the grubs, are being distributed in certain areas by beetle-control authorities.
Many birds eat the grubs and starlings are
known to eat the adult beetles.

**JAPANESE (or CHINESE) BELL-
FLOWER.** A common name for *Platycodon grandiflorum,* a hardy, blue- and
white-flowered perennial better known as
Balloon-flower, which see.

JAPANESE-CEDAR. Common name
for *Cryptomeria japonica,* a large evergreen tree of striking form and unique
foliage character.

JAPANESE CLAW FERN. Common
name for *Onychium japonicum,* also called
Carrot Fern. The botanical name (from
the Greek word for "nail") refers to the
recurved and claw-like segments of the
fertile fronds. A delicate, fennel-like fern
for cool greenhouse and ideal living-room
conditions, it has fronds 1 to 2 ft. long,
4-pinnate, with pointed segments bright
green in color. The fruit-dots are in a
continuous line, partly concealed by the reflexed margin of pinnules. Rootstock creeping. Pot loosely in leafmold, fibrous loam,

BEETLE GRUBS UNDER SOD
Where Japanese beetles are numerous, their
larvae injure lawns by eating the grass roots and
loosening the turf until it can be rolled back like
this. Poisoning the soil with lead arsenate will
kill them.

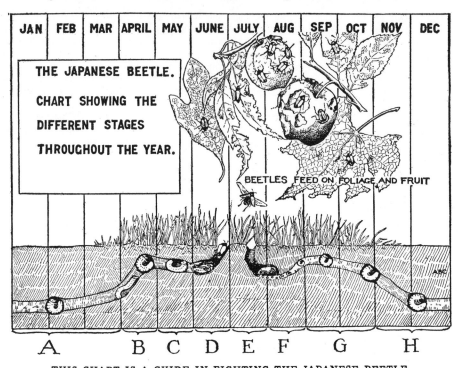

| JAN | FEB | MAR | APRIL | MAY | JUNE | JULY | AUG | SEP | OCT | NOV | DEC |

THE JAPANESE BEETLE.

CHART SHOWING THE

DIFFERENT STAGES

THROUGHOUT THE YEAR.

BEETLES FEED ON FOLIAGE AND FRUIT

A   B C D E F G   H

THIS CHART IS A GUIDE IN FIGHTING THE JAPANESE BEETLE

Stages in its history, indicated by the letters below are: (A) grub in winter cell; (B) moves nearer surface and feeds on roots; (C) begins to form cell. Then (D) rests as pupa; later changes to adult beetle and leaves ground; (E) during 2 months' active flying and eating period female beetles lay eggs in soil, preferably where vegetation is; (F) eggs hatch and young grubs feed on decaying plant matter and live roots; (G) grubs grow rapidly, feeding steadily, then (H) descend 3 to 12 in. and make winter cell. (From Bul. 473, Pennsylvania Dept. of Agriculture, with permission.)

and sand, keeping the crowns well above surface, the fronds free from direct water, and the plants in shade.

JAPANESE (or **KOREAN**) **CLOVER.** Common name for *Lespedeza striata,* one of the bush clovers grown as a hay and green manure crop in the S.

JAPANESE GARDEN. Garden design in Japan is so distinctive that this term seems hardly to need definition, however unlike the gardens of the Far East most of the so-called Japanese gardens seen in this country may be. Stone lanterns, half-moon bridges, bamboo retreats and dwarfed trees do not by or in themselves make such a garden, albeit these things are all found in the gardens of Japan. The essential difference between Japanese gardens at home and in other parts of the world lies much deeper.

THEORY AND PURPOSE

THE UNDERLYING IDEAL. The Japanese ideal of garden making, as expounded to

the writer by an eminent Japanese gentleman in the midst of his own garden, is to reproduce for intimate and constant enjoyment the loftiest aspects of Nature—those natural scenes which are not otherwise available for day-by-day contemplation. Scenes of wild and rugged splendor —mountains, forests, cascades, chasms, promontories, abysses—supreme features that stimulate the imagination by bringing the observer an experience of those emotions which such natural scenes arouse—these are the common denominator of Japanese garden design.

Hence for this reason the garden in Japan is much more than a pleasant retreat or an appropriate setting for the dwelling. Rather it is designed to be an enriching experience of things not otherwise comprehended by the untraveled man. Understood in this, its true aspect, the Japanese garden becomes something very different from the playful toy which its space limitations suggest and often make it resemble. In the U. S. or any other country of vast distances the toylike appearance remains, to be sure; but in an intelligently, sympathetically made garden it takes on meanings that toys do not possess, and one enters into the spirit of such a garden involuntarily, whether he will or no. In such a garden the sum total of natural beauty pervades the consciousness, even though the surroundings are cramped and the spirit of the individual is beset with the distraction and difficulties of daily round.

Such is the ideal which inspires even the simplest Japanese garden design. It has become formalized in that school of garden creators which insists upon definite features at fixed points—stones selected for their special forms which signify special things, placed meticulously with reference to each other and to all the rest; trees or a single tree similarly employed; a lantern and a shrine; a little stream (or the dry bed of a stream, where flowing water is not to be had), and so on. These formalities arise as Nature's aspects are, as it were, crystallized into conventionalized expression. They are not universally followed in Japanese gardens but the Nature aspects from which they derive are invariably followed.

EACH GARDEN A STORY. It is necessary to think simply and very directly and naturally in order to arrive at such a truly naïve result as is sought and intended in Japanese gardening. It is necessary to think in terms of meaning as well as in terms of appearance or looks. What is the garden going to mean; what definite Nature story is it going to tell? That of a mighty river, or of a great mountain, or of a wide-reaching plain? The story of love and lovers, or of war and warriors, or of mothers and children? The story of joy or sadness, of spiritual glories and triumphs, of temple bells and peace? Or the story of energy and ceaseless activity and conflict?

Some theme, which the gardener must decide upon, is to be expressed with all the art imaginable, in a Japanese garden. And, once the decision is made, there must be no discordant or warring elements. Everything that finds a place in the garden, each plant and shrine, and all that goes to make up the whole, must be selected and placed for the part it is to play in carrying out this supreme idea. Noth-

ing may be left to chance, nor is there space or place for a solitary knick-knack picked up in auction room, oriental shop, or in Japan itself—*unless this object fits in with the meaning of the whole,* unless it makes a definite contribution to the telling of the story that is being unfolded.

An austere and rigorous formula this, viewed in contrast with the casual gardening of western people. But there is no other concept in Japan. Such gardens as have been developed here and there in imitation of Japanese creations present merely a surface likeness to the true thing (and a very imperfect one at that). Being wholly objective and imitative in concept, they lack entirely the qualities which distinguish the humblest true Japanese garden and set it apart from all others.

It is hardly possible to sum up these qualities in a single phrase, but remembering that the Japanese people are largely of the Buddhist philosophy, there is clearly discernible the underlying principle of a mystical consciousness of Life embodied in an Idea—in this instance the Idea of the Garden—coupled with a mystical confidence in all lesser life to express the greater. If men think in these terms, men must set them forth in what they do—especially in making gardens. For every man's faith—or lack of faith—is inevitably set forth in the garden that he makes.

PRACTICAL CONSIDERATIONS

WHERE? This last fact makes it impossible to say where a Japanese garden may properly be undertaken. Wherever a garden enthusiast who is capable of fulfilling the exactions outlined above has a bit of ground that may be set apart and hidden completely from all conflicting sights, a Japanese garden is possible. Elsewhere, and under other auspices, it ought never to be undertaken. For there is nothing in the average community in the U. S. than can furnish a harmonious setting for such a delicately conceived creation; and no matter with what horticultural skill it may be designed and carried out, it will fail in effectiveness for lack of proper "frame." Within a Japanese garden one should be, in effect, in Japan—not in an American landscape at all!

MATERIALS. It is a dominant characteristic of Japanese craftsmen to utilize natural forms, letting fancy play with them and adapt them to the purpose of the moment. Hence it is to be expected that Nature forms will be largely used in the Japanese garden for such structures as design may require. Wood in its natural state, stone, bamboo—these are the building materials, augmented only as may be necessary with dressed timbers and slat work, both open and close-set, such as the design may demand. Quick to seize upon the suggestion in a gnarled branch or an unusual rock formation which may resemble an animal, a bird, or a human being, pleasant and poetic fancy is exercised by the Japanese artist to bring out such resemblance to the highest degree, even to the extent of making it dominate its immediate surroundings, which are then developed as adjuncts to it.

For example, in the garden already mentioned, near the top of a splendid towering hard maple tree, there was noted by the garden maker's keen eye, in an out-thrust branch the unmistakable half-size suggestion of a dainty woman in Japanese dress, her hands folded demurely within her sleeves, her eyes downcast. Not from every angle was this visible, but an approach to the spot from which it could be seen most clearly and in its loveliest aspect had been cunningly planned to bring out the silhouette with startling emphasis at the instant of one's arrival before a very small shrine erected in honor of this Lady of the Treetops. Here little tokens were placed on special occasions, and the Lady was taken quite seriously even though playfully; a festival in her honor being celebrated when the foliage and all the surrounding conditions brought out her presence sharply and clearly. Thus she brooded over her bit of the garden, wielding a pleasant influence.

WATER AND WATER COURSES. Water is always desired in the Japanese garden, but as it is not always possible to have a pool or rivulet, a dry brook or dry pool may be substituted. These are exactly what the name implies—a channel in the first instance, a depression in the second, where water would flow or rest if water were present, if the little stream or tiny lake had not "gone dry." Surprisingly enough it is possible to achieve a very convincing sense of water by such features. The dry brook is, of course, laid out to follow natural gradations of level if these exist, becoming wider here and narrowing there as a natural watercourse would. The lake

or pool likewise takes a natural form. And the bed of each is covered with gravel and stones disposed as high-water or currents would carry them, while the banks on either side are fringed with the plants that grow naturally in such spots. Somewhere along the course of the dry brook a path must cross it, just as it would probably cross a running one; either over a half-moon bridge or by stepping stones. In all but large gardens the latter are preferred as being more in keeping with the Nature theme prevailing throughout.

PLANTS AND PLANTING. The plant material used in a Japanese garden must be chosen with great care, whether the work is on a diminished scale or full size. Each specimen is selected for its particular place with careful consideration of its form, its tendency of growth, its present adaptability to the composition, and its general appropriateness. No gardeners in the world are as successful as the Japanese in creating immediately and at the moment of finishing a planting the effect of natural growth long undisturbed.

This is partly due to the skill with which they "surface" the earth after a hole has been dug, a plant set, and its roots covered (to detect the disturbance of the ground after a Japanese gardener has finished such a task is practically impossible). But it is also due to the individual selection of every plant for the exact spot it is to occupy. And also to the care with which it is placed so that its form shall conform to its surroundings—to neighboring plants if it is in the midst of a group, or to the conditions governing its growth if it is a single specimen standing apart. Any sparsity in branches, or the over-development of one side—any tendency in its growth—is studied and it is so placed that such tendency is accounted for in the immediate surroundings as they affect its exposure to light and wind.

There may be flowers in the Japanese garden on occasion—dramatic displays of masses at their season. But the flower borders so usual in gardens of the western world are unknown. One flower should be the feature of its season—the iris perhaps, azaleas, the ravishing beauty of cherry blossoms, the twilight-dreaming loveliness of wisteria, and so on. Evergreen material in both tree and shrub form should be strongly dominant—but *never* in assorted kinds. One species used in quantity as

Nature plants, supplemented by deciduous growth that is wholly secondary in numbers, position and importance in the composition, is the rule.

JAPANESE HYDRANGEA - VINE. Common name for *Schizophragma hydrangeoides* (which see), a tall climbing shrub from the Orient.

JAPANESE IVY. A common name for *Parthenocissus tricuspidata,* also called Boston Ivy. See also IVY.

JAPANESE PAGODA-TREE. A common name for *Sophora japonica,* also known as Chinese Scholar-tree.

JAPANESE QUINCE. Common name for *Chaenomeles lagenaria,* a handsome hardy shrub formerly known (and still listed in catalogs) as *Cydonia japonica.* See QUINCE.

JAPANESE-ROSE. Common name for *Kerria japonica,* a green-stemmed semi-hardy shrub with golden-yellow flowers.

JAPANESE SHIELD FERN (*Dryopteris erythrosora*). A broadly triangular 2-pinnate fern, 2 to 3 ft. tall, not native to America but hardy as far N. as N. Y. Its variegated coloring when young and its glossy green when mature make it desirable in the fern garden. Needs woods soil of peaty texture.

JAPANESE-SPURGE. Common name for *Pachysandra terminalis,* a valuable, hardy, evergreen, herbaceous ground-cover, especially useful in shady places where grass will not thrive.

JAPANESE VARNISH-TREE. Common name for *Firmiana simplex,* also known as Chinese Parasol-tree.

JAPONICA (ja-pon'-i-kah). A name often mistakenly applied to the Japanese Quince (*Chaenomeles lagenaria,* formerly *C. japonica*) in the N., to *Camellia japonica* in the S. and often to other unrelated plants. It is thus incorrectly used by those who do not know or who forget that in scientific plant names, the important word comes first. *Chaenomeles japonica* means "Flowering Quince from Japan" and *Camellia japonica* means "Camellia from Japan." Thus *japonica* as a specific name means simply Japanese, no matter to what generic name it may be attached. It is said that in one part of England gardeners are humorously called "Ponicas," presumably because they use the name Japonica for so many plants having this specific name.

JASIONE (jaz-i-oh'-ne). A genus of annual and perennial herbs of the Bell-flower Family, with blue or sometimes white flowers borne in heads. Useful in borders and rock gardens. All species are of easy culture in ordinary garden soils and do well in either sun or partial shade. *J. perennis,* commonly called Sheeps-bit or Shepherds- or Sheep-scabious, a perennial to 1 ft. tall, forms tufted rosettes of oblong leaves and produces globular heads to 2 in. across of numerous pale blue flowers.

JASMINE. Common name for Jasminum, a genus of tropical and subtropical deciduous or evergreen shrubs, sometimes climbing. Belonging to the Olive Family, they are widely distributed in warm countries, and can be grown outdoors in the warmer parts of the U. S. Some are often grown under glass for their showy fragrant flowers produced in winter. They grow well in good loamy soil and are propagated by cuttings and layers.

PRINCIPAL SPECIES

J. officinale (Jessamine) is a long slender grower to 30 ft., with glossy compound foliage, and clusters of white fragrant flowers in summer. It is good on a wall, arbor or fence, and is hardy about as far N. as Washington, D. C.

nudiflorum grows to 15 ft. and opens its yellow flowers in late winter or early spring, before the leaves appear. With protection it survives as far N. as S. N. Y.

primulinum is a rambling free-flowering grower, evergreen in mild regions, and

JASMINE IN EARLY SPRING
Opening its satiny yellow flowers at the first hint of warmth. Jasmine sometimes blooms even during mild spells in winter.

hardy to Washington, D. C. In early spring it produces large pale yellow flowers (often semi-double) with a darker center.

fruticans is half-evergreen, with weak stems to 12 ft. and yellow flowers.

beesianum is dwarf, usually not over 3 ft., with pink or rose fragrant flowers.

humile is an evergreen to 20 ft., with weak stems and clusters of yellow fragrant flowers. Hardy to Md., it is often grown in pots.

grandiflorum (Spanish Jessamine) is a bushy grower with slender branches and clusters of white fragrant flowers, tinged pink. It is much grown in Europe for perfumery, and is naturalized in Fla.

azoricum is a tender evergreen climber with white flowers; good in the cool greenhouse.

sambac (Arabian Jessamine) is a moderate climber, with fragrant white flowers, sometimes double, produced almost continually in the tropics.

JEFFERSONIA (jef-er-soh'-ni-ah) *diphylla.* A woods herb native to Va. and adjacent States, the genus having been named for Thomas Jefferson. See under its common name TWINLEAF.

JERUSALEM ARTICHOKE. A perennial small-flowered American species of sunflower (*Helianthus tuberosus*) with edible tubers resembling potatoes but starchless. The name Jerusalem is a corruption of "girasole," the Italian name for Sunflower, given to the plant when it was carried back to Europe by early explorers in N. America. See ARTICHOKE.

JERUSALEM - CHERRY. Common name for *Solanum pseudo-capsicum,* a small shrubby relative of the egg-plant, potato and bittersweet, whose small globular scarlet or yellow fruits make it an attractive pot plant for the house. Since the fruits ripen among the shiny dark leaves in December, the name Christmas-cherry is also given it. Though a dwarf form is generally grown, plants will sometimes attain 4 ft. A small related species, *S. capsicastrum,* sometimes known as the False Jerusalem-cherry, is equally attractive for indoor culture.

To produce well-fruited specimens, seed should be sown in February and the young seedlings potted up and later plunged outdoors (pots and all) after danger of frost has passed. Occasional shifts into larger pots during the spring and summer bring flowering-size plants into 5 or 6 in. pots by September, when they are brought indoors.

In the house, they are highly susceptible to damage from gas fumes and drafts, against which they should be carefully safeguarded. After their winter fruiting season is over, the branches may be cut back to within 2 or 3 in. of the main stem. When the weather grows warm the plants, still in their pots, are plunged outdoors in

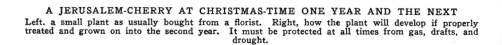

A JERUSALEM-CHERRY AT CHRISTMAS-TIME ONE YEAR AND THE NEXT
Left. a small plant as usually bought from a florist. Right, how the plant will develop if properly treated and grown on into the second year. It must be protected at all times from gas, drafts, and drought.

a sheltered spot for the summer. The shoots which have been pruned off may be rooted as cuttings to provide new plants.

JERUSALEM CROSS. Common name for *Lychnis chalcedonica,* a perennial with scarlet flowers in dense heads; also called Maltese Cross and Scarlet Lightning.

JERUSALEM-OAK. A common name for *Chenopodium botrys,* a strong-smelling annual of the Goosefoot Family grown for its feather-like spikes of small flowers sometimes used in bouquets.

JERUSALEM-SAGE. Common name for *Phlomis fruticosa,* a semi-woody herb with yellow flowers borne in whorls.

JERUSALEM - THORN. A common name applied to *Parkinsonia aculeata* and *Paliurus spina-christi,* two spiny but unrelated trees. The first named, a tropical legume with yellow fragrant pea-like flowers makes a good hedge; the latter, of the Buckthorn Family, has greenish-yellow flowers and brownish fruits. See both genera.

JESSAMINE. A common name for the genus Jasminum, and particularly *J. officinalis.*

Other plants called by this name are: Carolina Yellow-jessamine, which is *Gelsemium sempervirens;* Orange-jessamine which is *Murraea exotica;* Night-blooming-jessamine (*Gestrum nocturnum*); Confederate- Malayan- or African-jessamine (*Trachelospermum jasminoides*).

JETBEAD. The common name for *Rhodotypos tetrapetala* (better known as *R. kerrioides*). This is a deciduous upright spreading shrub to 6 ft., native to Asia and belonging to the Rose Family. It is hardy as far N. as New England and is a valuable ornamental shrub for general planting. Its clean bright green fóliage is particularly noticeable in the fall when many other shrubs are bare. The large white four-petaled flowers are borne singly, mostly in May and June, but sometimes sparingly during the summer. It has shiny black fruits which persist until spring, then lie dormant for a year, and finally give rise to seedlings which appear in abundance around an old plant.

JEW-BUSH. A common name for *Pedilanthus tithymaloides,* a succulent American shrub with red or purple flowers in spreading clusters.

JEWEL-WEED. A common name for two native species of Impatiens, namely *I. biflora* and *I. pallida.*

JIMSON-WEED. Colloquial corruption of Jamestown-weed (which see), the common name of *Datura stramonium,* a coarse native weed with prickly fruits.

JOBS TEARS. Common name for *Coix lachryma-jobi,* a tall ornamental grass grown as an annual in the S. The hard gray to pearly white seed is in the Orient eaten as a cereal ("adlay"). Saved from plants grown in the garden or greenhouse as a curiosity, the seeds are often made into necklaces. See ORNAMENTAL GRASSES.

JOE-PYE-WEED. Common name for *Eupatorium purpureum, E. maculatum* and *E. verticillatum,* N. Amer. species of Thoroughwort.

JOHNSON GRASS. Common name for *Holcus halepensis,* a perennial forage and pasture grass in the S. but often escaped as a pernicious weed. See WEEDS.

JOINT-FIR. A common name for Ephedra, a genus of mostly dry-region shrubs sometimes used as ground-covers.

JONQUIL. Often erroneously applied (as a synonym for daffodil) to any sort of hardy Narcissus (which see), this is really the name of a distinct species (*N. jonquilla*) which is distinguished by nearly round, rush-like foliage and small golden-yellow, medium to short-cupped flowers which are usually borne more than one on a stem and have a more marked fragrance than most other types.

JOSEPHINES-LILY. Common name for *Brunsvigia josephinae,* a summer-flowering bulbous S. African plant of the Amaryllis Family. Named after the Empress Josephine of France, who bought the original bulb after it flowered in the gardens at Malmaison.

JOSEPHS COAT. Common name for *Amaranthus tricolor,* a coarse annual grown for its large, often blotched and brilliantly colored leaves.

JOSHUA-TREE. Common name for *Yucca brevifolia,* a grotesque S. W. desert tree.

JOSS FLOWER. One of common names for *Narcissus tazetta orientalis,* one of the tender forms of Narcissus that bears small flowers in clusters; better known as Chinese Sacred-lily, which see.

JUBAEA (joo-bee'-ah) *chilensis.* A large unarmed Feather Palm, commonly called Syrup Palm or Coquito in Chile. It grows to 80 ft. with a stout columnar trunk 4 to 6 ft. in diameter, surmounted by a crown of feather-form leaves 6 to 12 ft. in length. A syrup or honey is made from the sap and the fruit is called "monkeys' coconuts." As a garden subject it is a handsome palm and grows well in Calif. but does not thrive in Fla. It is frequently grown under glass in the N. with a night temperature of 50 deg. F. Large specimens in tubs are seen in subtropical gardens.

JUDAS-TREE. A common name given to the genus Cercis—better known as Redbud (which see)—because tradition says that Judas hanged himself on a tree of this group.

JUGLANS (joo'-glans). The genus of deciduous trees, commonly called Walnuts, after which the Family Juglandaceae is named. It includes the Black Walnut, Butternut and some strains of the English or Persian Walnut which are hardy North, and other W. Coast species requiring a warm climate. The Walnuts are ornamental, with pinnate foliage markedly free from insect attack and commercially valuable for their edible nuts and their timber. Rich moist soils develop the finest specimens.

See also BUTTERNUT; WALNUT.

JUJUBE (joo'-joob). Deciduous or evergreen shrubs or trees (genus Zizyphus), of tropical and subtropical regions of both hemispheres, belonging to the Buckthorn Family. They are grown in warm climates for ornament and their edible fruits; propagated by seeds, root-cuttings and grafting. The principal species, *Z. jujuba* (Chinese Jujube) is the chief source of the jujube of commerce. This is a deciduous shrub or small tree with slender prickly branches and light green leaves, hardy as far N. as Mass. It is largely cultivated in warm climates, particularly in China, where a great many varieties are grown for the fruit, which is reddish-brown and about the size of an olive; *Z. mauritiana* (Cottony Jujube), a native of India, is an evergreen shrub with the young branches and the under side of the leaves white. It is hardy in the warmest parts of this country, but as yet is not so well developed for fruit production.

JUNCUS (jung'-kus). A genus of perennial, rather grass-like herbs found and adapted for planting in low damp places and commonly known as Rush, which see.

JUNE BEETLES. Also called May beetles, June bugs and May bugs, these are the large, clumsy, brown or blackish creatures that often fly against window screens in early summer evenings. The adults are not ordinarily serious pests, but the larval form is the destructive white grub which eats plant roots and damages lawns, strawberry beds, golf courses, etc. It is a white, curved soft-bodied, 6-legged grub $\frac{1}{2}$ in. to over 1 in. long, with a large brown head and a dirty white body, the dark contents showing through the translucent skin.

The winter is passed in either the larval or adult stage. In the late spring, the beetles become active at night, flying to such trees as poplar, oak, linden, willow, ash, maple and walnut. There they feed and mate, returning to the soil at dawn, where the females lay pearly-white eggs one to several inches below the surface in grass lands or patches of grassy weeds.

The young grubs which hatch in 2 or 3 weeks remain underground, feeding on roots until fall, when they work their way down below the frost line. As the soil warms up in the following spring they work their way up so that they are feeding near the surface by the time the plants are well started. They continue to feed throughout their second summer, pass a second winter deep in the soil, come up again and pupate late in the spring of the third season. Some adult beetles survive over winter and begin to feed on trees the next spring along with freshly emerged adults. The most severe damage thus occurs in three year cycles, the main injury from grubs occurring in the year after a heavy flight of beetles.

Corn, potatoes, strawberries and many vegetables are seriously injured by the grubs and such crops should not be planted on newly plowed sod land. On farms early fall plowing and thorough working of the ground will destroy many larvae and beetles and will bring others near the surface to be devoured by birds or destroyed over winter. Hogs and poultry allowed in newly plowed fields will eat many grubs. In gardens carbon bisulphide may be injected into the soil at the rate of 1 oz. per square yard and soil poisoning for the Japanese beetle (which see) will doubtless kill many. Both grubs and beetles are attacked by several natural parasites.

JUNEBERRY. A common name for the hardy shrub Amelanchier, which see.

JUNE GRASS. A common name for *Poa pratensis,* more often called Kentucky

Blue Grass and one of the best of grasses for pastures and lawns on soils that are not inclined to be sour or continually moist. See BLUE GRASS.

JUNIPER (the genus Juniperus), an ancient name meaning "forever young." Small or medium-sized evergreen trees and shrubs of the Pine Family with small leaves, mostly gray-green, and berry-like fruits blue or reddish. They include some of the best ornamentals, much used in landscaping. The majority are hardy even in the coldest parts of the U. S., preferring rather dry, sandy or gravelly soil, with full exposure to wind and sun, but tolerating average garden conditions and resenting only shade and wet ground; even less particular, and found sometimes in heavy clay and sometimes in marshes, is the Virginia Juniper or Red-cedar with its many varieties.

TYPES AND USES

In form junipers vary from dense columnar trees to trailing ground-cover. The taller columnar forms are used in both formal and informal planting, giving the same effect as the Italian cypress, which is not hardy. The dense, spire-like growth, however, is essentially a character of young trees; after 20 or 30 years the top growth tends to slow or stop, the branches spreading to a dome-like crown in the Red-cedar and Chinese Juniper and their varieties. Among the best slender forms are the Columnar Chinese, and the Red-cedar varieties: *canaerti, glauca* and *keteleeri.* Of the smaller upright forms, several dense, decorative ones have become popular but most of them are short-lived under average conditions: the Irish and Swedish Junipers are narrow and quick growing, the Greek and Variegated Chinese, slow and exceedingly compact.

Longer lasting is the irregularly spreading, massive Pfitzer Juniper, indispensable for evergreen border and foundation planting, especially as for a time it will endure some shade. Other spreading types of lower habit are the Savin and Japanese, and var. *depressa* of the Common Juniper.

For ground-cover in full sun, to hold steep banks, for the rock garden or an exposed evergreen border edging, a number of creeping junipers can be highly recommended, as Andorra, Sargent, Tamarix, Creeping, Waukegan, etc. Tiny junipers growing only an inch or two a year sometimes planted in European rock gardens are but little known in America.

Shades of color in juniper foliage should be studied in arboretums or nurseries as they are hard to describe though striking, and often changing with the seasons. From

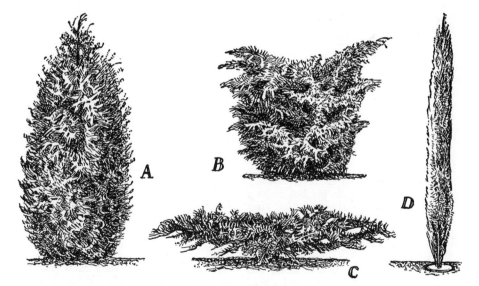

JUNIPERS ARE HARDY, ATTRACTIVE, AND VARIED IN FORM
These are but a few of the interesting types: (A) medium-size upright; (B) irregular bush form often seen in Pfitzer Junipers; (C) creeping or spreading type, fine in rock gardens; (D) narrow columnar type as illustrated by the Irish Junipers.

the black-green of Savin and Canaert to the pearl gray of Meyer, the junipers show all variations of blue-green and gray-green with pinkish and purplish tints and blooms, and deep purple winter color in some kinds. The fruits, though usually small, are ornamental, blue with a white bloom and plentiful on the Red-cedars. On the rare Formosa Juniper, they are orange-brown, while the Syrian Juniper bears brown edible fruits an inch in diameter. Fruits of the Common Juniper are used in making oil of juniper and gin.

FOLIAGE CHARACTERS. Juniper leaves are of two kinds: needle-shape on young seedlings and leading shoots and scale-like on the twigs of older trees. The young leaves spread wide from the twig, and are often bristle-tipped; the older, scale-shaped ones cling close to the twig, forming what is called whip-cord foliage, because it resembles a braided cord. In some forms, such as the Greek and Irish Junipers, all the leaves are of the spreading, juvenile type, not changing as the tree grows older; in others, like the Canaert Red-cedar, whip-cord foliage prevails even on the smallest plants; while still others, like the Male Juniper, have mixed foliage at all ages. None of these unnatural leaf forms can be reproduced from seed.

PROPAGATION. Juniper species are propagated from seed which does not usually germinate till the second or third year, and should therefore be stratified (kept a year in moist sand). Most juniper fruits do not ripen till the second year on the tree, but the Red-cedar and its varieties are ripe the first season, and the Common Juniper and its varieties nit till the third. Some forms are male and do not bear fruit.

In early spring, a year after stratifying the seed, prepare beds of loose, light, sandy soil shaded with lath and in them sow the stratified seed either broadcast or in rows 6 in. apart. As the full stand is not likely to come up until the year after sowing, seedlings should be left in the bed as long as possible without overcrowding; but after one year remove the shades. Two or three years after the first seed germinates seedlings should be dug in May and set two feet apart in nursery rows, where they should be cultivated deep and often, and transplanted every three years until placed permanently. Transplanting is not difficult, provided the fibrous roots are not exposed to sun or wind or allowed to dry. After the first transplanting they should usually be handled with a ball of earth.

Named varieties and the unnatural leaf forms mentioned above do not come true from seed, but are either grafted or grown from cuttings, which root slowly. Species also are thus propagated when seed is unobtainable or when a stock is wanted quickly. Because it saves time, grafting is preferred for most sorts, Red-cedar or Common Juniper being used as understock. Any gardener can root cuttings of the common varieties—Irish, Swedish, Greek, etc., in sand in a shaded coldframe. Tips 4 to 6 in. long are cut in August and, after the needles have been snipped away from an inch or two of the butt, are placed in a coldframe bed of sand 4 or 5 in. deep, spread over rich sandy soil. The bed must be watered thoroughly and covered with glass, and in cold climates earth should be heaped up a foot deep or more around the sides. This frame should be either placed where very little sun will strike it or properly shaded with lath, in which case no ventilation is necessary. By the following summer the cuttings will have rooted; the glass can then be removed and the frame treated like a seed bed. Arborvitae, yew and retinispora cuttings may be handled similarly.

PROTECTION. Junipers need little shearing, but may be trimmed back when out of shape or sheared in formal planting. Their chief requirements are sunlight, drainage and cultivation. When shaded even slightly, most varieties are subject to scale and red spider, which weaken and disfigure them. Dormant sprays of miscible oil about 1 to 40, or nicotine-soap solutions in the growing season control both these pests, but no control is really satisfactory in shade. Junipers placed in full sun and well cultivated will seldom suffer any infestation and the Columnar Chinese, Canaert, and some other junipers are nearly immune.

A condition that looks like blight may be caused by mice gnawing the bark of the roots. The Savin, and most of the ground-cover junipers often show dead branches in the growing season, the result more often of injury than of disease, for any cut or bruise will usually cause an entire branch to turn brown. When the dead part has been cut away the plant appears unaffected, and may last indefinitely. Juniper varieties of the past have originated in foreign countries, but more recent American-bred forms seem more resistant to disease. Continued selection should give junipers of increased variety and vigor. The red heart-wood of the larger trees is very durable in the ground, making red-cedar posts one of the most desirable kinds for rustic fences and arbors. Cedar chests are made not of true Cedar (an Old-World tree) but of red-cedar, whose aromatic oil repels moths.

ENEMIES

A serious twig blight prevalent in nurseries is also common on eastern ornamental red-cedars during wet springs. The tips of the twigs die, turning light tan and in young trees the fungus may extend into the trunk. During rains, spores are carried from diseased leaves and infect nearby trees. Prune out brown diseased twigs and spray two or three times fortnightly with bordeaux mixture beginning when the new growth starts.

CEDAR RUST. Several species of rust fungus cause diseases of the common red-cedar and other junipers. The life history of the ever present apple and cedar rust (*Gymnosporangium juniperi-virginianae*) is typical. See also RUSTS AND RUST FUNGI.) Chocolate brown, corky "cedar-apples" (actually galls) are the response of the cedar to the irritation caused by this fungus in the leaf tissues. Beginning in spring and during warm rains, for several months, gelatinous orange-yellow horns, made up of hundreds of spores, grow out from depressed areas on the surface of the "apples." As the weather clears, the spores are liberated and carried by the wind to the leaves and twigs of apples or flowering crabs, causing, on the leaves, light yellow spots on the upper surface. Later, swellings on the *under* leaf surfaces discharge spores which are blown back to cedars, on whose twigs or leaves the fungus lives over winter, forming a small rounded enlargement the next spring, which increases in size during the summer, and the second spring matures as a gall or "cedar-apple." Thus the fungus spends 4 or 5 months on the apple host and 18 or more on the cedar.

Three species of red-cedar are susceptible to this rust, namely, the eastern red-cedar (*Juniperus virginiana*), the western red-cedar (*J. scopulorum*), and the creeping red-cedar (*J. horizontalis*). Some

varieties of apples are susceptible and others more or less resistant, depending on the locality. The ornamental Bechtels crab is particularly susceptible, but foreign species of crabs (with the exception of *Malus sylvestris*) have been found immune and should be used in place of the native sorts in gardens. In apple-growing regions rust is controlled by eradicating all red-cedars within a mile of any orchard. In gardens this may not be possible, but susceptible varieties of the two hosts should be kept apart or separated by a windbreak.

On the apple, rust may be controlled with 4 to 6 applications of a sulphur fungicide, and a similar spray on the cedars during July and August will probably prevent reinfection. In any case, remove all galls

FRESH FROM THE NURSERY
Keep the burlap around the ball of soil to keep the roots moist until this young juniper is in place in a foundation or background planting. Then soak well and fill the hole with good soil.

from junipers *before* the "spore horns" are put out.

In the somewhat similar cedar-hawthorn rust the small round galls are perennial and produce a crop of spore horns each year. Besides hawthorn, mountain-ash and cultivated apple and pear are alternate hosts.

The quince rust which occurs on pear, apple, chokeberry, shad and hawthorn, causes long spindle-shaped swellings of the branches of red-cedar and common mountain juniper on which orange-yellow spore pustules develop. Removal of one of the hosts is the only way to control the disease.

To control the birds-nest rust, which causes tufts of branches (witches' brooms)

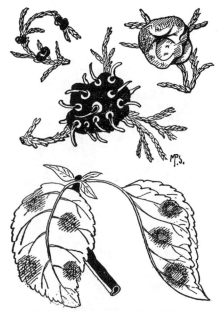

THE CEDAR-APPLE RUST
Above, 3 stages in growth of familiar galls on Red-cedar (Juniperus virginiana) from which the disease spreads to apples (below) causing serious leaf-spotting.

on red-cedar, remove shadbushes and quince trees from the vicinity.

PESTS. Among insect pests the, Juniper web-worm is becoming serious on *J. communis*. It forms webbed masses within which the reddish-brown, white-striped larvae feed. Spray with lead arsenate or dust with sulphur-lead arsenate during June and July while the caterpillars are small. Pyrethrum sprays applied with force enough to enter the webs are also effective.

The small circular snowy-white Juniper scale may be abundant (see SCALE INSECTS). Occasionally there is serious injury from bag-worm. See EVERGREENS; MITES.

SPECIES AND VARIETIES OF INTEREST

J. californica (Californian Juniper) to 40 ft. with large, reddish brown fruit.

chinensis (Chinese Juniper), to 60 ft., like red-cedar, but brighter green. Some varieties are: *aurea* (Golden Chinese Juniper), yellow tipped; *aureo-globosa*, dense, dwarf, with new growth yellow; *globosa*, rounded dwarf; *japonica* (Japanese Juniper), low, spreading, dark green; *mas* (Male Juniper), compact pyramid, light green; *pendula*, branches spreading, drooped; *pfitzeriana* (Pfitzer Juniper), massive spreading, dense, blue-green; *plumosa*, low, feathery; *pyramidalis*, narrow, compact column; *sargenti*, pale green ground-cover; *sheppardi*, dwarf nodding, with needle leaves; *variegata* (Whiteleaf Chinese Juniper), broad pyramid, dense upright branchlets streaked white.

communis (Common Juniper) shrub or tree, usually spreading, with needle leaves. Varieties are: *aurea* (Golden Juniper), with young leaves yellow; *compressa*, slow-growing dwarf; *cracovia* (Polish Juniper), with nodding tips; *depressa* (Prostrate Juniper), spreading, with ascending branches; *hibernica* (Irish Juniper), narrow, stiff upright, gray-green.

conferta (Shore Juniper), ground-cover; fruit black.

excelsa (Greek Juniper), to 60 ft., not hardy. Its var. *stricta* (Spiny Greek Juniper) makes a dense pyramid of gray-green juvenile foliage and is hardy.

horizontalis (Creeping Juniper), ground-cover. Var. *douglasi* (Waukegan Juniper), bluish, in winter purple.

sabina (Savin), spreading, rather low, dark green. Var. *cupressifolia*, low, trailing, blue-green; var. *fastigiata* (Column Savin), narrow, upright, dark green; var. *tamariscifolia* (Tamarix Savin), dense, low, spreading, gray-green.

scopulorum (Colorado Red-cedar), a W. form similar to red-cedar.

squamata, a pale blue-green ground-cover. Var. *meyeri* (Fishtail Juniper), dense, irregularly upright, pale blue-gray. Var. *prostrata*, flat to the ground.

virginiana (Red-cedar). Tree to 100 ft., common throughout E. U. S. Var. *canaerti* (Canaert Red-cedar), dark green columnar; var. *globosa* (Globe R.), dwarf, compact; var. *keteleeri,* dense upright; var. *kosteri,* dwarf; var. *pendula* (Weeping Red-cedar), branches pendulous.

JUPITERS BEARD. Common name for *Centranthus ruber,* a hardy perennial with, usually, crimson or light red fragrant flowers; also called Red-valerian. See CENTRANTHUS.

JUSSIAEA (jus-i-ee'-ah). Primrose-willow. Perennial herbs or woody plants, widely distributed in temperate and tropical regions, belonging to the Evening-primrose Family. One or two species are cultivated for aquatic or bog-garden planting, and may be treated as tender annuals. Propagate by seeds, submerging the seed-pans in shallow water; also by cuttings and division.

J. longifolia grows to about 2 ft. high and has narrow long-pointed leaves and yellow flowers. *J. repens* has creeping stems rooting at the nodes, with oval leaves and small yellow flowers.

JUSTICIA (jus-tish'-i-ah). Tropical shrubby plants belonging to the Acanthus Family and closely allied to Jacobinia. *J. secunda,* with heads of red flowers, is the best-known species at present. For cultural directions, see JACOBINIA.

K

KADSURA (kad-seu'-rah). Tender evergreen twining shrubs from Asia, belonging to the Magnolia Family. *K. japonica,* the principal species, can be grown outdoors only in warm climates. It climbs to about 10 ft., has dark green oval or oblong leaves, and small yellowish-white flowers, not showy. The clusters of scarlet berries make it a very striking plant in the fall.

KAFIR-LILY. Common name for two S. African genera both of fleshy-rooted herbs, namely Clivia and Schizostylis. The former includes good indoor pot subjects with showy red or yellow flowers like those of Amaryllis, to which they are related. Schizostylis, a member of the Iris Family, has tubular flowers of crimson usually grown for cutting.

KAFIR-PLUM (*Harpephyllum caffrum*). A South African tree, sometimes planted for ornament in the warmest parts of the U. S. It grows to 30 ft., and bears pinnate, thick glossy leaves, clusters of small greenish-white flowers, and dark red edible fruits about the size of an olive.

KAINIT. A low grade potash fertilizer obtained as a by-product from mines, mostly in Germany. As put on the market it contains from 12 to 14% of potash in the sulphate form, but this is adulterated with common salt (sodium chloride), which may make up as much as a third of the material, and other compounds. Unless it can be secured cheaply, kainit is not an economical or, for that matter, desirable way to supply potash to the soil. If used, it should be applied well in advance of planting—a full season or more if possible —so that the undesirable constituents which may injure young plant roots can leach out. On swamp or muck land, it can be applied at the rate of 400 lbs. per acre in the fall, as any injurious substances will probably be lost by spring while the potash will be retained.

KALANCHOË (kal-an-koh'-ee). A genus of succulent perennial herbs of the Orpine Family, shrubby in form, with fleshy oval leaves usually toothed, and a profusion of small bright-colored flowers that remain without fading for several weeks. While Kalanchoës are occasionally grown outdoors in the far S., they are best known as greenhouse and house plants.

Well known years ago, but neglected for some time, they have, since their recent reintroduction by florists, made progress toward becoming one of the principal pot plants for the Christmas season. Seed sown in spring in the greenhouse will produce flowering plants for the holidays. Propagation is also easily effected by cuttings. Cultural requirements are the same as for other succulents—a porous, gritty soil, ample moisture during the growing period. abundant sunshine, and freedom from drafts. If the potting soil is first sterilized, nematodes are not likely to infest the roots, and if excessive moisture is avoided, plants are less likely to be attacked by a Phytopthora wilt and stem rot that is favored by dampness.

K. coccinea and *K. globulifera* var. *coccinea* are most frequently seen. *K. coccinea* makes a bushy plant from 1 to 4 ft. tall, bearing long-lasting scarlet or orange flowers. *K. carnea,* 2 ft. tall, bears fragrant pink flowers. Many new species now being introduced give promise of other interesting subjects with purple, yellow and white flowers for indoor bloom. The pot plant known as *K. globulifera* var. *coccinea* is botanically *K. blossfeldiana.*

A POPULAR NEW POT PLANT

Kalanchoë. with brick-red flowers and heavy, succulent leaves, has recently come into wide use in both small and large sizes. The flowers last many weeks and the plants themselves are long-lived.

KALE. A hardy, biennial, non-heading kind of cabbage (*Brassica oleracea* var.

acephala) grown for its foliage, which is used as "greens." In home gardens it is generally grown during the fall and early winter, seed being sown in late spring, either where the plants are to mature or in seedbeds; in the latter case transplanting can be done 4 to 6 weeks later. Its culture differs in no way from that of cabbage (which see). Commercially the crop is grown mainly from Virginia southward for the winter and spring market. See BRASSICA.

KALMIA (kal'-mi-ah). (See illustrations, Plate 43.) Mostly evergreen shrubs, native of N. America, belonging to the Heath Family. Their leaves contain a poisonous principle that may prove fatal to sheep, goats and calves that browse on the plants. Some are among the best of broad-leaved evergreens for N. gardens, and very valuable for ornamental plantings, especially when massed. They thrive best in partial shade in sandy or peaty soils not too dry, but will also grow out in the open and in loam if free of lime. In sunny places a continuous mulch is invaluable. Propagated by seed, cuttings of half-ripened wood under glass, layers, and grafting, but plants may be successfully transplanted from the wild.

Enemies. Two leaf-spotting diseases that look somewhat alike are controlled by destroying infected leaves and spraying plants three or four times from June to September with bordeaux mixture. One causes circular, grayish white or silvery spots with a reddish border; the other causes larger spots lacking the silvery center. The flower-pot disease of azalea (which see) also attacks Kalmia.

PRINCIPAL SPECIES

K. latifolia (Mountain-laurel, Calicobush) is one of the most beautiful of shrubs, and perhaps the best broad-leaved evergreen for N. gardens. It is the State flower of Conn. and Penna. The showy flowers are borne in terminal clusters, varying in color from white to deep rose, with purple markings inside. There are several named forms, of which var. *polypetala* with narrow petals is conspicuous. Var. *myrtifolia* is a dwarf form with small leaves.

angustifolia (Sheep-laurel, Lambkill) grows to about 3 ft., with narrow light green leaves, pale beneath. It has purple or crimson flowers borne in lateral clus-

ters. The common names were given because the leaves were thought to be especially poisonous to sheep; actually there is more evidence of the dangerous nature of the better known Mountain-laurel.

polifolia (Bog Kalmia), formerly *K. glauca,* is a low straggling shrub, with leaves white beneath and rosy-purple flowers in terminal clusters. Var. *microphylla* is an alpine form from the Rocky Mountains, only a few inches high.

KANGAROO-THORN. Common name for *Acacia armata,* a spiny leguminous shrub with yellow flowers.

KANGAROO-VINE. A common name for *Cissus antarctica,* an Australian vine grown outdoors in warm countries and in greenhouses in the N.

KARANDA (kah-raun'-dah) or CARAUNDA. The common name for *Carissa carandas,* an evergreen, spiny shrub of India with white or pink, fragrant flowers and red fruits.

KARO (kay'-roh). Common name for *Pittosporum crassifolium,* an evergreen shrub or tree of New Zealand with red or purple flowers in terminal clusters.

KATSURA-TREE (kat-seu'-rah). Common name for *Cercidiphyllum japonicum,* a bushy deciduous tree from Japan sometimes planted for ornament because of its distinctive rounded leaves 4 in. across with heart-shaped bases. Its autumn color varies from yellow to scarlet. The flowers are inconspicuous. The female tree is more attractive, being of spreading habit, while the male is columnar. It grows best in moist rich soil and is propagated by seeds, cuttings of green wood in spring or by layers. Var. *sinense* is taller and may prove the better type.

KAURI-PINE (kou'-ri). Common name for *Agathis australis,* a tall New-Zealand tree somewhat grown in warmest parts of the U. S. See DAMMAR-PINE.

KEEL. A part of a flower forming a ridge shaped like a boat's keel; more particularly, the structure formed by the two lower petals of a sweet pea or other papilonaceous flower which are united along the lower edge.

KELP. A coarse, heavy, brown rubbery sea plant whose broad flat leaves are often many feet long. It is rich in potash (from 2.25 to 6.25%) and contains from 1.7 to 2.5% nitrogen and about .5% phosphoric acid. There are two principal commercial sources—Japan and the Pacific

Northwest—whose product when dried and ground is a valuable potash carrier. Thus far, however, the demand for other kelp constituents, as iodine, have prevented it from becoming an important fertilizer. Where a gardener is so located that he can obtain kelp for the hauling, he can well afford to compost it or otherwise put it in shape to be worked into the soil. It may, however, take a considerable time to rot and prove somewhat noisome while doing so.

KENILWORTH IVY. Common name for *Cymbalaria muralis,* a small trailing herbaceous perennial of Europe but naturalized in N. E. U. S. to Pa. It is somewhat grown as an evergreen ground-cover or to drape walls, but is even more common as a decorative trailer in greenhouses. Catalogs sometimes list it by its former name, *Linaria cymbalaria.*

KENNEDYA (ke-nee'-di-ah). Woody trailers or twining plants of Australia, belonging to the Pea Family. One or two species are grown outdoors in the warmer parts of the country, and sometimes in greenhouses for spring and summer bloom. They are fast growers and well adapted for draping pillars and rafters. Propagated by seeds and cuttings.

K. nigricans has flowers of deep purple, almost black, with a conspicuous green blotch. *K. prostrata* var. *major,* considered to be the best, is a free grower with scarlet flowers.

KENTIA (ken'-ti-ah). A genus of Feather Palms once comprising many species, now containing but two, neither in cultivation in this country. Other palms commonly called Kentia are now *Howea forsteriana* and *H. belmoreana,* and *Hedyscepe canterburyana* (the Umbrella Pine). These three palms are widely cultivated in the juvenile stage as pot plants. See HEDYSCEPE and HOWEA.

Rhopalostylis sapida (Nikau Palm) often listed as *Kentia sapida,* is a palm from New Zealand, growing over 25 ft. high; it thrives and fruits in the open in S. Calif. The Norfolk Island Palm (*R. baueri*) with a smooth trunk and feathery leaves 6 to 12 ft. long, is sometimes listed by its former name, *Kentia baueri.*

KENTUCKY BLUE GRASS. A common name for *Poa pratensis,* one of the best of pasture and lawn grasses for sweet or neutral soils. So called to distinguish it from the somewhat less valuable Canada

Blue Grass (*P. compressa*). See BLUE GRASS.

KENTUCKY COFFEE-TREE. Common name for *Gymnocladus dioica,* a majestic native deciduous tree found from N. Y. southward. See COFFEE-TREE.

KERNERA (ker-nee'-rah). A small genus of Old-World cruciferous perennials forming compact clumps from 2 to 12 in. high and bearing abundant white flowers all summer. They thrive in fairly fertile moist situations in full sun.

KEROSENE. A layer of kerosene on a pail or other vessel partly filled with water is useful in hand-picking such insects as the rose chafer and Japanese beetle, which are not readily controlled by spraying. A rag soaked in kerosene may be used in wiping out nests of the tent caterpillar (which see); this is less likely to damage trees than is the practice of burning out the webs.

Kerosene emulsion, though less used than formerly, is recommended as a spray for the four-lined plant bug (which see), the sod web-worm (see WEB-WORM) and some other insects. To make a stock emulsion dissolve 1 lb. soap chips or flakes in 1 gal. hot water; then add ½ gal. kerosene and stir rapidly until a creamy emulsion is formed. (A small butter churn is excellent, or effective churning can be done by pumping the mixture through a spray pump back into itself.) To use, mix 1 part of the emulsion with 50 parts of water. On grass apply at the rate of 1 gal. per square yard. On shrubs and trees apply thoroughly in fine mist form.

KERRIA (ker'-i-ah). A Chinese deciduous shrub, belonging to the Rose Family. It grows to 8 ft. high, and is not particular as to soil, but prefers a well-drained and sheltered position, doing well in partial shade. The light-green twiggy stems are very decorative in winter. They may be killed back at the top if exposed to much below zero temperatures. A disfiguring leaf and twig blight causes reddish-brown leaf spots; if it is severe the leaves may turn yellow and die prematurely. On stems, several spots may run together to form long cankers, the bark splitting and the twigs being gradually killed. Cut out diseased shoots; rake up dead leaves; spray with bordeaux mixture, or dust with sulphur.

K. japonica, the only species, has abundant single yellow flowers in late spring, and sometimes there is a scattering throughout the season. The double-flowered var. *pleniflora,* usually grows taller and may be trained to porches or against a wall. There are also varieties with white- and yellow-variegated leaves.

KEW GARDENERS IN AMERICA, THE ASSOCIATION OF. This professional organization was formed in 1916 as a social group of gardeners, teachers, investigators and others resident in the U. S. who graduated from The Royal Botanic Gardens at Kew, London, Eng. It forms a branch of the Kew Guild of Gardeners which meets each May in London and generally holds an informal meeting or dinner at the time of the International Flower Show in New York City.

Association news appears in a section of the "Journal of the Kew Guild," published annually in London.

There are no regular dues. The secretary is William H. Judd, Arnold Arboretum, Jamaica Plain, Mass.

KICKXIA (kik'-si-ah). A genus of creeping annual herbs from the Old World, sometimes used in rock gardens as groundcovers. The best known species are *K. elantine* and *K. spuria,* both with purplish and yellow flowers resembling those of Linaria. Both have become naturalized in E. N. America.

KIDNEY BEAN. In England, beans derived from *Phaseolus vulgaris;* in America, varieties whose ripe, purplish-red seeds are baked. See BEAN.

KILLARNEY FERN. A charming and diminutive member of the group called Filmy Ferns, which see.

KING PALM. Common name for the genus Archontophoenix, comprising tall, spineless Feather Palms from Australia, extensively grown in S. Fla. and Calif. They are attractive, not only for their feathery foliage, but also for their white or purple flower trusses which are followed by clusters of bright red pea-like fruits.

KINNIKINNICK. Colloquial name for several species of Cornus and other native American shrubs, the dried bark of which was smoked by the Indians.

KITAIBELIA (ki-tay-bee'-li-ah) *vitifolia.* An Old-World stout perennial mallow often 8 ft. high with grape-like leaves and showy, abutilon-like white or rose-colored flowers. It thrives in ordinary garden soils, where it is useful as background planting and among shrubbery.

KERRIA JAPONICA
This hardy, green-twigged shrub bears yellow rose-like flowers in June. In autumn the leaves turn golden-yellow.

KITCHEN GARDEN. The area where vegetables are grown by the occupant of a property for his own table. Strawberries, bush fruits, grapes, often flowers as edging or for cut flowers, and sometimes dwarf fruit trees are included, as well as vegetables. Where space is limited the most important vegetables to grow are salads, garnishes and culinary herbs—the first because their freshness is thus assured and the second because few or no kinds are available in the market. It should be located as close as possible to the kitchen and yet fit into the general plan of the property. See GARDEN DESIGN and compare TRUCK GARDENING and MARKET GARDENS.

KITTEN-TAILS. A catalog name for species of Synthyris (which see) perennial herbs of the Figwort Family, native to W. U. S. and sometimes grown in wild gardens or rock gardens.

KLEINIA (kly'-ni-ah). Former generic name for a group of succulent plants now considered a part of the genus Senecio, which see.

KNAPWEED. Common name for *Centaurea nigra,* a naturalized perennial with rose-purple flowers in heads; also called Hardheads.

KNEELING MATS. Rather flat cushions of various forms used to protect the knees when working in a kneeling position for weeding, thinning or other low garden tasks. They may be of thick sponge rubber or kapok, felt or other non-decaying material covered with burlap, or other tough fabric, preferably of open weave texture to facilitate drying. Another type is of woven cane or reed, with or without a raised front edge to prevent the knees from slipping off into the soil. Though such devices would probably be frowned on by old-time professional gardeners as "sissified," they can serve a useful purpose in making garden chores easier and in helping gardeners escape the possible ill effects of kneeling on damp ground.

KNIPHOFIA (nip-hoh'-fi-ah). One of the most startling of autumn-blooming plants, with dense cigar-shaped spikes of red and yellow tubular flowers rising like sky-rockets above other garden subjects so that it draws attention from everything around it. Appropriately called Torch-lily, Red-hot Poker, Poker-plant, or Flame-flower, Kniphofia is also often listed under its former botanical name of Tritoma. It belongs to the Lily Family and is a native of Africa.

Seed sown under glass in very early spring will sometimes produce flowering plants the following autumn. When set outdoors after all danger of frost is past, the young plants should be given a loose, well-drained, rather poor soil in a sheltered but sunny location. A dark green hedge provides an especially effective background as well as protection from strong winds which are likely to damage the tall, heavy flowered stalks. In the N., the rhizomes should be dug up in the fall and stored in dry earth in a cool, but not freezing, temperature. Seeds can also be sown outdoors in early summer, the plants being set in a permanent location the following spring. Old rhizomes may be divided to produce strong new plants, and when offsets arise they too may be used for propagation.

While there are many species, some dwarf ones for rock-garden use, blooming in summer, and other tender ones for the greenhouse, the species most often seen in cultivation is *K. uvaria* which has countless named and unnamed varieties. The brilliant flower-scapes rise several feet above the sword-shaped leaves. Kniphofia species are definite as they all hybridize freely when grown together in the garden.

THE REAL KITCHEN GARDEN CAN MEAN MUCH TO A HOME
It can provide interest, recreation and exercise, as well as better vegetables than the stores or stands can supply. See text.

KNOT-ROOT. A common name for *Stachys sieboldi,* also known as Japanese or Chinese Artichoke. See ARTICHOKE.

KNOTWEED. Common name for certain species in the genus Polygonum, mostly weedy herbs with close-set spikes of minute flowers, some of which are grown in wild gardens and borders.

KNOTWEED FAMILY. Another name for the Buckwheat Family or Polygonaceae, which see.

KOCHIA (koh'-ki-ah). A fast-growing, shrub-like, ornamental annual of the Goosefoot Family, known as Summer-cypress, Belvedere, Burning-bush, or Mexican Fire-bush. The small but dense foliage, which is a clear bright green in spring, and a somewhat deeper shade all summer, turns bronze-red after frost. The plants grow from 1½ to 4 ft. tall and are compactly pyramidal or rounded. They are of easy culture in moderately rich soil from seed sown in the open ground early in May or started indoors earlier. Their formal shape and uniform size adapt them for use as a temporary hedge or tall border for walks or drives, but they are inclined to become monotonous and are not especially distinguished or high class material. *K. scoparia,* the best-known species, and its var. *trichophila,* are most often used in borders and for semi-formal effects. *K. hyssopifolia* is a smaller plant with longer though still narrow leaves.

KOELREUTERIA (kel-roo-tee'-ri-ah). A genus of Oriental trees of great beauty when in flower. See GOLDEN-RAIN-TREE.

KOHLRABI. Sometimes called stem turnip. A hardy herb (*Brassica caulorapa*) of the cabbage group, which, though a biennial, is grown as an annual spring and fall vegetable for its pale green or purple, turnip-like swollen stem. This is ready for the table while tender and small (2 to 3 in. thick); when larger it becomes woody and strong flavored. Seed is usually sown in rows directly in the garden, though sometimes, for earliness, it is started in hotbeds, coldframes or outdoor seed beds. In any case the plants should stand a little farther apart than beets in rows 12 to 18 in. apart. The crop is managed like turnips. See BRASSICA; TURNIP.

KOLKWITZIA (kolk-witz'-i-ah) *amabalis.* An oriental deciduous shrub with white-throated pink flowers similar to weigela. Deservedly called Beauty-bush, which see.

KOHLRABI, FRESH FROM THE GARDEN
The tuberous stem should be less than 3 in. thick when harvested if the vegetable is to have the finest flavor.

KOREAN DAISY. Common name for the hardy horticultural Chrysanthemum, *C. coreanum,* with single white flowers.

KOREAN LAWN GRASS. Common name for *Zoysia japonica,* actually a Japanese creeping perennial grass sometimes used in S. lawns and golf courses.

KRIGIA (kri'-jah). A genus of small annual or perennial herbs of the Composite Family, commonly known as Mountain-dandelion. These bright, attractive, native plants, with heads of yellow or orange ray-flowers, are occasionally planted in the rock garden. See DANDELION.

KRUBI. Common name for *Amorphophallus titanum,* a tropical Asiatic plant reputed to bear the largest flowers known. Actually its "flower" is an inflorescence consisting, like that of the calla, of a petal-like sheath or *spathe* surrounding a spike-like *spadix* on which many real flowers are closely clustered. The flower of the plant that bloomed at the New York Botanical Garden in October, 1937, was 11 ft. 3 in. tall and nearly 8 ft. 10 in. in diameter.

KUDZU-VINE (kood'-zoo). Common name for *Pueraria thunbergiana,* a twining Asiatic perennial vine with large tuberous roots, belonging to the Pea Family. In the N. it usually dies to the ground in winter, but under favorable conditions it grows from 40 to 60 ft. long each summer. It has large three-part, somewhat lobed leaves, spikes of purple fragrant flowers, and large flat hairy seed-pods. Halo spot, a bacterial disease, causes conspicuous spotting of the leaves. To escape it plant roots from disease-free fields and avoid the use of· cuttings.

THE KUDZU VINE
A rank-growing, hardy climber, this purple-flowered vine will cover trellises and fences rapidly.

KUHNIA (keu'-ni-ah). A genus of variable American composite perennial herbs similar to Eupatorium, with small whitish flower-heads in late summer, thriving in any dry soil.

KUMQUAT (kum'-kwot). Common name for Fortunella, a small genus of Chinese evergreen shrubs differing only in small details from Citrus and grown in Fla. as one of the less important citrus fruits (which see). The trees, which attain 10 or 12 ft. and are somewhat hardier than the sweet orange, make ornamental tub plants for the N. and are grown outdoors in the S. for the elongated fruits about the size of small plums and the color of oranges. These are aromatic, edible raw, and good for preserving, besides being decorative on the table. Hybridized with various Citrus species, kumquats have given forms with such qualities as size, flavor and juiciness of fruit, more or less modified.

LABELS. Plants, bulbs, packets of seed and trees should always be labeled when bought, sold, or given away, or when moved to a new site, as it is easy to lose the name of a variety when out of the ground, and often impossible to identify it again with certainty. Labels for such temporary purpose are usually of wood or paper. When bought in quantity, wood labels are cheap, either those notched and wired for attaching to trees, stakes or cord, or larger sizes sharpened to be thrust in the ground or into a pot or bundle. Labels made of narrow strips of heavy waxed paper, printed or plain, and especially slit so they can be wrapped and quickly fastened around any stem or trunk, are even more convenient. Temporary labels of either type are also useful to mark single plants or flowers from which to propagate or collect seed. Newly sown rows, seed beds and seed pots are usually marked with wood labels, except seeds very slow in germinating, which may need more lasting markers. Names should be written with ordinary lead-pencil, not indelible pencil, because the latter blurs when wet.

For many purposes plants are labeled permanently, and gardeners have used such ingenuity in search of labels that will last that a host of forms, some of them excellent, are now in use. Labels for an arboretum, botanic garden, or nursery display-ground must be long-lived, not easy to remove or deface but easy to read in passing. They may be of painted wood with the name written in a lasting paint of lampblack and linseed oil. If stakes, the wood chosen should be cypress, cedar, or some species which will not rot off in the ground. A better method is to mount the label on a steel or wire frame. All-metal

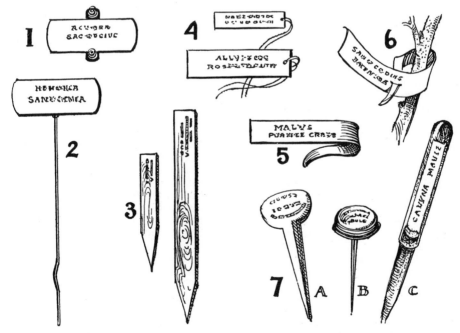

LABELS ARE INVALUABLE IN KEEPING PLANT IDENTITIES CORRECT

Here are a few of many available kinds. 1. Metal plate for large tree; spiral springs under nail or screw heads give room for bark expansion. 2. Metal or composition plate on metal rod "kinked" to prevent its turning in the ground. 3. Wooden labels, small for pots and flats, large for the garden. 4. Thin copper strips wired for attachment to plants. 5. Strip of lead with narrowed end to be wrapped around branch. 6. Paraffined paper label for temporary use. 7. Three modern garden types: (A) stamped metal, (B) with removable glass lens covering written label, (C) glass tube protecting written slip, fitted over wooden peg to stick in ground.

labels last longer than wood, with sheet zinc or aluminum first choice. A sheet of zinc stamped with raised letters and mounted on a rigid steel frame is probably best of all. In marking trees, labels are often nailed to the trunk, but this practice is not good, because it injures and eventually disfigures the tree.

In a small garden, valuable named varieties should be given permanent labels for reference only, not to be read from a distance. Especially in the rock garden, where numerous rare plants are used, labeling is most desirable and concealment of the label most urgent. Gardeners often depend on the shipping label, which, if a tree label of painted wood, and if the name is written distinctly in pencil, may last on a tree or shrub from 2 to 5 years, and still be read. But it must be taken off and reaffixed often so that the wire will not cut into the bark. Stake labels in the ground do not last as long, and are easily lost. The name is said to last much longer on wood labels if written with red wax crayon.

Permanent metal tree labels are of many kinds. Those of zinc may be written on with chemical ink (2 oz. verdigris, 2 oz. sal ammoniac, 1 oz. lampblack, 3 pints soft water) ; or, if weathered white, with ordinary lead-pencil. Paper-thin copper labels on which the name can be written with a metal stylus or large nail when the label is placed over a backing of soft cardboard, will last indefinitely, and the dark color of weathered copper is inconspicuous. Celluloid properly surfaced holds lead-pencil writing well, but even when tinted green is rather noticeable.

Labels on the ground are less easily made permanent than those on trees and shrubs. Frost loosens or pushes them out until they lie flat; then they become spattered with mud, and often, unnoticed, are raked up and thrown away with trash. Those of wood or celluloid tend to rot off at the base. Sometimes a label is moved to another plant in weeding, or kicked away by dogs or skunks. In these ways important varieties of herbaceous plants may be lost, or late-starting perennials like Platycodon may be dug out and destroyed in early spring cultivation. For economy some gardeners continue to use wood labels in border and rock garden, renewing them when the name wears off. In practice, however, the name often wears off completely before the new label is written. To overcome these objections, a number of permanent devices have been offered. Small zinc labels attached to metal pins last well. Paper labels enclosed in slender bottles or test tubes or covered with screwed-on glass lenses that magnify the writing, will often outlast the plants they name ; but they should be kept out of sight if possible. One of the most indestructible and least noticeable is a narrow, thick ribbon of lead, on which names can be stamped by machine or scratched easily with an awl, then rubbed with white paint which fills the depressions. The lead can be cut to any dimensions, bent or coiled in any form, hooked over a stem, or stuck in the ground by one end or both; and even after burying in the ground, it will always be readable.

LABIATAE (lay-bi-ay'-tee). Botanical name of the Mint Family, a widely distributed group of plants many of which are grown for their flavor or odor, for ornament, or as medicine. Most of the N. American kinds are garden subjects and sweet herbs. Mints have characteristically four-sided stems and are rich in a fragrant, volatile oil. Their flowers are grouped in flat heads or crowded into spikes, the petals of individual flowers fusing to form the characteristic irregular two lips. Among the genera cultivated are Rosmarinus, (rosemary), Salvia, Lavandula, Thymus, Monarda (bergamot), Nepeta, Physostegia, Mentha (mint), Leonotis, Marrubium, Scutellaria, Dracocephalum, Origanum, Hyssopus, Teucrium.

LABLAB (lab'.-lab). Another name for the Hyacinth-bean (*Dolichos lablab*), a purple-flowered tender vine grown as an annual.

LABRADOR-TEA. Common name for *Ledum groenlandicum,* a dwarf evergreen shrub with small white flowers in spring.

LABURNOCYTISUS (lah - bur - noh - sit'-i-sus). A compound generic name designating a hybrid between *Laburnum anagyroides* and *Cytisus purpureus.* One form, *L. adami,* formerly known as *Laburnum adami,* is interesting because it is a graft hybrid. Flower spikes are often produced bearing flowers of three different colors, the yellow of Laburnum, the purple of Cytisus, and others a fusion of both.

LABURNUM (lah-bur'-num). Goldenchain. Small deciduous trees from S. Europe and Asia, belonging to the Pea Family. Where hardy they rank among the most beautiful of flowering trees, with their 3-part leaves and long drooping clusters of yellow flowers. They thrive in any well-drained soil, and can stand city conditions very well. Propagated by seeds, layers, and in the case of choice vars. by budding and grafting.

PRINCIPAL SPECIES

L. anagyroides (Common Laburnum). Grows to 30 ft., but is not quite hardy where winters are severe. The showy yellow flowers are borne in pendulous clusters to about 8 in. long. There are several garden forms, of which the following are the best known—*aureum,* with yellow leaves; *bullatum,* with curled leaves; *pendulum,* with drooping branches; *quercifolium,* with lobed leaves; *autumnale,* which flowers a second time in late summer.

alpinum (Scotch Laburnum) is native in S. Europe and not Scotland as the common name might imply. It is the hardiest species and will stand as far N. as Mass. In habit it is of stiffer and more upright growth, with longer flower clusters that open about two weeks later.

vossi is a hybrid between these two species.

LACE-BARK. Common name for *Gaya lyalli* (formerly known as *Plagianthus lyalli*), a small deciduous tree of New Zealand, belonging to the Mallow Family. Hardy in the warmest parts of this country, it has medium-sized ovate leaves, and clusters of thin paper-like flowers, white with yellow stamens, about an inch across. Propagated by cuttings and layers.

LACE BUGS. These sucking insects are true bugs (which see) with broad, lacy wings in the adult stage. By robbing plants of their sap they cause a stippled, grayish or yellowish appearance on the upper surfaces of leaves and brownish discolorations on the under surfaces (due to feeding punctures, cast skins and excrement). Lace bugs are responsible for yellowed, sick-looking rhododendrons and azaleas, and unthrifty foliage on hawthorns and sycamores. Thorough spraying of the under surfaces of leaves with nicotine-sulphate and soap is the best means of control. See also RHODODENDRON; HAWTHORN.

LACE FERN. Common name for *Cheilanthes gracillima,* a densely tufted little Calif. fern, found in dry places. Needs porous soil, rock chips, and an open location, but moisture at the roots. The name

is also given to a handsome shield fern of S. Florida, *Dryopteris setigera.*

LACE- or **LATTICE-LEAF.** Common name for *Aponogeton fenestralis,* a greenhouse aquatic herb with submerged veiny leaves.

LACE-WINGED FLIES. Insects of the order Neuroptera that feed on other insects and are therefore the gardener's friends. The adults are delicate, weak-bodied, gauzy winged insects; the spindle shaped larvae have long jaws with which they grasp and puncture bodies of aphids, etc. They have the disgusting habit of piling up their own excrement and cast skins on their backs as a concealing or protective covering. See INSECTS, BENEFICIAL.

THE GAY LACHENALIA

Cape-cowslips rank among the most colorful of South Africa's small bulbs. Flowers occur in combinations of red, yellow, purple and green.

LACHENALIA (lak-e-nay'-li-ah). A genus of small S. African bulbous plants of the Lily Family closely related to the squills, in England called Leopard-lily, but in the U. S. Cape-cowslip, which see.

LACTUCA (lak-teu'-kah). A genus of mostly tall annual and perennial herbs of the N. hemisphere, belonging to the Composite Family. The species are generally weedy and not considered garden subjects in this country, but one (*L. sativa*) is the important salad plant, Lettuce, which see.

LADDER FERN. A common name for various types of Nephrolepis, which see.

LADIES GARTERS. A popular name for *Phalaris arundinacea,* var. *picta,* a striped ornamental perennial also called Ribbon Grass.

LADIES-TOBACCO. A common name for Antennaria, a large genus of small perennials sometimes grown for their rosettes of whitish leaves or their dry white flower-heads.

LADIES TRESSES. Common name for native, terrestrial orchids of the genus Spiranthes. They have small white flowers spirally arranged in spikes from 10 in. to 2 ft. high, and small leaves toward the base. Ladies tresses may be colonized in the wild garden in shady or semi-open grassy spots in acid soil. Two of the best known species are *S. cernua* (Nodding Ladies Tresses) with white flowers with strongly downward curving lips and *S. gracilis* with green-streaked, white flowers in several ranks of clusters on a tall slender stalk. See also ORCHIDS.

LADY BEETLES. Also called Ladybugs and Ladybird Beetles. Small hemispherical beetles with bright red, brown or tan bodies and, usually, conspicuous black spots, varying in number according to the species. This common beneficial insect is probably familiar to everyone in the beetle stage, both outdoors and in the house, where it is often seen over winter. The small larvae are carrot-shaped with tapering bodies, distinct body regions, long legs and warty or spiny backs. They may be colored with patches of blue, orange or black. Both larvae and adults are active and the number of scales or aphids they can devour in a single day is amazing. The orange industry in California was saved by the importation of the Australian lady beetle, and it is possible to buy quantities of commercially raised beetles of one species to be placed in greenhouses or in orchards in warm sections for the control of mealy bugs. See INSECTS, BENEFICIAL.

LADYBELL. Popular name for the genus Adenophora, perennial herbs grown for their campanula-like flowers.

LADY FERN (*Athyrium asplenoides*). A species of robust American ferns with finely cut fronds, succeeding in ordinary garden soil, but especially enjoying woods soil and a little lime. From 2 to 4 ft. tall, it often spreads rapidly. (See illustration, Plate 18.)

LADY-OF-THE-NIGHT. Common name for *Brunfelsia americand,* a greenhouse shrub with showy fragrant white flowers.

LADY - SLIPPER. (See illustrations, Plate 36.) This common name is given to plants of three genera of the Orchid Family because of a fancied resemblance of the inflated lip of the flower to a slipper. They are also sometimes called Venus-slipper. The genera so-called are Paphiopedilum, tropical epiphytic or terrestrial orchids from S. America; Cordula, stemless tropical epiphytic or terrestrial orchids from Asia and Malaya; and Cypripedium, which comprises hardy terrestrial orchids, growing in the N. hemisphere. Many of the greenhouse species are best known and usually listed as Cypripedium. See CORDULA; CYPRIPEDIUM and PAPHIOPEDILUM. See also ORCHIDS, for culture.

LADYS MANTLE. Common name for Alchemilla, a genus of low-growing evergreen perennials of the Rose Family, generally hardy, with matlike foliage and greenish or yellowish flowers. They are desirable for rock gardens or low borders, blooming in midsummer and of easy culture. Sow seed, where it is to grow, in autumn or spring, in well-drained soil with partial shade. Roots may be divided in November or early April. The species chiefly cultivated is *A. vulgaris,* to 1½ ft. tall, with gray woody foliage. Others of interest are *A. alpina,* 9 in., with silvery foliage and green flowers; and *A. arvensis* to 6 in. and *A. pratensis* much taller; the two last mentioned are naturalized in N. America and are annuals.

LADYS SMOCK. Common name for the species of Bitter-cress known as *Cardamine pratensis.* See CARDAMINE.

LADYS THUMB. Common name for *Polygonum persicaria,* an annual with 2-in. spikes of pink or purplish flowers.

LADY WASHINGTON GERANIUM. The name given to horticultural varieties of so-called "Show Pelargoniums" derived from *Pelargonium domesticum.* An old-fashioned window plant lately regaining favor.

LAELIA (lee'-li-ah). A genus of tropical epiphytic orchids with lovely flowers in rose, violet-rose, orange-red, golden-yellow, brownish, or white, with similar petals and sepals, a 3-lobed lip, and, often, a yellow throat. The handsome blossoms, almost equal in beauty to those of the Cattleya (which see), are borne throughout the winter, singly, or in loose racemes held high above the fleshy evergreen leaves. *L. anceps* from Mexico, with racemes 1½ ft. high of violet-rose flowers with purple-veined yellow throats, grows best in shallow orchid pans or baskets suspended from the rafters of the greenhouse. Many fine hybrids have been produced by crossing the Laelias with the general Cattleya and Brassavola; these hybrid forms are known as Laeliocattleyas and Brassocattlaelias. For culture see ORCHIDS.

LAGENARIA (laj-ee-nay′-ri-ah). From the Latin, *lagen,* a bottle. This name is given to a tender annual vine of the Gourd Family (Cucurbitaceae) with roundish leaves and slightly musk-scented white flowers which are followed by hard-shelled fruits which are decorative, curious and sometimes useful as utensils. It makes an excellent temporary screen, growing rampantly to 40 ft. Plant seeds 1 in. deep, four in. apart, in rich light soil in full sunshine. Water freely in dry weather and give liquid manure occasionally. Gather the gourds when yellow and hang indoors to dry. *L. leucantha,* the White-flowered Gourd, yields fruit in a great variety of shapes and sizes. See also GOURD.

LAGERSTROEMIA (lah-ger-stree′-mi-ah). A genus of woody plants blooming freely in greenhouses and known as Crape-myrtle, which see.

LAGURUS (lah-geu′-rus) *ovatus.* An annual grass of the Mediterranean region, now naturalized in Calif. and grown as a garden ornamental, sometimes indoors in pots and also for use in dry winter bouquets. Its common names are Hares-tail Grass (which see) and Rabbit-tail Grass. See also ORNAMENTAL GRASSES.

LALLEMANTIA (lal-e-mahn′-shi-ah). Annual or biennial plants of the Mint Family from Asia Minor and Persia averaging 1½ ft. high, with small, bluish two-lipped flowers set in whorls on the leafy stems. These are for a sunny border and supply bloom through July and August. Sow seed outdoors in April, ½ in. deep, in well-drained soil, thinning out later.

LAMARCKIA (lah-mar′-ki-ah) *aurea.* A tufted annual grass, grown for ornamental purposes, naturalized in Calif., though native in S. Europe; and commonly known as Golden-top, which see.

LAMBKILL. Common name for *Kalmia angustifolia,* a small evergreen shrub of E. N. America with purplish rose flowers; also called Sheep-laurel and Wicky.

LAMBS EARS. Common name for *Stachys lanata,* a purple-flowered hardy perennial with thick woolly leaves. It is largely used for bedding.

LAMBS-LETTUCE. A winter annual used as greens, generally under the name of Corn-salad, which see.

LAMBS QUARTERS. A common name for *Chenopodium album,* an annual weed used for greens.

LAMIUM (lay′-mi-um). Generic name for a group of border and rock-garden annual and perennial herbs, commonly known as Dead-nettle, which see.

LAMPRANTHUS (lam-pran′-thus). Succulent branching plants of the Aizoaceae or Carpetweed Family, resembling Mesembryanthemum (which see) in which genus they were formerly placed. Averaging 2 ft. high, with narrow, fleshy leaves and large, showy, brilliantly colored flowers, they are effective in sunny rockeries and dry borders. The seed is sown in spring in light, well-drained soil and the seedlings are thinned later to 6 in. Many varieties in golden yellow, red, violet or purple are offered by seedsmen.

LAMPWICK-PLANT. Common name for *Phlomis lychnitis,* a low woolly yellow-flowered shrub for the wild garden.

LANCEOLATE. Shaped like a spearhead; applied particularly to leaves several times longer than broad, narrowed toward each end, and broadest one-third of the distance from the base, like those of the pussy willow.

LAND PLASTER. A name given to calcium sulphate or gypsum (which see), a gray, cement-like powder sometimes used for modifying soil conditions, but not a fertilizer. See also AMENDMENT, SOIL.

LANDSCAPE ARCHITECTS, AMERICAN SOCIETY OF. A national organization whose membership, made up of fellows and junior fellows (both men and women) comprises experienced graduates from the advanced professional courses in the subject given at some of the country's institutions of higher education. Its objectives are: the maintaining of high professional and ethical standards; the maintaining of mutually beneficial relations with organizations of nurserymen and other horticulturists concerned with the use of plants in the landscape; and the promotion of greater public appreciation of the best in garden design and other subjects that make up landscape architecture, which see.

The Society has Chapters in different parts of the country. Its secretary's office is at 9 Park Street, Boston, Mass.

LANDSCAPE ARCHITECTURE and LANDSCAPE GARDENING. These two terms are used interchangeably and refer to the same thing. Yet each conveys a definite meaning which ought perhaps to be better understood than it is. Landscape architecture specifically designates that profession for which a student prepares himself by completing a course of academic training and receiving a degree from a college entitled to bestow it. Landscape gardening alludes more to the practice of professional garden-making carried on by those who have not had such college training, but who have fitted themselves for the work by special studies (along horticultural lines principally, and as much architecture and architectural drawing, composition and engineering as possible) and through practical experience.

Both are concerned with building gardens, hence each is architecture in the broad sense. Some of the greatest of our artists in garden building were never academically trained, because, in their day, there was no opportunity for academic training. Therefore it is sometimes questioned whether the college graduate alone is entitled to call his profession Landscape Architecture even though it is distinguished by being the subject of a collegiate degree.

LANDSCAPING. This covers the very broad field of outdoor composition or design. It embraces garden design but also the development of estates, public parks, cemeteries, boulevards, and public or private grounds of every kind—places in which gardens, in the more limited sense, have no part whatsoever. Thus it is possible to landscape a section of the earth without designing a garden thereon; while it is also possible (though not always advisable) to design or lay out a garden without giving consideration to the general landscape.

LANDSCAPING VS. GARDEN DESIGN

The distinction between landscaping and garden design (which see) is not too fine to be easily understood, for though no proper consideration of a garden site can wholly disregard the elements that make up the general landscape environment, garden design leaves to landscaping the broader field and concerns itself with certain of the particulars. In other words, landscaping deals with those elements which are outside the garden proper, but relate to it and to its surroundings. It has to do with large-scale matters and largely with composition in elevation rather than in ground plan, as distinguished from garden design, which must concern itself primarily with the ground plan or arrangement of beds, borders, paths and other areas.

In garden design it is first decided what is desired or needed; then the desired or needed things are given their best positions with respect to their own character and with relation to each other; and finally the whole is considered with regard to shaping it into a series of pictures—or what the landscape architect would term "elevations."

Landscaping proceeds the other way around. The elevation or "picture" is first conceived in the artist's mental view of the area under treatment—that is, what it will eventually offer as a picture. With this decided upon (and sometimes worked out in a hypothetical sketch or series of sketches), the plan is taken up, and developed wholly to carry out this picture-concept. Every element in the plan is introduced as a "how" and "where" of ground detail that shall support and carry out the preconceived elevation.

Thus the landscaping of an entire area (or section, to use the professional term) establishes the background for all the gardens that lie within it, even though every such garden is separate and apart from every other. Many and differing features are matters of landscaping and landscape service, such as: Highways of agreeable curve and yet continual advance movement so as to make the approach to a community a pleasing experience; the conservation of natural advantages and beauties and their emphasis by means of the cutting of vistas and other treatments; the planting on a broad scale of characteristic local plant material where such planting is needed, and all such general attention to the details of the country as make for its highest beauty development.

LANDSCAPING APPLIED

Yet landscaping is by no means limited to such public and semi-public service only. It is equally represented in the home owner's consideration of his own domain,

Plate 31.　　　　MAKE THE LANDSCAPE PART OF THE GARDEN

Top: Nearby trees form a background for the planting in the border which repeats and emphasizes their dominant lines.　Bottom: The lawn sweeps smoothly to the well-placed shrubs which lead the eyes to the stately ascending trunks of the overshadowing trees.　Insert right: Even though far beyond the limits of the garden itself, distant trees and hills should form an integral part of the garden picture.

and of the relation of this to all that adjoins it—and even to all that may be viewed from it. Even the tiniest home garden, given the right location, may include within its small plans the most splendid landscape; as where a panorama of mountains or sea or sweeping countryside visible from the garden's site is "planned in" to be a feature of the garden's design. (This, of course, it may be or it may prove not to be, depending upon the skill of the designer.) In such a situation the garden should be developed in relation to the panorama, never independently of it. Yet the garden design of itself must not be neglected. Rather it is "tuned in," as it were, to the greater element and influenced by it—and probably, if successfully treated, it is simplified and ennobled by it.

This principle applies also to great estates where broad and park-like lawn spaces often carry the vision on, beyond the estate boundaries, to greater spaces and wider perspectives, sometimes leading away to the very horizon. And at the other extreme it applies to the least of gardens. Without the keen sense of landscape which training is supposed to develop in the professional (but which is the natural endowment of many gardeners who are not professional at all), fine opportunities are often let slip, through failure to give this broad consideration to landscaping. Such failure is usually due, in all probability, to over-concentration on garden design.

If a formula were possible (which it is not) the rule would probably be to work from landscaping down to garden design— from the general to the particular. In a garden the landscape may be defined as "all that is within the range of vision regardless of whether it is within or without the boundaries of a particular property." The average garden is not large enough to permit its owner to exercise control over much that is thus a part of the landscape. In consequence he is not able literally to begin with the landscaping, except as he considers its effect, just as it is, upon his final garden pictures. In giving it this consideration he does, in a sense, begin at the right place; but he must also, at the same time, consider his garden design as viewed from his house, working outward from this in order to insure the continuity between house and garden which a well-organized design demands.

LANDSCAPING AND THE SMALL GARDENER

The practical approach for the small home gardener to any problem involving the making, remaking or enlarging of his garden is, therefore, a double one—a uniting of the landscaping problems with the individual garden problems which his particular house and grounds present. In other words, he must work down from landscaping, and up from garden design; and do this so well that the two meet and join or mingle without revealing that they are two. He must work "from out towards in" as well as "from in towards out" until the two become as one.

There is a growing appreciation of this dual demand in the garden-consciousness of the country generally. Hence more and more gardens are to be seen which reveal a regard for their landscape relations. When the time comes that these relations are everywhere considered as carefully as is the garden itself, the garden millenium will be at hand. For then every garden will be a picture or a series of pictures in itself, as well as a perfect element in the general landscape. (See illustration, Plate 31.)

ELEMENTS OF THE LANDSCAPE

In the study of the landscape everywhere, whether in relation to a garden or not, three things are to be specially observed. These are first, the distribution of the mass; second, the light and dark (or light and shade); third, the skyline. The *mass* is represented by the principle elements that compose the landscape—woods, meadows, water, hills or valleys, and undergrowth, as the case may be. Observing them it will be discovered that here one is dominant, there another; and that there is a proportion or ratio between them. Also that the lines defining the limits of each conform to a certain direction with reference to the line of vision—they may be perpendicular (parallel) to it, or transverse (across it), or fairly uniformly at any particular angle with it. These two things —proportion and direction—are the determinants of the effect of mass distribution. Incidentally, direction, in this sense, should always be adopted in developing a design, and never ignored or (worse still) opposed. Thus is the design developed in relation to the broad panorama as already mentioned. If the landscape directions are transverse to the line of vision, transverse development of the garden is indicated. If it is parallel or perpendicular to the line of vision—leading away from the observer —the leading lines of the garden should also follow that general direction.

Light is, of course, so closely related to shadow and shade—that is, to darkness— that it can not be thought of apart from them. These two elements—light and shade—present, in another fashion, a proportion—and one that concerns them in two ways. One way is the *total* of each, or the area and expanse of each as compared with that of the other, on the picture-plane; the other way is the *degree* of each in comparison with that of the other —the degree of dark or shadow compared with the degree of light. The character of a landscape is largely due to these proportions in it.

The *skyline,* which is the line of meeting between sky and earth (or sky and any objects on the earth—such as trees, hills, buildings, sea horizon and so on), is always dominant whatever the proportions of mass and of light (and dark) may be. Hence this will determine largely the prevailing effect of the landscape, as good or bad.

It is not, of course, possible to specify in advance the elements of a good landscape, any more than it is possible to say what the faults of a poor one may be. A study of fine landscapes or paintings of landscapes (and even of fine paintings not altogether landscape but classic in their qualities of line, form and proportion) will develop appreciation and, eventually, understanding of landscape composition. Then individual discrimination will assert itself with growing certainty until recognition of good and of bad becomes instinctive and, along with that recognition, more or less ability to design or create effects that are good—and beautiful.

LANTANA (lan-tah'-nah). Shrubby plants, resembling Verbena (to which they are related), natives chiefly of tropical America and N. to the Gulf States, and desirable both as greenhouse and garden plants.

L. camara, the principal species, originally tall and scraggly, has been developed into a number of low, compact, full-flowered varieties whose flowers in flattish clusters vary or change from brilliant yellow through orange to red. Widely grown as a greenhouse subject, being easily raised from either seeds or cuttings, it is excel-lent as a summer bedding plant, blooming continuously until nipped by the frost in autumn. Plants desired for indoor bloom in late spring may then be pruned back severely, potted in fresh soil, and kept in a cool greenhouse over winter. If new stock is wanted, prune the outdoor plants and pot them up in September and take cuttings from the new growth indoors. Give the young plants a fairly high temperature during their early growth.

L. sellowiana (Weeping or Trailing Lantana), a low sprawling plant with rosy-lilac flowers, makes an effective ground-cover in the S. or, when set out when continued warm weather is assured, also in N. States. Other good species are *L. lilacina, involucrata,* and *aculeata,* the last similar to *camara.*

ENEMIES. The greenhouse orthezia, sometimes called lantana bug, is a curious sucking insect resembling the mealy bug. Both are common on this plant, congregating on the leaves, along the veins and in the axils. The standard control for both these pests is a spray of nicotine and soap, but kerosene emulsion is known to be more effective against some mealy bugs.

LAPAGERIA (lap-ah-jee'-ri-ah) *rosea.* Chile-bells (which see), Chilean-bellflower. A choice, half-hardy, evergreen liliaceous vine with rosy or crimson flowers.

LAPEIROUSIA (lap-ay-roo'-zhi-ah). A genus of African bulbous plants having freesia-like red or blue flowers. They can be grown in the open N. if planted in light soil and given winter protection; are hardy S. of Washington, D. C. They are also frequently grown under glass for winter flowers. As the bulbs increase with great rapidity, they should be divided frequently. The two species grown are: *L. cruenta,* with bright scarlet flowers in a one-sided spike, 1 ft. high; and *L. juncea,* with rosy flowers growing on a 2-ft. stalk.

LAPPULA (lap'-eu-lah). Annual, perennial and biennial plants of the Borage Family, rough, rather weedy and ineffective. They are for rock gardens or edgings and will self-sow in ordinary soil. Small blue or whitish flowers on low spikes are succeeded by tiny burs. Of the two score species, some native to N. America, the most satisfactory are *L. consanguinea,* annual, with small blue flowers; and *L. floribunda,* perennial, with larger flowers.

LARCH. Common name for Larix, a genus of ornamental and timber trees which, belonging to the Pine Family and bearing cones, shed their leaves. They are thus deciduous conifers. In landscaping larches are planted for their stately form and soft texture, and for the pleasing delicate effect of the new growth early in the spring. Among the hardiest of all trees, they do well in almost any soil or location, preferring moderate moisture. Growth is very rapid, especially in young seedlings. The European Larch, though less often planted for ornament than the Japanese, is most grown for timber since its wood is very durable. The Tamarack of northern swamps is sometimes seen on lawns.

Larches usually take a Christmas-tree shape with long, straight branches, and short needles tufted like a pine. Species are grown from seeds sown in fall or spring in shaded beds and treated like spruce or pine. The seedlings, which should be given plenty of room to develop, are easily transplanted after the leaves have fallen. Varieties may be grafted on seedlings of European Larch either outdoors or under glass.

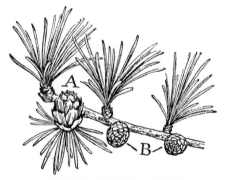

CONES OF THE LARCH

As on all conifers, they are of two kinds: the pistillate (A) that bear the seeds, and the staminate (B), seldom noticed, but also essential as producers of the pollen.

ENEMIES. The larch canker disease, serious in Europe, now exists in New England. The cankers (open wounds surrounded by rough and enlarged callus rolls) occur on the trunk, often near the base, and resinous material oozes from the tree. Specimens growing under adverse conditions are most likely to be attacked, the fungus gaining entrance through branch stubs and other wounds; healthy, vigorously growing trees cannot be directly infected. Prevent by careful pruning, wound protection (see TREE SURGERY), proper feeding and care.

Several rust fungi attack larch needles. (See RUSTS; also PINE.) One has willow as the alternate host; another is associated with poplar, while a third requires birch for the completion of its life cycle.

Needle-cast (see EVERGREENS) is common on larch, and the mistletoe that causes witches' broom of spruce (see SPRUCE) also attacks it.

The larch case-bearer and the woolly larch aphid are the principal insect enemies. The former, which may almost completely ruin early spring foliage, hibernates as a larva in a silk-lined case attached to the branches and main trunks. As new needles are put out the larvae drill and mine into them, eating as far as they can without leaving their cases. Filmy, gray moths are seen in June and July and in autumn a new brood of larvae is hatched. *Control:* Spray in the spring, while the larvae are feeding, with arsenate of lead plus nicotine. Lime-sulphur (1 to 10) applied as a dormant spray also helps.

Trees infested with the woolly aphis look as if they had been dusted with flour or small particles of woolly matter. Young hatch from eggs at the base of the leaves in May. Spraying with nicotine-soap solution at that time gives control.

The green, black-headed larva of the larch sawfly defoliates extensive areas of larch forests and occasionally injuries ornamental trees. (See SAWFLIES). Spray with arsenate of lead in June. The bagworm (which see) also attacks larch.

PRINCIPAL SPECIES

L. decidua (European Larch), 100 ft., strong-growing ornamental and valued for its lumber. Its var. *pendula* (Weeping Larch) has much drooped branchlets.

eurolepis (Dunkeld Larch). An attractive hybrid of the European and Japanese species.

gmelini (Dahurian Larch). To 70 ft., irregular and not ornamental.

kaempferi (Japanese Larch). To 90 ft. with striped bark and leaves bright yellow in fall. The most ornamental species.

laricina (American Larch, Tamarack, Hackmatack). A stiff swamp tree growing to 60 ft. and doing well also on drier ground.

occidentalis (Western Larch). To 180 ft. with bark cinnamon red.

Many names besides those listed above will be found in catalogs, as some species have been given a number of scientific names.

Golden-larch is *Pseudolarix amabilis.*

LARKSPUR. The name commonly applied to the annual species of Delphinium (which see), also to several native and Eurasian perennial species. While there is no particular structural distinction, it has of late become customary among gardeners to restrict the name Delphinium to the highly bred perennial species, hybrids and varieties in which the flower spikes have developed remarkable size, beauty and variability; the larkspurs are smaller, of looser form and less imposing.

Blue predominates in the annual larkspurs, but the colors range from white through pink and blue to deep purple; the wand-like spikes or loose racemes bear many flowers above the feathery, soft green foliage. Two of the native perennials, the Scarlet and Red Larkspurs (*D. cardinale* and *D. nudicaule*) bear bright red flowers loosely arranged in spike-like form; the leaves of the latter are more blunt. Coast Larkspur (*D. californicum*) grows man-high and bears hairy white, sometimes purplish, flowers in long spikes. Royal larkspur (*D. variegatum*), 1½ ft. tall, bears purple flowers. All are natives of Calif.

Garland Larkspur (*D. cheilanthum*) from Siberia is the supposed parent of many of the perennial garden types. Rocket Larkspur (*D. ajacis*) is the most popular garden annual, growing from 1 to 4 ft. high and bearing all summer a fine profusion of flowers of many blending tones. Bouquet Larkspur (*D. grandiflorum*) is a perennial that often blooms the first year with large blue or white flowers on plants about 3 ft. tall. Bee or Candle Larkspur (*D. elatum*) is the tall perennial species which has been so extensively bred, hybridized and improved and whose gigantic spikes of large, often double, flowers are known generally as Delphinium.

The annual larkspurs are easily raised from seed. This is sown, in the N. either indoors in early spring or in the open, in ordinary soil, in May; and, in the S., in fall. A disease peculiar to them is Diaporthe blight, characterized by premature withering of basal leaves at the approach of flowering and patches of dead tissue on stems at point of leaf attachment. Remove infected plants to save neighboring healthy ones; plant seed obtained from disease-free sources. and change the planting site

the year after an attack. Red aphids are exceedingly common on annual larkspur and require frequent spraying with a contact insecticide.

For culture of the perennial species and control of diseases, see DELPHINIUM.

LARVA (*plural larvae*). An insect in the first stage of its growth or metamorphosis after leaving the egg. It is the growing stage of an insect with complete metamorphosis whereas a *nymph* is the corresponding stage of an insect with gradual metamorphosis. (See INSECT). A larva is usually worm-like and strikingly different from the adult form, from which it is separated by a pupal, or resting, stage. The larvae of moths and butterflies are usually called caterpillars; those of beetles, grubs; and those of flies, maggots. Larvae grow in size by undergoing a series of molts; each successive stage is called an *instar*.

LASTHENIA (las-thee′-ni-ah). Hardy annual composites averaging 1 ft. high, bearing numerous inch-wide heads of yellow flowers in early summer. Sometimes grown in warm sheltered rockeries or low borders. Sow seed ⅛ in. deep where it is to grow, in light well-drained soil; in April for summer flowering, in October for spring bloom. The species, numbering about six, are native to California, Oregon and Chile.

LATANIA (lah-tay′-ni-ah). A genus of Fan Palms from the Mascarene Islands in the Indian Ocean. None of them become large trees, but many of them are remarkable for the brilliantly colored veins and mid-ribs of the leaves; hence and because they can be successfully grown in S. Fla. in heavy, fertile, but well-drained soil, with some lime in it, they are popular garden subjects there. They should be shaded when young and well watered. In the N. where they are extensively grown in a warm greenhouse in a light, well-drained soil, they require shading throughout the year, and an abundance of water. They are attractive house palms where conditions are satisfactory.

L. verschaffelti, a very slow growing sort, has 5 ft. leaves, with orange stalks; *L. loddigesi,* more rapid in growth, has leaves with bluish blades, sometimes tinged reddish in young plants; *L. commersoni,* one of the most striking species, has crimson leaf-stalks and leaf-ribs. The last named is sometimes listed in catalogs as

Latania borbonica, under which name are offered seeds that are generally of an entirely different plant, *Livistona chinensis.*

LATERAL. At the side, or on the side, of a part or organ, as a *lateral* arrangement of leaves, in contrast to a *terminal* position, which means at the end.

LATH or **SLAT HOUSE.** A more or less permanent structure of timber framework with top, sides, ends or all three covered with lath so spaced as to give broken shade. See Lath Shade, below. It is a valuable aid in both home gardening and commercial plant growing in California, Florida, and other sections where the intensity of the sunlight is a major problem. In such places a lath house often corresponds in usefulness to the greenhouse of colder localities, though it may also serve to supplement a small greenhouse in an especially well equipped garden layout. It also provides a pleasant place in which to do potting, grafting, flower arrangement, and other tasks that do not require indoor conditions and that cannot comfortably be performed out in the sunlight. The design and construction of lath houses are not standardized but usually worked out to suit the convenience of the user, the requirements of the location, or the demands of a crop, such as palms, camellias, begonias, Asparagus plumosus, etc., all of which are commonly grown under lath houses.

LATH SHADE. A simple and inexpensive method of protecting soil and plants from direct sunlight. Usually it is made by nailing plaster lath to supporting light boards or furring strips of convenient lengths—often 6 ft. to correspond with that of the regulation hotbed. The laths may be laid crosswise only, or in two directions at right angles. If spaced the width of a lath apart, the former arrangement casts strips, and the latter checks of shade, which sweep across the area covered as the sun moves. Such shades are sometimes fastened to permanent frames equipped with short legs, or with supports tall enough to stand beneath. The former are used mostly for protecting little plants, seedlings or cuttings; the latter, for sheltering potted plants or broad leaved evergreens from the summer sun outdoors. See SHADE.

LATHYRUS (lath'-i-rus). A leguminous genus of more than 200 species occurring throughout the world. The vines or erect plants, including both annuals and perennials, with tendrils and showy flowers ranging from white to shades of red, yellow and purple, are mostly cultivated for ornament, although a few species bear edible seeds. The perennials are propagated by seeds or cuttings in ordinary soil and will stand partial shade. The annuals require a deep moist soil and full sunlight. Ample support should be provided and the

L. BLAIR

THE LATH HOUSE IS A USEFUL WARM CLIMATE GARDEN FEATURE
Where plants need protection from intense sunlight rather than from cold. It can be simple and wholly functional, or more elaborate and fixed up as an outdoor garden room.

flowers should be kept picked to lengthen the blooming season. The better known species are the following:

L. odoratus is the familiar Sweet Pea (which see), an annual climber valued for its color and fragrance, now available in many shades, flower-forms and heights. It needs plenty of room and air and generous feeding.

latifolius is Perennial- or Everlasting-pea, not fragrant but excellent for general garden use as it can be trained on pillars, trellises or wires to fill in any gaps. Some of its vars. are *albus* with white flowers, *rosea* a clear pink, and *splendens* (dark red and purple).

sativus, the Grass-pea, has edible seeds.

maritima, the Beach-pea, is a widely distributed perennial species with attractive rosy-purple flowers, often used to bind sandy soils in seashore gardens.

LAURACEAE (lau-ray'-see-ee). The Laurel Family, a widely scattered group of aromatic trees and shrubs principally native to warm climates. Leaves are usually leathery and evergreen; flowers are petalless, with 6 sepals inserted below the ovary. A few are grown for ornament and some for the edible fruit and commercial spices, as avocado, nutmeg, cinnamon and camphor. Genera of horticultural interest treated here are Laurus (laurel), Persea (avocado), Sassafras, Umbellularia, Benzoin, Cinnamomum.

LAUREL. Used alone, this word refers to the genus Laurus (which see). However, it is also used in connection with plants of other genera to denote some particular kind of Laurel. Thus Alexandrian-laurel is *Danaë racemosa;* California-laurel, *Umbellularia californica;* Cherry-laurel, *Prunus laurocerasus* and *P. caroliniana;* Portugal-laurel, *Prunus lusitanica;* Mountain-laurel, *Kalmia latifolia* (see illustration, Plate 43); Sheep-laurel, *Kalmia angustifolia;* ground-laurel, *Epigaea repens* (better known as Trailing Arbutus), and Spurge-laurel, *Daphne laureola.*

LAURESTINUS (lau-res-ty'-nus) or LAURUSTINUS. Common name for *Viburnum tinus,* a tall evergreen shrub from the Mediterranean, with white or pinkish flowers and black fruit.

LAURUS (lau'-rus). Laurel; Sweetbay. A genus made up of two species of evergreen trees, of which only one, *L. nobilis,* appears to be in cultivation. This is native in S. Europe and is the laurel of

classical times. It grows to 50 ft. or more, and has rather large, lanceolate, leathery and aromatic leaves, greenish-yellow flowers and black berries. It can stand several degrees of frost, and thrives best in good loamy soil with leafmold. In mild regions it is a good hedge plant, and can stand hard pruning. It is the best evergreen for use on steps and terraces as a tub plant and can be trimmed into various shapes, the usual form being that of a round-headed, small standard tree.

LAVATERA (lav-ah-tee'-rah). A genus of usually tall, branching fast-growing herbaceous annuals and several shrubby perennials. The annual type is colorful with mallow-like flowers and is easily grown in any average garden. The perennial type is especially suited to W. Coast conditions. Raised from seed without special attention, even the perennials will bloom within a year. But they should never be transplanted.

L. trimestris, the principal annual species (often called *L. splendens* in catalogs), grows from 2 to 6 ft. high and bears large rose-red mallow-like blossoms in the axils of maple-shaped leaves. *L. mauritanica* is a smaller annual with purple flowers.

The principal shrubby species is *L. assurgentiflora,* a dense, round-headed plant 6 or more ft. tall, with large bright red flowers. It will stand dry sandy soil, wind and salty air.

L. arborea is a shrubby biennial 6 to 10 ft. tall with dark-veined magenta flowers.

Some splendid new hybrids of annuals have recently been made available from England.

LAVENDER. Common name for a genus (Lavandula) of fragrant herbs or shrubs of which a Mediterranean subshrub species (*L. spica,* formerly *officinalis* or *vera*) is grown for ornament in the garden and for its sweet scent when dried. The dried flowers are used to fill sachets and to perfume clothing or linens. Commercially they, and the green parts, are used for making "oil of spike," aromatic vinegar and lavender water. The name is also erroneously applied to *Chrysanthemum balsamita,* the "mint-geranium" or costmary. Sea-lavender or sea-pink is Limonium, which see.

True lavender, not being fully hardy, is little grown in northern gardens, where it must be protected over winter by mulching with straw. It is more popular, therefore, in the milder Pacific Coast and in the South. As seed produces variable plants, propagation is commonly by cuttings of selected plants. Taken of one-year-old "wood" in spring, these are set in a shady place, 4 in. apart, and kept cultivated for a year. Then they are transplanted not less than 2 ft. asunder in permanent quarters in dry, light, limy, friable soil and full sunlight. In such a location they thrive best, develop the maximum fragrance and are least likely to be injured in winter. In wet soils they grow but poorly; in rich ones, they become lush and sappy, and in both types they lack fragrance and easily succumb to frost.

LAVENDER-COTTON. Common name for *Santolina chamaecyparissus,* a stiff, broadly branching, fine-leaved subshrub growing 2 ft. tall with silvery-gray woolly foliage, remaining throughout the winter. The small globular yellow flower-heads are of less importance than the foliage. Native of the Mediterranean region, this old-fashioned plant, which is said to have been one of the first to be raised in American gardens, is easily cultivated in a sunny location. Propagation is by cuttings, taken either before frost or in the spring from plants which have been wintered in a cold-frame.

LAWN. With the increasing interest in gardening and the increased attention to landscaping the home grounds, the lawn is being recognized as the starting point or basis of garden design. No longer is it merely a checkerboard on which flower patterns and specimen trees are spotted. It is an integral part of the garden plan, an unbroken area on which the onlooker may gaze restfully, on which the shadows of clouds may form patterns of darker green, where one may rest, play and really enjoy the garden. To achieve this result the lawn should be bounded with trees, shrubs and perhaps occasional flower borders, but not broken up by them. Properly developed along these lines, not only does it give more pleasure to the eye and to the family, but also its upkeep is simpler, both mowing and the upkeep of neat edgings being facilitated. Furthermore, as the setting, frame, or approach to the dwelling, a good lawn appreciably increases the market value of any home place. (See illustrations, Plates 31 and 32.)

PREPARATION AND CONSTRUCTION

In planning and making a lawn keep in mind that it is a long-time proposition, and that a good foundation (including drainage, soil texture and food supply) is essential in providing a happy home for the grass plants. This calls for artificial drainage if necessary, thorough preparation of the soil, an ample supply of organic matter, grading which is artistically effective as well as practical from the point of view of upkeep, and the use of a good seed mixture and plenty of it.

Where the soil is already good and drainage conditions are satisfactory, preparation need not be deeper than 6 in. If the soil is heavy and inclined to stay wet, lines of 4 in. drain tile should be laid 20 ft. apart, and 18 to 24 in. below the surface. The fall of the tile should be 3 in. to 100 ft. and adequate provision for the discharge of the water must be provided. It is well to cover the tile with several inches of cinders or gravel, or at least to cover the joints with strips of building paper to prevent the soil from clogging up the passages. A slight grade (of 3 in. to 100 ft.) is also desirable in the surface leveling, when care should be taken that the top-soil is evenly distributed.

FITTING THE SOIL. If there is doubt as to the lime or food needs of the soil, samples should be sent (before any work is started) to the nearest State agricultural experiment station for analysis and recommendations. Heavy soils may be lightened by incorporating sand or some form of humus, such as peat moss; a bale to 300 sq. ft. worked into the upper 4 in. of soil is a good application. On the other hand, a light sandy soil is also improved and given more "body" by the addition of humus at the same rate.

If there is time, a green manure crop (which see) may be grown and plowed under to add to the supply of organic matter of the soil. Natural (animal or barnyard) manures are less desirable in making a lawn because they are likely to contain many weed seeds, which may continue to germinate over several years. Thoroughly rotted manure in which weed seeds have been killed by fermentation is safer, but its plant food value may be doubtful. A "balanced" commercial fertilizer of what is called a 5-10-5 formula (that is, containing 5% nitrogen, 10%

phosphates and 5% potash) worked into the upper 2 or 3 in. of soil at the rate of 25 to 40 lbs. to 1000 sq. ft., will supply available nourishment for the new grass as well as a supply of food later on. After the soil is thus prepared it is well to water it well to settle and firm it, then allow it to stand for two days before sowing.

If lime is needed to correct an acid condition, it should be applied on the surface and raked in at the rate of 35 lbs. of hydrated lime or 50 lbs. of ground limestone to 1000 sq. ft. If this can be done some months before the lawn is made, so much the better.

SEED MIXTURE. The seed mixture must be suited to the location and climate as well as to the soil and the sun or shade conditions. Reputable seed houses carry mixtures for special purposes, and it is generally more satisfactory for the amateur to use these than to mix his own. Good clean seed is never cheap, but the use of the highest quality mixture for a given purpose is a good investment.

Kentucky blue grass (*Poa pratensis*) is a standard sort for a neutral loam in a sunny situation. The fescues (Festuca) are particularly useful for dry slightly shady locations where the soil is neutral or mildly acid. For moisture, shade and a heavy soil rough-stalked meadow grass (*Poa trivialis*) is good. All these should be planted at the rate of 7 lbs. to 1000 sq. ft.

Redtop (*Agrostis palustris*) is useful as a "nurse crop," meaning that it comes up quickly and offers protection to the more permanent grasses in their early stages of development, besides crowding out the quick-starting weeds; it can be mixed with any of the above at the rate of 1 lb. to 7. The various bent grasses produce an exceptionally fine, velvety turf but require better conditions and more care than other lawn grasses in the way of more frequent mowing, watering and feeding. They like an acid soil and a moist condition and are much used for golf putting greens and on estates, being planted at the rate of 3 lbs. of seed to 1000 sq. ft. German, colonial, seaside and velvet bents are grown from seed; the improved Washington and Metropolitan strains are raised from stolons, or small cuttings of the underground rootstocks which, sown broadcast like seed, root at the joints. A good lawn may be established in a single season if bent grass stolons are used.

Many grass seed mixtures contain a small amount of white clover (*Trifolium repens*) which adds a variety of texture and helps keep weeds out during the first couple of years, after which it gives way to the more permanent grasses. If not in the mixture used, it may, if desired, be sown separately at the rate of ¼ lb. to 1000 sq. ft. (For grasses for southern lawns see the end of this article.)

SEED SOWING. The best time to sow lawn grass seed is in the fall; this practice cuts down the competition offered by weeds and takes advantage of the fall rains. Unless given a fine start a spring-sown lawn may burn out in summer. However, if necessary, spring seeding is entirely possible. Whatever the season, loosen the soil with a steel rake to the depth of 1 in. just before sowing. Then divide the seed into equal parts, half to be sown as the sower walks back and forth in one direction (north and south), and the rest as he walks back and forth at right angles over the same area. A calm day permits more even distribution and a cloudy one assures more moisture in the soil.

As soon as the seed is sown the surface can be raked with a fine tooth rake, or covered with not more than ½ in. of top-dressing (⅓ sand, ⅓ loam, and ⅓ compost or humus, well mixed). In either case the ground should be rolled (not too heavily) to firm the earth around the seeds and promote quick germination. On a small area the firming may be done with a plank or the back of a spade. If the sowing is done in late spring, a covering of brush, straw, burlap, or even newspapers may be laid over the area and moistened occasionally to prevent drying and baking; but this must be removed as soon as the young grass appears.

Watering should be done at first gently and with a fine sprinkler to prevent washing. It should be done often enough (depending on the weather) and generously enough to keep the soil and seeds from drying out. After the grass is well started, the waterings should be more thorough and less frequent. Deep watering encourages the development of deep roots upon which the future success of the lawn largely depends. Shallow watering or sprinkling tends to bring the roots near the surface where they are quickly affected by heat.

In mowing a new lawn set the blades to cut not less than 1½ in. to 3 in. above the ground. As the turf becomes thick it can be mown closer, although the longer it can be left consistent with good appearance, the better for the grass. If mowing is done frequently so that the clippings will not mat and smother the grass or turn brown and unsightly, they may be left on the ground to act as a mulch and add nutrition and humus.

An original method of lawn making, originated in England and introduced into the U. S. about 1938, involved the use of double sheets of thin paper glued together with grass seed distributed evenly between them. The idea was that the sheets would be spread over the prepared ground, covered with a thin layer of soil, and watered. This method, it was claimed, would remove the necessity for hand or machine sowing or sodding; insure even seeding and a uniform stand; prevent waste and lower costs; and promote a strong growth of grass since the paper would protect the seed against excess sunshine or rain and later decompose as the grass plants became established. There seems to be no evidence that this "pre-sown" method has received much attention or been widely adopted.

Care of the Lawn

An established lawn should be raked early in the spring to remove sticks, dead grass or leaves and other refuse. Then should follow an application of top-dressing composed of humus and the "5-10-5" fertilizer mentioned under Fitting the Soil at the rate of about 1 cu. yd. compost and 15 lbs. fertilizer to 1000 sq. ft. of lawn. This must be broadcast evenly to avoid causing a mottled, light and dark green, spotted appearance later on. Good soil should be used to level off any slight depressions and the lawn then rolled in two directions at right angles to one another. The roller should not be heavy enough to pack the earth so hard that it will bake during the first hot spell. For the first one or two mowings each spring the mower should be set high—about 2 in.

Summer maintenance consists mainly of: (1) thorough watering during dry spells; (2) mowing as often as necessary; and (3) preventing annual weeds from seeding. It is better to water thoroughly once a week than to sprinkle daily. If weeds are not allowed to seed they will, in the course of two or three seasons, be crowded out by vigorously growing grass. It is not advisable to fertilize during the hot summer months unless plenty of moisture is provided to make the food available. In such cases an application of half the spring quantity (say 20 lbs. per 1000 sq. ft.) may be broadcast evenly and at once watered in.

Early fall, however, is a particularly good time for lawn feeding. The current season's weed crop should have been eliminated by this time, so all the nourishment supplied will be available for the grass. Mowing should be done less frequently and only when absolutely necessary. Fallen leaves should not be allowed to remain on the lawn for they do not protect it as might be supposed, but, on the contrary, are inclined to suffocate it.

Under ordinary circumstances no winter mulch is needed, but if anything is used, granulated peat moss is best. Coarse manures are undesirable because of the weed seeds they contain, because they, too, have a tendency to smother the grass and because they make the lawn unsightly. Walking on lawns when the ground thaws during mild spells in winter should be avoided as it is likely to cut up the turf and leave holes and a rough surface.

When a lawn needs patching or renovating, do not merely sprinkle some seed on the bare spots, but rake them vigorously, or, better, loosen the soil with a spading fork, work in a little fertilizer and fresh compost, rake to a smooth, level surface, sow the seed thickly, and treat like a new lawn. Slight depressions in a good turf can be brought to grade by mulching them lightly and frequently with good compost. A hollow can thus be filled, without smothering the grass, in two or three seasons.

Special Problems

The Shaded Lawn. Lawns in the shade need special attention. Drain (with tile if necessary, or by grading) so that water will not stand there. For seeding use a special, good quality seed mixture of shade-enduring grasses. Three of the best shade-tolerant grasses in localities suited to them (as the N. E. part of the U. S.) are Chewing's New Zealand fescue, velvet bent grass, and rough blue grass (*Poa trivialis*). If the shade is cast by trees, deeper preparation of the soil and more frequent and more liberal feeding will

For Zoysia - Lime a Fertilize in Spring
Spectrocide & Fungicide in June
Fertilize 3 X a year

be needed to supply food for the grass as well as for the tree roots. A good plan is to work a fertilizer rich in organic matter into the soil 10 to 12 in. deep, from a point a ft. or so from the tree trunk out as far as the branches spread. Thereafter the top 6 in. of soil may be prepared as already directed for new lawn making.

Both in applying fertilizer and in mowing, remember that a lawn in the shade has a more delicate turf than one in the sun. However, weed control is usually simpler as most of the worst weeds also like a sunny exposure. Where the shade is so dense that grass cannot be made to grow, a ground-cover such as Japanese-spurge (*Pachysandra terminalis*), Periwinkle (*Vinca minor*), *Sedum ternatum*, English ivy (*Hedera helix*) or something of the sort will often give the desired green effect.

THE SLOPING LAWN. Slopes demand special attention. The home owner, in planning his grounds, should avoid making grassy slopes that are going to be difficult to mow or to keep from drying out. If grade conditions cannot be corrected, it may be best to give up the idea of grass and deliberately create a wild or "alpine" lawn. For this, the ground covers above mentioned could be used, or even rougher, more woody plants such as forms of Euonymus, Cotoneaster, or Juniper; or bearberry, *Lonicera japonica*, or some of the hardy, trailing roses, as Max Graf. However, if grass is decided on, the crest and the bottom of slope should be gently curved so as to avoid corners where the mower either will not cut or will gouge the soil. Special lawn grass mixtures for slopes are recommended because of their deep-rooting quality, but this is a good point in any grass mixture and deep preparation of the soil will encourage it.

A temporary trench around the top of a slope will help to prevent the soil washing while the grass is starting; or a nurse crop of oats or rye can be sown thinly with the grass seed to hold the earth until the grass roots are established. Such a nurse crop should not be allowed to grow more than 4 in. high or it will cut off air and light from the young grass; usually it is most conveniently mown with a scythe —as, indeed, fine lawns on Old-World estates always were.

Sometimes it is advisable to lay strips of sod at the top and bottom of the slope, and sow seed in between. The sown area can be covered with 2 or 3 in. of straw, which may remain until the grass is nearly tall enough to mow. Or burlap may be stretched across the seeded area and pegged securely to the sod strips. If the slope is very steep is may be necessary to sod it throughout. Here, or wherever sodding is done, sods should be cut 1 ft. wide, and as long as can be handled, and uniformly 1 in. deep as nearly as possible. They should be laid smoothly on a freshly raked seed bed, butted snugly together and, when all are in place, pounded down with the back of a spade, firmed with a sod-tamper, or rolled. Then water them thoroughly.

SUBSTITUTES FOR GRASS. The possibility of using other plants than grass for lawns in difficult locations, especially hot, dry ones, is a popular subject for conjecture. Some of the materials that have been suggested are these:

Zoysia matrella, or Manila grass, a real sub-tropical grass but quite rare, and of which the supply of both seed and stolons is very limited. It makes a good firm sod that remains green all summer and survives N. winters even though it turns brown with the first heavy frost.

Sagina subulata, a species of pearlwort and a member of the Pink Family. It grows about 1 in. high, thrives in either sun or shade, and does not need mowing save, perhaps, once in July to remove the small blossoms. However, it must be rolled frequently to keep the sod dense and firm— which might prove no less a bother than mowing grass.

Turfing-daisy (Matricaria) which also needs only an annual mowing, but which is of doubtful hardiness and will not stand even short periods of excessive moisture.

Chamomile (*Anthemis nobilis*), which is said to wear well, be pleasantly soft to the tread, and of a deep green color—at least, in England. But it needs regular, though not frequent mowing, even as does the common yarrow (*Achillea millefolium*), which stands severe drought and considerable usage.

Some forms of *Thymus serpyllum* might do in mild regions; and *Veronica filiformis* and *V. repens* have both been cautiously recommended, while *Mazuz reptans* is said to give a truly beautiful lawn effect except during the winter and early spring.

However, it must not be forgotten that no substitute can be expected to give the same beauty and character that marks a real lawn or greensward, well made and well cared for.

WEED CONTROL. There is no place in a healthy, well-kept lawn for weeds. Vigorous, well-fed grass will usually literally starve most of them out. However, there must be a constant lookout for newcomers, which must be removed and destroyed as soon as possible—certainly before seeding time. When a new colony of weeds is noticed the gardener should identify them, learn when they go to seed, and get rid of them before that time. Hand-pulling or cutting them out with a kitchen knife or weeder is effective and practicable against small colonies or isolated large weeds like dandelion, plantain, etc. In the case of creepers, such as ground-ivy, whose roots become entangled with those of the grass, their removal usually means digging up the spot and reseeding. Applications of sodium chlorate (see below) will kill ground-ivy without lasting injury to the grass.

Chickweed and pepper-grass are particularly troublesome because often they are not noticed until they have reached the seeding stage in early summer; and because of their many prostrate stems. Raking the lawn thoroughly with a steel rake before each mowing will lift the stems so the mower can cut them and thus help to prevent seeding. Applications in May of ammonium sulphate or iron sulphate are helpful and do not permanently injure the grass although they sometimes redden or brown it. Buckhorn, dandelion and plantain can also be stabbed in the crown with a stick which has been dipped in sulphuric acid or gasoline.

Sodium chlorate (*not* table salt, which is sodium *chloride*), iron sulphate, and ammonium sulphate all temporarily disfigure parts of the lawn where they are used, but the subsequent even-colored green of the weed-free lawn is a gratifying result. The sodium chlorate (obtainable under a trade name for garden use) is applied at the rate of 1 lb. to 1000 sq. ft., either dry or mixed with water and sprinkled or sprayed on. It is inflammable when it comes into contact with moisture and burnable material such as clothing, but is less dangerous when used as a dry application. If further treatments are necessary, the rate may a month later be increased to 2 lbs. to 1000 sq. ft.

Iron sulphate solution (1 lb. crystals to 1 or 1½ gals. water) can be sprayed or sprinkled over weedy lawns, 1 gal. being applied to 100 sq. ft. Ammonium sulphate should be sprinkled dry over the weed-infested areas after they have been watered, allowed to stand a day, and then watered again thoroughly. See also WEEDS.

Moss in grass is a sign, not of acidity, as once supposed, but of low soil fertility.

LAWNS IN THE SOUTH

Several points make the lawn of the S. a unique problem. What the S. home owner wants, and what is so difficult to find, is grass that will make a green lawn for the entire year, withstanding the hot summer (which is an even harder test than the N. winter). Preparation is a bigger job in the S., for a fairly good soil won't do: first class conditions are needed if a good lawn is wanted. A garden plot that has been fertilized and cared for for years would make a fine lawn. Otherwise, to give to the soil, in a comparatively short time, what the garden soil has acquired over years, one should, after a plowing or spading deeply, sow a green manure crop, such a cowpeas, in May. By August this will be ready to mow and a day or so later it may be turned under. Then work in a good, well-balanced fertilizer (see above). Over much of the S. the soil has an acid tendency, so an application of lime may also be needed.

For hot dry places, Bermuda grass, sown as seed or (like bent grass) chopped roots, is best. It makes a good lawn from June to October, but is discolored by the first heavy frost. If an annual such as Italian rye-grass is sown over the Bermuda lawn in the early fall, it will keep the lawn green until the Bermuda grass starts again in the spring, thus giving a good looking lawn throughout the year. White clover also may be added.

In the Piedmont and lower Piedmont regions a successful lawn seed mixture is 1 part white clover, 4 parts red top, 5 parts Italian rye-grass, and 10 parts Kentucky blue grass, sown at the rate of 1 lb. to 300 sq. ft. In the lower S., where the soil is sandy, St. Augustine, Charleston and Bermuda grasses are used. The first named is particularly well adapted to the coastal section. Grown from rootlets, it makes a presentable lawn if mowed frequently. Joint-grass may be used in situa-

Plate 32.   THE LAWN—INDISPENSABLE GARDEN ELEMENT

Top: The inviting sweep of the lawn leads naturally to the peaceful seclusion of the tea-house. Bottom: The varied hues of the border are enhanced by the harmonizing green of a smoothly-mown lawn.

tions too moist for Bermuda, but it can't be expected to make a dense turf.

Species of Zoysia, especially *Z. tenuifolia* (Mascarene or Velvet Grass) are sometimes used for lawns and golf grounds in the S. States.

It is well not to mow a new lawn in the S. until the grass is 3 or 4 in. high. During droughts a lawn should be watered thoroughly every three or four days (*never sprinkled*), and the grass clipping should be left on the lawn as a mulch.

LAWN TROUBLES

Brown spots on the lawn may be due to (1) unfavorable weather conditions, (2) burning from unequal distribution of fertilizers, (3) attacks of insects, or (4) fungous diseases.

BROWN PATCH. Of the latter, the best known is probably the so-called "large brown patch," caused by a common soil-inhabiting fungus. The browned area, which is usually more or less circular, may vary from an inch to several feet in diameter; it is usually bordered with a dark green ring of recently affected grass. Sometimes wefts of the fungus mycelium may be seen on the grass. The disease is most apt to develop in hot humid weather and is fostered by overwatering, excessive soil acidity and poor drainage. Mercury compounds are most satisfactory for control. Proprietary organic types in convenient form can be purchased under the names Semesan or Uspulun. They may be somewhat more expensive than the inorganic compounds of which mercuric chloride (corrosive sublimate) is the most effective. Calomel (mercurous chloride) is another food preventive of the disease but slower in action. The two chemicals are frequently mixed together (either half and half or two thirds calomel to one third mercuric chloride) and applied at the rate of 3 oz. to 1000 sq. ft. of lawn. If mixed with a peck or so of soil, this fungicide may be applied dry. For use with a sprinkler or sprayer, put 3 oz. in 50 gals. of water and apply to the same area. In either case, water the turf thoroughly afterwards. *Mercuric chloride* (see COR-ROSIVE SUBLIMATE) *is a virulent poison and should be handled with care.*

The disease called "small brown patch" or "dollar spot" is caused by another species of the fungus that causes large brown patch but differs in that the spots are a lighter brown, never more than 2 in. across. Control methods are the same.

Snowmold (caused chiefly by *Fusarium nivali*) is prevalent when the snow is melting off the grass, but it is serious only in the N. part of the country. Whitish-gray, dead, slimy areas appear in the grass often accompanied by a fluffy white growth of the fungus mycelium. The disease is favored by late fall feeding and winter mulching and may be checked or prevented by any treatment of the soil which tends toward rapid drying of the turf during spring thaws. If prevalent and repeatedly troublesome, the disease should be prevented by applying mercuric chloride or calomel in the fall at the rate of 2 to 5 oz. per 1000 sq. ft.

Damping off (which see) of new seedling grass may be caused by several fungi. To prevent it avoid overwatering or overfertilizing newly seeded areas.

GRUBS. Lawns may be "grub-proofed" against the larvae of the Japanese beetle, the Asiatic beetle, the Asiatic garden beetle and the so-called "white grubs" of the May beetle. The adults of all these insects usually lay their eggs in the soil during the summer months. The grubs at first feed on grass roots just below the surface, but on becoming full grown in the fall they burrow deeper and there pass the winter. Early fall injury may thus resemble drought injury, the turf being soft and spongy. If large numbers of grubs are present so much of the root system may be cut off that the turf can be lifted up from the soil like a loose, thick carpet. Such injury is usually most severe in exposed, unshaded sections of the lawn.

To grub-proof new lawns apply about 10 lbs. lead arsenate (the actual amount may vary from 5 lbs. for a very sandy, to 15 lbs. for a very heavy soil) to each 1000 sq. ft., raking it into the upper inch of soil *after* all grading and smoothing is done and just before the seed is sown. To treat an established lawn, apply the poison preferably in May or June, mixing 10 lbs. with a peck or more of sand, top-soil or humus and scattering this evenly over the 1000 sq. ft. As in seeding a lawn, this is best accomplished by using half the material while walking north and south and the rest while walking east and west. Apply only when the grass is dry and work down onto the soil with a broom or bamboo rake. For permanent protection against grubs, lead arsenate may be added to the top dressing each spring. See ASIATIC BEETLES; JAPANESE BEETLE; MAY-BEETLES.

The chinch bug (which see), formerly notorious as a corn and grass pest in the Middle West, has of late years caused serious damage to lawns in some parts of the East. The injured plants wither and turn brown, large areas being killed outright. The presence of the small black and white bugs may be proved by flooding a piece of lawn, which causes them to climb the grass stalks. Spray injured areas with nicotine-sulphate and soap or better, apply a derris dust analyzing 1% rotenone. If applied by hand, up to 25 lbs. per 1000 sq. ft. will be required but a special dusting machine makes an even application and reduces the amount to 8 to 10 lbs.

Sod web-worms (see WEB-WORMS) are most apt to cause injury in hot dry seasons, the young caterpillars feeding on grass leaves and forming protective silken webs and later building silk-lined tunnels along the surface of the soil into which cut-off blades of grass are dragged. Badly infested turf becomes ragged brown in appearance and much damage may be done in a short time. Kerosene emulsion (see KEROSENE) may be used at the rate of 1 gal. per sq. yd., but the latest recommendation is dichlorethyl ether, which see, to be applied according to manufacturer's directions.

Ants disfigure lawns with their mounds and may kill the grass in their neighborhood. The simplest way to destroy them is to inject a small amount of carbon bisulphide (which see) from a machine oil can into the openings or into holes made into the center of the nest with a smooth stick of pencil size. Calcium cyanide (which see) may be similarly used. In either case plug up the hole with a bit of soil or sod to confine the fumes. Various ant baits (see ANTS) may be purchased or prepared at home.

Earthworms are usually considered beneficial factors in soil building and conditioning and their injury to grass (if any) is debatable. Damage to lawns chiefly consists of heaving and having unsightly piles of castings. If so numerous that occasional raking or brushing of the surface is not sufficient, the worms can be destroyed by using either corrosive

sublimate as recommended above for brown patch or lead arsenate as in grubproofing. Another remedy is Mowrah meal, made from the ground seeds of the E. Indian madhuca-tree. Freshly bought (as it deteriorates on standing) this meal should be applied evenly at the rate of 15 lbs. per 1000 sq. ft. and then watered in.

Moles eat injurious insects but may themselves also do considerable damage to lawns by burrowing about and throwing up mounds above their tunnels. Besides being unsightly, these pull the earth away from the grass roots causing the turf to wilt and even die. Moles are hard to control, especially in loose soils, where they are less likely to constantly use a few routes or burrows. They may be combatted (1) by trapping, or (2) by poisoning with a teaspoonful of carbon bisulphide or calcium cyanide placed in the burrows every 5 ft. or so. See MOLE.

LAWN MOWER. Any mechanical device for expeditiously cutting the grass of a lawn to uniform, even height. The reel type mower consists of a series, usually 5, rarely 7, of curved, steel strip blades that are rapidly revolved by means of gears between two large metal driving wheels as the machine moves forward. The revolving blades draw and cut the grass leaves against a horizontal stationary sharpened blade held at the bottom, but adjustable as to the height the grass is to be left above the ground. A wooden roller behind the blades helps to support the machine and firm the turf after it has passed, ratchets in the wheels permit the blades to revolve in only one direction, slipping when the mower is drawn backward. This type of mower is made in various sizes and grades, some operated by pushing, others by a small motor. As to size, the choice should be in relation to the extent of the grass to be cut; blades 14 inches wide may suffice for a small lawn, but 18-inch mowers are more common, and 21 inches often preferred.

A modified mower of the reel type with only one wheel and blades about 6 inches long will cut grass close to walls, trees, and the edges of paths or beds. Another type working on a different principle of sharpened V-shaped teeth that move rapidly between a series of guards (practically a miniature edition of the cutting apparatus of a farm mowing machine) is useful for cutting tall grass and weeds. A heavy mower, it is not necessary for a well-kept lawn and it is much better adapted to the fairways of a golf course.

LAWN MOWER CARE. To get the best results with a lawn mower, assuming that it is a good one to start with, the gardener must give it intelligent care and usage. Oil it whenever it is taken out, and from time to time while in use. Brush it off before putting it away, and if it gets wet wipe it dry. Keep nuts and bolts tight and see that reel cutting blades are adjusted with just the right clearance. Learn from an expert how to make the necessary minor adjustment of the blades as they wear down.

The reel mower was invented in the 18th century when it was a wonderful improvement over the original method of laboriously trimming a lawn by scythe, hook and shears. Refinements have brought it to its present high degree of efficiency and reel cutting remains the best way to get a smooth, even surfaced lawn; a 5-inch blade being used for the standard grass mixtures, a 7-inch blade for bent grasses and wiry fescues.

The rotary mower was introduced in recent years and rapidly became highly popular for several reasons, one of which is its simplicity. It has only one blade, somewhat like a propeller in shape, with two cutting edges. This is revolved horizontally in the same plane as the surface of the soil at about 2,500 revolutions per minute, the cutting action being that of a knife or scythe, not the scissors-like operation of the reel mower. The high speed of the revolving blade requires a motor which leads some gardeners to prefer a reel mower of the personally-pushed type. The chassis of a rotary mower has four wheels instead of the reel's two.

One notable advantage of the rotary mower is that it will cut tall and coarse grasses through which a reel mower cannot be driven. Working on a lawn that is not entirely level, the rotary is less apt to scalp the top off any high spots. A disadvantage is that the rotary will not cut closer than an inch high, but few lawns, and those only of bent grass, require such close cropping. The rotary

blade can be removed and sharpened readily with a file; the reel blades require skilled attention and careful adjustment.

Some rotary mowers in cutting grass that is wet tend to discharge matted clumps of clippings. These can be dispersed if the machine is driven in the direction that will throw the clippings on the still uncut grass—that is, if it is desired to leave clippings on the lawn so that they may sink into the soil and turn into humus. This practice, however, is not as well regarded now as formerly, because lawn fertilizers are now more generally used.

With either type of mower it is important to see that the lawn is free from sticks, stones and dogs' bones before beginning to cut the grass. Such objects may knock chips out of reel blades. With a rotary mower they are very dangerous in that they may be picked up by the whirling blade and projected at high velocity causing serious injuries. Many gardeners will not allow children or pets anywhere near a rotary in operation. Another danger with the rotary lies in putting one's foot too far forward and jeopardizing one's toes.

Many kinds of both reel and rotary mowers are available, some equipped to carry the driver about; others requiring to be pushed. With a rotary, the latter requires effort justifying the extra cost of the self-propelled type.

LAYERING. A method of multiplying or propagating plants in which roots are caused or assisted to form on stems that are still a part of the parent plant. After the roots have formed, the section of stem bearing them is severed from the original plant and handled as a separate individual. As with other asexual propagation methods (in which no union of sexes or production of seeds is involved), layering reproduces a plant exactly, without variation such as may occur in plants raised from seed. As perfected and utilized by man, layering is a development of a wholly natural phenomenon, as many kinds of plants—especially vines, trailers and slender, drooping woody bushes—propagate themselves by simple layers. Periwinkle (Vinca) and other ground covers frequently take root at the joints; the strawberry sends out runners which root and thereby practice layering; and the dewberry and black raspberry do the same when the tips of their canes bend over, touch the ground, take root and establish new plants, by what is generally called "tip layering." In all cases the parent plant supplies the food until the new plant has an adequate root system and can "go it alone." So as to insure this continued food supply, layering outdoors is best done in spring.

Man has developed five principal methods of layerage from Nature's cruder forms.

SIMPLE LAYERING is done by bending and covering branches (except the tips, which must be kept uncovered to maintain circulation) with soil and holding them in position with pegs, stones or earth clods until rooted. In a modified form of this method the stems are laid in shallow trenches prior to anchoring or pegging. The branches are often twisted, scraped, cut, or otherwise slightly wounded on the under side at the points where rooting is desired, to encourage the quick formation of roots.

COMPOUND OR SERPENTINE LAYERING consists of bending flexible stems in a series of curves along the ground so that the "down" sections or "troughs" are in contact with and covered by soil and the "up" parts or "crests" are in the air. Otherwise the method is the same as simple layering.

CONTINUOUS LAYERING consists in burying whole branches, except the tips, of plants which root readily.

MODIFIED CONTINUOUS LAYERING is popular for the propagation of certain grape varieties and other vines whose cuttings root poorly. In spring, canes of the previous year's growth are pegged down in shallow, open trenches. When shoots several inches long have developed along these canes, the latter are wounded on the underside of the points where the shoots are, and soil is piled on these points and around the base of the shoots. After roots have formed the canes are cut between the rooted shoots, which are transplanted and carried on as separate plants.

MOUND, HILLOCK, or STOOL LAYERING is done by cutting bushes, such as quince, gooseberry and blueberry, back to within a few inches of the ground in spring and heaping earth over the stumps. These send up shoots which develop roots in the mound of earth. The following spring the rooted shoots are broken apart and planted in nursery rows or (if large enough) in their permanent positions. Rhododendrons are sometimes propagated by mound layering.

CHINESE, AIR, or POT LAYERING is a greenhouse or home practice employed chiefly on stiff, erect-growing plants, such as dracaena, croton, oleander and rubber-plant, which have become "leggy" and unsightly. The stem is wounded at the point where roots are wanted on the leafy top of the plant, generally by girdling or notching, a pebble or chip being placed in the cut to keep it open. The wounded place is then bound with soil, sphagnum moss or other moisture-retaining material held in place by a bandage of burlap, raffia or cloth or a special type pot and kept moist until roots have formed and penetrated the material. The whole top is then cut off below the new roots and potted. Sometimes (especially with rubber plants) the lower, bore part of the stem later sends out side shoots and develops a new head at a sufficiently low point to give a second attractive plant.

See AIR-LAYERING; PROPAGATION; RUBBER-PLANT.

LAYIA (lay'-yah). A genus of daisy-like annual plants native to W. America, easily grown in the open sunny border. For early blooms the seeds may be started in a hotbed, but they grow well if sown where the plants are to stand. The species most commonly grown include: *L. glandulosa* (white Daisy), an attractive plant to 1½ ft., having rather sticky narrow leaves and flowers in heads, the rays white or tinged with rose; *L. elegans* (Tidy Tips), a pretty Calif. wild flower, growing to 2 ft., and now often used in the border. The flowers have yellow rays, tipped with white.

LEAD ARSENATE. A chemical compound extensively used as a stomach poison against insects of the chewing ,type. See INSECTICIDES; ARSENICAL POISONS.

LEADER. The upright tip of any tree which grows with a central trunk. In spruce, fir, pine, etc., the leader is usually an unbranched shoot with buds at the top from which spring next year's extension of the leader and a new whorl of branches. When a tree of this type develops two or more leaders, all but one should be cut away. If the tip of the leader is injured, the tree stops growing in height until a new leader can develop, often two or three

HOW LEAVES SEEK THE LIGHT
By arranging themselves in a mosaic pattern so that the edges overlap little if at all, they obtain maximum light and sunshine by which to maintain the life and growth of the plant. This shows such mosaic arrangement in a begonia.

years later, and the trunk will be crooked at that point. A new and straight leader may be established in one growing season by immediately bending up the nearest branch (the strongest of a whorl) and tying it to a stake in as nearly a vertical position as possible. Thus aided, it will in time dominate the others and become the leader in fact.

LEAD-PLANT. Common name for one of the False-indigos, *Amorpha canescens.*

LEADWORT. Common name for Plumbago, a genus of shrubby plants hardy in the S. but in the N. cultivated under glass for the handsome phlox-like blossoms, blue, purplish-red, or white, on the branching tips. Propagated by seeds, by cuttings of nearly mature wood, or by division. They thrive in a turfy soil with some sand. Old plants should be cut back in the spring to within 1 in. of the base. Young plants need pinching back several times. *P. capensis,* with flowers of azure-blue, and *P. indica,* with purplish-red blossoms, both partial climbers, are the most familiar species. *P. scandens* is the white-flowered form.

LEADWORT FAMILY. Common name of the Plumbaginaceae, a herbaceous group of plants, some of value in medicine, but most of them grown for ornament.

LEAF. An expansion of or extension from the stem of a plant, its function being the turning of raw food material into real tissue-building substances. It consists, in the type form, of a broad *blade* connected to the branch by a *petiole* or stalk.

The vessels which transport food and materials from the root through the stem continue into the leaf and at its base (as well as on the stem where a leaf falls) are evident as tiny dots. In the leaf they appear as *veins.* Thus there is a continuous system throughout the plant for the bringing of raw materials to the leaves and the distributing of food manufactured from them throughout the entire organism.

The inner tissue of the leaf is thin-walled and with the aid of the vital substance *chlorophyll* (which also gives plant parts their green color), is equipped to manufacture food. In the presence of sunlight, the chlorophyll acts on the oxygen of the air and on the soil-solution brought up from the roots and builds up the basic food substance—*starch,* giving off carbon dioxide in the process.

Protecting the leaf is an *epidermis* covered with a waxy cuticle the *stomata* or pores of which regulate the giving off of excess water (see TRANSPIRATION). The epidermis, the structure and shape of the individual leaf, and even the whole plant organism—as in the arrangement of the many leaves on a plant—all are modified according to the habit of the plant, in order to protect the leaf against unfavorable external conditions and to obtain maximum amount of sunlight which it needs to do its work.

See also LEAVES.

LEAF CURL. A disease of the peach that results in thickened curled leaves with yellowish or reddish tints. For control, see PEACH.

LEAF-CUTTER BEE. The injury done by this bee (chiefly on rose foliage) is more interesting than serious. The bees nip out circular pieces of the leaves—the edge is always part of a smooth perfect circle—which they carry away to a tunnel in the stem of a plant and make into thimble-shaped cells. In each cell is placed an egg and a mass of nectar and pollen upon which the young bee feeds.

LEAF HOPPERS. These sucking insects belong to the same order (Homoptera) that includes the aphids. They occur throughout the world and attack nearly all wild and cultivated plants. When they are abundant, plants show lack of vigor and retarded growth, and the leaves usually have a whitened, stippled, or mottled appearance. Certain species, particularly the potato leaf hopper, causes the tips of the leaves to wither and die as if they had been scorched, the condition being called "hopperburn." Besides the direct injury they do, leaf hoppers are harmful because they carry the virus of certain plant diseases such as aster yellows. The adults are small, active, slender winged insects of various colors, usually found on the underside of leaves and hopping or flying for short distances when disturbed. The best control measure is the use of a contact insecticide with soap added. Since the insects move quickly not all will be hit with one application of spray.

LEAF MINER. Any of a number of kinds of insects small enough to live and feed between the upper and lower epidermis of a leaf. The tunnels they make show as winding white trails or broad whitish spots on the green leaf surface. They are difficult to control by spraying unless this is accurately timed to get the adult insect as it emerges from the leaf or to prevent egg laying. A nicotine molasses spray is used for the box leaf miner (see under BOX), and the birch miner is best controlled by spraying with nicotine just after the eggs are laid. On garden plants, as aquilegia, the most practicable plan is to remove and destroy unsightly mined leaves.

LEAFMOLD. A friable mixture of decayed leaves and varying quantities of earth, that accumulates naturally in forests and can be produced, in the garden, in compost heaps. See COMPOST; also LEAVES.

LEAF-PLANT, or LIFE-PLANT. Common names for a succulent tropical perennial (*Bryophyllum pinnatum*) noteworthy for the ease with which it can be propagated from new plants that develop in the notches of its leaves. It is an easily grown house-plant.

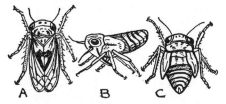

LEAF HOPPERS, TWO STAGES
A, an adult; B and C, nymphs, all much enlarged. Besides sucking leaf juices, some of these grotesque insects transmit serious plant diseases.

LEAF ROLL. The rolling of leaves may be caused by many agencies; waterlogged soil, excessive quantities of fertilizer, insects, bacteria, or fungi. The disease on potatoes specifically designated as leaf roll is a virus disease. See under POTATO.

LEAF ROLLER. A small green or bronze caterpillar which rolls up a single leaf, or fastens several together, and feeds within the resulting tent. Fruit tree leaf rollers with oblique bands, red-banded rollers and strawberry leaf rollers are among the common forms. Spray early with lead arsenate to poison the worms before the leaves become curled.

LEAF SPOT. A discolored area on a leaf with a more or less definite outline; a symptom of disease. When the areas involved are large and indefinite, the symptom is termed blotch or, sometimes, blight. Leaf spots frequently have centers of brown or light-colored or of dead tissue with a dark or reddish margin of more recently affected tissue. Small black dots in a leaf spot are the fruiting bodies of a fungus containing spores. If they are absent it may mean that the spot is of bacterial origin or merely that the fruiting stage has not been reached. Spraying with bordeaux mixture is the accepted control measure for most of the leaf-spotting fungi, although some of them can be controlled by sulphur sprays and dusts. Copper-lime dust, applied when the leaves are wet with dew, is effective. Spotted leaves should be raked up in the fall and burned, not added to the compost pile. During the growing season occasional spotted leaves on a plant should be removed, picked off and burned. See COPPER COMPOUNDS.

LEAF SPOT DAMAGE
The effect of one of the leaf-spot fungi on Japanese Ivy. Copper-lime dust is one good remedy.

LEAF TYER. The greenhouse leaf tyer is a moth whose active slender, green larvae cover several leaves with a light web or draw the parts of a single leaf together and eat the under surfaces of the leaves. They attack many plants in the greenhouse and also in the garden. The adult moths, brownish with wings crossed by dark wavy lines, emerge from cocoons formed within the rolled up leaves. Control by sanitary measures and fumigation in the greenhouse, and in the garden by spraying plants with lead arsenate.

LEATHER-LEAF (*Chamaedaphne calyculata*). An evergreen shrub of the Heath Family, found in boggy places in the colder parts of the northern hemisphere. It is of spreading habit and grows about 3 ft. high. A sandy-peat soil in a moist place is preferred, and it is most effective when planted in groups. The oblong leaves are rusty beneath, and the nodding white flowers are borne in terminal leafy racemes in early spring. Var. *angustifolia* has leaves more slender. Var. *nana* grows little more than a foot high. Propagated by seeds, cuttings of mature wood under glass, division or layers.

LEATHERWOOD. A common name given to both *Cyrilla racemiflora* and *Dirca palustris* on account of the tough fibrous bark, and the tough flexible shoots which can be bent and twisted without breaking. See both these genera.

LEATHER WOOD FERN. A common name for the Marginal Shield Fern (*Dryopteris marginalis*), which see.

LEAVES AND THEIR USES. No gardener who understands his business burns fallen leaves in the fall—or at any time—to make his place "tidy" *unless* they are badly infested with a serious plant disease and likely to spread it. He knows that they have real plant food value in their content of nitrogen, potash and phosphoric acid, and are even more valuable because of the vegetable matter that they add to the soil as they decay and become humus (which see). For humus increases the water-holding capacity of the soil and, in its acid reaction, helps break down the mineral elements of the soil. The accumulation of leaves (as leafmold) in forests is the explanation of the sustained soil fertility there even though no fertilizer is ever supplied. Therefore gather and save all disease-free leaves and use them either for mulching or for making compost, which see.

Where poultry or live stock are kept, plant-food value of leaves is enhanced by using them with (or instead of) straw or peat moss for litter and bedding; so used they absorb the liquid excrement which is especially rich in nitrogen (the most expensive and important of all fertilizer elements to buy), holding the nutritive materials in shape to be later applied to the soil directly or via the compost heap.

Useful as a winter mulch around shrubbery, leaves can also be stuffed into bottomless hampers, peach baskets, or crates placed around rose bushes; they can be piled on the rows to reduce or prevent the freezing of the ground where Jerusalem artichoke, salsify, parsnips, leeks, celery, and other tardy vegetables are left for winter digging; finally, if kept dry, they make good insulation for "pits" in which root vegetables, cabbage or apples are stored for winter use.

Leaves used as a winter mulch must not be allowed to pack down over the crowns of perennial plants like strawberries, delphinium, foxglove, etc., partly because they may smother the plants and also because a wet, soggy mat is not only poor insulation but, on the contrary, freezes and causes just the damage it is supposed to protect against. To avoid such damage, plants like Canterbury bells may be protected by inverting berry boxes or shallow grape trays over their crowns *before* the leaves are piled on the beds. Leaf mulches should not be applied until after the ground has frozen.

When oak, especially red oak, leaves are available, they make an excellent mulch for rhododendrons, mountain-laurel and other plants that require acid soil. Here, however, they should remain undisturbed from year to year, more being added on top as those beneath decay.

LEBBEK-TREE. A common name for *Albizzia lebbek,* a tropical tree with pea-like flowers.

LEDUM (lee'-dum). Hardy evergreen shrubs of N. America, belonging to the Heath Family. They are dwarf growers, not exceeding 3 ft. in height and often shorter. They have attractive narrow evergreen leaves with rolled edges, fragrant when bruised; and clusters of white flowers in early summer. They prefer a moist sandy peat soil, and seem to do equally well in sun or partial shade. Propagated by seed, layers and division. Seedlings are very slow growing.

L. palustre (Wild-rosemary) has narrow dark green leaves, densely covered with rusty hairs beneath. Var. *decumbens* is a low spreading form. *L. groenlandicum* (Labrador-tea) is very similar but has leaves a little larger, and flowers with 5-7 stamens instead of 10, as is usual in *L. palustre.* The leaves are said to have been used as a substitute for tea during the War of Independence.

LEEA (lee'-ah). Tropical shrubby plants belonging to the Grape Family. *L. amabilis,* the best known in cultivation, is a handsome plant for the warm greenhouse, either to drape a pillar or as a trained specimen in a pot. It does well in a rich loamy soil. The leaves are divided into 5 to 7 leaflets, bronzy green and of velvety texture, with a broad white stripe. Var. *splendens* has red stems and leaves with bright red markings. Propagated by cuttings.

LEEK. A hardy, biennial herb (*Allium porrum*) of the Onion genius, but of milder flavor, grown for its thick leaves and enclosed stems which are served like asparagus or used to season soups and meat dishes. (See illustration, Plate 56.)

A light, rich, friable, moist but well-drained soil is ideal, but any good garden loam will give good results. To grow leeks best, sow the seed thinly in a seed bed in early spring. When the seedlings are 3 in. high, prick them out, setting the thinnings 1 to 2 in. apart in other nursery or seed beds. When the plants are as plump as straws, cut their tops back about one-half and transplant to the garden 12 to 15 in. apart in shallow trenches, burying the shortened plants more than half their length. As the season advances gradually fill the trench and when cool fall weather arrives ridge the soil slightly each two weeks so as to blanch the stems.

For winter use dig the plants and set them in moist soil, either in a coldframe that can be protected during cold weather or in a cellar where the air is moist and the temperature low. See ONION.

LEGUME. Any plant of the Leguminosae or Pulse Family, which see, below.

LEGUMINOSAE (lee-geu-mi-noh'-see). Legumes. Botanical name of the Pea or Pulse Family, a large group comprising herbs (many of them climbing), widely distributed in diverse situations in most parts of the world. The family contributes many ornamental subjects, as well as food and forage plants, most if not all of which can be readily recognized by the form of their fruit, which is a *legume* or true pod, opening along two sutures. There are three sub-families distinguished by details of flower structure; those best known in the N. are *papilionaceous,* that is, with butterfly-like petals, as in the sweet pea.

But of even greater significance, horticulturally, is the fact that all leguminous plants have (in varying degree) the peculiar property of being agents in the transformation of atmospheric nitrogen into nitrogenous compounds available for the use of plants. This is accomplished by certain soil bacteria which invade the roots of legumes, form colonies and irritate the root tissues which develop characteristic *nodules.* Here the bacteria obtain carbonaceous food from the plant and carry on the nitrogen-fixation process, storing up the resulting nitrogenous food material. This, if not used by the plant itself, is added to the soil when the plant dies and its roots decay, thereby becoming available for other plants. Thus, besides being able to secure the nitrogen they need (even when there is an insufficient supply in the soil), legumes *actually add to that supply* and, as far as the nitrogen is concerned, leave the land more fertile than before they grew. For this reason legumes such as clovers, vetches, soy-beans, etc., are commonly included (to be plowed under) in crop rotations to increase the nitrogen content of the soil as well as to add humus as they decay. Often it is advisable to supply the beneficial bacteria at the start in the form of commercial cultures. See INOCULATION.

Among the many useful genera in this important family are: Pisum (pea), Lens (lentil), Vicia (vetch), Lathyrus (sweet pea), Phaseolus (bean), Vigna, Dolichos, Clitoria, Desmodium (trefoil), Lotus, Medicago (alfalfa), Trifolium (clover), Baptisia, Lupinus, Amorpha, Erythrina, Robinia (locust), Gliricidia, Cladrastis, Sophora, Clianthus, Colutea, Swainsona, Anthyllis, Coronilla, Indigofera, Wisteria, Chorizema, Laburnum, Cytisus, Genista, Cercis, Cassia, Tamarindus, Ceratonia, Adenanthera, Mimosa, Acacia, Calliandra, Albizzia.

LEIOPHYLLUM (ly-oh-fil'-um). Sand-myrtle. Dwarf compact shrubs of N. America, belonging to the Heath Family. They thrive best in a sandy, peaty soil and can stand partial shade as well as an open situation. They are useful in the rock garden and for bordering evergreen plantings. Propagated by seeds or layers.

L. buxifolium is a twiggy compact shrub to 2 ft. or so; very attractive in late spring when studded with small white or pinkish flowers. *L. lyoni* is very densely branched and of more prostrate habit.

LEMNA (lem'-nah) *minor.* Under the common name, Duckweed (which see), this tiny, floating aquatic plant is found in most aquaria and pools.

LEMON. A small, spiny, evergreen, semi-tropical tree (*Citrus limonia*) which in commercial importance leads all the acid fruit bearing citrus species. Though grown on a commercial scale in this country mainly in California it is an important garden fruit in the warmer parts of the whole citrus belt. The trees are more subject to frost injury than those of the orange but less than those of the lime. In conservatories and even in residences the trees are often grown in large flower pots or tubs for ornament. For culture, see CITRUS FRUITS.

Water-lemon is *Passiflora laurifolia,* an unrelated tropical American climbing plant (one of the Passion-flowers) which bears white flowers spotted with red and purple, and edible yellow fruit.

LEMON BALM or **BEE BALM.** Common names for *Melissa officinalis,* an aromatic herbaceous perennial. See BALM.

LEMON-VERBENA. Common name for *Lippia citriodora,* a Chilean shrub with terminal white flowers and lemon-scented foliage. Also applied (incorrectly) to *Isotoma petraea* var. *alba,* a blue-flowered perennial herb of Australia.

LEMON-VINE. Common name for *Pereskia aculeata,* a tropical American cactus of slender growth with lemon-like persistent leaves that bears edible fruit suggesting another name, Barbados-gooseberry. It is more used as a stock in grafting other cacti (especially Zygocactus) than grown for its own sake.

LENTIL. An annual, semi-climbing leguminous herb (*Lens esculenta*) extensively grown abroad but only occasionally in the U. S. for its small, flattened, nutritious seeds which are used like dried beans. For a garden crop seed is sown like peas in early spring in drills 18 to 30 in. apart and given ordinary cultivation. The crop does best in a sandy loam. The seed keeps best if left in the pods when harvested.

LEONOTIS (lee-on-oh'-tis). Lions Ear, and sometimes Lions Tail. Shrubby plants from S. Africa and the tropics with two-lipped, yellow or orange-scarlet flowers in dense whorls about the tall leafy, square stems—which mark the Mint Family. They are suited to bold effects in the border in warm locations or to pot cultivation in cool greenhouses to flower in midwinter. Seed of annuals should be sown early in the hotbed, ¼ in. deep, and set out later in well-drained sunny soil. Perennials are increased by division and cuttings, and the shrubby kinds by cuttings rooted under glass in early spring. During the summer the plants growing outdoors should be pinched frequently to produce a compact, uniform shape. Only a few of the score of species seem to be cultivated. *L. leonurus,* to 6 ft. tall, has orange-red flowers in September; its dwarf form (*L. l. globosa nana*) does not exceed 2½ ft. in height.

LEONTOPODIUM (le-on-toh-poh'-dium). The genus to which belong the much-prized Edelweiss (*L. alpinum*) of European mountain tops, and its larger Russian relative, *L. sibiricum.* See EDELWEISS.

LEONURUS (lee-oh-neu'-rus). About ten species of weedy herbs related to the mints, occasionally tolerated in borders. Commonly called Lions Tail or Motherwort, which see.

LEOPARD-FLOWER. A common name for *Belamcanda chinensis,* also called Blackberry-lily, which see.

LEOPARD MOTH. An enemy of elms, maples and other shade trees, a native of Europe, first found in the U. S. in 1882 and now well established along the Atlantic Coast. The pinkish-white larvae, with dark brown spots, winter, partly grown, in burrows in the heartwood of infected trees. In the spring they start feeding and burrowing, then pupate in their tunnels, the moths emerging from June to early fall. The latter, 2 to 3 in. across when the wings are expanded, are white, blotched and spotted with blue and black and very striking. Eggs are laid in dark crevices, hatch in 10 days, the young borers soon working their way into the heartwood of the branch. Two or 3 years are required for a life cycle.

Control by cutting and burning, during the fall and winter months, all infested branches, which may be recognized in early fall by the wilted leaves and the numerous holes through which sawdust is thrown out. It is possible that the larvae may be killed by painting accessible twigs with a pine-tar, creosote, paradichlorobenzene mixture.

LEOPARD-PLANT. A common name for the variety *aureo-maculatas* (which means golden-spotted) of the tall growing composite, *Ligularia kaempferi.* The name refers to its effective yellow (sometimes white or rose) spotted leaves.

LEOPARDS BANE. Common name for the genus Doronicum; also for *Senecio doronicum* (which see). Both are Old-World perennial herbs popular in borders.

LEPACHYS (lep'-ah-kis). A genus of annual and perennial herbs of the Composite Family, one of the several genera known as Cone-flower. The plants closely resemble the daisy-like black-eyed susan, having brownish disks and yellow ray-flowers, but the foliage is more delicately cut and the disk of the flowers is more than 1 in. high. Two species of these beautiful wild flowers from the W. prairies are now in common cultivation, both easily raised. The seed of the annual, *L. columnaris* and its purplish variety *pulcherrima,* may be sown early in the spring in the border where the plants are to grow. If the seeds of the perennial *L. pinnata* are started early in the greenhouse and the seedlings set in the open in a sunny position the plants will bloom continuously from June to Sept.

LEPIDIUM (lee-pid'-i-um). A genus of Asiatic annual, perennial or biennial herbs of the Mustard Family, commonly called Pepper-grass. They have small white or greenish flowers and much cut leaves and the species are of little horticultural interest, except *L. sativum,* the common Garden Cress, which is used for salad and garnishing. Though easily grown from seed, which usually gives leaves ready for cutting in less than two months (and later crops thereafter), the plants quickly run to seed in hot weather so should be started early in the spring or in midsummer for fall harvesting.

LEPTODACTYLON (lep-toh-dak'-ti-lon). Desirable border plants of the Phlox Family, mostly natives of Calif. and the N. W., growing about 2 ft. high, of neat shrubby habit, with delicate foliage and vari-colored blossoms in funnel or saucer-like forms. They are easily grown in mild climates, the hardy annuals from spring-sown seeds in a sunny location, the half-hardy biennials from seed started indoors in January, and the half-hardy shrubs from seed sown in the coldframe in late summer. *L. californicum* (formerly called

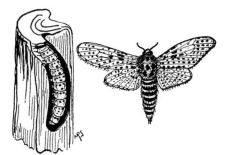

THE LEOPARD MOTH
The appropriately named adult (right) and its larva (left), both about half natural-size. The latter burrows in twigs and branches of many trees and branches, but the pest is as yet confined to the North Atlantic region.

Gilia), to 3 ft. with rose or lilac flowers, is one of the best-known sorts.

LEPTOSPERMUM (lep-toh-spur'-mum). Evergreen shrubs or small trees of Australia and New Zealand, belonging to the Myrtle Family. They are grown outdoors in the warmest parts of the U. S. and are also sometimes seen in collections of cool greenhouse plants. Those in cultivation are upright shrubs with slender branches and small stiff leaves. In spring they are most attractive with a profusion of white or pinkish flowers. Propagated by cuttings. *L. scoparium* is a good spring flowering woody plant for the greenhouse, producing a mass of white flowers when well grown. Its var. *bullatum* is an improved form with larger leaves and flowers, while a form with bright rose flowers is var. *chapmani. L. laevigatum* (Australian Tea-tree) has been much used in Calif. for the reclamation of loose, shifting sands.

LEPTOSYNE (lep-tos'-i-nee). Herbs or subshrubs, mostly native to Calif. and belonging to the Daisy Family. Some botanists describe them under Coreopsis. They have somewhat succulent, finely divided leaves and long-stemmed yellow flowers. In the North they are treated as annuals, and sometimes are grown under glass in winter; here they produce good flowers for cutting. They are easily and quickly grown from seed, and do well in a light soil and sunny place. The principal species are: *L. maritima* (Sea-dahlia) which grows to 3 ft. with a leafy stem and flowers 3 in. or more across; *L. stillmani* which also has leafy stems but is smaller in every way; *L. douglasi* which has basal leaves only and is still smaller.

LESPEDEZA (les-pe-dee'-zah). Bush Clover. Herbs or subshrubs belonging to the Pea Family. One or two of the Asiatic species are valuable in the garden for their late flowers. The roots at least are hardy N. and the plants thrive in light soils and a sunny place. *L. formosa* is a graceful and handsome plant with a profusion of rosy-purple flowers in September. *L. japonica* is similar but has white flowers.

LETTER-FLOWER. Common name for *Grammanthes dichotoma,* a half-hardy annual of the Crassulaceae or Orpine Family. The species has many variable forms, all about 6 in. high with fleshy leaves and yellow flowers. It is especially recommended for sunny rockeries. Sow seed indoors early on a sandy surface and plant out in sandy loam well limed. A V-like mark on the flower-petals accounts for the common name, which is a translation of the botanical name.

LETTUCE. A hardy, annual herb (*Lactuca sativa*) and the most important salad plant grown in America. In the case of so-called asparagus lettuce (var. *asparagina*), a variety little grown in this country, the thickened stem is used for food; in all the others the edible parts are the leaves. These latter kinds are grouped as (1) heading or cabbage lettuces (var. *capitata*), in which the leaves form cabbage-like heads; (2) leafing or loose lettuces (var. *crispa*), with crinkly leaves, not in heads; and (3) romaine or cos lettuce (var. *longifolia*), whose leaves form long, erect, columnar heads, the interiors more or less blanched.

Among these are numerous varieties and "strains" adapted for forcing under glass, for outdoor spring use or for summer culture. It is therefore of prime importance to study seed catalogs carefully and choose and sow seed of sorts adapted to the purpose in view.

Because lettuce is a salad plant it must be grown rapidly in what is called "quick" soil. This means well-drained, friable ground in which there is a constant supply of moisture and ample, readily available plant food. As the plant is hardy it may be started in a coldframe a month—or in a hotbed two months—before outdoor sowing is possible. A first planting of a 3 to 6 ft. row of thinly sown seed should give enough early plants for an ordinary family. Similar successional sowings should be made in outdoor seed beds at intervals of 10 or 15

days until midspring or later. The main reason for successional sowings is that as warm weather approaches the plants become bitter and quickly run to seed.

In the garden the lettuce rows should be far enough apart to permit tillage by wheel-hoe or hand tools—not less than 12 in. for small-growing kinds nor 15 in. for large ones. The plants should be thinned first while less than 2 in. tall to stand 2 in. asunder; a second time when they begin to crowd, each alternate plant being removed; and a third time in the same fashion when the remainder become crowded. The thinnings in the first two cases may be transplanted if not needed for the table.

In home gardens the loose-leaf varieties will usually be found most satisfactory because they are the easiest to grow to perfection, unless conditions are exceptionally favorable. Romaine or cos lettuce, though a so-called summer type, requires partial shade in our hot, sunny, dry summers. Shade may be provided by lath or cheese-cloth screens.

When garden space is restricted, lettuce plants may be set alternately with cabbage or similar plants or the rows may alternate with those of parsnips, salsify and other slow growing crops. In this case the lettuce is used first. On the other hand, quicker maturing crops like radish, spinach and onion sets may be grown between the lettuce plants. See COMPANION CROPPING.

Lettuce diseases, including two kinds of rots, a tipburn, and certain virus troubles, are sometimes very destructive. As the nature of the crop prevents spraying or dusting, removal of lettuce refuse, crop rotations, and the eradication of weeds in the vicinity are the chief control measures. Bottom rot starts in the bottom leaves lying on the ground and destroys first the blades and then the midribs. Drop or sclerotinia rot (which see) attacks chiefly greenhouse lettuce, as does the gray mold rot (see BOTRYTIS).

Tipburn results from high temperatures in combination with other unfavorable weather conditions and in midsummer may destroy many plants.

To control aphids (which carry a mosaic or virus disease of lettuce) spray with pyrethrum-soap. To check slugs, which are fond of lettuce, surround the plants with lime, fine coal ashes or soot.

To have lettuce reach the table in best condition the plants should be pulled or cut early in the morning while still wet with dew or at latest before the sun has wilted the leaves. The plants should then be washed and set in a cool place where the air does not circulate much. This will maintain the morning crispness. If the letture is shaken almost dry, placed in a tightly closed can, and kept in a refrigerator it will retain its crispness for a week.

Lambs-lettuce is *Valerianella officinalis.* Water-lettuce is *Pistia stratiotes.*

LEUCADENDRON (leu-kah-den'-dron). S. African trees or shrubs, belonging to the Protea Family. They are grown outdoors in Calif. and sometimes under glass. The best known, *L. argenteum* (Silver-tree), is one of the most noted trees of the Cape of Good Hope region, where it grows to 30 ft. It is a showy and interesting plant by reason of its narrow silvery-white leaves, closely set upon the stems. It is propagated by seeds. Dried leaves are shipped from S. Africa and used for decorative purposes.

LEUCOCORYNE (leu - koh - koh - ry'-nee) *ixioides.* A recently introduced bulbous herb of Chile, whose luminous blue flowers are called Glory-of-the-sun. Though still a novelty, even among florists who grow it under glass for cut flowers, the supply of bulbs (grown in Calif.) is increasing so it should in time become available for home greenhouses and perhaps as a half-hardy subject for mild sections.

LEUCOCRINUM (leu-koh-kry'-num) *montanum.* A native, spring-blooming herb of Western U. S. belonging to the Lily Family and commonly called Star-lily or Sand-lily, which see.

LEUCOJUM (leu-koh'-jum). Bulbous plants of the Lily Family having drooping white flowers and commonly known as Snowflake. In the N. they are hardy in the border, with winter protection, and in some sections of the S. they have become naturalized. They are easily grown, bulbs being planted 3 in. deep in well-drained soil in the perennial or shrubbery border or in the rock garden; they should remain undisturbed for as long as possible.

L. vernum (Spring Snowflake or St. Agnes Flower) has white blossoms, usually borne singly and appearing about a month after the early snowdrops.

aestivum (Summer Snowflake) has long strap-shaped leaves and bears 2 to 8 white, green-tipped blossoms clustered on a stalk 1 to 1½ ft. high, late in May.

autumnale has a very slender 9 in. flower-stalk bearing from 1 to 3 blossoms. This species is not as satisfactory as the other two in N. gardens, requiring a sheltered position and winter protection.

A PROMISING NEW BULB
Leucocoryne ixioides, called Glory-of-the-sun, recently introduced into North America from Chile.

LEUCOPHYLLUM (leu-koh-fil'-um). Spreading shrubs native in Tex. and N. Mex., belonging to the Figwort Family. *L. texanum* is apparently the only one cultivated. As sometimes seen in the S., usually as a hedge, it is a loose-growing shrub to 8 ft. or more, very attractive with its silvery leaves and large violet-purple flowers.

LEUCOTHOË (leu-koth'-oh-ee). Deciduous and evergreen shrubs, native in Asia and N. and S. America, belonging to the Heath Family. They do best in a moist sandy peat soil and partial shade, but will grow in the open if the soil is not too dry. Leucothoë sprays are much used by florists in design work. Only a few species can be grown outdoors N.

Brown blotches on the leaves are evidence of winter drying which may be followed by gray areas with conspicuous black fruiting bodies of a secondary fungus. Propagated by seeds, cuttings and division.

Principal Species

L. catesbaei, found from Va. S. and one of the handsomest broad-leaved evergreens, is hardy as far N. as Mass. It grows to 6 ft., with arching branches and large lustrous leaves, which in the open take on a bronze autumn tone. The nodding white flowers are borne in clusters along the stem in early spring. It is a good plant to use in protected places, and especially near the waterside or to mass in front of rhododendrons and kalmias.

axillaris differs only slightly from *L. catesbaei,* chiefly in having a smaller and shorter stemmed leaf, and flower buds greenish instead of reddish. It is not as hardy.

racemosa (Sweetbells) is a more upright grower to 10 ft., found in moist places from Mass to Fla. The leaves are deciduous and turn scarlet in fall.

recurva, found from Va. south, closely resembles *L. racemosa* but is of a rather more spreading habit. It can stand drier conditions than most and its leaves also turn scarlet before falling.

LEVELING. As a phase of landscaping, this is a more or less technical engineering operation beyond the scope of this work. In gardening, however, meaning the

THE HARDIEST LEUCOTHOË
L. catesbaei, whose drooping flowers adorn the bush in spring, will hold its purplish-green leaves all winter if given a sheltered position.

development of a uniform, horizontal surface by treating uneven ground to remove humps and fill hollows, it is a practical task that any gardener may have to undertake. It is especially necessary in connection with lawns, though it also is an important step in the construction of terraces.

The common mistake of merely cutting down the rises or humps to fill in the hollows results in soil of uneven depth and consequent uneven stands of plants, whether of grass, vegetables or flowers. For it shaves off a layer of good soil on the high spots (sometimes leaving little or no topsoil there) and piling up a perhaps unnecessarily deep bed of good soil in the hollows.

The proper way is: first, to remove and pile the sod by itself, either to be used in making compost or, if it is in good enough shape, for resodding later on; second, to remove the top-soil from the entire area and place it in convenient piles around the margins; third, to level the subsoil by shaving down the humps and filling and packing the hollows, and, at the same time loosening it thoroughly to improve both drainage and moisture-holding conditions; fourth, to soak the level area and let it settle for some days; fifth, to wheel back the top-soil and spread it evenly, adding more if necessary to bring the layer up to the desired depth; sixth, to roll or otherwise firm the top-soil, or to let it settle before seeding, sodding or planting it.

The best way to arrive at an even surface where a transit or surveyor's level cannot be used, is to use a system of pegs as follows: near the center, drive a peg with a notch in it or a mark on it to mark the desired final soil level there. Then at equal distances (say every 6 or 8 ft.) radiating from this point, drive other pegs and by means of a taut line or a straight edge and a spirit level, adjust them so that their tops are level with the mark on the center peg; or else make corresponding marks on all the pegs. When they are all in place and marked, the top soil may be brought in, spread and raked smooth. Then the pegs are pulled up and the holes filled with soil packed down and made level.

LEVISTICUM (lee-vis'-ti-kum). The generic name for an Old-World perennial herb commonly known as Lovage (which see), cultivated for its aromatic fruits.

LEWISIA (leu-is'-i-ah). A genus of low-growing perennial herbs of the Portulaca Family. They have narrow fleshy leaves, often in rosettes, and charming waxy, or satiny cactus-like flowers, white or in various shades of rose, borne singly or in clusters. The Lewisias, all native of the W. States, have recently come into cultivation as rock-garden plants, one of the species, *L. tweedyi*, being considered one of the four finest rock-garden plants in the world. They are perfectly hardy, but should be given an open, well-drained situation in the rock garden and a mulch of leaves during the winter. The thick, starchy roots require a period of rest, therefore perfect drainage must be assured. Propagation is by seed, which requires very careful handling, or by division in spring.

The evergreen Lewisias should be planted in sandy silt mixed with leafmold. The crown should be set 1 in. above the surface of the soil, and filled around with stone chips and pea-size gravel. This rough, loose material will assure perfect drainage of all water from the axils of the leaves. Evergreen species include:

L. columbianum var. *roseum,* with densely overlapping green leaves and branched clusters of lovely deep rose flowers 6 to 9 in. high. The species is white-flowered.

howelli, with somewhat ovate leaves, oddly crinkled and waved on the margin, and sometimes tinted red; and numerous clusters of pink violet-striped flowers, margined white, 6 in. above the foliage.

WESTERN LEWISIAS FOR ROCK GARDENS
Two types of this lovely pink-flowered American plant are shown here: (A) L. howelli, with clustered flowers on 6-inch stalks; (B) L. brachycalyx, with flowers close-set within the leaf rosette.

Lewisias may be considered under two divisions: deciduous and evergreen. The deciduous group requires a loose, gritty soil, full of humus, well-watered, but well-drained. The deciduous species include:

L. rediviva (Bitter-root), which has a dense rosette of narrow leaves above which rise beautiful silky short-stemmed blossoms 1½ in. across, varying in color from white to deep rose. This is the State Flower of Mont., where it covers acres of land with bloom in the spring.

brachycalyx, with oblong, light green leaves and white flowers veined with rose.

oppositifolia, with a few narrow leaves, and solitary white flowers, tinted rose, on stems 6 to 12 in. high.

nevadensis, with short-stemmed, white flowers tinted lavender.

tweedyi, with exquisite salmon-pink blossoms, nearly 2 in. across, 1 to 3 on a stem rising just above the thick fleshy leaves. As the root of this species is very large, plenty of room should be given it. This lovely plant has been known to have over 200 blossoms open during a season.

heckneri, with broad dark green leaves, red beneath and fringed with slender spines, and many flower-stalks bearing from 1 to 12 rose-pink blossoms.

LIATRIS (ly-ay'-tris). A genus of showy N. American perennial plants of the Composite Family, the small flower-heads being generally borne close against long wand-like stems. Attractive throughout midsummer and well into autumn in the wild, they are also effective when massed in the flower border. The flowers are usually purple, but white forms are also known. They are easily raised from seed or by division of the clumps, and do not resent transplanting.

Among the many species, the following are obtainable:

L. pycnostachya, to 5 ft. tall, has dense purple spikes to 1½ ft. long; unlike those of many tall plants they open their flowers from the top downward. Excellent when planted in masses.

spicata, to 6 ft. with long spikes of fluffy purplish-rose flowers. Var. *montana* has shorter spikes on dwarfer stouter plants.

scariosa, to 6 ft. is pubescent and bears bluish-purple flowers, often purple-tipped, in interrupted racemes.

graminifolia, to 3 ft. with purple flowers and long grass-like leaves. The flower stalks are sometimes branching.

ligulistylis, 1 ft. tall with rose-purple flower-heads in flattened clusters.

punctata, 1 ft. or more tall with small heads of rose-purple flowers in dense spikes.

LIBERTIA (li-bur'-ti-ah). Tender perennial plants of the Iris Family from Chile and New Zealand growing to 3 ft., with evergreen sword-like foliage and large white flowers in early summer. These lovely border subjects for S. U. S. should be planted in spring or fall in rich sandy soil and lightly covered in winter. The creeping fibrous-rooted rhizomes may be divided in April or seed may be sown in the coldframe from August to November. Most of the species have white flowers, *L. grandiflora* being especially free-flowering; but *L. caerulescens* has blue flowers. The plant is named after Marie A. Libert, a Belgian botanist.

LIBOCEDRUS (ly-boh-see'-drus). A genus of evergreen trees of the Pine Family called Incense-cedar, resembling the arborvitae (which see) but much larger, with heavy, fan-like foliage. Native to S. America and Asia, any of the half dozen or more species can be grown on the Pacific Coast and in the S. One species, the California Incense-cedar (*L. decurrens*), a columnar tree sometimes 200 ft. high, and with a massive trunk, is more or less successful in the N. E. near the coast.

LICHENS (ly'-kenz). Small plants ranking lower in the plant kingdom than the mosses and liverworts, but higher than the seaweeds and fungi. They are rootless, stemless, flowerless and leafless; usu-

ally gray-green or rusty-gray but sometimes brighter in color; clinging closely in flat or ruffled mats to rocks, old boards, tree bark and the bare ground where more complex forms of plant-life could obtain no foothold. Their fruits (containing spores) occur as knobs, disks, or cups usually brightly colored. Lichens are found in every zone and may conceivably have been the forerunners of other higher forms of vegetation; of very slow growth, they attain great age which may run into several centuries.

The lichen is unique among plants in that it is a dual organism, the result of the close association of two very different growths for their mutual advantage (called *symbiotic* association). One, an *alga* or minute green slime-plant with the power of manufacturing plant-food but easily dried by sun and wind, is fed upon by a white thread-like *fungus* unable to produce its own food but capable of absorbing and retaining moisture. In return for its food obtained from the alga which it enwraps completely, the fungus furnishes the necessary shade, moisture and protection for its companion. Between them, by chemical and mechanical action, they not only live and grow, but also gradually break down the rock and build up a thin layer of soil on which mosses can subsist; there they die, thus producing additional soil for higher orders of plants to grow in.

Lichens supply certain dyes and drugs and several species are edible; one supplies the so-called Iceland-moss. Another is believed identical with the manna of the Israelites. The so-called Reindeer-moss is a branching lichen. While not garden subjects to be cultivated, they are interesting when introduced as features of a rock- or wild-garden, or in miniature garden arrangements such as terraria, etc.

LICORICE or LIQUORICE. Common name for *Glycyrrhiza glabra,* a perennial herb of S. Europe growing to 3 ft. with pale blue, pea-like flowers in spikes and short flat pods. Of no special garden value, it is, however, grown in rich moist soils, from seed or division, and from its roots is obtained the licorice used in medicine and for flavoring.

LICORICE FERN. Common name for *Polypodium glycyrrhiza,* native from Alaska to Calif.

LICUALA (lik-eu-ay'-lah). A genus of small Fan Palms with single or clumped trunks and long-stemmed rounded fan-shaped leaves. These handsome palms, natives of tropical Asia and the islands of the Pacific, are not grown in the open in the U. S., but in the juvenile state make decorative specimens handled as tub plants in the warm greenhouse. They must have a plentiful supply of water and shade from intense sunlight.

The best known species is *L. grandis,* which has a single stem growing to 6 ft. and leafy, when young, for at least half its height. Propagation is by seed started in pans with bottom heat.

LIFTING. A gardening term for the digging of plants, not for harvesting purposes, but as a phase of their seasonal handling. Hardy bulbs, like tulips, narcissi, etc., are said to be lifted when dug after the foliage has died down so they can be ripened for a time and then replanted. Similarly perennial plants are "lifted" from time to time so they can be propagated by division of the clumps. Even annuals are sometimes lifted just before being hit by frost, if sufficiently stocky and vigorous to be potted up and grown on indoors for winter flowering.

LIGHT is of vital importance to all green plants; in fact, they cannot live without it. Plants feed themselves largely by turning the chemical elements contained in water and air into sugar, which supplies nearly all their needs and which they store for future use in the form of starch. Light is the fuel or source of energy by which water and air are thus combined in the cells of the leaf. Without light, no sugar or starch can be made; when the stored supply is used up, the plant dies.

Some plants require direct sunlight; others can use indirect or diffused light, such as that on the N. side of a rock or in the shade of thick woods, and may die if exposed to the direct rays of the sun. There are also plants which prefer some special combination of light and shade, a few hours full sunlight, shade the balance of the day, or scattered spots of sunlight falling through trees, or the light of the sky on a steep N. slope where direct sunlight never falls. But most plants adapt themselves to different degrees and kinds of light, by changing their leaf structure to suit conditions. Soft, thin leaves grown in shade often burn brown when moved into sunlight, later dropping off, when smaller, thicker leaves have grown to take

their place. It is therefore best not to move plants from shade to sun, or, if it must be done, to move them at a season when the sun is low.

The sun gives most light in June, when highest, and least in December, when it is lowest. The difference is made greater by the frequency of cloudy weather in winter. House and greenhouse plants, grown—or expected to go right on growing—in winter, suffer from lack of light, especially because not all the light passes through ordinary window glass. All possible light should be given these winter plants, though some need shielding from the unnatural heat of sunlight passing through glass.

House plants should be placed in the brightest part of the room, and hotbeds and coldframes so built that the sash slopes southward, to admit more direct light rays; and greenhouses should be laid out scientifically with the glass sloped so as to invite maximum light and to prevent the burning effect that results when light passes through a lens. Successful house and greenhouse plants are usually those which can adapt themselves easily to different amounts of light, or which prefer shade. Artificial light is helpful to supplement daylight in greenhouses and recent experiments tend to show that with the right size and type of bulbs used, electric light will help greatly in promoting the health and growth of plants that would soon die without it.

In spring, outdoor plants begin their growth more in response to light than to heat, with the result that early blossoms like those of magnolia, peach and dogwood, and the leaves of such evergreens as rhododendron, are sometimes injured by getting under way in advance of late spring frosts. Plants of these types should therefore be given less light by being placed on a N. slope or on the N. side of a building or woodland.

See also SHADE AND SHADING.

LIGNUM-VITAE (lig'-num vy'-tee). The common name of the genus Guaiacum, a small group of tropical American trees and shrubs with very hard, dense wood which is called by the same name and gives the plant commercial value. The name means "wood of life," perhaps in reference to medicinal properties. The rather ornamental plants have leathery, finely cut leaves and small purplish flowers. They can be grown in S. Calif. and S. Fla. *G. guatamalense,* growing to 10 to 16 ft., bears azure flowers in axillary clusters before the leaves. *G. officinale* has evergreen leaves and grows to 30 ft. in dry soil.

LIGULARIA (lig-eu-lay'-ri-ah). A genus of composite herbaceous perennials, some of them formerly grouped with Senecio, with broad basal leaves showily marked and numerous yellow flower-heads on 5 ft. stems. This is a striking subject for border-culture and is easily grown, seed being sown ⅛ in. deep in April in ordinary garden soil, and the plants thinned later. The species come from W. Europe and the Far East. *L. kaempferi* var. *aureo-maculata* (commonly called Leopard-plant) is hardy S. of Washington. *L. wilsoniana,* the Giant Groundsel, and *L. japonica,* a bold plant for landscaping, are hardy in N. Y.

LIGULE. A strap-shaped body, particularly the rain-guard where leaf-blade meets sheath in the grasses; and the narrow and moderately long corolla of the ray-flowers (which see) of composites. The term is derived from a Latin word meaning "little tongue."

LIGUSTICUM (li-gus'-ti-kum). A genus of hardy perennial herbs of temperate regions, belonging to the Parsley Family and characterized by smooth, compound leaves, aromatic roots, and compound flower clusters. None of the 20 known species possess much horticultural value. *L. latifolium* of New Zealand, with red flowers on branching 6 ft. stems, requires a mild climate. Two white-flowered species that occur in U. S., and may be used for naturalizing are *L. canadense,* 3 to 6 ft. high, found in rich, moist soil from Pa. southward, and *L. scothicum,* a smaller plant of salt marshes from N. Y. north.

LIGUSTRUM (li-gus'-trum). Deciduous or evergreen shrubs, native in Europe, Asia and Australia, belonging to the Olive Family and valuable especially as hedge material but also sometimes as specimens. See PRIVET.

LILAC. Common name for the genus Syringa. (See illustrations, Plate 33.) Lilacs are mostly large hardy shrubs of easy cultivation, free-flowering and very ornamental in bloom. The flowers are borne in large panicles, ranging in color from pure white to deep crimson, through many shades of lilac, with some near pink and blue. They may be single or double, and are usually very fragrant.

The common lilac (*S. vulgaris*) is one of the best-loved shrubs, and is often found in the countryside marking the site of a former dwelling. More than 200 named forms of this old favorite have been developed as the result of skilled work by plant breeders. Besides these (all of which flower in spring), there are several good Asiatic species which extend the season of bloom, ending with the so-called Tree Lilacs which flower in early summer.

Lilacs are good natured and tolerant of almost any soil and situation, but thrive best in a rich, well-drained soil and an open situation. They appreciate lime and respond well to applications of bonemeal and dressings of rotted manure from time to time. Should they get overgrown and scrawny, they can be completely renovated by being cut back almost to the ground in early spring. Lilacs force readily and are largely grown for this purpose in Europe. It is interesting to note that they respond more easily and quickly after being subjected to ether fumes for a certain period.

ENEMIES. Two diseases of lilac have much the same symptoms and are controlled in the same manner. They are bacterial blight which causes mostly black spots on succulent young leaves and stems, and Phytophthora blight in which the spots are dark brown. Either may kill suckers back to the parent stem. To avoid these troubles do not let bushes become crowded; cut out dead branches and prune to let in sun and air; and spray with bordeaux mixture beginning when leaves are opening.

The most common and conspicuous lilac disease is mildew but, coming in late summer, it is not very destructive. However, it is unsightly and if unchecked is apt to weaken the bushes. Dust with fine sulphur.

Both the oyster-shell and euonymus scales attack lilacs. Control with a dormant oil application before growth starts in the spring followed by a nicotine-soap spray in the summer if necessary. Presence of the lilac borer in stems is indicated by wilting of individual shoots and fresh borings hanging from the stem. Cut out infested canes or inject a nicotine paste (see BORERS). The giant hornet (see HORNETS) sometimes injures plants by tearing the bark from the stems to use for nests, and feeding on the sap. The lilac leaf miner is a recently introduced pest which first tunnels in the leaves and then webs them together and skeletonizes them. Spray with nicotine soap solution to kill the young larvae.

Plate 33.   LILACS IN PROFUSION AND VARIETY

Upper left: A fragrant Chinese lilac (Syringa pubescens). Center top: A typical pyramidal truss of lilac. Upper right: One of the fine double-flowered hybrids, Leon Gambetta. Center: A lilac hedge provides marvelous bloom as well as seclusion. Lower left: The charming Persian lilac makes a graceful, spreading specimen. Lower right: A single spray of Persian lilac, as delicate as old lace.

Lilacs are propagated by seed, by cuttings of half-ripened and mature wood, by suckers and by layers. Varieties are often budded or grafted on stock of common lilac or on privet for quicker growth, but generally own-root material is preferable. Grafting onto privet stock is frequently the cause of a graft-blight, which becomes progressively acute from year to year. There is yellowing, thickening, and brittleness of foliage, leaf roll, premature defoliation, a tendency for bark to overroll stock, and general malformation of bushes.

Principal Early-flowering Species

S. vulgaris (Common Lilac). A large shrub of stiff upright habit to 20 ft., with usually lilac-colored flowers. Var. *alba* is the common white form. The many named single and double forms in varying shades are commonly called French Lilacs; in general they have larger individual flowers and heavier clusters, but not all are as fragrant as the type. It is the State flower of N. H.

perisca (Persian Lilac) grows to 10 ft., with slender branches of more graceful

FOR EARLIER FLOWERING
Lilacs, forced in large pots in the greenhouse, give an abundance of bloom before winter is over.

habit. It is very showy in bloom with large loose clusters of pale lilac flowers. Var. *laciniata* is a smaller form with divided leaves.

chinensis is a supposedly natural hybrid between *S. vulgaris* and *S. persica*. For-

merly listed as *S. rothomagensis*, it is called Rouen Lilac, after the place of its origin. It is a fast grower and free bloomer, similar to *S. persica* in habit, but with more massive clusters of reddish-purple flowers.

oblata is a stout compact grower with broad leathery leaves, which turn wine-color in fall, an unusual happening with lilacs. It is one of the earliest to bloom, with compact roundish clusters of lilac-purple flowers. Var. *dilatata* is a good form of more graceful habit, with loose clusters of lilac-pink flowers.

meyeri is a small compact bush, very attractive early in the season, with small reddish-lilac flowers. It produces a second crop in fall.

pubescens is one of the most fragrant and free-flowering species. It has slender stems and large clusters of small pale lilac flowers.

Later-flowering Species

S. villosa makes a dense rounded shrub to 12 ft., with warty stems, large leaves and rosy-lilac to whitish flowers.

wolfi is somewhat similar but of larger growth, with large clusters of small violet-purple flowers.

josikaea (Hungarian Lilac) is a tall narrow grower with dark green lustrous leaves, and small violet-colored flowers in rather short clusters.

reflexa (Nodding Lilac) grows to 12 ft., and is very distinct with long drooping flower clusters, red in the bud, later rose, and white inside.

sweginzowi grows to 12 ft., with oblong dull green leaves and pale pink flowers in long narrow clusters. It flowers freely when quite small.

microphylla is of graceful spreading habit, with small leaves and loose clusters of pale lilac flowers.

julianae is a graceful spreading shrub to 6 ft., with lilac-purple flowers.

pekinensis is one of the so-called Tree Lilacs, but in cultivation it is usually a large shrub. The bark breaks into thin flakes as in the birch. It has rather flat clusters of yellowish-white flowers in June, freely produced when well established.

japonica grows to 30 ft. or more, with a short trunk and reddish-brown bark similar to a cherry. It is conspicuous in early summer with large panicles of creamy-white flowers.

LILIACEAE (li-li-ay'-see-ee). The Lily Family, a large, important group of plants widely distributed but most abundant in warm regions. Though most are perennial herbs, dying down after flowering to a crown of fleshy underground stems, some are woody or tree-like, as species of Dracaena. A few are grown for food, as species of asparagus and onion, but the family is most noted for contributing some of the finest of ornamentals. Flowers are large, regular and very showy, or sometimes, if small, in clusters. Flower-parts are typically in sixes; both petals and sepals are alike, colored and inserted below the ovary instead of above, as in the other families of the general lily alliance.

Genera commonest in cultivation are: Lilium (lily), Fritillaria, Tulipa (tulip), Calochortus, Brodiaea, Allium (onion), Colchicum, Bulbocodium, Ornithogalum, Camassia, Scilla, Lachenalia, Muscari, Hyacinthus (hyacinth), Galtonia, Chionodoxa, Aloe, Asparagus, Ruscus, Gloriosa, Tricyrtis, Agapanthus, Sansevieria, Rohdea, Convallaria (lily-of-the-valley), Hosta, Aspidistra, Hemerocallis, Yucca, Phormium, Liriope, Ophiopogon, Kniphofia, Asphodelus, Asphodeline, Anthericum, Smilax, Chlorophytum, Eremurus, Paradisea, Dracaena, Cordyline.

LILY. (The genus Lilium.) A large group of true bulbs whose original species are spread over a wider territory than is usual with other bulbous plants. As with most other bulbous subjects, the native sources of origin are largely confined to water-bound locations; thus we find the islands and coastal regions of the Orient and the Mediterranean Sea, together with both coast lines of this country, important contributors of different forms of this important and beautiful flower. (See illustrations, Plate 34.)

Lily bulbs, in all instances, are composed of fleshy, overlapping scales and are of a size usually proportionate to the stem and flowers produced. The erect stems bear both spear-shaped leaves and funnel- or bell-shaped flowers with 6 petals; the outer three are sometimes smaller than, and overlap to some extent, the inner three.

Lilies have long been known as "garden aristocrats" and certainly their stately splendor richly deserves such a name, for there is no other subject that adds such dignified glory to so many garden settings. When they are grown in pots or used as cut flowers, this same dignified beauty prevails; it has made them general favorites in various ways and at all sorts of festive occasions and, in the case of the chaste white species, particularly for the Easter season.

In this country horticultural trade custom has divided lilies into two main groups. The first takes in all of the garden kinds—both white and colored—and designates them as "hardy lilies"; the second comprises the tender white, so-called "Easter Lilies," some of which can, however, be flowered outdoors as summer bedding subjects and in the S. This article treats garden lilies first and in detail and then the tender group (and the production of its bulbs) more briefly.

PROPAGATION OF LILY BULBS. There are several ways by which lilies can be successfully propagated. With commercial growers the approved practice—which amateurs eager to raise large quantities of lilies can follow—is to select the finest appearing lily stalks at time of flowering and to use the bulbs that produce them as propagating stock. This insures constant improvement, which may not be attained when other means are employed. The plants marked at flowering time are carefully dug and the bulbs separated. When the normal planting time approaches, these bulbs are broken apart, scale by scale, and the scales are planted out in rows. Tiny bulbils form at the base of the scales where they were separated from the main bulb and each one produces a top growth. When this dies down in the normal manner the bulbils are lifted to be replanted the next season. Repeated replantings ultimately produce flowering-size bulbs, the time needed for this development differing with the variety of lily. In many types, the second year's planting will give a crop of a size suitable for garden planting.

Another method widely employed is the planting of seed. Here again the selection of seed-pods from the finest stalks is important. However, variations will likely occur in all lilies grown from seed. At the same time, most lilies are heavy seed producers so the planting of seed is the quickest way to develop a stock.

The seed, harvested during the summer, can be sown in greenhouses or coldframes in late fall or outdoors in the early spring. Bulbils, varying in size according to the variety and the treatment given them, will, with subsequent replantings, develop into flowering-size bulbs. The Regal Lily especially grows well from seed and this is the method chiefly employed in commercial production of vast quantities of this variety.

There are also three methods of what may be called natural propagation. The most intensive is by means of the small bulbs that form along the stalk underground from just above the bulb to the surface of the soil. Their number can be increased by deep planting or by hilling up the bulbs as the stalks grow so as to lengthen the portion below ground. The bulbs so formed are usually quite large, and in the case of many varieties will make flowering size after being grown on for one additional season.

Secondly, there are the aerial bulblets that form in the axils of the upper leaves of some species. In the Tiger Lily such bulbils are quite prolific and there are several other species that produce them about as freely. These bulbils should be carefully watched at about flowering time so they can be gathered when ripe, but before they fall to the ground. Planted whenever the bulbs of the parent stock are planted, the bulbils will increase in size annually and in two or three seasons produce flowering-size bulbs. Finally there is the natural division of the bulb itself, which is quite important to the gardener whose plantings are likely to remain undisturbed for several years. Under such conditions varieties that have become well established will be found to have increased considerably. The whole clump of bulbs should be then lifted after the foliage has died down naturally and the new bulbs that have formed about the original one can be pulled apart readily. Since all lily bulbs dry out quickly when exposed, immediate replanting should be done.

ENEMIES. Mosaic, the most serious lily disease, is prevalent in all parts of the world and all species of Lilium (and the related genus Fritillaria) are more or less susceptible; *L. longiflorum, L. speciosum* and *L. auratum* are more susceptible than *L. canadense, L. hansoni* or *L. regale*. It is caused by a virus (which see) which is carried from diseased to healthy lilies by the melon aphid. It is not transmitted through the seed nor by contaminated soil. Affected plants exhibit marked stunting, often with distortion and twisting of stems and leaves, deformed flowers and mottling of the foliage into light and dark areas.

The virus invades all parts of the plant except the seed and affected plants never recover, but die. Plant only bulbs known to be healthy, if possible, or, if practicable, raise lilies from seed. In plantings remove all mosaic-infected plants as soon as detected (this practice is known as "roguing"). In greenhouses, frequent fumigation to control aphids checks the spread of mosaic. Forcing at a slightly higher temperature increases the percentage of perfect bloom.

Another virus disease affecting the tops of lily plants is known as "yellow flat." The leaves become pale and curl downwards. The control is the same as for mosaic.

Botrytis blight, a serious fungous disease, appears first as conspicuous orange-brown spots on the foliage; these are followed by a blighted or burned appearance and rotted buds. Diseased areas may be covered with a gray mold. Small black spore-bearing bodies (sclerotia) formed on dead leaves and stems give rise to early spring infection, and the disease spreads very rapidly in moist weather. To control it, gather and burn all dead stalks and leaves in the autumn and spray with 4-4-50 bordeaux mixture in the spring as soon as new growth appears, repeating two or three times. Copper-lime dust may be used if applied while plants are wet with dew. In greenhouses keep the humidity low.

If bulb rots are seen when bulbs are dug, cut away any rotted portions and soak bulbs for one hour in formalin (1 tablespoon commercial—40 per cent—formaldehyde to 3 quarts water).

The bulb mite causes considerable injury to lily bulbs but no satisfactory method of control has been developed since methods used against mites in other bulbs may be injurious to lilies. Plant only sound, healthy bulbs; destroy infected plants, and, when bulbs are out of the ground, store them at low temperatures. A brown and yellow aphid is often present in great numbers on the under side of lily leaves from midsummer on into fall. Spray with contact insecticides directed at the undersurface of foliage. See also BULB ENEMIES under BULBS.

LILIES IN THE GARDEN

There are hardy lilies appropriate for every part of the garden and although some extra time and trouble is required for success with some of the species, their outstanding grace and beauty and the distinction they add to the garden picture make the extra effort well worth while. Growers agree that the most essential factor in the successful cultivation of lilies is good drainage. An ideal soil is a porous loam with a gravelly subsoil; but if a given soil is too heavy or too light and sandy, it should be dug out to a depth of 3 ft., a layer of stones or gravel placed in the bottom and this covered with a good, friable, fertile fibrous loam.

The depth of planting varies with the species; normally it should be about 3 times the height of the bulb. That is, if the bulb is 3 in. high, its base should be 9 in. deep when planted. According to rooting habits, there are two main classes of lilies. Those of one class produce roots from the base of the bulb only; the other kind develop feeding roots along the stem between the bulb and the surface of the ground.

Bulb-rooting lilies require shallow planting and depend on available plant humus food in the surface soil for their nourishment. It is advisable to mix well-rotted manure with the soil to a depth 6 in. below where the base of the bulb will be, to encourage the downward growth of the

TWO LARGER HARDY TYPES
The pure white Madonna Lily (left) and the attractive rose-spotted Japanese Lily (right).

basal roots. Base-rooting lilies often lie dormant the first year after planting or send up only a weak non-flowering shoot, because the heavy roots have been destroyed in storage and transit. Lilies care-

TWO SMALL HARDY LILIES
The dainty Coral Lily (left) and the Candlestick Lily (right) are both easily grown and have brilliant flowers.

fully transplanted do not suffer this damage and resulting check.

Stem-rooting lilies require deep planting so as to have maximum root-producing stem area. They usually bloom well the first year and it is desirable to incorporate bonemeal into the first 18 in. of soil, to add to the nourishment which they can derive from the humus and plant food already present.

Whether lilies are grown in a bed by themselves or in the border in combination with perennials, they require a year-round mulch to keep the soil mellow and to conserve moisture. Fresh manure should never be used, but partially decayed leaves are excellent if the soil is rich; well-rotted horse or cow manure is essential, if the soil lacks humus. Many lilies do well in the shrubbery border, where their roots are kept cool and their stems are supported by the surrounding plants, their blossoms reaching up into the sunlight.

In certain species the bulbs are composed of very loose scales under which water may collect and cause rotting. To prevent this, plant them on their sides on a layer of sharp sand. Indeed, a handful of sand placed in the bottom of the hole when planting any kind of lily, is an advisable rot preventive.

In the list of species that follows are noted the special cultural requirements of the important garden kinds which are also distinguished as to whether stem rooting or bulb rooting.

Lilies for American Gardens

The following list comprises the most important Lilium species suitable for garden culture in this country. As the principal ones are of foreign origin they are given first; then the native kinds, and finally some foreign sorts of value but requiring expert handling. At the end of each species description B R indicates base-rooting, and S R stem-rooting (see culture, above). The figures indicate planting depth measured from the base of the bulb to the surface of the soil.

Lilies from Other Lands

L. regale (Regal Lily). A useful and magnificent Chinese species introduced since the beginning of the century. From 3 to 4 ft. tall, it bears flowers in large terminal clusters. They are long trumpet-shaped, white with lilac and brown shadings on the outside and shading to yellow on the inside base. Unlike many lilies this species adapts itself well to garden conditions and propagates readily. S R, 12 in.

speciosum. An important showy species from Japan which includes several varieties grown commercially for cut flowers as well as in gardens. The white flowers flushed with rose are reflexed, slightly drooping and borne in groups on stems to 4 ft. This lily is easy to grow in the open sunny border or among small deciduous shrubs. S R, 8 to 12 in. Chief varieties are: *album,* pure white; *kraetzeri,* white tinged with green; *magnificum,* white with crimson shadings; *roseum,* carmine pink; and *rubrum,* deep rose.

candidum (Madonna or Annunciation Lily). A well-known and important garden species from S. Europe and Asia with pure white, horizontally borne flowers, with short, flared trumpets. The bulbs, obtained principally from France, are available in midsummer and should be planted then. They produce a rosette growth in the fall which begins to lengthen in early spring, the flowers appearing in late June on stems 3 to 4 ft. tall. B R, 4 to 5 in.

auratum (Golden-banded or Goldband Lily of Japan). Growing to 6 ft., this is one of the largest and handsomest of lilies. The large, fragrant flaring-trumpet flowers are ivory white with broad yellow bands down the center of each petal and purple blotches on the inner surface. Plant in soil rich in humus but free from lime. S R, 9 to 12 in. Of the several varieties, *platyphyllum* is large and especially vigorous; *rubrum* has crimson instead of yellow

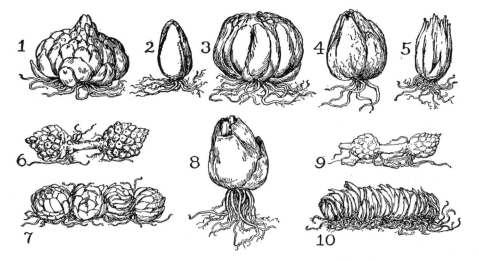

LILY BULBS VARY GREATLY IN SIZE AND SHAPE

Here are shown, in proportionate size, bulbs of the following: 1. Western Orange-cup Lily (L. umbellatum). 2. Coral Lily (L. tenuifolium), a jewel of the rock garden. 3. The easily grown Japanese Lily (L. speciosum). 4. The outstandingly beautiful Regal Lily (L. regale). 5. The old-time Martagon Lily (L. martagon). 6. Two bulb scale clusters of the American Turks Cap Lily (L. superbum) joined by a section of creeping rootstock. 7. The graceful native Leopard Lily (L. pardalinum), showing one year's natural increase. 8. The Himalayan Giant Lily (L. giganteum)—this bulb is bottle-green. 9. The Meadow Lily (L. canadense), which has fleshy creeping rootstocks and clusters of bulb scales. 10. The Mt. Hood Lily (L. washingtonianum) with its narrow, pointed bulb scales.

bands, and *pictum* has the tip of each band crimson.

elegans or *thunbergianum.* A dwarf Japanese species in which the orange-red flowers, with purple black spots, are held erect. There are many horticultural forms showing great variations in color and height. They grow well in sunny borders or in the rock garden. S R, 6 in.

tigrinum. Though native to China and Japan, the well-known Tiger Lily is now common in American gardens and elsewhere having naturalized in many places. It grows 3 to 4 ft. high with large heads of reflexed orange-red flowers with purplish-black dots and is easily established under average garden conditions over a wide range. S R, 9 in. (See illustration, Plate 6.) Var. *splendens* is taller and more highly colored, while var. *flore-pleno* is semi-double with several rows of petals.

browni. A beautiful Japanese species with trumpet-shaped flowers, the inside of the petals being creamy white and the outside rose-purple. It grows readily in the open border in light sandy soil. *Plant the bulb on its side* on a bed of sand so water will not collect under the scales and rot it. S R, 8 in.

hansoni. A fine Japanese species, growing to 5 ft. The drooping flowers with reflexed petals are bright yellowish-orange with purplish-brown spots. It grows readily in the border, but should be planted in partial shade to prevent flower bleaching. S R, 6 in.

henryi. A tall robust species (to 9 ft.) from China. The lemon to orange-yellow flowers are reflexed and look like those of *L. speciosum.* Sometimes 20 are borne on one stem making some support desirable; this lily is therefore an excellent species to plant among rhododendrons. S R, 10 in.

davidi. A tall (6 ft.) Chinese lily with cinnabar-red flowers spotted black. A hardy species, easily grown in the open border. S R, 6 in.

monadelphum. A sturdy Caucasian species with 5 to 6 ft. stems and golden yellow flowers often spotted with purple. It should be planted in partial shade but will not flower until the second year. B R, 5 in. Var. *szovitzianum* (also known as *colchicum*) is straw-colored with black spots.

croceum (Orange Lily). Native of the mountains of S. Europe, this species grows 6 ft. tall and bears chalice-shaped orange or saffron colored flowers spotted with

crimson. A robust species for the border, it grows well in any good garden soil and eventually forms dense clumps. S R, 5 in.

testaceum (Nankeen Lily). Generally considered a hybrid between *L. candidum*

AT EASTER TIME
The familiar Easter Lily as a pot plant in a basket arrangement bordered with Primulas.

and *L. chalcedonicum,* having foliage, habit and time of flowering like to those of the former. The flowers are flat, slightly reflexed and apricot colored. Plant in the open border among tall growing perennials. B R, 5 in.

rubellum. A species from Japan with fragrant, rosy-pink flowers borne horizontally on 2 ft. stems. It grows best in sandy or gravelly soil, and is excellent in a border of deciduous shrubs or in the rock garden. S R, 6 in.

tenuifolium (Coral Lily). A popular rock-garden species with nodding, brilliant scarlet flowers on slender stems from 18 in. to 3 ft. high. A hardy species for open border or rock garden. S R, 5 in.

chalcedonicum. Commonly known as "Scarlet Turks Cap Lily," this 4 ft. species, native to Greece, bears bright scarlet flowers with rolled back petals but a disagreeable odor. It is easily grown in a sunny position and will endure a limy soil. B R, 5 in. The var. *maculatum* is darker red spotted with purple.

dahuricum or *dauricum* (the "Candlestick" Lily). This species from Siberia has orange-red, black-spotted flowers borne erect on stems 2 to 3 ft. tall. There are many horticultural forms such as var. *venustum,* of which Batemanni is an improved form; S R, 5 in.

martagon (Martagon or Turks Cap Lily). The drooping flowers with recurved petals are produced in tiers or whorls along stems that grow 6 ft. tall. They are purplish-red to violet-rose spotted with deep red at the base. This species and its white and purple varieties will grow in sun or shade. S R, 5 in.

medeoloides (Wheel Lily). This Oriental species to 2½ ft. has drooping flowers with recurved petals, scarlet with apricot shadings and black spots. S R, 6 in.

japonicum. A Japanese species to 2 ft. bearing broad funnel-shaped flowers pale pink to rose in color. A beautiful lily, it thrives in the peaty soil under rhododendrons and kalmias, but is not reliably hardy in the New England States. S R, 8 in.

concolor (Star Lily). This species to 4 ft. from China and Japan, bears usually erect unspotted flowers which range in color from yellow to bright scarlet. Var. *pulchellum* frequently shows spotted flowers. It should be planted in the rock garden in full sun. B R, 4 in.

pomponium (Lesser Turks Cap Lily). An Italian species with 2 to 3 ft. stems and drooping, bright red flowers spotted with purple. It responds readily to cultivation in the garden in sunlight. B R, 5 in.

pyrenaicum (Yellow Turks Cap Lily). Native to the Pyrenees and attaining 3 to 4 ft. it has greenish-yellow, purple-spotted flowers. Easily grown in the open border. B R, 5 in. Var. *aureum* is deeper yellow.

Native Lilies for American Gardens

L. canadense (Meadow Lily). Found along the Atlantic Coast from Canada to Ga. The flowers on 3 to 5 ft. stems are small, drooping, funnel-shaped and vary in color from orange-yellow to red. There are several varieties including *rubrum, parvum* and *flavum.* In the wild it grows in damp meadows but when cultivated does well in sun or partial shade, or in a moist, well-drained situation. S R, 10 in.

superbum (American Turks Cap Lily). Native to the Atlantic Coast from New Brunswick to Ga. The tall stems bear orange-red flowers spotted with purple.

This beautiful lily should be grown on the edge of the woodland in moist peaty soil, near a stream or in shrubbery in the open. S R, 9 in.

philadelphicum (Orange-cup Lily). An E. N. American species with cup-shaped flowers of bright scarlet which shades to yellow at the base and has purple spots. Plant in acid, dry soil in sun or shade. S R, 5 in.

michiganense. Similar to *L. canadense* but native to Mich., Minn. and Mo. Red colors predominate in its flowers. It grows to 5 ft. in rocky woods and has a branching rhizome.

parvum (Sierra Lily). A native 5-ft. species of Ore. and Calif. with flowers bright orange-scarlet shading to orange at base, spotted purplish. The variety *luteum* has clear yellow spotted flowers. An easily grown lily if given dry soil and semi-shade. B R, 4 in.

washingtonianum. A grand lily from Calif. and Ore. with drooping, funnel-shaped sweet-scented flowers; pure white tinged purple or lilac borne on 4 to 6 ft. stems. Plant in well-drained but moist soil in partial shade. S R, 10 in.

umbellatum (Western Orange-cup Lily). This species, a native of the Midwestern States, bears erect red or orange flowers on stems up to 2 ft. Resembles *L. philadelphicum.*

pardalinum (Leopard Lily). A very fine species from Calif. and Ore. where it grows to 8 ft. The reflexed flowers, which droop on the stalk, are bright orange-red with dark crimson spots. There are several forms varying in color and height. It should be grown in a moist but well-drained peaty soil in full sun. It grows from a rhizome and requires shallow planting.

humboldti. A tall (6 ft.) species from Calif. with drooping reflexed flowers, rich orange-red with maroon spots. The var. *magnificum* is larger. Plant in open woodland or among tall shrubbery in peaty soil. B R, 5 in.

kelloggi. A Calif. species characterized by large trusses of delicate reflexed flowers of pinkish purple banded with yellow and maroon dots. Grows best in half sunlight in a mixture of sand and peat. B R, 5 in.

columbianum. This native of N. W. America has bright reddish-orange flowers with reflexed petals spotted purple. The blossoms droop. Not reliably hardy E., it should be grown in semi-shade in acid soil. B R, 6 in.

bolanderi (Thimble Lily). A Calif. species with bell-shaped, deep crimson flowers spotted purple. Grow amid shrubbery. S R, 6 in.

maritimum (Coast Lily). A Calif. species, found growing close to the shore. The stems, 3 to 5 ft. tall, bear reddish-orange flowers spotted purple. It should be grown in a moist, well drained spot, free from lime. B R, 4 in.

grayi. A native of Va. and N. C. and closely related to *L. canadense*. The drooping, funnel-shaped flowers are rich crimson blotched with purple at the base. It thrives in loose, peaty soil among rhododendrons or kalmias. B R, 5 in.

carolinianum to 4 ft. A pretty species native to Fla. and the Gulf States. The reflexed, orange-scarlet fragrant flowers droop on the stems. Plant in moist soil in half shade in protected situations. S R, 5 in.

catesbaei (Southern Red Lily). A native of the S. States from N. C. to Fla. Bright orange-red erect flowers with many spots of purple. B R, 4 in.

parryi. A Calif. species, 3 to 4 ft. tall with sweet-scented, pale, lemon-yellow flowers. Plant in shrubbery in loamy soil with a gravelly subsoil. B R, 5 in.

rubescens (Chaparral Lily). Native to Calif. and Ore. it bears its fragrant white flowers with purple shadings erect in large heads on 6 ft. stems. Should be grown in acid soil amid shrubbery. B R, 5 in.

FOREIGN LILIES FOR THE SPECIALIST

L. bakerianum. From Burma and China, this species grows 3 ft. high and bears broad funnel-shaped flowers to 2½ in. across, creamy white with many brown spots at the base. Should be handled in pots, plunged in summer and taken into a cool cellar for winter. S R, 8 in.

bulbiferum. A European species to 4 ft. with erect cherry-red flowers spotted with purple black. It will grow well in the border. S R, 4 in.

callosum. An Oriental species with small, drooping, orange-colored flowers borne abundantly on 2 to 3 ft. stems. Plant in full sun. S R, 8 in.

carniolicum. A S. European species with fragrant, recurved, orange-yellow and red flowers dotted purple-black, 2 in. or less in diameter. S R, 6 in.

duchartrei or *farreri*. A native of W. China producing from small bulbs slender stems to 4 ft. tall. The flowers are white with inside spots of reddish-brown. Grow in a well-drained, shaded part of the rock garden. S R, 4 in.

giganteum. To 12 ft. A beautiful tall-growing species from the Himalayas. The long, tubular, white flowers to 6 in. long with purple markings in throat are sweet-scented. It should be planted on the edge of the woodland or among shrubs, just below the ground surface. B R, 4 in. (Not to be confused with a white Easter Lily often called *giganteum*, but really a variety of *L. longiflorum*.)

lankongense. A species from W. China whose slender stems from 1 to 2 ft. tall support reflexed flowers that are white with a purplish cast, spotted crimson. This species is best grown in full sunlight. S R, 5 in.

leichtlini. A fine Japanese species with reflexed flowers of citron-yellow, heavily spotted with purple borne on stems to 6 ft. tall. Grow in light loamy soil in the open. S R, 6 in. There are several forms. Var. *maximowiczi* having salmon-red flowers.

leucanthum (Chinese White Lily). A beautiful species closely resembling *Lilium browni*, with long milky white, funnel-shaped drooping, fragrant flowers with a greenish cast on the outside and tinged with yellow in the throat. As it is not hardy it should be raised in the greenhouse. S R, 9 in.

myriophyllum. A Chinese species to 4 ft. in which the flowers are greenish-white with a yellow cast and often red outside. It should be grown in the open. S R, 10 in. The var. *superbum*, commonly called *L. sulphureum*, is a rare, vigorous form of exceptional beauty. The flowers are sulphur-yellow with streaks of claret-red on the outside of the petals. The name "myriophyllum" is often applied to *L. regale*.

neilgherrense. A tender species from India growing to 4 ft. with sweet-scented, pale sulphur-yellow flowers to 10 in. in length. S R, 9 in.

philippinense. A low-growing (to 1½ ft.) species from the Philippines rather easily produced from seed and, as a result, attracting considerable attention. The flowers are large, trumpet-shaped and pure white tinged with green. Var. *formosanum* is white with reddish-purple shadings on

LILY BULBS FROM THE ORIENT
Many kinds, both hardy and for forcing, are grown in Japan and shipped to horticultural markets all over the world.

the outside. Not hardy, but easily grown in the greenhouse. S R, 8 in.

sargentiae (Sargent Lily). A species from W. China in which the flowers, borne horizontally on 6 ft. stems, are milky-white occasionally with greenish throat and purple shadings on the outside. A hardy species but much subject to disease, which should be grown among low shrubbery in the sun. S R, 9 in.

szovitzianum. See *L. monadelphum,* above.

EASTER LILIES

The various forms of the well-known white Easter Lily are all developments of one Japanese species, *L. longiflorum.* For the most part they show only slight differences that would not be noticed by the layman, but that are important to the commercial grower who selects his varieties and strains on the basis of such factors as size and texture of flower, date of flowering, forcing temperature requirements, length of stem, etc.

Bermuda was the first region to grow bulbs of this species commercially and for many years it had the world's markets practically to itself. The sort grown there, though formerly—and sometimes still—referred to as a species (*L. harrisi*), is actually a variety—*L. longiflorum eximium.* It is a fine large lily of excellent texture and form, but for a time its culture was threatened with extinction by a serious disease that appeared on the island early in the

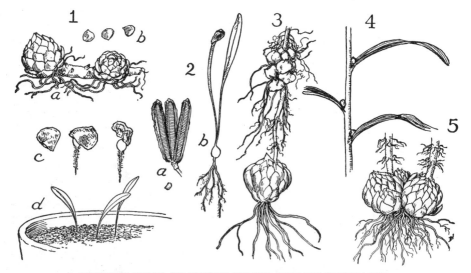

VARIOUS WAYS IN WHICH LILIES MAY BE INCREASED
1. By scales: (a) clusters of scales on a creeping rootstock; (b) 3 scales removed and (c) as they germinate and develop bulblets; (d) young plants growing from such bulblets. **2.** By seed: (a) typical lily pod and, below it, a single seed; (b) lily seedling with bulblet, withered cotyledon at top of its stem, and the first true leaf. **3.** By bulblets formed on the erect stem between the mother bulb and the ground surface. **4.** By bulbils formed in the leaf axils. **5.** By natural increase of bulbs themselves.

20th century. By the time measures for controlling and preventing it were perfected, the Japanese had begun to develop other varieties and had developed a world demand that they continue to supply, even though the Harrisi Lily is abundantly available in its former perfection. Some of the Japanese forms fit particularly well into the needs of the flower business because they can safely be kept in cold storage for long periods and taken out to be forced at any time, thereby providing for a succession of flowers throughout the year instead of only at Easter time as formerly. In some parts of this country progress is slowly being made toward the growing of bulbs for forcing; in the Gulf States especially *L. longiflorum* types known as "Floridi" and Creole Lily (var. *alexandrae*) are being produced in increasing numbers and proving acceptable to the florist trade.

Probably the best known of these Easter Lilies are the following varieties: Var. *alexandrae*, just referred to; *erabu*, a Japanese sort; *eximium*, the Bermuda variety, better known as *harrisi*; *multiflorum*, but slightly different from *eximium*; *giganteum*, often grown in gardens but *not* the same as *L. giganteum*; and *insulare*, also of Japan and frequently called by the name *formosum* first given it when it was thought to be a separate species.

For greenhouse culture, bulbs of any of the kinds mentioned are planted in pots— one to a 6 in. pot is the usual practice—and either placed under a bench in a coolhouse or plunged outdoors (away from frost) until the root system has developed and top growth begins to appear above the soil in the pots. They can then be brought in to full light and, gradually, to a forcing temperature. This is from 60 to 70 deg. F., at which flowers will open in from 110 to 120 days.

Though usually considered essentially greenhouse plants, Easter Lilies can be planted out in spring in the N. and will bloom well in the garden in summer. In the S. and in Calif. they are used extensively in the border.

OTHER "LILIES"

Many plants that resemble lilies but are not of the genus Lilium, and some that do not even belong to the Lily Family, commonly have the name lily applied to them. They include the following, which see:

Adobe-lily, African-lily, Checkered-lily, Daylily, Fawn-lily, Glory-lily, Mariposa-lily, Lily-of-the-Nile, Lily-of-the-valley, Plantain-lily, St. Bernards-lily, St. Brunos-lily, Sand-lily, Snake-lily, Star-lily, Toad-lily, Torch-lily, Triplet-lily, and Trout-lily, all belong to the Lily Family (Liliaceae).

Amazon-lily, Atamasco-lily, Belladonna-lily, Blood-lily, Chinese Sacred-lily, Guernsey-lily, Jacobean-lily, Josephines-lily, Kafir-lily, Mystery-lily, Prairie-lily, Rain-lily, St. James-lily, Scarborough-lily Sego-lily (State flower of Utah), Spear-lily, Spider-lily, and Zephyr-lily all belong to the Amaryllis Family (Amaryllidaceae).

Calla-lily, a wrong name for Calla (Zantedeschia) belongs to the Arum Family.

Mountain-lily belongs to the Crowfoot Family.

Ginger-lily belongs to the Ginger Family.

Blackberry-lily belongs to the Iris Family.

Cowlily, Pondlily, and Waterlily belong to the Waterlily Family.

LILY-OF-THE-NILE. Common name for *Agapanthus umbellatus*, a tender bulbous pot plant with bright blue flowers.

LILY-OF-THE-PALACE. Common name of *Hippeastrum aulicum*, a bulbous plant 2 ft. tall bearing 2 large red green-throated flowers.

LILY-OF-THE-VALLEY. Common name for *Convallaria majalis*, a low perennial herb of the Lily Family, native to Europe and Asia, but widely grown both in gardens (where it often becomes naturalized) and indoors. It has underground, creeping rootstocks and fleshy crowns popularly known as "pips," which develop two oblong leaves and a solitary, one-sided, graceful spike of fragrant, small white, bell-shaped blossoms that are excellent for small vase arrangements and much used for corsages, bride's bouquets and other decorative purposes.

The fleshy pips are bulb-like in their construction and action in that the flower embryo is actually present in all ripened, full-size specimens so that only water and moderate heat are needed for the development of flower stems. This makes "valley" one of the most easily handled of all floral subjects and largely accounts for its great popularity.

The commercial supply of lily-of-the-valley pips that is used by florists, and which runs into many millions annually, is mainly produced in Germany. Many are

LILY-OF-THE-VALLEY PIPS

Strong, well-rooted stock as delivered from cold storage at any time of year. For forcing in shallow containers, the roots may, without harm, be trimmed back to the point shown.

held in cold storage for flowering over a season, extending from Christmas to Easter or even throughout the whole year. When withdrawn from cold storage, they are thawed out gradually and then planted. Florists generally use sand and, in an enclosed chamber within a greenhouse where a temperature of 80 deg. can be maintained, bring them into bloom in about 3 weeks.

Because of its beauty, easy-flowering quality and availability over the whole year, the lily-of-the-valley is also a favorite subject for house culture. Almost any receptacle will answer and, where the roots are too long for use in shallow bowls, they can be cut off to the extent of one-half their length without injury. A bowl 6 in. in diameter will accommodate 10 to 12 pips which should be stood in an upright position with the fleshy tips extending above the bowl. Sand, sphagnum moss or peat moss should be firmly pressed between and around the roots and the receptacle filled with luke-warm water and placed near a light window where, if water is added as it evaporates so as to keep the moss or sand moist, the pips will flower in 3 or 4 weeks in usual room temperature.

For garden planting pips should be planted either in late fall or very early spring. For best results they insist upon a

cool, rather densely shaded spot and are perfectly hardy. They can be planted about 6 in. apart for as soon as they are established they will begin to increase and spread over a larger area every year. The planting should be kept free from weeds and not crowded out by other subjects. The flowers can be cut freely, but any removal of the foliage before it has completely died down will interfere with the flower crop the following season.

LILY-THORN (*Catesbaea spinosa*). A slow-growing evergreen shrub from the W. Indies, belonging to the Madder Family. It can be grown outside in the warmer parts of the United States where it reaches 15 ft. It has rather small leaves with spines that are longer. The showy, pale yellow, funnel-shaped flowers grow to 6 in. long and are followed by an oval, pale or whitish, edible berry.

LILY-TURF. Popular name for two genera of stemless perennial herbs—Liriope and Mondo—both prized as ground-covers.

LIMB. The expanded, flaring portion of an organ, particularly the upper, outspread portion of a corolla in which the petals are fused, the lower portion of which is the *tube;* or the flaring portion of an individual petal in such a corolla.

A NOVEL ARRANGEMENT

A modified form of strawberry-jar (a), in which valley pips are planted in light, fibrous soil or peat moss with one emerging from each opening (b) will in a few weeks produce the effect shown. Florists' smilax or other foliage can be grown around the base in a flower-pot saucer.

LIME. A small, tropical, thorny ever-green tree (*Citrus aurantifolia*) grown for its strongly acid fruit. Because of its ten-derness to frost it is restricted almost wholly to gardens in the S. tip of Florida and S. California. Several varieties popu-lar in home gardens bear larger finer qual-ity fruits than the seedling limes sold in markets. See CITRUS FRUITS.

LIME. A compound of calcium (which see). Limestone is the carbonate, quick-lime the oxide, slaked or hydrated lime the hydroxide. All three forms are used to improve soils and to reduce acidity or sour-ness, while quicklime and hydrated lime also have many uses in the preparation of sprays, dusts and whitewash.

Quicklime (or burned lime) is made from limestone by burning in a kiln, and should never be used directly on plants as it will burn them. It must first be slaked by add-ing water—*but carefully*—because the heat generated may cause a fire, and the ex-pansion will burst an ordinary box. When quicklime is used on fallow land, the lumps are slaked by dumping them in piles and exposing them to the weather.

For most garden purposes hydrated lime is preferred, as it comes finely powdered in convenient paper bags, and is easy to handle and is not caustic. It usually con-tains some magnesium in addition to the calcium, and the analysis printed on the bag should be noted, for lime with more than 25 per cent magnesium is not desirable. Nor should waste lime from chemical fac-tories be used unless analyzed and found free of injurious impurities. Hydrated lime should not be kept over from year to year, for it gradually turns back to limestone.

Most vegetables and some flower plants benefit if lime is spread in winter and mixed thoroughly with the soil as soon as it can be worked. Average soil will take 100 to 200 lbs. a year on a plot 50 ft. square; less should be applied on light, sandy soil and more on clay. It should *not* be used for acid-soil plants. It is valuable in com-bination with leafmold and compost, hasten-ing their decay, releasing plant food, and neutralizing acidity. Lawns of blue grass and a few other lime-loving grasses may be sprinkled with hydrated lime but other lawns are better without it. It is often scattered around the roots of iris, delphin-ium, and other lime-loving plants.

By liming, the soil is changed in chemical nature; not only is it made less acid, but also the potash and phosphorus salts are altered to forms that make better plant food, while some injurious elements are made harmless. The soil texture is also improved; clay is broken up and sand com-pacted. Lime also helps the complicated process by which soil bacteria, especially those that live in the roots of legumes, put valuable nitrogen in plant-food form.

Lime is an ingredient in spray materials, lime-sulphur, bordeaux, etc., and is also used for dusting. Plain hydrated lime is a convenient insecticide for currant and cabbage worms. Mixed with tobacco dust finely ground, it will control aphis and other insects if simply thrown over the plants by hand, 2 or 3 times at intervals of a few hours. Since it is harmless, the dust may be used freely except on acid-soil plants; what falls to the ground acts as good fertilizer. Lime alone or mixed with tobacco, if dusted on young peas, beans, etc., will repel rabbits. Whitewash made with lime and water, a little glue sometimes added as a binder, is sometimes painted on the trunks of orchard trees to destroy insect pests, on boards in cold-frames, greenhouses, etc., for the same pur-pose, and somewhat as a wood-preservative.

See also ALKALINE SOIL; CALCIUM; IM-PROVEMENT, SOIL; LIMESTONE; LIME-LOVING PLANTS.

LIME. British name for the genus Tilia, the Linden (which see). In America, it is frequently called Basswood and some-times (erroneously) Whitewood.

LIME-BERRY. A spiny evergreen shrub or small tree (*Triphasia trifolia*) of Asiatic origin rarely grown in the far S. as a hedge plant or ornamental. It bears solitary fragrant white flowers followed by dull red berries.

LIME-LOVING PLANTS. In some respects these are the same as alkaline-soil plants (which see), but some kinds that do not like alkaline soil, and some that are indifferent to either acidity or alkalinity, are helped by lime. Others naturally associated with soils made alka-line by serpentine rock, or rock other than limestone, may appear not to favor lime.

Lime (which see) not only makes soil alkaline, but acts on it in many other ways, for example altering compounds of potash, phosphorus, iron, and other elements affect-ing plant growth, and changing the soil texture. Results of experiments on lime-loving and alkaline-soil plants often disagree because of the difference between the presence of lime and actual alkalinity; and also because different soils are differently affected by lime. Gardeners should not only use lime for alkaline-soil plants, and avoid using it on acid-soil plants (to most of which it is poison) but should also try it in small amounts experimentally on plants not known to prefer either acidity or alkalinity—thus making practical tests the results of which will apply specifically to their own soils.

LIMEQUAT. A hybrid citrus fruit developed by W. T. Swingle of the U. S. Department of Agriculture; its parents being the West Indian lime and the kumquat (which see). The tree, which can be grown wherever the latter is hardy, bears abundant crops of small, pleasantly flavored fruits which may be eaten raw or used for ades or marmalades. See CITRUS FRUITS.

LIMESTONE. Natural rock consisting mainly of calcium carbonate mixed with some magnesium carbonate. It is the principal rock of large sections of country, giving rise to alkaline soil and "hard" water (where the acid rainwater, leaching through, dissolves the stone). Because alkaline or neutral soil improves most garden crops, finely ground limestone is often spread on the vegetable garden where it renders the same service as lime (which see), although more slowly. It is entirely safe and will not "burn" plants so can be used generously if needed.

Limestone is also much used for rock gardens, partly because large stones of it are comparatively light in weight and easily handled, and partly because many alpine plants prefer it. For these lime-loving alpines, a mulch of limestone chips proves effective.

See also ALKALINE SOIL; CALCIUM; LIME-LOVING PLANTS.

LIME-SULPHUR. A compound of lime and sulphur long used as a dormant spray against scales and other insects and some fungi; and also as a summer fungicide. See SULPHUR AND ITS COMPOUNDS; also FUNGICIDE.

LIMNANTHEMUM (lim-nan'-the-mum). A name sometimes used for Nymphoides (which see), a genus of flowering aquatics of the Gentian Family much used in the water garden and the aquarium.

LIMNANTHES (lim-nan'-theez) *douglasi.* Annual herb with white or pinkish fragrant flowers. Formerly in the genus Floerkea. See MEADOW FOAM.

LIMNOCHARIS (lim-nok'-ah-ris). A genus of tropical American aquatic herbs with large leaves lifted above the water, characterized by milky juice. The flowers, which open in July, are composed of 3 petals and 3 sepals. The principal species are *L. flava,* which stands 1 to 1½ ft. above water, has blunt velvet-green leaves, and green and yellow flowers, and *L. humboldti,* now often placed in a separate genus as *Hydrocleis commersoni* because of its floating leaves. Both are readily grown in the greenhouse in warm tanks or outdoors in shallow ponds through the summer. Propagated by root division or from runners.

LIMONIUM (li-moh'-ni-um). Known in gardens as Statice, this genus contains plants of decorative value in homes and greenhouses, rock gardens, borders, and in dried bouquets of "everlastings." Sea-lavender and Sea-pink are the common names for these plants. The small spiked or clustered flowers, of papery texture, are of white, yellow, rose, lavender or blue; whether left on the plants or cut for bouquets they are exceedingly long-lasting. Among nearly 200 species, the following are representative:

L. suworowi (Russian or Rat-tail Statice), is a lilac-flowered annual, easy of culture indoors, retaining its long, finger-like spikes of flowers in fresh-looking condition for many months. Seed sown in January gives flowering plants in spring.

latifolium; a perennial with flowers of delicate lavender, somewhat resembles Gypsophalia and is similarly used both fresh and dried. It favors a dry situation in the garden or greenhouse.

sinuatum, biennial or perennial, has white flowers with persistent blue calyxes, varieties appearing also in pink, lavender and yellow. A low rosette of dandelion-like leaves forms the base for the stiff, angular, branching flower stalks.

LINANTHUS (ly-nan'-thus). A genus of annual herbs of the Phlox Family, called Flax-flower and California-phlox. They have opposite leaves usually divided to the base and appearing to be whorled. The funnel-form flowers are arranged in more or less dense terminal heads, in soft tones of pink, violet, yellow, blush and white. Plants are grown from seed, chiefly in the W., where some of the species are native. It should be sown thickly in light soil. The best species are: *L. grandiflorus,* 1½ ft., with long flowers in lilac and pink; and *L. dianthiflorus,* with tufted 6 in. entire, thread-like leaves and smaller flowers. The genus is often listed as Gilia.

LINARIA (ly-nay'-ri-ah). A genus of rather low-growing annual, biennial and perennial herbs of the Figwort Family, some trailing and others erect. The flowers, which come in a wide variety of pastel shades, resemble miniature snap-dragons.

The annuals are of easy culture from seed, which is generally sown indoors. The perennials are equally simple to grow, the usual method of propagation being division, though seeds should produce flowering plants the second year. Kenilworth Ivy, usually listed in catalogs as *L. cymbalaria* is now classified as *Cymbalaria muralis* and some other species with single axillary flowers and palmately veined leaves are now placed in the same genus (which see).

While *L. vulgaris* (Toadflax or Butter-and-eggs), with 2-toned yellow flowers on erect plants, is a common roadside weed throughout most of the world, an improved variety was considered fine enough to be included among the 1934 All-America selection of the choice garden annuals.

Other garden species include: *L. marocanna,* a fast-growing hardy annual 15 in. tall which is offered in a mixture of shades of crimson, orange and blue; its var. Fairy Bouquet is shorter and more compact in growth; *L. alpina,* a low-spreading rock-garden plant with fine frosty leaves and bright violet flowers with an orange palate; *L. bipartita* (Cloven-lip Toadflax) an erect annual, also in violet and orange, with varieties all purple and all white; *L. dalmatica* and *L. macedonica,* both resembling Butter-and-eggs but showier; *L. triphylla,* a 2-ft. annual, its white and orange flowers having a violet spur; and *L. anticaria,* a low-branched plant for shady rock pockets, with blue and white lilac-spurred flowers.

LINDELOFIA (lin-de-lof'-i-ah). A genus of half-hardy perennial herbs having long racemes of small deep-blue flowers resembling forget-me-nots. *L. longiflora,* from the Himalayas, growing to 1½ ft., is occasionally grown in a sheltered spot in the rock garden in ordinary soil, well-drained, but in the N. it requires winter protection. Increased by seed or division.

LINDEN. Common name for the genus Tilia, the only northern representative of a

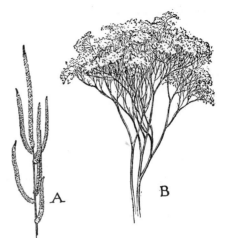

LIMONIUM—OFTEN CALLED STATICE
The long purplish finger-like spikes of L. suworowi (A) last many weeks on the plant or cut for dried bouquets. L. latifolium (B) is a favorite of florists and gardeners for its airy effect among other flowers.

mostly tropical family. There are numerous natural hybrids and horticultural varieties. The other common name, Basswood, comes from the *bast,* or fibre of the wood, which has long been used for the making of strong ropes. The name was formerly Bastwood.

All lindens are hardy N., thriving in rich soils not too wet; if the soil is too dry the leaves drop in warm weather, retarding growth. In youth they are generally pyramidal in form, some species becoming more irregular with age. They have been extensively planted because of their dense, attractive foliage and the abundant fragrant, yellowish flowers which add to their beauty. Also they produce uniformity along avenues or entrance driveways. Where numerous, lindens are important bee-forage trees and the hum of the insects in their tops is an added charm.

Several leaf spot fungi and a powdery mildew may be controlled by three or four applications of bordeaux mixture. Fungi entering the wood through woodpecker holes sometimes attack the sapwood and kill trees. The white-marked tussock moth (which see) can be controlled by collecting and burning the egg masses. Where the Japanese beetle (which see) is abundant, spray trees with lead arsenate. For red spider, which may cause leaf fall during dry seasons, spray with a sulphur compound.

The American Linden (*T. americana*) grows to great size and has been used extensively as a street tree; there are several desirable varieties. The European Linden (*T. vulgaris*) with smaller leaves and generally more pyramidal, has also long been a favorite street tree. *T. platyphyllos,* the large leaved species, grows to 120 ft. and has several varieties, some with colored branchlets, deeply cut leaves, pyramidal habit, etc. The White or Silver Linden (*T. tomentosa*) grows to 100 ft. and has more upright branches; it endures heat and dryness better than the other species. *T. petiolaris* resembles it closely but has attractive slender, pendulous branches.

Lindens are propagated by seeds (which require two years to germinate), layers, and cuttings. Named kinds of special value are sometimes grafted (in spring) or budded (in summer) on common stocks.

LINDEN FAMILY. Another name for the Basswood Family, Tiliaceae, which see.

LINDSAYA (lind'-say-ah). A genus of greenhouse ferns, difficult to cultivate. They have fronds 6 to 12 in. long, with curved segments of a semi-transparent texture. The creeping rhizomes are shallow-rooting, enabling one to provide plenty of drainage for potted specimens, as they require much water and a damp atmosphere. The best soil is fibrous loam and sand.

LINEAR. Narrow and more or less long, with margins parallel, as the leaves (or needles) of pines.

LINNAEA (li-nee'-ah) *borealis.* An evergreen trailer with pink or white fragrant flowers. See TWIN-FLOWER.

LINOSYRIS (lin-os'-i-ris) *vulgaris.* European perennial herb with heads of yellow flowers in late summer. Commonly called Goldilocks, which see.

LINUM (ly'-num). The botanical name for Flax (which see); narrow leaved herbs and shrubs, including several blue, white, yellow or red flowered annuals and perennials which are popular in gardens.

LIONS EAR or LIONS TAIL. Two common names for Leonotis, a genus of herbs and shrubs of the Mint Family, grown outdoors in S. Fla. and Calif.

LIP. One of the parts formed by the calyx or corolla of a flower when organized into (usually two) unequal divisions, as in plants of the Mint Family; also the labellum of an orchid. See ORCHIDS.

LIPARIS (lip'-ah-ris). A genus of terrestrial orchids commonly known as

Twayblade, a name also given to another genus, Listera. The hardy native species, *L. lilifolia,* is sometimes grown in the wild garden in rich vegetable humus, slightly acid. It has racemes of small yellow flowers veined with red, held about 10 in. above the broad flat leaves. *L. viridiflora* from India and China, has many-flowered racemes of yellowish-white flowers with a green lip. For culture see ORCHIDS.

LIP FERN. Common name for Cheilanthes (which see), a genus of woolly little ferns, many native to this country and of possible garden use.

LIPPIA (lip'-i-ah). A genus of tender herbs and shrubs of the Verbena Family having rose, purple or white flowers, closely clustered or in spikes. Only 2 species are well known horticulturally—*L. canescens* and *L. citriodora.*

L. canescens from S. America (often listed as *L. repens*), has a creeping spreading stem and small heads of lilac flowers. It is often grown as a ground-cover in Calif. and other warm-climate countries and, as it spreads rapidly in dry, poor soil, it is a very acceptable substitute for grass. The small flower-heads are easily removed by the lawn mower, and as the plant spreads by creeping branches and not by seed or underground stems, there is no danger of its becoming a dangerous weed.

L. citriodora (Lemon-verbena), a small shrub from S. America, has delightfully lemon-scented foliage, the long slender leaves growing in whorls. In Calif. and other warm climates it is grown in the open as a standard and may attain a height of 10 ft. In the N. it is grown mainly as a house, windowbox, or greenhouse plant. Lemon-verbenas in pots can be plunged in the garden over summer and taken into the house at the approach of frost. They make excellent foliage plants during the winter, and in mid-Victorian days no bouquet was considered complete without a spray of the deliciously scented leaves. They are increased by greenwood cuttings started in sand.

LIQUIDAMBAR (lik'-wid-am-bahr). *styraciflua.* Botanical name for Sweet Gum (which see), a noble tree with maple-like foliage that turns purple in autumn.

LIQUID MANURE. Since plants can use (that is, take in through the roots) only food that is in solution, solid manures and fertilizers take effect slowly, depending on rain or artificial watering to dissolve them. When quick results are wanted, such as flowers to be forced for sale or for exhibition, manure and fertilizers are often dissolved in water, and the resulting liquid manure is applied to the soil. This must be done carefully, using a weak solution, applying it only to soil that is already moist and, preferably, adding more water immediately afterward.

For ordinary garden needs, liquid manure is made by hanging a sack of rotted cow manure or sheep or chicken manure in a barrel of water for a couple of days, then dipping out the dark liquid (or drawing it off through a spigot) and diluting it to the color of weak tea, when it is safe to apply with a sprinkling can. Do not use it oftener than once a week. Any animal manure used in gardening will make liquid manure, but must be rotted or dried, not fresh. It is a mistake to use liquid manure or any other forcing treatment except at or just before flowering time, or on sickly plants, because forced growth is not hardy, and plants require weeks or months to recover from the strain of forcing.

See also MANURE.

LIRIODENDRON (lir-i-oh-den'-dron) *tulipifera*. Botanical name for the Tulip-tree (which see), often called Whitewood.

LIRIOPE (li-ry'-oh-pee). A genus of stemless, smooth, evergreen perennial herbs of the Lily Family having broad, grass-like foliage and small purplish to whitish flowers in spikes. They are of easy culture in tubs in the cool greenhouse or on the summer verandah, and are hardy to N. Y. Within their range they are useful as a ground cover over large areas, as they are indifferent to shade or sun, and are readily increased by root-division. They flower in late summer and fall and are sometimes listed under the name of Mondo (or Ophiopogon) which is an allied, more tender genus. Both are commonly called Lily-turf. The two principal species are:

L. muscari, 15 to 20 in. tall, with deep lilac flowers suggesting grape-hyacinths, and some with yellow-striped leaves.

spicata (Creeping Liriope). A small narrow-leaved form with pale lavender flowers, suitable for window boxes or hanging baskets.

LISTERA (lis'-ter-ah). A genus of small, native terrestrial orchids with inconspicuous greenish flowers. The two broad leaves on the stem give rise to the common name of Twayblade. *L. ovata* is some-

times planted in the wild garden in damp, acid soil.

LITCHI, or LEECHEE, or LYCHEE. Common name for a Chinese evergreen tree (*Litchi chinensis*) belonging to the Soapberry Family and popular in warm countries for its fruits which are there eaten fresh. In the N. it is better known in its dried state, the sweetish, raisin-like pulp and its single large seed being enclosed in a rough, thin, brown papery shell; the whole about 1 in. in diameter. In Southern Florida and California it is often planted as a garden tree. It should be given ample room, say 40 ft. Deep, loamy soils with ample moisture suit it best. When once established it will stand slight frosts.

LITHOCARPUS (lith-oh-kahr'-pus). A small genus of trees of the Beech Family, ranking half-way between the Oaks and the Chestnuts, and confined chiefly to the Orient. However, one species, *L. densiflora*, the Tanbark-oak, is native to the dry hillsides and ravines of Ore. and Calif., and makes a splendid garden tree in the far W. and S. Reaching a height of 80 ft., or more, it bears evergreen leaves yellow-downy in the spring, and a profusion of yellow flowers in erect catkins in midsummer. It is propagated by cuttings, layers or seeds.

LITHOSPERMUM (lith-oh-spur'-mum). A genus of hairy perennials or annuals related to forget-me-not and known as Gromwell. Common Gromwell has long been cultivated as a medicinal herb, and may be included in lists for the herb garden. Other species are occasionally used in the wild garden, border or rock garden. Collected plants and sometimes seeds of American species are offered by dealers in wildflowers. The striking and well known rock plant commonly called *Lithospermum prostratum*, is now classified as *Lithodora diffusa*.

The following Lithospermum species are all perennials: *L. angustifolium*, 1 ft. or more high, has yellow flowers. *L. canescens* (Puccoon), 1 ft., has orange flowers; the root is said to have given the Indians a red dye. *L. intermedium*, a shrubby plant 10 in. high, blue-flowered, is interesting for the rock garden. *L. multiflorum* to 2 ft. has light yellow blossoms. *L. officinale* (Common Gromwell) growing to 4 ft. is a medicinal plant only. *L. purpureo-caeruleum* attains 2 ft. and has flowers of a good blue, but not showy.

LITTLE FERN (*Cryptogramma acrostichoides*). A small rock fern of the N. States, rather difficult of cultivation. Has pod-like fertile segments, and parsley-like barren fronds.

LITTLE PICKLES. Common name for *Othonna crassifolia,* a hanging-basket plant with small succulent leaves suggesting little cucumbers.

LIVE-FOREVER. Common name of Sedum, a genus of mostly succulent, semi-evergreen perennials popular for use in rock gardens.

LIVERLEAF. Common name for Hepatica, a genus of small perennial herbs with white, pink, or blue flowers in early spring.

LIVERS OF SULPHUR. A name for potassium sulphide (which see), an old time fungicide used to some extent to check mildew in greenhouses but generally considered inferior to the modern, much finer sulphur dusts. See also SULPHUR AND ITS COMPOUNDS.

LIVERWORT. Common name for a member of the group of flowerless plants knowns as hepatics or, botanically, Hepaticae. These, together with a second large class, the Mosses (which see), make up the second main division (Bryophyta) of the plant kingdom. Liverworts are flat, green, red, or yellow-brown, ribbon-like, or stemmed and scaly-leafed, growths that creep closely along the bark of living trees in damp woods, or on shady banks or rocks. From a botanical standpoint they are of great importance, representing an evolutionary link between the lowest form of plant life (bacteria, fungi, algae, etc.) and the spore-bearing plants (ferns) which have well-developed stems, leaves and roots. Do not confuse with the genus Hepatica (which see), a group of true flowering plants of the Buttercup Family.

LIVING-ROCK. Common name for *Roseocactus fissuratus,* a succulent perennial of Mexico and Tex. with turnip-like roots, a flattened, thickened, half-buried stem suggesting the common name, and white or purple flowers to 1½ in. across.

LIVISTONA (liv-i-stoh'-nah). A genus of Fan Palms from Asia and Australia, comprising a number of beautiful and decorative sorts having large fan-shaped leaves with spiny stalks and panicles of small whitish flowers growing from the leaf-axils. A number of the species are grown in Calif. and Fla. among them *L. australis*

and *L. chinensis.* These palms require a heavy moist soil, made so, if it is sandy to start with, by incorporating clay and well-rotted manure. In the N. these two vigorous species are easily grown in the greenhouse in a rich light soil and a night temperature of 60 deg. F.

L. australis (Australian Fan Palm) growing to 80 ft., has a dense crown of dark green, almost round leaves.

chinensis (Chinese Fan or Fountain Palm) is a low-growing stout tree from Central China, surmounted by heavy crown of fan-shaped leaves 6 to 8 ft. in diameter. This is the source of the familiar palm leaf fans shipped to this country from China. In this country it is a popular subject grown in large pots or tubs for porch, terrace or garden decoration in summer. Plants of this species are often erroneously listed under another genus as *Latania borbonica.*

LIZARDS TAIL. Common name for *Saururus cernuus,* a hardy perennial wild-flower occasionally grown as a bog plant. It grows as much as 5 ft. tall, with a long rootstock, 6 in. heart-shaped leaves and slender, nodding spikes of feathery, white, fragrant flowers in midsummer. All the plants needed can be collected from the wild, but lizards tails may also be multiplied by division of the roots. In nature they are found in swamps and wet places. There is also a Chinese species, *S. loureiri,* of smaller size.

LOAM. A medium grade soil that does not answer to the description of either clay, muck, sand or gravel. It is a mixture coarser-grained than clay, finer than sand, and containing organic matter. Loam is easily worked, usually fertile, and acceptable to nearly all plants. Those which favor clay and will not thrive in sand, or those which demand sand and do not grow in clay, can usually be handled in loam with good success. Gradations in texture are often referred to as "sandy loam" or "clay loam." The word loam, sometimes (but incorrectly) pronounced *loom,* is less used in gardening than formerly, since top-soil is usually loam, and the better-known term. See also SOIL.

LOASA (loh-ay'-sah). Annual or perennial herbs of tropical America. They have stinging hairs like nettles, but one or two species are sometimes grown in flower gardens (being treated as half-hardy annuals) for their showy flowers.

L. urens grows about 18 in. high, with divided leaves and bright yellow flowers. *L. tricolor* grows to 2 ft., with prickly 2-pinnate leaves and yellow flowers with a red crown and white stamens. *L. vulcanica* is a bushy grower to 3 ft., with 3- to 5-lobed leaves and flowers white, marked red and yellow.

LOBELIA (loh-bee'-li-ah). A genus of annual and perennial herbs with mostly blue or red, irregular flowers in close, or long spike-like, clusters. As garden subjects, they fall naturally into two groups: the annual and the perennial.

The annual species, *L. erinus,* is one of the popular small plants for borders. The simplest way to grow it is from seed, which should be started under glass in January or February so as to have blooming-size specimens ready to set out in May. In a cool climate the border of annual lobelia will continue in bloom until fall. Even where the summer is hot, the plants, if cut back and given a plentiful supply of water, will usually keep on blooming. Annual lobelias can also be increased by cuttings, taken late in the winter from plants wintered in the greenhouse. The perennial species are increased by seed, by division or by offsets.

Yellow lower leaves, dark lesions on the stems, often followed by wilting and dying of the plants, indicate rhizoctonia rot. To avoid it, plant in sterile soil, space plants properly and give plenty of ventilation. If lobelia is attacked by a rust (*Puccinia lobeliae*), dust with sulphur during the growing season and destroy old plant parts in the fall.

PRINCIPAL SPECIES

L. erinus is a low-growing plant from S. Africa having blue or violet flowers. Some of the different forms include: var. *alba,* white; *gracilis* with long slender branches, more suitable for the cutting garden than an edging; *compacta,* of very short close growth, and *speciosa,* sky-blue with white throat.

cardinalis (Cardinal-flower or Indian-pink), a perennial plant growing to 4 ft., has narrow leaves and a spire of intense crimson flowers. This is one of the most beautiful of native plants, growing naturally in damp, half-shaded situations and sometimes in the shallow water of slowly moving streams. It is raised from seed, or increased by offsets and plants will grow in a well-watered border, although a woodland setting is more appropriate.

siphilitica is a sturdy native perennial plant growing to 3 ft. and found from Me. to La. It has a receme of flowers of a charming shade of clear blue and grows readily in moist soil in half-shaded situations.

LOBLOLLY-BAY. Common name for *Gordonia lasianthus,* a 60 ft. evergreen tree with showy white flowers native to S. E. U. S.

LOBULARIA (loh-beu-lay'-ri-ah) *maritima.* A popular perennial known as Sweet Alyssum (which see), grown as an annual in borders for its abundant little white or lavender flowers borne all summer. See also ALYSSUM.

LOCO-WEED. Common name for *Astragalus mollissimus* and *Oxytropis lamberti,* herbs of the Pea Family with feather-form leaves and small sweet-pea-like flowers in clusters. Both plants (of no horticultural interest) are found on the prairies of the W. States, and have gained their common name because of their poisonous effect on cattle, horses and sheep.

LOCUST. Common name for native deciduous trees and shrubs of the genus Robinia, a member of the Pea Family. Locusts are hardy subjects characterized by graceful, feather-form leaves and showy sweet-pea-like blossoms in long drooping clusters, which are followed by flattened glossy brown or nearly black pods. They are widely planted for decorative purposes and are easily transplanted and grow well under ordinary conditions; even in dry, thin soil. Propagation is by seed, cuttings, suckers, and root-cuttings and division.

ENEMIES. About the only disease of locust is wood decay that follows a borer injury, but several insects are very destructive. Black locusts have been ruined in certain sections by the borer, whose presence is first shown by sawdust protruding from holes that later become ugly scars. Cut and burn badly infested trees and spray the bark (not the foliage), of valuable specimens with soluble arsenate (¼ lb. in 5 gal. water, plus 1 qt. of miscible oil). The carpenter worm (which see) is fond of locust, and a general browning of black locust leaves from the vicinity of New York City southward is due to the feeding of leaf miners, small reddish, black-marked beetles. Spray just after the leaves are developed, with lead arsenate.

SPECIES

R. pseudoacacia (Black Locust, Honey Locust, False-acacia). A tall tree of E. and Central U. S. attaining 80 ft., with thorny branches and grayish-brown, heavy, deeply grooved bark. The very fragrant white flowers in long pendent racemes cover the tree in May and June, and the flat 4 in. pods hang on the tree all winter, rattling in the wind when they be-

with dark red calyxes it is often planted in the garden.

LOCUST. Correctly used, this means any kind of grasshopper, though it may be restricted to the migratory kinds that travel in huge armies. Popularly, the term is applied to various kinds of cicadas or harvest-flies, which, however, are not flies at all, but sucking insects, whereas grasshoppers are chewing insects. See CICADA.

THE YELLOW LOCUST SCENTS THE COUNTRYSIDE IN JUNE
Left, a spray of the fragrant white flowers of the locust, Robinia pseudoacacia. Right, its spineless variety inermis, trained to standard form.

come dry. As the Honey Locust stands severe prunning it is much used abroad in formal plantings; but in this country, although it has remarkable drought-resistant qualities, it is but little planted as it is attacked by borers (which see) and therefore likely to be short-lived. There are many varieties, among the most useful being *inermis,* which is thornless, and *umbraculifera,* with a compact head of unarmed branches.

hispida (Rose-acacia) a shrub of the S. E. region, sometimes reaching 9 ft., has charming rose-colored blossoms; the stems, branchlets and pods are covered with reddish bristles. Plants are often trained as standards when the drooping flowers are most decorative. The species suckers freely and may become a nuisance in the border, dominating and crowding out less aggressive shrubs.

viscosa (Clammy Locust) a small, irregular tree growing to 40 ft., native in S. U. S. but hardy N. Because of its attractive feathery foliage and pink flowers

LODOICEA (lod-oh-is'-ee-ah). A genus of unarmed (spineless) Fan Palms commonly known as Double-coconut because of the very large, double-lobed seed, said to be the largest in the vegetable kingdom. *L. maldivica* grows naturally only on the Seychelles Islands in the Indian Ocean, where it attains a height of 100 ft. with a straight slender trunk 1 ft. in diameter, crowned by the heavy fan-like leaves, 5 to 10 ft. long. The huge nuts, sometimes 18 in. in length, require 10 yrs. from the time of flowering to reach maturity. They were once called "Coco de mer" as they were often picked up on the seashore, prior to 1743 when the palm was discovered and the source of the mysterious objects revealed. Lodoicea is seldom cultivated either under glass or in gardens.

LOESELIA (loh-see'-li-ah). Herbs or subshrubs, found from Texas and Calif. to S. America, belonging to the Phlox Family. They are sometimes grown in pots under glass for their attractive flowers in winter. They thrive in a mixture of loam, peat, and sand and are propagated by cuttings, under close conditions. *L. mexicanum,* the species commonly cultivated, grows to 3 ft. and is handsome in bloom with tubular rose-red flowers.

LOESS (lo'-ess). A fine-grained, sticky soil (which see) found in various parts of the world and believed to be of wind-blown origin. Great deposits occur in N. China, hundreds of feet in depth, formed by the accumulation of dust blown over from Tibet and the Gobi Desert. Similar soil types are encountered in parts of W. U. S. Special management for loess soils may be planned from a study of the Chinese deposits, which are extremely dry in rainless periods and subject to severe flood erosion. They should be kept covered with crops, preferably deep-rooted ones. On mountain slopes, permanent sod or forest plantings are called for. See also CULTIVATION; IMPROVEMENT, SOIL.

LOGANBERRY. A blackberry-like bramble (*Rubus loganobaccus*) sometimes also called Phenomenal. It originated in Calif. and is extensively grown on the Pacific Coast for its red fruits, which are used for eating and cooking, fresh, dried, canned and for the production of juice. It is propagated by means of rooted cane tips planted at least 8 ft. asunder in rows 6 ft. or more apart and trained, like the dewberry (which see), on wire trellises as the canes are long and trailing. The plants are tender to frost and cannot be grown successfully in cold regions though the roots may live over winter.

See also RUBUS.

LOGGIA (loj'-ah). A permanent, usually elaborate, roofed garden shelter characterized by a wall (either blank or a house wall) along one side and a row of pillars to support the roof along the other side. See GARDEN SHELTERS.

LOISELEURIA (loh-i-se-leu'-ri-ah). Alpine-azalea. A low evergreen shrub of northern sub-arctic regions, belonging to the Heath Family. Rarely cultivated, it makes a mat of growth only a few inches high and bears very small white or pink flowers. A cool moist place in the rock garden, and sandy peaty soil is suitable.

LOLIUM (lol'-i-um). A genus of small annual and perennial meadow and pasture grasses called Rye Grass (which see). They are not suitable for lawns but are sometimes included in cheap seed mixtures —which are never a good investment.

LOMARIA (loh-may'-ri-ah). A genus of cool greenhouse and indoor ferns, whose name (from the Greek word for "hem") describes the indusia. The fronds are 6 to 24 in. long in most species, growing from creeping roots. They require moist atmosphere but tend to discolor if watered overhead. Use a soil mixture of equal parts loam, leafmold, and sand. Pot loosely; do not over-water.

SPECIES

L. alpina. Narrow, evergreen fronds, 4 to 10 in. long, once-pinnate; blunt pinnae, bright green when young. Excellent for greenhouse or terrarium.

ciliata. A very compact species rather like the following:

gibba. Fronds 2 to 3 ft. long, deeply cut, shining green; the scaly stripes from an upright fleshy stem, which sometimes grows to 3 ft., suggesting a tree fern. The most popular greenhouse species.

L. spicant (Deer Fern, Hard Fern). A dwarf, evergreen and robust species, hardy in England, adaptable to moist mild regions in the U. S. and sometimes listed as *Blechnum spicant.* Rich green clustered fronds, 1 ft. tall, once-pinnate, with fruit dots on either side of the mid-rib. Will grow in shale, gravel, or clay; dislikes limestone, and prefers half-shade. The fronds last a long time when cut.

LOMATIA (loh-may'-shi-ah). Trees or shrubs of Australia and Chile, belonging to the Protea Family. They are sometimes grown in the cool greenhouse or outdoors in warm regions. In pots they thrive in a mixture of equal parts loam, peat and sand. Good drainage is essential. They are of interest chiefly for their elegant foliage. *L. ilicifolia* has prickly holly-like leaves. *L. silaifolia* has attractive divided foliage which is dyed and used by floral decorators under the name of "crinkle-bush." *L. ferruginea,* from Chile, is a graceful plant with finely divided leaves, and yellow and scarlet flowers with rusty hairs.

LOMATIUM (loh-may'-shi-um). A group of perennial herbs of the Parsley Family, found in dry soil in W. U. S. Few of the 60 species have been developed in cultivation but some are adaptable to rock-work, the front of large borders, or to gravelly soil in the wild garden. They are nearly or quite stemless, varying according to species from 2 ins. to $2\frac{1}{2}$ ft.

tall, with dissected leaves and flat heads of small yellow or white flowers.

LOMBARDY POPLAR. Common name for *Populus nigra* var. *italica,* a variety of the Black Poplar, of tall, slender, columnar form useful for barrier planting or formal garden designs.

LONAS (loh'-nahs) *inodora.* A branching annual of the Composite Family (formerly called *Athanasia annua*), native in the Mediterranean region, and popularly known as African Daisy. (Do not confuse with Gerbera to which this name is more commonly applied.) Growing 1 ft. high, it bears small yellow heads composed entirely of disk-flowers.

LONDON PLANE. Common name for *Platanus acerifolia,* a hybrid of the Buttonwood and the Oriental Plane-tree valuable for street planting or large lawn areas. See PLANE.

LONDON PRIDE. Common name for *Saxifraga umbrosa,* a pink or white flowered perennial, to 1 ft. high.

LONDON PURPLE. A calcium-arsenic insecticide at one time almost as well known as Paris Green but now little used. See ARSENICAL POISONS.

LONG-DAY PLANT. Term applied to plants in which flower bud formation is initiated by exposure to relatively long day lengths (fourteen hours or more) and suppressed by exposure to shorter day lengths. Examples are Annual Hollyhock, Timothy, Tickseed (*Coreopsis tinctoria*), Cape Marigold (*Dimorphotheca aurantiaca*), Golden Glow (*Rudbeckia laciniata*), Bee Balm (*Monarda didyma*), Sedum spectabile, Oenothera missouriensis, Cheiranthus allioni, Rose of Sharon (*Hibiscus syriacus*), gladiolus, Clematis paniculata, China Aster, Calceolaria, Gaillardia lorenziana.

When it is desired to endeavor to bring long day plants into bloom at a time of year when short days are the rule, artificial lighting is resorted to. Tungsten filament lights of appropriate candle-power are used as a supplement to normal daylight, i.e., to extend the daylight period. See also PHOTOPERIODISM; SHADE; SHORT-DAY PLANT.

LONICERA (lon-is'-er-ah). A large genus of deciduous or evergreen shrubs, widely distributed throughout the N. hemisphere and known as Honeysuckle (which see). It comprises bushes, climbers and trailers, and includes some of the most popular and useful ornamental shrubs.

LOOPER. Name given to any caterpillar that humps up the middle of its body when it moves. Familiar examples are the cabbage and celery loopers. The term is also applied to the canker worm, or inch worm, both of which see.

LOOSESTRIFE. Common name for two genera of herbaceous plants—Lysimachia and Steironema—of the Primrose Family, that require similar handling and moist situations. They are perennial, summer-blooming herbs, with well-shaped corollas.

Species of Lysimachia, which are best propagated by division, include *L. barystachys,* to 2½ ft. high, with white flowers in loose racemes, drooping when first opening; *L. dubia,* to 2 ft., with rose flowers borne in spikes; *L. clethroides,* to 3 ft., with white flowers in terminal spikes and foliage which takes on attractive fall coloring, and *L. nummularia* (Moneywort or Creeping Charlie or Creeping Jenny), a low trailing round-leaved plant with bright yellow flowers, often found bordering ponds or ditches.

Steironema ciliatum, which bears whorled yellow flowers on fringed petioles, is a tall plant useful in the wild garden.

Purple Loosestrife is *Lythrum salicaria* and Swamp Loosestrife is *Decodon verticillatus;* both are of the Loosestrife Family.

LOOSESTRIFE FAMILY. Common name of the Lythraceae, which see.

LOPEZIA (loh-pee'-zi-ah). Herbs or shrubby plants, native in Mexico and S. America, belonging to the Evening-primrose Family, sometimes grown under glass and outdoors in warm climates. They are of slender bushy habit, with small attractive flowers in leafy racemes. Propagated by seeds and cuttings.

L. albiflora grows to 2 ft. with white flowers tinged pink. *L. lineata* is a bushy plant to 3 ft., with hairy stems and short clusters of red flowers. *L. macrophylla* has green succulent stems with larger leaves and bright red flowers.

LOQUAT (loh'-kwot). The Biwa of the Japanese. A small, oriental, subtropical, evergreen tree of the Rose Family (*Eriobotrya japonica*), grown as a home garden fruit from Florida westward to California, where it is also planted commercially for its plum-like, yellow or orange fruit, which is delicious whether eaten raw or in pies, preserves, etc. These develop in spring from fragrant white flowers borne in panicles in autumn. Plants are occasionally grown under glass in pots as ornamentals. Though the tree will grow in any good soil, it does best in clay loams. It needs an area 25 to 30 ft. in diameter, but calls for no special treatment.

LORANTHACEAE (loh-ran-thay'-see-ee). Botanical name of the Mistletoe Family, a widely distributed group of chiefly shrubby plants with jointed stems, parasitic upon trees. The leaves may be broad but are sometimes scale-like; the flowers are small and the fruit is a berry which germinates on the host plant, into which the parasite sends its feeding roots. They are not horticultural plants, though familiar through the species associated with Christmas.

LORDS-AND-LADIES. Common name for *Arum maculatum.* Also called Cuckoopint. See ARUM.

LORINSERIA (loh-rin-see'-ri-ah). A genus of ferns including the Net-veined Chain Fern, which is usually referred to the genus Woodwardia, which see.

LOROPETALUM (loh-roh-pet'-ah-lum). An attractive but tender evergreen from China, belonging to the Witch-hazel Family. Only one species (*L. chinense*) is in cultivation. A medium sized shrub, thriving best in a peaty and gritty soil, it can be grown outdoors only in the warmer parts of the country. In early spring it produces a mass of white flowers, with strap-shaped petals.

LOTUS. The common name for water-lilies of the genus Nelumbium (which see). The name is also often given to certain species of tropical waterlilies, notably *Nymphaea caerulea,* the Blue African Lotus, the rather similar *N. stellata,* of India, and *N. lotus,* the White Lotus of Egypt. See also AQUATIC PLANTS.

Lotus is also the name for a totally different genus of leguminous shrubs and herbs in the Pea Family, not native to this country but often thriving in sunny dry situations and valuable for groundcover in the rockery and on banks. They have irregularly pinnate leaves and yellow, purple or white pea-like flowers. Propagate by seed or, for those with woody stems, by cuttings.

SPECIES

L. corniculatus (Birds-foot Trefoil, Ladies Fingers). Perennial, introduced from Europe; of sprawling habit, with many small yellow flowers from usually red buds.

jacobaeus (St. James Trefoil). Taller, somewhat shrubby, with flowers varying from dark purple to yellow.

bertheloti. A tender much-branched dwarf shrub, with curious scarlet flowers. For conservatory use in Calif. gardens.

tetragonolobus (Winged Pea). A trailing annual, with sparse purplish-red flowers.

LOUSEWORT. A common name for the genus Pedicularis (which see), also called Wood-betony.

LOVAGE. The common name for plants of 2 closely related genera in the Parsley Family: the N. American species of Ligusticum (which see), and the Old-World genus Levisticum, which is confined to one species, *L. officinale.* The latter grows to 6 ft., with glossy, dark green, compound leaves and greenish-yellow flowers in umbels. Hardy in the U. S. as far north as Pa.; of easy cultivation, requiring little care but much root-room, and preferring deep rich soil.

LOVE-APPLE. Old-fashioned name for the tomato.

LOVE-ENTANGLE. One of the popular names for *Sedum acre.*

LOVE-IN-A-MIST. One of the common names for *Nigella damascena,* a blue-flowering garden annual.

LOVE-LIES-BLEEDING. Common name for *Amaranthus caudatus,* a coarse, erect annual with long, drooping tassels of small red flowers.

LOVE-PLANT. Catalog name for *Catananche caerulea,* also called Cupids Dart, which see.

LUCERNE. A common name for *Medicago sativa,* or Alfalfa, which see.

LUCULIA (leu-keu'-li-ah). A genus of tender shrubs from the Himalayas, with large leathery leaves and showy corymbs of salver-shaped flowers in white, rose or red. They are of easy cultivation under glass in moderate temperature and bloom through mid-winter. They can be set out-of-doors in summer. Keep well syringed to avoid attacks of red spider. Young plants may be raised from cuttings taken after the flowering period and should be gradually hardened off by reduced temperatures. Three species, *L. gratissima, L. speciosa,* and *L. intermedia,* are obtainable, of which the first is the most reliable, the second a variant with larger, deeper pink flowers, and the last a red-flowered form, which might well be cultivated for the Christmas season.

LUCUMA (leu-keu'-mah) *nervosa.* A small tropical American tree grown for its oblong edible yellow fruit, which gives it the common name Egg-fruit, which see.

LUDWIGIA (lud-wij'-i-ah). A genus of bog or water plants with rather small yellow flowers close to the stem. They can be grown from either seeds or cuttings but most Ludwigias are little known and seldom cultivated. They are related to the Evening-primrose. *L. alternifolia* is a 3 ft. perennial sometimes used in the wild garden. *L. mulertti* is an aquarium plant from the tropics, attractive for its brightly colored foliage.

LUETKEA (leu-et'-ki-ah). A trailing ground shrub of high altitudes from N. Calif. to Alaska. The only known species, *L. pectinata,* is rare in cultivation but a distinct rock-garden possibility. It forms dense carpets from 2 to 6 in. tall, with bright 3-lobed leaves and erect 2 in. racemes of small white spirea-like flowers. Propagate by division or green-wood cuttings.

LUFFA (luf'-ah). Loofah. A genus of tropical, climbing herbs with large white flowers and cylindrical or oblong fruits of the familiar cucurbitous type. These when ripe have dry, papery shells which contain a network of strong fibres. This may be detached entire from the softer tissues and used as a tough fabric for washing purposes. Hence the popular names wash-rag-, towel-, dish-cloth-, flesh-brush-, and vegetable-sponge-gourd. The young luffas are eaten in some tropical countires. Cultivation is the same as that of other gourds.

LUNARIA (leu-nay'-ri-ah). Honesty, Moonwort, Satin-flower. There are two cultivated species of this winter-bouquet plant which belongs to the Crucifer or Mustard Family. One is an annual or biennial and the other a perennial, but both are erect, branching and 2 to 3 ft. tall bearing single flowers ranging from purple to white, followed by interesting flat, papery seed-pods, which, when dried, provide a lasting ornamental material. Both species thrive in partial shade and are easily grown from seed. *L. annua* (or *L. biennis*) has pods rounded at both ends, 2 in. long and nearly as wide. While it can be grown as an annual, if started early enough, it is best treated as a biennial, the satiny pods being produced the second

season. In the perennial species (*L. rediviva*) the leaves are more closely and sharply toothed, and the pods taper at both ends and are much longer than broad.

See also EVERLASTINGS.

LUNGWORT. Common name for Pulmonaria, a genus of border perennials with blue or purplish flowers.

LUPINE. Common name for Lupinus, a genus of annual and perennial herbs, or sometimes shrubs, of the Pea Family, grown chiefly for ornamental purposes though some species are useful cover and forage crops. In the U. S. the ornamental forms are popular bed and border subjects. For many years catalogs and books have advised planting them in acid soils, but recent experiments and experience have shown that they often do just as well in lime soil.

Lupines are distinguished by their deeply cut foliage, which has many lance-like rays radiating from the end of the leaf stalk. The flowers, shaped like those of peas, are borne in great profusion on long-stemmed spikes. (See illustration, Plate 49.) The perennials are more popular than the annuals, though both are excellent for display purposes. The annuals often continue to bloom until August and are good in mixed beds or borders and also for cutting. The perennials for the best effects should be planted in masses.

The plants generally grow about 3 ft. tall, thriving in either sun or partial shade. The flowers, predominantly blue, yellow, white or rose, are usually borne in May and June. After the first bloom is over, if the plants are cut back, they will often produce a second showing of flowers.

Propagation is by seed sown in the open, where the plants are to grow, as they are tap-rooted and resent transplanting. The perennials can also be increased by division.

Many fine garden hybrids are constantly being made available in addition to a number of species that are well worth growing because they are of easy culture and make an attractive show of flowers.

PRINCIPAL SPECIES

L. perennis. A native hardy perennial, about 2 ft. tall, with downy foliage and abundant flowers, usually blue but varying to pink and white.

polyphyllus. A tall perennial with blue-winged purple flowers, or some varieties white and rose, blooming through most of the summer.

argenteus. A silvery-leaved perennial from the W., 2 or 3 ft. tall, with rose, violet or white flowers.

luteus. A European annual 2 ft. tall with fragrant yellow flowers, thriving even in the poorest soil and important as a green-manure crop, but also useful for garden ornament.

hirsutus. A blue-flowered annual, easily grown, and useful for ornament, as fodder and as a green manure crop.

arboreus. A tender shrub of the W., growing man-high and bearing numerous canary-yellow flowers in summer.

subcernosus. A blue-flower annual, native to Texas, of which it is the State flower.

False-lupine is Thermopsis, a yellow-flowered perennial, also of the Pea Family.

LUZULA (leu'-zeu-lah). A genus of about 40 very similar species of grass-like herbs to which the common name Woodrush is given. Many are native to various parts of the U. S. and though seldom offered by dealers should be useful for covering dry ground and colonizing large areas. The flowers are greenish and inconspicuous; the softly hairy and often variegated leaves are charming in the garden and in dried bouquets.

LYCASTE (ly-kas'-tee). A genus of tropical American terrestrial orchids having variously colored, solitary, spurred flowers with a 3-lobed lip, often crested or hairy, and rather large, plaited leaves. A number of the species and hybrids are very lovely and flower freely throughout the winter in the warmest part of the cool greenhouse. Among the species most popular and most widely grown are L. *aromatica,* with fragrant, orange-yellow flowers, 2½ in. across, with a crested lip spotted with rose; and L. *skinneri* with white or rose flowers to 6 in. across, with a purple lip, the middle lobe of the lip spotted with yellow or white. For culture see ORCHIDS.

LYCHNIS (lik'-nis). A large genus of brilliantly-colored garden flowers, including annuals, biennials and perennials, all easily raised from seed and usually propagating themselves readily when once established. While some species (as in the related genus Silene) are known as Campion, Lychnis also includes such familiar and satisfactory flowers as Mullein-

pink, Scarlet Lightning, Flower-of-Jove, Cuckoo-flower and others. The dominant color in the genus is red, and the five petals, which expand broadly at the top of the long calyx-tube, are characteristically notched in the center or sometimes deeply divided into segments.

If seeds are sown early indoors, most of the species will give their first bloom in the garden in June and July. They will do well in ordinary soil, even in rather dry situations, and they especially love the sun. Perennials may be increased by division.

PRINCIPAL SPECIES

L. coeli-rosa (Rose-of-Heaven). A free-flowering annual, 1 ft. or more tall, a single broad rose-red flower opening at the top of each stalk. A white-flowered plant is among the many garden forms developed.

coronaria (Mullein-pink, Rose Campion, or Dusty Miller). A much-branched plant, biennial or perennial, with white-woolly leaves and a large crimson flower terminating each branchlet. (Other plants are also called Dusty Miller, which see.)

coronata. An early summer bloomer with loosely clustered cinnabar or salmon-colored flowers 2 in. in diameter, the petals toothed; leaves smooth and green; plant somewhat tender, biennial in cultivation.

dioica (Morning Campion). A coarse, hairy, somewhat sticky plant with branched clusters of red flowers 1 in. across opening in the morning.

alba (Evening Campion). Bearing white flowers that open in the evening, the plant is more sticky than, but otherwise resembles, L. *diocia.* Both have double-flowered forms, and both in cultivation are perennial or biennial.

flos-cuculi (Cuckoo-flower or Ragged Robin). Hardy, rapidly spreading perennial with red to white flowers clustered at the top of an erect stem, each petal deeply cut into 4 segments.

flos-jovis (Flower-of-Jove). A hardy perennial, the flower-stalk rising erect from a rosette of coarse hairy leaves and bearing a cluster of small bright rose-red flowers.

chalcedonica (Scarlet Lightning, Maltese Cross, Jerusalem Cross). A perennial with gleaming scarlet flowers 1 in. across, each petal indented half its length, forming a large rounded cluster at the top of a 2- to 3-ft. stalk. Flowers sometimes occur from rose to white and there are double forms.

viscaria (German-catchfly). A tufted perennial with clustered small red flowers; white, pink, striped or double in its varieties.

alpina. A good species for rock-garden use, growing 1 ft. or less high, bearing bright rose-pink flowers with narrow 2-lobed petals, blooming in May. L. *pyrenaica* and L. *lagascae,* both small prostrate plants with pink and white flowers, are also recommended for rock crevices.

haageana. An early summer-flowering hybrid perennial with brilliant scarlet flowers 2 in. across, borne 2 or 3 together on plants 12 to 15 in. tall.

arkwrighti. Another large hybrid with star-shaped flowers of similar dazzling hue, several in a head.

walkeri. A long-blooming hybrid perennial with carmine flowers and silvery-hairy leaves.

LYCIUM (lis′-i-um). Matrimony-vine, Box-thorn. Deciduous or evergreen shrubs, distributed throughout the temperate and warmer regions of both hemispheres, belonging to the Nightshade Family. They are sometimes spiny and of a more or less loose and clambering habit, well suited for planting against walls and fences, and showing to good advantage on rocky slopes. They are not particular as to soil and do well in dry places. Some thought should be given their location on account of the suckering habit of most kinds, which would be a nuisance in some situations. Most species are tender, but a few are hardy. Propagated by seed, cuttings, layers and suckers.

PRINCIPAL SPECIES

L. *chinense* has slender arching and often prostrate branches to 12 ft. long, usually spineless and holding the leaves green until late in the fall. It bears a profusion of small purple flowers in early summer, followed by a showy display of orange-red berries about an inch long.

halimifolium is a more upright grower, with arching branches to 10 ft., usually spiny and also holding its leaves green quite late. The flowers and scarlet oval fruits are rather smaller than those of L. *chinense.*

pallidum is a much branched shrub to 6 ft., native from Utah to Mexico, but fairly

hardy North. It has pale and somewhat fleshy leaves, greenish-yellow flowers with a purple tinge, and showy scarlet round berries, not freely produced. It does not sucker as most other species do.

LYCOPERSICON (ly-koh-pur′-si-kon). Also spelled Lycopersicum. A genus of herbaceous annuals and perennials of S. America and other warm regions important in gardening because one species (L. *esculentum*) includes all forms of the familiar tomato. Var. *cerasiforme* is the cherry tomato with fruit about ¾ in. in diameter in clusters; var. *commune* is the common tomtato from which the different large red, and yellow named kinds have been developed; var. *grandifolium* is an uncommon large-leaved form; var. *pyriforme* bears pear-shaped fruit a little larger than the cherry type; and var. *validum* makes a sturdy, erect, very compact plant.

A second species (L. *pimpinellifolium*) is the Currant Tomato (which see). Though really perennials, all these plants are grown as annuals. Belonging to the Nightshade Family, they are related to the white potato.

LYCOPODIUM (ly-koh-poh′-di-um). A genus of evergreen, flowerless plants with scale-like leaves known as Club-moss, and the only horticulturally interesting member of the Club-moss Family (Lycopodiaceae). They are useful as a ground-cover in shady woods, but as it is difficult to transplant and establish a colony of mature plants, they should be increased by cuttings. Being allied to the ferns, they produce not seeds but minute spores, on spikes or in the leaf axils. Many native species were formerly ruthlessly collected for use as Christmas greens.

PRINCIPAL SPECIES

L. *clavatum,* the Running-pine, has creeping stems to 9 ft. long.

obscurum, the Ground-pine, has stems growing underground and sending up tree-like branches to 10 in. high.

complanatum, in which the branches are fan-like, is sometimes called Ground-cedar. The name Lycopodium is sometimes used by florists for Selaginella, which see.

LYCOPUS (ly′-koh-pus). A genus of moisture-loving aromatic herbs in the Mint Family, commonly known as Water-hoarhound. Many species, varying from 1 to 3 ft. high, are well distributed in moist ground throughout the U. S. and are of

Upper left: The classic simplicity of the bloom of the pale rose Lilium japonicum.   Upper center: The European Turks-cap lily holds high its delicate drooping blossoms.   Upper right: The brilliant L. elegans, Orange Queen, makes a striking note in the border.   Center: For centuries the Madonna lily's purity has graced the garden.   Lower left: Lilies of varied heights in a formal mass planting.   Lower right: The golden-banded lily of Japan fills the air with its fragrant breath.

use in the wild garden, preferring a deep, rich soil. The leaves are toothed or pinnatified; the tiny flowers bell-shaped, white or pale blue, clustered in axillary whorls in midsummer. Included are the Bugleweeds, *L. virginicus* and *L. uniflorus,* the latter of more slender habit and smoother; and the widespread *L. americanus,* distinguished by its deeply pinnatifid leaves.

LYCORIS (ly-koh'-ris). Bulbous plants of the Amaryllis Family having lily-like red, orange, white or pinkish-lavender flowers which appear after the narrow leaves have entirely disappeared. They are native to China and Japan, whence bulbs of several species are imported to this country. However, only one, *L. squamigera,* is common in gardens. Its bulbs are planted in the open border in soil rich in humus in order that they may attain the vigorous growth essential to the production of handsome clusters of flowers. The lush foliage appears in early summer but soon ripens and dies; and in August the lovely pink flowers suddenly appear on the naked stalks. On account of this habit of blooming without foliage, the plants should be surrounded by some type of ground-cover, such as snow-in-summer (*Cerastium tomentosum*) or lavender petunias.

Principal Species

L. squamigera (sometimes listed in catalogs as *Amaryllis halli*) has fragrant, clustered lavender-rose blossoms 3 in. long, rising on naked stalks from 2 to 3 ft. Sometimes called Mystery-lily and, in parts of the Middle W., Naked-lady, both names referring to the sudden appearance of the flower stalks with no foliage. Var. *purpurea* has darker flowers. Both are perfectly hardy in New England.

radiata, often treated as a pot plant, has small bright red blossoms in clusters. The leaves appear in winter and the flowers later in the year. It is probably perfectly hardy. Var. *alba* is white.

aurea (Golden-spider-lily), with narrow grayish-green foliage and bright orange or yellow blossoms, is usually grown under glass, but doubtless hardy in the border with winter protection.

LYGODIUM (ly-goh'-di-um). A genus of ferns distinguished by their climbing habit, mostly of the tropics, but including one American species hardy in New England. Some species in the wild

grow to 30 ft., but in greenhouses they seldom reach more than 8 ft. The fronds grow at intervals from creeping stems; each consists of a delicate twining stem-like rachis on which the blades are borne on long petioles, or stems. The broad blades varying from 3 to 12 in. wide, are triangular and deeply lobed; in some species spores are borne on the upper parts of the fronds, in others the fertile and sterile fronds are distinct. Lygodiums thrive in rich, wet, acid soil, of a porous and open texture. Equal quantities of loam, leafmold, and peat moss make the ideal compost. The plants climb best on twigs or other plants.

Species

L. dichotomum. This vigorous and long-lasting species is excellent for the warm greenhouse. It has 10 in. 3-pinnate, bright green fronds with the fertile divisions much contracted.

japonicum. The best known and most reliable species. The fronds are deeply divided and very decorative, up to 8 in. long and 4 in. wide. For greenhouse or other ideal indoor conditions only.

palmatum (Hartford Fern, Alices Fern). This species was formerly abundant on the low meadows and river banks of Conn. and N. J., but it was so extensively collected as decorative material that it was almost exterminated. It is now illegal to gather roots or fronds in Conn., so plants should be bought from the dealer. Growing to 3 or 4 ft., it requires the protection and support of other plants. The blades are 3 in. wide and equally long, branched into 5 equal radial lobes.

LYME GRASS. A common name for a genus of tall growing perennial grasses, also called Wild-rye. Some species are used as ornamentals in backgrounds and on bank, but they are more important as soil binders along beaches and in other sandy places.

LYONIA (ly-oh'-ni-ah). Deciduous or evergreen shrubs, native in N. America, the W. Indies and Asia, belonging to the Heath Family. They are bushy shrubs, not often planted, but suitable for massing, succeeding under the same conditions as Leucothoë. Only one or two species are hardy N. Propagated by seeds, cuttings and layers.

L. ligustrina (Male-berry, He-huckleberry) is a deciduous shrub to 12 ft., found from Me. to Fla. In early summer it bears small white flowers in leafless racemes, and in the fall the oval leathery leaves take on colored tints. *L. lucida* (Fetter-bush) is an evergreen to 6 ft., found from Va. S. with lustrous leaves and flowers in leafy racemes. *L. mariana* (Stagger-bush) found from R. I. to Fla., is deciduous and grows to 6 ft. Its nodding white or pink-ish flowers are borne in leafless racemes.

LYSIMACHIA (ly-si-may'-ki-ah). A genus of Old-World perennial herbs with white or yellow flowers, commonly called Loosestrife, which see.

LYTHRACEAE (lith-ray'-see-ee). Botanical name of the Loosestrife Family, a group of mostly tropical herbs, shrubs and trees. Several of the genera are grown for ornament, among them Lythrum, Lawsonia, Lagerstroemia and Cuphea. Others furnish timber, medicinal and dye products. Leaves are mostly arranged in whorls; the flowers are axillary or in whorled heads; the calyx is tubular and usually ribbed.

LYTHRUM (lith'-rum). A genus of slender perennial moisture-loving herbs of the Loosestrife Family, including several American species which are easy to grow and good subjects for naturalizing. The pink or magenta flowers may be borne singly or in clusters.

The Spiked or Purple Loosestrife, *Lythrum salicaria,* originally introduced from Europe, has wand-like spikes of deep magenta flowers that color broad stretches of marshland in the E. late in summer. This species, with its horticultural varieties, of which *roseum superbum* is most used, is a splendid border plant, and will grow 4 or 5 ft. tall in soil well drained but copiously supplied with water. It is sometimes known as Willow-herb, from the willow-like leaves.

L. hyssopifolia is a 2 ft. annual with scattered flowers of pinkish-purple.

M

MAACKIA (mak'-i-ah). A genus of oriental deciduous trees and some shrubs with attractive foliage and whitish pea-like flowers in erect panicles. The species imported and grown from seed are hardy in Mass. They thrive in any soil but bloom best when in sunny positions.

MABA (may'-bah). Tropical trees or shrubs, with hard ebony-like wood, closely related to Diospyros, but usually with smaller leaves. Two species have been introduced into the warmest parts of this country for ornamental planting: *M. natalensis,* from S. Africa, an evergreen shrub to 20 ft., with oval or oblong dark green leaves, and bunches of black berries; and *M. sandwicensis* (Lama), an Hawaiian tree to 40 ft., with thick leathery dull green leaves and reddish-yellow edible berries.

MACLEAYA (mah-klay'-ah) *cordata.* A tall-growing perennial herb often listed under its former name, *Bocconia cordata* or *B. japonica.* Its common names are Tree Celandine and Plume-poppy, which see.

MACLURA (mah-kloo'-rah) *pomifera.* A deciduous spiny tree found from Ark. to Tex., but hardy into New England. It grows well even on rather poor land and makes a fine dense hedge, for which purpose it is well known as Osage-orange, which see.

MADAGASCAR-JASMINE. Common name for *Stephanotis floribunda,* a well-known greenhouse climber, valued for its clusters of waxy white fragrant flowers. It requires a warm temperature, and thrives best in turfy loam. Good specimens may be grown in pots or planted out in a small bed. The shoots may be trained over a frame or carried along the rafters on wires. It has thick shining green leaves, with flowers freely produced and very lasting. It is a favorite plant of the mealy bug, and a grower may well feel proud of a really clean plant. Propagated by cuttings of half-ripened shoots.

MADDER FAMILY. Common name of the Rubiaceae, a large and important plant family, the source of many economic products and ornamental subjects.

MADEIRA-VINE. A common name for *Boussingaultia baselloides,* also called Mignonette-vine, a tropical American vine with tuberous roots, which may sometimes live over winter in the N., but can be lifted and stored. It is a tall, rapid grower, often used with good effect to clothe porches and arbors. The foliage is clean and attractive, and late in the summer the plant bears long spikes of small white fragrant flowers. It is easily propogated by seeds, root division or by small tubercles that develop along the stems in the leaf axils.

MADIA (may'-di-ah). A genus of sticky, strongly scented, annual and perennial herbs, commonly called Tarweed, whose yellow flowers close in strong sunlight but open early and late in the day. *M. elegans,* the common annual Tarweed, is useful as an ornamental in shady places. *M. sativa* var. *congesta* is important for sheep forage on dry ground.

MADONNA LILY. Popular name for *Lilium candidum,* a white-flowered hardy species. See LILY.

MADRE. Common name for *Gliricidia sepium,* a tree of warm regions with pink, white or lilac pea-like flowers in early spring before the foliage develops.

MADRONA (mah-droh'-nyah). Common name for *Arbutus menziesi,* an evergreen tree of the West Coast, bearing white flowers in panicles, and small red fruits.

MADWORT. An old name for the genus Alyssum. Annual and perennial herbs with small yellow or white flowers.

MAGGOTS. The soft, legless, grub-like larvae of flies. Some kinds of maggots injure various plants, as for instance apple, cabbage, onion, corn and wheat. See also FLIES.

MAGNESIUM. One of the chemical elements essential to plant growth, but also believed to be present in most average soils in sufficient quantities to meet the needs of crops. The magnesium compounds in which it occurs include carbonates, nitrates, sulphates, silicates, phosphates, and chlorides. Their function in plant life is not well understood but magnesium is known to be associated with nitrogen in protoplasm (the contents of living cells) and a component of chlorophyl, the green coloring matter of plants. Magnesium sulphate and magnesium carbonate have limited use as indirect fertilizer; like calcium, they help make potassium available. Kainit

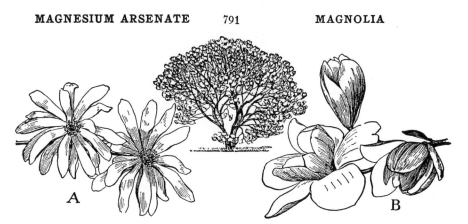

MAGNOLIAS BRING SOUTHERN BLOOM INTO NORTHERN GARDENS
Flowers of the Starry Magnolia (A) and of the hybrid M. soulangeana (B) and between them a typical tree of the latter type in bloom before the leaves appear.

(which see) contains magnesium phosphate.

MAGNESIUM ARSENATE. An arsenical poison extensively used in combating the Mexican bean beetle because it is less likely to injure the foliage than lead arsenate. For dusting use 1 lb. mixed with 5 lbs. hydrated lime; for spraying use 3 lbs. of the arsenate, 2 lbs. casein-lime, 100 gals. water. See ARSENICAL POISON; INSECTICIDE.

MAGNOLIA (mag-noh'-li-ah). Common and generic name of more than a score of trees and shrubs, deciduous and evergreen, of N. and Central America and Asia. (See illustration, Plate 35.) The evergreen sorts are not so hardy as the deciduous kinds. Many of them are spectacular in the blooming season, bearing probably the largest flowers of any cultivated tree; these range from white, through yellow and pink to purple. The tree is not especially graceful in form, but the astonishing spring transformation from naked branches to a mass of gorgeous, fragrant flowers never fails to win admiration. Since the flowers are not marketable, bruising easily and discoloring quickly, trees escape mutilation that would otherwise occur.

From the Orient come slow-growing, dwarfer species and hybrids, such as *M. kobus, stellata, soulangeana,* etc., that blossom before the leaves, and provide some of the most striking and useful garden types. In view of their early blossoming habit they are best placed against an evergreen background.

Most of the magnolias thrive in a rich porous soil that is moderately moist, pre- ferring sandy or peaty loam. They are difficult to transplant and must be carefully balled and wrapped and not trampled when reset, to avoid breaking and bruising the roots. The native kinds should be moved just as growth begins, and the Asiatic species and hybrids when in bloom, as the roots are tender and will not heal except when the plant is growing. Pruning must be done during the growing season as dormant trees do not easily heal their wounds.

Several leaf spots may occur on magnolia but they are rarely sufficiently serious to warrant spraying. In the S. E. States at the end of the rainy season a parasitic alga, entering through surface wounds, forms reddish-brown or orange cushion-like patches on leaves, twigs and fruit.

The magnolia scale is large ($\frac{1}{2}$ in. across), soft, and resembles the tulip-tree scale. As the young winter over in a partly grown state the best control is a dormant application of a safe miscible oil. The Comstock mealy bug, which is abundant on catalpa (which see), and sometimes injures magnolia can be controlled with a dormant spray.

Magnolias are propagated from seed and greenwood cuttings, and by layering or grafting on potted stock in the greenhouse; for the latter, *M. tripetala* is preferred because of its superior fibrous roots, although *M. acuminata* is also used.

PRINCIPAL SPECIES

In the following list those of Asiatic origin are indicated by (A).

M. acuminata, the Cucumber-tree, to 110 ft., is hardy from N. Y. West and South.

The large green flowers of this imposing pyramidal tree are distinguished with difficulty from the leaves.

campbelli (A) attains 80 ft. Its 10-in. flowers are white and pink within and purple outside. Hardy from Va. southward.

fraseri grows to 50 ft. and bears leaves 1½ ft. long and flowers 10 in. across. Hardy from Va. southward.

grandiflora (Bull Bay), to 100 ft., is the grandest tree of the tribe, with large lustrous evergreen leaves. It grows along the coast from N. C. to Texas but may survive in sheltered locations up to Phila. In bloom from April to August, it is very showy and its 8 in. flowers like giant roses cast their fragrance far and wide. It is the State flower of La. and Miss.

obovata (A), growing to 100 ft., is hardy from N. Y. City southward. Its large leaves are almost silvery white beneath and its fragrant 7 in. flowers are followed by scarlet cylindrical fruits 8 in. long.

macrophylla is the Large-leaved Cucumber-tree. It attains 50 ft. and is conspicuous for its 3-ft long leaves and its fragrant flowers often 1 ft. across. Its range is from Ky. to Fla. and La.

tripetala (Umbrella-tree), is hardy from Pa. southward; grows to 40 ft. and has leaves 2 ft. long. The 10 in. flowers are of unpleasant odor.

virginiana (Sweet or Swamp Bay), varies from shrub size to a tree of 60 ft. and is hardy from Mass. along the coast south to Texas, where it is evergreen. Its fragrant flowers are but 3 in. across.

(The following hardy kinds bloom before the foliage.)

kobus (A) to 30 ft., has a dense symmetrical habit; the white flowers, though small, stand well above the foliage.

soulangeana (A) to 12 ft., is a prolific bloomer and one of the kinds most planted. Its 6-in. fragrant flowers are white inside and brilliant purple outside. It is a hybrid having several varieties with white, rosy, red, and other shades.

stellata (A), the Starry Magnolia, is bushy and slow growing, to 15 ft. A showy plant with sweet, narrow-petaled flowers about 3 in. in diameter, it blooms with the early daffodils. In the north the blossoms are frequently frosted for their eagerness.

MAGNOLIACEAE (mag-noh-li-ay'-see-ee). The Magnolia Family, a group of trees, shrubs, or sometimes vines mostly native to N. America and Asia. The leaf margins are untoothed, and the flowers are fragrant and showy. The numerous pistils are packed about a fleshy prolongation of the receptacle forming a cone. Many shrubby forms of Magnolia and Illicium are valued as ornamentals because of the beauty of their flowers and foliage and their ready response to cultivation. A Chinese species of Illicium is the source of anise oil and the genus Liriodendron (tulip-tree) yields timber and fine ornamental trees.

MAHERNIA (mah-her'-ni-ah) *verticillata*. An African sub-shrub with drooping, yellow, fragrant bell-like flowers. See HONEY-BELL.

MAHOGANY. Common name for *Swietenia mahagoni*, a tropical evergreen tree whose dark red wood is valued for furniture and interior finish. It is often planted in warm countries for ornament and shade in gardens, parks and along streets.

Mountain-mahogany is Cercocarpus; Bastard-mahogany is *Eucalyptus botryoides;* Red-mahogany is *E. resinifera;* Swamp-mahogany is *E. robusta.*

MAHOGANY FAMILY. Common name of the Meliaceae, a group of tropical hardwood trees and shrubs.

MAHONIA (ma-hoh'-ni-ah). Handsome evergreen shrubs with yellow flowers and glossy foliage, found in N. and Central America, Europe and Asia, belonging to the Barberry Family. Most species are tender, but a few are hardy N., where they appreciate a position sheltered from wind and hot sun. They grow well under trees, especially where the soil is inclined to be moist, and are fine for massing. Some kinds spread freely by suckers. Propagated by seeds, suckers, layers and cuttings.

PRINCIPAL SPECIES

M. aquifolium (Holly-barberry), grows to 3 ft. or more. It has handsome spiny dark green lustrous leaves of 5 to 9 leaflets, which take on a bronzy tone in fall. The clusters of yellow flowers are showy in spring, and later the bluish-black bloomy fruits are attractive.

repens is a low grower of suckering habit, with bluish-green leaves of 3 to 7 leaflets.

Plate 35.   THE MAGNOLIA ANSWERS THE CALL OF SPRING

Upper left: The deliciously fragrant waxy bloom of the large-leaved cucumber-tree (Magnolia macrophylla).   Upper right: Delightful magnolia blossoms appearing with the leaves.   Center: The noble evergreen bull-bay (M. grandiflora) of the South has magnificent, heavily fragrant-cupped blossoms. Center right: The white, lavender-tinted flowers of Magnolia soulangeana appear before the foliage. Bottom: The spring garlands of the magnolia welcome the early flowering bulbs.

nervosa (Oregon-grape) is another dwarf and free suckering species, with large lustrous leaves with 11 to 19 leaflets. It is the State flower of Oregon.

bealei grows to 12 ft., with handsome leaves of 9 to 15 leaflets with a few spiny teeth, and large clusters of pale yellow flowers. It is not quite as hardy as the others mentioned, and is said to be often grown under the name of *M. japonica,* a species which authorities do not think is actually found in N. American gardens.

MAIANTHEMUM (may-yan'-the-mum). A genus of spring-blooming, low-growing perennials with white lily-of-the-valley-like flowers. The species are useful for planting in cool shady places and ordinary soils where they form mats of foliage.

MAIDENHAIR. Name given to any fern of the genus Adiantum (which see), the name probably being due to the delicate dark-brown or purplish-black branching stipes. They are among the best known and loveliest hardy and greenhouse foliage plants. One species is hardy N. of Washington, and others southward. Dealers list many varieties, but only the most dependable are listed under the generic name in this work. (See illustration, Plate 18.)

MAIDENHAIR-TREE. Common name for *Ginkgo biloba,* an attractive, hardy, deciduous Chinese tree, the deeply cut leaves of which are greatly enlarged reproductions of those of the familiar maidenhair fern (Adiantum).

MAIDENHAIR-VINE. A common name for *Calacinum complexum,* a twining vine popular in Calif. for covering rocks and structures.

MAINTENANCE OF THE GARDEN. Simple and specific as this subject sounds it can be subdivided into several phases. For one thing its objectives may be either esthetic—looking to the creation and perpetuation of lovely and artistic effects, or purely practical, looking to the health and growth of the plant materials, or the condition of the garden as a whole in relation to its use and enjoyment. At the same time, an important objective should be to see that the care of the garden does not take so much time and energy that none is left with which to enjoy and benefit from it.

Naturally garden upkeep is a seasonal proposition; but it should not be overlooked that there is plenty to be done in *each* of the seasons. (See AUTUMN, SPRING, SUMMER, and WINTER WORK IN THE GARDEN.) Also it should be realized that at any given time the work to be done may look either backward or forward—that is, it may have to do with the closing of the past season and the completion of its plant growth, or with preparation for a new season and a new generation of plants.

As with all complicated tasks that stretch over a long period, it is well to plan the year's work in the garden ahead and lay it out according to some sort of program or calendar. This may be divided so as to separate the parts or phases of the garden—such as front-yard and back-yard; or trees, shrubs, lawn, vegetable garden, flower garden, etc. Or it may segregate the mere chores that have to be done at more or less regular times or intervals from the special activities that have more interest and variety—such as planting, pruning, propagating of different plant subjects, construction of new features and the like.

Perhaps the chief necessity in planning any sort of garden-maintenance program is to visualize the garden as a whole, to realize the living nature of its plants and their needs, and to appreciate the value of getting the right thing done at the right time and in the right way.

Considering particularly the plant materials, garden maintenance in general involves especially spraying, pruning, mulching, feeding, watering, and cultivating.

SPRAYING is done for three general purposes: 1. As a preventive of trouble that might happen. 2. For the control of insects. 3. For the control of plant diseases. A March spraying of evergreens with water alone will stimulate leaf action and help remove the accumulation of winter smoke and gases. A late dormant spraying with a suitable solution (see SPRAYING) will clean up many insect eggs and larvae and many disease spores where they have overwintered on or around trees. During the growing season spray activities must be adapted to the circumstances as they arise.

PRUNING. There are four principal reasons for pruning: 1. The production of an abundance of flowers, foliage or fruit. 2. To modify natural forms or retain a desired form and height. 3. To rejuvenate old plants. 4. To balance•root and top growth, after transplanting.

A safe guide is to prune spring-flowering shrubs immediately after they bloom, before they develop the buds of the next year's flowers. Summer-flowering shrubs can be pruned in the fall or during early spring before active growth begins. Evergreens are best sheared after they have completed their first growth of the season and before they begin another, about June. To keep shrubs youthful and from becoming a tangled mass of sticks, all growths over five years should ordinarily be cut out right back to the ground.

MULCHING. This means covering the ground around the plants with light litter such as leaves, straw, well-rotted manure, compost, etc. A summer mulch should always be applied the first season on spring-planted stock; leaves, lawn clippings or compost can be used, but no fresh manure. The fall or winter mulch is necessary in all northern sections, especially for stock planted the same fall. It prevents heaving of heavy soil caused by alternate freezing and thawing, and conserves soil moisture by preventing excessive evaporation. In the spring if the mulch is fairly well decomposed it may be dug into the soil around the plants.

FEEDING. Commercial fertilizers supply plants with food, but add nothing of permanent value to the texture of the soil. Consequently manures and other organic fertilizers are used to supply humus. One of the sources of humus is the compost heap. The feeding of the lawn is one of the most important items of its maintenance, for few lawns are so well prepared when first made that they do not begin to need additional food by the second or third season.

WATERING must be thoroughly done if it is to be effective. If soil is kept cultivated, only during protracted dry spells will much watering be needed. At such times it is better to remove the hoze nozzle and soak the earth to a depth of 6 in. than to attempt to sprinkle it. As soon after watering as a crust begins to form, the soil should be cultivated to prevent evaporation.

GENERAL CULTURE. To keep a border or garden producing flowers, seed-pods must not be allowed to form, especially on annuals. *Careful staking is often necessary. Aside from the fact that neglect of any sort destroys the neatness and looks of the garden, it frequently leads to or opens the way for invasions of mildew or other troubles.

With the exception of peonies, dictamnus, Japanese anemones, trollius, and perhaps one or two other perennials, the plants in the border should be moved or thinned every three or four years. The entire border need not be disturbed at one time, though every perennial border is benefited by a thorough spading over and enriching at least once every three years. Divide and replant in the spring those fall-blooming sorts which continue to flower until late in the season, such as chrysanthemums and anemones, and all the fleshy-rooted plants except the peony. Otherwise, the best time for lifting and separating perennials in general is in the fall. Early-flowering perennials like some of the irises and leopards-bane give best results if divided and transplanted shortly after they have completed their flowering period.

No attempt should be made to develop an extensive garden until a careful estimate has been made of the probable cost of its future maintenance.

MAIZE. A native W. Indian name for *Zea mays,* the Corn (which see) of America, the term being more used in England than in the U. S.

MAJORANA (may-jor-ay'-nah) *hortensis.* A perennial culinary herb, commonly called Sweet (or Annual) Marjoram, grown for its fragrant foliage which is used to flavor various meat dishes. See MARJORAM; also HERBS.

MALABAR-NIGHTSHADE. Common name for *Basella alba* and *B. rubra,* twining vines whose young leaves are used as pot herbs in warm countries. When cooked it resembles spinach but is mucilaginous. It must not be sown until danger of frost has passed.

MALACOTHRIX (mal-ah-koth'-riks). A genus of annual and perennial herbs and sub-shrubs with white, pinkish or yellow thistle-like flowers in heads. Two species, *M. glabrata* and *M. californica,* are sometimes grown on sandy soils for ornament.

MALAY-APPLE. Common name for *Eugenia malaccensis,* a Malayan tree with a large thick head, reddish-purple flowers and fragrant, apple-flavored red berries; also called POMERACK.

MALAY JEWEL-VINE. Common name for *Derris scandens,* a woody vine of the Pea Family, native from China to Australia, and sometimes planted in other warm regions. A relative of the plant from which a modern contact insecticide is made. See DERRIS.

MALCOMIA (mal-koh'-mi-ah). A genus of low grayish annuals and perennials called Malcolm Stocks, of which 3 species are grown in American gardens for their small scentless flowers of white, lilac, or pinkish-purple. Seed is sown in the fall or started under glass for early blooming; outdoors for later flowers. Virginian Stock (*M. maritima*), the best known species, is a 12-in. annual of easy culture which may be sown bi-weekly for successional bloom, preferably in front of the border.

MALEBERRY. A common name for *Lyonia ligustrina,* a deciduous, ericaceous shrub also known as He-huckleberry.

MALE FERN. Common name for *Dryopteris filix-mas,* a large, once-pinnate species of Shield Fern, found only in the extreme N. parts of this country, and not recommended for gardens outside of its natural range. Its culture is the same as for other Dryopteris, which see.

MALLOW. Common name of annual, perennial and biennial herbs of the genus Malva; also applied (with descriptive adjectives) to various plants of related genera, all having the characteristic 5-parted rose or white, silky or papery-petaled flowers characteristic of the Mallow Family. Mallows may be grown without difficulty in any ordinary garden soil, preferring plenty of light and warmth. All are inclined to self-sow and escape from cultivation and some species have become familiar weeds.

PRINCIPAL SPECIES

M. moschata (Musk Mallow—but see also list of other genera below), an Old-World perennial with rose or white flowers and finely cut leaves. It is sometimes cultivated, and often seen as an escape both in England and America.

alcea, a perennial, with deep rose or white flowers similar to those of Musk Mallow, often found naturalized by the roadside.

rotundifolia (Common Mallow). This common biennial or perennial barnyard weed has very small white flowers followed by flat wrinkled green fruits called by children "cheeses."

crispa, a tall annual (to 8 ft.), is sometimes planted in the back of the border. The curly leaves are occasionally used as a garnish in place of parsley.

False-mallow is Malvastrum; Globe-mallow is Sphaeralcea; Jews-mallow is *Corchorus olitorius;* Marsh-mallow is *Althaea officinalis;* Musk-mallow is *Hibiscus abelmoschus;* Poppy-mallow is Callirhoë; Prairie-mallow is *Malvastrum coccineum;* Rose-mallow is Hibiscus; Tree-mallow is Lavatera.

MALMAISON (mal-may'-zon) **CARNATION.** A large-flowered type of Carnation, widely grown in England before the Winter- or Perpetual-flowering strain was introduced. Because of the great size of the flowers, hybridists have used it in breeding new strains, but it has proved of little value in producing improved forms.

MALNUTRITION. A physiological disease of plants caused by the lack of proper nutrients in the soil or their presence in unavailable form. A frequent cause of yellowing of foliage (chlorosis) is lack of iron in the tissues, not because it is lacking in the soil, but because an excess of lime or magnesium keeps the iron compounds in insoluble form. See PHYSIOLOGICAL DISEASES.

MALOPE (mal'-oh-pee). A genus of mallow-like annuals common in Old-World flower gardens. The large purple, rose or white flowers will continue to open from early summer till frost if the seeds are sown early in a good garden soil.

MALORTIEA (mal-or-ty'-ee-ah). A genus of small spineless palms from Central America, fairly popular outdoors in Calif. and elsewhere under glass. The three species *M. gracilis, M. simplex* and *M. tuerckheimi* are best known.

MALPIGHIA (mal-pig'-i-ah). Trees or shrubs of tropical America, sometimes grown under glass and outdoors in warm regions. Propagated by seeds and cuttings. *M. glabra* (Barbados-cherry), the principal species, grows to about 15 ft., with shining oval leaves and rose-red flowers with a fringed edge. The fruit is red, about the size of a cherry, and much esteemed in the tropics. *M. coccigera* is a bushy shrub to 3 ft. with small roundish spiny leaves and pale pink flowers; sometimes used for dwarf hedges in warm climates. *M. urens* (Cowage, Cow-itch), is a small shrub with oblong leaves clothed beneath with stinging bristles. It has pink or pale purple flowers, and edible fruit.

MALTESE CROSS. A common name for *Lychnis chalcedonica,* a favorite red-flowered perennial for centuries.

MALUS (may'-lus). The botanical name for all the apples. Unfortunately, botanists differ as to whether it should be applied to a genus or to a species. In the first case the apples would belong to two species, *Malus communis* and *M. sylvestris*. In the second case they would be merely varieties and forms of the species *malus* of the genus Pyrus, which also includes the crabapples and the pears. The latter system was proposed and followed by Linnaeus and it has been so generally adhered to by many botanical and horticultural authorities that it is followed in this book.

MALVA (mal'-vah). A genus of herbs, some useful in the flower garden and others persistent garden weeds. The common name for the group is Mallow, which see.

MALVACEAE (mal-vay'-see-ee). The Mallow Family, a widely distributed group of herbs and shrubs of economic and horticultural importance. The regular flowers have 9 sepals and 5 petals, and the many stamens are united to form a column about the pistils which are joined in a ring. The family yields many ornamental subjects, and a few grown for food, medicine and fibres. The outstanding representative is Gossypium, the source of commercial cotton. Among other genera in cultivation are Malva (mallow), Callirhoë, Althaea, Lavatera, Sidalcea, Malvastrum, Malvaviscus, Sphaeralcea, Abutilon, Malope and Hibiscus.

MALVASTRUM (mal-vas'-trum). A genus of herbs and sub-shrubs popularly called False-mallow, with yellow, orange or red ·flowers in spikes. The following popular species are of easy culture in any garden soil: *M. hypomadarum*, white with rosy-purple eye; *M. capense*, purple; *M. coccineum* (Prairie-mallow), red or copper-colored; *M. campanulatum*, rosy-purple; and *M. lateritium*, brick-red with yellow-based petals.

Propagation is usually by cuttings.

MALVAVISCUS (mal-vah-vis'-kus). Shrubby plants, mostly from tropical America, belonging to the Mallow Family. One or two species are well known in outdoor gardens in warm regions or under glass in the N. Propagated by cuttings.

M. arboreus, the principal species, is well known in greenhouses and is a good houseplant. In pots it grows 2 to 3 ft. high, and has a long season of bloom. The flowers are bright scarlet, resembling those of abutilon, but not fully opening.

M. mollis, with soft hairy leaves and scarlet flowers, has been used for low hedges in California.

MAMMEA (ma-mee'-ah). A genus of West Indian trees of which one large species, *M. americana*, is grown in warm countries for its globular, russet, rather rough, leathery-skinned, apricot-flavored fruit. It has generally failed in Calif. but in Fla. has succeeded as far north as Palm Beach. In rich soil the tree becomes one of the most striking of West Indian subjects, often attaining a height of 60 ft. with a trunk 3 to 4 ft. in diameter, displaying glossy thick foliage and abundant, white fragrant flowers. Among its common names are Mammee-apple and Santo-Domingo-apricot.

MAMMILLARIA (ma-mi-lay'-ri-ah). The cacti of this genus (whose name means nipple-cactus) are by some classified as Neomammillaria. The group includes more species than any other single genus. The greater number are Mexican, many of them plants of great beauty and interest, but quite a few are native to S. W. U. S. These plants are popular as dish-garden material. See also CACTUS.

MANDARIN ORANGE. The popular name of a small, loose-skinned botanical variety (*deliciosa*) of the King Orange (*Citrus nobilis*). This includes the horticultural variety called Tangerine Orange. The name is sometimes given to fruit of the Mangosteen, which see.

MANDRAKE. Common name for the old European medicinal herb, *Mandragora officinarum*, known also as Love-apple. From the thick tuberous roots, often branching into human-like shapes, an aphrodisiac used to be decocted in ancient times, and many superstitions still linger about the plant, which if eaten has poisonous qualities. The leaves are large and the solitary purple or yellowish bell-shaped flowers are almost hidden among the foliage. Plants grow readily to about 1 ft. high in rich warm loamy soil and are increased by seed or division. Formerly grown in herb collections, they are sometimes seen in wild gardens.

The name Mandrake is also, but incorrectly, applied to the American May-apple (*Podophyllum peltatum*).

MANETTI (mah-net'i). A variety of the China Rose (*Rosa chinensis*) with pink, single or semi-double flowers. It is valued and extensively used not, however, as a plant but as a stock upon which to grow (usually by budding) improved varieties of greenhouse roses for cut-flower production. Large quantities of the young seedling stocks are imported from Europe and some are produced in parts of the U. S., principally the Pacific N. W.

MANETTIA (mah-net'-i-ah). Tropical American twining plants, belonging to the Madder Family. One or two species are often grown under glass, and are useful to drape trellises and rafters or to train on forms. They may also be used for summer flowering outdoors in a sunny place. They have a long season of bloom, and some attention should be given to training and trimming to prevent the growth from becoming a tangle. Propagated by cuttings.

M. bicolor, perhaps the best known, has bright tubular flowers of red, tipped yellow, and somewhat swollen at the base. *M. inflata* is very similar, differing in the more reflexed leafy calyx-lobes, the base of the flower more swollen, and the yellow tip smaller. *M. glabra* has larger flowers, more than an inch long, and crimson throughout.

MANFREDA (man-free'-dah). A genus of fleshy bulbous herbs whose greenish or purplish-white flowers open at night. Their culture is the same as that of agave, which see.

MANGEL, Mangold, or Mangel-wurzel. Popular name for a group of beet varieties (*Beta vulgaris* var. *macrorhiza*) characterized by red or yellow roots of great size and coarse texture. They are used mainly for cattle feeding. See BETA and BEET.

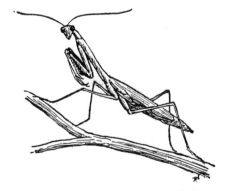

FRIEND OF THE GARDENER
The praying mantis lives on other insects, thus ridding the garden of many noxious pests.

MANGO. A tropical evergreen Asiatic tree (*Mangifera indica*) grown in southernmost Florida and California for its large, peach-like fruits. These, when of good varieties, are ranked among the world's choicest in color, aroma, flavor and food value; common ones are unfit to eat. In Nature, the tree often exceeds 75 ft. in height and 100 ft. in spread; in gardens by proper pruning it may be kept less than half as large. It needs well-drained but moisture-retentive soil. It may be grown from seed, but choice varieties are propagated by grafting (especially in arching) and budding. In the tropics the mango fills the place taken by the apple in temperate climates.

MANGOSTEEN (mang'-goh-steen). The common name for *Garcinia mangostana,* a pink-flowered Malayan tree whose reddish-purple fruits (sometimes called Mandarin-oranges) are among the world's choicest. Only in the warmest parts of the U. S. can the tree be grown. It needs well-drained but moist soil and complete freedom from cold.

MANIHOT (man'-i-hot). A genus of tropical American plants of which a shrub, *M. esculenta,* is the most important. It is cultivated for its long, thick tuberous starchy roots which furnish the tapioca of commerce. In S. Fla., where it thrives best in rich, light soil, its main use is for stock feed. Common names for the plant are Manioc and Cassava.

MANNA GRASS. Common name for Glyceria, a genus of mostly tall perennial grasses that grow in wet ground, and are sometimes planted in wild or bog gardens.

MAN-OF-THE-EARTH. A common name for *Ipomoea pandurata,* the Wild Sweet-potato-vine, a hardy perennial sometimes used for clothing stumps and fences, but generally a pernicious weed. It is sometimes applied to the Wild-cucumber (*Echinocystis lobata*).

MANTIS, PRAYING. A common name for a large, curious looking insect of the order Orthoptera, also called "mule killer." It lives entirely on other insects, including many injurious kinds for which reason the first part of the name is also spelled preying. But the other form was originally given because of the attitude taken by the creature when at rest, with its enormous grasping fore-legs held together in front as if in supplication. The insects appear in midsummer and the eggs winter over in rounded masses of hardened frothy substance an inch or so in diameter fastened to the twigs of shrubs and low-growing bushes. Fairly common from N. Y. City southward, the mantis (mantes, mantids or mantides in the plural) is highly beneficial as an insect destroyer both in garden and greenhouse, and neither the mantis nor the egg masses should be destroyed.

MANURE. Animal and vegetable matter used to enrich soil. Originally the word (coming from the same root as "maneuver" and "manual") meant much more; in Old French it meant "hand work" including tillage and cultivating as well as fertilizing. It can still sometimes refer to any substance used to improve the soil, even lime, though in recent years the tendency is to drop these older senses in favor of the special one. Today the word manure, unless accompanied by some other word (as green manure, which see), stands for stable, henhouse and barnyard droppings.

SOURCES OF MANURE. Except on virgin soil, manure in some form is usually necessary in gardening. Its scarcity and high price of late years are in part due to the replacement of horses in thickly settled communities by automobiles, but as the total number of horses in the country has not been greatly reduced, while that of cows and other livestock has increased, another cause is, no doubt, the increased use with the development of home and commercial gardening. With the spread of scientific knowledge among farmers, cow and hog manures are usually kept on the farm, and seldom sold in quantity except from stockyards. They are valuable because they do not generate much heat, and particularly desirable for making liquid manure. The manure usually sold is stable manure, from horses or mules, and varies in quality according to the bedding used. If bedded with sawdust, it is practically useless for gardening, the unrotted wood waste giving off harmful acids and encouraging fungous growth. Salt hay bedding gives a close-grained manure, a little hard to handle, but otherwise moderately satisfactory. Straw, and especially rye straw, makes the best manure for general purposes. Peat moss, also much used for bedding, gives a manure that rots slowly, but that has the additional soil-building (humus) properties of the peat moss.

Stable manure with straw bedding may consist of much straw and little dung,

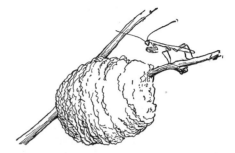

A MANTIS EGG MASS
Do not destroy these yellowish-white shiny masses found on twigs of shrubs. Next summer it will hatch out young ones like that shown at the right.

or the reverse, but not too much attention should be paid to this difference, as straw itself benefits the soil, particularly when saturated with urine. Such manure is in demand not only for spreading on the soil, but for use in hotbeds and mushroom houses. In hotbeds its fermentation furnishes heat to force growth and keep out frost. For the mushroom house, manure is composted, watered and forked over frequently for about three weeks, then placed in wooden beds for the mushroom spawn (planted in a covering layer of soil) to feed on. When, after 2 or 3 months, the mushroom crop has been gathered, the spent manure is removed from the beds along with about a quarter its bulk of the topsoil that was used for casing; it must be removed immediately to a distance or it will infect the next crop. In regions where many mushrooms are grown, this spent manure or mushroom soil may be had cheaply between January and June, and while most of the potash and some other valuable substances have been exhausted, the residue, rich in humus, is safe to use in any quantity on evergreens, plants of the Heath Family, and others which dislike fresh manure. All the heat has been removed from this mushroom manure by the composting and in most cases the alkalinity has also disappeared, making this the most desirable manure for acid-soil plants.

Fresh stable manure should not usually be placed on the soil, except in fall on plowed land or land to be turned in spring. It is better if first composted, watered and occasionally turned with a fork to avoid burning or "fire-fang" from too rapid fermentation of the pile, with loss of fertilizing value in the form of ammonia. Soil mixed through the manure as it is turned will slow up the fermentation and lessen the danger of overheating. When the interior of the pile is no longer warm to touch, the manure is ready for use on the garden. Poultry manure, which also heats if allowed to ferment, should be mixed with its own bulk of soil and composted before applying, for if spread on the ground fresh, it may injure plants that it touches.

MANURE FOR THE GARDEN
Three good rules are: 1. Use all you can get; 2. Be sure it is well-rotted; 3. Apply well in advance of planting, turn under, and incorporate thoroughly.

USING MANURES. Composted manure can be used more effectively than fresh because top-dressings can be placed where most needed in addition to the bulk applications turned under. In the vegetable garden, leaf crops such as lettuce, spinach and chard should be given much more manure than root crops, especially carrots, which are best not manured at all. In the flower border manure should be used sparingly on perennials subject to root-rot, such as iris or delphinium. Annuals thrive best when heavily manured. Plants of the squash and melon group like a large shovelful in the bottom of the hill, but this method should not be used except for rank-growing annuals. It is a mistake to place manure in the bottom of the hole when transplanting any woody subject. The quick growth that follows may mean disaster to the plant, which, instead of increasing the top, should be spending its energies on root-growth to prepare for drought and frost. Manure should be used on transplanted shrubs and trees only as a top-dressing, and only in late fall or winter, the purpose being to

keep out frost rather than to fertilize. Of course, incorporation of thoroughly rotted manure with soil in advance of planting is always in order.

Manure which has been dried and shredded, like the commercial sheep manure sold in bags, is usually highly concentrated, but much of the heating capacity has been removed by drying; also the shredding makes it safe to sprinkle thinly on lawns, or even on the perennial border, if care is taken to keep the particles well scattered, for even small piles may generate heat. Otherwise it should be handled like fresh manure. Rabbit manure, also sometimes available in quantity, should be treated the same as poultry manure. Stockyard products, as dried blood, tankage, etc., being organic materials, might be classed as manures, but are more conveniently considered with fertilizer (which see). Guano, accumulated deposits of the droppings of sea-fowl on the Chilean coast, is actually a manure, but more often called fertilizer.

MANURIAL VALUES. The value of manure depends on its ability to supply those plant foods which quickly disappear from the soil under cultivation and heavy cropping. Compounds of nitrogen, potash and phosphorus are the first to become exhausted, and of these nitrogen is hardest to replace. The soil content of organic matter or humus, though less accurately measurable and less fully explained by chemistry, is even more important to maintain. All these needs are supplied by ordinary manure. Chemical fertilizers often substituted are desirable in that they do not carry weed seeds, as even carefully composted manures do. But just as humans cannot keep healthy on a diet wholly of food in tablet form, plants, except in the laboratory, will not thrive indefinitely on chemical fertilizers alone. These should be used as stimulants and sources of special food in conjunction with manure. Some kinds can be added to the manure itself rather than to the soil. Superphosphate, phosphate rock and gypsum scattered lightly over fresh manure either in the stall or on the compost heap not only add their own fertilizing value to the value of the manure, but prevent the escape of important nitrogen compounds.

Green manure is the name for a growing crop turned under to rot in the soil. In small-scale gardening it is not usually possible, as on the farm, to give up the ground for a whole season to a green-manure crop, or to use crop rotations which call for the plowing under of grass or clover sod. In vegetable gardens, however, some manure can often be grown while the ground stands idle in late fall and early spring by sowing rye or rye and vetch. Those are the hardiest and most satisfactory crops for this purpose in the N., but several others will winter well enough on the average to give good value. Parts of the garden which fall into disuse in August or early September should immediately be sown to crimson clover, winter vetch, turnips, rye, or anything that will grow vigorously until frost, survive the winter if possible, and furnish a good quantity of succulent green stuff to turn under in spring. Even if it fails to winter, the crop will contribute fertility, especially if the root system is heavy, for the roots furnish green manure as well as the tops. Leguminous plants, as clover, vetch, etc., add additional nitrogen to the soil through the action of beneficial bacteria in their roots.

A *compost* (which see) of cornstalks, weeds, sods, grass clippings, green garbage, leaves and straw—in short, everything of vegetable (but not of woody) nature, can be made to supply nearly as much plant food as manure. None of these materials should be burned in the well-regulated garden, unless badly infected with especially serious plant pests. Slight infections can be largely destroyed if lime is added and the pile is occasionally wet down and forked over. If manure is scarce, the compost may be still further enriched in fertilizing value by adding now and then a little of the following mixtures of chemicals: 60 lbs. sulphate of ammonium, 30 lbs. superphosphate, 25 lbs. muriate of potash, 50 lbs. ground limestone. A little of this should be scattered lightly over the compost heap every few days as more material is added; the compost should be watered frequently, and the heap kept hollow-topped so it will not shed rain. Such compost, however, must not be used on acid-loving plants.

Every winter a new heap should be started, so that the old one will be ready to use as manure in spring. Wood shavings, sawdust, etc., should not be included in any compost; but if piled up separately in a damp spot and covered with leaves, they will, after three or four years, rot into an acid humus suitable for acid-soil plants.

Amounts of manure or compost to be used in the garden are not easily stated; nor, if stated, are the recommendations easily followed, because different lots will differ in strength. However, if it is properly rotted or composted, much manure can be used without danger and any excess plant food is carried for the most part from year to year, which is not true in the case of soluble fertilizers. On the other hand, every bit that is added is of help, so no gardener should spurn a supply of manure however small. A load or two of manure delivered late each winter is good fare for the average small garden, when supplemented with compost and fertilizers.

It is estimated that well-rotted manure weighs about 810 lbs. per cu. yd. On this basis one ton of such manure represents very close to 2½ cu. yds.

See also COMPOST; FERTILIZER; PLANT FOODS AND FEEDING; IMPROVEMENT, SOIL.

MANZANITA (man-zah-nee′-tah). Common name for Arctostaphylos, a genus of evergreen shrubs and small trees of the Heath Family, also called Bear-berry. See ARCTOSTAPHYLOS.

MAPLE. Common name for the handsome, deciduous, usually long-lived trees of the genus Acer, all having opposite, often lobed, leaves and bearing clusters of small flowers, followed by two-winged fruits, called *samaras* or keys. Nearly all the maples are hardy N., and many are among the most attractive street, lawn, and specimen trees. They are quite indifferent as to soil, although the Silver and Red Maples requiring considerable moisture, do best in swampy situations.

The Sugar Maple, valuable for its sap and timber, as well as for shade and ornament, is one of the most beautiful and symmetrical of hardy trees for average planting. The Red Maple is a most satisfactory tree for yard or street, beautiful at all times, but especially in the early spring when covered with its vivid red flowers, in May when hung with red keys, and in the fall because of the brilliant crimson coloration of the foliage. The Ash-leaved Maple, because of its rapidity of growth and abundant foliage, has been widely planted through the Middle W. States, but unfortunately it is a short-lived tree with brittle limbs; stronger species, or ash or elm should be grown in its place. The Silver Maple, a rapid-growing tree also, with easily broken limbs, has been extensively planted in the Mississippi Valley, where, however, the Red Maple should be given preference. The Japanese Maple species are most decorative dwarf trees for lawns, but restraint should be used in planting the varieties with finely cut or brightly colored leaves.

Most maples are grown from seed, sown as soon as ripe, or stratified and planted in spring; the Japanese species are commonly grafted. Occasionally shrubby types are increased by layers or greenwood cuttings.

ENEMIES

DISEASES. Maples are subject to various fungus diseases and insect pests but one of the commonest troubles—leaf scorch—is caused not by an organism but by unbalanced water relations, Sugar, Soft and Japanese Maples being especially susceptible. Since maples leaf out early and bear large, thin leaves, moisture may be lost from the foliage faster than it can be supplied by the roots, especially in early spring and in dry summers. The trouble appears as irregular blotches or a streaking of the veins and a yellowing of the entire leaf. The best treatment is to remove from trees subject to scorch 25 per cent of the foliage by winter pruning. Also stir the soil in the spring and fertilize well and during hot weather water thoroughly and frequently.

Maple wilt, caused by a fungus which enters mostly through wounds, is most destructive to Norway and Sugar Maples, the leaves and branches suddenly wilting while green; this is followed by the death of other branches and, usually, of the entire tree, which shows long conspicuous green streaks in the sapwood. Control by preventing wounds, painting fresh pruning cuts (see TREE SURGERY) and eliminating sources of infection by destroying diseased trees immediately, being sure to remove roots also.

Maples in N. J. are dying from a Phytopthora disease characterized by thin crown, decrease in number and size of leaves, and reddish discoloration of bark. In New England another species of this fungus causes bleeding canker, which begins with a reddish ooze coming from fissures in trunk and branches and eventually causes large trunk cankers.

All kinds of maples are subject to a number of leaf-spot diseases which may cause large brown spots bordered by a reddish-purple zone, small light brown or whitish spots, a scorched appearance (usually called anthracnose) or large tar-like blotches. Practically all of them can be controlled by keeping the foliage covered with bordeaux mixture.

PESTS. Several species of aphids infest maples and are particularly obnoxious because often followed by the black sooty mold fungus (which see). Spray with nicotine sulphate and soap. The cottony maple scale and the woolly maple-leaf scale are best controlled with a dormant oil spray. Maple foliage may be fed upon by canker worms, the green-striped maple worm, the forest tent caterpillar, gypsy moth, brown-tailed moth, bag-worm, white-marked tussock moth, and Japanese beetle, all of which are easily controlled by spraying thoroughly with arsenate of lead.

Several borers operate on maples. The maple borer, especially destructive to Sugar Maples, may be controlled by injecting carbon bisulphide or nicotine-sulphate into the burrows. There is no control for the leaf-stem borer which tunnels the leaf stalks and causes serious dropping of leaves. Galls on the leaves, caused by a mite, are more unsightly than injurious; spray in spring with dormant strength lime-sulphur at the blossom period.

PRINCIPAL SPECIES

A. rubrum (Red, Scarlet, or Rock Maple) grows to 120 ft. with strong, upright branches which make it resistant to storm and winds. The leaves, 3 to 4 in. long, are 3 to 5 lobed and turn scarlet or orange in the fall. Var. *columnare* of narrow upright growth is an interesting variation, as are var. *globosum* of rounded form and var. *magnificum,* whose leaves in the fall are vivid crimson veined with green.

saccharum (Sugar, or Rock Maple) is a large tree reaching over 100 ft. in height with lobed leaves 6 in. long, turning bright orange and red. It does well in any soil and is one of the most beautiful trees in the forests of the E. States.

platanoides (Norway Maple) is a large handsome European tree with broad, rounded head. The leaves turn yellow in the fall and remain long on the tree. It is used extensively as a street tree, especially in the Middle W.

pseudoplatanus (Sycamore Maple), growing to 70 ft. and an important hard-wood tree in Europe, has coarse-toothed leaves like those of the Buttonwood or Sycamore. It grows well, even in exposed situations, but unfortunately is short-lived in this country.

palmatum (Japanese Maple), a small tree, usually not over 20 ft. in height and of shrubby growth, has lobed leaves, almost circular in outline. The varieties are hardier than the type form and show beautiful and brilliant coloring, particularly noticeable in the early spring and fall. Some of the best of the horticultural varieties are: *atropurpureum* with purple leaves; *linearilobum* and *dissectum* with leaves finely cut and divided into segments; *sanguineum* and *rubrum* with foliage brilliant red from the moment it unfolds in the spring.

ginnala (Amur Maple), a graceful, shrubby tree from N. China and Japan, the foliage turning a vivid crimson in the fall. Extremely hardy, it may be planted where the Japanese Maple winter-kills.

nigrum (Black Maple), native of the Middle W., reaches 120 ft. in height. It resembles the Sugar Maple, but has thinner foliage, which does not color so brilliantly in the fall.

pennsylvanicum (Moosewood, or Striped Maple) is a charming species of slender growth, sometimes reaching a height of 40 ft. The graceful trunks are striped green and white and the large, rather long leaves turn clear yellow when mature. Found only in cool, rich woods, this maple may be grown in the shady shrubbery border, or naturalized in the wild garden as a shrub.

saccharinum or *dasycarpum* (Silver or White Maple), is a quick-growing tree that stands considerable heat and drought and that will grow on poor soils. In spite of being short-lived, brittle, and of no special timber value, it is sometimes used as a shade tree where quick results are sought in some of the more difficult sections of the S. W.

spicatum (Mountain Maple), a small tree to 30 ft. found usually only at high elevations in the E. States. As its foliage turns to lovely shades of scarlet and yellow in the fall, it is an attractive tree for underplanting with higher growing trees.

macrophyllum (Big-leaf Maple), a W. species, not hardy N. A forest tree of the W. Coast, it is now extensively planted in that region and abroad for outlying avenues and for shade in gardens. A stately, wide-spreading tree, it grows to 100 ft. in height, and bears remarkable large, lobed leaves.

circinatum (Vine Maple), a small tree to 40 ft., which, when growing in dense forests of larger trees, produces long, slender, trailing branches. In the open the circular, finely lobed leaves begin to color in August, turning brilliant orange and red.

MAPLEWORT. Common name for *Aceranthus diphyllus,* a low growing hardy Asiatic rock-garden perennial herb with small white or pink flowers in loose racemes. It is grown like Epimedium.

MARANTA (mah-ran'-tah). A genus of tropical American perennial herbs grown in warm countries and greenhouses for their ornamental foliage. Most plants so named are properly members of the genus Calathea (which see). One species, *M. arundinacea,* is cultivated like Manihot (which see) for its roots, which supply arrow-root.

MARANTACEAE (mar-an-tay'-see-ee). The Maranta or Arrowroot Family, a group of perennial herbs with rootstocks formed in clumps; many are cultivated for their very irregular interesting flowers and showy foliage, and from the starchy rootstocks of one a form of tapioca is obtained. Some are planted out, but others are grown under glass, principally species of Calathea and Maranta.

MARES TAIL. A common name for an aquatic herb of the genus Hippuris; its long slender stems stand erect in the shallow water of ponds or streams.

MARGINAL SHIELD FERN (*Dryopteris marginalis*). A common and very hardy woods fern of the E. U. S. with broad blue-green fronds and conspicuous marginal fruit dots. It readily transplants to ordinary garden soil. More fully discussed under DRYOPTERIS.

MARGUERITE. Common name for various daisy-like plants of different genera. Probably most used by florists for *Chrysanthemum frutescens,* also called Paris Daisy, a perennial herb grown by them as a pot plant for winter and early spring sales. Bearing white-rayed, yellow-disked flowers, it will bloom the year 'round, and is also grown in the garden in mild climates.

Blue Marguerite is *Felicia amelloides;* and Golden Marguerite is *Anthemis tinctoria.*

MARICA (ma'-ri-kah). A genus of tropical perennial herbs with long narrow

TWO BRILLIANT MARIGOLDS
The French type (A) bears outer rays or ruffles of maroon. The much larger African or Aztec form (B) is gleaming orange or yellow.

leaves and white, yellow or blue flowers on long flat leaf-like stalks. In Fla. they survive the winter when properly mulched. *M. northiana* is an excellent house plant, blooming in winter and spring. The flowers resemble those of the iris (to which the plant is related) but are short-lived. Propagation is by division of the clumps.

MARIGOLD. Common name for Tagetes, a popular genus of brilliantly colored, mostly strongly scented annuals, which succeed almost anywhere with little attention. Natives of Mexico and South America, they are thoroughly hardy throughout the U. S. and have been developed and hybridized to produce many forms, from the giant so-called "Africans" or Aztecs to the tiny French types. Varieties are available for nearly every garden purpose, whether bed, border, massing, or cutting. They bloom from July until frost, with solitary or sometimes clustered heads of yellow, orange, brownish or reddish ray and disk flowers borne profusely on branching plants 1 to 3 ft. tall. Realizing the popularity and wide applicability of the well known marigold forms, plant breeders and in particular one prominent American seedsman, have developed a great variety of improved and enlarged types. Of special interest are handsome hybrids in which the brilliant red tones of the French splash flowers of real African size and form; a unique race developed from plants found in the Far East which, because they lack the tiny oil sacs found in the leaves of most marigolds, are totally lacking in the characteristic, sharp fragrance; still another practically odorless variety in which the oil sacs are present in the leaves, but apparently do not function; and finally an extra large-flowered strain created by treating parent plants with colchicine (which see) and thus producing a so-called tetraploid condition. The resulting novelty was therefore named Tetra. Along with these flower developments have also come increased size and vigor of plant, greater bushiness, or other qualities favored in gardens.

They thrive in any ordinary garden soil in sunny locations; in fact, the French varieties do better in rather poor soil, as rich earth encourages rank growth of the finely cut foliage, which may subordinate the gay blossoms. The plants are propagated by seeds sown indoors in early spring or outdoors when danger of frost has passed. They are free from or withstand disease better than most other annuals.

If a bacterial wilt similar to that of tomatoes and related plants attacks marigolds, destroy diseased plants. A fungus wilt and stem rot appears as a blackening and shrivelling of stems near the soil line followed by wilting and death. Remove infected plants and sterilize soil before replanting. See DISINFECTION. In moist weather gray mold may attack flowers, which should be removed and burned. Slugs (which see) are fond of marigolds but can be checked by sprinkling lime on the soil. Derris sprays help repel the Japanese beetle.

PRINCIPAL SPECIES

T. erecta (Aztec or African Marigold). Once supposed to be a native of Africa, this is really a Mexican species. The compact, tubular or quilled petals of its flower-heads make a large globe of golden yellow or orange. The plants grow from 18 in. to 3 ft. tall. Yellow Supreme, the newest and most vigorous of the Aztec varieties, has fluffy double or semi-double blossoms, resembling carnations, without the disagreeable odor common to most marigolds.

Guinea Gold and All Double Orange, varieties which produce virtually all double flowers, are both free bloomers.

patula (French Marigold). More profuse than the Aztec type, the plants bear smaller flowers, often two-toned in yellow and red. The petals are flat and overlapping. Branching from the base, the plants grow about 18 in. tall and produce blossoms admirably suited for cutting. This species offers also dwarf varieties, compact little bushes with feathery dark foliage, covered with brilliant buttons of flowers and admirable for bedding and edging. Good sorts are Gold Striped, Golden Ball and Maroon. Among the dwarf singles, growing only 8 in. tall, the rich yellow petals blotched at the center with garnet, is Legion of Honor.

tenuifolia. A tall plant with few-rayed yellow flowers, this species is better known in its dwarf var. *pumila,* which makes a compact fern-like little bush of delicate fragrance, covered all summer with tiny single orange blossoms.

sigmata. An annual, best known to earth by its dwarf var. *sumila,* which has masses of small yellow flowers.

lucida (Sweet-scented Marigold). This, while botanically a perennial, is cultivated as an annual. The small orange-yellow heads grow in dense terminal clusters, and the leaves are toothed, not deeply cut. Plants grow about 18 in. tall.

Other plants not species of Tagetes are sometimes referred to as marigolds, namely: Pot-marigold, *Calendula officinalis;* Corn-marigold (which see), *Chrysanthemum segetum;* Cape-marigold (which see), Dimorphotheca; Fig-marigold, Mesembryanthemum; March-marigold, *Caltha palustris.*

MARINE IVY. Common name for *Cissus incisa,* a tall, fleshy-stemmed tendril-climbing shrub often planted in the S.

MARIPOSA - LILY, MARIPOSA-TULIP. Names popularly used for many species of Calochortus, attractive bulbous herbs with variously colored cup- or trumpet-shaped flowers, native to N. W. America.

MARJORAM, or SWEET MARJORAM. Perennial herbs usually grown as annuals for their fragrant foliage which is used to flavor dressings and meat dishes. The plants are variously designated as *Origanum vulgare, Majorana hortensis* (formerly *O. majorana*), and *M. onites.*

Since the seed is very small, sow it in a seed pan; prick out the seedlings into flats;

water them carefully and shield from strong sunlight until growing well, then transplant to the garden 12 in. asunder in rows 18 in. apart. Gather for drying just before flowering begins. See HERBS.

MARKER CROPPING. The practice of sowing quick-sprouting seed (especially of forcing radish varieties) in the same rows and at the same time with seed of plants that germinate slowly or whose seedlings are hard to see. The "marker" seed leaves appear in a few days and thus show the location of the permanent crop rows. See CROPPING SYSTEMS.

MARKET GARDEN. An area where vegetables are grown for near-by markets by men who make sales direct to retailers or consumers rather than to wholesalers. Before the advent of motor trucks the areas so utilized were mostly within a ten-mile radius of the market; today they are often 25 to 50 miles away. Compare KITCHEN GARDEN and TRUCK GARDEN.

SOME MODERN MARIGOLDS HAVE NO ODOR

Leaves of an ordinary variety (B) with oil sacs responsible for the pungent odor, and the modern Crown of Gold (A) without sacs or smell. Also a flower of Burpee Gold, whose leaves have oil sacs that don't function.

MARKETING GARDEN PROD-UCTS. When the home gardener makes high quality his standard he can usually dispose of any surplus vegetables, fruits and flowers he harvests and also any extra small vegetable or flowering plants for transplanting that he may have left over, because there is an unsatisfied demand for such things in nearly every community.

When he has proved this to be the case he may begin to plan so as to have still more of the best-selling or most profitable kinds. In time he may even build up a small local business which should more than repay him for the thought, energy and labor devoted to it. However, he must realize that it is folly to attempt to compete with established commercial growers, especially by shipping into a large city market. His safe and sane course is to seek special customers who want—and are willing to pay for—fresher, better products than they can buy in the stores and markets or from hucksters.

Until the products become known for their high quality, the most helpful factor in creating sales is attractiveness. This includes cleanliness, freshness, neatness, novel packages and "little artistic touches" that will catch the buyer's eye and immediately suggest superiority. This attractiveness should apply also to methods of offering the goods, such as a pleasingly designed road-side stand. Until the business is big enough to warrant the erection of a permanent structure, a neat pleasingly colored tent will serve every purpose. Two important things that should always be provided are (1) ample parking space well off the highway and (2) shade, preferably that of one or more large attractive trees. See also ROADSIDE STANDS.

Unless and until the quality of products to be sold warrants advertising in the local papers, or by means of "direct mail" circulars and postcards, the most practical way to attract customers is by well-worded signs erected beside the road in each direction from the sales place, but not such as will deface the landscape or offer a menace by taking motorists' attention unduly. The appearance of the stand and of the produce itself and all resulting "mouth to ear" publicity spread by pleased customers are also good. By keeping a record of sales and a mailing list, the grower can arrange to notify desirable customers when various products are going to be ready for sale.

When there are children in the family old enough to wait on customers and make sales, not only will their help mean a good deal, but also they themselves will gradually learn the fundamentals of good business and how to carry responsibility.

What products to grow in developing such a business will depend largely upon personal taste as well as local conditions, which must be studied and probably experimented with. However, some of the most easily produced and readily sold are the various berries, currants, gooseberries, grapes, peaches, plums, cherries and the dessert varieties of pears and apples. Among the vegetables, really ripe tomatoes, freshly gathered sweet corn and asparagus are probably the best. Long-lasting flowers are also good—gladiolus, dahlia, chrysanthemum, delphinium, aster, and peony. Small vegetable and flower plants for transplanting are also in demand, but these must usually be advertised to attract patrons; also they must be ready promptly when the planting season opens. The sale of perennial plants and divisions, and of iris clumps, dahlia tubers, etc., quickly tends to develop into a real profession rather than a mere sideline.

MARL. A crumbly lime deposit usually left under other deposits in the beds of streams or shallow lakes. It consists of calcium carbonate and clay and is one of the forms in which lime may be applied to the soil. It is slow acting, however, as far as correcting acidity is concerned.

See also CALCIUM; LIME.

MARLBERRY. Common name for *Ardisia paniculata,* a small tree with white flowers and glistening black berries.

MARMALADE-BOX. Common name for *Genipa americana,* a tropical American shrub whose brown berries are used for jams and beverages. See GENIP.

MARMALADE-FRUIT, MARMALADE-PLUM, SAPOTE. Common names for *Achras zapota,* a tropical American evergreen tree grown for its edible fruit. See SAPOTE.

MARROW, or VEGETABLE MARROW. Various types of the bush squash (*Cucurbita pepo*) widely popular in Europe but less known in America. This is unfortunate because their modest requirements and easy culture, ease of preparation for the table, minimum of waste, and high quality should commend them more highly than any other varieties to people who enjoy summer squash. The fruits are not scalloped, warted or irregular like simlin, pattypan or crookneck varieties, but oblong, uniform, thicker fleshed and much heavier when ready for use. While they can be and are served boiled like summer squash, they are especially good when cut in slices about a half-inch thick and fried like eggplant. See SQUASH; PUMPKIN.

MARRUBIUM (mah-roo'-bi-um). A genus of mint-like herbs popularly called Hoarhound, which see.

MARSDENIA (mahrz-dee'-ni-ah). Twining shrubs of warm regions, belonging to the Milkweed Family. The principal species is *M. erecta,* from S. Europe and Asia, and fairly hardy N. It is a deciduous, more or less twining shrub to 20 ft., with light green heart-shaped leaves and clusters of small white fragrant flowers. Propagated by cuttings.

MARSH FERN (*Thelypteris palustris*). A common fern of the E. U. S., growing in wet fields and woods. Not recommended for the garden because of its rampant growth. Formerly known as Aspidium, and more recently as Dryopteris.

MARSH-MALLOW. Common name for *Althea officinalis,* a perennial herb with large pink flowers.

MARSH-MARIGOLD. Popular name for *Caltha palustris,* a succulent perennial with yellow flowers common in wet ground. Sometimes incorrectly called Buttercup and Cowslip.

MARSH-PENNYWORT. Common name for *Hydrocotyle rotundifolia,* a creeping herbaceous perennial with small white flowers sometimes planted in moist areas as ground cover and for carpet bedding.

MARTINEZIA (mahr-ti-nee'-zi-ah). A genus of very spiny Feather Palms from Tropical America, called Spiny-maidenhair or Thorny-fishtail Palms. The ornamental feather-form leaves, with leaflets broader toward the tip, resemble those of the Fish-tail Palms, and the long clusters or orange, scarlet or rose-pink fruit are most decorative. Several species are grown in Fla., requiring well-fertilized soil. Some are occasionally grown in greenhouses, or used as pot plants, but are not attractive as small specimens because of the spiny growths on all parts of the plant. *M. caryotaefolia,* to 30 ft., with very slender trunk, ringed with long black spines, and leaves 3 to 6 ft. long, thrives in S. Fla.

MARTYNIA (mahr-tin'-i-ah). Old generic name (still used in seed catalogs) for the Unicorn-plant, which botanically is now called *Uroboscidea jussieui.*

MARVEL-OF-PERU. A common name for *Mirabilis jalapa,* or Four-o'clock, a tender perennial usually grown as an annual.

MARYLAND-DITTANY. A common name for *Cunila origanoides,* also called Stone-mint, a low herb with purplish-pink flowers in whorls.

MASDEVALLIA (mas-dee-val'-i-ah). A genus of epiphytic tropical American orchids, with yellow, white, violet-, orange- or yellowed-red blossoms, usually borne singly, but occasionally up to 8 to a stalk. The petals and lips are small and the sepals often prolonged into long tails making the flowers resemble insects. Native to high elevations in Central and S. America, Masdevallias are grown most successfully in a cool greenhouse, where they should be given an abundance of water at all times (particularly in summer) and overhead spraying twice daily. *M. coccinea* with violet-red and white flowers, is the most useful and easily grown species. For culture see ORCHIDS.

MASK-FLOWER. Common name for a small group of tender or half-hardy annual herbs and small shrubs of the Figwort Family, belonging to the genus Alonsoa. They have dark green foliage and bear an abundance of 2-lipped scarlet or orange flowers, turned upside down by the twisting of the pedicels.

Growing well in warm, open places, these natives of tropical America are best propagated by seeds sown indoors in spring. For winter bloom, seeds may be sown outdoors in summer or stem cuttings may be made. Young plants taken up in the fall will become shrubby in form and bloom for a long period. One of the best species is *A. warscewiczi,* a bushy type reaching a height of 3 ft. and bearing vermilion-scarlet blossoms. *A. caulialata* is a dwarf species growing 1 ft. tall and producing scarlet blooms. *A. meridionalis* is an orange-blooming species similar to *A. caulialata* in habit.

MASSACHUSETTS FERN (*Thelypteris simulata*). A fern of E. woods and wet places, much resembling the Marsh Fern and the New York Fern. Rare, and not desirable for gardens because of its rampant growth. Referred by some botanists to the genera Aspidium and Dryopteris.

MATHIOLA, or MATTHIOLA (mat-thy'-oh-lah). A genus of annuals and perennials of the Crucifer Family named for the Italian botanist, Matthioli, and generally known as Stock (which see). Two species with many horticultural varieties are cultivated for ornament in garden and greenhouse, both bearing flowers of many colors in terminal clusters.

MAT, HOTBED. A straw or fabric covering used to protect plants in cold-frames and hotbeds against cold. Homemade mats, made of small bundles of long, unbroken rye straw bound together side by side with stout cord, butt end outward and tops overlapping in the middle, are inexpensive, but cumbersome, especially when wet and frozen, and short lived. Fabric mats of quilted burlap, canvas or other waterproofed material have practically replaced them. Several styles of these available at garden supply stores have the advantages of costing little, being easy to handle and durable and giving more uniform and more reliable protection. See HOTBED.

MATILIJA POPPY (mah-til'-ee-hah). A common name for *Romneya coulteri,* the Canyon Poppy (which see), a tall Calif. and Mexican perennial herb with large white fragrant flowers.

MATRICARIA (mat-ri-kay'-ri-ah). A genus of rather weedy, mostly annual herbs of the Composite Family, known as Matricary. They have finely cut foliage, often disagreeably scented, and small flower-heads with yellow disk florets and sometimes white rays. A few of the species are grown in the border, the others in old-fashioned herb gardens for medicinal purposes. They grow readily to 2 ft. or less in any good garden soil. The perennials are increased by seed and division; the annuals and biennials by seed sown where the plants are to stand.

M. chamomilla (Sweet False-chamomile), an annual, has scented foliage and daisy-like flowers to 1 in. across; *M. aurea,* a smaller annual, has round heads of dull yellow flowers; *M. inodora* (Scentless False-chamomile), an annual, has rather pretty heads of flowers with white rays, 1½ in. across and almost scentless foliage; its var. *plenissima,* sometimes known as Bridal-rose, has very double heads; *M. tchihatchewi* (Turfing Daisy), a perennial, forms mats of finely cut leaves not over 1 ft. high and covered with little white-rayed "daisies"; it is most attractive as an edging plant. This species was formerly classed as a chrysanthemum.

MATRIMONY-VINE. Common name for Lycium, a genus of clambering shrubs with small inconspicuous flowers and scarlet or orange-red berries.

MATTOCK, or GRUB-HOE. A pick-axe-like hand tool in which one part of the head is a broad blade set at right angles to the handle like that of a hoe, while the other part is narrower and set to cut at right angles to the first—or axewise. It is used mainly for cutting roots, hummocks and heavy sods. See TOOLS.

MAURANDIA (mau-ran'-di-ah). Climbing perennial herbs of slender habit, natives of Mexico and adjoining areas in the U. S., belonging to the Figwort Family. They may be grown under glass for winter flowering, thriving in a mixture of fibrous loam with leafmold and a little old cow manure, and flowering well in 7-in. pots. They may also be treated as tender annuals for summer flowering outdoors, and are attractive in baskets and vases as well as trained on a trellis. Propagated by seeds or cuttings under glass.

M. barclaiana is the species best known in cultivation. It has angular heart-shaped leaves and purple flowers about 2 in. long. There are forms with white and rose colored flowers, sometimes listed as *M. varius. M. antirrhiniflora,* also known as *Antirrhinum maurandioides,* is widespread in Tex. and Calif. It climbs to 6 ft., with halberd-shaped leaves and purple flowers. *M. erubescens* has triangular leaves and large rose-colored flowers.

MAXILLARIA (mak-si-lay'-ri-ah). A genus of terrestrial and epiphytic orchids with small, rather dull-colored flowers, brownish or yellow and occasionally white or deep purple, borne singly or in few-flowered clusters. Only a few species are of horticultural value. *M. grandiflora,* an interesting sort from Peru or Ecuador, has 4-in. white flowers, with lemon-yellow lips streaked with dark red. The Maxillarias do best when grown in the intermediate temperature house. As they are evergreen they require much water in summer and should never be allowed to dry out at the roots.

MAY-APPLE. Common name for *Podophyllum peltatum,* a May-flowering native perennial, conspicuous for its large, lobed, shield-shaped leaves, which die down in midsummer. Hanging from the fork of the stem is a waxy-white cup-like flower with a rather disagreeable odor, followed by lemon-shaped fruits called the "apples" which have an insipid sweetish taste. The May-apple grows prolifically in many parts of the E. States and makes an excellent ground-cover on open sandy banks or under trees in partial shade. It thrives in rich, moist soil and is easily increased by division or seed.

This plant is also called Mandrake (which see), though the Mandrake of the Old World is a totally different plant.

MAY BEETLES. These familiar, large brown or blackish beetles, also called June Beetles, are the adult form of white grubs (which see). They feed on tree foliage at night but rarely do serious damage.

MAYBERRY. Common name for *Rubus palmatus,* a slender growing bramble, related to the raspberries and blackberries, with white flowers and yellow fruit. With protection the roots are hardy in the N. but for fruit production it needs a mild climate.

MAYFLOWER. Common name for the attractive, pink-flowered, trailing evergreen, *Epigaea repens,* found wild from Newfoundland to Ky. and sometimes successfully established in gardens. See ARBUTUS, TRAILING.

MAYPOP. A common name for the yellow edible fruit of the Wild Passionflower (*Passiflora incarnata*) native from Va. to Tex.

MAZE, GARDEN. An intricately tortuous path enclosed between high hedges, occupying a piece of circular, square or rectangular ground and leading, with many false blind-end turns along the way, from an entrance on the outer boundary to a central area or object. It was very popular in ancient gardens where it was representative of the elements known by the general term of "antick works"—playful devices to amuse visitors, rather than examples of horticultural beauty. The most famous garden maze in the world is probably that at Hampton Court, in England.

MAZUS (may'-zus). A genus of low creeping herbs grown as ground-covers on account of their mat-forming habits. *M. reptans,* most frequently used, has small, coarsely toothed, bright-green leaves and blue or purple and white mimulus-like flowers. *M. pumilio* has larger leaves and smaller flowers; *M. japonicus* has flowering stems up to 1 ft. tall. The first 2

species, which are quite hardy, spread so rapidly in the rock garden that they are best confined to rock crevices and steps.

MEADOW BEAUTY. Common name for the E. N. American genus Rhexia, consisting of several low-growing herbs suitable for summer bloom in moist spots in the wild garden. They are propagated by seeds or tubers. *M. virginica* is a most attractive little wild flower with a square, winged stem and clusters of rosy-purple blossoms 1 in. or more across. It grows naturally in sunny marshes but will thrive in neutral soil in the garden if given sufficient moisture. *R. mariana,* a taller plant with cylindrical hairy stems, has slightly smaller pale purple flowers.

MEADOW FOAM. Common name for *Limnanthes douglasi* (often known in the trade as Floerkea), an annual herb having finely cut yellowish-green leaves and fragrant white flowers which are shaded toward the base into pink and yellow. This attractive little plant grows in masses in low damp places in W. America and is lovely in the wild garden in that region, creating a charming effect in the early spring. It is easily raised from seed.

MEADOW-PARSNIP. Common name for *Thaspium aureum,* a perennial plant of the Parsley Family growing to 1½ ft. and having divided leaves and yellow flowers in umbels. Var. *atropurpureum* with dark purple flowers, much more attractive than the type, is a rather weedy plant which will grow in any ordinary soil, but prefers partial shade. It is easily increased by seed or division of the root.

MEADOW-RUE. Common name for the genus Thalictrum, comprising mostly tall perennial herbs with delicate foliage and minute tassel-like flowers. Of easy culture in well-drained soil.

MEADOW-SAFFRON. Common name for the genus Colchicum (which see), more often called Autumn-crocus, whose large flowers appear in fall but the foliage in spring.

MEADOW-SWEET. Common name for three species of Spiraea, namely *S. alba, S. latifolia,* and *S. salicifolia;* also sometimes applied to Filipendula, a genus of hardy perennials.

MEADOW-TULIP. Common name for *Calochortus nudus* and *C. uniflorus,* wet-meadow plants of W. U. S.

MEALY BUGS. White, cottony-appearing insects attacking many ornamental and

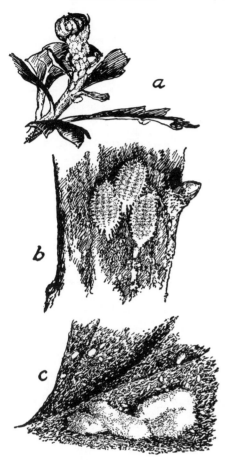

MEALY BUGS

Persistent pests of house and greenhouse plants. (a) massed below a chrysanthemum bud, life size; (b) three individuals enlarged; (c) females with characteristic woolly covering, and near them several small nymphs.

greenhouse plants and all citrus species. Of world-wide distribution they belong to the same family as scale insects (which see). They are of two types: the citrus or short-tailed mealy bugs which produce living young; and the long-tailed mealy bugs, which have long, waxy processes resembling tails, and which reproduce by means of eggs. These are carried by the females in cottony waxy sacs which are found chiefly at the axils of branching stems or leaves of infested plants. In greenhouses the eggs hatch in about 10 days; the young flattened, oval, smooth-bodied, light yellow, 6-legged bugs crawl over the plants, start sucking the sap and soon begin to secrete the white waxy covering. The young fe-

males (called nymphs) change little as they grow to ¼ in. long, but the males form a white case inside of which they transform into minute active 2-winged flies.

Mealy bugs, which are especially troublesome on soft-stemmed plants such as begonia, coleus, fuchsia and croton, but also on succulents, ferns, gardenias, etc., are best controlled by syringing the foliage with a fine spray forcefully applied. Plants may also be sprayed with a nicotine-soap or pyrethrum-soap solution. In greenhouses fumigation will kill young mealy bugs but not always affect the eggs or older insects. A white-oil spray, used with caution, will also control mealy bugs. On house plants mealy bugs may be taken off with a soft brush dipped in soapsuds or even picked off with a toothpick. See GREENHOUSE PESTS; HOUSE PLANTS.

MEASURING WORM. A common name given to the canker worm (which see) and sometimes to other caterpillars which progress by alternately looping up and straightening out the body as if measuring off distances. Other names are inchworm and looper.

MECONOPSIS (me-kon-op'-sis). A genus of annual, biennial and perennial herbs of the Poppy Family having yellow juice and yellow, reddish or blue flowers borne singly or in clusters. They make an attractive group of plants for the border or rock garden in climates where they can live. Generally requiring a cool, moist summer, they should be given a rich warm sandy loam and a sheltered half-shaded position. The perennials are increased by seeds or by division of the roots, and the annual and biennial sorts by seeds started early under glass. The annuals are planted out after danger of frost is over, and the biennials and perennial seedlings are carried over the summer in pots and planted out in the fall.

PRINCIPAL SPECIES

M. betonicifolia, a perennial to 6 ft., has blue or bluish-violet flowers to 2 in. across in flat-topped clusters; its var. *baileyi* is considered one of the finest blue flowers in cultivation, but is difficult to grow in the E. States. It should be sheltered from the intense heat and drying winds of summer and given applications of liquid manure at the flowering season.

wallichi (Satin Poppy), a perennial to 6 ft., forms a mound of finely cut, silvery foliage and bears pale blue flowers to 2 in. across.

cambrica (Welsh Poppy), perennial to 1½ ft., has much-cut leaves with a silvery bloom beneath and large solitary pale yellow flowers.

heterophylla (Wind or Flaming Poppy), annual to 2 ft., has solitary brick-red flowers with a purple center; it is a handsome decorative plant native to W. America.

pratti, annual, to 3 ft., bears bright blue flowers in racemes.

integrifolia (Yellow Chinese Poppy), biennial, 1½ to 3 ft., with long narrow leaves and clusters of yellow flowers each 6 in. across; unlike those of the other species which have 4 petals, the flowers have 5 to 10.

MEDICAGO (med-i-kay'-go). A genus of leguminous herbs and some shrubs commonly called Medick, bearing small pea-like flowers in heads or racemes. Some species are grown for ornament but the most important, *M. sativa*, known as Alfalfa or Lucerne, is a valued forage and hay crop, especially in irrigated sections. In orchards it is sometimes grown as a cover-crop, which see.

MEDINILLA (med-i-nil'-ah). Tropical shrubby plants, including some of the most striking for growing in the warm greenhouse. They are not happy in strong sunlight but, on the other hand, do not flower well in heavy shade. Good fibrous loam with sharp sand suits them well, and firm potting is necessary to produce good flowering wood. Propagation is by cuttings, best rooted singly in peat and sand.

M. magnifica, the outstanding species, has handsome evergreen-leathery leaves, and pendulous panicles of deep pink or reddish flowers, with showy rose-pink bracts. *M. teysmanni* bears upright panicles of rose-pink flowers without bracts. *M. curtisi* has much smaller leaves and terminal panicles of white flowers.

MEDITERRANEAN FRUIT FLY. The most feared of subtropical fruit pests. Distributed all over the world except in N. America, it was found in Florida in 1929 having apparently eluded the strict quarantine exclusion regulations. As a result of a vigorous compaign of extermination by State and Federal Governments, the infestation was subdued and prevented from spreading.

The fly, which is somewhat smaller than the housefly and yellowish in color, attacks citrus fruits particularly, but also the fruit of other trees, such as peach, and of garden vegetables, such as tomatoes. It lays eggs in cavities in the flesh of the fruit, through which the maggots bore, rendering it unfit for consumption. Needing a warm environment, the fly could become established only in the S. States. There is no control; all that can be done is to attempt to promptly exterminate the pest.

MEDLAR. A small deciduous hardy tree (*Mespilus germanica*) of Europe rarely grown in America for its edible but acid apple-shaped fruits. These are eaten raw when fully ripe, or may be preserved. The tree, which may attain 20 ft., may be grown from seed or grafted or budded on pear, quince or hawthorn stock.

MELALEUCA (mel-ah-leu'-kah). Bottle-brush. Shrubs or trees of Australia, belonging to the Myrtle Family. Several species are grown in the warmer parts of this country as lawn specimens and street trees. They have a pleasing habit, with attractive, somewhat leathery leaves, and dense spikes or heads of conspicuous flowers. They are well able to withstand drought.

M. armillaris is a graceful shrub or small tree, with slender drooping branches, soft slender *linear* leaves and round spikes of white flowers.

hypericifolia has bright green leaves and dense spikes of brilliant red flowers.

ericifolia has feathery heath-like foliage and spikes of yellowish-white flowers.

lateritia is a graceful shrub with slender branches and scarlet flowers.

leucadendra (Cajeput-tree, Punk-tree) sometimes grows to 80 ft., and is well able to withstand salt water and wind. It has thick spongy bark, which peels in thin layers and is used for many purposes. The flowers are creamy-white.

thymifolia is a dwarf, with thyme-like leaves and red flowers.

MELASTOMA (mee-las'-toh-mah). Tropical shrubby plants, sometimes grown in warm greenhouses for their showy flowers. They require partial shade with plenty of moisture during the growing season, and thrive in a mixture of loam and peat, with sand. Propagated by cuttings under close conditions. The names and identity of the species seem confused.

M. decemfidum (once known as *M. sanguineum*) has narrow or oblong leaves, shining green above with red markings beneath. It bears large rosy-purple flowers,

1 to 3 on a stem, in winter. *M. corymbosum* (also known as *Amphiblemma cymosum*) has roundish satiny leaves sharply toothed, and clusters of bright purple flowers.

MELIA (mee'-li-ah). Bead-tree. Deciduous or evergreen trees and shrubs native in tropical Asia and Australia. One species, *M. azedarach* (China-berry or Umbrella-tree), which has become widely distributed throughout warm regions, can stand a few degrees of frost. It is often a deciduous tree, growing to 50 ft., with graceful pinnate foliage. The fragrant lilac flowers are borne in loose panicles. The yellow oval fruits hang for a long time, and in some countries the seeds are threaded as beads. Var. *umbraculiformis* (Texas Umbrella-tree) grows with an umbrella-like effect. Var. *floribunda* is a very floriferous form, flowering when small.

MELIACEAE (mee-li-ay'-see-ee). The Mahogany Family, a group of tropical hardwood trees and shrubs, one genus (Swietenia) furnishing the mahogany of commerce and a few providing ornamental subjects. Species of Cedrela are used in warm regions as avenue trees and also grown for lumber; and the principal genus cultivated in the U. S. is Melia, species of which are popular·for shade and ornament.

MELIANTHUS (mel-i-an'-thus). A genus of strongly-scented S. African evergreen shrubs, of decorative value in warm regions. See HONEY-BUSH.

MELICOCCA (mel-i-kok'-ah) *bijuga.* A tropical American tree grown for its edible fruits. It is also called Mamoncillo, Spanish-lime, and Genip, which see.

MELILOTUS (mel-i-loh'-tus). A genus of hardy Old-World perennials of the Pea Family grown for forage as Sweet Clover, which see.

MELISSA (me-lis'-ah). A genus of perennial herbs of which one is cultivated under the common name Balm, which see.

MELITTIS (me-lit'-is) *melissophyllum.* A perennial Old-World herb of the Mint Family growing to 1½ ft. and bearing pink or variegated flowers in whorls.

MELON. The fruit of a number of Asiatic or African annual herbs of the species *Cucumis melo,* the name being also applied to the plant. The numerous varieties grown in America are of three general classes: (1) netted or nutmeg melon; (2) casaba or winter melon (to both of which the name muskmelon is given); and (3)

honey-dew. The first of these is the most adaptable to both commercial and garden production. One or more kinds can be grown in most of the states and the warmer parts of Canada as outdoor crops; or, in the colder sections, they do well in hotbeds and protected coldframes. The honey-dew and casaba varieties are grown commercially in warm sections, but require too long a season to be successful in the N. While the name cantaloupe (which see) is popularly used as synonymous with muskmelon, it correctly refers to a variety rarely if at all grown in America. See CUCUMIS.

REQUIREMENTS. Melons thrive best in highly fertile, light, sandy loams, sunny situations and warm weather. They "sulk" or become diseased in cold and damp weather and are easily killed by frost. With adequate protection at both ends of the season they can be grown successfully in home gardens, but they must be grown rapidly.

ENEMIES. Unless protected against insects, especially while young, melons may be killed by a wilt disease which these creatures carry from plant to plant not only of melons but also of other cucurbits. In fact melons are subject to all the same diseases and insect pests as cucumbers and the other cucurbits. In addition the melon worm is frequently injurious to melons in the S. and sometimes as far N. as N. Y. The adult is a white moth with brown bands along the wing margins; the caterpillar is mottled greenish yellow, about 1 in. long. Control by (1) planting some squashes ahead of melons to serve as a trap crop; (2) using arsenical sprays or dusts; (3) destroying vines and waste fruits as soon as the crop is harvested.

CULTURE. As melons are difficult to transplant seed is generally sown right in the garden. For early fruiting and to overcome a short season handicap, plants may be started indoors in flower pots, berry boxes or inverted sods a month or so earlier. In this case harden the plants off well before setting them out. When the weather has settled either sow a dozen seeds or set 2 to 4 plants in each "hill." Space the hills 5 by 5 or 4 by 6 ft. apart. If seed is sown destroy all but the best 2 to 4 plants in each hill when they are well started.

If the soil is not naturally rich, thoroughly mix a large forkful of well decayed manure or a pound of high grade complete fertilizer in each hill before sowing or transplanting. Cultivate the soil weekly, shallow near the plants, deeper farther away. When the plants begin to "run" lay the vines lengthwise of the rows to permit continued tillage and to facilitate fruit gathering.

HARVESTING. For market, melons are usually gathered too immature and, being chilled in refrigerator cars, fail to develop their natural flavor and are disappointing. But when allowed to ripen fully on the vine their flavor is also impaired. An experienced eye recognizes at a glance and by indescribable signs melons that are just "ready." The way to learn these signs is to examine the stem ends of the fruit. So long as no cracks appear around the stem union the fruit is too immature to gather. When cracks show all around the stem, it is the time to gather them. There are also differences in color, netting and a sort of "glisten" that one comes to recognize. After gathering, keep the fruit in a warm place one or two days before using it.

MELONS IN GREENHOUSES. English forcing varieties of melons are the best for growing in greenhouses. For early summer fruit sow seed in late February or early March and transplant from flower pots three or four weeks later; for November fruit, sow in mid-July. In each case grow the plants in raised benches so they can have bottom heat (which see). Set the plants 30 in. apart in beds 4 ft. wide, and train the vines by tying them to cords or trellises; in addition support the fruits with net slings or they may break the vines or pull them down. Unless bees have access to the plants, the flowers must be hand-pollinated or no fruit will set. During the ripening period keep the air rather dry.

Watermelon is also a cucurbit, but of a different genus, *Citrullus vulgaris;* one of its varieties (*citroides*) is called Citron or Preserving-melon and the latter name is also applied to a plant of still another cucurbitous genus, *Benincasa hispida.*

MELON-PEAR and MELON-SHRUB. Common names for *Solanum muricatum,* a S. American shrubby relative of the potato and egg-plant, also called Pepino. Its 6 in. yellow and purple fruits are edible.

MELON SPURGE. Common name for *Euphorbia meloformis,* so-called from the globular form of the main stem of the plant, which is deeply ribbed and practically leafless.

MENDELISM, MENDEL'S LAW. (1) A phenomenon in heredity whereby it is possible approximately to forecast the results of the breeding together of different characters; (2) the scientific principle on which it is based. Both are named after an Austrian monk, Gregor Mendel, who observed the phenomenon and formulated the law.

MENISPERMACEAE (men-i-spermay'-see-ee). The Moonseed Family, a largely tropical group of herbaceous or woody climbing vines, so named on account of the half-moon-shaped fruit. The flowers are small and inconspicuous but the foliage and fruit cause some forms to be employed as wall and arbor covers, principally the genera Menispermum and Cocculus.

MENISPERMUM (men-i-sper'-mum). A genus including two hardy, woody, climbing vines suitable for covering arbors and trellises. See MOONSEED.

MEN'S GARDEN CLUBS. A recent manifestation of the increasing interest in home gardening in America, garden clubs exclusively (or mainly) for men came into being in 1928 when, on March 15, the first such organization was formed in Chicago. Credit for the idea and its realization goes to Mr. Leo W. Nack of that city, whose 45 by 60 ft. garden had, the previous year, won the $1000 first prize in a garden contest sponsored by a Chicago newspaper. Two years later, Jay N. Darling, famous cartoonist, conservationist, and, later, chief of the U. S. Bureau of Biological Survey, was the organizer and first president of a similar group in Des Moines, Ia. The same year two more clubs were formed in Aurora, Ill. and Fort Wayne, Ind. and in September, 1932, representatives of the four clubs met in Chicago and organized the Men's Garden Clubs of America. With the spontaneous growth of the idea stimulated by annual conventions held in different cities, local clubs continued to spring up in all directions and join the national body until, when its 1940 Year Book was issued, it had 29 affiliated member clubs and an Illinois sectional group. The clubs are scattered from N. Y. State to Ore., Calif., Mo. and as far S. as Ga. The office of the secretary of the national body is at 212 West Michigan Ave., Jackson, Mich.

Men's garden clubs concern themselves primarily with practical "dirt gardening," although both in their own shows and occasionally in those staged by other organizations, members have demonstrated their interest, originality, and skill in the field of flower arrangement. Their organization is essentially elastic and informal, and meeting programs frequently take the form of inspection trips to members' gardens, lively round table discussions and vigorous debates. Most of the clubs issue small, monthly news bulletins for their members and for exchange with other clubs. A slogan quite generally favored by members is "More P(1)ants in the Garden."

MENTHA (men'-thah). A genus of herbs of the Mint Family having aromatic leaves and inconspicuous flowers. They are generally cultivated for their essential oils or, in the herb garden, for their leaves. They grow easily in any good garden soil, preferably in a moist and sunny position, and are easily raised from seed, cuttings, runners or division. In many parts of the E. States they have escaped from old gardens and become naturalized. *M. requieni,* a creeping species with small, roundish, peppermint-scented leaves and bluish-lavender flowers, is suitable as a ground-cover for the rock garden. *M. spicata* (Spearmint) to 2 ft. has strongly aromatic leaves and flowers in whorls on a spike. *M. piperita* (Peppermint) to 3 ft. with purple or white flowers, is extensively cultivated for the strong essential oil. *M. pulegium* (Pennyroyal) with stems lying on the ground and small bluish-lavender flowers, is grown in the herb garden; it is said to keep mosquitoes away from its vicinity. *M. citrata* (Bergamot Mint) with low-lying stems to 2 ft., and *M. rotundifolia* (Apple Mint) to 2½ ft. are often found as escapes from old gardens. See also MINT.

MENTZELIA (ment-zee'-li-ah). A genus of showy plants of W. America, often shrubby in growth with barbed hairs. The most frequently cultivated species is the annual *M. lindleyi,* commonly listed in catalogs as *Bartonia aurea.* Its large, single, fragrant, 5-petaled, golden-yellow flowers with bristling stamens open late in the afternoon during July and August. The foliage, in contrast to the blossoms, which produce a metallic effect in the sunlight, is gray and downy. The plants, which grow from 1 to 3 ft. high, are extremely effective when grown in masses in a sunny location. As they do not like to be moved, seed should be sown where the plants are to stand.

M. laevicaulis (Blazing Star) is a 3-ft. biennial with shining white stems and light yellow flowers 3 to 4 in. across. Another biennial is *M. decapetala,* with white or yellowish flowers 5 in. across, fragrant and also opening late in the day.

MENYANTHES (men-i-an'-theez) *trifoliata.* A large, showy, herbaceous perennial for wet situations, known as BOG-BEAN, which see.

MENZIESIA (men-zi-ee'-si-ah). Small deciduous shrubs of N. America and Japan, belonging to the Heath Family. They have clusters of small but attractive urn- or bell-shaped flowers, and are suitable for the rock garden or moist peaty borders. Propagated by seeds or cuttings.

M. pilosa, found in the mountains from Pa. to Ga., grows to 6 ft. and has hairy leaves and yellowish-white or pinkish flowers.

ferruginea, from the W. part of the country, is usually a low straggly grower with rusty-hairy leaves and small brownish flowers.

The following species from Japan may be found in cultivation: *M. ciliicalyx* with yellowish-green and purple flowers, *M. pentandra* with white flowers, and *M. purpurea* with bright red flowers.

MERATIA (mer-ay'-ti-ah). Deciduous or evergreen shrubs, natives of China, belonging to the Calycanthus Family. *M. praecox* (Wintersweet, formerly known as *Chimonanthus fragrans* and as *Calycanthus praecox*) is well worth growing in a mild climate for its very fragrant yellow flowers in winter. It can stand some frost, and may be grown as a bush or trained to a wall. It thrives in sandy loam with plenty of leafmold. Var. *grandiflora* has larger leaves and flowers, but is not as fragrant. Propagated by seeds and layers.

MERCURY. A common name for *Chenopodium bonus-henricus,* or Good-King-Henry, a naturalized perennial herb sometimes cultivated. Its young shoots are eaten like asparagus and its leaves like spinach.

MERCURY COMPOUNDS. These are used in gardening chiefly as disinfectants. Bichloride of mercury (corrosive sublimate) has many uses as a soil and seed disinfectant as, for example, in the treatment of seed potatoes and cabbage seed; for sprinkling on the soil around cabbage plants to control maggots and slugs; for drenching the crowns of plants

PLATE 33.   ORIENTAL POPPIES

Making a short but brilliant appearance in the perennial border, modern varieties of Oriental Poppies can be had in a varying palette. Reading from top to bottom, left, are Helen Elizabeth, Watermelon, and Cavalier. On the right are Indian Chief, Baris White, and Crimson Pompom.

Wayside Gardens Company

PLATE 34.   A COLORFUL BED OF PORTULACA

Related to the troublesome weed, Purslane, Portulaca does well in any good sunny position. The plants cannot be transplanted and must be sown where they are to remain.

T. H. Everett

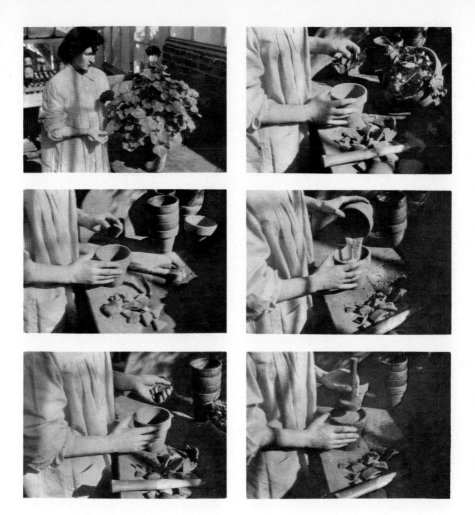

PLATE 35.   PROPAGATING GERANIUMS

Propagation by cuttings is most easily practised with the Geranium, which responds readily to this treatment. Top left is a fine healthy plant from which the cuttings are to be taken. The pot is prepared by placing a piece of broken crockery over the drainage hole, and then smaller bit of crockery or pebbles are put in place. A handful of leaf mold goes next, and then the pot is filled with sand. Lastly, this is tamped down firmly in place. The preparation of the cuttings is described on the next page?

T. H. Everett

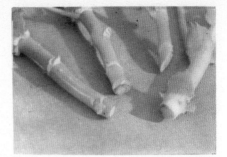

PLATE 36. PROPAGATING GERANIUMS

A branch of the parent plant is cut off and divided into small branchlets. Extra leaves are trimmed off and the base cut on the diagonal with a sharp knife. The top right picture shows a close-up of the prepared stems. A pencil makes a good dibber to form holes in the sand, and the slips are set in place and firmed down. Then the pot is given a good soaking.

T. H. Everett

PLATE 37.   RHODODENDRONS

Rhododendrons run the gamut from small shrubs to small trees, and from
varieties that are hardy in the extreme North to tender types suitable only for
the South. At the top is Catawbiense, the hardiest evergreen type, and beneath
it one of the Dexter Hybrids.

T. H. Everett

PLATE 38.   EVERBLOOMING HYBRID TEA ROSES

The most satisfactory roses for the garden are the Hybrid Teas which give a
succession of blooms through the summer. Reading from left to right, top row,
are President Hoover, Etoile de Hollande, and Phyllis Gold. In the center are
Edel and Edith Nellie Perkins. The three at the bottom are President Macia,
Mrs. E. P. Thom, and Poinsettia.

Wayside Gardens Company

PLATE 39.   INTERESTING ROSE SPECIES

Some of the most interesting shrubs for the garden are the various species of roses, native in many parts of the world. Above is the Rugosa Rose, Repens Alba. Below is the Moss Rose, Mousseaux Ancien.

Bobbink and Atkins

PLATE 40.   MORE ROSE SPECIES

Two more of the great variety of species roses are Rosa Mutabilis, shown at the
top, and Rosa Rubrifolia, below.

Bobbink and Atkins

PLATE 41.   CLIMBING AND RAMBLER ROSES

The distinction between Climbers and Ramblers is mainly one of the size of the flowers. Here are nine old favorites. 1. American Pillar; 2. Climbing American Beauty; 3. Hiawatha; 4. Silver Moon; 5. Tausendshon; 6. Paul's Scarlet Climber; 7. Gardenia; 8. Excelsa; and 9. Christine Wright.

Bobbink and Atkins

PLATE 42.   PROPAGATING SAINTPAULA

Saintpaulia, commonly known as the African Violet, is easily propagated by
plucking leaves which may be inserted in pots of moist sand. The new plant
develops from the base of the old leaf.

T. H. Everett

PLATE 43.   ANNUAL SCABIOSA
Also known as Pincushion Flower because of the way the stamens protrude from
the flower head, their odd dark colors make them interesting cut flowers.
W. Atlee Burpee Co.

PLATE 44.   THE WOOD HYACINTH

Scilla hispanica is larger and bears larger flowers than the English Bluebell. Three fine varieties are Rose Beauty, Alba Maxima, and Excelsior (blue).

Wayside Gardens Company

PLATE 45.   FALL COLOR EFFECTS

Two fine shrubs for Fall show are Euonymus elatus compactus, at the top, and
Pyracantha coccinea lalandi, shown below.

T. H. Everett

PLATE 46.   HYBRID SNAPDRAGONS

Members of the Antirrhinum family, Snapdragons have been hybridized to give showy plants from a few inches tall to giants several feet tall. Here are some of the handsome, tall-flowering varieties available today.

W. Atlee Burpee Co.

PLATE 47.   A COLLECTION OF SQUASHES

The varieties of Squash which may be raised in the garden are many. Here is a
representative collection ranging from pattypans to zucchini.

W. Atlee Burpee Co.

PLATE 48.   LOW PLANTS FOR THE BORDER

Two fine dwarf plants, Sweet Alyssum and a dwarf Marigold, make an attractive grouping in the border.

W. Atlee Burpee Co.

affected with crown rot, Sclerotinia rot and Rhizoctonia rot, and for the disinfection of iris rhizomes. It is also used generally as a disinfectant for tools and hands when working on plant material infected with certain diseases. It is obtainable in convenient tablet form, the usual solution being 1 tablet to 1 pint of water, which equals a 1 to 1000 dilution. A combination of mercuric chloride, mercuric cyanide and glycerine is used in the treatment of fire blight, which see.

Mercurous chloride (calomel) is used in the treatment of brown patch (see under LAWN). Various proprietary organic mercury compounds such as semesan, uspulun, dipdust and the like are used to treat seed or soil for the control of damping-off. See DISINFECTION.

MERRYBELLS. A common name for the genus Uvularia, perennial herbs with drooping yellow flowers, easily grown from divisions of the rootstocks in shady wild gardens. Also called Bellwort.

MERTENSIA (mer-ten′-si-ah). A genus of perennial herbs of the Borage Family having delightful blue, white or purple bell-shaped blossoms in graceful nodding clusters. They are plants for the shady informal border, or for naturalizing in the wild garden. Virginia-bluebells (*M. virginica*), the most widely planted species, is charming in combination with the pure white flowers of *Trillium grandiflorum* in a half-shady location and a soil abundantly supplied with humus. As the foliage disappears entirely after the plants bloom, it is well to plant them among Christmas or Oak Ferns which will conceal the bare soil. Mertensias are increased by seed and, with difficulty, by division.

PRINCIPAL SPECIES

M. virginica (Virginia-bluebells or Virginia-cowslip) grows to 2 ft. with smooth leaves and nodding clusters of blossoms; the pink buds contrast delightfully with the drooping blue flowers. Var. *rubra* has pink blossoms and a pure white form is occasionally found.

sibirica is an E. Asiatic form with long racemes of purplish or light blue flowers, sometimes varying to white.

ciliata, a Rocky Mountain type growing to 3 ft., with blue bell-shaped blossoms from bright pink buds, and a profusion of smooth grayish-green leaves.

nutans, with lovely azure blooms in slender graceful panicles, is found in the far W. and is charming grown among evergreen ferns in the wild garden.

MESCAL-BEAN. Common name for *Sophora secundiflora*, a shrub or tree of S.W. U. S. with fragrant blue pea-like flowers.

MESEMBRYANTHEMUM (mes-em-bri-an′-the-mum). A genus of low growing, fleshy, succulent herbs, commonly known as Fig-marigold. Many of them have striking, glistening ice-like points on the foliage. The group, originally very large, has gradually been broken up by botanists and so many species have been placed in other genera that few now go under the name Mesembryanthemum in botanical lists.

Mostly natives of hot, dry, barren portions of S. Africa, the plants are tender N. and if grown outside in the summer must be wintered in a cool, well-ventilated greenhouse. In Fla. and Calif. a number of species are grown in the open, doing particularly well on the West Coast because of the dry climate. When grown in pots they should be given a light, dry, gritty soil and excellent drainage, care being taken to water them from below.

Species of garden or greenhouse interest are the following:

M. deltoides with small rose flowers of a satiny texture, and toothed, triangular leaves misted with a gray bloom.

multiflorum, a white-flowered, rather woody plant, with straight branches covered with 3-angled grayish-green leaves.

speciosum, of shrubby growth to 2 ft., with showy, scarlet blossoms and short, flattened leaves, glistening when young.

spectabile, bearing purple flowers and trailing woody stems covered with pointed 3-angled gray-green leaves.

The annual ice-plant (which see), frequently listed as *Mesembryanthemum crystallinum*, is now properly *Cryophytum crystallinum*. Other Fig-marigolds grown in the open in Calif. are listed under the genera Carpobrotus, Cryophytum, Lamprantus and others.

METALDEHYDE BAITS. Poison baits obtainable in commercial preparations and particularly effective in attracting and killing snails and slugs. The use of metaldehyde for this purpose was discovered quite by accident in a park in France, when someone noticed that slugs were killed in large quantities by the remains of Meta heat tablets discarded by picnic parties.

METHYL BROMIDE. A colorless, heavy liquid used extensively for the fumigation of live plants for certification before shipment outside of quarantined areas, especially in the case of the Japanese beetle. It may also be used as a soil fumigant for certain greenhouse pests. Fumigation is carried out in a tight box; the dosage is $2\frac{1}{2}$ lbs. per 1000 cu. ft. of space for $2\frac{1}{2}$ hours at a temperature of 64 to 65 deg. F. Methyl bromide also offers promise as a soil fumigant for outdoor plants. Asiatic garden beetles in soil around azaleas have been killed without appreciable injury to plants when an emulsion of 50 cc. methyl bromide is 500 cc. methyl alcohol added to 3 gals water was applied to the soil.

METROSIDEROS (me-troh-si-dee'-ros). A genus of trees and shrubs, sometimes climbing, and mostly native in New Zealand. They belong to the Myrtle Family and are closely allied to Callistemon (which see), the Bottle-Brush of Australia, requiring the same treatment.

M. scandens is a climber, with leathery shining leaves and white flowers. It grows to about 5 ft. in pots, but in its native forest climbs to the tops of the tallest trees. *M. tomentosa* (New-Zealand Christmas Tree) is a tree to 70 ft., with dark red flowers. *M. tremuloides* is a small tree of Hawaii, with narrow shining leaves and bright red flowers.

MEXICAN BEAN BEETLE. One of the most destructive pests of garden beans, but controllable by careful, repeated use of magnesium arsenate (which see) as spray or dust. See also under BEAN.

MEXICAN-BREADFRUIT. Common name for *Monstera deliciosa,* sometimes called Ceriman, a hothouse climber with huge leaves cut and perforated, whose cone-like fruits are edible.

MEXICAN-, SPANISH-, or TEXAS BUCKEYE. A common name for *Ungnadia speciosa,* a S. shrub or tree bearing clusters of rose-colored flowers in spring. See BUCKEYE.

MEXICAN FIRE-PLANT. A common name for *Euphorbia heterophylla,* an easily grown annual of warm regions, whose upper leaves are red.

MEXICAN-ORANGE (*Choisya ternata*). A handsome evergreen shrub, growing to 6 ft. or more. It can stand only a few degrees of frost, but has leathery, bright green leaves, which show off to advantage the clusters of fragrant white flowers. These resemble orange blossoms and are produced over a period of several months.

MEXICAN POPPY. Another name for Argemone, a genus of prickly herbs of N. and S. America grown as annuals for their white, yellow, orange and sometimes purple flowers. Also called Prickly Poppy.

MEXICAN STAR. Common name for *Milla biflora,* a bulbous herb of the Lily Family often incorrectly referred to as *Bessera elegans.* It sends up a stalk $1\frac{1}{2}$ ft. tall bearing 1 to 5 star-shaped waxy flowers to $2\frac{1}{2}$ in. across. These are fragrant and will last for many days. The small bulbs should be planted in the border in the spring; then in late summer, after the foliage has matured, they should be taken up and stored in a frost-proof place until the following year. Mexican Star may also be grown indoors, a number of bulbs being placed in a pot and allowed to start into immediate growth.

MEXICAN-SUNFLOWER. A common name for the genus Tithonia, herbs and shrubs with brilliant sunflower-like blossoms grown in the S. and under glass.

MEZEREUM (mee-zee'-ree-um) **FAMILY.** Common name of the Thymelaeaceae, of which Daphne is the best known genus in gardening.

MICE. The meadow mouse and its allied species the pine mouse are responsible for most of the damage to orchards and shrubbery. The latter is particularly destructive in the winter when, hidden from sight by snow and protective mulches, its labyrinth of runways involves a havoc of ruined trees and other vegetation.

The only really effective remedies are, first, watchfulness; second, poison. Strychnine in minute doses inserted inside small raisins and dropped into the rodents' runways has been found particularly good. The mice are canny and have been known to refuse poison unskillfully prepared. They frequently fool the gardener's attempts to get them with poisoned grain by carefully peeling the wheat and leaving the deadly outer layer in a neat little pile while they consume the untainted inner kernel.

MICHAELMAS DAISY. A common name now loosely applied to all species of the genus Aster (the hardy Starworts of both hemispheres) but originally used in England for N. American species, notable *A. tradescanti* (native from Me. to Mo.), *A. novi-belgi* (the New-York Aster, native from Newfoundland to Ga.), and *A. novae-angliae* (the New-England Aster, native from Quebec to Va. and Colo.). These, introduced abroad, received far more recognition and attention than was ever accorded them in their native land and subsequently many fine named hybrids were developed, much planted in Europe, and sent back to the U. S. to receive generous acclaim. In recent years American plantsmen have also been giving them more attention, stimulating their more general use and also producing new and attractive forms of this splendid American plant.

See ASTER.

MICHAUXIA (mi-shauk'-si-ah). A genus of biennial and perennial herbs with white or pink bell-like flowers. One species, *M. campanuloides,* is sometimes grown from seed and planted in perennial borders.

MICHELIA (my-kee'-li-ah). Asiatic trees or shrubs, belonging to the Magnolia Family. The best known in cultivation is *M. fuscata* (Banana-shrub) which has also been known as *Magnolia fuscata.* It is a popular evergreen shrub in the S. States, where it grows to about 15 ft. The young growth is covered with soft brown hairs, but later the leaves are smooth. The brownish-purple flowers, an inch or more across, produced from April to June, emit a strong banana fragrance. Propagation is sometimes from seed, but mostly by cuttings of ripened wood, under glass.

MICONIA (my-koh'-ni-ah). Tropical American woody plants, sometimes grown in the warm greenhouse. The best known is *M. magnifica,* one of the most striking of tropical foliage plants. The broad leaves with wavy margins grow 2 ft. or more in length, are lustrous green above and reddish-bronze beneath, and have prominent, light-colored veins. The plant needs good fibrous loam with old manure or leafmold, plenty of water, and protection from direct sunlight. Propagation is from cuttings.

MICROGLOSSA (my-kroh-glos'-ah). Shrubby plants from Asia and Africa, belonging to the Daisy Family. Only one species, *M. albescens,* is likely to be found in cultivation. This grows to 3 ft. high, with narrow leaves gray beneath, and heads of pale blue or whitish aster-like

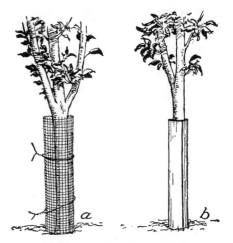

PROTECTION FROM MICE
To prevent rodents from gnawing the bark of young fruit trees, cylinders of fine wire netting (a) or wood veneer (b) are effective. Sink them in the ground a few inches to steady them.

flowers. It will stand some frost, and is not particular as to soil. Propagated by seeds or divisions of the roots.

MICROLEPIA (my-kroh-le'-pi-ah). A genus of tropical and subtropical ferns, of which *M. platyphylla* with long graceful leaves, is grown in greenhouses. It thrives best in a loose but rich compost with ample light, air, and moisture, in a temperature not over 65 degrees.

MICROMERIA (my-kroh-mee'-ri-ah). A genus of small perennial creeping herbs of the Mint Family, having small leaves and tiny 2-lipped flowers. They can be grown in the rock garden and are easily increased by seed or cuttings. Only two species are commonly known: *M. piperella* from S. Europe, semi-shrubby in growth and bearing small rosy-purple flowers in clusters; and *M. chamissonis* (Yerba Buena), the "good herb" of the early Spanish settlers in Calif. who made a tea of the delightfully aromatic leaves. The latter is a small trailing vine, charming when naturalized in the wild garden in sun or shade.

MICROSTYLIS (my-kros'-ti-lis) *unifolia.* A small, terrestrial native orchid bearing greenish flowers on a stalk 3 to 9 in. high, which rises from a single sheathing leaf. It is commonly known as Green Adders Mouth and is occasionally planted in the wild garden in moist, strongly acid soil. As rodents are fond of the bulbs, places where they are planted should be inclosed with quarter inch mesh wire-netting to keep the pests out. For culture, see ORCHIDS.

MIDGE. A small two-winged insect related to the fly and often called a gnat. Midges are chiefly troublesome as greenhouse pests and are fairly well controlled by fumigation with nicotine. The chrysanthemum midge is one of the most important. Leaves are mis-shapen and covered with cone-shaped galls, from which the adult flies emerge, always between midnight and morning.

MIDRIB. The large central vein of a leaf usually existing as a ridge-like extension of the petiole; or a similar main ridge on any leaf-like part.

MIDSUMMER EFFECTS. Because the life cycle of most garden plants requires the entire growing season—spring, summer and autumn—to fulfill itself, special selections must be made in order to have an abundance of flowers during the summer. Only plants that grow quickly and mature rapidly can postpone the important reproductive process of blooming as late as July, since this leaves them but a very brief time in which to mature their fruit, that is, their seed.

The plants answering to this requirement are mostly those known as annuals (which see). There are a good many perennials which bloom late, it is true; but with the exception of the daylilies (Hemerocallis) some of the true lilies, phlox, the earlier flowering hardy asters and a perennial salvia, these are not important in effect and therefore not to be relied on for midsummer display.

However, regardless of the kind of plants used for flowers alone, midsummer effects should be provided by the larger, more permanent plant materials as well. There are several fine shrubs, and of trees there are at least three kinds—one with two varieties, making four in all—which are not used in gardens as often as their merits deserve.

These trees should be used just as trees in general are utilized around the garden—for shade, as backgrounds and as specimens; the only restriction is that of climate in the case of the three foreign forms. The one native tree of the four (hardy in the N.) is the Yellow-wood (*Cladrastis lutea*), which blossoms in late June. Later-flowering is the Chinese species, *C. sinensis,* with pinkish racemes of small flowers in July.

Then there is the so-called Varnish-tree (*Koelreuteria paniculata*), which blooms in July and August and is used to a considerable degree in the central W. and S. This is hardy northward as far as Mass. and is a beautiful tree deserving to be used throughout its range, even though it does not live to an extreme age. It is especially good for hot, dry situations. The same is true of the representative of the third genus in the group, namely the Japanese Pagoda-tree (*Sophora japonica*), which is hardy within the same latitudes and an exceptionally beautiful sight when, in midsummer, its large white panicles of bloom are displayed against its deep green foliage.

Supplementing the summer-flowering trees are such shrubs as the two Hydrangeas *H. paniculata* and *H. arborescens grandiflora;* the Rose-of-Sharon (*Hibiscus syriacus*) ; *Vitex negundo incisa;* the Sweet Pepperbush (*Clethra alnifolia*) for cool, damp places and half shade; *Lespedeza bicolor; Hypericum prolificum;* and *Buddleia davidi veitchiana.* There are also such climbing plants as Clematis, of which four are superlative as summer bloomers—*C. paniculata, C. crispa, C. virginiana* and *C. texensis; Akebia quinata;* Fleece-vine (*Polygonum auberti*) ; *Bignonia radicans;* and *Lyceum chinense.*

With such heavy permanent material setting forth the midsummer emphasis, massed plantings of annual flowers in whatever colors and kinds are most liked will develop midsummer effects of superlative beauty and excellence.

MIGNONETTE. Common name for Reseda, a genus of tender herbs with thick stems and coarse foliage; and especially for *R. odorata,* an annual species grown outdoors and under glass for the fragrance of its stout, oval spikes of greenish, yellowish or sometimes reddish flowers which individually are inconspicuous. Yielding a large amount of excellent honey, it is often planted by bee-keepers. These sweet-scented plants are excellent for pots or boxes, valuable in the bed or border, and, in their newly developed, improved forms, suitable for culture as cut flowers.

CULTURAL NOTES

Adaptable and growing in either full sun or partial shade, mignonette thrives best in cool moderately rich soil. From 6 to 15 in. high, its vigorous branches spread gracefully and are well clothed with rather heavy, dark green leaves. Plants should be started from seed in the open ground, for they grow quickly and dislike transplanting. The blooming period is from June to frost, but, for a continuous supply of the delicate fragrance in the garden, successive sowings should be made, the last one in August. Plants should stand about 6 in. apart.

A leaf spot or blight may appear in gardens or greenhouses. The spots on the foliage are numerous, small, light brown, often with a darker border, and may have centers covered with a dense growth of the fruiting fungus threads. If the trouble has been noted before, start spraying plants while young with bordeaux mixture. The cabbage looper and the corn ear worm occasionally feed on this host. See control measures under CABBAGE and CORN.

In recent years a number of excellent large-flowered varieties of *R. odorata* have been introduced; among the best of them are the following:

Giant Machet, an improved strain of compact plants with large, reddish spikes; Goliath, with large, coppery red florets; White Pearl, with large spikes of fluffy white flowers; New York Market, with long-stemmed, reddish spikes; Golden Sunset, with golden-yellow flowers, and Bismarck, fragrant, with reddish flowers.

MIGNONETTE-TREE. A common name for *Lawsonia inermis,* a shrub of the Far E. which supplies the dye henna (which see); it is also grown for ornament in warm countries.

MIGNONETTE-VINE. A common name for *Boussingaultia basselloides,* a vigorous perennial twining plant of the American tropics but whose roots often prove hardy N. It is a popular ornamental for both greenhouse and outdoors, with fleshy leaves and long clusters of fragrant white flowers in late summer. Another common name is Madeira-vine, which see.

MIKANIA (mi-kay'-ni-ah) *scandens.* A native hardy twining vine known as Climbing-hempweed (which see), with white or pink flower heads.

MILDEW. The common name for certain types of fungi and for the diseases they cause. There are two groups: the powdery mildews (of the Ascomycete group) and the downy mildews (of the Phycomycete group). (See FUNGUS.) The chief characteristic of the latter is the tufts or downy masses of mycelium or white vegetative tissue, usually on the under surface of leaves. Downy mildew of grape is probably the most important disease in this group. See GRAPE; DOWNY MILDEW.

The powdery mildews live for the most part on the surface of host plants, making a cobwebby growth of mycelium which assumes a white powdery appearance with the formation of chains of minute spores (*conidia*). From the surface mycelium special root-like sucking organs (*haustoria*) penetrate the cells of the host plant and there obtain food. Small round, black bodies (*perithecia*) are scattered through the white mycelial growth.

Mildew is more prevalent in cloudy, humid weather and on plants grown in shade. The young shoots and buds may be curled and distorted and the entire plant may be somewhat dwarfed. Roses, phlox, and lilacs are especially subject to attack but powdery mildews can be readily held in check by dusting plants with fine sulphur. See DISEASES, PLANT; FUNGICIDE.

MILFOIL. A common name for *Achillea millefolium,* also called Common Yarrow. Water-milfoil is Myriophyllum.

MILK-BUSH. A common name for the Indian Tree Spurge, *Euphorbia tirucalli,* an easily grown but poisonous succulent.

MILK THISTLE. A common name for *Silybum marianum,* a thistle-like herb with large purplish flower-heads.

MILKWEED IN THE GARDEN
This common roadside plant can be brought into the wild garden or border to create striking mass effects.

MILK-VETCH. Common name for Astragalus, a large genus of herbs of the Pea Family.

MILKWEED. A common name for the genus Asclepias and for some species of Euphorbia (see both titles), given because of their milky juice.

MILKWEED FAMILY. Common name of the Asclepiadaceae (which see), a family of herbs and shrubs characterized by a milky juice, a few of which are used for ornament.

MILKWORT. Common name for the genus Polygala, comprising several ornamental herbs and shrubs; also the name of the family (Polygalaceae) to which the genus belongs.

MILLA (mil'-ah) *biflora.* A bulbous plant of the S. W. with large white fragrant flowers, sometimes mistakenly grown or listed as *Bessera elegans.* See MEXICAN STAR.

MILLEPEDES. These so-called "thousand-legged worms" are not true insects. They resemble centipedes but have two pairs of short legs on each body segment; also the body is round and not flat in cross section, and there are no poison legs. Millepedes generally feed on decaying vegetable matter but some species attack crops growing in damp soil, eating roots and leaves close to the ground, and sometimes becoming serious pests. They are often mistaken for wireworms (which see) and are controlled in similar fashion and by means of poison baits (see bran mash). They may also be killed by drenching the soil with a 1 to 1000 solution of corrosive sublimate.

MILLET. A common name used (usually with various qualifying words) for three groups of grasses grown by farmers mainly for hay and forage. They are excellent for getting new or neglected land under control as they choke out weeds; also as catch-crops to substitute for some earlier sown crop that has failed to make a good stand of plants. In gardening their chief uses are as green manures and cover-crops (both of which see).

MILTONIA (mil-toh'-ni-ah). A genus of tropical, epiphytic orchids having very beautiful, white, rose, orange, bright yellow, or dark purple pansy-shaped flowers variously marked with yellow, purple or red-brown. The lip is expanded but not 3-lobed, and the large flowers are borne singly or in loose racemes over the slender, sheathing, dark green leaves. Of easy culture, Miltonias grow well in the intermediate house and bloom profusely during May and June, the flowers remaining in perfection for at least a month.

M. vexillaria from the W. slope of the Andes and Colombia, is a popular species. It has large flat, pale or deep pink flowers with a deep rose, cleft lip, streaked with red and yellow. Many attractive hybrids have resulted from crosses between Miltonia and the closely related genus, Odontoglossum. For culture, see ORCHIDS.

MIMOSA (mi-moh'-sah). Shrubby or herbaceous plants, native mostly in tropical America, belonging to the Pea Family. Most of them are spiny and have attractive feathery leaves, which in some species are very sensitive. Some of the shrubby kinds are planted for ornament in warm regions. *M. pudica,* the so-called Sensitive-plant, is often grown as an annual in the flower garden or under glass. Mimosas thrive under the same treatment as acacias, some of which, by the way, are popularly known as Mimosas, particularly *A. decurrens* var. *dealbata.* Compare ACACIA.

A wilt that attacks the circulatory system of mimosa trees has spread rapidly throughout the Southeast since it was first noted in N. C. in 1935. Wilted leaves dry, shrivel, and fall, and the death of the tree follows within a year after such defoliation. Since there is, as yet, no cure, mimosa planting stock should come from areas known to be free from the disease. In regions where the wilt has become established, other kinds of trees will probably have to be used in place of this host.

PRINCIPAL SPECIES

M. pudica (Sensitive-plant) is perennial in the tropics, but in cultivation is usually grown as an annual. Its chief interest lies in the extremely sensitive leaves. It has round lavender-colored flower heads, and is easily grown from seed.

argentea is of slender climbing habit, with leaves and young shoots, silvery-gray and pinkish. An interesting plant for the warm greenhouse.

spegozzini is a spiny shrub with sensitive leaves and heads of rosy-purple flowers. It makes an interesting greenhouse plant, and is grown outdoors in warm sections.

MIMULUS (mim'-eu-lus). A genus of tender annual or perennial American herbs or shrubby plants of the Figwort Family commonly called Monkey-flower. They

have large, oddly shaped two-lipped flowers
of brilliant yellow, flesh, crimson, maroon
or white.

Excellent for boxes and baskets, for
house culture, or for garden borders, the
plants can also be cultivated in the greenhouse. When grown in the open border in
warm climates, they should have some
shade, protection from wind, and plenty of
water, though the semi-shrubby species do
well in the sun.

In the greenhouse plants are grown from
cuttings or divisions or, more often, from
seed sown from January to April in loam,
leafmold and sand, and kept in a temperature of 60 deg. F. until they germinate.
They will bloom the first year.

One of the best known species is *M.
moschatus* (Musk-plant), grown for the
musk-like fragrance of the leaves. It is a
yellow-flowered, low, spreading perennial.
The species generally listed in catalogs as
Monkey-flower is *M. tigrinus,* a hybrid
growing 1 ft. tall, and producing flowers
in many colors made more striking by contrasting stripes and spots. *M. luteus,* a
prostrate perennial, the source of most of
the garden varieties, bears yellow flowers
spotted with red or purple. *M. aurantiacus*
(Bush Mimulus) is a shrubby plant to
4 ft., with flowers of apricot or yellow.
Several species may be successfully transferred to the wild garden in regions where
they grow naturally.

Some species are listed in catalogs as of
the genus Diplacus.

MIMUSOPS (mi-meu'-sops). Tropical
evergreen trees of the Sapodilla Family,
with leathery leaves and milky juice;
planted in warm countries for ornament, as
well as for edible fruits, oil, rubber, and
other products. They are rarely seen in
botanical collections in this country. *M.
balata* grows to 100 ft. and yields rubber
of fair quality. *M. elengi* (Spanish-
cherry) is a much smaller tree, and is
valued for its yellow edible berries.

MINA (my'-nah). Former name (still
found in some seed catalogs) for the genus
Quamoclit.

MINER, LEAF. An insect, of any of
several kinds, that spends part or all of its
life between the upper and lower surfaces
of a leaf, getting its food from the tissues
and usually eating a tunnel that shows as
a narrow serpentine, pale or white area
against the normal green of the leaf. See
LEAF MINER.

PEPPERMINT
(a) A flowering stalk with its fragrant leaves;
(b) a section of the square stem typical of all
mints.

MINT, SPEARMINT. A hardy perennial herb (*Mentha spicata* or *M. viridis*)
of the Mint Family, grown for its leaves
which are used to flavor vinegar and jelly
(often served with roast lamb and other
meats) and to enhance thirst-quenching
cooling beverages.

The plant produces no seed but propagates itself by stolons so readily that, unless curbed, it is likely to become a pestiferous weed. It should therefore be
planted where it will not encroach on other
plants. It revels in deep, rich, moist
ground and requires no care except manuring or fertilizing in spring. However, as
the stems grow rapidly and the leaves become thin and small as the season advances, it is advisable to cut down from a
third to a half of the patch when 6 or 8 in.
high, drying the leaves and putting them in
tight jars for winter use. Then soak the
cut-over area with liquid manure to stimulate a second crop of foliage. A month
later treat another area similarly. Thus a
succession of succulent foliage may be had
all season. Orange spots on the backs of
mint leaves are caused by a rust which can
be controlled by dusting with sulphur. But
if the mint is to be for culinary, beverage
or other human consumption purposes, the
sulphur must be pure and not mixed with
arsenate of lead. The four-lined plant bug

(which see) disfigures the terminal leaves, but can be controlled by dusting with rotenone.

Peppermint, Water Mint, Bergamot Mint, Apple Mint and Pennyroyal are other species of Mentha (which see). Mountain-mint is Pycnanthemum; Stonemint is *Cunila origanoides,* and Horse-mint is a name for species of Monarda (which see) especially *M. didyma.*

MINT FAMILY. Common name of the Labiatae, which see.

MINT-GERANIUM. A common name for *Chrysanthemum balsamita* or Costmary, sometimes wrongly called Lavender.

MIRABILIS (my-rab'-i-lis). Perennial herbs of the American tropics grown in gardens as tender annuals. Some have tuberous roots, which can be taken up and stored over winter. Of the dozen species known in the warmer parts of the U. S. the most popular is the Four-o'clock or Marvel of Peru (*M. jalapa*), which takes the former common name from the fact that it does not open its flowers until about 4 o'clock except on dull, cloudy days. It is a well-branched plant about 3 ft. tall with bright foliage and fragrant long-tubed blossoms of good colors and markings, in shades of white, red, and yellow. It blooms from midsummer to frost and is useful as a summer hedge, plants then being set 1 ft. apart. In the border 2 ft. is the proper distance for maximum plant development. *M. longiflora* has much larger flowers of violet, white or red. Seed should be sown in the open ground. Cultural directions are the same for all species of Mirabilis.

MISCANTHUS (mis-kan'-thus) *sinensis.* A tall perennial grass grown for its ornamental plumes, commonly known as Eulalia, which see.

MISCIBLE OILS. Preparations of vegetable or mineral oils readily emulsifiable in water and used as insecticides. See OIL SPRAYS; SPRAYING.

MIST-FLOWER. Common name for *Eupatorium coelestinum,* a tall perennial with heads of blue or violet flowers.

MISTLETOE. Common name for the many members of a large family of green parasitic plants that infest the branches of various kinds of trees. In the U. S. they are represented mainly by the genus Phoradendron of which the species *P. flavescens* is found throughout the S. Atlantic States forming dense bunches 1 to 3 ft. across. The stems are smooth and green; the small

rounded leaves are yellowish-green, thick and persistent, and the inconspicuous flowers are followed by waxy-white berries. The plant is not cultivated, but is gathered by collectors for sale during the Christmas holidays because it resembles the traditional mistletoe (*Viscum album*) of Europe, which for centuries has been a romantic Yule-tide symbol with vague religious or sentimental significance. It is also the State "flower" of Okla.

The Oak Mistletoe of Calif. is *Phoradendron villosum.*

MISTLETOE AS A DISEASE. This is one of the few higher plants that are capable of causing plant disease (see also DODDER). In the S. and Pacific States it is a common pest of many shade trees, producing on their branches globular masses, from a few inches to several feet in diameter. These parasitic masses obtain food from their host by means of root-like parts called *haustoria.* If mistletoe is present in abundance it is a distinct menace to the host tree and in extreme cases may kill it. It can usually be kept under control by breaking off the brittle growths but sometimes the masses must be removed by pruning so as to get the haustoria embedded in the wood.

MISTLETOE CACTUS. Common name for *Rhipsalis cassutha,* a species of cacti not beautiful but odd and interesting and so-called because of the fancied resemblance of its stems, with their white berries, to those of the true Mistletoe.

See also CACTUS; RHIPSALIS.

MISTLETOE FAMILY. Common name of Loranthaceae, which see.

MITCHELLA (mit-chel'-ah) *repens.* Partridge-berry, Squaw-berry, Twin-berry. A very attractive, native, evergreen trailer, rooting along the stems. It can be used to good advantage to carpet shady places in the rock garden, and as a ground-cover under evergreen trees. Small berried specimens in glass bowls are featured by the florists at Christmas time. It has dark green rounded leaves, often marked with white lines. The twin flowers are white with a pinkish tinge, fragrant, and followed by scarlet berries ⅓ in. in diameter. Var. *leucocarpa* has white fruits. Plants are easily propagated by rooted portions of the stems.

MITELLA (mi-tel'-ah). A genus of delicate but hardy woodland herbs of the Saxifrage Family, known as Bishops Cap or Mitrewort. They have heart-shaped basal leaves and small white or greenish flowers. *M. diphylla,* the most pleasing species for the wild garden, has white flowers in a slender raceme sometimes 8 in. long. It is increased by seed or division and should be grown in rich leaf-mold or woods soil in the shade.

MITES. Exceedingly small animals ($\frac{1}{64}$ to $\frac{1}{32}$ in. long) belonging to the spider group and differing chiefly from insects in having 4 instead of 3 pairs of legs. Some mites are parasitic on animals—ticks and the itch-mite for example —but many infest living plants and live by sucking the juices from leaves and flower buds. Mites winter in the form of small oval pinkish eggs attached to twigs, the young hatching out in the spring with only three pairs of legs but soon acquiring four. There may be many generations, eggs being laid on the leaves in summer.

The common, wrongly named, red spider (which see) is the most widely distributed of the mites, infesting many flowering plants indoors and out, shrubs and trees. Its injury is apparent at a glance in the peculiar yellowing and reddish discoloration of the leaves and the mealy or powdery appearance of their under surface, which is covered with fine webs. Both the red spider and its near relative, the spruce mite, may cause the browning and death of needles of evergreens. Control with sulphur sprays or dusts, or by spraying with rotenone, or pyrethrum, or glue, which see.

The boxwood mite causes a fine stippled grayish discoloration of boxwood leaves and the oak mite turns the leaves of oak, chestnut, and birch brownish. The European red mite, chiefly a pest of fruit trees, is controlled by a dormant oil spray. The cyclamen mite which deforms and curls the leaves and blackens the buds of cyclamen, delphinium, and many other greenhouse and garden plants, is best controlled with rotenone sprays at 1-200 or 1-400 dilution, although sulphur dust is credited with some deterrent effect. Greenhouse plants may be effectively treated with hot water, held at 110 deg. F. for 15 minutes for cyclamen, and 108 deg. for 20 minutes for saintpaulia and begonia. Plants should be shaded with newspaper for two days after such treatment.

Certain mites, as the ash-flower gall mite and the hackberry mite, cause galls or overgrowths. A blister mite which causes brown swellings on pear and apple leaves may be controlled by spraying with a miscible oil before growth starts.

MITREWORT. A common name for the genus Mitella (Bishops Cap). False-mitrewort is Tiarella, which see.

SPRUCE MITE WORK ON TWIGS
Enlarged view of the smothering webs spun by these tiny insects. Thriving in hot dry weather, they can be killed by a sulphur spray then or by a dormant oil treatment earlier.

MOCCASIN-FLOWER. A common name for the orchid genus Cypripedium. Some native species are hardy and useful for planting in moist semi-shade in wild gardens. *C. spectabile,* better known as the showy Ladyslipper, is the State flower of Minn.

MOCK- or **WILD-CUCUMBER.** Common name for *Echinocystis lobata,* an annual vine with abundant small white flowers.

MOCKERNUT. A common name for *Carya alba,* the Big-bud Hickory. See HICKORY.

MOCK-HEATHER. Common name for *Ericameria ericoides,* a tender evergreen shrub, not related to the true heathers, but a member of the Composite Family. Growing to a height of 3 ft. or so, it has heath-like foliage and clusters of yellow flowers in daisy-like heads. A good seaside shrub where hardy, it is propagated by cuttings of half-ripened shoots, rooted under glass.

MOCKORANGE. The correct common name for Philadelphus, often, but wrongly, called Syringa (which is the botanical name for the Lilacs) ; and also an accepted

common name for *Prunus caroliniana.*
Deciduous shrubs mostly of medium size,
valued for their great display of white or
creamy, fragrant flowers in early summer.
Most of them are hardy N. They are not
particular as to soil, provided it is not
soggy or poor, and can stand shade better
than most flowering shrubs. Propagated
by seeds, layers, greenwood and hardwood
cuttings. (See illustration, Plate 48.)

Both the bean and spinach aphids may
infest tender shoots of the Mockorange.
A leaf miner makes a curved, linear tunnel
expanding into a blotch in the leaf. Control of the insect has not been worked out.

P. coronarius (European Mockorange),
is perhaps the oldest in cultivation. It
grows to 8 ft., and bears racemes of
creamy-white flowers, the most fragrant of
any species.

American Species

P. inodorus is a vigorous grower with
long arching branches bearing lustrous
green leaves and large pure-white scentless
flowers, usually borne singly.

lewisi, growing to 6 ft. with leaves up
to 3 in. long, is native from Mont. to
Wash. and Ore.

microphyllus is small and graceful, with
small leaves and very fragrant flowers
usually borne singly.

pubescens, formerly called *P. latifolius,*
is a vigorous grower to 10 ft., with dark
green leaves and racemes of slightly fragrant flowers.

grandiflorus is very similar to *P. inodorus*
but has larger leaves of dull green and
flowers less rounded in form.

gordonianus is a vigorous grower with
spreading lateral branches and large
slightly fragrant flowers in dense recemes.

Asiatic Species

delavayi is a strong grower to 15 ft., with
large very fragrant flowers, the petals
somewhat fringed.

sericanthus grows to 12 ft., with spreading branches and short clusters of drooping
fragrant flowers.

subcanus is somewhat similar but the
flowers have the odor of lemon-verbena.

THE MOCKORANGE PERFUMES THE SUMMER SHRUBBERY BORDER
Left, the partially double-flowered hybrid, Philadelphus virginalis. Right, a branch of its variety
Virginal in full bloom. The Mockorange is often improperly called Syringa.

incanus is an upright grower to 12 ft., one of the latest to bloom.

purpurascens is one of the best. It grows to 12 ft., with spreading and arching branches with small leaves, and rather small cupped flowers, very fragrant and set off with a bright purple calyx.

HYBRIDS

By crossing *P. coronarius* with *P. microphyllus,* Lemoine, the French nurseryman, laid the foundation for a new and valuable garden race. *P. lemoinei,* the first of this group, is a small graceful shrub, with slender stems, fine leaves, and a wealth of small fragrant flowers. Some of the best forms of this hybrid are Avalanche, Mont Blanc, Candelabra, Erectus, all with single flowers; and Boule d'Argent, a double.

P. virginalis, a vigorous hybrid of *P. lemoinei* and, presumably, *P. nivalis,* has large semi-double flowers. Good forms of this are Bouquet Blanc, Argentine, Glacier and Virginal. *P. splendens,* a chance hybrid, supposedly between *P. grandiflorus* and *P. gordonianus,* is one of the handsomest of the larger kinds, with clusters of pure white flowers to 3 in. across.

MOCK-PRIVET. Common name for the genus Phillyrea (sometimes wrongly spelled Filaria), evergreen shrubs and small trees with small white flowers and black fruits.

MOCK-STRAWBERRY. A common name for *Duchesnea indica,* the Indian-strawberry, which see.

MOLD. A term applied to loose, black, friable soil rich in humus and practically synonymous with leafmold (which see).

This term is frequently used loosely to cover certain fungi that do not belong in any one botanical group but that show some superficial resemblances. All of them are more or less cottony, cobwebby, velvety or powdery organisms occurring on decaying organic matter and frequently producing fermentation and decay. The black mold found on bread and the green mold on jelly and other foods are familiar to housekeepers. Botrytis blight (which see) of peonies is often called gray mold; the black sooty fungus often growing on aphid honeydew is called sooty mold (which see); fruits affected with brown rot are often said to be moldy. The black mold bread fungus mentioned above may cause a rot of sweet potatoes and some other crops; a

group of fungi characterized by abundant wefts of white mycelium are called water molds; and certain primitive fungi are termed slime-molds (which see).

For control, see the various types of mold and the host plants referred to.

MOLE-PLANT. Common name for the European annual, *Euphorbia lathyrus,* also known as Caper Spurge.

MOLES. These small mammals with minute eyes often covered with skin, small concealed ears and soft iridescent fur, live almost entirely underground, feeding on smaller animal life, especially earthworms. The related, somewhat similar shrews, have long pointed snouts and velvety fur. Both creatures are beneficial in gardens in so far as they feed on insects; but they may do considerable damage to lawns by heaving up the soil, causing the grass to dry out quickly, and by creating conspicuous, unsightly ridges or mounds which indicate the underground runways. (One species, the star-nosed mole, which has a long tail and curious finger-like appendages on its nose, does not make ridges but throws dirt up in a mound.)

TRAPPING AND POISONING

Several methods of control are in use. Strategically placed steel traps, one in the main burrow (if it can be determined) and several others in the various branching runs, are probably the best means of destruction. In handling the traps clean rubber gloves should be worn and care should be taken to press the soil firmly about the places where they are set so that as little evidence as possible of their presence is left.

Poison gas in the runs is a method in common use, but caution must be used as damage to the vegetation sometimes results. A teaspoonful of calcium cyanide or carbon bisulphide may be put into the burrows every 5 ft. or so, each opening being promptly closed with a bit of sod. Paradichlorobenzene (which see) can be applied every 6 to 10 ft. in the same way. Ordinary moth balls and castor oil beans dropped in the runs are said to drive moles away, even if they do not kill them. Garden hose or other rubber tubing can be attached to the exhaust pipe of an automobile, the other end inserted into the runway and the motor allowed to run for 20 minutes. Concentrated lye, obtainable at grocery stores, has also been suggested. The burrow is opened with a narrow trowel every four or five feet and a teaspoonful of the crystals poured into the opening which is then closed with a piece of sod.

Before becoming too excited about the inroads of moles, it might be well to check their damage against the very real damage done by the mice (which see) and the damage that would otherwise be done by the pests the moles devour. It must be remembered that the number of moles depends on the food supply—that is, insects —and if your garden has many, it probably needs them.

MOLINIA (moh-lin'-i-ah). A genus of tufted perennial grasses of which one, *M. caerulea,* is sometimes grown for ornament. See ORNAMENTAL GRASSES.

MOLTKIA (molt'-ki-ah). A genus of woody perennial herbs 1 ft. tall with purplish-blue flowers. Two species (*M. suffruticosa* and *M. petraea*) may be used in rock gardens.

MOLUCELLA (mol-eu-sel'-ah). A genus of annuals of the Mint Family. *M. laevis* is the popular Molucca-balm or Shellflower of old gardens, with whorls of fragrant white flowers. *M. spinosa* grows man-high. In the N. both plants are easily raised from seed started under glass in early spring; in the S. seed may be sown outdoors.

MOMORDICA (moh-maur'-di-kah). Annual or perennial tendril-climbing plants of the tropics, belonging to the Cucumber Family. Two species are sometimes grown in gardens as ornamental vines, being treated as tender annuals, that is, started outdoors after frost danger is past, or preferably, earlier indoors. They require a light rich soil and have deeply lobed leaves, yellow flowers, and fruits which are very decorative when they burst open after ripening. *M. balsamina* (Balsam-apple) is a moderate grower, bearing oval orange-colored fruits to 3 in. long. *M. charantia* (Balsam-pear) is larger in all its parts, and has orange-red oblong fruits to 8 in. long. It is the more common species.

MONARCH-OF-THE-VELDT. A seed-catalog name for *Venidium fastuosum,* a S. African annual of the Composite Family with large orange flowers.

MONARDA (moh-nahr'-dah). A genus of annual or perennial, rather coarse aromatic herbs, commonly known as Horsemint. They have the square stems and opposite leaves characteristic of the Mint Family, and bear showy (usually red or lavender) flowers in clusters. Easily grown, horse-mints can be naturalized in the wild garden and they are occasionally used in the border. They are easily propagated by division in the spring.

SPECIES

M. didyma (Oswego-tea, Bee- or Fragrant-balm), grows to 3 ft. with scarlet flowers, surrounded by red-tinted bracts, at the summit of the leafy stalks. A brilliant perennial plant with a long season of bloom, it is most appropriate grown in a natural setting. There is a white variety (*alba*), and var. *salmonea* has yellowish-pink blossoms.

fistulosa (Wild-bergamot) has lavender or lilac blossoms with purple or whitish bracts in clusters at the summit of 3 ft. stalks. Growing well on a dry sunny slope in the wild garden, it is also effective in the border planted in combination with perennial phlox.

MONARDELLA (mon-ahr-del'-ah). A genus of annual or perennial herbs of the Mint Family with fragrant foliage. Natives of Calif., they bear 2-lipped flowers in heads resembling those of Bee-balm or Horse-mint (Monarda). The plants are occasionally grown in the rock garden in a light sandy soil, where they are increased by seed or division in the spring. *M. villosa,* a perennial to 1½ ft., has purple, white or pink flowers ½ in. long. *M. macrantha,* not so tall, is a tufted plant with orange flowers 1½ in. long. *M. lanceolata,* an annual and larger, has soft-hairy foliage and rose-purple flowers.

MONDO (mon'-doh). A genus of Oriental low-growing, sod-forming plants of the Lily Family, with evergreen grass-like leaves and small bluish to whitish flowers in racemes. Called Lily-turf and Snakes Beard, they are used chiefly as greenhouse foliage plants but recently have come into use in S. Calif. as green turf and edging plants. They should prove valuable for formal and parterre gardening as they are easily grown in sun or shade and increased by root-division. The best known species is *M. jaburan,* which with its varieties, has leaves 2 to 3 ft. long and white flowers followed by bluish fruits. *M. japonicus,* which has smaller leaves, bears small flowers below the mat of foliage.

The botanical name for the group was formerly Ophiopogon.

MONESES (moh-nee'-seez) *uniflora.* A perennial evergreen herb of the Heath Family commonly known as One-flowered Shinleaf. It is a dainty little plant with a solitary fragrant white flower on a drooping stem 5 or 6 in. long and roundish leaves clustered at the base of the stem. It should be grown in rich acid soil in the shady wild garden. It is difficult to grow from seed but can be increased by cuttings.

MONEY. A common name for *Lunaria annua* and *L. rediviva,* better known as annual and perennial honesty.

MONEYWORT. Common name for *Lysimachia nummularia,* also called Creeping Jenny or Creeping Charlie. It is a creeping yellow-flowered perennial, good as a ground-cover in shady places but a pest in lawns.

MONKEY-COCONUT PALM. A common name for *Jubaea chilensis* (also called Syrup Palm or Coquito) suggested by the small fruits which look like miniature coconuts. They are actually one-seeded plumlike fruits with fibrous flesh and 1½ in. long; in Chile they are used in candymaking.

MONKEY-FLOWER. The common name for a genus of annual and perennial herbs of the Figwort Family (Scrophulariaceae) mostly native to the Pacific Coast. The name refers to the fancied resemblance of the spotted flowers to a grotesque face. See MIMULUS.

MONKEY PUZZLE. Common name for *Araucaria araucana,* a gaunt, rather grotesque tree related to the Norfolk Island Pine, with stiff, sharp-pointed leaves clothing branches and trunk and making it difficult to climb "even for a monkey."

MONKSHOOD. A common name for the genus Aconitum, perennial herbs grown in borders for their showy spikes of hooded blue (or sometimes white or yellow) flowers. (See illustration, Plate 40.) The plant is highly poisonous but yields the medicinal drug aconite.

MONKS PEPPER-TREE. A common name for *Vitex agnus-castus,* the Chastetree or Hemp-tree, a half-hardy shrub with lilac flowers.

MONOCARP. A plant that flowers and fruits but once, then dies soon after. All annuals and biennials are monocarps; also some perennials, such as the century-plant.

MONOCOTYLEDON. That class of flowering plants, including the Grasses, Sedges, Rushes, Lilies, Iris, Orchids, Aroids, Palms and their relatives, which have only one seed-leaf, or cotyledon (which see), as contrasted with the rest of the flowering plants, the *dicotyledons,* which have two seed-leaves. The monocotyledonous plants, or "monocots" as they are sometimes called, are further characterized by parallel-veining in the leaves; by having the food or water vessels vertical tubes scattered unevenly through the stem (not arranged in rings around it), and by having the parts of the flower characteristically (though not necessarily) arranged in threes.

Contrast DICOTYLEDON.

MONOECIOUS (moh-nee'-shus). A term applied to plants which bear flowers of different "sexes," that is, staminate and pistillate (which see), on the same individual.

Contrast DIOECIOUS.

MONSTERA (mon'-ster-ah). Strong handsome climbers of tropical America, belonging to the Arum Family. The best known is *M. deliciosa* (Ceriman) which may be grown in a pot, but is most imposing when planted out in a warm greenhouse, and allowed to grow at will against a wall or other support. It is conspicuous because of its large leathery perforated leaves, and long cord-like aerial roots. The club-like flower spike (*spadix*) rises from a creamy-white enveloping leaf or bract (*spathe*) about 1 ft. long; the spadix eventually develops into a cone-like edible fruit, with the flavor of pineapple and banana. It is propagated by cutting up the stem and rooting the pieces in a mixture of sand and leafmold, in heat.

MONTANOA (mon-tah-noh'-ah). Shrubs or small trees of Mexico and Colombia, belonging to the Daisy Family. They are sometimes grown under glass for winter bloom, or outdoors in summer for subtropical effect. *M. bipinnatifida,* the principal species, grows to 8 ft., with large handsome hairy leaves deeply cut, and 3 in. heads of flowers with white ray petals. It is easily grown from seeds sown under glass in spring.

MONTBRETIA (mont-bree'-ti-ah). Common and trade name (and former generic name) for the group of S. African cormus plants of the Iris Family now given the botanical name Tritonia (which see). Many horticultural forms blooming in midsummer and later have become important garden subjects. They produce narrow, sword-like leaves and slender spikes of small, funnel-shaped flowers in which red and yellow shades predominate.

Montbretias should be treated exactly the same as gladioli, for, despite belief to the contrary, they are not always hardy and for safety should be lifted every fall and kept over winter in frost-free storage. As the corms suffer from exposure, they should when stored, be covered with dry sand, fine sawdust, or slightly moist earth. Because of the perishable nature of the blossoms, Montbretias are not good cut-flower subjects, but, grown in clumps or mass plantings in the garden, each corm produces several flower spikes and provides a wealth of beauty over a long period. The corms propagate naturally by producing offsets—quite abundantly in some of the species but quite slowly in the case of many of the new hybrids. In the S. they can with benefit remain undisturbed for several years.

There are four principal species, and numerous named varieties are offered by bulb dealers. The species are: *T. crocata*, with orange-yellow or reddish flowers 2 in. across; *T. pottsi*, with bright yellow, long-tubed flowers about an in. long; *T. rosea* with bright red, yellow spotted flowers, and *T. crocosmaeflora*, with larger orange-red flowers, a hybrid of Tritonia and a related genus, Crocosmia.

MONTEZUMA-CYPRESS. Common name for *Taxodium mucronatum*, a Mexican cone-bearing evergreen planted for ornament in Calif. and the S.

MONTHLY ROSE. A term (now of only historical significance) formerly used to refer to that group of garden roses which bloomed for only about a month—usually June in the N. Atlantic States, where it originated—and represented by descendants of the China Rose (*Rosa chinensis*), the Tea Rose (*R. odorata*) and similar species possessing quality and beauty but limited hardiness and a relatively brief flowering period. See also ROSE.

MONTIA (mon'-ti-ah) *perfoliata*. A small annual herb, known as Winter-purslane, native to the Pacific Coast. See PURSLANE.

MOON, PLANTING BY THE. Belief that the moon exerts a definite and substantial influence, not only upon the earth (as evidenced by the tides), but also upon the physical welfare and comfort of men and the growth and development of plants, has existed from the earliest times. Unfortunately, the subject, although highly controversial, has never been subjected to careful, intensive, scientific investigation; consequently the theories involved and the claims made regarding them have never been conclusively proved or disproved. However, in addition to statements that have come down from the ancient philosophers, and traditions passed from generation to generation of peasants and practical gardeners as well as savage tribes (which might easily be scrutinized with some incredulity), there are constantly being reported by intelligent, unprejudiced modern plant growers experiences which tend to make it impossible to discredit or ignore the theory of lunar influence on the time of seed sowing, planting, and other cultural operations. It seems logical, therefore, to recognize the existence of this theory as something more than mere superstition, and to suggest that any gardener curious about it undertake careful, systematic, accurate tests that will assist him in making up his own mind regarding it. It should be understood that even strong supporters of the theory are not necessarily astrologists and do not consider planting by the moon astrological practice.

Briefly, the assumptions upon which arguments for planting by the moon are based are: (1) That the moon, in its monthly revolution around the earth, passes through twelve zones or "signs" of the zodiac, which is an imaginary belt in the heavens encircling the earth at right angles to its axis as related to the sun; thus the zodiacal belt does not coincide with the equator which is at right angles to the north and south pole axis. (2) That the influence of the moon varies according to the sign in which it happens to be at the time planting or other garden work is done. (3) That, in general, plants which bear the desired parts above ground (as beans, tomatoes, corn, flowers) benefit if planted during a waxing or increasing moon, that is up to the time of full moon; and that plants which yield below ground (potatoes, beets, parsnips, dahlias—if tubers are especially wanted—etc.) benefit if planted during a waning moon, that is, after the full.

According to one student of the subject, there are two systems used in determining the position of the moon in relation to the signs. One, the *heliocentric* derives from the sun and although it is the one on which most almanacs are calculated, it is not, he claims, accurate in determining the moon's influence on plant life. The other, or *geocentric*, which takes the earth as the center of reckoning, should always be used in calculating advantageous planting times. This latter system is used in making up astrological tables called *ephemerides* (singular, *ephemeris*) which can be obtained from publishers of such things.

The requirements for successful planting by the moon—or for a fair test of the theory—are, therefore: First, accurate location of the moon in the signs, through the consultation of reliable tables based on the geocentric system. Second, use of an "authoritative" guide to the moon's influence in the different signs; presumably the only wholly authoritative manual of this sort would be one based on exhaustive tests made under conditions similar to those under which the theory is to be applied. And, third, intelligent, common-sense management of soil, seeds, plants, etc. in line with good gardening theory under any system and in any locality.

For further study of this subject, readers are referred to publications of The Aries Press, Chicago, Ill.

MOONFLOWER. Common name for Calonyction, a genus of twining perennial herbs of tropical America, belonging to the Morning-glory Family. The principal species is *C. aculeatum* (formerly classified as *Ipomaea bona-nox*). This is the common Moonflower, sometimes grown under glass in the N., and outdoors in warm regions. In good soil it grows to 20 ft. high, bearing large heart-shaped leaves, and white, trumpet-shaped fragrant flowers to 6 in. across. These open in the evening and usually close before noon. Several forms are offered in the trade under various names. Plants are easily grown as tender annuals but the seeds germinate more readily if previously notched or soaked overnight in warm water.

MOONSEED. Common name for Menispermum, a genus of plants of the same family name (Menispermaceae), comprising two species of twining woody vines, one native in N. America and the other Asiatic, but both hardy N. and suitable for draping fences, arbors and trellises. Propagated by seeds and cuttings of ripened wood.

M. canadense is found in rich lowlands from Quebec to Ga. It grows to 10 ft. or more, with large heart-shaped lobed leaves, small greenish-yellow flowers, and bunches of black berries like tiny grapes. These contain a flattened crescent-shaped stone, from which the common name is derived. *M. dauricum,* from Asia, is very similar, but with smaller, more shield-shaped leaves, and smaller fruiting clusters.

MOONWORT (*Botrychium lunulatum*). A very small fern ally, having round-lobed fronds and a spike of naked fruit. Found in pastures throughout the U. S., it is difficult to cultivate. See BOTRYCHIUM.

MORACEAE (moh-ray'-see-ee). The Mulberry Family, a widely distributed group of herbs, shrubs, trees or sometimes vines, yielding many horticultural subjects and economic products. From it are obtained fibre, rubber, food for silkworms, hops and edible fruits, such as breadfruit, figs and mulberries. The osage-orange (Maclura) is widely used for hedges and others are of general interest. Principal cultivated genera are Morus (mulberry), Broussonetia (paper-mulberry), Maclura, Artocarpus, Ficus (fig), Cannabis (hemp), Humulus (hop). The small flowers are borne in heads or spikes; the male and female organs are on separate flowers, the pistils sometimes being borne on the inner surface of a hollow receptacle, as in the fig.

MORAEA (moh-ree'-ah). A genus of plants resembling and closely related to the iris, not hardy N. but grown extensively in Calif. and Fla. They have corms or rootstocks, narrow grass-like leaves, and clustered white, red, yellow or lilac flowers which last only a day. In cold climates the corms or rootstocks must be planted in the spring, lifted before frost in the fall and stored like those of the gladiolus. The majority of the species are from Africa. *M. robinsoniana,* to 8 ft., with loose clusters of white flowers spotted with red and yellow, is one of the most beautiful of the species, a native of Australia. *M. bicolor* to 2 ft. has lemon yellow flowers to 2 in. across, beautifully spotted with brown. *M. pavonia,* 1 to 2 ft. tall, has brilliant red flowers with a blue- or green-black mark at the base of each petal; its var. *lutea* is yellow and var. *villosa* purple.

MORAINE GARDEN. Usually seen as part of a rock garden, this is markedly different both in soil and in moisture conditions from what that term generally implies. The moraine garden affords place for many rare and beautiful plants which cannot live anywhere else; it must therefore be a perfect reproduction in miniature of a natural moraine, which is an accumulation of stone fragments deposited by a glacier at its terminus and exposed by the summer-melting of ice masses. Through such detritus icy water flows continually during warm weather from the melting ice higher up, but the open character of the mass does not retain water. Hence it is well aerated even though it is perpetually bathed in moisture. Since winter shuts off this water supply completely, moisture is wholly absent from the plant roots during the cold season when they are protected above ground by deep snow. Once they are understood, these condition are not difficult to reproduce in the garden.

See also ALPINE PLANTS; ROCK GARDEN.

MORINDA (moh-rin'-dah). A genus of trees, shrubs and climbers of the Madder Family, widely spread throughout the tropics. Some species have edible fruit, and others yield dyes. *M. citrifolia* (Indian-mulberry), the best-known species, is a small tree with large leaves and small heads of white flowers, followed by yel-

MORNING-GLORY VINE
The annual Ipomoea purpurea grows quickly from seed sown where the plants are to climb.

lowish fleshy fruit. A red dye is obtained from the flowers and a yellow one from the roots. *M. royoc,* native of Fla. and the W. Indies, is a low branching shrub with spreading and somewhat climbing stems.

MORNING-GLORY. Common name for various plants of the Morning-glory or Bindweed Family (Convolvulaceae), but particularly the whole genus Ipomoea (which see). This includes annual and perennial twining herbs some of which have long been garden favorites for covering trellises, fences, walls, etc. Their large, dark green, heart-shaped leaves make an excellent screen and the trumpet-shaped flowers of many beautiful clear colors are borne in great profusion all summer. Though they close at noon, their brightness and variety are a joy and a beauty all morning.

Morning-glories grow rapidly in almost any moderately rich garden soil. Seed should be sown where the plants are wanted as soon as danger from frost is passed; as they are very hard, germination is hastened by filing small holes or notches through the horny coat. Perennial kinds are readily propagated by cuttings rooted under glass. As they are of S. origin their tuberous roots should be dug in the fall in cold regions and stored like dahlia tubers over winter.

The larva of a small moth sometimes makes a serpentine mine in the leaves, but no control measure is known. In case of severe injury by tortoise beetles (which see), spray with lead arsenate.

Silver- or Woolly-morning-glory is Argyreia (which see).

MORUS (moh'-rus). The botanical name of the Mulberry (which see) a genus of hardy deciduous trees grown in the U. S. for the edible, though rather insipid, berry-like fruits and, in the Orient, for the leaves, on which silkworms are fed.

MOSAIC. A virus disease having as its chief symptom mottling of the foliage, caused by light yellow areas arranged on the leaves in a kind of mosaic pattern. This is accompanied by general dwarfing of the plant and sometimes by the curling and crinkling of the leaves.

See VIRUS DISEASES.

MOSES-IN-THE-CRADLE. A common name, probably local, for *Rhoeo discolor* (which see), an attractive form of spiderwort in which the small white flowers snuggle closely in boat-shaped green bracts.

MOSQUITOES. Although not plant pests, these insects deserve mention as familiar garden nuisances and, in some cases, as health menaces as carriers of malaria and other human diseases. It is the adult that annoys by "biting" (and "stinging"), the mouth parts being of the piercing-sucking type. In biting, the common mosquito holds its body parallel to the surface it rests on, while the malarial species stands with its body sloping upward to the rear; also the latter bites chiefly in the evening or early morning.

Mosquitoes winter either in the egg stage, as adults (females) in cellars, sheds, hollow trees, etc., or, in some cases, as larvae in the mud of stagnant ponds or even frozen in the ice. In any case, they develop only in water, the eggs forming tiny rafts resembling bits of soot floating on the surface wherever water stands for a few days. Hatching they produce the familiar "wrigglers" often seen in rain barrels and such places. These active little creatures breathe through openings at their posterior end which, when they are at rest, is at the surface while their large heads point downwards. After a few days they change to active pupae called "tumblers" and these in turn change to adults in anywhere from a few days to weeks.

Since mosquitoes cannot develop except in water, gardeners should make sure that their grounds are so well drained that there are no pools or standing water, and no old tin cans or other containers left around in out of the way places. Also pools and other garden water features should be well stocked with top-feeding minnows, goldfish or other kinds of fish which feed on the mosquito larvae. In the case of bodies of stagnant water that cannot be done away with and in which it is not possible or desirable to keep fish, a film of kerosene or other oil sprayed on the surface two or three times a summer will prevent the mosquito larvae from breathing and thus eliminate them. This is the method used in extensive campaigns.

If one must work in the garden when mosquitoes are particularly numerous, gloves, leggings and the use of a repellant such as oil of citronella give partial protection.

MOSQUITO-TRAP. Common name for *Cynanchum acuminatifolium*, a Japanese

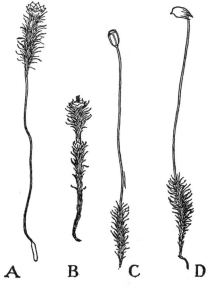

MOSS PLANTS, "FLOWERS" AND "FRUITS"

Male plants of two different types are shown at (A) and (B). Spores from the flower-like growth at their tips fertilize female plants, which send up long stalks (C) and (D), bearing capsules within which develop still other spores from which grow new plants.

twining perennial herb, sometimes shrubby, belonging to the Milkweed Family. It is more curious than beautiful, and perhaps its chief recommendation is that mosquitoes are caught in the flowers which are white and borne in clusters. It is easily grown in ordinary garden soil and is propagated by division of the rootstock.

MOSS CAMPION. A common name for the low-growing, bright pink flowered Cushion-pink, *Silene acaulis*.

MOSSES. Minute green plants with leafy stems and minute root-like parts, densely packed together to form velvety cushions or growing in clusters resembling tiny ferns or trees. They form the second of the two classes that make up the second great division (Bryophta) of the plant kingdom, the other class being the Hepatics or liverworts (which see). Mosses grow on rocks and damp banks, on dead or living trees, and on the surface of shallow waters, and are found in all humid climates, over a wide range of altitudes and degrees of heat or cold. It is believed that mosses, lichens and hepatics, the triple link between aquatic and land plants, may have been the first vegetation to appear on the earth and that they may have reigned supreme for a time.

Mosses build up plant-tissue and capture dust and débris from the wind, thus providing (with the decay of the older plants) sufficient soil for the sprouting of fernspores and later of the seeds of herbs, shrubs and, in time, trees. They thus play an important part in establishing plant growth in previously barren places. Indeed, the storage of dust by rock-mosses and of mud by aquatic mosses has actually directed the earth's covering of vegetation. There are many genera and hundreds of species. The main division is between those that live on land, including rocks and trees, and those that live in water.

The most important mosses from the gardener's standpoint are the peat or bog types. These are usually of large, loose growth, changing color with variations in the weather as they spread over the surface of swamps and ponds preparing a foothold for larger plants. The mossy surface shows only the tops of the very plants whose under parts died long before and are being gradually transformed into peat (which see). Bogs so formed, if eventually drained, make rich crop-lands. Ancient peat deposits are dug up and used for fuel in certain parts of the world, or ground and, as peat moss (which see), added to garden soil to increase its moisture-retaining quality and improve its texture. On account of its spongy, absorptive quality, moss of the genus Sphagnum (which see) is largely used in packing plants for shipping.

MOSS-PINK. A common name for *Phlox subulata,* a hardy mat-forming perennial with abundant pink, white or lavender flowers; also called Ground-pink.

MOSS ROSE. Common name for *Rosa centifolia* var. *muscosa,* a form of the old-time Cabbage Rose, in which the calyx and flower stem are roughened and "mossy." See ROSE.

MOTHER-OF-THOUSANDS. A common name for *Cymbalaria muralis,* better known as Kenilworth Ivy, a familiar ground-cover or trailing plant for vases or hanging baskets in greenhouses or mild places.

MOTHER-OF-THYME. A common name for *Thymus serpyllum.* See THYME.

MOTHERWORT. The genus Leonurus, which is also called Lions Tail. Weedy

herbs of the Mint Family from Eur. and Asia that have become naturalized in U. S. They are of coarse habit growing 2 to 3 ft. high, with small leaves and prickly two-lipped purplish, pink or white flowers closely set about a single spike. Though occasionally seen in gardens, their tendency to self-sow makes them dangerous guests. When desired, they are easily raised from spring-sown seed in any ordinary soil. *L. cardiaca vulgaris* is the common motherwort blossoming in waste places through the summer.

MOTH ORCHID. Common name for Phalaenopsis, a genus of epiphytic orchids of the Philippines and other Asiatic countries, grown in greenhouses.

MOTHS. These insects, also called millers, belong to the order Lepidoptera. They undergo what is known as complete metamorphosis in growing from egg to adult, the larvae being caterpillars. The adults have siphoning mouth-parts. Moths differ from butterflies (which see) by being chiefly night fliers, and in having large heavy abdomens, wings that usually lie horizontally when the creature is at rest, and, often, two *ocelli* or "eye-spots" on the wings. The pupae are often protected by cocoons.

Moths may be useful, as the silk-worm moths; destructive in the household, as the clothes moths; or plant pests, as the tent caterpillar, canker worm and many others. However, injurious moths are only destructive in the larval or caterpillar stage; the adult moth is usually harmless, except in laying eggs to produce more caterpillars. See also INSECTS.

MOUNTAIN-ASH. Common name for the genus Sorbus, a group of ornamental trees and shrubs, grown for their attractive foliage, showy clusters of white flowers, and decorative fruits, mostly red or orange. Members of the Rose Family, they are mostly hardy N., not particular as to soil, and able to endure dry conditions. They are propagated by seed, layers, budding and grafting.

The mountain-ash is subject to some of the diseases and insect pests found on apple, such as fire blight, rust of cedar and apple, scurfy and San José scales, woolly aphid and the round-headed apple-tree borer. (See APPLE.) The pear-leaf blister mite is occasionally abundant, causing brownish swellings on the under leaf surface. See PEAR.

PRINCIPAL SPECIES

S. americana (American Mountain-ash) growing to 30 ft., with leaves of 11 to 17 leaflets, is very showy in fall with bright red fruits. Its native range is from Newfoundland southward to N. C.

decora is another native species, found from Labrador southward to N. Y. It grows about the same size, but is often shrubby, with fewer (7 to 15) leaflets, and larger, showier fruit.

aucuparia (Rowan-tree) is a round-headed European tree growing to 50 ft. or more. Its 9 to 11 leaflets are shorter and more rounded than those of *S. americana* but it is equally showy in fruit. There are several forms of this species; var. *fastigiata* is of narrow pyramidal habit; var. *pendula* has long drooping branches, and var. *xanthocarpa* has orange-yellow fruit.

commixta is a small Asiatic tree, somewhat similar to *S. americana*, but with smaller leaves and fruit.

domestica (Service-tree) is a European tree growing to 60 ft., with 11 to 17 leaflets. The fruit is sometimes used in Europe for cider making.

torminalis (Wild Service-tree) is a wide-spreading European tree to 80 ft. It has attractive light green leaves with angular lobes, turning bright red in the fall.

aria (White Beam-tree) is a handsome European species to fifty feet tall, with entire leaves, sharply toothed, white beneath, and bearing orange-red fruits. It will stand dry and exposed positions.

hybrida is a hybrid between *S. aucuparia* and *S. intermedia*, growing to 40 ft. The young growth is whitish and the leaves are deeply lobed or sometimes quite divided. It is mostly cultivated under the name of *S. quercifolia*.

latifolia is hybrid between *S. aria* and *S. torminalis*, growing to 50 ft. It has ovate leaves, slightly lobed and pale beneath.

MOUNTAIN-DANDELION or DWARF-DANDELION. Common names for *Krigia virginica*. See DANDELION.

MOUNTAIN-EBONY. Common name for *Bauhinia variegata*, also called Orchid-tree, an Asiatic species popular in S. Fla. on account of its ornamental foliage and lavender pea-like flowers.

MOUNTAIN FLEECE. Common name for *Polygonum amplexicaule*, a perennial herb with rosy or white flowers in spikes.

MOUNTAIN FRINGE. Common name for *Adlumia fungosa*, or Allegheny-vine (which see), an attractive biennial climber of E. N. America, ornamental and useful in cool damp locations.

MOUNTAIN-HOLLY. Common name for *Nemopanthus mucronata*, an ornamental deciduous shrub of the Holly Family found from Newfoundland to Wis. and Va., mostly in moist ground. In habit it is a well-branched shrub to 10 ft.; the young branches are purplish but later turn gray. It has medium-sized bright green leaves which turn yellow in the fall. The whitish flowers are inconspicuous but the red berries make a good showing. It grows well in partial shade. Propagated by seeds.

MOUNTAIN HOLLY FERN (*Polystichum lonchitis*). A dark green prickly toothed fern of the N. States, once-pinnate. Suitable for gardens in its range, it prefers woods soil with limestone.

MOUNTAIN-LAUREL. (See the illustrations, Plate 43.) The common name for *Kalmia latifolia*, a hardy evergreen shrub of E. U. S. with showy pink flowers closely related to the rhododendrons and often called Calico-bush. It is the State flower of Conn. and Penna. See KALMIA.

MOUNTAIN-LILY. A common name in New Zealand for *Ranunculus lyalli*, an erect, showy, white- or cream-flowered relative of our wild buttercup native to that country.

MOUNTAIN-MAHOGANY. A small group of evergreen shrubs or semi-deciduous small trees of western N. America. The botanical name (Cercocarpus) comes from Greek words meaning long hairy tail, referring to the seed. The plants will thrive on dry rocky or gravelly slopes in arid temperate regions where conditions are unfavorable to other plants, and are sometimes used for hedges or shrubbery. Propagate by seeds or cuttings. The species *C. ledifolius* and *C. parvifolius* will endure temperatures to zero.

MOUNTAIN-MINT. Common name for Pycnanthemum, a N. American genus of perennial herbs with heads or flat-topped clusters of small white or purplish flowers. Members of the Mint Family and also called Basil. Of the easiest culture, they are often transferred to the wild garden. *P. virginianum*, which grows from 1 to 3 ft. high, has fragrant mint-like leaves and flowers in dense heads.

P. flexuosum, not so tall, has slender stems and whitish-lavender flowers. *P. incanum* has foliage with woolly hairs beneath and white flowers in loose clusters.

MOUNTAIN-PRIVET. Common name for Forestiera, a genus of hardy American shrubs and trees.

MOUNTAIN-ROSE, Rosa de Montana. Common names for *Antigonon leptopus,* a tendril-climbing vine with bright pink flowers, popular in the S. and in greenhouses. In too rich soil the plant runs to foliage and flowers poorly.

MOUNTAIN SHIELD FERN (*Dryopteris spinulosa* var. *americana*). A form of shield fern found in the N. States and in upland rocky woods. One of the best of the genus for gardens in its range.

MOUNTAIN SPRAY. Catalog name for *Holodiscus microphyllus,* a hardy W. ornamental shrub with creamy flowers on drooping stems.

MOUNTAIN-TOBACCO. A catalog name for *Arnica montana,* a hardy perennial of the Composite Family.

MOURNING BRIDE. A common name for Scabiosa (sometimes specifically *S. atropurpurea*), probably a fanciful modification of the older name, Mournful Widow; arising from a widow's fashion of adding bits of white to her costume after the pediod of deep mourning—the very dark purple of the flower being flecked with white. See SCABIOSA.

MOUSE-EAR CHICKWEED. Common name for the genus Cerastium, comprising low, tufted herbaceous plants, some used in borders, others mere weeds.

MOVING-PLANT. A common name for *Desmodium gyrans,* a tender leguminous plant with a peculiar property of being able to move its leaves, which has given it also the name Telegraph-plant.

MOWERS and MOWING. In present-day American gardening mowing refers to the cutting of an expanse of lawn by means of a lawn-mower either hand operated, drawn by a horse, or driven by a small gasoline engine mounted on the frame of the machine. The farmer thinks of mowing in terms of hay or other forage or grain crops as done with a regulation mowing machine, or with a hand scythe. It is interesting to recall that old-time gardeners—and perhaps many of Old-World training even today—have a high regard for the scythe as an implement for the mowing of lawns as well as roadsides, fence corners, etc. However, the delicate manipulation of a scythe for this purpose is something that the average home gardener is not likely to want or need to take the trouble to learn.

The mowing of a new lawn should begin when the young grass is between 2 and 3 in. tall; for the first few times it should not be too close or the soil will be so exposed to the sun that it may become baked and the grass roots killed. Later as the turf thickens the cutting may be closer, depending upon the condition and quality of the soil, the moisture supply, the weather, the vigor of the grass and the degree to which, and the purposes for which, the lawn is used.

The frequency of mowing should be such that the clippings will not at any one time be too heavy to leave on the surface; there they will gradually rot and add to the humus in the soil without tending to cause mold or mildew. Of course if the trimmings are long and coarse, it is better to rake them up—and add them to the compost heap. See COMPOST.

Do not mow a lawn when the ground is so wet and soft that the operator's feet will injure it or the pressure of the mower compact and puddle it. On the other hand, refrain from mowing during hot dry weather when the grass makes little growth; also as soon in the fall as vigorous growth stops, so that the lawn can go into the winter with a good protection of sod.

The use of the lawn mower should be supplemented around tree trunks and along beds and borders, paths and other boundaries by the use of the sickle or grass-hook, or suitable edging shears. While this is slower work and harder on the back, it is better than barking trees and shrubs by mowing too close to them or breaking down the sod edges of flower beds by constantly running the mower off them as is necessary in trimming the edges closely.

Needless to say, good mowing can be done only with a good machine, of adequate size, kept sharp, well oiled and in good mechanical condition. Learn how to keep it adjusted and in addition have it sharpened and gone over by an expert as often as may be necessary; once a year may be often enough—or it may not.

See also LAWN MOWER.

MOWRAH MEAL. A vegetable poison used particularly against earthworms.

Ground from seeds of the Madhuca tree of the E. Indies, the meal is sprinkled on lawns at the rate of 15 lbs. to 1000 sq. ft. and the area immediately given a good soaking. For best results use only when fresh. See also LAWN.

MUCK. Known also as meadow-peat or swamp-muck, this is a type of soil consisting mainly of ancient plant deposits that have undergone more complete decomposition than peat (which see). In color it is dark brown or black, thus closely resembling leafmold or humus. Its plant-food constituents are very slowly available and it is distinctly acid in reaction. It can be used to a limited extent in gardening as a mulch for acid-loving plants, or, in combination with lime, to modify heavy clay or loose sandy soils.

See SOIL.

MUEHLENBECKIA (meu-len-bek'-i-ah). Former name of certain plants of the Buckwheat Family now separated into two genera, Calacinum (Wire-plant) and Homalocladium (Ribbon-bush or Centipede-plant). The interesting shrubby plant with green ribbon-like stems, often grown in greenhouses as *Muehlenbeckia platyclados,* is now called *Homalocladium platycladum.*

MUGWORT. Common name for *Artemisia vulgaris* and *A. lactiflora,* species of Wormwood.

MULBERRY. Common name for the genus Morus, comprising a number of species of deciduous, long-lived trees or shrubs, native in temperate regions of the northern hemisphere. They are interesting as ornamental trees because of the variableness of their leaves, several forms being often found on the same tree. They are also cultivated for the edible fruits and in some parts for the leaves, which are used to feed silkworms. The flowers are not showy, and male and female are borne in separate catkins.

Mulberry foliage is well-known as the preferred food of the silkworm, but ordinarily it is not in this country seriously affected by either insect pests or diseases. The so-called popcorn disease is kept down by intensively cultivating the soil under the trees to kill the fungus fruiting bodies. Tiny moth-like adults of the mulberry white fly may be seen in numbers on the backs of the leaves, but control measures are not usually needed. Red spider (which see) and the Comstock mealy bug (see under CATALPA) may be prevalent. The

small lightning leaf hopper having dark wings with a whitish covering, is responsible for masses of white woolly matter which, dropping from the young insects, make the trees unsightly; but there is no satisfactory control. Propagated by seeds, cuttings, layers and grafting.

PRINCIPAL SPECIES

M. alba (White Mulberry) is a Chinese tree to 50 ft., of rounded form with shining light green leaves variously lobed. It bears in abundance very sweet white, pinkish or purple fruit. Seedlings showing a good deal of variation are often found along the roadside. Var. *tatarica* (Russian Mulberry) is a smaller and very hardy form, with dark red or sometimes white fruit. There are some other forms planted chiefly for ornamental purposes; of which *pendula,* with drooping branches; *pyramidalis,* of narrow upright habit; and *skeletoniana,* with deeply divided leaves, are the most outstanding.

nigra (Black Mulberry) is an Asiatic tree to 30 ft., with a short trunk and broad round head. It has large, rough, dull green leaves tapering into a point and usually not lobed. It bears large dark colored fruits and is not entirely hardy N.

rubra (Red Mulberry) is a native tree growing to 60 ft. or more, with large variable leaves which turn bright yellow in fall. It has dark purple fruit.

acidosa, also from Asia, is usually a large shrub with large leaves coarsely toothed and often variously lobed. It bears palatable dark red juicy fruits.

multicaulis, with very large rough and coarsely toothed leaves of dull green, seldom lobed, bears very sweet black fruits. It was introduced into this country from China, with the idea of fostering the silk-raising industry here.

The word Mulberry has been used in connection with other plants. French-mulberry is *Callicarpa americana.* Indian-mulberry is *Morinda citrifolia.* Paper-mulberry is Broussonetia. *Rubus odoratus,* the Flowering Raspberry, is sometimes improperly called Mulberry.

MULBERRY FAMILY. Common name of the Moraceae (which see), a family of plants of some horticultural and great economic importance, including the fig, the rubber-tree, and others.

MULCH. Originally, this meant merely an application of manure or other loose

GLASS WOOL, A NEW KIND OF MULCHING MATERIAL
Right, above, a new roll of the cottonlike mat; below, as applied on bed or border. Left, as used
to protect small evergreens; tie in place with soft cord.

material such as straw or leaves, spread thickly on the surface of the ground around newly planted trees and other plants to protect the roots from the drying effects of wind and sun. A further meaning is a layer of such material applied in winter or in late fall to keep frozen soil frozen and thereby protect plants from being lifted out of the ground by the "heaving" action of the soil in alternately expanding and contracting with changes in temperature. Similarly, winter mulches may be used to protect established plants against especially severe and deep freezing, or to keep a piece of ground frost-free so that bulbs, shrubs or trees can be planted after the close of the normal planting season.

Modern tillage practices have still further extended the meaning of summer mulch to include a loose layer of surface soil maintained by means of cultivators, "weeders," hand hoes, rakes and various wheelhoe attachments, and which, by breaking up the natural capillary action in soil, checks evaporation of moisture from the surface. (Such cultivation also, of course, serves to keep down weeds.) The advisability of this now almost universal practice is occasionally questioned by some scientists who claim that stirring the surface brings up moist soil from below and thereby increases instead of reduces the loss of water from the soil. Unquestionably in field culture when deep stirring is done with power cul-

tivators, this may be the case; but in gardens where the raking, hoeing, or cultivating (done, it is to be hoped, weekly or certainly after every rain) turns up probably less than an inch of surface soil, it is not true. At any rate, there is abundant experimental evidence that where so-called "dust mulches" are maintained, better crops are grown.

However, in vegetable and flower gardens a dust mulch is less desirable than one of such loose, organic material as buckwheat hulls, or other cereal chaff, shredded corn stover, finely chopped straw, lawn clippings (if not permitted to mat down and heat), or granulated peat moss, provided these are readily available and not too expensive. For not only do they similarly check evaporation, but also when dug or cultivated in they in time decay and thus increase the soil's content of humus (which see). Coarse materials, such as whole corn and other stalks, straw, and marsh or salt hay are especially suitable for mulching fruit trees, grape-vines, berry bushes and ornamental shrubbery. Clean straw spread between strawberry rows performs the additional function of keeping the ripening berries off the ground, clean and less liable to mildew or mold.

Nature may be encouraged to provide a winter mulch by spreading brush over the areas to be protected; the winds will blow leaves among the twigs which will hold them in place and also prevent them from becoming matted down and sodden. Otherwise winter mulches must be applied with caution and not until the ground has frozen. Sometimes, as in the strawberry bed, this is important mainly because it avoids running a loaded wheelbarrow (or wagon) down the rows until the frozen crust is thick enough to support it. In the case of hardy bulbs, the delay in mulching keeps mice from building nests in the material, burrowing in the soft ground beneath it and eating the bulbs. By the time the mulch is applied the creatures will have gone elsewhere. See PROTECTION OF PLANTS.

Mulches around fruit trees, bushes and vines may be removed in early spring or (if not too coarse) turned under according to the preference of the gardener and the soil's need of humus. Around some plants they may be left from year to year, and in the case of rhododendrons and related sorts they always should be. Coarse mulches on strawberry beds must be removed from off the plants either to the spaces between the rows or altogether as soon as grass in the neighborhood begins to show green. This rule also applies to hardy bulbs and perennials. Fine materials such as buckwheat hulls or the finer residue from well-rotted manure may be allowed to remain to be gradually incorporated with the soil by cultivation. It is well to remove mulches gradually, a little at a time over two weeks or more, so as to harden the new spring growth without exposing it to possible damage by late frosts.

With the growing realization of the importance and value of mulches (and with the reduced supply of stable litter and rough manure), new materials are constantly being sought, discovered or devised, sometimes with considerable success. Wherever obtainable at reasonable cost, salt marsh hay is highly thought of, mainly because it does not contain grass and weed seeds, but also because it is clean, does not mat down and become soggy, and can be gathered up in the spring and used year after year—as it regularly is on bulb fields in this country and abroad. Cranberry tops, trimmed from the bogs each fall, are being baled and marketed from the Mass. cranberry growing region. The tough, tangled stems are wiry and springy, letting light and air penetrate to the plants covered and making a very desirable and lasting mulch for perennials.

One of the newest offerings is glass wool, spun from glass marbles into long mats or strips looking very like absorbent cotton and marketed in bulky, but light, rolls. Originally planned as insulating material for houses, this "artificial snow" has been tested extensively at the N. Y. State Experiment Station and found quite practical for certain conditions if carefully used. Letting air, light, and moisture through, and remaining fluffy even under heavy snowfall, it is excellent for alpine plants and perennials that resent being "smothered." It can also be wrapped around valuable small evergreens or other specimens of questionable hardiness. It can be rolled up again in spring and made to last for several years. However, it should be handled with care and, preferably, with gloves, to lessen the chance of minute slivers of the glass filaments getting into the skin. While its final place in gardening probably has not been determined, it is well worth experimenting with.

PAPER-MULCHING. Within recent years mulching with paper, which had its inception in pineapple plantations of Hawaii, has become popular among amateur gardeners. The paper, especially made for the purpose, is an impervious, black, tough material which is spread upon the ground, either between or actually upon the rows. In the former case, the plants usually grow from seed sown before the paper is put in place; in the latter case they are transplanted from flats, flower pots or nursery beds and placed in the soil at desired intervals through holes cut in the paper. The paper is held down either by soil piled along the edges, or by wires or laths, or both stretched across it and fastened to firmly driven pegs or metal pins. Besides preventing loss of water by evaporation, such a mulch prevents the growth of weeds, and, being black, it tends to raise the temperature of the soil by absorbing heat from the sun, thus hastening plant development and maturity, increasing the size of the plants, improving the quality of the edible parts, and keeping clean of such crops as sprawl upon the ground.

MULLEIN. The common name for Verbascum, a genus of tall, usually biennial herbs of the Figwort Family having more or less woolly or downy foliage, and purple, red, or yellow flowers. Mulleins grow readily in any warm dry soil, and are familiar field and roadside weeds in the U. S. Nearly all the species thrive in full sunlight, one exception being *V. phoeniceum,* which prefers partial shade whether in the border or in the greenhouse. They are increased by seed, cuttings and division and hybridize readily with the genus Celsia, the result being many new color forms—pink, lilac, rose, or violet.

V. thapsus (Common Mullein), an Old-World plant, widely naturalized in N. America, has a densely woolly rosette of foliage and yellow flowers on stalks up to 6 ft. high. When grouped in the wild garden as a background, it creates a striking effect. *V. chaixi,* to 3 ft. with white-woolly leaves and yellow flowers with purple stamens, is an excellent border plant. *V. olympicum,* to 5 ft. with white-downy foliage and bright yellow flowers in tall racemes, is a stately species from Greece. *V. blattaria* (Moth Mullein), 3 to 6 ft. tall, with smooth leaves and yellow flowers with lilac throat, is also an Old-World plant often found as an escape from old gardens.

V. nigrum to 3 ft. has leaves smooth above, downy beneath, and densely clustered, small yellow flowers with lilac throat and woolly purple stamens. *V. phoeniceum* (Purple Mullein) to 5 ft. with leaves smooth above, soft-hairy beneath, and red or purple flowers with prominent purple stamens, is a parent of nearly all the pastel-colored hybrids. Some of the named hybrids are Miss Wilmott, which has 5-ft. spikes of pure white flowers, and *libani* with yellow flowers.

Cretan-mullein is *Celsia cretica;* Rosette-mullein is the genus Ramonda.

MULLEIN-PINK. A common name for *Lychnis coronaria,* also called Rose Campion, a woolly biennial with brilliant crimson flowers.

MUNDI-ROOT (*Chlorocodon whitei*). A twining African vine belonging to the Milkweed Family. It may be grown under glass, or outdoors in the far South. It has long oval leaves and panicles of purplish and white flowers about an inch across. Propagated by cuttings.

MURIATE OF POTASH. This chemical compound, also called potassium chloride, is a convenient commercial fertilizer for soil known to lack potash. While commercial grades differ in quality, the average potassium content is from about 35 to 50 per cent, which is equivalent to 44 to 60 per cent of potash. It is particularly beneficial to such plants as celery and potatoes. It is about as soluble as common salt, which it resembles, but it promptly combines with other substances in the soil and is not leached away by drainage water as is nitrogen. In other words, it remains until taken up by plants. When used alone, it should be applied not more than 3 lbs. to 100 square feet, and it is better to make several small applications at intervals than one large one.

See also POTASH ; FERTILIZER.

MUSA (meu'-zah). A genus of tropical tree-like herbs commonly known as Banana. The familiar edible yellow fruit is produced by a variety (*sapientum*) of the species *M. paradisiaca,* which is grown commercially in huge plantations in tropical America. The dwarf Chinese banana (*M. cavendishi*) is also grown for fruit and to a considerable extent for ornament in Fla. and Calif. where it is planted on the margins of lakes or on the banks of streams. It is easily handled in the home hothouse. Banana plants are usually included in botanical garden greenhouse collections, but most of them quickly outgrow the accommodations of small home greenhouses even if successfully started there. See BANANA.

MUSACEAE (meu-zay'-see-ee). The Banana Family, a group of stout tropical herbs often becoming woody and of great stature. The leaves are large and paddle-shaped; the flowers are borne in the axils of large bracts grouped in loose clusters. A few members are striking ornamentals; fibre is derived from a few, and two species yield the bananas of commerce. Genera usually cultivated are Musa (banana), Ravenala (travelers-tree), Strelitzia (bird-of-paradise) and Heliconia.

MUSCARI (mus-kay'-ry). A genus of small bulbous plants of the Lily Family, commonly known as Grape-hyacinths. Their charming tiny blue or white bell-shaped flowers in spike-like racemes appear very early in the spring. Grape-hyacinths should be planted in drifts in the border or rock garden or among shrubs, preferably in light loam, though they grow readily under almost any good garden conditions. They are increased by seeds or offsets and multiply naturally very rapidly.

M. botryoides, with its dark blue bead-like flowers, is well known in old gardens and has become naturalized in orchards and other grassy places in many sections. Its var. *album* has white, and its var. *caeruleum* blue flowers, while the named var. Heavenly Blue is much larger than the type and is exceedingly charming planted in combination with some of the species tulips, such as the pink and white *T. clusiana* or the primrose yellow *T. sylvestris.* Another species, *M. comosum,* is interesting because of the peculiar flowers of its variety *monstrosum,* which are sterile and cut into fringe-like shreds.

MUSHROOM. Properly speaking, this refers to any large, fleshy fungous growth whether edible, inedible or poisonous. However, it is often limited to those kinds which have conspicuous, umbrella-like "caps," which are also correctly called toadstools, though this term is popularly applied to poisonous or supposedly poisonous sorts as distinguished from edible mushrooms. Among the edible fungi that can loosely be called mushrooms but that do not form caps and therefore are not "toadstools" are chantrelles, puff-balls, morels, clavarias, truffles, and pore-, horse- and liver-fungi. As explained in the article on Fungus, all these varying forms are actually the spore-containing fruiting bodies of fungi whose growing parts are masses of threadlike tissue in the soil. The spores are small and dustlike when ripe—as may be seen by breaking open an old, brown puffball.

Though some species may be "cultivated" by dusting their spores or transplanting clumps (with more or less attached earth) to supposedly favorable spots in the garden, only the common mushroom (*Agaricus campestris*) has so far become a real "crop plant." It is extensively grown for market in caves, abandoned mines and quarries, cellars and special mushroom houses and since the introduction of special varieties and strains it has become an important commercial product.

The conditions under which it is so produced (mainly in beds or on shelves filled with manure compost) make its culture undesirable in residence cellars. It can be grown in barns and other outbuilding basements, if favorable conditions can be maintained. But in a beginner's hands the probability of failure in such places is so great and a family's needs are relatively so small, that the market had better be relied upon—except during the "natural" season when the lawn and other favorable

FOR EARLY SPRING BLOOM
Muscari, the Grape-hyacinth, opens its neat, compact spikes of blue flowers along with the squills, hoop-petticoat daffodils, and chionodoxas.

parts of the home grounds may produce enough to justify gathering them. Of course this should not be done indiscriminately or without assurance that the wild kinds are edible. "When in doubt, discard it," is an excellent first rule for mushroom gatherers.

Though mushrooms often fail in lawns, the cost of planting them there is so slight that every home gardener can afford to attempt to establish them there. All that is necessary is to plant 2 in. cubes of "mushroom spawn" or, preferably, bits of "mushroom cultures" (both obtainable from seedsmen) beneath the sod in spring and—trust to luck! When soil, moisture and seasonal conditions are favorable, plenty of mushrooms should appear during the fall for many years. Applications of horse, cow, or sheep manure will help increase both the number and the size of the "caps" and the "buttons" as the young mushrooms are called. Organic fertilizers, such as dried blood, cottonseed and bonemeal, also help.

MUSHROOM ROOT ROT. A common disease of fruit and forest trees caused by a honey colored mushroom. See ARMILLARIA ROOT ROT.

MUSK MALLOW. Common name for two plants of the Mallow Family. One is

Malva moschata, a true mallow (which see); the other is *Hibiscus abelmoschus,* one of the related Rose-mallows from which the large-flowered garden forms have developed.

MUSKMELON. Common name for the netted or nutmeg types and the Cassabas or winter melons, all originating from the species *Cucumis melo.* Compare CANTALOUPE. See CUCUMIS; MELON.

MUSK-PLANT. Common name for *Mimulus moschatus,* a perennial herb with a musky odor and pale yellow brown-dotted flowers.

MUSQUASH-ROOT. Common name for *Cicuta maculata,* a tall species of Water-hemlock (which see) sometimes grown in bog and wild gardens for striking effects. Its roots are poisonous.

MUSTARD. Various species and varieties of the genus Brassica. They are all

half-hardy annual herbs whose leaves are used for salads and pot-herbs; whose seeds —whole or ground, alone or mixed with other spices—are used to flavor foods and as a condiment; and from whose seeds is obtained "colza" or oil of mustard, a counter-irritant. Other species are pestiferous weeds, especially in grain fields.

The most commonly grown garden mustard in this country is *B. juncea,* Leaf or Chinese Mustard, especially its var. *crispifolia,* referred to as Southern Curled. Another type includes three oriental species often called Chinese Cabbages, namely *B. chinensis* (Pak-choi), *B. parachinensis* (False Pak-choi) and *B. pekinensis* (Petsai or Celery Cabbage).

For salad and pot-herb use sow seed of any of the mustards thinly, outdoors in rows 12 in. apart (a) in earliest spring and at weekly intervals until a month before hot weather; and (b) in the fall until six weeks before winter. For a winter supply, sow from November until March in coldframes or cool greenhouses. Gather by shearing the plants while young and tender—for salad when they are 4 in. high and for greens when 6 in. tall. If not sheared too closely, a planting will give two or three cuttings. Hot weather makes the leaves too strong for most tastes, espe-

EDIBLE

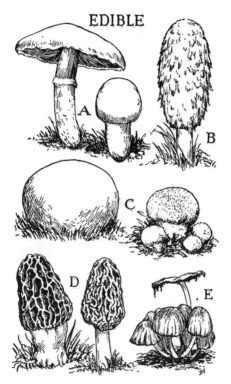

POISONOUS

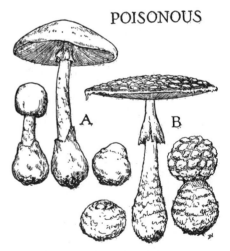

MUSHROOMS YOU SHOULD KNOW—I
Five common kinds all wholesome and delicious. A. The common pink-gilled Meadow Mushroom; note smooth, tapering base. B. The Shaggy Mane, with its scalpy cape. C. Puffballs, a large mature one and a clump of little ones. D. The unmistakable Morel. E. Inky Caps, delicate and short-lived. Contrast all these with the two shown in the next illustration.

MUSHROOMS YOU SHOULD KNOW—II
Safety first! When you see these—or others like them—leave them alone. A. The ghostly Destroying Angel (Amanita phalloides). B. The brilliant orange-colored Fly Amanita (A. muscaria). Note in both the swollen, cupped base and the fringe torn from it as the stem grows. Both these characters mark poisonous mushrooms **always.**

cially for salad. (See BRASSICA; GREENS, EDIBLE; POTHERBS; SALADS.) The mustard whose seeds are used as a condiment is chiefly *Brassica nigra*.

Hedge-mustard is a catalog name for a plant of a related genus, Erysimum, or Blister-cress, especially *E. pulchellum*.

MUTISIA (meu-tish'-i-ah). Interesting tendril climbers from S. America, belonging to the Daisy Family. They may be grown in greenhouses, or outdoors in the warmest parts of the country. They grow best in a sandy loam with leafmold added, and are propagated by cuttings. *M. clematis*, the best known, grows to 20 ft. or more, with pinnate leaves and 2 in. heads of red flowers. *M. illicifolia* grows to 15 ft. and has holly-like leaves and heads of white or rose flowers. *M. decurrens* grows to 12 ft. and has orange-scarlet flowers.

MYCELIUM (my-see'-li-um). The fundamental structure or vegetative part of a fungus, consisting of delicate, branched tubular or filamentous threads, called *hyphae*. See FUNGUS.

MYCORRHIZAL (my-kor-y'-zal) ASSOCIATION. A term used to describe the association of a fungus with a higher plant in which it acts not as a parasite, but as a partner to their mutual benefit. The mycelium, or underground vegetative part of the fungus, envelops the roots of the other plant and functions like root hairs, absorbing from the soil and giving to the plant substances necessary for the latter's nutrition. This relationship has long been known in connection with some of the tropical orchids, which cannot live without their fungus partners, unless certain chemicals are supplied to them artificially by the grower. Also many plants of the Heath Family, as rhododendron, kalmia, and *Epigaea repens* (Mayflower) and many wild flowers are greatly dependent on it. It has also been discovered that many of our forest trees cannot grow without proper mycorrhizal association. A recent experiment with white pine seedlings grown under similar conditions in their native and in sterilized soil showed that those in soil without the right fungi, dependent on their absorbing root-tips, grew yellow and spindling; those aided by the presence of a fungus were strong and healthy, with much larger and more vigorous root systems covered with celium.

The study of mycorrhizal association is in its infancy, but may in time revolutionize our ideas of forestry and many of our fertilizing practices.

MYOSOTIS (my-oh-soh'-tis). A genus of annual, biennial or perennial, blue, white, or pink-flowered herbs of the Borage Family, well known everywhere as Forget-me-not, and preferring cool locations, partial shade and plenty of moisture in the soil. (See illustration, Plate 19.)

While the dwarf varieties are among the most delightful of all edging plants bearing their bright small flowers early in the season, others are admirable for waterside planting or for naturalizing in the wild garden. In combination with pansies or English daisies they make an effective display. They also are good for the rock garden or as a ground-cover in the rose garden. The tall varieties, growing to 18 in., will spread and trail over a large area. Winter protection of all species is desirable.

If seed is sown early, blossoms may be produced the same year, though generally flowers are borne only the second year, appearing from early spring until late August. The foliage, which is rather small and smooth and of a clear light green, accentuates the delicate beauty of the flowers. The annual species will self-sow.

Branches of Myosotis cut and placed in water will continue blooming for a long time, and often will develop roots so they can be potted and grown on. Root clumps of the perennial kind can be divided.

Of the dozen or more species the following are of special interest:

M. sylvatica. Annual or biennial, growing from 8 in. to 2 ft., flowers, with yellow center, varying from blue to white or pink. There are many forms including plants often listed as *M. alpestris, M. dissitiflora, M. lithospermifolia* and *M. robusta grandiflora*.

M. arvensis, of similar habit, has blue or white flowers. *M. azorica* has blue flowers with whitish center, *M. laxa* with yellow-centers, and *M. scorpioides* (formerly *M. palustris*) with white, pink, or yellow centers. The last named 3 are perennials. *M. scorpioides* var. *semperflorens* is dwarf.

MYRICA (mi-ry'-kah). Wax-myrtle, Bayberry, Sweet Gale. Evergreen and deciduous shrubs or small trees, widely distributed in the temperate and warmer regions of both hemispheres. They are grown for their attractive aromatic foliage and decorative fruits. Wax is obtained from the fruit of some species, and the fruit of others is edible. They need a lime-free soil and most appreciate peat or leaf-mold, but *M. caroliniensis* and *M. californica* of the East and West coast regions, respectively, grow well in sandy sterile soil. Only one or two are hardy North. Propagated by seeds, layers and suckers.

PRINCIPAL SPECIES

M. caroliniensis (Bayberry) grows to 8 ft. and is found from Nova Scotia to Fla. It has dull green almost evergreen leaves, and in winter is conspicuous with its grayish-white fruits. It thrives in poor soil.

cerifera (Wax-myrtle) is a large evergreen shrub or small tree, native from N. J. to Fla. It does best in moist peaty soil and has small gray waxy fruits.

gale (Sweet Gale) is a deciduous shrub to 5 ft., hardy N. It suckers freely and also prefers a moist peaty soil. The yellowish fruit is borne in catkins.

californica (California Bayberry) is a large evergreen shrub or slender tree, with reddish-purple fruit. It will grow in poor soil but is not hardy in a cold climate.

rubra is an evergreen shrub from Asia with reddish-purple edible fruit from which a good drink is extracted.

MYRICARIA (mir-i-kay'-ri-ah). A genus of deciduous woody shrubs of Europe and Asia related to the Tamarisk and called False-tamarisk, which see.

MYRIOCEPHALUS (mir-i-oh-sef'-ah-lus). A genus of Australian herbs with tubular yellow flowers in dense heads surrounded by conspicuous bracts. One species, *M. stuarti* (sometimes listed as *Polycalymma stuarti*) a 2 ft. annual, is sometimes grown for winter bouquets. See EVERLASTINGS.

MYRIOPHYLLUM (mi-ri-oh-fil'-um). A genus of aquatic herbs of the Water Milfoil Family, several species of which are in common use in aquaria and pools. Their long, graceful stems are densely covered with the finely dissected leaves which make this group the most feathery of all the aquatics.

M. proserpinacoides, the Parrots Feather or Water Feather, is a favorite, not for its submerged foliage, but for the delicate green masses of foliage produced *above* the water. Potted in rich soil and submerged at the edge of the pool or in the aquarium, with adequate warmth and light, a plant quickly produces myriads of trailing stems, encircled with whorls or feathery leaves. It is particularly useful, planted in this fashion, for relieving the austere lines of the formal pool or the fountain basin. In the house, planted in a watertight hanging basket, it is as charming in effect as any fern.

See also AQUARIUM.

MYROBALAN (mi-rob'-ah-lan). Common name for *Phyllanthus emblica,* also known as Emblic; and for *Terminalia catappa,* the Tropical- or Indian-almond, both being aquatic trees. Myrobalan Plum is a common name for *Prunus cerasifera,* a slender small tree much used in England as a hedge-plant, but more in this country as a stock on which to bud plums and peaches for growing on heavy soils. It has varieties of weeping form and with variously colored leaves including var. *pissardi,* popular and frequently planted as the ornamental purple-leaved plum.

MYRRH. The common name for the perennial herb *Myrrhis odorata,* known in Europe as Sweet Cicely. A member of the Parsley Family, it has finely cut leaves and bears small white flowers in umbels. Formerly much esteemed as a pot herb or for salad, it is now occasionally grown in the border for its fragrant white flowers. It is easily propagated by seed or division.

MYRTACEAE (mur-tay'-see-ee). The Myrtle Family, an important distinctive group of tropical aromatic trees and shrubs with thick evergreen leaves. A number are grown as avenue trees in warm regions and many others yield economic products such as gums, oils, cloves, edible fruits and timber as well as many ornamental subjects. Genera most commonly cultivated are Myrtus (myrtle), Melaleuca, Eugenia, Pimenta, Rhodomyrtus, Feijoa, Psidium, Metrosideros, Leptospermum, Calothamnus, Tristania, Eucalyptus and Callistemon.

MYRTLE. Common name for Myrtus, a genus of attractive evergreen shrubs, found mostly in subtropical regions. They are very ornamental for outdoor planting in the milder parts of the country, and are often grown as pot plants in the N., thriving in well-drained loamy soil with leaf-mold added. Propagated by cuttings of half-ripened shoots under glass, and by layers.

PRINCIPAL SPECIES

M. communis is the Myrtle of the ancients who used it in different forms on

festive occasions. Native in the Mediterranean region, it is a handsome bushy evergreen to 10 ft., with glossy dark green
scented leaves and fragrant white flowers
followed by blue-black berries. It makes
a good hedge or screen plant in mild regions, and a good pot or tub plant for
summer porch or terrace decoration in the
N. There are a variegated leaved form
and several named varieties which differ
chiefly in the size and shape of the leaves.

ugni (Chilean Guava) is a handsome
evergreen shrub with leathery leaves, rose-
tinted flowers and a purple edible berry.

The word Myrtle is applied to several
other plants. Crape-myrtle is Lagerstroemia; Downy-myrtle is *Rhodomyrtus tomentosa;* Gum-myrtle is Angophora; Running-myrtle is *Vinca minor;* Sand-myrtle
is Leiophyllum and Wax-myrtle is *Myrica
cerifera,* all of which see.

MYSTERY-LILY. A common name
for the useful and attractive bulbous garden
plant, *Lycoris squamigera* (which see),
applied presumably because of its habit of
sending up a naked flower stalk in midsummer, some time after the lush spring
foliage has ripened, died and disappeared.

N

NAEGELIA (nay-jee'-li-ah). A genus of tropical American herbs of the Gesneria Family with soft, heart-shaped leaves and brilliant tubular flowers 1½ in. long in clusters. In the N. the plants, which grow about 20 in. tall, are raised in a warm greenhouse, the rootstocks being started into growth in boxes, lightly covered with soil, and later potted up in 5- or 6-in. pots filled with rich porous soil, with plenty of drainage material at the bottom. After blooming, the rhizomes should be stored under the benches in the greenhouse and given water occasionally. They are increased by runners or offsets. *N. zebrina* with soft-hairy leaves veined with purplered has spotted red and yellow flowers. *N. cinnabarina* has leaves covered with red or purple hairs and drooping cinnabar-red flowers spotted with white.

NAILWORT. A common name for the genus Paronychia, small annual and perennial herbs with tiny flowers.

NAKED-LADY. A local name in the Middle W. for the summer-blooming bulbous herb, *Lycoris squamigera,* which see.

NANDINA (nan-dy'-nah) *domestica.* A beautiful evergreen shrub, native of China and Japan, belonging to the Barberry Family. Though generally considered tender, it can stand some frost and near New York plants have survived below-zero temperatures and sent up new tops in spring. A light loamy soil, with plenty of leafmold, in a rather moist place suits it well. It is of rather slow growth with reed-like stems to 8 ft. The divided leaves are tinted pink when young, then in winter change from green to red. The large terminal clusters of white flowers are followed by bright red berries. Propagated by seeds or cuttings.

NANNY-BERRY, or Sheep-berry. Common names for *Viburnum lentago,* a tall bush with white flowers and edible black berries, native from N. Canada to Miss.

NAPHTHALENE. The active constituent of moth balls and flakes used to repel clothes moths and other household insects. It is also used in fumigating greenhouses for mites and thrips under certain conditions. For this purpose 1½ oz. for each 1000 cu. ft. of enclosed space are evaporated over slow steady heat under conditions of high humidity. Moth balls are sometimes inserted in the soil of pot plants as an aid in the control of cyclamen mite. Worked lightly into the soil around the crowns of plants naphtalene flakes are used as a preventive for crown rot (which see) in beds where this disease has been prevalent. They are also used to treat gladiolus corms for thrips (which see). Naphthalene is also employed in various proprietary forms, alone or combined with nicotine and other substances, for the control of various soil-infesting insects.

See also FUMIGATION.

NAPTHALENEACETIC ACID. An odorless white crystaline powder, insoluble in water, but freely soluble in alcohol and ether, this is one of the most powerful of the hormone-activating or hormone-like substance group. An increasing number of uses for it are constantly being discovered. It is good for forming roots on cuttings of many plant species. Sprays containing this material (1 part in 100,000 parts of water) are effective in the prevention of premature apple, peach, and avocado drop. Potatoes have been kept in a dormant condition for considerable time after being subject to treatment. Fruit trees, especially peaches, can be sprayed to retard the development of fruit buds until danger from late spring frosts has passed. Fruits and berries have with this chemical been made to set fruits without the need of pollination; this causes the fruits or berries to mature without seeds but with longer keeping qualities. This phenomenon (called by scientists *parthenocarpy*) offers interesting possibilities for growers of small fruits, tomatoes, etc., and also of small berried plants such as holly for ornamental purposes.

NARCISSUS (nahr-sis'-us). (See illustrations, Plates 5, 6, and 50.) A genus of chiefly spring-flowering bulbous plants, the hardy forms being commonly called Daffodils and sometimes Jonquils though that is correctly the name of a single species. They are universal favorites in N. temperate gardens and also popular subjects for indoor and greenhouse culture as well; tender kinds with smaller flowers in clusters are easily bloomed in bowls of pebbles

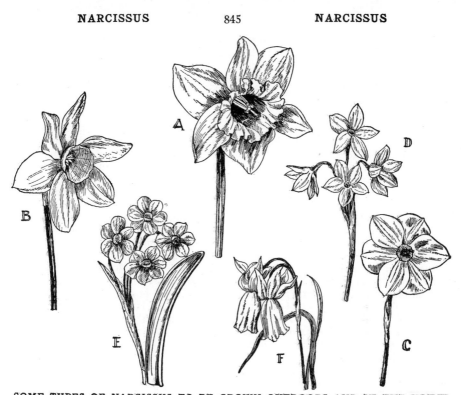

SOME TYPES OF NARCISSUS TO BE GROWN OUTDOORS AND IN THE HOUSE

A. The Trumpet Narcissus, commonly known as the Daffodil. B. One of the Barri hybrids, whose cup is one-third the length of the petals. C. Poets Narcissus, fragrant and hardy, marked by a short, red-rimmed crown. D. The tender Paper-white Narcissus, easily grown indoors in water, sand or soil. E. The true Jonquil, with small, brilliant yellow, sweet-smelling, clustered flowers and hollow, rush-like leaves. F. One of the diminutive Cyclamineus hybrids, with narrow, grooved leaves, drooping flowers, and petals sharply reflexed.

or peat moss in the living room. Members of the Amaryllis Family, narcissi are characterized by flowers of white, yellow, or orange with 6 flaring perianth-segments, that surround a central tube of varying lengths, known as the trumpet, cup, corona, or crown. The leaves, which are generally smooth and linear, appear with the flowers.

NARCISSUS TERMS AND TYPES. The greatest development of the narcissus has taken place in England and Ireland where professional gardeners and serious-minded amateurs have taken the original species and early hybrids, and, with ever-progressive cross-fertilization, developed many charming new forms in endless variety, showing improvement in size, form, color and flowering date. Similar work is being done by some of the expert bulb growers of Holland; and, during the last decade, the stimulation of narcissus growing in U. S. by plant quarantines that excluded foreign stocks, has brought about some progress in the same direction here.

In the early stages of narcissus development, botanists tried to classify the new types in accordance with wild species which they most nearly resembled; then in some cases, they named for the introducer some particular form (such as *Barri* or *Leedsi*) that had been developed by him. But, as hybridizing continued, the differences between the forms narrowed until the classification, by other than experts, became almost hopeless. Hence the clearest guide to narcissus identification today is found in the generally accepted terms used by bulb dealers in their catalogs. In most cases, these describe the form of the flower rather than the supposed parentage.

In this country confusion also exists because the generally accepted terms "narcissus", "daffodil" and "jonquil" are not clearly understood or differentiated. Narcissus, though actually the name of the entire genus, in this country usually applies to the sweet-scented usually tender cluster types of the Polyanthus classification.

Daffodil is the common name by which the trumpet varieties are usually known, but many people use it loosely for all of the hardy garden narcissi in which the yellow color predominates. Jonquil is a true classification (*N. jonquilla*) of the hardy Narcissus distinguished by nearly round, rush-like leaves and small, deep-yellow, sweet-scented flowers appearing in clusters on the stem. However, in some parts of the country, all the hardy trumpet narcissi are erroneously called jonquils.

CULTURE OF HARDY NARCISSI

Narcissi are not desirable subjects for formal plantings; they show off to best advantage when they give the impression of not having been planned or planted. Their color and gracefulness permit many charming effects at a season when little else is in bloom in the garden. For small gardens small group plantings of separate varieties are very effective. The Poets Narcissus is especially good among other perennials, accompanying the very earliest of them in flower.

USES AND SITES. Narcissi are largely employed to produce naturalized effects. For this purpose the older short-cup varieties and the smaller trumpet kinds are preferable to the newer more refined hybrids, which are less likely to continue in flowering condition over a period of years. Mass plantings in grassy slopes, meadows and woodland borders or along the banks of streams give an annual array of flowers with little attention until the bulbs become so crowded that both number and size of flowers diminish. The bulbs can then be taken up, separated and replanted.

In common with most true bulbous plants, narcissi thrive best in water-bound areas; thus we find our N. Atlantic and N. W. states, together with Mich., the principal larger commercial sources of hardy narcissi, and our S. E. and Gulf States and S. Calif. leading in the production of the tender varieties. Garden plantings of these types in these same locations can be màintained to the best advantage. However, because the flower-buds of narcissi are safely incased within the bulbs when dormant, it is possible to make bulbs bloom in any region where approximately similar climatic conditions prevail. But it should be remembered that the mere flowering of these bulbs is quite a different thing from their successful maintenance in a flowering condition from season to season.

With the exception of the Polyanthus kinds all narcissi are hardy, which means that they can be grown outdoors in the temperate zone though some winter covering is advocated in exposed places. It may consist of leaves, straw or salt hay, but it should be removed in the early spring when the bulbs come through the ground; it is not intended to keep the frost from penetrating down to the bulbs but to prevent the alternate quick freezing and thawing which occurs during some winters.

PLANTING. For new plantings, the bulbs, which are available from Semptember on through the fall months, should be planted as soon as possible. Early planting is an advantage in any location, and almost a necessity in the more N. States, as the bulbs should be given an opportunity of making their long roots before the cold weather sets in. A slightly sheltered spot without too much sun is best. Prepare the soil by digging deeply and enriching with well-rotted manure or bonemeal, but do not let any manure touch the bulbs. Place the bulbs upright and cover them with 3 in. or more of soil. They can be spaced in accordance with the arrangement desired and the length of time they are to remain in the same spot, for under good conditions they multiply rapidly.

It is important to keep the foliage in a green condition as long as possible, for it is between the flowering period and the dying of the foliage that the flower buds for the following season are made. If the bulbs are to be lifted, it should be done as soon as the foliage has entirely withered. The curing and storing of narcissus bulbs involves some risk and as there is nothing to be gained by keeping them out of the ground, digging and replanting should be carried on simultaneously. As the bulbs are lifted, those that fall apart readily should be separated, but no attempt should be made to pull apart those that adhere at the base. Care must be taken to prevent the sun from shining directly on the bulbs while harvesting is in progress, as this will result in scalded spots that may start decay. Care should also be taken to prevent bruising.

Where dormant storing is unavoidable, it can best be done in shallow wooden trays with an air space at the bottom. They should be placed away from moisture and where there is an abundance of air. A shed with low eaves but no sides is ideal. In the early stages of drying, the bulbs should be stirred frequently.

Growing Narcissus Indoors

The varieties of the tender Polyanthus or Cluster Narcissus (*N. tazetta*) are the most readily flowered indoors. The most popular variety is the pure white Paperwhite or *grandiflora;* Soleil d'Or, the pure yellow variety, ranks next in popularity, while the combination cream and yellow kind (var. *orientalis*), commonly known as Chinese Sacred-lily, is also used extensively. There is a double form of this latter type called Double Roman Constantinople that is very fragrant but with stems hardly strong enough to support the heavy flowers.

Bulbs of these varieties are available from early fall through to midwinter and can be planted at any time during this period. Early plantings will produce flowers in late November, but the time required for flowering shortens as the season develops so that plantings made at Christmas time will flower in about three weeks. Successive plantings will therefore provide flowers over a long period.

Blooming Narcissi in Water. Growing these bulbs in water is a favorite way of flowering them, and is really all that is required. Any additional material simply serves as a root anchorage to prevent the plants from toppling over. Therefore a thin layer of gravel, stones, sand, peat moss or similar material should be placed in the bottom of the receptacle and the bulbs arranged on it in an upright position. They can be placed almost touching and the spaces around and between them filled in with the same material. Shell chips and colored stones are considered by some to have a decorative value; or, when sand or peat moss is used, grass seed, which grows readily, can be sown on top. Water is then added and the bulbs will start to grow at once. It is better, however, to keep them in a cool dark place until an abundance of root growth is evident. Small pieces of charcoal placed in the water will prevent it from souring, but the same effect can be obtained by changing it each week. In any event, additional water (at room temperature) should be added as fast as noticeable evaporation occurs. Placed in a light sunny window with a uniform temperature of about 60 degrees, the bulbs will come into flower within a few weeks. They must never be allowed to freeze.

The hardy types are more difficult to handle in the house or conservatory, but they can be successfully flowered indoors with a preliminary outdoor planting. The bulbs should be planted in receptacles with drainage holes (clay flower-pots are best) in good garden soil or peat moss. The pots should be plunged outdoors (that is, buried so their rims are below the surface) and covered with a foot or more of leaves, straw or sifted ashes to prevent the frost from penetrating and the soil from drying out. If this is done before the ground freezes, the bulbs should have developed a good root system by the first of the year (this can be determined by examining one pot). They are then ready to be brought into the house where the atmosphere should be humid and the temperature not above 60 deg. for the first 10 days. Thereafter it can gradually be raised to 70 deg. Strong light should not be allowed until the shoots turn green. Abundant water is required.

Enemies

Most species are affected with mosaic or gray disease (a virus trouble) which causes streaking of flowers and foliage and smaller and fewer bulbs. Roguing (which see) just before and during blooming is probably the best control measure. Basal rot, caused by a species of fusarium (a fungus) inhabiting the soil, begins at the root plate or base of the scales and spreads into the central portion of the bulb, the rotted tissue being purplish brown, dry and spongy. The large Trumpet Narcissus is principally affected, the Jonquil, Poetaz and Polyanthus types being highly resistant. This is principally a problem for commercial growers; there is little that gardeners can do about it. A reported control on bulb farms is the use of yellow oxide of mercury applied in the bulb rows at the rate of 30 lbs. per acre. The acidity of the soil may be a factor.

Two other related fungi (forms of botrytis, which see) cause diseases. One is fairly common; the other has only recently become important in some fields in the Pacific N. W. where is has completely destroyed the foliage but has not caused bulb rot. Leaf scorch appears as yellowish, reddish or brown areas at the tips of the leaves followed by reddish-brown raised spots; it kills the leaves several weeks early.

For the control of the above fungous diseases and a discussion of narcissus pests —nematodes, bulb mites, and the greater and lesser narcissus flies, see BULB ENEMIES under BULBS.

NARCISSUS CLASSES

In setting up the following classification of the genus, the commonly accepted separations used by bulb dealers have been followed alphabetically, with references made to original species only where they have a bearing on varieties in commerce today.

AJAX. Under this heading are listed all of the single large trumpet varieties belonging to or derived from the botanical species *N. pseudonarcissus*. This is a native of Europe, but the fine large trumpet varieties available today are really hybrids and several times as large. This is the group correctly referred to as Daffodils. The large trumpet varieties with white petals and a yellow trumpet are known as Bicolors. King Alfred is a splendid solid yellow Ajax, while Spring Glory is a typical Bicolor.

barri. An important classification including the varieties with short cups instead of trumpets where the cup is usually not more than *one-third* the length of the perianth segments. This is a hybrid form and the flowers are always solitary. Varieties of this group are especially recommended for naturalizing on account of their free-flowering qualities. In the newer hybrids red-edged cups are appearing and the novelty of this trait is being stressed. An old and typical variety of the Barri group is *conspicuus.*

BICOLOR. See AJAX.

biflorus. Believed to be a natural hybrid between *N. poeticus* and *N. tazetta,* it has pure white petals and a pale yellow cup. Largely seen in the S. States where it is commonly known as Twin Sisters.

bulbocodium. Popularly known as the Hooped or Petticoat Narcissus because of the shape of the corona. A dwarf, pretty species from N. Africa and S. Europe, it has a solitary bright yellow flower with thin, inconspicuous petals. There are several varieties. This is a charming subject for rock gardens but does not establish itself as freely as most other narcissus.

campernelli (Campernelle). See *odorus,* below.

cyclamineus. A charming dwarf species from Portugal with drooping orange-yellow cup or trumpet and lemon-yellow petals extremely reflexed, as on a cyclamen.

DOUBLES. Double varieties exist in most forms of narcissus and to a great extent are mutations. The common double yellow *telamonius plenus* or Double Von Sion of the Ajax classification is widely distributed in gardens over the E. part of the U. S., where it loses its true yellow color and double trumpet form. The double white "Gardenia Narcissus" (var. *albo pleno odorata*) is the double form of *N. poeticus.* It needs a location where moisture is available during the flowering period; otherwise the buds will wither up instead of opening.

incomparabilis. Another European species that has benefited largely by hybridizing; here again the development of red in the cup is being stressed. It includes those varieties with cups that are often three-quarters as long as the perianth segments. Sir Watkin is a typical variety and there are many double forms.

jonquilla (Jonquil). A species from S. Europe and Algeria with characteristic rush-like foliage and deep yellow, fragrant flowers borne several on a stem. There is a double form with the same characteristics. While it is perfectly hardy, it seems to do best in warmer climates and will thrive further S. than other hardy narcissi.

leedsi. This is a beautiful hybrid form usually with a milky white perianth and a short sulphur-yellow cup; but in some of the newer hybrids the cup is much longer and broader and sometimes beautifully frilled. Queen of the North is one of the typical older varieties.

odorus. Commonly known as Campernelle, this species is closely related to *N. jonquilla* and may be a hybrid. The habit of growth is the same and, like the Jonquil, it will thrive under subtropical conditions though perfectly hardy in the N. It usually bears from 2 to 6 deep golden-yellow, very fragrant flowers on a stalk. Newer horticultural varieties have longer and larger trumpets showing the influence of Ajax blood.

poetaz. This, a hybrid between *N. tazetta* group and *N. poeticus,* retains the multiple-flowering quality of the former to some extent but the individual flowers are larger. In hardiness and in flowering dates it is like poeticus.

poeticus. The well known Poets Narcissus. A native of S. Europe, it has pure white petals and a shallow, saucer-like cup with an orange or red rim. All of the early flowering forms—of which var. *ornatus* is typical—have solitary flowers. A late form called *recurvus* or Pheasants Eye has recurved petals and frequently bears two flowers to the stem. The Poeticus Narcissus is very free flowering and, like the Barri group, well adapted to naturalizing or for planting where the bulbs are to remain undisturbed for years.

POLYANTHUS. See *tazetta,* below.

pseudonarcissus. See AJAX.

tazetta. This is the Polyanthus or Cluster Narcissus; the wild species is native to S. Europe, the Orient and the Canary Isles. It produces umbels of from 4 to 20 small, star-shaped flowers with small, short cups. Being tender, it is not suited to N. gardens, but in the S. States, particularly N. Florida, large commercial cultures exist and here the whole group is an admirable outdoor subject. Unlike the hardy types, this class does not like a naturalized or neglected garden situation, so the bulbs can only be maintained in good flowering condition by yearly digging and replanting. The bulbs are mainly used for indoor and greenhouse flowering, as explained above under GROWING NARCISSUS INDOORS.

triandus. A beautiful clustered species from Spain and Portugal, the drooping flowers (1 to 6 on a stem) being pure white with the petals bent sharply backward. Both bulbs and flowers are small. The plants are not especially thrifty and

APHIDS ON NASTURTIUM

These common pests—black or brown—can—and should—be destroyed with a nicotine spray.

under American garden conditions need better than average care. There are several forms and many new horticultural varieties which maintain the same drooping, graceful appearance and odd shape of the original species.

NARROW-LEAVED SPLEEN-WORT. Common name for *Athyrium angustifolium,* a desirable species of fern for gardens, to be planted in woods soil.

NASTURTIUM (nas-tur'-shum). The garden name for the genus Tropaeolum, which includes climbing and dwarf herbs from S. America with showy red, orange or yellow, funnel-shaped flowers consisting of 5 separate petals, the sepals produced into a long spur containing nectar.

T. majus, the species most widely grown, is an annual with fleshy stems, shield-shaped leaves, and bright blossoms which are produced continuously throughout the summer. The flowers and foliage make pleasing cut-flower arrangements, especially in clear glass bowls.

Seed is sown in the open in the spring, or earlier in a hotbed or in pots or boxes in the house. The plants will bloom most prolifically if given a rather poor soil in a N. exposure.

Nasturtiums may suffer

AN IMPROVED DWARF NASTURTIUM

The flowers are double and the leaves characterized by a slight rolling at the edges. An attractive, free-flowering border plant when given occasional shade.

from a bacterial wilt common also on tomatoes, egg-plant, potatoes and peppers, so they should not be grown in soil where any of those plants have previously been attacked by wilt. Destroy diseased plants and sterilize the soil. See DISINFECTION.

An almost inevitable pest of this plant seems to be the black bean aphid, which infests the stems and undersides of the leaves, curling and distorting them. Spray or dust with a contact insecticide (which see) as soon as the first aphid is seen. Leaf miners may make serpentine tunnels in the leaves. Destroy infested leaves.

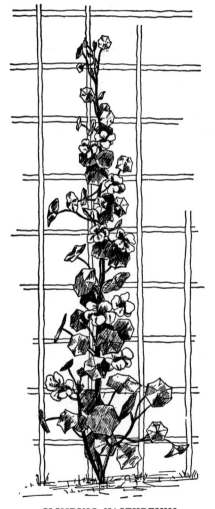

CLIMBING NASTURTIUM
Supporting a plant against a trellis will induce a nasturtium to reach considerable height during the summer.

While *T. majus* is naturally a climber, its var. *nanum* (Tom Thumb Nasturtium) is a dwarf hybrid which has proved excellent for edging a border. *T. minus* is a naturally dwarf form with smaller flowers and leaves than in *T. majus*.

Many horticultural varieties, showing most attractive colors, have been developed from both species, among them *atropurpureum,* deep crimson; *coccineum,* brilliant scarlet; and *hemisphericum* and *luteum,* yellow. Within the last few years a double-flowered nasturtium, called by the originator Golden Gleam, has created a great deal of interest. Even more recently, the doubling of flowers has been extended from the original yellow to many varieties in red and orange. The flowers, which are fragrant, are produced on plants throwing out only a few trailing branches. These new hybrids are as easily grown as the single nasturtium, but as some produce no seed they must be increased by cuttings.

Garden nasturtiums in England are known as Indian-cress, and often the seeds and leaves are pickled commercially and labeled with that name.

NATAL GRASS. Common name for *Tricholaena rosea,* also called Ruby Grass, a member of the Grass Family often grown in the S. either for forage or in garden border plantings. It is a perennial usually grown as an annual from seed, with leaves to 8 in. long, and shining, open racemose flower clusters either pink or reddish brown. See ORNAMENTAL GRASSES.

NATIONAL ASSOCIATION OF GARDENERS. See GARDENERS, NATIONAL ASSOCIATION OF.

NATIONAL PLANT, FLOWER AND FRUIT GUILD. This was organized in 1893 to distribute surpluses of flowers, fruits and vegetables to the poor and sick, and to institutions. It establishes gardens for children and adults on vacant city lots and in suburban areas and on the grounds of institutions. It also supplies nature material for study in schools.

The Guild, which is composed of branches and segregated members, was the first organization to tie garden clubs together nationally. Country branches collect material and conduct plant markets and turn over the surplus to city branches which distribute the produce where it is needed.

The active membership fee is $1, and donor, subscribing, patron, co-operative organization (for groups with the same aims), church-garden-club, and junior-guild memberships are available. The Executive Director is Mrs. Ida White Parker, 1192 Sixth Ave., New York City.

NATIVE. A term applied to a species, a genus, or even a family of plants, indicating its origin in a particular region. Do not confuse with "naturalized," i.e., introduced and "run wild" in a new place. A species of Lythrum (Purple Loosestrife) long ago introduced ínto American gardens from Europe where it was *native,* has now become completely naturalized in E. N. America, growing freely in the wild. Compare INDIGEN; contrast EXOTIC.

NATIVE PLANTS. In the search for novelty and as a result of the advertising of exotic and created materials, the charm of our native plants has been largely overlooked by the average gardener. We must go to England to see the full glory of our hardy asters (or Michaelmas daisies) which, taken abroad by keen eyed horticulturists, have been developed by the English growers through selection and hybridization to a high state of perfection. Even our lowly goldenrod is, abroad, an appreciated, improved and truly beautiful garden subject.

Every section of the U. S. has trees, shrubs and flowers particularly beautiful as a part of the natural topography and of recent years there has developed a growing appreciation of their suitability for landscape work, especially in informal plantings. Not long ago it was exceedingly difficult to obtain native plants from nurserymen, but now many dealers are making a specialty of them; and as the demand grows we shall see more and more of the rarer and lovelier plants preserved from extinction through their proper use and appreciation.

On the Atlantic seaboard the dogwood reaches its highest degree of loveliness. But whereas formerly people had to seek wild specimens and transplant them to their gardens (all too often unsuccessfully), plants may now be obtained from nurserymen, not only in the common white form, but in the rarer and lovely pink and double varieties. All through the E. States these and other species of dogwoods and many of the Viburnums, all attractive in flower and fruit, may be used most effectively. Full advantage should be taken of the charm of mountain-laurel and rhododendron, includ-

ing the lovely, pink, white, and flame-colored azaleas. Other shrubs—such as hollies, wild cherries, plums, chokeberries, shadbush, hawthorns, spicebush, sweet pepper-bush, gordonia, and fringe-tree—combined with plantings of native trees, are characteristic of this section.

And so it is in all the varying regions of the country: each has its characteristic plants that can, and should, be more used in home plantings and, to that end, be grown by commercial horticulturists.

See also CONSERVATION OF NATIVE PLANTS; WILD GARDEN.

NATURAL ENEMIES. If it were not for natural checks to insect populations they would soon inherit—or, more accurately, usurp—the earth. Fortunately, man is aided in his warfare against plant pests not only by climate and other environmental conditions, but also by birds, skunks, moles, shrews, snakes, toads, lizards and turtles, and, particularly, by other insects—both those which are predacious and devour their prey and those which live as parasites on or in insect hosts. Fungous diseases also take their toll of many injurious insects. See BIOLOGICAL CONTROL; INSECTS, BENEFICIAL.

NATURALIZING. The setting out of trees, shrubs, flowering plants, bulbs, etc., in such a manner as to reproduce the effect of natural wild growth. (See illustration, Plate 5.) In the case of plants which grow easily from seed, this may be broadcast thickly over the area. Plants should be chosen which can be largely left to care for themselves. They must be placed irregularly, which is a hard thing to accomplish since natural irregularity is an unbelievably elusive thing to copy. Try to avoid putting together plants that match up or are specimens. One way to determine the position of each plant in a group is the old device of tossing from a basket as many potatoes or other similar objects as you have plants to set out. Then plant one where each potato rests. This plan is successfully followed with bulbs, which, strewn by handfuls or from a basket (preferably in the direction of the prevailing wind—to suggest windborne distribution) are planted wherever they fall.

NAVELWORT, or NAVELSEED. Common names for Omphalodes, a genus of small herbs resembling Forget-me-nots, grown in the border and the rock gardén. Members of the Borage Family, they are of easy culture, thriving in sun or shade if given sufficient moisture. They are propagated from spring-sown seed or by division of the perennials. Two species, both perennials, are common in gardens. *O. verna* (Creeping-forget-me-not), with blue flowers, produces runners freely, spreading quickly over bare spots in the rock garden, or naturalizing readily on the edge of a pool. *O. luciliae,* with rose flowers turning bluish, should be grown in well-drained limestone soil.

Navelwort is also the common name for *Cotyledon umbilicus.*

NECTARINE. A peach with a smooth, not furry, skin. It may originate from a seed or from a bud ("bud sport") and its seeds or buds may give rise to either "peaches" or "nectarines." In American gardens it is grown more as a curiosity than for its merits, though in California it is planted commercially. Except that its fruit needs more protection against the curculio (which see) than does the peach its cultural handling is the same as for the peach, which see. See also PRUNUS.

NECTARY. A glandular surface or organ in a flower which secretes nectar to attract insects which by visiting different flowers bring about pollination.

NECTRIA CANKER. A diseased area caused by infection by a fungus of the cortex and cambium region of trees. It is generally localized in relatively small areas on the trunk, spreading slowly from year to year. Each year the cambium at the margin of the canker forms a new callus which is subsequently killed by the fungus (a species of the genus Nectria) so that the area consists of concentric rings of callus. At certain times of the year small scarlet fruiting bodies (*perithecia*) of the fungus are found on the recently killed bark near the margin of the canker.

Nectria cankers are common on nearly every species of hardwood and on many of the larger shrubs. Plants are seldom killed outright, but the open wound created furnishes entrance for insects and wood-destroying fungi. Cankers should be looked for and removed in their initial stages. See TREE SURGERY.

NEEDLE PALM. Common name for *Rhapidophyllum hystrix,* a dwarf Fan Palm, sometimes called Blue Palmetto, growing near the coast in S. C., Fla. and Miss. The handsomest of the native species, it has dark green, shiny leaves,

silvery-gray beneath; the stems, only 2 or 3 ft. high, are covered with long, erect spines, which also surround the bloom and protect it in its immature state, when it appears like a white egg. This interesting little palm is easily moved from its wild site to the garden, where it grows well even in dry, sandy soil without the use of fertilizer. When grown in the greenhouse in the N. the Needle Palm should be potted in a light, loamy soil and given a night temperature of from 55 to 60 deg. F.

NEILLIA (neel'-i-ah). A species of deciduous shrubs, native in Asia and closely allied to Spiraea, belonging to the Rose Family. They are graceful shrubs of spreading habit, with bright green leaves more or less lobed, and small pink or whitish flowers in terminal clusters. Fairly hardy N. Propagated by seed, and cuttings of green wood under glass.

N. sinensis grows to 6 ft. and has clusters of nodding pink flowers in late spring. It is the hardiest of the group, and a most attractive shrub.

longiracemosa is a taller grower, with larger flower clusters, also pink.

thyrsiflora grows to 6 ft. in mild regions and has white flowers. In the N. it is usually killed to the ground in severe winters, but renews itself with new growth.

NELUMBIUM (ne-lum'-bi-um). Nelumbo. Held sacred by the ancient Hindus, this waterlily (which we know better as the Lotus) found its way westward to receive new reverence at the hands of the old Egyptians. Its leaves, blooms and curious seed pods are perhaps the most striking single feature in all Egyptian architecture and decoration.

Nelumbiums bloom with us in the latter part of June, continuing well into August. The flowers are carried on high stems which tower above the wide, blue-green silver-sheened leaves. Like those of many waterlilies, the flowers open on three successive days before they fade.

In a good location with plenty of sun and rich soil, the plants thrive and good-sized roots will bloom the first season. Once set, Nelumbiums bloom freely and, unless the roots are actually frozen, suffer but little from the cold.

Planting should be done in the spring when warm weather has definitely arrived. Treatment should be much the same as for other waterlilies (which see). Like them they may be grown in half barrels or tubs successfully if a pond or other larger body of water is not available.

N. speciosum (or *N. nelumbo*), the East Indian Lotus (often known to the trade as Egyptian Lotus), has been the parent of a number of varieties whose showy, fragrant blooms range in color from pure white to dark rose-red. The size of leaf and bloom is equally varied, ranging from the small pure white bloom of var. *pygmaea alba* to the 12-in. bloom of var. *alba plena* (known as Shiroman).

N. luteum, the American Lotus or Water-chinquapin, the seeds of which were used by the American Indians for food, is perfectly hardy, easy of cultivation and rewards the grower with magnificent yellow blossoms as much as 10 in. in diameter.

See AQUATIC PLANTS; also NYMPHAEA.

NEMASTYLIS (nem-ah-sty'-lis). A genus of tender bulbous plants of the Iris Family, with grassy leaves and blue or purple flowers. Resembling Blue-eyed-grass, they are but little known in gardens. *N. acuta* has leaves to 1 ft. long and 2 or 3 bright blue flowers in clusters lasting only for a day. It is native from Tenn. to Texas.

NEMATODES. Microscopic worm-like animals, tubular or thread-like in form, called also nemas, eel-worms, or round-worms. They live in moist soil, water, decaying organic matter and tissues of other living organisms. Nematodes form a part of the normal soil fauna; some are pathogenic, causing diseases in man, animals and plants; others live on and destroy the pathogenic forms and are therefore beneficial. For example, one kind of eel-worm is being vigorously fought as a serious pest of narcissus, while another, which is a parasite of the Japanese beetle, is being grown and distributed by government agencies in the beetle-infested area as a possible factor in controlling that insect.

Nematodes puncture the tissues of their hosts with a hollow, spear-like organ imbedded in their mouth parts, then suck up the juices from the living cells by means of a bulbous apparatus at the base of the esophagus. Although any long-range movement of eel-worms requires external agencies, such as the shipment or other transfer of infested soil, surface water or plant material, the minute organisms can move through moist soil by threshing

about. In this way they may travel in the soil as much as 30 in. a year.

The female nema, after fertilization, is white, pear-shaped, and large enough to be seen with the naked eye. She lays 500 or more eggs which hatch in five days. As the life cycle is completed in 30 days, several generations may occur in a single season in the South, where the organisms are a serious pest.

NEMATODE INJURY
Root nodules on clematis, the result of eelworm infestation.

Three important nematodes affect ornamental plants: One is the stem and bulb nematode of hyacinth, phlox and narcissus; the second causes root knot on more than 500 different species of plants, and the third is the leaf nematode of ferns, begonia, coleus and other greenhouse plants.

BULB EEL-WORM CONTROL. The stem or bulb nematode causes discolored streaks or rings in dormant bulbs and dwarfing and distortion of foliage. To the experienced bulb grower its presence is disclosed by tiny swellings or "spicules" in the leaf blades which can be felt when a leaf is drawn between finger and thumb. Treat bulbs while dormant by immersing in water heated to 110° to 115° F., for two and a half hours. A fungicide (103 Semesan to 3 gallons water, or 1 oz. corrosive sublimate to 8 gallons water) should be added to the hot water to prevent spread of the basal rot disease. (See BULB ENEMIES under BULBS.) Infested phlox has stunted, swollen, cracked stems, and distorted, crinkled leaves, and flowering may be prevented. Remove and burn diseased plants as soon as observed.

Irregular swollen galls on roots are the chief symptoms of the root knot nematode but affected plants are usually dwarfed and a paler green than normally. On perennials the nematodes pass the winter in the galls and resume development in the spring. In summer they are usually found in the upper foot of soil and are more numerous in light sandy soils. Steam sterilization, or sometimes chemical fumigation, of soil gives control in greenhouses; field control is more difficult, but the use of some chemicals, such as chloro-picrin, or carbon bisulphide, is feasible in small areas. See FUMIGATION. Nitrogen-ous and potash fertilizers will also help. Dormant infected peony roots may be dipped in hot water at 120 deg. F. for 30 minutes.

To control the leaf nematode, which is confined to the leaves of various green-house plants, cut off and burn infected leaves and avoid wetting foliage when watering plants. Use steam sterilized soil for potting and sterilized sand for rooting cuttings. The leaf nematode is also a most serious pest of chrysanthemums grown outdoors. See CHRYSANTHEMUM.

NEMESIA (ne-mee'-si-ah). A genus of small half-hardy S. African annuals of the Figwort Family, having bright yellow, orange and red blossoms, resembling those of snapdragons in miniature. There are many intermediate shades and colors in cultivated strains, and a close planting of these brilliant little flowers makes an effect like a mosaic of jewels.

Nemesias are started in March in the hotbed or greenhouse and set out in the open at the end of May. They should be set close, so that the frail stems may sup-port one another. Where the summers are not too hot they will bloom continu-ously for several months. They are also charming in the window-box. The species most widely grown is *N. strumosa* to 2 ft. with racemes of white, yellow or purple blossoms with the throat spotted. Its var. *suttoni* has much larger flowers in more varied colors and var. *nana compacta,* one of the prettiest forms, is excellent for an edging. *N. versicolor, N. floribunda* and *N. lilacina,* are also grown occasionally in the garden.

NEMOPANTHUS (ne-moh-pan'-thus) *mucronata.* A native deciduous shrub found from Newfd. to Wis. and Va., with attractive fruit and autumn foliage. A member of the Holly Family, it is called Mountain-holly, which see.

NEMOPHILA (ne-mof'-i-lah). A genus of delicate annual herbs, mostly native of Calif., having cut leaves, some-times prickly or hairy, and blue or white flowers, borne singly or occasionally in racemes. If seeds are sown early in spring in a semi-shaded spot in the border, or on the edge of the wild garden, the small bright flowers will appear continuously all summer. The species most widely grown,

N. insignis (Baby Blue-eyes) has delight-ful clear blue wide-open or broadly bell-shaped blossoms held on short stems above the prettily cut leaves. Other species sometimes grown include *N. maculata* (Five-spot) with white blossoms, the tip of each petal marked with dark purple; and *N. aurita* (Fiesta-flower), a trailing plant which often climbs on others, sup-porting itself by means of the long bristles on the stem. It bears violet flowers 1 in. broad in loose clusters.

NEOMAMMILLARIA (nee-oh-ma-mi-lay'-ri-ah). The name sometimes pre-ferred for the large genus of cacti better known as Mammillaria, which see.

NEPENTHES (ne-pen'-theez). A genus of insectivorous plants found only in the tropical Orient. They are known as Pitcher-plants because the expanded midrib of the leaf forms a pitcher-like re-ceptacle, the hooded top, often being bril-liantly colored and furnished with winged fronts, lids and spreading collars. These characters apparently attract insects into the "pitchers" from which they cannot escape. Finally they fall to the bottom and are there dissolved and digested by a fluid secreted by the plant. The small flowers are borne in clusters.

Nepenthes are grown in greenhouses in pots or hanging baskets of sand, peat, and sphagnum moss in a temperature never be-low 65 deg. They are increased by seed or cuttings of ripened wood. *N. phyllam-phora* has pale or reddish-green pitchers to 6 in. long and 1½ in. across, with nar-row frontal wings. *N. hookeriana* has pale green pitchers marked with purple, to 6 in. long and 3 in. wide; the wings are sometimes doubly fringed. *N. veitchi* has hairy yellowish-green to red pitchers 8 in. long and 3 in. across, with very wide rims and fringed wings. Nepenthes hybridize readily, and there are many horticultural species.

See also INSECTIVOROUS PLANTS.

NEPETA (nep'-e-tah). Annual or perennial herbs of the Mint Family, some naturalized in U. S. Mostly odorous, with toothed or cut leaves and whorls of blue or white flowers borne in spikes or clusters. The genus is of importance chiefly as a source of medicinal products, but there are several species useful in the garden, par-ticularly as ground-covers in shady places. All are of easy culture and propagated by seeds or division.

PRINCIPAL SPECIES

N. cataria (Catnip or Catmint). A perennial, growing to 3 ft., with pale downy foliage, and whitish or pale purple flowers ¼ in. long borne in dense spikes to 5 in. long. The plant, common in old gardens and now widely naturalized, has a characteristic pungent odor, liked by cats.

hederacea (Ground Ivy, Field-balm, Gill-over-the-Ground). A creeping, mat-forming perennial useful as a ground-cover in either shady or exposed situations. The 1-in.-long light blue flowers are produced in sparse clusters. Var. *variegata* has variegated leaves.

mussini. A branching perennial to 1 or 2 ft., covered with whitish down. The flowers, blue with dark spots, grow to ½ in. long in long racemes.

wilsoni. A hairy perennial with wrinkled leaves, growing to 2½ ft. The dark blue flowers, 1 in. long, are borne in widely separated clusters.

NEPHROLEPIS (ne-frol'-e-pis). A genus of ferns whose name, from two Greek words meaning "kidney" and "scale," describes their indusia. Commonly known as Ladder Ferns, they are among the most vigorous and reliable of greenhouse and indoor ferns, including the Boston Fern. In Florida some species attain a length of 20 ft. The typical plant has indefinitely prolonged, simply pinnate fronds of a clear medium green, produced at intervals and in clusters on creeping rhizomes. In cultivated specimens propagation usually occurs by these creeping stems, but some kinds have wiry stolons as well. These ferns do best in a compost composed chiefly of peat moss and a little sandy soil.

SPECIES

N. bausei. Dwarf, with erect 1-ft. fronds on very brief stipes, once pinnate, with feathery pinnae. Requires more moisture than the Boston Fern, which see.

cordifolia (Tuber Fern). Has 1- to 2-ft. narrow fronds, once pinnate, with overlapping lobes eared on the upper side; the most reliable species for cool greenhouse.

davallioides. A superb plant for warm conditions, with curving, broad, 2- to 3-ft. fronds, from crowns sending out long stolons.

duffi. A compact form with shining, very slender 18-in. fronds, once pinnate, and the pinnae often forked or crested. Requires moisture and heat.

exaltata. The species from which originated the variety known as Boston Fern, which see.

NEPHTHYTIS. A small genus of W. African herbs of the Arum Family having thick rhizomes and long-petioled, arrow-shaped leaves. One species, *N. afzelli,* is being cultivated in Fla. and offered as a foliage plant for home, greenhouse, and conservatory decoration.

A YOUNG BOSTON FERN

A variety of the Sword Fern (Nephrolepis exaltata), this graceful plant has given rise to many decorative forms, all fine house plants. A single frond is shown below.

NERINE (ne-ry'-nee). A S. African genus of brilliantly flowered plants of the Amaryllis Family, favorites for greenhouse cultivation because of their mass of crimson or scarlet bloom in the late fall. White and rose blossoms are also occasionally seen. The flowers, with recurved petals about 1 in. in length and long bright red stamens, are borne in a large umbel at the top of a scape (leafless stem) 1 ft. or more in height.

The leaves appear after the flowers are gone, and at this time the plants need the greatest care, with plenty of sunshine, frequent sprinkling of the leaves, persistent watering of the roots, and occasional applications of liquid manure. When the leaves finally turn yellow, the pots should be laid on their sides in the sun for the bulbs to ripen. In August, top-dress the pots with rotted manure, soak them well, and return them to the greenhouse bench. Do not repot the plants for about 5 years; use the offsets to produce new plants.

N. sarniensis (Guernsey-lily) and *N. curvifolia* var. *fothergilli* are most often seen. The plant often listed as *Nerine japonica* is a species of Lycoris.

NERIUM (nee'-ri-um). A genus of attractive evergreen shrubs with showy flowers, native from S. Europe to Japan, belonging to the Dogbane Family, and popularly known as Oleander, which see.

NEROS CROWN. A common name for *Ervatamia* (or *Tabernaemontana*) *coronaria,* the Crape-jasmine, which see.

NETTLE. Common name for the genus Urtica, comprising about 30 annual and perennial weeds frequently found in waste places, but rarely troublesome except for their stinging hairs, which irritate the skin when touched. They are one of the genera in the Nettle Family (Urticaceae).

Dead-nettle (which see) is the common name for the genus Lamium, border or rock-garden plants of the Mint Family, not the Nettle Family.

NETTLE-TREE. A common name for Celtis, a genus of ornamental trees and shrubs whose fruits are a favorite food of birds. See HACKBERRY.

NET-VEINED CHAIN FERN. Common name for *Woodwardia areolata,* a vigorous fern of the E. States. Not recommended for garden use, except for naturalizing in marsh land.

NEUTRAL SOIL. Soil neither acid nor alkaline. Tests (as explained under ACID SOIL), give a pH reading of 7. Few soils are exactly neutral; all tend to become slightly acid in wet seasons, alkaline in dry. In practice, soils may be described as neutral when they vary between say pH 6.8 and 7.2. Acid soil can be made neutral by adding lime, alkaline soils by adding aluminum sulphate, sulphur or tannic acid. Except for scientific experiments, it is seldom important that soil should be exactly neutral; actually many ordinary garden soils are pretty close to that point.

See also ACID SOIL; ALKALINE SOIL.

NEVIUSIA (nev-i-eus'-i-ah) *alabamensis.* A deciduous shrub grown in the Gulf States for its feathery white flowers. See SNOW-WREATH.

NEW-JERSEY-TEA. Common name for *Ceanothus americanus,* a small hardy shrub with white flowers.

NEW-YORK FERN (*Thelypteris noveboracensis*). A common fern of the Atlantic States, with tapering basal pinnae, Growing in dense colonies in half-shade, and useful for naturalizing. Sometimes referred to the genus Aspidium or Dryopteris.

NEW-ZEALAND BUR. Common name for *Acaena microphylla,* a trailing perennial ground-cover with attractive leaves, used in rock gardens.

NEW-ZEALAND-FLAX. Common name for *Phormium tenax,* a large perennial herb with immense leaves and large red flowers; a fibre plant in its native land, but grown in other warm countries for ornament.

NEW-ZEALAND SPINACH. A prostrate, tender annual herb of the S. hemisphere (*Tetragonia expansa*) grown for its succulent leaves and branch tips which are used as summer "greens." While very similar to ordinary spinach when cooked, it has a much wider usefulness for home gardens because (1) it thrives in hot weather which spinach can not stand; (2) it is easy to grow and gives repeated cuttings all summer long; and (3) having a more open growth, it does not collect as much sand and require as much washing as spinach. It needs more space—15 to 18 in. between rows and 3 to 6 in. between plants, but is entitled to it in any garden where greens are wanted. In other respects cultivate like Spinach, which see.

NEW-ZEALAND WINEBERRY. Common name for *Aristotelia racemosa,* a small evergreen tree planted in Calif. for its ornamental foliage and rosy flowers in large panicles.

NICANDRA (ni-kan'-drah) A genus of Peruvian annual herbs similar to Physalis but with more showy flowers, somewhat grown for ornament in the S. and in N. greenhouses. *N. physalodes* (Apple-of-Peru) is an old-fashioned garden favorite with blue flowers, easily grown from seed and sometimes called Fly-poison-plant and Shoo-fly plant because of its reputed ability to kill house flies if some crushed leaves and shoots are mixed with milk and exposed in a saucer where the flies can get at it.

NICOTIANA (ni-koh-shi-ay'-nah). A genus of mostly New-World annual or perennial occasionally shrubby herbs of the Nightshade Family. One species (*N. tabacum*) supplies the tobacco leaves of commerce; another (*N. bigelovi*), called Indian Tobacco, of the S. W. was similarly used by the Indians. In the garden, the genus is of value because of several species commonly known as Flowering Tobacco. Like most of the others they have sticky, hairy foliage and long-tubed white, yellow, greenish or purple flowers which usually open at night, and almost invariably are delightfully fragrant. All the types commonly cultivated are natives of tropical S. America and are very sensitive to frost. They prefer light rich soil and need a warm sheltered situation. Although they frequently self-sow, it is advisable to start plants from seed sown early in the spring in greenhouse or hotbed; harden the plants off gradually and do not set them out until the weather has turned definitely warm.

The many diseases and insect pests of tobacco as a farm crop need not be mentioned here. But ornamental nicotiana is frequently infested late in the season with the greenhouse whitefly. Spraying with a contact insecticide (which see) is partially effective. Spray with lead arsenate to prevent foliage injury by Asiatic beetles and slugs.

SPECIES

N. alata grows to 5 ft., the flowers drooping as if wilted during the day, then opening in the evening. Var. *grandiflora* (Jasmine Tobacco) formerly listed as *N. affinis,* is the type usually grown, the blossoms giving forth in the dusk an exquisite jasmine- or narcissus-like perfume.

glauca is a quick growing plant of the dry hill regions of S. Calif. which attains heights of 20 ft., or more, becoming woody and tree-like. It has graceful, drooping foliage and attractive flower clusters and is sometimes planted for ornament and shade under the name, Bird-tobacco-tree.

sylvestris, a tall graceful plant, is topped with shower-like clusters of starry white flowers with long slender tubes which open in the daytime but are not fragrant.

sanderae is a hybrid strain growing to 3 ft., with carmine-rose flowers. Some of the named varieties, as Crimson King with velvety deep crimson-red blooms, are striking plants for the annual border.

NICOTINE. A yellowish oily liquid extracted from tobacco and widely used as a contact insecticide (see INSECTICIDE). It is obtainable in the form of nicotine-sulphate and free nicotine. The manufactured solution usually contains 40 per cent nicotine-sulphate or 40 or 50 per cent free nicotine. One teaspoon to a gallon of water (giving a 1 to 800 dilution) is the one most commonly used against aphids and other soft-bodied insects. Soap is generally added as a spreader. See SOAPS.

Nicotine-oleate, good for mealy bugs, is made by mixing 1¾ parts oleic acid to 2½ parts 40 per cent free nicotine and adding 4¼ parts soft water. This stock solution is diluted at the rate of 1 fluid oz. to 2 gals. water or 1 gal. water in the case of hardy plants.

Nicotine may also be used in the form of a 1 or 2 per cent dust (see DUSTING). Tobacco dust, made of waste parts of the tobacco plant dried and powdered, will give fair control of aphids if dusted on, and will repel some other insects.

Nicotine powder, liquid, and impregnated paper can be used in fumigating greenhouses. See FUMIGATION.

NIDULARIUM (nid-eu-lay'-ri-um). A genus of Brazilian epiphytic herbs of the Pineapple Family, with prickly edged leaves in rosettes, and, among the foliage, red, white or purple stemless flowers, surrounded by brightly colored bracts. In the N. they are grown in a warm greenhouse in pots, baskets or slatted cribs filled with fibrous material. They should be sparingly watered in the winter when dormant, but plentifully supplied with moisture in summer when growth is active. The two best known species are: *N. innocenti* with 1 ft. leaves and white flowers surrounded by brilliant scarlet bracts; and *N. fulgens* with thick clusters of white and lavender flowers with bright red bracts, set close in the axils of the white-spotted leaves.

NIEREMBERGIA (nee-rem-ber'-ji-ah). A genus of low-growing, half hardy perennials or subshrubs of the Nightshade Family, the garden forms of which are usually treated as annuals. One species (*N. rivularis*) is called White-cup, but the group as a whole is known as Cup-flower, which see.

NIGELLA (ny-jel'-ah). A genus of attractive hardy annual herbs of the Buttercup Family, with blue, yellow or white flowers, and very finely cut foliage, which probably suggested the common name, Fennel-flower. Seed can be sown in spring as early as the ground can be worked, or even in the fall, as the small plants from the fall-sown seed often survive the winter and bloom extra early in the summer.

N. damascena (Love-in-a-mist or Devil-in-a-bush) grows to 1½ ft. and has pale blue or white flowers, surrounded and partially concealed by the finely cut green leaves of the involucre. The flowers, which last well when cut, are most attractive in mixed bouquets. The variety Miss Jekyll, has deeper blue flowers, much prettier than those of the type. *N. sativa* (Fennel-flower) from the Mediterranean region, has solitary blue flowers without a surrounding lacy involucre. The seeds, called black cumin, are used for seasoning in the Old World. Not the same as those of cumin (*Cuminum cyminum*, a plant of the Parsley Family.

NIGHT-BLOOMING CEREUS. As many of the cereus type of cacti bloom at night, this term may apply to any one of many species of many genera. *Hylocereus undatus* and *Selenicereus macdonaldiae* are special favorites in this group.

NIGHT-PHLOX. Common name for *Zaluzianskya capensis*, a S. African annual with long tubular dark purple flowers, white inside, fragrant at evening. Easily grown from seed indoors in early spring.

NIGHTSHADE. Common name for *Solanum nigrum*, an annual weak-stemmed plant of the Nightshade Family, that sometimes lies on the ground and sometimes grows erect to 2 ft. It has small white flowers followed by black berries. Improved forms are offered and sometimes cultivated as Wonderberry and Sunberry, but the possibility of the berries having poisonous qualities is much discussed.

The Nightshade Family (Solanaceae, which see) is a warm-climate group furnishing important horticultural and economic subjects, including tomatoes, potatoes, egg-plants, peppers, etc.

Deadly-nightshade is *Atropa belladonna*, which is cultivated for medicinal purposes only. Enchanters-nightshade is *Circaea lutetiana;* Malabar-nightshade is the genus Basella.

NINEBARK. Common name for Physocarpus, a genus of hardy deciduous shrubs, native in N. America (and one in Asia) belonging to the Rose Family. They are good-natured shrubs of usually spreading habit, with leaves more or less lobed, and whitish flowers borne in dense umbels in late spring. Propagated by seed, and cuttings of growing or mature wood.

P. opulifolius grows to 10 ft., with wide spreading arching branches. Var. *lutea* has bright yellow leaves turning bronzy; var. *nanus* is a dwarf form with small dark-green leaves.

amurensis, the Asiatic species, is similar to *P. opulifolius* but more vigorous and with larger flowers.

monogynus is a neat shrub to 3 ft., with small leaves deeply lobed.

glabratus is of similar habit but with leaves less deeply lobed and with larger flowers.

bracteatus is a compact grower to 6 ft., and one of the most attractive in bloom.

NIPPON BELLS. Common name for *Shortia uniflora*, a low Japanese evergreen herb with nodding flowers, useful in shady rock gardens.

NIPPON DAISY or NIPPON CHRYSANTHEMUM (*Chrysanthemum nipponicum*). A 2-ft., hardy, shrubby-based, autumn-blooming perennial with thick leaves and large white flower-heads.

NITRATES. Chemical substances (salts) formed by the combination of nitric acid with various metallic bases. A number of them, being readily soluble and rich in the essential plant-food element nitrogen (which see), are important in gardening as quick-acting fertilizers, being mixed with other materials to form "complete fertilizers," or applied alone as plant stimulants. The nitrate sources of nitrogen most commonly used are: nitrate of soda, found as a crude salt in Chile and containing on the average about 16 per cent nitrogen, urea, and synthetic products in which atmospheric nitrogen is combined with mineral products as carriers. Potassium nitrate (saltpeter) is too much in demand for other purposes and too expensive to be used as a fertilizer.

Being so soluble, nitrates are soon leached or washed out of a soil so should not be applied except to growing plants during the growing season. They are best used in small quantities, sprinkled on the soil (2 lbs. per 100 sq. ft.) and cultivated in, or dissolved in water (1 oz. to 2 gals.) and applied around *but not on* the plants. Light applications every 2 weeks or so are better than heavier ones at long intervals. If used dry, the nitrate must not be allowed to touch plant tops or roots.

Plants most in need of and most benefited by nitrate fertilizers are those that make much leaf growth, as lettuce, celery, cabbage and such vegetables. If stimulated by nitrogenous tonics, especially after early summer, trees, shrubs, etc., are likely to make soft, sappy growth that is most likely to be injured by frost or other weakening conditions.

See also FERTILIZER; MANURE; PLANT FOODS.

NITRIFICATION. The changing of crude compounds of nitrogen (which see) into, first ammonia, then nitrites and finally nitrates, in which form the nitrogen becomes available for the use of plants as food. This progressive change is brought about in the soil or in other substances containing nitrogen in complex forms (as stable manures, humus, etc.), by the action of so-called *nitrifying* bacteria. If conditions are unfavorable for the activity of these organisms (one such condition being a lack of oxygen), then another sort of bacteria, the *denitrifying* kind, get to work and break down the valuable nitrates, releasing much of the nitrogen in gaseous form which is thus lost to the plants through the process of *denitrification.* An example is the burning ("fire-fanging") of horse-manure, as a result of which its plant-food value is largely lost. Recommended methods of handling manure, the compost heap and the soil are designed to foster nitrification, prevent denitrification and thereby improve the fertility of the soil.

NITROGEN. A colorless, tasteless, odorless gas which forms about 77 per cent of the air and is present in animal and vegetable life in the form of ammonium compounds and nitrates. Playing an important part in the cell activities of living plants, and contributing especially to the development of leaf and stem tissue, nitrogen is one of the essential plant-food elements. As it is one of the least stable, often the least abundant in combined forms that plants can use, and most easily lost, it is the most expensive and the one gardeners must make the greatest effort to supply to the soil.

Fortunately, nitrogen is carried in varying amounts by all, or most, organic manures, and by a number of commercial (mineral) fertilizers (which see) such as nitrate of soda, ammonium sulphate, and urea. By modern industrial processes it is also taken from the atmosphere and combined with certain minerals, and the same source is tapped by certain bacteria that live in the roots of plants called legumes (which see) and store up the nitrogen in nodules on the roots of the plants.

As a frequent "limiting factor" in plant growth, nitrogen is a material that the gardener should take particular pains to conserve in, and add to, his soil.

See also MANURE; NITRATES; PLANT FOODS.

NODE. That part of a stem at which leaves and buds have their origin. (The spaces between nodes are called *inter-*

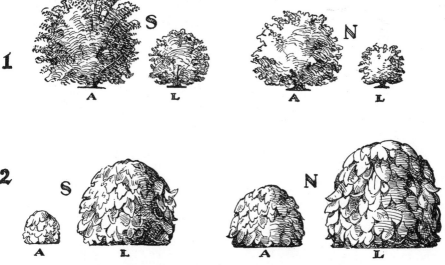

PLANTS SHOW INTERESTING NITROGEN PREFERENCES
Different kinds of nitrogen give different results with different plants. These diagrams represent:
1. Four cranberry plants; those marked S received sulphate of ammonia, those marked N, received nitrate of soda; in each case (A) is a plant grown in acid and (L) one grown in limestone soil.
2. Four spinach plants, the letters having the same meaning. Thus cranberry does best on an acid soil fed with sulphate of ammonia, while spinach needs a limestone soil and prefers nitrate of soda.

nodes.) It is from this area that new plants arise in propagation by suckers, stolons, rhizomes and runners (which see). Also it is the presence of nodes that distinguishes underground stems from roots, which branch, but not by the development of buds.

NOLANA (noh-lay'-nah). A genus of trailing herbaceous perennials grown as annuals, with flowers resembling morning-glories but of greater substance. Native in Peru and Chile, these basket plants (which are also useful in the border or among rocks) prefer a sunny exposure and will thrive in dry soils and hot situations. Seed is best sown where the plants are to grow, though it is possible to start it indoors and transplant later. Nolana combines well with portulaca, which requires about the same conditions.

There are two popular species: One is *N. atriplicifolia* with stems 1 ft. or more long, spotted and streaked with purple above. The showy tubular blue flowers, 2 in. across, have white throats, yellow inside. Var. *violacea* has violet blossoms. The second is *N. lanceolata.* The entire plant is covered with short whitish hairs and the deep blue blossoms, 2 in. across, have yellowish-white, spotted throats.

NOPALEA (noh-pay'-lee-ah). An interesting genus of cacti, whose peculiar red flowers set them apart from others of the Opuntia tribe. The flower does not open, but is erect at the edge of the flat joint, with exserted stamens, and with the pistil exserted beyond the stamens. One species at least should be in any large garden collection; this is *N. cochinellifera* (cochineal-plant), a rapid and rank grower, formerly of commercial importance as the host plant for the cochineal insect from which a brilliant red dye was made prior to the development of the cheaper aniline products.

NORFOLK-ISLAND-PINE. Common name for *Araucaria excelsa,* a handsome evergreen grown in warm countries for ornament and in greenhouses as pot plants.

NOTHOLAENA (noth-oh-lee'-nah). The name of a genus of ferns, commonly called Cloak Fern, native to sunny arid regions, to which they have adapted themselves by developing on the under surfaces a dense covering of moisture-retaining hairs. The name means "false wool" in Greek. Fruit dots are chiefly marginal and naked but soon covered by the reflexed

edges of the pinnules. Several species are native in the S. W. States and can be grown in gardens there. Greenhouse types from foreign regions include several with gold or silvery powder on the undersides; these are very delicate, needing well-ventilated, open and rather dry positions, and moisture from below only. Hence they are best grown in baskets.

Species

N. dealbata, an American species, has 6- to 8-in. tufted fronds on dark and wiry stipes, 3-pinnate, powdered snowy white below. The only one found E. to Mo.

flavens. The best warm-greenhouse species, suggesting a small Maidenhair in outline but coated below with golden farina.

hookeri. Has dark green star-shaped blades about 3 in. tall and wide, on 6-in. stipes. The under color varies from rich sulphur to pale yellow.

lanuginosa. A diminutive American species, useful also in the cool greenhouse. White, wooly scales cover the undersides.

newberryi (Cotton Fern). A native of S. Calif., with broad, pointed, feathery, 8- to 10-in. fronds on black stipes, from scaly rhizomes; its powdery leaf-surfaces very silvery. Enjoys more shade than the others.

NOTHOSCORDUM (noth-oh-skaur'-dum). A small genus of bulbous, onion-like plants of the Lily Family known as False-garlic. They have yellow or white flowers in flattish clusters and grass-like leaves. They are not hardy N. and if grown in the garden the bulbs should be dug in the fall; they can also be grown as pot plants. *N. bivalve,* to 16 in., has yellowish flowers. *N. fragrans* has leaves to 1 ft. and fragrant blush-white flowers lined with deep pink borne on stems to 2 ft. tall.

NURSERY. A place where trees and other plants are propagated for use in landscape, garden, orchard or forest. Nurseries may be private, State, Federal, or commercial. Commercial nurseries grow all manner of plants for sale, and are usually specialized to some degree for propagating, collecting, growing, breeding, distributing or landscaping. Propagating nurseries raise plants from seed or by cuttings, grafts, layers or division of the root. Some nurseries do their own propagating, others buy young stock from propagators or collectors. Native plants are usually dug from the wild and either sold directly or grown on in a nursery to the proper shape ,for landscaping. Growing and selling (either wholesale, retail or both) are usually combined in the same nursery, but some nurseries buy young plants, raise them to selling size, and then sell to a dealer who markets them. Until recent years most American nurseries specialized in fruit trees.

A home garden may include a small private "nursery" where plants are grown from seeds, cuttings, gift plants or otherwise for later planting to the garden. This area may be enclosed by a wall or fence, or blocked off by a building; it may, if there is room include a small greenhouse, hotbeds, coldframes, etc.

Many State Governments and the Federal Government maintain nurseries where forest trees are propagated by millions to reforest public lands or encourage private forestry. See REFORESTATION.

NUT. As commonly understood, any fruit whose seed is inclosed in a leathery, woody or bony "rind" or "shell" more or less separable from the seed itself; but the term is also applied to the "meat" or "kernel." Botanically speaking it is an indehiscent (irregularly opening), single-celled,

IN THE NURSERY ROW
Plants of various sizes and types growing into garden material. Make your nurseryman your friend and visit his place often; it is full of interest and information.

single-seeded hard fruit; in horticulture, it is any hard-shelled fruit which, when "cured" may be stored more or less indefinitely. Loosely, many fruits are called nuts—as the almond (which is the seed of a peach-like fruit), peanut, cashew and pinyon; also the pecan, brazil-nut, walnut, hazelnut, chestnut, acorn, and many others. But of those named only the *last six* are true nuts in the botanical sense.

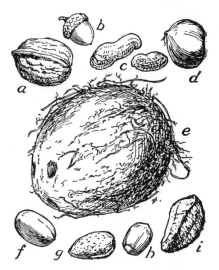

HOW MANY ARE TRUE NUTS?
Many fruits called nuts are not really nuts at all. Of the above, the true nuts are the walnut (a); acorn (b); chestnut (d); pecan (f); filbert (h); and brazil-nut (i). The others are peanut (c); coconut (e); and almond (g), really the kernel of a peach-like fruit.

NUTRIENT SOLUTION. A solution of chemical salts in water that will supply to a plant all of the mineral elements needed for growth, in proper proportions and at the proper concentration. The plant, in order to carry out its life processes, requires carbon, oxygen, hydrogen, nitrogen, phosphorus, potassium, calcium, magnesium, iron. Of these, carbon is derived almost entirely from the carbon dioxide of the air (see PHOTOSYNTHESIS). Oxygen and hydrogen are supplied by the water which enters through the roots. The next seven elements are mineral, and enter the plant in solution through the roots; they are called the essential elements. However, there are several other elements (called trace elements) that are equally essential, although their importance is often overlooked because they are used in minute quantities. These are boron, manganese, copper and zinc.

In any discussion of nutrient solutions, reference will be made to two groups, one containing six of the seven essential elements, and the other containing the trace elements together with iron.

The problem in making a satisfactory, practical nutrient solution is to find a few chemical salts that are completely soluble, that is, will leave no precipitate, and that will combine all the elements needed. In the research work in this field done up to 1914, four chemical salts were used to make what was called the four-salt solution. In 1915, a three-salt solution was evolved. Later on, combinations that contained certain partly soluble salts or of salts that would dissolve but would cause precipitation when mixed, were tried out successfully under certain circumstances. For any type of sand or gravel culture (which see) a complete or total solution is advisable. In tank culture, the precipitates do no harm and are often helpful.

When a three-salt solution is used, the chemicals usually employed are Primary Potassium Phosphate (KH_2PO_4), Calcium Nitrate [$Ca(NO_3)_2 \cdot 4H_2O$], and Magnesium Sulphate ($MgSO_4 \cdot 7H_2O$). Sometimes, and at certain seasons of the year, better growth is obtained by substituting some Ammonium Sulphate [$(NH_4)_2SO_4$] for a part of the calcium nitrate, as plants may absorb and utilize ammonium nitrogen.

The various nutritive elements must be in more or less definite proportions one with another. The relative proportions of nitrogen and phosphorus must be higher than those of potassium or magnesium.

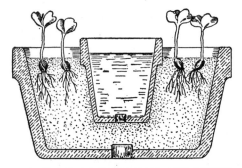

FOR GROWING SEEDLINGS AND BULBS
An arrangement which supplies nutrient solution without disturbing the growing medium.

Calcium must be relatively high, but the proportions of calcium and phosphorus have a direct relationship. If the calcium is high, then the phosporus must also be high.

Not only must the salts used to make the solution contain all the elements needed for plant growth in soluble form and in proper relationships; the growth of the plant is definitely affected by the *concentration* of the solution, that is, the relative proportion of salts to water. A plant ab-

sorbs materials into its system by what physicists call osmosis, which see. The contents of plant cells are in such form that they cannot readily pass through the cell wall membrane. But when the solution outside the roots is in a dilute form (or low concentration), it tends to pass readily into the cells. When growing conditions are ideal, the rapid absorption of solution gives the plant plenty of nitrogen and other nutrients to work with, and rapid growth ensues. On the other hand, when deficient sunlight, low temperature, etc., create growing conditions that are not so good, plants cannot utilize as much in the way of plant food materials. At such times a solution of higher concentration (a greater quantity of salts in the same amount of water) brings the outside solution nearer to the concentration of the cell sap, and less of it is absorbed. This phenomenon is utilized by the plant grower in modifying the concentration according to growth conditions. In summer, with growing conditions ideal, a solution of low concentration is used. In winter, when growing conditions are poor, the nutrient solution may contain four to eight times as much salts in the same quantity of water.

It is customary to make up a solution of the trace elements separately and add it as required to the bulk of the nutrient solution.

ACIDITY

The relative acidity of a nutrient solution must be watched more closely than that of soil, because soil contains more materials that act as "buffers," preventing rapid change. It is true that plants will grow well in nutrient solution of higher acidity than is required in soil. But change takes place rapidly, and this is one reason for changing a nutrient solution at intervals. As the plant grows, it may absorb and utilize only one part of a salt. For example, when ammonium sulphate is used in the solution, the plant takes out the ammonium and leaves most of the sulphuric acid radicle in the solution, thus increasing the acidity. Increased acidity is one of the causes of plants turning yellow.

TRACE ELEMENT AND IRON SOLUTIONS

A special trace-element solution will usually be found advisable in all solutions except those made up of crude fertilizer salts.

It is prepared as follows, and if kept tightly stoppered, will keep almost indefinitely:

Chemical	Amounts
Manganese sulphate	1 gram
Boric acid	1.5 grams
Copper sulphate	0.5 grams
Zinc sulphate	0.5 grams
Water	1 quart

Use one tablespoonful of this solution in each gallon of nutrient solution.

The iron solution is needed in nearly all nutrient solutions and should be made fresh each time the solution is changed. To make it, dissolve 5 grams of ferrous sulphate in a quart of water and add a tablespoonful to each gallon of nutrient solution. If the nutrient solution is used repeatedly for a long period and the growing tips of the plants turn light green or yellow, iron may be needed and should be added.

NUTRIENT SOLUTIONS

A number of typical nutrient solutions are herewith presented. While specific plants will give best results with specific salt combinations, the solutions suggested are satisfactory for a wide range of plants. There are also available in commerce a great many commercial salt mixtures, all based more or less upon the types given. The grower, then, can either purchase the ready mixed salts and experiment with them, or he can purchase the chemicals and mix his own. In making up the tables, weights and measures are given. A level teaspoonful is the unit of measure.

Solution Number 1. This will give generally good results with a wide range of plants. The salts should be dissolved in the order given.

Chemical	Amounts Grams	Teaspoons
Primary potassium phosphate..	2.3	½
Calcium nitrate	8.0	2
Magnesium sulphate	4.2	1½
Trace-element solution		3
Iron solution		3
Water	1 gallon	

Solution Number 2. This solution contains some ammonium nitrogen and will give generally better results for summer conditions, particularly in alkaline sands or with very hard water. For winter conditions the salts in this solution should be doubled or tripled.

Chemical	Amounts Grams	Teaspoons
Primary potassium phosphate..	2.30	½
Calcium nitrate	8.00	2
Magnesium sulphate	4.20	1½
Ammonium sulphate	1.00	¼
Trace-element solution		3
Iron solution		3
Water	1 gallon	

Solution No. 3. This is compounded for summer conditions where tank culture is being used for such plants as tomatoes. As large quantities are made up at a time the amounts of chemicals are given for 25

MODERN SOLUTION CULTURE
A clever device in which nutrient solution in lower receptacle is carried by the porous clay wick to the plant roots in the gravel in upper container.

gallons of water. If this solution becomes too acid, limewater, made up by adding slaked lime to water in small quantities until no more will dissolve, should be added. Do this by adding one teaspoonful per gallon of solution at a time until a slight precipitate or cloudiness appears.

Chemical	Amounts Grams	Teaspoons
Primary potassium phosphate...	5.0	1
Calcium nitrate	20.0	4
Magnesium sulphate	10.0	2
Ammonium sulphate	2.5	½
Trace-element solution		¾ pint
Iron solution		¾ pint
Water	25 gallons	

Solution Number 4. This is composed of fertilizer-grade salts and is recommended for tank culture. Some insoluble material will settle out, but this need cause no concern. It will gradually dissolve if the solution is agitated. The trace-element solution and the iron solution may not be needed.

This solution can also be used in drip cultures if it is well mixed and if, after the precipitate has settled to the bottom, the upper solution is decanted or poured off into a separate container.

Chemical	AMOUNTS Grams	Teaspoons
Triple superphosphate (44-48%)	6.0	1½
Sodium nitrate	4.0	1
Magnesium sulphate	6.0	1½
Muriate of potash	4.5	1
Ammonium sulphate	2.0	½
Trace-element solution (if used)	15	
Water	5 gallons	

Solution Number 5. This solution is particularly useful when alkaline sand or hard water is employed.

Chemical	AMOUNTS Grams	Teaspoons
Primary ammonium phosphate.	3.0	⅔
Potassium nitrate	14.0	3
Calcium nitrate	15.0	3
Magnesium sulphate	8.0	2
Trace-element solution	15	
Iron solution	15	
Water	5 gallons	

Even with the foregoing directions, the searcher for knowledge will necessarily use the trial and error method. He must decide upon the nutrient solution to use, the type depending upon the species of plant, the time of the year (available light), the reaction of the water and of the sand or other material used as a growing medium. Those plants that require a low relative acidity in soil (most of the garden plants) should have a solution high in calcium. Those that ordinarily grow in acid soils (as ferns) should have a solution that is lower in calcium. The solutions will have to be modified in concentration to meet growing conditions.

See also CHEMICAL GARDENING; GRAVEL CULTURE; SAND CULTURE; SOILLESS CULTURE; WINDOW BOX, SOILLESS.

NYCTAGINACEAE (nik-tah-jin-ay'-see-ee). The Four-o'clock Family, a group of herbs, shrubs and trees widely distributed in warm regions but chiefly confined to America. The characteristic flowers are petalless, and the colored corolla-like calyx nestles in an involucre composed of several bracts that exactly imitate a calyx. The base of the true calyx persists after flowering, enclosing the ovary to form a leathery fruit. A few genera are grown for ornament, chiefly Bougainvillea, Mirabilis and Abronia.

NYMPH. The name given during its growing stage to an insect that undergoes gradual or, as it is called, incomplete metamorphosis in its life cycle. The nymph corresponds to the larva (grub) of an insect that undergoes a complete metamorphosis. But whereas a larva, such as a caterpillar, differs greatly in appearance from the adult moth or butterfly, a nymph is similar in shape and body construction to its adult. Nymphs grow by molting or shedding their skin and each successive stage between two molts (called an *instar*) is more like the adult than the preceding one. With the final molt the nymphal stage passes over into the adult stage without the intervention of an inactive or pupal stage such as occurs in insects with complete metamorphoses. See also INSECTS; LARVA.

NYMPHAEA (nim-fee'-ah). A genus of large flowered fragrant plants, entirely aquatic in habit, and well known in both wild and cultivated forms as Waterlily (which see). Another common name is Nymphea, a simplified spelling of the generic name.

Genera in the Waterlily Family (Nymphaeaceae) besides Nymphaea include Victoria, Nelumbium, Nymphozanthus, Cabomba and Brasenia. The plants are perennial, arising from submerged rootstocks, and, except for the last two, which are small, have broad, floating foliage and mostly showy flowers.

NYMPHOIDES (nim-foh-y'-deez). Three species of this genus (formerly Limnanthemum), all perennial flowering aquatics of the Gentian Family, are in common use, not only in the garden pool, but also in tub garden and aquarium.

Commonly called Floating Heart (because of the leaf shape) and delicately flowered, their daintiness and similar habit of growth admirably supplement the major theme of the large waterlilies with a minor variation.

N. indicum, the Water Snowflake, has the typical, light green heart-shaped leaves and snowflake-like, minutely fringed, white flowers with yellow centers. It blooms profusely throughout the summer but is not hardy enough to leave in the outdoor pool over winter. *N. lacunosum* is also white but has smaller flowers. *N. peltatum* has the typical waterlily-like leaves and produces a profusion of rich yellow flowers. It is fairly hardy.

All 3 species propagate freely from those parts of the leaf which bear the flower buds. Because of their spreading habit, plants are best kept confined to a submerged box of rich soil.

See also AQUATIC PLANTS.

NYMPHOZANTHUS (nim-foh-zan'-thus). A genus of native Waterlilies found growing in still, mud-bottomed ponds and streams. More familiar names are Spatterdock or Cow-lily, which see.

NYSSA (nis'-ah). A genus of 3 species of N. American deciduous trees known as Tupelo. Their simple leaves turn a brilliant scarlet in autumn. The small greenish-white flowers are followed by purple or blue fruits. They grow naturally in moist situations in the S. half of the U. S. and since they have long roots and few rootlets, it is difficult to transplant large specimens. However, they are easily propagated from seed either stratified or sown as soon as ripe.

N. sylvatica (Pepperidge, Sour- or Black-gum) is a hardy, cylindrical tree attaining 100 ft. It is the most interesting of the species horticulturally; its foliage is excellent during the summer and turns a flaming red in the fall, and the bold crooked twiggy branches make a picturesque outline against the sky in the winter. *N. aquatica* (Tupelo- or Cotton-gum) and *N. biflora* are rather similar species native to the swamps of the S. States.

O

OAK. Common name for Quercus, a genus of noble trees, sometimes evergreen, but generally deciduous, members of the Beech Family. They have inconspicuous flowers borne in catkins or spikes and oblong or roundish fruits called "acorns," set in cup-like involucres. Beautiful in all their various forms, the oaks are usually wide-spreading with great trunks, often tall and majestic. They are valuable forest trees and most useful for ornamental purposes in street planting, in the park or on home grounds. Some of the low-growing species are excellent to plant on dry, rocky hillsides. The foliage, often beautifully cut, is always interesting, and in many species assumes brilliant autumn coloring. The evergreen species, with their holly-like leaves, grow only in the S. States, Calif. and Ore., but almost all the deciduous species are hardy. Many oaks grow in swamp ground but others, especially those of the Red Oak section, prefer drier soil. All are generally increased by seed sown as soon as gathered, but the varieties are grafted in the greenhouse on potted stock, preferably *Q. robur*. Sometimes in the S. the evergreen species are increased by layers or cuttings.

ENEMIES. Practically all species of oak are subject to leaf blister, caused by a fungus that is common throughout the U. S. but more injurious in the S. Blisters appear on the leaves before they are full-grown, often causing them to curl. Control measures used for peach leaf curl should be successful: a bordeaux spray after the leaves fall and before the buds swell.

Four species of powdery mildew attack oak leaves, and, where necessary, control may be obtained by spraying with wettable sulphur. Anthracnose or scorch, caused by a fungus, and common also on the plane tree, may cause complete or partial defoliation of White Oaks. Spray three times with bordeaux mixture at 2-week intervals, beginning when leaves are half grown; also destroy fallen leaves. Several species of blister rust fungi (see RUSTS) have their alternate stage on oak leaves. One of them injures 2- and 3-needled pines and, if the pines are the more valuable in a locality, oaks should be removed to eliminate the menace from the pines.

The list of insects attacking oaks is a long one but few are of great importance. Scales are controlled by dormant spraying with a miscible oil. For protection against the many leaf-eating insects the foliage should be thoroughly sprayed with lead arsenate in the spring. In certain localities and years the canker worm will practically denude the trees. Caterpillars of the cecropia moth, the American silkworm, the luna moth and the gypsy, brown tail, and buck moths, and the forest tent caterpillar, as well as the orange striped oak worm, may all feed on the leaves. The California oak-moth is a destructive pest of live oaks on the Pacific Coast. A late summer as well as a spring spray may be needed to control the two broods. Leaf rollers that may attack oak are controlled by spraying the trees with lead arsenate before the leaves begin to curl, but there is no known way to control several conspicuous leaf miners.

Various deformities known as galls are extremely common and often conspicuous on oak twigs and leaves but no control measures have been devised.

PRINCIPAL SPECIES

Q. alba (White Oak), to 100 ft., is one of the most characteristic and noble trees of the N. States. It should be planted where it will have room to show its majestic proportions when full grown and the full beauty of its autumn coloring, a beautiful wine-red or purple. It grows best in rather moist soil, though it is most adaptable.

borealis (Northern Red Oak), to 80 ft., is a rapid-growing tree, forming a large round head; the foliage becomes dark red in fall.

rubra (Spanish Red Oak), to 80 ft., a handsome round-topped tree with spreading branches and foliage becoming dark red in the fall, is not quite hardy N.

coccinea (Scarlet Oak), to 80 ft., is excellent for a dry situation. The bright green foliage becomes brilliant scarlet in autumn.

palustris (Pin Oak), to 80 ft. or more, forms a symmetrical pyramidal head with long pendulous branches. The foliage is much cut and assumes a bright red in autumn. Because of its erect, symmetrical and rather rapid growth, it is much used for avenues and as a specimen tree on lawns.

imbricaria (Shingle Oak), to 60 ft., has in youth slender drooping branches, but becomes round-topped in age. The foliage is glossy, dark green above, downy beneath, and becomes russet-red in the fall.

velutina (Black Oak), to 100 ft. or more, with slender branches and an open head, is a rapid-growing tree with glossy foliage assuming dull red or dark orange autumn coloring.

montana (Chestnut Oak), to 70 ft. or more, has deeply ridged bark in age and turns dull orange in autumn. It grows well in dry ground. It should not be confused with *Q. prinus* (Basket Oak) which grows farther S.

robur (English Oak), to 80 ft., a stout wide-spreading tree, greatly valued for its historical associations. It has many horticultural varieties, among them var. *atropurpurea* with purple leaves; var. *fastigiata* of upright growth; var. *pendula* with drooping branches.

virginiana (Live Oak), to 60 ft. and very wide-spreading, has elliptic evergreen leaves, glossy above and downy beneath. This species, native to the S. States, is much appreciated and planted there, but is not hardy N.

agrifolia (California Live Oak), to 100 ft., is a handsome tree with spiny-toothed glossy evergreen leaves, native of Calif.

ilicifolia (Scrub Oak), to 10 ft., much branched and generally of shrubby growth, can be used for dry banks or seaside planting.

Jerusalem-oak is *Chenopodium botrys.* Poison-oak is *Rhus toxicodendron;* also *R. diversiloba.* She-oak is Casuarina. Silk-oak is *Grevillea robusta.* Tanbark-oak is *Lithocarpus densiflora.*

OAK-APPLE. A large, globular gall 1 to 2 in. across, occurring on twigs of black, red, and scarlet oaks and caused by the gall wasp. Fortunately the galls are not especially injurious, as there is no control to be recommended.

OAK FERN. Common name for the genus Phegopteris, which see.

OAK-LEAVED FERN. A name sometimes given to the Sensitive Fern, which see.

OBEDIENT-PLANT. A common name for the genus Physostegia, also known as False-dragonhead (which see). The gaping small flowers, when turned in any direction on the stem, remain in that position without turning back.

OBLANCEOLATE. Shaped like a spearhead but with the broadest portion two-thirds of the distance toward the apex, like the leaves of *Ilex cassine* or *Myrica cerifera.* Compare LANCEOLATE.

OBOVATE. Egg-shaped in outline, like the leaves of the shellbark hickory, the broader portion of the leaf being toward the apex. Compare OVATE.

OCIMUM (os'-i-mum). A genus of annual or perennial very aromatic herbs or small shrubs of the Mint Family, commonly known as Basil (which see). Easily grown in the border or herb garden from plants started in the greenhouse or hotbed, they are esteemed for flavoring and for their pleasingly scented foliage. *O. basilicum* (Basil) to 2 ft. is grown as an annual. *O. minimum* (Bush Basil) is probably only another form. *O. suave* (Tree Basil) to 8 ft. is a branched shrub with white or purplish flowers in dense clusters.

See also HERBS.

OCONEE BELLS. Common name for *Shortia galacifolia,* an attractive little white-flowered evergreen herb suitable for shady spots, especially in a heath garden, which see.

OCOTILLO (oh-ko-teel'-yoh). A common name for *Fouquieria splendens,* a species of Candlewood (which see). Also called Coach-whip, Vine-cactus and Jacobs Staff.

ODONTOGLOSSUM (oh-don-toh-glos'-um). A genus of epiphytic, tropical American orchids with racemes of white, yellow, yellowish-green, purple, or dark brown flowers, with petals and sepals spotted with various colors, and a lip with a widely spreading mid-lobe, sometimes with a hairy crest. As the orchids of this genus are from the high Andes where a cool moist atmosphere prevails, their culture is difficult in parts of the U. S. where the summers are very hot. They can be grown successfully, however, in a specially constructed greenhouse fitted with a cold water pipe running along the ridge of the roof and equipped with spray nozzles set at intervals. In warm weather the water is turned on to cool the glass. The greenhouse should also be fitted with a double set of lath or slat shades, one designed to roll up and down, and the other lengthwise of the house; the lower shade should be 6 in. above the glass, and the upper one 6 in. higher. The house should also have ventilators at or below ground level. At all times the plants require abundant water at their roots.

O. crispum with wavy-margined, yellow-throated flowers, spotted with brown, and *O. pescatorei* with 3 ft. panicles of lovely white flowers, 2 in. across, are two species quite easily grown.

See also ORCHIDS.

ODONTONEMA (oh-don-toh-nee'-mah). Tropical American shrubby plants belonging to the Acanthus Family. *O. schomburgkianum,* better known in gardens by its former name, *Thyrsacanthus rutilans,* is the principal species. This is sometimes grown in warm greenhouses for the long drooping racemes of tubular red flowers in winter. It is best started anew each year from cuttings of basal shoots, and has to be well grown in order to have presentable plants flowering in 6 or 7 in. pots. Add some old manure to a mixture of fibrous loam, leafmold and sand, and feed with liquid manure when the flower stems show.

OEDEMA (e-dee'-mah). A physiological disease, also called dropsy, possibly due to too much water in the soil, that results in swellings on leaves and other organs, giving a blistered appearance. Over-fertilizing with nitrates is thought by some to induce the condition.

OENOTHERA (ee-noh-thee'-rah). A large genus of annual, biennial and perennial herbs of wide distribution, consisting of two distinct main groups. One includes the Evening-primroses, which open late in the day and close toward morning; and the other, the Sundrops (see illustration, Plate 38), which remain open during the sunlight hours, forming attractive clumps.

Peculiarly, the Evening-primroses open suddenly with a quick nervous motion that can be seen and heard, exposing yellow, red, pink, rose or white corollas and attracting night-flying moths. They are among the best of the evening garden flowers and are excellent for mixed beds and borders, growing in branching form from 1 to 3 ft. tall and producing large blossoms continuously. With their soft poppy-like blooms decorating the tops of the upright spikes, they give the effect of candelabras.

The sundrops, valuable especially in the perennial border, bear flowers generally yellow on plants 2 ft. tall. There are species in both groups that are stemless or more or less prostrate, and useful in the rock garden. The culture of both types is easy, so long as they are given dry soil and full sunlight. Propagation is by seed or in the perennial species by division of the clumps. There are about 70 species, of which the following are the more easily grown and the most popular:

O. acaulis (Dandelion-leaved Sundrop), biennial or perennial. At first without stems, it later develops spreading branches. Growing 6 to 12 in. tall and blooming in July and August, the plants bear long-tubed yellow, blue or white flowers 4 in. across.

biennis (Common Evening-primrose). Biennial. Coarse, erect, simple or branched, to 3 ft. tall. The yellow flowers are 2 in. across. This weedy species has naturalized widely and is common in fields and waste places. Var. *grandiflora* is a larger-flowered S. form.

fruticosa. Perennial, to 3 ft. Semi-woody at the base and with reddish stems. The showy yellow flowers, to 2 in. across, open during the day. Var. *major* bears flowers in profusion and is bushy in habit. Var. *youngi* is strong and stocky and also a prolific bloomer.

missouriensis. Trailing perennial, to 1 ft. The extremely showy flowers are 4 to 6 in. across and long-tubed.

mollissima. Branching annual, to 2½ ft. The night-blooming yellow flowers are small (¾ in. across). The plant is weedy.

rubricalyx (Afterglow Evening-primrose). Biennial. Has an attractive red calyx tube.

OFFSET. A plant which develops from the base of a "mother" plant, such as the small "chickens" of the common houseleek (*Sempervivum tectorum*), known as Hen-and-chickens.

OIL SPRAYS. These are used chiefly for spraying plants in a dormant condition, having, in many cases, replaced the older lime-sulphur solution. They are of two general types, called miscible oils (or stable emulsions) and oil emulsions in which the oil droplets are larger and break down or separate quickly; the main difference is in the kind or quantity of emulsifying agent used. Miscible oils are usually mineral and vegetable oil compounds, manufactured and sold under various trade names, and used at dilutions ranging from 1 part oil to

15 to 25 parts of water; but the manufacturer's directions should be followed exactly. Lubricating-oil emulsions, used against scale and other insects on deciduous orchard and shade trees and on some truck crops, may also be purchased ready prepared. The usual dilutions are 1 part oil to 25 to 35 parts water. If a layer of clear oil is found on top of an emulsion the material is not safe to use until it has been re-emulsified.

Deciduous trees should be sprayed with oil a week or two before the buds are due to break in the spring; evergreens somewhat later, just before their new growth starts, but usually with a weaker dilution, To avoid injury in using oil sprays, spray only on bright clear days when the temperature is above 45 deg. F. and not likely to fall below it for some hours. Severe injury may attend the use of oils in cloudy weather when the oil does not dry rapidly. Oil sprays should not be used on any plants where the stems or leaves form a cup or cavity from which the oil will not drain. They should not be used on hard maples or upright types of juniper such as *J. excelsa stricta* and *J. communis hibernica* which are susceptible to injury. Oils are hard on rubber gaskets and hose in sprayers.

Lightweight summer oils may be procured for certain greenhouse and garden purposes and are especially useful against mealy bugs, red spider and white fly.

See also SPRAYING.

OKRA or GUMBO. A tall, African, tropical annual herb (*Hibiscus esculentus*) whose long, ribbed pods are used, while green and tender, for thickening soups, catchups and stews, or as a vegetable. They may be canned, dried, or used fresh. The fully formed, but unripe, seeds of larger pods may be shelled and cooked like peas.

As the plants have large, striking leaves and handsome yellow, red-centered blossoms of typical hibiscus form, they may be used as ornamentals in the flower garden or the front of the shrubbery border.

Okra thrives in any well-drained, good garden soil in full sunlight and with clean culture.

The seeds tend to rot in wet soil, so good drainage is essential; as the plants are sensitive to frost the weather must be settled before they are started. They are hard to transplant unless started in flower pots, which should be done a month before

it is safe to set them outdoors. Outdoors sow seed an inch deep. Rows for tall varieties should be 24 to 36 in. apart; for dwarfs 18 in. The tall plants should stand 30 in. asunder; the shorter ones, 15 in.

The powdery mildew common on phlox occasionally infects okra, and a fusarium wilt causes yellowing and death. With a view to avoiding disease grow seedlings in uninfected seed beds and plant them in clean soil. The spinach aphid and the corn ear worm (see CORN) may feed on okra.

OKRA OR GUMBO

The plant, grown as a tender annual, is attractive; the mallow-like flowers are lovely, and the long, ribbed pods are delicious in cookery if picked while young.

OLD MAN. A common name applied to hoary, whitish plants of different genera, most frequently to *Artemisia abrotanum*. This is a shrubby plant of the Composite Family growing to 5 ft. with finely cut leaves and yellowish white flowers in heads growing in a loose cluster. Old-Man-and-Woman is *Sempervivum tectorum,* a small succulent plant that forms a rosette of foliage and is usually surrounded by the smaller rosettes of offsets. Old Mans Beard is one name for *Clematis vitalba,* given because of the feathery grayish fruits. The Old-man Cactus is *Cephalocereus senilis.* Rosemary (*Rosmarinus officinalis*) is also sometimes called Old man.

OLEACEAE (oh-lee-ay'-see-ee). The Olive Family, a group of temperate climate trees and shrubs a few of which are grown for ornament and one, the olive, for its fruit. The flowers, which have a 4-cleft calyx and a 4-cleft tubular corolla, are grouped in rather loose clusters. The family is subdivided into three tribes, their dominant genera being the ashes (Fraxinus), lilacs (Syringa), and olives (Olea). Among other genera widely cultivated are Osmanthus, Phillyrea, Ligustrum (privet), Jasminum, Chionanthus and Forsythia.

OLEANDER. Common name for plants of the genus Nerium. Oleanders are well-known evergreen shrubs, grown in pots or tubs in the N. for conservatory, window-garden, or porch decoration, and outdoors in warm climates. Despite the fact that the stems, leaves and flowers are poisonous to man and beast if eaten and are beloved by scale insects and mealy bugs, they have long been popular subjects. Plants thrive in good loamy soil, and it is not difficult to have good specimens if attention is paid to resting and cutting them back after flowering, and subsequent shaping and feeding when growth is active. Good well-ripened shoots are essential for free flowering, so they should be fully exposed to air and light. Propagated by cuttings of mature wood, which are often rooted in water.

Oleanders may be infested with mealy bugs, soft scale and white or oleander scale. To control all these, fumigate greenhouses or spray plants repeatedly with nicotine or pyrethrum and soap. In Fla. a fungus often causes witches brooms (which see) on this host. The plants are stunted and flower production ceases. Prune out all brooms together with 12 in. of the branches on which they are growing; then spray with 3-3-50 bordeaux mixture. Burn all prunings.

Principal Species

N. oleander (Oleander) native in S. Europe, is the one most widely grown. It may attain 20 ft., and is attractive at all times with its dark green leathery leaves, up to 8 in. long. The large showy flowers are borne in terminal clusters, rosy-red in the type. There are numerous varieties ranging in color from white to bright red, and with double as well as single flowers.

odorum (Sweet-scented Oleander), an Asiatic species, is a less robust grower with more slender leaves. It bears very large clusters of rosy-pink and musky scented flowers.

Yellow-oleander is the common name for *Thevetia nereifolia*.

O L E A R I A (oh-lee-ay'-ri-ah). Tree-aster, Daisy-tree. Evergreen shrubs and small trees of New Zealand and Australia, belonging to the Composite or Daisy Family. They can stand a few degrees of frost, but can be grown outdoors only in favored places in this country. They do well near the seaside if not too exposed. Propagated by seeds and cuttings.

Of the principal species, *O. haasti* is the hardiest. It makes a compact bush to 8 ft. with grayish-green small leathery leaves, silvery beneath, and clusters of white daisy-like flowers. *O. stellulata* grows to about 5 ft. and bears large leafy heads of white flowers. Seedling forms with flowers of rosy-pink to blue have been developed. *O. fragrantissima* has heads of yellowish fragrant flowers, and *O. ilicifolia* is distinguished by its holly-like leaves.

OLEASTER. A common name for the Russian-olive, *Elaeagnus angustifolia,* which see; also for the family, Elaeagnaceae.

OLIVE. Common name for the genus Olea, comprising evergreen trees or shrubs, often spiny, native in warm regions of Europe and Asia. *O. europaea* is the common wild Olive and its var. *communis* is the type of the cultivated forms. The latter is a gray-green thornless tree, with willow-like leaves and small egg-shaped edible fruits, shining black when ripe. Olives are grown in Calif, under orchard conditions, the best fruits being pickled and the remainder used in making olive oil.

O. chrysophylla is a small tree of tropical Africa, with leaves yellow beneath, producing large and blackish fruit and grown in S. Calif.

O M P H A L O D E S (om-fah-loh'-deez). A genus of low growing annuals and perennials with white or blue flowers resembling forget-me-nots. See NAVELWORT.

ONAGRACEAE (oh-nah-gray'-see-ee). The Evening-primrose Family, comprising mostly herbs principally limited to the temperate portions of the W. hemisphere. The flower parts are usually in fours; the four petals are distinct and clawed, and the stamens are inserted on the rim of an elongated ovary around which is the tubular calyx. Among the genera providing popular ornamental garden subjects, mostly of easy cultivation, are Zauschneria, Epilobium, Jussiaea, Clarkia, Oenothera (evening-primrose), Godetia, Fuchsia, Euchari-dium, Lopezia and Gaura. Ludwigia and Trapa are aquatic forms.

ONCIDIUM (on-sid'-i-um). A genus of tropical epiphytic orchids of the New World that bear long racemes or panicles of showy flowers, usually yellow, with a 3-lobed, crested lip. They bloom during the winter in the N. and only a few of the numerous species are easily grown in the cool greenhouse. The others, more difficult to handle, should only be attempted by experienced growers. All require heat and moisture while growing, but after growth is completed should be tested in a tempera-ture between 50 and 55 deg. F., and given only enough water to prevent shriveling.

The species most easily grown in the coolhouse are: *O. concolor* with citron-yellow flowers in pendent racemes 12 in. long. *O. marshallianum* with striking greenish-yellow blossoms 2½ in. across in 5-ft. erect panicles; *O. curtum* with branched panicles of yellow flowers, striped reddish-brown; *O. incurvum,* an unusual type with white flowers, spotted with purple-rose in panicles 2 ft. high.

Other popular types are *O. varicosum* var. *rogersi* with 5-ft.-long panicles of greenish-yellow blossoms, and *O. splen-didum* which has yellow flowers, spotted with brown, borne in 4-ft. erect panicles.

See also ORCHIDS.

ONE-FLOWERED PYROLA (pir'-oh-lah), or ONE-FLOWERED SHIN-LEAF. The common names for *Moneses uniflora,* a low evergreen perennial herb with white or pink fragrant flowers.

ONION. A hardy biennial herb (*Al-lium cepa*) grown usually for its firm, ripe, white bulbs, but also for its immature stems ("bunch onions") which are eaten raw as a relish or salad, and its tender young leaves which are used for seasoning.

The numerous varieties are propagated in four ways: (1) From seed; (2) from sets or little bulbs grown from seed the previous season but checked in their de-velopment by thick sowing, usually in poor soil; (3) from "multipliers" or "potato onions," each consisting of two to several "hearts" which when planted develop new stems and when mature contain one to several new hearts; (4) "top onions" or bulblets that develop in place of flowers, at the tops of flower stems.

Seed-raised onions are the most impor-tant commercially as it is their ripe bulbs

that can be shipped, stored for use during winter, etc. Top, "tree" and so-called "Egyptian" onions are useful in home gar-dens, the tops being broken apart and the bulblets planted like sets to produce early "young onions." The plants raised from bulblets, if allowed to mature, produce new tops crowded with more bulblets and per-haps a few flowers; those grown from sets should be used while young as they would otherwise most likely produce inferior bulbs.

SOIL AND SEED SOWING. The soil for onions should be loose and well drained but well supplied with humus and highly retentive of moisture. When possible, espe-cially if it is heavy, it should be plowed or dug in the fall and left rough over win-ter so the frost can mellow it. As early in spring as it can be worked it should be raked fine and the seed sown promptly. Seed sprouts slowly and the shallow rooted seedlings need moisture to help them through their baby stages. Late-sown onion seed is almost sure to fail.

The rows may be 12 in. apart for wheel-hoe culture or closer for hand-tool work. Though thick sowing is usually recom-

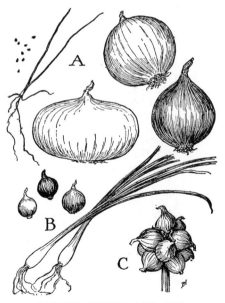

ONIONS, YOUNG AND OLD
The familiar large white, red and yellow sorts (**A**) are generally raised from tiny black seeds, the slender seedlings sometimes being transplanted. Green, spring, or bunch onions (**B**) or scallions grow from dwarfed bulbs or "sets," or from the bulblets (**C**) formed on the stalks of the so-called potato or multiplier types.

mended, thin sowing is more economical of seed and will involve less finger and thumb work in thinning. None but the best seed should be sown.

If desired, seedlings may be started in a coldframe or hotbed a month to six weeks earlier than outdoors and transplanted 4 to 6 in. apart in the garden when spring opens; they should then be but little larger than a "dance program" lead pencil or a piece of spaghetti. Seedlings started in nursery beds or even in the open garden rows may also be transplanted at about the same stage when the first thinning is done. In the home garden several thinnings are desirable, each one, after the first, giving young onions that can be used on the table either green or, somewhat later, as "boilers." Clean culture is essential throughout the season, but especially during the early stages.

When the tops of most of the bulbs in a row or bed begin to ripen and yellow, a light roller may be run over it to break down the rest of the crop and hasten the ripening of the bulbs. As "thick necks" or "scullions" do not keep well, they should be pulled and used as soon as possible. When all the tops have died, or just before cold weather arrives, pull or dig the crop in the early morning; leave the bulbs on the ground for a day or two to dry, then place them loosely in crates and store under cover where free air circulation will dry them still further. When thoroughly dry they should be cleaned and, for winter, stored in frost-proof, dry quarters.

Sets and bulblets of top onions are planted in early spring, an inch or two apart. In a month or six weeks they may be used as green onions.

ENEMIES. The most important of the diseases of onion are smut, downy mildew, pink root and neck rot. The fungus causing smut (probably the most destructive disease in the N.) lives from year to year in the soil. It injures chiefly seedlings which show black smutty lesions on the leaves and die early; onions grown from sets are not subject to smut. Control it by applying formaldehyde—1 pint to 16 gals. of water—in the furrow at time of seeding.

The downy mildew fungus lives on the seed as well as in old refuse, and affected plants turn yellow and die. A 3- or 4-year crop rotation is advised. Pink root (caused by another fungus) causes the roots to turn pink, shrivel and die. To offset the loss of those roots feed the plants well. Neck rot occurs in storage after the onions are dug. To prevent it store them in slatted crates under conditions of low temperature and humidity.

The chief insect pests are the onion thrips and maggot. The former blanch and deform the leaves, the injury being worse in hot dry weather. Spraying with nicotine kills many thrips but does not entirely control them; some success has followed applying crude naphthalene along the row. The onion maggot is the larva of a small fly. Hatching from eggs laid on the base of plants or in cracks in the soil, the young maggots feed in the stem. Young plants usually die, but in older plants the maggots work into the bulb. Control by spraying with a mixture of 1½ gals. of stock lubricating-oil emulsion to 50 gals. of a 4-6-50 bordeaux mixture. Burn all onion tops and trash and grass surrounding an onion field.

Sea-onion is *Urginea maritima;* also *Scilla verna.*

See also ALLIUM; CHIVES; LEEK.

ONOCLEA (on-oh-klee′-ah). A genus of ferns, represented by one common American species, useful for naturalizing, but too weedy for the garden. See under SENSITIVE FERN.

ONONIS (oh-noh′-nis). A genus of leguminous herbs and shrubs of the Old World bearing pink or yellow flowers and swollen pods and useful for borders and rock gardens. Commonly known as Rest Harrow, which see.

ONOPORDON (on-oh-paur′-don) or ONOPORDUM. A genus of coarse annual and perennial thistle-like herbs of the Composite Family with large, prickly leaves and white or purple flowers. Among species cultivated for ornament in wild gardens and borders, the best known is *O. acanthium,* the Scotch Thistle. All species are easily propagated by seed and grow in any well-drained garden soil.

The troublesome weedy thistles of fields and pastures belong to other genera, Carduus, Cirsium or Cnicus.

ONOSMA (oh-noz′-mah). A genus of annual, biennial and perennial herbs, sometimes shrubby, belonging to the Borage Family. Yellow, purple, or white flowers are borne in one-sided clusters from midsummer to autumn. The tubular or urn-shaped corollas with attached stamens make the blossoms extremely attractive, especially when grown in the rock garden among plants with light foliage. The taller species are good for borders. Propagation is by seeds or by cuttings taken in summer and plants do well in either full sunshine or partial shade. One of the tallest species is *O. echioides,* a biennial or perennial sort growing 1½ ft. high and bearing cylindrical, drooping pale yellow or whitish flowers. *O. stellulatum,* growing 8 in. tall, is the most commonly cultivated low species. Its tubular yellow flowers are 1 in. long.

ONYCHIUM (oh-nik'-i-um). A genus of ferns, including the Japanese Claw Fern (which see), characterized by nail-like pinnae on the fertile fronds and suitable for greenhouse cultivation only.

OPHIOGLOSSACEAE (of-i-oh-glos-ay'-see-ee). The Adders Tongue Family, a group of ferns two genera of which (Botrychium and Ophioglossum) are sometimes planted in rock or wild gardens. Some are very small. From a short underground rootstock rises an erect, fleshy, petioled leaf bearing a kind of spike on which are borne large sacs filled with spores. This peculiar arrangement of parts gives the family the snakelike appearance from which its common name is derived.

OPHIOGLOSSUM (of-i-oh-glos'-um). A genus of fern allies, known popularly as Adders Tongue (which see). Of doubtful use in gardens.

OPHIOPOGON (of-i-oh-poh'-gon). Former name, still found in literature, for the genus Mondo (which see), a small group of evergreen sod-forming perennials with lily-like flowers, useful as groundcovers.

OPUNTIA (oh-pun'-shi-ah). Probably the best known genus in the Cactus Family as it is the most widely distributed in its native habitat, which extends from Canada to the extremities of S. America. There are many interesting and beautiful species suitable for culture in both house and garden. There are two sections whose names are so descriptive that they effectively differentiate them. These are (1) Cylindropuntia, with cylindrical stems, and (2) Platyopuntia, with flat stems or pads.

The Cylindropuntia group includes the famed cholla (cho-ya) of the S. W. which, though of little value economically, is sometimes used as a supplementary forced forage in arid sections. Many species have barbed spines, often encased in a papery sheath. Because of this some forms of considerable beauty are not recommended for cultivation, as for instance the Silver Cholla (*O. bigelovi*). Many are, however, highly desirable.

The Platyopuntia or Prickly-pear group is of much greater value economically. Used to some extent as a forage it is also cultivated for its edible fruits, which are shipped to the markets of large eastern cities. Hardy forms are common along the Atlantic coast as far N. as Long Island, N. Y.

ORACH (or'-ach). Also called Seapurslane or French Spinach. A tender, annual herb (*Atriplex hortensis*), grown mainly as a pot herb. The red-leaved varieties, which often grow 6 ft. tall, are sometimes planted for ornament. Sow the seed in drills 12 in. apart in early spring and gather the seedlings when large enough to use and while still succulent. Though the plant resists heat better than spinach, it quickly runs to seed; so make successional sowings at bi-weekly intervals. See GREENS, EDIBLE.

ORANGE. Common name for both plant and fruit of several species of the genus Citrus (which see). The orange blossom is the Fla. State flower. The following are the most important:

Common or Sweet Orange (*C. sinensis*), by far the most popular, with many horticultural varieties including the Navels.

King Orange (*C. nobilis*) with its varieties called Mandarin or Tangerine (var. *deliciosa*) and Satsuma (var. *unshiu*). The last named is the hardiest of all. The fruits of this species are often called kidglove oranges because of their readily separable skins and segments.

Sour Orange (*C. aurantium*), widely used in America as a propagating stock but seldom planted for its fruit though it makes better ades and marmalades than other citrus species.

Trifoliate or Three-leaved Orange (*C.* or sometimes *Poncirus trifoliata*), an almost inedible-fruited species with deciduous leaves, used as stock for budding because of its hardiness and also grown as a hedge in those regions where it can survive the winters.

Otaheite Orange (*C. taitensis*) grown as a pot plant in N. greenhouses for its fragrant flowers and small, ornamental, though bitter, fruits.

The name Orange is also used in connection with the following non-citrus plants: Mexican-orange (*Choisya ternata*), an evergreen shrub grown outdoors in warm climates and in greenhouses for its showy, white, fragrant flowers; Osage-orange (*Maclura pomifera*), a tree often used for hedges on rather poor soils as far N. as S. Mich.; Mockorange (Philadelphus), a genus of hardy shrubs grown for their white or creamy flowers which in many species are fragrant; Wild- or Mock-orange (*Prunus caroliniana*), the Cherry-laurel, an evergreen tree native from N. C. to Texas.

See also CITRUS FRUITS.

ORANGE-JESSAMINE (*Murraea exotica*). A small evergreen tree of tropical regions, belonging to the Rue Family. It may be grown as a pot plant in the greenhouse, or outdoors in the warmest parts of the country. In pots it needs good soil and liberal feeding. It has glossy pinnate leaves, and very fragrant white flowers, produced in successive crops during the late spring and summer. These are followed by clusters of red fruits. Propagated by cuttings.

ORANGE-ROOT. A common name for *Hydrastis canadensis,* a low perennial herb native to moist, shady woods and cultivated under similar conditions for medicinal purposes. Also called Golden-seal, which see.

ORCHARD. This term originally applied to the general home garden in which vegetables, bush fruits, grapes and tree fruits were grown together. As methods of culture were changed by the development of improved tools and power implements, berry plants were gradually relegated to "patches," grapes to "vineyards," vegetables to kitchen or truck gardens, and the deciduous fruit and nut trees to "orchards." Citrus fruits (which are evergreens) are generally said to be grown in "groves" which, however, in lay-out and management are identical with orchards. Thus an orchard may be either a home or a commercial proposition depending upon its size and purpose.

Berries and vegetables are often grown between rows of trees in orchards to help defray the cost of bringing the trees to bearing-age. When the latter need the space or shade the ground, the short-lived crops are discontinued there. Grapes are not suited to such interplanting because,

being long lived, they would have to be removed while still in their prime. See also FRUIT IN THE GARDEN.

ORCHARD GRASS. Common name for *Dactylis glomerata,* a perennial grass planted in meadows and pastures and sometimes included in lawn-grass seed mixtures for shady places. Except that it is quick-growing and will withstand shade it is not a desirable lawn grass as it is coarse and makes a bunchy turf. Var. *variegata* with silver-striped leaves is a dwarf ornamental sometimes planted in borders.

ORCHIDS (aur'-kids). Common name (plural) for plants of the Orchidaceae, considered by many to be the most highly prized of all groups of plants. The flowers are always remarkably distinctive in form. (See illustrations, Plate 36.)

DESCRIPTION AND CHARACTERS. The Orchid Family (Orchidaceae) is a large and extensive group of epiphytic (air-growing) and terrestrial (land-growing) plants, belonging to the monocotyledons, or single seed-leaf class. There are between 500 and 600 known genera widely distributed throughout the world. The majority are mostly native of tropical and subtropical countries, and only about 25 genera are of practical value to the gardener.

The family may be recognized by its habit of growth which includes generally a thickened or bulbous root system and stems which are often characterized by peculiarly thickened internodes, called *pseudobulbs.* The flowers are entirely different in form from those of any other family or group of plants. They are irregular in shape, the perianth consisting of 3 sepals and 3 petals, only 2 of the latter being alike. The third petal (which is lip-shaped and termed the *labellum*) has many distinctive forms, some of which are pouched or sac-shaped (saccate), spurred, fringed and compound. Others take on the form of insects, as in *Oncidium papilio majus,* the Butterfly Orchid.

The pistils and stamens are united and form a column or *gynandrium,* which bears the masses of pollen. The ovary, which is inferior (below the floral parts) and capsular in shape, contains hundreds of very minute seeds. Even the more typical orchid plants vary greatly in shape and form, although the root systems of the two types are practically the same.

Members of the terrestrial group may have a fibrous, bulbous, or a tuberous root,

Plate 36.   ORCHIDS—ARISTOCRATS AMONG FLOWERS

Upper left: The yellow lady-slipper (Cypripedium parviflorum), a hardy orchid for the wild garden. Upper center: The rose and violet of Cattleya mossiae graces the conservatory.   Upper right: From Guatemala comes this odd, purple-spotted, yellow orchid, Epidendrum stamfordianum.   Center left: The elegance of the ever-popular Cattleya.   Center right: Greenhouse lady-slippers—some of them as easily grown as ordinary house-plants.   Lower left: The delicate Angraecum with its aerial roots. Lower right: The fragrant, ivory-white Cymbidium eburneum.

and some have a short rhizome, or creeping stem, from which each year's growth is produced.

A few terrestrial orchids, such as the native coral-root (Corallorhiza), possess no green in their leaves or stems. They are saprophytic, but none are ever parasitic (see both those terms).

In the epiphytes, the rhizome is more pronounced and elongated, and therefore more easily recognized than in the terrestrial group; an example is the Cattleya. Again the genus Vanda and allied types differ from Cattleya in having a long, wiry flower-stalk and a 2-ranked (distichous) leaf arrangement.

The Culture of Orchids

The culture of orchids need no longer be feared by the amateur and home gardener, as to the ultimate results of their labors, provided they have acquired some general knowledge of the habits of the various types, species and varieties that will grow in intermediate temperatures, and sometimes under adverse climatic conditions. The same may be said of other types that normally grow under tropical conditions and that, therefore, in temperate and cool climates, require greenhouse structures for protection and the required temperatures.

Orchids, as noted, are generally classed under one of two headings: "Epiphytal" and "Terrestrial." Epiphytes (from the Greek, *epi,* upon, and *phytos,* a plant) are air plants which live upon trees and other plants. They are not parasites, as they only cling to their hosts for support and do not take nourishment from them, as does mistletoe, but they get much of their food from the atmosphere. Such are the genera Aërides, Angraecum, Brassavola, Brassia, Cattleya, Dendrobium, Epidendrum, Laelia, Odontoglossum, Oncidium, Phalaenopsis, and Vanda. The genera Vanilla and Renanthera are climbing types, rarely seen in orchid collections in U. S.

The term Terrestrial is applied to all kinds of orchids that grow in, and derive all their nourishment from, the soil. To simplify further class distinctions, the Orchid Family is divided into the following classes according to the climatic conditions they require: First, Tropical and Subtropical; second, Temperate and Subtemperate; third, Hardy.

Tropical and subtropical orchids are rare, expensive, and very beautiful. Their beauty may be seen and enjoyed by flower loving people who live in or near large cities where there are botanical gardens with suitable greenhouse structures, and those who can attend flower shows held in various sections of the country. In both places one may see exhibits set up in natural form depicting the manner of growth and appearance of orchids in their native habitats.

Temperate species may and can be grown in small greenhouses attached to the home, or even in sun parlors and large bay windows, once the grower has acquired the practical and theoretical knowledge of how to grow and care for the plants and how to afford them congenial conditions so as to obtain the best results and avoid disappointments.

Hardy types may be enjoyed by all who have around or adjoining their homes an area where soil, shade and moisture conditions can be maintained. It is to be recommended that, wherever possible, commissioners of public parks instruct their superintendents to establish plantings of hardy orchids in suitable locations so that the general public may have the pleasure and enjoyment of seeing them growing and blooming under natural conditions and still protected from ruthless destruction.

How the Orchid Grows. The orchid plant has three distinct and important stages of growth during the entire year: First, the growing stage; second, the flowering stage, and third, the resting or dormant stage. Lack of knowledge on the grower's part of the plant's requirements during any of these stages is detrimental to the plant's life. Therefore, all who take up the culture of orchids, should first obtain a knowledge of their physical and natural requirements, and, second, begin by growing only a few plants so as to gain practical knowledge and experience.

In their native habitats, tropical epiphytal orchids grow on trees (some on rocks) from which they obtain little or no nourishment; this is the reason for calling them "air orchids" or air plants. Many are found at high elevations, such as the temperate genus Odontoglossum. This is a native of the Andes mountains at elevations of from 2,000 to 7,000 ft. above sea level, but more plentiful at the lower level among the oak trees of that section.

The Mexican Cattleya (*Cattleya citrina*) grows on rocks and low trees about 8 ft.

from the ground facing north or on the north side of a hill. Some orchids of this type grow on trees overhanging rivers, and others in damp shady woods where very little sunshine can reach them; therefore, they require a moist and shady atmosphere when grown under greenhouse cultivation. The species that grow on higher elevations do better under cultivation when exposed to the sun's rays during certain stages of their growth.

Terrestrial orchids (tropical species) are found growing on the lowlands in swamps and also on high elevations; but the higher up they grow the more varied are the temperature requirements of the different species. For example, the genus Paphiopedilum (known as the greenhouse Cypripedium or the Venus-slipper Orchid), growing on the lowlands, requires a higher temperature and moister atmosphere during all stages of its growth than does the genus Masdevallia, which is found at the higher elevations in New Granada.

Under cultivation, *Masdevallia harryana* (now listed as *M. coccinea*) flowers more freely during May and June if the temperature during the winter months is allowed to drop from 35 to 40 deg. F. when the temperature is zero outdoors, and if the plants are shaded from bright sunshine after the middle of February. This shading is even more essential as the days grow longer, for the rays of the sun penetrating through glass are greatly intensified.

A Small Greenhouse for Orchids

For successful orchid culture a small greenhouse attached to the dwelling (sometimes span-roofed), should run north and

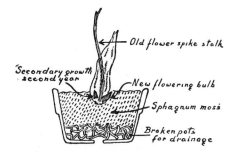

ORCHID STARTING NEW GROWTH
Diagram of a Calanthe potted up in February, to show parts and planting details.

south, so as to soften the rays of the midday sun. Lean-to structures should be built on the east or northeast side of the house, so as to escape the strong rays of the midday and afternoon sun. A similar location would be suitable for a bay window in which orchids are to be grown. The sun parlor, as the name applies, should be on the south and west sides of the home.

SHADING. Roller slat shades should be used on the span-roofed and lean-to greenhouse, so as to provide the proper amount of light and at the same time protect the foliage of the plants from the burning rays of the sun. Regular window slat shades can be used on bay windows and sun parlors so as not to exclude all the light. Ventilation should be provided for, as all orchids require fresh air when weather conditions are favorable. Ventilators should be built in at the top and bottom of the span-roofed and lean-to houses. The lower ones should be so constructed that they will open below the level of the benches; this will prevent the outside air from striking directly on the plants. Span-roofed houses should have top ventilators on both sides to permit ventilation under all conditions of weather, wind, etc.

The size of the greenhouse will depend greatly on the number of plants the grower intends to start with. However, allowance should be made for extensions and additions later as the stock increases. On the other hand, if there is only space available for a three-quarter span or lean-to house, then the grower can fit up the interior according to the requirements of his plants. That is, the terrestrial species can be grown on the lower levels, and the epiphytals on the higher levels. In building benches for orchids, the framework

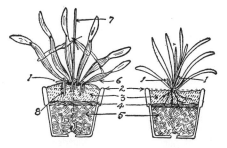

HOW TO POT ORCHIDS
Left, an epiphyte such as Cattleya; right, a terrestrial type, as Cypripedium. 1. New growths. 2. Rim of pot. 3. Compost. 4. Layer of sphagnum moss. 5. Drainage material. 6. Pseudobulb. 7. Supporting stake. 8. Wire pegs to hold plant down.

should be of iron and the shelves of cypress; this will give a bench that will last almost a lifetime.

The width of the house will depend on the amount of space available, but should not be less than 10 ft. The height, from the floor to the ridge, should be from 9 to 15 ft. and from floor to eaves from 5 to 6 ft. Sufficient heating pipes should be installed to insure the required temperature inside even though it is at zero outside; this gives a feeling of assurance that the plants are well protected in severe winters.

A good water supply is another important factor in maintaining the required conditions.

Rain conductors should be built along the eaves of both greenhouse and house and connected with a tank beneath the plant benches. The amateur who cannot afford a greenhouse, and who wishes to grow orchids in the sun parlor or bay window, can place a barrel in the basement or in a woodshed to which a pipe can conveniently be led from the rain conductors. Either plan will assure a supply of the right kind of water to meet the plant's requirements. Rain water is not only economical but also, as a natural product, very helpful in promoting the health of orchid plants.

INTERIOR CONSTRUCTION. Benches should be so spaced that it will be convenient for the grower to reach all his plants, without danger of hitting and knocking over any and thus causing considerable damage. The walk should be at least 2 ft. 6 in. wide, so that, in a span-roofed house, there would be space for benches 3 ft. 9 in. wide on either side of the walk. In lean-to houses a terraced or stepped bench 5 ft. wide should be built next to the back wall, and a front bench 2 ft. 6 in. wide built level. All benches to be used for orchids should be constructed with a space underneath to hold coke, gravel or other material for moisture-retaining purposes; in other words, a double bench should be built.

The upper part, on which the pots are set, should be made of 2 in. by ⅞ in. strips of cypress, with a 1 in. space between each two strips to allow for a free circulation of air underneath and around the plants; also to provide free drainage.

The lower part or bench may be built of pecky cypress boards (which are cheaper and very durable) with a ½ in. space between them. The space between the upper and lower benches should be from 12 in. to 15 in. and the distance from the floor to the top of the upper or plant bench 3½ ft. The same spacing applies to the terraced or stepped bench, of which each step should be 8 in. wide. These dimensions are applicable to the 10-ft.-wide house.

In wider houses, more space for extra benches can be allowed for. In the sun parlor and bay window sufficient heating radiation should be installed to prevent freezing during the winter months. Trays for holding water should be placed over the pipes and radiators, so as to provide the required congenial atmospheric conditions. Suitable benches and tables can be so placed that they will be attractive as well as serviceable.

After the beginner has acquired some practical knowledge about growing the species of any particular genus, he will then be better equipped to grow some of the hybrids, of which there are many.

CULTURAL DIRECTIONS

Genera, discussed elsewhere in this book in alphabetical order, call for widely varying methods of culture, including composts, potting, watering and temperature; also, in the case of outdoor hardy types, different soils and locations.

Epiphytal types need a compost consisting mainly of osmundine fiber (commonly called orchid peat) which should be broken up into pieces about 2 in. in diameter. All the fine particles should be shaken out so as to allow water to pass through quickly when the plants are watered; and also to allow for a free circulation of air through the compost. Lumps of charcoal (about 1 in. in size) mixed with the compost will help to keep it open. If at any time the plants look weak and sickly, add 25 per cent sphagnum moss to the compost. The aforementioned compost is suitable for Brassia, Cattleya, Coelogyne, Cymbidium, Dendrobium, Laelia and Masdevallia. For Odontoglossum add 25 per cent sphagnum moss and 10 per cent dried oak leaves; and for Miltonia, Oncidium, Phalaenopsis and Schomburgkia, add 20 per cent moss. Aërides, Angraecum, Epidendrum, Vanda and Vanilla do best when potted in straight sphagnum moss. For Paphiopedilum (the intermediate types), use a compost consisting of 2 parts peat, 1 part good fibrous loam with the fine particles shaken out, and 20 per cent sphagnum moss. This compost is also suitable for Anguloa, Catasetum, Lycaste and Zygopetalum. For the more tropical species of Paphiopedilum a compost consisting entirely of peat is best. Calanthe requires a compost consisting of 1 part good fibrous loam, 1 part peat, 10 per cent sphagnum, and 20 per cent well dried cow manure gathered from the pasture.

The best compost for hardy outdoor orchids is the one most nearly like that in which they are found growing naturally; in most cases this means a soil of high acidity. The species found growing in the swamps secure the necessary acid effect from decayed sphagnum moss; for those that thrive on higher ground the desired acidity is supplied by the decayed fallen leaves of trees.

The pink Lady-slipper Orchid or Moccasin-flower (*Cypripedium acaule*) is always associated with pine trees. Colonies of greater or less size may be found growing near isolated specimens of pine, though not under large, thickly planted groves.

POTTING AND TEMPERATURES. In preparing to pot orchids, thoroughly clean the pots and always provide sufficient drainage by first placing over the hole in the bottom an inverted piece of potsherd (fragment of pot). Then fill the pot about one-third full of more potsherds, leaving the other two-thirds to be taken up with the compost and the roots of the plants.

When potting or repotting a plant always make sure that all dead and decayed roots are cut off, and that all the rotted compost is removed, so that when the plants make new roots, they will have fresh compost to penetrate and adhere to. The same applies in planting or replanting hardy outdoor orchids.

There are various methods of potting different types of orchid plants, but if the horizontal stem or *rhizome* of a pseudo-bulbous epiphytal orchid is kept slightly above the rim of the pot, there is less chance of rot and decay; also less danger from overwatering.

The terrestrial group do best when the base of the plant is placed about 1 in. below the level of the rim of the pot. This permits a sufficient supply of water to be applied to the roots of the plant when required, and makes it possible to keep them in the desired moist condition that all terrestrial orchids (and especially the

evergreen species) love during the growing season. On the other hand, deciduous greenhouse types require little or no water at the roots during their flowering and resting periods.

The interesting hardy outdoor species are in nature governed more or less by climatic and soil conditions; under cultivation artificial watering makes it possible to provide what they need most. In potting, the compost should be pressed down firmly; by bearing downward and at the same time giving a slight twist of the hand holding the potting tool, you can firm the compost equally throughout, which is essential.

In preparing for outdoor planting, the grower must see that the proper amount of shade and light are provided by leaving or planting trees in the proper positions to create the necessary effect. The ground should be graded to suit the different kinds, as some require more moisture at their roots than others. The soil should be of a moist, retentive nature, and of a rather high degree of acidity; the latter can be brought about by the addition of well-decayed leaves, and black muck collected from the woods and swamps.

The proper time to pot or repot orchids is, in the case of epiphytal types, first,

MOCCASIN FLOWER
This priceless native orchid should be left untouched in the woods, for it seldom survives transplanting; even if only the flower is taken the root is usually pulled from the soil and dies.

when the new roots begin to appear and are about an inch long, or, second, when the compost in which they are growing has become soft and soggy. The terrestrial types, such as Calanthe, should be potted in February; Miltonia, during the fall months; Paphiopedilum, in March and April; Odontoglossum, when the new growths are about 2 in. long; Aërides, in February and March, and Vanda just as soon as they finish flowering.

Cypripediums and nearly all other hardy outdoor orchids should have their locations marked with a stake just after they have finished flowering. They should then be lifted with a good ball of compost attached to their roots during the latter part of September or the first three weeks of October, and placed in permanent quarters. Careful use of the watering pot and hose is very necessary after potting or transplanting. Spraying overhead twice daily during bright sunny weather is all that is required until the plants become well established and are rooting freely. When the new growths are about 2 in. long, the watering should be gradually increased until they are growing freely; then copious supplies of water should be given until the flower buds are well developed. From then on gradually decrease the supply of water at the roots and in the atmosphere.

As the terrestrial species require more moisture at their roots than the epiphytals, all hardy outdoor groups should be well watered after being planted so as to keep their roots and bulbs in a plump condition throughout the winter.

The Calanthe Orchid requires slightly different treatment from all other terrestrial orchids mentioned in this encyclopedia. When all the flower spikes have been cut off, the bulbs are taken out of the pots, and all the old compost is shaken off. Then the current year's flowering bulb has all the old roots cut off to within 1 in. of the base, the previous (or two-year-old) bulb being discarded; or it may be kept to increase the stock. The trimmed bulbs are then placed in flats or boxes containing a mixture of sphagnum moss and sand; they should be set at an angle of 85 degrees, with the bud (or new bulb eye that shows at the base of the bulb) facing the elevated side and about 1 in. deep in the compost. The flats should then be placed in the warmest part of the house and sprayed overhead every day to keep the compost moist. When the new lead or growth is about an inch long and the new roots are about the same length, pot the bulbs into 4½-in. pots in compost as recommended above under Cultural Directions (which see). Spray the pots overhead daily until the new growths are well developed and the pots are well filled with roots; then give copious supplies of water, and feed once a week with liquid cow manure which has been strained through a fine screen. A 6-in. potful to about 2 gallons of water will produce beautiful long spikes of flowers during the latter part of December, throughout January and sometimes well into February. Calanthes love a very high temperature and a humid atmosphere when in active growth, but a lower temperature, less humidity and a decreased water supply as soon as the first flowers begin to open. Finally stop all watering at the roots for the rest of the flowering period.

PROPAGATING ORCHIDS

There are various methods of propagating and increasing a stock of orchid. *First,* by division. This method is practiced largely in commercial establishments growing Cattleyas. The rhizome is cut through with a sharp knife so as to leave groups of three or four pseudo-growths six months or more previous to repotting the plants. At that time the plant is divided up into two, three or more parts (according to the number of cuts that were made) and each division is potted up singly. *Second,* Vandas, Aërides, Dendrobiums and Epidendrums are propagated by cutting the stems or pseudobulbs into various lengths and placing the fragments in sphagnum moss; also, by cutting off the young growths that oftentimes sprout out from the old stems or pseudobulbs and develop a root system. *Third,* the terrestrial species are propagated by division at the time of repotting, and likewise the hardy outdoor types, at the time of moving and transplanting.

Propagation from seed has greatly increased the number of new hybrids, and also some new generic and bi-generic types. The symbiotic or culture method of propagation from seed (in which the seeds are sprouted in glass flasks on a laboratory medium in the presence of certain bacteria) is rather an expensive thing for the average amateur to undertake, so I recommend that those who want to raise orchids from seed do it by the old method of germinating the seed on cheesecloth or sphagnum.

In one case some cheesecloth should be sterilized by boiling in water, and then cut into pieces. Each is made into a ball (by filling it with a mixture of equal parts of chopped peat and sphagnum moss) of such size that it will fit into a 3-in. or 4-in. pot. After sowing the seed on the surface of the ball, place the pot in a saucer of water to about half its depth and place a bell glass with a small hole in the top over it. See that the saucer is kept full of water, so as to prevent the ball of compost from becoming dry. Sphagnum moss can be used in the same manner without being enclosed in cheesecloth, but when gathering the moss for this purpose select only the best.

The terrestrial species are best and most easily raised from seed by preparing special seed beds under the parent plants. In the case of greenhouse species, the plants are repotted, and care is taken to have fresh, live sphagnum moss finish off the surface of the potting material; this should be neatly clipped three to four weeks previous to sowing the seed. The same method can be used with the outdoor hardy types. Special seed beds are prepared under the foliage and around the parent plants by chopping up peat, sphagnum moss and leafmold in equal parts.

It is interesting and helpful to know that in most types of orchids, the seed requires from 9 to 12 months after fertilization has taken place to develop in the seedpod and become fully ripe for harvesting and sowing. The beds must be carefully attended to as regards watering after the seeds have been sown, and kept free from slugs or snails, sow-bugs and cockroaches.

ENEMIES

In the greenhouse the most troublesome pest is thrips, but it can be easily controlled by spraying regularly, once a week, with a certified insecticide containing nicotine, of which there are several on the market. Late afternoon or early evening is the best time for spraying, as the ventilators can then be closed down to confine the fumes of the insecticide within the house for a longer period and kill any flying insects that happen to be around. It is also advisable to water all the plants that require it before spraying; this pro-

tects the roots that are on the surface or hanging over the sides of the pots, from any burning effect of the nicotine.

Red spider (really a mite) is another insect that does considerable damage to orchid foliage if not kept under control. The same method of spraying as recommended for thrips and free use of the hose will keep plants free of this insect. Cymbidiums suffer the most from this pest, which has a chance to accumulate during the long bulb-ripening period in the fall which induces flowering. During this time there is less moisture in the house; however, careful spraying once a week will keep the plants in a clean healthy state and free of red spider.

Scale is another highly injurious pest on orchid plants; it is found mainly on the bulbs underneath a protecting layer of tissue. This should be removed when scale is discovered, and the plants thoroughly sponged with an insecticide containing vegetable oil and nicotine; a small, soft-haired toothbrush can be used to remove the scale from the small crevices which are characteristic of the growth on orchid plants. Mealy bug is rarely seen on orchids except Oncidium and Phalaenopsis. It can be kept under control by frequent careful examination and sponging of the plants.

Cattleya fly is still another dreaded pest (especially on the genus after which it is named). When it is first discovered, steps should be taken to get rid of it as quickly as possible, for if allowed to increase it will destroy the plants in a very short time. C. trianaei, C. labiata and C. gigas are species most susceptible to this pest. The female fly pierces the new lead or bulb when it is in the bud stage, and lays eggs which hatch in a very short time. The larvae feed on the inside of the young growth, stunting it; and in some instances the bulb decays. The infected growths can easily be detected as they develop a swollen appearance. The larvae develop and pupate within the young growths. The adult flies then emerge through small holes in the tissues of the young growth, and fly to other plants where the females deposit eggs and start the process of reproduction over again.

The best methods of control are (1) cut off and immediately destroy infected young growths before the insects hatch out, and (2) spray regularly once a week with a highly concentrated solution of nicotine.

In the cases of a bad infestation, spray three times a week until there is assurance that the pest is under control.

The curculio beetle, a minute, black, very destructive insect, feeds on the roots, the tips of the young growths, and the inflorescence, both bud and flower, disfiguring it

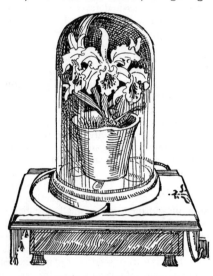

ORCHIDS IN THE HOME
A modern device combining a shallow tray for water, controlled electrical heating element, and a glass dome provides the warmth and humidity needed to keep a plant in perfect condition for weeks.

severely. The best way to control this pest is to go over the plants every morning and examine them carefully, especially the points of the young growth, the flower sheath and also the flowers. Hold a sheet of white paper or piece of white cloth under the plant. A beetle, on being disturbed, like all curculios, will fall off onto the white surface and "play possum." Any insects so collected should be destroyed.

Snails do considerable damage by eating the young flower stalks and destroying many of the flowers. Trap them on pieces of orange skin placed on a piece of cardboard and sprinkled with powdered alum. As they eat at night they can often be found with a flashlight.

Sow-bugs can be trapped by placing pieces of sliced raw potatoes on the benches. Examine them in the morning, and drop any bugs found into a pail of hot water. Cockroaches, also night prowlers of the orchid and plant house, enjoy chewing the luscious young root tips and freshly

opened flowers. Roach paste, of which several kinds are available, is the only effective means of control. Place small amounts on pieces of cardboard and distribute these among the plants.

The hardy outdoor species are more or less bothered by aphis, fly and red spider, all of which can be controlled by regular sprayings with an approved insecticide. Among larger animal pests, rats, mice and chipmunks destroy many outdoor hardy orchids, especially those of the bulbous types. The other methods of control are by using poison bait; by trapping; and by placing barriers of quarter-inch mesh wire netting around the beds.

A Selected List of Orchids for Different Purposes

1—For Outdoor Culture

Arethusa bulbosa
Bletilla striata
Calopogon (Grass-pink orchid)
Cypripedium (Moccasin-flower); especially *C. montanum, C. parviflorum, C. reginae* and *C. acaule,* which should be obtained from a dealer in native plants, rather than dug up from the wild.
Epipactis decipiens, E. pubescens, E. tesselata
Habenaria blephariglottis, H. ciliaris, H. fimbriata
Liparis liliifolia, L. loeseli
Listera ovata
Microstylis unifolia
Orchis spectabilis
Spiranthes cernua and *S. lucida*

2—For the Small Greenhouse or Dwelling

Cattleya warsewiczi var. *gigas* (known also as *C. gigas*); *C. labiata, C. mossiae*
Coelogyne cristata, C. pandurata
Cypripedium insigne and its varieties (now listed as Cordula): Harefield Hall and *sanderae*
Dendrobium nobile
Zygopetalum mackayi

3—For the Estate Owner or Orchid Fancier

Aërides lawrenciae
Angraecum eburneum, A. sesquipedale
Vanda tricolor var. *suavis*
Zygopetalum mackayi

Also the following genera in different species: Brassocattleya, Brassolaeliocattleya, Calanthe, Cattleya, Cymbidium, Cypripedium, Dendrobium, Epidendrum, Laelia, Laeliocattleya, Lycaste, Masdevallia, Miltonia, Odontoglossum, Oncidium, Phalaenopsis and Schomburgkia.

ORCHID SOCIETY, AMERICAN. This body was organized in 1921 to aid in the importation and improvement of exotic orchids and the preservation of native kinds. The membership consists largely of amateur collectors and fanciers, with some commercial growers. The Society sponsors exhibitions, lectures and publications with which it is spreading knowledge of, and use and love for, its flower. Its members receive all publications and free tickets to exhibitions.

The American Orchid Society Bulletin, issued quarterly, contains valuable information on all phases of orchidology.

Annual dues are $5. The secretary is Mr. David Lumsden, 115 Glenbrook Rd., Bethesda, Md.

ORCHID-TREE. A common name for *Bauhina variegata,* a tropical oriental tree popular in S. Fla. for its purple or white pea-like flowers.

ORCHIS (aur'-kis). A genus of native hardy, terrestrial orchids with small purple, lavender or white flowers that are borne in loose spikes on rather short heavy stems above the large smooth glossy leaves. *O. spectabilis* (Showy Orchis) to 1 ft., the commonest species, may be colonized in the wild garden in open woods in rich leafmold. There is confusion of names between these plants and others belonging to the genus Habenaria (which see), called the Rein or Fringed Orchis.

OREGON-GRAPE. A common name for *Mahonia nervosa,* a small W. evergreen shrub with yellow flowers and blue berries. It is the State flower of Ore.

ORGANIC. Living, as contrasted with inorganic, which means non-living. All living things are either plants or animals, possessing the capacities of growth, behavior, and reproduction of their kind; matter which has once been alive is also called organic. Thus, when a gardener is told to add organic matter to the soil, he should spade in barnyard or other manures, and the contents of his compost heap (made up of garden litter, sods, and other refuse, the manure well mixed and thoroughly decayed; or he can turn under

succulent green manures (which see), that is, crops of grasses, clovers, etc., grown for the purpose of contributing to the organic content of the soil as they decay.

ORGANIC FERTILIZER. Any substance or material of value as a plant food (or containing plant food) derived or manufactured from matter of living origin, as distinguished from matter of mineral, or inorganic, origin. The sources of such material are, of course, animal and vegetable remains, including barnyard manure, green crops grown to be turned under and incorporated with the soil, compost, humus and the natural accumulation of leafmold, etc., in woods or other undisturbed places; and also by-products such as bonemeal, cottonseed-meal, fish scrap, tankage, dried blood, and other refuse from slaughter houses, factories, etc.

In practical usage, however, the term fertilizer is usually restricted to the manufactured or processed and more or less concentrated types of the materials referred to, the other cruder and less prepared substances being classed as manure, which see.

See also FERTILIZER; INORGANIC; PLANT FOODS AND FEEDING.

ORIENTAL FRUIT MOTH. This insect, which attacks peach, quince, apple, pear, apricot, plum and several other fruits, was apparently brought into the U. S. from the Orient some time before 1915; it is now well established over the eastern part of the country. The earliest injury is a dying back of new twigs in the spring, caused by the burrowing of the pinkish or creamy white larvae with brown heads. Later the injury to .the fruit is similar to that done by the codling moth. The larvae pass the winter in cocoons on the bark of trees or in rubbish and the small gray moths with chocolate brown markings emerge in spring to lay eggs on leaves and twigs. There may be from one to seven generations a year. Spraying does not give sufficient control to warrant the expense. Orchard sanitation is of value and the use of paradichlorobenzene about the base of the tree as for the peach tree borer (see under PEACH) kills some of the overwintering larvae.

ORIGANUM (oh-rig'-ah-num). A genus of perennial herbs of which *O. vulgare* is grown for flavoring dressings and sauces. See MARJORAM; also HERBS.

ORIGINATION. The creation of a new plant variety. A plant breeder, nurseryman or gardener by hybridizing (cross-breeding), causes variations in the character of vegetables, fruits, flowers or trees, such as a new color in a dahlia, better flavor in an apple, etc. By study and selection he may find a new and superior form among these variations. Or he may come upon a spontaneous, natural variation or "sport" in which he perceives some desired improvement. He gives it a name, perhaps patents it, and thus becomes the originator of that variety. In the case of annuals, he must also "fix" the strain, so that it will come true from seed. The new variety is then ready to be propagated until there is a commercial supply, introduced, and disseminated.

See also DISSEMINATION; INTRODUCTION; PLANT BREEDING; PROPAGATION.

ORNAMENTAL GRASSES. A number of members of the Grass Family (Gramineae) are useful in landscaping and in the herbaceous border because of their distinctly decorative foliage and the pleasingly varied forms and soft colors of their spikes or plume-like flower clusters. (See illustrations, Plate 37.) Most of the annual forms of ornamental grasses and many of the perennials are also valuable for use in flower arrangements, both fresh and dried as in winter bouquets with everlastings (which see) or by themselves. These grasses are not used as extensively as they could be to advantage.

ANNUAL GRASSES. Annual ornamental grasses are easily raised from seed sown in early spring where the plants are wanted. They prefer an open sunny position and the seedlings should be thinned out when they are quite small so that each plant will have full chance to develop. The most common mistake in growing them is allowing the plants to become or remain crowded. On the average a foot between plants is none too much even though it is hard to believe that the young seedlings will ever need that much space.

Among the annuals suitable for edging the flower border or wherever the smaller, neater kinds are wanted, are the Harestail Grass (*Lagurus ovatus*), Cloud Grass (*Agrostis nebulosa*), and the small Quaking Grass (*Briza minor*). At the other size extreme is Rainbow Corn (*Zea japonica*) that may reach 10 or 12 ft., and there are all sizes in between.

In color, one may have the white downy tufts of Hares-tail Grass; the striped effects

in white, yellow and pink in the case of Rainbow Corn; or, among the Fountain Grasses, the rose or purple plumes and green foliage of *Pennisetum ruppeli,* and the copper bronze foliage and plumes of *P. macrophyllum atrosanguineum.* This is only a hint of the versatile appearance of these annual ornamentals. A list of kinds suitable for gardens would include these genera:

Agrostis, Anthoxanthum, Aspris, Avena, Brachypodium, Briza, Bromus, Chloris, Coix, Demazeria, Echinochloa, Eleusine, Eragrostis, Euchlaena, Festuca, Holcus, Hordeum, Koeleria, Lagurus, Lamarckia, Oryza, Panicum, Paspalum, Pennisetum, Phalaris, Polypogon, Scleropoa, Setaria, Synthterisma, Zea, and Zizania.

PERENNIAL GRASSES. The perennial sorts also range from plants suitable for edgings and rock gardens such as the 6-in. Cocks-foot Grass (*Dactylis glomerata*) to the gracefully majestic Giant Reed (*Arundo donax*) which sometimes reaches a height of 20 ft. According to their height and habit, these can be used in the flower border, in natural gardens, at the edge of ponds or streams, grouped in the shrub border, as temporary summer barriers, and as interesting accent points in the garden design.

Seeds for a large proportion of the perennials are available, from which they can easily be raised, the plants developing quickly. Others can be rapidly increased by division, by cutting a clump in pieces 3 or 4 in. across in early spring. This method should be followed with all the variegated sorts which cannot be depended upon to come true from seed. When transplanting seedlings, remember, as in the case of the annuals, that crowded plants will not thrive; furthermore, as the perennials keep on growing year after year, they will need even more space, or more or less regular thinning out.

For a striking effect in the landscape, the Giant Reed is excellent, doing well in a deep, rich soil. The general effect is somewhat like that of a slender hill of corn, but considerably more graceful. The bamboos, notably *Arundinaria simoni* and *Phyllostachys aurea,* attain 15 ft. or more and are effective, although not entirely hardy without protection in temperate climates. Another of the most beautiful of the perennial types, Pampas Grass (Cortaderia) is also not hardy; in most sections the roots

Plate 37.   ORNAMENTAL GRASSES IN VARIED EFFECTS

Upper left: Bamboos and grasses fringe the tranquil stream.   Upper right: Eulalia's silver and green
leaves cascade gracefully to the lawn.   Lower left: Bold, yet delicate and feathery, the tall plumes of
the pampas grass are excellent as accents.   Lower right: The slender, pale green stems of the
bamboo create striking, exotic effects.

must be stored in soil in a cellar during the winter. Resembling it, and nearly as beautiful, is the Plume Grass (Erianthus), occasionally called the hardy Pampas Grass. The perennial Fountain Grass (*Pennisetum japonicum*) with its fox-tail plumes is also effective in the landscape and border.

Supplying various color tones, there are among the perennials the silvery Beard Grass (*Andropogon argenteus*) growing about 3 ft., and the silver plumed, 8-ft. tall Plume Grass (*Erianthus ravennae*). The Blue Fescue (*Festuca glauca*) produces fine blue-gray foliage, about 9 in. high, and does well in a dry situation. Wild Rye, also called Lyme Grass in its blue form (*Elymus glaucus*), grows about 3 ft. The perennial Fountain Grass has mahogany plumes tipped with white.

There are also many variegated grasses in this group: Eulalia offers two; *Miscanthus sinensis variegatus* has green and white stripes, and Zebra Grass (*M. sinensis zebrinus*) green and yellowish stripes. There is also Ribbon Grass (*Phalaris arundinacea picta*) with green and white stripes. All of these grow about 5 ft. Among the smaller growing ones there are the Cocksfoot Grass (*Dactylis glomerata variegata*), and *Arrhenatherum elatius tuberosum.*

Perennials very useful for cutting are Feather Grass (*Stipa pennata*), Canary Reed (Phalaris), Spike Grass (Uniola); and those suited for dry bouquets include Bottle-brush Grass (Hystrix), Eulalia, and Pampas Grass.

Important genera containing ornamental perennial grasses are Agrostis, Aira, Alopecurus, Ammophila, Ampelodesma, Anatherum, Andropogon, Anthoxanthum, Arrhenatherum, Arundinaria, Arundo, Axonopus, Bambusa, Brachypodium, Briza, Bromus, Cephalostachyum, Chloris, Cortaderia, Cymbopogon, Cynodon, Cynosurus, Dactylis, Dendrocalamus, Elymus, Eragrostis, Eremochloa, Erianthus, Euchlaena, Festuca, Glyceria, Gynerium, Holcus, Hordeum, Hystrix, Koeleria, Leptochloa, Lolium, Melica, Miscanthus, Molinia, Neyraudia, Notholcus, Oplismenus, Panicum, Paspalum, Pennisetum, Phalaris, Phleum, Phragmites, Phyllostachys, Poa, Saccharum, Sasa, Setaria, Stenotaphrum, Stipa, Thamnocalamus, Thysolaena, Tricholaena, Trisetum, Uniola and Zoysia.

ORNITHOGALUM (aur-ni-thog'-ah-lum). Bulbous herbs of the Lily Family,

some from Europe and others from Africa, with white, reddish, or yellow lily-like flowers in clusters at the top of a leafless stalk. (See illustrations, Plate 38.) The hardy species are often left in the ground from year to year but tender sorts, grown in pots or in window gardens, are brought indoors as soon as cold weather arrives. Propagation is by offsets.

Some species, like *O. nutans* and *O. umbellatum*, are found wild in the N. States. The former, 2 ft. tall with leaves 18 in. long and ½ in. wide, bears nodding clusters of flowers 2 in. across that are white inside and green with white margins outside. The latter species, known commonly as Star-of-Bethlehem, is 1 ft. or less tall, with leaves about 1 ft. long and slightly wider than in *O. nutans*. The flowers 1 in. across are white inside, green margined with white outside, and are borne in flattened clusters. Other species of interest are:

O. arabicum. To 2 ft. with leaves 2 ft. long and 1 in. wide. The fragrant flowers borne in racemes are white with shining black pistils. This is a greenhouse plant.

caudatum. A good window plant to 3 ft., with leaves 2 ft. long and 1½ in. wide. The flowers 1 in. across in long racemes are white with green centers.

graminifolium. Has cylindrical leaves 1 ft. long and small white flowers borne in clusters 3 in. long.

narbonense. To 2 ft., with leaves 1½ ft. long and ½ in. wide and racemes of white flowers lined green on the outside.

pyramidale. Hardy, to 2 ft. The leaves and flowers much as in *O. narbonense,* but only half as large; the flower clusters are long and narrow.

thyrsoides. A fine greenhouse plant. To 1½ ft. with leaves 1 ft. long and 2 in. wide and dense clusters of white flowers about ¾ in. across. Var. *aureum,* with deep golden yellow flowers, is known as Chincherichee.

ORONTIUM (oh-ron'-shi-um) *aquaticum.* A handsome native perennial aquatic of the Arum Family whose conspicuous spike or spadix of yellow flowerets has given it the popular name of Golden-club, which see. See also AQUATIC PLANTS.

OROXYLON (oh-rok'-si-lon) or OROXYLUM *indicum.* An oriental tropical tree of the Bignonia Family with large white or purple bell-shaped flowers followed by pods 3 ft. long. It is popular in the Gulf States and Mexico, thriving best in rich, well-drained soils.

ORPINE. The common name for Telephium, a genus of European herbs of the Pink Family; also for the Family Crassulaceae (which see), a group of succulent herbs and shrubs. The name comes from *crassus,* meaning thick, in reference to the fleshy leaves and stems. Formerly Orpine was a common name for species of Sedum, particularly *S. telephium.*

ORTHEZIA (aur-thee'-zi-ah), **GREEN-HOUSE.** A sucking insect (related to the cicada) and even more closely to scales and mealy bugs (which see). The dark-green, wingless young (nymphs) about the size of pinheads have rows of minute waxy plates over their bodies; the adult female drags a white, waxy, fluted eggsac twice the diameter of her body. These insects, whose habits resemble those of mealy bugs, may be controlled by the same methods. See also GREENHOUSE PESTS.

OSAGE-ORANGE. Common name for *Maclura pomifera,* a deciduous tree, native in some of the S. States, but hardy as far N. as Mass. A member of the Mulberry Family, it is a medium-sized, spiny tree with fairly long bright green leaves. The flowers are not showy, but the female tree is conspicuous when bearing the large greenish-yellow orange-like fruits, which are inedible. It has been largely planted in the Middle West for hedges as it survives repeated browsing by livestock and is not particular as to soil. At one time it was largely grown for its leaves, used as a substitute for mulberry for feeding silkworms. The Osage Indians, who valued its wood for bow-making, called it Bow-wood. Because of its durability in the ground it is good for fence-posts and railroad ties. Propagated by seeds and also by greenwood and root cuttings under glass.

OSIER. A common name for those species of Salix (Willow) whose lithe stems or branches are used for wicker-work, especially *S. viminalis* and *S. purpurea.*

Cornus stolonifera, a N. American shrub of a different family, is known as Red-osier Dogwood.

OSMANTHUS (os-man'-thus). Evergreen shrubs or small trees, belonging to the Olive Family. They have attractive foliage and clusters of small, very fragrant flowers, but are too tender to grow out-side in the N. although *O. ilicifolius* may survive in N. Y. State in a sheltered position. They grow well in ordinary soil and can stand partial shade. Propagated by cuttings of half-ripened wood under glass.

PRINCIPAL SPECIES

O. americanus (Devil-wood) is native in the South and grows to 40 ft. It has whitish bark, long shining leaves, and greenish-white fragrant flowers in early spring.

illicifolius is a Japanese shrub to 20 ft., with spiny glossy-green oval leaves and small fragrant white flowers in summer. Var. *myrtifolius* has small narrow leaves, and var. *rotundifolius* is a dwarf form with roundish leaves. Vars. *argentea-marginatus* and *aureus* have white- and yellow-variegated leaves.

delavayi is a Chinese shrub to 6 ft. with small dark green leathery leaves and fragrant white flowers in early spring.

fortunei, a hybrid between *O. ilicifolius* and *O. fragrans,* grows to 6 ft. It has large oval spiny leaves and white flowers.

fragrans is an Asiatic tree to 30 ft., well known in cultivation as a greenhouse shrub, and valued for its yellowish-white fragrant flowers in winter and spring.

OSMOSIS. The absorption of one liquid into another. When two different liquids are separated by a thin membrane, the flow is not, as many would suppose, from the denser to the lighter liquid, but from the lighter to the denser. Thus the soil solution carrying plant food in weak solution is absorbed through the walls of the root hairs, because it is not so concentrated as the liquid sap inside the root cells. On this same principle, soluble plant food such as a concentrated commercial fertilizer should be applied *in small quantities* at a time, *not too close* to the plant roots, and in connection with *prompt generous applications of water;* otherwise the soil solution around the fine roots may be made more concentrated than the liquid in the roots which, as it is drawn out by osmotic pressure, ruptures the cell walls.

See PLANT FOODS AND FEEDING.

OSMUNDA (os-mun'-dah). A genus of ferns represented by three species common and hardy throughout the U. S. from Me. to N. C. and W. to Minn. They are excellent ferns for the garden, succeeding anywhere if given plenty of water, and responding nobly to ideal conditions of good drainage, fibrous soil mixed with swamp mud and a little sand. They differ from the true ferns in having the fertile blades so contracted that they lose all suggestion of a frond and resemble rather a spray of minute flowers going to seed, whence the common name, Flowering Fern. They grow from 3 to 5 ft. high and are unequalled for background plantings. Guard against heavy winds and do not remove old fronds or winter stubble. Principal species are:

O. cinnamomea (Cinnamon Fern). Once-pinnate, broad, blue-green sterile fronds, 2 to 4 ft. tall, and fertile ones bearing narrow spikes of spores, olive green when young and cinnamon-like when ripe in early June.

claytonia (Interrupted Fern). Once-pinnate, 1- to 3-ft. fronds, the fertile ones bearing, half-way to the summit, three or four pairs of abbreviated pinnae, contracted and covered with brown spores. These hang down when ripe and give the plant an appearance unique among all ferns.

regalis var. *spectabilis* (Royal Fern). One of the stateliest and most celebrated of all N. ferns. Fronds 1 to 5 ft., 2-pinnate below, the pinnae distant and again pinnate. The reddish pink fronds in early spring are particularly lovely. The fruit is borne in flower-like panicles at the tip of the fronds. Likes much moisture but must stand with its roots well drained.

OSMUNDINE. The fibrous root-masses of the Cinnamon Fern and the Interrupted Fern, two species of Osmunda common in the U. S. This tough fiber is an excellent and durable material in which to grow orchids and other epiphytes. Two grades are used: that from the upper part of the root mass is preferred for Cattleyas and the like, while the darker and more decayed portion is used for Cypripediums and other more or less terrestrial orchids. Much of the fiber is shipped to orchid growers abroad.

OSOBERRY (*Osmaronia cerasiformis*). A deciduous shrub, native in the western part of the country, belonging to the Rose Family. It grows to 15 ft. and is hardy as far north as Mass. in sheltered positions. Preferring moist soil in a partly shaded place, it has rather large, bright green leaves which open early. The pendulous racemes of small white fragrant blossoms appear with them. The male and female flowers are separate, and usually on different plants. The female plant bears attractive bluish-black fruits.

OSTEOMELES (os-tee-oh-mee'-leez). Ornamental evergreen shrubs of Asia, belonging to the Rose Family. They can stand some frost, but are not hardy where winters are severe. A light soil, with plenty of leafmold, in a sunny position suits them well. Propagation is by seeds, cuttings or layers.

O. anthyllidifolia is evergreen, to 6 ft. with silvery fern-like leaves, clusters of white flowers, and bluish-black berry-like fruits. *O. schwerinae* grows to 10 ft. and has more leaflets.

OSTRICH FERN (*Pteritis nodulosa*). A tall and vigorous fern of the N. E. States. It grows in shaded sandy swamps, often to a height of 7 ft. Though it seldom attains more than 4 or 5 ft. in cultivation, it is a beauty for moist situations. The sterile fronds are broad, tapering below, and palm-like; the fertile ones, which appear in July, are plume-like, shorter, stiff, and with the beaded pinnae rolled back and covering the spores. Prefers spongy soil. (See illustration, Plate 18.)

OSTROWSKIA (os-troh'-ski-ah) *magnifica.* A perennial herb with large lilac flowers known as Giant-bellflower, which see.

OSTRYA (os'-tri-ah) *virginiana.* A deciduous American tree called the Hophornbeam (which see) and also Ironwood.

OSWEGO-TEA. A common name for *Monarda didyma,* a tall, mint-scented herb with crimson flowers (or lighter tones in some of its horticultural varieties). Also called Horse-mint, Bee-balm, Fragrant-balm and Bergamot.

OTAHEITE-GOOSEBERRY (oh-tah-hee'-tee). A common name for *Phyllanthus acidus,* a tree of the Spurge Family with small panicles of reddish flowers and edible fruits that are used for preserves.

OTAHEITE ORANGE. Common name for *Citrus taitensis,* the small ornamental orange grown by florists as a pot plant. Its origin is unknown but the compact form, glossy, oblong leaves, fragrant white flowers, pink on the outside, and the inedible but decorative fruits, make the plant a favorite for indoor culture. The fruits, which are 2 in. in diameter, hang for a considerable period. Propagation is by seeds and by grafting on seedlings. The plant requires a very well drained, mellow soil, prefers a place in a sunny window, frequent watering, and occasional applications of commercial fertilizer.

OTHONNA (oh-thon'-ah). S. African herbs or shrubs, belonging to the Daisy Family. *O. crassifolia,* apparently the only one grown to any extent, makes a good hanging-basket plant for the conservatory or window garden. It has slender drooping stems, fleshy cylindrical leaves, and small heads of yellow flowers produced over a long season. It is easily grown, and propagated by pieces of the stem.

O U R I S I A (oo-ris'-i-ah). Perennial herbs of the Figwort Family, often grown in rock gardens and cool, shaded locations like those in which they are found in New Zealand, Tasmania and the Andes. Some grow erect, while others are decumbent or prostrate. Their flowers, ranging from white to purplish shades with yellow centers and occasionally to scarlet, are usually borne in clusters on mostly leafless stems, though sometimes they are axillary or solitary. The plants thrive in well-drained soil that is kept well watered. Propagation is by seeds or division.

The three species commonly grown are: *O. coccinea,* to 1 ft., with scarlet flowers drooping above the foliage; *O. macrocarpa* in which the thickish stems may attain 2 ft. and the white flowers in whorls have yellow centers; *A. macrophylla,* more slender than *O. macrocarpa* and pubescent.

OUTDOOR LIVING-ROOM. An effectively descriptive name given to that area in the garden devoted to the uses of a general family retreat and lounge, to be furnished with informal tables, seats, couches, swings and so on and sometimes featuring a "barbecue" or open fireplace where food may be cooked on occasion. A definite establishing of limits is essential to the privacy and success of an outdoor living-room; otherwise it will never invite use as a "room," any more than would an indoor room lacking walls—if such were possible—or with glass partitions.

This feature can be made more distinctive if it is some distance from the dwelling. Yet it must be convenient and of ready access, not only from the house but also from other portions of the garden; the ideal location places it sufficiently apart to make it an individual feature and yet sufficiently approachable so that it invites with compelling force. It fulfils its purpose only if lived in as continually as season and weather permit. It may be developed un-

der a large tree, under an arbor, or in the open. Wherever it is situated the space should be paved or otherwise made agreeable underfoot for use in the evening and after summer showers.

OUVIRANDRA (oo-vi-ran'-drah) *fenestralis.* A trade name (and formerly the botanical name) for *Aponogeton fenestralis,* a submerged aquatic commonly called Madagascar Lace-plant or Lattice-leaf.

OVARY. The more or less bulbous part of the pistil within which are contained one or more ovules. Flowers with stamens, petals and sepals originating around the base of, or below, the ovary are said to have a *superior ovary;* when these parts are inserted around the summit of the ovary and seem to rise from it, the ovary appears not within but beneath the flower, which is said to have an *inferior ovary.* See FLOWER.

OVATE. Term applied to leaves and leaf-like parts and meaning egg-shaped in outline, the point of attachment being at the broad end. Compare CORDATE; OBOVATE.

OVULE. A body contained within the ovary of the flower, which when fertilized by the sperm contained in the pollen-grain becomes a seed. See FLOWER.

OWLS-CLOVER. Common name for the genus Orthocarpus, annual and perennial herbs of W. N. and S. America. *O. purpurascens,* a Calif. species, is sometimes grown in gardens for its spikes of purple or crimson tubular flowers.

OXALIS (ok'-sah-lis). A genus of small, rather delicate plants, some useful

AN OTAHEITE ORANGE
The fruit is not edible but it and the plant make a handsome, cheerful decorative plant for the house.

in rock gardens, others for bedding, for hanging baskets, as pot plants, or greenhouse decoration. (See illustration, Plate 38.) The native species are characterized by their clover-like leaves which, like the flowers, close at night. The flowers, usually in pastel shades, have 5 petals which expand above a cone-shaped tube.

Whether being raised from tubers, rootstocks, or seeds, plants grown outdoors are best if started in spring. Both indoor and outdoor subjects require an acid soil composed of a porous mixture of leafmold, sand and loam. Liquid manure applied from time to time when the plants are nearly mature will encourage the production of good flowers.

Among the hardy species is the native one known as Wood-sorrel, especially *O. montana,* familiar in N. woods and useful for naturalizing. Another is its earlier-blooming European representative *O. acetosella* (naturalized in E. N. America). Still other hardy ones are *O. oregana,* from the Pacific Coast, rose-flowered, good for ground-cover in the shade; the S. African *O. bowieana,* whose rose-red flowers will continue to open all summer in the rock garden; and *O. rubra* (often sold as *O. rosea*), with rose, lilac or white flowers compactly clustered on long stalks. The true *O. rosea* has pink flowers more loosely clustered. The purple-leaved bedding oxalis with yellow flowers, generally sold as *O. tropaeoloides,* is *O. corniculata* var. *atropurpurea.*

Tender or half-hardy species include *O. cernua* (Bermuda-buttercup) from S. Africa but naturalized in Fla. and the W. Indies, bearing yellow flowers on stalks which rise above the often purplish leaves; *O. crenata* (Oka), raised as an annual from tubers (which are eaten in S. America), and bearing yellow flowers veined with purple; *O. hirta,* with deep violet, rose or purple flowers, the leaves with 3 narrow leaflets; *O. valdiviensis,* a perennial raised as an annual, with yellow flowers, brown striped inside, clustered on 6-in. stalks; *O. lasiandra* (often sold as *O. floribunda* in several color forms), having large leaves with 5 to 10 leaflets and the flowers crowded in umbels; *A. deppei,* with white flowers and dark green leaves with purple bands; *O. ortgiesi,* somewhat succulent, with yellow flowers, the leaflets having pointed instead of rounded lobes (the latter 2 are especially suitable for greenhouse

culture); and 2 interesting species with many narrow leaflets arranged like rays. One of these is *O. enneaphylla* and the other *O. adenophylla;* both are low, compact plants with large flowers, white or pinkish with darker veins.

Blue-oxalis is *Parochetus communis,* the Shamrock-pea, which see.

OXERA (ok-see'-rah). Shrubby climbing plants belonging to the Vervain Family. *O. pulchella,* apparently the only one cultivated, is usually grown in a warm greenhouse, or outdoors in the warmest parts of the country. It is an interesting winter-flowering climber, bearing clusters of white fragrant trumpet-shaped flowers, 2 in. or more long. It does well in a mixture of fibrous peat and loam with sand, and is propagated by cuttings.

OXEYE. A common name for the genus Buphthalmum, perennial herbs of the Composite Family with showy yellow flower-heads. Easy to grow from seed in any good garden soil.

OXEYE DAISY. A common name for *Chrysanthemum leucanthemum,* a European perennial sometimes grown for its large white flowers but more widely known as a pernicious weed on mis-managed land. It is the State flower of N. Caro.

OXIDE OF IRON. A chemical powder or dust recently found of value in preventing certain fungous diseases, notably damping-off of seedlings, and being increasingly used as a disinfectant. See IRON.

OXLIP. A common name for *Primula elatior,* an old-fashioned garden perennial valued for its abundant yellow flowers in early spring.

OXYDENDRUM (ok-si-den'-drum) *arboreum.* A large slow-growing tree with foliage which turns scarlet in autumn. Commonly called Sorrel-tree or Sourwood, which see.

OXYGEN. A colorless, odorless, tasteless gas, one of the non-metallic elements. Because gardening is based on the growth of plants in the soil, and because more than 47 per cent of the soil and some 42 per cent of any plant is oxygen, it is one of the vital substances in plant life. However, unlike nitrogen, phosphorous and potassium (the most important of the other essential elements), oxygen does not have to be supplied by the gardener since plants secure their supply from the carbon dioxide (CO_2) they take in through their leaves

Upper left: A study in black and white—the hothouse Ornithogalum arabicum. Upper right: Ornithogalum nutans with nodding green and white bells, often escapes the garden's bounds. Center left: The Star-of-Bethlehem graces the rock garden or the grassy field. Lower left: Rose-purple against the gray stone, Oxalis bowieana, from South Africa, fits well into the rock garden. Lower right: The handsome white flowers of Oenothera speciosa open with the morning sun.

from the air, and from the water (H_2O) they take in through their roots from the soil. At the same time, it is part of the gardener's task to keep a supply of moisture available and within reach of the roots, and to so manage the soil that it will contain enough oxygen-bearing air to promote the activity of plant root cells and of the beneficial micro-organisms that inhabit a fertile soil.

For the plant, oxygen performs two kinds of services. First, it combines with other elements to form various compounds from which plants get their nourishment; second, it is a vital factor in many life processes, such as the transformation of the sun's energy into plant tissue, the germination of seeds, the development of flowers, and many more. In short, without oxygen there would be no plants—and, probably, no animals to eat them or people to enjoy them.

OXYTROPIS (ok-sit'-roh-pis). Perennial herbs or small shrubby plants, found mostly in mountainous regions of Europe, Asia and N. America, belonging to the Pea Family. A few species are sometimes grown in rock gardens, where they thrive in sandy loam and a sunny place.

Of the principal species, *O. campestris* grows to 1 ft. with short spikes of pale yellow flowers tinged purple. *O. lamberti* is a low tufted plant covered with silky hairs, and with bluish-purple flowers; it is one of the loco-weeds of the W. *O. splendens* is of similar appearance, with deep purple flowers in dense spikes.

OYSTER-PLANT, or VEGETABLE-OYSTER. Names given (because of the flavor of the long, slender tap-root) to *Tragopogon porrifolius,* a species of Goats Beard or Salsify, which see.

Spanish-oyster-plant is *Scolymus hispanicus.*

OYSTER-SHELL SCALE. A common and widespread pest of various shrubs and trees so called because of the shape of the protective covering which suggests an oyster shell from ⅛ to ¼ in. long. See SCALE INSECTS.

P

PACHISTIMA (pak-is'-ti-mah). Low-growing evergreen shrubs in N. America, closely related to Euonymus. Hardy except in the coldest parts of the country, they seem to thrive in any well-drained soil, and are well suited for rock gardens and the foreground of evergreen shrub borders. Propagated by layers, cuttings, or rooted divisions.

P. canbyi, from the mountains of Va., forms a dense mat up to 1 ft. high, with trailing and rooting branches. It grows well in the open or partial shade. *P. myrsinites,* from Br. Col. and Calif., grows to 2 ft., is of somewhat stiffer habit, and prefers partial shade.

PACHYSANDRA (pak-i-san'-drah). Low, dense-growing hardy herbs or subshrubs, evergreen or partly so, belonging to the Box Family. *P. terminalis* (Japanese-spurge) is one of the most useful evergreen ground-cover plants available, especially for planting under trees. It can also be used to advantage to clothe terrace banks, and any spot where grass will not grow or is not desirable, particularly in shady places. It is easily propagated by cuttings. The terminal spikes of white flowers that open early in spring are attractive to bees. The fruit (not often seen) is a soft white berry. Var. *variegata* has leaves marked white.

P. procumbens (Allegheny-spurge) has less attractive foliage, and is usually deciduous. The greenish-white flowers with purple markings arise from the base of the stem in early spring.

Pachysandra in this country has only one known disease. A fungus may cause large, brown blotches on the leaves and cankers on the stems. The best control is to increase the general vigor of the plants and remove all diseased individuals. Spray with bordeaux mixture. The euonymous scale is frequently, and the San José scale occasionally, injurious. Control with a dormant spray, which see under SPRAYING.

PACKING AND SHIPPING. Gardeners often want to send seeds, plants, flowers, fruits and vegetables by mail or express. Unless they know the correct ways of packing, they are likely to make mistakes which result in spoiled shipments and disappointment. First of all, before getting the shipment ready, make sure that no quarantine regulations prohibit sending it or require inspection and certification by State or Federal officials. The local express agent and postmaster are kept advised of these regulations and can supply information about them and the address of the nearest quarantine headquarters.

Seeds (which see) must be well dried before they are packed for shipment, otherwise they may heat and lose their vitality. Small quantities may be sent in envelopes, which should always be of stout paper so as to avoid breakage of individual packages and disastrous mixing of varieties when several kinds are inclosed in a larger envelope. Extra packing and wrapping is advisable to prevent breakage of seed when the stamps are canceled.

Plants are more likely than seeds to suffer when improperly packed. So far as shipment is concerned they naturally fall into two classes: dormant and active. There is little risk in shipping well-packed dormant deciduous trees, shrubs and woody vines; but the following steps are important: (1) the plants should be carefully dug so as to save all the roots possible. (2) Except with a few species (for example, magnolias) the earth should be shaken off the roots to save weight. (3) The roots should be protected until packed. (4) The time between digging and packing should be as short as possible. (5) The largest specimens should be laid close together and the smaller ones then fitted among them as compactly as possible. (6) When all are in position they should be tied firmly with stout cords around both roots and tops in several places. (7) The inner wrapping material should be of stout oiled or waterproof paper, on which should be spread a liberal amount of excelsior or, better, sphagnum moss, damp but not wet. (8) The bundle should be placed with its roots on this damp material, more of which should be placed upon and among them. (9) The inner wrapper should then be drawn closely around the bundle and securely tied. (10) Apply the outer wrapper, tie securely and attach label firmly, also inspection certificate if required.

Upon arrival the package should be opened at once and, if the packing material is dry, the plants should be plunged, roots, branches and all, for 24 hours or more in water deep enough to cover them.

Evergreens, magnolias and a few other woody plants must be balled and burlapped; that is, dug with earth around the roots and placed on squares of burlap, the corners of which are drawn up over the ball and tied around the trunks. The soil must not be allowed to dry out. On arrival, if the earth ball feels dry and hard through the wrapper, the whole thing intact should be stood in water for several hours. Even when planting it is not necessary to remove all the burlap, but it is advisable to cut away the excess at the top and, if the material is dense and heavy, to cut several slashes in the sides to let the roots through.

Plants such as strawberry and annuals and perennial flowers may be shipped with or without earth. If with earth (plants from pots) the earth must be moist but not wet, and each plant should be wrapped separately in paper and the lot packed snugly in a suitable container—box, basket, or crate. If without earth, the foliage and stems must be dry and left open to the air, and the roots packed with damp, not wet, sphagnum moss, peat moss or similar light but absorbent material. If the foliage is wet, not sufficiently ventilated or too tightly packed, or if the packing is too wet, the plants are likely to "heat" and be destroyed.

Among wrapping materials for plants are waxed and oiled paper, nurserymen's crinkly, waterproof paper, and "parafilm," a kind of thin rubber sheeting which can be stretched but which will not contract to its original size. These can be purchased at garden or florist supply stores.

Flowers should be cut for shipment just as the buds reach maturity and are ready to open and, if possible, early in the morning while the stems and foliage are full of moisture. As cut they should be immersed in cold water. Packing is best done in light cardboard cartons lined with waxed paper, on which latter the flowers should be laid in layers, each layer with the blossoms or buds resting just below those of the layer below. In the case of exhibition stock a sheet of wax paper should go under each layer of bloom; and some sort of cleat across the stems is advisable to keep them from shifting. Otherwise soft tissue paper should be packed in to keep the shipment firm.

Berries, cherries, grapes and soft plums, apricots, etc., are most satisfactorily shipped in commercial packages—standard size berry boxes or "Climax" baskets—and these in crates. Such fruits should always be freshly gathered, dry, and freely ventilated in their packages.

Hard fruits such as apples and pears may be shipped in closed packages (boxes, barrels or caftons), preferably ventilated. Always they should be packed snugly to prevent shifting and bruising; and quality fruit, especially summer apples and pears, is worth wrapping individually in waxed or soft paper. Tomatoes and other soft vegetables should be similarly handled.

Green vegetables such as peas, corn and beans, and the various salad plants and culinary herbs require well-ventilated packages. Asparagus bundles should be stood with their square-cut butts on damp sphagnum moss, and their tips open to the air but protected from injury. Young beets, carrots and the like with tops intact ship best in crates; mature root crops and onions without tops can go in any convenient package and without special handling.

PADDY'S (or IRISHMAN'S) WIG. A common name for the small, creeping herb, *Helxine soleiroli,* grown as a ground cover in greenhouses and mild locations, and also known as Creeping-nettle, which see.

PAEONIA (pee-oh'-ni-ah). A genus of perennial herbaceous or shrubby plants of the Buttercup Family, with thickened rootstocks and large handsome flowers in white, pink and shades of red borne in early spring. Long a favorite garden subject, it is best known by its anglicized and common name, Peony, under which it is treated in this book.

PAGODA-TREE, JAPANESE. A common name for *Sophora japonica,* a large hardy, deciduous tree with yellowish flowers in long panicles. Also called Chinese Scholar-tree.

PAINTBRUSH. A common name for three plants: *Hieracium aurantiacum* (Devils Paintbrush or Hawkweed), a pestiferous weed in fields but sometimes grown for its orange-colored flowers; *Emilia sagittata* (Floras Paintbrush or Tasselflower), a garden annual with small red flowers; and *Castilleja californica* (Indian Paintbrush), a perennial with bright red flowers and floral bracts. See HAWK-WEED; EMILIA; CASTILLEJA.

PAINTED CUP. Common name for the genus Castilleja, also called Indian Paintbrush, native herbs with red-tipped floral leaves, mostly parasites on the roots of other plants.

PAINTED DAISY. A common name for *Chrysanthemum coccineum,* also called Painted Lady and sometimes Pyrethrum (its former generic name), a perennial with pink-, lilac- or white-rayed flowerheads.

PAINTED TONGUE. Common name for *Salpiglossis sinuata,* a half-hardy annual with large funnel-formed flowers of various colors and vein-like markings.

PAK-CHOI (pak-choi'). A pot herb (*Brassica chinensis*), one of the better known Chinese cabbages, which are really mustards. See BRASSICA; CHINESE CABBAGE; MUSTARD.

PALAFOXIA (pal-ah-fok'-si-ah). Former name (still seen in the trade) for Polypteris, a genus of native composite herbs, of which one species, *P. hookeriana,* is grown in gardens for its rose-colored flowers.

PALIURUS (pal-i-eu'-rus). Spiny deciduous trees or shrubs, from S. Europe and Asia, belonging to the Buckthorn Family. One species, sometimes grown in this country, but not hardy north of Washington, D. C., is *P. spina-christi* (Christthorn or Jerusalem-thorn). This is a spreading shrub or small tree to 20 ft. The dark green foliage is attractive, but the real interest is in the brownish fruits, shaped like a low-crowned, wide-brimmed hat. It needs a sunny position and well-drained soil. Propagated by seed, layers and root-cuttings.

PALMA CHRISTI (pal'-mah kris'-ty). A common name for *Ricinus communis,* the Castor-bean-plant, which see.

PALMETTO. Though loosely applied to several genera, this is properly the common name for Sabal, a group of New-World palms embracing about 20 species, spineless and often stemless. They are found from the marshy districts of N. C. to Fla. and then southward throughout Mexico to Venezuela. Found in some localities in groups of only a few trees, in the rich, black soil of Fla. river valleys, it grows by thousands, covering large areas.

The species most common in the U. S. is *S. palmetto,* known as the Cabbage Palmetto, or Cabbage Palm, from the fact that the terminal bud can be eaten, boiled, like a cabbage. In the wild it has an erect stem, from 20 to 60 or rarely 80 ft. tall and from 12 to 15 in. in diameter. The long-stemmed, deeply-cut, fan-shaped leaves measure from 5 to 8 ft. across the blade. This species is the most favored for cultivation. If well cared for, it will thrive on poor sandy soil. It is widely grown along avenues and roads in the S. States, and used generally in landscaping effects.

A tree of large size can be easily transplanted if the whole of the stem is carefully dug out and all the roots and leaves are cut off. The shorn stem is then set at least 3 ft. deep in a generously large hole, which is filled with the richest available soil well firmed. Then water abundantly until growth starts. While growing, it should have liquid nitrogenous fertilizers at frequent intervals and a plentiful supply of water.

All the species of Sabal which make trunks are of great beauty and in the N. several are grown as tub plants in the greenhouse, and moved outdoors in summer. South American palmettos require hothouse conditions. Propagation of all kinds is by suckers.

The Dwarf Palmetto or Blue Palm is *Sabal minor;* but the Blue-palmetto is *Rhapidophyllum hystrix;* and the so-called Saw- or Scrub-palmetto is a related genus, Serenoa, which see.

PALM GRASS. Common name for *Setaria palmifolia,* a perennial member of the Grass Family often grown as an ornamental plant in the far S. and in greenhouses N. It grows to 6 ft., has folded leaves 2 ft. long and 3 in. wide. The spikelets are borne in branching terminal racemes on stems 2 ft. long. One form has striped leaves. See ORNAMENTAL GRASSES.

PALMS. Decorative and useful tropical woody plants, mostly trees, some bushy, and a few climbers, forming the botanical family Palmaceae. This is one of the most outstandingly beautiful groups of the plant world. The stately trunks and feathery foliage of many of the 1,500 or more species give the characteristic note to the tropical landscape.

Those most frequently seen have a cylindrical trunk, from a few to 100 or more ft. in height, in some species smooth, in others armed or spiny, and in many covered with the sheaths of old leaves. Most palms bear their leaves in a crown at the top, and are divided according to the type of foliage and for horticultural convenience into two sections, quite broad in their inclusiveness. One comprises the so-called Fan Palms with broad leaves palmately divided; in some species they are 10 ft. across. The other is made up of the Feather Palms with leaves divided in feather-form, that is, cut into segments from the midrib; these are occasionally nearly 50 ft. in length. Sometimes the foliage, and occasionally the fruit, is armed with sharp spines, or prickles.

Many palms are grown outdoors in Fla., the Gulf States, and Calif., and a few species are native in the S. Among these, the sabals and other palmettos will endure several degrees of frost. Palms of the type of the Royal (which see) add immeasurable dignity when planted along avenues or driveways or to frame vistas, and the Coconut Palms are particularly lovely as they bend over the ocean beaches. The stiff fans of the Palmettos form a good evergreen background for the garden picture; and the plants used singly make excellent accents. The feathery plumage and beautiful flowers and fruit of other species add interest to the tropical and semi-tropical garden, which nothing else can supply.

Black scorch of date palms prevalent in the S. W. is reduced by destroying infected trunks, leaves, and litter. In Calif. a Penicillium disease which may kill ornamental palms appears as discolored linear streaks in leaves of *Phoenix canariensis;* as deformed leaves and retarded terminal growth in *Washingtonia filfera* (for which the resistant *W. robusta* should be substituted); and trunk cankers, which should be surgically treated as soon as noted, on *Cocos plumosa.*

A surprising number of palms are now grown in the U. S. and as experimenting is constantly being done with new species, and much data being accumulated, others will be found adaptable. Among those now frequently grown are the King, Rootspine, Grugru, European Fan Palms, Areca, Wine or Fish-tail Palms, Talipot and Linoma Palms, Assai, Coquito or Monkey Palms, Coconut Palms, Norfolk-Island, Umbrella and Nikau Palms, Spiny Maidenhair or Thorny Fish-tail Palm, Raphia Palms (also called Wine and Bamboo Palms), Silver Palms, Seaforthia, Washingtonia, Latania, Livistona, Date Palms, and others.

PALMS IN THE GARDEN. The outdoor culture of palms varies widely with the location and the species, but in general, most of them will not endure frost and should be planted in a somewhat protected position, sheltered from too intense sun, as well as from cold winds; many of the more tender types, indeed, suffer more from exposure to sun than from cold. The soil, which in most regions well suited to palms (as Fla. and Calif.) is inclined to be sandy, should be made rich with well-rotted manure; this should also be used to mulch the roots during the rainy season. Frequent applications of a well-balanced fertilizer will promote growth and enhance the beauty of the plants.

Many palms drop their leaves, which gradually rotting around the base of the trees provide a natural humus; this should not be raked away. Although palms are associated with sandy places water is required for their best success, especially in the dry season; lacking it, growth will be slow. It has been found that hardiness depends upon age, young specimens often perishing in a cold snap that older trees will come through unscathed even though it means several degrees of frost.

PALMS AS HOUSE PLANTS. Over most of the country palms are best known as house plants. A number of species can be easily grown by anyone under ordinary dwelling conditions. They require relatively little sun and often grow surprisingly well in the living-room, where the atmosphere is usually too hot and dry for most plants. The kinds most widely grown and most easily obtained from florists and nurserymen include: Areca (now listed botanically as Chrysalidocarpus), the Kentias (now classified in the genus Howea and other genera), Cocos (now known botanically as Syagrus), *Livistona chinensis, Phoenix roebeleni* and *P. canariensis.*

For success with palms in the house a few basic requirements should be remembered. Chief among them is never to allow a palm to be chilled by a sudden cold draft from an open door or window; this will cause the leaves to turn brown and eventually drop. As palms are not expensive in the small sizes, it is better to

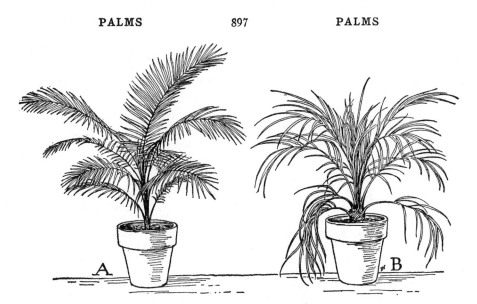

POTTED PALMS REQUIRE LITTLE CARE AS HOUSE PLANTS
A. One of the Coco Palms, Cocos weddelliana. B. A juvenile Date Palm, Phoenix roebeleni. These are two of the most successful types for indoor culture.

buy a new one than to endeavor to restore a chilled plant to normal beauty. Another requisite is to water thoroughly whenever necessary, but never to allow stagnant water to stand in the pot or in the saucer beneath it. It is best to water palms from below, by setting the pot in a basin of water, and leaving it there until the surface soil is damp. This treatment once a week is far better than a daily sprinkling of the soil. To keep the leaves free from dust and soot, sponge them frequently with clear water; regular syringing with a fine spray and considerable pressure will normally keep insects such as scale, thrips, red spider, etc., under control.

Repotting should be done only when absolutely necessary, and preferably in spring or early summer. In shifting do not move to too large a pot; one a single size larger than the former container is about right as palms do best when their roots are confined. A good potting soil consists of 1/3 turfy loam, 1/3 sand, 1/3 mold and dried cow manure in equal parts. Add a 4-in. pot of coarse bonemeal to each bushel of the above mixture.

IN THE GREENHOUSE. For years, palms have been stately greenhouse subjects in botanical garden collections and also in large private conservatories. They are also widely grown commercially in many sections, both in small sizes for sale as house plants and in larger sizes for use as decorative material in hotel lobbies, etc., and at functions.

In the greenhouse the majority of palms succeed best in a night temperature of 60 deg. F. and a day temperature of 70 to 80 deg. During the heat of summer they should be shaded and a humid atmosphere should be maintained by frequent watering and constant spraying of the foliage. However, adequate ventilation should be assured day and night in order to keep down fungous diseases, which thrive in a hot, moist atmosphere.

To control a leaf spot or anthracnose that may kill the tips of the leaves and cause spotting, carefully cut off all dead lower leaves and burn them; also spray with bordeaux mixture. Mealy bugs and many kinds of scales infest palms in greenhouses and dwellings but all can be controlled by cyanide fumigation or by repeated spraying with nicotine-sulphate and soap or other contact spray. The scales can be wiped off the leaves of a small stock of plants with a soft cloth dipped in the soapy solution.

ECONOMIC VALUE. In the tropics, palms are an essential part of the lives of the natives, besides being in several cases the source of important products used throughout the world. From palms people secure food, clothing and shelter; it has been estimated that the Palmyra Palm has 800 uses. The Coconut provides in its nuts a valuable food, an important source of oil and fat, and also a fibre which is manufactured into matting and many other useful articles. Other palms yield palm oil and wine, and from the starchy pith of some species is manufactured sago, an important foodstuff for thousands in the tropics. The Cabbage Palm develops an edible bud on the leafy shoot, dying when it is gathered; the betel-nut, widely chewed as a stimulant by the natives of S. Asia and the E. Indies, is the fruit of the palm called Areca; and the date, the dried fruit of a widely grown palm genus, is an important article of commerce.

PAMPAS GRASS. Common name for Cortaderia, a genus of tall-growing perennial grasses, native to S. America, and one of the showiest of the ornamental kinds. (See illustration, Plate 37.) The long silky plumes, borne in late summer, remain beautiful for many weeks. They may be cut and dried for winter house decoration as soon as they are fully developed.

Pampas Grass thrives in a rich, light, sandy soil in a sheltered position among shrubs or on the lawn. It is not hardy N. but can be grown there as an annual, from seeds sown under glass in spring. Seedlings are first transplanted to a coldframe for hardening, then when 1 to 2 ft. high to their permanent location. In warm sections clumps can be divided.

C. selloana grows to 20 ft., has very long leaves about ¾ in. wide, and white or pink panicles. *C. rudiuscula* grows to 6 ft., has leaves to 4 ft. long, and purple or yellow panicles.

Cortaderias are often called Gyneriums, the two genera being much alike, except for flower details. See UVA GRASS, which is *G. sagittatum;* also ORNAMENTAL GRASSES.

PAN. In gardening, a broad shallow flower pot (which see), either round or square, used for germinating limited quantities of seed or for forcing bulbs indoors.

PANAMA-HAT-PLANT. C o m m o n name for the tropical American palm, *Carludovica palmata.*

PANAX (pay'-naks). A genus of perennial herbs commonly called Ginseng (which see), grown for their roots, which are used in medicine.

PANCRATIUM (pan-kray'-shi-um). A genus of interesting white- or green-flowered bulbous plants of the Amaryllis Family; the white cup bearing the stamens in some species somewhat resembles the trumpet or crown of a daffodil. The cultivated species, some of which are mistakenly called and grown as Hymenocallis, require a rather high temperature, good ventilation without drafts, frequent syringing, abundant watering, and a rich loamy soil containing about ⅓ well-rotted cow manure. While flowering, they may be given a cooler, airier place; after flowering water should be gradually reduced until their resting period arrives. After a few weeks on a bench in a coolhouse where they are occasionally watered, they are ready to grow again. Unless crowded, it is better to top dress them than to disturb their roots. If offsets develop they may be used for propagation, rooting them in a mixture of sand, leafmold and peat. Seeds may also be used; young plants should be kept moist and given plenty of sun.

The hardiest species, useful for summer bloom in milder climates, is *P. illyricum,* bearing 6 or more flowers at the top of a scape 1 ft. tall. The evergreen, fragrant, white-flowered *P. maritimum* has a cup 1 in. long within a perianth which extends 1½ in. above the tube.

PANDANUS (pan-day'-nus). Screwpine. A large genus of trees or shrubs of the family of the same name, which comes from the spiral way in which the leaves are arranged. They are handsome, easily cultivated as potted plants for the house, succeeding best in sandy loam with charcoal and leafmold intermixed. They require good drainage with plenty of water in summer, but are best kept moderately dry in winter, when no water should be allowed to lodge in the axils of the leaves. The plants have a disposition to raise themselves out of the pots because of the downward course which the roots pursue.

One of the best and most useful species is *P. veitchi,* largely employed in a young state for table use. For this purpose, propagation is by offsets or suckers which, arising from the base, should be cut as soon as they are large enough to be detached. This should be done carefully with the point of a sharp knife. The cuttings are inserted singly in small pots, the crown of each cutting being kept well up, and the pots should be plunged in a close frame with but little water given until roots are formed. Propagation may also be from seed. During the winter the foliage will benefit from occasional gentle spongings with warm, slightly soapy water, dried off with a damp cloth.

PRINCIPAL SPECIES

P. baptisti. Short-stemmed, with green leaves about 1 in. wide, striped yellow or white.

caricosus. A shrub of dwarfy branching habit, with narrow, channeled leaves about 2 in. wide, a gray-green underneath and not very spiny.

gracilis. Shrubby, overlapping leaves with incurved prickles along the margins and midrib.

graminifolius (Grass-leaved Pandanus). Leaves narrow, 12 to 18 in. long, gray-green beneath.

pygmaeus (Pigmy Pandanus). A low spreading shrub, less than 2 ft. high in the center, sending out branches from the base in all directions, with the leaves at the ends of the branches, gray-green beneath.

sanderi. Short-stemmed, with leaves 2 in. or more wide and yellow bands running lengthwise of the margins.

variegatus. Green leaves striped, blotched or marked with white. Sometimes the whole leaf is white in young plants.

veitchi. Leaves 2 ft. long, up to 3 in. wide, spiny, dark green in the center and bordered with white. A very handsome decorative house plant.

PANDOREA (pan-doh'-ree-ah). Vigorous-growing evergreen vines from Australia and S. Africa, belonging to the Bignonia Family. They grow outdoors in warm regions, but can stand a few degrees of frost. A sunny location and rich soil suits them best. Propagated by seeds and cuttings of green wood. The principal species are as follows:

P. pandorana (Wonga-Wonga-vine) is the least showy, with many-flowered panicles of whitish-yellow flowers spotted purple; but it would be worth growing for the fine foliage alone. *P. ricasoliana* has loose clusters of pale pink flowers with red stripes; it is slow in getting established and reaching the flowering stage. *P. jasminoides* (Bower-plant) has few-flowered clusters of white blossoms with pink throat.

PANICLE. A loose, spire-like arrangement of flowers (*inflorescence*) on a stalk; a branched raceme (which see). Astilbe, often called Japanese-spirea, is an example.

PANICUM (pan'-i-kum). A rather large genus of annuals and perennials of the Grass Family. They are of little garden interest, but some are important grain and forage plants, and others are troublesome weeds. One species, *P. capillare,* a hairy plant often called Witch Grass (which see), has large loose spikes which are sometimes used in both living and everlasting bouquets. *P. virgatum* (Switch Grass), a perennial to 6 ft. but otherwise much the same as *P. capillare,* can be raised by seed for ornament. Millet (*P. miliaceum*) is the best-known species of agricultural interest.

PANSY. Under the old name of Heartsease, the Pansy (*Viola tricolor* var. *hortensis*) has long been grown in beds and borders because of its ease of culture and the wonderful diversity in color and markings. (See illustration, Plate 57.)

This is an anual or a perennial treated as an annual, with long and branching stems, oval leaves, coarsely notched, about 1½ in. long, and stipules ½ in. broad. The flowers are large for Violas, of purple, white or yellow but showing wide variation, not only in color but size and shape as well.

While Pansies will do well in any good light soil, they prefer a sandy, loamy, deep planting where the roots may be kept cool, and a location where they will not be overshadowed by trees or too much exposed to hot dry sun. Ordinary good garden soil to which has been added about ⅓ well decayed leafmold, humus or finely sifted coal ashes makes an ideal soil.

They are multiplied by seed, cuttings and sometimes by layering. Seed may be sown at any time but, as planting is best performed in spring or early autumn, it is advisable to sow in June for transplanting in autumn and in late August for the early spring transplants. Sow seed in light soil, cover slightly, and transplant to boxes as soon as large enough. It is important that good roots be formed and that balls of soil should adhere before the final setting. Cuttings from side-shoots start readily during late summer. If they are bent over, the side-shoots will also soon root as layers. In some instances the old plants may be divided carefully at the roots.

In planting, press roots firmly and deeply in the soil and, as soon as the flowering period begins, apply a top mulch of humus or leafmold. If exhibition flowers are wanted, from 4 to 6 shoots may be allowed each plant, the remaining ones being removed or pinched out. If all blossoms are removed up until about 3 weeks before the show, the plant will be strengthened and the size of the blossoms increased.

For two leaf spotting fungi that produce whitish spots spray with bordeaux mixture to which potassium oleate has been added as a sticker. If cutworms and slugs feed on leaves and flowers of plants in coldframes and in the garden they should be sprayed with lead arsenate. The celery leaf tyer may severely injure pansies under glass. See under CELERY.

PAPAVER (pah-pay'-ver). The genus known popularly as Poppy (which see). Containing both annuals and perennials, the group may be recognized by its large flowers with paper-like petals of clear color on long slender stems; and by its milky juice.

PAPAVERACEAE (pah-pa-ver-ay'-see-ee). The Poppy Family, a group of largely familiar herbs, many of them choice

MULCH PAPER FOR A YOUNG TREE
A square of mulch paper slit to an opening in the center, slipped around a newly planted tree and held down with soil on the edges conserves moisture and avoids the need of cultivating.

flower-garden subjects. Widely distributed, these plants are most abundant in the tropics; many are characterized by a milky or colored juice and showy flowers, the petals of which are often wrinkled; the numerous very slender stamens are arranged in whorls. (The closely related family *Fumariaceae* is distinguished by its watery juice.) Genera commonly culti-

vated are Papaver (poppy), Romneya, Platystemon, Meconopsis, Chelidonium (celandine), Glaucium, Dendromecon (tree poppy), Eschscholzia (California poppy), Hunnemannia (tulip poppy), Macleaya, Argemone.

PAPAYA (pah-pah'-yah). A common name for *Carica papaya,* a tropical American tree better known as Pawpaw (which see). Do not confuse with the N. American (though not entirely hardy) deciduous tree, *Asimina triloba,* also called Pawpaw or Papaw.

PAPER-BUSH (*Edgeworthia papyrifera*). A small deciduous shrub, also called Mitsumata, hardy only in warm-temperate regions. It has very flexible stems that can easily be tied into knots, and a soft tough paper is made from the inner bark. It has clusters of fragrant yellow flowers, usually in advance of the leaves, which are long, covered with silky hairs when young, and crowded at the ends of the branches. It will grow in any good garden soil, but is not happy in hot dry summers.

PAPER-MULBERRY. Common name for *Broussonetia papyrifera,* a deciduous tree, hardy in the Central States.

PAPER, MULCH. A type of heavy, black, durable paper made especially to be placed on the ground between crop rows and around plants, trees, etc., to check evaporation of soil moisture, prevent weed growth, obviate cultivation of crops, and stimulate and improve plant growth in various ways. Perfected as an aid in pineapple culture, it has been adapted to the cultivation of both commercial and home plantings of both food and ornamental crops. Sold in rolls of different widths and weights the paper is either spread on the ground in advance of planting and the plants or bulbs set in the soil through holes punched where needed, or laid down in the space between rows of seedlings, or cut into squares that are placed around individual shrubs or trees. In either case it is held down by pulling soil over the edges, or by means of arrangements of wires or laths or both attached to pegs driven into the soil beside the paper.

PAPER-PLANT or PAPER-REED. Common names for Papyrus, which see.

PAPHIOPEDILUM (pay-fi-oh-pee'-dilum). A genus of tropical American, epiphytic or terrestrial, orchids having leathery leaves and racemes or panicles of pale green, yellow-green, or white flowers with sac-like lips. These plants and those of the genus Cordula were formerly listed as Cypripedium and are still best known and frequently referred to under that name; or by the common name of Venus- or Lady-slipper. These tropical species and their numerous hybrids are usually grown in the hothouse; a few of them in a house of intermediate temperature where they require a copious supply of water at all times. Interesting species are *P. caricinum, P. caudatum* and *P. sargentian- um.* See also LADY-SLIPPER.

PAPYRUS (pah-py'-rus). Common name for the tall growing sedge, *Cyperus papyrus* (formerly *Papyrus antiquorum*), now a favorite in the water garden, but used by the ancient Egyptians as a source of their paper.

PARADICHLOROBENZENE. A white flaky or granular material, used as a re- pellent against clothes moths and other household insects. In the garden it is used chiefly to control the peach borer and the oriental fruit moth. For direc- tions see under PEACH.

PARADISEA (par-ah-dis'-ee-ah) *lilia- strum.* A perennial of the Lily Family with funnel-shaped flowers 2 in. long. See ST. BRUNOS LILY.

PARAFFIN. The use of melted paraf- fin to cover grafts instead of the familiar grafting wax (which see), received con- siderable attention following successful ex- periments with it in connection with work on nut trees reported about 1920 by Dr. Robert T. Morris of Connecticut. He found that it was convenient and cleanly to use, afforded protection to the graft from moisture and infection, admitted the helpful light rays and thereby hastened the union of stock and scion, and in gen- eral greatly simplified the previously dif- ficult problem of nut grafting.

From his work and recommendation that not only the graft but the entire scion be covered with the melted (but not hot) paraffin, developed the now quite common practice of dipping the entire top of dor- mant plants, such as rose bushes and some fruit trees, in paraffin to check evapora- tion and keep them in better condition between digging and storage. This treat- ment has become widespread among nurs- erymen, especially in connection with the so-called packaged roses, in which the roots are embedded and sealed in a mass of peat moss, the whole plant being en- closed in a carton for sale by department and hardware stores, etc.

Paraffining has also been practiced on budded plants, but with somewhat less suc- cess, owing to the greater susceptibility of the tender buds to injury. Neverthe- less, the use of paraffin, which can be ob- tained anywhere and kept in the right con-

MULCH PAPER FOR SMALL PLANTS
A strip of this durable paper can be spread on the row and plants set through holes cut out of or slit in it at the right intervals, as shown in front; or two strips can be laid down on either side of a planted row of larger plants. Weigh it down with soil along the edges or with cross wires fastened to pegs.

dition for application with a soft brush in a simple heating pot, as an easy method of covering any sort of propagation wound and of preventing evaporation and drying of the tops of dormant, deciduous plants, can well be investigated by home gar- deners. Information about the latest de- velopments and recommendations in the field can be obtained from State agricul- tural colleges and experiment stations.

PARASITE. The original meaning of this word is "one who frequents the table of a rich man and gains his favor by flattery." Biologically the word refers to a plant or animal nourished by an- other to which it attaches itself or within which it establishes itself. Generally the presence of the parasite produces a dis- eased condition but this is not always true. The term *pathogene* is used to cover all disease-producing organisms whether they are parasitic or not.

PARASOL - TREE, CHINESE. A common name for *Firmiana simplex,* the Phoenix-tree, a 50-ft. tree planted in S. gardens and streets for shade. See CHINESE PARASOL-TREE.

PARDANTHUS (pahr-dan'-thus). Catalogue name and former botanical name for the Asiatic perennial, *Belamcanda chinensis*, the Blackberry-lily, which see.

PARIS (pa'-ris). A genus of liliaceous plants similar to Trillian. See HERB-PARIS.

PARIS DAISY. A common name for *Chrysanthemum frutescens* (Marguerite), popular and much grown by florists as a pot plant for winter bloom.

PARIS GREEN. A familiar, widely used stomach poison (which see) known chemically as aceto-arsenite of copper. The insecticide is usually applied as a spray or used in making poison baits. See ARSENICAL POISONS; also INSECTICIDE.

PARKINSONIA (pahr-kin-soh'-ni-ah). Tropical or subtropical trees or shrubs, belonging to the Pea Family. The principal species is *P. aculeata* (Jerusalem-thorn or Ratama), a thorny evergreen small tree, with feathery, pendulous branches and loose clusters of fragrant yellow flowers. It is much used as a hedge plant in warm regions, and can stand very dry conditions. It has been tried as a warm greenhouse plant, but it is not easy to grow in pots. Propagated by seeds.

PARNASSIA (par-nas'-i-ah). Grass-of-Parnassus. Small perennial herbs, found in moist places in the north temperate zone, belonging to the Saxifrage Family. They are interesting for partly shaded moist places, blooming in late summer. The white flowers, marked with greenish or yellowish veins, are borne singly. Propagated by both seed and division.

P. caroliniana, common in moist meadows and swamps of the N., grows to 1 ft. or more with ovate leaves about 2 in. long, and flowers 1 in. or more across. *P. palustris,* found in Europe and Asia, as well as N. America, has smaller leaves and flowers. *P. asarifolia,* found in the mountains of Va. and N. C., grows to 20 in., with kidney-shaped leaves and flowers 1 in. across. *P. fimbriata* is native in the N. W., and is distinguished by its fringed-petaled flowers.

PAROCHETUS (pa-roh-kee'-tus) *communis.* A perennial tropical trailer with blue and pink pea-like flowers. See SHAMROCK-PEA.

PARONYCHIA (par-oh-nik'-i-ah). Whitlow-wort, or Nailwort. Small annual or perennial, mostly hardy tufted herbs of the Pink Family, well suited for rockwork, walls and carpet bedding. They thrive in light sandy soils and may be increased from seeds or, the perennials, by division of the roots.

P. argentea is a low prostrate perennial with egg-shaped leaves and small, whitish, crowded flowers. Free-growing plants forming neat patches 1 ft. or more in diameter. *P. argyrocoma* is an upright perennial to 8 in., forming broad mats covered with silvery downy hairs; straight leaves, and small flowers, in forked flat clusters. Native from Me. to Ga.

PARROTIA (pah-roh'-shi-ah) *persica.* A small deciduous tree, native of Persia and belonging to the Witch-hazel Family. It is hardy but in cultivation usually takes the form of a large shrub. It likes a well-drained, loamy soil in a protected place. The flowers are more curious than beautiful; they are without petals, but have conspicuous purple stamens, and appear before the leaves. The latter take on brilliant coloring in the fall. Propagated by seeds and layers.

PARROTS-BILL, or PARROT-BEAK. Common names for *Clianthus puniceus*, a vine-like shrub with large pea-like crimson flowers in drooping racemes; also called Red Kowhai.

PARROTS FEATHER. Common name for *Myriophyllum proserpinacoides*, a delicate, feathery-leaved, light-green aquatic herb used in fountain basins, aquaria and pools for its above-the-surface foliage.

PARSLEY. A biennial herb (*Petroselinum hortense*) grown as an annual. Its many horticultural varieties are grouped as curled-leaved (var. *crispum*) fern-leaved (var. *filicinum*) and Hamburg or "rooted" (var. *radicosum*). Though the leaves of all are used for flavoring meat dishes, soups, salads, etc., the curled varieties are most popular in America both for this purpose and for garnishing, though the fern-leaved are, equally attractive. Hamburg Parsley is generally cooked like parsnips.

As parsley seed germinates slowly (sometimes taking several weeks) it should be soaked in warm water over-night before planting. Sow outdoors in early spring in rows 10 to 12 in. apart, and cover ½ in. deep. Later thin the plants to stand about 6 in. apart. The leaves may be cut all season for use as needed. In the fall they may be dried and stored in tight jars, or roots may be transplanted into pots or boxes to be grown on indoors. The following spring remove the flower stems as fast as they appear so as to keep the plants producing leaves until those grown from a newly sown crop are ready.

The parsley stalk weevil sometimes hollows out the main stem, but no remedy or preventive is known. The celery worm also feeds on parsley. For control see under CELERY. See also HERBS.

PARSLEY FAMILY. Another name for the Carrot Family. See UMBELLIFERAE.

PARSLEY FERN (*Cryptogramma acrostichoides*). A small rock fern of the N. States, with narrow pod-like segments on the fertile fronds and parsley-like barren fronds.

PARSNIP. A biennial herb (*Pastinaca sativa*) grown for its long, thick, white, sweet roots which are used as a vegetable from late autumn to early spring. To produce straight, unbranched roots, the plants should be grown in deep, rich, moist soil. As they require a long season to develop and as the seed is slow to sprout, sow it in early spring in rows 18 in. apart, scattering seeds of a quick-growing forcing radish at 3-in. intervals to mark the rows. When these are of edible size, use them and weed and thin the parsnip seedlings to stand 6 in. apart. Cultivate cleanly all season until the foliage touches between the rows. Beginning in late fall dig as needed. Some may be stored in a root cellar or a pit for winter use when the ground is frozen; but leave enough in the ground for spring use as they are not injured by freezing. In spring dig as needed until new tops start to grow, then dig all that remain and store them in a cold place to prevent sprouting. So long as they do not start to grow, spring-dug parsnips are better than fall-dug ones.

Celery blight or leaf spot may also injure parsnips (see under CELERY). The carrot rust fly (see under CARROT) injures parsnip roots and the celery worm feeds on the foliage. The parsnip web-worm binds together and feeds on unfolding blossom-heads of both parsnips and celery. Spray or dust with calcium arsenate and cut injured flower-heads in August before moths emerge. Large green caterpillars with black cross bands (the larvae of the black swallowtail butterfly) also feed on parsnip and related root vegetables. Cow-parsnip is Heracleum; Meadow-parsnip is Thaspium.

PARTERRE (pahr-ter'). An area devoted to ornamental beds separated by paths, usually disposed in symmetrical arrangement and containing flowers or occasionally filled with selected pebbles of different colors, or even, in one or two famous instances, with colored glass chips. The mosaic effect suggests a great rug spread on the ground, this comparison being justified by the essential meaning of the term parterre, which is "flat on the earth." A broader treatment with lawns and pools is also designated by this term.

PARTHENOCISSUS (pahr-the-noh-sis'-us). Deciduous high-climbing vines, native in N. America and Asia, belonging to the Grape Family. They cling closely to walls and other supports, mostly by means of tendrils with adhesive tips. They thrive in any good soil not too dry and, when established, cover a large space. Propagated by seed, cuttings and layers.

Enemies are the same as for Ampelopsis (which see), with which the following species were formerly associated.

PRINCIPAL SPECIES

P. quinquefolia (Virginia creeper, American Ivy) is a handsome tall climber, native from New England southward. It clings to walls or tree trunks, and is also an excellent cover on steep banks. Its large 5-parted leaves, which clearly distinguish it from Poison Ivy (which see) with which it is sometimes confused, turn scarlet and crimson in fall. Var. *engelmanni* is a good form with smaller leaves.

tricuspidata (Boston Ivy, Japanese Ivy) is a high-climbing and close-clinging Asiatic vine. Its glossy 3-lobed or 3-parted leaves of varying size make a very dense flat covering especially on brick walls, and give a brilliant patch of orange and scarlet in fall. Var. *veitchi* is a form with smaller leaves, purple when young, and entire or 3-parted. Var. *lowi* has small leaves varying from entire to 3-parted or palmately lobed, turning deep red in fall.

henryana is a tender Chinese vine of moderate growth, with 5-parted leaves marked white along the veins, and purple beneath. The leaf coloring is developed best under glass or outdoors in a partly shaded place. See also IVY.

PARTNERSHIP CROPPING. The practice of growing two crops, that have the same season but that differ in habit of growth, on the same area at the same time. See CROPPING SYSTEMS.

PARTRIDGE - BERRY. A common name for *Mitchella repens;* also in the N. for *Vaccinium vitis-idaea.*

PASQUE-FLOWER. Common name for *Anemone pulsatilla,* an early spring perennial with lilac cup-shaped flowers.

PASSIFLORA (pas-i-floh'-rah). Passion-flower. A large genus of mostly tendril-climbing vines, the principal member of the Passion-flower Family (Passifloraceae). Some species are grown under glass or as climbing house plants, or outdoors in warm regions, for their interesting and ornamental flowers, and others are grown for their edible fruits. The flowers are of unusual structure, thought by early discoverers to be emblematic of the crucifixion of Christ. Under glass they may be grown in pots, or planted out in a border if intended to cover a large area. They do well in fibrous loam with leafmold, and appreciate liquid manure when growth is active. Propagated by seeds and cuttings.

PRINCIPAL SPECIES

P. caerulea is a slender but vigorous grower, with flowers 3 to 4 in. across in a mixture of white, blue, and purple, followed by egg-shaped yellow fruits. There are several named forms, Constance Elliot, with white fragrant flowers, being one of the best.

alata has winged stems, large fragrant flowers of crimson, purple and white, and yellow edible fruit about 5 in. long.

alata-caerulea is a hybrid between these two, with fragrant flowers of white and pink, the crown purple, blue and white.

racemosa, with deeply lobed leaves, is one of the best of the red-flowered species, and has been largely used in hybridizing.

coccinea, with ovate leaves not lobed, is a free-flowering species with scarlet and orange flowers.

laurifolia (Jamaica-honeysuckle) has entire leaves, white flowers spotted red, and yellow edible fruit.

manicata is a rapid and vigorous climber, suitable for outdoor planting in the warmer parts of the country. It makes a fine show with its profusion of bright scarlet flowers set off with a blue crown.

exoniensis, a hybrid between *P. vanvolxemi* and *P. mollissima,* has large showy flowers of brick-red and rose-pink.

quadrangularis (Granadilla) is one of the chief species grown for fruit. It is a tall strong grower, with large fragrant flowers of white, red and purple, and yellowish-green fruits to 9 in. long.

edulis (Passion-Fruit, Purple Granadilla) has white and purple flowers smaller than most, and purple fruit about the size of a hen's egg. It is grown as a commercial crop in Australia.

incarnata (Maypop) is a native; fruit edible; flowers white, pink and purple.

PATENT, PLANT. The granting of a patent for a new kind of plant—thereby putting the producer of that plant on the same basis in the eyes of the law as the inventor of a patentable device or method—was authorized for the first time in history on May 23, 1930, when President Hoover signed the Townsend-Purnell Act which amended those sections of the Federal Statutes known as the Patent Laws.

The amendments were comparatively slight, adding in one section after the granting of the right to "make, use, and vend the invention or discovery" the words "(including in the case of a plant patent the exclusive right to asexually reproduce the plant)." To the second section, describing those eligible to secure a patent, was added this phrase: "or who has invented or discovered and asexually reproduced any distinct and new variety of plant, other than a tuber-propagated plant."

Within 5 years from the enactment of the Plant Patent Act, about 150 patents had been issued, a good proportion of them for roses, a number for fruits, especially plums and apples, a few for small fruits, several for flowering plants and a scattering for evergreens, mushrooms, waterlilies, bulbous subjects and so on. Five years later (October, 1940) the number of patented plants was 430, roses still being strongly in the majority, and there being much the same scattered distribution among other kinds. The progress of the Act has, however, been accompanied by considerable controversy as to various important details—especially as to its interpretation in the U. S. Patent Office where the applications are handled and reviewed, with the assistance and coöperation of experts in the Department of Agriculture. Questions have been raised as to the right to issue a patent for a "sport," that is a new type or kind of plant produced naturally, not as the result of man's efforts, but observed, recognized as meritorious and propagated by him. Also there is disagreement as to whether patents or the formal patent descriptions should refer to, or cover, individual plants as such, their products, such as fruits or flowers, etc., or plant types or groups.

Irrespective of these discussions and their ultimate outcome, the fact remains that the legislation was introduced and enacted for the purpose of recognizing the value of the work of plant breeders and others who give to the world new and worthwhile plants; and of enabling such persons to secure some material reward for their work by giving them the right, for 17 years, to control by license or otherwise the production and sale of the offspring of their plant "invention." That such recognition and right were deserved and long overdue seems to be generally accepted by persons familiar with the history of the development of new plants and with the many cases in which the contributor of a vastly important variety not only failed to receive anything for it but actually died in want. The only question at issue is as to how best the desired objective can be attained so as to avoid future complications and litigation.

Meanwhile, as far as the average gardener is concerned, the plant patent situation is briefly this: The person who, through hybridization or other method, produces a new plant, or who first recognizes in one of his plants a new and desirable characteristic, and who thereupon propagates that plant asexually—this is, by any other method than by seed, is now able to apply to the U. S. Patent Office for a patent on that plant. The Patent Office will supply full information and instructions as to how this should be done; but since all patent matters are complicated and involve legal and technical points, it is usually desirable and advisable to employ an experienced patent lawyer to look after the filing of the patent application with the necessary description and drawing; to make the required search of previously issued patents, etc. There are certain set fees for some of these steps but it appears than $200 is an average total cost.

Once secured, the patent does not in itself confer any protection, but merely gives the holder standing in the eyes of the law and the Government if he should bring suit against any person who attempts to propagate and dispose of any plants of the patented variety without permission. This may involve the purchase of a license or the signing of an agreement for which the patentee can charge whatever he thinks is right. Payment can be required as a flat sum, or in the form of royalties on authorized sales.

Another value of a patent is that it can be used as a selling point in advertising a new plant. For it seems obvious that a new sort, for the protection of which the introducer is willing to spend some hundreds of dollars and go to considerable trouble, is possessed of more than average merit, and therefore is worth the premium price asked for it. Of course, the expectations of the producer of the plant may not be realized; again, after a few years, sales under license may have been so great that the value of the patent will lessen considerably. However, in either case, its holder will have secured far more than was ever possible before the enactment of the Plant Patent Act.

PATHOGENE. Any disease-producing organism, often parasitic but not necessarily so. See PARASITE; also HOST.

PATHS. See GARDEN PATHS.

PATIO (paht'-yoh) **GARDEN.** This refers to a garden within a court, which is the literal translation of "patio." Such a garden is sometimes loosely termed a "Spanish garden." The custom of building dwellings and other edifices around the four sides of an open and unroofed space, upon which the rooms all open—generally under the shelter of a continuous colonnade—probably came to Spain (with which it is generally associated) with the Moors. For the arrangement of an open area completely surrounded and protected by the house is a device of the Orient where absolute seclusion is a requirement for the women of the household, even though the climate makes outdoor living instinctive and puts a premium, especially in summer, on abundant circulation of air.

All regions of Spanish influence have adopted it; but in the freedom of the western world, the patio is usually open on one side—the opening being protected by a low wall or iron grill—the house occupying the other three. In this very intimate space, gardening is best confined to plants of special beauty and importance. In accordance with the Spanish custom of using potted plants lavishly, set wherever fancy dictates or the garden design invites, the handling of such material is most appropriate. It does not, however, preclude planting others in the earth. So a patio garden may properly include a tree or trees if desired, depending only on its spaciousness.

PAULLINIA (pau-lin'-i-ah). One species (*P. thalictrifolia*) of this genus of tropical climbing shrubs is sometimes grown in greenhouses for its attractive foliage. It is a twining plant with much divided, fern-like leaves, tinted bronze when young. The flowers are pale and inconspicuous. It thrives in a mixture of

ONE SEASON'S GROWTH
Besides being a handsome, sturdy shade tree, Paulownia tomentosa, the Empress-tree, is remarkably vigorous, as this one-year-old shoot from a stump proves.

loam and leafmold, and is useful for decorative draping purposes. Propagated by cuttings.

PAULOWNIA (pau-loh'-ni-ah). A genus of Asiatic trees of the Figwort Family having large leaves resembling those of catalpa and large erect clusters of beautiful violet, gloxinia-like flowers. *P. tomentosa* (formerly *P. imperialis*), the Empress-tree, a medium-sized tree to 40 ft., has conspicuous, fragrant flowers in 1-ft.-long clusters, followed by pods which remain on the tree all winter. It is much planted as a specimen tree or for avenues in mild climates, and is hardy in N. Y. It will withstand salt air and is therefore a good subject for shore properties. Farther N. it is root-hardy, dying to the ground each winter and sending up in the spring exceedingly vigorous shoots covered with huge leaves, which permits its use as a screening foliage plant as far N. as Montreal. If possible it should be sheltered from strong winds. It grows best in a light warm loam and may be increased by greenwood cuttings, rooted under glass, also by seeds and root cuttings.

PAVONIA (pah-voh'-ni-ah). A genus of tropical and warm climate herbs and shrubs of the Mallow Family, of limited horticultural value. They thrive in light rich soils in the S. and may be grown under glass in the N. from seed or from cuttings, which root readily in sand. Among the species sometimes grown are the following:

P. hastata, to 6 ft., with toothed leaves, and solitary pale-red dark-spotted flowers, is a S. American species naturalized in S. U. S.

multiflora, with oblong leaves, 6 to 10 in. long, in terminal clusters, has dull purple flowers to 1½ in. long.

praemorsa, shrubby, with broad oval leaves, has yellow, dark-centered flowers.

sepium, a shrub to 6 ft. with coarsely toothed oblong leaves, has small flowers in sparse clusters.

spinifex, a shrub to 20 ft. also naturalized in S. U. S., bears 1-in.-long yellow flowers.

PAWPAW or PAPAW. A common name for two American plants, one a tree of the genus Asimina (which see), the other a tough-stemmed herb of tree-like proportions (*Carica papaya*), known locally as Papaya. The latter grows erect, unbranched, and palm-like, often to 20 ft.

with a crown of 7-lobed leaves, each 2 ft. broad, from the axils of which hang 20 to 50 melon-like, yellow-skinned, pink or yellow-fleshed fruits which ripen successively for several weeks and may weigh 10 to 15 lbs. each. While immature these are cooked like squash; when ripe they are eaten like muskmelons, with which their flavor is sometimes compared. The unripe fruits yield the medicine, papain.

Though the plants are easily propagated from seed, the best varieties are grafted. They require sunny positions, well-drained, rich loam and frequent cultivation.

PEA. The genus Pisum. An annual, herbaceous, tendril-climbing vine grown mainly for its edible seeds and pods. Horticultural varieties fall into four groups: (1) The original species (*P. sativum*) which climbs about 6 ft. and bears pods 4 in. long or longer; (2) edible podded varieties (var. *macrocarpon*) also tall, with soft, 6-in. pods; (3) dwarf varieties (var. *humile*) 15 to 36 in. tall which bear small pods; and (4) field peas (var. *arvense*) grown as a source of "dried peas," as a forage crop, or as green manure (which see). The first three kinds have white flowers; the last, pinkish blossoms with lavender wings and greenish keels.

The tall varieties need to be supported by "brush" or a trellis; the dwarf kinds are usually allowed to sprawl on the ground, though it is much better to support them so they can more easily be cultivated and harvested. Garden varieties of peas are further divided into "smooth-seeded" and "wrinkle-seeded" kinds; as the former are somewhat hardier and not so likely to rot in cold damp soil, they can be sown about a week earlier. They are, however, of poorer quality so should be planted in only limited quantity to provide "the first taste of peas." Taking less space and yielding sooner, the dwarf and half-dwarf, wrinkle-seeded varieties are more popular than the tall kinds, but they are less prolific and have a much shorter season.

PEA BRUSH AND ITS USE. Birch branches or small saplings make the best pea-vine "brush" because they are very twiggy and when the season ends can be removed with the vines and burned. Branches from a severely pruned privet hedge are also good. Poultry netting (2-in. or larger mesh and the height depending on that of the variety) is popular,

being easily set up and tied to stout stakes. At the end of the season it can easily be taken down, rolled up and cleaned of dead vines by being held and turned over a hot fire. If stored under cover it will last for years.

To avoid damaging the plants and to stimulate their growth, the brush should be thrust firmly into place as soon as the peas are sown. Netting should be placed while the seedlings are not more than an inch or so high. The bottom of the wire or other trellis should be 2 or 3 in. above the soil. It is usual to sow tall varieties in double rows 6 or 8 in. apart with the trellis between them and with pairs of rows 30 to 36 in. apart. This space may be given over to short-season crops such as spinach, lettuce, onions (sets) and radishes sown at the same time as the peas but harvested before the pea-vines get tall enough to shade them.

Dwarf varieties are often sown in groups of 4 rows only 6 or 8 in. apart, 24 to 36 in. being left between the groups so as to permit picking two rows from each side. However, unless the vines are supported, this method generally results in a jungle of vines and difficult picking. If no support is to be given single-row sowing will be more satisfactory but in this case the vines must be turned first to one side and then to the other to allow of cultivation.

WHEN AND HOW TO SOW. Some gardeners prefer to make successional sowings of early wrinkle-seeded varieties, and a better plan is to sow all at one time, and early, several varieties that require different periods for maturing, for the reason that the pea is a cool-season crop and early sowings get a better start and yield more abundantly than those made after the ground has become drier and warmer. Tall kinds take longer to mature than dwarfs so the two types, even if planted at the same time, come into bearing at different periods.

Though peas are essentially a spring crop, some of the quick-growing varieties (especially the round-seeded ones) may be sown after midsummer for autumn use. But unless there are frequent showers or overhead irrigation is employed, the autumn crop is likely to be disappointingly small.

It is most important to sow peas—especially the tall varieties—thinly. Plants of the dwarf kinds should never be closer than 3 in. or those of the tall sorts less than

4 in. apart in the rows. If the amount of seed usually recommended (1 pound, or pint, to 100 ft. of single row) is sown to insure a good stand, the seedlings should be thinned to the distances mentioned. Thin planting will result in increased yields and also make the seed "go farther." The earliest sowing (round-seeded varieties only) should be made 3 or 4 in. deep; the later ones not more than 2 in.

Should the ground be somewhat dry at sowing time the seed may be soaked over night, then spread out in the morning until the surface water has evaporated. After sowing, firm the soil by treading on the rows. Soaking is especially advisable in growing an autumn crop, for soaked seed should sprout several days earlier than dry seed and the plants grow more lustily. However, if the soil is wet and the weather cold, the sowing of soaked seed might lead to decay rather than germination.

ENEMIES. Several diseases attack peas. Powdery mildew is most serious during warm humid weather, covering the plant with a dense white coating. To avoid it grow early and quick-maturing varieties, and dig vines and refuse under immediately after harvesting the crop. Spraying with bordeaux mixture or dusting with sulphur dust will kill the fungus. Root rot, caused by a soil infesting organism, can best be fought by planting peas on the same ground only once in 5 or 6 years. See ROTATION OF CROPS.

Foot-rot produces dark brown spots on leaves, pods, stems and tap-root, while the leaf and pod spot shows as light tan spots. The use of seed free from the fungus is the only preventive in either case. To control mycosphaerella blight which causes purplish-brown spots and a foot-rot and often kills plants, practise crop rotation and use disease-free seed.

The pea aphid and a weevil are the only insects likely to be serious. The aphid stunts the plants and causes severe crop losses. Apply nicotine dust on a warm day before plants are injured. The adult weevil, a brownish beetle, $\frac{1}{5}$ in. long, spotted with gray, dark-brown and white, lays eggs on the surface of newly formed pods; when they hatch the young larvae drill through the pods and into the peas. If their presence is known or suspected, peas wanted for seed should be fumigated in a tight box for 36 hours at a temperature at least 70 deg. F., using 1 lb. of carbon bisulphide per

100 cu. ft. Or small quantities of peas can be heated for 5 to 6 hours at 120 to 130 deg. F. which will kill the weevils without injuring the seed.

Sweet Pea (which see), Black-pea, Everlasting-pea and Perennial-pea are species of Lathyrus (which see). Australian-pea is *Dolichos lignosus;* Butterfly-pea is a name given to both Centrosema and Clitoria; Cowpea (which see) is Vigna, and Catjang-pea is *V. catjang;* Chick-pea (which see) is Cicer; Glory-pea is *Clianthus dampieri;* Rosary-pea is *Abrus precatorius;* Senna-pea is Swainsona; Shamrock-pea (which see) is *Parochetus communis;* Winged-pea is *Lotus tetragonolobus.*

PEA or PULSE FAMILY. Common name of the Leguminosae, which see. The ancient term pulse refers to a thick pottage of vegetables, which was probably originally made of peas or some related seed.

PEACH. A small tree (botanically *Prunus persica,* which see, but formerly *Amygdalus persica*), native to China, cultivated since ancient times for its fruit and in some forms especially for its ornamental bloom. Its principal botanical varieties are the flat or peen-to peach (var. *compressa* or *platycarpa*) grown in S. gardens and the nectarine (var. *nucifera*) which is produced either from seed or from "bud sports. See NECTARINE; PRUNUS.

The peach is the most adaptable of all tree fruits for home gardens. It may be grown nearly everywhere in the U. S., S. Ontario and coastal British Columbia, where the winters are not colder than 15 deg. below zero. However, unless the wood is well matured and remains dormant until spring it may be injured by even milder winters and spring frosts may destroy the blossom buds or the newly set fruits. The peach blossom is the State flower of Del., in whose agriculture the fruit is an important crop.

Under ordinary commercial management peach orchards rarely last longer than 12 years but with exceptional care they may be continued profitably for more than twice as long. Though individual trees may reach 30 or even 40 years it is advisable to plant new ones every five years as replacements.

PROPAGATION AND PLANTING. Peaches are propagated by summer-budding desired varieties on stocks grown from seed sown early the previous spring. In the S. where the work is done in early summer the trees (called "June buds") develop the same year and are ready to plant in the autumn. In the N. where the budding is done after midsummer the buds remain dormant until spring. They then grow the entire season and are called "one year" trees. Both types are good to plant, but the latter are usually the larger.

No older trees should be planted because the loss of roots of such trees would make recovery slow if at all. Peach trees should be spaced 25 ft. apart for spread.

Yearling trees usually have so many branches that favorably placed ones may be easily chosen, superfluous ones being cut off after the trees are planted. The three or four chosen ones should point in different directions and be spaced, if possible, 8 to 12 in. apart on the trunk to lessen the chance of splitting. These branches and the main stem above the topmost branch should be shortened so as to concentrate plant food in the remaining buds.

Though the peach does best in sandy loams and other light, well-drained soils it readily adapts itself to all but heavy and rich ones. In these, growth is likely to be excessive and to suffer in winter. Yet the possession of unfavorable soil should not deter anybody from planting peaches for home use because heavy soils may be lightened and rich ones reduced in richness by growing nitrogen-consuming crops beneath the trees.

In home gardens peach trees are best grown under clean culture until midsummer when the ground should be sown to cover-crops (which see). When this is not feasible a circle at least 2 ft. in diameter should be kept cultivated around each trunk to discourage borers.

FEEDING AND PRUNING. Peach trees must be fed sparingly because they tend to grow rankly. In none but the poorest sandy soils should nitrogenous fertilizers be used until they have borne their first crop. Then 1 lb. of nitrate of soda may be scattered thinly around each tree under the branch spread. When the trees are 5 or 6 years old the amount may be increased to 2 or 3 lbs. When fruit bearing starts 1 to 3 lbs. each of potash (sulphate or muriate) and superphosphate may be applied to ripen the wood and the fruit.

Before the buds swell in the second spring all shoots not needed to form the framework must be cut off. The only later pruning needed (until after the trees begin to bear fruit) is merely to encourage good form and to keep the interior open to admit light and air.

As the fruit is borne mostly on long, one-year shoots developed mainly from the terminal and adjacent buds, peach trees tend to extend rapidly and to break down from the weight of the crop. To prevent such accidents reduce these shoots 50 to 75 per cent each spring while the tree is still dormant. Often also after the trees are 6 years old some cutting of 2- and 3-year old branches should be done to reduce the spread and leverage.

No tree is less likely to be over-pruned than the peach. Heavy pruning of dormant trees tends to produce new shoots with blossom buds which the following season will bear fruit. These buds can easily be recognized because they are rounded, whereas branch buds are pointed. Other fruit buds are borne on short wiry shoots along the main branches. After the fruit has ripened these "spurs" generally die.

In selecting peach varieties for the home fruit garden, choose those recommended as (1) suitable for the region and (2) of highest dessert quality; avoid those described as long keepers, especially good for shipping, etc.

ENEMIES

DISEASES. There are two important fungous diseases of peaches. Peach leaf curl is most serious in the N. States where repeated attacks will kill a tree. The tissue of the leaves is puckered along the midvein, resulting in curling and distortion and a glistening yellow or reddish color. Most of the leaves soon fall and are replaced by a new crop,

PEACH LEAF CURL
A fungus disease causes this wrinkled distortion. Use a sulphur or copper-lime dust in early spring.

but this lowers the vitality of the tree, interferes with or prevents the setting of fruit and makes the trees more susceptible to winter-killing. The fungus spores live over the winter on the buds and can be readily killed by spraying with 1-15 lime-sulphur or 5-5-50 bordeaux mixture at any time during the dormant period when the temperature is well above freezing. Fall spraying is regarded as preferable. Since leaf curl is so common and its control so easy, all peaches should be sprayed each year.

The soft brown decay caused by the brown rot fungus is responsible for the familiar grayish brown spore masses and later the wizened mummied fruits. Cankers are often formed and gum is frequently exuded. (For control see BROWN ROT and the general spray schedule at end of this article.) Peach scab, also known as freckles and black spot, causes small, round olive-black spots on the fruits 6 weeks after the petals have fallen, followed by cracking and premature falling of diseased fruits. (See spray schedule below.) Powdery mildew, sometimes present on the young twigs and leaves, is readily controlled by a sulphur spray or dust. Two virus diseases, yellows and little peach, may kill infected trees. The former ripens fruit prematurely; the latter delays ripening and the leaves are rolled and turn red or yellow. The only thing to do in either case is to dig up and burn diseased trees as soon as detected. A disease called phony peach, prevalent in orchards in the S. Atlantic region, is being studied as to cause, nature and control.

A new virus disease, first discovered in Conn. in 1933 but now found nearly across the continent, and known as yellow-red or X disease, is transmitted from the choke cherry. In June leaves of infected trees suddenly develop yellow and red, ragged-edged spots, from which the tissue drops out; partial defoliation follows, and most of the fruit drops early. To prevent its occurrence eradicate all choke cherries near peach orchards.

INSECTS. The best known insect pest of peaches is the peach borer (*Aegeria exitiosa*). Its larvae work in the trunk, at or near the ground level, producing gummy masses of reddish borings. The adult is a brilliant yellow and black, hornet-like moth. Peach trees should be examined for signs of injury in June and September and any borers killed by inserting a flexible wire into the tunnels, enlarging the opening slightly with a sharp knife if necessary. Banding the lower portion of the trunk during the summer while the moths are in flight helps prevent infestation. For some years paradichlorobenzene has been widely used in late September or early October as soon as the eggs have hatched. The

soil about the base of the tree is leveled off and the fumigant in the form of fine crystals is spread in a ring around the base of the tree, but not less than 1½ in. from the trunk. It is then covered with fine soil to a depth of 2 to 3 in. This treatment is safe with trees 4 or more years old, but it is likely to injure younger ones. Ethylene dichloride emulsion is now superseding the treatment just described. It is effective over a greater temperature range and so can be applied later in the season. Commercially prepared emulsions are available and should be used strictly according to directions accompanying them.

The oriental fruit moth (which see) is a new and serious pest of peaches for which no satisfactory control has been devised. The plum curculio may also infest peach trees (see CURCULIO). Keeping trees in a vigorous condition is the best protection against the fruit bark beetle or shot-hole borer, although a dormant lime-sulphur spray helps and also controls the peach twig borer, and the San José and West Indian peach scales. Young shoots may be injured by the tarnished plant bug (which see) for which there is no adequate control on peach. Aphids may be kept in check by nicotine sprays or dusts.

SPRAY PROGRAM. A peach spray schedule for the home garden should be secured from the State experiment station in order to make sure of effective dates, etc. The following general schedule is safe in some states:

1. *In fall or spring before the buds swell.* Use 1 gal. concentrated lime-sulphur to 10 gal. spray solution. (Controls leaf curl and San José scale.)
2. *Just as the husks begin to split from the small fruits.* Dry-mix sulphur-lime 2½ lbs., lead arsenate 1 cup, lime 1 lb. to 10 gal. spray. (Controls scab, brown rot and curculio.)
3. *Two weeks after 2.* Repeat spray.
4. *Two or three weeks after 3.* Dry-mix sulphur-lime 2½ lbs. in 10 gal. spray. (Controls scab and brown rot.)

Sulphur-lime dust (80 to 20) may be substituted for the dry-mix sprays.

PEACOCK-FLOWER. A common name for *Delonix regia,* also called Royal Poinciana and Flamboyant.

PEACOCK FLOWER-FENCE. Another name for the tropical Bead-tree (*Adenanthera pavonina*).

PEACOCK GAZANIA (gah-zay'-ni-ah). A composite perennial, *Gazania pavonia,* so called from the bizarre coloring of the flower-heads.

PEANUT. The common name for a tender annual, herbaceous vine (*Arachis hypogaea*) of the Legume Family grown in the S. for forage and hay, as a soil improver and for its pods—the familiar peanuts that everyone knows. These are also called "goobers," "pindars" and "ground-nuts."

The plants will not stand frost and require a long season in which to mature. Commercially they are important only from Virginia southward and westward but they are sometimes grown as a garden novelty even as far N. as Mass. and Mich. However, in such places they ripen few or no pods unless the season is favorable.

At corn planting time seeds of thick-shelled varieties should be removed from the pods and scattered about 10 in. asunder in rows 30 in. apart. Thin-shelled varieties are usually sown without shelling. Sandy loam soils suit them best and clean cultivation is given until the plants are well established.

The showy yellow flowers that appear are the staminate ones. The productive, pistillate flowers are inconspicuous; after being fertilized they bury themselves in the ground, where the "peanuts" develop. When frost has killed the tops the plants are pulled or dug and allowed to dry for a while before the pods are removed. If the latter are fully grown they should be kept dry and carefully roasted for use.

When the peanut is grown as a forage crop, cattle and hogs are turned into the field, the former to browse the foliage and the latter to root for the nuts. For hay, the crop must be cut before frost; after drying it is stacked on slat platforms.

The Hog-peanut is *Amphicarpa* (which see) *monoica* or *A. pitcheri.*

PEAR. Trees (and their fruit) of the genus Pyrus, of which two species are grown in America: the European pear (*P. communis*), to which all the dessert and the best culinary varieties belong; and the Chinese sand pear (*P. pyrifolia,* formerly *P. serotina*), noted for the grittiness of its fruit, which has been passed on to a mongrel group of varieties of easy culture but whose poor quality has lowered pears in general in public estimation. (See illustrations, Plate 22.)

In localities where the pear can be grown, dessert varieties deserve outstanding popularity among home-garden fruits for several reasons. Early varieties cannot be successfully marketed in best, or usually

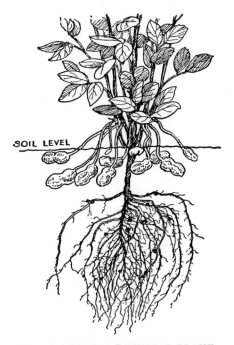

THE PEANUT, A PECULIAR PLANT
An easy and interesting legume to grow in the garden, the plant develops the typical nitrogen bacteria nodules on the roots. The "nuts" are not tubers but seed capsules that grow down into the soil after the flowers fade.

even in good, condition; no other temperate-climate fruit compares with them in aroma, lusciousness or range of flavors; they can always be grown to greater perfection in small plantings than in commercial plantings; assorted varieties ripening successively cover a season from midsummer to midwinter or later; where space is limited, several to many dwarf trees may be planted in the area needed by one standard tree.

Pears are more limited in their range than apples, because of less resistance to both cold and heat. They have a wider N. but more limited S. range than peaches. Commercially they succeed best from New England to Mich. and on the Pacific Coast; in home gardens, in both these regions and in mountainous areas and near rivers and lakes large enough to keep the air humid.

In the dry air and cold winters of the Prairie States failure is likely.

Though the pear succeeds best in heavy, moderately fertile soils retentive of moisture, no one need hesitate to plant it in any soil available if it is well drained.

As with the apple (which see), 1-year trees are best for planting because the frame branches may be trained to give a strong top; but since some varieties are highly susceptible to fire blight (which see), the trunk and the lower parts of the frame limbs should be kept free from small twigs and fruit spurs which can easily become infected.

Standard pear trees should be allowed spaces of 30 ft. diameter; dwarfs, 15 or perhaps 12 ft. Dwarfs, propagated on quince stocks, are specially desirable in home gardens.

Selection of varieties is more restricted than with apples because some do better as standards, others as dwarfs, and still others must be "double worked," that is, grafted on a pear stock already made dwarf by previously being grafted on quince.

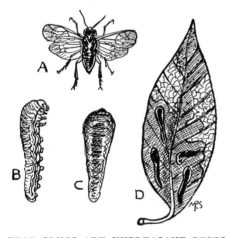

PEAR SLUGS ARE UNPLEASANT PESTS
A. An adult. B. A larva or slug without its usual slimy covering that makes it appear as in (C). D. Pear leaf with slugs at work. This insect also attacks the cherry.

Dessert varieties more desirable as dwarfs than standards include: Angoulême, Elizabeth, Glou Morceau, Louise Bonne, Diel, and Easter; some equally good as standards or dwarfs are: Anjou, Boussoc, Kingsessing, Colmar, Josephine de Malines, Rosteiser, Superfin, Tyson; varieties that should be double worked (if to be grown

as dwarfs) are Bosc, Washington, Winter Nelis, Sheldon, Dix; varieties best as standards are Seckel, Bartlett, Gray Doyenné, Belle Lucrative, White Doyenné, Summer Doyenné. As only a few of these varieties are listed by nurserymen, gardeners seeking pears are referred to suggestions under APPLE.

The fact that some varieties of pears are self-sterile need not alarm the home pear grower, provided that he (or his near neighbors) will plant several varieties so bees may carry pollen from flower to flower.

Tillage and fertilizing are the same as for the apple, except that nitrogenous fertilizers must be used more cautiously, to prevent lush growth, which is more likely to be attacked by blight than firmer tissues. For this reason mulching and sod culture are more desirable than clean cultivation.

Pruning and training are similar to that of apple except that a larger number of secondary branches may be allowed to remain as reserves in case of blight attack.

Pears should never be allowed to ripen on the trees. They should be gathered when, upon being bent upward, they separate at the union between the stems and the fruit spurs that bear them. The ripening process is completed in the house. As with other fruits cold retards and heat hastens ripening.

ENEMIES

DISEASES. Fire blight (which see) is the most prevalent and serious of pear diseases. The use of nitrogenous fertilizers increases susceptibility to it. During periods of rapid growth, it causes twigs and branches to die quickly, the leaves turning black and hanging to the twigs. Remove all blighted parts several inches below the diseased portions, disinfecting the pruning tools in corrosive sublimate between cuts.

There are two rust diseases of pear leaves and fruit. The one in the E. is similar to the apple rust and also has red-cedar as its alternate host; the W. form completes its cycle on incense-cedar. Several leaf spot diseases may occasionally cause defoliation; if they are prevalent, spray with lime-sulphur or wettable sulphur.

INSECTS. Injury by the pear psylla dwarfs the leaves, produces brown areas and often causes defoliation. This small sucking insect has at least four broods in a season. The reddish-brown tiny fly-like adults pass the winter under the bark and in trash and lay their eggs in early spring around the buds. The young (nymphs) during their first three stages are covered with honeydew which supports an infestation of sooty mold (which see). Spray with lime-sulphur (dormant strength) just before the blossom buds open to kill the eggs. Supplement this with nicotine-sulphate and soap sprays during the summer. A nicotine-bordeaux-lime spray is sometimes used.

The pear-leaf blister mite, which produces brownish blisters on the foliage, can be controlled by dormant applications of a miscible oil. This, or lime-sulphur, will also control San José scale. A carefully timed spray of 2% miscible oil and nicotine will control pear thrips which cause the developing buds to turn brown and shrivel. The pear midge infests small pears with maggots which cause them to drop. Kill the adult midges with contact sprays when the buds show pink. The larvae of pear slugs (which are slimy and swollen in form, rather like tadpoles) when abundant skeletonize the foliage. They are readily killed by stomach poisons or even by contact sprays if actually hit.

The sinuate pear borer is injurious in E. gardens, causing sinuous winding galleries in the inner bark and sapwood. Spray with lead arsenate during the flight period of the purplish-bronze beetles the latter part of May and during June.

Pears may also be attacked by aphids, brown-tail moth, codling moth, fall webworm, false tarnished plant bug, New-York weevil, quince curculio and scurfy scale, all discussed under their own names or the crops they especially infest.

Alligator-pear is *Persea americana,* or Avocado (which see). Balsam-pear is *Momordica charantia;* Prickly-pear is Opuntia, a genus of cacti; Vegetable-pear is *Sechium edule,* or Chayote, which see.

PEARL-BUSH. Common name for the genus Exochorda, consisting of several hardy spirea-like shrubs with white flowers.

PEARL EVERLASTING or PEARLY EVERLASTING. Common names for *Anaphalis margaritacea,* a woolly perennial often used for winter bouquets.

PEARL-FRUIT or PEARL-BERRY. Common names for *Margyricarpus setosus,* a S. American heath-like shrub belonging to the Rose Family. It is a little twiggy

evergreen about 1 ft. high, with inconspicuous flowers but showy white berries. Not hardy where winters are severe.

PEARLWORT. Common name for Sagina, a genus of small tufted annual or perennial herbs of the Pink Family and of the N. hemisphere. Mostly weeds, they are sometimes used as ground-covers, in which case they should be kept beaten flat with the spade. Sow seed in May or plant patches (divisions) in September.

S. glabra is a low creeping perennial suitable for rock work, with slender straight leaves and white flowers in late summer. *S. procumbens* grows 3 in. high, spreading and forming mats. *S. subulata* is a hardy evergreen perennial, creeping, branching, tufted and moss-like in growth. It bears abundant white (or, in one variety, yellow) flowers on slender stems.

PEA-SHRUB. A common name for the genus Caragana, the Pea-tree, which see.

PEAT or PEAT Moss. Obtained from extensive deposits of partly decomposed plant life laid down in ancient bodies of water, this material has come into wide use in recent years as a soil conditioner, mulching material and rooting medium. It is also invaluable in making temporary gardens, as in flower shows, where soil would be too heavy and hard to handle. Its value is based mainly on its ability to absorb and hold moisture; considerably less on its service as a source of humus or organic matter; and to only a slight degree on its plant-food content, this being small, slowly available and usually of an acid-forming nature. For the last mentioned reason it is most useful in growing ericaceous and other acid-loving plants and for maintaining cool, moist conditions in wild gardens, around shrubs, etc. Here it may be spread from 2 to 4 in. or more deep and either cultivated in or left undisturbed. (See MULCH.) In the propagating bench it is used alone or mixed with sand in different proportions depending on the kind of cuttings to be rooted. See PROPAGATION.

Three classes of peat moss are recognized: Grass peat, derived from swamp grasses, sedges, etc.; moss peat, composed mainly of decayed sphagnum (which see); and upland peat, which is less completely rotted and contains fragments of twigs, leaves, roots, etc. The second (and most important) type, formerly obtained commercially in Germany, Sweden and Holland, but now, in increasing quantities, in various parts of the U. S., is dug out of the beds in blocks, stacked to dry for some months, then ground, graded and baled. Commercial grades include: coarse (used for livestock bedding); poultry litter; horticultural, used for most garden purposes; and very fine, for mixing with potting soil, etc. The horticultural grade is sometimes used as bedding and given increased plant-food value through the admixture of manure, the whole being dried, ground and sold in bags as a convenient, effective substitute for barnyard manure.

As a bale of peat moss is dry and greatly compressed, it is often lumpy and slow to take up moisture at first. The bale should therefore be left outdoors with the binding wires cut so that it can absorb rain and become soft, loose and absorbent before needed for use. Otherwise a small quantity (for filling pots, flats, etc.) should be soaked in water, then squeezed partly dry in order to be easily handled and mixed with soil.

While the way peat is used should be determined by local conditions and needs, the following general directions can be noted: For new lawns and general gardening, use a 2 in. layer of peat moss, plus 1 lb. of ground limestone, and 5 lbs. of a balanced fertilizer analyzing approximately 5-8-7, per 100 sq. ft. working the materials well into the soil spade deep. For seed flats, mix one-third peat and two-thirds loamy soil; for house plants this same mixture with ¼ lb. of a good complete plant food added to each bushel is excellent. An established lawn is benefited by spreading 5 to 8 bushels of sifted or pulverized peat over each 1000 sq. ft. as soon as growth starts in the spring, and raking it in thoroughly with a steel rake; the spring application of fertilizer can be mixed with the peat, applied at the same time and then, of course, watered in. Peat moss bales usually contain from 20 to 22 cu. ft. tightly compressed; a cu. yd. of loose peat moss will contain about 20 bushels.

PEA-TREE or PEA-SHRUB. Common names for Caragana, a genus of ornamental hardy shrubs thriving in sunny places and light soils. They are grown chiefly for their bright yellow flowers and interesting habit of growth. *C. arborescens* is one of the best hedge and shelter plants for the prairies of the Northwest. Propagation is by seeds, layers, or grafting on seedling *C. arborescens.*

PRINCIPAL SPECIES

C. arborescens (Siberian Pea-tree). A tall shrub or small tree of stiff upright habit, conspicuous in spring when crowded with small, yellow pea-like flowers. Var. *pendula,* a weeping form with stiffly hanging branches, is usually grafted high. Var. *nana* is a dwarf, stunted form with contorted branches.

microphylla is a graceful Chinese shrub to 10 ft. with long spreading branches.

frutex, found in S. Russia, has slender yellowish branches.

pygmaea, from China and Tibet, is usually a prostrate spiny shrub, but sometimes is grafted high to form a graceful small standard tree.

maximowicziana. A handsome densely branched shrub from W. China, with bright green leaves and bronzy-yellow flowers.

PECAN (pee-kan'). Common name for *Carya pecan,* a valuable nut-bearing tree of the Walnut Family. Its natural range is from Ind. into Mexico; in Texas there are great natural groves and also extensive orchards. The pecan is not quite hardy N. but has been planted successfully from the 43rd parallel in the N. to the Gulf, and also in the W. States.

It is a deep-rooting, long-lived, vigorous tree growing best in fertile soil, rich in humus, on land that has been under cultivation for a number of years. In an orchard trees should be spaced widely—from 60 to 72 ft. apart in rich soil. Often intercropping with cotton, corn, peaches, etc., is resorted to until the trees come into bearing. A tree 8 to 10 years old will bear 5 to 25 lbs. of nuts.

Pecans do not come true from seed, and are difficult to start from cuttings, therefore much work has been done with budding and grafting in order to perpetuate desirable varieties.

The pecan is infested with many of the insect enemies of hickory (which see). Spraying with calcium arsenate during the spring and summer will control the pecan bud-moth and the pecan-leaf case-bearer. Trees should be sprayed with arsenate for case-bearers immediately after the nuts have set, and with bordeaux mixture for the fungous disease called pecan scab.

Carya aquatica (Bitter Pecan) is a small tree to 90 ft., found in swampy ground from Va. to Fla. and Tex.

See also HICKORY.

PEDICULARIS (pe-dik-eu-lay'-ris). A genus of the Figwort Family, commonly known as Wood-betony or Lousewort, comprising perennial and annual herbs with spiked clusters of whitish or reddish 2-lipped flowers, suitable for the wild garden. Care should be taken to give them plenty of their native wood soil, for some of the species are dependent on mycorrhizal association (which see). They are increased by seed and division.

P. canadensis (Wood-betony), to 1½ ft., with soft-hairy fern-like leaves which are more attractive than the rather dull reddish or yellowish flowers, is a common woodland plant. *P. lanceolata,* to 3 ft., has purple flowers with an occasional white-flowered form.

PEDILANTHUS (ped-i-lan'-thus). Small succulent plants of tropical America, belonging to the Spurge Family. *P. tithymaloides* (Redbird-cactus or Jew-bush), the principal species, is an attractive plant for the warm greenhouse, or outdoors in warm regions. It grows 4 to 6 ft. high, with fleshy stems and dark green leaves, the midrib being keeled below. The showy part of the flower cluster is the red or purple involucre. Vars. *variegatus* and *cucullatus* both have white-edged leaves, and in the latter the edge is turned up, somewhat cup-shaped. The plants are propagated by cuttings, which should first be dried at the base.

PELARGONIUM (pel-ahr-goh'-ni-um). The genus to which the common geranium (which see) belongs. It is quite distinct from but related to the genus Geranium. The occasionally used common name of Storksbill (also applied to the related Erodium, though that is more properly Heronsbill) is suggested by the shape of the fruit, like that of Cranesbill for the true Geraniums, these being also translations of the Latin names.

Besides the geranium, so much used for bedding and potting, often known as the Zonal or Horseshoe Geranium, Pelargonium includes the old-fashioned window plant known as the Lady Washington Geranium (*P. domesticum* in variety), which is now being brought back into more extensive culture. Other important house plants in the group include the Ivy-leaved Geraniums (*P. peltatum* and others), the Nutmeg Geranium (*P. odoratissimum*), the Rose Geranium (*P. graveolens*), and others with deeply cut, often

fragrant leaves, as well as a number of species of interest to fanciers.

For cultural directions see GERANIUM.

ENEMIES. Their chief diseases are (1) bacterial leaf spot, which shows first as a water-soaked dot, later brown and irregular or circular in outline, the leaf tissue between the spots finally turning yellow and dying; (2) botrytis blight or gray mold, which, under humid conditions, attacks both blossoms and leaves, quickly covering them with a soft gray mold; and (3) cercospora leaf spot, which causes small light brown or red spots with a darker border. Control all three by placing plants well apart and giving them plenty of light and air, picking off diseased flowers and leaves, watering carefully so as not to splash the tops, and keeping the humidity down.

Leaf crinkle, a virus disease serious in greenhouses, causes irregular yellow spots on ruffled dwarfed leaves which later drop off. Since the disease is known to be transmitted by infected cuttings, propagation stock should be carefully inspected.

Blackleg, a disease of cuttings and young plants, causes a blackening and rotting of stem and petioles; avoid it by using fresh or sterilized sand in the cutting bench. Dropsy, a physiological disease, causes water soaked spots, later brown and corky, on the leaves, which turn yellow around them and later drop off, checking the plant's growth. The disease is usually worse in late winter after dark weather and is thought to be due to warm moist soil stimulating root action while cool moist air prevents transpiration. Therefore keep the air dry and the temperature even and do not overwater. Diseased plants may recover when warm weather comes if set out-of-doors.

Spray with nicotine-sulphate and soap for aphids. For control of the greenhouse leaf tyer, white fly, mealy bugs, red spider and cyclamen mite, see GREENHOUSE PESTS. Outdoors geraniums may be eaten by garden slugs (which see) or have their stems tunneled out by termites (which see). In the latter event, destroy infested plants and treat soil with carbon bisulphide.

PELICAN-FLOWER. Common name or *Aristolochia grandiflora,* which see, a large-leaved ornamental vine with curiously shaped flowers.

PELLAEA (pe-lee'-ah). A genus of small ferns, known as Cliff-brakes, with marginal indusia, and differing from the Rock-brakes in that their sterile and fertile fronds are nearly alike. They grow in tufts, chiefly on limestone cliffs. The coloring of most species is dark or bluish green, with dark and polished stipes. Several species are native to the U. S., but they require ideal conditions for garden cultivation, preferring exposed situations, a light soil, and constant moisture at the roots, though none from above. Small chips of stone will help to retain the moisture. For greenhouse varieties provide a compost of 2 parts peat to 1 part loam and sand, with some lime.

SPECIES

P. andromaedaefolia (Coffee Fern). A western species, with deep rounded segments.

atropurpurea (Purple Cliff-brake). Fronds 6 to 20 in. long, of leathery texture, once-pinnate above, 2-pinnate below, with smooth, entire blue-green segments and purplish stems.

hastata. A good greenhouse species, having delicate textured 18-in. fronds, once-pinnate, and many of pinnae broadly 3-lobed.

densa. A western form much like *P. atropurpurea,* but with brownish stipes and smaller pinnae.

ornithopus (Birdsfoot Fern, Tea Fern). A S. Calif. species, liking gravelly soil or rock pockets. The small wiry pinnae are in threes.

viridis (Green Cliff-brake). The best greenhouse species, native to S. Africa; it has delicate, deeply pinnate 1- to 2-ft. fronds.

PELLIONIA (pel-i-oh′-ni-ah). Tender perennial herbs, belonging to the Nettle Family, creeping at the base, with ornamental foliage and variable leaves. They are valuable in window boxes and hanging baskets, and thrive in rich sandy loam, requiring a moist atmosphere. Propagation is by division of the roots and cuttings rooted in sandy soil.

P. daveauana has succulent prostrate creeping stems to 2 ft. long, with leaves alternate, long or elliptic-oblong, ½ to 2½ in. long, of a bronzy olive-green slightly tinged or marked with a broad irregular band of bright green. *P. pulchra* has leaves tinged dull purplish underneath.

PELTANDRA (pel-tan′-drah) *virginica.* An American bog plant called Arrow Arum

(which see), suitable for margins of water gardens.

PELTARIA (pel-tay′-ri-ah). A small genus of perennial herbs called Shieldwort, which see.

PELTATE. Shield- or target-shaped, as applied to circular leaves (like those of the East Indian Lotus) whose stalks are attached at a point within the circumference of the lower leaf-surface. *Peltately veined* refers to veins radiating in all directions from the point of attachment of the petiole, as in a peltate leaf, like the garden nasturtium.

PENNISETUM (pen-i-see′-tum). This genus of grasses comprises some species grown for grain and forage and also several graceful and highly ornamental annual and perennial kinds. They are native to the tropics and subtropics but are widely grown both as garden subjects and for cutting and drying for winter decoration. Seed should be started indoors or in hotbeds in March and the seedlings grown on in small pots with plenty of room to develop. When planting them in the garden, allow 12 to 18 in. between clumps.

PRINCIPAL SPECIES

P. latifolium, 5 ft. tall, or more, from S. America, has leaves 1 ft. long and 1 in. wide, and nodding green bristly spikes borne several on a stem and therein different from the others, which have solitary heads. It prefers a sandy loam in well-drained soil, and a sheltered site. In the N. plants can be lifted in the fall and wintered under glass. Perennial.

villosum (sometimes listed as *P. longistyllum*) is from Abyssinia, with short leaves and 4-in. purplish spikes at the end of 2-ft. stems, long feathery bristles giving a plume-like effect. Somewhat hardier than the preceding species, it will grow in any ordinary soil and is a good subject for the sunny border. It is best grown as an annual. Perennial.

ruppeli (Fountain Grass), 4 ft. tall, with very narrow leaves to 2 ft. long. The spikes 1 ft. or more long are strikingly colored—purple, coppery red, and rose.

alopecuroides, is from China, to 4 ft., with narrow 2-ft. leaves, and 6-in. silvery and purplish spikes. Perennial.

macrostachyum, from the East Indies, to 5 ft., with 1-ft. leaves and spikes to 1 ft.

The species grown for its grain is *P. glaucum* (Pearl, Indian, or African Millet), and the one grown as fodder is *P. purpureum* (Napier Grass).

See also ORNAMENTAL GRASSES.

PENNY-CRESS. Small annual and perennial herbs (Thlaspi), natives of temperate and cold climates and mountainous altitudes throughout the world. Some species are widely distributed weeds. Others are sometimes grown for their racemes of small flowers. Still others are raised for their large, flat, ornamental pods which are occasionally used as "strawflowers" in winter bouquets.

Though some of the perennials may be propagated by division and cuttings, they, and the annuals, are usually grown from seed, the seedlings being transplanted to partially shaded situations in naturally moist soil, usually in rock gardens. The species best known in America are all perennials, namely, *T. alpestre,* 12 in. high, with reddish tinged white flowers; *T. coloradense,* 6 in., larger flowered, white; *T. rotundifolium,* 8 in., lilac; and *T. stylosum,* 1 in., rose tinted.

PENNYROYAL. A common name given to a number of plants. European Pennyroyal is *Mentha pulegium* (which see), a member of the Mint Family, and one of the "sweet herbs," easily grown in the herb garden if given winter protection of straw or leaves. American Pennyroyal is *Hedeoma pulegioides,* a small purple-flowered annual herb, also belonging to the Mint Family, common along wood roads from Quebec to Kan. and occasionally transferred to the wild garden because the odor of the leaves (resembling that of the European Pennyroyal) is said to be offensive to mosquitoes.

Bastard-pennyroyal is *Trichostema dichotomum,* a species of Blue-curls, which see.

PENNYWORT. A common name for *Cotyledon umbilicus,* an Old-World succulent; also for Hydrocotyle, a genus of perennial herbs of the Parsley Family, and for *Obolaria virginica,* a small native American plant of the Gentian Family.

PENTAS (pen'-tas). African herbs and subshrubs, sometimes grown in the warm greenhouse for winter bloom, or as bedding plants in warm countries. In the early stages they do well in pots filled with a mixture of loam, peat and sand. At the final potting, in 6- or 8-in. pots, add some old cow manure. Water and spray freely when growth is active, and pinch the shoots to induce a compact habit. Propagate by cuttings in spring. The principal species is *P. lanceolata,* with clusters of flesh-pink flowers. Var. *kermesina* has showier flowers of carmine-rose.

PENTSTEMON (pent-stee'-mon). (Sometimes spelled Pensemon and Pentastemon.) A genus of perennial herbs or dwarf shrubby plants of the Figwort Family, mostly native in N. America and commonly called Beardtongue. They are good plants for the flower border and rock garden, thriving best in open situations in soil well-drained but not too dry. Only a few are entirely hardy in the N., but some others may survive in a favored spot.

The showy garden race known as *P. gloxinioides* can be handled as a tender bedding perennial in the same way as geraniums (which see), or raised as tender annuals from seed. It is a good summer- and fall-blooming plant for the flower garden where conditions are not too hot and dry. Pentstemon is subject to sudden wilt caused by the crown rot organism. For control see CROWN ROT.

Pentstemons are propagated by seed, cuttings and division.

PRINCIPAL SPECIES

P. barbatus makes tall slender stems to 6 ft., with flowers from pink to red.

torreyi is a form with scarlet flowers and a favorite in flower borders. Var. Pink Beauty is a newer form with shell-pink flowers.

digitalis grows to 5 ft., with white inflated flowers. It is a good border plant and often conspicuous in moist land from New England S.

grandiflorus has stout glaucous leaves and stems to 6 ft., carrying numerous large lavender-blue flowers.

acuminatus is of somewhat stiff habit to 2 ft., with glaucous leaves and good blue flowers.

angustifolius is smaller, with slender leaves and stems crowded with blue flowers.

glaber is a handsome plant to 2 ft., with large blue flowers.

cyananthus is closely related, with dense clusters of bright blue flowers.

cabaea grows to 2 ft., with large purple flowers.

unilateralis, blue, is tall and showy when grown in masses.

hartwegi makes stems to 4 ft., carrying large drooping rich red flowers.

gloxinioides, a hybrid race mostly derived from the two preceding species, is a good garden flower in many color shades.

menziesi, growing to 1 ft. high from a woody base, with violet-blue or purple flowers, is good in the rock garden.

scouleri is a low shrubby species with lilac-purple flowers.

heterophyllus grows to 5 ft. from a woody base, with pink or rose-purple flowers loosely arranged.

rupicola is a low spreading shrub usually under 6 in. It has rosy-crimson flowers and is excellent in the rock garden.

PEONY. Common name for Paeonia, a genus of hardy, handsomely flowered plants, members of the Buttercup Family and including some of the most decorative of garden subjects. (See illustrations, Plate 39.) The peonies most widely grown are divided by horticulturists into two classes: the herbaceous, which includes the numerous variations developed from *P. albiflora* and *P. officinalis;* and the Tree Peonies, forms of *P. suffruticosa,* a Chinese shrub to 6 ft., once widely grown, but now somewhat superseded in favor by the many new herbaceous forms.

The flowers of the herbaceous peonies show a multiplicity of variations in shape as well as in color and the types have been classified as follows: (1) *Single,* with few petals and profuse stamens; (2) *Japanese,* with wider, more conspicuous stamens; (3) *Bomb,* with some of the stamens changed to narrow petals; (4) *Semi-double,* with a number of stamens changed into broad, petal-like parts; (5) *Crown,* with both stamens and carpels petal-like; and (6) *Rose,* completely double flowers, both stamens and carpels having become petals.

Peonies are among the most popular and satisfactory of garden perennials. Their blooms are showy without being coarse and range in color from white through pink and red to the darkest purple, with a few yellows among the newer types. Their foliage is decorative from early spring to fall, and they are absolutely hardy N. They are effectively used in the border in combination with other perennials and especially grouped as accents.

They thrive best in a not too heavy soil which has been well dug and enriched. They should be planted (preferably in spring) so that the buds or "eyes" are not covered more than 3 in. deep. As the plants are heavy feeders it is well to give them an annual top-dressing of bonemeal or well-decomposed manure mixed with rich soil from the compost heap. Sometimes peonies do not produce characteristic blooms the first year after planting; but when once established and properly fed, they will increase in size and produce beautiful blooms for ten or twelve years without division.

Herbaceous peonies are easily forced in the greenhouse for winter bloom. The clumps are dug early in the fall and kept in a coldframe until needed, then brought into the greenhouse and kept in a temperature of about 60 deg. when the flowers will appear in 6 to 8 weeks.

ENEMIES

BOTRYTIS BLIGHT. This, the most common disease of peonies, is likely to be very destructive during wet seasons. The names bud blight, bud blast and gray mold have also been given it. In reality there are two blights, one early and one late, caused by different species of the same fungus (*Botrytis paeoniae* and *B. cinerea*). Early in the spring young shoots suddenly wilt and fall over, turning black and showing masses of gray-brown spores. If nothing is done, these spores are later carried to developing buds which turn black and cease growth; Botrytis blight is usually the unsuspected cause of the failure of peonies to bloom. Older buds may be blasted; the stems may take on brown appearance in places, there may be irregular dark areas on the leaves, spreading rapidly during wet weather, and decay and crown rot may extend all through the season.

Although spraying with weak bordeaux mixture several times in the spring, beginning when the young tips first show, is advisable, sanitary measures are the chief means of control. Therefore, in late fall cut all stalks just *below* the surface of the ground, removing as much of the stalk as possible without injuring the bud; this destroys many resting bodies (*sclerotia*) that would be sources of spring infection. Remove promptly any infected shoots in the spring and all diseased buds, flowers and leaves during the season. In doing this carry a paper bag and in it place all diseased material as gathered; then burn it. Diseased parts carried about uncovered will scatter spores.

OTHER ROTS. Occasionally other rots—phythophthora blight and sclerotinia stem

Plate 39.　　　　PEONIES AND TWO OTHER PERENNIALS

Upper left: Striking but never coarse, the peony is the glory of the early summer garden. Upper right: The rosy-pink false-dragonhead has a long season of bloom. Center left: The globular buds of the Japanese balloon-flower open into starry flowers. Lower left: A peony of the bomb type—its pink guard petals surround a creamy center. Lower right: The Bride—an exquisite single peony.

rot—may kill the shoots. The control measures just given will take care of them. Leaf blotch and other leaf diseases are usually held in check by the fall clean-up but bordeaux mixture can be used during the summer to advantage.

Nematode root knot caused by a microscopic eel-worm (which see) is especially serious in sandy soils in E. U. S. Affected roots are irregularly knotted or gnarled and the weak, spindling, stunted plants gradually die. Dig suspicious-looking plants in the fall, remove all infected roots, divide the healthy portions and replant them. Dormant roots may be treated in hot water at 120 deg. F. for 30 minutes. In planting new roots and treated ones avoid soil where the disease has occurred.

INSECTS. The insect pests of peony are not numerous. If stalks are left standing they are likely to be infested with oyster-shell scale. Ants are often seen on the buds, but they are merely feeding on a sticky secretion and cause no injury. The rose chafer (see CHAFER, ROSE) is especially fond of this plant and should be removed by hand-picking and the insects destroyed.

Propagation is by division of the clumps, done preferably in the fall, or by seed (the seedlings not blooming until the third year), and by grafting the eyes of improved varieties on the tubers of some strong-growing species.

PRINCIPAL SPECIES

P. officinalis, to 3 ft., with single flowers varying from white to dark crimson. This is the old garden favorite, usually seen in double white, rose, or red, and (in var. *festiva*) in white flowers with crimson centers.

albiflora, from which many of the garden forms have been derived, has flowers with 8 or more pink or white petals; also pink and white double varieties.

tenuifolia, to 1½ ft., has leaves cut into many segments and small, erect, dark crimson blossoms.

delavayi is a shrubby form to 3 ft., having crimson blossoms 2 in. across.

suffruticosa (Tree Peony), to 6 ft., has white, rose or red flowers to 12 in. across and a number of varietal forms.

lutea, a shrubby type with yellow flowers, is now being used by hybridists to bring more yellow into the color range of garden peonies.

PEONY, SOCIETY, THE AMERICAN. This society was organized in 1903 to spread information about peony culture; to encourage new varieties of merit; and to increase public interest in this flower. Membership is largely amateur although nearly all the prominent peony growers belong.

The Society publishes a quarterly bulletin covering new varieties, experiences in growing peonies in various localities, and reports of local and national shows, which is free to members. Also a profusely illustrated manual, actually a "peony encyclopedia," which costs $3.15 postpaid.

The annual dues are $3. The secretary is W. F. Christman, Northbrook, Ill.

PEPEROMIA (pep-er-oh'-mi-ah). Annual or perennial, herbaceous, fleshy, creeping, succulent plants of the Pepper Family. Small growing, with ornamental leaves, they are well suited for use as foliage plants in greenhouses or in hanging baskets. Equal parts of loam, leafmold and sand makes a satisfactory soil, and the plants should be given a warm temperature, watered carefully and kept shaded during summer. Propagate by cuttings or by leaves inserted in sand over bottom heat. Species generally cultivated include *P. maculosa* with egg-shaped leaves to 7 in. long, fleshy and bright, shining green, and erect stems spotted with brown or purple; and *P. sandersi,* stemless, with leaves to about 5 in. long, and dark reddish stems. A variety (*argyreia*) has light colored stripes between the leaf veins.

PEPINO. A common name for *Solanum muricatum,* a spiny herb with blue flowers and edible purple-marked yellow fruits.

PEPPER. Garden peppers are tropical shrubs grown as annuals in temperate climates. The original species (*Capsicum frutescens*) bears small, round or oblong, generally red, pungent fruits. Its botanical varieties include Cherry Peppers (Var. *cerasiforme*); Cone Peppers (Var. *conoides*); Red Cluster Peppers (Var. *fasciculatum*); and Long Peppers (Var. *longum*); all of them are more or less "hot" or highly pungent. Sweet or Bell Peppers (Var. *grossum*), much larger than any of the above, are the mild-flavored varieties used for salads and for stuffing with minced cabbage, celery and "forcemeat." The term Pimento (from the Spanish word *pimiento* meaning pepper) is loosely applied to forms of Capsicum, which see.

Pepper plants are started from seed sown under glass six to eight weeks before time to plant outdoors. The seed requires two to three weeks to germinate. Seedlings are pricked into small flower pots or flats (2 in. apart) and should be kept growing steadily, without check, until after all danger of frost has passed. Transplanted then to the garden, they should stand 12 to 18 in. asunder in rows 24 to 36 in. apart, and be given clean and frequent cultivation. They do best in well-drained but moist, light, warm soil well supplied with humus but not over-rich.

When gathering the fruits do not pull them off as this is likely to injure the plants. Instead cut them with a knife or pruning shears, but with only a short piece of stem, to avoid poking holes in other fruits. When the first fall frost threatens gather all the fruits both large and small into hampers and store in a cool cellar where the air is not dry, where they may keep until Christmas or later.

Of the several diseases of peppers anthracnose or fruit rot is the most widespread, causing depressed soft lesions in the fruit, covered with dark fungus mycelium and pink spore masses. As sunburnt fruits are the most seriously affected, spray with bordeaux mixture to hold the foliage.

For the spinach, melon and potato aphids which sometimes infest peppers, spray or dust with nicotine. Some control of the pepper maggot which infests the fruits and causes decay may be obtained by repeatedly dusting the plants with talc.

The black and white pepper of commerce is made from the berries of a tropical shrub (*Piper nigrum*).

The name Wall-pepper has been applied to stonecrop (*Sedum acre*).

PEPPERGRASS. Common name for Lepidium, a genus of annual, biennial and perennial cruciferous plants. An annual species (*L. sativum*) known as Gardencress is grown as a spring, autumn and winter salad, and for garnishing and flavoring. See CRESS; LEPIDIUM.

PEPPERIDGE. A common name for *Nyssa sylvatica*, the Black-gum. See NYSSA; GUM.

PEPPERMINT. Common name for *Mentha piperita*, a perennial whose essential oil is distilled and used for flavoring and as a medicine. See the reference under MINT.

PEPPER-ROOT. A common name for *Dentaria diphylla* or Toothwort, which see.

PEPPER-TREE. Common name for the genus Schinus, warm-climate trees to 50 ft. of which two species grow in Calif. The California Pepper-tree (*S. molle*) with graceful pendulous branches, long panicles of yellowish flowers followed by long-lasting rose colored berries, has been extensively planted as a lawn, park and street tree, but as it is subject to attack by black scale, a menace to citrus orchards, it is being replaced by *S. terebinthifolius*, the Brazilian Pepper-tree or Christmas-berry-tree. This is of more rigid habit, with leaves very dark above and lighter below and bright red fruit. Both species are dioecious (bearing male and female flowers on different plants). Propagated by seeds and cuttings.

Monks-pepper-tree is a totally unrelated shrub, *Vitex agnus-castus.*

PEPPER-VINE. A common name for *Ampelopsis arborea,* a native, tendril-climbing shrub found from Va. to Fla. and Mex.

PEPPERWORT. The common name for the genus Marsilea, a group of aquatic plants allied to the ferns. The leaves, their distinguishing feature, resemble those of four-leaf clovers. It reproduces by means of spores.

M. quadrifolia, growing wild in the E. States, makes an attractive water cover. If not controlled it is likely to be a nuisance.

M. drummondi, from Australia, has its leaflets covered with whitish hairs and is commonly cultivated in northern greenhouses. Pots of rich soil kept in water-filled saucers are best for it.

PERENNIALS. Plants which live more than two years are known as perennials, as distinguished from annuals and biennials. Though trees and shrubs are perennial in habit, the term is generally applied to herbaceous rather than woody plants; those whose roots continue to live, sending up year after year new branches and flower stems which die when winter comes. Some perennials live indefinitely; others, like sweet william, tend to die out after three or four years, unless the roots are taken up, divided and replanted every two or three years. The latter are known as "imperfect perennials."

In many old-time gardens most of the plants were hardy perennials, such as phlox, peonies, delphinium and bleeding heart; hence, although they are just as popular and probably even more widely grown in all well-balanced gardens, they are known as "old-fashioned" plants. Because of their hardiness, permanency and variations in color, height, foliage, and nature of bloom, these old-fashioned flowers form the background of modern gardens. They are often referred to as the "busy man's favorites," for they render unnecessary the sowing of seeds every year. While some perennials will flower the first season from seed if it is sown early, they often are not at their best until the second year. Differing from annuals in many respects, especially in their flowering habit, perennials offer the gardener many advantages.

For one thing, as new plants come into bloom and old ones pass, the garden scene presents changes almost from week to week, constantly giving the gardener something to look forward to. In a garden of annuals the picture of the same plants in blossom for long periods is apt to become monotonous. Only a few perennials bloom all season, and most of them in congenial surroundings increase in beauty with the passing of the years. With judicious selection and arrangement of plants one may be assured of continuous change from early spring until fall, and because of this ever-shifting picture the herbaceous border has become more and more a feature of American gardens.

The herbaceous border is also one of the most flexible parts of the garden, having no regular or formal design but lending itself to variations according to the taste of the individual gardener. Plants should be arranged with reference to the space allotted them. Place the tallest species in the background, especially those which provide a good display of foliage. Some of these tall sorts should, however, extend into the front, especially in the wider parts of the border, to provide interest and relieve any possible monotony. Dwarf edging plants of compact growth should be used in the foreground, with plants of intermediate height distributed throughout the rest of the border.

If a border is devoted entirely to perennials it should be at least 5 ft. wide. If the grounds are small and there is a hedge or a shrub border, the space between that feature and the lawn can be widened by

2 or 3 ft. and beautified by planting perennials in the bed so created. Perennials are always best when planted in masses or clumps; these are more interesting and attractive than a hit-or-miss planting, especially if consideration is given to color harmony or contrast. A generous use of white flowers is frequently advisable.

KINDS OF PERENNIALS

Understanding the nature of plants will aid materially in establishing a garden that will be a thing of beauty rather than a disappointment. Some are rather tender, some are evergreen, and every perennial has its own particular flowering period.

Tender perennials. Among the kinds that are somewhat tender to cold and do best in the N. when wintered over in coldframes are:

Caryopteris incana (bluebeard), *Cortaderia argentea* (pampas grass), early-flowered chrysanthemums, *Chrysanthemum maximum* (Shasta daisy), *Digitalis purpurea* (foxglove), *Geum chiloense* (avens), *Incarvillea delavayi* (incarvillea), *Kniphofia* (torch-lily), *Salva patens* (gentian sage), *S. farinacea* (mealy-cup sage), *Statice armeria* (thrift) and *Thalictrum dipterocarpum* (meadow-rue).

Evergreen perennials. A number of perennials retain their leaves the year around. They include:

Dianthus barbatus (sweet william), *D. plumarius* (grass pink), *Heuchera sanguinea* (coral-bells), *Iberis sempervirens* (evergreen candytuft), *Iris foetidissima* (Gladwin iris), *Linum perenne* (perennial flax), *Sedum* (stonecrop), *Teucrium chamaedrys* (germander), *Thymus serpyllum* (mother-of-thyme) and *Yucca filamentosa* (bayonet-plant).

Spring-flowering perennials. After the earliest flowering bulbs have gone spring color depends to a large degree upon perennials, with early iris, peonies and columbine among the predominant plants. They, together with Canterbury bells, delphinium and foxglove, keep the garden bright with color until the annuals add their contributions. It is in spring that perennials planted in a border or among shrubs will supply blossoms of beauty and color. The following list of spring-blooming perennials includes many of the long-time favorites:

Adonis amurensis (Amur Adonis), *Alyssum saxatile compactum* (dwarf golden-tuft), *Arabis alpina* (alpine rock-cress), *Aubreitia deltoidea* (purple rock-cress), *Bellis perennis* (English daisy), *Claytonia virginica* (spring beauty), *Convallaria majalis* (lily-of-the-valley), *Dicentra eximia* (plumy bleeding heart), *D. spectabilis* (bleeding heart), *Doronicum caucasicum* (leopards-bane), *Euphorbia epithymoides* (cushion spurge), *Hemerocallis flava* (lemon daylily), *Iberis sempervirens* (evergreen candytuft), *Mertensia virginica* (bluebells), *Myosotis sylvatica* (forget-me-not), *Polemonium reptans* (creeping polemonium), *Trollius europaeus* (globe-flower) and *Vinca minor* (common periwinkle).

Summer perennials. As the spring blossoms fade there come into flower a vast array of summer perennials, which because of their number may be classified in two groups: (1) the early summer species, blossoming from June to July, and (2) the late summer sorts, flowering from July to August. An excellent selection may be made from the following popular plants:

Early summer: *Anchusa azurea* (Italian bugloss), *Anthemis tinctoria* (golden marguerite), *Astilbe japonica* (Japanese astilbe), *Baptisia australis* (false-indigo), *Campanula persicifolia* (peach-leaf bellflower), *Centaurea montana* (mountain bluet), *Coreopsis lanceolata* (perennial coreopsis), *Echinops ritro* (globe thistle), *Geranium sanguineum* (cranes-bill), *Geum chiloense* (avens), *Gypsophila paniculata* (perennial babys breath), *Heuchera sanguinea* (coral-bells), *Lupinus polyphyllus* (perennial lupine), *Oenothera fruticosa* (evening-primrose), *Pentstemon* in variety, *Polemonium caeruleum* (Greek valerian), *Thalictrum aquilegifolium* (c o l u m b i n e meadow-rue), *Valeriana officinalis* (garden-heliotrope), *Veronica spicata* (spike speedwell), *Yucca filamentosa* (common yucca).

Late summer: *Achillea millefolium* (yarrow), *A. ptarmica* (sneezewort), *Macleaya (Bocconia) cordata* (plume poppy), *Campanula carpatica* (Carpathian harebell), *Echinacea* (or *Rudbeckia*) *purpurea* (purple coneflower), *Euphorbia corollata* (flowering spurge), *Gaillardia cristata* (perennial gaillardia), *Geranium ibericum* (Iberian cranesbill), *Hemerocallis fulva* (tawny daylily), *Hosta* (plantain-lily), *Liatris pycnostachya* (gay-feather), *Limonium latifolium* (sea-lavender), *Linum perenne* (perennial flax), *Oenothera speciosa* (sundrops), *Platycodon grandiflorum* (balloon-flower), *Rudbeckia*

laciniata (cutleaf coneflower), *Salvia nemerosa* (violet sage), *Thalictrum dipterocarpum* (Yunnan meadow-rue), *Viola cornuta* (tufted pansy).

Fall perennials. As summer's heat wanes and days grow perceptibly shorter, a number of perennials come into bloom, to give the garden the benefit of their beauty, and continue to blossom until frost nips them. Among them are the following: *Aconitum fischeri* (azure monkshood), *Anemone japonica* (Japanese anemone), Artemisia in variety (old man, old woman, mugwort), Aster in variety, *Boltonia asteroides* (boltonia), *Chelone glabra* (turtlehead) *Eupatorium coelestinum* (mistflower), *Helenium autumnale* (sneezeweed), *Helianthus maximiliani* (Maximilian sunflower), *H. rigidus* (prairie sunflower), *Hibiscus moscheutos* (rose mallow), *Lobelia cardinalis* (cardinal-flower), *L. syphilitica* (blue lobelia), *Rudbeckia speciosa* (showy coneflower), *Salvia azurea* (azure sage), Chrysanthemum in variety, *Sedum spectabile* (showy sedum).

How to Grow Perennials

PREPARATION OF THE SOIL. Because a perennial bed is permanent it should have a deep, adequate foundation involving drainage, texture and fertility. Spare no efforts to prepare the bed thoroughly, digging the soil to a depth of at least a foot and mixing with it a coating, at least 2 in. thick of well-rotted manure and 10 lbs. of bonemeal for every 100 sq. ft. Or use any available source of humus and reinforce it with a balanced, available plant food. Economy of effort lies in thorough preparation at the start, so that the soil will not require renewal or elaborate attention for several years.

SEED SOWING. The most inexpensive method of growing perennials is, of course, from seed, though for a first-year start, it is well to buy a few established plants. While not all perennials will come true to type from seed, especially plants which have been hybridized, most of them can be so handled. In the S. seed may be sown in the fall, so the plants will get a start and then make vigorous growth early in the spring and mature before the heat of summer. In the N. seed should be sown early enough to make good growth before winter; some are sown in the spring at the same time as many annuals, others in the summer and a few in the early fall.

For many years the general practice was to sow seeds in midsummer, but in recent years experts have been advocating April and May planting. One of the chief reasons is that then the weather is cool and moist, aiding germination which with many perennials is best accomplished in cool weather. Delphiniums, for example, start best in a temperature of about 40 deg. and in summer it is often difficult to obtain germination; also at that time seedlings must have extra attention to prevent their being scorched. When seeds are sown in spring the little plants should be shifted to the garden by July, to give them time and space to develop into sturdy plants, so that by fall they will be large enough to set in their permanent locations in the border.

Another advantage of spring sowing is that many perennials will produce flowers the first year, among them: *Anthemis nobilis* (c h a m o m i l e), *Bellis perennis* (English daisy), *Cerastium tomentosum* (snow-in-summer), *Delphinium grandiflorum* (Chinese larkspur) *Dianthus* (pinks, sweet william), *Glaucium luteum* (horned poppy), *Hesperis matronalis* (sweet rocket), *Malva moschata* (musk mallow), *Myosotis palustris* (forget-me-not), *Papaver nudicaule* (Iceland poppy) and *Salvia farinacea* (mealy-cup sage). On the other hand there are several perennials which must be three or more years old from seed before they bloom. They include: Aconitum (monkshood), Adonis, Baptisia (wild indigo), Dictamnus (gas-plant), Helleborus (Christmas-rose), Peony, Primula (polyanthus) and Trollius (globe-flower).

OTHER PROPAGATION METHODS. These include division of the roots; stolons or the rooting of the shoots; root cuttings and stem cuttings.

The best time to take cuttings is in the spring when the parent plants are about 6 or 8 in. high. Root cuttings are best made in the middle or late summer when they will grow into good plants by the next spring. On page 925 are listed popular perennials and favored methods of propagation, which see.

SUMMER CARE. If the perennial bed is made well in the beginning, thoroughly worked and well supplied with humus and plant food, it will require only occasional cultivation with hoe or other tool during the growing season—unless low groundcovers are planted among the perennials to keep down weeds and shade the soil

from the hot sun, or unless the bed is mulched with peat moss, buckwheat hulls or lawn clippings. Such a mulch keeps it cool, prevents baking, checks evaporation and prevents weed growth. Hence the most important cultivation is that done when the bed is uncovered each spring and when the fine part of a winter mulch can be dug under to keep up the humus supply.

One phase of perennial gardening often misunderstood is proper watering during the growing season. Casual spraying is not only inadequate, but actually worse than not watering at all, for it merely wets the top layer of the soil and has a tendency to bring the roots upward. To reach the deeper roots the watering must be thorough; continue it until water stands in puddles on the surface. Then don't give more water until it is definitely needed. Early in the morning is the best and most economical time to water, before the sun evaporates so much. Morning is better than late afternoon, for damp foliage overnight in warm close weather contributes to the spread of fungous diseases.

WINTER PROTECTION. When perennials are purchased from a local nursery they are likely to be hardy in that neighborhood. However, perennial gardens usually come through the winter better when given some sort of protection or mulch. This is given, not to keep the plants warm (for hardy perennials do not mind low temperatures), but to keep the ground at as near an even temperature as possible; as a matter of fact, to keep it cold. For that reason it should not be applied until the ground has frozen. A covering put on while the weather is mild and before the soil has frozen is likely to smother the plants, whereas if the ground is left uncovered alternate freezing and thawing tends to make the soil heave (especially a heavy soil) and to loosen or dislodge the plant roots. This occurs especially with recently planted perennials which have not yet established firm footholds.

Another purpose of mulching is to protect the evergreen foliage of plants like hollyhock, foxglove, candytuft and sweet william from damage caused by exposure to ice and snow. The simplest mulch is a loose layer of leaves of hardwood trees. Those of oak are better than those of maple, which being softer become soaked and mat down tightly. Cornstalks or

Propagation Methods for Popular Perennials

KEY: D, *division;* S, *stolons or shoots;* R, *root cuttings;* C, *stem cuttings;*

Acanthus D	Delphinium D,C	Lysimachia D,C	Sagittaria D
Achillea D	Dianthus D,C	Lythrum D,C	Salvia D,C
Aconitum D	Dicentra D,R	Menispermum D,C	Sambucus D,C
Adonis D	Dictamnus D	Mentha D,S,C	Sanguinaria D
Alyssum D,C	Digitalis C	Mertensia D	Saponaria D,R,C
Anemone D	Erigeron D	Miscanthus D	Sassafras D,S,R,C
Anthemis D	Eremurus D	Monarda D,R,C	Saxifraga D,S
Aquilegia D	Gaillardia D,R,C	Myosotis D,C	Scabiosa D
Arabis D,R	Gentiana D	Myrica D,R,C	Sedum D,C
Armeria D	Geum D	Oenothera D,S,C	Sempervivum S
Arnica D	Gypsophila D,R,C	Papaver D	Senecio D,C
Artemisia D	Helianthus D,S,C	Pentstemon D	Silene D,C
Arundo D	Helleborus D	Peony D,R	Solidago D,C
Asperula D	Hepatica D	Phlox D,R,C	Spiraea D,C
Aster D	Hemerocallis D	Physostegia D,C	Stokesia D,R
Aubrietia D,C	Hesperis D,C	Platycodon D	Syringa D,C
Auricula D	Heuchera D,C	Plumbago D,C	Tenacetum D,C
Baptisia D	Hosta D	Podophyllum D,R	Thalictrum D
Bellis D	Iberis D,C	Polemonium D	Trachymene D
Bocconia D,S,R	Iris D	Polygonatum D	Tradescantia D,C
Boltonia D	Liatris D	Polygonum D,R,C	Trollius D
Callirhoë D,C	Linaria D	Potentilla D	Uvularia D
Campanula D	Linum D	Primula R	Vaccinium D,C
Centaurea D,C	Lobelia D	Ranunculus D	Valeriana D
Centranthus D	Lonicera R,C	Rhus D,C	Verbascum D,C
Chrysanthemum D,C	Lunaria D	Romneya S,R	Veronica D
Coreopsis D	Lupinus D	Rose S,C	Viola D
Cynoglossum D	Lychnis D,C	Rudbeckia D	Yucca D,R,C

coarse strawy manure may be used, and also peat moss or compost. Keep the mulch light enough not to smother the plants; a few inches will be sufficient. A light covering may be kept in place by placing chicken wire, light boards or branches over it. In the spring the protection should be lifted gradually—a little at a time over several days—as soon as a reasonable amount of growth has appeared. Don't wait until the shoots are big enough to be damaged by the removal of the material and the forking over of the soil.

PEST CONTROL. Spraying is usually necessary to keep perennials free of insects and fungous diseases, but many gardeners spray indiscriminately, sometimes doing more damage than would be caused by the plant enemies. Three kinds of insect pests affect perennials: chewing, sucking and subterranean. Those of the first group are easily detected at work on foliage or flowers and can be fairly easily controlled by the use of a stomach poison containing arsenic, such as paris green or lead arsen-ate. Apply such a spray after the insect appears; earlier applications are wasted. Sucking insects, which pierce the plant's tissues and suck its vital juices, must be killed by being hit with a contact poison, such as kerosene emulsion, a soap mixture or a nicotine preparation. Subterranean pests, including cut-worms and root lice, may be eliminated to some degree by cultivation. Poison baits also help, but should be used carefully, to prevent harm to young children, birds or pets. A soil fumigant like tobacco dust or naphthalene compounds is recommended and other suggestions are carbon bisulphide or carbolic emulsion, discussed under INSECTICIDE.

Proper cultivation, adequate feeding and garden cleanliness will help keep perennials clear of fungous diseases. In general, when a plant is found to be diseased the tops should be cut down and destroyed. If a second attack is apparent when new growth comes from the roots, it is often wise to pull up and destroy the plant. Regular spraying with a good fungicide is a preventive, one of the best being the old standby, bordeaux mixture. Mildews can be controlled by applications of powdered sulphur. In all cases, the aim should be to prevent the occurrence of disease if possible; next its prompt cure when detected; and finally, if necessary, removal of a fatally diseased specimen before it spreads infection to other plants.

PERENNIALS FOR DIFFERENT PURPOSES

FOR CUT FLOWERS. Just as in the case of annuals, it is advisable to have a separate cutting garden in some out-of-the-way spot, where constant picking of blossoms will not spoil the general garden scene. Flowers suggested for such a garden include delphinium, peonies, most of the daisy-flowered kinds, iris, campanulas, dianthus, gaillardia, rudbeckia, platycodon, hemerocallis, salvia, pyrethrum, scabiosa and veronica.

AT THE SUMMER RESORT. Though the seaside or mountain home garden must depend chiefly upon annuals for its flower decorations, there are several perennials that can be grown with success in sandy soils and salty or high atmospheres, among them agrostemma, dusty miller, hardy asters, eryngium, hibiscus, *Phlox subulata* and *Sedum spectabile*.

FOR ROCK GARDENS. Perennials are the backbone of the rockery, and the gardener should include as many of them as possible. The following list includes plants which grow best in a setting of rocks and which have been grown with the greatest success as alpines: arabis, aquilegia, arenaria, anemone, anchusa, ajuga, *Aster alpinus,* alyssum, aubrietia, *Callirhoë involucrata, Bellis perennis,* cheiranthus, euphorbia, erinus, edelweiss, gentiana, gypsophila, helianthemum, hepatica, heuchera, hieracium, helleborus, iberis, mertensia, *Phlox subulata,* platycodon, pachysandra, plumbago primula, podophyllum, polemonium, potentilla, silene, spiderwort, statice, stokesia, trollius, veronica and vinca.

While the foregoing list includes only those which may be grown with ease, it by no means exhausts the genera available.

FOR SHADE. There are scores of perennials that can be grown in the shade, just as there are many annuals that will thrive under such conditions. The various plantain-lilies (Hosta) do especially well there. Others include *Anemone japonica, Anchusa azurea, Aruncus sylvester, Dicentra spec-*

tabilis, Hemerocallis flava, Lobelia cardinalis, Phlox subulata, and species of Ajuga, Aquilegia, Aconitum, Aegopodium, Digitalis, Monarda, Mertensia, Myosotis, Platycodon, Sedum, Thalictrum and Viola.

PERENNIAL CLIMBERS. Among the perennials that can be used to good advantage as vines or climbers are: *Adlumia fungosa* (Allegheny-vine, mountain fringe), *Aristolochia sipho* (Dutchmans pipe), *Celastrus scandens* (bittersweet), *Parthenocissus quinquefolia* (Virginia creeper), and species of Akebia, Clematis, Lonicera (honeysuckle), Lathyrus (perennial-pea), Campsis (trumpet creeper), wisteria and ivy.

FOR FRAGRANCE. Among the perennials the most delicious fragrance is obtained from such subjects as *Monarda didyma* (fragrant balm), *Lippia citriodora* (lemon-verbena), *Artemisia lactiflora* and *A. vulgaris* (mugwort), *Hosta grandiflora* (plantain-lily), *Convallaria majalis* (lily-of-the-valley), *Dianthus plumarius* (grass pink), *Iris germanica* and its varieties (bearded iris), *Hemerocallis flava* (lemon daylily), *Lavandula vera* (lavender), *Melissa officinalis* (bee balm), *Thymus citriodora* (lemon thyme), *Valerianella officinalis* (garden-heliotrope), *Hesperis matronalis* (sweet rocket).

See also SOIL, TRANSPLANTING, CUTTINGS, ROCK GARDEN, EDGING PLANTS, BACKGROUND PLANTING; PLANTS FOR SPECIAL PURPOSES.

PERESKIA (pe-res'-ki-ah). A Mexican, W. Indian and S. American genus of cacti in which the broad, flat leaves are persistent to the extent that they may be said to be evergreen. They are all succulent in appearance but possess the one unmistakable characteristic which marks them as cacti, namely the areole or center of growth. In the N. they are greenhouse or lathhouse subjects. Easily propagated from cuttings. They are much used as a stock for grafting. The flowers, which differ from those of other cacti in that they have stems (others are sessile) appear either singly or in drooping clusters. They are single and range from white to rose. *P. aculeata* (or *pereskia*) has an edible fruit which gives it the name of Barbados-gooseberry. Its manner of growth and the shape of its leaves suggest another common name, Lemon-vine.

PERFECT FLOWER. A flower having both stamens and pistils and therefore capable of both producing pollen and developing seeds—though it may not be able to fertilize itself. Because it possesses both male and female organs it may be called a hermaphrodite, or a bisexual flower. See also FLOWER.

PERGOLA. In its original meaning and in the true and best sense, this designates a simple arbor as designed in Italy, usually for supporting grape-vines. It is constructed with permanent and sometimes architectural and massive columns, but its overhead vine-supporting members are easily replaced by light saplings or slender boards such as furring-strips, replacement often being made necessary by the weight of the vines.

The elaborate structures often called "pergolas" in American gardens, approach nearer the cloister, colonnade, peristyle or loggia in character. All these differ from the true pergola principally in being fully protected by a roof.

See also GARDEN FIXTURES.

PERIANTH. The floral envelope as a whole; that is, normally the calyx and the corolla together or the calyx alone when there is no corolla. The term is generally used when the calyx and corolla are much alike, as in lilies.

PERILLA (pe-ril'-ah). A small genus of the Mint Family, consisting of half-hardy annual herbs, natives of India and China, grown and valued for their highly colored foliage which is sometimes used for summer bedding and subtropical effects in the garden. The plants thrive in any light loamy soil. They may be propagated by seeds in gentle heat in March, then gradually hardened off and placed in the border at the end of May.

P. frutescens (var. *crispa* or *nankinensis*) is the garden form, with dark bronzy-purplish foliage with margins crisped and fringed.

PERIPLOCA (pe-rip'-loh-kah). Deciduous or evergreen climbing shrubs belonging to the Milkweed Family and known as Silk-vine (which see). Though of tropical origin they are hardy in the U. S. if given winter protection in the N.

PERISTROPHE (pe-ris'-troh-fee). Herbs or shrubs of the tropics, belonging to the Acanthus Family. *P. speciosa,* the one commonly grown, is a bushy shrub, often grown in pots for winter flowering in the greenhouse. The flowers are violet-purple, and it thrives under the same treatment as Jacobinia (which see).

PERITHECIUM (per-i-thee'-shi-um). A closed fungous fruiting body, spherical

PERIWINKLE AS A CUT FLOWER
This modest sturdy little perennial (Vinca minor) is well known as a blue-flowered evergreen ground cover, but some of the improved, larger-flowered forms are worthy of other uses as suggested here.

or flask-shaped, containing sacs (*asci*) in which are the sexual spores. See FUNGUS; compare APOTHECIUM.

PERIWINKLE. Common name for the Vinca (which see), a genus of trailing herbs, useful as ground-covers and decorative window-box and urn plants. Common Periwinkle or Running-myrtle is the hardy evergreen *V. minor;* Madagascar Periwinkle is the tender *V. rosea.*

PERMANGANATE OF POTASH. Another name for potassium permanganate (which see) sometimes used in garden operations as a disinfectant.

PERNETIANA (per-net-i-ay'-nah). The name given to a large, but at present rather confused and indefinite, group of bush roses that is really a section of the Hybrid Tea class (see under ROSE). Some describe Pernetianas as "all the modern, highly colored Hybrid Tea Roses." The name was given after the famous French rosarian and hybridist, Pernet-Ducher, succeeded in doing what rosarians had long sought to do, namely infuse some real yellow into the hybrid tea roses, which heretofore had lacked that color. This he did by crossing the strongly yellow Austrian Brier species (*R. foetida*) on various H. T.'s. The resulting strain, of which the variety Daily Mail (or Willowmere) was one of the first noted ones, was called Pernetiana and thereafter was very freely rebred into existing hybrid-tea species until its brilliant color tendency, especially in yellow shades, is so well distributed through them that it is practically impossible to designate where it stops and the pure H. T. begins.

PERNETTIA (per-net'-i-ah) or PER-NETTYA. Prickly-Heath. Low evergreen shrubs from S. America, belonging to the Heath Family but not reliably hardy N. They do best in peaty, rather moist, soil in a sunny place, and are well placed in the rock garden or with evergreen shrubs. They have small spiny-pointed, glossy green leaves, and small white or pinkish nodding flowers in early summer. The pea-like fruits are very colorful, varying from white to red or dark purple. Propagated by seeds, cuttings, layers and suckers. *P. mucronata,* the principal species, is a bushy grower 2 to 3 ft. tall occurring in various forms with different colored berries.

PEROVSKIA (per-of'-ski-ah). (Often spelled PEROWSKIA.) Herbs or shrubby plants of Asia, belonging to the Mint Family. *P. atriplicifolia,* apparently the only one in cultivation, is a handsome little shrub with silver-gray stems, small oval leaves and spikes of violet-blue flowers. The entire plant gives off a sage-like odor when brushed. It should have well-drained soil and a sunny location, and in the N. usually behaves as an herbaceous perennial. Propagated by seeds and cuttings.

PERPETUAL or PERPETUAL-FLOWER-ING. A term applied to varieties of flowering plants which, instead of bearing flowers only during a brief period of their active growing season, continue to bloom as long as growth goes on. Perpetual Carnations long ago replaced the older, one-season varieties, as the continued yield proved much more profitable to the growers. Hybrid Perpetual Roses (H. P.'s), an improvement on the old Monthly Rose, bear flowers from early summer until hard freezing.

PERSEA (pur'-se-ah). A genus of broad-leaved evergreen trees some of which are planted extensively for ornament in warm countries. The most important species, however, is *P. americana,* which bears the so-called Alligator-pear or Avocado, which see.

PERSIAN INSECT POWDER. A name given to an insecticide made from the dried flower-heads of Asiatic species of Pyrethrum, which see.

PERSIMMON. The common name for a genus (Diospyros) of trees and shrubs of the Ebony Family, mostly of Asia but few native to the U. S.; and also for the edible fruit of certain species. Some are grown as ornamentals or in plant collec-

tions. The common American persimmon (*D. virginiana*) which grows wild in woods and fields from Conn. to Iowa and the Gulf States, has produced a score of choice varieties which ripen successively from late August to November and are good garden subjects though their fruit does not ship well and therefore is not grown commercially. *D. ebenaster,* the Black Sapote, native to Mex. and the W. Indies, may be grown in S. Fla. Two Asiatic species, *D. lotus,* the Date-plum, and *D. kaki,* the Japanese Persimmon or Kaki, are apparently hardy in the Cotton Belt. The last named is grown commercially in the S. and in Calif.

All those mentioned are excellent home garden fruit trees within their climatic ranges. They have deep-reaching tap roots, good foliage, and attractive flowers. However, the grower should keep in mind three important points: (1) Only grafted or budded varieties should be planted because seedlings bear often worthless fruit; (2) none but young and small trees should be planted because large ones are likely to die if moved; (3) to make sure of fruit, several different varieties of the same species must grow in the neighborhood because at least some require cross-pollination. Once established, in lawns or gardens, persimmons need no special cultural care; but leaf eating insects generally and especially the flat-headed borer (see under APPLE) should be watched for and controlled. In orchards persimmon trees may be planted and cultivated like peaches.

A Cephalosporium wilt of the native persimmon, first reported from Tenn. in 1937, has spread rapidly throughout the SE. Nearly all infected trees die, some as soon as two months after initial infection. There is no known control.

Except for those mentioned, the species of Diospyros are tropical or suited only to mild climates and are not of importance as garden subjects.

PERSISTENT. Remaining longer than usual, as parts of a flower which remain until the fruit is ripe, as the calyx of the apple; or leaves of deciduous plants which hang upon the twig into winter.

PERUVIAN-DAFFODIL. A common name for Ismene (*Hymenocallis calathina*), or basket-flower, a species of Spider-lily, which see.

PESTS. Broadly this term includes all garden enemies, but in garden literature it has been used chiefly to designate insects (which see) and related small animals such as mites and red spiders, sow-bugs and slugs, as opposed to diseases of plants caused by fungi and bacteria.

Larger pests, such as rodents, with which this article deals, often present a difficult problem. Besides the damage they do to plant material, the unsightly evidences of their presence—raised runways topped with yellowed grass and mounds of earth in the center of immaculate lawns—sometimes make their eradication imperative.

The mole (which see), though no eater of plant life, is a great offender in this respect. On the credit side he destroys great quantities of mice, beetles, grubs, etc., creatures which have no mercy on delicate roots and bulbs.

Meadow and field mice, like the mole, make ugly runways either on or just below the surface of the ground. In addition, they have an inordinate fancy for choice tidbits such as lily and tulip bulbs and the tender bark and young roots of tender trees and shrubs.

Poison gas (automobile exhaust directed into the burrows through a hose attached to the exhaust pipe) is a common and effective remedy, but has the disadvantage of being dangerous to plant material. The gas given off by commercial forms of calcium cyanide or by carbon bisulphide is also effective in many cases. (See under FUMIGATION.) For moles, the steel trap is probably the best control agent. For mice, strychnine, administered in small doses placed in raisins dropped into the runs, has proven good.

To defend especially precious bulbs and roots from burrowers, it is well to plant them in containers made of ½-in. galvanized wire mesh; or, if the pests are very bad, to even line the bed with such wire. This container method has the advantage of permitting easy moving and division of the tubers or bulbs.

In the winter, the gardener should be particularly watchful for signs of mice about the bases of shrubs and trees. Concealed by snow and protective mulches, they may work for weeks unnoticed and completely destroy a good planting by girdling the stems before their presence is known. Burrowers of as wide distribution as the mice are the pocket gophers, which live strictly on plant materials and are easily satisfied with the best of everything

—roots, bulbs, tubers, garden vegetables, grains, and the bark of shrubs and trees—especially fruit trees. Poison gas, steel traps and strychnine are all useful against them. Castor-beans (*Ricinus communis*) dropped by twos and threes into the runways through small holes immediately closed with a bit of sod have been effective as poison or as a repellent. *Do not leave these beans where children or domestic animals can get them.*

Rabbits in the garden are less of a problem in the summer months than in the winter months when they attack permanent planting material, not temporary vegetables. Rabbit-proof fences, of course, are effective at all times. A common method of winter protection is to enclose the trunk of each tree in fine wire mesh, tar paper, wood veneer or other tooth-resistant fabric. A comparatively new control method is the use of a repellent paint or spray, the following mixture being recommended by agricultural college investigators: Heat, in the open air, and in a container holding about 2 gals. 1 qt. linseed oil to 470 deg. F. or until a light bluish smoke appears. Take from the fire and stir in 3 oz. finely ground sulphur a very little at a time. If correctly made it will cool to a thick black fluid of most disagreeable odor. Paint on deciduous trees and shrubs as high as the rabbits can reach. To protect evergreens and low shrubs, make an emulsion of 1 qt. of the preparation to 2 qts. of water in which 2 oz. of finely shaved laundry soap has been dissolved. Stir or shake well and use as a spray.

PETAL. One of the inner series of floral leaves which together make up the *corolla,* which see. See also FLOWER.

PETALOSTEMUM (pet-ah-los-tee'-mum) or PETALOSTEMON. A genus of mostly perennial American herbs commonly called Prairie-clover. The pea-like flowers appear in small spikes. About a dozen species are grown in wild gardens and rock gardens.

PETASITES (pet-ah-sy'-teez) (from the Greek word for a hat, referring to the large leaves). A genus of easily grown herbaceous perennials, native to Europe and Asia, and to the N. temperate and sub-arctic regions of N. America, and popularly known as Butter-bur. About 20 species are recognized. Though coarse-growing and weedy-looking, their big, felty, round or kidney-shaped leaves and early

PETUNIAS PLEASING OUTDOORS
Free-flowering, vigorous, and graceful, petunias in a tub or urn are a splendid feature for the top or bottom of a flight of entrance steps.

flowering make them desirable for locations otherwise bare in early spring. Their flowers are produced in large purple to white clusters. Propagation is by division; also by seeds. *P. fragrans,* from the Mediterranean, known as Winter-heliotrope and Sweet-coltsfoot, grows to 1 ft. tall and blooms in winter in the greenhouse, affording an excellent lilac to purple cut flower of vanilla-like odor. *P. japonicus,* to 6 ft. with leaves 4 ft. across, in an Asiatic species; in its native territory the stalks are eaten as a vegetable and the flower buds as a condiment.

PETREA (pee-tree'-ah). Tropical American shrubby plants, belonging to the Vervain Family. The principal species is *P. volubilis* (Purple-wreath), a twining shrub grown outdoors in warm regions and sometimes farther N. under glass, where it is usually trained to a support or form. It thrives in a compost of equal parts fibrous loam and peat, with the addition of some old cow manure and sharp sand. It has oblong wavy leaves and very showy purple flowers in a slender cluster.

PETROCALLIS (pet-roh-kal'-is). A small alpine perennial of the Mustard Family, much favored in rockwork and on old walls where its mat-like mass may fill the cracks and crevices. It should be placed in the sunniest spot where the late autumn sun will mature the plant and return more abundant bloom in the spring. Propagated by root division in early spring.

P. pyrenaica (Rock Beauty) is matted, 2 to 3 in. tall, with simple stems, wedge-shaped leaves arranged in a rosette, and flowers at first white, later changing to purple or pink.

PETROCOPTIS (pet-roh-kop'-tis). Small low-growing perennials of the Pink Family, with leaves tufted or in rosettes. Suitable for the rock garden, they are of very easy culture in almost any garden soil but thrive best in a light, rich well-drained loam. Propagation is by seeds or division of roots, both in spring. *P. lagascae* (*Lychnis lagascae*) is a tufted, low plant to 4 in. high, with leaves straight and tapering to ¾ in., and flowers rose with a white center, ¾ in. in diameter.

PETROPHYTUM (pe-tro-fy'-tum). Low evergreen prostrate shrubs, native of the W. part of the country and belonging to the Rose Family. The principal species is *P. caespitosum,* which forms mats up to 3 ft. across, and bears short spikes of small white flowers. It thrives in limestone soil and a sunny place, is well adapted to the rock garden and is hardy N. Propagated by seeds or division.

PE-TSAI (pee'-tsy'). An oriental species of mustard (*Brassica pekinensis*) which, like several related plants, is incorrectly called a Chinese Cabbage. It is gaining in popularity in America on account of its dense, cylindrical heads of crisp green leaves with a tender, white central core. It can be eaten raw or cooked and, like other Brassicas, does better in the cool weather of spring and autumn than in winter. See BRASSICA; CHINESE CABBAGE; MUSTARD.

PETUNIA (pe-teu'-ni-ah). A genus of highly ornamental hardy or half-hardy annuals or perennials of the Nightshade Family. They are usually treated as annuals and are very showy and popular plants, effective in beds, borders, porch boxes and pots. They thrive in a mixture of 2 parts of loamy soil and 1 part of leafmold or well-decayed manure, and require plenty of water during summer.

They may be raised from seed or, in the case of the named varieties, may be readily propagated from cuttings. The seeds, which are minute, should be sown in March in light, finely sifted soil, very lightly covered and given gentle heat. When large enough, pot singly, and pinch back the points before they get too high, to induce compact growth. For planting out, these potted plants should be gradually hardened off early in May. Plants retained for flowering inside should be potted last and kept in frames where there is plenty of air. When cuttings are to be made, old plants may be preserved during the winter in a warm location and cut in the spring. Young shoots root readily in a close frame during Feb. and March.

The leaves of mosaic-infected plants are mottled with yellowish-green and dark-green areas and usually crinkled and deformed. Destroy all plants with these symptoms and keep down the aphid carriers of the trouble by using contact sprays and destroying all weeds in the vicinity. The greenhouse orthezia (which see) may infest bedding plants out-of-doors. The potato flea beetle and the yellow woolly bear (see under VERBENA) may feed on petunias. If an infestation becomes serious spray with lead arsenate.

Principal Species

P. hybrida (Common Garden Petunia). There are many varieties and strains of this species, said to consist of a series of hybrids between two or more of the older species. There are single and double, fringed and plain petaled varieties, some with flowers up to 5 in. across. There is also a compact dwarf strain that is well suited for the rock bed and for potting purposes. The colors vary from pure white to deep violet reds; some are striped, many are fringed, and one improved form has a clearly defined 5-pointed star-like markings.

axillaris (*P. nyctaginiflora*). A spreading or erect half-hardy perennial to 2 ft.; with a cylindrical tube and white flowers, often fragrant, borne in Aug.

violacea. Violet-flowered half-hardy perennial, with many prostrate or erect stems 6 to 10 in. long, oval leaves, and purplish-violet flowers to 1½ in. long.

PHACELIA (fa-see'-li-ah). A genus of small native herbs with blue, white or purple blossoms, clustered, or in racemes. They are rather charming in a mass but of somewhat straggling growth and fleeting bloom. Only a few annual species are in cultivation; they may be grown easily from seed sown where the plants are to stand, or started in the hotbed for very early bloom.

P. whitlavia (California-bluebell) growing to 1½ ft. has blue or purple bell-shaped blossoms; var. *alba* has white flowers. This species is often listed as Whitlavia. *P. campanularia* is a low-growing plant with clear blue flowers, suitable for edging.

PHALAENOPSIS (fal-e-nop'-sis). A genus of epiphytic, tropical orchids having racemes or panicles of white, rose or rose-purple flowers, with 3-lobed lips, often spotted and streaked, and long, thick leathery leaves. Many of the new hybrids surpass any of the species in the size and beauty of the flowers, *P. elizabethae* being one of the showiest crosses produced.

These rare and lovely plants from the Malay Peninsula and the Philippines are termed the aristocrats of the orchid world, and as they are difficult to grow, their culture should not be attempted except by those with special equipment. They need a draft-free greenhouse with a moist atmosphere, a minimum temperature of 65 deg. F., and a copious supply of water during growing season. Grows best in osmundine or sphagnum, in shallow pans or baskets.

PHALARIS (fal'-ah-ris). A genus of annual and perennial ornamental grasses of the Old World (and one species of N. America). One of the most commonly cultivated sorts, popular in old-time gar-

IMPROVED PETUNIAS AS CUT FLOWERS
Recent successful plant breeding efforts have turned the once simple, single petunia into a striking, ruffled colorful blossom especially effective for vase arrangements.

dens, is a variety (*picta*) of the perennial species *P. arundinacea,* known as Ribbon Grass or Gardners Garters, because of its yellow and white striped leaves. An annual species, *P. canariensis,* is grown for its shining yellow seeds which are fed to birds, giving it the name Canary Grass. Propagation of the perennial types is by division; of the annual types by seeds. See also ORNAMENTAL GRASSES.

PHASEOLUS (fah-see′-oh-lus). A genus of annual or perennial herbs of the Pea Family native in warm regions and including the familiar garden, lima, and other beans, though not the broad bean (Vicia) nor the soy-bean (Glycine). Mostly of twining habit, they are grown chiefly for their edible pods and seeds. For culture see BEAN.

PRINCIPAL SPECIES

P. caracalla (Snail-flower, Corkscrew-flower), a twining perennial to 20 ft. or more, with clusters of curious fragrant light purple or yellowish flowers, with the keel coiled like a snail-shell.

coccineus (Scarlet Runner) has a somewhat tuberous perennial root, but is grown mostly as an annual. A tall slender twiner, with bright scarlet flowers and long edible pods, it is often grown for ornament on porches and arbors.

limensis (Lima Bean) is a tender high climber with white or creamy flowers but valued for its edible and highly nutritious seeds. Var. *limenanus* is the Bush or Dwarf Lima.

vulgaris (Kidney Bean, Haricot) is a tall twining annual with white, yellowish or violet flowers. Var. *humilis,* a non-climbing form, is the common field and garden bean. There are a great many named varieties most of which are used in the green pod stage, though a few are grown for the dry seeds.

PHEASANTS-EYE. The c o m m o n name for the genus Adonis; also applied to the Poets Narcissus (*N. poeticus*). See NARCISSUS.

PHEGOPTERIS (fe-gop′-ter-is). Beech Fern. A genus of ferns of the temperate regions, the English name being a translation from the Greek. The deciduous, triangular fronds are produced from running underground stems. Some species common in rocky woods in the U. S. are suitable for the garden and desirable because they continue to produce new fronds

through the summer. They do well in ordinary well-drained woods soil, and semi-shade. Sometimes referred to Dryopteris,

SPECIES

P. dryopteris (Oak Fern). Fronds smooth and bright green, 6 to 10 in. tall, broadly triangular, and 3-divided, each division pinnate at the base; fruit-dots naked and near the margin. Splendid for the base of rockery or for massing under shrubbery in good soil. Must have excellent drainage, shade and moisture. In planting barely cover the running rhizomes.

hexagonoptera (Broad Beech Fern). Fronds broadly triangular, 7 to 12 in. wide, once-pinnate with deeply lobed pinnae, the lobes nearest the rachis uniting and forming a wing along it; fruit-dots tiny, round, at margins of lobes. More abundant in S.

polypodioides (Long Beech Fern). Fronds 5 to 12 in. long, much like those of the last named but narrower, without the markedly winged rachis, and distinguished by the noticeably downward and outward slant of the lowest pair of pinnae. Prefers the proximity of wet rocks.

robertiana (Limestone Polypody). Of the N. W. States, it is suitable for gardens in that region, liking chalks or limestone soils. Resembles the Oak Fern (see above), but is larger and stiffer in appearance, and duller green; the joints of the rachis and main divisions of frond often form split nodes.

PHELLODENDRON (fel - oh - den′-dron). Botanical name for the Cork-tree.

PHENOMENAL. A common name for the Loganberry, which see. See also RUBUS.

PHILADELPHUS (fil - ah - del′ - fus). (See illustration, Plate 48.) Familiar shrubs of Europe, Asia and N. America, of the Saxifrage Family. Graceful, free-flowering and deliciously fragrant, their popularity has increased since the introduction of numerous hybrids. Often mistakenly called Syringa (which is the name of the Lilac genus), they are properly referred to as Mockorange, which see.

PHILLYREA (fi-lir′-e-a) or FILARIA. A genus of evergreen shrubs or low trees with small white flowers and black fruits. Several species are grown for ornament in mild countries, from seed or grafted upon privet stocks.

PHILODENDRON (fil-oh-den′-dron). Tropical American shrubby plants, usually climbing, belonging to the Arum Family. They are sometimes grown under glass and do best in a warm temperature and moist atmosphere. They may be grown in pots, the climbing forms doing well planted out and trained to a wall or pillar. A compost of fibrous loam and peat, with sand, suits them well. Propagated by cuttings of the tops or stem lengths.

PRINCIPAL SPECIES

P. bipinnatifidum is a short-stemmed species with large divided leaves and a spathe or calla-like flower bract about 8 in. long, reddish-brown on the outside and whitish within.

giganteum is a climber with leaves to 3 ft. long and 2 ft. wide. The spathe is almost a foot long, purplish outside and red within.

grandifolium is also a climber, with arrow-shaped leaves 2 ft. or more long, and a yellowish spathe.

mamei is a dwarf, with large handsome leaves marked silvery-white.

verrucosum is a beautiful climber with medium-sized leaves of satiny-green with metallic shadings above, lined with bands of maroon beneath. The leaf-stems are red and bristly.

PHLOMIS (floh′-mis). Perennial herbs or shrubby plants, belonging to the Mint Family. They are rather coarse growers, suitable for the wild garden or shrubbery. Propagated by seeds, cuttings and division.

PRINCIPAL SPECIES

P. fruticosa (Jerusalem-sage) is a shrubby plant to 4 ft., with crinkled green sage-like leaves white beneath. It has many-flowered whorls of yellow flowers, opening in summer in the East and said to flower all winter in S. Calif.

lychnitis (Lampwick-plant) is a woody plant from 1 to 2 ft., with narrow leaves white beneath, and few-flowered whorls of yellow flowers. The slender basal leaves have been used as lamp-wicks.

tuberosa is a vigorous herbaceous perennial with tuberous roots and dense whorls of purple flowers. It is native in S. Europe, but has become naturalized in E. parts of the U. S.

PHLOX. Hardy erect or diffuse tall or tufted perennials or, rarely, half-hardy annual herbs, natives of N. America and Russian Asia, and members of the Phlox Family (Polemoniaceae). The flowers are in tones of red, pink, violet, blue, buff, or white, and usually are very showy. (See illustration, Plate 40.)

The perennial species and varieties are among the best and most popular of garden plants. Some of the species are dwarf creeping plants well suited for rockwork or in the front of the mixed border. The taller growing forms are well adapted for bedding purposes and at the rear of mixed border plantings. They are all very easily cultivated, the tall growing perennials succeeding best in rather heavy soils of good depth, thriving fairly well, however, in any good bed or border. During dry weather a top mulch of humus or peat is helful, as well as occasional drenching with water.

The dwarf species do not seed very readily, and are propagated mainly from cuttings or root division. Cuttings inserted in a coldframe during July and then shaded will form good plants for the following spring. If light soil has been shaken among them in summer, so that they have become rooted, the trailing branches of large, established plants may be divided in autumn to form new plants. Taller growing varieties may be propagated from seed (which should be saved from extra fine varieties only), or by cuttings of the young stems, shoots, or roots. The roots may be cut into

A LUSTY PHLOX
One year's growth from a November-made root cutting. All the long, straight roots seen here could similarly be cut into 2-in. pieces and rooted to yield 50 or more new plants and the original would still be there to grow on to flowering size.

short lengths and treated like seed. Old clumps may also be lifted, separated and replanted in early spring. It is advisable to destroy self-sown seedlings, as they have a strong tendency to revert back to the original lavender species shades.

ENEMIES. Aids in the control of most diseases of phlox are (1) the destruction of all plant tops and fallen leaves in the fall and (2) the proper division and spacing of the plants. Powdery mildew covers both top and bottom of the leaves in mid-summer with a white fungous growth whose black fruiting bodies (*perithecia*) may later be seen. It is more prevalent on phlox which is crowded and in damp or

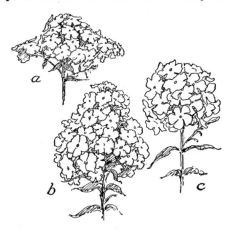

FLOWER ARRANGEMENT IN PHLOX
Three types of clusters, or panicles, are shown: (a) the flattened, spreading type; (b) pyramidal, as in the well-known perennial P. paniculata; (c) the globose form of certain varieties.

shady places but can easily be controlled by dusting with fine sulphur. Leaf spot appears as brown spots, first on the lower leaves, which may die, and progressively on other leaves up the stem. It may be very serious on certain varieties; but the cause is not known.

Phlox is subject to a nematode or eel-worm that causes root galls and also the more destructive stem nematode (the same that attacks narcissi) which causes stunted plants, swollen cracked stems and narrow crinkled leaves and may inhibit flowering. Remove and destroy diseased plants with surrounding soil.

Red spider (which see), the most serious of the pests of phlox, infests the under sides of the leaves, which become light yellow in color and give the plant a general unthrifty appearance. Looking closely on the under surface one can see the tiny red mites enclosed in a webby mass. Plants in full sun in hot dry weather are more subject to injury by red spiders. Dusting with sulphur as for mildew will

often keep them in check. Syringing with the hose is useful. For a very serious infestation spray with a summer oil. The phlox bug which punctures tender shoots and sucks the sap can be controlled with a nicotine-soap spray but this is not usually necessary. The common stalk borer (see under DAHLIA) occasionally tunnels in phlox stems.

PRINCIPAL SPECIES

P. bifida (Sand Phlox). A dwarf tufted hairy perennial with awl-shaped lower leaves about ¼ in. long; flowers violet to white with violet tube.

divaricata (*P. canadensis*). This is the Blue Phlox or Wild-sweet-william, the native Phlox of the woods. Height 9 to 18 in.; oblong leaves 2 in. long; flowers pale violet, blue, lavender to mauve, borne in clusters in spring and early summer. Color forms appear in several varieties, including *alba, lilacina, laphami*.

drummondi (Annual Summer Phlox or Drummond Phlox), from about 12 to 15 in. high, leaves oval to tapering; stem erect, a little branched at top; flowers red varying to rose, purple or white with a darker eye. This is a native of Texas, of strong sturdy growth with large heads of individually large flowers. It shows to best advantage when grown in masses. There are many color forms: snow-white, shell-pink, deep rose, bright scarlet, rich crimson, primrose and soft lilac.

paniculata (Summer Perennial Phlox). Perennials growing to 4 ft. in height; leaves oblong-oval, 4 or 5 in. in length; flowers originally purple in the type, now varying into many colors and shades, borne in large terminal clusters in summer and early autumn. With its many forms, which have been blended and intermixed to a great degree, it forms what is now commonly known as Garden Phlox.

stolonifera (*P. reptans*). A hairy creeping perennial; leaves tapering-oval, about 3 in. long; flowers purple or violet in flat clusters in spring and early summer.

subulata (Ground- or Moss-pink). Low perennial, forming mats about 6 in. high; leaves oval-shaped, about ½ in. long, evergreen; flowers pinkish, varying to purple and white, flowering in early spring. There are various color forms in cultivation. Grows best in an acid soil.

suffruticosa. The early flowering form of the summer-flowering Perennial Phlox, growing about 3 ft. high; leaves to 5 in. long; flowers from purple to rose and white.

Night-phlox is the common name for *Zaluzianskya capensis* (which see), a S. African annual grown indoors for its fragrance and as an ornament.

PHOENIX (fee'-niks). A genus of palms, commonly known as Date Palms. Some of the species have no evident stem; others have tall trunks nearly covered with the bases of old leaf-stalks; almost all sucker profusely from the base. They have plumy leaves and bear a profusion of edible fruit.

PRINCIPAL SPECIES

P. dactylifera, the date (which see), is now grown commercially in Calif., Ariz. and parts of Texas, as well as in the Old World, where it is one of the oldest and most valuable of cultivated trees. Several species are grown in Fla. and Calif.

canariensis (Canary-Island Date Palm). This is a tall strong tree with widespreading leaves with yellow stalks. It is extensively planted in Fla. and Calif. as an avenue tree or as a garden specimen. It requires regular watering and frequent applications of fertilizers rich in ammonia, phosphate and potash. As a pot plant it is excellent for porch, sun-room or patio decoration, enduring hot sun and severe summer storms.

roebeleni (Pygmy Date Palm) is a graceful dwarf palm, grown in Fla. in the shade in rich, moist, loamy soil. In the N. it is a popular greenhouse or house plant, easily handled, and very desirable because of its slow growth.

zeylanica (Blue Date Palm) grows in clumps, with foliage rivaling that of the Colorado Blue Spruce in color.

sylvestris (Date Sugar Palm) commonly planted in Fla. and Calif. gardens, resembles *P. dactylifera* but has more beautiful arching crowns of bluish-green leaves and great bunches of non-edible orange fruit. The trunks are studded with old leaf-stalks which furnish an excellent growing place for ferns and native orchids.

rupicola, a Himalayan species, is a small symmetrical tree with bright green, glossy foliage. It requires rich, moist soil, and protection from cold when young.

PHOENIX-TREE. A common name for *Firmiana simplex,* the Chinese Parasoltree, which see.

PHONY DISEASE OF PEACH. Occurring in the commercial peach growing regions of Georgia and Alabama, this trouble is probably caused by a virus. Affected trees produce short terminal growth, profuse lateral branching, deep green foliage and undersized fruits. The latter suggested "pony peach" as a name for the disease, but when it was mistakenly passed along as "phony" peach, that name stuck. Trees do not apparently die of this disease, but they never recover.

PHORMIUM (faur'-mi-um). A genus of tall perennial herbs of the Lily Family native to New Zealand, where they are valued for their very strong fibre. But they are planted out in Calif. and other warm climates as ornamentals, making striking lawn groups. In the N. they are grown in the greenhouse; or in tubs which are set outside in summer and wintered in a cool greenhouse. They are increased by seed or division. *P. tenax* (New-Zealand-flax) grows to 15 ft. with long narrow leaves and numerous dull red flowers clustered on a long stem; it has showy color forms, one variegated and one showing reddish-purple foliage. *P. colensoi,* to 7 ft., has less rigid leaves and bears yellow flowers.

PHOSPHATES. A general term for compounds of phosphorus, a waxy yellowish non-metallic element, one of the three most essential to all plant growth and frequently lacking in soils. The term phosphate used to be commonly, and incorrectly, applied to all kinds of commercial fertilizers, but this use is going out.

The only source of phosphates for use as plant food in the organic group is animal bone, which is obtainable in the form of bonemeal of different degrees of fineness and either raw or steamed, the latter containing less nitrogen as a result of the treatment.

Among commercial (inorganic) fertilizers the chief phosphate carrier is natural phosphatic rock ground and sold either raw or after treatment with sulphuric acid. The latter product, formerly called acid phosphate but now preferably superphosphate, is the more soluble and valuable. It usually contains about 6 per cent phosphorus (equivalent to 14 per cent phosphoric acid) though some grades run to only 5 or 4 per cent. Basic slag, a by-product of steel factories, is a fine black powder carrying a fair percentage of phosphorus, combined with calcium and other elements.

Phosphorus applied to the soil in the forms mentioned is not quickly lost, as is nitrogen, so can be added at any time in considerable quantities. Superphosphate is an excellent material to sprinkle in live-stock stalls or gutters of cow barns, in hen-houses, on manure piles and on the compost heap, where it absorbs liquid materials and adds to the food value of the resulting manure.

In plants, phosphorus hastens maturity, stimulates root growth and contributes to seed formation.

PHOTINIA (foh-tin'-i-ah). Evergreen and deciduous shrubs or small trees, native in Asia, belonging to the Rose Family. The deciduous species are mostly hardy N., and prefer a sunny position; the evergreen species can stand only a few degrees of frost. Both kinds do well in a light sandy loam and are propagated by seeds, cuttings of half-ripened wood under glass, and layers.

PRINCIPAL SPECIES

P. villosa is a large deciduous shrub with somewhat spreading branches, good clean foliage, and clusters of hawthorn-like flowers in early spring. The leaves are colorful in fall and the bright red berries persist into winter.

serrulata (Chinese-hawthorn) is an evergreen shrub or tree to 40 ft. with long leathery dark glossy green leaves, crimson tinted when young. The flower clusters, about 6 in. across, are followed by round red berries.

davidsoniae is a Chinese evergreen tree to 50 ft., with lustrous bright green leaves; very striking in spring with the colorful young growth, and, in fall, with orange-red fruit.

PHOTOGRAPHY IN THE GARDEN. The camera is fast becoming a universal tool. From year to year it seems more potent in its possible uses as a recorder of facts and accomplishments. It gives to us the ability to paint with light, the results being limited only by our skill.

As a garden accessory, it will record the succession of blooms or other effects throughout the year, and states of development over longer periods. If each picture is dated and the featured plants are recorded on the back, one has material for winter study that may improve the gar-

dening results in succeeding years. Winter aspects of a garden are also worthwhile recording; beautiful in themselves, they may help develop a better plan.

Where there are children, the garden is a desirable place in which to portray them. As one seeks a pleasing setting or composition, a better grouping of plants for next year's pictures may suggest itself. A camera can go hand in hand with an interest in insects, both useful and otherwise; and in birds and other garden denizens.

It will be profitable to give the camera a little study. The result will be fewer but better pictures. There is much reliable free literature published by manufacturers. There are many well-written elementary books obtainable for as little as 25 or 50 cents.

For serious work a folding type of camera is desirable in which the lens may be moved according to a distance scale. With a camera of this kind you can more easily photograph some of the choice flowers or plants individually. A film pack or plate camera will enable you to have single pictures finished without waiting to make a dozen as with the roll film. There are on the market numerous small-size, low priced, stereoscopic cameras. Taking two views simultaneously from slightly different angles, they portray the third dimension, giving much more information. In small sizes the pictures are more satisfying than the ordinary print.

A tripod is desirable for many subjects, particularly where a close view is made. With the color-sensitive films now commonly used, it is possible for the amateur to make better photographs of flowers and other highly colored subjects. A light yellow filter that fits over the lens will greatly improve the result. A supplementary inexpensive wide angle lens may be placed over the regular lens thereby extending the angle of view and increasing the value of a small camera. If a roll film camera has no distance scale for the wide angle lens, it will be impossible to use one. With either film pack or plate back the image may be focused sharply and the view judged more accurately than is possible with the small attached "finder."

If you would make attractive pictures consider the angle of the sun. The best time of day is from early morning until about 9:30 a.m. and from 4 p.m. on in summer. Exposures will have to be longer but the shadows will be full of light, the feeling of distance will be increased and the plant groups or shrubs will have a better appearance of roundness. Rarely can a good picture be made with the sun directly behind you. Let the shadows fall from left or right and choose the time of day to suit the subject, for good pictures are seldom made without care and study. In working with morning or afternoon shadows, and in using small lens openings for close views of flowers, some means of estimating the correct exposure will be necessary. There are numerous devices that will help avoid failures, varying in price from a cheap cardboard calculator to expensive instruments employing a photo-electric cell.

Wind is the greatest enemy of the garden photographer, but by working early and late he may find some calm periods. Flower groups or portraits taken close up, or near views of shrubs, may often be taken to better advantage when no sun is shining on them. Direct sunshine often spoils a picture by making a confused pattern of high lights and shadows. A more valuable record (as distinguished from an artistic composition) can be made by using a background to shut out the other plants. A gray or white card may be tacked to stakes or a piece of fine woven cloth may be stretched on a frame. Such backgrounds must be placed sufficiently far back to prevent their texture from showing. And if the sun is shining, place the background so that no plant shadows will fall upon it. An individual flower spike may be held still by tying it to a green wire rod. Cut specimens are more easily photographed by a well-lighted window, in an open shed, or just within an open door.

Photography may be pursued to the point of making direct color pictures, both still and motion, by several methods now possible. Such records of the garden leave little to be desired.

PHOTOPERIODISM. By this is meant the effect of relative length of daylight exposure (photoperiod) upon the growth and flowering (reproduction) of plants. It has been learned that flowering plants fall into four groups: (1) *short day plants* (which see), those in which flower bud formation is initiated in a relatively short day length (about 10 to 12 hours) and suppressed by increasing the length of day; (2) *long day plants* (which see), in which flower bud formation is initiated by exposure to a relatively long day length (14 hours or more) and suppressed by decreasing the length of day; (3) *indeterminate,* those which bloom with more or less readiness under all light periods; (4) *intermediates,* those plants in which flowering is initiated by a zone or band of day lengths of median duration, but inhibited by day lengths either above or below this band. Other features of plant growth, such as stature, bulk, production of seeds or oil, etc. are influenced by the photoperiod, although, of course, other factors, such as temperature, moisture, humidity, and food supply, have a bearing upon the behavior of all these plants.

An understanding of this phenomenon is important in determining whether a particular plant will bloom if taken to a new region that differs in latitude. It has been of importance in genetics, as it has been possible by varying length of day to secure more than one generation of certain plants within a year. By manipulating day length, it has been possible to bring into bloom simultaneously varieties or species that normally bloom in widely separated periods, and thus successful crosses have been made. Commercially, it has permitted the extending of the blooming period of many plants, thus making certain cut flowers available for much longer seasons than formerly. The lengthening or shortening of the daily exposure to light has become an accepted commercial practice with growers of greenhouse chrysanthemums, china asters, *Kalanchoë coccinea,* and other plants.

PHOTOSYNTHESIS. This comes from Greek words meaning "light" and "putting together" and refers to the process by which the green leaves of plants, in the presence and with the aid of sunlight, manufacture sugars and starches from the carbon dioxide absorbed from the air and the water and raw food materials taken in by the roots from the soil.

Fundamentally, food is a form of stored energy. Thus this manufacture of sugar and starch in the leaf is the conversion of the radiant energy of the sun into these compounds. This is effected by microscopic bodies called *chloroplasts,* which contain the green pigment (*chlorophyll*) which gives plants their characteristic color and without which the vital process of photosynthesis cannot go on.

PHYGELIUS (fi-jee'-li-us) *capensis.* A small S. African shrub formerly called Cape Figwort but now better known as Cape-fuchsia, which see.

PHYLLANTHUS (fil-an'-thus). Tropical herbs, shrubs or trees, belonging to the Spurge Family. One or two species are grown in the tropics for their edible fruits, and others are useful ornamental plants for the greenhouse. Propagated mostly by cuttings; sometimes by seeds and layers.

The principal species are as follows:

P. nivosus, or as called by some botanists, *Breynia nivosa* (Snow-bush). This is a slender little shrub, with oval leaves, mottled green and white. It is used as a hedge plant in the warmest parts of the country, and grown in greenhouses in the North. In its var. *roseo-pictus* the leaves are also mottled pink and red, and in var. *atropurpureus* they are dark purple.

acidus (Otaheite-gooseberry) has become naturalized in S. Fla., and is cultivated in the tropics for its fruits, used in preserves.

emblica (Myrobalan) grows to 30 ft. The branches are clothed with many small leaves, giving it the appearance of a fir or hemlock. It bears edible fruits.

PHYLLITIS (fi-ly'-tis). A genus of ferns with entire, leaf-like fronds, confined to one American species, the Harts Tongue Fern, which see.

PHYLLODOCE (fi-loh'-doh-see). Mountain-heath. Dwarf evergreen shrubs from the arctic regions of Europe, Asia and N. America, belonging to the Heath Family. They are suitable for the rock garden and require moist peaty soil in a partly shaded place. Propagated by cuttings or layers.

P. breweri is usually under a foot high with dark green leaves and rosy-purple flowers. *P. caerulea* grows about 6 in. high, with pink or purple urn-shaped flowers. *P. empetriformis* makes a low-growing mat of small dark green shining leaves, with heads of rosy-purple bell-shaped flowers; there are several horticultural varieties with white or pink flowers.

PHYLLOSTACHYS (fil-oh-stay'-kis). One of several genera of plants of the Grass Family, commonly known as Bamboo. It comprises tall grassy Chinese and Japanese shrubs with stems flattened on one side. *P. aurea* (Golden-bamboo), to 15 ft., has yellow canes and graceful leaves 5 in. long, smooth above with a bloom beneath. *P. nigra* (Blackjoint-bamboo),

hardy and slow growing, but reaching 25 ft., has canes that turn black the second year, and plume-like foliage. *P. violescens,* to 12 ft., has purplish canes and leaves to 6 in. with purple stems. See also BAMBOO.

PHYLLOXERA (fil-ok-see'-rah). Gall-forming plant lice, chiefly important on grape, which see.

PHYMATOTRICHUM (fy-mah-tot'-ri-kum) **ROOT ROT.** Also known as Texas or cotton root rot. A disease caused by the soil-inhabiting fungus, *Phymatotrichum omnivorum,* native to the semi-arid SW. and which, though especially destructive to cotton, may attack some 1700 other plant species. The monocotyledons (which see) and some of the crucifers, mints, and verbenas are immune. During the summer rain period, dense circular mats of fungus mycelium appear on the surface of the ground; the rest of the year the fungus lives in the soil, sclerotia carrying through unfavorable conditions. Plants in infested areas suddenly turn yellow and wilt, death following in a few days. Heavy applications of ammonium sulphate may save infected trees and shrubs, and fallow soil may be disinfected with formaldehyde or carbon bisulphide. See DISINFECTION. Apply to the Univ. of Arizona or the Texas Agr. Experiment Station for bulletins giving lists of plants susceptible to the disease.

PHYSALIS (fis'-ah-lis). A genus of tender annual or perennial herbs of the Nightshade Family, some grown in the garden for the large, bright colored inflated and papery calyxes and others for their small, edible, papery husked fruits, commonly known as Ground-cherry or Husk-tomato. Most of them are natives of warm climates and tender, so plants should be started early in the greenhouse, gradually hardened off, and set out in a warm sheltered spot after danger of frost is over.

P. alkekengi (Alkekengi, Winter-cherry or Chinese Lantern Plant), growing to 2 ft., bears small white flowers followed by large brilliant red calyxes becoming 2 in. long when the plant is in fruit. It is a perennial and forms long tuberous roots which are not killed by frost and spread all over flower-beds, becoming a great nuisance. The bright red "lanterns" are valued for winter bouquets, but the plants should be grown only on waste spots, where their aggressive attempts to occupy the earth will not become objectionable.

pruinosa (Strawberry-tomato or Dwarf Cape-gooseberry), a stout branched, gray-hairy native annual with buff-yellow flowers, followed by a yellow edible fruit about the size of a cherry and tomato-flavored, covered by a large hairy calyx.

peruviana (Cape-gooseberry), a tropical plant growing to 3 ft. with yellowish flowers followed by a yellow berry enclosed in a swollen, long-pointed calyx. Native of S. America, this species has been given its common name because it is widely cultivated in S. Africa.

ixocarpa (Tomatillo), an annual from Mexico, now grown N. The clear yellow flowers are followed by a round sticky purple berry surrounded by a purple-veined calyx.

PHYSIOLOGICAL DISEASES. These are non-parasitic but rather environmental troubles, due not to living organisms but to conditions under which the plants are growing, such as:

1. DEFICIENCIES OF FOOD MATERIAL IN THE SOIL. Lack of sufficient nitrogen causes yellowing and stunting; lack of iron prevents chlorophyll development and consequently causes poorly colored foliage; calcium is necessary for normal leaf development, phosphorus for the formation of proteins, and potassium for carbohydrate development (for example, there is a disease called "potash hunger" of potatoes). A deficiency of magnesium also causes chlorosis or poor foliage color, as in the "sand drown" of tobacco. For such diseases the remedy is of course to supply fertilizers rich in the deficient element but this must frequently be done by the trial and error method.

2. EXCESSES OF SOLUBLE SALTS IN THE SOIL. Symptoms of over-nourishment may be too dark foliage color, suppression of reproductive organs, or their transformation into other organs. An excess of nitrogen may cause rank, succulent plant growth and lower the quality of fruits and vegetables as well as resistance to disease. Plants fed too late in the season may be "soft" and unable to withstand winter.

3. IMPROPER SOIL ACIDITY. Too acid a soil may result in definite symptoms of disease in almost all plants except those requiring a special acid condition; on the other hand such plants as rhododendron and laurel which prefer acid conditions do exceedingly poorly in a neutral or alkaline soil.

4. UNFAVORABLE WATER RELATIONS. Much so-called "winter injury" is due to lack of available water, either through freezing of the soil or actual drought. Trees will show the effects of one or two seasons of drought for several years. But too much water in the soil may so reduce the supply of oxygen that the plants die.

5. UNFAVORABLE TEMPERATURE RELATIONS. Too high temperatures cause tipburn and scald; too low temperatures cause dieback, bud injury and frost cankers.

6. MANUFACTURING OR INDUSTRIAL PROCESSES are responsible for many diseases. Vapor or dust from tarred roads or fumes from melting tar compounds are distinctly injurious. Trees may suffer not only from lightning but from electrical discharges from transmission lines. Leakage of illuminating gas into the soil is a fairly common source of trouble in greenhouses and gardens and along streets. Even a slight leakage of gas causes a slow but very thorough poisoning from which there is not much chance of recovery. In detecting such leakage scientists use certain plants very sensitive to small amounts of gas, such as the tomato or sweet pea.

Smoke injury is another hazard near large industrial centers. The chief injury is done by sulphur dioxide; when large amounts are present in the air there is rapid disappearance of chlorophyll in the leaves followed by death. When small amounts are present symptoms are retarded growth, failure to blossom and set fruit, early shedding of leaves and eventual death. When it can be proved that industrial plants are responsible for crop damage, they can be held liable.

7. POOR PROTECTIVE MEASURES. Diseases due to practices employed in trying to control other diseases include injury during seed disinfection, fumigation or spraying. See SPRAY INJURY.

PHYSOCARPUS (fy-soh-kahr'-pus). A genus of spirea-like shrubs called Ninebark, which see.

PHYSOSTEGIA (fy-soh-stee'-ji-ah). False-dragonhead. (See illustration, Plate 38.) A small genus of hardy perennial herbs of the Mint Family, sometimes known as Obedient-plant, presumably because the flower remains at any angle to which it is turned. It succeeds in any good soil but thrives best in cool, moist positions. and in partial shade. Propagation is by seeds or by root division.

P. virginiana, also known as *Dracoceph-alum virginianum,* grows from 2 to 3 ft. high; with narrow-tapering leaves, 5 in. long, irregularly notched, and flowers flesh-colored to purplish, about 1 in. long, in spikes at the tips of branches. The stems are erect and herbaceous, dying down in winter. There are also white and pink varieties.

PHYTEUMA (fy-tu'-mah). A genus of perennial herbs of the Old World grown mostly in rock gardens under the common name Horned Rampion, which see.

PHYTOLACCA (fy-toh-lak'-ah). A genus of herbs, shrubs and trees, the best-known member being the showy but some-what poisonous Pokeberry, which see.

PICEA (pis'-e-ah). The genus of coni-fers known as Spruce (which see). It is a most important group of ornamental trees, with many species native of N. America.

PICKEREL-WEED. Common name for a genus of aquatic plants best repre-sented by *Pontederia cordata,* a fine, hardy native found in shallow waters. (See illus-tration, Plate 2.) Its leaves are large, arrow-shaped, and carried on long stalks rising a foot or so above the surface of the water. The spikes of blue-violet flowers are profuse and most attractive. It is use-ful for planting in shallow waters (about 10 or 12 in. deep) of pond or lake mar-gins. Propagation is largely by division. Most dealers in aquatic plants keep a good stock of the Pickerel-weed on hand.

PICOTEE. A type of carnation (which see) characterized by having a marginal band of color on each petal contrasting with the solid body color of yellow or white.

PIE-PLANT. Colloquial name for Rhu-barb, which see.

PIERIS (py-er'-is). Evergreen shrubs or small trees, native in N. America and Asia, belonging to the Heath Family. They thrive best in a sheltered position, and a rather moist sandy soil with peat or leafmold. Sometimes they are grown in pots and gently forced under glass, *P. japonica* being especially good for that pur-pose. Usually propagated by seeds and layers. Cuttings of nearly mature wood may be rooted under glass, but it is a slow process.

P. floribunda, found from Va. S., is a slow-growing dense shrub to 6 ft., desir-able for its hardiness and early flowering. It has dull green leaves, and nodding white flowers in upright panicles. The flower buds are conspicuous all winter.

P. japonica is larger and a faster grower, very handsome in form, with lustrous leaves delicately tinted when young. It is a beautiful sight in bloom, with droop-ing panicles of white flowers, but in the North these are often winter-killed. Var. *variegata* is of dwarfer habit, with leaves edged white.

PIGEON-BERRY. Common name for *Duranta repens,* commonly called Sky-flower, a decorative shrub or tree of warm regions.

PIGEON MANURE. The droppings of pigeons make a valuable manure for garden use. The composition and uses are similar to those of other manures. It should similarly be used with judgment as it is rather dry and concentrated and is likely to burn plants with which it comes in contact. See MANURE.

PIGEON-PEA. Common name for *Cajanus cajan,* a tropical shrub grown for its edible seeds.

PIGEON-PLUM. The small edible berry of *Coccolobis floridana,* a tropical tree sometimes grown in S. Florida.

PIG MANURE. This is not ordinarily obtainable by the average gardener, but when available it is a valuable source of plant food, especially if composted with horse manure or with any absorbent ma-terial such as peat moss or straw. It re-sembles cow manure in being rather cold and heavy which makes it decompose slowly. On the average its composition is about .55 per cent nitrogen, .5 per cent phosphoric acid and .4 per cent potash but there is considerable variation, depend-ing upon the way it has been handled, its age, and other factors.

PIGNUT. Common name for *Carya glabra,* a species of hickory with astrin-gent kernels; also for *Simmondsia cali-fornica* or jajoba, a subtropical evergreen shrub related to box (Buxus) and some-what grown for ornament, or for its edible fruits or oily seeds.

PIGWEED. A common name for spe-cies of Amaranthus, especially *A. retro-flexus* and *A. hybridus;* also for Goose-foot, the genus Chenopodium, especially *C. album.*

PILEA (py'-le-ah). A genus of trop-ical, annual or perennial, herbs of the Nettle Family. Some are creeping and many are weedy, only two species being worth growing in S. gardens or as pot plants or greenhouse bench edging material in the N. They thrive best in a moist compost of loam and leafmold to which a little sand has been added; they can be propagated by seeds, cuttings or division of the roots.

P. microphylla, annual or biennial, with much-branched, fleshy stems from prostrate to 12 in. high, has leaves not over ¼ in. long. It is called Artillery-plant because of its habit of forcibly discharging its pollen from the staminate flowers when mature. *P. nummulariae-folia* (Creeping Charlie) is a perennial with creeping stems that root at the joints. The oval leaves are as much as ¾ in. across.

PIMELEA (pi-mee'-le-ah). A genus of Australian shrubs commonly called Rice-flower, which see.

PIMENTO. A name derived from the Spanish *pimiento,* meaning pepper, applied to the genus Capsicum (which see) and to certain of its cultivated sorts. It is also the common name for *Pimenta officinalis* (Allspice) an aromatic, tropical American tree growing to 40 ft. in the W. Indies and Cent. America, with leathery foliage, white flowers, and dark brown fruits that provide the allspice of commerce.

PIMPERNEL. Common name for Anagallis, a genus of small herbs with axillary flowers generally of red or blue, occasionally white.

PIMPINELLA (pim-pin-el'-ah). A large genus of herbs, the seed of one of which yields anise (which see). One or two others are occasionally planted in borders.

PINACEAE (pi-nay'-see-ee). The Pine Family, the largest group of Gymnosperms or evergreen cone-bearing plants. (See CONIFER.) It comprises resinous trees and shrubs of wide distribution, including many ornamentals and timber-producers. The leaves are typically needle- or scale-like, mostly evergreen, and borne in condensed clusters. Male and female organs are in different flowers of the same plant and are borne on the upper surfaces of modified leaves which make up the characteristic cones. Many genera are of horticultural importance, among them Pinus (pine), Cedrus (cedar), Larix (larch), Tsuga (hemlock), Araucaria, Taxodium, Cryptomeria, Juniperus (juniper), Cupressus (cypress), Thuja (arborvitae), Abies (fir), Picea (spruce), Pseudotsuga, Sciadopitys, Sequoia, Chamaecyparis, Libocedrus, Thujopsis.

PINCHING. The shortening of young shoots, either to maintain a symmetrical plant form, to encourage the development of buds, or to enhance flower or fruit development. It is usually done without regard to bud position. See DISBUDDING.

PINCUSHION-FLOWER. A common name for the genus Scabiosa (which see) given because the florets suggest pins stuck in a globular cushion.

PINE. Common name for the large genus Pinus, after which the Pine Family (Pinaceae) is named, comprising many species of evergreen trees, distinguished from other conifers by bearing their needle-like leaves in clusters of definite numbers, and hard, woody cones which mature the second or third season. Widespread in their distribution, the pines are extremely adaptable to varied climatic conditions and, with their many forms and types supply indispensable material for ornamental use as well as the production of timber, turpentine, etc.

Pines, as a rule, will grow well in rather poor but well-drained sandy loams, as they prefer a light diet rather than an overabundance of plant food. In soil of this type they develop long tap-roots which serve to anchor them, but which make it difficult to transplant mature specimens. It is much better to plant nursery grown trees which have been frequently root pruned or transplanted and caused to develop a fibrous root system. Even then the roots should not be exposed to the air, unless protected by a ball of earth, but puddled as soon as dug in a thin mud.

They are most easily propagated by seed sown in spring in pots or pans, in prepared beds in frames, or in the open. Later the young seedlings should be shaded from intense sunlight. For forest planting 1-year-old seedlings are generally used.

For landscape work, in either parks or home grounds, there are Pine species for every situation, fast and slow growing kinds, types with light silvery foliage, and others showing a green of almost sombre darkness. While most of them grow to 100 ft. or more, a few are medium-sized or dwarf in habit.

One of the main things to remember in planting Pines is that they are lightloving, and therefore become scraggly and unsightly when shaded.

ENEMIES

WHITE PINE BLISTER RUST. The blister rust of white pine, introduced from Europe in 1906, is now firmly established in N. America, being generally prevalent in New England and N. Y. and found in certain areas in the middle-northern and N. W. States. All pines having their needles in *clusters of five* are susceptible. The rust fungus (*Peridermium strobi* on pine) destroys the bark, girdling twigs and branches; young trees are killed quickly, older ones more slowly. The rust cannot spread from one pine to another but must first infect a plant of one of the alternate hosts (currants and gooseberries), on which the fungus is called by another name (*Cronartium ribicola*). The various stages in the life history of a rust fungus are explained under RUSTS (which see). Spores from a plant of the two kinds just named infect pine needles, whence the fungus mycelium works down into the stems. By the third year small brown dead spots on the yellowed bark are filled with pycnio-spores (O-stage). In the spring

of the fourth year the bark cracks, and conspicuous white blisters form and break, discharging the yellow aecio-spores (I-stage). These two stages may occur year after year on a pine until the resulting canker surrounds the branch or trunk and kills all parts above. In spring I-stage spores carry the rust back to wild and cultivated currants or gooseberries and start another cycle of disease.

The only feasible control of blister rust lies in the eradication of currants and gooseberries, within a mile of valuable pine plantings in the case of black currant (which is especially susceptible), and for a distance of 300 yards in the case of other species. In some States it is illegal to grow or sell black currant bushes.

OTHER FUNGUS DISEASES. Other stem blister rusts attack two- and three-needled pines. The alternate hosts of one are the common sweet-fern and sweetgale which should be removed from a zone 200 ft. wide around western yellow, scrub, and pitch pines. Young pines in gardens or nurseries may be killed or stunted by this rust; from 10 years on they are more resistant. Young trees are also susceptible to the rust which infects 2- or 3-needled

ONE TRUE PINE AND A DISTANT RELATIVE
Left, the handsome, dark green Limber Pine (P. flexilis). Right, the so-called Umbrella-pine (Sciadopitys verticillata), an ornamental Japanese member of the Pine Family.

pines (except Pitch Pine) and has species of Comandra as alternate hosts. Another fungus is destructive to Shore, Lodgepole and Western Pine W. of the Rocky Mountains; the fungus affects weeds of the genus Castilleja but does not require them in order to spread. A stem blister rust is generally distributed throughout the U. S., causing witches' brooms (which see), bark swellings on pines and leaf pustules on oaks. Remove infected young pines.

Blister rust fungi sometimes cause the defoliation of pines. The most common of them completes its life cycle on aster and goldenrod.

Other fungus diseases, as well as diseases caused by drought and sun scorch, are discussed under Evergreens, which see.

PINE SHOOT MOTH. The European pine shoot moth is especially serious on red and Scotch pines but may infest other species. The brown caterpillars feed on the buds, tunnel in the new shoots, kill the terminal buds and make the lateral shoots leaders. A distinctive crooked condition known as bayonet growth results. Small reddish-brown moths emerge in June and lay eggs on the new buds; the presence of the larvae is indicated in the autumn by small masses of pitch over the entrance holes. *Control:* Remove and burn infested shoots; spray with nicotine and arsenate of lead when the moths are emerging and later when the young borers are hatching.

OTHER PESTS. The white pine weevil, a small brown, gray-mottled snout beetle, kills leaders of white and other pines during midsummer. Cut and burn infested discharging the yellow aecio-spores (I- to 9) in spring before growth starts. Banding the base of the leaders with cotton may help. Feeding trees to keep them in a vigorous condition is advisable since the weevil like certain other insects attacks the weaker trees first.

The small white, block-headed larvae of the pine tip moth burrow into the tips of shoots or buds causing side shoots to develop; often gummy resin collects at the injured place. Spray growing tips of young trees carefully with nicotine-sulphate at weekly intervals during June and July. Cut off and destroy infested twigs in fall and winter.

Pine needles are fed upon by various species of sawfly larvae (see SAWFLIES) which may do considerable damage before

their work is noticed. Hand-pick the caterpillars from small trees; spray larger specimens with arsenate of lead.

Webbed masses of brownish or greenish excrement on terminal twigs of various pines are caused by the green or brown larvae of the false pine web-worms. Control as directed above for sawfly larvae.

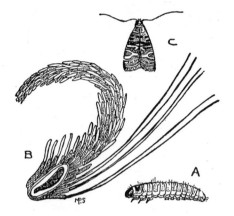

A BAD PINE PEST
The European pine shoot moth (C) attacks Red, Scotch, Mughus and similar kinds, the larva (A) tunneling in and deforming buds and new shoots in which it pupates as shown in (B).

Fluffy white masses on bark and shoots of white pine indicate the pine bark aphid which, by sucking the tree juices, causes poor growth, yellow needles, defoliation and sometimes death. Spray thoroughly with nicotine-sulphate. Another sucking insect is the spittle bug, whose grayish nymphs are found in the center of frothy masses of white spittle. Use derris dust.

The white, elongated pine leaf scale on needles of pines and related conifers may be controlled by spraying carefully in early spring with a miscible oil or oil emulsion, or with nicotine-sulphate when the young are hatching in May. See SCALE INSECTS.

See also EVERGREENS; BARK BEETLES.

TYPES FOR SPECIAL PURPOSES

For use in the E. States, in groves or as specimen trees, the White Pine (*Pinus strobus*) is eminently suitable, not only because it is the characteristic forest tree of the region, but because it is graceful in youth, sturdy and compact in middle life, and most picturesque in age with its great trunk and often widespread branches.

For background planting, the Red Pine with its glossy green needles makes a less

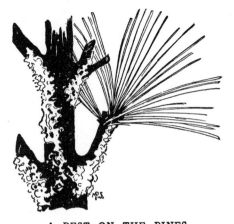

A PEST ON THE PINES

The pine bark louse or bark aphid being covered with a waxy secretion makes white patches on the trunks. Spray with a contact insecticide.

sombre effect than the rapid growing Austrian Pine, which is frequently used for that purpose. The short bluish-green needles of the Scotch Pine make a pleasing contrast when planted in front of darker pines or spruces. The Swiss Mountain Pine, usually shrubby, is frequently used for foundation planting, but is too coarse except for large formal buildings; it is better adapted for accent points in driveways. The open irregular growth of the Pitch Pine is often most picturesque in the wild garden, especially near the seashore, while many of the so-called scrub-pines, *P. virginiana* and *P. banksiana,* are useful soil-binders on dry sandy slopes.

Principal Species

P. strobus (White Pine). Symmetrical and pyramidal at first, later wide-spreading, with soft bluish-green needles to 5 in. long in clusters of 5; and brown, cylindric, pendent, often gracefully curved cones to 4 in. long. A sprig of leaves and cones constitutes the State flower of Me. Several horticultural varieties have been developed: var. *fastigiata* is of narrow, upright growth; *glauca* has grayish-green needles; *nana* is a bush form; *prostrata* has trailing branches; *umbraculifera* is shaped like an open umbrella.

resinosa (Red Pine). Upright and dome-like in youth, later wide-spreading with rather drooping branches, with dark green glossy needles in groups of 2 and light brown cones to 2½ in. Very hardy and useful for planting with the White Pine.

nigra (Austrian Pine). Has a pyramidal growth at first, later becoming flat-topped with stout branches. The needles are stiff, dark green, to 6½ in. long, 2 in a cluster, and the 3-in. cones are somewhat oval. Among the numerous varieties are *pendula* with drooping branches, *prostrata* with branches lying on the ground, and *pygmaea,* a very dwarf form.

thunbergi (Japanese Black Pine). Attains a broad pyramidal head with drooping branches and has bright green sharp-pointed needles, 2 in a bundle and 4½ in. long; the cones are 3 in. long. Native to Japan it is perfectly hardy N. In the var. *oculus-draconis* the needles are banded with two yellow stripes.

densiflora (Japanese Red Pine). A rapid growing tree, at length forming a rather wide-spread, strongly-branched head. The slender, sharp-pointed blue-green needles, 5 in. long, are in clusters of 2, and the cones are 2 in. long. It is quite hardy N., but sometimes suffers from winter injury.

peuce (Macedonian Pine), a slow-growing tree not attaining more than 50 ft., has a compact pyramidal growth, bluish-green needles to 4 in. long in bundles of 5; cylindric cones to 6 in. long.

koraiensis (Korean Pine). Of dense pyramidal growth, with dark green needles 4 in. long, 5 in a bundle, and long cones. This compact, slow-growing pine is excellent in the home grounds.

sylvestris (Scotch or Scots Pine). Has spreading, drooping branches; stiff bluish-green, often twisted, needles to 3 in. long in clusters of 2; and cones 2½ in. long. An extremely hardy and useful European tree, extensively planted in the E. States. Varieties are: *argentea,* with silvery needles; *aurea,* with leaves golden when young; *fastigiata,* of narrow, upright growth; *nana,* of dwarf growth; *watereri,* with bluish-gray leaves and columnar growth.

flexilis (Limber Pine). A hardy species found from Alberta to Texas and Calif. The needles, 3 in. long, are in bundles of 5 and the oval cones are 6 in. long.

mugo (Swiss Mountain Pine), usually shrubby in growth, has bright green leaves to 2 in. long, 2 in a bundle, and cones to 2½ in. Var. *compacta* is a dense rounded form, *mughus* a prostrate shrub, and *rostrata* a tree to 80 ft.

excelsa (Himalayan Pine). A graceful tree with soft grayish-green drooping needles to 8 in. long, in a bundle; and cylindric cones to 10 in. It is hardy as far N. as Mass. if planted in a sheltered situation.

parviflora (Japanese White Pine). To 80 ft. A hardy tree of dense growth with bluish-green needles to 1½ in. long in bundles of 5 forming tufts at the tips of the branches.

PINEAPPLE. A South American perennial herb (*Ananas sativus*) related to the ornamental bromelias of the Pineapple Family (Bromeliaceae). Its familiar aromatic fruit which suggests a pine cone is responsible for its common name. The plant consists of a rosette of stiff, thick, sharp-pointed, prickly edged leaves and resembles a century-plant. From the center rises a stem sometimes 4 ft. high; near its summit this swells into a fruit which consists of "a spike or head of flowers, all parts of which are consolidated into one succulent mass," surmounted by a crown or tuft of leaves.

The markets are supplied with fruit mainly from Hawaii, Puerto Rico and Cuba, but choice fruiting varieties and a few ornamental forms with variously striped leaves are grown in gardens in warm parts of the U. S. and sometimes in greenhouse collections.

Any well-drained, but moisture-retaining soil will grow good pineapples. Plants are propagated mainly from suckers (called ratoons) that develop at the bases of old stems; from slips that form along the stems of mature plants; and from slips taken from the base of the fruits. They are set 18 to 24 in. apart and cultivated only an inch deep to avoid root injury. Moderate dressings of fertilizers composed mostly of organic materials such as ground bone, tankage and cottonseed meal should be applied.

In greenhouses where the pineapple was formerly quite popular, it is now grown only occasionally as a pot or tub plant. For cultural directions see SUCCULENTS.

PINEAPPLE-FLOWER. Common name for *Eucomis punctata*, a half-hardy Cape bulb whose raceme of green and brown flowers is borne 1 ft. above a rosette of many large, purplish-spotted, lance-shaped leaves and is topped by a cluster of leafy bracts, somewhat as in the pineapple. Bulbs may be left in the ground

all year in the S.; in the N. they are treated only as greenhouse subjects.

PINEAPPLE-GUAVA. A common name for Feijoa, a genus of tropical trees and shrubs with edible fruits. One species is ornamental in S. gardens. See FEIJOA.

PINE-BARREN BEAUTY. Another name for *Pyxidanthera barbulata*, also called Pyxie (which see), a creeping evergreen shrub with white flowers in spring.

PINETUM (py-nee'-tum). A specialized tree garden for interest or education designed to include all species and varieties of the Pine Family that will grow in the different soils, exposures and other conditions afforded by a given location. It is thus a special kind of arboretum (which see), and might form a part of one, as is the case in some instances. If developed in a naturalistic, landscape style it may become a garden of most extraordinary beauty. Unfortunately such plantations open to the public are not common.

See EVERGREEN GARDEN.

PINGUICULA (pin-gwik'-eu-lah). A genus of stemless herbs, some of them native, whose sticky leaves attract and entrap insects. See BUTTERWORT.

PINGUIN (ping'-gwin). A common name for *Bromelia pinguin*, a tropical American herb.

PINK. Common name for the flowers of the genus Dianthus (which see); also for the family (Caryophyllaceae) to which the genus belongs. Maiden Pink, Clove Pink, Cheddar Pink, and Grass, Garden, and Scotch or Pheasants-eye Pink are all species of Dianthus.

The name is also applied to several species of the related genera Lychnis and Silene, such as Mullein-pink (*L. coronaria*), Fire-pink (*S. virginica*), Cushion-pink (*S. acaulis*) and Wild-pink or Peat-pink (*S. caroliniana* or *S. pennsylvanica*).

Other plants known by this common name include Thrift or Sea-pink (those members of the genus Statice which were formerly classed as Armeria); Swamp- or Stud-pink (*Helonias bullata*), and Moss- or Ground-pink (*Phlox subulata*).

PINK-ROOT. Common name for *Spigelia marilandica*, a perennial herb to 2 ft. with tufted stems, stemless leaves, and red tubular flowers to 2 in. with throats yellow inside borne in one-sided clusters. It is a handsome native plant, seldom seen in cultivation, but very easily grown in sun or shade and strikingly beautiful in color. It should be planted in rich deep soil and is easily increased by seed or division of the roots.

PINK SHOWER. A common name for *Cassia grandis,* a tropical tree, commonly called Senna, which see.

PINNA. One of the leaflets of a fern frond or similarly formed or *pinnately compound* leaf, which means one with an arrangement of leaflets on either side of a common petiole.

PINUS (py'-nus). An important genus of coniferous trees dominating and giving its name to the Pine Family. Its 80 species are confined largely to the temperate and N. temperate zones, but some are found on mountains in the tropics. The genus is most easily recognized by the needle-like leaves, which are generally longer than in other conifers, and always grouped in bundles or clusters, of from 2 to 5, the number being an important factor in distinguishing the species.

For further discussion of the genus, its characteristics, uses, and culture, see PINE.

PINXTER-FLOWER. Common name for *Rhododendron nudiflorum,* a deciduous pink-flowered Azalea of E. U. S.

PIP. In horticulture, a term of various meanings: 1. The small seed of the so-called "pip-fruits"—apple, pear, quince, etc. 2. Synonym for varieties of apples called Pippin. 3. One of the segments on the surface of a pineapple fruit. 4. The crown or dormant shoot, or rootstock of peonies, anemones and especially the pointed crown of lily-of-the-valley, as distinct from the growing clump of plants. This last applies most definitely to the "pips" used by florists for forcing. 5. An individual flower of the Auricula.

PIPEVINE. A common name for *Aristolochia durior,* the hardy woody climbing plant better known as Dutchmans Pipe on account of its yellowish-green flowers with curved tubes and spreading limb.

PIPSISSEWA (pip-sis'-e-wah). Common name for Chimaphila, a genus of small evergreen herbs of the Heath Family. They have nodding umbels of white or pink flowers. The leathery, evergreen, toothed, sometimes marbled, leaves grow in irregular whorls on the stem, and the creeping rootstock sends up branches at intervals, thus making these plants desirable as a ground-cover in plantations of conifers or broad-leaved evergreens, where they should be given an acid soil, rich in leafmold. They are propagated by soft wood cuttings, taken when the leaves are half-grown.

C. umbellata has shining dark green leaves and white or rose-pink flowers, 4 to 7 in a cluster. *C. maculata* has variegated foliage and very fragrant white flowers; *C. menziesi,* slightly smaller, has a more slender habit and white or pink nodding flowers.

PIPTANTHUS (pip-tan'-thus). Deciduous or partly evergreen shrubs of Asia, belonging to the Pea Family. They like a sunny, sheltered position but are not hardy North. Propagated by seeds or layers. *P. nepalensis* (Himalayan-laburnum) has glossy trifoliate leaves, and dense erect clusters of yellow flowers. *P. tomentosus* (Chinese-laburnum) is somewhat hardier and very distinct with silky silvery foliage. The flowers are similar except for long silky hairs on the calyx.

PIQUERIA (pi-kee'-ri-ah). A genus of tropical shrubs and herbs with small heads of whitish flowers. *P. trinervia* is the florists' "Stevia" (which see) grown for winter bloom.

PISTIA (pis'-ti-ah) *stratiotes.* A floating perennial much used in aquariums and warm ponds and commonly called Water-lettuce, which see.

PISTIL. The central organ of a flower, consisting of one or more parts (*carpels*), each of which consists of a *style,* or stem; *stigma,* or apex; and basal, ovule-bearing ovary. In compound pistils (composed of more than one carpel) the carpels are merged to form what appears to be a single organ, though the styles and stigmas may be either fused or independent. Because they contain the cells which when fertilized become seeds, pistillate flowers are often referred to as female flowers. See FLOWER.

PISUM (py'-sum). The genus of leguminous plants of which the common garden pea is the most important member. See PEA.

PITCAIRNIA (pit-kayr'-ni-ah). Greenhouse perennial herbs, rarely shrubs, natives of tropical America, generally stemless, members of the Pineapple Family. They have narrow leaves in rosettes with red, yellow or nearly white flowers, borne in spikes or clusters. They thrive in a well-drained mixture of rich loam and leafmold. Increase is by offsets.

P. corallina has tapering leaves 4 to 5 ft. long, about 4 in. broad, spiny edged; flowers bright red, edged with white, borne in clusters on red stalks 1 ft. long. *P. punicea* grows about 1 ft. high; leaves 1 ft. long, less than ½ in. wide, slightly spiny; flowers scarlet, in loose clusters 4 to 6 in. long.

PITCHER-PLANTS. General common name for a number of genera of carnivorous plants all having leaves modified into pitcher form into which insects are attracted and in which they are trapped and ultimately die and are "digested" in liquid in the hollow base. See also SARRACENIA; NEPENTHES; DARLINGTONIA; HELIAMPHORA; INSECTIVOROUS PLANTS.

PITTOSPORUM (pit-tos'-poh-rum). Evergreen trees and shrubs, mostly native in the S. hemisphere. Several species are grown outdoors in the warmest parts of this country, and one or two under glass, usually by professionals. They are of good habit with attractive foliage and clusters of small, mostly fragrant flowers. Useful for hedges, specimen planting, and some as avenue trees, they are propagated by seed and cuttings, or by grafting on *P. undulatum.*

Principal Species

P. crassifolium (Karo) is a tall shrub or small tree from New Zealand. It has thick leathery shining leaves and clusters of dark purple flowers. It is said to be a good windbreak for seaside gardens on the West coast.

tenuifolium (Tawhiwhi) is a symmetrical compact tree to 30 ft.; one of the best for screening purposes; stands close clipping.

tobira (Japanese Pittosporum), a good hedge plant in warm regions, is the one commonly grown under glass. It has thick leathery leaves and clusters of yellowish-white fragrant flowers. A form with leaves marked white is var. *variegata.*

undulatum (Victorian-box) is a shrub or tree to 40 ft.; often planted as an avenue tree in S. Calif. and highly prized for its very fragrant flowers.

eugenioides (Tarata), is a tall shrub or slender tree much used in Calif. for clipped hedges and ornamental groupings.

rhombifolium (Queensland Pittosporum) may be grown as a pot plant or an avenue tree. It has orange-yellow fruits which remain decorative for a long time.

phillyraeoides (Willow Pittosporum) is a tree of the Australian desert, resembling a weeping willow.

PITYROGRAMMA (pit-i-roh-gram'-ah). A genus of ferns, represented by one species in Calif. (*P. triangularis*) often known as *Gymnogramma triangularis* (which see). It is a small rock fern often called the Golden-backed Fern.

PLANE or PLANE-TREE. Common name for Platanus, a genus of handsome deciduous trees characterized by bark that peels off in large patches and by dense maple-like foliage. Frequently used for street-planting and other ornamental purposes, the trees grow to a massive shapeliness. Though they thrive best in rich moist soil, some species are most tolerant of city conditions, and they will stand severe pruning. They are excellent shade trees and their mottled white and gray trunks, from which the bark falls in shreds or plates, give them a most distinctive character. They are propagated by cuttings of ripened wood, by greenwood cuttings, sometimes by layers, and from seed.

ENEMIES. A killing disease of London plane, which may also occur on American plane, is spreading slowly through the E. States. First noted, in N. J. in 1929, it was reported officially only in 1935. Most prevalent around Philadelphia and Baltimore, where 10,000 or more trees have been lost, it is reported also in Del., Washington, D. C., Va., W. Va., N. C., Tenn., Ky., and Miss. The first symptoms are dark, discolored streaks on the bark; such lesions coalesce and as a result of complete girdling the branch, or the entire tree, is killed. Death may be delayed as much as three to five years after initial infection. The fungus, which belongs to the genus Ceratostomella, apparently gains entrance through injuries or pruning cuts.

This is primarily a city disease, and municipalities with incipient outbreaks should remove and burn all infested trees and require that all pruning tools used on planes be disinfected with denatured alcohol or other disinfectant. The planting of London planes in solid blocks should be discouraged, since a continuous stand of susceptible plants greatly aids the rapid progress of a disease.

A leaf and twig blight attacks both plane and oak. Large brown dead areas occur on the leaves soon after they expand and the trees appear scorched and may be completely defoliated. Carefully rake together and burn all infected leaves. Spray early in the spring with bordeaux mixture making the first application when the leaves are about half grown, *before* a rain, and the second about a week later.

Several leaf-eating insects attack plane foliage but do not cause serious injury. A lace-bug that may disfigure the leaves can be controlled with nicotine-sulphate.

PRINCIPAL SPECIES

P. orientalis (Oriental Plane), to 100 ft., with a short trunk and broad head, is the Old-World plane, not frequently seen in this country as it is not hardy N. of Mass.; *P. occidentalis* (Buttonwood), to 150 ft., is the hardy native species; *P. acerifolia* (London Plane), a hybrid between *P. orientalis* and *P. occidentalis,* is commonly planted as a street tree as it is hardy as far as Mass. and to a considerable extent free from disease. *P. racemosa* is the form found in S. Calif.

PLANERA (plan'-er-ah) *aquatica.* A deciduous tree of the Middle West, resembling the elm and called Water-elm, which see.

PLANT. Generally speaking, a plant is a living organism which for the most part manufactures its own food and 'is incapable of locomotion. Of special importance to gardeners are the *flowering plants;* although there are over 100,000 species of these, each with its distinctive habit, one form of structure, with modifications in the cases of air plants and aquatic plants (which see), is common to all:

The main axis of the typical plant body is in two parts: the root and the stem. The *root* is underground, holds the plant fast, and obtains from the soil the water and raw food materials without which the plant cannot live and grow. The *stem* is the above-ground portion; it bears a variety of structures, besides transporting food materials from the root to the leaves and thence to all other parts. On the stem are *buds* from which develop leaves, branches, and new stem-growth. The branches also develop buds, some of which become leaves or smaller branches while others become *flowers* which are special parts organized to reproduce the plant. After a flower is fertilized one or more *seeds* develop in the *fruit* whose function it is to bring about the dispersal of the seed. Upon the *leaf* (which see) devolves

the responsibility of feeding the plant, as it manufactures raw food with materials it takes from the air, and materials brought by the roots. See also ROOT, STEM, etc. for additional discussion of the parts of the plant body.

In their garden relations, plants may be *annual* (living for only one year), *biennial* (living for two years), or *perennial* (living for more than two years); they may be *herbaceous* (with soft above-ground parts lasting only one season) or *woody;* tender, semi-hardy, or hardy (depending, of course, upon the location, latitude and weather); and of various forms, as trailing, climbing, shrubby, tree-form, etc. All these and many other characteristics and variations determine their value and adaptability for garden use under different conditions. Hence the practical value of a knowledge of plant forms, types and other matters dealt with in what is known as *systematic* botany.

PLANTAIN. Common name for the genus Plantago of the Plantain Family, comprising herbs and shrubby plants, marked mostly by basal leaves and inconspicuous flowers in heads or spikes. They include several troublesome weeds, but a few are grown in the garden for ornament. All are easily propagated by seed.

P. patagonica, an annual to 1 ft., has very small flowers in dense spikes. *P. maritima,* annual, biennial, or perennial, with flowers in spikes to 5 in., is found by the seashores of Eurasia and N. America. *P. cynops,* a shrubby plant to 1½ ft., has whitish flowers in heads ½ in long. *P. lanceolata* is the ugly widespread weed on lawns, which should be dug out whenever seen but is only to be eradicated by growing so dense and vigorous a turf that it cannot find a foothold.

Plantain is also the common name of *Musa paradisiaca,* the species to which the common banana belongs. Plantain-lily is Hosta; Poor-Robins-plantain is *Erigeron pulchellus* (or sometimes *Hieracium venosum*); Rattlesnake-plantain is *Epipactis pubescens;* Water-plantain is Alisma; and Wild-plantain is *Heliconia bihai.*

See those references; also WEEDS.

PLANTAIN-LILY. Common name for Hosta, a genus of fleshy-rooted plants of the Lily Family, having large, conspicuously ribbed leaves and blue or white funnel-form flowers in loose clusters or racemes. (See illustration, Plate 28.)

Plantain-lilies, native of China and Japan, are widely planted for their foliage effect. The clumps of large glossy leaves make excellent accents at corners of beds, or in foundation plantings; while a row along a driveway gives a definite finish to the edge of the lawn. Many of the species grow well in shade. They are increased by seed and by division, and should be planted in rich soil.

Crown rot (which see) may occur, the reddish spore bodies of the fungus often being so numerous around the base of this plant that they actually color the ground. Control by removing any diseased plant and the surrounding soil and drenching the spot with corrosive sublimate solution 1 to 1000.

Species

H. plantaginea (Fragrant Plantain-lily) has graceful sprays of fragrant white flowers rising, late in summer, 2½ ft. above the large, heart-shaped, deeply-ridged leaves, 10 in. long and 6 in. wide.

caerulea (Blue Plantain-lily) has deep green leaves 9 in. long and 5 in. wide, and blue flowers in a long, loose raceme rising to nearly 3 ft.

Other species include *H. japonica* (Narrow-leaved Plantain-lily) of which the var. *albo-marginata* is even more widely grown than the type; *H. fortuneo* (Tall-cluster Plantain-lily) with blue-green foliage; and *H. undulata* with wavy-margined leaves, splotched with creamy white.

PLANT BREEDING. The creation of new horticultural varieties, or the improvement of existing varieties, by selection, hybridizing, etc. The best-known plant breeder of modern times—probably because the most publicized—was the late Luther Burbank, but breeding has been practised for hundreds of years in Europe and thousands in Japan and China; and hundreds of horticulturists—scientific, professional, commercial, and amateur—are carrying it on in all parts of the world, with all kinds of plants and with varying degrees of success. Nearly all popular flowers, vegetables, and fruits have been bred away from their natural condition, in some cases so far that scientists cannot decide what that natural condition was. The difference between a Delicious or a Winesap apple and the hard, sour, worthless fruit of a natural apple seedling, is due to plant breeding, as is the change from the weed Queen Annes Lace to the garden carrot.

A batch of seedlings of any wild plant, when carefully compared, will show considerable differences in size, habit, flower color, fruit, etc. The first step in practical plant breeding is to select from a great number of seedlings, of the plant to be improved, one or more that are better than all the rest. By this method alone, the pecan nut has been improved from something not much better than the hickory to the thin-shelled, full-meated pecan of commerce.

Selection plays a part in the breeding of all plants, but principally in connection with two other methods, both of which cause wider variations from the normal plant than are ordinarily found in nature.

One of these methods is cultivation. Seedlings of cultivated plants tend to vary more than those grown from seeds of similar plants found in the wild; and the higher the degree of cultivation, and the longer it is continued, the greater the variations will be. They may take the form of bud sports—sudden, unaccountable changes in the character of a single branch, such as a red-flowering branch of a white rose. Bud sports may occur anywhere, and not only plant breeders and nurserymen, but gardeners, too, should watch for them, because, when desirable, they can usually be propagated as new varieties. Dwarfing, variegation and other changes of the nature of bud sports may come in batches of cuttings, induced apparently by propagation. In all these cases the variation is provoked by some form of cultivation.

A second means of inducing variation is hybridizing. Plants produce seed naturally by pollination (which see). Pollen (the minute dust-like bodies on the stamens) from one flower falls or is carried by wind or insect to the pistil of that flower or another flower on the same or another plant. Fertilization then takes place, and seed begins to form at the base of the pistil. Some plants, like wheat, do not have to be crossed, but are self-pollinated; but the great majority of ordinary plants produce poorer seed or none at all when self-pollinated.

If the pollen comes, not from the same kind of plant, but from one of different variety or species, the offspring is called a hybrid (which see). Thus a wild blackberry and a red raspberry were crossed to produce the purple loganberry, which is therefore said to be a hybrid between the two. Hybrids, according to the laws of Mendel (see MENDELISM), are usually much alike in the first generation. Thus if, when the blackberry and raspberry were hybridized, hundreds of the resulting hybrid seedlings had been raised, all of them would probably have resembled the loganberry, in appearance about half way between the parents. But if a loganberry (already a hybrid) is crossed either with a similar hybrid or with a blackberry or a raspberry, seedlings showing much variation will result, some with purple fruit, some with black, some with red, and with various combinations of growth habit. To know just what variations may be expected, it is necessary to study the science of genetics, which is the accumulated, organized knowledge concerning the phenomena of heredity. But even after such scientific study, much uncertainty remains.

Plant breeders use various methods of artificial pollination to produce hybrids, depending on the kind of plant. Sometimes pollen is collected by touching one flower with a fine brush until the pollen clings to it, then touching the brush to the pistil of the flower to be pollinated. Sometimes pollen is collected in quantity by shaking or scraping the flowers over a sheet of paper. A simpler way is to take the stamen from one flower and touch its tip to the pistil of the other flower. With plants that bloom at different seasons, it is better to save the pollen of the earlier flower rather than force·the later one, but both methods are used. Some pollen will remain potent a month or more if the plucked flower is put in an envelope and allowed to dry. Luther Burbank, because he operated on a large scale, usually made no effort to protect the pollinated flower from further natural pollination; but most plant breeders usually cut away the stamens so that the flower's own pollen cannot reach the pistil, and tie transparent paper over the branch to keep insects from pollinating it with pollen from other flowers. A label is then attached, carrying a record of the cross or a number referring to a filed record.

Recent developments in the science of plant breeding including the treatment of parent plants or their reproductive cells in various ways to change the nature, arrangement, and number of the chromosomes and other bodies by which inheritance of characters is transmitted. Exposure to X-rays and high-frequency electrical currents has been experimented with and, more recently, treatment with a drug colchicine (obtained from the autumn-crocus) which so shocks a plant as to increase the number of its chromosomes. See POLYPLOIDY. These methods are interesting and may lead to developments in which gardeners may share (there is already available one polyploid marigold variety, named Tetra) but at present they are experimental rather than a part of practical gardening.

In the case of plants that can be propagated asexually (that is, by cuttings, grafts, layers, or divisions), the breeder keeps planting seeds of any crosses that promise improvement, and watching the seedlings as they develop. When a single plant of the desired form appears, the objective of that particular breeding effort is complete. It remains only to propagate a sufficient stock of plants from the one selected; to name it; perhaps to apply for a patent for the variety; and to disseminate it. The specialist breeder, however, continues to look for other and better types, leaving the propagation and distribution of the one obtained to commercial growers.

In the case of annuals, which are grown from seed, a new variety must be "fixed" (that is, made to reproduce dependably by seeds). Seeds of plants of the desired form or other characteristics are collected and sown. As the seedlings develop, those which do not keep the new form are weeded out at once, before their pollen can ripen. Only the best are allowed to set seed, which is again sown and the weeding out or "roguing" repeated. In from two to several years, when the number of rogues has been reduced to a few scattered plants, the variety is fixed, and the seed can be marketed.

Plants of very different nature cannot be hybridized. A hybrid between a tomato and a poppy (plants of different families) would be virtually impossible; one between a tomato and a potato (both of the Nightshade Family but of different genera) might be possible but would probably be useless. To be useful, hybrids must usually be made between species or varieties in the same genus, as two species of rose, or two varieties of squash. Hybrids between closely related plants will commonly set at least a few fertile seeds, while hybrids between distantly related plants rarely set any seed; the seeds if any are almost never fertile; or, if fertile, they usually produce feeble plants.

Some famous varieties have originated, not through the work of professional plant breeders, but in private gardens. It is said that no magnolia variety was ever produced intentionally, but that all have appeared by chance. Even gardeners working on a small scale may do interesting and valuable plant breeding by improving plants now of lesser importance, which professional breeders have neglected.

PLANT EXPLORATION. To most of us the term "hunter and explorer" suggests a rotogravure picture of a gentleman with a very large gun standing triumphantly beside the carcass of some jungle king he has brought to a glorious death and a stuffed future.

Fortunately for civilization and for us, there is another, altogether different, sort of hunter and explorer—the plant hunter. To men of this ancient and obscure order, notable for their courage and persistence, our orchards, tilled fields and gardens are living memorials. The mappers of new rivers and mountains and the travellers on unknown seas have always received due credit for their exploits, but, somehow, the pioneers who entered these same new regions in search of beautiful and useful plant material for man's pleasure and food have missed out in the distribution of public glories. Probably they were too busy to garner their share.

Plant hunting is a most ancient craft. When man left off his nomadic life and began to cultivate the soil, the plant hunter's work began with a search for new edible grains, and fruits, and medicinal plants. Much later new plant sources of fibres, timber and other utilitarian materials were sought; and gradually the appreciation of plants for their beauty of bloom and foliage alone came to stimulate and widen the plant hunter's work and scope.

Geographic explorations of the 15th Century not only brought a new world under Europe's dominion, but added enormously to man's fund of food and medicinal plants. And these early explorers, although not professional plant hunters, were, almost without exception, capable and interested amateurs. In the rich cargoes from the New World were strange fruits, seeds, roots and carefully tended plants. Medicinal plants were particularly sought after; and many plants, valued by the primitive medical science of the time for virtues inherent in curious form or coloring, found their way into the monastery herb gardens of Europe. Columbus himself was an enthusiastic plant hunter and in the journals of one of his later voyages we have the first description of the pineapple: "a fruit resembling green pine cones, with flesh like a melon, very fragrant and sweet."

Expeditions primarily for plant collecting began in the 17th Century, but reached their peak only in the 19th. All parts of the world were visited and thousands of new plants added to the wealth that already glorified European and American gardens. Plant-hunting expeditions were financed by governments, by private enterprises, by educational institutions and by individuals, and in spite of the extreme difficulties involved most of them returned with trophies that amply repaid their sponsors and personnel. A garden would have to be very carefully planned indeed *not* to include some of the plants brought into occidental cultivation through the work of those 19th-century men.

One reason that the work of the plant hunter is not easy is that the hardest part really begins where that of the game hunter ends. With the dressing of his quarry's hide, the latter can breathe a sigh of relief and consider the worst of his job done. But, with his game found, and apparently captured, the plant hunter's main problem and worry begins. Not at all seasons are roots, seeds, cuttings, or small plants to be had. Often, after locating a specimen of a new or desirable species, the plant hunter must stay in the region and make periodical visits to his trophy before he can collect the harvest. Having secured it—whether cuttings, seeds, roots or young plants—he must solve the problem of transporting it to, and establishing it in, the home garden. Any slight carelessness, neglect or imprudence on the part of his helpers, the shipping agent to whom the material is entrusted or those whose task it is to rear a stock from his small start, dooms the particular species to continued obscurity. Even though these obstacles are successfully overcome, months or even years must elapse before the actual value of the plant can be judged.

Interested in all sorts of trade, the English East India Company, under a charter from Queen Elizabeth, was one of the first agents in bringing to English (and American) gardens the wealth of useful and ornamental plants with which the Orient has enriched them. Through the work of its John Reeves in the late 18th Century, many new and beautiful Chinese plants— azaleas, camellias, chrysanthemums, peonies, wisteria and many others—were introduced into W. gardens. In England, the Royal Horticultural Society was the recipient of many of his shipments and itself sponsored many collecting expeditions. Two of its men, John Damper Potts and John Parks, visited the Orient about 1821 and brought back many notable forms especially of chrysanthemums and roses.

Between 1842 and 1861, Robert Fortune, working under the Horticultural Society of London and the East India Company, visited China many times and, disguised as a native, penetrated wild and dangerous areas, studying and collecting plants and seeds. Our gardens received from him nearly 200 species and varieties, most of them entirely new and the rest unknown except as herbarium specimens. Among them figure many, to us, old friends: roses, azaleas, peonies, chrysanthemums, clematis, the white wisteria, forsythias, viburnums, the bleeding heart and others equally familiar.

The Dutch East India Company was also instrumental in bringing to Europe many new plants. In Japan particularly its agents were active as early as 1680, studying and describing the unfamiliar flora. A legacy from a surgeon of that company, Carl Peter Thunberg, pupil of Linnaeus and later his successor as a teacher, is that indispensable hedge plant and shrub, the Japanese Barberry (*Berberis thunbergi*).

We are in particular debt to two other early plant hunters for Japanese plants. Philipp von Siebold, a Bavarian, lived in Japan for six year (1823-29) and in addition to his magnificent Flora Japonica, brought back to Europe with him many important contributions to European and American horticulture, among them *Lilium elegans* and *L. speciosum*. On a later trip, he brought out the crabapple which bears his name, *Malus sieboldi,* and a number of flowering cherries. Having won the admiration and liking of Japanese horticulturists, he was able to arrange to have plants previously unknown outside of Japan sent to him at his nursery and propagating garden in Leyden.

After von Siebold, it is to an Englishman, John Gould Veitch, and his firm of James Veitch and Sons that we are particularly indebted for Japanese plants. Collectors from various other nurseries have played a considerable part, but this firm is perhaps the most noteworthy for its service in making available to the gardener plants from all parts of the world, especially the Orient. Mr. Veitch visited Japan as early as 1860 and in the considerable amount of plant material he took to England were several forms of Japanese Maple, *Lilium auratum,* and the popular Japanese Ivy (*Parthenocissus tricuspidata*). He also visited the Pacific Islands and brought home many crotons, the pandanus which bears his name.

In our own day, there has been intensive plant collecting in the Orient. The similarity between the climatic conditions and flora of China and N. America has made introduction to American gardens from that country most practical and the work so ably begun by John Reeves and Thomas Fortune was carried on with the same competence and interest by such men as the late Frank N. Meyer of the Department of Agriculture, the late Ernest H. Wilson, originally of England, later of the Arnold Arboretum in Mass., and Reginald Farrar, another Englishman, during the early part of this century.

Although his collecting took him all over the world, Ernest Wilson spent so much time in the Orient as to earn the affectionate nickname of "Chinese" Wilson. Among his most notable introductions were the original group of Kurume azaleas (1917) and the Chinese Regal Lily (1910). It was on a second expedition for the latter plant that a sudden rock slide swept down upon his cavalcade and left him with a badly crushed leg. Several days of forced marches ensued before he could receive medical attention and the leg healed slowly so that, although it carried him thousands of miles in his later life, it was permanently crippled and shortened.

Next to the Orient, our gardens are most indebted to Africa, S. Africa especially, for a marvelous array of plant material, the fruits of the work of an intrepid group of plant hunters in investigating the horticultural possibilities of the dark continent.

Plate 40.   PERENNIALS EVERY GARDEN SHOULD POSSESS

Upper left: In early spring the evergreen candytuft drifts through the rock garden.   Upper right: The quaint blue blooms of monkshood.   Center left: Phlox—the framework around which other perennials may be grouped.   Center right: The Buddleia's arching, lavender sprays add grace to the perennial border.   Lower left: The charming, old-fashioned bleeding heart.   Lower right: The primrose brings a vision of spring in England.

Of these, Frederick Masson, first collector sent into the field by the famous Kew Gardens of England, is perhaps the most noteworthy. Arriving at Cape Town in 1772, he gathered, among many other things, the seeds of many species of beautiful heaths later raised successfully at Kew. He became associated with the same Thunberg mentioned above and on their combined trips they collected more than a hundred new species of plants including euphorbias, mesembryanthemums, aloes and others. In all Masson introduced into Kew over 400 new species of plants. To him and others like him we owe the fine available species of "Cape bulbs" and heaths, some of which, like the gladiolus and freesia, have become so common in gardens that it is difficult to believe that they ever were exotics.

The tropical forests of Africa, Malaysia and S. America have yielded many strange and beautiful species into the hands of the plant hunter, through whose persistence, care and indifference to discomfort and danger our greenhouses are enriched by the infinite beauty and variety of orchids and our ponds and tanks by the fragrant loveliness of the tropical waterlilies.

Plant exploration has, naturally, passed its golden age, for the world has become a small place and past activities in all regions have cut down the possibilities of any spectacular discovery. Nevertheless, plant hunting is being carried on with as much vigor as ever. Commercial growers are eager to find novelties. Wealthy individuals, government agencies and institutions continue to investigate both wild and cultivated plant materials of countries all over the world and are constantly adding to the list of those suitable for use in our gardens and greenhouses and on our farms, and those that promise to be useful as parents in plant-breeding work with forms already adapted to American conditions.

Special mention must be made of the office of Plant Introduction of the U. S. Department of Agriculture, which is systematically endeavoring to locate, bring to this country, test, propagate and aid in the distribution of new and worthy plants, both utilitarian and merely decorative. By itself or in coöperation with other agencies, it sponsors explorations; conducts trial grounds, as at Bell, Md., Chico, Calif., and in S. Fla.; distributes limited quantities of new things for trial among volunteer co-operating growers in different parts of the country; works up basic stocks of anything worthy of dissemination, and then, in some cases, works with organizations of growers to offer the novelty plants to the public— a step that the Government itself cannot, of course, take. Bulletins and other reports of the work of the office are available for those interested in the latest plant "immigrants."

PLANT FOODS and PLANT FEEDING. The actual nutriment of plants is largely sugar (a compound of carbon, hydrogen and oxygen) which they make in their leaf-cells by combining air and water with the help of energy from the sunlight. But they also need in small quantities compounds of nitrogen, potassium, phosphorus, calcium, magnesium, sulphur, sodium, iron, and a number of other elements. In nature the decay of accumulated vegetable matter in the surface soil and the disintegration of mineral parts of the subsoil maintain a balanced supply of these substances, the elements continually being returned to the soil as plants die and decay where they grew. Under cultivation, crops are not returned to the soil in this way. Hence, after a number of years, soil exhaustion sets in, and the supply of one or more of the elements becomes deficient. The minerals and humus carrying them must then be added to the soil to replace the elements taken out. This is the purpose of soil improvement: the adding of manure, compost, commercial fertilizers, lime and other materials. By feeding each crop the minerals it needs, and removes in growing, the soil is prevented from again becoming exhausted, and its fertility is maintained. Obvious signs of soil exhaustion are stunted and yellow growth, lack of flowers, fruit, or seeds, and poor root development.

Experienced gardeners keep on hand a supply of various plant foods, not only manure—which is a general soil builder containing both vegetable matter and many plant-food elements in limited amounts—but also special foods especially rich in certain elements and meeting the special needs of particular crops or unusual soil conditions. Manure is turned under by plowing or spading and mixed with the soil as it is cultivated; it is also added on the surface, to be cultivated in if fine enough or left as a mulch. Its preparation and use, and the use of soil conditioners, green manure, compost, peat, humus, lime, etc., are discussed under MANURE and IMPROVEMENT, SOIL. The art of plant feeding however depends on understanding the nature of the many mineral or commercial fertilizers and knowing how to apply them. Each vegetable, flower and tree has likes and dislikes, but certain general principles of fertilizing can be stated.

PLANT FOODS MUST BE SOLUBLE. Since plants can assimilate only materials that are dissolved in the water their roots take up, a substance that is not soluble in water (or in the weak solution of chemicals that makes up the moisture in the soil) is not a plant food. It may, however, be a "soil conditioner" or a fertilizer which gradually will become a plant food, or cause other substances to become plant foods. Some fertilizers dissolve quickly and, unless taken up by the plant and used at once, may be washed or leached away by rain. Others dissolve slowly, remaining in or near the place where applied, for months or years; they may require a chemical action in the soil to fit them for plant use.

Healthy soil is filled with bacteria, which perform an essential work in fermenting the humus and breaking down the different complex fertilizer substances into simpler ones which combine with mineral substances in the soil to produce new and more available compounds. Each added fertilizer plays a part in this activity of the living soil. And fertilizers also act on each other, some combining to produce beneficial results, others to interfere with the plant-feeding process. The most successful fertilizers or plant-food mixtures are those which not only furnish food themselves, but also help make the food in manure and humus more available.

Bonemeal, for example, dissolves slowly, furnishing phosphorus and some nitrogen, and has a beneficial action in combination with manure, which makes it desirable as a general plant food. It should be used on perennial and woody plants in generous quantity, but not on lawns, except straight blue grass, on acid-soil plants or on evergreens except boxwood. It is often added to a potting-soil mixture or applied as a top-dressing.

Dried blood, tankage, and fish-refuse fertilizers also contain nitrogen and phosphorus, and may be used like concentrated manure; they are convenient for use in potting soil or for feeding house and greenhouse plants. In the case of all animal and vegetable fertilizers, it is a good plan to use first one, then another, as they vary in nature and their good qualities, and the beneficial effects are likely to carry over from one crop to the next even if not realized at once.

COMMERCIAL FERTILIZERS. In the case of chemical fertilizers, the food value as a rule is available to the plants at once, and does not last over a winter except in the case of mineral products such as phosphate rock. Balanced commercial fertilizers are concentrated mixtures of the food materials likely to be needed by the average crop in the average soil; generally they enable the plants to also take full advantage of the crude food materials already present in the soil, manure, compost, humus, etc. It is sometimes said that commercial fertilizers exhaust the soil. This is not true, but they *do* help plants to exhaust the soil, by enabling them to use the food more rapidly. Therefore they should not be used alone, but in conjunction with soil-building, humus-forming materials. To get the greatest yield from the land, manures should be added each year to maintain general fertility and condition, supplemented by (1) both general and special fertilizers to furnish the minerals needed by the crop, and (2) stimulants to encourage use by the plants of these foods.

Commercial fertilizers have their analyses printed on the bag or other container, the important facts being the percentages of nitrogen, phosphoric acid, and potash. Thus a 4-8-5 fertilizer contains 4 per cent nitrogen, 8 per cent phosphoric acid, and 5 per cent potash, these being the elemental compounds most needed by plants, most commonly deficient in soils and most easily exhausted from them.

In the vegetable garden, a soil to which manure, compost and lime have been added and plowed (or, better, deeply spaded) in, can be made more productive by fertilizers scattered on the surface. For broadcasting in this way the following amounts may be used per 100 sq. ft.: muriate or sulphate of potash, sulphate of ammonia, or nitrate of soda, 1 lb.; hydrated lime, complete fertilizers, or cottonseed meal, 2 to 4 lbs.; superphosphate, horn shavings, ground limestone, or wood ashes, 5 to 10 lbs. Any such materials applied during the summer should be used in the smaller quantities recommended; indeed, it is always better to apply several small doses at intervals than a heavy application at one time.

Instead of broadcasting, some prefer to use fertilizers between the rows so that each crop may receive what it needs. Sweet corn is helped by liberal feeding—manure added to the surface at planting time, and any good commercial fertilizer being scattered between the rows about 2 weeks later, a handful to the sq. yd. If the soil tends to pack, a dressing of wood ashes or lime will help. Any of these materials should be worked in with the cultivator at once.

FEEDING KINDS OF PLANTS. Nitrates or any fertilizers very rich in nitrogen should not be used on corn or other crops in which seed or fruit production is desired rather than that of stem or leaf, as in celery, lettuce and cabbage. Potatoes should not be surface manured nor limed, but should receive a good application of balanced fertilizer. Root crops generally are helped by a top-dressing of sulphate or muriate of potash, and beets by lime and manure; but no lime, and especially no manure, should be applied for carrots. Onions relish some lime and either a balanced fertilizer or superphosphate and sulphate of potash.

For all leaf crops, especially lettuce, nitrates are particularly good, and general fertilizers and manure are also needed. Squash and melons also respond to nitrates, and benefit by large amounts of manure and balanced fertilizers. Nitrates are good on young tomato plants too, but should be given only at planting time, a balanced fertilizer being added soon after.

Annual flowers require heavy feeding with manure (preferably worked into the soil well in advance—or for the previous crop) and fertilizers, especially those that are quickly soluble. If grown for exhibition, they should receive applications in liquid form when the buds form. They can be given the maximum quantity of any plant foods except nitrates, which should be used (if at all) moderately on the young plants.

Perennials vary greatly in their requirements, but should not be fed as much as annuals, since they must grow at a moderate rate to prepare for winter. The more concentrated fertilizers, particularly nitrates, should be avoided. Commercial fertilizers are generally beneficial early in spring, and should be worked into the ground rather than left on the surface. Chief reliance should be placed on manure, compost and bonemeal rather than chemical stimulants. But as there are hundreds of kinds of perennial plants, there are naturally frequent exceptions—plants which respond to some special fertilizer and will not tolerate some other.

Lawns from which the new growth is constantly being removed are continually in need of feeding, and many special foods are recommended. The ground for new lawns should be thoroughly prepared, well-rotted manure being worked in to a depth of at least 10 in. and fertilizer raked into the surface 3 or 4 in. After a year or two, if no food were provided, the sod would become thin and poor with the exhaustion of the original food supply. Therefore even new lawns should be dressed with finely shredded manure, rich compost or peat moss in late fall, and a balanced fertilizer should be broadcast in early spring, about 40 lbs. per 1000 sq. ft. Water this in well immediately. To heighten the vigor and color of the grass, nitrate of soda or sulphate of ammonia may be added occasionally, not more than 2 lbs. per 1000 sq. ft.; it should be washed in with water immediately to prevent burning. As almost any good plant food will help a lawn, it is well to use first one, then another, rather than depend on a single kind.

Shrubs and trees do not need fertilizing if their roots can be kept covered at all times with a natural mulch of leaves. The root system of a tree or a spreading shrub usually reaches about as far as the spread of the branches, and the feeding roots will be found mainly in or near this outer zone. It is where the drip from the branches falls, therefore, that a mulch is most useful. Moisture-loving trees, such as elm and Lombardy poplar, and lusty-feeding shrubs like privet, send their roots out many yards farther than their branches, but these rank growers do not usually need mulching or special feeding. Sod is not a good cover for tree roots, especially those of evergreens. Large white pines will sometimes die in a few years on a lawn; but plant around them a wide bed of rhododendrons with a permanent heavy mulch of leaves, and they will flourish indefinitely. If a mulch is not practicable and the tree cannot get its normal supply of nitrogen nutrients as the mulch decays, it must be fed. Fertilizers may be scattered on the surface if it is loose soil, or placed in crowbar holes made about 2 ft. apart over the feeding root area. In the latter method the holes should not be more than a foot or at most 18 in. deep, as the active feeding roots lie mostly fairly near the surface, just below the layer of leafmold that would be their natural source of food in a forest. Rotted or composted manure, compost, and other animal and vegetable matter make the best tree foods. Rapid-growing kinds like maple and elm may do well on commercial fertilizers. But no tree should be forced with nitrates, which give a quick, succulent, nonresistant growth. Commercial tree foods high in nitrates also should not be used.

Acid-soil plants and shrubs, especially rhododendron, azalea and mountain-laurel, should be fed with leafmold, peat and old manure rather than with chemical fertilizers. Food on which they will thrive is contained in rotted oak leaves. Just before flowering time they may be fed with liquid manure, and thoroughly rotted manure may be added to their permanent mulch in winter. Acid-soil perennials such as trailing arbutus or wild orchids have the same needs. Boxwood, an exception, prefers bonemeal. Coniferous evergreens, most of which are acid-soil trees, should be given no mineral or chemical fertilizers, no lime, and no fresh manure. For heather the soil must be both acid and of sandy texture.

House plants in pots can be fed as outdoor plants are, by mixing the food with their potting soil and repotting when it is exhausted. Or a complete commercial fertilizer may be sprinkled on the surface, a teaspoonful to a 5-in. pot, once every few months. Prepared foods in tablet form are usually satisfactory and exceedingly convenient to use.

See also FERTILIZER; MANURE; SOIL.

PLANT GUILD. See NATIONAL PLANT, FLOWER AND FRUIT GUILD.

PLANTING. Although a planting is often used to mean the arrangement or design of plants—as in orchards, vineyards, groves, shrubberies, borders and landscape gardening—it is here restricted to the practical applications of fundamental principles involved in the handling of individual plants.

So considered, planting naturally starts with the sowing of the seed or, in some cases, of young plants developed from cuttings, layers, or other results of asexual propagation methods. In the home garden, planting carries through all stages from these starting points and the preliminary preparation of the plantlets to the final placement in permanent quarters; when the plants are procured from nurseries or other outside sources it starts with their care upon arrival and continues through several precautionary processes to the establishment of the plants in their new quarters.

SEED SOWING. Seedlings to be planted out are started in seed pans, flats and nursery beds and removed at suitable periods of development either to other flats or seed beds, or to greenhouse benches, hotbeds, coldframes or the open ground.

The soil for growing seedlings to transplanting size should never be more than moderately fertile because what is needed in a seedling is abundant and sturdy root development and comparatively small tops. Such plants are much more likely to survive the unavoidable loss of roots (often 75 per cent) suffered in even careful planting.

PREPARING A FLAT. Before it is placed in seed pans or flats the soil should be passed through two sieves, a course one ($\frac{1}{2}$ in. or $\frac{3}{4}$ in. mesh) and a fine one ($\frac{1}{4}$ in. mesh); the former removes large clods, stones, etc., the latter makes a second assortment of the material. The finely sifted part can be used to fill seed pans and to provide the surface inch or two in flats while the material removed by the second sifting is good to put in the bottom of the flat to serve as drainage.

Standard-size flats of cypress lumber are convenient and durable. Their length and width are made to fit into standard greenhouse benches, hotbeds and coldframes with minimum waste and their depth ($2\frac{3}{4}$ in. or $3\frac{3}{4}$ in.) has been proved most favorable for seedling development.

Special flats are made with compartments for individual plants, which can later be removed each with its cube of earth (and enclosed roots) intact. Such flats are of distinct advantage in amateur gardening.

Seed pans are generally used for only the smallest seeds which are scattered broadcast as evenly as possible. Flats are used for larger seeds which are sown thinly, generally in rows, so as to favor sturdy development. Several different species can be sown in the same flat, but it is not advisable to sow two or more varieties of the same species side by side or even in the same flat if it can be avoided, as seeds are easily misplaced or moved about in watering or otherwise, thus causing a mixture of varieties.

The soil for seed sowing should not be either wet or dry, but *moist*. A test is to squeeze a handful. If water comes from between the fingers, it is too wet. If, when the hand is opened, the soil does not hold its shape but falls apart, it is too dry. The soil should retain its shape but not in a putty-like mass.

SEED PLANTING. Having leveled and firmed the drainage material, and the sifted surface soil—especially in the corners and along the sides of the flat—with a rectangular block, place a straight-edge on the surface and with a pot label or pointed tool make straight rows from side to side (rather than from end to end) of the flat. A pane of glass slightly shorter than the width of the flat can be used to make the "drills" or rows, which will then be straight and of any desired uniform depth.

After the seeds are sown and covered with soil about twice as deep as their diameters, and firmed with the wooden block, the flat must be watered. This is best done by placing it about half its depth in water until the surface of the soil shows a wet spot. Then it must be removed, drained by slightly tilting it, and placed on a greenhouse bench, in a hotbed, a coldframe or some other place where the temperature is favorable for germination. It should be covered with a pane of glass to reduce evaporation and radiation of heat and a sheet of newspaper to keep out light. As soon as sprouting starts the paper must be removed and whenever moisture condenses on the glass this must be raised slightly for ventilation or removed altogether for a time.

PRICKING-OUT SEEDLINGS. When the seedlings have formed their second pair of leaves they must be "pricked out," which means gently removed and replanted a little farther apart—usually 1 in. each way. Generally done by lifting each one on a pointed stick, this is more speedily accomplished by means of a 6-in. garden label with a V-

shaped notch cut in the small end, with which the plantlets are lifted one by one. Larger seedlings, such as those of cabbage and tomato, are removed by cutting the earth away on each side of a row, loosening the plants and placing each one in a hole made with a dibble about twice as thick as a lead pencil in other prepared flats filled with soil or in open-ground nursery beds.

Always when the dibble or a trowel is used for planting, the soil must be pressed close to the roots of each plant, set all the way down, so as to avoid leaving air spaces around them.

SPOTTING BOARDS. To assure uniform spacing a "spotting board" can be used. This may consist of a board just the size of the space in the flat and with ½-in. holes bored in it, or of board of the same size but with pegs set at desired distances apart. In either case each hole or peg represents the position of a plant; a dibble can be thrust through the holes in the first board to make holes in the soil, while the peg style makes the holes when pressed on the soil.

Often it is a good plan to transplant a second time before putting the plants in their permanent locations. The main reason for doing this is to increase the number of roots and to confine them in limited space; also, of course, it prevents crowding of the seedlings and the development of spindly growth. Nearly as satisfactory and easier is to pass a knife, thrust the full depth of the soil into the flat, from side to side between each two rows and then from end to end between the plants 10 days or 2 weeks before and again immediately before the final planting. The first of these cuttings shortens the roots and tends to create thick bushy root masses; the second makes it easier to remove the individual plants with cubes of soil.

A still better way to insure getting a good, uninjured root ball is to use dirt bands or square paper pots which fit snugly in the flat, and each of which receives a single plant. At planting time the papers need not be removed, though slits should be cut in them or the bottoms removed (especially if the paper is tough) in order to let the roots out into the soil. Most paper used for such pots will decay in a few weeks in moist soil.

Plants such as melons and cucumbers, which are difficult to transplant either because of their brittleness, their tap-roots, or for other reasons, can be started in paper pots, dirt bands, berry boxes, flower pots, or 6-in. squares of inverted sod. Only those started in flower pots need have the receptacles removed at planting time. By starting such plants in this way, they can be kept protected against frost, insects and diseases; also 2 or more weeks can be saved over starting them outdoors in the open ground. However, it is important to harden-off early plants and prevent their suffering a shock when they are set out.

Handling Perennials. When herbaceous plants with leaves are received from nurseries or greenhouses, they should be unpacked at once and carefully examined to make sure that they are in good condition and not heated or dry. If heated they are probably spoiled and should be replaced. If dry, the roots should be either soaked or the plants heeled-in (which see) in wet soil for a few days. Nothing is gained and much may be lost if dry plants are planted without such previous soaking—except in *very* moist soil. Another good way to treat dry plants is to repack the roots in moist burlap or sphagnum moss for a day or two, leaving the tops exposed to the air.

Several hours before plants in flats, flower pots or other receptacles are planted in the open, the soil should be soaked; the excess water should then be allowed to drain away. Similarly, plants growing outdoors should be watered before they are moved, preferably the day previous to planting.

When small plants are to be planted out in rows it is a good plan to stretch a stout garden line tightly where the row is to be, lift it a few inches off the ground at two or more points and let it snap back into place. If the soil is in good seed-bed shape this snapping will leave a mark which can be used as a guide after the line has been removed. This saves the bother of trying to set the plants alongside the cord.

Balancing Root and Top. When vegetable and flower plants have been grown in such rich soil that they have developed large tops but relatively small roots; or when a straggly root system is injured or has to be reduced in transplanting, it is advisable to reduce the amount of foliage so as to create an approximate balance between root and top. A good plan is to cut off some of the lower, older leaves entirely and perhaps a part of the remaining large ones.

When plants have become spindling (or, as gardeners call it, "leggy") because of being crowded in the rows, they are almost sure to grow poorly after being transplanted unless a considerable part of the stems is placed below ground. If they are very leggy, the stems may be set on a slant in the soil; but always point them in the same direction in the row so as to keep them in line.

A TREE PLANTING BOARD IN USE
The board is placed with its center notch around a peg driven exactly where the tree is wanted. The two end pegs are then set, the board is removed and the hole dug. Then the board is replaced, and when the tree is placed in the center notch it will be exactly where the original locating peg stood.

Hardy vegetable and flower plants (as cabbage, columbine) when properly hardened-off can be planted in the open ground when peach and Japanese plum trees and forsythia bushes are in bloom; half-hardy kinds (lettuce, beardtongue) not until a week after those plants have dropped their flowers; tender ones (watermelon, Chinese primrose) not until after the usual date of the last local spring frost. Otherwise they may be killed by cold weather or so chilled that they will "sulk" for weeks.

Soil Treatment. Garden soil should always be well prepared for planting by deep digging and by thoroughly mixing in the manures and fertilizers (especially those of a chemical nature). Weather as well as soil conditions should govern planting. Not only should the soil be moist and

A PRECAUTION IN PLANTING

Always firm the soil well over a row of seeds planted in the garden. Do it with the feet, with a rake, with a plank or as you like—but do it. And then lightly scratch the surface soil to check evaporation.

fine, but advantage should be taken of cloudy days; or planting should be done toward evening so the plants will have the best chance to re-establish themselves before the hot sun strikes them. If the planting can be done immediately before a rain, so much the better—unless the plants are so small that they might be buried by a heavy downpour. After a rain it is essential to break the crust of surface soil for the reasons explained under cultivation (which see), especially around young, delicate plants.

When planting must be done during dry weather or in dry soil (as in midsummer) it is advisable to sow seeds more deeply than during spring (see SEEDS AND SEED-SOWING). At such times take extra precautions to prevent newly set plants from wilting; it is neither necessary nor desirable to have the surface soil moist, because the roots should be induced to develop more deeply than during spring when the soil is naturally more moist.

During summer and other "dry times" it is essential to maintain an effective mulch (which see) of loose surface soil or some applied material such as buckwheat hulls, peat moss, or straw. If the soil is exceedingly dry, make a shallow depression around each plant and fill it with water. Then, after the water has seeped away and a crust has formed, it must be broken and a new dust mulch established.

PLANTING DORMANT STOCK. Dormant perennial plants, such as rose bushes, can be handled and planted with less risk of loss, but that is no excuse for carelessness such as allowing their roots to become dry or failing to pack the soil firmly around them.

Trees, shrubs and woody vines in leaf require special care in digging and planting and only under exceptional circumstances should the amateur gardener undertake the work. Ordinarily the services of a skilled expert represent a good investment; the contract for any large tree-moving job should include a clause providing for attention and service for at least a full year after planting.

Dormant trees, shrubs and woody vines can, with few exceptions, be successfully planted from S. New England southward during autumn, with probable success, provided they are not made dormant artificially or prior to their natural times.

BUY RIPENED TREES. In ordering dormant nursery stock the buyer should insist that the plants be allowed to shed their leaves naturally and not be clipped or stripped. When they drop their leaves of their own accord they will have closed the tubes that carry sap between the twigs and the leaves, whereas when clipped or stripped a wound is made where each leaf is forcibly removed, through which much moisture is lost. This injures and may kill the trees before spring.

It is better to have dormant woody nursery stock arrive too late in the autumn for planting than to have the leaves removed. For it can safely be stored until spring—either being heeled-in (which see) or placed in an airy cellar and kept damp but not wet. Thus the advantages of early ordering can be enjoyed; namely, obtaining varieties and sizes desired, getting freshly dug stock, etc.

STEPS IN PLANTING. In the actual planting of dormant nursery stock the most important things to do are (1) to trim the broken and otherwise injured roots back to sound wood; (2) to pack the roots firmly in the ground and to reduce the number and length (or both) of the branches so as to balance the unavoidable reduction of roots by digging. Pruning the tops should never be done before planting. See PRUNING; TRAINING OF PLANTS.

To make sure that trees shall be in exact rows, as in an orchard or along a roadway, it is well to use a planting board. The most popular style is made and used as follows:

USING THE PLANTING BOARD. At each end of a 1-in. board 6-in. wide and not less than 5 ft. long cut a V-shaped notch half way through; then cut another notch midway along one side. When ready to plant a tree place the middle notch snugly against a stake already driven where the tree is to stand; then drive a temporary stake in each end notch. Take away the board and the tree stake; dig the hole for the tree (see below); replace the board with its notches against the temporary stakes; place the tree in the hole with the trunk erect and in the center notch (formerly occupied by the location stake), and fill in part of the earth. Finally remove the planting board after the roots are covered with earth tramped down so the tree will not shift. Then complete the filling in.

Actual planting should be performed as follows:

In well-prepared ground dig the holes wide enough to take in the trimmed roots without bending; throw the top-soil in one pile and the poorer sub-soil in another; hold the plant so its stem or stems will be about an inch deeper than it or they stood in the nursery (this can be judged by the difference in color of the stem at the ground level); have an assistant shovel in the good soil first so the new roots will have it to grow in; work the soil well down among the roots with the fingers and when these are covered 2 or 3 in. deep, tramp the loose soil down thoroughly to prevent the formation of air pockets and also to bring the earth into intimate contact with the roots and the lower moisture-holding soil; after the pile of top-soil has all been shoveled in and tramped down, throw in the sub-soil and tramp down most, but not all, of this; leave an inch or more of it loose on the surface to serve as a dust mulch and thus check evaporation of moisture from the tramped ground.

The main advantage of having the subsoil on top is that since it is of poorer quality than the surface soil, weeds have less opportunity to grow there, while the roots have a better chance to get plant food from the good top-soil around them.

Evergreens and a few deciduous species are sold by nurseries "balled and burlapped," that is with soil held around their roots by burlap wrapping. This protects them for a time against injury by drying.

On arrival, if the ball feels dry, it should be stood in water over night, allowed to drain, then planted, burlap and all.

If the burlap is heavy and of dense weave, make several slashes in its sides when the tree is in place, to allow the roots easy egress. Also cut away the excess wrapping on the top or spread it out so it will decay more quickly.

In packing the soil down care must be taken to avoid breaking the ball and the roots within it. If the ground is dry, the hole should be filled once or twice with water and this allowed to seep away before the plant is set. Finally, a thick mulch should be spread over the filled in soil well beyond the diameter of the specimen. Watering and mulching are of greatest importance with evergreens planted in late summer and early autumn, which is the best period in which to plant them, *provided* these precautions are taken and the staking of large specimens is practiced.

See also BALL; TRANSPLANTING.

PLANT LICE. A name for aphids, small soft sucking insects that attack many kinds of plants. See APHIDS.

PLANT NAMES AND CLASSIFICATION. One of the first and most important problems confronting the gardener is the identification of the plants he uses. Without it, adequate utilization and proper handling of plant materials is not practicable. The actual number of kinds of plants in the world is not known—probably it exceeds 350,000 species; when there are also considered the additional thousands of varieties and strains, it is apparent that identification, even of the relatively small numbers of garden plants, demands and presupposes a system of classification.

While plants exhibit highly diversified characteristics, definite relationships are soon apparent. Thus, different kinds of roses resemble each other so as to be recognized as roses, as do hawthorns, clovers and lilies. But all roses also have many (though less obvious) characteristics in common with hawthorns, perhaps a few in common with clovers, but none at all with lilies, unless we think of the bearing of flowers or some such generality. On this basis we therefore find roses and hawthorns quite closely related; both more distantly related to the clovers; and all three but very distantly related to the lilies.

Classification is the systematic arrangement of plant groups which expresses these relationships in terms of evolution, or descent from ancestors in common.

Plants differ most obviously in structure, and this is the principal basis of classification. Minor structural differences such as the size, shape, color and number of leaves, are regarded as "unstable characters" as they do not breed true. (See PLANT BREEDING.) The number, structure and arrangement of flower-parts, however, are more constant, and therefore are important factors in identifying and classifying plants.

Proper classification and identification calls for an orderly nomenclature or system of naming. Because names in Latin (the accepted scientific language) are of international usage, they are preferable to common names which may mean different things to different persons in different places. When their construction and significance are understood such "scientific" names are no more difficult to use than the "common" ones, and of course they are more definite and accurate. The real gardener makes use of both kinds. The unit of classification is the plant individual which is said to belong to a *species,* that is, a group of plants so nearly alike in their more stable characters that they differ no more than offsprings of the same parent.

The familiar White Birch (*Betula alba*) is such an individual. All birches taken together form a distinct and easily recognizable group called a *genus.* A species, then, is a collection of closely related individuals, and a number of such species (it may be many or few) make up the genus. The two categories, genus and species, in that order, give the individual plant its botanical or "official" name. *Betula* is the name of the Birch genus, that is, all birches; *alba,* the specific name, tells *what kind* of birch, thus classifying it. Thus, *Betula alba* is the name of a birch (Betula) which is like all other birches in general characteristics, but is further identified as a *white* birch.

VARIETIES AND THEIR NAMES

Within a species plants may also differ among themselves to some degree, by minor and less stable variations. These give rise to *varieties,* or subdivisions of a species; each member of a variety has the determining characteristics of its species but differs slightly from the species; *Betula alba* var. *papyrifera,* for example, is a variety of *B.*

alba differing from it by being somewhat larger, more restricted in locale and with much larger leaves. Often a variety bears the name of its discoverer or producer, as *Acer platanoides schwedleri,* or the Schwedler Maple. *Races, strains* and *clons* are other terms used to describe subdivisions along horticultural or cultural lines.

According to botanical usage the generic part of a plant name is capitalized. In the style followed in this book the specific and variety parts of the name are not; however, botanists and horticulturists are not agreed as to this latter point, so variation will be found in different publications. In strict botanical usage an abbreviation of the name of the person who first listed the plant is also a part of the name (as *Acer saccharum* Marsh.—meaning the Sugar Maple as named by Humphrey Marshall). As this information is rarely needed by practical gardeners it is usually omitted outside botanical works.

The practice of listing horticultural varieties in catalogues, etc., under names that have not been given some sort of official or general recognition and status is a cause of considerable confusion, as oftentimes the same name is applied to quite different varieties. Difficulty is also caused by uncertainty in classification or by a change of name made as a result of more knowledge than the original namer of the plant possessed. Thus, the peach is now generally called *Prunus persica,* whereas some stick to the former name *Amygdalus persica,* which was given when the plant was thought to belong to a separate genus. Today, most botanists consider it merely a species (persica) of the genus (Prunus) to which belong also the plums, cherries and other "stone fruits." Sometimes such confusion is due to mistaken identity, often to difference of opinion, and frequently it is an inevitable result of progress. So a system of classification can at best be but a somewhat arbitrary effort.

FAMILIES, ORDERS AND CLASSES

In classification by "blood" relationship similar species, *Betula alba, Betula lutea,* and so on, are, as already explained, grouped into a genus, in this case Birch (Betula). But the Birch genus is closely related to four other genera, namely, the alders (Alnus), hornbeams (Carpinus), ironwoods (Ostrya) and hazelnuts (Corylus). Such an aggregation of related genera is called a *family*—in this case the Betulaceae or Birch Family, named after its principal genus. The fact that the names of all plant families end in the letters *ae* or *aceae* makes it easy to recognize them.

A further, somewhat more distant, relationship is that between different families. The Rose Family (Rosaceae), for instance, is grouped with the Pea Family (Leguminosae), the Witch-hazel Family (Hamamelidaceae) and four other families to which it bears certain structural resemblances, to form the *Rose Order,* Rosales. Similarly the Birch Family (Betulaceae) is akin only to the Beech Family (Fagaceae), which, incidentally, includes the oaks, so these two families are grouped together into the order Fagales. Here also there is a distinguishing form of name, all plant orders ending in the letters *ales.*

Each order of flowering plants in turn falls into one of two great *Classes,* which are distinguished by profound structural differences. Grasses, palms, lilies, and orchids are members of Class I, the *Monocotyledons* (which see), but the bulk of garden plants falls into Class II, called *Dicotyledons,* which see.

These two great classes, each composed of orders, families, genera, and species, together comprise the *Angiosperms,* or plants which bear seeds inside a receptacle called an ovary. (See FLOWER.) These are the plants one thinks of when speaking of flowers, but the conifers, which belong to the other great subdivision, the *Gymnosperms,* or naked-seeded plants, also bear flowers, in the botanical sense of the word. The cones of the pine and the "berries" of the yew are the mature female flowers which bear the seeds, the male flowers being less conspicuous.

The entire group of flowering plants makes up the last and most complex of the four great Divisions into which the Plant Kingdom is divided, each of which is subdivided according to the system explained on page 962.

The Four Great Groups

Group I is composed of the simplest plants (Algae and Fungi) without stems, roots or leaves and, except in a primitive way, sexually unspecialized. Plants in Group II (Liverworts and Mosses) are distinguished by a highly specialized manner of reproduction; they also have the rudiments of roots, stems, and leaves. Group III is composed of plants (Ferns, Horsetails, Club-mosses, etc.) with true roots, stems, and leaves, but lacking seeds, which are the distinguishing character of Group IV, as already noted.

Applying the System

In applying the above classification system to the flowering plants, as in any analytical key to a group of plants, the distinguishing characters are usually grouped in pairs. Thus, leaves may be hairy or smooth, simple or compound, persistent (evergreen) or deciduous. Flowers may be staminate, or pistillate (or both); regular or irregular; simple or compound; with parts separate or fused. Stems may be woody or herbaceous. Roots may be fibrous or fleshy. Fruits may be fleshy or dry; simple or aggregate, and so on. There are, of course, many other characteristics, but this method of grouping by pairs greatly simplifies the identification of a plant specimen whether the key is simple and general or complex and exacting.

Applying the same method to other than structural characters, gardeners can—and constantly do—classify plants according to whether they are *annuals, biennials,* or *perennials;* that is, whether they live one season, or two seasons (flowering the second) or endure through many years. Any of these are further termed *hardy* and *half-hardy,* referring to the relative degree to which they endure cold, and, of course, indicating the sort of treatment they must receive.

The environment in which plants live, their *habitat,* is such an important factor in determining their manner of living and requirements that it forms the basis of other sorts of classification as into *aquatic, terrestrial* or *epiphytic;* or into *tropical, temperate* or *arctic;* or into acid-loving or lime-loving, etc. Again, plants fall fundamentally (as far as garden use is concerned) into such groups as *herbs, shrubs, vines,* and *trees.*

Because of the constant, even if unconscious use of these and other systems of classification, gardeners are much more "scientific" in their activities and decisions than they may realize. They can, therefore, well afford to lose the old-fashioned fear or distrust of scientific names, terms and methods of approach and, instead, take pride and pleasure in gradually accumulating and constantly utilizing scientific facts —which, after all, is merely another term for organized knowledge.

Throughout this book the attempt is made to supply such knowledge, along with practical cultural directions, in such a way as to make it attractive and helpful in enabling gardeners to get the most out of their gardens and their plants.

See also articles on FAMILY; GENUS; VARIETY, and other terms used in this article; also STANDARDS.

PLANTS FOR SPECIAL PURPOSES. An understanding of the natural adaptation of certain plants to certain purposes is necessary for successful planting. Too many failures are the result of trying to grow shade-loving plants in full sun, acid-loving plants in limestone regions and swamp-margin plants on dry hillsides. A little study of plant requirements will obviate losses, and improve the vigor and naturalness of the plant groupings. Some of the most common types of plants, with suggestions as to various situations in which they can be used, follow.

Annuals

Annuals (which see) are particularly useful to the home-gardener who wishes to have a great display of bloom for small expenditure. As they are grown each year from seeds, and bloom the same season, they are particularly valuable for the new garden in which perennials have not had time to become established. They also bloom most prolifically in midsummer when blossom effect from perennials is relatively sparse. Longer-lived plants which are grown as annuals are treated here as such.

FOR SUN AND DRY SOIL. Most annuals like full sun, and a few are particularly useful for hot, dry locations where the midsummer sun bakes out most other plants:

Portulaca	Shirley Poppy
California Poppy	Swan River Daisy

FOR PARTIAL SHADE. Some which will thrive and sometimes bloom longer in partial shade include:

Nasturtium	Torenia
Snapdragon	Nemophila
Pansy	Annual Stock

FOR CUTTING. Annuals are prolific and constant in bloom and vary widely in color

and size, so they naturally become the chief reliance in the cutting garden or border. Those particularly useful in view of their ease of growth and long season of bloom are:

Snapdragon	Blue Laceflower
Calendula	Annual Chrysanthemum
Cornflower	Pentstemon
Coreopsis	Border Pink
Cosmos	China Aster
Mealycup Sage	Cape-marigold
Larkspur	Clarkia
Hunnemannia	Lupine
California Poppy	Verbena
Annual Gypsophila	Nasturtium
Ageratum	Annual Phlox
Heliotrope	Salpiglossis
Sweet Pea	Mourning Bride
Gaillardia	Marigold
Zinnia	Stock

FOR CONTINUOUS BLOOM. Annuals which reach flowering size in a short period may be given several sowings, 2 or 3 weeks apart, during the summer. These include:

Annual Gypsophila	Phlox
Cornflower	Coreopsis
Poppy	Candytuft
Mignonette	

Sweet Alyssum and Edging Lobelia may be cut back to produce later bloom.

FOR WINDOW AND PORCH BOXES. As the plants in boxes must usually be replaced each year, the use of annuals here is inevitable.

For center of box	*To trail over edge*
Zinnia	Sweet Alyssum
Marigold	Verbena
Blue Salvia	Petunia
Half-dwarf	Thunbergia
Snapdragon	Lobelia
Lantana	

ANNUAL VINES. These offer an excellent group of plants for covering unsightly fences or walls quickly, or for filling bare spots against a new house or fence while the slower perennial vines are becoming established. The most interesting of the annual vines are:

Morning-glory—	Cardinal-climber
Heavenly Blue	Canary-bird-vine
Moonflower	Scarlet-runner-
Hyacinth-bean	bean
Hop-vine	Cypress-vine
Cup-and-saucer-vine	

Perennials

Perennials (which see) are those plants that bloom annually. Many may be grown from seeds; others are propagated by division of existing roots or by cuttings. They include many of our finest garden flowers and have the advantage of needing less yearly attention than annuals, in order to yield a succession of bloom from early spring till frost. Most flowering plants need sun, and except for those listed for shade, perennials should have at least a half day's full sun.

To Insure Succession of Bloom (In order of blooming season)

German Iris	Delphinium
Siberian Iris	Daylily
Bleeding Heart	Phlox
Columbine	Purple Coneflower
Peony	Boltonia
Oriental-Poppy	Aster
Japanese Iris	Chrysanthemum

For Shade. Few of our garden perennials will succeed in dense shade. Where no sun penetrates, the list must be restricted largely to those plants which are native to thick woodlands. Where there are two or three hours of sun, or flickering shade from trees, certain of our garden favorites will bloom satisfactorily.

DENSE SHADE:

Baneberry (*Actaea alba* and *A. rubra*)
Snakeroot (*Cimicifuga racemosa* and *C. simplex*)
Ferns—*Osmunda cinnamomea*
    O. claytonia
    Polystichum acrostichoides
    Adiantum pedatum

Plaintain-lily	Trillium
Lily-of-the-valley	Violets (native species)

SEMI-SHADE:

Japanese Anemone	Primrose (*Primula*
Foxglove	*vulgaris*)
Meadow-rue	Monkshood
Bleeding Heart	(Also list above)

For Light, Poor Soil.

Yarrow	Mistflower
Golden-tuft	Gaillardia
Golden Marguerite	Gayfeather
Rock-cress	Flax
Butterfly-weed	Sun-rose
False-indigo	Lupine
Harebell	Iceland Poppy
Meadow Sage	Moss-pink Phlox
	Yucca

For Heavy Clay Soil.

Amsonia	Perennial Pea
Siberian Iris	Tiger Lily

For Cutting. Perennials form an important part of the well-established cutting garden. Many may also be cut from the border to induce further bloom. Among those that are useful especially as cut flowers are the following:

Achillea "The Pearl"	Sweet William
Japanese Anemone	Mistflower
Aquilegia species	Babys Breath
Smooth Aster	Helenium
Peachleaf Bellflower	Coral-bells
Chrysanthemum	Iris—all species
"Shasta Daisy"	Royal Lily
Ground Clematis	Gold-banded Lily
(*Clematis recta*)	Peonies
Lily-of-the-valley	Pentstemon
Coreopsis	Trollius
Delphinium	Purple Coneflower

Easily Grown From Seed. While some perennials are most satisfactorily increased by division or cutting, others are easily grown from seed. A few will bloom the first year if seed is sown early indoors. The rest can be counted on for flowers the second summer. Among those thus easily raised from seed are the following:

Golden-tuft	Digitalis
Golden Marguerite	Eupatorium
Aquilegia	Gypsophila
Wall-cress	Common Sneezeweed
Butterfly-weed	Candytuft
New England Aster	Regal Lily
Blue Wild-indigo	Cardinal-flower
English Daisy	Iceland Poppy
Campanula—most	Oriental Poppy
species	Pentstemon
Mountain-bluet	Balloon-flower
Jupiters Beard	Rudbeckia
Chrysanthemum	Salvia
"Shasta Daisy"	Thalictrum
Delphinium	Tufted Pansy (*Viola*
Dianthus	*cornuta*)

Shrubs

The list of shrubs available for use on the home grounds is much larger than is generally realized. In addition to the too generally used flowering shrubs, like the hydrangea, spireas and weigelas, there are many more unusual varieties of well-known species, and many native shrubs which adapt themselves readily to refined plantings. Instead of confining oneself to flower-color alone the home owner should plan to include material (1) particularly valuable for color of fruit, leaves or stems at other than blooming season; (2) well-adapted to special conditions of soil, climate, shade and moisture; (3) whose natural shape and size at full maturity is in the proper relation to the given setting, thereby avoiding constant chopping and pruning for restraint. Choice of material with these requirements in mind will result in more varied and unusual plantings, and in economy of upkeep because of natural fitness to surroundings. See also SHRUBS.

SHRUBS FOR SUMMER EFFECT (July and August).

FLOWERS:

Chinese Abelia (*Abelia chinensis*)
Sweet-scented Buddleia (*Buddleia davidi*)
Japanese Beauty-berry (*Callicarpa japonica*)
Summersweet (*Clethra alnifolia*)
Shrub-althea (*Hibiscus syriacus*)
Bushy St.-Johnswort (*Hypericum densiflorum*)
Hardhack (*Spirea tomentosa*)
Japanese Storax (*Styrax japonica*)

FRUIT:

Honeysuckle (*Lonicera* in variety)
Shadbush (*Amelanchier canadensis*)
Blueberry (*Vaccinium* in variety)
Elder (*Sambucus racemosa* and *canadensis*)
Withe-rod (*Viburnum cassinoides*)

SHRUBS FOR FALL EFFECT (September and November).

FOLIAGE COLOR:

Barberry (*Berberis* species)
Dogwood (*Cornus florida*)
Necklace-flower (*Enkianthus campanulatus*)
Winged Burning-bush (*Euonymus alatus*)
Fragrant Sumac (*Rhus canadensis*)
Shining Sumac (*Rhus copallina*)
Staghorn Sumac (*Rhus typhina*)
Mapleleaf Viburnum (*Viburnum acerifolium*)
Withe-rod (*Viburnum cassinoides*)
Nannyberry (*Viburnum lentago*)
Doublefile Viburnum (*Viburnum tomentosum*)

FRUIT:

Red Chokeberry (*Aronia arbutifolia*)
Spicebush (*Benzoin aestivale*)
Barberry (*Berberis* species)
Chinese Beauty-berry (*Callicarpa purpurea*)
Flowering Dogwood (*Cornus florida*)
Winged Burning-bush (*Euonymus alatus*)
Sargent Crab (*Pyrus sargenti*)
American Elder (*Sambucus canadensis*)
Japanese Sweetleaf (*Symplocos paniculata*)
Ground Yew (*Taxus canadensis*)
Siebold Viburnum (*Viburnum sieboldi*)
Arrow-wood (*Viburnum dentatum*)
American Hazelnut (*Corylus americana*)
Hawthorn (*Crataegus* species)
Cockspur Thorn (*Crataegus crusgalli*)
Snowberry (*Symphoricarpos albus*)
Coral-berry (*Symphoricarpos orbiculatus*)
European Burning-bush (*Euonymus europaeus*)
Winterberry (*Ilex verticillata*)
Northern Bayberry (*Myrica carolinensis*)
Shrub Roses (Rosa—many species, such as *R. rugosa* and *R. eglanteria*)
Japanese Cranberry-bush (*Viburnum dilatatum*)
Nannyberry (*Viburnum lentago*)
Japanese Barberry (*Berberis thunbergi*)
European Barberry (*Berberis vulgaris*)
Evergreen Thorn (*Pyracantha coccinea*)
Shining Sumac (*Rhus copallina*)
Staghorn Sumac (*Rhus typhina*)
Smooth Sumac (*Rhus glabra*)
European Cranberry-bush (*Viburnum opulus*)

ACID-LOVING SHRUBS. Acid condition of the soil is unfavorable to the greater proportion of our shrubs. There are, however, certain of our most beautiful shrubs which are native to acid soils and can be grown only under acid conditions. They include Rhododendrons and all other members of the Heath Family as well as a number of others. For a list, see ACID-LOVING PLANTS.

For Dry Rocky Places. Certain shrubs are invaluable because they will thrive in dry rocky soil. These include several natives, such as Blueberry, Wild Raspberry, Wild Roses of several kinds, the Sumacs and the Locust. Also two of the handsomest of the lesser known flowering shrubs, Halimodendron and Kolkwitzia, will do well in an exposed situation where the soil is none too good.

Hedges

Hedges may be severely trimmed into geometric perfection, lightly trimmed to keep them within bounds, or left untrimmed for fruit and flowering effects. The material for the hedge should be selected in terms of the height and width and character desired.

Trimmed Hedge.

EVERGREEN :

(tall)	(low)
Arborvitae	Yew
Hemlock	Box
Cedar	Holly (*Ilex crenata*
Spruce	*microphylla*)

DECIDUOUS :

(tall)	(medium)
Pea-shrub	Privet
Russian-olive	Buckthorn
Osage-orange	Hawthorn of
English Beech	several kinds
European Hornbeam	Flowering Quince

Untrimmed.
Deutzia lemoineri
Honey-locust (*Gleditsia triacanthos*)
Spiraea vanhouttei
Rose (*Rosa rugosa, R. centifolia, R. rubiginosa*)
Hydrangea paniculata
Hemlock
Japanese Quince
Rose-of-Sharon (*Hibiscus syriacus*)
Lilac (*Syringa vulgaris* and *persica*)
Honeysuckle (*Lonicera fragrantissima, tatarica,* or *maacki*)

Vines

For Rapid Covering. Certain woody vines are useful for covering rocks or banks where grass is not possible or desirable. They are chosen for their hardiness and prolific growth under difficult conditions, and include :

Honeysuckle (*Lonicera japonica*)
Woodbine (*Parthenocissus quinquefolia*)
Bittersweet (*Celastrus scandens*)
Virgins Bower (*Clematis virginiana*)
Dutchmans Pipe (*Aristolochia durior*)

For Brick or Stone. Vines for use on brick or stone walls must be those which cling by "suckers' that adhere to the wall surface. The list includes :

Englemans Ivy	Trumpet-vine
Boston Ivy	Climbing Euonymus
English Ivy	Climbing Hydrangea

For vines to be treated as annuals, producing showy flowers, see the list under Annuals in this article.

Plants to Frame a House

The type of a house controls the planting placed against it, whether formal, requiring a balanced treatment, or unsymmetrical, permitting informal picturesqueness and irregularity. Restraint should be exercised in all instances, bareness being preferable to over-crowding.

Such shrubs as are chosen should be of good quality; neat, dense and not necessarily flowering; they should be selected for permanence and for dignity of appearance and must be calculated to withstand bad conditions. This is important, as in most cases the soil immediately next to foundation walls consists largely of construction refuse, and the more delicate shrubs will not survive. Confine your choice to those which are known to grow easily and well, and be sure to consider the ultimate height or spread and habit of growth.

A Formal Entrance demands a careful balance of design. Among shrubs which may be used on either side are :

EVERGREEN :

Box (not universally hardy)	Mountain-laurel
Yew	Leucothoë
Japanese Holly	Andromeda
Rhododendron	Cotoneaster (in variety)
Arborvitae	Juniper (especially Pfitzers)
Eunonymus japonicus (not hardy far N.)	

DECIDUOUS :

Ibota Privet	Snowberry
Japanese Privet	Witch-hazel
Inkberry	Hawthorns (in variety)
Russian-olive (in variety)	Spicebush

Dogwood	Azalea
Abelia	Mockorange
Japanese Quince	Viburnum (in variety, including the Japanese Snowball, Highbush-cranberry and Black-haw)
Rose-of-Sharon	
Lilacs (in variety)	
Barberries (in variety)	
Coral-berry	

TO TRAIN AGAINST WALLS:

Forsythia	Hawthorns (certain varieties)
Laland Firethorn	

An unsymmetrical house requires more subtle handling but less careful, obvious balance in the planting. Among the larger shrubs or small trees useful for placing against wide wall spaces are:

Dogwood	Fringe-tree
Laburnum	Red-bud
Washington Thorn	Magnolia (especially *M. soulangeana* and *M. stellata*)
Halesia	
Crab-apple (in variety)	

Vines are of great value, both for the ornamentation of entrances and for spaces too small for shrubs. They grow rapidly and cover large areas at small cost, giving permanent effects and having a close relation to the building. In choosing them it is necessary to analyze the type of vine, whether clinging or requiring support; on wooden houses vines should be grown on a trellis or on detachable wires, to permit painting the building at intervals. Boston Ivy, for example, clings closely, making a smooth blanket of leaves and accentuating the form of the structure against which it is trained. Virginia Creeper clings also, but loosely, falling into graceful curves. Both grow to a considerable height and require no support. The following are large:

Wisteria	Dorothy Perkins
Grape	Rose
Bittersweet	*Clematis paniculata*
Trumpet-vine	*Euonymus radicans* (evergreen)
Dutchmans Pipe	
Climbing Hydrangea	English Ivy (not hardy far N.)
Halls Honeysuckle	
Silver Moon Rose	

Small vines, delicate in foliage and generally clinging, include:

Akebia

Clematis (Vars. Ramona, Mme. Veillard)

Climbing Roses (Vars. Jacotte, Musk Everblooming, Mrs. Geo. C. Thomas)

Ampelopsis (*A. brevipedunculata* and *A. aconitifolia*)

Euonymus radicans var. *minimus*

It will be found possible and sometimes desirable to lighten the austerity near the house by the introduction of small bulbs such as Crocus, Chionodoxa, Grape-hyacinth, the lower-growing Scillas, and Snowdrops, which spread readily and, once established, require no further attention.

PLATANUS (plat'-ah-nus). A genus of large S. European, Asiatic and American ornamental deciduous trees commonly known as Plane-tree (which see). Other common names are Buttonwood, Buttonball, and, in the case of one species, Sycamore.

PLATYCERIUM (plat-i-see'-ri-um). A genus of ferns with broad and uniquely forking fronds, commonly known as Stags Horn Fern. They are chiefly tropical and require warm greenhouse care, though *P. alcicorne,* the commonest species, will grow under good living room conditions, and is hardy in S. California. The fertile fronds are winged almost to the rootstock, spreading into fan-shaped blades above, and the fruit-dots occupy small patches between the main lobes. The smaller, barren fronds are nearly round. Plants should have a preponderance of peat moss or leafmold, plenty of indirect light, and occasional syringing, with a thorough watering only when they begin to droop. They are best grown as basket ferns or fastened into pieces of charred wood or cork, as they produce numerous fronds from various parts of the rootstock.

P. alcicorne. The most popular and easiest to grow. Fronds 2 to 3 ft. long, clustered, leathery, covered with fine hairs below.

grande. A super type with 4- to 6-ft. arching fronds, in pairs; they have curious elongated lobes.

PLATYCODON (plat-i-koh'-don) *grandiflorum.* A favorite perennial of the Bluebell Family, with showy white or blue flowers. See BALLOON-FLOWER. (See illustration, Plate 39.)

PLEACH. This is the term for interweaving the slender branches of trees or shrubs to train them into a naturally covered green alley similar to an arbor but not requiring artificial support. Only species of tough and elastic wood are suitable for pleached alleys, and in regions of much snowfall a temporary supporting framework is needed for the first years. Hedges are sometimes pleached to make them secure and the practice is frequently followed where it is desired to bring hedge plants together over a gate, pathway or other opening.

PLEURISY-ROOT. A common name for *Asclepias tuberosa* or Butterfly-weed (which see), a hardy perennial with brilliant orange flowers in midsummer.

PLUM. Various small trees of the genus Prunus, cultivated for centuries for their smooth-skinned, bloom-covered fruit. American species have been important for about one hundred years. Their diverse origin explains the widely different cultural requirements and adaptations of the different groups.

TYPES. The common plum (*P. domestica*) probably originated in S. E. Europe. It includes most of the dessert varieties and all of the prunes cultivated in the commercial fruit-producing areas from New England to Mich. and on the Pacific Coast. As home-garden fruits various varieties may be grown farther N. and others in the mountains southward to Ga. They are less reliable in the S. and in the Prairie States.

Since the so-called Japanese (though probably Chinese), species (*P. salicina* or *P. triflora*) was first introduced into America in 1870, increasing numbers of its varieties have proved of far wider adaptability than the European kinds. They may be grown farther N. and S. and with greater prospect of success in the Prairie States. Among them are some of excellent dessert quality.

American plums have originated from several species whose natural range extends from the Canadian N. W. to the Gulf States and from the Mississippi River to the Rocky Mountains. Outside of this area they should not be planted because they are of lower quality than are the dessert varieties of both European and Japanese species and because the more humid atmosphere encourages brown rot.

Besides these three groups several other species are more or less grown in gardens for fruit or ornament but not commercially. Among them are the Apricot Plum or Simon Plum (*P. simoni*), popular mainly in California; the Beach Plum (*P. maritima*), native along the Atlantic Coast to Va. and planted in sandy soils for its flowers and rather astringent fruits used for making jam and jelly; and the Pacific Coast native plum (*P. subcordata*) somewhat grown for ornament and fruit.

VARIETIES. With perhaps no fruit is selection of varieties so likely to prove disappointing; unless guided the novice is almost sure to choose kinds unsuited to his region. Hence the following lists. As probably no nursery carries more than half of those named, the method of locating them given under APPLE should be adopted. It is highly important that different varieties be growing in the neighborhood to assure pollination, because some varieties are self-sterile.

European: Pearl, Peters, Washington, Imperial Gage, Jefferson, Italian Prune, Spaulding, Reine Claude, Middleburg, Tragedy, Imperial Epineuse, French, Shropshire, Damson, Purple Gage, McLaughlin, Golden Drop, German Prune, Bavay, Yellow Gage, Palatine.

Japanese: Red June, Abundance, Burbank, Satsuma, Kelsey, Wickson, Chabot, Gonzales, Japex, Kerr, Maynard, October.

American: Bixby, Opata, Cheney, Mankato, Emerald, Stoddard, Brackett, Omaha, Waneta, Surprise, Wild Goose, Wolf, Wood.

CULTURE. Plums may be grown in any well-drained garden soil. Where there is a choice, European varieties should be planted in heavy clay loams, Japanese and American kinds on lighter soils. Where fowl are kept the trees can well be planted in the yard so the chickens or ducks can eat the insects (curculios) that make the fruits wormy.

One-year trees give best results when planted and trained like apple (which see). Though Damsons may be planted closer, other European and American varieties should be given 20 ft. in which to spread and Japanese kinds 24 ft. When thoroughly cultivated (see APPLE) the trees will need no fertilizer on good land; when in sod or under mulch they will yield fairly well if bearing trees are given 1 to 2 lbs. of nitrate of soda in early spring.

For dessert use and for jam, plums should be allowed to ripen on the trees because they thus attain their best quality; for canning whole they should be ripe but firm. Mature trees well tended should yield from one to three or four bushels of fruit a year.

ENEMIES

DISEASES. The brown rot fungus is particularly destructive to plum fruits, rotting them, covering them with soft gray spore masses and turning them into mummies. Where possible remove infected fruit from the tree and destroy it, and rake up all fallen fruit. For a spray schedule see under PEACH; see also BROWN ROT.

The common black-knot disease, which may be destructive to both wild and cultivated plums and cherries, is hard to, control. The fungus causes hard swellings, covered with charcoal-like black fruiting bodies, on twigs, small branches and even on larger limbs. Prune off all affected twigs and branches during the winter and remove and destroy whole trees if badly infected. Spray with bordeaux mixture every 2 weeks beginning early in April until 5 applications have been made.

Two common leaf diseases (leaf blight and bacterial black-spot) cause brown spots which fall out, giving a shot-hole effect. For control see spray schedule under CHERRY.

INSECTS. The European fruit leucanium, a convex reddish-brown soft scale, and the San José scale are best controlled with a dormant application of a miscible oil. The several aphids which infest plums—the green apple, spinach, mealy plum and rusty plum aphids—are checked by spraying with nicotine-sulphate and soap. The fruit bark beetle and the peach borer (both discussed under PEACH) may attack plum. For the plum curculio (see CURCULIO) which cuts crescent-shaped marks in the fruit, spray with lead arsenate just after the petals fall and again a week or two later.

See also PRUNUS.

Coco-plum is *Chrysobalanus icaco;* Date-plum is *Diospyros lotus;* Governors-plum is *Flacourtia indica;* Hog-plum is *Spondias mombin;* Jambolan-plum is *Eugenia cumini;* Japan-plum is *Eriobotrya japonica;* Kafir-plum is *Harpephyllum caffrum;* Marmalade-plum is *Achras zapota;* Natal-plum is *Carissa grandiflora;* Pigeon-plum is *Coccolobis floridana;* Spanish-plum is *Spondias purpurea.*

PLUMBAGINACEAE (plum - baj - i - nay'-see-ee). The Leadwort Family, a group of widely distributed herbs and shrubs preferring salty soil conditions. Many species are useful out-of-doors in rockeries and borders or for bedding; a few are grown under glass and some have medicinal properties. Plumbago, Ceratostigma, Limonium and Statice are the genera most cultivated.

PLUMBAGO. A genus of subtropical herbs and small shrubs known as Leadwort (which see), with generally blue, sometimes white or red, flowers in spikes.

PLUMED THISTLE. Common name for Cirsium, a genus of coarse, prickly herbs sometimes planted for bold effects in borders.

PLUME GRASS. A common name for Erianthus, a genus of stout perennial grasses grown as ornaments. See ORNAMENTAL GRASSES.

PLUMELESS THISTLE. Common name for Carduus, a genus of stout herbs with spiny flower-heads.

PLUME-POPPY. Common name for *Macleaya cordata* (better known by its former name, *Bocconia cordata*) and sometimes called Tree-celandine. A member of the Poppy Family, it is very different from the ordinary poppy. The tall herb with feathery sprays of small petalless flowers held high above the large grayish-green, lobed leaves makes an effective background for perennials, or an excellent tall accent near the house and in the shrubbery border. The small flowers are followed by slender, drooping plumes of

PLUME-POPPY, A HARDY PERENNIAL
Known also as Tree-celandine, this old-fashioned plant bears feathery spikes of small flowers on leafy stalks up to 10 feet high.

seed vessels, quite as attractive as the flowers. The Plume-poppy is easily increased by removing and resetting the numerous suckers which form at the base of the plant; if set in rich soil, they will rapidly develop to blooming size.

PLUMERIA (ploo-mee'-ri-ah). Frangipani. Tropical American trees, belonging to the Dogbane Family, popular in warm climates for their large waxy and very fragrant funnel-shaped flowers. Propagated by cuttings.

P. acuminata is a tree to 20 ft. with leaves a foot or more long, and clusters of white flowers flushed yellow. It is a favorite graveyard tree in tropical countries. *P. rubra* is a small tree or shrub, with more or less rosy flowers.

PLUMOSE. Featherlike; as the plumy hairs or bristles making up the modified calyx (pappus) of certain composites like thistle and blazing star (Liatris).

PLUNGE. To sink the flower pot in which a plant is growing rim-deep in the soil or cinders of a greenhouse bench or a coldframe, or in the ground outside; usually done between its flowering periods.

POA (poh'-ah). A genus of small, mostly perennial grasses much used in lawns and in pastures. The principal species are *P. pratensis* and *P. compressa,* commonly known as Blue Grass, which see. See also LAWNS.

PODOCARPUS (pod-oh-kahr'-pus). Evergreen trees and shrubs, native of subtropical regions of Australasia, S. America, Asia and Africa, belonging to the Yew Family. Some species are grown outdoors in the warmest parts of this country, and occasionally under glass elsewhere, for their attractive foliage. They do well in a mixture of sandy loam and peat. Propagated by seeds or cuttings.

PRINCIPAL SPECIES

P. macrophylla, from Japan, grows to 60 ft., with narrow dark green glossy leaves in dense spiral formation. Var. *maki,* usually shrubby, has smaller leaves.

alpina, from Australia, is the hardiest and can stand considerable frost. It is usually a dense rounded bush.

elongata, from Africa, grows to 70 ft., with thin pointed leaves to 3 in. long. It is often grown as a decorative plant in pots or tubs.

totara, from New Zealand, grows to 100 ft., but in cultivation is often a bush less

than one-tenth that height. It has small rigid leathery leaves of a bronzy tone.

PODOLEPIS (poh-dol'-ee-pis). Hardy annual or perennial herbs of the Composite Family, usually treated as annuals and sometimes grown as everlastings (which see). They are well adapted for beds in full sun. A light and well-drained soil is most suitable. Seed may be sown in April in heat and the seedlings transplanted in June, about 1 ft. apart. Sowings may also be made in the open during May or June, being thinned later to 1 ft. apart.

P. aristata is an annual, about 1 ft. high, with yellow flower heads, 1 in. in diameter. *P. canescens* (*P. affinis*) is similar, with smaller flowers. *P. gracilis* is a delicate perennial to 3 ft., with purple or lilac flower-heads.

PODOPHYLLUM (pod-oh-fil'-um). A genus of perennial herbs native in shady places and called May-apple, which see.

POGONIA (poh-goh'-ni-ah) *ophioglossoides.* A small terrestrial, native orchid commonly known as Rose Pogonia or Snake Mouth. It has a single, dainty, pale rose to white, fragrant flower, 1 in. long, with oval sepals and petals and a pale pink lip, veined with rose and crested with yellow-brown hairs. It should be grown in the bog garden, in strongly acid soil, or in sphagnum moss.

POINCIANA (poin-si-ay'-nah). A genus of shrubs or small trees of the Pea Family, native to warm regions, sometimes confused with members of the genus Caesalpinia.

Poincianas are very popular in the tropics, and when in bloom rank with the showiest trees and shrubs. They will grow in the warmest parts of this country, and thrive in rather dry soil. Propagation is by seeds, which should be soaked in warm water before they are sown in sandy soil.

PRINCIPAL SPECIES

P. pulcherrima (Barbados Pride, Barbados Flower-fence. Dwarf Poinciana). This plant, formerly called *Caesalpinia pulcherrima,* is a somewhat prickly shrub to 10 ft., with feathery foliage and gaudy red and yellow flowers with conspicuous red stamens.

gilliesi is a shrub of straggling habit, with mimosa-like leaves and clusters of light yellow flowers with long stamens of brilliant red. It is known in Calif. as "Bird of Paradise."

The so-called Royal-poinciana, formerly classified as *P. regia*, is now *Delonix regia*.

POINSETTIA (poin-set′-i-ah). Common name for *Euphorbia pulcherrima*, a tropical American species of Euphorbia (which see) suitable for garden culture in frost-free regions but familiar throughout the country as one of the most popular and characteristic Christmas pot plants, its large, red, flower-like bracts conveying true holiday atmosphere.

Outdoors, the Poinsettia is a shrub to 10 ft. (or sometimes twice that height), with oval or tapering leaves, sometimes with pointed lobes, the upper ones narrower; it bears large bright red (or pink or white) bracts in a flat rosette, with a central cluster of small, yellow flowers. Grown as pot plants, Poinsettias do best in a mixture of one-half loam, a quarter dried cow manure, and a quarter leafmold. They are grown from cuttings, about 3 in. long, set 3 in a small pot, and kept in a close atmosphere in a warm frame until rooted. Afterwards they are shifted into

WATCH OUT FOR POISON IVY!
Three glossy leaflets (the middle one on a short stalk) and inconspicuous clusters of flowers and berries, are signs by which it may be recognized.

larger pots, disturbing the roots as little as possible so as to avoid the checks caused by abrupt shifting. One large plant or 2 or 3 small ones can be flowered in a 5- to 7-in. pot.

When flowering is over the plants should be dried off and allowed to rest in a warm place for 3 or 4 months; then they can be cut back, brought into light and heat, and in May, forced into growth to supply young cuttings. A gift plant, rested and cut back, if grown on slowly or plunged outdoors over summer will sometimes bloom again. Plants must receive full light and sunshine at all times. Avoid sudden changes of temperature.

Mealy bugs (which see) are a common pest. The poinsettia root aphid may be controlled on potted plants by dusting the earth ball and the inside of the pot with 5% nicotine dust, or by submerging the earth ball in a solution of nicotine sulphate (1 tbsp. per gal. of water) and soap that has been heated to 100 deg. F.

POISON-BULB. A common name for *Crinum asiaticum*, an Asiatic bulbous plant of the Amaryllis Family, with fragrant white flowers.

POISON-HEMLOCK. Common name for *Conium maculatum*, a coarse, rank-growing biennial herb of the Parsley Family, sometimes known as "Winter-fern." Growing to 4 ft. with finely cut leaves and small white flowers in compound umbels, it is a disagreeable smelling Old-World herb, now naturalized in both N. and S. America, and of value only as a source of medicine. The root is very poisonous and a decoction made from it is said to have been the death drink of the Greek philosopher Socrates.

POISON IVY. Common name for *Rhus toxicodendron*, also called Poison-oak, a shrub that clambers over rocks or fences and often climbs high on trees by means of aerial rootlets. The leaves consist of 3, somewhat oval, pointed leaflets, glossy above, slightly hairy beneath; the small greenish flowers, in loose clusters, are followed by small grayish round fruits remaining on the plant during the winter. The foliage takes on red and orange hues in the fall.

Poison Ivy or Poison-oak is a widespread pest throughout the U. S., growing not only in waste places, where its sinister beauty might be enjoyed at a distance, but also along the roadside and frequently in the garden, where it is a real menace. In the far W. *Rhus diversiloba,* which takes the place of *R. toxicodendron,* is more shrubby in growth, but has the same poisonous qualities.

Poison Ivy causes much distress every year, for many persons are susceptible to the poisonous oil called toxicodendrol contained in the leaves, bark, root and fruit. This causes in those not immune to it extreme itching and burning of the skin, and often swelling and a feeling of extreme lassitude. Severe cases often incapacitate the victim and fatal consequences are not unknown.

REMEDIES. Different authorities (and victims) recommend different remedies and doubtless the personal element is important. But the following suggestions are based on wide experience: After coming in touch with Poison Ivy, wash the hands and all parts that have been exposed thoroughly with a strongly alkaline soap, such as a yellow laundry soap. Make a profuse lather, apply with a soft brush or cloth and rinse well, repeating the process 3 or 4 times, taking care not to break the skin. Then dab the skin with cotton wet with grain alcohol and water, equal parts, and repeat this several times, using fresh cotton each time. *Never use poisonous wood alcohol.*

Another remedy to use after exposure is to bathe with a 5 per cent solution of permanganate of potash in water. A 5 per cent solution of ferric chloride in equal parts of water and glycerine is also effective. Ferric chloride solution is also a preventive, if applied to hands and face and allowed to dry thoroughly, before going where Poison Ivy is prevalent. The most modern method of protection is, however, by injections by a competent physician of a solution prepared from the plant itself.

ERADICATION. Poison Ivy may be killed by spraying or otherwise treating the plants as follows: Soak with 3 lbs. of common salt to 1 gal. of water. Or use 2 lbs. of sodium chlorate per gal. of water; of this apply 1 to 1½ gals. per sq. rod.

This material can also be dusted on the foliage where it absorbs moisture from the air, goes into solution and is taken up by the plant. Do not let powder or solution touch the clothing, for when it dries spontaneous combustion may result.

A thorough wetting with kerosene oil is effective but keep the oil off other plants and the surrounding soil if plants are to be grown there.

1 lb. of sodium arsenite to 5 gals. of water; this is a very poisonous solution and should not be used where cattle might have access to nearby foliage.

Large plants may be killed by cutting the vines at or below ground level and saturating the bases with brine, giving a second application after two weeks. A few drops of crude sulphuric acid applied to the roots every few days will also destroy the plants within a short time.

BEWARE OF POISON SUMAC!
Even more poisonous to the touch than poison ivy, this showy shrub of swampy ground whose leaves turn to brilliant scarlet in the fall is to be admired only at a distance.

POISON SUMAC. Common name for *Rhus vernix,* a tree or shrub to 20 ft. with leaves consisting of 7 to 13 leaflets, smooth above, soft-hairy beneath. It bears greenish-white flowers in loose panicles, followed by somewhat pendent clusters of grayish-white flattened fruits ⅕ in. across. Poison Sumac grows in damp marshy ground, and though the foliage turns a most brilliant scarlet in autumn, it should not be planted, for it is extremely poisonous to many people.

See also POISONOUS PLANTS.

POISONOUS PLANTS. Plants with poisonous qualities may be divided into 2 classes: (1) those causing irritation of the skin when touched, and (2) those poisonous when eaten, either in whole or in part. This article deals only with those kinds likely to be encountered in the garden or nearby woods, or eaten by mistake for an edible species or by experimenting children.

PLANTS POISONOUS TO TOUCH

POISON IVY (*Rhus toxicodendron*) is responsible for a great deal of unhappiness and discomfort. All who frequent the country or undeveloped suburban areas should learn to recognize its glossy leaves of 3 (never 5) leaflets and dull gray berries, and carefully avoid the plant, even those who consider themselves immune to its irritating effects.

POISON SUMAC (*Rhus vernix*) is closely allied to Poison Ivy both botanically and in poisonous properties. It is a tall shrub or small tree, often growing in clumps. The leaves are divided into 7 to 13 leaflets (the odd leaflet at the end), oval or oblong, smooth above and slightly hairy beneath, turning a most attractive, brilliant scarlet in the fall. The greenish flowers, in clusters 8 in. long, are followed by small gray or whitish, rounded or flattened fruits which distinguish it from the harmless red-fruited sumacs which make gay the autumn fields. Poison Sumac grows in the E. States and as far S. as Fla. and La., but is not as widespread as Poison Ivy. The same remedies and methods of eradication should be employed as those recommended under POISON IVY.

POISON-OAK (*Rhus diversiloba*) is the western form of Poison Ivy and occasionally has 5 leaflets instead of 3. It is more shrubby in growth, and the whitish fruit drops soon after ripening, thus doing away with an excellent means of identification. The poisonous qualities are the same as those of *R. toxicodendron*.

COW-PARSNIP (*Heracleum lanatum*), another plant poisonous to touch, is a large herb of the Parsley Family growing to 8 ft. tall in moist soil near streams or in damp meadows. It has large, finely cut leaves and white flowers in broad coarse umbels at the top of tall, stout, grooved white-hairy stems. The whole plant has a disagreeable odor and if touched often causes poisoning like that caused by Poison Ivy. The poisonous agent is called heraclin; the irritation it causes can be treated as recommended under POISON IVY.

PRIMROSE. Different species of Primula, including *P. vulgaris, sinensis, obconica, farinosa, mollis, reticulata* and *auricula*, produce a decided red rash on the skin of certain persons, which can be treated with Poison Ivy remedies. Certain salves are also said to be helpful but this type of poisoning is a difficult problem. See PRIMROSE.

NETTLE. This common wayside weed when touched produces burning and itching, which is caused by the formic acid in the hairs on the leaves; these penetrate the skin and break. The irritation can be relieved by applications of ammonia. Mayweed or Dog-fennel (*Anthemis cotula*), another irritant weed of the Daisy Family, affects some people seriously, others less severely. It was a bane of former harvest workers who reaped and bound grain crops by hand.

The juice of daffodils is distinctly irritant to growers handling the flowers in quantity. *Cypripedium parviflorum* and some Euphorbias (that most likely to be encountered is Snow-on-the-mountain) are irritating in varying degrees to many persons. Little is known about the nature and cure of these effects. It is suggested that local commercial growers of any of these plants be questioned as to the results of their experiences.

PLANTS POISONOUS WHEN EATEN

MUSHROOMS. Plants poisonous when eaten include some mushrooms found at times on shady lawns or in the woodland where a wild garden has been developed. The two poisonous species most often eaten in mistake for the safe and edible meadow mushroom, or because of their attractive appearance, are the Destroying Angel or Death-cup (*Amanita phalloides*) and the so-called Fly Agaric, Fly Amanita, or Fly Mushroom (*Amanita muscaria*). If it appears that either of these plants has been eaten, a doctor should be called immediately, for 98 per cent of those that eat the Destroying Angel die if not given immediate attention, and many hundred deaths are attributable each year to the eating of the Fly Mushroom.

The Destroying Angel has a white, brownish, greenish or yellowish cap, white gills and a ringed stem rising from a cup at the base. Thus it differs from the common Meadow Mushroom, which always has pink or brown gills beneath the cap and *no cup at the base.* (See illustrations under MUSHROOMS.)

The Fly Amanita has a brilliant orange or yellow cap, spotted with white warts; white gills and a ringed stem, rising from a swollen base covered with concentric rings of the fluffy cup. It is frequently found under planted or native birch trees and in open pine-woods where its bright color makes it attractive to children who frequently eat it as an experiment.

Other poisonous plants are:

POISON IVY, POISON SUMAC, AND SOME HARMLESS PLANTS RESEMBLING THEM
Learn to know them apart, and teach others how to do so. 1 and 5 are sprays of Poison Ivy and Poison Sumac, respectively. Beware of them! 2. The 5-lobed Woodbine (Virginia Creeper) leaf. 3. Silky Dogwood (Cornus amomum). 4. Fragrant Sumac (Rhus canadensis). 6, 7, 8. Dwarf, Smooth and Staghorn Sumacs, all harmless. 9. Mountain-ash (Sorbus americana). 10. Black Ash (Fraxinus nigra). 11. Elderberry (Sambucus canadensis). This and the two preceding illustrations reproduced from Cornell Extension Bulletin 191.

Bittersweet (*Solanum dulcamara*), berries sometimes fatal. *Not* False-bittersweet (*Celastrus scandens*).

Boxwood (*Buxus sempervirens*), the whole plant.

Castor-oil-bean (*Ricinus communis*), fatal. Wild Black Cherry or Rum Cherry (*Prunus serotina*), withered leaves quite poisonous.

Christmas-rose (*Helleborus niger*), all parts poisonous, especially the leaves.

Deadly Nightshade (*Solanum nigrum*), berries of some plants very poisonous, especially when green.

Death-camas (*Zygadenus venenosus*), all parts poisonous; root fatal.

Dogwood (Cornus), fruit slightly poisonous.

English Ivy (*Hedera helix*), berries.

False-hellebore (*Veratrum viride* and other species), all parts poisonous, root fatal.

Foxglove (*Digitalis purpurea*), leaves.

Holly (*Ilex aquifolium, opaca, vomitoria*), leaves and berries.

Jack-in-the-pulpit (*Arisaema triphylla*), root is irritant and astringent.

Jimson-weed (*Datura stramomium*), all parts fatal.

Lambkill (*Kalmia angustifolia*), foliage.

Larkspur (Delphinium), foliage and root.

Lily-of-the-valley (*Convallaria majalis*), berries.

Lupine (Lupinus), seeds.

Monkshood (Aconite), foliage and root.

Mountain-laurel (*Kalmia latifolia*), young leaves and shoots fatal to children.

Oleander (*Nerium oleander*), foliage.

Poison-hemlock (*Conium maculatum*), seeds, foliage and root.

Pokeweed (*Phytolacca americana*), root.

Rhubarb (*Rheum rhaponticum*), leaves.

Water-hemlock (*Cicuta maculata*), whole plant, particularly root.

If any of the above plants are known to have been eaten, administer a strong emetic and call a physician immediately. Prompt action is vitally essential in all plant-poisoning cases.

POKEBERRY or POKEWEED. Common names for the genus Phytolacca, a group of New-World herbs, shrubs and trees, occasionally climbers; with undivided leaves, small flowers in terminal clusters followed by fleshy berries.

P. americana (Poke or Skoke), native from Me. to Fla. or Mexico, grows to 12 ft., dying to the ground each fall. It is a strong-smelling plant, but bears attractive small purplish-white flowers in long racemes, followed by reddish-purple berries with a staining juice. The stems and leaves are smooth, often with a bloom or purplish tinge and the plant makes a clean attractive foliage growth for the wild garden. The roots are decidedly poisonous as are the seeds of the berries. The young growth is sometimes used as a substitute for asparagus, but great care should be taken in gathering it in order not to include any of the poisonous root.

Indian-poke is *Veratrum viride*.

POKER-PLANT. A common name for Kniphofia (which see), a genus of ornamental half-hardy perennial herbs known as Torch-lily.

POLEMONIACEAE (pol-ee-moh-ni-ay'-see-ee). The Phlox Family, a group of occasionally woody, widely distributed herbs principally native to N. America. It supplies many flower-garden ornamentals and subjects for greenhouse treatment, principally from the genera Polemonium, Loeselia, Gilia, Collomia, Cantua, Phlox and Cobaea. The regular flowers, borne in heads or clusters, have a tubular, funnel-form, bell- or saucer-shaped perianth; the calyx is cleft in 5 segments, there are 5 petals, and 5 stamens are inserted on the corolla tube.

POLEMONIUM (pol-ee-moh'-ni-um). A small genus of ornamental, tall or dwarf hardy perennials, rarely annuals, belonging to the Phlox Family. The blue, violet or white flowers are showy; the finely cut foliage resembles fern fronds. They are of easy cultivation in any ordinary good garden soil but flourish best in a deep, rich and well-drained loamy soil. The low-growing forms fit well in the rock garden, the taller ones being better suited for backgrounds in the border. They may be grown from seeds or increased by division of the roots.

PRINCIPAL SPECIES

P. caeruleum. Jacobs Ladder, Charity, Greek-valerian. Grows 2 to 3 ft. high; has feather-shaped leaves; leaflets egg-shaped and narrow; flowers bright blue with yellow stamens. There are also varieties bearing white and lilac-blue flowers and one with variegated foliage.

humile (*P. richardsoni*). Dwarf, 6 to 9 in. high with 15 to 21 leaflets; stems many, leafy and downy; bears a faint odor of musk. Var. *pulchellum* has smaller flowers, violet, or in some forms, white.

reptans. Six in. to 1 ft. high; narrow leaves with 7 to 11 egg-shaped leaflets, sharp pointed, smooth; stems leafy and smooth; roots creeping; flowers light blue, sometimes white, drooping, in loose clusters. Equally well suited for the front of the border or on rockwork.

viscosum. To about 4 ft., with sticky, downy leaves of 30 to 40 leaflets about ⅓ in. long; flowers blue or violet, about ¾ in. long.

POLIANTHES (pol-i-an'-theez). A genus of Mexican tuberous herbs of the Amaryllis Family, called the Tuberose (which see), with racemes or spikes of intensely fragrant white flowers.

POLLARD. To cut a tree back to its crown or trunk, or to cut out the main central branch, in order to induce the luxuriant growth of new shoots. Only certain species respond satisfactorily. In America willow trees are perhaps the most familiar subjects, the resulting shoots—called osiers, withes or wickers—being used in making furniture, baskets and other wickerwork. The olive is handled similarly, old trees being thus renewed.

POLLEN. This dusty substance, seen in many opening flowers and inconspicuous in others, consists of the male sex cells of flowering plants. Developed in the anthers or receptacles that surmount the stamens of a flower, pollen grains exhibit great diversity in size, character and design, so that many species may be identified by their distinctive pollens when these are studied under a microscope. They are variously adapted to conveyance by the wind or by insects, depending upon the species.

POLLINATION. The transfer of pollen from the anther of one flower to the stigma of another. Accomplished in nature by wind, insects, etc., it may also be brought about by man by artificial means, in which case the process is called *hand-pollination* or *artificial pollination*. Although pollination is one of the steps in the process of reproduction by seed, fertilization (which see) is also necessary. The two terms are often confused, but should be sharply distinguished, for fertilization does not always follow pollination. For the explanation of "cross-pollination," "self-pollination" and other terms, see FLOWER; PLANT BREEDING.

Plants exhibit many wonderful adaptations and mechanisms developed for the purpose of aiding pollination. Many species are entirely dependent upon bees and other insects for the transfer of their pollen and, hence, for the perpetuation of their kind. This is especially true of those forms with imperfect flowers or that are self-sterile. Others depend upon the wind for pollination; wind-borne pollen will sometimes float for hundreds of miles on the wind currents of the upper atmosphere. Pollen from species normally insect-pollinated is generally unadapted to flying in the wind and often possesses special features, which aid insects. Flower colors and odors, and the nectar of blossoms are considered adaptations for the purpose of attracting insects and aiding cross-pollination.

See FERTILIZATION; FLOWER.

POLYANTHUS (pol-i-an'-thus). A term of Greek origin meaning rich in flowers or many-flowered. It is applied especially to the most popular primrose grown in America—*Primula polyantha,* a hybrid group of garden varieties supposed to have originated from *P. acaulis, P. elatior* and *P. veris,* though credited by some botanists to *P. elatior* alone, by others to *P. acaulis.*

It is also the common name of a species of Narcissus (*N. tazetta*) including the Paperwhite, Soleil d'Or and *orientalis* varieties whose small, fragrant flowers are borne in clusters.

See NARCISSUS.

POLYGALA (poh-lig'-ah-lah). Milkwort. Annual and perennial herbs and shrubs, widely distributed through the temperate and warmer regions of the world. They comprise the principal cultivated genus of the Milkwort Family (Polygalaceae), the flowers of which are irregular, somewhat in the manner of the orchids. Some of the shrubby tender species are grown under glass and outdoors in the warmest parts of the country. The hardy native species do well in light soil and partial shade. Propagated by seeds and cuttings.

P. paucifolia (Fringed Polygala, or Flowering-wintergreen) is a pretty native trailing perennial with light rosy-purple flowers. *P. chamaebuxus* is a hardy creeping evergreen shrub from Europe, with yellow flowers. Its var. *grandiflora* has yellow flowers with purple wings. *P. dalmaisiana,* said to be a hybrid, is a free-blooming bushy plant with rosy-purple flowers, sometimes grown under glass.

POLYGONACEAE (pol-i-goh-nay'-see-ee). The Buckwheat or Knotweed Family, a group of erect or climbing herbs, shrubs and trees widely distributed in both warm and cold climates. The name, derived from the Greek for "many-kneed," refers to the jointed stems. Flowers are individually small and inconspicuous but often showy in mass. Species of several genera are cultivated for ornament and a few for food; among these are Polygonum, Rheum (rhubarb), Rumex, Antigonon, Coccolobis, Muehlenbeckia. Many forms are weeds, such as the docks and various species of Polygonum, like the knotweeds and smartweeds.

POLYGONATUM (pol-i-gon'-ah-tum). A genus of perennial herbs with greenish pendulous flowers. See SOLOMONS SEAL.

POLYGONUM (poh-lig'-oh-num). A very large genus of annual or perennial greenhouse or hardy herbs, rarely undershrubs, of variable habits, found throughout the world but rare in the tropics, belonging to the Buckwheat Family. A large number of them have no ornamental value whatever, particularly Knotweed or Knotgrass (*P. aviculare*), which is a troublesome weed. Several, however, are well worth growing. Silver Lace-vine (*P. auberti*), which has of late become better known, grows to 25 ft. with a wealth of foamy white flower sprays. (See illustration, Plate 58.) It has been found hardy as far north as N. Y. and appears to be entirely free from plant diseases. Leaves of most species are typically large; the flowers minute but often massed in showy spikes or clusters.

The desirable species are of easy culture in any ordinary good garden soil. The annuals, such as the W. dwarf white- or pink-flowered *P. polygaloides* and the tall *P. orientale* (Princes Feather), may be grown from seed sown in the open in spring. If Princes Feather is raised in slight heat and given rich soil, finer plants will result. The perennials such as those listed below may be increased by division.

PERENNIAL SPECIES

P. multiflorum. A Japanese climber with tuberous roots; evergreen in mild climates, with greenish-white flowers in slender clusters.

auberti (China Fleece-vine, Silver Lace-

vine) is a fast-growing climber to 25 ft.; covered with greenish-white, fragrant flowers which are borne in long clusters in late summer.

baldschuanicum is of similar form, but better suited to W. and S. States.

sachalinense (Sacaline) is a coarse, rampant vine which must be used, if at all, with discretion.

sieboldi comes up anew from the roots each year, forming a large, dense shrub.

alpinum grows to 3 ft., with narrow leaves and white flowers in clusters in summer.

amplexicaule (Mountain-fleece) also grows to 3 ft. high; leaves heart- to egg-shaped, up to 6 in. long; stems 2 to 3 ft.; flowers bright rose-red or white, single or in clusters 2 to 6 in. long, borne in September and October.

POLYPLOIDY (pol'-i-ploid-ee). A modern term in the science of genetics given to the condition that exists when a plant (or animal) has a greater number of chromosomes, or microscopic heredity-transmitting bodies, in its cells than are normally found in an individual of that species or variety. Starting with any family or genus, the species having the lowest number of chromosomes would be considered a *diploid*. If that same species has a variety with chromosomes in any multiple of that lowest number (twice, three times, four times as many, etc.), that variety would be considered a *polyploid*. Since the number of chromosomes is an influential factor in their ability to combine and pair off during the process of reproduction, a polyploid may have, or be able to transmit, qualities that a diploid cannot possess or pass on. Thus a hybrid, normally unable to reproduce at all, if a polyploid, might be able to do so.

All this would be of little practical interest to gardeners were it not that plant breeders are finding ways to create polyploids, such as by treating plants with the drug colchicine, which see. The marigold variety, Tetra, much larger than the type from which it was developed, was introduced as a polyploid resulting from such treatment. Although progress in this field is in its infancy, developments of significance and importance may result in due course.

POLYPODIACEAE (pol-i-poh-di-ay'-see-ee). The Common Fern Family, which embraces three-fourths of the ferns of the world. The members are mostly low plants of varying habits, without distinct trunks and growing mostly from prostrate rhizomes. The fronds or leaf-like parts are usually feather-formed, always bearing tiny spore-cases on the under side (when fertile). By this latter characteristic they are distinguished from the so-called Flowering Ferns, Grape Ferns, and other fern-allies. The Polypodiaceae is sometimes known as the True Fern Family. It includes most of the cultivated forms discussed under FERNS.

POLYPODY (pol-i-poh'-dy). Common name for Polypodium, a large genus of ferns including three N. American species and several excellent greenhouse plants. The usually evergreen fronds, rather coarse and leathery, are borne abundantly on surface-creeping rhizomes. The fruit-dots are large and circular, without indusia, and in one or more rows halfway between the midvein and margin. The hardy kinds are shallow rooting, require leafmold and plenty of space; the tender sorts should have a soil of 2 parts loam to 1 part leafmold, and some sand.

The Limestone Polypody belongs to a group formerly included under Polypodium but now placed in the genus Phegopteris, which see. See also FERNS.

HARDY SPECIES

P. incanum (Resurrection Fern, Gray Polypody). Stiff, 2- to 6-in. fronds, with long rounded entire pinnae extending into a wing on either side of the rachis, and gray and hairy on the under side. This species closely resembles *P. virginianum* but is smaller and of S. distribution. It often grows on tree trunks, and is excellent for S. rockeries in woods soil. The first given common name comes from its ability to recover after long extended periods of drought.

scouleri. The W. form of *P. virginianum,* somewhat larger but requiring the same cultivation.

virginianum. Common everywhere in the E. and N. States, on shaded cliffs and boulders and decaying logs. The fronds are from 6 to 10 in. long, dark green, with entire rounded pinnae joined along their bases. Evergreen and delightful for filling in spaces in the rockery, it transplants readily, but should be cut, *not torn,* from the tangled mats in which it grows. (See illustration, Plate 18.)

TENDER SPECIES

P. aureum (Golden Polypody). A vigorous and bold species for warm conditions, with broad 3- to 4-ft. fronds, once-pinnate but of curious shape, the terminal segment being much the longest, and the rachis winged. The abundant, raised, rich yellow fruit-dots give the plant its common name. It needs plenty of water and occasional waterings with weak liquid manure.

conjugatum. A species for the cool greenhouse, with long 2-ft. tapering and glossy fronds, the pinnae entire and waved.

heracleum. A large hothouse species from Java, the stiff 3- to 6-ft. fronds having a densely haired rachis and rising directly from the rhizome in clusters without stipes.

meyenianum (Bears Paw Fern). A curious hothouse species, the fronds 2 to 3 ft. long and once-pinnate. The lower pinnae are sterile, broad and pointed; the upper ones fertile, contracted and recurved, suggesting open claws, and covered with bright yellow sori. Best grown in peat alone, in a basket or hollowed log, with room for the surface rhizomes to spread.

phymatodes. Has bold and deeply lobed fronds, often showing bronze and brownish colors, with large orange fruit-dots below.

plumula (Strap Fern). A curious species from S. Fla., the long entire 2-ft. fronds curled tight like thongs in the dry season.

subauriculatum. A superb plant for the large hothouse, the mature fronds sometimes reaching 6 ft. in length, and the pinnae more than 6 in., with eared lobes at the base. The spores are sunk below the surface. Needs half fibrous loam and half peat; and plenty of light.

vulgare var. *cambricum* (Welsh Polypody). A variety of the hardy British polypody, which very closely resembles our *P. virginianum.* This variety, however, has fronds 18 in. long, deeply serrated and plumed, of a delicate feathery texture and clear light green color. One of the most beautiful of all ferns for the cool greenhouse. Always barren.

POLYPTERIS (poh-lip'-ter-is). Hardy or nearly hardy erect herbs, natives of Mexico and Fla., belonging to the Composite Family. They should be treated as half-hardy annuals. *P. hookeriana,* the single cultivated species, thrives best in warm sandy soil in the border. Seed is sown in April in gentle heat and plants set out in the open, about 1 ft. apart, in June. This species grows 2 to 4 ft. high; narrow leaves, to 4 in. long; small flower-heads, 1 in. or more in diameter, and purple-tipped bracts.

POLYSCIAS (poh-lis'-i-ahs). Tropical shrubs or trees, formerly known as Aralias. They make attractive foliage plants for the warm greenhouse, and grow well in a mixture of fibrous loam, leafmold, and a little old manure, with sand and charcoal to make it porous. Propagated by cuttings of the leafy tops, or heel cuttings from an old cut-back plant.

PRINCIPAL SPECIES

P. filcifolia has very variable leaves, from oblong and entire to very narrow and deeply cut.

fruticosa has coarse, divided leaves, also of variable appearance. Var. *plumata* is a form with fine and narrow leaves.

guilfoylei has long divided leaves mostly edged white. Var. *laciniata* has the white margins cut into narrow pronged teeth. Var. *victoriae* is a good compact form with much divided leaves, often sending up stout suckers.

POLYSTICHUM (poh-lis'-ti-kum). The name (from the Greek meaning "many-tiered," probably in reference to the numerous pinnae) for a genus of ferns commonly called Holly Ferns, closely allied to Nephrolepis (which see), and including species native to the U. S. and others ranging well over the world. They are usually once- or 2-pinnate, toothed, and of a rich dark color, with running rhizomes. The N. American sorts are evergreen, occur in deep woods, and prefer limestone and leafmold. The exotic species, which are among the most reliable greenhouse plants, should have a compost of 3 parts sandy peat and 1 part loam, and must be kept from strong light.

The Tender Holly Fern, a standard house plant, belongs to another genus, Cyrtomium (which see), but resembles the true Holly Ferns in its glossy rich color and prickly lobes.

PRINCIPAL SPECIES

P. acrostichoides (Christmas Fern). One of the most familiar American ferns, its narrow 1- to 2-ft. once-pinnate fronds suggesting the Boston Fern. The round fruit dots appear on the upper third of the blade and nearly cover that surface when ripe. There is much variation in the pinnae, some being deeply toothed, others conspicuously eared at the base, some pointed, and others forked.

brauni (Brauns Holly Fern). Thick, rigid, shining fronds, tapering at both ends, 2-pinnate, the stipe covered with chaff. Confined to the N. States and Canada.

coriaceum (Leather Fern). A tall-growing sort from S. Africa, suitable for the cool greenhouse. Its broadly triangular 2- to 3-ft. fronds are shining and once-pinnate, very tough and lasting. Water thoroughly only when moisture is needed.

lonchitis (American Holly Fern). Rigid, 8- to 16-in. fronds, once-pinnate, the pinnae curved below like a scythe blade and prickly edged. A N. species, chiefly of Canada.

mucronatum. A dwarf species for the warm greenhouse, much like *P. lonchitis* but of a richer, darker color and less rigid.

munitum (Giant Holly Fern, Dagger or Sword Fern). The far W. species corresponding to the Christmas Fern but with fronds 3 to 4 ft. long and more rigid and leathery.

tensemense (Tsushima Holly Fern). A Japanese species for the cool greenhouse producing compact tufts of slender, erect, 12- to 15-in. 2-pinnate fronds. Likes a stiffer soil than the other species.

POMADERRIS (poh-mah-der'-is). Trees and shrubs of Australia and New Zealand, belonging to the Buckthorn Family. One or two species are grown for ornament in the warmest parts of this country. Propagated by cuttings of half-ripened shoots.

P. apetala (Victorian-hazel) grows to 15 ft. or more, with leaves white beneath, and long clusters of greenish-white flowers without petals. *P. elliptica* grows to 8 ft., with leaves white beneath and clusters of bright yellow flowers. *P. lanigera* is a tall shrub with the young branches and under side of leaves covered with soft rusty hairs. It has large clusters of pale yellow flowers.

POME. A fleshy fruit composed of several parts (carpels) naturally grown together, containing a parchment-like inner layer (endocarp) in which are the seeds (popularly called "pips"). Typical examples are the apple, pear and quince. Pomes do not open in any regular manner, as do peas and beans, or poppy or radish pods. See also BERRY; DRUPE; FRUIT.

POMEGRANATE. A large tropical and subtropical bush (*Punica granatum*) grown for its brilliant orange-red flowers and its large, hard-rinded, juicy, pulpy fruits, about the size of oranges and with many seeds. There is a dwarf form (var. *nana*) suitable for greenhouse culture and small gardens; other varieties have white, red, variegated, and double, striped flowers. In the Gulf States and other warm areas the pomegranate is a popular garden subject and somewhat grown commercially in deep, heavy loams. In orchards, bushes are set about 15 ft. apart; for hedges, they are set 6 to 8 ft. apart. They are propagated by seeds and layers, but chiefly by hardwood cuttings taken in spring.

POMELO (pom'-e-loh). An American synonym for the Grapefruit (which see), erroneously applied in the E. Indies to the pummelo or shaddock, which see. See also CITRUS FRUITS.

PONCIRUS (pon-sy'-rus). Trifoliate-orange. A small, spiny deciduous tree of China, belonging to the Rue Family. It is largely grown as a stock on which to graft citrus fruits to increase their hardiness, but in warm regions it is also used for hedges and lawn planting, and can stand as far N. as N. J. The fragrant white flowers, which open in advance of the leaves, are followed by very aromatic, very acid, small orange-like fruit. Propagated by seeds.

POND. As distinguished from a pool or water garden, a pond is a natural body of water included within the garden area, or a water feature made to appear natural.

In making a natural pond one of the features of the garden consideration must first be given to the source and quantity of the water supply. Contrary to general opinion, a steady and robust stream of water passing through it is *not* desirable. In addition to floating out valuable surface vegetation, running water is likely to damage the tender waterlilies and other plants and prevent their attaining full perfection. The idea that the pond must be supplied with a steady flow rises from the fear that standing water may become stagnant and a breeding place for malaria-bearing mosquitoes. But if it is well-stocked with plant- and fish-life, this danger is completely avoided. The only incoming water needed is just enough to replace losses through evaporation or leakage.

In view of this, streams entering the pond should be diverted around it at a con-

siderable distance, if possible by an open ditch; or perhaps, if it is not too expensive an undertaking, carried through it by a terra cotta or cement pipe. The diversion pipe or ditch must be large enough to carry any sudden flood water and prevent an overflow of muddy and unpleasant muck to pollute the pond. The ditch itself may be made an extremely ornamental part of the landscaping by the judicious use of aquatic and semi-aquatic plants. See AQUATIC PLANTS; BOG GARDEN.

To provide automatic replenishing of the pond waters and protect against flooding, it is advisable to install a floating ball valve at the inlet. Obtainable at any hardware or plumbing store, this can be installed without difficulty.

Before planting a natural pond to tender tropical lilies, it might be well to investigate the water temperature so as to make sure that it is not fed by underwater springs too cold to permit the pond warming up to a healthy temperature for the plant materials considered.

POND CYPRESS. Common name for *Taxodium ascendens,* a deciduous cone-bearing tree.

POND-LILY. A common name for Waterlily (which see). The Yellow Pond-lily is Nymphozanthus, the Cow-lily (which see) or Spatterdock.

PONDWEED. Common name for a large genus of aquatic herbs, the Potamogetons. It includes more than 100 species of the tropical and temperate regions, all attractive enough in appearance. Some have elliptic and others strap-like leaves, beautifully veined; still others long grass-like leaves. However, they have not been very satisfactory in cultivation and are most likely to come to the gardener's attention by being a nuisance in the lily pond.

Cape-pondweed is another genus, Aponogeton, which see.

PONTEDERIA (pon-te-dee'-ri-ah) *cordata.* A fine, native aquatic, blue-flowered, with large arrow-shaped leaves, found growing in shallow waters from Nova Scotia to the Gulf. See PICKEREL-WEED.

POOL, GARDEN. See GARDEN POOL.

POOR-MANS-ORCHID. Another name for Schizanthus or Butterfly-flower, a genus of large annual or biennial herbs of easy culture in greenhouse or garden, bearing innumerable showy variously colored flowers.

POOR - MANS WEATHER - GLASS. Common name for Anagallis (which see), also called Pimpernel.

POPLAR. Common name for Populus, a genus of soft-wooded deciduous trees of rapid growth, members of the Willow Family. They have alternate leaves and bear flowers in catkins, followed by seeds often surrounded by cottony hairs. Because of their rapid growth, they are extensively planted in dry prairie regions for windbreaks and avenues, and also for ornamental purposes. But they are not generally long-lived and as their long roots are likely to find their way into drains and clog them up, or upheave pavements, they should be placed with care. Their graceful trunks and their light airy leaves, rustling in the slightest breeze, combine to make them cheerful companionable trees, but those species with conspicuously white-lined leaves should be placed among darker-leaved deciduous trees or before evergreens to get the full beauty of their form and coloring. Because of its symmetrical columnar effect the Lombardy Poplar has been much planted for accents and boundaries, but in the E. States it is short-lived and within a few years becomes unsightly. In the W. States it attains great size and beauty and may be used in landscape work with confidence, always remembering that a tree of such pronounced type of growth should be planted among other types to avoid monotony.

ENEMIES. Poplars are subject to several types of diseases. At least four leaf rusts, with alternate hosts on hemlock, larch and fir, may interfere with the growth of young trees. The European poplar canker frequently kills Lombardy poplars in the nursery and trees recently set out; the general effects are the death of twigs and small limbs and disfiguring open wounds on trunk and larger limbs. Prune off limbs and cut out cankered areas. Cytospor, a canker which is destructive during periods of drought, may be prevented by keeping trees in a vigorous healthy condition by proper feeding and watering.

Insects that feed on poplar foliage include the willow leaf-beetle, satin moth, spiny elm caterpillar and cottonwood leaf-beetle; use a poison spray if they become serious. The oyster-shell scale is a common pest; and the poplar and willow curculio, the native poplar borer and the cottonwood borer may be very injurious. For the latter two use carbon bisulphide or calcium cyanide in the burrows, or cut and burn badly infested trees.

The poplars grow readily in any soil, though the species called Cottonwood are found growing naturally in low land near rivers. They are easily propagated by seed or hardwood cuttings, and often will reach a height of 90 ft.

PRINCIPAL SPECIES

P. balsamifera (Cottonwood), with glossy heart-shaped leaves, is native from Quebec to Fla. and Tex. A moderately long-lived tree of stately appearance, it is one of the most widely planted of all, being especially valuable in dry regions. On the home grounds the staminate form should be planted, as the seeds borne by the pistillate tree are surrounded by a dense cotton which becomes unsightly if it accumulates on the ground.

alba (White Poplar, Abele). An Old-World tree, to 90 ft. or more, with lobed leaves, having whitish or grayish down beneath. Its var. *nivea,* with leaves densely white beneath, is found in many regions as an escape in the U. S., where, suckering freely, it has become quite a nuisance. Other varieties are *pyramidalis,* of close columnar form; *globosa,* small with a rounded head; and *pendula,* with drooping branches.

nigra (Black Poplar) has triangular leaves, light green beneath. It is best known through its var. *italica* (Lombardy Poplar), of distinct columnar growth, which is frequently planted.

canadensis (Carolina Poplar) probably a hybrid between *P. nigra* and *P. balsamifera,* is a beautiful rapid-growing tree, also best known by its pyramidal var. *eugenei.*

candicans (Balm-of-Gilead), a strong-growing tree extensively planted in Europe. It makes an excellent shade tree on the lawn and is good for avenue planting, but is liable to attack by oyster-shell scale.

tremula (European Aspen), to 60 ft. with leaf-stalks flattened, tilting the leaves and causing them to flutter in the slightest breeze. Var. *pendula* is an extremely graceful tree with drooping branches; notable in the very early spring for the profuse growth of slender pendent catkins.

tremuloides (American Aspen) is a small tree with leaves hung on such slender stalks that they flutter restlessly. The clear yellow of the autumn foliage, especially in

Plate 41.   POPPIES PLEASE THROUGHOUT THE SEASON

Upper left: The crinkled silky bloom of the oriental poppy, Perry's White.   Upper right: Shirley poppies with their varied rosy hues add great charm to the annual border.   Lower left: Striking color accents are contributed by the very double blossoms of the carnation poppy.   Lower right: New and interesting developments in the attractive race of annual poppies.

the W. forms, in contrast with the silvery white trunks and limbs, makes a most pleasing note in a woodland planting.

POPPY. Common name for the genus Papaver, which comprises a number of annual and perennial herbs having showy flowers of much decorative value in the garden; also applied to other genera in the Poppy Family (Papaveraceae). (See illustrations, Plate 41.) The graden species and their varieties have a great range of color, and as they are of easy culture, they are very widely used in beds, borders, and in the rock garden. *P. orientale* and *P. bracteatum* are true perennials; all the others are annuals, or perennials that bloom the first year from seed. Seed for the annual species is sown in the fall or very early in the spring in light warm soil in an open, sunny position in the spot where the plants are to stand, and the seedlings thinned out, for it is exceedingly difficult to transplant the annual types. The perennial *P. orientale* is increased by seed, by division and by root-cuttings in August. It should be planted in full sun, and in gritty, well-drained soil, as standing water causes the roots to rot.

Bacterial blight causes black lesions on stems, leaves, floral organs and seed pods of Oriental and Shirley Poppies. The leaf tissues between the black spots turn yellow, then brown, and the leaf falls; if the stems are girdled the plants die. The only known control is to destroy the plants in infected beds and to disinfect the soil.

The black bean aphid and the spinach aphid both infest poppies but can be controlled by throughly spraying the under side of leaves with nicotine-sulphate or dusting with nicotine dust.

PRINCIPAL SPECIES

P. orientale, 3 ft. tall or more, has large coarsely cut leaves, covered with bristly hairs, and brilliant scarlet flowers, blotched with black at the base of each petal. Within recent years many new varieties have been developed, carrying the color range from pale pink through salmon to maroon. Oriental Poppies, though their blooming season is short, give a most brilliant effect in the border, and later their fading foliage may be concealed if perennial babys breath is planted among them.

bracteatum, Perennial. Is one of the parents of the new hybrid Oriental Poppies, differing from *P. orientale* in having solid color petals and leafy bracts below the flowers.

rhoeas (Corn or Flanders Poppy) is the common Field Poppy of Europe and Asia, usually having cinnabar-red flowers, blotched with black. It is known in the garden under various forms, the most popular being the Shirley Poppy, a strain now available in shades varying from pure white through pink and rose, to bright scarlet, without the dark base.

nudicaule (Iceland Poppy), to 1 ft., a perennial blooming the first year from seed, and rarely lasting more than three years in the garden. It has charming white, orange, or reddish, fragrant flowers with a number of brilliant varietal forms.

somniferum (Opium Poppy), a handsome annual plant, native of Greece and the Orient, growing to 4 ft. with grayish-green foliage and large flowers from white to purple in color. Among its horticultural forms are the carnation-flowered type with fringed petals and the peony-flowered type which has very double blossoms. Among the single forms, one of the most attractive is Danebrog, or Danish Cross, in which the white spots at the bases of the petals form a cross.

alpinum (Alpine Poppy). Perennial, from the Alps, a low-growing delicate plant with finely cut grayish foliage and fragile, white or yellow, delightfully scented blossoms. It should be planted in a sunny, well-drained part of the rock garden, in soil composed largely of rock chips and sand.

glaucum (Tulip Poppy) has grayish-green foliage and cup-shaped scarlet flowers, 4 in. across, borne on 2 ft. stems.

pavoninum (Peacock Poppy), to 1 ft., has small scarlet, black-spotted blossoms.

californicum (Western Poppy) has brick-red flowers, marked with green at the base of the petals. It should not be confused with the true California Poppy (*Eschscholzia californica*), which see.

rupifragum, with finely cut leaves, has pale red blossoms borne on 1½ ft. stalks. It should be planted in poor sandy soil in the rock garden, as it becomes weedy when grown in rich ground.

For other kinds of poppy see: Argemone (Mexican or Prickly Poppy); Bush- or Tree-poppy (Dendromecon); Celandine-poppy (Stylophorum); Echscholzia (California Poppy); Glaucium (Horned or Sea Poppy); Meconopsis; Plume-poppy (Macleaya); Romneya (Matilija Poppy); Snow Poppy (Eomecon); Water-poppy (Hydrocleis).

POPPY-MALLOW. Common name for Callirhoë, a genus of N. American herbs with showy pink or purple flowers.

POPULUS (pop'-eu-lus). Generic name for Poplar, which see.

PORCELAIN-BERRY. A common name for *Ampelopsis brevipedunculata* (formerly considered a variety of *A. heterophylla*), a useful, hardy vine or climbing shrub whose berries take on in fall beautiful shades of lilac, green, blue, etc., clearly suggestive of the name. See AMPELOPSIS.

PORTUGAL-LAUREL. Common name for *Prunus lusitanica,* a small broad-leaved evergreen often grown in cold climates as a tub plant, and in warm ones as an outdoor ornamental.

PORTUGUESE DAISY. Common name for *Chrysanthemum lacustre,* a tall perennial with long-stemmed white flower-heads. Also called Portuguese Chrysanthemum.

PORTULACA (paur-teu-lay'-kah). A genus of hardy, mostly perennial, fleshy, more or less succulent, low-growing or ascending herbs distributed all over the world. Commonly called Purslane, they are members of the Purslane Family, which includes Claytonia and Talinum. The flowers, which open only in sunlight, are single or double and may be purple, yellow, or pink. Treated usually as half-hardy annuals, purslanes may be used for massing in beds, as edging plants, on rock work and walls and on bare sunny banks. They succeed in any good garden soil, preferring a mixture of loam, leafmold and coarse sand and a sunny position. Seed should be sown where plants are to grow, but as it is very fine, a more even distribution may be obtained by mixing it with dry soil or sand before sowing.

The common wild sort (*P. oleracea* var. *sativa*), usually called "pusley," is often a troublesome, persistent garden weed. Small portions of the fleshy pink stems will take root under adverse conditions and whole plants pulled up and thrown aside will often stay alive long enough to permit the taproot to bend over and re-enter the ground. The weed can be destroyed by spraying with iron sulphate (which see). But its tender young tips and fleshy leaves make very acceptable greens, resembling New Zealand spinach (which see), so it

may be worth while to leave a few plants in some corner where they will not cause trouble.

P. grandiflora (Rose-moss, Sun-plant). Low growing to 1 ft. high; leaves scattered, about 1 in. long; flowers red, white and yellow, sometimes striped, up to 1 in. or more in diameter. A popular subject for warm sunny locations in the garden.

P. oleracea var. *sativa* (Kitchen-garden Purslane). Low, spreading by thick, succulent reddish stems radiating from the crown. Flowers small, bright yellow. An ornamental form (var. *giganthes*) bears double flowers.

Winter-purslane is *Montia perfoliata,* a white-flowered annual herb of the same family sometimes grown as a salad or pot herb.

PORTULACACEAE (paur-teu-lah-kay'-see-ee). Botanical name of the Purslane Family, a group of widely distributed fleshy herbs, chiefly native to the tropics of the W. hemisphere. The flowers, of 2 sepals and either 4 or 5 petals, usually open only in the sunshine, the petals soon withering. A few genera are grown for ornament or as pot herbs, among them Portulaca, Montia, Calandrinia, Claytonia and Talinum.

POSSUM-HAW. Common name for one of the S. Hollies (*Ilex decidua*), a shrub or tree with orange or red berries, found in swampy situations.

POTASH. A compound (oxide) of potassium. The name was given when it was obtained by steeping wood ashes in an iron pot, a method rarely used today. In addition to the natural oxide and carbonate so obtained, the name potash has been extended to include the sulphate and muriate now used as fertilizers.

Potash is necessary to healthy plant growth; under ordinary cultivation the supply in the soil becomes exhausted, calling for the use of manure, compost and special potash fertilizers. The oldest and one of the best sources is wood ash, for any vegetable matter yields potash when burned. Ashes from the open fireplace or chunk-burner, though small in bulk, contain as much as 7 per cent potash, and should be scattered on the soil of the vegetable and flower gardens whenever available in winter, or stored in a dry place for use in spring. Small quantities may be applied to the lawn also if sprinkled thinly, but none should be used on any acid-soil plant or evergreen, as the ash contains some lime.

Of the chemical potash fertilizers, the sulphate is usually the best, the muriate cheapest. These should be applied at the rate of not more than 3 lbs. to 100 sq. ft. and frequent smaller applications are best.

Potash helps strengthen stem and leaf growth, improves flower, fruit, seed and root crops generally. It is specially valuable on potatoes, beets and onions.

POTASSIUM PERMANGANATE. A granular crystalline chemical of deep purple color occasionally used in garden operations as a disinfectant. Sometimes recommended for treating iris rhizomes in the control of soft rot; and as a cure for ivy poisoning. See POISON IVY.

POTASSIUM SULPHIDE. A chemical compound known as livers of sulphur and used in the control of mildew. See FUNGICIDE.

POTATO. A tropical and subtropical, perennial herb (*Solanum tuberosum*) now extensively grown in temperate countries for use as a vegetable, a source of starch and for other commercial purposes. It is closely related to egg-plant, tomato and pepper (Capsicum) and like them is tender to frost.

Commercially potatoes are produced by two classes of growers: (1) truckers, mostly in the South, who grow for the early markets; and (2) farmers, mainly in the North, who supply the late and winter demands. Among both groups are specialists who grow selected, improved varieties and use machinery especially devised for large-scale planting, fertilizing, culti-

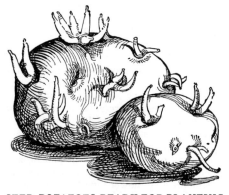

SEED POTATOES READY FOR PLANTING
These tubers have sprouted just enough to facilitate growth—and not too much. Take care in cutting and planting not to break off the tender shoots.

vating, spraying, digging and sorting. Potatoes are therefore abundant and, generally, inexpensive.

For these reasons and because the crop requires considerable hand-work when grown on a small scale, it is less popular in gardens than formerly. Also the space it requires over the entire season can be more satisfactorily used for crops that cannot be obtained in as good condition from markets, stores, etc., such as salads, herbs, and so on. Nevertheless, where space is available potatoes are a good home-garden crop, particularly for an early season supply to which this article especially refers.

SOIL AND PLANTING. Potatoes thrive best in sandy loam soils rich in humus, well drained but retentive of moisture and well supplied with potash. However, a satisfactory crop can be grown in any good garden soil. Stable manure if used is best applied to the previous crop; or plowed under the previous autumn so it may become well decayed before the potatoes are planted. Should the soil need sweetening, it should not be limed within a year prior to planting because lime, as well as wood ashes (which are 30 per cent lime) and fresh manure, tend to make the tubers scabby. Plowing under clover-sod or other leguminous green-manure crop is a good preparation for potatoes. The land should be deeply plowed or dug and made fine by harrowing or raking or both. Also commercial fertilizer rich in potash should be worked in either over the whole area or in the furrows (or hills). But keep it from coming in direct contact with the "seed" (cut tubers) or it may burn them. Always mix the fertilizer with the soil *below* where the tubers are to be placed; the roots will go down and get it.

In the home garden potatoes are generally planted in "hills," scooped out with a hoe, 3 to 4 in. deep and 18 to 24 in. apart. But planting in drills involves less labor (especially if they are made with hand or power machines) and generally gives more satisfactory results. In this case the seed pieces are dropped in furrows 3 to 5 in. deep at intervals of 6 or 8 in.; or, preferably, two pieces together at intervals of 15 to 18 in., thus forming "hills." The space between rows should be not less than 18 in. for wheelhoe culture or 30 in. for horse or garden tractor tillage.

The former practice of earthing up the hills or rows not only wastes time and labor but also, except in wet land, produces poorer results than level culture. However, at the last cultivation slight earthing up may be advisable to prevent exposing any tubers to the light, which makes them green, tough and undesirable—and possibly dangerous—for consumption.

For "seed" purposes choose tubers that are well formed, of moderate to large size and with shallow eyes (this type is better for peeling). Small tubers and the tip ends of large ones (the end where the eyes are crowded together) should be discarded because they produce many shoots that compete with one another and thus reduce the yield. The remainder of each tuber should be cut in large pieces each bearing at least one eye, preferably two, and not more than three. If any pieces must be kept a day or more before planting, dust the cut surfaces with gypsum.

The most important step in securing early potatoes is choosing a quick maturing variety. The time between planting and harvest may be shortened still further by spreading the seed potatoes one layer deep where they will be in strong sunlight and a temperature of 60 degrees or more for two or three weeks before planting. Instead of developing long, brittle, white shoots, as potatoes usually do toward spring when stored in dark, damp cellars, these light-exposed tubers develop short, tough, dark colored rosettes which, if not broken off when planted, will rapidly develop into plants. In warm, rich, sandy loams the time between planting and harvesting may thus be reduced to seven or even six weeks in the case of the earliest varieties.

Main-crop potatoes should be kept green and vigorous throughout the season, being cultivated (not too deep nor too close), and sprayed regularly. When the vines die or are killed by frost, and before the ground freezes, dig carefully with a spading fork when the soil is not wet. Let the tubers dry for a few hours, then gather them, taking care not to bruise them, and store in a dark, moist, cool (just above freezing) cellar or pit. Early potatoes may be dug as soon as they are large enough to use, a few hills at a time as needed.

Potato Enemies

DISEASES. The potato seems to be subject to more diseases than other vegetables but the severity of any one trouble depends largely on the section of the country and on weather conditions. Late blight (due to *Phytophthora infestans*) which caused the great Irish famine of 1844, is probably most generally destructive. Wet seasons favor the disease, which first shows as

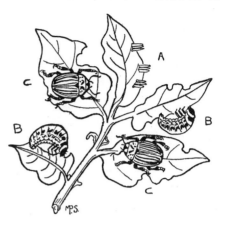

POTATO BUGS AT WORK
Actually they are beetles. From eggs (A) attached to the leaves, hatch unpleasant grubs (B), which develop into the familiar hard-shelled adults (C). Both the latter stages attack plants and should be poisoned.

water-soaked areas on the leaves, with a white mold on the under side. Tubers are rotted as a result of spores being washed down into the soil. Protect by spraying with 5—5—50 bordeaux mixture every 10 to 14 days throughout the season.

Rhizoctonia, another fungus, appears as brown corky sclerotia (spore bodies) on the potato skins, often thought to be merely dirt. The cooking quality is not affected but if such potatoes are used for seed the seedlings may be girdled and die. Soak seed potatoes before cutting in corrosive sublimate 1 to 1000 for 1½ hours.

Common scab affects chiefly the appearance of the tubers. Treat seed potatoes as for rhizoctonia and keep the soil acid by using sulphate of ammonia as the source of nitrogen in feeding the crop, or by adding inoculated sulphur to the soil.

For black leg, which is a bacterial soft rot of the base of the stem, treat seed as for rhizoctonia.

Fusarium wilt causes rapid collapse of the plant. In cutting seed discard tubers showing discoloration. The symptoms of the several virus diseases of potatoes are indicated by the names—mosaic, leaf roll, spindle tuber, and yellow-dwarf. Control consists in use of seed from clean fields and the control of the insect carriers, namely, aphids and leaf hoppers.

INSECTS. About six are likely to be serious. The best known is the Colorado potato beetle; both the larvae (soft, dark red with black head and spots) and the adults (convex hard-shelled yellow beetles with black stripes) feed on the foliage, and there are two generations a year. Spray or dust the foliage with arsenate of lead or calcium arsenate.

The very small, shiny, jet-black potato flea beetle eats small round holes in the leaves until they appear sieve-like. Repel them by spraying with bordeaux mixture which also controls the leaf hopper, which sucks out the plant juice sometimes until the margins and tips of the leaves die, causing what is called "hopper burn." For the potato aphid, a large pink or green plant louse, spray with nicotine-sulphate and remove wild rose-bushes from the vicinity. White grubs (which see) and wireworms (which see) may eat the tubers.

Air-potato is *Dioscorea bulbifera.* Sweet potato (which see) is *Ipomoea batatas.*

POTATO-VINE. Common name for *Solanum jasminoides* (also known as Jasmine Nightshade), a shrubby Brazilian vine with star-shaped, bluish-white flowers.

P O T E N T I L L A (poh-ten-til'-ah). Cinquefoil; Five-finger. A genus of mostly hardy sub-shrubs or herbs, rarely annuals, natives of the N. hemisphere, and belonging to the Rose Family. The flowers are usually yellow, and sometimes white, but in the newer hybrid forms there are shades of orange, red, crimson and pink in both single and double forms. They are suitable for beds and borders and some of the species are good subjects for rockwork and bare banks. They thrive in sunny positions in any ordinary good garden soil but prefer sandy soils. They may be readily increased by seed or by division of the roots. The newer hybrid forms are of more importance than the species, both for appearance in the garden and for cutting, the flowers being borne from July to September.

PRINCIPAL SPECIES

P. alpestris. Perennial, from 6 to 12 in. high; basal leaves of 5, sometimes 7 wedge-shaped leaflets, deeply cut in the upper half; bright yellow flowers about 1 in. across, borne in July.

nepalensis. Rose-colored; variety Miss Willmott especially recommended.

atrosanguinea. Blood-red; 18 in. tall.

warrensi. Tall; clear yellow flowers.

recta. Large plant; sulphur flowers.

nitida. Rose-colored; for rock garden.

anserilla (Silverweed). Low, creeping, with yellow flowers.

fruticosa (*Dasiphora fruticosa*). From 2 to 4 ft. high; feather-shaped leaves, narrow, tapering, downy leaflets up to 1 in. long; sparse yellow flowers, 1½ in. across, borne in summer. There are several varieties of this species not now so well known but listed as: *albicans, dahurica, friedrichseni, ochroleuca, parvifolia, purdomi, tenuifolia, veitchi, vilmoriniana.*

villosa. A native of China, about 1 ft. high; leaves parted into 3 leaflets, coarsely toothed, silky above, hairy beneath; flowers creamy.

POT HERB. Any plant whose young succulent parts are boiled and eaten as "greens"—such as spinach, mustard, fetticus, and possibly cabbage. See HERBS.

POTHOS (poh'-thos). A trade name for the genus Scindapsus, commonly called Ivy-arum (which see) because of the climbing habit and calla-like flowers (spathes). It comprises tropical climbing shrubs grown in greenhouses in cold countries.

POT MARJORAM. A little used common name for *Origanum vulgare,* perennial herb grown for its fragrant foliage. See MARJORAM.

POT PLANTS. A term commonly used by florists and commercial plant growers for plants produced and handled to be sold and grown on in flower pots for their decorative effect. The term "potted plants" is often used by laymen in the same sense. Such plants may be either flowering subjects, as Calceolarias, Cyclamens, Begonias, Primulas, Kalanchoë; bulbous materials such as Easter lilies, tulips, hyacinths, etc.; or foliage plants, as ferns, dracenas, crotons, palms, aspidistras, etc. In all cases they are carried in pots from their earliest stages until they are discarded, and are not grown in greenhouse benches or used as a source of cut flowers.

Pot plants may be grown from seed, from cuttings or as grafted specimens, They are essentially greenhouse subjects, although in the course of their growth some of them may spend part of the summer out of doors or perhaps in a cool storage shed or cellar. Representing many genera they naturally differ greatly in their cultural requirements, and as they often represent also the results of the highest skill in plant management they are in many cases not logical subjects for the home gardener to attempt. In other cases, however, a pot plant may be merely the Boston fern, the English ivy, the Jerusalem-cherry, or the wax-plant that remains year after year an attractive feature of the home conservatory or even the living-room. See HOUSE PLANTS.

Factors in the production of quality pot plants include: Choice of suitable, improved varieties that will meet with popular favor; propagation methods that will give the desired stock of uniformly vigorous, thrifty young plants; preparation of the best soil mixture; proper handling as regards shifting, pinching, watering, feeding, and all other cultural details; development of the plants to just the right stage at the time when they are most in demand—as at Christmas, Easter, etc.; and placing them on the market in such condition that they will attract buyers and, when bought, give the purchaser maximum satisfaction.

POTTING or POTTING-UP. The transferring of plants from seedling flats, cutting benches and other propagating quarters to flower pots; also the re-potting or shifting (which see) of larger plants from one pot to another. Though the operation is simple, failure to perform it properly is a common cause of failure with pot plants.

For a proper start, seeds should be sown thinly in seed pans or flats so the seedlings will have room to grow, without becoming spindly, until they have formed their second pair of true leaves. At this stage they may either be pricked-out into other flats to develop for 2 to 4 weeks more or potted directly into 2-in. pots—never larger. See PRICKING-OUT; TRANSPLANTING.

Cuttings should also be given plenty of space while striking root. The best stage at which to pot them is when their roots are not more than ¼ in. long. If done much sooner they are likely to develop slowly; if done later, they are more difficult to handle and they are liable to suffer a check through the breakage of roots.

Soil for potting should be light, well supplied with humus and sand, moderately fertile, well sifted, uniformly mixed and damp, but not wet. A good test is to squeeze a handful hard; if any water comes out the soil is too wet; if it falls apart quickly when the hand is opened, it is too dry; if it retains its shape as squeezed and merely cracks slightly, it is damp enough.

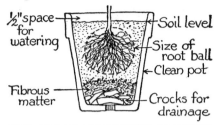

POT PLANT CORRECTLY PLANTED
Idealized diagram to show the important points to look out for in potting: Cover drainage hole in pot with pieces of broken crock, and this with a layer of moss or other fibre to prevent the soil washing through. Be sure the pot is clean and of the right size for the root mass. And leave half an inch above the soil level to hold water until it sinks in.

Correct potting of cuttings and seedlings consists in (1) placing each little plant in the center of its 2-in. flower pot at the same depth at which it stood in the seed bed or the cutting bench; (2) firming the soil around the roots, and (3) refraining from filling the pot with soil. In a 2-in. pot, ¼ in. (proportionately more in larger pots) must be left between soil surface and pot rim to hold water. If the soil is even with the rim the water runs off instead of soaking in and the plants suffer or die from thirst.

After-care until the little plants have become established is important. The pots must be set *level,* preferably on an inch of sand on a bench or, if out of doors, an inch deep in sifted coal ashes. Unless they are level the pots will not hold enough water. Shade the newly potted plants for from 3 days to a week, the time and density depending on the season and the strength of the sunlight. Less shade is needed in winter than in summer.

Never let the plants suffer for lack of moisture. Herein lies the value of the sand and the ashes under or around the pots; both retain moisture well and at the same time provide good drainage. Water early in the morning so any excess will have drained off or evaporated before night.

KNOCKING-OUT. Just as soon as the developing plant has used all the food in the small pot and filled the soil space with its roots, it must be *shifted* to a larger container or it will be stunted. Experienced growers can recognize the shifting stage at a glance; the novice can determine it by "knocking out" the plant thus: place one hand, palm down, on top of the pot with the plant stem between the first and second fingers; turn the pot and plant upside down (steadying it with the other hand) and rap the rim of the pot on the edge of a bench or any solid wooden surface. The ball of soil will slide into the one hand and the pot remain in the other. If only a few roots are visible the plant is not ready for a shift and should be replaced in the pot, the *bottom* of which should then be rapped on the bench to firm the ball of soil back into the pot. Never press the loosened ball back into the pot (as is done in potting a plant the first time) as it might break the roots. If however, the roots have formed a dense network around the outside of the earth ball, and especially if they are becoming dark colored, the plant is ready to be shifted at once. In all cases shift only to the next larger size pot.

Be sure the soil is merely moist when a plant is knocked out. If very dry the ball may fall apart; if wet the soil may puddle and later bake.

SHIFTING. Always have the ball of soil moist when it is repotted. If it is dry no amount of watering later will wet it. Always use clean pots.

Before placing a plant in the next larger size pot, break and shake the surface soil off as far down as the roots because it has been depleted of its original supply of plant food by the plant and by leaching. The plant is then placed on some good soil in the new pot, more soil is added around the sides and on top of the root ball, the soil is gently firmed with the thumbs and the bottom of the pot is then given a sharp rap on the bench to further firm the soil. As before, avoid setting the plant either too deep or too shallow.

While the plants are in 2-, 3- or 4-in. flower pots they need little or no special drainage, but from the time they are in 5-in. pots, they require it. Drainage is provided by placing a curved piece of broken pot, convex side up, over the drainage hole and a few other pieces on top of it. This not only allows excess water to pass out, but also admits the necessary air to the soil. An inch of drainage material is enough for a 5- or 6-in. pot;

larger sizes need 2 in. or more. Cinders, fine gravel, or broken stone on the greenhouse bench or in the coldframe supply drainage and aëration for the pots placed upon them. If plants must be left on the bench for long, they should be lifted occasionally to prevent their rooting through the drainage hole. See also PLANTING.

POTTING SHED. That part of a greenhouse or other garden workshed (or, sometimes, a separate structure) in which such indoor gardening operations as potting up plants and bulbs, making cuttings and grafts, and the like are done, and where the necessary supplies and appliances for such work are kept. In large greenhouse establishments the potting shed is centrally located with respect to the different houses and usually is near the boiler room for comfort in winter. In the small garden the potting shed can often be conveniently combined with the tool shed.

In addition to arrangements for the convenient placing of tools where they will be out of the way yet ready to hand, the potting shed should provide bins for the storage of soil-mixture ingredients that cannot be secured in winter; places for the safe storage of seeds, bulbs, spray materials, commercial fertilizers, flower pots and saucers, flats and the hundred and one other things that permit gardening to be done with maximum efficiency and enjoyment. As a successful garden is neat and orderly, so its potting shed is kept clean and in order; this assists in keeping all the tools in the bright keen condition that enables them to do the best work.

POULTRY MANURE. Poultry droppings are at least twice as valuable a plant food as cow manure on the basis of the nutrients they contain, an average analysis being nitrogen, 1.6 per cent, phosphoric acid 1.75 per cent, potash .9 per cent. They are, however, much drier and lighter and tend to ferment much more rapidly with accompanying loss of nitrogen in the form of ammonia. Also they are more concentrated and, if applied directly on crops or allowed to come in contact with their roots, may cause injury by burning.

For these reasons it is desirable to use an absorbent material such as gypsum, superphosphate, kainit, dry earth, peat moss, or leafmold in connection with them, preferably by keeping it on the floors and dropping-boards of hen-houses, or else by mixing it well with the poultry manure as soon as the latter is collected from the houses. Poultry manure is also a good material to mix with cow or pig manure which are of the "cold" type; and it can be used to make liquid manure, which see.

Applied to the soil, poultry manure is quite rapidly soluble, soon becoming available for plant use. It is best applied as a top-dressing an inch or so thick (after all lumps have been broken down to a uniform fineness) and raked or cultivated in.

PRAIRIE-CLOVER. Common name for Petalostemum, a genus of mostly perennial leguminous herbs used in rock gardens and borders.

PRAIRIE-DOCK. Common name for *Silphium terebinthinaceum,* a tall sunflower-like perennial herb with yellow flowerheads. See ROSINWEED.

PRAIRIE-GENTIAN. Common name for *Eustoma russellianum,* an annual herb to 3 ft. with erect wide-open bell-shaped purple flowers 2 in. across. An attractive plant, native to the prairies in Neb. and Tex., it is little cultivated but worthy of a place in the border. Although an annual, seeds can be sown in summer and the seedlings carried over winter in a frame; the plants then come into bloom early the following summer. It should be planted in dry loamy soil in an open sunny position.

PRAIRIE-LILY. A common name for Cooperia, a genus of fragrant-flowered night-blooming bulbous perennials of the S. W.; they are related to Amaryllis.

PRAIRIE-MALLOW. A common name for the genus Sidalcea (which see); also for *Malvastrum coccineum,* a species of False-mallow, which see.

PRATIA (pray'-shi-ah) *angulata.* A perennial creeping herb of New Zealand, the stems growing to 1 ft. long with 1-in. leaves and small white, purple-streaked flowers. A member of the Lobelia Family, it is a good subject for the rock garden or for use over walls. It prefers a rich soil and a sunny position and can be grown from seed; or plants can be divided in spring.

PRAYING MANTIS. A beneficial, predacious insect. See MANTIS.

THE POTTING SHED—AN IMPORTANT ADJUNCT OF THE ALL-YEAR GARDEN
Especially if connected with a small greenhouse, a garden workshop where one can putter and plan, propagate and experiment and get closer to his plants, can be a joy indeed.

PRENANTHES (pre-nan'-theez). A genus of tall perennial leafy-stemmed plants of the Composite Family bearing small heads of flowers in spike-like panicles. Known as Rattlesnake-root, they have little horticultural value, but are occasionally planted in the border, though more appropriate in the wild garden. They are easily grown in any light loamy soil and are increased by seed. *P. purpurea,* to 5 ft., has narrow leaves with a bloom beneath and purple flowers on slender drooping stems. *P. aspera,* growing to 4 ft., is a coarse hairy plant with erect short-stemmed yellow flowers.

PRESERVING MELON. Common name for *Citrullus vulgaris citroides,* a variety of Watermelon (which see) ; also for *Benincasa hispida,* another tropical cucurbit relative especially popular among the Chinese.

PRETTY-FACE.. Common name for *Brodiaea ixioides,* a Pacific Coast herb growing from a corm and bearing purple-veined yellow flowers.

PRICKING-OUT, PRICKING-OFF. Two terms for the process of transferring tiny seedling plants from seed pans to flats or from crowded rows in one flat to another flat, where they are spaced about an inch apart each way. The purpose is to give them room for normal development until large enough to transplant and also to prevent them becoming spindly and weak as they inevitably will if left crowded. It is usually done with a stick with a V-shaped notch cut at its small end, the plantlet being lifted between the points and set where wanted. See TRANSPLANTING.

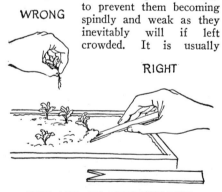

WRONG

RIGHT

THE ART OF PRICKING-OUT
Which is simply the transplanting of tiny seedlings from where they start to a flat or hotbed where they can really grow. A small label with a notched end, as shown, is a handy tool for the work. Don't pull tender plantlets out by the roots.

PRICKLY-ASH. Common name for *Zanthoxylum americanum,* a prickly shrub or tree sometimes planted for ornament.

PRICKLY-PEAR. Common name for the best known members of the Cactus Family, making up the flat-stemmed group of the genus Opuntia. So called because of its pear-shaped edible fruits. See OPUNTIA ; also CACTUS.

PRICKLY POPPY. Common name for Argemone, a genus of S. W. herbs with yellow juice, grown for their large variously colored flowers.

PRIDE-OF-CALIFORNIA. Common name for *Lathyrus splendens,* a shrubby perennial with violet or magenta pea-like flowers.

PRIDE-OF-INDIA. A common name for *Melia azedarach,* a tropical tree with purple or white flowers.

PRIM. A name sometimes used for Privet (which see) botanically *Ligustrum vulgare.*

PRIMROSE. Common name for Primula, a large genus of usually low-growing perennial herbs belonging to the Primrose Family (Primulaceae). (See illustration, Plate 40.) The flower-parts always occur in 5's, the tubular corolla being topped by 5 spreading lobes.

Primroses are exceedingly useful plants, being adapted for various decorative purposes and positions, under glass, as houseplants, and in the open. They are mostly perennial herbs, growing from underground stems, with flowers of nearly any color or combination desired, though white, pink and yellow predominate. There are several hundred species of varying habits, all but about five native to the N. temperate zone.

HARDY SPECIES

The primulas native to England and widely cultivated there are not always successful in N. America, because of our usually hot dry summers. However, where proper conditions can be provided, they thrive, and as gardeners are gradually understanding their requirements, they are becoming increasingly popular. Unless suitable spots in rock gardens are available, the E. slope of a hill seems to be the ideal situation, for there they are sheltered from wind and midday sun and have good drainage. Coolness, some shade, ample moisture and drainage must always be provided ; and once the plants are established, they are best not disturbed. Species to be treated in this fashion include *P. acaulis* (the Common, or English, Primrose), *P. veris* (Cowslip), *P. elatior* (Oxlip) and *P. polyantha* (Polyanthus).

Some of the Asiatic Primulas, larger and showier than the British species, may also be used successfully outdoors if treated correctly. They include *P. japonica;* the robust *P. sieboldi;* water-loving *P. pulverulenta* with tall silvery scapes; *P. bulleyana,* with deep reddish-orange flowers; and *P. beesiana,* with yellow-eyed carmine flowers. They like especially a low moist spot among the rocks, sheltered and partly shaded.

ALPINE SORTS. The alpine species, which virtually demand a rock-garden situation, will do well enough if sheltered from heat and given a rich moist soil, preferably exposed to the E. or N. Pebbles or rock chips placed under the leaves will give them needed protection from the dampness of the soil.

Among the alpine species are *P. denticulata,* with dense heads of pale blue-purple flowers; *P. cortusoides,* its rosy flowers in loose clusters; the low-growing *P. rosea;* bog-loving, yellow and fragrant *P. sikkimensis;* mealy-leaved *P. farinosa* with yellow-throated purple blooms; small *P. mistassinica,* with flesh-colored flowers; startling *P. littoniana* with heavy spikes of scarlet and violet; and *P. auricula,* ever fascinating with its multitudinous colors, which include tones of brown, plum, and green. This last is the flower commonly known as Auricula, a bit difficult to grow outdoors in this country, but well worth attention where it will survive the heat of summer. Greenhouse forms of Auricula have mealy markings that enhance the color-patterns of the flowers.

CULTURAL DIRECTIONS. Any of the above plants may be raised from seed sown in a warm greenhouse in February, though the alpine species are preferably sown in July, when the seed is ripe. The English types may be started in April or May in a coldframe.

The soil should be light and the seeds should be covered with 1/4 in. of finely sifted compost, then kept shaded until germination occurs. As the seedlings appear they should be pricked off to a position near the glass and later shifted singly into small pots. Later, humus or leafmold may be added to the soil, the established plants preferring a deep, moist, rich, loamy medium, well drained. September is the best time to transplant seedlings to their permanent site, though alpine species sown in a frame in July may be set out in spring.

Hardy species may also be propagated by division, which merely means pulling a large plant gently apart at the base, and replanting the two parts; this also is best done in September.

Over winter a light mulch or a covering of evergreen boughs will be adequate protection for hardy Primulas.

GREENHOUSE PRIMROSES

Some of the above named species, as well as numerous others, may also be grown in a greenhouse as pot plants, but *Primula japonica, P. sinensis, P. malacoides, P. obconica, P. kewensis,* and *P. floribunda* are the most popular for greenhouse culture. Many varieties of each of these species are available.

P. japonica, one of the finest, strong-growing species, whose umbels of flowers appear one above the other in early summer, succeeds well in pots for house or greenhouse decoration as well as when planted on rockwork or in the open border. Seed of this species should be sown as soon as ripe and the plants grown on to flower in their second spring. They are strong growers, and indoors after the first winter should have rich soil and large pots. All flower buds should be pinched off the first year and some during the second winter. *P. japonica* does not require heat. After the leaves die down in winter the pots may be stored in a cold-frame and kept moderately, but not absolutely, dry.

The Fairy Primrose (*P. malacoides*), a delicate-looking plant with tones of rose or lilac in its long-stemmed flower-umbels, is known as a good winter-bloomer in the greenhouse. In fact, it now often supplants the long-popular Chinese Primrose (*P. sinensis*), which is rather sensitive to moving or a change of temperature during the blooming period. Seeds of either of these sown in March will produce flowering plants in late fall.

P. kewensis is a well-known hybrid with tall scapes of fragrant yellow flowers and slightly whitish foliage.

Blooming at the same time in winter is *P. obconica,* originally with small lilac flowers, but now available in improved forms with large blooms in many tones and sometimes with fringed petals. Except for its irritating hairs, which are poisonous to some people, *P. obconica* makes an excellent house plant. Washing with alcohol, followed by soap and water, will relieve the irritation of primula poisoning. Another treatment recommended by an English gardener is this: Make a paste of old fashioned lump starch and smear it on the affected areas with a spoon handle. If this is not effective consultation of a doctor is advised. Those known to be susceptible to primrose poisoning are cautioned not even to smell the flowers, let alone touch the plants.

The Buttercup Primrose (*P. floribunda*) is also recommended as a pot plant for winter bloom, its fragrant yellow flowers being attractively small and compact.

These last three named are all easily grown plants.

CULTURE UNDER GLASS. The general culture of greenhouse primroses requires well-drained shallow pans filled with light sandy soil but with no added humus of any kind. They are best started between January and March. Fill the pans nearly full, cover the seed very lightly, place the pans in a warm frame covered with a pane of glass, and keep them shaded to prevent evaporation. Water will not be needed until the seed has germinated, when the glass must be removed immediately.

In about 2 weeks the seedlings may be potted singly—always with care that the crown of the plant is exactly even with the soil—placed in the coldframe near the light and given plenty of air, to insure a compact, sturdy growth. As the small pots fill with roots, shift into larger sizes, the 5-in. pot being about right for flowering. For this final potting, the soil should be rich and rather open, consisting of 2 parts loam to 1 each of old, well-decayed manure and leafmold, with enough sand or charcoal to insure porosity. Pots must be clean and perfectly dry, and when planted they must afford thorough drainage.

Ventilation, shading and watering are all important. While in the outdoor frame in summer, a light shading from the sun's rays is essential through the hottest part of the day. Heavy shading, however, is harmful. Liberal amounts of water are required in summer but, toward autumn and during the winter, it must be carefully applied. In early winter a temperature of from 50 to 55 deg. F. is better than a higher one.

ENEMIES

Primroses are subject to attacks from the primrose flea bettle, a metallic blue insect which is rather plentiful, usually first appearing in June. A second generation from eggs laid in July winters over in adult form in protected locations. Arsenate of lead is the most useful treatment; bordeaux mixture may be used with it as a preventive. Plants in the garden are sometimes eaten by slugs (which see) and the white fly may be troublesome in greenhouses. See GREENHOUSE PESTS.

The tiny mite, commonly called red spider (which see) is a persistent primrose pest, particularly bothersome indoors where, however, as a rule, it will be sufficient to spray several times with clear water, or for bad infestations with a contact insecticide, such as nicotine-sulphate, or soap solutions; plants can be dusted with sulphur. Outdoors a good spraying, plus the cleaning up and burning of all rubbish and weeds, will keep down all kinds of pests.

Damping-off (which see) sometimes causes heavy losses among young plants. Careful attention to soil conditions, watering and ventilation are effective preventives.

Botrytis blight or gray mold is most prevalent under glass but may occur in the garden during humid weather and rapidly rot the plants. In the greenhouse destroy badly diseased plants, remove infected parts from others and reduce the water supply. If possible water from underneath so as not to wet the leaves.

OTHER "PRIMROSES"

The plant sometimes known as Arabian-primrose is *Arnebia cornuta;* Evening-primrose, with large yellow flowers in summer, is Oenothera; Cape-primrose, a greenhouse plant, is Streptocarpus.

PRIMROSE-WILLOW. Common name for Jussiaea, a genus of tender annuals grown in damp soils, especially *J. longifolia.*

PRIMULA (prim'-eu-lah). A genus of several hundred species of herbs widely distributed through the temperate zone and commonly called Primrose (which see). Many of them are in cultivation as greenhouse and garden subjects.

PRIMULACEAE (prim-eu-lay'-see-ee). The Primrose Family, comprising widely distributed herbs abundant principally in the N. hemisphere. The flowers are borne in irregular or rounded clusters at the summit of a leafless stalk; the 5-lobed corolla is tubular and bell- or wheel-shaped, and the 5-part calyx persists after blooming. Many of the genera are showy and widely grown in rockeries, gardens and under glass; among the best known are Anagallis, Androsace, Cyclamen, Dodecatheon, Lysimachia, Primula and Soldanella.

PRINCES FEATHER. Common name for *Amaranthus hybridus* and *A. hypochondriacus;* also for *Polygonum orientale.*

PRINSEPIA (prin-see'-pi-ah). Deciduous shrubs from Asia, belonging to the Rose Family. *P. sinensis,* native to Manchuria and the best-known species, is a spiny, slender-branched shrub to 6 ft. or more, thriving in a sunny position and well-drained soil. It is hardy N. and about the first shrub to come into leaf, which makes it conspicuous when most others are still bare. The small bright yellow flowers appear in clusters from the axils of the opening leaves. The fruit is cherry-like and edible, but not freely produced. Propagated by seeds and layers.

PRIVET. Common name for Ligustrum, a genus of deciduous or evergreen shrubs of the Olive Family, very useful for hedges, screening purposes, and general ornamental planting. (See illustration, Plate 26.) They are not particular as to soil, and are well adapted to stand shade, city, and seaside conditions. They have good clean foliage, spikes of white flowers in summer, and usually black or bluish-black berries, borne in great profusion and mostly remaining all winter. The evergreen species are not hardly N., and some of the deciduous ones are killed back in severe winters; but if cut back severely, they usually grow up vigorously and even more bushy than before. Some species are well adapted for close clipping and trimming in fancy shapes. *L. ovalifolium* (California Privet) is largely used for this purpose, but is killed to the ground till below-zero weather. *L. amurense,* while not quite as good-looking, is very much hardier. For a tall hedge or screen, *L. vulgare* is good, holding its leaves green until quite late.

A fungus may kill the tips of twigs and produce small, dark fruiting bodies on the dead wood. Dormant spraying with a fungicide and a later spray to protect new growth is sometimes advisable. Cut out and burn infected wood.

The Japanese scale (which resembles the oyster-shell scale) and the olive scale (which is small and circular) may infest privet. Control both by dormant spraying with a miscible oil. For the privet mite that may cause yellowing or fading of the leaves, use a sulphur spray.

Propagated by seeds, cuttings, and, in the case of choice varieties, by grafting on *L. vulgare* or *L. ovalifolium.*

PRINCIPAL SPECIES

L. vulgare (Common Privet), native of Europe, grows to 15 ft., with slender spreading branches, dense panicles of flowers and lustrous black berries. There are many garden forms, running mostly to leaf variegation. Var. *xanthocarpum* has yellow berries.

ovalifolium (California Privet), a native of Japan, is of upright rather stiff habit to 15 ft. It has handsome shining foliage and creamy-white flowers, the odor of which is unpleasant to many. Var. *aureo-marginatum* (Golden Privet) is less vigorous, and needs good soil in a sunny place to show to best advantage.

obtusifolium (commonly grown and offered as *L. ibota*) is a hardy Japanese shrub with wide-spreading and curving branches, bearing small nodding panicles of flowers, and heavily laden all winter with bloomy-black berries. Var. *regelianum* is a low dense form with almost horizontal branches, making a very handsome shrub for foreground planting.

ibolium is a hybrid between *L. ovalifolium* and *L. obtusifolium,* somewhat hardier than the first-named parent.

amurense (Amur Privet) is a Chinese shrub of upright habit to 15 ft., with light green leaves held late, and slightly bloomy berries. It is one of the hardiest, and a good hedge plant for the N.

quihoui, also from China, grows to 6 ft., with spreading stiff branches. It is fairly hardy N. in light soil and a favored position, and is very striking in midsummer with its long panicled flower spikes.

sinense (Chinese Privet) grows to 12 ft. or more, and makes a very showy flowering specimen in summer. Not hardy N.

acuminatum is a Japanese species of somewhat spreading habit to 6 ft. The leaves drop early in fall but it has shining black berries. Var. *macrocarpum* is of more upright habit, with larger leaves.

japonicum is a handsome bushy evergreen to 10 ft., with flower panicles to 6 in. long. Hardy only in mild climates.

lucidum (Glossy Privet) is a large shrub or small tree, sometimes used for street planting in warm regions. Very showy in bloom with panicles about 10 in. long, it is cultivated in China for the white wax exuded from the bark as the result of insect work.

Mock-privet is Phillyrea (which see); and Mountain-privet is a name given to *Forestiera neo-mexicana*. Both are members of the Olive Family.

PROBOSCIDEA (proh-bo-sid'-ee-ah). Proboscis-Flower. A genus of sticky-hairy annual and perennial herbs, also called Unicorn-plant, with large, long-stemmed leaves, large purple flowers and okra-like fruits that, when ripe, become woody with long curved sharp-pointed beaks. The most important species *P. jussieui*, generally listed by seedsmen under its former generic name, Martynia, is a native American plant growing from Del. to Ill., southward and westward to N. Mex. It is grown as both an ornamental and a vegetable. In the latter rôle its soft, immature fruits are pickled, either alone or mixed with other vegetables. In the N. seed must be sown under glass and the plants set in the open ground and spaced about like cucumber hills after danger of frost has passed; in the S. it may be started outdoors, later all but 3 or 4 seedlings being thinned out of each hill.

A LAYERING POT

A handy device in propagation is a 2 or 3 in. flower pot made or carefully broken away like this for use in increasing house plants by what is called "air-layering," which see.

PROPAGATING BENCH, or FRAME. A greenhouse bench or portion of one in which cuttings are rooted and grafts placed while making unions. Until recent years it was invariably filled with clean, sharp sand. Lately granulated peat moss has been found an excellent rooting medium for some plants, and mixtures of peat moss and sand (in different proportions) for others.

Hence the modern propagating bench may contain either or all of these in its several sections. The bench may or may not be boxed or curtained-in below to conserve bottom heat (which see), and it may or may not be closed in above and covered with a glass sash to both raise the temperature and increase the humidity of the air around the plant materials. See COLD-FRAME; HOTBED.

PROPAGATION, PLANT. The increase in number, or multiplication, of plants to perpetuate the species or variety. Also the processes and methods employed by man to promote natural increase in some plants and to bring increase about under conditions when it would not otherwise take place. As controlled by man it is based on natural principles or laws which constitute the science of propagation and upon methods of handling which constitute the "art."

Methods, of which there are many, can be grouped in two classes: (1) those dependent upon seeds and spores; and (2) those which employ buds. Because reproduction by seeds is dependent upon the previous activity of the reproductive organs (stamens and pistils) it is called sexual. Reproduction by buds (which includes cuttings) is termed asexual because no union of parent plants is involved. Spores are asexual, usually one-celled, reproductive bodies of flowerless plants. Practically speaking, however, reproduction by spores (as, for instance, in mushrooms and ferns) is considered a sexual process.

Nearly all farm and garden crops and many flowers are grown from seeds. Notable exceptions are Irish potatoes and sugar cane which, though they produce some seed, are propagated asexually; so also are American ("Jerusalem") artichokes, tarragon, sweet-potatoes and horse-radish, and most of the tree and bush fruits whose seedlings, though true to the species characteristics, rarely reproduce true to variety, the fruit of the seedlings being inferior to that of the parent variety. Hence the necessity of producing all such plants by asexual methods.

The propagation of plants by asexual methods depends primarily upon the activity of the *cambium*. This is a layer of very thin tissue composed wholly of young, easily broken cells filled with protoplasm ("the physical basis of life") from which new plant tissues are formed. This vital layer separates the bast and sieve tissues (phloëm) from the wood (xylem) and in most common trees forms a continuous sheath between bark and wood extending from root tips to topmost buds. Upon it depends all growth of woody plants—the lengthening of roots and branches and the increase in girth of all parts. Also upon cambium activity depends the healing of wounds that penetrate deeper than the bark, since it develops over them protective callus tissue.

In propagation by cuttings (which see), a callus must form over the severed base prior to the development of roots; in layering (which see), cambium action hastens root development if the buried parts of the stems were previously wounded. In successful grafting (which see), the cambium of stock and of scion unite and the callus formed from the edges of these wounds covers the exposed internal tissues and protects them from drying and decay.

In both sexual and asexual propagation methods, gardeners and nurserymen from time immemorial have relied largely upon traditional rules which have proved only partially successful. Seeds of many plants have taken months or even years to germinate, and cuttings have failed altogether or have given poor results when handled by ordinary methods. However, thanks to experiments and investigations, many propagation problems have been solved in recent years and further improvements are clearly on the way. So the alert propagator should keep abreast of new discoveries and become familiar with at least some of the methods worked out by scientists and proved in the trial grounds of different institutions.

See also BULBS; SEEDS AND SEEDSOWING; DIVISION.

PROPHET-FLOWER. Common name for *Arnebia echioides,* a perennial with purple-spotted yellow flowers.

PROSTANTHERA (pros - tan - thee'-rah). Shrubby plants of Australia, belonging to the Mint Family. They are studded with resinous glands and are usually strong-scented. Sometimes grown under glass and outdoors in warm regions. Propagated by cuttings. *P. nivea* is a handsome shrub to 6 ft., with slender leaves and snow-white flowers sometimes tinged blue, in leafy racemes. *P. lasianthos* (Victorian-dogwood) has toothed oblong leaves pale beneath, and white flowers tinged red. *P. rotundifolia* has small roundish leaves and purple flowers in short close clusters.

PROTEA (proh-tee-ah). Trees, shrubs or stemless perennials, outstanding plants of the Cape of Good Hope. At one time they were amongst the most popular greenhouse plants, but today are seldom seen under glass outside a botanical garden. They are unusual-looking plants, with leathery leaves and large round flowerheads featured by scaly and usually colored bracts. Sandy peat, with good drainage, careful watering, and a sunny, airy position, are the chief cultural requirements.

P. cynaroides, one of the outstanding species in their native habitat, has white flowers and pink-tipped bracts. When the

Outer sash
Height 2'
Height 18"
Inner sash
Height 11" Level of Peat Height 12"
4" of Peat Level of soil in frame
Level of ground outside

A SIMPLE PROPAGATING FRAME FOR THE SMALL GARDEN
It consists merely of one coldframe within another—or the inner one can be supplied with a foundation of fermenting manure (or with electric heat) and be made into a hotbed. The surrounding air space and the double sash insulate the inner area.

2 × 4" Stud   *Side of outer frame*   *Stud*

Space between frames   *Side of inner frame*

End of inner frame

End of outer frame

Space between frames

Dimensions { Inner frame – '6' × 3'
             Outer frame – 6'6" × 3'6" }

PLAN OF THE PROPAGATING FRAME SHOWN IN THE PRECEDING ILLUSTRATION

flower-heads first open they are full of a honey-like substance which is collected and made into sugar. *P. speciosa,* with silky-white flowers and bracts, was formerly one of the most popular cultivated species.

PROTECTION OF PLANTS. This subject includes the prevention of damage by sun, wind, cold, snow, domestic and other animals, insects, diseases and humans.

SUN INJURY

Sun may be responsible for injuries of various kinds. Shade-loving plants cannot thrive, in fact, may even be killed by strong sunshine. This is especially true of both broad-leaved and coniferous evergreens which in winter must be protected by shading either provided naturally by trees or artificially by lath or similar screens, or by burlap-covered frames. Young plants—cuttings or seedlings—on propagating benches are easily injured by sun, and should be covered by newspapers or cheesecloth spread over them until they have struck root. See SHADE AND SHADING.

Sun often does injury also by "burning" the trunks and main branches of trees, more especially those growing in well-cultivated orchards. Usually such injury is on the south side, though often also on the east, less often on the west and never on the north in the Northern Hemisphere. The damage is generally not confined to these exposed areas, but, because the tissues in the inner bark are destroyed, the downward flow of elaborated plant food is interfered with and the roots below these areas are more or less deprived of sustenance. The wider the injured area, therefore, the more seriously do the roots suffer and, in consequence, the tops also, for improperly functioning or inactive roots fail to supply the necessary "sap" to the tops.

When the injury penetrates more deeply than the cambium (which see), it kills the young wood through which the upward flow of sap is carried to the leaves. Often the injury is so great that the trees are killed.

Sun scald may be brought about by any one of several causes; for instance, heavy pruning of branches which provided shade for the trunk, or the removal of tall weeds or other protection which played the same rôle. Probably, however, the most common condition that precedes sun scald is the failure of the trees to ripen up the young tissues made during late summer and early autumn. Almost invariably such growth is the result of abundant rain during these months, following an extended period of dry weather. If winter sets in early, that growth has insufficient time to become mature and therefore resistant to injuries by the sun.

Such damage may usually be prevented by inducing the maturity of this growth developed late in the season in one or, preferably, both of two ways: first, by having abundant soluble potash and phosphoric acid in the soil from August forward; second, by sowing in mid-August certain nitrogen-consuming crops, such as buckwheat, millet, rape, turnips or rye, or a combination of one of the first two with one of the last three.

The first two are quick to start and grow but as they are killed by early frost their period of usefulness is short; the others are much slower, but are hardy, usually surviving the winter. Each of them can be counted upon to reduce the content of nitrogen and water in the soil, thus reducing danger of late growth of the trees, which will then tend to ripen the wood already formed.

Another way to reduce risk of damage by strong sunlight, both in winter and summer, is to provide shade for the trunks and main branches on the south and east sides. The objection to this, however, is that it tends to prevent the formation of thickened bark by the trees themselves as natural protection. Should such artificial protection be removed the trees would suffer more than if it had never been used. However, where heavy pruning has been given to trees that have produced abundant and dense shade, it is advisable to establish temporary protection by means of wood splints, burlap or other conveniently applied materials.

Wind Damage

Damage by wind is of two general kinds; first, the one that makes newly planted trees, especially those such as evergreens with large tops, tilt to one side. Usually this is due to faulty planting, the soil not having been properly packed around the roots and trunks. Preventive measures in such cases are firm packing and staking. Three stakes are arranged in a triangle with the true trunk held centrally by means of wires or stout non-stretching cords which are passed between the stakes and around the trunk. The bark is protected from cutting by pieces of rubber hose, automobile shoe, or a thick wrapping of several layers of burlap.

The second class of damage by wind is breakage of branches. Much of this may be prevented by training the trees while young so as to avoid weak crotches, especially those in which two branches of practically uniform development form a capital Y with the trunk. These arms are almost certain to break down under stress of heavy loads of fruit or snow or rain that freezes on them and weighs them down. Preventive measures are discussed under PRUNING.

Damage by Cold

Cold damages plants that are natives of warm climates, likewise so-called "hardy" plants whose tissues have not been properly prepared to resist such damage. Those started under glass in spring may, because of rapid growth, become succulent and thin-celled and therefore have poor resistance to late spring frosts when they are placed outdoors. Damage to such plants may be prevented by hardening-off (which see). Also, trees, and bushes that have failed to ripen their wood before the advent of winter will be damaged by cold. Such winter injury may be avoided by the methods already outlined to prevent sun scald.

Often the effects of late spring and early autumn frosts upon tender plants growing outdoors may be prevented by simple, inexpensive, easily applied precautions or by prompt treatment in the early morning after a cold snap. In a small way, individual plants may be covered with newspapers, sheets, large inverted flower pots, crocks, or peach baskets which will reduce the radiation of heat from them and the earth so covered.

On a larger scale, a more satisfactory way is to fill the atmosphere with water vapor shortly after nightfall. The object of this is to assure the deposition of dew with its accompanying action of liberating its latent heat and thus checking the fall of temperature as the freezing point is approached.

The easiest way to assure this moisture in the air is to spray the plants and the ground in a wide area so that the warmth of the earth will induce evaporation. When an overhead irrigation system is available it may be turned on during the evening and, if hand-operated, re-set at least two, preferably more, times before midnight so as to cover the widest possible area with moisture.

Smouldering fires of damp straw, weeds and similar materials (when they will not annoy the neighbors) will fill the air with steamy smoke which will both check radiation and provide water vapor for deposition as dew. Bright fires of coal, wood or oil, though highly effective when in large numbers, are not satisfactory upon a small scale because they are too few and small on a small property to affect the great bulk of air.

When frost occurs: It is comparatively easy to predict a local frost so as to know when the protection of plants may be instituted. The following signs are characteristic of an approaching frosty night in late spring and early autumn: A fall of temperature from fifty degrees Fahrenheit to forty or less between the hours of 4 in the afternoon and 9 in the evening; a cessation of wind between those times; and a cloudless sky with brilliant stars.

Fortunately, frost does not invariably occur even when all these signs seem to predict that it will. The reason is that these conditions may be counteracted by changes beyond human prognostication. For instance, before morning a wind may arise and thus stir up the atmosphere, mixing relatively warm upper air with the colder air near the ground surface, thus keeping the temperature above the freezing point; or clouds may form low in the sky or (what amounts to the same thing), a fog may collect near the ground and thus check the radiation of heat into space as well as deposit dew.

When a slight frost does occur, especially in the absence of such precautions as those mentioned, it is often possible to save plants, provided the efforts are made before the sun strikes them. The treatment consists in drenching the foliage with cold water in order to "draw the frost." Even such tender plants as dahlias, cannas, tomatoes and melons may thus be saved, provided the temperature has not been more than a degree or two below freezing.

Because these methods of preventing frost injuries are so easily applicable to small gardens it is worth taking the risk of loss in spring by sowing or planting tender vegetables a week or even two weeks earlier than the locally popular date, protecting them when required, and thus giving the plants an extra early start and probably beginning to gather the crops earlier in consequence. In autumn the plants must be similarly protected to prevent loss of such tender ones as peppers, egg-plants, and geraniums.

When the ground freezes: As freezing the ground deeply may damage even well-established trees, shrubs and vines of various species, including many generally considered relatively hardy, it is advisable to adopt precautionary measures that will reduce the depth of frost penetration and prevent alternate freezing and thawing. Such plants in sod ground are less likely to suffer than those growing where the ground is bare. Hence one advantage of mulching and the growing of a cover crop.

Where neither of these is feasible it is a good plan to pile manure or litter a foot or more deep and at least a yard wide around the bases of trunks just before winter sets in, previously protecting these trunks by wrapping with galvanized wire cloth. The material must be removed in early spring.

Snowing and thawing: Snow seldom does injury to the hardy plants it covers on the ground, though it may do so when it thaws and freezes as sheets of ice. It much more frequently causes injury when it collects and freezes on the branches, especially of evergreens. Under such conditions breakage is common; yet it may be prevented in either of two ways.

First, as soon as a storm has stopped and while the snow is soft and fluffy the excessive loads may be jarred from the branches. This should never be done by striking the branches from above, because such blows would increase the strain and often would break the branches. The proper way is to lift each branch, give it a slight shake from side to side, then a stronger one, and two or more until at least half the snow has fallen off. Branches beyond arm's reach may be raised with a pitch-fork or a garden rake and each given a series of jarrings from below. Higher branches are generally more pliable than the lower ones so are less likely to be injured.

The second method is specially adapted to the treatment of branches that have become coated with frozen snow and rain. It consists in spraying the trees with a saturated solution of muriate or sulphate of potash or of nitrate of soda. Such solutions, preferably made in advance of the storm, are most easily prepared by hanging a quantity of either of these chemicals in a burlap bag just below the surface of water in a barrel or a large deep crock. This position favors rapid and complete solution and provides a sure test of saturation; for if any chemical is left in the bag the solution is saturated; whereas if all is dissolved it probably is not. In the latter case more chemical must be placed in the bag for dissolving.

Best results will be obtained when the saturated solution is sprayed, a little at a time, as high up as can be conveniently reached, a small area at a time at intervals of 5 or 10 minutes. The strong liquid will dissolve part of the ice, and crack and break off other parts, so that in a short time, when enough has been sprayed, the branches will be bare. Very little of this fertilizer will be wasted (unless the land is so steep it will flow over the surface) because it will usually find its way into the ground and thus feed the trees.

Injury by Animals

Domestic animals often cause damage to trees. When hogs, horses or mules on a farm are fed rations which lack some necessary element they may be expected to tear the bark and young wood from the trunks and branches as high up as they can reach; the hogs often grub and eat the bark of the roots as deep down in the soil as they can burrow.

Whenever it becomes necessary to keep these animals among trees, such injuries can be prevented by supplying them with an adequate ration and by encasing the trunks and branches in galvanized wire cloth (or half-inch mesh wire netting) as high up as the creatures can reach and 4 to 6 in. below the ground surface. Sheep and cows do no such damage. When fed well-balanced rations domestic animals of all kinds may be allowed to graze among trees without fear of damage.

Among other animals that often injure trees the four worst are deer, rabbits, hares and mice. In states where deer are protected by law they are often the cause of heavy losses and serious mutilation of trees, especially young ones. Complaints must be lodged with the State Game Commission, which has the right to issue permits to kill. Nothing but very high, strong, woven wire fences can keep the animals out, though shooting blank cartridges is fairly effective in frightening them away.

Rabbits often destroy such low-growing plants as raspberries and low-headed fruit trees. They likewise gnaw the bark from tree trunks during winter when food is scarce. Trapping and shooting are the best controls, though the wire netting method already described is highly effective. They should be not only as high as the animals can reach from the soil surface but as high in addition as the estimated depth of the snow.

Mice gnaw the bark near the ground level, both above and below the surface, when they cannot get other food during winter. The wire cloth method is the best protection, though a 12-in. mound of earth around each tree trunk is a fair, but temporary substitute. So is snow tramped down hard.

Humans do damage by the careless use of power implements and hand tools; but probably more frequently by erroneous cutting of large branches—the sort of improper sawing which tears strips of wood off the trunks or leaves stubs which induce decay. See PRUNING.

Protection of an individual tree near a drive or a road may be gained by placing a boulder 3 or 4 ft. away from the tree in such a position that an automobile or a carriage would strike it before reaching the tree. Drivers will respect a boulder whereas they might not mind striking the tree trunk.

Though injuries due to diseases and insects are more serious than perhaps all other causes combined, they are easiest to control.

Protection here means the interposition of a barrier between the plant and the insects, bacteria or fungi that are capable of initiating injury or disease. Occasionally this may consist of an actual barrier such as a windbreak or a cheesecloth screen or tent, but the method most used consists of keeping the plant covered at critical periods with fungicidal or insecticidal sprays or dusts. Since protection implies prevention rather than cure, such control measures must be taken in advance of the presence of the enemy. See also DISEASES, PLANT; FUNGICIDE; INSECTICIDE; SPRAYING; DUSTING; FUMIGATION.

PROVENCE (prov'-ens) **ROSE.** A term which, in the present confused relationship of rose species and types, is sometimes applied to the old French garden roses (*Rosa gallica*), which make persistent bushes to 4 ft. with pink or crimson flowers borne singly. Formerly it designated a so-called "garden group," including *R. gallica* and numerous varieties which have since been shifted to other species. The Moss Rose, for instance—formerly *R. gallica muscosa* and classed as one of the Provence Roses—is now considered a variety of *R. centifolia,* the Cabbage Rose. See ROSE.

PRUNE. Originally, this term referred to any plum; in modern, American usage, it means a dried plum or any meaty, not juicy, variety of plum which can be easily dried without spoiling. Though various prune varieties are grown in the Eastern States they are not dried there commercially because the air is too humid. The American prune industry is practically confined to the Pacific Coast States.

PRUNELLA (proo-nel'-ah). A genus of small perennial herbs (sometimes called Brunella) of the Mint Family, bearing purple or violet flowers in close-set heads or spikes. They are rather weedy plants, but can be used in the shady part of the border or rock garden. They grow well in any garden soil, are easily naturalized in the wild garden, and increased by seed or division.

P. vulgaris (Self-heal or Heal-all), to 2 ft., with stems often lying on the ground, is an Old-World herb naturalized in America. It has purple or blue flowers but there are occasional white forms and its var. *laciniata* has greatly cut leaves. *P. grandiflora,* to 1 ft., is a European plant with purple flowers, showing various color forms listed as vars. *alba, carminea* and *rubra.*

PRUNING. The removal of dead or living plant-parts to benefit those that remain, to increase flower or fruit production, or to improve the form of the pruned tree, bush or vine. The term is generally applied to what man does in his efforts to grow plants as he wants them, yet Nature prunes ruthlessly using such "tools" as shade, wind and over-loads of fruit, ice or snow. Thus pruning is a "natural" operation; but as such it often destroys trees by permitting the entrance of decay through wounds where branches break off. Human methods are an improvement in this respect, for they (1) remove badly placed branches so as to increase the structural strength of those that remain; (2) make clean wounds whose healing is facilitated so that disease infection is prevented; (3) enhance the beauty of form and abundance of flowers and fruit; and (4) maintain and extend the life of specimens beyond their normal span.

Every decaying branch and stub is a menace to the life of a tree because through it decay may work into and destroy the heartwood and make the trunk hollow and weak. Hence the importance not only of removing all dead, dying and diseased branches, but also of detecting in advance those that are likely to be starved by being shaded or to become broken or diseased or to otherwise threaten the well-being of the tree. The smaller such branches are when removed and the more carefully the cuts are made (as directed below) the quicker will be the healing and the less the chance of disease gaining entrance.

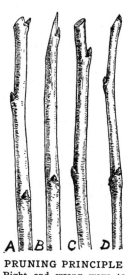

Though wrong pruning methods may result in the death of trees, pruning as an operation is not harmful. As plants have neither nerves nor a blood system they do not suffer as animals do from "shock" when important limbs are removed. Even the so-called "bleeding" of some plants when pruned late in the dormant period does no harm.

PRINCIPLES OF PRUNING

The underlying principles of pruning may be grouped under three heads: 1. True pruning, or the removal of plant parts to increase either the number or improve the quality of the flowers (and therefore the fruit) or to improve the character of the plant. 2. Simple training, or the location of individual branches in structurally favorable positions and the removal of those less favorably placed. 3. Training the plant in some more or less unnatural form.

Gardening literature is full of pruning rules, but since many apply to specific aims conditions or plant species, apparent contradictions are common. It is therefore important to understand the following fundamental principles, rather than to adopt mere rules.

1. Constant good management of plants is of primary importance; pruning is secondary. It will not offset abuse or neglect of necessary tillage, plant feeding or control of plant pests.

2. Climate and locality influence both the need for and the effects of pruning; methods that are right under one set of conditions must be avoided or modified under others. For instance, from Del. southward, along the seaboard where the air is humid winter pruning may do no harm; but in the Prairie States where it is dry and cold so much water may be lost through winter-made wounds that trees may be killed; again, in hot, dry regions, sun scald of the trunks and branches may follow heavy pruning of trees previously neglected.

3. Pruning does not change the natural habit of a plant; pruned plants resume their normal habit when left to themselves. A sprawling tree like that of the Rhode Island Greening Apple cannot be made to grow erect like one of Northern Spy, or *vice versa*. Pruning should seek merely to correct faults and maintain the natural form of the variety.

4. Plants of the same variety or species vary in habit according to their age, so must be pruned more or less differently at different ages. Plants when young tend to make rapid, erect growth; as they approach bearing age they reduce this rate, preliminary to flower and fruit production.

5. Drastic pruning of branches stimulates or favors stem or wood production because the supply of food taken up by the full root system is forced into a smaller percentage of top with the result that latent buds develop into branches. Gardeners prune weak shrubs and trees to promote increased top growth.

6. Drastic pruning of the roots reduces wood production, so may be used to induce fruitfulness. Its effects resemble the withholding of food, for it reduces the quantity of sap supplied. A plant thus or otherwise checked in its normal growth promptly sets about reproducing itself—that is, forming flower buds.

7. Watersprouts and suckers develop because of some disturbance of a plant's physiological balance, especially after excessive pruning or the destruction of large amounts of top by insects or diseases. They indicate vigor of root and a more or less inactive top.

8. The uppermost buds on branches usually grow most vigorously, particularly in young plants. When a shoot is shortened, a side or "axillary" bud (one formed in the angle of a leaf stalk) becomes an "uppermost" bud and, instead of remaining dormant, develops a shoot to take the place of the lost leader. This will be larger than any shoot produced from a bud lower down on the same stem.

9. Shoots developed from terminal (end) buds usually grow straight ahead; those from branch buds on the sides of shoots, always at an angle. Advantage may be taken of this to spread or to contract a tree or bush or to fill gaps between branches by so pruning that the topmost bud remaining points in the desired direction.

10. Pruning trees in summer favors flower and fruit production; pruning in winter stimulates leaf and branch produc-

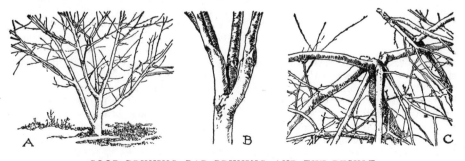

GOOD PRUNING, BAD PRUNING, AND THE RESULT
A. A low-headed fruit tree well pruned when young so as to develop a balanced head. B. Poor pruning left this triple crotch—a weak point as shown in (C) where it has been split apart by the combined strain of winds and heavy snows; or even a heavy load of fruit might do it.

tion. Trees and shrubs pruned while dormant strive to replace the parts removed with new ones; the result is the forced development not only of flower buds, but also of leaf and shoot buds that would otherwise have remained dormant. Thus severe dormant pruning is followed by much top growth but often reduces yield.

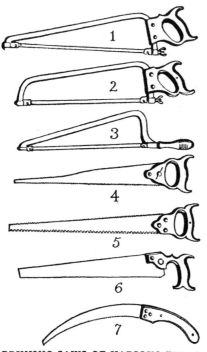

PRUNING SAWS OF VARIOUS TYPES
All these forms are satisfactory and adapted for special purposes except 5, with teeth on both edges. Never use that kind; it is likely to do more damage than good. 1, 2, and 3 are especially convenient because swivel arrangements permit the blade to be turned to different angles.

This does *not* apply in the case of the grape, which see.

11. Excessive growth may be converted into flowering or fruiting "spurs" by shortening them.

12. Removal of small branches and twigs may be used as a means of thinning the fruit and thus promoting annual bearing. To practice it the pruner must know how the variety bears its blossom buds. It is a less costly method of thinning than the removal of the developing fruit in midsummer but it requires careful determination of the proportion of flower buds that will set fruit. (See illustrations under BLUEBERRY and BUD.

13. The healing of wounds is affected by the kind and vigor of the plant, the length and location of the stubs, the smoothness or roughness of the cut surfaces, the health of the wood, and the season when made.

If pruning wounds are small and made shortly before or during spring, growth may be so speedy as to close them before midsummer. But if they are large with ragged surfaces, decay organisms are likely to enter, especially if the pruning is done between July and February, after active spring growth has stopped. In such cases not only does the wound-surface dry but the dryness penetrates beneath the bark, which raises, widens the wound and delays healing. The sooner the edges of ragged wounds are trimmed and protected from drying the more likely is healing to occur.

Swabbing the wound-surface with an antiseptic and covering it with the following lotion will prevent drying: Melt 1 lb. first grade resin and 1 oz. beef tallow over a gentle fire; then add 8 oz. alcohol. Keep tightly corked in a wide-mouthed bottle and apply with a small brush. Should the lotion become thick add a little alcohol.

The healing of tree wounds differs from that of animal wounds in that the callus or scar tissue has no connection with the tissues beneath. Its only functions are to stop the loss of water and prevent the entrance of decay. Its formation often is so slow that, unless the wound is protected, decay starts before the callus seals the surface.

14. Though wound dressings do not themselves hasten healing, they may serve to prevent the entrance of disease, are harmless to growing tissues, antiseptic, and serve to protect the wound-surface until the callus forms. Properly made wounds smaller than 2 in. across, especially those made just before spring opens, heal so quickly they need not be dressed. Larger wounds may be dressed advantageously provided the young tissues are not injured.

As formation of a callus over extra large wounds requires several years, the heartwood may be sparingly brushed with creosote or carbolineum once or twice a year in the interim. But these fluids are powerful antiseptics and penetrate both deeply and widely so use them carefully and apply them so thinly that they will not reach the marginal ring of young wood, which they might kill.

Paints, varnishes, shellac, grafting wax and paraffin are worthless as permanent dressings, being neither antiseptic nor protective for any length of time.

Types of Pruning

REMOVING LARGE LIMBS. To remove a large branch make three separate cuts as follows: (1) About a foot from the main trunk saw from below through the limb until the saw binds—possibly a third of the branch diameter; (2) a few inches beyond this cut, saw downward through the limb until it falls—the undercut will prevent the branch tearing off a strip of bark down the tree, as almost always happens if the first cut is made from above; (3) remove the stub so left by again sawing from above and so close to the main trunk that a smooth, flush wound results. While this will be larger than if the branch were cut farther out, it will heal more quickly with little chance of the decay infection that almost always attacks a stub.

PRUNING NURSERY STOCK. This should be done as soon as the plants are delivered and unpacked.

Before planting, shorten slightly every root of the thickness of a lead-pencil, and cut back any injured roots to sound wood. Make the cuts with a sharp knife and preferably on a slant with the surface of the wound facing down.

After planting reduce the tops of all except 1-year trees at least 50 per cent, and preferably 75 per cent, to balance the reduction of the feeding-root area suffered even under the most careful handling. But before reducing the top decide which branches to retain so as to develop a structurally strong specimen. Whenever possible let the main branches start a foot or more apart on the trunk and point in different directions. Three or 4 are enough to start with—others may be developed later. Shorten these "frame" limbs 30 to 50 per cent and cut off all the others.

It is not advisable to cut the leader or main stem because if that is done, branches tend to develop in a bunch just below the cut and to make the tree structurally weak at that point. If a young tree exhibits such a bunch of branches, cut off all but the best one. But to avoid receiving such stock insist that the nursery supply you with trees that have not had their leaders cut. Better still, buy only 1-year "whips," which are usually branchless, permitting the development of branches exactly where wanted by the simple expedient of pinching off any others during the first spring and summer.

CORRECTING A Y-CROTCH. If an otherwise desirable tree has two main branches forming a sort of Y with its tendency to split when the tree gets older, the condition can be corrected in 3 ways: (1) Remove one branch (the smaller) close to the

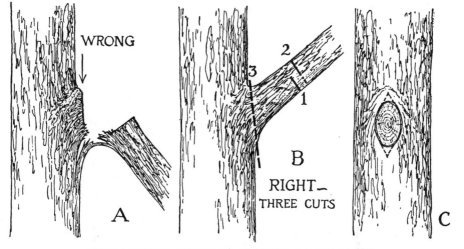

FUNDAMENTAL RULES IN PRUNING LARGE LIMBS

A. Never try to cut a big branch from the top with one sawing; its weight will break it off and leave a long, ragged wound. Instead, (B) Make three separate cuts in the order and to the depths shown—(1) from below (2) and (3) from above. C. To insure clean, quick healing, cut the bark of pruning wounds flush with the trunk pointed at top and bottom, so as to stimulate the flow of healing sap.

trunk, i.e. close to the other that is to be left as the leader. But as this is likely to cause a rather large wound and serious drying that may injure the tree, a better plan is: (2) Shorten the smaller branch considerably and the larger one only a little. This makes the former a subordinate side branch on the latter. (3) Often the best plan of all in the case of a newly planted tree is to cut back the poorer branch to a 6-in. stub which is left for 2 years and then trimmed off close to the main trunk the second spring. The small wound at the end of the stub does not dry out the trunk or interfere with the sap movement, and, as the stub does not increase in size, the wound left when it is finally cut off is proportionately smaller

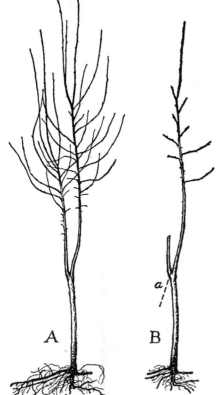

PRUNING TO PREVENT TROUBLE

There is one condition in which a pruning stub can be left—temporarily. That is (A) when a tree develops two almost equal leaders to form a bad crotch. Cut off the smaller branch, leaving a 6-in. stub (B). The following season, when sap is no longer flowing into it, cut off the stub close to the main stem (a).

and more likely to heal over rapidly. See illustration above.

SPUR PRUNING. This consists of the reduction of shoots to only a few joints and buds. It is practiced mostly on dwarf fruit trees and usually in late spring or summer, though sometimes in winter. It consists of pinching off the young shoots. See GRAPE.

HEADING-IN, or shortening young growths, is done to correct bad habits or to promote fruit bearing. In the former case the main governing factors are extent or rate of growth, distance between trees, character of trees (dwarf or standard), and preference as to form. Annual growths of 3 ft. in young or unfruitful trees may be shortened 30 to 50 per cent to make the head thicken up. In rampant, mature trees such treatment may aggravate the trouble which may have been caused by excess of plant food or previous excessive or faulty pruning. In such cases checking the growth is essential. Heading-in is often practiced with dwarf trees to maintain good proportion of top to root and to keep the trees small and fruitful.

PINCHING-OFF is a form of heading-in, the immature shoots being shortened while still small. Its chief purposes are to foster flower and fruit bud development, keep the trees small, maintain desired forms of plants, thin the fruit, and insure balance between the tops and roots of dwarf trees. Properly, it consists of pinching the soft shoots with the thumb nail.

DISBUDDING, the pinching-out of buds that would become branches or flowers where not desired, is mostly employed to produce "specimen" or "exhibition" flowers such as roses, chrysanthemums and dahlias. Within recent years it has been employed to develop structurally strong trees. See TRAINING OF PLANTS.

CLIPPING (or shearing) is the removal of small growths so as to develop and maintain plants in more or less unnatural forms, as in hedges. Strictly speaking, it is not pruning.

PRUNING ORNAMENTALS. Ornamental trees, shrubs and woody vines, when pruned at all, are more often wrongly pruned than are fruit trees. All too often they are sheared or clipped in fantastic or formal shapes while dormant and thus shorn of their greatest beauty—their flowers. Usually, all they need is annual attention.

When a branch grows beyond the bounds of balance, beauty of form or convenience, cut it off at its starting point so as not to leave an ugly prong. Any "hole" left in the plant by such a step will soon fill up with new growth.

Cut out dead, diseased and dying stems whenever they are seen because they menace the health of other parts, prevent the entrance of sunlight and air, and waste the water pumped into them by the roots. Similarly, when bushes become crowded with stems, thin out the old, failing, puny and worthless ones.

To obtain the finest display of bloom it is necessary to know how and where the individual species produce their blossom buds, which might otherwise be pruned off. On this basis they fall into 2 classes:

1. All shrubs and trees that bloom during early spring develop their flower buds during the previous year. If they are pruned while dormant, and especially if clipped to some set shape, many blossom buds are destroyed. The correct time to prune them is within a week or two after the flowers have fallen—while the plants are in leaf. They then have the balance of the growing season in which to develop more and better blossom buds for the following year.

2. Shrubs and trees that blossom from late spring forward develop their blossom buds earlier during the *same season*. They may therefore be pruned to advantage while dormant or just as growth is starting.

EVERGREENS. Never prune evergreens, either coniferous or broadleaved, in winter, because the additional evaporation from the cut surfaces might kill them. Prune them just as growth is starting in spring. Rampant shoots appearing during the growing season may be pinched back or headed when noticed. Usually evergreens require little other pruning beyond the removal of dead, diseased or injured branches.

Winter-killing of branches often upsets the pruning program because it necessitates heroic cutting. When it occurs, wait until the living parts can be distinguished from the dead ones, then prune accordingly. Trees whose branches apparently matured the previous autumn are benefited by heavy pruning, while those which did not ripen their wood well may be injured by such treatment. In cases of severe winter-killing, delaying the needed pruning until the trees are growing well permits the shade of their foilage to protect the

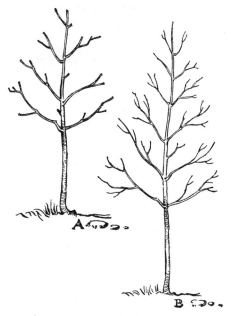

PRUNING NEWLY PLANTED TREES IS IMPORTANT
A—Wrongly done, because top has been cut off and stubs are left. B—Correct, because leader and form remain even though considerable wood has been thinned out.

trunks from sun scald. Whitewash sprayed on the sunny side decreases the risk of sun scald by reflecting the sun's rays.

PRUNUS (proo'-nus). The Stone Fruits. An important group of mostly deciduous shrubs and small trees, found chiefly in the north temperate zone and belonging to the Rose Family. It includes valuable orchard fruits as well as purely decorative kinds. (See illustrations, Plate 42.) Many are hardy N. and very showy when flowering in spring, although after a severe winter most of the flower buds may be killed. They thrive best in a well-drained loamy limy soil; to avoid injury by late frosts it is desirable to plant them in northern exposures where they will be less likely to start into growth early. Propagation is by seed, by grafting, and budding. See also ALMOND; APRICOT; CHERRY; NECTARINE; PEACH; PLUM.

PRINCIPAL SPECIES

PLUM GROUP

P. americana, a native plum, usually a small twiggy and thorny tree, has small yellow and red fruit.

maritima (Beach Plum) is a native sometimes thorny bush, found chiefly in coastal areas and well adapted for planting in sandy soil. The profuse small white flowers are followed by mostly red or deep purple bloomy fruit rather bitter for eating raw but excellent for jelly or jam.

hortulana, native in Kentucky and adjoining areas, is a small tree with red and yellow fruit.

domestica, from Europe and Asia, is the parent of many garden plums. Its var. *insititia* has smaller leaves and fruit; to it belong the Bullace and Damson sorts.

cerasifera (Cherry Plum, Myrobalan) is a small slender tree much used as a stock for grafting, and a useful hedge plant. Var. *pissardi* is a handsome purple-leaved form, often grown to provide colorful shoots for cutting.

spinosa is the Sloe or Blackthorn, a bush with short stiff thorny branches, and small blue-black very acid fruit.

salicina (Japanese Plum) is a spreading tree, very hardy and cultivated in several vars.

CHERRY GROUP

P. avium (Sweet Cherry) is a tall pyramidal tree, with birch-like bark and clusters of white flowers. It is cultivated in many named forms, the common seedling forms with small fruit being known as Mazzard Cherries, and much used as stocks.

cerasus (Sour Cherry) is a small round-headed tree, cultivated in many forms for the acid fruit used for pies, preserves, etc. Var. *persiciflora* is a form with double pink flowers; var. *rhexi* has double white flowers; var. *semperflorens* (All Saints Cherry) blooms a second time in summer on young growth.

lannesiana, serrulata, and *sieboldi* are Japanese species from which have been derived the many beautiful Flowering Cherries.

subhirtella is the spring cherry of Japan, a large shrub or small tree, bearing a profusion of blush or pink flowers. Var. *pendula* is the well-known weeping form.

mahaleb (Mahaleb Cherry) grows to 30 ft., with small white fragrant flowers opening after the leaves are well out; it is much used as a stock for cherries.

tomentosa is a spreading shrub to 10 ft., with white or tinted flowers early, and reddish edible fruit.

glandulosa is an ornamental Asiatic shrub, commonly grown in the double white and double pink forms, that are known and usually listed in catalogs as Flowering Almonds.

besseyi (Western Sand Cherry) is a dwarf spreading species, valued on the Plains for its sweet fruit. It has been used for crossing with other species, and also as a stock, to give hardiness and induce dwarfing.

pennsylvanica (Wild Red Cherry) is a bushy shrub or tree to 40 ft., with slender red-barked branches, small white flowers in umbels, and light-red fruit in summer.

BIRD CHERRY GROUP

P. padus (European Bird Cherry) is a tree to 40 ft., with fragrant white flowers in loose drooping clusters, followed by black fruit. Varieties well known in cultivation are *pendula,* with drooping branches; *acubaefolia,* with yellow spotted leaves; and *plena* with double flowers.

serotina (Black Cherry) is a fine native timber tree, to 100 ft., the outer bark dark brown, the inner bitter and aromatic. The flowers are in long loose racemes, opening when the leaves are well out and followed by purplish-black fruit.

virginiana (Chokecherry) is a shrub or tree to 30 ft., with rough speckled bark. white flowers in short dense racemes with the leaves, and red fruit.

CHERRY-LAUREL GROUP

P. caroliniana is the native Cherry-laurel, an evergreen tree to 40 ft., found from N. C. southward. It has small creamy-white flowers and is known as Wild-orange and Mock-orange.

laurocerasus (English-laurel) is an evergreen shrub or small tree, with large glossy leaves and short clusters of white fragrant flowers. It is much used for hedge and screening purposes in mild climates. Var. *schipkaensis,* a smaller form, is hardy in sheltered places in Mass.

lusitanica (Portugal-laurel) is a handsome evergreen shrub with thick leathery leaves and white flowers in clusters longer than the leaves. Not hardy N.

ALMOND, APRICOT AND PEACH GROUP

P. communis (Almond) is a peach-like tree, one of the showiest in early spring with its delicate pink flowers but not hardy in cold climates.

Plate 42.   PRUNUS AND PYRUS—TWO OUTSTANDING PLANT GROUPS

Upper left: The simple beauty of the blossom of the apple (Pyrus malus).   Upper right: The weeping Japanese cherry (Prunus subhirtella var. pendula) becomes a veritable fountain of spring bloom. Lower left: In the double-flowering Japanese cherry close-set rosettes of rosy blossoms garland the reddish-brown boughs.   Center right: The flowering crabapple is fragrant as well as beautiful. Lower right: Double-flowering almond and spring bulbs—a lovely and inspiring combination.

nana (Russian Almond), is a hardy dwarf compact bush, with pink flowers early. Var. *georgica* has darker colored but smaller flowers.

triloba (Flowering Almond) is a hardy bush with clear pink flowers. Var. *plena* with double rosy-pink flowers, is the form usually grown, generally on plum stock.

armeniaca (Apricot) is a round-headed tree with pinkish or white flowers, and cultivated for its choice fruit in many named varieties.

mume (Japanese Apricot) is hardy N. when worked on plum stock. Very decorative forms with double white and double pink flowers are known as Japanese Flowering Plums.

persica (Peach) is a small tree bearing pink flowers, very showy when in bloom, and valued for its choice slightly downy fruit in many named varieties. There are also double pink- and white-flowered forms, and one with purple leaves. Var. *nucipersica* is the Nectarine, with smaller, smooth-skinned, very choice fruit.

davidiana is a slender peach-like tree with blush flowers very early. It is hardy N., but the flower buds are often winter-killed.

PSEUDERANTHEMUM (pseu-der-an'-thee-mum). Tropical shrubby plants, belonging to the Acanthus Family. They make good free-flowering subjects for the warm greenhouse. After flowering, old plants may be rested, cut back and grown on into good specimens. Propagated by cuttings.

P. atropurpureum is a showy plant with purple leaves about 6 in. long, and clusters of white purple-centered flowers. *P. reticulatum* has green wavy leaves to 10 in. long, marked with a yellow network. The flowers are white, spotted reddish-purple. *P. tuberculatum* is a neat white-flowering shrub with small leaves, and branches covered with small wart-like growths.

PSEUDOBULB. The thickened and fleshy base of the stem of certain orchids (like Cattleya, Coelogyne and Odontoglossum) having the appearance of a bulb but the structure of a true stem. See ORCHID.

PSEUDOLARIX (seu-doh-la'-riks) *amabilis.* A deciduous cone-bearing tree called Golden-larch, which see.

PSEUDOTSUGA (seu-doh-tseu'-gah). A genus of evergreen coniferous trees of the Pine Family having needle-like leaves and drooping cones with trident-shaped bracts.

They are of symmetrical pyramidal growth, resembling the true firs (Abies) but easily distinguished from them by the drooping cones and more flexible leaves. In their natural habitat they are valuable forest and timber trees, but they take kindly to cultivation. They are propagated by seed. One species, *P. douglasi,* the Douglas-fir (which see) is one of the fastest growing and most satisfactory of evergreens for parks or home grounds. It has horizontal branches with drooping branchlets, bluish-green needles and cones to 4½ in. *P. macrocarpa* (Big-cone-spruce) has drooping branches and cones to 7 in. *P. japonica* has glossy leaves notched at the tip and 2-in. cones. *P. sinensis* also has notched leaves and 2½ in. cones.

PSIDIUM (sid'-i-um). A genus of trees and shrubs commonly called Guava (which see), grown in tropical and subtropical countries for their fruit which is made into jelly.

P T E L E A (tee'-lee-ah) *trifoliata.* A small unimportant American tree-like shrub called Hop-tree, which see.

PTERIDIUM (tee-rid'-i-um). A genus of ferns well distributed through the world, belonging to the group which has linear fruit-dots concealed under the margins of the pinnae. The only species of possible garden use is *P. latiusculum,* the common Bracken, which grows in dry soil all over this country, and is excellent for covering waste land but too rampant for mixed plantings in beds.

PTERIS (tee'-ris). A large genus of ferns of world-wide distribution known as Brakes and characterized by the continuous linear fruit-dots under the reflexed margins of the pinnae. The only species native to this country, outside of Fla., is *P. aquilina* which grows only in the W. and is so closely related to the Bracken (*Pteridium latiusculum*) as to need no further comment here. Some exotic species are decorative greenhouse plants and a few will endure living-room conditions. These should have a compost of ordinary loam and peat with a little sand, and should stand in subdued light. The generic name is from a Greek word for "wing," later applied to many ferns.

SPECIES

P. argyrea (Silver Brake). Each pinna and each lobe of the pinnae of its

2- to 3-ft. fronds is marked by a broad band of purest white. For cool or warm greenhouse, but requiring special care.

aspericaulis. A dwarf species from India. The fronds are 1½ ft. tall, once-pinnate, the lowest pair of pinnae again divided, and the rest deeply lobed. A fern of very handsome color, being bright red when young and changing through bronze shades, to a clear glossy green. Some fancy varieties are variegated in color.

cretica (Cretan Brake). A reliable cool-greenhouse and living-room plant with many horticultural varieties available. Next to the Boston Fern (which see) and Chinese Brake (see below) it is probably the most satisfactory indoor fern, if the atmosphere can be kept reasonably moist. The broad fronds are 1 to 2 ft. long, once-pinnate but deeply lobed, and sometimes toothed.

ensiformis var. *victoriae* (Queen Fern). A warm-greenhouse species, 12 to 18 in. tall, slender, elaborately forked and highly variable.

serrulata (Chinese Brake). One of the easiest of house plants to grow, and interesting because of its habit of producing unexpected forked, crested, plumed and other forms. The texture is thin and papery, the color is a pleasing dull green, and the 9 to 18 in. fronds are deeply divided into winged segments, with pale brown wiry stipes. It grows naturally on certain old walls at Charleston, S. C., and is thought to have been introduced accidentally in shipments of tea from China.

vittata (Ribbon Fern). A curious fern of S. Fla., suitable for the warm greenhouse. The long, blue-green, ribbon-like fronds are produced in great abundance from a rootstock with golden hairs. Best grown on the stumps of old tree ferns or in hollowed logs.

PTERITIS (tee-rit′-is). A genus of ferns, including one N. American species, *P. nodulosa,* the Ostrich Fern (which see); excellent for garden cultivation.

PTEROCARYA (ter-oh-kay′-ri-ah). A genus of Asiatic trees known as Wing-nut (which see), grown for ornament.

PTEROSTYRAX (ter-oh-sty′-raks.) A genus of Asiatic trees and shrubs with white flowers, commonly called EPAULET-TREE, which see.

PTYCHOSPERMA (ty-koh-spur′-mah). A genus of Feather Palms from Australia and nearby islands. The most interesting species is *P. elegans,* a slender tree to 20 ft. with gracefully arching featherform leaves 3 ft. in length. It is grown in S. Fla. in rich moist soil. This is probably the palm often called *Seaforthia elegans,* the plant listed by dealers under that name being usually *Archontophoenix alexandrae.*

PUBESCENT. Covered (but not matted) with hairs, particularly short, soft, downlike and not very dense hairs, like those on the under side of the leaves of hardy catalpa, the twigs of the flowering dogwood, or the throat of the flower of *Crocus vernus. Puberulent* means somewhat pubescent.

PUCCOON. Common name for *Lithospermum canescens,* a perennial with orange-yellow flowers.

PUDDING - PIPE - TREE. Another name for the Golden-shower (*Cassia fistula*), a tropical tree with large racemes of yellow flowers. It is a kind of Senna, which see.

PUDDLE. A thick mixture of clay and water; also the dipping of roots of newly dug trees, bushes and woody vines

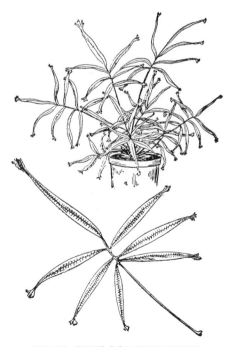

SMALL FERN FOR THE HOUSE
Cretan Brake (Pteris cretica) is an intriguing plant to raise indoors; its finger-like fronds take various shapes. It needs plenty of water, but never on the leaves.

in such a mixture to check loss of moisture between digging and replanting.

Using the word in quite another sense, clay soils "puddle" if worked while too wet. Their texture is changed and they tend to bake, become hard and then crack open into brick-like clods on drying. To prevent this, do not work clay when it glistens with moisture or sticks to the spade, fork or plow. To offset it or lessen a soil's tendency to puddle, work in sand, sifted coal ashes, any available sort of humus or vegetable matter, and lime. See also PLANTING; TRANSPLANTING.

PUERARIA (peu-er-ay'-ri-ah) *thunbergiana.* A hardy twining vine with fragrant purple flowers, called KUDZU-VINE, which see.

PULMONARIA (pul-moh-nay'-ri-ah). A genus of European perennial herbs with creeping rootstocks; they belong to the Borage Family and are closely related to the forget-me-not. Commonly known as Lungwort they have large basal leaves, often mottled, and bear blue or purple flowers in flat-topped clusters. Attractive, decorative plants for the border, they thrive best in a semi-shaded position in rich moist soil. They may be grown from seed, but are easily increased by division of the clumps.

P. saccharata (Bethlehem-sage), to 1½ ft., has white-spotted leaves and whitish or reddish-violet flowers. *P. angustifolia,* to 1 ft., with dark blue flowers, has two other color forms, var. *aurea,* and var. *azurea. P. montana,* to 1½ ft., has bright green leaves and violet flowers. *P. officinalis* has spotted leaves and odd reddish flowers fading to violet.

PUMMELO, SHADDOCK and POMPELMOUS. Popular names for *Citrus maxima,* sometimes misapplied to the grapefruit or pomelo (*C. paradisi*). The two are distinguished by the fact that the pummelo bears larger, coarser-grained fruits singly instead of in clusters as does the grapefruit. See CITRUS FRUITS.

PUMPKIN. A name loosely applied, sometimes interchangeably with "squash," to the plants and edible fruits of several species of Cucurbita, which see.

Pumpkins thrive best in the full sun, and in rich, well-drained, light soils. Generally the seed is sown where the plants are to mature. Often, however, where the seasons are short growth is hastened by sowing them on inverted sods, or in berry

boxes or flower pots, whence the plants are transplanted to the open ground after danger of frost has passed. Frequently field varieties are planted (as partner crops) in vacant hills in corn fields. Bush varieties are set 4 or 5 ft. apart, and vining kinds, 10 or 12 ft. Generally only one plant is allowed to a "stand" or hill. In soil less than moderately rich a forkful of well-decayed manure should be mixed with the soil at each stand.

The fruits must be gathered before frost touches them, handled as carefully as eggs to prevent bruising and consequent decay, laid in a sunny place or in a coldframe or deep straw, covered in cold and wet weather until the shells become hard (in about two weeks), and then stored where the air is dry and the temperature does not fall below 50 deg. So handled they should keep until after midwinter.

Pumpkin vines may be attacked by downy mildew, bacterial wilt and anthracnose but are not often seriously injured. The squash bug and squash vine borer are the worst insect pests. See under CUCURBITA. See also SQUASH.

PUNCTATE. Dotted with pits such as the resinous depressions on Wax-myrtle leaves; they may be colored or translucent, on the surface or internal.

PUNK-TREE. A common name for *Melaleuca leucadendra,* an Austrialian tree with creamy flowers in spikes.

PUPA. The form during which an insect, which undergoes "complete metamorphosis" (see INSECTS), changes from the larval or grub to the adult state. During this stage (sometimes erroneously called a "resting stage") locomotion and feeding cease, respiration is reduced, and all available energy is devoted to the development of wings, legs, mouth parts and other appendages of the adult and to the maturing of the reproductive organs. A pupa may be naked and exposed (in which state it is called a *chrysalis*), or enclosed in a case, which may be anything from a folded leaf to a silken cocoon. See also BEETLES; INSECTS; CHRYSALIS; COCOON.

PURPLE-BELLS. Common name for *Rhodochiton volubile,* a tender, free-flowering Mexican vine of graceful habit, belonging to the Figwort Family. More vigorous than Maurandia (which see), to which it is closely related, it thrives under the same treatment. The leaves are heart-shaped and toothed, and the red-stemmed drooping purplish-red flowers, more than 2 in. long, are borne singly. If seed is sown early it will flower the first season.

PURPLE-WREATH. Common name for *Petrea volubilis,* a tropical woody vine with blue flowers and showy fruits.

P U R S H I A (pur'-shi-ah) *tridentata.* Antelope-brush. A shrubby plant from the western part of the country, belonging to the Rose Family. A gray-leaved deciduous shrub to 6 ft. with small yellow, not very showy flowers, it is fairly hardy N. if given a sunny well-drained place. Propagated by layers and cuttings.

PURSLANE, or PUSLEY. Common name for *Portulaca oleracea,* a persistent succulent annual weed of E. vegetable gardens, sometimes used as a pot herb. See WEEDS.

Winter-purslane is *Montia perfoliata,* a small herb sometimes grown in moist ground for salad and cooking.

The Purslane Family (Portulacaceae) includes several useful garden subjects, such as Claytonia, Lewisia, Montia, etc., as well as Portulaca.

PUSCHKINIA (push-kin'-i-ah). A genus of small bulbous plants of the Lily Family. They resemble the early-flowering squills (which see), but are not so brilliantly blue, the small nodding blossoms in loose clusters being striped pale blue and white. Only one species, *P. scilloides,* is commonly grown; it is charming in the rock garden or on the edge of the border. It increases slowly if left undisturbed.

PUSLEY, or PUSSLEY. Colloquial name for Purslane (*Portulaca oleracea*), a persistent garden weed. The tips, if gathered young before the flower buds develop, make an excellent pot herb, like New-Zealand spinach. See PURSLANE.

PUSSY-TOES. A common name for Antennaria, a genus of small woolly perennial herbs. See also EVERLASTINGS.

PUSSY WILLOW. Common name throughout the E. States for the deciduous tree, *Salix discolor,* whose large silvery catkins or *aments* appear before the leaves in late winter or early spring. It grows to 20 ft., sometimes in tree form, but more often forms a shrub to about 10 ft. In either form it is attractive, not only because of the catkins but because of its symmetrical growth. It does well in dry ground as well as moist locations and is easily propagated by cuttings. Where cut sprays of "pussies" are more important

than garden or landscape effect, plants can be severely cut back each spring, year after year.

PUTTY-ROOT. Common name for *Aplectrum hyemale,* a native hardy orchid also called Adam-and-Eve in some places. It has yellowish-brown flowers with 3-lobed lips, borne in racemes on 12 in. stems, with one leaf at the base. It is occasionally grown in the bog garden in very moist, acid soil. The common name, Putty-root, is given on account of the consistency of the sticky substance of the old bulbs, which is sometimes used to mend broken china.

PUYA (peu'-yah). A genus of large S. American dry-region herbs with dense rosettes of spiny edged leaves and spikes of yellow, purple or blue flowers. Related to Bromelia (which see), they require the same sort of treatment whether in Calif. gardens or, as sometimes grown, in greenhouses.

PYCNANTHEMUM (pik-nan'-thee-mum). A genus of native perennial herbs called Mountain-mint (which see), bearing small purple or white flowers in late summer or fall.

PYRACANTHA (pir-ah-kan'-thah). A genus of evergreen, mostly thorny, shrubs of the Rose Family called Firethorn (which see). Their masses of white flowers are followed by many brilliant orange-red "berries"—really diminutive apples or pomes.

PYRETHRUM (py-ree'-thrum). The name of a former genus of plants of the Composite Family now considered as part of the genus Chrysanthemum (which see). As a common name it is applied by florists to *Chrysanthemum coccineum* (or *C. roseum*) a perennial with finley cut foliage, bearing in spring or summer flower-heads of white to lilac or crimson on long erect stems; and sometimes to *C. cinerariaefolium.* See PYRETHRUM, below. In gardens the name is also applied to *C. parthenium,* better known as Feverfew, which see.

PYRETHRUM. An insecticide manufactured from the dried daisy-like flowers of three species of chrysanthemum. The form produced in Asia, known as "Persian insect powder," is made from *C. roseum* and *C. carneum;* Dalmatian powder is made from *C. cinerariaefolium,* a plant being grown for the purpose on a large scale in Calif. and other parts of the U. S.; the American product is also known as Buhach. Against fleas, pyrethrum is used as a dust; on plants, it is usually used with soap as a spreader. Follow the manufacturers' directions. See also IN-SECTICIDE.

PYROLA (pir-oh'-lah). A genus of evergreen, dwarf perennial herbs with waxy whitish flowers called Shinleaf, which see.

PYROLACEAE (pir-oh-lay'-see-ee). The Shinleaf Family. The name, a diminutive form of Pyrus, the pear genus, refers to a fancied resemblance in foliage. Some scientists combine this group with others in the Ericaceae or Heath Family. Its members, mostly evergreens, are low herbs found in N. regions. Their flowers are small and regular and in Pyrola, the genus principally cultivated, are borne on an upright, leafless stalk.

PYROSTEGIA (pir-oh-stee'-ji-ah). Evergreen climbing shrubs, belonging to the Bignonia Family. *P. ignea* (formerly *Bignonia venusta*), the principal species, is a popular vine outdoors in the warmest parts of the country and is sometimes grown under glass. The leaves have 2 to 3 leaflets, and the tendrils, by which it climbs, are 3-parted. It has showy drooping clusters of reddish-orange flowers with reflexed lobes. Propagated by cuttings.

PYRUS (py'-rus). THE POME FRUITS. An important group of mostly deciduous trees, rarely shrubs, native in cool temperate regions of the N. hemisphere and belonging to the Rose Family. The genus includes valuable orchard fruits and many good ornamentals, showy in spring when in bloom, and attractive in fall with their colorful fruit. (See illustrations, Plate 42.) Most of them are hardy N., and of easy culture in well-drained soil. Propagation is by seed and, in the case of named varieties, by budding and grafting. See also APPLE; CRAB; PEAR.

PRINCIPAL SPECIES

APPLE GROUP—*Sometimes called genus Malus*

P. coronaria (Wild Sweet Crab) grows to 30 ft., very handsome in spring with pink and white fragrant flowers. The fruits are like small green apples, hard and sour but good for jelly making.

ioensis (Prairie Crab-Apple) is a tree to 30 ft., with large blush or pink flowers. Var. *plena,* known as Bechtels Crab, has very showy double pink flowers.

The foregoing are native kinds and very subject to cedar rust.

malus (Apple, which see). A round-headed tree to 40 ft. or more, native in Europe and Asia and long and widely cultivated for its fruit, in many named varieties. Var. *paradisiaca* is the Paradise Apple, a dwarf form of great value as a dwarfing stock. Var. *aldenhamensis* is a form with leaves marked with a purple midrib, semi-double light red flowers, and purplish-red fruit. Var. *niedzwetzkyana* is a very conspicuous form with reddish bark and wood, purplish leaves, and reddish-purple flowers and fruit.

atrosanguinea makes a small bushy tree, very floriferous and showy with rosy-carmine flowers.

baccata (Siberian Crab-Apple) is a handsome tree to 40 ft., with snowy-white flowers and small red or yellow fruit.

eleyi is a vigorous hybrid, with reddish purple leaves, light red flowers and purple-red fruit.

floribunda is a large shrub or small tree, very floriferous with carmine-tipped buds but pale flowers; especially showy in fall with pea-size red and yellow fruit. Var. *arnoldiana* is a form with larger lighter colored flowers and yellow fruit; var. *scheideckeri* is a compact form with showy pale pink flowers, often semi-double, and yellow fruit.

halliana is usually of bushy habit, with glossy leaves and deep-rose flowers. Var. *parkmani* is a form with double pink flowers.

micromalus makes a shapely little tree, one of the showiest with its pink flowers and red fruit.

prunifolia is very showy in bloom with large white flowers; also and in fall with yellow and red fruit.

sargenti is a spreading compact bush, very ornamental with red-tipped buds and white flowers, and again later with small, dark red small fruit.

spectabilis (Chinese Flowering Apple) grows to 25 ft., and has showy pink flowers, fading to white.

theifera is of stiff upright growth, with fragrant white or tinted flowers, resembling a cherry tree when in bloom.

toringoides has lobed leaves, creamy-white flowers, and yellow and red fruit.

zumi is a shapely tree of pyramidal habit to 20 ft., with pink buds and white flowers, followed by small red fruit.

Pear Group

P. communis (Common Pear) is a large upright long-lived tree, showy in spring with clusters of white flowers and cultivated for its fruit in many named varieties.

calleryana is a handsome free-flowering Chinese species, with glossy leaves very colorful in fall.

nivalis (Snow Pear) is very ornamental, the young growth being white, and the white flowers large and showy. It has small acid fruit, used in Europe for making perry, a cider-like beverage.

salicifolia is a small tree with slender, more or less drooping branches, silvery willow-like leaves, and creamy-white flowers.

PYXIDANTHERA (pik-si-dan'-ther-ah) *barbulata*. Known as Pyxie, Pine-barren Beauty and Flowering-moss, this is a creeping evergreen plant that forms cushion-like masses. It is found in sandy pine barrens from N. J. to N. C. but is rarely seen in cultivation, and apparently is not easy to get established. Its branches, about 1 ft. long, are clothed with very small leathery leaves; and it bears small white starry flowers in early spring. It belongs to the Diapensia Family.

QUAIL-BUSH. Common name for *Atriplex lentiformis,* one of the Saltbushes, a Calif. shrub that grows naturally in salty soil. It is related to the vegetable Orach (which see) grown as greens.

QUAKE GRASS. Common name for *Bromus brizaeformis,* a European ornamental grass now naturalized in U. S., often dried and used in bouquets of everlastings, which see.

QUAKING GRASS. Popular name for the genus Briza, which embraces a number of small annual and perennial ornamental grasses, so called because of the trembling of the spikelets in the lightest breeze. They are natives of the Old World and Mexico but several have been naturalized in the U. S. When dried, these grasses add much to the beauty of bouquets of everlastings. They are easy to grow from seeds sown in the early spring in any garden soil. See ORNAMENTAL GRASSES.

QUAMASIA (kwah-may'-zhi-ah). An alternative spelling of Camassia (which see), a genus of hardy N. American bulbous herbs of the Lily Family.

QUAMOCLIT (kwam'-oh-klit). Tropical annual or perennial twining vines, belonging to the Morning-glory Family and often called Star Glory. They are frequently grown from seed as tender annuals, making useful summer-flowering vines of light and rapid growth, thriving best in rather light soil in the sun.

PRINCIPAL SPECIES

Q. pinnata (Cypress-vine) is a slender annual twiner to 20 ft., with leaves divided into fine thread-like segments, and showy scarlet flowers. There is a white form called *alba.*

coccinea (Star-ipomoea) is an annual to 20 ft., with heart-shaped leaves and scarlet flowers with a yellow throat. Var. *hederifolia* is a form with 3- to 5-lobed or divided leaves and larger flowers. Var. *luteola* is a form with yellow or orange flowers.

lobata is a robust perennial with 3-lobed heart-shaped leaves and crimson flowers fading to pale yellow.

sloteri (Cardinal-climber) is a hybrid between *Q. coccinea* and *Q. pinnata.* It has palmately-lobed leaves and crimson flowers with a white throat.

QUARANTINE, PLANT. A regulation or statute promulgated and administered under the law by an authorized official of a local, State or Federal government for the purpose of preventing the introduction or spread of injurious insects or plant diseases. It may either completely prohibit the entry or movement of plant or other material known or suspected to be a host or carrier of the pest or disease (in which case it is an embargo), or merely regulate by requiring preliminary inspection and certification either of the material itself or, in the case of plants, bulbs, etc., of the premises or locality where they were grown.

REASONS FOR QUARANTINES. The individual grower combats the insects and diseases that threaten his crops by spraying, dusting, fumigating and, if necessary, destroying the most seriously infested individuals. The community—meaning the States and the United States as well as smaller divisions—employs these same methods in fighting pests on public land. But in addition, it attempts to protect all citizens and plant growers—commercial and amateur—from preventable loss by checking the spread of pests from heavily to lightly infested areas, and by preventing the introduction into "clean" territory of troubles not previously known there.

That is the basic principle behind the Federal and State plant quarantines, both foreign (that is, affecting products from foreign countries) and domestic, about which there is considerable controversy in horticultural circles. There seems no reason to doubt that the operation of quarantines in the various countries on both hemispheres has greatly retarded the spread of many serious insects and diseases, even if it may not have absolutely prevented the transfer of some of them from one land or section to another. On the other hand, as with all man-administered regulations, there are unanswered—and perhaps unanswerable—questions as to whether certain quarantines have been necessary, fair to all concerned, handled with maximum efficiency, etc. Unfortunately, there is a tendency among plant growers, as among humans generally, to approve of restrictions that appear to benefit us by controlling "the other fellow," but to vigorously protest against regulations that curtail our liberties.

The fact remains that there are in force, with the power of law, regulations as to what plants and plant products can be brought into this country or shipped from certain parts of it, and also as to when and how products that may be moved shall be handled, packed, labeled and treated at point of destination. Any' gardener likely to purchase plants from a distance, or to have occasion to ship plants or plant parts out of his immediate neighborhood, whether in small or large quantities, and whether as sales or gifts, should secure the latest information about the quarantines affecting his region and in the event of wanting to "import" or "export" such materials from his place take the necessary steps to prevent his being liable for violation of State or Federal quarantine laws.

How QUARANTINES ARE HANDLED. Federal quarantine matters are in the hands of the Bureau of Entomology and Plant Quarantine of the U. S. Department of Agriculture which has a force of scientists, inspectors, etc. in Washington, and other research workers and inspectors scattered about the country. Quarantines are promulgated by the Secretary of Agriculture when he becomes convinced that a certain situation or danger warrants such action, and after a public hearing has been held at which the situation is reviewed and the opinion of citizens heard. A quarantine is administered and enforced by the Bureau already referred to. Such a Federal quarantine takes precedence over any existing or contemplated State quarantine dealing with the same insect pest or disease; that is, a certificate permitting the movement of plant material under a Federal quarantine must be accepted and respected by a State. If, however, the Federal Department fails to find justification for a quarantine, or removes one already in force, the way is open for any State to promulgate and enforce a quarantine or embargo of its own.

State quarantines—of which there are many more than there are Federal orders—are generally administered by a State Department of Agriculture, of Farms and Markets, or of Nursery Inspection, after having been enacted as State statutes.

Often a State will coöperate with the Federal Government in seeking to control or study a pest situation, as well as in inspecting infested or suspected territory, certifying certain properties or plant materials as free and fit for shipment, etc. Sometimes such inspection activities involve the patrolling of highways and the examination of vehicles from infested areas to see that no prohibited or regulated plant materials are being carried into clean territory. In some extreme emergencies authority is given State and Federal employees to destroy, or oversee the destruction of, infested plants or plantings—as was necessary in Florida in fighting an epidemic of the fatal citrus canker that almost destroyed the citrus industry of that State. In some cases the officials find it impossible to maintain an efficient quarantine barrier with the funds provided and thereupon lift the quarantine, such as that against the European corn borer; or the trouble may be found insufficiently serious to warrant the expense and inconvenience of a general quarantine, as in the case of the phony peach disease.

SOME IMPORTANT QUARANTINES. While there are in all several hundred plant quarantines—Federal and State—now in effect, many of them are relatively local or limited in application, and a number deal with staple crops rather than those of interest to the home gardener. Some of those with which he is or might easily become concerned may be briefly mentioned herewith. Additional information can—and should—be secured from the Department of Agriculture in Washington, and from the corresponding State department, either direct or through the nearest plant inspector or quarantine headquarters.

FOREIGN QUARANTINES. The most important and sweeping of these is No. 37, issued in 1919, involving all nursery stock, plants and bulbs (with certain specified exceptions) from all foreign countries. Serving to cut off supplies of many kinds of plant materials previously imported in great quantities from Europe, this caused a great change in the horticultural situation, affecting the trend in the use of plants and stimulating attempts to produce in this country many materials that foreign competition had theretofore made unprofitable. The subject of much vigorous discussion, this order is still a moot question, made recently more so by the announcement by the Government that in December, 1936, its provision prohibiting the importation of many kinds of Narcissus would be revoked.

Other foreign quarantines are No. 7, affecting all 5-leaved pines, on account of the White Pine blister rust (see under PINE); No. 20, affecting all European pines on account of the European pine shoot moth; and No. 70, affecting elm trees, logs, etc., from Europe on account of the Dutch elm disease.

DOMESTIC QUARANTINES. These are of 2 kinds as already explained: Federal and State. The latter are too numerous to discuss here. Of the former the following are perhaps the most important:

No. 38, controlling the movement of barberry and mahonia plants (which are intermediate hosts of the black stem rust of grains) into and out of some 13 states; No. 45, affecting the movement of various host plants, quarry products, Christmas trees, lumber, etc., from New England on account of the gypsy moth (which see); No. 48, affecting nursery and greenhouse products (and also cut flowers and vegetables at certain periods) produced in a large part of E. U. S., on account of the Japanese beetle (which see); No. 60, regulating the movement of sand, soil or earth, alone or around the roots of plants from the Japanese beetle area, on account of that pest; No. 63, affecting currants and gooseberries as alternate hosts of the white pine blister rust; and No. 72, affecting certain S. crops on account of the white-fringed beetle.

QUEEN ANNES LACE. Common name for an herb (*Daucus carota*) of the Parsley Family, having finely-cut foliage and filmy white flowers in umbels. It is a weed, widely naturalized through N. A.

QUEEN FERN (*Pteris ensiformis* var. *victoriae*). An Australian brake, excellent for warm greenhouse conditions, growing 12 to 18 in. tall.

QUEEN-LILY. Common name for *Curcuma petiolata*, an Asiatic tuberous-rooted perennial herb of the Ginger Family, grown in warm greenhouses for its yellowish-white flowers.

QUEEN-OF-ORCHIDS. Common name of an epiphytic Malayan orchid, *Grammatophyllum speciosum;* also called Letter-plant. See ORCHIDS.

QUEEN-OF-THE-MEADOWS. Common name for *Filipendula ulmaria,* a tall (6 ft.) perennial herb of Asia naturalized in the U. S. and grown in hardy borders for its panicles of white flowers.

QUEEN-OF-THE-PRAIRIE. Common name for *Filipendula rubra,* another hardy perennial form of Meadow-sweet growing to 8 ft. with peach-pink spirea-like blossoms.

QUEENSLAND-NUT. Common name for *Macadamia ternifolia,* an evergreen Australian tree belonging to the Protea Family. Cultivated in the warmest parts of the U.' S. for its large edible nuts, it also has merit for an ornamental tree. It can stand some frost and dry conditions, but grows best in deep moist loamy soil, where it may attain 50 ft. It has whorls of shining leaves to a foot long, and bears white flowers in clusters about as long as the leaves and nuts that are smooth and shining.

QUERCUS (kwer'-kus). A genus of magnificent, mostly deciduous hardwood trees, widely known and admired as the Oak (which see). It is characterized by the capped nuts called acorns and includes some of the finest and strongest trees of the N. temperate zone.

QUICKLIME. A popular term for freshly burned limestone, containing up to 95 per cent or more of calcium oxide, depending on the purity of the original rock. It is finer, lighter and in better shape for even application to the land than ground limestone, and much quicker in its characteristic lime action, namely the modification of the texture of both clay and sandy soils and the liberation or making available of plant food, especially nitrogen. The name quicklime is given because, when water is added, there is an immediate, vigorous reaction with the evolution of much heat. This process is called "slaking" and the resulting powdery, noncaustic material is slaked or hydrated lime. If water is not added, slaking takes place very gradually through action of the moisture in the air, producing air-slaked lime. See SOIL; AMENDMENT, SOIL.

QUINCE. Various shrubs grown for fruit or ornament or both. The common quince (*Cydonia oblonga,* but formerly included with apples and pears as *Pyrus cydonia*) is a wide-spreading shrub or small crooked tree of slow growth. It thrives best in deep, heavy, moist, not over-rich soil, where, however, the fruit produced is dull greenish-yellow instead

QUINCE IN FLOWER AND FRUIT
The quince (Cydonia oblonga) makes an attractive low tree for gardens and the fruit is prized for jam and preserve making. The variety pictured is Orange Quince.

of the rich golden-yellow characteristic of lighter soils.

For home use one or two specimens should yield an ample supply, for a mature bush should bear 2 to 4 pecks of fruit annually. Because of the beauty of the flowers and of the ripe fruit, too, quinces deserve a place as ornamental subjects, provided a circular space 15 ft. or more in diameter is allowed for each plant.

As they are shallow rooted plants they do better under mulch than if the soil is cultivated. So treated, they are also less liable to fire blight because the growths are less sappy and therefore more resistant to attack. The aim should always be moderate, not luxuriant, growth and this may be gained partly by the sparing use of nitrogenous fertilizers and manures and liberal dressings of potash and phosphoric acid.

As the quince blossoms rather late in spring and bears its flowers on green shoots of the current season, it is a regular, annual cropper. However, it is prone to set more fruit than it can develop to full size, so all defective and crowded ones (and often others) should be removed while small. This is easily done a week or two after the flowers fade while the stems are still soft enough to permit pinching them off.

One-year or two-year bushes are better to plant than older ones. They can then be trained in either tree or bush form. The advantage of the tree form is that in it borers are more easily controlled; that of the bush form is that fire blight can more easily be kept in check and new stems can be induced and encouraged when necessary. See control of these and other quince enemies under APPLE.

Pruning consists merely of removing dead, dying and superfluous branches while the plants are dormant.

ENEMIES. Fire blight (which see) is a common disease of both common and flowering quinces. Infected wood must be removed with great care. The quince rust has juniper as its alternate host. (See RUSTS; also JUNIPER.) It produces deep orange spores in white cluster cups on the backs of the leaves and on the fruit. A leaf and fruit blight common on pear (which see) may seriously injure quince trees and the black rot of apple (which see) may occur.

Until the advent of the Oriental fruit moth (which see) the quince curculio was the most destructive pest of this tree. These small gray snout beetles appear in midsummer and the flesh-colored grubs tunnel through the fruit. Two thorough applications of arsenate of lead, when the beetles appear and begin to lay eggs, give some control. Several aphids, the codling moth and the San José scale commonly in-

THE HANDSOME FLOWERING QUINCE
Formerly called Cydonia, but now Chaenomeles lagenaria, it is a charming spiny shrub and hedge plant with flowers in white, pink, or red, and fragrant green fruit, inedible raw but usable for jellies, etc.

fest quince. See control measures under those subjects.

The Flowering or Japanese Quince (*Chaenomeles lagenaria,* but often listed in catalogs as *C. japonica*) has long been a favorite ornamental in home gardens because of its pink to scarlet flowers. These, appearing before the leaves or with the earlier ones, suggest one of its popular names, Burning-bush, though this properly belongs to species of Euonymus (which see). The Flowering Quince sometimes attains a height of 10 ft. and a spread of 20 ft. The hard, greenish-yellow, highly fragrant fruit is often placed in bureaus and chests to perfume bedding and clothing. It is not palatable raw but is sometimes used to make jelly. Nurseries offer several varieties which differ mainly in the colors of their flowers, which range from white through blush, pink and striped to crimson and salmon; there are also double forms.

The Dwarf Japanese Quince (*C. japonica*) grows only 3 ft. high and bears orange-scarlet flowers. It has a prostrate variety (var. *alpina,* or *C. sargenti*) which is useful for planting on slopes.

The Chinese Quince (*C. sinensis*), a large shrub or small tree to 20 ft. high, bears light pink flowers in spring and yellow, woody, fragrant fruits often 7 in. long in autumn. Though hardy along the Atlantic Coast to Long Island, N. Y., it is tender inland N. of Philadelphia.

QUINCULA (kwin'-keu-lah) *labata.* A low, spreading, purple-flowered perennial herb of the S. W. suitable for dry sunny areas in the garden.

QUISQUALIS (kwis-kway'-lis) *indica.* A tropical climbing shrub of S. Asia, called RANGOON-CREEPER, which see.

RABBIT-TAIL GRASS. A common name for *Lagurus ovatus,* an annual grown for ornament; also called Hares-tail Grass.

RACE. A term often loosely used but which in plant breeding means a strongly marked group of individuals, capable of coming true from seed in so far as the distinguishing racial characters are concerned. Cultivated races are somewhat similar to botanical varieties; but they are usually highly developed forms, originating in cultivation and generally requiring more or less selection to keep them from degenerating. See PLANT BREEDING; STRAIN; VARIETY; CLON.

RACEME (rah-seem'). An elongated, slender flower cluster in which each flower is borne not close against the main stalk (*peduncle*) as in a spike (which see), but on a stalk or *pedicel* of its own. A raceme may be erect or drooping, and loose or compact, depending on the length of the pedicels.

RACHIS (ray'-kis). The continuation of the twig into the flower cluster so as to form the main axis on which are borne the flowers (and individual flower stalks if they are present) making up the inflorescence. See also FERNS.

RADISH. An annual herb (*Raphanus sativus*) grown for its crisp-fleshed roots of various sizes, shapes and colors; and, in the case of the rat-tailed or aërial radish, for its long, soft, thick pods which are pickled or used as a salad. Root radishes are of three classes: (1) Small, globular, or oblong spring varieties, white, pink or red in color, which reach edible size in from 3 to 5 weeks; (2) somewhat larger, oblong or slender, pink or white summer varieties that stand hot weather well; and (3) white or black winter varieties that require cool conditions, grow to large (sometimes enormous) size and are used fresh or stored like turnips. Small radishes are invariably eaten raw as a relish; the larger kinds are occasionally boiled and served like turnips.

To be crisp, mild and of the best quality radishes should grow rapidly and be used as soon as large enough. This means frequent small sowings which fit well into the garden scheme as interplantings between larger, slower growing crops and also to mark rows of seed which start slowly. Forcing radishes may be grown an inch or two apart in rows only 6 or 8 in. apart; the larger kinds need up to 12 in. or more between the rows and correspondingly more space between the plants. Before planting sift out and discard small, light seeds. Make successional sowings every week or so, first in the hotbed from late winter until early spring; then outdoors until late spring, using the summer sorts for the later plantings.

After midsummer sow the large winter kinds which become hard, stringy and strong-flavored if started in hot weather. Dug before frost and stored in a cool place, these will keep for several weeks. For use, peel and cut the tender, crisp roots lengthwise in thin slices.

A white rust occurring on many crucifers is most serious on radish, causing prominent white blisters on the leaves and the thickened and distorted stems. Spraying is not usually justified, but crop rotation, cultivating to keep down cruciferous weeds and burning of all infected crop refuse are advisable preventive measures against this and other radish troubles, which are chiefly those discussed under CRUCIFER. The most common insects are plant lice, the cabbage root maggot and flea beetles. The maggot may be kept out of small

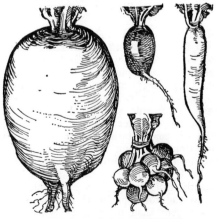

FOUR KINDS OF RADISHES
Left, the large Winter Radish—there are black and white kinds; right, the slender white Icicle type. Between the two, above, the Olive type, and below, the Early Forcing Radish, both red-skinned varieties.

plantings by screening the bed; or corrosive sublimate (which see) may be applied in a stream along the rows.

Horse-radish (which see) is *Armoracia rusticana.*

RAFFIA. Dried vegetable fibre made from the peeled cuticle of the leaves of a

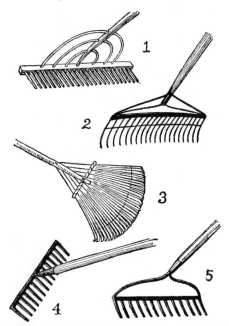

USE THE RIGHT RAKE FOR EACH TASK
Here are styles that might well be called indispensable. 1. Wooden leaf and lawn rake. 2. Spring-tooth lawn-comb or broom, easy to use for light litter. 3. Japanese bamboo rake—use with a sweeping motion. 4. Standard steel rake for soil working. 5. Bow rake, a variation of (4) preferred by some.

Madagascar palm (*Raphia ruffia*) and used for tying plants to stakes, for bunching vegetables, in budding and for various other gardening purposes. Sold in woven plaits by the pound at seed and garden supply stores, it is light, inexpensive, clean, easy to use and surprisingly strong. It gradually rots under the influence of moisture and weather so should not be used for permanent tying, but it is usually good for a season in the flower garden. It is somewhat easier to handle if slightly moistened. It is obtainable dyed green and some prefer this form as less conspicuous than the natural yellow; but it is not so strong or durable when so treated and colored raffia is less used in gardens than as a weaving material in handcraft work.

RAGGED ROBIN. A common name for *Lychnis flos-cuculi,* a herbaceous perennial with red or pink flowers.

RAGGED SAILOR. A common name for *Centaurea cyanus,* the familiar Cornflower, a hardy blue-flowered annual widely used in beds and borders.

RAGWORT. A common name for the genus Senecio, comprising herbs, shrubs and trees, some of which are grown for ornament.

RAIN-LILY. Common name for Cooperia, a genus of native bulbous plants sometimes called Prairie-lily. It is also applied to the related genus Zephyranthes. Belonging to the Amaryllis Family, the Rain-lilies are delightfully fragrant, summer-blooming bulbs with grassy leaves and waxy, long-tubed, flat flowers which open only in the evening. They are grown in the open in the S. and W. States. Plant the bulbs in the garden in early spring, lift them in the fall and pack them in dry soil so they will not shrivel.

The two species grown are *C. pedunculata* and *C. drummondi,* both having white flowers tinged red on the outside; those of *C. drummondi* are slightly larger and have longer tubes.

RAISIN. Originally a term for grape clusters; now popularly it means dried grapes of different, usually small, varieties. Probably the Muscat varieties are the most important. See GRAPE.

RAISIN-TREE, JAPANESE. Common name for *Hovenia dulcis,* a hardy deciduous tree with greenish flowers and small fruits with fleshy, edible stems.

RAKES and RAKING. The rake is primarily a tillage tool, which, in its simplest form, consists of short metal or wooden teeth, or tines, attached to a bar set at right angles to a long handle. Its principal uses are (1) to draw loose materials (as leaves, grass-clippings, etc.) together; (2) to break up soil clods, and (3) to level and make soil surfaces fine. The simple form is varied in many ways to adapt the tool to special purposes. the variations involving differences in size, number, shape, length, closeness and arrangement of the teeth and the material of which the tool is made.

TYPES. Some styles are strongly built for heavy duty, such as raking gravel, breaking clay clods and removing stones from garden beds; others are made for light work, such as gathering grass clippings on lawns: still others are especially adapted for gathering leaves, some of these including various kinds of self-cleaning devices. Although the teeth are usually of rigid steel or in the form of wooden pegs, some are of flexible metal, split bamboo, or rubber-covered flexible wire. No one style is adapted to all duties, so every gardener should have an assortment of styles, each adapted to a specific kind of work and the physique of the worker.

For the average garden, this assortment should include a wide and a narrow "ordinary" steel garden rake with a 5- or 6-ft. handle, preferably of "clear" white ash; a wooden "lawn rake," with either wood or metal bows, for clearing up twigs, litter, etc., and "dressing" drives and paths; several light bamboo or "lawn-broom" type rakes whose long, flexible tines literally sweep up grass clippings and leaves, without injuring the grass; and, possibly, one with flexible rubber tines.

How to Rake. The correct and efficient use of the rake so as to conserve effort while doing good work is a real art. In gathering leaves and twigs, the large wooden rake should be used with long sliding strokes, the tines being lifted only enough to clear the debris; the light bamboo or steel spring kind is better used like a broom to "brush" the litter along. The steel rake is used differently, whether smoothing newly dug soil, breaking a surface crust or destroying young weeds.

In fitting soil and preparing a seed bed use alternating push and pull strokes, letting the teeth touch only the top of the clods at first, then sinking them gradually until finally they work freely in the pulverized soil. Sometimes it helps to turn the rake over and use the flat top to break large clods and fill hollows and uneven spots. To break up a crust and create a dust mulch rake only 1 in. or less deep, letting part of the weight of the tool come on the hand nearest the head and propelling it with the other. This same delicate action is most effective in destroying a new crop of weeds, especially if the rake is moved backward and forward with a slight sidewise movement so as to cover every inch of surface. Where seeds are planted a full inch or more deep, this raking can be done in two directions, at right angles, over the whole planted area, thereby getting rid of a host of weeds that would otherwise call for much close, or perhaps hand, work later.

Even the raking of gravel or ashes, as in making a path or drive, has a technique which, if followed, means a better job. The trick consists of constantly pulling forward from the back and top of the pile the larger stones and clinkers so that they form a layer in front and at the bottom. Then as the process is continued, the finest material is left on the top where it can be smoothly leveled or crowned and then rolled to a firm, even surface.

See also CULTIVATION; LAWN.

RAMERO. A local name in S. Calif. for *Trichostema lanatum,* a desirable shrubby perennial of the Mint Family. See BLUE CURLS.

RAMONDA (rah-mon'-dah). A genus of herbs of the Gesneria Family having rosette-like leaves and broadly bell-shaped flowers to 1 in. across, usually violet or purple. The Ramondas are exquisite rock-garden plants, and though difficult to grow are worth the care that must be given them. *R. pyrenaica,* a perennial growing to 3 in., the most popular species, is hardy in the E. States. Seeds should be sown in the spring and the small plants wintered over in the coldframe, then placed in rock crevices in a cool shaded position in acid peaty soil. They need perfect drainage and will often grow splendidly on the shady side of a rock wall. When once estab-

ANOTHER WAY TO USE A RAKE
Unorthodox, perhaps, but helpful when you have a long ladder to raise alone. Just hook the head over the lower rung and stand on the rake handle to keep the ladder end on the ground.

lished they will self-seed freely, but old plants can be divided. After freezing weather arrives they should be lightly mulched to prevent alternate freezing and thawing. Var. *alba* has white flowers. *R. nathaliae,* from Serbia, has hairy oval leaves and lavender flowers with yellow centers.

RAMPION (ram'-pi-un). Common name for *Campanula rapunculus,* a biennial species of Bellflower whose roots and leaves are eaten raw as salad.

Horned-rampion (which see) is the common name for the genus Phyteuma.

RANGOON-CREEPER. Common name for *Quisqualis indica,* a tropical shrub of vigorous climbing habit, sometimes grown in warm greenhouses. It thrives best when planted out in a bed of fibrous loam, peat and sand. In summer it bears loose clusters of fragrant flowers, with long green calyx-tubes and petals varying from pink to red. After flowering it needs a resting period and later a severe pruning to induce a good growth again. Propagated by soft wood cuttings.

RANUNCULACEAE (rah-nun-keu-lay'-see-ee). The Buttercup or Crowfoot Family, a hardy group of mainly herbaceous, but sometimes shrubby and woody climbing plants, widely distributed over temperate and arctic regions. The name comes from the Latin for "little frog," referring to the moisture-loving character of the typical genus. All the flower-parts are generally present and regular, but there are many departures from the type, as in monkshood and larkspur. Many of the genera supply favorite flower-garden subjects and some, as Aconitum, yield powerful drugs. See also ADONIS; ANEMONE; AQUILEGIA; CIMICIFUGA; CLEMATIS; DELPHINIUM; ERANTHIS; HELLEBORE; NIGELLA; PEONY; RANUNCULUS; TROLLIUS.

RANUNCULUS (rah-nun'-keu-lus). A widely distributed genus of annual, biennial or perennial herbs of the Crowfoot Family, including both wild plants and others grown in the flower garden, border or rockery under the familiar names of Crowfoot and Buttercup. Most of the species are perennial, and only a few have been modified into variously colored forms and doubles, the common plants bearing yellow, white or red blossoms with mostly 5 sepals and petals and many stamens. Most of the Buttercups are propagated from seeds or by division of the plants in the spring. Most of the Crowfoots are yellow, but there are several white species, especially in the Batrachium group, which includes bog or aquatic plants. Many Crowfoots are adaptable to rock-garden use, all preferring well-drained soil and a sunny location.

The florists' species is *R. asiaticus* (Turban or Persian Buttercup). It is grown in the greenhouse or outdoors in the summer and propagated by the peculiar, tooth-like tuberous roots, which should be taken up and stored over winter. It is not generally considered hardy but if the soil is well drained so that surface water will run off easily success may be achieved. The plant likes a cool, moist atmosphere and indoors success cannot be obtained in a hot, dry room. Like the cape bulbs, it should be put in a temperature of between 40 and 50 deg. F. immediately after potting, for root and top growth are simultaneous. Other features of this species are its simple or only slightly branched habit of growth to a height of 1½ ft., the long-stalked bright yellow flowers, and the hairy sepals. Horticultural forms are very hairy. A new variety, *superbissimus,* is taller and produces larger flowers.

One of the best rock-garden species is *R. repens,* known as Creeping Buttercup, growing from 6 to 12 in. tall, and bearing yellow flowers from May to August. The runners root at the joints and the flower sepals are slightly hairy. Var. *pleniflorus* has double flowers.

Both *R. asiaticus* and *R. repens* are perennial. An annual form is *R. ophioglossifolius,* with hollow stems, undivided leaves, small pale yellow flowers and smooth sepals, and a biennial form is *R. abortivus,* growing 2 ft. tall, with broad, toothed basal leaves and small yellow flowers.

RAOULIA (ray-oo'-li-ah). A genus of small herbs of the Composite Family that make dense mats of foliage, useful as a ground-cover for bulb plantings in mild climates. They are extensively grown in the sunny rock gardens of Calif. They may be raised from seed or increased by division and should be planted in a well-drained open position. *R. tenuicaulis,* with prostrate stems to 10 in., has grayish-downy foliage and very small heads of inconspicuous flowers. *R. australis,* with matted stems to 6 in., is valued for its yellowish, downy foliage. *R. glabra* has smooth yellowish-green foliage.

RAPE. A common name for *Brassica napus*, a hardy annual herb of the Mustard Family, grown for forage and as a cover-crop. In home gardens the seed is best sown in August or early September among standing crops at the rate of 1 to 2 oz. per 1000 sq. ft. It is not necessary to prepare the land as for most crops, although loosening the surface with a rake or a wheelhoe when possible will help get a good stand. As soon as the ground can be worked in spring, the crop should be dug or plowed under.

See also BRASSICA.

RAPHANUS (raf'-ah-nus) *sativus.* The cruciferous species from which the cultivated radish (which see) has been developed.

RAPHIA (ray'-fi-ah) **PALMS.** Feather Palms of the genus Raphia, mostly native to tropical Africa. They have short trunks and magnificent, spreading leaves, sometimes 65 ft. long by 8 ft. wide. Several species are grown in S. Fla., among them *Raphia ruffia* from Madagascar, a tree to 30 ft., bearing among the leaves 6-ft. clusters of fruit sometimes weighing 300 lbs. From the young, folded leaves of this plant is obtained the fibre called raffia (which see), a favorite material for tying up plants, bunches of vegetables, etc., and also used commercially for making baskets, woven fabrics, etc.

RAPHIOLEPIS (raf-i-ol'-e-pis). Evergreen shrubs, native of China and Japan, belonging to the Rose Family. They can only be grown outdoors where the climate is mild, but their range may be extended a little if they are trained to a wall. A well-drained soil with plenty of humus suits them well. Propagated by seeds, cuttings, or layers.

P. umbellata (Yeddo-hawthorn) grows to 12 ft. or more, and is the hardiest. It has thick, lustrous, dark green leaves and dense clusters of fragrant white flowers. *R. indica* (Indian-hawthorn) grows to 5 ft., and bears clusters of fragrant white flowers tinged pink. *R. delacouri* is a hybrid between these two species, intermediate in habit and with pink flowers.

RASPBERRY. Erect perennial plants of the Bramble genus (see RUBUS) and therefore closely related to the blackberries and dewberries. They have woody, usually prickly, biennial stems and are cultivated for their delicious fruits. (See illustration, Plate 4.) Though some red and yellow sorts grown in America belong to the European species (*R. idaeus*), the majority belong to its American variety (*R. idaeus, var. strigosus*). All these propagate themselves naturally by suckers which develop from the roots, especially when the latter are injured or broken. The many varieties of black raspberries belong to the native American species (*R. occidentalis*), called blackcap raspberry or thimbleberry, and propagate by the tips of their young canes bending over to the ground and there taking root. Purple sorts, which are hybrids of these two species, may propagate by one or the other of the two methods described.

Red, white and black varieties are most desirable and popular as dessert fruits, purple ones less so because of their color. All four kinds, but especially the last, are excellent for canning, jam and juice. Every home garden should include at least one variety of each group, and preferably three —an early, a late and a midseason one— with enough plants of each to meet family needs. Of the red varieties, American kinds should be chosen when possible because they are hardier than the European. Black varieties are less hardy than the reds; purple sorts follow the "blood" or characters of the dominant parent. Raspberries will not stand drought or heat, so they cannot be grown successfully in the South except in high altitudes or with special care as to moisture and partial shade.

CULTURE. Raspberries thrive in any well-drained soil if liberally supplied with humus and moisture. Black kinds do better than red ones in light soils. When plants are set out the stems should be cut back close to the ground. This tends to develop sturdy new shoots and a strong root system, whereas if the original stems are left the plants may die, even though they seem at first to thrive and may even bear some fruit the first season.

Though raspberry (as well as blackberry) plants produced from suckers may be planted with safety in the fall, those grown from tips (like the dewberries) should be planted only in spring. The reason is that the former may be set deeply enough to withstand any heaving of soil over winter, whereas the latter, which must be set with their buds no deeper than the soil surface, are likely to be heaved out of the ground and killed by alternate thawing and freezing. Spring setting is, therefore, best for all bramble fruits.

Varieties that propagate only by stem tips tend to form clumps or hills and are easily kept in place if the tips are not allowed to root at will and thus give rise to a veritable jungle. This is easily prevented by pinching the succulent young tips when they reach 30 to 36 in. high and by frequently moving the ends of any shoots that reach the ground if it is not desired to cut them off. See BLACKBERRY.

Popular distances to set suckering varieties are 3 ft. between plants and 5 or 6 ft. between rows. The spaces between plants in the rows may be allowed to fill up with new ones (developed from suckers), or others may be transplanted there, being set about 12 in. asunder. Black caps are generally spaced 4 or 5 ft. apart with 6 or 7 ft. between the rows. Raspberries are often planted in checks or squares so they may be cultivated in two directions. The first year, strong plants may be allowed to develop two shoots; weak ones should be permitted only one.

As soon as the last fruit has been gathered, the old canes and the puny new ones should be cut out; the former will die during winter anyway; and the latter will pro-

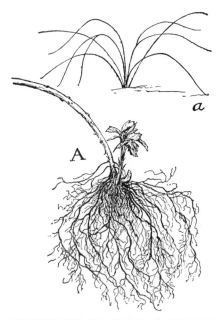

TIP-ROOTING OF BLACK RASPBERRY
This is one of the plants that naturally increases by rooting of the tips (a). At (A) is shown a tip that has rooted well, is developing new shoots and is ready to be cut lose from the parent stem and handled as a new plant.

duce no fruit. Three to five sturdy stems should be left on each plant to fruit each year. In gardens it is often more desirable to grow all raspberries (and blackberries) under a permanent, year-around mulch than to attempt constant cultivation. This conserves moisture, supplies humus, saves the labor of cultivation and reduces the bother of suckers starting up from cut roots.

In early spring, while the stems are dormant, any old dead canes should be removed and the long stems of red and yellow raspberries reduced to 3 or 3½ ft. In fact, the branches of all kinds can be shortened somewhat at this time. When flower buds can be seen, the branches may be again cut back if it is desired to increase the size and improve the equality of the fruit by reducing the size of the crop.

ENEMIES. The four chief diseases of raspberries, as well as other brambles, are yellows, anthracnose, orange-rust and cane-blight. Yellows is a virus disease which dwarfs and stunts the plants and causes the berries to dry or ripen prematurely. Remove and destroy diseased plants. Anthracnose causes small purplish spots, which later form irregular cankers with grayish-white centers; black raspberries are most susceptible. Plant only disease-free plants, cut out old and diseased canes and remove trash and weeds from around the bushes. Several sprayings with bordeaux mixture help in the control of the disease.

Cane blight, another fungous disease, causes sudden wilting. The only control of orange rust is the destruction of all diseased plants, rooting them out carefully. Crown gall (which see) is often found on raspberry bushes and in wet seasons fruits may be covered with a gray mold. See BOTRYTIS.

The most serious insect pests are two borers—the raspberry cane borer, which is the grub of a long-horned beetle; and the root borer, the adult of which is a clear-winged moth. Cut out and burn wilted canes and dig the root borers from the canes or burn infested plants. Eggs can be killed by spraying foliage with oil twice in the fall—after September 10 in the N. E. states. The raspberry cane maggot girdles the canes and causes wilted tips. Control it by cutting several inches below the girdled zone and burning all wilted tips. The fruit worm, a light yellow grub, causes the fruit to dry up; the adult is a light brown, hairy beetle that feeds on tender terminal leaves and blossoms. Spray with lead arsenate several times before the blossoms open. This treatment will also control the sawfly, whose green spiny larvae devour the foliage.

EVERBEARING RASPBERRIES. In addition to the different colored raspberry varieties (purples, scarlets, yellows and blacks) there are a few autumn-fruiting kinds, all of the red type. These are highly desirable for the home garden provided they are given the slight extra attention they need (and deserve) to make them bear in the autumn. This means plenty of plant food and, especially, sufficient moisture in the soil to make the plant food available during hot, dry weather. Unless the ground is moist the buds that produce the autumn crop will fail to develop or the fruit to ripen. A constantly maintained mulch is perhaps the easiest and cheapest means of assuring fall fruiting, though overhead irrigation where available is even better. As the fruit is borne in the fall on young shoots of the current season's development, these shoots must not be treated like old canes and cut out after fruiting; if they are, the following summer's crop will be reduced.

RATAMA (rah-tah'-mah). Common name for *Parkinsonia aculeata,* a tropical spiny tree, with fragrant, pea-like yellow flowers in loose racemes. It is used in the S. for hedges.

RAT-TAIL CACTUS. Common name for *Aporocactus flagelliformis,* a slender succulent plant with hanging, branching stems that send out aërial roots, and bear small bright red flowers. It is often grafted on other species and trained into fantastic and often grotesque forms.

RATTLEBOX. Common name for the genus Crotalaria, a member of the Pea Family, comprising herbs and shrubs having sweet-pea-like flowers and swollen pods which give rise to the common name. Some species are grown as cover-crops in the S. and others in N. greenhouses. The shrubby kinds can be increased by cuttings, but plants are usually raised from seed, which must first be soaked in warm water. *C. retusa,* an annual to 3 ft., sometimes listed as "Golden-yellow-sweet-pea," has about 12 flowers in a raceme, the yellow blossoms being streaked with purple. *C. capensis,* to 5 ft. with golden yellow flowers to 1 in. long, is a native of S. Africa widely grown

in S. Fla. *C. striata,* a perennial to 8 ft., has yellow flowers striped with brown; in the S. it is grown to be turned under for green manure. *C. lanceolata,* to 3 ft., has narrow leaves and yellow flowers with purple veins, followed by pods 1 or more in. long.

The name Rattlebox is also applied to *Rhinanthus crista-galli* (which see), an annual herb sometimes grown in rock gardens.

RATTLESNAKE FERN (*Botrychium virginianum*). The largest and commonest American species of the Grape Ferns (which see), with a single, triangular, and deeply cut blade, and a separate fruiting spike. Suitable for shaded locations in woods soil.

RATTLESNAKE MASTER. A common name for *Eryngium aquaticum,* a perennial herb with white or blue flowers and spiny bracts, useful in borders and rock gardens. See ERYNGIUM.

RATTLESNAKE-PLANTAIN. A common name for *Epipactis pubescens,* a terrestrial orchid with variegated leaves and yellowish-white flowers borne in spikes.

RATTLESNAKE-ROOT. Common name for Prenanthes, a genus of hardy perennial herbs with variously colored composite flowers, useful in wild gardens and borders.

RAVENNA GRASS. Common name for *Erianthus ravennae,* a stout ornamental perennial grass. See ERIANTHUS; also ORNAMENTAL GRASSES.

RAY FLOWER. One of the large, usually bright-colored, petal-like, strap-shaped florets that form the radiating border of the flower-head of many composite plants, such as the daisy, marguerite, sunflower, or massed together, a head, as in the dandelion. When associated with disk flowers (which see), as in the daisy, ray flowers lose their reproductive function, only the disk flowers being pollinated and bearing seed. The ray flower thus becomes primarily an organ of insect attraction, the petals of its corolla fusing into a flattened, showy, ray.

RECEPTACLE. The apex of the flower stalk upon which the floral parts are borne. It is also called *torus* and is often remarkably modified. The "fruit" of the strawberry, for instance, is an enlarged receptacle in which the seeds (called *achenes*) are embedded. In the East Indian Lotus the receptacle is greatly enlarged, but so as to enclose the seeds, not to form a berry.

RED-BAY. A common name for *Persea borbonia,* or Bull-bay, a large evergreen tree of the S. sometimes planted for ornament.

RED-BERRY. Common name for *Rhamnus crocea,* one of the Buckthorns.

REDBIRD-CACTUS. A common name for *Pedilanthus tithymaloides,* not really a cactus but a tropical American spurge with red or purple flowers.

RED-BUD or JUDAS-TREE. Common name for Cercis, a genus of deciduous shrubs or trees, native in N. America, S. Europe and Asia, belonging to the Pea Family. They are very showy in early spring, with a profusion of rose-pink flowers opening before, or as, the leaves unfold. Clusters of flowers are produced on the old stems as well as on younger growth. The foliage is handsome, and plants are well suited for the background of shrubberies. They do well in ordinary well-drained soil but are best transplanted when small, older plants being rather difficult to get established. Propagated by seeds or layers, also by greenwood cuttings under glass.

PRINCIPAL SPECIES

C. canadensis, found from N. J. to Fla., is a tall shrub or sometimes a tree to 40 ft., with a broad round head. It is the only one really hardy North, and is very showy in early spring with short clusters of rosy-pink flowers. Var. *alba,* with white, and var. *plena,* with double flowers, are listed, but apparently not common in gardens.

chinensis is an Asiatic tree to 50 ft., but in cultivation is usually shrub-like. It has glossier leaves and deeper colored flowers than *canadensis,* but is not so hardy.

racemosa, also from Asia, growing to 30 ft., is considered to be the most handsome, with pendulous racemes of rosy-pink flowers. Not hardy North.

siliquastrum (to which the name Judas-tree is sometimes restricted) is a shrub or tree of S. Europe, with large rosy-purple flowers. It is effective when trained against a wall, in which case the laterals are pruned back after flowering.

RED BUGS, APPLE. These sucking insects, which cause a pitting or dimpled appearance, dwarfing and hardening of apple, pear, and haw fruits, are well distributed east of the Mississippi River but most destructive in New England and N. Y. The eggs, laid on the bark of fruit trees, hatch in early spring and the young nymphs feed on the foliage and later on the young apples; whenever they insert their beaks the surrounding tissue becomes hardened and stops growing. Control by spraying with nicotine-sulphate at the cluster-bud period (see APPLE) and again at the time of petal-fall. Apply on warm days with two men working simultaneously on opposite sides of the trees; the bugs are so active that they can escape from a spray applied from one side only.

RED-CEDAR. A name applied to species and varieties of Juniperus which are not really cedars at all. *J. virginiana* and its varieties are called just Red-cedar; *J. scopulorum* is Colorado Red-cedar, and *J. lucayana* is Southern Red-cedar. See JUNIPER.

RED-FIR. A common name for Pseudotsuga taxifolia, the Douglas-fir or Douglas-spruce, a large W. American cone-bearing evergreen timber tree attractive and ornamental.

RED-HOT POKER. A common name for Kniphofia (which see), a genus of semi-hardy perennial herbs grown for their showy red and yellow flower spikes. Also called Torch-lily.

REDMAIDS. Common name for *Calandrinia caulescens* var. *menziesi,* an annual fleshy herb with rose or crimson flowers.

RED-OSIER DOGWOOD. Common name for *Cornus stolonifera,* a native shrub with red branches. See DOGWOOD.

RED RIBBONS. Common name for *Eucharidium concinnum,* a dainty annual plant of the Evening-primrose Family. It grows to 2 ft., has charming rose flowers with 3-lobed petals and grows readily in ordinary garden soil.

RED-ROBIN. A common name for *Geranium robertianum,* an annual or biennial herb used as a ground-cover in the moist soil of rock gardens.

REDROOT. A common name for *Lithospermum canescens,* a perennial with orange-yellow flowers used in borders and rock gardens.

RED SPIDER. Not really a spider or even an insect, but a tiny eight-legged mite (*Tetranychus telarius*), this pest is common in greenhouses, on house plants, vegetables and ornamental plants in the garden and on many trees and shrubs, both decidu-ous and evergreen. The leaves show the results of its sucking of the juices, becom-ing blotched with pale yellow and reddish brown spots and gradually dying and drop-ping. The underside of the leaves appears to have been dusted with fine white powder, but this examined through a lens is seen to consist of empty wrinkled skins and minute eggs suspended on strands of fine silk webbing along which move the small green, yellow, black or red mites.

Red spiders can often be held in check, especially in house and greenhouse, by syringing plants with a forceful stream of water; but unless this is done early in the day the watering may make conditions more favorable for disease infections by leaving the atmosphere moist at night. For greenhouse use proprietary compounds based on such chemicals as selenium, dinitrophenols or derris thiocyanate are available in spray or dust form. Spraying with lime-sulphur, summer strength, or with rotenone or pyrethrum, is quite effec-tive. Dusting with very fine sulphur is often successful, especially on evergreens. See also MITES.

REDTOP. Common name for *Agrostis palustris,* a species of Bent Grass (which see), sometimes known as Fiorin and, in the S., as Herds Grass. Useful in pastures and lawns, it will grow in good soil almost anywhere except in the extreme S. and in arid regions. It is tolerant of, if not ac-tually benefited by, an acid soil. A stand-ard lawn grass seed mixture may consist of 1 part redtop and 2 to 5 parts of Ken-tucky Blue Grass and some white clover. See also LAWN.

RED-VALERIAN. A common name for *Centranthus ruber,* a perennial 3 ft. tall bearing flat-topped clusters of fragrant red flowers.

RED-WHITE-AND-BLUE-FLOW-ER. Common name for *Cuphea miniata,* a greenhouse shrub grown as an annual for its showy red flowers with purple and green calyxes.

REDWOOD. Popular name for the giant evergreen trees of the Pacific Coast (*Sequoia sempervirens*), given on account of the color of the wood. See SEQUOIA.

REED. A common name for various plants of the Grass Family, some of which are used for ornamental effects near water.

The Great or Giant Reed (which see) is *Arundo donax,* a native of S. Europe,

capable of making from 10 to 20 ft. of growth in a season.

Southern Cane, or Cane-reed (which see), is *Arundinaria macrosperma,* a large shrubby grass belonging to the Bamboo group of the Grass Family. Native from Va. to Fla. and La., it grows to 25 ft., in swamps and by rivers. See BAMBOO.

Sea-sand-reed is *Ammophila arenaria.*

REED-MACE. One name for the genus Typha, more commonly known as Cat-tail, which see.

REFORESTATION. The restocking of cut-over or burnt-over forest lands, or the planting of abandoned fields and so-called "marginal" farm land with trees which will develop into valuable forests. Reforestation is not only of vital impor-tance as a governmental activity, but also offers a real opportunity to individuals who wish to add to the beauty and value of their country property by (1) providing for a future source of revenue from sales of timber, and (2) preventing erosion and conserving soil and water resources which are sadly depleted when hilly land is left bare.

Recognizing the desire of such individu-als to reforest waste land, many states now distribute seedling trees to private tree planters at cost of production, which usu-ally ranges from $1 to $5 per 1000 trees; the cost per acre of such reforestation, including stock and planting, may run from $10 to $15. In most states such purchases involve an agreement that the trees so planted will not be used or resold as orna-mentals; this is to prevent infringement of the legitimate nursery industry by the state-operated, tax-supported forest-tree nurseries. New York State has 6 such nurseries with an output of 50,000,000 seedlings annually, as well as a nursery for the production of shade trees for state highway planting work which, as a sort of "reforestation," adds materially to the value of adjoining property as well as to the beauty of the highways.

The U. S. Forest Service also has tree nurseries scattered through the country and the Clarke-McNary law provides special allotments to coöperating states interested in reforestation. As a phase of the New Deal conservation policy, the Federal Gov-ernment greatly extended its reforestation activities, starting new nurseries for the production of plants for the control or pre-vention of erosion, and, especially, trees for the vast shelter-belt planned to cover a 100-mide wide area extending along the 100th meridian from the Canadian border to Okla. and Texas.

REGULAR. A flower of which all the members of any one set of floral organs are like each other, all sepals alike, all petals alike, all stamens alike, the carpels alike. Looking at the center of the flower, the parts are repeated or radiate about it, as in the lilies and most members of the Crowfoot Family.

REHMANNIA (ray-man'-i-ah). A genus of perennial herbs of the Figwort Family comprising plants with sticky-hairy foliage and showy 2-lipped tubular brownish or pale-colored flowers with brilliant colored throats. They are grown as greenhouse plants N. but are suitable for the outdoors in the S. and in Calif. and can be increased by seeds or cuttings. *R. elata,* to 6 ft., has rose-purple flowers to 3 in. across, the throat dotted with yellow and red. *R. angulata* to 3 ft. has smaller red flowers banded with scarlet on the upper lip and dotted with orange on the lower. *R. glutinosa* has large solitary yellowish flowers, purple-veined and with a purple throat.

REINECKIA (ry-nek'-i-ah). A genus of the Lily Family represented by one species, *R. carnea,* native to China and Japan, having tufted foliage to 1½ ft. growing from a rootstock, and bearing dull-pink fragrant flowers in clusters at the tip of a leafless stem only a few inches high; these are followed by round berries. Grown as a house plant N. and in the open in mild climates, it is an attractive foliage-plant, easily increased by division.

REIN-ORCHIS. A common name for Habenaria, a genus of terrestrial orchids with flowers of various colors, well suited to bog gardens; also called Fringed Orchis.

REINWARDTIA. Small shrubby plants of the Flax Family, native in India. The important species is *R. indica,* known as Yellow-flax, which see, and sometimes as East-Indian-flax.

REPELLENTS. Various substances used alone or as ingredients of spray mixtures, which tend to protect plants, not by killing, but by driving away pests because of disagreeable odor, color or other physical characteristics. Bordeaux mixture, a popular fungicide, and some of the copper dusts are valuable repellents for certain beetles and for leaf hoppers. Tobacco dust or ground up stems may be mixed with the soil about the roots of plants to repel root aphids; lime is sometimes useful, especially against slugs. Any fine dust (such as soot) sprinkled on foliage acts as a mechanical repellent. Naphthalene is much used against household insects and certain bulb and corm pests, as the gladiolus thrips. Coal-tar, creosote and similar compounds act both as mechanical and chemical repellents, as do most oils, oily substances and soaps. Tree tanglefoot and other kinds of barriers placed around tree trunks act as mechanical repellents. Derris dust and sprays are much used to repel the Japanese beetle.

RESEARCH IN GARDENING. Investigations into the nature, structure, habits, identity and other characteristics of plants, as such, have been going on for centuries, but studies of their value, adaptability and culture as elements in the garden are of much more recent development. One reason is that whereas plants have long been recognized as of great importance to man as foods, medicines and so on, and have therefore occupied the attentions of persons primarily interested in medicine, art, and divers industrial activities as well as botanists, interest in gardens was for many years restricted to those of considerable means; and even they were usually inclined to leave the professional details to their employed gardeners and content themselves with merely enjoying and showing off the results of the labors of others.

Gradually, however, the garden has attained an entirely different importance as a place from which the individual and the family can derive not only material rewards in the form of flowers, vegetables and fruits, but also physical benefit through exercise in the open air, recreation, pride in accomplishment and the joy of an outdoor accession to their living quarters. With this change in its status and with the tremendous increase in the numbers of people who garden because they want to and are interested in the problems involved as well as the results, has come an increasing demand for practical, helpful information along those very lines; information based, not on mere tradition and rule of thumb methods, but on scientific knowledge and experimental proof. In short, gardening in all its phases is attaining in the general scheme of things a new status, a dignity which, while it was always appreciated by the gardening fraternity, has often not even been suspected by those figuratively "outside the garden wall."

In response to that demand scientists, educators, professional men, and men and women primarily associated with commercial activities are giving increasing attention to practical problems, or to the scientific factors and principles upon which the solution of those problems depends. A complete roll call of such workers and the institutions and agencies with which they are connected is out of the question here. But there may be mentioned as typical of the places where such work is going on, arboretums and botanical gardens in various countries; state colleges and affiliated or independent experiment stations; special test gardens and research institutions operated on private endowments or with the funds of horticultural societies, garden clubs, flower societies, etc.; the trial grounds of seed firms, nurseries and concerns that manufacture different spray materials, fertilizers, garden implements, etc., and which have a sincere desire to prove the efficiency of their products before offering them to the gardening public; the gardens of broad-minded private individuals who may well be termed "patrons of horticulture," and different branches of the agricultural departments of State and Federal Governments.

In line with their different methods of working, all these agencies put on record and distribute more or less widely the results of their investigations through regular or occasional bulletins, memoirs, yearbooks, news releases and other publications; through reading courses sent to the homes of gardeners; through the lecturing activities of members of their staffs; through commercial advertising; through displays and demonstrations at flower shows, fairs and other exhibitions; and, in some cases, through classes for amateur and professional gardeners conducted either as parts of their regular curricula or in various places more convenient for the students, according to the modern "extension" idea.

The facts thus being learned and spread abroad can prove of tremendous help to gardeners and plant lovers everywhere if they will but take advantage of them. But however far afield the enthusiast may go or look for helpful information about what to grow and where and how to grow it, he should never forget that within the con-

fines of his own garden—no matter how small—and in the gardens of his neighbors, lie countless invaluable opportunities for research that he cannot afford to overlook or neglect.

See also ARBORETUM; BOTANIC GARDEN; EDUCATION IN GARDENING; EXTENSION COURSES; GOVERNMENT AGENCIES; GARDEN CLUBS; HORTICULTURAL SOCIETIES.

RESEDA (re-see′-dah). A genus of herbs grown in gardens and indoors for their dense, fragrant spikes. See MIGNONETTE.

RESISTANCE. The ability of plants to withstand adverse conditions, such as disease, insect attacks, winter cold, sun scald, or drought. Plants may be resistant or susceptible to disease in varying degrees, *immunity* implying 100 per cent resistance. Resistance to certain conditions is increased either by natural or artificial selection, or by breeding, that is, crossing desirable but susceptible species and varieties with more hardy forms. See also PLANT BREEDING.

REST HARROW. The genus Ononis. Herbs or shrubs of Europe, Asia and Africa, belonging to the Pea Family. They are well adapted for sunny places in the border or rock garden, requiring no special treatment and flowering well in summer; propagated by division and seed.

Principal species include: *O. fruticosa,* a shrubby plant to about 2 ft., with three-part leaves and clusters of pink to whitish flowers; *O. rotundifolia,* somewhat smaller with bright rose flowers; *O. spinosa,* dwarf and spiny, with pink flowers, showing well on a slope; *O. natrix* (Goat-root), a dwarf perennial with yellow flowers.

REST-PERIOD. A natural season of inactivity in plant growth, due to internal causes (such as chemical or physiological factors) and not necessarily to cold weather or other external factors. During the rest-period most plants are incapable of active vegetative growth, no matter how favorable the external environment. This prevents plants from breaking into active growth during warm spells in midwinter and thus protects them from injury which might otherwise occur. Plants having a short rest-period are in greater danger of being injured by early spring frosts than those whose rest-period continues until danger of frost is past. But plants in warm climates or in the greenhouse also often undergo a regular rest-period. After the rest-period is completed, plants may still be kept "dormant" by external conditions, such as cold temperature or lack of moisture. The "after ripening" of seeds (see SEEDS) is not unlike the rest-period of plants. See DORMANT.

RESURRECTION FERN (*Polypodium incanum*). A small, coarse-textured fern of the S. States, found on rocks and trees, creeping extensively and useful in the rock garden. The name refers to its ability to revive after severe dry spells.

RESURRECTION-PLANT. A common name given to two unrelated plants that have the common habit of curling up when dry and opening out again when supplied with moisture. One is *Anastatica hierochuntica,* an annual plant of the Mustard Family, called also Rose-of-Jericho, native to sandy deserts from Arabia to Syria and Algeria. It grows 6 in. tall and has small, broadly oval leaves and small white flowers borne in spikes and followed by a short broad fruit bearing two seeds. After forming this fruit the little plant sheds its leaves and rolls up into a dry ball consisting of the interlaced branches. This is soon unrooted by the winds and rolls rapidly over the desert sands until it reaches some damp soil or until rain falls, when the dry branches soften and unroll and the seeds fall out and immediately start to germinate.

This Resurrection-plant may be raised in the house from seeds started in February in light soil. Transplant seedlings to 4 in. pots when they have formed their true leaves, then let the plants stay in the pots until they have bloomed and fruited. For ages fantastic stories have been told about these plants, which were first brought to Europe by the crusaders; by some they are thought to be "the rolling thing before the whirlwind" mentioned in the Bible.

The other Resurrection-plant is *Selaginella lepidophylla,* a small, moss-like, flowerless herb native from Tex. to S. America with rather stiff branches to 4 in. long covered with small scale-like leaves and forming flattened tufted rosettes. When dry the plant curls up into a tight grayish ball, in which form it is sold in shops and by peddlers in cities. When put in water, it expands and becomes green, and it can thus be alternately dried and "resurrected" a number of times. Or, it can be grown on in soil as a decorative plant indoors.

RETINISPORA (ret-i-nis'-poh-rah). A horticultural name given to juvenile forms

of members of two genera of the Pine Family, namely, Chamaecyparis (False-cypress) and Thuja (Arborvitae). These plants in their immature state have linear leaves resembling those of the Junipers; later the foliage gradually changes to the scale-like leaves and frond-like branchlets of the mature Chamaecyparis or Thuja. For a long time this transition in form confused botanists who assumed that the young plants were of a separate genus to which they gave the name Retinispora (sometimes spelled Retinospora), which is still used in catalogs.

The so-called Retinisporas are easily propagated by cuttings, which are much slower-growing than seedlings of the parent form and therefore valuable for foundation plantings, as accent plants or to create evergreen effects in the rock garden. Unfortunately they are short-lived, soon losing the foliage from the lower limbs and becoming straggly.

Two of the plants formerly listed as Retinispora are *Chamaecyparis thyoides* var. *ericoides* (formerly *R. ericoides*), a stiff, close-growing columnar evergreen, green in summer but turning to grayish-violet in winter; and *Thuja occidentalis* var. *ericoides* (known as *R. dubia*), which forms a round bush with linear dull green leaves that change to brownish in winter.

REVOLUTE. Rolled backward or downward, as a coiled tendril, or a leaf or petal whose margin rolls backward from the apex (as in the cactus or quilled form of dahlia). Compare INVOLUTE.

RHAMNACEAE (ram-nay'-see-ee). The Buckthorn Family, a group of widely distributed erect or climbing, often spiny, small trees and shrubs, some grown for ornament and a few for their edible fruit. Flowers are small, greenish or whitish, and usually borne in broad flat heads; the cup-shaped receptacles are lined with a fleshy disk in which the flower sepals and petals are inserted. Important genera are Ceanothus, Colletia, Hovenia, Pomaderris, Rhamnus, Zizyphus.

RHAMNUS (ram'-nus). Buckthorn. Deciduous or evergreen shrubs or small trees, found chiefly in the temperate regions of the northern hemisphere; a few in the tropics. Several of them are quite hardy North, and well worth a place in shrub borders for their handsome foliage and attractive fruits. They are not particular as to soil and can stand some shade. They

Plate 43.   RHODODENDRON AND MOUNTAIN-LAUREL IN SPRING

Top: The enchantment of the delicate bloom of rhododendrons against the green of pines. Center left and center: Varying types of rhododendron flowers. Center right: The individual flowers of mountain-laurel are of exquisite shape and texture. Bottom: The massed rosiness of the laurel illuminates the woodland glades.

are propagated by seeds, best sown in fall; also by cuttings and layers.

Principal Species

R. cathartica (Common Buckthorn), native to Europe and Asia, has become naturalized in parts of this country. It is a vigorous grower to 12 ft. and bears glossy black berries. It does well in dry soil and is a good hedge plant.

frangula (Alder Buckthorn) has also become naturalized. It is a wide-spreading shrub to 12 ft., with lustrous leaves held late in the fall, and attractive berries changing from red to black. Var. *asplenifolia* is an interesting form with narrow feathery foliage.

fallax (Carniolian Buckthorn) grows to 10 ft. and is one of the handsomest, with large, finely-toothed leaves and black berries.

imeretina is very similar but not quite as hard. It has larger leaves, which take on a bronzy tone in fall.

caroliniana (Indian-cherry), a shrub or tree to 30 ft., has attractive finely-toothed leaves, and berries turning from red to black.

purshiana is a handsome small tree from the western part of the country, not quite hardy North. It is the source of Cascara Sagrada.

infectoria (Avignon-berry) is a European spiny shrub to 6 ft. with black berries.

alaternus is a good bushy evergreen from S. Europe, but is not hardy North.

crocea (Red-berry) is a Californian dwarf evergreen with stiff spiny branches, handsome foliage, and red berries.

ilicifolia, also from California, is a much larger evergreen, with larger leaves and berries, also red.

RHAPIS (ray'-pis) (often incorrectly spelled and pronounced Raphis). A genus of reed-like oriental palms of which two species (*R. humilis* and *R. excelsa* or *R. flabelliformis*) are popular subjects for moderately heated greenhouses or, in warm countries, as lawn specimens. See PALMS.

RHEUM (ree'-um). A genus of strong-growing Asiatic perennials, of which the most important is *R. rhaponticum,* the vegetable Rhubarb (which see). Other species, notably *R. officinale,* are used for bold foliage effects.

RHEXIA (rek'-si-ah). A genus of N. American perennial, mostly purple-flowered herbs known as Meadow Beauty (which

see). They are successfully grown in moist wild gardens and sometimes in borders.

RHINANTHUS (ry-nan'-thus). A genus of the Figwort Family comprising annual herbs with blue, yellow or violet 2-lipped flowers. The species most commonly grown in the rock garden is *R. crista-galli,* known as Rattlebox, because its seeds rattle within the capsules or seed vessels. It grows to 1½ ft. and bears yellow, purple-spotted flowers. It can be raised from seed very easily, and should be planted in light, loamy soil in a sunny part of the rock garden.

RHINEBERRY. A common name for *Rhamnus cathartica,* a shrub or small tree with inconspicuous flowers and black fruits; popular in shrubbery plantings.

RHIPSALIS (rip'-sah-lis). A genus of cacti unique in many ways among the members of the Cactus Family. The plants in nature are epiphytic or semi-epiphytic, trailing over trees and rocks without rooting; but in cultivation they are quite happy when potted. They are in no sense beautiful, the blossoms being small and insignificant, but they are interesting because of their odd, different and unusual appearance. All are greenhouse subjects and grow readily from seed or cuttings. *R. cassutha* is sometimes known as the Mistletoe Cactus because of the similarity in appearance between it when in fruit and the familiar mistletoe; the fruit is in the form of small white berries borne along the stem.

Rhipsalis presents the one possible exception to the statement that the distribution of cacti is restricted to the W. hemisphere, for it is found in Africa and some other places; it has been supposed to be native there, but this is now considered doubtful.

RHIZOCTONIA (ry-zok-toh'-ni-ah) **ROT.** A root and stem rot common to many cultivated plants, caused by a fungus known both as *Rhizoctonia solani,* and, in another stage, as *Corticium vagum.* Infection may extend from the diseased roots up the stem, causing a brown sunken canker at or just above the soil line. The same fungus often destroys cuttings in greenhouses, is a frequent cause of damping-off of seedlings and seed rotting, and is responsible for the small brown corky specks (sclerotia) on potato tubers. It seems to thrive especially in an acid soil.

Seed treatment and the use of fresh or sterilized soil are the chief control measures. In the garden seeds may be planted in soil freshly treated with formaldehyde dust; in the greenhouse they may be treated with 5 per cent formaldehyde solution for 5 minutes, then planted in steam-sterilized soil. When root rot develops on growing plants affected individuals should be immediately removed and destroyed and the vacant space and the crowns of surrounding plants drenched with a 1 to 1000 solution of corrosive sublimate, which see.

RHIZOME (ry'-zohm). An underground or rootlike stem, from the joints (nodes) of which spring roots and stems of new plants, which can be cut from the parent and treated as separate individuals. While some rhizomes are as slender as the overground stem, most are thickened by the storage of food material which sustains the plant over winter, during rest periods, etc. While the function of rhizomes as a means of propagation is especially apparent in the rapid underground spread of many grasses, notably quack grass and witch grass, it is also a valuable method of reproducing plants in the garden, as, for example, Solomons Seal, Sanguinaria, *Gentiana lutea*, etc.

RHIZOMORPH (ry'-zoh-maurf). When the microscopic threads (*hyphae*) of the growing part (*mycelium*) of a fungus combine to form thread-like strands or "cables" the latter are called rhizomorphs. White or brown in color, they mingle with tree roots and penetrate the bark and wood, causing rotting of the tissues. See under ARMILLARIA ROOT ROT.

RHODES GRASS. Common name for *Chloris gayana,* an African perennial, grown for forage in the S.

RHODODENDRON * (roh-doh-den'-dron). From the Greek, meaning "tree rose." Hardy or tender showy flowering shrubs, usually evergreen, varying in size from dwarf shrublets to small trees. (See illustrations, Plate 43 and 53.) Azalea (which see) is properly included within this group. All are characterized by their preference for acid soils, most of them enjoy semi-shade and the evergreen sorts need wind protection. All dislike hot, scorching sunshine. Given a few simple

* EDITOR'S NOTE: Rhododendron enthusiasts, led by the Rhododendron Society of England, have gone far in standardizing rhododendron nomenclature and the style they have adopted has been followed in this article and the one on Azaleas, even though in some respects it differs from that adhered to elsewhere throughout this book.

requirements, Rhododendrons are easy to grow, but they are peculiar in some respects and hence cannot be treated exactly as most common shrubs and garden flowers. Their gorgeous blossoms and magnificent foliage amply repay the gardener who is willing to give them the required special care in planting. Little subsequent care is needed in most situations. Nearly every color but blue is found in the genus. The well known Great Rhododendron (*R. maximum*) of the E. States is the State flower of W. Va.; the Coast Rhododendron (*R. macrophyllum*) is that of Washington.

The "true" or evergreen rhododendrons (as distinguished from azaleas, the hardiest of which are deciduous) may be grown over a wide range along the Atlantic Seaboard and also upon the Pacific Coast. They may be grown in gardens in the N. Central States and occur naturally in the S. Central States, east of the Mississippi River. With protection from sweeping winds, hot drying sunshine and alkaline soil, their present range of culture might be considerably extended. Only the hardiest sorts should be attempted in New England or north of the Mason-Dixon line in the Central States. On the Pacific Coast, however, is an opportunity to grow hundreds of oriental species and scores of the finest half-hardy hybrids, which are just too tender to endure the cold winters of the Northeast or the summer heat of the Southeast. Most rhododendrons enjoy a moist, equable climate and it would probably be difficult to grow them in arid regions.

SOIL REQUIREMENTS. An acid soil is required for all ordinary species. By this is meant a soil such as blueberries, trailing arbutus, wintergreen, laurel and other acid-loving plants naturally inhabit. Technically, such a soil should test between pH 4.5 and pH 5.2 as indicated in the simple soil-testing devices now on the market. (See ACID SOIL.) The ideal soil should also contain much fibrous material, rendering it spongy and retentive of moisture, but filled with air spaces and never sodden or soggy. Rhododendron roots are very delicate and lie near the surface, so they should always have moisture enough nearby to prevent injury from drought; but they dislike actual "wet feet." If oak leafmold or one of the several kinds of acid peat comprises about 50 per cent of the soil in which the rhododendrons are planted, the problem of soil acidity and those of moisture, aeration and drainage will all be automatically solved in most cases. Ordinary garden soil is commonly not acid enough for rhododendrons and it seldom contains enough organic matter.

It usually pays to dig a hole of generous width and about 18 in. deep at the place you intend to plant a rhododendron. Loosen up the soil below to insure good drainage and, when planting, refill the hole with a mixture of half-and-half loam and peat. Cinders are sometimes placed in the bottom of the hole to keep out angleworms. A pailful of water in the hole before the plant is set is helpful. When several plants are placed in a group, a bed of prepared soil may be made. Local conditions sometimes determine procedures. It is not difficult to "make" proper rhododendron soil, so shortcomings of the native soil should be no deterrent to their culture. In Rochester, N. Y., almost pure peat is used. In regions where rhododendrons grow naturally little soil preparation may be needed. If your neighbors are growing rhododendrons successfully, it is always a good practice to copy their methods. You can almost always grow rhododendrons on huckleberry soil or top-soil from oak woods, but it is frequently too heavy and needs peat. Rhododendrons prefer sandy or gravelly soil formations, but will grow on clay if enough organic matter is present.

SITE AND EXPOSURE. The site chosen should afford wind protection, semi-shade and adequate moisture if possible. Where conditions are not ideal, adaptations may be made at given seasons, such as wind protection in winter and artificial watering during dry spells. Oaks, fruit trees, conifers and other non-competing trees make good cover for rhododendrons, but maples and elms should usually be avoided, because their strong surface-feeding roots will enter the rhododendron beds and ruin the plants. Oaks are especially desirable, because of the enduring acidity of their leaves, their non-competing "tap" roots and the lightness of their shade. A "speckled" interplay of sunlight and shadow is ideal. Conifers are useful in cold climates, because of the protection they give from winter winds and too-early spring sun.

G. G. NEARING'S NEW TYPE PROPAGATING FRAME AND SHADE STRUCTURE
In which, using a specially prepared soil mixture excellent results in propagating hybrid rhododendrons and other difficult subjects can be obtained. (*From Bul. 666, N. J. Agricultural Experimen Station, Dec. 1939*)

Rhododendrons will flourish on the shady sides of buildings and will, upon occasion, tolerate complete shade, which makes them sometimes useful in city courtyards. But they do not enjoy total shade and need at least an hour or two of good sunshine per day in order to grow and bloom satisfactorily. They should never be planted against sunny south walls or in hot dry sites. Avoid drafts and air currents around the corners of buildings, or check such currents by planting windbreaks. A hardy conifer, such as pine, spruce, hemlock or Douglas-fir, planted nearby, can be made to cut off an air current. Large-growing conifers may be kept dwarf, if desired, merely by clipping back the new growth to one inch in July. Winter protection by covering with burlap of evergreen boughs will keep off wind and sun.

PLANTING AND MULCHING. In New England and New York the best time to plant rhododendrons is perhaps in April, although experts can transplant them at almost any time. Next to spring, early autumn is advised. The plants should always be moved with a tight, undisturbed ball of soil about their roots and handled with the utmost care. After the soil has been prepared (as indicated above), the plants should be set firmly enough to insure good anchorage, but without injury to the roots by too close stamping. Set the plants no deeper than they were previously growing. Ordinarily, leave a shallow depression in the ground above them and fill this basin with a mulch of leaves, which should be maintained at all seasons. This mulch may be built up to a depth of 6 or 8 in. with advantage to the plant, which is thus protected against the drying out of the roots and given nourishment from the decaying leaves.

A mulch should be left on throughout the year, adding new leaves every fall and removing the excess, if any, in the spring. In time of summer drought, a uniform moisture condition is maintained under the mulch, while during the winter the roots are protected. Oak leaves or peat make the best mulch. If peat becomes so dry on the surface as to resist water, put on a thin covering of leaves to keep the peat moist. Oak leaves make a superior mulch because they become acid upon decomposing and remain acid for a long time, whereas maple leaves, garden litter and other thin leaves decompose quickly and soon become alka-

line, and poisonous to rhododendrons. Manure, likewise, should almost always be avoided, unless the soil is so very acid as to make its use safe. The use of a mulch to conserve rainwater in summer is of special advantage in regions of "hard" or alkaline water, since it relieves the need of artificial irrigation with unsuitable water.

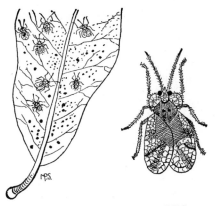

RHODODENDRON LACE-BUG
This curious-looking fly, shown greatly enlarged at right, peppers the under sides of rhododendron leaves with brown specks, as it sucks the juice from the tissues. Use a nicotine or kerosene emulsion spray.

FEEDING. Rhododendrons will grow fairly well if not artificially fertilized where a leafmold mulch is maintained, but they will grow more vigorously and perhaps be hardier if fed. Ordinary commercial fertilizers should not be used unless especially recommended for rhododendrons, since they often contain nitrate of soda or lime, both of which are very bad for the plants. Tankage (not over $\frac{1}{4}$ lb. to one sq. yard of soil) is one of the best fertilizers and might be improved by the use of a little acid phosphate. One successful grower advocates the use of one part of potassium nitrate to two parts of acid phosphate (superphosphate), mixed and applied at the rate of one trowelful to each 3-ft. plant. Ammonium sulphate in dilute solutions—perhaps not over 1 tablespoonful to 12 qts. of water—sprinkled around a plant, is a fairly good nitrogenous fertilizer.

As a rule, no applications of any fertilizer should be applied in the North later in the year than June first. The plants stop growing in July and need to harden off for winter. Fresh manure should never be applied, because of the ammonia it contains, although well-rotted cow manure may be applied as a top-dressing in winter or early spring if the soil is acid enough to withstand its alkaline effect. In case of doubt, test the soil. Peat has little or no nutritional value and must be supplemented if vigorous growth is wanted. Small but frequent applications of fertilizer are preferable to large doses.

Do Not Cultivate. Do not cultivate rhododendrons or azaleas, as the roots are shallow and will be injured. If weeds occur, pull them out by hand; but if the soil is properly mulched there will be few weeds. If the mulch looks untidy, conceal it with an evergreen ground-cover or edging. Dwarf rhododendrons, evergreen azaleas and many other acid-loving plants are good for this. Low-hanging kalmias or other species, if planted in the foreground, are also good. Or a fine-textured substance, like Michigan peat, may be substituted for leaves.

In planting the coarser leaved rhododendrons, do not get them too much in the foreground or in front of a light wall where their unattractive rolled-up leaves in cold weather will be conspicuous. The finer leaved sorts, such as *R. carolinianum,* are better for foregrounds than *R. maximum* and *R. catawbiense.* Use the latter for bold effects. Conifers make an excellent setting for rhododendrons in winter.

Rhododendrons beyond the seedling stage are seldom injured by diseases. A very common insect is the lace-bug, which gets on the underside of the leaves in warm weather, sucks the juices, and leaves the foliage rusty or speckled. It mainly affects plants in warm sunshine. Some varieties, like Boule de Neige, are especially susceptible. For control measures, see ENE-MIES, farther on.

Pale or yellowish leaves may, in rare cases, indicate a virus disease, but are usually caused by a soil insufficiently acid. To check this, test the soil with one of the simple, inexpensive outfits available—or consult your county farm bureau agent or State experiment station. Tannic acid, applied to the soil in a dilute solution with plenty of water, will acidify it; the amount used should be governed by the soil test. Aluminum sulphate, up to ½ lb. per sq. yard, may be applied with safety for the same purpose, but it is less esteemed than formerly.

PROPAGATION METHODS. Rhododendron species in America are commonly either collected plants or seedlings. Hybrids and other clonal varieties (see CLON) are raised by grafting, layering or cuttings. The Catawba hybrids are often grafted upon rootstocks of *R. ponticum,* a process which is best accomplished by specialists who are familiar with it. In England, layerage is the usual method of propagation and this method (and also cuttings to a limited extent) is now employed in America to produce "own-root" plants. While no hardier than the grafted sorts, own-root rhododendrons are superior in that a bushy plant may be developed from "suckers"; graft-union troubles are eliminated and the top, if injured, will be replaced by wood of the identical variety rising again from the roots.

A new and original method of propagating desirable hybrid rhododendrons from cuttings, perfected by Mr. G. G. Nearing of N. J., is described in detail in Bulletin 666 of the N. J. Agricultural Experiment Station (December, 1939). Its essential features are the maintenance of correct and exact moisture and light conditions, and the use of a special rooting medium built up in layers made respectively of peat moss and mushroom manure on the bottom, peat moss and sand next, and sand on top. The propagating frame used has a bottom in which "no intentional drainage is provided," and a shading and reflecting system consisting of a wide hood opening directly N., which prevents the sun from shining on the cuttings except in early morning and late afternoon. The method, which one year gave 50 or more per cent of rooted cuttings from nine varieties and 25 to 50 per cent from eight other varieties, has also been used successfully with a large number of species of ericaceous and other broadleaved evergreens and conifers.

Collecting rhododendrons is a large industry in the Appalachian Mountains. Collected plants are excellent when properly cut back and re-grown in a nursery before being sold. Buyers should be wary, however, of poorly collected plants in buying stock that has not been re-grown, because plants are seldom vigorous in the wild and often have scraggly roots and old, inactive stems which are apt to die back to the ground. Old stems seldom become vigorous again and are hard to establish. Vigorous plants become established more quickly and also have greater winter hardiness. It is often good economy to purchase carefully collected, re-grown material, although some of the other type will succeed when well handled; and it is often low priced.

HARDINESS AND ADAPTABILITY

A most important consideration is to fit the proper species or variety to the climate, for inherent hardiness or tenderness is a determining factor. In the list of species and varieties given here farther on, the approximate hardiness of each is designated by an alphabetical symbol. Those marked **(AA)** are the hardiest and are generally the only ones that should be attempted in New England, New York State and the North Central States. Those marked **(A)** may be grown at New York City or its equivalent. **(B)** and **(C)** are for the regions of Philadelphia and southward, except for a few warm gardens on Long Island and Cape Cod. It seems probable that everything from **(AA)** to **(D)** may be grown in the Pacific Northwest, but little testing has been done in this country and most ratings below **(A)** are made from British records. In the South, ability to stand summer conditions may be significant, although local situations may offer mitigating features. Given protection, many species may be grown, both North and South, quite outside their natural ranges. Those listed as **(E)** and **(F)** are properly just greenhouse shrubs.

HARDY SPECIES. For the **(AA)** region, the best evergreen species now available are probably: *R. carolinianum* (pink) and its variety *album* (white); *R. catawbiense* (lilac); *R. maximum* (apple-blossom pink); *R. minus* (lilac-purple); *R. racemosum* (light rose, dwarf, see page 1042); and *R. smirnowii* (rosy lilac).

HARDY HYBRIDS. At present there is only one important group of hybrids in the hardiest evergreen class and these are known collectively as the Catawba hybrids, although some are predominantly of *R. maximum* or *R. caucasicum* type. They have much more brilliant colors than the species above mentioned and must be propagated as clons because they do not "come true" from seed. The following are the best varieties of the **(AA)** class, with the writer's choice in each color group marked (*): *atrosanguineum* * (red); Charles Dickens (red); Mrs. Charles Sargent * (deep rose); Henrietta Sargent (deep rose); Lady Armstrong * (rose); *roseum*

elegans (rose); *purpureum grandiflorum* * (purple lilac); *purpureum elegans* (purple lilac); *everestianum* * (lilac, frilled edges); *catawbiense album* * (white); *album grandiflorum* (white); *album elegans* (white); Boule de Neige (early white); *delicatissimum* (blush); and *candidissimum* (blush).

RHODODENDRONS NEED ACID SOIL
These two lots of plants in 2 in. pots are three years old from seed. Those above are in ordinary garden soil; those below, in soil made acid with aluminum sulphate.

There are a few other kinds of hardy hybrids, such as *myrtifolium* and *Wilsonii*.

HALF-HARDY KINDS. In sheltered gardens of the **(A)** region and more extensively in the range of **(B)** and **(C)**, *R. fortunei* in some of its seedling forms will grow satisfactorily and is well worth while because of its clear colors, size and fragrance. *R. decorum*, *R. yunnanense*, *R. Fargesii* and *R. hippophaeoides* are promising for **(B)** and **(C)**, but are too little tested for definite recommendation.

There are several fine races of half-hardy hybrids which should prove valuable south of Philadelphia and on the Pacific Coast. Some of the Fortunei hybrids might be hardy at New York. The Griffithianum hybrids are less hardy and varieties like *Loderi*, *kewense*, Pink Pearl, Bagshot Ruby and Ascot Brilliant belong in this class. The Arboreum hybrids are tender, too, and this includes the Penjerrick group. The Campylocarpum hybrids bear yellow color and are promising in the **(C)** region or milder places. The same may be said of the Thomsonii hybrids. Almost all of these races surpass the Catawba rhododendrons where they can be grown and should be extensively tested for use in mild regions.

Some of the best of these half-hardy hybrid varieties—**(B)** class—are as follows— Armistice Day, Beauty of Littleworth, Blue Peter, Britannia, Butterfly, Corona, Countess of Derby, Elspeth, Faggetter's Favourite, Goldsworth Yellow, Lady Primrose, Mars, Mother of Pearl, Mrs. Furnival, Mrs. Mary Ashley, Mrs. Philip Martineau, Mrs. W. C. Slocock, Praecox, Princess Elizabeth, Purple Splendour, Souvenir of W. C. Slocock. The following belong in the **(C)** class: Earl of Athlone, Gill's Crimson, *Loderi* (King George), Penjerrick. Others in **(C)** are: Cornish Cross, Corry Koster, Dr. Stocker, Duke of Cornwall, *Edmundii,* J. G. Millais, Lady Bligh, Lady Stuart of Wortley, Loder's White, *Luscombei,* Mme. F. T. Chauvin, Mrs. A. M. Williams, Mrs. A. T. de la Mare, Mrs. Henry Agnew, Nanette, Queen Wilhelmina, Rosamond Millais, *Shilsonii* and Sir Charles Lemon. In America, those listed as **(C)** appear about equal to those of **(B)** in hardiness.

The Javanicum hybrids and the Maddenii Series are greenhouse shrubs, suitable for conservatories and of considerable beauty. Although there are many dwarf alpine species, some coming from relatively cold regions, few seem to endure American garden conditions, as tested thus far.

Azaleodendrons are sterile hybrids between "true" rhododendrons and azaleas, usually intermediate in character. Good varieties of **(B)** and **(C)** hardiness are: Glory of Littleworth, *Broughtonii aureum* and *Smithii aureum,* all yellow.

RHODODENDRON SOURCES. There are some 850 species in the genus Rhododendron, not counting over 2,000 named varieties. The world's greatest center for rhododendrons is in the mountains of Western China and the Himalayan region. The American headquarters is in the mountains of North Carolina. Hundreds of oriental species are of recent introduction and up-to-date knowledge of them can be found in the annual Yearbook of the Rhododendron Association (of England). For convenience, the genus has been temporarily subdivided into about 44 Series. Each Series consists of a group of related species clustering around one central type from which the Series takes its name. The genus might also be classified according to those sorts which have large leaves (Grande and Falconeri Series), the tropical kinds (Javanicum and its allies), the alpines (Lapponicum and its allies), the other evergreen rhododendrons and the azaleas.

The species here marked **(B)** and **(C)** are the choicest sorts in those classes.

SPECIES FOR AMERICAN GARDENS *

R. arborescens (Smooth Azalea), 8-20 ft. Best hardy, white American azalea. The flowers are 1½-2 in. across, with heliotrope scent; branches and foliage smooth. Blooms June 7 at N. Y. Pink and cream color forms are known. Hardiness **(AA)**.

atlanticum (Coast Azalea), 1½ ft. A twiggy, dwarf American azalea, spreading by runners and very floriferous. Flowers 1¼ in. across, white (best form) or pink, sweet scented, May 30 at N. Y. Plants from N. Car. are **(A)**, while those from S. Penn. are **(AA)** in hardiness.

barbatum, 30 ft. From the Himalayas, with bright crimson scarlet flowers **(C)**.

bullatum, 8 ft. greenhouse species with white or blush, scented flowers **(D)**.

calendulaceum (Flame Azalea), 4-10 ft. American azalea with typically orange flowers, sometimes pure yellow or vermillion. Perfectly hardy and one of the very best. Blooms June 7 at N. Y. **(AA)**.

californicum (West-Coast Rhododendron), 6-12 or 20 ft. The Western prototype or *R. catawbiense,* more showy but not so hardy. Ponticum Series. Rosy purple **(B or C)**.

calophytum (Fortunei Series), to 30 ft. White or pink flowers, early spring **(B)**.

campylocarpum (Thomsonii Series), 4 ft. Because of its canary yellow flowers, one of the most striking evergreen species, but rather difficult. Hardiness **(B)** in England, but probably **(C)** or **(D)** in U. S.

camtschaticum, 6 inches. A very dwarf arctic species, hard to grow. Purple **(AA)**.

canadense (Rhodora), 1-3 ft. An azalea of compact habit, with finely divided lilac flowers about May 1 **(AA)**.

canescens, 12 ft. This is not a plant from the Piedmont, but a tender azalea of Florida, utterly useless in the North. It has been confused in the trade with the Virginia form of *R. roseum,* a better plant, sold as *R. canescens.* Flowers whitish **(D)**.

* AUTHOR'S NOTE: All azaleas belong to the Azalea Series. In the case of other species in this list, the series to which each belongs is given in parentheses following the species name *unless* the series and species names are the same, in which case it is omitted.

cantabile (Lapponicum Series), 3 ft. A small alpine, with violet flowers (A?).

carolinianum (Carolina Rhododendron), up to 6 ft. A compact plant with smallish evergreen leaves and pinkish flowers, May 20 at N. Y. One of the best American hardy species. Its var. *album* is perhaps still better, as it has pure white flowers without any tinge of purple. In some plants the buds are tinged with creamy yellow. Suitable also for greenhouse forcing (AA).

catawbiense (Catawba Rhododendron), 6-15 ft., broader than high. Flowers, lilac, about June 7, at N. Y. The most important and showiest American evergreen species. Its chief drawback is its lilac-magenta color, but this is attractive in woodlands or wherever it does not clash with brighter hues. Var. *album* is white, excellent. It belongs to the Ponticum Series (AA).

cinnabarinum, 6 ft. Has tubular flowers sometimes orange red. It is tender in the N. E., but is esteemed in England (C to D).

dauricum (Dahurian Rhododendron), up to 6 or 8 ft. One of the species on the borderline between Rhododendron and Azalea, usually deciduous, but sometimes evergreen. It is the first to bloom, about April 1, at N. Y. Looks like an azalea. Flowers bright magenta. Korea (AA).

Degronianum (Ponticum Series), 3-4 ft. Formerly confused with *R. Metternichii*. Hardy evergreen; flowers pink. Japan (A).

dichroanthum (Neriiflorum Series), 6 ft. A low shrub with orange or salmon flowers, evergreen leaves. Yunnan, China (B).

discolor (Fortunei Series), to 20 ft. A desirable Chinese species with whitish flowers, 4 in. across, delightfully scented. Probably less hardy than *R. Fortunei* (C).

Falconeri, 40 ft. A big-leaved sort with creamy flowers for warm gardens (D).

Fargesii (Fortunei Series), 6-20 ft. A floriferous sort with rosy pink flowers (B).

ferrugineum (Alpine Rose), 3 ft. Small rosy purple flowers. Switzerland (A).

Forrestii (Neriiflorum Series), 1 ft. Creeping evergreen; flowers crimson (B).

Fortunei, 15 ft. Large, fragrant pink or lilac flowers, with possibilities for use in sheltered gardens as far north as Boston. Flowers 3 in. across. China (B).

Griersonianum (Auriculatum Series), 7 in. Flowers beautiful geranium scarlet but too tender for use in cold regions. China (D).

Griffithianum (Fortunei Series), 14 ft. Large, white scented flowers. Himalayas (E).

haematodes (Neriiflorum Series), 10 ft. Slow growing shrub with brilliant scarlet-crimson flowers. China (B).

hippophaeoides (Lapponicum Series), 3 ft. Miniature trusses of lilac flowers in April. Lives at New York with protection. China (B).

indicum (Indica Azalea, but *not* the "Indian Azalea" of the greenhouse), 3 ft. A low, Japanese species, almost hardy at New York. Semi-evergreen. Rose to red (B).

japonicum (Japanese Azalea), 6 ft. A hardy deciduous species with large flowers of orange, yellow or apricot. One of the very best. Hardier than *R. molle* (AA).

Kaempferi (Torch Azalea), 3-5 ft. A fine, deciduous species from Japan with brilliant salmon-red flowers, fading in sunlight. Does well at Boston, but some strains are hardier than others. There is an evergreen form which is tender (A to AA).

Keiskii (Triflorum Series), 3 ft. A low rock-garden species with greenish yellow flowers and semi-evergreen leaves (C).

lacteum, to 30 ft. A fine yellow rhododendron for mild climates. Yunnan (C).

lapponicum, 6 in. A little arctic species, with lilac flowers, growing also on Mt. Washington, but not easy to cultivate in gardens. Evergreen (AA).

luteum (Pontic Azalea), 12 ft. A deciduous, yellow-flowered azalea, no better than *R. calendulaceum* and not nearly so hardy. Used as grafting stock (B).

Maddennii, 6 ft. A greenhouse species.

maximum (Rosebay Rhododendron; Great-laurel; 12-20 ft. The large, evergreen rhododendron of the Northern U. S. and the Appalachian Mts., with flowers of apple-blossom pink in July (AA).

micranthum (Manchurian Rhododendron), 4 ft. A low bush useful only for its hardy evergreen foliage; tiny white flowers like those of a spiraea. No floral value (AA).

minus (Piedmont Rhododendron), 6-20 ft. Fast growing hardy American species, tall, loose, with magenta-rose flowers. Close to *R. carolinianum* but six weeks later (AA).

molle (Mollis Azalea), 6 ft. A Chinese yellow azalea, resembling *R. japonicum* but less hardy. Co-parent of Mollis hybrids (B).

mucronatum (Snow Azalea), 4 ft. Called also *R. indica alba* and *R. ledifolia.* A species from Japan with large white flowers, fine for south of New York City. Varieties with crimson spots are Sekidera, *magnifica* and Damask Rose; *amethystinum* is flushed lilac, Viola is mauve and *indica rosea* blush (A).

mucronulatum (Korean Rhododendron), 7 ft. A deciduous rhododendron (Dauricum Series) blooming early April at N. Y. with bright rosy purple flowers, 1½ in. across. Rather better than *R. dauricum.* Korea (AA).

neriiflorum, 3 ft. A little Chinese species with scarlet flowers, tender (C).

nudiflorum (Pinxter-flower), 3-6 ft. An American azalea with pale pink flowers, often whitish, with purplish red at base of tube. Sweet-scented, but insipid and not spicy. Inferior to *R. roseum* (AA).

obtusum (Kurume Azalea), 2-3 ft. The species from which the cultivated Kurume race has come. White, pink, purple. Japan (B).

occidentale (Western Azalea), 6 ft. A fine, large white flower with yellow spot, but too tender for cold places. Calif. (B).

pentaphyllum (Fiveleaf Azalea), 12 ft. Bright rose-pink, large flowers, very early on small, deciduous tree. April 25 at N. Y. Very handsome. Japan (A).

ponticum (Pontic Rhododendron), 15 ft. Used as grafting stock. Purple (B).

poukhanense (Korean Azalea), 3 ft. A broad, low, deciduous, hardy azalea with lilac flowers. (Syn. *R. yedoense.*) Its double flowered variety is Yodagawa (AA).

prunifolium, to 8 ft. An azalea from Georgia; crimson flowers in July (D).

pulchrum (Phoenician Azalea), under 6 ft. Purple. Close to *R. indicum* (B or C).

racemosum (Virgatum Series), 1 ft. A fine little rock-garden plant, evergreen, with pink and white flowers in May. Only one form, Number 59717, is hardy (A or C).

roseum (Mayflower Azalea), 2-8 ft. Often called a form of *R. nudiflorum,* this is a much better azalea. Flowers bright rose, strongly close-scented. Leaves sometimes downy. New England to Virginia. A Southern form has been much sold as *R. canescens.* May 20 to 30 at N. Y. (AA).

Schlippenbachii (Royal Azalea), 6 ft. A pale pink species with large flowers. Blooms early with *R. Vaseyi.* Korea (AA).

Simsii, 5 ft. Parent of Indian Hybrid Azaleas (F).

Smirnowii (Smirnow Rhododendron), 6 ft. An excellent hardy species of the same type as *R. catawbiense,* but with better rose flowers and foliage covered with a white wool. Caucasus Mts. (AA).

speciosum (Scarlet Azalea), 1-6 ft. An azalea from Georgia, much like the red form of *R. calendulaceum,* but probably not so hardy nor desirable (C?).

Thomsonii, 6-10 ft. A Himalayan species with red flowers, slow grower (B or C).

Ungernii (Ponticum Series), 12 ft. A hardy, slow growing Caucasian species with pale pink flowers, blooming in July (AA).

Vaseyi (Pink-shell Azalea), 5-15 ft. One of the very best American azaleas. Flowers clear, light rose or white, early May (AA).

viscosum (Swamp Azalea), 6 ft. Slender, clove-scented, white flowers in July with sticky buds. The latest to bloom. U. S. (AA).

yunnanense (Triflorum Series), 10 ft. Pale pink flowers. China (B).

RHODODENDRON ENEMIES

DISEASES. Plants in good growing condition, well mulched, with the proper acid-soil conditions and protected from drying winds and a southern exposure, rarely suffer from plant diseases. Sun scald and winter drying are, however, common when rhododendrons are exposed to strong sun and wind in early spring, and following such injury and that produced by insects, fungi may cause leaf spots—some silvery gray dotted with black fruiting bodies, others brown and associated with cankers, and still others silvery with raised margins and prominent oval fruiting bodies. Prevent such diseases by proper cultural care A generous mulch and watering late in the fall will prevent winter drying while a windbreak of coniferous evergreens will ward off sun scald.

Rhododendrons may be attacked by a blight or die-back caused by the same fungus that is responsible for lilac blight. Infected through the terminal bud, lateral bud scales, or wounds, the tissue becomes a chocolate brown, and infection advances rapidly down the twigs. Girdling cankers may form at the base of infected twigs or branches and cause sudden death and wilting of the parts above; and leaves roll downward along the midrib. Prune out diseased stems well below the brown portions and avoid planting rhododendrons near old or diseased lilacs.

Another species of the same fungus causes a very serious wilt of seedling rhododendrons and grafted plants up to 4 years old, *R. ponticum* and its hybrids being most susceptible. The first symptoms are a yellowing and wilting of the upper foliage and when plants so affected are lifted, the roots are found to be dead and brown. Remove and destroy all infected plants and increase the soil acidity to the condition described as pH 4.0 in which the organism is inactive.

The mushroom fungus (*Armillaria mellea*) may attack rhododendron roots and kill the plants; to ward it off increase their vigor by feeding. A bud blast and a large white leaf gall are sometimes seen on rhododendrons in their native mountain habitat but are not garden troubles.

INSECTS. A common and troublesome insect pest is the lace-bug, whose nymphs and adults feed on the undersides of the leaves; they puncture the leaf tissue and suck out the sap, causing a light spotting and stippling of the upper surface, often followed by shriveling and drying of the leaves. The under leaf surface shows spots of varnish-like excrement and brownish scabs covering the eggs along the midrib. Around New York the first brood hatches about the end of May, the second during July. Rhododendrons in shady places are not often infested, but it is rare to find a plant in the sun which does not have this pest. *Thorough spraying of the undersides of the leaves* with nicotine (1-600) and soap, or pyrethrum and soap, easily controls the insect, though two or more sprayings may be necessary to get all the bugs. The Azalea lace-bug, a related species, also attacks rhododendrons; life-history and control measures are as given above. The adults of both insects have wings with beautiful lace-like patterns.

The rhododendron clear-wing causes wilting of the leaves and death of branches. The larvae are whitish boring caterpillars who work just under the bark a foot or more above the ground, pushing out borings in the form of fine sawdust. The adult, wasp-like, clear-winged moths appear in May. The stem borer causes the death of branches or entire plants, the adult beetles emerging in June and depositing eggs at the tips of branches. The first year the young larvae bore down through the twigs for a foot or so; the second year they bore down through the main stem, pushing out sawdust; thence they pass into the base of the stem, after girdling the plant 6 in. or so above soil level so that infested plants die and are easily blown over by the wind. Destroy in the autumn all parts of plants infested by borers. If the latter are in the main trunk of a valuable bush, inject nicotine paste into the openings of their burrows.

To control weevils which may eat holes in the edges of the leaves, use lead arsenate in the soil, 3 lbs. to 100 sq. ft., to kill the grubs, or scatter on the surface a commercial apple bait to kill the adults.

Two recently noticed pests of rhododendron are the midge and a whitefly peculiar to this host. The midge, noted in N. Y. and New England, produces swollen greenish-yellow marginal rolls on the leaves and later brownish markings resembling a fungous disease. Minute white maggots develop into yellow-brown flies. Spray tips after growth starts with a molasses and nicotine sulphate spray similar to that used for the boxwood leaf miner (see BOX), but with soap added. The rhododendron whitefly produces a mottling of the leaf and secretes copious quantities of honeydew in which sooty mold develops. Spraying in early fall or spring with a summer oil combined with nicotine sulphate is said to give control. This pest is known not only in several E. States but also on the Pacific Coast.

RHODORA (roh-doh′-rah). Common name for *Rhododendron canadense* (formerly *Rhodora canadensis*), a small deciduous shrub of boggy regions in the N. E., bearing showy rose-purple flowers in spring.

RHODOTHAMNUS (roh-doh-tham′-nus) *chamaecistus*. A dwarf evergreen shrub from the European Alps, belonging to the Heath Family. It is adapted to a moist, partly shady place in the rock garden, and requires a peaty porous soil. It has pinkish flowers an inch across, usually borne singly. Propagated by seeds, layers, and cuttings of ripened wood.

RHODOTYPOS (roh-doh-ty′-pus) *tetrapetala*. A shrub of China and Japan, sometimes called White-flowered Kerria but usually Jetbead, which see.

RHOEO (ree′-oh) *discolor*. A Mexican and W. Indian plant of the Spiderwort

Family closely resembling Tradescantia having dark green leaves, purple beneath, to 1 ft. long and somewhat flattened clusters of small white flowers partly hidden by 2 boat-shaped bracts. Var. *vittata* has the leaves attractively striped with yellow. Both forms make decorative foliage plants for the warm greenhouse and may be grown in the open in the S. where they are occasionally found naturalized.

RHUBARB, or PIE-PLANT. A stout, hardy perennial herb (*Rheum rhaponticum*) whose thick leaf-stalks are used principally in spring and early summer, stewed or made into pies and preserves. The leaves are not edible, either raw or cooked. Plants in the garden may be forced for winter and extra early spring use by covering them with. drain tiles, peach baskets, barrels or deep boxes around which fresh horse manure is packed to create warmth; or deep coldframes may be placed over them. Again, clumps may be dug in late fall after freezing weather and planted in soil in a cellar or beneath greenhouse benches for a forced winter crop.

Rhubarb requires rich soil, well supplied with moisture. Propagation is easily done in spring by dividing established clumps; each piece should have at least one "eye." Set plants 4 to 5 ft. apart each way with their crowns 4 in. below the surface; tramp them in place, give clean cultivation and feed generously. No stalks should be pulled till the second year, and then only sparingly. Thereafter they may be pulled until peas are ready—or until the stalks become dry and hollow. So treated, clumps should produce well for at least 20 years, though it may be advisable to dig, divide and replant some of them in new well-prepared soil every 8 or 10 years. Calculate one or two clumps for each member of the family for an ample supply. In gathering do not break off the stalks but grasp firmly close to the base and, with a quick jerk, remove it whole. When flower stems appear, remove them promptly to conserve the strength of the plants.

Leaf spot produces conspicuous reddish-brown circular spots, but the only control measure called for is the removal of old leaves in the fall.

The bean and spinach aphids, the European corn borer, the common stalk borer and the yellow woolly bear (see under VERBENA) may infest rhubarb. The rhubarb curculio when feeding and laying eggs makes punctures in the stalks from which exude drops of sap. There is no remedy except gathering the black snout beetles.

Spinach-rhubarb is Sorrel or Dock (*Rumex abyssinicus*), a hardy perennial. Its leaf-stalks are used like rhubarb and its leaves like spinach.

RHUS (rus). A genus of deciduous or evergreen shrubs or small trees, widely distributed in temperate and subtropical regions, belonging to the Cashew Family. Known as Sumac (or Sumach), they are grown chiefly for the handsome foliage, which takes on brilliant coloring in the fall. They are useful for the shrub border or for massing for naturalistic effects on slopes, doing quite well on dry banks.

The native deciduous kinds are hardy N., and most of the others fairly so. Two of them are, however, virulently poisonous. The evergreen species require a warm climate. All are propagated by seed, root-cuttings or layers.

PRINCIPAL NATIVE SPECIES

R. canadensis (Fragrant Sumac). A low spreading shrub, one of the best cover plants for dry rocky slopes. It has highly aromatic 3-part leaves, short spikes of yellow flowers in spring, and red hairy fruit.

copallina (Shining Sumac) grows to 30 ft., and is conspicuous with dark-green glossy leaves with a winged leaf-axis.

glabra (Smooth Sumac) grows to 15 ft., with smooth and bloomy stems; very handsome in fall with bright red foliage and scarlet fruit-heads.

typhina (Staghorn Sumac) grows to 30 ft., with branches densely covered with velvety hairs, and bearing handsome foliage, especially colorful in fall. Var. *dissecta* is handsome with finely-cut leaves.

toxicodendron (Poison Ivy) is a high climber on tree trunks, and common along roadsides, scrambling over fences. It is sometimes mistaken for, but can easily be distinguished from the harmless Virginia Creeper (*Parthenocissus quinquefolia*) by its shining leaves of 3 leaflets, whereas Virginia Creeper leaves have 5 parts. A beautiful vine but extremely irritating to most people.

vernix (Poison Sumac) grows to 20 ft., with leaves of 7 to 13 leaflets, turning orange and scarlet in fall, and gray fruit. It grows mostly in swamps and is very poisonous.

Plate 44.   A REAL ROCK GARDEN

The stern gray rocks are masked with drifts of alpine plants, the clustered blooms accented and emphasized by erect dwarf evergreens. (Garden by Alderson and Dell, Landscape Architects. Photograph by Richard Averill Smith.)

ASIATIC SPECIES

R. javanica grows to 25 ft., and is distinguished by having the leaf-axis and often the leaf-stem winged. It is the showiest in bloom, with large panicles of creamy-white flowers in late summer.

verniciflua (Lacquer-tree) is an ornamental but poisonous Asiatic tree to 60 ft., with large leaves of 11 to 15 leaflets and drooping clusters of pale-yellow fruit. It yields the famous varnish or lacquer of Japan.

succedanea (Wax-tree) is a tender Japanese species growing to 30 ft., with 9 to 15 lustrous leaflets and also poisonous. From the whitish fruit a wax-like substance is expressed and used in candle making.

See also POISON IVY; SUMAC.

RIBBON-BUSH. Common name for *Homalocladium platycladum,* a tropical shrub of the Buckwheat Family with broad ribbon-like, shiny stems, often leafless in the flowering stages; and small, inconspicuous greenish flowers, followed by a decorative red berry-like fruit, which later turns dark purple. Also called centipede-plant because of its numerous long straggling branches, it is a native of the Solomon Isles, but is grown under glass in the N., principally for its curious appearance, as well as outdoors in the extreme S. As a pot plant it attains a height of 4 ft. but as a garden subject it may reach 12 ft. Easily grown, it is propagated by cuttings and occasionally survives light frosts.

RIBBON FERN (*Pteris vittata*). A strange fern for the warm greenhouse, with long narrow entire fronds from creeping, and often climbing rhizomes.

RIBBON GRASS. A common name for *Phalaris arundinacea* var. *picta,* an attractive form with slender green and white striped foliage.

RIBES (ry'-beez). A large genus of mostly deciduous shrubs, native in temperate regions and belonging to the Saxifrage Family. Some (currants and gooseberries, which see) are grown for their edible fruits; others for the decorative value of their flowers and foliage. Most are hardy N. and grow well in any good loamy soil. They can be propagated by seed, cuttings of green and mature wood, and layers.

Currants and Gooseberries are alternate hosts of the destructive white pine blister rust disease (see PINE) and therefore should not be grown in the vicinity of valuable white pine stands. Some species being especially susceptible are barred from interstate commerce by plant quarantine regulations; the Black Currant is also "outlawed" by organized nursery interests which refuse to grow or supply it.

PRINCIPAL SPECIES

R. odoratum (Buffalo Currant) is a bushy shrub to 6 ft., very ornamental in early spring with yellow fragrant flowers which appear with the leaves. It is sometimes confused with *R. aureum,* which is very similar but smaller in every way and with less fragrant flowers.

sanguineum grows to 12 ft., and is very showy with a profusion of rosy-red flowers. Its vars. *atrorubens* and *splendens* are less vigorous forms with darker flowers.

speciosum, native in Calif., is one of the showiest species, with long pendulous bright-red fuchsia-like flowers; but it is tender N.

americanum (American Black Currant) has drooping racemes of whitish flowers. The leaves turn yellow and crimson in fall.

nigrum (European Black Currant) is the parent of the Black Currants of gardens.

sativum, a W. European species, has given rise to the cultivated Red and White Currants. Var. *macrocarpum,* the Cherry Currant, has larger red fruits.

grossularia, to 3 ft. with spiny stems and larger, hairy green, yellow or red veined fruits, is the European Gooseberry from which the garden varieties have been developed.

RICCIA (rik'-si-ah). A genus of small plants belonging to the group called Liverworts or Hepatics, often found on stagnant pools associated with Duckweed. The small flattened part (*thallus*) is only ⅛ in. broad, but may be 1 or 2 in. long and branched. *R. fluitans* is grown in indoor pools and aquaria, the plant bodies floating on the surface (sometimes forming mats). Though at such times without roots, they develop root hairs if they come in contact with soil.

RICE-FLOWER. Common name for Pimelea, a genus of evergreen shrubs, of which a few species are sometimes grown in American greenhouses and outdoors in S. Calif. and S. Fla. They are raised from semi-ripe wood cuttings, taken in spring, kept in a moderate temperature in partial shade until well rooted, then potted. Thereafter they are kept in moist but well-drained soil, and shifted to larger pots when necessary. They should begin to bloom the second spring.

RICE, WILD-. A common name for water-loving grasses of the genus Zizania. See WILD-RICE.

RICHARDIA (ri-chahr'-di-ah). Former name (still sometimes used in catalogs) for the genus Zantedeschia, grown by florists as Calla, which see.

RICINUS (ris'-i-nus). A genus of tropical plants of which one species, *R. communis,* is an attractive annual foliage plant for gardens and also important as a source of medicinal products. This is the Castor-bean or Castor-oil-plant, which see.

RICOTIA (ri-koh'-ti-ah). A small genus of the Mustard Family of little horticultural interest, represented principally by one species, *R. lunaria,* a much-branched plant to 20 in. tall with finely cut leaves and bearing lavender flowers, like those of the radish, followed by large flat pods resembling those of the well-known honesty or moonwort (*Lunaria annua*). A native of Syria and Egypt, it is occasionally used in the rock garden. The seed may be sown in the spring in an open sunny position where the plants are to stand.

RIDGING. The practice of pulling up earth around the base of vegetables whose stems are to be blanched (bleached) or whose underground parts, as potato tubers, must be kept protected from light. When only a few plants are to be ridged the work is easily done with a hoe; if several rows must be done, the plow attachment of the wheelhoe will save labor. On a large scale special ridgers drawn by horse or tractor are used. See DIGGING.

RIMU (ree'-moo). Common name for *Dacrydium cupressinum,* a tall New-Zealand evergreen tree of the Yew Family grown in Calif.

RINGING. Removing a narrow strip of bark from around the stem of a growing plant without, however, cutting through into the wood. It is done to induce the formation of flowers or fruits, or both, at points above the cut, a result achieved through the fact that the elaborated plant food descending from the leaves cannot pass the gap so created and is consequently utilized in the parts above. Grape canes

are often ringed to produce large berries and exhibition clusters of fruit. But the quality of such fruit is usually inferior to that normally produced.

RIVINA (ri-vy'-nah). A genus of delicate herbs of the Pokeweed Family, native to S. U. S. and tropical America. The cultivated species, *R. humilis,* called Rouge-plant, grows to 3 ft. and bears white or rosy flowers followed by attractive red berry-like fruits. Grown in the greenhouse or as a summer annual outdoors. It is increased by seed or by cuttings started over heat in the spring.

ROADSIDE PLANTING. The essential elements of a roadside treatment should be sought in the adjoining natural or developed environment. Where a highway passes through rural landscape, it should be treated with corresponding planting and plants; where it traverses a wilderness, thickets of native material are the proper adornment of its right-of-way; where it enters town or city or village, the planting should be modified to conform to the gardens adjoining—or to the general character of the place if gardens are lacking. Thus a traveler should be able to judge, by a glance at the roadside, what his immediate surroundings are, even if he cannot see them in detail.

Thus the same laws which prevail in garden design and execution apply to roadside planting. If these are observed, and if reliance is placed on native plant material suited to the particular conditions of each different section of highway—as regards kind of soil, exposure, etc.—the whole matter of roadside planting becomes so simple and practical that it ceases to be a problem in any community. The individual gardener may not often have occasion or opportunity to attempt roadside planting, but he can be a valuable guiding influence in an organization or community project of this sort.

ROADSIDE STANDS. For the amateur gardener who finds himself with an oversupply of flowers, fruit or vegetables a roadside stand is a convenient way to dispose of the surplus. This type of marketing does away with the necessity of packing or shipping, both serious problems of the large commercial grower.

The roadside stand, however, has other problems to solve. Chief among these is that of location. It may not be absolutely necessary (though it is usually desirable) to be on a main travel highway. On a side road the parking problem is less hard to solve. On the main road space should be provided on both sides of the road in order to avoid traffic congestion in busy hours.

The type of stand to use is another important question. Here ingenuity should be brought into play so that, by novelty or attractiveness, the display will catch the eye of the passer-by. For an amateur grower, the stand is usually of a temporary nature, to be used through the summer only; or perhaps only when certain special products, such as green corn or tomatoes, are in season. These temporary stands may vary from rows of tiered shelves, push-carts or wheelbarrows, loaded with bright vegetables, to an artistic shingled or thatched shelter where flowers and other home products are ingeniously displayed. If possible the stand should be placed beneath the shade of trees and a supply of drinking water should be conveniently accessible.

This type of stand gives an excellent opportunity for the display and disposal of the more perishable types of fruits—cherries, raspberries, or strawberries. Early in the season, before vegetables in the garden have reached maturity, seedling tomatoes, cabbages, egg-plants, etc., can be sold. Potted plants in flower also meet with a ready sale.

Later in the year cut flowers add greatly to the display of vegetables and fruits. Some annuals easily grown and handled in this way include: Aster, bachelors buttons, calendula, candytuft, cosmos, love-in-a-mist, marigolds (both African and French), verbenas and zinnias. All these flowers last well when cut and when loosely bunched or combined with annual babys breath aid materially in giving a cool, light and airy effect to the stand.

The roadside stand also provides a means of disposing of the by-products of the garden—extra honey, home-made pickles, jellies, jams, preserves and cider. Pies, cakes and biscuits are often sold and find a ready market. Such easily cared-for products of the dairy as buttermilk or cottage cheese may be added to the list.

All articles to be sold should be fresh, for the passer-by expects this quality beyond all else when he buys in the country, and often is willing to pay well for it. All prices should be clearly marked. This obviates the need of discussion and facilitates sales.

Packages and containers should, as a rule, be small. People from the city are used to buying in small quantities and are much more likely to buy a peck of apples and, if they are of the finest quality, return for more, than to take a bushel basket back to a city apartment. On the other hand, many suburban dwellers depend on the wayside stand for their preserving supplies and will often buy peaches, strawberries, cherries, etc., in large quantities.

The name by which the stand or products are known deserves special attention. Also the signs pointing out its whereabouts. These signs should be located far enough away on the road so that the stand will not be passed; human nature is against turning back when there may be another stand beyond the next turn. A stand is usually operated 7 days a week, the height of the trade coming on Saturdays and Sundays when the week-end rush is on. The long hours of attendance and the unremitting attention which must be given to maintain the high quality and give good service, are some of the disadvantages of the roadside stand, but many families enjoy the contacts and the friends they make, as well as the remuneration and the business training for the children that it provides.

The roadside stand has now assumed a definite business status and is recognized as an important factor in home economics. In many sections coöperative stands are maintained, thus providing an outlet for a wide diversity of products. Several States have endeavored to enforce regulations, Massachusetts probably leading the way. In that State stands are inspected, and those meeting the requirements are given signs which testify to the quality of their products. Other states follow this plan and others favor inspection by local organizations, as by chambers of commerce or county boards of agriculture.

ROBINA (roh-bin′-i-ah). A genus of highly ornamental American trees and shrubs with pea-like flowers commonly called Locust, which see.

ROCAMBOLE (rok′-am-bohl). A common name for *Allium scorodoprasum,* the Giant Garlic, a close relative of the onion; it produces long pointed bulbs or "cloves" used for flavoring, like those of the true garlic, *A. sativum.*

ROCK BEAUTY. Common name for *Petrocallis pyrenaica* (formerly *Draba pyrenaica*), a rock-garden perennial which forms mats of foliage and bears white flowers which change to pink.

ROCK-BRAKE. A genus of ferns (Cryptogramma) included in the group with marginal fruit-dots and distinguished from the Cliff-brakes (Pellaea) by having unlike fertile and sterile fronds. A few species, native to the N. and far W. States, are charming rock plants but are difficult to grow.

ROCK-CRESS. Common name for the genus Arabis, widely used annual biennial and perennial herbs with white, purple or pink flowers.

ROCKET-SALAD. or Roquette. A half-hardy annual herb (*Eruca sativa*) grown like spinach as a spring and fall salad because in hot weather it quickly runs to seed. Seed is sown outdoors when the weather is settled and in early fall. In six to eight weeks the leaves may be used. To reduce their natural strong flavor they must be grown rapidly and cut often. Sometimes listed in catalogs as Rucola. See GREENS, EDIBLE.

ROCKET, SWEET. A common name for *Hesperis* (which see) *matronalis,* also called Dames-violet. Rocket is the common name for the genus Diplotaxis. Rocket-salad or Roquette is *Eruca sativa*.

ROCKFOIL. A common name for the genus Saxifraga, mostly perennials of many forms and colors suitable to rock gardens.

ROCK GARDEN. A rock garden is one intended primarily for the culture of alpine plants and other more or less small species which cannot properly or successfully be grown in the herbaceous border. Its construction should be an attempt to reproduce as nearly as possible the conditions under which these plants thrive in the wild state and to present to the eye a natural and pleasing appearance. (See illustrations, Plates 44 and 45.)

Location. A successful rock garden can be made almost anywhere except in dense shade or on marshy ground; it may be of any size from a few square yards up to several acres. A rather sunny slope is probably the best location as sun is essential to the success of many rock plants and the slope makes possible an effect of height without troublesome or costly construction. It is of no particular advantage in the small rock garden to have a natural outcropping of rock as this definitely limits the depth of soil or drainage and almost invariably it is inconveniently placed and difficult to deal with.

If there is any choice the garden should have an eastern exposure, that is, it should be open to or slope toward the

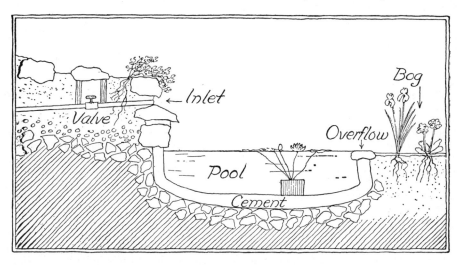

COMBINING ROCK, WATER AND BOG GARDENS

Water supplied through the pipe carried from the rock garden (beyond at the left) is controlled by a valve hidden underneath a rock. A cement lining, laid on rock, will keep the water clear and within bounds, while the overflow at the farther edge can soak the ground in the area just outside to create the bog garden where certain iris and other bog-loving plants may be raised.

east. South, west and north are the next choices in the order of desirability. The reason for this is that, while most of the plants enjoy sun, they prefer not to be subjected to its direct rays during the hottest part of the day. However, a western exposure can be made very satisfactory by the judicious planting of some such tree as the White Birch which will cast thin and scattered shade during the early afternoon. Apple trees, kept very much thinned out, are also effective as well as decorative.

Aside from the matter of exposure, some judgment should be exercised in choosing a site for the rock garden. Such a garden can be built in the middle of a flat lawn but great skill is required to give it a natural appearance in such a location. It is far better at the edge of the lawn with a background of small trees and shrubs.

Materials and Construction

The Rock. Practically any kind of rock will do for the construction, weathered limestone being probably the best, and round field boulders the least desirable. Many gardeners and all suitable plants favor tuffa, a native porous volcanic rock which holds moisture like a sponge and is full of little channels for the roots of plants. Tuffa, however, must be imported into most neighborhoods at considerable expense and always has an artificial appearance unless carefully used by an expert. The safest rule is to use whatever rock prevails in the neighborhood and attempt to have it all of the same character, although this is not essential.

The beginner's commonest faults in constructing a rock garden are a tendency to place stones on end in a way that never occurs in nature, or to place them formally at regular intervals, which is equally unnatural. A little time spent in examining a natural outcropping before beginning the construction will be well spent. By always recalling the fact that whatever looks artificial is wrong, you will steer clear of a great many pitfalls.

When a site has been chosen and its limits marked off, the area should be dug out to a depth of at least a foot, or preferably more, especially in low ground. One condition that rock plants almost invariably demand is good drainage. The excavation should, therefore, be filled a little

more than half full with broken stone, broken bricks or tile, well-washed cinders (*not* ashes), or coarse gravel; this material may be piled a little higher in the spots where the final construction will be high. Next add a layer of sand, gravel or finer cinders and thoroughly wash this in with the hose. This matter of drainage cannot be stressed too strongly and can scarcely be overdone. It is a comparatively easy matter to water a rock garden when it is too dry but, if it is improperly drained and a spell of wet weather occurs, nothing can be done and the choicest plants will rot away overnight.

The Soil. A good light black garden loam makes the best foundation for the rock-garden soil mixture, but any reasonably good top soil will do. Use one-third soil, one-third leafmold and one-third sand, with a liberal admixture of limestone chips or a little old mortar rubble. This will give a soil that is light and friable, that cannot bake hard in the sun and that can not become muddy or hold too much moisture. The leafmold supplies plenty of organic nourishment besides lightening the mixture; the sand provides drainage but retains a film of moisture around each particle, and the limestone or mortar rubble sweetens the mix, counteracting the acid of the leafmold. The proportions given may be varied greatly without ill effects; if leafmold is not available, commercial humus, obtainable at comparatively small expense, can be used in less amount, or this factor may be left out entirely. Ordinary slaked lime, if used very carefully in small amounts, may be substituted for limestone chips.

There are several principles that must be followed to get the best results in the above-ground construction. In the first place, a large proportion of rock plants send their roots to a surprising depth, even down into the drainage material. There should, therefore, be a good depth of soil (at least a foot) wherever there is to be planting. Rocks set into a slope should slant in and down as they are thus less likely to come loose and will also throw the moisture inward toward the roots of the plants. Steep slopes should be avoided as they wash out badly in heavy rain, burying the plants below as well as uncovering the roots of those above. A terraced construction, with gentle slopes on the terraces and miniature cliffs or ledges separating them, is probably the most satisfactory. Steeper slopes may be used if occasional flat rocks are sunk into the slope in a vertical position with just their top edges showing so they will check the wash. Planting of dense creeping plants such as thyme is also helpful, but nothing will completely prevent the erosion of a steep slope.

TERRACE CONSTRUCTION. The making of a terraced rock garden, particularly on a small scale, is quite simple. When the drainage has been built up almost to the ground level, a layer of soil is thrown over this and thoroughly washed in. This washing-in is important throughout the construction as it prevents any possibility of air pockets into which roots might stray and reduces to a minimum later settling which would otherwise quite alter the contours of the finished garden. Next lay an irregular rim of rock around the edge of the area, some stones being almost flush with the ground and others rising well above it. Fill this enclosure with the soil mixture and thoroughly soak it with the hose as before.

On the low plateau thus formed construct another terrace in the same way, sinking all rocks firmly so that they do not move when used as stepping-stones. Remember that irregularity in the width and height of the terraces is essential and that the grain of the rock should tend to run in one general direction. This terracing process may be continued until the desired height is reached. Occasional gaps in the terrace walls, one above the other, give the impression of minature valleys or gulleys.

When the construction has been completed, the soil should be plentifully scattered over with limestone or other stone chips. Gravel will serve the same purpose —which is to slow down the evaporation of moisture, keep the foilage of the plants off the ground and prevent spattering of mud onto low-growing blooms during heavy rains.

Paths in the rock garden are best made of flat stepping-stones sunk flush with the ground level as they look more natural than gravel and require less care than grass.

MORAINES AND SCREES. As the rock gardener becomes more experienced he will probably want a *moraine.* In nature this is the mass of rocks, stones and gravel plus a small amount of silt which is deposited at the foot of a melting glacier. The proportion of soil in this débris is almost negligible, yet there are some plants which thrive under just such conditions. A moraine is usually a sunny siope watered from underneath by the melting snow an ice of the glacier. This watering from underneath as well as the manner of its deposit is what distinguishes the moraine from the *scree,* which is the mass of broken rock at the base of a cliff, formed by the accumulation of fragments torn loose from above by frosts and rock slides. In other words, the scree is a "dry moraine" as far as the rock garden is concerned; it is, generally speaking, too dry a type of construction for this country although extensively used in England.

Many gardeners prefer to have a sloping concrete basin a foot or so below the surface as a foundation for the moraine, but this is not really necessary unless the ground below is very sandy and likely to drain off the supply of moisture too rapidly. Otherwise the foundation of drainage is the same as for the rest of the rock garden. But instead of building up with the regular soil mixture, use one part of that to four or more parts of gravel, sand and broken stone. The moraine feature should be a gentle slope in a valley of the rock garden with cliffs on each side and higher construction at the top.

The underground watering is supplied in various ways. If the concrete foundation is used, a trickle of water in at the top is sufficient. Otherwise, one of the best methods is to run a perforated pipe up the middle of the valley a few inches below the surface. This pipe should be fitted with a valve so that only a very little water will flow, otherwise the moraine will turn into a swamp. The water may be turned off entirely in wet weather and, of course, in the winter.

See also ALPINE PLANTS.

WATER. Water is always an addition to the rock garden; a little trickle of a stream running into a small pool and overflowing into a bit of boggy ground offers great possibilities both in construction and planting. Eight or 10 in. is deep enough for a pool of this type and, while ordinary waterlilies will find this rather shallow, such plants as the water snowflake and the water-poppy will be ideally suited. (Certain primulas, irises, etc., will enjoy

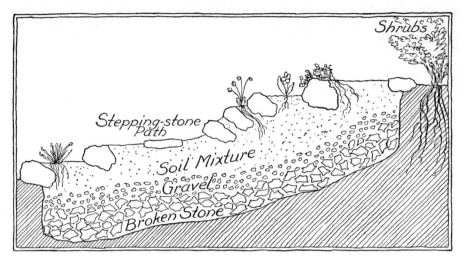

GIVING ROCK PLANTS THE CONDITIONS THEY REQUIRE

Note in this cross section of ordinary, simple rock work, the protecting shrubs at the top of the slope; the underlying drainage layer of rubble or broken stone overlaid with gravel and 6- to 12-in. layer of the type of soil preferred by the plants used; the rocks set into the slope at an incline so moisture will seep into, not away from, the plant roots.

the bog. See also BOG GARDEN; WATER GARDEN.

CARE AND PLANT MATERIALS

The care of a rock garden is rather easier than that of an ordinary herbaceous garden. Of course it should be kept free of weeds as it does not take long for a strong-growing weed to smother some of the more delicate rock plants.

Such plants as arabis, aubrietia and alyssum should be well cut over after flowering to keep them neat and in good condition.

Watering is, at times, essential, as the soil is likely to dry out due to its porous nature; and it is quickly affected by the wind as well as the sun. Incidentally, rock plants are not as quick to show the effects of drought as are ordinary garden plants. They turn brown slowly and seldom wilt but show their displeasure rather in lack of growth and scantiness of bloom.

The rock garden should be covered in the fall as soon as the ground has well started to freeze. This covering is less to keep the garden warm than to keep the soil frozen and prevent alternate freezing and thawing, which is ruinous to many plants. Salt hay (that is, hay cut from the salt marshes) is one of the best coverings as it is not likely to scatter weed seeds which will germinate in ordinary

ground; also it is light and pervious to the air. It should be applied loosely to a depth of about 2 in. Leaves of any hardwood trees may be used although they tend to blow off the heights unless held down with brushwood or otherwise. Evergreen boughs also make a very satisfactory covering.

Removal of the covering in the spring requires more care. It is best taken off gradually as the days become milder and the frosts light. Certain precocious plants should be uncovered earlier to allow them full development; the early crocuses, snowdrops and winter aconites are examples. It is well to put a light covering back over these at night for a time, especially when there is prospect of a heavy frost. Leaving the covering on too long is as dangerous as taking it off too soon, as some of the early blooming plants will become distorted or may even flower unseen. There is also great danger of their rotting when spring rains begin and the covering becomes sodden and heavy. Gradual uncovering and shaking up of the cover to admit air largely eliminate both of these hazards.

When the garden is finally uncovered, it will often be found that some plants have been forced out of the ground by the heaving action of frost. These should be pressed back into place or actually taken up and replanted if necessary. At this time it is just as well to top-dress the whole garden, that is, add a thin layer of good soil mixture with possibly a little more leafmold than the one-third originally recommended. In the case of plants that form dense mats, this layer of soil may be spread right over them and washed in with a little sprinkling or worked in with the fingers. This insures thorough covering of the roots and supplies fresh nourishment for the spring growth.

PLANTING. In planting the rock garden there is a great wealth of material upon which to draw. Someone has said that there are 40,000 different plants suitable for this type of culture; whether this is so or not, there are a great many very beautiful and interesting plants which are easily grown under these special conditions and which are easily procurable. There are whole genera all of whose numerous members are typical and desirable rock plants, except the few which are not hardy. Notable among these are sedums, sempervivums, saxifrages, dianthus, drabas, androsaces, etc.

The ideal rock plant should be a freely flowering hardy perennial of neat habit and dwarf stature, easily grown but not a rampant spreader. Below is given a list of plants which, generally speaking, fulfill these conditions. Some exceptions have been included either on account of their beauty of foliage and neatness of habit alone, even though the bloom is insignificant, or because, while somewhat difficult of culture, they possess exceptional beauty that more than offsets this disadvantage.

The list is divided by seasons but many plants flower on into the next season, particularly from late spring into summer and from summer into autumn. Also many spring-flowered species bloom again in the fall. Following the name of each plant are given the method of propagation if other than seed (as bulb, corm, etc.), the color, height and habit, type of soil preferred, and best exposure. With this information the gardener can make a good start.

The best times to plant are in the spring as soon as frosts are over and the ground becomes workable, and in the early autumn. Bulbs and corms should be planted in autumn except those of colchicum, which must be planted in August during their dormant season.

EXCELLENT CONSTRUCTION AND PLANTING IN A ROCK GARDEN
The rocks are set naturally (and firmly) to stimulate a ledge, the strata all running in the same direction. Between them, suitable plants are placed in such a way that the roots find ample soil in which to spread and can receive the moisture they require. At the top, larger plants and shrubs find the best situation, while on the level floor of the garden, especially if underground water can be obtained from a nearby stream, moraine or alpine plants find a happy home.

Plant Material for Rock Gardens
EARLY SPRING FLOWERING

Adonis amurensis, yellow, 1 ft., sun or light shade.

Anemone pulsatilla (Pasque-flower), blue to purple, 9 in., dry, sun.

Arabis albida, white, to 8 in., sun.

Aubrietias, blue to purple, 3 in. mat, sun.

Chionodoxa luciliae, bulb, blue, 6 in., sun.

Crocus imperati, corm, lavender, 6 in., dry, sun.

Crocus sieberi, corm, lavender, 3 in., dry, sun.

Crocus susianus, corm, yellow, 4 in., dry, sun.

Crocus tomasinianus, corm, lavender, 4 in., dry, sun.

Dicentra formosa, pink, 10 in., sun or light shade.

Eranthis hyemalis (Winter Aconite), yellow, 3 in., shade.

Erythronium hendersoni (Trout-lily), bulb, purple, to 1 ft., light shade.

Fritillaria meleagris, alba, bulb, white, to 1 ft., light shade.

Galanthus elwesi (Snowdrop), bulb, white, to 6 in., sun.

Galanthus nivalis (Snowdrop), bulb, white, 4 in., dry, shade.

Gentiana acaulis, blue, 4 in., sun.

Helleborus niger (Christmas-rose), white, 1 ft., rich, part shade.

Iris atroviolacea, purple, 4 in., sun.

Narcissus minimus, bulb, yellow, 2 in., sun.

Narcissus minor, bulb, yellow, 4 in., sun.

Phlox subulata G. F. Wilson, pink, 4 in. mat, sun.

Primula denticulata, various, to 8 in., sun.

Pulmonaria angustifolia (Lungwort), blue, to 8 in., sun or light shade.

Trillium grandiflorum, white, to 16 in., acid, shade.

Tulipa kaufmanniana, bulb, yellow to red, to 8 in., sun.

Tulipa dasystemon, bulb, yellow and white, 4 in., dry, sun.

LATE SPRING FLOWERING

Ajuga metallica crispa (Bugle-weed), blue, 4 in., sun or light shade.

Allium moly, yellow, 1 ft., sun or light shade.

Alyssum saxatile citrinum, yellow, to 10 in., dry, sun.

Armeria maritima (Thrift), pink, to 10 in., dry, sun.

Bellis rotundifolia (English Daisy), white, 5 in., sun.

Campanula garganica, blue, 6 in., sun.

Campanula portenschlagiana, blue, 5 in., crevice, sun.

Cerastium alpinum, white, 4 in. trailer, sun.

Chrysanthemum alpinum, white, to 8 in., sun.

Chrysogonum virginianum, yellow, to 6 in., sun or light shade.

Corydalis lutea, biennial, yellow, 8 in., sun or shade.

Cymbalaria aequitriloba, lavender, ½ in. mat, light shade.

Dianthus arenarius, white, to 8 in., dry, sun.

Dianthus neglectus, pink, 5 in., dry, sun.

Erythronium revolutum, bulb, white or lavender, to 1 ft., light shade.

Geranium cinereum, pale pink, 6 in., sun.

Globularia nudicaulis, blue, to 8 in., sun.

Gypsophila repens rosea, pink, to 6 in., sun.

Helianthemum vulgare, various, 8 in., lime, sun.

Hypoxis hirsuta (Star-grass), yellow, to 10 in., sun or light shade.

Iberis sempervirens (Candytuft), white, to 1 ft., sun.

Iris cristata, blue, to 4 in., dry, sun or light shade.

Linum alpinum (Flax), blue, to 6 in., sun.

Lychnis alpina, pink, 3 in., sun.

Muscari botrioides alba, bulb, white, to 8 in., sun.

Myosotis rupicola (Forget-me-not), blue, 6 in., sun.

Oenothera caespitosa, white, 6 in., sun.

Oenothera missouriensis, yellow, to 10 in., sun.

Papaver alpinum, various, 6 in., dry, sun.

Phlox divaricata, lavender, to 1 ft., dry, sun or light shade.

Potentilla alba, white, 4 in., sun.

Potentilla verna nana, yellow, 2 in. mat, sun.

Primula japonica, various, to 18 in., moist, sun or light shade.

Primula juliae, red, 4 in., sun.

Saxifraga aizoon brevifolia, white, 6 in., dry, sun.

Saxifraga macnabiana, white, to 16 in., dry, sun.

Sedum dasyphyllum, white, 3 in. mat, sun.

Sedum pulchellum, rose-purple, 4 in. trailer, sun or light shade.

Sedum ternatum, white, 4 in., sun.

Silene pennsylvanica (Wild-pink), pink, to 6 in., sun or light shade.

Stachys corsica, white, ½ in. mat, dry, sun.

Thymus serpyllum album, white, 2 in. mat, rocks, sun.

Tiarella cordifolia, white, 6 in., shade.

Tulipa linifolia, bulb, red, to 6 in., dry, sun.

Veronica rupestris, blue, 3 in. trailer, sun.

Viola gracilis, lavender, 8 in., sun.

Viola pedata, violet, 4 in., acid, sun or light shade.

SUMMER FLOWERING

Allium carinatum, bulb, pink, to 18 in., dry, sun.

Allium cyaneum, bulb, blue, 6 in., sun.

Allium stellatum, bulb, pink, to 18 in., sun.

Astilbe simplicifolia, pale pink, 8 in., dry or moist, sun or shade.

Astilbe sinensis pumila, pink, to 1 ft., moist, sun or light shade.

Campanula carpatica, blue, 1 ft., sun.

Campanula pusilla, blue, 5 in., crevice, sun.

Campanula rotundifolia, blue, to 14 in., dry, sun.

Campanula tomasiniana, purple-blue, to 6 in., sun.

Ceratostigma plumbaginoides, blue, to 1 ft., sun or light shade.

Cyclamen europaeum, crimson, 4 in., sun.

Dianthus gallicus, pink, to 8 in., sun.

Digitalis ambigua (Foxglove), yellow, 2 ft., sun or light shade.

Erodium chamaedryoides, pink, 2 in., sun.

Eryophyllum caespitosum, yellow, 1 ft., sun.

Gentiana lagodechiana, blue, 4 in., sun or light shade.

Gentiana septemfida, blue, 5 in., sun or light shade.

Gentiana sino-ornata, blue, 4 in., sun or light shade.

Geranium sanguineum lancastriense, pink, 6 in., sun.

Hypericum reptans, yellow, trailer, sun.

Inula ensifolia, yellow, to 9 in., sun.

Lavandula Munstead Dwarf, lavender, to 18 in., sun.

Mentha requieni, white, ½ in. mat, sun or light shade.

Nierembergia rivularis, white, 3 in. trailer, light shade.

Parnassia palustris, white, 6 in., moist, sun.

Potentilla tonguei, orange-pink, 6 in., sun or light shade.

Saponaria ocymoides, pink, 6 in., sun.

Saxifraga cortusifolia, white, 8 in., light shade.

Scutellaria alpina, violet, 6 in. trailer, sun.

Sedum ewersi, purple, 5 in. trailer, sun.

Sedum sieboldi, pink, 4 in., prostrate, sun.

Sedum spurium, bright pink, 4 in. trailer, sun.

Sempervivum (Houseleek), in variety.

Silene schafta, pink, 6 in., sun.

Teucrium chamaedrys, pink, 8 in., sun.

Thymus citriodorus, pink, 6 in. mat, sun.

SUMMER BLOOMING ANNUALS

All these need sun.

Asperula azurea-setosa, blue, 9 in.

Gypsophila muralis, pink, 6 in.

Ionopsidium acaule, lilac, 2 in.

Linanthus hybridus, varicolored, 4 in.

Oenothera tetraptera, white, to 8 in., night blooming.

Sedum caeruleum, blue, 5 in.

Verbena chamaedryoides, brilliant red, prostrate.

AUTUMN FLOWERING

Aster linariifolius, blue, 4 in. trailer, sun.

Chrysanthemum arcticum, white, to 14 in., sun.

Colchicum autumnale album, corm, white, to 6 in., light shade.

Colchicum autumnale roseum plenum, corm, pink, 6 in., light shade.

Colchicum bornmuelleri, corm, rose or lilac, to 8 in., light shade.

Crocus longiflorus, corm, lilac, 5 in., dry, sun.

Crocus speciosus, corm, lilac, 6 in., dry, sun.

SHRUBS

Berberis verruculosa (Barberry), yellow flowers, black berries, spiny to 3 ft., evergreen.

Calluna vulgaris (Heather), pink to purple, summer, to 3 ft., dry, sun.

Cytisus kewensis (Broom), white, spring, 2 ft., sun.

Erica carnea (Heath), red, spring, 1 ft., dry, sun.

Genista dalmatica (Broom), yellow, spring, 6 in., dry, sun.

Genista sagittalis (Broom), yellow, spring, prostrate, rocks, sun.

Juniperus horizontalis procumbens (Juniper), 8 in., prostrate, evergreen.

Picea glauca albertiana (Spruce), conical evergreen, slow-growing.

Rhododendron racemosum, pink, to 18 in., acid, light shade.

Rosa rouletti, pink, spring and summer, to 8 in., sun.

ROCK GARDEN SOCIETY, AMERICAN.

This was organized in March, 1934, to meet the rapid increase of interest in rock gardening in North America and to promote the cause of "the right plants rightly used," as well as to handle the esthetic problems of proper design. Its aim is to be truly American in scope, considering the climatic and other conditions of different sections of the country. Shortly after its organization several regional groups became active. Membership is about equally professional and amateur.

The society's official organ is the *Gardeners' Chronicle*, a subscription to this monthly magazine being included with membership. In the *Chronicle* are included extensive reports of meetings, exhibitions and activities of the Society, sometimes illustrated; also a list of rock gardens of members which are open to other members. In addition to this, occasional pamphlets are published.

Annual dues are $3.50. Sustaining and Life memberships are available. The secretary is Mrs. D. E. Hansell, 1270 Sixth Ave., New York City.

ROCK-JASMINE. Common name for Androsace, a genus of small tufted perennials with red and white primrose-like flowers. They are useful in rock gardens, where they must have good drainage, yet must not lack water.

ROCK-ROSE. The genus Cistus. Shrubs bearing a profusion of showy flowers, but only hardy where frosts are light. They are sun lovers and do well in rather dry light soil where lime is present. The large handsome flowers resemble single roses, but are very delicate in texture and fleeting in character. An individual flower lasts only about a day, but a succession keeps up a display for some time. The plants resent much pruning and do not transplant well except as young plants from pots. Propagated by seeds, cuttings and layers. Principal species include:

C. laurifolius, the hardiest, is also the tallest. The leaves are usually whitish beneath, and the white flowers are marked with yellow blotches.

villosus is a small shrub with hairy leaves and reddish-purple flowers.

crispus grows only 2 ft. high; has crinkled leaves and rose-colored flowers.

albidus is distinctive with the young growth covered with soft white hairs. The flowers are rosy-lilac.

ladaniferus is a handsome medium shrub with clammy leaves, dark green above and white beneath. The flowers are white with a purple blotch.

purpureus is a hybrid form with purple flowers blotched maroon.

cyprius, also a hybrid, has leaves whitish beneath, and white flowers blotched purple.

loreti, another hybrid, has sticky leaves and white flowers with a crimson blotch.

ROCK-SPIREA (spy-ree'-ah). Common name for *Holodiscus discolor,* a deciduous shrub with small creamy flowers borne in erect panicles.

ROCKSPRAY. Common name for *Cotoneaster microphylla,* a trailing evergreen shrub with small white flowers and abundant red berries; a good rock-garden plant. The name is less correctly used for other trailing Cotoneasters.

RODENTS. Gnawing mammals, including rats, mice, squirrels and rabbits, all of which are characterized by sharp, chiseledged front teeth. Rabbits and mice attack the roots and crowns of fruit trees and may do considerable damage to many woody shrubs. The injury to the plant consists not only in gnawing of the bark, which may girdle the trunk and cause death, but also in making wounds through which bacteria and spores of fungi can gain entrance and cause disease. These small animals sometimes carry fungus spores on their feet and thus both injure and inoculate a tree at one time. When straw and similar materials are used for protecting roses and other shrubs it should not be put on until the ground has frozen so that mice will not nest in it. Mice from fields and meadows may use mole tunnels in the lawn and borders and eat the tender grass and plant roots and bulbs. In fact they are often responsible for the damage blamed on the moles.

Mice and chipmunks can be controlled by placing small snap-back traps in the runways. Mice in the garden may be poisoned with the following bait: ⅛ oz. strychnine mixed with ⅛ oz. baking soda and sifted over 1 quart rolled oats; heat the mixture in an oven and sprinkle with 6 tablespoons of a mixture of 3 parts melted beef fat and 1 part melted paraffin; the whole is then stirred until the cereal is evenly coated. A teaspoonful of the poisoned mash should be placed in a piece of drain tile, a wide-mouthed bottle

Plate 45.   A FEW ROCK GARDEN PLANTS

Upper left: Starry spikes of Scilla japonica, a newly introduced species. Upper right: A touch of
spring makes the pasque-flower (Anemone pulsatilla) unloose its furry buds. Center left: The
amethyst fleabane (Erigeron compositus), is a jewel from the western mountains. Center right: The
surprise of the frail chalices of the autumn-crocus. Below center right: The beloved English daisy,
Bellis rotundifolia. Lower left: The newly introduced Saxifraga tennesseensis. Lower right: Wild-pink
(Silene caroliniana) softens the rocky steps.

or a covered wooden bait box and these traps then distributed about the orchard or garden. Young trees may be protected against rabbits by protectors of wire screening or wood veneer placed around the trunk for 2 ft. or so from the ground, into which they are inserted for an inch or two.

See also PROTECTION OF PLANTS.

RODGERSIA (ro-jer'-si-ah). Hardy ornamental shrubby herbs of the Saxifrage Family, native to China and Japan. Their 5-lobed leaves spread like a wide-open hand and they bear showy terminal clusters of small white or yellowish-white flowers resembling those of the astilbe. The most commonly grown species is *R. podophylla,* whose foliage, light green in spring, changes to metallic bronze in summer. The plant reaches a height of 3 to 5 ft. and the leaves average 20 in. across. It will grow in sun or shade if sheltered from high winds, and prefers a moist and peaty soil. Propagation is by division or seeds.

ROGUE. A name given by plantsmen and plant breeders to a variation, usually inferior, from a given standard or type.

Roguing, in plant breeding, is the removal of such undesired or deviating individuals as they occur in a seedling population, in order to purify or "fix" the variety, race or strain. See PLANT BREEDING.

Roguing of individual plants affected by infectious diseases is also done to control and prevent the spread of the diseases. It is especially important in fighting virus diseases, which see. See also DISEASES, PLANT.

ROHDEA (roh'-dee-ah) *japonica.* An Asiatic herb of the Lily Family grown indoors in the N. and outdoors in mild climates as a reliable foliage plant. It has broad leathery basal leaves to 2 ft. long but only 3 in. broad; small rounded bell-shaped flowers in short spikes almost hidden in the foliage and followed by large round red berries. There are a number of varieties with variegated leaves. Rohdeas are hardy as far N. as Washington, D. C., and make excellent house plants, doing well even in a cool window. They are highly thought of in China and Japan, where the many varieties are intensively grown by wealthy enthusiasts.

ROLLER. A cylinder of wood, concrete or metal mounted movably on an axle and equipped with a handle, used to compact loose soil. Though deep preparation of the soil is desirable, excessive air spaces interfere with the upward passage of moisture from the subsoil reservoir. But the surface of a seed bed should be loose, hence the roller should be followed by a scarifier (weeder, harrow or rake) to create a dust mulch that will check loss of moisture by evaporation.

The efficiency and ease of operation of rollers depend more upon their height and width than upon their weight. Of two rollers of equal weight, the higher, narrower one will press the soil harder and also be easier to operate because less of its surface is in contact with the ground and the longer distance between axle and rim affords greater leverage in moving it.

Rollers consisting of two or more cylinders mounted on one axle are easier to operate, especially around curves and when turning, than one-piece types, because the sections turn independently and there is no dragging or scraping.

Rollers with platforms on which stones can be piled and those in which water or sand can be placed for ballast are convenient because their weight can be varied to fit the work to be done. Except for rough work, concrete rollers are undesirable, but they are easy and inexpensive to make.

Rollers should be pulled, not pushed, over soft ground because they will thus cover foot-marks.

To firm a winter-heaved and water-loosened lawn prior to the first spring mowing, a roller should be used as soon as the frost is out of the ground.

See also TOOLS.

ROMANZOFFIA (roh-man-zof'-i-ah). A genus of perennial but delicate saxifrage-like herbaceous plants with round basal leaves and long-stemmed pale pink or purple flowers, varying to white, in several-flowered clusters. Members of the Waterleaf Family, they are increased by seed, or by planting the small tubers; they should be grown in rich woodland soil in the wild garden. *R. sitchensis,* to 9 in. with white flowers, is native to the W. Coast from Alaska to Calif.

ROMNEYA (rom'-ni-ah) *coulteri.* A S. Calif. and Mex. plant commonly called Matilija or Canyon Poppy, which see.

RONDELETIA (ron-dee-lee'-shi-ah). Tropical evergreen shrubs or trees, some of which are grown in the warm greenhouse and outdoors in warm regions. They bear large, many-flowered clusters of showy fragrant flowers, but, in common with most woody plants for the greenhouse, are not grown as much as in former years. They thrive in a mixture of loam, peat and sand. Young shoots need pinching to induce a bushy habit, and old plants can be grown year after year. Propagated by cuttings. *R. odorata* has showy clusters of red flowers with a yellow throat; *R. cordata* has pink flowers, also with a yellow throat; *R. gratissima* has very fragrant long-tubed pink flowers.

ROOF GARDEN. The roof garden need not and should not be restricted to the penthouse of a city building. By a little careful planning the small home in the suburbs or country can have an outdoor living room on the second or third floor, where all the advantages of the city roof can be had, with none of the problems of high wind, smoke, and inaccessibility which make the city penthouse an expensive pleasure. With the increased use of the flat roof for modern dwellings, the possibilities of the subject should certainly be considered by small home-owners.

The deck above an enclosed porch, the flat roof of a low wing connecting two parts of the house, even the top of the garage, may be used for a roof garden. The practical essentials are that the supports of the construction underneath be made strong enough to allow the extra weight of flooring, furniture, plants, flower boxes and people; and that the area be provided with means for draining off surface water, so that the hose can be used both for watering plants and for cleaning floor and furniture. In a new house the architect can plan for such a space; in an existing house the local builder or architect can investigate and make the necessary improvement to allow its use.

With drainage and supports provided for, the next essential is a good floor. Least expensive is a floor of boards spaced a half inch apart to allow for drainage. This, however, will rot out in a few years in spite of constant painting or oiling. Much more pleasing and less expensive in upkeep and replacement is a floor of flagstone, slate, tile or brick.

The edge of the area must have some sort of railing, parapet, or screen, both for safety and for privacy. If the architecture of the house allows, a wood, brick, or stone parapet from 2 ft. 8 in. to 3 ft. high is most satisfactory. Where this is not possible or too expensive, boxes of cypress, redwood, or white-cedar planted with shrubs or evergreens give a very pleasant and durable green hedge background.

Inside the parapet or hedge, the treatment depends largely on the use to which the roof garden is to be put. If designed primarily for a quiet place in which to rest and be secluded, the furniture is the important item. Really comfortable chairs, seats and couches can be had, of iron, wire, wood, or outdoor wicker, with waterproof cushions, which will stand rain and bad weather. No furniture should be used which requires a rush to the roof whenever a cloud appears, and sturdy furniture that can be cleaned with the hose will make the roof a relief instead of a housekeeping burden. Where the roof garden is largely an outdoor living-room, very few plants are necessary or desirable. They should consist of hardy things in tubs in the corners, and flowers in boxes, tubs or pots, easily replaced and requiring little attention, but giving the garden illusion.

If, on the other hand, the roof is a real garden adjunct it can be a gay and colorful spot from May to November. Boxes of durable wood, tarred inside and reinforced with steel rods and corner angle-irons, can be built to fit the corners and other places where plant material is needed. For shrubs, the boxes should be at least 18 in. to 2 ft. deep and 2 ft. wide. For flowers they need be only from 6 in. to a foot deep, depending on the kind of plant, and of whatever width the space allows. The bottom of each box should have half-inch holes bored in it about a foot apart for drainage, and there should be small blocks at the corners to allow a circulation of air under the box. The bottom 2 in. should be filled with broken stone or gravel; on this should go a layer of sphagnum moss or anything to keep the soil from settling into the drainage material. Rich loam or compost should fill the box except for half an inch or so at the top to prevent the soil washing out when watered.

In the larger boxes, allowing ample root growth, many garden shrubs will last for years. Forsythia, wisteria, honeysuckle, flowering quince, flowering almond, and lilacs will provide a moderate amount of bloom, and yews, arborvitae, cedars, and small hemlocks will give the dark foliage tones and winter effect. As the soil depth is restricted all plants will need more feeding than an ordinary garden setting; a good mulch of well-rotted manure each spring should be supplemented by doses of stimulating fertilizer when needed. The kind of fertilizer depends on the plant, but liberal applications of bonemeal are usually in order in early spring and fall. After a few years the roots of quickly growing plants will become cramped, making replacement with younger ones necessary; the slower growing evergreens will continue in good shape for considerably longer. In a very windy or smoky location, like a city roof, privet is often almost the sole survivor after a year.

Among flowering plants, annuals are most satisfactory. Sweet alyssum, ageratum, heliotrope, zinnias, marigolds, calendulas, nasturtiums—all will thrive where the soil is properly prepared each year and there is plenty of sun. In a northern exposure the shade will make annuals spindly and weak in bloom. Where the winters are not too severe tulips and other small

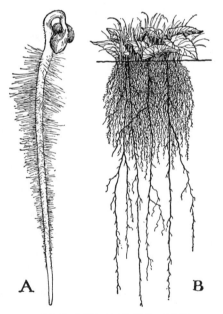

ROOTS BENEATH THE SOIL

A. Root of a mustard seedling, showing the fine root hairs that clothe the feeding roots of all plants except at the growing tip. The plant's nourishment is absorbed dissolved in water. B. Contrast between the short fibrous grass roots in a lawn and the deep-reaching wiry tough roots of a persistent weed, like plantain.

spring flowering bulbs, like grape-hyacinth, crocus, and scillas, can be planted in the boxes in the fall, just as in the garden. They will bloom somewhat earlier than those in the ground, particularly if on a south roof, with a heated room underneath.

There are other garden possibilities for a roof. It may be developed as a propagating place, with a coldframe or benches for flats in which to harden off seedlings started in the house before the ground outside can be worked. Or, if the architecture and heating system permit, a small lean-to greenhouse can be built. These, however, are such specialized uses that they cannot be classed as roof gardens, though they would be a great joy to the garden-minded owner.

ROOT. The descending axis of a plant. It penetrates the soil, absorbs moisture and raw materials later to be converted into food by the leaves; and acts as a support and anchor for the stem. Its structure is particularly adapted to fulfill these twin functions of nutrition and support. The *pith* region is a storage place for reserve foods; and this concentration of food gives many roots (such as the carrot) a high food value. About the pith is a cylinder of *vessels,* which either carry manufactured food down to build up the growing root tips or pump raw material up the stem. Surrounding this cylinder is a thick layer of tissue which strengthens the root and over all is a protecting *epidermis.* Long, thread-like *root hairs* branch out into the soil increasing the absorptive surface of the root, and at the tip of each root is the delicate yet surprisingly strong growing point. It is the growing point and the root hairs which are most frequently damaged in careless or ignorant gardening, especially in transplanting, which see.

The roots of plants of the Legume Family often carry little nodules called *tubercles,* composed of stored up nitrogen gathered by a kind of bacteria that have the peculiar power of taking this food material out of the air. For this reason legumes are of the greatest value in building up worn-out or nitrogen-depleted soil.

ROOT APHIDS. White or green plant lice which suck the sap from plant roots. Asters are particularly susceptible, the injury showing as a gradual yellowing of the foliage and weakened growth. Because they are underground, root aphids are hard to control. The soil around each plant may be pushed back and nicotine sulphate and soap solution poured into the depression; or tobacco dust may be worked into the soil around the plant. Because of the close association between ants and aphids it is particularly important to wage war on the ants simultaneously with any type of aphid control. Weeds which may harbor aphids' eggs should also be eliminated.

ROOT-FORMING SUBSTANCES. These materials, which are receiving much attention at the hands of scientists, commercial plantsmen, and gardeners, too, are of two kinds: natural, made by plants themselves, and synthetic, or man made. Other names applied to them are growth substances, growth regulators, growth-promoting substances, plant hormones, auxins, etc., several of which see. Besides inducing or speeding up the formation of roots, which gives them their chief value, they can be made to influence plant growth generally in a number of other ways, either promoting or retarding it.

Probably everyone has noticed that if a plant is grown in a window where strong light comes from one side, the tips of the shoots will bend toward the light. If it is turned around, the tip partially straightens, then once again bends lightward. But this bending occurs only *below* the tip; furthermore, a beheaded plant does not react, nor will bending take place if the tip is shaded from light. These observations led to the discovery that a growth substance is manufactured in the growing tips of plants and thence flows down through them. Under experimental conditions, if a cut is made across a stem, the substance (auxin) collects just above the cut, forms a callus, and causes the formation of roots there.

The first pure chemical to be used successfully for forming callus and roots was carbon monoxide gas, the deadly constituent of automobile exhaust vapor. When once certain chemicals were found to affect growth, especially of roots, scientists began to investigate the action of various other substances. Of many tried only a few were found both effective and easy to use. *Indoleacetic acid* (which see) was one of the first. It was once thought to be the natural hormone, but actually it is not found in green plant tissue, though a growth requirement for some fungi and lower plants. Very effective, it is still less valuable for inducing roots than *Indole-*

butyric acid, which accelerates the increase of cells and the initiation of root primordia (the starting places of roots) to almost unbelievable speeds. *Naphthaleneacetic acid* is considered one of the most powerful of the root-inducing group, but it is also used for other purposes, such as preventing apple and peach drop, retarding fruit buds, artificial setting of fruits, prevention of early leaf shedding, both from trees and from Christmas wreaths of holly.

All the foregoing growth substances can be applied in different ways to suit different needs and conditions. The chemicals can be incorporated in lanolin, oil, or other suitable carriers and rubbed or otherwise applied on plants. This salve method is restricted to small scale propagation or when callus formation directly on the plants is desired. A solution of some of the substances can be used for soaking the base of large numbers of cuttings at one time. The number of hours needed for them to take up the proper amount varies with different species; detailed instructions have been worked out and are supplied with the commercial preparations. The chemicals can be used in powder form (mixed with talc or other suitable carrier), which possesses certain advantages, especially ease of application and convenience. Cuttings are merely dipped into the powder, tapped gently to remove any excess, and placed in the propagating bed. Usually they should be moistened to insure the right amount of powder sticking to them, but plants with pulpy or hairy stems, like geranium and poinsettia, contain enough moisture to make this unnecessary.

While the root-inducing qualities of these chemicals have been their major asset, new uses are being and will continue to be found for them.

ROOT KNOT, or Root Gall. Names of a disease caused by eel-worms, or nematodes (which see), which may occur on more than 500 wild or cultivated species of plants.

ROOT NODULES. Small swellings or enlargements on the roots of leguminous plants caused by nitrogen-fixing bacteria which have the power of taking nitrogen from the atmosphere and "fixing" it in a form available for the use of plants. See INOCULATION.

ROOT-PRUNING. The reduction of root length as an horticultural operation is of three types: It may occur as an unavoidable trimming of the roots of nursery stock when being dug; it may mean the trimming of the injured roots of such stock back to sound wood to favor healing and the establishment of new feeding roots; and it may involve the cutting of roots without digging in order to check vegetative growth or to restrict the space in which the plants are allowed to develop. This last method is used in the "block system" of growing vegetable seedlings at regularly spaced intervals in flats, the soil being cut between them in both directions at weekly intervals. Specimen nursery trees are often similarly treated by special tools in order to stimulate the formation of a compact "ball" well supplied with fine roots. Root-pruning is also a preliminary step in moving a large tree; in that case it consists in digging a trench a foot or so wide and twice as deep around the tree as far from the trunk as the radius of the desired ball. This is done a full season ahead of the actual transplanting, by which time the severed roots will have developed enough young feeding roots to make the moving operation less of a shock to the tree.

ROOTSPINE PALM. Common name for Fan Palms of the genus Acanthorhiza, medium-sized trees with trunks clothed with spines, which are the hardened aërial roots.

ROQUETTE. A common name for the rather strong-flavored salad plant, *Eruca sativa,* better known as Rocket-salad, which see.

ROSA (roh'-zah). The botanical name of the important genus discussed in this book under the heading Rose.

ROSACEAE (roh-zay'-see-ee). The Rose Family, an important group of trees, shrubs and herbs of various habits, widely distributed throughout the N. Temperate Zone and contributing many major ornamental forms and fruit-yielding subjects, besides a few of medicinal value. The flowers are of many colors with white and shades of pink predominating; the petals are borne on the margin of a usually hollow receptacle which in some species becomes fleshy and enlarged, to form the apple and strawberry fruits. Most of the cultivated forms are hardy; some of the most important genera in gardening are: Rosa, Alchemilla, Sanguisorba, Kerria, Rhodotypos, Holodiscus, Filipendula,

Geum, Potentilla, Fragaria (strawberry), Duchesnea, Rubus (the brambles), Exochorda, Spiraea, Sibiraea, Stephanandra, Physocarpus, Aruncus, Gillenia, Sorbaria, Prunus (the stone fruits), Cotoneaster, Pyracantha, Osteomeles, Crataegus (hawthorn), Mespilus, Cydonia, Chaenomeles, Raphiolepis, Amelanchier, Eriobotrya, Photinia, Heteromeles, Stranvaesia, Sorbus (mountain-ash), Aronia, Pyrus (the pome fruits—apple and pear).

ROSA-DE-MONTANA (mohn-tahn'-yah). A common name for *Antigonon leptopus,* a Mexican climbing plant with bright pink flowers borne in racemes.

ROSARY-PEA. Common name for *Abrus precatorius,* a tropical woody vine bearing scarlet seeds used for necklaces and rosaries.

ROSE.* Probably the best known and best beloved of all flowers. Garden roses have been developed from less than a dozen of the hundred or more species which grow wild all around the world N. of the equator.

The history of cultivated roses begins in antiquity. They have been found in the dry bouquets taken from Egyptian tombs; they are mentioned in the oldest known writings; the Chinese have grown them for countless centuries. The fact that the name is the same (or nearly so) in all modern European languages testifies that the plant was known to the ancient, prehistoric tribes from which most people of the white race have descended.

Roses are grown under glass in huge quantities of cutting to supply the florists' trade, and millions of plants are sold to amateur gardeners every year that they may grow and enjoy their own flowers, outdoors and in their homes. Modern specialists' catalogs list both new and old standard sorts classified according to the scheme given hereafter.

Kinds of Garden Roses

The many kinds of roses may be roughly grouped into three main classes—Bedding Roses, Climbers, and Shrubs. (See illustrations, Plates 46 and 47.)

Bedding Roses. These are grown for display in gardens and for cut flowers, both

---

* This article is in three main parts: A brief description of the kinds or classes of garden roses (beginning on page 1062); directions for growing roses in the garden (page 1066); a descriptive list of the important species in the genus Rosa (page 1068); and special supplementary notes on rose enemies—diseases and insects (page 1072).

out-of-doors and under glass. There are several types, of which the Hybrid Teas (commonly referred to as H.T.'s) are by far the most important.

Hybrid Teas are descended from the older Tea (T.) roses, originally crossed with Hybrid Perpetuals (H.P.). These old teas are now less popular except in S. and Pacific Coast gardens. The flowers of Hybrid Teas vary from thin, few-petaled forms valued chiefly because they are produced abundantly or are brilliantly colored, to large full flowers with fine symmetrical centers. Some have the "old-fashioned" rose fragrance, some have tea and fruit-like scents, while others are practically without perfume. The color may be white (as Mme. Jules Bouche), various tones of pink (Katherine T. Marshall, the older Picture), scarlet, crimson (Christian Dior), cream, lemon, buff, yellow (King's Ransom), bicolors (Peace and Kordes Perfecta), flesh, salmon and coppery tones, orange, and even brownish shades, or any of these in all possible variations, tints, and combinations. Colors like violet and purple exist in some classes, but no clear blue rose has yet appeared in any class. Green varieties have been reported, but the only one commonly known is a hideous mass of sepals instead of petals. The so-called "black roses" (as Nigrette) are all deep shades of crimson or purple with a sooty sheen; none is really black.

Most of the yellow, brilliant orange, and orange-scarlet roses belong to a section of the Hybrid Teas called Pernetiana. In fact, almost all modern Hybrid Teas are Pernetianas, and no consistent distinction can be made between them.

The outstanding merits of the Hybrid Teas are that they combine the ever-blooming quality of the Teas with some hardiness of the Hybrid Perpetuals, and have added to the color range of both the vivid hues of the Pernetianas. They are by far the most important roses grown today, and most of the cultural directions, notes, and comments on roses refer directly to them.

Teas. The Teas from which the Hybrid Teas are descended are valued only by enthusiasts especially in milder parts of the country. They are liable to damage by frost, and are generally killed by

N. winters. Their flowers are much like those of the Hybrid Teas.

Hybrid Perpetuals. These, representing the other parent of the Hybrid Teas, are sturdy bushes 3 to 6 ft. high or more. Their color range includes tones of red (legendary American Beauty, the "state" flower of the District of Columbia), pink

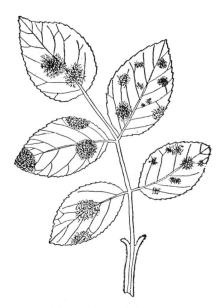

BLACK SPOT OF ROSES
This is how it appears on the leaves, but don't wait for it—start dusting or spraying as the leaves open and prevent the disease so you will not have to cure it.

(Mrs. John Laine) and white (Frau Karl Druschki), but there are no yellow varieties except a few of the earlier Pernetianas which resemble Hybrid Perpetuals more than Hybrid Teas. They are definitely hardier than the Hybrid Teas, but they appreciate some protection in severe climates. The flowers are large and generally fragrant, and are produced freely only once in the season, although a few scattering flowers may come in the fall.

Polyanthas. Also of somewhat lesser importance is the Polyantha (P.) tribe. This type began as shrubby little bushes somewhat hardier than the Hybrid Teas, but bearing very small, generally scentless, flowers in bunches, almost continually throughout the season. Varieties have been steadily improved until some compare more favorably in size and quality with the H.T.'s; but the blooms are invariably borne in clusters. The Polyanthas are much used for massed beds, for edging, and for low, everblooming hedges. The color range is not quite equal to that of the H.T.'s, for there is no good, clear yellow, and the coppery and rosy-orange shades are missing; but there are blues, after a sort, and a very peculiar, harsh shade of orange-scarlet unlike any color in any other class. Examples are Gloria Mundi (orange) and Sparkler (red) with small flowers, and Kirsten Poulsen (scarlet), Cécile Brunner (pink) and Gruss an Aachen (flesh pink) with large blooms.

Floribundas. This new class of roses, made first for the creations of the late Dr. J. H. Nicolas, exhibits highly desirable garden qualities including hardiness, compact, shrubby growth, long blooming period, and the production of thick clusters of moderately to quite double blossoms of Hybrid Tea size. Thus it demonstrates the combination of good traits of both the H.T. and the Polyantha blood that it carries. The plants are vigorous and easy to grow, the flowers look well on them and are also good for cutting, and the color range thus far available is generous and beautiful. Among the outstanding Floribundas are World's Fair (deep scarlet), Donald Prior (rich red with Damask-like fragrance), Smiles (salmon-pink), Betty Prior (opening red to light pink).

Grandifloras. Newest and an outgrowth of the Floribunda group these are still more like the Hybrid Teas. Though generally stronger growers and somewhat more trouble-free than the Hybrid Teas, the clusters of flowers are smaller than the Floribundas but the flowers larger, better formed, and more Hybrid Tea-like. They are profuse bloomers and their color range is expanding fast. They include vibrant reds like John S. Armstrong, pinks like Queen Elizabeth, and yellows like Gold Coast.

CLIMBING ROSES. These fall naturally into two big groups: Those with large flowers (L.C. or Large-flowered Climbers), and those with small flowers in clusters (R.—Ramblers). Thus they resemble in a way the Hybrid Teas and the Polyanthas of the bedding roses, and to some extent they are similar in origin. Over most of N. America success with these roses depends almost entirely upon their hardiness. As a rule, climbers with large flowers are less hardy than members of the small-flowered type.

Large-flowered Climbers. Many large flowered climbers have been derived directly from other large-flowered groups, the principal one of which is at present the Hybrid Teas, either as seedlings or as sports or mutations; and most of these are likely to be just as tender to frost as their parents. These roses are (C.H.T.) regardless of origin, and are more or less everblooming, chiefly more.

Some varieties are the Climbing Crimson Glory, the Climbing Peace (mixed tones), the Climbing Coral Dawn, the Climbing Golden Showers, and the Climbing Summer Snow.

Other forms of large-flowered climbers have been developed from the small-flowered type by cross-breeding with Hybrid Teas, Hybrid Perpetuals, etc. They are likely to inherit some of the tenderness of their large-flowered parents, although as a rule they are hardier than C.H.T.'s. They are seldom everblooming.

Ramblers. The small-flowered climbers or Ramblers are descended from the species *Rosa multiflora* and *R. wichuraiana.* They are frequently classified as Hybrid Multiflora (H.M.) or Hybrid Wichuraiana (H.W.). Typical varieties are Dorothy Perkins (shell pink), Crimson Rambler and White Dorothy.

These are true Ramblers, with small flowers in clusters, like the Polyanthas which are descended from them. Their wood is willowy so that they can be trained easily on arches or trellises, or into garlands and festoons. There are slender, trailing varieties which will creep over the ground rooting as they run, bedecked in season with clusters of charming little flowers of many hues.

Ramblers are generally hardy throughout the rose-growing sections of N. America, although in very severe winters they may be damaged somewhat in exposed situations. But they renew themselves very quickly.

There are other types of climbers such as the Noisettes, which are scarcely of any consequence at all today, and rather tender; forms derived from *Rosa bracteata,* the Macartney Rose, such as the lovely variety Mermaid, which is almost hardy; the Giganteas, several of which also appeared; and the Banksias which are tender and useful only in the S.

Among the hardier forms are Ayrshire types (*Rosa arvensis*); the Evergreen Roses from *R. sempervirens;* and a few descended from our own Prairie Rose (*R. setigera*), which has large bright pink flowers. These three species are reported to be absolutely hardy everywhere.

Hardiness is so important a factor in growing climbing roses that success depends almost entirely upon it. Roughly speaking, the Ramblers are the hardiest, and may be expected to endure

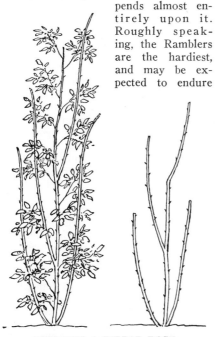

BUILDING A PILLAR ROSE
Left, a pillar or climbing rose as it might appear the second fall after planting, when it is time to form the permanent frame work. Cut back to about four strong main stems and tie these to the support. Thereafter, merely head back sideshoots each summer after they bloom and take out dead wood when it appears.

the coldest winters where peaches can be successfully grown as a commercial crop. Next to them are their large-flowered descendants such as the famous Dr. W. Van Fleet, Mary Wallace, and such roses which have been produced directly from Hybrid Teas as Climbing Peace.

All climbing roses are adaptable for many uses. Besides the ground-cover types mentioned among the Ramblers, there are stiffer forms which may be al-

lowed to stand alone as huge specimen shrubs; and all of them can be trained on arches, pergolas, trellises and fences.

Shrub Roses. These may be used in the same manner as spireas, forsythias, hydrangeas, lilacs and such other familiar plants, in borders, shrubbery plantings, and landscape schemes generally. The flowers may be single or double, and the color range is narrower than that of the bedding types or the climbers.

The *Rugosas,* both species and hybrids (H.R.), are tough, stiffly upright bushes, from 6 to 15 ft. tall, with very spiny or thorny stems, rough, wrinkled foliage, and generally fragrant, although somewhat irregular flowers. For rustic use and naturalizing, the species *Rosa rugosa* and *R. rugosa alba,* purple-red and white respectively, are probably best. In more sophisticated surroundings the double hybrids are useful and attractive. There are two varieties (called F. J. Grootendorst and Pink Grootendorst) which seem to be a blend of the Rugosa and Polyantha types, and which are particularly good where shrubs of moderate height and everblooming tendency are needed.

Rugosas, in the species and those hybrids which most closely resemble them, are very hardy and endure much cold, heat, dryness and even the poor soil and salt air of the seaside. Agnes (yellow), Conrad Ferdinand Meyer (pink) and Sarah Van Fleet (pink) are typical hybrids.

Hybrid Sweet-briers, or Penzance Briers are forms of the common Sweetbrier (*Rosa rubiginosa*). They make tall, arching bushes, with gracefully bending stems, bearing small, single or semidouble flowers in bright red, pink, white, and blended tints. There is one fawn yellow variety and one of a striking copper hue. Their outstanding characteristic is their scented foliage, the fragrance of which is particularly fine when the leaves are wet.

Scotch Roses, descended from *Rosa spinosissima,* the Burnet of N. Europe, are very spiny, with small leaves and generally moderate stature rarely over 5-6 ft. high. The most familiar of this group is the old Harisons Yellow, whose fragrant bright yellow flowers are among the earliest roses to open. The form known as Altai has large, flat milk-white flowers borne most profusely and is probably the best form of the species. All Scotch roses are extremely hardy, and may be planted almost anywhere in the N. with safety.

The original Austrian Yellow (*R. foetida*) is a lovely shrub with clear, brilliant yellow, single flowers in late spring; but it is less frequently grown than its double form known as Persian Yellow, the ancestor of the Pernetiana type of Hybrid Teas. Persian Yellow is a bush 6 ft. high or more with pale sickly green foliage, which is very subject to disease. The smallish, double flowers are brilliant yellow and very attractive. It is not common; most plants called Persian Yellow are really Harisons Yellow.

Austrian Copper is like Austrian Yellow, except that the inside surface of the petals is shining copper red which makes a striking contrast with the yellow on the back of the petals. It is one of the most startlingly beautiful of all flowering shrubs, but like all of this group should be planted in open, sunny places, and left mostly alone. *Do not prune any of them.*

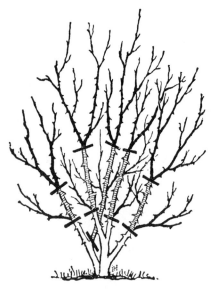

PRUNING A BEDDING ROSE

The more severely a rose is pruned, the more vigorous the resulting growth. In late fall this Hybrid Tea should be cut back to the shaded area. If not injured over winter and if a large number of medium size flowers are wanted, it can be left so. But if any branches are killed back, or if a smaller number of finer, larger blossoms are desired, cut back again in early spring to the part shown in white.

Other forms are occasionally met with, such as Le Rêve, which is really a Climber; Star of Persia, which is similar; and Buisson d'Or, which probably belongs here.

Practically all wild roses have some attractiveness if used as shrubs. See list of species, below.

GROWING GARDEN ROSES

The culture of roses does not differ materially from that of most other decorative plants. They enjoy the best soil they can be given. They need a reasonable supply of water, and the soil *must not be saggy*. They like plenty of fresh air and regular feeding.

SOIL. The ground should be deeply prepared for roses; 2 ft. is sufficient, but deeper is better. (See TRENCHING.) Manure or garden compost should be worked liberally into the soil. Preparation need not be carried to extravagant lengths, for roses will tolerate ordinary conditions; but generally they deteriorate after several seasons if the ground has not been reasonably well prepared for them.

Cow manure is an excellent fertilizer but commercial fertilizers may be freely used if cow manure is not obtainable. Commercial fertilizers (which see) give excellent results if used in connection with compost, peat, or other vegetable matter.

PLANTING. Roses may be planted at any time when they are dormant. In N. climates, fall-planted roses should be heavily protected through the ensuing winter. Spring planting is successful everywhere. But it is advisable to plant *early* in the spring. And in the S., planting should not be delayed beyond late winter.

The best plants are 2-year-old, field-grown, budded stock. They can be bought in the autumn, winter, and early spring. They should be cut back sharply at planting time, taking away at least two-thirds of their tops (usually done by nursery).

The secrets of successful rose planting are: to do it early; to keep the roots from drying out while they are being handled; and to tramp the ground very firmly around the plant to make the roots firm in the soil.

CARE THROUGH THE SEASONS. Keep the rose beds cultivated at all times. Water when the weather is dry, soaking the ground deeply and cultivating the surface as soon as it dries.

Where the winters are severe, Climbers should be taken down from their supports in late autumn, and the canes gathered into a bundle, laid on the ground and covered with earth, leaves, or some other protection. Hybrid Teas should be hilled up as high as possible, and the hills covered with leaves, evergreen boughs, or some material which will not pack into a wet, soggy mass. The Shrub Roses are generally hardy enough to take care of themselves.

PRUNING. When the covering is removed in the spring, cut out all diseased and dead wood first, making clean cuts and leaving no stubs. Then shorten the remaining canes, remembering that the more wood there is left on the plants, the more flowers will be produced, but the less perfect they will be.

For the finest flowers the plants may be cut almost to the ground and only one, two, or three flowers allowed to develop on each bush. Only the most ardent enthusiasts and exhibitors go to that extreme; most gardeners are satisfied to cut away about half of last year's growth.

The time to prune Ramblers is immediately after flowering. All old canes which have borne flowers should be removed at the base of the plant; and the strong, new shoots appearing from the ground or the bottom of the old stems should be trained up to take their places. Ramblers always produce the best flowers on wood which is only one year old.

Large-flowered climbers should be left unpruned, but old, worn-out or disease-ridden stems may be removed. Obstreperous, dangling ends, unwanted canes, and old blooms may be removed, but the best flowers are usually borne on the older wood. This is particularly true of the Climbing Teas, Climbing Hybrid Teas, Noisettes, and their kin. The large-flowered Climbers developed from the Wichuraiana Ramblers may require a modification of this pruning by occasionally cutting them back severely. The grower must learn these points by experience.

Shrub roses ought to be looked over every spring for weak, sickly, or worn-out canes, which should be cut out at the base of the plant. If this is done every year there is little danger of the bushes becoming over-grown.

PROTECTIVE MEASURES. Beginning as soon as the foliage begins to unfold, precautions should be taken against the diseases. Two comparatively new and effective materials are Phaltan and Mildex. An older material "Massey Dust," developed by Cornell University and the American Rose Society, is 9 parts dusting sulphur and 1 part finely divided arsenate of lead. This is still mentioned and is moderately effective in protecting roses against leaf diseases and attacks of chewing insects.

Aphids or plant lice, which gather at the ends of the shoots and on the young buds and leaves, may be destroyed by a solution of Lindane, Malathion, or non-poison rotenone. These materials are available at supply stores under various trade names.

All kinds of dusts, new or old, should be applied to the rose plants lightly but thoroughly, covering both surfaces of the leaves. It is best to do it when the air is still and the foliage is dry; late afternoon is generally an ideal time. If dusts are showy and objectionable turn to the much less conspicuous spray materials.

Special insects, such as the rose-bug and Japanese beetle, were once endured or driven away by covering the plants with arsenate of lead. Especially valuable plants in infested areas also had to be covered by screens until the attacks were over. Now with DDT, Malathion, and Sevin, they can be controlled.

PROPAGATING ROSES

Roses are rarely grown from seed, except to obtain new varieties. The simplest method of reproducing a certain plant is by cuttings or "slips" (see PROPAGATION), but this is a slow, tedious method, and is adopted only by those who have plenty of time and limited resources, or who want to amuse themselves. It is more successful in the S. States than in the N. The commercial production of such rooted cuttings, called "one-year own-root roses," used to be enormous, but they have just about disappeared from the market.

Most shrub roses and some climbers stool out by underground stems, or from roots; when these appear above ground they may be severed from the main plant and started off in life as new individuals. Similarly, some Climbers and Shrubs may be propagated by layering (see PROPAGATION); in fact many of the creeping Ramblers take root wherever they touch the ground.

Grafting (which see) is rarely resorted to for garden roses; but it is practiced to some extent under glass, and some of the roses grown in greenhouses for florists' use are grafted, the stock used being principally *R. chinensis* var. *manetti;* large quantities are imported, but some are being grown in the Pacific N.W.

Budding (which see) is the quickest, most economical, and commonest method of propagating out-door roses. Millions of budded roses are grown annually for sale to gardeners. The most popular understock upon which to bud outdoor roses is a Japanese form of *Rosa multiflora*. In the N. and E., this understock is generally grown from seed; in the S.W. and far W., it is grown from cuttings.

THE GENUS ROSA

This may be described as a large group of shrubs native to the N. hemisphere, chiefly deciduous, and characterized by prickly stems and alternate, compound leaves, with an odd number of leaflets. The flowers, which are borne singly or in clusters, have normally five petals and may be any color, except blue. The fleshy fruit (called a "hip") contains hard, bony seeds encased in silky wool. More than 100 species are recognized, but garden roses have been developed from less than a dozen Eurasian species, as already outlined. A few others are cultivated to some extent as ornamental shrubs. The most important species, from a horticultural standpoint, are:

R. acicularis. Erect, very spiny stems, 3 to 7 leaflets, rather large, pink, fragrant flower. N. America and N. Asia.

alba. Old garden form with large white or pale pink, single or double flowers. Foliage gray-green, large.

altaica. Variety of *R. spinosissima.*

arvensis (Ayrshire Rose). Climbing; prickly; 7 leaflets, fairly large; white, solitary flowers. Parent of the old Ayrshire climbers. Europe.

banksi. Climbing; thornless, or nearly so; 3 leaflets; flowers small in clusters. Double white form is fragrant. Both single and double flowers are otherwise scentless. Hardy only in S., and China.

blanda. Erect, thornless, red-stemmed shrub; pale pink flowers in small clusters. N.E.N. America.

bracteata (Macartney Rose). Semi-climbing, evergreen shrub with big hooked prickles; 5 to 9 small smooth leaflets; large single, saucer-shaped, white flowers, with big feathery bracts. Parent of a few garden forms. China, but naturalized in the S.

brunoni (Himalayan Musk Rose). Half-climbing shrub with 5 or 7 large leaflets, and big, fragrant white flowers in clusters. Not hardy. Himalayas.

californica. A 10-ft. shrub with 5 or 7 leaflets and big clusters of single pink flowers. There is a double form. Pacific Coast.

canina (Dog Rose). Tall shrub with dog-tooth prickles; 10 to 12 ft. high; 5 or 7 leaflets; light pink flowers in big clusters. Very showy. Many forms and variations exist. Much used as an understock formerly and in Europe. Suckers badly. Europe.

centifolia (Cabbage Rose). Ancient garden rose; single form not known. Grows 6 ft. with 5 or more broad leaflets. Flowers nodding, pink, very double, very fragrant. Many garden roses are descended from it; and the moss rose is a form of it; see *R. mucosa.*

cherokeensis. See *R. laevigata.*

chinensis (China Rose). Twiggy shrub of variable height; evergreen; 3 or 5 leaflets; flowers white to deep pink or red, usually scentless, everblooming; not reliably hardy N. Ancestor of most modern roses; a very variable species. China.

cinnamomea (Cinnamon Rose). Prickly shrub 6 ft. high; 5 or 7 leaflets; deep pink, single or double flowers, very fragrant. Europe, W. Asia.

damascena (Damask Rose). One ancestor of the H. P.'s. Big shrub, 8 ft. high with 5 pale green leaflets; flowers pale pink or red, fragrant and double. Probably Asiatic. A pink and white striped variety is known as York and Lancaster.

ecae. Graceful, upright shrub with brown stems and reddish thorns; 7 to 15

Plate 46.   SOME OF THE OUTDOOR ROSE TYPES

Upper left: A hybrid double rugosa rose, a sturdy, spiny-stemmed shrub type. Upper right: The brilliant cherry-red American Pillar. Center left: The rosy wreaths of Dorothy Perkins. Center right: Paul's Scarlet Climber glows against a neutral background. Lower left: Killarney—an exquisite example of the everblooming hybrid tea rose. Lower right: The fragrant, buff-pink Gloire de Dijon—a favorite climber in southern gardens.

small leaflets; aromatic when wet; flowers cream-white, 1 in. across, borne in late spring. Very handsome shrub. Asia.

eglanteria (*R. rubiginosa*). Known as Eglantine and Sweet-brier. Semi-climbing shrub with many branchlets; 5 or 7 leaflets; strongly scented like green apples when wet; pale pink flowers 2 in. across. Ancestor of the Penzance Briers. Europe.

foetida (*R. lutea*). The Austrian Brier. An upright, brown-stemmed shrub with straight, sharp spines; 5 to 9 small leaflets; flowers deep yellow with a strong odor. Asia. The variety *bicolor* is the famous Austrian Copper, brilliant copper-red on the inside of the petals. Persian Yellow is a double variety of *R. foetida* and is the ancestor of the so-called Pernetiana strain of Hybrid Teas.

gallica (French Rose). Dwarf shrub 4 ft. or less, with 5 thick, rough leaflets and deep pink or crimson flowers, usually semi-double. One of the ancestors of the H. P.'s. Striped and spotted forms are frequently found, and many garden roses derived from this species were popular a century ago. Europe and W. Asia.

hugonis (Father Hugos Rose). Very tall, graceful shrub with brownish stems and many spines; 5 to 13 leaflets; single, pale yellow flowers 2 in. across, borne along the stems with great freedom in late spring. China.

laevigata (*R. camellia, R. cherokeensis*). The Cherokee Rose. Vigorous, evergreen climber with 3 leaflets and large, white,

fragrant flowers. Not hardy N. China. The State flower of Ga.

lheritierana (Boursault Rose). Old-fashioned garden forms, hybrids of *R. pendulina* and *R. chinensis*. Blooms early with double flowers, pink or red and very fragrant.

manetti. A variety of *R. chinensis*, much used as an understock, especially for greenhouse roses.

microphylla. See *R. roxburghi*.

moschata (Musk Rose). Semi-climbing shrub; 5 or 7 leaflets; clusters of fragrant white flowers. Not hardy N. One of the ancestors of the Noisettes. Europe.

moyesi. Big shrub with 7 to 13 leaflets and deep blood-red single flowers. A very handsome rose species but difficult to grow in most gardens. China.

multibracteata. Enormous shrub with 7 or 9 tiny leaflets and very small pink flowers in clusters. Attractive shrub for its acacia-like foliage. China.

multiflora. Trailing or climbing shrub with 5 to 11 leaflets, with fringed stipules. The fragrant white flowers like clustered blackberry blossoms. Ancestor of many climbing roses, and the Polyanthas. There are pink-flowered variations of the species, and the variety *japonica* is much used as an understock for garden roses. Japan.

muscosa (Moss Rose). Strictly a variety of *R. centifolia* with double, fragrant flowers set in a mossy or fringed calyx. Once a very popular garden type, with many varieties.

WHAT BLACK SPOT WILL DO TO A NEGLECTED ROSE

The plant at the left was protected against infection by regular dusting or spraying throughout the growing season. That at the right, left untreated, has been almost completely defoliated by the fungus and not only is it a flowerless eyesore, but also it has been sadly weakened and its future welfare jeopardized.

PLATE 49.   A GARDEN FAVORITE

Beloved for their fragrance and beautiful flowers, larger and more attractive varieties are being introduced almost yearly. This is a representative collection of fine varieties for the home gardener.

W. Atlee Burpee Co.

PLATE 50.   TRANSPLANTING SEEDLINGS

The secret of successful transplanting is to disturb the plant as little as possible.
In this series, the seedling is knocked out of the pot, set immediately into a hole
and the earth tamped well around the little plant.

T. H. Everett

PLATE 51.   FLOWERING TREES AND SHRUBS

Some of the most attractive additions to the garden are the flowering trees and
shrubs. At the top left is the Silk-tree, Albizzia julibrissin. Top right is one of
the forms of Barberry which bears attractive yellow blossoms, as well as the red
berries. Below, left, is the strikingly beautiful Dove Tree, Davidia involucrata,
and, right, Enkianthus campanulatus which bears striking blossoms and is one
of the most brilliantly colored shrubs in the fall.

T. H. Everett

PLATE 52.   FINE TREES FOR GARDEN EFFECTS

At the top is Colorado Blue Spruce used effectively with other types of evergreens.
Below, fine specimens of the European and Copper Beech.

T. H. Everett

PLATE 53.   PLANTING TULIPS

When planting tulips, the soil should be enriched with bonemeal or other fertilizer
and spading it deeply. Then rake the surface until it is level and finely pulverized.
Lay out the bulbs on the prepared soil, spacing as desired. Then dig the holes and
set the bulbs individually.

T. H. Everett

PLATE 54.   TULIP SPECIES

Many tulips which grow wild in various parts of the world make interesting garden specimens and are available through nurseries. Reading from left to right, top row, are Tulipa Marjoletti, Tulipa Eichleri, and Tulipa Persica. Middle row, Tulipa Kaufmanniana, Tulipa Acuminata, Tulipa Daystemon. Lower row, Tulipa Australis, Tulipa Clusiana, and Tulipa Praestans.

Wayside Gardens Company

PLATE 55.   A FINE SPRING DISPLAY

One of the loveliest of spring effects is a mass of tulips, here planted in front of lilacs.

Associated Bulb Growers of Holland

PLATE 56.   TULIPS IN MASS EFFECT

Tulips seem to show to best advantage when used in mass plantings rather than isolated bulbs or straight rows.

Associated Bulb Growers of Holland

PLATE 57.   SPRING VISTA

While this picture is obviously not one of a small garden, the use of bulbs and flowering shrubs offers suggestions to the home gardener for creating spring displays.

Associated Bulb Growers of Holland

PLATE 58.   THE VEGETABLE GARDEN

There is no doubt that the home gardener who has room for a vegetable garden can enjoy fresher and finer vegetables than he can buy in the markets. Here is a collection of garden vegetables, all easily handled by the amateur.

W. Atlee Burpee Co.

PLATE 59. BRILLIANT VERBENA

Delightfully fragrant and appearing in the most attractive color forms, Verbena furnishes continuous bloom through the summer.

W. Atlee Burpee Co.

PLATE 60. DECORATIVE VINE AND POISONOUS PEST

At the top is a vine of American Ivy, also known as Virginia Creeper, with its characteristic five petals. Below is the equally decorative, but dangerous Poison Ivy with its three petals.

T. H. Everett

PLATE 61.   JAPANESE WISTERIA

One of the most striking of the vines is the Wisteria, of which there are several
species. The floribunda, shown here, bears the largest flower clusters.

Bobbink and Atkins

PLATE 62.   HYBRID ZINNIAS

Seedmen have constantly improved the strains of Zinnia so that hybrids of large
flower size and brilliant coloring are available and easily grown.

W. Atlee Burpee Co.

PLATE 63.   PERENNIAL DELPHINIUM

Considered a garden gem, perennial delphinium come in every shade of pink, blue and
purple. They need lots of sun and a little lime, but otherwise need little care to bloom
radiantly twice a year.

PLATE 64. A FINE PANSY PLANT

Although Pansies are often bought as blooming plants and set in place in the border, they are not very difficult to grow from seed. Many attractive varieties, bearing giant blossoms, are available.

W. Atlee Burpee Co.

nitida. Very dwarf shrub, less than 2 ft. high, with 7 or 9 glossy leaflets and deep pink flowers borne in midsummer, or later. An excellent low garden shrub. Atlantic coast from Newfoundland to New England.

nutkana. Vigorous, upright shrub with brownish stems, 5 to 9 leaflets and deep rose pink, solitary flowers. Used somewhat as an understock for standard roses, it is the ancestor of several recent garden hybrids. Alaska to Calif.

odorata (Tea Rose). Evergreen shrub of partially climbing habit; 5 or 7 large leaflets of waxy texture; ever-blooming flowers white, pale pink, or yellow, 3 in. across. Hardy only in the far S. Ancestor of the Tea roses, and one of the parents of the Noisettes. China.

omeiensis. Vigorous, branching shrub with 9 to 17 small leaflets and four-petaled white flowers, nearly 2 in. across. The variety *pteracantha* has enormous deep red prickles with wide winged bases. A very handsome garden shrub. China.

palustris (Swamp Rose). A 6-ft. shrub with 7 leaflets and pale pink flowers in corymbs. Native to E. U.S.

pendulina (*R. alpina*). A 3-ft. shrub with 7 or 9 leaflets and pink or deep rose flowers. Ancestor of Boursault roses. Europe.

pernetiana. See *R. foetida.*

polyantha. Garden hybrids of *R. multiflora* and *R. chinensis.*

roxburghi (*R. microphylla*). The Bur Rose. An 8-ft. shrub with pale green, sharp-prickled stems, 7 to 15 waxy green leaflets and pale pink, double flowers, followed by spiny hips. A single flowered variety is known. Not reliably hardy N. China, Japan.

rubiginosa. See *R. eglanteria.*

rubrifolia. Vigorous, upright shrub with 7 or 9 purplish red leaflets and tiny star-shaped, deep pink flowers. Europe.

rugosa. Vigorous, erect shrub with 5 to 9 large, coarse leaflets and purplish pink or white fragrant flowers 4 in. across; almost everblooming. Ancestor of Hybrid Rugosas. Much used in landscape planting, enduring difficult conditions where other shrubs will not survive. China, Japan.

sempervirens. Of trailing or climbing habit, with 5 or 7 evergreen leaflets, and clusters of fragrant white flowers. Not hardy N. Ancestor of a group of garden hybrids now rarely seen.

setigera (Prairie Rose). Bold, arching shrub of almost climbing habit, with normally 3 rough pale green leaflets and flowers bright pink, borne in midsummer

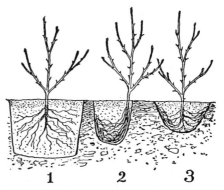

GOOD AND BAD PLANTING OF ROSES
1. A bush correctly placed in the center of a broad, deep hole filled with good rich soil. 2. Shrub badly crowded to one side in a much too narrow hole. 3. The hole is too shallow, allowing the roots no chance to spread.

or later. Ancestor of a group of old-fashioned hardy climbing roses now not much seen, and of a more recent group in somewhat wider use. It is the State flower of Iowa.

soulieana. Vigorous climbing shrub with 7 small, waxy leaflets and huge clusters of white flowers. A very decorative species but not reliably hardy. N. China.

spinosissima (*R. pimpinellifolia*). The Scotch or Burnet Rose. Densely spiny shrub; erect stems with 5 to 11 tiny leaflets and black or purple fruits; flowers white, pink or pale yellow. Its best variety is the white *altaica.* Formerly represented by many garden hybrids.

stellata (Gooseberry Rose). Straggly shrub with very spiny gray stems and curious foliage like that of a gooseberry; flowers large purple-pink. *R. mirifica* is a larger form of the same. Texas and Arizona.

virginiana (*R. lucida*). The common E. species up to 6 ft. high, with 7 or 9 leaflets and pale pink or rose-colored flowers. There is a white and also a double-flowered variety. Newfoundland to Va. and Mo. The State flower of N.Y.

watsoniana (Willow-leaved Rose). Arching shrub with 3 or 5 very narrow leaflets and insignificant flowers. A decorative drooping or weeping shrub. Japan.

wichuraiana (Memorial Rose). Creeping, glossy-leaved, almost evergreen climber with 7 or 9 leaflets and fragrant white flowers in clusters. Ancestor of most of the hardy climbers or Hybrid Wichuraiana roses.

willmottiae. Handsome, graceful shrub to 10 ft. high, with 7 or 9 tiny gray-green leaflets and purplish pink flowers set closely along the branches. China.

xanthina. Very spiny, stout, 10-ft. shrub with 7 to 13 small leaflets. Large double or semi-double deep yellow flowers in late spring. N. China.

Rose Enemies

The control of rose enemies is simpler than it sounds in the telling. A few minutes of care once a week, the time being religiously set aside for the purpose, will give luxuriant foliage and (in the case of Hybrid Teas) practically continuous bloom from early June until after frost.

Black Spot. This is probably most widely distributed of all rose troubles, present wherever the rose is grown, practically all varieties being susceptible in some degree. The fungus (*Diplocarpon rosae*) causes black irregularly circular spots with a radiating margin (formed of the dark mycelium) on the leaves which may turn yellow and drop off. Many gardeners do not realize that this defoliation in July and August is due to a fungus disease in the mistaken idea that rose bushes always look bad in midsummer. Not only are the spotting and defoliation unsightly, but also they seriously weaken the plants and make them more susceptible to winter injury. Very susceptible varieties, such as Los Angeles and many of the Pernetianas, show lesions on the canes as well as on the leaves.

Black spot can be controlled either by spraying or dusting. It does not matter too much which you use so long as you apply thoroughly and frequently—every week or 10 days—during the more active growing seasons. Tender new growth, especially, must be well protected. Properly applied—sprayed or dusted up from underneath through the plant and in proper amounts—neither form is unsightly. While it is possible to apply controls for sucking insects like aphids, thrips, and mites or chewing insects like beetles and worms, it is much easier to apply them in combination sprays or dusts. Now practically all garden marts carry an assortment of trade brands which are not only effective in controlling the insects, but will also check all common diseases as well. The important thing is to start the spraying or dusting program *early,* soon after the leaves come out, and certainly by the first of May, and to apply the fungicide thoroughly once a week while the bushes are growing rapidly, and once in ten days during hot dry midsummer weather, continuing the program until frost. Spray particularly the *underside* of the leaves.

Mildew is prevalent on ramblers in June and usually on bedding roses in late summer; new growth is covered with a white powdery coating, the buds and leaves are dwarfed and distorted and patches of white felt may also appear on the canes. Spraying regularly with either Mildex or Karathane as a preventive measure will prove effective in controlling mildew. Rust, sometimes present on rose leaves, may be recognized by orange-brown powdery spore masses on the under leaf surfaces. To control it gather and burn all fallen leaves in the fall; measures given for black spot are also effective.

Leaf spots of rose may be caused by several different fungi. Anthracnose, prevalent in late summer in many sections, may be very disfiguring. Strangely, Dr. Van Fleet and related varieties which seem resistant to most diseases, are quite susceptible to this one. The conspicuous spots are ashen in the center with a reddish-brown border and may be present on the canes as well as the leaves. Modern sprays control the disease. Chlorosis or mosaic is a virus disease of greenhouse roses in the E. but affects garden roses in the W.; the leaves are yellow along the veins and frequently distorted. Destroy diseased plants.

Cankers. The several rose cankers are best controlled at the time of uncovering and pruning plants in the spring. If a dormant spray of lime-sulphur (1 to 9) can be applied before the buds break, it will be useful. Brown canker, the most serious cane disease, causes small, circular reddish spots with white centers on the young canes. In late winter and early spring the spots enlarge to form a cinnamon-buff oval canker, which frequently girdles the canes and causes death of all portions above it. During wet weather yellowish spore tendrils project from the cankers. Stem canker, called frequently common canker, kills many rose canes in the garden and sometimes entire plants in the greenhouse; infection takes place through wounds.

A graft canker caused by the same fungus is common. In early spring stem cankers appear as reddish black lesions; later they turn brown and look smutty from the liberation of dark colored spores. Brand canker caused by another species of fungus is very serious where found but fortunately these places are relatively few. The symptoms resemble those of stem canker but the fruiting bodies appear through tiny longitudinal slits in the bark. Stem canker is most serious from N.Y. southwards while brand canker is more northern in its habits.

Prompt pruning out of all cankered canes in early spring is the first step in the control of rose cankers. Spraying or dusting as recommended for black spot will also keep down canker diseases. Too much "coddling" of roses over the winter makes them more susceptible to fungus attacks. In most localities some hilling up with earth is necessary, but burlap, straw, or thick blankets of leaves should be used sparingly since they provide ideal temperature and moisture conditions for fungous infection, and also may smother the plants.

Crown canker, which attacks only greenhouse roses, forms reddish-brown hard cankers near the union of stock and scion. Destroy diseased plants. Both greenhouse and out-door plants may be subject to crown gall, which see.

INSECTS. There are hundreds of insects that may attack roses but most of them also are easily controlled. New shoots and leaves may be coated in spring and fall with any of several varieties of aphids. If the spray or dust used for black spot contains a contact insecticide, the aphids will be taken care of automatically; if not, a separate application of Lindane, Malathion, or the older rotenone should be made. Leave an interval of 2 or 3 days between dusting with sulphur-lead arsenate and using any preparation containing soap. The rose leaf hopper, another sucking insect (especially injurious in spring) is controlled by the spray used for aphids. Both nymphs and adults cause a white stippled effect on the upper surface of leaves. See LEAF HOPPER.

Most of the chewing insects that attack roses can be controlled by DDT, Malathion, or Sevin, applied either alone, or combined with a fungicide. Among these pests are three species of rose sawflies, the slimy, slug-like larvae of which skeletonize the leaves and turn them brown. Foliage sprayed with above ma-

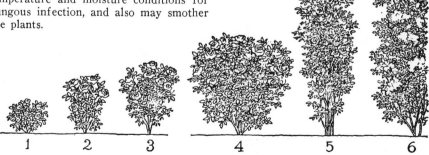

COMPARATIVE PLANT FORMS OF THE MAIN TYPES OF GARDEN ROSES
1. Polyantha or "Sweetheart" Roses—small bushes bearing all season clusters of small flowers; 2. Tea and Hybrid Tea Roses, with large flowers, usually scented, borne from early summer until late fall. 3. Hybrid Perpetuals, making larger plants but blooming only for about a month. 4. Shrub type, such as Rosa rugosa. 5. Pillar Rose, tall-growing, blooming in June on branches developed during the preceding summer. 6. Climbing Rose, producing large single blooms, or masses of small ones, some varieties growing to great height when well supported.

terials is protected against the rose chafer (see CHAFER, ROSE) and the Japanese beetle (which see). The flowers may also be protected by hand-picking the insects. During periods of heavy beetle infestations it is well to cut the roses while in bud.

The rose curculio is a snout beetle which eats holes in the buds, as does one of the climbing cut-worms. Modern sprays will discourage both of these; also the leaf-cutter bee which nips out circular pieces with which to line its nest and several leaf rollers which tie up the leaves. The rose stem-girdler which tunnels in the twigs causing swellings is the grub of a small metallic beetle. Clip off and burn infested twigs. Destroy stems badly infested with the rose scale and spray those lightly infested with lime-sulphur in spring.

In greenhouses Fuller's rose beetle, a brown, gray-marked snout beetle, feeds on the leaves at night and hides during the day. To destroy it, spray foliage with a modern spray, and treat soil with a fumigating material. The rose smidge is a small fly which lays its eggs near the flower buds on which the young larvae feed. Since the life cycle is only 2 weeks long there are many generations. Fumigate houses regularly. (See FUMIGATION.)

Recently the rose midge has escaped from greenhouses and become a real pest of outdoor roses. A mulch of tobacco dust is probably the easiest method of control. In a dry season thrips may discolor and "ball" the blooms. Frequent applications of contact insecticides are the only solution, but the insects are well protected between the petals so that wherever these pests exist rose growers must spray thoroughly and faithfully.

ROSE-ACACIA. Common name for *Robinia hispida,* an attractive shrub belonging to the Pea Family, native from Va. south, but hardy N., and growing to 9 ft. It thrives in sandy soil and suckers freely, a habit which may make it a nuisance in some places. Sometimes it is grafted to form a small standard, in which case it needs a sheltered position as the wood is brittle and easily broken. It is densely clothed with bristly hairs, has pinnate leaves with 7 to 13 leaflets, and racemes of showy pink flowers in May and June. Var. *macrophylla* is al-

most free of bristles, with larger leaflets and flowers. Propagated by seeds and suckers.

ROSE-APPLE. A common name for *Eugenia jambos,* a tropical tree grown in warm countries for its fruit, which is eaten fresh or used for confectionery and preserves.

ROSE-BAY. A little used common name for the genus Rhododendron; also sometimes applied to *Nerium oleander,* better known as Oleander, which see.

ROSE CAMPION. A common name for *Lychnis coronaria,* the familiar woolly white perennial also called Dusty Miller and Mullein-pink; and sometimes listed in catalogs as *Agrostemma coronaria.*

ROSELLE. Common name for *Hibiscus sabdariffa,* a stout tropical annual grown in warm countries (and somewhat in S. Fla. and S. Calif.) for its yellow flowers, whose large, thick fleshy calyxes supply a juice which makes a delicious beverage and, when cooked, a sauce or jelly with cranberry-like flavor.

The plant is as easily grown as the tomato, the plants being set 18 to 24 in. apart in rows 3 to 4 ft. apart. The bolls are gathered before they become woody and used either fresh or dried.

ROSE-MALLOW. Common name for Hibiscus, a genus of showy-flowered herbs, shrubs and small trees with large, papery or silky blossoms of white, pink or crimson.

ROSEMARY. Common name for *Rosmarinus officinalis,* a hardy evergreen sub-shrub grown chiefly for its aromatic leaves which are used in seasoning and which yield an oil used in medicine. Small light blue flowers are borne in April and May, in loose clusters that spring from the leaf axils. The foliage is white and woolly on under side and dark and shiny above. Plants grow to a height of 6 ft. and last for years if given winter protection. They prefer dry, well-drained soil and in Pacific Coast States where soil is dry and rocky, they are planted as hedges.

The plant called Bog-rosemary is Andromeda; the name Wild-rosemary is sometimes given to *Sedum palustre.*

ROSE-MYRTLE. A common name for *Rhodomyrtus tomentosa,* better known as Downy-myrtle (which see), an Asiatic tropical shrub grown for its rose-pink flowers and edible purple berries.

Plate 47.   HOW CLIMBING ROSES ADORN THE GARDEN

Top: The heavy severity of a stone wall softened by garlands of Dorothy Perkins, a hardy rambler rose.   Center left: At intervals, great glowing clusters of the American Pillar arch across the garden path.   Center right: A rambler wreathes and shades the arbor.   Lower left: Roses at the entrance welcome the visitor.   Lower right: An arch of roses terminating a perennial border.

ROSEOCACTUS (ròh-zee-oh-kak'-tus). A genus of Cacti having large turnip-like roots and a flat or half-round body covered with angular, spineless tubercles. *R. fissuratus* (Living-rock) from the limestone regions of W. Texas and Mexico, is a rounded plant 5 to 6 in. across, growing half-buried in the sand. White or purple flowers, 1½ in. across, grow from the center of the top. Roseocactus was formerly included in the genus Ariocarpus and is still often listed under that name.

See also CACTUS.

ROSE-OF-HEAVEN. Common name for *Lychnis coeli-rosa,* an annual with clear rose-red, or white, or purple-eyed flowers.

ROSE-OF-JERICHO. A common name for *Anastatica hierochuntica,* a small annual herb which at maturity becomes rounded and closely curled. If soaked, it will open, but if dried it will return to its tight, ball-like shape. See RESURRECTION-PLANT.

ROSE-OF-SHARON. A common name for the upright summer-flowering hardy shrub, *Hibiscus syriacus* (which is also called Rose-of-China and Chinese-rose); and for *Hypericum calycinum,* a low shrubby species of St. Johnswort. See HIBISCUS and HYPERICUM.

ROSE-ROOT. Common name for *Sedum roseum,* a succulent perennial with fragrant roots.

ROSE SOCIETY, AMERICAN. This was organized in 1899 by commercial florists and remained professional and semi-professional until Dr. J. Horace McFarland was invited to edit its publications in 1915. Since then its chief effort has been devoted to encouraging amateur and non-professional rose-growing in American gardens, although it has members throughout the world.

The Society keeps records of rose names to avoid duplication and endeavors to debar difficult and unpronounceable names. It has set up a standard for judging this flower at shows, offers its medals and special prizes at various outstanding flower shows throughout the country and gives gold and silver certificate awards at the society's test gardens in Portland, Ore.

Members are entitled to borrow books from the circulating library by paying postage expenses, and may have free advice on all matters pertaining to roses. Lantern slide lectures are available to members at a rental fee. The membership card admits members without charge to rose shows in which the Society participates and serves as an introduction to members throughout the world.

"What Every Rose Grower Should Know," an illustrated manual issued by the Society, tells the beginner much of what he needs to know about practical rose culture; the "Members' Handbook" contains the Society's regulations and laws, suggestions for rose shows, a catalog of the circulating library, a list of gardens open to members, and a geographical list of members; "The American Rose Annual," a comprehensive, well illustrated record and survey of rose progress, published every spring, contains many articles as well as a critical review of recent varieties and advice concerning all new roses; *The American Rose Magazine,* issued six times a year, gives up-to-date information about rose events, Society news, pilgrimages, and announcements. All the above are free to paid-up members and extra copies may be secured at a small charge, except in the case of the Members' Handbook.

Annual dues are $3.50; three years' dues are $10.00. Life, sustaining, commercial and research memberships are also available. The secretary is R. M. Hatton, Harrisburg, Pa.

ROSETTE. A clustering habit of growth which may be a natural arrangement of the foliage, as in the live-forever (Sempervivum), the dandelion and other plants, or else a symptom of certain virus diseases, such as peach rosette and the rosette of wheat. See VIRUS DISEASES.

ROSETTE-MULLEIN. Common name for *Ramonda* (or *Ramondia*) *pyrenaica,* a dwarf herb with purple (occasionally white) flowers, suitable for specialized rock plantings.

ROSINWEED. Common name for the genus Silphium, comprising tall perennial herbs of the Composite Family with heads of yellow disk and ray flowers. Silphiums resemble the perennial sunflowers and being rather coarse are suitable for the back of the sunny open border. They are easily propagated by seed or division.

S. laciniatum (Compass-plant) to 12 ft. has rough leaves and large heads to 5 in. across; it blooms continuously from July to Sept. In *S. perfoliatum* (Cup-plant, Indian Cup) to 8 ft. the upper leaves surround the stem, giving rise to the common names; the heads are 3 in. across. *S. in-*

tegrifolium has entire leaves and heads of flowers to 2 in. across borne in Aug. and Sept. *S. terebinthinaceum* (Prairie Dock) to 10 ft. has almost smooth foliage and many 3 in. flower-heads that make it one of the most decorative of the species. *S. trifoliatum* to 7 ft. has long narrow leaves and heads to 2 in. across from july to Oct.

ROSMARINUS (roz-mah-ry -nus) *officinalis.* A low, hardy, evergreen shrub of S. Europe, belonging to the Mint family, well known as Rosemary (which see). A source of aromatic leaves used in flavoring and a volatile oil.

ROT. A disintegration of tissues; decay; putrefaction. As a symptom of plant disease a rot may be hard, soft, wet or dry. See DISEASES, PLANT.

ROTATION OF CROPS, or CROP RO-TATION. The practice of alternating various crops on a given area as a matter of convenience in operating, or to enhance soil fertility, control pests or diseases, or increase crop yields. See CROPPING SYSTEMS.

As one means of controlling plant diseases caused by bacteria or fungi living in the soil, this practice "starves out" the disease-producing organism by keeping susceptible crop plants off the area for a sufficient number of years. On lands inhabited by the club root organism, cabbage and other cruciferous plants should be grown only once in 4 to 6 years. A long rotation should also be practiced for the control of black rot of cabbage and cauliflower. A three-year rotation of corn helps to avoid corn smut.

Although long-time crop rotation is often impracticable in the small home garden, changing the planting site each year or even the shifting of individual crops from place to place prevents accumulation in the soil of the pathogenes of aster wilt, gladiolus corm diseases, tulip blight and nematodes. If all types of rotation are impossible, the only way to overcome a serious soil infestation is to remove the soil to the depth of 6 to 8 in. and either sterilize it or replace it with fresh, uninfected soil.

ROTENONE. An insecticide extracted from the ground roots of derris and cubé (which see), tropical plants, used in tropical countries to paralyze fish in streams and make them easy to catch. Of value both as stomach poison and as a contact insecticide, it is being increasingly used because it is not toxic to man. It may be used as a dust or a spray and is available in various proprietary compounds, sometimes combined with pyrethrum or some kind of fungicide. See also INSECTICIDE.

ROUGE-PLANT. Common name for *Rivina humilis,* a slender annual of S. U. S. and the tropics grown in greenhouses and outdoors in warm sections for its ornamental berry-like fruits.

ROWAN-TREE. A common name for *Sorbus aucuparia,* the European Mountain-ash (which see). The name is sometimes used also for related species.

ROYAL FERN (*Osmunda regalis* var. *spectabilis*). A common and luxuriant N. American fern, belonging to the "flowering fern" family and bearing its fruit clusters in terminal racemes. Most desirable for the garden, at the back of the border, it grows 3 to 4 ft. tall, requiring much moisture and good drainage.

ROYAL PALM. Common name for spineless Feather Palms of the genus Roystonea, native to Fla. and the W. Indies. They bear heads of long arching leaves surmounting trunks, often swollen in the middle, that rise from 50 to 100 ft.

The Royal Palms, because of their extremely rapid growth, their resistance to fire, disease and winds, and their adaptability to a variety of soils, are valued for street and specimen planting in the S. States. They grow readily from seed and often take root in the wild on plate rock, the roots getting their nourishment from the fallen leaves and flowers.

ROYAL WATERLILY. Common name for the showy Amazonian aquatic, *Victoria regia.*

ROYENA (roi-ee'-nah). Evergreen trees or shrubs, native of Africa. One species, *R. lucida,* is sometimes grown under glass, and outdoors in S. Calif. It is a shrub to 12 ft. high, with shiny leaves and small white flowers, followed by fleshy red or purple fruit.

ROYSTONEA (roy-stoh'-nee-ah). A genus of majestic Feather Palms, with tall trunks and widespread, arching leaves commonly known as Royal Palms (which see). Native to the W. Indies and Fla., they are widely planted in those sections.

RUBBER-PLANT. Common name for *Ficus elastica,* a close relative of the fig and one of the most popular of house plants. Its sturdy, enduring growth, long life, simple cultural requirements, and large, handsome leaves, anywhere from 3 to 12 in. long and about one-third as wide, have offset its stiff, sometimes ungainly form and made the rubber-plant a favorite for years. Oblong or elliptical in shape, with small, abrupt points, the leaves are glossy and dark green above and dull or lighter green on the under side. The plant's requirements are simple; if given sunlight, rich potting soil and an ample supply of water during the growing season, it will thrive in spite of the dry air of the modern home. During the summer it will benefit from being placed outdoors (in the pot) in a sheltered corner where it will not be damaged by wind. Because it grows rapidly, especially if occasionally fed with liquid manure, it should be repotted once a year. Rubber-plants are generally grown to single stems or sometimes two. But excellent specimens can be obtained by pinching them back to make them branch and training them into compact, sturdy plants.

When a plant becomes too large or the long stems ungainly, it is desirable to alter its habit. This may be done in two rather simple ways. One is to cut it back to within a foot of the soil, whereupon new shoots will appear at the base. Many persons, however, object to losing the rest of the plant and prefer the so-called Chinese or air-layering system, which enables them to make two plants out of one. There are two easy ways to do this. One is to tie a

TWO RUBBER-PLANTS FOR INDOORS
Left, the common rubber-plant, Ficus elastica. Right, the less known but more decorative F. pandurata. Both will endure the conditions of poorly lighted living-rooms.

ball of sphagnum moss about the base of a young shoot at a point where the stem has been notched or scarred to stimulate the formation of roots. Keep the moss moist and when new roots are found spreading through it, cut the shoot from the parent branch and pot it up as a new plant.

The other, and generally practiced, method is to make an upward incision about half way through the stem at a point near the lowest leaves and keep the cut open by inserting a pebble or small piece of wood. Then split a 3-in. or 4-in. flower pot in two vertically, place it around the cut portion, fill it with moss or loose, absorbent soil and bind the pot tightly in place with wire. Keep the material moist at all times and within several weeks young roots will develop from the wound. Then sever the rooted specimen from the old stem, pot it up carefully in a new, whole pot and you will have two plants, as the parent will develop side branches.

The gardener who has a propagating box may increase his stock of plants by cutting off the upper part of a stem and making short pieces of it, with one leaf to each piece. Put these cuttings in sand in the propagating box in which bottom heat and a humid atmosphere must be maintained.

Mealy bugs and scale insects commonly infest this plant. The circular scale is dark, reddish and stands out prominently from the leaf. In greenhouses, cyanide fumigation will control this scale and Morgan's scale which is somewhat similar but flatter. For control of soft scale which also infests this plant, see under FERNS. However, all these pests can be controlled by spraying with nicotine or pyrethrum and soap. See also under HOUSE PLANTS.

Ficus lyrata is a more recently introduced rubber plant of lower, more compact form, with large, oblong cabbage-like leaves of irregular outline and deep green color, with conspicuous veins.

RUBBER-TREE. Common name for *Castilla elastica,* a tropical American tree of the Mulberry Family valuable commercially for its milky juice from which rubber is made. It grows to 60 ft. and has large leaves to 1½ ft., with dense soft hair beneath, and flowers in close clusters. A native of Mexico, Central America and northern S. America, it is extensively grown in the tropics, being raised from seed and the seedlings being set in their permanent positions when 12 in. tall. The trees may be tapped when they are 8 years old.

This plant belongs to the same family as the familiar rubber-plant though the latter is more closely related to the fig.

RUBBER-VINE. The genus Cryptostegia. Tropical climbing evergreen shrubs, grown for ornament in a warm greenhouse. Propagated by cuttings, they are easy to grow in a mixture of loam and peat.

C. grandiflora has thick glossy leaves and twisted flower buds. The funnel-shaped reddish-purple flowers turn pale with age. This plant has been widely cultivated in India for rubber obtained from the juice.

madagascariensis is a good climber with showy flowers of white or pink.

RUBIACEAE (roo-bi-ay'-see-ee). The Madder Family, a large, distinct group of plants mostly tropical. It furnishes many ornamental forms, chiefly greenhouse subjects, and yields many economic products, such as coffee, quinine, dyes and medicine. Genera commonly cultivated include Rubia, Asperula, Ixora, Coffea, Coprosma, Serissa, Manettia, Bouvardia, Luculia, Cinchona, Pentas, Rondeletia, Hoffmannia, Hamelia, Gardenia, Genipa, besides the native Houstonia.

RUBUS (roo'-bus). Brambles. A large genus of shrubby plants, native mostly in the temperate and colder regions of the northern hemisphere, belonging to the Rose Family. Most have prickly, and usually biennial, stems. Some are grown for their edible fruit; others for their ornamental stems, foliage and flowers. They thrive in open situations and good loamy soil and are propagated by seed, layers, suckers, and root-cuttings.

See also BLACKBERRY; DEWBERRY; LOGAN-BERRY; RASPBERRY.

PRINCIPAL NATIVE SPECIES

R. alleghentensis is a Highbush Blackberry, with leaves of 3 or 5 leaflets, from which have originated some of the cultivated varieties.

deliciosus (Rocky Mountain Flowering Raspberry) is a good hardy ornamental shrub, with currant-like leaves and showy rose-like white flowers.

flagellaris (American Dewberry) is a trailer with stems usually several feet long; one parent of the cultivated Dewberries.

frondosus is a Highbush Blackberry, with (usually) leaves of 3 leaflets; it is cultivated in improved forms.

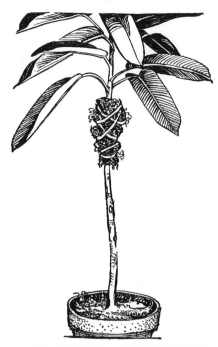

AIR-LAYERING A RUBBER-PLANT
When it gets tall and lanky, cut a notch in the stem just below the leaves, and wrap the place in sphagnum moss kept moist. When roots begin to show through, cut the old stem just below the moss and pot up the "new" stocky plant.

hispidus (Swamp Dewberry) is a slender trailer without prickles, and with glossy half-evergreen leaves; a good ground-cover for moist places.

occidentalis (Blackcap Raspberry) is an erect moderate grower with glaucous prickly canes which arch to the ground where the tips root producing new plants. It is the source of good cultivated varieties.

odoratus (Flowering Raspberry) grows to 6 ft. or more, without prickles, and with large lobed leaves and showy rosy-purple flowers. It thrives in partial shade and moist soil.

ASIATIC SPECIES

R. biflorus (Whitewash Bramble) has leaves of 3 or 5 leaflets and yellow fruit. It is conspicuous in winter with its white stems but it is not hardy N.

giraldiana, with 7 or 9 leaflets, is a stronger and hardier species, also with white stems. The fruit is black.

illecebrosus (Strawberry Raspberry) is a dwarf prickly shrub forming patches. The stems kill to the ground in the N., but new shoots flower and produce the large scarlet fruit late.

phoenicolasus (Wineberry) is ornamental with stems covered with reddish glandular hairs; it bears small red edible fruit.

EUROPEAN RUBUS SPECIES

R. idaeus (European Raspberry) is the source of some of the cultivated forms. Var. *strigosus* is the American Red Raspberry, which is also cultivated in improved forms.

laciniatus (Cutleaf Bramble) grows to 20 ft. in a mild climate. With finely cut leaves and large black fruit, it makes an attractive plant for furnishing an arch.

ulmifolius var. *bellidiflorus* is an ornamental form with double pink flowers. Var. *inermis* is the Evergreen Thornless Blackberry, often grown in mild regions.

loganobaccus (Loganberry) is a vigorous hybrid, cultivated in mild regions for its large red acid fruit, good for preserves.

RUBY GRASS. A common name for *Tricholaena rosea,* a perennial ornamental and forage grass of the S. See NATAL GRASS.

RUDBECKIA (rud-bek'-i-ah). One of several genera given the common name Coneflower because of the conical shape of the disks of the daisy-like flowers. Natives of North America, these coarse, summer-blossoming, annual, biennial or perennial herbs of the Composite Family generally have showy terminal heads of yellow ray flowers and cone-shaped, brown, yellowish or purplish-black disks. Thriving in any soil and doing equally well in full sun or partial shade, they make welcome additions to the yellow border, continuing their bloom until well into the fall. Propagation is by seeds, sown indoors or outdoors; by cuttings, or by division of the roots. Their sturdiness is indicated by the fact that *R. hirta* is the well-known Black-eyed Susan of the fields, which is also the Maryland State flower. In pioneer days Rudbeckias were mainly familiar wild flowers of the S. W., but today their descendants are popular garden flowers.

Of the many species, the most familiar are the Black-eyed Susan (*R. hirta*), with its vivid yellow, dark-centered flower-heads, abundantly borne on rough-hairy plants 2 to 3 ft. tall, and the tall, smooth Golden Glow (*R. laciniata* var. *hortensia*). Some species grow man-high, and many have yellow rays shaded to brownish

purple at the base. Among these is the Erfurt Coneflower (*R. bicolor* var. *superba*), a horticultural form recommended for the garden. One of the most attractive of the Rudbeckias is the much-branched Brown-eyed Susan (*R. triloba*), which bears quantities of small but showy flowers.

RUE. Common name for the genus Ruta, comprising a few species of perennial aromatic herbs, of medicinal rather than horticultural interest, but a common subject in the herb garden. All are hardy and can be increased by seeds or division. *R. graveolens* (Common Rue), a shrubby plant to 3 ft. with yellowish flowers to 1½ in. across and much divided fragrant leaves, is found in the E. States escaped from old gardens. *R. patavina,* to 6 in., has undivided leaves and yellow blossoms.

Goats-rue is *Galega officinalis.* a perennial leguminous herb; and Meadow-rue is the common name for the genus Thalictrum.

RUE-ANEMONE. Common name for *Anemonella thalictroides* (formerly known as Syndesmon), a delicate perennial herb of the Crowfoot Family, with tuberous roots, native in the E. part of N. America. It can be grown in colonies and is often transferred to the wild garden. Plants grow about 9 in. tall and bear pink or white flowers 1 in. across in spring. Thriving in light, moist soil, they prefer partial shade. Propagation is by division of the roots in spring or fall. Double flowers are produced on the var. *flore-pleno.*

RUELLIA (roo-el'-i-ah). A genus of widely distributed, generally hairy herbs or shrubs of the Acanthus Family bearing flat or funnelform flowers in shades of blue, violet, white, rose, red, and occasionally yellow or orange. The tropical species known collectively in England as Christmas Pride, are easily grown in the conservatory. Seeds should be sown in the spring in sandy soil and the seedlings potted in soil composed of sand, peat, leafmold and loam. They should be watered freely in summer and when in bud in the fall be given liquid manure as a stimulant. Plants may be also increased by cuttings taken in spring or summer and by division. They are frequently grown outdoors in the S.

R. macrantha from Brazil grows to 6 ft. with rosy-purple bell-shaped flowers to 3 in. borne singly in the leaf-axils; it is an excellent easily grown plant for the greenhouse. *R. amoena* to 2 ft. has clusters of bright red flowers. *R. ciliosa* to 2½ ft. is a native species found from N. J. to Tex., hardy N. with stemless blue flowers to 2 in. across borne singly or in clusters.

RUGOSA (roo-goh'-sah) **ROSE.** The anglicized name of a valuable species (*Rosa rugosa*), characterized by its extreme hardiness, its continuous blooming habit, its extremely prickly nature and its "rugose," downy leaves. The species itself and numerous varieties are grown as specimens, and in borders and hedges. See also ROSE.

RUGOSE. Wrinkled, or marked by fine depressed lines, as the leaves of *Prunus tomentosa*.

RUMEX (roo'-meks). A genus of about 100 species of widely distributed hardy herbs of the Buckwheat Family, mostly biennial and perennial, and many of them troublesome weeds. Some inhabit dry areas; others prefer marshy lands. They are popularly known as Dock, and Sorrel. Some authorities divide the docks from the sorrels, placing all tall-growing species under the first title, and low-growing ones under the second. One of the attributes of the Sorrels is their acidity, which has led to their being considered (perhaps to an unwarranted degree) as unquestionable evidence of acid soil conditions. See also DOCK; SORREL; WEEDS.

RUNNER. A long, slender trailing stem which may take root and produce new plants wherever its leaf and bud parts come in contact with the soil. Runners are especially valuable in propagating some plants quickly and inexpensively, as the strawberry, which forms runners in July after the blooming period. Many ornamental plants also spread and increase naturally by runners, or may be induced to do so. Of course where increase in size or number is not wanted, the frequent removal of the runners is a necessary phase of the culture of the plant in question.

RUSCUS (rus'-kus). Low evergreen shrubby plants from the Mediterranean region, belonging to the Lily Family. They are valuable for undergrowth in dark places and under trees, spreading by suckers, but are not hardy where winters are severe. The best known species is *R. aculeatus* (Butchers-broom), which grows to about 3 ft. It has green stems and glossy leaf-like flattened stem branches from the middle of which the small white flowers are borne in clusters; the male and female usually on separate plants. The

fruit is a large red berry. Dried and dyed sprays of foliage are much used by florists and sold for decorative purposes by seed stores, especially during the Christmas holiday period. *R. hypoglossum* is a dwarfer sort with larger leaves.

RUSH. Common name for Juncus, a genus of stiff, perennial herbs resembling grasses. They grow in wet places and have unbranched, round stems, narrow, flat, grassy leaves and small clusters of greenish or brownish flowers. Some of the smaller rushes (sometimes obtainable from dealers) are grown in pots or planted in the bog garden. Two of the more interesting species are:

J. effusus (Common Rush) with a soft stem to 4 ft. high, widely distributed in the N. temperate zone; it is used for making woven mats. Its varieties *spiralis* and *vittatus,* the latter yellow-striped, are decorative forms. *J. balticus* is tufted in growth, with greenish flowers edged white.

RUSSELIA (ru-see'-li-ah). Coralblow. Shrubby plants of the American tropics, belonging to the Figwort Family. They are often grown in greenhouses and outdoors in warm regions. They have a long season of bloom and, by reason of their pendulous habit, are well adapted for hanging baskets. They thrive in rich light soil, and are easily propagated by cuttings. *R. equisetiformis* (formerly called *R. juncea*) is the principal species. It is a muchbranched plant to 4 ft. with drooping rushlike stems, bearing a profusion of small tubular scarlet flowers.

RUSSIAN-OLIVE. A common name for the Oleaster (*Elaeagnus angustifolia*) a hardy shrub grown for its fragrant but inconspicuous flowers and its ornamental foliage. See ELAEAGNUS.

RUSSIAN-THISTLE. Common name for *Salsola pestifer,* a rampant, bushy annual herb which at maturity dries into a rounded mass of stems and becomes a "tumble-weed" to be blown along by the wind, scattering its seed as it goes. It is most common in the Prairie States, along railways and waste land. In gardens it is not likely to become troublesome if destroyed before it can go to seed.

RUSTIC WORK. This refers to all kinds of garden structures—fences, arbors, furniture, etc.—constructed of wood as it grows, using the natural forms, sometimes without stripping off the bark. Ingenuity in selecting each piece is demanded, for durable with a coat of spar varnish or one of plain boiled linseed oil. If a touch of color is wanted a little yellow ochre or red lead can be worked into the oil. Creosote helps to preserve the parts of any permanent rustic structures that have to be inserted in the ground.

See also GARDEN FIXTURES; GARDEN FURNITURE.

RUSTS. A name used to designate either a group of fungi (see below) or the diseases produced by them. The name is taken from the easily recognized iron rust color of the spore pustules. Many of the rusts occurring in garden and greenhouse, such as those on hollyhock, snapdragon, etc., can be controlled by dusting with fine sulphur. Other rusts, which require two different hosts on which to complete their life cycle, are more frequently controlled by the removal of that host which is of least importance in the garden or larger area being protected. Control of some rusts is also being achieved by breeding resistant varieties, as in the case of wheat, asparagus, and snapdragon. Plants attacked by rusts do not usually die, but may be dwarfed and yellowed. Certain rusts cause accelerated growth in the form of galls or formations known as witches' brooms, which see.

DEVELOPING RUST-RESISTANCE

Both of these snapdragons were exposed to Antirrhinum rust. The plant at the left, an ordinary variety, became infected and dwarfed, the foliage being badly spotted. The specimen at the right, of a newly developed rust-resistant hybrid form, was not affected, and grew and blossomed normally.

RUST FUNGI

The common name, "rust," of the fungous order Uredinales is suggested by the conspicuous reddish-orange spore pustules observed in certain stages of the life cycle of typical forms. Rust fungi are *obligate parasites,* that is, they cannot grow unless in contact with living plant tissue. The vegetative part (*mycelium*) which is made up of thread-like *hyphae* (see FUNGI) grows between the cells of the host plant and feeds by means of specialized sucking organs (*haustoria*) which penetrate the cell walls.

Five different types of spores (reproductive bodies) may be formed during the life of a single rust, but not all are found in every species. For aid in classifying and describing rusts these spore forms have been given the symbols O, I, II, III, IV, which represent different stages in the life cycle. Rusts are of two general types; first, those which pass all the stages of their life cycle on a single host and are called *autoecious;* and, second, those which spend part of their life on one kind of plant

each must be naturally of the form and size (diameter) which its position requires.

Design of rustic work should always be severely plain and functional. The rough character of the material is suited only to expressing the purpose of the object in direct and simple terms, and when more than this is attempted the effect is labored and the spirit of the idea—which is devotion to Nature-forms—is wholly lost. Rustic work is likewise out of its element when placed in a finished environment in the garden. Natural and even wilderness surroundings furnish the setting in which it is seen at its best.

Any kind of wood free from oozing sap is suitable for making rustic furniture, hickory, ash, larch, fir, red-cedar (Juniper), willow and birch being satisfactory examples. If the bark is to be left on, the wood should be cut in winter if possible. Except in the case of birch and other smooth barks, peeled material is less likely to become dirty and soil the clothing. Rustic work from which the bark has been removed can be made more attractive and

and the rest on another kind of plant called an "alternate host." Hollyhock and asparagus rusts are well known garden examples of autoecious rusts, no alternate hosts being necessary.

The important black stem rust of wheat, barley, rye and many grasses (caused by the fungus *Puccinia graminis*) is an excellent example of a rust of the second type (heteroecious) and may be used to demonstrate a typical life cycle with its different stages. While the details are of interest mainly to scientists, it is well for gardeners to know the complicated history of some of their plant troubles.

First or red spore stage (*Urediniospores* or summer spores of the II group are formed in spore pustules called *uredinia*). Reddish-brown streaks or pustules on the cereal hosts are the first signs of this rust. Successive crops of spores formed are carried by the wind to healthy plants.

Second or black spore stage (*Teliospores* or winter spores of the III group

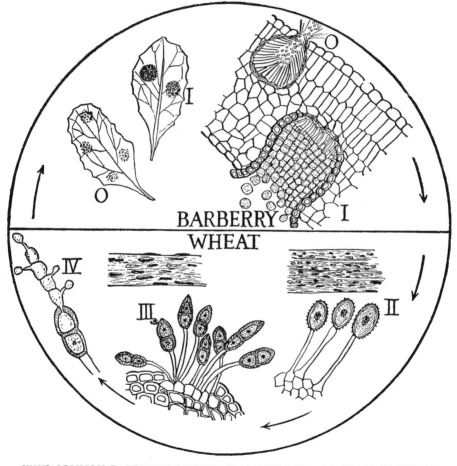

WHY COMMON BARBERRY SHOULD BE DESTROYED TO PROTECT WHEAT

This diagram illustrates the life cycle of the devastating rust disease of wheat, in which the common barberry (not the Japanese species) plays an important role. (Everything but the plant leaves is shown greatly enlarged.) The spores (reproductive bodies) which cause the infection on leaves of wheat are borne in orange-colored pustules on barberry leaves. They are of two kinds and are borne separately on the upper (O) and lower (I) leaf surfaces. The latter are blown by the wind to nearby wheat fields, where they cause red rusty patches on leaves of the grain (II). The spores which develop there (shown enlarged) infect the stems of the grain causing black roughened areas (III). From these develop resistant or "resting" spores which keep the fungus alive over winter on the stubble. In spring, they give rise to still another kind of spores (IV) which blow to and infect more barberry leaves and start the cycle over again. If barberry is not present, the life of the wheat rust can not continue, and many acres of grain may be saved from destruction.

are formed in *telia*). Dark-colored spore cases (*sori*) appear on the wheat in late summer or early fall but the spores do not germinate until spring, when they produce small colorless sporidia.

THIRD or SPORIDIUM STAGE (*Sporidia* or *basidiospores* of the IV group develop). These spores cannot reinfect wheat but germinate *only if the wind carries them to leaves, twigs, or fruit of certain species of barberry.*

FOURTH or PYCNIAL or SPERMAGONIAL STAGE (*Pycniospores* of the O group are formed in *pycnia*). Yellowish areas appear on the upper surface of barberry leaves. Spores that formed in the minute flask-shaped bodies in these areas are necessary for the development of the next stage.

FIFTH or CLUSTER CUP STAGE (*Aeciospores* of the I group are formed in *aecia*). Clusters of tiny yellow-orange cups form on the under surface of barberry leaves and are filled with chains of yellow spores. These spores *cannot reinfect barberry but must return to wheat* where they start a new life cycle.

The blister rust of white pine (see PINE) is another heteroecious rust of great economic importance, currants and gooseberries being alternate hosts. The rust affecting cedar and apple (see JUNIPER) is particularly injurious to the apple fruit;

Important Rust Diseases and Their Hosts

Disease (common name) and rust (*scientific name*).	Spore Stages and Hosts on Which They Occur			
	O	I	II	III
Orange rust of aster and goldenrod (*Coleosporium solidaginis*)	Pine species		Aster and goldenrod	
Blister rust of 5-needle pines (*Cronartium ribicola*)	White pine and other five-needle species		Species of currants and goose-berries	
Poplar rust (*Melampsora medusae*)	Species of larch		Species of poplar	
Witches' broom of fir and spruce (*Melampsorella elatina*)	Fir and spruce		Various species of the Pink Family	
Rust of apple (*Gymnosporangium juniperi-virginianae*)	Wild crabs and cultivated apple varieties		Red-cedar and *Juniperus barbadensis*	
Quince rust (*Gymnosporangium germinale*)	Quince, hawthorn and apple		Juniper (*Juniperus communis* and *J. virginiana*)	
Hawthorn rust (*Gymnosporangium globosum*)	Hawthorn (many species) and apple		*Juniperus virginiana*	
Pea rust (*Uromyces pisi*)	Spurge (*Euphorbia cyparissias*)		Common pea	
Rust of stone fruits (*Transschelia punctata*)	Hepatica, Thalictrum and Anemone species		Almond, apricot, cherry, peach and plum	
Corn rust (*Puccinia sorghi*)	Oxalis		Indian corn	
Rust of beet and spinach (*Puccinia sarcobati*)	Beet, spinach and many wild plants of 22 families		Salt grass (*Distichlis spicata*)	
Stem rust of cereals (*Puccinia graminis*)	Species of Mahonia and the common barberry, but *not* Japanese barberry.		Wheat, oats, barley, rye and grasses	

on the cedar it produces the gall-shaped deformations commonly known as cedar-apples. Deformations caused by other rusts may take the form of excessively bushy growths of shoots at the end of tree limbs; these are known as witches' brooms.

Getting down to the control or prevention of such rusts, removal of the alternate host from the vicinity of the one that is economically more important is the principal method. The table on page 1084 lists some of the more important examples of such rusts and shows on which plants the different stages (spore groups) occur. This information may be of value to the gardener in enabling him to determine which plants should be removed, for much needless eradication of worth-while plant material has been caused through a misunderstanding of the relationships of some of these rusts. On the other hand, removal of a dangerous alternate host may be the only way to save a valuable crop.

RUTA (roo'-tah). A genus of aromatic perennial herbs and sub-shrubs known as Rue, which see.

RUTABAGA (roo-tah-bay'-gah). Swedish turnip. A hardy, biennial herb (*Brassica napobrassica*) cultivated as an annual vegetable. It differs from the turnip structurally in having bloom-covered leaves, a more elongated and leafy top and much more fibrous roots. As to habit, it requires 4 to 6 weeks longer to mature and somewhat more liberal distance between plants and rows. Because it needs cool weather and moist soil to develop, it is sown in early summer for winter use.

See BRASSICA; TURNIP.

RUTACEAE (roo-tay'-see-ee). The Rue Family, a group of frequently evergreen, mostly woody, aromatic plants, distributed in tropical and sub-tropical regions. Most of the genera yield a characteristic pungent or aromatic oil and some include medicinal, ornamental and odorous species. However, the family is best known for the important citrus fruits. Some species, the fruits of which are not edible, are nevertheless of value for hybridizing purposes. Genera commonly cultivated are: Ruta, Dictamnus, Evodia, Diosma, Boronia,

Choisya, Correa, Ptelea, Casimiroa, Phellodendron, Murraea, Severinia, Skimmia, Triphasia, Citrus, Fortunella, Citropsis, Poncirus.

RUTLAND BEAUTY. Common name for *Convolvulus sepium,* a perennial trailing herb of the bindweed group.

RYE. A hardy annual grass (*Secale cereale*) grown on farms for its grain and straw, but in orchards and gardens as a green manure and cover-crop (see both titles) for the purpose of adding to both the humus and the plant food content of the soil. In the vegetable garden seed can be scattered among maturing crops during August and September (1 oz. to 25 sq. ft.) and lightly raked or cultivated in, care being taken not to injure the growing crops. The resulting green crop can be dug or plowed under in the late fall, or it may be left as a cover-crop and dug in early in the spring.

On land from which a fall crop is harvested any time before freezing weather, rye may be broadcast at the same (or a little heavier) rate, for even if it does not germinate immediately, it will be ready to sprout at the first warm spell and make some growth before time to plow in the spring. Winter or hairy vetch (*Vicia villosa*) is often sown (1 oz. to 50 sq. ft.) with rye to augment the supply of nitrogen (see LEGUME). Fall-sown rye will usually make a good start and survive any ordinary winter. In spring it must be plowed or dug under while soft and succulent and less than 1 ft. high. If left too long there may be difficulty in covering it; also woody stems take longer to rot and are a much poorer source of humus.

Wild-rye is Elymus.

RYE GRASS. Common name for Lolium, a genus of Grasses grown in pastures and meadows, and sometimes in lawns (which see) to give a quick green covering to the soil and to supply moderate shade for other slower growing sorts. *L. multiflorum* (Italian Rye Grass) and *L. perenne* (Perennial or English Rye) are used in lawns. *L. temulentum* (Darnel), supposedly the tares of the Bible, is a weed with poisonous properties if eaten.

SABAL (say'-bal). A genus of about 20 species of palms, distinguished by their spineless leaves, and of varying heights, up to 90 ft.; some have no stem above the ground level. See PALMETTO.

SABATIA (sa-bat'-i-ah). A genus of hardy annual or biennial herbs of the Gentian Family, with white, rose-pink or rose-purple wheel-shaped flowers, in flat-topped clusters. Native to E. N. America they are seldom seen in cultivation; but they are handsome plants well worth a place in the border or rock garden, where they should be planted in a moist, peaty soil. They are sometimes called Rose-gentians.

SACRED-LILY, CHINESE. See CHINESE SACRED-LILY, which is *Narcissus tazetta* var. *orientalis.*

SAFFLOWER. A common name for *Carthamus tinctorius,* or False-saffron, an annual grown for its orange flowers which are used for dyeing and rouge-making.

SAFFRON. Common name for *Crocus sativus,* a lilac-flowered fall-blooming species grown also as a source of a dye and culinary and medicinal products.

SAGE. Common name for the two genera Salvia and Audibertia; but most popularly for the hardy sub-shrub *Salvia officinalis,* which is extensively grown for seasoning dressings used with rich meats, and for flavoring sausage and cheese.

Sow the seed thinly indoors or in outdoor seed beds. Transplant when plants are large enough to move, setting them at least 18 in. apart, and giving clean cultivation. Holts Mammoth is the best variety, but as it bears no seed, it is propagated by layers and cuttings. As the plants often exceed 3 ft. in diameter they should be planted that far apart. See SALVIA; HERBS.

Bethlehem-sage is *Pulmonaria saccharata.* Jerusalem-sage is *Phlomis fruticosa.* Crimson, Purple, White, and Black Sages are species of Audibertia.

Sagebrush, whose blossom is the State flower of Nevada, is *Artemisia tridentata,* a native shrub of the arid S. W.

SAGERETIA (saj-ee-ree'-shi-ah). Deciduous or evergreen shrubs of Asia and N. America, belonging to the Buckthorn Family. They have little ornamental value, but might be used for hedges. *S. pycnophylla* from China is hardy N. It is a spiny shrub to 6 ft. with slender drooping branches, bearing tiny white flowers in slender spikes, followed by blackish berries. *S. minutiflora,* native to the S. E. States, is a spiny straggly shrub of no particular ornamental value.

SAGINA (sah-jy'-nah). A genus of annual and perennial herbs used for rock-garden edgings. See PEARLWORT.

SAGITTARIA (saj-i-tay'-ri-ah). A genus of aquatic herbs, mostly with arrow-shaped leaves, known as Arrowhead, which see. See also AQUARIUM.

SAGITTATE. Shaped like an arrowhead, such as the leaves of the genus Sagittaria; that is, long-triangular with the sharp basal lobes projecting downward. Compare HASTATE and CORDATE.

SAGO-PALM. A common but misleading name for *Cycas revoluta,* which is not a palm but a cycad, which see.

SAGUARO (sah-gwah'-roh). Common name for *Carnegeia* (formerly *Cereus*) *giganteus,* one of the giant cacti of the S. W. deserts, whose blossom is the State flower of Ariz. See CARNEGEIA.

ST. ANDREWS CROSS. Common name for *Ascyrum hypericoides,* a low herb-like branching native shrub of the St. Johnswort Family. It grows about 2 ft. tall, with golden-yellow flowers ½ in. across, particularly attractive because of the profuse stamens. It is not always hardy in the E. States, requiring winter covering, but in the S. and the W. States it is evergreen and is often used for a ground-cover in landscape work where a considerable extent of sandy soil has to be covered. It is increased by seeds or division.

ST. AUGUSTINE GRASS. Common name for *Stenotaphrum secundatum,* a creeping perennial member of the Grass Family, sometimes used in S. lawns. See LAWN.

ST. BERNARDS LILY. Common name for *Anthericum liliago,* a tuberous-rooted herb that bears small flowers.

ST. BRUNOS LILY. Common name for *Paradisea liliastrum,* a hardy perennial herb with long grassy leaves and white flowers in loose racemes on stems 2 ft. high. The effect when the plants are in flower makes them most attractive in the hardy border in combination with meadow-rues or speedwells.

ST. DABEOCS HEATH. Another name for the Irish Heath (*Daboëcia cantabrica*), a little evergreen shrub useful in rock gardens though requiring winter protection.

ST. JAMES LILY. Another name for *Sprekelia formosissima,* the Jacobean-lily (which see), a Mexican amaryllis-like greenhouse plant, grown outdoors in warm climates.

ST. JOHNS BREAD. Common name for the dried fleshy seed pods of *Ceratonia siliqua,* an evergreen, warm-country tree of the Pea Family. Also known as Carob (which see). It is grown in S. Calif. and Fla., where the pods are fed to stock, but they are also used to some extent as human food, being sold from city street stands as "honey locust."

ST. JOHNSWORT. Common name for Hypericum, a genus of yellow-flowered herbs and small shrubs grown in borders and rock gardens.

ST. MARYS THISTLE. A common name for *Silybum maritimum,* an annual or biennial, thistle-like herb with purple flowers. Also called Blessed, Holy and Milk Thistle.

SAINTPAULIA (saynt-pau'-li-ah) *ionantha.* African- or Usambara-violet. This native of Africa is a greenhouse and terrarium subject, occasionally grown as a house plant. Its pale or deep lavender flowers, about ¾ in. across, with a bright yellow, bead-like center, grow 3 to 6 in. above shiny, hairy, dark green foliage. The plant has no main stem, the oblong leaves, 1½ in. long, with a suggestion of a point on the ends, growing on separate leaf stems from the base or crown. The main flower stalks branch into 2-in.- or 3-in.-long stems, each carrying one flower. A thriving plant has several of these flower sprays at one time.

When used as a house plant the African-violet likes a position at a light window protected from the direct rays of the sun. Although the roots want a fair amount of moisture, water should not be splashed or spilled on the leaves or crown. Once a week, however, the leaves should be treated to a misty spray.

As the plant may be expected to last for only about a year, leaf cuttings should be made in March. Pick the leaves at the base of the plant and insert them in pots or boxes of sand which are kept wet. Keep these containers covered with glass until the leaves take root and new plants start. These will grow to flowering size in about 8 months.

ST. PETERSWORT. Common name for *Ascyrum stans,* an herb-like shrub with yellow flowers.

SALADS. Plants whose leaves or stems or both are eaten raw, either alone or mixed with other ingredients. They may be grouped under three heads: Neutral (such as fetticus); bitter (endive, chicory, dandelion); and piquant or warm (watercress, pepper-grass, nasturtium, chives). Lettuce properly belongs with the bitter salads, but when well grown and not old it is almost a neutral. In America it is easily the leading salad plant with chicory (witloof) and endive far behind. In Europe many other plants are popular, especially pepper-grass and mustard, which are grown in every home garden as well as extensively for market.

Since salads must be fresh when served, the home garden is the ideal place to grow them. They do best in rich, friable soil well supplied with moisture and should be grown rapidly with no check. For the earliest spring crop make the bed in the sunniest, driest place to promote quick growth and best flavor; for late crops, choose partially shaded, moist spots to provide moisture and shelter from beating sunlight. For water-cress a stream is not essential—merely continuously moist soil. See GREENS, EDIBLE; LETTUCE; CHICORY; ENDIVE.

SALAL (sal'-al). Common name for *Gaultheria shallon,* a small shrub related to wintergreen with white or pink bell-shaped flowers and purple fruits.

SALIX (say'-liks). A genus of trees and shrubs comprising the Willow (which see) and Osier. They are deciduous, usually hardy and useful for planting in wet ground, to hold banks of streams and dams, as well as for ornament.

SALLOW. A common name for *Salix caprea,* a species of Willow (which see). Also called Goat Willow.

SALMON-BERRY. Common name for *Rubus spectabilis,* an almost spineless, hardy, perennial-stemmed bramble with purple or rose-colored flowers and salmon-colored edible fruit.

SALPIGLOSSIS (sal-pi-glos'-is). Painted Tongue. This half-hardy, branching annual from Chile, growing about 2 ft. high, produces funnel-shaped flowers 2½ in. long and wide, of velvety texture and in many colors, the interior of the blossoms being strikingly veined. (See illustration, Plate 49.) The suggested name, "paisley flower" gives an idea of their exotic beauty. The background colors include exceedingly rich tones, the purples, blues and reds being particularly good. However, the colors, though beautiful, should not be used where a definite color effect is wanted, because they are too subtle.

The plant thrives best in a sandy soil and in half shade; a soil that is not excessively rich gives the best and most colorful flowers. The branches do not spread much, so individual plants need comparatively little elbow room and are easily tucked between perennials where they get the desired amount of shade. Pinching out

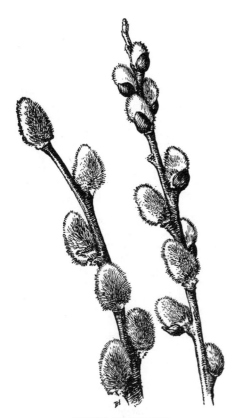

PUSSY WILLOWS

The "pussies" which emerge from the shining brown winter scales long before the leaves appear are the male and female catkins or flowers of the native willow, Salix discolor.

the center while the plant is small encourages branching. The stems are wiry and slender and few annuals have greater lasting qualities as a cut flower. Salpiglossis is as decorative indoors as out.

The seeds are extremely fine and unless carefully handled are likely to be buried too deep or washed away. Whether started in a seed box in the house during March, or planted in a carefully marked row outdoors when the soil has started to warm, they should be merely sprinkled on the surface and pressed into the soil, then covered with newspaper or muslin which is kept moist. After the seeds have germinated the plants mature without difficulty but should not be allowed to suffer a check or be stunted. For winter flowering indoors, sow seed in midsummer and pot up the young plants carefully in the fall.

Salpiglossis belongs to the Nightshade Family. All cultivated sorts are of the species *S. sinuata* or its var. *superbissima,* which is unbranching and therefore more upright or columnar.

SALSIFY. A hardy biennial, *Tragopogon porrifolius,* also called Vegetableoyster or Oyster-plant, and grown for its long, fleshy, edible white roots. In form they resemble but are smaller than parsnips; in flavor they suggest oysters.

As the plants require a long season to develop usable roots, seed must be sown as soon as the ground can be worked in spring. They are hardy, so some of the roots may be left in the ground like parsnips until the following spring; they must then be dug for use before growth starts. This practice is even better than digging and storing them in the fall, because they tend to shrivel even more than parsnips and to become tough if stored indoors. Winter supplies should be dug late and stored preferably in outdoor pits. See STORING OF CROPS.

Oyster-plant succeeds best in light, rich, mellow, deep soil. Sow seed thinly an inch deep in rows 15 in. apart. When the seedlings are 3 in. high they should be thinned to 4 in. apart and thereafter be given clean cultivation.

Black-salsify is *Scorzonera hispanica.* Spanish-salsify or Golden Thistle is *Scolymus hispanicus.*

SALT. Common salt, either in household form or as crude commercial sodium chloride, is sometimes used as an indirect fertilizer and to destroy weeds. Its main effect on soil fertility seems to be that of changing potassium from an insoluble to a soluble form. It was long recommended and used as a stimulant on asparagus, but any benefit it may have on this crop is now attributed to its prevention of weeds. For this purpose it should be scattered lightly between the rows (not more than 1 lb. to 100 sq. ft.). To kill poison ivy, destroy weeds in paths and drives, etc., it must be applied much more heavily and directly on the undesired plants, either dry or as a strong brine.

In chemistry a *salt* is a compound in which a metal element has replaced the hydrogen of an acid. Many such salts are important fertilizers or spray materials, as sodium nitrate, copper sulphate, etc.

SALTBUSH. Common name for the genus Atriplex, consisting of herbs and shrubs native to salty lands. One species, *A. hortensis,* or Orach, is grown for greens.

SALT HAY. Hay cut on salt marshes is exceedingly valuable for mulching, first because it is inclined to be firm and stiff and not so likely to mat down and freeze solid; second, because it is free from seed, both of its own kind and of weeds; and third, because, where obtainable, it is usually cheap and abundant. Large quantities are used on commercial bulb farms, the hay being carefully raked from off the rows in spring, stacked, and used year after year. It is equally useful for mulching perennial borders, strawberry beds, etc., in the home garden, but is not so suitable for use as a cover-crop or source of humus to be plowed under or added to the compost heap. See MULCH.

SALT-TREE (*Halimodendron halodendron*). An ornamental hardy deciduous Asiatic shrub growing to about 6 ft. It does well in a light sandy soil, and is a good subject for the seaside garden. In habit it is wide-spreading with slender branches. Its pinnate and silky-silvery leaves give it a very graceful appearance, and in early summer it is covered with pale purple flowers. Propagation is usually from seeds or layers, but it is sometimes grafted on *Caragana arborescens,* another member of the Pea Family.

SALVER-SHAPED. A corolla in which the limb (which see) or border is flat and flares abruptly from the long slender tube, as in phlox and flowering tobacco (Nicotiana).

SALVIA (sal'-vi-ah). Sage. This large genus of herbs, subshrubs and shrubs

belonging to the Mint Family is represented practically throughout the world. It includes several valuable garden perennials whose flowers grow in spikes, racemes, or panicles on tall stems in blue, red, pale-yellow or white, and variations. They range from 2 to 4 ft. high. Some species are only half-hardy in temperate climates and must be treated as annuals. Some of the best, however, are extremely hardy, and this, combined with their simple cultural requirements, makes them model border plants. Any average garden position suits them, although they are at their best when planted in an enriched loamy soil where they get sun most of the day. Some of the species are grown as culinary or medicinal herbs. See HERBS.

The scarlet sage (*Salvia splendens*) is the best known and most used; in fact, it tends to be over-used and misused. Its vivid color does not combine easily with other flower shades; it is therefore advisable to use the plant by itself against a background of green. The same applies to many of its vivid varieties such as Bonfire, Harbinger, and Scarlet Dragon, though not to the white var. *alba.* All are usually treated as annuals, being started in seed boxes indoors during February or March and set out in the garden when the soil is warm.

There are two other adaptable species in this class, the blue sage (*S. patens*) and the mealy or mealycup sage (*S. farinacca*). The former grows about 2 ft. high and has flowers of a fine ultramarine blue. Some amateur growers dig its roots up in the fall and store them out of reach of frost until time to replant in spring, thus making the plants last for several years. The mealycup sage grows nearly 4 ft. tall and makes a large soft clump of silver (foliage) and lavender (flowers).

The finest of the truly hardy salvias, which remain in the garden for years, is *S. pitcheri,* native in the Midwest States and sometimes cataloged and sold as a variety (*grandiflora*) of the lower-growing, S. species, *S. azurea.* It provides the deepest and purest of salvia blues, coming into bloom in late summer and continuing to bear until frost its 1-in. flowers along thin, nimble stems about 4 ft. high. If not staked from early summer on, the plant takes on a semiprostrate and less tidy appearance. Also when once allowed to grow on the ground the stems cannot be straightened up. As the new growth appears late in the spring, the stakes should remain in place from year to year to prevent the plants from being spaded up, and as a reminder to tie the stems to them. Where lighter blue flowers and slightly shorter plants are desirable *S. azurea* can be used.

Another extremely hardy species is *S. argentea.* Its large (to 8 in.) woolly leaves form rosettes in early spring, are responsible for the common name "silver salvia," and make it a plant of high decorative value throughout the season. Graceful sprays of white, yellowish, pale rose, or blue flowers are borne in midsummer on stems about 3½ ft. high, which should be staked so they will not be broken off by wind or storms. The same caution applies to the violet salvia (*S. nemorosa* or *S. virgata* var. *nemorosa*), a hardy perennial growing to 3 ft. or more with large loose clusters of flowers that range from light blue to purple.

These hardy salvias should be increased by division when the clumps become large. The best time to do this is in spring, as soon as the plants appear above the ground.

There are many other species of interest and beauty but lesser ornamental value, including *S. officinalis,* common or garden sage, a hardy European sub-shrub with aromatic leaves which are used, dried, in cooking. Plants once established persist for years. See SAGE.

SALVINIA (sal-vin'-i-ah). A small and interesting genus of floating, flowerless annuals which form large colonies on the surface of quiet waters. *S. natans,* the species found commonly in ponds and aquaria, soon spreads over a large tank although each plant consists of but two very small, oval leaves.

See AQUARIUM and AQUATIC PLANTS.

SAMARA (sam'-ah-rah). A hard, dry, winged fruit, as of the ash or elm. Two samaras may be joined together forming a *double samara,* as in the maple.

SAMBUCUS (sam-beu'-kus). Deciduous shrubs or small trees known as Elder (which see), widely distributed in temperate and subtropical regions. Both the large flat heads of white flowers and the dense clusters of small berries are effective; the latter are a favorite bird food.

SAMPHIRE (sam'-fyr). Common name for *Crithmum maritimum,* a fleshy herb of the Parsley Family, 1 ft. high or less, with cut leaves and inconspicuous flowers in umbels. An Old-World seashore plant, it is occasionally grown in the border or in the herb garden for salad. It thrives best in dry sandy or gravelly soil, in an open sunny position, and is increased by division or by seed sown as soon as ripe.

SAMUELA (sam-eu-ee'-lah). A genus of S. W. tree-like plants of the Lily Family, growing to 18 ft., with basal clusters of sharp-pointed narrow leaves and dense clusters of white bell-like flowers. Closely related to and resembling the Yucca (which see), they are called Date-yucca because of the 3-in. fruits. However, they have a soft-pulped stem instead of a woody trunk. They are somewhat grown in Calif.

SANCHEZIA (san-kee'-zi-ah). S. American herbs or shrubs, one species of which is grown for ornamental purposes in the warm greenhouse and outdoors S. This is *S. nobilis,* a shrubby plant to 5 ft. with attractive leaves and flowers. It requires good soil, and young plants are more decorative than old ones, which soon get straggly. The leaves grow to a foot long, and the yellow flowers are borne in dense terminal panicles from the axils of bright red bracts. Var. *glaucophylla* has showier leaves, glaucous and striped white or yellow. Propagated by cuttings.

SAND. From the gardener's standpoint, sand consists of the mineral part of the soil—minute rock-fragments ranging from very fine (which still is coarser than clay or silt) to coarse (which is finer than the smallest grade of gravel). Chemically, it is almost pure quartz or silica and consequently plays little or no part in providing plants with food. Also, since its structure is very porous, it cannot hold moisture, but dries out and warms up quickly. These qualities make it, alone, impracticable as a garden soil; but they render it a valuable material to add to stiff, heavy clays to make them looser and more friable; or to loose, over-fibrous peaty soils to give them more body and substance. For many crops, what is known as a sandy loam cannot be surpassed, provided it is kept supplied with humus and the essential plant-food elements.

Such a soil is easy to cultivate, well drained, quick to dry off after rains so as to permit cultivation, ready for planting moderately early in the spring, free from stones, and not inclined to "puddle" and bake when dried out by the sun. If it becomes extreme in any of these respects, it can easily be improved by generous additions of stable manure, by turning under green manure crops, or by otherwise incorporating additional humus, which see.

Sands vary in character according to their origin. Those formed by the action of water consist of individual grains rounded like tiny boulders—as found on ocean or lake beaches and in river beds; those not subjected to water action have sharp grains, as found in builders' sand and gravel pits. The former kind (if not impregnated with sea salt) can be used to lighten and aërate heavy soils. The latter type is an excellent medium for the rooting of many kinds of cuttings; for some plants it should be mixed with peat moss for this purpose. It is also used for stratifying hard seeds over their "ripening" period.

Within recent years, sand has gained a new importance as a medium for growing both experimental and commercial crops of various greenhouse plants, such as carnations, sweet peas and others. This sand culture, however, requires that the plants be fed regularly and constantly with a weak solution of certain chemical substances so compounded as to supply exactly the diet demanded by that particular kind of plant. As the sand can be cleaned by flooding with water, or sterilized by means of heat or chemicals between crops without being taken out of the benches, it does away with much work required in removing and replacing soil every year or so. It is even suggested that with the perfection of feeding methods, such "sand culture" will become a simple and satisfactory method of growing many kinds of plants in the house. See also SOIL.

SAND CULTURE. This term may be used in a general way to refer to cultures in sand, fine gravel or cinders, but here it applies specifically to cultures of plants in sand, using nutrient solutions to supply the mineral elements required for plant growth. Sand is adapted for such use where free drainage is possible, as in the constant-drip and flush or "slop" techniques described under CHEMICAL GARDENING. In small installations, coarser grades of sand may be used with sub-irrigation, which see. In larger installations, it is not suitable for the subirrigation method because of slow drainage, but it can be used in a greenhouse bench with free drainage and the surface application of the nutrient solution.

The best type of sand is a quartz sand of the grade used for making concrete. It should be washed clean. This can be done by placing the sand in a pail or tub and forcing water up through it by delivering the water through a hose at the bottom of the receptacle so the flooding will carry out clay and silt particles. Washing is especially important if the sand is fine. If the sand is too coarse, it will require more nutrient solution to maintain the proper moisture relation.

If the only source of sand available is a limestone sand, it may be advisable to use cinders, for the lime sand contains much calcium which, in excess, will cause plant foliage to turn yellow. However, by using a more acid nutrient solution, or by running the nutrient solution daily through the limestone sand for two weeks before placing the plants in the medium, the sand grains can be given a coating of

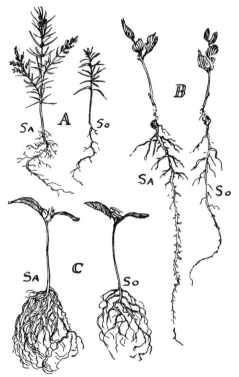

SAND CULTURE STIMULATES ROOT GROWTH
Comparative development of seedlings of (A) Oriental arborvitae, (B) sweet pea, and (C) cucumber when germinated in sand (left in each pair) and soil (right in each pair). (*From Bul. 380, Conn. Agricultural Experiment Station, Jan. 1936*)

phosphates and be made safe for growing plants.

Growing Seedlings in Sand

Seedlings can be raised by sand culture either to be transferred to cultures for chemical gardening or for use in the outdoor garden. By this method seedlings with very fine root systems can be produced; if handled properly they will transplant into soil readily and, given proper care, start to grow promptly. In addition, losses from damping-off are minimized, while another advantage is that if the seedlings are not too crowded, they can remain in the sand if supplied with nutrient solution in the proper concentration.

A good way to handle them is to construct a box not less than 4 in. deep on the inside with openings in the bottom so excess solution can drain out. These spaces between the bottom boards or small drainage holes can be covered with cheesecloth, burlap, or glass wool to prevent the sand from sifting through. Fill the box with clean sand and flush it well with water to settle the sand thoroughly. Then flush with nutrient solution diluted with five times as much water.

The seeds may be sown in drills or rows or broadcast; if in rows, make the furrows barely deep enough so that the seeds can be covered after being sown thinly. If the broadcast method is used, spread the seeds uniformly and not too thickly over the surface, and cover with about one-fourth inch of sand. In either case, firm or compact the sand, then apply the dilute nutrient solution until the sand is saturated. Cover the box with newspaper to reduce evaporation and place in the proper temperature for the kind of seed sown.

Since it would be fatal to the embryo of the seed if the surface should become dry, the sand must be kept moist. The dilute nutrient solutions should be applied as a fine spray, to prevent disturbing the surface; a rubber bulb syringe with a fine rose nozzle is excellent for this purpose.

As soon as the seeds have germinated and the shoots appeared above the surface, remove the newspaper covering. When the seedlings have grown to suitable size, they may be transplanted to a permanent location or to other vessels where they can be more widely spaced. If it is desired to leave them in the flat, thin them out to a proper spacing. They are now able to manufacture food in their leaves, and the nutrient solution should be applied in a stronger concentration—one part of nutrient solution to one part of water.

Should it be desired or necessary to remove the seedlings from the sand medium, flood it with nutrient solution and gently pull the plants out one by one, assisting the removal with some instrument thrust under the root. A label, spatula, or case knife will be suitable.

See also NUTRIENT SOLUTION; SEEDS AND SEED SOWING.

SAND-LILY. Common name for *Leucocrinum montanum,* a native, spring-blooming herb of the Lily Family, also known as Star-lily. It has a rootstock or rhizome, narrow grass-like leaves, and fragrant tubular white flowers, star-like in form, growing in clusters just above the surface of the soil. Sand-lilies may be planted in sandy soil in the rock garden or as an underplanting or border for beds of other bulbs. Native from Neb. to Calif., they may be collected in the wild or procured from dealers. The plants make a charming addition to a dry open portion of the wild garden.

SAND-MYRTLE. Common name for Leiophyllum, a genus of small evergreen shrubs with little pink or white flowers; useful in borders and rock gardens supplied with peaty soil.

SAND-VERBENA. Common name for the genus Abronia, low or trailing annual and perennial herbs with fragrant, variously colored, showy flowers. They prefer sunny locations.

SANDWORT. Common name for the genus Arenaria, dwarf mat-forming annuals and perennials useful in rock, wall and alpine gardens.

SANGUINARIA (san-gwi-nay'-ri-ah) *canadensis.* A perennial, woodland plant with white flowers in the spring. It is known as Bloodroot (which see) in eastern and central N. America.

SANGUISORBA (san-gwi-saur'-bah). A genus of herbs of the Rose Family, commonly called Burnet (which see). They have cut leaves and small inconspicuous flowers in heads or dense spikes and are sometimes grown in the border. One species (*S. minor*) is an herb-garden subject and some are pasture plants.

SANITATION. The removal of all materials capable of harboring diseases or insect pests is a most important, but one of the least practiced phases of gardening. The control of practically all garden enemies properly begins in the autumn when most other garden operations cease. In raking up leaves for the compost pile *do not include* those from horsechestnut trees covered with brown blotches, or the fallen rose leaves yellowed by the black spot fungus. . Burn all obviously diseased leaves; rake up and burn fallen mummied fruits under plum trees; remove all dried and spotted leaves from the iris bed. When the peony tops turn yellow in late fall cut the stalks *below the ground surface,* making a clean slanting cut as deep as possible without injuring the buds; then burn these tops, *never* using them for a mulch if you wish to be free from botrytis blight.

Most gardeners feel that cutting off dead stalks with the pruning shears a nice neat distance above the ground is sufficient for fall care. True, this is easier, and the garden looks all right; but it is wasted effort as far as getting rid of the plant enemies is concerned. The few inches left standing will harbor plenty of insects, insect eggs, and pupae; and all the fungus mycelium, spores and resting bodies necessary to turn the garden into a shambles in early spring. Four hollyhock stalks, pulled from one clump in March, yielded a slug, a millipede, a sowbug, numerous fly puparia and the ever present pustules of the rust fungus—all alive after a cold winter and ready to start work on the first warm spring day.

Be thorough, therefore, in your fall clean-up campaign. Pull and burn annuals that have ceased blooming and, especially, all weeds; cut perennial stalks back to the ground. If canker worms were bad in the spring, band the trees they attacked in September (see BANDING, TREE). During the fall and winter prune out fire-blight cankers, cut and burn the egg masses of tent caterpillars, the aphid galls on spruce, crooked tips infested by the European pine shoot moth and cedar galls.

Dormant spraying (see SPRAYING) is an important part of the sanitation program. And, after beginning so well, do not relax too much during the growing season. It is easy to carry a paper bag and scissors or pruning shears as you walk around to admire the garden. And if, as you do so, you pick off a blighted head here or a spotted leaf there; pull up this plant stricken with wilt, that one mottled with

mosaic; get the first delphinium bud deformed by mites, and so on, you will be surprised and gratified to see how such a program of inspection supplemented by routine spraying and dusting will keep your garden vigorous, healthy and beautiful with a minimum of extra effort.

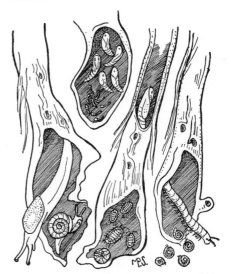

SANITATION ELIMINATES SUCH PESTS
Garden refuse is the harboring place of garden enemies. This shows old hollyhock stalks, left standing over winter, and some of the insects and other harmful creatures found alive in them in March.

SAN JOSÉ SCALE. An insect pest of many fruit and ornamental trees and shrubs, formerly considered exceedingly harmful and dangerous but now easily kept under control by systematic correctly planned spraying. See SCALE INSECTS.

SANSEVIERIA (san-se-vi-ee′-ri-ah). A genus of perennial herbs with stiff, very thick leaves, often mottled with white, and clustered flowers on slender stalks. Members of the Lily Family, they are popularly known as Snake-plants or Bowstring-hemp. In the N. they are grown as house or porch plants, requiring little sun and doing best in a rather heavy soil. They are grown as garden subjects in the S. Propagation is by division or by leaf-cuttings set in sand which send out shoots which root and develop into new plants. When grown indoors the leaves should be washed frequently with warm soapy water and then sponged off with clear water. The species most frequently seen are: *S. zeylanica,* to 2½ ft., from Ceylon, with hollowed leaves banded across with white; and *S. trifasciata* var. *laurenti,* from Africa, whose leaves are striped creamy-yellow, lengthwise.

Fusarium leaf spot appears as roundish, sunken, reddish-brown lesions with yellow borders. Destroy diseased leaves and use care in watering to prevent splashing spores about. Burgundy mixture (which see) has been recommended as a spray.

SANTOLINA (san-toh-ly'-nah) *chamaecyparissus.* A low evergreen shrubby plant, native to Europe and Asia, belonging to the Daisy Family. See LAVENDER-COTTON.

SANVITALIA (san-vi-tay'-li-ah). A genus of small American herbs of the Composite Family, with heads of flowers resembling Rudbeckias. They are easily grown as annuals in any warm rich soil, and if given winter protection often survive and bloom a second year. They are increased by seed. *S. procumbens,* to 6 in., is of branching habit and has a purple disk- and yellow ray-flowers. It is a pretty little hardy annual from Mexico, blooming through the late summer and fall.

SAPINDUS (sah-pin'-dus). A genus of tropical trees and shrubs grown for ornament and for the leathery fruits used in warm countries as soap substitutes. See SOAPBERRY.

SAPIUM (say'-pi-um) *sebiferum.* A tropical tree planted in warm parts of the U. S. for ornament and in equatorial countries for its fruits. Formerly called Stillingia.

SAPODILLA (sap-oh-dil'-ah). Common name for an American tropical evergreen tree (*Sapota achras,* formerly *Achras sapota*) which attains 50 ft. or more and bears abundant scurfy, brown fruits which when mellow-ripe contain yellowish, translucent, melting, sweet flesh. It is popularly cultivated in Mexico and the West Indies, naturalized in the southern tip of Florida, and often grown in southern gardens, especially those with fertile sandy loam soils. Trees are planted 30 ft. apart. Do not confuse with SAPOTE, below.

SAPONARIA (sap-oh-nay'-ri-ah). A genus of hardy annual and perennial Old-World herbs of the Pink Family, commonly known as Soapworts. They have white, pink or red flowers in clusters and are very easily cultivated in the border, some species in the rock garden. Increase is by seed or division.

S. officinalis (Bouncing Bet), a perennial often 3 ft. tall, widely naturalized along roads and railroad tracks in E. N. America, has profuse clusters of white or pinkish flowers to 1 in. across. *S. ocymoides,* a perennial to 9 in. tall, is a trailing, soft-hairy plant with pink flowers in flat-topped clusters, much used on walls and in the rock gardens; its var. *alba* has white flowers and var. *splendens,* larger flowers of an intense pink; *S. racemosa* (Cow-herb), an annual to 3 ft., also found as an "escape," has large rose-pink flowers in loose clusters. *S. lutea,* small, tufted, with clusters of yellow flowers with violet stamens, is a charming plant for the rock garden, while *S. caespitosa,* to 6 in., a tufted plant with rose flowers, can be tucked in the crevices of a dry stone retaining-wall.

SAPOTA (sah-poh'-tah) *achras.* A tropical American evergreen tree called Sapodilla (which see), grown in warm countries for its delicious brown fruit.

SAPOTE. One of the common names for *Achras zapota,* also called Marmalade-plum, an evergreen tropical tree of the Sapota Family having broadly oval leaves to 16 in. and white flowers to ½ in. across, followed by brownish fruit with red flesh and one hard seed. Native to Central and S. America, it cannot endure any frost. It is propagated by seed, which after the husk is removed is planted in heavy clay soil.

Owing to similarity in names this tree is likely to be confused with the Sapodilla (which see), a member of the same family whose botanical name was formerly *Achras sapota,* but was later changed to *Sapota achras.*

Black-sapote is *Diospyros ebenaster,* of the Ebony Family; a tree to 60 ft. with lustrous leaves to 8 in., small white flowers and olive-green fruit with dark brown edible pulp. It is a tropical fruit, but will withstand a few degrees of freezing.

White-sapote is *Casimiroa edulis,* a Mexican tree of the Rue Family growing to 50 ft. and having leathery divided leaves, greenish flowers and round yellow-green fruit with creamy-white edible flesh. A tropical fruit easily raised in warm climates in ordinary garden soil, it is propagated by seed and by shield-budding.

SAPROPHYTE. A plant without chlorophyll (the green coloring matter that gives most plants their characteristic color) and therefore lacking the power to manufacture its own food. It obtains nourishment from *dead* decaying organic matter and therein differs from a *parasite* (which see) which is nourished by a *living* host. But many fungi are both parasitic and saprophytic.

SARCOCOCCA (sahr-koh-kok'-ah). Attractive evergreen shrubs from Asia, belonging to the Box Family. They are not particular as to soil, and can stand the shade and drip of trees. They need a mild climate to grow at their best, but one or two species can survive N. winters in a sheltered position. The glossy green leaves are their chief attraction, the clusters of small whitish fragrant flowers, which open early in spring, being inconspicuous. Propagated by division or cuttings under glass. *S. hookeriana* grows to 6 ft. in a mild climate. It has narrow leaves to 3 in. long and blue-black fruits. Its var. *humilis* is smaller and said to be somewhat hardier. *S. ruscifolia* may also grow to 6 ft.; it has roundish leaves and red fruits.

SARRACENIA (sar-ah-see'-ni-ah). A genus of small insectivorous herbs known as Pitcher-plants because their basal leaves (often attractively mottled or splashed with various colors) are hollow, forming receptacles, sometimes with a wing along one side and a lid at the top. Insects trapped within them are drowned in the liquid held in the hollow base and gradually absorbed, thereby supplying the plant with nitrogenous food. The flowers are nodding, single, and range from yellow to purple.

Some species are hardy and can be grown in the bog garden; other tender kinds can be grown in the greenhouse in pots filled with sandy muck covered with sphagnum moss and kept standing in saucers of water in full sunlight. They are grown from seed and hybridize easily.

Principal Species

S. purpurea is a widespread native species, found in cold mountain bogs from the E. Coast to the Rocky Mts. Its leaves are often 10 in. long and its purple or greenish flowers 2 in. across.

drummondi, an attractive S. species, has trumpet-shaped pitchers to 4 ft., green veined with purple and equipped with an erect wavy-margined lid; the flowers are purple.

sledgei has erect lidded pitchers to 2½ ft., green with purple veins, and yellowish, fragrant flowers.

flava, with erect trumpet-shaped, crimson-throated pitchers to 3 ft., veined yellow-green to green or entirely crimson, has pungent-smelling yellow flowers to 4 in.

ruba, with erect pitchers to 20 in., veined with purple and with a bent-over lid, has crimson, violet-scented flowers.

minor has veined purple and blotched white and yellow pitchers to 2 ft., and pale yellow flowers.

psittacina, with prostrate leaves to 6 in., splotched and veined purple and white and a strongly bent lid, has purple to greenish-purple flowers to 2 in. across.

See also INSECTIVOROUS PLANTS.

SASA (sas'-ah). A genus of dwarf or medium-sized shrubs of the Grass Family; one of those popularly known as Bamboo. Distinguished from the other Bamboos by their small size, they have cylindrical stems and graceful leaves, often toothed or hairy. Some are hardy enough to be planted as far N. as Washington, D. C. For culture see BAMBOO.

S. japonica is an attractive shrub to 15 ft. with leaves 10 in. long, shining above and with a bloom beneath.

pygmaea to 2 ft. is much branched and has hairy leaves.

variegata to 3 ft. has toothed leaves striped with white.

auricoma to 4 ft. has purplish-green leaves striped green and yellow.

SASSAFRAS (sas'-ah-fras). Both the common and the generic name of three species of aromatic deciduous trees of the Laurel Family. They are handsome pyramidal trees with light green peculiarly lobed foliage which assumes brilliant hues in the autumn. The yellow flowers, borne in racemes, are followed by beautiful blue fruits on fleshy red stems. Trees should be planted in light soil in an open sunny position and may be increased by seed, sown immediately on ripening, or by root cuttings or suckers. It is very difficult to transplant other than very young trees on account of their long tap-roots.

This tree is ordinarily not seriously injured by insects, but the Japanese beetle (which see) is especially fond of it. In beetle regions spray with lead arsenate in late June.

S. variifolium, the American species, attains 60 ft. or more and is hardy in the N. Its leaves vary in shape from entire to 3-lobed and its fruit is highly ornamental. Much planted for the decorative effect of its form and foliage, it will stand severe trimming and can be used for a windbreak near salt water. *S. tzuma* is a Chinese species similar to the foregoing, but taller growing and not so hardy.

SATIN-FLOWER. A common name for Lunaria, a genus of herbs grown principally for their round flat, papery pods which are used in winter bouquets. Some catalogs list Godetia as Satin-flower.

SATIN-LEAF. Common name for *Chrysophyllum oliviforme,* a tropical tree somewhat grown for ornament in S. Fla. and other warm regions. Related to Star-apple, which see.

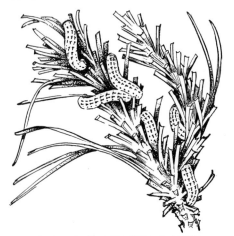

SAWFLIES ATTACKING PINE
Note how the needles have been almost completely devoured by the ravenous larvae.

SATIN POPPY. A common name for *Meconopsis wallichi,* a tall perennial with large, pale blue flowers.

SATUREJA (sat-eu-ree'-jah), or SATU-REIA. A genus of hardy, aromatic herbs and small evergreen shrubs of the Mint Family, natives chiefly of the Mediterranean region but in some cases escaped from culture and widely distributed in E. U. S. Known generally as Savory (which see), the genus includes Summer Savory (*S. hortensis*) and Winter Savory (*S. montana*), which are grown as pot herbs; also several species grown in the border for their attractive fragrant bloom. Because of their low growth, they are of special value in the rock garden, and also useful in the wild garden. They do well in any common soil and can be propagated by seeds, or by division in the spring.

SAUROMATUM (sau-roh-may'-tum). A genus of tropical herbs of the Arum Family having large flowers resembling the Jack-in-the-pulpit. One species, *S. guttatum,* has a long, pointed greenish spathe marked with dark purple spots and one long leaf, cut into segments. It is sometimes grown as an oddity in the greenhouse, but the large tubers of this curious dull-colored arum will survive in the open border if given winter protection. One form of this species is sometimes grown under the name of "red calla."

SAURURUS (sau-roo'-rus). A genus of wet-ground perennials with small fragrant white flowers in dense racemes or spikes. See LIZARDS TAIL.

SAUSAGE-TREE. Common name for *Kigelia pinnata,* a tropical African tree of the Bignonia Family, having leaves in threes and claret-colored bell-shaped flowers in drooping panicles, followed by rough, gourd-like fruits to 1½ ft. that hang on cord-like stems several feet long. It is occasionally grown in the S. States and Calif. or in the West Indies, as an oddity, and is sometimes referred to as the "fetish tree" because it is considered sacred by the natives in some parts of Africa.

SAUSSUREA (sau-seu'-ree-ah). A genus of temperate zone herbs of the Composite Family, having heads of blue or purple disk-flowers clustered on the stems. Occasionally planted in the garden, they are easily increased from seed or by division. *S. deltoides,* a perennial to 8 ft., has leaves that are white and downy beneath and rather showy heads of purple flowers 1½ in. across in leafy clusters.

SAVANNAH-FLOWER. Common name for *Echites tomentosa,* a tropical American twining vine with large red-centered yellow flowers, grown in S. Calif.

SAVIN. Common name for *Juniperus sabina,* a spreading evergreen species of Juniper, which see.

SAVORY, SUMMER. A hardy annual (*Satureja hortensis*), an important and useful culinary herb, whose aromatic leaves are used, either green or dried, for flavoring salads, sauces, stuffings, soups, and stews. As the seed is minute it should be sown indoors in seed pans, and the seedlings pricked off into flats and later transplanted outdoors when large enough. The plants should stand 15 in. asunder. They will thrive in any good garden soil in full sunlight. See HERBS.

SAVORY, WINTER. A perennial herb or sub-shrub (*Satureja montana*) grown and used like summer savory.

SAW FERN. A common name for the Deer Fern (*Lomaria spicant*), native only to the N. W. but hardy elsewhere in gravelly soil and a moist mild climate. It has stiff, comb-like fronds, excellent for cutting.

SAWFLIES. Insects belonging to the same order as the bees and wasps and so named because of the sawlike egg-laying apparatus of the female, who uses it to cut pockets in the plant tissue in which the eggs are placed. Actual injury (usually a skeletonizing of the leaves) is done only by the larvae, which are called false caterpillars or slugs, since they are usually covered with a slimy coating. Many kinds of shade trees and shrubs may be attacked by the sawfly larvae, which will be noted coiled over the edges of the leaves. Important members of this group are the cherry and pear slug, the three rose slugs and the imported currant sawfly. Sawflies on conifers are becoming increasingly destructive. Mugho and Austrian pines may have lost nearly all their needles and be near death before the well-camouflaged larvae are discovered. Other sawflies attack white pine and spruce. For control suggestions see discussions under the host plants.

SAW- or **SCRUB-PALMETTO.** Common name for *Serenoa repens,* a member of the Palm Family, having a trailing, branching stem, fan-like leaves to 2½ ft. across, cut into 20 or more parts, and fragrant flowers followed by an almost round black fruit. This plant covers vast areas of sandy soil from S. C. throughout Fla. and in La., where it has to be cleared before the land can be cultivated. The cut tops, or "crowns," are sent N. for Christmas decorations, remaining fresh and green for a long period. Plants are occasionally grown in the cool conservatory in the N. and small specimens make good slow-growing pot plants.

SAXIFRAGACEAE (sak-si-frah-gay'-see-ee). The Saxifrage Family, a mostly temperate and sub-arctic zone plant group of widely varied characters supplying many ornamental herbs and sub-shrubs for borders, rockeries and the greenhouse; also the currant and goosebery grown for their edible fuits. It is closely allied to the Rose Family. Genera frequently cultivated include: Saxifraga, Bergenia, Astilbe, Heuchera, Hydrangea, Schizophragma, Deutzia, Philadelphus (mockorange), Carpenteria, Escallonia, Itea, Ribes.

SAXIFRAGE or ROCKFOIL. Common names for Saxifraga (sak-sif'-rah-gah) meaning "rock-splitter," a genus of mostly hardy perennial (and very rarely annual) plants, native to the N. and S. temperate and arctic zones, with the exception of S. America, Africa and Australia. The flowers are white or yellow, rarely purple or rose; the leaves are variable but usually at the base of the plant, frequently forming rosettes. (See illustration, Plate 45.) Nearly all are beautiful and highly interesting subjects very desirable in the rock garden or on walls, being valued as highly for the decorative appearance of the compact foliage masses as for the flowers. The taller growing kinds, if not wanted in the rock garden, may be grown to good effect in sunny positions in the mixed border.

Saxifrages used in connection with sempervivums and sedums really make rock gardens possible almost anywhere, their odd and interesting forms contrasting with other subjects and providing constant attraction for young and old gardeners.

CULTURAL NOTES

Where seed is obtainable, plants may easily be started in late summer and protected over winter to be set in their permanent places in early spring. Old established plants may readily be increased from the offsets or by division of the tufts in early spring. Once established, saxifrages need little winter protection. Many of the rosettes with their bright green leathery leaves turn to even brighter colors at the approach of cold weather. Later in the season, when the soil is frozen, they may receive a light covering of leaves or other litter, its purpose being mainly to prevent alternate freezing and thawing of the soil.

Food may be applied two or three times during the growing season in the form of a complete fertilizer scattered thinly around the plants *but not touching any part;* this should be lightly cultivated into the soil where the rains will carry it to the roots. When well grown among the rocks and when weeds are kept out, the plants seem markedly free of disease. If chewing or sucking insects from neighboring plants attack them, spray with a combined insecticide and fungicide preparation.

SPECIES

S. aizoon. Forms rosettes of silvery leaves 5 to 9 in. high; small white flowers speckled with purple or crimson on stems attaining 20 in. Varieties have variously colored leaves and flowers.

aquatica. Fleshy leaves to 2 ft. White flowers ¾ in. across, July and August.

burseriana. Densely tufted plant with beautiful milk-white, usually solitary flowers 1 in. across, March to June.

camposi, leaves variable to 6 in.; glossy leaves; flowers white in May.

decipiens (Crimson-moss). Dwarf, mossy plant to 1 ft.; white flowers in May and June; foliage turns to beautiful crimson as winter approaches; numerous varieties.

florulenta. A striking alpine species, but hard to grow. Leaf rosettes 5 to 7 in. in diameter, flowers pale lilac but rarely produced.

geranioides. A 6-in. alpine with numerous small white flowers in July.

granulata (Meadow Saxifrage). To 20 in.; stems erect, bulbous at base, branched and bearing many white, drooping flowers 1 in. across in May. Many bulblets form in leaf axils. There is also a double-flowered form.

longifolia. To 2 ft. tall; leaves 3 in. long, thick and heavy, forming handsome rosettes; flowers white spotted with red, July.

macnabiana. A hybrid whose green rosettes turn to rich autumn shades; 1 ft. high; flowers white, spotted crimson in early spring.

pygmaea. One of the smallest alpines, from 1 to 2 in. with very small yellowish flowers, May and June.

retusa. Another alpine, about 2 in., with purple flowers, May and June.

sarmentosa (Strawberry - geranium). Popular for vase and basket culture. To 9 in. tall, flowers white, spotted yellow and scarlet, in June and July. Spreads by strawberry-like runners. Has several common names, including Mother-of-Thousands, Aarons Beard, Old Mans Beard, etc.

umbrosa (London Pride). A low growing (to 1 ft.) spreading sort, with white flowers sometimes sprinkled with red; blooms freely, June and July.

virginiensis. A native mountain form found from N. B. to Ga. and Tenn. About 1 ft. high with white flowers, April to June.

Some popular species have been transferred to other genera as, for example: *S. cordifolia* and *S. crassifolia* which are now listed as Bergenia (which see) and *S. peltata* (the Umbrella-plant) now called

Peltiphyllum peltatum. A group of low-growing varieties listed as Guilford's seedlings have unusual reddish foliage.

SCAB. Definite, more or less circular, usually slightly raised and roughened ulcer-like lesions on fruits, tubers, leaves or stems of plants, resulting from the overgrowth of epidermal and cortical tissues. The name is also used for the disease as well as for the symptom, as apple scab and potato scab. For control measures, see under the various host plants affected.

SCABIOSA (skay-bi-oh'-sah). A genus of annual or perennial herbs of the Teasel Family with showy flowers in heads. They are commonly known as Mourning-bride or Pincushion-flower, the first name referring to the very dark colors of some of the species, and the second to the fact that the knobbed stamens protrude beyond the florets. Scabiosas are easily grown in an open sunny position from seed started indoors or planted in the open ground in May. Seedlings of the annual sorts (forms of *S. atropurpurea*) should be set 6 to 8 in. apart. Pinched back while small they will make bushy 12 ft. plants. If seed-heads are not allowed to form, flowers will be produced all summer. As cut flowers Scabiosas last well, and their odd color range makes them effective in bouquets.

PRINCIPAL SPECIES

S. atropurpurea has cut leaves and dark, rose or white flowers. Horticultural varieties show interesting differences in height and form.

caucasica is a perennial growing to 2 ft. with pale blue flowers in rather flat heads, surrounded by a grayish involucre. Varieties, handsomer than the type, include: *goldingensis* with large deep lavender blossoms; *magnifica,* bluish-lavender, and *alba,* white.

japonica is a very attractive plant, perennial, growing to 2 ft., with finely cut foliage and large heads of dark purple-blue flowers.

SCABROUS. Rough or gritty to the touch because of short, stiff hairs or points, as the surface of certain leaves, those of Echium, for example.

SCALD. A blanching of the epidermis and adjacent tissues of a plant part making them look as if injured by scalding water. The injury is frequently caused by too much exposure to the sun. See DISEASES, PLANT.

SCALE. A much reduced leaf, generally without chlorophyll (green coloring matter) and usually modified to perform a protective function. Often, however, a scale may be vestigial, that is, a survivor of an ancestral character and without function on the plant.

A pine cone is composed of scales which bear and protect the bodies which later produce seed; the scales of buds are old-growth leaves investing the embryo shoot and leaves with a protective covering capable of many modifications to shield them against severe weather, birds and insects. See BUD; LEAF.

SCALE INSECTS. These are sucking insects, all belonging to the order Homoptera, and mostly quite small, but varying considerably in form and appearance. Some look like mere pinhead dots of gray or brown, others resemble tiny oyster shells ⅛ in. or less long, still others are disguised in waxy or woolly coverings suggesting bits of cotton or fluff rather than living creatures. While the young (and, in some cases, certain of the adults) can move about, they spend most of their lives affixed to the leaves, stems, or branches of their hosts. Scales attack many kinds of plants both indoors and out, from small pot plants to the largest of orchard and shade trees, and constitute an important group of economically destructive pests.

In general they are controlled out-of-doors by the use of an oil spray (a miscible oil or an oil emulsion), or by spraying with lime-sulphur at 1 to 7 or 1 to 8 dilution before growth starts in the spring. Sometimes, when the young appear in late spring, they can be best controlled with a nicotine spray. Fumigation is done in greenhouses and under tents in citrus orchards.

Scales are difficult to control on house plants (which see). Young ones may be killed with weekly applications of a contact insecticide used about three times as strong as recommended for aphids. Heavy leaved plants such as palms and rubber-plants may be brushed with a strong contact spray and soap suds, and afterwards syringed with clear water. Soft scales and mealy bugs may be picked off succulent plants, cacti, etc., with a toothpick or small toothbrush, but this will not prevent the development of more thereafter. Natural enemies are helpful control measures; see INSECTS, BENEFICIAL.

Some of the common scale insects are described below. Others, together with their control measures, are described under GREENHOUSE PESTS; CITRUS FRUITS; and under various host plants. See also FUMIGATION; SPRAYING.

Scale insects may be divided into two groups: (1) the armored scales, which have distinct, hard, separable shells or scales over their delicate bodies, and (2) the tortoise or soft scales, in which the hard shell is not separable from the body. Armored scales usually reproduce by means of eggs, which are protected under the mother's shell, but in some cases the young are born alive. In either case the young crawl about actively for a time, then settle down in a favorable location, insert their thread-like mouth parts through the epidermis of the leaf or bark and start sucking the sap. After a short time they molt, the cast skin being incorporated into the scale which forms on the insect's body, being composed of fine threads of wax exuded from the body wall. The female

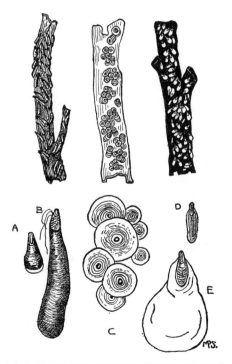

SCALES WHICH INJURE MANY PLANTS
Shown in reduced size above and enlarged below. Left, oyster-shell scale, (A) male and (B) female. Center, San José scale; (C) the individuals enlarged. Right, scurfy scale; (D) male and (E) female.

scales molt twice but always remain under their shells. The male scales are smaller, more elongated and after several molts become two-winged yellowish insects with a long appendage projecting from the tip of the abdomen. They move about and mate with the female scales.

The life history of the tortoise scales is the same, but the protective shell is made of the hard (chitinous) body wall instead of wax and cast skins. The body is generally smooth and brown, black or mottled. Reproduction is either by eggs or living young.

Some Common Scale Insects

Black Scale. Probably the most destructive citrus pest of California. But the principal damage is caused not by the feeding of the insect but by the sooty mold fungus which grows on the honeydew secreted by the scale. See under CITRUS; also SOOTY MOLDS.

Cottony Cushion Scale. Appears as large, white, cottony fluted masses on citrus twigs and as smaller, oval, yellowish brown scales on leaves. Introduced into California in 1868, it threatened the entire citrus industry until its natural enemy, the Australian ladybug, was introduced. See INSECTS, BENEFICIAL.

Cottony Maple Scale. A very destructive scale on soft maple and other trees. Cottony-appearing masses appear on the undersides of twigs and branches in late spring, the foliage often turns a sickly yellow, and branches may die. Though distributed throughout the U. S., it is most destructive in the northern part. Over winter the insect is a small brown flattened scale that puts out large quantities of wax as the eggs are laid in the spring. Spray with a dormant oil just before leaves open.

Juniper Scale. A very small, circular, snowy-white scale often abundant or juniper and occasionally on arbor-vitae. Give a dormant application of a miscible oil, or use a summer oil with nicotine in June.

Pine Leaf Scale. This occurs on pine, spruce, fir and hemlock throughout northern U. S., the elongated whitish scales being attached to the needles which become yellow. The most effective control measure is to spray with a dilute oil emulsion when the eggs are hatching in midspring. Use an oil especially recommended for use on evergreens, as some kinds, though effective scaleicides, may injure plants.

Oyster-shell Scale. Small, brownish-gray, curved scales, about ⅛ in. long, resembling a minute oyster shell; they may cover the bark of many trees and shrubs. Occurring generally throughout the U. S., they are very common on the balm-of-gilead (*Populus candicans*) and lilacs (with the exception of the white lilac), often occur on roses and may be found in abundance on old peony stems.

Each female shell shelters over winter 50 to 60 elliptical white eggs which hatch after shrubs come into full foliage. After crawling about for a few hours, the young start sucking sap, molting and secreting the wax which forms the brown protective scale. About midsummer the two-winged adult males develop, mate and die. After the female lays her eggs she dies, leaving them protected so that spraying with oils during the dormant season will only kill 80 or 90 per cent of them. A very thorough application of a summer miscible oil when the young are hatching is more effective. Spraying with 1 to 7 lime-sulphur before the leaves come out for three or four years in succession will keep down this scale.

San José Scale. Formerly considered a very serious orchard pest, this is now generally kept well under control. The necessary spraying has also helped grow healthier, cleaner orchards and produced finer fruit. Introduced from China, the scale was first noticed in this country near San José, Calif., about 1880, but gradually spread over the country before effective control measures were developed.

This scale is the size and shape of a small pinhead with a nipple rising from a slight central depression. It is black or brown, covered with a grayish bloom; its young, produced alive, are lemon yellow. Its sap-sucking action interferes with the growth and vigor of the tree, and sometimes causes death. Also the spotting of infected fruit greatly reduces its market value. Dormant applications of lime-sulphur, of miscible oil or of an oil emulsion will readily control this scale.

Scurfy Scale. This grayish-white scale about ⅛ in. long is rounded at one end and tapers to a sharp point at the other. Various species attack apple and other fruit trees and are often serious on small elms, willows and dogwoods. Reddish-purple eggs, just discernible with the naked eye, may be found in the winter under the scales; they hatch late in the spring after the trees come into full leaf. Dormant spraying is satisfactory.

TERRAPIN SCALE. This pest attacks all the common fruits and many shade trees and shrubs in E. and S. States. The shiny, convex, brownish females that adhere to the bark over winter give birth to living young in late spring. Control with dormant applications of a miscible oil or oil emulsion. Lime-sulphur is not satisfactory.

SCALLION. A name popularly used in U. S. for young or "bunch" onions, which are eaten raw, whether grown from sets or from seeds sown thickly and not thinned until of edible size. Sometimes it is applied to young or small leeks. It is a corruption of the botanical name of the shallot (*Allium ascalonicum*), another member of the onion group little known here.

SCAPE. A stalk arising directly from the crown of the root, and bearing one or more flowers but no foliage leaves, as in the shinleaf (Pyrola) and bloodroot (Sanguinaria).

SCARBOROUGH-LILY. One of the common names for *Vallota speciosa,* a S. African bulbous plant of the Amaryllis Family, having strap-shaped leaves to 2 ft. long and scarlet lily-like flowers to 2½ in. across in rounded clusters. Var. *alba* has white flowers.

The Scarborough-lily is grown in the N. in the greenhouse or as a window plant; it blooms in summer and should be rested in the winter, but not entirely dried out, even during its resting period. The bulbs are planted in pots in a mixture of a well-rotted manure, sand, fibrous peat and loam as much below the surface of the soil as their diameter. Repot only after they have flowered or when a shift is absolutely necessary, and in doing this do not disturb or break the roots. It is much better for the bulbs to be crowded than to have too much room, and they should always have full sunshine even during the resting period. Water with liquid manure after the buds have started. Scarborough-lilies are grown in the open in the S. and in Calif., where they bloom several times a year.

SCARLET BUGLER. Common name for *Pentstemon centranthifolius,* a Calif., and Ariz. perennial with scarlet flowers.

SCARLET-BUSH. Common name for *Hamelia erecta,* a small tree with orange or scarlet flowers and purple or dark red fruits.

SCARLET LIGHTNING. A common name for *Lychnis chalcedonica,* a scarlet-flowered perennial useful for planting in borders. Also called Maltese, or Jerusalem Cross.

SCARLET PLUME. Common name for Euphorbia fulgens, a greenhouse shrub with scarlet petal-like flower parts.

SCARLET RUNNER. Common name for *Phaseolus coccineus,* a perennial twining bean grown as an annual in cold countries for its brilliant flowers and large edible seeds.

SCARLET SAGE. Common name for *Salvia splendens,* a small, tender shrub grown in N. gardens as an annual for its brilliant flowers.

SCHINUS (sky'-nus). Several species of semi-tropical (southwestern and S. American) trees, two of which are common outdoors in California and sometimes grown in greenhouses N. mainly for their ornamental fruits. See PEPPER-TREE.

SCHISANDRA (sky-san'-drah) or SCHIZANDRA. A small genus of deciduous twining shrubs of Asia and N. America, belonging to the Magnolia Family. Propagated by seeds, greenwood and root cuttings, layers and suckers.

S. chinensis, the principal species, is hardy N. and useful for draping trees and fences. Thriving in a rather moist sandy loam and partial shade, it grows to 20 ft., and has bright medium-sized leaves, clusters of small fragrant pink flowers, and small bright red berries. The flowers being dioecious, plants of both sexes must be planted together to insure fruit. *S. coccinea,* the only species native in N. America, can only be grown S. It has purplish-crimson flowers and scarlet berries.

SCHIZAEA (sky-zee'-ah). A genus of ferns in which the fertile fronds are thread-like and topped by a tiny cluster of branching contracted pinnae, and the sterile fronds are grasslike. The only American species, restricted to the N. J. pine barrens, is *Schizaea pusilla,* the Curly-grass. Needing acid soil, this is of doubtful use in the garden, for it is only 2 in. tall—too small to be seen readily among the other bog plants with which it grows.

SCHIZANTHUS (sky-zan'-thus). A genus of showy annual or biennial plants of the Nightshade Family, having finely-cut foliage and white, lilac, bluish, or pink flowers. The daintily graceful blossoms give them the names, Butterfly-flower and

Poor-mans-orchid. Plants are grown out-doors in the summer or as large specimens in pots in the greenhouse for winter and early spring bloom. For summer bloom in the garden seed can be started under glass in March, or planted outdoors in May when the soil is warm. When transplant-ing pinch out the tops of the young plants to make them bushy. Spray with water when the weather is hot, for they do better in a cool summer climate than where the heat is intense. For greenhouse culture sow seeds in pots in September in light rich soil, shifting the seedlings as they grow and eventually to 12 in. pots, again pinching out the tops and staking. These plants will bloom from February to May.

SPECIES

S. pinnatus, to 4 ft., varies greatly in color and markings; the lower lip is usu-ally lilac or violet.

grahami, to 5 ft., has rose or violet flowers.

wisetonensis, a hybrid between *S. pin-natus* and *S. grahami,* shows many inter-esting variations in form and color.

retusus, a dwarfer form, has more orange on the notched upper lip, and a number of beautiful color variations.

SCHIZOBASOPSIS (skiz-oh-bah-sop'-sis) *volubilis.* A member of the Lily Fam-ily from S. Africa, grown as a green-house curiosity in America, and known (by utilizing its former generic name) as Twining Bowiea. From its large green bulb above the ground springs a slender, leafless, climbing stem which twines around the support provided. The flowers are small, and greenish-white. The bulbs require a brief resting period in summer. Propagation is by seeds, or division of the bulbs.

SCHIZOCENTRON (skiz-oh-sen'-tron) *elegans.* A Mexican creeping vine, rooting at the joints, which forms thick carpets on the ground. It is a charming plant with deep blue flowers, 1 in. broad, worthy of being more widely cultivated in mild sections as well as under glass or in porch baskets and window boxes. It can be grown in shade or sun in any light, warm soil and is easily increased from seed or cuttings.

SCHIZOPETALON (skiz-oh-pet'-ah-lon) *walkeri.* A little South American annual of the Mustard Family, having purple or white flowers with fringed petals

and growing to about 1 ft. It is fre-quently grown in the border or in frames for its fragrant white flowers borne in erect racemes. Seeds may be sown in the open in May, and the plants will bloom throughout the summer; or plants from later sowings may be carried in cold frames over winter for early spring bloom.

SCHIZOPHRAGMA (skiz-oh-frag'-mah). Climbing-hydrangea. Tall climb-ing deciduous shrubs of E. Asia, belong-ing to the Saxifrage Family. They climb by means of aërial rootlets, and are slow in getting established; but they are well worth waiting for if wanted to cover a wall or tree trunk. Propagation is by seeds, greenwood cuttings under glass, and layers.

The best known is *S. hydrangeoides* which is often confused with *Hydrangea petiolaris.* It is, however, easily distin-guished when in flower because the sterile marginal flowers consist of only one sepal an inch or more long, instead of four as in the Hydrangea. It also flowers later in the summer and the leaves are thicker and more coarsely toothed. This species, also called Japanese Hydrangea-vine, grows to 30 ft. and bears its loose white flower clusters in July.

S. integrifolium is not nearly so tall, but bears larger flower clusters and larger sterile flowers. It is not hardy N.

SCHIZOSTYLIS (ski-zos'-ti-lis) *coc-cinea.* A S. African fleshy-rooted herb with red flowers commonly known as Crim-son Flag (which see) and as Kafir-lily.

SCHLUMBERGERA (shlum-ber-gee'-rah) *gaertneri.* This plant, known as the Easter Cactus, is one of the old-time favorites. It grows best when grafted, making large and beautiful specimens, but it also grows well on its own roots, re-quiring a mixture of peat, loam and sand and standing the addition of some fertilizer. It can easily be propagated from cuttings.

SCHOMBURGKIA (shom-bur'-ki-ah). There are many hybrids. See also CACTUS. A genus of epiphytic, tropical American orchids bearing many-flowered racemes of brownish blossoms from 1 to 4 in. across. A few species are quite easily grown in the same manner as Cattleya (which see), others are of little horticultural value. One of the loveliest is *S. tibicinis* from Hon-duras, with long erect racemes of hand-some, purplish-brown flowers, the lips with yellow centers and veined with dark brown.

SCHRANKIA (shran'-ki-ah). A genus of perennial prickly herbs or shrubs of the Pea Family, with small divided leaves that droop when touched like those of the "sensitive plant," and small, pink or purple flowers in dense clusters. However, they are of little horticultural value, because of the abundant sharp spines or prickles borne by the prostrate stems and the seed pods. One species, *S. roemeriana,* native to southern Texas, is sometimes grown in the S. States.

SCIADOPITYS (sy-ah-dop'-i-tis) *verticillata.* A slow-growing ornamental Japanese evergreen tree of unusual appearance. See UMBRELLA-PINE, and illustration under PINE.

SCILLA (sil'-ah). A genus of small bulbous plants of the Lily Family, commonly known as Squill, Wild-hyacinth, or Blue-bell. The flowers of some of the species provide perhaps the most beautiful blue in the garden. The hardy types are of the simplest culture, increasing rapidly by offsets and self-sown seeds. Blooming early in the spring, they are lovely in the border or rock garden, or naturalized in the grass where they should be fed occasionally with top dressings of well-rotted manure. (See illustration of a novelty species, Plate 45.)

PRINCIPAL SPECIES

sibirica (Siberian Squill) has 1 to 3 small, drooping, intensely blue flowers on a rather short stalk rising above the narrow leaves which are 4 to 6 in. long. Blooming very early, it should be given a sheltered position.

nonscripta (Common Blue Squill, English-bluebell) grows to 1 ft. with leaves 18 in. long and racemes of 6 to 15 drooping blue, white, or rose flowers. The blue form is effective planted in drifts among the mid-season tulips. The white var. *alba,* a little more delicate in growth, is charming in groups in the rock garden but the pink form of this species is a rather muddy, unsatisfactory shade of lavender-rose.

hispanica has blue to rose-purple bell-shaped flowers on stems 20 in. high. They are larger than those of the English-bluebell, but bear larger flowers.

autumnale (Autumn Squill, Starry-hyacinth) growing to only 6 in., has wheel-shaped rose-colored blossoms appearing in autumn.

peruviana, a greenhouse species from S. Europe, despite its name. It has long broad leaves and a many-flowered cluster of blue blossoms. It is often planted in the border in mild climates.

SCINDAPSUS (sin-dap'-sus). Climbing perennials of the tropics, belonging to the Arum Family and grown in greenhouses as Pothos or Ivy-arum, which see.

SCION. An alternative way to spell cion, which is the piece of an improved variety of plant (bud or cutting) that is inserted into the rooted "stock" in the process of grafting, which see.

SCIRPUS (sur'-pus). A genus of large, coarse, grass-like perennials called Bulrush (which see) and sometimes planted in bog gardens as a background. See also AQUATIC PLANTS.

SCLEROTINIA (skle-roh-tin'-i-ah) ROT. A stem rot and wilt of various garden vegetables and ornamental plants caused by a fungus. It is common on lettuce (where it is known as lettuce-drop), carrots, beans, celery, cucurbits, crucifers and tomatoes, and it occurs on aquilegia, calendula, peony, delphinium, sunflower and other perennials and annuals. The symptoms are chiefly a soft rot at the base of the plant, involving also the lower leaves, followed by a wilting of the entire plant. In moist weather the crown of the plant may be covered by a thick weft of white mycelium and black resting bodies, called *sclerotia,* in the rotting tissues. The fungus may be distinguished from that causing crown rot (which see) by the black color of the sclerotia, the size (up to ½ in.), and the more luxuriant and prominent mycelium. The control measures for the two diseases are the same—removal of diseased individuals and drenching of the soil and surrounding plants with corrosive sublimate in a 1 to 1000 solution.

SCLEROTIUM (skle-roh'-shi-um). A dense compact mass of fungus threads (*hyphae*) combined with food materials in the form of oil and other compounds. The name comes from a Greek word meaning hard, as sclerotia are generally more or less rounded, elongated, cylindrical, globular or ellipsoidal masses with usually a hard outer covering. They vary in size from a pinhead to some unusual forms as big as a cantaloupe, and may be reddish-brown, brown, or black in color. They are resting bodies which serve to carry the fungus over periods unfavorable for its growth. Loose in the soil or in bits of plant debris they live through the winter and are ready to initiate infection in the spring. Plant diseases common in the garden which depend chiefly on sclerotia for overwintering are crown rot, sclerotinia rot, rhizoctonia rot and botrytis blight, all of which see. See also FUNGUS.

SCOKE. A common name for the showy, strong-smelling poisonous herb, *Phytolacca americana,* also known as POKE.

SCOLYMUS (skol'-i-mus). A hardy, biennial herb (*Scolymus hispanicus*), known also as Spanish-oyster-plant or Golden Thistle, and grown like parsnip (which see) for its long edible roots. These are larger than those of salsify but are used in the same ways as a fall, winter and spring vegetable.

SCOLYTUS (skol'-i-tus). A genus of bark beetles two species of which carry the fungus of the Dutch Elm disease, which see.

SCORCH. The sudden death and browning of large, indefinite areas in leaves and fruits; a symptom of disease caused by drought, excessive heat, toxic action of fungicides or insecticides, or, sometimes, by bacteria or fungi. See DISEASES, PLANT.

SCORPION-SENNA. Common name for a half-hardy shrub, *Coronilla emerus,* which blooms abundantly from May to July with large pea-like flowers of yellow tipped with red.

SCORZONERA (skaur-zoh-nee'-rah). A hardy perennial herb (*Scorzonera hispanica*) raised as an annual vegetable for its long, slender roots, known also as Black or Spanish-salsify. The young leaves are also sometimes used as a salad. Grown like parsnip or ordinary salsify (which see) it may be used in the fall or left in the ground until spring, then, before growth starts, dug and stored in a cold place.

SCOTCH THISTLE. Common name for a tall, prickly biennial herb *Onopordon* (or *Onopordum*) *acanthium.*

SCOURING-RUSH. Common name for some species of Equisetum, a genus of practically leafless plants with hollow, jointed stems, found in waste moist ground; also known as Horsetail, which see.

SCREE. A geological term meaning the broken, rocky or pebbly surface of a high mountain slope, spreading downward in a fan-shaped manner, and formed by the accumulation of fragments weathered

from outcropping rocks or cliffs above. Usually water from melting snows is continually seeping slowly just beneath the surface of the loosely piled material, supplying abundant moisture for many lovely alpine plants that grow in such places. With the increased interest in rock gardening and alpine plants the term has come into general horticultural use and now "scree garden" is often used as a synonym for moraine garden, which see.

SCREENING. In gardening this term has several applications.

Soil for filling pots, flats, greenhouse benches or hotbeds may be screened or sifted to get rid of stones and débris and to make uniform mixtures. Sand and gravel may be similarly treated in making concrete or in connection with various construction jobs.

In the sense of shading, screening is done to reduce the heating and drying effects of the sun on the soil in which seed has been sown, where young plants are set or where especially susceptible plants are being grown. It is, for instance, used to modify the growth or especially the blooming of plants, as in growing tobacco beneath canvas "sheds" and in protecting dahlias for the production of exhibition blooms.

As such sheds or tents also tend to check radiation of heat from the ground they serve as protectors of tender crops during cold snaps in late spring and early fall. Thus dahlias which are easily killed by temperatures only a degree or two below the freezing point may be saved from damage and often maintained in thrifty condition for several weeks after near-by plants not so protected are dead.

Such protection also prevents the attacks of insects which may both injure the plants themselves and also inoculate them with even more destructive diseases. A striking instance of this is the exclusion of the tiny leaf hopper which carries the organism causing the "yellows" disease of asters that at times has made the growing of these plants difficult or impossible in home gardens and unprofitable commercially. See ASTER.

Screening of individual hills of cucumbers, melons, squashes and pumpkins is done to exclude the two worst enemies of these plants—spotted and striped cucumber beetles—which not only destroy young plants but also carry infection from diseased to healthy plants and thus often ruin the whole crop. When such protectors—at least 12 in. in diameter—keep these insects away until the plants need additional space, they so delay infection as to give the plants a chance to mature their fruits before death overtakes them or may even permit the plants to become so large and sturdy as to be highly resistant.

SCREENS. Three purposes are served by screen-plantings in the garden. (1) Privacy is afforded by boundary or other divisional screens: (2) the general landscape, or particular vistas are perfected by groups of plants blocking out undesirable objects or views that cannot be removed or controlled by the gardener; (3) protection from winter wind and rigors or prevailing storms at any season is achieved by heavy planting of windbreak material.

By the simple law of optics involving the angle of vision, the size of a screen needed to hide an objectionable view or object diminishes as the screen comes nearer the observer. Hence the closer a screen planting can be placed to the area it is desired to serve by blocking out an eyesore, the less space it will have to occupy. Yet it is never good composition to screen anything with merely a straight, flat line of trees or shrubs wholly lacking in group interest. All forms of screen are most effective when, in addition to performing their function as a screen, they offer the charm and interest of a group of trees or shrubs (or both) that appear to "happen," to occupy naturally their particular position. For they then arouse no suspicion of something beyond them which they have been planted to hide.

For all-year effectiveness a combination of deciduous and evergreen material is desirable in every screen planting.

See also PROTECTION; WINDBREAK.

SCREW-PINE. Common name for the genus Pandanus, ornamental tropical shrubs and trees with prickly-margined, sword-like leaves closely set in a spiral arrangement on the main stem. Grown mostly in greenhouse and dwellings where they thrive under conditions suitable for palms; but they are considerably "tougher."

SCROPHULARIA (skrof-eu-lay'-ri-ah). A genus of strong-smelling perennial herbs grown mainly for medical purposes but sometimes in borders. See FIGWORT.

SCROPHULARIACEAE (skrof-eu-lay-ri-ay'-see-ee). Botanical name (often contracted by gardeners to "Scrophs") of the Figwort Family, given by Linnaeus because of the supposed ability of its members to cure scrofula. Found in all climates, the plants—mostly temperate herbs and rarely shrubs or trees—include many with medicinal value, chiefly Digitalis (foxglove). Many other genera are cultivated, among them Calceolaria, Pentstemon, Euphrasia, Verbascum and Collinsia.

SCULPTURE FOR THE GARDEN. In considering this very realistic form of art expression in its garden relation, it must be remembered that fundamentally, in gardens, fantasy prevails, and it should prevail throughout every medium employed to develop the garden's beauty. In other words, the garden is not the place for literal renderings in any terms. This, interpreted in the terms of image-making (which is what sculpture is), means that the garden is *not* the place for commonplace statues of commonplace, everyday folk. Rather it is the haunt of those unreal creatures—or are they unreal only to dull eyes and perceptions?—of legend and myth and old song and tales: fauns, satyrs, the great god Pan, nymphs, elves, gnomes—all kinds of fairy beings who have naught to do with houses and humans and their stupidities.

The best garden sculpture has always demonstrated this principle and always will. A definite rule that will guide one in judging and selecting sculpture for the garden may therefore be set forth as follows: Garden sculpture must be both timeless and impersonal, regardless of whether its proportions are heroic or exquisitely lilliputian. Supplementing this may be added the caution that, if human forms are used to carry out a concept, everything demands that they shall be unclad, undraped forms—that is, the human being minus artificialities and conventional observances. Animals of all kinds are, of course, suitable subjects, providing such trappings as men have imposed on them—harness, reins, and so on—are eliminated.

In this connection it is interesting to note that sculpture of the advanced modern type—wholly abstract creations—is extremely fine for garden adornment; providing, of course, that the objects are fine examples of this type with significance and meaning—not spurious monstrosities.

In every garden great or small there is room and a place for at least one good example of ornamental or garden sculpture. City gardens usually make use of such a bit, often as the leading motif; and from this it seems evident that very small and restricted areas may be more agreeably developed through use of one fine composition of this kind than in any other way. Both formal and informal design—as these terms are generally understood—may be developed in such a way that each makes equally good provision for a piece of marble or bronze. However both the piece of sculpture and the garden design must be studied and they must be united. The piece of sculpture must not be regarded and treated as a pretty ornament to be set here or there as fancy alone indicates, but must be recognized as an important feature for which a very special place and space commensurate with its importance is provided in the design and suitably prepared.

SCULPTURE'S FUNCTION

When it is thus recognized and given importance, its surroundings must, it is clear, take their key from it; they must be developed in the same spirit and accompany its theme as a musical accompaniment follows the lead of a soloist. In the general design the approach to the special place which the statue or other feature is to occupy should be so subtle that there is no suspicion of special purpose until one has come quite near. Then it should so develop as to stimulate curiosity and arouse anticipation; so that the senses are prepared for something. Then the sculpture itself shortly comes into view, fulfilling the expectancy. Thus it gives a psychological satisfaction and one's reaction to its beauty is immeasurably intensified.

As to the material for such decorative pieces, it is well to recognize that the startling gleam of white is too melodramatic for limited spaces. So bronze or some other rich metal, which has color, depth and values of shadowy character, is better suited to the small garden than marble. The latter may, of course, be supremely beautiful in the right places. Lovely things are made also in modern porcelains, in terra cotta and in some instances in cement. All are permanent and endure the elements without hurt.

Whether such things as huge glass bottles, brightly colored figurines of gnomes, mushrooms, etc., iron urns, curious boulders (outside the limits of the rock garden), shells and other objects sometimes placed in gardens for the sake of their decorative character or interest should be considered in the category of sculpture is, perhaps, a matter for argument. But certainly in any case their use could—and should—be determined and controlled according to the principles discussed above.

SCURFY SCALE. Common name of one of the scale insects, which see.

SCURVY-GRASS. Common name for *Cochlearia officinalis,* a small N. herb of the Mustard Family, with heart- or kidney-shaped leaves, and small white flowers in spring. Of some medicinal value, it is also sometimes grown as a salad plant in spite of a peculiar flavor of tar. It prefers cool or partially shaded soil.

SCUTELLARIA (skeu-te-lay'-ri-ah). A genus of usually perennial herbs or shrubby plants of the Mint Family, commonly known as Skullcap. They have scarlet, yellow, blue or violet flowers, and are sometimes planted in the border or rock garden, where they grow 1 ft. or less tall. One tender species, *S. ventenati,* with scarlet flowers in long racemes, is grown in the greenhouse. The herbaceous kinds are grown from divisions or seed and the shrubby forms from cuttings. *S. orientalis,* low growing, has gray-green foliage and yellow flowers over a long season; *S. resinosa* has soft-hairy gray foliage and charming blue or purplish flowers; *S. indica* has bluish flowers in dense clusters to 4 in., while its var. *japonica* is lower with bluer flowers. *S. alpina* spreads rapidly and has purple and white flowers 1 in. long in thick clusters; *S. angustifolia* to 6 in. has rather large solitary violet-blue flowers in the axils of the leaves.

SCYTHIAN LAMB. Common name for *Cibotium barometz,* a trunkless tree fern from China, the down-covered root of which gave rise to a 17th century widely credited rumor about a plant that bore living lambs of wool, flesh and blood.

SEA-BUCKTHORN. Common name for Hippophaë, a genus of hardy spiny shrubs and small trees with ornamental foliage and fruit.

SEAFORTHIA (see-faur'-thi-ah). An alternative name for the small feather palm, *Ptychosperma elegans,* native to E. Australia, growing to 20 ft. with bright

Plate 48. SHRUBS PROPERLY USED AND CARED FOR

Top: Hydrangeas formally massed against an evergreen background. Center left: The Japanese Snowball shows its creamy bloom to best advantage when planted as an isolated specimen. Center right: The fragrant mockorange, beloved shrub of New England dooryards. Lower left: Viburnum tomentosum, a shrub with excellent foliage and showy flowers, followed by scarlet fruit. Lower right: A well-grown specimen of the blue Hydrangea used as a formal accent on a terrace.

green leaves 3 ft. long and frequently planted in S. Fla. The name is sometimes applied to another palm, *Archontophoenix alexandrae*.

SEA-GRAPE. A common name for *Coccolobis* (or *Coccoloba*) *uvifera*, a S. Fla. tree with large, red-veined, leathery leaves, white flowers and purple fruits in grape-like clusters.

SEA-HOLLY. A common name for *Eryngium maritimum*, a perennial herb 1 ft. high with heads of pale blue flowers and spiny blue foliage.

SEA-KALE. A hardy perennial herb (*Crambe maritima*) whose young shoots are eaten like asparagus after being blanched by being earthed up or otherwise covered to exclude light. It is a highly desirable home-garden vegetable because once established, it will yield well for eight or ten years if well fed. Plants are grown from seeds or root cuttings, the latter being preferred because they begin to yield the second year, a year before seedlings. Set plants 3 or 4 ft. apart and treat like rhubarb, which see.

SEA-LAVENDER. A common name for the genus Limonium, also called Sea-pink (and, in gardens, Statice, though that is correctly the name of another related genus). They are stiff, much-branched herbs with white, yellow, pink or lavender flowers, ornamental in gardens and dried for winter bouquets. See EVERLASTINGS.

SEA-OAT. Common name for *Uniola paniculata*, a perennial plant of the Grass Family, growing to 8 ft., bearing showy clusters of spikelets in long drooping panicles, and extensively used for winter bouquets. It is native to the sand-hills of the S. States, but may be planted as far N. as Canada.

SEA-ONION. Common name for *Urginea maritima*, whose bulbs are the "squill" of druggists; also for *Scilla verna*, and sometimes incorrectly used for *Ornithogalum caudatum*. *U. maritima* is a bulbous plant of the Lily Family growing to 3 ft. with leaves 4 in. wide and to 1½ ft. long. It bears a 50- to 100-flowered raceme of small whitish flowers at the top of a 1½-ft. leafless stem. It is not hardy N. but is occasionally grown in the greenhouse where it needs light soil and cool conditions. The flowering spikes, which appear before the leaves, last in good condition for many weeks. Propagation is by offsets.

SEA-PINK. A common name for two genera—Limonium (sea-lavender) and Statice (also called thrift), both members of the Leadwort Family. The variously colored flowers of both are used in dried winter bouquets.

SEA POPPY. A common name for *Glaucium flavum*, also called Horned Poppy, whose large orange or yellow flowers are borne on long stems above bluish foliage.

SEASIDE-DAISY. One of the common names for *Erigeron glaucus*, a perennial species of Fleabane with violet flower-heads. For culture see ERIGERON.

SEASIDE GARDEN. At a distance of 500 ft. or more from the shore line, there is often little difference between a seaside garden and any other, save that created by more or less persistent wind from one direction. A slight advantage may be the dampness, which compensates during the height of summer for lack of rain, if there is such lack. Also the presence of any large body of water has a stabilizing effect on temperature, tending to reduce the extremes of both heat and cold.

But, on the other hand, salt spray may be an element of the special conditions that prevail close to the oceanside, while soil that is light and sandy (if not indeed pure sand) is characteristic, unless the location is on an elevated coast which sometimes provides fairly good soil. These things affect the choice of plant material, as mentioned farther on.

Design is influenced everywhere by the dominating element of sea landscape wherein the horizon plays such an important part. Because of it everything partakes of the horizontal, making the keynote of design in gardens at the seaside a combination of width and low-lying lines and masses as extended as may be, all harmonizing with the sweep of sea and horizon line.

This does not, however, imply or require the absence of trees or other material that may rise against the sky. It merely states of what the prevailing effect should aim to be. Naturally it involves the use of a majority of plants which grow rather close to the ground; but as this is desirable wherever strong winds prevail, it simply proves that to carry out the prevailing rhythm of the situation, it is necessary to use plant material especially suited to exactly that kind of situation.

Many plants grow well by the sea, so there is no reason to undertake the impossible or even the very difficult. To make a garden that shall embody the best of Nature's offerings in the particular place and conditions and preserve the character of the environment should always be the governing thought. When native seaside vegetation is supplemented by those exotics that literally "take to the sea," the garden will lack nothing that is needed to make it delightful—and unmistakably a seaside garden.

In both the construction and maintenance of a seaside garden the two main problems are, probably, first, the improvement of the soil, and, second, the prevention of its blowing or drifting—which involves both its loss where it is needed and the possible burying of plants or whole plantings. Drainage is rarely, if ever, a problem, so soil improvement in the seaside garden means the overcoming of a too sandy condition by the incorporation of humus, both as a preliminary operation and as a feature of the annual care. The best way to do this will vary with local conditions, but the generous use of peat moss is a practical solution anywhere; striking evidence of its effectiveness can be seen in the plantings of the Long Island Park Commission in connection with the south (or ocean) shore New York State Parks.

SOIL-BINDING METHODS

The prevention of blowing is, of course, also effected as the soil is made heavier and given more body and moisture-holding capacity. But beyond the flower bed or garden area so treated it may be desirable, if not absolutely necessary, to establish coarse grasses and other soil-binding plants (which see) as well as, sometimes, windbreaks or other forms of protection.

There are places where a lawn is possible without undue effort; and many other places where it is impossible to have a good lawn no matter how much effort is expended. In the latter instance it is infinitely better to use a ground-cover (which see) that will thrive on the sandy wastes, than it is to struggle for the conventional turf. The native bearberry (*Arctostaphylos uva-ursi*) is as fine a prostrate growth as can be found for this purpose. It establishes itself on the driest sandy spots, including railroad embankments; it is hardy throughout N. America and it re-

quires no care once it is established in any open, airy, sandy place. Wide areas or small are alike effective when covered by its compact, evergreen growth; and it is eloquent of the sea and its sandy reaches.

Of similar character, among the shrubs, are bayberry (*Myrica cerifera*) and beach plum (*Prunus maritima*), which grow close to tidewater. Other native shrubs which endure seaside conditions are groundsel-tree, chokecherry, two of the cornels (*Cornus amomum* and *C. paniculata*), the shiny sumac, and two plants not native but perfectly at home in the U. S., namely, the tamarisk and the sea-buckthorn (*Hippophaë rhamnoides*).

For flowers it is better to rely on vigorous annual plants set out each spring than on perennials—unless the garden is an all-year-round enterprise where careful attention may be continuous. Even then, near salt water, fresh plants of quick growth and continuous bloom will give better results. Petunia, salpiglossis, nicotiana, ageratum, *Phlox drummondi,* marigold, zinnia, calliopsis, physostegia and annual larkspur are excellent in broad massed plantings.

SEA URCHIN. Common name for *Hakea laurina,* an Australian shrub or tree bearing crimson flowers with long yellow styles.

SEA-URCHIN CACTUS. Common name for the genus Echinopsis, which see.

SEAWEED. Various kinds of seaweed are gathered, allowed to decay in heaps and then used as manure, since they provide humus, some nitrogen and a fair amount of potash. Plenty of water should be applied to the pile while it is rotting to wash out salt from the seawater; rain and freezing weather will hasten this desirable conditions. Seaweed, when well rotted, can be spread 3 or 4 in. deep and plowed or spaded into the soil. It varies considerably in its composition but on the average may contain 0.50 per cent nitrogen, 0.20 per cent phosphorus and 1 per cent potash.

SECATEURS (sek'-ah'-turs'). A name (from the French) sometimes found in catalogs, for hand pruning shears. See TOOLS.

SEDGE. The common name of a plant family (Cyperaceae, which see), and also of the genus Carex (which see), a group of some 900 species of perennial grass-like herbs, with long, narrow leaves. They inhabit temperate and arctic regions, most of them growing on marsh lands and often yielding crops of bog hay. Some species are used in gardening, as edgings for aquatic gardens; or, in the case of the broad-leaved type, in rock gardens or as a feature in corners, or beside walls. Sometimes they are grown in pots as house or conservatory plants; and in the arts some species are utilized in making grass rugs and other fabrics. Propagation is by division of the clumps, or from seeds sown in the fall.

SEDUM (see'-dum). Derived from the Latin word meaning to sit, this name refers to a genus of plants which characteristically "sit" or affix themselves on rocks and walls. Common names are Stonecrops and Live-for-ever. They are mostly hardy, all succulent or fleshy, erect or prostrate members of the Orpine Family (Crassulaceae). Some are herbaceous perennials, dying to the ground in winter, while many are evergreens. Native of the temperate and frigid zones, they are easy to raise in America and with the growing interest in rock and indoor gardening are attaining increased popularity. (See illustration, Plate 51.) The flowers are usually white or yellow, rarely pink or blue; the leaves are very variable—opposite, alternate and sometimes in whorls. They succeed in almost any position—on made rock-work and walls or old ruins, in the mixed border, and are especially useful for carpet bedding. In naturalistic plantings they are sometimes allowed to spread extensively.

Like most plants, sedums have preferences, doing particularly well in a light, loamy soil in open sunny positions. No rock garden can be considered quite complete without its quota of sedums, along with saxifrages and sempervivums and no class of plants appeals more to children than these three, all being easily grown. Encouraged to set young plants in chinks in the walls or use them as carpet bedding in the paths, children will often develop interest that will extend to many other plants.

All sedums are easily grown from seed which can be sown in late summer, the seedlings being wintered over with slight covering, ready to be transplanted to their permanent places in spring; or the seed may be spring sown. Stock may also be multiplied by division of the tufts in early spring or it may be propagated from cuttings rooted in sandy soil and kept shaded until well started.

To suggest the adaptability of different species to meet all situations, here are outstanding examples: *S. acre* is greatly favored for its spreading capacity, *S. lydium,* an evergreen, is used for rock-work edging and *S. spectabile,* because of its greater height, is grown largely in the mixed border and is frequently utilized as a pot plant.

Humus or well rotted leafmold with which a good complete fertilizer has been mixed, may be worked lightly into the soil about the plants to good advantage, and if weeds are kept out the plants seem to remain noticeably free from disease.

Insects, both sucking and chewing, from neighboring plants will sometimes attack. Occasional light spraying with a combined insecticide and fungicide will act as a preventive. Being quite hardy, sedums need little winter protection other than a few leaves put on late in the season to prevent heaving of the soil.

SPECIES

S. acre (Wall-pepper). A low, creeping evergreen with leaves less than $\frac{1}{4}$ in. long and yellow flowers in summer. In var. *aureum* the leaves are bright yellow in spring, the plant providing a mossy, golden carpet for use on walls, rocky ledges and stone garden paths.

aizoon. Numerous small, yellow to orange flowers in late summer; useful for edging.

album. Dark green creeping evergreen that forms compact mats. Handsome flat heads of white flowers in midsummer. Several varieties with foliage of different shades.

anglicum. A biennial which, as it self-sows, gives an evergreen effect about 2 in. high. Compact gray foliage; white flowers in summer.

brevifolium. Another creeping evergreen with small leaves densely crowded along the stems and small, whitish flowers in July.

dasyphyllum. Makes tiny gray-green evergreen tufts; flowers are pinkish in July. Fits in well and is considered one of the best of the group.

ewersi. To 1 ft., stocky with short thick leaves and pink to purple flowers.

Somewhat tender evergreen but good for pot culture.

hispanicum. Annual or biennial, with gray-green leaves, and pink flowers in midsummer. Var. *minus* is a dwarf form (to 2 in.) often used in carpet bedding.

kamtschaticum. Evergreen to 6 to 9 in. Dark glossy green foliage makes strong clumps; stems prostrate; orange-yellow flowers in July and August.

lydium. A dwarf, shapely, evergreen, the leaves tipped red, and the tiny white or pink flowers in late summer. A well-fitted little evergreen for carpet bedding or rock edgings.

pulchellum. A handsome but little known native evergreen, to 1 ft., with slender trailing or ascending branches and rosy-purple flowers.

rupestre. A creeping evergreen that reddens with age and in dry weather; flowers golden yellow in July.

rhodanthum. Erect perennial, of the Rocky Mountains, to 1 ft. with stout rootstock, very leafy stems and rose-colored flowers in summer.

spectabile. Commonly grown robust upright perennial, to 1 ft., with light green foliage and numerous small pink flowers in September.

sarmentosum. A fast spreading prostrate evergreen of yellowish tinge with bright yellow flowers.

sexangulare. Dwarf, rich green creeping evergreen with leaves densely crowded and yellow flowers in July.

populifolium. An evergreen sub-shrub with white to pinkish fragrant flowers in late summer.

SEED DISINFECTION. Treatment of seed before planting with either a dust or a liquid disinfectant to prevent infection by bacterial or fungous disease. See DISINFECTION.

SEED PRODUCTION. The growing and saving of seed of garden crops for sowing purposes is such a highly developed activity and demands such intimate knowledge of the plants concerned that the grower of vegetables or flowers—and especially the home gardener—may well leave the work to seed growers, hybridists and other specialists who devote their lives to originating new varieties or to the maintenance of the purity of established strains.

The principal reason that amateur seed growing is unsatisfactory is that the desirable characteristics of a variety are likely to disappear after a year or two and give way to other, less desirable qualities. Unless careful selection of the best is constantly practiced, retrogression of improved sorts is almost inevitable. And it takes skill, knowledge and experience to recognize and segregate the most valuable seed-bearing plants.

There is also the fact that reputable seedsmen offer reliable, standard varieties and strains at such reasonable prices, and the quantities of seed needed by the home gardener are so small that the time required for producing and saving them might far better be devoted to other gardening tasks.

Seed production is carried on along two lines. One involves plant breeding and the selection and multiplication of new, improved varieties so produced; the other is the maintenance of stocks of seed true to type, strain or variety by rigorous roguing—which means the ruthless removal from the growing seed crop of all plants that differ from the definite ideal or fall below the standard established.

In both directions there are unlimited opportunities for the skilled professional or commercial grower. For there is always a demand for both new and improved varieties and for good seed true to variety. Quality product in both classes of seed commands premium prices; but to develop the one and maintain the other, a working knowledge of the laws of plant breeding and selection, and familiarity with complicated practices are essential.

Of the two activities, the former is likely to appeal most to the beginner, mainly because of the appeal to his inexperienced eye of the possibility of becoming a second Luther Burbank. Actually, however, this possibility is remote and the work is likely to be disappointing and unprofitable, as is any difficult specialty undertaken by the unequipped person.

The amateur gardener who may want to save the seed of some especially fine plant should realize, first, that the progeny of a plant is almost certain to differ more or less widely from its parent. Probably less than one per cent will "come true." If only seed from these true ones is saved and planted, and if this process is repeated year after year the percentage of "true to type" plants will increase until, in time, the stock of seed so built up may be practically 100 per cent true. To help anyone who is willing to start slowly and work gradually and carefully toward such a result the following rules are offered: 1. Make sure that the seed is fully ripe before gathering the heads, pods or other "fruit." 2. Spread the heads, pods or other parts thinly on cloth or clean boards or trays, preferably in the shade or indoors where the air is dry and in motion. 3. Make sure that these enclosing parts are thoroughly dry before separating the chaff and waste from the seed itself. 4. After removing the trash, place the clean seed in containers that permit free access of air —cotton sacks are good. 5. Store where the air will be dry and the temperature not higher than is comfortable for a human being; be sure they are out of reach of mice and other pests. If there is any likelihood of insect infestation (weevils are especially common as seed pests) treat seed as directed under DISINFECTION.

The length of time seed will remain viable (that is, able to sprout strongly and produce sturdy seedlings) varies widely with the species and the care taken in harvesting and storing the seed. Some seeds, such as those of chervil and martynia, rarely retain their germinating power longer than one year; whereas seed of celery, cabbage, cucumber and various other vegetables and flowers may sprout well when ten years old or even more. Seed not fully mature when gathered or that stored before fully dry, or kept at too high a temperature, may sprout very poorly or not at all whenever planted. In any case it is well to make tests before doing any actual planting. See SEED TESTING.

SEEDS AND SEEDSOWING. Seeds are fertilized, ripened ovules or "eggs" of flowering plants. Each contains a rudimentary plant (the embryo) which while dormant is protected by various coats and is supplied, either in or around its seed leaves (cotyledons), with stored-up food sufficient to start its active life and carry the seedling until its roots and true leaves begin to function. Since seed development results from the fertilization of the ovules by pollen produced in the stamens of the same or some other flower, reproduction of plants by seed is termed "sexual" as distinguished from the "asexual" processes of division, rooting cuttings, etc.

Seeds vary widely in size, from those of the begonia, which are dust-like, to those

SEEDLINGS IN DOUBLE POT

By packing the space between the two pots with sphagnum or peat moss and keeping it moist, the soil in the small pot in which seed is planted is kept from drying out yet does not become too wet.

of the "double coconut" (*Lodoicea maldivica*), which are often 12 to 18 in. long and weigh up to 40 lbs. each. They also exhibit a marvelous diversity of form. In many cases the form is a special adaptation to assist in the distribution of the seed, as the "wings" of the maple and tulip-tree and the "parachutes" of dandelion and milkweed, for wind transportation, and various burs and hooks which attach their seeds to animals. In other instances they have impervious coats enabling them to survive digestion in animals' stomachs, as those of tomato and blackberry; still others are suited for transportation by water, by being buoyant and waterproof for long periods.

Relatively few seeds will sprout as soon as mature. Even under ideal germinating conditions most of them remain dormant for what is called a "rest period," which varies in length in different plant groups. Such periods are thought to be necessary for certain chemical changes related to the "ripening" of the foods stored in the seed.

Mangrove seeds sprout while still attached to the branches and some cereal grains germinate during wet weather while still in the heads. Some vegetable and flower seeds of the Mustard, Grass, Lily, Bean and Sunflower Families, start into growth within a few days; others (carrots and parsnips) require about a month, and in many species of shrubs, trees and perennials, the rest-period often exceeds a year.

Recent investigations have disclosed means of shortening these periods, in some cases thus reducing the cost of starting the plants and the risk of losses from drying, decay, and the depredations of mice and other pests. Agencies used to hasten germination include chemicals, combined moisture and heat, moisture and freezing, and different combinations of all these and other treatments. One important and long-practiced method is stratification, which consists of placing alternating layers of seed and sand in a box or flat and keeping them wet, or in some cases, subjecting them to freezing and thawing by leaving them outdoors all winter. This breaks down or cracks hard shells.

Such methods, however, are exceptional, because most "garden seeds" keep best in a dry and cool condition. It should be kept in mind that seeds, though dormant, are living organisms and must be properly treated if they are to give satisfactory results. Naturally, all they need in order to grow is favorable conditions. Their vitality (or lack of it) is established by their maturity, the weather conditions during harvest time and their treatment during harvesting and storing.

Well-ripened seeds harvested under favorable (dry) conditions and properly stored should retain their vitality for the maximum time characteristic of the species. Seeds of some plants germinate poorly if more than a few weeks old; those of others sprout well even after being stored for 10 years or more. But stories about seeds sprouting after having been in tombs or the pyramids for centuries are usually publicity schemes or newspaper "yarns."

Seeds harvested during muggy weather are usually less viable (capable of growth) than those gathered under dry conditions. Seeds once injured never regain their vigor. Heating always reduces vitality.

How Seeds Germinate

The popular idea is that seed germination or sprouting is the first step in plant growth; actually it is merely the resumption of activity by the dormant young plant in the seed. The factors essential to germination are: viable seed, moisture, air and favorable temperature. The degrees of the last three factors needed vary considerably with different kinds of plants. Briefly, the process of germination is as follows: The seed absorbs water which enables certain substances in the seed (called *enzymes*) to convert stored starches into sugars. These contribute to the growth of plant cells and tissues; this increases the size of the embryo, which, becoming active, bursts through the water-softened seed coats—and a seedling plant is started on its way.

Both the time and the depth to sow seed out of doors are influenced by the moisture in the soil and the temperature there. Seeds sown deeply in moist cool soil in early spring often decay, because, even though the air is mild, evaporation of soil water keeps the soil too cold for them. Seeds sown too shallow in summer, especially if the soil is not packed firmly around them, find so little moisture to absorb that they remain practically dry and fail to sprout. Hence, early spring sowing should be much shallower than late spring and summer sowing of the same kind of seed.

Other than this, the only general rules to follow are (1) that seeds of hardy plants may be sown earlier in spring, in wetter ground and deeper than those of tender plants; (2) that strongly viable and fresh seed may be sown more deeply than weak and old stock; (3) that in spring, when the soil is damp, it should be firmed but lightly over the seeds (if at all), whereas in summer when the ground is dry—perhaps powdery—it must be packed hard to permit the rise of moisture from the subsoil; and (4) that seeds of large size may be sown deeper than small ones, especially when the ground is dry.

A general statement as to the depth at which to plant is: sow 2 to 4 times the diameter of the seed; but merely press very small seeds into the surface, allowing subsequent sprinkling to cover them.

Too deep sowing reduces the supply of oxygen necessary for germination and makes it hard for the seedlings to reach the surface. In greenhouses where conditions are under control, seed may be sown twice as deep as out of doors. When seeds are sown in a pot, pan or flat, caking of the surface soil can be prevented by watering them by setting the container almost its full depth in water until the moisture rises through it and is apparent on the surface. Then cover it with newspaper and a pane of glass. When the seeds begin to sprout, remove the paper; when the temperature rises too high or the air gets too moist, forming mist on the glass, tilt or remove the glass for ventilation and to prevent "damping-off" (which see), or the "drawing" of the seedlings into tall, weak, spindly plants.

The popular practice of soaking pea, bean, corn and other garden seeds is not always desirable; if continued too long the seed may become water-logged and decay when planted in moist or cold soil.

Though seeds that sprout strongly usually make the best plants, there are exceptions. Double-flowering ruffled petunia seed produces both lusty and puny seedlings; the former develop into sturdy plants which bear single flowers and later produce seed; the less vigorous seedlings produce the desired double flowers *but no seed.*

Since the value of seed depends first of all on its ability to germinate, the testing of seed before planting is well worth while. Under the laws of most States this must be done and the approximate germination percentage certified to by the dealer before the seed is sold. State departments also take samples of seed on the open market and test them both for viability and for purity—that is, trueness to variety and also freedom from chaff, dirt and weed seed, etc., as a check against the dealers' representations. These activities are a safeguard and a help for gardeners, but often the latter find it interesting or desirable to make their own tests—of surplus seed that has been stored for a year or more, or of home-grown seed.

Simple Seed Testing

Commercial seed testers and those of State departments have special apparatus for making delicate tests of many lots of seed, but for home testing of seed purity all that are really needed are: stout white paper or cardboard on which to spread samples, tweezers to pick out small seeds, a 6-in. plant label whittled to a thin edge and point for separating them from impurities, and a pocket lens with which to examine seeds for impurities and identification.

To make a simple but adequate germination test, place a disk of white blotting paper in a saucer or soup plate, wet it, and on it scatter 25, 50 or 100 seeds; cover with another matching disk of moistened blotting paper, and then with an inverted saucer or soup plate. Keep the device in a living-room temperature and apply water gently to the paper often enough to keep it moist. After the third day gently remove the upper blotter, count any seeds that have sprouted and do so from day to day for a couple of weeks. The percentage of seeds that actually sprout will give an idea of the viability of the seed; the relative numbers that sprout before and after the middle of the test period supply a guide as to whether the seed should be sown thickly or thinly.

Seed-Sowing Pointers

Seedage, as the sowing of seeds is called, involves all the fundamentals so far considered and includes the following practical points:

Seeds may be classified as large and small; and, according to the kind of plants they produce, as hardy or tender to frost, and annual, biennial or perennial.

So far as size is concerned, the main considerations are depth of planting. Most large seeds may be sown in the open ground. Medium sized ones may be sown either out of doors or under glass. Minute seeds, as those of thyme and petunia, should always be sown in seed pans or flats, as directed above.

Seeds of hardy plants like radish and poppy may be sown as early in the spring as the ground can be worked—and should be, in order to get the benefit of the cool moisture of the soil at the time. Seeds of tender plants must not be sown outdoors until the ground is warm and only just moist.

Seeds of tropical and subtropical plants, such as egg-plant, tomato, and Cobæa, are best sown under glass several weeks before it would be safe to sow them out of doors.

Seeds of half-hardy and tender annuals may be treated the same way for early results or sown out of doors, either in nursery beds for transplanting or direct in the open ground, when the flowers are wanted in their normal summer season.

Biennials, such as Canterbury bells and dandelion for greens, may be sown at any time between early spring and midsummer; given necessary protection over winter, they will mature the following spring or summer. Biennials are often started outdoors in midsummer for the following season's bloom, but more, larger and finer flowers should result from spring-sown seed.

Seeds of hardy perennials are often sown in greenhouses, hotbeds and coldframes during winter. Home gardeners without such facilities can use seed pans or flats in a sunny window, or may prepare special sheltered outdoor seedling beds in which to sow as early as possible in spring. The seedlings started indoors are pricked-out into flats and a month or so later transplanted to "nursery rows" where they are grown for one season so as to be a good size for planting in their permanent quarters that fall or the following spring.

It is usually advisable to sow seeds more thinly than the seedsman recommends. This avoids crowding the seedlings and making them spindly and weak. For the same reason it is essential to prick out or transplant the seedlings *before they begin* to crowd. This work is best done on cloudy days, in the evening or just before a rain. When done under glass, the seedlings should be given some shade for a day or two.

Soil in which seeds are sown should be freshly sifted or dug and finely raked so as to be porous while still retaining enough moisture to favor germination. Always firm the soil over the seeds to bring them in contact with the moisture film that envelops the soil particles. Soils for merely starting seedlings should be only moderately. fertile—poor is better than rich—because this will stimulate root rather than top development and facilitate transplanting later.

Out doors the cultivation should be given 3 or 4 days after sowing in order to kill weeds whose seeds, being already in the soil and moist, are sure to germinate before the crop seeds can start. This first cultivation is the most important of all because by killing the first crop of weeds one tends largely to reduce the number of later weeds.

Advantage may be taken of the difference in speed of germination by sowing a few seeds of a quick-starting kind in the rows of slow-growing kinds to show where the rows are. The best crop for this purpose is a forcing variety of radish because its seeds (dropped 3 in. apart) will sprout within 3 or 4 days. The roots will reach edible size in less than a month, and the foliage will shade the rows just enough to help the growth of the more permanent or full season crop. When the radishes are removed (and used), the regular crop may be given its first thinning and weeding.

SEED TESTING. The practice of estimating the purity and germinating power (viability) of seed samples by sprouting them under favorable, controlled conditions. By determining the percentage that start, the value of the seed from which the samples are taken, as well as the proportion of chaff, dirt, weed seed and other impurities, can be ascertained in advance of planting. While seed testing is one of the regular activities of large, reputable seed firms and also of governmental agencies seeking to protect public interests, it can often be done on a small scale by home gardeners with interest and profit. A simple method is explained under SEEDS AND SEEDSOWING, which see.

SEGO-LILY. Common name for *Calochortus nuttalli* (which see), whose white blossom, lined and spotted at the throat with purple, is the State flower of Utah.

SELAGINELLA (sel-ah-ji-nel'-ah). A genus of flowerless herbs with scale-like leaves, grown for the beauty of their mossy foliage. Some species are hardy, but those most interesting horticulturally are grown in the greenhouse to cover the soil in benches, pots or baskets, as specimen plants for table decoration, or in the terrarium. The hardy kinds are easily cultivated in damp, shady woods. In the

TWO WAYS TO PROMOTE SEED GERMINATION
Seed sown in a flower pot or "pan" may be covered with a piece of glass and shaded with newspaper for a few days (a). In a flat (b) the broadcast seed can be covered with an inverted flower pot which provides both shade and the desired close atmosphere.

greenhouse new growth will start readily from old plants chopped up and scattered over the soil, which is then covered with a glass and kept at 70 deg. F.

S. kraussiana, from Africa, is a bright green mossy perennial with creeping stems, often used to carpet soil. *S. emmeliana,* from tropical America, grows to 1 ft., with bright green leaves, and makes a fern-like specimen for the table. *S. brauni,* with straw-colored foliage and an erect stem over 1 ft. high, is often used in porch boxes. *S. martensi,* with long graceful stems and very fine pale green leaves, is often grown for cut foliage.

S. lepidophylla, found from Tex. to S. America, is the curious Resurrection-plant, which see.

SELECTION. The process of choosing an individual or a group of individuals for the preservation of desirable characters or for further breeding operations, eliminating all others. In a systematic attempt to develop an improved variety or strain, a plant breeder might first cross (or hybridize) two plants showing certain desirable characters; then by practicing selection he would separate out from the progeny of that cross the individuals showing the closest approach to the desider ideal. These he might use for further crossing; or, if of sufficient merit, they could be propagated by cuttings, division or other asexual methods, so as to build up a stock of plants of the new kind. See also PLANT BREEDING.

SELENIA (see-lee'-ni-ah). A genus of small native herbs of the Mustard Family, with finely cut foliage and yellow flowers. They are interesting annuals which can be readily grown from seed in any sunny spot in the wild or rock garden. *S. aurea,* with golden-yellow flowers, bears flat seed-pods similar to those of Honesty or Lunaria, which see.

SELENICEREUS (sel-ee-ni-see'-ree-us). The name (meaning moon-cereus) of a genus of slender cacti, climbing in habit. To it belong some of the best known and most beautiful of those given the name "night-blooming cereus."

S. macdonaldie is a most wonderful sight when in bloom, with flowers 15 in. in diameter. It is a very rapid grower, its slender, cylindrical stems reaching to lengths of 15 or 20 ft. in a single season. Semi-aërial in character, it roots easily and under cultivation is happy in the soil.

Of tropical origin, it should receive greenhouse or lath-house treatment in the colder climates. Several other species of the genus are also favorites in cultivation.

SELF. In plant breeding, self-pollination, or "selfing," means the use of a plant's own pollen upon its own stigmas to produce self-fertilized progeny. This results in seed production without crossing or hybridizing. (See PLANT BREEDING.) The term self is also used by florists to denote a flower of a single, solid color.

SELF-HEAL. A common name for *Prunella vulgaris,* a low, weedy, perennial herb, with purple flowers in flat-topped spikes.

SEMELE (sem'-ee-lee). A shrubby vine from the Canary Islands, belonging to the Lily Family. See CLIMBING BUTCHERS-BROOM.

SEMPERVIVUM (sem-per-vy'-vum). This name for the plants popularly called houseleeks comes from Latin words meaning "live for ever," alluding to the well known tenacity of many of the species, especially *S. tectorum,* the common or roof houseleek. (See illustration, Plate 51.)

The genus comprises 50 or more species of succulent herbs or sub-shrubs of variable habits, often stemless and developing young plants or offsets in the leaf axils. Those grown in the U. S. are mostly hardy, and many seem to be hybrids of, or derived from, a few basic species. The alternate leaves are thick and fleshy, frequently form compact rosettes and often are red spotted toward the tips. In the so-called spider-web forms, the entire plant appears to be covered with silvery cobwebs. The flowers, borne in dense heads, are variously colored—white, pink, greenish, yellow or purplish. All the hardy forms are well suited for rock work and borders; the more tender or greenhouse kinds are valuable as succulents indoors and as summer carpet-bedding plants outdoors. The smaller sorts are popular material for use in dish gardens, terraria and other miniature arrangements.

CULTURAL DIRECTIONS

Sempervivums succeed well in any ordinarily good garden soil, and will thrive even in sandy wastes. Consequently they are unsurpassed for rock gardens, for covering dry banks or embedded in or on old walls. They were formerly largely used in formal gardening as edging plants.

Plants are easily raised from seed which may be sown in spring or late summer and carried over winter with slight protection to be permanently planted out the following spring. The young plants which spring up about the base of the old ones can be easily separated and grown on as new individuals.

No plants are more easily grown and cared for than the houseleeks. They require no care other than to prevent weeds from crowding them out; but at the same time they respond well to a shallow cultivation of the soil surrounding them. They are shallow rooted and enjoy a light mulch of humus or peat moss during severe hot weather, but do not require further feeding. Ocassionally plants are found covered with orange-red rust pustules. Remove and destroy individuals if badly rusted and dust the others with fine sulphur. Crown rot (which see) may also occur. But, generally speaking, sempervivums are pleasingly free from pests and plant diseases and, like many other shallow-rotted rock plants, need no winter protection other than a thin covering of leaves or other light litter applied in early winter to prevent the "heaving" or lifting of the roots out of the soil. Where children have gardens of their own, some of these easily grown, highly interesting plants should by all means be included in them.

Useful Garden Species

S. arenarium. To 9 in., forming tiny, globular clumps of 60 to 80 bright green leaves; flowers pale yellow. A sand-loving species.

arachnoideum (Cobweb Houseleek). Only 3 to 4 in. high. Gray-green hairy leaves joined by a lacy, silvery web; flowers red, in June. Fine for rock gardens and for edging borders.

brauni. To 9 in., has leaf rosettes about 2 in. across and dull yellow flowers in July.

calcareum. From France; attains 1 ft., has smooth leaves with red-brown tips, and pale red flowers in summer.

fimbriatum. An 8- to 10-in. hybrid with reddish leaves tipped with hairs and the outer ones reddish; bright red flowers in July.

flagelliforme. Low-growing (4 in.) with tiny rosettes of woolly leaves and 1-in. red flowers close against them.

globiferum. To 1 ft., with rather few, 1-in. yellow flowers flushed purple inside in summer.

montanum. Tightly packed leaf rosettes, and bright purple flowers in June, on 6-in. stems.

schotti. Pale red flowers on 1-ft. stems in summer; leaves tipped with reddish-brown.

soboliferum. A popular form with pale yellow flowers in dense heads 4 in. across in summer. New rosettes are attached to the parent plants by slender threads.

tectorum. The best known species with many names, including Roof Houseleek, Hen-and-chickens, Old Man, Old Woman, etc. Leaf rosettes to 4 in. across; hairy stems to 1 ft. high; flowers pink to red, about 1 in. across.

triste. A rarer form of the preceding with the upper part of the leaves suffused with red brown, and the bright red flowers on 1-ft. stems.

atlanticum. Pale red, 1-in. flowers in summer on 1-ft. stems; the slender smooth, pale green leaves are tipped with reddish brown when mature.

SENECIO (se-nee'-shi-oh). Groundsel. A very large and variable genus, comprising herbs, shrubs and small trees, widely distributed throughout the world and belonging to the Daisy Family. It includes some climbers, some fleshy kinds (actually succulents), some hardy herbaceous perennials, and the pot plant that florists call Cineraria. Some species formerly included under Senecio are now listed under Ligularia. The woody species are native in S. Africa, Central and S. America, and Australia.

In general, Senecios are easy to grow in good loamy soil. They are propagated by seed, cuttings and division.

Principal Herbaceous Species

S. articulatus (Candle-plant) is of branching habit to 2 ft., with flat-lobed leaves and heads of white flowers, minus ray petals. It is often grown in succulent collections.

mikanioides (German Ivy) is a slender twiner with dark green angled leaves and heads of small yellow flowers; a popular window-garden plant.

scandens is a woody climber to several feet, with grayish green leaves and heads of yellow flowers. It is often confused with the preceding species.

macroglossus (Cape Ivy) is an herbaceous climber with handsome ivy-like leaves, good in the cool greenhouse.

auriculatissimus, a climbing perennial, is also an interesting plant for the greenhouse, with attractive foliage and bright yellow flowers.

cruentus is a short-stemmed perennial with large soft leaves and reddish purple flowers. This is the source of the florists' Cineraria, which see.

cineraria (Dusty Miller) is a tender branching perennial with white-woolly stems and leaves often used in bedding arrangements.

leucostachys is better known in gardens as *S. cineraria* var. *candidissimus.* It is used in the same way, and is less stiff in habit, with more finely cut leaves.

petasites (Velvet Groundsel, Californian-geranium) is a robust, tender perennial to 8 ft., with large soft-lobed leaves and many-headed panicles of yellow flowers; a good winter-blooming plant for the greenhouse.

speciosus is also a good plant for the greenhouse, with showy heads of bright purple flowers.

aureus (Golden Ragwort) is a hardy herbaceous perennial growing to 2 ft. or so, with golden flower-heads in late spring.

doronicum (Leopards-bane) is also a hardy herbaceous perennial, with heads of orange-yellow flowers 2 in. or more across.

pulcher is of erect habit to 4 ft., fairly hardy in well-drained soil. It is of white cobwebby appearance, with showy flower-heads to 3 in. across, the disk flowers yellow and ray petals reddish purple.

tanguticus is a stout herbaceous perennial to 7 ft., with broadly ovate leaves divided into toothed segments, and numerous heads of yellow flowers borne in a terminal pyramidal panicle.

elegans (Purple Ragwort) is an old-time garden annual with yellow disk flowers and purple ray petals. There are forms with white, rose, and crimson flowers, and some double forms.

jacobaea (Tansy Ragwort) is a biennial or perennial, with divided leaves and heads of yellow flowers. Naturalized along the coast of E. N. America.

Principal Shrubby Species

These are interesting in mild climates. *S. grandifolius,* native in Mexico, is a large shrub to 15 ft., with leaves to 18 in.

long, and heads of yellow flowers. *S. greyi* is a New Zealand shrub with leathery leaves about 3 in. long, white beneath, and yellow flowers.

hectori, also from New Zealand, grows to 12 ft., with leaves to 1 ft. long, white beneath, and with heads of white flowers.

compactus is a dwarf dense grower from the same part of the world, with small leaves and yellow flowers in leafy clusters.

SENNA. Common name for the genus Cassia, which includes herbs, shrubs and trees common in tropical countries. The leaves and pods of several are useful in medicine and a few species are grown for ornamental purposes, but only one or two can stand more than a few degrees of frost. They are sun lovers, preferring a sandy loam, and are very attractive with finely cut foliage and showy flowers. Propagated by seeds.

Principal Species

C. corymbosa. A half-hardy shrub from S. America, sometimes grown in pots or tubs for conservatory decoration. The yellow flowers are freely produced all through the summer.

fistula (Golden Shower). A small tree from India, with long racemes of showy yellow flowers and pods 1 to 2 ft. long; these are the cassia pods of commerce.

grandis (Pink Shower). A tropical American tree to 50 ft. with long drooping racemes of rose-pink flowers.

marylandica (Wild Senna). A hardy perennial herb to 4 ft., native from New England southward. It has bright yellow flowers in summer.

tomentosa. A Mexican shrub with deep golden flowers and leaves whitish beneath.

artemisioides. An Australian shrub with silvery, thread-like leaves and pale yellow flowers. Grows and flowers well in dry places in California.

SENNA-PEA. Common name for the genus Swainsona, Australian herbs and sub-shrubs with pea-like flowers and swollen pods; grown out of doors in warm regions and as pot plants in N. greenhouses.

SENSITIVE FERN (*Onoclea sensibilis*). A coarse and abundant fern of marshes and wet woodlands throughout the U. S., needing much moisture and good drainage, and useful primarily for naturalizing, because of its rank growth. The barren fronds are 10 to 20 in. long, broadly once-pinnate, and winged along the rachis, turning brown at the first touch of frost. The fertile fronds are contracted and appear late in summer. Because of their stiff erect habit they and the terminal fruit are often dyed and used in winter bouquets.

SENSITIVE-PLANT. Common name for *Mimosa pudica,* a tropical perennial of the Pea Family, also known as Humbleplant. It has a spiny stem, long-stemmed leaves cut into leaflets, and purplish flowers in rounded heads. The name refers to the action of the leaves, the leaflets folding together and the leaf-stalk drooping at the slightest touch; after a time they slowly assume their original form. The Sensitive-plant, frequently grown as a curiosity, is treated as an annual in the N., seed being sown in ordinary garden soil in full sunshine. Grown in the house or cool greenhouse as a pot plant it is easily increased by cuttings rooted in sandy soil.

SEPAL. One of the outer set of floral leaves which collectively make up the *calyx.* See FLOWER.

SEQUOIA (se-kwoi'-ah). A genus of immense American coniferous evergreen trees, valued for their massive beauty and as natural wonders, and considered to be among the oldest living things. Some are estimated to be 3000 or more years old. Thriving only where sea fogs occur they now occupy only a narrow belt along the Pacific. In past ages they grew as far E. as Arizona, but were exterminated by geological and climatic changes. The wood does not decay and is difficult to burn. Sequoias are not garden subjects, but rounded protuberances (burls) cut from the trunks and placed in water in flat dishes send out graceful, feathery frond-like shoots and make attractive table decorations that last for months.

S. gigantea, the Giant Sequoia, will grow to 30 ft. in sheltered sections of the central States.

S. sempervirens, the true Redwood, will live only in very mild sections.

SERPENT GOURD, or SNAKE GOURD. Common name for *Trichosanthes anguina,* an annual vine of the Gourd Family, raised in India for its edible fruits and in the U. S. as an oddity. It has large, almost round, lobed leaves, racemes of flowers with finely cut petals, and very slender gourd-like fruits from 1 to 6 ft. long, usually curved and coiled like a serpent. It can be raised in the N. if

treated as a tender annual; start the seeds under glass and set the plants out in very rich soil after all danger of frost is over.

SERVICE AREA. All that part of the grounds or plot which is devoted to the administration of a home. In its simplest form it may be merely a place for the ash barrel or trash bin, or the clothes-drying area; as the size of the establishment increases it may take on additional functions and features. The secondary entrance—or one of the secondary entrances—to the dwelling is from the service area or yard; goods and provisions are received through it, the garage and outbuildings adjoin it and, on large estates, there may be an entirely separate driveway connecting it with the highway. This driveway would then be included in the term. The entire area should be enclosed in any preferred way to insure its being private.

SERVICE-BERRY. A common name for Amelanchier, which see.

SERVICE-TREE. Common name for species of Sorbus, the Mountain-ash (which see), especially *S. domestica* and *S. torminalis.*

SESSILE. Without a stalk and seated directly upon the support; a term applied to any stalkless organ which is commonly stalked, as a flower or leaf.

SET. This term in gardening has several meanings. A tree is said to "set" fruit when the petals of the pollinated flowers have fallen and the flower bases or receptacles have begun to swell and take on the form of a tiny apple, pear or whatever. An onion "set" is a small, actually dwarfed bulb, the result of seeding thickly and growing a crop for a season without thinning. The resulting undersized bulbs, ranging from $\frac{1}{8}$ to $\frac{1}{2}$ in. in diameter, are harvested, dried and, the following spring, sold as sets, to be planted out early, especially for the production of green bunch onions or "scallions," although if left to mature they will give fair sized bulbs.

The term set is also sometimes applied to a rooted "slip" or sprout of the sweet-potato, by which the plant is propagated.

SETARIA (see-tay'-ri-ah). A genus of warm country annual and perennial grasses. *S. palmifolia* or Palm Grass (which see) and *S. italica* or Foxtail Millet, in numerous varieties with colored spikes, are grown as ornamentals. See ORNAMENTAL GRASSES.

CLOTH SHADE IN A GREENHOUSE
By spreading opaque black cloth over a temporary frame like this for a certain number of hours each day, the flowering period of some plants can be advanced or retarded by as much as several weeks.

SHADBUSH, or SHADBLOW. Common names for Amelanchier, which see.

SHADDOCK, PUMMELO, POMPELMOUS. Common names applied to *Citrus maxima* but sometimes mistakenly used for the pomelo or grapefruit (*C. paradisi*). The shaddock is a smaller tree but bears much larger, coarser grained fruits singly; the pomelo bears its finer grained fruits in clusters, suggesting the popular American name, grapefruit, which see. See also CITRUS FRUITS.

SHADE AND SHADING. As applied in gardening this cannot be defined by any single term such as "obscuration of light," because it may refer to natural unavoidable shadows; to the desired protection of seeds, seedlings, cuttings or newly pricked-out or transplanted plants indoors or out; to the coating of greenhouse or conservatory glass with whiting, white lead or whitewash during late spring and summer to reflect the sun's rays and thus reduce the inside temperature and glare; and to the various materials used to produce the shade in these and other cases.

Natural shade, such as that cast in the morning and evening by high hills, shortens the duration of direct sunlight often to the extent of an hour or two a day. In amateur summer gardening this is not a serious objection, but in commercial greenhouse operation it may be such a handicap as to make the growing of various crops unprofitable. Shade cast by trees and buildings is objectionable in greenhouse operation in proportion to its extent and duration and in a garden may be so dense or wide-spreading as to preclude the growing of many sun-loving plants or a good lawn. On the other hand, it may provide favorable conditions for the development of plants that thrive in shade; conditions particularly desired for a certain effect. When such shade is caused by obstructions on a neighboring property it is advisable to choose such plants as are known to thrive best under these conditions; if the tree casting shade is on one's own grounds, it may become necessary to decide which is most wanted—the tree or the smaller plants that its presence precludes.

Shading of seeds newly sown in seed pans and flats is necessary to prevent excessive heating of the surface soil and to check evaporation, especially when the seeds require a long time to germinate. It is similarly necessary to protect and keep moist greenwood cuttings while they are striking root and various kinds of grafted plants while kept in propagating quarters.

Seedlings pricked out into flats or transplanted to other flats, also freshly potted cuttings, similarly need shading for two or three days to prevent excessive wilting. Such shade is generally supplied by cotton cloth stretched on light frames made by nailing four plaster laths together at their ends, or by a long strip of the cloth rolled lengthwise above the bed on a temporary

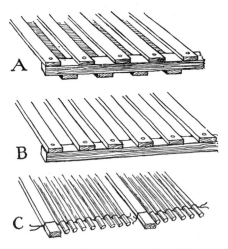

THREE KINDS OF SLAT SHADE
that cause belts of shade to sweep across plants as the sun moves. A. Double lath screen made by nailing laths alternately on upper and lower side of side strips. B. Single lath screen throwing less shade. C. Woven cane screen easily made at home, light and giving fairly dense shade.

wood or wood and wire, or cord, frame raised 6 or 8 in. above the plants.

Out-of-door frames of the first type just described are sometimes used to shade beds of seedlings and rooted cuttings, but more often "lath shades" are employed. These are usually made by first nailing the ends of four laths together to form a square, then nailing other laths at lath-wide intervals from side to side in one or both directions. The former arrangement casts narrow strips, and the latter small squares, of light and shade which change position constantly as the sun moves across

side of each plant, and boards held supported by blocks or bricks. However, such precautions are generally unnecessary with well-grown plants properly planted on cool, cloudy days and in moist soil.

In greenhouses as spring advances and the sun rises higher, the temperature is likely to become so high as to make plants of many kinds "draw" or become "leggy" and weak. Also during summer, plants, even those of tropical origin, left in the

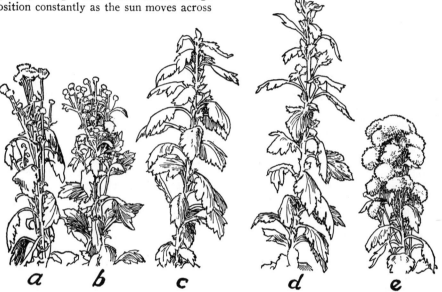

HOW DIFFERENT DAY LENGTHS AFFECT CHRYSANTHEMUM BLOOMING

These plants (variety Bokhara) are of the same age and were grown in the same greenhouse under different degrees of shading with black cloth. Note the variation in flower development. Four extra hours of darkness were given daily to each of the three at the left: (a) 4 to 8 p.m.; (b) 5 to 9 a.m.; (c) 9 a.m. to 1 p.m. The bench where the tall plant (d) grew was not darkened at all, while the plant in full bloom (e) came from a bench darkened each day from 6 p.m. to 7 a.m.

the sky. For permanent use such frames can be made of stronger side members and larger, so as to cover one or even two standard (3 by 6 ft.) hotbeds or cold-frames.

On a large scale, lath screens are made by machine in rolls with flexible wire replacing the cross-boards. These are easily placed upon and removed from temporary or permanent quarters above the beds by unrolling and rolling them up as needed.

In gardens individual newly set plants are often shielded from the sun by various kinds of home-made protectors—such as newspapers rolled into cones, berry boxes, shingles stuck in the ground on the south

house are likely to suffer from excessive heat. The necessary shading is sometimes provided by cloth or slat blinds on rollers inside the house, or by lath or similar frames laid and fastened on the roof outside; but most often it is applied by spraying the glass outside with whitewash, whiting or thin white lead paint. By autumn much of the material will have been removed by scaling off and by rains. The balance must be removed by scrubbing with stiff brushes.

Of recent years the effect of shading upon the flowering season of ornamental plants has been extensively investigated and the remarkable results obtained are being applied to an increasing extent by commercial growers of cut flowers. The advancing or retarding of blossoming by subjecting plants to regular periods of darkness by shading them with opaque black cloth is associated with a natural grouping of such plants into so-called long-day and short-day kinds. Thus certain plants grow most successfully and flower quickest when the normal amount of daylight is regularly augmented by a few hours of electric or other artificial illumination; such plants include those that are essentially midsummer garden materials. Others do best when relatively short days alternate with long nights, and these (which are naturally spring or fall flowering) are aided by darkening their surroundings during the early evening or late morning hours for a part of their growing season.

Under such treatment the fomer flowering seasons of chrysanthemums, dahlias and numerous other garden and greenhouse subjects are being lengthened in both directions, and further interesting developments may well be looked for. As yet, however, shading for this purpose is a commercial greenhouse practice rather than a garden activity, so those interested are referred to the publications of agricultural colleges and experiment stations.

SHADE, PLANTS FOR. See PLANTS FOR SPECIAL PURPOSES.

SHADE TREE COMMISSION. A group of citizens of a county, municipality, etc. appointed to look after the trees of the community, formulate and recommend legislation for their protection, superintend their planting, care and removal when necessary and otherwise provide for the maximum benefits for the citizens from the presence of trees, consistent with other needs and interests. The first such body was apparently created about 1900, and some of the most effective have been in N. J. where, in 1925, a State Federation of Shade Tree Commissions was formed to "establish contact and closer cooperation between the Commissions of the State; encourage an interchange of experience on mutual problems; promote the establishment of municipal and county shade tree commissions; work out a solution of the general problems confronting all such commissions, and encourage and stimulate an intelligent interest and activity on the part of the general public in the need and value of organized shade tree work."

One of the outstanding accomplishments of this Federation was the successful endorsement of a bill "for the licensing and supervision of tree experts" generally called the "Certified Tree Experts' Law," which was enacted by the N. J. Legislature in 1940 after several years of discussion. Conceived and worked on by members of the National Shade Tree Conference, a law of this sort had been sought in various places, but N. J. was the first State to actually get one, though it is expected that its example will be followed in different parts of the country where there is advanced professional and public interest in trees. The federation publishes a monthly bulletin, *The Shade Tree,* at Kearney, N. J.

SHADE TREE CONFERENCE. The National Shade Tree Conferences are annual meetings of scientists and commercial workers in the field of the protection and conservation of shade trees through knowledge of their habits and requirements, the pests, diseases, and other dangers that threaten them, and means of controlling, preventing, or mitigating these troubles. The first one, held about 1924, was or grew out of an informal gathering planned to combine a chance to discuss problems and developments in the field with a social summer meeting. Conferences have since been held at different points throughout the E. part of the country with steadily growing attendance and programs of addresses, demonstrations, round table discussions, and exhibitions of tree care equipment. They have also been the annual conventions of the national organization of tree experts or arborists. From the National Conference came the idea of similar regional meetings for representatives of the profession in the W. and S. Since the Conferences are open only to those concerned, they are only of indirect interest to gardeners. But in contributing new facts about tree care and promoting higher standards for the profession, they have worked for more and better trees around homes and in parks, along highways, and in other public grounds. Information can be obtained from the secretary of the National Shade Tree Conference at Ohio State University, Columbus, O.

SHAGBARK. Common name for *Carya ovata,* one of the hickories; a handsome deciduous tree to 120 ft. with gray bark breaking up into shaggy shreds, pinnate leaves with usually 5 leaflets, and a nearly round nut of excellent flavor. A highly ornamental, picturesque tree for estate or park planting, it is also the best nut-bearing tree for sections where the pecan is not hardy. There are a number of unproved named forms. See CARYA; HICKORY.

SHALLOT. A small, mild-flavored species of onion (*Allium ascalonicum*) used for flavoring, but little grown in the U. S.

SHAMROCK. Common name applied to *Oxalis acetosella,* the European Woodsorrel, and *Trifolium repens,* the White Clover. Both are plants with 3 leaflets, said to have been used by St. Patrick as a symbol for and explanation of the Trinity. And both are extensively used in celebrating St. Patrick's Day in Ireland and other countries. Several other plants having 3 leaflets are claimed to be the true Shamrock, and cress also has its supporters as a candidate for the honor.

SHAMROCK-PEA. Common name for *Parochetus communis,* also known as Blue-oxalis, a low-growing creeper of the Pea Family, with cobalt-blue flowers with pink wings. It is useful as a pot plant and for hanging baskets, as it blooms nearly the whole year. The soil should be a mixture of sand and humus and the pots should be placed in a partially shaded position. Plants can also be grown in a cool sheltered position in the rock garden, but they are of doubtful hardiness N.

SHARPENING GARDEN TOOLS. Four important points are gained by keeping garden tools well sharpened: (1) the work done is more workmanlike; (2) it is done with less effort; (3) the workman can do a larger amount in a given time; and (4) he will be less fatigued at the end of the day or job.

The expression "sharp as a razor" should apply to all knives, shears, saws and other tools used in pruning, in budding and other forms of grafting, and in gathering garden flowers, because the keener the "edge" the cleaner the cut and the quicker the healing—provided, of course, that the cut is made in the right place. See PRUNING.

On the other hand, any spade, hoe, sickle, scythe or other tool used in similar ways that suggests the simile "dull as a hoe" (which never originated in a good gardener's domain), not only reproaches the owner but makes him pay for his short-sightedness. Here especially bright, sharp tools will reduce work, perhaps more than any other one thing.

In using tools, slight, frequent regular attention to sharpening throughout the season is far easier and better than one general, spring or fall sharpening. Usually all that is needed for the larger, heavier implements is a flat file, though a

SAFETY FIRST IN SHARPENING
A better grip and protection for the fingers can be afforded by wrapping the handle of a scythe stone or "rifle" (used also for keeping an edge on sickles, etc.) with a strip of old inner tube, folding back about an inch to form a guard, and tying the whole firmly with twine.

carborundum wheel will save time and effort, especially in keeping spades and hoes in condition. For sickles and scythes a whetstone is best, and for "edged" tools such as knives and shears, an oilstone.

The technique of using whetstone, oilstone or other sharpening agent cannot be satisfactorily explained in a short article. It will well repay any gardener to seek out an experienced practical worker and take some lessons in this important subject. Also manufacturers of saws and other implements often have helpful literature giving detailed directions for the care of their (and, of course, other) tools, that they will gladly supply on request.

If bent corners or nicks occur on spades, hoes and the like, they should be filed down and the blade given an edge, preferably on a short rather than a long bevel because this will be less likely to become injured again on striking unseen obstructions such as stones.

Nicks in knives and shears, usually being due to brittle steel and twisting the blade while making cuts, do not necessarily mean "grinding them out." Small ones may be disregarded because later sharpening will eliminate them; large ones may, however, ruin the tool or make heavy grinding necessary. Nothing can take the place of experience in deciding such a question.

As a precaution and a help in maintaining an edge on tools, clean off all damp earth and grass and remove all moisture after using. This also wards off rust. Wiping with an oily rag after a period of use also prevents rust, keeps the tool blade bright and insures the easiest possible operation. See also TOOLS.

SHASTA DAISY. Common name given to certain hardy, summer-flowering species of chrysanthemum and their improved hybrids; in catalogs it is sometimes applied to *C. leucanthemum.*

Shasta Daisies are sometimes attacked by a leaf blotch as a result of which the leaves are covered with large circular zoned blotches of dead tissue. Spray with bordeaux mixture.

TYPES OF SHASTA DAISIES
These popular flowers, which are in reality summer-blooming chrysanthemums, have been developed into a number of decorative forms since they first appeared in gardens scarcely a generation ago.

SHEARS. In gardening, a cutting tool which consists (1) of a beveled blade, pivoted and operating against a flattened "anvil" or (2) of two beveled blades facing each other and similarly pivoted. They are used for various cutting tasks, as gathering flowers or fruits, pruning, thinning, hedge trimming, edging of beds and borders and so on.

Countless styles and sizes of one-hand and two-hand shears (the latter often called lopping shears or "loppers") are obtainable at garden supply stores, some of them excellent, and others objectionable for one or more reasons such as poor design or material, faulty or cheap construction, etc.

When choosing pruning shears the following features should be noted or sought:

1. First class steel in the blades, because a keen edge is essential to good work and to prevent unnecessary damage to the plant being pruned.

2. The tool should work freely and, after a cut has been made, open promptly through the action of a spring. The style of spring is mainly a personal preference; it should be sufficiently, but not too, strong and so shaped and attached that it is not likely to catch in twigs, snap out of place or pinch the user's hand.

3. The blades when closed should unite to form one narrow point that can be easily inserted between branches without barking them.

4. The handles should be alike and without projections so that the tool can easily be reversed in the hand, allowing the cutting blade to be placed against the plant part from which a piece is to be severed; this avoids bruising that part.

5. The blade should not enter a slot but should engage its opposing jaw like the blades of a scissors (or close down on it like a knife on an anvil), because slots are likely to become clogged and interfere with speedy operation.

6. For general tree work pruning shears should be fairly heavy. A 10-in. size is suitable for an average man; for women and children smaller sizes are better and these are also better (because less tiring) for trimming twigs and small branches and for flower gathering. A special type of shears for picking flowers, grapes, etc., grasps and holds the cut stem so as to prevent dropping blossom or fruit.

Two-handled shears are also of many styles and sizes. Those in which slender short metal shanks are inserted in long wooden handles are all objectionable because, in spite of ferrules, they are weakest where they should be strongest. In the best style only the hand grips are of wood, the blades being extensions of the lever-handles.

Unless shears (especially lopping blades) are kept sharp, they are prone to injure the tree on which used. They should not be used to cut branches that are obviously larger than they were made for. A pruning saw will handle these more easily, and with less danger of injuring the tree. See PRUNING; TOOLS.

Grass shears are mostly single-hand clippers. They may work like spring-equipped scissors, they may be made of one piece of spring steel, so shaped as to keep the blades apart except when hand pressure is applied, or they may be so shaped and pivoted that the blades work horizontally as the handles are worked vertically in a somewhat easier position. One such device includes a long handle and lever arrangement that permits the operator to stand erect while trimming grass edges.

Hedge shears are mostly two-hand tools with blades about as long as the handles, so that, operated like scissors, they make a long cut and permit rapid work. Recently electrically operated shears of various styles have been placed upon the market. Some have series of teeth that work back and forth like those of a mowing-machine; others have motor-driven curved blades that revolve at high speed. Where current is available within the range of the 100 ft. or longer cable supplied with these tools they are, though rather heavy, great time savers. They are not suitable for other than light work or small growth.

SHEATH. Any tubular part surrounding or encasing another part; as the leaves of the bromeliads which sheathe one another; or the leaf-base surrounding the stem in the grasses.

SHEEP-BERRY. A common name for *Viburnum lentago,* a large hardy native shrub with white flowers and blue-black berries covered with a bloom.

SHEEP-LAUREL. A common name for *Kalmia augustifoli,* small rose-flowered evergreen shrub of E. N. America, the leaves of which are liked by sheep but poisonous to them; hence sometimes called Lambkill.

SHEEP MANURE. A quick-acting natural or organic fertilizer, convenient to use whether freshly obtained from the farmyard or secured in dried and pulverized form as it is often advertised and sold. Containing, on the average, about 2.25 per cent nitrogen, 1 per cent phosphoric acid and 2 per cent potash, sheep manure is rather more valuable than horse manure and also less liable to ferment and lose its nitrogen in the form of ammonia. At the same time it is a drier and lighter manure than cow or pig manure and can therefore be added to either of them to good advantage. When used alone it can well be applied as a top-dressing (which see) and cultivated in beside the plant rows or around the individual plants; or it can be used to make an effective liquid manure, which see.

SHEEPS-BIT. A common name for *Jasione perennis,* also known as Sheep- or

Shepherds-scabious, a small herbaceous perennial with blue flowers in globular heads.

SHELL-FLOWER. Common name for 3 widely differing plants: (1) *Alpinia speciosa,* a perennial herb of the Ginger Family with fragrant white purplish-tinged flowers mottled with brownish red; (2) *Molucella laevis,* an old-fashioned annual of the Mint Family with fragrant white flowers; and (3) *Tigridia pavonia,* a bulbous plant of the Iris Family with yellow and purple-spotted blossoms.

SHELTERS. See GARDEN SHELTERS.

SHEPHERDIA (she-pur'-di-ah). Shrubs or small trees of N. America, belonging to the Oleaster Family. They

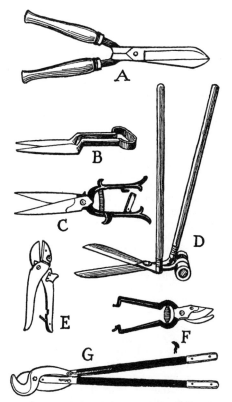

STRONG SHEARS FOR GOOD SERVICE
A. Standard hedge clipping shears—use with a guiding line to get a smooth surface. B, C. Two types of grass or edging shears. D. Edging shears on wheels are easy on the back. E, F. Two good types of pruning shear—if kept sharp, as all tools should be. In (E) the blade cuts down onto a soft metal "anvil." G. All-metal lopping shears with compound hinge action, needed for heavy tree or hedgerow work; they are much stronger than the customary wooden handled ferrule type.

are very hardy, able to withstand extreme cold and dry conditions, and do well near the seaside. Male and female flowers are borne on separate plants. Propagated by seeds, best sown in fall.

S. *argentea* (Buffalo-berry) is a tall thorny shrub, with silvery leaves and red oval edible fruits, valued for jellies and conserves. It is very attractive for contrast in a mixed shrub planting, and is a useful hedge plant in the N. W. S. *canadensis* is a twiggy thornless shrub to 8 ft., with leaves green above and silvery mixed with brown scales beneath. It is a useful shrub for dry rocky banks.

SHIELD FERN. Common name given to a large group of ferns on account of the shape of the indusium. They are now placed in the genus Dryopteris (which see) and are also known as Wood Ferns. They include several species from 2 to 4 ft. tall, native to America and of easy cultivation in woods soil, if well-drained, and shade. The best sorts are the Toothed Wood Fern, with deeply cut fronds, much used by florists; and the Marginal Shield Fern, also known as the Evergreen Wood Fern, which has leathery, blue-green fronds and conspicuous fruit dots.

SHIELDWORT. Common name for *Peltaria alliacea*, a member of the Mustard Family. It is a perennial herb 1 ft. or more tall, bearing small white clustered flowers with an onion-like odor, and almost round, flat seed-pots which give the plant its name. It is occasionally planted in the border for its profusion of white flowers in the summer. Easily grown in any good garden soil, it is increased by division or by seed.

SHIFTING. The transfer of plants from pot to pot, usually to successively larger sizes. See FLOWER POT; POTTING; TRANSPLANTING.

SHINLEAF. Common name for Pyrola, a genus of small evergreen herbs of the Heath Family, growing from root stocks and bearing white, purple, or greenish flowers at the top of a slender stalk. As they need very acid soil, it is impossible to grow them in the average border; but if very carefully handled they can be transplanted and colonized in the wild garden in a soil kept continuously acid with a mulch of oak leaves. They are likely to do well under pine trees. *P. elliptica* has white flowers; *P. rotundifolia*, the European form, has white flowers; *P. chlor-*

antha, with greenish-white flowers, is found in both N. America and Europe. One-flowered-shinleaf is *Moneses uniflora.*

SHOE-BLACK-PLANT. A name sometimes given to *Hibiscus rosa-sinensis* (Chinese Hibiscus) because the flowers are used in some tropical regions for dyeing hair and blacking shoes.

SHOOTING STAR. A common name for the genus Dodecatheon, small American perennials with clusters of cyclamen-like flowers. Good rock-garden plants.

SHORT-DAY PLANT. Term applied to plants in which flower bud formation is normally initiated by relatively short day lengths (10 to 12 hours) and suppressed by exposure to longer day lengths.

Typical plants of this category are Chrysanthemum, Poinsettia, Cosmos (late varieties), certain varieties of Dahlias, African marigold, Ageratum, Tithonia, most of the Goldenrods, most of the native Asters, and Aquilegia.

Such plants can be forced into earlier bloom by shading them with opaque black cloth. This is a common commercial practice with growers of chrysanthemums, especially under glass. The shading is started just prior to the time of normal bud-setting, the cloth covering being applied at an appropriate hour in the afternoon and left on till nightfall. The practice is continued for several weeks, the length of time and the time of starting the shading depending upon the latitude and variety being grown. Conversely, the use of artificial light to supplement daylight will delay bud setting in this type of flower. By following these practices, a certain variety of chrysanthemum may be brought in early by shading, at a normal period by treating it naturally, and at a later period by the use of supplementary artificial light.

See also LONG-DAY PLANT; PHOTOPERIODISM; SHADE.

SHORTIA (shaur'-ti-ah). A genus of low evergreen stemless herbs of the Diapensia Family, with nodding white, bell-shaped flowers. They are delightful little plants for the rock garden, or as an underplanting for rhododendrons and kalmias. They require a shaded position in acid soil, rich in humus, and should be mulched regularly with oak leaves. They seldom set seed and should be propagated by division or runners. The American species *S. galacifolia* (Oconee Bells) has roundish, wavy-margined, rather leathery leaves, similar to those of Galax, and charming white flowers nearly 1 in. across; its var. *rosea* has rose-pink blossoms. First discovered in 1788 in the mountains of Carolina, it has never been found wild anywhere else. *S. uniflora* (Nippon Bells), native to Japan, differs only in the more heart-shaped leaves.

Another plant sometimes listed as *Shortia californica* is the Composite, *Baeria coronaria,* popularly called Gold-fields.

SHOT-HOLE. A symptom of disease in plants, that may be a result of fungus infection or of spray injury. It results from the dropping out of dead areas, making the foliage appear as if peppered with shot. Certain plants, especially cherries and peaches, are more inclined than others to show such an effect.

SHOWER-OF-GOLD. A common name for *Cytisus scoparius* (Scotch-broom), a semi-hardy shrub with abundant yellow pea-like flowers.

SHRIMP-PLANT. Common name for an interesting greenhouse plant, *Beloperone guttata,* whose many branches are terminated with pinkish overlapping bracts enveloping the inconspicuous flowers.

SHRUB-ALTHEA. A common name for *Hibiscus syriacus,* also called Rose-mallow and Rose-of-Sharon, a tall shrub with large white, pink or purple, single or double flowers set close against the erect leafy branches. (See illustrations, Plates 1 and 27.)

SHRUBS. Shrubs are woody plants of bushy habit in varying sizes, developing several stems instead of a single trunk, as does a tree. The use of shrubs in garden making is, of course, taken for granted; everyone knows about shrubs in a general way. But far too often they have not received the consideration to which they are rightly entitled. Considering their permanent character and importance in the garden and landscape picture, less imagination has been displayed in the selection and arrangement of shrubs than in that of any other group of garden plants. As a result, too many plantings are dull and uninteresting for the greater part of the year.

One reason for this is the monotonous repetition of a few well known kinds. Every shrub has a value for some particular use and place, but when planted without regard to position, or with little or no consideration given to harmonious arrangement, a pleasing result can scarcely be expected. One need only point to the indiscriminate over-planting of the sterile form of *Hydrangea paniculata.*

Every place has its own special problem as to what and where to plant. However,

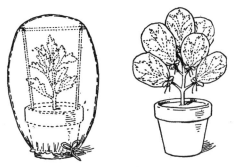

ARTIFICIAL DARKNESS
Two methods of excluding light from a plant. A bag may be supported so as to enclose the entire plant, or smaller bags may be tied around shoots.

regardless of the purpose for which shrubs are to be used in the garden, there is a wealth of material to choose from, and no good excuse for the small variety found in the shrub plantings of most localities.

SELECTING AND USING SHRUBS

Before the selection is finally made there are several important things to be considered: first, the location and exposure; whether high or low, and whether open to air and sunlight, or subject to various degrees of shade. Then the character of the soil: whether naturally heavy and retentive of moisture, or light and dry. The amount of space to be filled determines the proportion of dwarf, medium, and large growing kinds.

Among the various purposes for which shrubs can be used, which range from carpeting the ground to clothing a high wall, are: To screen out unsightly objects or to tie the foundation walls of a building to the ground. To display individual charm and beauty as a single specimen; to group together for mass effect; or to squeeze close together in hedge form. To cheer with flowers before the official arrival of spring, or later to prolong the garden interest with a bright display of fruits or colored stems after the icy breath of winter has laid low nearly all other plants.

Soil and Planting. While most shrubs, with the exception of those belonging to the Heath Family, are not specially particular as to the composition of the soil, they do appreciate thorough preparation in the form of deep digging, especially where there is a hard sub-soil. This is really more important than adding manure at planting time, and it pays to break up the soil at least 2 ft. deep. The shrubs are likely to be in their station for a long time, and feeding can be taken care of later on when established. However, the addition of organic matter in the form of really old, rotted manure or leafmold, placed below the roots at planting time, will not be amiss.

Planting of most kinds can be safely done in the fall when growth is mature, except perhaps in low wet places. A generous mulch of littery manure or half-rotted leaves will protect the plants from the bad effects of freezing and thawing, so common in our northern winters. Spring planting can be started as soon as the soil is dry enough to work freely.

How to Select Kinds. The very wealth of material makes the selection a matter of careful study. In a large garden it is possible to use greater variety and to plant for mass effect. For a small garden make the selection from a few choice and favorite kinds. In planting shrub borders a common fault is a too close spacing for proper development of good growth, although it is recognized that the individual plant is not expected to develop as fully when grouped as when planted as a single specimen. Close planting for immediate effect is all very well if thinning out and rearrangement is taken care of as soon as crowding takes place. Too often, however, this is entirely neglected, and the resulting tangle is not only a mass but a mess. The proper spacing will depend of course on the ultimate size of the particular kinds. It will vary from 2 to 3 ft. with the smaller growers, up to 6 ft. or more for the more vigorous kinds. Some of the more robust herbaceous perennials make good temporary fillers among shrubs.

There is much to be considered in shrub planting besides the great burst of growth and flower in the early part of the season. Some thought should be given to year-round effects, which means a study of form, foliage and fruiting values, as well as floral display. An attempt to secure brilliant pictures with fall coloring is well worth while. Some kinds gain added value by holding their leaves green for some time after others are bare. In this connection the hybrid snowberry, *Symphoricarpos chenaulti,* might well replace some of the expressively common bridal-wreath, *Spiraea vanhouttei.* Then there are the numerous berried kinds that have continued interest long after the leaves have fallen.

Arrangement Hints. Something to consider in the grouping of various kinds is harmony of composition with respect to habit of growth and quality of foliage. A gradual transition from coarse to fine foliage is more restful than too great a contrast. In arranging the planting a more pleasing effect is obtained by grouping three or more of a kind together and avoiding the appearance of lining up. Certain large upright growers such as *Caragana arborescens, Chionanthus virginica, Cornus alternifolia, Cotoneaster actuifolia* var. *villosula, Halesia carolina, Hibiscus syriacus,* and *Viburnum sieboldi,* may be used to good effect singly as accent plants to relieve flatness. The use of dwarf and spreading kinds in the front of a border, to hide the bare legs of taller specimens and tie the planting to the ground, must also be considered. Such examples as *Kerria japonica, Itea virginica, Stephanandra incisa, Symphoricarpos chenaulti, Spirea thunbergi, S. bumalda, Deutzia gracilis* and *Abelia grandiflora,* are admirable for the purpose.

Pruning. The general appearance and well-being of shrubs depend a good deal on the manner in which pruning is practiced. Every one knows that pruning is necessary, but many do not understand the principles which should govern the use of pruning shears. Too often the natural form is marred by a general trimming instead of a judicious thinning out of old wood sufficient to keep up a renewal of vigorous young growth. Except where desirable for architectural effects, sheared specimens all over the place give a spotty and unnatural appearance.

Study the habits of the individual kind before beginning any pruning operation. In general, shrubs which flower before midsummer should receive most of their pruning *immediately after flowering.* This will consist chiefly in the removal of a certain amount of old growth from the centre, and perhaps a little shortening back to suit the position. Those which flower later need pruning *before growth starts,* as their flowers are borne on wood of the current season's gowth.

In dealing with neglected or overgrown specimens it is sometimes necessary to be very drastic, and to cut everything back to within a foot or so of the ground just before growth starts. Sad-looking specimens can be wonderfully renewed in this way, especially if the soil is stirred up and enriched at the same time. In pruning shrubs for the effect of colored stems in winter, they may be entirely cut back close to the ground in spring. If the gap thus made for a time is objectionable, cut back only a part each year.

A style of planting now popular is that known as foundation planting (which see), in which the chief object is to tie the building to the ground and create a well furnished appearance in harmony with the architectural style. This requires careful consideration in selecting plants for year-round effect. Foliage and form are more important than the fleeting floral display, and it is not generally necessary to completely hide the foundation walls. Pleasing and interesting arrangements can be worked out with selections of broad-leaved evergreens, dwarf forms of the coniferous type, and the choicest dwarf and medium growing deciduous shrubs.

Shrubs for Various Purposes

The groups suggested below are not to be regarded as complete for every place and purpose, but rather as examples. In favored climates a much wider selection of course is possible.

BROAD-LEAVED EVERGREENS. Unfortunately only a comparatively few can be safely used in N. gardens, which makes these few all the more important. They are worth special care, and mostly prefer a sheltered and partly shaded place. Examples are the native rhododendrons and certain hybrids; mountain-laurel, *Leucothoë catesbaei;* and the native and Japanese species of Pieris. The many forms of heather (Calluna) are fine to furnish sandy places in the open, as are several species of heath (Erica), though not quite as hardy. The native sand-myrtle (Leiophyilum) looks well clumped in front of azaleas, and a healthy patch of trailing

arbutus would be choice in any garden where it could be made to thrive. Other prostrate and easier plants in this group are the bearberry and the partridgeberry. All the foregoing abhor lime in the soil and object to surface cultivation. A mulch of peat moss keeps the surface in good condition.

Several of the evergreen species of Euonymus are hardy and useful for various purposes, from carpeting bare spots under trees to clothing walls, making informal hedges or good individual specimens. The related *Pachistima canbyi* makes a very desirable evergreen mat. In a sheltered place the evergreen barberries and the allied mahonias may do very well. The same can be said of box and certain of the hollies. The only evergreen viburnum that can stand much frost is *V. rhytidophyllum,* a very handsome shrub where it can be grown. The lovely *Daphne cneorum* is a choice plant for rock gardens and edging foundation plantings.

SHRUBS WITH LASTING FOLIAGE. Deciduous shrubs which retain their leaves green late in the fall are often desirable, and the following are good in this as well as other respects: *Acanthopanax sieboldianus, Buddleia alternifolia, Cotoneaster hupehensis, C. simonsi, Forsythia spectabilis, F. viridissima, Kerria japonica, Kolkwitzia amabilis, Ligustrum vulgare, L. amurense, L. ovalifolium, Lonicera fragrantissima, L. morrowi, L. maacki* var. *podocarpa, L. syringantha, L. xylosteum, Lycium chinese, Rhamnus frangula, Stephanandra incisa, Symphoricarpos chenaulti, Viburnum alnifolium, V. lantana,* and *V. tomentosum.*

SHRUBS FOR SHADY PLACES. The following do well in shady places under ordinary soil conditions: Large shrubs— *Ligustrum amurense, L. vulgare, L. obtusifolium, Viburnum alnifolium, V. dentatum, V. cassinoides, Benzoin aestivale, Cornus alternifolia, C. mas, C. stolonifera, Berberis vulgaris, Euonymus* (any of the deciduous kinds), *Hamamelis virginiana,* and *Philadelphus,* which may not flower freely but grows well in shade. Medium and smaller growers: *Berberis thunbergi, Deutzia gracilis, Kerria japonica, Rhodotypos tetrapetala, Clethra alnifolia, Calycanthus floridus, Diervilla lonicera,* all kinds of *Forsythia, Hydrangea radiata, Rubus odoratus, Symphoricarpos albus,* and *Zanthorrhiza apiifolia.*

EARLY FLOWERING SHRUBS. In regions where winter clamps down hard, no flowers are more welcome than those which appear early in the year. A few shrubs belong with this advanced group which herald the season's display. *Dephne mezereum* sometimes opens its fragrant flowers in February. Some of the witch-hazels may show even before that, such as *Hamamelis vernalis, H. japonica* and *H. mollis.* The showy flowers of the related *Corylopsis* open in advance of the leaves, *C. gotoana* being considered the hardiest and best. One of the several good qualitics of *Lonicera fragrantissima* is that its sweetly scented flowers make their presence known before winter has quite gone. *Prinsepia sinensis* is distinguished by its early leaves and flowers, and often in March its arching shoots are clustered with soft yellow bloom. A dwarf early bloomer with yellow flowers is *Dirca palustris,* and two tall ones are *Benzoin aestivale* and *Cornus mas. Forsythia ovata* is the earliest of this showy group. *Viburnum carlesi* is a delightful shrub that should be in every garden for its fragrant and handsome early flowers.

SUMMER AND LATE FLOWERING SHRUBS. After the great burst of spring and early summer bloom has passed there still remain a few flowering kinds to carry along the display well into autumn. For mid-summer there are several forms of *Spiraea japonica* and *S. bumalda,* particularly the var. Anthony Waterer. *Cytisus nigricans* and *C. supinus* are neat shrubs for a sunny place, as are also the garden forms of *Potentila fruticosa,* which continue in flower more or less all summer. Of larger growth and very showy are *Hypericum aureum* and *H. prolificum. Itea virginica* and, later, *Clethra alnifolia* are conspicuous with their fragrant white flowers in erect racemes. *Hydrangea quercifolia* is outstanding with its huge panicles, and *H. radiata* with its flat white heads and leaves silvery beneath gives a cool appearance in a shady place. Later in the season *H. paniculata* is conspicuous with its long loose white panicles. *Stewartia pentagyna* is so beautiful in midsummer that one marvels at its rarity in gardens. *Abelia grandiflora* begins to show well at this time and continues until frost. The forms of *Hibiscus syriacus* give a striking display of color in late summer. *Clerodendron trichotomum* is valued for its late flowers,

which are quickly followed by colorful fruit.

In some sections the following are subject to more or less winter-killing of the top but they usually flower well on young shoots from below: *Buddleia davidi, Caryopteris incana, Elshotzia stauntoni, Lespedeza formosa,* and *Vitex agnus-castus.*

SHRUBS WITH COLORFUL FRUIT. There is a wealth of good material in this group, and it is rightfully receiving more attention from planters, as the several kinds do much to prolong the interest beyond the actual growing season. Such genera as Berberis, Cotoneaster, Cornus, Euonymus, Ilex, Lonicera, Ligustrum and Viburnum contain many species that will give a varied and colorful display, in some cases lasting throughout the winter. Some of the shrubby roses, such as *R. rubrifolia, P. rugosa, R. multiflora, R. moyesi* and *R. omeiensis,* are also valuable in this respect. Species of Callicarpa have lilac and violet-colored fruits, and the brightest blue is found in *Symplocos paniculata. Hippophaë rhamnoides* is outstanding with orange-colored fruit, and some of the species of Eleagnus have orange and silvery fruits. *Symphoricarpos albus* has the most conspicuous white fruit.

SHRUBS WITH COLORED STEMS AND TWIGS. This group is outstanding for providing color masses in winter, and the intensity of the color increases as spring approaches. They are often well placed in association with waterside plantings, but will do well in drier places. The brightest coloring is developed in the open. Various dogwoods and willows have brilliant red and yellow stems. *Kerria japonica* and *Forsythia viridissima* show well with stems of bright green, and *Berberis dictyophylla,* with old and new shoots, shows reddish brown and white.

SHRUB YELLOW-ROOT. Common name for *Xanthoriza apiifolia,* a little shrub 2 ft. or less tall, of the Buttercup Family. It bears drooping racemes of small, star-shaped, brown-purple flowers in early spring, and its sharply cut leaves turn a clear yellow in autumn. The yellow wood of root and stems gives the plant its name. Producing a profusion of suckers, it is a good subject for under-planting the shrubbery border, or as a ground-cover in damp shady positions, or even in sandy soil. But it is not reliably hardy in the N. It will grow from seed, but as the seedlings are delicate and hard to handle, it is easier to divide old, vigorously growing plants, the pieces soon taking hold and spreading rapidly.

SIBBALDIA (si-bal'-di-ah). A genus of low growing perennials of the Rose Family, occasionally used as carpeting plants in the rock or alpine garden. *S. procumbens*, which hugs the ground, has 3-part leaves and small yellow flowers and is native to the arctic and alpine regions of Eurasia and N. America. It may be grown from seed or division.

SIBERIAN PEA-TREE. A common name for Caragana, a genus of hardy shrubs or small trees. See PEA-TREE.

SIBERIAN WALLFLOWER. Catalog name for a perennial bearing brilliant orange flowers over a long season, commonly listed as *Cherianthus allioni,* but properly *Erysimum asperum.* See WALLFLOWER.

SIBTHORPIA (sib-thaur'-pi-ah). A genus of small trailing perennial herbs of the Figwort Family with roundish leaves and yellowish or red flowers. They are frequently grown under glass in the N. but used as a ground-cover in mild climates. They root readily at the nodes and may be propagated by cuttings in sand or by division. *S. europaea,* a small creeping plant with yellowish-pink flowers grows in cool shady woods in England and on the Continent and with its slender graceful habit of growth is there frequently cultivated as a ground-cover in bog gardens or rock gardens. In this country it is a good subject for hanging baskets in the greenhouse or sun porch.

SICANA (si-kay'-nah) *odorifera.* A vine belonging to the Cucumber Family, known as Curuba and, more commonly, as Cassabanana, which see.

SIDALCEA (si-dal'-see-ah). A genus of perennial and annual herbs of the Mallow Family, growing 2 or 3 ft. tall and bearing white, pink or purple flowers like miniature hollyhocks, in spikes or clusters. Grown from seed, cuttings or divisions, it should be planted in rich sandy soil. The cultivated species are perennial and many of them bloom over a long season. *S. malvaeflora* (Checkerbloom) has rosy blossoms in many-flowered racemes; its var. *atropurpurea* has purple flowers, and var. *listeri* mallow-like blossoms of silky pink. *S. nervata* has rose flowers 1½ in.

across. *S. candida* is a pure white form from the Rocky Mountains. A number of horticultural hybrids are offered as *S. hybrida,* some having attractive pink or satiny-rose flowers.

SILENE (sy-lee'-nee). Plants of the Pink Family, known as Catchfly or Campion, the genus comprising many species of annual, biennial, or perennial herbs, some of them clustered, others erect, and some vine-like in form. (See illustration, Plate 45.) Many have showy flowers—red, pink, or white—and are of great decorative value in the border or rock garden; a few are good greenhouse subjects. They have a long season of bloom, through the summer and well into the fall, and are easily grown in a light, warm soil. The annuals, notably *S. armeria* and *S. pendula,* are increased by seed, and the perennials from seed and by division and cuttings. If the seed of the annual sorts is sown in the fall much earlier bloom will be secured.

USEFUL SPECIES

S. armeria (Sweet-william Catchfly). A smooth plant to 2 ft. with clusters of rose or white flowers from July to September. The seed should be sown where the plants are to stand in the border in the fall or very early spring.

pendula. Grows to 10 in. with soft hairy foliage and flesh-colored flowers in graceful, drooping racemes in summer. Var. *alba* is pure white; var. *bonnetti* is purplish.

maritima. An attractive plant to 1 ft., the foliage having a bloom and the white flowers balloon-like calyxes. There is a very double variety.

alpestris (Alpine Catchfiy). From 4 to 6 in., with sticky foliage and glistening white flowers from June to August. It is best suited to the rock garden or the edge of the border.

virginica (Fire-pink). To 2 ft. the brilliant scarlet or crimson flowers with notched petals are borne in nodding clusters from May until early fall. It provides an excellent note of color in the border and does well in the wild garden.

caroliniana (Wild-pink). Growing to 10 in. with white or rose flowers in flat clusters in spring, it is good in the border as well as in the wild garden. Sometimes listed as *S. pennsylvanica.*

schafta (Moss Campion). Grows to only

6 in. with soft-haired leaves in rosettes and rose or purple flowers. Fine for the rock garden.

hookeri. To 5 in.; the beautifully fringed rose or salmon pink flowers are 2 in. across. Difficult to grow in the E. but where successful remarkably fine in the rock garden.

laciniata (Mexican Campion or Indianpink). To 5 ft. with glowing red flowers. The dwarf form (var. *purpusi*) has cardinal-red flowers and is much better for the border than the type.

regia (Royal Catchfly). To 4 ft. with deep, glowing scarlet flowers in panicles in midsummer. Exceptionally fine when naturalized in the wild garden.

stellata (Starry Campion). A woodland plant with white, nodding flowers to 3 ft. tall all summer. It is more appropriate in the wild garden than in the border.

acaulis (Cushion-pink or Moss Campion). Hardly more than 2 in. high, it has reddish purple flowers ½ in. across over a long summer season. Very good in the rock garden. There is a white form, var. *alba.*

pumilio. To 3 in.; a low tufted plant with rose flowers, 1½ in. across.

quadrifida. To 4 in. with white flowers with 4-lobed petals.

flavescens. To 8 in.; foliage is yellowish hairy and flowers are bright yellow.

compacta. A biennial to 2 ft. best increased by seed. Foliage has a bloom, and pink flowers are in heads 3 in. across, surrounded by the upper leaves.

SILK-COTTON-TREE. Common name for *Ceiba pentandra,* a tropical tree to 120 ft. belonging to the Bombax Family. It has immense widespreading branches, a very large buttressed trunk, sometimes 30 ft. in diameter, compound, deciduous leaves, and white or rose-colored flowers (the petals hairy outside), followed by capsular fruit, woolly inside and containing many woolly seeds. The cottony material inside the seed capsules is the kapok of commerce widely used for stuffing pillows, life-preservers, etc. Interesting as well as valuable, this tree is frequently planted as a shade tree in warm climates.

The name Silk-cotton-tree is also applied to *Bombax malabaricum,* another member of the same tropical family whose seed capsules are similarly lined with silky lint. The bark of some species of Bombax also produces a fibre.

SILK-OAK. Common name for *Grevillea robusta,* an Australian tree, seedling specimens of which are grown as pot plants in greenhouses for their delicate foliage.

SILK-TASSEL-BUSH. Common name for the genus Garrya, evergreen ornamental shrubs of W. America, where, when cultivated, they demand a sunny, sheltered situation.

SILK-TREE. Common name for *Albizzia julibrissin,* a unique ornamental Asiatic tree, allied to Acacia; it has become established in parts of S. U. S.

SILK-VINE. The genus Periploca, consisting of mostly twining shrubs from warm countries, one or two species of which are fairly hardy as far north as Mass. They need well-drained soil in a sunny position, and are well adapted to clothe arbors and trellis-work. Propagated by seeds, cuttings and layers.

P. graeca is a vigorous deciduous vine to 40 ft., with dark green shining leaves held late, and loose clusters of greenish and brownish-purple flowers. *P. sepium,* a shorter and more slender grower, with smaller leaves and flowers, is the hardiest; its leaves turn yellow in the fall.

SILKWEED. Another name for the genus Asclepias, or Milkweed; some species are grown for ornament, while others are familiar pasture and roadside weeds, sometimes troublesome or even pernicious.

SILPHIUM (sil'-fi-um). A genus of tall coarse perennials with yellow sunflower-like heads, commonly called Rosinweed, which see.

SILT. A term applied to a soil type intermediate in texture between sand and clay. While, when rubbed between the fingers, it has a soft smooth feeling like clay, rather than a gritty feeling like sand, it does not tend to puddle and bake to the same extent as clay, nor does it dry out as quickly as sand. Ordinarily, however, it is deficient in humus or organic matter, so can be greatly improved for crop production purposes by having manure, peat moss, leafmold or other vegetable matter incorporated with it. As it usually contains a fair amount of mineral matter it is a good basis for a useful garden soil. In fact, a good silt loam is an excellent type for most garden plants except those that are expected to make quick, early spring growth.

SILVER-BELL. A common name for the genus Halesia, which includes some most attractive hardy and half-hardy shrubs and trees, covered with drooping, bell-shaped white flowers in spring. Also called Snowdrop-tree.

SILVERBERRY. Common name for *Elaeagnus argentea,* a silvery-leaved shrub of N. U. S. and Canada with inconspicuous but fragrant flowers in spring, followed by silvery fruits.

SILVER BRAKE (*Pteris argyrea*). A highly decorative greenhouse fern, marked by bands of silvery white, requiring subdued light and plenty of peat with some sand.

SILVER FERN. A name given to species of the genera Cheilanthes, Gymnogramma, and Notholaena on account of the silvery whitish powder or hairs that cover the under side of the fronds and retard evaporation, as they are all native to rather dry climates. Suitable for cool greenhouse, except in the S. W., where some are native and can be grown outdoors. Water from below only and give plenty of indirect light.

SILVER-LACE-VINE. A common name for *Polygonum auberti,* a fast-growing, woody, twining vine with profuse, greenish-white, fragrant flowers.

SILVER-ROD. Common name for *Solidago bicolor,* a species of Goldenrod (which see) with whitish instead of yellow flowers.

SILVER-TREE. Common name for *Leucadendron argenteum,* a S. African tree popular in Calif., with large leaves closely set along the branches and densely covered with silky white hairs.

SILVER-VINE. Common name for *Actinidia polygama,* a twining shrub with variegated white or yellowish leaves, inconspicuous flowers and yellow fruit.

SILVER-WEED. Common name for *Potentilla anserina,* a tufted herb which spreads by runners; the leaves silky underneath, the yellow flowers on long stems. The name is also applied to the genus Argyreia, which see.

SILVERY SPLEENWORT (*Athyrium acrostichoides*). A choice American wood fern, with once-pinnate, 2- to 3-ft. fronds, whose under sides are covered with whitish fruit-dots that gleam in the wind and give the plant its name. Of easy culture in good woods soil and shade.

SILYBUM (sil'-i-bum). A genus of thistle-like herbs of the Composite Family, having spiny white-spotted leaves and large heads of purplish flowers. They grow well in a sunny spot in any good garden soil and will bloom the first year from seed. *S. marianum* (St. Marys, Blessed, Holy or Milk Thistle), an annual or biennial up to 4 ft., has spiny glossy leaves and rose-purple heads of flowers to 2½ in. across, surrounded by spiny bracts. An Old-World plant, it has become naturalized in Calif.

SINNINGIA (si-nin'-ji-ah) *speciosa.* A species of showy greenhouse pot plants which florists call Gloxinia, which see.

SISYRINCHIUM (sis-i-rin'-ki-um). A genus of American grass-like perennials with small blue or yellow flowers. See BLUE-EYED-GRASS.

SIUM (sy'-um). A genus of the Parsley Family comprising herbs with small white flowers in umbels and much-divided leaves. One species, *S. sisarum* (Skirret), growing to 3 ft., is cultivated for its edible tuberous roots which are used as a vegetable. Plant seed in fall or early spring in rich soil; the roots can be dug in the fall and stored like beets in a cool place, or left in the ground over winter.

SKIMMIA (skim'-i-ah). Evergreen shrubs from Asia, belonging to the Rue Family. They are handsome dwarf shrubs of slow growth, well able to stand city conditions where hardy. They prefer a rather moist loam and partial shade. In the N. they are not hardy, but are sometimes grown in pots for their attractive foliage and decorative berries. They grow well in sandy loam with peat or leafmold. Propagated by seeds or cuttings.

S. japonica, the most commonly grown species, is a dense shrub to 5 ft., with pale yellowish green leaves. In this species male and female flowers are borne on separate plants, the staminate flowers being very fragrant. One or two of these plants should be planted with a group in order to insure a crop of the round scarlet berries, which remain in good condition for some time. *S. reevesiana* is of dwarfer habit, with dark green leaves, perfect flowers, and oval dark red berries freely produced.

SKULLCAP. Common name for the genus Scutellaria, consisting mostly of perennials 1 ft. or less in height, bearing small 2-lipped flowers of purple, yellow, red or blue. Several species are suitable for rock gardens or borders.

SKUNK-CABBAGE. Common name for *Symplocarpus foetidus,* a coarse perennial herb of the Arum Family, with heavy roots, broad leaves 3 ft. long and a bloom consisting of a spadix or spike rising from a brownish colored calla-like spathe, interesting in form but with a heavy fetid odor. Skunk-cabbages, found in low swampy places throughout E. N. America, are often transferred to the wild or bog garden for the ornamental effect of the large leaf clumps and the colored inflorescence.

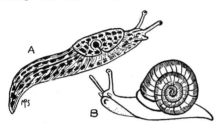

SLUGS AND SNAILS
Slugs, illustrated here by the black land slug (A) are much more of a pest in American gardens than their shell-carrying relatives the snails, of which a typical specimen is shown at (B).

Yellow-skunk-cabbage is *Lysichitum camtschatensis,* another member of the Arum Family, a native of W. America and E. Asia. The leaves are 5 ft. long, both spadix and spathe are a clear bright yellow and the odor is not as disagreeable as in the true skunk-cabbage.

SKUNKWEED. Common name for *Polemonium confertum,* a low growing, blue-flowered perennial of the S. Rocky Mountain region; also for *Navarretia squarrosa,* an evil-smelling annual of W. N. America.

SKYFLOWER. A common name for *Duranta repens,* sometimes called Pigeon-berry, a shrub or tree with sometimes drooping branches, small lilac flowers and yellow fruits.

SLAT HOUSE. A garden (or commercial plant grower's) structure made of timber framework covered with lath so spaced as to give broken shade beneath. Also called lath house, which see.

SLIME FLUX. A fluid or semi-fluid outflow from the bark or wood of various deciduous trees. It does not set or harden in solid masses like gum and may be not only unsightly but also malodorous due to fermentation processes carried on by various yeasts, fungi and bacteria which find the ooze a good nutrient medium in which to grow. Wounds in certain kinds of trees, such as birch, elm and maple, may bleed profusely producing the slime-flux condi-

tion, which, however, may also appear near the base of some trees without the previous presence of wounds.

The true nature and cause of slime-flux are not known but it is believed to be connected with positive gas and water pressure in the heart-wood which can be relieved by inserting a pipe into the heart-wood at the base of the tree. Bracing trees and feeding them to insure rapid growth will help to stop bleeding from wounds, which should always be treated immediately—shaped and so handled as to induce rapid healing. See TREE SURGERY.

SLIME MOLDS. Common name for a group of lower plants—called by scientists Myxomycetes—somewhat intermediate between animals and plants but classed as the latter. Few of the slime molds are of importance to the plant grower. One causes club root of cabbage and other crucifers; another, powdery scab of potatoes; and a third is doubtfully connected with a sweet-potato disease. See CLUB ROOT; CRUCIFER.

SLIP. Old-fashioned name for a Cutting, which see.

SLIPPER-FLOWER. A common name for *Pedilanthus tithymaloides,* also called Slipper-plant or Slipper-spurge, a succulent tropical American shrub with small red or purple flowers.

SLOE. A common name for *Prunus spinosa,* the Blackthorn, a shrub or tree with plum-like white flowers and small blue or black bloomy fruits.

SLUGS. Garden slugs are related to snails, clams and oysters, belonging to the animal group popularly called mollusks; the snail and slug members are known as gastropods (meaning "stomach in the foot"). Snails—or at least their shells—are familiar objects to everyone although less common in gardens than the soft slimy slugs which are similar except that the protecting shell has been reduced to a very small plate on the back. At least two species of garden slugs are troublesome. The more common is the gray field slug; the other is the giant or spotted garden slug.

Slugs hide under rubbish during the day and feed at night on tender leaves of many garden plants, leaving a slimy trail where they have crawled. Jelly-like eggs are laid in fall and spring in the soil or under stones, sticks and clods of earth. Plants not to be used for food can be protected by spraying with lead arsenate; bordeaux mixture is also recommended. Among vegetables slugs may be trapped beneath shingles or other pieces of board and then killed. As they do not like to crawl through dry or caustic material, plants and flower beds can be protected by sprinkling hydrated or air-slaked lime, fine coal ashes, or soot about. Metaldehyde baits (which see) are the most recently developed means for getting rid of them.

Pear, cherry and rose slugs are not mollusks but the slimy-coated larvae of insects. See under PEAR; ROSE.

SMARTWEED. Common name for several weedy native species of Polygonum, a group of herbs and vines called in general Knotweed, and including some pleasing garden forms.

SMILACINA (smy-lah-sy'-nah). A genus of perennial woodland herbs called False-Solomons-Seal (which see), with small whitish flowers and shiny berries in terminal racemes.

SMILAX (smy'-laks). A genus of widely distributed, mostly woody tendril-climbing vines belonging to the Lily Family and commonly called Greenbrier. They are little cultivated, but some of the native species are cut and used for decorative purposes especially by florists. However, the true smilax of florists is *Asparagus asparagoides.* The sharp-thorned *S. glauca* spreads rapidly and may form cruel and bothersome thickets.

S. lanceolata (Florida Smilax), native in the S. States, is a high-climbing evergreen, with large fleshy tubers. Its leafy stems are extensively cut and used for decorative work.

rotundifolia (Horse-brier) is a common weedy deciduous vine, spreading rapidly by underground stems.

glauca (Cat-brier) is partially evergreen with its underground stems spiny and tuberous and its slender smooth aërial stems armed with stout, hooked, viciously sharp prickles; the leaves are smooth beneath.

herbacea (Carrion-flower) is an herbaceous perennial, distinguished by the foul odor of its flowers.

walteri, found in swamps in sandy regions, bears coral-red berries, useful in winter decorations.

All the above are native species.

SMILAX, FLORISTS'. This name is given to *Asparagus asparagoides,* an ornamental relative of the familiar garden vegetable. It is a popular greenhouse vine, valued for its long trails of rich green foliage useful for many decorative purposes. It is usually grown in solid beds, the growths being trained to strings and cut as needed. After cutting, plants need but little water until new growth starts. In good soil and with liberal feeding, it is possible to keep the plants in good production for 3 or 4 years. Propagation is by seed, best sown early in the year. Do not confuse with the two other decorative species of asparagus, namely, *A. sprengeri* and *A. plumosus;* or with the genus Smilax, which see.

SMOKE INJURY. Conspicuous injury to vegetation in and around industrial centers is caused by smoke and poisonous gases discharged from chimneys of manufacturing plants, office buildings, apartments, private residences, railroad locomotives, smelters, furnaces, kilns and so on. Certain species of plants may be killed and others chronically injured for miles around; acute injury has been traced for distances of 10 to 15 miles from the source and chronic injury up to 100 miles. The most important toxic gas is sulphur dioxide, but carbon monoxide, acetylene, ethylene, arsenic and other toxic compounds may be carried in smoke.

When the smoke is very dense more damage may result from the coating of soot deposited on the leaves than from the gases accompanying the smoke. The combination of soot and gases causes the leaves to turn brown in spots, then to die, and the plant to make little growth. Coniferous trees are particularly susceptible. The common garden bean succumbs quickly to smoke injury and can be used as an indicator or detector of possible smoke damage to valuable trees.

Control of the cause of smoke injury is usually outside the power of the individual but there should be some sort of community consideration of the problem to prevent its reaching the nuisance stage.

As to prevention of smoke injury, investigations at the Mellon Institute in Pittsburgh have led to recommendations that trees and plants (especially evergreens) in cities and other smoke-ridden places should be given an annual spring cleaning to rid them of the oily, sooty deposits. Under average conditions plants up to 6 ft. tall need only sponging with a tepid suds of pure soap. For larger specimens and especially heavy smoke coatings, spraying with a solution of sodium metaphosphate (obtainable under the trade name Calgon) is advised; sometimes more than one treatment will be needed.

The crystals should be dissolved in water at the rate of 2½ lbs. to 1 gal., making a saturated solution. To this is added a bar of pure soap dissolved in water. The mixture is thoroughly stirred into from 25 to 50 gals. of water, the strength of the spray depending on the condition of the trees, which should be kept wet with the solution for 20 to 30 minutes, after which they are given a hard rinsing with the hose. The solution is said to be harmless to both plant tissue and human skin; moreover, in soaking into the ground it adds available phosphate plant food.

SMOKE-TREE. Common name for *Cotinus coggygria* (formerly Rhus cotinus), treated hereunder, but also used for *Dalea spinosa,* a small tree of the Colo. desert. The genus Cotinus, a member of the Cashew Family, comprises two species, one in N. America and the other found from S. Europe into China. They thrive in well drained soil, not too rich, the native *C. americanus* especially doing well in poor soil. Propagated by seeds, root-cuttings and layers.

C. coggygria (European Smoke-tree). This, the European species, is the hardiest, and produces the best "smoky" effect. It is a bushy shrub to 15 ft., outstanding in summer with large panicles of feathery filmy fruiting panicles. The foliage takes on good coloring in fall. Var. *purpureus* is a form with purplish leaves and panicles with dark purple hairs.

C. americanus (*Rhus cotinoides*), called American Smoke-tree or Chittam Wood, is native in the S. part of the country, but fairly hardy N. It is a large shrub or small tree to 30 ft. or more. Its fruiting panicles make very little show, but it is one of the most brilliant woody plants in fall when the leaves turn orange and scarlet.

SMUT FUNGI. A group of disease-causing organisms, so named because of the sooty black ripe spore masses which usually break up into a fine dust-like powder. Smuts attack many cultivated hosts as well as wild plants. The corn and onion smuts are probably most familiar to the gardener but those affecting wheat, oats, barley, rye, rice and sorghum are of great economic importance. The parts most frequently destroyed are either the kernels (seeds) or the entire flower cluster. The fungi can live and grow only on their hosts, but the spiny, heavy-walled, dark spores serve as resting bodies and are able to live in refuse for a long time and then infect plants with which they come in contact.

In corn smut infection results in large boil-like overgrowths on ears and sometimes tassels. In the loose smuts of cereal grains the young kernels are reduced to a smutty mass consisting of disintegrated flower parts, mycelium and spores. There is also a "stinking smut" of wheat, so called because of its foul odor. Onion smut causes dark pustules on the seedlings.

Corn smut is controlled by the removal and burning of the smut boils before the masses break; onion smut by wetting the soil with formalin as the onions are planted. Cereal smuts are prevented or controlled by the use of clean seed, by crop rotation and by seed disinfection.

SNAIL-FLOWER. Another name for *Phaseolus caracalla,* a perennial twining vine naturalized in Calif. with fragrant flowers coiled like snail shells; also called Corkscrew-flower.

SNAILS. Although many species of snails are known to science, only one group really concerns the American gardener. This is the slug, a snail that has degenerated and lost his "house" or shell, only a vestige of which remains. The slug devours decaying vegetation and, to some extent, live plant material; in addition it is an unpleasant creature to have around. Night is its active time, but it may be traced to some cranny under log or rock by the trail of viscid slime he leaves behind. One method of eliminating slugs is to encourage a garter snake (which is completely harmless) to haunt the premises.

Fresh water snails of several types, notably the so-called red ramshorn snail and the speedy little pond snail, are used in aquaria and in outdoor pools as scavengers. The little pond snail (Physa) should not be confused with the slower moving Limnaea, which is a voracious plant eater; if introduced to the aquarium it raises havoc in the tank.

See also SLUGS.

SNAILSEED. Common name for the genus Cocculus, a member of the Moonseed Family, comprising herbs or woody plants, usually vine-like in habit, having inconspicuous flowers, attractive foliage and red or black fruit hanging in clusters. A few of the evergreen species are grown in pots; others can be grown outdoors in the N. in rich moist soil. They are sometimes used to trail over gateways and arbors and can be propagated by seed, or by cuttings of half-ripened wood started under glass with bottom heat.

C. trilobus is hardy N., forming a slender vine with soft-hairy, 3-lobed leaves and black fruit. *C. carolinus* (Carolina Moonseed), a native plant with brilliant red fruit, is also hardy N. *C. laurifolius,* to 15 ft., is an evergreen shrub with black fruit adapted only to warm climates or to the conservatories in the N.

SNAKE GOURD. A common name for *Trichosanthes anguina,* a climbing annual vine with white flowers and long, slender, contorted fruits. See SERPENT GOURD.

SNAKEHEAD. A common name sometimes given to *Chelone glabra,* a hardy, shade- and moisture-loving perennial, better known as Turtlehead.

SNAKE-LILY. Common name for *Brodieae volubilis* (which see), a pink-flowered herb of the Lily Family native to the W. Coast and grown in gardens there and in the S.

SNAKEROOT, BLACK. Common name for *Cimicifuga racemosa,* also called Bugbane or Black Cohosh, a tall perennial herb of the Buttercup Family, with large divided leaves and small, white, ill-smelling flowers borne in a wand-like raceme. It is found in semi-shaded situations on the edge of wooded lands from Me. to Mo., and when transferred to the border or wild garden makes striking groups, often man-high, especially if planted in moist soil, rich in humus. It may be increased by division of roots or by seed sown as soon as ripe.

Button Snakeroot is a name for *Eryngium aquaticum* and also the genus Liatris; Canada Snakeroot is Asarum; Seneca Snakeroot is *Polygala senega;* Virginia Snakeroot is *Aristolochia serpentaria;* White Snakeroot is *Eupatorium urticaefolium.*

SNAKES. Notwithstanding the natural aversion of many people to all kinds of snakes, and the well-warranted fear of the poisonous kinds, snakes as ordinarily found in gardens merit entirely different consideration. For the most part they are harmless to man and desire merely to be left alone to carry on their search for insects, field mice and other creatures that are definitely injurious to plant life. Consequently, while there is no reason for a gardener trying to develop a desire to handle snakes against his natural inclinations, he will be contributing to his garden's success and beauty if he resists the all too common tendency to kill or have killed every snake he sees.

For more detailed information about both harmful and beneficial snakes, see ANIMALS IN THE GARDEN.

SNAKES-HEAD. A common name for *Fritillaria meleagris,* a hardy spring-flowering bulb with curiously marked flowers; sometimes called Guinea-hen-flower.

SNAKEWEED. Common name for *Polygonum bistorta,* a perennial with pink or white flowers in compact spikes.

SNAPDRAGON. Common name for the popular genus Antirrhinum, a member of the Figwort Family, comprising a dozen or more species of erect perennial herbs that are usually treated as annuals, as they flower from seed the first year. *A. majus,* the snapdragon of our gardens and greenhouses, is the most beautiful and most interesting species horticulturally. From the original type with its white to purplish, sac-like, 2-lipped flowers, hybridists have developed a number of strains outstanding in beauty of form, color and even fragrance (see ANTIRRHINUM). The dwarf varieties are excellent for edging, the half-dwarf

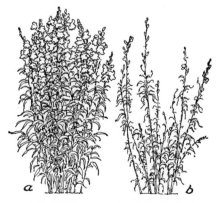

AN ARGUMENT FOR DUSTING

A serious enemy of snapdragon is the rust fungus which destroys the foliage, stunting the plants. Fine sulphur dusted on frequently, beginning early, will control it as shown by this dusted plant (a) as compared with the undusted one (b). See also under RUST.

sorts for massing in beds, and the taller types for use in groups in the border.

Seed should be sown indoors in March or April. It may be slow in germinating but after the true leaves have formed the growth is usually rapid. The small plants can be transplanted to the open as soon as danger of frost is over; they will flower from July until frost if the blossoms are picked as soon as they fade. Seed may also be planted in the open in August, and the seedlings transplanted to pots for winter bloom, or the plants can be covered with a mulch over winter to give earlier summer flowers.

To encourage the growth of flower-bearing side branches, the central bud should be pinched out when transplanting; followed by occasional pinching of other too-vigorous shoots, this will result in a compact oval plant covered with short racemes of flowers.

ENEMIES. Rust, the most serious snapdragon disease, is found all over the United States on both greenhouse and outdoor plants. Dusty, chocolate-brown pustules (spore masses) are produced on the under side of the leaves and on stems. Weekly applications of dusting sulphur during rainy periods and fortnightly applications in dry weather will effectively control rust if a start is made early in the season. Keep sulphur off the flowers when in bloom. Beds should be surface irrigated if possible, rather than watered with a hose or sprinkler so as to keep the foliage dry and prevent the spores from being spread by splashing water. Commercially desirable rust resistant strains, testing 75 per cent rust proof, are now on the market.

Blight, showing up as dark spots on leaves and water-soaked spots on stems; and anthracnose, recognized by the grayish white leaf spots with a reddish border and sunken areas on stems, may be prevented by cleaning up all plant débris in the fall and spraying with bordeaux mixture during the growing season. Destroy plants attacked by wilt and disinfect the soil or select a new location for subsequent plantings. Cyclamen mite and red spider (which see) are important greenhouse pests of snapdragon.

SNAPWEED. Common name for Impatiens, a genus of succulent herbs (including the familiar garden balsam) whose seed pods burst suddenly when ripe and forcibly expel the seeds.

SNEEZEWEED. Common name for the genus Helenium, coarse, erect annual and perennial composite herbs with yellow or bronze flowers in late summer and fall.

SNEEZEWORT. Common name for *Achillea ptarmica,* a perennial with small white flowers. See ACHILLEA.

SNOUT BEETLES. In this group of beetles the head is prolonged forward and downward, forming a cylindrical snout that may range in length from a short beak to one much longer than the entire rest of the body. With the mouth parts at the end of the long snout, the insect makes a hole deep into the tissues of plants and in the hole lays its eggs. The snout also enables the beetle to eat the soft underlying plant tissues. The larvae are footless grubs.

Many species of snout beetles are very destructive. The plum curculio also attacks apples and many stone fruits, the well-known cherry "worm" being the grub of this snout beetle. The cotton boll weevil is probably the most destructive southern pest of this group. The imbricated snout beetle, dull silvery white with brown markings, gnaws holes in many kinds of garden vegetables and fruits and also in the bark of trees and shrubs. See CURCULIO; WEEVILS; BEETLES.

A SNOUT BEETLE
Drawn more than four times natural size to show the long proboscis with which it bores into plant stems, fruits, seeds, etc.

SNOWBALL. One of the common names for *Viburnum opulus* var. *roseum,* a variety of the European Cranberry-bush, which has large round white clusters of sterile flowers. Chinese Snowball is *V. macrocephalum* var. *sterile,* and Japanese Snowball is *V. tomentosum* var. *sterile* (formerly called var. *plenum*).

SNOWBERRY. Common name for *Symphoricarpos albus,* a hardy, deciduous white-berried shrub of N. America, also called Waxberry; also applied to Chiococca, a genus of tropical American shrubs and vines with leathery leaves and globular white fruits.

SNOWDROP. Common name for the genus Galanthus, early spring-blooming hardy bulbous herbs with drooping white flowers.

SNOWDROP-TREE. A common name for the genus Halesia, deciduous shrubs with drooping, bell-like white flowers; also called Silver-bell.

SNOWFLAKE. Common name for the genus Leucojum, small hardy bulbous herbs with red- or green-tinted white flowers. Water-snowflake is *Nymphoides indicum.*

SNOW-IN-SUMMER. Common name for *Cerastium tomentosum,* a hardy creeping perennial with grayish downy foliage and abundant white flowers in late spring.

SNOWMOLD. A lawn or turf disease most severe in the N. part of the U. S. White patches, due to the cottony growth of the fungus, appear on the grass just as the snow is melting in early spring. For control, see LAWN.

SNOW-ON-THE-MOUNTAIN. Common name for *Euphorbia marginata,* a 2-ft. annual with white-margined upper leaves and small flowers with white petal-like parts.

SNOW POPPY. Common name for *Eomecon chionantha,* a perennial herb of the Poppy Family, growing from a rootstock and bearing white, poppy-like flowers in clusters on reddish, branching stalks from 9 to 12 in. high. These are surrounded by pale green, heart-shaped leaves, grayish beneath. Hardy as far N. as New York City, it may be increased by division of the rootstock.

SNOW-WREATH. Common name for *Neviusia alabamansis,* a deciduous shrub of the Rose Family, native only tò Sand Mountain in Ala. It grows to 6 ft. tall and though the flowers, clustered on the slender graceful branches, have no petals, their profuse stamens produce a feathery, snowy appearance. Outdoors, the flowers are sometimes discolored or greenish, but forcing readily under glass, it there develops great beauty. It is increased by green-wood cuttings started in heat, or by seed.

SOAP-BARK-TREE. Common name for *Quillaja saponaria,* an evergreen member of the Rose Family, with small, shining, leathery leaves, and white flowers ¾ in. across in terminal clusters. Its bark has saponaceous and medicinal qualities. Not hardy N., it is sometimes grown as a greenhouse tree or outdoors in the S. States and Calif. It is increased by cuttings rooted under glass.

SOAPBERRY. Common name for Sapindus, a genus of trees or shrubs bearing fruit containing a soapy substance (saponin) used for cleansing purposes by the natives of tropical countries. A few species are grown in the S. as ornamentals, doing well even in dry rocky soil. They are increased by seeds or cuttings in the spring. *S. saponaria,* to 30 ft., is evergreen, with pinnate leaves, small white flowers in racemes to 10 in. long and a small round, shining orange-brown fruit. *S. mukorossi,* to 60 ft., is a brittle evergreen tree whose orange-brown fruit has a very soapy quality. *S. drummondi,* to 50 ft., is deciduous with yellowish-white flowers and round yellow fruit becoming black.

SOAP-PLANT. Common name for *Chlorogalum pomeridianum,* also called Amole, a tall bulbous herb of the Lily Family, with basal leaves to 1½ ft. and small white flowers with purple veins, opening only in the afternoon. The bulb is used by the Indians and Mexicans for soap-making. Easily grown, it thrives in any good (but not too rich) garden soil. Plant the bulbs in the fall 3 or 4 in. deep, preferably in groups of 5 or 7. Plants may also be increased by seed.

SOAPS AS SPRAYS. Soaps are of value as contact insecticides, having been one of the earliest poisons for soft-bodied insects. At the present time soap is not often used alone as a spray, except perhaps against a few aphids on house plants; but it is used to a considerable extent as a flux in making oil emulsions and as a spreader for nicotine and pyrethrum sprays. Whale-oil soap or fish-oil soap is made by combining fish-oil with water and caustic potash or soda. Sodium soaps are hard or laundry soaps.

The amount of soap which can be safely used varies from ½ oz. to 3 oz. per gallon of diluted spray, depending on the insect to be controlled and the kind of plant to be sprayed. Soaps are safe to use with all contact sprays but *should never be used with stomach poisons,* such as lead or calcium arsenate, since free arsenic will be liberated and burning may result.

See also INSECTICIDE; SPREADERS AND STICKERS.

SOAPWORT. Common name for the genus Saponaria, hardy annual and perennial herbs with white, pink or red flowers.

SOD. The surface layer of a lawn or other stretch of closely mown grass; also a small section cut out of such an area to be used elsewhere. Thus used the word corresponds to "turf," as used in English gardening. Sodding (the operation of placing sods to cover an area of bare ground), while more expensive than raising grass from seed, is a convenient and valuable method of securing a good turf almost immediately; also in places where seed cannot well be sown, or where the soil is likely to wash, as on terrace slopes, along narrow borders, etc. Even in developing a

TOOLS FOR WORK WITH SOD
A. Half-moon edges for cutting strips of turf. B. Flat spade, useful for lifting sod and for beating it down when laid. C. Sod-cutting iron, used like a spade to cut loose sods of uniform thickness. D. Sod beater, easier to use than a spade in firming newly laid sod.

larger stretch of greensward than could economically be sodded, sods can often be used to advantage to outline the area, or perhaps cut it up into squares. The soil within the strips is then brought to the exact level of the grass ready for seeding.

SOD CUTTING. Sods may be cut from out of the way corners of a large lawn for use in more important places, or from good dense sod in a pasture or orchard. Some nurserymen and landscape gardeners grow sod as a crop, replacing a plot with rich top-soil and reseeding it as soon as it has been stripped of its turf. Sods are usually cut 1 ft. wide and of uniform thickness (usually 2 or 3 in.), depending on the depth of the root growth. Horse-drawn sod-cutting tools are used for large scale work, but for ordinary garden jobs the strips should be cut with a regular half-moon edger kept very sharp, and worked along the edge or edges of a heavy plank. Each strip is cut free by sliding the edger, a sharp spade, or a special sod-cutting tool under it at a uniform depth. The strips are then cut in 1-ft. to 3-ft. lengths de-

pending on the denseness and strength of the turf. To handle well, sod should be neither dry nor wet; the important thing is to have a good loamy soil that will not shake loose from the roots at the slightest movement. Good sod cannot be cut from sandy soil.

It is best, of course, to reset sods without delay, but they can be piled (not more than 2 ft. deep) and left for a few days without danger, so long as the grass is not damp enough to heat or mold.

LAYING SOD. Before laying sod prepare the soil as in making a lawn, rake it smooth and leave it, when loose and uncompacted, just about as high as the desired finished level. Lay the sods carefully, first along the margin of the area, then side by side toward the center. Fit the edges *close* together, adding or removing a little soil beneath as may be necessary to produce a level surface. When an area a few sods wide is laid (or the whole area is only a few square yards in extent, as in a lawn-patching job), pound it down hard, using either a heavy flat wooden block on a handle, or the flat back of a spade. A plank should be laid to walk on while doing this so as to avoid making footprints in the new turf. Do not attempt to roll the sod down; but pound it well, especially where the edges join. Then soak it thoroughly. When it is all firmly in place, the edge can be trimmed to its correct finish; or, better still, this can be delayed until the grass takes root and begins to grow and the sods merge into a solid mass. Thereafter treat the area like a regular lawn or grass border.

SOIL. This is the surface layer of the earth that supports plant life. It is the composite result of (1) disintegration and decomposition of diverse kinds of rocks; (2) the effects of climatic and other physical conditions; (3) the activities during their lives, and the decay after the deaths, of animals and plants existing upon or in the ground. As these conditions vary, so do the composition, character, color and depth of the soil.

SOIL CHARACTERISTICS

KINDS OF SOIL. Of the four main contributing factors the composition of the fundamental rock is generally the most influential in deciding the type of a soil. When limestone rock disintegrates it forms clay soil with an alkaline reaction. Such soils are often so fine grained that the particles "run together" and thus make drainage, plowing, digging and cultivation difficult. However, upon being improved and lightened, they become retentive of moisture and plant nutrients and as a rule constitute a class of highly desirable soils for tree, bush and vine fruits. Also when properly managed they are among the most productive for grains and vegetables.

On the other hand, when granites or sandstone disintegrate they form sandy soils which, unless carefully treated, allow too rapid passage of water and with it the loss of dissolved plant nutrients. Soils formed from sandstone rocks contain little or no alkali and, in fact, are usually more or less acid. Hence they are especially adapted to such plants as rhododendrons, azaleas, blueberries and other acid soil types. See ACID SOIL.

SOIL CONSTITUENTS. Soils vary not only according to their basic mineral (rock) composition, but also according to the size of the particles (fine or coarse) and the proportion of decaying animal and vegetable matter or humus (which see) that they contain. This latter constituent varies widely in amount in different soils and from time to time. A peat or muck soil may be nearly all humus; a clay may contain

practically none; and a loam may be said to have just the right amount for average garden requirements. Humus is, however, restricted to the upper layer of cultivated soil, or (in nature) the zone in which plant roots live—and die. The underlying subsoil is usually devoid of it. As humus is constantly breaking down into simpler substances, cultivation tends to hasten this change as does the heat of southern regions. In these places, it more frequently needs to be replaced than in the North.

From the soil specialist's standpoint, there are seven grades of soil based on the size of the mineral particles, as follows: *Fine gravel*—diameter 2 to 1 millimeter; *coarse sand*—diameter 1 to $\frac{1}{2}$ mm.; *medium sand*—$\frac{1}{2}$ to $\frac{1}{4}$ mm.; *fine sand*—$\frac{1}{4}$ to $\frac{1}{10}$ mm.; *very fine sand*—$\frac{1}{10}$ to $\frac{1}{20}$ mm.; *silt*—$\frac{1}{20}$ to $\frac{1}{200}$ mm.; *clay*—less than $\frac{1}{200}$ mm. Based on that classification, types of soil are defined in this way:

Sands contain less than $\frac{1}{5}$ silt and clay.

Sandy loams—from $\frac{1}{5}$ to $\frac{1}{2}$ silt and clay but not more than 20 per cent clay.

Silt loams—more than 50 per cent silt and clay with less than $\frac{1}{5}$ of clay and more than $\frac{1}{2}$ silt.

Clay loams—more than $\frac{1}{2}$ clay and silt with less than $\frac{1}{2}$ silt and 20 to 30 per cent clay.

SODDING SAVES TIME AND IF WELL DONE GIVES A HIGHLY SATISFACTORY TURF
The worker at the left is using a sod cutting iron to loosen the strips of sod as cut along the edges of a 12-in.-wide plank by the man at the right. Cut in, usually, 3-ft. lengths, sods can be piled (grass side up) as shown in the background for several days if not allowed to get wet enough to heat and mold.

Clays—more than 50 per cent silt and clay combined and more than 30 per cent of clay.

Two other types are *peat,* with 65 per cent or more of organic matter; and *muck,* with from 25 to 65 per cent well-decomposed organic matter mixed with much clay, silt, or sand.

Soils of glacial origin are of mixed composition because they have been developed from confused mixtures of various kinds of rock collected from various places. Other soils are built up by the action of water which carries the eroded mineral fragments from high to lower levels as in river valley and, especially, deltas. Still others, formed along sea and lake coasts, result from the depositing of sand and finer soils carried by the water currents and dropped when the force of the movement abates.

Soil Origins. Soils that form and remain where the "bed rocks" are located are said to be "sedimentary." Their character is typical of the rocks from which they are developed. Soils that form mainly from the decomposition of vegetable matter in swamps must be thoroughly drained before they can be used for cultivated plants. They are generally too acid for most vegetables and flowering plants so must be dressed liberally with lime and made "neutral" or somewhat alkaline before being used.

Soils that are or were carried by water, wind, glacier or other agency are called "transported" and naturally differ considerably from the types just described.

Soil Color. It is generally believed that dark colored soils are of better quality than lighter types; but this is not necessarily so, because dark soils may have acquired their color from particles of dark rock instead of the humus that also is black or dark brown and that usually represents fertility and good physical condition. Iron compounds also contribute to soil color, producing yellows, reds, blues and in some cases gray, while humus usually causes brown to black shades. Red generally indicates good drainage; black, brown and yellow, poor drainage.

Soil Depth. This varies greatly. A soil may be a mere film formed upon rocks partly by the decay of lichens, algae, and other lowly plants, and partly by the destruction of the rocks by these plants and by frost action. Or soil may be several or many feet deep as in river valleys, that of the Mississippi, for instance, where Nature has laid down rich deposits.

From the farmer's and gardener's viewpoint, soils are divided into two parts: (1) the upper surface, or *top-soil* (or soil proper), a generally dark layer, richer in plant nutrients and especially in humus than (2) the lower, or *sub-soil.* Though most cultivated plants distribute their roots mainly if not altogether in the surface layer, many crops and trees penetrate the sub-soil to an astonishing depth—field corn often more than 5 ft., alfalfa to 10 or even 75 ft.

Soil Fertility. The capacity of soils to produce plants differs widely, and can be judged with a fair degree of accuracy by mere observation. Even without the knowledge that certain species of plants are associated with specific soil types or conditions, it is possible for a person without a knowledge of botany to roughly determine the general character of a given soil area.

Where the natural vegetation is luxuriant the soil quality is almost sure to be good; where the growth is sparse and scrawny the opposite is usually true—though the cause may be abuse of a formerly good soil by man. Such superficial methods of judging soils may be a real help when several places are being considered in the search for a prospective home; or when one is trying to find the best site on a piece of property for a vegetable garden or special landscape feature.

No matter how poor a soil is, it can almost always be improved, though in some cases the cost would be so high or the time required so long that it would be more economical to replace the worthless earth with top-soil brought in.

If a soil is wet, "cold" and late, drainage (which see) will dry and aerate it and make it warmer. If it is heavy and sticky, it will be helped by the addition of sand, sifted coal ashes and humus in the form of manure, green manures, compost or cover-crops, plus late autumn plowing or digging and early spring top-dressing with lime or wood ashes. These operations will tend to lighten it, and make it more retentive of moisture, warmer, and easier to work. If it is excessively sandy, additions of humus reinforced with lime will give it more body. If it is lacking in plant nutrients, these may be added in many forms. See MANURE; FERTILIZER; PLANT FOODS AND FEEDING.

Soil Management

In the great majority of cases the gardener must make the best of what soil he happens to have. Next in order to draining (when this is necessary) comes the removal of superficial, undesirable materials upon or in the surface layer—such things as stumps, roots, stones and boulders, etc., and, in the case of recently built houses, as builders' and other rubbish.

TILLAGE. Next comes the treatment of the earth itself. As a general rule only a few inches (4 to, perhaps, 7) are plowed or dug. In gardens, soils are sometimes deepened and greatly improved by double digging or trenching (which see). These practices, together with the subsequent harrowing and raking, are done not only to bury sod and trash and to mix manures and fertilizers with the top-soil, but also to loosen the soil mass so that the roots of plants may penetrate it and various helpful microörganisms (bacteria) find it a suitable medium in which to perform their functions. They also increase the porosity of the ground, its capacity to absorb and retain water. They also increase the aeration of the soil, its ability to admit air, which is as necessary to root development and activity as are water and plant nutrients.

PUDDLING. When soil (especially clay, adobe and loess) is mismanaged by being tilled while too wet, the finer particles become wedged between the coarser ones, the moisture and air are driven out, the soil mass becomes dense, the roots of plants find it hard to penetrate the soil and the latter soon becomes hard and difficult to plow or dig. When it is turned up it forms clods which, on drying, bake to almost brick-like hardness. Sée PUDDLE.

HARDPAN. Another undesirable condition in a soil is the existence of hardpan—which is a layer of impermeable soil just below the top-soil. It may be a natural condition or it may have been induced by plowing the soil when too wet, or repeatedly at the same depth until a "floor" is formed. A hardpan prevents the downward passage of water after a rain, and also the normal upward passage of water from lower levels to the surface layer.

This makes the surface soil cold in spring, as a result of the chilling effect of the evaporation of the excess water retained above the hardpan, and later dry in summer because after the excess surface moisture has evaporated, too little comes up from below to replace it.

A hardpan should therefore be broken up. On a small scale this may be done by using a pick-axe in the bottoms of the furrows, or by double digging (see TRENCHING). On a larger scale it may be done by following the ordinary plow by a deep-tilling sub-soil plow which penetrates several inches below the bottom of the furrow, and lifts, breaks, and loosens, but does not invert the hard layer. Moderate charges of dynamite are sometimes used to accomplish the same object.

Another cause of poor soils is lumpiness, which may result (as already explained) from working the soil when too wet. More often, however, it is due to plowing or digging when too dry.

To prevent the condition, therefore, study the soil type and choose that time for plowing or digging when the soil is just moist enough to turn and crumble nicely, and before it tends to turn up in the form of dry clods. It is important that the newly plowed furrows (or the freshly rough dug soil), be harrowed or raked into uniform friability with the least possible delay so as to conserve as much moisture as possible in the soil. In a small garden or a bed or border raking should be done as soon as a few square yards have been dug with the spading fork—which should be used to break each clod as it is turned. See DIGGING.

SOIL FILLING. Just when to dig or plow can be determined—after practice—in several ways: (1) By the appearance of the soil surface; if it glistens with moisture, it is too wet. (2) By digging up chunks of soil here and there in the area to be worked and examining the surfaces for the condition mentioned in (1). (3) By squeezing a handful; if it holds its shape fairly well, when the hand is opened, only a few cracks showing, it is in good condition; but if it leaves mud on the hand it is too wet; and if it falls apart readily and is more or less dusty, it is too dry.

MAINTAINING HUMUS. Soils are often made poor by depleting their supply of the humus through mismanagement or the failure to obtain and add manure. With the growing scarcity of manure and its rising cost, gardeners have been too prone to rely upon chemical fertilizers for the needed plant food, and to neglect to provide any other kind of humus. Actually it is comparatively easy to do this in several inexpensive ways. First, all fallen leaves, cut and pulled weeds, lawn clippings and trimmings, stems of plants, vegetable waste from the kitchen and similar organic materials should be utilized; either bury it directly in a part of the garden allotted for the season to that use, or compost it. (See COMPOST.) Second, grow catch crops, cover-crops, and green manures (see these titles) and dig or plow under while still green and soft to supply the necessary succulent vegetable matter. Such materials, upon decaying, become humus.

Remember that losses of humus are due partly to "burning" somewhat (though not exactly) as fuel is burned in a stove. Gaseous products of oxidation are constantly being given off from decomposing humus and, unless reabsorbed by the soil, are usually lost into the air. Also the activities of microscopic forms of life in the soil help to break down the complicated organic materials into simpler compounds which are taken up by plants, leached away or released into the air until nothing is left in the soil except the mineral constituents.

The loss of humus is generally most rapid in sandy soils because of their more open structure, better drainage and therefore higher temperature.

SOIL LIFE. Finally soils may become unproductive for other reasons, the most common of which is probably lack of nutritive substances. When it is understood that the soil is not "just dead dirt" but both a complicated chemical laboratory and a theater in which myriads of microscopic creatures play important roles, it is easy to understand that mismanagement and neglect will quickly impair, if not destroy, the very purpose for which man uses soil—namely, for growing plants.

Available plant nutrients are reduced in a soil by continuous cropping and by losses of soluble materials in the drainage water. These and similar losses can be replaced through the addition of composts, manures, and fertilizers (see these titles), by green manures and cover-crops. Soils become less productive as they become either too acid for certain plants or too alkaline for others. The accumulation of "alkali" salts at or near the surface may create soil solutions too strong for plants to thrive in. But such conditions, at least in humid climates, can usually be corrected by drenching the soil surface so as to dilute and wash the undesirable materials to levels below the reach of plant roots.

Materials actually poisonous to plants are sometimes developed in soils as the result of life processes of certain plants or animals. Some of these may be poisonous to other plants. Their presence is not characteristic of any particular kind or condition of soil because the interminable natural changes in soils effect constant variation in the amounts of the poisonous substances. Such toxic conditions may be caused by (1) poor drainage and ineffective ventilation or aeration of the soil—for which the remedy is evident (see DRAINAGE); (2) deficiency of lime (which see); (3) continuous cropping with the same crop or with crops that belong to the same botanical family or to a special class of crops such as roots—this can be corrected by rotation of crops (see CROPPING SYSTEMS); (4) undesirable minerals in the soil, as aluminum, manganese and silica compounds—but these seem to be one result of insufficient lime; (5) the presence of unfavorable, or the absence of favorable, microscopic organisms, especially bacteria, which see.

SOIL-BINDING PLANTS. These may be divided into two classes: those planted to hold the shores of rivers and lakes against the force of the waves or current; and those planted in dry, exposed situations to counteract the effect of erosion (which see). Foremost among the trees planted for the former purpose stand the willows (*Salix alba* and *S. nigra*). The former (white willow) is extensively planted through the E. States and has become so generally naturalized that many think of it as an indigenous tree. *S. nigra* (black willow) reaches its greatest growth in the Mississippi valley, where it has been instrumental in preventing floods in many districts. The alders, notably *Alnus incana* and *A. maritima* in the E. States and *A. rubra* in the N. W., are trees of the river banks. Other trees often planted for shelter belts and to prevent erosion are the cottonwoods, especially *Populus balsamifera* and *P. canadensis;* and also in many parts of the W. the Lombardy Poplar (*P. nigra* var. *italica*) which may be seen in long rows sheltering vast fields. Other trees planted in the Central Plains, where the need of holding the soil in place is great, are the quick-growing but short-lived box-elder (*Acer negundo*), the hackberry (*Celtis laevigata*), the ash (*Fraxinus lanceolata*), the American elm (*Ulmus americana*), the honey locust (*Gleditsia triacanthos*) and such evergreens as *Abies concolor, Picea abies, P. glauca, P. pungens, Pinus nigra* and *P. sylvestris*.

On dry sandy banks the gray birch (*Betula populifolia*) or the red-cedar (*Junipers virginiana*) may be planted; and if larger trees are wanted, the sassafras (*Sassafras variifolium*), the pignut (*Carya glabra*) or the mockernut (*C. alba*) should be underplanted with scrub oak (*Quercus ilicifolia*), *Junipers communis* and coltsfoot (*Tussilago farfara*).

Near the seashore the pitch pine (*Pinus rigida*), often gnarled and twisted and very deep-rooting, should be combined with the black oak (*Quercus velutina*) and underplanted with the shadbush (*Amelanchier canadensis*), the hawthorn (*Crataegus tomentosa*), the beach plum (*Prunus maritima*). All can be interlaced with dwarf huckleberry (*Gaylusaccia dumosa*), mats of bearberry (*Arctostaphylos uva-ursi*), Hudsonia, the beach-pea (*Lathyrus maritima*), and beach wormwood (*Artemisia stelleriana*). In the most exposed dunes beach-grass (*Ammophila breviligulata*) combined with panic grass (*Panicum*) and sometimes with the prickly-pear (*Opuntia vulgaris*) will anchor the shifting sands. Other plants extensively used in sandy situations of this type are the lupine (*Lupinus perennis*) and in the W. *L. arboreus;* also Bush-clover (Lespedeza).

For planting on steep banks or terraces above the garden, the climbing hydrangea (*H. petiolaris*) staked down at intervals may be used; also English ivy (*Hedera helix*), the native bittersweet (*Celastrus scandens*), the Japanese honeysuckle (*Lonicera halliana*), the Japanese memorial rose (*Rosa wichuraiana*) and various other rambler roses, the winter creeper (*Euonymus radicans*) and its varieties, the perennial-pea (*Lathyrus perennis*) and, in a sheltered spot, *Vinca minor,* or periwinkle. For more shrubby effects forsythia, especially *F. suspensa*, makes excellent effects, as do various dwarf junipers, among them *J. conferta, J. chinensis* var. *sargenti, J. sabina, J. squamata, J. horizontalis.* Likewise *Cotoneaster adpressa, C. horizontalis,* and, where it is hardy, *C. microphylla, Pachysandra terminalis* and *P. canbyi*.

Among trees the Canadian yew (*Taxus canadensis*) may be used, and in slightly more open situations, the Japanese yew (*T. cuspidata*), mountain-laurel (*Kalmia latifolia*), dwarf hemlock (*Tsuga canadensis* var. *pendula* and var. *nana*). In sun, on a bank too steep for grass, *Iberis sempervirens* or *Arabis alpina* will hold the soil, as will the various Sedums—*S. spectabile, S. septangulare, S. telephium* and *S. acre;* also *Phlox subulata* and *Nepeta mussini*.

All plants on banks should be placed deep in a pocket of good, rich soil. If practical, each should be anchored with small stones. Sandy soils are made more retentive of moisture and less likely to blow away while the plants are becoming established by the addition of peat moss. On exposed shores, clumps of beach-grass and low-growing shrubs should be covered with light boughs until they are well rooted. Planting should be done in the spring or early fall, and whenever possible water should be given until growth is well established.

See also EROSION; SEASIDE GARDEN.

SOIL CONSERVATION. In the broad sense, this means the "permanent maintenance of the productive capacity of the land." But of late years, as men have begun to realize how sadly they have been wasting and destroying the land's resources, more emphasis has been placed upon the narrow meaning that implies the control and prevention of destructive agencies and practices involved in man's use of the soil. One of the worst of these is erosion, whether by wind, water or other cause. Because many of man's farming and pioneering methods have, through ignorance, shortsightedness or indifference, caused or promoted erosion—such as one-crop farming with tilled crops; the clearing of wooded watersheds of timber and the absorbent forest floor; the plowing of prairie sod lands where normal rainfall and crop growth are not sufficient to hold the top soil in place; the up-and-down tillage of sloping land, and the failure to keep the soil supplied with sufficient humus —the problem is a vast one combining investigation and survey work on the one hand, the development of erosion-control methods on the other, and the education of agriculturists, lumbermen, industrialists, and the public in general to the seriousness of the situation and the need of improving conditions and adopting a policy of constructive conservation.

While all those larger considerations affect every home gardener as a citizen, there are conservation problems that he can attack right on his own home grounds. Heavy rains, water discharged from house leaders, etc., can in a small way, do the same sort of erosion on sloping lawns or gardens as can huge freshets on sloping farm lands. The burning of leaves in the fall, and the failure to add manure or some form of humus to cultivated beds and gardens both contribute to the weakening of the vigor of a soil. The failure to sow a cover crop, or grass, or even to let a crop of weeds grow (to be cut down before it goes to seed, however) on vacant land, is likely to lead to soil-blowing and the accumulative deterioration of a good soil. Yet all these destructive tendencies can be checked, and the garden soil kept more productive by the practice of what are recognized as sane, conservation practices whether on farms, on estates, or in back yards.

**SOIL TESTING IS SIMPLE, INTEREST-
ING, HELPFUL**
Inexpensive outfits enable any gardener to learn
new facts about his soil and what it needs. To
solve more difficult problems, there are professional sources of advice.

For information about soil conservation, apply locally to county farm agents, to State colleges and departments of agriculture, and to the Soil Conservation Service of the U. S. Dept. of Agriculture, Washington, D. C. or to any of its district offices located in various parts of the country.

SOILLESS CULTURE. This term is loosely applied to growing plants in nutrient solutions, no matter what the method. It may correctly be applied to growing in water cultures; but when sand or cinders is used, it is difficult to draw the line where soilless culture leaves off and soil culture begins. Soil, as generally defined, is made up of sand, silt, clay and colloids, which see. In sand culture, if the sand is thoroughly washed, there may be no clay particles, but colloids may develop from the decay of roots. Cinders will contain sand, silt, clay and colloids, which through chemical and physical reaction may become free. Actually, the only difference between soilless culture and culture in soil is the technique of handling the nutrient solution.

See CHEMICAL GARDENING; NUTRIENT SOLUTION; SAND CULTURE; WINDOW BOX.

SOIL TESTING. Thorough analysis of soil is not practicable for the ordinary gardener; he had better send samples to the nearest state agricultural experiment station, or to his county agricultural agent. In doing this, he should take care to supply a typical, representative sample by collecting small quantities from at least half a dozen places in the area in question, mixing them thoroughly, and then sending in about a pint of the mixture. A good way to collect the soil is to make borings with a soil auger or large carpenter's auger (not needed for delicate wood work), to the full depth of the cultivated layer of the plot. Or a hollow pipe an inch or two in diameter can be driven into the soil, withdrawn, and tapped until the core of soil falls out. Even a small trowel can be used, the point being to mix all such samples well in a pail or box before putting the test sample in a tin can for shipment.

In submitting such a soil sample, it is helpful to describe the piece of land, tell how it has been handled, if possible, and also state to what use it is to be put, so that the report can include recommendations as to any treatment needed (such as liming, fertilizing, etc.), to make it suitable for the contemplated crop or planting. But conditions as to acidity or alkalinity are constantly changing, and they can be easily tested by anyone. Not only may acidity be increased or decreased by the fertilizers used and the plants grown, but it may also be much greater in one part of the garden than in another. When to use lime or where to put an acid-soil plant are, therefore, questions that are continually before the gardener.

Litmus tests are only partly satisfactory but interesting. Strips of red and blue litmus paper can be had at the drug store. Placed in contact with moist samples of the soil for a few minutes, they may change color. If the blue paper turns red, the soil is acid; if the red paper turns blue, it is alkaline; if both turn purple, it is neutral. The degree of acidity or alkalinity is not shown, though it may be guessed from the speed of the color change.

Better, because more delicate, are the results obtained with inexpensive testing sets now sold in seed stores. With the simplest of them, a sample of dry soil is saturated with a green liquid and allowed to stand for a minute; then the liquid is run off and examined. If it has turned blue, the soil is alkaline; if red or yellow, the soil is acid. By a color chart furnished with the set, a pH reading (explained unded ACID SOIL) can be taken approximately from the shade of color. A reading of 7 is neutral, higher than 7 alkaline, and lower than that, acid.

Tests should be made before planting definitely acid- or alkaline-loving plants; also whenever such plants show signs of lowered vitality. If the pH reading of soil samples taken from near their roots has shifted towards neutral since the last test, corrective additions of either lime or aluminum sulphate or oak leaves should be made to the soil immediately, according to whether less or more acidity is wanted.

See also ACID SOIL; ALKALINE SOIL.

SOLANACEAE (sol-ah-nay'-see-ee). The Nightshade Family, a large group of more or less poisonous plants abundant in the warmer regions of the earth. It furnishes important drug and food products as well as many ornamental forms; among them are red pepper, tobacco, belladonna, the tomato, potato and egg-plant. The members are mostly rank-scented, round stemmed herbs with a watery sap, but some are woody shrubs, trees or climbing vines.

Principal cultivated genera are: *Solanum* (egg-plant, potato, etc.), *Lycopersicon* (tomato), *Cyphomandra, Atropa, Physalis, Iochroma, Lycium, Grabowskia, Mandragora, Capsicum* (pepper), *Cestrum, Salpichroa, Solandra, Fabiana, Hyoscyamus, Nicotiana* (tobacco), *Datura, Nierembergia, Petunia, Salpiglossis, Brunfelsia, Browallia, Streptosolen, Schizanthus.*

SOLANDRA (soh-lan'-drah). Three or four species of tall woody plants, native to tropical America and grown mostly in greenhouses. See CHALICE-VINE.

SOLANUM (soh-lay'-num). A genus of herbs, shrubs, vines and trees of the Nightshade Family; many are of horticultural value, others are used medicinally or as vegetables. Examples are the potato, egg-plant and showy Jerusalem-cherry. The species have compound or simple leaves, white, blue, yellow, or purple, bell- or wheel-shaped flowers, followed by berries which are often decorative. Most Solanums can be raised from seed; others from cuttings or by division.

IMPORTANT SPECIES

S. pseudo-capsicum (Jerusalem-cherry). A shrubby Old-World plant with white flowers, followed by round red or yellow fruit ½ in. across. Much grown in pots as a decorative house plant, it is very susceptible to drafts and even more so to gas, dropping its leaves immediately if there is even a faint trace in the atmosphere.

capsicastrum (False Jerusalem-cherry, sometimes called Ornamental-pepper). A Brazilian species resembling the preceding but with scarlet or deep orange, oval or pointed fruits, lasting only a short time.

dulcamara (Bitter-sweet). An Old-World shrubby vine to 8 ft. with violet flowers followed by red poisonous berries. Naturalized throughout N. America, it makes an attractive climber in the wild garden.

jasminoides. A shrubby climber to 10 ft. with starry, bluish-white flowers. Grown under glass in the N. and outdoors in the S. and California.

crispum. A small shrubby tree, the fragrant lavender flowers being followed by round yellow fruit. Tender N., it can be grown in the S. and Calif.

nigrum. A widely distributed sprawling weedy plant with white flowers, followed by black berries which may be quite poisonous, especially if eaten green. A number of cultivated forms grown for their edible fruit are known as Wonderberry, Sunberry or Garden-huckleberry.

wendlandi is a showy climber grown in greenhouses in the N. and outdoors in warm regions. It has lilac-blue flowers 2½ in. across and in Calif. reaches 50 ft. if planted in full sun.

giganteum, known in S. Calif. as "African-holly," is an Asiatic shrubby plant growing to 25 ft. It has lavender or blue flowers followed by round red berries.

integrifolium (Scarlet or Tomato Eggplant). Growing to 3 ft. tall with white flowers and scarlet or yellow fruit, this species makes an ornamental annual garden plant.

melongena, a shrubby plant to 3 ft. with lavender flowers and purple fruit. Var. *esculentum* is the common Egg-plant (which see) in which the fruit is usually purple but may be white, striped or yellowish. Var. *depressum* is the Dwarf Eggplant and var. *serpentinum* the Snake Egg-plant, its fruit being long, slender and curled at the end.

tuberosum, the "Irish" potato (see POTATO), a food plant of worldwide importance. Its original habitat was the Andes.

SOLDANELLA (sol-dah-nel'-ah). A genus of perennial herbs of the Primrose Family, having nodding blue, violet or white fringed flowers. Natives of the Alps, these beautiful little flowers should be grown in moist shady positions in the rock garden. They are increased by ·division or seeds. *S. alpina,* growing to 6 in., has roundish leaves and pale blue flowers in umbels; *S. pusilla,* to 6 in., has deep blue or violet flowers ½ in. across, usually solitary; *S. montana,* to 15 in., the showiest of the group, has clear blue flowers in umbels from May to July.

SOLIDAGO (sol-i-day'goh). A genus of erect, perennial herbs of the Composite Family well known as Goldenrod (which see). Many minute heads of golden-yellow flowers make plume-like showy masses throughout late summer and fall.

SOLLYA (sol'-yah). Evergreen climbing shrubs, natives of Australia. They are hardy outdoors in the S., and are sometimes grown under glass. *S. heterophylla* (Bluebell Creeper), the principal species, grows to 6 ft. high, with slender twining stems and variable leaves from narrow to oval. Very attractive when in bloom with bright blue flowers in loose clusters. In the S. it is a popular plant for scrambling over banks, boulders, and low fences. Propagated by seeds and cuttings.

SOLOMONS SEAL. Common name for the genus Polygonatum, a member of the Lily Family. They have creeping roots, on which each year's growth scars show prominently, giving rise to the common name. From the roots rise graceful, arching, leafy stems, with small white or greenish bell-shaped flowers hanging from the axils of the leaves; these are followed by handsome blue or black fruits. Plants should be grouped in soil rich in humus in a shady part of the wild garden, or among ferns at the north side of the house. They are easily propagated by seed or division. *P. commutatum,* growing to 8 ft., makes outstanding groups; *P. biflorum,* less than half as tall, and with fewer flowers to a cluster, is the species most frequently seen in the wild; its var. *majus* is larger. *P. latifolium* and *multiflorum* are Old-World species.

SOOT. This familiar black deposit found in chimneys and flues has value as a nitrogenous fertilizer, containing an average of about 3 per cent nitrogen. It may be applied dry or in water as a liquid manure. Because of its dark color it absorbs heat when sprinkled dry on the surface of the soil and appreciably raises the temperature of the latter. It is also effective in lightening heavy soils and, sprinkled among plants, it kills or at least repels slugs and snails. Its use in gardening is, however, necessarily limited because of the small supply.

SOOTY MOLDS, or SOOTY FUNGI. The leaves of many trees often become coated with a black, sooty covering in midsummer. The damage is chiefly to their appearance unless the coating is so heavy as to shut out sunlight and interfere with the normal leaf processes. The condition is caused by fungi related to the powdery mildews but in which the mycelium is dark colored instead of white. These fungi are not parasitic to the extent of sending feeding rootlets into the leaf tissue, but obtain nourishment either from sugary solutions exuded from the leaves or from insect secretions, known as "honeydew." Sooty molds, which frequently follow infestations of aphids and the citrus white fly, can, if serious, be controlled by spraying or dusting as for powdery mildew (see MILDEW); or by destroying the insects with suitable contact poisons, which see.

Plate 49.   SOME EMINENTLY SATISFACTORY SUBJECTS

Upper left: Great delicacy of form and beauty of marking characterize salpiglossis blooms.   Upper right: The hybrid strains of perennial lupines show a wide range of color.   Lower left: Spirea Anthony Waterer is a dependable bloomer even under trying conditions.   Lower right: The double stock is exceedingly fragrant, making the garden in the evening a place of delight.

SOPHORA (soh-foh'-rah). A genus of mostly deciduous trees, belonging to the Pea Family. They have decorative pinnate foliage and conspicuous, long panicles of fragrant flowers of yellow, white, or violet. Some are evergreen and grow only south. They thrive in soils varying from rather dry to moist, well-drained sandy loam. Those which are a little tender north should be planted by a sheltering building or wall. Showy when in bloom, they have much ornamental value for lawn or garden. Propagated by seeds, greenwood cuttings, layers and grafting.

S. japonica, the Japanese Pagoda-tree, or Chinese Scholar-tree, grows to 75 ft. or more, is hardy north. The dense, round-headed tree bears yellowish flowers in panicles 15 in. long. It is particularly desirable in the garden because of its late flowering (from July to Sept.) when most woody plants are out of bloom. Against a background of evergreens the long chains of flowers are even more effective. There is a narrow columnar var. (*columnaris*) and a much used weeping var. (*pendula*) with contorted branches.

viciifolia, growing only to 8 ft., is also hardy north and a useful garden plant. Its terminal racemes are of pale violet.

secundiflora, called the Mescal-bean, is an evergreen growing to 40 ft. but not hardy north. It has fragrant violet-blue flowers 1 in. long.

tetraptera and *microphylla* are tender evergreens to 40 ft., with small leaves and abundant good-sized golden yellow blossoms.

SORBARIA (saur-bay'-ri-ah). A genus of Asiatic deciduous shrubs with attractive leaves and flowers. See FALSE-SPIREA.

SORBUS (saur'-bus). A genus of deciduous trees or shrubs with ornamental foliage and clustered fruits, native in temperate regions of the N. hemisphere and belonging to the Rose Family; commonly called Mountain-ash, which see.

SORREL. One common name for the genus Rumex, sometimes applied particularly to the low-growing species with spearhead-shaped, fleshy, sour but edible leaves which are sometimes used as a salad, or to flavor other salads of other leaves. Two or three of these sorrels are cultivated in Calif. and some of the S. States. They are long-lived perennials, sustaining frequent and severe cutting. The earliest of these "greens" (*Rumex patientia*) is called

Patience or Spinach-dock. It may be followed by Belleville-dock or Garden Sorrel (*R. acetosa*) as a succession crop.

Jamaica-sorrel is *Hibiscus sabdariffa,* and Wood-sorrel a species of Oxalis.

SORREL-TREE. Another name for Sourwood (which see), *Oxydendrum arboreum.*

SOTOL (soh'-tohl). Common name for Dasylirion, a genus of tree-like desert plants with whitish lily-like flowers in dense panicles.

SOURBERRY. Common name for *Rhus integrifolia,* an evergreen Sumac (which see), with green flowers and hairy scarlet fruit.

SOUR-GUM. Another name for *Nyssa sylvatica,* the Tupelo, Black-gum or Pepperidge, a large tree whose foliage turns brilliant scarlet in, autumn. See GUM; NYSSA.

SOURSOP. A common name for *Annona muricata,* a tropical American fruit tree.

SOURWOOD. One name for *Oxydendrum arboreum,* a hardy, slow-growing tree of the Heath Family, also known as Sorrel-tree. It has thick, fissured bark; long, slender, pointed leaves with a sour taste, and small white flowers in conspicuous semi-drooping panicles, followed by grayish capsules. It is frequently planted in front of larger trees, or as a background for the shrubbery border, as the bright glossy green leaves turn a brilliant scarlet in the fall. Sourwood is propagated by seeds sown, as soon as ripe, in pots or pans filled with sandy peat soil, and sometimes covered with cut sphagnum. It thrives best in a rather acid soil in a partially shaded situation.

SOUTH AFRICAN PLANTS. Americans are always on the lookout for new flowers for their gardens. It is rather odd, therefore, that they have been slow in finding out what an enormous number of beautiful plants are to be found in S. Africa, many of which they could grow. These plants, with few exceptions, will not be hardy in the latitude of New York but will grow out of doors in the S. and S. W.; in the N. many can be grown as winter or summer bulbs or as garden annuals. Many of the succulent sorts can be grown during the summer in rock gardens, but they are especially to be recommended for house windows or sunrooms. The latter, with their abundance of light and rather cool temperature, are liked especially by most

S. African bulbs and succulents which generally prefer the cooler air to the hot temperature of greenhouses.

Many of these plants are established already in Fla. and Calif. gardens, but many are still unknown, and in the N. the variety available is small, though growing rapidly. Nurserymen each year include more and more kinds in their catalogs, and what promises to be a "boom" in S. Africans is already on the way. An exhibition of such plants at the 1935 International Flower Show in New York City gave many people a realization of their beauty and interest.

SOME FAMILIAR ONES. Some plants of S. African origin have been favorites in the U. S. for years, for example, freesias and some of the daisies. A handsome bulbous plant, called the Mexican-lily, but really *Crinum moorei,* from S. Africa has been grown in New England farmhouses for many years. Not hardy as far N. as New York, it will bloom in the house in winter or on the verandah in summer and its tall, 3- to 4-ft. stalks bear 8 to 10 big lily-like flowers, white and pink, and fragrant. It is almost fool-proof, the huge bulbs growing in the same pot or tub for years; the only care it needs when resting after flowering is to have the pot laid on its side under a bush or set in a cellar window without water until it is ready to start again. There are many other fine Crinums.

Other familiar S. African plants are the callas (*Zantedeschia africana*), which grow easily indoors. They need a moist soil containing peat moss or any other material that holds water, as they must not be allowed to dry out. Few people realize how attractive they look out of doors in a damp spot or by a pool where, grown in clumps, they are very desirable. They must in the N. be taken up at the approach of frost, but they are no more trouble than gladioli. Unlike most of the S. Africans (which generally need a long drying out), they should be kept slightly damp in pots or boxes in the cellar. After a very short rest, they can, if desired, be brought up to a sunny window, where they will grow till it is time to set them out again. Yellow callas of two kinds (*Z. elliottiana* and *Z. albo-maculata,* the latter with white-spotted leaves) need much the same treatment but rather less moisture. The charming dwarf Pink Calla (*Z. rehmanni*) must have still drier soil and conditions. It is not quite so easy to grow but rewards care and attention.

The Red-hot Pokers (Kniphofia) grow well in long grass by a pond and need much the same treatment as the tall callas. They are said to be hardy if planted deep, but it is better to take them up in the N.

SMALL BULBS. Other bulbs which make good winter subjects include a group of low-growing ones (8 to 10 in.) called Babiana (which see) and known by their plaited leaves. The flowers are white, bright blue or crimson, with 6 rather widely opened petal-like segments. One fine variety (*B. stricta* var. *rubro-cyanea*) has blue petals each with a deep crimson blotch at the base. In their habitat, Babianas are irrepressible, coming up in all sorts of unexpected places, sometimes squeezing through a minute crack between two rocks.

Sparaxis is another of the smaller bulbs, growing about a foot high with flowers of brilliant colors, generally with a dark spot at the base of the 6 widely opened segments. The colors range from creamy white through yellow and orange to deep crimson, purple, velvety brown, mauve, etc., in an immense variety. The plants are of the easiest culture and do well in pots in the window or sunroom.

Another fine bulbous plant is Ixia, with many starry 6-petaled flowers on rather long stalks. These too come in a great variety of colors, often with the dark blotch at the base of the segments. With these flowers, as with Babiana and Sparaxis, one is safe in ordering any kind, for all are attractive. Perhaps the strangest and most beautiful is *I. viridiflora,* the Green Ixia, which has petals of a queer metallic blue-green with a black blotch at the base. Ixias can also be grown as summer bulbs outdoors.

These are all cousins of the well-known freesias and are treated in much the same way. There are also many kinds of gladiolus—not the huge hybrids of the flower shops, but delicate, dainty wild ones, in exquisite colors and often fragrant. *G. tristis* has pale creamy flowers with purple markings, the variety *concolor* being a clearer cream color. Only a few of these wild gladioli are to be had in this country, but they are well worth cultivating.

Handsome tall Watsonias belong also to the big Iris tribe, though there are no true irises in S. Africa. They are grown indoors in winter or in the garden in summer.

Tritonias (incorrectly called Montbretias) are summer or winter bulbs of the easiest growth with bright flowers, generally salmon or orange on 1-ft. to 2-ft. stalks.

The Kafir-lily (*Schizostylis coccinea*) has crimson flowers on long stalks; its pink variety, Mrs. Hagerty, is earlier and very fine. They are best grown in pots in a cold frame and brought indoors when ready to bloom in the late fall or early winter. In warmer regions they will live out of doors and make large clumps.

The handsome big blue Agapanthus, sometimes called the Blue-lily-of-the-Nile, is fairly common, being grown usually in tubs on verandas.

The S. African Chincherichee is related to our Star-of-Bethlehem. The 6-petaled, wide-opened flowers in white or orange, borne along stalks from 6 in. to 18 in. tall, last for months. They are *Ornithogalum thyrsoides* (white) and *O. aureum* (yellow) and both are easy to grow.

Other bulbs are Lachenalias, like small hyacinths, good for hanging baskets and coming in many varieties. A queer bulbous subject is Haemanthus (Blood-lily or Snake-lily) with a mass of brilliant stamens surrounded by bright colored sheaths and suggesting a snake with head upraised.

Amaryllis belladonna, the Belladonna-lily, the only true Amaryllis, has big crimson lily-like flowers and is the hardiest of the group.

Nerines come generally in exquisite shades of coral, salmon, or crimson and glitter as if the flowers were set with thousands of tiny mirrors; at night they look as if powdered with gold dust.

GROWING THE BULBS. These bulbs are not hard to grow. The climate of S. Africa is one of heavy rainfall followed by a long dry period, so the bulbs must, generally, after flowering, have a long rest, when no water at all is given them. Laying a pot on its side under a bush will often be satisfactory treatment, but a sunny dry place getting absolutely no water is better; such would be an upper greenhouse shelf (the pots being covered with a little straw if left upright), a covered coldframe, or a sunny cellar window. The plants are not at all fussy about soil, but will repay the gardener with finer flowers in return for a moderately rich soil and weekly doses of liquid fertilizer while growing. They do not need to be put in the dark to make

roots when first planted as do tulips and hyacinths. Warmth and water are all they need and amateurs will find them easy to grow.

SOUTH AFRICAN DAISIES. Many kinds of daisies make fine garden annuals or greenhouse plants in winter. There are Ursinias, generally yellow or orange with a dark green zone at the base of the petals; Arctotis, in many shades of color, orange, red, purple and deep crimson and white, etc., some with deeper color on the back of the petals or zoned. *Arctotis stoechadifolia* (known as *A. grandis*) has long been grown in our gardens. Venidium, the Namaqualand Daisy, has huge flowers of flaming orange-red with a maroon base, and there are many hybrids. Dimorphotheca is another fine one with white, purple, yellow or orange flowers. Gazanias are handsome daisies of many colors with exquisite markings, and the Gerberas or Jamestown Daisies come in shades of salmon-pink and crimson. Then there are two lovely blue ones—Felicia, with yellow centers, now often included among the Asters, and Charieis, with dark blue centers.

Most of the flowers are annuals or will bloom the first year from seed. The rest are perennial and in the N. must be kept over winter in a frame or greenhouse. They like a light soil and full sun. If planted in a box or flat and set in the sun in a window or frame without water for 2 or 3 weeks and then watered, they will be more likely to germinate freely. They should not be allowed to dry out when growing as they may become stunted and never recover.

Geraniums (or Pelargoniums) grow wild in Africa and there are many varieties, not large-flowered as a rule, but interesting.

Nemesias are also S. African plants and are grown as garden annuals or for winter flowers under glass; there are many hybrids in a great variety of colors.

There is a vast number of Succulents (which see) for which ordinary cultivation, as practiced in gardens or greenhouses or sunrooms (with the usual spraying for pests), is suitable for the S. African plants, with the extra points noted above.

SOUTHERNWOOD. A common name for *Artemisia abrotanum,* a sub-shrub with yellowish flowers, also called Old Man.

SOW-BUG. Common in old or neglected greenhouses, in hotbeds and wherever there are dampness and rotting wood, this creature is not a true insect but a crustacean, related to the crayfish. Sow-bugs have five pairs of walking legs, two pairs of antennae and, unlike insects, they have no tracheae and breathe by blood gills. Sometimes called pill-bugs, they are flat bodied, oval, light gray or slate colored, up to ½ in. long, and roll up into a small ball resembling a pill when disturbed. They are usually found in damp warm places at the surface of the ground, under boards or trash and in other protected places. They injure greenhouse plants by feeding on the roots but are often found in gardens as well. About one year is required for the life cycle, but all stages may be found in a greenhouse at the same time. The easiest method of control is the use of poisoned bran mash as recommended for cut-worms, which see.

In greenhouses, a mixture of 9 parts sugar and 1 part paris green, or a combination of 2 parts white flour, 2 parts sugar and 1 part paris green can be used as poison bait; or fine tobacco dust will serve as a repellent.

SOY-BEAN. Common name for *Glycine max* (also called Soya- or Soja-bean), an erect annual leguminous herb of China and Japan, growing sometimes to 6 ft., with inconspicuous white or purple flowers and pendent, brownish hairy pods. An important human food crop and source of various commercial products in the Orient, it is, in this country, a valuable forage crop in the S. and a valuable warm weather green manure or cover-crop throughout the country. See also COVER-CROP.

SPADES AND SPADING. The spade and the spading-fork are tools used to dig the soil in preparation for sowing and planting. The chief objects are (1) to bury weeds and manures—both applied dressings and green manure crops; (2) to fine and thus aerate the soil and increase its porosity and water-absorbing and holding capacity; (3) to bring plant food from lower levels nearer to the surface and thus favor plant development; and (4) to provide a deep, loose, friable seed bed or growing medium.

The common spade has a rather thick, usually flat, steel or wrought iron blade. The straight (or rarely curved) cutting edge, guided by the wooden handle, is pressed into the ground with the foot placed on its upper end. In general form the shovel resembles the spade but is usually rounded in outline, of more concave form,

has low, raised sides and is made of thinner metal; thus it is adapted more for scooping and throwing sand, gravel or loose earth than for cutting dense soil.

Both spades and shovels are made in many forms. The four most used in home gardening have long or short handles, either straight or with a D-shaped hand

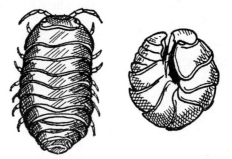

SOW-BUGS OR PILL-BUGS
Actually not bugs at all but relatives of crayfish and lobsters, these hard-shelled creatures infest damp places feeding on rotting wood and living plants. This shows one seen from above (left) and from the side as it curls up when disturbed. Both greatly enlarged.

hold. The styles with long, straight handles are less effective than the others, as their shorter curved blades do not penetrate the soil as deeply as do the straight spade blades; also their smooth, round handles are harder to manipulate, especially in turning soil over. The short or D-handled spade and digging-fork penetrate the soil deeply when their blades or tines are thrust vertically downward, and are well designed to pry up and turn over the "spits," as the lumps or clods of earth are called. For all soils except dry, sandy ones the D-handled spading-fork (which see) is the best digging tool; where the soil is sandy and loose, the solid blade of the spade is better.

The common (but wrong) way to dig with either fork or spade is to thrust the tool slantingly into the ground. This not only removes or loosens a shallower layer of soil but also demands more stooping than does the correct way; it is much harder work, does not adequately bury the weeds, grass, manure and other surface material and yet demands fully as much time and effort as the right way. The shallow stratum of soil does not provide as good a rooting medium and dries out quickly, the plants in it suffering more or less or dying in consequence.

The right way is to thrust the tines or blade *vertically full depth* into the soil; with the foot force the cross-piece at the top of the blade down flush with the soil surface; then pry up the spit, invert it completely in the air and dump it upside down in the furrow. Finally slice or crumble it with glancing blows of the tool. Thus all trash will be buried deeply where it will most readily decay and the clods will be broken up ready for the rake to make the soil surface still finer in readiness for seeding and planting. A well-spaded plot is level, clean, uniform and a joy to the gardener's eye.

In heavy soils the work may be lightened by making the spits only half as wide as in medium and light ones, where the spade is usually thrust in from 6 to 10 or more inches from the edge of the undug soil. But always it should be to full spade depth, except that shallow soils should not be either dug or plowed full depth the first time. This would bring up too much inert unaerated sub-soil. Deepen a new soil gradually, digging about an inch deeper each year and mixing this thin layer of new sub-soil with manure or humus and the richer surface earth as it is turned up.

Never dig more ground in one day than can be sown or planted that same day, because seeds and plants will start best in freshly turned soil and if a rain should occur before seeding or planting the surface might become so heavily caked that re-digging might be necessary. This rule is especially important when the ground is very dry (as in midsummer). Seed sown then in freshly dug ground and well firmed may be expected to give a full stand of plants, whereas, if the soil dries out, the seed, when planted, is at a distinct disadvantage.

Another good plan to follow when digging is always to use the steel rake as soon as four or five furrows have been dug across the area. The gardener may thus stand on firm, undug ground while raking and thereby avoid tramping on the soft, newly turned soil; more important still, it will mean a more thorough job and retain the maximum amount of moisture in the soil. In any case always rake immediately after digging; never postpone this work from morning until afternoon.

See PLANTING; RAKES AND RAKING; SEEDS AND SEEDSOWING; TRENCHING.

Plowing, even where practicable in a small garden, is less satisfactory than digging because it is generally much shallower; in large areas, of course, it saves time and labor.

SPADING-FORK. A digging tool on the lines of a spade but with four or five flat-faced tines instead of a single, broad flat blade. To use it correctly, push the tines vertically downward full depth into the soil and from 6 to 10 in. from the edge, lift the "spit" (which see), turn it upside down, and dump it in the furrow. Then break any large chunk with one or two sidewise blows of the tines, which will slice it thin and prepare it for the rake. The sign of an expert wielder of a fork is a smooth uniform surface with no weeds or litter showing; moreover, this result should be accomplished at the first effort, not in a series of diggings.

See PLANTING; RAKES AND RAKING; SPADES AND SPADING; SEEDS AND SEEDSOWING; TRENCHING.

SPADIX. A form of spike (which see) formed of a fleshy axis in which the flowers are frequently deeply imbedded, as in the aroids; the whole is subtended or shielded by a large, arching, and frequently colored bract called the *spathe,* which see.

SPANISH BAYONET, or SPANISH DAGGER. Common names for *Yucca aloifolia* and *Y. gloriosa;* sometimes applied to other species.

SPANISH-BROOM, or WEAVERS-BROOM. Common name for *Spartium junceum,* a shrub of the Pea Family, growing upright to 10 ft. with slender rush-like branches and racemes of large golden-yel-

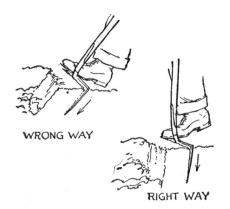

WRONG WAY

RIGHT WAY

HOW TO SPADE THE SOIL
Insert the spade vertically (not diagonally) so as to dig its full depth; then lift the earth and in throwing it down, invert and break it up well.

low sweetly fragrant pea-like flowers. Hardy as far N. as Philadelphia, it is much planted in the W. States on dry rocky banks, where it blooms almost the year around. It is increased by seed or by cuttings of green wood started under glass.

SPANISH-CHERRY. Common name for *Mimusops elengi,* a tropical tree, grown for its yellow berries.

SPANISH GARDEN. A type of garden design in which the planted area is surrounded by the dwelling on 3, or even 4, sides. Although much used by, and associated with, the Spanish, it originated in N. Africa whence the Crusaders brought it to Europe. As seen in the U. S. (especially the S. W.) it is more commonly referred to as Patio Garden, which see.

SPANISH-LIME. A common name for *Melicocca bijuga,* a tropical tree grown for its juicy fruit and more often called Genip, which see.

SPANISH-MOSS. Common name for *Tillandsia usneoides,* an epiphytic herb of the Pineapple Family, having long slender gray moss-like stems covered with tiny leaves, and very small inconspicuous flowers. In its native S. States and tropical America its long strands hanging gracefully from the branches of trees (especially Live Oaks) are a characteristic feature of the landscape. The "moss" is used commercially for packing and in the manufacture of various materials.

SPARAXIS (spah-rak'-sis). A genus of S. African, spring-blooming bulb-like herbs known as Wandflower, which see.

SPARKLEBERRY. A common name for *Vaccinium arboreum,* a large evergreen shrub with white flowers and black fruits.

SPARMANNIA (spahr-man'-i-ah). African-hemp. Handsome shrubs of the Linden Family from S. Africa, with dense hairy foliage and heavy heads of white bloom in early summer, rivaling the viburnums. Under greenhouse culture in the N. they average 6 ft. in height, but outdoors in S. Calif. they may attain 20 ft. They require full sunlight and a rich loam soil with peat and sand. Cuttings are propagated under unshaded glass in April.

Of the two species *S. africana* is the more desirable; its var. *flore-pleno* (double-flowered) is less free-flowering. *S. palmata,* with deeply-lobed leaves, is of lower growth.

SPARTIUM (spahr'-shi-um) *juncea.* An ornamental S. European shrub with fragrant yellow pea-like flowers, and known as Spanish-broom, which see.

SPATHE. A large, hood-like bract subtending and arching over a spike or other inflorescence usually in such cases called a *spadix* (which see). The spathe is frequently colored and somewhat petal-like, as in the calla.

SPATHODEA (spa-thoh'-dee-ah). A genus of strikingly handsome tropical trees of the Bignonia Family, with evergreen pinnate leaves and clustered, bell-shaped, scarlet or orange flowers with a leathery calyx. One species, *S. campanulata,* is occasionally planted in the S. States and commonly used as a street tree in the tropics. It requires a rich moist soil and is increased by seed or cuttings.

SPATTERDOCK. One of several common names applied to *Nymphozanthus advena,* the native yellow pond-lily, generally known as the Cow-lily, which see.

SPAWN. The common name for the whitish, fibrous vegetative part (*mycelium*) of certain fungi, from which the conspicuous, above-ground spore-bearing parts, called mushrooms, toadstools, shelf fungi, etc., are developed. In seed catalogs it refers to this material prepared in the form of dry "bricks" of peat-like appearance or in other forms. It is planted in the cultivation of edible mushrooms, which see.

SPEAR GRASS. A common name for Stipa, a genus of tall perennial grasses grown for ornament; also called Feather Grass.

See also ORNAMENTAL GRASSES.

SPEARHEAD FERN (*Phegopteris polypodioides*). A small and fairly common American fern of open woods, with long triangular fronds and conspicuous basal pinnae turned outward and downward. Good for garden use where rocks and woods soil can be provided. More often known as the Long Beech Fern.

SPEAR-LILY. Common name for Doryanthes, a genus of large succulent Australian desert plants somewhat grown in Calif.

SPEARMINT. Common name for *Mentha spicata,* a hardy perennial used for flavoring.

SPECIES. A group of plants comprising a subdivision of a genus and including individuals which are so nearly alike in their more stable characteristics that they all might have come from a single parent.

In a plant name the first word indicates the genus, and the second the species it belongs to. Thus the familiar white oak is *Quercus alba,* "Quercus" signifying the whole oak genus, and "alba" (Latin for "white") the group or *species* of which any member resembles in essential characters all other *white* oaks more than it does any other kind of oak.

Because of the natural variation of plants it is almost impossible to separate them into absolute categories; thus small (though sometimes striking) differences between plants of one species—as in shape, color, or number of leaves—give rise to smaller groups called *varieties.* Stable characters on which grouping into species is based include such constant features as number, structure and arrangement of flower-parts; these are retained and passed on from generation to generation when members of the same species mate. The mating of members of different species constitutes what is called "crossing" or hybridizing, the result being a cross or hybrid. Species, therefore, although an arbitrary term used to indicate close relationship, really represents a primary "blood" relationship and is regarded as the unit of Classification, which see.

See also FAMILY; GENUS; VARIETY.

SPECULARIA (spek-eu-lay'-ri᠊ah). A genus of small annual herbs closely resembling bellflowers (Campanula). They have blue, violet, or white wheel-shaped or broadly bell-shaped flowers and are used in the rock garden or the border, growing from seed sown where they are to stand. *S. speculum* (Venus Looking-glass), often used as an edging plant, has violet-blue or white toothed flowers to 1½ in. long, borne 1 to 3 together in the axils of the leaves; *S. pentagonia* is a hairy-leaved plant with 5-angled buds and small solitary blue flowers.

SPEEDWELL. Common name for a large genus of herbs with blue, violet, or white flowers in tightly packed racemes. See VERONICA.

SPENT HOPS. A by-product of brewing, the residue from hops is useful for lightening soil or performing other beneficial functions of humus. It also makes a good summer mulch, and carries a small amount of rather slowly available nitrogen. With the repeal of the Eighteenth Amendment the way was cleared for a larger supply than during the previous decade, and those gardeners situated where they can secure spent hops at a low price should find them valuable, especially if their soils tend to extremes of lightness or heaviness.

SPHAERALCEA (sfee-ral'see-ah). A genus of herbs and shrubs grown in warm countries and greenhouses for their mallow-like flowers. See GLOBE-MALLOW.

SPHAGNUM. A name given to moss-like plants of some 300 species found in all N. temperate countries and also called bog-moss or sometimes, loosely, peat moss (which see). Although occasionally used while alive and green on the surface of pots of orchards, etc., it is more familiar to gardeners in its dried form in which it is largely used in making compost for growing water-loving plants, like pitcher-plant, for propagating certain greenhouse subjects, for mulching, and, especially, for wrapping the roots of plants, such as roses, perennials, etc., before shipping them. Its value is based on its high absorbent and water-holding capacity, due to its peculiar cell construction and sponge-like texture. Even as it decays and loses some of its body, it continues useful for mulching and lightening soil, thereby becoming more like real peat moss which is largely made up of decomposed sphagnum deposits laid down centuries ago.

SPHENOGYNE (sfee-noh-gy'-nee). A name frequently used in catalogs for the S. African plant correctly called Ursinia, which see.

SPHINX MOTH. One name for a large, heavy-bodied moth with long, narrow wings, also called hawk moth or humming-bird moth. It flies at twilight and poises in the air to sip nectar from deep throated flowers in the manner of a humming-bird. The larva, called a horn-worm, is a large, smooth caterpillar, usually green, about 3 in. long when full grown, and with a prominent backward projecting horn near the tip of the abdomen. Injurious members of this group are the tomato and tobacco worms and the catalpa sphinx. For control see under those host plants.

SPICEBUSH. Common name for *Benzoin aestivale,* a native shrub with small yellowish, highly fragrant flowers and scarlet fruits.

SPIDER-FLOWER, or SPIDER-PLANT. The common names for *Cleome spinosa,* a tall tropical annual with white or purple flowers having slender protruding stamens.

SPIDER-LILY. Common name for Hymenocallis, a genus of bulbous plants of the Amaryllis Family. Their leaves are narrow or strap-shaped and the strange flowers with their long segments and stamens are borne in umbels at the top of a rather stout, leafless stem. Some species are grown in the greenhouse for winter bloom, others are grown in the garden for summer bloom, and the bulbs lifted after flowering and stored over winter. They are increased by offsets.

H. calathina (Basket-flower, or Spider-lily), a summer-blooming plant from S. America, has white flowers with a funnel-shaped, fringed crown, striped with green, and long, thread-like stamens. Some catalogs and gardeners still call it by its former generic name, Ismene. *H. caribaea* with long, narrow, shining leaves and fragrant white flowers with very narrow petals, blooms in winter under glass. Two natives, spring-flowering species—*H. occidentalis* and *H. rotata*—are charming naturalized in wild gardens in the S. States.

In the S., Spider-lily is *Lycoris radiata*, and Yellow Spider-lily is *L. aurea* (see LYCORIS).

SPIDERWORT. Common name for the genus Tradescantia, a common herb with grass-like leaves and generally purple flowers. Also for the family, Commelinaceae (which see), to which belong Tradescantia and other herbaceous garden subjects.

SPIKE. An elongated spire-like flower cluster (inflorescence) in which the individual flowers are without stalks (that is, sessile) and borne close against the main flower stalk. A head of timothy or wheat is an example; also that of Blazing Star. The Willow catkin is a form of spike.

SPIKE GRASS. Common name for three different plants of the Grass Family. One is *Demazeria sicula,* an annual, native to the Mediterranean region, sometimes grown for its feathery sprays which are used in either green or everlasting bouquets. It is a small plant, about 1 ft. tall, with narrow leaves to 6 in. long, and flowering heads 2 to 3 in. long made up of small individual spikelets. Seed should be sown where the plants are to grow. The other species, sometimes called Spike Grass, are *Uniola latifolia* and *Leptochloa fascicularis.* The former is a native American perennial grass to 5 ft., ranging from Pa. to Tex., and occasionally planted for

landscape effects. The latter, used for the same purpose, is a native of warm and temperate parts of E. U. S. It grows to 2½ ft., has thread-like leaves 8 in. long, and panicles to 1 ft. in length.

SPIKE-HEATH. Common name for *Bruckenthalia spiculifolia,* a small evergreen shrub of the Heath Family, with needle-like leaves in whorls, and spikes of small nodding bell-shaped flowers. Resembling in growth the dwarf Ericas (heaths), it is hardy N. and an excellent plant for the rock garden, as its freely produced rosy blossoms come in summer when bloom is needed. Thriving in an acid soil, it grows readily from seed or cuttings.

SPIKENARD, AMERICAN. Common name for *Aralia racemosa,* a woodland perennial of E. U. S. with small whitish flowers and purplish berries and aromatic roots.

SPILANTHES (spil-an'-theez). A genus of small, often weedy, herbs of the Composite Family, with white or yellow rayed flower-heads. The toothed leaves of one species (*S. oleracea*) are used to flavor salads. Few others are known in the garden, but *S. americana* is a rather showy native yellow-flowered plant.

SPINACH. A short-season herb grown and used as "greens." Its horticultural varieties are grouped as prickly-seeded (*Spinacea oleracea*) and round-seeded (var. *inermis*).

As the plants are hardy, seed may—and indeed should—be sown as soon as the ground can be worked; successional sowings may follow until midspring. Plants from later sowings quickly run to seed, so for summer greens New-Zealand Spinach (which see) should be substituted. In the North sowings of the true spinach may be made again in August and September for autumn use.

The soil should be well drained and abundantly supplied with both humus and quickly available plant food. Because it keeps the leaves freer from sand and lessens the necessary washing, a peat or muck soil is especially desirable; large commercial crops are grown in muck-bed areas in the northern States. After putting the soil in fine condition, make rows 12 in. apart and sow the seed thinly (one every inch) to reduce the labor of thinning, which, done when the plants get their first true leaves, should leave them 3 to 6 in. apart. Cutting can usually start in 6 to

8 weeks, the plants being harvested successively as they become big enough to use until the crop is cleaned up.

Spinach can be (as it used to be before shipped up from the South) carried over winter either beneath light straw mulches or in uncovered coldframes. By covering the frames with sash a few weeks before a crop was wanted, the plants could be started into growth and supplies could be had all winter. For early spring use, seed was often sown during February in hot-beds or coldframes.

There are several leaf diseases of spinach but no spraying can be advised because of the nature of the crop. Seed treatment with red copper oxide (see DISINFECTION) has been very successful in controlling damping off. The most common pest is the spinach aphid and the best control is probably nicotine dust. There is no control for the spinach flea beetle, a tiny greenish-black beetle which eats holes in the leaves. A leaf miner is sometimes quite destructive but no control can be recommended except burning the injured leaves.

SPINACH-BEET. A name sometimes used for Swiss Chard. See CHARD.

SPINDLE-TREE. Common name for Euonymus, a genus of ornamental shrubs, small trees and climbers of many forms.

SPINE. A sharp-pointed and rigid process of indeterminate size usually arising as a direct outgrowth of the stem or branch, as on the honey locust, or, less often, on leaf margin, as a holly. Less woody than a *thorn.*

SPINY MAIDENHAIR PALM. A name for trees of the genus Martinezia. They are spiny, tropical American palms with leaves pinnately divided, the leaflets expanded in fishtail form toward the end of the frond. See PALMS.

SPIRAEA (spi-ree'-ah). Spirea. A large group of deciduous shrubs, native in temperate regions of the N. hemisphere, belonging to the Rose Family. Many of the species, as well as numerous hybrids and horticultural forms, are hardy. They are mostly small or medium-sized shrubs of good habits, and very profuse bloomers with white the dominant color. (See illustration, Plate 49.) The early-flowering group is all white, but the late-flowering group comprises some with pink or reddish flowers. Those in the first group should be pruned right after flowering, the pruning consisting of thinning out old wood rather than cutting back. Those in the latter group are best cut back fairly hard in spring.

Spireas prefer a sunny position and will grow in any good soil, but thrive best in a rich moist loam. They are propagated by seed, cuttings of green and mature wood, and layers.

SPIRAEA HAS MANY FORMS WITH WHICH TO ORNAMENT THE GARDEN
1. The arching sprays of Spiraea vanhouttei, one of the type popularly called Bridal Wreath, are covered with countless white flowers toward the end of spring. 2. Spiraea billiardi, a shrub 6 feet in height, is a garden hybrid bearing spires of brilliant pink flowers after midsummer. 3. Anthony Waterer, a frequently used variety of Spiraea bumalda, is a low shrub bearing flattened clusters of crimson flowers in late summer.

Although occasionally troubled by a bacterial leaf spot, powdery mildew, chlorosis (loss of color) due to a virus, and a root rot, these shrubs are relatively free from disease. The most common insect pest is the spirea aphid, of which at least two species may be present. Control both by thorough spraying with nicotine-sulphate and soap or other contact insecticide. A leaf-rolling caterpillar sometimes draws the leaves together and fastens them with silken threads, but it is rarely serious. If necessary, spray with lead arsenate in July and clip off and burn any webby nests. The mealy white spirea scale may be controlled by a nicotine-sulphate and soap spray. The late-flowering spireas are particularly subject to attack by Japanese beetles in areas infested by that pest.

PRINCIPLE EARLY-FLOWERING SPECIES

S. thunbergi is the first to bloom, often before spring has really arrived. It is a twiggy shrub to 5 ft., with slender arching branches, feathery bright green leaves which turn orange to scarlet in fall, and small pure white flowers.

prunifolia var. *plena* grows to 6 ft., with upright slender branches, dark green shining leaves, brilliant orange-scarlet in fall, and double flowers.

arguta, a hybrid between *S. thunbergi* and *S. multiflora,* is very similar to the former but showier in flower.

multiflora is a hybrid between *S. crenata* and *S. hypericifolia.* It has slender arching stems and flowers a bit later than *S. arguta.*

cantoniensis is a bushy grower to 4 ft., with dense showy umbels of flowers, and blue-green leaves held late. Not quite hardy N. Its var. *lanceata,* with narrow leaves and double flowers, is still more tender.

trilobata grows to 4 ft. with slender spreading branches and leaves usually 3-lobed.

vanhouttei, a hybrid between *S. cantoniensis* and *S. trilobata,* resembles the latter but is larger and showier. It is one of the most floriferous and popular of shrubs.

nipponica follows in bloom, a vigorous shrub of rather stiff habit to 8 ft. It has dark green leaves, bluish beneath, held late in the fall, and showy umbels of white flowers.

trichocarpa is somewhat similar, making a dome-shaped bush to 6 ft.

henryi comes into bloom as the two preceding species pass out. It is very hardy, of vigorous upright growth to 8 ft. or more, with dark green leaves gray beneath, and flower clusters to 5 in. across.

veitchi, the latest of this group to flower, grows to 12 ft., with spreading arching branches, dark green leaves and flat clusters of creamy-white flowers in June and July.

LATE-FLOWERING SPECIES

S. japonica is a bushy upright shrub to 4 ft., with flat clusters of pink flowers. A variable species with several named forms.

albiflora is a dwarf compact Japanese shrub with a profusion of white flowers.

bumalda is a hybrid between *S. japonica* and *S. albiflora,* with flowers white to deep pink. Two of the best known forms are Anthony Waterer, dwarf and compact with crimson flowers; and Froebeli, of taller growth but also with crimson flowers.

billiardi, a hybrid between *S. douglasi* and a S. European species, grows to 6 ft., and bears pink flowers in July-Aug.

bullata is a dwarf Asiatic shrub with crinkled leaves and pink flowers, suitable for the rock garden and sometimes listed as *S. crispifolia.*

decumbens is a European species of prostrate growth with white flowers.

NATIVE SPECIES

S. tomentosa (Hardhack, Steeple-bush) is a low shrub common in moist places and showy in late summer with steeple-like panicles of rosy-purple flowers.

alba (Meadowsweet) grows to 6 ft., with white flowers in long leafy clusters.

virginiana grows to 4 ft., with slender arching stems, and rounded clusters of white flowers.

douglasi, native in the W. part of the country, grows to 8 ft., and is very handsome with rosy-pink flowers in long dense panicles. It spreads by suckers.

menziesi is somewhat similar but of lower growth.

densiflora, also a W. species, is a dwarf bushy shrub with attractive clusters of rose-colored flowers.

The so-called Spirea or Japanese Spirea forced by florists for late winter and early spring sale is Astilbe. Rock-spirea is *Holodiscus discolor.* False-spirea is the genus Sorbaria. Blue-spirea is *Caryopteris incana.*

SPIRANTHES (spy-ran′-theez). A genus of terrestrial native orchids known as Ladies Tresses, which see.

SPIRONEMA (spy-roh-nee′-mah) *fragrans.* A small Mexican perennial herb of the Spiderwort Family, with long fleshy drooping stems, clasping translucent leaves, and delicate fragrant white flowers in clusters. It is occasionally raised under glass as a basket plant in the N. and is planted in the open in the subtropics. It is sometimes grown and listed as *Tradescantia dracaenoides.*

SPIT (in digging). A garden synonym for spade; hence to spit the ground is to dig it. Spit also means the depth of the blade of a spade as well as a cubical chunk of earth one spade-length in each dimension—depth, width and length—that

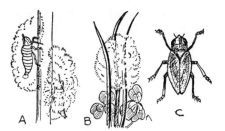

SPITTLE INSECTS AND THEIR WORK
These tiny green creatures (C) of the leaf hopper group live on grass and low herbage in masses of froth (B) consisting of a fluid that they secrete, then whip to a foam by rapid violent motion of their bodies.

is, the maximum amount that can be removed with a spade in one load. "One spit deep" and "two spits deep" mean respectively once and twice the depth of a spade blade. Spading a bed two spits deep is sometimes called "double digging."

SPITTLE BUGS. Small sucking insects of the family Cercopidae, which on grass and plant stems produce (and live in) masses of frothy, whitish foam often called "frog-spittle." Ordinarily only species found on grass and on pine are common, but in the summer of 1935 an unprecedented epidemic of them occurred in N. Y. and N. J. They are also considered a serious pest in parts of the Pacific N. W. The pine spittle insect (*Aphrophora parallela*) produces in the nymph stage masses of white frothy matter on Scotch Pine especially. The nymphs (white or flesh colored bugs, about ¼ in. long) secrete the spittle masses and beat them into foam, drawing in bubbles of air through their spoon-shaped posterior extremities. The adult is brownish gray, about ½ in. long with golden, oblique bands. Spittle bugs cannot be controlled by the ordinary contact sprays but derris dust has been found to be very effective.

In the 1935 epidemic spittle masses were found in great numbers even in penthouse gardens high up above N. Y. City streets. In N. J. they were especially numerous on legumes and strawberries. The adults were present all season on chrysanthemum plants but seemed to cause no particular damage.

SPLEENWORT. A common name for any fern of the genus Asplenium (which see), including several little American lime-loving kinds, excellent for transplanting to the rock garden but needing good

SPOONFLOWERS FROM THE DESERT
These stiff but interesting gray-green stalks with ivory, curved tops make striking arrangements (A). Actually they grow the other way up as the basal leaves of a desert plant resembling yucca (B).

drainage. The Silvery Spleenwort and Narrow-leaved Spleenwort, however, belong to the genus Athyrium, which see.

The name, spleenwort, is an old name, referring to the supposed value of these ferns for diseases of the spleen. The characteristics by which true spleenworts are distinguished include *sori* of linear shape, firm tissue, and a special type of scales sometimes called *clathrate*, (lattice-like). The genus Athyrium also has sori of linear shape, but always short, and often bent over the veins to which they are attached, in comma shapes or even horseshoe shape. Leaves of Athyrium species usually have a softer texture and the stem and leaves of scales are thin and chaffy.

The most common true spleenworts, or Asplenium are the wall rue, maidenhair, mountain, ebony, mother, Belanger's, and the Bird's Nest Fern.

The Athyrium species are the Lady Fern, Narrow-leaved, silvery, Japanese and a north Eurasian species, *A. crenatum.*

Because the species of Athyrium are no longer regarded by botanists as closely related to the true spleenworts, it has been recommended that the scientific name be used as a common name, and they are referred to as Athyriums.

SPOONFLOWERS. Name given to the leaves of *Dasylirion wheeleri,* a N. American desert plant of the Lily Family, locally called Sotol. They are long, stiff, and very slender except at the base which is broad, ivory colored and spoon-shaped where they overlap one another. In recent years these leaves, with the blades and bases cleaned and polished, have become popular for decorative use and in flower arrangements; placed *upside down,* the polished bases are interesting and clearly suggest the name given them. So widespread has the fad become that conservationists, fearing the extinction of the wild plants in the S. W. by collectors, are considering protective statutes and meanwhile urging gardeners to grow the plants from seed. These may be sown in sand during warm weather and covered with moist burlap until they sprout. Seedlings are grown on in partial shade and later in full sun. Although they will stand light frost, the plants cannot survive N. winters so should be grown indoors like other plants of similar habitat.

In Fla. the name spoonflower is applied to *Peltandra sagittaefolia,* a close relative of the Arrow Arum, which see.

SPORE. A body of microscopic size which serves to disseminate and reproduce a fungus, thus corresponding to a seed in the higher plants. Spores are of two types: those formed as a result of the union of two elements which represent male and female and termed *sexual* or *perfect spores,* and those formed directly from hyphae (fungus threads) without the intervention of a breeding act and called *asexual* or *imperfect spores.*

See FERNS; FUNGUS: see also under SEEDS and SEEDSOWING.

SPORT. Name given to an abrupt deviation from type; in scientific language a mutation. The term usually refers to a bud sport (*somatic mutation*), such as the sudden, unexplainable occurrence of a branch bearing pink roses on a bush normally having only red flowers. This usually implies a genetic or hereditary change within the affected plant cells, so that the new character becomes fixed, that is self-perpetuating and heritable. Many popular kinds of roses, carnations, apples and other valuable plants called by scientists *clonal varieties* have risen as bud sports.

See CLON; PLANT BREEDING; and, for contrast, HYBRID.

SPOTTED-WINTERGREEN. A common name for the genus Chimaphila. See PIPSISSEWA.

SPRAGUEA (spray'-gee-ah). A genus of small half-hardy perennial herbs of the Purslane Family, having fleshy leaves and small white, fleeting flowers borne in umbels at the top of a spike-like stem.

S. umbellata to 1 ft. with white flowers, occasionally tinged rose, is native to the mountains of W. America and can be grown in the rock garden if treated as an annual. It is increased by seed.

SPRAYING AND SPRAYERS. There are several methods of applying insecticides and fungicides to plants—spraying; dusting (which see), and systemics (which see). Spraying is the application of suspensions or solutions of pesticides under pressure through nozzles which distribute the liquid in very fine drops over the surface to be treated.

Most spray materials are available in two forms—wettable powders which go into suspension when mixed with water and emulsifiable concentrates, solutions of the pesticides in an organic solvent which, in turn, is made to disperse in water as an emulsion. A few are in the form of water miscible solutions. Wettable powders must be kept in suspension while spraying by shaking or an agitator in the sprayer. They are generally safer on foliage than emulsifiable concentrates, but leave more of a conspicuous residue. Emulsifiable concentrates generally do not require agitation once they are dispersed in the water and may have a slight edge in effectiveness on insects. Most fungicides are purchased in wettable powder form and only a few (mainly some mercurials) are available as water miscible liquids.

The choice of the spray material depends on accurate identification and knowledge of the habits of the plant enemy to be combatted, as well as a knowledge of how the pesticide acts. The modern organic insecticides with a few exceptions are specific for certain pests or groups of pests and are not necessarily limited by the insects' method of feeding on plants. By way of example, both lindane and malathion are useful on many insects that chew or suck. Chlordane is recommended specifically for lawn pests such as white grubs and ants; dieldrin for garden soil pests, leaf chewers, thrips, leaf miners and tree borers; and heptachlor for garden soil pests. Two phosphate compounds TEPP (tetra ethyl pyrophosphate) and parathion because of their highly poisonous nature on man and animals are recommended only for commercial growers who are acquainted with all necessary precautions to take. TEPP is excellent for mites, aphids, and most other sucking pests as a contact insecticide with no residual effectiveness; while parathion is a most effective insecticide for practically all above ground pests.

When it comes to the control of plant diseases, it is frequently not enough to know that the trouble is a fungous leaf spot or a blight, since the fungicide needed may depend on the actual species of organisms causing it. Certain well known diseases can be readily identified by the gardener, but the determination of others and the identification of the organisms causing them must be left to the scientist. When in doubt, send specimens of affected plants to your local agricultural extension service.

Ferbam is especially good for rust diseases, apple scab and black spot of roses, but does not take care of the mildews. Captan and maneb are effective on many fruit, vegetable and flower diseases but not on powdery mildew; thiram is specific for some lawn diseases; sulphur is used mainly for tree fruit diseases; nabam for potato diseases; and crude streptomycin for fire blight and other bacterial plant diseases.

SELECTING PESTICIDES. The number of pesticides appearing under trade names is constantly increasing. Many of these products are similar and control the same pests, according to the information given on the labels. This is most confusing to home gardeners and growers who are trying to find the most effective and economical material for certain pests or groups of pests. Insects and diseases vary greatly in their susceptibility to different chemicals in the formulations. Some plants also react adversely to some ingredients in pesticides. It is of great importance to read all the information on labels carefully and to know what to look for on a label when making a selection.

The analysis or active ingredient statement on a label is of primary importance as a basis of spray selection; not the trade name which is generally of little value. In order to purchase intelligently the gardener should familiarize himself with the characteristics and uses of the common basic pesticides.

An increasing number of combination insecticides and fungicides are being put on the market as general purpose fruit sprays, vegetable sprays or flower sprays. They are usually in the form of dusts (which see) or wettable powders but some emulsifiable liquid concentrates are also available. Their periodic use saves time and effort and eliminates the need for identifying or controlling any specific foliage or fruit insect or disease, even though their use may be wasteful when only one ingredient is required. Homemade combinations such as methoxychlor, malathion, and captan; or lindane, ferbam, and sulphur are easy to prepare when spraying and allow for formula adjustment for the particular problems to be dealt with.

The time of application and the number of sprays necessary depend on the enemy to be controlled. Most ornamental trees and shrubs can profit from a general purpose spray as soon as their leaves are nearly fully out to take care of such pests as tent caterpillars, canker worms, aphids, and leaf blight diseases. Two more applications at monthly intervals are generally sufficient under normal conditions to keep foliage healthy.

But the timing of applications is particularly important in controlling plant diseases; for once a fungus has entered the plant most fungicides are helpless in stopping the infection. Most fungicides are protectants and must be used, before a disease has started, to form a protective barrier between the plant and the disease producing organisms.

A few fungicides such as liquid lime-sulphur and some of the organic mercury compounds are also eradicants and may destroy the disease or prevent its sporulation and spread. It is always important to spray before wet rainy periods since it may only take several hours of such weather for spores to germinate and enter plant tissues—then it is too late for a protective application.

Both home gardeners and commercial growers can obtain spray schedules for various crops or plants in their area from their state agricultural service. These give the pesticide combinations to be used and the timing of the applications based on the stage of plant development or the time of year.

Dormant Sprays

Applications of spray materials to plants for pest control when they are dormant or inactive, normally after leaf drop in the fall and before the start of new growth in the spring, are called dormant sprays. In practice they are usually applied in the early spring from a month before right up to the time new growth begins. Dormant spraying is a sort of protective insurance against some insects and diseases that spend the winter on trees and shrubs in their hibernating or dormant stages.

Dormant sprays must act as contact poisons to kill the overwintering eggs and insects, hidden in cracks or bark crevices, on the undersides of twigs and around leaf scars and buds. Many, but not all, dormant pest stages on plants are susceptible to dormant spray materials. For the few that are not, such as canker worm and tent

SPRAYING BY WATER PRESSURE—1
This convenient sprayer screws onto the garden hose, the water flow being controlled by a trigger. A concentrated solution placed in the mason jar is drawn out by the suction of the water playing across a small opening and diluted to just the right strength as it is delivered.

caterpillar eggs, sprays must await their active stages.

There are only three basic compounds to consider for dormant spraying. The most time-honored of the three is liquid lime-sulphur. It was once widely used at dilutions of 1 to 7 to 1 to 10 for aphid eggs, red mite eggs, scale insects, and peach leaf curl. In recent years it has lost favor with the public because it is not particularly effective against most of the dormant pests and is in addition malodorous and discoloring to painted surfaces. With a few exceptions it is now replaced by either dormant oils or dormant dinitro products.

The oils used in dormant spraying are highly refined petroleum oils purchased as miscible oils under numerous trade names. When mixed with water they produce a milky suspension. The so-called "superior" oils—highly refined paraffinic oils from the eastern oil fields—are safer on plants, and more effective on insects than the mixed mid-continent or far western asphaltic oils widely used at one time. Dosage ranges from two to four gals. per 100 gals. of water or six to nine tablespoonsful per gal. of water. Before adding the miscible oil to the spray tank, first stir it vigorously in a small amount of water—this will produce a well-dispersed emulsion. Some agitation in the spray tank is desirable to prevent the oil separating out with possible plant injury.

Even though plants are sprayed when they are dormant, oils may still produce injury to susceptible species. The lower recommended dosages only should be used carefully on such deciduous trees as beech, hickory, walnut, butternut, Japanese maple, sugar maple and magnolia; and on such evergreens as hemlock, cryptomeria, retinospora, Douglas fir, and larch. Oils will also remove the bloom of blue spruces temporarily until the new growth appears. Superior oil may be used safely up to the delayed dormant stage of apple growth— that is when the leaves are about one-fourth inch out. Since mite eggs are more susceptible the closer they are to hatching, it is best to wait as late as possible before applying dormant oils.

The oils are chiefly used to control red mite eggs and the soft scales which are usually hemispherical when mature and have the protective scale as part of their body. They have less effectiveness against the hard or armored scales whose protective scales are actually separate from their bodies like a shell. By themselves dormant oils are of little use against aphid eggs.

The dinitro compounds are yellow dye-like materials which may be obtained under several trade names in the form of thin pastes or powders to be dissolved in water or miscible oils. They are not as agreeable to use as oils. The paste forms require stirring before dilution to obtain an even distribution of the chemical. Old clothes and rubber gloves are also necessary to avoid yellow hands and permanently stained woolens. But it does wash out of cottons and off painted surfaces. To avoid burning they should be applied only when the plants are fully dormant, before green tips appear. They should not be used on needled evergreens, but are safe on fully dormant boxwood for Nectria canker control.

The dinitros are highly effective against aphid eggs, the armored scales, the pear psyllid and the pear leaf blister mite.

Since the dinitros are effective on some dormant pests and the oils on others it may be desirable to apply a dinitro in the fully dormant period and to follow this with an oil spray in the green tip stage of development; or to combine both ingredients into one fully dormant spray using 2 gals. of miscible oil and 1½ qts. or lbs. of dinitro per 100 gals. of water (6 tbsp. of oil and 1 tbsp. of dinitro per gal. of water).

The same dormant spray should be applied only once per year. Repeat applications may be harmful and are not necessary when done right. Select a mild calm day when there is no danger of a freezing night. Do not attempt to spray at temperatures below 40° F. or late in the day when temperatures may drop below freezing that night. Once the spray dries on the tree there is no danger of freezing injury or a rain making it ineffective.

Spraying Equipment

Modern gardeners have a number of types of sprayers from which to make a selection—hose applicators of the proportioner type, aerosol applicators, hand atomizers, slide sprayers, compressed air sprayers, knapsack sprayers, bucket pumps, hydraulic power sprayers, and mist blowers. More than one type may be necessary to take care of all situations around the home or garden.

Hose applicators of the proportioner type are very popular with home gardeners for they make spraying relatively easy. They consist of a glass jar with a siphoning device in the cover attachable either at the faucet end or at the nozzle end of the hose. When the water is turned on the concentrated spray material is taken up and diluted with the water in a predetermined proper dilution for spraying. They come equipped with a nozzle that is adjustable for both a fan-shaped spray for close-up spraying or a long stream suitable for the upper parts of trees that are not too tall. Many liquid pesticides are now obtainable in bottles equipped with a disposable plastic proportioner that produces the right dilution for spraying that particular material. Some hose sprayers produce a more uniform spray than others and those equipped with a shut-off valve are preferable.

Aerosol applicators are relatively new and simple but comparatively expensive devices for applying pesticides in the air in the form of a fog, mist, or smoke. A liquid aerosol is formed when a volatile liquid under pressure disperses the pesticide mixed with it; and a solid or smoke aerosol is formed when a combustible material mixed with a pesticide burns and disperses it in the smoke. Practically all the pesticides that are soluble in organic solvents may be applied in liquid aerosol form. Those aerosols used in the garden or on house plants are fairly coarse and wet the foliage readily, but those for use against flies and mosquitoes in enclosed places or out in the open for space treatments are very fine and hang in the air for a considerable time.

Aerosols containing one or more insecticides, combinations of insecticides and fungicides, or weed killers are available for dispersal in pint-sized or larger metal containers, *bombs*, with a valve spray release for home, garden, and greenhouse use; in cardboard or metal containers for combustion in greenhouses; and with mobile fog generators for space application outdoors. They should be held at least a foot away from the plants when in use to avoid plant injury.

The hand atomizer sprayer is a handy type of spray applicator for house plants or a limited number of the smaller outdoor plants. It usually comes from pint to quart size and produces a fine mist with suspensions, emulsions or solutions by operating a hand plunger.

Slide or trombone sprayers are of two types. One type is attached to the cover of a quart container; the other type is equipped with a four to six foot hose that can be placed in any convenient bucket containing the spray. The nozzle is adjustable for close up or long distance spraying but the pumping action becomes tiring and it is difficult to get good coverage on the undersides of low growing plants with such sprayers.

The compressed-air type of sprayer is still popular for general garden use. It consists of an air-pump mounted in an airtight chamber, which is never filled more than three-fourths full with the spray material. Pressure is secured by pumping air into the tank like blowing up a tire. The high pressure gives a good spray at first but as the pressure goes down the spray gets poorer and frequent stops for pumping more air into the tank are necessary.

Knapsack sprayers, carried slung on the back and operated by pushing a handle up and down with one hand and manipulating the spray gun with the other, are too heavy and tiring for the average home gardener. Their advantages over the compressed air sprayers are that they are equipped with an agitator to keep the spray mixed and a large air chamber to produce a steady spray pressure.

Bucket pumps are simple or double-acting, that is they produce either an intermittent or a constant spray. They are clamped into a bucket or other suitable spray container. Two people are usually

COMPRESSED AIR SPRAYER
How one type already pictured is used in the garden. The pressure should be maintained by pumping often enough to make a fine misty spray.

required for efficient operation, one pumping and the other spraying. There should be a long enough hose to enable the latter to move around a tree or bush without having to move the bucket too frequently.

SPRAY SUPPLEMENTS

Any substance that, when combined with a pesticide, enhances its sticking, spreading or wetting qualities, makes it safer to foliage, aids in its dilution or uniform dispersion, or increases its toxicity to pests. Included are adhesive or sticking agents, wetting and spreading agents, emulsifying agents, safeners or correctives, diluents or carriers, and synergists (which see).

A good sticker has the function of prolonging the retention of sprays or dusts on plants. Spreaders and wetters aid liquid sprays in wetting waxy surfaces and spreading evenly over them by reducing the surface tension of the water. All three characteristics are desirable in most spray applications and substances having all three are generally employed.

Safeners or correctives are compounds added to sprays to reduce the danger of injury to foliage. Common examples are the use of hydrated lime with arsenicals, and activated charcoal with parathion.

Diluents or carriers are used to decrease

the amount of an active ingredient in a spray or dust so that it may be evenly dispersed in small quantities over a given surface. Water is the usual diluent for sprays but a number of finely ground inert materials may be used in dusts. These include clays such as pyrophyllite, kaolin or bentonite; talcs; and botanical flours such as walnut shell flour, redwood bark flours, soybean flour and peanut shell flour. Alkaline diluents including water from limestone areas should not be used with pesticides that are not compatible with alkalis. See SPREADERS AND STICKERS.

SPRAY INJURY

The application of chemical compounds in the form of sprays or dusts to leaves and other plant parts may produce various types of injury when label directions are not followed, weather conditions are not right or applications are made carelessly. Crops differ in their sensitivity to spray chemicals and may exhibit varying responses such as, spots, shot holes, burning, stunting, yellowing, and defoliation, cankers, die-back, blight and even death. Frequently the symptoms of such injury resemble those of true diseases.

The dormant dinitro compounds are not safe on needled evergreens and should not be used on them. Peach trees and Persian walnuts are very sensitive to arsenicals which produce yellowing of the foliage, defoliation, cracking and cankered areas on the twigs.

DDT will kill Kalenchoes; Squash and cucumbers may be severely stunted by both DDT and toxaphene, but the pure aerosol grade of DDT is safe on them. TEPP injures tomatoes and cyclamens and parathion may burn the leaves or spot the fruit of McIntosh, Cortland and related apple varieties in their early stages of growth.

Lime-sulphur may cause yellowing and leaf drop on apples, russeting of fruit, especially in hot weather, and is too injurious on peaches in the summer to be used at all.

Copper sprays, including Bordeaux mixture, may cause russeting of fruit and defoliation and are not recommended on them, except low soluble copper on sour cherry after picking. Their weekly use in the vegetable garden may produce stunting of young plants and paling of leaf margins and brittleness and spotting of older plants.

The newer organic fungicides also vary in their safety on plant species. Young cucumbers and squash will be stunted if maneb, zineb, or nabam is used on young plants before runners form. Captan applied before the third cover spray on Red Delicious and Baldwin apples may cause early leaf spotting, yellowing and leaf drop. Ferbam causes russeting and lenticel enlargement on Golden Delicious Apple and to a lesser degree on others.

A number of spray chemicals are incompatible when used in mixtures or in sprays immediately preceding each other and may produce mild to severe injury to foliage and fruit. Oils and sulphurs should never be mixed together or follow one another in a spray schedule. Sulphur sprays immediately preceding captan increase the possibility of captan injury.

SPRAY RESIDUE AND HEALTH.

This refers to the amount of poisonous material left on edible plant parts at harvest. This problem usually arises when residual sprays are applied too close to the harvest period for the control of a pest or disease or when a pest or disease becomes troublesome just before or as the crop ripens and must be stopped. The residue of some of the new chemicals as well as of lead arsenate may affect man and animals, in more than one way.

If enough is present and eaten at one time it may produce acute oral toxicity; but even if only very small apparently harmless doses are taken daily or periodically over a varying period of time, some tend to accumulate in the body and sooner or later bring on the symptoms of poisoning.

Those gardeners who do not wish to use any poisonous materials on their plants should turn to the old favorites, rotenone and pyrethrum and a newer synthetic, affethrin-insecticides. These have been made more potent through the incorporation of synergists, compounds such as piperonyl butoxide, piperonyl cyclonene, and sesmolin which double their insect killing powers. With these insecticides there is no need to worry about spray drift or poisonous residues.

More care will be required in applying newer insecticides such as methoxychlor, lindane, and malathion. With these, spraying leafy vegetables should be avoided and the safe interval between the last application and harvest should be respected (methoxychlor, and lindane—3 weeks; malathion—3 days).

Dieldrin, chlordane endrin, parathion and heptachlor require still greater care in use and about a month for weathering before harvest. This means that they can be used safely only in the early stages of vegetable growth and fruit development.

The older copper and sulphur fungicides are also considered safe. But the newer ferbam, captan, maneb, ziram and zineb require some care, but are usually preferable for all around disease control.

Mercury compounds are not to be used on vegetables at all, and only in the early stages of fruit tree growth before the fruit forms.

No washing of fruits and vegetables for any pesticides is necessary when safe spraying margins before harvest are followed.

SPREADERS AND STICKERS. Materials for increasing the spreading and adhesive qualities of certain fungicides and insecticides. They are especially necessary where fruit or foliage has a waxy surface, on which the spray material tends to collect in spots. Soap, oil emulsions, glue and in recent years, milk products, resin and flour, are used. Their addition results in smaller-sized particles in the mixtures, which permit a more even distribution of the spray.

Soap spreaders are ordinarily used with contact insecticides. Of dry soaps use 1 oz. to 2 gals. of the liquid spray; of liquid soap use 1 oz. to 1 gal. *Do not use soaps with lead arsenate or lime-sulphur.*

Fish oil is sometimes added to lead arsenate; for gypsy moth on shade trees, 1 pint of oil to 3 lbs. lead arsenate in 100 gals. water. Potash fish-oil soap may be used with lime-sulphur or bordeaux mixture at the rate of 1 oz. (2 tablespoonfuls) to 1 gal. spray.

Oil emulsions are unsatisfactory as spreaders because they cause some burning and destroy the bloom on ornamentals.

Casein spreaders may be combined with bordeaux mixture, lime-sulphur and arsenical sprays. Calcium caseinate, a finely ground mixture containing about 20 per cent casein and 80 per cent hydrated lime, is sold under various trade names. In mixing wettable sulphurs 2 qts. of skim milk may be used in place of ½ lb. of calcium caseinate.

Resin (rosin) is used to a limited extent as a sticker in bordeaux mixture, and in a resin wash for spraying plants with waxy leaves; it does not mix readily with water.

Common flour and billboard pastes are good spreaders and stickers having no chemical reaction with any spray solution. Flour is frequently mixed with lead arsenate in sprays for the Japanese beetle— 1½ oz. to 1 gal. of spray.

Glue may be used as an adhesive in any spray solution at the rate of 1 oz. to 100 gals.

SPREKELIA (sprek-ee'-li-ah) *formosissima.* A bulbous herb of Mexico and S. America, belonging to the Amaryllis Family and grown in the open border in mild regions under the common names Jacobean-lily (which see) and St. James-lily.

SPRING BEAUTY. Common name for Claytonia, a genus of small spring-blooming wild flowers.

SPRING EFFECTS IN THE GARDEN. In planning for special seasonal effects it is important to realize that all parts and details of a garden are dependent, in their effect, on things that are not really a part of them. This is peculiarly applicable to spring effects. Springtime is a season of bare earth—and much mud!— as well as a season of flowers and abounding life. Hence, whether it is an entire garden devoted to spring effects that is being planned, or just a small portion of a garden, the sparseness of vegetation generally must be considered, and dealt with. Bare, soggy earth must be concealed, either by spring flowers themselves or by something which will supplement and, if possible, emphasize their character and special beauty, which is in general elusive, delicate and high in key. (See illustration, Plate 50.)

One reason for this high pitch is the strong light due to the bare trees and shrubs which not only cast no shade but also do not absorb any light. Shadows being few on the ground as well as in the tree and shrub masses, there is little contrast. And this brings up a most important element in spring effects. Shadow must be provided one way or another, not only as contrast or foil to the high lights but also as background.

Inasmuch as coniferous evergreens (as well as one or two others of fine foliage) retain their shadows at all times, it becomes a kind of rule that some evergreen material is a necessity in spring effects. It may be of low and comparatively unimportant ground-covers, growth such as that of prostrate junipers; or it may be lofty and majestic, as the pine tree beneath which snowdrops cluster to make a lovely picture. In one instance there is depth and shadow in the mass itself, in the other there is shade—both furnishing the required contrast.

DESIGN. Springtime demands freedom of expression; it is not to be subjected to forms and conventionalities. Spring effects, therefore, should be naturalistic—surprising as nature is surprising, startling with their unexpectedness. Little sheltered spots where the sun shines warmly and wind do not reach, especially those within view of the house (for it may be too chilly to walk in the garden even when much bloom is out) and which give no sign of a gardener's touch, are the ideal toward which to plan. Happily it is as easy to achieve this result in very tiny gardens as in large ones; and no season lends itself to miniature display more satisfactorily than springtime.

PLANT MATERIAL. This will differ of course in different regions. The bulbs usually dominate, however, everywhere, introducing the season and staying with it to its end. And no class of flowers is better adapted to naturalistic plantings—with the possible exception of tulips and hyacinths. The early iris, trillium, dogtooth-violet, anemone, many of the wild flowers suited to rock gardens (which will grow also in colonies in the border or some chosen spot without the usual rock surroundings), the familiar creeping phlox, hardy candytuft, and many other early flowering perennials should supplement whatever bulbs are planted. With them use such spring blooming shrubs as the natice azaleas, benzoin or spicebush, lilacs in the colder regions, and, where a vine is needed, wisteria.

SPRING STAR-FLOWER. Common name for *Brodiaea uniflora*, a bluish-white, flowered, onion-scented, bulb-like plant.

SPRING WORK IN THE GARDEN. Almost all of the various garden operations must be performed, in certain phases, in the spring time.

If you did not spade up your garden in the fall, do it now, first spreading a good thick layer of compost (or well-rotted manure), then digging it in deeply. (See SPADES AND SPADING; TRENCHING.) The object is to break the soil up well, deepen it and mix the compost evenly through it. The compost or finer part of a winter mulch can be worked into the beds after the rough part is removed and added to the new compost heap.

If seeds are to be sown directly, the soil will have to be even more carefully raked and leveled and freed of sticks or stones. To sow seeds in poorly prepared soil is a waste of time and money. See PLANTING; SEEDS AND SEEDSOWING.

Seeds for both flower and vegetable garden that are not hardy enough to stand early spring temperatures outdoors should be sown in hotbeds, or in flats indoors or in the greenhouse. The seedlings will later go into the coldframe to harden off and then be transplanted to their permanent locations. (See TRANSPLANTING.) Just as soon as frost is out of the ground, you can sow sweet peas in a 5-in.-deep trench. The soil should be well enriched with manure a foot or 18 in. below the bottom of the trench so as to provide a supply of moisture and food that will attract the roots down to where it is cool and favorable for them.

Start preparations for a new lawn, or for renewing an old one. The deeper the soil is prepared the better. See LAWN.

Discontinue spraying with dormant spray materials (lime-sulphur, certain miscible oils, etc.) for scale and some fungous diseases, but don't stop spraying altogether; change to the type of insecticide (which see) and fungicide (which see) suitable for young and tender foliage. (See SPRAYING.) Almost any sort of woody tree or shrub (evergreens included) can be moved in the early spring before growth starts. Mulch well after transplanting to prevent heavy loss of moisture. If strong winds dry the soil soon after moving a plant or setting out new ones, water well and keep the surface loose by cultivating.

Rhododendrons that are scraggly may be cut back severely.

Plant all kinds of hardy climbers, too, such as clematis, Virginia creeper, honeysuckle, etc. In the case of established vines, cut out all dead wood and weak branches, trim back vigorous stems and fasten them up where they are wanted. See TRAINING OF PLANTS; VINES.

Plate 50.   THE GLORY OF THE GARDEN IN SPRINGTIME

Top: The ever-young, dancing joy of the spring-flowering bulbs. Lower left: The Trillium's triad of petals proclaims its faith in the age-old miracle of spring. Lower right: Frank, open-faced flowers of the Japanese dogwood (Cornus kousa) which needs a sheltered, half-shaded position.

Handle climbing roses the same way, pruning severely if much new growth is desired, and proportionately less if the size and form of the plant are satisfactory. See PRUNING.

Start uncovering bulbs as soon as shoots appear above the ground. Do this gradually, taking off part of the mulch every other day over a week or more to avoid too sudden changes. Do the same with the mulch on the perennial borders.

Reset or firm any rock plants that have heaved, and top-dress with equal parts leafmold, sand, and stone chips. New rock gardens can be planted; also ferns can be set out. Give them a mulch of rotted leaves or soil from the woods.

Plants in the herbaceous border that appeared crowded last summer can be lifted, divided and replanted as soon as the soil is workable. After gradually taking the protection from the bush roses, give them a good mulch of rotted manure. Cut them back hard if you want to develop new tops and control flowering so as to get extra fine blooms. Plant new roses in soil well prepared in advance.

Start staking herbaceous plants early; before they actually need the support; with sweet peas it is well to put the brush in place at planting time. Set out plants started last summer or fall and wintered over in the coldframes. As the weather settles and the soil becomes warm, plant summer flowering bulbs such as gladiolus and dahlias. When it is time to mow the lawn, first rake it clear of rubbish, then roll it not too heavily, then mow with the blade of the machine set about 2 in. above the ground.

IN VEGETABLE AND FRUIT GARDEN. The hotbed is of great value here in starting early vegetables—peppers, egg-plants, early cabbage, tomatoes, lettuce, cucumbers, and melons. Outdoors, can be planted late cabbage, beets, lettuce, salsify, parsnips and the hardier, round-seeded varieties of green peas. Later plantings of peas—the higher quality wrinkled-seeded sorts—can follow every 2 weeks. Sow seeds of herbs in a corner of the garden. Corn planting begins, the old rule says, when the oak leaves are the size of squirrels' ears. Make successive plantings of an early variety every 2 weeks until, say July.

Thin out the early sown vegetables and continue to sow quick-growing ones such as lettuce, carrots, radishes, etc. Top-dress the asparagus bed and all leafy vegetables like lettuce with nitrate of soda.

Spray tomatoes, potatoes, cucumbers and any vegetables subject to blights with bordeaux mixture. Plant currants, raspberries and blackberries, cutting them back and cultivating the young plants enough to keep the soil loose, but not deep enough to damage the new roots. Prune established currant bushes enough to let in the sun and air. Dig up around apple trees as far as the spread of the limbs. If a cover-crop was sown in the fall turn it under while it is green and succulent.

Grapes require only a moderately fertile soil. Any feeding should be done early, soon after the buds break. In pruning newly planted grapes, the vine is kept the first year to a single shoot which is trained on a stake or strong string support. Later something stronger and more permanent is needed.

Strawberries prefer a strong, rich soil. Plant them on land that has been cultivated for one or more years, or there is likely to be much trouble with white grubs.

LATE SPRING TASKS. Window boxes, porch baskets, etc., can be planted. If bedding plants are used, they should have been hardened off before moving them outside. Annuals may be sown directly in the boxes or transplanted from flats.

When young seedlings (as lima beans) or newly set plants (flowers or vegetables) collapse over night, look for cut-worms, which can usually be found near the base of the destroyed plants. Kill them and surround remaining plants with fine coal ashes; or scatter poison bran mash among them.

The earliest tulips can be dug (or moved) if necessary, as soon as the foliage becomes yellow.

Nip back chrysanthemums and any other perennials that seem to be growing too tall, to make them branch and become stocky.

Stake all tall perennials; and keep faded flowers removed to prevent seeds from forming and making a drain on the plants.

Make lists of hardy bulbs to be bought and planted next fall. Note the garden results generally and make notes for fall work that will improve next spring's picture.

If bad patches appear in the lawn, look to see if white grubs or the larvae of some kind of Asiatic beetle are responsible.

If so poison the soil with lead arsenate. Otherwise dig up, loosen and enrich the soil in the bare places and reseed. Water these places until the grass is well started. Other than this, a well-made lawn on a good, deep soil should not need much watering except in severe drought periods. But when water is needed, apply plenty, soaking the soil.

SPRINKLERS AND SPRINKLING. Devices by which streams of water are broken up into rain-like drops provide one good means for watering gardens and lawns. Sprinklers are of many patterns and types, from adjustable hand nozzles in which the opening can be changed so as to emit anything from a long solid stream to a short, broad cone of fine spray, to mechanical devices that are placed on the lawn and automatically operated by the water pressure so as to revolve or otherwise throw fine streams over a wide area without needing further attention. The type or types used should be selected according to the nature and amount of work to be done and the money that can be invested. See IRRIGATION.

Two objections attach to sprinkling as generally done in gardens. (1) It is started too early in the season before the moisture is needed; (2) during really dry weather too little water is applied. In both cases more harm than good generally results.

Sprinkling should never be started until after the season is well advanced because the water stored deep in the soil during winter keeps working upward toward the surface from the time the ground thaws until early summer. The time to begin will depend largely upon the winter's precipitation *and* the amount and frequency of the rains that fall during this spring period. Sprinkling started too early keeps the surface soil so moist that plants are stimulated to develop their roots close to the surface instead of going down into the deeper more permanent reservoir of soil moisture where they will be more likely to find water throughout the season even if the surface dries and is baked by the sun.

The second wrong practice often results because, in dry weather, after a few minutes sprinkling, the surface soil becomes muddy and deceives the inexperienced gardener into believing that enough water has been applied. Actually the water has not even reached the roots, which may be in an

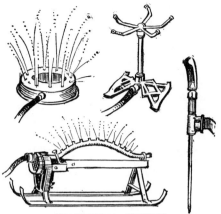

SPRINKLER STYLES

Whether of the simple perforated ring or whirling type (above), the fan-spray type with a spike to be plunged in the ground (right), or the automatic, oscillating "water-fan" type (below), a lawn sprinkler is valuable only if used long enough in one place to soak the soil thoroughly.

almost powdery dry earth below a thin layer of mud from which the water quickly evaporates. Deep roots thus get no benefit while shallow ones, as in a lawn, are attracted to the surface stratum and then, when it dries, are worse off than if no sprinkling had been done.

Sprinkling should always be continued on any one spot until the soil has become thoroughly drenched. Then do not sprinkle that place again until the plants appear definitely in need of more water.

The best time of day to sprinkle is toward or during the evening; not that the water applied then is of any more benefit than an adequate amount applied during midday, but because usually the air then being cooler and stiller, evaporation losses and waste will be reduced to a minimum.

Though precautions must be taken when sprinkling plants in greenhouses to avoid burning the foliage, as a result of the concentration or focusing of the sun's rays, no such precaution is needed in the case of plants outdoors. Sprinkling may be done at any hour of the day.

It is no unfair criticism of sprinkling even when it is done correctly, to suggest that, as a rule, the practice of watering (which see) or irrigation—both of which imply the more abundant use of water in line with principles above outlined—is to be preferred to sprinkling as a phase of garden management.

SPRUCE. Common name for Picea, a genus of evergreen trees (some with shrubby varieties) of the Pine Family, with whorled branches, narrow needle-like leaves, and fruit usually a pendent cone but occasionally berry-like. (The drooping cones distinguish the spruces from the firs, which bear upright cones.)

In their various forms, spruces are exceedingly useful and ornamental. The large types are especially valuable for park or estate planting and the slower-growing species for the home ground.

Most of them are hardy and, being tolerant of shade, may be used on N. slopes. They will grow in almost any kind of soil if there is good drainage and sufficient moisture; because of their shallow rooting habit, they are easily transplanted. Their dense close foliage and strong branches make them excellent for windbreaks or shelter belts, and the species (such as *P. abies* and *P. polita*) that endure severe pruning are often used as hedge plants.

Spruces are raised from seed and cuttings, and the rarer varieties are grafted on seedling stock of *P. abies*.

ENEMIES

DISEASES. Spruces grown as ornamentals are fairly free from diseases. Several rust fungi (see RUSTS) may attack leaves, twigs or cones. Three of them causing blisters on spruce needles have alternate hosts in members of the Heath Family—Labrador-tea, bog-rosemary and leather-leaf; others have wild red raspberries and *Rubus pubescens*. A different type rust, requiring only one host, causes the falling of one-year-old needles of Engelmann spruce in the N. W. Large witches' brooms are caused by a rust of which the alternate host has not been discovered.

The dwarf mistletoe (*Arceuthobium pusillum*) is fairly common on Black Spruce and occasionally seen on the Red and White Spruces and may kill or dwarf trees. Pecky wood-decay prevalent in forests may attack large ornamental spruces. See EVERGREENS; BRACKET FUNGI.

INSECT PESTS. One of the most serious is the gall aphid which attacks especially Norway Spruce but may infest Red and Black Spruces, causing cone-shaped galls at the base of young shoots that prevent twig growth. These are caused by the feeding of the young nymphs, which remain in the gall pockets until late summer. Then they emerge and lay eggs from which the overwintering females are hatched. Control by removing infested twigs during the winter and by spraying with nicotine-sulphate and soap before growth starts in the spring. Or a miscible oil spray may be carefully applied at that time. See DORMANT SPRAYING, under SPRAYING.

For control of the spruce mite that webs over the needles after the manner of the common red spider, see EVERGREENS; also MITES.

The light green larvae of the spruce leaf-miner mine in, and web together, the needles. For this and other leaf miners spray with arsenate of lead in early summer. Caterpillars of the spruce bud-worm feed on new needles and those of the preceding season, webbing them together and severing them at the base. Spray early with lead arsenate.

Sawflies are of increasing concern. The European spruce sawfly has become well distributed in Canada since its introduction a few years ago, and the yellow-headed spruce sawfly occurs both in Canada and across northern U. S. A pest of forest trees, it also occurs on ornamental spruces which can be sprayed with lead arsenate to which fish oil or linseed oil has been added at the rate of 4 oz. for each lb. of lead arsenate. See also SAWFLIES.

Bark beetles (which see) infest weak trees of red, white and black spruce, which should be removed and destroyed. And leaders may be attacked by the white pine weevil. See PINE.

PRINCIPAL SPECIES

P. abies (Norway Spruce), to 150 ft., is a tall pyramidal tree with horizontal branches and drooping branchlets, shiny dark-green needles and long drooping brown cones to 7 in. Although a native of Europe, it is one of the commonest of cultivated evergreens in the E. States, even though, while attractive in youth, it becomes unkempt in age. It is often used for hedges. Among its many varietal forms, some with variegated foliage, are *argentea*, green and white; *aurea*, golden-yellow; and dwarf varieties suitable for the rock garden, such as *pumila* and *pygmaea*, not exceeding 2 ft.

glauca (White Spruce), to 70 ft., has ascendant branches and drooping branchlets; leaves somewhat bluish-green with a strong aromatic odor when crushèd; and small glossy light-brown cones to 1½ in. The foliage is dense and close in young trees, making them highly ornamental. Var. *caerulea* has leaves with a decided whitish bloom.

engelmanni (Engelmann Spruce), to 150 ft., has slender branches in close whorls, and bluish-green foliage. It forms a slender pyramidal tree much more graceful than the widely planted *P. pungens,* which, like it, is a native W. species. Var. *glauca* has steel-blue needles.

pungens (Colorado Spruce), from 80 to 150 ft., has horizontal branches forming a regular pyramidal growth. The rigid, spiny leaves are bluish-green, silvery-white or occasionally dull green; the cones are to 4 in. long. The foliage color is so striking that the species should be used with discretion; it has been badly abused in indiscriminate foundation groupings. Var. *kosteriana* is the frequently seen blue-leaved form.

breweriana, to 120 ft., has the upper branches ascending, the lower ones horizontal with many whip-like branchlets creating a most graceful appearance. One of the most beautiful of the spruces, but not hardy N.

polita (Tiger-tail Spruce), to 90 ft., has stout rigid branches in youth and grows irregular with age. The needles are dark shining green, rigid and curved and the branchlets droop, giving rise to the common name. A hardy tree which stands pruning into hedge form.

Big-cone-spruce is *Pseudotsuga macrocarpa.* Hemlock-spruce is Tsuga.

SPUD. A long-handled, chisel-like tool used for cutting the tap-roots of such weeds as burdock and dandelion deeply below the soil surface by thrust strokes so the plants may be easily pulled or raked up. See TOOLS.

SPUR. A modification of one or more petals or sepals so that they are fused to form a tube-like structure, as in larkspur or columbine. The tube is usually filled with a sweet fluid, nectar, so the spur is (or at some time was) a pollination device; for insects, in order to reach the nectar, must first brush over the stamens and pistil and thereby bring about pollination, which see.

A *fruit spur* is a dwarf shoot terminated by a cluster of fruits, as in the apple.

SPURGE. Common name for plants of the genus Euphorbia, which comprises

a great variety of herbs, shrubs and tree-like forms, some of them closely resembling Cacti, though quite unrelated to them. Their milky juice is sometimes irritating.

There are small hardy species, suitable for the rock garden and border, many of them quite weedy; and other larger succulent species are grown in the greenhouse in the N. or planted out in the S. One species, *E. pulcherrima,* the Poinsettia with its brilliant scarlet bracts surrounding the small yellow flowers, is one of the most popular of winter-flowering florists' plants, especially for the Christmas season. See EUPHORBIA.

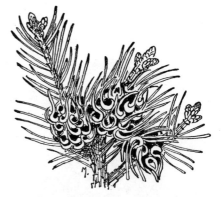

GALLS ON NORWAY SPRUCE
These familiar malformations at the base of new growth are caused by a kind of aphid. To control it, spray in late winter or very early spring with a strong contact insecticide.

Mountain- and Japanese-spurge are *Pachysandra procumbens* and *P. terminalis* respectively.

Spurge Family is the common name of the Euphorbiaceae, which see.

SPURGE-LAUREL. Common name for *Daphne laureola,* an evergreen spring-blooming shrub with yellowish-green flowers.

SPURGE-OLIVE. Common name for *Cneorum tricoccon,* an evergreen shrub of the Mediterranean region and the Canary Isles, useful for outdoor planting in the S. States and in Calif. The shining, leathery, entire leaves are 2 in. long, and the deep yellow flowers growing from the leaf-axils are followed by greenish black 3-lobed fruits.

SQUASH. The corrupted, abbreviated Indian name for the fruit and the plant of several annual cucurbits or members of the Gourd Family. For practical purposes, squashes may be grouped in two ways. One division would be into so-called "bush" and running varieties; the other, into summer and winter sorts. The "bush" and summer kinds comprise relatively small plants with small fruits which are eaten while immature; the other kinds (running and winter) occupy wide spaces and produce larger fruits, which are used mature, during autumn and winter. The name Guinea-squash is sometimes applied to the Egg-plant, which see.

All squashes are tender to frost, so they must be sown or planted neither before the weather is warm, nor so late that early or fall frost will destroy them before their fruits mature. As they are difficult to transplant, seed is best sown where the plants are to remain, though sometimes

BOTTLE-FED SQUASH
Thread a length of yarn or wicking through the stem of a young fruit, put the ends in a jar of water (some suggest milk), and watch the squash grow to vast proportions. Use a Hubbard or other winter variety. (The practicability of this procedure has been challenged since the cut first appeared; but, although he has not had opportunity to test or prove it, the Editor believes reports that he has read and heard concerning it and is leaving their endorsement or otherwise to gardeners who care to try it out.)

it is started on inverted sods or in berry boxes or flower pots so as to artificially lengthen short seasons.

Squashes revel in well-drained, rich, light, soils and full sunlight. Bush varieties are usually spaced 4 or 5 ft. apart, and running kinds, 10 or 12 ft. Clean cultivation is necessary until the plants occupy the ground.

Fruits of summer squashes should be gathered as soon as large enough to use—while their rinds are still soft enough to indent easily with the fingernail. If allowed to mature, the fully ripe fruits will be less desirable for the table, and also the plants will tend to stop bearing. Winter kinds, on the other hand, should be allowed to remain until frost threatens, then gathered and handled as carefully as ripe peaches to avoid bruises; for these soon result in rot. To harden the rinds lay them singly on straw in a sunny exposure for two weeks; but protect them in cold and wet weather. If then stored in dry air and at a temperature above 50 degrees, they will often keep until spring; in humid air and at lower temperatures they may decay in a few weeks.

Squashes are not especially subject to disease, but may be attacked by downy mildew, bacterial wilt and anthracnose. The most important insect pests are the squash bug (which see) and the squash-vine borer, whose presence is disclosed by piles of sawdust. To control it cover the main stem with soil or spray the basal 4 ft. of each vine with nicotine-sulphate, 1 to 100, weekly during July. See also under CUCURBITA.

SQUASH BUG. This reddish-brown to black, flattened true bug (*Anasa tristis*), ¾ in. long, feeds on squash, melons and other cucurbits. Leaves attacked by it soon wilt and become blackened and crisp. Because, when the insects are crushed, they give off a disagreeable odor, they are sometimes called "stink bug," which name is, however, correctly applied only to a related group of insects. See BUGS; CUCURBITA; STINK-BUGS.

SQUAW-BERRY. Another name for the Partridge-berry (*Mitchella repens*), an evergreen trailing herb with scarlet berries.

SQUILL. Common name for Scilla, a genus of mostly small early spring blooming bulbous plants with white, blue or purple flowers in racemes.

Medicinal squill is the genus Urginea.

SQUIRREL-CORN. Common name for *Dicentra canadensis,* an American woodland perennial, useful in shady rock gardens.

SQUIRRELS FOOT FERN. Common name for *Davallia bullata,* a handsome fern for the greenhouse, the name suggested by its hairy, reddish-brown creeping stems. The broad fronds are about 10 in. long, dark, shining, and 4-pinnate. It needs a wide shallow pot or basket, and very peaty compost with some sand. Do not bury the rhizomes; and give the plant plenty of diffused light.

SQUIRREL-TAIL GRASS. Common name for *Hordeum jubatum,* a biennial or perennial grass grown for ornament. See HORDEUM; also ORNAMENTAL GRASSES.

SQUIRTING-CUCUMBER. Common name for *Ecballium elaterium,* a trailing annual grown as a curiosity because of its curious habit of ejecting its seeds.

STACHYS (stay'-kis). A genus of rather coarse weedy herbs or shrubs of the Mint Family, commonly known as Betony or Woundwort. They have white, yellow, purplish or scarlet flowers in whorls or spikes. A few species are of interest in the garden, and one, *S. sieboldi,* is sometimes grown for its edible tubers, called Japanese artichokes. (See ARTICHOKE.) They thrive in a rich sandy loam in full sunshine, and may be increased by seeds, cuttings, or rooted runners. Other species are:

S. lanata (Lambs-ears), a hardy, strong-growing perennial clothed with a dense white wool, valued chiefly as a foliage bedding plant; *S. coccinea,* a perennial to 2 ft., with vivid rose-red or scarlet flowers; *S. corsica,* a soft-hairy annual with small leaves making a close carpet covered with large pale-pink blossoms; *S. grandiflora,* a perennial to 3 ft., with soft-hairy leaves and violet flowers 1 in. long; its varieties *superba* (intense purple), *superba alba* (white) and *robusta,* with rose-pink spikes; and *S. germanica,* a white-woolly perennial with small white or rose-purple flowers, to 4 ft. tall.

STACHYURUS (stak-i-eu'-rus). Early flowering deciduous shrubs or small trees, natives of China and Japan. Of spreading habit to 12 ft., they grow well in sandy loam with leafmold. They are hardy as far N. as Mass. but the flower buds are killed in severe winters. *S. praecox,* the principal species, bears drooping clusters of bell-shaped greenish-yellow flowers before the leaves. These are large, more or less oval, toothed and long pointed. The yellowish berry-like fruits ripen at the end of summer. Propagated by seeds, cuttings and layers.

STAFF-TREE. Common name for Celastrus, a genus of twining shrubs with greenish white flowers and capsule-like fruits containing showy crimson "berries."

Commonly called Bittersweet. The STAFF-TREE FAMILY (Celastraceae) which see.

STAGBUSH. A common name for *Viburnum prunifolium,* a stout shrub with white flowers and bloomy blue-black berries.

STAGGER-BUSH. Common name for *Lyonia mariana,* a deciduous shrub bearing nodding pinkish flowers in May or June.

STAGGER-WEED. Common name for *Delphinium tricorne,* a succulent-stemmed perennial herb with blue and yellow flowers.

STAGS HORN FERN. A name applied to various species of Platycerium (which see), a genus of large and tropical looking ferns with forking fronds. They are for indoor use only, preferring baskets or woody wall pockets and needing a very peaty compost, careful watering, and abundant indirect light.

STAKING. The practice of supporting tall plants and vines with stakes may be done for one or more of the following objects: to keep vines from sprawling on the ground; to save space; to prevent tall stems or flowers (as dahlia) being broken by wind; to facilitate gathering a crop (as climbing beans); or to keep clean, improve the quality, and reduce the tendency to disease of the fruit (as tomato).

Staking includes keeping individual plants off the ground with a single stake or with several (though the latter if connected are generally called collectively a "support"); and also "brushing" sweet peas and tall-growing varieties of garden peas by placing twiggy branches or small saplings beside the rows for the vines to clamber upon. (The use of lattice or chicken wire might not be termed "staking" but would have the same object.)

Brush, stakes and "bean poles" should always be put in position as soon as seed sowing has been done. If this step is delayed there is risk of injuring the roots, a risk that increases with every day's delay as the root growth increases. When setting out dahlia tubers or any kind of plants, the stakes should be put in place before or when the planting is done so as to avoid injuring the bulbs or root balls as often happens when pointed stakes are driven into the ground after planting.

Stakes should, of course, be chosen with relation to the height and size the plants can be expected to make, as well as the exposure and the strength of prevailing winds. In the herbaceous border bamboo canes of finger thickness or less are often sufficient and desirably inconspicuous. For hollyhocks and delphiniums larger bamboo sticks up to an inch in diameter at the base and 6 ft. tall may be required; while for dahlias a one-inch-square stake 6 to 8 ft. long, to be set 1 to 2 ft. deep, is often used. A fairly successful alternative is made of two or three slender bamboo canes bound together at two or three points with copper wire. Except in the case of bamboo, it is highly desirable to paint garden stakes both to protect them against decay and to improve their appearance. White and dark green are the colors commonly used.

STALK. The stem or support of an organ, as the *petiole* of a leaf, the *peduncle* of a flower or flower cluster, the *pedicel* of one flower in a flower cluster, the *filament* of a stamen, or the *stipe* of a pinnately-compound leaf.

STALK BORER. The common stalk borer is the larva of a moth which is an almost universal pest, working in stems of any plants large enough to shelter it and soft enough so it can bore into them. It is distributed generally throughout the U. S. from the Rocky Mountains E. and is particularly injurious to corn and dahlia (both of which see). The mature larva is 1½ in. long, grayish brown with one white stripe down its back and two stripes along its sides. There is only one generation. The moths emerge from pupae in early fall and lay eggs on the stalk of food plants into which the larvae bore in spring. Destruction of all old stalks in the fall is therefore the best control measure. Sometimes the borers may be killed by slitting the stalk with a knife or by injecting a few drops of carbon bisulphide, or nicotine paste, into it near the small hole above the ground, which, with the sawdust or borings thrown out, indicates the presence of the pest.

STAMEN. That part or organ of a flower that bears pollen-grains. It is composed of a thread-like stem (*filament*) bearing a two-celled sac (*anther*) containing reproductive bodies or pollen-grains in which are germ cells. When a pollen grain reaches the pistil of a flower, it grows, penetrates the pistil and releases the sperms which fertilize the egg cells in the ovary. Consequently the stamens are often called the *male organs* of the flower. They are arranged around the pistil and just within the corolla or circle of petals. See also FLOWER.

STAMINATE. A term used to describe a flower containing only the stamens, or male reproductive organs, as distinguished from one that is either *pistillate* (which see), that is, possessing the female organs, or *perfect* (which see), possessing both kinds of organs. The term is also applied to an individual plant or tree all the flowers of which are staminate. When the two kinds of flowers are borne separately, the plant is called *dioecious*.

STANDARD. Botanical term for the more or less erect upper petal of the sweet pea or similar papilionaceous flower. The term is also applied to each of the three inner segments of iris flowers which are erect and narrow to a claw, in contrast to the three relaxed and hanging outer segments known as *falls*. Iris standards are variously described according to their position, as domed, cupped, flat, arching, etc.

Horticulturally, the term has several applications, chiefly, perhaps, in connection with fruit trees. A "standard" fruit tree, as popularly understood in America, is a tree allowed to attain the natural size and development of its species. (Contrast with DWARF PLANTS.) Among British gardeners, though sometimes similarly used, the term also has a more specific designation; namely, a dwarf tree trained to stand without the support of wall, trellis or stake; (contrast with ESPALIER and CORDON). See also TRAINING OF PLANTS.

Still another application is to rose bushes trained in tree form, whether grown on own roots or grafted or budded. In each case the "trunk" or stem is grown to the desired height before flowering branches are allowed to develop to form a head. Other shrubs, both flowering and fruit-bearing, are similarly trained. Among the more common are quince, currant and gooseberry. In America, however, the standard or tree form is not desirable because of the attacks of borers.

Florists grow various shrubs and some of the sturdier herbaceous plants such as fuchsia, geranium and pelargonium, single stems bearing many-branched heads. The crab cactus (Zygocactus, normally a drooping or sprawling plant, is often grafted on erect species, notably Pereskia.

With ornamental shrubs the object is to increase attractiveness through formality and uniformity. Its achievement demands frequent and intelligent attention on the part of the gardener so as to prevent the development of branches where they are not wanted and encourage it where desired, check rampant growths, etc.

Standard roses and other semi-hardy shrubs require special winter protection. Popular ways of providing it include bending the plants down to the ground (usually first digging away some soil on the "down side" to lessen the strain on the stem) and covering them before the ground freezes; and wrapping the stems with straw or other material. See PROTECTION.

STANDARDS. Various organizations in the nursery and florist trades have formulated and endorsed standards of size, quality and condition for many of their products and these are being increasingly adapted and adhered to by responsible firms. They are especially beneficial to purchasers in connection with estimates for contract work, tending to bring bids for the same grade of work into greater uniformity. Efforts have also been made to establish standards and rules of business methods, and these have had an appreciable effect, although there is room for further progress.

Confusion in the matter of plant names has been a most difficult problem owing to differences of opinion between botanists and the casual application of the same common name to different plants, different names to the same plant, etc. A valiant effort was made to start a reform here with the publication in 1923 of "Standardized Plant Names," a check list of recommended names for plants in the horticultural trades. Described as a "Catalogue of Approved Scientific and Common Names of Plants in American Commerce," this work has been of much value in standardizing catalogs even though not all horticulturists—commercial or amateur—have as yet accepted it. With the progress in plant discovery and production, need for its revision, modernization, and enlargement became so pressing that the task was finally begun by representatives of the original editorial committee, in cooperation with the U. S. Department of Agriculture and the Arnold Arboretum. It has been announced that a completely new, second edition will be published early in 1941.

STANDING-CYPRESS. Common name for *Gilia rubra,* a tall scarlet-flowered

pyramidal herb, biennial or perennial, native from the Carolinas to Fla. and Tex.

STANLEYA (stan-lee'-ah). A genus of hardy perennial herbs of the Mustard Family, occasionally grown in the border, but more appropriate in the wild garden. They can be grown from seed or increased by division. *S. pinnata,* 4 ft. or more tall, has variously divided or entire leaves and golden-yellow flowers in a spike-like cluster; it is much like Cleome in general appearance.

STAPELIA (stah-pee'-li-ah). A genus of cactus-like plants of the Milkweed Family, with odd showy flowers often with a disagreeable odor which has gained them their common name of Carrion-flower. Natives of Africa, they are grown in greenhouses in the N. and a light open sandy soil with excellent drainage. During our winter they rest and should have little water; in summer as they come into flower they need more. They are increased by cuttings.

S. variegata has fleshy 4-angled stems to 6 in. and dark yellowish-green flowers to 3 in. across, marked with purplish spots. *S. gigantea* has fantastic hairy brown and buff blossoms 11 in. across, barred with dark purple.

STAPHYLEA (staf-i-lee'-ah). Bladder-nut. Deciduous shrubs or small trees, found in temperate regions of the northern hemisphere. They have attractive compound foliage, white flowers in mostly nodding clusters, and inflated bladder-like fruits. They are useful subjects for a mixed shrub planting; not very particular as to soil and location, but preferring a rather moist and partly shaded location. Propagated by seeds, layers and cuttings.

PRINCIPAL SPECIES

S. trifolia (American Bladder-nut) is an upright shrub to 15 ft., found from Quebec to Ga. It has leaves composed of 3 leaflets, flowers in nodding clusters about 2 in. long and fruit up to 3 in. long.

pinnata (European Bladder-nut) grows about the same size, but has 5 or 7 leaflets, longer flower clusters and smaller fruits.

bumalda, from Japan, grows to about 6 ft., with slender spreading branches, 3 leaflets, and flower clusters erect.

colchica, from the Caucasus region, is not quite so hardy, but may stand as far N. as Mass. It grows to 12 ft., has 3 or 5 leaflets, flower clusters erect or nodding, and fruits about 4 in. long. It is sometimes grown in pots for forcing.

holocarpa, from China, considered to be the most handsome, has white or pinkish flowers opening before the leaves. It grows to 25 ft. or more, has 3 leaflets, and pear-shaped fruit about 3 in. long.

STAR-ANISE. Common name for *Illicium verum,* a small aromatic evergreen Chinese tree somewhat grown in warm parts of the U. S.

STAR-APPLE. One of the common names for *Chrysophyllum cainito,* a tropical evergreen tree of the Sapodilla Family, growing to 50 ft. tall. It has shining leaves golden-brown and silky beneath, purplish-white flowers, and almost round, smooth, light-purple or green fruit 4 in. across, with a white, usually edible, pulp. The star-apple can be grown in the N. in a conservatory where it requires a moist hot atmosphere and rich sandy soil. It is propagated by seed, and by cuttings of ripe wood over heat.

STAR-CUCUMBER. A common name for *Sicyos angulatus,* an American cucumber-like vine sometimes grown for ornament but more often fought as a weed. Also called Bur-cucumber, which see.

STARFLOWER. Common name for Trientalis, a genus of small herbs of the Primrose Family with white or pink starry flowers on very slender stems. They are native to rich shady woods of N. America and Europe and are sometimes transferred to the wild or rock garden. *T. borealis* has slender creeping rhizomes, thin, whorled leaves, and white wheel-shaped flowers; *T. europea* has white to pink star-like flowers and its var. *latifolia,* found in W. America, has exceedingly charming little blossoms, white to rose-red.

Spring-starflower is *Brodiaea uniflora.*

STAR GLORY. Common name for the genus Quamoclit, tropical herbaceaus vines with yellow or red flowers several species of which are grown in gardens, especially *Q. coccinea* (Star-ipomoea), *Q. sloteri* (Cardinal-climber) and *P. pinnata,* Cypress-vine.

STAR-GOOSEBERRY. A common name for *Phyllanthus acidus,* also called Otaheite-gooseberry.

STAR-GRASS. A common name for two unrelated genera of herbaceous flowering plants and also for a species of ornamental grass, *Chloris truncata,* which see.

One of the genera is Aletris, a group of perennial herbs with fibrous roots, native in N. America and Asia and belonging to the Lily Family. *A. farinosa,* the principal species of N. America, is found from Me. to Fla. The leaves form a spreading grass-like cluster, and the flower stem grows to 3 ft., bearing a spike of small white flowers. It prefers a moist sunny place and is suitable for the wild garden. Propagated by seed and division.

The other genus called Star-grass is Hypoxis, a group of small herbs of temperate and tropical regions, members of the Amaryllis Family. *H. hirsuta,* the common Star-grass of N. America, is found from Me. to Fla. in grassland and dry open woods. It has hairy grass-like leaves and flower stems to 1 ft. high, bearing 1 to 6 bright yellow star-like flowers. It is of interest in the wild garden or a dry border and is propagated by division.

STAR-HYACINTH. Common name for *Scilla amoena,* a white- or blue-flowered spring-blooming bulbous herb.

STAR-JASMINE, or STAR-JESSAMINE. Common names for *Trachelospermum jasminoides,* a woody evergreen vine of the Dogbane Family, with opposite leaves and very fragrant salver-shaped white flowers to 1 in. across in flat-topped clusters. Var. *variegatum,* with green and white leaves, sometimes tinged reddish, is said to be hardier. In the N. it is grown in greenhouses, making a most satisfactory climber although it takes several years to develop a large-sized specimen. It may also be grown in tubs, trimmed to bush form and wintered in a coolhouse or sunporch. In the S. States where it is one of the favorite vines, it is grown in the open and known also as Confederate-jasmine.

STAR-LILY. A common name for *Leucocrinum montanum,* a Pacific Coast plant with fragrant white lily-like flowers.

STAR-OF-BETHLEHEM. Common name for *Ornithogalum umbellatum,* a hardy spring-blooming white flowered bulbous herb; also for the Amazon-lily (*Eucharis grandiflora*), a greenhouse bulb with highly fragrant white flowers.

STAR-OF-THE-VELDT. A common name for the genus Dimorphotheca, more generally known as Cape-marigold, which see.

STAR-TULIP. A common name for the certain species of Calochortus whose bell-shaped flowers, borne erect, are lined with hairs and variously streaked or spotted. They are native in W. N. A., from Mex. to Ore. See CALOCHORTUS.

STARWORT. A common name sometimes applied to the genus Aster.

STATE FLOWERS. The flowers chosen as symbolic of the various States are in some cases native wild flowers or trees, in others garden flowers, and in still others introduced plants which have become associated with the region. They have been selected for divers reasons—through sentiment, because of their prevalence, or to give the State prominence commercially. Also they have been selected in various ways. In many States the flower has been named by the legislature; in others it has been officially proclaimed by the Governor; and in many sections it was voted for by the people or the school children.

Some States seek to preserve wild flowers in danger of extinction by bringing them to public notice, as Arizona did with the saguaro and New Mexico with the yucca; while others merely wish to commemorate the beauty of certain plants at blooming season, as illustrated by the magnolias of Louisiana and the rhododendrons of West Virginia.

The list on page 1180 is reported to have the sanction of the Governors of the States and Territory mentioned.

STATICE (stat'-i-see). A genus of dwarf perennial plants of the Leadwort Family with narrow leaves in rosettes and small flowers in heads. Known as Seapink, or Thrift, they are used in the rock garden or as edgings for beds or borders. They grow readily in ordinary garden soil and may be easily increased by seed or division. The genus has been enlarged to take in plants formerly called Armeria. But the well-known garden or florists' Statice so widely used for dried flowers in winter bouquets belongs to the genus Limonium, which see.

SPECIES

S. armeria (Common Thrift) has narnow tufted leaves and heads of rose-purple flowers growing to 1 ft. There are several color variations—var. *alba* with white, and vars. *laucheana* and *splendens,* with rose flowers.

caespitosa, has a compact growth of tiny, prickly rosettes studded with almost stem-less heads of pure pink flowers, and is charming in a sunny crevice in the rock garden.

pseudo-armeria, with bright pink flowers in heads to 2 in. across borne on wiry stems to 1½ ft. tall, makes an excellent edging for the border.

STAUNTONIA (staun-toh'-ni-ah) *hexaphyla.* A tender woody vine from E. Asia. It has evergreen leaves and clusters of small white, very fragrant flowers, followed by round green berries, splashed with scarlet. This handsome plant is used in Fla. to cover old stumps or small trees, and if planted in moist rich ground will eventually reach a height of 40 ft.

STEAM. One of several agencies used for disinfecting greenhouse soils. See DISINFECTION.

STEEPLE-BUSH. A common name for *Spiraea tomentosa,* a native shrub of E. U. S. with purple or rose colored flowers; also called Hardhack.

STEIRONEMA (sty-roh-nee'-mah). A genus of N. American yellow-flowered perennials commonly called Loosestrife, which see.

STELLARIA (ste-lay'-ri-ah) *holostea.* A perennial species of a group of white-flowered, temperate-region plants of the Pink Family, commonly called Easter Bells, which see.

STEM. The ascending axis of a plant from which leaves, flowers and fruits develop. Since the stem is the continuation of the root, the internal structure of that part is carried up into the stem. The principal modification is the addition of tissue that adds rigidity to the stem and enables it to fulfill its chief function of support.

Stems take special forms according to different functions they sometimes perform, such as food storage, propagation, and specialized kinds of support. Examples of these are tubers, rhizomes, stolons, crowns, bulbs and tendrils, all of which see.

STEM ROT. Any plant disease (or the symptom or phase of a disease) that causes the destruction of stem tissue, either by dry or soft decay. See under ROT.

STENANTHIUM (sten-an'-thi-um). A genus of tall herbs of the Lily Family with grass-like leaves and clusters to 2 ft. long of small whitish or greenish flowers. Some of the tropical species are grown in the greenhouse, others are decorative in the wild garden or border. Grown

STATE FLOWERS

State	Common Name	Botanical Name
Alabama	Goldenrod	Solidago canadensis
Arizona	Giant cactus	Carnegeia giganteus
Arkansas	Apple blossom	Malus sp.
California	California poppy	Eschscholtzia californica
Colorado	Colorado columbine	Aquilegia caerulea
Connecticut	Mountain-laurel	Kalmia latifolia
Delaware	Peach blossom	Prunus persica
District of Columbia	American beauty rose	Rosa (hybrid)
Florida	Orange blossom	Citrus sinensis
Georgia	Cherokee rose	Rosa laevigata
Idaho	Lewis mockorange	Philadelphus lewisi
Illinois	Native wood violet	Viola sp.
Indiana	Zinnia	Zinnia elegans
Iowa	Wild rose	Rosa pratincola
Kansas	Sunflower	Helianthus annuus
Kentucky	Goldenrod	Solidago patula
Louisiana	Southern magnolia	Magnolia grandiflora
Maine	Pine cone and tassel	Pinus strobus
Maryland	Black-eyed susan	Rudbeckia hirta
Massachusetts	Trailing arbutus	Epigaea repens
Michigan	Apple blossom	Malus sp.
Minnesota	Showy ladyslipper	Cypripedium spectabile
Mississippi	Southern magnolia	Magnolia grandiflora
Missouri	Downy hawthorn	Crataegus mollis
Montana	Bitterroot	Lewisia rediva
Nebraska	November goldenrod	Solidago serotina
Nevada	Sagebush	Artemisia tridentata
New Hampshire	Purple lilac	Syringa vulgaris
New Jersey	Violet	Viola sp.
New Mexico	Yucca	Yucca sp.
New York	Rose	Rosa carolina
North Carolina	Oxeye daisy	Chrysanthemum leucanthemum
North Dakota	Prairie rose	Rosa arkansana
Ohio	Scarlet carnation	Dianthus caryophyllus
Oklahoma	Mistletoe	Phoradendron flavescens
Oregon	Oregon hollygrape	Mahonia nervosa
Pennsylvania	Mountain-laurel	Kalmia latifolia
Rhode Island	Violet	Viola sp.
South Carolina	Carolina jessamine	Gelsemium sempervirens
South Dakota	American pasqueflower	Pulsatilla hirsutissima
Tennessee	Iris	Iris sp.
Texas	Texas bluebonnet	Lupinus subcarnosus
Utah	Sego-lily	Calochortus nuttalli
Vermont	Red clover	Trifolium pratense
Virginia	Flowering dogwood	Cornus florida
Washington	Coast rhododendron	R. macrophyllum
West Virginia	Great rhododendron	R. maximum
Wisconsin	Native violet	Viola sp.
Wyoming	Indian paintbrush	Castilleja coccinea
Alaska	Forget-me-not	Myosotis sp.
Hawaii	Hibiscus	Hibiscus rosa-sinensis

from seed, they should be planted in light rich soil in partial shade. *S. robustum* (Feather-fleece), grows to 5 ft. tall and has long narrow leaves and greenish flowers: *S. gramineum* has still narrower grassy leaves and pure white flowers.

STEPHANANDRA (stef-ah-nan'-drah). Deciduous shrubs from Asia, belonging to the Rose Famliy. They are of graceful habit, well suited for the front of shrub borders or to plant on rocky slopes. Propagated by cuttings and division.

S. incisa grows to 8 ft., with wide-spreading slender branches densely arranged, and triangular, deeply-lobed leaves which take on reddish purple tints in the fall. Its small clusters of tiny white flowers are freely produced. In severe winters the stems may be killed back, but young growth springs freely from the base. *S. tanakae* is a more vigorous grower with larger leaves, very handsome in fall when they turn shades of orange, scarlet and yellow.

STEPHANOTIS (stef-ah-noh'-tis). Twining shrubs of the tropics belonging to the Milkweed Family. *S. floribunda,* the Madagascar-jasmine (which see), is the best known.

STEPPING STONES. An adaptation to the garden of the ancient method provided in rural districts for crossing shallow streams on foot. Just when they began to be used in gardens where there is no water to be crossed is uncertain, but in old gardens as well as modern ones they often take the place of continuous paths, where it is desired to provide a definite route across a turf area without interrupting the sweep of the green.

Flagstones naturally are the best for stepping stones; their flat surface makes walking on them safe and easy. But as they are beginning to be rare in many places, there has been developed an artificial flagging which closely resembles them, and serves the purpose perfectly. Searching out stones here and there appeals to many gardeners, and excellent stepping stones are often found—not uniform in thickness to be sure, but made to appear so by fitting them into depressions made to conform to their under sides. Thus their upper surfaces are brought flush with the ground and made level. Whatever their shape, stepping stones should always be embedded firmly so they cannot tilt.

Very effective "stones" may be made right where they are wanted by pouring a rich cement concrete mixture into depressions shaped out in the line of the path, as regularly or irregularly as taste dictates. The distance between them—and between stones of any kind used in a path —should be determined always to the centers; it is best fixed by walking deliberately over the route and noting what constitutes a comfortable stride. It is as bad to have them too close together as it is to have them too far apart, so this matter should be very carefully worked out in every garden and according to the stature of those who are to live in and use the garden.

In ordinary places stepping stones are best set flush with the surface of the ground. In wet and boggy areas they are better laid on its surface. Whatever their position, the grass at their edges should be kept trimmed by hand; otherwise it will gradually encroach on and work over them, giving them the effect of being submerged little by little, which is very unpleasant. Whatever their shape, their size in general should never be less than 200 sq. in.

See also GARDEN PATHS.

STEPS IN THE GARDEN. Differences in ground level, even slight ones, are given added interest and themselves add interest to the garden if made definite by a step or steps. The simplest form possible, suitable where conditions are generally naturalistic, is merely a log riser, held in place by driving sharpened stakes well into the ground in front of it, 2 in. from each end, and filling in behind it with earth which forms the tread. Often a single step of this sort will greatly relieve the grade of a path and make walking over it easier and pleasanter. When it is possible to rest the riser against trunks of existing trees near either end, instead of using stakes, the entire construction takes on a casual spirit delightfully in keeping with natural woodland trails.

For a little more finished effect, plank risers held in place by stakes are good. They should be 2 in. thick by 6 in. wide, and the treads whether of soil, stone or whatever not less than 12 in. deep—from back to front. They may be still deeper if desired, though too great depth may be unpleasant to one walking up and down.

Stone steps are equally good in wild or sophisticated surroundings but the method of construction will not be the same, since the latter demands greater finish than the former. It takes much patience and skill to lay safe dry stone steps of natural stones. Each one must be chosen for its place and tested in that place, then fitted to it carefully, to make certain it cannot tilt or slip or move in any way whatsoever when stepped upon. Also it must be brought to an exact and proper level in order to be in every way satisfactory.

Rough stone underwork or risers topped with flagstone treads offers less difficulty, though with this type also it is necessary to proceed slowly in order to make sure of the firmness and security of each foundation stone as well as of the topping flagstone tread. An easier construction is a combination of flagstone tread with the plank or log riser (in this instance a smaller log or a sapling) held in place with deeply driven stakes at each end, as already explained. Such steps approach architectural effect more than any yet mentioned, and yet preserve at the same time the integrity of natural materials.

Where the soil is reasonably heavy and grows a sod dense and strong enough to hold together firmly, steps of turf, laid as bricks are laid, make an unrivaled garden feature. There remain in one or two very old gardens examples of such sod steps— in one instance they are considerably more than a hundred years old, so their permanence is beyond question. If they are made with the treads concave instead of straight across their front, it is an extra insurance; for this incurved form braces itself to a very helpful extent. It also makes for added beauty in their elevation.

For steps made of brick a deep foundation, extending 2 in. below normal frost line, is absolutely necessary. Bricks must be well laid, ends out, and preferably on edge, in strong cement mortar. Finally there is cement (concrete), convenient and plastic as regards construction, and capable, when handled by an artist in design, of being developed into beautiful features for those parts of a garden where architectural forms are demanded. The character of such steps demands spacious and dignified surroundings; hence they are never advisable in small gardens, and are permissable in any garden only under the skillful handling of a trained designer. One exception exists in the making of slabs to be used like flagstones, that is, for treads

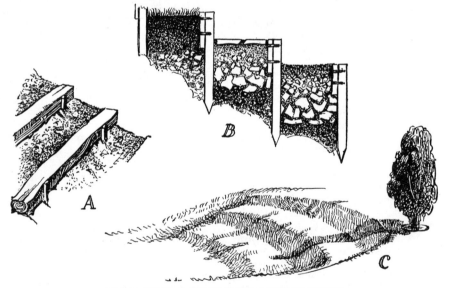

SOME SIMPLE STYLES IN GARDEN STEPS

One of the easiest, and well suited to wild and woodland gardens, consists of roughly squared logs (old railroad ties are good) set into a niche in the bank and held with firmly driven stakes (A); sow grass seed or plant ground covers around them. Slightly more formal steps can be made with plank risers nailed or screwed to strong stakes (B) and the space behind them filled in with broken stone and gravel for drainage and a surface layer of sod (top step), flagstone (second step), or fine gravel (bottom step). Steps made all of turf (C) are beautiful in a formal garden and if concave in outline are durable; but they take a lot of careful mowing and trimming.

upheld either by natural stone or sapling risers, as described. These slabs should be 2 in. thick by 12 in. broad and as long as desired. Reinforce each one by placing a layer of chicken wire or metal lath in the form when it is half filled and covering it with the concrete.

A reflection of the modern trends in architecture is seen in the occasional suggestions (usually in flower shows or publications) that heavy glass brick could be used effectively for garden steps and walks. Here is an idea for garden designers to work on as glass for construction becomes more available and less expensive.

cial fibres, and several are grown for ornament. The flowers are usually clustered in panicled or axillary whorls, often without petals, and with five or more stamens forming a tube. Among the cultivated genera are Brachychiton, Firmiana, Cola, Theobroma (cacao), Dombeya, Mahernia.

STERILITY IN PLANTS. Unfruitfulness, or failure of plants to bloom, set seed or produce functional offspring, may

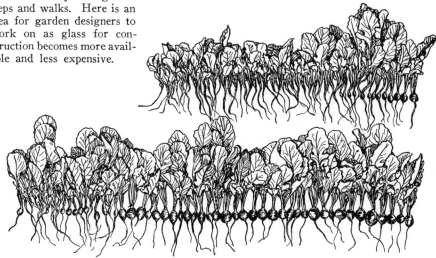

STERILIZING SOIL MAY MAKE ALL THE DIFFERENCE BETWEEN SUCCESS AND FAILURE
Here the the yields from two plantings of radishes made at the same time and with equal amounts of seed. One lot was sown in soil that had been growing other crops in a greenhouse bench for eight months; it produced the radishes shown above. The other lot was sown in some of the same soil after it had been sterilized to kill growth-hindering organisms and poisons; it produced the splendid crop shown below.

PLANTS FOR STEPS. Specialists offer collections of plants for use in the crannies of walks and steps as well as dry walls. One cannot do better than trust to such a specialist, who is always glad to help with advice about the planting of such special character. Supply full information about the soil, the extent of air and soil moisture, the degree of exposure to sun or degree of shade (if in the shade), etc., and a selection of suitable materials will be made by any reputable grower without extra charge.

STERCULIACEAE (ster-keu-li-ay'-see-ee). The Sterculia Family, a tropical group of soft-wood shrubs and trees, rarely herbs and sometimes vines. One member furnishes cocoa and chocolate, another the cola-nut; the bark of some yields commer-

be of many kinds and degrees. Anything that causes a break in the chain of events necessary for flowering, pollination, fertilization, or fruition may be a factor. The condition may be inherent or may result from environmental influence; or both circumstances may be partly responsible.

Some plants produce no seed because they are impotent. The pollen cells may be imperfect, or one or both of the sex organs may have been lost as in certain double flowers. Or seeds may fail to form, as in certain grapes which are inherently seedless.

Two plants, normal in every other respect, may refuse to set seed or fruit when crossed, perhaps because they are so unlike that they are unsuited to one another. Sometimes two species may cross, but produce feeble offspring, a living hybrid plant, which, in turn, may be unable to produce good seed.

When plants cannot be crossed successfully because some inherent physiological or chemical factor prevents fertilization, they are said to be *incompatible,* and the condition is called *cross-incompatibility.* If, as commonly occurs, a plant will not set seed to its own pollen, it is said to be *self-incompatible* or *self-sterile.* Again, certain plants are *unisexual* and will not set fruit if planted alone; others ripen their essential organs at different times, so that the pollen, ripening first, is all shed before the stigmas become mature. All such forms should be grown alongside others which are capable of acting as pollinators.

Among the environmental factors affecting fruitfulness are the weather, the season, nutritional conditions, diseases and insects. Some crosses may be successful under greenhouse conditions although found impossible outdoors.

Sterilities and their causes are of great practical importance to plant breeders, fruit growers, seedsmen and all who wish to raise superior seedlings. See also PLANT BREEDING.

STERILIZATION. The act or process of rendering a medium sterile or free from living bacteria or other organisms. Complete sterilization of soil for the control of disease-causing agents (*pathogenes*) in it is seldom desirable since the word implies the death of *all* organisms, beneficial as well as harmful. The usual aim is, therefore, only a partial sterilization or disinfection, which see.

STERNBERGIA (stern-bur'-gi-ah). A genus of Old-World bulbous plants of the Amaryllis Family with narrow leaves and crocus like flowers, generally appearing in autumn. Plant them 6 in. deep in a rather heavy soil in full sun where the bulbs may ripen thoroughly in summer. *S. lutea,* growing very profusely throughout Palestine, is thought by some to have been the Biblical "lilies of the field." It has golden-yellow, funnel-shaped flowers, and resents transplanting, increasing in numbers if left undisturbed.

Other species, less well known, but charming in the rock garden, are *S. colchiciflora,* with fragrant, yellow flowers, and *S. fischeriana* from the Caucasus, which blooms in the spring.

STEVIA (stee'-vi-ah). A name given by florists to *Piqueria trinervia,* a tender perennial herb of the Composite Family, extensively grown under glass for its graceful sprays of small white clustered flowers which are combined with bolder blossoms in bouquets; it is also sometimes grown as a bedding plant. It is easily raised from seed, cuttings or division and will thrive in sun or shade; but it should be grown in a coolhouse. Pinching back makes for floriferous and compact plants. Early in January the plants should be cut back; in March the new growth can be rooted as cuttings and later potted. The plants are set outdoors after danger of frost is over, and grown there until fall when they are again potted up and grown on for winter bloom in the coolest house.

The true Stevia is another sturdy perennial of the Composite Family with purple or white flowers in clusters, but it is only occasionally grown in gardens. *S. ivaefolia* and *S. purpurea* are the species usually seen there.

STEWARTIA (steu-ahr'-shi-ah). (Sometimes spelled STUARTIA.) Deciduous shrubs or trees of N. America and Asia, belonging to the Tea Family. They are among the most outstanding of summer-flowering shrubs, with their large flowers like single roses; but they are not commonly planted. *S. pentagyna* and *S. pseudo-camellia* are hardy as far north as Mass. They thrive in a sandy loam with peat or leafmold added. Propagated by seeds, cuttings of almost mature wood, and layers.

PRINCIPAL SPECIES

S. pentagyna, native from N. C. southward, grows to 15 ft. and has white wavy petaled flowers 2 to 3 in. across, with white stamens and yellow anthers. Var. *grandiflora* is a rare form with larger flowers and conspicuous purple stamens.

malacodendron, native from Va. southward, is a handsome shrub to 12 ft., with flowers up to 4 in. across with purple stamens. Not hardy N.

pseudo-camellia is a Japanese shrub or tree to 50 ft. It has showy flowers with orange colored anthers. In fall the leaves turn brilliant red, orange and yellow.

sinensis is a Chinese shrub or tree to 30 ft., with flowers 2 in. across.

STICKTIGHTS. A common name for the genus Bidens, called Bur-marigold, some species of which are grown in flower gardens but most of which are fought because they are weedy and produce large numbers of troublesome burs.

STIGMA. In flowering plants, the apex or terminal extension of the pistil (usually at the summit of a stalk, called the *style*). It may or may not be enlarged but is usually roughened, sticky or otherwise prepared to receive and retain pollen grains. See FLOWER.

STINGBELLS. Common name for *Fritillaria agrestis,* a bulbous herb of Calif. whose yellowish-green flowers have a disagreeable odor.

STINK-BUGS. Properly this refers to certain shield-shaped true bugs (which see) with an offensive odor. However, the name is often wrongly applied to the related squash bugs (which see). Some stinkbugs attack and kill other insects; others are pests of rice and cotton. The southern green stink-bug injures a variety of garden vegetables. As they are sucking insects, stink-bugs must be fought with contact poisons (which see) such as kerosene emulsion, nicotine-sulphate, or pyrethrum.

STIPA (sty'-pah). A genus of perennial grasses often called Spear, Feather or Needle Grass. They grow to 3 ft. tall, have leaves rolled inward at the edges, and small bearded spikelets borne in clusters. Two species, *S. elegantissima,* with bearded purple spikelets in panicles half the height of the plant, and *S. pennata,* conspicuously feathered, are among the most beautiful of the small ornamental grasses for garden or border. They can be grown from divisions of the clumps, or from seed, See ORNAMENTAL GRASSES.

STIPULE. One of the two small leaflike appendages sometimes appearing at the base of a leaf-stalk. Their function seems to be to protect the buds, as in tulip-tree, but sometimes they exist as prickles, glands or tendrils; occasionally they take on the form of leaves, as in the pansy.

STOCK. The stocks as gardeners know them comprise at least 3 unlike plants. Two of them are species of Mathiola (also spelled Matthiola), and the third is the single species of Malcomia. Both are members of the Crucifer Family. The name Gilliflower, sometimes applied to one species of Mathiola, now refers also to the related genus Cheiranthus, the Wallflower, though the original Gilliflower was the Carnation.

SPECIES

Mathiola bicornis (Evening or Grecian Stock) is a straggling branchy annual grown for its small fragrant lilac blossoms which open toward evening; the mature seed pods bear two conspicuous horns.

M. incana (Queen or Brompton Stock, or Gilliflower) is a perennial or biennial grown for late summer and autumn blossom in the open or under glass. A sturdy,

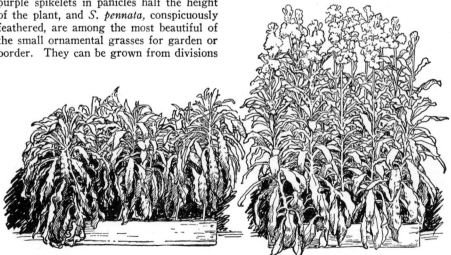

STOCKS GROW BEST IN A MODERATELY COOL TEMPERATURE

These two flats of stocks were planted at the same time and handled exactly the same except that the one at the left was kept in a greenhouse where the temperature never went below 60 deg. F., while the one at the right was kept in a temperature that ranged between 50 and 60 deg. Obviously a southern border fully exposed to the summer sun is no place for this plant.

erect plant 1 to 2½ ft. tall, it bears flowers usually double and in a wide range of colors, with purples and pinks predominating. (See illustration, Plate 49.) The race known as Ten-weeks or Intermediate Stock is the var. *annua,* usually grown as an annual.

The third kind of stock is *Malcomia maritima,* popularly called Malcolm, Mahon or Virginian Stock, a diffuse annual, with flowers lilac and reddish to white. It grows 6 to 12 in. high and the pods are not horned.

The 3 subjects are best considered separately because they differ widely in character.

Culture of Stocks

M. incana should be grown from seed sown in May or June in the open air for bloom about 15 months later. When the seedlings are 2 in. high, they should go into separate pots to be set in a frame for protection from possible rainy weather and later from the cold. The following spring they can be transplanted to the spot where they are to bloom. For greenhouse culture, they may be started in flats in August, taken inside at the end of October and the earliest brought into bloom in March. Var. *autumnalis,* the latest blooming type, is the one known as the Brompton Stock.

Among horticultural varieties are Beauty of Nice, a soft pink on a branching plant 16 in. tall, excellent both for cutting and bedding; Perpetual Branching, also known as Dresden Stock or Cut-and-Come-Again, a later variety requiring a longer period before reaching flowering size, but available in almost any color desired. Var. *annua* is the most popular type. As its common name, "Ten-weeks Stock," implies, it is quick to come into bloom. The fragrant flowers, ranging from white through lilac to crimson, are borne on handsome spikes, the double flowers forming rosettes. The doubles produce no seed; but seed from a vigorous single, grown in rich soil under as nearly perfect conditions as possible, will usually produce double flowers. These last for a long period and the side shoots give a succession of blossoms from July to frost. The plants require a plentiful amount of moisture and do best in cool locations and seasons. Seeds are best sown in the hotbed from February on, pricking out the

young seedlings into shallow pans when their second leaves appear, and into small pots 3 or 4 weeks later. By the end of April they can usually go outdoors 1 ft. apart in deep, rich soil in a sunny location. Seeds sown in summer make good winter-flowering plants.

Dwarf Ten-weeks Stock is a compact plant excellent for edging or for low beds; it is not more than 1 ft. high.

White maggots destroy the roots of these stocks if watering is not judiciously done. In the early stages, a fine spray should be used,—in the morning if weather is cold, or at night when warm. Later only the soil should be watered, a straight spout being attached to keep moisture off the foliage. The earlier spraying with water helps to check the flea beetle, which sometimes eats the leaves of young plants. Stocks may suffer from bacterial blight, mosaic or stem rot, and in all cases diseased plants should be removed as soon as noticed.

Mathiola bicornis (Evening Stock) is a hardy annual, 15 in. high, sweetly fragrant after twilight hours or after a shower. The plants bear many small single lilac flowers which are inconspicuous by day. The blooming period is from July to September. Plants are grown from seeds sown indoors or outdoors.

Malcomia maritima (Virginian Stock). Its graceful sprays of small white, lilac or crimson flowers make this Old-World annual a garden favorite. With successional sowings of seed, it will bloom throughout most of the summer. Seeds sown in the fall will give flowers early in spring. The plants thrive best in a sunny location, and are especially suitable for edging.

STOCK. The axis, or shortened base of a stem; a tuberous, underground stem thickened for the storage of reserve foods, as in the iris. In grafting, the stock is the plant (often a seedling) into which the scion or bud of another plant has been inserted; it thus fulfils the root functions of the new plant, the scion doing the work of the top. For best· results the stock should belong to a species closely related to the scion and be chosen with regard to (1) similarity of habit and (2) its adaptation to the soil and climate conditions under which it is to grow.

STOKESIA (stoh-kee′zhi-ah) *laevis.* A native perennial herb of the Composite Family, found from S. C. to La. and known as Stokes-aster. It bears blue or purplish-blue flowers in heads to 4 in. across and has grayish green foliage. Var. *alba* has white, *lutea,* yellowish, and *rosea* pink flowers. Stokes-aster is a charming erect branched plant growing to about 15 in., most attractive in groups in the middle of the border. It blooms freely over a long period and is easily grown from seed or increased by division. It requires an open sunny position in light rich soil and should not be allowed to become too dry.

STOLON. A form of stem or, more accurately, a branch or shoot given off at the summit of a root. It may grow either just above or just below the soil surface, take root at the tip or at several joints, and form one or more new plants. This kind of stolon is commonly called a *runner;* and it is by runners that strawberries (which see) are propagated.

STOMACH POISON. An insecticide (which see) used to destroy chewing insects, either mixed with edible materials to form a bait, or applied as a spray or dust which covers plants so thoroughly that the insect, in making a meal of the plant tissue, will get a fatal dose. Stomach poisons are chiefly composed of some form of arsenic, especially lead arsenate, but non-arsenicals such as hellebore, fluorine compounds, rotenone and nicotine tannate are also used. See INSECTICIDE.

STONE-CRESS. Common name for the genus Aethionema, dwarf herbs and subshrubs similar to candytuft, with pink, purple or white flowers in terminal racemes.

STONECROP. Common name for the genus Sedum, often called Live-forever, low growing succulent perennials, favorites in rock gardening and, the smaller kinds, for dish gardens.

STONE FRUIT. A common name for what is botanically a *drupe,* that is, a fruit developing from one simple pistil or the elements (carpels) of a compound pistil, each drupe generally containing one seed or kernel, surrounded by a bony shell (endocarp) called a pit or stone. Typical examples are the peach, cherry, apricot and other fruits of the genus Prunus; hence the term is often used for any or all of them. Forms intermediate between drupes and nuts are walnut and coconut.

For comparison see FRUIT; BERRY; POME; DRUPE; PRUNIS.

STONE MINT. Common name for *Cunila origanoides,* a hardy native perennial of the Mint Family, growing to 1 ft. and having small purplish two-lipped flowers in flat-topped clusters, and small oval leaves. It is grown in the border for its profusion of bloom, or in the herb garden for its foliage, the leaves being occasionally used for a tea. It needs a light dry sandy soil, and is increased by seed or division. It is sometimes known as Maryland-dittany.

STONE-ROOT. A common name for Collinsonia, a genus of aromatic N. American herbs of which *C. canadensis* (Citronella) is sometimes planted in moist shady wild gardens.

STONE WORK. This includes all the uses in gardens of natural or artificial stone. This may be in walls, walks, pavements, steps, rock gardens and rockeries. The desirability of resorting to artificial forms (such as concrete) in regions where natural stone and rock are lacking, is a matter which each must decide for himself. As with all imitations, perhaps the most important thing to look out for is to see that the substitute does not attempt to pose as the real thing, but frankly acknowledges its artificiality. Otherwise it may be better to forego stone effects where natural stones are not to be had.

The possibilities of stone in the garden are great. So also are the pitfalls and hazards. It requires great patience, skill and imagination to build it into a structure that shall be firm and enduring. And even greater skill is demanded in assembling rocks or stones in a rock garden, a stream bed and cascade, or any such feature in which absolute fidelity to the Nature-model is essential. Moreover, in a garden the relation between the stone work and the plant materials must be correctly maintained, which makes greater demands upon the ingenuity of the builder.

STOOL. A clump of suckers together with the plant base from which they spring. A grass or grain plant is said to be "stooling" when it throws up stalks other than the primary stalk. In some cases (as in the gooseberry) suckers so formed are used as a means of propagation, the method being *layering* (which see). Surplus suckers above those wanted for reproduction should be removed

STOPPING. The practice of nipping "leader" shoots while soft to prevent further elongation and thus strengthen the remaining parts and induce the production of lateral branches. It is often done with trained dwarf fruit trees, blackberries, black raspberries, chrysanthemums, dahlias and other plants, indoors and out. Though somewhat practiced with European varieties of grapes, especially those grown under glass, it is *not* a desirable practice in growing American varieties because it induces worthless, that is, non-bearing, lateral growths. See PINCHING.

STORAX (stoh'-raks). Common name for the genus Styrax, decorative shrubby plants with beautiful, usually drooping, white flowers in clusters, followed by inconspicuous fleshy or dry fruits. These are most attractive shrubs, a handsome addition to the shrubbery border and charming planted as single specimens on the lawn. Only a few of the species are hardy N. and they should be planted in a warm sandy loam in a sheltered position. They are increased by seed, by grafting on *Halesia carolina,* or by layers. Great difficulty is experienced in starting cuttings.

S. japonica, to 30 ft., a shrub with light open graceful branches and fragrant drooping bell-shaped flowers, is hardy to Mass.

obassia, also to 30 ft. and hardy to Mass., has almost round leaves, velvety beneath, and many-flowered racemes of pure white blossoms in May.

americana, to 10 ft., with oval leaves and few-flowered racemes of fragrant blossoms to ½ in. long, although found wild from S. Va. to Fla., is hardy in N. Y.

grandifolia, to 12 ft., with fragrant many-flowered racemes, is hardy to Philadelphia.

wilsoni, to 10 ft., a compact much-branched little shrub with 3 to 5 flowers in a cluster, is remarkable for its tendency to bloom when very small.

STORING OF CROPS. As popularly understood, this refers to the saving of the less perishable fruits and vegetables; in a more general sense and as considered here, it includes also the storage of seeds (see SEED PRODUCTION) and that of flowers. In the latter connection it may mean the keeping of living flowers in water for as long as possible or that of dried flowers and seed-pods (see EVERLASTINGS). Cut flowers keep best if gathered just as they are beginning to open, in the early morning, while they are cool from the night air, and while their stems and foliage are filled with sap; they should at once be plunged almost the full depth of the stems in cold water and kept out of the sunlight, preferably in a dark cellar where the temperature is relatively low, until they are to be arranged in vases or packed for shipment. (See CUT FLOWERS; FLOWER ARRANGEMENT.)

Flowers that "dry well" should be cut just as the buds are fully developed and beginning to open; otherwise they may "shatter" or fall apart when dry and thus become worthless. After cutting they should be hung heads downward in warm, dry quarters, out of strong sunlight and where there is good ventilation. If stored in an upright position the heads will bend over and dry in contorted or distorted shapes, but if hung as suggested they will dry in an almost, if not quite, natural position.

Successful storage of vegetables and fruits depends upon the maintenance of low temperature, sufficient ventilation and relatively high humidity of the air surrounding them, although the exact requirements vary more or less widely with the various kinds of products stored.

Nuts, like seeds, must be thoroughly "cured" and dry before being stored in bulk. They must be kept in dry quarters where the ventilation is good and the temperature is not high. If they are well cured, a low temperature will not injure their quality, but if the temperature is high they may turn rancid and if not well cured they will mold.

To keep other fruits in good condition the temperature must be maintained as low as possible (above freezing), the humidity must be relatively high and the ventilation good. The first of these factors, cold, checks the ripening process; for though fruit should be relatively "ripe" when gathered, the ripening continues and gradually blends into decay, the speed of the change increasing directly with the temperature.

Under home storage conditions, the temperature cannot be reduced much below 50 deg. F. until mid-autumn. Then it may be lowered further by opening windows and doors at night, closing them in the morning, and keeping them shut all day, except when the outdoor temperature is lower than the inside. During winter this same method of regulation can be followed, care being taken to prevent the temperature falling more than a degree or two below the freezing point. Remember that cool air is heavier than warm, so that to insure ventilation—that is, air in motion—there should be an outlet for the warm air somewhere near the ceiling of the room or cellar.

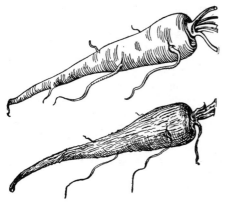

SUITABLE STORAGE CONSERVES QUALITY

Above is a parsnip freshly dug in the fall; below as it looked after 5 days in the open air. Correctly stored, it would have remained in good condition for months.

From the storage standpoint vegetables may be classified into two groups, namely, those that require warm and dry conditions and those that must be kept in cool quarters and a relatively humid atmosphere. Typical of the former are pumpkins, winter squashes and sweet-potatoes, which require a temperature of 50 deg. or higher. Hence the advisability of storing them near the house heater or in an upstairs properly warmed room. Examples of the second group are cabbage, potatoes and all the so-called "root crops"—beets, carrots, turnips, etc., which keep best at 38 deg. or lower, but which suffer injury at below 32 deg.

Though ventilation is less important for cool vegetables than for warm ones (except during the first month or two of storage), vegetables requiring warm conditions must not be allowed to "sweat," for this generally precedes decay. It may be prevented by raising the temperature somewhat until the dew-like dampness has been evaporated.

The best way to assure the most favorable humidity is to have in the storage room a natural earth or sand floor, or one of porous brick, because through these materials moisture slowly evaporates into the air. Incidentally this evaporation tends to lower the temperature, for evaporation is a cooling process.

The worst kind of floor for storage quarters is concrete because practically no moisture can pass through it. If this condition exists, the best way to overcome it is to sprinkle the floor at frequent intervals, to keep it covered with a layer of moist sand or peat moss, or to provide "humidifiers" of some sort.

Storage rooms constructed in house cellars should be thoroughly insulated to prevent the passage of heat from the furnace room. They should also be provided with some method of ventilation that will not only remove the characteristic odors of the vegetables and fruits, but also keep the temperature under control. When the storage room can be placed beneath the bay window of a ground floor room its insulation can usually be more effective than when it must be built in a corner; for in the former case only one wall need be insulated as against two in the latter case. Still better is the storage space built as a separate room off the main cellar and entered by an insulated door.

When possible, the storage room should have two windows facing the different directions to assure ample ventilation. Another good scheme is to remove two small panes from the window sash. Then lead a tube from the lower opening directly down almost to the floor, and from the upper one lead another tube horizontally across the ceiling almost to the side wall opposite to the window. The heavy cool air will flow in through the first tube and the lighter warm air will escape through the other out of the upper one.

Or, one large pane can be removed from the window and replaced with a piece of board or metal with two holes bored in it, one above the other, to serve as inlet and outlet for two tubes as just described. In either case each tube should be equipped with a simple damper to regulate the inflow and outflow of the air.

When it is not feasible to have a storage room in the cellar, a substitute may be provided out of doors. This may be a series of receptacles buried in a corner of the garden or a "mound." Nail kegs are convenient receptacles because each can be lined with straw or newspaper and filled with an assortment of vegetables to last a week or two, so it may be taken up without disturbing the others. The covering of soil and litter held down by boards will vary in depth with the degree of cold weather that can be expected.

The mound type of storage is better adapted to holding over larger quantities of produce. The main objection to it is that once it is opened (between winter and early spring) all the vegetables must be removed because it is next to impossible to close it effectively with frozen soil. The best way to make a mound storage pit is as follows:

Choose a well-drained spot, preferably one from which surface water will flow to a lower level. Smooth off a circular area 4 to 6 ft. in diameter. Dig two trenches at right angles across it for ventilation and drainage and cover them with ½-in. mesh galvanizing netting or "hardware cloth." Where the two trenches intersect in the center place a cylinder of the same material erect to serve as a ventilator; its length will depend upon the height of the mound, above which it should extend 4 to 6 in. Cover the bottom of the mound with a 6-in. layer of fallen leaves, straw or similar material and on this pile vegetables or apples and pears in a conical pile around the ventilator.

When the pile is about 30 in. high cover it with 4 to 6 in. of leaves or straw, then 6 to 10 in. of soil, leaving 4 to 6 in. of the chimney; this must be covered with a board or building paper to shed rain and snow. Keep the outer ends of the trenches open until the arrival of freezing weather makes it necessary to close them. To prevent water entering the mound from the side make a trench all the way around it with a lead off to a lower level.

Root crops, cabbage and other hardy vegetables as well as apples and winter pears can be kept in such mound storages until spring.

STORKSBILL. A common name for the genus Erodium (also called Heronsbill) of the Geranium Family; also sometimes applied to the genus Pelargonium, which includes the common bedding geranium which is much grown as a house plant.

STOVEHOUSE. Originally this (sometimes called merely "stove") was the glass-house or section of a greenhouse range in which the tropical plants were grown. Before the days of hot water and steam pipes, such a structure was heated by stoves and hot-air flues, generally of brick. Today

the term, though not much used, similarly applies to the section of a greenhouse containing the tropical plants (formerly called "stove plants") in which the highest heat and humidity are maintained. See also GREENHOUSE; HOTHOUSE; COOLHOUSE; CONSERVATORY.

STRAIN. A group of individuals within a variety or race, which constantly differ in one or more characters from the varietal or racial type. An illustration would be an improved sort of pea, bean or other vegetable developed from a well-known variety by a grower or seedsman who would work up a supply of seed or plants to be sold as his "strain" of the given variety. However, it should be kept in mind that a catalog variety or strain bearing the name of a grower or firm can not always be clearly differentiated from the variety of which it is supposed to be an improvement. See also VARIETY; RACE; SPORT.

STRANVAESIA (stran-vee'-si-ah). Evergreen shrubs or small trees, native in Asia, belonging to the Rose Family. They have handsome foliage and clusters of small white flowers resembling those of the hawthorn; the fruit is in the form of small red or orange berries. They thrive in a well-drained loamy soil with humus, but are not hardy North. *S. davidiana,* the principal species, grows up to 20 ft. with oblong leaves to 4 in. long, and scarlet berries. Var. *undulata* has wavy leaves and orange-red berries, and is hardier.

STRAP FERN. Common name for *Polypodium phyllitidis,* a good plant for the greenhouse, with long, leathery, shining fronds and running stems. Grow in shallow pots, using plenty of peat or half-decayed leafmold, and water generously; but provide good drainage.

STRATIFICATION. The practice of storing large seeds in alternate layers with sifted sand, soil, granulated peat moss or similar materials that are kept moist to prevent the seeds from drying out and thereby promote germination. Seeds so treated are mostly bony ones such as plum pits, hickory nuts, and thorn seeds, which in nature are kept damp by the pulp of the fruit. Usually stratification is done in flats or boxes that can be placed where rain will keep the material wet; and in general it is done over winter so that frost action will help split the shells. See SEEDS AND SEEDSOWING.

STRATIOTES (strat-i-oh'-teez) *aloides.* A perennial aquatic herb, commonly called the Water Soldier, which see.

STRAWBERRY. A low-growing, stemless, perennial that increases rapidly by long runners and bears delicious, highly prized, red berries in late spring. The cultivated strawberry resulted from the hybridizing in Europe of the Virginian strawberry, *Fragaria virginiana,* of eastern North America, and the Chilean strawberry, *F. chiloensis,* of the Pacific coast of South America. It is the most widely grown of all our fruits and there are varieties suited to every state and Canadian province.

The strawberry bed should be a sunny site without shade of trees or buildings or the competition of tree roots. Less trouble from frost, leaf spot and fruit rot will be experienced if good soil drainage and air circulation are present. Avoid planting after tomatoes until two years have elapsed, and eliminate perennial weeds before planting.

Soils that will grow good vegetables, if well-drained and in good physical condition, are suitable for strawberries. Organic matter should be added if needed either as manure compost or by turning under a sod crop.

Plants should be purchased from nurseries specializing in producing strawberry plants. Special methods have recently been developed for producing virus-free, nematode-free dormant plants from cold storage and these are much superior and no more expensive than plants not produced by these methods.

PLANTING AND CARE. Strawberries are usually set as early in the spring as soil condition and weather permits, but dormant plants from cold storage make delays less hazardous. Fall planting, late October and early November, is also successful. Mid-summer planting of freshly dug plants, although often practiced, is much less satisfactory than early spring planting.

Strawberries are usually grown in the matted-row. The plants, which are set in a row, produce many runner plants which take root around the mother plant and bear fruit the following year. With vigorous varieties that produce many runners and favorable growing conditions, the row becomes overcrowded and the crop and berries are much smaller than where the number of runners are limited. For best results with the matted row the runner plants should be spaced around the mother plant as they develop until they are spaced about 6 in. apart in a row 18 in. wide. Thereafter all runner plants are removed.

A better method is the hill system. The plants are set a foot apart in the row and all runner plants are removed as they appear. Two, three or four rows may be set this way with a foot between rows. An alley three feet wide is left and additional beds may be set.

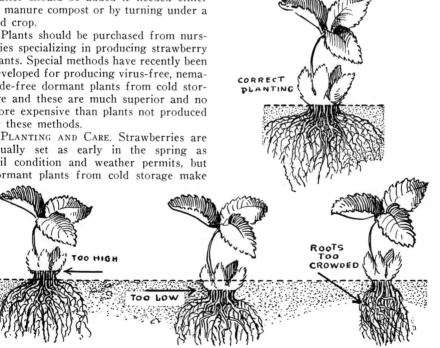

CORRECT PLANTING

TOO HIGH

TOO LOW

ROOTS TOO CROWDED

HOW TO PLANT—AND HOW NOT TO PLANT—A STRAWBERRY

This method results in maximum production per unit of area and the berries are larger than with the crowded matted row.

Strawberry plants are set with the crown (the solid part from which the leaves arise) even with the surface of the ground. Dormant plants set early will not need watering, but freshly dug plants may need watering, especially if set late, and the weather is dry. Fertilizers, unless used very carefully, should not be used at planting time. Starter solutions used for vegetables may be used at planting to start the plants off quickly.

Summer care is mostly weed control which may be done with the hoe. Chemical herbicides, such as Crag Sesone, are useful to reduce the amount of hoeing. Sprayed on the soil according to instructions on the package they kill the germinating weed seeds and lengthen the interval between hoeings.

The blossoms, which appear a few weeks after planting, should be removed to prevent fruiting which reduces plant vigor. Any fruit obtained from first year fruiting is at the expense of the crop a year later.

Fertilizers may not be needed on fertile garden soils that have grown well-fertilized vegetables for several years. On less fertile soils a pound of ammonium nitrate or two pounds of sodium nitrate may be applied as a side dressing to 100 feet of row at the first hoeing. In mid-August another application is desirable to stimulate fruit bud formation which occurs during the fall months. Fertilizers should not be applied to the bed in the spring of the fruiting year.

The bed should be mulched with straw or marsh hay in late fall before temperatures drop below 20° F. and after a few hard frosts have occurred. The straw is spread over the plants to a depth of three inches. In the spring part of the straw is raked into the alley between the rows. The leaves and blossoms push through the remaining straw which keeps the berries clean during splashing rains.

In the bearing year irrigation may be needed if the weather is dry. Rainfall and water from irrigation should total about an inch a week. If applied with a porous canvas hose less rotting of the berries is likely.

Plantings in good vigor may be renewed for a second crop by cleaning up the weeds after harvest, fertilizing and caring for the bed as during the first year.

Everbearing strawberries fruit more or less continuously during the summer and fall. They are best grown in hills with all runners removed. Mulching with sawdust, high fertility, and ample moisture are essential for good crops. Blossoms are removed until about July 1 after which they are permitted to develop.

ENEMIES. Diseases are not likely to be a problem with present day varieties and nursery practices.

The tarnished plant bug, which causes malformed, seedy-ended berries is controlled by spraying the plants just before they bloom with an insecticide.

White grubs feed on the roots of strawberry plants planted on freshly turned under grass sod, but chlordane dust applied to the ground at the rate of 10 pounds per acre before planting will control the grubs. Various other insects may be locally troublesome and control measures are available from agricultural colleges. Slugs often feed on the berries and they may be controlled with a slug bait containing metaldehyde which is placed in small piles in the bed at dusk, being careful not to get it on the berries.

VARIETY SELECTION. Many good varieties are available, each region having its own list. North of the latitude of Washington, D.C., Sparkle is one of the best varieties, being of excellent dessert quality and suitable for freezing. Catskill, Midland, Fairfax and Empire are also good sorts. South of Washington, D.C., Blakemore is widely cultivated, but Dixieland, Pocahontas, Earlidawn, Redglow and Surecrop are considered favorably. Albritton is grown in North Carolina, Klonmore in Louisiana while in Florida, the long-grown Missionary and newer Florida 90 are favorites.

The Mid-West grows many of the northern varieties as well as Robinson, Armore and Vermilion. Marshall has long been a West Coast favorite because of its high quality and suitability for preserving and freezing.

Everbearing varieties are Gem (Superfection, Brilliant) Streamliner, Redrich, Arapahoe and others.

Baron Solemacher, a runnerless form of the Alpine strawberry, *Fragaria vesca*, is occasionally grown in gardens. The berries

Plate 51.　　　　SUCCULENTS—AN INTERESTING PLANT GROUP

Upper left: The heavy leaves of the Echeveria store moisture and enable it to live under arid conditions. Upper right: Conophytum bears a daisy-like flower larger than the plant itself. Center left: The thick foliage of Sedum alboroseum proclaims its membership in the group. Center: The century-plant, the largest of all, stores enough food in its roots and enormous leaf rosette to support a flower stalk sometimes 40 ft. high. Center right: Crassula lactea, a shrub from South Africa, makes an excellent pot plant. Lower left: In the dry, sunny rock garden, sedums are invaluable, Sedum album being one of the best. Lower right: The hen-and-chickens (Sempervivum) thrives in dry crevices in the rock garden.

are small, long pointed, soft, and with a mild characteristic flavor. The plants fruit throughout the summer and fall.

Strawberry breeders are bringing out good new varieties at frequent intervals and these may be found in the catalogues of strawberry plant growers.

STRAWBERRY - BUSH. Common name for *Euonymus americanus* and *E. obovatus,* deciduous American shrubs with inconspicuous flowers and pink fruits. It is sometimes applied to other species.

STRAWBERRY FERN. Common name for *Hemionitis palmata,* a species of small fern whose 5-lobed, blades 2 to 6 in. long, resembling ivy leaves, are borne on long brownish hairy stipes 6 to 12 ins. tall. Excellent for the terrarium or greenhouse, in 2 parts peat moss and 1 part sand. Having few roots, they do best in small pots which insure good drainage.

STRAWBERRY-GERANIUM. A common name for *Saxifraga sarmentosa,* given because of its strawberry-like method of propagation by runners. See SAXIFRAGE.

STRAWBERRY-RASPBERRY. Common name for *Rubus illecebrosus,* also called Balloon-berry. It is a Japanese nearly woody herbaceous bramble planted for its ornamental foliage, large, fragrant, white flowers and scarlet fruit which is good for stewing or canning.

STRAWBERRY-TOMATO. A common name for several species of Physalis, especially *P. alkekengi.* Also called Winter-cherry or Chinese Lantern Plant. This is a perennial usually grown as an annual for the inflated, balloon-like form of its red calyx. Sprays are ornamental additions to winter bouquets.

STRAWBERRY - TREE. Common name for *Arbutus unedo,* a medium-sized European evergreen tree with small flowers and berry-like red fruits.

STRAWFLOWER. Common name for *Helichrysum bracteatum,* a tall annual whose variously colored flower-heads when dried are used for winter bouquets. See EVERLASTINGS.

STRELITZIA (stre-lit'-si-ah). A genus of S. African herbs of the Banana Family, popularly known as Bird-of-paradise Flowers. They have showy blossoms borne in rigid boat-like bracts with several petals united to form the "tongue"; these are being increasingly seen in florist shops and flower shows. Several of the species may be grown under glass in tubs, or outdoors

in warm climates, being increased by division or suckers, and occasionally by seed started in moist heat. *S. reginae,* to 3 ft., is a trunkless plant with long leaves and yellow flowers with dark blue tongues and purple boat-like bracts. *S. parvifolia* has shorter leaves and bright orange flowers with blue tongues and green bracts edged with red. *S. angusta,* a tree-like form, to 18 ft., has white flowers with purplish bracts sometimes 15 in. long.

STREPTOCARPUS (strep-toh-kahr'-pus). A genus of stemless S. African herbs of the Gesneria Family with blue or purple gloxinia-like blooms, commonly known as Cape-primrose, which see.

STREPTOPUS (strep'-toh-pus). A genus of small native woodland herbs called Twisted-stalk, which see.

STREPTOSOLEN (strep-toh-soh'-len) *jamesoni.* This evergreen shrub, native to S. America and belonging to the Nightshade Family, is a popular plant for outdoor grouping in the warmest parts of the country, and an old favorite in N. greenhouses. It is sometimes grown in standard form for summer bedding arrangements but does well in pots, thriving in a sandy loam with leafmold or old manure. It is very showy when in bloom with clusters of orange-red flowers at the ends of slender shoots. Old plants may be cut back and grown on year after year. Propagated by cuttings.

STROBILANTHES (stroh-bi-lan'-theez). A genus of tropical Asiatic herbs and shrubs, known as Conehead, grown under glass in the N. and requiring abundant heat and moisture. They are sometimes used as bedding plants in the S. and are propagated by cuttings started in sandy soil under heat. *S. isophyllus* has pink, or blue and white, flowers growing in clusters from the axils of the long narrow leaves. *S. dyerianus,* to 3 ft., is a shrubby greenhouse plant with purplish iridescent leaves and violet flowers in spikes.

STROMANTHE (stroh-man'-thee). A genus of tropical herbs of the Maranta Family, grown principally for their foliage. *S. porteana,* the only species commonly cultivated, has broad green leaves to 1 ft. long, barred with white above, and purple beneath. The blood-red flowers are borne in racemes to 6 ft. long. It should be grown in a warm greenhouse where the night temperature does not drop below 65 deg., in soil composed of rich loam, leafmold and sand; it should be shielded from direct sunlight. Propagation is by division of the rootstocks or by cuttings.

STRUTHIOPTERIS (stroo-thi-op'-ter-is). Former generic name of members of the Common Fern Family, some now called Bleehnum, and of the Ostrich Fern, now Pteretis (which see). This has 3- to 5-ft. fronds, once-pinnate and plume-like. It grows in wet sandy soil supplied with leafmold.

STUARTIA. An occasional, but not preferred, spelling of Stewartia, which see.

STUD-FLOWER, STUD-PINK. Common names for *Helonias bullata,* the Swamp-pink (which see), a tuberous-rooted herb with long-stalked racemes of purplish or pink flowers. Doing well in sun or shade, it is good for bog gardens and for late winter flowering in pots indoors.

STUNT. A name given to diseases whose chief symptom is a dwarfing of the plant with shortened internodes (spaces between the stem joints). The condition is usually produced by a virus (which see) but sometimes eel-worms (which see) are the primary cause. There are, for example, two stunts of dahlia (which see), one a virus and the other a nematode or eel-worm disease.

STYLE. The column, or pillar, in a flower, which extends above the ovary and is capped by the stigma (which see). The style varies considerably in length, or may be absent in some flowers, as the poppy.

STYLOPHORUM (sty-lof'-oh-rum) *diphyllum.* A perennial herb with yellow or red flowers, called Celandine-poppy, which see.

STYRAX (sty'-rax). A genus of deciduous or evergreen trees or shrubs, widely distributed in tropical and warm-temperate regions of America, Asia and Europe, and commonly called Storax. They are of attractive habit and handsome in bloom with racemes or clusters of showy white flowers. They do best in light well-drained soil, but only one or two are fairly hardy N. Propagated by seed, layers, grafting, and rarely by cuttings. See STORAX.

SUB-IRRIGATION. Most of the commercial installations for the use of nutrient solutions make use of the sub-irrigation method, in which the solution is applied to the gravel, cinders, or other root medium from beneath. Concrete is usually used for bench construction and the benches (about

6 or 8 in. deep) should be made in relatively short units, as a slope of not less than 1 in. in 100 ft. is necessary to secure drainage flow. The bottom of the bench should slope from both sides toward the middle, where a trough one to two in. deep is formed. This is covered with a U-shaped tile. At the end of each unit a level chamber should be constructed, in

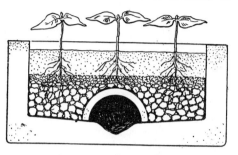

FOR SUB-IRRIGATION
This is a cross-section representation of a greenhouse bench which is described in the text.

order that the root medium may become saturated with the nutrient solution. A storage tank is constructed under the bench or at some convenient place below the bench level. Both the inside of the bench and the tank should be coated with some water-proofing material, such as hot asphalt. Certain asphalt emulsions have proved satisfactory. It is also necessary to have a pump of some sort to deliver the solution to the level chamber; an automatic pump is often used. By-pass valves permit drainage of the solution back to the tank after the roots have been flooded.

After these preparations, the bench is filled to the top with a suitable growing medium. If cinders are used, they should be carefully washed to get rid of all fine particles. Fine gravel is also a good medium. Then, if limestone material is used, the medium is prepared for the plants as described under SAND CULTURE. The medium is then saturated, the plants all set in place, and the medium is saturated yet again. Subsequent applications of the nutrient solution should be stopped when the level reaches to within one inch of the top of the growing medium. This will help to prevent growth of algae on the surface. The number of daily applications needed cannot be given arbitrarily, as they will vary with the type of plant, the nature of the medium (its ability to hold water), the temperature, light, and other factors that affect growth.

In the home, sub-irrigation may be practiced on a smaller scale. For example, a window box can be constructed that will have a capacity of 12 qt. of nutrient solution and a 12 qt. pail connected to the bottom of the box by means of a rubber tube. To operate the apparatus, raise the pail and hang it on a hook (previously provided) until the solution runs into the growing medium and saturates it and the plant roots. Then lower the pail and let the solution drain back into it to remain until time for the next application. See under WINDOW BOX.

See also CHEMICAL GARDENING; NUTRIENT SOLUTION.

SUB-SHRUB. A term used to designate a partly shrubby plant, one having persistent but not hard-wooded stems. Examples are Southernwood, Japanese-spurge, and Lavender-cotton.

SUBSISTENCE GARDENS. This term refers to vegetable gardens designed to furnish food for those persons and families planting and tending them, who, during periods of unemployment and public relief, would otherwise be unable to obtain it. Similar efforts were made during the World War to insure against food shortage and at that time the results were known as War or Emergency Gardens. They were largely the result of voluntary activity, though prompted usually by organized and official efforts to induce householders to grow their own food or at least a part of it. Large corporations with many employees also put unused lands at their disposal or established such gardens as community enterprises. In other places, organizations were formed, land was leased from (or lent, rent free, by) private owners and the whole project was considered a patriotic measure.

In many foreign countries such gardens remained, after the emergency was over, as a permanent economic contribution. In America the enthusiasm died out as necessity ceased to urge and such effort was generally abandoned. But the impressive figures of emergency garden production were not lost or entirely forgotten; and interest in them revived as, with the deepening of the depression shadows of 1928-29 and thereafter, the need for a similar general garden movement to aid the able unemployed became apparent.

During the World War emergency period, it was demonstrated on experimental plots that an abundant supply for one adult person for an entire year, can be grown in a space 25 by 30 ft. in size, if intensively cultivated and if the soil is of average fertility. In round figures, and with abundant margin allowance, this means that an acre of ground will produce the food for 50 people. The potential value of a subsistence garden to an average family on which it lays no great burden for planting and maintenance, is, therefore, evident.

Records to date encourage those associated with social work to continue to urge this type of activity. Such gardens do not compete with the truck gardener or farmer and do not affect the demand for the fresh vegetables they produce, since this demand comes chiefly from cities and congested regions with little or no land available for cultivation. On the other hand, subsistence gardens provide healthful and vital food for those who would otherwise lack vegetables altogether and suffer the effects of an unbalanced and inadequate diet.

SUB-SOIL. A term applied to the layer of soil next beneath that of ordinarily cultivated and frequently enriched "top-soil." Lying anywhere from a few to 12 in. or more below the surface it is not generally penetrated by plant roots, except those of large and exceptionally vigorous subjects. Because it has long been undisturbed and is poorly aërated, and devoid of humus or organic matter, the sub-soil cannot support the beneficial micro-organisms essential to the manufacture of plant food in the soil and therefore is unsuited to growing crop plants. This condition can, however, be gradually corrected by (1) sub-soil plowing, trenching (which see), or other deep cultural operations; (2) the incorporation of manures and other kinds of humus, and (3) the growing of sturdy, especially deep rooting plants for a few seasons.

The stiff, lifeless type of sub-soil just described is naturally associated with heavy clay-soil formations. A sandy or gravelly sub-soil may be just as lacking in humus and just as unsuitable for most crops, but it is easier to break up and improve; and it does not interfere with the drainage of excess water as does a clay sub-soil or hardpan (which see). On the other hand, it may sometimes be so porous as to make it hard to keep the top-soil sufficiently moist for the needs of the plants grown in it. Added humus improves this condition. See SOIL; IMPROVEMENT SOIL.

SUCCESSION CROPPING. The practice of replacing an early crop when harvested with one which will occupy part or all of the balance of the growing season. See CROPPING SYSTEMS.

SUCCORY. A common name for *Cichorium intybus*, or Chicory, which see.

SUCCULENTS. Succulents are fleshy plants of the desert, or semi-desert, places of the world. Because of the dry conditions under which they live, and their need to store up water, they have adapted themselves to their necessity in many different ways, often by taking all sorts of queer shapes. Some are as round as an orange, as *Euphorbia obesa* and *E. meloformis*. Others of the Cissus group are like old tree stumps, causing surprise by suddenly bursting forth into a crown of leaves and flowers. The well-known Joshua-tree of the W. holds up its arms to heaven and another Yucca, known as "Our Lord's Candle," is beautiful when in bloom with its great pyramid of white flowers.

The thin, broad leaves that serve plants of regions that have abundant rainfall would give off too much water in the dry air of desert areas, so leaves of the succulents are likely to be very thick and fleshy, small, or even entirely absent, their place being taken sometimes by thorns or spines. The stems, too, are frequently thick and sometimes many-angled.

INTERESTING TYPES. Among the succulents are plants with stems like a series of organ pipes. One of these, strangely enough, is a so-called geranium (really Pelargonium), but recognizable as

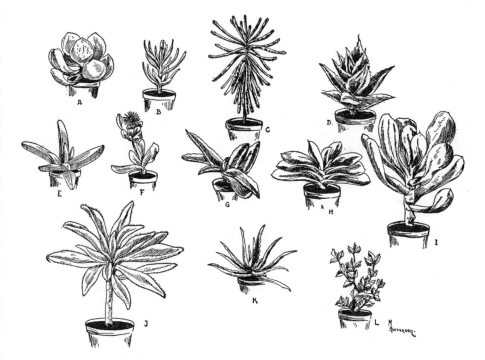

A DOZEN DECORATIVE SUCCULENTS FOR A SUNNY WINDOW
People who fancy these fleshy-leaved plants will find in them many curious colors and forms. The rosette of Crassula leaves (A) represents a juvenile form of a 10-foot South African desert plant. The Kalanchoë (C) will also grow to great size, bearing handsome, brilliantly colored flowers. The tubular leaves, which develop young plants on their tips, are mottled in brown, green, gray, purple and red. The small Kleinia (now called Senecio) (B) also has tubular leaves. Two characteristic Aloes are shown (D and K). The thick leaves of Corpuscularia (E) are always 3-angled, while those of Mesembryanthemum maximum (F) are half-moon shape. The latter bears a bright pink flower. Another Kalanchoë is shown (G), and beside it the strange opposite arrangement of leaves on Gasteria mollis (H). The glaucous leaf-rosettes of Cotyledon (I) and Echeveria (J) are always ornamental, as are the frosted-green, pointed leaves of Oscularia (L), which are as thick as they are broad.

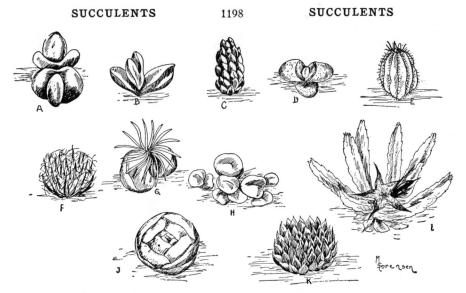

FROM SOUTH AFRICA COME THESE MANY AMUSING SUCCULENTS

Rimaria (A), with whitish globose leaves; Cheiridopsis (B), which is purplish; Pleiospilos (D), which resembles bits of gravel; and Conophytum (G and H), whose flowers are larger than the rest of the plant, used to be members of the genus Mesembryanthemum. Haworthia, shown in three widely different forms (C, F and K), is a member of the Lily Family. The cactus-like globe (E) is a Euphorbia. Stapelia (I), with its carrion-scented but attractive flowers, is botanically related to the common milkweed. The species of Crassula shown at (J) is a rare one. Note that none of these plants, despite its appearance and fleshy stem and leaves, is a cactus. See also other succulents in the illustrations on the opposite page and in Plate 51.

such only when it sends out its characteristically shaped leaves. There are succulent plants so like the stones among which they grow that it is a difficult task to find them. These are the interesting "Stoneplants" or "Living Rocks" of S. Africa. In these same deserts may be found the curious "Window-plants," such as the Lithops, Fenestrarias and others. These, because of the climatic conditions, or for some other reason, long ago retired into the ground, their only connection with the outer world (except when they bloom) being through the flat translucent tops of their leaves which lie on the surface and let in to the plant all the light it receives.

Haworthias, Crassulas and others are sometimes formed of fleshy leaves laid so closely one upon another that they form a solid column or sphere. Some of the succulents protect themselves by turning the edges of their leaves toward the sun.

In the last few years great interest in these queer plants has grown up and they have been planted extensively indoors and out. It is not strange that they have become popular for, besides their curious shapes, many of them have large and beautiful flowers. Deserts glow at times with the blossoms of these succulents, in shades of pink or crimson, scarlet, orange and yellow or white. Some of the tiny ones are almost completely hidden by their large flowers, and these are fine for indoor gardens.

KINDS OF SUCCULENTS. We find a surprising number of plant families represented among the succulents. The great family of cacti (Cactaceae) includes many of the better known genera. They are found with few exceptions in the W. hemisphere, especially S.W. U. S., Mexico, and S. America. Here are the true cacti, the Echinocactus and Cereus, often of large growth; the Echinocereus, with low growth, sometimes hanging over rocks; the Ferocactus, globular to cylindric in shape; the Neomammillaria, with many globular or cylindrical species, covered with tubercles; the Opuntias or prickly-pears which run riot in many desert places; the Epiphyllums (Phyllocactus), mostly epiphytes or air plants, with branches often flat and leaf-like, and many others.

In the Lily Family we find Aloe, Apicra, Gasteria, Haworthia and Yucca, as well as our old friend Sansevieria, so familiar in the dark entrance halls of houses and apartments. These plants, which are not true lilies but related to them, occur in many forms, from tree Aloes, such as *A. cooperi* and *A. bainesi,* to low-growing ones. Among the Apicras, Haworthias and Gasterias are many small types suitable for rock gardens in the milder parts of the country and for sunrooms in the N. They are streaked and striped, turned and twisted, flattened and angled in an enormous variety of interesting shapes.

In the Amaryllis Family we find the Agaves, to which group the century-plant belongs, as well as many of the more familiar ones. The Milkweed Family has a fascinating collection of odd forms, found generally in S. Africa. There are carrion-flowers (Stapelia), with stiff angled stems bearing large and strangely beautiful star-shaped flowers along or at the top of the stems and attractive in spite of the sometimes unpleasant odor. Others are Hoodia, with flat, widely-opened flowers in exquisite shades of creamy pink or buff; and Huernia and Trichocaulon.

The Orpine Family (Crassulaceae) includes Cotyledon, Crassula, Kalanchoë. Rochea, Sedum, and Sempervivum. The first four genera have many species with handsome flowers which are often fragrant. The last two are well-known rock garden plants, stonecrop and hen-and-chickens being found here. Valuable plants for indoor or outdoor gardens, they sometimes smother everything else with their rapid growth.

Then there is the big Euphorbia or Spurge Family, including the well-known crown-of-thorns (*Euphorbia splendens*), and the medusas head (*E. caput-medusae*), with its snaky-looking stems, as well as the two mentioned above at the beginning—*E. obesa* and *E. meloformis,* the fat, and the melon-shaped, Euphorbias.

Even the daisies contribute some species known as Kleinia, Senecio and Othonna, while the Portulaca Family contributes some queer ones called Anacampseros; some of these are covered with a white wool.

There is also the immense group formerly called Mesembryanthemum, but now divided into many different genera. The stone-plants and the window-plants belong here and the greatest variety of almost unbelievably strange forms. The true Mesembryanthemums of S. Africa make thick carpets of growth, their small succulent leaves being very green and attractive and their masses of daisy-like flowers covering the plants with white, yellow, orange, pink, scarlet, or magenta. The flowers have a glittering effect, due to their surface texture which acts like thousands of tiny mirrors in reflecting the light. These are easily grown indoors and in Calif. and Fla., but the S. African succulents are not hardy in the N.

CULTURAL DIRECTIONS. Some of the American succulents are hardy in the latitude of New York and many are already being grown there. The warmer parts of the country furnish conditions suitable for nearly all of them, but even there the smaller S. African ones will be improved by a little shelter from summer rains. Both kinds (American and S. African) do well as sunroom subjects. They grow easily and like the fairly cool temperature of sunrooms better than the hot air of greenhouses. They must, however, be protected from frost. They must have fresh air; this is very important. Water may be given when the plants are growing but must be withheld almost entirely when they are resting. They should be watered from below.

They do well in ordinary soil but must have good drainage. They grow easily from cuttings but these should be laid on a shelf or put in completely dry sand for a week or more, or the cut end should be dipped in powdered charcoal; otherwise they will be likely to rot. Nicotine preparations will protect from aphids. Fumigation with naphthalene vapor at a temperature of 88 to 95 deg. F. is effective for eradicating red spider. For mealy bug and woolly aphids, use alcohol on cotton.

SUCKER. A short or subordinate stem springing from a bud at the summit of the root; but the term is also applied to shoots that arise from buds located anywhere along the trunk of a tree, as water-sprouts on an apple. True suckers are sometimes used to propagate the plant, as their leaf nodes take root when bent into the soil. (See LAYERING; PROPAGATION.) Suckers on grafted plants are particularly objectionable, since they represent the stock (usually an unimproved seedling) rather than the desired variety grafted upon it. They should therefore be removed as soon as they appear by cutting them off as close to the root as possible, not merely cutting them back. See also STOOL.

SUFFRUTICOSE. Half-herbaceous and half-shrubby (in the sense of woody);

the condition found in so-called sub-shrubs which have herbaceous stems and branches that die down yearly to a woody base.

SUGARBERRY. Common name for *Celtis laevigata,* the Mississippi Hackberry, but sometimes applied to *C. occidentalis.* Both are ornamental shade or lawn trees. See HACKBERRY.

SUGAR-BUSH. Common name for *Rhus ovata,* a S.W. U.S. evergreen sumac with light yellow flowers and dark red hairy fruits. Sugar-bush is also the popular term in the U. S. for a grove of sugar maple trees.

SULPHUR AND ITS COMPOUNDS. Sulphur is one of the ten or more chemical elements believed to be essential to the growth of plants. It apparently ranks close to phosphorus in both the amount used by crops and the supply in the soil (which often seems below the theoretical requirements), but it does not appear as important a factor; and it is rarely if ever necessary (as far as soil fertility is concerned) to add sulphur to the soil, especially under garden conditions. (See also FERTILIZER; PLANT FOODS; SOIL.) It is much more important in gardening as a material for plant protection.

As A SPRAY MATERIAL. Sulphur, the only fungicidal or insecticidal material now in use which was known to the ancients, was used by Cato to fumigate trees as far back as 200 B.C. Flowers-of-sulphur were being used against plant lice in 1787 and for peach mildew in 1821, and a self-boiled lime-sulphur was made in 1833.

Lime-sulphur as known today, first used in Australia as a sheep dip, was introduced into California about 1880 as an insecticide to control San José scale. The fact that peach trees so sprayed for scale were free from leaf curl revealed its fungicidal value. But its possibilities as a summer fungicide were not discovered until nearly 30 years later when it was substituted for bordeaux mixture in the control of apple scab. It is now the standard fungicide for use on pome fruits (apple, pear, quince).

Lime-sulphur may be purchased as a concentrated liquid or as a dry powder. For *dormant spraying* the usual dilution is 1 part liquid concentrate to 7 parts water, or 1 lb. powder to 4 gals. water. For *summer spraying* the dilution is usually 1 part liquid to 49 parts or 1 lb. powder to 16⅔ gals. water. It may safely be com-bined with lead and calcium arsenate and with nicotine-sulphate.

Where the amount needed justifies the messiness and evil odor involved, lime-sulphur solution may be prepared at home. The ingredients are 50 lbs. lump or stone lime, 100 lbs. commercial ground sulphur, and water to make 50 gals. Heat one-third of the water and add to the lime; when this starts slaking add the sulphur which has been mixed with enough water to make a thick paste. Add the rest of the water and boil for about an hour, keeping the liquid up to its original level by adding more water as necessary. The concentration of the solution must be tested by means of a hydrometer which should show about 33 deg. on the Baumé scale. Diluted for dormant spraying the solution should test about 5 deg. Be. and for summer spraying just under 1 deg. Be.

To prepare *self-boiled lime-sulphur,* which is sometimes used as a summer spray for stone fruits and for certain varieties of apples, use 8 lbs. sulphur flour, 8 lbs. stone lime and 50 gals. water. Place the lime in a barrel and add enough water to start slaking; when well started dump in the sulphur and stir vigorously, adding water in small amounts to continue the slaking. Add the rest of the water as soon as vigorous boiling ceases.

Dry-mix sulphur-lime is a recent substitute for self-boiled lime-sulphur for use on peaches, plums and cherries. The formula calls for 8 lbs. sulphur, 4 lbs. lime (8 if lead arsenate is to be added), ½ lb. calcium caseinate or powdered skim milk and 50 gals. water. Mix the dry ingredients (or purchase a ready prepared mixture) and sift into the spray tank partly filled with water and with the agitator running. This material, though not potent enough for the pre-pink and pink-bud applications against apple scab, is used for the later sprays.

Potassium sulphide (livers of sulphur) is an old compound used as a stainless spray on ripening fruit and by some florists in combating mildew. Use at the rate of 1 oz. in 3 gals. water, spraying immediately after mixing.

So-called "wettable sulphurs" are dry preparations or pastes which mix readily with water and are obtainable ready for dilution. They are prepared by mixing the sulphur with various fluxes, such as calcium caseinate, oleic acid, glue, diatomaceous earth, flour or dextrin, and are more noticeable on the plants than sulphur dusts (see below).

Colloidal sulphur is a manufactured, extremely finely divided form in which the particles are much smaller than could be produced by grinding; 'when mixed with water they form a very fine suspension.

Dusting sulphurs are specially prepared sulphur powders fine enough to pass through a 300-mesh sieve. Ordinary flowers-of-sulphur should never be used for dusting as the particles are too coarse for adequate coverage and may cause burning. Usually some substance called a "fluffer" is added to the sulphur dust to prevent its packing and make it flow evenly. It may be talc or lead arsenate; if the latter, the dust controls not only fungous diseases but chewing insects as well. The usual proportion is 9 parts sulphur to 1 part lead arsenate; or sometimes 8 sulphur, 1 lead arsenate and 1 lime.

Sulphur dusts are particularly useful against powdery mildews and rusts and rose diseases, especially black spot. Red spider and the broad mite (see MITES) are also controlled with sulphur dusts applied when the temperature is 70 deg. F. or above. The dust may be obtained colored green which makes it less conspicuous on the foliage, but, properly applied, the cheaper yellow sulphur is not objectionably noticeable and it is better for ornamental plantings than sulphur sprays. Nicotine dust may be added to the sulphur-lead-arsenate combination but is more efficient against aphids if applied as a separate contact insecticide.

SUMAC, or SUMACH (seu'-mak). Common name for most members of the genus Rhus, which comprises numerous trees and shrubs, many of them familiar natives of N. America. Some are used for commercial purposes; others are poisonous; but the majority are decorative and suitable for ornamental planting. Most of the sumacs have compound leaves which assume brilliant scarlet colorings in the fall, though a few W. species have simple, evergreen leaves. The flowers, usually small, occur in large panicles; in many species these are followed by dense fruit-heads, often a fine deep red, soft and velvety and retaining their beauty well into winter. Many of the native kinds grow well in dry poor soil and are useful for massing on barren hillsides. Even *R. toxicodendron*, the baneful

poison ivy (which see), is attractive in foliage, but it should be eradicated wherever possible. *R. vernix,* the poison sumac (which see), the only moisture-loving species, should at least be strictly avoided.

Sumacs are increased easily by seed sown in autumn or stored at freezing temperature in a box of sand for spring germination; or by root cuttings. They grow in any soil except a damp one. Some of the species sucker so readily that they become a nuisance in shrubbery borders.

Cultivated sumac may be troubled with a powdery mildew, which, if severe, can be cured with sulphur dust. Two kinds of aphids may infest plants; one feeds on the under side of leaves, while the other forms a sac-like gall projecting downward from a leaflet. No control has been worked out. Psyllids or jumping plant lice may also infest sumac, and the flower spikes may be injured by gall mites. See MITES.

PRINCIPAL SPECIES

R. typhina (Staghorn Sumac). A tall shrub or tree, gaining its common name because of the velvety hairs on the twigs. Its leaves, consisting of many small leaflets, turn scarlet in autumn; the large clusters of greenish flowers, followed by hairy crimson fruit, last late. Ornamental shrubs, especially when planted in connection with lower-growing species.

glabra (Smooth Sumac). A shrub or tree. Also with brilliant fall coloring, and panicles of green flowers followed by red fruit.

copallina (Shining Sumac) is a shrub or tree to 20 ft. with dark green glossy foliage becoming brilliant scarlet, green flowers and hairy red fruit.

canadensis (Fragrant Sumac) is a smaller shrub, with aromatic 3-part leaves, yellowish flowers appearing before the leaves, and hairy red fruit.

toxicodendron (Poison Ivy or Poison-oak). A partly erect or vine-like shrub, climbing by aerial rootlets. *The leaves have 3 leaflets* (a distinguishing character) and the foliage becomes glowing scarlet and orange in the fall. The flowers are green and fruits are small, round, grayish berries.

vernix (Poison Sumac or Poison-elder). A marsh-land shrub or tree to 20 ft., the leaves consisting of 7 to 13 leaflets, which turn bright scarlet. The loose panicles of greenish flowers are followed by flattened, roundish gray fruit. This plant is even more poisonous than *R. toxicodendron*.

javanica, an Asiatic shrub or tree, has attractive creamy white flowers in panicles in August and September, followed by red fruit. It is hardy to Mass.

verniciflua (Varnish-tree or Lacquer-tree). Another large Asiatic tree with whitish flowers in loose clusters, followed by a smooth yellowish fruit. Hardy into New England and useful commercially as a source of varnish, but not a garden subject as it, too, is poisonous.

SUMMER-CYPRESS. A common name for *Kochia scoparia,* also called Belvedere, a quick growing annual of compact, symmetrical rounded form grown for its formal effect and its dense, fine, light green foliage that turns red in fall. A good temporary hedge plant, but as it self-sows it may become a troublesome weed.

SUMMER EFFECTS. See MIDSUMMER EFFECTS IN THE GARDEN.

SUMMER-FIR. Common name for *Artemisia sacrorum* var. *viride,* a very tall annual or biennial herb with rich green lacy ornamental foliage.

SUMMER HOUSE. A structure usually open (or partly so) on all sides but provided with a roof and a floor, built in the garden as a shelter and place to rest in hot weather. Summer houses of rustic construction were a popular feature of large dooryards in the mid-Victorian period, though it is doubtful if they were actually used to any extent. Those old-fashioned and often cumbersome structures have been modernized in the gardens of today until they are so inviting that often the garden interests center in them and revolve around them. Now they are put to constant use, and appropriately furnished, not infrequently to the extent of including a fireplace for barbecues.

In this modern form the summer house is designated by various architectural terms such as loggia, cloister, peristyle, belvedere, bower, or gazebo. But these are not used correctly unless the design conforms to classic models—which, as a matter of fact, are, in the main, too ambitious for the average garden.

SUMMER-SWEET. A common name for *Clethra alnifolia,* better known as Sweet Pepper-bush, an American shrub with small fragrant white flowers in late summer.

SUMMER WORK IN THE GARDEN. The most important work at this season is careful cultivation. It should not be deep, but should keep the surface soil loose. The objectives are: (1) Conservation of soil moisture. (2) Aëration of soil. (3) Modification of soil temperature. (4) Stimulation of bacterial action. (5) Destruction of weeds, which rob the soil of both moisture and food at the expense of the plants.

It is now warm enough to sow any annuals and tender bulbs; also start seed of perennials in coldframe or outdoor seedbed. When dahlias are about a foot tall, side shoots may be pinched out to develop a stronger main stalk and larger finer flowers.

Continue to pinch back all quick-growing herbaceous plants to make them compact. Later disbud (see DISBUDDING) for larger blooms.

Set tender waterlilies in the pools. Feed roses frequently with quite weak liquid manure. Dust leaves with very fine sulphur for mildew and to prevent black spot. Prune climbing roses after they have finished blooming. Aphids are likely to appear in large numbers at this time. Watch for them and spray promptly with a contact insecticide. Keep all tall plants well staked, for appearance and to prevent them from falling or being blown over. One summer storm can undo the careful work of weeks.

Many perennials, as delphiniums, phlox, and anchusa will give a second crop of flowers if the first faded blossoms are removed promptly. Perennials from seed sown early in the season are or will soon be ready for transplanting.

Divide Japanese and bearded iris after they bloom. Tulips may be lifted now and the bulbs stored for fall planting.

Take cuttings of hollyhocks, pinks, and all early carpet plants such as arabis, aubrietia, etc. Most early flowering rock plants can be propagated in this way. Carnations may be propagated either by layering or by cuttings at this time.

Top-dress the lawn with a light dose of plant food—say 2 lbs. per 100 ft. or half the usual spring dose of 4 lbs. Keep hedges clipped, and prune shrubs after they have flowered and before they have made the wood on which next year's blossoms will be borne. This is a good time to make cuttings of easily grown shrubs.

Cut out dead wood of climbing plants and keep shoots trained up as may be necessary. Keep watered with mulched newly transplanted trees, shrubs, and perennials. Iris, peonies, oriental poppies and madonna lilies may be transplanted now.

Pinch out side shoots of evergreens to induce bushiness. Such trees may be moved in August, if dug with good balls of earth and if carefully mulched and watered. Prune the roots of large trees that are to be moved next winter. Thin shoots of raspberries, blackberries and currants. Dust the latter for worms.

Continue to spray cucumbers, tomatoes, potatoes and all vegetables subject to blight, with bordeaux mixture. Spray potatoes with arsenate of lead for potato bugs. For clean, perfect fruit, stake.

Transplant late cauliflower, kale, broccoli, and brussels sprouts to their permanent quarters. Sow seed of fall crops of carrots, turnips, winter radishes, and late celery.

Remove some of the leaves from the grape-vines to let the sun in. Bagging is an excellent practice to protect the bunches of fruit from insects, diseases, sunburn and birds.

Harvest fruit before it gets too ripe.

Cut out old shoots of raspberries and blackberries.

Whenever a patch of land becomes vacant—if it is not to be used again the same season—sow a quick-growing cover-crop to protect it over winter and be turned under next spring.

In gathering the onion crop, leave the bulbs in the sun to cure for a day or so, then store in ventilated trays in a cool, dry place.

Sow parsley seed for a next spring crop and remove old parsley plants to frames.

Make a final sowing of peas, spinach, cress, radishes, lettuce, turnips, and the like.

Keep a lookout for asparagus beetle.

By the end of August stop cultivating so that the plants will mature and not be in a growing and tender state when the first cold weather of fall comes.

SUNDEW. Common name for the genus Drosera, small insectivorous herbs bearing white, red or pink flowers in clusters on slender stems above rosettes of leaves that are covered with glistening sticky hairs. Insects become entangled in these hairs, which gradually bend inward toward the center, effectively trapping the victim. Their sticky excretion then turns to an acid substance that acts on the insect and permits it to be digested, much as gastric juice acts on human food. Sometimes grown in the greenhouse, sundews should be planted in pots in mucky soil covered with sphagnum and the pots set in saucers of water that will assure a constant supply of moisture at the roots. They must have full sunshine and are easily propagated by seeds, by cuttings of the rootstock or by division. One of the common species, found throughout Eurasia and N. America, is *D. rotundifolia;* it has round glistening hairy leaves to 1½ in. and white to red flowers on stems to 10 in. *D. filiformis* has thread-like leaves covered with glistening purple hairs and white to purple flowers on stems to 2 ft. tall.

SUNDIAL. The sundial was originally developed as a utilitarian outdoor clock. From its simple beginning as a flat plane with a simple arm slanted to show by its shadow the correct time, it was gradually ornamented and elaborated, both on the dial itself and on its base or pedestal. Today its usefulness has been so subjugated to its decorative value that the sundial and its pedestal are frequently in unsuitable positions or where it cannot perform its primary function of recording the sun's movement. It should always be placed where it will get the full rays of the sun and the dial itself should be orientated to the location (according to latitude), so that it actually does tell correct sun time. It should also be placed where the dial can be easily read—in other words, with walking space around it, not in the center of a flower bed or surrounded by a barrier hedge.

The sundial is one of the accents best suited to the small garden as it may be of various materials and sizes and so adapted to the location and surroundings. The dial itself is best made of bronze or lead for permanence, although occasional dials are found carved in teak or other long-lasting woods, or cast in iron. The pedestal may be of carved wood, painted or left to weather; stone; terra-cotta; iron, or bronze. For the average garden the simple wood or stone or good terra-cotta pedestal is best, selected carefully for proportion, size and simple decoration. The cheap-looking concrete objects seen along the highways are almost invariably badly proportioned.

The location of the sundial in the garden should be a point where accent is needed. It may be at the center of a geometric garden, at the intersection of two main paths, or at the end of a cross or a diagonal path. While it should have planting near it as a contrast or a background, this should be far enough away to allow walking close to the dial face. Most pedestals gain by having a brick or stone base under them, either flush with the ground, or 4 to 6 in. high, projecting far enough to allow the observer to stand on the base to look at the dial. Where the pedestal is unusually tall this base may form steps to raise the observer to the proper level. Under this base, for security, it is best to have a concrete foundation extending below frost, so that there will be no danger of winter tipping. In very windy locations it is advisable to dowel the pedestal to its foundation.

SUNDROPS. Common name for various annual and perennial species of Oenothera (the evening-primrose), grown for their large yellow flowers.

SUN FERN (*Phegopteris polypodioides*). More often known as the Long Beech Fern, this is a fairly common plant of open and rocky woods in America. It has pointed fronds about 1 ft. high, once-pinnate, the lowest pair of pinnae turned outward and downward, and the whole frond often tilted

"SONNY" AND SOME SUNFLOWERS
The striking size range in this typically American plant is illustrated by the single flower-head (gone to seed) in the youngster's lap, and the blossom in his hand from the small-flowered plants behind them.

on its stipe to catch the sunlight. A good garden species.

SUNFLOWER. Common name for Helianthus, a genus of tall, coarse annual or perennial herbs of the Composite Family. They have typical daisy heads, the ray flowers yellow and the disks, brown, yellow, purple or almost black in some of the hybrids. The common garden sunflower (*H. annuus*) sometimes reaches a height of 12 to 15 ft. and develops huge heads over 1 ft. across. A native plant, widespread over the W. prairies, it is at times a pernicious weed in Kansas and adjacent States; nevertheless, it is the Kansas state flower. Several horticultural forms have been developed with attractive wine-red and chestnut shades and combinations of lemon-yellow and orange. These plants are smaller and more appropriate for the border; the taller type should be planted only as background material or on the edge of the vegetable garden where pole beans can be allowed to climb the stalks and where the heads will furnish valuable poultry food or winter provender for the birds. Sunflowers are widely cultivated in Russia, India and Egypt, an oil being extracted from the seeds, and the resulting oil-cake being fed to stock. The ripened seeds are also eaten by some peoples as we eat nuts.

Some of the hardy sunflowers—among them *H. decapetalus* (Twinleaf Sunflower) —have numerous small heads of yellow flowers which, in the horticultural varieties, vary through coppery and purplish tones. They bloom over a long period, and though rather coarse for the herbaceous border, make striking groups in shrubbery.

Applications of sulphur dust will control not only the sunflower rust, which produces yellow-brown spore pustules on the backs of the leaves, but also the powdery mildew which appears late in the season. Plants affected by Sclerotinia rot (which see) should be removed and burned and the soil drenched with corrosive sublimate. Signs of this fungus are white mycelium and large black spore bodies (*sclerotia*) at the base of the plant. The larvae of the sunflower maggot may occur in such numbers inside the stalks as to cause them to fall over; the adult fly may be controlled by spraying the leaves with lead arsenate.

See also HELIANTHUS.

SUNKEN GARDEN. A space developed on a lower level than the general surroundings and not necessarily devoted to the culture of any special thing, although it may be. Where the natural grade of a property falls off, or is irregular, so that an expensive fill is required to level the ground, a design which includes such a feature may be a happy solution. Around the sunken garden walls of brick or stone or sloping banks of earth are used, according to circumstances, materials available and cost limitations. Walls, of course, allow delightful opportunity for making a real wall garden (which see), in front of which no flower borders would be required. Sloping banks of earth may be covered with evergreen or flowering ground-cover plants or other prostrate growth, which provides a background for a flower border, if desired, around the entire sunken area.

A pool is very desirable in a sunken garden, since its surface can be better seen from the higher surrounding level and reflections thereon appear to greater advantage than when seen from nearer the water level.

There is an advantage also in looking down upon the entire composition, the effect being comparable to viewing a stage from a balcony seat. Thus a sunken garden may exhibit dramatic qualities which do not always exist in gardens on a level with the observer.

It is never advisable to introduce a sunken garden, however, unless there is wide, unobstructed space around it—an area much wider than its own. It should give an impression of a rather precious gem, set in the midst of a proportionately broad landscape.

SUN-ROSE. Common name for the genus Helianthemum, low herbs and sub-shrubs useful in rock gardens and sunny borders for their relatively large, brilliantly colored, rose-like flowers.

SUN SCALD. Plant injury caused by exposure to excessive sunlight, especially after recent planting or transplanting. See SCALD; HEAT INJURY.

SUPERPHOSPHATE. A popular name, now coming into almost universal use in American gardening and farming, for a valuable fertilizer—the product resulting from the treating of ground phosphatic rock (found in large deposits in the S. Atlantic States) with sulphuric acid. This render the phosphoric acid it contains readily soluble and available as plant food and makes the material well worth its

added cost over the raw ground rock or "floats." Its former name, "acid phosphate," was never applicable, since the addition of this material to the soil does not increase its acidity.

Superphosphate varies somewhat in quality, but on the average contains from 14 to 16 or 18 per cent phosphoric acid, equivalent to 5 to 8 per cent phosphorus. In view of the importance of this element in plant growth, and of the fact that it is deficient in many soils, superphosphate is used in large quantities, either applied directly to the land at the rate of about 10 lbs. per 100 sq. ft., or indirectly, by being mixed with vegetable matter or manure in making compost, or by being used on the floors of cow-barns, hen-houses, etc., to absorb the liquid plant-food materials and, in general, reinforce the manure in its phosphorus content. Of course, being purely a mineral product, it provides no humus, so if used on the land either alone or as part of a complete fertilizer, it should be accompanied—or, better, preceded—by stable manure, green manures, or cover-crops plowed or dug under.

See also FERTILIZER; PHOSPHATES; PLANT FOODS AND FEEDING.

SUPPLE-JACK. Common name for *Berchemia scandens,* an American twining shrub with greenish-white flowers and bluish-black fruits.

SURINAM-CHERRY. A common name for *Eugenia uniflora,* a tropical shrub or small tree, also called Pitanga, with white fragrant flowers and eight-ribbed, crimson, edible fruits.

SUTURE. A line along which a fruit (more especially a pod or capsule) splits open to emit its seeds. Milkweeds, pea, radish and garden balsam supply examples.

SWAINSONA (swayn-soh'-nah). Herbs or shrubby plants of Australia, belonging to the Pea Family. They are grown outdoors in warm regions, and one or two are old greenhouse favorites. Under glass they thrive in a mixture of sandy loam with leafmold. If given a sunny position, and with the root area restricted in a pot tub, or narrow border, they produce flowers freely over a long period. Old plants may be cut back and grown on again, but young plants generally give best results. They appreciate liquid manure when established. Propagated by seeds and cuttings.

S. galegifolia has long supple branches and is usually trained as a climber. It has graceful leaves composed of 11 to 21 leaflets, and long-stemmed clusters of deep red flowers. Var. *albiflora,* with pure white flowers, is more generally grown for decorative purposes. Other forms sometimes grown are var. *rosea,* with pink flowers; and var. *violacea,* with flowers of rosy-violet. *S. greyana* (Darling River Pea) grows to 3 ft., with the young growth whitish; it bears large pink flowers in long upright racemes.

SWAMP BAY. A common name for *Magnolia virginiana,* a native shrub or tree with fragrant white flowers and red fruits, half hardy in the S.

SWAMP-HONEYSUCKLE. A common name for *Rhododendron viscosum,* a summer-blooming American shrub with fragrant white flowers which are sticky and give it the name Clammy Azalea.

SWAMP LOCUST, or WATER LOCUST. A common name for *Gleditsia aquatica,* a large spiny tree with lacy foliage, inconspicuous pea-like flowers, and large pods.

SWAMP LOOSESTRIPE. A common name for *Decodon verticillatus,* a woody perennial with rose-purple flowers, native to the Atlantic Coast. See WATER-WILLOW.

SWAMP-PINK. Common name for *Helonias bullata,* a native spring-flowering, tuberous-rooted herb with pink or purplish flowers in long-stemmed racemes. Useful in bog gardens, it also does well as a pot plant flowering in late winter.

SWAN RIVER DAISY. Common name for *Brachycome iberidifolia,* a hardy herbaceous annual 10 to 18 in. tall with branching stems, making an excellent plant for the rock garden or border, or for edging. The popular name comes from its native habitat, the Swan River in Australia, along whose banks its blue, rose and white daisy-like flowers, about an inch across, first attracted attention. Its deeply cut, lacy foliage, compact growth and free flowering quality (which makes the plant resemble a cineraria) have long combined to make it a garden favorite. It is easy to grow under any normal garden conditions, being started from seed (preferably rather early, indoors) and handled like any other hardy annual.

SWEET ALYSSUM (ah-lis'-um). One of the most satisfactory of dwarf border plants, the small rounded spikes of minute flowers, usually white, being abundant, long-blooming and sweet. Long known botanically as *Alyssum maritimum,* it has

recently been transferred to the genus Lobularia, which see. But for culture see ALYSSUM.

SWEET-BAY. A common name for the genus Laurus (Laurel), a group of trees of the Mediterranean region and Canary Islands, one of which is used as evergreen tub specimens. The name is also applied to *Magnolia virginiana.*

SWEETBELLS. Common name for *Leucothoë racemosa,* a native evergreen shrub found from Mass. to La. and planted in moist areas for its ornamental white or pale-pink flowers in spring.

SWEET-BRIER. A common name for *Rosa eglanteria,* or Eglantine, a favorite old-fashioned rose with fragrant foliage. See ROSE.

SWEET CICELY. A common name for *Myrrhis odorata,* a perennial herb grown for its fragrant foliage which is used in cooking. See MYRRH.

SWEET-CLOVER, or MELILOT. Common name for Melilotus, a genus of annual and biennial leguminous herbs of Asia and the Mediterannean region where they have long been prized as forage crops. Naturalized in the U. S., they have generally been regarded as weeds or, at best, valuable bee plants, though improved strains are being increasingly grown as a hay, green forage and pasture crop. Dried shoots and flower-heads are often used to scent linen shelves and bureau drawers, but in gardening sweet clovers are of value mainly as green manures to be plowed under while soft and succulent as a source of humus. The best known species is *M. alba* (Bokhara or White Sweet-clover). *M. officinalis,* with yellow flowers, is also a biennial.

SWEET-COLTSFOOT. A common name for *Petasites fragrans,* also called Winter-heliotrope, a lilac-flowered herbaceous perennial with felt-like, evergreen foliage.

SWEET CORN. A name given to the smaller-growing garden varieties of *Zea mays,* grown to provide green "roasting ears," as distinguished from the different kinds of "field corn" grown either as forage or for the ripe grain. See CORN.

SWEET-FERN. Common name for *Comptonia asplenifolia,* really not a fern at all, but a flowering plant of the Sweet-gale Family. A sweet-smelling deciduous shrub growing to 5 ft., it has finely cut fern-like leaves and bears inconspicuous flowers in catkins. It is valuable chiefly as a ground-cover or soil-binder on dry sandy slopes and is particularly good in the wild garden when planted at the base of sumac bushes. It is easily grown from seed, division or layers.

SWEET FLAG. Common name for *Acorus calamus,* a hardy marsh perennial herb sometimes grown in bog gardens for its grass-like foliage.

SWEETGALE. Common name for *Myrica gale,* a deciduous shrub found in peaty soil; it bears catkins and small fruits.

SWEET GUM. Popular name for *Liquidambar styraciflua,* a large deciduous tree with shining maple-like leaves that turn brilliant scarlet and deep crimson in early fall. In winter the tree is conspicuous for its erect branches, its deeply fissured bark, its persistent spiny fruit-balls. It is exceedingly ornamental, useful and strikingly free from pests and diseases. Excellent for park and street planting, it is much used in the W. and S. It is best propagated by seed. The name Liquidambar refers to the fragrant juice exuded by the tree when wounded.

SWEET HERBS. A collective name for various aromatic plants, such as parsley, thyme, marjoram, and sage, which are grown for the flavor their leaves add to cookery. See HERBS.

SWEETLEAF. Common name for the genus Symplocos which gives its name to the Sweetleaf Family. Only one of the many species is hardy N. This is *S. paniculata* (Asiatic Sweetleaf), a large shrub or small tree with slender spreading branches. In spring it produces an abundance of small white flowers in short panicles, and in fall it is conspicuous with bright blue fruits. It is best transplanted when small, and thrives in good ordinary soil and a sunny place. Propagated by seeds, which are slow to germinate; cuttings under glass, and layers. *S. tinctoria* (Sweetleaf, Horse Sugar) is an evergreen species growing from Del. south. It has dense clusters of yellowish fragrant flowers and orange-brown fruit.

SWEET MARJORAM. A common name for *Majorana hortensis,* a perennial herb grown as an annual for its aromatic foliage which is used in cookery. See also HERBS.

SWEET PEA. Common name for *Lathyrus odoratus,* a popular hardy annual climbing plant attaining a height of 6 ft.

or more but requiring trellis, wire or other kind of support upon which to climb. There is a wide range of solid, striped and mottled colors and of forms in the beautiful, sweet-scented flowers, which may be plain-petaled, wavy-petaled or ruffled. (See illustration, Plate 12.)

The remarkable improvement that has taken place in this highly favored flower dates back to about the beginning of the twentieth century. Two separate and distinct forms have been developed, one the summer-flowering sweet pea, which must

TWO TYPES OF SWEET PEA
The familiar, large-flowered, annual *Lathyrus odorous* (A) and the hardy, free-growing, perennial *L. maritima* (B) with clusters of smaller blossoms. The latter sometimes becomes a nuisance.

be sown as early as the ground can be worked in the spring, and the other a winter-flowering type chiefly used for the greenhouse production of cut flowers but which can also be successfully grown outside in the S. States. There is also a non-climbing form (var. *nanellus*) that forms low compact plants suitable for use in beds and borders where they bloom from June until late summer. These are called Cupid, Dwarf, or Bedding Sweet Peas.

SOIL PREPARATION. Sweet peas require a rich deeply worked soil, preferably one containing clay, but with good drainage. Thin sandy soils are not suitable since they dry out too quickly. Open sunny locations are desirable, for plants grown in too much shade will be weak and spindling.

If the ground where sweet peas are to be planted has been in cultivation for a long time without having been limed, it may possibly be acid; in that event it should receive a liberal top-dressing of a slow acting form of lime—marl, ground oyster shell, or finely ground limestone. This should be cultivated in after the soil has been prepared in the fall, and the application of any commercial fertilizer withheld until early spring.

Outdoor sweet peas to be at their best must make their growth early, during the cool spring months. The ground should be prepared deeply as late in the fall as the soil remains in a workable condition. If possible, quantities of well-decayed stable manure should be worked into it; or if commercial fertilizer be used to provide plant food, plenty of humus should be added and thoroughly mixed with the soil to a depth of 18 in. or 2 ft.

PLANTING. As early in the spring as the ground can be worked, prepare trenches about one spade wide. Sow the seed an inch or two apart in furrows 3 or 4 in. deep, covering them with not more than 2 in. of the soil. If the white-seeded varieties (which are more tender and likely to rot) are placed in heavy soil, it is well to sow them in a 1-in. bed of sand in the bottom of the furrow. As the young plants grow, fill the trench gradually by cultivating the soil in around them a little at a time; but leave a slight depression to catch the water and carry it down to the roots until they grow down into the lower stratum of cool, moist, enriched soil.

If brush (that of birch is excellent) is to be used as a support, it should be placed in or beside the trench securely enough to withstand heavy winds. It should be put in place while the plants are less than 2 in. high; doing it later may injure the sweet pea roots. Any extensive planting will warrant the use of a trellis consisting of 4 x 4 in. posts set in the trench at intervals of about 8 ft. and joined top and bottom on each side by 1 x 2 in. furring strips or shingle lath in which galvanized nails have been driven in about halfway every 6 in. Heavy string is run up and down from nail to nail, providing a support to

which the vines cling readily and which cannot blow over or wash down in hard storms. When such a support is used, the trench should be wide enough to allow for a row of seed to be planted on each side of the trellis. Such a trellis is easily taken down and can be used over and over; it is far superior to chicken wire, which may become so hot in midsummer as to actually injury the vines by burning them.

Seed may be planted 1 in. apart or one every 3 in., but in either case they should afterward be thinned out so the plants will stand not less than 6 in. apart in the row. This should be the minimum distance in rich soils so as to allow for proper root expansion; if the distance be increased to 12 in. larger plants and more and better flowers will result.

FALL PLANTING. In the N., if one cares to take a chance with uncertain seasons, the seed may be sown in the fall just before frost. At that time it should be covered about 3 in. deep; then, as soon as the soil is frozen, cover the trench with a 3-in. layer of manure or rough litter to be removed early in the spring when cultivation will gradually fill in the trench as already explained. In normal winters the freezing will not injure the seed; in mild winters excess moisture may rot it, or it may be started into growth and the seed or the young plants frozen during later cold spells. But this is a risk worth taking for the sake of the results that may be achieved.

A more certain method of starting sweet peas in the fall is by using a coldframe. Here the seed should be sown thinly in flats or 3 seeds to a 3-in. pot, in either case covering them with not more than 1 in. of soil. This should be 5 or 6 weeks prior to the average date for severe weather in the locality. Give water as needed but do not cover the frames with sash until the nights begin to get cold and the plants are about 2 in. high. Even then remove the sash during mild weather to keep the growth as strong and sturdy as possible. Later, during very severe weather, the frames may be covered with straw or burlap mats.

As spring approaches, gradually harden the plants off by ventilating at all possible occasions; then set them outdoors in a fall-prepared trench as soon as freezing weather has departed, disturbing the roots as little as possible in the process. At least two or three weeks will be gained in bringing them into flower.

SEASONAL CARE

Whatever method is followed, flowers must be kept closely picked. As soon as seed pods develop, the vine stops growing and dies, as it has then performed its function of insuring its reproduction.

During dry seasons the roots must not suffer for want of water; when applying it, soak the soil to a depth of 8 or 10 in. Let it flow directly on the soil in a gentle stream rather than as a spray, which does more harm than good. For one thing it takes a long time to really wet the soil by sprinkling; in the second place, it tends to create a thin crust as the soil dries, which cracks open later, allowing unnecessary loss of moisture. All during the growing season and especially during hot dry weather, while water is beneficial, it will not take the place of a loose surface mulch maintained by constant shallow cultivation. The sweet pea, like other plants of the Legume Family, is a deep rooter, and in deep, well-prepared soils the roots *can* penetrate deeply and find water. But a continuous mulch conserves moisture, helps the soil and makes plant food available, keeps the roots cool and prevents weeds from competing with the plants. When the latter are well developed, a 2- or 3-in. mulch of leafmold or other humus or old well-decayed manure can take the place of cultivation and the dust mulch.

Sweet peas benefit from being fed at 3 or 4 week intervals with a complete plant food, in which, however, the nitrogen content is low and phosphoric acid and potash contents are relatively high. Like other legumes, sweet peas do not need much added nitrogen, as, with the help of beneficial bacteria, they can obtain it from the air and store it up in nodules on the roots.

ENEMIES. Streak, a bacterial disease, may occur on both outdoor- and indoor-grown sweet peas, causing reddish-brown to blackish streaks along the stem from the base upwards. On the leaves water-soaked areas enlarge and turn brown and the plants may be killed finally. Treat seed in a 5 per cent formaldehyde solution for 5 minutes and plant in clean or sterile soil; then burn all plant parts in the fall. The same control measures are used for anthracnose, which appears at blossom time and is the most troublesome disease of sweet peas outdoors. Leaves show white areas and infected shoots dry up before any flowers form. As the same fungus causes bitter rot of apples, sweet peas near apple orchards are apt to be most seriously attacked. The black root rot and rhizoctonia root rot are controlled by soil sterilization (see DISINFECTION), which also is the only control measure for the nematode root knot which dwarfs the plants. See NEMATODES.

Mildew, which is troublesome mostly in the greenhouse in spring, may be controlled by painting the heating pipes with sulphur. White blight, another greenhouse trouble, may be controlled by dusting with sulphur. Plants infected with mosaic, a virus disease that occurs both inside and outdoors, should be destroyed immediately.

Insects commonly seen on sweet peas are the pea aphid (controlled by dusting or spraying with a contact insecticide), the greenhouse leaf tyer and the corn ear worm. See GREENHOUSE PESTS and under CORN.

The Perennial, or Everlasting, Pea (or-sometimes Sweet Pea) is a related species, *Lathyrus maritima,* which see. Although the blossoms, which are like those of the annual Sweet Pea in shape and are borne in small, short-stemmed clusters, lack the size, beauty, varied colorings and fragrance of those of *L. odoratus,* the foliage is

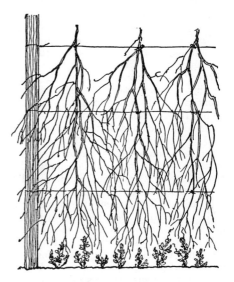

STAKING SWEET PEAS

A departure from the usual method consists of attaching the brush, butts upward, to horizontal wires. The bushy tops give the tendrils of the young plants more to get hold of and when the flowers open up above the brush ends they are easily picked.

attractive and the plant is easy to grow and hardy. So it is well worth a place in the garden.

SWEET PEA SOCIETY, AMERICAN. An organization of both amateur and commercial enthusiasts in which, however, the former have played the dominant part especially in connection with the annual exhibitions staged by the Society. For some years, owing to curtailed activities on many private estates where exhibition sweet peas were formerly grown, the Society has been practically dormant, but its officers and more interested members continue to look forward to its rejuvenation when conditions are propitious. The secretary when the organization last functioned was Mrs. S. G. Van Hoesen, Fanwood, N. J.

SWEET PEPPER-BUSH. Another name for Summer-sweet (*Clethra alnifolia*), a native shrub of moist shady woods, planted for its small fragrant flowers. See CLETHRA.

SWEET-POTATO. A tropical, perennial, trailing herb (*Ipomoea batatas*) grown for its swollen, tuber-like roots which are a popular (principally winter) vegetable. It is grown commercially from New Jersey southward and westward; but it will sometimes mature in gardens from Conn. to S. Mich. However, it is not suited to the small garden because the vines of individual plants often extend 10 ft. or more.

The crop thrives best in a sandy loam, but in any warm, well-drained soil will give good yields. It is grown from rooted "draws" or "sprouts" which are broken or slipped from tubers planted in hotbeds about a month before the last expected spring frost. Manure is spread in furrows made 6 in. deep and 4 ft. apart, then covered with soil raised about 6 in. by plowing from each side of each furrow toward it so as to form a ridge. The plants (then about 6 in. long) are set 5 in. deep and 15 in. apart in these ridges and given clean cultivation. To prevent the vines from taking root after they start to run they are lifted and moved every couple of weeks.

When frost has killed the tender tips of the vines the crop is dug and allowed to dry on the ground for a few days. Bruised and frosted roots are discarded and the perfect ones placed in barrels in layers alternating with layers of dry sand and stored in dry, warm quarters.

Sweet-potatoes are subject to some diseases in the field and to storage rots which are of more interest to the housekeeper than to the gardener. Soft-rot is widely known as the cause not only of the soft decay of the potato tuber, but also of the black bread mold. The disease spreads from one infected tuber to all in contact with it; hence in handling the tubers, take care not to bruise or break the skin.

Numerous garden diseases of this crop include Fusarium stem-rot, black rot, foot-rot, scurf, Texas root-rot and leaf blight and spot. Seed selection, use of clean plant beds and crop rotation are the general control measures recommended. The leaf diseases are not serious enough to call for protective measures.

Aphids, blister beetles, leaf hoppers and tortoise beetles are pests, but the sweet-potato weevil is of chief importance. This snout beetle feeds on leaves, vines and roots of this host and of morning-glory. Thoroughly clean fields at harvest time so as to leave nothing for the insect to winter in.

Wild-sweet-potato-vine or Man-of-the-earth is another perennial species of Ipomoea (*I. pandurata*) native from Conn. to Texas. It sometimes becomes a bad weed if neglected. The roots are not eaten, but the vine is ornamental in a rough way and, if kept under control, makes a good cover for stumps, back fences, etc. Also it is very hardy, the roots surviving below-zero temperatures if well mulched. On this account it is sometimes offered as "wild-" or "Perennial Morning-glory."

SWEET SCABIOUS (skay'-bi-ous). Common name for *Scabiosa atropurpurea*, an erect annual whose flowers are fine for cutting.

SWEET-SHRUB, or SWEET-SCENTED-SHRUB. A common name for Calycanthus, a genus of deciduous American shrubs noted for the fragrance of their chocolate colored flowers.

SWEETSOP. Another name for the Sugar-apple, *Annona squamosa*, a tropical American tree with edible fruits.

SWEET SPIRE. Common name for *Itea virginica*, a native American deciduous shrub with racemes of small fragrant white flowers.

SWEET SULTAN. Common name for *Centaurea moschata*, an annual herb with fragrant white, yellow or purple flowers; an old-fashioned garden favorite of easiest culture. (See illustration, Plate 9.)

SWEET WILLIAM. Common name for *Dianthus barbatus*, a species of hardy pinks and an old and popular garden flower. Flowers in many beautiful colors and combinations are produced in clusters in great profusion on plants 18 in. tall in June and July. (See illustration, Plate 14.) Though strictly a hardy herbaceous perennial, it should be treated as a biennial; sow seeds outdoors in May and transplant them in August to flower the second season. See DIANTHUS.

Wild-sweet-william is *Phlox divaricata.*

SWEET WIVELSFIELD. The name of a recently developed English strain of hardy pink (Dianthus), the result of crossing *D. barbatus* (sweet william) and *D. allwoodi.*

SWISS CHARD. A variety of leaf or spinach beet See CHARD.

SWORD FERN. A name given to various plants of the type of the Boston Fern (which see) and also, in the far W., to *Polystichum munitum,* a superb once-pinnate tall wood fern, suitable for gardens in good well-drained soil and shade.

SWORD-LILY. A little used common name for the genus Gladiolus, which see.

SYAGRUS (sy-ay'-grus). A genus of Brazilian Feather Palms, usually small and some species stemless. They have graceful feathery leaves, not armed, or spiny except, occasionally, on the stems of the leaves. The species of most importance is *S. weddelliana,* formerly classified as *Cocos weddelliana,* and still so called by florists. In Brazil it grows to 7 ft. with slender, frond-like foliage, dropping nearly to the ground. In Fla., where it is grown occasionally outdoors, it requires abundant moisture; although it has withstood temperatures of 26 deg., it should be protected during cold weather with a covering of evergreen branches. The slow symmetrical growth of this species makes it the most popular of dwarf palms for house culture. In the juvenile state the glossy deep green leaves spread in an almost perfect circle.

For culture see PALMS.

SYCAMORE. Common name for a number of deciduous trees, the most interesting in America being the Plane-tree (*Platanus occidentalis*). In Europe, *Acer pseudoplatanus* is called Sycamore. The Sycamore of the Bible, however, is a small fig-tree of Egypt and Syria, botanically *Ficus sycamorus* (or *Sycamorus antiquorum*), but commonly known today as Pharaohs Fig. It has lately been somewhat grown in S. Fla.

SYMMETRICAL. Term applied to a flower of which each circle of floral organs has the same number of parts or a multiple of that number; the number of stamens is commonly a multiple of one of the other parts, as in the geranium, which has 5 petals, 5 sepals and 5 parts (carpels) to the pistil, but twice 5, or 10, stamens.

SYMPHORICARPOS (sim-foh-ri-kahr'-pos). Deciduous shrubs of N. America, belonging to the Honeysuckle Family. They are good-natured shrubs as far as soil conditions are concerned, and do equally well in sun or shade. Not all are entirely hardy N. They are of slender upright or spreading habit, well suited for the front of a shrub border or for under planting. The flowers are rather inconspicuous, the chief decorative value being in the clustered fruits.

Anthracnose causes a conspicuous reddish to black discoloration of the berries, with the appearance of flesh-colored spore masses during wet periods. Berries infected with fruit rot turn yellow to brown, then decay. Control these diseases by pruning out all dead canes during the dormant period, spraying with lime sulphur (1 to 10) before growth starts, and dusting with copper-lime dust in late summer.

Both aphids and San José scale infest this shrub. Caterpillars of the snowberry clear-wing are horn-worms; hand pick them or spray the foliage with lead arsenate.

Symphoricarpos is propagated by seeds, cuttings and suckers.

PRINCIPAL SPECIES

S. albus (Snowberry, Waxberry) is a slender shrub to 3 ft., with oval leaves, sometimes lobed on young shoots, small pinkish tubular flowers, and round snow-white berries. Var. *laevigatus,* which grows to 6 ft., and has larger leaves and fruit clusters, is often known as *S. racemosus.*

orbiculatus (Coral-berry, Indian-currant) is a twiggy grower to 6 ft., with dull green oval leaves and white bell-shaped flowers. The leaves are held green late, and the plant is conspicuous well into winter with its dense clusters of dark red berries.

microphyllus is an upright grower to 10 ft., with pink flowers and fruit. Not hardy.

chenaulti, a hybrid between *S. orbiculatus* and *S. mycrophyllus,* is quite hardy. It has slender spreading branches and graceful foliage which hangs on and remains green quite late. It is one of the best *facers* for a shrub planting. The usually not abundant berries are red with whitish streaks.

occidentalis (Wolfberry) is an upright grower of rather stiff habit, with leaves grayish beneath, pinkish flowers and white berries.

oreophilus grows to 4 ft., with slender spreading branches and oval leaves whitish beneath. The pink, tubular flowers are larger than most, and followed by white ovoid berries.

SYMPHYTUM (sim'-fi-tum). A genus of coarse herbaceous perennials called Comfrey, which see.

SYMPLOCOS (sim'-ploh-kos). A large genus of deciduous or evergreen trees or shrubs, mostly distributed in tropical and subtropical regions, and popularly known as Sweetleaf, which see.

SYNERGIST. Synergists are chemicals that are added to pesticides to increase their toxic effectiveness. Their use may permit a reduction in the amount of active ingredient in a spray, a greater dilution of the spray, or increase the potency of a spray. Rotenone, pyrethrum and allethrin have been made more potent by the addition of such compounds as piperonyl cyclonene, piperonyl butoxide or sesmolin which double and even triple their insect killing powers. Synergists in the new organic insecticides may help overcome house fly resistance to them to some degree. Hydrated lime may be considered a synergist for nicotine sulfate.

See SPRAYERS AND SPRAYING.

SYSTEMICS. Systemic insecticides are chemicals which, when applied to leaves or roots, are absorbed by the plant. These make the plant poisonous to insects which feed on them.

One of the most powerful of these at present is Systox (Schraeden) discovered originally in Germany. It is used on ornamental nursery stock. Due to its highly poisonous nature, Federal Authorities are reluctant to permit its general use.

Sodium selenate is also used as a systemic. In capsule form, it is useful in treating African violet soil. However, because of its poisonous nature, it must not be used on any soil which might eventually reach the vegetable garden.

More extensive use of systemic insecticides is growing with the development of safer chemicals and methods for use which do not expose the user to their hazards.

SYNTHYRIS (sin'-thy-ris). A genus of small perennial herbs of the Figwort Family, bearing white or purple flowers in very early spring. Charming in the rock or wild garden, they should be planted in an acid soil, rich in humus, and in partial shade. Increase by seed or division of clumps. *S. reniformis* to 9 in. is from W. America and has almost round leaves and small blue or purple flowers in clusters. *S. rotundifolia,* often found growing under evergreens, has round leaves and white flowers.

SYRINGA (si-rin'-gah). A genus of deciduous shrubs or small trees belonging to the Olive Family, native in S. E. Europe and Asia, and widely known and loved under the familiar name of Lilac. An important and popular group of hardy ornamental woody plants, its members are valued for their large and showy flower panicles, borne mostly in spring. The name Syringa, derived from a word meaning "pipe," has been applied to mockorange (Philadelphus) because shepherd's pipes used to be made from the pithy stems. Hence Pipe-tree is also an old common name for the plant. See LILAC.

TABERNAEMONTANA (tah-bur-nee-mon-tay'-nah). A genus of evergreen trees or shrubs of the tropics, belonging to the Dogbane Family. They are attractive plants for the shrub borders in warm regions, and are sometimes grown in pots under glass. Propagated by cuttings.

T. citrifolia grows to 6 ft., with leaves about 5 in. long, and clusters of white fragrant flowers an inch across. *T. grandiflora* is of similar habit and size, but has clusters of larger yellow flowers.

TACAMAHAC (tak'-ah-mah-hak). A common name for *Populus tacamahacca* (formerly but erroneously *P. balsamifera*), a large deciduous tree of N. America, sometimes called Balsam Poplar. See POPLAR.

TACCA (tak'-ah). A genus of tropical, tuberous-rooted perennial herbs having large leaves at the base of stems which are surmounted by brown or greenish flowers in dense, round-topped clusters. Below there are showy, leaf-like bracts from which arise long, thread-like flower stems which, however, bear no flowers. In the N. the plants can be grown in greenhouses and should be given rich soil with excellent drainage. As they bloom in summer, water should be withheld and the plants rested over winter. They are increased by division. *T. pinnatifida*, with finely cut leaves sometimes 4 ft. across, is grown in the tropics as a source of arrowroot, which is obtained from the ground tubers. It has greenish and purplish flowers.

TAGETES (tah-jee'-teez). A genus of strong-scented annual herbs much grown in the garden for midsummer bloom as Marigold (which see). The plants have finely cut leaves and either single or clustered heads of ruffled flowers in brilliant yellow, orange, deep red and sometimes brownish shades. Easily grown in any soil in a sunny situation from seed started either outdoors or, earlier, under glass, they are but little troubled by enemies and provide splendid, long-lasting cut flowers. Tagetes are native in Mexico and S. A.

TAIL-FLOWER. A common name for the genus Anthurium, tropical American perennials grown in warm greenhouses for their long-lasting, brilliantly colored flower bracts and attractive foliage.

TALINUM (tah-ly'-num). A genus of small fleshy herbs popular in rock gardens, commonly called Fame-flower, which see.

TALIPOT PALM. Common name for *Corypha umbraculifera*, one of the Fan Palms, a tree to 80 ft. having enormous fan-shaped leaves.

TALLOW-TREE. Another name for *Sapium sebiferum*, the Chinese Tallow-tree, which see.

TAMARACK. A common name for *Larix laricina*, a species of Larch (which see), a hardy deciduous coniferous tree also known as Hackmatack.

TAMARISK. The common name for Tamarix, a genus of deciduous shrubs or trees, native to Europe and Asia. They are of graceful habit and unusual appearance, with their long slender branches and heath-like leaves. The small pinkish flowers, freely borne in loose racemes or panicles, give the plants a very feathery appearance. In gardens it is generally best to keep them in bushy form by annually cutting back the long growth. They grow well near the sea, and may be used as windbreaks. A few kinds are hardy as far north as Mass. They are propagated by seed and cuttings of growing wood.

The hardiest three Tamarisk species are: *T. parviflora*, to 15 ft., which has reddish bark and pink flowers in spring; *T. pentandra*, an equally strong grower, with purple branches and large panicles of pink flowers in late summer; and *T. odessana*, to 6 ft., with upright slender branches and pink flowers in midsummer.

T. anglica (English Tamarisk) grows to 10 ft., with reddish-brown stems and white flowers, tinged pink, in early summer. *T. gallica* (French Tamarisk), the common Tamarisk of the Mediterranean region, grows to 30 ft. with white or pink flowers in early summer; the leaves turn reddish-yellow in fall. *T. articulata*, to 30 ft., often used as a windbreak in dry regions of Calif., is distinguished by jointed branches and tiny sheathing leaves. *T. chinensis*, growing to 15 ft., is conspicuous with slender drooping branchlets bearing bluish-green leaves and pink flowers in large loose pendulous panicles.

False-tamarisk is the common name for the genus Myricaria, which see.

TANACETUM (tan-ah-see'-tum). A genus of annual and perennial herbs of the Composite Family, well known as Tansy (which see). They are plants with strong-scented foliage and clusters of small heads made up entirely of disk flowers. The plant sometimes listed as *Tanacetum balsamita* is correctly *Chrysanthemum balsamita*.

TANBARK-OAK. Common name for *Lithocarpus densiflora,* a tall tree of the Beech Family, intermediate between the oaks and the chestnuts. It is valued commercially as a source of tannin, and is of distinct merit for ornamental planting. It was formerly placed in the oak genus (Quercus).

TANGELO. A hybrid citrus fruit whose parents were the pomelo and the tangerine (both of which see). The fruit is smaller than that of the former, which it resembles in appearance; but it suggests that of the latter in the looseness of its skin; in favor it shows a resemblance to both. See also CITRUS FRUITS.

TANGERINE. Popular name for fruit of a form of Mandarin or Kid Glove Orange (*Citrus nobilis var. deliciosa*). See CITRUS FRUITS.

TANKAGE. This comparatively quick-acting organic fertilizer consists of a mixture of miscellaneous slaughter-house refuse. The materials, such as bone, waste, flesh, blood, hides scraps, etc., are treated to remove the fat, then dried and ground. When bone materials are present in large quantities it is high in phosphorus and is usually called bone-tankage. When softer, more highly nitrogenous materials predominate, it is called meat-tankage. Its composition varies greatly, the nitrogen ranging from 4 to 10 per cent and the phosphoric acid from 7 to 12 per cent. See FERTILIZER.

TANSY. Common name for the genus Tanacetum, comprising annual and perennial herbs of the Composite Family, with aromatic, pinnately cut foliage and clusters of small, tight heads of very small yellow disk flowers. A few are grown in the garden for ornament and in the herb garden for medicinal purposes and, occasionally, for flavoring. They may be easily increased by seed or division and require no special care or soil conditions.

T. vulgare (Common Tansy), a perennial to 3 ft., is an Old-World plant, but has escaped and become naturalized all over the U. S. in waste places and along roadsides. Its var. *crispum* has much more finely cut foliage.

huronense, also a perennial to 3 ft. but native to the N. States, has soft hairy leaves and is much less floriferous than *T. vulgare.*

TAPE-GRASS. A common name for the genus Vallisneria (which see), also called Eel-grass, a group of aquatic perennials used in aquaria.

TAPER FERN (*Thelypteris noveboracensis*). A light colored, deciduous fern of the N. E. States, with 18-in. once-pinnate fronds, narrowed below. Growing in dense colonies in open woods, it is ideal for naturalizing in moist well-drained soil and semi-shade but apt to over-run the garden.

TARA-VINE. A common name for *Actinidia arguta,* a hardy climbing Asiatic shrub with attractive foliage and edible fruit.

TARAXACUM (tah-rak'-sah-kum). A genus of stemless herbs of the Composite Family with bright yellow flat flower-heads followed by fluffy balls formed by the plumes of the seeds. Familiar everywhere as Dandelions (which see). While the plants are sometimes grown for greens, they are widely distributed as weeds.

TARE. Historical name for *Vicia sativa,* the common or spring vetch, an annual or biennial legume grown for forage and as a cover-crop especially in orchards. See VETCH.

TARNISHED PLANT BUG (*Lygus pratensis*). An inconspicuous brown plant bug, a true bug, generally distributed throughout the U. S. injuring many kinds of cultivated plants as well as many weeds and grasses. The adults are about ¼ in. long, flattened, oval in outline and in general mottled brown with flecks of gold giving the "tarnished" effect. They hibernate under leaves, stones and the bark of trees and among weeds, and early in the spring begin to attack the buds of fruit trees. The eggs are laid, not on trees, but in the stems, midribs and buds of herbaceous plants. There are from three to five generations a year but the abundance of these pests is often overlooked because of their protective coloring and their shy, hiding habits.

Owing to their activity control by spraying is difficult. Pyrethrum sprays are probably best and dusting with sulphur has been recommended. Destroy weed hosts, such as pigweed, ragweed, mallow, goldenrod, evening-primrose and aster.

The false tarnished plant bug (*L. communis*) closely resembles the tarnished plant bug but is more elongated and differently marked. Pears and other fruits punctured by it often fail to develop or become knotty and gritty. This insect winters under bark in the egg stage. Control by adding nicotine-sulphate to the fruit tree spray applied immediately after the petals fall and again a week later.

TARO. Common name for *Colocasia esculenta,* a tropical Asiatic herb, introduced into the U. S. by the Department of Agriculture and cultivated in the S. for its edible starchy tubers (also known as eddo), which are cooked in as many ways as potatoes. The sprouts are gathered outdoors in spring and, known as dasheen, are used like asparagus; in winter they are forced, blanched and similarly served.

TARRAGON. Common name for *Artemisia dracunculus,* a perennial herb the leaves of which are used for seasoning, especially vinegar. See also HERBS.

TARTAR EMETIC. A standard drug, also known as antimony and potassium tartrate, which is replacing paris green as a means of controlling thrips. It is recom-

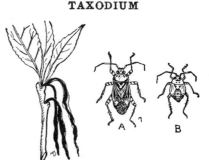

DAMAGED PEACH LEAVES
Characteristic wilting and blackening of twigs and leaves is caused by the feeding of the tarnished plant bug (A) and its nymph (B).

mended particularly for the gladiolus thrips but some gardeners have also used it successfully on roses. It is combined with brown sugar in varying amounts, a popular formula for small quantities being 4½ tsps. tartar emetic, 1⅔ cups brown sugar, and 3 gals. of water. Even less sugar may be effective. Tartar emetic is a poison for which no antidote is known, so care should be exercised in its use.

TARWEED. Common name for the genus Madia, a group of sticky annuals and perennials of W. N. and E. America with yellow daisy-like flowers that close in strong sunlight.

TASSEL-FLOWER. Common name for garden flowers of three different genera. One is *Amaranthus caudatus,* better known as Love-lies-bleeding; the other two, both members of the Daisy Familiy, are *Brickellia grandiflora,* a perennial, and *Emilia sagittata,* an annual, also called Floras Paintbrush.

TAXACEAE (tak-say'-see-ee). The Yew Family, a group of resinous evergreen trees and shrubs distributed in warm regions throughout the world. The leaves are needle- or scale-like; the male and female organs are in separate flowers on the same plant, the staminate flowers being cone-like; the fruit is a hard-coated seed surrounded by a fleshy disk, the whole resembling a berry. Some species are grown for landscape planting, mostly of the genera Taxus (Yew), Torreya, Cephalotaxus, Podocarpus.

TAXODIUM (tak-soh'-di-um). A genus of evergreen and deciduous trees and shrubs of the Pine Family planted for their picturesque effect and their feathery, ornamental foliage. The best known species is *T. distichum,* the Bald-cypress, a deciduous

TARNISHED PLANT BUG INJURY
A normal aster plant (a) contrasted with one of the same age (b) that has been stunted and deformed by the feeding of uncontrolled tarnished plant bugs in the young central shoots.

tree growing to 150 ft. with a trunk sometimes 12 ft. in diameter, light brown, flaky bark, small light green needle-like leaves, and a head, at first narrow, then broad and rounded. As the trees grow older the trunks grow large and give rise to the cypress "knees" which bring air to the roots when the swamps are flooded. The Bald-cypress grows naturally in swamps from Del. to Fla., but it is hardy as far N. as New England and is excellent planted in parks or in extensive home grounds, especially where there is wet, swampy soil.

TAXUS (tak'-sus). A genus of evergreen trees or shrubs with broad, flat leaves (needles) native throughout the N. hemisphere and commonly called Yew (which see). Until recent years they were included in the Pine Family; now they are placed in a separate group called, after the genus, the Yew Family.

TEA. The tea of commerce is derived from the leaves of *Thea sinensis,* a tender evergreen shrub or tree to 30 ft., with leaves to 5 in. long, and white fragrant flowers more than an inch across. Of distinct ornamental as well as commercial value, it can be grown in the S. States under the same conditions as camellia. Cultivated for its leaves especially in China and India, it has produced several forms, and certain districts are noted for specializing in particular varieties. However, the kinds of tea offered as "black" and "green" are the results of different ways of treating the leaves after picking, not the product of special varieties. Tea plantations are continually renewed by setting out young vigorous plants, which are raised from seed.

The word Tea is also applied to several other plants, the leaves of which have been used in the same way at some time or other. Appalachian-tea is *Viburnum cassinoides;* New-Jersey-tea is *Ceanothus americanus;* Oswego-tea, *Monarda didyma;* Crystal-tea, *Ledum palustre;* Labrador-tea, *Ledum groenlandicum;* Paraguay-tea, or Yerba de maté, *Ilex paraguariensis;* Mexican-tea, Ephedra and *Chenopodium ambrosioides;* Philippine-tea, *Ehretia microphylla.* The Australian-tea-tree is *Leptospermum laevigatum.*

TEABERRY. One common name for *Gaultheria procumbens,* a small native creeping shrub with glossy leaves, bell-like white flowers and scarlet fruits. Also called Wintergreen and Checkerberry.

TEA FERN (*Pellaea ornithopus*). A small wiry, 3-divided fern of S. California, with fruit-dots marginal under the overlapping lobes. For gravelly soil in that region, or for the cool greenhouse.

TEA ROSE. Common name for *Rosa odorata,* a species of Chinese origin, too tender to be grown outdoors except in the extreme S. where it is evergreen, partly climbing and continuous blooming. The flowers range from white to yellow and pale pink and are characteristically tea-scented. Formerly grown in greenhouses, this species is today mainly of historical interest as a parent of the much hardier and otherwise improved Hybrid Tea roses, which form the most important group of bedding roses. Some horticultural varieties of *R. odorata* are hardier than the type and grown in mild regions. See ROSE.

TEAR GAS. The vapor of chloropierin (which see), a chemical developed to be used as a weapon for warfare or in quelling mobs, but now used as a soil sterilizing material. See DISINFECTION.

TEASEL. Common name for the genus Dipsacus, a group of coarse, prickly biennial herbs of the Teasel Family (Dipsaceae), thistle-like in appearance. A few species are grown as ornamentals in the wild garden or shrubbery border. Started from seed, they are easily established and, indeed, are likely to escape and become weeds. *D. fullonum* (Fullers Teasel), to 6 ft., has lavender flowers in dense heads and the bracts on the seed heads are sharp and spine-like. These heads are still used in the textile industry to raise the nap of woollen cloth, no machinery ever having been invented to take their place. *D. sylvestris* (Common Teasel) differs but slightly from the above and both species have additional value as bee plants. *D. pilosus,* to 4 ft., is a bristly plant with yellowish-white flowers in round heads.

TEASEL GOURD. Common name for the bristly-fruited *Cucumis dipsaceus,* an Arabian relative of the cucumber, grown as an ornamental or curiosity.

TEA-TREE, AUSTRALIAN. Common name for species of Leptospermum, especially *L. laevigatum,* a white-flowered shrub somewhat planted in the S. and Calif., especially to prevent the blowing of sandy soils.

TECOMA (te-koh'-mah). A genus of upright shrubs, native from Fla. to S. America, belonging to the Bignonia Family.

They are grown outdoors in the warmest parts of the country, and sometimes in pots under glass for their showy flowers. Several species formerly listed under Tecoma have been referred to other genera. Propagated by seeds and cuttings.

T. garrocha is a graceful plant to 5 ft. or so, with leaves of 7 to 11 leaflets, and clusters of scarlet and yellow tubular flowers. *T. smithi* is a supposed hybrid of Australian origin. It has 11 to 17 leaflets and large showy panicles of yellow flowers tinged orange.

TECOMARIA (tek-oh-may′-ri-ah). Half-climbing shrubby plants of the tropics. *T. capensis,* the species commonly grown, is known as Cape-honeysuckle, which see.

TEFF. Common name for *Eragrostis abyssinica,* an annual grass grown as an ornamental and for bouquets. See ORNAMENTAL GRASSES.

TELANTHERA (tel-an′-ther-ah). Former name of a genus of tropical herbs and shrubs now included with the popular bedding and foliage plants in the genus Alternanthera, which see.

TELEGRAPH-PLANT. Common name for *Desmodium gyrans,* a purple-flowered perennial species of Tick-trefoil from tropical Asia, grown as an annual in greenhouses as a curiosity because of the peculiar jerking of its leaflets.

TELEPHIUM (tel-ee′-fi-um) *imperati.* A low-growing perennial herb of the Pink Family, with small white flowers. Known as Orpine, but little used in the garden.

TELLIMA (tel′-a-mah) *grandiflora.* A hairy herbaceous perennial of W. N. America with greenish flowers. See FALSE-ALUM-ROOT.

TEMPLETONIA (tem-p′l-toh′-ni-ah) *retusa.* An Australian shrub with leathery leaves and pea-like red flowers. See CORAL-BUSH.

TENDER HOLLY FERN (*Cyrtomium falcatum*). An excellent and reliable indoor and cool greenhouse fern, with once-pinnate fronds, 1½ to 2½ ft. tall, of rapid growth. The pinnae are broadly sickle-shaped and glossy dark green and the stipes are clothed with light brown scales. The ideal soil is leafmold, peat and sand in equal parts. Do not pot tightly; water sparingly in winter, and rest occasionally in a cool dark place. Var. *rochfordianum* is a dwarf; var. *mayi* has crested tips; var. *pendulum,* with large drooping fronds, is a splendid plant for the living room.

TENDRIL. A very slender, flexible appendage which serves to support a plant by clinging to or winding around some other object, as in cucurbits and sweet peas. Tendrils are sometimes provided with disk-like attachments that permit them to cling to flat surfaces, as in the Virginia creeper; being coiled like a spiral spring they are able to hold a plant and still allow some "play" without pulling loose, and, by contracting, to draw closer.

TENT CATERPILLAR, EASTERN. Also called the apple tree tent caterpillar. The larvae of certain species of moth common throughout the U. S., often completely defoliating in spring unsprayed orchards and sometimes ornamental trees and shrubs, and filling wild cherry, apple and other trees along roadsides with large unsightly nests. The winter is passed in the egg stage, gray or dark-brown, shiny egg masses about ½ in long encircling small twigs as though a bit of gum had been wrapped around them and varnished. The eggs hatch just as the apple leaves unfold and the tiny worms at once attack them, at the same time forming a colony in the nearest branch fork and building a web-like nest for protection at night and in wet weather. As the caterpillars crawl out to feed, they leave a silken trail behind which may connect several nests over the tree. In about a month the caterpillars, fullgrown, and 2 in. long, black, with bluish markings and a white stripe down the back, leave the nests, crawl along the ground, fences, buildings, etc., and pupate in dirty whitish dusty cocoons fastened on tree trunks, under bark or shingles or on any sort of trash. The small heavy-bodied moths, appearing in early summer, have short, reddish-brown wings with white bands. There is but one brood a year and "tents" seen in midsummer or later are caused not by this pest but by the fall webworm, which see.

A regular spray program (as recommended under APPLE) will control the tent caterpillar in orchards. In gardens and home grounds the nests may be removed by burning with a torch—if the work is done carefully, so as not to injure the tree. A better plan is to wipe them out of the crotches with rags moistened with kerosene, gasoline or some full strength contact spray. The sooner this is done, the easier, pleasanter and more effective it is. But the best means of control is by pruning off and burning the twigs carrying egg masses. Do this any time while the leaves are off the trees, when the masses can be easily seen against the sky. Birds and other insects (including parasites) are natural enemies of the tent caterpillar and a natural balance is gradually established so that after the pest has been abundant for four or five years it usually disappears for the same length of time.

The related forest tent caterpillar is a pest of woodlands but may defoliate shade trees such as poplar, maple and oak. The blue-headed caterpillar has a line of silvery, diamond-shaped spots down the middle of the back. Again the winter stage is the egg, ½-in. long light-brown masses being laid on the twigs of host plants. No web

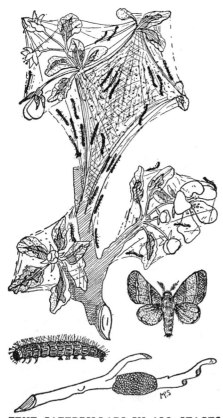

TENT CATERPILLARS IN ALL STAGES

Attacking principally wild cherry and apple but many other trees as well, these repulsive, voracious "worms" deface them in early spring with tough whitish webs to which they retreat at night after eating leaves all day. Burning out the webs and destroying the dusty yellow cocoons before the moths emerge are helpful measures but better still is collecting egg masses from bare twigs in winter (shown at bottom) and burning them.

is formed so control consists of spraying with lead arsenate in spring, as the egg masses are rarely within reach.

See also SPRAYING AND SPRAYERS.

TEN-WEEKS STOCK. Common name for the annual variety of Brompton Stock or Gilliflower (*Mathiola incana* var. *annua*). It refers, approximately, to the period between seedsowing and flowering which in this variety is considerably shorter than in the biennial or perennial species to which it belongs. See MATHIOLA; STOCK.

TERMINAL. The end or apex of a stem, foliage branch, or shoot bearing a flower cluster. The term is commonly used as an adjective as "the terminal bud" meaning the one at the end of a shoot. Because this bud is responsible for the continuation of the growth of the stem in its original direction, the shape of the plant can be modified by removing or destroying it. See also BUD; DISBUDDING.

TERMINALIA (tur-mi-nay'-li-ah). Tropical trees, mostly of S. Asia, where they are valued for ornamental and economic purposes. *T. catappa,* the Tropical-almond or Myrobalan (which see), has been introduced into southern Florida for street planting. It is a deciduous tree of stately appearance, up to 80 ft. with horizontal branches in whorls. The leaves grow to a foot long, are clustered at the ends of the branches, and turn a rich red before falling. The fruit is a nut of good flavor, and in the tropics yields a valuable oil.

TERMITES. Wood-infesting insects which are called white ants but which differ from true ants by not having a slender waist. They occur in all parts of the world but are much more numerous in the tropics. They may attack woody plants in the garden but are more seriously destructive to buildings, fence posts and any type of structure made of wood or with wooden framework. The fact that they work within the wood, giving no sign of their presence until much damage may have been done, makes them all the more dangerous.

To prevent infestation, great care should be taken to avoid having woodwork come in contact with the earth. The foundations and framework of infested buildings should be replaced with metal or stone, or wood treated with creosote. Exterminator companies now make a special business of finding the colonies, killing the termites and treating all woodwork against infestation.

Termite colonies resemble those of ants in organization, but the male helps to start the nest and remains with the queen throughout life. The adults are of three types—workers, soldiers, and kings and queens. The workers, which are the destructive forms, are soft bodied, white and wingless. The males and females are black, rather narrow, with long brittle wings; they leave the nests in swarms at certain times of the year and are then mistaken for "flying ants."

TERRACE GARDEN. This may refer to a hillside garden developed by terracing a slope into a series of narrow level areas; or it may be used in reference to the garden treatment of a terrace—paved or grassed—before the dwelling, or of the space immediately adjacent to and below this terrace.

In the first instance it implies the breaking up of a slope, whether steep or gentle, (by the method known as "cut-and-fill") into level spaces large enough to be planted with flowers (and sometimes also with trees and shrubs), and to allow for a pathway the length of each level, with steps at some point descending and ascending to the levels below and above. Retaining walls are a necessity in such a terrace garden and are, indeed, a feature of its development, wherein are combined opportunity for wall gardening and for the culture of the more usual garden flowers and fruits.

In the garden treatment of a terrace, potted plants may be largely depended upon. In the space adjacent to and below it, semi-formal effects are desirable since this is the zone uniting the house and what may be called the outer garden.

TERRARIUM (ter-ay'-ri-um). (Plural terraria.) A container, chiefly of glass, and usually rectangular (though it may be of any shape), in which are grown small plants so arranged as to suggest a bit of natural landscape.

The discovery of the terrarium is credited to the late Dr. Nathaniel Ward, who, so the story goes, on a walk through the dry woods one day found a bottle containing a bit of soil in which was a lush, green growth of fern indifferent to the drought and heat outside. His pondering over the secret of the bottle—controlled heat, humidity and light—resulted in the development of the Wardian case, a cherished feature of the fashionable Victorian home and a frequent adjunct of the nature-study class room.

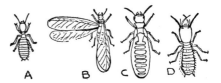

TERMITES, A THREAT TO GARDEN STRUCTURES
These creatures, often wrongly called "flying ants," may attack some woody plants, but are more likely to enter and destroy wooden foundations of buildings where they are in contact with moist soil. A. Worker; B. Winged male; C. Female; D. Soldier.

Almost any type of glass-sided container may be the foundation of a successful terrarium. The most usual and the easiest to plant and care for is a leaky, discarded aquarium or other rectangular glass case. Or, panes of window glass may be fastened together with adhesive tape (painted green before applying) and placed in a base made of a baking or roasting pan.

Like any other garden, a terrarium depends for its success on its design and the suitability and practicability of the plant material used. The native woodland terrarium is perhaps the easiest and most interesting to make.

MAKING A TERRARIUM. The first step is the preparation of the container. Place an inch or so of gravel in the bottom. On this sprinkle a layer of ground or broken-up charcoal to keep the terrarium sweet. Then add leafmold or humus to receive the actual planting.

A trip to familiar woods will not only provide the opportunity to collect the small flowering plants, small ferns, moss and rocks needed, but also afford a chance to study the associations in which these materials are found and thus learn how to plant them.

In gathering these materials, select small plants of small species unless your terrarium is larger than the usual size. As you collect them, fold each plant in a bit of oiled paper or a paper towel before placing in a basket or box. Moss should be stripped in large pieces from logs or the ground and packed with the green surfaces together, sandwich fashion. If for any reason it is impossible to use the plant material as soon as you get home, put it in the refrigerator and even after several days it will still be in good condition for planting. Whenever out in the woods watch for interesting bits of bark, lichens, sticks, pebbles and other bits that might work into your terrarium scheme.

As in a larger garden, differences of level add charm and character to the terrarium, and serve to better display the plants. Set small rocks in place to help attain this effect and pile the leafmold up behind them in the desired contours. Pockets should be made to hold the larger plants. In this "landscaping" the shape of the container must govern the design. If it be square or rectangular the contours will probably slope upward from front to back. If round or globular, a center elevation will perhaps be most satisfactory.

If you have selected a small seedling evergreen, plant it and any other large rooted plants first, being careful to tamp the leafmold well about the roots. This material will no doubt be most effective at the back and at the ends. Small ferns are particularly good in the terrarium and should be planted with their crowns just above the soil.

With the large plants and ferns in place, the terrarium is ready for the surface covering of moss which should be packed tightly around the protruding rocks and on top of the raw humus. Next lay in the bits of lichen-covered bark and other decorative accessories. A light sprinkling from a fine spray and the terrarium is set up and ready to live as a little world by itself. Naturally, it must be provided with a glass cover. Experience will teach the owner

GARDENS IN BOTTLES AND BOWLS

These modern and popular developments of the original oblong terraria, usually restricted to school rooms and museums, are especially adapted to dwellings where they supply just the moisture and temperature conditions required by a variety of dainty and interesting plants, and protect them from drafts and other dangers.

whether the cover should be kept tight, partly open or entirely off. When the glass becomes clouded with condensed moisture, give more ventilation; as long as the air is clear the terrarium can be kept covered, or nearly so.

For the woodland terrarium, an almost endless list of plants is available. All of the small ferns (particularly the maidenhair) are good; also the striped rattlesnake-plantain, mayflower, columbines, violas, trilliums, hepatica and (if your terrarium is very large) jack-in-the-pulpit, Solomons seal and larger ferns.

The most important thing is to see that the plant material and accessories are in scale with one another and that the relationship in which you have placed them is such as might easily occur in nature. In this way, your terrarium becomes a bit of outdoors which you can enjoy in those days when the real woods are inaccessible.

ADDING A WATER FEATURE. If a tiny pool and a water planting is a part of the scheme some provision must be made for concealing the edges of the water container; also take care to prevent the woodland part from becoming mildewed or waterlogged. If a combination terrarium-aquarium is desired, a good method is to divide a square or rectangular aquarium diagonally or lengthwise by a low strip of glass well fastened in place. This is best done by providing a backing of plaster of paris on the side that is to receive the earth planting. Perhaps a further reinforcement of aquarium cement at the corners and seams will be advisable. With a background planting of woodland material well banked on one side of the partition and an arrangement of rocks, sand and aquatic plants in the other, the side of a small stream can be beautifully reproduced with its typical plant and, if you choose, its animal life. A terrarium of this type is especially suitable as a home for small toads, baby turtles and other semi-aquatic animals.

The so-called "bottle garden" is simply a terrarium in which a large bottle is used as the container. Its planting differs from the planting of a regular terrarium only in that (1) the work must be done with long wooden forceps and tamping sticks (these may be home made); and (2) the original plant material must be small enough to go through the neck of the bottle without injury or cramming. Once set in place, it tends to rapidly grow and fill the entire space. A little more ingenuity and patience are required to make one of these, but the effect is worth the trouble.

A desert- or arid-terrarium is started in much the same way as the woodland type except that the drainage layer of gravel and charcoal is hardly necessary, while the soil is of sandy gravelly character rather than loamy and rich in humus. Cacti vary so greatly in shape and color that they lend themselves to many pleasing arrangements. Associated with them, little bunches of grass, like the clumps found in desert regions, and western wild flowers raised from seed in places where they are wanted (the California poppy, for instance), make a charming effect.

The desert-terrarium needs more sun and air than the woodland type. The latter will do with partial sunlight unless flowering plants are the feature. Then it needs plenty of sun.

TETRAGONIA (tet-rah-goh′-ni-ah) *expansa.* New-Zealand-spinach, a hot weather substitute for spinach, which see.

TEUCRIUM (teu′-kri-um). A genus of herbs or shrubby plants, widely dispersed throughout the temperate and warmer parts of the earth, belonging to the Mint Family, and known as Germander. A few species are hardy in the N. and well adapted for rock-garden and flower-border planting. They are not particular as to soil but a light sandy soil seems to suit them best. Propagated by seeds, cuttings, or root divisions.

PRINCIPAL SPECIES

T. chamaedrys is a procumbent shrubby plant with stems about 1 ft. high and loose spikes of reddish-purple or rose flowers. *fruticans* (Tree Germander) grows to 6 ft. in a mild climate, and is a very attractive shrub with silvery foliage and blue flowers. In mild regions it has a long flowering season and is recommended for dry places. *montanum* is a low prostrate shrub, with creamy or pale yellow flowers, making a fine effect in mass. *marum* (Cat-thyme) is a small much-branched tender shrub from the Mediterranean region with short spikes of purplish pink flowers; cats are said to be very much stimulated by it.

TEXAS-BUCKEYE. Common name for *Ungnadia speciosa,* also called Spanish- and Mexican-buckeye, a tender shrub or small tree of the S. W. with rosy flowers opening before the leaves. See BUCKEYE.

THALIA (thay′-li-ah). A genus of large, perennial herbs of the Maranta Family. They do best planted in wet ground or in shallow water, but most species are suited only to the greenhouse or to very mild climates, although several are hardy as far N. as Philadelphia.

T. dealbata has leaves from 6 to 9 in. long, lightly powdered like those of a canna, and borne on stalks from 1 to 4 ft. tall. The small purple flowers are carried high on a very long stem. Where the climate is mild enough, this is a splendid subject for a waterside planting.

T. divaricata is similar to the foregoing, but much larger. It grows from 5 to 10 ft. in height and its leaves are as much as 2 ft. long.

THALICTRUM (thah-lik′-trum). A genus of perennial plants of the Buttercup Family commonly known as Meadow-rue. Some are very decorative in the border and others are charming when naturalized in the wild garden. They have attractive cut foliage and numerous clustered flowers, without petals, but with numerous large, drooping stamens and sometimes showy sepals. They create a remarkably fine effect in the border in combination with plants of heavier growth, such as iris or peonies. Almost all the species are easily grown in a light, rich loamy soil, but a few of the tall-growing, native kinds thrive in moist, swampy land. Propagation is by seed or division.

PRINCIPAL SPECIES

T. aquilegifolium (Feathered-columbine), to 3 ft., has rosy-purple clustered flowers blooming in early summer. *flavum,* to 4 ft., has creamy-yellow flowers with numerous bright yellow stamens. *glaucum,* with grayish-blue foliage and yellow flowers borne on 4 ft. stems, blooms late in June or early in July. *delavayi,* with purple or lavender flowers on tall stems, provides light feathery bloom in the back of the border. *dipterocarpum* is a tall, late blooming species with pyramidal clusters of rosy-mauve or purple flowers brightened by drooping golden stamens. *minus,* low-growing with greenish-yellow flowers, is excellent in the rock garden. *dioicum,* a native plant to 2 ft., is easily grown in dry woodland soil.

polygamum, to 8 ft., is another native species growing naturally in damp open meadows and easily colonized on the edge of the bog garden. It has large clusters of feathery white flowers.

THATCHING. The desire for the picturesqueness associated with English cottages has led to a revival of thatching for roofs of garden shelters and tool-houses. Unfortunately the revival has not always been attended with either a sense of appropriateness or a knowledge of construction. The thatched roof is a village or farm development and should be restricted to country surroundings where the straw is a naturally-available material and looks appropriate. It is also better on an enclosed structure like a tool-house or playhouse than on an open arbor where the necessary thickness of the thatching is all too likely to give the appearance of a haystack on stilts.

Thatch is best made of wheat or rye straw, thoroughly cleaned of weeds and slightly dampened before applying. It is applied to the roof by tying bunches or "yealms" or straw onto the battens of the roof, starting at the eaves and working to the ridge. The straw is overlapped both laterally and vertically, and when completed should be 12 to 15 in. thick. Properly made thatch will last for several years in N. temperate climates, and is interesting in certain locations.

THEA (thee'-ah). A genus of evergreen shrubs and trees from Asia, known as Tea (which see). Some are grown in mild climates for ornamental purposes, but the most important species is *T. sinensis,* which is widely cultivated in subtropical countries for the leaves, which yield the tea of commerce. It was formerly known as *Camellia thea,* but Camellia and Thea are so closely allied that at one time all the species of both were listed under Thea. The chief difference appears to be that in Camellia the practically stemless flowers are upright with deciduous sepals, whereas in Thea the flowers are stalked, and nodding and have persistent sepals.

THELESPERMA (thel-e-spur'-mah). A group of some ten annual or perennial herbs or sub-shrubs of the Composite or Daisy Family, the flowers, with light-colored yellow or orange rays and purple disks, later turning brown, being a good deal like those of Coreopsis (which see). The one species grown in gardens (*T. bur-*

ridgeanum), often called by a former name, Cosmidium, was at one time supposed to be a hybrid between Thelesperma and Coreopsis. Of easy culture in any good garden soil if given a sunny location, this plant branches freely and blossoms all summer. Propagation is by seed.

THELYPTERIS (the-lip'-ter-is). A genus of ferns, sometimes placed with the Shield Ferns in the genus Dryopteris. Three species, found in the E. States, are recognized by their deciduous texture, rampant growth, and favorite location, which is an open marshy place, often in full sun. They are not recommended for other purposes than naturalizing, being much too weedy and robust. The Marsh Fern (*T. palustris*) is 1 to 2½ ft. tall, with the fertile fronds much contracted as the margins overlap behind; the Massachusetts Fern (*T. simulata*) is less common and found on drier ground; the New York Fern (*T. noveboracensis*), with pinnae spaced out and tapering at the base, grows in open woods and is useful as a ground cover in clearings or under shrubbery.

THEOBROMA (thee-oh-broh'-mah) *cacao.* The tropical tree from whose seeds, borne in large, woody fruits, are obtained the cocoa and chocolate of commerce. Common names for it are Chocolate-tree and Cacao, which see.

THERMOPSIS (ther-mop'-sis). A genus of perennial herbs of the Pea Family, comprising a number of lupine-like plants having racemes of yellow flowers. Useful in the garden, they are easily grown in light rich soil in an open sunny position and are propagated by seeds or by division. The best known species is *T. caroliniana,* which grows to 4 ft. bearing its yellow pea-like blossoms in midsummer. Though a rather coarse plant, it is good for bold effects in the perennial border.

THIMBLEBERRY. Popular name loosely applied to blackberries and raspberries generally, but properly to the Blackcap Raspberry (*Rubus occidentalis*).

THIOUREA (thy'-oh-yoo-ree-ah). A chemical compound in the form of white crystals, partially soluble in water, which has been used in connection with seed and cutting treatments. When mixed with some of the root-growth substances (which see) it seems to increase root forming activity. Some seeds have been greatly benefited by the application of thiourea prior to planting, but the same varieties of seeds from different sources do not show identical reactions to Thiourea applications. Its use is still chiefly experimental.

THISTLE. Common name given to different genera of plants, many of them troublesome weeds, but applied particularly to the genus Onopordum of the Composite Family, a group of woolly, prickly-leaved herbs with attractive rounded heads of white or purple flowers. They are Old-World plants and a few are grown in the border, where they are easily propagated from seed sown where the plant is to stand. *O. acanthium* (Scotch Thistle), a biennial growing sometimes to 9 ft., has prickly leaves covered with white down and heads of lavender flowers 2 in. across. This is the Thistle of song and story, inseparably associated with Scotland. It makes an effective picture when planted against an evergreen background, but should not be allowed to seed promiscuously for fear it will become a pest, as it is in many neglected fields.

Blessed, Holy, or St. Marys Thistle is *Cnicus* (or *Silybum*) *marianum;* Fishbone Thistle is *Cirsium diacantha;* Globe Thistle is the genus Echinops; Golden Thistle is *Scolymus hispanicus;* Plumed Thistle is Cirsium; Plumeless Thistle is Carduus; Russian-thistle is *Salsola pestifer.* See those references, and, for eradication measures, see WEEDS.

THLASPI (thlas'-py). A genus of annual and perennial herbs of the Mustard Family, with white, pink or purple flowers in loose clusters. See PENNY-CRESS.

THORN. Alone this is generally used as a common name for the genus Crataegus. Combined with other words it is applied to various species of that and other genera. White Thorn is a common name for *Crataegus oxyacantha,* the English Hawthorn; Cockspur Thorn is *C. crus-galli* and Washington Thorn is *C. phaenopyrum.* Black-thorn is *Prunus spinosa;* Box-thorn is Lycium; Broom-thorn is *Ulex europaea;* Camel-thorn is *Acacia giraffae,* and Kangaroo-thorn, *A. armata;* Goats-thorn, is *Astragalus tragacanthus;* Christ-thorn is *Paliurus spina-christi;* Jerusalem-thorn, *Parkinsonia aculeata;* Lily-thorn, *Catesbaea spinosa;* Hedge-thorn, *Carissa arduina;* Firethorn and Evergreen-thorn, Pyracantha; Mysore-thorn, *Caesalpinia sepiaria.*

THORNAPPLE. Popular name for Crataegus, a genus of spiny shrubs with rose-like flowers and apple-like fruits. Also applied to species of Datura, ill-smelling shrubs, trees and coarse growing annuals with trumpet-shaped flowers and prickly or spiny fruits. See both genera.

THORNY FISHTAIL PALM. A common name for Martinezia, a genus of tropical American palms bearing spines on trunk or foliage (or both) and sometim called Spiny Maindenhair Palm. See P

THOROUGH-WAX. Popular name Bupleurum, a genus of yellow-flowere herbs and shrubs of the Old World; useful in warm sections where the soil is poor.

THOROUGHWORT. Popular name for Eupatorium (which see), a genus of tropical American, mostly perennial herbs, including both garden and greenhouse subjects. Also called Boneset.

THRIFT. Common name for Statice (also called Sea-pink), a genus of dwarf evergreen, hardy perennials which bear abundant small pink, white, lilac or red flowers throughout the season. They are good edging plants.

Prickly-thrift is Acantholimon, which see.

THRINAX (thry'-naks). A genus of slender, spineless Fan Palms commonly known as Silver Palms because of the light colored under surface of the leaves. Several species are native to Fla. or nearby islands, and are extensively planted in that region. One of the most beautiful is *T. microcarpa,* which has a trunk to 30 ft., sometimes elevated 3 ft. above the ground by the massed roots, and surmounted by a wide head of fan-shaped leaves, silvery-white beneath. This lovely palm thrives in sun or shade, preferring rich moist loam; but if planted in sand it responds readily to applications of organic fertilizers.

THRIPS. The name (singular and plural) for minute insects with rasping-sucking mouth-parts belonging to the order Thysanoptera, which means bristle-wings. They are slender, rarely as long as $\frac{1}{8}$ in. and agile. They feed on flowers and other plant parts and may be serious pests of fruits, vegetables, flowers and field crops; the gladiolus, greenhouse, onion and pear thrips are among the particularly destructive species. Thrips injury is sometimes called white blast, the surface of the leaves becoming whitened and flecked; then the tips wither, curl up and die.

The greenhoue thrips deposits eggs in slits in the leaf; these hatch within a week into active white nymphs which feed by first rasping the leaves and then sucking the sap. After four molts, the nymph changes to a yellowish to brown adult with four narrow wings fringed with long hairs. Fumigation with nicotine or cyanide is effective; or a spray consisting of 2 lbs. brown sugar, 2 tablespoons paris green and 3 gals. water may be used. The gladiolus thrips overwinters on the corms and may be killed by placing these in tight paper bags containing 1 oz. of naphthalene flakes to each hundred corms. During the growing season spray with the paris green-brown sugar mixture just described; or with the following improvement on that formula: Tartar emetic (which see), 2 oz. or 4½ tsp., brown sugar 8 oz. or 1⅔ cups, water 3 gals. Spray weekly from the time the shoots are 6 in. high. Some gladiolus growers report excellent thrips control through the soaking of the corms for six hours in a solution (4 tsps. to 1 gal. water) of a well known household disinfectant which is now being advertised for that purpose.

THROATWORT. Common name for Trachelium, a genus of S. European herbs and shrubs of the Bellflower Family, having simple leaves and bearing tubular blue flowers. Only the species *T. caeruleum* is commonly seen. Sometimes growing to 3 ft., it has clusters of small flowers varying from dark blue to white. A perennial plant, it is grown outdoors in the S. or as a greenhouse plant or a garden annual in the N. It is grown from seed or cuttings.

THUJA or THUYA (thoo'-yah). A genus of evergreen coniferous trees of the Pine Family, well known in many forms as Arborvitae. Their foliage is scale-like, flattened on the stem, soft and waxy to the touch, with a pleasant aromatic odor when crushed. The native American species (*T. occidentalis*) grows to 60 ft. especially in cool regions and in a well-drained soil with abundant water below. It will also grow in soil that is thoroughly wet. The many compact dwarf forms that have been developed—some of them highly colored—are extensively used. See ARBORVITAE.

THUJOPSIS (thoo-yop'-sis) *dolobrata.* The single representative of a genus of evergreen trees of the Pine Family closely related to Thuja (which see) and sometimes called False-arborvitae. It grows to 50 ft., with graceful frond-like branchlets. A native of Japan it is hardy in the U. S. except in N. New England. There are

several forms, var. *nana* being dwarf with lighter colored leaves; var. *variegata* having white-tipped branchlets, and var. *hondai* being taller with smaller leaves.

The plant sometimes referred to as *T. borealis* is correctly *Chamaecyparis nootkatensis.*

THUNBERGIA (thun-bur'-ji-ah). A genus of about 75 species of tender climbing plants from tropical regions, belonging to the Acanthus Family and known by the name Clock-vine. Several are grown for greenhouse decoration; when planted out they grow and flower freely, the blossoms being white, buff, blue, scarlet, purple, etc. In the warmest parts of the country some are grown as attractive vines on trellises, verandas and arbors. *T. alata* and its varieties are the hardiest forms, although a slight frost cuts their top growth to the ground. In the North they are often grown as annuals, and show to advantage in hanging baskets or when draping the front of window boxes. Thunbergias bloom mostly in late summer and autumn. Propagation is by seeds, cuttings or layers. The principal species are the following:

T. alata (Black-eyed Susan). A twining perennial to 8 ft., often grown as an annual for greenhouse bloom or outdoors where it flowers in late summer. The flowers are mostly buff with a dark purple throat. Two good varieties are *alba*, white; and *aurantiaca*, orange, both with dark centers.

coccinea is a tall woody climber, bearing scarlet flowers with a yellow throat.

grandiflora is the commonest of the blue kinds. It is a tall climber with large heart-shaped leaves and bell-shaped flowers, borne singly or in short drooping racemes.

laurifolia is a strong woody climber, one of the best for winter flowering in the greenhouse. The large pale-blue flowers are borne in clusters.

erecta is a medium shrub of rather straggly habit. The dark purple flowers with yellow markings are borne singly, but in great profusion.

THYME. The common name for Thymus, a genus of aromatic herbs or shrubby plants of the Mint Family, long cultivated and valued as both ornamentals and sweet herbs. They have small lavender or pink flowers and are planted in the rock garden and the border for ornament, or in the herb garden, to be used for seasoning. They grow easily in ordinary garden soil and are easily increased from cuttings or seed. See also HERBS.

T. serpyllum (Mother-of-Thyme or Creeping Thyme), is a small sprawling shrub with rooting stems and small, purplish flowers which appear from June to September. An Old-World plant, it has escaped from gardens in many parts of America. Some of the many varieties that have been developed under cultivation are: *albus,* flowers white; *splendens,* flowers red; *aureus,* with yellow variegations on the leaves; *argenteus,* leaves variegated with white; *vulgaris* (Lemon Thyme), leaves small and lemon-scented; *coccineus,* tall (to 3 ft.) with crimson flowers; *roseus,* flowers rose.

vulgaris (Common Thyme) is an erect shrubby plant to 8 in. with white hairy branches and small leaves.

nitidus, is a Sicilian shrub of compact growth with shining leaves and small bright pink flowers borne over a long period.

Spanish-thyme is a name given to *Coleus amboinicus.*

THYMELAECEAE (thi-mee-lee-ay'-see-ee). The Mezereum Family, is a group of warm-climate trees and shrubs with tough, acrid bark. Flowers are borne in clusters with petals lacking or reduced to scales and the calyx a petal-like tube, often colored. Some forms are poisonous or sources of drugs; and several are grown in borders and greenhouses for their beautiful, sweet-scented flowers. Useful genera in the garden are Pimelea, Daphne, Dirca.

TIARELLA (ty-ah-rel'-ah). A genus of small perennial woodland herbs of the Saxifrage Family, known as False-mitrewort. They have small delicate flowers in racemes, and their simple or compound leaves assume beautiful bronzy red tones in the autumn. False-mitreworts are delightful colonized in the wild garden, or the rock garden, and they are easily propagated by seed or division. *T. cordifolia* (Foam-flower) to 1 ft. the form found in the E. States, has small white flowers. There are interesting color differences in var. *purpurea* with reddish-purple flowers and var. *marmorata* with marbled foliage. *T. unifoliata* to 2 ft., the W. form, bears feathery flowers in panicles.

TIBOUCHINA (ti-boo-ky'-nah). A genus of tropical shrubs and herbs with large purple flowers, commonly called Glory-bush, which see.

TICKSEED. A popular name for Bidens and Coreopsis, closely related genera of the Composite Family. American species of the former are weeds; some foreign ones are ornamentals.

TICK-TREFOIL. Common name for Desmodium, a genus of herbs with small pea-like flowers in loose clusters.

TIDY TIPS. Common name for *Layia elegans,* a daisy-like annual of W.N. America, whose yellow ray flowers are often tipped with white.

TIGER LILY. (see illustration, Plate 6.) Common name for *Lilium tigrinum,* a popular old-fashioned hardy orange-flowered species of Lily, which see.

TIGRIDIA (ty-grid'-i-ah). A small genus of tender herbs native to Mexico and Peru, known as Tiger-flower. Growing from bulbs or corms, they produce short, sabre-like foliage and a forked, leafy stalk which bears several iris-like flowers in quick succession. They are strikingly beautiful members of the Iris Family, few flowers equaling them in brilliance. While the individual blossoms last only a day, there are enough on each stalk to provide a display over a considerable period.

Flowering in midsummer, they are well adapted to American garden conditions though they will not survive a freezing temperature. The corms should be planted in the spring when the soil is thoroughly warm, dug in fall before frost, and stored, like gladiolus corms, over winter. Rodents are particularly fond of them, both while in the soil and when stored, but can be kept away with naphthalene flakes.

The most important species is *T. pavonia,* which grows to 2½ ft. in great profusion in the Mexican hills. Its flowers are red, spotted yellow and purple, but there are varieties providing interesting yellow, white and lilac effects. Var. *grandiflora* has very large flowers.

TILIA (til'-i-ah). The genus of handsome hardy deciduous trees known as Linden, Lime, and Basswood. Distributed through the N. temperate zone, they are valuable timber and ornamental subjects and in some places important sources of honey. Though easily suited as to soil, they need plenty of moisture in order to thrive. See LINDEN.

TILIACEAE (til-i-ay'-see-ee). The Linden or Basswood Family, a group of trees and shrubs widely distributed in warm and tropical regions but with some range into the temperate zone. The sap is mucilaginous and the bark tough, that of the genus Tilia yielding commercial fibre and a species of Corchorus being the source of jute. Sparmannia is a greenhouse subject and forms of Tilia (linden) are among the best known shade and ornamental trees.

TILLAGE. In general, this means all practices relating to the management of land in crop production—manuring, plowing, harrowing, disking, rolling and cultivation (as used to indicate the loosening of the surface soil between plants in order to aerate the soil, cónserve moisture, and destroy weeds). In this sense synonyms are: Culture, Cultivation generally, and Husbandry.

In a more limited sense, tillage means merely the hoeing or cultivating of orchards, vineyards and gardens where the trees, vines and other crops are already in place, the land between the plants being stirred by various tillage tools.

See CULTIVATION ; DIGGING.

TILLANDSIA (ti-land'-zi-ah) *usneoides*. A slender, drooping American "air plant" of the Bromelia Family. Known as Spanish-moss (which see) it is common on trees, especially live oaks, in the S.

TIMOTHY. Common name for *Pheleum pratense,* a perennial grass and one of the most important hay plants. Sometimes called Herds Grass, it has leaves to 1 ft. long and cylindrical short bearded spikes, sometimes 6 in. or more long at the end of stiff stems that may attain 5 ft. in rich soils. Seed is sometimes included in low-priced lawn-grass mixtures because it is cheap and starts quickly, giving a good green growth soon after seeding. But it is in no way desirable as a lawn grass and mixtures containing it should be avoided. Also timothy hay should not be used as a winter mulch as it will scatter seed in the beds and require interminable weeding thereafter.

TITHONIA (ti-thoh'-ni-ah). A genus of robust herbs or shrubby plants, native in Mexico and further S., called Mexican-sunflower and belonging to the Daisy Family. The principal species is *T. rotundifolia,* better known as *T. speciosa.* This is a very robust grower, sometimes attaining a height of 12 ft. in six months from seed. The flowers are brilliant orange-red about 3 in. across, with the top part of the flower stem inflated. The usual type flowers late in the summer, but an early-flow-

ering strain is now offered. A dwarf strain would make this a plant of much greater value in the garden.

TITI (tee'-tee). A common name for *Cliftonia monophylla,* an evergreen shrub with pinkish-white flowers found in swamps of S. U.S. Better known as Buckwheat-tree, which, see.

TOADFLAX. Common name for *Linaria vulgaris,* a widespread perennial weed with yellow and orange flowers; the familiar "Butter-and-eggs" of roadsides.

TOAD-LILY. Common name for Tricyrtis, a genus of perennial herbs of the Lily Family, with root-stocks, leafy stems, and spotted, somewhat bell-shaped flowers. They are usually grown in pots in the N., but can be used outdoors if given adequate winter protection. They are increased by division.

The species most generally grown are: *T. macropoda,* from China and Japan, with violet flowers spotted purple, borne in clusters on 2- to 3-ft. stems; *T. hirta,* with hairy leaves and white, purple and black spotted blossoms, and *T. flava,* with yellow flowers, not spotted.

TOADS. Ugly though they may appear, these curious creatures are true friends of the gardener—both in disposition and in their habits, which include the devouring of many, many injurious insects, worms, and slugs, both plant pests and annoyers of humans, such as mosquitoes. Also, while they are probably happier if not handled, there is no truth in the old belief that contact with toads causes warts. In short, toads are distinct assets in the garden and should be protected and induced to make their residence there. They are land animals usually burrowing in the earth in the daytime and coming out to feed at night. During the breeding season they seek water, in which the eggs are laid and in which the tailed, swimming young, called tadpoles, live for a few weeks.

See also ANIMALS IN THE GARDEN.

TOBACCO. In gardening, the name of several species of herbaceous annual and perennial plants of the W. hemisphere grown for their attractive, fragrant flowers. They belong to the genus Nicotiana (which see). The species *N. tabacum* supplies the tobacco leaves of commerce but is not grown as an ornamental.

Indian-tobacco is *Lobelia inflata;* Ladies-tobacco is Antennaria; Mountain-tobacco is a catalog name for *Arnica montana.*

TOBACCO PREPARATIONS. These have insecticidal value as repellants and also as contact and stomach poisons. Nicotine is extracted from tobacco stems and refuse which are also used raw, or ground, or in compounds for fumigating greenhouses. Tobacco stems or dust is sometimes used as a mulch indoors and in gardens because of the repellant effect on root aphids.

Containing from 2 to 4 per cent nitrogen, ½ to 1 per cent phosphoric acid and 4 to 10 per cent potash, any form of tobacco waste, but especially if finely ground, has a distinct plant food value in addition to its insecticidal usefulness. The relatively high content of potash makes it especially good on sandy or muck soils that are usually deficient in that element.

See also FUMIGATION; INSECTICIDE; NICOTINE.

TOBIRA. A common name for *Pittosporum tobira,* a Japanese evergreen shrub with whitish fragrant flowers, good for hedges in S. U.S.

TOCOCA (toh-koh'-kah). A genus of S. American shrubby plants, sometimes grown in warm greenhouses for their attractive leaves and flowers. They thrive in a sandy loam with peat or leafmold, and require a moist and shady position. Propagated by single eye cuttings or side shoots, placed in sand and kept in a close atmosphere. *T. platyphylla* is a striking plant with a bristly succulent stem, broad leaves growing to 1 ft. long, and panicles of showy pink or red flowers. *T. imperialis* has very large, handsome, rich dark green leaves with a velvety surface, and the principal veins marked red.

TODAEA (toh'-dee-ah). A genus of ferns found in temperate parts of the S. hemisphere and known as Crape Fern; often placed in the genus Leptopteris. They are semi-transparent in texture, and produced from erect fibrous stems, which in some species are thickened and woody and give the plants the character of tree ferns. All species but *T. barbara* require an atmosphere sufficiently moist to condense on the fronds, and greenhouse conditions. The soil should be chiefly of peat moss and coarse sand.

T. barbara has 2- to 3-ft. fronds, broad, dark and glossy, 2-pinnate, and spreading from short thickened stems. It is a good fern for the living-room, and will withstand a dryer air than the other species.

pellucida has 1½- to 2½-ft. fronds, 2-pinnate, with pointed pinnae 4 to 6 in. long, of delicate texture.

superba (New Zealand Filmy Fern). A splendid miniature tree fern. The trunk, from 6 to 18 in. tall, is crowned by numerous fronds 2 to 4 ft. long, 3-pinnate and plume-like, woolly below.

TOLMIEA (tohl-mee'-ah) *menziesi.* A hardy herb of the Saxifrage Family with rounded toothed leaves and small green and brown flowers in slender racemes; good material for the rock garden. It reproduces by buds which form at the base of the leaf stalks, grow into little plants and send out roots as the old leaves wither. A native of cool forests of the W. Coast, it is known as Youth-on-age.

TOLPIS (tol'-pis). A genus of Composite plants with yellow flowers in heads. Seed of one species, *T. barbata,* an annual to 1 ft. from S. Europe, is sometimes sold under the name of "Golden-yellow-hawkweed." It is occasionally used in the border, where it is easily grown from seed sown where the plants are to stand.

TOMATO. A tropical herb (*Lycopersicon esculentum*) related to the egg-plant, pepper (Capsicum) and potato. It is sometimes grafted on the potato for curiosity's sake; the resulting freak plant, which may produce tubers below ground and tomatoes above, is sometimes called a "potomato."

Tomato varieties offer a wider range of choice and uses than those of most other vegetables. In size the "fruits" vary from the so-called "currant" varieties, weighing less than an ounce, to mammoth meaty sorts weighing over a pound apiece. The "plum," "pear," and "cherry," varieties (so-called because of their shapes) and others somewhat larger are so desirable for individual salads and for preserving that every home garden should have a few plants. In flavor some are highly acid, others almost sweet. Many are exceedingly juicy, so are well adapted to cocktail making; others are meaty and almost seedless, hence desirable for slicing or for canning whole. Four distinct colors are represented—scarlet, purple, yellow and orange—making attractive salad combinations possible. Every home gardener can find among the 20 to 30 varieties carried by leading seedsmen sorts that will suit his preference, meet his needs and add to the interest and enjoyment of his gardening activities.

CULTURAL DIRECTIONS

In its native habitat the tomato is a perennial; in temperate climates it is grown as an annual. But as it requires a longer season than occurs in the North between late spring and early fall frosts, the plants are usually started under glass or in shel-

SUPPORTS FOR TOMATO PLANTS
One way to train tomatoes is to place a strong stake near each of four plants and fasten them together tent-pole-wise at the top. They help support each other and make harvesting easy.

tered beds from 4 to 8 weeks before the earliest date when they can be safely planted outdoors. The seed-bed soil should be light and friable, but not rich, as forced growth is likely to be spindling and weak.

If seed is sown thinly in flats or beds (not more than three to the inch), much stronger plants will result than from thicker seeding. When the seedlings have their second pair of true leaves they should promptly be pricked into other flats 4 by 4 in. apart, or into 3-in. flower pots. Delay leads to crowding, stunting and unsatisfactory plants. It is also better to grow them slowly but steadily at a rather low temperature (50 degs.) than at higher heat because they then suffer less of a

check when set outdoors in less favorable surroundings.

Set the plants in the open after all danger of frost has passed; they should then be stocky, sturdy and dark green. Spindling, tall, yellowish plants are not worth planting—and certainly not worth buying.

Any well-drained garden soil will grow good tomatoes, especially if well supplied with humus. Manures and nitrogenous fertilizers must be used with caution because they tend to develop over-sized plants and but few, small inferior fruits. Ground bone and superphosphate tend to make sturdy plants and sulphate and muriate of potash and wood ashes foster abundant high quality fruit, so they can be used freely.

Where cultivation can be done in two directions the plants may stand as close as 3 by 3 ft., though up to 1 ft. farther apart is better. In home gardens the plants can well be trained on trellises, stakes or other supports for appearance's sake, to save space, and because the fruit supported up in the light and air is better able to resist diseases than if the plants sprawl on the ground. If to be trained to stakes and cultivated in only one direction, plants may be set 24 in. apart or even less.

In home gardens space is often too precious to allow tomato vines to sprawl at will over the ground as in commercial plantations; so supports of many kinds have been devised to keep the plants more upright and compact. They also tend to keep the fruit clean, to prevent premature decay and to facilitate gathering. Wire supports can be bought, but entirely satisfactory ones can be made at home of laths, barrel hoops, etc.

Many home gardeners also prune their vines pinching or cutting out the shoots that arise from the leaf axils, in the belief that they thus obtain larger, finer quality fruit or increased quantities. Such pruning, however, has been repeatedly proved a waste of time because it accomplishes none of these aims.

Even in the North fresh tomatoes may be had until Thanksgiving Day or later by either of the following methods, the second being the better: (1) When frost threatens pull up the plants and hang them, tops downward in a warm place where the air is not too dry. Cut off all the small green fruits for pickling, but leave on the vines all that show any pink or that are whitening. Most of these should ripen. (2) Gather all fruits that are turning pink and lay them singly on deep straw in a cold frame. Ripening may be hastened by keeping the frame covered with sash, or retarded by uncovering it whenever the weather is not cold.

TOMATOES UNDER GLASS With a greenhouse the normal tomato season can be greatly extended. For a late fall crop sow seed in June; for a winter crop, in September; for an early spring crop, in December; and for an early summer crop in February. Only forcing varieties should be so used. The seedlings are handled as already described, except that they should be transplanted from the second flat or the small flower pots to larger sizes once or twice before being set in the greenhouse benches (for the winter crop) or in open beds (for spring, summer or fall use).

In the greenhouse the soil must be supplied with ample quickly available plant food not too rich in nitrogen. Plants may be set as close as 24 in. apart each way. Generally they do best when pruned to single stems, tied to vertical wires or cords fastened above and below. Night temperatures must not be less than 60 degs. F.

Watering must not be overdone, especially in cloudy weather. In sunny weather when the air in the greenhouse is dry the pollination of the flowers (which outdoors is done by bees) may be accomplished by jarring the vines several times daily to scatter the ripened pollen; otherwise they must be hand-pollinated by collecting the pollen in a watch-glass and applying it with a camel's hair brush to the pistils of all open flowers. Winter yields should average about 5 lbs. per plant and those at other seasons somewhat more.

TOMATO ENEMIES

A number of tomato diseases may be controlled to a large extent by using clean seed (see SEED DISINFECTION), burning all crop refuse and thoroughly cleaning the area in the autumn. Certain diseases are best prevented by growing resistant varieties. This is especially true of Fusarium wilt which shows first as a wilting, yellowing and dying of the leaves from the lower part of the plant upward, followed by death of the entire plant.

Two leaf diseases—leaf spot and early blight (caused by the fungus responsible for potato blight) both of which are characterized by dark-brown, circular spots on the leaves—may be controlled by spraying with 3-5-50 bordeaux mixture or by dusting with 20-80 copper-lime dust accompanied by general sanitary precautions. During wet weather the disease organisms may be spread by contact so that all cultivation should be avoided until the plants are dry.

The familiar blossom-end rot, appearing as water-soaked areas that later turn black, on the blossom ends of fruit, is due to unfavorable environmental conditions. Plant in good moisture-retentive soil, cultivate well and give plenty of water. Plants showing the virus disease, mosaic (which may be recognized by yellowing and mottling of the leaves and stunting of the plant), should be burned. Many other diseases of tomatoes may be serious in

TOMATOES ARE A GOOD CHEMICAL GARDENING CROP
Growth and yields like this have been secured in both experimental and commercial greenhouses. But they require real knowledge and skill and adequate equipment.

certain localities but those mentioned here are the most generally distributed.

Cut-worms (which see) are one of the most serious pests of young plants. The potato and spinach aphids, which commonly infest tomato, may be controlled by spraying with nicotine-sulphate and soap. The same spray may be used against the greenhouse white fly (see WHITE FLIES) which may bother outdoor tomatoes as well. Small black jumping beetles (see FLEA BEETLES) eat tiny holes in the leaves of newly set plants. When transplanting dip tops of plants in bordeaux mixture to which is added 5 level tablespoons of lead arsenate pergallon.

Large green worms with a projection or horn on the back (the tomato warm and the related tobacco worm) that feed on the leaves should be picked off or plants can be sprayed (before the fruits set) with lead arsenate. The adult moth is mottled gray-brown with a wing spread of 4 to 5 in. If stems are infested by a striped caterpillar (the common stalk borer) the only course is to destroy the plants and set out new ones. See also under DAHLIA.

Strawberry- or husk-tomato is *Physalis pruinosa*. Tree-tomato is *Cyphomandra betacea*, a S. American shrub.

TOMENTOSE. Covered with a rather dense matting of short, soft, woolly hairs, as on the leaves of mullein. Compare WOOLLY.

TONGUE FERN (*Cyclophorus linqua*). One of a genus of ferns for the greenhouse, having simple, oblong or linear fronds 6 to 18 in. tall, rarely lobed, rather fleshy and hairy, on creeping, scaly rhizomes. It likes peaty soil and coarse sand and does best in shallow pots.

TOOLS, GARDEN. Mechanical devices by which work is lightened, improved or done more expeditiously than is possible by hand alone. In this general category are included not only "hand tools" such as spades and rakes, but also implements or machines which may or may not operate on wheels but which require "power" supplied either by additional man labor, by horse, or by garden tractor.

In amateur gardening the one factor usually at a premium is time. Hence money spent for tools that enable a larger amount of work to be done in a specified time is really an investment in time. From another standpoint one of the greatest satisfactions in amateur gardening is to use the best adapted tool for each type of work; for such tools lessen the labor involved, speed up the work, and thus add to the pleasure of doing it in the best possible manner. A skilled workman may be able to make poor tools do a good job but he would never consider purchasing such, because no one so well as he knows the satisfaction and possibilities of owning and using the best.

GOOD TOOLS PAY. A good tool may cost slightly more than a poor one, but this difference is more than offset by the better work it does and the increased length of time it will last; it is therefore deserving of better care than a cheaper and poorer tool—and under such care it gives even longer and better service. Because a good tool is made of better materials than a poor one it will keep its edge better, give better service and wear out rather than "give out." Its initial cost will almost certainly be less than that of the two or three cheap ones that it will mostly likely outlive.

A poor tool is poor from one or both of two standpoints: first, the low quality of materials (especially the metal) used in its working parts, and, second, the method of its construction. The latter is not so clearly undesirable; the former advertises its own undesirability, as in the case of the "one piece" trowel. This is made of sheet metal pressed into shape to form blade, hand-grip and shank all in one; it is weak and is likely to break under hard usage.

Most other cheap tools with handles (such as hoes and rakes) are made by forcing the metal shank into a hole in the wooden handle, then covering the wood with a metal ferrule to prevent splitting. The frequent result is either that the wood dries and shrinks so that it and the metal pull apart, or the wood breaks where it has been weakened. The ferrule is an attempt to remedy this weakness but, except as noted below, it is not an unqualified success.

To offset the tendency of such a tool to pull apart, some manufacturers flatten and lengthen the metal shank and, after inserting it in the wood, drive a pin through the ferrule, the wood and the shank, thus making it impossible to separate the parts. Such construction makes it cost more than the style first described, but the slight difference in cost is more than offset by the greater durability of the tool.

STRONG CONSTRUCTION. An even better construction, especially in spading forks, spades and shovels, involves the expansion and shaping of the metal shaft to form a hollow cone into which the conically tapered wooden handle is firmly driven and then securely fastened with a pin extending through one or both sides of the metal as well as through the wood. Not only is it impossible to pull the wood and the metal apart but it is almost impossible to break the shank by any ordinary use. Spades and forks for extra heavy work are still further strengthened by having the metal socket lengthened to form a strap extending up the wooden handle; or there may even be two such straps, above and below.

Until they begin to appreciate the time- and labor-saving characteristics of good tools designed for specific purposes most amateur gardeners either buy blindly or restrict themselves to fewer and poorer tools than the nature of their work would warrant. Generally it is not essential or even advisable to spend a large sum of money on the start for a complete assortment. After the few fundamental tools such as digging fork, hoe and rake have been bought, others may be added on a budgeting basis of one or two dollars a month.

CARE OF TOOLS. Because of their relatively high first cost and because keeping them in good condition adds to the satisfaction of their use, tools should always be properly stored in a specific place. Exposure to the weather soon rusts them; so does storing them in a cellar or a basement. Dampness soon destroys the "edge" of cutting tools (and spades and hoes, too) and rusts other parts. Hence the toolshed or other quarters should always be dry (to prevent rusting) and light—to aid in placing and finding them. Every tool should have its individual place.

An excellent way to store tools with long, straight handles such as rakes and hoes is upright in racks with holes bored for the handles in the lower horizontal member. D-handled spades and forks are best hung on hooks screwed into the wall. Others such as lawn mowers, wheelhoes and wheelbarrows should be placed against the wall with their wheels held in place by cleats on the floor and their handles kept upright by means of hooks attached to the wall. Sometimes space can be saved by rigging ropes, with loops to take the handles of such implements, over pulleys attached to overhead beams, so the mower or cultivator can be hoisted up to hang against the wall.

Small tools such as saws, trowels, shears and hand weeders are best stored in well ventilated, book-like cupboards, hung on hooks screwed into both front and back surfaces. This doubles the storage space without requiring much increased depth.

Another time-saving scheme is to paint the wooden part of all hand tools some distinctive, vivid color, as red, orange, or light blue, so that if one is carelessly left lying around the garden it will be conspicuous against the earth or foliage background. Extending this idea, the positions of tools stored on or against a wall may be indicated by outlining them in paint of some contrasting color so that the absence of any item will be noticed at a glance.

Because tools cost money and because care increases their useful "life," it is important to clean every tool promptly after it has been used or, in any event, at the end of the day or the completion or temporary interruption of a job. Soil is easily removed from metal parts while moist by scraping with a flat-ended stick, but after it has dried it is difficult to budge, especially if it contains much clay, and the longer soil is allowed to adhere to a tool the greater will be the development of rust. When all the soil possible has been removed with the stick or an old broom a piece of rough burlap or old carpet should be used to remove any remaining traces. Finally the metal parts should be rubbed with an oily rag to protect them against rust.

At the close of each season all tools should be examined and all machines overhauled; worn-out and broken parts should be replaced and every implement repaired, sharpened, oiled, repainted or otherwise renovated and put in shape as may be necessary. Oiling all bearing parts (especially of lawn mowers when in use, but still more at the season's end) is one of the most important but most commonly neglected of all tool care essentials. Lack of lubrication is one of the chief reasons why machines wear out.

Care of tools also includes maintaining an "edge" on spades, hoes, sickles, scythes, weeders, wheelhoe blades and the like, because sharp blades increase efficiency and

A Good Outfit of Garden Tools

Basket, Picking	Knife, Asparagus	Shovel, D-handle
Cultivator, Norcross	Knife, Budding	Shovel, Long handle
Dibble	Knife, Pruning	Sickle
Dusting machine	Labels, garden, pot and tree	Spade, D-handle
Edger, Grass	Ladder, Step	Spade, Long handle
Flower pots	Lawn mower	Sprayer, atomizer
Fork, digging	Lawn roller	Sprayer, knapsack
Fork, Manure	Lawn sprinklers	Stakes, Bamboo and
Fork, Transplanting	Line, Garden	Wooden
Grafting chisel	Pruners, Hand and Pole	Supports, Plant
Grafting mallet	Rake, Bamboo	Trowels
Grafting wax	Rake, Steel	Tying material
Hoe, Common	Rake, Wooden	Watering-pot
Hoe, Scuffle	Saw, Pruning (swivel style)	Weeders, hand and hoe types
Hoe, Warren	Scythe	Wheelbarrow
Hose with nozzle and reel	Shears, Grass, Hedge,	Wheelhoe, with seed-drill
Hotbed mats	Pruning	attachment

lighten the labor of using them. In ordinary cases a file or a whetstone will serve, but if a tool is allowed to become very dull it will be necessary to use an emery or a carborundum wheel to develop a new edge. See SHARPENING GARDEN TOOLS.

More important still: rust must be fought constantly, not merely because it interferes with and makes work more difficult but because it shortens the life of the tools. Therefore, when the tools are overhauled at the close of the season they should be thoroughly cleaned with kerosene to remove grease, caked oil and dirt. Similarly all nuts and bolts should be soaked in kerosene and then, before being replaced, given a few drops of heavy oil or vaseline so they will work easily. Finally all metal parts should be swabbed with oil (waste oil from the crank case of an automobile will do) before they are put away for the winter.

One convenient way to do this oiling of such tools as spades and rakes is to put clean sand in a long narrow box, saturate it with the oil and work the tools back and forth in it a few times before hanging them up. Otherwise use an oily rag.

NOTES ON BUYING TOOLS. Points of construction are of special importance when purchasing machines for garden work. For instance, the lawn mower made with bronze bushings in the axles, though usually somewhat more costly than one of equal size with ball bearings, is the better to buy because it is more durable, less costly to repair and (after being used for several years) easier to operate.

Another point in choosing a lawn mower is to avoid getting a size too large, which means, unless the person who is to operate it is exceptionally strong, any size above 16-in. for any but the most perfectly made, level lawn. This same point applies to other hand-power machines, especially the garden roller, which see.

It is always advisable to buy tools by personally selecting them at least a month prior to the opening of the season, when stocks in the seed, garden supply and department stores are most complete and when the regular better informed tool department clerks are free to answer questions and give advice. Extra clerks put on during the rush spring season are less reliable and often they know little or nothing about gardening or the construction, workmanship, quality of materials, advantages and (particularly) disadvantages of many tools they offer for sale.

TOOLS TO AVOID. For instance, they may laud a combination rake-and-hoe on the ground that it provides "two tools for the price of one"; whereas the fact is that such combinations are usually made of poorer metal than tools designed for a single purpose; and, more important still, the hoe blade must be carried along idle while the rake is being used and *vice versa,* thus adding to the effort needed to use either tool.

One of the worst "combination tools" is the double-bladed pruning saw toothed on both edges. Not only it is usually too light for cutting large limbs but it is also too heavy and thick for removing small ones; it commonly does poor work with both sets of teeth and the teeth on the edge not being used are very likely to wound the tree badly whenever the saw is used in close quarters, or even when it is being gotten into position for cutting. Incidentally it may be said that one of the best of all general-purpose pruning saws is the "Pacific Coast" style which somewhat resembles a slightly pointed butcher's saw but which has a swivel and thumb nut at each end of the thin, narrow blade. This permits the blade to be turned in any direction so as to cut at any desired angle to the back and in cramped quarters without damaging adjacent branches or the trunk.

Every season new tools, including improvements and modifications of old ones, are advertised but rarely are some of these obtainable in garden stores until two or three years later, because they have to prove their worth and popularity before many of the stores will list them. Hence it is advisable to watch for such advertisements in the better garden magazines, examine the tools at the spring flower shows, consult other gardeners about them and then buy promptly such as promise to lighten work, save time or otherwise enhance the pleasure of gardening.

So far as materials are concerned two classes of hand sprayers are available: those made with brass and those made with galvanized iron tanks. The former cost about 50 per cent more but are well worth the difference because of their naturally longer life. The latter are sometimes quickly ruined by various spray chemicals, especially if the materials are allowed to remain in them for any time. With all, but especially with them, it is imperative that the sprayer tank be thoroughly rinsed and all tubes and nozzles cleaned immediately after every spraying.

One way to lengthen the life of a galvanized iron tank is to pour hot black asphaltum into it after removing the pump, turning it in every direction so as to coat the inside thoroughly, and then turning it upside down to drain off the excess. Then place the tank in the sun for several days to allow the asphaltum to harden. A galvanized iron tank so treated should last about as long as one of brass—ten years at least.

TOOTHACHE-TREE. Common name (based on its medicinal properties) for *Zanthoxylum clava-herculis,* a spiny tree

of the S. Atlantic and Gulf States with small flowers and shining black seeds.

TOOTHWORT. Common name for Dentaria, a genus of small woodland herbs of the Crucifer Family with white tooth-like roots and clustered, white, rose, or lavender flowers. They are used in the rock garden or for colonizing in the wild garden. The two species most commonly seen are: *D. diphylla,* with clustered white flowers, and *D. laciniata,* with white or lavender blossoms.

The name Toothwort is also applied to the genus Lathraea, which includes root-parasitic plants without green leaves, little known horticulturally.

TOP-DRESSING. Manure, compost. fertilizer or other plant-food material placed on the surface of the ground, as opposed to that plowed or spaded under. Any plant food added after growth begins must naturally be applied as a top-dressing —unless dissolved in water. Fertilizer spread between rows in the vegetable garden is sometimes spoken of as "side-dressing." Top-dressing differs from mulching in that a mulch is meant primarily to protect the roots from weather, and remains on the surface; its feeding effect is secondary. A top-dressing is principally for feeding, and may be (indeed, usually is) cultivated into the ground. Top-dressings are also used on potted plants.

See also MULCH.

TOPIARY WORK. This is the training or pruning of plant material into unnatural geometric, or fantastic, shapes. It has been practiced in gardens since the Middle Ages, and is seen at its best in some of the present day English gardens. Very little of it exists in the U. S. in its more elaborate forms and as a part of a real garden plan. (Too often the specimens seen are merely crude, grotesque results of shearing docile quick-growing plants.) This scarcity of representative topiary work is due partly to the fact that it belongs to the most formal type of garden, of which we have comparatively few; and partly to the length of time and the infinite amount of patience it takes to bring a specimen to full beauty. In its simple forms it may consist of clipping and forming the end plants of a hedge into balls or piers or pyramids; or of accenting a clipped hedge at intervals or regular spacing with a round or square finial. This breaks the monotony of a long regular hedge, and serves to ac-

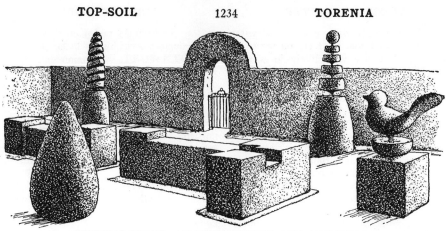

**TOPIARY WORK—AN INTERESTING ART ASSOCIATED
WITH OLD TIME GARDENING**
The shearing of living plants into all manner of odd—sometimes outlandish—forms reflects ingenuity
on the gardener's part, but certainly tolerance and docility on that of the plants. Practiced abroad on
slow-growing subjects like box and yew, it may be tried in American gardens with the friendly
familiar privet.

cent entrances or frame vistas, and is highly desirable when done with discretion.

More advanced specimen topiary pieces in geometrical cubes, balls, pyramids, or combinations of such forms, or in figure pieces like peacocks, chickens, rabbits, squirrels and the like, are interesting accents, but must be used only in tidy, formal gardens and on places where the gardener has time to keep the training and pruning severely in hand.

The best evergreen materials for the work are box (*Buxus suffruticosa*), yew (*Taxus cuspidata, T. brevifolia,* and hybrids), and hemlock (*Tsuga caroliniana*); the best deciduous material is found in the privets (Ligustrum, in variety). Beech (Fagus), hornbeam (Carpinus) and hawthorn (Crataegus) may also be used for large simple forms. English ivy trained over wire supports is also available and very beautiful. Topiary pieces in yew, box and privet are available in a few of the E. nurseries and it is usually wise to buy the already-trained plants, particularly in the case of the more difficult forms.

TOP-SOIL. The upper layer—usually from 6 in. to about 10 in. in depth—of normally fertile, arable, loamy soil found in well cared for gardens or in uncultivated, undisturbed fields, pastures, etc. Its ability to grow plants is due largely to its humus content and the fact that it is aerated and contains the bacteria and other microscopic organisms that give life to a soil, and which are lacking in the subsoil, which see. Sometimes, in suburban com-

munities, avaricious contractors (unless prevented by statutes) will buy or take the right to "skin" the top-soil off large areas of vacant land and sell it to gardeners for the improvement of their properties. This is all right for the latter, but hard on future purchasers of the "skinned" land.

TOP-WORKING. Completely changing over the top of a seedling or other tree that bears poor fruit, by grafting it to one or more desired varieties, usually by the cleft method (see GRAFTING). This operation, usually done to old or at least well-developed trees, is naturally a severe one so it is generally done gradually. That is, perhaps a third of the large branches are grafted one year, another third the second year and the remainder the third year, by which time the initial grafts will have probably begun to make growth. This progressive method parallels a similar practice followed when a large, old, neglected tree is to be subjected to severe pruning.

TORCH-LILY. Common name for Kniphofia, a genus of thick-rooted perennial plants of the Lily Family, also called Poker-plant because of its slender red and yellow spikes.

TORENIA (toh-ree'-ni-ah). A genus comprising annual and perennial herbs of the Figwort Family bearing 2-lipped flowers resembling small gloxinias. Native to tropical Asia and Africa, they are treated as garden annuals in the N., or occasionally grown in the greenhouse. In

Fla., as they spring up readily from self-sown seed, they are used as the pansy is in the North, grown along water-courses but also in dry sandy situations. They succeed best, however, in a partially shaded position and require regular watering. They are propagated from seed or cuttings and plants should not be set outdoors until the ground is warm.

Species of interest are: *T. fournieri*, with violet and blue flowers marked with yellow; *T. flava*, with flowers predominantly yellow marked with red-purple; and *T. asiatica*, with dark bluish-purple flowers 1½ in. long.

TORTOISE BEETLES. The feeding of these turtle-shaped beetles, also called sweet-potato beetles or gold bugs because they are golden, striped, mottled or spotted with black, is confined chiefly to plants of the Morning-glory Family. The larvae have conspicuous horny spines (including two extra long ones at the posterior end) on which they pack all of their dirt and excrement. They eat rounded holes in the leaves or devour them completely. Spray with lead arsenate, 1 oz. to 3 gals. of water.

TORUS. The extremity of the stalk on which the floral organs are borne; the receptacle, which see.

TOUCH-ME-NOT. A common name for species of Impatiens, which see.

TOWNSENDIA (toun-sen'-di-ah). A genus of perennial N. American herbs of the Composite Family, closely resembling asters. The rather large heads have ray flowers varying in color from white to violet and rose-color. They are little known horticulturally, but a few of the species may be grown in the wild garden. *T. exscapa*, known as Easter Daisy in Colorado, is stemless, the 2-in. flower-heads nestling in a bed of very narrow leaves. *T. grandiflora*, to 8 in. tall, has large heads of flowers and linear leaves.

TOYON, or Tollon. Common names for *Heteromeles arbutifolia* (formerly Photinia), a large evergreen shrub or small tree, native in Calif. where it is largely used for ornamental planting, being prized for its profusion of bright red berries. These are in great demand for decorations at Christmas time, for which reason the plant is also known as Christmas-berry. It has shining dark green sharp-toothed leaves and panicles of white flowers. It is extremely susceptible to injury by lacebugs (which see), for which an oil and nicotine spray is recommended.

TRACE ELEMENTS. Certain chemical elements which, investigations have shown, are needed by the plant to carry on its life cycle only in minute amounts. Manganese, boron, copper, and zinc are the chief trace elements. If technical or commercial grades of salts are used to make up the nutrient solutions used in chemical gardening (which see), it may not be necessary to add trace elements. This is also true if the common inorganic fertilizer materials, such as superphosphate, muriate of potash, and so on, are used to make the solution.

See also NUTRIENT SOLUTION.

TRACHELIUM (tra-kee'-li-um). A genus of perennial herbs or small shrubs of the Bellflower Family commonly known as Throatwort, which see.

TRACHELOSPERMUM (tray-kel-oh-spur'-mum). A genus of S. Asiatic evergreen vines with white, fragrant flowers. See STAR-JASMINE.

TRACHYMENE (tray-ki-mee'-nee). A genus of Australasian herbs with delicate blue or white flowers in flattish clusters resembling those of the common wild carrot or Queen Annes lace. They are represented in America by *T. caerulea*, popular for garden and greenhouse culture under the name Blue Lace-flower (which see) and listed in many catalogs under the former generic name, Didiscus.

TRADESCANTIA (trad-es-kan'-ti-ah). A genus of herbs of the Spiderwort Family. They are of various habits, some erect, others trailing; some are grown in the open, others under glass or in hanging baskets. The indoor species are usually grown for their foliage, but several of the hardy species make attractive border plants with white, rose-purple or blue flowers. All are easily grown from seed, division or cuttings.

PRINCIPAL SPECIES

T. fluminensis (Wandering Jew) is a trailing S. American plant, rooting at the joints of the stem, and often seen edging benches in greenhouses as a window-box plant, or in plant boxes in the house. It requires a constant supply of moisture in order to grow luxuriantly. Cuttings of the fleshy stems root easily in water and can then be potted up. Var. *variegata* has yellow and white striped leaves, but this coloration is seen only when the plant grows in full light, the foliage returning to the ordinary green form when shaded.

virginiana (Common Spiderwort). A hardy native plant growing to 3 ft. with long, reed-like leaves, and dark violet-purple flowers, 1 to 2 in. across, produced nearly all summer. Var. *alba,* with white flowers, and var. *coccinea* with red flowers are interesting variations.

pilosa, to 3 ft., is another species native from S. Pa. to Mo. It has lilac-blue flowers.

reflexa, native to the Central and S. States in damp situations, has very narrow grass-like leaves and blue or white flowers on 3-ft. stems.

TRAGOPOGON (trag-oh-poh'-gon). A genus of Old-World biennial or perennial herbs with yellow or purple heads of ray-flowers, commonly known as Goatsbeard, and widely naturalized throughout N. America. *T. pratensis,* a biennial plant growing to 3 ft. with yellow flowers 2¼ in. across, is occasionally cultivated for ornament. *T. porrifolius,* a purple-flowered biennial, is grown as a vegetable for its oyster-flavored root as Salsify, which see.

TRAILING ARBUTUS. Common name for *Epigaea repens,* the Mayflower. See ARBUTUS, TRAILING.

TRAILING-HOLLYHOCK. A common name for *Hisbiscus trionum,* an annual yellow or white-flowered species of Rose-mallow, also called Flower-of-an-hour.

TRAILING QUEEN, or TRAILING FUCHSIA. Common names for *Fuchsia procumbens,* a New Zealand trailing vine with orange and purple flowers.

TRAINING OF PLANTS. The methods and practices of developing plants according to specific aims, either for constructional strength, as in the disposition of framework branches of trees and shrubs; for the developing of symmetrical forms as in the shaping of pot plants; for the arrangement of the stems of vines according to systems that promote flower or fruit production; for the restriction of the development of certain plants to dwarf stature; and for various other objects.

TRAINING TREES

Properly understood and conducted, training is an "educational" rather than a "corrective" process. It endeavors to prevent, or at least reduce, the necessity for pruning. With no group of plants is this objective so important, but at the same time so frequently neglected, as in the growing of shade trees. Though, as a rule, nurserymen cut off the lower branches of such trees, either to facilitate cultivation of the soil around them or to develop branchless trunks up to desired heights, probably not one tree in a hundred is ever afforded further training as to the position, arrangement, direction, length or balance in size of its branches.

The all too common result of such neglect is that when such dead or crowded branches are cut out, the cutting is incorrectly done, leaving stubs through which decay enters the main trunks and thus dooms the abused trees to untimely breakdown. In other cases where two main branches are allowed to develop to practically uniform size in the form of a Y, the result is that when loaded heavily with ice or snow and especially when subjected to the extra strain of high wind, one or both of these branches may crash to the ground, thus leaving a lop-sided tree or merely a stump.

These same remarks apply with less force to fruit trees, at least as grown by well informed commercial and amateur fruit growers. For modern fruit growers demand either 2-year trees that have never been "topped" (that is, had their "leaders" or main stems cut), or 1-year-old unbranched "whips" on which they may develop branches exactly where wanted and suppress all others before they have become woody or even before they have developed from the buds.

The most recently developed and most satisfactory method of training fruit trees is to restrict the number of buds to groups of three at various desired heights and specific distances apart on the whips, to destroy all others and, commencing in the spring of the following season, to select the best placed branch in each group, cutting off all the others with a sharp knife close to the stem.

This plan permits the grower (1) to have the framework (sometimes erroneously called "scaffold") branches located so far apart—a foot or more—that no two will pull directly against each other and thus tend to break down; and (2) to have the branches point in different directions so that when viewed from above they suggest the spokes of a wheel, thus laying the foundation for systematic development

Plate 52.   TRAINED TREES FOR RESTRICTED AREAS

Upper left: The combination of thickly blossomed trees, a trellis and a low wall makes a handsome garden boundary. Upper right: Pear trees trained in simple diagonal cordon style on wires. Center left: A perfect specimen of a six-armed palmette verrier, suitable for apples, pears and plums. Lower left: How trained trees enhance a garden vista. Lower right: Spreading in a single plane, trained trees economize space, benefit from the shelter afforded and yield more and finer fruit.

which can be further promoted by selecting the secondary branches by the same method.

Though these same principles are equally applicable to shade trees, most planters of such ornamentals prefer to plant specimens with at least some branches already developed. In that case choose specimens that have no Y-crotches, in which the main branches are far apart, that have the leader or tip intact, that have no ugly crooks in trunks or branches and, always, those that are of small size because they are easier to train, most certain to grow and least costly to buy.

After planting such trees, cut out cleanly close to the trunk all inferior and badly placed branches and reduce the number of secondary branches. This will produce better results than shortening the branches, which is almost certain to create undesirable crooks and bunches of branches.

On side hills and in narrow quarters fruit trees are sometimes trained in conventionalized fan form by restricting the branches to a narrow area the widest way of the area or at approximate right angles to the slope of the hill. A second advantage of this system is the increased distribution of light and air, which results in fruit of higher color and quality.

A disadvantage of the system is that it demands attention several times each season; for branches which start to develop at right angles to the desired form must be suppressed. Preferably, this should be done while the shoots are green and succulent—during May or early June. While succulent they can be bent over and pulled off with scarcely any effort, whereas if allowed to mature they must be cut. When they are pulled off no new branches are likely to develop at the same points, but when cut watersprouts are likely to appear around the wounds and call for additional later pruning.

To produce and maintain fruit trees in dwarf form requires, first, grafting or budding the desired varieties on dwarfing stocks; second, the annual removal of all roots that develop above the graft (if a root operation) and, third, frequent attention during the growing season to pinching out superfluous shoots and preventing undue extension of those that are desired; for, unless restricted, supposedly dwarf trees will probably become "half" or even "full standard" size.

Dwarf trees are trained in three general forms: namely (1) as so called "standards"; (2) the cordon and (3) the espalier, each open to various modifications. The term "standard" in this case indicates that the specimen stands without support of any kind except the straight unbranched trunk that carries a definite head on its summit. Training may make this head more or less globular, pyramidal, oval, oblong or other form; the style is essentially formal and conducive to that sort of garden design. The cordon, which requires support such as a stake or a wall, is a dwarf tree whose trunk may be erect or oblique and single (with short fruit spurs) or with 2 to several branches all in one vertical plane. An espalier is a dwarf tree trained on a trellis with arms trained in opposite pairs at right angles to the main trunk, but otherwise managed like a cordon. See CORDON; ESPALIER. (See also the illustrations, Plate 52.)

TRAINING VINES

Vines can be satisfactorily trained only when their individual nature is understood and when methods are adopted to meet the specific characteristics of each. They naturally fall into three general groups: (1) those which cling to walls, trees and other supports, by means of root-like organs on their stems (English ivy; trumpet creeper); (2) those which hold fast to supports by means of tendrils (grape, wholly; Virginia creeper, partly); or by modified leaves (clematis, coiling leaf stems; garden pea, tendrils at the ends of the leaves); and (3) those that coil around their supports (wisteria, false-bittersweet or Celastrus).

Training of clinging vine species consists mainly in leading the growing tips in desired directions on masonry walls. Do not let such vines attach themselves to wooden walls or they may wedge themselves beneath or between the clapboards or shingles and pry them off.

Tendril-climbing vines require supports around which their tendrils can twist or to which the hold-fasts on these tendrils can become attached. They rarely give trouble such as clinging or twining vines do.

Coiling or twining vines must also be given supports around which they can twist. They must not be allowed to grow around shrubs, saplings. or tree limbs because they do not "give" and in time will "strangle" and often kill such support growths. They can, however, be grown over dead trees or stumps. Rampant vines like wisteria if trained on verandas or other attached parts of a house may actually pull their supports apart. In general, the training of vines (except grapes) consists mainly in directing the growth where wanted and in reducing the branches to desired numbers.

In grape training the main object is to secure abundant fruit. Though this is generally considered as pruning it is equally a matter of training because the underlying principles are modified to meet the ideas of the grower. Thus there are dozens of systems followed, most of which produce fruit in abundance. See GRAPE.

Training Shrubs

So called "climbing" roses and other shrubs such as weeping forsythia (*F. suspensa*), which are not strictly climbers, may be trained to reach heights of 10 to 15 ft. by restricting the stems to few or only one, to be tied loosely at various points to stakes or arbors or on the front of (*not led through*) trellises. By pinching off the lower shoots these stems will become trunk-like below and very branching above. To cover the lower parts of the trellises, other plants (of the same or of different kinds) may be employed and similarly treated, but with shorter trunks. Even such sturdy shrubs as Japanese flowering quince may be trained on walls in this fashion.

Bush roses may be trained in almost any form desired. One popular form is the so called "standard" or tree-like form. This is accomplished by tying the single stem to a stake and preventing the development of branches below the point decided upon for the "head." The suppression of such branches should occur just as the buds are starting to develop into shoots. Standard-form plants are often created by grafting the desired sort at the top of an erect growing plant of the desired height.

One of the simplest but most pleasing styles of training is that of making stiff-stemmed, erect-growing annuals (zinnia and cosmos) and perennials grown as annuals (dahlia and delphinium) grow tree-like. All that is necessary is to pinch off the growing tip (an inch or less) of the young stem just above a leaf stalk when the plant is only 4 to 6 in. high. Branches will soon develop from the buds in the angles of the remaining leaves and will extend outward and upward in somewhat shrub-like form. After these branches have grown 3 or 4 in. long they also may, if desired, have their tips similarly pinched to increase the number of branches. This will tend to thicken the tops and increase the number of blossoms, though the size of each flower will probably be smaller than on plants not so trained. However, the effect will be more striking because of the abundance of flowers.

One precaution is necessary when this type of training is done: the plants must be set farther apart, because they will need the extra space in which to spread.

Training Pot Plants

This same method, though more carefully and repeatedly employed, is often practiced by florists with pot plants in wide variety. It is most easily done with soft-wooded plants as geranium and fuchsia, but is more exacting as to the amount of attention required to make "exhibition specimens" of chrysanthemums, roses and especially of such shrubs as azaleas, gardenias and camellias.

In training of this character where symmetrical form is the object the trainer must remember, (1) that the stem must be pinched while soft, short and succulent; (2) that each pinch must be just above a leaf stem so as to compel the bud in the angle of the leaf stalk to grow; (3) that he may take advantage of the position of the outermost bud, thus left, to expand or contract the specimen or to fill in gaps between the branches. This is because each new branch tends to avoid somewhat the direction of the branch from which it grows; thus if the outermost bud left on a pinched branch is on the underside the new shoot will tend to grow somewhat downward and outward before ascending, thereby tending to widen the specimen.

Conversely, if the bud is on the upper side the shoot developed from it will incline inward toward the center of the specimen, then upward and more or less parallel with the central axis of the plant, thereby tending to make the plant more compact and erect.

When the outermost bud is on the side of the stem the shoot developed from it will extend on that side, thus tending to fill in any gap between its parent branch and the one nearest to it on the same side.

To have such plants develop most effectively demands considerable experience and skill in the pinching and the disbudding (which see) so as to have the plants develop symmetrically and blossom abundantly and uniformly.

In many cases, especially with exhibition chrysanthemums and bush roses, it is necessary to use wire frames with radiating ribs, circles or other set forms to which to tie the branches in the positions desired. Many conventional styles are available at florist supply stores but similar, simpler or special styles may easily be made at home.

TRANSPIRATION. The process by which excess water is given off by the leaves of a plant. It is accomplished and regulated by the *stomata* or minute openings or pores on the surface of the leaf (which see). These openings are formed or bounded by two sacs or kidney-shaped cells which, with an abundance of water in the leaf, become turgid and distend the pore, permitting moisture to be given off. When the leaf's supply of water is low, they become flaccid and collapse, thus diminishing the opening and checking transpiration. This regulation assists the plant in keeping the correct temperature for the performance of its life functions.

It is estimated that a large sunflower plant can thus give off a quart of water daily, and an average oak tree during its five active months, about 28,000 gallons. From this can readily be imagined the effect of transpiration on the temperature and humidity of forest, garden, park or wherever plants grow.

The greatest transpiration activity takes place during full sunshine; for that reason flowers should not be cut at such times as there is likely to be insufficient water in the stems to prevent flagging.

TRANSPLANTING. The process of removing plants from one place and resetting them in another. When small seedlings are lifted from the rows in a flat or from seed pans, separated and replaced at uniform distances in other pans or flats, the term "pricking out" (which see) is generally used. This first transplanting is done to give them space in which to develop until, a few weeks later, they are either potted or planted in more

permanent quarters. Crowded seedlings quickly become slender or spindly, weak and useless.

For early spring planting outdoors, seedlings can be started in greenhouse benches or hotbeds, pricked out into flats or coldframes and later moved to the garden, or sometimes, as with melons, onions, etc., they are transplanted but once —to the open ground. For later use, seed can be sown thinly in outdoor nursery beds when the weather is favorable and the seedlings later transplanted to their permanent quarters.

Transplanting almost invariably injures some of the delicate feeding rootlets and thereby checks the growth of the plant to some extent. However, it offers various advantages—including that of stimulating the development of a good, compact root system, so the most improved methods should be used.

First, plants to be pricked out or transplanted should be prepared for the operation. With seedlings and small plants this means watering them well several hours before they are to be moved; this makes them plump and tends to prevent the soil from falling from their roots. Second, the soil where they are to be placed should be freshly dug, finely raked and moist (but not wet) so as to help them become established and soon resume normal growth activity. Third, should considerable loss of roots be unavoidable, part of the top (leaves) should be removed to balance such root loss. Fourth, transplanted plants, especially succulent seedlings, should be shaded from the full sun for a few days.

Within limits, the younger the plant the more likely is it to survive the operation and suffer little check. Short, stocky, herbaceous plants transplant better than weak, spindly ("leggy") ones. Those started under glass but gradually inured to outdoor conditions such as lower temperatures and strong sunlight (see HARDENING-OFF) will resist unfavorable weather better than those not so prepared. Further, those that have been pricked out and transplanted once or twice while small, or root-pruned (see ROOT PRUNING), will withstand the shock of final transplanting because the preliminary processes restrict the roots to a smaller area than they would otherwise occupy. Consequently they suffer less root injury when moved.

Always transplant in cloudy, cool and damp weather if possible; or at least wait until the cool of the evening. If the next day proves hot or windy, cover the plants to prevent excessive evaporation.

Firming the soil about the roots of transplanted plants is important because it stimulates the rise of water by capillary action from the deeper sources of supply to within reach of the roots. But as a compacted soil surface evaporates more water than a loose one, the surface soil should be stirred and loosened immediately after the plant is definitely planted. On top of the layer of loose soil so created it is well to spread an additional mulch (which see) of peat moss, compost, buckwheat hulls or other loose material to effect the same result.

Sprinkling newly set plants is never advisable because it wets only the immediate surface. Whenever necessary, watering should be deep and thorough. For best results, form a shallow basin of loose soil around each plant and fill it once or more before mulching the plant. Wait until the water has sunk in and the soil formed a slight crust; then loosen it an inch or so deep before it really bakes.

Plants with tap-roots transplant with difficulty, unless the main vertical root is cut while small and made to send out horizontal side roots. Plants carrying considerable foliage for the size of roots —as lettuce, cabbage, etc. may also prove difficult, unless the amount of leaf surface is reduced by about ⅓.

When a considerable number of plants are to be set out, a hand transplanting machine is a great saver of time and backaches. A well known type makes a hole in well prepared soil, and sets, firms and waters a plant all in one operation whenever the operator thrusts it into the ground. It can be operated about as fast as he can stroll across the garden. To insure even setting the rows should be marked out, and unless the operator is expert, it will be well to indicate the desired spacing for the plants, at least at first.

Potted plants and those grown in transplanting boxes transplant easily because each has its roots compactly surrounded by a ball of earth. This should be well moistened before the plant is set out. Shrubs, woody vines and trees from a nursery are usually transplanted while dormant. Any broken or injured roots should be cut back to sound wood. The holes for them should be dug wide and deep enough to accommodate *all* the roots without having to bend or overlap them. The top-soil and sub-soil from the hole should be placed in separate piles, and in filling the hole use the top-soil first, working it well around the roots with the fingers or a blunt stick. Settle it well by watering or tramping firmly. Then add the sub-soil and firm that well also. Leave a depression around the plant so that rain or water applied in dry spells will soak into the roots and not away from them. After planting, the branches should be pruned to balance any loss of roots and to start the formation of the top of the plant. See PRUNING.

Large trees may be moved in winter with balls of frozen soil if prepared for the operation in advance. This is, however, more a task for an expert tree mover than for the gardener. Similarly it is better to transplant nursery grown trees with compact root system than wild plants with spreading roots that are sure to be injured.

TRANSVAAL DAISY. Common name for *Gerbera* (usually spelled *Gerberia*) *jamesoni,* also called Barberton Daisy. A popular S. African perennial with large, pastel-colored flowers.

TRAPA (tray'-pah). A genus of Asiatic aquatic herbs producing nut-like fruits commonly known as Water-chestnut, which see.

TRAUTVETTERIA (traut-vee-tee'-ri-ah). A genus of tall hardy perennial herbs of the Buttercup Family, occasionally planted in the wild garden. *T. carolinensis* has small white flowers to ½ in. across in clusters and large lobed leaves. It will grow readily if planted in rich soil, and is easily increased by division of the roots in early spring or late fall.

TRAVELERS JOY. Common name for *Clematis vitalba,* a tall climbing vine with fragrant greenish-white flowers Sometimes called Old Mans Beard.

TRAVELERS TREE (*Ravenala madagascariensis*). A tropical plant of remarkable appearance, having a palm-like trunk and large banana-like leaves arranged to form a large fan-shaped head. Small specimens are sometimes seen under glass, and it may be grown outdoors in the warmest parts of the country. In the tropics it grows to 30 ft. high. It received its popular name from the fact that water held in the flower bracts and leaf stalks is likely to be a lucky find for any thirsty traveler that comes upon the tree.

TYPES OF TREES—1
Natural effects call for natural, unhampered forms like those provided by conical evergreens such as the hemlock (A), or by the graceful white birch (B).

TRAVELING FERN (*Woodwardia areolata*). A rank-growing marsh fern with coarse once-pinnate fronds. It resembles the Sensitive Fern but has taller fronds, and spores are borne in parallel rows on the underside of the narrower and taller fertile fronds. Good for covering low acid bogs, but too difficult and too rampant for other locations. It is known also as the Narrow-leaved Chain Fern.

TREE. A tree, in a strict sense, is a woody plant with a single stem or trunk, usually without branches to a height of 10 ft., but crowned at the top with spreading branches. There are numerous exceptions to the latter part of this definition, as in many firs, spruces, the red-cedar, etc., which for much of their life have close-set branches from the ground up. Another type of exception is found in trees of shrubby or declining form, often with a number of weedy stems.

The term "tree form" or standard (which see) is applied to plants, both woody and herbaceous, pruned, grown and trained, or grafted, to form a single stem with a compact and globular, or weeping top.

Trees may be divided into two broad main classes: evergreen and deciduous.

Evergreen trees hold their foliage—which may be either needle-shaped or broad-leaved—throughout the year; though it is usually completely replaced in from 3 or 4 to several years, the young leaves are constantly growing to replace the old ones so the tree is never bare. Deciduous trees shed their foliage in the fall. They are usually broad-leaved, but a few needle-leaved (coniferous) trees belong in this class.

The question of the color and texture of foliage of plant material must be carefully considered in every planting, but in the case of trees the greatest importance to both landscape architect and the home gardener lies in the type or shape of plant in accordance with the composition considered as a whole.

Broadly speaking, both evergreen and deciduous trees fall into two divisions: the columnar and the spreading types. (See illustrations, Plate 17.) In the former, the leading bud of the main stem

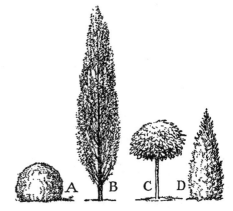

TYPES OF TREES—2
There are formal shapes in trees and, where desired, these can be accentuated by training or shearing. Squatty globe forms (A) are seen in several species of arborvitae, pine (as in the Mugho pine), etc. The Lombardy poplar (B) is one of the few strictly columnar deciduous trees. Along a formal pathway, the round-headed Catalpa bungei (C) gives the effect that used to be gained with sheared bay-trees. The red-cedar (D) is typical of the medium sized conical evergreen so much used in foundation and border plantings.

grows faster than the side shoots, thus producing a slim, upright form, or one broad at the older base but progressively narrowing toward the top. Many evergreens illustrate the second of these; the popular red-cedar and the deciduous Lombardy poplar are of the first type and both are much used for framing vistas and outlining paths or driveways, or as accents. In the spreading type the branches grow more or less equally or broader toward the top than at the base, producing a round-topped tree of some sort. The Norway or red maples, so useful for lawn or shade-trees, show this form to perfection.

Taking the columnar form as a type, variations from it are seen in the gradually widening shapes of the tall, stately tulip-tree and the pin oak among deciduous trees; and in the beautifully symmetrical pyramidal forms of the firs, hemlocks and spruces, so often used for specimens or in background plantings.

The typical example of the spreading form is seen in the familiar white oak of the N. and the live oak of the S.,

TYPES OF TREES—3. EVER VARYING, MANY ARE MAJESTIC AND INSPIRING
A. The American elm, especially beloved of New England, is popular over a wide territory. **B.** The pin oak is one of the cleanest and most orderly of medium-sized shade trees for home grounds or roadsides. **C.** The white oak typifies true dignity, strength and endurance. **D.** The weeping willow combines massive beauty and grace. **E.** The Norway maple, trim, symmetrical, docile, is deservedly one of the most popular street trees.

in both of which the horizontal dimension of the branches is often greater than the height of the tree; this renders them ideal where a wide area of shade is desired.

The spreading type also is subject to infinite variations. One is provided by the American elm, whose lovely "wineglass" shape silhouetted against the sky is such a familiar sight in the New England landscape especially. Other variations are seen in the slender, airy growth of the white birch, so charming when its silvery trunks stand out against a grove of hemlocks or other evergreens.

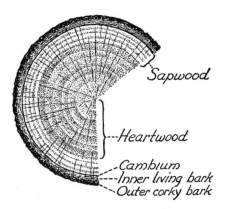

Sapwood

---Heartwood

--Cambium
---Inner living bark
--Outer corky bark

A TREE TRUNK'S STRUCTURE

This diagrammatic cross section shows the approximate proportions of the several layers of tissue. The very thin cambium is the actual growing portion. From it develops, on the inside, the sapwood through which the "lifeblood" of the tree moves up; this gradually becomes the dense inner heartwood. On the outside, the cambium gives rise to the inner living bark through which the sap moves down, and the outer, protective corky bark that is constantly being split and shed by the growth of the tissues within.

Another division of the rounded-topped trees contains those of weeping habit. The weeping willow, a Chinese tree, has been cultivated for years for the beauty of its graceful pendent branches. The long, flowing lines of groups of this tree planted along the edge of a pond or stream make an outstandingly beautiful composition. The weeping form has also been developed in horticultural varieties of well-known trees, such as the beech, mulberry and cherry, but on these the effect inclines to be somewhat artificial and they should be used with restraint, as should all horticultural developments with finely or grotesquely cut, brightly colored, or peculiarly variegated leaves.

Dwarf trees constitute a subdivision of both columnar and spreading classes. They may be natural forms, or horticulturally created varieties or specimens of trees naturally of tall growth; or, as in the retinisporas, they may be juvenile forms showing wide variations in shape and foliage from the mature tree.

Dwarf spruces and firs are extensively used in rock gardens. Some of them are truly pyramidal in growth, but permanently of pygmy form, growing only a few inches in a year. Dwarf retinisporas, because of their slow growth, are used both for foundation plantings and for backgrounds in the perennial border. Dwarf fruit trees result from the grafting of standard, full-size varieties on stocks that exert a dwarfing effect, and subsequent careful continuous pruning and training. They are both ornamental in form and productive of extra fine quality fruit, even though in less quantity than that yielded by longer lived trees which have been kept of standard size.

See also TREES IN THE GARDEN.

TREE-ASTER. A common name for a genus of evergreen shrubs and trees of the Composite Family, also called Daisytree. See OLEARIA.

TREE BLACKBERRY. Common name for *Rubus probabilis,* a sturdy, spiny bush with clustered white flowers and edible fruit, native from Del. to Fla.

TREE-CELANDINE. Common name for *Macleaya cordata,* a tall, large-leaved perennial with plume-like panicles of small petal-less flowers; generally listed in catalogs as Bocconia, which see.

TREE FERN. The name of a large group of plants (far more abundant in prehistoric times than at present) that differ from the low growing ferns in possessing true elongated erect stems which bear fronds at their summits, whereas in the other types the fronds are produced from horizontal creeping stems or much abbreviated surface crowns. Some sorts reach a height of 30 ft. and the Giant Dicksonia (*D. antarctica*) of Victoria, Australia, reaches 60 ft. In cultivation they will seldom grow to more than 10 or 15 ft.

Some require a hothouse, others only a cool greenhouse, but none will endure our variable out-of-doors climate. Species of various genera are included in this group, the best known belonging to Al-

THE CONTRAST IN TREES TELLS A WONDERFUL STORY

What greater privilege and satisfaction could the gardener ask than that of planting a slender sapling, such as the Chinese elm shown at the left, in the knowledge that, given a little care and attention, it will grow on through the ages giving pleasure, protection and comfort to generation after generation, as has the noble old oak shown at the right?

sophila, Blechnum, Cibotium, Cyathea, and Dicksonia (all of which see). They are not as a rule difficult to grow if replanted regularly, as they develop, in a porous soil composed of rough peat, coconut fibre and some sand; and if they are kept shaded. The stems should be moistened constantly except during an annual period of rest. Smaller species are available for limited space and the stems or trunks of all are useful as domiciles for many smaller ferns.

TREE-GUARD. Any device employed to protect an individual tree from possible or probable injury. Guards are most used on street trees, especially young ones, to prevent their being damaged by careless passers-by or by horses that gnaw the bark and cause wounds that soon become infected with disease. The protection can be merely two or more stakes placed around the trunk and to which it is tied (thereby receiving support as well as protection); or a more or less complicated frame of wood or grill-work of wire or metal. It should be firmly fixed in the ground and the tree should be so tied or braced by means of pieces of rope or

wire run through lengths of old hose (so they will not cut into the bark) that it will not rub against any sharp edge. All too often, a well-meant guard does more harm than good because this point is neglected.

A tree-guard may also be a strip of metal affixed around a tree trunk so as to form a downward sloping projection that will prevent cats climbing the tree to get at birds nesting in it. See BIRDS.

TREE-MALLOW. Common name for the genus Lavatera, a group of herbs and shrubs with flowers like single hollyhocks.

TREE-MOVING. When young trees are moved, the work is usually called transplanting (which see). Tree-moving implies trees from the size that 3 or 4 men can handle to those requiring a gang of men, power winches, and special hauling equipment.

Large trees are moved with a ball of earth including as much as possible of the root system. The size of the ball depends on the kind of tree to be moved, evergreens requiring a larger one in proportion to height and caliber, because the leaves continue to throw off moisture which the root system must supply even while the plant is in transit. The most careful method involves following the long main roots to their extremities, uncovering them with a spading fork and, instead of cutting them off, wrapping them in burlap, which is kept moist.

Surface-rooting trees like maple require only a shallow ball, and are more easily moved than those (like fir) which develop a tap-root, which is not infrequently so injured that the tree does not survive. In any case, the ball is cut by skilled workmen and enclosed in burlap or canvas, which is then laced tightly with ropes, usually on a heavy wooden platform or skid. The tree is then dragged on rollers to a low-bodied truck on which it is mounted and tied in a slanting position; or it may be fastened to a specially designed framework on wheels equipped with a lifting device to raise the ball from the ground. A route must, of course, be chosen to avoid narrow bridges and low-hanging wires.

Trees moved with a comparatively small ball must be cut back when planted. It is not good practice to put coarse sods, strawy manure or such things in the bottom of the hole, as these tend to interrupt the upward movement of moisture. A mulch of straw in spring or of manure in winter will protect the roots from weather changes, and applications of fertilizer will

TREES DESERVE GOOD CARE
If it becomes necessary to attach any sort of guy wire to a tree, lead it around (or through) stout wooden blocks that will prevent its cutting into the bark—and perhaps strangling the tree.

furnish the tree food needed. Trees can be moved at any season if enough care is taken, but summer moving is more difficult and expensive. All deciduous trees are most easily handled when dormant and evergreens when they are least active —in early spring or, even better, in August. Both kinds can also be moved with comparative safety in winter, with a frozen ball. But this calls for preparatory root pruning the previous season.

TREE OF HEAVEN. Common name for *Ailanthus altissima,* a coarse quick-growing tree much used for planting in crowded cities.

TREE PEONY. Common name for *Paeonia suffruticosa,* a shrubby peony from China, widely grown throughout the Orient and more sparingly cultivated in this country. It is a low, much-branched shrub, bearing large flowers in shades of purplish-red, rose and white. Var. *humei* has whitish, semi-double flowers with dark centers and var. *papaveracea* has poppy-like blossoms with dark-blotched, satiny petals. Propagation is done by grafting the improved (often named) sorts on non-blooming tubers of herbaceous peonies. The Tree Peony is often listed in catalogs as *P. moutan.*

TREE-POPPY. A common name for *Dendromecon rigida,* a yellow-flowered Calif. evergreen shrub, also called Bush-poppy, which see.

TREES IN THE GARDEN. Because of the close intimacy that results when trees are used in the garden, the kinds to be planted, as well as their placing, should be decided on with care and with special reference to qualities which are of less importance in the case of trees composing the general landscape. Litter—such as large leaves, coarse leaf-stems, burs or seed pods, etc.—is most undesirable at any season of the year, hence those kinds which scatter it in any form are to be avoided. Similarly, forms that have any strong and decided odor, especially if it tends to be unpleasant, should be ruled out. Trees of neat habit and form are more appropriate to small gardens than the majestic forest type, and should usually be chosen.

Considerations of soil make it impossible sometimes to use trees otherwise most desirable. But from the list of small, highly ornamental trees, which comprises such species as the flowering dogwood, redbud, yellowwood, the flowering crab-apples, the hawthorns, varnish-tree, sour-wood, the European linden and the katsura tree of Japan, it is possible to choose for any conditions. Of these the linden and katsura tree are the largest, reaching heights of 75 and 50 ft. respectively when mature. The others range from little more than large shrubs of 15 ft. to charming small trees of about 30 ft.

The same considerations of trim appearance are equally important in the case of evergreens. Here it is also desirable to avoid those showing definite color peculiarities or abnormalities, even though they may be interesting in themselves. Their emphatic note often overreaches in a composition and drowns out other interests.

The functions of trees in the garden are, of course, those of trees anywhere—with certain of them intensified by the space limitations. The providing of shade is a most important service—but it can be overdone, to the detriment of lawn, flowers, the dwelling and the comfort of the family. Trees of course are background and frame material; the rustling of their leaves is a pleasing reaction on a sense not ordinarily appealed to in a garden. Flowering trees can delight with both their color and their fragrance; and fruit in season is a further boon. Most certainly plan for trees in the garden. (See illustrations, Plate 53.) See also TREE.

TREE-SPIREA (spy-ree'-ah). Common name for *Sorbaria arborea,* a deciduous Asiatic shrub with panicles of little white flowers. Also called False-spirea, which see.

TREE SURGERY. A few years ago this meant chiefly the cleaning out and filling of cavities and the strengthening of old trees with chains or cables to prevent branches splitting off. Nowadays the attitude seems to be that a hundred pounds of tree food is worth more than a hundred hours of cavity work. Up-to-date tree surgeons (or, better, tree experts) spend more time keeping trees in good health by proper attention to small wounds and pruning cuts, by fertilizing and overcoming drought conditions and by spraying for the control of insect pests and plant diseases, and less time than formerly in making handsome, expensive fillings in trees which may die anyway in a short time and which might better be replaced by younger healthy trees.

Failure to properly treat fresh wounds causes much needless expense in later years. Fungi, gaining entrance through neglected wounds and spreading, cause extensive decay inside the tree. Practically all cavities would therefore be prevented if the initial injury were sterilized and the wounded area protected so that healing callus tissues could grow over it. *All* pruning wounds should be treated, notwithstanding the former (and still widely accepted) theory that it is unnecessary to paint scars less than a half inch in diameter. For small cuts a coat of shellac or grafting-wax may be sufficient. The ideal dressing for large wounds is yet to be discovered, but there are many fairly satisfactory proprietary tree paints on the market, most of them with a coal-tar or creosote base. A bordeaux paint, made fresh as needed by stirring dry bordeaux mixture into raw linseed oil to make a thick paste, makes a very good dressing with fungicidal properties.

All broken branch stubs should be removed and all pruning cuts should be made smooth and flush with the surface of the supporting trunk. In removing large limbs three cuts should be made (see illustration, PRUNING) to prevent the

A TREE'S DEFENSE AGAINST ABUSE
This plank, thoughtlessly wedged against the tree to make a seat, gradually wore a deep wound in the trunk which the tree sought to heal by growing new bark out over the obstruction. Recognize trees as living things and you can save them much unnecessary injury.

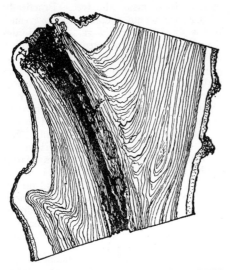

HOW DECAY ENTERS THROUGH A STUB
When a branch is not cut off flush with the trunk, bark cannot grow over the surface and decay organisms enter and grow down into the heartwood. Below at left is the healed over wound of a proper pruning job.

tearing of the bark when the limb falls. The surface of the cut should be left smooth and the cut (or any other wound in a tree trunk) should be somewhat pointed at top and bottom to encourage callus formation. All dressed surfaces should be watched for tendencies to blister, crack or check, and repaired annually.

Cavity work involves cutting out decayed wood. With heartwood decay it

is usually impossible to tell when all the infected wood has been removed; and often, if all of the decayed matter were removed, the tree would be so weakened as to be a menace. Decay of the sapwood, on the other hand, can usually be taken care of efficiently. Excavate discolored and water-soaked wood until the sound portion is reached; smooth the surface of the cavity and so shape it that water cannot remain in any hollow; make the final cutting along the edge of the bark and sapwood with a sharp knife; cover the cambium immediately with a coat of shellac; then paint the remainder of the cavity with a good wound dressing.

It is not necessary to fill the cavity. The only reasons for so doing are to give improved appearance and to provide a foundation surface for the callus growth. Contrary to popular belief, filling a cavity does not increase the strength of the tree. Bolts and cables are used to brace cavities and to keep crotches from splitting in high winds or under pressure of ice and snow. It should be remembered that large scars will always be conspicuous, that the tree may never entirely heal, and that, unless the tree is particularly valuable sentimentally or otherwise, the cost of extensive cavity work might better be spent in replacing the tree with a sound specimen.

Ordinarily the home owner will find it more satisfactory to employ an experienced tree surgeon than to attempt a major operation himself. But before signing a con-

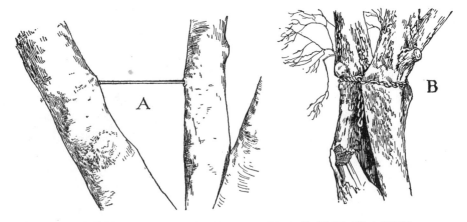

RIGHT AND WRONG WAYS OF BRACING A CROTCH IN A TREE
Never attempt to strengthen a tree or prevent it splitting by binding a metal strap or chain around it, as at (B); as the tree grows it will gradually strangle itself. The correct way is to drill in a straight line through both limbs and connect them with a steel rod threaded and equipped with washers and bolts at each end. Or two short bolts connected by wire or chain can be used.

tract for the work he should insist on many if not all of the following provisions being agreed upon: 1. No climbing spurs shall be used on any part of the tree. 2. The shoes worn by workmen shall have soft soles. 3. After all diseased, rotten, discolored or insect-eaten wood has been removed the cavity shall be inspected by the owner or his agent before it is dressed and filled. 4. Ordinary commercial shellac or other efficient covering shall be applied to cut edges of sapwood, bark and cambium within 5 minutes after final trimming cuts have been made. 5. All cut surfaces shall be painted with shellac or creosote, followed by thick coal-tar, asphalt or other equally permanent covering. 6. The contractor shall repair free of expense any defects in the work developing within 2 years.

Tree owners should regard with suspicion all persons who claim that tree work is a secret art, and no unknown self-styled "tree doctor" should be allowed under any circumstances to bore holes in trees for the injection of some reputed cure-all. Trees oftentimes add thousands of dollars to the value of the home properties and the small amount of money needed to have them inspected and taken care of—about twice yearly—should be thought of as legitimate, well-warranted insurance.

TREE-TOMATO. Common name for *Cyphomandra betacea*, a S. American shrub with fragrant pinkish flowers sometimes grown in N. greenhouses or outdoors in warm sections for its egg-shaped, mildly acid fruits.

TREFOIL. A word meaning threefold, applied to various plants having leaves divided into three leaflets. Correctly it is a common name for species of Lotus (*not* the water plant of Egypt), known as Birdsfoot Trefoil (*L. corniculatus*); but it is loosely applied to other leguminous clover-like plants. Tick-trefoil is the common name for Desmodium, which see. See also TRIFOLIUM.

TRELLIS WORK. This is any open structure of wood erected usually for the support of climbing plants, though sometimes used alone as a screen. The simplest form is composed of light strips nailed vertically and horizontally to a framework of heavier wood, with the spaces between the parallel laths about equal to the strips themselves. This forms an open mesh resembling a very open weav-

ing. From this simple basic effect, more elaborate designs develop the mesh into oblique or diamond patterns, or into oval or circular forms sometimes centering in diamond pattern panels. Trellis of this highly ornamental type is obviously intended to be kept free of vines or other covering growth; otherwise it represents a lot of unnecessary, wasted effort and expense.

The gardens of France carried such ornamental patterns to their finest development. Their *treillage* became something that was in itself superb; and their *treillageurs* or trellis makers were craftsmen as skilled as fine cabinet makers. Naturally this sort of thing is appropriate only to the most ornate, stately and elegant gardens; it is not to be considered as a model for the trellis work which the average American garden may need today. On the contrary, there is almost nothing that can be introduced into the average garden which will clash as hopelessly with every other element in its composition as even a very small amount of such highly developed trellis construction.

It is always well to keep the color of trellis work subdued rather than striking. If rightly designed and colored, its open character merges it with the garden's greens and shadows until its presence is just the unobtrusive accompaniment and aid to vegetation that is desirable. (See illustrations, Plates 3, 32, 44 and 46.)

TRENCHING. A method of digging or spading soil to greater depth than ordinary digging reaches. It thereby creates an increased volume of loose, aerated earth for plant roots to spread through, and an increased supply of plant food and moisture. Its advantages amply justify the extra labor involved, especially in the small home garden where maximum plant growth and products are sought from a limited area. The essential feature of trenching is that it works over the soil 2 "spits" deep, that is, twice the depth of the spade blade. There are 3 types or variations of the operation.

SUBSTITUTE TRENCHING. In this, the simplest and least effective, the surface spit (spade-depth) is dug in the usual way (see SPADES AND SPADING) each spadeful being merely inverted and broken up. But, in addition, the sub-soil is loosened by frequently thrusting the spade (or spading fork) straight down and as deep as pos-

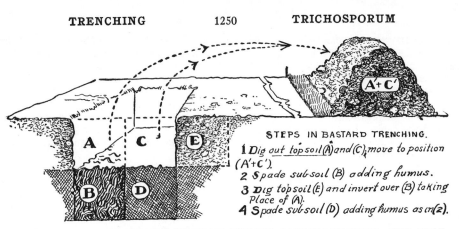

STEPS IN BASTARD TRENCHING.

1 *Dig out top soil (A) and (C), move to position (A'+C').*

2 *Spade sub-soil (B) adding humus.*

3 *Dig top soil (E) and invert over (B) taking Place of (A).*

4 *Spade sub-soil (D) adding humus as in (2).*

TRENCHING IS ONE OF THE WAYS TO INSURE GARDEN SUCCESS—NOT EASY TO DO, BUT HIGHLY EFFECTIVE

The operation shown here, called bastard trenching, is designed to deepen by 100 per cent the fertile topsoil from which most plants derive their nourishment. It is a necessary preparation for true trenching shown in the next illustration. Study the legend carefully and in connection with the text.

sible. Done every few inches, this opens up the sub-soil, improves its drainage and also increases its water absorbing capacity.

BASTARD TRENCHING. This is the next stage in thorough soil preparation. The steps are as follows: (1) Dig out the soil across the end of the bed or border, two spits wide and one spit deep and move it in a wheelbarrow to the farther end of the area, piling it along the edge, but not on the bed. (2) Dig a trench 1 spit wide and deep in the bottom of the double trench just made, inverting the soil and mixing with it a generous quantity of rotted manure or other humus. (3) Dig the next adjoining spit of surface soil and use it to fill in the first trench covering the soil just enriched as directed in (2). (4) Dig the lower spit of this trench, moving it to the left, inverting it, and working in humus as was done in (2). (5) Repeat this sequence of operations until the whole area has been dug over. At the far end of the bed, the trench left when the whole area has been dug over is then filled with the soil previously piled there, mixing manure in the lower half of the trench and using the rest of the soil on top.

This method of trenching is especially effective in deepening and enriching shallow, unproductive soils. It should be done annually for at least 2 years in such a soil before the type of trenching next described is attempted.

TRUE TRENCHING. This is advisable only where the soil is already deep, either naturally or as a result of good management (including bastard trenching). (1) Start as in bastard trenching but dig a trench 1 spit wide and 2 spits deep, taking the earth as before to the other end of the bed and piling it there. (2) Dig the next parallel spit 1 spit deep, invert and throw it in the bottom of the trench, mixing manure or humus with it. (3) Dig the lower half of this spit, invert it, and throw it on top of the soil enriched as told in (2) thus filling the trench 1 spit wide to the top. Repeat this sequence the length of the bed and at the far end fill in the final trench with the soil previously placed there. Note that in true trenching the lower layer or spit of soil is brought to the top, whereas in bastard trenching it is broken up, inverted and enriched, but retains its lower position.

TRICHOLAENA (trik-oh-lee′-nah). A genus of grasses, mostly perennials, grown for forage and ornament and known as Natal Grass, which see.

TRICHOMANES (tri-kom′-ah-neez). A genus of delicate and diminutive ferns in the Filmy Fern Family (which see), known as Irish Fern or Killarney Fern. Requiring constant moisture, they are best used in the terrarium. One species, native to damp parts of the S. States and northward to Ky., is known as *T. radicans* or *T. boschianum.* It has 4- to 10-in. fronds, finely cut, from threadlike rooting stems. In growing it use very little earth and provide sandstone for the roots to fasten upon.

TRICHOSPORUM (tri-kos′-poh-rum). Shrubby climbing plants from the tropics, belonging to the Gesneria Family. In cultivation they are usually grown in pans or baskets and hung from the roof of a warm greenhouse. They can also be grown as pyramids, by training them to moss-covered blocks of wood. A mixture of osmundine, sphagnum moss and broken charcoal suits them well. When growing freely they appreciate liquid manure now and again. They have attractive foliage and showy flowers. Propagated by cuttings.

Principal Trichosporum Species

T. lobbianum, perhaps the most commonly grown, has ovate leaves and scarlet flowers with yellow throats emerging from large bell-shaped purple calyxes.

pulchrum has broadly ovate toothed leaves and scarlet flowers about three times as long as the greenish calyx.

cordifolium has heart-shaped leaves and deep red flowers striped black.

fulgens has slender oval pointed leaves and long pointed bright crimson flowers.

tricolor has small oval leaves and flowers of deep red with orange and black markings.

TRICHOSTEMA (trik-oh-stee'-mah). A genus of native herbs called Bluecurls.

TRICYRTIS (try-sir'-tis). A genus of half-hardy Asiatic plants of the Lily Family, whose purple-spotted flowers give it the name of Toad-lily, which see.

TRIENTALIS (try-en-tay'-lis). A delicate woodland plant called Star-flower, which see.

TRIFOLIATE ORANGE. Common name for *Poncirus trifoliata,* a semi-hardy citrus species used as a stock for grafting.

TRIFOLIUM (try-foh'-li-um). A genus of annual or perennial herbs of the Pea Family commonly known as Clover (which see). They have divided leaves, consisting of 3 leaflets, and very small white, red, purple, or yellow flowers pea-like in form but borne in dense, soft, rounded heads. A few species are grown for ornament; others are important forage, cover-crop, green-manure, or lawn plants. They are grown from seed sown broadcast in very early spring, sometimes before the frost is out of the ground.

T. repens (White Clover), a creeping perennial with small round white heads, is often included in lawn-seed mixtures with the idea that the plants will start quickly, shade the ground and later die out as the more permanent grasses spread. *T. incarnatum* (Crimson Clover), to 3 ft. with tall, deep crimson spikes, is one of the most ornamental species; it and the lower growing *T. pratense* (Red Clover) and *T. hybridum* (Alsike Clover) are some of the more important kinds grown for forage and soil-improvement purposes.

Other garden species of clover include *T. alpestre,* about 10 in. tall, with purple flowers, and *T. rubens,* with purplish-red flowers, usually in paired heads. Yellow and yellow-white forms include *T. agrarium, T. alexandrinum* (Egyptian Clover), and *T. filiforme.*

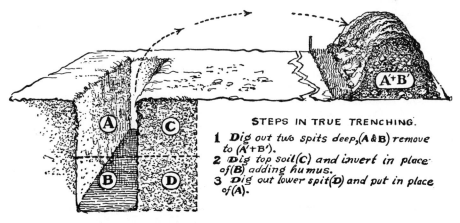

STEPS IN TRUE TRENCHING.

1 *Dig out two spits deep, (A & B) remove to (A'+B').*

2 *Dig top soil (C) and invert in place of (B) adding humus.*

3 *Dig out lower spit (D) and put in place of (A).*

TRUE TRENCHING—A METHOD OF BUILDING A LONG-TIME CONGENIAL HOME FOR DEEP-ROOTING PLANTS

Thoroughly done it provides abundant food and moisture to a depth of two feet or more, insuring maximum growth of roses, shrubs, vines, large perennials, etc. It should, however, be preceded by bastard trenching, as shown in the other illustration and explained in the text.

TRILISA (tril'-i-sah) *odoratissima.* A fibrous-rooted perennial of the S. Atlantic States with foliage sweet-scented when bruised. See CAROLINA-VANILLA.

TRILLIUM (tril'-i-um). A genus of hardy perennial herbs of the Lily Family, having short, thick rootstocks, leaves in threes, and three-parted flowers that may be white, pinkish, violet, or greenish. (See illustration, Plate 50.) They are beautiful woodland plants, growing naturally in semi-shade in moist soil, rich in humus; they are easily transferred to the wild garden, and some species grow well in the border, even in city gardens. The best time to transplant trilliums from the woods is midsummer after the foliage has ripened, but they can be moved successfully even when in full bloom, and also grown from seeds sown as soon as ripe.

A rust that attacks trillium has a grass (Brachyelytrum) as its apparent alternate host; see RUSTS. Crown rot, which see, is also known on this host.

T. grandiflorum, to 1½ ft., with white flowers changing to rose-pink, is one of the handsomest species, responding readily to cultivation and increasing rapidly in the wild garden or shady border. The flowers are scentless.

erectum (Wake-robin), to 1 ft., has flowers purplish-red with a disagreeable odor. It is most effective in groups in the wild garden.

ovatum, to 1½ ft., has fragrant white flowers changing to rose-pink. Similar to *T. grandiflorum,* it is less easily grown and is more suitable for the wild garden than the border.

undulatum (Painted Trillium), to 2 ft., has a white flower veined with purple at the base of the petals and followed by a brilliant red berry, most attractive in the summer.

cernuum (Nodding Trillium), to 1½ ft., has a small white drooping flower.

sessile, to 1 ft., has a purplish or greenish erect flower, set without a stem in the midst of three mottled leaves. Var. *californicum* has purple, rose or white flowers to 4 in. across and spotted leaves; var. *rubrum* has red-purple flowers.

Other less common species are: *T. nivale,* to 6 in., with erect or drooping white flowers to 1 in.; *T. stylosum,* to 1½ ft., with rose or pink flowers to 2½ in. on drooping 2-in. stems; *T. recurvatum,* to 1½ ft., with erect brown-purple blossoms;

T. petiolatum, to 6 in., whose purple stemless flowers to 2 in. scarcely show above the forest floor; *T. rivale,* to 8 in., with erect white purple-marked flowers, and *T. pusillum,* to 8 in., with erect pink flowers about 1 in. across.

TRIOSTEUM (try-os'-tee-um). A weedy, perennial herb known as Horsegentian (which see), or Feverwort.

TRIPLET-LILY. A common name for *Brodieaea laxa* (which see), a sturdy white- or purple-flowered herb, also known as Ithuriels spear.

TRISTANIA (tris-tay'-ni-ah). Trees and shrubs of Australia, belonging to the Myrtle Family, sometimes grown in greenhouse collections, and hardy in the warmest parts of the U. S. *T. conferta* (Brisbane-box), the principal species, is a handsome evergreen tree to 150 ft., very valuable in hot dry regions, whose difficult conditions it can well withstand. The conditions it can well withstand. The leaves, which grow to 6 in. long, are crowded at the ends of the branches. The small fringed white and spotted flowers are borne in clusters.

TRITOMA (try-toh'-mah). Former name of the genus Kniphofia, which see.

TRITONIA (try-toh'-ni-ah). A genus of half-hardy S. African bulbous plants of the Iris Family that produce slender spikes of bright red, orange, or yellow flowers in summer. They are commonly listed in catalogs by their former botanical name, Montbretia (which see). They are also sometimes called Blazing Star, which name is, however, more often associated with either Liatris, Mentzelia or Chamaelirium.

TROLLIUS (trol'-i-us). A genus of perennial herbs with lobed or cut leaves and white, orange or yellow flowers resembling large double buttercups. Members of the Buttercup Family and called Globe-flower, they grow naturally in swampy situations, but adapt themselves well to garden conditions, if planted where the soil is not too dry. They may be placed also on the edge of a bog garden or near a pool. They are increased by seed or by division.

Species

T. europaeus, to 15 in., has large rounded, lemon-yellow flowers. It blooms from May to July and is attractive in the border.

ledebouri, a larger species from Siberia, has more open, clear yellow flowers.

Plate 53.   TREES—THE IDEAL BACKGROUND

Top: Enclosing trees make the garden a world within itself; their foliage provides an admirable foil for blossoming shrubs. Bottom: The spreading branches of trees on the edge of the lawn cast areas of restful shade in delightful contrast to the patches of sunlight that play on the velvety grass.

caucasicus is a still taller plant from W. Asia, bearing golden globe-shaped flowers on 3-ft. stalks.

Many named forms listed in catalogs are apparently varieties or hybrids of the above species. *T. laxus,* a native of swampy meadows in the N. E. States, is sometimes grown in rock gardens.

TROPAEOLUM (troh-pee'-oh-lum). A genus of tender S. American dwarf or climbing herbs with showy flowers, popularly known as Nasturtium (which see). They have succulent stems, shield-shaped, lobed, or finely cut leaves and usually orange, red or yellow spurred flowers, often with fringed lower petals and in both single and double forms. Many of the species are perennials in mild climates, but all are treated as annuals in the N. See NASTURTIUM for culture.

SPECIES

T. majus (Garden Nasturtium) is a somewhat succulent annual vine with large blossoms, which in the species are orange or yellow, but which in the many horticultural varieties show a wide range of colors from pale straw to dark reddish-purple. The rounded, ribbed green seed pods have a peppery flavor and are sometimes pickled while young.

minus, a dwarf form with flowers 1½ in. across.

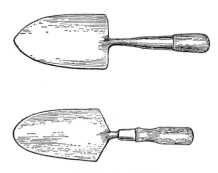

GARDEN TROWELS

Some gardeners prefer the modern, all-metal, non-rusting type. Of these two, the upper tool, with the solid wooden handle driven into a socket, is much stronger than the ordinary ferrule style shown below.

peregrinum (Canary-bird-flower), a graceful annual vine with dainty yellow blossoms and small lobed leaves.

speciosum, a slender, perennial vine with small, attractive scarlet flowers and finely divided foliage. It is hardy in the S. and W. For summer bloom in the N. the small tuberous roots may be planted out after danger of frost is over.

TROUT-LILY. One of the common names for species of Erythronium, which see.

TROWEL. A small tool consisting of handle and blade of metal or metal and wood for use in one hand. The blade resembles a curved spade or scoop, many styles and sizes being carried by garden supply stores, each adapted for some more or less specific purpose in the planting or transplanting of bulbs, plants, cuttings, and so on.

The best style is that made of one piece of steel with a cone-shaped socket into which a wooden handle is driven and firmly held by a riveted pin extending through both. It usually costs more than the type made with a ferrule, the "one piece" pressed metal style or any of the double-ended combinations of trowel and weeder, etc. But a strong, well-shaped, well-balanced trowel is a tool of many uses and long service; it is worth paying a good price for and deserves good care.

TRUCK GARDENING. A term for vegetable growing in favored regions on a large or field scale, the produce being shipped in wholesale quantities by rail or boat to distant markets. Sales are made either to "buyers" at points of production or through commission merchants in the cities. The most notable trucking regions are the seaboard States from Virginia to Texas. Important areas are also found in California, Colorado, Arizona, New Mexico, Cuba, Puerto Rico, Mexico and the States of the lower Mississippi Valley. Compare KITCHEN GARDEN and MARKET GARDEN.

TRUMPET-BUSH. Common name for *Tecoma garrocha,* a tender shrub with fragrant yellow or pink, scarlet-tubed flowers in panicles or racemes.

TRUMPET-CREEPER. Common name for Campsis, a genus of ornamental deciduous shrubs, usually grown as climbers, but adapted also for covering banks and rambling over rocky places. They prefer rich soil in a sunny situation and as climbers show to best advantage on posts and old tree trunks. If allowed on wooden buildings they are likely to do damage by loosening shingles. To keep these plants in good form the long lateral shoots should be cut back to about two nodes before growth begins. Propagated by seeds, cuttings, of both green and mature wood, root-cuttings, and layers.

Two species are known, one found from Pa. southward, the other in China. The native Trumpet-vine (*C. radicans*) is the hardiest and can be grown into New England. It climbs to 30 ft. or more by means of stem rootlets and bears orange-red tubular flowers in terminal clusters in late summer. (See illustration, Plate 58.) It spreads rapidly and may become a troublesome weed if not controlled. Var. *speciosa* is more of a bush than a climber.

C. chinensis is not such a high climber as *radicans* and produces fewer aërial roots, but has larger and more brilliant flowers. Not hardy N. *C. hybrida,* a hybrid from the two species, is intermediate in hardiness and habit, with flowers almost as large and showy as those of the Chinese parent.

TRUMPET-FLOWER. A common name for *Bignonia capreolata, Solandra grandiflora* and (in Fla.) *Thevetia nereifolia.* East Indian Trumpet-flower is *Oroxylon indicum.*

TRUMPET HONEYSUCKLE. Common name for *Lonicera sempervirens,* a climbing shrub with scarlet, yellow-tubed flowers and red fruits. The name is also sometimes applied to *Campsis radicans.*

TRUMPET-VINE. A common name for *Campsis radicans,* also called TRUMPET-CREEPER, which see.

TSUGA (tseu'-gah). An important genus of N. American and Asiatic evergreen, coniferous trees of the Pine Family, with graceful drooping branches clothed with short usually flattened needles, giving a softer effect than that of the firs and spruces. They are extensively planted for groves, windbreaks and hedges as well as occasionally for specimens. See HEMLOCK.

TSUSIMA HOLLY FERN (*Polystichum tensemense*). A slender Japanese Shield Fern with dark green fronds, suitable for the cool greenhouse, and preferring a soil containing clay.

TUBER. A short, swollen, underground stem gorged with reserve food. Being really a kind of stem, a true tuber bears buds (called "eyes") which are small and covered with tiny scales. Because of these buds and its large content of stored food, a tuber is able to give rise to a new plant and support it until its own feeding roots develop. A perfect example of a true tuber

is an "Irish" potato. Horticulturists speak of "root-tubers," "stem-tubers" and "crown-tubers," but only the stem type truly merits the name.

TUBER FERN (*Nephrolepis cordifolia*). An excellent greenhouse fern, with fronds 1 to 2½ ft. tall, rather like the Boston Fern, to which it is closely related, but with more erect and wiry fronds and blunter, darker pinnae. The small tubers at the base of the fronds give rise to new plants. Grows best in wide, shallow pots, but is splendid in baskets, in a compost composed chiefly of peat moss, and kept moist.

TUBEROSE. The common name for *Polianthes tuberosa,* a Mexican herb that forms a fleshy, bulb-like rootstock or tuber (hence the name). The top part of this stock is covered with the broadened bases of the old leaves. From its short, rosette-like growth of spear-shaped grass-like foliage arises a solitary flower stalk which bears in summer and autumn many waxy-white, funnel-shaped, usually double flowers, whose chief claim to fame is an intensely sweetish odor.

Tuberoses are one of the few so-called bulbous stocks that are produced commercially almost exclusively in this country. For a great many years a small section in E. North Carolina has been the chief source of supply, not only for this country but for Europe, where many are sent annually.

In gardens bulbs should be planted in light soil, about 1 in. deep, after danger from frost is over. In fall they can be dug before frost and stored in a dry, warm place. Ordinarily, however, they are difficult to maintain in a flowering condition from year to year; annual replacement is therefore recommended. The bulb that has flowered is often worthless the next season and the many small bulbs that it produced must be grown on for another year under favorable conditions in order to attain flowering size. For the gardener this procedure is hardly justified in view of the low cost of new bulbs. Where a temperature of up to 80 deg. can be maintained flowers can he had in spring from forced bulbs planted in pots in January. Or, if they can be kept cool so they will not start into growth, a few can be held for summer planting (in pots) and forced for early winter flowers.

There are several varieties, the most popular being the double form called Dwarf

Pearl Excelsior; Mexican Single is freer flowering. There are also several varieties with more or less variegated foliage.

TULIP. This, the genus Tulipa, is probably the most popular of the bulbous spring flowers of the N. temperate zone. It is a group of true bulbs of the Lily Family, developing several long, broad pointed leaves and a single scape, bearing, usually, one erect cup-shaped or bell-shaped flower with 6 so called "petals" (actually both petals and sepals). (See illustrations, Plates 5, 6 and 54.) The flowers, of satiny texture, occur in a wide range of colors, pure, broken and combined; they appear with the leaves in spring from bulbs planted in the fall.

TULIPS IN THE GARDEN

Bulbs can be planted as soon as they are available from dealers, which is about Sept. 1; or they may be set out any time thereafter until the ground actually freezes. The size of the bulb has a definite bearing on the size of the flower that will be produced. With most varieties, bulbs measuring 1½ in. in diameter will make the best showing the first year.

Prepare the soil thoroughly by spading it deeply and enriching it with bonemeal or well-rotted manure. If possible, do not use a location that was planted to tulips the year before.

Tulips should be set out in accordance with a prearranged plan to bring out the effect desired. The planting of mixed colors rarely produces a satisfactory result. For those who wish a wide assortment of colors, group or spot planting of individual varieties is best. Where formal bedding is desired, the Single Early or Double Early sorts (see below) will be preferable as their stems are shorter and therefore do not need a background to show them off to best advantage. The longer-stemmed, later flowering groups make their best appearance when planted in front of shrubbery or evergreens or when massed in a perennial border. With the wide range of colors available in practically all classes of tulips any desired color scheme (except one depending on blue) can be planned and worked out. When formal designs are required, it is well to consult catalogs that give the height of each variety so as to achieve uniformity.

PLANTING AND AFTER-CARE. In carrying out design planting, a good plan is to dig out the whole space that the bulbs are to occupy to the depth of 4 or 6 in., place the bulbs in the desired position about 6 in. apart, and replace the soil.

Although tulips are hardy in the N. temperate zone, a slight winter covering is always an advantage and sometimes a necessity in exposed places. However, it must not be applied until the ground has frozen. It can be of leaves, hay or straw, and it should be removed in the spring as the bulbs peep through. But for the growing of exhibition flowers, nothing is better than a liberal covering of rotted cow manure; this can be left on the planting next year to act as a mulch as well as a fertilizer. When the practice of buying new tulip bulbs every year is followed, the bulbs should be dug as soon as they finish flowering, for the longer they stay in the ground, the smaller will be the chances of producing good quality flowers in the same location next year. Those who desire to use the bulbs again should realize that the second-year bulbs will not be likely to give as good results as would new ones because, even with the best care, the cultural conditions in the average garden do not compare with those used in commercial bulb-growing fields.

Tulip bulbs produce their leaves and flowers on the same stem, and if the blooms are cut so low as to remove part of the foliage the future flowering quality of the bulbs will be lessened. Except for special cutting, therefore, the faded flowers should be removed close to the top of the stem and before they begin to form seed pods, as seeding draws heavily upon the stored-up vitality of the bulb. The foliage should then be encouraged to remain green as long as possible, for during the growing period after flowering the new bulbs are being formed for the next year.

As soon as the foliage is completely withered the bulbs should be lifted. Several smaller bulbs (bulblets) will be found in place of the large one planted. These should be stored in an airy, dry location; in a few weeks they can be cleaned, sorted as to sizes, and replanted. Any bulb that measures 1 in. or more in diameter will likely provide a flower the next season. The smaller sizes can be planted in rows in a separate part of the garden, to grow into flowering-size bulbs in 1, 2 or 3 years, depending on soil and other conditions which may affect their growth.

Plate 54.   TYPICAL TULIPS AND SOME VARIANTS

Upper left: The long-stemmed Darwins lead in stately, formal grace.   Upper right: April coaxes out the gay, pink and white Tulipa kaufmanniana.   Lower left: Rembrandts like their Darwin ancestors in form, but curiously "broken" and variegated in color.   Center right: Darwin tulips edge a formal path.   Lower right: The daintily reflexed petals of the Picotee or Maidens Blush tulip are softly suffused with carmine.

TULIPS INDOORS

Although forced by florists both for cut flowers and as pot plants for midwinter and early spring trade, and grown to marvelous perfection in the greenhouses of large estates, tulips are not as satisfactory for ordinary home forcing as are hyacinths and narcissi. This is principally because tulips require a longer period of preparation which is best given by burying the pots or flats in which the bulbs are planted, 18 in. to 2 ft. deep outdoors, and covering them with soil, or better, sifted coal ashes. Here they can be—and indeed should be—subjected to hard freezing temperatures until time to bring them indoors, by which time they will be well rooted. While the gardener with facilities and willingness to give the necessary effort will probably get results, there is for most people a sufficient reward in the varied beauty of tulips grown outdoors.

ENEMIES

The most common tulip trouble is a spotting and rotting disease known as "fire." Small circular spots on petals and leaves increase in size, the margins appearing water-soaked and the centers gray. In moist weather the leaves and blossoms quickly decay and become covered with the brownish-gray mold typical of Botrytis blights (which see). The fungus spores are carried to healthy tulips by tools, animals running through the garden, splashing rain and air currents. Plants wounded in digging are easily infected.

Rogue out all infected plants as soon as noticed; cut off each blossom as soon as it has finished blooming and cut the leaves down to the surface of the soil as soon as they turn yellow. Before planting bulbs, examine them carefully and remove all bulb scales containing the small black sclerotia of the fungus. It is better not to plant tulips on the same land two years in succession. Spraying two or three times in early spring with a weak bordeaux mixture will help to control the disease.

Gray rot of bulbs is only occasionally destructive in the United States. Soil disinfection with formalin is advised.

A virus disease is responsible for the sudden color change in tulips known as "breaking" (which see). The odd flowers resulting were long considered and named as a distinct type—and some growers still so regard them.

The only insect generally destructive to tulips is the bulb mite. For control see BULB ENEMIES under BULBS.

TULIP HISTORY AND TYPES

Introduced into Europe from Turkey in 1554, tulips have figured prominently in floral history ever since and have gained increasing favor everywhere. The famous "tulipomania" of Holland in the 17th century, during which fortunes were invested in the bulbs and their culture and vast sums lost through wild speculation, is school-book history. But while fabulous prices such as were then paid for a single bulb of a new variety have never been equaled, there has continued a strong desire on the part of tulip growers to create or possess new kinds of outstanding merit.

Tulips grow readily from seed, and this is the means chiefly employed for producing new varieties. However, many new kinds also appear naturally as mutations (commonly known as "sports"). That is, a bulb, for some unaccountable reason, suddenly bears a flower that is different in either form or color from that of its variety and what it normally would produce. If grown on for another season, the bulb retains this difference, it may become the nucleus of another new kind, a stock of which is built up by the natural tendency of the plant to develop small new bulbs at the base of a large one. These (except in the case of sports) reproduce their parent.

Holland is the home of commercial tulip production, for reasons explained under DUTCH BULBS. But tulips thrive in other water-bound regions of the N. temperate zone.

Unfortunately there is no simple rule to guide the average gardener in correctly classifying the many tulip types, for constant crossing has served to narrow or even eliminate many of the former differences.

Relative flowering dates have influenced tulip classification and offer perhaps the most convenient basis on which to discuss the principal types. First to appear in the spring is the Single Early group as used so generally for formal bedding in parks. The flower stems are relatively short and the flowers do not have the keeping qualities of the late-flowering types. A typical variety is Keiserskroon, with its striking color combination of yellow and red. Practically all tulip colors and many combinations are available in this class.

Closely following is the Double Early group with large, peony-like flowers that make the varieties very showy and are worth placing in any garden; Peach Blossom, a handsome pink, is a favorite.

Following the Doubles come two groups of recent introduction: the Triumph and Mendel types, developed in an effort to combine the early-flowering qualities of the early tulips with the long stems and large flowers of the later bloomers. Then, closely grouped as to flowering season, come the glorious large-flowered later types. These include the long-stemmed globular-flowered Darwins, the pure-toned Breeders, and the Cottage or May-flowering sorts. The Darwins consist mainly of the solid or "self" colored sorts ranging from pure white through nearly all the colors of the rainbow to the purple, almost black, Le Noire.

The Breeders are so called because their self-coloring makes them especially good for hybridizing. The variety Louis XIV of purple and bronze is typical.

The Cottage Tulips, the last to bloom, are distinguishable, to some extent, by their more slender stems and narrower foliage and often by their more graceful flowers with pointed petals reflexed in some varieties. Mrs. Moon, a tall handsome yellow, is typical.

Parrot (or Dragon) Tulips are midseason bloomers. Their ragged, queer-shaped petals, usually multi-colored, are as odd as they are beautiful, but their stems are often too weak to hold the gigantic flower aloft. The favorite variety, Fantasy, in which pinks predominate, is a mutation from the Darwin variety Clara Butt.

No attempt is made here to give a representative list of even the leading varieties, for constant improvement goes on in all of the classes. Reference must be made to current catalogs of bulb dealers for names and descriptions of the prevailing favorites.

Tulip Species

The name *Tulipa gesneriana* has been given to the tulip which, it is believed, is the parent of most of our modern garden tulips—as the Darwins, Parrots, and other hybrid races of today—but which has never been known in its original wild form. It is characterized by its cup-shaped flowers whose perianth segments are rounded across the top.

Another species long cultivated is *T. suaveolens,* the type of the modern Duc van Thol Tulips of today. These are known by their fragrance and by the pointed tips of the "petals."

Where their odd colorings and shapes have not been surpassed by hybrids, many of the wild species now are popular garden subjects. Some of them defy all attempts to produce them commercially, so the yearly supply is gathered from the original wild locations. Among the more popular of these are:

T. clusiana—often called Lady Tulip or Candy-stick Tulip. A dainty variety, from the N. Mediterranean shores, produces a graceful slender flower on a tall stem. The outer petals are cherry-rose and the inner ones white. Not only does it bloom perfectly in our N. gardens, but it is one of the very few tulips that does well in the extreme S. States. The very small bulb has a hard shell covering unlike that of any other species.

kaufmanniana. A beautiful early flowering species from Turkestan with several color variations though yellow and red predominate.

greigi. Fine early-flowering species distinguishable by the gray-green leaves spotted with purple-brown dots. There are several forms, the most common being fiery red with a dark yellow-edged blotch, at the base of each petal.

eichleri. Like *T. greigi,* large-flowered.

dasystemon. A small, early-flowering, yellow tulip, suitable for rock use.

acuminata. Flowers light yellow, streaked with red; each petal long and extremely narrow, the edge sometimes rolled back, a long point at the tip.

biflora. Small tinted white flowers on branching stalks, early blooming.

praestans. Leaves slightly hairy; flower light scarlet, each petal pointed at the tip.

fosteriana. A recently discovered species from Bokhara; probably the most brilliant red of all.

Many other tulip species, especially the smaller ones, are being sought for rock-garden planting.

Other Tulips

Members of the genus Calochortus (which see) are often referred to as tulips, the added qualifying names indicating different groups of species within the genus. Among them are Mariposa-tulips (or lilies), Globe-tulips, Star-tulips, and Meadow- and Butterfly-tulips.

TULIP POPPY. Common name for *Hunnemannia fumariaefolia,* a Mexican herbaceous perennial resembling Eschscholzia, grown as an annual in warm, sunny locations in the N.

TULIP-TREE. Common name for *Liriodendron tulipifera,* a deciduous tree of the Magnolia Family having bluish-green foliage, the leaves lobed and abruptly cut off at the tips, and bearing in May or June solitary bell-shaped greenish-yellow flowers, marked with orange at the base and followed by long cone-like fruits. A number of varieties have originated, among them *pyramidale,* with a tall narrow, pyramidal growth; *aureo-marginatum* with leaves margined with yellow, and *integrifolium* with leaves not lobed.

One of the finest forest trees of the E. seaboard and the Middle W., the Tulip-tree grows to 200 ft., in congenial surroundings and is a handsome subject with a beautiful clean straight trunk, sometimes as much as 10 ft. in diameter, admirably adapted for park or street planting. It thrives best in rich moist soil, and is increased by seed and rarely by layers; the varieties are grafted or budded on seedlings. It is known in the S. as Tulip-poplar, and sometimes as Whitewood.

ENEMIES. Several leaf diseases may appear as brown blotches or small brown spots, but they are not usually serious enough to call for control measures. The tulip-tree scale, however, may become a serious pest. A large hemispherical soft scale, it can be best controlled by a dormant miscible-oil spray. A green aphid may be numerous on the underside of the leaves, and a black sooty mold fungus lives on the honey dew secreted by the aphid and the scale. Spraying with nicotine-sulphate and soap will control the aphid. The circular brown leaf spots of the tulip-tree spot gall are caused by a tiny gnat-like fly. Although infested leaves may fall, this is not a serious pest and no control is known.

TUNA. Mexican name for Opuntia (which see), a large genus of the Cactus Family, commonly called Prickly-pear. Also for the species *O. tuna* and, in markets, for its reddish edible fruits.

TUNBRIDGE FERN (*Hymenophyllum tunbridgensis*). A very delicate little plant of the Filmy Fern Family (which see), with forking pinnae. Needs a moist atmosphere, shallow soil and sandstone chips. The best place for it is the terrarium.

TUNIC-FLOWER, or Coat-flower. Common name for *Tunica saxifraga,* a hardy perennial herb of the Pink Family, growing 6 to 10 in. tall with delicate, wiry stems and white, lavender or rosy flowers. It is frequently used as an edging plant in the border, or in the rock garden, and is easily increased from seed or by division. Var. *florepleno* has double flowers.

TUPELO. Common name for Nyssa, a genus of handsome deciduous trees, whose leaves turn scarlet in fall. Often known also in S. U. S. as Gum-tree.

TURF. The mat of grass plants, their interwoven roots and the entangled soil that forms the body of any stretch of greensward—lawn, putting green, ballfield, etc. The term is often used interchangeably with sod, although the latter refers particularly to the grass mat when removed in strips or squares to be used elsewhere in sodding an area to get results quicker than could be achieved by seeding.

TURFING-DAISY. Common name for *Matricaria tchihatchewi,* a mat-making perennial with white flowers and finely cut leaves.

TURKEY-BEARD. Common name for Xerophyllum, a genus of hardy perennial herbs, with thick woody rootstocks, native in N. America and belonging to the Lily Family. *X. asphodeloides,* the principal species, is found in pine barrens from N. J. S. From the center of a tuft of long narrow leaves it sends up a stem to 5 ft., bearing a raceme about 6 in. long of yellowish-white fragrant flowers, from May to July. It is a good plant for the wild garden. *X. tenax,* native in the Pacific Coast region, bears larger racemes of white flowers with violet-colored stamens. Propagated by seed or division.

TURMERIC. A condiment and dye made from the roots of *Curcuma longa,* an Asiatic perennial herb of the Ginger Family.

TURNIP. A semi-hardy biennial herb (*Brassica rapa*) grown as an annual for its enlarged roots which are served as a vegetable or used for flavoring soups and stews. It differs from the Swedish turnip or rutabaga (often popularly called "baga" and "Swede") by its closer grouping of leaf stems, its hairy (not bloom-covered) leaves, the flatter or more globular form of the swollen root, an almost naked tap-root and light colored flesh (purple on the upper surface in some varieties).

To grow quality tender roots for summer use, sow seed thinly in early spring in well-prepared, moderately fertile, well-drained soil. Make the drills 12 to 15 in. apart. When the seedlings are 4 to 6 in. high thin them to stand 6 or 8 in. asunder. Cultivate every 7 to 10 days until the foliage touches between rows. Gather the roots for use when 2 to 3 in. thick; if allowed to grow larger they may become woody and strong flavored or the plants may go to seed, especially if the weather is hot.

For autumn and winter use, sow after midsummer but manage like the spring crop. When cold weather approaches dig the roots, cut off the tops and store the roots in a cellar. Keep the air moist and the temperature as near 32 degrees as possible without reaching that point; these conditions prevent shriveling and decay. An outdoor pit can be used if well protected. See STORING OF CROPS.

The diseases and insects that commonly affect turnips are discussed under Crucifer (which see). The most serious diseases are club-root and black-rot, and the most injurious insect pests are the turnip aphis, root maggot and flea beetles.

Indian-turnip or Jack-in-the-pulpit (which see) is *Arisaema triphyllum.*

See also BRASSICA; RUTABAGA.

TURNIP-ROOTED CELERY. Thick-rooted celery varieties used for flavoring. See CELERIAC.

TURNIP-ROOTED CHERVIL. A biennial vegetable grown for its small dark gray carrot-like roots. See CHERVIL.

TURTLE-HEAD. Common name for Chelone, a genus of perennial herbs with showy tubular flowers of white, rose-purple, or rose.

TUSSOCK MOTH, WHITE-MARKED. Usually considered a shade-tree pest, this insect sometimes may be destructive in orchards. Foliage of all kinds of trees except conifers is skeletonized by the yellowish-black, hairy, striped caterpillar which has a long, narrowed tuft of black hairs projecting from each side of the head and one from the tail, and two bright red spots on the back. The eggs, laid in the fall in conspicuous white stiff masses attached to trunk, branches or dead leaves, hatch in late spring, the larvae becoming full-grown in July and spinning cocoons on the trunk. The male moths are dark brown with strong wings; the females, like those of the canker worm, are

wingless. Larvae of a second generation feed on the trees late in August and early in September. Control by daubing over-wintering egg masses with creosote. Especially valuable trees may also be sprayed with lead arsenate as soon as the caterpillars appear.

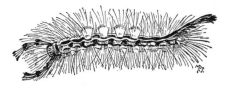

AN EASY-TO-RECOGNIZE-PLANT PEST
This hairy caterpillar of the white marked tussock moth, with its long black plumes "fore and aft," its striped sides, and the four white tufts on its back, devours the leaves of several kinds of shade trees.

TWAYBLADE. Common name for the native hardy orchid, *Liparis liliifolia,* good for the wild garden in a shady spot in damp soil full of humus. It has broad leaves nearly 6 in. long, and a many-flowered raceme of small red-veined yellow blossoms, rising 10 in. above the foliage.

TWINBERRY. Another name for Partridge-berry (*Mitchella repens*), a small native trailing evergreen vine with "double" scarlet fruits.

TWINFLOWER. Common name for *Linnaea borealis,* a dainty trailing plant of the Honeysuckle Family, native in cool northern woods of Europe and N. America. It has small glossy evergreen leaves, and small pink bell-shaped very fragrant flowers, nodding in pairs from slender erect stems. Var. *americana* has more tubular flowers to ½ in. Twinflower can be naturalized in the wild or rock garden, if given a cool moist situation and an acid soil rich in peaty humus. It can be transplanted from the wild and then increased by division or by cuttings of green or half-ripened wood rooted under glass. The name comes from Linnaeus, whose favorite flower it was said to be. The name Twinflower is also given in Mexico to *Bravoa geminiflora,* a handsome plant, closely resembling the tuberose.

TWINLEAF. Common name for *Jeffersonia diphylla,* a hardy perennial N. American herb of the Barberry Family, named for Thomas Jefferson. An attractive plant, to 1 ft., with 2-parted leaves and dainty white flowers 1 in. across, it can be easily transplanted from the woods to the wild garden or rock garden, where

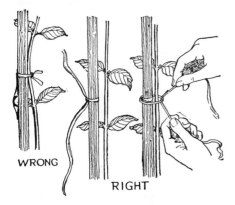

WRONG

RIGHT

TYING A PLANT TO A STAKE

Do not bind the stem close against stake as shown at the left. First tie the cord tightly around the stake with the knot on the side away from the plant; then, bring the ends back around stake and stem and tie.

it should be given a moist soil, rich in humus.

TWIN-SPUR. Common name for *Diascia barberae,* a slender, low-growing, half-hardy S. African annual bearing its sprays of rose or violet two-lipped flowers on leafy 1-ft. stems. Two conspicuous round spurs on the flower's lower lip account for the common name. The mottled yellow throat suggests the plant's kinship to the better known Nemesia. This is a good border or pot plant, easily raised from seed in light well-drained soil and sunlight. It should be started in the house and then transplanted to stand 6 in. apart. Pink and orange hybrids are now available.

TWIST-ARUM. Common name for *Helicodiceros muscivorus,* a tuberous-rooted plant of the Arum Family, growing to 1½ ft. with leaves parted into finger-like divisions and a hairy spadix or spike-like flower cluster shaded by a purple-hairy spathe twisted at the throat into a horizontal position. Though a floral curiosity, this plant is seldom grown because of the vile odor of the flowers, which attracts carrion-flies and other insects. Started in autumn under glass, it will flower in the spring; it is increased by division.

TWISTED-STALK. Common name for Streptopus, a genus of perennial herbs of the Lily Family, resembling Solomons Seal, but branching in habit. They have small pink or white bell-shaped flowers growing

from the point where each leaf clasps the stem. They are excellent material for the wild garden, requiring partial shade and rich moist soil. The flowers are followed by bright red berries which hang like tiny Japanese lanterns, making a bright color note amidst the green. They are increased by seed or by division of the creeping rootstock. *S. amplexifolius* which grows 2 to 3 ft. tall, has 2 greenish-white flowers and later scarlet berries hanging from each leaf-axil, each flower stem appearing as if knotted; *roseus,* to 2 ft., has solitary rosy purple flowers.

TYING. This, in gardening, means the fastening of plants to stakes, trellises and other supports. When done improperly or with wrong materials it may do more harm than good. Undesirable materials are hard strings and wires because, being thin, they tend to cut or girdle the relatively soft stems of plants. Soft, coarse white cord is not so bad. Raffia (which see) is somewhat better though not very durable; but ¼ or ½ in. tape or strips of cotton cloth are better still, being broad enough to avoid such cutting and also good for a full

A HANDY WAY TO CARRY CORD FOR TYING PLANTS

Cut two vertical slits in the side of an ice-cream or beverage container for the belt to run through. Then lead the end of a ball of string through a hole punched in the cover—and the cord is ready at hand and never tangles. Use soft string for tying plants.

season or more. A simple, convenient tying device that has become quite popular since its recent introduction, consists of a strip of tough green paper about 10 in. long folded lengthwise and glued, with a reinforcing piece of soft copper wire down the center. It can be quickly twisted into place and provides satisfactory support for vines, stems, etc., for a season or two. Ordinary flexible pipe cleaners, dyed green, are also being sold as tying material.

The proper steps in tying, whatever material is used, are as follows: 1. Place the tape or other strip between the plant stem and the stake. 2. Bring the ends around the stake and tie them firmly so the knot is on the side of the stake away from the plant. 3. Bring the ends *back* around the stake and the plant stem, and finally tie them in a tight knot but so as to leave the stem in a loose loop to allow for its expansion as the plant grows. A tie so made keeps its position on the stake without slipping but allows "play" for the stem.

Incidentally, when trees, vines, and shrubs are received from nurseries the labels should be removed and replaced with loops enough larger to allow for expansion in stem girth. If left as attached by the nurseries they will girdle and kill the stems above the constrictions.

Tying of such plants as climbing and pillar roses, wisteria, grape and the like to trellises is the same as fastening them to stakes; but for fastening them to solid walls the so-called "wall nails"—steel nails with pliable soft metal strips attached to their heads—are best because the stems, though held firmly where wanted, will spread the soft metal as they grow. These plants and non-clinging vines may be held against brick and masonry walls by using "vine supports" of various kinds. Some of these combine the flexible metal strip with a nail that can be driven into a

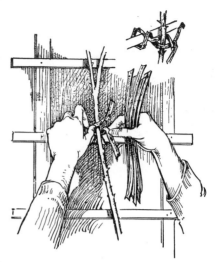

A MODERN AID IN TYING PLANTS
Short lengths of green-paper covered wire make quick work of supporting vines, rose canes, etc. on trellises. Make a twist between stem and support (see small sketch) to avoid strangling the growth.

wooden plug inserted in a drilled hole, or with some sort of so-called expansion bolt.

TYPE. To botanists this means an herbarium specimen upon which a species is based. To belong to the same species, other plants must approximate this "type specimen" in certain general characteristics. Thus it is the ideal representation of a species.

In gardening and plant growing, however, the word is often used loosely, in its general sense, to refer to a kind of plant or group; as, for instance, a "bushy type" of shrub, an "upright type" of evergreen, an "improved type" of geranium, etc.

TYPHA (ty'-fah). Botanical name for the hardy swamp plant commonly called Cat-tail, which see.

U

UDO (oo'-doh). A hardy perennial herb (*Aralia cordata*), recently introduced from Japan as a desirable home-garden vegetable. Its culture resembles that of asparagus, except that the spring shoots must be blanched by earthing-up the crowns; the development of green color injures their flavor. The shoots are boiled in salt water for a few minutes to extract the turpentine flavor; then drained and served like asparagus.

Plants, grown from seed started under glass, are set outdoors 4 ft. apart. To propagate a specially good plant, 5-in. cuttings of green shoots may be used. When the spring gathering season ends, the crowns must be uncovered so the plants may grow normally. Except when seed is wanted, the flower clusters must be cut while small.

ULEX (eu'-leks). Furze, Gorse, Whin. Much-branched shrubs with rigid, dark green spiny branches, native in Europe and belonging to the Pea Family. They are not entirely hardy North, but may survive in favored spots with protection. The principal species is *U. europaeus,* which grows to 4 ft. or more, growing and flowering well in sandy or gravelly soil in a sunny situation. It is a good seaside plant where hardy. The yellow fragrant flowers are very showy and in mild climates are produced almost continuously. Var. *plenus* has double flowers. Propagated by cuttings or by seeds, which should be sown where they are to grow, as it is a difficult subject to transplant.

ULMACEAE (ul-may'-see-ee). The Elm Family, sometimes listed as a tribe of the Nettle Family (Urticaceae). It includes deciduous trees and shrubs with a watery juice, widely distributed throughout temperate climates. Species of Celtis (hackberry) are sometimes planted, and the elm (Ulmus) is extensively grown as an important shade and ornamental tree.

ULMUS (ul'-mus). The genus of tall, long-lived deciduous trees popularly known as Elms. Because of their graceful shape and handsome foliage consisting of small alternate, toothed leaves, Elms are extensively used for ornamental purposes and for street-planting, especially in the E. States. They are increased by seed or layering and are easily transplanted. See ELM.

UMBEL. An umbrella-shaped flower cluster (*inflorescence*) in which the flower-stalks (*peduncles*) all spring from the same point at the summit of the main stem. The rays so formed, being of nearly equal length, give to the cluster its characteristic shape, which may range from nearly flat to domed. Umbels are *compound* when the flower-stalks in turn branch into *pedicels* on which the individual flowers are borne, as in the carrot. The umbel gives its name to the Umbelliferae or Parsley Family, to which belong the carrot, blue lace-flower, caraway, poison-hemlock, fennel, harbinger-of-spring, parsnip, and many other familiar plants. Milkweed and onion flowers also occur in umbels.

UMBELLIFERAE (um-be-lif'-er-ee). The Carrot or Parsnip Family, a distinctive group of hollow-stemmed herbaceous plants sometimes reaching great size, widely distributed throughout temperate and subtropical regions. The family takes its name from its typical inflorescence, an *umbel,* or flattened cluster in which the several flower stalks spring like rays from one point; many forms have "compound umbels" in which this arrangement is repeated in the branches of the clusters. Many species are ornamental; others are grown for food and medicine, as celery, asafetida, anise and caraway. The family also includes some bad weeds. Important genera are: Eryngium, Trachymene (blue lace-flower), Astrantia, Daucus (carrot), Cuminum, Coriandrum, Ferula, Anethum, Foeniculum, Levisticum, Petroselinum, Aegopodium, Apium (celery), Pimpinella, Pastinaca (parsnip), Sium, Myrrhis, Anthriscus. Chaerophyllum, Conium, Carum (caraway).

UMBRELLA FERN. A name for species of Gleichenia, a tropical genus of ferns for the cool greenhouse. They have uniquely branching, spoke-like fronds, from 1 to 6 ft. long, and require rough peat and sand, and plenty of indirect light and air.

UMBRELLA-LEAF. Common name for *Diphylleia cymosa,* a perennial herb of the Barberry Family. It has but 3 leaves —1 large, shield-shaped, lobed and toothed, as much as 2 ft. across, and two smaller ones on the stalk (sometimes up to 4 ft. high), which bears small white flowers followed by blue berries nearly ½ in. long. This interesting plant, which is occasionally grown in the wild garden, is increased by seed or division of the thick creeping rootstock. In damp moist soil it attains its maximum size, but it will grow in a dwarf form in a dry situation.

UMBRELLA PALM. A tall and broad-fronded palm (*Hedyscepe canterburyana*) native only to the Lord Howe Islands but of proven value in S. Fla. and S. Calif. gardens, and also under glass in the North. (See HEDYSCEPE.) The name is sometimes given popularly to *Cyperus alternifolius,* an ornamental sedge plant, better known as Umbrella-plant, which see below.

UMBRELLA-PINE. C o m m o n name for *Sciadopitys verticillata,* a Japanese tree of the Pine Family, growing to 100 ft., and hardy in Me. It is a slow-growing pyramidal evergreen with handsome foliage, the glossy needles 5 or 6 in. long growing in whorls of 15 to 35. Its name comes from the shape it assumes in age, when the branches become more loose and drooping and the head grows broader. It thrives best in a rather sheltered position in partial shade in a well-watered loam or clay soil. It is propagated principally from seed.

UMBRELLA-PLANT. A common name for *Cyperus alternifolius,* a cultivated sedge used in the aquarium, the water garden and sometimes as a pot plant. Sometimes called Umbrella-palm.

UMBRELLA-TREE. Common n a m e for *Magnolia tripetala,* a deciduous ornamental tree growing to 40 ft. in height. It has leaves nearly 2 ft. long and white flowers to 10 in. across with a most dis-agreeable odor; these are followed by large rose-red fruits. See MAGNOLIA.

Texas-umbrella-tree is *Melia azedarach* var. *umbraculiformis.*

UNDERSHRUB. Any woody plant suf-ficiently shade-tolerant to permit its planting at the base and in the shade of other, larger subjects to mask their bare trunks and create an effect comparable to that of natural underbrush. The term is relative rather than specific and may apply to dif-ferent kinds and sizes of plants, depending upon the conditions under which they are used.

UNICORN-PLANT. Common name for Proboscidea, a genus of herbs grown for the curious seed pods used while young as pickles.

UNIOLA (eu-ny´-oh-lah). A genus of native perennial grasses known as Spike Grass (which see). One species (*U. lati-folia*) is grown for ornament. The showy drooping and flattened panicles of *U. pani-culata* are unusually handsome when dried, being faintly tinged with pink. Native to the S. E. Coast, it can be grown as far north as S. Canada in sandy soil. See also ORNAMENTAL GRASSES.

URCEOLINA (ur-see-oh-ly´-nah). A genus of bulbous plants of the Amaryllis Family, with strap-shaped leaves, which appear after the scarlet or yellow urn-shaped flowers borne in umbels on a stem 1 ft. tall. Urceolinas are beautiful lily-like subjects, easily grown in the green-house or for summer or autumn bloom in the garden if brought indoors in the fall in their pots or tubs and stored for the winter. *U. miniata* has umbels of 2 to 6 bright scarlet flowers; *U. pendula* has 4 to 6 golden, green-tipped flowers and rather broad leaves.

URGINEA (ur-jin´-i-ah) *maritima.* A bulbous herb of the Lily Family from which is obtained the "squill" of druggists. Only half-hardy outdoors, it is sometimes grown in greenhouses for its yellow or rose flowers, and called Sea-onion, which see.

URSINIA (ur-sin´-i-ah). A genus of S. African composites numbering about 60 annuals, perennials and sub-shrubs. Their vivid orange "daisies" on long wiry stems stand 2 to 3 ft. above low tufts of finely-cut foliage. The plants bloom profusely from midsummer to late fall, making a colorful addition to the sunny border, and may be potted for continued flowering indoors. The blooms last well when cut.

The few species that are available, with the new hybrids, are treated as annuals and as easily raised as zinnias (which see), with the same requirements as to well-drained soil and hot sunshine. They include the following: *U. anethoides* and its hybrids, called Jewels-of-the-veldt, 1 to 2 ft. tall, have orange flowers with deep purple centers. *U. calendulacea,* 2 ft. high and 3 ft. wide, has rich orange flowers. *U. pulchra* (sometimes listed as *Spheno-gyne speciosa*) to 1½ ft., has orange flow-ers with brown centers. *U. pygmaea,* 4 in. tall, has flowers with orange, pointed rays, and is a treasure for low borders.

URTICA (ur-ty'-kah). A genus of Old-World herbs bearing stinging hairs; one species sometimes grown under glass. See NETTLE.

URTICACEAE (ur-ti-kay'-see-ee). The Nettle Family, a group of herbs, shrubs and trees often bearing stinging hairs, chiefly native to the tropics. The small, inconspicuous flowers are variously disposed in clusters. A few species (mostly of the genera Boehmeria, Pilea and Helxine) are cultivated for their ornamental foliage, and one is a source of fibre. The family includes several noxious weeds, particularly the Great or Stinging Nettle.

UTRICULARIA (eu-trik-eu-lay'-ri-ah). A genus of aquatic plants and some land-growing air plants. See BLADDERWORT.

UVA GRASS. Common name for *Gynerium sagittatum,* a perennial member of the Grass Family growing up to 40 ft. and bearing silky plume-like terminal pan-

icles 3 ft. long with drooping branches. It is much like Cortaderia (Pampas Grass) except for botanical details of the flowers. The leaves, 3 by 6 in., have finely toothed edges. The plant is used as an ornamental in warm sections. See ORNAMENTAL GRASSES.

UVULARIA (eu-veu-lay'-ri-ah). A genus of hardy herbs of the Lily Family, popularly known as Bellwort or Merry-bells. They are erect perennials growing from a rootstock and having clasping or stemless leaves and graceful drooping yellow flowers 1½ in. long borne at the ends of the stalks. They grow naturally in the shade in rich moist woods and may be easily transferred to the wild garden, where they may be increased by division. *U. sessilifolia* to 1 ft. has greenish-yellow flowers; *U. grandiflora* to 1½ ft. has pointed leaves and pale yellow flowers; and *U. perfoliata* to 1½ ft. has clasping leaves and clear yellow blossoms.

V

VACCINIUM (vak-sin'-i-um). A genus of deciduous or evergreen shrubs, belonging to the Heath Family and of wide distribution from the Arctic Circle to mountains of the tropics. Common names given to different species are Blueberry, Cranberry, Cowberry, Whortleberry and sometimes Huckleberry, which, however, correctly applies to the genus Gaylussacia (which see). Some Vacciniums are grown especially for the beauty of their colored leaves in fall, others for their edible fruits. They must have a lime-free soil, and thrive best in a rather moist sandy peat. In recent years free and large fruiting forms of *V. corymbosum* have been developed, making blueberries a good garden crop where soil conditions are right. Propagated by cuttings, layers and division.

PRINCIPAL SPECIES

V. corymbosum (Highbush Blueberry) is a bushy deciduous shrub to 12 ft., found from Me. to Fla. There are numerous forms with blue-black berries of fine flavor. One of the handsomest shrubs in fall, when the leaves turn orange and scarlet. See also BLUEBERRY.

pennsylvanicum (Lowbush Blueberry) is a dwarf shrub to 2 ft., common in E. N. America. It grows well on dry sandy hills, and furnishes most of the blueberies of the markets.

macrocarpon (Large or American Cranberry) is a creeping evergreen, extensively cultivated for its large berries, used for sauce or jelly. See also CRANBERRY.

oxycoccus (Small or European Cranberry) is a slender creeping evergreen of smaller growth and fruit than the preceding species.

stamineum (Deerberry) is a much-branched deciduous shrub to 3 ft., with pale leaves, white or purple-tinged flowers, and large greenish berries.

myrtillus (Whortleberry) is a small upright shrub, with drooping pink flowers and bloomy-black edible berries.

vitis-idaea (Cowberry) is a low creeping evergreen with small dark green shining leaves and dark red berries. Attractive for edging in the evergreen shrub border. Var. *majus* has larger leaves and

fruit, and *minus* is a smaller form, making a dense mat. Berries edible when cooked.

VALERIANA (vah-lee-ri-ay'-nah). A genus of hardy herbs or shrubs with small white or rose flowers in spikes or flat-topped clusters, commonly known as Valerian. Easily grown for either garden effects or for cut flowers, they are propagated by seeds or division. Valerian is subject to crown rot (which see) and plants showing sudden wilting should be removed immediately together with surounding soil. Black aphids may appear on the plants in large numbers but they can be controlled with a nicotine sulphate and soap spray.

V. officinalis (Common Valerian, Garden-heliotrope), with cut leaves and pinkish-lavender fragrant flowers, is an old-time

VALERIAN OR GARDEN-HELIOTROPE
Given the latter name because of its fragrance, this is a good, hardy border perennial. The flowers are pinkish-lavender or, in variety alba, white. The plant grows about 4 feet tall.

garden favorite, growing to about 4 ft. Var. *alba* with white flowers, and *rubra* with red, are pleasing variations.

supina, a little 6-in. pink-flowered species from Austria, which can be tucked in a hot sunny spot in the rock garden.

arizonica, a small plant with pale pink or white flowers, native to the W. States.

sitchensis, to 2 ft., not as coarse as *V. officinalis* but like it has delicate, fragrant lavender flowers.

African-valerian is *Fedia cornucopiae;* Greek-valerian is *Polemonium caeruleum;* Red-valerian is *Centranthus ruber.*

VALERIANELLA (vah-lee-ri-ah-nel'-ah). A genus of annual herbs with small rose, blue, or white flowers in flat-topped clusters, grown principally as salad plants, only a few species being used in the border or rock garden. The former should be raised like lettuce as a cool-weather crop in the spring or fall, or in the greenhouse in the winter; they require about 7 weeks to become usable. The species used in the border may be raised from seed sown where they are to grow. *V. locusta* var. *olitoria* growing 1 ft. tall with leaves 3 in. long, raised as a salad crop, is Corn Salad (which see); *V. eriocarpa* (Italian Corn Salad) is similar, but with longer leaves; *V. echinata,* of S. Europe, has small rose-pink flower-clusters; and *V. congesta,* slightly taller, is a pretty pink-flowered species from the prairies.

VALLARIS (vah-lay'-ris). Twining tropical shrubs, belonging to the Dogbane Family. One species, *V. heyni,* is grown outdoors in the far S. It is a tall climber, suitable for porch and arbor decoration, bearing clusters of white fragrant flowers.

VALLISNERIA (val-is-nee'-ri-ah). Also known as Eel-grass, Tape-grass and Wild-celery, the two common species (*V. americana* and *V. spiralis*) of this aquatic perennial with submerged leaves are prime favorites of the aquarist and, to a lesser degree, the water gardener. In addition to its special value as an oxygenator (see AQUARIUM), the long slender grass-like leaves are extremely decorative. The tiny, 3-petaled, pure white, pistillate flowers are carried to the surface on spiral stalks. Staminate flowers are produced on the submerged stem and, breaking loose, float to the surface to scatter pollen to accomplish a somewhat haphazard fertilization. The plant propagates freely, however, by means of runners.

VALLOTA (val-loh'-tah) *speciosa.* The Scarborough-lily (which see), a showy amaryllis-like flowering bulb for the greenhouse.

VALVE. One of the parts in which a fruit splits when it opens at maturity, as the two *valves* of a pea pod.

VANCOUVERIA (van-koo-vee'-ri-ah). A genus of small perennial herbs of the Barberry Family, having compound leaves and rather small white flowers. Closely related to Epimedium, they are most attractive in the rock garden or used as a ground-cover in the wild garden. Natives of the deep forests of the W. States, they should be given partial shade and an acid soil. Plants can be increased by division or grown from seeds. *V. hexandra* (Inside-out-flower), 1 ft. or more tall, has graceful rue-like foliage and delicate sprays of dainty white flowers.

VANDA (van'-dah). A genus of handsome tropical epiphytic orchids with racemes of fragrant white, lilac, blue, or greenish flowers, sometimes with sacs or spurs, growing from the axils of the leaves, which are arranged on the stems and branches in 2 opposite rows. Natives of the tropics of the E. hemisphere, they require a high temperature and a humid atmosphere during the growing season, but in the winter months should be exposed to the sun in a drier, cooler place. For further cultural details see ORCHIDS.

Among the outstandingly beautiful species are: *V. tricolor* from Java, with 11-in. racemes of yellow, brown-spotted flowers, with violet lips, streaked with purple; and *V. caerulea* (the Blue Orchid) from the Himalayas, with light blue blossoms 4 in. across in erect racemes 18 in. high. Some of the hybrids of *V. caerulea* are remarkable for their decided dark blue color.

VANILLA. A genus of climbing, tropical epiphytic orchids with racemes or spikes of greenish-yellow flowers. The plants are of little importance horticulturally, but *V. planifolia* (*V. fragrans*), from the W. Indies, has commercial value. From its large seed pods is made the extract of vanilla used for flavoring. This plant should not be confused with Carolina-vanilla (which see) which is *Triliso odoratissima,* a member of the Composite Family, with leaves vanilla-scented when bruised.

VANILLA GRASS. Common name for *Hierochloë odorata,* a fragrant perennial member of the Grass Family native to temperate regions of Europe and N. America. It grows to 2 ft. high, has short flat leaves, and a brownish spreading terminal panicle 2 to 4 in. long. The pleasing fragrance of the plants is responsible for the common name and for the frequent use of the leaves and stems for making woven baskets, mats and boxes, which remain fragrant for years.

VAPORIZED SULPHUR. This is frequently used in greenhouses to prevent mildew, being made in this way: Equal parts sulphur and hydrated lime are mixed with enough water to give a creamy texture and painted on the heating pipes whose heat slowly vaporizes the sulphur which condenses on the plants. See SULPHUR AND ITS COMPOUNDS.

VARIETY. A group of individuals within a species, but with differences too slight to constitute another species. An ordinary *botanical variety* is similar to a race or strain of plants which come true from seed to their distinguishing varietal characteristics. A *horticultural variety* (often indicated in botanical books by the term "Hort.," meaning *hortensis,* after it) is practically the same as the foregoing except that it has originated under cultivation, that is, in garden, greenhouse or nursery, often from hybrid ancestry. A *geographical variety* is a wild group which likewise comes true from seed, but which is localized in a certain region.

Individuals which are *not* thus "seed-constant" and which therefore require to be propagated vegetatively are commonly called varieties in commerce, but are properly *clons* or *clonal varieties.* Differences between varieties and species are often hard to determine. Races, strains and clons are usually subordinate to varieties and are terms seldom applied except to cultivated plants. See RACE; STRAIN; CLON SPECIES.

VARNISH-TREE. A name applied to at least four Asiatic genera, namely, Ailanthus, Aleurites, Firmiana and Koelreuteria (all of which see), but most correctly to the true Varnish-tree or Lacquer-tree, *Rhus verniciflua.* This, also a native of China and Japan, is a tree to 60 ft. with leaves consisting of 11 to 15 leaflets, followed by whitish flowers in long loose clusters, followed by smooth yellow fruit ¼ in. broad, from the oil of which lacquer used on highly polished wooden ware is made. The

tree is exceedingly poisonous like its American relatives, poison ivy (*R. toxicodendron*) and poison sumac (*R. vernix*).

VEGETABLE. As popularly understood, any plant cultivated for its edible parts. This loose definition includes roots (as beet, carrot), tubers (potato, Jerusalem artichoke), stems (celery, cardoon), leaves used raw as salad (pepper-grass, lettuce), leaves cooked as pot herbs or "greens" (mustard, spinach), flower buds and heads (French artichoke, cauliflower), fruits (tomato, watermelon) and seeds (peas, sweet corn).

By another popular definition, a vegetable is any plant whose edible part is used in some culinary way, as distinguished from a "fruit" which is used as a dessert. Botanically considered, all "vegetables" whose edible parts result from development of pollinated flowers are fruits —cucumber, pepper, "green" beans. (See FRUIT.) And in the soil-handling phase of gardening "vegetable matter," such as humus, is synonymous with plant material, whatever parts or kinds of plants it is derived from.

VEGETABLE GARDEN. (See illustrations, Plates 55 and 56.) The advantages of a vegetable garden are: 1. Choicer varieties may be grown in it than can be bought from stores, markets or hucksters. 2. The products can always be freshly gathered and when they have attained edible perfection. 3. Kinds not obtainable from commercial sources can be grown. 4. The products are not contaminated by exposure for sale. 5. It may be made to reduce the expenditure of money for food, often to the extent of 5 to 10 per cent of an "average" salary. 6. It combines the foregoing benefits with those of an enjoyable hobby and a healthful, useful recreation.

HOME-GARDEN SORTS ARE BEST. To amplify two of the points just made: First, varieties of the same species differ greatly in quality. To be satisfactory commercially they must have a tough, coarse texture so they can withstand packing and shipping and rough handling in markets and stores. This durability always sacrifices some delicacy and toothsomeness. Varieties originated for the home table, on the other hand, are characterized by fine texture, and flavor, and they develop over relatively long periods, thus extending their season.

Second, freshness, though of minor importance in some vegetables, is an outstanding factor in many others. Potatoes, turnips, late cabbage and the like may be just as nutritious and palatable 1 month or 6 months after being gathered as when fresh; but unless the salad crops such as leaf lettuce, pepper-grass, and mustard, are in the mouth within an hour of being gathered, they will have lost their delightful crispness and much of their appetizing flavor. Garden peas fresh from the vines and cooked rapidly in an open kettle are a different vegetable from any that can be bought; and sweet corn is best when gathered, steam-cooked (for less than 15 minutes) and placed on the table within half an hour of its being pulled.

Recognizing these things, choice kinds for the garden of limited size should be governed by the following considerations: 1. Those that the family does not enjoy will naturally be eliminated at once. 2. Where space is at a premium elimination should begin with those kinds that require excessive space and of which the family can use only limited quantities— for example, pumpkin, sweet-potato, watermelon, cantaloupe, winter squash, and cucumber (though the last named may be trained on trellises). 3. Staple, winter vegetables that can always be purchased in the stores and markets should be discarded next—late potatoes and cabbage, kale, turnips, rutabagas and late celery. 4. Species that occupy the ground over the whole season—parsnip, salsify, chicory, black salsify and leek—should be next omitted because from 2 to 4 short-season crops can be grown in the place of any one of them. Of course this elimination program should not exclude any desired vegetables of the types mentioned if there is space to include them. Nor should it rule out asparagus, which demands considerable space and occupies the ground for many years; for this area can be utilized annually for some 8 or 10 weeks to produce short-season crops between the asparagus rows before the asparagus will need the space.

CHOOSING VARIETIES. In many cases, varieties, especially of garden peas, sweet corn and bush beans require different lengths of time in which to reach edible maturity. These may be started according to two plans: (1) by making successional sowings of a quick-maturing variety at intervals of ten days or two weeks; or, (2) by sowing, all at one time, several varieties that require different lengths of time to mature, thus securing a succession.

Except where there is irrigation, successional sowings of one variety of garden peas are not as satisfactory as sowing several varieties with different ripening periods at one time. This is because the pea makes its best growth and sets the best crop of the finest pods in cool weather, while the soil is moist. With bush beans and sweet corn both plans work well, provided the sowings are made long enough before the usual date of the earliest autumn frost to permit their reaching edible maturity.

Having restricted the selection of both species and varieties to fit the available space, the next thing is to sort them into groups according to their hardiness and tenderness, their sowing dates, and their short and long growing seasons. This is essential to the most satisfactory arrangement of the available space so as to gain maximum use of the minimum area, by utilizing cropping systems, which see.

MAKING THE GARDEN. As to the garden itself it is impossible to do more than present generalizations and suggestions because environment and other circumstances vary so greatly that almost no statement can be made to fit all conditions. Nothing can compare with experience which, fortunately, can be gained in gardening at trifling expense.

SOIL AND SITE. As to soil and situation, make the best of what you have. Few of us can pick and choose the ideal site, soil and other factors so emphatically emphasized by most writers on gardening. Yet it is advisable to know what these are so that they may be recognized and as nearly as possible established.

For convenience in both cultivation and gathering the produce, locate the garden as near the kitchen door as the general arrangement of the property and its beauty, balance and unity will permit. See CULTIVATION; HARVESTING GARDEN CROPS.

It is highly desirable to have a conveniently available water supply, distributed preferably by means of an overhead irrigation system; otherwise by hose. See IRRIGATION; WATERING.

If a choice of exposure is possible, choose a gentle slope toward the E., the S. E. or the S., because there are the "early fac-

Plate 55.   DON'T OVERLOOK THE VEGETABLE GARDEN

Top: Too spreading in growth for the very small garden, the cucumber grows marvelously in rich soil where given elbow room.   Center left: The well-planned, well-cared-for vegetable garden is a source of joy to the whole family.   Center right: The bush bean requires no support and yields an abundant harvest of tender, stringless pods.   Bottom: Long straight rows, properly spaced, make easier the task of cultivating.

ings." Other conditions being equal, vegetables on such slopes will mature earlier and be of higher quality. Supplementing this, if possible, protect the area on the N., W. and N. W. from cold winds. This can often be afforded by woods, buildings, evergreen hedges or tight-board fences.

FRESH VEGETABLES IN WINTER
The benefits of the vegetable garden do not end when winter comes. Besides the canned surplus of tender products there are the hardy crops such as kales, brussels sprouts, parsnips, etc,. which not only survive freezing temperatures but are in some cases improved by them.

A vegetable garden should be away from shallow-rooted trees such as maples, elms, willows and poplars, which will not only shade the ground if situated on the E., S. or W., but also steal plant food (and especially water) from the soil.

Always the ground should be well drained, either naturally or artificially, for well-drained land is warmer and earlier. It is also more retentive of moisture, which constantly ascends from lower levels bringing the plants supplies of necessary plant food. If the drains cannot discharge to some lower level, they can converge on a "blind well," preferably built of loose stones, at the lowest available point, and protected with a strong cover. See DRAINAGE.

SOIL HANDLING. Though the gardener must often make the best of the soil he has, where a choice is possible it is best governed by the physical character of the soil because this is the hardest to modify.

Clay, adobe and loess soil do not readily absorb moisture, or easily assimilate plant nutrients; yet they are retentive of both. As they retain moisture, they are cold and late in spring; they are also heavy, sticky, plastic and difficult to work when wet, and tend to bake hard when dry.

However, they can be lightened and made more workable by draining, autumn plowing or digging (the furrows or clods being left over winter for the frost to break down), by additions of sifted coal ashes and humus and, in spring, by top dressings of lime or wood ashes. See HUMUS; LIME.

Very light sandy soils are easy to work, even when wet. They are loose and friable, readily receptive but not retentive of water and plant nutrients, which consequently tend to wash out and be lost. Combinations of these two extreme types, known as loams, especially the sandy loams, are better than either type.

ADDING PLANT FOOD. Though plant nutrients are sometimes abundant in readily available form in a garden soil they can be added as needed. In general, dark colored soils are usually (though not necessarily) more fertile than lighter ones; the latter are generally deficient in humus, which must be added to improve their water and plant-food-holding capacity.

House builders generally injure what surface soil there may be on a property by spreading the earth and stones from excavations and foundations over the surface and by burying their débris in it. Yet such a condition is rarely hopeless.

The first step in reclamation is to get rid of the débris, and—if possible and not too expensive—of the worthless excavated earth, too. The bringing in of fertile top-soil may seem too costly to consider, yet it is often the quickest, most economical way to insure a satisfactory garden. Otherwise heavy soils can be ameliorated and rendered productive as already outlined and light ones improved by the liberal use of green manures and cover-crops.

Though level culture is generally better than ridging (which see), in special cases and with heavy soils it is an advantage to raise and prepare in the autumn an area in the sunniest part of the garden 3 to 6 in. above the general level. This will thaw out and be ready to work as soon as spring opens.

THE NEED OF PLANNING. Apart from the preceding considerations, nothing is more conducive to success than careful planning and arrangement of the garden. Having the rows extend the long way of the area will save much time because fewer turns will be necessary when cultivating with a wheelhoe, horse-drawn implement or a garden tractor. In small areas the rows may extend either lengthwise or crosswise, as far as convenience is concerned. But in the interests of the crops it is advisable (theoretically at least) to have the rows extend N. and S. because thereby they receive more even distribution of sunlight. Otherwise, the tallest growing vegetables—sweet corn, pole beans and okra—should be placed on the N. side of the plot so they will not cast shadows on the lower sorts growing beside them. On a slope, run the rows— and cultivate—around, not up and down, to prevent washing and erosion.

Perennial vegetables, such as asparagus, rhubarb, Globe and Jerusalem artichoke and cardoon, should be grouped at one end or side of the garden. This is also the logical place for the hotbeds and coldframes, provided it is convenient to the house, tool-house or workshed, water supply, etc.

Various phases of vegetable gardening are discussed elsewhere in this book under the following titles, which should be consulted: SEEDS AND SEEDSOWING; PLANTING; TRANSPLANTING; DRILL; WHEELHOE; CULTIVATION; TILLAGE; MULCH; WATERING; IRRIGATION.

Vegetable-growing Notes

The following cultural notes upon various vegetables will be of special help to the novice gardener when planning his lay-out and should help him to (1) get the largest returns from his limited area; (2) avoid having related plants succeed themselves or their close relatives on the same space either the same season or that immediately following; and (3) choose good combinations for companion, succession and other systems of cropping. See also discussions of the different vegetables under their respective headings.

ARTICHOKE, GLOBE. Semi-hardy perennial. Start seeds in late winter under glass; transplant to rich soil outdoors in spring. Replace winter-killed plants each spring with new plants so started. Needed: 2 packets of seed the first year and one annually thereafter.

ARTICHOKE, JERUSALEM. Hardy perennial. Produces no seed. Plant tubers in early spring in some odd corner where the soil is rich and absorbent. No culture required. Needed: a quart of tubers enough for permanent stocking.

ASPARAGUS. Hardy perennial. Start with one-year (never older) plants; set them in trenches in early spring in rich ground. Do not cut until the third spring. Needed: 100 to 200 plants.

BEAN, BUSH. Tender annual. After danger of frost in spring has passed, sow successively at bi-weekly intervals until after midsummer—that is, 6 to 8 weeks before the date of the earliest recorded autumn frost in the locality; this gives the variety time to reach edible maturity. Needed: 1 lb. of seed sown 2 in. apart will plant 100 ft. of row and produce 2 to 4 pecks of snap beans.

BEAN, BUSH LIMA. Tender annual. Start plants in 2-in. flower pots, 2 to 4 weeks before usual date of last local spring frost and transplant to the garden after that date has passed; set 8 to 12 in. apart in 24- to 30-in. rows. Or plant outdoors when ground has become warm. Needed: 1 lb. of seed will plant 100 to 150 ft.

BEAN, POLE. Tender annual. Manage like bush bean, except: sow in hills 3 or 4 ft. apart each way or in drills with plants 12 in. apart. Most varieties are more prolific and of longer season than bush beans, so less seed is needed.

BEAN, POLE LIMA. Tender annual. Manage like bush limas, except: place the plants 12 to 15 in. apart in rows where plants grow over trellises, or only 3 or 4 around each pole. Much more prolific than dwarfs, so half the quantity of seed will be enough.

BEET. Semi-hardy biennial, grown as an annual. For the earliest crop sow globe varieties in early spring; for summer sow from mid-May to mid-June; for winter, from mid-July to mid-August; sow "long" and "half-long" varieties in midspring. Drop the "seeds" (actually seed clusters) 2 or 3 in. apart and cover 1 in. deep. Thin (and, if desired, transplant) seedlings when in second true leaf. Needed: 1 oz. for 75 to 100 ft. of drill.

BROCCOLI. Hardy annual (as grown). Start seedlings and handle like cabbage (see below), except: give more space between plants and rows. Needed: 2 to 3 doz. plants, enough for average family.

BRUSSELS SPROUTS. Hardy annual (as grown). Start seedlings and handle like late cabbage, except increase space between plants and rows. Needed: 2 or 3 doz. plants.

CABBAGE. Hardy—grown as an annual. Sow early varieties in late winter under glass. Prick out in flats 2 in. apart, set in garden in early spring, 24 in. apart each way. For late crop start in nursery beds in early June and transplant in July, 24 to 30 in. apart. Needed: 2 to 4 doz. plants of early and late sorts.

CARROT. Hardy biennial grown as an annual. Sow thinly ½ in. deep in early spring with radishes as row marker. Make one or two successional sowings at biweekly intervals; then more in July for autumn and winter crop. In dry weather irrigate to produce size and succulence and prevent splitting and woodiness. Needed: 1 oz. of seed will supply a family.

CAULIFLOWER. Semi-hardy. Start plants for early and late crops like cabbage. As white (flower) heads form, gather up leaves and tie up over head—when it is dry—to protect and bunch it. Needed: 2 or 3 doz. plants.

CARDOON. Half-hardy perennial. Start seedlings and handle like French Globe artichoke, except that stalks must be blanched by banking with earth in autumn. Needed: 1 or 2 doz. plants.

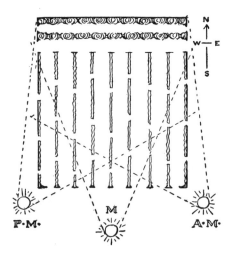

NORTH AND SOUTH ROWS ARE BEST
This diagram shows why. As the summer sun moves from east to west, it shines on both sides of north-south rows, but on only one side of east-west rows.

CELERY. Half-hardy; a staple crop. Requires so much work that supplies might better be bought.

CELERIAC. Half-hardy. Sow seed in nursery bed in spring. Thin the seedlings to 1 in. asunder. When large enough to handle transplant 6 in. asunder in rows 18 to 24 in. apart. One packet enough.

CHARD, SWISS. Hardy biennial grown as annual. Sow and grow like beet, except to thin the plants to stand 15 or 18 in. apart. Required: 2 or 3 doz. plants.

CHICORY, WITLOOF. Hardy perennial grown as an annual. See CHICORY.

CORN, SWEET. Tender annual. Sow seed 1 in deep after danger of frost has passed, 8 to 12 in. apart, preferably (in home garden) in drills 24 to 36 in. apart, depending on size of variety. Needed: 1 lb. of seed will plant 500 ft. of drill; preferably sow in ¼-lb. lots of one early variety at bi-weekly intervals.

CUCUMBER. Tender annual. Sow in hills 4 or 5 ft. apart, a dozen seeds in each, after frost danger has passed. Thin plants to 2 or 3 to the hill when rough leaves have developed. Needed: 1 packet. This crop often disappoints as disease may kill the vines before the fruit reaches edible size.

DANDELION. Hardy perennial usually grown as an annual. Seed is generally sown in late summer in drills 12 or 15 in. apart and seedlings are protected over winter with brush or straw to give spring crop. Needed: 1 packet.

EGG-PLANT. Tender annual. Sow under glass in late March. Prick out seedlings into 2-in. pots when they have the second pair of leaves; shift to larger pots when necessary and transplant outdoors after danger of frost. Needed: 12 plants.

ENDIVE. Hardy annual. For early use sow seed thinly under glass in early spring and transplant outdoors in mid-spring. For autumn, sow in nursery bed during June or early July and transplant 12 in. apart each way. Needed: 2 to 4 doz. plants.

KALE. Hardy annual. Grow like late cabbage.

KOHLRABI. Hardy annual. Grow like cabbage for early or late use.

LEEK. Biennial grown as an annual. Sow seed thinly in early spring in drills 18 in. apart and thin seedlings to 4 in.; or sow in nursery bed and transplant when about ⅛ in. in diameter. Blanch stems

Plate 56.　　　　VEGETABLES—USEFUL AND BEAUTIFUL, TOO

Top: Tempting and artistic as well, is this arrangement of vegetables at a flower show.　Bottom: A variety of crisp, succulent greens ready for the salad bowl and French dressing.

in autumn with earth or paper. Usually the few leeks wanted are bought at market; moreover, crop uses space all season. Needed: 1 packet enough for a family.

LETTUCE. Half-hardy annual. Start earliest crop under glass; harden plants and transplant between early cabbage plants, etc. Make succession sowings until mid-May and again during August. Choose varieties listed in catalogs as adapted to the seasons. Needed: 1 packet of any one variety.

MARROW, VEGETABLE. Tender annual. Grow like bush squash, see below.

MUSKMELON. Tender annual. May be grown like cucumber, takes much space and is susceptible to disease.

MUSTARD. Hardy annual. Sow seed thinly ½ in. deep in early spring in rows 12 or 15 in. apart. Make succession sowings bi-weekly until mid-May and again in late summer and early fall. Thin seedlings when 2 or 3 in. high and use as salad or greens; and later at intervals as wanted. Needed: 1 oz. of seed.

OKRA. Tender annual. Start plants like tomato. After frost danger has passed transplant to the garden 24 to 36 in. apart. Needed: 1 packet.

ONION. Hardy biennial, grown as an annual from seed or "sets." For green bunch onions or scallions, plant sets 1 to 2 in. apart in 10 to 12 in. rows as soon as soil can be worked; harvest when ready to eat. For bulb production, sow seed in early spring in rows 12 in. apart for wheel-hoe cultivation or less for hand weeding and soil stirring. Thin gradually to two or three per foot. Or sow in flats or benches under glass six weeks earlier and transplant out of doors when of pencil size. Cultivate cleanly all season and when tops ripen (yellow) break them down with light roller or barrel. Just before cold weather, pull or dig and leave on surface to dry for a day or two. Then remove tops, ripen thoroughly in a cool, airy place, clean, and store in a frost-proof place. Needed: 1 packet seed, 1 pint sets.

PARSLEY. Hardy biennial. Sow thinly in shallow drills with some forcing-radish seed to mark rows. In 4 weeks remove the last radishes and weed and thin the rows. Use successively thinned out seedlings for flavoring until remaining plants are 8 to 12 in. apart; thereafter cut dark green leaves as needed or for drying. Needed: 1 packet.

PARSNIP. Hardy biennial. Grown as annual. Sow seed outdoors in early spring with forcing-radish row markers. Remove latter in 4 weeks and thin parsnips to stand 4 in. apart. Not an advisable crop for the small garden because it occupies the land all season and can be bought. Needed: 1 packet.

PEA. Sow in early spring, seeds 2 or 3 in. apart, 2 in. deep and in 18- to 24-in. rows for dwarf varieties and 4-ft. rows for tall ones. Needed: 1 lb. of seed will sow 75 to 100 ft. of row and should yield 1 to 2 pecks of pods.

PEPPER. Tender annual. Sow seed under glass, prick out into small pots, shift as necessary and transplant to the garden after frost danger has passed. Set 24 in. apart with 30 in. between rows. Needed: 12 plants of hot varieties and 24 of sweet.

PEPPER-GRASS. Short-season annual. Sow seed thickly in rows 8 or 10 in. apart in early spring; make weekly succession sowings until mid-spring and again through September and early October. When plants are 3 or 4 in. high cut with shears.

POTATO. Tender perennial grown as annual. Not desirable for small garden because it occupies too much space, demands too much attention, yields too little in proportion to the area and is obtainable in the markets.

POTATO, SWEET-. Tender perennial grown as an annual. Takes too much space for the small garden.

PUMPKIN. Tender annual. Not desirable for small garden; uses too much space and good fruits can be bought.

RADISH. Hardy annual. Sow seed of forcing varieties in early spring 1 in. apart in 12-in. rows; make succession sowings until mid-May, using larger varieties; repeat in late summer for autumn use; in August sow winter varieties in rows 24 to 30 in. apart and thin seedlings to 3 in. Needed: 1 oz. of spring sorts; ½ oz. of winter kinds.

RHUBARB. Hardy perennial. Set plants or root divisions 3 to 4 ft. apart each way in spring. Feed lavishly. Gather no stalks until second spring following. Needed: 6 or 8 plants enough, unless also desired for jams and forcing.

RUTABAGA. Hardy biennial grown as annual. Broadcast seed thinly among tomato, corn and other tender crops in early July and let the plants shift for themselves. Needed: 1 packet.

SPINACH. Hardy annual. Sow thinly in drills 12 to 15 in. apart in early spring and again in late summer for fall use. Needed: 1 oz. will sow 100 ft. of drill.

SPINACH, NEW-ZEALAND. Start seedlings under glass in small pots 2 to 4 weeks before latest local frost date; then transplant to the garden after that 3 or 4 ft. apart. Needed: 6 to 12 plants.

SQUASH, BUSH. Tender annual. Sow in hills 4 ft. apart after danger of frost has passed. Needed: 6 to 12 plants.

SQUASH, WINTER. Tender annual. Needs too much space for small garden; better buy fruits.

TOMATO. Tender annual. Sow seeds under glass 6 to 8 weeks before latest local spring frost date. Prick out seedlings into small pots, shift as necessary and transplant after last frost 3 or 4 ft. apart. Needed: 3 or 4 doz. plants.

TURNIP. Hardy biennial grown as an annual. Sow seed thinly in early spring in rows 15 or 18 in. apart; thin seedlings to stand 4 or 6 in. apart. For autumn use scatter seed thinly among tender crops (corn, tomatoes, etc.) in early August and let the plants shift for themselves. Needed: 1 packet enough for both sowings.

WATERMELON. Tender annual. Handle like cucumber; uses much space and often succumbs to disease.

WITLOOF. See Chicory, above.

VEGETABLE LAMB (*Dicksonia barometz*). A giant cool-greenhouse fern, with massive prostrate hairy rhizomes (which are responsible for the common name) and 3-pinnate, 6- to 8-ft. fronds, of a dark glossy green above, paler below. Provide a soil of two parts peat, and one part sphagnum moss in a pot rather small for the size of the roots, so as to insure good drainage.

VEGETABLE MARROW. Bush squash varieties characterized by large size, elongated form, smooth skins either solid colored or striped, and meatiness. See MARROW; PUMPKIN; SQUASH.

VEGETABLE OYSTER. A long-season root vegetable. Botanically *Tragopogon porrifolius,* a species of Goatsbeard, it is best known as Salsify, which see.

VEGETABLE TALLOW. A common name for *Sapium sebiferum,* also called Chinese Tallow-tree, which see.

VEGETATIVE REPRODUCTION. Another term of asexual reproduction, (which see) or propagation without the use of seeds, which does not require the "mating" of two parent individuals. See also PROPAGATION, PLANT.

VELTHEIMIA (velt-hy'-mi-ah). Bulbous herbs of the Lily Family from S. Africa, with sword-like foliage in basal rosettes and tubular, drooping flowers in dense terminal clusters. Though little known in the U. S. they are of easiest culture, either in a moderately warm greenhouse or out-of-doors in the S. Bulbs planted in the fall will blossom the following spring and summer. A rich, fibrous soil with charcoal and sand gives best results.

There are but few species grown. *V. viridifolia,* bearing clusters of flowers yellow or tinged with red or purple on 1½-ft. stalks, and *V. glauca,* with flowers bright yellow or red, are the best known.

VELVET-LEAF. Common name for *Cissampelos pareira,* a tender vine with round, shield-shaped or lobed, downy leaves and small flowers followed by a round red drupe. It is widely grown in warm climates, including S. Fla.

VELVET-PLANT. One name for *Gynura aurantiaca,* a stout branching tropical herb belonging to the Composite Family. It has inconspicuous yellow or orange flowers in clusters and its appeal is in the large velvety green leaves which are covered with purple hairs, that produce a lovely effect when seen in certain lights and from certain angles. Not hardy N., it is grown as a pot plant in the greenhouse in the same general manner as coleus (which see). Good light is needed for the handsome color of the leaves to fully develop. It is increased by cuttings or from seed. A native of Java, it has occasionally escaped from cultivation in warm regions where it grows to 3 ft. Under glass it rarely exceeds 18 in.

VENATION. The kind of pattern formed by the veins of a leaf (which see). There are three main types: The grasses, lilies, and related plants that make up the monocotyledons (which see) are *parallel-veined;* while all the dicotyledons (which see) are usually *net-veined,* the multiple branches uniting throughout the leaf, like the cords of a fishnet, and ending freely in the margin.

Net-veined leaves are said to be *pinnately veined* when there is one principal vein (the midrib) giving rise to minor veins, as in sumac, and *palmately veined* when several midribs start at the base and diverge through the blade, as in the maple, The repeatedly two-forked veining characteristic of the ferns is called *dichotomous.*

VENIDIUM (ve-nid'-i-um). A small genus of hardy annuals and perennials of the Composite Family, native to S. Africa and allied to the arctotis. Their brilliant orange or yellow flowers, with short broad petals and large centers, suggest small sunflowers. The foliage is densely hairy, the plant compact, averaging 2 ft. in height. The venidium is valuable as a color accent in the border or greenhouse and the flowers last well when cut. Though several of the available species are hardy in greenhouses, and some are occasionally grown as perennials in Calif. they are generally grown from seed sown indoors in early spring and treated as annuals. A foot all around should be allowed each plant, which asks only elbow-room, full sun and well-drained soil in return for abundance of bloom from summer to late autumn.

V. fastuosum (Monarch-of-the-veldt), the choicest species, has silky grayish foliage and bright orange flowers 4 in. across, with a purplish-black zone around a dark center. *V. decurrens* (also listed as *V. calendulaceum*) has 2-in. yellow heads with black centers; it is the best known but rather weedy. Less important are *V. cinerarium; V. hirsutum,* with hairy stems and yellow flowers; and *V. speciosum,* with showy orange-yellow flowers.

VENTILATION. In horticulture, "ventilation" is synonymous with "airing." In the case of hotbeds heated by fermenting materials, especially manure, it is done partly to replace the air that has become more or less vitiated by the gases of decomposition. In other hotbeds and in cold-frames its object is to remove excessive heat and moisture so the plants will develop stockily. (See illustrations under COLDFRAME and HOTBED.

No essential phase of coldframe and hotbed management requires as much judgment as does ventilation. In late winter and early spring alternate sash must not be slid down and up (as can be done later in warmer weather) because this would result in drafts upon the plants immediately beneath the openings.

To avoid such drafts, ventilation of frames is done in two ways, both good.

The upper end of the sash may be raised and held up an inch or more by a block made with steps, each an inch higher than the preceding; or the sash may be raised on the sides from which the wind is *not* blowing. By these methods, no draft will be created.

However, no method relieves the gardener of responsibility; ventilation given when the sun is shining brightly must be reduced or shut off promptly if the sky becomes overcast, the wind rises or the air becomes colder.

During cold weather ventilation may start on sunny days at 9 o'clock or even earlier, but the sash should be closed in the afternoons while the sun is still shining brightly—not later than 4 o'clock, often at 3—so as to retain as much of the sun's heat as possible. With the advance of the season the ventilation should increase so as to make the plants grow sturdy. See also WATERING.

Ventilation of greenhouses and rooms in dwellings where plants are grown is just as important as, but less difficult than, the hotbed ventilation described. Again the essential thing is to prevent drafts of cold air hitting the plants. See DRAFTS; GREENHOUSE; HOUSE PLANTS.

VENUS FLYTRAP. Common name for *Dionaea muscipula,* an insectivorous, perennial herb of the Sundew Family, found only in swamps in N. and S. Carolina. The plants have white flowers to 1 in. across on stems to 1 ft. tall and rosettes of leaves consisting of two hinged blades set with sensitive hairs. When these are touched by an insect, the halves of the leaf close to form a trap. The entrapped insect dies and its juices are absorbed by the plant.

Dionaeas are sometimes grown in botanical collections in greenhouses where they should be potted in silver sand and black silt, with a surface of chopped sphagnum. The pots should be set in an inch of water and kept in a moist atmosphere in full sunshine.

See also INSECTIVOROUS PLANTS.

VENUS-HAIR FERN. A name for *Adiantum capillus-veneris,* an attractive fern of mild climates also known as Southern Maidenhair. See ADIANTUM; FERNS.

VENUS LOOKING-GLASS. Common name for *Specularia speculum-veneris,* an annual herb of the Bellflower Family.

VERATRUM (vee-ray'-trum). A genus of hardy, perennial herbs of the Lily Family, known as False-hellebore. They grow to 9 ft. tall and have large clasping ribbed leaves and small white, greenish or purplish flowers in panicles at the top of the stalk. They are very decorative planted along the margin of a stream or pond in the wild garden, and they are occasionally used for bold foliage effects in the shady part of the border. They are increased by division or seeds. *V. viride* (American White-hellebore), to 8 ft., has yellowish-green flowers; some of the names by which it is or has been called are Duck-ratten, Earth-gall, Devil's-bit, Bear-corn, Poor Annie, Itchweed, and Indian Poke. *V. album* (European White-hellebore), to 4 ft., has greenish-white flowers; and *V. californicum*, to 6 ft., a handsome species from W. N. America, has white flowers marked green. The roots are poisonous.

VERBASCUM (ver-bas'-kum). A genus of tall, hardy, mostly biennial herbs with variously colored flowers; several species are useful ornamentals but some have become weeds. See MULLEIN.

VERBENA (ver-bee'-nah). A genus of perennial herbs (sometimes known by the ancient name Vervain) grown in gardens for their white, red or lilac flowers in broad flat clusters. There are also some shrubby wild forms.

The species most widely grown is *V. hortensis* (Garden Verbena), a hybrid race with variously colored flowers and varying habits of growth, usually semi-trailing, the shoots rooting readily. The color forms usually seen are one-color, eyed, and striped. They are brilliant and decorative plants, frequently delightfully fragrant and furnish continuous bloom from June until late fall. They are used for massing in beds, for edgings, to fill in spaces in the border left vacant by spring bulbs, and as a ground-cover among summer or fall bulbs, such as gladiolus and lycoris.

Although perennial in the S., they are treated as annuals N., being grown from seed sown in boxes or flats in a sunny window in the house, in a hotbed, or in the greenhouse. The seedlings after being transplanted at least once are set outdoors in May, about 12 in. apart. Seed may also be sown in the open in April or May to bloom about midsummer.

ENEMIES. If powdery mildew should appear on verbena leaves, dust with sulphur. For the spinach aphids which may infest plants, spray with nicotine-sulphate and soap or some other contact insecticide. The verbena bud-worm bores in the new shoots causing them to wither; the larva, less than ½ in. long, is greenish yellow with a black head; the adult is a purplish-brown moth. To control it clip off and burn infested tips. A leaf miner is probably more disfiguring than destructive.

The "woolly bear," a white, yellow or brown caterpillar 2 in. long and covered with long yellow to reddish brown hairs, feeds on the leaves in late summer and spins cocoons under rubbish. Control by picking off and destroying the caterpillars or spraying with lead arsenate.

Many varieties of Verbena have been developed and as they do not come true from seed they must be increased by cuttings, usually taken late in September and rooted in moist sand.

Other species of Verbena, all perennials, but likewise treated as annuals are: *V. rigida* (often listed as *V. venosa*), the tuber verbena, blooming the first year from seed and spreading rapidly, bearing many short spikes of purplish flowers; *V. laciniata* (Moss Verbena), a low-growing plant with finely cut leaves and lavender flowers in small heads; *V. pulchella*, also with cut leaves and blue or lilac flowers; *V. canadensis* (Clump Vervain), more erect in habit, with rose, white or purple blossoms in spikes; *V. hastata*, a tall native plant growing in damp ground, with small dark blue flowers in spikes; and *V. officinalis*, with pale lavender flowers on 2-ft. spikes, the only Old-World species, though found as an escape in N. America.

Lemon- or Lemon-scented-verbena is *Lippia citriodora;* Sand-verbena is Abronia.

VERBENACEAE (ver-bee-nay'-see-ee). The Vervain Family, a group of herbs, shrubs and trees distributed throughout temperate and tropical regions. It is closely related to the Labiatae, as shown by the lobed, two-lipped corolla tube of the verbena flower. The genus Tectona yields teak wood, and many others provide fine garden plants, as Verbena, Lippia, Duranta, Petrea, Vitex, Callicarpa, Clerodendron, Lantana, Caryopteris.

VERNATION. The manner in which leaves are arranged in the bud. Determined by cutting the bud at an angle.

it is often a valuable guide in identifying plants. The blade may be folded along the veins like a closed fan (*plicate*), as in maples; or folded lengthwise along the midrib (*conduplicate*), as in the Magnolia Family; or rolled lengthwise (*convolute*), as in the Rose Family; the margins may be variously rolled (*involute* and *revolute*), as in violets and azaleas; or the midrib may unroll from base to tip (*circinate*), as in the ferns.

VERNONIA (ver-noh'-ni-ah). Tropical perennial herbs with showy flowers in heads. See IRONWEED.

VERONA FERN. A very feathery form of the Boston Fern, with pale green fronds 8 to 12 in. long; one of the best house plants. Give N. light and porous soil and water only as necessary.

TWO FORMS OF VERONICA
Illustrative of the wide range among the many useful perennial species, are shown above, **V.** spicata, an excellent border subject, and, below, **V.** bidwilli, a prostrate, leathery-leaved, white-flowered type good for sheltered rock gardens.

VERONICA (ve-ron'-i-kah). A genus of annual and perennial plants of the Figwort Family, highly useful and decorative in the border and rock garden. Commonly known as Speedwell, they are hardy, free-flowering, thrive in an open sunny position or light shade, and are easily grown from seed or increased by division.

PRINCIPAL SPECIES

V. maritima (sometimes listed as *V. longifolia*), with long racemes of deep lavender-blue flowers, is a useful plant for the perennial border and is naturalized in E. U. S. Var. *subsessilis,* with deeper blue flowers, blooms for a long period in moderate shade.

spicata, to 1½ ft., has blue or pink flowers in spike-like racemes; var. *albo* has white flowers; var. *erica,* pink heather-like blossoms.

incana, to 2 ft., with white hoary foliage and porcelain-blue flowers, is one of the most charming species for the border.

orchidea, to 1½ ft., has lavender-blue or pinkish flowers and glossy foliage.

gentianoides, has long loose spike-like clusters of pale lavender flowers veined with blue; those of var. *pallida* are Wedgwood blue.

multifida is a pale blue- or pink-flowered spreading species, good in the rock garden.

peduncularis, to 5 in., has small pink-veined, white blossoms and bronzy-green foliage forming mounds.

teucrium, to 1½ ft., is a valuable species with long racemes of clear blue flowers; var. *prostrata,* low-growing and with rich blue flowers, is excellent in the rock garden.

repens, a small creeping perennial with shiny mossy leaves and blue, or pink almost stemless flowers, is desirable planted between paving-stones or used as a ground-cover among small spring-blooming bulbs.

bidwilli is a low growing New-Zealand species with leathery leaves and white flowers.

hookeriana, with stiff leathery leaves and clustered purplish or white flowers, is another low-growing perennial for the rock garden.

filiformis, with mats of pale green foliage and pinkish lavender flowers in spring, makes a good ground-cover.

VERTICILLIUM (ver-ti-sil'-i-um) **WILT.** A serious wilt disease of shade trees, especially maple, elm and ailanthus, and a few other woody hosts. Commonly known as maple wilt, it does not generally occur on plants growing naturally in the wild. More maples are being lost each year as a result of this disease but although trees attacked do not usually recover there is not the rapid spread to surrounding trees characteristic of the Dutch elm disease. External symptoms are sudden wilting and dying of the foliage on one or more limbs, frequently on one side of the tree or in the top. Sometimes large trees die suddenly as if their moisture supply had been suddenly cut off. The wood of infected twigs shows characteristic green or brown streaks. Experiments are now being carried on to see if a program of generous feeding will arrest the disease.

VERVAIN. A common name for Verbena, usually applied to native species not generally cultivated.

The name is also given to the Vervain Family (Verbenaceae), which includes a number of fine garden plants.

VETCH. Common name for those species of the genus Vicia (which see) that are grown as forage crops and green-manure crops. They are low-growing, trailing or climbing herbs with profuse foliage made up of small leaflets and, like other members of the Pea Family, they add both nitrogen and humus to the soil when dug or plowed under. Though primarily farm crops, they are useful for improving garden soil, the hardy Winter or Hairy Vetch (*Vicia villosa*) being most used for this purpose. It is usually sown with rye, equal parts, at the rate of 1 pint of the mixture per 100 sq. ft. any time during the fall wherever land is vacant. Common or Spring Vetch, also called Tare, is sometimes similarly used, but as it will not survive freezing it is sown in the spring as a soil conditioner over summer. Vetches will grow in any average soil but prefer one well supplied with lime. In farm sections, escaped vetch has at times proved a troublesome weed.

Crown-vetch is *Coronilla varia;* Kidney-vetch is *Anthyllis vulneraria;* Milk-vetch is Astragalus.

VIBURNUM (vy-bur'-num). A large genus of deciduous or evergreen shrubs or small trees, widely distributed throughout the northern hemisphere, belonging to the Honeysuckle Family. They rank among the most ornamental and useful shrubs for general planting purposes. (See illustration, Plate 48.) In habit they are mostly compact and bushy with attractive foliage, which in many cases takes on good fall coloring.

Most of them also have showy flowers, followed by decorative fruits. They are well suited for shrub borders and roadside planting and some make handsome single specimens on the lawn. They are not very particular as to soil and situation, although most of them prefer a place not too dry. Several can stand considerable shade. The deciduous species are mostly hardy, but only one evergreen species (*V. rhytidophyllum*) can survive the northern winters. The snowball aphis sucks the sap from new leaves and shoots in the spring, ruining the bloom and causing leaves and shoots to curl. Since the curling starts almost before the aphids are visible to the naked eye, control is difficult. But a late dormant spray with a miscible oil followed by a spray of nicotine-sulphate and soap as soon as the leaves start to unfold should greatly reduce the infestation. Dusting with nicotine will probably get aphids within curled leaves better than a spray. Where possible dipping the ends of the twigs in nicotine soap mixture is effective.

Propagation is by seeds, best sown when ripe or stratified; by greenwood cuttings under glass; hardwood cuttings; layering and grafting.

Principal N. American Species

V. acerifolium (Dockmackie) grows to about 5 ft. with slender upright branches and maple-like leaves. It is good under-shrub, and does fairly well in dry places. The yellowish-white flowers are borne in small clusters, and the fruit is almost black; neither is very showy. The leaves take on a rosy-purple tone in fall.

alnifolium (Hobblebush, American Way-faring Tree) is a vigorous grower to 10 ft. or more, with large handsome dark green wrinkled leaves, turning reddish purple in fall. It has conspicuous flat clusters of white flowers, the outer ones large and sterile, followed by purple-black berries. It is somewhat slow to get established, and prefers a moist and half-shady place.

affinis is a compact shrub to 6 ft., with dense clusters of white flowers freely produced, followed by bluish-black berries.

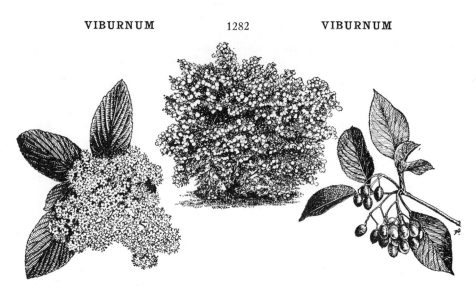

VIBURNUMS—ORNAMENTAL IN FORM, FOLIAGE, FLOWER AND FRUIT—ARE
DESERVEDLY AMONG THE MOST POPULAR OF SHRUBS
Center, the familiar, widely used Snowball or Guelder-rose (V. opulus sterile); left, handsome leaves
and one of the creamy flower clusters of the Japanese V. sieboldi; right, a cluster of the blue-black
fruits of the Black-haw (V. prunifolium).

cassinoides (Withe-rod) is one of the handsomest of native shrubs. In the wild it is usually found in moist places, sometimes 15 ft. or more high. In cultivation in the open it makes a compact round-headed specimen. It has finely toothed leaves and clusters of creamy-white flowers in June. In the fall it is outstanding in fruit, with heavy clusters of berries varying in color from yellowish-green to pink and blue-black.

dentatum (Arrow-wood) is an upright bushy grower to 15 ft. or more, with roundish coarsely-toothed leaves, wide clusters of white flowers in June, and blue-black berries. It does well in moist ground, and is also good for shady places and under trees.

lentago (Sheep-berry, Nanny-berry) is a tall shrub or small tree with large lustrous leaves, clusters of creamy-white flowers and juicy black berries. It is distinguished in winter with its long pointed buds.

molle is a very dense grower to 12 ft., with coarsely-toothed leaves, white flowers and blue-black berries. It is distinguished in winter by the flaky bark and light gray young stems.

prunifolium (Black-haw) is a large shrub or small tree with wide spreading branches; often the outstanding feature of rocky hillsides in the East. It has handsome foliage, clusters of pure white flowers, followed by blue-black and bloomy berries.

rufidulum (Southern Black-haw) makes a tree to 40 ft., with wide-spreading branches in the South, but in the North is usually a shrub. It has dark green shining leaves, and is distinguished by rusty brown hairs on the leaf and flower stalks. The flowers are pure white in a broad cluster, and the berries are dark blue and bloomy.

pubescens is a good free-flowering shrub in early summer. It has small compact clusters of white flowers followed by black fruits. Var. *canbyi* has larger leaves and flower clusters, and is the latest to bloom.

trilobum, better known as *V. americanum,* (Cranberry-Bush) is the native form of the European *V. opulus*. It is a large handsome shrub with 3-lobed leaves which turn a brilliant color in fall. It has showy clusters of white flowers, the outer ones large and sterile. The large heavy clusters of scarlet, juicy berries color early and remain decorative until spring.

Principal Asiatic Species

V. carlesi is one of the most desirable shrubs, valued for its very fragrant pink and white flower clusters, opening with the leaves. It is of rounded form to 5 ft. or so, and is sometimes grafted, so sucker growths should be checked. Its blue-black berries are not freely produced.

bitchuiense is somewhat similar to *V. carlesi*, but is of rather straggly habit, with smaller leaves and flower clusters. Not as desirable for general planting.

fragrans grows to 10 ft. and has short panicles of very fragrant pink and white flowers in advance of the leaves.

dilatatum is a large and handsome shrub to 10 ft. or more, free flowering and very conspicuous in fall with an abundance of small scarlet berries, often remaining well into winter.

hupehense grows to about 6 ft. and is of rounded form; very showy in fall with a profusion of small round scarlet berries.

lobophyllum grows to 15 ft. and is a striking plant in fall with its heavy clusters of bright scarlet berries. The young growth has a waxy bloom.

wrighti is similar to *V. dilatatum*, but with smaller flower clusters and larger berries often so freely produced that the branches are weighted to the ground. The fruit and foliage are retained in good condition for some time.

theiferum is a narrow upright grower with very handsome leaves but rather plain flower clusters. It is very decorative in fruit with clusters of large ovoid scarlet berries. The tops are likely to be killed back in severe winters. The specific name comes from the fact that in China Buddhist monks make from the leaves an infusion known as Sweet Tea.

tomentosum is one of the handsomest of the family. It is outstanding in form with its wide-spreading horizontal branches, bearing handsome leaves and showy clusters of white flowers along the upper side. The clusters are conspicuous with an outer ring of large and sterile flowers. It is also attractive in fruit, which changes from scarlet to black. Var. *sterile*, better known as *plicatum,* and the most familiar of the "Snowball" forms, is a dense grower with compact heads of white sterile flowers. It is not always entirely hardy or easy to transplant.

sieboldi is a tree-like shrub with bright green lustrous leaves which give off a disagreeable odor when bruised. It is very showy in bloom with large clusters of white flowers, followed by berries changing from red to black and soon falling.

sargenti is the Asiatic form of *V. opulus*, and much like the N. American *V. trilobum*. It has larger sterile flowers than these, and is the handsomest of the

three in bloom. It is of good compact habit. Var. *flavum* has yellow fruit.

rhytidophyllum is a handsome evergreen species growing to about 10 ft. with long dark green wrinkled leaves, yellowish and felt-like beneath. It bears large flat clusters of yellowish-white flowers and fruit changing from red to black. It needs a protected position for the sake of the foliage and kills back in below-zero weather. It is the only evergreen species that may be kept alive outdoors in the North.

Principal European Species

V. lantana (Wayfaring-tree) is a vigorous shrub to 15 ft. with light green wrinkled leaves, white beneath, turning deep red in fall. It has clusters of white flowers and berries which change from red to black. It will thrive in drier places than most and is much used as a stock for grafting purposes.

opulus (European Cranberry-bush) is a vigorous grower to 12 ft. with 3-lobed leaves turning crimson and orange in fall. It has clusters of showy white flowers and scarlet juicy fruit. Var. *nanum* is a dwarf compact non-flowering form with small leaves, useful in foundation plantings. Var. *roseum* (Common Snowball, Guelder-rose) has all the flowers sterile in a globose head. It is often attacked by black aphis. Var. *xanthocarpum* is a yellow-fruited form.

tinus (Laurestinus) is the most useful of the evergreen species where hardy. A bushy grower to 10 ft. or more, it has dark, glossy-green leaves and clusters of pinkish-white flowers, which, in mild climates, open during the winter. It may be grown in pots for winter flowering in the cool greenhouse.

VICIA (vis'-i-ah). A genus of trailing or tendril-climbing, rather weedy herbs of the Pea Family. They have purple, white, or scarlet flowers and abundant feather-form leaves. Some species known as Vetch (which see) are used as forage or green-manure crops. One, *V. faba,* the Broad, Windsor, English Dwarf, or Horse Bean, is a vegetable grown as human food for centuries. It is an erect annual plant about 3 ft. high, bearing broad pods, sometimes 18 in. long, containing almost round, flat seeds. It is not much grown in American gardens but is used in the W. to fatten cattle. It dislikes extreme heat.

A few species are rather decorative and sometimes grown in the flower garden. They are *V. cracca* var. *gerardi,* a hardy annual with purple flowers in short racemes, occasionally grown in the border; *V. gigantea,* a W. species with reddish-purple blossoms, offered by dealers in native plants; and *V. caroliniana,* with loose racemes of white blossoms, an attractive trailer for sunny slopes in the wild garden.

VICTORIA. Royal or Victoria Water-lily. The first specimen of this truly royal S. American waterlily to be studied and described was called *Victoria regia* in honor of England's then reigning Queen. The fragrant, night-blooming flowers, from 6 to 18 in. across, and the large platter-like leaves as much as 7 ft. in diameter give the plant an overpowering beauty and magnificence. The flowers, opening white, change to pink which, on the second night of bloom, becomes a deep rose; their fragrance is like the odor of pineapples. The enormous, rich green, circular leaves have a curiously turned up rim from 5 to 6 in. high; the underside is heavily netted with a cross veining of air pockets of deep purplish green. Stem and veinings are spined.

In addition to *V. regia,* one other species and a horticultural variety of *V. regia* are cultivated in the U. S. *V. cruziana* (also called *V. trickeri*), from Paraguay, is the most easily cultivated as it does well in a lower temperature (70 to 75 deg. F.), whereas *V. regia* and its var. *randi* demand 85 deg. or more and almost always require additional heat in the pool for best results.

A pool 25 to 30 ft. in diameter is none too large for a single Victoria, and it hardly need be said that it needs full sun at all times.

Seeds must never be allowed to dry. As soon as gathered (the plants seldom bloom early enough to ripen seed in a N. climate) they must be put in bottles of water and kept there until planted.

VICTORIAN-HAZEL. Common name for *Pomaderris apetala,* a 20-ft. tree of Australasia with greenish flowers. Popular in Calif. for street and yard planting.

VIGNA (vig'-nah). A genus of annual herbs of the Pea Family with leaves in 3's and yellowish-white or purplish, sweetpea-like blossoms. Most of the species are tender N. and are grown only in the S. (or as short-season, midsummer subjects for cover-crops or forage in the N.). *V.*

sinensis is the Cowpea (which see); and *V. sesquipedalis,* the Yard-long or Asparagus Bean, is raised both N. and S. for its edible pods from 1 to 3 ft. long.

VILLOUS. Covered with a nap of fine soft hairs, not matted and rather more shaggy than velvety. Many of the flea-banes (Erigeron) exhibit this characteristic.

VINCA (vin'-kah). Periwinkle. Erect or trailing herbs or sub-shrubs, mostly from warm regions, belonging to the Dogbane Family. The best known species—and also one of the most useful of garden plants—is *V. minor* (Running-myrtle). This is a native of Europe but it has run wild in some parts of the country. It is very hardy, thrives under shaded conditions, and is one of the best plants to grow beneath trees and other places where a carpeting effect is desired. It has shining evergreen leaves and attractive violet-blue flowers in spring. There are several varieties, including white rosy-purple and double-flowered forms, also some with variegated leaves. Var. *bowlei,* a recent introduction, is superior to the type in foliage effect and has flowers of a deeper shade of blue, freely produced in spring and again lightly in the fall. *V. major* is larger in every way than *V. minor* but not as hardy. The variegated form which is usually grown, is much used for furnishing baskets, vases and window boxes. These two species and their varieties are propagated by cuttings and division.

V. rosea (Madagascar Periwinkle) is a tender perennial which may be grown in the North as an annual. It is a good flower-garden subject with rosy-purple flowers and is often used in parks with good effect as a bedding plant. There are varieties with white flowers and white ones with a reddish eye. Seeds should be sown early in the year in a warm greenhouse and transplanted several times before being set outdoors.

VINE-CACTUS. A common name for *Fouquieria splendens,* a spiny shrub of the S. W. with scarlet flowers. A species of CANDLEWOOD, which see.

VINE FAMILY. Another name for the Grape Family. See VITACEAE.

VINES. Under this general heading is included a large and varied group of plants. In England, the term would be taken to refer only to grape-vines, but here it is used to include all kinds of climbing plants, and also certain shrubs with long flexible shoots which may be trained to serve as vines.

The group comprises a wealth of plant material available for various situations and purposes. (See illustrations, Plate 58.) Outdoors, vines are used to clothe porches, trellises, arbors, pergolas and posts; to clamber up old tree-trunks or cover the bare ground beneath; to sprawl over rocks and to cover steep banks. Under glass they are useful to drape pillars and roof rafters, to cover walls, and

Some vines are supported by their leaves; the stems or petioles, being sensitive to contact with a supporting object, curl around it. Clematis is notable in this group. Many plants have stems which twine about a support, and it has long been a matter of interest that not all twine in the same direction. The hop, for example, turns or winds to the right, or clock-wise; while the morning-glory turns to the left, or counter clock-wise.

SUPPORTS FOR VINES. With the exception of the stem-rooting type, vines used

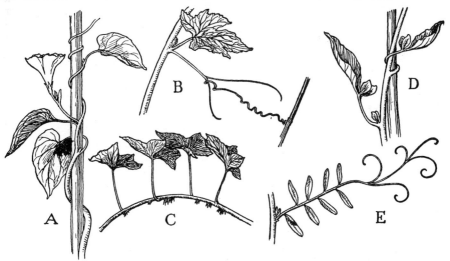

VINES CLIMB BY VARIOUS MEANS AND METHODS

Some twine around a support, as the morning-glory (A); some hold on by means of tendrils like spiral springs, as the grape (B), while others cling by means of stem roots, as the English ivy (C). In Clematis and species of Solanum (D) the leaf petioles themselves twine about the support, while in various legumes like vetches and peas (E) the leaf is elongated into a branched tendril for the same purpose.

in general to add to the floral and foliage effect of a well-kept greenhouse or conservatory. Some are also used to embellish window and porch boxes and hanging baskets in or around the dwelling.

How VINES CLING. Vines have developed different methods of supporting their stems. Some produce adventitious roots along one side of the stem, which serve to fix and hold them to such objects as a wall or tree. English ivy and trumpet-vine are good examples of this group. Many cling by means of tendrils, which are often twisted like a spiral spring so as to combine security with a certain amount of flexibility or "give." Gourds, grapes and peas climb this way. The Boston ivy attaches itself by means of disks at the ends of the tendrils.

to cover walls will require some kind of support attached to the wall. The old-time cloth shreds and wall nails are still used in some places. Modified forms of this idea are found in wire clips cemented to the wall surface, in wall nails with pliable tips to bend over the stems, and in staples (driven into wooden plugs which in turn are driven into drilled holes) to which the stems are tied. Stout wires run through screw-eyes projecting a few inches from the wall afford a good means of support in many cases. For porches and against walls that have to be painted from time to time, a good plan is to construct an iron-pipe frame with wire cross strands or wire-netting, and attach it to the wall by means of hooks. The entire section can then be unhooked, lowered to the ground and laid there out of the way of the painters and without damage to the vines. Various forms of wood lattice-work may best serve the purpose under certain conditions. To form a screen away from buildings, posts with wires threaded through them may be used, and for individual vines out in the open cedar posts with the branch stubs left on are very satisfactory. In place of a low fence or along a walk or drive, vines can be grown on chains or heavy wires looped in long curves between wood, metal, or masonry posts.

PREPARATION FOR VINES. An important item in the growing of vines, and one often slighted, is the proper preparation of a good station. Most vines are vigorous growers and are expected to remain in the same place for many years. If simply stuck into the ground without regard for soil quality and condition, most kinds are pretty sure to be stunted and become an easy prey to insects and diseases. Therefore, break up the soil at least 2 ft. deep and over an area 3 ft. or more across for each plant; entirely replace the soil with good loam if need be, and in any case enrich it with old manure or leafmold. If close to a building watch out for buried piles of brickbats, mortar and other rubbish that might interfere with both moisture and food supply for the plants.

As a general rule, planting is best done in spring, and in most cases it is a good plan to cut the plants back pretty severely so as to induce a good basal growth. Watch the young shoots and see that they are properly secured from the start. Vines close to a wall are likely to suffer from dryness at the roots; and thorough soakings from time to time will be well worth while. Established vines appreciate a mulch of manure and feeding with some good complete fertilizer now and again when growth is active.

PRUNING. Due consideration should be given to the space to be covered when selecting kinds of vines. A vigorous grower planted where there is only space for one of moderate growth means a lot of cutting back, which detracts from the natural beauty of the plant. Some pruning, of course, is necessary, but as always the pruning shears should be used with discretion and good judgment. Vines which flower early should be looked over right after flowering, the laterals should be shortened and perhaps some of the old main shoots removed to make way for young ones. Vines which flower on shoots of the current season's growth are properly pruned in spring just before new growth starts. It is sometimes advisable to give old plants of English ivy a hard shearing, and if this is done in spring the stems will soon be clothed again with new leaves. Old plants of *Euonymus vegetus* will remain more compact and better furnished if some of the laterals are shortened back in spring. Do not allow vines to cover up good architectural features, but by all means let them conceal poor ones. Select vines with consideration for their habits.

VINES FOR VARIOUS PURPOSES
(For detailed information refer to the various genera mentioned)

HARDY VINES. Self-clinging on walls: *Campsis radicans, Euonymus radicans* and var. *vegetus, Hedera helix,* in variety, *Hydrangea petiolaris, Parthenocissus tricuspidata, P. quinquefolia, Schizophragma hydrangeoides.*

Requiring supports and training on walls; good on trellises, fences and arbors: *Actinidia arguta, A. polygama, Akebia quinata, Ampelopsis aconitifolia, A. brevipedunculata* and var. *elegans, Aristolochia durior, Celastrus articulatus, C. scandens,* Clematis, most kinds, *Forsythia suspensa, Lonicera caprifolium, L. heckrotti, L. japonica, L. periclymenum, L. sempervirens, L. tragophylla, Lycium chinense, Polygonum baldschuanicum, Vitis kaempferi, Wisteria floribunda, W. sinensis.*

VINES GOOD ON SLOPES. *Celastrus articulatus, Campsis radicans, Clematis virginiana, Euonymus radicans* var. *coloratus* (in shade), *Lonicera japonica* var. *halliana, L. henryi* (in shade), *Hedera helix* (in shade), *Parthenocissus quinquefolia.*

ANNUAL VINES (or may be grown as such). Useful for quick effects: *Cardiospermum halicacabum, Cobaea scandens, Cucurbita pepo* var. *ovifera, Dolichos lablab, Eccremocarpus scaber, Echinocystis lobata, Humulus japonicus, Ipomaea hederacea, I. tricolor, Phaseolus coccineus, Quamoclit pinnata, Tropaeolum majus, T. peregrinum.*

HERBACEOUS VINES (or usually so). *Apios tuberosa, Clematis jackmani, Boussingaultia basselloides, Dioscorea batatas, Humulus lupulus, Lathyrus latifolius, Pueraria thunbergiana.*

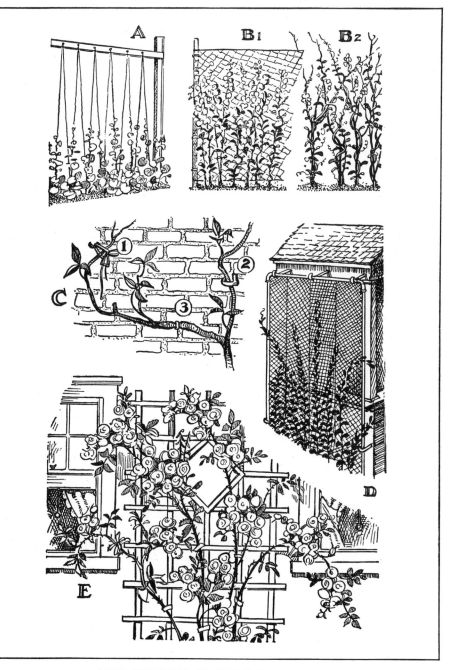

SOME METHODS OF SUPPORTING VINES

A. A simple, temporary framework and strings or wires for annuals like morning glory. B. Sweet peas will cling well to poultry wire (1) but twiggy brush (2) is better. C. Non-clinging vines can be held against brick walls by tying them to nails or staples (1), or with the flexible ends of "wall-nails" (2); but never drive a staple over a stem (3) or it soon will choke and kill it. D. Against a house wall or porch a wire-covered pipe frame can be hung on brackets and lifted down when painting is necessary without removing or injuring the vine. E. For climbing roses against a house, an attractive slat trellis is always effective.

For Window Boxes and Hanging Baskets. *Hedera helix, Cymbalaria muralis, Maurandia barclaiana, Nepeta hederacea, Pelargonium peltatum, Senecio mikanioides, Thunbergia alata, Vinca major.*

For Greenhouses (or outdoors in warm regions). *Antigonon leptopus, Bignonia capreolata, Doxantha unguis-cati, Clematis flammula, C. indivisa, Gelsemium sempervirens, Jasminum officinale, J. grandiflorum, J. primulinum, Lapageria rosea, Dipladenia boliviensis, Passiflora caerulea, P. edulis, Solanum jasminoides, S. wendlandi, Trachelospermum jasminoides, Plumbago capensis.*

Vines Requiring Tropical Conditions. *Allamanda grandiflora, Aristolochia elegans, A. grandiflora, Bougainvillea glabra, B. spectabilis, Beaumontia grandiflora, Clerodendron thomsonae, Stephanotis floribunda, Stigmaphyllon ciliatum, Solandra grandiflora, Thunbergia laurifolia, Ipomaea horsfalliae* var. *briggsi.*

VIOLET. The genus Viola, which includes a number of species of small, generally perennial herbs, having attractive blue, white, lavender or yellow, spurred flowers in the early spring or summer. Among them are the plants better known as Pansies, the attractive garden Violas and the still more familiar Violets of the florist shops and the woods. Violets, the species not designated but presumably native wild types, are the State flowers of Ill., N. J., R. I., and Wis. (See illustrations, Plate 57.) All are propagated by seeds, divisions or offsets. See also PANSY.

The Sweet, Garden, or Florists Violet is *V. odorata,* an Old-World species widely cultivated in the garden and grown in the N. in frames or cool greenhouses for winter and early spring cut flowers. In the garden the single forms of *V. odorata* in blue or white are easily grown as border plants, or they may be naturalized on the edge of the woodland. Set the young plants in rich loamy soil in a sheltered position in the late spring or early fall and mulch well with leafmold or light decomposed material from the compost heap. With this simple treatment they will bloom for a month or six weeks in the spring. They tend to set runners freely—in fact too much so, and to prevent their becoming a matted mass and rapidly "running out" they should be lifted every year after flowering, and pulled apart, and the young plants reset.

ENEMIES. Several leaf-spot diseases may kill the tissues, forming small or large, circular or irregular, ashy white or brown areas; and mildew and rust may occur. One leaf spot, known as scab, although officially recorded only recently, is so widespread that it must have flourished unnoticed for years. It causes small red and white spots which change to light-colored scalded or blistered areas on leaves and petioles. All such diseases are usually held in check by destroying old leaves in the fall. If much spotting is noticed during prolonged periods of wet weather, spray with 2-4-50 bordeaux mixture. Gray mold (see BOTRYTIS) is sometimes prevalent in wet weather. Two root rots affecting violet and other Viola species, one mostly outdoors, the other in greenhouses, can be controlled only by changing the soil, by soil sterilization, and by the selection of healthy plants for propagation. Affected plants are yellow, dwarfed, and eventually die, the roots decaying and becoming jet black.

Eel-worms may infect violet roots (see NEMATODES); slugs (which see) may feed on the leaves and aphids and red spiders may suck the juices. The yellow woolly bear caterpillar may also feed on the leaves (see under VERBENA). In the greenhouse twisting and distortion of the leaves is due to the gall midge, which can be controlled by occasionally fumigating for two hours (*not for all night*) with calcium cyanide (see FUMIGATION). The blue-black grubs of the violet sawfly eat the leaves at night and the adult, a small, 4-winged black fly, lays its eggs in blister-like incisions in the leaves. Control by spraying or dusting with hellebore or lead arsenate.

A number of varieties of *V. odorata* have been developed especially for cultivation under glass. Among the double forms the favorites are Marie Louise and Lady Hume Campbell, and in the singles, Princess of Wales, California, and Baroness Rothschild.

Growers now prefer the cheaper form of glass houses to frames for forcing violets for winter bloom. They are grown in solid beds; the young plants being set in the late spring 8 to 12 in. apart in rows 10 in. apart, in soil composed of 4 parts light loam to 1 part well-rotted manure, the whole well mixed and made definitely alkaline (sweet) with lime. During the summer the house is shaded and kept cool

Plate 57.   THE VIOLET AND SOME RELATIVES

Top: The white form of the fragrant English violet naturalizes readily on the edge of the woodland. Center left: Quaint pansy faces smile at the sun. Lower left: One of the new developments in bedding violas—the petals deep and rich in color, their texture velvety and lasting. Lower right: The long-stemmed, single violet—always a favorite cut flower.

and well-ventilated. The plants are watered in moderation but never soaked; a mulch of spent manure is excellent to conserve moisture. All runners should be removed, thus inducing a compact growth and stimulating flowers to come into bloom in October. Very little heat is required during the winter as violets succeed better when the temperature does not exceed 50 deg. Propagation is by division, or preferably, by offsets rooted in sand.

From the species *V. cornuta,* which has a flower with a very long spur, the garden Violas, also called Tufted Pansies, have been developed. They are most valuable and decorative for edging the border or for ground-cover under roses. Some of the best named forms include G. Wermig, forming clumps of rich purple flowers in bloom throughout the summer, Jersey Gem, a fine dwarf, free-flowering plant, Suttons Apricot with large flowers, buff, tinted orange, Golden Yellow, and a number of others.

VIOLETS IN A ROCK GARDEN
In a location like this violets not only look at home but also show that they are at home and happy.

V. tricolor var. *hortensis,* with large, short-spurred flowers in shades and combinations of blue, white and yellows, is the familiar Pansy (which see) or Heartsease.

Other species of Viola used in the rock and wild garden are as follows:

V. gracilis from E. Europe, having delightful starry, purple flowers.

elegantula, with purplish-pink blossoms. often listed as *V. bosniaca.*

blanda, a native species with white, sweet-scented flowers which is charming planted as a ground-cover for early spring-flowering bulbs.

canina (Dog Violet), a European plant having purple flowers with yellow spurs.

pedata (Birdsfoot Violet) with finely cut leaves and purple blossoms, requiring an open position in acid, sandy soil.

African- and Usambara-violet are names for *Saintpaulia ionantha;* Dames-violet is *Hesperis matronalis;* Dogs-tooth-violet is *Erythronium dens-canis.*

VIPERS-BUGLOSS. Common name for Echium, a genus of bristly herbs or shrubs with rose, blue or purple flowers.

VIRGINIA CHAIN FERN (*Woodwardia areolata*). A tall once-pinnate marsh fern of the E. States, good for naturalizing in acid and wet but well-drained soil. Rather too robust for the mixed garden.

VIRGINIA-COWSLIP. A common name for *Mertensia virginica,* also known as Virginia blue-bell, a spring-flowering perennial herb with blue, sometimes purple, flowers.

VIRGINIA CREEPER. Common name for *Parthenocissus quinquefolia;* also called American Ivy. See IVY.

VIRGINIAN STOCK. Common name for *Malcomia maritima,* a spreading annual plant of the Crucifer Family with abundant white, lilac or pinkish flowers.

VIRGINS BOWER. A common name for several small-flowered forms of Clematis, a genus of many diverse species of handsome herbaceous perennial and woody flowering vines.

VIRUS DISEASES. A group of plant diseases due to some infectious principle, called a *virus,* which may be transmitted from diseased to healthy individuals. No visible organisms (even with the ultramicroscope) or casual agents are known, as the viruses can pass through fine filters. However, since the behavior of this group of diseases closely resembles those known to be caused by germs it is probable that the virus contains some living entity.

Virus diseases take the form of infectious chlorosis or foliage or flower variegation (see chlorosis); yellows, as exemplified in peach or aster yellows; leaf roll (of pota-

toes); curly top (of sugar beets); rosetting; stunting and the various so-called
mosaics, whose chief symptom is a mottling
of the leaves often accompanied by dwarfing or malformation of the flowers.

Some virus diseases, such as tobacco
mosaic, may be transmitted merely by
touching. Others are transmitted only by
budding or grafting, as peach yellows. A
few are transmitted through the seed, as
bean mosaic; some both by grafting and
insects, and many chiefly by insects. Most
mosaics are carried by insects: aster yellows is carried by leaf hoppers, cucumber
mosaic by the melon aphis and the striped
cucumber beetle, curly top by a leaf
hopper, and so on through a long list.

There are no protective measures known
by which virus diseases may be controlled
so the chief precaution against them and
their spread is the immediate removal of all
diseased individuals, a practice known as
"roguing." Special crops such as tobacco
or asters are often grown under cheesecloth tents to prevent their infection with
disease by the agency of insects.

VISTAS. These are paths or stretches
of unobstructed vision restrained from
wandering by a frame planting on each
side (and sometimes by borders of foliage
above and below), and terminating in
scenes or objects of beauty. As a whole
a vista may be planned or natural, and
the terminal feature may be near at hand
or at a great distance. In planning any
garden it is of primary importance to
learn, first of all, whether the possibility
of vistas as landscape features exists, in
directions which make them accessible
from any place or places in that garden.

Sometimes the cutting out of certain
trees or parts of trees will immeasurably
enrich the entire composition by bringing
into it a vista of distant sea or mountains,
or of sweeping meadows and rural landscape. If so, it is mistaken sentiment to
preserve the trees at the garden's expense.
On the other hand, to plant trees and
shrubs where they will hide or break up a
monotonous horizon and create a vista—
or vistas—focused on the choicest portion
of that horizon, is equally important on
occasion.

Within the smallest garden little vistas
are possible—as where a rose arch centers
the vision on a tiny pool beyond it; and
as a medium of increasing the apparent
size of any place they are invaluable.

For by narrowing the vista as it extends
into the distance the perspective is deepened. And deep perspective (even when
illusory) conveys the impression of greater
distance and, therefore, of larger size.

VITACEAE (vy-tay'-see-ee). The
Grape or Vine Family, a group of erect
shrubs and rarely small trees, but better
known as woody vines climbing by means
of tendrils. The family is largely one of
tropical and subtropical latitudes, but many
forms are hardy and easy of cultivation.
The family includes, besides the wild and
cultivated grapes (the genus Vitis), the
genera Parthenocissus, Ampelopsis and Cissus, species of which are cultivated as ornamental vines and wall and trellis covers.

VITAMINS. These much publicized
substances are important regulators for
plant growth as well as for the health of
the human body. We consume a considerable amount when we eat vegetables and
fruits, many of which are rich in the vitamin source. However, in plant life they
are actually hormones (which see) because
they are substances produced in one part
of the plant that regulate the function of
another part. A number have been isolated
and studied and more maybe discovered in
the future. *Vitamin B₁* (Thiamin chloride) has been definitely demonstrated to
be an essential for root development in
plants. It would seem that the vitamin is
produced in the leaves and gradually works
downward to the roots where it has a
stimulating influence on the growing root
tips. It is *not* a plant nutrient or fertilizer nor can its effect be considered similar to that of such materials. The vitamin
activates cell growth on the tip end of the
root, thereby enabling more food to be
taken in for the nourishment of the entire
plant.

Most plants growing under normal, satisfactory conditions manufacture sufficient
Vitamin B₁ for their needs in their own
leaves. On the other hand, some species
of plants seem to be incapable of building
up, or synthesizing, the vitamin in sufficient quantities to satisfy their root requirements. The growth of such plants therefore has definite limitations, and they must
therefore, rely on external sources for their
vitamin supply. Obviously, if the amount
of vitamin synthesized by the plant leaves
is large (as in many fast growing plants
like tomatoes), then the roots receive a
sufficient amount. Under these conditions

the addition of any more would be wasteful and superfluous. If the amount synthesized by the leaves is small, as it appears to be in some plants, then there is a strong possibility of increasing the growth by adding vitamin to the soil.

Manure, rotting vegetation, seed meal, and humus-making materials generally all contain considerable amounts of Vitamin B_1. When such materials are used or find their way into the soil, a rich source of the vitamin has been supplied. It is logical to suppose that under favorable growing conditions most plants either create or have access to enough Vitamin B_1 for all their requirements. Where growing conditions are poor, or the soil is deficient in a vitamin, its addition will probably serve as a stimulus. However, any influence Vitamin B_1 might exert on shoot growth, seems to be primarily the result of its effect upon the root growth.

Vitamin C (Ascorbic acid) is present in oranges, lemons, tomatoes and black currants in good quantities. Manufactured by nature, it is stored in the fruit and there is some indication that it improves the keeping qualities of seeds.

Vitamin B_2 (Riboflavin) seems to be a root growth factor similar to Vitamin B_1. Smaller amounts produce effective results, but on a fewer number of plant species. *Vitamin B_6* is another of the vitamins probably normally present in plants and affecting root growth. It has been known to cause cuttings to root more readily when it is sprayed over the green tops in the propagating bench.

Nicotinic acid is another vitamin of the B group. Greatly increased root length has been noted in some plants after it has been applied under laboratory conditions.

VITEX (vy'-teks). Deciduous or evergreen shrubs or trees, widely distributed in warm and temperate regions, belonging to the Vervain Family. One or two species, although not entirely hardy, can be grown N. They are valued for their showy flower spikes produced late in the season and are not particular as to soil, providing it is well-drained and the situation is open. Propagated by layers and greenwood cuttings.

V. agnus-castus (Chaste-tree, Hemptree, Monks Pepper-tree) is a native of S. Europe. Under favorable conditions it grows to 10 ft. high, but the shoots are usually killed far back in severe climates.

Young shoots from the base flower the same year. It has very dark green divided leaves, gray on the under side, and long dense spikes of lilac or lavender flowers. There is a white form, var. *alba*. *V. macrophylla* as listed in catalogs is said to be just a broad-leaved form of *V. agnus-castus*. It is a vigorous and very good shrub, with fine spikes of blue flowers. *V. negundo* is a Chinese shrub growing to 15 ft., with four-sided stems and loose panicles of lavender flowers. The finely cut-leaved var. *incisa* is of more graceful habit, and also hardier.

VITIS (vy'-tis). A genus of fast-growing, tendril-climbing deciduous vines, natives of the N. hemisphere, mostly in temperate regions, and known in this country as Grape (which see), but often in the Old World as Vine. Some are grown for their ornamental foliage, which in many cases takes on brilliant coloring in fall; others are important vineyard and home-garden plants grown for their edible luscious fruit. Propagation is by seed, cuttings of ripened wood, and layers.

Principal American Species

V. aestivalis (Summer Grape) is a tall climber found from N. Y. southward, distinguished in foliage by the large lobed leaves, reddish-brown beneath. The berries are bloomy-black.

berlandieri (Spanish or Winter Grape) is a southern vine of moderate growth, with large lustrous leaves and compact clusters of purple berries, ripening late.

candicans (Mustang Grape), another native of the S., is a strong high climber with the young growth and the under side of leaves white. The berries are light purple with tough skin and an unpleasant flavor.

cordifolia (Frost Grape), native from Pa. southward, is a strong high climber with large lustrous leaves scarcely lobed, and dull black berries, edible after frost.

labrusca (Fox Grape), native from New England to S. U. S., is a strong grower with large thick felt-like leaves dull-white to reddish-brown beneath. The fruit is purplish-black with a strong musky odor. This is the principal parent of American cultivated grapes.

leconteana (Blue Grape), found from New England to S. U. S., is a strong climber resembling *V. aestivalis* but with leaves glaucous beneath and smaller berries.

Plate 58.   THE VARIED LUXURIANCE OF VINES

Top: Like a fragrant living springtime snow, the white wisteria clings to the overhanging eaves.
Insert right: The orange bugles of the trumpet-vine call the humming-bird to a feast of nectar.
Bottom: The fleece-flower (Polygonum auberti) veils an unsightly fence or quickly makes the arbor a
shady retreat.

rotundifolia (Muscadine, Southern Fox Grape) is found along river banks and in rich woodlands of the S., often growing to 100 ft. It has rather small heart-shaped leaves and dull purple musky berries.

vulpina (Riverbank Grape) is a vigorous climber found from Nova Scotia southward. It has fragrant flowers, attractive bright green leaves, and small purple-black berries.

PRINCIPAL ASIATIC SPECIES

V. amurensis (Amur Grape) is a strong grower with large leaves which turn crimson and purple in fall.

kaempferi (formerly *V. coignetiae*) is a vigorous hardy grower, with heavy foliage turning brilliant scarlet in fall, and giving it the name Crimson-glory Vine.

thunbergi is a slender grower, with the young growth and the under side of leaves covered with a rusty hairy growth. The leaves turn crimson in fall.

romaneti is a stout grower, distinguished by the young growth covered with purple glandular bristles.

vinifera (Wine Grape) is the cultivated grape of history, now largely grown in Europe and Calif. in many varieties. (See illustrations, Plate 24.)

VRIESIA (vree'-si-ah). A genus of striking greenhouse subjects of the Pineapple Family, native to tropical America, but succeeding in the open in S. Florida. The stiff, spiny leaves, barred or variegated often 2 ft. long, grow in dense rosettes; the flowers, borne in flattened spikes, are conspicuous for their brightly-colored bracts or sheaths. In nature these are mostly air plants (epiphytes) but under glass a rich, fibrous soil is required and liberal watering throughout the summer, when growth is chiefly made. A light sprinkling should be given in the winter, until flowers form in earliest spring. Propagation is by suckers from around the base of old plants.

V. duvaliana, to 1 ft., has leaves tinged with red beneath, flowers yellow tipped with green, and bracts scarlet and green. *V. fenestralis,* to 1½ ft., has leaves dark-veined, tipped with brown and flowers pale yellow while the bracts are spotted green. *V. hieroglyphica* has leaves banded and irregularly marked with dark green and purple; its flowers are purplish.

WAFER-ASH. Common name for *Ptelea trifoliata,* a shrub or small tree of E. U. S. with small greenish flowers and dry winged fruits; a species of Hop-tree, which see.

WAHLENBERGIA (wahl-en-bur'-ji-ah). A genus of small annual or perennial plants of the Bellflower Family with nodding, bell-shaped, blue flowers. They resemble the Bellflowers (which see) and should be given the same culture. They are grown in rock gardens, preferably in the open, in a well-drained situation. The annuals are increased by seed, the perennial by seed or division.

W. gracilis is an annual to 1 ft., with solitary blue flowers ½ in. long. *W. congesta* is a creeping perennial, with round leaves and small pale blue blossoms. *W. saxicola,* another annual, has small leaves and solitary white, blue-veined flowers.

Wahlenbergia is often listed as Edraianthus, which see.

WAHOO. Common name for *Euonymus atropurpureus,* a deciduous shrub with small purple flowers and scarlet fruits.

WAKE-ROBIN. Common name for the genus Trillium, familiar woodland perennials with white, pink or purple three-part flowers and lily-like leaves.

WALKING FERN (*Camptosorus rhizophyllus*). A curious rock fern of the E. States, having 4- to 12-in. fronds, long, simple, and narrowed to a tip that often takes root and produces a new plant. Thus large colonies are formed on mossy boulders. The fruit-dots are narrow-oblong, scattered at random. Excellent in the rock garden, in shade, moisture, and rich woods soil with some lime.

WALKING-STICK. A slender, extremely elongated, cylindrical, wingless insect with long stiff legs and long feelers belonging to the same order as the grasshoppers (Orthoptera). Sometimes called also walking leaf and devil's darning needle, though the latter name is generally applied to species of dragon-flies. It feeds on the foliage of trees and in its resemblance to a dry twig or stick it is a good example of the phenomenon known as "protective resemblance." Walking-sticks are considered non-injurious in the garden although they may do some injury to trees and shrubs in feeding.

WALKS, GARDEN. Discussed under GARDEN PATHS AND DRIVES, which see.

WALL FERN (*Polypodium virginianum*). A small and vigorous fern abundant locally in rocky woods in the E. States, and easily cultivated in the garden. The fronds, 6 to 12 in. tall, are once-pinnate or nearly so, from densely matted creeping stems. Especially useful for wall gardens and rock slides, preferring limestone and requiring moisture. In transplanting from the wild do not tear, but cut the rooting stems.

WALLFLOWER. Common name for *Cheiranthus cheiri,* a perennial herb of the Crucifer Family having fragrant yellow or orange flowers in racemes. It is a native of S. Europe and its showy velvety blossoms are favorites in gardens especially abroad. The many horticultural varieties show charming shades of yellow, brown and ruby-red and purple; also double and dwarf branching forms.

In the E. States the seed should be sown early in summer and the seedlings transplanted once or twice and pinched back to induce bushy growth. The young plants are then wintered over in a coldframe and set out in the spring to bloom before hot summer weather. The plants are often found growing naturally (in England) in crannies, ruins and limestone walls, so should be planted in light loamy soil made sweet with ground limestone. In mild climates they will live through the winter in the open, coming into full bloom in early spring. Annual strains may now be obtained which bloom the first year from seed, but they are more successfully grown in the far W. than in the E.

C. kewensis is a hybrid strain with flowers 1 in. across, with yellow or orange petals, brownish purple on the outside.

The Siberian-wallflower, often listed as *C. allioni,* is properly *Erysimum asperum.* It is a short-lived perennial with small vivid orange blossoms continuing in bloom over a long season. It is grown more easily than the true wallflower, blooms freely about tulip time, and is so bright and cheerful and self-sows so readily that it is an addition to any garden.

Beach-wallflower is *Erysimum suffru-tescens;* and Coast-wallflower *E. capitatum.*

WALL GARDEN. This is the result of the culture, against the vertical face of a retaining wall of stone, of plants especially adapted to such a location. Actually, of course, they grow into the soil between and behind the rocks and boulders; but, as they drift against the stony irregularities, sometimes conforming to them to a surprising degree, they create charming and picturesque effects. (See illustration, Plate 59.)

There are, of course, marked similarities between wall gardens and rock gardens. But the wall garden does not provide those separated enlarged pockets in which specially prepared soil for special plants may be isolated, as does a rock garden. All of the vegetation in a wall garden must accept the same conditions as regards soil, namely, cool moisture at deep levels whence roots may travel away from heat and glare. Rock gardens often afford these, it is true, but they do not necessarily stop there; the wall garden must.

One advantage that the wall garden has and the rock garden lacks, is appropriateness to any place, however small, and adaptability to any environment. Even where there is no natural variation of level in the land, it is possible to excavate a space and build a low wall around it against the earth of the original level; thus one creates a ·sunken wall garden. And where the grade is naturally sloping one of the simplest of tasks is to break the slope with a cut-and-fill and retain the higher portion with a stone wall. In every case field stones or quarried stones that are roughly squared may be used. The former suit the informal, naturalistic environment; the latter are more harmonious in surroundings of some finish and dignity.

BUILDING THE WALL. Such walls are of course laid dry—without mortar or cement—and this must be carefully done in order to insure their resistance to the action of frost in the earth behind them, as well to its normal pressure at all times. For this reason the face of a retaining wall should slope backward from the bottom toward the top at the rate of from 10 to 15 per cent, depending on the height of the wall. This means that a low wall will depart from the perpendicular 1 in. for every 10 in. of height, while a wall 2 ft. or more in height will fall back 1½ in. for every 10 in.

In addition to being laid to produce this backward slope of the wall itself, the individual stones must be laid to slope downward at the back towards and into the earth. This further strengthens the entire structure, but more especially it carries rain back into the soil and the water from melting snow. Every aperture between the stones must afford direct contact with the mass of earth behind; must be, as it were, a vein of earth leading to the main body.

In laying the wall, therefore, it is imperative to fill around each stone as it is settled into place, packing the earth firmly. The soil may well be specially prepared by mixing equal parts of good loam with humus or leafmold and adding broken sandstone in small quantity.

Always keep in mind that such a wall is being built to retain an earth bank, not primarily to develop a wall garden (though this may be the real objective); the required precautions to prevent dirt washing out between the stones and undermining the structure will then suggest themselves. Above all, stones must *rest on stones* and not on earth except as they reach back into it, and come in contact with it. Thus the wall rightly built should be able to stand by itself even if there were no earth bank behind it, notwithstanding its sloping face; for its units are fairly interlocking.

It is not necessary to start from a foundation below the surface of the lower ground, though irregular stones in the first tier should be fitted into the earth as may be necessary to provide a uniform beginning. Flat stones may start the work laid on the ground instead of into it. Finally, as the wall rises, be sure that the stones are laid with broken joints, as bricks are, and that 70 per cent of them are placed with their longest dimension *across* the wall, so that they extend back into the earth and are locked into it by its weight resting on their ends. A wall laid according to these directions will never bulge and should never need to be rebuilt.

PLANTING THE WALL. Planting should proceed as the wall is being built, if growing plants are to be used. These should be on hand, in pots or flats, to be laid in place wherever desired. Spread the roots out fanwise on the soil that has been packed into place behind each layer of stones, placing the crown or growing center where a joint rather than a stone will come directly over it. This insures freedom for the crown from too great weight as well as continual support of the plant on the stone underneath. If a plant is placed above a joint, it has a tendency to work downward along the vein of earth, and sometimes it grows unsightly above as a consequence. This is one of those small things which if attended to do a good deal for the result as a whole. Of course there are many plants which will (and do usually) grow between stones where seemingly they are squeezed unmercifully. But to plant them in such situations is very difficult, not to say risky. They must choose them for themselves.

Do not overplant a wall in the beginning. The stone background is every bit as important as the flowers that drift across it, and for the best effect at least one part wall to two parts plants should always be maintained. In some locations, indeed, a reversal of these proportions will be best, but in the main they are about right. Many of the things suited to wall gardens grow luxuriantly and cover an astonishing area when they become well established. Plant sparingly as you build, wait for this original planting to show what it is, then, if necessary, introduce additional material.

LATER PLANTING. The only practical way of doing this is by seeds, since thrusting a live plant into a cranny seldom results in anything except the plant's eventual death. Introduce seeds directly to the earth well back by rolling several in a little ball of mud the consistency of putty, and pushing this against the earth underneath a vertical joint; otherwise place it at the bottom of a cranny between two of the stones of a layer, which brings it on top of a stone of the layer next below.

PLANT MATERIALS. In the group of plants which thrive in the conditions which a wall affords there are two divisions. One is better adapted to growing on the flat earth at the top of the wall where the growth may overhang as well as creep along the wall's direction; the other prefers the crevices and the sidewise position which they involve. Within these two divisions there is the further usual one of shade-loving and sun-loving; also the semi-shade-loving which means a preference for a little sunlight during a part of the day.

Depending upon the direction they face, walls are entirely shaded, entirely exposed to sun, or shaded for a third of the daylight hours in summer; and they may, of course, be under the shade of trees or tall shrubs. But it is not alone the full sun which must be considered in wall exposure; it is the sun's reflected light and heat. In America we have a great intensity of both; consequently, even during freezing winter weather, plants burn when growing in or against a wall exposed to the sun. Witness the English ivy which thrives on shady northern exposures but seldom endures on a wall facing south.

The best exposure for a wall garden is unquestionably northward or northeast. Around a rectangular sunken area, however, there will, of course, be four different exposures. Selections of plants must therefore be made especially for each, for even overhead shade, provided by planting trees, will not altogether overcome the conditions consequent upon the wall's facing south or southwest—the most trying direction of all. It may be necessary to try out many things before a completely satisfactory planting is accomplished and the desired effect assured.

A selection for full sun may include Aethionema; Alyssum in variety; Arabis; *Gypsophila repens;* Helianthemums; Iberis; *Linaria alpina;* Nepeta; Plumbago; Saponaria; Santolina; Thymus; *Tunica saxifraga; Veronica incana.*

For a shaded wall a good beginning is made with Aquilegia; *Arenaria montana; Aubrietia; Campanula carpatica; Corydalis lutea;* Hypericum; Lewisia; *Linaria hepaticaefolia;* Ramonda; Saxifrages of the mossy group; *Sedum nevi.*

WALL-PEPPER. Common name for *Sedum acre,* a small-leaved, yellow-flowered succulent perennial.

WALL-RUE (*Asplenium ruta-muraria*). A tiny cliff fern of the N. States, having tufts of linear, forking fronds, light green in color, with clustered fruit-dots at the tips. Difficult to grow, requiring limestone, perfect drainage and sheltered location.

WALLS, GARDEN. See GARDEN WALLS.

WALNUT. The genus Juglans, of the Walnut Family; it includes some 10 species of mostly hardy, deciduous, noble trees of the N. temperate zone. Generally clean branched, with strong trunks, they make large domes and swing their graceful foliage close to the ground. One species is grown commercially in California for its nuts; several yield superior timber for furniture, gun stocks, etc., and all walnuts are desirable ornamentals because of their attractive form and cheerful airy appearance. The vibrating foliage permits breezes to pass through, yet casts an ample shade. The delicious nuts and comparative freedom from leaf-eating insects add greatly to their value.

Brown leaf spot causes a generally unthrifty condition of black walnut and butternut trees. The irregular brown spots appear on the leaves in early summer and the fungus winters in the dead leaves. Ornamental black walnuts and butternuts should be sprayed annually with bordeaux mixture, using two or three applications at two week intervals beginning when the leaves are half grown.

The walnut caterpillar is a serious pest. The black 1½-in.-long caterpillars with white spiny hairs feed in groups on the leaves and rear up both ends when disturbed. Spray with lead arsenate. Pick up and burn nuts that drop prematurely after being injured by the butternut and walnut curculios. Spray before leaf growth starts in the spring with a miscible oil to control oyster-shell and walnut scales. The walnut aphid, which may produce extensive honeydew, can be controlled with nicotine dust.

Walnuts were formerly grown entirely from seed but improved sorts are now commonly grafted or budded on seedlings of the Black or California species.

Principal Species

J. nigra (Black Walnut) is best known and most planted as a shade or avenue tree because of its majestic form and general beauty. Given rich soil, room and sunlight it will attain 150 ft. Spreading, round-headed and long lived, it provides abundant shade and background for home or garden. The roots of black walnut, or soil conditions caused by them, have a toxic effect on rhododendrons and other ornamentals, so the two kinds of plants should not be planted in close proximity.

cinerea (Butternut or White Walnut) is also a worthy ornamental but it has a more spreading form and is not so long lived; however, it endures a moister soil.

regia (English or, properly, Persian Walnut) is more compact as befits an orchard tree, but it deserves a place in the lawn or garden background. The bark is silvery gray and smooth as compared with the rough, dark barks of other species. Hardy

from Calif. through the south and along the Atlantic coast to Mass., if grafted on roots of *J. nigra,* it becomes hardy in the northern states, ripening its nuts before frost. A shrubby variety (*laciniata*) with cut leaves is particularly ornamental and suited to use in garden designs. Var. *pendula* has pendulous branches that add grace to this usually stiff-branched species.

californica (California Walnut) varies from a 50-ft. tree in rich soil to a shrub at 3000 ft. elevation. It has been extensively used as a street tree and as stock for budding the English Walnut on.

sieboldiana, the very hardy Japanese Walnut, has in recent years been much planted in the northern States. It grows rapidly, has dense luxuriant foliage, and is a desirable ornamental for garden and grounds.

WANDERING JEW. Common name for *Tradescantia fluminensis,* a perennial herb of the Spiderwort Family, having smooth stems and leaves, and bearing white flowers, hairy inside. The leaves of the type species are very green, especially when the plants grow where there is little light, but var. *variegata* has leaves striped green and yellow. In order that this color variation may be maintained plants should be kept in full sunlight. They are easily increased by cuttings rooted in water or light soil, but require plentiful moisture at all times in order to thrive.

Two other plants, both of the Spiderwort Family but of different genera (*Zebrina pendula* and *Commelina nudiflora*) are so like Wandering Jew that it is difficult to distinguish between them and the different forms of *T. fluminensis* when the plants are not in bloom. *Z. pendula,* a tender plant used for hanging baskets, has red flowers and leaves always striped above and red below. It, too, is often called Wandering Jew. *Commelina nudiflora* has blue flowers, makes a good ground-cover and is hardy as far N. as Central N. Y.

WANDFLOWER. Common name for Sparaxis, a genus of S. African herbs of the Iris Family growing from corms and having narrow grass-like leaves and flowers in clusters. *S. tricolor,* to 1½ ft., the species most commonly grown, has purplish flowers with yellow throats, each segment marked with dark spots.

Wandflowers are planted outdoors in the spring for summer bloom as they are not hardy N. After the plants have blossomed, allow the foliage to ripen until the end of July, then lift the corms and store them in a dry place until the following spring. When forced under glass 5 or 6 corms are planted in a 6-in. pot and the pots placed in a cool frost-free pit for several weeks in order that roots may form. They are then brought into a cool greenhouse and kept at a temperature of 55 deg. until after flowering, when the foliage is allowed to ripen before the bulbs are removed from the pots and stored.

WARDIAN CASE. A London physician of the early 19th century, Dr. Nathaniel Ward, one day came across a bottle in which a tiny fern flourished in spite of dry weather which was causing severe damage to larger and hardier plants. Inspired by this chance find, he developed the horticultural philosophy of controlled light, heat and humidity. In time glass cases of ferns and exotics became a feature of the Victorian drawing room and were called "Wardian cases" after their originator. Later they were considerably used in connection with botany courses.

Today the word "terrarium" (which see) has largely come into use to describe such a case and modern, more ornamental derivatives from it. See also TERRARIUM.

WASHINGTONIA (wah-shing-toh'-ni-ah). A genus of American Fan Palms, extensively grown in Fla., Calif. and the Gulf States. They have wide fan-shaped leaves and tall trunks covered with the dead drooping foliage as if with a skirt. In the juvenile stage they make excellent specimen plants and the large trees are often used for avenue planting.

W. robusta (Washington Palm) is tall and slender, sometimes reaching 100 ft., with a crown of fan-shaped leaves 3 to 5 ft. across, first erect, then spreading and at length drooping. At home in Fla., it is resistant to salt air and flourishes near the seashore; but as it requires a rich moist soil it cannot be grown successfully in the high pineland sections.

W. filifera, native near water on the border of Colo. Desert, Calif., is planted in Fla. but does not thrive near the coast.

WASHINGTON-PLANT. C o m m o n name for *Cabomba caroliniana,* an aquatic with tiny white flowers.

WASPS. Common name for a well-known group of stinging insects belonging to the same order (Hymenoptera) as the bees. They are four-winged, swift flying and usually conspicuously marked with yellow. To many people the term suggests only the larger, familiar, stinging sorts, but there are many other kinds of wasps (some quite minute) with various garden relationships, both beneficial and harmful.

Beneficial wasps include the mostly small, parasitic types which lay their eggs near or actually within the bodies of various plant pests which the wasp larvae later destroy by feeding on them. Another useful kind is the tiny fig wasp whose presence is essential to the pollination of certain kinds of fig (which see) and the development of its fruit.

Among the harmful activities of wasps is the causing of galls or unsightly leaf or stem swellings in which the larvae or other stages of the insect are passed; also the injuring of fruit, out of which they sometimes eat large cavities, and the gnawing of twigs of woody plants in their search for bark fibre to use in making nests. See HORNETS.

According to their manner of living there are two kinds of wasps—solitary and social. The former include the beneficial parasitic forms (see INSECTS, BENEFICIAL). The social wasps live in colonies like bees and ants and construct the familiar nests out of a special tough paper made by them from wood. This group includes the hornets, yellow jackets and paper-nest wasps which are useful in destroying flies and other insects, but sometimes bothersome because of their painful stinging propensities. They do not sting unless provoked but the provocation does not have to be intentional. The best first aid treatment for stings is the immediate application of compresses of ammonia water.

With due precautions wasp nests can be burned out or the wasps can be killed by blowing calcium cyanide dust into the nest after the insects have all settled in it for the night.

A large predacious wasp (*Sphecius speciosus*), called the cicada-killer, makes holes in lawns and gravel paths, throwing up mounds of earth at the entrances to its underground nests. The wasp, more than an inch long and with a wing spread of nearly two inches, is black with yellow bands on the abdomen. It stings and paralyzes the large green cicada and drags it into the nest to feed the young wasp which later hatches from an egg laid in the cicada's body. The paralyzing venom apparently "preserves" the carcass until the offspring is old enough to devour it. If such wasps are present in quantity, so that they scare or bother passers-by or disfigure fine lawns, they can be killed while in slow flight by hitting them with a wire bat, made somewhat like a tennis or badminton racket; or by putting a small amount of carbon bisulphide in the opening of every nest found, and then closing it with a bit of sod.

WATER-ALOE. Common name for Stratiotes, a genus of aquatic perennials with white flowers which rise above the water. Better known as Water Soldier, which see.

WATER-ARUM. A common name for *Calla palustris,* a small, white-flowered bogland perennial. Do not confuse with the calla of florists which is the genus Zantedeschia. See CALLA.

WATER-CHESTNUT. Common name for Trapa, a genus of aquatic herbs of the Evening-primrose Family, and also for their distinctive nut-like fruit. They have both floating and submerged leaves and small flowers and are grown in this country in aquaria.

T. natans, to which the name Waterchestnut is usually applied, has dainty mottled, pinnate floating foliage in a rosette, and small, inconspicuous white flowers. The fruit, nut-like, with 4 spiny angles, is formed under the leaves and drops off when ripe. It is edible and in Europe is roasted and eaten. An Old-World plant, it has become naturalized in the E. U. S.

T. bicornis (Ling-nut) has a fruit with 2 strongly curved spines shaped like a bull's horns. It is often sold on the streets by fakers, who display one in a jar of water with large pink, red or yellow azalea-like (artificial) flowers rising from it which, they assert, have been produced by it.

T. bispinosa (Singhara-nut) is said to yield very large, sweet, usually 2-horned nuts, much used by the natives of Ceylon. It is also found naturalized in the E. States.

WATER-CHINQUAPIN. Common name for *Nelumbium luteum,* an aquatic perennial with large yellow flowers.

WATER-CRESS. A hardy, perennial, European herb (*Nasturtium officinale*) which grows naturally in wet soil along and in spring brooks, ditches and pond margins and is cultivated under such conditions for use as a garnish and a piquant salad. See CRESS.

WATER-ELM. Common name for the small deciduous tree, *Planera aquatica,* a member of the Elm Family, but not hardy N. of S. Ill., whence its range extends to Fla. and Tex. It has small, smooth, rather leathery leaves and is seldom seen in cultivation, as it has little beauty of form or foliage to recommend it. If planted, it should be given a moist soil. It is propagated by seed, by layers, or by grafting on the elm.

WATER FEATHER. One common name for *Myriophyllum proserpinacoides,* usually known as Parrots Feather, an aquatic herb much used in pools, etc., for its delicate, light-green, above-the-surface foliage.

WATER FERN. Common name for Ceratopteris, a genus of small tropical and subtropical ferns, with inflated fronds, suitable only for expert greenhouse cultivation.

WATER GARDEN. Strictly this refers to a garden featuring water in any form, as fountains, cascades, canals, pools, and so on; or to bodies of water, such as natural ponds or artificial pools, in the open or under glass, devoted to the culture of aquatic plants. However, it is loosely applied to a garden or portion of a garden where water and aquatics are a feature, even though terrestrial plants share largely in the composition. See illustrations, Plate 23.)

DESIGN. The design of a water garden is subject to the same general laws of landscape development as all others. In a natural environment, the introduced features should be in accord with Nature models and their arrangement such as to reproduce natural effects so that there is no suggestion of "design." But in restricted surroundings, close to architectural structures, pools will instead take exact forms. Rivulets will become canals of definite pattern in the design; tumbling waterfalls will be replaced by fountains and planned arching cascades; and the whole will be pervaded by architectural feeling and purpose.

It is important to recognize that neither one of these types is better than the other. Each is the only suitable thing for its particular environment; a deplorable mistake if forced into the conditions to which it is unsuited. As prevailing conditions, even in well-settled communities, are more often naturalistic than architectural, the type should most often be adopted.

THE FORMAL TYPE. The formal water garden, implying dignity and considerable splendor, is not usually as appropriate, though it may find suitable surroundings in the city, where a courtyard within brick or stone walls invites garden treatment, yet affords no opportunity for setting plants into the earth. Here a simple pool conforming to the scale as well as the shape of the space, with choice waterlilies, perhaps one kind of floating plant and a little school of goldfish, will turn the otherwise rather dreary spot into a charming place, requiring comparatively little attention.

While water alone may be handled elaborately to constitute a water garden ("garden of waters"), this does not mean that a pool or pond is in itself a water garden. It merely supplies the essential element, in and around which the objective may be developed. In it aquatic plants are set out in different depths of water, according to their requirements, and around it moisture-loving terrestrial plants which naturally haunt watersides. If there is a bit of halfway ground, wet and soggy, a further variation is provided and a bog garden (which see) can be included.

Particularly difficult garden problems involving ground that is always wet and soggy (either from surrounding drainage or underground springs) can often be solved only by means of a water garden. By excavating such an area at its lowest spot sufficiently to induce the formation there of a natural pond, the surrounding ground will be made normally dry and useful for cultivation. Thus what has been a liability may be turned into a valuable asset.

THE NATURAL POND TYPE. To build a naturalistic pond where this form is appropriate is a task requiring as great skill as to make a fine rock garden, with one important difference: the form of such a pond will usually be determined by the irregularities of the ground where it is to be. Hence the builder will need only to waterproof the depression, instead of having first to decide upon the pool's shape and size. If desired, a bog area can be added beside such a pond by waterproofing a separated shallow space into which the water may be turned and allowed to spread, which is then filled with earth.

WATER-GARDEN PLANTS (see also AQUATIC PLANTS). There are many beautiful plants for the waterside, the water itself and the bog area. The leading water plants are the waterlilies (Nymphaea) and the lotus (Nelumbium) (both of which see). Nothing is finer than the native pondlily (*Nymphaea odorata*) with its pink and yellow varieties. The flowers of the yellow kind are raised somewhat above the water. For small ponds or pools there is a very desirable dwarf Chinese form (*N. pygmaea*). These are all sweet-scented. Then there is a race of night-blooming tender Nymphaeas as well as tender daytime bloomers, both cultivated in the open but brought into greenhouse or indoor temperature before cold weather.

Their simple cultivation in tubs sunk in the earth is a kind of water gardening which does not require pond or pool, yet yields much satisfaction. However, a better term for such endeavors would be water-lily or tank or tub gardens.

See also GARDEN POOL; POND.

WATER-HAWTHORN. Common name for *Aponogeton distachyus,* an Asiatic aquatic herb with tuberous rootstocks, floating leaves and white or violet flowers in spikes.

WATER-HEMLOCK. Common name for *Cicuta maculata,* a perennial herb of the Parsley Family, having small white flowers in flat or round-topped clusters, strongly scented foliage and a large poisonous root. It grows to 6 ft. and its finely cut foliage and numerous white flowers make it a bold and striking specimen in the bog or wild garden. It grows naturally in marshes and swampy places in eastern N. America, where it is also known as Musquash-root. See also POISONOUS PLANTS.

WATER-HOARHOUND. Common name for the genus Lycopus, moisture-loving, mint-like perennials with small white or tinted flowers.

WATER-HYACINTH. The common name for *Eichhornia crassipes,* a showy tender perennial floating plant much used in tanks and ponds for its attractive foliage and bloom. (See illustration, Plate 2.) Though easily checked by frost, it has in the S. (Florida particularly) attained the status of a major pest, growing so luxuriantly as to completely obstruct traffic in certain rivers. Its control requires constant attention and labor and great expenditures.

In the tank or pond, its submerged hanging roots are valuable as a refuge for newly spawned fish. The enlarged leaf stems are enlarged to form bladders or floats which sustain the heavy masses of leaves and bloom at the water's surface. In shallow water the plants root in the soil and grow and flower more freely than when floating unattached. The beautiful flowers, pale blue with markings of darker blue and yellow, are borne in groups of 6 or 8 on a loose spike rising about a foot above the mass of leaves.

See also AQUATIC PLANTS ; AQUARIUM.

WATERING. The application of water to plants, both outdoors and indoors, requires more understanding of fundamental principles, more judgment and more skill than any other gardening practice; yet it is perhaps more often wrongly done than any other gardening task. Too much water is given or too little; or at wrong times, wrong temperatures, and so on. And the results, though often unsuspected (or at least not associated with their true cause) are frequently serious. Just how to water growing plants cannot be satisfactorily told in mere words, but the principal rules can perhaps be stated, as follows:

1. Avoid watering until the soil has become fairly dry, *not powdery;* then soak it thoroughly. Outdoors this means from several inches to a foot or more deep; indoors, it means enough to wet the soil in

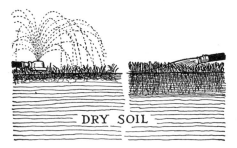

DRY SOIL

SPRINKLING VERSUS WATERING

Sprinkling a lawn, unless long continued, moistens only a shallow surface layer of soil as shown at the left. Here the grass roots concentrate and are quickly affected by drought and hot summer sun. Deep, thorough soaking, as indicated at the right, results in the roots going down where they are out of reach of ordinary surface drying.

the pot or the greenhouse bench from top to bottom. In the latter case the excess can, of course, drain off, but as this means the loss of soluble plant food by leaching, frequent overwatering is wasteful even though it may not always prove injurious.

2. Avoid keeping the soil continuously wet. To learn when plants in clay flower

pots need water, fillip the pot with the finger and note whether the sound is a "thud" or a perceptible "ring." The former indicates the presence of plenty of water; the latter, the need of thorough soaking. However, that is only a tyro's test; the experienced grower knows when to water by the appearance of the plants, of the flower pots, the surface of the soil, and the conditions under which the plants are growing.

3. Avoid light—even though frequent— surface-sprinkling of outdoor plants and lawns. Such applications of water are worse than giving none at all because the moistened stratum of soil is very shallow; the plants are thereby encouraged to develop roots near the surface, and the result is disaster when sprinkling is discontinued for even a few days or when an exceptionally hot spell occurs to dry and almost literally bake the roots.

4. Water actively growing, soft-stemmed large- and succulent-leaved plants abundantly, but dormant and "resting," hardwooded, slow-growing and small-leaved subjects with restraint. The former may show signs of flagging and yet recover fully when water is again applied; the latter are likely to suffer seriously, if not die, if allowed to become too dry. A safe rule to apply to plants in active growth is to water at the first suggestion of flagging.

5. As the amount and character of foliage affect water-using capacity, plants that have been cut back, that have lost their foliage from any cause, or that have become unhealthy must be kept drier than normal until new foliage begins to develop. Similarly, cuttings and newly potted or recently transplanted plants need to be kept fairly dry so as to encourage the development of root hairs and fibres, which is indicated by the commencement of new leaf and shoot development. One soaking at the time of potting or planting is generally enough, provided the plants are shaded for a few days from strong sunlight.

6. The quantity and character of soil should influence water applications. Loose and warm soils dry out more rapidly than do clays, so they are less likely to become sour if given an excess of water. This principle applies especially in regard to the growing of small plants in flower pots. Such plants should be kept in small pots until the soil becomes filled with roots, then shifted to the next size pot—not a

much larger one. Thus the amount of water needed to wet the soil is not likely to be enough as to induce souring.

7. During cloudy and muggy weather, watering indoors must not be heavy because it is likely to injure the roots and to produce such humidity of the confined air that the plants will be weakened and made subject to disease and insect attack.

8. Watering greenhouse plants in the morning should be the rule especially during the winter, in order that ventilation may remove the excess before night, when the foliage should always be dry and the air relatively so. Watering of cutting benches and seedlings late in winter afternoons is almost sure to prove disastrous, for damping-off (which see) is prone to attack plants so conditioned. In moderate winter weather, the humidity in a tight greenhouse is likely to be greater than when it is cold, for ventilation is less effective than when the cold outside condenses much of the excess moisture on the glass, thus making the air relatively dry. Therefore water sparingly during mild winter weather; when it gets cold and clear you can be more liberal.

9. Usually the only times when watering may be safely done late in the day are during clear weather in summer when there is free ventilation and relatively low humidity. At that season and on bright days watering during the middle half of the day is likely to produce scalding of the leaves

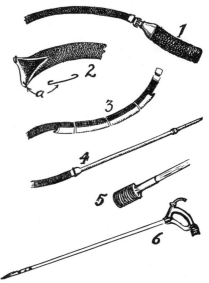

WATERING DEVICES USEFUL IN GREENHOUSE AND GARDEN

1. Short piece of auto radiator hose attached by means of reducing nipple to ordinary hose to produce larger, gentler stream. 2. Radiator hose can be slit up 4 inches, flared and held flat with piece of heavy wire (a). 3. Piece of curved, grooved wood wired to hose end enables user to reach across bench or bed. 4. Brass extension between hose and nozzle serves the same purpose, as does the new "Waterwand" (5), a metal tube with an end like an auto muffler that breaks the force of the flow. 6. One of several types of sub-surface or root-waterer.

of such plants as Chinese primrose and rex begonias, unless the plants are adequately shaded.

10. Air temperatures, the location of heating pipes, the strength of the light, and the amount of ventilation must all be considered in greenhouse or conservatory watering practice. So must the temperature of the water, which, if much more than 10 deg. lower than the air temperature, is likely to produce serious effects on plant growth, flowering and fruiting.

To reduce evaporation (and hence the watering requirements), especially during summer, flower pots in greenhouses are often plunged rim deep in sifted coal ashes, sand, tanbark, spent hops or peat moss, which absorb and hold excess water, thus checking evaporation and maintaining a desirably humid atmosphere. A parallel practice in dwellings or apartments where the air is even more likely to be dry consists of either placing a plant, pot and all, in a jardinière and filling the space between with peat moss, which is deliberately kept

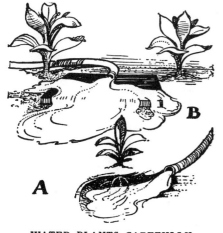

WATER PLANTS CAREFULLY

Flooding directly from the hose end is more effective than sprinkling. But to avoid washing out the soil from around the roots (A), let the hose flow onto a square board (B); or a piece of extra-heavy canvas would serve.

moist; or standing the pot in a deep enough saucer or other receptacle to hold an inch or two of peat moss or pebbles, which permit water to be kept there without waterlogging the soil in the pot.

The best time of day to water lawns, flower beds, borders and outdoor plantings generally is the evening, not because the water might burn the foliage during the strong sunshine but because the loss from evaporation is less. Outdoors, too, watering should be delayed until the plants are actually in need of water as indicated by slight flagging; and then done generously. Usually it is most effective to remove the

the tube. Leave until the ground around the roots is well saturated, then move to another spot. This method greatly reduces waste of water by evaporation on run-off and gets the water down where the plant roots can get it.

See also IRRIGATION; SPRINKLERS.

WATERING POT. A partially covered, galvanized iron or copper pail with a long tubular neck or spout ending in what is called a "rose"—that is, a flattened enlargement with numerous small perforations through which the water flows in little streams when the can is tilted forward. These streams can be made to fall more

TWO MODERN WATERING DEVICES IN OPERATION
Left, getting water down to the root system of a newly planted shrub without waste or delay.
Right, the "Waterwand" supplies a generous flow of water without washing the soil or spattering the base of the plants.

hoze nozzle or sprinkler and let the water flow in a gentle stream until a fair sized area is soaked, then move it to another spot. To avoid washing holes in lawn or bed, place a piece of board under the end of the hose, or a square of heavy cloth.

For watering large shrubs and trees, especially after being transplanted, an excellent device is some type of subsoil irrigator, several of which are on the market. Consisting of a long, sharp-pointed, hollow steel rod with a few holes near the tip, and a grip or handle, a hose connection and a shut-off valve, this tool is attached to the hose and thrust into the soil at the base of the plant while the valve is opened a little. The gentle flow of water helps it penetrate to the depth of the feeding roots when the valve is opened just enough so that the water will not spout out beside

lightly and in rain-like drops by holding the can higher to increase the distance between the apertures and the points where the water strikes. Roses with various sized apertures supplied with the more expensive cans permit safe watering of smaller, more delicate plants.

Watering pots are useful in a small way for wetting soil in seed pans, flats, cold frames, hotbeds and seedling beds and for sprinkling foliage. By the removal of the perforated screw top of the rose (or in some cans of the entire rose) the water may be applied in a solid stream to wet the soil of plants in flower pots and other receptacles. But care must be taken to apply the stream gently to newly potted plants to prevent gouging holes in the loose soil.

Many styles of watering pots are offered by garden supply stores. The commonest has a handle across the top at right angles to the direction of the spout and another on the side opposite to and parallel with the spout. A more convenient and adaptable style has a single tubular handle attached to the top near the spout and extending to form a large circle over the top and well down to the rear where its opposite end is attached. The advantage of this style is that it can be readily tilted as much or as little as desired without cramping or straining the hand and wrist.

See also SPRINKLERS; WATERING.

WATER IN THE GARDEN. There is, of course, a large place for water in the garden as an essential factor in plant growth. But here it is considered in any one of the several forms possible in garden design or composition, rather than as used for irrigation or sprinkling. It considers pools, basins of various kinds, fountains, water gardens, artificial watercourses and natural springs, ponds and streams—and the effects they create. The last three, it is true, may not often occur in a garden problem, but where they do, they afford rich opportunities. Usually they suggest, in themselves, the most appropriate general treatment for the entire project.

The garden pool (which see) is the simplest and also, in a sense, the safest water feature that can be chosen for any garden. It accommodates itself to every circumstance in size, shape, method of construction and maintenance; and adjusts itself so readily that even if it is not located in the one best spot it still enriches the whole picture. Furthermore, it is very little more trouble to acquire than the popular bird-basin, while it offers an infinitely greater degree of charm and water interest.

Basins of another sort are those set only slightly above the terrace or ground surface and also sinking below it on the inside; they are sometimes used for goldfish display. In them, while water is a requirement, it is not the only feature, for ornamental tiling is usually also important. The combined effect in general is comparable to a well of classic type, especially where the raised coping is broad enough to rest on.

The term "fountain" may mean a quiet basin or, usually, a jet of water thrown into the air above a surrounding basin. Bubbling fountains are more suitable to the small garden than tall jets, which suggest rather more pretentious surroundings. Wall fountains, bubbling, spouting, or merely overflowing from one level to another provide the pleasant sound of murmuring water which to many makes greater appeal than the actual sight of water spread before them.

WATERING POTS
1. Ordinary type, with a rose spray. 2. French type, good for conservatories, greenhouses and wherever in the garden it is desired to reach a certain plant or clump.

The only general principles applicable to both natural and artificial water features are restraint and simplicity. Allow water to have undisputed leadership, without unnecessary interruptions, at all times. This is the essence of its nature and must be assured if it is to serve its purpose in creating beauty. See also POND; WATER GARDEN.

WATER-LEAF. The name commonly applied to the several species of showy perennial herbs of the genus Hydrophyllum (which see), used as a planting about shrubbery and as a wild planting in rich, shady locations.

WATER-LEMON. A common name for *Passiflora laurifolia,* a species of Passion-flower (which see) with large red-spotted white flowers and yellow edible fruits.

WATER-LETTUCE. The popular name for *Pistia stratiotes,* a small, tender, floating perennial herb of the Arum Family much used in aquaria and warm ponds. Its floating rosette of pale green, fluted leaves, velvety to the touch, and the pendent mass of feathery roots are mostly ornamental. It prefers a partly shaded location and a temperature of from 70 to 80 deg. F. Young plants develop from side runners.

See AQUATIC PLANTS and AQUARIUM.

WATERLILY. The most familiar name for the genus Nymphaea, or Nymphea, justly the most prized of all aquatic plants. (See illustrations, Plate 2.) About 40 species from all parts of the tropic and temperate zones with their many hybrids offer a range of color and size of bloom and leafage to satisfy any need or desire.

From the gardener's point of view, waterlilies fall into two classes—tender (tropical) and hardy. The latter are perennial in the U. S. and may be kept over from year to year in outdoor ponds if the roots are protected from actual freezing. The flowers of most hardy lilies float on the surface of the water, but a few varieties hold their blooms well above it. In color they range from pure white to deep vermilion with all sorts of variations in yellow and its allied colors—bronze and copper.

The tropicals, which are usually considered as annuals and replaced yearly, are favored and generally considered superior to the hardy sorts, but the fancier usually includes both types in his planting. The blooms of the tropicals are the larger and the better for cutting; and the plants make a quick growth during the summer and bloom until hit by frost. Their flowers stand high above the water on stout stalks and are more fragrant than those of the hardy kinds. Their color range is an infinitely varied palette of blues, all shades of violet and purple, pinks and deep rose, and dark red. But they lack the yellow and copper tints of the hardy lilies, so most color schemes of any extent call for the planting of both types.

The tropicals themselves are divided into the two classes of day-blooming and night-blooming. Consequently, by judicious planting, the owner of even a very small pool may have lilies in flower 24 hours a day.

To grow waterlilies successfully, plenty of good rich soil is imperative. They are gross feeders and the large night-bloomers especially make a heavy leaf growth and must have plenty of food to keep them at their best through the entire summer.

Top-soil of a somewhat heavy texture should be, over a period of months, first piled in layers and then thoroughly mixed with cow manure (if available) in a half-and-half mixture; horse manure (used in the same proportion) is not quite as good. If neither is to be had, sheep manure at the rate of 1 part to 8 or 10 parts of top-soil is excellent. In addition to the manure, ground bonemeal, dried blood or other concentrated fertilizer may be added.

Lily roots, when unconfined, tend to spread and the more delicate species are often choked by the rank growth of stronger varieties. To check this tendency

and to make their general culture easier, the common practice is to plant each individual lily in a box, tub, or other suitable container and submerge the whole. The size of the container should naturally vary according to the need of the occupant; but generally speaking, at least a cubic foot of good rich soil must be allowed each lily; larger species demand more root room and more soil. With small boxes, the soil must be renewed each year, at which time the root may be divided.

To raise lilies from seed, sow in small pots of well-sieved sandy loam and submerge in water in a warm sunny place. When sufficient growth has been made, pot up the seedlings in fertilized soil. If seed is to be sown directly in a pond, roll each one in a ball of clay and drop in the desired location.

Hardy lilies are usually grown from dormant rootstocks, which should be planted just below the soil surface at an angle slightly off horizontal. They may be set out as early as the middle of April. If planted directly in the pool rather than in a container, either put them in a small basket of soil or press them down into the bottom and weigh with a small stone. Direct planting may be done in from 1 to 2 ft. of water.

Tropicals are usually bought from the grower as growing plants. When the average temperature runs around 70 deg. F. they should be set out with the leaf crown just above the top of the soil. Growers commonly put a shallow layer of clean sand or fine gravel on top of the soil to hold it down and keep the pool clean. The depth of water above the crown should be from 8 to 16 in. Shallow water allows the sun to warm the young plants. One of the great advantages of container planting is that by putting blocks under the box, any desired depth of water may be had.

Waterlilies should not be too crowded; plant from 3 to 6 ft. apart—more for larger varieties—in a position receiving maximum sunlight. Plenty of light and heat are essential to bring them to perfection. If they need extra food during the growing season, they may be given additional nourishment by shoving a paper bag full of dried blood or one of the special lily fertilizers now on the market down among the roots.

Hardy lilies may be wintered in the pond or pool unless it freezes solid. A small pool should be covered with boards and a blanketing of straw or leaves placed on that. If the pool has to be drained, fill it with straw, etc., being careful to amply protect your boxes of roots (if left in place) against the invasion of rats and mice. Containers are best cared for by removing them to the cellar and covering them with burlap, which should be moistened often so as to keep the soil damp enough to ward off dry rot.

Useful Nymphea Varieties

Growers list many fine varieties of both hardy and tropical lilies and each season sees the list augmented with new hybrids. The following selections are all well-proven and easily obtained types:

Hardy Nympheas

White: *Nymphaea marliacea albida; N. gladstoniana; N. odorata gigantea* (less hardy N.).
Yellow: *N. tetragona (N. pygmaea); N. marliacea chromatella; N. odorata sulphurea grandiflora.*
Apricot to copper-red: Nymphaea varieties Aurora and Comanche.
Pink: *N. marliacea rosea* and Nymphaea vars. W. B. Shaw, Attraction and Rose Arey.

Tropical Nympheas—Day-Blooming

White: *N. gracilis* and Nymphaea var. Mrs. George H. Pring.
Blue: *N. caerulea; N. gigantea hudsoniana; N. pennsylvanica; N. zanzibariensis azurea;* and Nymphaea var. Mrs. Edwards Whittaker.
Pink: *N. zanzibariensis rosea* and Nymphaea vars. General Pershing and Mrs. C. W. Ward.
Purple: *N. zanzibariensis* and Nymphaea vars. Panama-Pacific and August Koch.

Tropical Nympheas—Night-Blooming

White: *N. lotus dentata; N. lotus dentata superba.*
Pink and red: *N. devoniensis* and Nymphaea vars. Frank Trelease and Bissett. See also AQUATICS.

WATERLILY FAMILY. Common name for the Nymphaeaceae, aquatic herbs, much used in garden pools, of which Nymphaea, the waterlily, is the typical genus.

WATERMELON. An African, tropical, annual, trailing vine (*Citrullus vulgaris*) of the Cucurbit Family, cultivated for its large, globular to cylindrical green, mottled or striped fruits which are a sweet, refreshing midsummer delicacy.

Watermelon vines are tender to frost, so seed must not be sown in the open or plants transplanted there until the weather has settled. They grow best in full sunshine and do well in any good garden soil well supplied with humus, and moisture during hot weather. Though they are faster growing than muskmelons they require longer to mature. Hence, where seasons are short only early varieties should be grown. It is good garden practice to start these in hotbeds or coldframes on rotted sods or in berry boxes or flower pots a month before safe time to set them outdoors.

Small-growing kinds may be planted 8 ft. apart; larger kinds need 10 or 12 ft. To avoid weed trouble, it is advisable to prepare the soil in early spring and either keep it cultivated or grow early maturing vegetable crops in it until melon-planting time. Cultivate like melons and cucumbers.

Anthracnose is one of the most troublesome watermelon diseases. (For control see under CUCURBITS.) Stem-end rot and blossom-end rot are common and ground-rot is destructive in the S. The chief control measure for any of these rots is the destruction of infected fruit. Watermelon is affected by the same insects as cucumber (which see) and the melon aphis is more serious on watermelon than on cucumber or muskmelon. See also MELON.

Watermelons are best if left on the vines until really ripe. This condition is indicated by certain changes in appearance which are hard to describe but which with experience are easy to recognize, such as hardening and yellowing of the underside, and blackening and shriveling of the tendril nearest to the fruit. Also a ripe melon gives a characteristic dull, thudding sound when flicked with the finger. See HARVESTING GARDEN CROPS.

C. vulgaris var. *citroides,* called the Citron or Preserving Melon, produces smaller, white, hard-fleshed fruits which are used only for preserving. The candied citron, however, is the peel of the fruit of a tree (*Citrus medica*).

The Chinese-watermelon (also sometimes called Preserving Melon) is another cucurbitous plant, *Benincasa hispida,* which see. See also CITRULLUS.

WATER MILFOIL. Common name for Myriophyllum, a genus of aquatic plants—feathery, graceful, submerged herbs—used for their oxygenating power in the aquarium, which see.

WATER-PENNYWORT. Common name for Hydrocotyle, or Marsh-pennywort, which see.

WATER-PLANTAIN. Common name for Alisma (which see), a genus of hardy perennial aquatic herbs good for the bog garden or the margins of ponds and streams.

WATER PLANTS. Another name for Aquatic Plants (which see), which include both those that live submerged and those that grow with only their roots in or under water. They supply material for both indoor aquaria and outdoor pools, ponds, bog gardens and water gardens, all of which see.

WATER-POPPY. Common name for *Hydrocleis nymphoides,* a Brazilian aquatic herb with showy foliage and bloom. The large, glossy, oval leaves floating on the water make an attractive background for the large, yellow, poppy-like flowers. (See illustration, Plate 2.) The latter last only a single day, but the plant continues in profuse bloom almost throughout the summer.

It grows well in shallow ponds or in the aquarium. In natural ponds, an edge planting soon spreads although the plant is somewhat susceptible to frosts. It grows well in tubs filled ⅔ full of rich, manured soil, covered with sand. Two or three roots should be clustered in the center and the tub filled with water. Propagation is by division of the rooting stems.

WATER SHIELD. Common name for *Brasenia schreberi,* a hardy, aquatic plant belonging to the Waterlily Family, found in N. America, Asia, Africa and Australia, and grown as an edging plant in small aquatic gardens. Its leaves float on the water surface, and the under parts are coated with a transparent colloidal jelly. It has small purple flowers. Except in the warmer sections it should receive some winter protection. It is propagated by division of the roots, or by seeds.

WATER SNOWFLAKE. Common name (suggested by its dainty, minutely fringed flowers) for *Nymphoides indicum,* an aquatic of the Gentian Family.

WATER SOLDIER. Common name for *Stratiotes aloides,* a hardy, perennial European aquatic herb related to the Eel-grass. It is made up of a cluster of narrow, pointed, tooth-edged leaves, stiff and spiny enough to give it in some localities the name of Crabs Claw.

In addition to its ornamental value in the aquarium, it has an interesting and unique habit. In winter it remains submerged entirely and rooted in the bottom mud; as the water becomes warmer in spring, aided by the buoyant growth of new leaves, it floats to the surface to display its 3-petaled white flowers. In the fall, its blooming over, it sinks again to the bottom.

WATER SPROUT. A succulent shoot or branch produced in a single season from the base, or along the trunk or a main limb, of an established tree. It is a natural sequence of severe pruning or other disturbance of the tree's natural equilibrium. As water sprouts are soft and weak and ordinarily develop where branches are not needed or wanted, they should be cut off close to the trunk as soon as noticed. This does not, of course, apply to the annual growth made by willows grown and cut back annually for the production of withes or "pussy willow" sprays.

WATER-VIOLET. A common name for water plants of the Primrose Family belonging to the genus Hottonia, which see.

WATERWEED. Common name for the useful, whitish-flowered aquarium plant, *Elodea canadensis.*

WATER-WILLOW. A name sometimes applied to *Decodon verticillatus,* the Swamp Loosestrife, a tall, woody-stemmed perennial with long leaves and showy rose-purple flowers. See DECODON.

The same name is given to plants of the genus Dianthera because of the shape of the leaves. Belonging to the Acanthus Family, they are, with but few exceptions, tropical or sub-tropical and adapted for outdoor use only in mild climates. One species, *D. pectoralis,* sometimes called Garden-balsam (but not to be confused with the popular annual *Impatiens balsamina*), grows from 1 to 3 ft. high and has most attractive one-sided spikes of rose or pale blue flowers with parti-colored throats amid the profusion of long green leaves. *D. americana,* with purplish flowers, grows in wet places and swamps as far N. as Quebec and is useful in the bog garden and for planting along stream margins.

WATSONIA (waht-soh'-ni-ah). A genus of sturdy summer-blooming bulbs of the Iris Family, differing from Gladiolus only in small botanical characteristics. From 1 ft. to 6 ft. tall, they have long sword-shaped leaves and bear scarlet, rose or white flowers in racemes. Strong plants often branch into several stalks. Plant the bulbs 3 to 6 in. deep, with a little sand under each, in the border about the first of May in an open sunny position. The soil should have been enriched the year before with stable manure; do not use fresh manure where it will touch the corms. Bonemeal is an excellent fertilizer for them. Lift the bulbs before freezing weather, remove the tops, and store in a cool, dry frost-proof place. Watsonias bloom from July to September, and are a popular source of summer bloom in Calif. gardens. They can also be grown under glass and as the blooms continue to open after the spike has been cut, they make excellent cut flowers. They may be increased by seed or the offsets of the corms. The principal species are:

W. iridifolia, to 4 ft., with pink flowers to 3 in.; var. *obrieni*, with pure white flowers, is very desirable for greenhouse culture; *W. rosea*, to 6 ft., with rose flowers; *W. longifolia*, to 5 ft. or more, with many-flowered spikes in white, pale pink or rose; *W. pillansi*, to 6 ft., brick-red flowers in a spike to 1 ft. long; *W. meriana*, to 4 ft., bright rose, 12- to 20-flowered spikes; *W. marginata*, to 5 ft., rose-red, very fragrant flowers; *W. bulbillifera*, with bright rose flowers, develops bulbils in the upper leaves and bracts; *W. beatricis*, to 3 ft., flowers glowing yellowish-red; *W. brevifolia*, to 1½ ft., rose-red flowers.

WATSONIA SOCIETY OF AMERICA. A young organization, as yet national in name only, formed to promote this flower, its cultivation, breeding, and appreciation. The secretary's address as last reported was San Fernando, Calif.

WATTLE. Common Australian name for species of *Acacia*, mostly yellow-flowered trees and shrubs grown for ornament in the S. and in Calif.

WAXBERRY. Common name for *Symphoricarpos albus*, a hardy deciduous shrub whose inconspicuous flowers are followed by showy white fruits that last into winter.

WAX EMULSIONS. A number of wax preparations which emulsify readily when mixed with water have been devised to be sprayed on woody plants of different types for the purpose of reducing winter injury. At least one of them is now on the market

and being used to some extent by nurserymen. Tests carried out by a N. Y. institution sought to ascertain the protective efficiency of the available materials (1) as an aid to recently transplanted subjects; (2) as a protection against actual freezing of the plant tissues; (3) as a preventive of desiccation (drying) and winter browning of evergreens; (4) the best time or times to apply the wax, as determined by season and temperature.

In general, transplanted yews, arborvitaes, red and white pines, Norway spruce, etc., showed better spring color when "waxed" before being moved. Deciduous trees moved while dormant showed no apparent effect, while treated Norway maples and catalpas moved in full leaf did not hold their leaves any longer in the fall, but did open their buds earlier the following spring. Except for some California privet and forsythias, the wax seemed to have no effect in reducing or preventing frost injury. But it did seem to help in preventing winter browning on narrow-leaved evergreens. Wax is used by some rose growers who dip all the above-ground part of a plant in it while still warm; this is thought to keep the plant in better condition over winter while in storage. The treatment is mainly of indirect benefit to gardeners as yet, but the future may bring new and extended applications and uses that they, too, can employ.

WAX FOR GRAFTING. See GRAFTING WAX.

WAX GOURD. One of the common names for the Chinese-watermelon or Preserving-melon, *Benincasa hispida*, an annual pumpkin-like vine bearing a culinary fruit.

WAX-MYRTLE. Common name for *Myrica cerifera*, a fairly hardy evergreen shrub with grayish-white fruits native from N. J. to Tex.

WAX-PLANT. Common name for *Hoya carnosa*, a climbing greenhouse shrub of Asia; and rarely for Indian Pipe (*Monotropa uniflora*), a curious white woodland saprophytic herb. It was formerly applied to shiny-leaved begonias, and is sometimes incorrectly applied to *Crassula arborescens* and other glossy-leaved succulents.

WAX-WORK. Common name for *Celastrus scandens*, a twining shrub with showy orange-yellow fruits, also called False-bittersweet.

WAYFARING-TREE. Common name for *Viburnum lantana*, an Old-World shrub with white flowers in early summer and black fruits in autumn. The American wayfaring-tree is *V. alnifolium*.

WAYTHORN. Another name for the common buckthorn (*Rhamnus cathartica*), a spiny shrub with greenish flowers and black fruits.

WEATHER. In outdoor gardening, thought must be given continually to changing weather. Moderate heat and sunshine interspersed with frequent rains make the most favorable conditions for plant growth, and when other conditions arrive the garden suffers. Intense heat brings need of shade for certain plants; drought calls for sprinkling, and cold for protection.

Weather brings sunshine, heat, drought, clouds, fog, rain, wind, lightning, hail, frost, snow, sleet, with, occasionally, flood, tornado or blizzard. Work in the garden must be planned to suit it: planting when rain is expected, cultivating and weeding when the sun is shining. Sowing of ten-

WEATHER AFFECTS EVEN THE STURDIEST PLANTS

This shows a frost crack in the trunk of a mature tree. Ordinarily it calls for no treatment and heals up without attention. But if a valuable lawn specimen is repeatedly affected, expert protective tree surgery may be needed to prevent infection with disease.

der annuals must be delayed 'till danger of frost is past. For these and a hundred such reasons, a study of weather is important to gardening.

Some persons, by observing local conditions and without the aid of any scientific data, often gain considerable skill at forecasting weather for a day or so in advance. Direction of wind, cloud formations, sunset color, clearness or mistiness of the air and rise or fall of temperature indicate what may be expected. Old sayings like "Rain before seven, clear before eleven," "Thunder in the morning, sailors take warning," etc., are founded on sound principles, though they may often fail. But forecasting the weather months ahead, predicting a cold winter or a dry summer, appears to be guesswork only.

In all of the U. S. except the Pacific slope, there is an almost uninterrupted movement of weather conditions from S. W. to N. E.; thus storms move at the rate of about 600 miles a day, faster in winter, slower in summer. If it rains in St. Louis on Wednesday, rain may reasonably be expected in New York about Friday. Storms, which are circular depressions in the atmosphere, may be small or a thousand miles in diameter. They follow one another as whirlpools follow an oar in the water, but irregularly, changing their courses toward the S. or the N. but almost always shifting rapidly eastward. The wind blows from all directions toward these storm centers (which are called cyclones), not directly at the center, but with a whirling motion opposite to that taken by the hands of a clock. (In the S. hemisphere their direction is just the opposite.) Thus, in the U. S. as a storm approaches from the W., the wind blows from the S. E. or S. If the center passes to the N. of the observer, the wind veers to the W. and then to the N. If the storm passes to the S., the wind shifts E., then N. In the exact center of a storm (and often for some distance around it) there is no wind. The storm area usually brings rain, always cloudiness, and a tendency to higher temperatures. When it has passed, the sky clears and the air turns colder, unless other following storm areas interfere. The position of cyclones is shown by comparing air pressure (barometer readings) at different points.

The United States Weather Bureau twice daily charts weather conditions showing regions of high and low pressure, storm areas, temperatures, wind directions and precipitation conditions. The maps based on these reports are published in many newspapers and displayed in post offices and other public places. They are the basis of forecasts issued by the Weather Bureau, which also are printed in newspapers and announced on the radio. These forecasts are not always correct, because sudden and unexpected storm movements often occur, new storms develop, or old ones fill up and lose their force. New storms originating on the S. Atlantic coast move northeastward, often bringing violent N. E. winds and heavy rains extending a short distance inland. Occasionally a storm of unusual power starts in the tropical (Caribbean) region and moves westward for hundreds of miles before sweeping toward the N. E. In their early stages, such storms are known as hurricanes and their forecasting is of the greatest significance to agriculture, horticulture, shipping and the public in general.

Frost and hail are the weather disasters most feared in gardening. Frost (which see) can be predicted, and its damage to

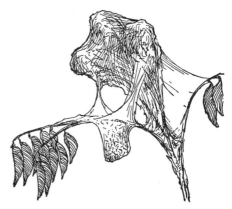

FALL WEB-WORM NEST
Made by hairy caterpillars on fruit and shade trees, it resembles that of the tent caterpillar (which see) but appears later and at the ends, not in the crotches, of branches. Prune off and burn while young and full of worms.

some extent forestalled, but hail storms and tornadoes come with little warning and cannot be prevented. Greenhouse owners can, however, protect themselves financially with insurance.

Wood and stones exposed to the weather for a long time take on pleasing shades of gray, due to the action of sunshine, frost and rain, and small forms of plant life. Described as "weathered," such material is in demand for rock gardens and rustic work. Rock gardens can, however, be built of unweathered stone, and a fair degree of weathered effect obtained in a few months by sprinkling once or twice daily.

See also CLIMATE, which might be described as, in any region, the result or composite of accumulated weather conditions; and WIND.

WEB-WORM. A general name for various widely distributed caterpillars which work under the protection of silken webs. The fall web-worm (see below) feeds on many kinds of trees. The garden web-worm is a special pest of clover, alfalfa and some other crops. The parsnip web-worm binds together the flower-heads of parsnip, celery and many weeds. Sod web-worms are particularly injurious to corn. Some of the web-worms may be controlled by spraying or dusting with calcium arsenate.

FALL WEB-WORM. The presence of this caterpillar (*Hyphantria cunea*) is indicated by loosely-woven, dirty white webs enclosing the ends of the branches and not filling crotches as do the tougher, usually larger

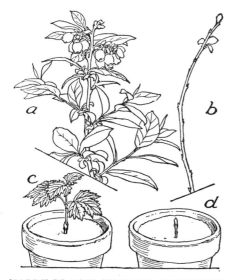

HARDY PLANTS NEED COLD WEATHER
Above: the blueberry branch (a) shows normal spring growth after a winter outdoors. The other branch (b) from a plant kept in a greenhouse over winter refuses to grow and the upper two buds are dead while the third is weak. Below: the vigorous Viburnum americanum seedling (c), wintered in a temperature of 32 to 40 deg. F., made this growth in early spring. The other (d) was kept in a greenhouse of 55 to 70 degrees and did not respond to the seasonal advance.

(spring) nests of the tent caterpillar, with which they are sometimes confused. The worms are pale-yellow, black-spotted and very hairy; they feed on the leaves within the webs, excreting quantities of unsightly black pellets. They attack more than 100 fruit, shade and woodland trees (but *not* evergreens) over the U. S. and S. Canada generally.

The winter is passed as a pupa inside a silken cocoon under trash on the ground or under bark of trees. The nearly snow-white moths emerge at intervals during the spring and lay their eggs in masses covered with white hairs on the leaves. The caterpillars feed for a month or 6 weeks in midsummer, then pupate and produce a second generation in early fall. Control by pruning off and burning the webs or by spraying with lead arsenate.

WEEDS, WEEDING, and WEEDERS. Weeding means the removal, from among crops, of obnoxious plants, that is, undesired plants growing in competition with desired ones. However, the term weed (see list below) is a relative one because many plants may be useful, beautiful or interesting where they are wanted, but pernicious elsewhere. White clover, for instance, is a useful and often highly desirable plant in a lawn, but a pest in a strawberry bed.

THE HARM WEEDS DO. Weeds are not only useless, but usually result in direct loss to the crop grower in the following ways: 1. They contend with the crop plants growing on the same area for plant food and moisture. 2. Thus they reduce the yields of the crop. 3. They provide hosts for diseases that attack related crop plants, also shelter and food for insects which multiply and attack the desired plants. 4. They increase the amount of labor necessary to bring cultivated crops from planting to harvest. 5. When allowed to grow uncontrolled, they injure the appearance and value of the property and the community.

About the only advantages that might be claimed for them are: 1. They occupy and cover ground which if allowed to remain bare (fallow) might be eroded by rain or melting snow or lose much soluble plant food by seepage. 2. When plowed or dug under they add their vegetable matter to the soil and thus increase its humus content. 3. They may serve as a volunteer winter cover-crop (which see) in orchards,

berry patches and vineyards. However, in this last capacity weeds are less desirable than a sown cover-crop because if allowed to become established they may become serious pests.

KINDS OF WEEDS. From the standpoint of their duration, weeds are of three classes. The first class consists of the *Annuals,* which, like goosefoot and pusley, complete their life cycles within one year. In this class belong the "winter annuals," such as shepherds purse and chickweed, which start to grow in the autumn but complete their life cycle during the following spring when they bear seed and die. From the latter it is an almost imperceptible step to the second class of *Biennials.* These are slow-growing plants such as burdock and wild carrot which produce only vegetative parts (roots and rosettes of leaves) during one season and bear seed the following year. The third class comprises the *Perennials,* plants like Canada thistle and milkweed, whose underground parts live for an indefinite number of years and normally produce seed every year except the first.

WEED CONTROL

As annual and biennial plants propagate themselves solely by seeds they may be controlled, first, by preventing their going to seed; second, by cultivating to prevent their getting established; and, third, by weeding, that is, the removal one by one of plants that have made a start. Perennials may be similarly controlled while young, but if they are allowed to gain a root-hold they must be fought by destruction of the underground root parts, by chemical treatment, by exposing them to the action of the sun, air or frost, by choking them out with a "smother crop"; or by starving them by preventing the development of their green parts by which their food is manufactured.

When weeds are allowed to approach maturity seed production can of course be prevented by cutting the tops close to the ground. But they are far easier to control during the sprouting or young seedling stage; for then only a slight disturbance of the surface soil in which they are starting to grow is enough to expose their tender rootlets to the sun and air where in perhaps a very few minutes they will shrivel beyond possibility of resuscitation.

Herein lie the chief advantages of the steel garden rake, the rake attachments of the wheelhoe and of the horse- or tractor-drawn "weeder," an implement resembling a miniature old-fashioned hay rake but with spring teeth that penetrate the ground for only a couple of inches.

WEEDERS. For removing weeds close to desired plants hand weeders are essential. They are of many styles, some suggesting the bent fingers of the open hand, others like hooks or claws, still others like knives bent in various forms. All are good for their respective purposes.

Individual weeds in lawns and other areas that cannot be cultivated can be destroyed by using a spud (which see) to cut the roots several inches below the ground surface. This tool must *not,* however, be used in lawns to *pry up* the weeds as this would leave ugly holes and injure the lawn; pulling up the plants after the roots have been severed is the correct practice. Though the sooner this is done the better, in no case should it be postponed later than the blossoming stage of the plant, otherwise a fresh crop of weed seeds will result. There are also devices combining a hollow cone-like receptacle for an acid or corrosive solution, and a sharp hollow point through which some of the material can be injected into the weed.

Weed killing in fence rows, walks, drives and similar places can be effectually done with a gasoline or kerosene torch which throws a strong hot flame. In some cases perennial weeds will require a second or even a third burning before they are completely destroyed. By applying the flame to the ground around the weed long enough to thoroughly heat it, any weed seeds can also be destroyed. For best results the ground should be dry when this is done.

There are various proprietary weed-killing preparations that can be sprayed on walks or drives where there is no desirable vegetation that would be killed along with the weeds. For some weeds a solution of iron sulphate is often used. While this may temporarily stain the crop plants, it does them no permanent harm.

Weeds commonly found in the garden are listed below in four classes as follows: (1) Weeds of the Lawn; (2) Weeds of the Vegetable Garden; (3) Weeds of the Flower Garden; (4) Intruders. The life duration is indicated to assist in choosing the type of extermination method, as discussed in the article above. Roman numerals in the column headed Treatment refer to chemicals or other spray materials.

FIRE IS AN EFFECTIVE WEED DESTROYER
And a portable pressure oil-burning flame gun is a convenient way to apply it along paths or stone walls, or wherever weeds become militant.

I indicates *iron sulphate,* which is used as a solution at the rate of 2 lbs. to 1 gal. of water. The solution should be poured into the spray tank through a strainer that will remove any impurities or undissolved particles of the chemical. II indicates *sodium* or *calcium chlorate* which is applied either in solution or as a dust. For scattered weeds with fairly large leaves, dust the powder on from a perforated container when the foliage is moist with dew. For a larger infestation the chlorate in dry form can be applied in fall at the rate of 2½ lbs. per sq. rod or in solution at strengths recommended by the manufacturer of the brand used. III refers to *sulphuric acid,* more used for weed control on extensive farm or range areas than in gardens, although a few drops placed on the cut surface of the root of a dock or dandelion will kill it. Do not let the acid touch clothes or skin as it will cause a burn, for which bicarbonate of soda (baking-soda) is a good neutralizing agent.

Kerosene is sometimes used on stubborn weeds, as is a strong brine of either common table salt or ice-cream salt. However, except where the material is applied carefully and only to the foliage of the weeds, land treated with chemicals will not be in shape to grow crops for months or, possibly, years.

WEEDS OF THE LAWN.

Common Name and Duration	Features and Distribution	Treatment	Scientific Name and Family
Barnyard Grass, Annual	Coarse, resembling millet. E. except far N.	Mow often to prevent seeding	*Echinochloa crus-galli.* Grass Family
Bermuda Grass, Perennial	Rough, coarse leaves Md. and S.	Dig out and burn	*Cynodon dactylon.* Grass Family
Chess or Cheat, Annual or Biennial	Flat-leaved grass	Dig out	*Bromus secalinus.* Grass Family
Chickweed, Common, or Winter, Annual	In tufts, slender, weak, hairy stalks, small oval leaves, white flowers	Hoe or hand weed, or spray with I or II	*Stellaria media.* Pink Family
Chickweed, Mouse-ear, Perennial or Annual	Clustered, clammy, hairy leaves, small white flowers	Cultivate. Clover will crowd it out	*Cerastium vulgatum.* Pink Family
Crab Grass, Annual	Stems flat on ground, branches rooting at joints	Prevent seeding; cultivate out; or use II	*Syntherisma sanguinalis.* Grass Family
Dandelion, Perennial	Yellow flowers in heads, cut foliage in flat rosettes	Dig out with spud; jab with ice-pick and use I or III	*Taraxacum officinale.* Composite Family
Dock, Perennial	Coarse leaves, large deep root	Dig out or cut off and apply III	*Rumex* spp. Buckwheat Family
Foxtail, Pigeon Grass, Annual	Rough, coarse leaves. Upper Miss. valley	Cultivate out	*Setaria italica.* Grass Family
Garlic, Perennial	Clustered grass-like leaves, small flowers in umbels, bulblets	Dig out bulb and destroy	*Allium vineale.* Lily Family
Johnson Grass, Perennial	Coarse leaves, running rootstocks. Va., Tex. and W.	Dig out	*Holcus halepensis.* Grass Family
Nut-grass, Perennial	Triangular stems, nutlike tubers. S. States	Dig out and destroy	*Cyperus esculentus.* Sedge Family
Orange Hawkweed or Devils Paintbrush, Perennial	Hairy foliage, bright orange flowers. E. U. S.	Dig out and destroy	*Hieracium aurantiacum.* Composite Family
Plantain, English or Buckhorn, Perennial	Narrow ribbed leaves, clustered fibrous roots	Dig out; apply I	*Plantago lanceolata.* Plantain Family
Plantain, Large, Perennial	Prominently veined oval leaves, clustered fibrous roots	Take out with spud; cut off at surface and apply salt, or I or III with ice-pick	*Plantago major.* Plantain Family
Quack Grass, Perennial	Creeping stems. E. States to Minn.	Dig out, or apply II	*Agropyron repens.* Grass Family
Ragweed, Annual	Finely cut, hairy leaves	Cut down before seeds ripen	*Ambrosia elatior.* Composite Family
Shepherds Purse, Annual	Small white flowers, flat whorl of leaves	Pull out	*Capsella bursa-pastoris.* Crucifer Family
Smartweed, Annual	Light rose flowers in short clusters, narrow leaves. E. and S. U. S.	Cut back before flowering	*Polygonum pennsylvanicum.* Buckwheat Family

WEEDS OF THE VEGETABLE GARDEN.

Common Name and Duration	Features and Distribution	Treatment	Scientific Name and Family
Bermuda Grass, Perennial	Rough, coarse leaves. Md. and S.	Dig out and burn	*Cynodon dactylon.* Grass Family
Bindweed, Perennial	Pink or white flowers like small morning-glory	Pull out and apply salt	*Convolvulus arvensis.* Morning-glory Family
Canada Thistle, Perennial	Heads of purple flowers, spiny foliage	Dig out before seeding and destroy roots	*Cirsium arvense.* Composite Family
Chess or Cheat, Annual	Flat-leaved grass	Cultivate out	*Bromus secalinus.* Grass Family
Chickweed, Common, or Winter, Annual	In tufts, slender, weak, hairy stalks, small oval leaves, small white flowers	Hoe, hand-weed, or use I	*Stellaria media.* Pink Family

(Weeds of the Vegetable Garden—Continued.)

Chickweed, Mouse-ear, Perennial or Annual	Clustered, clammy, hairy leaves, small white flowers	Cultivate or pull out	Cerastium vulgatum. Pink Family
Cocklebur, Annual	Coarse-toothed or -lobed leaves, prickly burs	Dig out before it seeds	Xanthium spp. Composite Family
Crab Grass, Annual	Branched stem roots at joints	Pull or cultivate out to prevent seeding	Syntherisma sanguinalis. Grass Family
Dandelion, Perennial	Yellow flowers; flat rosette of toothed leaves	Dig out or apply I and destroy before seeds form	Taraxacum officinale. Composite Family
Dock, Perennial	Coarse leaves, large root	Dig out; cut off leaves and apply III	Rumex spp. Buckwheat Family
Foxtail or Pigeon Grass, Annual	Coarse, grayish leaves	Cultivate out	Setaria glauca. Grass Family
Garlic, Perennial	Clustered grass-like leaves, small bulbs	Dig out and destroy bulbs	Allium vineale. Lily Family
Horse-nettle, Perennial	Yellow flowers, coarse yellowish foliage	Pull out	Solanum carolinense. Nightshade Family
Johnson Grass, Perennial	Coarse leaves, running rootstocks. Va., Tex. and W.	Dig out and burn	Holcus halepensis. Grass Family
Ladys Thumb, Annual	Narrow leaves, flowers in spikes	Pull out before seeding	Polygonum persicaria. Buckwheat Family
Lambs-quarters or Pigweed, Annual	Erect, mealy leaves, small green flowers	Cultivate out	Chenopodium album. Goosefoot Family
Lettuce, Wild, Annual	Prickly leaves, milky juice, small yellow flowers	Cultivate early to prevent seeding	Lactuca scariola var. integrata. Composite Family
Morning-glory, Annual	Heart-shaped leaves, white, purple or blue flowers	Dig out before it flowers	Ipomoea hederacea. Morning-glory Family
Mustard Charlock, Annual	Cut foliage, yellow flowers	Pull out before it seeds	Brassica arvensis. Crucifer Family
Orange Hawkweed or Devils Paintbrush, Perennial	Hairy foliage, red-orange flowers. E. U. S.	Dig out or apply I	Hieracium aurantiacum. Composite Family.
Nut-grass, Perennial	Triangular stems, nut-like tubers. S. States	Cultivate out entirely	Cyperus esculentus. Sedge Family
Pigweed, Annual	Rough, dull green leaves, small dull flowers in spikes	Pull out before it seeds	Amaranthus spp. Amaranthus Family
Plantain, English, or Buckhorn, Perennial	Narrow, ribbed leaves, clustered fibrous roots, flowers in spikes	Hand-weed and destroy	Plantago lanceolata. Plantain Family.
Plantain, Large, Perennial	Oval, prominently ridged leaves, fibrous roots	Dig out and destroy	Plantago major. Plantain Family
Purslane, Pusley, Annual	Fleshy, pink stems, small, round leaves	Pull out and destroy	Portulaca oleracea. Purslane Family
Quack Grass	Creeping stems. E. S. to Minn.	Dig out or apply II	Agropyron repens. Grass Family
Ragweed, Annual	Finely cut, hairy leaves, green seeds	Cut off before seeds ripen	Ambrosia elatior. Composite Family
Russian-thistle	Prickly cut foliage, creeping roots	Dig out completely with spud	Salsola pestifer. Goosefoot Family
Shepherds Purse, Annual	Small white flowers, flat whorl of leaves	Cut off before it seeds	Capsella bursa-pastoris. Crucifer Family
Smartweed, Annual	Rose flowers in clusters, narrow leaves	Cut off before it flowers	Polygonum pennsylvanicum. Buckwheat Family
Sorrel, Sheep, Perennial	Arrow-shaped leaves, small reddish flowers in spikes	Dig out thoroughly, getting all long roots	Rumex acetosella. Buckwheat Family

WEEDS OF THE FLOWER GARDEN.

Common Name and Duration	Features and Distribution	Treatment	Scientific Name and Family
Beggarsticks or Sticktights, Annual	Small yellow flowers, later small burs. N. States	Pull out before seeding	Bidens frondosa. Composite Family

(Weeds of the Flower Garden—Continued.)

Bermuda Grass, Perennial	Rough coarse leaves. Md. and S.	Dig out and destroy	Cynodon dactylon. Grass Family
Bindweed, Perennial	White or pink flower, like morning-glory	Pull out and apply salt	Convolvulus arvensis. Morning-glory Family
Carrot, Wild, Biennial	White flowers in umbels. E. States to Miss.	Dig out and destroy fleshy roots	Daucus carota. Parsley Family
Chess or Cheat, Annual or Biennial	Flat-leaved grass	Dig out	Bromus secalinus. Grass Family
Chickweed, Common, or Winter, Annual	Small white flowers, slender, weak, hairy stems	Hoe or hand-weed or spray with I	Alsine media. Pink Family
Chickweed, Mouse-ear, Perennial or Annual	Small white flowers, clustered, clammy, hairy leaves	Cultivate or pull out or spray with I	Cerastium vulgatum. Pink Family
Crab-Grass, Annual	Branched, roots at joints	Pull or cultivate out to prevent seeding	Syntherisma sanguinalis. Grass Family
Dandelion, Perennial	Yellow flower, rosette of leaves on ground	Pull out by hand	Taraxacum officinale. Composite Family
Fleabane or Horseweed, Annual	Bristly, small flowers in heads; white ray-flowers	Pull out before blossoming	Erigeron canadensis. Composite Family
Purslane or Pusley, Annual	Small round leaves; spreading fleshy stems	Dig out and destroy to prevent re-rooting	Portulaca oleracea. Purslane Family
Quack Grass, Perennial	Creeping stems. E. states to Minn.	Cultivate out thoroughly	Agropyron repens. Grass Family
Shepherds Purse, Annual	Small white flowers, flat whorl of leaves	Weed out	Capsella bursa-pastoris. Crucifer Family
Smartweed, Annual	Light rose flowers in clusters. E. states and S.	Pull out before it flowers	Polygonum pennsylvanicum. Buckwheat Family
Sorrel, Sheep, Perennial	Arrow-shaped leaves	Dig out roots thoroughly	Rumex acetosella. Buckwheat Family
Yellow Wood-sorrel, Perennial	Yellow flowers; leaves in threes	Dig out	Oxalis corniculata. Wood-sorrel Family

INTRUDERS.

COMMON NAME AND DURATION	FEATURES AND DISTRIBUTION	TREATMENT	SCIENTIFIC NAME AND FAMILY
Beggarsticks, Annual	Small yellow flowers, later small burs	Pull out before seeding	Bidens frondosa. Composite Family
Black-eyed Susan, Biennial or Annual	Flowers in heads, yellow rays, brown disks	Destroy before seeding	Rudbeckia hirta. Composite Family
Bouncing Bet	Pinkish-white flowers. E. States	Dig and expose roots	Saponaria officinalis. Pink Family
Butter and-eggs, Perennial	Yellow and white flowers like small snapdragons	Uproot before it spreads	Linaria vulgaris. Figwort Family
Bracken, Perennial	Coarse ferns, long running rootstocks	Dig out and destroy roots	Pteridium latiusculum. Polypodiaceae
Buffalo Bur, Annual	Yellow flowers, rough, yellowish leaves	Destroy before it seeds	Solanum rostratum. Nightshade Family
Carrot, Wild, Biennial	White flowers in flat clusters, long root	Dig out and destroy root	Daucus carota. Parsley Family
Catnip, Perennial	Grayish foliage, spikes of pale purple flowers	Dig out before it spreads	Nepeta cataria. Mint Family
Cheeses, Biennial	Round-heart-shaped leaves, rounded fruit	Dig roots before fruits are formed	Malva rotundifolia. Mallow Family
Chicory, Perennial	Bright blue flowers against stems	Cut and apply III	Cichorium intybus. Composite Family
Chinese Lantern Plant, Perennial	Large red calyx around small fruit. E. States	Dig out large root and burn	Physalis alkekengi. Nightshade Family
Daisy Fleabane or Winter, Annual	Tall stem, small white daisies	Cut before seeding	Erigeron annuus. Composite Family
Goldenrod, Perennial	Tall yellow, plume-like clusters of flowers	Dig out roots	Solidago spp. Composite Family
Ground-ivy, Perennial	Trailing stem, roundish leaves, small purple flowers	Dig out or apply II	Nepeta hederacea. Mint Family
Heal-all, Perennial	Small purple flowers in heads	Pull out or apply II	Prunella vulgaris. Mint Family
Japanese Honeysuckle, Perennial	Rampant vine with white flowers	Uproot and burn	Lonicera japonica. Honeysuckle Family

(Intruders—Continued.)

Common Name and Duration	Features and Distribution	Treatment	Scientific Name and Family
Jerusalem Artichoke, Perennial	Tall weeds, small sunflower-like blossoms	Dig and burn roots	*Helianthus tuberosus.* Composite Family
Jimpson Weed, Annual	Large white flowers and coarse leaves, prickly fruit	Poisonous. Destroy plant and fruit	*Datura stramonium.* Nightshade Family
Knotweed, Annual or Perennial	Coarse leaves, small flowers in clusters	Uproot while small	*Polygonum* spp. Buckwheat Family
Live-forever, Perennial	Thick oval leaves, purple flowers in flat-topped clusters	Weed out where not desired	*Sedum triphyllum.* Orpine Family
May-weed, Dog-fennel, Annual	Daisy-like, finely cut, ill-scented foliage	Cut before seeding	*Anthemis cotula.* Composite Family
Michaelmas Daisies, Perennial	White or lavender daisy-like flowers	Hoe out roots	*Aster* spp. Composite Family
Moneywort, Creeping Jenny or Charlie, Perennial	Yellow flowers, creeping stem	Destroy in rock garden	*Lysimachia nummularia.* Primrose Family
Nettle, Perennial	Coarse, stinging leaves	Pull out with gloved hands and burn	*Urtica dioica.* Nettle Family
Orange Hawkweed, Perennial	Hairy foliage, brilliant orange flowers	Dig roots and burn	*Hieracium aurantiacum* Composite Family
Oxeye Daisy	Yellow disk, white rays, growing to 3 ft.	Dig out and destroy root	*Chrysanthemum leucanthemum.* Composite Family
Poison Ivy, Perennial	Woody climber, three leaflets, gray fruit	Dig and burn roots or use II	*Rhus toxicodendron.* Sumac Family
Pokeweed, Perennial	Large leaves, tall racemes of dark purplish-red fruits	Dig and destroy poisonous roots	*Phytolacca americana.* Pokeweed Family
Sow Thistle, Annual	Tall coarse weed with pale yellow flowers	Cut before it seeds	*Sonchus oleraceus.* Composite Family
Speedwell, Perennial	Trailing stem, small blue or white flowers in clusters	Dig out or apply II	*Veronica serpyllifolia.* Figwort Family
White Cockle, Biennial or Perennial	Narrow leaves, white flowers opening in the evening	Weed out before it seeds	*Lychnis alba.* Pink Family
Wild Potato-vine, Man-of-the-earth, Perennial	Fiddle-shaped leaves, white, funnel-shaped flowers	Dig out and burn large root	*Ipomea pandurata.* Morning-glory Family

WEEPING TREES. A term for all kinds of trees, large and small, which have pendulous, downward sweeping branches. It includes two distinct forms, one a natural departure, the other an artificially developed one. The former is exemplified by the weeping willow, weeping beech, camperdown elm and occasional freakish growing trees of practically all species. The artificially produced weeping trees are seen in the weeping mulberry and the many varieties of flowering crab and almond which have always been favorite subjects for this sort of use. These are made by grafting naturally drooping or prostrate-growing varieties or forms upon straight, woody trunks of an upright form of the same species.

Obviously trees of this distinct form, whether natural or artificially produced, and whether large or small, are very striking. They therefore arrest attention instantly and must be introduced into the garden very carefully, so that they take exactly the right place in the picture. They do not group well either with their own kind or with more conventional material, but are usually best when planted as single specimens or accents (which see) where it is desired to focus attention. They may easily become the feature of their portion of the garden when treated thus.

WEEVILS. These insects are properly beetles belonging to two types: those that attack stored seed, such as the bean and pea weevils; and the typical weevils, snout beetles or curculios which attack growing plants, especially, in many cases, the fruits. See also INSECTS; BEETLES.

The pea weevil is short and chunky, about ⅕ in. long, brownish and flecked with white, black and grayish patches. Old peas may be found with neat circular holes in the shell and the contents eaten entirely away. The various bean weevils are similar in appearance and action. The best control is fumigation of the seed when harvested with carbon bisulphide (which see). Place the seed in bags in a tight box, cover with gunny sacks and pour the heavy, colorless, ill-smelling—and *highly inflammable*—liquid over the sacks. Then leave the box closed for 24 to 36 hours. Use 1 oz. bisulphide for each bushel of seed.

For treatment of typical weevils see SNOUT BEETLES; CURCULIO.

WEIGELA (wy-gee'-lah). Deciduous shrubs, belonging to the Honeysuckle Family and native to Asia. Until recently they were included in the genus Diervilla. They are of spreading habit, with more or less pendulous branches, and the clusters of bell-shaped flowers are very showy in spring and early summer. They thrive in any good garden soil that does not get too dry. While generally considered hardy, most kinds are likely to be killed back somewhat in severe winters unless protected. The tender terminal leaves are sometimes attacked by the four-lined plant bug, which see.

A number of free-flowing and colorful hybrids produced by crossing the different species are now the most popular kinds in gardens. To keep them well furnished, thin out old and straggly wood after flowering. Propagated by greenwood and hardwood cuttings.

PRINCIPAL SPECIES

W. florida, the best known, grows 6 ft. or more high, with showy flowers of rose-pink. Var. *venusta,* from Korea, is the hardiest and earliest to bloom. It has smaller leaves, and a profusion of dark rose-purple flowers on arching branches.

coraeensis is the tallest grower, reaching 15 ft. It has large leaves and flowers, but is not a profuse bloomer. The color varies from pale pink to carmine.

praecox is not unlike *florida,* the flowers not quite as handsome but opening earlier.

floribunda grows to 10 ft., with slender branches and flowers of dark crimson.

hybrida is a collective name for the numerous hybrids between these species. Some of the best are the following: flowers white or nearly so—Avalanche, Dame Blanche, Vestale, Mme. Lemoine, Candida,

Mont Blanc; flowers pink to carmine—Abel Carrière, André Thouin, Esperance, Gustave Mallot, Seduction, Styriaca; flowers red or dark crimson—Congo, Eva Rathke, Henderson, Incarnata, Lavalle, P. Duchartre. Vars. with variegated leaves: yellow markings—*kosteriana variegata, luteo-marginata;* white markings—*nana variegata, sieboldi argenteo-marginata.*

WELSH POPPY. Common name for *Meconopsis cambrica,* a yellow-flowered perennial herb to 1½ ft. suitable for borders and the rock garden.

WETTABLE SULPHUR. Sulphur prepared in such a way that it mixes readily with water for use as a spray. See SULPHUR AND ITS COMPOUNDS.

WHALE-OIL SOAP. An old name (now largely superseded by the more accurate "fish-oil soap" for a material used in spray form as a contact insecticide, in the preparation of emulsions and spreaders, and sometimes as a repellent in the form of a wash to be applied to trunks of trees. See SOAPS AS SPRAYS.

WHEELBARROW. A shallow, box-like or bowl-like receptacle of wood or metal supported in front by a wheel (or more rarely two wheels) placed between two shafts, and in the rear by a pair of legs or braces. It is pushed or pulled by one man who stands between the rear ends of the shafts and grasps them, one in each hand, with the arms full length. The wheel was the inspiration of Leonardo da Vinci, who added it to the ancient hand barrow, a box with shafts at each end for two men to carry (still occasionally used in some industries).

Wheelbarrows are of two general forms. One has a body made of wood or metal bent into bowl-like form; the other, more common in gardens, has a usually flat bottom and removable straight sides. The former is most used for rough work such as moving gravel, sand and earth; the latter for carrying lighter and more bulky materials—manure, straw, weeds, etc., as well as earth. With the sides removed, the barrow can be used to move poles, planks and other long objects placed crosswise; or it can be equipped with a light framework of wood and wire netting in which to carry large loads of leaves, trash, and other loose material.

One of the most helpful developments in modern gardening has been the adaptation of the pneumatic tire to wheelbarrows of the better type as optional equipment. The tire makes the barrow push more easily, run more smoothly and do less damage to lawns, edges, etc.

WHEELHOE. A hand-operated cultivator consisting of a frame mounted on one or two wheels and equipped for carrying one or more interchangeable attachments or sets of soil-stirring tools. Each of the latter is especially adapted to a specific type of work, as shallow plowing, furrowing, seeding, ridging, cultivating, disking, hoeing, scarifying, raking, weeding, and even lifting and putting aside overhanging foliage.

As a time and labor saver the wheelhoe (both with and without a special seed-drill attachment) is not only part of the essential equipment for commercial gardening, but also a boon, if not indispensable, to the amateur gardener with a plot 50 ft. square or smaller. Its value can be enhanced by starting to cultivate with it soon after seedsowing instead of waiting until the seedlings appear above ground. The use of the drilling or seeding attachment makes this possible, as it leaves a distinct mark when the seed has been placed which can be avoided in the early cultivations that destroy many weed seedlings that otherwise would compete with and perhaps smother the young crop plants.

The trick of using a wheelhoe in cultivating consists of pushing it in a series of quick, short thrusts rather than a steady forward movement. The operator's steps can be synchronized with these thrusts and the alternate effort and pause is far less tiring than a sustained drive. Also it is desirable to keep the arms bent at the elbow so as to get the cushioning effect of pushing with the muscles instead of with stiff, straight arms. The handles of a wheelhoe are adjustable to permit just the right angle for the individual operator. See also CULTIVATION; TOOLS.

WHIN. A common name for the genus Ulex, also called Furze and Gorse; it includes spiny shrubs with yellow pea-like flowers.

WHISPERING BELLS. Common name for *Emmenanthe penduliflora*, a dwarf Calif. desert herb with drooping racemes of yellow flowers.

WHITE-ALDER. Common name for *Clethra alnifolia*, a fragrant white-flowered N. shrub blooming in late summer.

WHITE BAY. Common name for *Magnolia virginiana*, a semi-evergreen tree with fragrant white flowers 3 in. across. Also called Sweet Bay.

WHITE BEAM-TREE. The common name for *Sorbus aria*, a large European Mountain-ash (which see) with white flowers in spring and red "berries" in autumn.

WHITE-CEDAR. Common name given to two different trees of the Pine Family, neither of which is a true cedar. One is *Chamaecyparis thyoides*, a species of False-cypress; the other is *Libocedrus decurrens*, a species of Incense-cedar.

WHITE-CUP. Common name for *Nierembergia rivularis*, a low early blooming perennial with white, blue or rose-tinted flowers. See CUP-FLOWER.

WHITE DAISY. Common name for *Layia glandulosa*, an early blooming annual of W. U. S., with white or rose-tinted flower-heads, to 18 in. tall.

WHITE FLIES. A name given to several kinds of insects, small and troublesome, principally in greenhouses or warm regions.

The greenhouse white fly (*Trialeurodes vaporariorum*) infests many kinds of plants under glass and is often carried into the garden when greenhouse house-grown plants are set out. The tiny moth-like adult is given a mealy appearance by small particles of wax which it secretes. It lays eggs on the underside of leaves where the nymphs remain sucking the sap. These, somewhat resembling scale insects, are oval in shape with a marginal fringe of short wax rods; they are white at first, becoming yellow when grown, at which time the skin splits open and the adult emerges. About 5 weeks are necessary for each generation and there may be several broods. Fumigate greenhouses with cyanide (see CYANIDE COMPOUNDS); spray house or garden plants with nicotine or pyrethrum and soap.

Other species are the mulberry white fly, which may be numerous on many kinds of trees and shrubs; and the azalea white fly. The citrus white fly (*Dialeurodes citri*) is injurious mainly in Fla., where it not only sucks the sap but also produces quantities of honeydew in which grows the sooty mold fungus (which see). Other fungi, parasitic on the white fly, have been introduced in the hope of controlling it.

WHITE GRUBS. A name for the larvae of so-called June bugs or, more accurately, May or June beetles (which see). They have smooth curved bodies, white except for the swollen dark colored posterior portion; six legs, large brown heads, and distinct jaws. They range from $\frac{1}{2}$ to 1 in. long, being thereby distinguished from the smaller, but otherwise quite similar, larvae of Japanese, Asiatic and other smaller beetles. They feed on the roots of grass, corn, wheat, potatoes, strawberries and other plants and are likely to be numerous in sod land or long-established strawberry beds. If serious they can be destroyed by poisoning the soil with lead arsenate (see ARSENICAL POISONS). Chickens are fond of them and will devour many if allowed to run where the ground is being dug or plowed.

WHITE-HELLEBORE. A common name for species of Veratrum or False-hellebore; hardy perennial herbs with whitish or greenish flowers.

WHITE MOUNTAIN-LILY. A common name for *Leucocrinum montanum,* stemless liliaceous herb of the N. W. with fragrant white flowers borne in clusters in spring. See SAND-LILY.

WHITE SNAKEROOT. Common name for *Eupatorium urticaefolium,* a hardy perennial herb with white flower-heads, native from Me. to Fla. and La.

WHITEWEED. One of the popular names for *Chrysanthemum leucanthemum,* a common perennial weed in mismanaged land, also known as Oxeye Daisy.

WHITEWOOD. One of the names given to the *Liriodendron tulipifera,* the Tulip-tree (which see). Formerly applied also to Tilia, the Linden, which see.

WHITLAVIA (whit-lay'-vi-ah). Common name sometimes applied to *Phacelia whitlavia,* an 18-in. Calif. annual with blue or purple flowers.

WHITLOW-GRASS. Common name for *Draba verna,* a variable annual herb grown in rock gardens.

WHITLOW-WORT. Common name for Paronychia, a genus of little annuals and perennials with tiny flowers, easily grown in the rock garden.

WHORL. A set of 3 or more leaves or flowers, arranged in a complete circle around the stem; such as the leaves of the Indian Cucumber-root (*Medeola virginiana*), or the flowers of Spearmint. Compare ALTERNATE.

WHORL-FLOWER. Common name for *Morina longifolia,* a perennial, thistle-like herb of the Teasel Family, growing to 4 ft. with spiny foliage. The showy flowers, deepening in color from white to pink and finally crimson, grow in a whorled spike, each whorl surrounded by spiny bracts. Whorl-flowers are useful in the border and should be planted in a light rich soil in a warm sheltered position. They can be increased by seed or division.

WHORTLEBERRY. Rarely used common name for *Vaccinium myrtillus* and *V. corymbosum,* which are, respectively, low-bush and highbush blueberries, with pinkish flowers. See BLUEBERRY.

WICKY. A common name for *Kalmia angustifolia,* also called Sheep-laurel and Lamb-kill. See KALMIA.

WICOPY. Common name for *Dirca palustris,* the Leatherwood (which see), an American shrub so named because of its tough pliable branches.

WIDOWS-TEARS. A common name in some parts of the U. S. for members of the spiderwort genus, Tradescantia, which see.

WIGANDIA (wi-gan'-di-ah). A genus of coarse perennial tropical American shrubby plants or herbs, having large bristly leaves and bell-shaped blue or violet flowers in one-sided spikes. They are not hardy N. and do not make good greenhouse subjects, but are used for bedding plants in subtropical parts of the S. They are increased by root-cuttings taken in the spring or from seeds sown under glass. *W. caracasana,* a woody shrub to 10 ft. or more, has toothed wrinkled leaves 18 by 10 in. and violet bell-shaped flowers with a white tube; its var. *macrophylla* is the form usually grown. *W. urens,* to 12 ft., has 1-ft. leaves and violet flowers. Other forms, sometimes listed as species, are probably only varieties of *W. caracasana.*

WILD-BERGAMOT. Common name for *Monarda fistulosa,* a strongly scented perennial of the Mint Family with terminal heads of lilac flowers, native from N. E. to Colo., and easily transplanted.

WILD BUCKWHEAT. Common name for *Eriogonum fasciculatum,* a sub-shrub of Calif. and Nev. to 3 ft. tall, with white flowers in flat clusters.

WILD-CHAMOMILE. Common name for *Matricaria chamomilla* (also called Sweet False-Chamomile), a branching annual composite with finely cut foliage, white ray flowers and yellow disks.

Plate 59.   WELL-PLANTED WALL GARDENS

Top: The terraced garden with dry rock retaining walls gives an opportunity for much interesting plant material.   Insert: The retaining wall makes an ideal home for many rock garden plants.
Bottom: In fascinating variety the tiny cliff-dwellers cling precariously in niche and crevice.

WILD FLOWERS. Term usually applied to native plants of a country which grow in the fields and woods without cultivation, but which often offer rich possibilities as garden subjects when either carefully transplanted to suitable locations or grown from seed as cultivated plants. See NATIVE PLANTS.

WILD GARDEN. A wild garden is, in the highest sense, a collection, ecologically correct, of the plants native to that portion of the country in which the garden is located. It is no longer a heterogeneous collection of so-called wild flowers from various parts of the world, but a harmonious grouping of plants flourishing in their own native conditions, or in an environment which, by careful thought and study of their natural growth, has been made to simulate those conditions.

Thus, in the desert States, the wild garden should contain the cacti and other plants thriving in arid conditions; in the S. States, especially Fla. or La., swamp conditions might be duplicated; in the Middle West a collection of prairie flowers would be appropriate; or in the Rocky Mountains the use of the alpines of that region; and so on, throughout our widespread country. Conditions vary so greatly from place to place that it is absurd to expect (for sentimental reasons) that trailing arbutus will thrive in the desert or a Joshua-tree look at home on a New England hillside.

WILD-GARDEN POSSIBILITIES. For a wild garden on a large scale in a portion of the country where forest conditions still prevail (or where they once existed) a bit of land on a hillside, sloping to a natural meadow, watered by a stream flowing into a marshy lake, is an ideal site. If the trees are still intact and the smaller plants have been destroyed or removed, those native to the region should be secured and planted. If it is impossible to secure land with trees already existing, a wild garden may even be made on cleared land, building it from the very beginning. First a study must be made of what was there before it was cleared and "civilized"; then trees, shrubs and other plants must be grouped in a natural planting. Such a wild garden, if well done, can be worked out so successfully that it appears as a piece of untouched woodland.

To get an idea of wild-garden possibilities on a large scale in N. Y. or southern New England, let us make a study of a hillside typical of that region. Such a garden may occupy an acre or more; or it may be duplicated in miniature on a portion of the home grounds.

At the highest point grow chestnut oaks, a few white pines and dwarf pitch pines. Here, where the soil has washed away from the rocks for years, we find an acid condition in which grow mountain-laurel, dwarf blueberry, mats of polypody fern, wintergreen, occasional colonies of rattlesnake-plantain, pipsissewa, shinleaf and prince's pine, and, on northern hillsides, patches of trailing arbutus. In the more open spots we may discover groups of the stemless lady-slippers (sometimes with their roots spread over the mossy rocks) which will not grow except where acid soil prevails and where there is proper mycorrhizal association (which see). Here, with confidence, we may establish more colonies of the rarer and choicer plants, such as the lady-slipper and dainty mayflower.

Lower on the slope we find more neutral soil and an association of other oaks, hickories, ashes, different birches and maples. Among them grow the striped maple, occasionally patches of Canadian yew, witch-hazel, shadbush, maple-leaved viburnum and, here and there, carpets of partridge-berry. In spring the wake-robin parts the fallen leaves, accompanied by bloodroot, anemones, the showy orchis, true and false Solomons seal, Jack-in-the-pulpit, various violets, wild-ginger; hepaticas and yellow lady-slippers; while in open stretches the dutchmans breeches nod among their finely cut leaves. In the rock crevices sway vivid groups of the red and yellow columbine, and the early saxifrage foams in snowy drifts. The marginal shield fern will unfurl its chaffy fronds in graceful clusters, and there are masses of the delicately green interrupted, New-York and hay-scented ferns; also the silvery new growth of the Christmas fern, and in damp spots frail fronds of maidenhair. Later the bellworts will swing their yellow blossoms, the red and the white baneberries will bloom and bear their conspicuous fruits, and their near relative, the bugbane, will raise its wand-like stems of feathery white, ill-smelling flowers higher than the nearby shrubs. Toward the edge of the woodland, the flowering dogwood will be covered with drifts of snowy blossoms, and the alternate-leaved dogwood with creamy flat-topped clusters; both will be followed later in the season by the attractive vari-colored scarlet-stemmed fruits.

Following the little brook to the open meadow we find a dancing company of yellow trout-lilies among their mottled leaves. Willows and alders outline the stream, and early in the spring, just as the cinnamon and royal ferns are unfurling their croziers, the marsh-marigolds glorify the margin. Here calamus-root and iris, monkey-flower, blue lobelia and cardinal-flower grow almost in the water; and where it is moist (but not too wet) the turtle-head and the great purple-fringed orchis bloom later in the year. If the stream flows into a marshy lake, we shall find a new grouping of plants, dominated by the feathery growth of larches and the silver trunks of swamp red maples, interspersed with a varied collection of shrubs—hardhack, black alder, sweet pepper-bush, button-bush, osier dogwood and willow; and mingled with them marsh, sensitive, cinnamon, and royal ferns.

In the summer will rise great tall heads of Joe-Pye-weed, swamp milkweed, white boneset, and Turks Cap lily and, in the more open spots, the swamp lily. On grassy hummocks in the marsh, in the light shade of the larches, will grow in leafy groups the showy lady-slipper, always in reach of water but never quite in it. Here also will flourish the skunk-cabbage, buck-beans and, if there is sphagnum moss, the tiny insectivorous sundew. Under similar conditions in higher mountain swamps we would find masses of bunchberry, pitcher-plant, wild-calla and golden-club, while on the edge of the pond grows the pickerel-weed with its vivid blue spikes, the swamp loosestrife, the arrow-head and the dainty white flowers of the water-buttercup. Out in the open water the golden buds of the spatterdock and the fragrant white cups of the water-lily stand out against the blue.

DUPLICATING NATURAL PLANTINGS. In any section of the country this type of study of near-by woods and swamps will help more than anything else in planning a wild garden, large or small. If on the available site one has only to supplement the natural growth, the task is simple; it then means merely enlarging the colonies already established with additional plants procured from nurseries or raised from seed or cuttings. But if the area has to be planted with trees, shrubs and herbs from the beginning, care should be taken to banish too vigorous, weedy growths which always hasten to crowd in when man has upset the balance of nature. Next prepare the soil for the different plant associations, and in doing so make careful use of one of the inexpensive soil-testing outfits now on the market.

In the small wild garden, where conditions are necessarily artificial, the soil-tester is indispensable in order to be sure whether the soil is acid, alkaline, or neutral before setting out the various types of plants. It is much simpler in the small wild garden to specialize in small groups of plants having the same soil requirements, placing the acid-soil lovers in one part of the yard or border, those requiring lime in another, and those that thrive in neutral conditions somewhere else. Thus, in one corner, under a hemlock tree, an appropriate and harmonious grouping would include rhododendron and mountain-laurel, kept mulched with red oak leaves; and beneath their shelter a happy company of stemless lady-slippers and vigorously growing trailing arbutus (*Epigaea repens*), while on a lichen-covered boulder the common polypody fern and Canadian may-flower (*Maianthemum canadense*) would mingle with a ground-cover of wintergreen and various club-mosses.

In a more open spot in the shrubbery border a group of the native viburnums, so attractive in flower and fruit, could supply the light shelter needed for a group of easily grown spring-blooming wild flowers. The soil should be rich in woodland humus, but quite neutral in reaction. Here, in the earliest sunny days, hepaticas would open, followed by bloodroot, anemones, dutchmans breeches, bleeding heart and various trilliums, all intermingled with the delicate little oak fern. Near an artificial pool a collection of the ferns of the region could be grouped about a number of showy lady-slippers and purple- and yellow-fringed forms of orchis. Hundreds of combinations can be worked out—always considering the natural habitats and soil requirements of the different plants.

WILD GARDENS BY THE SEA. The sea-side wild garden is another interesting variation, but it should be attempted only in its natural environment and never planned as a part of the shrubbery border. Here, the native pitch pines, gnarled and dwarfed, should form the main feature; or various oaks and sassafras, underplanted with shadbush, beach plum, hawthorn, inkberry, sweet-fern, wild roses and mats of bearberry. In the more exposed portions the sand should be anchored with beach grass and bear-grass, and there should be widespread clumps of rose-purple beach-pea, wild lupine, beach worm-wood and hudsonia. In more sheltered spots there could be colonies of birdsfoot violet, pixie, the brilliant orange milkweed and the wood lily, aided and supported by the vast company of native asters and goldenrods.

SECURING PLANTS. Whenever possible, wild flowers should be raised from seeds or cuttings, or bought from nurseries which specialize in growing them, rather than collected. The reason is that wild specimens, because of their widespread root systems, are difficult to transplant; also as an aid to conservation efforts we should endeavor to preserve rare plants in their own habitats. The only exception to this policy would be when we learn that a given area is to undergo real estate development; then it certainly would be an aid to conservation to salvage as many plants as possible before the land is invaded and built upon. Many wild flowers are easily raised from seed. Others, such as arbutus and gentian (which see), require special treatment.

PATH CONSTRUCTION. In the large-scale wild garden, if paths do not already exist, they should be cut, following carefully the slope of the land, so that the higher parts may be reached by easy stages. If the path leads through a grove of birches they may be thinned so that they stand in groups to show their full beauty. Always remember, though, that a wood with the underbrush all neatly removed is not natural woodland, for many trees cannot thrive without shrubs and low-growing wild flowers for ground-cover. If at the highest point of the path there is a widespread outlook, interfering trees should be removed, carefully choosing the survivors so they will frame the vista. At other points on the path the removal of underbrush may open up other delightful views of surrounding country.

The brook may be spanned by a small rustic bridge, or, preferably, by stepping-stones, and flat-topped boulders may be used for resting-places, for even rustic benches seem out of place in a wild garden.

With a little ingenuity paths may be built even through the swampland, taking advantage of the high spots and setting in flat rocks and heavy sods.

The best time to start a wild garden is in the early fall. Most of the spring flowers are most easily transplanted at that time and will become established before winter, rewarding the gardener with airy bloom early the following spring, often before there is a single flower in the border. If given proper soil conditions, they will bloom more beautifully and increase more rapidly than when they have to struggle against adverse conditions. In dry seasons rare plants in the larger wild garden should be mulched with leaves, and in the smaller garden should be watered in order to assure them the advantages of natural sheltered forest conditions.

For further cultural details, see articles on the various plants mentioned. See also NATIVE PLANTS; CONSERVATION.

WILD-PINK. Common name for *Silene caroliniana* (sometimes called *S. pennsylvanica*), a perennial species of Catchfly or Campion native to E. U. S.

WILD-RICE. The most common name for *Zizania palustris,* an aquatic grass also called Indian-rice, Water-rice and Water-oats. Growing along the swampy borders of streams and ponds, it attains, in some regions, a height of 10 ft., and used in the water garden it is a splendid and very handsome grass for a marginal planting. (In grocery stores catering to the so-called "luxury trade," wild-rice brings a good price, as epicurean traditions demand that it be served with certain wild fowl.)

Hunt clubs and individuals, especially throughout the S., have been sowing great quantities of wild-rice about ponds and in marshes to attract duck and other game birds. The seed is obtainable from almost any seed house. Before planting, it is advisable to put the seed in a coarse cotton bag, attach a rock or other ballast and soak in water for 24 hours. Sow in water from 6 in. to 5 ft. deep or in any marsh where water stands the year round.

See also AQUATIC PLANTS.

WILD-ROSEMARY. A common name for *Ledum palustre,* a low evergreen ericaceous shrub with small white flowers borne in spring.

WILD-RYE. Common name for Elymus, a genus of tall perennial grasses grown as background plants in borders.

WILD-SWEET-POTATO-VINE. The common name for *Ipomoea pandurata,* a pestiferous weed native from Conn. to Fla. and Tex. It has a tuberous perennial root, trailing or twining stems, and purple-throated white flowers. See also WEEDS.

WILLOW. Common name for the genus Salix, comprising soft-wooded trees and shrubs related to the poplars. Some forms are erect, others are weeping or even prostrate. All have deciduous leaves and bear staminate and pistillate flowers on separate trees, in the form of catkins (*aments*) which, because of the covering of silky hairs developed in some species, are often conspicuous in the spring before the leaves open. Willows differ widely in size, from the White Willow with lofty furrowed trunk and spreading branches, to a tiny prostrate shrub of the Arctic regions.

Willows are planted as ornamental trees and valued for their quick growth, pleasing form, graceful foliage; the silvery catkins or "pussies" of some species and the bright golden or orange twigs of others, which make a bright and cheering spot of color in the winter landscape.

Because of its extensive root system the willow is exceedingly valuable for soil binding and to prevent erosion along river courses; it is often planted near lakes and ponds to hold the shore-line. Preferring moist locations but able to grow in unfavorable locations, willows naturalize readily. While not especially long lived, they grow so rapidly that they are often used as nurse trees for others slower in growth that need partial shade while young. The slender pliant twigs of some species (*S. viminalis* principally) are used extensively abroad in basket-making, the "pollarded" willows (those of which the tops have been repeatedly cut back) forming a characteristic note of the European countryside. Willows are also cultivated for basket-making in this country, especially through central N. Y.

Growing readily from cuttings (sometimes broken branches lodging along the shore of a stream strike root and start new plants without human help), willows can also be raised from seed, which should be planted as soon as ripe.

The weeping types are sometimes grafted on upright stocks to create a standard form. Special care should be taken in placing willows of the drooping type, for appropriate surroundings accentuate their charm. One willow leaning over a pool may be artistic, whereas a dozen in a row may create a crowded and confused effect.

ENEMIES. A leaf and twig blight recently found in the New England States is the most serious willow disease. The fungus (*Fusicladium saliciperdum*) has killed or injured hundreds of large trees, but will probably not be serious except in N. New England. It overwinters in cankers on the twigs and blights the young leaves as they emerge from the bud. Four or 5 applications of bordeaux mixture will give protection: the first should be made before the buds open, another 2 weeks later, a third as the leaf tips emerge, one when the leaves are half to two-thirds grown and the last when they are full size.

Leaf rusts are common on willow and occasionally a "tar spot" occurs similar to that on maple. Rusts and one or two leaf-spotting fungi may cause defoliation, but raking up and burning all fallen leaves will ordinarily keep them under control.

The imported willow beetle is a common pest. Both the dark metallic blue, shiny, $\frac{1}{8}$-in.-long beetles and the bluish-black alligator-like larvae feed on the leaves, the former chewing holes and the latter skeletonizing them. There are two broods. Spray with lead arsenate. Many other insects feed on willow, among them aphids, the fall web-worm, gypsy moth, poplar leaf beetle, poplar tent maker, satin moth, and spiny elm caterpillar. The oyster-shell scale commonly infests willow and the poplar and willow curculio bores into the trunks and twigs of pussy willows.

All trees badly infested with any of these pests should be cut down, but two sawflies that may be injurious, the currant stem girdler (see CURRANT) and the yellow-spotted willow slug, can be controlled by spraying with lead arsenate.

PRINCIPAL SPECIES

S. alba (White Willow), to 75 ft., has lance-shaped leaves to 4 in. long; the catkins appear with the leaves. An Old-World tree, it has become widely naturalized in N. America. A number of variations are listed as: var. *calva,* of upright growth; var. *chermesina,* with brilliant red twigs; var. *sericea,* with leaves very silky beneath; var. *tristis,* with yellow drooping branches; var. *vitellina,* with leaves bloomy beneath, and very yellow branches.

viminalis (Common Osier), to 30 ft., has lance-shaped silvery leaves to 10 in. and catkins that appear before the leaves. It is another Eurasian plant that has become established in America; it is the species most commonly used in basket-weaving.

babylonica (Weeping Willow), to 30 ft., has exceedingly long graceful drooping branches, narrow leaves to 6 in. long and catkins with the leaves. A curious form (var. *crispa*) has twisted and curled leaves.

pentandra (Bay or Laurel Willow), to 60 ft., has shining green leaves to 5 in., whitish beneath; the catkins come with the leaves. Much used in landscape work in the E., it has escaped from cultivation in many places.

caprea (Goat Willow or Sallow), to 25 ft., has rather broad leaves to 4 in. and large, handsome catkins before the leaves. Var. *pendula* (Kilmarnock Willow) has crooked branches; var. *variegata* has variegated leaves.

purpurea (Purple Osier), a shrub to 9 ft. with leaves whitish beneath, has also escaped in many places. Var. *lambertiana* has thick purple branches; var. *pendula* has drooping branches and var. *gracilis* has narrow leaves and delicate branches.

fragilis (Brittle or Crack Willow), to 60 ft., has lance-shaped leaves to 7 in., and catkins with the leaves. It is so called because of the brittleness of the long slender twigs. Posts cut from this species often take root and establish themselves as trees.

discolor (Pussy Willow), to 20 ft. Well known for its silvery catkins, and worthy of being more extensively planted.

scouleriana (Western Pussy Willow), to 30 ft., with leaves to 4 in., often silvery beneath, bears its large catkins long before the leaves, giving an effect of a fruit tree in blossom.

Desert- or Flowering-willow is *Chilopsis linearis;* Primrose-willow is Jussiaea; Water-willow is *Decodon verticillatus.*

WILLOW-HERB. The common name for Epilobium, a genus of herbs or sub-shrubs with willow-like leaves. They are among the easiest plants to grow, but although one or two may be grown in borders, for the most part they are better placed in the wild garden and by the water-side. They have small, white or sometimes yellow flowers and long fruit pods or capsules. Propagated by seeds, division and runners. Principal species are:

E. angustifolium (Fireweed), found all across the northern part of the country, is a tall robust perennial, spreading rapidly by means of underground runners. It bears long terminal spikes of rosy-purple flowers. Var. *album* has been improved in cultivation, and is a useful white-flowering plant for the border.

hirsutum (Codlins-and-cream) is a soft hairy clammy plant with leafy clusters of pale purple to white flowers. It grows to about 4 ft., and also spreads rapidly and widely by underground runners.

dodonaei is a smaller grower with rosemary-like leaves and reddish flowers crowded at the ends of the branches.

nummularifolium, a little creeping plant from New Zealand, with tiny white flowers, is of value as a ground-cover in the rock garden.

The name Willow-herb is sometimes applied to *Lythrum salicaria.*

WILTING. The drooping of a plant, caused chiefly by the collapse of cells, may be due to lack of water but is in many cases a typical disease symptom (see DISEASES, PLANT). Bacteria may cause wilting by stopping up the water-conducting system, and fungi may secrete toxic substances into the plant vessels. Wilting is one of the first symptoms in many root and crown diseases. See CROWN ROT; SCLEROTINIA ROT; FUSARIUM; VERTICILLIUM WILT.

WIND. Changes in the weather (which see) depend partly on wind, which is therefore useful. Some trees such as pine and juniper require wind to keep them in health. It helps or stimulates the flow of sap, may rid them of certain insect pests and fungous diseases, helps distribute their pollen and seeds and tends to prevent or ward off frost, which see.

On the other hand some plants, especially broad-leaved evergreens, will not grow in exposed, windy places; and the majority of all plants do better if protected from the strong winds of winter, which may injure through their force and cold, and more often through their drying effect. For this reason, largely, protection (which see) is frequently vital to gardening. Sometimes the contour of the ground will serve: a valley running N. E. and S. W., or a ravine or pocket in the hillside. Elsewhere windbreaks should be created. Rhododendrons and their kind should be placed where little or no wind reaches them, for, like all broad-leaved evergreens, their tops are dried out much more rapidly in wind than in still air, and when the ground is frozen their roots find it difficult to maintain a supply of moisture. In places subject to disastrous storm winds, trees such as silver maple and locust, with their brittle branches, should be avoided.

See also WINTER PROTECTION.

WINDBREAK. This designates any planting of trees or shrubs on the windward side of a garden, orchard, field or buildings as protection from the wind. (See illustration, Plate 27.) Much garden material that is not injured by extreme cold suffers greatly and may be damaged beyond repair by the drying effect (as well as the buffeting) of strong winds blowing full on it, in summer as well as winter. Gardens near the sea are especally subject to this sort of injury and often the only possible way of having a garden there is to plant extensive windbreaks between it and the direction of the prevailing wind—usually the water.

Where there is ample ground space, the best form for a windbreak is that of a natural, close-set grove of evergreen trees, carried far enough in both directions to stay the wind over an area considerably wider than the protected space itself. This width is needed because the protection is based on the principle of shredding up the wind force and scattering it, rather than actually stopping it. The garden or picture effect of such a planting is of course much more agreeable than that of a series of straight rows of trees, since it is always better to do necessary things in garden design in such a way that they shall seem to be natural.

Evergreen trees are obviously the preferred material for large-scale windbreaks. One large conifer placed in just the right place will afford a surprising degree of protection to a dwelling; a group of three or more, according to the situation, may shelter it so completely that even high winds will not be felt, although the sound of their passage through the branches may be an additional source of pleasure in the garden. In close quarters, a hedge of either evergreen or dense deciduous material serves well, especially if the plants are set, staggered, in a double row and given sufficient pruning and other regular care to keep it compact and thick.

See also HEDGE; PROTECTION; PRUNING.

WINDFLOWER. A common name for Anemone, a genus of useful perennial herbs with white, pink, red, or lavender flowers. The hardier species are grown mostly in borders, and some, more tender, are forced for cut-flower production.

WINDOW BOXES. Whether of wood or metal, window boxes should measure 8 in.. in depth, inside measurement; they may be from 8 to 12 in. in width; the length is ordinarily determined by the distance between window casements; but for convenience in handling, a long box may be made in short lengths to be placed end to end.

If made of wood it should be of 1-in. stock and strongly constructed, with brass or galvanized screws to resist rusting. It should be lined with zinc or well protected against decay by several coats of paint both inside and out. Holes should be provided in the bottom three or four inches apart for drainage purposes. Broken flower pots should be placed over the drainage holes to prevent loss of soil, and an inch of coarse drainage material, broken pots, cinders, clinkers, etc., spread over the bottom before filling with soil. Metal boxes are obtainable equipped with false bottoms and special provision for drainage and for watering at extended intervals.

Location in the room is important since flowering plants require exposure to direct sunlight while foliage plants prefer shaded or subdued light. Plants may be set directly in the soil or be allowed to remain as potted plants in the box. The plants or groups selected should have the same soil preferences, temperature requirements and needs as to water and spraying. Boxes may be planted to solid varieties of plants, to mixed plantings or combinations, but generally the central portion is occupied by upright plants while trailing vines or drooping plants are used about the sides or edges. The soil must be well supplied with humus; a good mixture is one-half good loamy garden soil, one-quarter old well-rotted leafmold or finely sifted humus and one-quarter sand. To this should be added a 4-in. potful of high grade commercial fertilizer (which see) (analyzing about 5-8-7 or 4-12-4) to the wheelbarrow load. All must be well mixed and screened through a $\frac{1}{2}$-in. mesh wire screen; it must not be wet or sticky when used in planting.

At times window boxes are planted solidly with cactus and succulent plants, in which case both treatment and preparations would be different. In such case the box should contain a 2-in. layer of coarse drainage material in the bottom, and the soil should be two-thirds loamy soil and one-third sand, with a layer of moss or fibre between the drainage material and the soil. In planting, the soil should be pressed firmly about the shallow-rooted plants, and no water given until growth shows. Later watering should be done only when the soil shows dryness.

The natural resting period of such plants is from September on through the winter.

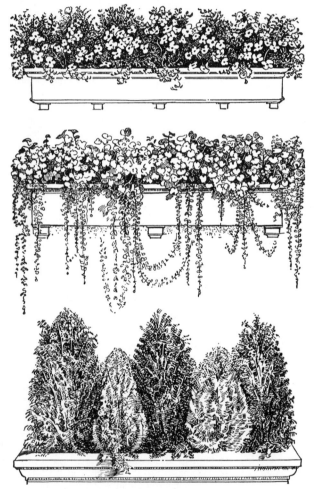

WINDOW-BOX PLANTING STYLES FOR SUMMER AND WINTER EFFECTS

Top, compact growth with abundance of flowers, especially suitable for a southern exposure. Center, foliage and trailing vines are featured instead of flowers; a type of planting that will thrive even if facing north. Bottom, low evergreens will keep the box green all winter.

February, when active growth is about to begin, is the best month for planting or transplanting operations. While they may be raised from seed the operation is slow, so cuttings and grafted plants are usually used. Cuttings may be taken at any time but preferably as growth starts. Allow them to lie exposed in a sunny position for ten days, by which time they should be callused; then insert them in sand where roots will quickly form, after which they may be transplanted to their permanent quarters.

Cultivation of cacti as window-box plants will vary according to the type. Natives of the temperate climate require different treatment from tropical specimens, but all call for dry temperatures and for this reason should be kept separate from flowering plants and most of the foliage plants that need a moist atmosphere.

With the latter, it is always advisable to keep in the vicinity either flat shallow pans of water on radiators or narrow deep water containers behind them, as a help in preserving the desired humidity.

Plants growing in window boxes are subject to disease and insects about the same as are most plants grown indoors. Careful attention to location, keeping temperatures within bounds (70 deg. in the daytime and 10 deg. less at night is best), care in watering, keeping all dead foliage removed and not allowing seed pods to form—all these practices tend to keep plants thriving and help in warding off disease.

Syringing of the foliage with clear water at weekly intervals is beneficial. If palms and ferns are attacked by scale, these may be removed with a toothbrush and warm soapy water, which is then washed off by spraying with clear water. Mealy bug, which attacks various windowbox plants, especially succulents, can be controlled with oil solutions and other commercial preparations. Aphids, both black and green, may be overcome with nicotine solutions, pyrethrum extracts or home-made solutions of fish-oil soap. Red spider, the common enemy of all indoor plants where high temperatures and dry conditions prevail, may be overcome by spraying with clear water followed later by dusting with fine sulphur (flowers of sulphur).

Selection of subjects is largely a matter of choice, location and surrounding conditions. Too great variety should be avoided. Boxes may be made up to contain only ferns, palms and English ivy if they are to occupy a shady or northern exposure, since those plants will get along without sunlight; or they may contain flowering plants exclusively, in which event they would require all the sunlight which they can possibly get.

Among the upright flowering sorts may be included abutilon, begonia, heliotrope, fuchsia, geranium, petunia (single) and lantana. Upright foliage plants, in addition to palms and ferns, include *Dracaena indivisa,* coleus, croton, pandanus (screwpine), *Ficus elastica* (rubber-plant) aspidistra, sansevieria, and umbrella-plant. Useful climbing plants are *Asparagus plumosus,* smilax, and two less well known but beautiful subjects. One is known as wax-plant (*Hoya carnosa*), and grows several feet tall, with thick leaves and white flowers with a pinkish brown eye, sweetly perfumed. The other is philodendron, with large, heart-shaped, glossy leaves. In the trailing or drooping flowering plants are sweet alyssum, lobelia, *Fuchsia procumbens,* and oxalis, these being equally suitable for window box and hanging basket. Drooping foliage plants include wandering jew, English ivy, vinca and *Saxifraga sarmentosa.*

Soil in confined spaces such as window boxes soon becomes depleted of its plant food, which must be replaced. Weak solution of liquid manure applied at monthly intervals is good, or complete, balanced fertilizers can be purchased in powder or tablet form and dissolved in water to be applied according to directions on the package.

All that has been said above as to construction and general care will apply also to outside window or porch boxes. However, because of the relatively shallow soil and the increased exposure to cold, plants are so likely to freeze in such containers that it is rarely advisable to plant subjects of a permanent nature in them except in warm regions. They may, however, be planted to annuals for summer effects and winter effects can be secured with the aid of various dwarf evergreens. Such subjects should have good, compact root-balls, should be planted carefully and allowed to become established before the boxes are placed in exposed locations, and thereafter given regular watering, feeding and care instead of being neglected as they are in so many cases.

THE SOILLESS WINDOW BOX

In order to provide some sort of a container or structure in which plants could be grown in the home, even in the living room, without making any dirt or spilling water or nutrient solution on the floor, a structure similar to a window box was invented, to be used in front of a window. This structure, as shown in the illustration, is self-contained, although the growing box and the nutrient-solution tank are of separate construction, hinged together and connected by a rubber tube. When the reservoir is lifted, the nutrient solution is poured over the cinders or gravel in the plant box; when the reservoir is returned to its normal position, the nutrient solution drains out of the plant box and, through the hose, back into the solution tank. Plants have been grown in such structures for six months at a time without changing the solution, simply by adding fresh material so as to maintain the water level where it was at the start.

The structure, as made by the inventor, is of Toncan steel, galvanized, and coated on the inside with a bakelite varnish to prevent corrosion. However, one of these structures was set up experimentally without the bakelite varnish to find out whether the products of corrosion would harm the roots of plants; after six months, the plants were still growing satisfactorily. If the cinders are flushed twice a month there should be no danger of toxic concentrations of iron salts. The use of phosphates in the nutrient solution also would tend to prevent the heavy metals from becoming poisonous to the plants.

The structure can be made with four legs to stand on the floor; or by extending the ends of the growing box eight inches to serve as legs, it can be made to stand on a low table; or it can be equipped with brackets and hung on the wall, or handled as a regular window box and attached to the window outside. Its size can be just right to fit on the window sill. If it stands alone the plant box may be of any length, but 24 in. seems a good average. It is 8 in. deep, 6 in. wide at the top, and 4 in. wide at the bottom. The solution tank is the same length as the plant box, 14 in. deep, 4 in. wide at the bottom and 1 in. wide at the top with a half-inch slit most of the way so as to permit the solution to run out along its entire length. The rubber tube is attached in the middle at the bottom of the plant box and to a nipple near the bottom of the solution tank midway between one end and the center.

The solution is made up in three-gallon lots and enough is poured over the washed cinders in the plant-growing box to saturate them completely. The solution is then allowed to drain into the solution tank, where it is ready for a feeding the following day. Feeding once a day or once every other day is sufficient. The nutrient

A WINDOW BOX FOR SOILLESS GARDENING

The hinged metal tank holds enough nutrient solution to flood the gravel, cinders or other medium in which the plants are growing, when it is raised as shown. When the tank is lowered (insert), the solution drains back through the hose into the tank until time for another application.

solution is renewed once every three or four weeks during the winter and every two weeks during the summer. Water should be added at frequent intervals to maintain the initial volume in the solution tank; during dry days this may require a quart every other day. Whenever the plants indicate that they are not getting the proper nutrients, the solution should be changed. This is better than to change the solution at definite intervals.

A box this size will accommodate any ordinary house plant. A good arrangement is to set in three large growing plants and four low growing types with four vines to hang over the edge, if desired, right over the solution tank. Raising the solution tank to transfer the nutrient solution to the plant box, if done carefully, so that no leaves happen to be over the edge of the box, will not interfere with the growth of the vines.

See CHEMICAL GARDENING; GRAVEL CULTURE; NUTRIENT SOLUTION; SAND CULTURE.

WINEBERRY. A bramble (*Rubus phoenicolasius*) related to, and grown like the Dewberry (which see), preferably on a trellis, and usually more for ornament than for its small, soft, red, rather insipid, though sometimes acid, fruit. In cold localities and when grown on wet soils it often winter-kills, but it then generally sends up new shoots from the crown.

New-Zealand-wineberry is a name given to an evergreen shrub of the S. hemisphere, *Aristotelia racemosa*.

WINE PALM. Common name for *Caryota urens,* a graceful tree to 60 ft., having finely cut leaves, and yielding a sap called toddy or palm wine.

WINGED-PEA. Common name for *Lotus tetragonolobus,* a creeping annual leguminous herb of S. Europe with purplish red flowers and pods, edible when young.

WINGNUT. Common name for Pterocarya, a genus of deciduous trees of the Walnut Family. They are valuable, rapid-growing trees with divided leaves and winged nutlets, some of them not quite hardy N. when young. They are increased by seeds, layers or suckers. *P. rhoifolia,* to 100 ft., an important forest tree in Japan, has proved perfectly hardy in the Arnold Arboretum in Mass. *P. fraxinifolia,* to 60 ft., often develops several trunks.

WINTER-ACONITE. Common name for Eranthis, a genus of small hardy herbaceous perennials bearing yellow flowers in early spring.

WINTERBERRY. Common name applied to various species of Ilex, especially the evergreen, black-berried *I. glabra* (Inkberry) and the deciduous, red-berried *I. verticillata* (Black-alder). See HOLLY.

WINTER BOUQUET. An arrangement of dried flowers, grasses, leaves, seedpods, or berried twigs, or a mixture of any of them, for use in a vase, without water, for indoor decoration in winter. See EVERLASTINGS.

WINTER-CHERRY. A common name for *Physalis alkekengi*, the Chinese Lantern Plant, a hardy perennial, sprays of whose inflated papery red pods are used for winter bouquets.

WINTER CREEPER. Common name for *Euonymus radicans*, a slow growing vine, excellent for covering walls.

WINTER-CRESS. Common name for Barbarea, a genus of mostly biennial and perennial weeds. See CRESS.

WINTER EFFECTS IN THE GARDEN. It is desirable to clear away the habitual thought of evergreens as the dominant feature in the winter landscape before attempting to consider the many other elements which relate particularly to such special seasonal effects. This is not to imply that evergreens are not important, or that they should be ignored. But they must not obscure the value of other material or give the impression that only the lavish use of conifers and the broad-leaved type will create winter beauty.

It should be recognized first of all that it is not only impossible to maintain the garden in winter as in summer, but also undesirable. Winter brings a complete change in the picture, and the planning should seek to emphasize this change between the active and the rest periods in the year's cycle. This at once precludes the overplanting of evergreens with the idea of keeping up plant activity and growth. Such an effort may lead to one of the worst faults a garden can have, namely, monotony.

The basis of fine effects in winter as in summer lies in the garden design. Simple direct treatment which results in broad spaces and contrasting rich masses of vegetation is the framework required. The dominant thought in the planting should be warmth—an abiding sense of snugness and shelter and protection; of being "tucked in." To look out from windows of snug rooms and see birds flitting in and out of sheltering masses of growth is one of the happiest winter effects possible.

Such masses may—and usually should—have perhaps one evergreen specimen related to if not actually a part of them; but it is the ruddy stems of deciduous growths, richly interwoven until they form an impenetrable barrier to snow and wind, that give the most desirable effect.

These valuable winter characteristics of deciduous trees and shrubs lie in the green, golden, or bright red bark of some; in the bright more or less persistent fruits or berries of others; and in the density of growth and interesting and agreeable sweep of branches as these are exposed to view as the leaves fall.

Shrubs notable for these qualities are the cornels, viburnums, barberries, many of the species of rose, euonymus, cotoneaster, ilex (which includes holly and winterberry), bayberry, callicarpa, eleagnus, malus, hawthorn, vaccinium and symphoricarpos. Thickets composed of from 3 to 5 species of such subjects planted from 3 to 5 ft. apart in as great number as space and the design allow (including those at the foundation of dwelling and other buildings) are a revelation of beauty when their bare interlaced branches and twigs have developed into real snow and wind barriers. And their rounded and swelling irregularities of form, either bare or covered with snow, provide a flowing boundary effect which does not seem to limit lawn spaces as strictly as the more upstanding and always individualistic evergreens.

Hedges of privet or the richer Japanese yew are very useful in carrying out plans for winter beauty. A secluded sunny expanse enclosed with such a hedge, backed on the windward side with adequate windbreak material, makes a delightful winter feature where exercise, play and rest in the open may be enjoyed even in cold weather.

WINTERGREEN. One of the common names for Gaultheria, a genus of attractive, evergreen rock-garden plants, and also sometimes applied to the genus Pyrola (which see) or Shinleaf. Both are members of the Heath Family. Flowering-wintergreen is one of the common names for *Polygala paucifolia*, a member of the Milkwort Family.

WINTER-HAZEL. Popular name for Corylopsis, a genus of half-hardy deciduous

Asiatic shrubs grown for their fragrant yellow flowers.

WINTER-HELIOTROPE. Common name for *Petasites fragrans,* an herbaceous evergreen perennial 12 in. high, grown for its fragrant pale lilac to purple flowers.

WINTER INJURY. Damage done to plants by low temperature occurring after the end of the growing season or before growth starts in the spring, as distinguished from frost injury (see FROST). Symptoms of winter injury vary from immediate death of a plant to such localized injury as twig blight, dieback, root killing, bud injury, frost cracks, cankers, winter sun scald, crown or collar rot, and internal necrosis or black heart. It is not only the degree of cold but also the time in the period of dormancy that influences the amount of injury. Severe weather in early winter causes more injury because plant tissues have not yet become hardened; also sudden cold following moderate weather which starts tissues into activity is likely to cause heavy freezing. The presence or absence of a snow cover at the time of freezing also influences the amount of injury. Winter-drying of evergreens is caused by the rapid loss of water from leaves at a time when the water in the soil is frozen and cannot be taken up by the plant roots. See also DISEASES, PLANT; PHYSIOLOGICAL DISEASES.

WINTER PROTECTION. This refers to diverse methods of preventing various kinds of injury to shrubs, trees, vines, perennials, etc.

In localities where deer abound and are protected by law, they often do considerable damage to orchards and even in home gardens by eating the branches and even gnawing the trunks of young trees and shrubs. About the only effective protection is fencing or a hedge so high that the animals cannot jump over it and so strong or dense they cannot break through.

Rabbits sometimes destroy young trees, shrubs and other woody plants by nibbling the twigs and stems as far up as they can reach above the snow. Small tree trunks can be protected against them for several months by swabbing with a mixture of cayenne pepper and lard or other soft fat (one ounce to the pound); it is well to wear rubber gloves to protect the hands against pepper-burning.

Field mice, which work beneath the snow and mostly near the surface of the ground, may gnaw away patches of bark, often completely girdling the trunks and killing the tree—unless bridge-grafting is resorted to promptly the spring after the injury is done (see under GRAFTING).

Several methods of protection are effective against these creatures. Keeping the ground clear of grass and weeds for at least 2 ft. around the trunks is a help, but heaping earth, sifted coal ashes or sand around each trunk to form a conical pile 12 to 15 in. high is better since it tends to keep the mice away.

If this is not done before the ground freezes, some protection may be had by keeping up and tramping or pounding snow around the tree trunks after every snow storm. However, if the ground has been kept bare during the autumn and there is no coarse mulch around the trees to harbor the mice, this need not be done because the animals rarely travel far from home during winter.

The best and most permanent way to protect tree trunks against both rabbits and mice is to wrap around them cylinders of ½-in.-mesh galvanized wirecloth or of wood veneer sold for the purpose. For roped growing trees these cylinders may have to be 6 or 8 in. in diameter. They should extend 2 or 3 in. below the surface of the ground and at least a foot higher than a rabbit can reach allowing for the average snow level. See illustration under MICE.

When rhododendrons, azaleas and other broad-leaved evergreens are placed in exposed positions they need protection against strong sunshine to prevent the burning of the leaves. This may be given by covering or enclosing them with rough wooden frames, tents of burlap or other material or evergreen boughs, or by wrapping them as described below.

Protection of coniferous evergreens and densely branched deciduous shrubs against breakage under the weight of snow is best done immediately after each snow storm by lifting each branch separately and shaking it from side to side. *Never strike loaded branches downward* as this would increase the strain on them. Branches out of reach may be raised with a pitchfork and given two or three upward jars. Those branches beyond pitchfork reach are normally more supple than the lower ones and more acted upon by winds, so are less likely to be broken.

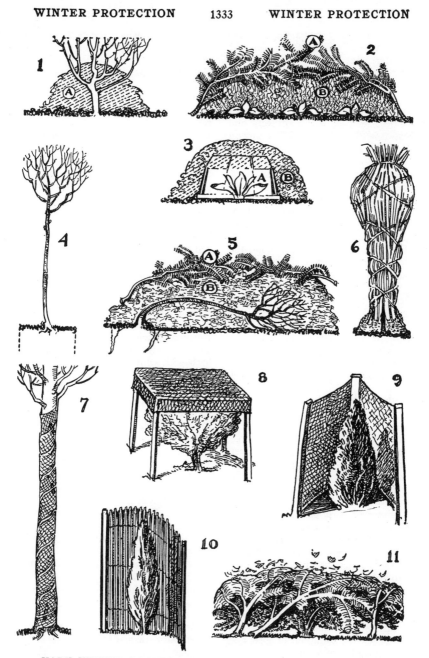

VARY WINTER PROTECTION METHODS TO FIT PLANT NEEDS

1. Rose with soil mound (A) around base.   2. Perennials covered with leaves or litter (B) held down with evergreen boughs (A).   3. A berry box (A) will prevent a mulch (B) from smothering a plant. 4. Root-prune a standard rose (see dotted lines), then bend it gently over and cover completely with litter (B) and boughs (A); or else, wrap the whole plant in straw or cornstalks (6).   7. Wrap trunks of transplanted trees in burlap for one winter or, better, two.   8. Coarse burlap above a boxwood may be enough protection; or it can be added around the frame as well.   9. Exposed evergreens should be screened against wind and strong winter sun.   10. Imported cane matting makes an equally effective and better-looking screen.   11. Protect low-growing conifers with evergreen boughs from snow, ice, sun and wind.

When snow partially melts then freezes again, and when rain freezes on the branches after sleet storms, breakage can be prevented by spraying the encrusted branches with a saturated solution of nitrate of soda. It is best to apply a little at a time on any one area. The solution will crack the ice, melt it, break off bits and bring most of it to the ground. The nitrate in the solution soaking into the soil will act as plant food.

Dwarf evergreens, especially the more or less erect or pyramidal specimens, can be protected against breakage under the weight of snow or ice by wrappings of burlap. The best way to do this is, first to start at the bottom and tie a stout cord to one of the branches, then walk around the specimen, lifting each branch and holding it in place with the cord till the top is reached, when the end of the cord is tied to the next lower strand.

Then apply the burlap, starting at the bottom and fastening its end to the first round of cord with wire nails used like pins. Next walk around the specimen as before, winding the burlap spirally upward and fastening each lap in several places with the nails. If desired the top may be covered with a square of burlap also pinned in place or with any other cap that will shed the snow.

When tender, semi-hardy or even hardy plants that have been growing in the open during summer need a resting period between autumn and spring, or are to be used as stock plants to yield cuttings, they are often stored in "pits" or coldframes until late winter or early spring, when they are taken into the greenhouse and gotten in shape for the following season's activity.

Of the two carrying-over storage places the pit is the better because, as it goes deeper into the ground, the temperature is more easily kept uniform, just above the freezing point. However, in severe weather, adequate protection can be assured by covering the sash of the frame with mats and shutters to check the radiation of heat and prevent the entrance of cold.

The trunks and main branches of semi-hardy and tender (not too tender) trees can be protected against sun scald and winter injury by wrapping them and the main branches, especially those most exposed to the sun, with straw or such like materials.

Rose bushes and the smaller shrubs can be covered with bushel hampers or peach baskets from which the bottoms have been removed and which are then filled with dry leaves; if desired, especially valuable roses —such as standards—can previously be wrapped with straw. It is important, however, to delay the application of all such protections until the weather has become really cold; for if done too early, the heat from the sun is likely to swell the protected buds in the fall, in which case the cold which follows is almost certain to kill them if not the whole bush. In spring the protection must be gradually removed just about the time that grass begins to grow.

A mulch (which see) is important winter protection for strawberries, roses, many shrubs and hardy perennials because it prevents the alternate heaving and settling of the ground due to intermittent freezing and thawing. Two recently introduced protective materials—cranberry tops and glass wool—are discussed under MULCHES.

WINTER-PURSLANE. A c o m m o n name for *Montia perfoliata* (known in the European trade as *Claytonia perfoliata*), a dwarf Pacific Coast annual fleshy-leaved herb with white flowers.

WINTER WORK IN THE GARDEN. Although we ordinarily think of winter as a time to rest so far as the garden is concerned—the plants being covered over and the ground frozen hard—nevertheless, there is plenty to be done.

OUTDOOR WORK

Any last bit of protection needed by plants of doubtful hardiness should be attended to right now. A layer of sifted coal ashes on the lily beds may be better than a cover of vegetable matter that will mat down. But be careful not to cover any plants too much.

Begin dormant pruning and spraying as the weather permits, spraying apple trees with lime-sulphur for San José scale, for instance. Some varieties of grapes can be pruned.

Examine lilacs and other shrubs for scale. Cut off and burn wild cherry twigs carrying tent caterpillar egg masses.

Top-dress the lawn with compost or peat moss; and protect fruit tree trunks from mice and rabbits (see PROTECTION). Knock snow or sleet from evergreens so the added weight will not break the branches.

The lawn and porch furniture, now in garage or cellar, should be looked over and repaired. A coat of paint will help it.

Tools can be repaired, oiled and then put away.

Large trees can be moved now, but this is usually a job for experts or professional firms. With the ground frozen, manure can be hauled to bare areas and spread at once to be plowed under in spring.

INDOOR TASKS

Make up lists of plants, bulbs, and tools you will want and need for next year. Winter is the time to make a plan for a new garden or to revise an old one. Consult good garden books and catalogs, for they contain much information of specific nature. But make use also of the notes made in your garden from time to time during the growing seasons.

Examine stored gladiolus corms and dahlia tubers now and then. Paper-white narcissus and hyacinths can be brought out of the dark and started into growth.

Pay close attention to house plants. They need more moisture and fresh air than the average steam-heated apartment can supply without aid. Do not use cold from the tap on plants; let it stand for a few hours. Feed plants in pots and boxes with plant foods made for the purpose. Cultivate the soil frequently by scratching the surface lightly. Wash the leaves of foliage plants every few days. Watch for mealy bug and spray with soap or nicotine preparations for them.

Order shrubs for spring delivery. Nurserymen are glad to discuss plans with you, and by ordering early you get the pick of the stocks.

As the winter wanes, sow seeds of tomatoes, egg-plants, peppers and other tender plants—flowering subjects, too—in flats, or pots, kept in a warm, well-lighted place.

Cut a few branches of early-flowering shrubs where they will not be missed for forcing in the house. Look up a supply of manure for the hotbed and arrange to have it delivered in February or March—unless you use electricity to heat your hotbed.

Look the rock garden over and note any rocks that may have to be replaced or rearranged. Watch out for any soil washing that may leave plants bare.

Get your order for plants and seeds in early. Look over—and test—any seed you have saved over. Get ready for real work when, some morning, you wake up and find that spring has arrived before you expected it.

WIRE GRASS. Common name for *Eleusine indica,* sometimes also known as Crab, Goose, or Yard Grass. Another species, *E. coracana,* is known as African-millet. All consist of annual flat-leaved species, tufted in character, with spikelets borne in 5-branched umbrella-shaped form. They are essentially forage plants, though sometimes grown for ornament. *E. coracana* grows to 4 ft. and bears broad spikes 1½ in. long. *E. indica* from 1 to 2 ft. has spreading spikes to 4 in. long. *E. tristachya* is dwarfer with very narrow leaves.

WIRE-VINE. A common name for *Calacinum complexum,* a twining New Zealand vine grown in warm countries over rocks and elsewhere in greenhouses. Also called Maidenhair-vine. See CALACINUM.

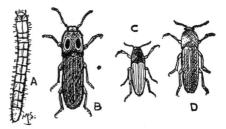

WIREWORMS ARE WORSE THAN THEIR PARENTS

The slim, brown, shiny worms (A) injure roots, bulbs and tubers. The adults, of different shapes and sizes (as B, C and D), are called click beetles and are not themselves harmful.

WIREWORMS. These larvae of the so-called click beetle (which see) are familiar to most gardeners as slender, smooth, usually dark brown and hard-shelled, but sometimes soft and yellow, creatures varying from ½ to 1½ in. in length. Distributed throughout N. America they attack most crops belonging to the Grass Family as well as many other plants such as corn, clovers, beans, potatoes, turnips, etc. feeding on the roots and tubers. Infested plants have a sickly-stunted appearance and sometimes wilt and die; if pulled up they are found to have little or no root system. The life cycle covers from 2 to 6 years so control is difficult. In large fields long crop rotations are advisable. Later summer or fall plowing helps by killing the pupae and also adult beetles before they emerge from the soil. In small gardens or flower beds the worms can be destroyed by disinfecting the soil with carbon bisulphide. In the vegetable garden rows of corn planted here and there will often attract many of the worms and keep them away from other crops.

WISTERIA (wis-tee'-ri-ah). (Sometimes spelled Wistaria.) Deciduous twining shrubs, native in N. America and Asia, belonging to the Pea Family. They rank among the best of the ornamental vines for temperate regions, and often attain a good old age and large size. (See illustration, Plate 58.) While they will grow in almost any soil, they thrive best in a deep rich loam that does not get too dry. They are at their picturesque best when allowed to grow at will up an old tree. On a wall or building it is best to pay some attention to training the growth. They are sometimes grown in standard form, and also force readily in pots. As their roots are long but not fibrous, the plants are best transplanted when small or from pots rather than from the field.

Wisterias often disappoint by not flowering for many years. These non-producers are seedlings, and it is highly uncertain as to when they will reach the flowering stage. Restriction of the root run and shortening back the long shoots in midsummer may aid in the formation of flower buds. But the best thing is to plant only grafted or layered plants from flowering specimens. The spring crop of flowers is borne on spurs, and in severe climates the buds are often winter-killed. A small crop of flowers is often produced in late summer on young growth of the current season.

Large sucking bugs called lantern flies are often found on wisteria as well as on lilies and a variety of herbaceous plants and shrubs. They lay their eggs in slits in the bark and cover them with masses of a white wax secretion. If the injury becomes serious, spray plants with nicotine-sulphate and soap. Larvae of the large silver-spotted skipper (a butterfly) feed on leaves of wisteria and locust, fastening several leaflets together to make a case. Spray with lead arsenate.

Wisteria is propagated by seeds, but better by cuttings, layers and grafts.

PRINCIPAL WISTERIA SPECIES

W. sinensis (Chinese Wisteria) is one of the more vigorous climbers of the N. hemisphere, growing to 100 ft. in mild climates. It has 7 to 13 leaflets and showy clusters of violet-blue flowers.

floribunda (Japanese Wisteria) is hardier than the Chinese species; has 13 to 19 leaf-

lets, and smaller and more fragrant flowers which open some days later. Of the several forms available var. *macrobotrys* (formerly known as *W. multijuga*) often bears racemes 3 ft. long, and in Japan clusters over 5 ft. long have been grown. Forms with white and pink flowers are also available.

venusta (Silky Wisteria), a Chinese species, one of the hardiest, grows to 30 ft. It has 9 to 13 velvety leaflets, white flowers in short racemes, and velvety pods.

frutescens, native from Va. S. is also hardy. It has 9 to 13 leaflets and short compact clusters of lilac-purple flowers.

macrostachya, found in swampy places from Ill. S., is hardy as far N. as Mass. It is much showier than the other native species, having larger flowers and clusters of light blue flowers. Its var. *albo-lilacina* has white and bluish flowers. Both the last-mentioned species flower later than the Asiatic kinds.

WITCHES' BROOM. The apt and descriptive name given to a closely grouped cluster of fine slender branches usually arranged more or less parallel to each other and originating from an enlarged axis. Witches' brooms occur on various kinds of woody plants at the ends of branches and are definite disease symptoms. They may be caused by some of the leaf-curl fungi, various species of rusts, and the scaly or dwarf mistletoe. Mostly they are caused by parasitic plant organisms but that of hackberry is due to a mite followed by a fungus. See also DISEASES, PLANT.

WITCH GRASS. Common name for *Panicum capillare,* usually a weed but sometimes grown for use in dry bouquets. An annual, it grows to 2 ft., with leaves 1 ft. long and ½ in. wide. The branches of the panicles, which may be 14 in. long, are extremely slim and spreading. See also WEEDS.

WITCH-HAZEL. Common name for Hamamelis, a genus of small American and Asiatic deciduous trees or shrubs which bear yellow flowers between late autumn and very early spring and are planted for their ornamental and screen effect.

WITCH-HAZEL FAMILY. Common name for the Hamamelidaceae, which see.

WITHE-ROD. A common name for *Viburnum cassinoides* and *V. nudum,* tall deciduous American shrubs which bear white flowers in June and blue-black fruits in autumn.

WITLOOF. Name (Dutch for "white leaf") given to heads of blanched leaves resembling cos lettuce produced by forcing mature chicory roots. See CHICORY.

WOAD. Common name for Isatis, a genus of annual, biennial and perennial herbs of the Crucifer Family. They are erect or branching plants with small yellow or yellowish flowers. The two species cultivated for ornament or interest are easily grown from seed. *I. tinctoria* (Dyers Woad), a biennial to 3 ft., bears yellow flowers in terminal clusters. It was formerly grown as a source of a blue dye used to color woolen cloth. *I. glauca*, a perennial to 4 ft., sometimes used in the border, has very large clusters of mustard-yellow flowers.

WOADWAXEN. An old name for Dyers Greenweed (*Genista tinctoria*), grown in dry ground for its abundant yellow pea-like flowers. See GENISTA.

WOLF-BERRY. Popular name for *Symphoricarpos occidentalis*, a hardy deciduous W. American shrub grown for its white berries.

WOLFSBANE. A popular name for *Aconitum lycoctonum*, a tall European herbaceous perennial grown as a specimen plant in borders.

WOMANS-TONGUE-TREE. A common name for the *Albizzia lebbek*, a tropical Asiatic tree naturalized in the W. Indies. Also called Siris-tree and Lebbek-tree.

WONDERBERRY, or SUNBERRY, or GARDEN-HUCKLEBERRY. Trade names for forms of Black Nightshade or Stubbleberry, an annual, half-hardy herb (*Solanum nigrum*, var. *guineense*) grown for its ½-in. black fruits which are used for pies and preserves. See SOLANUM.

WONGA-WONGA. Common name for *Pandorea pandorana*, a tropical vine grown outdoors in the S. U. S. for its yellowish-white purple-spotted flowers.

WOOD-APPLE. Common name for *Feronia limonia*, a spiny deciduous Asiatic tree of the Rue Family, having small cut leaves. The hard-shelled fruit, 3-in. in diameter with pinkish agreeably acid, edible pulp, is frequently used for jelly. The plant is not hardy N., but has been planted in Fla. and Calif. and is being tested by the Department of Agriculture as a stock on which to graft citrus fruits.

WOOD-BETONY. Popular name for *Pedicularis canadensis*, a hardy native perennial somewhat planted in borders and rock gardens.

WOODBINE. Popular Old-World name for a species of Honeysuckle (*Lonicera periclymenum*). In America the name is often applied to Virginia Creeper (*Parthenocissus quinquefolia*). See also under IVY.

WOOD FERN. A common name for the Shield Ferns or Buckler Ferns, now placed in the genus Dryopteris (which see). Species are distributed all over the world, including several native to the U. S., chiefly the familiar Toothed Wood Fern or "fancy fern" of the florist, and the Evergreen Wood Fern, with coarse blue-green fronds. These and others discussed under Dryopteris are among the best of all standard ferns in the hardy garden, needing only woods soil, drainage, shade, and lime.

WOODLAND STAR. Common name for *Lithofragma affinis*, a small perennial herb of the Saxifrage Family, growing to 16 in. with reddish, hairy stems, small bronzy leaves, and starry white flowers. It is native to W. N. America where it grows in rich prairie soil on the edge of the woodland. It is an attractive little plant for the wild or rock garden, and the tuberous roots may be transferred to the garden from the wild or plants may be propagated from seed.

WOOD-LOUSE. Another name for sow-bug (which see), a small, hard-shelled creature that infests damp soil, rotting wood, etc. and feeds on tender plants, sometimes doing considerable damage.

WOODRUFF. Common name for Asperula, a genus of herbaceous perennials grown in semi-shady locations in borders and rock gardens.

WOOD-RUSH. Common name for Luzula, a genus of native grass-like or rush-like perennial herbs.

WOODSIA (wood'-zi-ah). A genus of soft textured, small, tufted ferns of temperate regions. The fronds have wiry stipes, more or less covered with chaff, produced from densely matted rootlets. They grow on rock ledges, chiefly granite or sandstone, often in full sun. The scattered fruit-dots are covered by indusia that split at maturity into roughly star-shaped lobes. Several species are found in the U. S. and can be grown in the rock garden in porous soil mixed with peat and a little charcoal. Sandstone chips on the surface will aid in simulating the natural environment.

SPECIES

W. glabella (Smooth Woodsia). Has linear, once-pinnate fronds with roundish-lobed pinnae and straw-colored stipes. A small and very rare species occurring only in mountains of the N. States, but of easy cultivation.

ilvensis (Rusty Woodsia). With woolly-looking 2 to 6 in. fronds, the pinnae deeply round-lobed and covered below with fine hairs that turn brown by midsummer. Grows in dense clumps near the summit of hills.

obtusa (Common Woodsia). Grows 6 to 14 in. tall, with distant rounded pinnae; native throughout the Appalachians, ever-green in S. range.

scopulina. A very similar, slightly smaller species of the N. W.

WOOD-SORREL. Common name for Oxalis, a genus of bulbous or tuberous herbs many of which are grown as house plants for their red, yellow, or pink flowers.

WOODWARDIA (wood-wahr'-di-ah). A genus of ferns characterized by their parallel rows of large linear fruit-dots, suggesting the common name, Chain Fern. They are acid-loving, chiefly of marshy land, and rank growers. Three species only are found in the U. S., the first two along the E. coast, the last in the far W. Used for naturalizing over large areas.

W. areolata (Narrow-leaved Chain Fern). Has fronds 1 to 2 ft. tall, once-pinnate, rich green, the fertile ones taller and contracted; root-stems creeping.

virginica (Virginia Chain Fern). Has 2- to 4-ft. fronds, with deeply cut rounded pinnae. Less rampant than *W. areolata,* therefore better for the garden. Use much peat and some sand and mulch with oak leaves.

radicans (California Chain Fern). Has 3- to 7-ft. arching fronds, once-pinnate, the lower pinnae partly again pinnate, and the tip of the fronds often producing bulbils which give rise to new plants. A superb fern of the Far W., good in the garden in a soil of fibrous loam, peat moss, and some sand, with plenty of water. This fern can also be grown in the cool greenhouse.

WOOLFLOWER, CHINESE. Common name for a type of cockscomb (*Celosia argentea* var. *cristata*). An annual grown for its fluffy crimson, pink or yellow flowers, it is often cataloged as *C. childsi* or *C. cristata.*

WOOLLY. Provided with long curly and matted hairs, as in *Stachys lanata.* Compare TOMENTOSE; VILLOUS.

WOOLLY APHIDS. These are purplish aphids or plant lice which cover themselves with white cottony masses. The most important are the woolly apple aphid, occurring on apple, pear, hawthorn, mountain-ash and elm; and the woolly beech aphid. Control by spraying with nicotine-sulphate when the leaves first show green. See also APHIDS; APPLE; BEECH.

WORM. A name popularly given to the larvae of many kinds of insects although true worms (see EARTHWORMS) are not insects at all. We speak of canker worms, bud-worms, army worms, cabbage worms and many others. "Hundred-legged worms" are centipedes and "thousand-legged worms" are millepedes. Round-worms or eel-worms are names for minute creatures correctly called nematodes.

WORMWOOD. Common name for the genus Artemisia (which see) especially *A. absinthium,* a European perennial used for making absinthe. See also HERBS.

WOUNDS. All wounds suffered by plants, whether made by insects, rodents, pruning or cultivating tools, wind, ice, snow or other agencies, are potential avenues for infection by spores or germs of plant diseases (which see). While the chances of infection increase in proportion to the extent of the wound, its form and location are also significant factors as they affect the plant's ability to heal the lesion by growing new bark or protective tissue over it before infection occurs. Thus a smooth pruning wound made close to a branch so as to leave no stub, or a surface wound on a tree trunk cleaned and trimmed into a vertical oval shape, will heal much more rapidly than a ragged, neglected one. In general all pruning wounds are best treated with a protective dressing. See TREE SURGERY.

WOUNDWORT. Popular name for the genus Stachys, also called Betony; also for *Anthyllis vulneraria,* the Kidney-vetch. The former comprises herbs or small shrubs sometimes grown in borders; the latter is a legume grown for forage on poor European soils.

WULFENIA (wool-fee'-ni-ah). A genus of low-growing, hardy perennial herbs of the Figwort Family, bearing tubular blue flowers on stems to 2 ft. tall rising from a clump of basal leaves. They are suitable for a shady corner of the rock garden or the border and need a rich moist soil. But they should be given excellent drainage, for, as some of the species have evergreen foliage, they decay easily in wet weather or in winter. They may be increased by division in spring or autumn or by seeds. *W. carinthiaca* has small blue flowers in clustered, slender racemes.

WYETHIA (wy-ee'-thi-ah). A genus of perennial W. American herbs of the Composite Family, having long slender leaves and yellow flowers. Though of but little horticultural interest, they are occasionally transferred to the garden, where they are easily increased by seed or division. *W. amplexicaulis* to 2 ft. has long glossy leaves and bright yellow flowers with rays 1½ in. long; *W. angustifolia,* to 2 ft., is a hairy plant with yellow flower heads, the rays being 2 in. long.

XANTHISMA (zan-thiz'-mah.) A genus of annual or biennial American herbs of the Composite Family, having narrow leaves and yellow flower-heads, consisting of ray flowers only. They are suitable for planting in dry, open places in the wild garden, and grow readily from seed which should be sown where the plants are to stand. In *X. texanum* to 4 ft., a native to Texas, the showy yellow heads about 2 in. across consist of about 20 slender rays.

XANTHOCERAS (zan-thos'-er-as) *sorbifolia.* A large handsome deciduous shrub from China, thriving in any good soil in a sunny place and hardy N. The attractive dark green and glossy pinnate leaves are held until late in the season. In May it is conspicuous with its upright panicles of showy white flowers, each petal having a yellow to red blotch at the base. Their resemblance to large hyacinths has suggested the common name Hyacinth-shrub. It is propagated by seeds, which are similar to those of the horse-chestnut; they are best stratified (buried in sand and subjected to freezing over winter) and sown in spring. It is also propagated by root cuttings under glass.

XANTHORRHIZA (zan-thoh-ry'-zah). An alternative spelling of the older name Zanthorhiza. *Z. apiifolia* is a native deciduous woody plant better known as Shrub Yellow-root, which see.

XANTHOSOMA (zan-thoh-soh'-mah). Tropical American herbs of the Ginseng Family with large thick leaves on long stalks, and calla-like flowers; popularly known as Yautia, Tanier and Malanga. In the tropics they are grown for their thick edible tuber-like underground stems; in temperate climates they are ornamental greenhouse subjects. Of the half-dozen species *X. lindeni* (known to florists as *Phyllotaenium lindeni*) has bright green leaves a foot long with white midribs and veins. *X. saggitaefolium,* which often exceeds 3 ft. in height, has green leaves 3 ft. long and almost as wide on stems equally long.

XANTHOXYLUM (zan-thok'-si-lum). An alternative spelling of the original name Zanthoxylum (which see), for a genus of aromatic, often prickly, shrubs and trees.

XERANTHEMUM (zee-ran'-thee-mum). A genus of annual herbs of the Composite Family, grown mainly for their papery flowers, used as "everlastings." They are easily grown from seed, the most common species being *X. annuum.* This is the Common Immortelle, to 3 ft., with white downy foliage and pink, purple and white flowers to 1½ in. across. It has varieties with semi-double and double flowers.

XEROPHYLLUM (zee-roh-fil'-um). A genus of native perennial liliaceous herbs with white flowers in racemes, often called Turkey-beard, which see.

XYLOPHYLLA (zy-loh-fil'-ah). Tropical American shrubs with deciduous leaf-like branches, belonging to the Spurge Family. They are sometimes grown in greenhouse collections for their curious appearance. *X. angustifolia* is a small shrub with narrow, flattened branches and reddish flowers along the margins. In *X. speciosa* the branches are about twice as wide and the flowers are whitish.

YAM. Properly this refers to various vines, mostly tender ornamentals, species of Dioscorea (which see). In the U. S. it is often wrongly applied to large varieties of sweet-potato (which see). Tubers of the Winged Yam (*D. alata*) often exceed a yard in length and a weight of 100 lbs. They are of coarse texture and inferior flavor to the smaller varieties, which rarely exceed a pound. True yams are occasionally grown as vegetables in Fla. but scarcely elsewhere in the U. S. The Chinese Yam (*D. batatas*), popularly grown as an ornamental even in the N., is best known as the Cinnamon-vine (which see). Its tubers are of excellent quality but difficult to dig.

YAMPEE. One of the common names for *Dioscorea trifida,* also called Cush-Cush, a tender vine with small tuberous roots.

YANGTAO. One of the common names for *Actinidia chinensis,* a shrubby but tender vine with yellow flowers that are followed by an edible fruit having a gooseberry flavor.

YARD-LONG BEAN, or ASPARAGUS BEAN. Common name for *Vigna sesquipedalis,* an herb related to the cowpea. It is grown as an annual mainly for forage and green manure, but also for its sparsely borne edible, rather flabby pods often 3 ft. long. It is tender and adapted only to warm climates, though sometimes started under glass and grown in the N. States as a curiosity.

YARROW. Popular name for Achillea, a genus of hardy spring- and summer-blooming herbaceous composite perennials, some grown in borders and rock gardens for their white, yellow or pink flowers. Golden-yarrow is *Eriophyllum confertiflorum.*

YAUPON. A common name for *Ilex vomitoria,* a species of Holly (which see). It is an evergreen shrub or small tree (to 25 ft.) with red berries, native from Va. to Fla. and Tex.

YEDDO-HAWTHORN. Common name for *Raphiolepsis umbellata,* an attractive tender shrub of the Rose Family.

YELLOW-BELLS. A common name (perhaps not in general use) for *Emmenanthe penduliflora* (which see) ; and also for Uvularia, a native herb of the Lily Family.

YELLOW DAISY. One of the common names for *Rudbeckia hirta,* also known as Black-eyed Susan.

YELLOW-ELDER. Common name for *Stenolobium stans,* an erect shrub or small tree with showy bell-shaped yellow flowers borne in loose clusters. Native along the Gulf Coast to Fla., where it is popular for ornamental planting.

YELLOW-FLAX, or EAST-INDIAN-FLAX. Common name for *Reinwardtia indica* (formerly known as *Linum trigynum*), a small shrubby plant of Asia suitable for outdoor planting in warm regions, and sometimes grown under glass for its bright yellow flowers in winter. For pot culture, a sandy loam with leafmold and a little old manure is suitable for growing nice specimens in 5- or 6-in. pots. Pinching the shoots now and then induces a compact growth. It is a plant that must be well grown, and protected all the time from the ravages of red spider. Propagated by cuttings taken from the basal shoots.

YELLOW-OLEANDER. A common name for *Thevetia nereifolia,* a tropical American tree with fragrant yellow flowers, known in Fla. as Trumpet-flower.

YELLOW POND-LILY. One of the common names for *Nymphozanthus advena,* also known as Cow-lily. See NYMPHOZANTHUS.

YELLOWS. A name given to certain fungous, and, particularly, certain virus, diseases. The fungous leaf spot on cherry (which see) has been called yellows; another fungus causes cabbage yellows (see under CRUCIFER). Peach yellows is a virus disease which may be transmitted from diseased to healthy trees by budding, and in which the stems of the shoots are short and the leaves generally pale green or yellow, reduced in size, and drooping, rolled or curled. Aster yellows, another virus disease, transmitted by leaf hoppers, causes yellowing and stunting of aster plants and many other garden plants and weeds. See ASTER. Yellows of gladiolus (which see), caused by a Fusarium fungus, has been called the coming most important disease of this plant. It causes yellow foliage in the field and often a rotting of stored corms; and, as it cannot be detected until damage has been done, can remain virulent

Plate 60.   THE YEW SHOULD BE MORE WIDELY USED

Top: The yew, shorn into a hedge, or used as a specimen is always restful in color and satisfying in outline.   Center left: A single plant of Irish yew (Taxus baccata var. fastigiata), dark green in color and columnar in habit.   Center right: A branch of yew showing the crimson, honey-sweet fruit.
Bottom: Some handsome spreading specimens of English yew (Taxus baccata).

in the soil for some years, and cannot be cured by any known method, the greatest present hope of a gladiolus grower is to prevent its getting into his plantings by being exceedingly careful to buy only healthy stock.

YELLOW STAR-OF-BETHLEHEM. Common name for *Gagea lutea,* a spring-blooming bulbous plant with flat clusters of yellow flowers.

YELLOW-TUFT. Common name for *Alyssum argenteum,* a yellow-flowered perennial species, lighter colored and taller growing than the familiar *A. saxatile,* but also of dwarf form, to 15 in.

YELLOW-WOOD. Common name for the genus Cladrastis but mostly applied to *C. lutea,* which will grow much farther N. than its native range, which is S. E. U. S. It is a deciduous smooth-barked tree with shining leaves and open branches that give an airy effect. Its white flowers in racemes a foot long fill the air with fragrance for a great distance. Deep-rooting and drought-resistant, this tree deserves to be more widely planted as a street and park tree and particularly in the home grounds because of its showy flowers. Grown from seeds sown in spring and root cuttings kept cool and moist over winter.

YERBA BUENA. Common name for *Micromeria chamissonis,* a Pacific Coast trailing perennial herb of the Mint Family grown in rock gardens.

YEW. Common name for Taxus, a genus of evergreen trees or shrubs of slow growth and variable form and of great value for many planting purposes. (See illustrations, Plate 60.) They range in height from a dwarf bush a foot or so high to a 60-ft. tree. The low-growing forms are among the most useful of evergreens for small gardens. Their leaves (needles) are broader than those of fir or spruce and extend on either side of the stems, producing a flattened soft effect. The rich dark green foliage remains uniform in coloring throughout the year, and the pistillate plants are colorful in fall with scarlet berry-like fruits.

Yews stand hard clipping well and, being of dense habit, make good hedge plants and are first-rate for any form of topiary work. A rather moist loam suits them best, but they grow well in ordinary soil with plenty of humus, and do well in sun or shade. Horses and cattle have been poisoned by eating the young growth.

The most important pest of Yew is the black vine weevil whose larvae feed on the roots. The tops of the plants turn yellow and then brown, and severely injured plants may die. The adult black beetles hide by day and feed on foliage at night, when they may be jarred off onto a cloth and dropped into a pail of kerosene and water. A bait consisting of a mixture of dried ground apple pulp and sodium fluosilicate is sold under a trade name. Lead arsenate (3 lbs. to 100 sq. ft.) may be worked into the soil, or a pyrethrum extract applied in solution.

Yews are propagated by seeds, cuttings of half-ripened or fully matured shoots under glass, and, in the case of varieties, sometimes by grafting.

PRINCIPAL SPECIES

T. baccata (English Yew) grows to 60 ft. with a short wide trunk and a broad head. It lives to a great old age, but is not quite hardy N. There are numerous named varieties, some of which are hardier

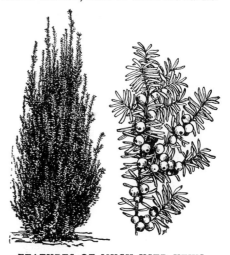

FEATURES OF MUCH USED YEWS
Left, Typical specimen of the handsome erect Hicks yew (Taxus media hicksi), developed in America from the result of crossing the English and Japanese yews. Right, a spray of the Japanese species (T. cuspidata) with its clean foliage and bright red "berries."

than the type. Var. *adpressa,* usually of irregular habit, has long spreading branches; good forms of this are *erecta,* of bushy columnar habit, and *aurea,* one of the best of the so-called Golden Yews. Var. *dovastoni* is widespreading with pendulous branches, making a handsome lawn specimen. Var. *elegantissima* is a compact and ornamental form with young leaves striped pale yellow. Var. *fastigiata* (Irish Yew) is a handsome columnar form with heavy growth and very dark green leaves. Var. *repandens* makes a low spreading mound, and is one of the hardiest. Var. *washingtoni* is a vigorous golden-leaved form, somewhat hardier than the type.

cuspidata (Japanese Yew) is a large shrub or tree to 50 ft., somewhat similar to *T. baccata,* but with darker green leaves, yellowish beneath. There are both upright and spreading forms. Var. *nana* is a good shrubby form of slow growth with short needles. It is very dense and compact when young, later becoming widespreading.

brevifolia (Western Yew) is native to the N. W. coastal region, but rarely cultivated. It grows to 40 ft. or more, with slender horizontal branches.

canadensis (Canadian Yew, Groundhemlock) is a very hardy low-spreading grower, usually found in dense shade. In cultivation it will grow in the open and become less straggly, but the foliage is likely to be discolored by the winter sun.

media is a hybrid race between *T. baccata* and *T. cuspidata.* Two of its outstanding forms are *hatfieldi,* of dense bushy form, and *hicksi,* of columnar habit. Its seedlings show interesting differences in leaf form and habit of growth.

YEW FAMILY. The Taxaceae, which see.

YOUNGBERRY. A vigorous, half-hardy, thorny vine bearing dark purple berries of the blackberry type that turn black when thoroughly ripe. Produced over a long period of several months, they are of pleasant sub-acid flavor and excellent shippers. The plant originated in Louisiana as a cross between the Phenomenal berry (*Rubus loganobaccus*) and the Mayes-Austin dewberry. The vines should be planted 7 or 8 ft. apart and trained on tall stakes or trellises. A thornless "sport" of this hybrid was one of the early plants to be granted a patent, which see.

YOUTH-AND-OLD-AGE. A name popularly applied to Zinnia because the flowers are long lasting on the plant, some remaining attractive even when others have ripened seed. Also, locally, to the calla begonia (which see) presumably because

it bears green leaves, suggesting youth, and white ones, suggesting age, at the same time. Do not confuse with Youth-on-age, below.

YOUTH-ON-AGE. Common name for *Tolmiea menziesi* (which see), a hardy herb of the Pacific N.W., given because young plants develop right on the growing old ones from buds that form at the base of the leaves. Formerly considered only as a rock garden subject, it is now being offered and grown in some places as a house plant, under the name, "pick-a-back plant."

YUCCA (yuk'-ah). Herbaceous and tree-like plants of striking character, members of the Lily Family and native to N. America and the W. Indies. Some are stemless, others have woody, scaly trunks, often of majestic height, rising from clumps of stiff, sword-shaped leaves. The white or violet cup-shaped flowers, like huge lilies-of-the-valley, are borne mostly in erect clusters or along most of the stalks; some shed a heavy fragrance when open at night. Yuccas are fine for bold, subtropical effects, especially in dry areas. The hardy sorts may be grown out-of-doors in the N.; others are excellent greenhouse specimens, while many species flourish throughout the S. and W. A rich, but well-drained, fibrous soil is best and a sunny exposure. Propagation is from seed (plants often self-sowing), or by rhizome or stem cuttings, or offsets.

Y aloifolia, to 25 ft. is the true Spanish Bayonet, and *Y. brevifolia,* to 30 ft., is the grotesquely-shaped Joshua-tree. *Y. gloriosa,* to 8 ft., is called Spanish Dagger, and *Y. glauca,* to 8 ft., with short prostrate trunk, and *Y. filamentosa* (Adams Needle), to 12 ft., in which the leaves are edged with fine white threads, are the species commonly seen in the N. The great yuccas of S. Calif., known as "Candles of the Lord" and a glorious sight in bloom, are *Y. arborescens.*

The name Date-yucca is applied to Samuela (which see), another genus of S. plants of similar appearance, but with a soft-pulped trunk and certain botanical differences.

YULAN. Common name for *Magnolia denudata,* a 50-ft. Chinese tree which bears 6-in. fragrant flowers before the leaves.

ZALUZIANSKYA (za-loo-zee-an'-ski-ah). A genus of S. African annual or perennial herbs or shrubby plants of the Figwort Family, bearing tubular flowers that are very fragrant in the evening. The annual species are quite frequently cultivated for their ornamental effect as well as for their fragrance. They are grown from seed started in the fall, the plants being wintered over in a coldframe; or from seed started early in the spring in a greenhouse. If planted in light, rich soil, Zaluzianskyas will start to bloom in ten weeks from the time they are set out and continue in flower during July and August. *Z. capensis* (Night-phlox), to 1½ ft., has soft-hairy tubular flowers, white inside and purple-black outside.

ZAMIA (zay'-mi-ah). A genus of perennial tropical and subtropical plants of the Cycad Family, resembling both ferns and palms. The leaves of one species known as Coontie (which see) are used as decorative foliage by florists.

ZANTEDESCHIA (zan-te-des'-ki-ah). A genus of herbaceous, stout-rooted S. African plants with heart- or spear-shaped long-stemmed leaves and striking white, yellow, reddish, or spotted lily-like spathes (see INFLORESCENCE). In the N., where they are much grown by florists as pot plants and for cut flowers (popular with severe and formal wedding costumes), they are known and invariably referred to as Callas or Calla-lilies, although there is a genus Calla—an unrelated, small, water-loving N. herb. Zantedeschias are also widely grown in gardens in warm regions. For their species and culture, see CALLA.

ZANTHORHIZA (zan-thoh-ry'-zah) *apiifolia.* A small deciduous shrub of E. N. America, found in damp shady places; known as Shrub Yellow-root, which see.

ZANTHOXYLUM (zan-thok'-si-lum). Deciduous or evergreen shrubs, widely spread in tropical and temperate regions, belonging to the Rutaceae. They are mostly prickly, and are grown chiefly for their decorative foliage. The flowers—small and white or greenish—are followed by small pods with shining black seeds. Several species have medicinal value. They are not particular as to soil, and are propagated by seeds and root-cuttings.

The principal species are: *Z. americanum* (Prickly-ash), a vigorous native shrub, the hardiest of the group; *Z. clavaherculis* (Hercules Club, Toothache-tree), a native tree of the South with prickly trunk and branches; *Z. schinifolium,* bearing handsome leaves, with 13 to 21 leaflets, and the hardiest of the Asiatic kinds, doing fairly well as far N. as Mass. in protected places; *Z. piperitum,* similar but not as handsome in foliage and more tender. In Japan almost every part of the last-named plant seems to have a useful purpose.

ZAUSCHNERIA (zaush-nee'-ri-ah). Several species of low-growing, perennial herbs belonging to the Evening-primrose Family. One or two are grown in the flower garden, mainly as wall-covers, or in steep places in rockeries, where their drooping habit is of advantage. As they are not vigorous growers, several plants set close together and pinched back at intervals give the best results. The species most in cultivation (*Z. californica*) is known as California-fuchsia; it has several varieties, all of which bear drooping scarlet flowers. A light, rich soil is best. Propagation may be by division, cuttings in autumn, or seeds sown in the spring.

ZEA (zee'-ah) *mays.* A plant of the Grass Family known the world over as corn (which see) or maize. Presumably of Mexican origin, it now consists of many botanical, and countless agricultural, varieties and strains. Some are cultivated for the succulent stalks and large, coarse leaves used as forage and fodder; others for the ripened grain to be used as food for humans and animals (in some cases after "popping"); still others for the young tender ears cooked and eaten as a vegetable; and a few as ornamentals, for their colorful, variegated foliage.

ZEBRA GRASS. Common name for *Miscanthus sinensis* var. *zebrinus,* a variety of Eulalia (which see). The long leaves are banded with yellowish-white.

ZEBRA-PLANT. Common name for *Calathea zebrina,* a perennial herb of Brazil, grown in greenhouses for its velvety green-striped foliage.

ZEBRINA (ze-bry'-nah) *pendula.* A trailing plant of the Spiderwort Family, commonly known as Wandering Jew (which see). It is frequently grown in greenhouses are a hanging foliage plant.

ZELKOVA (zel-koh'-vah). Deciduous shrubs or trees, native of Asia, belonging to the Elm Family. They resemble twiggy, small-leaved elms and thrive under the same conditions that favor those trees. *Z. serrata,* the principal species, is a good-looking tree attaining 100 ft. It usually has a short trunk, dividing into many stems with slender spreading branches, forming a round-topped head. *Z. carpinifolia,* growing to 80 ft., also has a short trunk divided into many stems, but forms an oval head.

ZENOBIA (ze-noh'-bi-ah) *pulverulenta.* (See illustration, Plate 1.) A small deciduous or partly evergreen shrub, native to N. America, belonging to the Heath Family, and one of the plants called Andromeda. It thrives best in a sandy peaty soil, and is very conspicuous with its bluish-white foliage. The clusters of nodding white flowers open in May and June. Var. *nuda* has green leaves and smaller flowers. Propagated by seeds and layers.

ZEPHYRANTHES (zef-i-ran'-theez). A rather large genus of bulbous plants, most of which are native to the Americas from Pa. southward into the tropics. They produce narrow, strap-shaped leaves and funnel-shaped flowers borne erect on slender, hollow stems. Although they resemble some lilies and are commonly called Zephyr-lilies, they are actually members of the Amaryllis Family. In the S. States another common name is Rain-lily, given because the flowers appear in great numbers as if by magic as soon as a rainy season starts.

The Zephyr-lily is a beautiful and interesting subject and deserves to be more popular, as it doubtless will be as more is learned regarding its habits. The similarity in appearance of several forms that have different growing habits has not only led to botanical confusion but has also hindered its garden culture and horticultural development. Some kinds are hardy enough to come through the winter if well protected, but in general the bulbs should be lifted in fall and stored like gladiolus.

PRINCIPAL SPECIES

Z. atamasco. The common white species native in the S., is of doubtful hardiness in the N. It blooms in spring.

candida. The fall-flowering white species, which grows very prolifically in warm regions, but is not hardy. It is dormant in early summer but if then planted, either in the garden or in the house, it can be quickly and easily flowered.

carinata. With flowers rose-red or pink and appearing in early summer, this species, if handled as a tender, summer-flowering bulb, can be used in N. gardens. The bulbs should be lifted in the fall, stored frost-free over winter, and planted out in early spring.

rosea. This species is a rose-red autumn-bloomer native to Cuba, but most of the bulbs sold under this name are really *Z. carinata.*

robusta. A very large and beautiful rosy-lavender variety from S. America. Blooming in May, it is very fine for garden planting in the S. or for conservatory or house culture in the N.

texana. A native of Texas with coppery-yellow flowers with purple markings borne in summer.

ZINGIBER (zin'-ji-ber). A genus of tropical perennial herbs of the Ginger Family, grown in greenhouses in the N., for summer bedding in the S., and as the source of true ginger root in the tropics. Do not confuse with Asarum, a native genus known as Wild-ginger. See also GINGER.

ZINGIBERACEAE (zin-ji-ber-ay'-see-ee). The Ginger Family, a group of tropical herbs, some cultivated for their ornamental foliage and habit, and many for dyes, spices, perfumes and medicinal products. Nearly all are perennials with clumps of short, cane-like stems rising from tuberous rootstocks. The most commonly grown are: Zingiber (ginger), Amomum, Alpinia, Curcuma and Hedychium, all grown in the N. only under glass.

ZINNIA (zin'-i-ah). A genus of herbs and small shrubs of the Composite Family, native to N. and S. America, much grown as annuals in N. gardens for their abundant, cheery, double flowers in a wide range of colors. (See illustration, Plate 61.) The zinnia (type and variety not indicated) is the state flower of Ind.

These forms have been developed from the Mexican species (*Z. elegans*), the many varieties being decorative in the border, valuable for massing or for edging and fine for cutting. They are particularly rich in shades of rose and orange, and new, greatly improved varieties show many lovely harmonious color variations. They are divided according to height into *Tall*

Upper left: A new type, fascinatingly quilled and twisted and showing many subtle shades and tones. Center left: The large double zinnia, striking and effective in color but rather coarse. Upper right: Brilliant colors and lasting qualities make zinnias general favorites. Bottom: In a copper container, orange and apricot zinnias lend themselves admirably to artistic arrangement.

(30 in. or more), *Medium* (to 20 in.), and *Dwarf* (from 12 to 15 in.).

Zinnias are grown from seed, started in flats indoors about the end of March, or they may be started in the open at the same time as other hardy annuals. If indoors, prick out the seedlings into other flats and later transplant them to the open after the last frost. The tall varieties should be set 2 ft. apart and the smaller sorts 12 to 14 in. They grow best in light well-fertilized loam in full sun, but will bloom in partial shade. Applications of a complete fertilizer at 3 or 4 week intervals help produce larger, more perfect flowers. All types blossom from early summer until hard frost. The profuse foliage sets off their varied colors both outdoors and when cut and arranged in the house.

Several leaf diseases are common on zinnias in the late summer. Powdery mildew may be controlled by dusting with fine sulphur. A leaf spot and a leaf blight, both caused by fungi, may mar the appearance of plants but except in very wet seasons do not prevent normal flowering. If necessary spray with bordeaux mixture. Mosaic (which see) is sometimes found on zinnia, and plants with mottled leaves should be removed and burned.

The common stalk borer (see under DAHLIA) may infest zinnia, and blister beetles (see under ASTER) and cut-worms (which see) are sometimes troublesome. Other species not so well known as *Z. elegans* are: *Z. pauciflora,* with yellow heads, sometimes with purple or yellow ray flowers; *Z. angustifolia,* smaller than *Z. elegans,* with bright orange heads; and *Z. multiflora* which has small heads to 1 in. across with narrow red or purple rays.

ZONAL GERANIUM. A name sometimes applied loosely to the common bedding or pot geraniums which are actually species, varieties and hybrids of Pelargonium. The name, derived from one of the parent species (*P. zonale*) is suggested by the leaf markings.

ZOYSIA (zoh'-i-si-ah). A small genus of creeping perennial grasses of S. Asia, whose fine, compact foliage fits them for use in lawns in the S. States. The species are *Z. matrella* (Manila Grass), *Z. tenuifolia* (Mascarene Grass), and *Z. japonica* (Korean Lawn Grass). They may be grown from seeds or root divisions.

ZYGADENUS (zig-ah-dee'-nus). A genus of lily-like perennials, some with and some without bulbs, growing about 2 ft. tall, and having grass-like leaves and white, greenish or yellow flowers in clusters. Sometimes grown as pot plants, they are also occasionally seen in the rock or wild garden. They are propagated by division or seed. Some of the species have poisonous seeds, leaves and bulbs. *Z. venenosus* (Death Camas), with small greenish-white flowers, is a W. species with a very poisonous bulb. *Z. angustifolius* has leaves 1½ ft. long and racemes to 4 in.; *Z. elegans* has very narrow leaves with a silvery bloom and greenish flowers in clusters to 1 ft. long; *Z. paniculatus,* another W. species, has yellow flowers and an exceedingly poisonous bulb; *Z. nuttalli* has rather large flowers ½ in. across, in loose clusters.

ZYGOCACTUS (zy-goh-kak'-tus) *truncatus.* A popular species of Brazilian epiphytic cactus with flattened, glossy joints which suggest one of its common names, Crab or Lobster Cactus. Its drooping branches are tipped with handsome red, sometimes double, flowers which, appearing from just before the winter holiday season until early spring, suggest another common name, Christmas Cactus. An attractive, easily-grown house plant, it has been popular and a feature of most cactus collections ever since it was introduced into cultivation more than a century ago. A common practice is to graft it on a more robust stock—often an upright stem of a plant of the genus Pereskia,—which results in a large bushy plant, very showy when in bloom. It is also used in hanging pots or baskets; if cuttings are inserted a few inches apart they soon produce a thick, graceful mass of foliage. As it is a tropical plant, this cactus prefers a richer soil than is needed for types of desert origin. See also CACTUS.

ZYGOPETALUM (zy-goh-pet'-ah-lum). A genus of tropical American epiphytic orchids having rather large, fragrant flowers, solitary, or in racemes, in shades of violet, rose or greenish-yellow. A number of lovely species, popular because of their winter-blooming habit, are grown in the N., requiring an intermediate-temperature greenhouse. They can be potted in the same manner as terrestrial orchids, but care should be taken to see that the foliage is dry at night, as moisture causes discoloration of the leaves and rots out the young growth which appears just before the flowering stage. For culture details see ORCHIDS.

Your First Garden

Your First Garden

A GUIDE FOR THE BEGINNER

By Carol H. Woodward

CONTENTS

Frontispiece. Spring in your first garden can be as lovely as this. The daisies, tulips and daffodils have been interplanted to produce a light and cheerful mood. The picture is from The Netherlands Flower Bulb Institute.

FOREWORD

A garden may be started at any time of year. If the inspiration comes in January, it may be momentarily satisfied with some potted plants for the window. In the northern states it is far too early to commence sowing seeds for the outdoor garden, but the important long-range work of planning can be begun.

The season's colorful catalogs will soon be in the mail, and every gardener, whether a novice or a veteran, can profit by acquiring a large supply of these. The garden advertising columns of the magazines and newspapers tell where to send for seed and nursery catalogs.

If the urge to start a garden comes in March or April, the time is right for spading up the ground as soon as a plan has been made for the planting. Without a design on paper, the gardener runs the risk of having a hodgepodge instead of the artistic composition of flowers, shrubs, and trees of which he has dreamed.

For a garden started in summer a plan in advance is equally desirable. Summer is not the ideal time to make a new garden, but an array of flowers can, nevertheless, be achieved while work is being initiated on the future plan for the property.

Those who can commence preliminary work for next year's garden in the fall are fortunate, for the results in flowers, fruits, and vegetables then are likely to be the best of all.

But no matter what time of year a garden is undertaken, the beginner will find helpful suggestions and instructions under the following titles on the pages ahead:

Opposite. The smaller chrysanthemums should be considered for planting close to the house. They tend to stay neater and require little or no staking. Early varieties start to bloom in midsummer.

STARTING IN THE FALL

PLANNING THE GARDEN

From the beginning, a garden should be planned for the *future*. There should be a design for the entire property, a harmonious planting scheme that will link the house to its surroundings.

In developing this design, the first consideration should be the trees, and they should be chosen with the greatest of care, for they may outlive the occupants of the house.

You may not decide at once that you want a pin oak here and a flowering cherry there. You will be merely thinking, "I'd like a nice sturdy tree, but not too large, at that corner, and a small flowering tree where I can see it from the east bedroom window." With ideas like these in mind—or, better yet, on paper—your local nurseryman can help you choose the best varieties for your purposes.

The shrubbery comes next in the plan, then the special gardens, and the herbaceous flowering plants last. This Encyclopedia's list of PLANTS FOR SPECIAL PURPOSES will be of help.

To make a plan on paper is not as complicated as you think, and it has great value. It is easy to get the dimensions of the property. Pace off the distances if you don't know them and haven't a tape on hand. Mark the boundaries of the area on a sheet of square-ruled paper, each quarter-inch representing one foot. Do the same for the house and any other buildings, also for driveways and paths, and put their outlines on the paper.

If you already have trees, mark an irregular circle to indicate the spread of their branches. Darken an area to the north of each to show the extent of the shade.

Start your plan on paper by marking circles for your new trees first, then plot positions for your shrubs, special gardens and borders. Here are some points to keep in mind while making the plan for your garden and grounds:

Consider the direction and amount of shade from buildings and trees.

Save sunny areas for flowers and vegetables.

Try to have at least one vista—a long, pleasant view from living-room, dining-room, or street.

Select trees with consideration for their durability, future size, rate of growth, and year-round appearance.

Arrange shrubs in groups at the borders of the property.

Use trees and shrubs with dense foliage to hide unsightly objects and views.

Keep the lawn free of flower beds and specimens.

Do not buy plants until you know exactly where you wish to place them.

START WITH THE SOIL

Every garden soil, whether new or old and whether for trees, shrubs, flowers, or a lawn, needs attention, and the first thing one should do is to dig it deeply and treat it to a good application of organic matter and whatever other amendments and nutrients it needs. For general directions, see pages 1377-1380.

The deeper the spade goes into the soil, the better the results will be in next year's garden. And the greater the quantity of humus (partially decayed organic matter) that is added to the soil, the happier the plants will be—and the gardener too. In your first year of gardening it may be a problem to locate a source of humus, and you may have to beg, borrow, or buy whatever you can get. Old leaves, piles of grass clippings, garbage that has been buried—all are useful. Manure, best of all and once easily obtainable, is at a premium today.

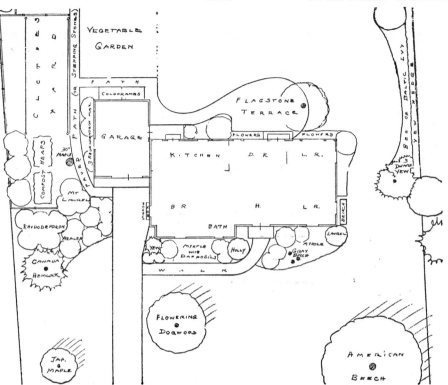

HOW TO DRAW A PLAN FOR YOUR GROUNDS

First, measure the property, then the outlines of the house, garage, driveway and paths, and mark their contours on squared paper. Then put in the trees and shrubs existing and the plants desired. Evergreens for the plan are shown by circles of invested scallops; deciduous trees and shrubs by rounded outlines.

Partial plan adopted from Alice L. Dustan

After you have gardened for a year you will have your own mulch pile, or compost heap (see page 1379). This is like having a bank account for your garden soil. It will give you a fine feeling of independence.

Soil which is deeply dug and enriched in the autumn (see pages 1355 and 1377), then left rough for the winter, will be in excellent shape for raking and planting in spring.

If, however, you have some fall planting to do, the ground may be raked level as soon as it has been dug.

A LAWN IN SHORT ORDER

September is the recommended month for seeding a lawn, but even November, except in the extreme north, is better than spring or summer. Better yet is the second September after starting to prepare the ground, but if green grass in three weeks means more to you than greener grass a year from now, dig the soil well, improve it as needed (see page 1378) and add an extra quantity of extra fine humus. Then rake and rake and rake some more, until every stone is out, every clod of earth pulverized, and the entire surface level and smooth. The only roughness should be the fine corrugations left by the teeth of a lightly held rake, and these will help to hold the seed in place.

If you want about 1,000 square feet of lawn (say an area 32 x 32 or 25 x 40 feet), four pounds of seed should give you a heavy stand of grass. To make sure you sow it evenly, divide it into four portions, then divide your ground into four equal parts. Select a calm day with a shower in the offing, if possible, and scatter the seed slowly, holding the hand close to the ground. Then tamp or roll the ground to press the tiny seeds into close contact with the earth. If the shower doesn't come, wet the soil thoroughly—but with the finest possible spray. Then be patient and wait for the first signs of green to appear.

PLANTING DATA for BULBS

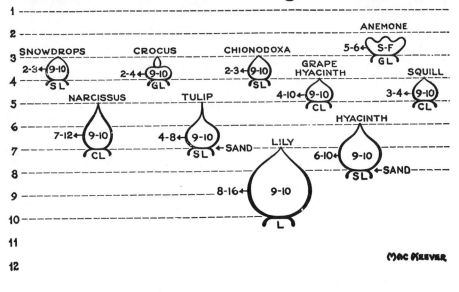

DEPTH AND DISTANCES FOR PLANTING BULBS

Figures in the left column show the depth for planting; those beside the bulbs show the proper distances apart. Figures within each bulb tell the month to plant. The letters indicate the ideal soil for the bottom of the hole. CL stands for clay loam; SL, sandy loam, GL, gravelly loam, and L, loam.

Chart designed by Frank C. MacKeever

Bulbs for Spring Cheer

One of the most miraculous acts in gardening is to tuck firm brown bulbs beneath the soil in the fall, let winter obliterate their hiding places and then awake some fine spring morning to find the garden gleaming with color where there had been only brown grass or spring-wet earth before.

In a place where you are willing to let the grass remain uncut until the leaves of bulbs have disappeared, there is nothing pleasanter than naturalized crocuses and daffodils.

Bulbs in front of shrubbery also give delight. Some fit well in a special border; smaller ones belong in the rock garden.

Tulips can be planted just before the ground freezes, crocuses also late, and daffodils whenever they are available from August through October. The smaller flowering bulbs—squills, snowdrops, snowflakes, glories-of-the-snow, grape-hyacinths —are rewarding in the spring if planted in mid-autumn. On grape-hyacinths foliage appears in the fall.

The secret of planting them is to set them firmly, *flat* in the bottom of a hole that measures three times the height of the bulb itself. Fill the hole with soil, press it fairly firmly, and level off the top. Spring will bring the miracle of bloom.

Head Start on Annuals

Flowering in early summer can be hastened on a few of the annuals by sowing the seeds in the fall. Unless the seedlings can endure the rigors of winter, it is best to sow them just before the ground freezes, so that they will not germinate before spring. You can keep the bed in readiness for them by mulching it heavily after the soil is prepared. When the surrounding soil has frozen, lift the mulch and sow your seeds in the still soft earth. Replace the mulch and in spring remove it gradually.

Among the hardiest of plants for late October sowing are annual larkspur, bachelors buttons, and sweet alyssum.

Annual seeds which may be sown in late November to spend the winter dormant include calendulas, petunias, snapdragons, and the annual forms of candytuft, coreopsis, dianthus (pinks), and babys breath.

In less severe regions, balsam, cosmos, four o'clocks, love-in-a-mist, nicotiana, poppies, sweet peas, and sunflowers may be sown just before the start of winter.

PLANTING TREES AND SHRUBS IN AUTUMN

Deciduous woody plants—that is, shrubs and trees that lose their leaves before winter comes—may be set in the ground with equal advantage in the fall or early spring, except in the most northerly regions. The main requirement at either season is to keep their roots constantly moist.

If evergreens have not been transplanted by late September (in the north), it is better to wait until April.

To make sure that the kinds of trees and shrubs you want are suited to your vicinity, buy them from a nearby nurseryman. If he can grow them, you can too.

They should always be dug with their original soil held tightly around their roots with burlap to minimize the shock of moving. If, however, you are planting a specimen with its roots exposed, *be sure to keep them wet.*

Holes should be dug to receive trees and shrubs in advance of their arrival, and each hole should be larger than the depth and spread of the roots. The subsoil should be worked over, improved and tamped down, then covered with 2 or 3 inches of humus-enriched soil. The shrub or tree is set in place so that the surface of the soil will be the same as it was originally.

If the roots are bare, they are spread out naturally, broken ones are cut off sharply, and good soil is packed around the roots until the hole is filled. If roots are pruned, branches should be pruned to balance.

If the plant is "balled and burlapped," the burlap is loosened, pressed flat in the hole, and left to decay. The roots should not be disturbed. After the hole is filled in with good earth, the plant must be thoroughly watered and kept reasonably moist to the end of the season.

PRELUDE TO SPRING

The first few weeks of the new year are the weeks of a gardener's dreams. While waiting impatiently for the mailman to bring the first seed catalogs, he pores over gardening books, reads the gardening magazines, and builds up a bulwark of knowledge to use as soon as spring brings him the opportunity.

The catalogs come ... and what a temptation they are! Each glowing picture represents new possibilities. This is the time for the dreamer to awaken to realities and recognize the size of the garden he has planned. He must be strict with himself; or his garden will overflow its boundaries and give him additional problems of summer care when the weather is hot and he wants to relax.

For the first garden it is wisest to order familiar flowers, those which are known to bloom in abundance almost everywhere. After that, let the gardener experiment with novelties. Each year will bring him new treasures in experience and in beauty.

SOWING SEEDS INDOORS

At the end of February in the northern states, spring seems very far away, for it is not yet planting time unless one has a greenhouse available. In milder regions outdoor work can be initiated now; but for a vast section of the country only the slowest-growing plants should be started, even indoors.

If you are ambitious to grow your own border flowers such as lobelia, torenia, browallia, ageratum, and petunias and verbenas, instead of buying plants, their seeds may be sown the last of the month. Most other plants, however, will become spindly and weak if they are started early, for their never is enough bright sun in any house to meet the demands of fast growing seedlings.

After the middle of March the impatient gardener may start other annuals indoors, among them nasturtiums, garden balsam, stock, mignonette, scarlet sage (which looks better in a border than in a circular bed), scarlet runner and hyacinth beans, and several other annual vines.

The most up-to-date method for sowing seeds indoors is to use vermiculite (obtainable wherever you buy your seeds), either alone or with half sifted peatmoss. Another good medium is finely chopped sphagnum. These substances hold moisture well and prevent damping-off disease, which often kills seedlings.

For small quantities of seeds, broad low pots called "bulb pans" are best. Put pieces of broken crockery over the drainage hole, a layer of clean pebbles if you can get them readily, then fill the pot with vermiculite or other medium, leaving up to an inch at the top. Stand the pot in a pan of water at room temperature until moisture appears at the top.

Scatter the seeds thinly and sift vermiculite over them to cover them twice their height.

Cover the pots with a pane of glass, which should be dried daily, then with a newspaper. Keep the medium slightly moist. As soon as the first sign of green appears, remove the newspaper, then the glass; and give the containers light but not full sun. Increase the strength of light gradually as the seedlings grow.

When watering, wait till the medium looks dry, then give a gentle soaking.

The first pair of leaves to appear will be the cotyledons, which are part of the seed structure. Wait for the plant's true leaves to expand before transplanting.

A tool for lifting the seedlings can be improvised by notching the end of a small wooden label or sneaking a steel fork out of the kitchen drawer. Lift each individual seedling carefully out of its medium, and give it more room in another pot containing fine, moist soil of one third sand, one third loam, and one third peatmoss or leafmold. If you do not have these materials on hand, they can be bought in small quantities from some of the one-time "ten-cent" stores or from garden supply houses.

If you have many seedlings, transplant them into a flat, which is a box about 4 inches high with slats or drainage holes on the bottom. Make the soil firm around their roots. Transplanting is advantageous to the later growth of seedlings.

Be patient as the days grow warm; cold nights are almost sure to come through May. Get your plantlets used to them by giving them some outdoor air each day. The end of the month is time enough to set out the house-grown seedlings. They should then give abundant reward with early bloom.

TOOLS FOR THE BEGINNING GARDENER

It pays to buy good tools and to keep them in good shape, cleaning and drying

BRIGHT FLOWERS IN SPRING FROM FALL PLANTING OF BULBS
Left, trumpet daffodils and grape-hyacinths; *above,* Chionodoxa, or glory-of-the-snow; *below,* one of several kinds of squills.
Photos by Gottscho-Schleisner

them after every use, storing them in a dry, protected place, and sharpening at intervals those that require an edge.

Here is a list of essential tools. A beginner needs them just as much as a gardener of long experience. More will be required as the garden becomes more elaborate and the owner's activities increase.

For preparing the soil: Spade, spading fork, hoe, mattock, rakes (both steel and bamboo).

For sowing and planting: Trowel (with strong wooden handle), dibber (or dibble) for making small holes in soil for seedlings, watering pot, atomizer spray, labels.

For garden maintenance: Scuffle hoe for cultivating, weeding fork, pruning knives and shears, stakes and raffia for supporting tall plants, lawn mower, grass and hedge shears, hose with nozzle and sprinkler, lawn roller.

For disease and pest control: Sprayers and dusters.

And, for the gardener's convenience: Wheelbarrow and carrying baskets.

YOUR CLIMATIC ZONE

Planting dates in spring are largely determined in each region by the latest recorded killing frost. With many local variations, zones can be mapped which correspond roughly to the zones of hardiness recognized for woody plants.

The procedures recommended in this Supplement are in practice in the gardening region adjacent to New York City, where April 20 is considered as the date of the last killing frost. They will also apply in central New Jersey, southeastern Pennsylvania, northern Maryland and Virginia, West Virginia, Kentucky, northern Arkansas, central Oklahoma, a narrow belt of Texas, central New Mexico, northeastern Arizona, and from there northwestward.

The belt starting directly north of New York City, where frosty nights can be expected 10 days longer, includes Connecticut and Massachusetts, Pennsylvania, Ohio, Indiana, southern Illinois, central Missouri, a diagonal corner of Kansas and Oklahoma, northwestern Texas, northern New Mexico, Utah, Nevada, and northward.

STARTING IN THE SPRING

FIRST, THE PLAN

As in the fall, it is essential to *plan* the garden before starting to plant it (see page 1350). The earlier you begin to put your ideas on paper, the better garden you will have.

First comes the background in the landscape plan—and this includes all the trees. After woody plants have begun new growth in spring, it is unwise to try to bring them into the garden; they are most satisfactorily moved when they are dormant. Therefore it may be best to wait until fall before acquiring them, unless a skilled nurseryman can guarantee their continued growth. The place where they are to be, however, should be clearly marked on the plan, so that flower beds, which are more temporary affairs, can be located according to the sun they will receive when the planting is finished. They should have about 6 hours of sun a day.

The view of the flowers from vantage points such as the dining-room windows or from the terrace, and their freedom from competition with the vigorous roots of woody plants, are among other deciding factors in the plan.

ATTENTION TO THE SOIL

You will need warm gloves and overshoes when you start to work your soil in spring, for the air will still be cold. If a garden has never been made on the site before, dig the soil deeply, pushing the spade in vertically to the full length of the blade, opening a trench into the bottom of which you fork manure, compost, or any kind of organic matter you can get (see pages 1350 and 1377), then fill the trench with the soil from the trench you dig beside it, and continue this performance to the end.

It is always better if this work can be done in the fall, but early spring is the next best season. The job can be started as soon as the soil can be worked without clinging, clay-like, to the spade.

If it is already time to sow the first seeds (the end of March at the very earliest in the north, as described on page 1357), rake the ground level, add a sprinkling of lime, if needed, about like powdered sugar on a coffee cake, rake it again, and put in the seeds. But if there is time to wait, let the ground settle a bit, then rake it again before sowing. In this repetitive job of raking, draw the implement lightly over the soil surface with an even stroke. If you thrust it into the ground, you will achieve a permanent wave in your bed.

TREES AND SHRUBS FOR SPRING PLANTING

If you buy large trees and shrubs for your property, you miss all the pleasure of watching them grow from year to year until they finally attain the size and aspect that you had visualized. Also, you pay more for each plant and for the handling of it, and you run a greater risk of its failure.

While it is fine to get a head start by setting some of the hardiest of the woody plants in the ground in the fall, in the more northerly climates early spring is a better time for planting trees and shrubs.

If their first response to their new environment can be in slowly warming earth, they may adjust themselves as readily as though they had not been moved.

Planting of shrubs and trees in spring is done the same way as in the fall (see page 1353). After a plant is set and the hole is filled with well tamped soil (the feet make the best tampers), a slight depression may be made to hold the water until it soaks down to the roots. Water well, but never keep a specimen permanently wet. Remember that air also must reach the roots, and this can happen only between waterings by bucket, hose, or rain.

Pruning of newly set shrubs is desirable —first of the roots, removing all broken, diseased, or excessively long ones; then of the top, to balance the underground trimming. Old, worn-out branches, as well as damaged ones, should be removed and the tips should be trimmed back to give the plant good shape and induce more vigor in the new growth (see page 1375).

Roses, by the way, can go into the garden the earliest of any shrubs. As soon as the ground is capable of being dug, they may be pruned and planted. (See page 1364 for more about roses.)

If you are unfamiliar with most types of flowering shrubs, the best thing to do is to plan the colors and sizes you would like in each location, then take your plan to a well established nursery, and let the nurseryman help you make your selections. It is

---

WHERE TO BUY SUPPLIES FOR YOUR GARDEN
(A list of recommended sources)

Seeds and bulbs: Select from catalogs (try to find out which are most reliable) and order by mail.

Annual and perennial plants: From a nearby nursery or florist.

Shrubs and trees: Also from a nearby nursery, or, for rarer specimens, from a nursery specializing in the material you want.

Topsoil*: From a nearby nursery or farmer.

Humus*: From a nursery, farmer, or feed store.

Peatmoss*: From a nursery or feed store.

Sand*, gravel, and clay: From a building supply firm or a road contractor.

Vermiculite: From a garden supply store or through a seed catalog.

Fertilizers, sprays, dusts, weedkillers, and tools: From your neighborhood hardware store, garden supply house, or through seed and nursery catalogs.

Mulching materials: Ask your local nurseryman or feed store, or a neighbor with gardening experience.

*In small quantities from ten-cent stores and florists.

In a pleasant garden which is intimately close to the house, the flowers of annuals, biennials, perennials and vines are cheefully combined.
Photos by Gottscho-Schleisner

ideal if you can first see the shrubs in bloom, but this often means waiting nearly a year before they can be moved into your garden.

Here are some factors to consider in selecting the shrubs and small trees to ornament your property:

Plan to have something in flower at every season. Even in March there are dogwoods (not the "flowering" kind, but species with clouds of yellow along the branches), and in November there is the cheerful yellow of the native witch-hazel.

If your soil and climate will support the flowering evergreens, such as rhododendron and andromeda, include as many of these as you can. (They require acid soil.)

Consider leaf textures as well as flowers in planning for harmony.

Have several varieties with attractive autumn fruits and foliage.

Consider the winter effect of shrubs that lose their leaves; some have interesting lines and colors.

Purchase only hardy material. Few people want to take time to coddle their plants with winter overcoats of burlap.

SOWING SEEDS OUTDOORS

Even though one must often wait two months or more for flowers, the actual sowing of flower seeds in outdoor beds in spring is one of the most exciting of all garden tasks, because it gives promise of such immediate result. It may take a magnifying glass to see the first sign of green above the brown soil, but once it is visible, growth increases daily, and with each expanding leaf the day of flowering advances. Was ever a prettier design created than a symmetrical pattern of young leaves across an expanse of fine earth?

To prepare the ground for the flower bed, follow the same process that has been described on pages 1350 and 1355. (Also see pages 1377-1380.)

The plants which are sown in spring for summer flowering are the annuals—those which die completely at the end of the season and need to be started anew each year. Some persist in the garden by reseeding themselves, but they are in the minority.

Perennial plants—those whose roots live over winter and send up new shoots annually—seldom bloom before the second year. (See page 1359.)

Only the hardiest plants, which will not object to unpredicted cold weather after they have sprouted, can be sown outdoors in the northern states as early as mid-April. Gardeners in milder regions can best judge time of planting by their local weather conditions and by the customs of the region.

Among the first flower seeds to sow are such sturdy, reliable sorts as cornflower or bachelors buttons, snow-on-the-mountain, poppies (which should never be transplanted), candytuft, sweet alyssum, sweet sultan, and the annual forms of babys breath, lupine, and coreopsis, often known as "calliopsis."

A few that are only half hardy—such as portulaca, petunia, garden balsam, nicotiana, and cleome or spider-flower—are also worth risking with an early sowing date, if they have not already been started indoors.

Two weeks later, snapdragons, morning glories, calendulas, cockscombs, annual chrysanthemums, nasturtiums, mignonette and scabiosa may go into the ground.

Still later—not before mid-May in the north—those all-time favorites, zinnias and marigolds, may at last be sown outdoors, and with them cosmos, annual gaillardia, and a number of others.

If the seeds are very fine, they can be evenly scattered by mixing them with four times their bulk of sand. A little fine soil sifted over them is the only covering they will need. Larger seeds may be raked in until they are covered, or, if they are sown in drills, the earth may be drawn over them with the back of the rake, a board, trowel, or the hand. Vermiculite sprinkled in the drills is a safeguard for survival, especially in early seed-sowing. The largest seeds should have individual holes about four times their diameter, but not more.

The location of every kind of seed planted should be clearly marked. For annuals, a small wooden label is sufficient for the name and the date of sowing. Either there or in a notebook (which in time will become the gardener's indispensable companion), the source of the seed should be noted, and later its progress and behavior.

The annuals will look most attractive in the garden if they are placed in clumps rather than rows. Since not every seed will germinate, it is essential to sow more than you think you will need. But don't be excessive! Leave space for each seedling to sprout if the seed does germinate. A practical scheme is to determine the final spacing of the plants, then sow three or four seeds in each spot. When they start to grow, the sturdiest one in each group can be saved

HOW SOON DO ANNUALS SPROUT FROM SEED OUTDOORS?

Average number of days required for germination is given here. The length of time varies with temperature, moisture, and soil condition.

Flowers	Days (approx.)	Flowers	Days (approx.)
Cosmos	6	Snapdragon	14
Marigold	6	Verbena	18
Zinnia	6		
Morning Glory	10	*Vegetables*	
Sweet Alyssum	10	Beans	7
Nasturtium	10	Lettuce	10
Portulaca	10	Beets	12
Sweet Pea	10	Carrots	14
Larkspur	14	Onions	14
Petunia	14	Peas	14
Poppy	14	Parsley	18

ANNUAL FLOWERS FOR SHOWY, RELIABLE BLOOM
Zinnias in the garden are zestful, while Shirley poppies, in contrast, are fragile lookings, though they abound in flowers. These are among the most popular and easiest to grow of all the annuals.

Photos by Roche

and some of the others used for replacements where needed. Most plants will require 9 inches of spacing. Small ones, such as sweet alyssum and portulaca, will give good bloom at 4 to 6 inches; the largest specimens need up to 24.

When seedlings are transplanted, make sure their roots do not dry out from the time they are lifted until they show by their renewed growth that they have become established.

As with seedlings grown indoors, transplanting is not done until the plant's true leaves appear—the first pair after the cotyledons, or seed leaves. Then it should not be delayed.

June, to the uninitiated, connotes masses of brilliant garden flowers. As a matter of fact, except for roses, June in the northern states is one of the poorest months in the garden. The spring perennials will be gone and the earliest annuals sown outdoors will barely begin to bloom before the end of the month. June is a month for patience—and hope.

EARLY COLOR IN THE BORDER

Color can be achieved during the otherwise barren weeks of early summer by buying some plants that have been grown in a nearby nursery. These can usually be found already bearing their first blossoms, so they can be fitted into the color scheme of the garden. The blue of lobelia and ageratum, white, pink, red, and purple of verbena and petunia flowers, and the delicate blue and velvety purple combined in the blossoms of torenia will happily initiate a season of increasing bloom from all these reliable plants.

If you started these flowers yourself indoors, you are ahead of the season and have your reward. It is with special pride that a gardener, showing off his border, remarks, "I grew them all myself from seed!"

PERENNIALS FOR PERMANENCE

When perennials are brought into the garden, they are brought to stay. Their arrangement, as to color combinations, height and spread, time of bloom, leaf color, shape and texture, and their appearance after they have gone to seed can make the grounds look like a weed patch or a place of distinctive beauty. Clashing colors can be effectively offset with masses of white and with foliage.

The plants should be studied in books and catalogs before being ordered. (For lists and suggestions see Perennials in this Encyclopedia.) If you have space for a border, place the tallest at the back, but not in a straight unbroken line, and graduate them, somewhat irregularly, down to the front of the border. Use several plants of one kind together for effect.

The tall plants—and some of the others too—will need staking to keep them held upright. Use tall stakes set well into the ground and tie the main stems at intervals, not directly to the stakes, but with a loose figure 8 of raffia—or with a flexible plastic or metal strip. Lower plants, especially bushy ones, can be held upright with twiggy dry branches of birch thrust into the ground beside their main stems. Staking should be done *before* the plant needs it. Afterward may be too late.

Perennials, being long-lived, generally require more than a year to develop their first flowers. The beginning gardener, therefore, will do well to buy at least a few perennial plants of one-year growth in order to get his garden started.

Meanwhile, seeds of perennials may be sown almost any time outdoors from May to August, or even earlier in a coldframe or protected bed. In hot, dry weather, summer-sown seedlings will have a struggle. Spring sowing is therefore preferable.

The plants are most easily handled if they are started in pots or flats (see page 1353), which can be protected in a coldframe or a sheltered bed in a sunny spot. In early spring, the coldframe must be covered with a window sash, then with burlap, weighted down.

As soon as the seeds have germinated the burlap may be removed and the sash lifted a trifle for ventilation. When the second pair of true leave has appeared, it is time for thinning and transplanting an inch apart in flats, or in individual pots of the smallest size. Transplants should have part shade until they become established.

When they are 3 inches high, weather permitting, they may be moved outdoors— but not into their permanent quarters; they are not yet grown up enough to join the adults of the garden family. There should always be a nursery bed in a hidden part of the grounds where such plants can pass their adolescence unobserved.

When fall comes they may either be moved to their permanent place or left in the nursery until spring. Wherever they are, these young things should have a mulch of dry, airy material—such as newly fallen leaves held in place by branches—*after* (not before) the ground is frozen.

SPRINGTIME AND LATE SUMMER SCENES WITH PERENNIALS
Left, bleeding heart, foamflower, and blue phlox bloom together in the spring. *Right*, plantain-lilies flower well in the shade.
Photos by Gottscho-Schleisner

BIENNIALS FOR BEAUTY
The transparent seed-pods of honesty, or money-wort, are its attractive feature.

Biennials in the Border

Halfway between the ranks of the annuals and perennials are those plants which bloom customarily the second year from seed, then die. These are the biennials, or two-year plants.

The most familiar ones are Canterbury bells, hollyhocks, wallflowers, pansies, forget-me-nots, sweet william, honesty, sweet rocket, and foxglove (which, because of its poisonous quality, should not be grown where children are likely to nibble any part of the plant).

These are started and eventually planted in the garden the same as perennials, but the process must be repeated every year if the species are to be kept blooming in the garden. A few, if the soil around them is not cultivated, will persist from seeds that the plants themselves have dropped; but there is no assurance of this behavior.

Some biennials behave as annuals or as perennials in different locations. If they take kindly to your situation you are fortunate, for the biennials are among the handsomest of the summer flowers.

Lawn Work in Spring

While it is admitted that the ideal time to start a lawn is in the fall, it is not always possible. If your grounds are new and it is early spring, dig the soil well (see pages 1350, 1355 and 1377), enrich it, remove roots and stones, rake it level, and sow a cover crop of rye-grass, rye, or vetch.

In July spade this under. Throughout August keep the weeds controlled. Add a good commercial fertilizer (see page 1378). Rake the ground level, and in September sow the grass seed, roll the lawn, and wait for next year's reward.

It takes an experienced sower to spread the grass seed evenly over the soil. In addition to dividing both seed and area into four or more equal portions (see page 1351), it is a good idea to divide each lot of seed again. Sow the first half walking east and west across the plot and the second half walking north and south.

Fallen leaves should not be left on a newly sprouted lawn over winter. Flick them off with a bamboo rake, and save them for a mulch around the shrubbery.

If the grass reaches 3 inches in height before the end of the season, it should be cut with the lawnmower blades set 2 inches high. Otherwise it should be left until spring.

Hollyhocks, always a favorite, by seeding themselves often bloom year after year.
Photos by Roche

STARTING IN SUMMER

MAKING A PLAN FOR THE FUTURE

In a way, the easiest time to make a plan for a garden is in midsummer, when you can see things growing and blooming all around you, instead of having to rely on catalog pictures and descriptions in gardening books—indispensable though these may be. First and foremost to consider is the plan for the entire property. The effect of shade trees in your neighborhood will give you an idea of how and with what you wish to start. If the streets in your part of town are too sunny, here is an occasion for you to set a glorious example with appropriate shade and flowering trees in your yard.

Visiting the gardens of neighbors and friends and visiting nurseries, arboretums, and botanical gardens where plants are growing in quantities will be of immeasurable aid when you go to select materials for your new garden. A notebook should be in your pocket all the time, for wherever you go you will pick up ideas to be treasured.

Your plan should be for the future, and it should be as complete before you start as you, a beginner, can make it. Don't expect too much this year; midsummer is not the time to rush into planting. You can have flowers, however, before fall, and each of these first blooms will have the value of ten in your eye.

YOUR GARDEN SOIL

Any soil needs attention before it is planted. Even a professional gardener who has maintained plants in the same spot year after year will keep on constantly improving the soil, to replace the elements that have been used up by his plants. On a newly built property that is taken over in midsummer there is little to be done with the soil before fall—unless one wants to plant a cover crop on the bare ground to be plowed under at the end of the season. (See page 1361.)

For those small areas where you wish to have some quick bloom, do a temporary job on the soil by spading it well, adding plenty of well-decayed compost, sand if needed to lighten the texture, and a sprinkling of a commercial fertilizer. Rake the soil fine, make the beds level, water the areas well, and do your planting as soon as the water has subsided from the surface enough to make the soil workable. Then sow some of the quick-growing annuals.

WHERE TO FIND OUT . . .

County Agents and the staffs of State Agricultural Experiment Stations, Botanical Gardens, Arboretums, and Garden Centers all are eager to help in solving problems for the home gardener. Their success in functioning often is measured in terms of such co-operation. *Ask them without hesitancy:*

What type of soil you have and what it needs.
What plants are hardy in your region.*
How early seeds may be sown and plants set out.*
What disease or pest is bothering your plants.

Consult this Encyclopedia to find out:

The address of your nearest Experiment Station or Botanical Garden.
How to perform various gardening operations.
How to handle each kind of plant throughout the season.
How to combat specific pests and diseases.

Follow the advertising columns in the gardening sections of newspapers and magazines to find out where to send for seed, bulb, and nursery catalogs. From your neighbors try to find out which are the most reliable.

---

*Your gardening neighbors and your local nurseryman also can help.

SPECTACULAR FLOWERS AND FOLIAGE FOR LATE SUMMER
Lycoris (*left*) is a hardy bulb which will bloom in October if planted in July. Fancy-leaved caladiums (*right*) in red and white and green may be set out for a showy effect in the late garden.   Photos by Roche

Summer-sown Annuals

Four to six weeks from seed should bring you bloom from a number of annuals sown in July. They will need more attention than seeds started in spring, because the summer sun will quickly parch their small sphere of earth, but the results of your care will be gratifying. Unless you live in a climate where frosts come early in September, you may have late summer flowers from candytuft, Cape marigold (also known as African daisy), scarlet flax, babys breath, poppies, sweet alyssum, dwarf marigolds and zinnias.

If you have a friend whose garden needs thinning, you may benefit by receiving some full-grown plants. Care in transplanting them quickly with soil still around their roots, watering well, and protecting them from sun until they start to look perky again, should give you a fair degree of survival. But never try to move poppies, portulaca, mignonette, larkspur, lupine, nasturtiums, or sweet peas. They will simply turn up their toes and die if they are disturbed.

Quick Flowers for Late Starters

The really resourceful person who is obliged to start his garden in July may end with an astonishingly brilliant show of flowers.

If you have a shady spot, find a nurseryman or florist who still has a stock of tuberous begonias. You can have a glorious display immediately from the brilliant scarlet, salmon, pink, and glistening white or yellow blooms.

As showy as flowers in shady areas are the decorative leaves of the elephants ear, which sprout immediately after the bulky tubers are planted and grow rapidly to enormous size. Even the fancy-leaved caladiums, ordinarily grown indoors, may be set outside to adorn the late summer garden with their foliage of marbled red and white and green.

In regions where frosts do not come until late November, calla lilies make interesting outdoor subjects. They can be planted up to August in pots of exceedingly rich soil, which are then buried among other plants in the border.

In sun, you can have gladioli, planting the corms as late as mid-July, about 4 inches deep and 6 inches apart. With faithful cultivation and watering, they will flower for you in about two months. Pick some quick-flowering varieties.

Tigridia, the tiger-flower of Mexico, may

also be planted up to mid-July for late summer bloom. The mottled orange flowers are striking.

The most astonishing bulb in speed of flowering is the Peruvian daffodil, or basket-flower (Ismene, also called *Hymenocallis calathina.*) Set deeply in the ground any time in summer up to late July, it will send forth within a few weeks a cluster of fragrant white lily-like flowers, tinged with pale green.

All of the above plants must be dug before killing frosts, carefully dried, and their corms or tubers stored until next spring, the Peruvian daffodil in a higher temperature than the others. Wait until the foliage has died down and then carefully take out the plant, as illustrated at the bottom of the page.

Those who lack facilities for cool winter storage may use hardy bulbs which can be planted after the middle of summer. The lavender amaryllis-like flowers of Lycoris ordinarily appear in late July or August, but if the bulbs are planted in midsummer, they will scent the garden at a correspondingly later time.

Sternbergia, which is like a large yellow crocus, likewise the autumn-flowering species of the crocus itself, will bloom gratifyingly in September and October if they are planted as late as August.

Even in September, corms of Colchicum, the meadow saffron, also known as autumn crocus, can be planted. They are so eager to bloom at this time of year that within a month you will doubtless see flowers of shimmering white or delicate lavender, looking much like the true crocus. All of these, left in the ground, will increase year after year, flowering in autumn and sending forth their foliage every spring.

If you can find some lily bulbs (such as *speciosum*) which have been kept in cold storage, you may plant these in the garden in July and be assured of September bloom.

The finest autumn flower of all, the chrysanthemum, can be moved full-grown into the garden up to the time that the buds begin to open.

SPECIAL PLANTS AND GARDENS

ROSES FROM SPRING TILL FALL

When they are planted in variety, roses are capable of giving a longer season of bloom than any other plant; and nothing is more delightful in the garden than the early single flowers of the species roses, such as the yellow *Rosa Hugonis,* or the

late effulgence of bloom on the sturdy hybrid tea roses, which sometimes provide bouquets for the Thanksgiving table. June is, of course, the peak period, but there can be bloom for six additional months in the well planned rose garden.

The species roses—those that represent

END-OF-SEASON CARE OF TENDER BULES
Ismene (shown above) and other bulbs which are not hardy must be dug just before frost and stored in a dry, cool place over winter.   Photo by Roche

wild forms from some part of the world—require little attention. The hybrids demand care throughout the season.

Autumn is the time to plant roses *except* in the north, where spring is considered a safer time to plant. Actually, attention to soil, mulching, and pruning has more effect than a calendar date on the rose. Follow the directions for planting any shrub (see page 1353), spreading the roots out well in the hole, and tamping—or even stamping—the earth over them, as it is shoveled in. The hybrids are generally grafted onto a hardy stock, and the union should be set barely below the soil line. They must be pruned of weak and excess growth as soon as they are planted.

Except in mild climates roses need protection in winter, preferably with a mound of earth about 6 inches high, often with leaves (held in place with evergreen branches) piled on top of this. Remove the protection gradually in the spring. Then mulch the plants with some organic matter, such as peatmoss, that can be dug in to benefit the soil as it decays.

In May start dusting the undersides of the leaves with a fungicide containing ferbam (see page 1377) to keep blackspot under control. Add some rotenone to it to combat the insects too. Never let blackspot on leaves get a head start on you. Every week or so inspect your plants and dust again. With conscientious care they will be the glory of your garden.

The Rock Garden

An untouched piece of land in the country sometimes contains a ready-made location for a rock garden. The rocks themselves are present, there are small trees for shade if shade is desired, and perhaps there are some attractive native shrubs in the background. The setting is apt to be more ideal in appearance than for practice. Tree roots will doubtless have to be pruned away from beneath the sod; deep pockets of humusy soil will have to be furnished for the plants. But still, this is probably easier than to build a rock garden up from level ground, for this takes skillful planning and maneuvering of earth and rocks to give an effect that successfully imitates nature.

A sensible scheme is first to design a path, just slightly winding; then build up the soil at an easy and irregular slope on either side. Next set in the rocks—native ones, preferably, and as large as can be handled. Study the outcroppings in your neighborhood, and imitate them. Slant the rocks in your banks of earth so that they will catch the rain water and let it run to the roots of the plants.

The rock garden is the place for low, spreading mats of bloom and foliage and for individual gems of plants that would be lost in a showy border. It is a place for perennials—not for annual flowers. The early spring phloxes, rockcress, perennial candytuft, golden alyssum and miniature bulbs are standbys for spring bloom followed by veronicas, campanulas, and gentians, among countless other summer flowers. From here on, the rock gardener will begin to choose his own favorites, each one of which will arouse a new ecstasy.

Waterlilies and Their Companions

Whether the aquatic garden is a tub only large enough to hold a single waterlily, or a genuine pool, either a natural or an artificial one, it will provide the restful effect that water always brings to a garden. But if it is artificial, it must look natural, or its pleasant effect will be destroyed. The water surface must be lower than the surrounding ground, and there should be a bank, at least on one side. Rocks at the edge may be both picturesque and practical.

Hardy waterlily roots may be set in tubs of richly manured soil on the bottom of a pool any time from April to the first of June. They need not be removed in winter. Maximum depth should be 2 feet; the distance from the top of the tub to the surface of the water, 6-12 inches. Along the shallower margins of the pool other aquatics may be planted — parrotfeather, floating heart, water snowflake; also water lettuce and water fern, which float. Beside the pool water-loving plants can be grown—cardinal flower, arrowhead, water-plantain, marsh-marigold, blue flag, and other irises —Siberian and Japanese.

Reliable Vegetables

Even though you live in the country where you can get fresh vegetables from a nearby farm, there is nothing quite so good to the taste as your own home-grown tomatoes, carrots, and beans.

If you have an area that gets full sun for 6 hours or more a day, and if you are willing to give your plants at least 8 inches of good soil, by all means grow some vegetables.

Soils that have tested as acid will require lime—up to 10 pounds per 100 square feet. But if you have dug manure into the soil— an excellent practice—don't add lime at the same time. Wait a few days, at least, and then mix it into the upper few inches of soil just before planting.

Before adding lime another year, have your soil tested again. One application in three years is generally sufficient to keep the required alkalinity.

In some regions, the northeastern states particularly, superphosphate in the soil will benefit vegetable crops.

For a vegetable garden a planting plan on paper is particularly necessary. The succession of crops is one of several aspects to consider. Here is a sample schedule for the region around New York City.

Vegetable	Start	Begin to harvest
Late March		
Tomatoes	seed indoors, set out pl. late May	10 wk. later (early Aug.)
Cabbage	seed indoors, set out pl. late May	8 wk. later (late July)
Broccoli	seed indoors, set out pl. mid-May	6 wk. later (July 1)
Radishes	seed outdoors	5 wk. later
Beets	seed outdoors	3 mo. later
Carrots	seed outdoors	3 mo. later
Lettuce	seed outdoors	2 mo. later
Onions	seed outdoors	4 mo. later
Onions	sets outdoors	2 mo. later
Mid-May		
Cabbage	seed in nurs. bed, transpl. in 6 wk.	9 wk. later
Beets	seed outdoors	2 mo. later
Carrots	seed outdoors	2 mo. later
Snap beans	seed outdoors	6 wk. later
Wax beans	seed outdoors	7 wk. later
New Zealand spinach	seed outdoors	9 wk. later
Early June		
Broccoli	seed in nurs. bed, transpl. in 4 wk.	7 wk. later
Kale	seed in nurs. bed, transpl. in 4 wk.	4 mo. later
Radishes	seed outdoors	5 wk. later
Mid-June		
Snap beans	seed outdoors	6 wk. later
Late June		
Carrots	seed outdoors	3 mo. later
July 10		
Beets	seed outdoors	10 wk. later
Carrots	seed outdoors	4 mo. later (for winter use)
Early August		
Radishes	seed outdoors	4 wk. later
Beets	seed outdoors	11 wk. later
Carrots	seed outdoors	3 mo. later
Snap beans	seed outdoors	8 wk. later
Lettuce	seed in nurs. bed, transpl. in 2 wk.	2 mo. later

ROCK GARDEN AND POOL

These two naturalistic features can often be combined where the terrain of a garden can be adapted to rock and water plantings. In both the effect should be natural, not artificial; perennial plants should be encouraged to fit themselves into the picture.   Photos by Gottscho-Schleisner

Roses (*left*), if varieties are well selected, will provide bloom in the garden from May until November.   Photo by New York Botanical Garden

Other vegetables are worth trying too, particularly if they are your favorites—and if you have room. Peas can be started during March or early April; peppers and egg-plants are treated much like tomatoes; lima beans are generally sown only once, in May or June; Swiss chard in April or early May, for a long season of harvesting; kohlrabi and turnips may be sown along with beets and carrots; and corn may be planted in succession any time from May to July.

The Mexican bean beetle will bother your beans, but you can bother him with a frequent dusting of rotenone, especially on the undersides of the leaves.

HERBS FOR THE FANCIER

The thought of herbs is likely to give the nose a twitch, either in pleasant anticipation or in fear of an unfamiliar flavor in tomorrow's salad or soup. Yet every garden has a decorative row of parsley, started anew each spring, and parsley is an herb in every sense.

Chives are a perennial herb, and, with their balls of lavender blossoms, they make an ornamental border plant. A clump may be divided and planted any time of year.

Other easy, pleasant herbs for the beginner are anise, basil, dill, and savory, which are annuals, sown in spring; and the various mints, which are perennials, and may become garden pests.

PLANTS AT THE HOUSE FOUNDATION

A house that sits stark upon its foundation with no softening lines of plants to blend it into its foreground is a cold and uninviting place. A dwelling whose windows are hidden behind a darkening screen of overgrown shrubbery is dismal within.

Between these two extremes are many pleasing ways of planting the front and sides of a house that will leave the windows free for sun and views, enhance the architecture, and furnish bloom and foliage for the equal delight of passer-by and owner.

Evergreens are always in good taste, both the needle type with cones or berries and the leafy ones that bear attractive flowers. Other flowering shrubs, especially those of compact growth, can be effectively used with them to prolong the season of bloom. It is not required to hide the foundation completely, but merely to break the line between the house and the ground with plants that offer beauty the year

around. When deciduous shrubs are used, the pattern of branches in winter should be considered as part of their effect. Azaleas, for instance, are interesting; forsythia has no design in its branch arrangement. But if azaleas or the flowering evergreens are used, it must be remembered that they require an acid soil, and either the soil or the rest of the planting must be tempered accordingly.

Here are some points to keep in mind when selecting and planting shrubbery for the house foundation:

Avoid symmetrical planting, and don't imitate your neighbors.

If you buy evergreens, make *sure* they are dwarf or very slow-growing varieties, not merely young plants of tall, fast-growing species. If you have been fooled, be ruthless and replace them with plants that are more appropriate.

Seek plants that have brightly hued berries in fall, or foliage that changes color, or both—such as Japanese barberry.

Before buying, find out how and when a plant may be pruned in order to keep it within bounds.

Set plants at least 2 feet away from the house foundation, and also away from the drip of rain from the roof.

Give the plants plenty of root room in good soil and allow plenty of space for the spread of their branches as they grow.

Mulch them with clean, inconspicuous material and treat them occasionally to some commercial fertilizer.

WINDOW-BOXES

The variety of plants that may be used in a window-box rivals the choice that one has for an entire garden, but with the limited space available, the selection must be made with special care. The soil should be well fertilized, and watered frequently. A mulch will help to retain the moisture.

Drainage holes are needed in the bottom of a window-box, besides a 2-inch layer of broken crocks and pebbles. Even though the soil you provide is rich, after the plants are established they will need extra nourishment—for the box beneath each window, 1 ounce of a commercial fertilizer in a gallon of water once a month, applied after the plants have been watered.

Window-boxes must be replenished every spring.

In the shade the leaves of the rex begonia are striking. For continuous bloom in either shade or sun, the wax begonia is indispensable. To hang over the edge of the box, the variegated vinca, wandering Jew, and various ivies are always reliable, and there are other vines too, while petunias gracefully bridge the gap between the trailers and the upright plants.

Window-boxes are most attractive when they are longer than the window is wide. They should be at least 8 inches deep and 10 or 12 inches from front to back. The most practical way to be assured of pleasing arrangement is to buy full-grown plants from a florist or nursery and arrange them for greatest effect from the outside of the house.

In winter the boxes may be filled with evergreens.

Vines and window-boxes together ornament the exterior of a house. *Clematis Jackmani*, on the trellis, is one of the handsomest of perennial climbers.   Photo by Gottscho-Schleisner

HOUSE PLANTS

Most indoor plants thrive best in an atmosphere that would also benefit the human occupants of the house. That is, they like the air moderately cool, more moist than they are usually allowed, and fresh but completely free of drafts.

One of the best ways of achieving this medium for plants and people alike is to set a long, flat, shallow pan of pebbles on the radiator, keep it nearly filled with water, and place the potted plants on top. This is not a means of watering the plants, but of providing the desired moisture in the atmosphere.

When to water house plants always is a question. The only answer is: *when they need water.* When the soil in the pots is obviously dry—but before the plants show signs of wilting—water thoroughly. Set the pots in a pan of water, if practicable, and leave them until wetness shows on the surface. Otherwise pour water in the pots until it starts coming out of the bottom.

Glossy-leaved plants need their leaves washed occasionally; a small bulb syringe, or atomizer spray, is helpful. Use water of room temperature; do not wipe them with oil. Protect fuzzy leaves, like those of African violet, from water; the least drop may make a permanent spot.

Each pot should have broken crocks or pebbles on the bottom, then good loamy soil mixed with equal parts of sand and leafmold to within half an inch of the top.

Small amounts of fertilizer for house plants can be bought in powder or in tablet form, with directions on the package.

If you have only a north window, don't expect to have flowers. There are several foliage plants, however, such as English ivy, grape-ivy, Chinese evergreen, ivy-arum (also called pothos), and small dracaenas which can make a pleasant window garden. Starting with a few plants from a florist or a friend, the indoor garden will grow, and with it your knowledge.

THE OUTDOOR LIVING-ROOM

Every family needs to have a comfortable spot for relaxation within sight of flowering trees and shrubs, the blending tones of foliage, or an array of bloom in the borders. For some this is the area where the outdoor fireplace is built; for others, it is a flagstone terrace adjoining the house, or a pleasantly shaded part of the lawn furnished with outdoor lounging chairs.

Strategically placed plants should be a part of this picture—the choicest shrubs, a flowering cherry or dogwood, a symmetrical evergreen, or whatever one most enjoys. If the terrace is paved with flagstones, the plants between them must be thoughtfully chosen. Grass requires constant cutting; clover sprawls into a tangled mat. Moss, when established, is excellent, but it is slow and uncertain. There are several moss-like plants, such as a small arenaria, which one can obtain from a nursery for filling in the spaces. Most plants grow too high and are constantly underfoot, but a clinging form of thyme is attractive and sturdy, and fragrant when bruised by the foot.

At the edges, small flowering plants can be placed—violets in shade or sun, portulaca in full sun, creeping veronicas, and others. Pot-plants give an Old World Mediterranean effect. Vines can be effectively used in some situations (see page 1369).

The outdoor living-room should assure coolness on summer afternoons, pleasant plant surroundings, and convenience to at least one door of the house.

VINES

To soften the lines of a house, mask the unsightly boards of a fence or the wall of a building, or to shade a walk, a balcony or terrace, vines provide the obvious answer. Some are annual, being grown from seed anew each season. Others, with woody stalks, are perennial, and some of those, like wisteria, become venerable specimens with age. Here are a few that are easy to grow in any temperate climate.

Annuals, needing strings for twining:

Morning glory and cypress vine should be sown where they are to remain. Soak the seeds for a day or file a notch in their coats.

Balloon-vine and moonflower, best in milder regions, are handled much like morning glory.

Gourds may be started in mid-April in a strawberry box of good rich soil, box and all planted out around the first of June.

Perennials, needing a trellis:

Clematis Jackmani is one of the easiest and showiest of this group.

Woody vines:

English ivy, Virginia creeper (woodbine) and Boston ("Japanese") ivy will cling to wood or masonry.

China fleece-vine (silver lace-vine)

FOR ENJOYMENT OF THE GARDEN

To lounge in comfort beneath a tree, gazing on smooth green lawn and beds of flowers, is due reward for a gardener on a summer day. As one version of the outdoor living-room, a spot like this can give the entire family added pleasure in the garden.   Photo by Gottscho-Schleisner

twines around long wires, blooms twice a year, and endures neglect.

Akebia needs wires for climbing; is attractive with clusters of five leaflets.

Dutchmans pipe is fast-growing, and will screen a porch in a season, especially if given a limey soil.

Wisteria and trumpet-creeper are both vigorous, showy, and long-lived.

Ground Covers

Under trees and on steep banks where grass to be maintained or mown presents a series of problems, creeping and low-growing plants can be used to advantage. Besides the ubiquitous gout-weed (or bishops-weed), vinca (also called myrtle) and pachysandra, many kinds of small plants will cover the ground gracefully, adding interest while they save on labor.

In spring, beneath a group of flowering cherry trees, nothing is more charming than flowering bulbs emerging from a carpet of English ivy (the hardy Baltic variety in the north). Bugle (Ajuga), sometimes with metallic-purple leaves, will cover the ground solidly in sun or shade and will endure mowing.

Ferns, especially the maidenhair and hay-scented, will thrive and spread in shady spots in place of grass.

Gill-over-the-ground, with scalloped rounded leaves an inch across, will carpet the earth particularly well in shaded places. A white mottled form is more attractive but more slow in spreading.

Some sedums make a solid mat of growth, most of them doing best in barren places in the sun.

The Wild Garden

To dig up an orchid from the woods is not the way to start a wild garden. Most of the orchids are protected by law; very few survive transplanting successfully, and a languishing lady-slipper does not make a wild garden any more than a swallow makes a spring.

It is easiest and most appropriate to create a wild flower garden in a spot where nature has been left more or less unmolested; but with native shrubs or a small tree brought in to simulate the woodland (for most wild flower gardens are composed of woodland flowers), a compact bit of native scenery can be reproduced on any property.

First, study the natural surroundings of the plants you wish to grow, and duplicate them as nearly as possible as to quality of soil, degree of moisture or dryness, and amount of sun or shade. Most wild plants, you will find, survive best in a soil composed largely of leafmold.

Use plenty of ferns, the small ones especially; most of them transplant readily. Avoid the trailing ground-pines, which are almost impossible to move and keep alive—and which are on most conservation lists.

Among the easiest woodland subjects with which to start a wild-flower garden are jack-in-the-pulpits, columbines, violets, anemones, wild ginger, the native saxifrages, bellwort, and bloodroot, all of which are easily transplanted. Trilliums are among the finest flowers of all, but they should be obtained from a nursery, to save the native stands.

Many wild plants resent transplanting—notably lupine, baneberry, and orchids. If there is a nearby nursery which handles native material, buy your plants from there instead of stealing them from the woodland.

If you frequent a particular spot in the countryside, you can mark plants that are in flower and gather the seed later. Here, as in planting, it is best to follow nature's proceedings, and sow the seed shallowly as soon as it is ripe.

To Attract the Birds

When a robin nests in the pin oak that shades the south dining-room window and when a hummingbird hovers over the bee-balm in the border, the home gardener can rightly feel that his garden is a success. To keep the birds coming, it is desirable to plant trees and shrubs whose fruits they will enjoy, and whose branches will give them peaceful shelter.

The fallen seeds of ash trees will bring a bevy of birds in wintertime. Junipers (red-cedars) are a favorite, too, also birches and pines. Among others to be planted for birds are hawthorn, sassafras, mulberry, and mountainash. Ornamental shrubs which are useful as food for the birds include holly, elder, spicebush, bayberry, blackberry, blueberry, and honeysuckle.

Birdhouses of the right kind for the nesting season, and seed and suet put outdoors in winter, will be additional attractions, but the trees and shrubs that are selected with a dual purpose will be the greatest asset of all.

THE GARDENER'S CHORES

Care of the Plantings

If the garden chores are regularly done, they can be a pleasure instead of a task, for outside of the self-satisfaction of accomplishment, each moment of labor among one's plants gives opportunity for increased enjoyment of them.

The close view of a blossom, as one cultivates the soil beneath it, will reveal new beauties in its form and coloring. The underside of a leaf, when it is inspected for signs of pests, will be seen to have a unique quality, often far more interesting than its upper surface.

The perfection of form of a single plant can be seen from a new point of view when one's knees are on the ground. One can observe the often identical angles of branches on the same kinds of plants; the frequently regular spacing of the leaves; the gradual change in size and shape of the leaves as they proceed from the base to the top; the mosaic effect of arrangement by which each leaf is assured a maximum of sunlight on its surface. The weeding may take longer when you stop to look, but the time will seem to be cut in half.

The best way to keep the garden free of weeds is to cultivate the soil once a week from May until September. In small areas, a hand weeder will be satisfactory. In a larger garden, especially where the plants are set in rows, a scuffle hoe is most efficient. Always walk backward with it, cutting off the weeds below the surface of the soil and pushing them under as you go along. Weeds left growing rob the flowers of food; those pushed under will enrich the soil. Weeds that have gone to seed should not be buried in this manner; but if one has cultivated conscientiously all summer long, none of the weeds will have

THE MARSH-MARIGOLD THRIVES FROM

THE CAROLINAS TO CANADA

The marsh-marigold may be grown successfully in moist spots in the border. The double-flowered variety is especially attractive when planted near the edge of a pool. They are easy to grow from freshly gathered seeds.

THE GARDEN MAKES THE HOME

. . . And a garden like this is not difficult to achieve. An open lawn, a simple fountain, flowers blending into the borders of shrubbery, a flowering tree by the terrace, answer the requirements of pleasure for the owner, season-to-season beauty, and long life in the fine trees that form the background.

Photograph by Gottscho-Schleisner

DAHLIAS ARE A GOOD
SELECTION FOR
BEGINNING GARDENERS

Dahlias are easy to grow and very reliable, so they are useful for the beginner. Some varieties such as "Queen of Moorland" have very dark foliage that blends well with evergreens planted near the house. If started indoors in February, Dahlias will start blooming in June and continue all summer.

passed the seedling stage when they are apprehended.

Cultivating has another useful purpose: by breaking up the surface it keeps the soil below in better condition.

Watering, like cultivating, is best done once a week. Then soak the ground so that every plant will have enough moisture to last until the next watering-day. A good way to let the water penetrate is to lay the nozzle of the hose on a flat board, then move the board when soaking is completed.

At the sight of any plant that does not seem to be at its prime, it is time to seek the cause of the trouble—which will most often be a fungus or an insect causing damage. For preliminary suggestions on procedure, see page 1376; for details, look up the name of the plant in this Encyclopedia.

A mulch is often desirable in summer. Shrubs, particularly, will benefit from a dressing of leaves, peatmoss, lawn clippings, buckwheat hulls, or other materials over the soil. The ground will thus stay moist and cool even during a drought, and as the mulch decays it may be spaded in to enrich the soil.

LAWN PATROL

Old-fashioned methods of pulling weeds have all gone out of style. An herbicidal spray containing 2,4-D will control most of them, and crab grass gives promise of succumbing to several new chemicals with which experiments still are being made. In using weed-killers, follow directions on the packages carefully; and, above all, keep one sprayer *exclusively* for the use of herbicides. The slightest trace of the chemicals they contain will mean death to other plants.

Care of the lawn does not end with cutting it periodically. The least that should be done is in late fall to spread over it a layer of screened organic material — leafmold, peatmoss, dried or decayed manure, or a commercial lawn food. Bonemeal, which is slow-acting, also makes a good lawn dressing.

When summer comes, don't cut your lawn too closely. It will thrive better if the mower blades are set 1½ inches high. Clippings, if not too long, may be left on the ground or they may be gathered for a mulch around the shrubbery.

PROPAGATION OF GARDEN PLANTS

The seeds that develop from a flower are formed for the specific purpose of propagating the species, and the gardener takes advantage of their production by using them for the start of many of his plants. There are, however, other and speedier methods of acquiring several plants from one. These vegetative types of propagation also ensure reproduction of the identical form if one is dealing with hybrids or with sports.

For example, many gardeners like to grow chrysanthemums and dahlias from seed, starting them early indoors. The result is a festive mixture of colors and forms, representing all the parents in the strain. If there is one that the gardener particularly likes, he obtains more plants of that form and coloring by vegetative propagation the following year. Were he to sow the seeds, he would get the same sort of array of flowers as before.

Some plants which have fibrous or somewhat fleshy roots and numerous stems are most easily multiplied by dividing the clump into two or more parts when it is dormant—either in late fall or early spring. Daylilies, peonies, phlox, chives, and mockorange are examples. Always replant in a more porous soil—that is, a soil containing more coarse sand and humus — than the original. Keep the plants well watered (but not continuously soaked) and partially shaded until new growth begins.

Various parts of a plant, both below and above ground, may be used for propagating.

Below-ground parts include various types of stems and roots. Be sure there is a live bud on each segment used.

Rhizomes are more or less horizontal underground stems. Iris rhizomes may be lifted, cut and replanted shortly after flowering.

Tubers are fleshy underground stems, as on potatoes.

Tuberous roots (dahlias) will give several new plants in spring, after being stored in a cool dry place over winter. Started in April, they may be planted out the first of June.

Bulbs (tulips, daffodils, lilies) will form new bulbs beside the old one. These may be removed and used to start new plants.

Bulb scales of lilies may also be used individually for propagation.

Corms (crocus and gladiolus) form small cormels which can be planted.

Above-ground parts can be most satisfactorily developed into new plants by starting them in a propagating case. It is easy to make one with an aquarium tank. Drill some holes in the bottom for drainage and set it on the tray of wet pebbles that you keep for house plants on your radiator. Place 2 inches of coarse sand or cinders in the bottom. On top of this have a firm rooting medium of moist sand, vermiculite, or of sand and finely sifted peatmoss mixed half and half. Kept covered with a pane of glass, it will require very little attention. The plants should have light but little sun until they have grown enough to be transplanted.

The plants mentioned below are only examples; others too are propagated by the methods described.

Leaves: Rex begonias. Trim the leaf to half size. Cut the main veins on the underside with a razor blade; lay the leaf on the rooting medium and weight it down with pebbles. With African violets and gloxinias, insert the leak-stalk in the moist rooting medium.

Slips or cuttings: Geraniums, wax begonias, chrysanthemums, shrubs. Take from the parent plant a healthy young shoot containing several leaves; cut it diagonally a little below the point where a leaf arises; remove the lower leaves and insert the base firmly in the moist rooting medium. Chrysanthemum cuttings in very early spring may be taken with or without a segment of the root.

Offsets—such as the small rosettes on hen-and-chickens and the tiny plantlets that form on the leaves of some houseplants. Remove at any time and set in small pots of sandy, porous soil.

Bulbils, formed along the stems of a tiger lily, are best developed in a marked-off area of the nursery bed where they will get good sun.

Runners or *stolons,* as on strawberry plants, will easily take root where they are or they can be induced to root in a small pot buried beneath them, for eventual removal to another bed. In the rock garden, pinks, saxifrages, and other plants may be propagated by this method.

Layering: Forsythia, blackberries, and other shrubs with wand-like stems. Allow the stem to touch the earth, make a fine cut on the underside (unless it is only the tip that touches), weight it down, cover it with soil, and sever from the parent plant when it is rooted.

In starting cuttings, particularly of woody plants, better success can often be assured by the use of growth hormones. They are helpful, rather than essential. If your dealer in garden supplies does not yet stock them, watch for advertisements in gardening periodicals, or write to your favorite gardening magazine for information.

PRUNING

Why and how and when to prune are important to understand before you take your shears, saw or clippers in hand. A pruner must understand a plant's needs and its natural habits of growth and flowering.

The reasons for pruning may be:

To eliminate dead wood and thus give the plant more light and air, as well as better appearance.

To remove diseased portions or branches infested with scale insects or invaded by borers—always cutting to the very base of the shoot.

To cut out old wood which would no longer flower.

To relieve the plant of weak shoots.

To destroy suckers from the rootstocks of grafted plants, such as roses, lilacs, flowering almonds, and some rhododendrons.

To induce larger flowers.

To give a shrub or tree a more desirable shape.

To compensate for loss and inactivity of roots at the time of transplanting.

Unless there is good reason, *do not prune.* Many shrubs, as well as trees, are just as well off if the pruning tools never touch them. Evergreens, particularly, seldom should be cut back, except to keep them within bounds in foundation plantings.

Some fundamental rules and a few suggestions for pruning are:

Use clean, sharp tools.

Never leave a stub, but always trim close to the bark of the parent stem; otherwise, disease will enter which may infect the entire plant.

When pruning for shape, cut branches close to buds which are pointing in the direction desired for the shrub's eventual outline.

Prune the spring-flowering shrubs *after* they have bloomed, then remove

ROSES WILL GROW WELL FOR THE NOVICE

What would a garden be without roses? Even though they take extra care, the thrill they provide cannot be matched by any other flowers. Deep digging, full sun and plenty of water in dry spells are the major ingredients for successful rose growing. The beautiful rose above is from J. Horace McFarland and is called "Signora."

CHRYSANTHEMUMS TAKE CARE OF THEMSELVES

Chrysanthemums are easy to grow and produce an abundance of flowers in the fall. In order not to be straggly, they must be pinched back to six inches several times during the early summer. The above variety is Jackson & Perkins "Flicker."

WHEN TO PRUNE WHAT

In winter, when they are dormant, prune:
Deciduous trees, also shrubs that need thinning or shaping.

In early spring, before growth starts, prune:
Young wood of rose-of-Sharon and Peegee hydrangea back to 2 eyes;
Snowberry and Hills-of-Snow hydrangea close to the ground;
French hydrangea very slightly, if at all; only enough to remove spindling shoots;
Buddleia, either close to the ground or only enough to remove dead wood and to shape the plant;
Climbing roses by removing dead and 2-year-old wood;
Hybrid tea and hybrid perpetual roses by removing winter-killed wood and weak growths.

In spring, after flowering, prune:
Forsythia, deutzia, weigela, beauty-bush, mockorange, lilac, by removing old wood from base;
Flowering almond by thinning out old wood.

In summer, after flowering, prune:
Rambler roses, by cutting off spent flower heads and removing wood of 2 years' growth.

Any time, prune:
Previously overlooked dead, diseased, or weak, worthless stems or branches.

---

the oldest stems and branches. Next spring's flowers will come on new wood that has not yet developed.

Summer-flowering shrubs need little pruning except to shorten trailing branches and remove dead or worn-out wood.

When pruning a large limb from a tree, first make an undercut at least 6 inches from the trunk; then cut it off from above, 2 inches closer to the trunk. This will prevent the weight of the limb from stripping the bark as it falls. Finally, trim the stub close to the bark and parallel to it, to ensure the bark's quickly growing over the open wound.

Winter Protection

Unless one has a surplus of time for playing nursemaid to his plants, there is little point in growing shrubs that have to be coddled over winter, handsome though they may be as specimens. Winter protection then, for the average gardener, will consist mainly in keeping herbaceous perennials from being heaved out of the ground during winter thaws. As long as their roots remain firm in the frozen soil, they will be safe. This means that they should not be covered until the ground has frozen a couple of inches deep.

Biennials and perennials which form winter rosettes of leaves need only a light, dry covering.

For mulching material use whatever is common in the neighborhood. In the south it may be cornstalks or bagasse from sugar mills; on the east coast, salt-marsh hay; in middle western farming regions, straw; and in other places leaves and branches. Remove such mulches gradually as growth starts and spring advances.

A winter mulch that can be left to decay will benefit shrubs not already provided for.

Hybrid roses need to have soil thrown around them to a height of at least 6 inches. Climbing roses should have their stalks tied firmly to their support.

Newly planted young trees may need their bark protected the first year by wrapping it in burlap.

Sun and wind are the greatest sources of danger to evergreens. Avoid planting them in exposed places. Snow can also damage them. Shake it from their branches during a storm before it permanently bends them. Soak their roots thoroughly late in the fall, for they need water over winter.

For the garden as a whole, the best preparation for winter is to leave it cleaned of all debris.

Disease and Pest Control

Plants that are grown in well-drained,

weed-free soil where they get all the sun and air they need have good insurance against attacks by fungi, insects, and other parasites and pests. But no amount of caution provides a guarantee against invasion, so the gardener had best be prepared with sprays and dusts and the equipment with which to apply them. He also needs to be on the alert for the first sign of trouble, if he is to wage successful combat against the enemies in his garden.

One dust gun and at least one sprayer (but preferably two or three) are sufficient at the beginning, unless one's place is very large. One or two hand sprayers the size of flit guns, kept on a convenient shelf and always filled with mixtures that may be needed, will mean that plants in trouble will receive prompt attention. For larger jobs, a knapsack sprayer holding several gallons is desirable. Quick action often will avoid a long-term program of control and may mean the saving of the plants.

The principal enemies of plants are the insects which infest them and the fungi, bacteria, and viruses which infect them just as a child may be infected with measles. Viruses are particularly difficult to control. Removing all infected plants or parts of plants is the first step; then attack the insect which is believed to have brought the virus infection into the garden.

Whenever you are removing diseased plants, pop them quickly into a bag, close it tight, and burn them. Do not touch healthy plants with hands or tools that have been in contact with infectious organisms.

Insects which damage plants are of two main sorts—(1) those that suck the juices from the leaves and (2) those that chew. The sucking insects are attacked by what is called a *contact* spray; that is, it kills them when it hits their bodies. The chewers are attacked by covering the surfaces of the leaves on which they feed, causing them to die of internal poisoning. Most often, they feed on the undersides of the leaves, so it is especially important to spray from beneath.

It is possible to use a combination spray which will attack most fungi and most insects together. Several are on the market under trade names. If the list of ingredients on the container mentions sulfur, rotenone, DDT, and ferbam, it will be an efficient all-around spray, though it may not be a satisfactory control for some *specific* fungus or pest.

WHAT AILS YOUR PLANTS

Appearance	*Cause*	*Control*
Leaves powdery-gray	mildew (a fungus)	sulfur compound
Dark or orange spots or patches on leaves	rust or some other fungus	ferbam compound
Blackened sections of stems	fungus or bacterial infection	may require special treatment
Light mottling of leaves	mosaic (a virus)	destroy the plant or remove infected parts
Gray or rusty speckling on leaves	any of various sucking insects, general on underside	DDT or nicotine sulfate
Serpentine tunnels in leaves	leaf miners	DDT or nicotine sulfate
Tiny soft-bodied insects in great numbers	aphids	nicotine sulfate
Tiny red spider-like insects on undersides of leaves	mites	nicotine sulfate
Shell-like growths on woody twigs	scale insects	miscible oil
Hard-shelled insects	beetles	DDT or rotenone
Soft-bodied "worms"	caterpillars (larvae, chiefly of moths)	rotenone

Most of the chewing insects, such as beetles and caterpillars, will succumb to rotenone, either a dust containing ¾ of 1 percent of the substance, or a liquid spray of the same.

For sucking insects, such as aphids, mealy bugs, leafhoppers, lacebugs, thrips, and mites, nicotine sulfate remains one of the most effective compounds for destroying them, though rotenone may also be used against some of them.

For either kind of insect, DDT may also be recommended, though it is not effective against all. But do *not* use household DDT, which is dissolved in oil. From your garden supply store get 50 percent wettable DDT powder, and follow directions on the package.

DDT is especially effective against leafhoppers, which often carry virus diseases from plant to plant. Follow it with nicotine sulfate or rotenone, to combat the redspider mites which are certain to appear after their enemies have been destroyed by the DDT.

Scale insects, which are also of the sucking type, are best attacked when trees and shrubs are dormant, by using a miscible oil (obtainable under a number of trade names) and diluting in water as directed.

To combat most of the common fungus infections, the recommendation is for any spray containing "ferbam" (a name lately adopted by plant pathologists for the black powder which is the basis of fermate and other trade products).

Ferbam is especially good for keeping blackspot of roses under control.

Mildews are also fungus infections, but they respond better to a sulfur compound.

How does the gardener know what is ailing his plants when they begin to look sick? A few clues and some recommended remedies are given in the box on the facing page.

YOUR GARDEN SOIL AND ITS NEEDS

To Improve the Soil

The beauty of your flowers springs from the earth which supports and nourishes their roots.

As garden soil, the earth needs to be both structurally and chemically improved before it is suitable for planting. Two things are added to it: *amendments* and *fertilizers*.

Amendments are substances that improve its condition, helping to make it more friable, and giving it good tilth when ready for planting.

Fertilizers are the substances which furnish nutrients. They may be either organic or inorganic—that is, derived from once-living material or from inert substances. The latter are known as chemical or "commercial" fertilizers. Made readily available to the plants in measurable quantities, they provide the identical chemicals that the plant-roots extract from organic material spaded into the soil. Both are needed.

The proportions of each substance to incorporate into the soil vary with the type of soil. Along the eastern seaboard, lime is generally needed, but in the Great Lakes area there is already lime enough in the soil to meet all garden needs. The Experiment Station in each state is always prepared to analyze a sample of soil and give advice on its needs.

General Procedure

Supposing you are starting with an average plot of ground—a few scant inches of topsoil supporting weedy growth, a little clay, a number of small stones and a few large ones, roots of woody plants—nothing very bad about it, nothing very good.

The best treatment it can receive is to dig it thoroughly—not just turning it over, but digging a series of parallel trenches, each one marked off with a carefully measured line. As each trench is dug to the full depth of the spade, organic matter and other substances are forked or spaded deeply into the bottom of it, then covered with the soil dug from the next trench.

Drainage Problems

When you strike your spade deep in the soil, if you find a layer of impervious hardpan, you have a job ahead of you in breaking it up with a pick or mattock or even with explosive powder. To keep the clay sub-soil from cementing itself together again, coal ashes may be forked in deeply. No garden plants can thrive unless there is porous ground for drainage beneath their roots.

Standing water beneath the topsoil is another condition that plants resent. A subsoil plow may help the condition. Otherwise, have a local contractor put in field drains for you or make a stone ditch leading to a main drain.

Organic Matter

Where do you get your organic matter? If you have been gardening for a year or more, you have a compost pile (see page 1379). But if you are just beginning you must rely on other sources. The most nearly perfect organic matter is well rotted cow manure, but this is both rare and expensive for the small home gardener. Any animal manure available is good, and poultry manure, which is especially strong and high in nitrogen, is generally procurable. Otherwise, sewage sludge is an acceptable substitute.

Any kind of plant growth, as long as it is not diseased and does not contain weed seeds, may be spaded into the soil—crop residues, spent annual or perennial plants, weeds, old hay or straw, mowings and clippings, shavings, sawdust, and such. Cover crops, called "green manures"—generally of rye, rye-grass, millet or such legumes as vetch or clover—are another source of organic matter. Peatmoss, which is a leading product for this purpose, can be bought in bales.

If these bulky materials make a loose layer 6 inches high in a trench, the gardener can feel he is doing well.

Soil Amendments

If lime is required, this is the time to start adding it. Ground limestone is safest to use. If hydrated (agricultural) lime or burned (caustic) lime is used, less is needed. These are both faster in their action on the soil.

One thing to remember is not to apply lime and manure together, unless they are completely spaded under. In the open air the effect of both will be lost by their chemical action upon one another.

Wood ashes also supply lime, as well as potash and phosphoric acid.

Perhaps your soil already contains too much lime for your needs. To make it more acid, or to increase the acidity for the culture of rhododendrons and their relatives, add aluminum sulfate.

If your whole soil structure is principally of clay, sand will improve it, so will lime.

If, on the other hand, you find yourself digging in sand, you will need clay with abundant organic matter.

SOIL AMENDMENTS AND HOW TO APPLY THEM

Type of soil to be improved	What to add	Depth of layer if spread over surface or in trench	Quantity per 1,000 square feet
CLAY	Sand	1"–2", spaded in 8" deep	3–6 cu. yd.
	Hydrated lime		100 lb., raked into surface
	Organic matter Coal ashes	6" in 12" trench 1"–2"	3–6 cu. yd.
SAND	Clay		4 cu. yd.
	Organic matter Coal ashes	6" in 12" trench 1"–2"	3–6 cu. yd.
EXTREMELY ACID SOIL	Lime (in one of 3 forms): Ground limestone Hydrated lime Caustic lime		50–100 lb. 37–75 lb. 25–50 lb.
EXTREMELY ALKALINE SOIL	Aluminum sulfate		100 lb.

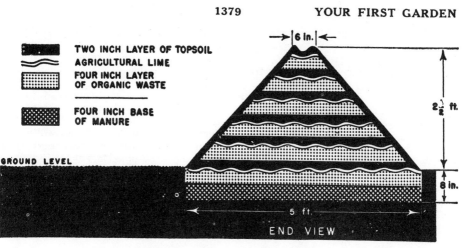

TWO INCH LAYER OF TOPSOIL

AGRICULTURAL LIME

FOUR INCH LAYER OF ORGANIC WASTE

FOUR INCH BASE OF MANURE

GROUND LEVEL

6 in.

2½ ft.

8 in.

5 ft.

END VIEW

HOW TO MAKE A COMPOST HEAP

This diagram, designed with instructions for procedure by Mrs. John M. Whitaker of Huntington, N. Y., is reproduced here by courtesy of the North Shore Garden Club, Long Island, member of the Garden Club of America.

In either sand or clay, hard coal ashes are advantageous. They help the sandy soil to retain water and they reduce the stickiness of the clay.

If all this work is one in the fall (the ideal time), the ground should be left rough over winter: then, as soon as the soil ceases to stick to the tools in spring, it may be raked smooth, commercial fertilizer added, and either immediately or later, it may be planted.

Humus and Chemicals

A great deal is written and said about the importance of organic matter as a complete fertilizer in the garden soil, and every gardener who has provided abundant humus —decayed or decaying organic matter—has had the pleasure of watching his plants respond with vigorous, healthy growth.

Quite as important as the chemical compounds that humus provides for plant growth, is the effect of humus on the working condition or tilth of the soil. It helps to maintain a balance between air and moisture in the earth by holding water more readily than sand, but less than clay. Plant roots need air as well as water, and humus makes both accessible in the right proportion.

Although spading humus into the earth is the least expensive way of furnishing a suitable growing medium for plants, it is often difficult to obtain enough to provide all the chemical elements that a plant re-

quires for optimum growth. Therefore, the addition of chemical or "commercial" fertilizers—particularly those that are designated as complete plant foods, simplifies the process of gardening and greatly benefits the plants.

These fertilizers bear three figures on the package, to indicate their contents. One that reads 5-10-5, which is the usual combination for a complete plant food, contains 5 percent of nitrogen, 10 percent of phosphoric acid, and 5 percent of potassium, or potash. (The chemicals are listed in alphabetical order.) A larger percentage of any one element is reflected in the figure. The balance of the ingredients is a carrier, for these chemicals would damage the plants if they were applied full strength.

Extra Chemicals

Sometimes the garden soil needs one chemical more than another. If an undecayed mulch is being spaded in, such as straw, sawdust, or a green cover crop, nitrogen should be added. This can be in the form of a nitrate (such as sodium nitrate), an ammonium salt (such as ammonium sulphate), or poultry manure, which is rich in nitrogen. Cottonseed meal is a valuable combination mulch and nitrogen provider.

Abundance of nitrogen results in exuberant leaf growth and good green color.

Fruit and seed crops need additional phosphorous in the soil, either superphosphate for immediate effect, or bonemeal for slow action.

Root crops benefit from potash, which can be obtained from wood ashes or from muriate of potash.

For the most advantageous proportion of these important plant foods, the relation of the three percentage figures on the container should be noted when a commercial fertilizer is being used.

EARTHWORMS

You have heard about earthworms and their supposed benefits. If you have a soil that is rich in humus, the earthworms will invade it without urging. Their burrows help to keep the soil porous and their castings make certain nutrient elements more readily available to the roots of plants. They do not *add* nutrients, they merely prepare them for the plants to absorb. But if you have a poor soil, no amount of introduction of earthworm colonies will induce them to remain. To the gardener who provides the finest possible soil for his plants shall be given a reward of handsome, healthy flowers, vegetables to delight the palate, and a lawn to inspire envy.